D1266205

COLLINS

SHORTER DICTIONARY & THESAURUS

COLLINS

SHORTER DICTIONARY & THESAURUS

HarperCollins*Publishers*

First Published 1991
First published in this edition 1995
Reprinted 1996, 1997
Latest reprint 1998
4 5 6 7 8 9
© HarperCollins Publishers 1991, 1995

ISBN 0 00 470907-1

Editorial Staff

Managing Editor
Marian Makins

Chief Lexicographer
Diana Adams

Lexicographers
Lorna Knight
Alice Grandison, Danielle McGinley, Tom Shearer, Elspeth Summers

A catalogue record for this book is available from the British Library.

All rights reserved. No part of this publication may be reproduced, stored in a retrieval system or transmitted, in any form or by any means, electronic, mechanical, photocopying, recording or otherwise, without prior permission of the publisher.

Entered words that we have reason to believe constitute trademarks have been designated as such. However, neither the presence nor absence of such designation should be regarded as affecting the legal status of any trademark.

Typeset by Barbers Ltd.
Wrotham, Kent

Printed and bound in Great Britain by
Caledonian International Book Manufacturing Ltd,
Glasgow, G64

CONTENTS

FOREWORD

COLLINS SHORTER DICTIONARY AND THESAURUS provides two kinds of language help, arranged on the same page for quick and easy reference. In the top section of each page, you will find dictionary text, while the lower half of each page provides a thesaurus.

The dictionary entries are simply and clearly laid out, to enable you to check at a glance spelling, meaning, pronunciation, and grammatical function. If you then look at the lower half of the page, you will find, for many of the words covered by the dictionary, lists of synonyms, that is words of the same or similar meaning. These synonym lists offer you a choice of alternative words to use in place of the one which you have in mind.

Suppose, for instance, you want to find another word for **difficult**. Perhaps you have used it already, or perhaps you feel that it is not quite suited to the tone or context of what you want to write or say.

The entry for **difficult** in the thesaurus text provides you with a choice of words that can be used in its place, covering the various contexts in which **difficult** might occur. So, from the many alternatives given, you could, for example, substitute: an *onerous* task; *straitened* circumstances; a *ticklish* situation.

Because the two texts are arranged in parallel format, you can refer from dictionary to thesaurus entries and then back again with ease. All the information on any one word in all its aspects is contained at one place.

COLLINS SHORTER DICTIONARY AND THESAURUS is a uniquely helpful book, an ideal companion for everyone who wants to increase their command of English.

HOW THE DICTIONARY ENTRIES ARE ARRANGED

1. All main entries are given in a single alphabetical listing that includes abbreviations, foreign words, and prefixes and suffixes (combining forms). Each such entry consists of a paragraph with the main word printed at the beginning in large bold type.

2. Within each entry, different meanings of the main word are numbered. After the meanings of the main word come words that are derived from it, printed in smaller bold type, in alphabetical order. These in turn are followed by compounds (if any) formed by the main word with the addition of another word. Derived words and compound words are explained, except when their meaning is obvious from the sense of the main word. Idiomatic phrases associated with the main word come at the end of the entry.

3. The part of speech is shown by an abbreviation placed after the word (or its pronunciation). When a word can be used as more than one part of speech, the change is indicated by a new part-of-speech label. Spellings of irregular noun plurals and verb parts are shown within brackets, printed in bold type.

4. In English many easily understood words are formed by adding prefixes such as *non-*, *re-*, *un-*, etc., to existing words. Such words are included, without definition, at the foot of the page on which the prefix in question is entered as a main entry and on following pages if necessary.

HOW THE THESAURUS ENTRIES ARE ARRANGED

1. Under each main-entry word, the synonyms are arranged alphabetically. When a word has distinctly separate meanings, separate numbered lists are given for the different senses, eg

   distinct 1. apparent, clear, clear-cut . . .
   2. detached, different, discrete . . .

2. Where it is desirable to distinguish between different parts of speech, labels have been added as follows: *n.* (noun), *v.* (verb), *adj.* (adjective), *adv.* (adverb), *pron.* (pronoun), *conj.* (conjunction), *prep.* (preposition), *interj.* (interjection). When a headword has more than one meaning and can function as more than one part of speech, a new part-of-speech function is shown by a large swung dash (~), eg

   local *adj.* **1.** community, district . . .
   2. confined, limited . . . ~*n.*
   3. character (*Inf.*), inhabitant . . .

3. Usually the synonyms for a particular part of speech are grouped together. Thus, in the entry *catch* synonyms for all the verb senses are given first, followed by synonyms for all the noun senses. Sometimes, however, noun and verb functions are very closely associated in specific meanings, and where this is the case the synonyms are grouped by meanings, as in the entry for *cover.*

4. Much-used phrases appear as main entries; for instance, *blow out* comes after *blow.* Expressions such as *en route,* and compounds such as *highly strung* or *high-spirited,* are also given as main entries within the alphabetical listing. Short idiomatic phrases are entered under their key word and are to be found either at the end of the entry or immediately following the sense with which they are associated. Thus, the phrase *on the face of it* appears as sense 6 of the entry *face,* since the synonyms in sense 5 most closely approximate to the meaning of the phrase.

5. Plural forms that have a distinctly separate meaning, such as *provisions,* are entered at their own alphabetical position, while those with a less distinct difference, such as *offices,* are given as a separate sense under the singular form, eg

   office . . . **2.** *Plural* . . .

6. A label in brackets applies only to the synonym preceding it while one which is not bracketed relates to the whole of that particular sense. Labels have been abbreviated when a readily understandable shortened form exists, such as *Sl.* (Slang), *Inf.* (Informal), and *Fig.* (Figurative).

ABBREVIATIONS USED IN THE TEXT

a.	adjective
abbrev.	abbreviation
Acc.	Accounting
adv.	adverb
Aeron.	Aeronautics
Afr.	Africa(n)
Amer.	America(n)
Anat.	Anatomy
Archaeol.	Archaeology
Archit.	Architecture
Arith.	Arithmetic
Astrol.	Astrology
Astron.	Astronomy
Aust.	Australia(n)
Biochem.	Biochemistry
Biol.	Biology
Bot.	Botany
Brit.	Britain, British
Bus.	Business
Canad.	Canada, Canadian
cent.	century
Ch.	Church
Chem.	Chemistry
Cine.	Cinema
Class. lit.	Classical literature
Class. myth.	Classical mythology
cm.	centimetre(s)
Comm.	Commerce
comp.	comparative
Comp.	Computers
conj.	conjunction
cu.	cubic
dial.	dialect
dim.	diminutive
E	East
Eccles.	Ecclesiastical
Ecol.	Ecology
Econ.	Economics
Educ.	Education
eg	for example
Elec.	Electricity
Electron.	Electronics
esp.	especially
fem.	feminine
fig.	figuratively
Fin.	Finance
Fr.	French
g	gram(s)
Geog.	Geography
Ger.	German
Gr.	Greek
Gram.	Grammar
Her.	Heraldry
Hist.	History
Hort.	Horticulture
ie	that is
impers.	impersonal
ind.	indicative
inf.	informal
interj.	interjection
It.	Italian
k	kilogram(s)
km	kilometre(s)
l	litre(s)
Lat.	Latin
Linguis.	Linguistics
lit.	literally
Lit.	Literary, Literature
m	metre(s)
masc.	masculine
Maths.	Mathematics
Mech.	Mechanics
Med.	Medicine
Met.	Meteorology
Mil.	Military
Min.	Mineralogy
mm	millimetre(s)
Mus.	Music
Myth.	Mythology
n.	noun
N	North
Naut.	Nautical
N.T.	New Testament
N.Z.	New Zealand
obs.	obsolete, obsolescent
offens.	offensive
oft.	often
orig.	originally
O.T.	Old Testament
Pathol.	Pathology
pers.	person
pert.	pertaining
Philos.	Philosophy
Phonet.	Phonetics
Photog.	Photography
Phys.	Physics
Phys. Ed.	Physical Education
Physiol.	Physiology
pl.	plural
pl.n.	plural noun
Poet.	Poetic, Poetry
Pol.	Politics

ABBREVIATIONS USED IN THE TEXT (*cont.*)

poss.	possessive	*sl.*	slang
pp.	past participle	*Sociol.*	Sociology
prep.	preposition	Sp.	Spanish
pres.t.	present tense	sq.	square
Print.	Printing	*St.Ex.*	Stock Exchange
pron.	pronoun	*sup.*	superlative
pr.p.	present participle	*Surg.*	Surgery
Psych.	Psychiatry	*Surv.*	Surveying
Psychoanal.	Psychoanalysis	*Theat.*	Theatre
Psychol.	Psychology	*Trig.*	Trigonometry
pt.	past tense	*T.V.*	Television
Rad.	Radio	usu.	usually
R.C.	Roman Catholic	*v.*	verb
refl.	reflexive	*v.aux.*	auxiliary verb
Rel.	Religion	*Vet.*	Veterinary Medicine
S	South	*vi.*	intransitive verb
Sc.	Science	*vt.*	transitive verb
Scot.	Scottish	W	West
sing.	singular	*Zool.*	Zoology

R	Registered Trade Mark
A	Australian
C	Canadian
NZ	New Zealand
SA	South African
UK	United Kingdom
US	United States

PRONUNCIATION KEY

The symbols used in the pronunciation transcriptions are those of the International Phonetic Alphabet. The following consonant symbols have their usual English values: ***b, d, f, h, k, l, m, n, p, r, s, t, v, w, z.*** The remaining symbols and their interpretations are listed below.

English Sounds

ɑː as in ***father*** (ˈfɑːðə), ***alms*** (ɑːmz)

æ as in ***act*** (ækt), ***plait*** (plæt)

aɪ as in ***dive*** (daɪv), ***aisle*** (aɪl), ***guy*** (gaɪ)

aɪə as in ***fire*** (faɪə), ***buyer*** (ˈbaɪə), ***liar*** (ˈlaɪə)

aʊ as in ***out*** (aʊt), ***bough*** (baʊ)

aʊə as in ***flour*** (flaʊə), ***cower*** (ˈkaʊə)

ɛ as in ***bet*** (bɛt), ***ate*** (ɛt), ***bury*** (ˈbɛrɪ)

eɪ as in ***paid*** (peɪd), ***day*** (deɪ), ***deign*** (deɪn)

ɛə as in ***bear*** (bɛə), ***dare*** (dɛə), ***prayer*** (prɛə)

g as in ***get*** (gɛt), ***give*** (gɪv), ***ghoul*** (guːl)

ɪ as in ***pretty*** (ˈprɪtɪ), ***build*** (bɪld)

iː as in ***see*** (siː), ***aesthete*** (ˈiːsθiːt)

ɪə as in ***fear*** (fɪə), ***beer*** (bɪə), ***mere*** (mɪə)

j as in ***yes*** (jɛs), ***onion*** (ˈʌnjən)

ɒ as in ***pot*** (pɒt); ***botch*** (bɒtʃ), ***sorry*** (ˈsɒrɪ)

əʊ as in ***note*** (nəʊt), ***beau*** (bəʊ), ***hoe*** (həʊ)

ɔː as in ***thaw*** (θɔː), ***broad*** (brɔːd)

ɔɪ as in ***void*** (vɔɪd), ***boy*** (bɔɪ)

ʊ as in ***pull*** (pʊl), ***good*** (gʊd), ***should*** (ʃʊd)

uː as in ***zoo*** (zuː), ***do*** (duː), ***queue*** (kjuː)

ʊə as in ***poor*** (pʊə), ***skewer*** (ˈskjʊə)

ə as in ***potter*** (ˈpɒtə), ***alone*** (əˈləʊn)

ɜː as in ***fern*** (fɜːn), ***burn*** (bɜːn), ***fir*** (fɜː)

ʌ as in ***cut*** (kʌt), ***flood*** (flʌd), ***rough*** (rʌf)

ʃ as in ***ship*** (ʃɪp), ***election*** (ɪˈlɛkʃən)

ʒ as in ***treasure*** (ˈtrɛʒə), ***azure*** (ˈæʒə)

tʃ as in ***chew*** (tʃuː), ***nature*** (ˈneɪtʃə)

dʒ as in ***jaw*** (dʒɔː), ***lodge*** (lɒdʒ)

θ as in ***thin*** (θɪn), ***strength*** (strɛŋθ)

ð as in ***these*** (ðiːz), ***bathe*** (beɪð)

ŋ as in ***sing*** (sɪŋ), ***finger*** (ˈfɪŋgə)

ᵊ indicates that the following consonant (***l*** or ***n***) is syllabic, as in ***bundle*** (ˈbʌndᵊl) and ***button*** (ˈbʌtᵊn).

PRONUNCIATION KEY (*cont.*)

Foreign Sounds

Certain common foreign sounds require additional symbols, as follows:

a   *a* in French *ami,* German *Mann,* Italian *pasta:* a sound between English /æ/ and /ɑ:/.

e   *é* in French *été, eh* in German *sehr, e* in Italian *che:* similar to the Scottish vowel in *day.*

i   *i* in French *il,* German *Idee,* Spanish *filo,* Italian *signor:* similar to English /i:/, but shorter.

ɔ   *o* in Italian *no,* French *bonne,* German *Sonne:* a vowel resembling English /ɒ/, but with a higher tongue position and more rounding of the lips.

o   *o* in French *rose,* German *so,* Italian *voce:* similar to the Scottish vowel in *so.*

y   *u* in French *tu, ü* in German *über:* similar to English /i:/ made with closely rounded lips.

ø   *eu* in French *deux, ö* in German *schön:* similar to /e/ made with closely rounded lips.

œ   *œu* in French *œuf, ö* in German *zwölf:* similar to English /ɛ/ made with open rounded lips.

~   above a vowel indicates nasalization, as in French *un* (œ̃), *bon* (bɔ̃), *vin* (vɛ̃), *blanc* (blɑ̃).

x   *ch* in Scottish *loch,* German *Buch.*

ç   *ch* in German *ich:* similar to the first sound in *huge.*

ß   *b* in Spanish *Habana:* similar to /v/ but made by the two lips.

ʎ   *ll* in Spanish *llamar, gl* in Italian *consiglio:* similar to the /lj/ sequence in *million.*

ɥ   *u* in French *lui:* a short /y/.

ɲ   *gn* in French *vigne,* Italian *gnocchi, ñ* in Spanish *España:* similar to the /nj/ sequence in *onion.*

ɣ   *g* in Spanish *luego:* a weak /g/ made with voiced friction.

Length

The symbol : is shown with certain vowel symbols when the vowels are typically long.

Stress

The main stress is shown by ', immediately *before* the stressed syllable.

Notes

(i) Though words like *castle, path, fast* are shown as pronounced with an /ɑ:/ sound, many speakers use an /æ/. Such variations are acceptable and are to be assumed by the reader.

(ii) The letter "r" in some positions is not sounded in the speech of Southern England and elsewhere. However, many speakers in other areas do sound the "r" in such positions. Again, such variations are to be assumed.

(iii) Though the widely received pronunciation of words like *which, why* is with a simple /w/ sound and is so shown in the dictionary, many speakers, in Scotland and elsewhere, preserve an aspirated sound: /hw/. Once again this variation is to be assumed.

a *or* **A** (eɪ) *n.* **1.** first letter of English alphabet **2.** any of several speech sounds represented by this letter, as in *take, calm* **3.** first in series, *esp.* highest mark (*also* ˈ**alpha**) (*pl.* **a's, A's,** *or* **As**) —**from A to Z** from start to finish

a (ə; *emphatic* eɪ) *a.* the indefinite article meaning one; *an* is used before vowel sounds, and sometimes before unaccented syllables beginning with *h* aspirate

A **1.** *Mus.* sixth note of scale of C major; major or minor key having this note as its tonic **2.** human blood type of ABO group **3. UK** major arterial road **4. UK** formerly, (film) certified for viewing by all age groups **5.** ampere **6.** absolute (temperature) **7.** area **8.** alto **9.** (*comb. form*) atomic, as in *A-bomb, A-plant*

Å angstrom unit

a. **1.** acre **2.** adjective **3.** answer **4.** are

a-[1] *or before vowel* **an-** (*comb. form*) not; without; opposite to, as in *atonal, asocial, anaesthetic*

a-[2] (*comb. form*) **1.** on; in; towards, as in *aground, aback* **2.** in state of, as in *afloat, asleep*

A1, A-1, *or* **A-one** (ˈeɪˈwʌn) *a.* **1.** physically fit **2.** *inf.* first-class; excellent **3.** (of vessel) in first-class condition

AA **1.** Alcoholics Anonymous **2.** anti-aircraft **3.** Automobile Association **4. UK** formerly, (film) that may not be shown to child under fourteen

A.A.A. **1. UK** Amateur Athletic Association **2. US** Automobile Association of America

aardvark (ˈɑːdvɑːk) *n.* nocturnal Afr. mammal which feeds on termites

A'asia Australasia

AB Alberta

A.B. able-bodied seaman

ab-[1] (*comb. form*) away from; opposite to, as in *abnormal*

ab-[2] (*comb. form*) cgs unit of measurement in electromagnetic system, as in *abampere, abvolt*

aback (əˈbæk) *adv.* —**taken aback** startled

abacus (ˈæbəkəs) *n.* **1.** counting device of beads on wire frame **2.** flat tablet at top of column

abaft (əˈbɑːft) *Naut. adv./a.* **1.** towards stern of vessel —*prep.* **2.** behind; aft of

abalone (æbəˈləʊnɪ) *n.* edible shellfish, yielding mother-of-pearl

abandon (əˈbændən) *vt.* **1.** desert **2.** give up altogether —*n.* **3.** freedom from inhibitions *etc.* —**aˈbandoned** *a.* **1.** deserted, forsaken **2.** uninhibited **3.** wicked —**aˈbandonment** *n.*

abase (əˈbeɪs) *vt.* humiliate, degrade —**aˈbasement** *n.*

abash (əˈbæʃ) *vt.* (*usu. passive*) confuse, make ashamed —**aˈbashment** *n.*

abate (əˈbeɪt) *v.* make or become less, diminish —**aˈbatement** *n.*

abattoir (ˈæbətwɑː) *n.* slaughterhouse

abbé (ˈæbeɪ) *n.* **1.** French abbot **2.** title used in addressing any French cleric

abbess (ˈæbɪs) *n.* female superior of convent

abbey (ˈæbɪ) *n.* **1.** dwelling place of community of monks or nuns **2.** church of an abbey

abbot (ˈæbət) *n.* head of abbey or monastery (ˈ**abbess** *fem.*) —ˈ**abbacy** *n.* office, rights of abbot

abbr., abbrev. abbreviation

abbreviate (əˈbriːvɪeɪt) *vt.* shorten, abridge —**abbreviˈation** *n.* shortened form of word or phrase.

ABC *n.* **1.** (*oft. pl. in Amer.*) the alphabet **2.** (*pl. in Amer.*) rudiments of subject **3.** alphabetical guide

abdicate (ˈæbdɪkeɪt) *v.* formally give up (throne *etc.*) —**abdiˈcation** *n.*

abdomen (ˈæbdəmən) *n.* belly —**abdominal** (æbˈdɒmɪnᵊl) *a.*

abduct (æbˈdʌkt) *vt.* carry off, kidnap —**abˈduction** *n.*

abeam (əˈbiːm) *adv.* abreast, in line

abele (əˈbiːl, ˈeɪbᵊl) *n.* white poplar

Aberdeen Angus (ˈæbədiːn ˈæŋgəs) breed of cattle, *orig.* Scottish

aberration (æbəˈreɪʃən) *n.* **1.** deviation from what is normal **2.** flaw **3.** lapse —**aˈberrant** *a.*

abet (əˈbɛt) *vt.* assist, encourage, *esp.* in doing wrong —**aˈbetter** *or* **aˈbettor** *n.*

THESAURUS

abandon *v.* **1.** desert, forsake, jilt, leave, leave behind **2.** evacuate, quit, vacate, withdraw from **3.** abdicate, cede, give up, relinquish, renounce, resign, surrender, waive, yield **4.** desist, discontinue, drop, forgo ~*n.* **5.** careless freedom, dash, recklessness, unrestraint, wantonness, wild impulse, wildness

abandoned **1.** cast aside, cast away, cast out, derelict, deserted, discarded, dropped, forlorn, forsaken, jilted, left, neglected, outcast, rejected, relinquished, unoccupied, vacant **2.** corrupt, debauched, depraved, dissipated, dissolute, profligate, reprobate, sinful, wanton, wicked **3.** uncontrolled, uninhibited, unrestrained, wild

abandonment **1.** dereliction, desertion, forsaking, jilting, leaving **2.** evacuation, quitting, withdrawal from **3.** abdication, cession, giving up, relinquishment, renunciation, resignation, surrender, waiver **4.** desistance, discontinuation, dropping

abbey cloister, convent, friary, monastery, nunnery, priory

abbreviate abridge, abstract, clip, compress, condense, contract, curtail, cut, digest, epitomize, précis, reduce, shorten, summarize, trim, truncate

abbreviation abridgment, abstract, clipping, compendium, compression, condensation, conspectus, contraction, curtailment, digest, epitome, précis, reduction, résumé, shortening, summary, synopsis, trimming, truncation

abdicate abandon, abjure, abnegate, cede, forgo, give up, quit, relinquish, renounce, resign, retire, surrender, vacate, waive, yield

abdication abandonment, abjuration, abnegation, cession, giving up, quitting, relinquishment, renunciation, resignation, retiral (*esp. Scot.*), retirement, surrender, waiver, yielding

abdominal gastric, intestinal, stomachic, stomachical, visceral

abduct carry off, kidnap, make off with, run away with, run off with, seize, snatch (*Sl.*)

abet **1.** aid, assist, back, condone, connive at, help, promote, sanction, second, succour, support, sus-

abeyance (əˈbeɪəns) *n.* condition of not being in use or action

abhor (əbˈhɔː) *vt.* dislike strongly, loathe **—abˈhorrence** *n.* **—abˈhorrent** *a.* hateful

abide (əˈbaɪd) *vt.* **1.** endure, put up with *—vi.* **2.** *obs.* stay, reside (**aˈbode** *or* **aˈbided** *pt./pp.*, **aˈbiding** *pr.p.*) **—abide by** obey

ability (əˈbɪlɪtɪ) *n.* **1.** competence, power **2.** talent

ab initio (æb ɪˈnɪʃɪəʊ) *Lat.* from the start

abject (ˈæbdʒɛkt) *a.* **1.** humiliated, wretched **2.** despicable **—abˈjection** *or* **ˈabjectness** *n.*

abjure (əbˈdʒʊə) *vt.* give up by oath, renounce **—abjuˈration** *n.*

ablation (æbˈleɪʃən) *n.* **1.** surgical removal of organ or part **2.** *Astrophysics* melting or wearing away of part **3.** wearing away of rock or glacier

ablative (ˈæblətɪv) *n.* case in (*esp.* Latin) nouns indicating source, agent, instrument of action

ablaut (ˈæblaʊt) *n.* vowel change within word, indicating modification of use, *eg sink, sank, sunk*

ablaze (əˈbleɪz) *a.* burning

able (ˈeɪbᵊl) *a.* capable, competent **—ˈably** *adv.* **—able-bodied** *a.* **—able-bodied seaman** seaman, *esp.* one in merchant navy, trained in certain skills (*also* **able seaman**)

-able (*a. comb. form*) **1.** capable of or deserving of (being acted upon as indicated), as in *enjoyable, washable* **2.** inclined to; able to; causing, as in *comfortable, variable* **—-ably** (*adv. comb. form*) **—-ability** (*n. comb. form*)

ablution (əˈbluːʃən) *n.* (*usu. pl.*) act of washing (oneself)

ABM antiballistic missile

abnegate (ˈæbnɪgeɪt) *vt.* give up, renounce **—abneˈgation** *n.*

abnormal (æbˈnɔːməl) *a.* **1.** irregular **2.** not usual or typical **3.** freakish, odd **—abnorˈmality** *n.* **—abˈnormally** *adv.*

aboard (əˈbɔːd) *adv.* on board, on ship, train or aircraft

abode (əˈbəʊd) *n.* **1.** home **2.** dwelling *—v.* **3.** *pt./pp. of* ABIDE

abolish (əˈbɒlɪʃ) *vt.* do away with **—aboˈlition** *n.* **—aboˈlitionist** *n.* one who wishes to do away with something, *esp.* slavery

A-bomb *n.* atomic bomb

abominate (əˈbɒmɪneɪt) *vt.* detest **—aˈbominable** *a.* **—aˈbominably** *adv.* **—abomiˈnation** *n.* **1.** loathing **2.** the object loathed **—abominable snowman** large legendary apelike creature said to inhabit the Himalayas

THESAURUS

tain, uphold **2.** egg on, encourage, incite, prompt, spur, urge

abeyance adjournment, deferral, discontinuation, inactivity, intermission, postponement, recess, reservation, suspense, suspension, waiting

abhor abominate, detest, execrate, hate, loathe, recoil from, regard with repugnance *or* horror, shrink from, shudder at

abhorrent abominable, detestable, disgusting, distasteful, execrable, hated, hateful, heinous, horrible, horrid, loathsome, obnoxious, odious, offensive, repellent, repugnant, repulsive, revolting

abide 1. accept, bear, brook, endure, put up with, stand, stomach, submit to, suffer, tolerate **2.** dwell, linger, live, lodge, reside, rest, sojourn, stay, stop, tarry, wait

abide by acknowledge, agree to, comply with, conform to, follow, obey, observe, submit to

ability adeptness, aptitude, capability, capacity, competence, competency, dexterity, endowment, energy, expertise, expertness, facility, faculty, flair, force, gift, knack, know-how (*Inf.*), potentiality, power, proficiency, qualification, skill, talent

abject 1. base, contemptible, cringing, debased, degraded, despicable, dishonourable, fawning, grovelling, humiliating, ignoble, ignominious, low, mean, servile, slavish, sordid, submissive, vile, worthless **2.** deplorable, forlorn, hopeless, miserable, outcast, pitiable, wretched

abjectness 1. abjection, baseness, contemptibleness, debasement, degradation, dishonour, humbleness, humiliation, ignominy, lowness, meanness, servility, slavishness, sordidness, submissiveness, vileness, worthlessness **2.** destitution, forlornness, hopelessness, misery, pitiableness, pitifulness, squalor, wretchedness

ablaze 1. afire, aflame, alight, blazing, burning, fiery, flaming, ignited, lighted, on fire **2.** aglow, brilliant, flashing, gleaming, glowing, illuminated, incandescent, luminous, radiant, sparkling

able accomplished, adept, adequate, adroit, capable, clever, competent, effective, efficient, experienced, expert, fit, fitted, gifted, highly endowed, masterful, masterly, powerful, practised, proficient, qualified, skilful, skilled, strong, talented

abnormal aberrant, anomalous, atypical, curious, deviant, eccentric, erratic, exceptional, extraordinary, irregular, monstrous, odd, peculiar, queer, singular, strange, uncommon, unexpected, unnatural, untypical, unusual, weird

abnormality aberration, anomaly, atypicalness, bizarreness, deformity, deviation, eccentricity, exception, extraordinariness, flaw, irregularity, monstrosity, oddity, peculiarity, queerness, singularity, strangeness, uncommonness, unexpectedness, unnaturalness, untypicalness, unusualness, weirdness

abolish abrogate, annihilate, annul, blot out, cancel, destroy, do away with, eliminate, end, eradicate, expunge, exterminate, extinguish, extirpate, invalidate, nullify, obliterate, overthrow, overturn, put an end to, quash, repeal, repudiate, rescind, revoke, stamp out, subvert, suppress, terminate, vitiate, void, wipe out

abolition abrogation, annihilation, annulment, blotting out, cancellation, destruction, elimination, end, ending, eradication, expunction, extermination, extinction, extirpation, invalidation, nullification, obliteration, overthrow, overturning, quashing, repeal, repudiation, rescission, revocation, stamping out, subversion, suppression, termination, vitiation, voiding, wiping out, withdrawal

abominable abhorrent, accursed, atrocious, base, contemptible, despicable, detestable, disgusting, execrable, foul, hateful, heinous, hellish, horrible, horrid, loathsome, nauseous, obnoxious, odious, repellent, reprehensible, repugnant, repulsive, revolting, terrible, vile, villainous, wretched

Aboriginal (æbəˈrɪdʒɪnᵊl) *a.* **1.** of, relating to the Aborigines of Aust. **2.** (**a-**) indigenous, earliest —*n.* **3.** Aborigine

Aborigine (æbəˈrɪdʒɪnɪ) *n.* **1.** one of race of people inhabiting Aust. when European settlers arrived **2.** (**a-**) original inhabitant of country *etc.*

abort (əˈbɔːt) *v.* **1.** (cause to) end prematurely (*esp.* pregnancy) —*vi.* **2.** give birth to dead foetus **3.** fail —**aˈbortion** *n.* **1.** operation to terminate pregnancy **2.** something deformed —**aˈbortionist** *n.* one who performs abortion, *esp.* illegally —**aˈbortive** *a.* unsuccessful —**aˈbortively** *adv.*

abound (əˈbaʊnd) *vi.* **1.** be plentiful **2.** overflow —**aˈbounding** *a.*

about (əˈbaʊt) *adv.* **1.** on all sides **2.** nearly **3.** up and down **4.** out, astir —*prep.* **5.** round **6.** near **7.** concerning —**about to** ready to —**about-turn** *n.* reversal, complete change

above (əˈbʌv) *adv.* **1.** higher up —*prep.* **2.** over **3.** higher than, more than **4.** beyond

abracadabra (æbrəkəˈdæbrə) *n.* supposedly magic word

abrade (əˈbreɪd) *vt.* rub off, scrape away

abrasion (əˈbreɪʒən) *n.* **1.** place scraped or worn by rubbing (*eg* on skin) **2.** scraping, rubbing —**aˈbrasive** *n.* **1.** substance for grinding, polishing *etc.* —*a.* **2.** causing abrasion **3.** grating

abreast (əˈbrɛst) *adv.* side by side —**abreast of** keeping up with

abridge (əˈbrɪdʒ) *vt.* cut short, abbreviate —**aˈbridgment** *or* **aˈbridgement** *n.*

abroad (əˈbrɔːd) *adv.* **1.** to or in a foreign country **2.** at large

abrogate (ˈæbrəʊgeɪt) *vt.* cancel, repeal —**abroˈgation** *n.*

abrupt (əˈbrʌpt) *a.* **1.** sudden **2.** blunt **3.** hasty **4.** steep —**aˈbruptly** *adv.* —**aˈbruptness** *n.*

abscess (ˈæbsɛs) *n.* gathering of pus in any part of the body

abscissa (æbˈsɪsə) *n. Maths.* distance of point from the axis of coordinates (*pl.* **-s, -sae** (-siː))

abscond (əbˈskɒnd) *vi.* leave secretly, *esp.* having stolen something

abseil (ˈæbsaɪl) *vi.* descend vertical slope by means of rope

absent (ˈæbsənt) *a.* **1.** away **2.** not attentive —*v.refl.* (æbˈsɛnt) **3.** keep away —**ˈabsence** *n.* —**absenˈtee** *n.* one who stays away, *esp.* habitually —**absenˈteeism** *n.* persistent absence from work *etc.* —**ˈabsently** *adv.* —**absent-minded** *a.*

THESAURUS

abominate abhor, detest, execrate, hate, loathe, recoil from, regard with repugnance, shudder at

abomination 1. abhorrence, antipathy, aversion, detestation, disgust, distaste, execration, hate, hatred, horror, loathing, odium, repugnance, revulsion 2. anathema, *bête noire,* bugbear, curse, disgrace, evil, horror, plague, shame, torment

aboriginal ancient, autochthonous, earliest, first, indigenous, native, original, primary, primeval, primitive, primordial, pristine

abound be jammed with, be packed with, be plentiful, crowd, flourish, increase, infest, luxuriate, overflow, proliferate, superabound, swarm, swell, teem, thrive

abounding abundant, bountiful, copious, filled, flourishing, flowing, flush, full, lavish, luxuriant, overflowing, plenteous, plentiful, profuse, prolific, rank, replete, rich, superabundant, teeming

about *prep.* 1. anent (*Scot.*), as regards, concerned with, concerning, connected with, dealing with, on, re, referring to, regarding, relating to, relative to, respecting, touching, with respect to 2. adjacent, beside, circa (*used with dates*), close to, near, nearby 3. around, encircling, on all sides, round, surrounding ~*adv.* 4. almost, approaching, approximately, around, close to, more or less, nearing, nearly, roughly 5. from place to place, here and there, hither and thither, to and fro

about to intending to, on the point of, on the verge *or* brink of, ready to

above 1. *prep.* atop, beyond, exceeding, higher than, on top of, over, upon 2. *adv.* atop, in heaven, on high, overhead

abrasion 1. *Medical* chafe, graze, scrape, scratch, scuff, surface injury 2. abrading, chafing, erosion, friction, grating, rubbing, scouring, scraping, scratching, scuffing, wearing away, wearing down

abrasive *adj.* 1. chafing, erosive, frictional, grating, rough, scraping, scratching, scratchy, scuffing 2. annoying, biting, caustic, cutting, galling, grating, hurtful, irritating, nasty, rough, sharp, unpleasant ~*n.* 3. abradant, burnisher, grinder, scarifier, scourer

abreast 1. alongside, beside, level, shoulder to shoulder, side by side 2. **abreast of** acquainted, *au courant, au fait,* conversant, familiar, informed, in touch, knowledgeable, up to date

abridge abbreviate, abstract, clip, compress, concentrate, condense, contract, curtail, cut, cut down, decrease, digest, diminish, epitomize, lessen, précis, reduce, shorten, summarize, synopsize (*U.S.*), trim

abridgment abbreviation, abstract, compendium, condensation, conspectus, contraction, curtailment, cutting, decrease, digest, diminishing, diminution, epitome, lessening, limitation, outline, précis, reduction, restraint, restriction, résumé, shortening, summary, synopsis

abroad 1. beyond the sea, in foreign lands, out of the country, overseas 2. about, at large, away, circulating, current, elsewhere, extensively, far, far and wide, forth, in circulation, out, out-of-doors, outside, publicly, widely, without

abrupt 1. blunt, brisk, brusque, curt, direct, discourteous, gruff, impolite, rough, rude, short, snappish, snappy, terse, unceremonious, uncivil, ungracious 2. precipitous, sharp, sheer, steep, sudden 3. hasty, headlong, hurried, precipitate, quick, sudden, surprising, swift, unanticipated, unexpected, unforeseen

abscond bolt, clear out, decamp, disappear, do a bunk (*Sl.*), escape, flee, flit (*Inf.*), fly, make off, run off, slip away, sneak away, steal away

absence 1. absenteeism, nonappearance, nonattendance, truancy 2. absent-mindedness, abstraction, distraction, inattention, preoccupation, reverie

absent *adj.* 1. away, elsewhere, gone, lacking, missing, nonattendant, nonexistent, not present, out, truant, unavailable, wanting 2. absent-minded, ab-

absinthe *or* **absinth** (ˈæbsɪnθ) *n.* potent aniseed-flavoured liqueur

absolute (ˈæbsəluːt) *a.* **1.** complete **2.** not limited, unconditional **3.** pure (as **absolute alcohol**) —*n.* **4.** something that is absolute —**absoˈlutely** *adv.* **1.** completely —*interj.* **2.** certainly —**ˈabsoluteness** *n.* —**ˈabsolutism** *n.* political system in which unrestricted power is vested in dictator *etc.*; despotism —**ˈabsolutist** *n.* —**absolute zero** lowest temperature theoretically attainable

absolve (əbˈzɒlv) *vt.* free, pardon, acquit —**absolution** (æbsəˈluːʃən) *n.*

absorb (əbˈsɔːb) *vt.* **1.** suck up, drink in **2.** engage, occupy (attention *etc.*) **3.** receive (impact) —**abˈsorbent** *a.* —**abˈsorption** *n.* —**abˈsorptive** *a.*

abstain (əbˈsteɪn) *vi.* (*usu. with* from) keep (from), refrain (from drinking alcohol, voting *etc.*) —**abˈstainer** *n.* —**abstention** (əbˈstɛnʃən) *n.* —**abstinence** (ˈæbstɪnəns) *n.* —**abstinent** (ˈæbstɪnənt) *a.*

abstemious (əbˈstiːmɪəs) *a.* sparing in food or *esp.* drink, temperate —**abˈstemiously** *adv.* —**abˈstemiousness** *n.*

abstract (ˈæbstrækt) *a.* **1.** existing only in the mind **2.** not concrete **3.** not representational —*n.* **4.** summary, abridgment —*vt.* (æbˈstrækt) **5.** draw (from), remove **6.** deduct —**abˈstracted** *a.* preoccupied —**abˈstraction** *n.* —**ˈabstractly** *adv.*

abstruse (əbˈstruːs) *a.* obscure, difficult to understand, profound —**abˈstrusely** *adv.*

absurd (əbˈsɜːd) *a.* contrary to reason —**abˈsurdity** *n.* —**abˈsurdly** *adv.*

abundance (əˈbʌndəns) *n.* great amount —**aˈbundant** *a.* plentiful —**aˈbundantly** *adv.*

THESAURUS

sorbed, abstracted, bemused, blank, daydreaming, distracted, dreamy, empty, faraway, heedless, inattentive, musing, oblivious, preoccupied, unaware, unconscious, unheeding, unthinking, vacant, vague ~*v.* **3. absent oneself** abscond, depart, keep away, play truant, remove, stay away, truant, withdraw

absently absent-mindedly, abstractedly, bemusedly, blankly, distractedly, dreamily, emptily, heedlessly, inattentively, obliviously, unconsciously, unheedingly, vacantly, vaguely

absent-minded absent, absorbed, abstracted, bemused, distracted, dreaming, dreamy, engrossed, faraway, forgetful, heedless, in a brown study, inattentive, musing, oblivious, preoccupied, unaware, unconscious, unheeding, unthinking

absolute 1. complete, consummate, downright, entire, out-and-out, outright, perfect, pure, sheer, thorough, total, unadulterated, unalloyed, unmitigated, unmixed, unqualified, utter **2.** absolutist, arbitrary, autarchical, autocratic, autonomous, despotic, dictatorial, full, peremptory, sovereign, supreme, tyrannical, unbounded, unconditional, unlimited, unqualified, unquestionable, unrestrained, unrestricted

absolutely completely, consummately, entirely, fully, perfectly, purely, thoroughly, totally, unmitigatedly, utterly, wholly

absoluteness 1. consummateness, entirety, perfection, purity, thoroughness, totality, unmitigatedness, wholeness **2.** arbitrariness, autonomy, despotism, dictatorialness, fullness, peremptoriness, supremacy, tyranny, unboundedness, unquestionability, unrestrainedness, unrestrictedness

absolution acquittal, amnesty, deliverance, discharge, dispensation, exculpation, exemption, exoneration, forgiveness, freeing, indulgence, liberation, mercy, pardon, release, remission, setting free, shriving, vindication

absolutism absoluteness, arbitrariness, autarchy, authoritarianism, autocracy, despotism, dictatorship, totalitarianism, tyranny

absolutist arbiter, authoritarian, autocrat, despot, dictator, totalitarian, tyrant

absolve acquit, clear, deliver, discharge, exculpate, excuse, exempt, exonerate, forgive, free, let off, liberate, loose, pardon, release, remit, set free, shrive, vindicate

absorb 1. assimilate, consume, devour, digest, drink in, exhaust, imbibe, incorporate, ingest, osmose, receive, soak up, suck up, take in **2.** captivate, engage, engross, enwrap, fascinate, fill, fill up, fix, hold, immerse, monopolize, occupy, preoccupy, rivet

abstain avoid, cease, decline, deny (oneself), desist, forbear, forgo, give up, keep from, refrain, refuse, renounce, shun, stop, withhold

abstemious abstinent, ascetic, austere, continent, frugal, moderate, self-denying, sober, sparing, temperate

abstinence abstemiousness, asceticism, avoidance, continence, forbearance, moderation, refraining, self-denial, self-restraint, soberness, sobriety, teetotalism, temperance

abstinent abstaining, abstemious, continent, forbearing, moderate, self-controlled, self-denying, self-restraining, sober, temperate

abstract 1. *adj.* abstruse, arcane, complex, conceptual, deep, general, generalized, hypothetical, indefinite, intellectual, nonconcrete, occult, philosophical, profound, recondite, separate, subtle, theoretic, theoretical, unpractical, unrealistic **2.** *n.* abridgment, compendium, condensation, digest, epitome, essence, outline, précis, recapitulation, résumé, summary, synopsis **3.** *v.* detach, dissociate, extract, isolate, remove, separate, steal, take away, take out, withdraw

abstracted absent, absent-minded, bemused, daydreaming, dreamy, faraway, inattentive, preoccupied, remote, withdrawn, woolgathering

abstruse abstract, arcane, complex, dark, deep, enigmatic, esoteric, hidden, incomprehensible, mysterious, mystical, obscure, occult, perplexing, profound, puzzling, recondite, subtle, unfathomable, vague

absurd crazy (*Inf.*), daft (*Inf.*), farcical, foolish, idiotic, illogical, incongruous, irrational, laughable, ludicrous, meaningless, nonsensical, preposterous, ridiculous, senseless, silly, stupid, unreasonable

absurdity craziness (*Inf.*), daftness (*Inf.*), farce, farcicality, farcicalness, folly, foolishness, idiocy, illogicality, illogicalness, incongruity, irrationality, joke, ludicrousness, meaninglessness, nonsense, preposterousness, ridiculousness, senselessness, silliness, stupidity, unreasonableness

abundance affluence, ampleness, bounty, copiousness, exuberance, fullness, heap (*Inf.*), plenitude, plenteousness, plenty, profusion

abundant ample, bounteous, bountiful, copious, exu-

abuse (əˈbju:z) *vt.* **1.** misuse **2.** address rudely —*n.* (əˈbju:s) **3.** improper use **4.** insulting speech —**aˈbusive** *a.* —**aˈbusively** *adv.* —**aˈbusiveness** *n.*

abut (əˈbʌt) *vi.* adjoin, border (on) (-tt-) —**aˈbutment** *n.* support, *esp.* of bridge or arch

abuzz (əˈbʌz) *a.* noisy, busy with activity *etc.*

abysmal (əˈbɪzməl) *a.* **1.** immeasurable, very great **2.** *inf.* extremely bad —**aˈbysmally** *adv.*

abyss (əˈbɪs) *n.* very deep gulf or pit

Ac *Chem.* actinium

AC 1. aircraftman **2.** alternating current

a/c account

acacia (əˈkeɪʃə) *n.* gum-yielding tree or shrub

academy (əˈkædəmɪ) *n.* **1.** society to advance arts or sciences **2.** institution for specialized training **3.** secondary school —**acaˈdemic** *a.* **1.** of academy **2.** belonging to University *etc.* **3.** theoretical —**acaˈdemically** *adv.* —**acadeˈmician** *n.*

acanthus (əˈkænθəs) *n.* **1.** prickly plant **2.** architectural ornament like leaf of acanthus plant (*pl.* **-es, -thi** (-θaɪ))

ACAS (ˈeɪkæs) Advisory Conciliation and Arbitration Service

acc. 1. accompanied **2.** account **3.** accusative

accede (ækˈsi:d) *vi.* (*usu. with* to) **1.** agree, consent **2.** attain (office, right *etc.*)

accelerando (æksɛləˈrændəʊ) *a./adv. Mus.* becoming faster

accelerate (ækˈsɛləreɪt) *v.* (cause to) increase speed, hasten —**acceleˈration** *n.* —**acˈcelerative** *a.* —**acˈcelerator** *n.* mechanism to increase speed, *esp.* in car

accent (ˈæksənt) *n.* **1.** stress or pitch in speaking **2.** mark to show such stress **3.** local or national style of pronunciation **4.** particular attention or emphasis —*vt.* (ækˈsɛnt) **5.** stress **6.** mark with accent

accentor (ækˈsɛntə) *n.* sparrowlike songbird

accentuate (ækˈsɛntʃʊeɪt) *vt.* stress, emphasize —**acˈcentual** *a.* —**accentuˈation** *n.*

accept (əkˈsɛpt) *vt.* **1.** take, receive **2.** admit, believe **3.** agree to —**acceptaˈbility** *n.* —**acˈceptable** *a.* —**acˈceptably** *adv.* —**acˈceptance** *n.* —**accepˈtation** *n.* common or accepted meaning of word *etc.* —**acˈcepter** *n.* —**acˈceptor** *n.* **1.** *Comm.* person or organization on which bill of exchange is drawn **2.** *Electron.* impurity added to semiconductor to increase its p-type conductivity

access (ˈæksɛs) *n.* **1.** act, right or means of entry —*vt. Comp.* **2.** obtain or retrieve (information) from storage device **3.** place (information) in storage device —**accessiˈbility** *n.* —**acˈcessible** *a.* easy to approach —**acˈcessibly** *adv.* —**access time** *Comp.* time required to retrieve stored information

accessary (əkˈsɛsərɪ) *see* ACCESSORY

THESAURUS

berant, filled, full, lavish, luxuriant, overflowing, plenteous, plentiful, profuse, rank, rich, teeming, well-provided, well-supplied

abuse *v.* **1.** damage, exploit, harm, hurt, ill-treat, impose upon, injure, maltreat, manhandle, mar, misapply, misuse, oppress, spoil, take advantage of, wrong **2.** calumniate, castigate, curse, defame, disparage, insult, inveigh against, libel, malign, revile, scold, slander, smear, swear at, traduce, upbraid, vilify, vituperate ~*n.* **3.** damage, exploitation, harm, hurt, ill-treatment, imposition, injury, maltreatment, manhandling, misapplication, misuse, oppression, spoiling, wrong **4.** blame, calumniation, castigation, censure, contumely, curses, cursing, defamation, derision, disparagement, insults, invective, libel, opprobrium, reproach, revilement, scolding, slander, swearing, tirade, traducement, upbraiding, vilification, vituperation

abusive calumniating, castigating, censorious, contumelious, defamatory, derisive, disparaging, insulting, invective, libellous, maligning, offensive, opprobrious, reproachful, reviling, rude, scathing, scolding, slanderous, traducing, upbraiding, vilifying, vituperative

abysmal bottomless, boundless, complete, deep, endless, extreme, immeasurable, incalculable, infinite, profound, thorough, unending, unfathomable, vast

abyss abysm, bottomless depth, chasm, crevasse, fissure, gorge, gulf, pit, void

academic *adj.* **1.** bookish, campus, college, collegiate, erudite, highbrow, learned, lettered, literary, scholarly, scholastic, school, studious, university **2.** abstract, conjectural, hypothetical, impractical, notional, speculative, theoretical

accede 1. accept, acquiesce, admit, agree, assent, comply, concede, concur, consent, endorse, grant, yield **2.** assume, attain, come to, enter upon, inherit, succeed, succeed to (*as heir*)

accelerate advance, expedite, forward, further, hasten, hurry, pick up speed, precipitate, quicken, speed, speed up, spur, step up (*Inf.*), stimulate

acceleration expedition, hastening, hurrying, quickening, speeding up, spurring, stepping up (*Inf.*), stimulation

accent *n.* **1.** beat, cadence, emphasis, force, pitch, rhythm, stress, timbre, tonality **2.** articulation, enunciation, inflection, intonation, modulation, pronunciation, tone ~*v.* **3.** accentuate, emphasize, stress, underline, underscore

accentuate accent, draw attention to, emphasize, highlight, stress, underline, underscore

accept 1. acquire, gain, get, have, obtain, receive, secure, take **2.** accede, acknowledge, acquiesce, admit, adopt, affirm, agree to, approve, believe, concur with, consent to, cooperate with, recognize, swallow (*Inf.*) **3.** bear, bow to, brook, defer to, put up with, stand, submit to, suffer, take, yield to **4.** acknowledge, admit, assume, avow, bear, take on, undertake

acceptance 1. accepting, acquiring, gaining, getting, having, obtaining, receipt, securing, taking **2.** accedence, accession, acknowledgment, acquiescence, admission, adoption, affirmation, agreement, approbation, approval, assent, belief, compliance, concession, concurrence, consent, cooperation, credence, O.K. (*Inf.*), permission, recognition, stamp *or* seal of approval **3.** deference, standing, submission, taking, yielding **4.** acknowledgment, admission, assumption, avowal, taking on, undertaking

access admission, admittance, approach, avenue, course, door, entering, entrance, entrée, entry, gateway, key, passage, passageway, path, road

accessibility approachability, attainability, availability, handiness, nearness, obtainability, possibility, readiness

accessible achievable, at hand, attainable, available,

accession (əkˈsɛʃən) *n.* **1.** attaining of office, right *etc.* **2.** increase, addition

accessory (əkˈsɛsərɪ) *n.* **1.** additional or supplementary part of motorcar, woman's dress *etc.* **2.** person inciting or assisting in crime *—a.* **3.** contributory, assisting

accidence (ˈæksɪdəns) *n.* the part of grammar dealing with changes in the form of words

accident (ˈæksɪdənt) *n.* **1.** event happening by chance **2.** misfortune or mishap, *esp.* causing injury **3.** nonessential quality **—acciˈdental** *a.* **—acciˈdentally** *adv.*

acclaim (əˈkleɪm) *vt.* **1.** applaud, praise *—n.* **2.** applause **—acclamation** (ækləˈmeɪʃən) *n.* **—acclamatory** (əˈklæmətərɪ) *a.*

acclimatize *or* **-tise** (əˈklaɪmətaɪz) *vt.* accustom to new climate or environment **—acclimatiˈzation** *or* **-tiˈsation** *n.*

accolade (ˈækəleɪd) *n.* **1.** praise, public approval **2.** award, honour **3.** token of award of knighthood

accommodate (əˈkɒmədeɪt) *vt.* **1.** supply, *esp.* with board and lodging **2.** oblige **3.** harmonize, adapt **—acˈcommodating** *a.* obliging **—accommoˈdation** *n.* **1.** lodgings **2.** agreement **3.** adjustment of lens of eye **4.** loan **—accommodation address** address on letters *etc.* that is not permanent or actual address

accompany (əˈkʌmpənɪ) *vt.* **1.** go with **2.** supplement **3.** occur with **4.** provide a musical accompaniment for (**-panied, -panying**) **—acˈcompaniment** *n.* that which accompanies, *esp.* in music, part which goes with solos *etc.* **—acˈcompanist** *n.*

accomplice (əˈkɒmplɪs, əˈkʌm-) *n.* one assisting another in criminal deed

accomplish (əˈkɒmplɪʃ, əˈkʌm-) *vt.* **1.** carry out **2.** finish **—acˈcomplished** *a.* **1.** complete, perfect **2.** proficient **—acˈcomplishment** *n.* **1.** completion **2.** personal ability

accord (əˈkɔːd) *n.* **1.** agreement, harmony (*esp. in* **in accord with**) *—v.* **2.** (cause to) be in accord *—vt.* **3.** grant **—acˈcordance** *n.* **—acˈcordant** *a.* **—acˈcordingly** *adv.* **1.** as the circumstances suggest **2.** therefore **—according to 1.** in proportion to **2.** as stated by **3.** in conformity with

THESAURUS

get-at-able (*Inf.*), handy, near, nearby, obtainable, on hand, possible, reachable, ready

accessory *n.* **1.** abettor, accomplice, assistant, associate (*in crime*), colleague, confederate, helper, partner **2.** accent, accompaniment, addition, adjunct, adornment, aid, appendage, attachment, component, convenience, decoration, extension, extra, frill, help, supplement, trim, trimming *~adj.* **3.** abetting, additional, aiding, ancillary, assisting in, auxiliary, contributory, extra, secondary, subordinate, supplemental, supplementary

accident 1. blow, calamity, casualty, chance, collision, crash, disaster, misadventure, mischance, misfortune, mishap, pile-up **2.** chance, fate, fluke, fortuity, fortune, hazard, luck

accidental adventitious, casual, chance, contingent, fortuitous, haphazard, inadvertent, incidental, inessential, nonessential, random, uncalculated, uncertain, unessential, unexpected, unforeseen, unintended, unintentional, unlooked-for, unplanned, unpremeditated, unwitting

accidentally adventitiously, by accident, by chance, by mistake, casually, fortuitously, haphazardly, inadvertently, incidentally, randomly, unconsciously, undesignedly, unexpectedly, unintentionally, unwittingly

acclaim 1. *v.* applaud, approve, celebrate, cheer, clap, commend, eulogize, exalt, extol, hail, honour, laud, praise, salute, welcome **2.** *n.* acclamation, applause, approbation, approval, celebration, cheering, clapping, commendation, eulogizing, exaltation, honour, laudation, plaudits, praise, welcome

acclamation acclaim, adulation, approbation, cheer, cheering, cheers, enthusiasm, laudation, loud homage, ovation, plaudit, praise, salutation, shouting, tribute

acclimatization acclimation, accommodation, acculturation, adaptation, adjustment, habituation, inurement, naturalization

acclimatize accommodate, acculture, accustom, adapt, adjust, become seasoned to, get used to, habituate, inure, naturalize

accommodate 1. billet, board, cater for, entertain, harbour, house, lodge, put up, quarter, shelter **2.** afford, aid, assist, furnish, help, oblige, provide, serve, supply **3.** accustom, adapt, adjust, comply, compose, conform, fit, harmonize, modify, reconcile, settle

accommodating complaisant, considerate, cooperative, friendly, helpful, hospitable, kind, obliging, polite, unselfish, willing

accommodation 1. adaptation, adjustment, compliance, composition, compromise, conformity, fitting, harmony, modification, reconciliation, settlement **2.** board, digs (*Inf.*), harbouring, house, housing, lodging(s), quartering, quarters, shelter, sheltering

accompany 1. attend, chaperon, conduct, convoy, escort, go with, squire, usher **2.** belong to, coexist with, coincide with, come with, follow, go together with, join with, occur with, supplement

accompanying accessory, added, additional, appended, associate, associated, attached, attendant, complementary, concomitant, concurrent, connected, fellow, joint, related, supplemental, supplementary

accomplice abettor, accessory, ally, assistant, associate, coadjutor, collaborator, colleague, confederate, helper, henchman, partner

accomplish achieve, attain, bring about, bring off (*Inf.*), carry out, complete, conclude, consummate, do, effect, effectuate, execute, finish, fulfil, manage, perform, produce, realize

accomplished 1. achieved, attained, brought about, carried out, completed, concluded, consummated, done, effected, executed, finished, fulfilled, managed, performed, produced, realized **2.** adept, consummate, cultivated, expert, gifted, masterly, polished, practised, proficient, skilful, skilled, talented

accomplishment 1. achievement, attainment, bringing about, carrying out, completion, conclusion, consummation, doing, effecting, execution, finishing, fulfilment, management, performance, production, realization **2.** ability, achievement, art, attainment, capability, gift, proficiency, skill, talent

accord *v.* **1.** agree, assent, be in tune (*Inf.*), concur, conform, correspond, fit, harmonize, match, suit, tally **2.** allow, bestow, concede, confer, endow, give, grant, present, render, tender, vouchsafe *~n.* **3.**

accordion (əˈkɔːdiən) *n.* portable musical instrument with keys, metal reeds and a bellows —**acˈcordionist** *n.* —**piano accordion** accordion in which right hand plays piano-like keyboard

accost (əˈkɒst) *vt.* approach and speak to, ask question *etc.*

account (əˈkaʊnt) *n.* **1.** report, description **2.** importance, value **3.** statement of moneys received, paid or owed **4.** person's money held in bank **5.** credit available to person at store *etc.* —*vt.* **6.** reckon **7.** judge —*vi.* **8.** give reason, answer (for) —**accountaˈbility** *n.* —**acˈcountable** *a.* responsible —**acˈcountancy** *n.* keeping, preparation of business accounts, financial records *etc.* —**acˈcountant** *n.* one practising accountancy —**acˈcounting** *n.* skill or practice of keeping and preparing business accounts

accoutre *or U.S.* **accouter** (əˈkuːtə) *vt.* equip —**accoutrements** *or U.S.* **accouterments** (əˈkuːtrəmənts, əˈkuːtər-) *pl.n.* **1.** equipment, *esp.* military **2.** trappings

accredit (əˈkrɛdɪt) *vt.* **1.** ascribe, attribute **2.** give official recognition to **3.** certify as meeting required standards **4.** (*oft. with* at, to) send (envoy *etc.*) with official credentials; appoint as envoy *etc.* **5.** believe —**acˈcredited** *a.*

accretion (əˈkriːʃən) *n.* **1.** growth **2.** something added on

accrue (əˈkruː) *vi.* **1.** be added **2.** result

acct. account

acculturate (əˈkʌltʃəreɪt) *vi.* assimilate traits of another cultural group —**acculturˈation** *n.*

accumulate (əˈkjuːmjʊleɪt) *v.* **1.** gather, become gathered in increasing quantity **2.** collect —**accumuˈlation** *n.* —**acˈcumulator** *n.* type of rechargeable battery, as in car

accurate (ˈækjərɪt) *a.* exact, correct, without errors —**ˈaccuracy** *n.* —**ˈaccurately** *adv.*

accursed (əˈkɜːsɪd, əˈkɜːst) *or* **accurst** (əˈkɜːst) *a.* **1.** under a curse **2.** hateful, detestable

accuse (əˈkjuːz) *vt.* **1.** charge with wrongdoing **2.** blame —**accuˈsation** *n.* —**acˈcusative** *n.* grammatical case indicating the direct object —**acˈcusatory** *a.* —**acˈcuser** *n.*

accustom (əˈkʌstəm) *vt.* make used (to), familiarize —**acˈcustomed** *a.* **1.** usual **2.** used (to) **3.** in the habit (of)

THESAURUS

accordance, agreement, concert, concurrence, conformity, congruence, correspondence, harmony, rapport, sympathy, unanimity

accordance **1.** accord, agreement, assent, concert, concurrence, conformity, congruence, correspondence, harmony, rapport, sympathy, unanimity **2.** according, allowance, bestowal, concession, conferment, conferral, endowment, gift, giving, granting, presentation, rendering, tendering

accordingly **1.** appropriately, correspondingly, fitly, properly, suitably **2.** as a result, consequently, ergo, hence, in consequence, so, therefore, thus

according to **1.** commensurate with, in proportion, in relation **2.** as believed by, as maintained by, as stated by, in the light of, on the authority of, on the report of **3.** after, after the manner of, consistent with, in accordance with, in compliance with, in conformity with, in harmony with, in keeping with, in line with, in obedience to, in step with, in the manner of, obedient to

account *n.* **1.** chronicle, description, detail, explanation, history, narration, narrative, recital, record, relation, report, statement, story, tale, version **2.** *Commerce* balance, bill, book, books, charge, computation, inventory, invoice, ledger, reckoning, register, score, statement, tally **3.** advantage, benefit, consequence, distinction, esteem, honour, import, importance, merit, note, profit, rank, repute, significance, standing, use, value, worth ~*v.* **4.** appraise, assess, believe, calculate, compute, consider, count, deem, esteem, estimate, explain, gauge, hold, judge, rate, reckon, regard, think, value, weigh

accountability answerability, chargeability, culpability, liability, responsibility

accountable amenable, answerable, charged with, liable, obligated, obliged, responsible

account for answer for, clarify, clear up, elucidate, explain, illuminate, justify, rationalize

accredit **1.** appoint, authorize, certify, commission, depute, empower, endorse, entrust, guarantee, license, recognize, sanction, vouch for **2.** ascribe, assign, attribute, credit

accredited appointed, authorized, certified, commissioned, deputed, deputized, empowered, endorsed, guaranteed, licensed, official, recognized, sanctioned, vouched for

accrue accumulate, amass, arise, be added, build up, collect, enlarge, ensue, flow, follow, grow, increase, issue, spring up

accumulate accrue, amass, build up, collect, cumulate, gather, grow, hoard, increase, pile up, stockpile, store

accumulation aggregation, augmentation, build-up, collection, conglomeration, gathering, growth, heap, hoard, increase, mass, pile, stack, stock, stockpile, store

accuracy accurateness, authenticity, carefulness, closeness, correctness, exactitude, exactness, faithfulness, faultlessness, fidelity, meticulousness, niceness, nicety, precision, strictness, truth, truthfulness, veracity, verity

accurate authentic, careful, close, correct, exact, faithful, faultless, just, meticulous, nice, precise, proper, regular, right, scrupulous, spot-on (*Inf.*), strict, true, truthful, unerring, veracious

accurately authentically, carefully, closely, correctly, exactly, faithfully, faultlessly, justly, meticulously, nicely, precisely, properly, regularly, rightly, scrupulously, strictly, truly, truthfully, unerringly, veraciously

accursed **1.** bedevilled, bewitched, condemned, cursed, damned, doomed, hopeless, ill-fated, ill-omened, jinxed, luckless, ruined, undone, unfortunate, unlucky, wretched **2.** abominable, despicable, detestable, execrable, hateful, hellish, horrible

accusation allegation, arraignment, attribution, charge, citation, complaint, denunciation, impeachment, imputation, incrimination, indictment, recrimination

accuse allege, arraign, attribute, blame, censure,

ace (eɪs) *n.* **1.** the one at dice, cards, dominoes **2.** *Tennis* winning serve, *esp.* one untouched by opponent **3.** very successful fighter pilot **4.** *inf.* person expert at anything —*a.* **5.** *inf.* excellent

-aceous (*comb. form*) relating to, having the nature of, or resembling, as in *herbaceous*

acerbate (ˈæsəbeɪt) *vt.* **1.** make worse **2.** make sour, bitter —**aˈcerbity** *n.* **1.** severity, sharpness **2.** sourness, bitterness

acetaldehyde (æsɪˈtældɪhaɪd) *n.* colourless volatile pungent liquid used as solvent

acetate (ˈæsɪteɪt) *n.* salt of acetic acid —**acetate rayon** synthetic textile fibre

acetic (əˈsiːtɪk) *a.* derived from or having the nature of vinegar —**acetic acid** colourless pungent liquid used in manufacture of plastics *etc.* (*see also* VINEGAR)

aceto- *or before vowel* **acet-** (*comb. form*) containing acetyl group or derived from acetic acid, as in *acetone*

acetone (ˈæsɪtəʊn) *n.* colourless liquid used as solvent

acetylene (əˈsetɪliːn) *n.* colourless, flammable gas used *esp.* in welding metals

acetylsalicylic acid (æsɪtaɪlsælɪˈsɪlɪk) *Chem.* aspirin

ache (eɪk) *n.* **1.** continuous pain —*vi.* **2.** be painful **3.** be in pain —**ˈaching** *a.*

achieve (əˈtʃiːv) *vt.* **1.** accomplish, perform successfully **2.** gain —**aˈchievement** *n.* something accomplished

Achilles heel (əˈkɪliːz) small but fatal weakness

Achilles tendon fibrous cord that connects muscles of calf to heelbone

achromatic (ækrəˈmætɪk) *a.* free from or not showing colour, as of a lens, colourless

acid (ˈæsɪd) *a.* **1.** sharp, sour —*n.* **2.** sour substance **3.** *Chem.* one of a class of compounds which combines with bases (alkalis, oxides *etc.*) to form salts —**aˈcidic** *a.* —**aˈcidify** *v.* (**-fied, -fying**) —**aˈcidity** *n.* —**aˈcidulate** *vt.* make slightly acid —**aˈcidulous** *a.* —**acid rain** rain acidified by atmospheric pollution —**acid test** conclusive test of value

ack-ack (ˈækæk) *n.* anti-aircraft guns or gunfire

acknowledge (əkˈnɒlɪdʒ) *vt.* **1.** admit, own, recognize **2.** say one has received —**acˈknowledgment** *or* **acˈknowledgement** *n.*

aclinic (əˈklɪnɪk) *a.* without inclination, said of the magnetic equator, on which the magnetic needle has no dip

acme (ˈækmɪ) *n.* highest point

acne (ˈæknɪ) *n.* pimply skin disease

acolyte (ˈækəlaɪt) *n.* follower or attendant, *esp.* of priest

aconite (ˈækənaɪt) *n.* **1.** genus of plants related to the buttercup, including monkshood **2.** drug, poison obtained from such

acorn (ˈeɪkɔːn) *n.* nut or fruit of the oak tree

acoustic (əˈkuːstɪk) *or* **acoustical** *a.* pert. to sound and to hearing —**aˈcoustics** *pl.n.* **1.** (*with sing. v.*) science of sound **2.** features of room or building as regards sounds heard within it

acquaint (əˈkweɪnt) *vt.* make familiar, inform —**acˈquaintance** *n.* **1.** person known **2.** personal knowledge —**acˈquaintanceship** *n.*

acquiesce (ækwɪˈɛs) *vi.* agree, consent without complaint —**acquiˈescence** *n.* —**acquiˈescent** *a.*

acquire (əˈkwaɪə) *vt.* gain, get —**acˈquirement** *n.*

THESAURUS

charge, cite, denounce, impeach, impute, incriminate, indict, recriminate, tax

accustom acclimatize, acquaint, adapt, discipline, exercise, familiarize, habituate, inure, season, train

accustomed 1. acclimatized, acquainted, adapted, disciplined, exercised, familiar, familiarized, given to, habituated, in the habit of, inured, seasoned, trained, used 2. common, conventional, customary, established, everyday, expected, fixed, general, habitual, normal, ordinary, regular, routine, set, traditional, usual, wonted

ace *n.* 1. *Cards, dice, etc.* one, single point 2. *Inf.* adept, champion, dab hand (*Inf.*), expert, genius, master, star, virtuoso, winner, wizard (*Inf.*) ~*adj.* 3. *Inf.* brilliant, champion, excellent, expert, fine, great, masterly, outstanding, superb, virtuoso

ache 1. *v.* hurt, pain, pound, smart, suffer, throb, twinge 2. *n.* hurt, pain, pang, pounding, smart, smarting, soreness, suffering, throb, throbbing

achieve accomplish, acquire, attain, bring about, carry out, complete, consummate, do, earn, effect, execute, finish, fulfil, gain, get, obtain, perform, procure, reach, realize, win

achievement 1. accomplishment, acquirement, attainment, completion, execution, fulfilment, performance, production, realization 2. accomplishment, act, deed, effort, exploit, feat, stroke

acid acerbic, acidulous, acrid, biting, pungent, sharp, sour, tart, vinegarish, vinegary

acidity acerbity, acidulousness, acridity, acridness, bitterness, pungency, sharpness, sourness, tartness, vinegariness, vinegarishness

acknowledge 1. accede, accept, acquiesce, admit, allow, concede, confess, declare, grant, own, profess, recognize, yield 2. address, greet, hail, notice, recognize, salute 3. answer, notice, react to, recognize, reply to, respond to, return

acknowledgment 1. acceptance, accession, acquiescence, admission, allowing, confession, declaration, profession, realization, yielding 2. addressing, greeting, hail, hailing, notice, recognition, salutation, salute 3. answer, appreciation, credit, gratitude, reaction, recognition, reply, response, return, thanks

acme apex, climax, crown, culmination, height, high point, optimum, peak, pinnacle, summit, top, vertex, zenith

acquaint advise, announce, apprise, disclose, divulge, enlighten, familiarize, inform, let (someone) know, notify, reveal, tell

acquaintance 1. associate, colleague, contact 2. association, awareness, cognizance, companionship, conversance, conversancy, experience, familiarity, fellowship, intimacy, knowledge, relationship, social contact, understanding

acquiesce accede, accept, agree, allow, approve, assent, bow to, comply, concur, conform, consent, give in, go along with, submit, yield

acquiescence acceptance, accession, agreement, approval, assent, compliance, concurrence, conformity, consent, giving in, obedience, submission, yielding

—**acquisition** (ækwɪˈzɪʃən) *n.* **1.** act of getting **2.** material gain —**acquisitive** (əˈkwɪzɪtɪv) *a.* desirous of gaining —**acquisitiveness** (əˈkwɪzɪtɪvnɪs) *n.* —**acquired immuno-deficiency syndrome** disease that breaks down the body's natural immunity, oft. resulting in fatal infection

acquit (əˈkwɪt) *vt.* **1.** declare innocent **2.** settle, discharge, as a debt **3.** behave (oneself) (-tt-) —**acˈquittal** *n.* declaration of innocence in court —**acˈquittance** *n.* discharge of debts

acre (ˈeɪkə) *n.* **1.** measure of land, 4840 square yards —*pl.* **2.** lands, estates **3.** *inf.* large area or plenty —**ˈacreage** *n.* extent of land in acres

acrid (ˈækrɪd) *a.* **1.** pungent, sharp **2.** irritating —**aˈcridity** *n.*

acrimony (ˈækrɪmənɪ) *n.* bitterness of feeling or language —**acriˈmonious** *a.*

acrobat (ˈækrəbæt) *n.* one skilled in gymnastic feats, *esp.* as entertainer in circus *etc.* —**acroˈbatic** *a.* —**acroˈbatics** *pl.n.* (*with sing. v.*) any activity requiring agility

acronym (ˈækrənɪm) *n.* word formed from initial letters of other words, *eg* UNESCO, ANZAC, NATO

acrophobia (ækrəˈfəʊbɪə) *n.* abnormal fear of being at great height

acropolis (əˈkrɒpəlɪs) *n.* citadel, *esp.* in ancient Greece

across (əˈkrɒs) *adv./prep.* **1.** crosswise **2.** from side to side **3.** on or to the other side —**get (*or* put) something across** explain something, make something understood

acrostic (əˈkrɒstɪk) *n.* word puzzle in which the first, middle, or last letters of each line spell a word or words

acrylic (əˈkrɪlɪk) *n.* variety of synthetic materials, *esp.* textiles, derived from an organic acid —**acrylic resin** any of group of polymers of acrylic acid, its esters or amides, used as paints, plastics *etc.*

act (ækt) *n.* **1.** thing done, deed **2.** doing **3.** law, decree **4.** section of a play —*v.* **5.** perform, as in a play —*vi.* **6.** exert force, work, as mechanism **7.** behave —**ˈacting** *n.* **1.** performance of a part —*a.* **2.** temporarily performing the duties of another —**ˈaction** *n.* **1.** operation **2.** deed **3.** gesture **4.** expenditure of energy **5.** battle **6.** lawsuit —**ˈactionable** *a.* subject to lawsuit —**ˈactivate** *vt.* **1.** make active, put into operation **2.** make radioactive **3.** make chemically active —**actiˈvation** *n.* —**ˈactivator** *n.* —**ˈactive** *a.* **1.** moving, working **2.** brisk, energetic —**ˈactively** *adv.* —**ˈactivism** *n.* —**ˈactivist** *n.* one who takes (direct) action to achieve political or social ends —**acˈtivity** *n.* —**ˈactor** *n.* one who acts in a play, film *etc.* (-**tress** *fem.*) —**action painting** type of abstract painting characterized by smeared or spattered paint (*also* **ˈtachisme**) —**action replay** rerunning of section of television film or tape of match *etc.*, oft. in slow motion —**action stations** *pl.n.* **1.** *Mil.* positions manned instantly in preparation for battle —*interj.* **2.** *Mil.* command to take up such positions **3.** *inf.* warning to get ready for something —**activated sludge** aerated sewage added to untreated sewage to hasten bacterial decomposition —**active list** *Mil.* list of officers available for full duty —**Act of God** *Law* unavoidable occurrence, such as earthquake, caused by natural forces

A.C.T. Australian Capital Territory

actinide series (ˈæktɪnaɪd) series of 15 radioactive elements with increasing atomic numbers from actinium to lawrencium

actinism (ˈæktɪnɪzəm) *n.* chemical action of sun's rays —**acˈtinic** *a.*

actinium (ækˈtɪnɪəm) *n.* radioactive element occurring as decay product of uranium

---

THESAURUS

acquire achieve, amass, attain, buy, collect, earn, gain, gather, get, obtain, pick up, procure, realize, receive, secure, win

acquisition **1.** buy, gain, possession, prize, property, purchase **2.** achievement, acquirement, attainment, gaining, learning, obtainment, procurement, pursuit

acquisitive avaricious, avid, covetous, grabbing, grasping, greedy, predatory, rapacious

acquisitiveness avarice, avidity, avidness, covetousness, graspingness, greed, predatoriness, rapaciousness, rapacity

acquit **1.** absolve, clear, deliver, discharge, exculpate, exonerate, free, fulfil, liberate, release, relieve, vindicate **2.** discharge, pay, pay off, repay, satisfy, settle **3. acquit oneself** bear, behave, comport, conduct, perform

acquittal absolution, clearance, deliverance, discharge, exculpation, exoneration, freeing, liberation, release, relief, vindication

acquittance acknowledgment, discharge, payment, receipt, release, settlement, settling

acrid acid, astringent, biting, bitter, burning, caustic, harsh, irritating, pungent, sharp, stinging

acrimonious acerbic, astringent, biting, bitter, caustic, censorious, churlish, crabbed, cutting, irascible, mordant, peevish, petulant, pungent, rancorous, sarcastic, severe, sharp, spiteful, splenetic, tart, testy, trenchant

acrimony acerbity, asperity, astringency, bitterness, churlishness, harshness, ill will, irascibility, mordancy, peevishness, rancour, sarcasm, spleen, tartness, trenchancy, virulence

act *n.* **1.** accomplishment, achievement, action, blow, deed, doing, execution, exertion, exploit, feat, move, operation, performance, step, stroke, undertaking **2.** bill, decree, edict, enactment, law, measure, ordinance, resolution, statute ~*v.* **3.** acquit, bear, behave, carry, carry out, comport, conduct, do, enact, execute, exert, function, go about, make, move, operate, perform, react, serve, strike, take effect, undertake, work **4.** act out, characterize, enact, impersonate, mime, mimic, perform, personate, personify, play, play *or* take the part of, portray, represent

acting **1.** *adj.* interim, *pro tem*, provisional, substitute, surrogate, temporary **2.** *n.* characterization, dramatics, enacting, impersonation, performance, performing, playing, portrayal, portraying, stagecraft, theatre

action **1.** accomplishment, achievement, act, blow, deed, exercise, exertion, exploit, feat, move, operation, performance, step, stroke, undertaking **2.** activity, effect, effort, exertion, force, functioning, influence, motion, movement, operation, power, process, work, working **3.** battle, combat, conflict, fighting, warfare **4.** affray, battle, clash, combat, contest, encounter, engagement, fight, fray, skirmish, sortie

actual (ˈæktʃʊəl) *a.* **1.** existing in the present **2.** real —**actuˈality** *n.* —**ˈactually** *adv.* really, indeed

actuary (ˈæktʃʊərɪ) *n.* statistician who calculates insurance risks, premiums *etc.* —**actuˈarial** *a.*

actuate (ˈæktʃʊeɪt) *vt.* **1.** activate **2.** motivate —**actuˈation** *n.*

acuity (əˈkjuːɪtɪ) *n.* keenness, *esp.* in vision or thought

acumen (ˈækjʊmɛn, əˈkjuːmən) *n.* sharpness of wit, perception, penetration

acupuncture (ˈækjʊpʌŋktʃə) *n. orig.* Chinese medical treatment involving insertion of needles at various points on the body —**ˈacupuncturist** *n.*

acute (əˈkjuːt) *a.* **1.** keen, shrewd **2.** sharp **3.** severe **4.** less than 90° —*n.* **5.** accent (´) over a letter to indicate the quality or length of its sound, *eg* abbé —**aˈcutely** *adv.* —**aˈcuteness** *n.*

ad (æd) *n.* advertisement —**ˈadman** *n. inf.* man who works in advertising

A.D. anno Domini

ad- (*comb. form*) **1.** to; towards, as in *adverb* **2.** near; next to, as in *adrenal*

adage (ˈædɪdʒ) *n.* much-used wise saying, proverb

adagio (əˈdɑːdʒɪəʊ) *a./adv./n. Mus.* leisurely, slow (passage) (*pl.* **-s**)

Adam (ˈædəm) *a.* in neoclassical style made popular by Robert Adam, Scottish architect and furniture designer

adamant (ˈædəmənt) *a.* very hard, unyielding —**adaˈmantine** *a.*

Adam's apple projecting part at front of the throat, the thyroid cartilage

adapt (əˈdæpt) *v.* **1.** alter for new use **2.** fit, modify **3.** change —**adaptaˈbility** *n.* —**aˈdaptable** *a.* —**adapˈtation** *n.* —**aˈdapter** *or* **aˈdaptor** *n. esp.* appliance for connecting two parts (*eg* electrical)

A.D.C. **1.** aide-de-camp **2.** analogue-digital converter

add (æd) *v.* **1.** join **2.** increase by **3.** say further —**adˈdition** *n.* —**adˈditional** *a.* —**ˈadditive** *n.* something added, *esp.* to foodstuffs

THESAURUS

5. case, cause, lawsuit, litigation, proceeding, prosecution, suit

activate actuate, animate, arouse, energize, galvanize, impel, initiate, mobilize, motivate, move, prompt, propel, rouse, set going, set in motion, set off, start, stimulate, stir, switch on, trigger (off), turn on

active **1.** acting, astir, at work, doing, effectual, functioning, in action, in force, in operation, live, moving, operative, running, stirring, working **2.** bustling, busy, engaged, full, hard-working, involved, occupied, on the go (*Inf.*), on the move, strenuous **3.** alert, animated, diligent, energetic, industrious, lively, nimble, on the go (*Inf.*), quick, spirited, sprightly, spry, vibrant, vigorous, vital, vivacious

activity action, activeness, animation, bustle, enterprise, exercise, exertion, hurly-burly, hustle, labour, life, liveliness, motion, movement, stir, work

actor actress, dramatic artist, leading man, performer, play-actor, player, Thespian, tragedian, trouper

actress actor, dramatic artist, leading lady, performer, play-actor, player, starlet, Thespian, tragedienne, trouper

actual **1.** absolute, categorical, certain, concrete, corporeal, definite, factual, indisputable, indubitable, physical, positive, real, substantial, tangible, undeniable, unquestionable **2.** authentic, confirmed, genuine, real, realistic, true, truthful, verified **3.** current, existent, extant, live, living, present, present-day, prevailing

actually absolutely, as a matter of fact, de facto, essentially, indeed, in fact, in point of fact, in reality, in truth, literally, really, truly, veritably

actuate animate, arouse, cause, dispose, drive, excite, impel, incite, induce, influence, inspire, instigate, motivate, move, prompt, quicken, rouse, spur, stimulate, stir, urge

acumen acuteness, astuteness, cleverness, discernment, ingenuity, insight, intelligence, judgment, keenness, penetration, perception, perspicacity, perspicuity, sagacity, sharpness, shrewdness, smartness, wisdom, wit

acute **1.** astute, canny, clever, discerning, discriminating, incisive, ingenious, insightful, intuitive, keen, observant, penetrating, perceptive, perspicacious, piercing, sensitive, sharp, smart, subtle **2.** critical, crucial, dangerous, decisive, essential, grave, important, serious, severe, sudden, urgent, vital **3.** cutting, distressing, excruciating, exquisite, fierce, intense, overpowering, overwhelming, piercing, poignant, powerful, racking, severe, sharp, shooting, shrill, stabbing, sudden, violent

acuteness **1.** acuity, astuteness, canniness, cleverness, discernment, discrimination, ingenuity, insight, intuition, intuitiveness, keenness, perception, perceptiveness, perspicacity, sensitivity, sharpness, smartness, subtleness, subtlety, wit **2.** criticality, criticalness, cruciality, danger, dangerousness, decisiveness, essentiality, gravity, importance, seriousness, severity, suddenness, urgency, vitalness **3.** distressingness, exquisiteness, fierceness, intenseness, intensity, poignancy, powerfulness, severity, sharpness, shrillness, suddenness, violence

adamant **1.** determined, firm, fixed, immovable, inexorable, inflexible, insistent, intransigent, obdurate, resolute, rigid, set, stiff, stubborn, unbending, uncompromising, unrelenting, unshakable, unyielding **2.** adamantine, flinty, hard, impenetrable, indestructible, rock-hard, rocky, steely, stony, tough, unbreakable

adapt acclimatize, accommodate, adjust, alter, apply, change, comply, conform, familiarize, fashion, fit, habituate, harmonize, make, match, modify, prepare, qualify, remodel, shape, suit, tailor

adaptability adaptableness, adjustability, alterability, changeability, compliancy, convertibility, flexibility, malleability, modifiability, plasticity, pliability, pliancy, resilience, variability, versatility

adaptable adjustable, alterable, changeable, compliant, conformable, convertible, easy-going, flexible, malleable, modifiable, plastic, pliant, resilient, variable, versatile

adaptation adjustment, alteration, change, conversion, modification, refitting, remodelling, reworking, shift, transformation, variation, version

add **1.** adjoin, affix, amplify, annex, append, attach, augment, enlarge by, include, increase by, supplement **2.** add up, compute, count up, reckon, sum up, total, tot up

addendum (əˈdɛndəm) *n.* thing to be added (*pl.* **-da** (-də)) **—ˈaddend** *n.* any of set of numbers that form sum

adder (ˈædə) *n.* small poisonous snake

addict (ˈædɪkt) *n.* **1.** one who has become dependent on something, *eg* drugs (*drug addict*) *—vt.* (əˈdɪkt) **2.** (*usu. passive*) cause to become dependent (on something, *esp.* drug) **—adˈdicted** *a.* **—adˈdiction** *n.* **—adˈdictive** *a.* causing addiction

addle (ˈædˀl) *v.* make or become rotten or muddled

address (əˈdrɛs) *n.* **1.** direction on letter **2.** place where one lives **3.** speech *—pl.* **4.** courtship *—vt.* **5.** mark destination on **6.** speak to **7.** direct **8.** dispatch **—addresˈsee** *n.* person addressed

adduce (əˈdjuːs) *vt.* **1.** offer as proof **2.** cite **—adˈducible** *a.* **—adduction** (əˈdʌkʃən) *n.*

-ade (*comb. form*) sweetened drink made of fruit, as in *lemonade*

adenoids (ˈædɪnɔɪdz) *pl.n.* tissue at back of nose **—adeˈnoidal** *a.*

adept (əˈdɛpt) *a.* **1.** skilled *—n.* (ˈædɛpt) **2.** expert

adequate (ˈædɪkwɪt) *a.* **1.** sufficient, enough, suitable **2.** not outstanding **—ˈadequacy** *n.* **—ˈadequately** *adv.*

à deux (a ˈdø) *Fr.* of or for two persons

adhere (ədˈhɪə) *vi.* **1.** stick **2.** be firm in opinion *etc.* **—adˈherent** *n./a.* **—adˈhesion** *n.* **—adˈhesive** *a./n.*

ad hoc (æd ˈhɒk) **1.** for a particular occasion only **2.** improvised

ad hominem (æd ˈhɒmɪnɛm) *Lat.* directed against person rather than his arguments

adieu (əˈdjuː) *interj.* **1.** farewell *—n.* **2.** act of taking leave (*pl.* **-s, adieux** (əˈdjuːz))

ad infinitum (æd ɪnfɪˈnaɪtəm) *Lat.* endlessly

ad interim (æd ˈɪntərɪm) *Lat.* for the meantime

adipose (ˈædɪpəʊs) *a.* of fat, fatty

adit (ˈædɪt) *n.* almost horizontal entrance into a mine

adj. **1.** adjective **2.** adjourned **3.** adjutant

adjacent (əˈdʒeɪsˀnt) *a.* lying near, next (to) **—adˈjacency** *n.*

adjective (ˈædʒɪktɪv) *n.* word which qualifies or limits a noun **—adjectival** (ædʒɪkˈtaɪvˀl) *a.* of adjective

adjoin (əˈdʒɔɪn) *v.* **1.** be next (to) **2.** join **—adˈjoining** *a.* next (to), near

adjourn (əˈdʒɜːn) *vt.* **1.** postpone temporarily, as meeting *—vi.* **2.** *inf.* move elsewhere **—adˈjournment** *n.*

adjudge (əˈdʒʌdʒ) *vt.* **1.** declare **2.** decide **3.** award **—adˈjudgment** *or* **adˈjudgement** *n.*

adjudicate (əˈdʒuːdɪkeɪt) *v.* **1.** try, judge *—vi.* **2.** sit in judgment **—adjudiˈcation** *n.* **—adˈjudicator** *n.*

adjunct (ˈædʒʌŋkt) *a.* **1.** joined, added *—n.* **2.** person or thing added or subordinate **—adˈjunctive** *a.*

THESAURUS

addendum addition, adjunct, affix, appendage, appendix, attachment, augmentation, codicil, extension, extra, postscript, supplement

addict **1.** dope-fiend (*Sl.*), fiend (*Inf.*), freak (*Sl.*), head (*Sl.*), junkie (*Sl.*), user (*Inf.*) **2.** adherent, buff (*Sl.*), devotee, enthusiast, fan, follower, freak (*Sl.*), nut (*Sl.*)

addicted dedicated, dependent, devoted, fond, habituated, hooked (*Sl.*), obsessed, prone

addiction craving, dependence, enslavement, habit, obsession

addition **1.** accession, adding, adjoining, affixing, amplification, annexation, attachment, augmentation, enlargement, extension, inclusion, increasing **2.** addendum, additive, adjunct, affix, appendage, appendix, extension, extra, gain, increase, increment, supplement **3.** adding up, computation, counting up, reckoning, summation, summing up, totalling, totting up

additional added, affixed, appended, extra, fresh, further, increased, more, new, other, over-and-above, spare, supplementary

address *n.* **1.** abode, domicile, dwelling, home, house, location, lodging, place, residence, situation, whereabouts **2.** direction, inscription, superscription **3.** discourse, disquisition, dissertation, harangue, lecture, oration, sermon, speech, talk ~*v.* **4.** accost, apostrophize, approach, greet, hail, invoke, salute, speak to, talk to **5.** discourse, give a speech, give a talk, harangue, lecture, orate, sermonize, speak, talk

adduce advance, allege, cite, designate, mention, name, offer, present, quote

adept **1.** *adj.* able, accomplished, adroit, dexterous, expert, masterful, masterly, practised, proficient, skilful, skilled, versed **2.** *n.* dab hand (*Inf.*), expert, genius, master

adequacy capability, commensurateness, competence, fairness, requisiteness, satisfactoriness, sufficiency, suitability, tolerability

adequate capable, commensurate, competent, enough, fair, passable, requisite, satisfactory, sufficient, suitable, tolerable

adhere **1.** attach, cement, cleave, cling, cohere, fasten, fix, glue, glue on, hold fast, paste, stick, stick fast, unite **2.** abide by, be attached, be constant, be devoted, be faithful, be loyal, be true, cleave to, cling, follow, fulfil, heed, keep, keep to, maintain, mind, obey, observe, respect, stand by, support

adhesive **1.** *adj.* adhering, attaching, clinging, cohesive, gluey, glutinous, gummy, holding, mucilaginous, sticking, sticky, tacky, tenacious **2.** *n.* cement, glue, gum, mucilage, paste

adieu congé, farewell, goodbye, leave-taking, parting, valediction

adjacent abutting, adjoining, alongside, beside, bordering, close, contiguous, near, neighbouring, next door, touching

adjoin abut, add, affix, annex, append, approximate, attach, border, combine, communicate with, connect, couple, impinge, interconnect, join, link, neighbour, touch, unite, verge

adjoining abutting, adjacent, bordering, connecting, contiguous, impinging, interconnecting, joined, joining, near, neighbouring, next door, touching, verging

adjourn defer, delay, discontinue, interrupt, postpone, prorogue, put off, recess, stay, suspend

adjournment deferment, deferral, delay, discontinuation, interruption, postponement, prorogation, putting off, recess, stay, suspension

adjudge adjudicate, allot, apportion, assign, award, decide, declare, decree, determine, distribute, judge, order, pronounce

adjudicate adjudge, arbitrate, decide, determine, judge, referee, settle, umpire

adjure (əˈdʒʊə) *vt.* beg, entreat earnestly —**adjuˈration** *n.*

adjust (əˈdʒʌst) *v.* **1.** make suitable, adapt **2.** alter slightly, regulate —**adˈjustable** *a.* —**adˈjuster** *n.* —**adˈjustment** *n.*

adjutant (ˈædʒətənt) *n.* military officer who assists superiors —**ˈadjutancy** *n.* his office, rank

ad-lib (ædˈlɪb) *v.* **1.** improvise, speak *etc.* without previous preparation —*n.* **2.** such speech *etc.* —*a.* **3.** improvised —**ad lib** without preparation; freely

ad libitum (æd ˈlɪbɪtəm) *Mus.* at performer's discretion

Adm. **1.** Admiral **2.** Admiralty

admin (ˈædmɪn) *n. inf.* administration

administer (ədˈmɪnɪstə) *vt.* **1.** manage, look after **2.** dispense, as justice *etc.* **3.** apply —**adˈministrate** *v.* manage (business, institution, government department *etc.*) —**adminiˈstration** *n.* —**adˈministrative** *a.* —**adˈministrator** *n.* (**-atrix** *fem.*)

admiral (ˈædmərəl) *n.* naval officer of highest sea rank (*also* **admiral of the fleet**) —**Admiralty (Board)** department in charge of Royal Navy

admire (ədˈmaɪə) *vt.* **1.** look on with wonder and pleasure **2.** respect highly —**admirable** (ˈædmərəbᵊl) *a.* —**admirably** (ˈædmərəblɪ) *adv.* —**admiration** (ædməˈreɪʃən) *n.* —**adˈmirer** *n.* —**adˈmiringly** *adv.*

admit (ədˈmɪt) *vt.* **1.** confess **2.** accept as true **3.** allow **4.** let in (-tt-) —**adˈmissible** *a.* —**adˈmissibly** *adv.* —**adˈmission** *n.* **1.** permission to enter **2.** entrance fee **3.** confession —**adˈmittance** *n.* permission to enter —**adˈmittedly** *adv.* willingly conceded

admixture (ədˈmɪkstʃə) *n.* **1.** mixture **2.** ingredient —**adˈmix** *vt.*

admonish (ədˈmɒnɪʃ) *vt.* **1.** reprove **2.** advise **3.** warn **4.** exhort —**admoˈnition** *n.* —**adˈmonitory** *a.*

ad nauseam (æd ˈnɔːzɪæm) *Lat.* to a boring or disgusting extent

ado (əˈduː) *n.* fuss

adobe (əˈdəʊbɪ) *n.* sun-dried brick

adolescence (ædəˈlɛsəns) *n.* period of life just before maturity —**adoˈlescent** *n.* **1.** a youth —*a.* **2.** of adolescence **3.** immature

Adonis (əˈdəʊnɪs) *n.* a beautiful youth beloved of Venus

adopt (əˈdɒpt) *vt.* **1.** take into relationship, *esp.* as one's child **2.** take up, as belief, principle, resolution —**aˈdoption** *n.* —**aˈdoptive** *a.* due to adoption

THESAURUS

adjust acclimatize, accommodate, accustom, adapt, alter, arrange, compose, dispose, fit, fix, harmonize, make conform, measure, modify, order, reconcile, rectify, redress, regulate, remodel, set, settle, suit, tune (up)

adjustable adaptable, alterable, flexible, malleable, modifiable, mouldable, movable, tractable

adjustment adaptation, alteration, arrangement, arranging, fitting, fixing, modification, ordering, rectification, redress, regulation, remodelling, setting, tuning

ad-lib **1.** *v.* extemporize, improvise, make up, speak extemporaneously, speak impromptu, speak off the cuff **2.** *adj.* extemporaneous, extempore, extemporized, impromptu, improvised, made up, off-the-cuff (*Inf.*), unprepared, unrehearsed **3.** **ad lib** *adv.* extemporaneously, extempore, impromptu, off the cuff, off the top of one's head (*Inf.*), without preparation, without rehearsal

administer **1.** conduct, control, direct, govern, manage, oversee, run, superintend, supervise **2.** apply, contribute, dispense, distribute, execute, give, impose, mete out, perform, provide

administration administering, application, conduct, control, direction, dispensation, distribution, execution, governing, government, management, overseeing, performance, provision, running, superintendence, supervision

administrative directorial, executive, governmental, gubernatorial (*Chiefly U.S.*), management, managerial, organizational, regulatory, supervisory

admirable choice, commendable, estimable, excellent, exquisite, fine, laudable, meritorious, praiseworthy, rare, superior, valuable, wonderful, worthy

admiration adoration, affection, amazement, appreciation, approbation, approval, astonishment, delight, esteem, pleasure, praise, regard, respect, surprise, veneration, wonder, wonderment

admire **1.** adore, appreciate, approve, esteem, idolize, look up to, praise, prize, respect, think highly of, value, venerate, worship **2.** appreciate, delight in, marvel at, take pleasure in, wonder at

admirer adherent, devotee, disciple, enthusiast, fan, follower, partisan, supporter, votary, worshipper

admissible acceptable, allowable, allowed, passable, permissible, permitted, tolerable, tolerated

admission **1.** acceptance, access, admittance, entrance, entrée, entry, ingress, initiation, introduction **2.** acknowledgment, admitting, affirmation, allowance, avowal, concession, confession, declaration, disclosure, divulgence, profession, revelation

admit **1.** accept, allow, allow to enter, give access, initiate, introduce, let in, receive, take in **2.** acknowledge, affirm, avow, concede, confess, declare, disclose, divulge, profess, reveal **3.** agree, allow, grant, let, permit, recognize

admittance acceptance, access, admitting, allowing, entrance, entry, letting in, passage, reception

admonish advise, berate, caution, censure, check, chide, counsel, enjoin, exhort, forewarn, rebuke, reprimand, reprove, scold, tell off (*Inf.*), upbraid, warn

admonition advice, berating, caution, chiding, counsel, rebuke, remonstrance, reprimand, reproach, reproof, scolding, telling off (*Inf.*), upbraiding, warning

admonitory admonishing, advisory, cautionary, rebuking, reprimanding, reproachful, reproving, scolding, warning

adolescence boyhood, girlhood, juvenescence, minority, teens, youth

adolescent **1.** *adj.* boyish, girlish, growing, immature, juvenile, puerile, teenage, young, youthful **2.** *n.* juvenile, minor, teenager, youngster, youth

adopt **1.** accept, appropriate, approve, assume, choose, embrace, endorse, espouse, follow, maintain, ratify, select, support, take on, take over, take up **2.** foster, take in

adoption **1.** acceptance, approbation, appropriation, approval, assumption, choice, embracing, endorsement, espousal, following, maintenance, ratification,

adore (əˈdɔː) *vt.* **1.** love intensely —*v.* **2.** worship —**aˈdorable** *a.* —**adoˈration** *n.* —**aˈdorer** *n.* lover

adorn (əˈdɔːn) *vt.* beautify, embellish, deck —**aˈdornment** *n.* ornament, decoration

A.D.P. automatic data processing

ad rem (æd ˈrɛm) *Lat.* to the point

adrenal (əˈdriːnˀl) *a.* near the kidney —**adrenal gland** —**adrenaline** *or* **adrenalin** (əˈdrɛnəlɪn) *n.* **1.** hormone secreted by adrenal glands **2.** this substance used as drug

adrift (əˈdrɪft) *a./adv.* **1.** drifting free **2.** *inf.* detached **3.** *inf.* off course

adroit (əˈdrɔɪt) *a.* **1.** skilful, expert **2.** clever —**aˈdroitly** *adv.* —**aˈdroitness** *n.* dexterity

adsorb (ədˈsɔːb) *v.* (of gas, vapour) condense and form thin film on surface —**adˈsorbent** *a./n.* —**adˈsorption** *n.*

adulation (ædjʊˈleɪʃən) *n.* flattery —**ˈadulate** *vt.* flatter —**ˈadulator** *n.* —**ˈadulatory** *a.*

adult (ˈædʌlt, əˈdʌlt) *a.* **1.** grown-up, mature —*n.* **2.** grown-up person **3.** full-grown animal or plant

adulterate (əˈdʌltəreɪt) *vt.* make impure by addition —**aˈdulterant** *n./a.* —**aˈdulterated** *a.* —**adulterˈation** *n.* —**aˈdulterator** *n.*

adultery (əˈdʌltərɪ) *n.* sexual unfaithfulness of a husband or wife —**aˈdulterer** *n.* (**aˈdulteress** *fem.*) —**aˈdulterous** *a.*

adumbrate (ˈædʌmbreɪt) *vt.* **1.** outline **2.** give indication of —**aˈdumbrant** *or* **aˈdumbrative** *a.* —**adumˈbration** *n.*

adv. **1.** adverb(ial) **2.** advertisement

ad valorem (æd vəˈlɔːrəm) *Lat.* in proportion to the value of goods in question

advance (ədˈvɑːns) *vt.* **1.** bring forward **2.** suggest **3.** encourage **4.** pay beforehand —*vi.* **5.** go forward **6.** improve in position or value —*n.* **7.** forward movement **8.** improvement **9.** loan —*pl.* **10.** personal approach(es) to gain favour *etc.* —*a.* **11.** (*with* of) ahead in time or position —**adˈvanced** *a.* **1.** at a late stage **2.** not elementary **3.** ahead of the times —**adˈvancement** *n.* promotion —**Advanced level** *formal name for* A LEVEL

advantage (ədˈvɑːntɪdʒ) *n.* **1.** superiority **2.** more

THESAURUS

selection, support, taking on, taking over, taking up **2.** adopting, fosterage, fostering, taking in

adorable appealing, attractive, captivating, charming, darling, dear, delightful, fetching, lovable, pleasing, precious

adoration admiration, esteem, estimation, exaltation, glorification, honour, idolatry, idolization, love, reverence, veneration, worship, worshipping

adore admire, bow to, cherish, dote on, esteem, exalt, glorify, honour, idolize, love, revere, reverence, venerate, worship

adorn array, beautify, bedeck, deck, decorate, embellish, emblazon, enhance, enrich, garnish, grace, ornament, trim

adornment **1.** accessory, decoration, embellishment, frill, frippery, ornament, trimming **2.** beautification, decorating, decoration, embellishment, ornamentation, trimming

adrift **1.** afloat, drifting, unanchored, unmoored **2.** amiss, astray, off course, wrong

adroit able, adept, apt, artful, clever, cunning, deft, dexterous, expert, ingenious, masterful, neat, nimble, proficient, quick-witted, skilful, skilled

adroitness ability, ableness, address, adeptness, aptness, artfulness, cleverness, cunning, deftness, dexterity, expertise, ingeniousness, ingenuity, masterfulness, mastery, nimbleness, proficiency, quickwittedness, skilfulness, skill

adulation blandishment, bootlicking (*Inf.*), extravagant flattery, fawning, fulsome praise, servile flattery, sycophancy, worship

adulatory blandishing, bootlicking (*Inf.*), fawning, flattering, obsequious, praising, servile, slavish, sycophantic, worshipping

adult **1.** *adj.* full grown, fully developed, fully grown, grown-up, mature, of age, ripe **2.** *n.* grown *or* grown-up person (man *or* woman), grown-up, person of mature age

adulterate *v.* attenuate, bastardize, contaminate, corrupt, debase, depreciate, deteriorate, devalue, make impure, mix with, thin, vitiate, water down, weaken

adumbrate **1.** delineate, indicate, outline, silhouette, sketch, suggest **2.** augur, forecast, foreshadow, foretell, portend, predict, prefigure, presage, prognosticate, prophesy

adumbration **1.** delineation, draft, indication, outline, rough, silhouette, sketch, suggestion **2.** augury, forecast, foreshadowing, foretelling, omen, portent, prediction, prefiguration, prefigurement, presage, prognostication, prophecy, sign

advance *v.* **1.** accelerate, bring forward, bring up, come forward, elevate, go ahead, go forward, go on, hasten, move onward, move up, press on, proceed, progress, promote, send forward, send up, speed, upgrade **2.** benefit, further, grow, improve, multiply, prosper, thrive **3.** adduce, allege, cite, offer, present, proffer, put forward, submit, suggest **4.** increase (*price*), lend, pay beforehand, raise (*price*), supply on credit ~*n.* **5.** advancement, development, forward movement, headway, onward movement, progress **6.** advancement, amelioration, betterment, breakthrough, furtherance, gain, growth, improvement, progress, promotion, step **7.** appreciation, credit, deposit, down payment, increase (*in price*), loan, prepayment, retainer, rise (*in price*) **8. advances** approach, approaches, moves, overtures, proposals, proposition ~*adj.* **9.** beforehand, early, foremost, forward, in front, leading, prior

advanced ahead, avant-garde, extreme, foremost, forward, higher, late, leading, precocious, progressive

advancement advance, amelioration, betterment, gain, growth, improvement, preferment, progress, promotion, rise

advantage aid, ascendancy, asset, assistance, avail, benefit, blessing, boon, convenience, dominance, edge, gain, good, help, interest, lead, precedence, preeminence, profit, service, start, superiority, sway, upper hand, use, utility, welfare

advantageous **1.** dominant, dominating, favourable, superior **2.** beneficial, convenient, helpful, of service, profitable, useful, valuable, worthwhile

favourable position or state **3.** benefit **—advan'tageous** *a.* **—advan'tageously** *adv.*

advent ('ædvɛnt, -vənt) *n.* **1.** a coming, arrival **2.** (**A-**) the four weeks before Christmas **—'Adventist** *n.* one of number of Christian sects believing in imminent return of Christ **—the Advent** the coming of Christ

adventitious (ædvɛn'tɪʃəs) *a.* **1.** added, artificial **2.** accidental, occurring by chance

adventure (əd'vɛntʃə) *n.* **1.** risk **2.** bold exploit **3.** remarkable happening **4.** enterprise **5.** commercial speculation *—v.* **6.** (take) risk **—ad'venturer** *n.* **1.** one who seeks adventures **2.** one who lives on his wits (**ad'venturess** *fem.*) **—ad'venturism** *n.* recklessness, *esp.* in politics and finance **—ad'venturous** *a.* **—ad'venturously** *adv.* **—ad'venturousness** *n.* **—adventure playground UK** playground for children that contains building materials *etc.*, used to build with, climb on *etc.*

adverb ('ædvɜːb) *n.* word added to verb, adjective or other adverb to modify meaning **—ad'verbial** *a.* **—ad'verbially** *adv.*

adverse ('ædvɜːs) *a.* **1.** opposed **2.** hostile **3.** unfavourable, bringing harm **—'adversary** *n.* enemy **—ad'versative** *a.* **—'adversely** *adv.* **—ad'versity** *n.* distress, misfortune

advert[1] (əd'vɜːt) *vi.* **1.** turn the mind or attention **2.** refer **—ad'vertence** *n.* **—ad'vertently** *adv.*

advert[2] ('ædvɜːt) *n. inf.* advertisement

advertise *or U.S. (sometimes)* **-tize** ('ædvətaɪz) *vt.* **1.** publicize **2.** make known **3.** give notice of, *esp.* in newspapers *etc.* *—vi.* **4.** make public request (for) **—advertisement** *or U.S. (sometimes)* **-tizement** (əd'vɜːtɪsmənt) *n.* **—'advertiser** *or U.S. (sometimes)* **-tizer** *n.* **—'advertising** *or U.S. (sometimes)* **-tizing** *a./n.*

advice (əd'vaɪs) *n.* **1.** opinion given **2.** counsel **3.** information **4.** (formal) notification

advise (əd'vaɪz) *vt.* **1.** offer advice **2.** recommend a line of conduct **3.** give notice (of) **—ad'visable** *a.* expedient **—ad'vised** *a.* considered, as in *well-advised* **—advisedly** (əd'vaɪzɪdlɪ) *adv.* **—ad'viser** *or* **ad'visor** *n.* **—ad'visory** *a.*

advocaat ('ædvəʊkɑː) *n.* liqueur with raw egg base

advocate ('ædvəkɪt) *n.* **1.** one who pleads the cause of another, *esp.* in court of law **2.** barrister *—vt.* ('ædvəkeɪt) **3.** uphold, recommend **—'advocacy** *n.* **—advo'cation** *n.*

advowson (əd'vaʊz'n) *n. English eccles. law* right of presentation to vacant benefice

advt. advertisement

adze *or U.S.* **adz** (ædz) *n.* carpenter's tool, like axe, but with arched blade set at right angles to handle

A.E.A. Atomic Energy Authority

aegis *or U.S. (sometimes)* **egis** ('iːdʒɪs) *n.* sponsorship, protection (*orig.* shield of Zeus)

aegrotat ('aɪgrəʊtæt, 'iː-) *n.* in British university, exemption *esp.* from final examinations because of illness

-aemia, -haemia, *or U.S.* **-emia, -hemia** (*comb. form*) blood, *esp.* specified condition of blood in diseases, as in *leukaemia*

Aeolian (iː'əʊlɪən) *a.* acted on by the wind, as **Aeolian harp**

aeon *or U.S.* **eon** ('iːən, 'iːɒn) *n.* **1.** age, very long period of time **2.** eternity

THESAURUS

advent appearance, approach, arrival, coming, entrance, occurrence, onset, visitation

adventitious accidental, casual, chance, extraneous, foreign, fortuitous, incidental, nonessential, unexpected

adventure 1. *n.* chance, contingency, enterprise, experience, exploit, hazard, incident, occurrence, risk, speculation, undertaking, venture **2.** *v.* dare, endanger, hazard, imperil, jeopardize, risk, venture

adventurer 1. daredevil, hero, heroine, knight-errant, soldier of fortune, swashbuckler, traveller, venturer, voyager, wanderer **2.** fortune-hunter, gambler, mercenary, opportunist, rogue, speculator

adventurous adventuresome, audacious, bold, dangerous, daredevil, daring, enterprising, foolhardy, hazardous, headstrong, intrepid, rash, reckless, risky, temerarious (*Rare*), venturesome

adversary antagonist, competitor, contestant, enemy, foe, opponent, opposer, rival

adverse antagonistic, conflicting, contrary, detrimental, disadvantageous, hostile, inexpedient, inimical, injurious, inopportune, negative, opposing, opposite, reluctant, repugnant, unfavourable, unfortunate, unfriendly, unlucky, unpropitious, unwilling

adversity affliction, bad luck, calamity, catastrophe, disaster, distress, hardship, hard times, ill-fortune, ill-luck, misery, misfortune, mishap, reverse, sorrow, suffering, trial, trouble, woe, wretchedness

advertise advise, announce, apprise, blazon, declare, display, flaunt, inform, make known, notify, plug (*Inf.*), praise, proclaim, promote, promulgate, publicize, publish, puff, push (*Inf.*), tout

advertisement ad (*Inf.*), advert (*Inf.*), announcement, bill, blurb, circular, commercial, display, notice, placard, plug (*Inf.*), poster, promotion, publicity, puff

advice 1. admonition, caution, counsel, guidance, help, injunction, opinion, recommendation, suggestion, view **2.** information, instruction, intelligence, notice, notification, warning, word

advisable appropriate, apt, desirable, expedient, fit, fitting, judicious, politic, profitable, proper, prudent, recommended, seemly, sensible, sound, suggested, suitable, wise

advise 1. admonish, caution, commend, counsel, enjoin, recommend, suggest, urge **2.** acquaint, apprise, inform, make known, notify, report, tell, warn

adviser aide, authority, coach, confidant, consultant, counsel, counsellor, guide, helper, lawyer, mentor, right-hand man, solicitor, teacher, tutor

advisory advising, consultative, counselling, helping, recommending

advocate *v.* **1.** advise, argue for, campaign for, champion, countenance, defend, encourage, favour, hold a brief for (*Inf.*), justify, plead for, press for, promote, propose, recommend, speak for, support, uphold, urge *~n.* **2.** apologist, apostle, backer, campaigner, champion, counsellor, defender, pleader, promoter, proponent, proposer, speaker, spokesman, supporter, upholder **3.** *Law.* attorney, barrister, counsel, lawyer, solicitor

aegis advocacy, auspices, backing, favour, guardianship, patronage, protection, shelter, sponsorship, support, wing

aerate (ˈɛəreɪt) *vt.* **1.** charge liquid with gas, as effervescent drink **2.** expose to air —**aerˈation** *n.* —**ˈaerator** *n.* apparatus for charging liquid with gas

aerial (ˈɛərɪəl) *a.* **1.** of the air **2.** operating in the air **3.** pertaining to aircraft —*n.* **4.** part of radio *etc.* receiving or sending radio waves —**ˈaerialist** *n. chiefly* US trapeze artist

aerie (ˈɛərɪ) *n. see* EYRIE

aero-, aeri-, *or before vowel* **aer-** (*comb. form*) air or aircraft, as in *aero engine*

aerobatics (ɛərəʊˈbætɪks) *pl.n.* stunt flying

aerobics (ɛəˈrəʊbɪks) *pl. n.* (*with sing. v.*) exercises designed to increase oxygen in blood

aerodrome (ˈɛərədrəʊm) *n.* UK airfield

aerodynamics (ɛərəʊdaɪˈnæmɪks) *pl.n.* (*with sing. v.*) study of air flow, *esp.* round moving solid bodies

aero engine engine for powering aircraft

aerofoil (ˈɛərəʊfɔɪl) *n.* surfaces of wing *etc.* of aircraft designed to give lift

aerogram *or* **aerogramme** (ˈɛərəgræm) *n.* airmail letter form (*also* **air letter**)

aerolite (ˈɛərəlaɪt) *n.* meteoric stone

aerometry (ɛəˈrɒmɪtrɪ) *n.* measurement of weight or density of gases

aeronaut (ˈɛərənɔːt) *n.* pilot or navigator of lighter-than-air craft —**aeroˈnautical** *a.* —**aeroˈnautics** *pl.n.* (*with sing. v.*) science of air navigation and flying in general

aeroplane (ˈɛərəpleɪn) *or U.S.* **airplane** (ˈɛəpleɪn) *n.* heavier-than-air flying machine

aerosol (ˈɛərəsɒl) *n.* (substance dispensed as fine spray from) pressurized can

aerospace (ˈɛərəspeɪs) *n.* **1.** earth's atmosphere and space beyond —*a.* **2.** of missiles, space vehicles *etc.*

aerostatics (ɛərəˈstætɪks) *pl.n.* (*with sing. v.*) **1.** study of gases in equilibrium and bodies held in equilibrium in gases **2.** study of lighter-than-air craft

aesthetic (iːsˈθɛtɪk, ɪs-), **aesthetical** *or U.S.* (*sometimes*) **esthetic, esthetical** *a.* relating to principles of beauty, taste and art —**aesˈthetics** *or U.S.* (*sometimes*) **esˈthetics** *pl.n.* (*with sing. v.*) study of art, taste *etc.* —**aesthete** *or U.S.* **esthete** (ˈiːsθiːt) *n.* one who affects extravagant love of art —**aesˈthetically** *or U.S.* (*sometimes*) **esˈthetically** *adv.* —**aesˈtheticism** *or U.S.* (*sometimes*) **esˈtheticism** *n.*

aestivate *or U.S.* **estivate** (ˈiːstɪveɪt) *vi.* spend the summer, *esp.* in dormant condition —**aestival** *or U.S.* **estival** (iːˈstaɪvᵊl) *a. rare* of summer —**aestiˈvation** *or U.S.* **estiˈvation** *n.*

aether (ˈiːθə) *n. see* ETHER

aetiology *or U.S.* **etiology** (iːtɪˈɒlədʒɪ) *n.* study of causes, *esp.* inquiry into origin of disease —**aetioˈlogical** *or U.S.* **etioˈlogical** *a.*

a.f. audio frequency

afar (əˈfɑː) *adv.* from, at, or to, a great distance

A.F.C. **1.** Air Force Cross **2.** Association Football Club **3.** automatic frequency control

affable (ˈæfəbᵊl) *a.* easy to speak to, polite and friendly —**affaˈbility** *n.* —**ˈaffably** *adv.*

affair (əˈfɛə) *n.* **1.** thing done or attended to **2.** business **3.** happening **4.** sexual liaison —*pl.* **5.** personal or business interests **6.** matters of public interest

affect (əˈfɛkt) *vt.* **1.** act on, influence **2.** move feelings of **3.** make show, pretence of **4.** assume **5.** have liking for —**affecˈtation** *n.* show, pretence —**afˈfected** *a.* **1.** making a pretence **2.** moved **3.** acted upon —**afˈfectedly** *adv.* —**afˈfecting** *a.* moving the feelings of —**afˈfectingly** *adv.* —**afˈfection** *n.* fondness, love —**afˈfectionate** *a.* —**afˈfectionately** *adv.*

afferent (ˈæfərənt) *a.* bringing to, *esp.* describing nerves which carry sensation to the brain

affiance (əˈfaɪəns) *vt.* betroth —**afˈfianced** *a./n.* (one) promised in marriage

affidavit (æfɪˈdeɪvɪt) *n.* written statement on oath

affiliate (əˈfɪlɪeɪt) *vt.* (*with* to *or* with) **1.** connect, attach (with larger body, organization) **2.** adopt —**affiliˈation** *n.* —**affiliation order** *Law* order that putative father of illegitimate child contribute towards its maintenance

THESAURUS

affability amiability, amicability, approachability, benevolence, benignity, civility, congeniality, cordiality, courtesy, friendliness, geniality, good humour, good nature, graciousness, kindliness, mildness, obligingness, pleasantness, sociability, urbanity, warmth

affable amiable, amicable, approachable, benevolent, benign, civil, congenial, cordial, courteous, friendly, genial, good-humoured, good-natured, gracious, kindly, mild, obliging, pleasant, sociable, urbane, warm

affair **1.** activity, business, circumstance, concern, episode, event, happening, incident, interest, matter, occurrence, proceeding, project, question, subject, transaction, undertaking **2.** amour, intrigue, liaison, relationship, romance

affect **1.** act on, alter, bear upon, change, concern, impinge upon, influence, interest, involve, modify, prevail over, regard, relate to, sway, transform **2.** disturb, impress, move, overcome, perturb, stir, touch, upset **3.** adopt, aspire to, assume, contrive, counterfeit, feign, imitate, pretend, put on, sham, simulate

affectation act, affectedness, appearance, artificiality, assumed manners, façade, fakery, false display, insincerity, mannerism, pose, pretence, pretension, pretentiousness, sham, show, simulation, unnatural imitation

affected **1.** afflicted, altered, changed, concerned, damaged, deeply moved, distressed, hurt, impaired, impressed, influenced, injured, melted, stimulated, stirred, touched, troubled, upset **2.** artificial, assumed, conceited, contrived, counterfeit, feigned, insincere, la-di-da (*Inf.*), mannered, mincing, phoney (*Inf.*), pompous, precious, pretended, pretentious, put-on, sham, simulated, spurious, stiff, studied, unnatural

affecting moving, pathetic, piteous, pitiable, pitiful, poignant, sad, saddening, touching

affection amity, attachment, care, desire, feeling, fondness, friendliness, good will, inclination, kindness, liking, love, passion, propensity, tenderness, warmth

affectionate attached, caring, devoted, doting, fond, friendly, kind, loving, tender, warm, warm-hearted

affiliate ally, amalgamate, annex, associate, band together, combine, confederate, connect, incorporate, join, unite

affinity (əˈfɪnɪtɪ) *n.* **1.** natural liking **2.** resemblance **3.** relationship by marriage **4.** chemical attraction —**afˈfinitive** *a.*

affirm (əˈfɜːm) *v.* **1.** assert positively, declare **2.** maintain (statement) —*vi.* **3.** make solemn declaration —**affirˈmation** *n.* —**afˈfirmative** *a.* **1.** asserting —*n.* **2.** word of assent —**afˈfirmatively** *adv.*

affix (əˈfɪks) *vt.* **1.** fasten **2.** attach, append —*n.* (ˈæfɪks) **3.** addition, *esp.* to word, as suffix, prefix

afflatus (əˈfleɪtəs) *n.* impulse of creative power or inspiration

afflict (əˈflɪkt) *vt.* **1.** give pain or grief to, distress **2.** trouble, vex —**afˈfliction** *n.* —**afˈflictive** *a.*

affluent (ˈæfluənt) *a.* **1.** wealthy **2.** abundant —*n.* **3.** tributary stream —**ˈaffluence** *n.* wealth, abundance

afford (əˈfɔːd) *vt.* **1.** be able to buy **2.** be able to spare (the time *etc.*) **3.** produce, yield, furnish

afforest (əˈfɒrɪst) *vt.* turn into forest, plant trees on —**afforesˈtation** *n.*

affray (əˈfreɪ) *n.* fight, brawl

affront (əˈfrʌnt) *vt.* **1.** insult openly —*n.* **2.** insult **3.** offence

aficionado (əfɪʃjəˈnɑːdəʊ) *n.* **1.** ardent supporter or devotee **2.** devotee of bullfighting (*pl.* **-s**)

afield (əˈfiːld) *adv.* **1.** away from home **2.** in or on the field

afire (əˈfaɪə) *adv.* on fire

aflame (əˈfleɪm) *adv.* burning

afloat (əˈfləʊt) *adv.* **1.** floating **2.** at sea **3.** in circulation

A.F.M. Air Force Medal

afoot (əˈfʊt) *adv.* **1.** astir **2.** on foot

afore (əˈfɔː) *prep./adv.* before, usu. in compounds —**aˈforementioned** *a.* chiefly in legal documents stated or mentioned before —**aˈforethought** *a.* premeditated (*esp. in* **malice aforethought**)

a fortiori (eɪ fɔːtɪˈɔːraɪ) *adv.* for a stronger reason

afoul (əˈfaʊl) *a./adv.* into difficulty

Afr. Africa(n)

afraid (əˈfreɪd) *a.* **1.** frightened **2.** sorry

afresh (əˈfrɛʃ) *adv.* again, anew

African (ˈæfrɪkən) *a.* **1.** belonging to Africa —*n.* **2.** native of Africa —**Afriˈcana** *pl.n.* objects of cultural or historical interest of southern Afr. origin —**African lily** S Afr. plant with funnel-shaped flowers —**African violet** house plant with pink or purple flowers and hairy leaves

Africander (afrɪˈkændə, æf-) *n.* breed of humpbacked S Afr. cattle

Afrikaans (afrɪˈkɑːns, -ˈkɑːnz, æf-) *n.* language used in S Afr., derived from 17th-cent. Dutch —**Afriˈkaner** *n.* White native of S Afr. with Afrikaans as mother tongue

Afro (ˈæfrəʊ) *n.* fuzzy, bushy hairstyle

Afro- (*comb. form*) Africa or African, as in *Afro-Asiatic*

afrormosia (æfrɔːˈməʊzɪə) *n.* hard teaklike wood obtained from tropical Afr. tree

aft (ɑːft) *adv.* towards stern of ship

after (ˈɑːftə) *adv.* **1.** later **2.** behind —*prep.* **3.** behind **4.** later than **5.** on the model of **6.** pursuing —*conj.* **7.** at a later time than that at which —*a.* **8.** nearer ship's stern —**ˈafters** *pl.n. inf.* course after main course; dessert —**ˈafterwards** *or* **ˈafterward** *adv.* later

afterbirth (ˈɑːftəbɜːθ) *n.* membrane expelled after a birth

aftercare (ˈɑːftəkɛə) *n.* care, *esp.* medical, bestowed on person after period of treatment, and *esp.* after childbirth

THESAURUS

affiliation alliance, amalgamation, association, banding together, coalition, combination, confederation, connection, incorporation, joining, league, merging, relationship, union

affinity **1.** alliance, analogy, closeness, compatibility, connection, correspondence, kinship, likeness, relation, relationship, resemblance, similarity **2.** attraction, fondness, inclination, leaning, liking, partiality, rapport, sympathy

affirm assert, asseverate, attest, aver, avouch, avow, certify, confirm, declare, maintain, pronounce, ratify, state, swear, testify

affirmation assertion, asseveration, attestation, averment, avouchment, avowal, certification, confirmation, declaration, oath, pronouncement, ratification, statement, testimony

affirmative agreeing, approving, assenting, concurring, confirming, consenting, corroborative, favourable, positive

afflict beset, burden, distress, grieve, harass, hurt, oppress, pain, plague, rack, smite, torment, trouble, try, wound

affliction adversity, calamity, cross, curse, depression, disease, distress, grief, hardship, misery, misfortune, ordeal, pain, plague, scourge, sickness, sorrow, suffering, torment, trial, tribulation, trouble, woe, wretchedness

affluence abundance, exuberance, fortune, opulence, plenty, profusion, prosperity, riches, wealth

affluent **1.** loaded (*Sl.*), moneyed, opulent, prosperous, rich, wealthy, well-heeled (*Inf.*), well-off, well-to-do **2.** abundant, copious, exuberant, plenteous, plentiful

afford **1.** bear, spare, stand, sustain **2.** bestow, furnish, give, grant, impart, offer, produce, provide, render, supply, yield

affront **1.** *v.* abuse, anger, annoy, displease, insult, offend, outrage, pique, provoke, slight, vex **2.** *n.* abuse, indignity, injury, insult, offence, outrage, provocation, slap in the face (*Inf.*), slight, slur, vexation, wrong

aflame **1.** ablaze, afire, alight, blazing, burning, fiery, flaming, ignited, lighted, lit, on fire **2.** afire, aroused, excited, fervent, impassioned, passionate, stimulated

afoot about, abroad, afloat, astir, brewing, circulating, current, going on, hatching, in preparation, in progress, in the wind, on the go (*Inf.*), operating, up (*Inf.*)

afraid **1.** alarmed, anxious, apprehensive, cowardly, faint-hearted, fearful, frightened, intimidated, nervous, reluctant, scared, suspicious, timid, timorous **2.** regretful, sorry, unhappy

afresh again, anew, newly, once again, once more, over again

after afterwards, behind, below, following, later, subsequently, succeeding, thereafter

aftereffect (ˈɑːftərɪfɛkt) *n.* subsequent effect of deed, event *etc.*

afterglow (ˈɑːftəgləʊ) *n.* light after sunset

afterlife (ˈɑːftəlaɪf) *n.* life after death or at later time in person's lifetime

aftermath (ˈɑːftəmæθ) *n.* result, consequence, *esp.* difficult one

afternoon (ɑːftəˈnuːn) *n.* time from noon to evening

afterpains (ˈɑːftəpeɪnz) *pl.n.* pains caused by contraction of uterus after childbirth

aftershave (lotion) (ˈɑːftəʃeɪv) *n.* lotion applied to face after shaving

afterthought (ˈɑːftəθɔːt) *n.* idea occurring later

Ag *Chem.* silver

again (əˈgɛn, əˈgeɪn) *adv.* **1.** once more **2.** in addition **3.** back, in return **4.** besides

against (əˈgɛnst, əˈgeɪnst) *prep.* **1.** in opposition to **2.** in contact with **3.** opposite **4.** in readiness for

agape (əˈgeɪp) *a./adv.* open-mouthed as in wonder *etc.*

agar (ˈeɪgə) *n.* gelatinous carbohydrate obtained from seaweeds, used as culture medium for bacteria in food *etc.* (*also* **agar-agar**)

agaric (ˈægərɪk) *n.* **1.** any of various fungi, *eg* mushroom —*a.* **2.** fungoid

agate (ˈægɪt) *n.* coloured, semiprecious, decorative form of quartz

agave (əˈgeɪvɪ) *n.* plant native to tropical Amer.

age (eɪdʒ) *n.* **1.** length of time person or thing has existed **2.** time of life **3.** period of history **4.** maturity **5.** long time —*v.* **6.** make or grow old —**aged** (ˈeɪdʒɪd) *a.* **1.** old —*pl.n.* **2.** old people —ˈ**ageless** *a.* —**age-old** *a.*

-age (*comb. form*) **1.** collection, set or group, as in *baggage* **2.** process or action or result of action, as in *breakage* **3.** state or relationship, as in *bondage* **4.** house or place, as in *orphanage* **5.** charge or fee, as in *postage* **6.** rate, as in *dosage*

agenda (əˈdʒɛndə) *pl.n.* (*with sing. v.*) **1.** things to be done **2.** programme of business meeting

agent (ˈeɪdʒənt) *n.* **1.** one authorized to carry on business or affairs for another **2.** person or thing producing effect **3.** cause **4.** natural force —ˈ**agency** *n.* **1.** instrumentality **2.** business, place of business of agent

agent provocateur (aˈʒã prɔvɔkaˈtœːr) *Fr.* police spy who tries to provoke persons to act illegally

agglomerate (əˈglɒməreɪt) *v.* **1.** gather into a mass —*n.* (əˈglɒmərɪt, -reɪt) **2.** confused mass **3.** rock consisting of volcanic fragments —*a.* (əˈglɒmərɪt, -reɪt) **4.** formed into a mass —**agglomerˈation** *n.* —**agˈglomerative** *a.*

agglutinate (əˈgluːtɪneɪt) *vt.* **1.** unite with glue *etc.* **2.** form (words) into compounds —*a.* (əˈgluːtɪnɪt, -neɪt) **3.** united, as by glue —**agglutiˈnation** *n.* —**agˈglutinative** *a.*

aggrandize *or* **-dise** (əˈgrændaɪz) *vt.* make greater in size, power or rank —**aggrandizement** *or* **-disement** (əˈgrændɪzmənt) *n.*

aggravate (ˈægrəveɪt) *vt.* **1.** make worse or more severe **2.** *inf.* annoy —ˈ**aggravating** *a.* —**aggraˈvation** *n.*

aggregate (ˈægrɪgeɪt) *vt.* **1.** gather into mass —*a.* (ˈægrɪgɪt) **2.** gathered thus —*n.* (ˈægrɪgɪt, -geɪt) **3.** mass, sum total **4.** rock consisting of mixture of minerals **5.** mixture of gravel *etc.* for concrete —**aggreˈgation** *n.*

aggression (əˈgrɛʃən) *n.* **1.** unprovoked attack **2.** hostile activity —**agˈgress** *vi.* —**agˈgressive** *a.* —**agˈgressiveness** *n.* —**agˈgressor** *n.*

aggrieve (əˈgriːv) *vt.* pain, injure —**agˈgrieved** *a.*

THESAURUS

aftermath after-effects, consequences, effects, end, outcome, results, upshot

again **1.** afresh, anew, another time, once more **2.** also, besides, furthermore, in addition, moreover, on the contrary, on the other hand

against **1.** counter, hostile to, in contrast to, in defiance of, in opposition to, in the face of, opposed to, opposing, resisting, versus **2.** abutting, close up to, facing, fronting, in contact with, on, opposite to, touching, upon **3.** in anticipation of, in expectation of, in preparation for, in provision for

age *n.* **1.** date, day(s), duration, epoch, era, generation, lifetime, period, span, time **2.** advancing years, decline (*of life*), majority, maturity, old age, senescence, senility, seniority ~*v.* **3.** decline, deteriorate, grow old, mature, mellow, ripen

aged age-old, ancient, antiquated, antique, elderly, getting on, grey, hoary, old, senescent, superannuated

agency **1.** action, activity, auspices, efficiency, force, influence, instrumentality, intercession, intervention, means, mechanism, mediation, medium, operation, power, work **2.** bureau, business, department, office, organization

agenda calendar, diary, list, plan, programme, schedule, timetable

agent **1.** advocate, deputy, emissary, envoy, factor, go-between, negotiator, rep (*Inf.*), representative, substitute, surrogate **2.** actor, author, doer, executor, mover, officer, operative, operator, performer, worker **3.** agency, cause, force, instrument, means, power, vehicle

aggravate **1.** exacerbate, exaggerate, heighten, increase, inflame, intensify, magnify, make worse, worsen **2.** *Inf.* annoy, exasperate, get on one's nerves (*Inf.*), irk, irritate, needle (*Inf.*), nettle, pester, provoke, tease, vex

aggravation **1.** exacerbation, exaggeration, heightening, increase, inflaming, intensification, magnification, worsening **2.** *Inf.* annoyance, exasperation, irksomeness, irritation, provocation, teasing, vexation

aggregate **1.** *v.* accumulate, amass, assemble, collect, combine, heap, mix, pile **2.** *n.* accumulation, agglomeration, amount, assemblage, body, bulk, collection, combination, heap, lump, mass, mixture, pile, sum, total, whole **3.** *adj.* accumulated, added, assembled, collected, collective, combined, composite, corporate, cumulative, mixed, total

aggression **1.** assault, attack, encroachment, injury, invasion, offence, offensive, onslaught, raid **2.** aggressiveness, antagonism, belligerence, destructiveness, hostility, pugnacity

aggressive belligerent, destructive, hostile, offensive, pugnacious, quarrelsome

aggressor assailant, assaulter, attacker, invader

aggrieved afflicted, distressed, disturbed, harmed, hurt, ill-used, injured, peeved (*Inf.*), saddened, unhappy, woeful, wronged

aggro (ˈægrəʊ) *n. sl.* aggression
aghast (əˈgɑːst) *a.* overcome with horror or amazement
agile (ˈædʒaɪl) *a.* **1.** nimble **2.** active **3.** quick —**ˈagilely** *adv.* —**agility** (əˈdʒɪlɪtɪ) *n.*
agin (əˈgɪn) *prep. inf., dial.* against
agitate (ˈædʒɪteɪt) *vt.* **1.** disturb, excite **2.** keep in motion, stir, shake up **3.** trouble —*vi.* **4.** stir up public opinion (for or against something) —**agiˈtation** *n.* —**ˈagitator** *n.*
agitprop (ˈædʒɪtprɒp) *n.* political agitation and propaganda, *esp.* of Communist nature
agley (əˈgleɪ, əˈgliː, əˈglaɪ) *a. Scot.* awry
aglitter (əˈglɪtə) *a.* sparkling; glittering
aglow (əˈgləʊ) *a.* glowing
A.G.M. Annual General Meeting
agnostic (ægˈnɒstɪk) *n.* **1.** one who holds that we know nothing of things outside the material world —*a.* **2.** of this theory —**agˈnosticism** *n.*
Agnus Dei (ˈægnʊs ˈdeɪɪ) **1.** figure of a lamb emblematic of Christ **2.** part of Mass beginning with these words
ago (əˈgəʊ) *adv.* in the past
agog (əˈgɒg) *a.* eager, astir
agony (ˈægənɪ) *n.* extreme suffering of mind or body, violent struggle —**ˈagonize** *or* **-ise** *vi.* **1.** suffer agony **2.** worry greatly —**ˈagonizing** *or* **-ising** *a.* —**agony column 1.** magazine feature offering advice to readers on personal problems **2.** *inf.* newspaper column containing personal messages *etc.*
agoraphobia (ægərəˈfəʊbɪə) *n.* fear of open spaces
AGR advanced gas-cooled reactor
agrarian (əˈgrɛərɪən) *a.* of agriculture, land, or its management —**aˈgrarianism** *n.*
agree (əˈgriː) *v.* **1.** be of same opinion **2.** consent **3.** harmonize **4.** determine, settle **5.** suit (**aˈgreed, aˈgreeing**) —**agreeaˈbility** *n.* —**aˈgreeable** *a.* **1.** willing **2.** pleasant —**aˈgreeableness** *n.* —**aˈgreeably** *adv.* —**aˈgreement** *n.* **1.** concord **2.** contract
agriculture (ˈægrɪkʌltʃə) *n.* art, practice of cultivating land —**agriˈcultural** *a.* —**agriˈculturist** *n.*
agrimony (ˈægrɪmənɪ) *n.* yellow-flowered plant with bitter taste
agronomy (əˈgrɒnəmɪ) *n.* study of management of land and scientific cultivation of crops —**aˈgronomist** *n.*
aground (əˈgraʊnd) *adv./a.* (of boat) touching bottom
agt. agent
ague (ˈeɪgjuː) *n. obs.* **1.** malarial fever with periodic attacks of chills and sweating **2.** fit of shivering
ah (ɑː) *interj.* exclamation of pleasure, pain *etc.*
A.H. (indicating years in Muslim system of dating, numbered from Hegira (622 A.D.)) anno Hegirae
aha (ɑːˈhɑː) *interj.* exclamation of triumph, surprise *etc.*
ahead (əˈhɛd) *adv.* **1.** in front **2.** onwards
ahem (əˈhɛm) *interj.* clearing of throat to attract attention *etc.*
ahoy (əˈhɔɪ) *interj.* shout used at sea for hailing
A.I. **1.** artificial insemination **2.** artificial intelligence
aid (eɪd) *vt.* **1.** to help —*n.* **2.** help, support, assistance
A.I.D. artificial insemination by donor
aide (eɪd), **aide-de-camp**, *or* **aid-de-camp**

THESAURUS

aghast afraid, amazed, appalled, astonished, astounded, awestruck, confounded, frightened, horrified, horror-struck, shocked, startled, stunned, thunder-struck
agile active, acute, alert, brisk, clever, limber, lithe, lively, nimble, prompt, quick, quick-witted, sharp, sprightly, spry, supple, swift
agility activity, acuteness, alertness, briskness, cleverness, litheness, liveliness, nimbleness, promptitude, promptness, quickness, quick-wittedness, sharpness, sprightliness, spryness, suppleness, swiftness
agitate 1. beat, churn, convulse, disturb, rock, rouse, shake, stir, toss **2.** alarm, arouse, confuse, disconcert, disquiet, distract, disturb, excite, ferment, fluster, incite, inflame, perturb, rouse, ruffle, stimulate, trouble, upset, work up, worry
agitation 1. churning, convulsion, disturbance, rocking, shake, shaking, stir, stirring, tossing, turbulence **2.** alarm, arousal, clamour, commotion, confusion, discomposure, disquiet, distraction, disturbance, excitement, ferment, flurry, fluster, incitement, lather (*Inf.*), outcry, stimulation, trouble, tumult, turmoil, upset, worry
agitator agent provocateur, demagogue, firebrand, inciter, instigator, rabble-rouser, revolutionary, troublemaker
agog avid, curious, eager, enthralled, enthusiastic, excited, expectant, impatient, in suspense, keen
agony affliction, anguish, distress, misery, pain, pangs, suffering, throes, torment, torture, woe
agree 1. accede, acquiesce, admit, allow, assent, be of the same mind, comply, concede, concur, consent, engage, grant, permit, see eye to eye, settle **2.** accord, answer, chime, coincide, conform, correspond, fit, get on (together), harmonize, match, square, suit, tally
agreeable 1. acceptable, delightful, enjoyable, gratifying, pleasant, pleasing, pleasurable, satisfying, to one's liking, to one's taste **2.** acquiescent, amenable, approving, complying, concurring, consenting, in accord, responsive, sympathetic, well-disposed, willing
agreement 1. accord, accordance, affinity, analogy, compatibility, compliance, concert, concord, concurrence, conformity, congruity, consistency, correspondence, harmony, similarity, suitableness, union **2.** arrangement, bargain, compact, contract, covenant, deal (*Inf.*), pact, settlement, treaty, understanding
agriculture agronomics, agronomy, cultivation, culture, farming, husbandry, tillage
aground ashore, beached, foundered, grounded, high and dry, on the rocks, stranded, stuck
ahead along, at an advantage, at the head, before, forwards, in advance, in front, in the foreground, in the lead, in the vanguard, leading, on, onwards, to the fore, winning
aid 1. *v.* abet, assist, befriend, encourage, favour, help, promote, relieve, second, serve, subsidize, succour, support, sustain **2.** *n.* assistance, benefit, encouragement, favour, help, relief, service, succour, support

(ˈeɪd də ˈkɒŋ) *n.* military officer personally assisting superior (*pl.* **aides(-de-camp)** *or* **aids-de-camp**)

AIDS (eɪdz) acquired immuno-deficiency syndrome

aigrette *or* **aigret** (ˈeɪgrɛt) *n.* **1.** long plume worn on hats or as headdress, *esp.* one of egret feathers **2.** ornament in imitation of plume of feathers

aiguille (eɪˈgwiːl) *n.* **1.** sharp, slender peak **2.** blasting drill

A.I.H. artificial insemination by husband

ail (eɪl) *vt.* **1.** trouble, afflict, disturb —*vi.* **2.** be ill —**ˈailing** *a.* sickly —**ˈailment** *n.* illness

aileron (ˈeɪlərɒn) *n.* movable section of wing of aircraft which gives lateral control

aim (eɪm) *v.* **1.** give direction to (weapon *etc.*) **2.** direct effort (towards) —*n.* **3.** direction **4.** object, purpose —**ˈaimless** *a.* without purpose

ain't (eɪnt) *nonstandard* **1.** am not **2.** is not **3.** are not **4.** has not **5.** have not

air (ɛə) *n.* **1.** mixture of gases we breathe, the atmosphere **2.** breeze **3.** tune **4.** manner —*pl.* **5.** affected manners —*vt.* **6.** expose to air to dry or ventilate —**ˈairily** *adv.* —**ˈairiness** *n.* —**ˈairing** *n.* time spent in the open air —**ˈairless** *a.* stuffy —**ˈairy** *a.* —**air bag 1.** bag in car, that inflates automatically in accident and prevents passengers from being thrown forwards **2.** inflatable bag for restraining loads in partly filled containers —**air base** —**air bed** —**ˈairborne** *a.* flying, in the air —**air brake 1.** brake worked by compressed air **2.** method of slowing down an aircraft —**ˈairbrick** *n. chiefly* **UK** brick with holes in it, for ventilation —**ˈairbus** *n.* airliner operated over short distances —**air commodore** —**air-condition** *vt.* —**air conditioner** —**air conditioning** system for controlling temperature and humidity of air in building —**ˈaircraft** *n.* **1.** collective name for flying machines **2.** aeroplane —**aircraft carrier** —**air curtain** air stream across doorway to exclude draughts *etc.* —**air cushion 1.** pillow which can be inflated **2.** pocket of air supporting hovercraft —**ˈairfield** *n.* landing and taking-off area for aircraft —**air force** strength of country in military aircraft —**air gun** gun discharged by force of compressed air —**air hostess** stewardess on aircraft —**air letter** air-mail letter, aerogram —**ˈairlift** *n.* transport of goods *etc.* by aircraft —**ˈairline** *n.* company operating aircraft —**ˈairliner** *n.* large passenger aircraft —**ˈairlock** *n.* **1.** air bubble obstructing flow of liquid in pipe **2.** airtight chamber —**air mail** —**ˈairman** *n.* —**air pocket** less dense air where aeroplane drops suddenly —**ˈairport** *n.* airfield for civilian aircraft —**air pump** machine to extract or supply air —**air raid** attack by aircraft —**air rifle** rifle discharged by compressed air —**air sac** any of air-filled extensions of lungs of birds —**ˈairscrew** *n.* propeller of any aircraft —**air shaft** passage for air into a mine *etc.* —**ˈairship** *n.* lighter-than-air flying machine with means of propulsion —**ˈairsickness** *n.* nausea caused by motion of aircraft in flight —**ˈairspeed** *n.* speed of aircraft relative to air —**ˈairstrip** *n.* small airfield with only one runway —**ˈairtight** *a.* not allowing passage of air —**air-to-air** *a.* operating between aircraft in flight —**air trap** device to prevent escape of foul gases —**air valve** —**ˈairway** *n.* **1.** regular aircraft route **2.** passage for ventilation, *esp.* in mine —**ˈairworthiness** *n.* —**ˈairworthy** *a.* fit for service in air

Airedale (ˈɛədeɪl) *n.* large rough-coated terrier dog

aisle (aɪl) *n.* passageway separating seating areas in church, theatre *etc.*

aitch (eɪtʃ) *n.* letter *h* or sound represented by it

aitchbone (ˈeɪtʃbəʊn) *n.* **1.** rump bone in cattle **2.** cut of beef from rump bone

ajar[1] (əˈdʒɑː) *a./adv.* partly open

ajar[2] (əˈdʒɑː) *a.* not in harmony

AK Alaska

akimbo (əˈkɪmbəʊ) *adv.* with hands on hips and elbows outwards

akin (əˈkɪn) *a.* **1.** related by blood **2.** alike, having like qualities

Al *Chem.* aluminium

AL Alabama

-al[1] (*a. comb. form*) of; related to, as in *functional, sectional*

-al[2] (*n. comb. form*) act or process of, as in *renewal*

-al[3] (*n. comb. form*) **1.** aldehyde, as in *salicylal* **2.** pharmaceutical product, as in *phenobarbital*

à la (ɑː lɑː) **1.** in the manner of **2.** as prepared in, by or for

alabaster (ˈæləbɑːstə) *n.* soft, white, semitransparent stone —**alaˈbastrine** *a.* of, like this

à la carte (ɑː lɑː ˈkɑːt) *Fr.* selected freely from menu

alack (əˈlæk) *or* **alackaday** (əˈlækədeɪ) *interj. obs., poet.* cry of sorrow

alacrity (əˈlækrɪtɪ) *n.* quickness, briskness, readiness

à la mode (ɑː lɑː ˈməʊd) *Fr.* in fashion

alarm (əˈlɑːm) *n.* **1.** sudden fright **2.** apprehension **3.** notice of danger **4.** bell, buzzer **5.** call to arms —*vt.* **6.** frighten **7.** warn of danger —**aˈlarming** *a.* —**aˈlarmist**

THESAURUS

aim 1. *v.* aspire, attempt, design, direct, draw a bead (on), endeavour, intend, level, mean, plan, point, propose, purpose, resolve, seek, set one's sights on, sight, strive, take aim (at), train, try, want, wish **2.** *n.* ambition, aspiration, course, design, desire, direction, end, goal, intent, intention, mark, object, objective, plan, purpose, scheme, target, wish

aimless chance, directionless, erratic, frivolous, goalless, haphazard, pointless, purposeless, random, stray, undirected, unguided, unpredictable, vagrant, wayward

air *n.* **1.** atmosphere, heavens, sky **2.** blast, breath, breeze, draught, puff, waft, whiff, wind, zephyr **3.** ambience, appearance, atmosphere, aura, bearing, character, demeanour, effect, feeling, flavour, impression, look, manner, mood, quality, style, tone **4.** aria, lay, melody, song, tune ~*v.* **5.** aerate, expose, freshen, ventilate

airiness breeziness, draughtiness, freshness, gustiness, lightness, openness, windiness

airing aeration, drying, freshening, ventilation

airless breathless, close, heavy, muggy, oppressive, stale, stifling, stuffy, suffocating, sultry, unventilated

airs affectation, affectedness, arrogance, haughtiness, hauteur, pomposity, pretensions, superciliousness, swank (*Inf.*)

airy blowy, breezy, draughty, fresh, gusty, light, lofty, open, spacious, uncluttered, well-ventilated, windy

aisle corridor, gangway, lane, passage, passageway, path

n. one given to prophesying danger or exciting alarm *esp.* needlessly **—alarm clock** clock which sounds a buzzer or bell at a set time, as to wake someone up

alas (əˈlæs) *interj.* cry of grief

alate (ˈeɪleɪt) *a.* having wings

alb (ælb) *n.* long white priestly vestment, worn at Mass

albacore (ˈælbəkɔː) *n.* tunny occurring *esp.* in warm regions of Atlantic and Pacific

albatross (ˈælbətrɒs) *n.* large oceanic bird of petrel family

albeit (ɔːlˈbiːɪt) *conj.* although

albert (ˈælbət) *n.* watch chain usu. attached to waistcoat

albino (ælˈbiːnəʊ) *n.* person or animal with white skin and hair, and pinkish eyes, due to lack of colouring matter (*pl.* **-s**) **—albinism** (ˈælbɪnɪzəm) *n.*

Albion (ˈælbɪən) *n. obs., poet.* **1.** Britain **2.** England

album (ˈælbəm) *n.* **1.** book of blank leaves, for photographs, stamps, autographs *etc.* **2.** one or more longplaying gramophone records

albumen (ˈælbjʊmɪn) *n.* egg white

albumin *or* **albumen** (ˈælbjʊmɪn) *n.* constituent of animal and vegetable matter, found nearly pure in white of egg **—alˈbuminous** *a.*

alchemy (ˈælkəmɪ) *n.* medieval chemistry, *esp.* attempts to turn base metals into gold and find elixir of life **—ˈalchemist** *n.*

alcohol (ˈælkəhɒl) *n.* **1.** intoxicating fermented liquor **2.** class of organic chemical substances **—alcoˈholic** *a.* **1.** of alcohol *—n.* **2.** one addicted to alcoholic drink **—ˈalcoholism** *n.* (disease caused by) habitual heavy consumption of alcoholic drink

alcove (ˈælkəʊv) *n.* recess

aldehyde (ˈældɪhaɪd) *n.* one of a group of organic chemical compounds

alder (ˈɔːldə) *n.* tree related to the birch

alderman (ˈɔːldəmən) *n.* formerly, member of governing body of a municipality **—alderˈmanic** *a.*

ale (eɪl) *n.* fermented malt liquor, type of beer, *orig.* without hops **—ˈalehouse** *n. obs.* public house

aleatory (ˈeɪlɪətərɪ) *or* **aleatoric** (eɪlɪəˈtɒrɪk) *a.* **1.** dependent on chance **2.** *Mus.* involving elements chosen at random

alembic (əˈlɛmbɪk) *n.* **1.** formerly, retort used for distillation **2.** anything that distils or purifies

alert (əˈlɜːt) *a.* **1.** watchful **2.** brisk, active *—n.* **3.** warning of sudden attack or surprise *—vt.* **4.** warn, *esp.* of danger **5.** draw (someone's) attention to something **—aˈlertness** *n.* **—on the alert** watchful

A level **UK 1.** advanced level of General Certificate of Education **2.** pass in subject at A level

Alexandrine (ælɪgˈzændraɪn) *n.* verse of six iambic feet

alexandrite (ælɪgˈzændraɪt) *n.* green chrysoberyl used as gemstone

alexia (əˈlɛksɪə) *n.* impaired ability to read

alfalfa (ælˈfælfə) *n.* plant of Europe and Asia used as fodder (*also* **luˈcerne**)

alfresco (ælˈfrɛskəʊ) *adv./a.* in the open air

alg. algebra

algae (ˈældʒiː) *pl.n.* various water plants, including seaweed (*sing.* **alga** (ˈælgə))

algebra (ˈældʒɪbrə) *n.* method of calculating, using symbols to represent quantities and to show relations between them, making a kind of abstract arithmetic **—algebraic(al)** (ældʒɪˈbreɪɪk(ᵊl)) *a.* **—algebraist** (ældʒɪˈbreɪɪst) *n.*

-algia (*n. comb. form*) pain in part specified, as in *neuralgia* **—-algic** (*a. comb. form*)

algid (ˈældʒɪd) *a. Med.* chilly, cold

ALGOL (ˈælgɒl) computer programming language designed for mathematical and scientific purposes

algorism (ˈælgərɪzəm) *n.* **1.** Arabic or decimal system of counting **2.** skill of computation **3.** algorithm

algorithm (ˈælgərɪðəm) *n.* procedural model for complicated calculations

alias (ˈeɪlɪəs) *adv.* **1.** otherwise *—n.* **2.** assumed name (*pl.* **-es**)

alibi (ˈælɪbaɪ) *n.* **1.** plea of being somewhere else when crime was committed **2.** *inf.* excuse (*pl.* **-s**)

alien (ˈeɪlɪən) *a.* **1.** foreign **2.** different in nature **3.** repugnant *—n.* **4.** foreigner **—alienaˈbility** *n.* **—ˈalienable** *a.* able to be transferred to another owner **—ˈalienate** *vt.* **1.** estrange **2.** transfer **—alieˈnation** *n.* **—ˈalienist** *n.* **US** psychiatrist who specializes in legal aspects of mental illness

THESAURUS

alarm *v.* **1.** daunt, dismay, distress, frighten, give (someone) a turn (*Inf.*), panic, put the wind up (someone) (*Inf.*), scare, startle, terrify, unnerve **2.** alert, arouse, signal, warn *~n.* **3.** anxiety, apprehension, consternation, dismay, distress, fear, fright, nervousness, panic, scare, terror, trepidation, unease, uneasiness **4.** alarm-bell, alert, bell, danger signal, distress signal, siren, tocsin, warning

alarming daunting, dismaying, distressing, disturbing, dreadful, frightening, scaring, shocking, startling, terrifying, unnerving

alcoholic **1.** *adj.* brewed, distilled, fermented, hard, inebriant, inebriating, intoxicating, spirituous, strong, vinous **2.** *n.* bibber, boozer (*Inf.*), dipsomaniac, drunk, drunkard, hard drinker, inebriate, soak (*Inf.*), sot, sponge (*Inf.*), tippler, toper, tosspot (*Inf.*), wino (*Inf.*)

alcove bay, bower, compartment, corner, cubbyhole, cubicle, niche, nook, recess

alert **1.** *adj.* active, agile, attentive, brisk, careful, circumspect, heedful, lively, nimble, observant, on guard, on one's toes, on the ball (*Inf.*), on the lookout, on the watch, perceptive, quick, ready, spirited, sprightly, vigilant, wary, watchful, wide-awake **2.** *n.* alarm, signal, siren, warning **3.** *v.* alarm, forewarn, inform, notify, signal, warn

alertness activeness, agility, attentiveness, briskness, carefulness, circumspection, heedfulness, liveliness, nimbleness, perceptiveness, promptitude, quickness, readiness, spiritedness, sprightliness, vigilance, wariness, watchfulness

alias **1.** *adv.* also called, also known as, otherwise, otherwise known as **2.** *n.* assumed name, *nom de guerre*, nom de plume, pen name, pseudonym, stage name

alibi defence, excuse, explanation, justification, plea, pretext, reason

alien **1.** *adj.* adverse, conflicting, contrary, estranged, exotic, foreign, inappropriate, incompatible, incongruous, not native, not naturalized, opposed, out-

alight[1] (əˈlaɪt) *vi.* 1. get down 2. land, settle

alight[2] (əˈlaɪt) *a.* 1. burning 2. lit up

align (əˈlaɪn) *vt.* bring into line or agreement —**aˈlignment** *n.*

alike (əˈlaɪk) *a.* 1. like, similar —*adv.* 2. in the same way

aliment (ˈælɪmənt) *n.* something that nourishes or sustains body or mind —**aliˈmentary** *a.* of food —**alimentary canal** food passage in body

alimony (ˈælɪmənɪ) *n.* allowance paid under court order to separated or divorced spouse

aline (əˈlaɪn) *vt. rare see* ALIGN —**aˈlinement** *n.*

A-line (ˈeɪlaɪn) *a.* (of garments) flaring out slightly from waist or shoulders

aliped (ˈælɪpɛd) *a.* 1. wing-footed —*n.* 2. animal, like the bat, whose toes are joined by membrane that serves as wing

aliphatic (ælɪˈfætɪk) *a.* (of organic compound) not aromatic, *esp.* having open chain structure

aliquant (ˈælɪkwənt) *a. Maths.* (of quantity or number) that is not exact divisor of given quantity or number

aliquot (ˈælɪkwɒt) *a. Maths.* of or signifying an exact divisor of a quantity or number

alive (əˈlaɪv) *a.* 1. living 2. active 3. aware 4. swarming

alizarin (əˈlɪzərɪn) *n.* brown-to-red crystalline solid used as dye

alkali (ˈælkəlaɪ) *n.* substance which combines with acid and neutralizes it, forming a salt; potash, soda *etc.* are alkalis (*pl.* **-s, -lies**) —**ˈalkaline** *a.* —**alkalinity** (ælkəˈlɪnɪtɪ) *n.* —**ˈalkalize** *or* **-ise** *vt.* —**ˈalkaloid** *n./a.*

Alkoran *or* **Alcoran** (ælkɒˈrɑːn) *n. see* KORAN

all (ɔːl) *a.* 1. the whole of, every one of —*adv.* 2. wholly, entirely —*n.* 3. the whole 4. everything, everyone —**All Black** member of international Rugby Union football team of N.Z. —**all found** (of accommodation charges) inclusive of meals, heating *etc.* —**all fours** hands and feet —**all in** exhausted —**all-in** *a. Wrestling* of style of professional wrestling with no internationally agreed set of rules —**all out** *inf.* to one's maximum capacity —**all-out** *a. inf.* using one's maximum powers —**all right** *a.* 1. adequate; satisfactory 2. unharmed; safe —*adv.* 3. very well 4. satisfactorily 5. without doubt (*also* (*nonstandard*) **alˈright**) —**all-right** *a.* **US** *sl.* acceptable; reliable (*also* (*nonstandard*) **alˈright**) —**all-round** *a.* 1. efficient in all respects, *esp.* in sport 2. comprehensive; many-sided —**all-rounder** *n.* person with ability in many fields —**All Saints' Day** Christian festival celebrated on Nov. 1st to honour all saints —**All Souls' Day** *R.C.Ch.* day of prayer (Nov. 2nd) for the dead in purgatory

alla breve (ˈælə ˈbreɪvɪ) *Mus. a./adv.* 1. with two beats to the bar —*n.* 2. formerly, time of two or four minims to the bar

Allah (ˈælə) *n.* Moslem name for the Supreme Deity

allay (əˈleɪ) *vt.* lighten, relieve, calm, soothe

allege (əˈlɛdʒ) *vt.* 1. state without or before proof 2. produce as argument —**allegation** (ælɪˈgeɪʃən) *n.* —**alˈleged** *a.* —**allegedly** (əˈlɛdʒɪdlɪ) *adv.*

allegiance (əˈliːdʒəns) *n.* duty of a subject to his sovereign or state, loyalty

allegory (ˈælɪgərɪ) *n.* 1. story with a meaning other than literal one 2. description of one thing under image of another —**alleˈgoric(al)** *a.* —**alleˈgorically** *adv.* —**ˈallegorist** *n.* —**ˈallegorize** *or* **-rise** *vt.*

allegretto (ælɪˈgrɛtəʊ) *adv./a./n. Mus.* lively (passage) but not so quick as allegro

allegro (əˈleɪgrəʊ, -ˈlɛg-) *adv./a./n. Mus.* fast (passage)

THESAURUS

landish, remote, repugnant, separated, strange, unfamiliar **2.** *n.* foreigner, newcomer, outsider, stranger

alienate **1.** break off, disaffect, divert, divorce, estrange, make unfriendly, separate, set against, turn away, withdraw **2.** *Law* abalienate, convey, transfer

alienation **1.** breaking off, disaffection, diversion, divorce, estrangement, indifference, remoteness, rupture, separation, setting against, turning away, withdrawal **2.** *Law* abalienation, conveyance, transfer

alight[1] *v.* come down, come to rest, descend, disembark, dismount, get down, get off, land, light, perch, settle, touch down

alight[2] *adj.* **1.** ablaze, aflame, blazing, burning, fiery, flaming, flaring, ignited, lighted, lit, on fire **2.** bright, brilliant, illuminated, lit up, shining

align **1.** arrange in line, coordinate, even, even up, line up, make parallel, order, range, regulate, straighten **2.** affiliate, agree, ally, associate, cooperate, join, side, sympathize

alignment **1.** adjustment, arrangement, coordination, evening, evening up, line, lining up, order, ranging, regulating, sequence, straightening up **2.** affiliation, agreement, alliance, association, cooperation, sympathy, union

alike **1.** *adj.* akin, analogous, corresponding, duplicate, equal, equivalent, even, identical, parallel, resembling, similar, the same, uniform **2.** *adv.* analogously, correspondingly, equally, evenly, identically, similarly, uniformly

alive **1.** animate, breathing, having life, in the land of the living (*Inf.*), living, subsisting **2.** active, existent, existing, extant, functioning, in existence, in force, operative, unquenched **3.** active, alert, animated, awake, brisk, cheerful, eager, energetic, full of life, lively, quick, spirited, sprightly, spry, vigorous, vital, vivacious, zestful

all *adj.* **1.** every bit of, the complete, the entire, the sum of, the totality of, the total of, the whole of **2.** each, each and every, every, every one of, every single **3.** complete, entire, full, greatest, perfect, total, utter ~*n.* **4.** aggregate, entirety, everything, sum, sum total, total, total amount, totality, utmost, whole, whole amount ~*adv.* **5.** altogether, completely, entirely, fully, totally, utterly, wholly

allegation accusation, affirmation, assertion, asseveration, averment, avowal, charge, claim, declaration, deposition, plea, profession, statement

allege advance, affirm, assert, asseverate, aver, avow, charge, claim, declare, depose, maintain, plead, profess, put forward, state

alleged affirmed, asserted, averred, declared, described, designated, professed, stated

allegorical emblematic, figurative, parabolic, symbolic, symbolizing

allegory apologue, emblem, fable, myth, parable, story, symbol, symbolism, tale

allergic **1.** affected by, hypersensitive, sensitive, sensitized, susceptible **2.** *Inf.* antipathetic, averse, disinclined, hostile, loath, opposed

alleluia (ælɪˈluːjə) *interj.* praise the Lord

allergy (ˈælədʒɪ) *n.* abnormal sensitivity to some food or substance innocuous to most people —**ˈallergen** *n.* substance capable of inducing an allergy —**allerˈgenic** *a.* —**alˈlergic** *a.* 1. having or caused by an allergy 2. *inf.* having an aversion (to)

alleviate (əˈliːvɪeɪt) *vt.* 1. ease, lessen, mitigate 2. make light —**alleviˈation** *n.* —**alˈleviator** *n.*

alley (ˈælɪ) *n.* 1. narrow street 2. walk, path 3. enclosure for skittles 4. fine marble (*pl.* -s)

Allhallows (ɔːlˈhæləuz) *n. see* **All Saints' Day** *at* ALL

alliance (əˈlaɪəns) *n.* 1. state of being allied 2. union between families by marriage, and states by treaty 3. confederation

alligator (ˈælɪgeɪtə) *n.* animal of crocodile family found in Amer.

alliteration (əlɪtəˈreɪʃən) *n.* beginning two or more words in close succession with same sound, *eg* Sing a Song of Sixpence —**alˈliterate** *v.* —**alˈliterative** *a.*

allocate (ˈæləkeɪt) *vt.* 1. assign as a share 2. place —**alloˈcation** *n.*

allocution (æləˈkjuːʃən) *n.* formal address

allogamy (əˈlɒgəmɪ) *n.* cross-fertilization

allomorphism (æləˈmɔːfɪzəm) *n.* 1. variation of form without change in essential nature 2. variation of crystalline form of chemical compound

allopathy (əˈlɒpəθɪ) *n.* 1. orthodox practice of medicine 2. opposite of homeopathy

allot (əˈlɒt) *vt.* 1. distribute as shares 2. give out (-tt-) —**alˈlotment** *n.* 1. distribution 2. portion of land rented for cultivation 3. portion allotted

allotropy (əˈlɒtrəpɪ) *or* **allotropism** *n.* property of some elements of existing in more than one form, *eg* carbon in the form of diamond and graphite —**ˈallotrope** *n.* —**alloˈtropic** *a.*

allow (əˈlau) *vt.* 1. permit 2. acknowledge 3. set aside —*vi.* (*usu. with* for) 4. take into account —**alˈlowable** *a.* —**alˈlowably** *adv.* —**alˈlowance** *n.* —**allowedly** (əˈlauɪdlɪ) *adv.* 1. by general agreement 2. admittedly

alloy (ˈælɔɪ, əˈlɔɪ) *n.* 1. mixture of two or more metals —*vt.* (əˈlɔɪ) 2. mix (metals) to form an alloy 3. debase by mixing with something inferior

allspice (ˈɔːlspaɪs) *n.* 1. berry of W Indian tree 2. spice made from this berry

allude (əˈluːd) *vi.* 1. mention lightly, hint (at), make indirect reference (to) 2. refer (to) —**alˈlusion** *n.* —**alˈlusive** *a.* —**alˈlusively** *adv.*

allure (əˈluə) *vt.* 1. entice, win over, fascinate —*n.* 2. attractiveness —**alˈlurement** *n.* —**alˈluring** *a.* charming, seductive —**alˈluringly** *adv.*

alluvial (əˈluːvɪəl) *a.* deposited by rivers —**alˈluvion** *n.* land formed by washed-up deposit —**alˈluvium** *n.* water-borne matter deposited by rivers, floods *etc.* (*pl.* -**s**, -**via** (-vɪə))

ally (əˈlaɪ) *vt.* 1. join in relationship by treaty, marriage or friendship *etc.* (**alˈlied, alˈlying**) —*n.* (ˈælaɪ) 2. state or sovereign bound to another by treaty 3. confederate (*pl.* **ˈallies**) —**allied** (əˈlaɪd, ˈælaɪd) *a.* —**ˈAllies** *pl.n.* 1. (in World War I) powers of the Triple Entente (France, Russia and Britain) together with nations allied with them 2. (in World War II) countries that fought against the Axis, *esp.* Britain and Commonwealth countries, Amer., Soviet Union and France

THESAURUS

allergy antipathy, hypersensitivity, sensitivity, susceptibility

alley alleyway, backstreet, lane, passage, passageway, pathway, walk

alliance affiliation, affinity, agreement, association, coalition, combination, compact, concordat, confederacy, confederation, connection, federation, league, marriage, pact, partnership, treaty, union

allied affiliated, amalgamated, associated, bound, combined, confederate, connected, hand in glove (*Inf.*), in cahoots (*U.S. inf.*), in league, joined, joint, kindred, leagued, linked, married, related, unified, united, wed

allocate allot, apportion, appropriate, assign, budget, designate, earmark, mete, set aside, share out

allocation allotment, allowance, apportionment, appropriation, grant, lot, measure, portion, quota, ration, share, stint

allot allocate, apportion, appropriate, assign, budget, designate, earmark, mete, set aside, share out

allotment 1. allocation, allowance, apportionment, appropriation, grant, lot, measure, portion, quota, ration, share, stint 2. kitchen garden, patch, plot, tract

all-out complete, determined, exhaustive, full, full-scale, maximum, optimum, resolute, supreme, thorough, thoroughgoing, total, undivided, unlimited, unremitting, unrestrained, unstinted, utmost

allow 1. acknowledge, acquiesce, admit, concede, confess, grant, own 2. approve, authorize, bear, brook, endure, give leave, let, permit, put up with (*Inf.*), sanction, stand, suffer, tolerate 3. allocate, allot, assign, deduct, give, grant, provide, remit, spare

allowable acceptable, admissible, all right, appropriate, approved, permissible, sanctionable, sufferable, suitable, tolerable

allowance admission, concession, sanction, sufferance, toleration

allow for arrange for, consider, foresee, keep in mind, make allowances for, make concessions for, make provision for, plan for, provide for, set (something) aside for, take into account, take into consideration

alloy *n.* 1. admixture, amalgam, blend, combination, composite, compound, hybrid, mixture ~*v.* 2. admix, amalgamate, blend, combine, compound, fuse, mix 3. adulterate, debase, devalue, diminish, impair

all right *adj.* 1. acceptable, adequate, average, fair, O.K. (*Inf.*), passable, satisfactory, standard, unobjectionable 2. hale, healthy, safe, sound, unharmed, unimpaired, uninjured, well, whole ~*adv.* 3. acceptably, adequately, O.K. (*Inf.*), passably, satisfactorily, unobjectionably, well enough

allure 1. *v.* attract, beguile, cajole, captivate, charm, coax, decoy, enchant, entice, inveigle, lead on, lure, persuade, seduce, tempt, win over 2. *n.* appeal, attraction, charm, enchantment, enticement, glamour, lure, persuasion, seductiveness, temptation

allusion casual remark, glance, hint, implication, indirect reference, innuendo, insinuation, intimation, mention, suggestion

ally 1. *n.* abettor, accessory, accomplice, associate, coadjutor, collaborator, colleague, confederate, co-worker, friend, helper, partner 2. *v.* affiliate, associate, band together, collaborate, combine, confeder-

alma mater ('ælmə 'mɑːtə, 'meɪtə) *Lat.* one's school, university, or college

almanac ('ɔːlmənæk) *n.* yearly calendar with detailed information on year's tides, events *etc.*

almighty (ɔːl'maɪtɪ) *a.* **1.** having all power, omnipotent **2.** *inf.* very great —**the Almighty** God

almond ('ɑːmənd) *n.* **1.** edible kernel of the fruit of a tree related to the peach **2.** tree bearing this fruit

almoner ('ɑːmənə) *n.* **UK** in hospitals, formerly, trained social worker dealing with patients' welfare

almost ('ɔːlməʊst) *adv.* very nearly, all but

alms (ɑːmz) *pl.n.* gifts to the poor —**'almshouse** *n.* **UK** privately supported house offering accommodation to the needy

aloe ('æləʊ) *n.* **1.** genus of plants of medicinal value —*pl.n.* (*with sing. v.*) **2.** bitter drug made from plant

aloft (ə'lɒft) *adv.* **1.** on high **2.** overhead **3.** in ship's rigging

alone (ə'ləʊn) *a.* **1.** single, solitary —*adv.* **2.** separately, only

along (ə'lɒŋ) *adv.* **1.** in a line **2.** together with one **3.** forward —*prep.* **4.** over the length of —**along'side** *adv./prep.* beside (something)

aloof (ə'luːf) *a.* **1.** withdrawn **2.** distant **3.** uninvolved —**a'loofness** *n.*

alopecia (ælə'piːʃɪə) *n.* baldness

aloud (ə'laʊd) *adv.* **1.** loudly **2.** audibly

alp (ælp) *n.* high mountain —**'alpine** *a.* **1.** of the Alps **2.** of high mountains —*n.* **3.** mountain plant —**'alpinist** *n.* mountain climber —**'alpenstock** *n.* iron-shod staff used by climbers —**the Alps** high mountain range in S central Europe

alpaca (æl'pækə) *n.* **1.** Peruvian llama **2.** its wool **3.** cloth made from this

alpha ('ælfə) *n.* **1.** first letter in Greek alphabet (Α, α) **2.** **UK** highest grade or mark, as in examination —*a.* **3.** involving helium nuclei; denoting isomeric or allotropic form of substance —**alpha particle** helium nucleus emitted during some radioactive transformations —**alpha ray** ionizing radiation consisting of stream of alpha particles —**alpha and omega** the first and last

alphabet ('ælfəbɛt) *n.* the set of letters used in writing a language —**alpha'betic(al)** *a.* in the standard order of the letters —**alpha'betically** *adv.* —**'alphabetize** *or* **-ise** *vt.* **1.** arrange in alphabetical order **2.** express by alphabet

alphanumeric (ælfənjuː'mɛrɪk) *or* **alphameric** (ælfə'mɛrɪk) *a.* consisting of alphabetical and numerical symbols

already (ɔːl'rɛdɪ) *adv.* **1.** before, previously **2.** sooner than expected

alright (ɔːl'raɪt) *adv. nonstandard see* **all right** *at* ALL

Alsatian (æl'seɪʃən) *n.* large dog of wolfhound breed, German shepherd dog

also ('ɔːlsəʊ) *adv.* **1.** as well, too **2.** besides, moreover —**also-ran** *n.* **1.** contestant *etc.* failing to finish among first three **2.** *inf.* loser

alt. **1.** alternate **2.** altitude **3.** alto

Alta. Alberta

altar ('ɔːltə) *n.* **1.** raised place, stone *etc.*, on which sacrifices are offered **2.** in Christian church, table on which priest consecrates the Eucharist —**altar boy** boy serving as an acolyte —**'altarcloth** *n.* —**'altarpiece** *n.*

alter ('ɔːltə) *v.* change, make or become different —**altera'bility** *n.* —**'alterable** *a.* —**'alterably** *adv.* —**alte'ration** *n.* —**'alterative** *a.*

altercation (ɔːltə'keɪʃən) *n.* dispute, wrangling, controversy —**'altercate** *vi.*

alter ego ('æltər 'iːgəʊ, 'ɛgəʊ) *Lat.* **1.** second self **2.** close friend

alternate ('ɔːltəneɪt) *v.* **1.** occur or cause to occur by turns —*a.* (ɔːl'tɜːnɪt) **2.** one after the other, by turns —**al'ternately** *adv.* —**alter'nation** *n.* —**al'ternative** *n.* **1.** one of two choices —*a.* **2.** presenting choice, *esp.* between two possibilities only **3.** (of two things) mutually exclusive **4.** denoting lifestyle *etc.* regarded as preferable to that of contemporary society because it is less conventional, materialistic or institutionalized —**al'ternatively** *adv.* —**'alternator** *n.* electric generator for producing alternating current —**alternating current** electric current that reverses direction with a frequency independent of characteristics of circuit —**alternative society** group of people who agree in rejecting traditional values of society around them

THESAURUS

ate, connect, join, join forces, league, marry, unify, unite

almighty **1.** absolute, all-powerful, invincible, omnipotent, supreme, unlimited **2.** *Inf.* awful, desperate, enormous, excessive, great, intense, loud, severe, terrible

almost about, all but, approximately, as good as, close to, just about, nearly, not far from, not quite, on the brink of, practically, virtually, well-nigh

alone abandoned, apart, by itself, by oneself, deserted, desolate, detached, forlorn, forsaken, isolated, lonely, lonesome, only, separate, single, single-handed, sole, solitary, unaccompanied, unaided, unassisted, unattended, uncombined, unconnected, unescorted

aloof **1.** chilly, cold, cool, detached, distant, forbidding, formal, haughty, indifferent, remote, reserved, standoffish, supercilious, unapproachable, unfriendly, uninterested, unresponsive, unsociable, unsympathetic **2.** above, apart, at a distance, away, distanced, distant

aloud **1.** audibly, clearly, distinctly, intelligibly, out loud, plainly **2.** clamorously, loudly, noisily, vociferously

already as of now, at present, before now, by now, by that time, by then, by this time, even now, heretofore, just now, previously

also additionally, along with, and, as well, as well as, besides, further, furthermore, in addition, including, into the bargain, moreover, on top of that, plus, to boot, too

alter adapt, adjust, amend, change, convert, diversify, metamorphose, modify, recast, reform, remodel, reshape, revise, shift, transform, transmute, turn, vary

alteration adaptation, adjustment, amendment, change, conversion, difference, diversification, metamorphosis, modification, reformation, remodelling, reshaping, revision, shift, transformation, transmutation, variance, variation

alternate **1.** *v.* act reciprocally, alter, change, follow in turn, follow one another, interchange, intersperse, oscillate, rotate, substitute, take turns, vary **2.** *adj.* alternating, every other, every second, interchanging, rotating

althorn (ˈælthɔːn) *n.* a tenor saxhorn

although (ɔːlˈðəʊ) *conj.* despite the fact that

altimeter (ælˈtɪmɪtə, ˈæltɪmiːtə) *n.* instrument for measuring height

altitude (ˈæltɪtjuːd) *n.* height, eminence, elevation, loftiness

alto (ˈæltəʊ) *n. Mus.* **1.** male singing voice or instrument above tenor **2.** contralto (*pl.* **-s**) **—alto clef** clef that establishes middle C as being on third line of staff

altogether (ɔːltəˈgɛðə, ˈɔːltəgɛðə) *adv.* **1.** entirely **2.** on the whole **3.** in total

altruism (ˈæltruːɪzəm) *n.* principle of living and acting for good of others **—altruˈistic** *a.* **—altruˈistically** *adv.*

alum (ˈæləm) *n.* mineral salt, double sulphate of aluminium and potassium **—aluminous** (əˈluːmɪnəs) *a.*

aluminium (æljʊˈmɪnɪəm) *or U.S.* **aluminum** (əˈluːmɪnəm) *n.* light silvery nonrusting metal **—alumina** (əˈluːmɪnə) *n.* oxide of aluminium **—aluminize** *or* **-ise** (əˈluːmɪnaɪz) *vt.* coat with aluminium **—aluminous** (əˈluːmɪnəs) *a.*

alumnus (əˈlʌmnəs) *or* (*fem.*) **alumna** (əˈlʌmnə) *n.* US graduate of college (*pl.* **-ni** (-naɪ) *or* **-nae** (-niː))

always (ˈɔːlweɪz) *adv.* **1.** at all times **2.** for ever

alyssum (ˈælɪsəm) *n.* garden plant with small yellow or white flowers

am (æm; *unstressed* əm) *first person sing. pres. ind. of* BE

Am *Chem.* americium

AM *or* **am** amplitude modulation

Am. America(n)

a.m. *or* **A.M.** ante meridiem

Amadhlozi *or* **Amadlozi** (æmæˈhlɒʒiː) *pl.n.* **SA** ancestral spirits

amah (ˈɑːmə) *n.* in East, *esp.* formerly, nurse or maidservant

amain (əˈmeɪn) *adv. obs., poet.* with great strength or haste

amalgam (əˈmælgəm) *n.* **1.** compound of mercury and another metal **2.** soft, plastic mixture **3.** combination of elements

amalgamate (əˈmælgəmeɪt) *v.* mix, combine or cause to combine **—amalgaˈmation** *n.*

amanuensis (əmænjʊˈɛnsɪs) *n.* **1.** person employed to take dictation **2.** copyist **3.** secretary (*pl.* **-ses** (-siːz))

amaranth (ˈæmərænθ) *n.* **1.** imaginary purple everlasting flower **2.** genus of flowering plants **—amaˈranthine** *a.* never fading

amaryllis (æməˈrɪlɪs) *n.* lilylike plant

amass (əˈmæs) *vt.* collect in quantity **—aˈmassable** *a.*

amateur (ˈæmətə) *n.* **1.** one who carries on an art, study, game *etc.* for pleasure rather than for financial gain **2.** unskilled practitioner **—*a.* 3.** not professional or expert **—ˈamateurish** *a.* imperfect, untrained **—ˈamateurishly** *adv.* **—ˈamateurism** *n.*

amatol (ˈæmətɒl) *n.* high explosive consisting of ammonium nitrate and trinitrotoluene (TNT)

amatory (ˈæmətərɪ) *or* **amatorial** (æməˈtɔːrɪəl) *a.* relating to love

amaze (əˈmeɪz) *vt.* surprise greatly, astound **—aˈmazement** *n.* **—aˈmazing** *a.* **—aˈmazingly** *adv.*

Amazon (ˈæməzᵊn) *n.* **1.** female warrior of legend **2.** tall, strong woman **—Amaˈzonian** *a.*

ambassador (æmˈbæsədə) *n.* senior diplomatic representative sent by one state to another (**amˈbassadress** *fem.*) **—ambassaˈdorial** *a.* **—amˈbassadorship** *n.*

amber (ˈæmbə) *n.* **1.** yellowish, translucent fossil resin **—*a.* 2.** made of, coloured like amber

ambergris (ˈæmbəgriːs, -grɪs) *n.* waxy substance secreted by the sperm whale, used in making perfumes

ambi- (*comb. form*) both, as in *ambidextrous, ambivalence*

ambiance (ˈæmbɪəns) *n. see* AMBIENCE

ambidextrous (æmbɪˈdɛkstrəs) *a.* able to use both hands with equal ease **—ambidexˈterity** *n.*

THESAURUS

alternative 1. *n.* choice, option, other (*of two*), preference, recourse, selection, substitute **2.** *adj.* alternate, another, different, other, second, substitute

alternatively as an alternative, by way of alternative, if not, instead, on the other hand, or, otherwise

although albeit, despite the fact that, even if, even supposing, even though, notwithstanding, though, while

altitude elevation, height, loftiness, peak, summit

altogether 1. absolutely, completely, entirely, fully, perfectly, quite, thoroughly, totally, utterly, wholly **2.** all in all, all things considered, as a whole, collectively, generally, in general, *in toto,* on the whole **3.** all told, everything included, in all, in sum, *in toto,* taken together

always consistently, constantly, continually, eternally, ever, everlastingly, evermore, every time, forever, *in perpetuum,* invariably, perpetually, repeatedly, unceasingly, without exception

amalgamate alloy, ally, blend, coalesce, combine, commingle, compound, fuse, incorporate, integrate, intermix, merge, mingle, unite

amalgamation admixture, alliance, alloy, amalgam, amalgamating, blend, coalition, combination, commingling, composite, compound, fusion, incorporation, integration, joining, merger, mingling, mixing, mixture, union

amass accumulate, aggregate, assemble, collect, compile, garner, gather, heap up, hoard, pile up, rake up, scrape together

amateur dabbler, dilettante, layman, nonprofessional

amateurish amateur, bungling, clumsy, crude, inexpert, unaccomplished, unprofessional, unskilful

amaze alarm, astonish, astound, bewilder, bowl over (*Inf.*), confound, daze, dumbfound, electrify, flabbergast, shock, stagger, startle, stun, stupefy, surprise

amazement admiration, astonishment, bewilderment, confusion, marvel, perplexity, shock, stupefaction, surprise, wonder

ambassador agent, consul, deputy, diplomat, emissary, envoy, legate, minister, plenipotentiary, representative

ambiguity doubt, doubtfulness, dubiety, dubiousness, enigma, equivocacy, equivocality, equivocation, inconclusiveness, indefiniteness, indeterminateness, obscurity, puzzle, tergiversation, uncertainty, unclearness, vagueness

ambience *or* **ambiance** (ˈæmbɪəns) *n.* atmosphere of a place

ambient (ˈæmbɪənt) *a.* surrounding

ambiguous (æmˈbɪgjʊəs) *a.* **1.** having more than one meaning **2.** obscure —**ambiˈguity** *n.* —**amˈbiguously** *adv.*

ambit (ˈæmbɪt) *n.* **1.** circuit **2.** compass

ambition (æmˈbɪʃən) *n.* **1.** desire for power, fame, honour *etc.* **2.** the object of that desire —**amˈbitious** *a.* —**amˈbitiously** *adv.* —**amˈbitiousness** *n.*

ambivalence (æmˈbɪvələns) *or* **ambivalency** *n.* simultaneous existence of two conflicting desires, opinions *etc.* —**amˈbivalent** *a.*

amble (ˈæmbᵊl) *vi.* **1.** move along easily and gently **2.** move at an easy pace —*n.* **3.** this movement or pace —**ˈambler** *n.*

ambrosia (æmˈbrəʊzɪə) *n.* **1.** *Myth.* food of the gods **2.** anything smelling or tasting particularly good

ambulance (ˈæmbjʊləns) *n.* conveyance for sick or injured

ambulatory (æmbjʊˈleɪtərɪ) *a.* **1.** of or for walking **2.** not fixed **3.** able to walk (*also* **ˈambulant**) —*n.* **4.** place for walking, such as cloister

ambuscade (æmbəˈskeɪd) *n.* **1.** act of hiding to launch surprise attack **2.** ambush

ambush (ˈæmbʊʃ) *n.* **1.** act of lying in wait —*vt.* **2.** waylay, attack from hiding, lie in wait for

ameliorate (əˈmiːljəreɪt) *v.* make better, improve —**amelioˈration** *n.* —**aˈmeliorative** *a.*

amen (eɪˈmɛn, ɑːˈmɛn) *interj.* **1.** surely **2.** so let it be

amenable (əˈmiːnəbᵊl) *a.* easy to be led or controlled —**amenaˈbility** *or* **aˈmenableness** *n.* —**aˈmenably** *adv.* —**amenable to 1.** likely to respond to **2.** answerable to

amend (əˈmɛnd) *vt.* **1.** correct **2.** improve **3.** alter in detail, as bill in parliament *etc.* —**aˈmendment** *n.* —**aˈmends** *pl.n.* reparation

amenity (əˈmiːnɪtɪ) *n.* (*oft. pl.*) useful or pleasant facility or service

amenorrhoea *or esp. U.S.* **amenorrhea** (æmɛnəˈrɪə, eɪ-) *n.* abnormal absence of menstruation

American (əˈmɛrɪkən) *n./a.* (native or inhabitant) of the American continent or the U.S.A.

americium (æməˈrɪsɪəm) *n.* white metallic transuranic element artificially produced from plutonium

amethyst (ˈæmɪθɪst) *n.* bluish-violet semiprecious stone

Amharic (æmˈhærɪk) *n.* **1.** official language of Ethiopia —*a.* **2.** denoting this language

amiable (ˈeɪmɪəbᵊl) *a.* friendly, kindly —**amiaˈbility** *or* **ˈamiableness** *n.* —**ˈamiably** *adv.*

amicable (ˈæmɪkəbᵊl) *a.* friendly —**amicaˈbility** *n.* —**ˈamicably** *adv.*

amicus curiae (æˈmiːkʊs ˈkjʊərɪiː) *Law* person, not directly engaged in case, who advises court (*pl.* **amici curiae** (æˈmiːkaɪ))

amid (əˈmɪd) *or* **amidst** *prep.* in the middle of, among

amidships (əˈmɪdʃɪps) *adv.* near, towards middle of ship

amino acid (əˈmiːnəʊ) organic compound found in protein

amiss (əˈmɪs) *a.* **1.** wrong —*adv.* **2.** faultily, badly —**take amiss** be offended by

amity (ˈæmɪtɪ) *n.* friendship

ammeter (ˈæmmiːtə) *n.* instrument for measuring electric current

ammo (ˈæməʊ) *n. inf.* ammunition

ammonia (əˈməʊnɪə) *n.* pungent alkaline gas containing hydrogen and nitrogen —**amˈmoniac** *or* **ammoniacal** (æməˈnaɪəkᵊl) *a.* —**amˈmoniated** *a.* —**amˈmonium** *n.*

ammonite (ˈæmənaɪt) *n.* whorled fossil shell like ram's horn

THESAURUS

ambiguous cryptic, doubtful, dubious, enigmatic, enigmatical, equivocal, inconclusive, indefinite, indeterminate, obscure, puzzling, uncertain, unclear, vague

ambition 1. aspiration, avidity, desire, drive, eagerness, enterprise, get-up-and-go (*Inf.*), hankering, longing, striving, yearning, zeal **2.** aim, aspiration, desire, dream, end, goal, hope, intent, objective, purpose, wish

ambitious aspiring, avid, desirous, driving, eager, enterprising, hopeful, intent, purposeful, striving, zealous

amble dawdle, meander, mosey (*Inf.*), ramble, saunter, stroll, walk, wander

ambush 1. *n.* ambuscade, concealment, cover, hiding, hiding place, lying in wait, retreat, shelter, trap, waylaying **2.** *v.* ambuscade, bushwhack (*U.S.*), ensnare, surprise, trap, waylay

amenable able to be influenced, acquiescent, agreeable, open, persuadable, responsive, susceptible, tractable

amend alter, ameliorate, better, change, correct, enhance, fix, improve, mend, modify, rectify, reform, remedy, repair, revise

amendment 1. alteration, amelioration, betterment, change, correction, enhancement, improvement, mending, modification, rectification, reform, remedy, repair, revision **2.** addendum, addition, adjunct, alteration, attachment, clarification

amends apology, atonement, compensation, expiation, indemnity, recompense, redress, reparation, requital, restitution, restoration, satisfaction

amenity advantage, comfort, convenience, facility, service

amiable affable, agreeable, attractive, benign, charming, cheerful, delightful, engaging, friendly, genial, good-humoured, good-natured, kind, kindly, lovable, obliging, pleasant, pleasing, sociable, sweet-tempered, winning, winsome

amicable amiable, brotherly, civil, cordial, courteous, fraternal, friendly, good-humoured, harmonious, kind, kindly, neighbourly, peaceable, peaceful, polite, sociable

amid amidst, among, amongst, in the middle of, in the midst of, in the thick of, surrounded by

amiss 1. *adj.* awry, confused, defective, erroneous, fallacious, false, faulty, improper, inaccurate, inappropriate, incorrect, mistaken, out of order, unsuitable, untoward, wrong **2.** *adv.* as an insult, as offensive, erroneously, faultily, improperly, inappropriately, incorrectly, mistakenly, out of turn, unsuitably, wrongly

ammunition (æmjʊˈnɪʃən) *n.* **1.** any projectiles (bullets, rockets *etc.*) that can be discharged from a weapon **2.** any means of defence or attack, as in argument

amnesia (æmˈniːzɪə, -ˈniːzjə, -ˈniːʒjə) *n.* loss of memory

amnesty (ˈæmnɪstɪ) *n.* **1.** general pardon *—vt.* **2.** grant amnesty to

amnion (ˈæmnɪən) *n.* innermost of two membranes enclosing embryonic reptile, bird or mammal (*pl.* **-s, amnia** (ˈæmnɪə)) **—amniˈotic** *a.* **—amniotic fluid** fluid surrounding baby in womb

amoeba *or U.S.* **ameba** (əˈmiːbə) *n.* microscopic single-celled animal able to change its shape, found in ponds *etc.* (*pl.* **-s, -bae** (-biː))

amok (əˈmʌk, əˈmɒk) *adv. see* AMUCK

among (əˈmʌŋ) *or* **amongst** *prep.* mixed with, in the midst of, of the number of, between

amoral (eɪˈmɒrəl) *a.* nonmoral, having no moral qualities **—amoˈrality** *n.*

amorous (ˈæmərəs) *a.* **1.** inclined to love **2.** in love **—ˈamorously** *adv.* **—ˈamorousness** *n.*

amorphous (əˈmɔːfəs) *a.* without distinct shape **—aˈmorphism** *n.*

amortize *or* **-tise** (əˈmɔːtaɪz) *vt.* pay off (a debt) by a sinking fund

amount (əˈmaʊnt) *vi.* **1.** come (to), be equal (to) *—n.* **2.** quantity **3.** sum total

amour (əˈmʊə) *n.* (illicit) love affair

amour-propre (amuːrˈprɔpr) *Fr.* self-respect

amp. **1.** amperage **2.** ampere

ampere (ˈæmpɛə) *n.* unit of electric current **—amperage** (ˈæmpərɪdʒ) *n.* strength of electric current measured in amperes

ampersand (ˈæmpəsænd) *n.* the sign & (and)

amphetamine (æmˈfɛtəmiːn) *n.* synthetic liquid used medicinally mainly for its stimulant action on central nervous system

amphi- (*comb. form*) **1.** on both sides; at both ends; of both kinds, as in *amphipod, amphibious* **2.** around, as in *amphibole*

amphibious (æmˈfɪbɪəs) *a.* living or operating both on land and in water **—amˈphibian** *n.* **1.** animal that lives first in water then on land **2.** vehicle able to travel on land or water **3.** aircraft that can alight on land or water

amphitheatre *or U.S.* **amphitheater** (ˈæmfɪθɪətə) *n.* building with tiers of seats rising round an arena

amphora (ˈæmfərə) *n.* two-handled jar of ancient Greece and Rome (*pl.* **-rae** (-riː), **-s**)

ample (ˈæmpᵊl) *a.* **1.** big enough **2.** large, spacious **—ˈamply** *adv.*

amplify (ˈæmplɪfaɪ) *vt.* **1.** increase **2.** make bigger, louder *etc.* (**-fied, -fying**) **—amplifiˈcation** *n.* **—ˈamplifier** *n.*

amplitude (ˈæmplɪtjuːd) *n.* spaciousness, width, magnitude **—amplitude modulation** *Rad.* method of transmitting information in which amplitude of carrier wave is varied

ampoule (ˈæmpuːl, -pjuːl) *or* (*esp. U.S.*) **ampule** *n.* container for hypodermic dose

ampulla (æmˈpʊlə) *n.* **1.** *Anat.* dilated end part of duct or canal **2.** *Christianity* vessel for wine and water used at the Eucharist; small flask for consecrated oil **3.** Roman two-handled bottle (*pl.* **ampullae** (-ˈpʊliː))

amputate (ˈæmpjʊteɪt) *v.* cut off (limb *etc.*) **—ampuˈtation** *n.*

amuck (əˈmʌk) *or* **amok** *adv.* **—run amuck** rush about as in murderous frenzy

amulet (ˈæmjʊlɪt) *n.* something carried or worn as a charm

amuse (əˈmjuːz) *vt.* **1.** divert **2.** occupy pleasantly **3.** cause to laugh or smile **—aˈmusement** *n.* entertainment, pastime **—aˈmusing** *a.* **—aˈmusingly** *adv.*

THESAURUS

ammunition armaments, cartridges, explosives, materiel, munitions, powder, rounds, shells, shot, shot and shell

amnesty absolution, condonation, dispensation, forgiveness, general pardon, immunity, oblivion, remission (*of penalty*), reprieve

amok *see* AMUCK

among, amongst **1.** amid, in association with, in the middle of, in the midst of, in the thick of, midst, surrounded by, together with, with **2.** between, to each of **3.** in the class of, in the company of, in the group of, in the number of, out of

amorous affectionate, amatory, ardent, attached, doting, enamoured, erotic, fond, impassioned, in love, lovesick, loving, lustful, passionate, tender

amount **1.** bulk, expanse, extent, lot, magnitude, mass, measure, number, quantity, supply, volume **2.** addition, aggregate, entirety, extent, lot, sum, sum total, total, whole

amount to add up to, aggregate, become, come to, develop into, equal, grow, mean, purport, total

ample abounding, abundant, big, bountiful, broad, capacious, commodious, copious, enough and to spare, expansive, extensive, full, generous, great, large, lavish, liberal, plenteous, plentiful, plenty, profuse, rich, roomy, spacious, substantial, unrestricted, voluminous, wide

amplify augment, boost, deepen, develop, dilate, elaborate, enlarge, expand, expatiate, extend, flesh out, go into detail, heighten, increase, intensify, lengthen, magnify, raise, round out, strengthen, stretch, supplement, widen

amply abundantly, bountifully, capaciously, completely, copiously, extensively, fully, generously, greatly, lavishly, liberally, plenteously, plentifully, profusely, richly, substantially, thoroughly, unstintingly, well

amputate curtail, cut off, lop, remove, separate, sever, truncate

amuck, amok berserk, destructively, ferociously, frenziedly, in a frenzy, insanely, madly, maniacally, murderously, savagely, uncontrollably, violently, wildly

amuse beguile, charm, cheer, delight, divert, enliven, entertain, gladden, gratify, interest, occupy, please, recreate, regale, tickle (*Inf.*)

amusement **1.** beguilement, cheer, delight, diversion, enjoyment, entertainment, fun, gladdening, gratification, hilarity, interest, laughter, merriment, mirth, pleasing, pleasure, recreation, regalement,

amylase (ˈæmɪleɪz) *n.* enzyme that hydrolyses starch and glycogen to simple sugar

amylum (ˈæmɪləm) *n. see* STARCH

an (æn; *unstressed* ən) *see* A

an- *or before consonant* **a-** (*comb. form*) not; without, as in *anaphrodisiac*

-an, -ean, *or* **-ian** (*comb. form*) **1.** belonging to; coming from; typical of; adhering to, as in *European, Elizabethan, Christian* **2.** person who specializes or is expert in, as in *dietician*

Anabaptist (ænəˈbæptɪst) *n.* member of Protestant movement that rejected infant baptism and insisted adults be rebaptized

anabolism (əˈnæbəlɪzəm) *n.* metabolic process in which complex molecules are synthesized from simpler ones with storage of energy **—anaˈbolic** *a.* **—anabolic steroid** any of various hormones that encourage muscle and bone growth

anabranch (ˈɑːnəbrɑːntʃ) *n.* stream that leaves a river and re-enters it further downstream

anachronism (əˈnækrənɪzəm) *n.* **1.** mistake of time, by which something is put in wrong historical period **2.** something out of date **—anachroˈnistic** *a.*

anacoluthon (ænəkəˈluːθɒn) *n.* a sentence or words faulty in grammatical sequence (*pl.* **-tha** (-θə))

anaconda (ænəˈkɒndə) *n.* large snake which kills by constriction

anadromous (əˈnædrəməs) *a.* (of salmon *etc.*) migrating up rivers to breed

anaemia *or U.S.* **anemia** (əˈniːmɪə) *n.* deficiency in number of red blood cells **—aˈnaemic** *or U.S.* **aˈnemic** *a.* **1.** suffering from anaemia **2.** pale, sickly, lacking vitality

anaerobe (ænˈɛərəʊb) *or* **anaerobium** (ænɛəˈrəʊbɪəm) *n.* organism that can live without free oxygen (*pl.* **-obes** *or* **-obia** (-ˈəʊbɪə)) **—anaerˈobic** *a.*

anaesthetic *or U.S.* **anesthetic** (ænɪsˈθɛtɪk) *n./a.* (drug) causing loss of sensation **—anaesthesia** *or U.S.* **anesthesia** (ænɪsˈθiːzɪə) *n.* loss of sensation **—anaesˈthetically** *or U.S.* **anesˈthetically** *adv.* **—anaesthetist** *or U.S.* **anesthetist** (əˈniːsθətɪst) *n.* expert in use of anaesthetics **—anaesthetize, anaesthetise,** *or U.S.* **anesthetize** (əˈniːsθətaɪz) *vt.*

Anaglypta (ænəˈglɪptə) *n.* **R** thick, embossed wallpaper

anagram (ˈænəgræm) *n.* word or words made by arranging in different order the letters of another word or words, *eg ant* from *tan* **—anagramˈmatical** *a.* **—anaˈgrammatist** *n.*

anal (ˈeɪnᵊl) *a. see* ANUS

analects (ˈænəlɛkts) *or* **analecta** (ænəˈlɛktə) *pl.n.* selected literary passages from one or more works

analgesia (ænᵊlˈdʒiːzɪə) *or* **analgia** (ænˈældʒɪə) *n.* absence of pain **—analˈgesic** *a./n.* (drug) relieving pain

analogue *or U.S.* (*sometimes*) **analog** (ˈænᵊlɒg) *n.* **1.** something analogous to something else **2.** *Biol.* analogous part or organ **—***a.* **3.** using analogue (such as dial and pointer) to represent data or information **—analogue computer** computer that uses voltages to represent numbers of physical quantities

analogy (əˈnælədʒɪ) *n.* **1.** agreement or likeness in certain respects **2.** correspondence **—anaˈlogical** *a.* **—anaˈlogically** *adv.* **—aˈnalogist** *n.* **—aˈnalogize** *or* **-gise** *v.* explain by analogy **—aˈnalogous** *a.* **1.** similar **2.** parallel **—aˈnalogously** *adv.*

analysis (əˈnælɪsɪs) *n.* separation of something into its elements or components (*pl.* **-yses** (-ɪsiːz)) **—ˈanalyse** *or U.S.* **-lyze** *vt.* **1.** examine critically **2.** determine the constituent parts of **—ˈanalyst** *n.* one skilled in analysis, *esp.* chemical or psychiatric analysis **—anaˈlytic(al)** *a.* **1.** relating to analysis **2.** capable of or given to analysing **—anaˈlytically** *adv.*

anapaest *or* **anapest** (ˈænəpɛst, -piːst) *n.* metrical foot of two short syllables followed by one long

anaphora (əˈnæfərə) *n.* **1.** *Rhetoric* repetition of word or phrase at beginning of successive clauses **2.** *Gram.* use of word such as pronoun to avoid repetition

anarchy (ˈænəkɪ) *n.* **1.** lawlessness **2.** lack of government in a state **3.** confusion **—anˈarchic(al)** *a.* **—anˈarchically** *adv.* **—ˈanarchism** *n.* **—ˈanarchist** *n.* one who opposes all forms of government

anastigmat (æˈnæstɪgmæt, ænəˈstɪgmæt) *n.* lens corrected for astigmatism **—anastigˈmatic** *a.* (of lens) not astigmatic

anastomosis (ənæstəˈməʊsɪs) *n.* interconnection of veins, arteries *etc.* (*pl.* **-ses** (-siːz))

anat. **1.** anatomical **2.** anatomy

anathema (əˈnæθəmə) *n.* **1.** anything detested, hateful **2.** ban of the church **3.** curse **—aˈnathematize** *or* **-tise** *v.*

THESAURUS

sport **2.** distraction, diversion, entertainment, game, hobby, joke, lark, pastime, prank, recreation, sport

amusing charming, cheerful, cheering, comical, delightful, diverting, droll, enjoyable, entertaining, facetious, funny, gladdening, gratifying, humorous, interesting, jocular, laughable, lively, merry, pleasant, pleasing, witty

anaemic ashen, bloodless, characterless, colourless, dull, enervated, feeble, frail, infirm, pale, pallid, sickly, wan, weak

anaesthetic **1.** *n.* analgesic, anodyne, narcotic, opiate, painkiller, sedative, soporific, stupefacient, stupefactive **2.** *adj.* analgesic, anodyne, deadening, dulling, narcotic, numbing, opiate, pain-killing, sedative, sleep-inducing, soporific, stupefacient, stupefactive

analogy agreement, comparison, correlation, correspondence, equivalence, homology, likeness, parallel, relation, resemblance, similarity, similitude

analyse **1.** assay, estimate, evaluate, examine, interpret, investigate, judge, test **2.** anatomize, break down, consider, dissect, dissolve, divide, resolve, separate, study, think through

analysis anatomization, anatomy, assay, breakdown, dissection, dissolution, division, resolution, separation, sifting, test

analytic, analytical detailed, diagnostic, discrete, dissecting, explanatory, expository, inquiring, inquisitive, interpretative, interpretive, investigative, logical, organized, problem-solving, questioning, rational, searching, studious, systematic, testing

anarchist insurgent, nihilist, rebel, revolutionary, terrorist

anarchy chaos, confusion, disorder, disorganization,

anatomy (əˈnætəmɪ) *n.* **1.** science of structure of the body **2.** detailed analysis **3.** the body —**anaˈtomical** *a.* —**anaˈtomically** *adv.* —**aˈnatomist** *n.* —**aˈnatomize** *or* **-mise** *vt.*

-ance *or* **-ancy** (*comb. form*) action, state or condition, or quality, as in *utterance, resemblance*

ancestor (ˈænsɛstə) *n.* **1.** person from whom another is descended **2.** early type of later form or product —**anˈcestral** *a.* —**ˈancestry** *n.*

anchor (ˈæŋkə) *n.* **1.** heavy (*usu.* hooked) implement dropped on cable, chain *etc.* to bottom of sea to secure vessel **2.** source of stability or security —*vt.* **3.** fasten by or as by anchor —**ˈanchorage** *n.* act of, place of anchoring —**anchor man 1.** *Sport* end member of tug-of-war team; last runner in relay team **2.** in broadcasting, compere who links different parts of programme —**weigh anchor** haul up anchor and set sail

anchorite (ˈæŋkəraɪt) *n.* hermit, recluse (**ˈanchoress** *fem.*)

anchovy (ˈæntʃəvɪ) *n.* small savoury fish of herring family

anchusa (æŋˈkjuːsə) *n.* plant with hairy leaves and blue flowers

ancien régime (ɑ̃sjɛ̃ reˈʒim) *Fr.* political and social system of France before the Revolution of 1789 (*pl.* **anciens régimes** (ɑ̃sjɛ̃ reˈʒim))

ancient (ˈeɪnʃənt) *a.* **1.** belonging to former age **2.** old **3.** timeworn —*n.* **4.** (*oft. pl.*) one who lived in an earlier age —**ˈanciently** *adv.* —**ancient monument** notable building or site preserved as public property

ancillary (ænˈsɪlərɪ) *a.* subordinate, subservient, auxiliary

-ancy (*comb. form*) condition or quality, as in *poignancy* (*see also* **-ance**)

and (ænd; *unstressed* ənd, ən) *conj.* connecting word, used to join words and sentences, to introduce a consequence *etc.* —**and/or** *conj.* used to join terms when either one or other or both is indicated

andante (ænˈdæntɪ) *Mus. a./adv.* **1.** at moderately slow tempo —*n.* **2.** passage or piece performed in this manner

andantino (ændænˈtiːnəʊ) *Mus. a./adv.* **1.** slightly faster or slower than andante —*n.* **2.** passage or piece performed in this manner (*pl.* **-s**)

andiron (ˈændaɪən) *n.* iron bar or bracket for supporting logs in fireplace

andro- *or before vowel* **andr-** (*comb. form*) **1.** male; masculine **2.** in botany, stamen or anther

androgen (ˈændrədʒən) *n.* steroid that promotes development of male sexual characteristics

androgynous (ænˈdrɒdʒɪnəs) *a.* **1.** *Bot.* having male and female flowers in same inflorescence **2.** hermaphrodite

android (ˈændrɔɪd) *n.* **1.** in science fiction, robot resembling human being —*a.* **2.** resembling human being

anecdote (ˈænɪkdəʊt) *n.* very short story dealing with single incident —**anecˈdotal** *or* **anecˈdotic** *a.*

anemia (əˈniːmɪə) *n.* **US** *see* ANAEMIA

anemograph (əˈnɛməʊgrɑːf) *n.* self-recording anemometer

anemometer (ænɪˈmɒmɪtə) *n.* instrument for recording force and direction of wind —**anemoˈmetric** *a.* —**aneˈmometry** *n.*

anemone (əˈnɛmənɪ) *n.* flower related to buttercup —**sea anemone** plantlike sea animal

anent (əˈnɛnt) *prep. obs.* concerning

aneroid (ˈænərɔɪd) *a.* denoting a barometer which measures atmospheric pressure without the use of mercury or other liquid

aneurysm *or* **aneurism** (ˈænjərɪzəm) *n.* swelling out of a part of an artery

anew (əˈnjuː) *adv.* afresh, again

angel (ˈeɪndʒəl) *n.* **1.** divine messenger **2.** ministering or attendant spirit **3.** person with the qualities of such a spirit, as gentleness, purity *etc.* —**angelic** (ænˈdʒɛlɪk) *a.* —**angelically** (ænˈdʒɛlɪkəlɪ) *adv.* —**angel cake** *or esp. U.S.* **angel food cake** light sponge cake made without egg yolks —**ˈangelfish** *n.* **1.** small tropical marine fish which has brightly coloured body **2.** S Amer. freshwater fish which has large dorsal and anal fins **3.** shark with flattened pectoral fins (*pl.* **-fish, -fishes**)

angelica (ænˈdʒɛlɪkə) *n.* **1.** aromatic plant **2.** the candied stalks of this plant used in cookery

Angelus (ˈændʒɪləs) *n.* devotional service in R.C.

THESAURUS

lawlessness, misgovernment, misrule, rebellion, revolution, riot

anathema 1. ban, condemnation, curse, damnation, denunciation, excommunication, execration, imprecation, malediction, proscription, taboo **2.** abomination, bane, *bête noire,* bugbear, enemy, pariah

anathematize abominate, ban, condemn, curse, damn, denounce, excommunicate, execrate, imprecate, proscribe

anatomize analyse, break down, dissect, dissolve, divide, examine, resolve, scrutinize, separate, study

anatomy analysis, dismemberment, dissection, division, examination, investigation, study

ancestor forebear, forefather, forerunner, precursor, predecessor, progenitor

ancestry ancestors, antecedents, blood, derivation, descent, extraction, family, forebears, forefathers, genealogy, house, line, lineage, origin, parentage, pedigree, progenitors, race, stock

ancient aged, age-old, antediluvian, antiquated, antique, archaic, bygone, early, hoary, obsolete, old, olden, old-fashioned, outmoded, out-of-date, primeval, primordial, superannuated, timeworn

ancillary accessory, additional, auxiliary, contributory, extra, secondary, subordinate, subsidiary, supplementary

and along with, also, as well as, furthermore, in addition to, including, moreover, plus, together with

anecdote reminiscence, short story, sketch, story, tale, yarn

anew afresh, again, another time, from scratch, from the beginning, once again, once more, over again

angel 1. archangel, cherub, divine messenger, guardian spirit, seraph, spiritual being **2.** *Inf.* beauty, darling, dear, dream, gem, ideal, jewel, paragon, saint, treasure

angelic 1. celestial, cherubic, ethereal, heavenly, seraphic **2.** adorable, beatific, beautiful, entrancing, innocent, lovely, pure, saintly, virtuous

Church in memory of the Incarnation, said at morning, noon and sunset

anger (ˈæŋgə) *n.* **1.** strong emotion excited by a real or supposed injury **2.** wrath **3.** rage —*vt.* **4.** excite to wrath **5.** enrage —**ˈangrily** *adv.* —**ˈangry** *a.* **1.** full of anger **2.** inflamed

angina pectoris (ænˈdʒaɪnə ˈpɛktərɪs) severe pain accompanying heart disease

angiosperm (ˈændʒɪəspɜːm) *n.* any plant having a seed vessel

angle[1] (ˈæŋgˈl) *vi.* fish with hook and line —**ˈangler** *n.* **1.** fisherman **2.** sea fish with spiny dorsal fin (*also* **angler fish**) —**ˈangling** *n.*

angle[2] (ˈæŋgˈl) *n.* **1.** meeting of two lines or surfaces **2.** sharp corner **3.** point of view **4.** *inf.* devious motive —*vt.* **5.** bend at an angle —**angle of incidence 1.** angle of line or beam of radiation to line perpendicular to surface at point of incidence **2.** angle between chord line of aircraft wing or tailplane and longitudinal axis

Anglican (ˈæŋglɪkən) *a./n.* (member) of the Church of England —**ˈAnglicanism** *n.*

anglicize *or* **-cise** (ˈæŋglɪsaɪz) *vt.* express in English, turn into English form —**ˈAnglicism** *n.* English idiom or peculiarity

Anglo (ˈæŋgləʊ) *n.* C English-speaking Canadian (*pl.* **-s**)

Anglo- (ˈæŋgləʊ-) (*comb. form*) English, as in *Anglo-American*

Anglo-French *a.* **1.** of England and France **2.** of Anglo-French —*n.* **3.** Norman-French language of medieval England

Anglo-Norman *a.* **1.** relating to Norman conquerors of England or their language —*n.* **2.** Norman inhabitant of England after 1066 **3.** Anglo-French language

Anglophile (ˈæŋgləʊfɪl, -faɪl) *or* **Anglophil** *n.* person having admiration for England or the English

Anglophobia (æŋgləʊˈfəʊbɪə) *n.* dislike of England *etc.*

Anglo-Saxon *n.* **1.** member of West Germanic tribes that settled in Britain from 5th century A.D. **2.** language of these tribes (*see* **Old English** *at* OLD) **3.** White person whose native language is English **4.** *inf.* plain blunt English —*a.* **5.** forming part of Germanic element in Modern English **6.** of Anglo-Saxons or Old English language **7.** of White Protestant culture of Britain and Amer.

angora (æŋˈgɔːrə) *n.* (*sometimes* **A-**) **1.** goat with long white silky hair which is used in the making of mohair **2.** cloth or wool made from this hair —**angora cat** *or* **rabbit** varieties of cat and rabbit with long, silky fur

angostura bitters (æŋgəˈstjʊərə) **R** (*oft.* **A-**) bitter tonic, used as flavouring in alcoholic drinks

angstrom (ˈæŋstrəm) *n.* unit of length for measuring wavelengths of electromagnetic radiation

anguish (ˈæŋgwɪʃ) *n.* great mental or physical pain

angular (ˈæŋgjʊlə) *a.* **1.** (of people) bony, awkward **2.** having angles **3.** measured by an angle —**anguˈlarity** *n.*

anhydrous (ænˈhaɪdrəs) *a.* (of chemical substances) free from water

anil (ˈænɪl) *n.* leguminous West Indian shrub (*also* **ˈindigo**)

aniline (ˈænɪlɪn, -liːn) *n.* product of coal tar or indigo, which yields dyes

animadvert (ænɪmædˈvɜːt) *vi.* (*usu. with* on *or* upon) criticize, pass censure —**animadˈversion** *n.* criticism, censure

animal (ˈænɪməl) *n.* **1.** living creature, having sensation and power of voluntary motion **2.** beast —*a.* **3.** of, pert. to animals **4.** sensual —**aniˈmalcular** *a.* —**aniˈmalcule** *n.* very small animal, *esp.* one which cannot be seen by naked eye —**ˈanimalism** *n.* —**ˈanimally** *adv.* —**animal husbandry** science of breeding and rearing farm animals —**animal magnetism 1.** quality of being attractive, *esp.* to opposite sex **2.** *obs.* hypnotism

animate (ˈænɪmeɪt) *vt.* **1.** give life to **2.** enliven **3.** inspire **4.** actuate **5.** make cartoon film of —**ˈanimated** *a.* **1.** lively **2.** in form of cartoons —**aniˈmation** *n.* **1.** life, vigour **2.** cartoon film —**ˈanimator** *n.*

animato (ænɪˈmɑːtəʊ) *a./adv. Mus.* lively; animated

animism (ˈænɪmɪzəm) *n.* belief that natural effects are due to spirits or that inanimate things have spirits —**ˈanimist** *n.* —**aniˈmistic** *a.*

animosity (ænɪˈmɒsɪtɪ) *n.* hostility, enmity

THESAURUS

anger 1. *n.* annoyance, antagonism, choler, displeasure, exasperation, fury, ill humour, ill temper, indignation, ire, irritability, irritation, outrage, passion, pique, rage, resentment, spleen, temper, vexation, wrath **2.** *v.* affront, annoy, antagonize, displease, enrage, exasperate, excite, fret, gall, incense, infuriate, irritate, madden, nettle, offend, outrage, pique, provoke, rile, vex

angle[1] *v.* cast, fish

angle[2] *n.* **1.** bend, corner, crook, crotch, cusp, edge, elbow, intersection, knee, nook, point **2.** approach, aspect, outlook, perspective, point of view, position, side, slant, standpoint, viewpoint

angry annoyed, antagonized, choleric, displeased, enraged, exasperated, furious, heated, hot, hot under the collar (*Inf.*), ill-tempered, incensed, indignant, infuriated, irascible, irate, ireful, irritable, irritated, mad (*Inf.*), nettled, outraged, passionate, piqued, provoked, raging, resentful, riled, splenetic, tumultuous, uptight (*Sl.*), wrathful

anguish agony, distress, grief, heartache, heartbreak, misery, pain, pang, sorrow, suffering, throe, torment, torture, woe

angular bony, gaunt, lank, lanky, lean, rangy, rawboned, scrawny, skinny, spare

animal 1. *n.* beast, brute, creature **2.** *adj.* bestial, bodily, brutish, carnal, fleshly, gross, physical, sensual

animate *v.* activate, embolden, encourage, energize, enliven, excite, fire, gladden, impel, incite, inspire, inspirit, instigate, invigorate, kindle, move, quicken, revive, rouse, spark, spur, stimulate, stir, urge, vitalize, vivify

animated active, airy, ardent, brisk, buoyant, dynamic, ebullient, elated, energetic, enthusiastic, excited, fervent, gay, lively, passionate, quick, spirited, sprightly, vibrant, vigorous, vital, vivacious, vivid, zealous, zestful

animation action, activity, airiness, ardour, briskness, buoyancy, dynamism, ebullience, elation, en-

animus (ˈænɪməs) *n.* **1.** intense dislike; hatred **2.** animosity

anion (ˈænaɪən) *n.* ion with negative charge

anise (ˈænɪs) *n.* plant with aromatic seeds, which are used for flavouring

aniseed (ˈænɪsiːd) *n.* liquorice-flavoured seed of anise

ankle (ˈæŋkᵊl) *n.* joint between foot and leg —**ˈanklet** *n.* ornamental chain *etc.* worn around ankle

ankylosis *or* **anchylosis** (æŋkɪˈləʊsɪs) *n.* abnormal adhesion or immobility of bones in joint

anna (ˈænə) *n.* formerly, Indian coin worth one sixteenth of rupee

annals (ˈænᵊlz) *pl.n.* historical records of events —**ˈannalist** *n.*

anneal (əˈniːl) *vt.* **1.** toughen (metal or glass) by heating and slow cooling **2.** temper (determination, will *etc.*) —**anˈnealing** *n.*

annelid (ˈænəlɪd) *n.* one of class of invertebrate animals, including the earthworm *etc.*

annex (æˈnɛks) *vt.* **1.** add, append, attach **2.** take possession of (*esp.* territory) —**annexˈation** *n.*

annexe *or esp. U.S.* **annex** (ˈænɛks) *n.* **1.** supplementary building **2.** something added

annihilate (əˈnaɪəleɪt) *vt.* reduce to nothing, destroy utterly —**annihiˈlation** *n.* —**anˈnihilative** *a.* —**anˈnihilator** *n.*

anniversary (ænɪˈvɜːsərɪ) *n.* **1.** yearly recurrence of a date of notable event **2.** celebration of this

anno Domini (ˈænəʊ ˈdɒmɪnaɪ, -niː) *Lat.* in the year of our Lord

annotate (ˈænəʊteɪt, ˈænə-) *vt.* provide notes for (literary work *etc.*), comment —**annoˈtation** *n.* —**ˈannotator** *n.*

announce (əˈnaʊns) *vt.* make known, proclaim —**anˈnouncement** *n.* —**anˈnouncer** *n.* broadcaster who announces items in programme, introduces speakers *etc.*

annoy (əˈnɔɪ) *vt.* **1.** vex **2.** make slightly angry **3.** tease —**anˈnoyance** *n.*

annual (ˈænjʊəl) *a.* **1.** yearly **2.** of, for a year —*n.* **3.** plant which completes its life cycle in a year **4.** book published each year —**ˈannually** *adv.*

annuity (əˈnjuːɪtɪ) *n.* sum or grant paid every year —**anˈnuitant** *n.* holder of annuity

annul (əˈnʌl) *vt.* make void, cancel, abolish (-**ll**-) —**anˈnulment** *n.*

annular (ˈænjʊlə) *a.* ring-shaped —**ˈannulate** *a.* having or marked with rings —**ˈannulated** *a.* formed in rings —**annuˈlation** *n.* —**ˈannulet** *n.* small ring or fillet

Annunciation (ənʌnsɪˈeɪʃən) *n.* **1.** angel's announcement to the Virgin Mary **2.** (**a-**) announcing —**anˈnunciate** *vt.* proclaim, announce

anode (ˈænəʊd) *n. Elec.* the positive pole, or point of entry of current —**ˈanodize** *or* **-dise** *vt.* cover metal object with protective film by using it for anode in electrolysis

anodyne (ˈænədaɪn) *a.* **1.** relieving pain, soothing —*n.* **2.** pain-relieving drug

anoint (əˈnɔɪnt) *vt.* **1.** smear with oil or ointment **2.** consecrate with oil —**aˈnointment** *n.* —**the Anointed** the Messiah

anomalous (əˈnɒmələs) *a.* irregular, abnormal —**aˈnomaly** *n.* **1.** irregularity **2.** deviation from rule

THESAURUS

ergy, enthusiasm, excitement, exhilaration, fervour, gaiety, high spirits, life, liveliness, passion, pep, sparkle, spirit, sprightliness, verve, vibrancy, vigour, vitality, vivacity, zeal, zest, zing (*Inf.*)

animosity acrimony, animus, antagonism, antipathy, bad blood, bitterness, enmity, hate, hatred, hostility, ill will, malevolence, malice, malignity, rancour, resentment, virulence

annals accounts, archives, chronicles, history, journals, memorials, records, registers

annex 1. add, adjoin, affix, append, attach, connect, fasten, join, subjoin, tack, unite **2.** acquire, appropriate, arrogate, conquer, expropriate, occupy, seize, take over

annexe 1. ell, extension, supplementary building, wing **2.** addendum, addition, adjunct, affix, appendix, attachment, supplement

annihilate abolish, destroy, eradicate, erase, exterminate, extinguish, extirpate, liquidate, nullify, obliterate, root out, wipe out

annihilation abolition, destruction, eradication, erasure, extermination, extinction, extinguishing, extirpation, liquidation, nullification, obliteration, rooting out, wiping out

annotate commentate, comment on, elucidate, explain, footnote, gloss, illustrate, interpret, make observations, note

annotation comment, commentary, elucidation, exegesis, explanation, explication, footnote, gloss, illustration, interpretation, note, observation

announce advertise, broadcast, declare, disclose, divulge, give out, intimate, make known, proclaim, promulgate, propound, publish, report, reveal, tell

announcement advertisement, broadcast, bulletin, communiqué, declaration, disclosure, divulgence, intimation, proclamation, promulgation, publication, report, revelation, statement

announcer anchor man, broadcaster, commentator, master of ceremonies, newscaster, news reader, reporter

annoy anger, badger, bedevil, bore, bother, bug (*Inf.*), displease, disturb, exasperate, gall, get (*Inf.*), harass, harry, incommode, irk, irritate, madden, molest, needle (*Inf.*), nettle, peeve, pester, plague, provoke, rile, ruffle, tease, trouble, vex

annoyance aggravation, anger, bedevilment, bother, displeasure, disturbance, exasperation, harassment, irritation, nuisance, provocation, trouble, vexation

annually by the year, each year, every year, once a year, per annum, per year, year after year, yearly

annul abolish, abrogate, cancel, countermand, declare *or* render null and void, invalidate, negate, nullify, recall, repeal, rescind, retract, reverse, revoke, void

annulment abolition, abrogation, cancellation, countermanding, invalidation, negation, nullification, recall, repeal, rescindment, rescission, retraction, reversal, revocation, voiding

anodyne 1. *n.* analgesic, narcotic, painkiller, painreliever, palliative **2.** *adj.* analgesic, deadening, dulling, narcotic, numbing, pain-killing, pain-relieving, palliative

anoint 1. daub, embrocate, grease, oil, rub, smear,

anomie *or* **anomy** (ˈænəʊmɪ) *n. Sociol.* lack of social or moral standards
anon (əˈnɒn) *adv. obs.* **1.** in a short time, soon **2.** now and then
anon. anonymous
anonymous (əˈnɒnɪməs) *a.* nameless, *esp.* without an author's name **—anoˈnymity** *n.* **—aˈnonymously** *adv.*
anopheles (əˈnɒfɪliːz) *n.* genus of the malarial mosquito
anorak (ˈænəræk) *n.* lightweight, warm, waterproof, *usu.* hooded jacket
anorexia (ænɒˈrɛksɪə) *n.* loss of appetite **—anorexia nervosa** (nɜːˈvəʊsə) psychological condition characterized by refusal to eat
another (əˈnʌðə) *pron./a.* **1.** one other **2.** a different (one) **3.** one more
ans. answer
anserine (ˈænsəraɪn) *a.* **1.** of or like goose **2.** silly
answer (ˈɑːnsə) *v.* **1.** reply (to) **2.** be accountable (for, to) *—vt.* **3.** solve; reply correctly **4.** meet **5.** match **6.** satisfy, suit *—n.* **7.** reply **8.** solution **—ˈanswerable** *a.* accountable
ant (ænt) *n.* small social insect, proverbial for industry **—ant bear** *see* AARDVARK **—ˈanteater** *n.* animal which feeds on ants by means of long, sticky tongue **—ant hill** mound raised by ants
-ant (*comb. form*) causing or performing action or existing in certain condition, as in *pleasant, deodorant, servant*
antacid (æntˈæsɪd) *n.* **1.** substance used to treat acidity, *esp.* in stomach *—a.* **2.** having properties of this substance
antagonist (ænˈtægənɪst) *n.* opponent, adversary **—anˈtagonism** *n.* **—antagoˈnistic** *a.* **—antagoˈnistically** *adv.* **—anˈtagonize** *or* **-nise** *vt.* arouse hostility in
antalkali (æntˈælkəlaɪ) *n.* substance that neutralizes alkalis (*pl.* **-s, -lies**)
Antarctic (æntˈɑːktɪk) *a.* **1.** of south polar regions *—n.* **2.** region round South Pole **—Antarctic Circle** imaginary circle around earth at latitude 66° 32′ S
ante (ˈæntɪ) *n.* **1.** player's stake in poker *—v.* **2.** place stake
ante- (*comb. form*) before, as in *antechamber*. Such words are not given here where the meaning may easily be inferred from the simple word
antecedent (æntɪˈsiːdᵊnt) *a./n.* (event, person or thing) going before
antedate (ˈæntɪdeɪt) *vt.* **1.** be or occur at earlier date than **2.** affix or assign date to (document *etc.*) earlier than actual date **3.** cause to occur sooner *—n.* **4.** earlier date
antediluvian (æntɪdɪˈluːvɪən) *a.* **1.** before the Flood **2.** ancient
antelope (ˈæntɪləʊp) *n.* deerlike ruminant animal, remarkable for grace and speed
ante meridiem (məˈrɪdɪəm) *Lat.* before noon
antenatal (æntɪˈneɪtᵊl) *a.* of care *etc.* during pregnancy
antenna (ænˈtɛnə) *n.* **1.** insect's feeler **2.** aerial (*pl.* **-ae** (-iː))
antepenultimate (æntɪpɪˈnʌltɪmɪt) *a.* **1.** third last *—n.* **2.** anything third last
anterior (ænˈtɪərɪə) *a.* **1.** to the front **2.** earlier
anteroom (ˈæntɪruːm, -rʊm) *n.* room giving entrance to larger room, oft. used as waiting room
anthem (ˈænθəm) *n.* **1.** song of loyalty, *esp.* to a country **2.** Scripture passage set to music **3.** piece of sacred music, orig. sung in alternate parts by two choirs
anther (ˈænθə) *n.* sac in flower, containing pollen, at top of stamen **—ˈantheral** *a.*
anthology (ænˈθɒlədʒɪ) *n.* collection of poems, literary extracts *etc.* **—anˈthologist** *n.* maker of such **—anˈthologize** *or* **-gise** *vt.* include (poem *etc.*) in anthology

THESAURUS

spread over **2.** anele (*Archaic*), bless, consecrate, hallow, sanctify
anomalous aberrant, abnormal, atypical, bizarre, deviating, eccentric, exceptional, incongruous, inconsistent, irregular, odd, peculiar, rare, unusual
anomaly aberration, abnormality, departure, deviation, eccentricity, exception, incongruity, inconsistency, irregularity, oddity, peculiarity, rarity
anonymous incognito, innominate, nameless, unacknowledged, unattested, unauthenticated, uncredited, unidentified, unknown, unnamed, unsigned
answer *n.* **1.** acknowledgment, comeback, defence, explanation, plea, reaction, refutation, rejoinder, reply, report, resolution, response, retort, return, riposte, solution, vindication ~*v.* **2.** acknowledge, explain, react, refute, rejoin, reply, resolve, respond, retort, return, solve **3.** conform, correlate, correspond, do, fill, fit, fulfil, measure up, meet, pass, qualify, satisfy, serve, suffice, suit, work
answerable accountable, amenable, chargeable, liable, responsible, subject, to blame
answer for be accountable for, be answerable for, be chargeable for, be liable for, be responsible for, be to blame for, take the rap for (*Sl.*)
answer to be accountable to, be answerable to, be responsible to, be ruled by, obey
antagonism antipathy, competition, conflict, contention, discord, dissension, friction, hostility, opposition, rivalry
antagonist adversary, competitor, contender, enemy, foe, opponent, opposer, rival
antagonistic adverse, antipathetic, at odds, at variance, averse, conflicting, contentious, hostile, ill-disposed, incompatible, in dispute, inimical, opposed, unfriendly
antagonize alienate, anger, annoy, disaffect, estrange, insult, irritate, offend, repel, rub (someone) up the wrong way (*Inf.*)
antecedent anterior, earlier, foregoing, former, preceding, precursory, preliminary, previous, prior
antecedents **1.** ancestors, ancestry, blood, descent, extraction, family, forebears, forefathers, genealogy, line, progenitors, stock **2.** background, history, past
antediluvian **1.** prehistoric, primeval, primitive, primordial **2.** ancient, antiquated, antique, archaic, obsolete, old-fashioned, out-of-date, out of the ark (*Inf.*), passé
anteroom antechamber, foyer, lobby, outer room, reception room, vestibule, waiting room
anthem **1.** canticle, chant, chorale, hymn, psalm **2.** paean, song of praise

anthracene (ˈænθrəsiːn) *n.* colourless crystalline solid used in manufacture of chemicals *etc.*

anthracite (ˈænθrəsaɪt) *n.* hard coal that burns slowly almost without flame or smoke

anthrax (ˈænθræks) *n.* **1.** malignant disease in cattle, communicable to man **2.** sore caused by this

anthropo- (*comb. form*) man, human, as in *anthropology*

anthropocentric (ænθrəpəʊˈsɛntrɪk) *a.* regarding man as central factor in universe

anthropoid (ˈænθrəpɔɪd) *a.* **1.** like man —*n.* **2.** ape resembling man

anthropology (ænθrəˈpɒlədʒɪ) *n.* scientific study of origins, development of human race —**anthropoˈlogical** *a.* —**anthroˈpologist** *n.*

anthropomorphize *or* **-ise** (ænθrəpəˈmɔːfaɪz) *vt.* ascribe human attributes to (God or an animal) —**anthropoˈmorphic** *a.* —**anthropoˈmorphism** *n.* —**anthropoˈmorphous** *a.* shaped like human being

anti (ˈæntɪ) *inf. a.* **1.** opposed to party *etc.* —*n.* **2.** opponent

anti- (*comb. form*) against, as in *anti-aircraft, antispasmodic.* Such words are not given here where meaning may easily be inferred from simple word

antibiosis (æntɪbaɪˈəʊsɪs) *n.* association between two organisms that is harmful to one of them

antibiotic (æntɪbaɪˈɒtɪk) *n.* **1.** any of various chemical, fungal or synthetic substances, *esp.* penicillin, used against bacterial infection —*a.* **2.** of antibiotics

antibody (ˈæntɪbɒdɪ) *n.* substance in, or introduced into, blood serum, which counteracts growth and harmful action of bacteria

Antichrist (ˈæntɪkraɪst) *n.* **1.** *Bible* the antagonist of Christ **2.** (*sometimes* **a-**) an enemy of Christ or Christianity

anticipate (ænˈtɪsɪpeɪt) *vt.* **1.** expect **2.** take or consider beforehand **3.** foresee **4.** enjoy in advance —**anticiˈpation** *n.* —**anˈticipative** *or* **anˈticipatory** *a.*

anticlerical (æntɪˈklɛrɪkˀl) *a.* **1.** opposed to influence of clergy, *esp.* in politics —*n.* **2.** supporter of anticlerical party

anticlimax (æntɪˈklaɪmæks) *n.* **1.** disappointing conclusion to series of events *etc.* **2.** sudden descent to the trivial or ludicrous

anticline (ˈæntɪklaɪn) *n.* formation of stratified rock folded into broad arch so that strata slope down on both sides from common crest

antics (ˈæntɪks) *pl.n.* absurd or grotesque movements or acts

anticyclone (æntɪˈsaɪkləʊn) *n.* system of winds moving round centre of high barometric pressure

antidote (ˈæntɪdəʊt) *n.* counteracting remedy

antifreeze (ˈæntɪfriːz) *n.* liquid added to water to lower its freezing point, as in car radiators

antigen (ˈæntɪdʒən, -dʒɛn) *n.* substance stimulating production of antibodies in the blood

antihero (ˈæntɪhɪərəʊ) *n.* central character in novel *etc.*, who lacks traditional heroic virtues

antihistamine (æntɪˈhɪstəmiːn, -mɪn) *n.* drug used *esp.* to treat allergies

antiknock (æntɪˈnɒk) *n.* compound added to petrol to reduce knocking in engine

antilogarithm (æntɪˈlɒgərɪðəm) *n.* number whose logarithm is the given number (*also* **ˈantilog**)

antimacassar (æntɪməˈkæsə) *n.* cover to protect chairs from macassar oil

antimatter (ˈæntɪmætə) *n.* hypothetical form of matter composed of antiparticles

antimony (ˈæntɪmənɪ) *n.* brittle, bluish-white metal

antinomy (ænˈtɪnəmɪ) *n.* **1.** opposition of one law *etc.* to another **2.** *Philos.* contradiction between two apparently indubitable propositions

antinovel (ˈæntɪnɒvˀl) *n.* prose fiction in which conventional novelistic elements are rejected

antiparticle (ˈæntɪpɑːtɪkˀl) *n.* any of group of elementary particles that have same mass as corresponding particle but have charge of equal magnitude but opposite sign

antipasto (æntɪˈpɑːstəʊ, -ˈpæs-) *n.* course of hors d'œuvres in Italian meal (*pl.* **-s**)

antipathy (ænˈtɪpəθɪ) *n.* dislike, aversion —**antipaˈthetic** *a.*

antiperspirant (æntɪˈpɜːspərənt) *n.* substance used to reduce sweating

antiphon (ˈæntɪfən) *n.* **1.** composition in which verses, lines are sung alternately by two choirs **2.** anthem —**anˈtiphonal** *a.*

antipodes (ænˈtɪpədiːz) *pl.n.* countries, peoples on opposite side of the globe (oft. refers to Aust. and N.Z.) —**anˈtipodal** *or* **antipoˈdean** *a.*

antipope (ˈæntɪpəʊp) *n.* pope elected in opposition to the one regularly chosen

antipyretic (æntɪpaɪˈrɛtɪk) *n./a.* (remedy) effective against fever

antique (ænˈtiːk) *n.* **1.** relic of former times, usu. piece of furniture *etc.* that is collected —*a.* **2.** ancient **3.** old-fashioned —**antiquary** (ˈæntɪkwərɪ) *or* **antiquarian** (æntɪˈkwɛərɪən) *n.* student or collector of old

THESAURUS

anthology analects, choice, collection, compendium, compilation, digest, garland, miscellany, selection, treasury

anticipate 1. apprehend, await, count upon, expect, forecast, foresee, foretell, hope for, look for, look forward to, predict, prepare for **2.** antedate, beat (someone) to it (*Inf.*), forestall, intercept, prevent

anticipation apprehension, awaiting, expectancy, expectation, foresight, foretaste, forethought, hope, preconception, premonition, prescience, presentiment

anticlimax bathos, comedown (*Inf.*), disappointment, letdown

antics buffoonery, capers, clowning, escapades, foolishness, frolics, larks, mischief, monkey tricks, playfulness, pranks, silliness, skylarking, stunts, tomfoolery, tricks

antidote antitoxin, antivenin, corrective, counteragent, countermeasure, cure, neutralizer, preventive, remedy, specific

antipathy abhorrence, animosity, animus, antagonism, aversion, bad blood, contrariety, disgust, dislike, distaste, enmity, hatred, hostility, ill will, incompatibility, loathing, opposition, rancour, repugnance, repulsion

antiquated antediluvian, antique, archaic, dated, obsolete, old-fashioned, old hat, outmoded, out-of-date, outworn, passé

things —**antiquated** (ˈæntɪkweɪtɪd) *a.* out-of-date —**antiquity** (ænˈtɪkwɪtɪ) *n.* **1.** great age **2.** former times

antirrhinum (æntɪˈraɪnəm) *n.* genus of plants including snapdragon

antiscorbutic (æntɪskɔːˈbjuːtɪk) *n./a.* (agent) preventing or curing scurvy

anti-Semitic *a.* discriminating against Jews —**anti-Semitism** (-ˈsɛmɪtɪzəm) *n.*

antiseptic (æntɪˈsɛptɪk) *n./a.* **1.** (substance) preventing infection —*a.* **2.** free from infection

antisocial (æntɪˈsəʊʃəl) *a.* **1.** avoiding company of other people; unsociable **2.** contrary to interests of society in general

antistatic (æntɪˈstætɪk) *a.* (of textile *etc.*) retaining sufficient moisture to provide conducting path, thus avoiding effects of static electricity

antithesis (ænˈtɪθɪsɪs) *n.* **1.** direct opposite **2.** contrast **3.** opposition of ideas (*pl.* **-eses** (-ɪsiːz)) —**antiˈthetical** *a.* —**antiˈthetically** *adv.*

antitoxin (æntɪˈtɒksɪn) *n.* serum used to neutralize disease poisons

antitrades (ˈæntɪtreɪdz) *pl.n.* winds blowing in opposite direction from and above trade winds

antitrust (æntɪˈtrʌst) *a.* *chiefly* **US** regulating or opposing trusts or similar organizations

antitype (ˈæntɪtaɪp) *n.* **1.** person or thing foreshadowed or represented by type or symbol **2.** opposite type

antivenin (æntɪˈvɛnɪn) *n.* antitoxin to counteract specific venom, *eg* of snake or spider

antler (ˈæntlə) *n.* branching horn of certain deer —**ˈantlered** *a.*

antonym (ˈæntənɪm) *n.* word of opposite meaning to another, *eg cold* is an antonym of *hot*

antrum (ˈæntrəm) *n.* *Anat.* natural cavity or sinus, *esp.* in bone (*pl.* **-tra** (-trə))

anuresis (ænjʊˈriːsɪs) *n.* inability to urinate

anus (ˈeɪnəs) *n.* the lower opening of the bowels —**ˈanal** *a.* of or near the anus

anvil (ˈænvɪl) *n.* heavy iron block on which a smith hammers metal into shape

anxious (ˈæŋkʃəs, ˈæŋʃəs) *a.* **1.** troubled, uneasy **2.** concerned —**anxiety** (æŋˈzaɪɪtɪ) *n.* —**ˈanxiously** *adv.*

any (ˈɛnɪ) *a./pron.* **1.** one indefinitely **2.** some **3.** whatever, whichever —**ˈanybody** *pron.* —**ˈanyhow** *adv.* —**any more** *or esp. U.S.* **anyˈmore** *adv.* any longer; still; nowadays —**ˈanyone** *pron.* —**ˈanything** *pron.* —**ˈanyway** *adv.* —**ˈanywhere** *adv.*

Anzac (ˈænzæk) *a.* **1.** of Australian-New Zealand Army Corps in WWI —*n.* **2.** soldier of that corps, Gallipoli veteran —**Anzac Day** Apr. 25th, public holiday in Aust. and N.Z. commemorating Anzac landing at Gallipoli in 1915

ANZUS (ˈænzəs) Aust., N.Z. and U.S., with reference to security alliance between them

a.o.b. *or* **A.O.B.** any other business

aorist (ˈeɪərɪst, ˈɛərɪst) *n.* *Gram.* tense of verb, *esp.* in classical Greek, indicating past action without reference to whether action involved was momentary or continuous.

aorta (eɪˈɔːtə) *n.* great artery rising from left ventricle of heart —**aˈortal** *a.*

apace (əˈpeɪs) *adv.* swiftly

Apache (əˈpætʃɪ) *n.* **1.** member of N Amer. Indian people of SW U.S. and N Mexico (*pl.* **-s, Aˈpache**) **2.** language of this people

apart (əˈpɑːt) *adv.* **1.** separately, aside **2.** in pieces

apartheid (əˈpɑːthaɪt, -heɪt) *n.* *esp.* in S Afr., official government policy of racial segregation

apartment (əˈpɑːtmənt) *n.* **1.** room **2.** *esp.* **US** a flat —*pl.* **3.** lodgings

apathy (ˈæpəθɪ) *n.* **1.** indifference **2.** lack of emotion —**apaˈthetic** *a.* —**apaˈthetically** *adv.*

apatite (ˈæpətaɪt) *n.* common mineral consisting basically of calcium fluorophosphate

ape (eɪp) *n.* **1.** tailless primate (*eg* chimpanzee, gorilla) **2.** coarse, clumsy person **3.** imitator —*vt.* **4.** imitate —**ˈapish** *a.* —**ˈapishly** *adv.* —**ˈapeman** *n.* apelike primate thought to have been forerunner of modern man

aperient (əˈpɪərɪənt) *a.* **1.** mildly laxative —*n.* **2.** any mild laxative

aperiodic (eɪpɪərɪˈɒdɪk) *a.* *Elec.* having no natural period or frequency

apéritif (əpɛrɪˈtiːf) *n.* alcoholic appetizer

aperture (ˈæpətʃə) *n.* opening, hole

THESAURUS

antique *adj.* **1.** aged, ancient, elderly, old, superannuated **2.** archaic, obsolete, old-fashioned, outdated ~*n.* **3.** bygone, heirloom, object of virtu, relic

antiquity **1.** age, ancientness, elderliness, old age, oldness **2.** ancient times, distant past, olden days, time immemorial

antiseptic **1.** *adj.* aseptic, clean, germ-free, hygienic, pure, sanitary, sterile, uncontaminated, unpolluted **2.** *n.* bactericide, disinfectant, germicide, purifier

antisocial **1.** alienated, asocial, misanthropic, reserved, retiring, uncommunicative, unfriendly, unsociable, withdrawn **2.** antagonistic, belligerent, disorderly, disruptive, hostile, menacing, rebellious

anxiety angst, apprehension, care, concern, disquiet, disquietude, distress, foreboding, fretfulness, misgiving, nervousness, restlessness, solicitude, suspense, tension, unease, uneasiness, watchfulness, worry

anxious apprehensive, careful, concerned, disquieted, distressed, disturbed, fearful, fretful, in suspense, nervous, overwrought, restless, solicitous, taut, tense, troubled, uneasy, unquiet (*Chiefly literary*), watchful, worried

apart **1.** afar, alone, aloof, aside, away, by itself, by oneself, cut off, distant, distinct, divorced, excluded, independent, independently, isolated, piecemeal, separate, separated, separately, singly, to itself, to oneself, to one side **2.** asunder, in bits, in pieces, into parts, to bits, to pieces

apartment accommodation, chambers, compartment, flat (*U.S.*), living quarters, penthouse, quarters, room, rooms, suite

apathetic cold, cool, emotionless, impassive, indifferent, insensible, listless, passive, phlegmatic, sluggish, stoic, stoical, torpid, unconcerned, unemotional, unfeeling, uninterested, unmoved, unresponsive

apathy coldness, coolness, emotionlessness, impassibility, impassivity, indifference, insensibility, listlessness, passiveness, passivity, phlegm, sluggishness, stoicism, torpor, unconcern, unfeelingness, uninterestedness, unresponsiveness

apex (ˈeɪpɛks) *n.* **1.** top, peak **2.** vertex (*pl.* **-es, ˈapices**) —**ˈapical** *a.* of, at, or being apex

APEX (ˈeɪpɛks) **1.** Advanced Purchase Excursion (reduced airline fare, paid for at least 30 days before departure) **2.** Association of Professional, Executive, Clerical and Computer Staff

aphasia (əˈfeɪzɪə) *n.* dumbness or loss of speech control, due to disease of brain

aphelion (æpˈhiːlɪən, əˈfiː-) *n.* point of planet's orbit farthest from sun (*pl.* **-lia** (-lɪə))

aphis (ˈeɪfɪs) *n.* any of various sap-sucking insects (*pl.* **aphides** (ˈeɪfɪdiːz)) —**ˈaphid** *n.* an aphis

aphorism (ˈæfərɪzəm) *n.* maxim, pithy saying —**ˈaphorist** *n.* —**aphoˈristic** *a.*

aphrodisiac (æfrəˈdɪzɪæk) *a.* **1.** exciting sexual desire —*n.* **2.** substance which so excites

apiary (ˈeɪpɪərɪ) *n.* place where bees are kept —**apiˈarian** *or* **ˈapian** *a.* —**ˈapiarist** *n.* beekeeper —**ˈapiculture** *n.* breeding and care of bees

apices (ˈæpɪsiːz, ˈeɪ-) *n., pl. of* APEX

apiece (əˈpiːs) *adv.* for each

aplomb (əˈplɒm) *n.* self-possession, coolness, assurance

apo- *or* **ap-** (*comb. form*) **1.** away from; off, as in *apogee* **2.** separation of, as in *apocarpous*

apocalypse (əˈpɒkəlɪps) *n.* **1.** prophetic revelation, *esp.* of St. John **2.** (**A-**) last book of New Testament —**apocaˈlyptic** *a.* —**apocaˈlyptically** *adv.*

apocrypha (əˈpɒkrɪfə) *n.* religious writing of doubtful authenticity —**aˈpocryphal** *a.* spurious —**the Apocrypha** collective name for 14 books orig. in Old Testament

apodosis (əˈpɒdəsɪs) *n.* consequent clause in conditional sentence, as distinct from protasis or *if* clause (*pl.* **-oses** (-əsiːz))

apogee (ˈæpədʒiː) *n.* **1.** point of moon's or satellite's orbit farthest from the earth **2.** climax

apolitical (eɪpəˈlɪtɪkˈl) *a.* politically neutral

apologia (æpəˈləudʒɪə) *n.* written defence of one's beliefs, conduct *etc.*

apologue (ˈæpəlɒg) *n.* allegory, moral fable

apology (əˈpɒlədʒɪ) *n.* **1.** acknowledgment of offence and expression of regret **2.** written or spoken defence **3.** (*with* for) poor substitute —**apoloˈgetic** *a.* —**apoloˈgetically** *adv.* —**apoloˈgetics** *pl.n.* (*with sing. v.*) branch of theology charged with defence of Christianity —**aˈpologist** *n.* —**aˈpologize** *or* **-gise** *vi.*

apophthegm *or* **apothegm** (ˈæpəθɛm) *n.* terse saying, maxim —**apophthegmatic** *or* **apothegmatic** (æpəθɛgˈmætɪk) *a.*

apoplexy (ˈæpəplɛksɪ) *n.* loss of sense and oft. paralysis caused by broken or blocked blood vessel in brain —**apoˈplectic** *a.*

apostasy (əˈpɒstəsɪ) *n.* abandonment of one's religious or other faith —**aˈpostate** *n./a.*

a posteriori (eɪ pɒstɛrɪˈɔːraɪ, -rɪ, ɑː) **1.** denoting form of inductive reasoning which arrives at causes from effects **2.** empirical

apostle (əˈpɒsˈl) *n.* **1.** (*oft.* **A-**) one sent to preach the Gospel, *esp.* one of the first disciples of Jesus **2.** founder of Christian church in a country **3.** leader of reform —**aˈpostleship** *n.* —**apostolic(al)** (æpəˈstɒlɪk(ˈl)) *a.* —**Apostles' Creed** concise statement of Christian beliefs —**Apostolic See** see of pope

apostrophe (əˈpɒstrəfɪ) *n.* **1.** mark (') showing omission of letter or letters in word **2.** digression to appeal to someone dead or absent —**aˈpostrophize** *or* **-phise** *v.*

apothecary (əˈpɒθɪkərɪ) *n.* *old name for* one who prepares and sells drugs, *now* chemist —**apothecaries' measure** system of liquid volume measure used in pharmacy in which 20 fluid ounces equal 1 pint

apothegm (ˈæpəθɛm) *n. see* APOPHTHEGM

apothem (ˈæpəθɛm) *n.* perpendicular from centre of regular polygon to any of its sides

apotheosis (əpɒθɪˈəusɪs) *n.* deification, act of raising any person or thing to status of a god (*pl.* **-ses** (-siːz)) —**aˈpotheosize** *or* **-ise** *vt.* **1.** deify **2.** glorify, idealize

appal *or U.S.* **appall** (əˈpɔːl) *vt.* dismay, terrify (**-ll-**) —**apˈpalling** *a.* dreadful, terrible

appanage *or* **apanage** (ˈæpənɪdʒ) *n.* **1.** land or other provision granted by king for support of *esp.* younger son **2.** customary perquisite

apparatus (æpəˈreɪtəs, -ˈrɑːtəs) *n.* **1.** equipment, instruments, for performing any experiment, operation *etc.* **2.** means by which something operates

THESAURUS

ape affect, caricature, copy, counterfeit, echo, imitate, mimic, mirror, mock, parody, parrot

aperture breach, chink, cleft, crack, eye, eyelet, fissure, gap, hole, interstice, opening, orifice, passage, perforation, rent, rift, slit, slot, space

aphorism adage, apothegm, axiom, dictum, gnome, maxim, precept, proverb, saw, saying

apiece each, for each, from each, individually, respectively, separately, severally, to each

aplomb balance, calmness, composure, confidence, coolness, equanimity, level-headedness, poise, sang-froid, self-assurance, self-confidence, self-possession, stability

apocryphal doubtful, dubious, equivocal, fictitious, legendary, mythical, questionable, spurious, unauthenticated, uncanonical, unsubstantiated, unverified

apologetic contrite, penitent, regretful, remorseful, rueful, sorry

apologize ask forgiveness, beg pardon, express regret, say one is sorry, say sorry

apology **1.** acknowledgment, confession, defence, excuse, explanation, extenuation, justification, plea, vindication **2.** caricature, excuse, imitation, makeshift, mockery, stopgap, substitute, travesty

apostle **1.** evangelist, herald, messenger, missionary, preacher, proselytizer **2.** advocate, champion, pioneer, propagandist, propagator, proponent

apotheosis deification, elevation, exaltation, glorification, idealization, idolization

appal alarm, astound, daunt, dishearten, dismay, frighten, harrow, horrify, intimidate, outrage, petrify, scare, shock, terrify, unnerve

appalling alarming, astounding, awful, daunting, dire, disheartening, dismaying, dreadful, fearful, frightening, frightful, ghastly, grim, harrowing, hideous, horrible, horrid, horrific, horrifying, intimidating, petrifying, scaring, shocking, terrible, terrifying, unnerving

apparel (əˈpærəl) *n.* **1.** clothing —*vt.* **2.** clothe (**-ll-**)

apparent (əˈpærənt) *a.* **1.** seeming **2.** obvious **3.** acknowledged, as in *heir apparent* —**apˈparently** *adv.*

apparition (æpəˈrɪʃən) *n.* (appearance of) ghost

appeal (əˈpiːl) *vi.* **1.** make earnest request **2.** be attractive **3.** refer, have recourse **4.** apply to higher court —*n.* **5.** request **6.** reference **7.** supplication —**apˈpealable** *a.* —**apˈpealing** *a.* **1.** making appeal **2.** pleasant, attractive —**apˈpealingly** *adv.* —**apˈpellant** *n.* one who appeals to higher court —**appellate** (əˈpɛlɪt) *a.* of appeals

appear (əˈpɪə) *vi.* **1.** become visible or present **2.** seem, be plain **3.** be seen in public —**apˈpearance** *n.* **1.** an appearing **2.** aspect **3.** pretence

appease (əˈpiːz) *vt.* pacify, quiet, allay, satisfy —**apˈpeasable** *a.* —**apˈpeasement** *n.*

appellant (əˈpɛlənt) *n. see* APPEAL

appellation (æpɪˈleɪʃən) *n.* name —**apˈpellative** *a./n.*

append (əˈpɛnd) *vt.* join on, add —**apˈpendage** *n.*

appendix (əˈpɛndɪks) *n.* **1.** subsidiary addition to book *etc.* **2.** *Anat.* projection, *esp.* small worm-shaped part of intestine (*pl.* **-dices** (-dɪsiːz), **-es**) —**appendiˈcectomy** *or* **appenˈdectomy** *n.* surgical removal of any appendage, *esp.* vermiform appendix —**appendiˈcitis** *n.* inflammation of vermiform appendix

apperception (æpəˈsɛpʃən) *n.* **1.** perception **2.** apprehension **3.** the mind's perception of itself as a conscious agent —**apperˈceive** *vt.*

appertain (æpəˈteɪn) *vi.* belong, relate, be appropriate

appetence (ˈæpɪtəns) *or* **appetency** *n.* **1.** desire, craving **2.** sexual appetite —**ˈappetent** *a.*

appetite (ˈæpɪtaɪt) *n.* desire, inclination, *esp.* desire for food —**apˈpetitive** *a.* —**ˈappetizer** *or* **-iser** *n.* something stimulating to appetite —**ˈappetizing** *or* **-ising** *a.* —**ˈappetizingly** *or* **-isingly** *adv.*

applaud (əˈplɔːd) *v.* **1.** express approval (of) by hand-clapping —*vt.* **2.** praise; approve —**apˈplauder** *n.* —**apˈplause** *n.* loud approval

apple (ˈæpᵊl) *n.* **1.** round, firm, fleshy fruit **2.** tree bearing it —**apple-pie bed UK** way of making bed to prevent person from entering it —**apple-pie order** *inf.* perfect order —**apple of one's eye** person or thing very much loved

appliance (əˈplaɪəns) *n.* piece of equipment, *esp.* electrical

THESAURUS

apparatus 1. appliance, contraption (*Inf.*), device, equipment, gear, implements, machine, machinery, materials, means, mechanism, outfit, tackle, tools, utensils **2.** bureaucracy, chain of command, hierarchy, network, organization, setup, structure, system

apparent 1. clear, conspicuous, discernible, distinct, evident, indubitable, manifest, marked, obvious, open, overt, patent, plain, understandable, unmistakable, visible **2.** ostensible, outward, seeming, specious, superficial

apparently it appears that, it seems that, on the face of it, ostensibly, outwardly, seemingly, speciously, superficially

apparition 1. appearance, manifestation, materialization, presence, vision, visitation **2.** chimera, ghost, phantom, revenant, shade (*Literary*), spectre, spirit, spook (*Inf.*), visitant, wraith

appeal *n.* **1.** adjuration, application, entreaty, invocation, petition, plea, prayer, request, solicitation, suit, supplication ~*v.* **2.** adjure, apply, ask, beg, beseech, call, call upon, entreat, implore, petition, plead, pray, refer, request, resort to, solicit, sue, supplicate **3.** allure, attract, charm, engage, entice, fascinate, interest, invite, please, tempt

appear 1. arise, arrive, attend, be present, come forth, come into sight, come into view, come out, come to light, crop up (*Inf.*), develop, emerge, issue, loom, materialize, occur, show (*Sl.*), show up (*Inf.*), surface, turn out, turn up **2.** look (like *or* as if), occur, seem, strike one as **3.** be apparent, be clear, be evident, be manifest, be obvious, be patent, be plain **4.** become available, be created, be developed, be invented, be published, come into being, come into existence, come out

appearance 1. advent, appearing, arrival, coming, debut, emergence, introduction, presence, showing up (*Inf.*), turning up **2.** air, aspect, bearing, demeanour, expression, face, figure, form, image, look, looks, manner, mien (*Literary*) **3.** front, guise, illusion, image, impression, outward show, pretence, semblance

appease allay, alleviate, assuage, blunt, calm, compose, conciliate, diminish, ease, lessen, lull, mitigate, mollify, pacify, placate, quell, quench, quiet, satisfy, soften, soothe, subdue, tranquillize

appeasement abatement, alleviation, assuagement, blunting, easing, lessening, lulling, mitigation, mollification, pacification, quelling, quenching, quieting, satisfaction, softening, solace, soothing, tranquillization

append add, adjoin, affix, annex, attach, fasten, hang, join, subjoin, tack on, tag on

appendage accessory, addendum, addition, adjunct, affix, ancillary, annexe, appendix, appurtenance, attachment, auxiliary, supplement

appendix addendum, addition, adjunct, appendage, codicil, postscript, supplement

appertain *Usually with* **to** apply, bear upon, be characteristic of, be connected, belong, be part of, be pertinent, be proper, be relevant, have to do with, inhere in, pertain, refer, relate, touch upon

appetite appetence, appetency, craving, demand, desire, hankering, hunger, inclination, liking, longing, passion, proclivity, propensity, relish, stomach, taste, willingness, yearning, zeal, zest

appetizing appealing, delicious, inviting, mouthwatering, palatable, savoury, scrumptious (*Inf.*), succulent, tasty, tempting

applaud acclaim, approve, cheer, clap, commend, compliment, encourage, eulogize, extol, laud, magnify (*Archaic*), praise

applause acclaim, acclamation, accolade, approbation, approval, cheering, cheers, commendation, eulogizing, hand, hand-clapping, laudation, ovation, plaudit, praise

appliance apparatus, device, gadget, implement, instrument, machine, mechanism, tool

applicable apposite, appropriate, apropos, apt, befitting, fit, fitting, germane, pertinent, relevant, suitable, suited, to the point, to the purpose, useful

applicant aspirant, candidate, claimant, inquirer, petitioner, postulant, suitor, suppliant

appliqué (æˈpliːkeɪ) *n.* **1.** ornaments, embroidery *etc.*, secured to surface of material —*vt.* **2.** ornament thus

apply (əˈplaɪ) *vt.* **1.** utilize, employ **2.** lay or place on **3.** administer, devote —*vi.* **4.** have reference (to) **5.** make request (to) (**-lied, -lying**) —**applicability** (æplɪkəˈbɪlɪtɪ) *n.* —**applicable** (ˈæplɪkəbˀl, əˈplɪkə-) *a.* relevant —**applicably** (ˈæplɪkəblɪ, əˈplɪkə-) *adv.* —**applicant** (ˈæplɪkənt) *n.* —**application** (æplɪˈkeɪʃən) *n.* **1.** applying something for a particular use **2.** relevance **3.** request for job *etc.* **4.** concentration, diligence —**applicator** (ˈæplɪkeɪtə) *n.* device, such as spatula, for applying medicine, glue *etc.* —**apˈplied** *a.* (of skill, science *etc.*) put to practical use

appoint (əˈpɔɪnt) *vt.* **1.** name for, assign to job or position **2.** fix, settle **3.** equip —**apˈpointment** *n.* **1.** engagement to meet **2.** (selection for a) job —*pl.* **3.** fittings

apportion (əˈpɔːʃən) *vt.* divide out in shares —**apˈportionment** *n.*

appose (əˈpəʊz) *vt.* **1.** place side by side **2.** place (something) near or against another thing

apposite (ˈæpəzɪt) *a.* suitable, apt —**ˈappositely** *adv.* —**ˈappositeness** *n.* —**appoˈsition** *n.* **1.** proximity **2.** the placing of one word beside another

appraise (əˈpreɪz) *vt.* set price on, estimate value of —**apˈpraisable** *a.* —**apˈpraisal** *or* **apˈpraisement** *n.* —**apˈpraiser** *n.*

appreciate (əˈpriːʃɪeɪt, -sɪ-) *vt.* **1.** value at true worth **2.** be grateful for **3.** understand **4.** enjoy —*vi.* **5.** rise in value —**apˈpreciable** *a.* **1.** estimable **2.** substantial —**apˈpreciably** *adv.* —**appreciˈation** *n.* —**apˈpreciative** *or* **apˈpreciatory** *a.* capable of expressing pleasurable recognition —**apˈpreciator** *n.*

apprehend (æprɪˈhɛnd) *vt.* **1.** seize by authority **2.** take hold of **3.** recognize, understand **4.** dread —**appreˈhensiˈbility** *n.* —**appreˈhensible** *a.* —**appreˈhension** *n.* **1.** dread, anxiety **2.** arrest **3.** conception **4.** ability to understand —**appreˈhensive** *a.*

apprentice (əˈprɛntɪs) *n.* **1.** person learning a trade under specified conditions **2.** novice —*vt.* **3.** bind as apprentice —**apˈprenticeship** *n.*

THESAURUS

application 1. appositeness, exercise, function, germaneness, pertinence, practice, purpose, relevance, use, value **2.** appeal, claim, inquiry, petition, request, requisition, solicitation, suit **3.** assiduity, attention, attentiveness, commitment, dedication, diligence, effort, hard work, industry, perseverance, study

apply 1. administer, assign, bring into play, bring to bear, carry out, employ, engage, execute, exercise, implement, practise, put to use, use, utilize **2.** appertain, be applicable, be appropriate, bear upon, be fitting, be relevant, fit, pertain, refer, relate, suit **3.** anoint, bring into contact with, cover with, lay on, paint, place, put on, smear, spread on, touch to **4.** appeal, claim, inquire, make application, petition, put in, request, requisition, solicit, sue

appoint 1. allot, arrange, assign, choose, decide, designate, determine, establish, fix, set, settle **2.** assign, choose, commission, delegate, elect, install, name, nominate, select **3.** equip, fit out, furnish, provide, supply

appointment 1. arrangement, assignation, consultation, date, engagement, interview, meeting, rendezvous, session, tryst (*Archaic*) **2.** allotment, assignment, choice, choosing, commissioning, delegation, designation, election, installation, naming, nomination, selection **3.** assignment, berth (*Inf.*), job, office, place, position, post, situation, station **4.** *Usually plural* accoutrements, appurtenances, equipage, fittings, fixtures, furnishings, gear, outfit, paraphernalia, trappings

apportion allocate, allot, assign, deal, dispense, distribute, divide, dole out, measure out, mete out, parcel out, ration out, share

apportionment allocation, allotment, assignment, dealing out, dispensing, distribution, division, doling out, measuring out, meting out, parcelling out, rationing out, sharing

apposite appertaining, applicable, appropriate, apropos, apt, befitting, germane, pertinent, proper, relevant, suitable, suited, to the point, to the purpose

appraisal 1. assessment, estimate, estimation, evaluation, judgment, opinion, sizing up (*Inf.*) **2.** assay, pricing, rating, reckoning, survey, valuation

appreciable ascertainable, clear-cut, considerable, definite, detectable, discernible, distinguishable, evident, marked, material, measurable, noticeable, obvious, perceivable, perceptible, pronounced, recognizable, significant, substantial, visible

appreciate 1. be appreciative, be grateful for, be indebted, be obliged, be thankful for, give thanks for **2.** acknowledge, be alive to, be aware (cognizant, conscious) of, comprehend, estimate, know, perceive, realize, recognize, sympathize with, take account of, understand **3.** admire, cherish, enjoy, esteem, like, prize, rate highly, regard, relish, respect, savour, treasure, value **4.** enhance, gain, grow, improve, increase, inflate, raise the value of, rise

appreciation 1. acknowledgment, gratefulness, gratitude, indebtedness, obligation, thankfulness, thanks **2.** admiration, appraisal, assessment, awareness, cognizance, comprehension, enjoyment, esteem, estimation, knowledge, liking, perception, realization, recognition, regard, relish, respect, responsiveness, sensitivity, sympathy, understanding, valuation **3.** enhancement, gain, growth, improvement, increase, inflation, rise

appreciative 1. beholden, grateful, indebted, obliged, thankful **2.** admiring, aware, cognizant, conscious, enthusiastic, in the know (*Inf.*), knowledgeable, mindful, perceptive, pleased, regardful, respectful, responsive, sensitive, supportive, understanding

apprehend 1. arrest, bust (*Inf.*), capture, catch, collar (*Inf.*), nab (*Inf.*), nick (*Sl.*), pinch (*Inf.*), run in (*Sl.*), seize, take, take prisoner **2.** appreciate, believe, comprehend, conceive, grasp, imagine, know, perceive, realize, recognize, think, understand **3.** be afraid of, dread, fear

apprehension 1. alarm, anxiety, apprehensiveness, concern, disquiet, doubt, dread, fear, foreboding, misgiving, mistrust, premonition, suspicion, unease, uneasiness, worry **2.** arrest, capture, catching, seizure, taking **3.** awareness, comprehension, grasp, intellect, intelligence, ken, knowledge, perception, understanding **4.** belief, concept, conception, conjecture, idea, impression, notion, opinion, sentiment, thought, view

apprehensive afraid, alarmed, anxious, concerned,

apprise *or* **-ize** (əˈpraɪz) *vt.* inform

appro (ˈæprəʊ) *inf.* approval

approach (əˈprəʊtʃ) *v.* **1.** draw near (to) —*vt.* **2.** set about **3.** address request to **4.** approximate to —*n.* **5.** a drawing near **6.** means of reaching or doing **7.** approximation **8.** (*oft. pl.*) friendly overture(s) —**approachaˈbility** *n.* —**apˈproachable** *a.*

approbation (æprəˈbeɪʃən) *n.* approval

appropriate (əˈprəʊprɪeɪt) *vt.* **1.** take for oneself **2.** put aside for particular purpose —*a.* (əˈprəʊprɪɪt) **3.** suitable, fitting —**apˈpropriately** *adv.* —**apˈpropriateness** *n.* —**appropriˈation** *n.* **1.** act of setting apart for purpose **2.** parliamentary vote of money —**apˈpropriative** *a.* —**apˈpropriator** *n.*

approve (əˈpruːv) *vt.* **1.** think well of, commend **2.** authorize, agree to —*vi.* **3.** (*usu. with* of) take favourable view —**apˈproval** *n.* —**apˈprover** *n.* —**apˈprovingly** *adv.*

approx. approximate(ly)

approximate (əˈprɒksɪmɪt) *a.* **1.** very near, nearly correct **2.** inexact, imprecise —*vt.* (əˈprɒksɪmeɪt) **3.** bring close **4.** be almost the same as —*vi.* (əˈprɒksɪmeɪt) **5.** come near —**apˈproximately** *adv.* —**approxiˈmation** *n.* —**apˈproximative** *a.*

appurtenance (əˈpɜːtɪnəns) *n.* **1.** less significant thing or part **2.** accessory

Apr. April

après-ski (æpreɪˈskiː) *n.* social activities after day's skiing

apricot (ˈeɪprɪkɒt) *n.* **1.** orange-coloured stone-fruit related to plum —*a.* **2.** of the colour of the fruit

April (ˈeɪprəl) *n.* fourth month —**April fool** victim of practical joke performed on Apr. 1st (**April Fools' Day** *or* **All Fools' Day**)

a priori (eɪ praɪˈɔːraɪ, ɑː prɪˈɔːrɪ) *a.* **1.** denoting deductive reasoning from general principle to expected facts or effects **2.** denoting knowledge gained independently of experience

apron (ˈeɪprən) *n.* **1.** cloth, piece of leather *etc.*, worn in front of body to protect clothes, or as part of official dress **2.** in theatre, strip of stage before curtain **3.** on airfield, tarmac area where aircraft stand, are loaded *etc.* **4.** *fig.* any of a variety of things resembling these —**tied to someone's apron strings** dominated by one's mother or wife

apropos (æprəˈpəʊ) *adv.* **1.** to the purpose **2.** by the way —*a.* **3.** apt, appropriate —**apropos of** concerning

THESAURUS

disquieted, doubtful, fearful, foreboding, mistrustful, suspicious, uneasy, worried

apprentice beginner, learner, neophyte, novice, probationer, pupil, student, tyro

approach *v.* **1.** advance, catch up, come close, come near, come to, draw near, gain on, meet, move towards, near, push forward, reach **2.** appeal to, apply to, broach the matter with, make advances to, make a proposal to, make overtures to, sound out **3.** begin, begin work on, commence, embark on, enter upon, make a start, set about, undertake **4.** approximate, be comparable to, be like, come close to, come near to, compare with, resemble ~*n.* **5.** access, advance, advent, arrival, avenue, coming, drawing near, entrance, nearing, passage, road, way **6.** approximation, likeness, semblance **7.** *Often plural* advance, appeal, application, invitation, offer, overture, proposal, proposition **8.** attitude, course, manner, means, method, mode, modus operandi, procedure, style, technique, way

approachable accessible, attainable, come-at-able (*Inf.*), get-at-able (*Inf.*), reachable

appropriate *adj.* **1.** adapted, applicable, apposite, appurtenant, apropos, apt, becoming, befitting, belonging, congruous, correct, felicitous, fit, fitting, germane, meet (*Archaic*), opportune, pertinent, proper, relevant, right, seemly, suitable, to the point, to the purpose, well-suited, well-timed ~*v.* **2.** allocate, allot, apportion, assign, devote, earmark, set apart **3.** embezzle, filch, misappropriate, pilfer, pocket, steal

appropriateness applicability, appositeness, aptness, becomingness, congruousness, correctness, felicitousness, felicity, fitness, fittingness, germaneness, opportuneness, pertinence, properness, relevance, rightness, seemliness, suitability, timeliness, well-suitedness

appropriation allocation, allotment, apportionment, assignment, earmarking, setting apart

approval **1.** acquiescence, agreement, assent, authorization, blessing, compliance, concurrence, confirmation, consent, countenance, endorsement, imprimatur, leave, licence, mandate, O.K. (*Inf.*), permission, ratification, recommendation, sanction, the go-ahead (*Inf.*), the green light (*Inf.*), validation **2.** acclaim, admiration, applause, appreciation, approbation, commendation, esteem, favour, good opinion, liking, praise, regard, respect

approve **1.** acclaim, admire, applaud, appreciate, be pleased with, commend, esteem, favour, have a good opinion of, like, praise, regard highly, respect, think highly of **2.** accede to, accept, advocate, agree to, allow, assent to, authorize, bless, concur in, confirm, consent to, countenance, endorse, give the go-ahead (*Inf.*), give the green light (*Inf.*), go along with, mandate, O.K. (*Inf.*), pass, permit, ratify, recommend, sanction, second, subscribe to, uphold, validate

approximate *adj.* **1.** almost accurate, almost exact, close, near **2.** estimated, inexact, loose, rough ~*v.* **3.** approach, border on, come close, come near, reach, resemble, touch, verge on

approximately about, almost, around, circa (*used with dates*), close to, generally, in the neighbourhood of, in the region of, in the vicinity of, just about, loosely, more or less, nearly, not far off, relatively, roughly

approximation approach, correspondence, likeness, resemblance, semblance

apron pinafore, pinny (*Inf.*)

apropos *adj.* **1.** applicable, apposite, appropriate, apt, befitting, belonging, correct, fit, fitting, germane, meet (*Archaic*), opportune, pertinent, proper, related, relevant, right, seemly, suitable, to the point, to the purpose ~*adv.* **2.** appropriately, aptly, opportunely, pertinently, relevantly, suitably, timely, to the point, to the purpose **3.** by the bye, by the way, incidentally, in passing, parenthetically, while on the subject

apropos of *prep.* in respect of, on the subject of, re, regarding, respecting, with reference to, with regard to, with respect to

apse (æps) *n.* arched recess, *esp.* in church —ˈ**apsidal** *a.*

apsis (ˈæpsɪs) *n.* either of two points lying at extremities of eccentric orbit of satellite *etc.* (*pl.* **apsides** (æpˈsaɪdiːz)) (*also* **apse**)

apt (æpt) *a.* **1.** suitable **2.** likely **3.** prompt, quick-witted **4.** dexterous —ˈ**aptitude** *n.* capacity, fitness —ˈ**aptly** *adv.* —ˈ**aptness** *n.*

APT Advanced Passenger Train

apteryx (ˈæptərɪks) *n. see* KIWI (sense 1)

aqua (ˈækwə) *n.* **1.** water (*pl.* **aquae** (ˈækwiː), **-s**) —*a.* **2.** *see* AQUAMARINE (sense 2)

aqualung (ˈækwəlʌŋ) *n.* breathing apparatus used in underwater swimming

aquamarine (ækwəməˈriːn) *n.* **1.** variety of beryl used as gemstone —*a.* **2.** greenish-blue, sea-coloured

aquanaut (ˈækwənɔːt) *n.* person who works or swims underwater

aquaplane (ˈækwəpleɪn) *n.* **1.** plank or boat towed by fast motorboat —*vi.* **2.** ride on aquaplane **3.** (of car) be in contact with water on road, not with road surface —ˈ**aquaplaning** *n.*

aquarium (əˈkwɛərɪəm) *n.* tank or pond for keeping aquatic animals or plants (*pl.* **-s**, **-ria** (-rɪə))

Aquarius (əˈkwɛərɪəs) *n.* (the water-bearer) 11th sign of zodiac, operative c. Jan. 20th–Feb. 18th

aquatic (əˈkwætɪk) *a.* living, growing, done in or on water —**aˈquatics** *pl.n.* water sports

aquatint (ˈækwətɪnt) *n.* etching, engraving imitating drawings *etc.*

aqua vitae (ˈviːtaɪ, ˈvaɪtiː) *Lat. obs.* brandy

aqueduct (ˈækwɪdʌkt) *n.* **1.** artificial channel for water, *esp.* one like bridge **2.** conduit

aqueous (ˈeɪkwɪəs) *a.* of, like, containing water —**aqueous humour** *Physiol.* fluid between cornea and lens of eye

aquilegia (ækwɪˈliːdʒɪə) *n.* columbine

aquiline (ˈækwɪlaɪn) *a.* **1.** relating to eagle **2.** hooked like eagle's beak

Ar *Chem.* argon

AR Arkansas

ar. **1.** arrival **2.** arrive(s)

Ar. **1.** Arabic **2.** Aramaic

Arab (ˈærəb) *n.* **1.** native of Arabia **2.** general term for inhabitants of Middle Eastern countries **3.** Arabian horse (small breed used for riding) —**Arabian** (əˈreɪbɪən) *a.* **1.** of Arabia —*n.* **2.** Arab —ˈ**Arabic** *n.* **1.** language of Arabs —*a.* **2.** of Arabia or Arabs —**Arabic numeral** one of numbers 1,2,3,4,5,6,7,8,9,0

arabesque (ærəˈbɛsk) *n.* **1.** classical ballet position **2.** fanciful painted or carved ornament of Arabian origin —*a.* **3.** (in style) of arabesque

arabis (ˈærəbɪs) *n.* low-growing garden plant with white, pink or lilac flowers

arable (ˈærəbᵊl) *a.* suitable for ploughing or planting crops

Araby (ˈærəbɪ) *n. obs., poet.* Arabia

arachnid (əˈræknɪd) *n.* one of the Arachnida (spiders, scorpions and mites) —**aˈrachnoid** *a.* —**arachˈnology** *n.*

arak (ˈærək) *n. see* ARRACK

Aramaic (ærəˈmeɪɪk) *n.* **1.** ancient Semitic language of Middle East —*a.* **2.** of, relating to or using this language

Aran (ˈærən) *a.* (of sweaters *etc.*) made with naturally oily, unbleached wool, oft. with complicated pattern

arbiter (ˈɑːbɪtə) *n.* judge, umpire (**-tress** *fem.*) —**arˈbitrament** *n.* —ˈ**arbitrarily** *adv.* —ˈ**arbitrary** *a.* **1.** not bound by rules, despotic **2.** random —ˈ**arbitrate** *vt.* **1.** decide (dispute) **2.** submit to, settle by arbitration —*vi.* **3.** act as umpire —**arbiˈtration** *n.* hearing, settling of disputes, *esp.* industrial and legal, by impartial referee(s) —ˈ**arbitrator** *n.*

arbor (ˈɑːbə) *n.* **1.** rotating shaft in machine on which grinding wheel is fitted **2.** rotating shaft

arboreal (ɑːˈbɔːrɪəl) *a.* relating to trees —**arboˈrescent** *a.* having characteristics of tree —**arboˈretum** *n.* place for cultivating specimens of trees (*pl.* **-s**, **-ta** (-tə)) —ˈ**arboriculture** *n.* forestry, cultivation of trees

arbour (ˈɑːbə) *n.* leafy glade *etc.*, sheltered by trees

arbutus (ɑːˈbjuːtəs) *n.* shrub having evergreen leaves and strawberry-like berries (*pl.* **-es**)

arc (ɑːk) *n.* **1.** part of circumference of circle or

THESAURUS

apt **1.** applicable, apposite, appropriate, apropos, befitting, correct, fit, fitting, germane, meet (*Archaic*), pertinent, proper, relevant, seemly, suitable, timely, to the point, to the purpose **2.** disposed, given, inclined, liable, likely, of a mind, prone, ready **3.** astute, bright, clever, expert, gifted, ingenious, intelligent, prompt, quick, sharp, skilful, smart, talented, teachable

aptitude **1.** ability, aptness, capability, capacity, cleverness, faculty, flair, gift, giftedness, intelligence, knack, proficiency, quickness, talent **2.** applicability, appositeness, appropriateness, fitness, relevance, suitability, suitableness

aptness **1.** applicability, appositeness, appropriateness, becomingness, congruousness, correctness, felicitousness, felicity, fitness, fittingness, germaneness, opportuneness, pertinence, properness, relevance, rightness, seemliness, suitability, timeliness, well-suitedness **2.** aptitude, bent, disposition, inclination, leaning, liability, likelihood, likeliness, predilection, proclivity, proneness, propensity, readiness, tendency **3.** ability, capability, capacity, cleverness, faculty, fitness, flair, gift, giftedness, intelligence, knack, proficiency, quickness, suitability, talent

arable cultivable, farmable, fecund, fertile, fruitful, ploughable, productive, tillable

arbiter adjudicator, arbitrator, judge, referee, umpire

arbitrary **1.** capricious, chance, discretionary, erratic, fanciful, inconsistent, optional, personal, random, subjective, unreasonable, whimsical, wilful **2.** absolute, autocratic, despotic, dictatorial, dogmatic, domineering, high-handed, imperious, magisterial, overbearing, peremptory, summary, tyrannical, tyrannous, uncontrolled, unlimited, unrestrained

arbitrate adjudge, adjudicate, decide, determine, judge, pass judgment, referee, settle, sit in judgment, umpire

arbitration adjudication, arbitrament, decision, determination, judgment, settlement

arbitrator adjudicator, arbiter, judge, referee, umpire

arc arch, bend, bow, crescent, curve, half-moon

similar curve **2.** luminous electric discharge between two conductors —*vi.* **3.** form an arc (**arced, 'arcing** *or* **arcked, 'arcking**) —**arc lamp** —**arc light**

arcade (ɑːˈkeɪd) *n.* **1.** row of arches on pillars **2.** covered walk or avenue, *esp.* lined by shops

Arcadian (ɑːˈkeɪdɪən) *a.* **1.** of idealized Arcadia of pastoral poetry **2.** rustic, bucolic —*n.* **3.** person who leads simple rural life

arcane (ɑːˈkeɪn) *a.* **1.** mysterious **2.** esoteric

arch[1] (ɑːtʃ) *n.* **1.** curved structure in building, supporting itself over open space by pressure of stones one against the other **2.** any similar structure **3.** curved shape **4.** curved part of sole of foot —*v.* **5.** form, make into, an arch —**arched** *a.* —**ˈarchway** *n.*

arch[2] (ɑːtʃ) *a.* **1.** chief **2.** experienced, expert **3.** superior, knowing; coyly playful —**ˈarchly** *adv.* —**ˈarchness** *n.*

arch. **1.** archaic **2.** architecture

arch- *or* **archi-** (*comb. form*) chief, as in *archangel, archenemy.* Such words are not given here where the meaning may easily be inferred from the simple word

-arch (*comb. form*) leader; ruler; chief, as in *patriarch, monarch*

archaeology *or* **archeology** (ɑːkɪˈɒlədʒɪ) *n.* study of ancient times from remains of art, implements *etc.* —**archaeoˈlogical** *or* **archeoˈlogical** *a.* —**archaeˈologist** *or* **archeˈologist** *n.*

archaeopteryx (ɑːkɪˈɒptərɪks) *n.* extinct bird of Jurassic times, with teeth, long tail and well-developed wings

archaic (ɑːˈkeɪɪk) *a.* old, primitive —**arˈchaically** *adv.* —**ˈarchaism** *n.* obsolete word or phrase

archbishop (ˈɑːtʃˈbɪʃəp) *n.* chief bishop —**ˈarchˈbishopric** *n.*

archdeacon (ˈɑːtʃˈdiːkən) *n.* chief deacon, clergyman next to bishop —**ˈarchˈdeaconry** *n.* —**archidiaconal** (ɑːkɪdaɪˈækənˀl) *a.*

archdiocese (ɑːtʃˈdaɪəsiːs) *n.* diocese of archbishop

archduke (ˈɑːtʃˈdjuːk) *n.* duke of specially high rank (**ˈarchˈduchess** *fem.*) —**ˈarchˈducal** *a.* —**ˈarchˈduchy** *n.*

archery (ˈɑːtʃərɪ) *n.* skill, sport of shooting with bow and arrow —**ˈarcher** *n.*

archetype (ˈɑːkɪtaɪp) *n.* **1.** prototype **2.** perfect specimen —**ˈarchetypal** *a.*

archfiend (ɑːtʃˈfiːnd) *n.* (*oft.* **A-**) the devil; Satan

archiepiscopal (ɑːkɪɪˈpɪskəpˀl) *a.* of archbishop —**archieˈpiscopate** *n.*

archipelago (ɑːkɪˈpɛləgəʊ) *n.* **1.** group of islands **2.** sea full of small islands, *esp.* Aegean (*pl.* **-es**) —**archipelagic** (ɑːkɪpəˈlædʒɪk) *a.*

architect (ˈɑːkɪtɛkt) *n.* **1.** one qualified to design and supervise construction of buildings **2.** contriver —**architecˈtonic** *a.* of or resembling architecture —**archiˈtectural** *a.* —**ˈarchitecture** *n.*

architrave (ˈɑːkɪtreɪv) *n. Archit.* **1.** lowest division of entablature **2.** ornamental band round door or window opening

archives (ˈɑːkaɪvz) *pl.n.* **1.** collection of records, documents *etc.* about institution, family *etc.* **2.** place where these are kept —**arˈchival** *a.* —**archivist** (ˈɑːkɪvɪst) *n.*

archpriest (ˈɑːtʃˈpriːst) *n.* **1.** formerly, chief assistant to bishop **2.** senior priest

Arctic (ˈɑːktɪk) *a.* **1.** of northern polar regions **2.** (**a-**) very cold —*n.* **3.** region round North Pole —**Arctic Circle** imaginary circle around earth at latitude 66° 32′ N

ardent (ˈɑːdˀnt) *a.* **1.** fiery **2.** passionate —**ˈardency** *n.* —**ˈardently** *adv.* —**ˈardour** *or U.S.* **ˈardor** *n.* **1.** enthusiasm **2.** zeal

arduous (ˈɑːdjuːəs) *a.* **1.** hard to accomplish, difficult **2.** strenuous; laborious —**ˈarduously** *adv.* —**ˈarduousness** *n.*

are[1] (ɑː; *unstressed* ə) *pres. ind. pl. of* BE

are[2] (ɑː) *n.* unit of measure, 100 square metres

area (ˈɛərɪə) *n.* **1.** extent, expanse of any surface **2.** two-dimensional expanse enclosed by boundary (area

THESAURUS

arch[1] *n.* **1.** archway, curve, dome, span, vault **2.** arc, bend, bow, curvature, curve, semicircle ~*v.* **3.** arc, bend, bow, bridge, curve, embow, span

arch[2] **1.** accomplished, chief, consummate, expert, finished, first, foremost, greatest, highest, leading, main, major, master, pre-eminent, primary, principal, top **2.** artful, frolicsome, knowing, mischievous, pert, playful, roguish, saucy, sly, waggish, wily

archaic ancient, antiquated, antique, behind the times, bygone, obsolete, old, olden (*Archaic*), old-fashioned, old hat, outmoded, out of date, passé, primitive, superannuated

arched curved, domed, embowed, vaulted

archer bowman (*Archaic*), toxophilite (*Formal*)

archetype classic, exemplar, form, ideal, model, original, paradigm, pattern, prime example, prototype, standard

architect **1.** designer, master builder, planner **2.** author, contriver, creator, deviser, engineer, founder, instigator, inventor, maker, originator, planner, prime mover, shaper

architecture architectonics, building, construction, design, planning

archives **1.** annals, chronicles, documents, papers, records, registers, rolls **2.** museum, record office, registry, repository

arctic **1.** far-northern, hyperborean, polar **2.** *Inf.* chilly, cold, freezing, frigid, frost-bound, frosty, frozen, gelid, glacial, icy

ardent avid, eager, enthusiastic, fervent, fervid, fierce, fiery, hot, hot-blooded, impassioned, intense, keen, lusty, passionate, spirited, vehement, warm, warm-blooded, zealous

ardour avidity, devotion, eagerness, earnestness, enthusiasm, feeling, fervour, fierceness, fire, heat, intensity, keenness, passion, spirit, vehemence, warmth, zeal

arduous backbreaking, burdensome, difficult, exhausting, fatiguing, formidable, gruelling, hard, harsh, heavy, laborious, onerous, painful, punishing, rigorous, severe, steep, strenuous, taxing, tiring, toilsome, tough, troublesome, trying

area **1.** district, domain, locality, neighbourhood, patch, plot, realm, region, sector, sphere, stretch, territory, tract, zone **2.** breadth, compass, expanse, extent, range, scope, size, width **3.** arena, department, domain, field, province, realm, sphere, territory **4.** part, portion, section, sector **5.** sunken space, yard

of square, circle *etc.*) **3.** region **4.** part, section **5.** subject, field of activity **6.** small sunken yard

areca (ˈærɪkə, əˈriːkə) *n.* genus of palms, including betel palm

arena (əˈriːnə) *n.* **1.** enclosure for sports events *etc.* **2.** space in middle of amphitheatre or stadium **3.** sphere, scene of conflict

arenaceous (ærɪˈneɪʃəs) *a.* **1.** composed of sand **2.** growing in sandy soil

aren't (ɑːnt) **1.** *contraction of* are not **2.** *inf., chiefly* **UK** (used in interrogative sentences) *contraction of* am not

areola (əˈrɪələ) *n.* **1.** *Biol.* space outlined on surface, such as area between veins on leaf **2.** *Anat.* any small circular area, such as pigmented ring around human nipple (*pl.* **-lae** (-liː), **-s**)

arête (əˈreɪt) *n.* sharp ridge that separates glacial valleys

argent (ˈɑːdʒənt) *n.* **1.** silver —*a.* **2.** silver, silvery-white, *esp.* in heraldry

argon (ˈɑːgɒn) *n.* a gas, inert constituent of air

argosy (ˈɑːgəsɪ) *n. Poet.* large richly-laden merchant ship

argot (ˈɑːgəʊ) *n.* slang

argue (ˈɑːgjuː) *vi.* **1.** quarrel, dispute **2.** offer reasons —*vt.* **3.** prove by reasoning **4.** discuss —**ˈarguable** *a.* —**ˈarguably** *adv.* as can be argued —**ˈarguer** *n.* —**ˈargument** *n.* **1.** quarrel **2.** reasoning **3.** discussion **4.** theme —**argumenˈtation** *n.* —**arguˈmentative** *a.*

Argus (ˈɑːgəs) *n.* fabulous being with a hundred eyes —**Argus-eyed** *a.* watchful

aria (ˈɑːrɪə) *n.* air or rhythmical song in cantata, opera *etc.*

arid (ˈærɪd) *a.* **1.** parched with heat, dry **2.** dull —**aˈridity** *n.*

Aries (ˈɛəriːz) *n.* (the ram) 1st sign of zodiac, operative c. Mar. 21st–Apr. 21st

aright (əˈraɪt) *adv.* rightly

arise (əˈraɪz) *vi.* **1.** come about **2.** get up **3.** rise (up), ascend (**aˈrose, arisen** (əˈrɪzᵊn), **aˈrising**)

aristocracy (ærɪˈstɒkrəsɪ) *n.* **1.** nobility **2.** upper classes **3.** government by the best in birth or fortune —**ˈaristocrat** *n.* —**aristoˈcratic** *a.* **1.** noble **2.** elegant —**aristoˈcratically** *adv.*

arithmetic (əˈrɪθmətɪk) *n.* **1.** science of numbers **2.** art of reckoning by figures —**arithˈmetic(al)** *a.* —**arithˈmetically** *adv.* —**arithmeˈtician** *n.* —**arithmetic mean** average value of set of terms or quantities, expressed as their sum divided by their number (*also* **ˈaverage**) —**arithmetic progression** sequence, each term of which differs from succeeding term by constant amount

ark (ɑːk) *n.* Noah's vessel

Ark (ɑːk) *n. Judaism* **1.** most sacred symbol of God's presence among Hebrew people, carried in their journey from Sinai to Promised Land (*also* **Ark of the Covenant**) **2.** receptacle for the scrolls of the Law (*also* **Holy Ark**)

arm[1] (ɑːm) *n.* **1.** limb extending from shoulder to wrist **2.** anything projecting from main body, as branch of sea, supporting rail of chair *etc.* **3.** sleeve —**ˈarmlet** *n.* band worn round arm —**ˈarmchair** *n.* —**ˈarmful** *n.* —**ˈarmhole** *n.* —**ˈarmpit** *n.* hollow under arm at shoulder

arm[2] (ɑːm) *vt.* **1.** supply with weapons, furnish **2.** prepare (bomb *etc.*) for use —*vi.* **3.** take up arms —*n.* **4.** weapon **5.** branch of army —*pl.* **6.** weapons **7.** war,

THESAURUS

arena 1. amphitheatre, bowl, coliseum, field, ground, park (*Inf.*), ring, stadium, stage **2.** area, battlefield, battleground, domain, field, field of conflict, lists, province, realm, scene, scope, sector, sphere, territory, theatre

argot cant, dialect, idiom, jargon, lingo (*Inf.*), parlance, patois, slang, vernacular

argue 1. altercate, bandy words, bicker, disagree, dispute, fall out (*Inf.*), feud, fight, have an argument, quarrel, squabble, wrangle **2.** assert, claim, contend, controvert, debate, discuss, dispute, expostulate, hold, maintain, plead, question, reason, remonstrate **3.** convince, persuade, prevail upon, talk into, talk round **4.** demonstrate, denote, display, evince, exhibit, imply, indicate, manifest, point to, show, suggest

argument 1. altercation, barney (*Inf.*), bickering, clash, controversy, difference of opinion, disagreement, dispute, falling out (*Inf.*), feud, fight, quarrel, row, squabble, wrangle **2.** assertion, claim, contention, debate, discussion, dispute, expostulation, plea, pleading, questioning, remonstrance, remonstration **3.** argumentation, case, defence, dialectic, ground(s), line of reasoning, logic, polemic, reason, reasoning **4.** abstract, gist, outline, plot, story, story line, subject, summary, synopsis, theme

argumentative belligerent, combative, contentious, contrary, disputatious, litigious, opinionated, quarrelsome

arid 1. barren, desert, dried up, dry, moistureless, parched, sterile, waterless **2.** boring, colourless, dreary, dry, dull, flat, jejune, lifeless, spiritless, tedious, uninspired, uninteresting, vapid

aright accurately, appropriately, aptly, correctly, duly, exactly, fitly, in due order, justly, properly, rightly, suitably, truly, without error

arise 1. appear, begin, come into being, come to light, commence, crop up (*Inf.*), emanate, emerge, ensue, follow, happen, issue, occur, originate, proceed, result, set in, spring, start, stem **2.** get to one's feet, get up, go up, rise, stand up, wake up **3.** ascend, climb, lift, mount, move upward, rise, soar, tower

aristocracy body of nobles, elite, gentry, *haut monde*, nobility, noblesse (*Literary*), patricians, patriciate, peerage, ruling class, upper class, upper crust (*Inf.*)

aristocrat grandee, lady, lord, noble, nobleman, noblewoman, patrician, peer, peeress

aristocratic 1. blue-blooded, elite, gentle (*Archaic*), gentlemanly, highborn, lordly, noble, patrician, titled, upper-class, well-born **2.** courtly, dignified, elegant, fine, polished, refined, stylish, well-bred

arm[1] *n.* **1.** appendage, limb, upper limb **2.** bough, branch, department, detachment, division, extension, offshoot, projection, section, sector **3.** branch, channel, estuary, firth, inlet, sound, strait, tributary

arm[2] *v.* **1.** *Esp. with weapons* accoutre, array, deck out, equip, furnish, issue with, outfit, provide, rig, supply **2.** mobilize, muster forces, prepare for war, take up arms

military exploits 8. official heraldic symbols —ˈ**armament** *n.*

armada (ɑːˈmɑːdə) *n.* large number of ships or aircraft

armadillo (ɑːməˈdɪləʊ) *n.* small Amer. burrowing mammal protected by bands of bony plates (*pl.* -**s**)

Armageddon (ɑːməˈgedˀn) *n.* **1.** *Bible* place designated as scene of final battle at end of world **2.** catastrophic and extremely destructive conflict

armature (ˈɑːmətjʊə) *n.* part of electric machine, *esp.* revolving structure in electric motor, generator

armistice (ˈɑːmɪstɪs) *n.* truce, suspension of fighting —**Armistice Day** anniversary of signing of armistice that ended World War I (*see also* **Remembrance Day** *at* REMEMBER)

armoire (ɑːmˈwɑː) *n.* large cabinet, orig. used for storing weapons

armour *or U.S.* **armor** (ˈɑːmə) *n.* **1.** defensive covering or dress **2.** plating of tanks, warships *etc.* **3.** armoured fighting vehicles, as tanks —**arˈmorial** *a.* relating to heraldic arms —ˈ**armourer** *or U.S.* ˈ**armorer** *n.* —ˈ**armoury** *or U.S.* ˈ**armory** *n.* —**armour plate** tough heavy steel oft. hardened on surface, used for protecting warships *etc.*

army (ˈɑːmɪ) *n.* **1.** large body of men armed for warfare and under military command **2.** host, great number

arnica (ˈɑːnɪkə) *n. Bot.* genus of hardy perennials. A tincture of *Arnica montana* is used for sprains and bruises

aroma (əˈrəʊmə) *n.* **1.** sweet smell, fragrance **2.** peculiar charm —**aroˈmatic** *a.* —**aˈromatize** *or* **-tise** *vt.*

arose (əˈrəʊz) *pt. of* ARISE

around (əˈraʊnd) *prep.* **1.** on all sides of **2.** somewhere in or near **3.** approximately (of time) —*adv.* **4.** on every side **5.** in a circle **6.** here and there, nowhere in particular **7.** *inf.* present in or at some place

arouse (əˈraʊz) *vt.* **1.** awaken **2.** stimulate

arpeggio (ɑːˈpedʒɪəʊ) *n. Mus.* **1.** notes sounded in quick succession, not together **2.** chord so played (*pl.* **-s**)

arquebus (ˈɑːkwɪbəs) *or* **harquebus** *n.* portable gun dating from 15th century

arr. 1. arranged **2.** arrival **3.** arrive(d)

arrack *or* **arak** (ˈærək) *n.* coarse spirit distilled from rice *etc.*

arraign (əˈreɪn) *vt.* accuse, indict, put on trial —**arˈraigner** *n.* —**arˈraignment** *n.*

arrange (əˈreɪndʒ) *vt.* **1.** set in order **2.** arrive at agreement about **3.** plan **4.** adapt, as music **5.** settle, as dispute —**arˈrangement** *n.*

arrant (ˈærənt) *a.* downright, notorious —ˈ**arrantly** *adv.*

arras (ˈærəs) *n.* tapestry

array (əˈreɪ) *n.* **1.** order, *esp.* military order **2.** dress **3.** imposing show, splendour —*vt.* **4.** set in order **5.** dress, equip, adorn

arrears (əˈrɪəz) *pl.n.* amount unpaid or undone

arrest (əˈrest) *vt.* **1.** detain by legal authority **2.** stop **3.** catch (attention) —*n.* **4.** seizure by warrant **5.** making prisoner —**arˈresting** *a.* attracting attention, striking —**arˈrestor** *n.* **1.** person who arrests **2.** mechanism to stop or slow moving object

THESAURUS

armada fleet, flotilla, navy, squadron

armaments ammunition, arms, guns, materiel, munitions, ordnance, weaponry, weapons

armour armour plate, covering, protection, sheathing, shield

armoury ammunition dump, arms depot, arsenal, magazine, ordnance depot

arms 1. armaments, firearms, guns, instruments of war, ordnance, weaponry, weapons **2.** blazonry, crest, escutcheon, heraldry, insignia

army 1. armed force, host (*Archaic*), land forces, legions, military, military force, soldiers, soldiery, troops **2.** *Fig.* array, horde, host, multitude, pack, swarm, throng, vast number

aroma bouquet, fragrance, odour, perfume, redolence, savour, scent, smell

aromatic balmy, fragrant, odoriferous, perfumed, pungent, redolent, savoury, spicy, sweet-scented, sweet-smelling

around *prep.* **1.** about, encircling, enclosing, encompassing, environing, on all sides of, on every side of, surrounding **2.** about, approximately, circa (*used with dates*), roughly ~*adv.* **3.** about, all over, everywhere, here and there, in all directions, on all sides, throughout, to and fro

arouse agitate, animate, awaken, call forth, enliven, excite, foment, foster, goad, incite, inflame, instigate, kindle, move, provoke, quicken, rouse, sharpen, spark, spur, stimulate, stir up, summon up, waken, wake up, warm, whet, whip up

arrange 1. align, array, class, classify, dispose, file, form, group, line up, marshal, order, organize, position, put in order, range, rank, set out, sort, sort out (*Inf.*), systematize, tidy **2.** adjust, agree to, come to terms, compromise, construct, contrive, determine, devise, fix up (*Inf.*), organize, plan, prepare, project, schedule, settle **3.** adapt, instrument, orchestrate, score

arrangement 1. alignment, array, classification, design, display, disposition, form, grouping, line-up, marshalling, order, ordering, organization, ranging, rank, setup (*Inf.*), structure, system **2.** *Often plural* adjustment, agreement, compact, compromise, construction, deal, devising, organization, plan, planning, preparation, provision, schedule, settlement, terms **3.** adaptation, instrumentation, interpretation, orchestration, score, version

array *n.* **1.** arrangement, collection, display, disposition, exhibition, formation, line-up, marshalling, muster, order, parade, show, supply **2.** *Poetic* apparel, attire, clothes, dress, finery, garb, garments, raiment (*Archaic*), regalia ~*v.* **3.** align, arrange, display, dispose, draw up, exhibit, form up, group, line up, marshal, muster, order, parade, place in order, range, set in line (*Military*), show **4.** accoutre, adorn, apparel (*Archaic*), attire, bedeck, caparison, clothe, deck, decorate, dress, equip, fit out, garb, outfit, robe, supply, wrap

arrest *v.* **1.** apprehend, bust (*Inf.*), capture, catch, collar (*Inf.*), detain, lay hold of, nab (*Inf.*), nick (*Sl.*), pinch (*Inf.*), run in (*Sl.*), seize, take, take into custody, take prisoner **2.** block, check, delay, end, halt, hinder, hold, inhibit, interrupt, obstruct, re-

arrière-pensée (arjɛrpɑ̃ˈse) *Fr.* hidden meaning or purpose

arris (ˈærɪs) *n.* sharp ridge or edge

arrive (əˈraɪv) *vi.* **1.** reach destination **2.** (*with* at) reach, attain **3.** *inf.* succeed —**arˈrival** *n.*

arrivederci (arriveˈdɛrtʃi) *It.* goodbye

arriviste (æri:ˈvi:st) *n.* person who is unscrupulously ambitious

arrogance (ˈærəgəns) *n.* aggressive conceit —**ˈarrogant** *a.* **1.** proud **2.** overbearing —**ˈarrogantly** *adv.*

arrogate (ˈærəgeɪt) *vt.* **1.** claim for oneself without justification **2.** attribute to another without justification

arrow (ˈærəʊ) *n.* pointed shaft shot from bow —**ˈarrowhead** *n.* **1.** head of arrow **2.** any triangular shape

arrowroot (ˈærəʊru:t) *n.* nutritious starch from W Indian plant, used as a food

arsenal (ˈɑ:sənᵊl) *n.* magazine of stores for warfare, guns, ammunition

arsenic (ˈɑ:snɪk) *n.* **1.** soft, grey, metallic element **2.** its oxide, a powerful poison —**arˈsenical** *a.* —**arsenious** (ɑ:ˈsi:nɪəs) *a.*

arson (ˈɑ:sᵊn) *n.* crime of intentionally setting property on fire

art (ɑ:t) *n.* **1.** skill **2.** human skill as opposed to nature **3.** creative skill in painting, poetry, music *etc.* **4.** any of the works produced thus **5.** profession, craft **6.** knack **7.** contrivance, cunning, trick **8.** system of rules —*pl.* **9.** certain branches of learning, languages, history *etc.*, as distinct from natural science **10.** wiles —**ˈartful** *a.* wily —**ˈartfully** *adv.* —**ˈartfulness** *n.* —**ˈartist** *n.* **1.** one who practises fine art, *esp.* painting **2.** one who makes his craft a fine art —**arˈtiste** *n.* professional entertainer, singer, dancer *etc.* —**arˈtistic** *a.* —**arˈtistically** *adv.* —**ˈartistry** *n.* —**ˈartless** *a.* natural, frank —**ˈartlessly** *adv.* —**ˈartlessness** *n.* —**ˈarty** *a.* ostentatiously artistic

art. 1. article **2.** artificial

artefact *or* **artifact** (ˈɑ:tɪfækt) *n.* something made by man, *esp.* by hand

arteriosclerosis (ɑ:tɪərɪəʊsklɪˈrəʊsɪs) *n.* hardening of the arteries (*pl.* **-ses** (-si:z))

artery (ˈɑ:tərɪ) *n.* **1.** one of tubes carrying blood from heart **2.** any main channel of communications —**arˈterial** *a.* **1.** pert. to an artery **2.** main, important, as in *arterial road*

artesian well (ɑ:ˈti:zɪən) deep well in which water rises by internal pressure

arthritis (ɑ:ˈθraɪtɪs) *n.* painful inflammation of joint(s) —**arthritic** (ɑ:ˈθrɪtɪk) *a./n.*

arthropod (ˈɑ:θrəpɒd) *n.* animal with jointed limbs and segmented body, *eg* insect, spider

artic (ɑ:ˈtɪk) *inf.* articulated lorry

artichoke (ˈɑ:tɪtʃəʊk) *n.* **1.** thistlelike perennial **2.** its edible flower —**Jerusalem artichoke** sunflower with edible tubers like potato

article (ˈɑ:tɪkᵊl) *n.* **1.** item, object **2.** short written piece **3.** paragraph, section **4.** *Gram.* words *the, a, an* **5.** clause in contract **6.** rule, condition —*vt.* **7.** bind as apprentice

articular (ɑ:ˈtɪkjʊlə) *a.* of joints or structural components in joint

articulate (ɑ:ˈtɪkjʊlɪt) *a.* **1.** able to express oneself fluently **2.** jointed **3.** (of speech) clear, distinct —*vt.* (ɑ:ˈtɪkjʊleɪt) **4.** joint **5.** utter distinctly —*vi.* (ɑ:ˈtɪkjʊleɪt) **6.** speak —**arˈticulated** *a.* jointed —**arˈticulately** *adv.* —**arˈticulateness** *n.* —**articuˈlation** *n.*

artifice (ˈɑ:tɪfɪs) *n.* **1.** contrivance **2.** trick **3.** cunning; skill —**arˈtificer** *n.* craftsman —**artiˈficial** *a.* **1.** manufactured, synthetic **2.** insincere —**artificiˈality** *n.* —**artiˈficially** *adv.* —**artificial respiration** method of restarting person's breathing after it has stopped

THESAURUS

strain, retard, slow, stall, stay, stop, suppress **3.** absorb, catch, engage, engross, fascinate, grip, hold, intrigue, occupy ~*n.* **4.** apprehension, bust (*Inf.*), capture, cop (*Sl.*), detention, seizure

arresting conspicuous, engaging, extraordinary, impressive, noticeable, outstanding, remarkable, striking, stunning, surprising

arrival advent, appearance, arriving, coming, entrance, happening, occurrence, taking place

arrive 1. appear, attain, befall, come, enter, get to, happen, occur, reach, show up (*Inf.*), take place, turn up **2.** *Inf.* achieve recognition, become famous, make good, make it (*Inf.*), make the grade (*Inf.*), reach the top, succeed

arrogance bluster, conceit, conceitedness, contemptuousness, disdainfulness, haughtiness, hauteur, high-handedness, imperiousness, insolence, loftiness, lordliness, overweeningness, pomposity, pompousness, presumption, pretension, pretentiousness, pride, scornfulness, superciliousness, swagger, uppishness (*Brit. inf.*)

arrogant assuming, blustering, conceited, contemptuous, disdainful, haughty, high and mighty (*Inf.*), high-handed, imperious, insolent, lordly, overbearing, overweening, pompous, presumptuous, pretentious, proud, scornful, supercilious, swaggering, uppish (*Brit. inf.*)

arrow bolt, dart, flight, quarrel, reed (*Archaic*), shaft (*Archaic*)

arsenal ammunition dump, armoury, arms depot, magazine, ordnance depot, stock, stockpile, store, storehouse, supply

art 1. adroitness, aptitude, artifice (*Archaic*), artistry, craft, craftsmanship, dexterity, expertise, facility, ingenuity, knack, knowledge, mastery, method, profession, skill, trade, virtuosity **2.** artfulness, artifice, astuteness, craftiness, cunning, deceit, duplicity, guile, trickery, wiliness

artful adept, adroit, clever, crafty, cunning, deceitful, designing, dexterous, foxy, ingenious, intriguing, masterly, politic, proficient, resourceful, scheming, sharp, shrewd, skilful, sly, smart, subtle, tricky, wily

article 1. commodity, item, object, piece, substance, thing, unit **2.** composition, discourse, essay, feature, item, paper, piece, story, treatise **3.** branch, clause, count, detail, division, head, heading, item, matter, paragraph, part, particular, passage, piece, point, portion, section

articulate *adj.* **1.** clear, coherent, comprehensible, eloquent, expressive, fluent, intelligible, lucid, meaningful, understandable, vocal, well-spoken ~*v.* **2.** enounce, enunciate, express, pronounce, say, speak, state, talk, utter, verbalize, vocalize, voice **3.** connect, couple, fit together, hinge, join, joint

artillery (ɑːˈtɪlərɪ) *n.* **1.** large guns on wheels **2.** troops who use them

artisan (ˈɑːtɪzæn, ɑːtɪˈzæn) *n.* craftsman; skilled mechanic; manual worker

artiste (ɑːˈtiːst) *n. see* ART

Art Nouveau (ˈɑː nuːˈvəʊ; *Fr.* ar nuˈvo) style of art and architecture of 1890s, characterized by sinuous outlines and stylized natural forms

arum lily (ˈɛərəm) plant with large white flower

-ary (*comb. form*) **1.** of; related to; belonging to, as in *cautionary* **2.** person or thing connected with, as in *missionary, aviary*

Aryan (ˈɛərɪən) *a.* relating to Indo-European family of nations and languages

as (æz; əz) *adv./conj. denoting* **1.** comparison **2.** similarity **3.** equality **4.** identity **5.** concurrence **6.** reason

As *Chem.* arsenic

AS **1.** Anglo-Saxon (*also* **A.S.**) **2.** antisubmarine

A.S.A. **1. UK** Amateur Swimming Association **2. US** American Standards Association

asafoetida *or* **asafetida** (æsəˈfɛtɪdə) *n.* bitter resin with unpleasant smell, obtained from roots of some umbelliferous plants

asap as soon as possible

asbestos (æsˈbɛstɒs) *n.* fibrous mineral which does not burn —**asbestosis** (æsbɛsˈtəʊsɪs) *n.* lung disease caused by inhalation of asbestos fibre

ascend (əˈsɛnd) *vi.* **1.** climb, rise —*vt.* **2.** walk up, climb, mount —**asˈcendancy** *or* **asˈcendency** *n.* control, dominance —**asˈcendant** *or* **asˈcendent** *a.* rising —**asˈcension** *n.* —**asˈcent** *n.* rise

Ascension Day (əˈsɛnʃən) 40th day after Easter, when Ascension of Christ into heaven is celebrated

ascertain (æsəˈteɪn) *vt.* get to know, find out, determine —**ascerˈtainable** *a.* —**ascerˈtainment** *n.*

ascetic (əˈsɛtɪk) *n.* **1.** one who practises severe self-denial —*a.* **2.** rigidly abstinent, austere —**asˈcetically** *adv.* —**asˈceticism** *n.*

ascorbic acid (əˈskɔːbɪk) vitamin C, present in green vegetables, citrus fruits *etc.*

ascribe (əˈskraɪb) *vt.* attribute, impute, assign —**asˈcribable** *a.* —**ascription** (əˈskrɪpʃən) *n.*

aseptic (əˈsɛptɪk, eɪ-) *a.* germ-free —**aˈsepsis** *n.*

asexual (eɪˈsɛksjʊəl) *a.* without sex

ash[1] (æʃ) *n.* **1.** dust or remains of anything burnt —*pl.* **2.** ruins **3.** remains, *eg* of cremated body —**ˈashen** *a.* **1.** like ashes **2.** pale —**ˈashy** *a.* —**ash can US** dustbin (*also* **garbage can, ash bin, trash can**) —**ˈashtray** *n.* receptacle for tobacco ash, cigarette butts *etc.* —**Ash Wednesday** first day of Lent —**the Ashes** symbol of victory in cricket test-match series between England and Australia

ash[2] (æʃ) *n.* **1.** deciduous timber tree **2.** its wood —**ˈashen** *a.*

THESAURUS

artifice **1.** contrivance, device, dodge, expedient, hoax, machination, manoeuvre, ruse, stratagem, subterfuge, tactic, trick, wile **2.** artfulness, chicanery, craft, craftiness, cunning, deception, duplicity, guile, scheming, slyness, trickery **3.** adroitness, cleverness, deftness, facility, finesse, ingenuity, invention, inventiveness, skill

artificer artisan, craftsman, mechanic

artificial **1.** man-made, manufactured, non-natural, plastic, synthetic **2.** bogus, counterfeit, ersatz, fake, imitation, mock, phoney (*Inf.*), sham, simulated, specious, spurious **3.** affected, assumed, contrived, false, feigned, forced, hollow, insincere, meretricious, phoney (*Inf.*), pretended, spurious, unnatural

artillery battery, big guns, cannon, cannonry, gunnery, ordnance

artisan artificer, craftsman, handicraftsman, journeyman, mechanic, skilled workman, technician

artistic aesthetic, beautiful, creative, cultivated, cultured, decorative, elegant, exquisite, graceful, imaginative, ornamental, refined, sensitive, stylish, tasteful

artistry accomplishment, art, artistic ability, brilliance, craftsmanship, creativity, finesse, flair, genius, mastery, proficiency, sensibility, skill, style, talent, taste, touch, virtuosity, workmanship

artless **1.** candid, direct, fair, frank, genuine, guileless, honest, open, plain, sincere, straightforward, true, undesigning **2.** humble, natural, plain, pure, simple, unadorned, unaffected, uncontrived, unpretentious

as *conj.* **1.** at the time that, during the time that, just as, when, while **2.** in the manner that, in the way that, like **3.** that which, what **4.** because, considering that, seeing that, since **5.** in the same manner with, in the same way that, like **6.** for instance, like, such as

ascend climb, float up, fly up, go up, lift off, mount, move up, rise, scale, slope upwards, soar, take off, tower

ascendancy, ascendency authority, command, control, dominance, domination, dominion, hegemony, influence, mastery, power, predominance, pre-eminence, prevalence, reign, rule, sovereignty, superiority, supremacy, sway, upper hand

ascendant, ascendent *adj.* ascending, climbing, going upwards, mounting, rising

ascent **1.** ascending, ascension, clambering, climb, climbing, mounting, rise, rising, scaling, upward movement **2.** acclivity, gradient, incline, ramp, rise, rising ground, upward slope

ascertain confirm, determine, discover, establish, ferret out, find out, fix, identify, learn, make certain, settle, verify

ascetic **1.** *n.* abstainer, anchorite, hermit, monk, nun, recluse, self-denier **2.** *adj.* abstemious, abstinent, austere, celibate, frugal, harsh, plain, puritanical, rigorous, self-denying, self-disciplined, severe, Spartan, stern

asceticism abstemiousness, abstinence, austerity, celibacy, frugality, harshness, mortification of the flesh, plainness, puritanism, rigorousness, rigour, self-abnegation, self-denial, self-discipline, self-mortification

ascribe assign, attribute, charge, credit, impute, put down, refer, set down

ashamed abashed, bashful, blushing, chagrined, conscience-stricken, crestfallen, discomfited, distressed, embarrassed, guilty, humbled, humiliated, mortified, prudish, reluctant, remorseful, shamefaced, sheepish, shy, sorry

ashamed (əˈʃeɪmd) *a.* affected with shame, abashed

ashlar *or* **ashler** (ˈæʃlə) *n.* hewn or squared building stone

ashore (əˈʃɔː) *adv.* towards or on shore

ashram (ˈæʃrəm) *n.* religious retreat or community where Hindu holy man lives

Asian (ˈeɪʃən, ˈeɪʒən) *a.* **1.** pert. to continent of Asia —*n.* **2.** native of Asia or descendant of one —**Asiˈatic** *a.*

aside (əˈsaɪd) *adv.* **1.** to or on one side **2.** privately —*n.* **3.** words spoken in an undertone not to be heard by some person present

asinine (ˈæsɪnaɪn) *a.* of or like an ass, silly —**asininity** (æsɪˈnɪnɪtɪ) *n.*

ask (ɑːsk) *vt.* **1.** request, require, question, invite —*vi.* **2.** make inquiry or request

askance (əˈskæns) *or* **askant** (əˈskænt) *adv.* **1.** sideways, awry **2.** with a side look or meaning —**look askance** view with suspicion

askew (əˈskjuː) *adv./adj.* awry

aslant (əˈslɑːnt) *adv.* on the slant, obliquely, athwart

asleep (əˈsliːp) *a.* sleeping, at rest

ASLEF (ˈæzlɛf) Associated Society of Locomotive Engineers and Firemen

asocial (eɪˈsəʊʃəl) *a.* **1.** avoiding contact **2.** unconcerned about welfare of others **3.** hostile to society

asp (æsp) *n.* small venomous snake

asparagus (əˈspærəgəs) *n.* plant whose young shoots are a table delicacy

aspect (ˈæspɛkt) *n.* **1.** look **2.** view **3.** appearance **4.** expression

aspen (ˈæspən) *n.* type of poplar tree

asperity (æˈspɛrɪtɪ) *n.* **1.** roughness **2.** harshness **3.** coldness

aspersion (əˈspɜːʃən) *n.* **1.** (*usu. in pl.*) malicious remarks **2.** slanderous attack

asphalt (ˈæsfælt) *n.* black, hard bituminous substance used for road surfaces *etc.* —**asˈphaltic** *a.*

asphodel (ˈæsfədɛl) *n.* plant with clusters of yellow or white flowers

asphyxia (æsˈfɪksɪə) *n.* suffocation —**asˈphyxiate** *v.* —**asˈphyxiated** *a.* —**asphyxiˈation** *n.*

aspic (ˈæspɪk) *n.* **1.** jelly used to coat meat, eggs, fish *etc.* **2.** *Bot.* species of lavender

aspidistra (æspɪˈdɪstrə) *n.* plant with broad tapered leaves

aspire (əˈspaɪə) *vi.* **1.** desire eagerly **2.** rise to great height —**aspirant** (ˈæspɪrənt) *n.* **1.** one who aspires **2.** candidate —**aspirate** (ˈæspɪreɪt) *vt.* pronounce with full breathing, as 'h' —**aspiration** (æspɪˈreɪʃən) *n.* —**aspirator** (ˈæspɪreɪtə) *n.* device employing suction, such as jet pump or one for removing fluids from body cavity —**asˈpiring** *a.* —**asˈpiringly** *adv.*

aspirin (ˈæsprɪn) *n.* (a tablet of) drug used to allay pain and fever

ass (æs) *n.* **1.** quadruped of horse family **2.** stupid person

assagai (ˈæsəgaɪ) *n. see* ASSEGAI

assail (əˈseɪl) *vt.* attack, assault —**asˈsailable** *a.* —**asˈsailant** *n.*

assassin (əˈsæsɪn) *n.* **1.** one who kills, *esp.* prominent person, by treacherous violence **2.** murderer —**asˈsassinate** *vt.* —**assassiˈnation** *n.*

assault (əˈsɔːlt) *n.* **1.** attack, *esp.* sudden —*vt.* **2.** attack —**assault and battery** *Law* threat of attack to person followed by actual attack

assay (əˈseɪ) *v.* **1.** test (*esp.* proportions of metals) in alloy or ore —*n.* (əˈseɪ, ˈæseɪ) **2.** analysis, *esp.* of metals **3.** trial, test —**asˈsayer** *n.*

THESAURUS

ashore aground, landwards, on dry land, on land, on the beach, on the shore, shorewards, to the shore

aside *adv.* alone, alongside, apart, away, beside, in isolation, in reserve, on one side, out of mind, out of the way, privately, separately, to one side, to the side

asinine brainless, daft (*Inf.*), dunderheaded, fatuous, foolish, gormless (*Inf.*), halfwitted, idiotic, imbecile, imbecilic, inane, moronic, obstinate, senseless, silly, stupid, thickheaded, thick-witted

ask **1.** inquire, interrogate, query, question, quiz **2.** appeal, apply, beg, beseech, claim, crave, demand, entreat, implore, petition, plead, pray, request, seek, solicit, sue, supplicate **3.** bid, invite, summon

askance awry, indirectly, obliquely, out of the corner of one's eye, sideways, with a side glance

askew *adv./adj.* aslant, awry, cockeyed (*Inf.*), crooked, crookedly, lopsided, oblique, obliquely, off-centre, to one side

asleep crashed out (*Sl.*), dead to the world (*Inf.*), dormant, dozing, fast asleep, napping, sleeping, slumbering, snoozing (*Inf.*), sound asleep

aspect **1.** air, appearance, attitude, bearing, condition, countenance, demeanour, expression, look, manner, mien (*Literary*) **2.** bearing, direction, exposure, outlook, point of view, position, prospect, scene, situation, view

asperity acerbity, acrimony, bitterness, churlishness, crabbedness, crossness, harshness, irascibility, irritability, moroseness, peevishness, roughness, ruggedness, severity, sharpness, sourness, sullenness

asphyxiate choke, smother, stifle, strangle, strangulate, suffocate, throttle

aspirant *n.* applicant, aspirer, candidate, hopeful, postulant, seeker, suitor

aspiration aim, ambition, craving, desire, dream, eagerness, endeavour, goal, hankering, hope, longing, object, objective, wish, yearning

aspire aim, be ambitious, be eager, crave, desire, dream, hanker, hope, long, pursue, seek, wish, yearn

aspiring *adj.* ambitious, aspirant, eager, endeavouring, hopeful, longing, striving, wishful, would-be

ass **1.** donkey, jennet, moke (*Sl.*) **2.** blockhead, bonehead (*Sl.*), dolt, dope (*Sl.*), dunce, fool, halfwit, idiot, jackass, nincompoop, ninny, nitwit, numskull, simpleton, twerp (*Inf.*), twit (*Inf.*)

assail assault, attack, beset, charge, encounter, fall upon, invade, lay into, maltreat, set about, set upon

assassin eliminator (*Sl.*), executioner, hatchet man (*Sl.*), hit man (*Sl.*), killer, liquidator, murderer, slayer

assassinate eliminate (*Sl.*), hit (*U.S. sl.*), kill, liquidate, murder, slay

assault **1.** *n.* aggression, attack, charge, incursion, invasion, offensive, onset, onslaught, storm, storming, strike **2.** *v.* assail, attack, beset, charge, fall

assegai *or* **assagai** (ˈæsəgaɪ) *n.* slender spear of S Afr. tribes

assemble (əˈsɛmbᵊl) *v.* **1.** meet, bring together **2.** collect —*vt.* **3.** put together (of machinery *etc.*) —**asˈsemblage** *n.* —**asˈsembly** *n.* **1.** gathering, meeting **2.** assembling —**assembly line** sequence of machines, workers in factory assembling product

assent (əˈsɛnt) *vi.* **1.** concur, agree —*n.* **2.** acquiescence, agreement, compliance

assert (əˈsɜːt) *vt.* **1.** declare strongly **2.** insist upon —**asˈsertion** *n.* —**asˈsertive** *a.* —**asˈsertively** *adv.*

assess (əˈsɛs) *vt.* **1.** fix value of **2.** evaluate, estimate, *esp.* for taxation **3.** fix amount of (tax or fine) **4.** impose tax or fine on (a person *etc.*) —**asˈsessable** *a.* —**asˈsessment** *n.* —**asˈsessor** *n.*

asset (ˈæsɛt) *n.* **1.** valuable or useful person, thing —*pl.* **2.** property available to pay debts, *esp.* of insolvent debtor —**asset-stripping** *n. Comm.* practice of taking over a company at low price and then selling assets piecemeal

asseverate (əˈsɛvəreɪt) *vt.* assert solemnly —**asseveˈration** *n.*

assiduous (əˈsɪdjʊəs) *a.* persevering, attentive, diligent —**assiˈduity** *n.* —**asˈsiduously** *adv.*

assign (əˈsaɪn) *vt.* **1.** appoint to job *etc.* **2.** allot, apportion, fix **3.** ascribe **4.** transfer —*n.* **5.** assignee —**asˈsignable** *a.* —**assignation** (æsɪgˈneɪʃən) *n.* **1.** secret meeting **2.** appointment to meet —**assignee** (æsɪˈniː) *n. Law* person to whom property *etc.* is transferred —**asˈsignment** *n.* **1.** act of assigning **2.** allotted duty —**assignor** (æsɪˈnɔː) *n.*

assimilate (əˈsɪmɪleɪt) *vt.* **1.** learn and understand **2.** make similar **3.** absorb into the system —**asˈsimilable** *a.* —**assimiˈlation** *n.* —**asˈsimilative** *a.*

assist (əˈsɪst) *v.* **1.** give help **2.** work as assistant (to) —**asˈsistance** *n.* —**asˈsistant** *n.* helper

assizes (əˈsaɪzɪz) *pl.n.* formerly, law court held in each area or county of England and Wales

assn. association

assoc. **1.** associated **2.** association

associate (əˈsəʊʃɪeɪt, -sɪ-) *vt.* **1.** link, connect, *esp.* as ideas in mind **2.** join —*vi.* **3.** keep company **4.** combine, unite —*n.* (əˈsəʊʃɪɪt) **5.** companion, partner **6.** friend, ally **7.** subordinate member of association —*a.*

THESAURUS

upon, invade, lay into, set about, set upon, storm, strike at

assay *v.* **1.** analyse, appraise, assess, evaluate, examine, inspect, investigate, prove, test, try, weigh ~*n.* **2.** *Archaic* attempt, endeavour, essay, try, venture **3.** analysis, examination, inspection, investigation, test, trial

assemble **1.** accumulate, amass, bring together, call together, collect, come together, congregate, convene, convoke, flock, forgather, gather, marshal, meet, muster, rally, round up, summon **2.** build up, connect, construct, erect, fabricate, fit together, join, make, manufacture, piece together, put together, set up

assembly **1.** accumulation, aggregation, assemblage, body, collection, company, conclave, conference, congregation, convocation, council, crowd, diet, flock, gathering, group, mass, meeting, multitude, rally, synod, throng **2.** building up, connecting, construction, erection, fabrication, fitting together, joining, manufacture, piecing together, putting together, setting up

assent **1.** *v.* accede, accept, acquiesce, agree, allow, approve, comply, concur, consent, fall in with, go along with, grant, permit, sanction, subscribe **2.** *n.* acceptance, accession, accord, acquiescence, agreement, approval, compliance, concurrence, consent, permission, sanction

assert **1.** affirm, allege, asseverate, attest, aver, avouch (*Archaic*), avow, contend, declare, maintain, predicate, profess, pronounce, state, swear **2.** claim, defend, insist upon, press, put forward, stand up for, stress, uphold, vindicate

assertion **1.** affirmation, allegation, asseveration, attestation, avowal, contention, declaration, predication, profession, pronouncement, statement **2.** defence, insistence, maintenance, stressing, vindication

assertive aggressive, confident, decided, decisive, demanding, dogmatic, domineering, emphatic, firm, forceful, forward, insistent, overbearing, positive, pushy (*Inf.*), self-assured, strong-willed

assess **1.** appraise, compute, determine, estimate, evaluate, fix, gauge, judge, rate, size up (*Inf.*), value, weigh **2.** demand, evaluate, fix, impose, levy, rate, tax, value

assessment **1.** appraisal, computation, determination, estimate, estimation, evaluation, judgment, rating, valuation **2.** charge, demand, duty, evaluation, fee, impost, levy, rate, rating, tariff, tax, taxation, toll, valuation

asset **1.** advantage, aid, benefit, blessing, boon, help, resource, service **2.** *Plural* capital, estate, funds, goods, holdings, means, money, possessions, property, reserves, resources, valuables, wealth

assiduous attentive, constant, diligent, hardworking, indefatigable, industrious, laborious, persevering, persistent, sedulous, steady, studious, unflagging, untiring, unwearied

assign **1.** appoint, choose, delegate, designate, name, nominate, select **2.** allocate, allot, apportion, consign, distribute, give, give out, grant, make over **3.** appoint, appropriate, determine, fix, set apart, stipulate **4.** accredit, ascribe, attribute, put down

assignment **1.** appointment, charge, commission, duty, job, mission, position, post, responsibility, task **2.** allocation, allotment, appointment, apportionment, appropriation, ascription, assignation (*Law, chiefly Scot.*), attribution, choice, consignment, delegation, designation, determination, distribution, giving, grant, nomination, selection, specification, stipulation

assist abet, aid, back, benefit, boost, collaborate, cooperate, expedite, facilitate, further, help, reinforce, relieve, second, serve, succour, support, sustain, work for, work with

assistance abetment, aid, backing, benefit, boost, collaboration, cooperation, furtherance, help, helping hand, reinforcement, relief, service, succour, support, sustenance

assistant abettor, accessory, accomplice, aide, aider, ally, associate, auxiliary, backer, coadjutor (*Rare*), collaborator, colleague, confederate, cooperator, helper, helpmate, henchman, partner, right-hand man, second, supporter (əˈsəʊʃɪɪt) 8. affiliated —**associˈation** *n.* society, club —**association football** 1. *see* SOCCER 2. A Australian Rules played in football association rather than league

assonance (ˈæsənəns) *n.* 1. likeness in sound 2. rhyming of vowels only —**ˈassonant** *a.*

assort (əˈsɔːt) *vt.* 1. classify, arrange —*vi.* 2. match, agree, harmonize —**asˈsorted** *a.* mixed —**asˈsortment** *n.*

ASSR Autonomous Soviet Socialist Republic

asst. assistant

assuage (əˈsweɪdʒ) *vt.* 1. soften, pacify 2. soothe —**asˈsuagement** *n.*

assume (əˈsjuːm) *vt.* 1. take for granted 2. pretend to 3. take upon oneself 4. claim —**assumption** (əˈsʌmpʃən) *n.* —**assumptive** (əˈsʌmptɪv) *a.*

assure (əˈʃʊə) *vt.* 1. tell positively, promise 2. make sure 3. insure against loss, *esp.* of life 4. affirm —**asˈsurance** *n.* —**asˈsured** *a.* sure —**assuredly** (əˈʃʊərɪdlɪ) *adv.*

A.S.T. US, C Atlantic Standard Time

astatic (æˈstætɪk, eɪ-) *a. Phys.* having no tendency to take fixed position

astatine (ˈæstətiːn) *n.* radioactive element that occurs naturally in minute amounts and is artificially produced by bombarding bismuth with alpha particles

aster (ˈæstə) *n.* 1. plant with starlike flowers 2. Michaelmas daisy

asterisk (ˈæstərɪsk) *n.* 1. star (*) used in printing —*vt.* 2. mark thus —**ˈasterism** *n.*

astern (əˈstɜːn) *adv.* 1. in or towards the stern 2. backwards

asteroid (ˈæstərɔɪd) *n.* 1. small planet —*a.* 2. star-shaped

asthma (ˈæsmə) *n.* illness in which one has difficulty in breathing —**asthˈmatic** *a./n.* —**asthˈmatically** *adv.*

astigmatism (əˈstɪgmətɪzəm) *or* **astigmia** (əˈstɪgmɪə) *n.* inability of lens (*esp.* of eye) to focus properly —**astigˈmatic** *a.*

astilbe (əˈstɪlbɪ) *n.* plant with ornamental pink or white flowers

astir (əˈstɜː) *a.* 1. on the move 2. out of bed 3. in excitement

A.S.T.M.S. Association of Scientific, Technical, and Managerial Staffs

astonish (əˈstɒnɪʃ) *vt.* amaze, surprise —**aˈstonishing** *a.* —**aˈstonishment** *n.*

astound (əˈstaʊnd) *vt.* 1. astonish greatly 2. stun with amazement —**aˈstounding** *a.* startling

astraddle (əˈstrædˀl) *a.* 1. with a leg on either side of something —*prep.* 2. astride

astrakhan (æstrəˈkæn) *n.* lambskin with curled wool

astral (ˈæstrəl) *a.* of the stars or spirit world —**astral body**

astray (əˈstreɪ) *adv.* 1. off the right path 2. in error

THESAURUS

associate *v.* **1.** affiliate, ally, combine, confederate, conjoin, connect, correlate, couple, identify, join, league, link, lump together, mix, pair, relate, think of together, unite, yoke **2.** accompany, befriend, be friends, consort, fraternize, hang about, hang out (*Inf.*), hobnob, mingle, mix, run around (*Inf.*) ~*n.* **3.** ally, collaborator, colleague, companion, compeer, comrade, confederate, confrère, co-worker, follower, friend, mate, partner

association affiliation, alliance, band, clique, club, coalition, combine, company, confederacy, confederation, cooperative, corporation, federation, fraternity, group, league, organization, partnership, society, syndicate, union

assort arrange, array, categorize, classify, dispose, distribute, file, grade, group, range, rank, sort, type

assorted different, diverse, diversified, heterogeneous, miscellaneous, mixed, motley, sundry, varied, variegated, various

assortment 1. array, choice, collection, diversity, farrago, hotchpotch, jumble, medley, *mélange*, miscellany, mishmash, mixed bag (*Inf.*), mixture, potpourri, salmagundi, selection, variety **2.** arrangement, categorizing, classification, disposition, distribution, filing, grading, grouping, ranging, ranking, sorting, typing

assume 1. accept, believe, expect, fancy, guess (*Inf., chiefly U.S.*), imagine, infer, presume, presuppose, suppose, surmise, suspect, take for granted, think **2.** adopt, affect, counterfeit, feign, imitate, impersonate, mimic, pretend to, put on, sham, simulate **3.** accept, acquire, attend to, begin, don, embark upon, embrace, enter upon, put on, set about, shoulder, take on, take over, take responsibility for, take up, undertake **4.** acquire, appropriate, arrogate, commandeer, expropriate, pre-empt, seize, take, take over, usurp

assumption 1. acceptance, belief, conjecture, expectation, fancy, guess, hypothesis, inference, postulate, postulation, premise, premiss, presumption, presupposition, supposition, surmise, suspicion, theory **2.** acceptance, acquisition, adoption, embracing, entering upon, putting on, shouldering, takeover, taking on, taking up, undertaking **3.** acquisition, appropriation, arrogation, expropriation, pre-empting, seizure, takeover, taking, usurpation

assurance affirmation, assertion, declaration, guarantee, oath, pledge, profession, promise, protestation, vow, word, word of honour

assure 1. affirm, attest, certify, confirm, declare confidently, give one's word to, guarantee, pledge, promise, swear, vow **2.** clinch, complete, confirm, ensure, guarantee, make certain, make sure, seal, secure

assured beyond doubt, clinched, confirmed, dependable, ensured, fixed, guaranteed, indubitable, irrefutable, made certain, sealed, secure, settled, sure, unquestionable

astonish amaze, astound, bewilder, confound, daze, dumbfound, flabbergast (*Inf.*), stagger, stun, stupefy, surprise

astonishing amazing, astounding, bewildering, breathtaking, impressive, staggering, striking, stunning, stupefying, surprising

astonishment amazement, awe, bewilderment, confusion, consternation, stupefaction, surprise, wonder, wonderment

astounding amazing, astonishing, bewildering, breathtaking, impressive, staggering, striking, stunning, stupefying, surprising

astray *adv.* **1.** adrift, afield, amiss, lost, off, off course, off the mark, off the right track, off the subject **2.** into error, into sin, to the bad, wrong

astride (əˈstraɪd) *adv.* 1. with the legs apart —*prep.* 2. straddling

astringent (əˈstrɪndʒənt) *a.* 1. severe, harsh 2. sharp 3. constricting (body tissues, blood vessels *etc.*) —*n.* 4. astringent substance —**asˈtringency** *n.*

astro- (*comb. form*) indicating star or star-shaped structure

astrol. astrology

astrolabe (ˈæstrəleɪb) *n.* instrument used by early astronomers to measure altitude of stars *etc.*

astrology (əˈstrɒlədʒɪ) *n.* 1. foretelling of events by stars 2. medieval astronomy —**asˈtrologer** *n.* —**astroˈlogical** *a.*

astrometry (əˈstrɒmɪtrɪ) *n.* determination of apparent magnitudes of fixed stars

astron. astronomy

astronaut (ˈæstrənɔːt) *n.* one trained for travel in space —**astroˈnautics** *pl.n.* (*with sing. v.*) science and technology of space flight

astronomy (əˈstrɒnəmɪ) *n.* scientific study of heavenly bodies —**asˈtronomer** *n.* —**astroˈnomical** *a.* 1. very large 2. of astronomy —**astronomical unit** unit of distance used in astronomy equal to the mean distance between the earth and the sun

astrophysics (æstrəʊˈfɪzɪks) *n.* the science of the chemical and physical characteristics of heavenly bodies —**astroˈphysical** *a.* —**astroˈphysicist** *n.*

astute (əˈstjuːt) *a.* perceptive, shrewd —**asˈtutely** *adv.* —**asˈtuteness** *n.*

asunder (əˈsʌndə) *adv.* 1. apart 2. in pieces

asylum (əˈsaɪləm) *n.* 1. refuge, sanctuary, place of safety 2. *old name for* home for care of the unfortunate, *esp.* of mentally ill

asymmetry (æˈsɪmɪtrɪ, eɪ-) *n.* lack of symmetry —**asymˈmetric(al)** *a.*

asymptote (ˈæsɪmtəʊt) *n.* straight line that continually approaches a curve, but never meets it

asyndeton (æˈsɪndɪtən) *n.* omission of conjunctions between parts of sentence (*pl.* **-deta** (-dɪtə)) —**asynˈdetic** *a.* without conjunctions or cross-references

at (æt) *prep./adv. denoting* 1. location in space or time 2. rate 3. condition or state 4. amount 5. direction 6. cause

At *Chem.* astatine

at. 1. atmosphere 2. atomic

ataraxia (ætəˈræksɪə) *or* **ataraxy** (ˈætəræksɪ) *n.* calmness, emotional tranquillity

atavism (ˈætəvɪzəm) *n.* appearance of ancestral, not parental, characteristics in human beings, animals or plants —**ataˈvistic** *a.*

ataxia (əˈtæksɪə) *or* **ataxy** (əˈtæksɪ) *n.* lack of muscular coordination

A.T.C. 1. air traffic control 2. UK Air Training Corps

ate (ɛt, eɪt) *pt. of* EAT

-ate[1] (*comb. form*) 1. having appearance or characteristics of, as in *fortunate* 2. chemical compound, *esp.* salt or ester of acid, as in *carbonate* 3. product of process, as in *condensate* 4. forming verbs from nouns and adjectives, as in *hyphenate*

-ate[2] (*comb. form*) office, rank or group having certain function, as in *episcopate*

atelier (ˈætəljeɪ) *n.* workshop, artist's studio

atheism (ˈeɪθɪɪzəm) *n.* belief that there is no God —**ˈatheist** *n.* —**atheˈistic(al)** *a.*

athenaeum *or U.S.* **atheneum** (æθɪˈniːəm) *n.* 1. institution for promotion of learning 2. building containing reading room or library

atherosclerosis (æθərəʊsklɪəˈrəʊsɪs) *n.* degenerative disease of arteries characterized by thickening of arterial walls, caused by deposits of fatty material (*pl.* **-oses** (-əʊsiːz))

athlete (ˈæθliːt) *n.* 1. one trained for physical exercises, feats or contests of strength 2. one good at sports —**athletic** (æθˈlɛtɪk) *a.* —**athletically** (æθˈlɛtɪkəlɪ) *adv.* —**athleticism** (æθˈlɛtɪsɪzəm) *n.* —**athletics** (æθˈlɛtɪks) *pl.n.* (*with sing. v.*) sports such as running, jumping, throwing *etc.* —**athlete's foot** fungal infection of skin of foot, *esp.* between toes and on soles

at-home *n.* 1. social gathering in person's home 2. occasion when school *etc.* is open for inspection by public (*also* **open day**)

athwart (əˈθwɔːt) *prep.* 1. across —*adv.* 2. across, *esp.* obliquely

Atlantic (ətˈlæntɪk) *n.* 1. (*short for* **Atlantic Ocean**) world's second largest ocean —*a.* 2. of or bordering Atlantic Ocean 3. of Atlas or Atlas Mountains

Atlantis (ətˈlæntɪs) *n.* in ancient legend, continent said to have sunk beneath Atlantic west of Gibraltar

atlas (ˈætləs) *n.* volume of maps

atm. 1. atmosphere 2. atmospheric

atmosphere (ˈætməsfɪə) *n.* 1. mass of gas surrounding heavenly body, *esp.* the earth 2. prevailing tone or mood (of place *etc.*) 3. unit of pressure in cgs system —**atmospheric** (ætməsˈfɛrɪk) *a.* —**atmospherics** (ætməsˈfɛrɪks) *pl.n.* noises in radio reception due to electrical disturbance in the atmosphere

THESAURUS

astronaut cosmonaut, spaceman, space pilot, space traveller, spacewoman

astute adroit, artful, bright, calculating, canny, clever, crafty, cunning, discerning, foxy, insightful, intelligent, keen, knowing, penetrating, perceptive, politic, sagacious, sharp, shrewd, sly, subtle, wily

astuteness acumen, adroitness, artfulness, brightness, canniness, cleverness, craftiness, cunning, discernment, foxiness, insight, intelligence, keenness, knowledge, penetration, perceptiveness, sagacity, sharpness, shrewdness, slyness, subtlety, wiliness

asylum 1. harbour, haven, preserve, refuge, retreat, safety, sanctuary, shelter 2. *Old-fashioned* funny farm (*Sl.*), hospital, institution, loony bin (*Sl.*), madhouse (*Inf.*), mental hospital, nuthouse (*Sl.*), psychiatric hospital

atheism disbelief, freethinking, godlessness, heathenism, infidelity, irreligion, nonbelief, paganism, scepticism, unbelief

atheist disbeliever, freethinker, heathen, infidel, irreligionist, nonbeliever, pagan, sceptic, unbeliever

athlete competitor, contender, contestant, games player, gymnast, player, runner, sportsman, sportswoman

athletic 1. *adj.* able-bodied, active, brawny, energetic, fit, herculean, husky (*Inf.*), lusty, muscular, powerful, robust, sinewy, strapping, strong, sturdy, vigorous, well-proportioned 2. *pl. n.* contests, exercises,

at. no. atomic number

atoll (ˈætɒl) *n.* ring-shaped coral island enclosing lagoon

atom (ˈætəm) *n.* **1.** smallest unit of an element which can enter into chemical combination **2.** any very small particle **—aˈtomic** *a.* of, arising from atoms **—atoˈmicity** *n.* number of atoms in molecule of an element **—ˈatomize** *or* **-ise** *vt.* reduce to atoms or small particles **—ˈatomizer** *or* **-iser** *n.* instrument for discharging liquids in fine spray **—atom bomb** *or* **atomic bomb** bomb whose immense power derives from nuclear fission or fusion, nuclear bomb **—atomic energy** nuclear energy **—atomic number** the number of protons in the nucleus of an atom **—atomic pile** *see* **reactor** *at* REACT **—atomic theory 1.** any theory in which matter is regarded as consisting of atoms **2.** current concept of atom as entity with definite structure **—atomic weight** the weight of an atom of an element relative to that of carbon 12

atonality (eɪtəʊˈnælɪtɪ) *n.* **1.** absence of or disregard for established musical key in composition **2.** principles of composition embodying this

atone (əˈtəʊn) *vi.* **1.** make reparation, amends **2.** give satisfaction **—aˈtonement** *n.*

atonic (eɪˈtɒnɪk, æ-) *a.* unaccented

atop (əˈtɒp) *adv.* **1.** at or on the top *—prep.* **2.** above

atrocious (əˈtrəʊʃəs) *a.* **1.** extremely cruel or wicked **2.** horrifying **3.** *inf.* very bad **—aˈtrociously** *adv.* **—atrocity** (əˈtrɒsɪtɪ) *n.* wickedness

atrophy (ˈætrəfɪ) *n.* **1.** wasting away, emaciation *—vi.* **2.** waste away, become useless

atropine (ˈætrəpiːn) *n.* poisonous alkaloid obtained from deadly nightshade

att. 1. attention **2.** attorney

attach (əˈtætʃ) *v.* **1.** join, fasten **2.** unite **3.** be connected **4.** attribute **5.** appoint **6.** seize by law **—atˈtached** *a.* (*with* to) fond (of) **—atˈtachment** *n.*

attaché (əˈtæʃeɪ) *n.* specialist attached to diplomatic mission (*pl.* **-s**) **—attaché case** small leather handcase for papers

attack (əˈtæk) *vt.* **1.** take action against (in war, sport *etc.*) **2.** criticize **3.** set about with vigour **4.** affect adversely *—n.* **5.** attacking action **6.** bout

attain (əˈteɪn) *vt.* **1.** arrive at **2.** reach, gain by effort, accomplish **—attainaˈbility** *n.* **—atˈtainable** *a.* **—atˈtainment** *n. esp.* personal accomplishment

attainder (əˈteɪndə) *n. Hist.* loss of rights through conviction of high treason

attar (ˈætə), **otto** (ˈɒtəʊ), *or* **ottar** (ˈɒtə) *n.* fragrant oil made *esp.* from rose petals

attempt (əˈtɛmpt) *vt.* **1.** try, endeavour *—n.* **2.** trial, effort

attend (əˈtɛnd) *vt.* **1.** be present at **2.** accompany *—vi.* (*with* to) **3.** take care (of) **4.** give the mind (to), pay attention (to) **—atˈtendance** *n.* **1.** an attending **2.** presence **3.** persons attending **—atˈtendant** *n./a.* **—atˈtention** *n.* **1.** notice **2.** heed **3.** act of attending **4.** care **5.** courtesy **6.** alert position in military drill **—atˈtentive** *a.* **—atˈtentively** *adv.* **—atˈtentiveness** *n.*

THESAURUS

games of strength, gymnastics, races, sports, track and field events

atmosphere 1. aerosphere, air, heavens, sky **2.** air, ambience, aura, character, climate, environment, feel, feeling, flavour, mood, quality, spirit, surroundings, tone

atom bit, crumb, dot, fragment, grain, iota, jot, mite, molecule, morsel, mote, particle, scintilla (*Rare*), scrap, shred, speck, spot, tittle, trace, whit

atone 1. *With* **for** answer for, compensate, do penance for, make amends for, make redress, make reparation for, make up for, pay for, recompense, redress **2.** appease, expiate, make expiation for, propitiate, reconcile, redeem

atrocious 1. barbaric, brutal, cruel, diabolical, fiendish, flagrant, heinous, infamous, infernal, inhuman, monstrous, nefarious, ruthless, savage, vicious, villainous, wicked **2.** appalling, detestable, execrable, grievous, horrible, horrifying, shocking, terrible

atrocity atrociousness, barbarity, barbarousness, brutality, cruelty, enormity, fiendishness, grievousness, heinousness, horror, infamy, inhumanity, monstrousness, nefariousness, ruthlessness, savagery, shockingness, viciousness, villainousness, wickedness

attach 1. add, adhere, affix, annex, append, bind, connect, couple, fasten, fix, join, link, make fast, secure, stick, subjoin, tie, unite **2.** accompany, affiliate, associate, become associated with, combine, enlist, join, join forces with, latch on to, sign on with, sign up with, unite with **3.** ascribe, assign, associate, attribute, connect, impute, invest with, lay, place, put **4.** allocate, allot, appoint, assign, consign, designate, detail, earmark, second, send

attached affectionate towards, devoted, fond of, full of regard for, possessive

attack *n.* **1.** aggression, assault, charge, foray, incursion, inroad, invasion, offensive, onset, onslaught, raid, rush, strike **2.** access, bout, convulsion, fit, paroxysm, seizure, spasm, spell, stroke ~*v.* **3.** assail, assault, charge, fall upon, invade, lay into, raid, rush, set about, set upon, storm, strike (at) **4.** abuse, berate, blame, censure, criticize, impugn, malign, revile, vilify

attain accomplish, achieve, acquire, arrive at, bring off, complete, earn, effect, fulfil, gain, get, grasp, obtain, procure, reach, realize, reap, secure, win

attainment 1. accomplishment, achievement, acquirement, acquisition, arrival at, completion, feat, fulfilment, gaining, getting, obtaining, procurement, reaching, realization, reaping, winning **2.** ability, accomplishment, achievement, art, capability, competence, gift, mastery, proficiency, skill, talent

attempt 1. *n.* assault, attack, bid, crack (*Inf.*), effort, endeavour, essay, experiment, go, shot (*Inf.*), trial, try, undertaking, venture **2.** *v.* endeavour, essay, experiment, have a crack (go, shot) (*Inf.*), seek, strive, tackle, take on, try, try one's hand at, undertake, venture

attend 1. appear, be at, be here, be present, be there, frequent, go to, haunt, make one (*Archaic*), put in an appearance, show oneself, show up (*Inf.*), turn up, visit **2.** care for, look after, mind, minister to, nurse, take care of, tend **3.** follow, hear, hearken (*Archaic*), heed, listen, look on, mark, mind, note, notice, observe, pay attention, pay heed, regard, take to heart, watch **4.** accompany, arise from, be associated with, be connected with, be consequent on, follow, go

attenuate (əˈtɛnjʊeɪt) *v.* **1.** weaken or become weak **2.** make or become thin —**atˈtenuated** *a.* —**attenuˈation** *n.* reduction of intensity

attest (əˈtɛst) *vt.* bear witness to, certify —**atteˈstation** *n.* formal confirmation by oath *etc.* —**atˈtested** *a.* **UK** (of cattle *etc.*) certified free from disease, *esp.* tuberculosis

attic (ˈætɪk) *n.* space within roof where ceiling follows line of roof

Attic (ˈætɪk) *a.* **1.** of Attica, *esp.* its dialect **2.** classically pure

attire (əˈtaɪə) *vt.* **1.** dress, array —*n.* **2.** dress, clothing

attitude (ˈætɪtjuːd) *n.* **1.** mental view, opinion **2.** posture, pose **3.** disposition, behaviour —**attiˈtudinize** *or* **-nise** *vi.* assume affected attitudes

attorney (əˈtɜːnɪ) *n.* one legally appointed to act for another, *esp.* a lawyer (*pl.* **-s**)

attract (əˈtrækt) *vt.* **1.** draw (attention *etc.*) **2.** arouse interest of **3.** cause to come closer (as magnet *etc.*) —**atˈtraction** *n.* **1.** power to attract **2.** something offered so as to interest, please —**atˈtractive** *a.* —**atˈtractively** *adv.* —**atˈtractiveness** *n.*

attribute (əˈtrɪbjuːt) *vt.* **1.** (*usu. with* to) regard as belonging (to) or produced (by) —*n.* (ˈætrɪbjuːt) **2.** quality, property or characteristic of anything —**atˈtributable** *a.* —**attriˈbution** *n.* —**atˈtributive** *a.* —**atˈtributively** *adv.*

attrition (əˈtrɪʃən) *n.* **1.** wearing away of strength *etc.* **2.** rubbing away, friction

attune (əˈtjuːn) *vt.* **1.** tune, harmonize **2.** make accordant

A.T.V. UK Associated Television

at. wt. atomic weight

atypical (eɪˈtɪpɪkᵊl) *a.* not typical

Au *Chem.* gold

aubergine (ˈəʊbəʒiːn) *n.* edible, purple fruit of the eggplant

aubrietia *or* **aubretia** (ɔːˈbriːʃə) *n.* trailing plant with purple flowers

auburn (ˈɔːbᵊn) *a.* **1.** reddish-brown —*n.* **2.** this colour

au courant (o kuˈrã) *Fr.* **1.** up-to-date **2.** acquainted

auction (ˈɔːkʃən) *n.* **1.** public sale in which bidder offers increase of price over another and what is sold goes to one who bids highest —*vt.* **2.** (*oft. with* off) sell by auction —**auctioˈneer** *n.* —**auction bridge** card game —**Dutch auction** auction in which price starts high and is reduced until purchaser is found

audacious (ɔːˈdeɪʃəs) *a.* **1.** bold **2.** daring, impudent —**audacity** (ɔːˈdæsɪtɪ) *n.*

audible (ˈɔːdɪbᵊl) *a.* able to be heard —**audiˈbility** *n.* —**ˈaudibly** *adv.*

audience (ˈɔːdɪəns) *n.* **1.** assembly of hearers **2.** act of hearing **3.** judicial hearing **4.** formal interview

THESAURUS

hand in hand with, issue from, occur with, result from **5.** *With* **to** apply oneself to, concentrate on, devote oneself to, get to work on, look after, occupy oneself with, see to, take care of **6.** accompany, chaperon, companion, convoy, escort, guard, squire, usher

attendance 1. appearance, attending, being there, presence **2.** audience, crowd, gate, house, number present, turnout

attendant 1. *n.* aide, assistant, auxiliary, chaperon, companion, custodian, escort, flunky, follower, guard, guide, helper, lackey, menial, servant, steward, underling, usher, waiter **2.** *adj.* accessory, accompanying, associated, concomitant, consequent, related

attention 1. concentration, consideration, contemplation, deliberation, heed, heedfulness, intentness, mind, scrutiny, thinking, thought, thoughtfulness **2.** awareness, consciousness, consideration, notice, observation, recognition, regard **3.** care, concern, looking after, ministration, treatment **4.** *Often plural* assiduities, care, civility, compliment, consideration, courtesy, deference, gallantry, mindfulness, politeness, regard, respect, service

attentive 1. alert, awake, careful, concentrating, heedful, intent, listening, mindful, observant, regardful, studious, watchful **2.** accommodating, civil, conscientious, considerate, courteous, devoted, gallant, gracious, kind, obliging, polite, respectful, thoughtful

attic garret, loft

attitude 1. approach, disposition, frame of mind, mood, opinion, outlook, perspective, point of view, position, posture, stance, standing, view **2.** air, aspect, bearing, carriage, condition, demeanour, manner, mien (*Literary*), pose, position, posture, stance

attract allure, appeal to, bewitch, captivate, charm, decoy, draw, enchant, endear, engage, entice, fascinate, incline, induce, interest, invite, lure, pull (*Inf.*), tempt

attraction allure, appeal, attractiveness, bait, captivation, charm, come-on (*Inf.*), draw, enchantment, endearment, enticement, fascination, inducement, interest, invitation, lure, magnetism, pull (*Inf.*), temptation, temptingness

attractive agreeable, alluring, appealing, beautiful, captivating, charming, comely, engaging, enticing, fair, fascinating, fetching, good-looking, gorgeous, handsome, interesting, inviting, lovely, magnetic, pleasant, pleasing, prepossessing, pretty, seductive, tempting, winning, winsome

attribute 1. *v.* apply, ascribe, assign, blame, charge, credit, impute, lay at the door of, put down to, refer, set down to, trace to **2.** *n.* aspect, character, characteristic, facet, feature, idiosyncrasy, indication, mark, note, peculiarity, point, property, quality, quirk, sign, symbol, trait, virtue

auburn chestnut-coloured, copper-coloured, henna, nutbrown, reddish-brown, russet, rust-coloured, tawny, Titian red

audacious 1. adventurous, bold, brave, courageous, daredevil, daring, dauntless, death-defying, enterprising, fearless, intrepid, rash, reckless, risky, valiant, venturesome **2.** assuming, brazen, cheeky, defiant, disrespectful, forward, impertinent, impudent, insolent, pert, presumptuous, rude, shameless

audacity 1. adventurousness, audaciousness, boldness, bravery, courage, daring, dauntlessness, enterprise, fearlessness, guts (*Sl.*), intrepidity, nerve, rashness, recklessness, valour, venturesomeness **2.** audaciousness, brass neck (*Inf.*), cheek, defiance, disrespectfulness, effrontery, forwardness, gall (*Inf.*), impertinence, impudence, insolence, nerve, pertness, presumption, rudeness, shamelessness

audible clear, detectable, discernible, distinct, hearable, perceptible

audio- (*comb. form*) relating to sound or hearing

audio frequency (ˈɔːdɪəʊ) frequency in audible range of 50 hertz to 20 000 hertz

audiometer (ɔːdɪˈɒmɪtə) *n.* instrument for testing hearing

audiotypist (ˈɔːdɪəʊtaɪpɪst) *n.* typist trained to type from dictating machine

audiovisual (ɔːdɪəʊˈvɪzjʊəl) *a.* (*esp.* of teaching aids) involving, directed at, both sight and hearing, as film *etc.*

audit (ˈɔːdɪt) *n.* **1.** formal examination or settlement of accounts —*vt.* **2.** examine (accounts) —**ˈauditor** *n.*

audition (ɔːˈdɪʃən) *n.* **1.** screen or other test of prospective performer **2.** hearing —*v.* **3.** conduct or be tested in such a test —**audiˈtorium** *n.* **1.** place where audience sits **2.** hall (*pl.* **-s, -ia** (-ɪə)) —**ˈauditory** *a.* pert. to sense of hearing

A.U.E.W. Amalgamated Union of Engineering Workers

au fait (o ˈfɛ) *Fr.* **1.** fully informed **2.** expert

auf Wiedersehen (aʊf ˈviːdərzeːən) *Ger.* goodbye

Aug. August

Augean (ɔːˈdʒiːən) *a.* extremely dirty

auger (ˈɔːgə) *n.* carpenter's tool for boring holes, large gimlet

aught *or* **ought** (ɔːt) *Lit., obs. n.* **1.** anything —*adv.* **2.** UK *dial.* to any extent

augment (ɔːgˈmɛnt) *v.* increase, enlarge —**augmenˈtation** *n.* —**augˈmentative** *a.* increasing in force

au gratin (o graˈtɛ̃) *Fr.* with browned breadcrumbs and sometimes cheese

augur (ˈɔːgə) *n.* **1.** among the Romans, soothsayer —*v.* **2.** be a sign of future events, foretell —**augural** (ˈɔːgjʊrəl) *a.* —**augury** (ˈɔːgjʊrɪ) *n.*

august (ɔːˈgʌst) *a.* majestic, dignified

August (ˈɔːgəst) *n.* eighth month

Augustan (ɔːˈgʌstən) *a.* **1.** of Augustus, the Roman Emperor **2.** classic, distinguished, as applied to a period of literature

auk (ɔːk) *n.* northern web-footed seabird with short wings used only as paddles

au lait (əʊ ˈleɪ) with milk

auld lang syne (ˈɔːld læŋ ˈsaɪn) times past, *esp.* those remembered with nostalgia

au naturel (o natyˈrɛl) *Fr.* **1.** naked; nude **2.** uncooked or plainly cooked

aunt (ɑːnt) *n.* **1.** father's or mother's sister **2.** uncle's wife —**ˈauntie** *or* **ˈaunty** *n.* **1.** *inf.* aunt **2.** (**A-**) *sl.* British Broadcasting Corporation —**Aunt Sally UK 1.** figure used as target in fairground **2.** person who is target for insults or criticism

au pair (əʊ ˈpɛə) young foreigner who receives free board and lodging in return for housework *etc.*

aura (ˈɔːrə) *n.* **1.** quality, air, atmosphere considered distinctive of person or thing **2.** medical symptom warning of impending epileptic fit *etc.*

aural (ˈɔːrəl) *a.* of, by ear —**ˈaurally** *adv.*

aureate (ˈɔːrɪɪt) *a.* **1.** covered with gold; gilded **2.** (of style of writing or speaking) excessively elaborate

aureole (ˈɔːrɪəʊl) *or* **aureola** (ɔːˈriːələ) *n.* **1.** gold disc round head in sacred pictures **2.** halo

au revoir (o rəˈvwaːr) *Fr.* goodbye

auricle (ˈɔːrɪkˀl) *n.* **1.** outside ear **2.** upper cavity of heart —**auˈricular** *a.* **1.** of the auricle **2.** aural

auricula (ɔːˈrɪkjʊlə) *n.* **1.** widely cultivated alpine primrose with leaves shaped like bear's ear (*also* **bear's ear**) **2.** *Biol.* ear-shaped part (*also* **ˈauricle**) (*pl.* **-lae** (-liː), **-s**)

auriferous (ɔːˈrɪfərəs) *a.* gold-bearing

aurochs (ˈɔːrɒks) *n.* species of wild ox, now extinct

aurora (ɔːˈrɔːrə) *n.* **1.** lights in the atmosphere seen radiating from regions of the poles. The northern is called **aurora borealis** and the southern, **aurora australis 2.** *Poet.* dawn (*pl.* **-s**)

auscultation (ɔːskəlˈteɪʃən) *n.* listening to movement of heart and lungs with stethoscope —**ˈauscultator** *n.* —**ausˈcultatory** *a.*

auspice (ˈɔːspɪs) *n.* **1.** omen, augury —*pl.* **2.** patronage —**ausˈpicious** *a.* of good omen, favourable —**ausˈpiciously** *adv.*

Aussie (ˈɒzɪ) *n./a. inf.* Australian

austere (ɒˈstɪə) *a.* **1.** harsh, strict, severe **2.** without luxury —**ausˈterely** *adv.* —**austerity** (ɒˈstɛrɪtɪ) *n.*

THESAURUS

audience 1. assemblage, assembly, congregation, crowd, gallery, gathering, house, listeners, onlookers, spectators, turnout, viewers **2.** consultation, hearing, interview, meeting, reception

au fait abreast of, *au courant,* clued up (*Sl.*), conversant, expert, familiar, fully informed, in the know, in touch, knowledgeable, on the ball (*Inf.*), well-acquainted, well up

augment add to, amplify, boost, build up, dilate, enhance, enlarge, expand, extend, grow, heighten, increase, inflate, intensify, magnify, multiply, raise, reinforce, strengthen, swell

augmentation accession, addition, amplification, boost, build-up, dilation, enhancement, enlargement, expansion, extension, growth, heightening, increase, inflation, intensification, magnification, multiplication, reinforcement, rise, strengthening, swelling

augur 1. *n.* auspex, diviner, haruspex, oracle, prophet, seer, soothsayer **2.** *v.* be an omen of, bespeak (*Archaic*), betoken, bode, foreshadow, harbinger, herald, portend, predict, prefigure, presage, promise, prophesy, signify

augury 1. divination, prediction, prophecy, soothsaying **2.** auspice, forerunner, forewarning, harbinger, herald, omen, portent, precursor, presage, prognostication, promise, prophecy, sign, token, warning

august dignified, exalted, glorious, grand, high-ranking, imposing, impressive, kingly, lofty, magnificent, majestic, monumental, noble, regal, solemn, stately, superb

auspice *n.* **1.** *Usually plural* advocacy, aegis, authority, backing, care, championship, charge, control, countenance, guidance, influence, patronage, protection, sponsorship, supervision, support **2.** augury, indication, omen, portent, prognostication, prophecy, sign, token, warning

auspicious bright, encouraging, favourable, felicitous, fortunate, happy, hopeful, lucky, opportune, promising, propitious, prosperous, rosy, timely

austere 1. cold, exacting, forbidding, formal, grave, grim, hard, harsh, inflexible, rigorous, serious, se-

austral (ˈɔːstrəl) *a.* southern

Australasian (ɒstrəˈleɪzɪən) *a./n.* (native or inhabitant) of Australasia (Australia, New Zealand and adjacent islands)

Australian (ɒˈstreɪlɪən) *n./a.* (native or inhabitant) of Australia —**Australian Rules** game resembling rugby football, played in Aust. between teams of 18 men each on oval pitch, with ball resembling large rugby ball

Austro-[1] (*comb. form*) southern, as in *Austro-Asiatic*

Austro-[2] (*comb. form*) Austrian, as in *Austro-Hungarian*

autarchy (ˈɔːtɑːkɪ) *n.* despotism, absolute power, dictatorship

autarky (ˈɔːtɑːkɪ) *n.* (*esp.* of political unit) policy of economic self-sufficiency

auth. **1.** author **2.** authority **3.** authorized

authentic (ɔːˈθɛntɪk) *a.* **1.** real, genuine, true **2.** trustworthy —**auˈthentically** *adv.* —**auˈthenticate** *vt.* **1.** make valid, confirm **2.** establish truth, authorship *etc.* of —**authentiˈcation** *or* **authenticity** (ɔːθɛnˈtɪsɪtɪ) *n.*

author (ˈɔːθə) *n.* **1.** writer of book **2.** originator, constructor (**-ess** *fem.*) —**ˈauthorship** *n.*

authority (ɔːˈθɒrɪtɪ) *n.* **1.** legal power or right **2.** delegated power **3.** influence **4.** permission **5.** expert **6.** (*oft. pl.*) body or board in control —**authoriˈtarian** *a.* **1.** favouring or characterized by strict obedience to authority or government by small elite **2.** dictatorial —*n.* **3.** person who favours or practises authoritarian policies —**auˈthoritative** *a.* —**auˈthoritatively** *adv.* —**authoriˈzation** *or* **-riˈsation** *n.* —**ˈauthorize** *or* **-rise** *vt.* **1.** empower **2.** permit, sanction —**Authorized Version** English translation of the Bible published in 1611 under James I (*also* **King James Version**)

autistic (ɔːˈtɪstɪk) *a.* withdrawn and divorced from reality

auto- *or sometimes before vowel* **aut-** (*comb. form*) self, as in *autograph, autosuggestion.* Such words are not given here where the meaning may easily be inferred from the simple word

autobahn (ˈɔːtəbɑːn) *n.* German motorway

autobiography (ɔːtəʊbaɪˈɒgrəfɪ) *n.* life story of person written by himself —**autobiˈographer** *n.* —**autobioˈgraphical** *a.* —**autobioˈgraphically** *adv.*

autochthon (ɔːˈtɒkθən) *n.* primitive or original inhabitant —**auˈtochthonous** *a.*

autocrat (ˈɔːtəkræt) *n.* **1.** absolute ruler **2.** despotic person —**auˈtocracy** *n.* —**autoˈcratic** *a.* —**autoˈcratically** *adv.*

autocross (ˈɔːtəʊkrɒs) *n.* motor-racing sport over rough course

auto-da-fé (ɔːtəʊdəˈfeɪ) *n.* **1.** *Hist.* ceremony of Spanish Inquisition including pronouncement and execution of sentences passed on heretics **2.** burning to death of people condemned as heretics by Inquisition (*pl.* **autos-da-fé**)

autoeroticism (ɔːtəʊɪˈrɒtɪsɪzəm) *or* **autoerotism** (ɔːtəʊˈɛrətɪzəm) *n.* self-produced sexual arousal

autogamy (ɔːˈtɒgəmɪ) *n.* self-fertilization

autogenous (ɔːˈtɒdʒɪnəs) *a.* self-generated

autogiro *or* **autogyro** (ɔːtəʊˈdʒaɪrəʊ) *n.* aircraft like helicopter using horizontal airscrew for vertical ascent and descent

autograph (ˈɔːtəgrɑːf) *n.* **1.** handwritten signature **2.** person's handwriting —*vt.* **3.** sign —**autoˈgraphic** *a.*

autogyro (ɔːtəʊˈdʒaɪrəʊ) *n. see* AUTOGIRO

autointoxication (ɔːtəʊɪntɒksɪˈkeɪʃən) *n.* poisoning of tissues of the body as a result of the absorption of bodily waste

automat (ˈɔːtəmæt) *n.* vending machine

automate (ˈɔːtəmeɪt) *vt.* make (manufacturing process *etc.*) automatic

THESAURUS

vere, solemn, stern, stiff, strict, stringent, unfeeling, unrelenting **2.** abstemious, abstinent, ascetic, chaste, continent, economical, exacting, puritanical, rigid, self-denying, self-disciplined, sober, solemn, Spartan, strait-laced, strict, unrelenting **3.** bleak, economical, plain, severe, simple, spare, Spartan, stark, subdued, unadorned, unornamented

austerity **1.** coldness, exactingness, forbiddingness, formality, gravity, grimness, hardness, harshness, inflexibility, rigour, seriousness, severity, solemnity, sternness, stiffness, strictness **2.** abstemiousness, abstinence, asceticism, chasteness, chastity, continence, economy, exactingness, puritanism, rigidity, self-denial, self-discipline, sobriety, solemnity, Spartanism, strictness **3.** economy, plainness, severity, simplicity, spareness, Spartanism, starkness

authentic accurate, actual, authoritative, bona fide, certain, dependable, factual, faithful, genuine, legitimate, original, pure, real, reliable, simon-pure (*Rare*), true, true-to-life, trustworthy, valid, veritable

authenticity accuracy, actuality, authoritativeness, certainty, dependability, factualness, faithfulness, genuineness, legitimacy, purity, realness, reliability, trustworthiness, truth, truthfulness, validity, veritableness, verity

author architect, composer, creator, designer, doer, fabricator, father, founder, framer, initiator, inventor, maker, mover, originator, parent, planner, prime mover, producer, writer

authoritarian **1.** *adj.* absolute, autocratic, despotic, dictatorial, disciplinarian, doctrinaire, dogmatic, domineering, harsh, imperious, rigid, severe, strict, tyrannical, unyielding **2.** *n.* absolutist, autocrat, despot, dictator, disciplinarian, tyrant

authority **1.** ascendancy, charge, command, control, domination, dominion, force, government, influence, jurisdiction, might, power, prerogative, right, rule, say-so, strength, supremacy, sway, weight **2. the authorities** administration, government, management, officialdom, police, powers that be, the establishment **3.** authorization, justification, licence, permission, permit, sanction, say-so, warrant **4.** arbiter, bible, connoisseur, expert, judge, master, professional, scholar, specialist, textbook

authorization **1.** ability, authority, power, right, say-so, strength **2.** approval, credentials, leave, licence, permission, permit, sanction, say-so, warrant

authorize **1.** accredit, commission, empower, enable, entitle, give authority **2.** accredit, allow, approve, confirm, countenance, give authority for, give leave, license, permit, ratify, sanction, vouch for, warrant

autocrat absolutist, despot, dictator, tyrant

autocratic absolute, all-powerful, despotic, dictatorial, domineering, imperious, tyrannical, tyrannous, unlimited

automatic (ɔːtəˈmætɪk) *a.* **1.** operated or controlled mechanically **2.** done without conscious thought —*a./n.* **3.** self-loading (weapon) —**autoˈmatically** *adv.* —**automation** (ɔːtəˈmeɪʃən) *n.* use of automatic devices in industrial production —**auˈtomatism** *n.* involuntary action —**auˈtomaton** *n.* self-acting machine, *esp.* simulating a human being (*pl.* **-ata** (-ətə)) —**automatic transmission** transmission system in motor vehicle, in which gears change automatically

automobile (ˈɔːtəməbiːl) *n.* motor car —**automoˈbilist** *n.* motorist

automotive (ɔːtəˈməʊtɪv) *a.* **1.** relating to motor vehicles **2.** self-propelling

autonomy (ɔːˈtɒnəmɪ) *n.* self-government —**auˈtonomous** *a.*

autopsy (ɔːˈtɒpsɪ, ˈɔːtəp-) *n.* **1.** post-mortem examination to determine cause of death **2.** critical analysis —**auˈtoptic(al)** *a.*

autoroute (ˈɔːtəʊruːt) *n.* French motorway

autostrada (ˈɔːtəʊstrɑːdə) *n.* Italian motorway

autosuggestion (ɔːtəʊsəˈdʒɛstʃən) *n.* process of influencing the mind (towards health *etc.*), conducted by the subject himself

autumn (ˈɔːtəm) *n./a.* (typical of) the season after summer —**autumnal** (ɔːˈtʌmnˀl) *a.* typical of the onset of winter —**autumnally** (ɔːˈtʌmnəlɪ) *adv.*

aux. auxiliary

auxiliary (ɔːgˈzɪljərɪ, -ˈzɪlə-) *a.* **1.** helping, subsidiary —*n.* **2.** helper **3.** something subsidiary, as troops **4.** verb used to form tenses of others

av. average

A.V. Authorized Version (of the Bible)

avail (əˈveɪl) *v.* **1.** be of use, advantage, value (to) —*n.* **2.** benefit (*esp. in* **of no avail, to little avail**) —**availˈbility** *n.* —**aˈvailable** *a.* **1.** obtainable **2.** accessible —**avail oneself of** make use of

avalanche (ˈævəlɑːntʃ) *n.* **1.** mass of snow, ice, sliding down mountain **2.** sudden overwhelming quantity of anything

avant-garde (ævɒŋˈgɑːd) *a.* markedly experimental or in advance

avarice (ˈævərɪs) *n.* greed for wealth —**avaˈricious** *a.* —**avaˈriciously** *adv.*

avast (əˈvɑːst) *interj.* stop

avatar (ˈævətɑː) *n.* **1.** *Hinduism* manifestation of deity in human or animal form **2.** visible manifestation of abstract concept

avaunt (əˈvɔːnt) *interj. obs.* go away, depart

avdp. avoirdupois

Ave. *or* **ave.** Avenue

Ave Maria (ˈɑːvɪ məˈriːə) *R.C.Ch.* prayer to Virgin Mary, based on salutations of angel Gabriel and Elisabeth to her

avenge (əˈvɛndʒ) *vt.* take vengeance on behalf of (person) or on account of (thing) —**aˈvenger** *n.*

avenue (ˈævɪnjuː) *n.* **1.** wide street, oft. lined with trees **2.** approach **3.** double row of trees

aver (əˈvɜː) *vt.* affirm, assert (**-rr-**) —**aˈverment** *n.*

average (ˈævərɪdʒ, ˈævrɪdʒ) *n.* **1.** the mean value or quantity of a number of values or quantities —*a.* **2.** calculated as an average **3.** medium, ordinary —*vt.* **4.** fix or calculate an average of —*vi.* **5.** exist in or form a mean

averse (əˈvɜːs) *a.* disinclined, unwilling —**aˈversion** *n.* (*usu. with* to *or* for) dislike, person or thing disliked —**aversion therapy** *Psychiatry* way of suppressing undesirable habit by associating unpleasant effect, such as electric shock, with it

THESAURUS

automatic **1.** automated, mechanical, mechanized, push-button, robot, self-acting, self-activating, self-moving, self-propelling, self-regulating **2.** habitual, mechanical, perfunctory, routine, unconscious **3.** instinctive, instinctual, involuntary, mechanical, natural, reflex, spontaneous, unconscious, unwilled

autonomous free, independent, self-determining, self-governing, self-ruling, sovereign

autonomy freedom, home rule, independence, self-determination, self-government, self-rule, sovereignty

autopsy dissection, necropsy, postmortem, postmortem examination

auxiliary **1.** *adj.* accessory, aiding, ancillary, assisting, back-up, emergency, helping, reserve, secondary, subsidiary, substitute, supplementary, supporting **2.** *n.* accessory, accomplice, ally, assistant, associate, companion, confederate, helper, partner, reserve, subordinate, supporter

available accessible, applicable, at hand, at one's disposal, attainable, convenient, free, handy, obtainable, on hand, on tap, ready, ready for use, to hand, vacant

avalanche **1.** landslide, landslip, snow-slide, snow-slip **2.** barrage, deluge, flood, inundation, torrent

avant-garde *adj.* experimental, far-out (*Sl.*), innovative, innovatory, pioneering, progressive, unconventional, way-out (*Inf.*)

avaricious acquisitive, close-fisted, covetous, grasping, greedy, mean, miserable, miserly, niggardly, parsimonious, penny-pinching, penurious, rapacious, stingy

avenge even the score for, get even for, punish, repay, requite, retaliate, revenge, take satisfaction for, take vengeance

avenue access, alley, approach, boulevard, channel, course, drive, driveway, entrance, entry, pass, passage, path, pathway, road, route, street, thoroughfare, way

average *n.* **1.** common run, mean, medium, midpoint, norm, normal, par, rule, run, run of the mill, standard ~*adj.* **2.** common, commonplace, fair, general, indifferent, mediocre, middling, moderate, normal, not bad, ordinary, passable, regular, run-of-the-mill, so-so (*Inf.*), standard, tolerable, typical, undistinguished, unexceptional, usual **3.** intermediate, mean, median, medium, middle ~*v.* **4.** balance out to, be on average, do on average, even out to, make on average

averse antipathetic, backward, disinclined, hostile, ill-disposed, indisposed, inimical, loath, opposed, reluctant, unfavourable, unwilling

aversion abhorrence, animosity, antipathy, detestation, disgust, disinclination, dislike, distaste, hate, hatred, horror, hostility, indisposition, loathing, odium, opposition, reluctance, repugnance, repulsion, revulsion, unwillingness

avert (əˈvɜːt) *vt.* 1. turn away 2. ward off

aviary (ˈeɪvjərɪ) *n.* enclosure for birds —**ˈaviarist** *n.*

aviation (eɪvɪˈeɪʃən) *n.* 1. art of flying aircraft 2. design, production and maintenance of aircraft —**ˈaviator** *n.*

avid (ˈævɪd) *a.* 1. keen, enthusiastic 2. (*oft. with* for) greedy —**aˈvidity** *n.*

avocado (ævəˈkɑːdəʊ) *n.* 1. tropical tree 2. its green-skinned edible fruit

avocation (ævəˈkeɪʃən) *n.* 1. vocation 2. employment, business

avocet *or* **avoset** (ˈævəsɛt) *n.* wading bird of snipe family with upward-curving bill

avoid (əˈvɔɪd) *vt.* 1. keep away from 2. refrain from 3. not allow to happen —**aˈvoidable** *a.* —**aˈvoidance** *n.*

avoirdupois *or* **avoirdupois weight** (ævədəˈpɔɪz) *n./a.* (of) system of weights used in many English-speaking countries based on pounds and ounces

avouch (əˈvaʊtʃ) *vt. obs.* affirm, maintain, attest, own —**aˈvouchment** *n.*

avow (əˈvaʊ) *vt.* 1. declare 2. admit —**aˈvowable** *a.* —**aˈvowal** *n.* —**aˈvowed** *a.* —**avowedly** (əˈvaʊɪdlɪ) *adv.*

avuncular (əˈvʌŋkjʊlə) *a.* of or resembling an uncle, genial

await (əˈweɪt) *vt.* 1. wait or stay for 2. be in store for

awake (əˈweɪk) *v.* 1. emerge or rouse from sleep 2. become or cause to become alert (**aˈwoke** *or* **aˈwaked, aˈwoken** *or* **aˈwaked, aˈwaking**) —*a.* 3. not sleeping 4. alert —**aˈwakening** *n.*

award (əˈwɔːd) *vt.* 1. give formally (*esp.* prize or punishment) —*n.* 2. prize 3. judicial decision

aware (əˈwɛə) *a.* informed, conscious —**aˈwareness** *n.*

awash (əˈwɒʃ) *a.* 1. level with surface of water 2. filled or overflowing with water

away (əˈweɪ) *adv./a.* 1. absent, apart, at a distance, out of the way —*n.* 2. *Sport* game played on opponent's ground

awe (ɔː) *n.* dread mingled with reverence —**ˈawesome** *a.*

aweigh (əˈweɪ) *a. Naut.* (of anchor) no longer hooked into bottom; hanging by its rope or chain

awful (ˈɔːfʊl) *a.* 1. very bad, unpleasant 2. *obs.* impressive 3. *inf.* very great —**ˈawfully** *adv.* 1. in an unpleasant way 2. *inf.* very much

awhile (əˈwaɪl) *adv.* for a time

awkward (ˈɔːkwəd) *a.* 1. clumsy, ungainly 2. difficult 3. inconvenient 4. embarrassed —**ˈawkwardly** *adv.* —**ˈawkwardness** *n.*

THESAURUS

aviation aeronautics, flight, flying, powered flight

aviator aeronaut, airman, flier, pilot

avid 1. ardent, devoted, eager, enthusiastic, fanatical, fervent, intense, keen, passionate, zealous 2. acquisitive, athirst, avaricious, covetous, grasping, greedy, hungry, insatiable, rapacious, ravenous, thirsty, voracious

avoid avert, bypass, circumvent, dodge, duck (out of) (*Inf.*), elude, escape, eschew, evade, fight shy of, keep aloof from, keep away from, prevent, refrain from, shirk, shun, sidestep, steer clear of

avoidance circumvention, dodging, eluding, escape, eschewal, evasion, keeping away from, prevention, refraining, shirking, shunning, steering clear of

avowed acknowledged, admitted, confessed, declared, open, professed, self-proclaimed, sworn

await 1. abide, anticipate, expect, look for, look forward to, stay for, wait for 2. attend, be in readiness for, be in store for, be prepared for, be ready for, wait for

awake *v.* 1. awaken, rouse, wake, wake up 2. activate, alert, animate, arouse, awaken, call forth, enliven, excite, fan, incite, kindle, provoke, revive, stimulate, stir up, vivify ~*adj.* 3. alert, alive, aroused, attentive, awakened, aware, conscious, heedful, not sleeping, observant, on guard, on the alert, on the lookout, vigilant, wakeful, waking, watchful, wide-awake

awakening *n.* activation, animating, arousal, awaking, birth, enlivening, incitement, kindling, provocation, revival, rousing, stimulation, stirring up, vivification, waking, waking up

award *v.* 1. accord, adjudge, allot, apportion, assign, bestow, confer, decree, distribute, endow, gift, give, grant, present, render ~*n.* 2. adjudication, allotment, bestowal, conferment, conferral, decision, decree, endowment, gift, order, presentation 3. decoration, gift, grant, prize, trophy, verdict

aware acquainted, alive to, appreciative, apprised, attentive, *au courant,* cognizant, conscious, conversant, enlightened, familiar, hip (*Sl.*), informed, knowing, knowledgeable, mindful, sensible, sentient, wise (*Inf.*)

awareness acquaintance, appreciation, attention, cognizance, consciousness, enlightenment, familiarity, knowledge, mindfulness, perception, realization, recognition, sensibility, sentience, understanding

away *adv.* 1. abroad, elsewhere, from here, from home, hence, off 2. apart, at a distance, far, remote 3. aside, out of the way, to one side ~*adj.* 4. abroad, absent, elsewhere, gone, not at home, not here, not present, not there, out

awe *n.* admiration, amazement, astonishment, dread, fear, horror, respect, reverence, terror, veneration, wonder

awful 1. alarming, appalling, deplorable, dire, distressing, dreadful, fearful, frightful, ghastly, gruesome, harrowing, hideous, horrendous, horrible, horrific, horrifying, nasty, shocking, terrible, tremendous, ugly, unpleasant, unsightly 2. *Archaic* amazing, awe-inspiring, awesome, dread, fearsome, majestic, portentous, solemn

awfully 1. badly, disgracefully, disreputably, dreadfully, inadequately, reprehensibly, shoddily, unforgivably, unpleasantly, wickedly, woefully, wretchedly 2. *Inf.* badly, dreadfully, exceedingly, exceptionally, excessively, extremely, greatly, immensely, quite, terribly, very, very much

awhile briefly, for a little while, for a moment, for a short time, for a while

awkward 1. all thumbs, artless, blundering, bungling, clownish, clumsy, coarse, gauche, gawky, graceless, ham-fisted, ham-handed, ill-bred, inelegant, inept, inexpert, lumbering, maladroit, oafish, rude, skill-less, stiff, uncoordinated, uncouth, ungainly, ungraceful, unpolished, unrefined, unskilful, unskilled 2. cumbersome, difficult, inconvenient, troublesome, unhandy, unmanageable, unwieldy 3.

awl (ɔːl) *n.* pointed tool for boring wood, leather *etc.*

awn (ɔːn) *n.* any of bristles growing from flowering parts of certain grasses and cereals

awning (ˈɔːnɪŋ) *n.* (canvas) roof or shelter, to protect from weather

awoke (əˈwəʊk) *pt. of* AWAKE —**aˈwoken** *pp. of* AWAKE

A.W.O.L. *or* **AWOL** (*when acronym* ˈeɪwɒl) absent without leave

awry (əˈraɪ) *adv.* 1. crookedly 2. amiss 3. at a slant —*a.* 4. crooked, distorted 5. wrong

axe *or U.S.* **ax** (æks) *n.* 1. tool with sharp blade for chopping 2. *inf.* dismissal from employment *etc.* —*vt.* 3. *inf.* dismiss, dispense with

axel (ˈæksəl) *n. Skating* jump of one and a half turns, taking off from forward outside edge of one skate and landing on backward outside edge of other

axes[1] (ˈæksiːz) *n., pl. of* AXIS

axes[2] (ˈæksɪz) *n., pl. of* AXE

axil (ˈæksɪl) *n.* upper angle between branch or leaf stalk and stem

axiom (ˈæksɪəm) *n.* 1. received or accepted principle 2. self-evident truth —**axioˈmatic** *a.*

axis (ˈæksɪs) *n.* 1. (imaginary) line round which body spins 2. line or column around which parts of thing, system *etc.* are arranged (*pl.* ˈ**axes**) —ˈ**axial** *a.* —ˈ**axially** *adv.* —ˈ**Axis** *n.* coalition of Germany, Italy and Japan, 1936–45

axle (ˈæksəl) *n.* rod on which wheel turns

axolotl (ˈæksəlɒtᵊl) *n.* aquatic salamander of N Amer.

ay *or* **aye** (eɪ) *adv. Poet., obs.* always

ayah (ˈaɪə) *n.* in parts of former British Empire, native maidservant or nursemaid

ayatollah (aɪəˈtɒlə) *n.* one of class of Islamic religious leaders

aye *or* **ay** (aɪ) *adv.* 1. yes —*n.* 2. affirmative answer or vote —*pl.* 3. those voting for motion

AZ Arizona

azalea (əˈzeɪljə) *n.* genus of shrubby flowering plants, allied to rhododendron

azimuth (ˈæzɪməθ) *n.* 1. vertical arc from zenith to horizon 2. angular distance of this from meridian

AZT azidothymidine: drug that prolongs life and alleviates symptoms in AIDS sufferers

Aztec (ˈæztɛk) *a./n.* (member) of Indian race ruling Mexico before Spanish conquest

azure (ˈæʒə, ˈeɪ-) *n.* 1. sky-blue colour 2. sky —*a.* 3. sky-blue

THESAURUS

compromising, delicate, difficult, embarrassed, embarrassing, ill at ease, inconvenient, inopportune, painful, perplexing, sticky (*Inf.*), thorny, ticklish, troublesome, trying, uncomfortable, unpleasant, untimely **4.** annoying, bloody-minded (*Inf.*), difficult, disobliging, exasperating, hard to handle, intractable, irritable, perverse, prickly, stubborn, touchy, troublesome, trying, uncooperative, unhelpful, unpredictable, vexatious, vexing

awkwardness 1. artlessness, clownishness, clumsiness, coarseness, gaucheness, gaucherie, gawkiness, gracelessness, ill-breeding, inelegance, ineptness, inexpertness, maladroitness, oafishness, rudeness, skill-lessness, stiffness, uncoordination, uncouthness, ungainliness, unskilfulness, unskilledness **2.** cumbersomeness, difficulty, inconvenience, troublesomeness, unhandiness, unmanageability, unwieldiness **3.** delicacy, difficulty, discomfort, embarrassment, inconvenience, inopportuneness, painfulness, perplexingness, stickiness (*Inf.*), thorniness, ticklishness, unpleasantness, untimeliness **4.** bloody-mindedness (*Inf.*), difficulty, disobligingness, intractability, irritability, perversity, prickliness, stubbornness, touchiness, uncooperativeness, unhelpfulness, unpredictability

axe *n.* **1.** chopper, hatchet **2. the axe** *Inf.* cancellation, cutback, discharge, dismissal, termination, the boot (*Sl.*), the chop (*Sl.*), the sack (*Inf.*), wind-up ~*v.* **3.** *Inf.* cancel, cut back, discharge, dismiss, dispense with, eliminate, fire (*Inf.*), get rid of, remove, sack (*Inf.*), terminate, throw out, turn off (*Inf.*), wind up

axiom adage, aphorism, apophthegm, dictum, fundamental, gnome, maxim, postulate, precept, principle, truism

axiomatic 1. absolute, accepted, apodictic, assumed, certain, fundamental, given, granted, indubitable, manifest, presupposed, self-evident, understood, unquestioned **2.** aphoristic, apophthegmatic, epigrammatic, gnomic, pithy, terse

axis axle, centre line, pivot, shaft, spindle

axle arbor, axis, mandrel, pin, pivot, rod, shaft, spindle

B

b *or* **B** (biː) *n.* **1.** second letter of English alphabet **2.** speech sound represented by this letter, as in *bell* **3.** second in series, class or rank (*also* ˈ**beta**) (*pl.* **b's, B's,** *or* **Bs**)

B 1. *Mus.* seventh note of scale of C major; major or minor key having this note as its tonic **2.** less important of two things **3.** human blood type of ABO group **4.** UK secondary road **5.** *Chem.* boron **6.** magnetic flux density **7.** *Chess* bishop **8.** (of pencils) black **9.** *Phys.* bel (*also* **b**) **10.** *Phys.* baryon number

b. *or* **B. 1.** *Mus.* bass; basso **2.** (on maps *etc.*) bay **3.** (**B.**) Bible **4.** book **5.** born **6.** (**b.**) *Cricket* bowled; bye **7.** breadth

Ba *Chem.* barium

B.A. Bachelor of Arts

baa (bɑː) *vi.* **1.** make cry of sheep; bleat (ˈ**baaing, baaed**) —*n.* **2.** cry made by sheep

B.A.A. British Airports Authority

baas (bɑːs) *n.* **SA** boss

baba (ˈbɑːbɑː) *n.* small cake, usu. soaked in rum

babble (ˈbæbᵊl) *vi.* **1.** speak foolishly, incoherently, or childishly —*n.* **2.** foolish, confused talk —ˈ**babbler** *n.* **1.** one who babbles **2.** tropical bird with incessant song —ˈ**babbling** *n./a.*

babe (beɪb) *n.* **1.** *old-fashioned* baby **2.** guileless person

babel (ˈbeɪbᵊl) *n.* confused noise or scene, uproar

baboon (bəˈbuːn) *n.* large monkey of Afr. and Asia —**ba**ˈ**boonish** *a.*

baby (ˈbeɪbɪ) *n.* very young child, infant —ˈ**babyhood** *n.* —ˈ**babyish** *a.* —**baby grand** small grand piano —**baby-sit** *vi.* —**baby-sitter** *n.* one who cares for children when parents are out

baccarat (ˈbækərɑː, bækəˈrɑː) *n.* gambling card game

bacchanal (ˈbækənᵊl) *n.* **1.** follower of Bacchus **2.** (participant in) drunken, riotous celebration

bacchanalia (bækəˈneɪlɪə) *pl.n.* **1.** (*oft.* **B-**) orgiastic rites associated with Bacchus **2.** drunken revelry —**baccha**ˈ**nalian** *a./n.*

bacchant (ˈbækənt) *or* (*fem.*) **bacchante** (bəˈkæntɪ) *n.* **1.** priest or priestess of Bacchus **2.** drunken reveller

baccy (ˈbækɪ) *n.* **UK** *inf.* tobacco

bachelor (ˈbætʃələ, ˈbætʃlə) *n.* **1.** unmarried man **2.** holder of lowest university degree **3.** *Hist.* young knight —ˈ**bachelorhood** *or* ˈ**bachelorship** *n.* —**bachelor girl** young unmarried woman, *esp.* one who is self-supporting

bacillus (bəˈsɪləs) *n.* minute organism sometimes causing disease (*pl.* **-cilli** (-ˈsɪlaɪ)) —**ba**ˈ**cilliform** *a.*

back (bæk) *n.* **1.** hinder part of anything, *eg* human body **2.** part opposite front **3.** part or side of something further away or less used **4.** (position of) player in ball games behind other (forward) players —*a.* **5.** situated behind **6.** earlier —*adv.* **7.** at, to the back **8.** in, into the past **9.** in return —*vi.* **10.** move backwards —*vt.* **11.** support **12.** put wager on **13.** provide with back or backing —ˈ**backer** *n.* **1.** one supporting another, *esp.* in contest **2.** one betting on horse, *etc.* in race —ˈ**backing** *n.* **1.** support **2.** material to protect the back of something **3.** musical accompaniment, *esp.* for pop singer —ˈ**backward** *a.* **1.** directed towards the rear **2.** behind in education **3.** reluctant, bashful —*adv.* **4.** backwards —ˈ**backwardness** *n.* —ˈ**backwards** *adv.* **1.** to the rear **2.** to the past **3.** into a worse state (*also* ˈ**backward**) —ˈ**back**ˈ**bencher** *n.* Brit. or Aust. member of Parliament not holding office in government or opposition —ˈ**backbite** *v.* slander (absent person) —ˈ**backbiter** *n.* —ˈ**backbiting** *n.* —ˈ**backboard** *n.* **1.** board that is placed behind something to form or support its back **2.** board worn to support back, as after surgery **3.** *Basketball* flat upright surface under which basket is attached —**back boiler** tank or series of pipes at back of fireplace for heating water —ˈ**backbone** *n.* **1.** spinal column **2.** strength of character —ˈ**backbreaking** *a.* exhausting —ˈ**backchat** *n.* *inf.* impudent answer —ˈ**backcloth** *or* ˈ**backdrop** *n.* painted cloth at back of stage —ˈ**backcomb** *v.* comb under layers of (hair) towards roots to add bulk to hair style (*also* **tease**) —**back**ˈ**date** *vt.* make effective from earlier date —**back door 1.** door at rear or side of building **2.** means of entry to job *etc.* that is secret or obtained through influence —**back**ˈ**fire** *vi.* **1.** ignite at wrong time, as fuel in cylinder of internal-combustion engine **2.** (of plan, scheme *etc.*) fail to work, *esp.* to the cost of the instigator **3.** ignite wrongly, as gas burner *etc.* —ˈ**backgammon** *n.* game played with draughtsmen and dice —ˈ**background** *n.* **1.** space behind chief figures of picture *etc.* **2.** past history of person —ˈ**backhand** *n.* *Tennis etc.* stroke with hand turned backwards —**back**ˈ**handed** *a.* (of compliment *etc.*) with second, uncomplimentary meaning —ˈ**backhander** *n.* **1.** blow with back of hand **2.** *inf.* a bribe —ˈ**backlash** *n.* sudden and adverse reaction —ˈ**backlog** *n.* accumulation of work *etc.* to be dealt with —**back marker** competitor who is at back of field in race —**back number 1.** issue of newspaper *etc.* that appeared on a previous date **2.** *inf.* person or thing considered old-fashioned —**back pack** *n.* **1.** type of knapsack —*vi.* **2.** travel with knapsack —**back-pedal** *vi.* **1.** turn pedals of bicycle backwards **2.** retract previous opinion *etc.* —**back room** place where important and usu. secret research is done —**back seat 1.** seat at back, *esp.* of vehicle **2.** *inf.* subordinate or inconspicuous position (*esp. in* **take a back seat**) —**back-seat driver** *inf.* **1.** passenger who offers unwanted advice to driver **2.** person who offers advice on matters that are not his concern —**back**ˈ**side** *n.* rump —ˈ**backslide** *vi.* fall back in faith or morals —**back**ˈ**stage** *adv.* **1.** behind part of theatre in view of

THESAURUS

babble 1. *v.* blab, burble, cackle, chatter, gabble, gibber, gurgle, jabber, mumble, murmur, mutter, prate, prattle **2.** *n.* burble, clamour, drivel, gabble, gibberish, murmur

babe 1. baby, bairn (*Scot.*), child, infant, nursling, suckling **2.** babe in arms, ingénue, innocent

baby *n.* babe, bairn (*Scot.*), child, infant, newborn child

babyish baby, childish, foolish, immature, infantile, juvenile, namby-pamby, puerile, silly, sissy, soft (*Inf.*), spoiled

audience —*a.* 2. situated backstage —ˈ**backˈstairs** *pl.n.* 1. secondary staircase in house —*a.* 2. underhand (*also* ˈ**backˈstair**) —ˈ**backstroke** *n. Swimming* stroke performed on the back —ˈ**backtrack** *vi.* 1. return by same route by which one has come 2. retract or reverse one's opinion *etc.* —ˈ**backup** *n. chiefly* US 1. support; reinforcement 2. reserve; substitute —ˈ**backwash** *n.* 1. water thrown back by ship's propellers *etc.* 2. a backward current 3. a reaction —ˈ**backwater** *n.* still water fed by back flow of stream —ˈ**backwoods** *pl.n.* remote forest areas —**back yard** yard at back of house *etc.* —**back up** 1. support 2. (of water) accumulate 3. *Comp.* make copy of (data file) —**in one's own back yard** close at hand

bacon (ˈbeɪkən) *n.* cured pig's flesh

Baconian (beɪˈkəʊnɪən) *a.* 1. pert. to English philosopher Francis Bacon or his inductive method of reasoning —*n.* 2. follower of Bacon's philosophy

bacteria (bækˈtɪərɪə) *pl.n.* microscopic organisms, some causing disease (*sing.* **-rium** (-rɪəm)) —**bacˈterial** *a.* —**bacteriˈologist** *n.* —**bacteriˈology** *n.* study of bacteria

Bactrian camel (ˈbæktrɪən) two-humped camel, used in deserts of central Asia

bad (bæd) *a.* 1. of poor quality 2. faulty 3. evil 4. immoral 5. offensive 6. severe 7. rotten, decayed (**worse** *comp.*, **worst** *sup.*) —ˈ**badly** *adv.* —ˈ**badness** *n.* —**bad blood** feeling of intense hatred or hostility; enmity —**bad debt** debt which is not collectable

bade (bæd, beɪd) *or* **bad** *pt. of* BID

badge (bædʒ) *n.* distinguishing emblem or sign

badger (ˈbædʒə) *n.* 1. carnivorous burrowing mammal, about the size of a fox —*vt.* 2. pester, worry

badinage (ˈbædɪnɑːʒ) *n.* playful talk, banter

badminton (ˈbædmɪntən) *n.* game like tennis, played with shuttlecocks over high net

baffle (ˈbæfᵊl) *vt.* 1. check 2. frustrate 3. bewilder —ˈ**baffler** *n.* —ˈ**baffling** *a.* —**baffle plate** device to regulate or divert flow of liquid, gas, soundwaves *etc.*

bag (bæg) *n.* 1. sack, pouch 2. measure of quantity 3. woman's handbag 4. *offens.* unattractive woman —*pl.* 5. *inf.* lots (of) —*vi.* 6. swell out 7. bulge 8. sag —*vt.* 9. put in bag 10. kill as game *etc.* (**-gg-**) —ˈ**bagging** *n.* cloth —ˈ**baggy** *a.* loose, drooping —ˈ**bagman** *n.* commercial traveller

bagasse (bəˈgæs) *n.* sugar cane refuse

THESAURUS

back *n.* 1. backside, end, far end, hind part, hindquarters, posterior, rear, reverse, stern, tail end ~*adj.* 2. end, hind, hindmost, posterior, rear, tail 3. *From an earlier time* delayed, earlier, elapsed, former, overdue, past, previous ~*v.* 4. backtrack, go back, move back, regress, retire, retreat, reverse, turn tail, withdraw 5. abet, advocate, assist, champion, countenance, encourage, endorse, favour, finance, sanction, second, side with, sponsor, subsidize, support, sustain, underwrite

backbone 1. *Medical* spinal column, spine, vertebrae, vertebral column 2. bottle (*Sl.*), character, courage, determination, firmness, fortitude, grit, hardihood, mettle, moral fibre, nerve, pluck, resolution, resolve, stamina, steadfastness, strength of character, tenacity, toughness, will, willpower

backbreaking arduous, crushing, exhausting, gruelling, hard, killing, laborious, punishing, strenuous, toilsome, wearing, wearying

backfire boomerang, disappoint, fail, flop, miscarry, rebound, recoil

background breeding, circumstances, credentials, culture, education, environment, experience, grounding, history, milieu, preparation, qualifications, tradition, upbringing

backhanded ambiguous, double-edged, equivocal, indirect, ironic, oblique, sarcastic, sardonic, two-edged

backing abetment, accompaniment, advocacy, aid, assistance, championing, encouragement, endorsement, funds, grant, moral support, patronage, sanction, seconding, sponsorship, subsidy, support

backlash backfire, boomerang, counteraction, counterblast, kickback, reaction, recoil, repercussion, resentment, resistance, response, retaliation, retroaction

backlog accumulation, excess, hoard, reserve, reserves, resources, stock, supply

backslide fall from grace, go astray, go wrong, lapse, regress, relapse, renege, retrogress, revert, sin, slip, stray, weaken

backward *adj.* 1. behind, behindhand, dense, dull, retarded, slow, stupid, subnormal, underdeveloped, undeveloped 2. bashful, diffident, hesitating, late, reluctant, shy, sluggish, tardy, unwilling, wavering ~*adv.* 3. aback, behind, in reverse, rearward

backwoods back of beyond, outback, sticks (*Inf.*)

bacteria bacilli, bugs (*Sl.*), germs, microbes, microorganisms, pathogens, viruses

bad 1. defective, deficient, erroneous, fallacious, faulty, imperfect, inadequate, incorrect, inferior, poor, substandard, unsatisfactory 2. base, corrupt, criminal, delinquent, evil, immoral, mean, sinful, vile, villainous, wicked, wrong 3. decayed, mouldy, off, putrid, rancid, rotten, sour, spoiled 4. disastrous, distressing, grave, harsh, painful, serious, severe, terrible

badge brand, device, emblem, identification, insignia, mark, sign, stamp, token

badger bully, chivvy, goad, harass, harry, hound, importune, nag, pester, plague, torment, worry

badly 1. carelessly, defectively, erroneously, faultily, imperfectly, inadequately, incorrectly, ineptly, poorly, shoddily, wrong, wrongly 2. criminally, evilly, immorally, improperly, naughtily, shamefully, unethically, wickedly 3. acutely, deeply, desperately, exceedingly, extremely, gravely, greatly, intensely, painfully, seriously, severely

baffle 1. amaze, astound, bewilder, confound, confuse, daze, disconcert, dumbfound, elude, flummox, mystify, nonplus, perplex, puzzle, stump, stun 2. balk, check, defeat, foil, frustrate, hinder, thwart, upset

bag *v.* 1. balloon, bulge, droop, sag, swell 2. acquire, capture, catch, gain, get, kill, land, shoot, take, trap

baggage accoutrements, bags, belongings, equipment, gear, impedimenta, luggage, paraphernalia, suitcases, things

baggy billowing, bulging, droopy, floppy, ill-fitting, loose, oversize, roomy, sagging, seated, slack

bagatelle (bægə'tɛl) *n.* **1.** trifle **2.** game like pinball played with nine balls and cue on a board

baggage ('bægɪdʒ) *n.* **1.** suitcases *etc.*, packed for journey **2.** *offens.* woman

bagpipes ('bægpaɪps) *pl.n.* musical wind instrument, of windbag and pipes —**'bagpiper** *n.*

bah (bɑː, bæ) *interj.* expression of contempt or disgust

Bahaism (bə'hɑːɪzəm) *n.* religious system founded in 1863, emphasizing value of all religions and spiritual unity of mankind —**Ba'haist** *or* **Ba'haite** *a./n.*

bail[1] (beɪl) *n.* **1.** *Law* security given for person's reappearance in court **2.** one giving such security —*vt.* **3.** release, or obtain release of, on security —**bail out** *inf.* help (person, firm *etc.*) out of trouble

bail[2] (beɪl) *n.* **1.** *Cricket* crosspiece on wicket **2.** bar separating horses in stable

bail[3] *or* **bale** (beɪl) *vt.* empty out (water) from boat —**bail out** leave aircraft by parachute

bailey ('beɪlɪ) *n.* outermost wall of castle

Bailey bridge ('beɪlɪ) bridge composed of prefabricated sections

bailie ('beɪlɪ) *n. Scot.* municipal magistrate

bailiff ('beɪlɪf) *n.* **1.** land steward, agent **2.** sheriff's officer

bailiwick ('beɪlɪwɪk) *n.* jurisdiction of bailiff

bain-marie (bẽma'ri) *Fr.* vessel for holding hot water, in which sauces *etc.* are gently cooked or kept warm (*pl.* ***bains-marie*** (bẽma'ri))

bairn (bɛən) *n. Scot.* infant, child

bait (beɪt) *n.* **1.** food to entice fish **2.** any lure or enticement —*vt.* **3.** set a lure for **4.** annoy, persecute

baize (beɪz) *n.* smooth woollen cloth

bake (beɪk) *vt.* **1.** cook or harden by dry heat —*vi.* **2.** make bread, cakes *etc.* **3.** be scorched or tanned —**'baker** *n.* —**'bakery** *or* **'bakehouse** *n.* —**'baking** *n.* —**baked beans** haricot beans, baked and tinned in tomato sauce —**baker's dozen** thirteen —**baking powder** raising agent containing sodium bicarbonate *etc.* used in cooking

Bakelite ('beɪkəlaɪt) *n.* **R** hard nonflammable synthetic resin, used for dishes, trays, electrical insulators *etc.*

baksheesh *or* **backsheesh** ('bækʃiːʃ) *n.* in some Eastern countries, *esp.* formerly, money given as tip

Balaclava helmet (bælə'klɑːvə) close-fitting woollen helmet covering head and neck

balalaika (bælə'laɪkə) *n.* Russian musical instrument similar to guitar

balance ('bæləns) *n.* **1.** pair of scales **2.** equilibrium **3.** surplus **4.** sum due on an account **5.** difference between two sums —*vt.* **6.** weigh **7.** bring to equilibrium —**balance of payments** difference over given time between total payments to and receipts from foreign nations —**balance of power** distribution of power among countries so that no nation can seriously threaten another —**balance sheet** tabular statement of assets and liabilities —**balance wheel** regulating wheel of watch

balcony ('bælkənɪ) *n.* **1.** railed platform outside window **2.** upper seats in theatre

bald (bɔːld) *a.* **1.** hairless **2.** plain **3.** bare —**'balding** *a.* becoming bald —**'baldly** *adv.* —**'baldness** *n.*

balderdash ('bɔːldədæʃ) *n.* idle, senseless talk

baldric ('bɔːldrɪk) *n.* shoulder-belt for sword *etc.*

bale[1] (beɪl) *n.* **1.** bundle or package —*vt.* **2.** make into bundles or pack into cartons —**'baler** *n.* machine which makes bales of hay *etc.*

bale[2] (beɪl) *vt. see* BAIL[3]

baleen (bə'liːn) *n.* whalebone

baleful ('beɪlfʊl) *a.* menacing —**'balefully** *adv.*

balk *or* **baulk** (bɔːk, bɔːlk) *vi.* **1.** swerve, pull up —*vt.* **2.** thwart, hinder —*n.* **3.** hindrance **4.** square timber, beam —**balk at 1.** recoil from **2.** stop short at

Balkan ('bɔːlkən) *a.* of or denoting large peninsula in SE Europe, its inhabitants, countries *etc.*

ball[1] (bɔːl) *n.* **1.** anything round **2.** globe, sphere, *esp.* as used in games **3.** *Cricket* ball as delivered **4.** bullet —*vi.* **5.** clog, gather into a mass —**ball-and-socket joint** *Anat.* joint in which rounded head fits into rounded cavity —**ball bearings** steel balls used to lessen friction on bearings —**ball boy** *esp.* in tennis, person who retrieves balls that go out of play —**ball cock** device for regulating flow of liquid into cistern *etc.*, consisting of floating ball and a valve —**ball game 1.** any game played with a ball **2.** US game of baseball

THESAURUS

bail[1] *n.* bond, guarantee, guaranty, pledge, security, surety, warranty

bail[2], **bale** *v.* dip, drain off, ladle, scoop

bail out, bale out 1. aid, help, relieve, rescue **2.** escape, quit, retreat, withdraw

bait *n.* **1.** allurement, attraction, bribe, decoy, enticement, inducement, lure, snare, temptation ~*v.* **2.** annoy, gall, harass, hound, irk, irritate, needle (*Inf.*), persecute, provoke, tease, torment **3.** allure, beguile, entice, lure, seduce, tempt

balance *v.* **1.** level, match, parallel, poise, stabilize, steady **2.** adjust, compensate for, counteract, counterbalance, counterpoise, equalize, equate, make up for, neutralize, offset **3.** assess, compare, consider, deliberate, estimate, evaluate, weigh ~*n.* **4.** correspondence, equilibrium, equipoise, equity, equivalence, evenness, parity, symmetry **5.** composure, equanimity, poise, self-control, self-possession, stability, steadiness **6.** difference, remainder, residue, rest, surplus

balance sheet account, budget, credits and debits, ledger, report, statement

balcony 1. terrace, veranda **2.** gallery, gods, upper circle

bald 1. baldheaded, baldpated, depilated, glabrous (*Biol.*), hairless **2.** barren, bleak, exposed, naked, stark, treeless, uncovered **3.** bare, blunt, direct, downright, forthright, outright, plain, severe, simple, straight, straightforward, unadorned, unvarnished

balderdash bunk (*Inf.*), bunkum, claptrap (*Inf.*), drivel, gibberish, nonsense, poppycock (*Inf.*), rot, rubbish, tommyrot, trash, twaddle

baldness 1. alopecia (*Pathology*), baldheadedness, baldpatedness, glabrousness (*Biol.*), hairlessness **2.** barrenness, bleakness, nakedness, sparseness, starkness, treelessness **3.** austerity, bluntness, plainness, severity, simplicity, spareness

balk 1. demur, dodge, evade, flinch, hesitate, jib, recoil, refuse, resist, shirk, shrink from **2.** baffle, bar, check, counteract, defeat, disconcert, foil, forestall, frustrate, hinder, obstruct, prevent, thwart

3. US *inf.* any activity —**ball-park figure** rough estimate; guess —**'ballpoint** *or* **ballpoint pen** *n.* pen with tiny ball bearing as nib (*also* **'Biro**)

ball[2] (bɔːl) *n.* assembly for dancing —**'ballroom** *n.*

ballad ('bæləd) *n.* **1.** narrative poem **2.** simple song

ballade (bæ'lɑːd) *n.* **1.** short poem with refrain and envoy **2.** piece of music

ballast ('bæləst) *n.* **1.** heavy material put in ship to give steadiness **2.** that which renders anything steady —*vt.* **3.** load with ballast, steady

ballet ('bæleɪ, bæ'leɪ) *n.* theatrical presentation of dancing and miming —**balle'rina** *n.* female ballet dancer

balletomania (bælɛtəʊ'meɪnɪə) *n.* enthusiasm for ballet —**bal'letomane** *n.*

ballista (bə'lɪstə) *n.* ancient catapult for hurling stones *etc.* (*pl.* **-tae** (-tiː)) —**bal'listic** *a.* moving as, or pertaining to motion of a projectile —**bal'listics** *pl.n.* (*with sing. v.*) scientific study of ballistic motion —**ballistic missile** missile that follows ballistic trajectory when propulsive power is discontinued

balloon (bə'luːn) *n.* **1.** large, airtight bag that rises when filled with air or gas —*vi.* **2.** puff out —**bal'looning** *n.* —**bal'loonist** *n.*

ballot ('bælət) *n.* **1.** method of voting secretly, usu. by marking ballot paper and putting it into box —*v.* **2.** vote or elicit a vote from —**ballot box 1.** sealed receptacle for completed ballot papers **2.** *fig.* the democratic process

ballyhoo (bælɪ'huː) *n.* **1.** noisy confusion or uproar **2.** vulgar, exaggerated publicity or advertisement

balm (bɑːm) *n.* **1.** aromatic substance obtained from certain trees, used for healing or soothing **2.** anything soothing —**'balminess** *n.* —**'balmy** *a.*

baloney *or* **boloney** (bə'ləʊnɪ) *n. inf.* foolish talk; nonsense

BALPA ('bælpə) British Airline Pilots' Association

balsa ('bɔːlsə) *n.* Amer. tree with light but strong wood

balsam ('bɔːlsəm) *n.* **1.** resinous aromatic substance obtained from various trees and shrubs **2.** soothing ointment —**bal'samic** *a.*

Baltic ('bɔːltɪk) *a.* **1.** denoting or relating to the Baltic Sea or the states bordering it **2.** of or characteristic of Baltic as a group of languages

baluster ('bæləstə) *n.* short pillar used as support to rail of staircase *etc.* —**'balustrade** *n.* row of short pillars surmounted by rail

bamboo (bæm'buː) *n.* large tropical treelike reed

bamboozle (bæm'buːz'l) *vt.* **1.** mystify **2.** hoax

ban (bæn) *vt.* **1.** prohibit, forbid, outlaw (**-nn-**) —*n.* **2.** prohibition **3.** proclamation —**bans** *or* **banns** *pl.n.* proclamation of marriage

banal (bə'nɑːl) *a.* commonplace, trivial, trite —**ba'nality** *n.*

banana (bə'nɑːnə) *n.* **1.** tropical treelike plant **2.** its fruit —**banana republic** *inf.* small country, *esp.* in Central Amer., that is politically unstable and has economy dominated by foreign interest

band[1] (bænd) *n.* **1.** strip used to bind **2.** range of values, frequencies *etc.*, between two limits —**'bandage** *n.* strip of cloth for binding wound —**band saw** power-operated saw consisting of endless toothed metal band running over two wheels

band[2] (bænd) *n.* **1.** company, group **2.** company of musicians —*v.* **3.** (*with* together) bind together —**'bandmaster** *n.* —**'bandsman** *n.* —**'bandstand** *n.*

bandanna *or* **bandana** (bæn'dænə) *n.* coloured silk or cotton handkerchief

b. and b. bed and breakfast

bandbox ('bændbɒks) *n.* light box of cardboard for hats *etc.*

bandeau ('bændəʊ) *n.* band, ribbon for the hair (*pl.* **-deaux** (-dəʊz))

bandicoot ('bændɪkuːt) *n.* ratlike Aust. marsupial

bandit ('bændɪt) *n.* **1.** outlaw **2.** robber, brigand (*pl.* **-s, banditti** (bæn'dɪtɪ))

bandoleer *or* **bandolier** (bændə'lɪə) *n.* shoulder belt for cartridges

bandwagon ('bændwægən) *n.* —**climb, jump, get on the bandwagon** join something that seems assured of success

bandy ('bændɪ) *vt.* **1.** beat to and fro **2.** toss from one to another (**'bandied, 'bandying**) —**'bandy** *or* **bandy-legged** *a.* having legs curving outwards

THESAURUS

ball 1. drop, globe, globule, orb, pellet, sphere, spheroid **2.** ammunition, bullet, grapeshot, pellet, shot, slug

ballast balance, counterbalance, counterweight, equilibrium, sandbag, stability, stabilizer, weight

balloon *v.* belly, billow, bloat, blow up, dilate, distend, enlarge, expand, inflate, puff out, swell

ballot election, poll, polling, vote, voting

ballyhoo 1. babble, commotion, fuss, hubbub, hue and cry, hullabaloo, noise, racket, to-do **2.** advertising, build-up, hype (*Sl.*), promotion, propaganda, publicity

balm 1. balsam, cream, embrocation, emollient, lotion, ointment, salve, unguent **2.** anodyne, comfort, consolation, curative, palliative, restorative, solace

bamboozle 1. cheat, con (*Sl.*), deceive, defraud, delude, dupe, fool, hoax, hoodwink, swindle, trick **2.** baffle, befuddle, confound, confuse, mystify, perplex, puzzle, stump

ban 1. *v.* banish, bar, debar, disallow, exclude, forbid, interdict, outlaw, prohibit, proscribe, restrict, suppress **2.** *n.* boycott, censorship, embargo, interdiction, prohibition, proscription, restriction, stoppage, suppression, taboo

banal clichéd, cliché-ridden, commonplace, everyday, hackneyed, humdrum, old hat, ordinary, pedestrian, platitudinous, stale, stereotyped, stock, threadbare, tired, trite, trivial, unimaginative, unoriginal, vapid

banality bromide (*Inf.*), cliché, commonplace, platitude, triteness, trite phrase, triviality, truism, vapidity

band[1] *n.* bandage, belt, binding, bond, chain, cord, fetter, fillet, ligature, manacle, ribbon, shackle, strap, strip, tie

band[2] *n.* **1.** assembly, association, body, clique, club, company, coterie, crew (*Inf.*), gang, horde, party, society, troop **2.** combo, ensemble, group, orchestra ~*v.* **3.** affiliate, ally, consolidate, federate, gather, group, join, merge, unite

bandage *n.* compress, dressing, gauze, plaster

bandit brigand, crook, desperado, footpad, freebooter,

bane (beɪn) *n.* person or thing causing misery or distress —**ˈbaneful** *a.* —**ˈbanefully** *adv.*

bang[1] (bæŋ) *n.* **1.** sudden loud noise, explosion **2.** heavy blow —*vi.* **3.** make loud noise —*vt.* **4.** beat, strike violently **5.** slam —**ˈbanger** *n.* **UK 1.** *sl.* sausage **2.** old decrepit car **3.** firework that explodes loudly

bang[2] (bæŋ) *n.* fringe of hair cut straight across forehead

bangle (ˈbæŋgᵊl) *n.* ring worn on arm or leg

banian (ˈbænjən) *n. see* BANYAN

banish (ˈbænɪʃ) *vt.* **1.** condemn to exile **2.** drive away **3.** dismiss —**ˈbanishment** *n.* exile

banisters (ˈbænɪstəz) *pl.n.* railing and supporting balusters on staircase

banjo (ˈbændʒəʊ) *n.* musical instrument like guitar, with circular body (*pl.* **-s, -es**) —**ˈbanjoist** *n.*

bank[1] (bæŋk) *n.* **1.** establishment for keeping, lending, exchanging *etc.* money **2.** any supply or store for future use, as blood bank —*vt.* **3.** put in bank —*vi.* **4.** transact business with bank —**ˈbanker** *n.* —**ˈbanking** *n.* —**bank account** account created by deposit of money at bank by customer —**ˈbankbook** *n.* book held by depositor, in which bank enters record of deposits, withdrawals *etc.* (*also* **ˈpassbook**) —**bank card** *or* **banker's card** card guaranteeing payment of cheques by bank up to an agreed amount —**bank holiday** day(s), usu. public holiday(s), when banks are closed by law —**bank note** written promise of payment —**bank rate** (*sometimes* **B- R-**) minimum rate by which central bank is obliged to rediscount bills of exchange —**bank on** rely on

bank[2] (bæŋk) *n.* **1.** mound or ridge of earth **2.** edge of river, lake *etc.* **3.** rising ground in sea —*vt.* **4.** enclose with ridge —*v.* **5.** pile up **6.** (of aircraft) tilt inwards in turning

bank[3] (bæŋk) *n.* **1.** tier **2.** row of oars

bankrupt (ˈbæŋkrʌpt, -rəpt) *n.* **1.** one who fails in business, insolvent debtor —*a.* **2.** financially ruined —*vt.* **3.** make, cause to be, bankrupt —**ˈbankruptcy** *n.*

banksia (ˈbæŋksɪə) *n.* genus of Aust. shrubs with dense, usu. yellow, cylindrical heads of flowers

banner (ˈbænə) *n.* **1.** long strip with slogan *etc.* **2.** placard **3.** flag used as ensign

bannisters (ˈbænɪstəz) *pl.n. see* BANISTERS

bannock (ˈbænək) *n.* round flat cake orig. in Scotland, made from wheat or barley

banns *or* **bans** (bænz) *pl.n. see* BAN

banquet (ˈbæŋkwɪt) *n.* **1.** feast —*vi.* **2.** hold or take part in banquet —*vt.* **3.** treat with feast —**ˈbanqueter** *n.*

banquette (bæŋˈkɛt) *n.* **1.** raised firing step behind parapet **2. US** upholstered bench

banshee (ˈbænʃiː, bænˈʃiː) *n.* Irish fairy with a wail portending death

bantam (ˈbæntəm) *n.* dwarf variety of domestic fowl —**ˈbantamweight** *n.* **1.** professional boxer weighing 112-118 lbs. (51-53.5 kg); amateur boxer weighing 112-119 lbs. (51-54 kg) **2.** wrestler weighing usu. 115-126 lbs. (52-57 kg)

banter (ˈbæntə) *v.* **1.** speak or tease lightly or jokingly —*n.* **2.** light, teasing language

Bantu (ˈbɑːntʊ) *n.* **1.** collective name for large group of related native tribes in Afr. **2.** family of languages spoken by Bantu peoples

bantubeer (ˈbɑːntʊbɪə) *n.* **SA** malted drink made from sorghum

banyan *or* **banian** (ˈbænjən) *n.* Indian fig tree with spreading branches which take root

baobab (ˈbeɪəʊbæb) *n.* Afr. tree with thick trunk and angular branches

bap (bæp) *n.* **UK** soft bread roll

baptize *or* **-ise** (bæpˈtaɪz) *vt.* **1.** immerse in, sprinkle

THESAURUS

gangster, gunman, highwayman, hijacker, marauder, outlaw, pirate, racketeer, robber, thief

bandy 1. *v.* barter, exchange, interchange, pass, shuffle, swap, throw, toss, trade **2.** *adj.* bandy-legged, bent, bowed, bow-legged, crooked, curved

bane affliction, *bête noire*, blight, burden, calamity, curse, despair, destruction, disaster, downfall, misery, nuisance, pest, plague, ruin, scourge, torment, trial, trouble, woe

baneful baleful, calamitous, deadly, deleterious, destructive, disastrous, fatal, harmful, hurtful, injurious, noxious, pernicious, pestilential, ruinous, venomous

bang *n.* **1.** boom, burst, clang, clap, clash, detonation, explosion, peal, pop, report, shot, slam, thud, thump **2.** blow, box, bump, cuff, hit, knock, punch, smack, stroke, wallop (*Inf.*), whack ~*v.* **3.** bash (*Inf.*), beat, bump, clatter, crash, hammer, knock, pound, pummel, rap, slam, strike, thump **4.** boom, burst, clang, detonate, drum, echo, explode, peal, resound, thump, thunder

banish 1. deport, drive away, eject, evict, exclude, excommunicate, exile, expatriate, expel, ostracize, outlaw, shut out, transport **2.** ban, cast out, discard, dislodge, dismiss, dispel, eliminate, eradicate, get rid of, oust, remove, shake off

banishment deportation, exile, expatriation, expulsion, proscription, transportation

banisters balusters, balustrade, handrail, rail, railing

bank[1] **1.** *n.* accumulation, depository, fund, hoard, repository, reserve, reservoir, savings, stock, stockpile, store, storehouse **2.** *v.* deal with, deposit, keep, save, transact business with

bank[2] *n.* **1.** banking, embankment, heap, mass, mound, pile, ridge **2.** brink, edge, margin, shore, side ~*v.* **3.** amass, heap, mass, mound, pile, stack **4.** cant, incline, pitch, slant, slope, tilt, tip

bank on assume, believe in, count on, depend on, lean on, look to, rely on, trust

bankrupt broke (*Inf.*), depleted, destitute, exhausted, failed, impoverished, insolvent, lacking, ruined, spent

bankruptcy disaster, exhaustion, failure, indebtedness, insolvency, lack, liquidation, ruin

banner banderole, burgee, colours, ensign, fanion, flag, gonfalon, pennant, pennon, standard, streamer

banquet dinner, feast, meal, repast, revel, treat

banter 1. *v.* chaff, deride, jeer, jest, joke, kid (*Inf.*), make fun of, rib (*Inf.*), ridicule, taunt, tease, twit **2.** *n.* badinage, chaff, chaffing, derision, jeering, jesting, joking, kidding (*Inf.*), mockery, persiflage, pleasantry, raillery, repartee, ribbing (*Inf.*), ridicule, wordplay

with water ceremoniously **2.** christen —**ˈbaptism** *n.* —**bapˈtismal** *a.* —**bapˈtismally** *adv.* —**ˈBaptist** *n.* member of Protestant Christian denomination believing in necessity of baptism by immersion, *esp.* of adults —**ˈbaptistry** *or* **ˈbaptistery** *n.* place where baptism is performed —**baptism of fire 1.** soldier's first experience of battle **2.** any initiating ordeal

bar[1] (bɑː) *n.* **1.** rod or block of any substance **2.** obstacle **3.** bank of sand at mouth of river **4.** rail in law court **5.** body of lawyers **6.** counter where drinks are served, *esp.* in hotel *etc.* **7.** unit of music —*vt.* **8.** fasten **9.** obstruct **10.** exclude (-rr-) —*prep.* **11.** except —**ˈbarring** *prep.* excepting —**bar code** arrangement of parallel lines, readable by computer, printed on, and giving details of, merchandise in shop *etc.* —**bar graph** graph consisting of bars whose lengths are proportional to quantities —**ˈbarmaid** *n.* —**bar sinister 1.** (*not in heraldic usage*) *see* **bend sinister** *at* BEND **2.** condition of being of illegitimate birth —**ˈbartender** *n.*

bar[2] (bɑː) *n.* unit of pressure

bar. 1. barometer **2.** barrel **3.** barrister

barb (bɑːb) *n.* **1.** sharp point curving backwards behind main point of spear, fish hook *etc.* **2.** cutting remark —**barbed** *a.* —**barbed wire** fencing wire with barbs at close intervals

barbarous (ˈbɑːbərəs) *a.* **1.** savage, brutal **2.** uncivilized —**barbarian** (bɑːˈbɛərɪən) *n.* —**barbaric** (bɑːˈbærɪk) *a.* —**ˈbarbarism** *n.* —**barbarity** (bɑːˈbærɪtɪ) *n.* —**ˈbarbarously** *adv.*

Barbary ape (ˈbɑːbərɪ) tailless macaque that inhabits NW Afr. and Gibraltar

barbecue (ˈbɑːbɪkjuː) *n.* **1.** meal cooked outdoors over open fire **2.** fireplace or grill used for this —*vt.* **3.** cook (meat *etc.*) in this manner (**-cued, -cuing**)

barbel (ˈbɑːbᵊl) *n.* **1.** spine or bristle that hangs from jaws of certain fishes **2.** any of several European fishes resembling carp

barbell (ˈbɑːbɛl) *n.* metal rod to which heavy discs are attached at each end used for weightlifting exercises

barber (ˈbɑːbə) *n.* one who shaves beards and cuts hair

barberry (ˈbɑːbərɪ) *n.* **1.** any spiny Asian shrub, having yellow flowers and orange or red berries **2.** fruit of these plants

barbican (ˈbɑːbɪkən) *n.* **1.** outwork of fortified place, *esp.* to defend drawbridge **2.** watchtower projecting from fortification

barbiturate (bɑːˈbɪtjʊrɪt, -reɪt) *n.* derivative of barbituric acid used as drug —**ˈbarbitone** *or U.S.* **ˈbarbital** *n.* —**barbituric acid** crystalline solid used in preparation of barbiturate drugs

barcarole *or* **barcarolle** (ˈbɑːkərəʊl, -rɒl; bɑːkəˈrəʊl) *n.* gondolier's song

bard (bɑːd) *n.* **1.** formerly, Celtic poet **2.** wandering minstrel —**ˈbardic** *a.* —**the Bard** Shakespeare

bare (bɛə) *a.* **1.** uncovered **2.** naked **3.** plain **4.** scanty —*vt.* **5.** make bare —**ˈbarely** *adv.* only just, scarcely —**ˈbareness** *n.* —**ˈbarebacked** *a.* on unsaddled horse —**ˈbarefaced** *a.* shameless

bargain (ˈbɑːgɪn) *n.* **1.** something bought at price favourable to purchaser **2.** contract, agreement —*vi.* **3.** haggle, negotiate **4.** make bargain

barge (bɑːdʒ) *n.* **1.** flat-bottomed freight boat **2.** state or pleasure boat —*vi. inf.* **3.** (*with* into *or* in) interrupt **4.** (*with* into) bump (into), push —**barˈgee** *or U.S.* **ˈbargeman** *n.* —**ˈbargepole** *n.* long pole used to propel barge —**not touch with a bargepole** *inf.* refuse to have anything to do with

baritone (ˈbærɪtəʊn) *n.* **1.** (singer with) second lowest

THESAURUS

baptism christening, immersion, purification, sprinkling

baptize 1. besprinkle, cleanse, immerse, purify **2.** call, christen, dub, name, title

bar *n.* **1.** batten, crosspiece, paling, pole, rail, rod, shaft, stake, stick **2.** barricade, barrier, deterrent, hindrance, impediment, obstacle, obstruction, rail, railing, stop **3.** boozer (*Inf.*), canteen, counter, inn, lounge, pub (*Inf.*), public house, saloon, tavern **4.** bench, court, courtroom, dock, law court **5.** *Law* barristers, body of lawyers, counsel, court, judgment, tribunal ~*v.* **6.** barricade, bolt, fasten, latch, lock, secure **7.** ban, exclude, forbid, hinder, keep out, obstruct, prevent, prohibit, restrain

barb 1. bristle, point, prickle, prong, quill, spike, spur, thorn **2.** affront, cut, dig, gibe, insult, rebuff, sarcasm, scoff, sneer

barbarian *n.* **1.** brute, hooligan, lout, ruffian, savage, vandal, yahoo **2.** bigot, boor, ignoramus, illiterate, lowbrow, philistine

barbaric 1. primitive, rude, uncivilized, wild **2.** barbarous, boorish, brutal, coarse, crude, cruel, fierce, inhuman, savage, uncouth, vulgar

barbarism coarseness, crudity, savagery, uncivilizedness

barbarity brutality, cruelty, inhumanity, ruthlessness, savagery, viciousness

barbarous 1. barbarian, brutish, primitive, rough, rude, savage, uncivilized, uncouth, wild **2.** barbaric, brutal, cruel, ferocious, heartless, inhuman, monstrous, ruthless, vicious **3.** coarse, crude, ignorant, uncivilized, uncultured, unlettered, unrefined, vulgar

bare 1. denuded, exposed, naked, nude, peeled, shorn, stripped, unclad, unclothed, uncovered, undressed **2.** barren, blank, empty, lacking, mean, open, poor, scanty, scarce, unfurnished, vacant, void, wanting **3.** austere, bald, basic, cold, essential, hard, literal, plain, severe, sheer, simple, spare, stark, unadorned, unembellished, unvarnished

barefaced audacious, bold, brash, brazen, impudent, insolent, shameless

barely almost, hardly, just, only just, scarcely

bargain *n.* **1.** agreement, arrangement, business, compact, contract, convention, engagement, negotiation, pact, pledge, promise, stipulation, transaction, treaty, understanding **2.** (cheap) purchase, discount, giveaway, good buy, good deal, good value, reduction, snip (*Inf.*) ~*v.* **3.** agree, contract, covenant, negotiate, promise, stipulate, transact **4.** barter, buy, deal, haggle, sell, trade, traffic

barge canal boat, flatboat, lighter, narrow boat, scow

barge in break in, burst in, butt in, infringe, interrupt, intrude, muscle in (*Inf.*)

barge into bump into, cannon into, collide with, hit, push, shove

adult male voice —*a.* **2.** written for or possessing this vocal range

barium ('bɛərɪəm) *n.* white metallic element —**barium meal** preparation of barium sulphate, which is opaque to x-rays, swallowed by patient before x-ray of upper part of alimentary canal

bark[1] (bɑːk) *n.* **1.** sharp loud cry of dog *etc.* —*v.* **2.** make, utter with such sound —'**barker** *n.* crier outside fair booth *etc.*

bark[2] (bɑːk) *n.* **1.** outer layer of trunk, branches of tree —*vt.* **2.** strip bark from **3.** rub off (skin), graze (shins *etc.*)

bark[3] (bɑːk) *n. see* BARQUE

barley ('bɑːlɪ) *n.* grain used for food and in making malt —'**barleycorn** *n.* **1.** (grain of) barley **2.** *obs.* unit of length equal to a third of an inch —**barley sugar** sweet originally made with barley —**barley water** drink made from infusion of barley

barm (bɑːm) *n.* **1.** *obs.* yeast **2.** froth —'**barmy** *a. inf.* silly, insane

bar mitzvah (bɑː 'mɪtsvə) (*sometimes* **B- M-**) *Judaism* **1.** ceremony marking 13th birthday of boy, who then assumes full religious obligations **2.** the boy himself

barn (bɑːn) *n.* farm building, used to store grain, hay *etc.* —**barn dance** (party with) country dancing —**barn owl** owl with pale brown and white plumage —'**barnstorm** *vi. chiefly* **US** tour rural districts putting on shows or making speeches in political campaign —'**barnstormer** *n.* —'**barnyard** *n.* farmyard

barnacle ('bɑːnək°l) *n.* shellfish which adheres to rocks and ships' bottoms —**barnacle goose** N European goose that has black-and-white head and body

barney ('bɑːnɪ) *inf. n.* **1.** noisy argument **2.** fight —*vi.* **3.** argue or fight

barograph ('bærəgrɑːf, -græf) *n.* recording barometer

barometer (bə'rɒmɪtə) *n.* instrument to measure pressure of atmosphere —**baro'metric** *a.* —**ba'rometry** *n.*

baron ('bærən) *n.* **1.** member of lowest rank of peerage (**-ess** *fem.*) **2.** powerful businessman —'**baronage** *n.* —**ba'ronial** *a.* —'**barony** *n.* —**baron of beef** cut of beef consisting of double sirloin joined at backbone

baronet ('bærənɪt, -nɛt) *n.* lowest British hereditary title, below baron but above knight —'**baronetage** *n.* —'**baronetcy** *n.*

baroque (bə'rɒk, bə'rəʊk) *a.* extravagantly ornamented, *esp.* in architecture and art

baroscope ('bærəskəʊp) *n.* any instrument for measuring atmospheric pressure —**baroscopic** (bærə'skɒpɪk) *a.*

barouche (bə'ruːʃ) *n.* four-wheeled carriage with folding top over rear seat

barque (bɑːk) *n.* sailing ship, *esp.* large, three-masted one —'**barquentine** *n.* small barque

barrack[1] ('bærək) *n.* **1.** (*usu. pl.*) building for lodging soldiers **2.** huge bare building

barrack[2] ('bærək) *inf. vi.* **1.** (*usu. with* for) encourage by cheering, *esp.* at sporting events —*vt.* **2.** criticize loudly —*v.* **3.** jeer —'**barracking** *n.*

barracouta (bærə'kuːtə) *n.* type of large, elongated, predatory fish, mostly tropical

barrage ('bærɑːʒ) *n.* **1.** heavy artillery fire **2.** continuous and heavy delivery, *esp.* of questions *etc.* **3.** dam across river —**barrage balloon** one of number of tethered balloons with cables or net suspended from them, used to deter low-flying air attack

barratry *or* **barretry** ('bærətrɪ) *n.* **1.** fraudulent breach of duty by master of ship **2.** stirring up of law suits —'**barrator** *n.* —'**barratrous** *a.*

barre (baːr) *Fr.* rail used for ballet practice

barrel ('bærəl) *n.* **1.** round wooden vessel, made of curved staves bound with hoops **2.** amount that barrel can hold (*also* '**barrelful**) **3.** anything long and hollow, as tube of gun *etc.* —*vt.* **4.** put in barrel (**-ll-**) —'**barrelled** *a.* —**barrel organ** instrument consisting of cylinder turned by handle, having pins that interrupt air flow to certain pipes or pluck strings, thereby playing tunes —**barrel vault** *Archit.* vault in form of half cylinder

barren ('bærən) *a.* **1.** unfruitful, sterile **2.** unprofitable **3.** dull —'**barrenness** *n.* —**Barren Grounds** sparsely inhabited tundra region in N Canada

barricade (bærɪ'keɪd, 'bærɪkeɪd) *n.* **1.** improvised fortification, barrier —*vt.* **2.** protect by building barrier **3.** block

barrier ('bærɪə) *n.* fence, obstruction, obstacle, boundary —**barrier cream** cream to protect skin —**barrier reef** coral reef lying parallel to shore

barrister ('bærɪstə) *n.* advocate in the higher law courts

barrow[1] ('bærəʊ) *n.* **1.** small wheeled handcart **2.** wheelbarrow

barrow[2] ('bærəʊ) *n.* **1.** burial mound **2.** tumulus

Bart. Baronet

barter ('bɑːtə) *v.* **1.** trade by exchange of goods —*n.* **2.** practice of bartering

THESAURUS

bark[1] **1.** *n./v.* bay, growl, howl, snarl, woof, yap, yelp **2.** *v. Fig.* bawl, bawl at, berate, bluster, growl, shout, snap, snarl, yell

bark[2] **1.** *n.* casing, cortex (*Anat., bot.*), covering, crust, husk, rind, skin **2.** *v.* abrade, flay, rub, scrape, shave, skin, strip

barmy crazy, daft, foolish, idiotic, insane, loony (*Sl.*), nuts (*Sl.*), nutty (*Sl.*), odd, silly, stupid

baroque bizarre, convoluted, elaborate, extravagant, flamboyant, florid, grotesque, ornate, overdecorated

barracks billet, camp, cantonment, casern, encampment, garrison, quarters

barrage 1. battery, bombardment, cannonade, curtain of fire, fusillade, gunfire, salvo, shelling, volley **2.** assault, attack, burst, deluge, hail, mass, onslaught, plethora, profusion, rain, storm, stream, torrent

barren 1. childless, infecund, infertile, sterile, unprolific **2.** arid, desert, desolate, dry, empty, unfruitful, unproductive, waste **3.** boring, dull, flat, fruitless, lacklustre, stale, uninformative, uninspiring, uninstructive, uninteresting, unrewarding, useless, vapid

barricade 1. *n.* barrier, blockade, bulwark, fence, obstruction, palisade, rampart, stockade **2.** *v.* bar, block, blockade, defend, fortify, obstruct, protect, shut in

barrier 1. bar, barricade, blockade, boundary, ditch, fence, fortification, obstacle, obstruction, railing,

baryon ('bærɪɒn) *n. Phys.* elementary particle of matter

baryta (bə'raɪtə) *n.* **1.** barium oxide **2.** barium hydroxide

barytes (bə'raɪti:z) *n.* barium sulphate

basalt ('bæsɔ:lt) *n.* dark-coloured, hard, compact, igneous rock —**ba'saltic** *a.*

bascule ('bæskju:l) *n.* **1.** lever apparatus **2.** drawbridge on counterpoise principle

base[1] (beɪs) *n.* **1.** bottom, foundation **2.** starting point **3.** centre of operations **4.** fixed point **5.** *Chem.* compound that combines with an acid to form a salt **6.** medium into which other substances are mixed **7.** *Maths.* number that when raised to a certain power has logarithm equal to that power —*vt.* **8.** found, establish —**'basal** *a.* of base —**'baseless** *a.* —**'baseline** *n.* **1.** *Surv.* measured line through survey area from which triangulations are made **2.** line at each end of tennis court that marks limit of play —**'basement** *n.* lowest storey of building

base[2] (beɪs) *a.* **1.** low, mean **2.** despicable —**'basely** *adv.* —**'baseness** *n.* —**'baseborn** *a.* illegitimate

baseball ('beɪsbɔ:l) *n.* game, orig. Amer., played with bat and ball

bases ('beɪsi:z) *n., pl. of* BASIS

bash (bæʃ) *inf. vt.* **1.** strike violently —*n.* **2.** blow **3.** attempt

bashful ('bæʃfʊl) *a.* shy, modest —**'bashfully** *adv.* —**'bashfulness** *n.*

basic ('beɪsɪk; *Austral. also* 'bæsɪk) *a.* **1.** relating to, serving as base **2.** fundamental **3.** necessary —**'basically** *adv.* —**basic slag** slag produced in steel-making, containing calcium phosphate

BASIC ('beɪsɪk) *Comp.* Beginners' All-purpose Symbolic Instruction Code

basil ('bæz'l) *n.* aromatic herb

basilica (bə'zɪlɪkə) *n.* type of church with long hall and pillars —**ba'silican** *a.*

basilisk ('bæzɪlɪsk) *n.* legendary small fire-breathing dragon

basin ('beɪs'n) *n.* **1.** deep circular dish **2.** harbour **3.** land drained by river

basis ('beɪsɪs) *n.* **1.** foundation **2.** principal constituent (*pl.* **'bases**)

bask (bɑ:sk) *vi.* lie in warmth and sunshine —**basking shark** large plankton-eating shark

basket ('bɑ:skɪt) *n.* vessel made of woven cane, straw *etc.* —**'basketry** *or* **'basketwork** *n.* —**'basketball** *n.* ball game played by two teams —**basket chair** wickerwork chair —**basket weave** weave of yarns, resembling that of basket

basque (bæsk) *n.* tight-fitting bodice for women

Basque (bæsk, bɑ:sk) *n.* **1.** one of race from W Pyrenees **2.** their language

bas-relief (bɑ:rɪ'li:f, 'bæsrɪli:f) *n.* sculpture with figures standing out slightly from background

bass[1] (beɪs) *n.* **1.** lowest part in music **2.** bass singer or voice —*a.* **3.** relating to or denoting the bass —**bass clef** clef that establishes F a fifth below middle C on fourth line of staff

bass[2] (bæs) *n.* any of large variety of fish, *esp.* sea perch

basset ('bæsɪt) *n.* type of smooth-haired dog

basset horn obsolete woodwind instrument

bassinet (bæsɪ'nɛt) *n.* wickerwork or wooden cradle or pram, usu. hooded

bassoon (bə'su:n) *n.* woodwind instrument of low tone —**bas'soonist** *n.*

bast (bæst) *n.* fibrous material obtained from phloem of jute, flax *etc.* used for making rope *etc.*

bastard ('bɑ:stəd, 'bæs-) *n.* **1.** child born of unmarried parents **2.** *inf.* person, as in *lucky bastard* —*a.* **3.**

THESAURUS

rampart, stop, wall **2.** *Fig.* check, difficulty, drawback, handicap, hindrance, hurdle, impediment, limitation, obstacle, restriction, stumbling block

barter bargain, exchange, haggle, sell, swap, trade, traffic

base[1] *n.* **1.** bed, bottom, foot, foundation, groundwork, pedestal, rest, stand, support **2.** basis, core, essence, essential, fundamental, heart, key, origin, principle, root, source **3.** camp, centre, headquarters, home, post, settlement, starting point, station ~*v.* **4.** build, construct, depend, derive, establish, found, ground, hinge, locate, station

base[2] **1.** abject, contemptible, corrupt, depraved, despicable, dishonourable, disreputable, evil, ignoble, immoral, infamous, scandalous, shameful, sordid, vile, villainous, vulgar, wicked **2.** downtrodden, grovelling, low, lowly, mean, menial, miserable, paltry, pitiful, poor, servile, slavish, sorry, subservient, worthless, wretched

baseless groundless, unconfirmed, uncorroborated, unfounded, ungrounded, unjustifiable, unjustified, unsubstantiated, unsupported

baseness 1. contemptibility, degradation, depravation, depravity, despicability, disgrace, ignominy, infamy, notoriety, obloquy, turpitude **2.** lowliness, meanness, misery, poverty, servility, slavishness, subservience, vileness, worthlessness, wretchedness

bash 1. *v.* biff (*Sl.*), break, crash, crush, hit, punch, slosh (*Sl.*), smash, sock (*Sl.*), strike, wallop (*Inf.*) **2.** *n.* attempt, crack, go, shot, stab, try

bashful abashed, blushing, confused, constrained, coy, diffident, easily embarrassed, nervous, overmodest, reserved, reticent, retiring, self-conscious, self-effacing, shamefaced, sheepish, shrinking, shy, timid, timorous

basic central, elementary, essential, fundamental, indispensable, inherent, intrinsic, key, necessary, primary, underlying, vital

basically at bottom, at heart, *au fond*, essentially, firstly, fundamentally, inherently, in substance, intrinsically, mostly, primarily, radically

basis 1. base, bottom, footing, foundation, ground, groundwork, support **2.** chief ingredient, core, essential, fundamental, heart, premise, principal element, principle, theory

bask laze, lie in, loll, lounge, relax, sunbathe, swim in, toast oneself, warm oneself

bass deep, deep-toned, grave, low, low-pitched, resonant, sonorous

bastard *n.* **1.** illegitimate (child), love child, natural child ~*adj.* **2.** baseborn, illegitimate, misbegotten **3.** adulterated, counterfeit, false, imperfect, impure, inferior, irregular, sham, spurious illegimate 4. spurious —ˈ**bastardize** *or* **-ise** *vt.* 1. debase 2. declare illegitimate —ˈ**bastardy** *n.*

baste[1] (beɪst) *vt.* 1. moisten (meat) during cooking with hot fat 2. beat with stick —ˈ**basting** *n.*

baste[2] (beɪst) *vt.* sew loosely, tack

bastinado (bæstɪˈneɪdəʊ) *n.* 1. beating with stick, *esp.* on soles of feet (*pl.* **-es**) —*vt.* 2. inflict a bastinado on (**-doing, -doed**)

bastion (ˈbæstɪən) *n.* 1. projecting part of fortification, tower 2. strong defence or bulwark

bat[1] (bæt) *n.* 1. any of various types of club used to hit ball in certain sports, *eg* cricket, baseball —*v.* 2. strike with bat or use bat in sport (**-tt-**) —ˈ**batting** *n.* performance with bat —ˈ**batsman** *n.*

bat[2] (bæt) *n.* nocturnal mouselike flying animal

bat[3] (bæt) *vt.* flutter (one's eyelids) (**-tt-**)

batch (bætʃ) *n.* group or set of similar objects, *esp.* cakes *etc.* baked together

bated (ˈbeɪtɪd) *a.* —**with bated breath** anxiously

bath (bɑːθ) *n.* 1. vessel or place to bathe in 2. water for bathing 3. act of bathing —*pl.* 4. place for swimming —*v.* 5. wash —**bath cube** cube of soluble scented material for use in bath —ˈ**bathrobe** *n.* loose-fitting garment of towelling, for wear before or after bath or swimming —ˈ**bathroom** *n.* 1. room containing bath and usu. washbasin and lavatory 2. US lavatory —**bath salts** soluble scented salts for use in bath

Bath chair (bɑːθ) invalid chair

bathe (beɪð) *vi.* 1. swim —*vt.* 2. apply liquid to —*v.* 3. wash 4. immerse or be immersed in water (**bathed, ˈbathing**) —*n.* 5. a swim or paddle —ˈ**bather** *n.*

bathometer (bəˈθɒmɪtə) *n.* instrument for measuring depth of water —**bathoˈmetric** *a.*

bathos (ˈbeɪθɒs) *n.* ludicrous descent from the elevated to the ordinary in writing or speech

bathyscaph (ˈbæθɪskæf), **bathyscaphe** (ˈbæθɪskeɪf, -skæf), *or* **bathyscape** *n.* vessel for deep-sea observation

bathysphere (ˈbæθɪsfɪə) *n.* strong steel deep-sea diving sphere, lowered by cable

batik *or* **battik** (ˈbætɪk) *n.* dyeing process using wax

batiste (bæˈtiːst) *n.* fine plain-weave cotton

batman (ˈbætmən) *n.* military officer's servant

baton (ˈbætɒn) *n.* 1. slender stick used by conductor of an orchestra 2. policeman's truncheon 3. staff serving as symbol of office

batrachian (bəˈtreɪkɪən) *n.* any amphibian, *esp.* frog or toad

battalion (bəˈtæljən) *n.* military unit consisting of three or more companies

batten[1] (ˈbætən) *n.* 1. narrow piece of board, strip of wood —*vt.* 2. (*esp. with* down) fasten, make secure

batten[2] (ˈbætən) *vi.* (*usu. with* on) thrive, *esp.* at someone else's expense

batter (ˈbætə) *vt.* 1. strike continuously —*n.* 2. mixture of flour, eggs, milk, used in cooking —**battered baby** young child who has sustained serious injuries through violence of parent or other adult —**battering ram** *esp.* formerly, large beam used to break down fortifications

battery (ˈbætərɪ) *n.* 1. connected group of electrical cells 2. any electrical cell or accumulator 3. number of similar things occurring together 4. *Law* assault by beating 5. number of guns 6. place where they are mounted 7. unit of artillery 8. large number of cages for rearing poultry *etc.*

batting (ˈbætɪŋ) *n.* cotton fibre, used as stuffing

battle (ˈbætᵊl) *n.* 1. fight between armies, combat —*vi.* 2. fight 3. struggle —ˈ**battlement** *n.* wall, parapet on fortification with openings or embrasures —**battle-axe** *n. inf.* domineering woman —**battle cruiser** high-speed heavily armed warship of battleship size but with light armour —**battle dress** ordinary uniform of soldier —**battle fatigue** mental disorder characterized by anxiety and depression, caused by stress of warfare —ˈ**battlefield** *or* ˈ**battleground** *n.* place where battle is fought —**battle royal** 1. fight involving more than two combatants 2. long violent argument —ˈ**battleship** *n.* heavily armed and armoured fighting ship

battledore (ˈbætᵊldɔː) *n.* 1. ancient racket game 2. light racket used in this game (*also* **battledore and shuttlecock**)

batty (ˈbætɪ) *a. inf.* crazy, silly

THESAURUS

bastion bulwark, citadel, defence, fastness, fortress, mainstay, prop, rock, stronghold, support, tower of strength

bat bang, hit, rap, smack, strike, swat, thump, wallop (*Inf.*), whack

batch accumulation, aggregation, amount, assemblage, bunch, collection, crowd, group, lot, pack, quantity, set

bath 1. *n.* ablution, cleansing, douche, douse, scrubbing, shower, soak, soaping, sponging, tub, wash, washing 2. *v.* bathe, clean, douse, lave (*Archaic*), scrub down, shower, soak, soap, sponge, tub, wash

bathe 1. *v.* cleanse, cover, dunk, flood, immerse, moisten, rinse, soak, steep, suffuse, wash, wet 2. *n.* dip, swim

bathos anticlimax, false pathos, mawkishness, sentimentality

baton club, mace, rod, staff, stick, truncheon, wand

battalion army, brigade, company, contingent, division, force, horde, host, legion, multitude, regiment, squadron, throng

batten[1] board up, clamp down, cover up, fasten, fasten down, fix, nail down, secure, tighten

batten[2] fatten, flourish, gain, grow, increase, prosper, thrive wax

batter assault, bash, beat, belabour, break, buffet, dash against, lash, pelt, pound, pummel, smash, smite, thrash, wallop (*Inf.*)

battery 1. chain, ring, sequence, series, set, suite 2. assault, attack, beating, mayhem, onslaught, physical violence, thumping 3. artillery, cannon, cannonry, gun emplacements, guns

battle *n.* 1. action, attack, combat, encounter, engagement, fight, fray, hostilities, skirmish, war, warfare 2. agitation, campaign, clash, conflict, contest, controversy, crusade, debate, disagreement, dispute, strife, struggle ~*v.* 3. agitate, argue, clamour, combat, contend, contest, dispute, feud, fight, strive, struggle, war

battlefield battleground, combat zone, field, field of battle, front

bauble (ˈbɔːbᵊl) *n.* showy trinket

baulk (bɔːk) *see* BALK —**baulk line** *or* **balk line** *Billiards* straight line across table behind which cue balls start game

bauxite (ˈbɔːksaɪt) *n.* clay yielding aluminium

bawd (bɔːd) *n.* **1.** prostitute **2.** brothel keeper —ˈ**bawdy** *a.* obscene, lewd

bawl (bɔːl) *v.* **1.** cry **2.** shout —*n.* **3.** loud cry or shout

bay[1] (beɪ) *n.* **1.** wide inlet of sea **2.** space between two columns **3.** recess —**bay window** window projecting from wall and forming alcove of a room

bay[2] (beɪ) *n.* **1.** bark **2.** cry of hounds in pursuit —*vi.* **3.** bark —**at bay 1.** cornered **2.** at a distance

bay[3] (beɪ) *n.* **1.** laurel tree —*pl.* **2.** honorary crown of victory —ˈ**bayberry** *n.* tropical Amer. tree that yields oil —**bay rum** aromatic liquid, used in medicines *etc.*, orig. obtained by distilling leaves of bayberry tree with rum

bay[4] (beɪ) *a.* reddish-brown

bayonet (ˈbeɪənɪt) *n.* **1.** stabbing weapon fixed to rifle —*vt.* **2.** stab with this (ˈ**bayoneted**, ˈ**bayoneting**)

bazaar *or* **bazar** (bəˈzɑː) *n.* **1.** market, *esp.* in Orient **2.** sale of goods for charity

bazooka (bəˈzuːkə) *n.* antitank rocket launcher

B.B. 1. Boys' Brigade 2. (of pencils) double black

B.B.C. British Broadcasting Corporation

BC British Columbia

B.C. before Christ

BCG Bacillus Calmette-Guérin (anti-tuberculosis vaccine)

B.Com. *or* **B.Comm.** Bachelor of Commerce

B.D. Bachelor of Divinity

B/D bank draft

B.D.S. Bachelor of Dental Surgery

be (biː; *unstressed* bɪ) *vi.* **1.** live **2.** exist **3.** have a state or quality (I **am**, he **is**; we, you, they **are**, *pr. ind.* —**was**, *pl.* **were**, *pt.* —**been** *pp.* —ˈ**being** *pr.p.*)

Be *Chem.* beryllium

be- (*comb. form*) **1.** surround; cover, as in *befog* **2.** affect completely, as in *bedazzle* **3.** consider as; cause to be, as in *befriend* **4.** at, for, against, on, or over, as in *bewail, berate*

B.E. 1. bill of exchange 2. Bachelor of Engineering

beach (biːtʃ) *n.* **1.** shore of sea —*vt.* **2.** run (boat) on shore —ˈ**beachcomber** *n.* one who habitually searches shore debris for items of value —ˈ**beachhead** *n.* **1.** area on beach captured from enemy **2.** base for operations

beacon (ˈbiːkən) *n.* **1.** signal fire **2.** lighthouse, buoy **3.** (radio) signal used for navigation

bead (biːd) *n.* **1.** little ball pierced for threading on string of necklace, rosary *etc.* **2.** drop of liquid **3.** narrow moulding —ˈ**beaded** *a.* —ˈ**beading** *n.* —ˈ**beady** *a.* small and bright

beadle (ˈbiːdᵊl) *n. Hist.* church or parish officer

beagle (ˈbiːgᵊl) *n.* small hound

beak (biːk) *n.* **1.** projecting horny jaws of bird **2.** anything pointed or projecting **3.** *sl.* magistrate

beaker (ˈbiːkə) *n.* **1.** large drinking cup **2.** glass vessel used by chemists

beam (biːm) *n.* **1.** long squared piece of wood **2.** ship's cross timber, side, or width **3.** ray of light *etc.* **4.** broad smile **5.** bar of a balance —*vt.* **6.** aim (light, radio waves *etc.*) in a certain direction —*vi.* **7.** shine **8.** smile benignly —**on her beam-ends** (of vessel) heeled over through angle of 90° —**on one's beam-ends** out of resources; destitute

bean (biːn) *n.* any of various leguminous plants or their seeds —ˈ**beano** *n. inf.* celebration —ˈ**beanbag** *n.* **1.** small cloth bag filled with dried beans and thrown in games **2.** large cushion filled with foam rubber or polystyrene granules and used as seat —ˈ**beanfeast** *n.* **UK** *inf.* **1.** annual dinner given by employers to employees **2.** any festive occasion —**full of beans** *inf.* lively

bear[1] (bɛə) *vt.* **1.** carry **2.** support **3.** produce **4.** endure —*vi.* **5.** (*with* upon) press (upon) (**bore** *pt.*, **born** *or* **borne** *pp.*, ˈ**bearing** *pr.p.*) —ˈ**bearable** *a.* endurable; tolerable —ˈ**bearer** *n.*

THESAURUS

battleship capital ship, gunboat, man-of-war, ship of the line, warship

batty barmy (*Sl.*), bats (*Sl.*), bonkers (*Sl.*), cracked (*Sl.*), crackers (*Sl.*), cranky (*Inf.*), crazy, daft, dotty (*Sl.*), eccentric, insane, loony (*Sl.*), lunatic, mad, nuts (*Sl.*), nutty (*Sl.*), odd, peculiar, potty (*Inf.*), queer, screwy (*Inf.*), silly, touched

bauble bagatelle, gewgaw, gimcrack, kickshaw, knickknack, plaything, toy, trifle, trinket

bawd brothel-keeper, madam, pimp, procuress, prostitute, whore

bawdy blue, coarse, dirty, erotic, gross, indecent, indecorous, indelicate, lascivious, lecherous, lewd, libidinous, licentious, lustful, obscene, prurient, ribald, risqué, rude, salacious, suggestive, vulgar

bawl **1.** bellow, call, clamour, halloo, howl, roar, shout, vociferate, yell **2.** blubber, cry, sob, squall, wail, weep

bay[1] **1.** bight, cove, gulf, inlet, natural harbour, sound **2.** alcove, compartment, embrasure, niche, nook, opening, recess

bay[2] **1.** bark, bell, clamour, cry, growl, howl, yelp **2. at bay** caught, cornered, trapped

bayonet *v.* impale, knife, run through, spear, stab, stick, transfix

bazaar **1.** exchange, market, marketplace, mart **2.** bring-and-buy, fair, fête

be be alive, breathe, exist, inhabit, live

beach coast, littoral, margin, sands, seaboard (*Chiefly U.S.*), seashore, seaside, shingle, shore, strand, water's edge

beachcomber forager, loafer, scavenger, scrounger, tramp, vagabond, vagrant, wanderer

beacon beam, bonfire, flare, lighthouse, pharos, rocket, sign, signal, signal fire, smoke signal, watchtower

bead blob, bubble, dot, drop, droplet, globule, pellet, pill, spherule

beak **1.** bill, mandible, neb (*Archaic or dialect*), nib **2.** nose, proboscis, snout

beam *n.* **1.** girder, joist, plank, rafter, spar, support, timber **2.** bar, emission, gleam, glimmer, glint, glow, radiation, ray, shaft, streak, stream ~*v.* **3.** broadcast, emit, glare, gleam, glitter, glow, radiate, shine, transmit **4.** grin, laugh, smile

bear **1.** bring, carry, convey, move, take, tote, transport **2.** cherish, entertain, exhibit, harbour, have, hold, maintain, possess, shoulder, support, sustain,

bear[2] (bɛə) *n.* **1.** heavy carnivorous quadruped **2.** other bearlike animals, *eg* Aust. koala bear —**bear garden** scene of tumult —**bear hug 1.** wrestling hold in which arms are locked round opponent's chest and arms **2.** any similar tight embrace —**ˈbearskin** *n.* Guards' tall fur helmet

beard (bɪəd) *n.* **1.** hair on chin —*vt.* **2.** oppose boldly

bearing (ˈbɛərɪŋ) *n.* **1.** support or guide for mechanical part, *esp.* one reducing friction **2.** relevance **3.** behaviour **4.** direction **5.** relative position **6.** device on shield

beast (biːst) *n.* **1.** animal **2.** four-footed animal **3.** brutal man —**ˈbeastliness** *n.* —**ˈbeastly** *a.*

beat (biːt) *vt.* **1.** strike repeatedly **2.** overcome **3.** surpass **4.** stir vigorously with striking action **5.** flap (wings) **6.** make, wear (path) —*vi.* **7.** throb **8.** sail against wind (**beat** *pt.*, **ˈbeaten** *pp.*) —*n.* **9.** stroke **10.** pulsation **11.** appointed course **12.** basic rhythmic unit in piece of music —*a.* **13.** *sl.* exhausted —**ˈbeater** *n.* **1.** instrument for beating **2.** one who rouses game for shooters

beatify (bɪˈætɪfaɪ) *vt.* **1.** make happy **2.** *R.C.Ch.* pronounce in eternal happiness (first step in canonization) (**-fied, -fying**) —**beaˈtific** *a.* —**beatifiˈcation** *n.* —**beˈatitude** *n.* blessedness

beatnik (ˈbiːtnɪk) *n.* **1.** member of Beat Generation of 1950s, rebelling against conventional attitudes **2.** *inf.* person with long hair and shabby clothes

beau (bəʊ) *n.* suitor (*pl.* **-s, beaux** (bəʊ, bəʊz))

Beaufort scale (ˈbəʊfət) system of indicating wind strength (from 0, calm, to 17, hurricane)

beaujolais (ˈbəʊʒəleɪ) *n.* (*sometimes* **B-**) red or white wine from southern Burgundy, France

beauty (ˈbjuːtɪ) *n.* **1.** loveliness, grace **2.** beautiful person or thing —**ˈbeauteous** *a.* —**beauˈtician** *n.* one who works in beauty parlour —**ˈbeautiful** *a.* —**ˈbeautifully** *adv.* —**ˈbeautify** *vt.* —**beauty parlour** *or* **salon** establishment offering hairdressing, manicure *etc.* —**beauty sleep** *inf.* sleep, *esp.* before midnight —**beauty spot 1.** small dark-coloured patch worn on lady's face as adornment **2.** mole or similar natural mark on skin **3.** place of outstanding beauty

beaver (ˈbiːvə) *n.* **1.** amphibious rodent **2.** its fur —**beaver away** work hard

bebop (ˈbiːbɒp) *n. see* BOP (sense 1)

B.Ec. Bachelor of Economics

becalmed (bɪˈkɑːmd) *a.* (of ship) motionless through lack of wind

became (bɪˈkeɪm) *pt. of* BECOME

because (bɪˈkɒz, -ˈkəz) *conj.* since —**because of** on account of

béchamel sauce (beɪʃəˈmɛl) thick white sauce

bêche-de-mer (bɛʃdəˈmɛə) *n.* edible sea slug

beck[1] (bɛk) *n.* —**at someone's beck and call** subject to someone's slightest whim

beck[2] (bɛk) *n.* stream

beckon (ˈbɛkən) *v.* (*sometimes with* to) summon or lure by silent signal

become (bɪˈkʌm) *vi.* **1.** come to be —*vt.* **2.** suit (**beˈcame** *pt.*, **beˈcome** *pp.*, **beˈcoming** *pr.p.*) —**beˈcoming** *a.* **1.** suitable to **2.** proper

THESAURUS

uphold, weigh upon **3.** abide, admit, allow, brook, endure, permit, put up with (*Inf.*), stomach, suffer, tolerate, undergo **4.** beget, breed, bring forth, develop, engender, generate, give birth to, produce, yield

bearable admissible, endurable, manageable, passable, sufferable, supportable, sustainable, tolerable

beard 1. *n.* bristles, five-o'clock shadow, stubble, whiskers **2.** *v.* brave, confront, dare, defy, face, oppose

bearer agent, carrier, conveyor, messenger, porter, runner, servant

bearing 1. air, aspect, attitude, behaviour, carriage, demeanour, deportment, manner, mien, posture **2.** *Naut.* course, direction, point of compass **3.** application, connection, import, pertinence, reference, relation, relevance, significance

beast 1. animal, brute, creature **2.** barbarian, brute, fiend, monster, ogre, sadist, savage, swine

beastly barbarous, bestial, brutal, brutish, coarse, cruel, depraved, inhuman, monstrous, repulsive, sadistic, savage

beat *v.* **1.** bang, batter, break, bruise, buffet, cane, cudgel, drub, flog, hit, knock, lash, maul, pelt, pound, punch, strike, thrash, thwack, whip **2.** best, conquer, defeat, excel, outdo, outrun, outstrip, overcome, overwhelm, subdue, surpass, vanquish **3.** flap, flutter, palpitate, pound, pulsate, pulse, quake, quiver, shake, throb, thump, tremble, vibrate ~*n.* **4.** blow, hit, lash, punch, shake, slap, strike, stroke, swing, thump **5.** flutter, palpitation, pulsation, pulse, throb **6.** accent, cadence, measure, metre, rhythm, stress, time **7.** circuit, course, path, rounds, route, way ~*adj.* **8.** *Sl.* exhausted, fatigued, tired, wearied, worn out

beaten 1. baffled, cowed, defeated, disappointed, disheartened, frustrated, overcome, overwhelmed, thwarted, vanquished **2.** much travelled, trampled, trodden, well-trodden, well-used, worn **3.** blended, foamy, frothy, mixed, stirred, whipped, whisked

beau admirer, boyfriend, escort, fiancé, lover, suitor, swain, sweetheart

beautiful alluring, appealing, attractive, charming, comely, delightful, exquisite, fair, fine, good-looking, gorgeous, graceful, handsome, lovely, pleasing, radiant, ravishing, stunning (*Inf.*)

beautify adorn, array, bedeck, deck, decorate, embellish, enhance, garnish, gild, glamorize, grace, ornament

beauty 1. allure, attractiveness, bloom, charm, comeliness, elegance, exquisiteness, fairness, glamour, grace, handsomeness, loveliness, pulchritude, seemliness, symmetry **2.** belle, charmer, cracker (*Sl.*), goddess, good-looker, lovely (*Sl.*), stunner (*Inf.*), Venus

becalmed motionless, settled, still, stranded, stuck

because as, by reason of, in that, on account of, owing to, since, thanks to

beckon 1. bid, gesticulate, gesture, motion, nod, signal, summon, wave at **2.** allure, attract, call, coax, draw, entice, invite, lure, pull, tempt

become 1. alter to, be transformed into, change into, develop into, evolve into, grow into, mature into, metamorphose into, ripen into **2.** embellish, enhance, fit, flatter, grace, harmonize, ornament, set off, suit

becoming 1. attractive, comely, enhancing, flattering, graceful, neat, pretty, tasteful **2.** appropriate,

becquerel (bɛkəˈrɛl) *n.* SI unit of activity of radioactive source

bed (bɛd) *n.* **1.** piece of furniture for sleeping on **2.** garden plot **3.** place in which anything rests **4.** bottom of river **5.** layer, stratum —*vt.* **6.** lay in a bed **7.** plant (**-dd-**) —**ˈbedding** *n.* —**ˈbedbug** *n.* any of several blood-sucking wingless insects infesting dirty houses —**ˈbedclothes** *pl.n.* sheets, blankets, and other bed coverings —**bedding plant** immature plant that may be planted out in garden bed —**bed linen** sheets, pillowcases *etc.* —**ˈbedpan** *n.* container used as lavatory by bedridden people —**ˈbedridden** *a.* confined to bed by age or sickness —**ˈbedrock** *n.* **1.** solid rock beneath surface soil **2.** basic principles or facts —**ˈbedroom** *n.* —**ˈbedsitter** *n.* one-roomed flat —**ˈbedsore** *n.* chronic ulcer on skin of bedridden person, caused by prolonged pressure —**ˈbedspread** *n.* top cover on bed —**ˈbedstead** *n.* —**bed and breakfast** *chiefly* **UK** in hotel, boarding house *etc.*, overnight accommodation and breakfast

B.Ed. Bachelor of Education

bedaub (bɪˈdɔːb) *vt.* **1.** smear with something thick, sticky or dirty **2.** ornament in gaudy or vulgar fashion

bedeck (bɪˈdɛk) *vt.* cover with decorations; adorn

bedevil (bɪˈdɛvᵊl) *vt.* **1.** confuse **2.** torment —**beˈdevilment** *n.*

bedew (bɪˈdjuː) *vt.* wet as with dew

bedizen (bɪˈdaɪzᵊn, -ˈdɪzᵊn) *vt. obs.* dress gaudily or tastelessly —**beˈdizenment** *n.*

bedlam (ˈbɛdləm) *n.* noisy confused scene

Bedlington terrier (ˈbɛdlɪŋtən) woolly-coated terrier with convex head profile

Bedouin *or* **Beduin** (ˈbɛduɪn) *n.* **1.** member of nomadic Arab race —*a.* **2.** nomadic

bedraggle (bɪˈdræɡᵊl) *vt.* dirty by trailing in wet or mud —**beˈdraggled** *a.*

Beds. (bɛdz) Bedfordshire

bee[1] (biː) *n.* insect that makes honey —**bee-eater** *n.* insect-eating bird —**ˈbeehive** *n.* —**ˈbeeline** *n.* shortest route —**ˈbeeswax** *n.* wax secreted by bees —**ˈbeeswing** *n.* filmy crust of tartar that forms in some wines after long keeping in bottle

bee[2] (biː) *n. chiefly* **US** social gathering for specific purpose, as to carry out communal task

Beeb (biːb) *n. inf.* the B.B.C.

beech (biːtʃ) *n.* **1.** European tree with smooth greyish bark and small nuts **2.** its wood —**ˈbeechen** *a.*

beef (biːf) *n.* **1.** flesh of cattle raised and killed for eating **2.** *inf.* complaint —*vi.* **3.** *inf.* complain —**ˈbeefy** *a.* fleshy, stolid —**beeves** *pl.n.* cattle —**ˈbeefburger** *n.* *see* HAMBURGER —**ˈbeefeater** *n.* **1.** yeoman of the guard **2.** warder of Tower of London —**beef tea** drink made by boiling pieces of lean beef

Beelzebub (bɪˈɛlzɪbʌb) *n.* Satan or any devil

been (biːn, bɪn) *pp. of* BE

beep (biːp) *n.* **1.** short, loud sound of car horn *etc.* —*vi.* **2.** make this sound

beer (bɪə) *n.* fermented alcoholic drink made from hops and malt —**ˈbeery** *a.* —**beer parlour C** licensed place where beer is sold to the public —**beer and skittles** *inf.* enjoyment or pleasure

beestings, biestings, *or U.S.* **beastings** (ˈbiːstɪŋz) *pl.n.* (*with sing. v.*) first milk secreted by cow or similar animal after giving birth

beet (biːt) *n.* any of various plants with root used for food or extraction of sugar —**ˈbeetroot** *n.* variety of beet that has bulbous dark red root that may be eaten as vegetable

beetle[1] (ˈbiːtᵊl) *n.* class of insect with hard upper-wing cases closed over the back for protection —**beetle-browed** *a.* with prominent brows

beetle[2] (ˈbiːtᵊl) *vi.* **1.** overhang; jut —*a.* **2.** overhanging; prominent

befall (bɪˈfɔːl) *v.* happen (to) (**beˈfell, beˈfallen**)

befit (bɪˈfɪt) *vt.* be suitable to (**-tt-**) —**beˈfittingly** *adv.*

befog (bɪˈfɒɡ) *vt.* perplex, confuse (**-gg-**)

before (bɪˈfɔː) *prep.* **1.** in front of **2.** in presence of **3.** in preference to **4.** earlier than —*adv.* **5.** earlier **6.** in front —*conj.* **7.** sooner than —**beˈforehand** *adv.* previously

befoul (bɪˈfaʊl) *vt.* make filthy

befriend (bɪˈfrɛnd) *vt.* make friend of

THESAURUS

befitting, *comme il faut*, compatible, congruous, decent, decorous, fit, fitting, in keeping, meet (*Archaic*), proper, seemly, suitable, worthy

bed *n.* **1.** bedstead, berth, bunk, cot, couch, divan, pallet **2.** area, border, garden, patch, plot, row, strip **3.** base, bottom, foundation, groundwork, substratum ~*v.* **4.** base, embed, establish, fix, found, implant, insert, plant, settle, set up

bedclothes bedding, bed linen, blankets, coverlets, covers, eiderdowns, pillowcases, pillows, quilts, sheets

bedeck adorn, array, bedight (*Archaic*), bedizen (*Archaic*), decorate, embellish, festoon, garnish, ornament, trim

bedevil afflict, annoy, confound, distress, fret, frustrate, harass, irk, irritate, pester, plague, torment, torture, trouble, vex, worry

bedlam chaos, clamour, commotion, confusion, furore, hubbub, madhouse (*Inf.*), noise, pandemonium, tumult, turmoil, uproar

bedraggled dirty, dishevelled, disordered, drenched, dripping, messy, muddied, muddy, sodden, soiled, stained, sullied, unkempt, untidy

bedridden confined, confined to bed, flat on one's back, incapacitated, laid up (*Inf.*)

bedrock 1. bed, bottom, foundation, nadir, rock bottom, substratum, substructure **2.** basics, basis, core, essentials, fundamentals, roots

beef *Sl.* complaint, criticism, dispute, grievance, gripe (*Inf.*), grouse, grumble, objection, protestation

beefy *Inf.* **1.** brawny, bulky, burly, hulking, muscular, stalwart, stocky, strapping, sturdy **2.** chubby, corpulent, fat, fleshy, heavy, obese, overweight, paunchy, plump, podgy, portly, pudgy, rotund

beetle, beetling *adj.* jutting, leaning over, overhanging, pendent, projecting, protruding, sticking out, swelling over

befall bechance, betide, chance, come to pass, ensue, fall, follow, happen, materialize, occur, supervene, take place, transpire (*Inf.*)

before 1. *adv.* ahead, earlier, formerly, in advance, in front, previously, sooner **2.** *prep.* earlier than, in advance of, in front of, in the presence of, prior to

befuddle (bɪˈfʌdˀl) *vt.* **1.** confuse **2.** make stupid with drink —**beˈfuddlement** *n.*

beg (bɛg) *vt.* **1.** ask earnestly, beseech —*vi.* **2.** ask for or live on alms (**-gg-**) —**ˈbeggar** *n.* —**ˈbeggarly** *a.*

began (bɪˈgæn) *pt. of* BEGIN

beget (bɪˈgɛt) *vt.* produce, generate (**beˈgot, beˈgat** *pt.*, **beˈgotten, beˈgot** *pp.*, **beˈgetting** *pr.p.*) —**beˈgetter** *n.*

begin (bɪˈgɪn) *v.* **1.** (cause to) start —*vt.* **2.** originate **3.** initiate (**beˈgan, beˈgun, beˈginning**) —**beˈginner** *n.* novice —**beˈginning** *n.*

begone (bɪˈgɒn) *interj.* go away

begonia (bɪˈgəʊnjə) *n.* genus of tropical plant

begot (bɪˈgɒt) *pt./pp. of* BEGET

begrudge (bɪˈgrʌdʒ) *vt.* grudge, envy someone the possession of

beguile (bɪˈgaɪl) *vt.* **1.** charm, fascinate **2.** amuse **3.** deceive —**beˈguiler** *n.*

beguine (bɪˈgiːn) *n.* **1.** dance of S Amer. origin **2.** music in rhythm of this dance

begum (ˈbeɪgəm) *n. esp.* in India, Muslim woman of high rank

begun (bɪˈgʌn) *pp. of* BEGIN

behalf (bɪˈhɑːf) *n.* favour, benefit, interest (*esp. in* **on behalf of**)

behave (bɪˈheɪv) *vi.* act, function in particular way —**beˈhaviour** *or U.S.* **beˈhavior** *n.* conduct —**beˈhaviourism** *or U.S.* **beˈhaviorism** *n.* school of psychology that regards observable behaviour as the only valid subject for study —**behave oneself** conduct oneself (well)

behead (bɪˈhɛd) *vt.* cut off head of

beheld (bɪˈhɛld) *pt./pp. of* BEHOLD

behemoth (bɪˈhiːmɒθ) *n.* **1.** *Bible* gigantic beast described in Job **2.** huge person or thing

behest (bɪˈhɛst) *n.* charge, command

behind (bɪˈhaɪnd) *prep.* **1.** further back or earlier than **2.** in support of —*adv.* **3.** in the rear —**beˈhindhand** *a./adv.* **1.** in arrears **2.** tardy

behold (bɪˈhəʊld) *vt.* watch, see (**beˈheld** *pt.*, **beˈheld, beˈholden** *pp.*) —**beˈholder** *n.*

beholden (bɪˈhəʊldˀn) *a.* bound in gratitude

behove (bɪˈhəʊv) *vt.* (*only impers.*) be fit, necessary for

beige (beɪʒ) *n.* **1.** undyed woollen cloth **2.** its colour

being (ˈbiːɪŋ) *n.* **1.** existence **2.** that which exists **3.** creature —*v.* **4.** *pr.p. of* BE

bejewel (bɪˈdʒuːəl) *vt.* decorate as with jewels (**-ll-**)

bel (bɛl) *n.* unit for comparing two power levels

belabour *or U.S.* **belabor** (bɪˈleɪbə) *vt.* beat soundly

belated (bɪˈleɪtɪd) *a.* **1.** late **2.** too late

belay (bɪˈleɪ) *vt.* fasten (rope) to peg, pin *etc.*

belch (bɛltʃ) *vi.* **1.** void wind by mouth —*vt.* **2.** eject violently **3.** cast up —*n.* **4.** emission of wind *etc.*

beldam *or* **beldame** (ˈbɛldəm) *n. obs.* old woman

THESAURUS

beforehand ahead of time, already, before, before now, earlier, in advance, in anticipation, previously, sooner

befriend advise, aid, assist, back, benefit, encourage, favour, help, patronize, side with, stand by, succour, support, sustain, uphold, welcome

beg 1. beseech, crave, desire, entreat, implore, importune, petition, plead, pray, request, solicit, supplicate **2.** cadge, call for alms, scrounge, seek charity, solicit charity, sponge on

beggar *n.* **1.** cadger, mendicant, scrounger (*Inf.*), sponger (*Inf.*), supplicant, tramp, vagrant **2.** bankrupt, down-and-out, pauper, starveling

beggarly abject, base, contemptible, despicable, destitute, impoverished, inadequate, indigent, low, meagre, mean, needy, niggardly, pitiful, poor, poverty-stricken, vile, wretched

begin 1. commence, embark on, inaugurate, initiate, instigate, institute, prepare, set about, set on foot, start **2.** appear, arise, be born, come into being, come into existence, commence, crop up (*Inf.*), dawn, emerge, happen, originate, spring, start

beginner amateur, apprentice, fledgling, freshman, greenhorn (*Inf.*), initiate, learner, neophyte, novice, recruit, starter, student, tenderfoot, trainee, tyro

beginning 1. birth, commencement, inauguration, inception, initiation, onset, opening, origin, outset, preface, prelude, rise, rudiments, source, start, starting point **2.** embryo, fountainhead, germ, root, seed

begrudge be jealous, be reluctant, be stingy, envy, grudge, resent

beguile 1. befool, cheat, deceive, delude, dupe, fool, hoodwink, impose on, mislead, trick **2.** amuse, charm, cheer, delight, distract, divert, engross, entertain, occupy, solace

behalf account, advantage, benefit, defence, good, interest, part, profit, sake, side, support

behave 1. act, function, operate, perform, run, work **2.** act correctly, conduct oneself properly, mind one's manners

behaviour actions, bearing, carriage, comportment, conduct, demeanour, deportment, manner, manners, ways

behest bidding, charge, command, commandment, decree, dictate, direction, expressed desire, injunction, instruction, mandate, order, precept, wish

behind *prep.* **1.** after, at the back of, at the rear of, following, later than **2.** backing, for, in agreement, on the side of, supporting ~*adv.* **3.** after, afterwards, following, in the wake (of), next, subsequently

behindhand backward, behind time, dilatory, late, remiss, slow, tardy

behold *v.* consider, contemplate, discern, eye, look at, observe, perceive, regard, scan, see, survey, view, watch, witness

beholden bound, grateful, indebted, obligated, obliged, owing, under obligation

beige biscuit, buff, *café au lait,* camel, cinnamon, coffee, cream, ecru, fawn, khaki, mushroom, neutral, oatmeal, sand, tan

being 1. actuality, animation, existence, life, living, reality **2.** entity, essence, nature, soul, spirit, substance **3.** animal, beast, body, creature, human being, individual, living thing, mortal, thing

belabour batter, beat, flog, lambaste, thrash, whip

belated behindhand, behind time, delayed, late, overdue, tardy

belch 1. burp (*Inf.*), eruct, eructate, hiccup **2.** discharge, disgorge, emit, erupt, give off, gush, spew forth, vent, vomit

beleaguer (bɪˈliːgə) *vt.* besiege

belfry (ˈbɛlfrɪ) *n.* bell tower

Belial (ˈbiːlɪəl) *n.* the devil, Satan

belie (bɪˈlaɪ) *vt.* **1.** contradict **2.** misrepresent (**beˈlied** *pt./pp.*, **beˈlying** *pr.p.*)

believe (bɪˈliːv) *vt.* **1.** regard as true or real —*vi.* **2.** have faith —**beˈlief** *n.* —**beˈlievable** *a.* credible —**beˈliever** *n. esp.* one of same religious faith

Belisha beacon (bəˈliːʃə) flashing light in orange globe marking a pedestrian crossing

belittle (bɪˈlɪtᵊl) *vt.* regard, speak of, as having little worth or value —**beˈlittlement** *n.*

bell (bɛl) *n.* **1.** hollow metal instrument giving ringing sound when struck **2.** electrical device emitting ring or buzz as signal —**bell-bottomed** *a.* —**bell-bottoms** *pl.n.* trousers that flare from knee —**ˈbellboy** *n.* pageboy in hotel —**bell jar** bell-shaped glass cover to protect flower arrangements *etc.* or to cover apparatus in experiments (*also* **bell glass**) —**bell metal** alloy of copper and tin, used in casting bells —**ˈbellwether** *n.* **1.** sheep that leads flock, oft. bearing bell **2.** leader, *esp.* one followed blindly

belladonna (bɛləˈdɒnə) *n.* deadly nightshade

belle (bɛl) *n.* beautiful woman, reigning beauty

belles-lettres (*Fr.* bɛlˈlɛtr) *pl.n.* (*with sing. v.*) literary works, *esp.* essays and poetry —**belˈletrist** *n.*

bellicose (ˈbɛlɪkəʊs, -kəʊz) *a.* warlike

belligerent (bɪˈlɪdʒərənt) *a.* **1.** hostile, aggressive **2.** making war —*n.* **3.** warring person or nation —**belˈligerence** *n.*

bellow (ˈbɛləʊ) *v.* **1.** roar like bull **2.** shout —*n.* **3.** roar of bull **4.** any deep cry or shout

bellows (ˈbɛləʊz) *pl.n.* instrument for creating stream of air

belly (ˈbɛlɪ) *n.* **1.** part of body which contains intestines **2.** stomach —*v.* **3.** swell out (**ˈbellied, ˈbellying**) —**belly ache** *inf.* stomachache —**ˈbellyache** *vi. sl.* complain repeatedly —**ˈbellybutton** *n. inf.* navel (*also* **tummy button**) —**belly dance** sensuous dance performed by women, with undulating movements of abdomen —**belly-dance** *vi.* perform belly dance —**belly flop** dive into water in which body lands horizontally —**belly-flop** *vi.* perform belly flop —**ˈbellyful** *n.* **1.** as much as one wants or can eat **2.** *sl.* more than one can tolerate —**belly laugh** *inf.* hearty laugh

belong (bɪˈlɒŋ) *vi.* **1.** (*with* to) be the property or attribute (of) **2.** (*with* to) be a member or inhabitant (of) **3.** have an allotted place **4.** pertain —**beˈlongings** *pl.n.* personal possessions

beloved (bɪˈlʌvɪd, -ˈlʌvd) *a.* **1.** much loved —*n.* **2.** dear one

below (bɪˈləʊ) *adv.* **1.** beneath —*prep.* **2.** lower than

belt (bɛlt) *n.* **1.** band **2.** girdle **3.** zone or district —*vt.* **4.** surround, fasten with belt **5.** mark with band **6.** *inf.* thrash

beluga (bɪˈluːgə) *n.* large white sturgeon

belvedere (ˈbɛlvɪdɪə, bɛlvɪˈdɪə) *n.* building, such as summerhouse, sited to command fine view

B.E.M. British Empire Medal

bemoan (bɪˈməʊn) *vt.* grieve over (loss *etc.*)

bemuse (bɪˈmjuːz) *vt.* confuse, bewilder

ben[1] (bɛn) *Scot. n.* **1.** inner room in cottage —*prep./adv.* **2.** in; within; inside

ben[2] (bɛn) *n. Scot., Irish* mountain peak

bench (bɛntʃ) *n.* **1.** long seat **2.** seat or body of judges *etc.* —*vt.* **3.** provide with benches —**bench mark** fixed point, criterion

bend (bɛnd) *v.* **1.** (cause to) form a curve (**bent** *pt./pp.*) —*n.* **2.** curve —*pl.* **3.** decompression sickness —**ˈbender** *n. inf.* drinking bout —**bend sinister** *Her.* diagonal line on shield, typically indicating bastard line

beneath (bɪˈniːθ) *prep.* **1.** under, lower than —*adv.* **2.** below

Benedictine (bɛnɪˈdɪktiːn, -taɪn) *n.* **1.** monk or nun of order of Saint Benedict **2.** (bɛnɪˈdɪktiːn) liqueur first made at Benedictine monastery

benediction (bɛnɪˈdɪkʃən) *n.* invocation of divine blessing

benefit (ˈbɛnɪfɪt) *n.* **1.** advantage, favour, profit, good

THESAURUS

belief 1. admission, assent, assurance, confidence, conviction, credit, feeling, impression, judgment, notion, opinion, persuasion, presumption, reliance, theory, trust, view **2.** credence, credo, creed, doctrine, dogma, faith, ideology, principles, tenet

believable acceptable, authentic, credible, creditable, imaginable, likely, plausible, possible, probable, reliable, trustworthy

believe accept, be certain of, be convinced of, count on, credit, depend on, have faith in, hold, place confidence in, presume true, rely on, swear by, trust

believer adherent, convert, devotee, disciple, follower, proselyte, supporter, upholder, zealot

bellow bawl, call, clamour, cry, howl, roar, scream, shout, shriek, yell

belly 1. *n.* abdomen, breadbasket (*Sl.*), corporation (*Inf.*), gut, insides (*Inf.*), paunch, potbelly, stomach, tummy, vitals **2.** *v.* billow, bulge, fill, spread, swell, swell out

belong 1. *With* **to** be at the disposal of, be held by, be owned by, be the property of **2.** *With* **to** be affiliated to, be allied to, be a member of, be associated with, be included in **3.** attach to, be connected with, be fitting, be part of, fit, go with, have as a proper place, pertain to, relate to

belongings accoutrements, chattels, effects, gear, goods, paraphernalia, personal property, possessions, stuff, things

beloved admired, adored, cherished, darling, dear, dearest, loved, pet, precious, prized, revered, sweet, treasured, worshipped

below *adv.* beneath, down, lower, under, underneath

belt 1. band, cincture, cummerbund, girdle, girth, sash, waistband **2.** *Geog.* area, district, layer, region, stretch, strip, tract, zone

bench 1. form, pew, seat, settle, stall **2.** court, courtroom, judge, judges, judiciary, magistrate, magistrates, tribunal

bend 1. *v.* bow, buckle, contort, crouch, curve, deflect, diverge, flex, incline, incurvate, lean, stoop, swerve, turn, twist, veer, warp **2.** *n.* angle, arc, bow, corner, crook, curve, hook, loop, turn, twist, zigzag

beneath *adv.* below, in a lower place, underneath

beneficial advantageous, benign, favourable, gainful, healthful, helpful, profitable, salubrious, salutary, serviceable, useful, valuable, wholesome

2. money paid by a government *etc.* to unemployed *etc.* —*vt.* 3. do good to —*vi.* 4. receive good (**ˈbenefited, ˈbenefiting**) —**beneˈfaction** *n.* —**ˈbenefactor** *n.* 1. one who helps or does good to others 2. patron (**ˈbenefactress** *fem.*) —**ˈbenefice** *n.* an ecclesiastical living —**beˈneficence** *n.* —**beˈneficent** *a.* 1. doing good 2. kind —**beˈneficently** *adv.* —**beneˈficial** *a.* advantageous, helpful —**beneˈficially** *adv.* —**beneˈficiary** *n.* —**benefit society US** *see* **friendly society** *at* FRIEND

benevolent (bɪˈnɛvələnt) *a.* 1. kindly 2. charitable —**beˈnevolence** *n.* —**beˈnevolently** *adv.*

Bengali (bɛnˈgɔːlɪ, bɛŋ-) *n.* 1. member of people living chiefly in Bangladesh and West Bengal 2. their language —*a.* 3. of Bengal, Bengalis or their language

benighted (bɪˈnaɪtɪd) *a.* ignorant, uncultured

benign (bɪˈnaɪn) *a.* 1. kindly 2. mild 3. favourable 4. *Pathol.* (of tumour *etc.*) not malignant —**benignancy** (bɪˈnɪgnənsɪ) *n.* —**benignant** (bɪˈnɪgnənt) *a.* —**benignantly** (bɪˈnɪgnəntlɪ) *adv.* —**benignity** (bɪˈnɪgnɪtɪ) *n.* —**beˈnignly** *adv.*

benison (ˈbɛnɪzᵊn, -sᵊn) *n. obs.* blessing

bent (bɛnt) *v.* 1. *pt./pp. of* BEND —*a.* 2. curved 3. resolved (on) 4. *inf.* corrupt 5. *inf.* deviant 6. *inf.* crazy —*n.* 7. inclination, personal propensity —**ˈbentwood** *n.* wood bent in moulds after being heated by steaming

bent grass low-growing perennial grass which has spreading panicle of tiny flowers

benumb (bɪˈnʌm) *vt.* make numb, deaden

Benzedrine (ˈbɛnzɪdriːn, -drɪn) *n.* **R** amphetamine

benzene (ˈbɛnziːn) *n.* one of group of related flammable liquids used in chemistry and as solvents, cleaning agents *etc.*

benzoin (ˈbɛnzɔɪn, -zəʊɪn) *n.* gum resin obtained from various tropical Asian trees, used in ointments, perfume *etc.*

bequeath (bɪˈkwiːð, -ˈkwiːθ) *vt.* leave (property *etc.*) by will —**bequest** (bɪˈkwɛst) *n.* 1. bequeathing 2. legacy

berate (bɪˈreɪt) *vt.* scold harshly

Berber (ˈbɜːbə) *n.* 1. member of Caucasoid Muslim people of N Afr. 2. language of this people —*a.* 3. of this people or their language

berberis (ˈbɜːbərɪs) *n.* shrub with red berries

berceuse (*Fr.* bɛrˈsøːz) *n.* 1. lullaby 2. instrumental piece suggestive of this

bereave (bɪˈriːv) *vt.* (*usu. with* of) deprive (of), *esp.* by death (**-ˈreaved, -ˈreft** *pt./pp.*) —**beˈreavement** *n.* loss, *esp.* by death

beret (ˈbɛreɪ) *n.* round, closefitting hat

berg (bɜːg) *n.* 1. large mass of ice 2. **SA** mountain

bergamot (ˈbɜːgəmɒt) *n.* 1. type of pear with strong flavour 2. type of orange 3. fragrant oil produced from this, used in perfumery

beriberi (bɛrɪˈbɛrɪ) *n.* tropical disease caused by vitamin B deficiency

berk (bɜːk) *n.* **UK** *sl.* stupid person

berkelium (bɜːˈkiːlɪəm, ˈbɜːklɪəm) *n.* radioactive transuranic element

Berks. (bɑːks) Berkshire

Bermuda shorts (bəˈmjuːdə) close-fitting shorts that come down to knees

berry (ˈbɛrɪ) *n.* 1. small juicy stoneless fruit —*vi.* 2. look for or pick berries

berserk (bəˈzɜːk, -ˈsɜːk) *a.* frenzied

berth (bɜːθ) *n.* 1. ship's mooring place 2. place to sleep in ship or train —*vt.* 3. moor

beryl (ˈbɛrɪl) *n.* variety of crystalline mineral including aquamarine and emerald

beryllium (bɛˈrɪlɪəm) *n.* corrosion-resistant toxic metallic element

beseech (bɪˈsiːtʃ) *vt.* entreat, implore (**beˈsought** *pt./pp.*)

beset (bɪˈsɛt) *vt.* assail, surround with danger, problems (**beˈset, beˈsetting**)

beside (bɪˈsaɪd) *prep.* 1. by the side of, near 2. distinct from —**beˈsides** *adv./prep.* in addition (to)

besiege (bɪˈsiːdʒ) *vt.* surround (with armed forces *etc.*)

besmirch (bɪˈsmɜːtʃ) *vt.* 1. make dirty; soil 2. reduce brightness of 3. sully

besom (ˈbiːzəm) *n.* broom, *esp.* one made of bundle of twigs tied to handle

THESAURUS

benefit 1. *n.* advantage, aid, asset, assistance, avail, betterment, blessing, boon, favour, gain, good, help, interest, profit, use 2. *v.* advance, advantage, aid, ameliorate, assist, avail, better, enhance, further, improve, profit, promote, serve

bent *adj.* 1. angled, arched, bowed, crooked, curved, hunched, stooped, twisted 2. *With* **on** determined, disposed, fixed, inclined, insistent, predisposed, resolved, set ~*n.* 3. ability, aptitude, facility, faculty, flair, forte, inclination, knack, leaning, penchant, preference, proclivity, propensity, talent, tendency

bequeath bestow, commit, endow, entrust, give, grant, hand down, impart, leave to by will, pass on, transmit, will

bequest bequeathal, bestowal, dower, endowment, estate, gift, heritage, inheritance, legacy, settlement, trust

bereave afflict, deprive of kindred, dispossess, divest, make destitute, strip, take away from, widow

bereavement affliction, death, deprivation, loss, misfortune, tribulation

berserk crazy, enraged, frantic, frenzied, insane, mad, maniacal, manic, rabid, raging, uncontrollable, violent, wild

berth *n.* 1. bed, billet, bunk, cot (*Naut.*), hammock 2. anchorage, dock, harbour, haven, pier, port, quay, slip, wharf ~*v.* 3. *Naut.* anchor, dock, drop anchor, land, moor, tie up

beseech adjure, ask, beg, call upon, crave, entreat, implore, importune, petition, plead, pray, solicit, sue, supplicate

beside abreast of, adjacent to, alongside, at the side of, close to, near, nearby, neighbouring, next door to, next to, overlooking

besides 1. *adv.* also, as well, further, furthermore, in addition, moreover, otherwise, too, what's more 2. *prep.* in addition to, over and above

besiege beleaguer, beset, blockade, confine, encircle, encompass, environ, hedge in, hem in, invest (*Rare*), lay siege to, shut in, surround

besotted 1. befuddled, drunk, intoxicated, stupefied 2. doting, hypnotized, infatuated, smitten, spellbound 3. confused, foolish, muddled, witless

besotted (bɪˈsɒtɪd) *a.* **1.** drunk **2.** foolish **3.** infatuated

besought (bɪˈsɔːt) *pt./pp. of* BESEECH

bespangle (bɪˈspæŋgˈl) *vt.* cover with or as if with spangles

bespatter (bɪˈspætə) *vt.* **1.** splash, as with dirty water **2.** defile; besmirch

bespeak (bɪˈspiːk) *vt.* engage beforehand (**beˈspoke** *pt.*, **beˈspoke, beˈspoken** *pp.*) —**beˈspoke** *a.* **1.** (of garments) made to order **2.** selling such garments

Bessemer process (ˈbɛsɪmə) process for producing steel by blowing air through molten pig iron in refractory-lined furnace to remove impurities

best (bɛst) *a./adv.* **1.** *sup. of* GOOD *and* WELL —*vt.* **2.** defeat —**best man** (male) attendant of bridegroom at wedding —**best seller 1.** book or other product that has sold in great numbers **2.** author of one or more such books *etc.*

bestial (ˈbɛstɪəl) *a.* like a beast, brutish —**bestiˈality** *n.*

bestiary (ˈbɛstɪərɪ) *n.* moralizing medieval collection of descriptions of real and/or mythical animals

bestir (bɪˈstɜː) *vt.* rouse to activity

bestow (bɪˈstəʊ) *vt.* give, confer —**beˈstowal** *n.*

bestrew (bɪˈstruː) *vt.* scatter over (surface)

bestride (bɪˈstraɪd) *vt.* **1.** sit or stand over with legs apart **2.** mount (horse) (**beˈstrode, beˈstridden, beˈstriding**)

bet (bɛt) *v.* **1.** agree to pay (money *etc.*) if wrong (or win if right) in guessing result of contest *etc.* (**bet** *or* **ˈbetted** *pt./pp.*, **ˈbetting** *pr.p.*) —*n.* **2.** money risked in this way

beta (ˈbiːtə) *n.* **1.** second letter in Gr. alphabet (Β or β) **2.** second in group or series

beta-blocker *n.* drug that decreases activity of heart: used in treatment of high blood pressure and angina pectoris

betake (bɪˈteɪk) *vt.* —**betake oneself** go; move

beta particle electron or positron emitted by nucleus during radioactive decay

betatron (ˈbiːtətrɒn) *n.* particle accelerator for producing high-energy beams of electrons by magnetic induction

betel (ˈbiːtˈl) *n.* species of pepper, chewed in parts of Asia as a narcotic —**betel nut** the nut of the areca palm

bête noire (bɛt ˈnwaːr) *Fr.* pet aversion

bethink (bɪˈθɪŋk) *obs., dial. v.* **1.** cause (oneself) to consider or meditate —*vt.* **2.** (*oft. with* of) remind (oneself)

betide (bɪˈtaɪd) *v.* happen (to)

betimes (bɪˈtaɪmz) *adv. obs.* **1.** in good time; early **2.** soon

betoken (bɪˈtəʊkən) *vt.* be a sign of

betony (ˈbɛtənɪ) *n.* plant with reddish-purple flower spike

betray (bɪˈtreɪ) *vt.* **1.** be disloyal to, *esp.* by assisting an enemy **2.** reveal, divulge **3.** show signs of —**beˈtrayal** *n.* —**beˈtrayer** *n.*

betroth (bɪˈtrəʊð) *vt.* promise to marry —**beˈtrothal** *n.* —**beˈtrothed** *n./a.*

better (ˈbɛtə) *a./adv.* **1.** *comp. of* GOOD *and* WELL —*v.* **2.** improve —**ˈbetterment** *n.*

between (bɪˈtwiːn) *prep./adv.* **1.** in the intermediate part, in space or time **2.** indicating reciprocal relation or comparison

betwixt (bɪˈtwɪkst) *prep./adv. obs.* between

THESAURUS

best *adj.* **1.** chief, finest, first, first-class, first-rate, foremost, highest, leading, most excellent, outstanding, perfect, pre-eminent, principal, superlative, supreme, unsurpassed **2.** advantageous, apt, correct, golden, most desirable, most fitting, right **3.** greatest, largest, most ~*adv.* **4.** advantageously, attractively, excellently, most fortunately **5.** extremely, greatly, most deeply, most fully, most highly ~*v.* **6.** beat, conquer, defeat, get the better of, lick (*Inf.*), outclass, outdo, surpass, thrash, triumph over, trounce

bestial animal, barbaric, barbarous, beastlike, beastly, brutal, brutish, carnal, degraded, depraved, gross, inhuman, low, savage, sensual, sordid, vile

bestow accord, allot, apportion, award, commit, confer, donate, entrust, give, grant, honour with, impart, lavish, present, render to

bestride bestraddle, bridge, dominate, extend, mount, span, step over, straddle, tower over

bet 1. *n.* ante, gamble, hazard, long shot, pledge, risk, speculation, stake, venture, wager **2.** *v.* chance, gamble, hazard, pledge, punt (*Brit.*), put money on, risk, speculate, stake, venture, wager

bête noire abomination, anathema, aversion, bugbear, pet hate

betide bechance, befall, chance, come to pass, crop up (*Inf.*), ensue, happen, occur, overtake, supervene, take place, transpire (*Inf.*)

betimes anon, beforehand, before long, early, first thing, in good time, punctually, seasonably, soon

betoken augur, bespeak, bode, declare, denote, evidence, indicate, manifest, mark, portend, presage, prognosticate, promise, represent, signify, suggest, typify

betray 1. be disloyal (treacherous, unfaithful), break one's promise, break with, double-cross (*Inf.*), inform on *or* against, sell down the river (*Inf.*), sell out (*Inf.*) **2.** blurt out, disclose, divulge, evince, expose, give away, lay bare, let slip, manifest, reveal, show, tell, tell on, uncover, unmask

betrayal 1. deception, disloyalty, double-cross (*Inf.*), double-dealing, duplicity, falseness, perfidy, sell-out (*Inf.*), treachery, treason, trickery, unfaithfulness **2.** blurting out, disclosure, divulgence, giving away, revelation, telling

better *adj.* **1.** bigger, excelling, finer, fitter, greater, higher quality, larger, more appropriate (desirable, expert, fitting, suitable, useful, valuable), preferable, superior, surpassing, worthier **2.** cured, fitter, fully recovered, healthier, improving, less ill, mending, more healthy, on the mend (*Inf.*), progressing, recovering, stronger, well **3.** bigger, greater, larger, longer ~*adv.* **4.** in a more excellent manner, in a superior way, more advantageously (attractively, competently, completely, effectively, thoroughly), to a greater degree ~*v.* **5.** advance, ameliorate, amend, correct, enhance, forward, further, improve, meliorate, mend, promote, raise, rectify, reform

between amidst, among, betwixt, halfway, in the middle of, mid

bevel (ˈbɛvᵊl) *n.* **1.** surface not at right angle to another **2.** slant —*vi.* **3.** slope, slant —*vt.* **4.** cut on slant (-ll-) —*a.* **5.** slanted —**bevel gear** gear having teeth cut into conical surface

beverage (ˈbɛvərɪdʒ, ˈbɛvrɪdʒ) *n.* drink

bevy (ˈbɛvɪ) *n.* flock or group

bewail (bɪˈweɪl) *vt.* lament

beware (bɪˈwɛə) *v.* be on one's guard (against), be wary (of)

bewilder (bɪˈwɪldə) *vt.* puzzle, confuse —**beˈwildering** *a.* —**beˈwilderingly** *adv.* —**beˈwilderment** *n.*

bewitch (bɪˈwɪtʃ) *vt.* **1.** cast spell over **2.** charm, fascinate —**beˈwitching** *a.* —**beˈwitchingly** *adv.*

bey (beɪ) *n.* **1.** in Ottoman Empire, title given to provincial governors **2.** in modern Turkey, title of address, corresponding to *Mr.* (*also* **beg**)

beyond (bɪˈjɒnd) *adv.* **1.** farther away **2.** besides —*prep.* **3.** on the farther side of **4.** later than **5.** surpassing, out of reach of

bezel (ˈbɛzᵊl) *n.* **1.** sloping face adjacent to working edge of cutting tool **2.** oblique faces of cut gem **3.** grooved ring or part holding watch crystal *etc.*

bezique (bɪˈziːk) *n.* **1.** card game for two or more players **2.** in this game, queen of spades and jack of diamonds declared together

b.f. **1.** UK *inf.* bloody fool **2.** *Print.* bold face

B/F *or* **b/f** brought forward

BFPO British Forces Post Office

bhang *or* **bang** (bæŋ) *n.* preparation of leaves and flower tops of Indian hemp, much used as narcotic in India

b.h.p. brake horsepower

Bi *Chem.* bismuth

bi- *or sometimes before vowel* **bin-** (*comb. form*) **1.** two; having two, as in *bifocal* **2.** occurring every two, as in *biennial* **3.** on both sides *etc.*, as in *bilateral* **4.** occurring twice during, as in *biweekly* **5.** indicating acid salt of dibasic acid, as in *sodium bicarbonate*

biannual (baɪˈænjuəl) *a.* occurring twice a year —**biˈannually** *adv.*

bias (ˈbaɪəs) *n.* **1.** slant **2.** personal inclination or preference **3.** one-sided inclination (*pl.* **-es**) —*vt.* **4.** influence, affect (**-s-**, **-ss-**) —**ˈbiased** *a.* prejudiced —**bias binding** strip of material cut on bias, used for binding hems or for decoration

biaxial (baɪˈæksɪəl) *a.* (*esp.* of crystal) having two axes

bib (bɪb) *n.* **1.** cloth put under child's chin to protect clothes when eating **2.** top of apron or overalls

bibcock (ˈbɪbkɒk) *or* **bibb** (bɪb) *n.* tap with nozzle bent downwards

bibelot (ˈbɪbləʊ) *n.* attractive or curious trinket

bibl. **1.** bibliographical **2.** bibliography

Bibl. Biblical

Bible (ˈbaɪbᵊl) *n.* the sacred writings of the Christian religion —**biblical** (ˈbɪblɪkᵊl) *a.* —**biblicist** (ˈbɪblɪsɪst) *n.*

biblio- (*comb. form*) book or books, as in *bibliography*

bibliography (bɪblɪˈɒgrəfɪ) *n.* **1.** list of books on a subject **2.** history and description of books —**bibliˈographer** *n.* —**biblioˈgraphical** *a.*

bibliomania (bɪblɪəʊˈmeɪnɪə) *n.* extreme fondness for books —**biblioˈmaniac** *n./a.*

bibliophile (ˈbɪblɪəfaɪl) *or* **bibliophil** (ˈbɪblɪəfɪl) *n.* lover, collector of books —**bibliˈophily** *n.*

bibulous (ˈbɪbjʊləs) *a.* given to drinking

bicameral (baɪˈkæmərəl) *a.* (of legislature) consisting of two chambers —**biˈcameralism** *n.*

bicarb (ˈbaɪkɑːb) *n.* bicarbonate of soda

bicarbonate (baɪˈkɑːbənɪt, -neɪt) *n.* chemical compound releasing carbon dioxide when mixed with acid —**bicarbonate of soda** sodium bicarbonate, *esp.* as medicine or raising agent

bicentenary (baɪsɛnˈtiːnərɪ) *or U.S.* **bicentennial** (baɪsɛnˈtɛnɪəl) *n.* **1.** two hundredth anniversary **2.** its celebration

biceps (ˈbaɪsɛps) *n.* two-headed muscle, *esp.* muscle of upper arm

bicker (ˈbɪkə) *vi./n.* quarrel over petty things —**ˈbickering** *n.*

bicolour (ˈbaɪkʌlə), **bicoloured** *or U.S.* **bicolor, bicolored** *a.* two-coloured

bicuspid (baɪˈkʌspɪd) *or* **bicuspidate** (baɪˈkʌspɪdeɪt) *a.* **1.** having two points —*n.* **2.** bicuspid tooth; premolar

bicycle (ˈbaɪsɪkᵊl) *n.* vehicle with two wheels, one in front of other, pedalled by rider —**ˈbicyclist** *n.*

bid (bɪd) *vt.* **1.** offer **2.** say **3.** command **4.** invite (**bad, bade** *or* **bid, ˈbidden**) —*n.* **5.** offer, *esp.* of price **6.** try **7.** *Cards* call —**ˈbiddable** *a.* **1.** having sufficient value to be bid on **2.** docile; obedient —**ˈbiddableness** *n.* —**ˈbidder** *n.* —**ˈbidding** *n.*

THESAURUS

beverage draught, drink, libation (*Facetious*), liquid, liquor, potable, potation, refreshment

bevy **1.** band, bunch (*Inf.*), collection, company, crowd, gathering, group, pack, troupe **2.** covey, flight, flock

bewail bemoan, cry over, deplore, express sorrow, grieve for, keen, lament, moan, mourn, regret, repent, rue, wail, weep over

beware avoid, be careful (cautious, wary), guard against, heed, look out, mind, refrain from, shun, steer clear of, take heed, watch out

bewilder baffle, befuddle, bemuse, confound, confuse, daze, mix up, mystify, perplex, puzzle, stupefy

bewitch allure, attract, beguile, captivate, charm, enchant, enrapture, entrance, fascinate, hypnotize, spellbind

beyond above, apart from, at a distance, away from, before, farther, out of range, out of reach, over, past, remote, superior to, yonder

bias *n.* **1.** bent, bigotry, favouritism, inclination, intolerance, leaning, narrow-mindedness, one-sidedness, partiality, penchant, predilection, predisposition, prejudice, proclivity, proneness, propensity, tendency, turn, unfairness **2.** angle, cross, diagonal line, slant ~*v.* **3.** distort, influence, predispose, prejudice, slant, sway, twist, warp, weight

biased distorted, embittered, jaundiced, one-sided, partial, predisposed, prejudiced, slanted, swayed, twisted, warped, weighted

bicker argue, disagree, dispute, fight, quarrel, row (*Inf.*), scrap (*Inf.*), spar, squabble, wrangle

bid *v.* **1.** offer, proffer, propose, submit, tender **2.** call,

biddy (ˈbɪdɪ) *n. dial.* chicken or hen

bide (baɪd) *vi.* **1.** remain **2.** dwell —*vt.* **3.** await (**ˈbided** *or* **bode, ˈbided**) —**ˈbiding** *n.*

bidet (ˈbi:deɪ) *n.* low basin for washing genital area

biennial (baɪˈɛnɪəl) *a.* **1.** happening every two years **2.** lasting two years —*n.* **3.** plant living two years —**biˈennially** *adv.*

bier (bɪə) *n.* frame for bearing dead to grave

biff (bɪf) *sl. n.* **1.** blow with fist —*vt.* **2.** give (someone) such a blow

bifid (ˈbaɪfɪd) *a.* divided into two lobes by median cleft —**biˈfidity** *n.*

bifocal (baɪˈfəʊkᵊl) *a.* having two different focal lengths —**biˈfocals** *pl.n.* spectacles having bifocal lenses for near and distant vision

bifurcate (ˈbaɪfəkeɪt) *vi.* **1.** divide into two branches —*a.* (ˈbaɪfəkeɪt, -kɪt) **2.** forked or divided into two branches —**bifurˈcation** *n.*

big (bɪg) *a.* of great or considerable size, height, number, power *etc.* (**ˈbigger** *comp.*, **ˈbiggest** *sup.*) —**ˈbigness** *n.* —**Big Brother** person or organization that exercises total dictatorial control —**big dipper** (in amusement parks) narrow railway with open carriages that run swiftly over route of sharp curves and steep inclines —**big end UK** larger end of connecting rod in internal-combustion engine —**big shot** *sl.* important person —**big stick** *inf.* force or threat of force —**big time** *sl.* highest level of profession, *esp.* entertainment —**big-timer** *n.* —**big top** *inf.* **1.** main tent of circus **2.** circus itself —**ˈbigwig** *n. sl.* important person

bigamy (ˈbɪgəmɪ) *n.* crime of marrying a person while one is still legally married to someone else —**ˈbigamist** *n.* —**ˈbigamous** *a.*

bight (baɪt) *n.* **1.** curve or loop in rope **2.** long curved shoreline or water bounded by it

bigot (ˈbɪgət) *n.* person intolerant or not receptive to ideas of others, *esp.* on religion *etc.* —**ˈbigoted** *a.* —**ˈbigotry** *n.*

bijou (ˈbi:ʒu:) *n.* **1.** something small and delicately worked (*pl.* **-joux** (-ʒu:z)) —*a.* **2.** *oft. ironic* small but tasteful

bike (baɪk) *n.* **1.** bicycle **2.** motor bike

bikini (bɪˈki:nɪ) *n.* woman's brief two-piece swimming costume

bilateral (baɪˈlætərəl) *a.* two-sided

bilberry (ˈbɪlbərɪ) *n.* small European moorland plant with edible blue berries

bile (baɪl) *n.* **1.** fluid secreted by the liver **2.** anger, ill-temper —**biliary** (ˈbɪlɪərɪ) *a.* of bile, ducts that convey bile, or gall bladder —**bilious** (ˈbɪlɪəs) *a.* nauseous, nauseating —**biliousness** (ˈbɪlɪəsnɪs) *n.*

bilge (bɪldʒ) *n.* **1.** bottom of ship's hull **2.** dirty water that collects in vessel's bilge (*also* **bilge water**) **3.** *inf.* nonsense —*vi.* **4.** spring a leak

bilingual (baɪˈlɪŋgwəl) *a.* speaking, or written in, two languages —**biˈlingualism** *n.*

bilk (bɪlk) *vt.* **1.** balk; thwart **2.** (*oft. with* of) cheat, deceive **3.** escape from; elude —*n.* **4.** swindle, cheat **5.** person who swindles or cheats —**ˈbilker** *n.*

bill[1] (bɪl) *n.* **1.** written account of charges **2.** draft of Act of Parliament **3.** poster **4.** commercial document —*vt.* **5.** present account of charges to **6.** announce by advertisement —**ˈbilling** *n.* degree of importance, *esp.* in theatre *etc.* —**ˈbillboard** *n. chiefly* **US** *see* HOARDING —**ˈbillposter** *or* **ˈbillsticker** *n.* person who sticks advertising posters to walls *etc.* —**ˈbillposting** *or* **ˈbillsticking** *n.* —**bill of exchange** document instructing third party to pay stated sum at designated future date or on demand —**bill of fare** menu —**bill of lading** document containing full particulars of goods shipped —**clean bill of health** *inf.* **1.** good report of one's physical condition **2.** favourable account of person's or company's financial position

bill[2] (bɪl) *n.* **1.** bird's beak —*vi.* **2.** touch bills, as doves **3.** caress

bill[3] (bɪl) *n.* **1.** tool for pruning **2.** hooked weapon —**ˈbillhook** *n.* hatchet with hook at end of cutting edge

billabong (ˈbɪləbɒŋ) *n.* A pool in intermittent stream

THESAURUS

greet, say, tell, wish **3.** ask, call, charge, command, desire, direct, enjoin, instruct, invite, require, solicit, summon, tell ~*n.* **4.** advance, amount, offer, price, proposal, proposition, submission, sum, tender **5.** attempt, crack (*Inf.*), effort, endeavour, try, venture

bidding 1. behest, call, charge, command, demand, direction, injunction, instruction, invitation, order, request, summons **2.** auction, offer, offers, proposal, tender

big 1. bulky, burly, colossal, considerable, enormous, extensive, gigantic, great, huge, hulking, immense, large, mammoth, massive, ponderous, prodigious, sizable, spacious, substantial, vast, voluminous **2.** eminent, important, influential, leading, main, momentous, paramount, powerful, prime, principal, prominent, serious, significant, valuable, weighty **3.** adult, elder, grown, grown-up, mature

bigot dogmatist, fanatic, persecutor, sectarian, zealot

bigoted biased, dogmatic, illiberal, intolerant, narrow-minded, obstinate, opinionated, prejudiced, sectarian, twisted, warped

bigotry bias, discrimination, dogmatism, fanaticism, ignorance, injustice, intolerance, mindlessness, narrow-mindedness, prejudice, provincialism, racialism, racism, sectarianism, sexism, unfairness

bigwig big cheese (*Sl.*), big gun (*Sl.*), big noise (*Sl.*), big shot (*Sl., chiefly U.S.*), celebrity, dignitary, heavyweight (*Inf.*), nob (*Sl.*), notability, notable, panjandrum, personage, somebody, V.I.P.

bile anger, bitterness, churlishness, ill humour, irascibility, irritability, nastiness, peevishness, rancour, spleen

bilious liverish, nauseated, out of sorts, queasy, sick

bilk bamboozle, cheat, con (*Sl.*), deceive, defraud, do (*Sl.*), fleece, rook (*Sl.*), swindle, trick

bill[1] *n.* **1.** account, charges, invoice, note of charge, reckoning, score, statement, tally **2.** advertisement, broadsheet, bulletin, circular, handbill, handout, leaflet, notice, placard, playbill, poster **3.** agenda, card, catalogue, inventory, list, listing, programme, roster, schedule, syllabus **4.** measure, piece of legislation, projected law, proposal ~*v.* **5.** charge, debit, figure, invoice, reckon, record **6.** advertise, announce, give advance notice of, post

bill[2] beak, mandible, neb (*Archaic or dialect*), nib

billet 1. *n.* accommodation, barracks, lodging, quarters **2.** *v.* accommodate, berth, quarter, station

billet[1] (ˈbɪlɪt) *n.* **1.** civilian quarters for troops **2.** resting place —*vt.* **3.** quarter, as troops

billet[2] (ˈbɪlɪt) *n.* **1.** chunk of wood, *esp.* for fuel **2.** small bar of iron or steel

billet-doux (bɪlɪˈduː) *Fr.* love letter

billiards (ˈbɪljədz) *n.* game played on table with balls and cues

billion (ˈbɪljən) *n.* million millions (*U.S., France* thousand millions)

billow (ˈbɪləʊ) *n.* **1.** great swelling wave —*pl.* **2.** the sea —*vi.* **3.** surge **4.** swell out

billy (ˈbɪlɪ) *or* **billycan** (ˈbɪlɪkæn) *n.* can with wire handle used for boiling water on open fire —**billy goat** male goat

biltong (ˈbɪltɒŋ) *n.* SA thin strips of meat dried in sun

B.I.M. British Institute of Management

bimetallism (baɪˈmɛtəlɪzəm) *n.* use of two metals, *esp.* gold and silver, in fixed relative values as standard of value and currency

bimonthly (baɪˈmʌnθlɪ) *adv./a.* **1.** every two months **2.** twice a month

bin (bɪn) *n.* **1.** receptacle for corn, refuse *etc.* **2.** one particular bottling of wine

binary (ˈbaɪnərɪ) *a.* **1.** composed of, characterized by, two **2.** dual —**binary star** double star system containing two associated stars revolving around common centre of gravity

bind (baɪnd) *vt.* **1.** tie fast **2.** tie round, gird **3.** tie together **4.** oblige **5.** seal **6.** constrain **7.** bandage **8.** unite **9.** put (book) into cover —*v.* **10.** (cause to) cohere (**bound** *pt./pp.*) —**ˈbinder** *n.* one who, or that which binds —**ˈbindery** *n.* —**ˈbinding** *n.* **1.** cover of book **2.** tape for hem *etc.* —**ˈbindweed** *n.* convolvulus

bine (baɪn) *n.* climbing or twining stem of any of various plants, such as bindweed

binge (bɪndʒ) *n. inf.* **1.** excessive indulgence in eating or drinking **2.** spree

bingo (ˈbɪŋgəʊ) *n.* game of chance in which numbers drawn are matched with those on a card

binnacle (ˈbɪnək[ə]l) *n.* box holding ship's compass

binocular (bɪˈnɒkjʊlə, baɪ-) *a.* seeing with, made for both eyes —**biˈnoculars** *pl.n.* telescope made for both eyes

binomial (baɪˈnəʊmɪəl) *a./n.* (denoting) algebraic expression consisting of two terms —**binomial theorem** general formula that expresses any power of binomial without multiplying out

bio- *or before vowel* **bi-** (*comb. form*) life, living, as in *biochemistry.* Such words are not given here where the meaning may easily be inferred from the simple word

bioastronautics (baɪəʊæstrəˈnɔːtɪks) *pl.n.* (*with sing. v.*) study of effects of space flight on living organisms

biocoenosis (baɪəʊsiːˈnəʊsɪs) *n.* relationships between animals and plants subsisting together

biodegradable (baɪəʊdɪˈgreɪdəb[ə]l) *a.* capable of decomposition by natural means

bioengineering (baɪəʊɛndʒɪˈnɪərɪŋ) *n.* **1.** design and manufacture of aids to rectify defective body functions **2.** design, manufacture and maintenance of engineering equipment used in biosynthetic processes —**bioengiˈneer** *n.*

biog. **1.** biographical **2.** biography

biogenesis (baɪəʊˈdʒɛnɪsɪs) *n.* principle that living organism must originate from similar parent organism —**biogeˈnetic(al)** *a.*

biography (baɪˈɒgrəfɪ) *n.* story of one person's life —**biˈographer** *n.* —**bioˈgraphical** *a.* —**bioˈgraphically** *adv.*

biol. **1.** biological **2.** biology

biology (baɪˈɒlədʒɪ) *n.* study of living organisms —**bioˈlogical** *a.* —**bioˈlogically** *adv.* —**biˈologist** *n.* —**biological control** control of destructive organisms by nonchemical means —**biological warfare** use of living organisms or their toxic products as weapon of war

biomedicine (baɪəʊˈmɛdɪsɪn) *n.* medical and biological study of effects of unusual environmental stress

bionics (baɪˈɒnɪks) *pl.n.* (*with sing. v.*) study of relation of biological and electronic processes —**biˈonic** *a.* having physical functions augmented by electronic equipment

biophysics (baɪəʊˈfɪzɪks) *pl.n.* (*with sing. v.*) physics of biological processes and application of methods used in physics to biology —**bioˈphysical** *a.* —**biophysicist** (baɪəʊˈfɪzɪsɪst) *n.*

biopsy (ˈbaɪɒpsɪ) *n.* examination of tissue removed surgically from a living body

biorhythm (ˈbaɪəʊrɪðəm) *n.* complex repeated pattern of physiological states, believed to affect physical, emotional, or mental states

bioscope (ˈbaɪəskəʊp) *n.* SA cinema

bioscopy (baɪˈɒskəpɪ) *n.* examination of body to determine whether it is alive

biosphere (ˈbaɪəsfɪə) *n.* part of earth's surface and atmosphere inhabited by living things

biosynthesis (baɪəʊˈsɪnθɪsɪs) *n.* formation of chemical compounds by living organisms —**biosynthetic** (baɪəʊsɪnˈθɛtɪk) *a.*

biotin (ˈbaɪətɪn) *n.* vitamin of B complex, abundant in egg yolk and liver

bipartisan (baɪpɑːtɪˈzæn, baɪˈpɑːtɪzæn) *a.* consisting of or supported by two political parties

bipartite (baɪˈpɑːtaɪt) *a.* consisting of two parts or parties

biped (ˈbaɪpɛd) *n.* two-footed animal —**bipedal** (baɪˈpiːd[ə]l, -ˈpɛd[ə]l) *a.*

biplane (ˈbaɪpleɪn) *n.* aeroplane with two pairs of wings

bipolar (baɪˈpəʊlə) *a.* **1.** having two poles **2.** of North

THESAURUS

billow **1.** *n.* breaker, crest, roller, surge, swell, tide, wave **2.** *v.* balloon, belly, puff up, rise up, roll, surge, swell

bind *v.* **1.** attach, fasten, glue, hitch, lash, paste, rope, secure, stick, strap, tie, tie up, truss, wrap **2.** compel, constrain, engage, force, necessitate, obligate, oblige, prescribe, require **3.** confine, detain, hamper, hinder, restrain, restrict **4.** bandage, cover, dress, encase, swathe, wrap

binge bender (*Sl.*), blind (*Sl.*), bout, fling, jag (*Sl.*), orgy, spree

biography account, life, life history, life story, memoir, profile

and South Poles **3.** having two opposed opinions *etc.*—**bipo'larity** *n.*

birch (bɜːtʃ) *n.* **1.** tree with silvery bark —*vt.* **2.** flog —**'birchen** *a.* —**the birch** rod made of birch twigs used, *esp.* formerly, for punishment

bird (bɜːd) *n.* **1.** feathered animal **2.** *sl.* young woman or girl —**'birdlime** *n.* **1.** sticky substance smeared on twigs to catch small birds —*vt.* **2.** smear with birdlime —**bird of paradise** any of various songbirds of New Guinea and neighbouring regions, males having brilliantly coloured plumage —**bird of passage 1.** bird that migrates seasonally **2.** transient person —**bird's-eye** *a.* **1.** seen from above; summarizing (*esp. in* **bird's-eye view**) **2.** having markings resembling birds' eyes

birdie ('bɜːdɪ) *n.* **1.** *Golf* score of one stroke under par for hole **2.** *inf.* bird, *esp.* small bird

biretta *or* **berretta** (bɪ'rɛtə) *n.* square cap worn by Catholic clergy

Biro ('baɪrəʊ) *n.* **R** ballpoint pen

birth (bɜːθ) *n.* **1.** bearing, or the being born, of offspring **2.** parentage, origin **3.** noble descent —**birth control** limitation of childbearing usu. by artificial means —**'birthday** *n.* —**'birthmark** *n.* blemish, *usu.* dark, formed on skin before birth —**birth rate** ratio of live births in specified area *etc.* to population, usu. expressed per 1000 population per year —**'birthright** *n.* **1.** privileges that person is entitled to as soon as he is born **2.** privileges of first-born son **3.** inheritance —**'birthstone** *n.* precious or semiprecious stone associated with month or sign of zodiac and thought to bring luck if worn by person born in that month

biscuit ('bɪskɪt) *n.* dry, small, thin variety of cake

bisect (baɪ'sɛkt) *vt.* divide into two equal parts —**bi'sector** *n.*

bisexual (baɪ'sɛksjʊəl) *a.* **1.** sexually attracted to both men and women **2.** of both sexes

bishop ('bɪʃəp) *n.* **1.** clergyman governing diocese **2.** chess piece —**'bishopric** *n.* diocese or office of a bishop

bismuth ('bɪzməθ) *n.* reddish-white metal used in medicine *etc.*

bison ('baɪsᵊn) *n.* **1.** large wild ox **2.** Amer. buffalo

bisque[1] (bɪsk) *n.* thick rich soup made from shellfish

bisque[2] (bɪsk) *n.* **1.** pink to yellowish tan colour **2.** earthenware or porcelain that has been fired but not glazed

bistre *or U.S.* **bister** ('bɪstə) *n.* **1.** transparent water-soluble brownish-yellow pigment made by boiling soot of wood **2.** yellowish-brown to dark brown colour

bistro ('biːstrəʊ) *n.* small restaurant

bit[1] (bɪt) *n.* **1.** fragment, piece **2.** biting, cutting part of tool **3.** mouthpiece of horse's bridle —**'bitty** *a.* **1.** lacking unity; disjointed **2.** containing bits, sediment *etc.*

bit[2] (bɪt) *pt./pp. of* BITE

bit[3] (bɪt) *n. Comp.* smallest unit of information

bitch (bɪtʃ) *n.* **1.** female dog, fox or wolf **2.** *offens. sl.* spiteful woman **3.** *inf.* complaint —*vi.* **4.** *inf.* complain —**'bitchy** *a.*

bite (baɪt) *vt.* **1.** cut into, *esp.* with teeth **2.** grip —*vi.* **3.** rise to bait —*v.* **4.** (of corrosive material) eat away or into (**bit** *pt.*, **bit, 'bitten** *pp.*, **'biting** *pr.p.*) —*n.* **5.** act of biting **6.** wound so made **7.** mouthful —**'biter** *n.* —**'biting** *a.* **1.** piercing; keen **2.** sarcastic; incisive —**'bitingly** *adv.*

bitter ('bɪtə) *a.* **1.** sharp, sour tasting **2.** unpleasant **3.** (of person) angry or resentful **4.** sarcastic —**'bitterly** *adv.* —**'bitterness** *n.* —**'bitters** *pl.n.* essence of bitter herbs —**bitter end** final extremity —**'bittersweet** *n.* **1.** N Amer. climbing plant **2.** woody nightshade —*a.* **3.** being mixture of bitterness and sweetness **4.** pleasant but tinged with sadness

bittern ('bɪtən) *n.* wading bird like heron

bitumen ('bɪtjʊmɪn) *n.* viscous substance occurring in asphalt, tar *etc.* —**bi'tuminous** *a.*

bivalent (baɪ'veɪlənt, 'bɪvə-) *a.* **1.** *Chem. see* DIVALENT **2.** (of homologous chromosomes) associated together in pairs —**bi'valency** *n.*

bivalve ('baɪvælv) *a.* **1.** having a double shell —*n.* **2.** mollusc with such shell

bivouac ('bɪvʊæk, 'bɪvwæk) *n.* **1.** temporary encampment of soldiers, hikers *etc.* —*vi.* **2.** pass the night in temporary camp (**'bivouacked, 'bivouacking**)

biz (bɪz) *n. inf.* business

bizarre (bɪ'zɑː) *a.* unusual, weird

Bk *Chem.* berkelium

THESAURUS

birth 1. childbirth, delivery, nativity, parturition **2.** beginning, emergence, fountainhead, genesis, origin, rise, source **3.** ancestry, background, blood, breeding, derivation, descent, extraction, forebears, genealogy, line, lineage, nobility, noble extraction, parentage, pedigree, race, stock, strain

bisect bifurcate, cross, cut across, cut in half, cut in two, divide in two, halve, intersect, separate, split, split down the middle

bishopric diocese, episcopacy, episcopate, primacy, see

bit 1. atom, chip, crumb, fragment, grain, iota, jot, mite, morsel, mouthful, part, piece, scrap, segment, slice, small piece, speck, tittle, whit **2.** brake, check, curb, restraint, snaffle

bitchy catty (*Inf.*), cruel, malicious, mean, nasty, rancorous, snide, spiteful, venomous, vindictive, vixenish

bite *v.* **1.** champ, chew, clamp, crunch, crush, cut, gnaw, grip, hold, masticate, nibble, nip, pierce, pinch, rend, seize, snap, tear, wound **2.** burn, corrode, eat away, eat into, erode, smart, sting, tingle, wear away ~*n.* **3.** itch, nip, pinch, prick, smarting, sting, tooth marks, wound **4.** food, light meal, morsel, mouthful, piece, refreshment, snack, taste

biting 1. bitter, blighting, cold, cutting, freezing, harsh, nipping, penetrating, piercing, sharp **2.** caustic, cutting, incisive, mordant, sarcastic, scathing, severe, stinging, trenchant, withering

bitter 1. acid, acrid, astringent, sharp, sour, tart, unsweetened, vinegary **2.** acrimonious, begrudging, crabbed, embittered, hostile, morose, rancorous, resentful, sore, sour, sullen, with a chip on one's shoulder

bitterness 1. acerbity, acidity, sharpness, sourness, tartness, vinegariness **2.** animosity, grudge, hostility, pique, rancour, resentment **3.** acrimoniousness, asperity, sarcasm, venom, virulence

bizarre comical, curious, eccentric, extraordinary, fantastic, freakish, grotesque, ludicrous, odd, offbeat, outlandish, outré, peculiar, queer, ridiculous, strange, unusual, weird

bk. 1. bank 2. book

B.L. 1. Bachelor of Laws 2. Bachelor of Letters 3. Barrister-at-Law 4. British Library

blab (blæb) *v.* 1. reveal (secrets) —*vi.* 2. chatter idly (-bb-) —*n.* 3. telltale 4. gossip —**ˈblabber** *n.* 1. person who blabs 2. idle chatter —*vi.* 3. talk without thinking; chatter

black (blæk) *a.* 1. of the darkest colour 2. without light 3. dark 4. evil 5. sombre 6. dishonourable —*n.* 7. darkest colour 8. black dye, clothing *etc.* 9. (B-) person of dark-skinned race —*vt.* 10. boycott (specified goods *etc.*) in industrial dispute —**ˈblacken** *v.* —**ˈblacking** *n.* substance used for blacking and cleaning leather *etc.* —**ˈblackamoor** *n. obs.* Negro or other person with dark skin —**black-and-blue** *a.* 1. (of skin) discoloured, as from bruise 2. feeling pain, as from beating —**black-and-white** *n.* photograph *etc.* in black, white, and shades of grey rather than in colour —**black art** black magic —**ˈblackball** *vt.* vote against, exclude —**black belt** *Judo, karate* black belt worn by instructor or expert; person entitled to wear this —**ˈblackberry** *n.* plant with thorny stems and dark juicy berries, bramble —**ˈblackbird** *n.* common European songbird —**ˈblackboard** *n.* dark-coloured surface for writing on with chalk —**black book** book containing names of people to be punished, blacklisted *etc.* —**black box** *inf.* flight recorder —**ˈblackcap** *n.* type of warbler —**ˈblackcock** *n.* male of the black grouse —**blackˈcurrant** *n.* 1. N temperate shrub having edible black berries 2. its fruit —**black eye** *inf.* bruising round eye —**ˈblackhead** *n.* dark, fatty plug blocking pore in skin —**black hole** *Astron.* region of space resulting from collapse of star, and surrounded by gravitational field that neither matter nor radiation could escape from —**ˈblackleg** *n.* 1. one who works during strike 2. disease of cattle —**ˈblacklist** *n.* 1. list of people, organizations considered suspicious, untrustworthy *etc.* —*vt.* 2. put on blacklist —**black magic** magic used for evil purposes —**ˈblackmail** *vt.* 1. extort money from (a person) by threats —*n.* 2. act of blackmailing 3. money extorted thus —**ˈblackmailer** *n.* —**Black Maria** (məˈraɪə) police van for transporting prisoners —**black mark** indication of disapproval *etc.* —**black market** illegal buying and selling of goods —**black mass** travesty of Christian Mass performed by practitioners of black magic —**ˈblackout** *n.* 1. complete failure of electricity supply 2. sudden cutting off of all stagelights 3. state of temporary unconsciousness 4. obscuring of all lights as precaution against night air attack —**Black Power** social, economic, and political movement of Black people to obtain equality with Whites —**black pudding** sausage made from minced pork fat, pig's blood *etc.* (*also* **blood pudding**) —**black sheep** person regarded as disgrace or failure by his family or group —**ˈBlackshirt** *n.* member of fascist organization, *esp.* It. Fascist party before and during World War II —**ˈblacksmith** *n.* smith who works in iron —**black spot** dangerous place, *esp.* on a road —**ˈblackthorn** *n.* shrub with black twigs —**black tie** *n.* 1. black bow tie worn with dinner jacket —*a.* 2. denoting occasion when dinner jacket should be worn —**black widow** highly poisonous Amer. spider —**black out** 1. obliterate or extinguish (lights) 2. create a blackout in (a city *etc.*) 3. lose consciousness, vision or memory temporarily —**in black and white** in print or writing; in extremes —**in someone's black books** *inf.* out of favour with someone —**the Black Country** heavily industrialized West Midlands of England —**the Black Death** form of bubonic plague pandemic in Europe and Asia during 14th cent. (*see* BUBONIC PLAGUE)

blackguard (ˈblægɑːd, -gəd) *n.* 1. scoundrel —*a.* 2. unprincipled, wicked —*vt.* 3. revile —**ˈblackguardism** *n.* —**ˈblackguardly** *a.*

bladder (ˈblædə) *n.* membranous bag to contain liquid, *esp.* urinary bladder

blade (bleɪd) *n.* 1. edge, cutting part of knife or tool 2. leaf of grass *etc.* 3. sword 4. *obs.* dashing fellow 5. flat of oar

blain (bleɪn) *n.* 1. inflamed swelling 2. pimple, blister

blame (bleɪm) *n.* 1. censure 2. culpability —*vt.* 3. find fault with 4. censure —**ˈblamable** *or* **ˈblameable** *a.* —**ˈblameless** *a.* —**ˈblameworthy** *a.*

THESAURUS

blab blurt out, disclose, divulge, gossip, let slip, reveal, tattle, tell, tell on

blabber 1. *n.* busybody, gossip, informer, rumourmonger, scandalmonger, talebearer, tattler, telltale 2. *v.* blather, blether (*Scot.*), chatter, gab (*Inf.*), jabber, prattle

black *adj.* 1. coal-black, dark, dusky, ebony, inky, jet, murky, pitchy, raven, sable, starless, stygian, swarthy 2. *Fig.* atrocious, depressing, dismal, distressing, doleful, foreboding, funereal, gloomy, hopeless, horrible, lugubrious, mournful, ominous, sad, sombre 3. bad, evil, iniquitous, nefarious, villainous, wicked ~*v.* 4. ban, bar, blacklist, boycott

blackball *v.* ban, bar, blacklist, debar, drum out, exclude, expel, ostracize, oust, repudiate, snub, vote against

blackguard bastard (*Offensive*), blighter (*Inf.*), bounder (*Brit. inf.*), miscreant, rascal, rogue, scoundrel, swine, villain, wretch

blacklist *v.* ban, bar, blackball, boycott, debar, exclude, expel, ostracize, preclude, proscribe, reject, repudiate, snub, vote against

black magic black art, diabolism, necromancy, sorcery, voodoo, witchcraft, wizardry

blackmail 1. *n.* bribe, exaction, extortion, hush money (*Sl.*), intimidation, milking, pay-off (*Inf.*), protection (*Inf.*), ransom, slush fund 2. *v.* bleed (*Inf.*), bribe, coerce, compel, demand, exact, extort, force, hold to ransom, milk, squeeze, threaten

blackout *n.* 1. coma, faint, loss of consciousness, oblivion, swoon, syncope (*Pathology*), unconsciousness 2. power cut, power failure

black sheep disgrace, ne'er-do-well, outcast, prodigal, renegade, reprobate, wastrel

blame *n.* 1. accountability, culpability, fault, guilt, incrimination, liability, onus, rap (*Inf.*), responsibility 2. accusation, castigation, censure, charge, complaint, condemnation, criticism, recrimination, reproach, reproof ~*v.* 3. accuse, admonish, censure, charge, chide, condemn, criticize, disapprove, express disapprobation, find fault with, hold responsible, reprehend, reproach, reprove, tax, upbraid

blameless above suspicion, clean, faultless, guiltless, immaculate, impeccable, innocent, in the clear, irreproachable, perfect, stainless, unblemished, unim-

blanch (blɑːntʃ) *vt.* **1.** whiten, bleach, take colour out of **2.** (of foodstuffs) briefly boil or fry —*v.* **3.** turn pale

blancmange (bləˈmɒnʒ) *n.* jellylike dessert made with milk

bland (blænd) *a.* **1.** devoid of distinctive characteristics **2.** smooth in manner

blandish (ˈblændɪʃ) *vt.* **1.** coax **2.** flatter —**ˈblandishments** *pl.n.*

blank (blæŋk) *a.* **1.** without marks or writing **2.** empty **3.** vacant, confused **4.** (of verse) without rhyme —*n.* **5.** empty space **6.** void **7.** cartridge containing no bullet —**ˈblankly** *adv.* —**blank cheque 1.** cheque that has been signed but on which amount payable has not been specified **2.** complete freedom of action —**blank verse** unrhymed verse, *esp.* in iambic pentameters

blanket (ˈblæŋkɪt) *n.* **1.** thick (woollen) covering for bed **2.** concealing cover —*vt.* **3.** cover with blanket **4.** cover, stifle —**blanket stitch** strong reinforcing stitch for edges of blankets and other thick material

blare (blɛə) *v.* **1.** sound loudly and harshly —*n.* **2.** such sound

blarney (ˈblɑːnɪ) *n.* flattering talk

blasé (ˈblɑːzeɪ) *a.* **1.** indifferent through familiarity **2.** bored

blaspheme (blæsˈfiːm) *v.* show contempt or disrespect for (God or sacred things, *esp.* in speech) —**blasˈphemer** *n.* —**blasphemous** (ˈblæsfɪməs) *a.* —**blasphemously** (ˈblæsfɪməslɪ) *adv.* —**blasphemy** (ˈblæsfɪmɪ) *n.*

blast (blɑːst) *n.* **1.** explosion **2.** high-pressure wave of air coming from an explosion **3.** current of air **4.** gust of wind or air **5.** loud sound **6.** *sl.* reprimand —*vt.* **7.** blow up **8.** remove, open *etc.* by explosion **9.** blight **10.** ruin —**ˈblasted** *a.* **1.** blighted, withered **2.** damned —**blast furnace** furnace for smelting ore, using preheated blast of air —**ˈblastoff** *n.* **1.** launching of rocket **2.** time at which this occurs —**blast off** be launched

blatant (ˈbleɪtᵊnt) *a.* obvious —**ˈblatancy** *n.*

blather (ˈblæðə) *vi.* **1.** speak foolishly —*n.* **2.** foolish talk; nonsense

blaze[1] (bleɪz) *n.* **1.** strong fire or flame **2.** brightness **3.** outburst —*vi.* **4.** burn strongly **5.** be very angry

blaze[2] (bleɪz) *v.* **1.** mark (trees) to establish trail —*n.* **2.** mark on tree **3.** white mark on horse's face

blaze[3] (bleɪz) *vt.* **1.** proclaim, publish (as with trumpet) —*n.* **2.** wide publicity

blazer (ˈbleɪzə) *n.* type of jacket, worn *esp.* for sports

blazon (ˈbleɪzᵊn) *vt.* **1.** make public, proclaim **2.** describe, depict (arms) —*n.* **3.** coat of arms

bleach (bliːtʃ) *v.* **1.** make or become white —*n.* **2.** bleaching substance —**bleaching powder** white powder consisting of chlorinated calcium hydroxide (*also* **chloride of lime, chlorinated lime**)

bleak[1] (bliːk) *a.* **1.** cold and cheerless **2.** exposed —**ˈbleakly** *adv.*

THESAURUS

peachable, unoffending, unspotted, unsullied, untarnished, upright, virtuous

blameworthy discreditable, disreputable, indefensible, inexcusable, iniquitous, reprehensible, reproachable, shameful

bland 1. boring, dull, flat, humdrum, insipid, monotonous, tasteless, tedious, undistinctive, unexciting, uninspiring, uninteresting, unstimulating, vapid, weak **2.** affable, amiable, congenial, courteous, friendly, gentle, gracious, smooth, suave, unemotional, urbane

blandishments blarney, cajolery, coaxing, compliments, fawning, flattery, ingratiation, inveiglement, soft soap (*Inf.*), soft words, sweet talk (*Inf., chiefly U.S.*), wheedling, winning caresses

blank *adj.* **1.** bare, clean, clear, empty, plain, spotless, uncompleted, unfilled, unmarked, void, white **2.** deadpan, dull, empty, expressionless, hollow, impassive, inane, lifeless, poker-faced (*Inf.*), vacant, vacuous, vague **3.** at a loss, bewildered, confounded, confused, disconcerted, dumbfounded, muddled, nonplussed, uncomprehending ~*n.* **4.** emptiness, empty space, gap, nothingness, space, tabula rasa, vacancy, vacuity, vacuum, void

blanket *n.* **1.** afghan, cover, coverlet, rug **2.** carpet, cloak, coat, coating, covering, envelope, film, layer, mantle, sheet, wrapper, wrapping ~*v.* **3.** cloak, cloud, coat, conceal, cover, eclipse, hide, mask, obscure, suppress, surround

blare blast, boom, clamour, clang, honk, hoot, peal, resound, roar, scream, sound out, toot, trumpet

blarney blandishment, cajolery, coaxing, exaggeration, flattery, honeyed words, overpraise, soft soap (*Inf.*), sweet talk (*Inf., chiefly U.S.*), wheedling

blasé apathetic, bored, cloyed, glutted, indifferent, jaded, lukewarm, nonchalant, offhand, satiated, surfeited, unconcerned, unexcited, uninterested, unmoved, weary, world-weary

blaspheme abuse, anathematize, curse, damn, desecrate, execrate, profane, revile, swear

blasphemous godless, impious, irreligious, irreverent, profane, sacrilegious, ungodly

blasphemy cursing, desecration, execration, impiety, impiousness, indignity (*to God*), irreverence, profanation, profaneness, profanity, sacrilege, swearing

blast *n.* **1.** blare, blow, clang, honk, peal, scream, toot, wail **2.** bang, blow-up, burst, crash, detonation, discharge, eruption, explosion, outburst, salvo, volley **3.** gale, gust, squall, storm, strong breeze, tempest. ~*v.* **4.** blow up, break up, burst, demolish, destroy, explode, ruin, shatter **5.** blight, kill, shrivel, wither

blasted blighted, desolated, destroyed, devastated, ravaged, ruined, shattered, spoiled, wasted, withered

blastoff *n.* discharge, expulsion, firing, launch, launching, lift-off, projection, shot

blatant bald, brazen, conspicuous, flagrant, flaunting, glaring, naked, obtrusive, obvious, ostentatious, outright, overt, prominent, pronounced, sheer, unmitigated

blaze *n.* **1.** bonfire, conflagration, fire, flame, flames **2.** beam, brightness, brilliance, flare, flash, glare, gleam, glitter, glow, light, radiance **3.** blast, burst, eruption, flare-up, fury, outbreak, outburst, rush, storm, torrent ~*v.* **4.** beam, burn, fire, flame, flare, flash, glare, gleam, glow, shine **5.** boil, explode, flare up, fume, seethe

bleach blanch, etiolate, fade, grow pale, lighten, peroxide, wash out, whiten

bleak 1. bare, barren, chilly, cold, desolate, exposed,

bleak[2] (bli:k) *n.* small, silvery fish

bleary (ˈblɪərɪ) *a.* with eyes dimmed, as by tears or tiredness —**bleary-eyed** *or* **blear-eyed** *a.* having bleary eyes

bleat (bli:t) *vi.* **1.** cry, as sheep —*v.* **2.** say, speak plaintively —*n.* **3.** sheep's cry

bleed (bli:d) *vi.* **1.** lose blood —*vt.* **2.** draw blood or liquid from **3.** extort money from (**bled** *pt./pp.*)

bleep (bli:p) *n.* short high-pitched sound —ˈ**bleeper** *n.* small portable electronic signalling device

blemish (ˈblɛmɪʃ) *n.* **1.** defect **2.** stain —*vt.* **3.** make (something) defective, dirty *etc.* —ˈ**blemished** *a.*

blench (blɛntʃ) *vi.* start back, flinch

blend (blɛnd) *vt.* **1.** mix —*n.* **2.** mixture —ˈ**blender** *n.* one who, that which blends, *esp.* electrical kitchen appliance for mixing food

blende (blɛnd) *n.* **1.** a zinc ore **2.** any of several sulphide ores

blenny (ˈblɛnɪ) *n.* small fish with tapering scaleless body

blesbok *or* **blesbuck** (ˈblɛsbʌk) *n.* S Afr. antelope

bless (blɛs) *vt.* **1.** consecrate **2.** give thanks to **3.** ask God's favour for **4.** (*usu. pass.*) endow (with) **5.** glorify **6.** make happy (**blessed, blest** *pp.*) —**blessed** (ˈblɛsɪd, blɛst) *a.* **1.** made holy **2.** worthy of deep reverence **3.** *R.C.Ch.* (of person) beatified by pope **4.** characterized by happiness **5.** bringing great happiness **6.** damned —**blessedness** (ˈblɛsɪdnɪs) *n.* —ˈ**blessing** *n.* **1.** (ceremony asking for) God's protection, aid **2.** short prayer **3.** approval **4.** welcome event, benefit

blether (ˈblɛðə) *n.* nonsense, gossip (*also* ˈ**blather**)

blew (blu:) *pt. of* BLOW[1]

blight (blaɪt) *n.* **1.** plant disease **2.** harmful influence —*vt.* **3.** injure as with blight

blighter (ˈblaɪtə) *n. inf.* fellow, person

Blighty (ˈblaɪtɪ) *n.* **UK** *sl.* **1.** Britain; home **2.** *esp.* in World War I, wound that causes recipient to be sent home to Britain (*also* **blighty one**)

blimey (ˈblaɪmɪ) *interj.* **UK** *sl.* exclamation of surprise or annoyance

blimp (blɪmp) *n.* small, nonrigid airship used for observing

blind (blaɪnd) *a.* **1.** unable to see **2.** heedless, random **3.** dim **4.** closed at one end **5.** *sl.* very drunk —*vt.* **6.** deprive of sight —*n.* **7.** something cutting off light **8.** window screen **9.** pretext —ˈ**blindly** *adv.* —ˈ**blindness** *n.* —**blind alley 1.** alley open at one end only; cul-de-sac **2.** *inf.* situation in which no further progress can be made —**blind date** *inf.* social meeting between man and woman who have not met before —**blind flying** navigation of aircraft by use of instruments alone —ˈ**blindfold** *vt.* **1.** cover the eyes of, so as to prevent vision —*n.* **2.** piece of cloth *etc.* used to cover eyes —**blindman's buff** game in which one player is blindfolded —**blind spot 1.** small area of retina, where optic nerve enters, in which vision is not experienced **2.** area where vision is obscured **3.** subject about which person is ignorant or prejudiced

blink (blɪŋk) *vi.* **1.** wink **2.** twinkle **3.** shine intermittently —*n.* **4.** gleam —ˈ**blinkers** *pl.n.* leather flaps to prevent horse from seeing to the side —**blink at** see, know about, but ignore —**on the blink** *inf.* not working (properly)

THESAURUS

gaunt, open, raw, unsheltered, weather-beaten, windswept, windy **2.** cheerless, comfortless, depressing, discouraging, disheartening, dismal, dreary, gloomy, grim, hopeless, joyless, sombre, unpromising

bleary blurred, blurry, dim, fogged, foggy, fuzzy, hazy, indistinct, misty, murky, rheumy, watery

bleed 1. exude, flow, gush, lose blood, ooze, run, seep, shed blood, spurt, trickle, weep **2.** deplete, drain, draw *or* take blood, exhaust, extort, extract, fleece, leech, milk, phlebotomize (*Medical*), reduce, sap, squeeze

blemish 1. *n.* blot, blotch, blur, defect, disfigurement, disgrace, dishonour, fault, flaw, imperfection, mark, smudge, speck, spot, stain, taint **2.** *v.* blot, blotch, blur, damage, deface, disfigure, flaw, impair, injure, mar, mark, smirch, smudge, spoil, spot, stain, sully, taint, tarnish

blend 1. *v.* amalgamate, coalesce, combine, compound, fuse, intermix, merge, mingle, mix, synthesize, unite **2.** *n.* alloy, amalgam, amalgamation, combination, composite, compound, concoction, fusion, mix, mixture, synthesis, union

bless 1. anoint, consecrate, dedicate, exalt, extol, give thanks to, glorify, hallow, invoke happiness on, magnify, ordain, praise, sanctify, thank **2.** bestow, endow, favour, give, grace, grant, provide

blessed 1. adored, beatified, divine, hallowed, holy, revered, sacred, sanctified **2.** blissful, contented, glad, happy, joyful, joyous

blessedness beatitude, bliss, blissfulness, content, felicity, happiness, heavenly joy, pleasure, sanctity, state of grace, *summum bonum*

blessing 1. benediction, benison, commendation, consecration, dedication, grace, invocation, thanksgiving **2.** approbation, approval, backing, concurrence, consent, favour, good wishes, leave, permission, regard, sanction, support **3.** advantage, benefit, boon, bounty, favour, gain, gift, godsend, good fortune, help, kindness, profit, service, windfall

blight *n.* **1.** canker, decay, disease, fungus, infestation, mildew, pest, pestilence, rot **2.** affliction, bane, contamination, corruption, curse, evil, plague, pollution, scourge, woe ~*v.* **3.** blast, destroy, injure, nip in the bud, ruin, shrivel, taint with mildew, wither **4.** *Fig.* annihilate, crush, dash, disappoint, frustrate, mar, nullify, ruin, spoil, wreck

blind *adj.* **1.** destitute of vision, eyeless, sightless, stone-blind, unseeing, unsighted, visionless **2.** *Fig.* careless, heedless, ignorant, inattentive, inconsiderate, indifferent, indiscriminate, injudicious, insensitive, morally darkened, neglectful, oblivious, prejudiced, thoughtless, unaware of, unconscious of, uncritical, undiscerning, unmindful of, unobservant, unreasoning **3.** hasty, impetuous, irrational, mindless, rash, reckless, senseless, uncontrollable, uncontrolled, unthinking, violent, wild **4.** closed, concealed, dark, dead-end, dim, hidden, leading nowhere, obscured, obstructed, without exit ~*n.* **5.** camouflage, cloak, cover, façade, feint, front, mask, masquerade, pretext, screen, smoke screen

blindly 1. aimlessly, at random, confusedly, frantically, indiscriminately, instinctively, madly, pur-

blip (blɪp) *n.* repetitive sound or visible pulse, *eg* on radar screen

bliss (blɪs) *n.* perfect happiness —ˈ**blissful** *a.* —ˈ**blissfully** *adv.* —ˈ**blissfulness** *n.*

blister (ˈblɪstə) *n.* **1.** bubble on skin **2.** surface swelling, *eg* on paint —*v.* **3.** form blisters (on) —ˈ**blistering** *a.* (of verbal attack) bitter —**blister pack** package for goods with hard, raised, transparent cover

blithe (blaɪð) *a.* happy, gay —ˈ**blithely** *adv.* —ˈ**blitheness** *n.*

blithering (ˈblɪðərɪŋ) *a.* **1.** talking foolishly; jabbering **2.** *inf.* stupid; foolish

B.Litt. *or* **B.Lit. 1.** Bachelor of Letters **2.** Bachelor of Literature

blitz (blɪts) *n.* sudden, concentrated attack —**blitzkrieg** (ˈblɪtskriːg) *n.* intensive military attack designed to defeat opposition quickly

blizzard (ˈblɪzəd) *n.* blinding storm of wind and snow

bloat (bləʊt) *v.* **1.** puff or swell out —*n.* **2.** distension of stomach of cow *etc.* by gas —ˈ**bloated** *a.* swollen —ˈ**bloater** *n.* smoked herring

blob (blɒb) *n.* **1.** soft mass, *esp.* drop of liquid **2.** shapeless form

bloc (blɒk) *n.* (political) grouping of people or countries

block (blɒk) *n.* **1.** solid (rectangular) piece of wood, stone *etc., esp. Hist.* that on which people were beheaded **2.** obstacle **3.** stoppage **4.** pulley with frame **5.** large building of offices, flats *etc.* **6.** group of buildings **7.** area enclosed by intersecting streets —*vt.* **8.** obstruct, stop up **9.** shape on block —ˈ**blockage** *n.* obstruction —**block and tackle** hoisting device in which rope or chain is passed around pair of blocks containing one or more pulleys —ˈ**blockbuster** *n. inf.* **1.** large bomb used to demolish extensive areas **2.** very forceful person, thing *etc.* —ˈ**blockhead** *n. derogatory* fool, simpleton —ˈ**blockhouse** *n.* **1.** formerly, wooden fortification with ports for defensive fire *etc.* **2.** concrete structure strengthened for protection against enemy fire, with apertures for defensive gunfire **3.** building constructed of logs or squared timber —**block letters** written capital letters —**block release** UK release of trainees from work for study at college for several weeks at a time —**block vote** *see* **card vote** *at* CARD —**block in** sketch in

blockade (blɒˈkeɪd) *n.* **1.** physical prevention of access, *esp.* to port *etc.* —*vt.* **2.** subject to blockade

bloke (bləʊk) *n. inf.* fellow, chap

blond (blɒnd) *a.* **1.** (of hair) light-coloured —*n.* **2.** someone with blond hair (**blonde** *fem.*)

blood (blʌd) *n.* **1.** red fluid in veins **2.** race **3.** kindred **4.** parental heritage **5.** temperament **6.** passion —*vt.* **7.** initiate (into hunting, war *etc.*) —ˈ**bloodily** *adv.* —ˈ**bloodless** *a.* —ˈ**bloody** *a.* **1.** covered in blood **2.** slaughterous —*a./adv.* **3.** *sl.* common intensifier —*vt.* **4.** make bloody —**blood bank** (institution managing) store of human blood preserved for transfusion —**blood bath** indiscriminate slaughter; massacre —**blood count** determination of number of red and white blood corpuscles in sample of blood —ˈ**bloodcurdling** *a.* terrifying; horrifying —**blood group** any of various groups into which human blood is classified (*also* **blood type**) —ˈ**bloodhound** *n.* breed of large hound noted for its keen powers of scent —**bloodletting** *n.* **1.** therapeutic removal of blood **2.** bloodshed, *esp.* in feud —**blood money 1.** compensation paid to relatives of murdered person **2.** money paid to hired murderer —**blood poisoning** disease in which blood contains poisonous matter (*also* **septiˈcaemia**) —**blood pressure** pressure exerted by blood on inner walls of arteries —**blood relation** *or* **relative** person related by birth —ˈ**bloodshed** *n.* slaughter, killing —ˈ**bloodshot** *a.* (of eyes) inflamed —**blood sport** sport in which animals are killed, *eg* fox-hunting —**blood stream** flow of blood through vessels of living body —ˈ**bloodsucker** *n.* **1.** parasite (*eg* mosquito) living on host's blood **2.** parasitic person —**blood test** examination of sample of blood —ˈ**bloodthirsty** *a.* murderous, cruel —**blood transfusion** transfer of blood from one person to another —**blood vessel** artery, capillary or vein

THESAURUS

poselessly, wildly **2.** carelessly, heedlessly, impulsively, inconsiderately, passionately, recklessly, regardlessly, senselessly, thoughtlessly, unreasonably, wilfully

blink 1. bat, flutter, glimpse, nictate, nictitate, peer, squint, wink **2.** flash, flicker, gleam, glimmer, scintillate, shine, sparkle, twinkle, wink **3. blink at** condone, connive at, disregard, ignore, overlook, pass by, turn a blind eye to **4. on the blink** *Inf.* faulty, malfunctioning, not working (properly), out of action, out of order, playing up

bliss beatitude, blessedness, blissfulness, ecstasy, euphoria, felicity, gladness, happiness, heaven, joy, paradise, rapture

blissful delighted, ecstatic, elated, enchanted, enraptured, euphoric, happy, heavenly (*Inf.*), in ecstasies, joyful, joyous, rapturous

blister abscess, blain, bleb, boil, bubble, canker, carbuncle, cyst, furuncle (*Pathology*), pimple, pustule, sore, swelling, ulcer, welt, wen

blithe animated, buoyant, carefree, cheerful, cheery, debonair, gay, gladsome, happy, jaunty, light-hearted, merry, mirthful, sprightly, sunny, vivacious

blitz assault, attack, blitzkrieg, bombardment, offensive, onslaught, raid, strike

blizzard blast, gale, snowstorm, squall, storm, tempest

bloat balloon, blow up, dilate, distend, enlarge, expand, inflate, puff up, swell

blob ball, bead, bubble, dab, dewdrop, drop, droplet, glob, globule, lump, mass, pearl, pellet, pill

bloc alliance, axis, cabal, clique, coalition, combine, entente, faction, group, league, ring, union, wing

block *n.* **1.** bar, brick, cake, chunk, cube, hunk, ingot, lump, mass, piece, square **2.** bar, barrier, blockage, hindrance, impediment, jam, obstacle, obstruction, stoppage ~*v.* **3.** bung up (*Inf.*), choke, clog, close, obstruct, plug, stop up **4.** arrest, bar, check, deter, halt, hinder, impede, obstruct, stop, thwart

blockade barricade, barrier, closure, encirclement, hindrance, impediment, obstacle, obstruction, restriction, siege, stoppage

blockage block, blocking, impediment, obstruction, occlusion, stoppage, stopping up

blockhead bonehead (*Sl.*), dolt, dullard, dunce, fool, idiot, ignoramus, numskull, simpleton

blond, blonde fair, fair-haired, fair-skinned, flaxen, golden-haired, light, light-coloured, light-complexioned, tow-headed

—**bloody-minded** *a.* UK *inf.* deliberately obstructive and unhelpful —**in cold blood** cruelly and ruthlessly; deliberately and calmly —**make one's blood boil** cause to be angry —**make one's blood run cold** fill with horror

bloom[1] (blu:m) *n.* **1.** flower of plant **2.** blossoming **3.** prime, perfection **4.** glow **5.** powdery deposit on fruit —*vi.* **6.** be in flower **7.** flourish —'**blooming** *a.*

bloom[2] (blu:m) *n.* rectangular mass of metal obtained by rolling or forging cast ingot

bloomer ('blu:mə) *n. inf.* ludicrous mistake

bloomers ('blu:məz) *pl.n.* wide, baggy knickers

blossom ('blɒsəm) *n.* **1.** flower **2.** flower bud —*vi.* **3.** flower **4.** develop

blot (blɒt) *n.* **1.** spot, stain **2.** disgrace —*vt.* **3.** spot, stain **4.** obliterate **5.** detract from **6.** soak up (ink *etc.*) from (-tt-) —**blotting paper** absorbent paper, used *esp.* for soaking up surplus ink

blotch (blɒtʃ) *n.* **1.** dark spot on skin —*vt.* **2.** make spotted —'**blotchy** *a.*

blotto ('blɒtəʊ) *a. sl.* unconscious, *esp.* through drunkenness

blouse (blaʊz) *n.* light, loose upper garment

blouson ('blu:zɒn) *n.* loosely fitting but tight-waisted jacket

blow[1] (bləʊ) *vi.* **1.** make a current of air **2.** pant **3.** make sound by blowing **4.** (of whale) spout —*vt.* **5.** drive air upon or into **6.** drive by current of air **7.** sound **8.** fan **9.** *sl.* squander (**blew, blown**) —*n.* **10.** blast **11.** gale —'**blower** *n.* —'**blowy** *a.* windy —**blow-by-blow** *a.* explained in great detail —**blow-dry** *vt.* **1.** style (hair) after washing, using hand-held hair dryer —*n.* **2.** this method of drying hair —'**blowfly** *n.* fly which infects food *etc.* (*also* '**bluebottle**) —'**blowhole** *n.* **1.** nostril of whales, situated far back on skull **2.** hole in ice through which seals *etc.* breathe **3.** vent for air or gas —'**blowlamp** *n.* small burner with very hot flame, for removing paint *etc.* (*also* **blow torch**) —**blow-out** *n.* **1.** sudden puncture in tyre **2.** uncontrolled escape of oil or gas from well **3.** *sl.* large meal —'**blowpipe** *n.* dart tube —**blow out 1.** extinguish **2.** (of tyre) puncture suddenly **3.** (of fuse) melt —**blow up 1.** explode **2.** inflate **3.** enlarge (photograph *etc.*) **4.** *inf.* lose one's temper

blow[2] (bləʊ) *n.* **1.** stroke, knock **2.** sudden misfortune, loss

blown (bləʊn) *pp. of* BLOW[1]

blowzy *or* **blowsy** ('blaʊzɪ) *a.* **1.** slovenly, sluttish **2.** red-faced

blubber ('blʌbə) *vi.* **1.** weep —*n.* **2.** fat of whales **3.** weeping

bludgeon ('blʌdʒən) *n.* **1.** short thick club —*vt.* **2.** strike (as) with bludgeon **3.** coerce

blue (blu:) *a.* **1.** of colour of sky or shades of that colour **2.** depressed **3.** indecent —*n.* **4.** the colour **5.** dye or pigment **6.** indigo powder used in laundering —*vt.* **7.** make blue **8.** dip in blue liquid (**blued** *pt./pp.*) —**blues** *pl.n. inf.* (*oft. with sing. v.*) **1.** depression **2.** form of Amer. Negro folk song in slow tempo, employed in jazz music —'**bluish** *a.* —**blue baby** baby born with bluish skin caused by heart defect —'**bluebell** *n.* wild spring flower —'**blueberry** *n.* N Amer. shrub with blue-black edible berries —**blue blood** royal or aristocratic descent —'**bluebook** *n.* UK government publication bound in blue cover —'**bluebottle** *n.* blowfly —**blue-collar** *a.* denoting manual industrial workers —**blue-eyed boy** *inf., chiefly* UK favourite of person or group —**blue-pencil** *vt.* alter, delete parts of, *esp.* to censor —**blue peter** signal flag of blue with white

THESAURUS

blood 1. gore, lifeblood, vital fluid **2.** ancestry, birth, consanguinity, descendants, descent, extraction, family, kindred, kinship, lineage, noble extraction, relations **3.** *Fig.* anger, disposition, feeling, passion, spirit, temper

bloodcurdling appalling, chilling, dreadful, fearful, frightening, hair-raising, horrendous, horrifying, scaring, spine-chilling, terrifying

bloodless anaemic, ashen, chalky, colourless, pale, pallid, pasty, sallow, sickly, wan

bloodshed blood bath, bloodletting, butchery, carnage, gore, killing, massacre, murder, slaughter, slaying

bloodthirsty barbarous, brutal, cruel, ferocious, inhuman, murderous, ruthless, savage, vicious, warlike

bloody 1. bleeding, blood-soaked, blood-spattered, bloodstained, gaping, raw, unstaunched **2.** cruel, ferocious, fierce, sanguinary, savage

bloom *n.* **1.** blossom, blossoming, bud, efflorescence, flower, opening (*of flowers*) **2.** *Fig.* beauty, blush, flourishing, flush, freshness, glow, health, heyday, lustre, perfection, prime, radiance, rosiness, vigour ~*v.* **3.** blossom, blow, bud, burgeon, open, sprout **4.** develop, fare well, flourish, grow, prosper, succeed, thrive, wax

blossom *n.* **1.** bloom, bud, floret, flower, flowers ~*v.* **2.** bloom, burgeon, flower **3.** *Fig.* bloom, develop, flourish, grow, mature, progress, prosper, thrive

blot *n.* **1.** blotch, mark, patch, smear, smudge, speck, splodge, spot **2.** blemish, blur, defect, disgrace, fault, flaw, spot, stain, taint ~*v.* **3.** bespatter, disfigure, disgrace, mark, smudge, spoil, spot, stain, sully, tarnish **4.** absorb, dry, soak up, take up **5. blot (out)** cancel, darken, destroy, efface, erase, expunge, obliterate, obscure, shadow

blow[1] *v.* **1.** blast, breathe, exhale, fan, pant, puff, waft **2.** bear, buffet, drive, fling, flutter, sweep, waft, whirl, whisk **3.** blare, mouth, pipe, play, sound, toot, trumpet, vibrate ~*n.* **4.** blast, draught, flurry, gale, gust, puff, strong breeze, tempest, wind

blow[2] *n.* **1.** bang, bash (*Inf.*), belt (*Inf.*), buffet, clomp (*Sl.*), clout (*Inf.*), clump (*Sl.*), knock, punch, rap, slosh (*Sl.*), smack, sock (*Sl.*), stroke, thump, wallop (*Inf.*), whack **2.** *Fig.* affliction, bolt from the blue, bombshell, calamity, catastrophe, comedown (*Inf.*), disappointment, disaster, jolt, misfortune, reverse, setback, shock, upset

blow out 1. extinguish, put out, snuff **2.** burst, erupt, explode, rupture, shatter

blow up 1. bloat, distend, enlarge, expand, fill, inflate, puff up, pump up, swell **2.** blast, bomb, burst, detonate, dynamite, explode, go off, rupture, shatter **3.** enlarge, enlarge on, exaggerate, heighten, magnify, overstate **4.** *Inf.* become angry, become enraged, erupt, go off the deep end (*Inf.*), hit the roof (*Inf.*), lose one's temper, rage

bludgeon *n.* **1.** club, cudgel, shillelagh, truncheon ~*v.* **2.** beat, beat up, club, cudgel, knock down, strike **3.** browbeat, bulldoze (*Inf.*), bully, coerce, force, hector, steamroller

square at centre, displayed by vessel about to leave port —ˈ**blueprint** *n.* **1.** copy of drawing **2.** original plan —**blue ribbon 1.** UK badge of blue silk worn by members of Order of the Garter **2.** badge awarded as first prize in competition —ˈ**bluestocking** *n.* scholarly, intellectual woman —ˈ**bluetit** *n.* common European tit having blue crown, wings, and tail, and yellow underparts —**blue whale** largest mammal: bluish-grey whalebone whale

bluff[1] (blʌf) *n.* **1.** cliff, steep bank **2. C** clump of trees —*a.* **3.** hearty **4.** blunt **5.** steep **6.** abrupt

bluff[2] (blʌf) *v.* **1.** deceive (someone) by pretence of strength —*n.* **2.** pretence

blunder (ˈblʌndə) *n.* **1.** clumsy mistake —*vi.* **2.** make stupid mistake **3.** act clumsily

blunderbuss (ˈblʌndəbʌs) *n.* obsolete short gun with wide bore

blunt (blʌnt) *a.* **1.** not sharp **2.** (of speech) abrupt —*vt.* **3.** make blunt —ˈ**bluntly** *adv.* —ˈ**bluntness** *n.*

blur (blɜː) *v.* **1.** make, become less distinct (**-rr-**) —*n.* **2.** something vague, indistinct —ˈ**blurry** *a.*

blurb (blɜːb) *n.* statement, advertising or recommending book *etc.*

blurt (blɜːt) *vt.* (*oft. with* out) utter suddenly or unadvisedly

blush (blʌʃ) *vi.* **1.** become red in face **2.** be ashamed **3.** redden —*n.* **4.** this effect —ˈ**blusher** *n.* cosmetic applied to cheeks to give rosy colour

bluster (ˈblʌstə) *vi./n.* (indulge in) noisy, aggressive behaviour —ˈ**blusterer** *n.* —ˈ**blustering** *or* ˈ**blustery** *a.* (of wind *etc.*) noisy and gusty

B.M. British Museum

B.M.A. British Medical Association

B.Mus. Bachelor of Music

B.O. 1. *inf.* body odour **2.** box office

boa (ˈbəʊə) *n.* **1.** large, nonvenomous snake **2.** long scarf of fur or feathers —**boa constrictor** very large snake of tropical Amer. and W Indies, that kills prey by constriction

boar (bɔː) *n.* **1.** male pig **2.** wild pig

board (bɔːd) *n.* **1.** broad, flat piece of wood **2.** sheet of rigid material for specific purpose **3.** table **4.** meals **5.** group of people who administer company **6.** governing body **7.** thick, stiff paper —*pl.* **8.** theatre, stage **9. C** wooden enclosure where ice hockey, box lacrosse is played —*vt.* **10.** cover with planks **11.** supply with regular meals **12.** enter (ship *etc.*) —*vi.* **13.** take daily meals —ˈ**boarder** *n.* —**boarding house** lodging house where meals may be had —**boarding school** school providing living accommodation for pupils —ˈ**boardroom** *n.* room where board of company meets —**above board** beyond suspicion —**on board** in or into ship

boast (bəʊst) *vi.* **1.** speak too much in praise of oneself, one's possessions *etc.* —*n.* **2.** something boasted (of) —ˈ**boaster** *n.* —ˈ**boastful** *a.* —ˈ**boastfully** *adv.* —ˈ**boastfulness** *n.* —**boast of 1.** brag of **2.** have to show

boat (bəʊt) *n.* **1.** small open vessel **2.** ship —*vi.* **3.** sail about in boat —ˈ**boater** *n.* flat straw hat —ˈ**boating** *n.* —ˈ**boathook** *n.* —ˈ**boathouse** *n.* —ˈ**boatman** *n.* —**boatswain** (ˈbəʊsᵊn) *n.* ship's officer in charge of boats, sails *etc.* —**boat train** train scheduled to take passengers to or from particular ship

bob (bɒb) *vi.* **1.** move up and down —*vt.* **2.** move jerkily **3.** cut (hair) short (**-bb-**) —*n.* **4.** short, jerking motion **5.** short hair style **6.** weight on pendulum *etc.* **7.** *inf.* formerly, shilling —**bobbed** *a.*

bobbejaan (ˈbɒbəjɑːn) *n.* **SA** baboon

THESAURUS

blue 1. azure, cerulean, cobalt, cyan, navy, sapphire, sky-coloured, ultramarine **2.** *Fig.* dejected, depressed, despondent, dismal, downcast, downhearted, down in the dumps (*Inf.*), fed up, gloomy, glum, low, melancholy, sad, unhappy **3.** *Inf.* bawdy, dirty, indecent, lewd, naughty, near the knuckle (*Inf.*), obscene, risqué, smutty, vulgar

blueprint design, draft, layout, outline, pattern, pilot scheme, plan, project, prototype, scheme, sketch

blues dejection, depression, despondency, doldrums, dumps (*Inf.*), gloom, gloominess, glumness, low spirits, melancholy, moodiness

bluff 1. *v.* deceive, defraud, delude, fake, feign, humbug, lie, mislead, pretend, sham **2.** *n.* bluster, boast, braggadocio, bragging, bravado, deceit, deception, fake, feint, fraud, humbug, idle boast, lie, mere show, pretence, sham, show, subterfuge

blunder *n.* **1.** error, fault, inaccuracy, mistake, oversight, slip, slip-up (*Inf.*) **2.** boob (*Sl.*), clanger (*Inf.*), faux pas, gaffe, gaucherie, howler (*Inf.*), impropriety, indiscretion, mistake ~*v.* **3.** botch, bungle, err, slip up (*Inf.*) **4.** bumble, confuse, flounder, misjudge, stumble

blunt *adj.* **1.** dull, dulled, edgeless, pointless, rounded, unsharpened **2.** *Fig.* bluff, brusque, discourteous, explicit, forthright, frank, impolite, outspoken, plain-spoken, rude, straightforward, tactless, trenchant, uncivil, unpolished ~*v.* **3.** dampen, deaden, dull, numb, soften, take the edge off, weaken

blur 1. *v.* becloud, bedim, befog, cloud, darken, dim, fog, make hazy, make indistinct, make vague, mask, obscure, soften **2.** *n.* blear, blurredness, cloudiness, confusion, dimness, fog, haze, indistinctness, obscurity

blurt out babble, blab, cry, disclose, exclaim, gush, reveal, spill, spout (*Inf.*), sputter, tattle, utter suddenly

blush 1. *v.* colour, crimson, flush, redden, turn red, turn scarlet **2.** *n.* colour, flush, glow, pink tinge, reddening, rosiness, rosy tint, ruddiness

bluster 1. *v.* boast, brag, bulldoze, bully, domineer, hector, rant, roar, roister, storm, swagger, swell, vaunt **2.** *n.* bluff, boasting, boisterousness, bombast, bragging, bravado, crowing, swagger, swaggering

blustery boisterous, gusty, squally, stormy, tempestuous, violent, wild

board *n.* **1.** panel, piece of timber, plank, slat, timber **2.** daily meals, food, meals, provisions, victuals **3.** advisers, advisory group, committee, conclave, council, directorate, directors, panel, trustees ~*v.* **4.** embark, embus, enplane, enter, entrain, mount **5.** accommodate, feed, house, lodge, put up, quarter, room

boast 1. *v.* blow one's own trumpet, bluster, brag, crow, exaggerate, puff, strut, swagger, talk big (*Sl.*), vaunt **2.** *n.* avowal, brag, gasconade (*Rare*), rodomontade (*Literary*), swank (*Inf.*), vaunt

boastful bragging, cocky, conceited, crowing, egotistical, puffed-up, swaggering, swanky (*Inf.*), swollen-headed, vainglorious, vaunting

bob bounce, duck, hop, jerk, leap, nod, oscillate, quiver, skip, waggle, weave, wobble

bobbin (ˈbɒbɪn) *n.* cylinder on which thread is wound
bobble (ˈbɒbᵊl) *n.* small, tufted ball for decoration
bobby (ˈbɒbɪ) *n. inf.* policeman
bobcat (ˈbɒbkæt) *n.* Amer. wild cat, bay lynx
bobolink (ˈbɒbəlɪŋk) *n.* Amer. songbird
bobsleigh (ˈbɒbsleɪ) *n.* **1.** racing sledge for two or more people, with steering mechanism —*vi.* **2.** ride on bobsleigh (*also* (*esp.* US) **bobsled** (ˈbɒbslɛd))
bobtail (ˈbɒbteɪl) *n.* **1.** docked or diminutive tail **2.** animal with such tail —*a.* **3.** having tail cut short (*also* ˈ**bobtailed**) —*vt.* **4.** dock tail of **5.** cut short; curtail
BOC British Oxygen Company
bode[1] (bəʊd) *vt.* be an omen of
bode[2] (bəʊd) *pt. of* BIDE
bodega (bəʊˈdiːgə) *n.* shop selling wine, *esp.* in Spanish-speaking country
bodge (bɒdʒ) *vt. inf.* make mess of; botch
bodice (ˈbɒdɪs) *n.* upper part of woman's dress
bodkin (ˈbɒdkɪn) *n.* **1.** large blunt needle **2.** tool for piercing holes
body (ˈbɒdɪ) *n.* **1.** whole frame of man or animal **2.** main part of such frame **3.** corpse **4.** main part of anything **5.** substance **6.** mass **7.** person **8.** number of persons united or organized **9.** matter, opposed to spirit —ˈ**bodiless** *a.* —ˈ**bodily** *a./adv.* —ˈ**bodyguard** *n.* escort to protect important person —**body politic** people of nation or nation itself considered as political entity —**body stocking** one-piece undergarment, usu. of nylon, covering torso —ˈ**bodywork** *n.* shell of motor vehicle
Boer (bʊə) *n.* a S Afr. of Dutch or Huguenot descent —**boerbul** (ˈbʊəbəl) *n.* **SA** crossbred mastiff —**boerewors** (ˈbʊərəvɔːs) *n.* **SA** mincemeat sausage —**boerperd** (ˈbʊəpɜːt) *n.* S Afr. breed of horse
boet (bʊt) *or* **boetie** *n.* **SA** *inf.* friend
boffin (ˈbɒfɪn) *n. inf.* scientist, technical research worker
bog (bɒg) *n.* **1.** wet, soft ground **2.** *sl.* lavatory —ˈ**boggy** *a.* marshy —**bog down** stick as in a bog
bogan (ˈbəʊgən) *n.* **C** sluggish side stream
bogey *or* **bogy** (ˈbəʊgɪ) *n.* **1.** evil or mischievous spirit **2.** standard golf score for good player —ˈ**bogeyman** *n.*
boggle (ˈbɒgᵊl) *vi.* stare, be surprised
bogie *or* **bogy** (ˈbəʊgɪ) *n.* **1.** low truck on four wheels **2.** pivoted undercarriage, as on railway rolling stock
bogus (ˈbəʊgəs) *a.* sham, false
Bohemian (bəʊˈhiːmɪən) *a.* **1.** unconventional —*n.* **2.** (*oft.* **b-**) one who leads an unsettled life —**Boˈhemianism** *n.*
boil[1] (bɔɪl) *vi.* **1.** change from liquid to gas, *esp.* by heating **2.** become cooked by boiling **3.** bubble **4.** be agitated **5.** seethe **6.** *inf.* be hot **7.** *inf.* be angry —*vt.* **8.** cause to boil **9.** cook by boiling —*n.* **10.** boiling state —ˈ**boiler** *n.* vessel for boiling —**boiler suit** garment covering whole body —**boiling point** temperature at which boiling occurs (100°C for water)
boil[2] (bɔɪl) *n.* inflamed suppurating swelling on skin
boisterous (ˈbɔɪstərəs, -strəs) *a.* **1.** wild **2.** noisy **3.** turbulent —ˈ**boisterously** *adv.* —ˈ**boisterousness** *n.*
bold (bəʊld) *a.* **1.** daring, fearless **2.** presumptuous **3.** striking, prominent —ˈ**boldly** *adv.* —ˈ**boldness** *n.*
bole (bəʊl) *n.* trunk of tree
bolero (bəˈlɛərəʊ) *n.* **1.** Spanish dance **2.** short loose jacket

---

THESAURUS

bode augur, betoken, forebode, foreshadow, foretell, forewarn, impart, omen, portend, predict, presage, prophesy, signify, threaten
bodiless disembodied, ghostly, immaterial, incorporeal, insubstantial, spectral, spiritual, supernatural
bodily **1.** *adj.* actual, carnal, corporal, corporeal, fleshly, material, physical, substantial, tangible **2.** *adv.* altogether, as a body, as a group, collectively, completely, en masse, entirely, fully, totally, wholly
body **1.** build, figure, form, frame, physique, shape, torso, trunk **2.** cadaver, carcass, corpse, dead body, relics, remains, stiff (*Sl.*) **3.** being, creature, human, human being, individual, mortal, person **4.** bulk, essence, main part, mass, material, matter, substance **5.** association, band, bloc, collection, company, confederation, congress, corporation, society **6.** crowd, horde, majority, mass, mob, multitude, throng **7.** consistency, density, firmness, richness, solidity, substance
bog fen, marsh, marshland, mire, morass, moss (*Northern Eng. & Scot.*), peat bog, quagmire, slough, swamp, wetlands
bog down delay, halt, impede, sink, slow down, slow up, stall, stick
bogey apparition, bogeyman, goblin, hobgoblin, imp, spectre, spirit, spook (*Inf.*), sprite
boggle be alarmed (confused, surprised, taken aback), shy, stagger, startle, take fright
boggy fenny, marshy, miry, muddy, oozy, quaggy, soft, spongy, swampy, waterlogged, yielding
bogus artificial, counterfeit, dummy, fake, false, forged, fraudulent, imitation, phoney (*Sl.*), pseudo (*Inf.*), sham, spurious
bohemian **1.** *adj.* alternative, artistic, arty (*Inf.*), avant-garde, eccentric, exotic, left bank, nonconformist, offbeat, unconventional, unorthodox, way-out (*Inf.*) **2.** *n.* beatnik, dropout, hippie, iconoclast, nonconformist
boil[1] *v.* **1.** agitate, bubble, churn, effervesce, fizz, foam, froth, seethe **2.** be angry, be indignant, foam at the mouth (*Inf.*), fulminate, fume, rage, rave, storm
boil[2] *n.* blain, blister, carbuncle, furuncle (*Pathology*), gathering, pustule, tumour, ulcer
boisterous **1.** bouncy, clamorous, disorderly, impetuous, loud, noisy, obstreperous, riotous, rollicking, rowdy, rumbustious, unrestrained, unruly, uproarious, vociferous, wild **2.** blustery, gusty, raging, rough, squally, stormy, tempestuous, tumultuous, turbulent
bold **1.** adventurous, audacious, brave, courageous, daring, dauntless, enterprising, fearless, gallant, heroic, intrepid, lion-hearted, valiant, valorous **2.** barefaced, brash, brazen, cheeky, confident, forward, fresh (*Inf.*), impudent, insolent, pert, presumptuous, rude, saucy, shameless **3.** bright, colourful, conspicuous, eye-catching, flashy, forceful, lively, loud, prominent, pronounced, showy, spirited, striking, strong, vivid

boll (bəʊl) *n.* seed capsule of cotton, flax *etc.*

bollard (ˈbɒlɑːd, ˈbɒləd) *n.* **1.** post on quay or ship to secure mooring lines **2.** short post in road or footpath as barrier or marker

Bolshevik (ˈbɒlʃɪvɪk) *n.* violent revolutionary —**ˈbolshie** *or* **ˈbolshy** *a. inf.* **1.** rebellious, uncooperative **2.** left-wing

bolster (ˈbəʊlstə) *vt.* **1.** support, uphold —*n.* **2.** long pillow **3.** pad, support

bolt[1] (bəʊlt) *n.* **1.** bar or pin, *esp.* with thread for nut **2.** rush **3.** discharge of lightning **4.** roll of cloth —*vt.* **5.** fasten with bolt **6.** swallow hastily —*vi.* **7.** rush away **8.** break from control

bolt[2] *or* **boult** (bəʊlt) *vt.* **1.** pass (flour *etc.*) through sieve **2.** examine and separate —**ˈbolter** *n.*

bomb (bɒm) *n.* **1.** explosive projectile **2.** any explosive device **3.** *sl.* large amount of money —*vt.* **4.** attack with bombs —**bomˈbard** *vt.* **1.** shell **2.** attack (verbally) —**bombarˈdier** (bɒmbəˈdɪə) *n.* artillery noncommissioned officer —**bomˈbardment** *n.* —**ˈbomber** *n.* aircraft capable of carrying bombs —**ˈbombshell** *n.* **1.** shell of bomb **2.** surprise **3.** *inf.* very attractive girl —**the bomb** nuclear bomb

bombast (ˈbɒmbæst) *n.* **1.** pompous language **2.** pomposity —**bomˈbastic** *a.*

Bombay duck (bɒmˈbeɪ) fish eaten dried with curry dishes as savoury (*also* **ˈbummalo**)

bombazine *or* **bombasine** (bɒmbəˈziːn, ˈbɒmbəziːn) *n.* twilled fabric, *esp.* one of silk and worsted

bona fide (ˈbəʊnə ˈfaɪdɪ) *Lat.* **1.** genuine(ly) **2.** sincere(ly) —**bona fides** (ˈfaɪdiːz) good faith, sincerity

bonanza (bəˈnænzə) *n.* sudden good luck or wealth

bonbon (ˈbɒnbɒn) *n.* sweet

bond (bɒnd) *n.* **1.** that which binds **2.** link, union **3.** written promise to pay money or carry out contract —*vt.* **4.** bind **5.** store (goods) until duty is paid on them —**ˈbonded** *a.* **1.** placed in bond **2.** mortgaged —**ˈbonding** *n.* process by which individuals become emotionally attached to one another —**ˈbondsman** *n.* **1.** *Law* person bound by bond to act as surety for another **2.** serf, slave (*also* **ˈbondservant**)

bondage (ˈbɒndɪdʒ) *n.* slavery

bone (bəʊn) *n.* **1.** hard substance forming animal's skeleton **2.** piece of this —*pl.* **3.** essentials —*vt.* **4.** remove bones from —*vi.* **5.** *inf.* (*with* up) study hard —**ˈboneless** *a.* —**ˈbony** *a.* —**bone china** porcelain containing bone ash —**bone-dry** *a. inf.* completely dry —**ˈbonehead** *n. inf.* stupid person —**bone meal** dried and ground animal bones, used as fertilizer or in stock feeds —**ˈboneshaker** *n.* **1.** early type of bicycle having solid tyres **2.** *sl.* any rickety vehicle

bonfire (ˈbɒnfaɪə) *n.* large outdoor fire

bongo (ˈbɒŋgəʊ) *n.* small drum, usu. one of pair, played with fingers (*pl.* **-s, -es**)

bonhomie (ˈbɒnəmiː) *Fr.* good humour, geniality

bonk (bɒŋk) *inf. vt.* **1.** hit —*v.* **2.** have sexual intercourse (with) —**ˈbonking** *n.*

bonkers (ˈbɒŋkəz) *a. sl.* crazy

bon mot (*Fr.* bɔ̃ ˈmo) clever and fitting remark (*pl.* **bons mots** (bɔ̃ ˈmo))

bonnet (ˈbɒnɪt) *n.* **1.** hat with strings **2.** cap **3.** cover of motor vehicle engine

bonny (ˈbɒnɪ) *a.* beautiful, handsome —**ˈbonnily** *adv.*

bonsai (ˈbɒnsaɪ) *n.* (art of growing) dwarf trees, shrubs

bontebok (ˈbɒntɪbʌk) *n.* S Afr. antelope

bonus (ˈbəʊnəs) *n.* extra (unexpected) payment or gift

bon vivant (bɔ̃ viˈvɑ̃) *Fr.* person who enjoys luxuries, *esp.* good food and drink (*pl.* ***bons vivants*** (bɔ̃ viˈvɑ̃))

bon voyage (*Fr.* bɔ̃ vwaˈjaːʒ) phrase used to wish traveller pleasant journey

bonze (bɒnz) *n.* Chinese or Japanese Buddhist priest or monk

boo (buː) *interj.* **1.** expression of disapproval or contempt **2.** exclamation to surprise *esp.* child —*v.* **3.** make this sound (at)

boob (buːb) *n. sl.* **1.** foolish mistake **2.** female breast

booby (ˈbuːbɪ) *n.* **1.** fool **2.** tropical marine bird —**booby prize** mock prize for poor performance —**booby trap 1.** harmless-looking object which explodes when disturbed **2.** form of practical joke

boodle (ˈbuːdᵊl) *n.* **US** *sl.* money

boogie-woogie (ˈbʊgɪˈwʊgɪ, ˈbuːgɪˈwuːgɪ) *n.* kind of jazz piano playing, emphasizing a rolling bass in syncopated eighth notes

book (bʊk) *n.* **1.** collection of sheets of paper bound together **2.** literary work **3.** main division of this —*v.* **4.**

THESAURUS

bolster aid, assist, boost, brace, buoy up, buttress, cushion, help, hold up, maintain, pillow, prop, reinforce, shore up, stay, strengthen, support, uphold

bolt *n.* **1.** bar, catch, fastener, latch, lock, sliding bar **2.** peg, pin, rivet, rod **3.** bound, dart, dash, escape, flight, rush, spring, sprint **4.** shaft, thunderbolt ~*v.* **5.** bar, fasten, latch, lock, secure **6.** cram, devour, gobble, gorge, gulp, guzzle, stuff, swallow whole, wolf **7.** abscond, bound, dash, escape, flee, fly, hurtle, jump, leap, make a break (for it), run, run for it, rush, spring, sprint

bomb 1. *n.* bombshell, charge, device, explosive, grenade, mine, missile, projectile, rocket, shell, torpedo **2.** *v.* attack, blow up, bombard, destroy, shell, strafe, torpedo

bombard 1. assault, blast, blitz, bomb, cannonade, fire upon, open fire, pound, shell, strafe **2.** assail, attack, barrage, batter, beset, besiege, harass, hound, pester

bombardment assault, attack, barrage, blitz, bombing, cannonade, fire, flak, fusillade, shelling, strafe

bona fide actual, authentic, genuine, honest, lawful, legal, legitimate, real, true

bond *n.* **1.** band, binding, chain, cord, fastening, fetter, ligature, link, manacle, shackle, tie **2.** affiliation, affinity, attachment, connection, link, relation, tie, union **3.** agreement, compact, contract, covenant, guarantee, obligation, pledge, promise, word ~*v.* **4.** bind, connect, fasten, fix together, fuse, glue, gum, paste

bonny beautiful, comely, fair, handsome, lovely, pretty, sweet

bonus benefit, bounty, commission, dividend, extra, gift, gratuity, hand-out, honorarium, plus, premium, prize, reward

bony angular, emaciated, gangling, gaunt, lanky, lean, rawboned, scrawny, skinny, thin

reserve (room, ticket *etc.*) —*vt.* **5.** charge with legal offence **6.** enter name in book —'**booking** *n.* reservation —'**bookish** *a.* studious, fond of reading —'**booklet** *n.* —'**bookbinder** *n.* —'**bookcase** *n.* —**book club** club that sells books at low prices to members —**book end** one of pair of ornamental supports for holding row of books upright —**book-keeping** *n.* systematic recording of business transactions —'**bookmaker** *n.* person whose work is taking bets (*also* (*inf.*) '**bookie**) —'**bookmark** *or* '**bookmarker** *n.* strip of material put between pages of book to mark place —'**bookplate** *n.* label bearing owner's name and design, pasted into book —**book value 1.** value of asset of business according to its books **2.** net capital value of enterprise as shown by excess of book assets over book liabilities —'**bookworm** *n.* great reader

boom[1] (bu:m) *n.* **1.** sudden commercial activity **2.** prosperity —*vi.* **3.** become active, prosperous

boom[2] (bu:m) *vi./n.* (make) loud, deep sound

boom[3] (bu:m) *n.* **1.** long spar, as for stretching the bottom of a sail **2.** barrier across harbour **3.** pole carrying overhead microphone *etc.*

boomerang ('bu:məræŋ) *n.* **1.** curved wooden missile of Aust. Aborigines, which returns to the thrower —*vi.* **2.** recoil **3.** return unexpectedly **4.** backfire

boon (bu:n) *n.* something helpful, favour

boor (bʊə) *n.* rude person —'**boorish** *a.*

boost (bu:st) *n.* **1.** encouragement, help **2.** upward push **3.** increase —*vt.* **4.** encourage, assist or improve —'**booster** *n.* person or thing that supports, increases power *etc.* —**booster shot** *inf.* supplementary injection of vaccine given to maintain immunization

boot[1] (bu:t) *n.* **1.** covering for the foot and ankle **2.** luggage receptacle in car **3.** *inf.* kick —*vt.* **4.** *inf.* kick —'**booted** *a.* —'**bootee** *n.* baby's soft shoe

boot[2] (bu:t) *n.* profit, use —'**bootless** *a.* fruitless, vain —**to boot** in addition

booth (bu:ð, bu:θ) *n.* **1.** stall **2.** cubicle

bootleg ('bu:tlɛg) *v.* **1.** make, carry, sell (illicit goods, *esp.* alcohol) (**-gg-**) —*a.* **2.** produced, distributed or sold illicitly —'**bootlegger** *n.*

booty ('bu:tɪ) *n.* plunder, spoil

booze (bu:z) *n./vi. inf.* (consume) alcoholic drink —'**boozer** *n. inf.* **1.** person fond of drinking **2.** bar, pub —'**boozy** *a. inf.* inclined to or involving excessive consumption of alcohol —**booze-up** *n. inf.* drinking spree

bop (bɒp) *n.* **1.** form of jazz characterized by rhythmic and harmonic complexity (*also* '**bebop**) —*vi.* **2.** *inf.* dance to pop music (**-pp-**) —'**bopper** *n.*

borage ('bɒrɪdʒ, 'bʌrɪdʒ) *n.* Mediterranean plant with star-shaped blue flowers

borax ('bɔ:ræks) *n.* white soluble substance, compound of boron —**boracic** (bə'ræsɪk) *a.*

Bordeaux (bɔ:'dəʊ) *n.* any of several red, white or rosé wines produced around Bordeaux in SW France —**Bordeaux mixture** *Hort.* fungicide consisting of solution of copper sulphate and quicklime

border ('bɔ:də) *n.* **1.** margin **2.** frontier **3.** limit **4.** strip of garden —*vt.* **5.** provide with border **6.** adjoin —'**borderline** *n.* **1.** border; dividing line **2.** indeterminate position between two conditions —*a.* **3.** on edge of one category and verging on another

bore[1] (bɔ:) *vt.* **1.** pierce —*vi.* **2.** make a hole —*n.* **3.** hole **4.** calibre of gun —'**borer** *n.* **1.** instrument for making holes **2.** insect which bores holes

bore[2] (bɔ:) *vt.* **1.** make weary by repetition *etc.* —*n.* **2.** tiresome person or thing —'**boredom** *n.* —'**boring** *a.*

bore[3] (bɔ:) *n.* tidal wave which rushes up river estuary

bore[4] (bɔ:) *pt. of* BEAR[1]

THESAURUS

book *n.* **1.** manual, publication, roll, scroll, textbook, tome, tract, volume, work **2.** album, diary, exercise book, jotter, notebook, pad ~*v.* **3.** arrange for, bill, charter, engage, line up, make reservations, organize, procure, programme, reserve, schedule **4.** enrol, enter, insert, list, log, mark down, note, post, put down, record, register, write down

bookish academic, donnish, erudite, intellectual, learned, literary, pedantic, scholarly, studious

boom[1] **1.** *v.* develop, expand, flourish, gain, grow, increase, intensify, prosper, spurt, strengthen, succeed, swell, thrive **2.** *n.* advance, boost, development, expansion, gain, growth, improvement, increase, jump, push, spurt, upsurge, upswing, upturn

boom[2] **1.** *v.* bang, blast, crash, explode, resound, reverberate, roar, roll, rumble, thunder **2.** *n.* bang, blast, burst, clap, crash, explosion, roar, rumble, thunder

boomerang backfire, come back, come home to roost, rebound, recoil, return, reverse, ricochet

boon *n.* advantage, benefaction, benefit, blessing, donation, favour, gift, godsend, grant, gratuity, present, windfall

boorish awkward, barbaric, bearish, churlish, clownish, coarse, crude, gross, gruff, ill-bred, loutish, lubberly, oafish, rude, rustic, uncivilized, uncouth, uneducated, unrefined, vulgar

boost *n.* **1.** encouragement, help, improvement, praise, promotion **2.** heave, hoist, lift, push, raise, shove, thrust **3.** addition, expansion, improvement, increase, increment, jump, rise ~*v.* **4.** advance, advertise, assist, encourage, foster, further, improve, inspire, plug (*Inf.*), praise, promote, support, sustain

boot *v.* drive, drop-kick, kick, knock, punt, shove

border *n.* **1.** bound, boundary, bounds, brim, brink, confine, confines, edge, hem, limit, limits, lip, margin, rim, skirt, verge **2.** borderline, boundary, frontier, line, march ~*v.* **3.** bind, decorate, edge, fringe, hem, rim, trim

borderline *adj.* ambivalent, doubtful, equivocal, indecisive, indefinite, indeterminate, inexact, marginal, unclassifiable

bore[1] **1.** *v.* burrow, drill, gouge out, mine, penetrate, perforate, pierce, sink, tunnel **2.** *n.* borehole, calibre, drill hole, hole, shaft, tunnel

bore[2] **1.** *v.* annoy, be tedious, bother, exhaust, fatigue, jade, pall on, pester, send to sleep, tire, trouble, vex, wear out, weary, worry **2.** *n.* bother, drag (*Sl.*), dull person, headache (*Inf.*), nuisance, pain (*Inf.*), pain in the neck (*Inf.*), pest, tiresome person, wearisome talker

boredom apathy, doldrums, dullness, ennui, flatness, irksomeness, monotony, sameness, tedium, tediousness, weariness, world-weariness

boring dead, dull, flat, humdrum, insipid, monotonous, repetitious, routine, stale, tedious, tiresome, tiring, unexciting, uninteresting, unvaried, wearisome

born (bɔːn) *pp. of* BEAR[1] —**born again** having undergone a conversion, *esp.* to new spiritual life

borne (bɔːn) *pp. of* BEAR[1] —**be borne in on** *or* **upon** (of fact *etc.*) be realized by

boron (ˈbɔːrɒn) *n.* chemical element used in hardening steel *etc.* —ˈ**boric** *a.* of or containing boron (*also* **boˈracic**) —**boric acid** white weakly acid crystalline solid, used as mild antiseptic (*also* **orthoboric acid**)

borough (ˈbʌrə) *n.* town

borrow (ˈbɒrəʊ) *vt.* **1.** obtain on loan or trust **2.** appropriate —ˈ**borrower** *n.*

borsch, borsh (bɔːʃ), **borscht** (bɔːʃt), *or* **borshch** (bɔːʃtʃ) *n.* Russian and Polish soup based on beetroot

borstal (ˈbɔːstəl) *n.* reformatory for young criminals

borzoi (ˈbɔːzɔɪ) *n.* breed of tall hound with long, silky coat

bosh (bɒʃ) *n. inf.* nonsense

bo's'n (ˈbəʊsᵊn) *n. Naut. see* **boatswain** *at* BOAT

bosom (ˈbʊzəm) *n.* **1.** human breast **2.** seat of passions and feelings

boss[1] (bɒs) *n.* **1.** person in charge of or employing others —*vt.* **2.** be in charge of **3.** be domineering over —ˈ**bossy** *a.* overbearing

boss[2] (bɒs) *n.* **1.** knob or stud **2.** raised ornament —*vt.* **3.** emboss

bosun (ˈbəʊsᵊn) *n. Naut. see* **boatswain** *at* BOAT

bot. **1.** botanical **2.** botany **3.** bottle

botany (ˈbɒtənɪ) *n.* study of plants —**boˈtanic(al)** *a.* —ˈ**botanist** *n.*

botch (bɒtʃ) *vt.* (*oft. with* up) spoil by clumsiness

botfly (ˈbɒtflaɪ) *n.* fly, larvae of which are parasites of man, sheep and horses

both (bəʊθ) *a./pron.* **1.** the two —*adv./conj.* **2.** as well

bother (ˈbɒðə) *vt.* **1.** pester **2.** perplex —*vi./n.* **3.** fuss, trouble —**botheˈration** *n.* **1.** state of worry, trouble, or confusion —*interj.* **2.** *chiefly* **UK** exclamation of slight annoyance —ˈ**bothersome** *a.* causing bother; troublesome

bo tree (bəʊ) Indian tree sacred to Buddhists

bottle (ˈbɒtᵊl) *n.* **1.** vessel for holding liquid **2.** its contents **3.** **UK** *sl.* courage; nerve; initiative —*vt.* **4.** put into bottle —ˈ**bottler** *n.* —ˈ**bottlebrush** *n.* cylindrical brush for cleaning bottle —ˈ**bottleneck** *n.* narrow outlet which impedes smooth flow of traffic or production of goods —**bottle party** party to which guests bring drink —**bottle up** **1.** restrain (powerful emotion) **2.** *inf.* keep (army or other force) contained or trapped

bottom (ˈbɒtəm) *n.* **1.** lowest part of anything **2.** bed of sea, river *etc.* **3.** buttocks —*vt.* **4.** put bottom to **5.** base **6.** get to bottom of —ˈ**bottomless** *a.* —**bottom drawer UK** young woman's collection of linen, cutlery *etc.* made in anticipation of marriage —**bottom line** last line of financial statement that shows net profit or loss of company *etc.* —**bottom out** reach lowest point

botulism (ˈbɒtjʊlɪzəm) *n.* type of food poisoning

bouclé (ˈbuːkleɪ) *n.* looped yarn giving knobbly effect

boudoir (ˈbuːdwɑː, -dwɔː) *n.* **1.** lady's private sitting-room **2.** bedroom

bouffant (ˈbuːfɒŋ) *a.* **1.** (of hair style) having extra height through backcombing **2.** (of skirts *etc.*) puffed out

bougainvillea (buːgənˈvɪlɪə) *n.* (sub)tropical climbing plant with red or purple bracts

bough (baʊ) *n.* branch of tree

bought (bɔːt) *pt./pp. of* BUY

bouillabaisse (buːjəˈbɛs) *n.* rich stew or soup of fish and vegetables

bouillon (ˈbuːjɒn) *n.* plain unclarified broth or stock

boulder (ˈbəʊldə) *n.* large weatherworn rounded stone —**boulder clay** unstratified glacial deposit consisting of fine clay, boulders, and pebbles

boulevard (ˈbuːlvɑː, -vɑːd) *n.* broad street or promenade

boult (bəʊlt) *vt. see* BOLT[2]

bounce (baʊns) *v.* **1.** (cause to) rebound (repeatedly) on impact, as a ball —*n.* **2.** rebounding **3.** quality in object causing this **4.** *inf.* vitality, vigour —ˈ**bouncer** *n.* *sl.* man, *esp.* one employed at club *etc.* to evict undesirables (forcibly) —ˈ**bouncing** *a.* vigorous, robust —ˈ**bouncy** *a.* lively

THESAURUS

borrow **1.** cadge, scrounge (*Inf.*), take and return, take on loan, use temporarily **2.** acquire, adopt, appropriate, copy, filch, imitate, obtain, pilfer, pirate, plagiarize, simulate, steal, take, use, usurp

bosom *n.* **1.** breast, bust, chest **2.** affections, emotions, feelings, heart, sentiments, soul, spirit, sympathies

boss[1] **1.** *n.* administrator, chief, director, employer, executive, foreman, gaffer (*Inf.*), governor (*Inf.*), head, leader, manager, master, overseer, owner, superintendent, supervisor **2.** *v.* administrate, command, control, direct, employ, manage, oversee, run, superintend, supervise, take charge

boss[2] knob, nub, nubble, point, protuberance, stud, tip

bossy arrogant, authoritarian, despotic, dictatorial, domineering, high-handed, imperious, lordly, overbearing, tyrannical

botch *v.* blunder, bungle, butcher, cobble, fumble, mar, mend, mess, mismanage, muff, patch, spoil

bother **1.** *v.* alarm, annoy, concern, dismay, distress, disturb, harass, inconvenience, irritate, molest, nag, perplex, pester, plague, put out, trouble, upset, vex, worry **2.** *n.* aggravation, annoyance, bustle, difficulty, flurry, fuss, inconvenience, irritation, molestation, nuisance, perplexity, pest, problem, strain, trouble, vexation, worry

bothersome aggravating, annoying, distressing, exasperating, inconvenient, irritating, tiresome, troublesome, vexatious, vexing

bottleneck block, blockage, congestion, hold-up, impediment, jam, obstacle, obstruction

bottle up check, contain, curb, keep back, restrain, restrict, shut in, suppress, trap

bottom *n.* **1.** base, basis, bed, deepest part, depths, floor, foot, foundation, groundwork, lowest part, pedestal, support **2.** backside, behind (*Inf.*), bum (*Sl.*), buttocks, fundament, posterior, rear, rear end, rump, seat, tail (*Inf.*)

bottomless boundless, deep, fathomless, immeasurable, inexhaustible, infinite, unfathomable, unlimited

bounce *v.* **1.** bob, bound, bump, jounce, jump, leap, rebound, recoil, resile, ricochet, spring, thump ~*n.* **2.** bound, elasticity, give, rebound, recoil, resilience,

bound[1] (baʊnd) *n./vt.* limit —**ˈboundary** *n.* —**ˈbounded** *a.* —**ˈboundless** *a.*

bound[2] (baʊnd) *vi./n.* spring, leap

bound[3] (baʊnd) *a.* on a specified course, as *outward bound*

bound[4] (baʊnd) *v.* **1.** *pt./pp. of* BIND —*a.* **2.** committed **3.** certain **4.** tied

bounden (ˈbaʊndən) *a.* morally obligatory (*obs. except in* **bounden duty**)

bounder (ˈbaʊndə) *n. old-fashioned* **UK** *sl.* morally reprehensible person; cad

bounty (ˈbaʊntɪ) *n.* **1.** liberality **2.** gift **3.** premium —**ˈbounteous** *or* **ˈbountiful** *a.* liberal, generous

bouquet (buːˈkeɪ) *n.* **1.** bunch of flowers **2.** fragrance of wine **3.** compliment —**bouquet garni** (ˈbuːkeɪ gɑːˈniː) bunch of herbs tied together and used for flavouring stews *etc.* (*pl.* **bouquets garnis** (ˈbuːkeɪz gɑːˈniː))

bourbon (ˈbɜːbᵊn) *n.* **US** whiskey made from maize

bourgeois (ˈbʊəʒwɑː) *n./a. oft. disparaging* **1.** middle class **2.** smugly conventional (person) —**bourgeoiˈsie** *n.* **1.** middle classes **2.** in Marxist thought, capitalist ruling class

bourn[1] *or* **bourne** (bɔːn) *n. obs.* **1.** destination; goal **2.** boundary

bourn[2] (bɔːn) *n. chiefly S Brit.* stream

Bourse (bʊəs) *n.* stock exchange of continental Europe, *esp.* Paris

bout (baʊt) *n.* **1.** period of time spent doing something **2.** contest, fight

boutique (buːˈtiːk) *n.* small shop, *esp.* one selling clothes

bouzouki (buːˈzuːkɪ) *n.* Greek stringed musical instrument

bovine (ˈbəʊvaɪn) *a.* **1.** of the ox or cow **2.** oxlike **3.** stolid, dull

bow[1] (bəʊ) *n.* **1.** weapon for shooting arrows **2.** implement for playing violin *etc.* **3.** ornamental knot of ribbon *etc.* **4.** bend, bent line **5.** rainbow —*v.* **6.** bend —**bow-legged** *a.* bandy —**bow tie** tie tied in bow —**bow window** window with outward curve

bow[2] (baʊ) *vi.* **1.** bend body in respect, assent *etc.* **2.** submit —*vt.* **3.** bend downwards **4.** cause to stoop **5.** crush —*n.* **6.** bowing of head or body

bow[3] (baʊ) *n.* **1.** fore end of ship **2.** prow **3.** rower nearest bow —**bowline** (ˈbəʊlɪn) *n. Naut.* **1.** line for controlling weather leech of square sail when vessel is close-hauled **2.** knot for securing loop —**bowsprit** (ˈbəʊsprɪt) *n.* spar projecting from ship's bow

bowdlerize *or* **-ise** (ˈbaʊdləraɪz) *vt.* expurgate

bowel (ˈbaʊəl) *n.* (*oft. pl.*) **1.** part of intestine (*esp.* with reference to defecation) **2.** inside of anything

bower (ˈbaʊə) *n.* **1.** shady retreat **2.** inner room —**ˈbowerbird** *n.* Aust. bird that hoards decorative but useless things

bowie knife (ˈbəʊɪ) stout hunting knife with short hilt and guard for hand

bowl[1] (bəʊl) *n.* **1.** round vessel, deep basin **2.** drinking cup **3.** hollow

bowl[2] (bəʊl) *n.* **1.** wooden ball —*pl.* **2.** game played with such balls —*v.* **3.** roll or throw (ball) in various ways —**ˈbowler** *n.* —**ˈbowling** *n.* **1.** game in which heavy ball is rolled down alley at group of wooden pins **2.** game of bowls **3.** *Cricket* delivering ball to batsman —**bowling alley** —**bowling green**

bowler (ˈbəʊlə) *n.* man's low-crowned stiff felt hat

bowser (ˈbaʊzə) *n.* fuel tanker

box[1] (bɒks) *n.* **1.** (wooden) container, usu. rectangular with lid **2.** its contents **3.** small enclosure **4.** any boxlike

THESAURUS

spring, springiness **3.** animation, dynamism, energy, go (*Inf.*), life, liveliness, pep, vigour, vitality, vivacity, zip (*Inf.*)

bouncing blooming, bonny, healthy, robust, thriving, vigorous

bound[1] **1.** *n. Usually plural* border, boundary, confine, edge, extremity, fringe, limit, line, march, margin, pale, periphery, rim, termination, verge **2.** *v.* circumscribe, confine, define, delimit, demarcate, encircle, enclose, hem in, limit, restrain, restrict, surround, terminate

bound[2] *v./n.* bob, bounce, caper, frisk, gambol, hurdle, jump, leap, pounce, prance, skip, spring, vault

bound[3] *adj.* **1.** cased, fastened, fixed, pinioned, secured, tied, tied up **2.** certain, destined, doomed, fated, sure **3.** beholden, committed, compelled, constrained, duty-bound, forced, obligated, obliged, pledged, required

boundary barrier, border, borderline, bounds, brink, confines, edge, extremity, fringe, frontier, limits, march, margin, precinct, termination, verge

boundless endless, illimitable, immeasurable, immense, incalculable, inexhaustible, infinite, limitless, measureless, unbounded, unconfined, unending, unlimited, untold, vast

bountiful beneficent, bounteous, generous, liberal, magnanimous, munificent, open-handed, princely, unstinting

bouquet **1.** boutonniere, bunch of flowers, buttonhole, corsage, garland, nosegay, posy, spray, wreath **2.** aroma, fragrance, perfume, redolence, savour, scent

bourgeois conventional, hidebound, materialistic, middle-class, traditional

bout **1.** course, fit, period, round, run, session, spell, spree, stint, stretch, term, time, turn **2.** battle, boxing match, competition, contest, encounter, engagement, fight, match, set-to, struggle

bovine dense, dull, slow, sluggish, stolid, stupid, thick

bow[1] *v.* **1.** bend, bob, droop, genuflect, incline, make obeisance, nod, stoop **2.** accept, acquiesce, comply, concede, defer, give in, kowtow, relent, submit, surrender, yield **3.** cast down, conquer, crush, depress, overpower, subdue, subjugate, vanquish, weigh down ~*n.* **4.** bending, bob, genuflexion, inclination, kowtow, nod, obeisance, salaam

bow[2] *Naut.* beak, fore, head, prow, stem

bowdlerize blue-pencil, censor, clean up, expurgate, mutilate

bowels **1.** entrails, guts, innards (*Inf.*), insides (*Inf.*), intestines, viscera, vitals **2.** belly, core, deep, depths, hold, inside, interior

bowl[1] *n.* basin, deep dish, vessel

bowl[2] *v.* fling, hurl, pitch, revolve, roll, rotate, spin, throw, trundle, whirl

cubicle, shelter or receptacle, *eg* letter box —*vt.* **5.** put in box **6.** confine —**box girder** girder that is hollow and square or rectangular in shape —**Boxing Day UK** first weekday after Christmas —**box junction UK** road junction having yellow cross-hatching on road surface —**box lacrosse C** indoor lacrosse —**box number** number given to newspaper advertisements to which replies may be sent —**box office 1.** office at theatre *etc.* where tickets are sold **2.** public appeal of actor or production —**box pleat** double pleat made by folding under fabric on either side of it —**ˈboxroom** *n.* small room or large cupboard —**the box UK** *inf.* television —**box the compass** make complete turn

box[2] (bɒks) *v.* **1.** fight with fists, *esp.* wearing padded gloves —*vt.* **2.** strike —*n.* **3.** blow —**ˈboxer** *n.* **1.** one who boxes **2.** breed of large dog resembling bulldog —**ˈboxing** *n.* art or profession of fighting with fists

box[3] (bɒks) *n.* evergreen shrub used for hedges

boy (bɔɪ) *n.* **1.** male child **2.** young man —*interj.* **3.** exclamation of surprise —**ˈboyhood** *n.* —**ˈboyfriend** *n.* male friend with whom person is romantically or sexually involved —**boy scout** *see* SCOUT (sense 2)

boycott (ˈbɔɪkɒt) *vt.* **1.** refuse to deal with or participate in —*n.* **2.** act of boycotting

boysenberry (ˈbɔɪzˀnbərɪ) *n.* **1.** type of bramble, cross of loganberry, various blackberries and raspberries **2.** edible fruit of this plant

B.P. **1.** British Petroleum **2.** British Pharmacopoeia

Br *Chem.* bromine

B.R. British Rail

br. **1.** branch **2.** bronze **3.** brother

Br. **1.** Breton **2.** Britain **3.** British

bra (brɑː) *n. short for* BRASSIERE

brace (breɪs) *n.* **1.** tool for boring **2.** clasp, clamp **3.** pair, couple **4.** strut, support —*pl.* **5.** straps worn over shoulders to hold up trousers —*vt.* **6.** steady (oneself), as before a blow **7.** support, make firm —**ˈbracelet** *n.* **1.** ornament for the arm —*pl.* **2.** *sl.* handcuffs —**ˈbracing** *a.* invigorating —**brace and bit** tool for boring holes, consisting of cranked handle and drilling bit

brachiopod (ˈbreɪkɪəpɒd, ˈbræk-) *n.* any marine invertebrate animal having ciliated feeding organ and shell consisting of dorsal and ventral valves

bracken (ˈbrækən) *n.* large fern

bracket (ˈbrækɪt) *n.* **1.** support for shelf *etc.* **2.** group —*pl.* **3.** marks [ ], ( ) used to enclose words *etc.* —*vt.* **4.** enclose in brackets **5.** connect

brackish (ˈbrækɪʃ) *a.* (of water) slightly salty

bract (brækt) *n.* small scalelike leaf

brad (bræd) *n.* small nail —**ˈbradawl** *n.* small boring tool

brae (breɪ) *n. Scot.* hill(side); slope

brag (bræg) *vi.* **1.** boast (**-gg-**) —*n.* **2.** boastful talk —**ˈbraggart** *n.*

braggadocio (brægəˈdəʊtʃɪəʊ) *n.* **1.** vain empty boasting **2.** braggart (*pl.* **-s**)

Brahma (ˈbrɑːmə) *n.* **1.** Hindu god, the Creator **2.** *Hinduism* ultimate and impersonal divine reality of universe (*also* **ˈBrahman**)

Brahman (ˈbrɑːmən) *n.* **1.** member of priestly Hindu caste (*also esp.* (*formerly*) **ˈBrahmin**) **2.** breed of beef cattle

braid (breɪd) *vt.* **1.** interweave **2.** trim with braid —*n.* **3.** length of anything interwoven or plaited **4.** ornamental tape

Braille (breɪl) *n.* system of printing for blind, with arrangements of raised dots instead of letters

brain (breɪn) *n.* **1.** mass of nerve tissue in head **2.** intellect —*vt.* **3.** kill by hitting on head —**ˈbrainless** *a.* —**ˈbrainy** *a.* —**ˈbrainchild** *n.* invention —**brain death** irreversible cessation of respiration due to irreparable brain damage —**brain drain** *inf.* emigration of scientists, academics *etc.* —**ˈbrainstorm** *n.* sudden mental aberration —**brains trust** group of knowledgeable people who answer questions in panel games, quizzes *etc.* —**ˈbrainwash** *vt.* change, distort ideas or beliefs of —**brain wave** sudden, clever idea

braise (breɪz) *vt.* stew in covered pan

brake[1] (breɪk) *n.* **1.** instrument for retarding motion of wheel on vehicle —*vt.* **2.** apply brake to —**brake horsepower** rate at which engine does work, expressed in horsepower, measured by resistance of applied brake —**brake shoe** curved metal casting to which brake lining is riveted in drum brake

---

THESAURUS

box[1] **1.** *n.* carton, case, chest, container, pack, package, portmanteau, receptacle, trunk **2.** *v.* pack, package, wrap

box[2] *v.* **1.** exchange blows, fight, spar **2.** buffet, butt, clout (*Inf.*), cuff, hit, punch, slap, sock (*Sl.*), strike, thwack, wallop (*Inf.*), whack ~*n.* **3.** blow, buffet, clout (*Inf.*), cuff, punch, slap, stroke, thumping, wallop (*Inf.*)

boxer fighter, prizefighter, pugilist, sparrer, sparring partner

boxing fisticuffs, prizefighting, pugilism, sparring, the fight game (*Inf.*), the ring

boy fellow, junior, lad, schoolboy, stripling, youngster, youth

boycott ban, bar, black, blackball, blacklist, embargo, exclude, ostracize, outlaw, prohibit, proscribe, refrain from, refuse, reject, spurn

boyfriend admirer, beau, date, follower, lover, man, steady, suitor, swain, sweetheart, young man

brace **1.** *n.* bracer, bracket, buttress, prop, reinforcement, stanchion, stay, strut, support, truss **2.** *v.* bandage, bind, bolster, buttress, fasten, fortify, hold up, prop, reinforce, shove, shove up, steady, strap, strengthen, support, tie, tighten

bracing brisk, chilly, cool, crisp, energizing, exhilarating, fortifying, fresh, invigorating, lively, refreshing, restorative, reviving, rousing, stimulating, tonic, vigorous

brag blow one's own trumpet, bluster, boast, crow, swagger, talk big (*Sl.*), vaunt

braggart bigmouth (*Sl.*), bluffer, blusterer, boaster, brag, braggadocio, bragger, show-off, swaggerer, swashbuckler

braid entwine, interlace, intertwine, interweave, lace, plait, ravel, twine, weave

brainless foolish, idiotic, inept, mindless, senseless, stupid, thoughtless, unintelligent, witless

brainy bright, brilliant, clever, intelligent, smart

brake **1.** *n.* check, constraint, control, curb, rein, restraint **2.** *v.* check, decelerate, halt, moderate, reduce speed, slacken, slow, stop

brake[2] (breɪk) *n.* **1.** fern **2.** bracken **3.** thicket **4.** brushwood

bramble (ˈbræmbᵊl) *n.* **1.** prickly shrub **2.** blackberry —**ˈbrambly** *a.*

brambling (ˈbræmblɪŋ) *n.* type of finch

bran (bræn) *n.* sifted husks of corn

branch (brɑːntʃ) *n.* **1.** limb of tree **2.** offshoot or subsidiary part of something larger or primary —*vi.* **3.** bear branches **4.** diverge **5.** spread —**branched** *a.* —**ˈbranchy** *a.*

brand (brænd) *n.* **1.** trademark **2.** class of goods **3.** particular kind, sort **4.** mark made by hot iron **5.** burning piece of wood **6.** sword **7.** mark of infamy —*vt.* **8.** burn with iron **9.** mark **10.** stigmatize —**brand-new** *a.* absolutely new

brandish (ˈbrændɪʃ) *vt.* flourish, wave (weapon *etc.*)

brandy (ˈbrændɪ) *n.* spirit distilled from wine —**brandy snap** crisp, sweet biscuit

brash (bræʃ) *a.* bold, impudent

brass (brɑːs) *n.* **1.** alloy of copper and zinc **2.** group of brass wind instruments forming part of orchestra or band **3.** *inf.* money **4.** *inf.* (army) officers —*a.* **5.** made of brass —**ˈbrassy** *a.* **1.** showy **2.** harsh —**brass hat UK** *inf.* top-ranking official, *esp.* military officer —**brass tacks** *inf.* basic realities; hard facts (*esp. in* **get down to brass tacks**)

brasserie (ˈbræsərɪ) *n.* restaurant specializing in food and beer

brassica (ˈbræsɪkə) *n.* plant of cabbage and turnip family

brassiere (ˈbræsɪə, ˈbræz-) *n.* woman's undergarment for supporting the breasts

brat (bræt) *n. disparaging* child

bravado (brəˈvɑːdəʊ) *n.* showy display of boldness

brave (breɪv) *a.* **1.** bold, courageous **2.** splendid, fine —*n.* **3.** warrior —*vt.* **4.** defy, meet boldly —**ˈbravely** *adv.* —**ˈbravery** *n.*

bravo (brɑːˈvəʊ) *interj.* well done

bravura (brəˈvjʊərə, -ˈvʊərə) *n.* **1.** display of boldness or daring **2.** *Mus.* passage requiring great spirit and skill by performer

brawl (brɔːl) *vi.* **1.** fight noisily —*n.* **2.** noisy disagreement or fight —**ˈbrawler** *n.*

brawn (brɔːn) *n.* **1.** muscle **2.** strength **3.** pickled pork —**ˈbrawny** *a.* muscular

bray (breɪ) *n.* **1.** donkey's cry —*vi.* **2.** utter this sound **3.** give out harsh or loud sounds

braze[1] (breɪz) *vt.* decorate with or make of brass

braze[2] (breɪz) *vt.* make joint between (two metal surfaces) by fusing layer of high-melting solder between them —**ˈbrazer** *n.*

brazen (ˈbreɪzᵊn) *a.* **1.** of, like brass **2.** impudent, shameless —*vt.* **3.** (*usu. with* out) face, carry through with impudence —**ˈbrazenness** *n.* effrontery

brazier[1] *or* **brasier** (ˈbreɪzɪə) *n.* brassworker

brazier[2] *or* **brasier** (ˈbreɪzɪə) *n.* pan for burning charcoal or coals

brazil nut (brəˈzɪl) **1.** tropical S Amer. tree producing globular capsules, each containing several triangular nuts **2.** its nut

B.R.C.S. British Red Cross Society

breach (briːtʃ) *n.* **1.** break, opening **2.** breaking of rule, duty *etc.* **3.** quarrel —*vt.* **4.** make a gap in —**breach of promise** *Law* formerly, failure to carry out promise to marry

bread (brɛd) *n.* **1.** food made of flour or meal and then baked **2.** food **3.** *sl.* money —**ˈbreadfruit** *n.* breadlike fruit found in Pacific Islands —**ˈbreadline** *n.* queue for free food —**ˈbreadwinner** *n.* person supporting dependants by his earnings —**bread and butter** *inf.* means of support or subsistence; livelihood —**on the breadline** *inf.* living at subsistence level

THESAURUS

branch 1. arm, bough, limb, offshoot, prong, ramification, shoot, spray, sprig **2.** chapter, department, division, local office, office, part, section, subdivision, subsection, wing

brand *n.* **1.** cast, class, grade, kind, make, quality, sort, species, type, variety **2.** emblem, hallmark, label, mark, marker, sign, stamp, symbol, trademark **3.** blot, disgrace, infamy, mark, reproach, slur, smirch, stain, stigma, taint ~*v.* **4.** burn, burn in, label, mark, scar, stamp **5.** censure, denounce, discredit, disgrace, expose, mark, stigmatize

brandish display, exhibit, flaunt, flourish, parade, raise, shake, swing, wave, wield

brash bold, brazen, cocky, forward, heedless, impertinent, impudent, insolent, rude

bravado bluster, boast, boastfulness, boasting, bombast, brag, braggadocio, fanfaronade (*Rare*), swagger, swaggering, swashbuckling, vaunting

brave 1. *adj.* bold, courageous, daring, dauntless, fearless, gallant, heroic, intrepid, plucky, resolute, undaunted, valiant, valorous **2.** *v.* bear, beard, challenge, confront, dare, defy, endure, face, stand up to, suffer, withstand

bravery boldness, courage, daring, dauntlessness, doughtiness, fearlessness, fortitude, gallantry, grit, guts (*Inf.*), hardihood, hardiness, heroism, indomitability, intrepidity, mettle, pluck, pluckiness, spirit, spunk (*Inf.*), valour

bravura animation, audacity, boldness, brilliance, brio, daring, dash, display, élan, energy, exhibitionism, ostentation, panache, punch (*Inf.*), spirit, verve, vigour, virtuosity

brawl 1. *n.* affray (*Law*), altercation, argument, battle, broil, clash, disorder, dispute, donnybrook, fight, fracas, fray, free-for-all (*Inf.*), melee, punch-up (*Sl.*), quarrel, row (*Inf.*), ruckus (*Inf.*), rumpus, scrap (*Inf.*), scuffle, squabble, tumult, uproar, wrangle **2.** *v.* altercate, argue, battle, dispute, fight, quarrel, row (*Inf.*), scrap (*Inf.*), scuffle, tussle, wrangle, wrestle

brawn beef (*Inf.*), beefiness, brawniness, flesh, might, muscle, muscles, muscularity, power, robustness, strength, vigour

brawny athletic, beefy (*Inf.*), bulky, burly, fleshy, hardy, hefty (*Inf.*), herculean, husky (*Inf.*), muscular, powerful, robust, sinewy, stalwart, strapping, strong, sturdy, thewy, vigorous, well-knit

breach 1. aperture, break, chasm, cleft, crack, fissure, gap, hole, opening, rent, rift, rupture, split **2.** contravention, disobedience, infraction, infringement, noncompliance, nonobservance, offence, transgression, trespass, violation **3.** alienation, difference, disaffection, disagreement, dissension, division, estrangement, falling-out (*Inf.*), parting of the

breadth (brɛdθ, brɛtθ) *n.* **1.** extent across, width **2.** largeness of view, mind

break (breɪk) *vt.* **1.** part by force **2.** shatter **3.** burst, destroy **4.** fail to observe **5.** disclose **6.** interrupt **7.** surpass **8.** make bankrupt **9.** relax **10.** mitigate **11.** accustom (horse) to being ridden **12.** decipher (code) —*vi.* **13.** become broken, shattered, divided **14.** open, appear **15.** come suddenly **16.** crack, give way **17.** part, fall out **18.** (of voice) change in tone, pitch (**broke, ˈbroken**) —*n.* **19.** fracture **20.** gap **21.** opening **22.** separation **23.** interruption **24.** respite **25.** interval **26.** *inf.* opportunity **27.** dawn **28.** *Billiards* consecutive series of successful strokes **29.** *Boxing* separation after a clinch **30.** *Cricket* deviation of a ball on striking the pitch —**ˈbreakable** *a.* —**ˈbreakage** *n.* —**ˈbreaker** *n.* **1.** one that breaks, *eg* electrical circuit breaker **2.** wave beating on rocks or shore —**ˈbreakaway** *n.* loss or withdrawal of group of members from association, club *etc.* —**break dance** acrobatic dance style of 1980s —**break-dance** *vi.* perform break dance —**break dancer** —**break dancing** —**ˈbreakdown** *n.* **1.** collapse, as nervous breakdown **2.** failure to function effectively **3.** analysis —**breakfast** (ˈbrɛkfəst) *n.* first meal of the day —**break-in** *n.* illegal entering of building, *esp.* by thieves —**ˈbreakneck** *a.* dangerous —**break-out** *n.* escape, *esp.* from prison —**ˈbreakthrough** *n.* important advance —**break-up** *n.* **1.** separation or disintegration **2.** in Canad. north, breaking up of ice on body of water that marks beginning of spring **3.** this season —**ˈbreakwater** *n.* barrier to break force of waves —**break away** (*oft. with* from) **1.** leave hastily; escape **2.** withdraw, secede —**break out 1.** begin suddenly **2.** make escape, *esp.* from prison **3.** (*with* in) (of skin) erupt (in rash *etc.*) —**break up 1.** (cause to) separate **2.** put an end to (a relationship) or (of a relationship) to come to an end **3.** dissolve or cause to dissolve **4.** *sl.* lose control of emotions

bream (briːm; *Austral.* brɪm) *or Austral.* **brim** (brɪm) *n.* broad, thin fish

breast (brɛst) *n.* **1.** human chest **2.** milk-secreting gland on chest of human female **3.** seat of the affections **4.** any protuberance —*vt.* **5.** face, oppose **6.** reach summit of —**ˈbreastbone** *n.* thin flat structure of bone to which most of ribs are attached in front of chest (*also* **ˈsternum**) —**breast-feed** *v.* feed (baby) with milk from breast —**ˈbreastplate** *n.* piece of armour covering chest —**ˈbreaststroke** *n.* stroke in swimming —**ˈbreastwork** *n.* temporary defensive work, usu. breast-high

breath (brɛθ) *n.* **1.** air used by lungs **2.** life **3.** respiration **4.** slight breeze —**breathe** (briːð) *vi.* **1.** inhale and exhale air from lungs **2.** live **3.** pause, rest —*vt.* **4.** inhale and exhale **5.** utter softly, whisper —**breather** (ˈbriːðə) *n.* short rest —**breathing** (ˈbriːðɪŋ) *n.* —**ˈbreathless** *a.* —**ˈbreathtaking** *a.* causing awe or excitement —**breath test UK** chemical test of driver's breath to determine amount of alcohol he has consumed

Breathalyser *or* **-lyzer** (ˈbrɛθəlaɪzə) *n.* **R** device that estimates amount of alcohol in breath —**ˈbreathalyse** *or* **-lyze** *vt.*

THESAURUS

ways, quarrel, schism, separation, severance, variance

bread 1. aliment, diet, fare, food, necessities, nourishment, nutriment, provisions, subsistence, sustenance, viands, victuals **2.** *Sl.* cash, dough (*Sl.*), finance, funds, money

breadth 1. beam (*of a ship*), broadness, latitude, span, spread, wideness, width **2.** broad-mindedness, freedom, latitude, liberality, open-mindedness, openness, permissiveness

break *v.* **1.** batter, burst, crack, crash, demolish, destroy, disintegrate, divide, fracture, fragment, part, rend, separate, sever, shatter, shiver, smash, snap, splinter, split, tear **2.** breach, contravene, disobey, disregard, infract (*Law*), infringe, renege on, transgress, violate **3.** abandon, cut, discontinue, give up, interrupt, pause, rest, stop, suspend **4.** bust (*Inf.*), degrade, demote, discharge, dismiss, humiliate, impoverish, make bankrupt, reduce, ruin **5.** announce, come out, disclose, divulge, impart, inform, let out, make public, proclaim, reveal, tell **6.** *Of a record, etc.* beat, better, cap (*Inf.*), exceed, excel, go beyond, outdo, outstrip, surpass, top **7.** appear, burst out, come forth suddenly, emerge, erupt, happen, occur, open **8.** cushion, diminish, lessen, lighten, mitigate, moderate, reduce, soften, weaken ~*n.* **9.** breach, cleft, crack, division, fissure, fracture, gap, gash, hole, opening, rent, rift, rupture, split, tear **10.** breather (*Inf.*), halt, hiatus, interlude, intermission, interruption, interval, let-up (*Inf.*), lull, pause, recess, respite, rest, suspension **11.** alienation, breach, disaffection, dispute, divergence, estrangement, rift, rupture, schism, separation, split **12.** *Inf.* advantage, chance, fortune, opening, opportunity, stroke of luck

breakable brittle, crumbly, delicate, flimsy, fragile, frail, frangible, friable

break away 1. decamp, escape, flee, fly, make a break for it, make a run for it (*Inf.*), make off, run away **2.** break with, detach, part company, secede, separate, withdraw

breakdown 1. collapse, crackup (*Inf.*), disintegration, disruption, failure, mishap, stoppage **2.** analysis, categorization, classification, detailed list, diagnosis, dissection, itemization

break-in breaking and entering, burglary, invasion, robbery

break out 1. appear, arise, begin, commence, emerge, happen, occur, set in, spring up, start **2.** abscond, bolt, break loose, burst out, escape, flee, get free **3.** burst out, erupt

break-up breakdown, breaking, crackup (*Inf.*), disintegration, dispersal, dissolution, divorce, ending, parting, rift, separation, split, splitting, termination, wind-up (*Inf., chiefly U.S.*)

break up adjourn, disband, dismantle, disperse, disrupt, dissolve, divide, divorce, end, part, scatter, separate, sever, split, stop, suspend, terminate

breast 1. boob (*Sl.*), bosom, bust, chest, front, teat, thorax, udder **2.** being, conscience, core, emotions, feelings, heart, seat of the affections, sentiments, soul, thoughts

breath 1. air, animation, breathing, exhalation, gasp, gulp, inhalation, pant, respiration, wheeze **2.** faint breeze, flutter, gust, puff, sigh, slight movement, waft, zephyr **3.** animation, energy, existence, life, lifeblood, life force, vitality

breathe 1. draw in, gasp, gulp, inhale and exhale,

bred (brɛd) *pt./pp. of* BREED

breech (briːtʃ) *n.* **1.** buttocks **2.** hinder part of anything, *esp.* gun —**breeches** (ˈbrɪtʃɪz, ˈbriː-) *pl.n.* trousers —**breech delivery** birth of baby with feet or buttocks appearing first —**breeches buoy** ring-shaped life buoy with support in form of pair of breeches —**ˈbreech-loader** *n.*

breed (briːd) *vt.* **1.** generate, bring forth, give rise to **2.** rear —*vi.* **3.** be produced **4.** be with young (**bred** *pt./pp.*) —*n.* **5.** offspring produced **6.** race, kind —**ˈbreeder** *n.* —**ˈbreeding** *n.* **1.** producing **2.** manners **3.** ancestry —**breeder reactor** nuclear reactor that produces more fissionable material than it consumes

breeze (briːz) *n.* gentle wind —**ˈbreezily** *adv.* —**ˈbreezy** *a.* **1.** windy **2.** jovial, lively **3.** casual

breeze block light building brick made of ashes bonded by cement

Bren gun (brɛn) air-cooled gas-operated submachine gun, used by Brit. in World War II

brent (brɛnt) *or esp. U.S.* **brant** (brænt) *n.* small goose that has dark grey plumage and short neck and occurs in most northern coastal regions (*also* **brent goose**)

brethren (ˈbrɛðrɪn) *n., pl. of* BROTHER, *obs.* except in religious contexts

Breton (ˈbrɛtᵊn) *a.* **1.** of Brittany, its people or their language —*n.* **2.** native or inhabitant of Brittany

breve (briːv) *n.* long musical note

breviary (ˈbrɛvjərɪ, ˈbriː-) *n.* book of daily prayers of R.C. Church

brevity (ˈbrɛvɪtɪ) *n.* **1.** conciseness of expression **2.** short duration

brew (bruː) *vt.* **1.** prepare (liquor, as beer) from malt *etc.* **2.** make (drink, as tea) by infusion **3.** plot, contrive —*vi.* **4.** be in preparation —*n.* **5.** beverage produced by brewing —**ˈbrewer** *n.* —**ˈbrewery** *n.* —**ˈbrewing** *n.*

briar[1] *or* **brier** (ˈbraɪə) *n.* prickly shrub, *esp.* the wild rose

briar[2] *or* **brier** (ˈbraɪə) *n.* European shrub —**briar pipe** tobacco pipe made from its root

bribe (braɪb) *n.* **1.** anything offered or given to someone to gain favour, influence —*vt.* **2.** influence by bribe —**ˈbriber** *n.* —**ˈbribery** *n.*

bric-a-brac (ˈbrɪkəbræk) *n.* miscellaneous small objects, used for ornament

brick (brɪk) *n.* **1.** oblong mass of hardened clay used in building —*vt.* **2.** build, block *etc.* with bricks —**ˈbrickbat** *n.* **1.** piece of brick *etc., esp.* used as weapon **2.** *inf.* blunt criticism —**ˈbricklayer** *n.*

bride (braɪd) *n.* woman about to be, or just, married —**ˈbridal** *a.* of, relating to, a bride or wedding —**ˈbridegroom** *n.* man about to be, or just, married —**ˈbridesmaid** *n.*

bridge[1] (brɪdʒ) *n.* **1.** structure for crossing river *etc.* **2.** something joining or supporting other parts **3.** raised narrow platform on ship **4.** upper part of nose **5.** part of violin supporting strings —*vt.* **6.** make bridge over, span —**ˈbridgehead** *n.* advanced position established on enemy territory —**bridging loan** loan to cover period between two transactions, such as buying of another house before sale of first is completed

bridge[2] (brɪdʒ) *n.* card game

bridle (ˈbraɪdᵊl) *n.* **1.** headgear of horse harness **2.** curb —*vt.* **3.** put bridle on **4.** restrain —*vi.* **5.** show resentment —**bridle path** path suitable for riding horses

Brie (briː) *n.* soft creamy white cheese

brief (briːf) *a.* **1.** short in duration **2.** concise **3.** scanty

THESAURUS

pant, puff, respire, wheeze **2.** articulate, express, murmur, say, sigh, utter, voice, whisper

breathless choking, exhausted, gasping, gulping, out of breath, panting, short-winded, spent, wheezing, winded

breathtaking amazing, astonishing, awe-inspiring, awesome, exciting, heart-stirring, impressive, magnificent, moving, overwhelming, stunning (*Inf.*), thrilling

breed *v.* **1.** bear, beget, bring forth, engender, generate, hatch, multiply, originate, procreate, produce, propagate, reproduce **2.** bring up, cultivate, develop, discipline, educate, foster, instruct, nourish, nurture, raise, rear **3.** arouse, bring about, cause, create, generate, give rise to, induce, make, occasion, originate, produce, stir up ~*n.* **4.** brand, class, extraction, family, ilk, kind, line, lineage, pedigree, progeny, race, sort, species, stamp, stock, strain, type, variety

breeding **1.** ancestry, cultivation, development, lineage, nurture, raising, rearing, reproduction, training, upbringing **2.** civility, conduct, courtesy, cultivation, culture, gentility, manners, polish, refinement, urbanity

breeze air, breath of wind, capful of wind, current of air, draught, flurry, gust, light wind, puff of air, waft, whiff, zephyr

breezy **1.** airy, blowing, blowy, blustery, fresh, gusty, squally, windy **2.** airy, animated, blithe, buoyant, carefree, casual, cheerful, debonair, easy-going, free and easy, informal, jaunty, light, light-hearted, lively, sparkling, spirited, sprightly, sunny, vivacious

brevity **1.** conciseness, concision, condensation, crispness, curtness, economy, pithiness, succinctness, terseness **2.** briefness, ephemerality, impermanence, shortness, transience, transitoriness

brew *v.* **1.** boil, ferment, infuse (*tea*), make (*beer*), prepare by fermentation, seethe, soak, steep, stew **2.** breed, concoct, contrive, develop, devise, excite, foment, form, gather, hatch, plan, plot, project, scheme, start, stir up ~*n.* **3.** beverage, blend, concoction, distillation, drink, fermentation, infusion, liquor, mixture, preparation

bribe **1.** *n.* allurement, backhander (*Sl.*), boodle (*Sl., chiefly U.S.*), corrupting gift, enticement, graft, hush money (*Sl.*), incentive, inducement, kickback (*U.S.*), pay-off (*Inf.*), payola (*Inf.*), reward for treachery **2.** *v.* buy off, corrupt, get at, grease the palm *or* hand of (*Sl.*), influence by gifts, lure, oil the palm of (*Inf.*), pay off (*Inf.*), reward, square, suborn

bribery buying off, corruption, graft, inducement, palm-greasing (*Sl.*), payola (*Inf.*), protection, subornation

bridge *n.* **1.** arch, flyover, overpass, span, viaduct **2.** band, bond, connection, link, tie ~*v.* **3.** arch over, attach, bind, connect, couple, cross, cross over, extend across, go over, join, link, reach across, span, traverse, unite

bridle *v.* **1.** check, constrain, control, curb, govern, keep in check, master, moderate, repress, restrain, subdue **2.** be indignant, bristle, draw (oneself) up, get angry, get one's back up, raise one's hackles, rear up ~*n.* **3.** check, control, curb, restraint, trammels

—*n.* **4.** summary of case for counsel's use **5.** papal letter **6.** instructions —*pl.* **7.** underpants **8.** panties —*vt.* **9.** give instructions —ˈ**briefly** *adv.* —ˈ**briefness** *n.* —ˈ**briefcase** *n.* hand case for carrying papers

brier (ˈbraɪə) *n. see* BRIAR[1], BRIAR[2]

brig (brɪg) *n.* two-masted, square-rigged ship

Brig. 1. Brigade **2.** Brigadier

brigade (brɪˈgeɪd) *n.* **1.** subdivision of army **2.** organized band —**brigaˈdier** *n.* high-ranking army officer, usu. in charge of a brigade

brigand (ˈbrɪgənd) *n.* bandit, *esp.* member of gang in mountainous areas

brigantine (ˈbrɪgəntiːn, -taɪn) *n.* two-masted vessel with square-rigged foremast and fore-and-aft mainmast

bright (braɪt) *a.* **1.** shining **2.** full of light **3.** cheerful **4.** clever —ˈ**brighten** *v.* —ˈ**brightly** *adv.* —ˈ**brightness** *n.*

Bright's disease (braɪts) chronic inflammation of kidneys; chronic nephritis

brill (brɪl) *n.* European food fish

brilliant (ˈbrɪljənt) *a.* **1.** shining **2.** sparkling **3.** splendid **4.** very clever **5.** distinguished —ˈ**brilliance** *or* ˈ**brilliancy** *n.* —ˈ**brilliantly** *adv.*

brilliantine (ˈbrɪljəntiːn) *n.* perfumed hair oil

brim (brɪm) *n.* margin, edge, *esp.* of river, cup, hat —**brimˈful** *a.* full to the brim —ˈ**brimless** *a.* —ˈ**brimming** *a.*

brimstone (ˈbrɪmstəʊn) *n.* sulphur

brindled (ˈbrɪndᵊld) *a.* spotted and streaked

brine (braɪn) *n.* **1.** salt water **2.** pickle —ˈ**briny** *a.* **1.** very salty —*n.* **2.** *inf.* the sea

bring (brɪŋ) *vt.* **1.** fetch **2.** carry with one **3.** cause to come (**brought** *pt./pp.*)

brink (brɪŋk) *n.* **1.** edge of steep place **2.** verge, margin —ˈ**brinkmanship** *n.* practice of pressing dangerous situation, *esp.* in international affairs, to limit of safety in order to win advantage

briquette *or* **briquet** (brɪˈkɛt) *n.* block of compressed coal dust

brisk (brɪsk) *a.* active, vigorous —ˈ**briskly** *adv.* —ˈ**briskness** *n.*

brisket (ˈbrɪskɪt) *n.* joint of meat from breast of animal

brisling (ˈbrɪslɪŋ) *n. see* SPRAT

bristle (ˈbrɪsᵊl) *n.* **1.** short stiff hair —*vi.* **2.** (of hair) stand erect **3.** show temper —ˈ**bristliness** *n.* —ˈ**bristly** *a.*

Brit (brɪt) *n. inf.* British person

Brit. 1. Britain **2.** Britannia **3.** British

Britannia (brɪˈtænɪə) *n.* **1.** female warrior carrying trident, personifying Great Britain or British Empire **2.** in ancient Roman Empire, southern part of Great Britain —**Britannia metal** alloy of tin with antimony and copper, used for decorative purposes and for bearings

THESAURUS

brief *adj.* **1.** compendious, compressed, concise, crisp, curt, laconic, limited, pithy, short, succinct, terse, thumbnail, to the point **2.** ephemeral, fast, fleeting, hasty, little, momentary, quick, short, short-lived, swift, temporary, transitory ~*n* **3.** argument, case, contention, data, defence, demonstration ~*v.* **4.** advise, explain, fill in (*Inf.*), gen up (*Brit. inf.*), give (someone) a rundown, give (someone) the gen (*Brit. inf.*), inform, instruct, prepare, prime, put (someone) in the picture (*Inf.*)

briefly abruptly, briskly, casually, concisely, cursorily, curtly, fleetingly, hastily, hurriedly, in a few words, in a nutshell, in brief, in outline, in passing, momentarily, precisely, quickly, shortly, temporarily

brigade band, body, company, contingent, corps, crew, force, group, organization, outfit, party, squad, team, troop, unit

bright 1. beaming, blazing, brilliant, dazzling, effulgent, flashing, gleaming, glistening, glittering, glowing, illuminated, intense, lambent, luminous, lustrous, radiant, resplendent, scintillating, shimmering, shining, sparkling, twinkling, vivid **2.** acute, astute, aware, brainy, brilliant, clear-headed, clever, ingenious, intelligent, inventive, keen, quick, quick-witted, sharp, smart, wide-awake **3.** cheerful, gay, genial, glad, happy, jolly, joyful, joyous, light-hearted, lively, merry, vivacious

brighten 1. enliven, gleam, glow, illuminate, lighten, light up, make brighter, shine **2.** become cheerful, buck up (*Inf.*), buoy up, cheer, encourage, enliven, gladden, hearten, make happy, perk up

brilliance, brilliancy 1. blaze, brightness, dazzle, effulgence, gleam, glitter, intensity, luminosity, lustre, radiance, refulgence, resplendence, sheen, sparkle, vividness **2.** acuity, aptitude, braininess, cleverness, distinction, excellence, genius, giftedness, greatness, inventiveness, talent, wisdom **3.** éclat, glamour, gorgeousness, grandeur, illustriousness, magnificence, splendour

brilliant 1. ablaze, bright, coruscating, dazzling, glittering, glossy, intense, luminous, lustrous, radiant, refulgent, resplendent, scintillating, shining, sparkling, vivid **2.** celebrated, eminent, exceptional, famous, glorious, illustrious, magnificent, outstanding, splendid, superb **3.** accomplished, acute, astute, brainy, clever, discerning, expert, gifted, intellectual, intelligent, inventive, masterly, penetrating, profound, quick, talented

brim border, brink, circumference, edge, lip, margin, rim, skirt, verge

brimful brimming, filled, flush, full, level with, overflowing, overfull, packed, running over

bring 1. accompany, bear, carry, conduct, convey, deliver, escort, fetch, gather, guide, import, lead, take, transfer, transport, usher **2.** cause, contribute to, create, effect, engender, inflict, occasion, produce, result in, wreak

brink border, boundary, brim, edge, fringe, frontier, limit, lip, margin, point, rim, skirt, threshold, verge

brisk active, agile, alert, animated, bustling, busy, energetic, lively, nimble, no-nonsense, quick, speedy, sprightly, spry, vigorous, vivacious

briskly actively, brusquely, coolly, decisively, efficiently, energetically, firmly, incisively, nimbly, promptly, quickly, rapidly, readily, smartly, vigorously

bristle *n.* **1.** barb, hair, prickle, spine, stubble, thorn, whisker ~*v.* **2.** horripilate, prickle, rise, stand on end, stand up **3.** be angry, be infuriated, be maddened, bridle, flare up, get one's dander up (*Sl.*), rage, see red, seethe, spit (*Inf.*)

Britannic (brɪˈtænɪk) *a.* of Britain; British (*esp. in* **His or Her Britannic Majesty**)

britches (ˈbrɪtʃɪz) *pl.n. see* **breeches** *at* BREECH —**too big for one's britches** *inf.* overconfident; arrogant

British (ˈbrɪtɪʃ) *a.* **1.** of Great Britain or the British Commonwealth **2.** relating to English language as spoken in Britain —*n.* **3.** natives or inhabitants of Britain —ˈ**Briton** *n.* native or inhabitant of Britain —**British thermal unit** unit of heat equal to 1055 joules

brittle (ˈbrɪtᵊl) *a.* **1.** easily broken, fragile **2.** curt, irritable —ˈ**brittleness** *n.*

broach (brəʊtʃ) *vt.* **1.** pierce (cask) **2.** open, begin —*vi.* **3.** *Naut.* turn beam-on to wind and waves

broad (brɔːd) *a.* **1.** wide, spacious, open **2.** plain, obvious **3.** coarse **4.** general **5.** tolerant **6.** (of pronunciation) dialectal —ˈ**broaden** *v.* —ˈ**broadly** *adv.* —ˈ**broadness** *n.* —**broad bean 1.** Eurasian plant cultivated for its large edible seeds **2.** its seed —ˈ**broadcast** *v.* **1.** transmit (broadcast) by radio or television —*vt.* **2.** make widely known **3.** scatter, as seed —*n.* **4.** radio or television programme —ˈ**broadcaster** *n.* —ˈ**broadcloth** *n.* **1.** fabric woven on wide loom **2.** closely woven fabric of wool *etc.* with lustrous finish —**broad-minded** *a.* **1.** tolerant **2.** generous —ˈ**broadsheet** *n.* **1.** newspaper with large format **2.** ballad or popular song printed on one side of sheet of paper, *esp.* in 16th-cent. England (*also* **broadside (ballad)**) —ˈ**broadside** *n.* **1.** discharge of all guns on one side of ship **2.** strong (verbal) attack —ˈ**broadsword** *n.* broad-bladed sword for cutting rather than stabbing

B-road *n.* secondary road in Britain

brocade (brəʊˈkeɪd) *n.* rich woven fabric with raised design

broccoli (ˈbrɒkəlɪ) *n.* type of cabbage

brochure (ˈbrəʊʃjʊə, -ʃə) *n.* pamphlet, booklet

broderie anglaise (ˈbrəʊdəriː ɑːŋˈglɛz) open embroidery on white cotton *etc.*

brogue (brəʊg) *n.* **1.** stout shoe **2.** dialect, *esp.* Irish accent

broil[1] (brɔɪl) *n.* noisy quarrel

broil[2] (brɔɪl) *vt.* **1.** cook over hot coals **2.** grill —*vi.* **3.** be heated

broke (brəʊk) *v.* **1.** *pt. of* BREAK —*a.* **2.** *inf.* penniless —ˈ**broken** *pp. of* BREAK —**broken chord** *see* ARPEGGIO —**broken-down** *a.* **1.** worn out, as by age; dilapidated **2.** not in working order —**brokenˈhearted** *a.* overwhelmed by grief or disappointment

broker (ˈbrəʊkə) *n.* **1.** one employed to buy and sell for others **2.** dealer —ˈ**brokerage** *n.* payment to broker

brolly (ˈbrɒlɪ) *n. inf.* umbrella

bromide (ˈbrəʊmaɪd) *n.* chemical compound used in medicine and photography —**bromide paper** photographic printing paper, treated with silver bromide

bromine (ˈbrəʊmiːn, -mɪn) *n.* liquid element used in production of chemicals —ˈ**bromic** *a.*

bronchus (ˈbrɒŋkəs) *n.* either of two main branches of trachea (*pl.* **bronchi** (ˈbrɒŋkaɪ)) —ˈ**bronchial** *a.* —**bronˈchitis** *n.* inflammation of bronchi

bronco *or* **broncho** (ˈbrɒŋkəʊ) *n.* half-tamed horse (*pl.* **-s**)

brontosaurus (brɒntəˈsɔːrəs) *or* **brontosaur** (ˈbrɒntəsɔː) *n.* very large herbivorous dinosaur

bronze (brɒnz) *n.* **1.** alloy of copper and tin —*a.* **2.** made of, or coloured like, bronze —*vt.* **3.** give appearance of bronze to —**bronzed** *a.* **1.** coated with bronze **2.** sunburnt —**Bronze Age** era of bronze implements

THESAURUS

brittle 1. breakable, crisp, crumbling, crumbly, delicate, fragile, frail, frangible, friable, shatterable, shivery **2.** curt, edgy, irritable, nervous, prim, stiff, stilted, tense

broach 1. approach, bring up, hint at, introduce, mention, open up, propose, raise the subject, speak of, suggest, talk of, touch on **2.** crack, draw off, open, pierce, puncture, start, tap, uncork

broad 1. ample, beamy (*of a ship*), capacious, expansive, extensive, generous, large, open, roomy, spacious, vast, voluminous, wide, widespread **2.** all-embracing, comprehensive, encyclopedic, far-reaching, general, inclusive, nonspecific, sweeping, undetailed, universal, unlimited, wide, wide-ranging **3.** *As in* **broad daylight** clear, full, obvious, open, plain, straightforward, undisguised **4.** broad-minded, liberal, open, permissive, progressive, tolerant, unbiased **5.** blue, coarse, gross, improper, indecent, indelicate, near the knuckle (*Inf.*), unrefined, vulgar

broadcast *v.* **1.** air, beam, cable, put on the air, radio, relay, show, televise, transmit **2.** advertise, announce, circulate, disseminate, make public, proclaim, promulgate, publish, report, spread ~*n.* **3.** programme, show, telecast, transmission

broaden augment, develop, enlarge, expand, extend, fatten, increase, open up, spread, stretch, supplement, swell, widen

broad-minded catholic, cosmopolitan, dispassionate, flexible, free-thinking, indulgent, liberal, open-minded, permissive, responsive, tolerant, unbiased, unbigoted, undogmatic, unprejudiced

broadside abuse, assault, attack, battering, bombardment, censure, criticism, denunciation, diatribe, philippic

brochure advertisement, booklet, circular, folder, handbill, hand-out, leaflet, pamphlet

broke bankrupt, bust (*Inf.*), cleaned out (*Sl.*), flat broke (*Sl.*), impoverished, insolvent, on one's uppers, penniless, penurious, ruined, skint (*Brit. inf.*), stony-broke (*Sl.*)

broken 1. burst, demolished, destroyed, fractured, fragmented, rent, ruptured, separated, severed, shattered, shivered **2.** defective, exhausted, feeble, imperfect, kaput (*Inf.*), not functioning, out of order, ruined, run-down, spent, weak **3.** disconnected, discontinuous, disturbed, erratic, fragmentary, incomplete, intermittent, interrupted, spasmodic **4.** dishonoured, disobeyed, disregarded, forgotten, ignored, infringed, isolated, retracted, traduced, transgressed

broken-down collapsed, dilapidated, in disrepair, inoperative, kaput (*Sl.*), not functioning, not in working order, old, on the blink (*Inf.*), out of commission, out of order, worn out

brokenhearted crestfallen, desolate, despairing, devastated, disappointed, disconsolate, grief-stricken, heartbroken, heart-sick, inconsolable, miserable, mournful, prostrated, sorrowful, wretched

broker agent, dealer, factor, go-between, intermediary, middleman, negotiator

brooch (brəutʃ) *n.* ornamental pin or fastening

brood (bruːd) *n.* **1.** family of young, *esp.* of birds **2.** tribe, race —*vi.* **3.** sit, as hen on eggs **4.** meditate, fret —ˈ**broody** *a.* moody, sullen

brook[1] (brʊk) *n.* small stream —ˈ**brooklet** *n.*

brook[2] (brʊk) *vt.* put up with, endure, tolerate

broom (bruːm, brʊm) *n.* **1.** brush for sweeping **2.** yellow-flowered shrub —ˈ**broomstick** *n.* handle of broom

bros. *or* **Bros.** brothers

brose (brəuz) *n.* *Scot.* porridge made by adding boiling liquid to meal, *esp.* oatmeal

broth (brɒθ) *n.* thick soup

brothel (ˈbrɒθəl) *n.* house of prostitution

brother (ˈbrʌðə) *n.* **1.** son of same parents **2.** one closely united with another —ˈ**brotherhood** *n.* **1.** relationship **2.** fraternity, company —ˈ**brotherliness** *n.* —ˈ**brotherly** *a.* —**brother-in-law** *n.* **1.** brother of husband or wife **2.** husband of sister

brougham (ˈbruːəm, bruːm) *n.* **1.** four-wheeled horse-drawn closed carriage having raised open driver's seat in front **2.** *obs.* early electric car

brought (brɔːt) *pt./pp. of* BRING

brouhaha (bruːˈhɑːhɑː) *n.* loud confused noise; uproar

brow (brau) *n.* **1.** ridge over eyes **2.** forehead **3.** eyebrow **4.** edge of hill —ˈ**browbeat** *vt.* bully

brown (braun) *a.* **1.** of dark colour inclining to red or yellow —*n.* **2.** brown colour, pigment, or dye—*v.* **3.** make, become brown —ˈ**brownie** *n.* **1.** in folklore, elf said to do helpful work at night, *esp.* household chores **2.** *chiefly* **US** flat, nutty, chocolate cake —**Brownie Guide** *or* ˈ**Brownie** *n.* junior Girl Guide —**brown rice** unpolished rice —**brown study** mood of deep absorption; reverie —**brown sugar** unrefined or partially refined sugar —**browned off** *inf.* bored, depressed

browse (brauz) *vi.* **1.** look (through book, articles for sale *etc.*) in a casual manner **2.** feed on shoots and leaves

brucellosis (bruːsɪˈləusɪs) *n.* infectious disease of cattle, goats, and pigs, caused by bacteria and transmittable to man (*also* **undulant fever**)

bruin (ˈbruːɪn) *n.* name for a bear, used in children's tales *etc.*

bruise (bruːz) *vt.* **1.** injure without breaking skin —*n.* **2.** contusion, discoloration caused by blow —ˈ**bruiser** *n.* strong, tough person

brumby (ˈbrʌmbɪ) *n.* Aust. wild horse

brunch (brʌntʃ) *n.* *inf.* breakfast and lunch combined

brunette (bruːˈnɛt) *n.* **1.** woman of dark complexion and hair —*a.* **2.** dark brown

brunt (brʌnt) *n.* **1.** shock of attack, chief stress **2.** first blow

brush (brʌʃ) *n.* **1.** device with bristles, hairs, wires *etc.* used for cleaning, painting *etc.* **2.** act, instance of brushing **3.** brief contact **4.** skirmish, fight **5.** bushy tail **6.** brushwood **7.** (carbon) device taking electric current from moving to stationary parts of generator *etc.* —*vt.* **8.** apply, remove, clean, with brush —*v.* **9.** touch lightly —ˈ**brushoff** *n.* *inf.* **1.** dismissal **2.** refusal **3.** snub **4.** rebuff —**brush-up** *n.* **UK** act or instance of tidying one's appearance (*esp.* *in* **wash and brush-up**) —ˈ**brushwood** *n.* **1.** broken-off branches **2.** land covered with scrub —**brush up** *inf.* **1.** (*oft. with* on) refresh one's knowledge, memory of (subject) **2.** make person or oneself clean or neat as after journey

brusque (bruːsk, brʊsk) *a.* rough in manner, curt, blunt

Brussels sprout (ˈbrʌsəlz) **1.** variety of cabbage, having stem with heads resembling tiny cabbages **2.** head of this plant, eaten as vegetable

THESAURUS

bronze brownish, chestnut, copper, copper-coloured, metallic brown, reddish-brown, reddish-tan, rust, tan

brood *v.* **1.** agonize, dwell upon, fret, meditate, mope, mull over, muse, ponder, repine, ruminate, think upon **2.** cover, hatch, incubate, set, sit upon ~*n.* **3.** breed, chicks, children, clutch, family, hatch, infants, issue, litter, offspring, progeny, young

brook beck, burn, gill (*Dialect*), rill, rivulet, runnel (*Literary*), stream, streamlet, watercourse

brother **1.** blood brother, kin, kinsman, relation, relative, sibling **2.** associate, chum (*Inf.*), colleague, companion, compeer, comrade, confrère, fellow member, mate, pal (*Inf.*), partner

brotherhood **1.** brotherliness, camaraderie, companionship, comradeship, fellowship, friendliness, kinship **2.** alliance, association, clan, clique, community, coterie, fraternity, guild, league, society, union

brotherly affectionate, altruistic, amicable, benevolent, cordial, fraternal, friendly, kind, neighbourly, philanthropic, sympathetic

brow **1.** eyebrow, forehead, front, temple **2.** brim, brink, crown, edge, peak, rim, summit, tip, top, verge

browbeat badger, bulldoze (*Inf.*), bully, coerce, cow, domineer, dragoon, hector, intimidate, lord it over, oppress, overawe, overbear, threaten, tyrannize

brown *adj.* auburn, bay, brick, bronze, bronzed, browned, brunette, chestnut, chocolate, coffee, dark, donkey brown, dun, dusky, fuscous, ginger, hazel, nigger brown, rust, sunburnt, tan, tanned, tawny, toasted, umber

browse **1.** dip into, examine cursorily, flip through, glance at, leaf through, look round, look through, peruse, scan, skim, survey **2.** crop, eat, feed, graze, nibble, pasture

bruise **1.** *v.* blacken, blemish, contuse, crush, damage, deface, discolour, injure, mar, mark, pound, pulverize **2.** *n.* black-and-blue mark, black mark, blemish, contusion, discoloration, injury, mark, swelling

brunt burden, force, full force, impact, pressure, shock, strain, stress, thrust, violence

brush *n.* **1.** besom, broom, sweeper **2.** clash, conflict, confrontation, encounter, fight, fracas, scrap (*Inf.*), set-to (*Inf.*), skirmish, slight engagement, spot of bother (*Inf.*), tussle ~*v.* **3.** buff, clean, paint, polish, sweep, wash **4.** caress, contact, flick, glance, graze, kiss, scrape, stroke, sweep, touch ~**5.** *n.* brushwood, bushes, copse, scrub, shrubs, thicket, undergrowth, underwood

brushoff *n.* cold shoulder, cut, dismissal, go-by (*Sl.*), rebuff, refusal, rejection, repudiation, repulse, slight, snub

brush up cram, go over, polish up, read up, refresh one's memory, relearn, revise, study

brute (bruːt) *n.* **1.** any animal except man **2.** crude, vicious person —*a.* **3.** animal **4.** sensual, stupid **5.** physical —**ˈbrutal** *a.* —**bruˈtality** *n.* —**ˈbrutalize** *or* **-ise** *vt.* —**ˈbrutally** *adv.* —**ˈbrutish** *a.* bestial, gross

bryony *or* **briony** (ˈbraɪənɪ) *n.* wild climbing hedge plant

bryophyte (ˈbraɪəfaɪt) *n.* any moss or liverwort —**bryophytic** (braɪəˈfɪtɪk) *a.*

BS British Standard(s)

b.s. **1.** balance sheet **2.** bill of sale

B.Sc. Bachelor of Science

B.S.C. **1.** British Steel Corporation **2.** British Sugar Corporation

BSI British Standards Institution

B.S.T. British Summer Time

Bt. Baronet

btu *or* **B.Th.U.** British Thermal Unit

bubble (ˈbʌbᵊl) *n.* **1.** hollow globe of liquid, blown out with air **2.** something insubstantial, not serious **3.** transparent dome —*vi.* **4.** rise in bubbles **5.** make gurgling sound —**ˈbubbly** *a.* —**bubble and squeak** **UK** dish of cabbage and potatoes fried together —**bubble gum** chewing gum that can be blown into bubbles

bubonic plague (bjuːˈbɒnɪk) acute infectious disease characterized by swellings and fever

buccaneer (bʌkəˈnɪə) *n.* pirate, searover —**buccaˈneering** *n.*

buck[1] (bʌk) *n.* **1.** male deer, or other male animal **2.** act of bucking **3.** **US, A** *sl.* dollar —*vt.* **4.** (of horse) attempt to throw rider by jumping upwards *etc.* **5.** resist, oppose —**ˈbuckshot** *n.* lead shot in shotgun shell —**ˈbuckskin** *n.* **1.** skin of male deer **2.** strong greyish-yellow leather, orig. made from deerskin but now usu. made from sheepskin **3.** starched cotton cloth **4.** strong satin-woven woollen fabric —**ˈbuckteeth** *pl.n.* projecting upper teeth

buck[2] (bʌk) *n.* *Poker* marker in jackpot to remind winner of some obligation when his turn to deal —**pass the buck** *inf.* shift blame or responsibility

buckboard (ˈbʌkbɔːd) *n.* **US** open four-wheeled horse-drawn carriage with seat attached to flexible board between front and rear axles

bucket (ˈbʌkɪt) *n.* **1.** vessel, round with arched handle, for water *etc.* **2.** anything resembling this —*vt.* **3.** put, carry, in bucket —**ˈbucketful** *n.* —**bucket seat** seat with back shaped to occupier's figure —**bucket shop** *chiefly* **UK** firm specializing in cheap airline tickets —**bucket down** rain very hard

buckle (ˈbʌkᵊl) *n.* **1.** metal clasp for fastening belt, strap *etc.* —*vt.* **2.** fasten with buckle —*vi.* **3.** warp, bend —**ˈbuckler** *n.* shield —**buckle down** start work

buckram (ˈbʌkrəm) *n.* coarse cloth stiffened with size

Bucks. (bʌks) Buckinghamshire

buckshee (bʌkˈʃiː) *a.* *sl.* free

bucolic (bjuːˈkɒlɪk) *a.* rustic

bud (bʌd) *n.* **1.** shoot or sprout on plant containing unopened leaf, flower *etc.* —*vi.* **2.** begin to grow —*vt.* **3.** graft (**-dd-**)

Buddhism (ˈbʊdɪzəm) *n.* religion founded in India by the Buddha —**ˈBuddhist** *a./n.*

buddleia (ˈbʌdlɪə) *n.* shrub with mauve flower spikes

buddy (ˈbʌdɪ) *n.* *chiefly* **US** *sl.* mate, chum

budge (bʌdʒ) *v.* move, stir

budgerigar (ˈbʌdʒərɪgɑː) *n.* small Aust. parakeet (*also* **ˈbudgie**)

budget (ˈbʌdʒɪt) *n.* **1.** annual financial statement **2.** plan of systematic spending —*vi.* **3.** prepare financial statement —*v.* **4.** plan financially

buff[1] (bʌf) *n.* **1.** leather made from buffalo or ox hide **2.** light yellow colour **3.** bare skin **4.** polishing pad —*vt.* **5.** polish

buff[2] (bʌf) *n.* *inf.* expert on some subject

buffalo (ˈbʌfələʊ) *n.* any of several species of large oxen (*pl.* **-es, -s, -lo**)

buffer[1] (ˈbʌfə) *n.* contrivance to lessen shock of concussion —**buffer state** small, usu. neutral state between two rival powers

buffer[2] (ˈbʌfə) *n.* **UK** *inf.* stupid or bumbling man (*esp.* *in* **old buffer**)

buffet[1] (ˈbʊfeɪ) *n.* **1.** refreshment bar **2.** meal at which guests serve themselves **3.** (ˈbʌfɪt, ˈbʊfeɪ) sideboard —**buffet car** **UK** railway coach where light refreshments are served

THESAURUS

brutal **1.** barbarous, bloodthirsty, cruel, ferocious, heartless, inhuman, merciless, pitiless, remorseless, ruthless, savage, uncivilized, vicious **2.** beastly, bestial, brute, brutish, carnal, coarse, crude, sensual **3.** bearish, callous, gruff, harsh, impolite, insensitive, rough, rude, severe, uncivil, unfeeling, unmannerly

brute *n.* **1.** animal, beast, creature, wild animal **2.** barbarian, beast, devil, fiend, monster, ogre, sadist, savage, swine ~*adj.* **3.** bodily, carnal, fleshly, instinctive, mindless, physical, senseless, unthinking **4.** bestial, coarse, depraved, gross, sensual

bubble *n.* **1.** air ball, bead, blister, blob, drop, droplet, globule, vesicle **2.** bagatelle, delusion, fantasy, illusion, toy, trifle, vanity ~*v.* **3.** boil, effervesce, fizz, foam, froth, percolate, seethe, sparkle **4.** babble, burble, gurgle, murmur, purl, ripple, trickle, trill

bubbly carbonated, curly, effervescent, fizzy, foamy, frothy, lathery, sparkling, sudsy

buccaneer corsair, freebooter, pirate, privateer, searover

buckle *n.* **1.** catch, clasp, clip, fastener, hasp ~*v.* **2.** catch, clasp, close, fasten, hook, secure **3.** bend, bulge, cave in, collapse, contort, crumple, distort, fold, twist, warp

buckle down apply oneself, exert oneself, launch into, pitch in, put one's shoulder to the wheel, set to

bud **1.** *n.* embryo, germ, shoot, sprout **2.** *v.* burgeon, burst forth, develop, grow, pullulate, shoot, sprout

budge dislodge, give way, inch, move, propel, push, remove, roll, shift, slide, stir

budget **1.** *n.* allocation, allowance, cost, finances, financial statement, fiscal estimate, funds, means, resources **2.** *v.* allocate, apportion, cost, cost out, estimate, plan, ration

buff[1] *v.* brush, burnish, polish, rub, shine, smooth

buff[2] addict, admirer, aficionado, connoisseur, devotee, enthusiast, expert, fan, fiend (*Inf.*), freak (*Sl.*)

buffer bulwark, bumper, cushion, fender, intermediary, safeguard, screen, shield, shock absorber

buffet[1] *n.* café, cafeteria, cold table, counter, cupboard, refreshment counter, salad bar, sideboard, snack bar

buffet[2] (ˈbʌfɪt) *n.* **1.** blow, slap **2.** misfortune —*vt.* **3.** strike with blows **4.** contend against —**ˈbuffeting** *n.*

buffoon (bəˈfuːn) *n.* **1.** clown **2.** fool —**bufˈfoonery** *n.* clowning

bug (bʌg) *n.* **1.** any small insect **2.** *inf.* disease, infection **3.** *inf.* concealed listening device —*vt. inf.* **4.** install secret microphone *etc.* in **5.** irritate (**-gg-**)

bugbear (ˈbʌgbɛə) *n.* **1.** object of needless terror **2.** nuisance

bugger (ˈbʌgə) *n.* **1.** sodomite **2.** *vulg. sl.* unpleasant person or thing —*vt. sl.* **3.** tire **4.** (*with* up) ruin, complicate

buggy (ˈbʌgɪ) *n.* light horse-drawn carriage having two or four wheels

bugle (ˈbjuːgᵊl) *n.* instrument like trumpet —**ˈbugler** *n.*

bugloss (ˈbjuːglɒs) *n.* shrub with blue flower clusters

build (bɪld) *v.* **1.** make, construct, by putting together parts or materials (**built** *pt./pp.*) —*n.* **2.** make, form —**ˈbuilder** *n.* —**ˈbuilding** *n.* —**building society** cooperative banking enterprise financed by deposits on which interest is paid and from which mortgage loans are advanced on homes —**build-up** *n.* **1.** progressive increase in number *etc.* **2.** extravagant publicity or praise **3.** *Mil.* process of attaining required strength of forces and equipment —**built-in** *a.* **1.** made as integral part **2.** essential; inherent —*n.* **3.** A built-in cupboard —**built-up** *a.* having many buildings —**build up 1.** construct gradually **2.** increase, *esp.* by degrees **3.** improve health of **4.** prepare for climax, as in story

bulb (bʌlb) *n.* **1.** modified leaf bud emitting roots from base, *eg* onion **2.** anything resembling this **3.** globe surrounding filament of electric light —**ˈbulbous** *a.*

bulbul (ˈbʊlbʊl) *n.* tropical songbird

bulge (bʌldʒ) *n.* **1.** swelling, protuberance **2.** temporary increase —*vi.* **3.** swell out —**ˈbulginess** *n.* —**ˈbulgy** *a.*

bulk (bʌlk) *n.* **1.** size **2.** volume **3.** greater part **4.** cargo —*vi.* **5.** be of weight or importance —**ˈbulkiness** *n.* —**ˈbulky** *a.*

bulkhead (ˈbʌlkhɛd) *n.* partition in interior of ship

bull[1] (bʊl) *n.* **1.** male of cattle **2.** male of various other animals —**ˈbullock** *n.* castrated bull —**ˈbulldog** *n.* thickset breed of dog —**ˈbulldoze** *vt.* —**ˈbulldozer** *n.* powerful tractor with blade for excavating *etc.* —**ˈbullfight** *n.* traditional Spanish spectacle in which matador baits and usu. kills bull in arena —**ˈbullfighter** *n.* —**ˈbullfighting** *n.* —**ˈbullfinch** *n.* **1.** European finch, male of which has bright red throat and breast **2.** any of similar finches —**bull-headed** *a.* blindly obstinate; stupid —**ˈbullring** *n.* arena for bullfighting —**bull's-eye** *n.* middle part of target —**bull terrier** breed of terrier developed by crossing bulldog with English terrier

bull[2] (bʊl) *n.* papal edict

bull[3] (bʊl) *n. sl.* nonsense

bullet (ˈbʊlɪt) *n.* projectile discharged from rifle, pistol *etc.*

bulletin (ˈbʊlɪtɪn) *n.* official report

bullion (ˈbʊljən) *n.* gold or silver in mass

bully (ˈbʊlɪ) *n.* **1.** one who hurts, persecutes, or intimidates weaker people —*vt.* **2.** intimidate, overawe **3.** ill-treat (**ˈbullied, ˈbullying**) —**bully beef** corned beef

bully-off *n. Hockey* method of starting play, in which two players strike sticks together and against ground three times before trying to hit ball (*also* **ˈbully**) —**bully off** *Hockey* start play with bully-off (*also* **ˈbully**)

bulrush (ˈbʊlrʌʃ) *n.* tall reedlike marsh plant with brown velvety spike

THESAURUS

buffet[2] **1.** *v.* bang, batter, beat, box, bump, clobber (*Sl.*), cuff, flail, knock, pound, pummel, push, rap, shove, slap, strike, thump, wallop (*Inf.*) **2.** *n.* bang, blow, box, bump, cuff, jolt, knock, push, rap, shove, slap, smack, thump, wallop (*Inf.*)

buffoon clown, comedian, comic, droll, fool, harlequin, jester, joker, merry-andrew, silly billy (*Inf.*), wag

bug *n.* **1.** *Inf.* bacterium, disease, germ, infection, microorganism, virus ~*v.* **2.** *Inf.* annoy, badger, bother, disturb, get on (someone's) wick (*Sl.*), harass, irk, irritate, needle (*Inf.*), nettle, pester, plague, vex **3.** eavesdrop, listen in, spy, tap, wiretap

bugbear anathema, bane, *bête noire*, bogey, bugaboo, devil, dread, fiend, horror, nightmare, pet hate

build 1. *v.* assemble, construct, erect, fabricate, form, make, put up, raise **2.** *n.* body, figure, form, frame, make, physique, shape, structure

building 1. domicile, dwelling, edifice, fabric, house, pile, structure **2.** architecture, construction, erection, fabricating, raising

build-up 1. accumulation, development, enlargement, escalation, expansion, gain, growth, increase **2.** ballyhoo (*Inf.*), hype (*Sl.*), plug (*Inf.*), promotion, publicity, puff **3.** accretion, accumulation, heap, load, mass, stack, stockpile, store

built-in essential, implicit, in-built, included, incorporated, inherent, inseparable, integral, part and parcel of

bulge *n.* **1.** bump, lump, projection, protrusion, protuberance, swelling **2.** boost, increase, intensification, rise, surge ~*v.* **3.** bag, dilate, distend, enlarge, expand, project, protrude, puff out, sag, stand out, stick out, swell, swell out

bulk 1. amplitude, bigness, dimensions, immensity, largeness, magnitude, massiveness, size, substance, volume, weight **2.** better part, body, generality, lion's share, main part, majority, major part, mass, most, nearly all, plurality, preponderance

bulldoze demolish, flatten, level, raze

bullet ball, missile, pellet, projectile, shot, slug

bulletin account, announcement, communication, communiqué, dispatch, message, news flash, notification, report, statement

bull-headed headstrong, inflexible, mulish, obstinate, pig-headed, stiff-necked, stubborn, stupid, tenacious, uncompromising, unyielding, wilful

bully 1. *n.* big bully, browbeater, bully boy, coercer, intimidator, oppressor, persecutor, ruffian, tormentor, tough **2.** *v.* bluster, browbeat, bulldoze (*Inf.*), bullyrag, coerce, cow, domineer, hector, intimidate, oppress, overbear, persecute, push around (*Sl.*), ride roughshod over, swagger, terrorize, tyrannize

bulwark 1. bastion, buttress, defence, embankment, fortification, outwork, partition, rampart, redoubt **2.** buffer, guard, mainstay, safeguard, security, support

bulwark (ˈbulwək) *n.* **1.** rampart **2.** any defence or means of security **3.** raised side of ship **4.** breakwater

bum (bʌm) *sl.* *n.* **1.** buttocks, anus **2.** US loafer, scrounger —*vt.* **3.** get by scrounging —*a.* **4.** useless —**bumˈbailiff** *n.* UK *derogatory* formerly, officer employed to collect debts and arrest debtors

bumble (ˈbʌmbᵊl) *vi.* speak or proceed clumsily —ˈ**bumbler** *n.*

bumblebee (ˈbʌmbᵊlbiː) *or* **humblebee** *n.* large bee

bump (bʌmp) *n.* **1.** heavy blow, dull in sound **2.** swelling caused by blow **3.** protuberance **4.** sudden movement —*vt.* **5.** strike or push against —ˈ**bumper** *n.* **1.** horizontal bar at front and rear of motor vehicle to protect against damage **2.** full glass —*a.* **3.** full, abundant —**bump off** *sl.* murder

bumph *or* **bumf** (bʌmf) *n.* *inf.* useless documents, information *etc.*

bumpkin (ˈbʌmpkɪn) *n.* rustic

bumptious (ˈbʌmpʃəs) *a.* offensively self-assertive

bun (bʌn) *n.* **1.** small, round cake **2.** round knot of hair

bunch (bʌntʃ) *n.* **1.** number of things tied or growing together **2.** cluster **3.** tuft, knot **4.** group, party —*vt.* **5.** put together in bunch —*vi.* **6.** gather together —ˈ**bunchy** *a.*

bundle (ˈbʌndᵊl) *n.* **1.** package **2.** number of things tied together **3.** *sl.* lot of money —*vt.* **4.** tie in bundle **5.** send (off) without ceremony

bundu (ˈbundu) *n.* SA wild uninhabited country

bung (bʌŋ) *n.* **1.** stopper for cask **2.** large cork —*vt.* **3.** stop up, seal, close **4.** *inf.* throw, sling —ˈ**bunghole** *n.*

bungalow (ˈbʌŋgələʊ) *n.* one-storeyed house

bungle (ˈbʌŋgᵊl) *vt.* **1.** do badly from lack of skill, botch —*vi.* **2.** act clumsily, awkwardly —*n.* **3.** blunder, muddle —ˈ**bungled** *a.* —ˈ**bungler** *n.* —ˈ**bungling** *a./n.*

bunion (ˈbʌnjən) *n.* inflamed swelling on foot or toe

bunk[1] (bʌŋk) *n.* narrow, shelflike bed —**bunk bed** one of pair of beds constructed one above the other

bunk[2] (bʌŋk) *n.* *sl.* hasty departure

bunk[3] (bʌŋk) *n.* *see* BUNKUM

bunker (ˈbʌŋkə) *n.* **1.** large storage container for oil, coal *etc.* **2.** sandy hollow on golf course **3.** (military) underground defensive position

bunkum *or* **buncombe** (ˈbʌŋkəm) *n.* nonsense

bunny (ˈbʌnɪ) *n.* *inf.* rabbit

Bunsen burner (ˈbʌnsᵊn) gas burner, producing great heat, used for chemical experiments

bunting[1] (ˈbʌntɪŋ) *n.* material for flags

bunting[2] (ˈbʌntɪŋ) *n.* bird with short, stout bill

buoy (bɔɪ; *U.S.* ˈbuːɪ) *n.* **1.** floating marker anchored in sea **2.** lifebuoy —*vt.* **3.** mark with buoy **4.** keep from sinking **5.** support —ˈ**buoyancy** *n.* —ˈ**buoyant** *a.*

BUPA (ˈbjuːpə, ˈbuːpə) British United Provident Association

bur (bɜː) *n.* head of plant with prickles or hooks (*also* **burr**)

burble (ˈbɜːbᵊl) *vi.* **1.** gurgle, as stream or baby **2.** talk idly

burden[1] (ˈbɜːdᵊn) *n.* **1.** load **2.** weight, cargo **3.** anything difficult to bear —*vt.* **4.** load, encumber —ˈ**burdensome** *a.*

burden[2] (ˈbɜːdᵊn) *n.* **1.** chorus of a song **2.** chief theme

burdock (ˈbɜːdɒk) *n.* plant with prickly burs

bureau (ˈbjʊərəʊ) *n.* **1.** writing desk **2.** office **3.** government department (*pl.* **-s, -reaux** (-rəʊz)) —**bureaucracy** (bjʊəˈrɒkrəsɪ) *n.* **1.** government by officials **2.** body of officials —ˈ**bureaucrat** *n.* —**bureauˈcratic** *a.*

THESAURUS

bump *v.* **1.** bang, collide (with), crash, hit, knock, slam, smash into, strike ~*n.* **2.** bang, blow, collision, crash, hit, impact, jar, jolt, knock, rap, shock, smash, thud, thump **3.** bulge, contusion, hump, knob, knot, lump, node, nodule, protuberance, swelling

bumper *adj.* abundant, bountiful, excellent, exceptional, full, jumbo (*Inf.*), massive, prodigal, spanking (*Inf.*), teeming, unusual, whacking (*Inf.*), whopping (*Inf.*)

bump off assassinate, dispatch, do away with, do in (*Sl.*), eliminate, finish off, kill, knock off (*Sl.*), liquidate, murder, remove, wipe out (*Inf.*)

bumptious arrogant, boastful, brash, cocky, conceited, egotistic, forward, full of oneself, impudent, overbearing, overconfident, presumptuous, pushy (*Inf.*), self-assertive, showy, swaggering, vainglorious, vaunting

bunch *n.* **1.** assortment, batch, bouquet, bundle, clump, cluster, collection, heap, lot, mass, number, parcel, pile, quantity, sheaf, spray, stack, tuft **2.** band, crew (*Inf.*), crowd, flock, gang, gathering, group, knot, mob, multitude, party, swarm, team, troop ~*v.* **3.** assemble, bundle, cluster, collect, congregate, cram together, crowd, flock, group, herd, huddle, mass, pack

bundle *n.* **1.** accumulation, assortment, batch, bunch, collection, group, heap, mass, pile, quantity, stack **2.** bag, bale, box, carton, crate, pack, package, packet, pallet, parcel, roll ~*v.* **3.** bale, bind, fasten, pack, package, palletize, tie, tie together, tie up, truss, wrap **4.** *With* **out, off, into,** *etc.* hurry, hustle, push, rush, shove, throw, thrust

bungle blunder, bodge (*Inf.*), botch, butcher, cock up (*Sl.*), foul up, fudge, louse up (*Sl.*), make a mess of, mar, mess up, miscalculate, mismanage, muff, ruin, screw up (*Inf.*), spoil

bungling awkward, blundering, botching, cack-handed (*Inf.*), clumsy, ham-fisted (*Inf.*), ham-handed (*Inf.*), incompetent, inept, maladroit, unskilful

bunk, bunkum balderdash, baloney (*Inf.*), bilge (*Inf.*), bosh (*Inf.*), garbage, havers (*Scot.*), hooey (*Sl.*), horsefeathers (*U.S. inf.*), nonsense, piffle (*Inf.*), poppycock (*Inf.*), rot, rubbish, stuff and nonsense, tarradiddle, tomfoolery, tommyrot, tosh (*Inf.*), trash, truck (*Inf.*), twaddle

buoy **1.** *n.* beacon, float, guide, marker, signal **2.** *v.* *With* **up** boost, cheer, cheer up, encourage, hearten, keep afloat, lift, raise, support, sustain

buoyant afloat, floatable, floating, light, weightless

burden *n.* **1.** affliction, anxiety, care, clog, encumbrance, grievance, load, millstone, obstruction, onus, responsibility, sorrow, strain, stress, trial, trouble, weight, worry **2.** *Naut.* cargo, freight, lading, tonnage ~*v.* **3.** bother, encumber, handicap, load, oppress, overload, overwhelm, saddle with, strain, tax, weigh down, worry

burette *or* **buret** (bjʊˈrɛt) *n.* graduated glass tube with stopcock on one end, for dispensing known volumes of fluids

burgee (ˈbɜːdʒiː) *n.* small nautical flag

burgeon *or* **bourgeon** (ˈbɜːdʒən) *vi.* **1.** bud **2.** develop rapidly

burgess (ˈbɜːdʒɪs) *n.* inhabitant of borough, *esp.* citizen with full municipal rights

burgh (ˈbʌrə) *n.* Scottish borough —**burgher** (ˈbɜːgə) *n.* citizen

burglar (ˈbɜːglə) *n.* one who enters building to commit crime, *esp.* theft —**ˈburglary** *n.* —**ˈburgle, ˈburglarize** *or* **-ise** *vt.*

burgundy (ˈbɜːgəndɪ) *n.* name of various red or white wines produced in the Burgundy region of France

burin (ˈbjʊərɪn) *n.* chisel of tempered steel used for engraving metal, wood, or marble

burlap (ˈbɜːlæp) *n.* coarse canvas

burlesque (bɜːˈlɛsk) *n.* **1.** (artistic) caricature **2.** ludicrous imitation —*vt.* **3.** caricature

burly (ˈbɜːlɪ) *a.* sturdy, stout, robust —**ˈburliness** *n.*

burn[1] (bɜːn) *vt.* **1.** destroy or injure by fire —*vi.* **2.** be on fire (*lit.* or *fig.*) **3.** be consumed by fire (**burned** *or* **burnt** *pt./pp.*) —*n.* **4.** injury, mark caused by fire —**ˈburner** *n.* **1.** part of stove *etc.* that produces flame **2.** apparatus for burning fuel, refuse *etc.* —**ˈburning** *a.* —**burning glass** convex lens for concentrating sun's rays to produce fire

burn[2] (bɜːn) *n.* small stream

burnish (ˈbɜːnɪʃ) *vt.* **1.** make bright by rubbing **2.** polish —*n.* **3.** gloss, lustre —**ˈburnisher** *n.*

burnoose, burnous, *or* **burnouse** (bɜːˈnuːs, -ˈnuːz) *n.* long circular cloak with hood, worn *esp.* by Arabs

burnt (bɜːnt) *v.* **1.** *pt./pp.* *of* BURN[1] —*a.* **2.** affected as if by burning; charred

burp (bɜːp) *n./v. inf.* (cause to) belch

burr[1] (bɜː) *n.* soft trilling sound given to letter *r* in some dialects

burr[2] (bɜː) *n.* rough edge left after cutting, drilling *etc.*

burro (ˈbʊrəʊ) *n.* donkey (*pl.* **-s**)

burrow (ˈbʌrəʊ) *n.* **1.** hole dug by rabbit *etc.* —*v.* **2.** make holes in (ground) —*vt.* **3.** bore **4.** conceal

bursar (ˈbɜːsə) *n.* official managing finances of college, school *etc.* —**ˈbursary** *n.* scholarship

burst (bɜːst) *vi.* **1.** fly asunder **2.** break into pieces **3.** rend **4.** break suddenly into some expression of feeling —*vt.* **5.** shatter, break violently (**burst** *pt./pp.*) —*n.* **6.** bursting **7.** explosion **8.** outbreak **9.** spurt

bury (ˈbɛrɪ) *vt.* **1.** put underground **2.** inter **3.** conceal (**ˈburied, ˈburying**) —**ˈburial** *n./a.*

bus (bʌs) *n.* **1.** large motor vehicle for passengers (*orig.* omnibus) —*v.* **2.** travel or transport by bus (**bused** *or* **bussed** *pt.*, **ˈbusing** *or* **ˈbussing** *pr.p.*) —**busman's holiday** *inf.* holiday spent doing same as one does at work

bus. business

busby (ˈbʌzbɪ) *n.* tall fur hat worn by certain soldiers

bush[1] (bʊʃ) *n.* **1.** shrub **2.** woodland, thicket **3. A, SA** *etc.* uncleared country, backwoods, interior —**bushed** *a.* **1.** tired out **2. A** lost, bewildered —**ˈbushy** *a.* shaggy —**ˈbushbaby** *n.* tree-living, nocturnal Afr. animal —**bush fire** widespread destructive fire in the bush —**bush jacket SA** shirtlike jacket with patch pockets —**bush line C** airline operating in bush country —**ˈBushman** *n.* member of hunting and gathering people of southern Afr. —**bush pilot** —**bush telegraph** *inf.* means of spreading rumour *etc.* —**bushveld** (ˈbʊʃfɛlt) *n.* **SA** bushy countryside

bush[2] (bʊʃ) *n.* **1.** thin metal sleeve or tubular lining serving as bearing —*v.* **2.** fit bush to (casing *etc.*)

bushel (ˈbʊʃəl) *n.* dry measure of eight gallons

business (ˈbɪznɪs) *n.* **1.** profession, occupation **2.**

THESAURUS

bureau **1.** desk, writing desk **2.** agency, branch, department, division, office, service

bureaucracy **1.** administration, authorities, civil service, corridors of power, directorate, government, ministry, officialdom, officials, the system **2.** bumbledom, officialdom, officialese, red tape, regulations

bureaucrat administrator, apparatchik, civil servant, functionary, mandarin, minister, office-holder, officer, official, public servant

burglar cat burglar, filcher, housebreaker, picklock, pilferer, robber, sneak thief, thief

burglary break-in, breaking and entering, filching, housebreaking, larceny, pilferage, robbery, stealing, theft, thieving

burial burying, entombment, exequies, funeral, inhumation, interment, obsequies, sepulture

buried **1.** coffined, consigned to the grave, entombed, interred, laid to rest **2.** covered, forgotten, hidden, repressed, sunk in oblivion, suppressed **3.** cloistered, concealed, hidden, private, sequestered, tucked away

burlesque **1.** *n.* caricature, mock, mockery, parody, satire, send-up (*Brit. inf.*), spoof (*Inf.*), takeoff (*Inf.*), travesty **2.** *v.* ape, caricature, exaggerate, imitate, lampoon, make fun of, mock, parody, ridicule, satirize, send up (*Brit. inf.*), spoof, (*Inf.*), take off (*Inf.*), travesty

burly beefy, big, brawny, bulky, hefty, hulking, muscular, powerful, stocky, stout, strapping, strong, sturdy, thickset, well-built

burn **1.** be ablaze, be on fire, blaze, flame, flare, flash, flicker, glow, smoke **2.** brand, calcine, char, ignite, incinerate, kindle, light, parch, reduce to ashes, scorch, set on fire, shrivel, singe, toast, wither **3.** be excited (angry, aroused, inflamed, passionate), blaze, desire, fume, seethe, simmer, smoulder, yearn

burrow **1.** *n.* den, hole, lair, retreat, shelter, tunnel **2.** *v.* delve, dig, excavate, hollow out, scoop out, tunnel

burst *v.* **1.** blow up, break, crack, disintegrate, explode, fly open, fragment, puncture, rend asunder, rupture, shatter, shiver, split, tear apart ~*n.* **2.** bang, blast, blasting, blowout, blow-up, breach, break, crack, discharge, explosion, rupture, split **3.** eruption, fit, gush, gust, outbreak, outburst, outpouring, rush, spate, spurt, surge, torrent

bury **1.** consign to the grave, entomb, inearth, inhume, inter, lay to rest, sepulchre **2.** conceal, cover, cover up, enshroud, hide, secrete, shroud, stow away

bush **1.** hedge, plant, shrub, shrubbery, thicket **2.** backwoods, brush, scrub, scrubland, the wild, woodland

busily actively, assiduously, briskly, carefully, diligently, earnestly, energetically, industriously, intently, purposefully, speedily, strenuously

commercial or industrial establishment **3.** commerce, trade **4.** responsibility, affair, matter **5.** work —**ˈbusinesslike** *a.* —**ˈbusinessman** *n.* person engaged in business, *esp.* as owner or executive (**ˈbusinesswoman** *fem.*)

busker (ˈbʌskə) *n.* one who makes money by singing, dancing *etc.* in the street —**busk** *vi.*

buskin (ˈbʌskɪn) *n.* **1.** formerly, sandal-like covering for foot and leg, reaching calf **2.** thick-soled laced half boot worn *esp.* by actors of ancient Greece **3.** (*usu. with* the) tragic drama

bust[1] (bʌst) *n.* **1.** sculpture of head and shoulders of human body **2.** woman's breasts

bust[2] (bʌst) *inf. v.* **1.** burst **2.** make, become bankrupt —*vt.* **3.** raid **4.** arrest —*a.* **5.** broken **6.** bankrupt —*n.* **7.** police raid or arrest

bustard (ˈbʌstəd) *n.* large swift-running bird

bustle[1] (ˈbʌsᵊl) *vi.* **1.** be noisily busy, active —*n.* **2.** fuss, commotion

bustle[2] (ˈbʌsᵊl) *n. Hist.* pad worn by ladies to support back of skirt

busy (ˈbɪzɪ) *a.* **1.** actively employed **2.** full of activity —*vt.* **3.** occupy (**ˈbusied, ˈbusying**) —**ˈbusily** *adv.* —**ˈbusybody** *n.* meddler —**busy lizzie** (ˈlɪzɪ) house plant

but (bʌt; *unstressed* bət) *conj.* **1.** yet **2.** still **3.** besides ~*prep.* **4.** except ~*adv.* **5.** only — **but for** without

butane (ˈbjuːteɪn, bjuːˈteɪn) *n.* gas used for fuel

butch (butʃ) *a./n. sl.* markedly or aggressively masculine (person)

butcher (ˈbutʃə) *n.* **1.** one who kills animals for food, or sells meat **2.** ruthless or brutal murderer —*vt.* **3.** slaughter, murder **4.** spoil (work) —**ˈbutchery** *n.*

butler (ˈbʌtlə) *n.* chief male servant

butt[1] (bʌt) *n.* **1.** the thick end **2.** target **3.** object of ridicule **4.** bottom or unused end of anything —*v.* **5.** lie, be placed end-on to

butt[2] (bʌt) *vt.* **1.** strike with head 2. push —n. 3. blow with head, as of sheep —*butt in* interfere, meddle

butt[3] (bʌt) *n.* large cask

butter (ˈbʌtə) *n.* **1.** fatty substance made from cream by churning —*vt.* **2.** spread with butter **3.** flatter —**butter bean** lima bean with large pale edible seeds —**ˈbutterfingered** *a.* —**ˈbutterfingers** *n. inf.* person who drops things inadvertently —**ˈbuttermilk** *n.* milk that remains after churning —**ˈbutterscotch** *n.* kind of hard, brittle toffee

buttercup (ˈbʌtəkʌp) *n.* plant with glossy, yellow flowers

butterfly (ˈbʌtəflaɪ) *n.* **1.** insect with large wings **2.** inconstant person **3.** stroke in swimming —**butterfly nut** *see* **wing nut** *at* WING

buttery (ˈbʌtərɪ) *n.* storeroom for food or wine

buttock (ˈbʌtək) *n.* (*usu. pl.*) rump, protruding hinder part

button (ˈbʌtᵊn) *n.* **1.** knob, stud for fastening dress **2.** knob that operates doorbell, machine *etc.* —*vt.* **3.** fasten with buttons —**ˈbuttonhole** *n.* **1.** slit in garment to pass button through as fastening **2.** flower, spray worn on lapel *etc.* —*vt.* **3.** detain (reluctant listener) in conversation

buttress (ˈbʌtrɪs) *n.* **1.** structure to support wall **2.** prop —*vt.* **3.** support (wall) with buttress

THESAURUS

business **1.** calling, career, craft, employment, function, job, line, métier, occupation, profession, pursuit, trade, vocation, work **2.** company, concern, corporation, enterprise, establishment, firm, organization, venture **3.** bargaining, commerce, dealings, industry, manufacturing, merchandising, selling, trade, trading, transaction **4.** affair, assignment, concern, duty, function, issue, matter, point, problem, question, responsibility, subject, task, topic

businesslike correct, efficient, matter-of-fact, methodical, orderly, organized, practical, professional, regular, routine, systematic, thorough, well-ordered, workaday

businessman, businesswoman capitalist, employer, entrepreneur, executive, financier, industrialist, merchant, tradesman, tycoon

bust[1] bosom, breast, chest, torso

bust[2] *v.* **1.** break, burst, fracture, rupture **2.** bankrupt break, crash, fail, impoverish, ruin **3.** arrest, catch, collar (*Inf.*), cop (*Sl.*), nab (*Inf.*), raid, search ~*n.* **4.** arrest, capture, cop (*Sl.*), raid, search, seizure

bustle **1.** *v.* bestir, dash, flutter, fuss, hasten, hurry, rush, scamper, scramble, scurry, scuttle, stir, tear **2.** *n.* activity, ado, agitation, commotion, excitement, flurry, fuss, haste, hurly-burly, hurry, pother, stir, to-do, tumult

busy *adj.* **1.** active, assiduous, brisk, diligent, employed, engaged, engrossed, hard at work, industrious, in harness, occupied, on duty, persevering, slaving, working **2.** active, energetic, exacting, full, hectic, hustling, lively, on the go (*Inf.*), restless, strenuous, tireless, tiring ~*v.* **3.** absorb, employ, engage, engross, immerse, interest, occupy

busybody eavesdropper, gossip, intriguer, intruder, meddler, nosy parker (*Inf.*), pry, scandalmonger, snoop, snooper, troublemaker

but **1.** *conj.* further, however, moreover, nevertheless, on the contrary, on the other hand, still, yet **2.** *prep.* bar, barring, except, excepting, excluding, notwithstanding, save, with the exception of **3.** *adv.* just, merely, only, simply, singly, solely

butcher *n.* **1.** destroyer, killer, murderer, slaughterer, slayer ~*v.* **2.** assassinate, cut down, destroy, exterminate, kill, liquidate, massacre, murder, put to the sword, slaughter, slay **3.** bodge (*Inf.*), botch, destroy, mess up, mutilate, ruin, spoil, wreck

butchery blood bath, blood-letting, bloodshed, carnage, killing, massacre, mass murder, murder, slaughter

butt[1] *n.* **1.** haft, handle, hilt, shaft, shank, stock **2.** base, end, fag end (*Inf.*), foot, leftover, stub, tail, tip **3.** Aunt Sally, dupe, laughing stock, mark, object, point, subject, target, victim ~*v.* **4.** abut, join, jut, meet, project, protrude

butt[2] **1.** *v./n. With or of the head or horns* buck, buffet, bump, bunt, jab, knock, poke, prod, punch, push, ram, shove, thrust **2.** *v. With* **in** or **into** chip in (*Inf.*), cut in, interfere, interrupt, intrude, meddle, put one's oar in, stick one's nose in

butt[3] barrel, cask, pipe

buttonhole *v. Fig.* accost, bore, catch, detain in talk, grab, importune, persuade importunately, take aside, waylay

buxom (ˈbʌksəm) *a.* **1.** full of health, plump, gay **2.** large-breasted

buy (baɪ) *vt.* **1.** get by payment, purchase **2.** bribe (**bought** *pt./pp.*) —ˈ**buyer** *n.*

buzz (bʌz) *vi.* **1.** make humming sound —*n.* **2.** humming sound of bees **3.** *inf.* telephone call —ˈ**buzzer** *n.* any apparatus that makes buzzing sound

buzzard (ˈbʌzəd) *n.* bird of prey of hawk family

B.V.M. Beata Virgo Maria (*Lat.*, Blessed Virgin Mary)

bwana (ˈbwɑːnə) *n.* in E Afr., master, oft. used as form of address corresponding to *sir*

by (baɪ) *prep.* **1.** near **2.** along **3.** across **4.** past **5.** during **6.** not later than **7.** through use or agency of **8.** in units of —*adv.* **9.** near **10.** away, aside **11.** past —**by and by** soon, in the future —**by and large 1.** on the whole **2.** speaking generally —**come by** obtain

by- *or* **bye-** (*comb. form*) subsidiary, incidental, out-of-the-way, near, as in *bypath, by-product, bystander*

bye (baɪ) *n.* **1.** *Sport* situation where player, team, wins by default of opponent **2.** *Cricket* run scored off ball not touched by batsman

by-election *or* **bye-election** *n.* parliamentary election caused by death or resignation of member

bygone (ˈbaɪgɒn) *a.* **1.** past, former —*n.* **2.** (*oft. pl.*) past occurrence **3.** small antique

bylaw *or* **bye-law** (ˈbaɪlɔː) *n.* law, regulation made by local subordinate authority

by-line *n.* **1.** line under title of newspaper or magazine article giving author's name **2.** *see* **touchline** *at* TOUCH

bypass (ˈbaɪpɑːs) *n.* road for diversion of traffic from crowded centres

by-play *n.* diversion, action apart from main action of play

byre (baɪə) *n.* cowshed

Byronic (baɪˈrɒnɪk) *a.* of, like, or characteristic of Byron, his poetry, or his style

bystander (ˈbaɪstændə) *n.* person present but not involved; spectator

byte (baɪt) *n. Comp.* sequence of bits processed as single unit of information

byway (ˈbaɪweɪ) *n.* **1.** secondary or side road **2.** area, field of study *etc.* that is of secondary importance

byword (ˈbaɪwɜːd) *n.* well-known name, saying

Byzantine (bɪˈzæntaɪn, -tiːn, baɪ-; ˈbɪzəntiːn, -taɪn) *a.* **1.** of Byzantium or Byzantine Empire **2.** of Orthodox Church **3.** of style of architecture developed in Byzantine Empire, characterized by domes, mosaics *etc.* **4.** complicated —*n.* **5.** inhabitant of Byzantium

THESAURUS

buttress 1. *n.* abutment, brace, mainstay, pier, prop, reinforcement, shore, stanchion, stay, strut, support **2.** *v.* back up, bolster, brace, prop, prop up, reinforce, shore, shore up, strengthen, support, sustain, uphold

buy *v.* **1.** acquire, get, invest in, obtain, pay for, procure, purchase, shop for **2.** *Often with* **off** bribe, corrupt, fix (*Inf.*), grease someone's palm (*Inf.*), square, suborn

by *prep.* **1.** along, beside, by way of, close to, near, next to, over, past, via **2.** through, through the agency of, under the aegis of ~*adv.* **3.** aside, at hand, away, beyond, close, handy, in reach, near, past, to one side

by and by before long, eventually, in a while, in the course of time, in the future, one day, presently, soon

bystander eyewitness, looker-on, observer, onlooker, passer-by, spectator, viewer, watcher, witness

C

c *or* **C** (siː) *n.* **1.** third letter of English alphabet **2.** speech sound represented by this letter, usu. either as in *cigar* or as in *case* **3.** third in series, *esp.* third highest grade in examination **4.** something shaped like C (*pl.* **c's, C's** *or* **Cs**)

C **1.** *Mus.* first degree of major scale containing no sharps or flats (**C major**); major or minor key having this note as tonic; time signature denoting four crotchet beats to bar (*see also* ALLA BREVE (sense 2), **common time** *at* COMMON) **2.** *Chem.* carbon **3.** capacitance **4.** heat capacity **5.** cold (water) **6.** *Phys.* compliance **7.** Celsius **8.** centigrade **9.** Conservative **10.** century, as in *C20* **11.** Roman numeral, 100

c. **1.** carat **2.** cent **3.** circa **4.** copyright

Ca *Chem.* calcium

CA California

ca. circa

C.A. chartered accountant

C.A.A. UK Civil Aviation Authority

cab (kæb) *n.* **1.** taxi **2.** driver's enclosed compartment on locomotive, lorry *etc.* —**ˈcabman** *or* **ˈcabby** *n.*

cabal (kəˈbæl) *n.* **1.** small group of intriguers **2.** secret plot

cabaret (ˈkæbəreɪ) *n.* floor show at nightclub or restaurant

cabbage (ˈkæbɪdʒ) *n.* vegetable with large head of green or reddish leaves

cabbala, cabala, kabbala *or* **kabala** (kəˈbɑːlə) *n.* **1.** ancient Jewish mystical tradition **2.** any secret or occult doctrine —**ˈcabbalist, ˈcabalist, ˈkabbalist** *or* **ˈkabalist** *n.* —**cabbaˈlistic, cabaˈlistic, kabbaˈlistic** *or* **kabaˈlistic** *a.*

caber (ˈkeɪbə) *n.* heavy wooden pole tossed as trial of strength at Highland games

cabin (ˈkæbɪn) *n.* **1.** hut, shed **2.** small room, *esp.* in ship —*vt.* **3.** cramp, confine —**cabin boy** boy who waits on officers and passengers of ship —**cabin cruiser** power boat with cabin, bunks *etc.*

cabinet (ˈkæbɪnɪt) *n.* **1.** piece of furniture with drawers or shelves **2.** outer case of television, radio *etc.* **3.** (*oft.* **C-**) committee of politicians governing country **4.** *obs.* small room —**cabinet-maker** *n.* craftsman who makes fine furniture

cable (ˈkeɪbᵊl) *n.* **1.** strong rope **2.** wire or bundle of wires conveying electric power, telegraph signals *etc.* **3.** message sent by this **4.** nautical unit of measurement (100–120 fathoms) —*v.* **5.** telegraph by cable —**cable car** passenger car on cable railway, drawn by strong cable operated by motor —**ˈcablegram** *n.* cabled message

caboodle (kəˈbuːdᵊl) *n. inf.* —**the whole caboodle** the whole lot

caboose (kəˈbuːs) *n.* **1.** ship's galley **2.** US guard's van on train

cabriolet (kæbrɪəʊˈleɪ) *n.* early type of hansom cab

cacao (kəˈkɑːəʊ, -ˈkeɪəʊ) *n.* tropical tree from the seeds of which chocolate and cocoa are made

cachalot (ˈkæʃəlɒt) *n.* sperm whale

cache (kæʃ) *n.* **1.** secret hiding place **2.** store of food *etc.*

cachet (ˈkæʃeɪ) *n.* **1.** mark, stamp **2.** mark of authenticity **3.** prestige, distinction

cachinnate (ˈkækɪneɪt) *vi.* laugh loudly —**cachinˈnation** *n.*

cachou (ˈkæʃuː, kæˈʃuː) *n.* **1.** lozenge eaten to sweeten breath **2.** substance obtained from certain tropical plants and used in medicine *etc.* (*also* **ˈcatechu, cutch**)

cack-handed (kækˈhændɪd) *a. inf.* **1.** left-handed **2.** clumsy

cackle (ˈkækᵊl) *vi.* **1.** make chattering noise, as hen —*n.* **2.** cackling noise or laughter **3.** empty chatter —**ˈcackler** *n.*

caco- (*comb. form*) bad, unpleasant, incorrect, as in *cacophony*

cacoethes (kækəʊˈiːθiːz) *n.* uncontrollable urge or desire

cacophony (kəˈkɒfənɪ) *n.* **1.** disagreeable sound **2.** discord of sounds —**caˈcophonous** *a.*

cactus (ˈkæktəs) *n.* spiny succulent plant (*pl.* **-es, cacti** (ˈkæktaɪ))

cad (kæd) *n.* UK *inf., old-fashioned* dishonourable, unchivalrous person —**ˈcaddish** *a.*

cadaver (kəˈdeɪvə, -ˈdɑːv-) *n.* corpse —**cadaverous** (kəˈdævərəs) *a.* **1.** corpselike **2.** sickly-looking **3.** gaunt

caddie *or* **caddy** (ˈkædɪ) *n.* **1.** golfer's attendant —*vi.* **2.** act as caddie

caddis fly (ˈkædɪs) small mothlike insect having two pairs of hairy wings —**caddis worm** *or* **ˈcaddis** *n.* aquatic larva of caddis fly, which constructs protective case around itself made of silk *etc.* (*also* **ˈcaseworm, ˈstrawworm**)

caddy (ˈkædɪ) *n.* small box for tea

cadence (ˈkeɪdᵊns) *or* **cadency** *n.* fall or modulation of voice in music or verse

cadenza (kəˈdɛnzə) *n.* *Mus.* elaborate passage for solo instrument or singer

cadet (kəˈdɛt) *n.* youth in training, *esp.* for officer status in armed forces

cadge (kædʒ) *v.* get (food, money *etc.*) by sponging or begging —**ˈcadger** *n.* sponger

THESAURUS

cab hackney, hackney carriage, minicab, taxi, taxicab

cabin **1.** berth, bothy, chalet, cot, cottage, crib, hovel, hut, lodge, shack, shanty, shed **2.** berth, compartment, deckhouse, quarters, room

cabinet **1.** case, chiffonier, closet, commode, cupboard, dresser, escritoire, locker **2.** administration, assembly, council, counsellors, ministry **3.** apartment, boudoir, chamber (*Archaic*)

cackle babble, blather, chatter, chuckle, cluck, crow, gabble, gibber, giggle, jabber, prattle, snicker, snigger, titter

cad bounder (*Brit. inf.*), churl, cur, dastard (*Archaic*), heel (*Sl.*), knave, rat (*Sl.*), rotter (*Sl.*)

caddish despicable, ill-bred, low, ungentlemanly, unmannerly

cadi *or* **kadi** (ˈkɑːdɪ, ˈkeɪdɪ) *n.* judge in Muslim community (*pl.* **-s**)

cadmium (ˈkædmɪəm) *n.* metallic element

cadre (ˈkɑːdə) *n.* nucleus or framework, *esp.* skeleton of regiment

caduceus (kəˈdjuːsɪəs) *n.* **1.** *Class. myth.* winged staff entwined with two serpents carried by Hermes (Mercury) **2.** insignia resembling this, used as emblem of medical profession (*pl.* **-cei** (-sɪaɪ))

caecum *or U.S.* **cecum** (ˈsiːkəm) *n. Anat.* pouch, *esp.* at beginning of large intestine (*pl.* **-ca** (-kə))

Caenozoic (siːnəʊˈzəʊɪk) *see* CAINOZOIC

Caerphilly (kɛəˈfɪlɪ) *n.* creamy white mild-flavoured cheese

Caesarean, Caesarian, *or U.S.* **Cesarean, Cesarian** (sɪˈzɛərɪən) *a.* **1.** of any of Caesars, *esp.* Julius Caesar *—n.* **2.** (*sometimes* **c-**) *Surg.* Caesarean section **—Caesarean section** surgical incision through abdominal wall to deliver baby

caesium *or U.S.* **cesium** (ˈsiːzɪəm) *n.* ductile silvery-white element of alkali metal group, used in photocells *etc.*

caesura (sɪˈzjʊərə) *n.* **1.** in modern prosody, pause, *esp.* for sense, usu. near middle of verse line **2.** in classical prosody, break between words within metrical foot (*pl.* **-s, -rae** (-riː))

café (ˈkæfeɪ, ˈkæfɪ) *n.* small or inexpensive restaurant serving light refreshments **—cafeˈteria** *n.* restaurant designed for self-service

caff (kæf) *n. sl.* café

caffeine *or* **caffein** (ˈkæfiːn) *n.* stimulating alkaloid found in tea and coffee plants

caftan (ˈkæftæn, -tɑːn) *n. see* KAFTAN

cage (keɪdʒ) *n.* **1.** enclosure, box with bars or wires, *esp.* for keeping animals or birds **2.** place of confinement **3.** enclosed platform of lift, *esp.* in mine *—vt.* **4.** put in cage, confine **—ˈcagey** *or* **ˈcagy** *a.* wary, not communicative

cagoule (kəˈguːl) *n.* lightweight, usu. knee-length type of anorak

cahoots (kəˈhuːts) *pl.n. sl.* partnership (*esp. in* **in cahoots with**)

caiman (ˈkeɪmən) *n. see* CAYMAN

Cainozoic (kaɪnəʊˈzəʊɪk, keɪ-), **Cenozoic** *or* **Caenozoic** *a.* **1.** of most recent geological era characterized by development and increase of mammals *—n.* **2.** Cainozoic era

cairn (kɛən) *n.* heap of stones, *esp.* as monument or landmark **—cairn terrier** small rough-haired terrier orig. from Scotland

cairngorm (ˈkɛəngɔːm) *n.* yellow or brownish-coloured gem

caisson (kəˈsuːn, ˈkeɪsᵊn) *n.* **1.** chamber for working under water **2.** apparatus for lifting vessel out of water **3.** ammunition wagon

caitiff (ˈkeɪtɪf) *obs. n.* **1.** mean, despicable fellow *—a.* **2.** base, mean

cajole (kəˈdʒəʊl) *vt.* persuade by flattery, wheedle **—caˈjolement** *n.* **—caˈjoler** *n.* **—caˈjolery** *n.*

cake (keɪk) *n.* **1.** baked, sweetened, breadlike food **2.** compact mass *—vt.* **3.** make into cake *—vi.* **4.** harden (as of mud) **—ˈcakewalk** *n.* **1.** dance orig. performed by Amer. Negroes for prize of cake **2.** piece of music for this dance

cal. **1.** calendar **2.** calibre **3.** (small) calorie

Cal. (large) Calorie

calabash (ˈkæləbæʃ) *n.* **1.** tree with large hard-shelled fruit **2.** this fruit **3.** drinking, cooking vessel made from gourd

calaboose (ˈkæləbuːs) *n.* **US** *inf.* prison

calamine (ˈkæləmaɪn) *n.* pink powder used medicinally in soothing ointment

calamity (kəˈlæmɪtɪ) *n.* **1.** great misfortune **2.** deep distress, disaster **—caˈlamitous** *a.*

calceolaria (kælsɪəˈlɛərɪə) *n.* Amer. plant with speckled, slipper-shaped flowers

calces (ˈkælsiːz) *n., pl. of* CALX

calciferol (kælˈsɪfərɒl) *n.* fat-soluble steroid, found *esp.* in fish-liver oils and used in treatment of rickets (*also* **vitamin D_2**)

calcium (ˈkælsɪəm) *n.* metallic element, the basis of lime **—calcareous** (kælˈkɛərɪəs) *a.* containing lime **—calˈciferous** *a.* producing salts of calcium, *esp.* calcium carbonate **—ˈcalcify** *v.* convert, be converted, to lime **—ˈcalcine** *vt.* **1.** reduce to quicklime **2.** burn to ashes **—ˈcalcite** *n.* crystalline calcium carbonate **—calcium carbonate** white crystalline salt occurring in limestone, chalk *etc.*

calculate (ˈkælkjʊleɪt) *vt.* **1.** estimate **2.** compute *—vi.* **3.** make reckonings **—ˈcalculable** *a.* **—ˈcalculated** *a.* **1.** undertaken after considering likelihood of success **2.** premeditated **—ˈcalculating** *a.* **1.** able to perform calculations **2.** shrewd, designing, scheming **—calcuˈlation** *n.* **—ˈcalculator** *n.* electronic device for

THESAURUS

café cafeteria, coffee bar, coffee shop, lunchroom, restaurant, snack bar, tearoom

cage **1.** *v.* confine, coop up, fence in, immure, impound, imprison, incarcerate, lock up, mew, restrain, shut up **2.** *n.* corral (*U.S.*), enclosure, pen, pound

cajole beguile, coax, decoy, dupe, entice, entrap, flatter, inveigle, lure, manoeuvre, mislead, seduce, sweet-talk (*U.S. inf.*), tempt, wheedle

cake **1.** *v.* bake, cement, coagulate, congeal, consolidate, dry, encrust, harden, inspissate (*Archaic*), ossify, solidify, thicken **2.** *n.* bar, block, cube, loaf, lump, mass, slab

calamitous blighting, cataclysmic, catastrophic, deadly, devastating, dire, disastrous, fatal, pernicious, ruinous, tragic, woeful

calamity adversity, affliction, cataclysm, catastrophe, disaster, distress, downfall, hardship, misadventure, mischance, misfortune, mishap, reverse, ruin, scourge, tragedy, trial, tribulation, woe, wretchedness

calculate **1.** adjust, compute, consider, count, determine, enumerate, estimate, figure, gauge, judge, rate, reckon, value, weigh, work out **2.** aim, design, intend, plan

calculated considered, deliberate, intended, intentional, planned, premeditated, purposeful

calculating canny, cautious, contriving, crafty, cunning, designing, devious, Machiavellian, manipulative, politic, scheming, sharp, shrewd, sly

calculation answer, computation, estimate, estimation, figuring, forecast, judgment, reckoning, result

making calculations —ˈ**calculus** *n.* **1.** branch of mathematics **2.** stone in body (*pl.* **calculi** (ˈkælkjʊlaɪ))

caldron (ˈkɔːldrən) *n. see* CAULDRON

calèche (*Fr.* kaˈlɛʃ) *n.* **C** horse-drawn carriage for taking tourists around

Caledonian (kælɪˈdəʊnɪən) *a.* **1.** relating to Scotland —*n.* **2.** *Lit.* native of Scotland

calendar (ˈkælɪndə) *n.* **1.** table of months and days in the year **2.** list of events, documents, register —*vt.* **3.** enter in list **4.** index

calender (ˈkælɪndə) *n.* **1.** machine in which paper or cloth is smoothed by passing between rollers —*vt.* **2.** subject to such process

calends *or* **kalends** (ˈkælɪndz) *pl.n.* first day of each month in ancient Roman calendar

calendula (kæˈlɛndjʊlə) *n.* marigold

calf[1] (kɑːf) *n.* **1.** young of cow and of other animals **2.** leather made of calf's skin (*pl.* **calves**) —**calve** *vi.* give birth to calf —**calf love** infatuation of adolescent for member of opposite sex

calf[2] (kɑːf) *n.* fleshy back part of leg below knee (*pl.* **calves**)

calibre *or U.S.* **caliber** (ˈkælɪbə) *n.* **1.** size of bore of gun **2.** capacity, character —ˈ**calibrate** *vt.* mark (scale of measuring instrument) so that readings can be made in appropriate units —**caliˈbration** *n.*

calices (ˈkælɪsiːz) *n., pl. of* CALIX

calico (ˈkælɪkəʊ) *n.* cotton cloth

californium (kælɪˈfɔːnɪəm) *n.* transuranic element artificially produced from curium

caliper (ˈkælɪpə) *n.* **US** *see* CALLIPER

caliph, calif *or* **khalif** (ˈkeɪlɪf, ˈkæl-) *n. Islam* title of successors of Mohammed as rulers of Islamic world —**caliphate, califate** *or* **khalifate** (ˈkeɪlɪfeɪt) *n.* office or reign of caliph

calix (ˈkeɪlɪks, ˈkæ-) *n.* cup; chalice (*pl.* ˈ**calices**)

calk[1] (kɔːk) *vt. see* CAULK

calk[2] (kɔːk) *or* **calkin** (ˈkɔːkɪn, ˈkæl-) *n.* **1.** metal projection on horse's shoe to prevent slipping —*vt.* **2.** provide with calks

call (kɔːl) *vt.* **1.** speak loudly to attract attention of **2.** summon **3.** (*oft. with* up) telephone **4.** name —*vi.* **5.** shout **6.** pay visit —*n.* **7.** shout **8.** animal's cry **9.** visit **10.** inner urge, summons, as to be priest *etc.* **11.** need, demand —ˈ**caller** *n.* —ˈ**calling** *n.* vocation, profession —**call box** kiosk for public telephone—**call girl** prostitute with whom appointments are made by telephone —**call up 1.** summon to serve in army **2.** imagine

calligraphy (kəˈlɪgrəfɪ) *n.* handwriting, penmanship —**calliˈgraphic** *a.*

calliper *or U.S.* **caliper** (ˈkælɪpə) *n.* **1.** metal splint for leg —*pl.* **2.** instrument for measuring diameters

callisthenics *or* **calisthenics** (kælɪsˈθɛnɪks) *pl.n.* light gymnastic exercises —**callisˈthenic** *or* **calisˈthenic** *a.*

callosity (kəˈlɒsɪtɪ) *n.* **1.** hardheartedness **2.** callus

callous (ˈkæləs) *a.* hardened, unfeeling —ˈ**callously** *adv.* —ˈ**callousness** *n.*

callow (ˈkæləʊ) *a.* **1.** inexperienced **2.** immature

callus (ˈkæləs) *n.* area of thick, hardened skin

calm (kɑːm) *a.* **1.** still **2.** quiet **3.** tranquil —*n.* **4.** stillness **5.** tranquillity **6.** absence of wind —*v.* **7.** become, make, still or quiet —ˈ**calmly** *adv.* —ˈ**calmness** *n.*

calomel (ˈkæləmɛl, -məl) *n.* colourless, tasteless powder used medicinally, *esp.* as cathartic

Calor Gas (ˈkælə) **R** butane gas liquefied under pressure in portable containers for domestic use

calorie *or* **calory** (ˈkælərɪ) *n.* **1.** unit of heat **2.** unit of energy obtained from foods —**caˈloric** *a.* **1.** of heat or calories —*n.* **2.** *obs.* hypothetical elastic fluid, embodiment of heat —**caloˈrific** *a.* heat-making —**caloˈrimeter** *n.*

calumet (ˈkæljʊmɛt) *n.* **1.** tobacco pipe of N Amer. Indians **2.** pipe of peace

calumny (ˈkæləmnɪ) *n.* slander, false accusation —**caˈlumniate** *vt.* —**calumniˈation** *n.* —**caˈlumniator** *n.* —**caˈlumnious** *a.*

Calvary (ˈkælvərɪ) *n.* place outside walls of Jerusalem where Jesus was crucified (*also* **Golˈgotha**)

calves (kɑːvz) *n., pl. of* CALF[1], CALF[2]

Calvinism (ˈkælvɪnɪzəm) *n.* theological system of Calvin, characterized by emphasis on predestination and justification by faith —ˈ**Calvinist** *n./a.* —**Calvinˈistic(al)** *a.*

calx (kælks) *n.* **1.** powdery metallic oxide formed when ore or mineral is roasted **2.** calcium oxide (*pl.* **-es,** ˈ**calces**)

THESAURUS

calibre 1. bore, diameter, gauge, measure **2.** *Fig.* ability, capacity, distinction, endowment, faculty, force, gifts, merit, parts, quality, scope, stature, strength, talent, worth

call *v.* **1.** announce, arouse, awaken, cry, cry out, hail, halloo, proclaim, rouse, shout, waken, yell **2.** assemble, bid, collect, contact, convene, convoke, gather, invite, muster, phone, rally, ring up, summon, telephone **3.** christen, denominate, describe as, designate, dub, entitle, label, name, style, term ~*n.* **4.** cry, hail, scream, shout, signal, whoop, yell **5.** announcement, appeal, command, demand, invitation, notice, order, plea, request, ring (*Brit. inf.*), summons, supplication, visit **6.** cause, claim, excuse, grounds, justification, need, occasion, reason, right, urge

calling business, career, employment, life's work, line, métier, mission, occupation, profession, province, pursuit, trade, vocation, walk of life, work

callous apathetic, case-hardened, cold, hard-bitten, hard-boiled (*Inf.*), hardened, hardhearted, heartless, indifferent, indurated (*Rare*), insensate, insensible, insensitive, inured, obdurate, soulless, thick-skinned, torpid, uncaring, unfeeling, unresponsive, unsusceptible, unsympathetic

calm *adj.* **1.** balmy, halcyon, mild, pacific, peaceful, placid, quiet, restful, serene, smooth, still, tranquil, windless **2.** collected, composed, cool, dispassionate, equable, impassive, imperturbable, relaxed, sedate, self-possessed, undisturbed, unemotional, unexcitable, unexcited, unflappable (*Inf.*), unmoved, unruffled ~*v.* **3.** hush, mollify, placate, quieten, relax, soothe ~*n.* **4.** calmness, hush, peace, peacefulness, quiet, repose, serenity, stillness

calmness 1. calm, composure, equability, hush, motionlessness, peace, peacefulness, placidity, quiet, repose, restfulness, serenity, smoothness, stillness, tranquillity **2.** composure, cool (*Sl.*), coolness, dispassion, equanimity, impassivity, imperturbability, poise, sang-froid, self-possession

calypso (kəˈlɪpsəʊ) *n.* W Indian improvised song on topical subject

calyx (ˈkeɪlɪks, ˈkælɪks) *n.* covering of bud (*pl.* **-es, calyces** (ˈkælɪsiːz, ˈkeɪlɪ-))

cam (kæm) *n.* device to change rotary to reciprocating motion —**ˈcamshaft** *n.* in motoring, rotating shaft to which cams are fixed to lift valves

camaraderie (kæməˈrɑːdərɪ) *n.* spirit of comradeship, trust

camber (ˈkæmbə) *n.* **1.** convexity on upper surface of road, bridge *etc.* **2.** curvature of aircraft wing

Cambrian (ˈkæmbrɪən) *a.* **1.** of first 100 million years of Palaeozoic era **2.** of Wales —*n.* **3.** Cambrian period or rock system **4.** Welshman

cambric (ˈkeɪmbrɪk) *n.* fine white linen or cotton cloth

Cambs. (kæmbz) Cambridgeshire

came (keɪm) *pt. of* COME

camel (ˈkæməl) *n.* animal of Asia and Afr., with humped back, used as beast of burden —**camel's hair** *or* **ˈcamelhair** *n.* **1.** hair of camel, used in rugs *etc.* **2.** soft cloth made of this hair, usu. tan in colour —*a.* **3.** (of painter's brush) made from tail hairs of squirrels

camellia (kəˈmiːlɪə) *n.* ornamental shrub

camelopard (ˈkæmɪləpɑːd, kəˈmɛl-) *n. obs.* giraffe

Camembert (ˈkæməmbɛə) *n.* soft creamy cheese

cameo (ˈkæmɪəʊ) *n.* **1.** medallion, brooch *etc.* with profile head or design carved in relief **2.** single brief scene or appearance in film *etc.* by (well-known) actor

camera (ˈkæmərə) *n.* apparatus used to take photographs —**ˈcameraman** *n.* photographer, *esp.* for television or cinema —**camera obscura** (ɒbˈskjʊərə) darkened chamber in which views of surrounding country are shown on sheet by means of lenses —**in camera** (of legal proceedings *etc.*) conducted in private

camiknickers (ˈkæmɪnɪkəz) *pl.n.* women's knickers attached to camisole top

camisole (ˈkæmɪsəʊl) *n.* underbodice

camomile *or* **chamomile** (ˈkæməmaɪl) *n.* aromatic creeping plant, used medicinally

camouflage (ˈkæməflɑːʒ) *n.* **1.** disguise, means of deceiving enemy observation, *eg* by paint, screen —*vt.* **2.** disguise

camp (kæmp) *n.* **1.** (place for) tents of hikers, army *etc.* **2.** cabins *etc.* for temporary accommodation **3.** group supporting political party *etc.* **4.** SA field, pasture —*a. inf.* **5.** homosexual **6.** consciously artificial —*vi.* **7.** form or lodge in camp —**ˈcamper** *n.* **1.** person who lives or temporarily stays in tent *etc.* **2.** US vehicle equipped for camping out —**ˈcamping** *n.* —**camp follower 1.** civilian, *esp.* prostitute, who unofficially provides services to military personnel **2.** nonmember who is sympathetic to group *etc.*

campaign (kæmˈpeɪn) *n.* **1.** series of coordinated activities for some purpose, *eg* political or military campaign —*vi.* **2.** serve in campaign —**camˈpaigner** *n.*

campanile (kæmpəˈniːlɪ) *n. esp.* in Italy, bell tower, not usu. attached to another building

campanology (kæmpəˈnɒlədʒɪ) *n.* art of ringing bells musically

campanula (kæmˈpænjʊlə) *n.* plant with blue or white bell-shaped flowers

camphor (ˈkæmfə) *n.* solid essential oil with aromatic taste and smell —**ˈcamphorated** *a.* —**camˈphoric** *a.* —**camphorated oil** liniment consisting of camphor and peanut oil, used as counterirritant

campion (ˈkæmpɪən) *n.* white or pink wild flower

campus (ˈkæmpəs) *n.* grounds of college or university

can[1] (kæn; *unstressed* kən) *vi.* **1.** be able to **2.** have the power to **3.** be allowed to (**could** *pt.*)

can[2] (kæn) *n.* **1.** container, usu. metal, for liquids, foods —*vt.* **2.** put in can (**-nn-**) —**canned** *a.* **1.** preserved in can **2.** (of music, programmes *etc.*) previously recorded —**ˈcannery** *n.* factory where food is canned

Can. **1.** Canada **2.** Canadian

Canadian (kəˈneɪdɪən) *n./a.* (native) of Canada —**Caˈnadianize** *or* **-ise** *v.* make, become Canadian —**Canada balsam** (ˈkænədə) **1.** yellow transparent resin obtained from balsam fir **2.** balsam fir —**Canada Day** Jul. 1st, anniversary of day in 1867 when Canad. received dominion status —**Canada goose** large greyish-brown N Amer. goose —**Canadian Shield** wide area of rock extending over most of E and Central Canad.: rich in minerals (*also* **Laurentian Shield**)

canaille (kaˈnɑːj) *Fr.* masses; mob; rabble

canal (kəˈnæl) *n.* **1.** artificial watercourse **2.** duct in body —**canaliˈzation** *or* **-liˈsation** *n.* —**ˈcanalize** *or* **-lise** *vt.* **1.** convert into canal **2.** direct (thoughts, energies *etc.*) into one channel

canapé (ˈkænəpɪ, -peɪ) *n.* small piece of toast *etc.* with savoury topping

canard (kæˈnɑːd) *n.* **1.** false report; rumour, hoax **2.** aircraft in which tailplane is mounted in front of wing

canary (kəˈnɛərɪ) *n.* yellow singing bird

canasta (kəˈnæstə) *n.* card game played with two packs

cancan (ˈkænkæn) *n.* high-kicking (orig. Fr. music-hall) dance

cancel (ˈkænsəl) *vt.* **1.** cross out **2.** annul **3.** call off (**-ll-**) —**cancelˈlation** *n.*

THESAURUS

camouflage 1. *n.* blind, cloak, concealment, cover, deceptive markings, disguise, false appearance, front, guise, mask, masquerade, mimicry, protective colouring, screen, subterfuge **2.** *v.* cloak, conceal, cover, disguise, hide, mask, obfuscate, obscure, screen, veil

camp 1. *n.* bivouac, camping ground, camp site, cantonment (*Mil.*), encampment, tents **2.** *adj.* affected, artificial, camped up, campy (*Inf.*), effeminate, mannered, ostentatious, poncy (*Sl.*), posturing

campaign attack, crusade, drive, expedition, jihad (*Rare*), movement, offensive, operation, push

cancel abolish, abort, abrogate, annul, blot out, call off, countermand, cross out, delete, do away with, efface, eliminate, erase, expunge, obliterate, quash, repeal, repudiate, rescind, revoke

cancellation abandoning, abandonment, abolition, annulment, deletion, elimination, quashing, repeal, revocation

cancer blight, canker, carcinoma (*Pathol.*), corruption, evil, growth, malignancy, pestilence, rot, sickness, tumour

cancer (ˈkænsə) *n.* malignant growth or tumour —ˈ**cancerous** *a.*

Cancer (ˈkænsə) *n.* **1.** (crab) 4th sign of zodiac, operative c. Jun. 21st–Jul. 21st **2.** constellation —**tropic of Cancer** parallel of latitude 23½° N of the equator

candela (kænˈdiːlə, -ˈdeɪlə) *n.* basic SI unit of luminous intensity

candid (ˈkændɪd) *a.* **1.** frank, open **2.** impartial —ˈ**candidly** *adv.* —ˈ**candidness,** ˈ**candour** *or U.S.* ˈ**candor** *n.* frankness —**candid camera** small camera used to take informal photographs of people

candidate (ˈkændɪdeɪt) *n.* **1.** one who seeks office, appointment *etc.* **2.** person taking examination or test —ˈ**candidacy** *or* ˈ**candidature** *n.*

candle (ˈkændᵊl) *n.* **1.** stick of wax with wick **2.** light —**candelabrum** (kændɪˈlæbrəm) *n.* large, branched candle holder (*pl.* **-bra** (-brə)) —ˈ**candlepower** *n.* unit for measuring light —ˈ**candlestick** *n.* —ˈ**candlewick** *n.* cotton fabric with tufted surface

Candlemas (ˈkændᵊlməs) *n. Christianity* Feb. 2nd, Feast of Purification of Virgin Mary and presentation of Christ in Temple

candy (ˈkændɪ) *n.* **1.** crystallized sugar **2.** **US** confectionery in general —*vt.* **3.** preserve with sugar —*vi.* **4.** become encrusted with sugar (ˈ**candied,** ˈ**candying**) —ˈ**candied** *a.* —ˈ**candyfloss** *n.* **UK** light fluffy confection made from coloured spun sugar, usu. held on stick

candytuft (ˈkændɪtʌft) *n.* garden plant with clusters of white, pink or purple flowers

cane (keɪn) *n.* **1.** stem of small palm or large grass **2.** walking stick —*vt.* **3.** beat with cane —**cane sugar 1.** sucrose obtained from sugar cane **2.** *see* SUCROSE

canine (ˈkeɪnaɪn, ˈkæn-) *a.* like, pert. to, dog —**canine tooth** one of four sharp, pointed teeth, two in each jaw

canister (ˈkænɪstə) *n.* container, *usu.* of metal, *esp.* for storing dry food

canker (ˈkæŋkə) *n.* **1.** eating sore **2.** thing that eats away, destroys, corrupts —*vt.* **3.** infect, corrupt —*vi.* **4.** decay —ˈ**cankered** *or* ˈ**cankerous** *a.* —ˈ**cankerworm** *n.*

canna (ˈkænə) *n.* tropical flowering plant

cannabis (ˈkænəbɪs) *n.* **1.** hemp plant **2.** drug derived from this

cannel coal *or* **cannel** (ˈkænᵊl) *n.* dull coal burning with smoky luminous flame

cannelloni *or* **canneloni** (kænɪˈləʊnɪ) *pl.n.* tubular pieces of pasta filled with meat *etc.*

cannibal (ˈkænɪbᵊl) *n.* **1.** one who eats human flesh —*a.* **2.** relating to this practice —ˈ**cannibalism** *n.* —**cannibalˈistic** *a.* —ˈ**cannibalize** *or* **-ise** *vt.* use parts from (one machine *etc.*) to repair another

cannon[1] (ˈkænən) *n.* large gun (*pl.* **-s,** ˈ**cannon**) —**cannoˈnade** *n./vt.* attack with cannon —ˈ**cannonball** *n.* —**cannon bone** horse's leg bone —**cannon fodder** men regarded as expendable in war because they are part of huge army

cannon[2] (ˈkænən) *n.* **1.** billiard stroke, hitting both object balls with one's own —*vi.* **2.** make this stroke **3.** rebound, collide

cannot (ˈkænɒt, kæˈnɒt) *negative form of* CAN[1]

canny (ˈkænɪ) *a.* **1.** shrewd **2.** cautious **3.** crafty —ˈ**cannily** *adv.*

canoe (kəˈnuː) *n.* very light boat propelled with paddle or paddles —**caˈnoeist** *n.*

canon[1] (ˈkænən) *n.* **1.** law or rule, *esp.* of church **2.** standard **3.** body of books accepted as genuine **4.** list of saints —**canoniˈzation** *or* **-iˈsation** *n.* —ˈ**canonize** *or* **-ise** *vt.* enrol in list of saints

canon[2] (ˈkænən) *n.* church dignitary, member of cathedral chapter —**caˈnonical** *a.* —**caˈnonicals** *pl.n.* vestments worn by clergy when officiating —**canonˈistic** *a.* —**canonical hour 1.** *R.C.Ch.* one of seven prayer times appointed for each day by canon law **2.** *Ch. of England* any time at which marriages may lawfully be celebrated —**canon law** body of laws enacted by supreme authorities of Christian Church

canoodle (kəˈnuːdᵊl) *vi.* (*oft.* **with** with) *sl.* kiss and cuddle

canopy (ˈkænəpɪ) *n.* **1.** covering over throne, bed *etc.* **2.** any overhanging shelter —*vt.* **3.** cover with canopy (**-opied, -opying**)

can't (kɑːnt) *v.* cannot

cant[1] (kænt) *n.* **1.** hypocritical speech **2.** whining **3.** language of a sect **4.** technical jargon **5.** slang, *esp.* of thieves —*vi.* **6.** use cant

cant[2] (kænt) *vt.* **1.** tilt, slope **2.** bevel —*n.* **3.** inclination from vertical or horizontal plane

Cantab. (kænˈtæb) Cantabrigiensis (*Lat.,* of Cambridge)

cantabile (kænˈtɑːbɪlɪ) *Mus. a./adv.* **1.** singing —*n.* **2.** piece or passage performed in this way

Cantabrigian (kæntəˈbrɪdʒɪən) *a.* **1.** of Cambridge or Cambridge University —*n.* **2.** member or graduate of Cambridge University **3.** inhabitant or native of Cambridge

THESAURUS

candid blunt, fair, forthright, frank, free, guileless, impartial, ingenuous, just, open, outspoken, plain, sincere, straightforward, truthful, unbiased, unequivocal, unprejudiced

candidate applicant, aspirant, claimant, competitor, contender, contestant, entrant, nominee, possibility, runner, solicitant, suitor

candour artlessness, directness, fairness, forthrightness, frankness, guilelessness, honesty, impartiality, ingenuousness, naïveté, openness, outspokenness, simplicity, sincerity, straightforwardness, truthfulness, unequivocalness

canker 1. *v.* blight, consume, corrode, corrupt, embitter, envenom, inflict, poison, pollute, rot, rust, waste away **2.** *n.* bane, blight, blister, cancer, corrosion, corruption, infection, lesion, rot, scourge, sore, ulcer

cannon artillery piece, big gun (*Inf.*), field gun, gun, mortar

canny acute, artful, astute, careful, cautious, circumspect, clever, judicious, knowing, perspicacious, prudent, sagacious, sharp, shrewd, subtle, wise, worldly-wise

canon catalogue, criterion, dictate, formula, list, precept, principle, regulation, roll, rule, standard, statute, yardstick

canopy awning, baldachin, covering, shade, sunshade, tester

cant[1] *n.* **1.** affected piety, humbug, hypocrisy, insincerity, lip service, pious platitudes, pretence, pretentiousness, sanctimoniousness, sham holiness **2.** argot, jargon, lingo, slang, vernacular

cant[2] *v.* angle, bevel, incline, rise, slant, slope, tilt

cantaloupe *or* **cantaloup** (ˈkæntəluːp) *n.* variety of muskmelon

cantankerous (kænˈtæŋkərəs) *a.* ill-natured, quarrelsome

cantata (kænˈtɑːtə) *n.* choral work like, but shorter than, oratorio

canteen (kænˈtiːn) *n.* **1.** place in factory, school *etc.* where meals are provided **2.** small shop in military camp **3.** case of cutlery **4.** mess tin

canter (ˈkæntə) *n.* **1.** easy gallop —*v.* **2.** move at, make to canter

Canterbury bell (ˈkæntəbərɪ) cultivated campanula

cantharides (kænˈθærɪdiːz) *pl.n.* diuretic and urogenital stimulant prepared from dried bodies of Spanish fly (*sing.* **ˈcantharis**) (*also* **Spanish fly**)

canticle (ˈkæntɪkᵊl) *n.* short hymn

cantilever (ˈkæntɪliːvə) *n.* beam, girder *etc.* fixed at one end only

canto (ˈkæntəʊ) *n.* division of poem (*pl.* **-s**)

canton (ˈkæntɒn, kænˈtɒn) *n.* division of country, *esp.* Swiss federal state

Cantonese (kæntəˈniːz) *n.* **1.** Chinese language spoken in Canton *etc.* **2.** native or inhabitant of Canton (*pl.* **-ese**) —*a.* **3.** of Canton or Chinese language spoken there

cantonment (kənˈtuːnmənt) *n.* quarters for troops

cantor (ˈkæntɔː) *n.* **1.** *Judaism* leading singer in synagogue liturgy **2.** *Christianity* leader of singing in church choir

Canuck (kəˈnʌk) *n./a.* C *inf.* Canadian

canvas (ˈkænvəs) *n.* **1.** coarse cloth used for sails, painting on *etc.* **2.** sails of ship **3.** picture —**under canvas** in tents

canvass (ˈkænvəs) *vt.* **1.** solicit votes, contributions *etc.* from **2.** discuss, examine —*n.* **3.** solicitation

canyon *or* **cañon** (ˈkænjən) *n.* deep gorge

caoutchouc (ˈkaʊtʃʊk) *n. see* RUBBER[1] (sense 1)

cap (kæp) *n.* **1.** covering for head **2.** lid, top or other covering —*vt.* **3.** put cap on **4.** outdo **5.** select for a team (**-pp-**)

cap. **1.** capacity **2.** capital **3.** capitalize **4.** capital letter

capable (ˈkeɪpəbᵊl) *a.* **1.** able, gifted **2.** competent **3.** having the capacity, power —**capaˈbility** *n.*

capacity (kəˈpæsɪtɪ) *n.* **1.** power of holding or grasping **2.** room **3.** volume **4.** character **5.** ability, power of mind —**capacious** (kəˈpeɪʃəs) *a.* roomy —**caˈpacitance** *n.* (measure of) ability of system to store electric charge —**caˈpacitor** *n.*

caparison (kəˈpærɪsᵊn) *n.* **1.** ornamental covering, equipment for horse —*vt.* **2.** adorn thus

cape[1] (keɪp) *n.* covering for shoulders

cape[2] (keɪp) *n.* point of land running into sea, headland —**Cape Coloured SA** *see* **Coloured** (sense 2) *at* COLOUR —**Cape pigeon** pied petrel of southern oceans —**Cape salmon SA** geelbek —**Cape sparrow** common S Afr. bird

caper[1] (ˈkeɪpə) *n.* **1.** skip **2.** frolic **3.** escapade —*vi.* **4.** skip, dance

caper[2] (ˈkeɪpə) *n.* pickled flower bud of Sicilian shrub

capercaillie *or* **capercailzie** (kæpəˈkeɪlɪ) *n.* large black grouse

capillary (kəˈpɪlərɪ) *a.* **1.** hairlike **2.** of capillarity —*n.* **3.** tube with very small bore, *esp.* small blood vessel —**capilˈlarity** *n.* phenomenon caused by surface tension and resulting in elevation or depression of surface of liquid in contact with solid (*also* **capillary action**)

capital (ˈkæpɪtᵊl) *n.* **1.** chief town **2.** money, stock, funds **3.** large-sized letter **4.** headpiece of column —*a.* **5.** involving or punishable by death **6.** serious **7.** chief **8.** leading **9.** excellent —**ˈcapitalism** *n.* economic system which is based on private ownership of industry —**ˈcapitalist** *n.* **1.** owner of capital **2.** supporter of capitalism —*a.* **3.** run by, possessing, capital —**ˈcapitalize** *or* **-ise** *vt.* **1.** convert into capital —*vi.* **2.** (*with* on) turn to advantage —**ˈcapitally** *adv.* —**capital gain** amount by which selling price of financial asset exceeds cost —**capital levy** tax on capital or property as contrasted with tax on income —**capital punishment** punishment of death for crime; death penalty —**capital stock** **1.** par value of total share capital a company is authorized to issue **2.** total physical capital existing in economy at any time —**capital transfer tax UK** tax payable on total of gifts of money or property made during donor's lifetime or after his death

THESAURUS

cantankerous bad-tempered, captious, choleric, contrary, crabby, cranky (*U.S. inf.*), crotchety (*Inf.*), crusty, difficult, disagreeable, grouchy (*Inf.*), grumpy, ill-humoured, irascible, irritable, peevish, perverse, quarrelsome, testy

canter *n.* amble, dogtrot, easy gait, jog, lope

canvass *v.* **1.** analyse, campaign, electioneer, examine, inspect, investigate, poll, scan, scrutinize, sift, solicit, solicit votes, study, ventilate **2.** agitate, debate, discuss, dispute ~*n.* **3.** examination, investigation, poll, scrutiny, survey, tally

canyon coulee (*U.S.*), gorge, gulch (*U.S.*), gulf, gully, ravine

cap *v.* beat, better, complete, cover, crown, eclipse, exceed, excel, finish, outdo, outstrip, overtop, surpass, top, transcend

capability ability, capacity, competence, facility, faculty, means, potential, potentiality, power, proficiency, qualification(s), wherewithal

capable able, accomplished, adapted, adept, adequate, apt, clever, competent, efficient, experienced, fitted, gifted, intelligent, masterly, proficient, qualified, skilful, suited, susceptible, talented

capacious ample, broad, comfortable, commodious, comprehensive, expansive, extended, extensive, generous, liberal, roomy, sizable, spacious, substantial, vast, voluminous, wide

capacity **1.** amplitude, compass, dimensions, extent, magnitude, range, room, scope, size, space, volume **2.** ability, aptitude, aptness, brains, capability, cleverness, competence, competency, efficiency, facility, faculty, forte, genius, gift, intelligence, power, readiness, strength

cape chersonese (*Poetic*), head, headland, ness (*Archaic*), peninsula, point, promontory

caper **1.** *v.* bounce, bound, cavort, dance, frisk, frolic, gambol, hop, jump, leap, romp, skip, spring **2.** *n.* antic, dido (*Inf.*), escapade, gambol, high jinks, hop, jape, jest, jump, lark (*Inf.*), leap, mischief, practical joke, prank, revel, shenanigan (*Inf.*), sport, stunt

capital *adj.* **1.** cardinal, central, chief, controlling, essential, foremost, important, leading, main, major, overruling, paramount, pre-eminent, primary, prime,

capitation (kæpɪˈteɪʃən) *n.* **1.** tax or grant per head **2.** census

Capitol (ˈkæpɪtˀl) *n.* **1.** U.S. Congress House **2.** a U.S. state legislature building **3.** temple of Jupiter in Rome

capitulate (kəˈpɪtjʊleɪt) *vi.* surrender on terms, give in —**capituˈlation** *n.*

capo (ˈkæpəʊ) *n.* device fitted across all strings of guitar *etc.* to raise pitch of each string simultaneously (*pl.* **-s**) (*also* **capo tasto** (ˈtæstəʊ))

capon (ˈkeɪpən) *n.* castrated cock fowl fattened for eating —**ˈcaponize** *or* **-ise** *vt.*

cappuccino (kæpʊˈtʃiːnəʊ) *n.* coffee with steamed milk

caprice (kəˈpriːs) *n.* whim —**capricious** (kəˈprɪʃəs) *a.* —**capriciousness** (kəˈprɪʃəsnɪs) *n.*

Capricorn (ˈkæprɪkɔːn) *n.* **1.** (sea-goat) 10th sign of zodiac, operative c. Dec. 21st–Jan. 19th **2.** constellation —**tropic of Capricorn** parallel of latitude 23½° S of the equator

capriole (ˈkæprɪəʊl) *Dressage n.* **1.** upward but not forward leap made by horse with all four feet off ground —*vi.* **2.** perform capriole

caps. **1.** capital letters **2.** capsule

capsicum (ˈkæpsɪkəm) *n.* tropical vegetable with mild peppery flavour, sweet pepper

capsize (kæpˈsaɪz) *vt.* **1.** (of boat) upset —*vi.* **2.** be overturned —**capˈsizal** *n.*

capstan (ˈkæpstən) *n.* machine to wind cable, *esp.* to hoist anchor

capsule (ˈkæpsjʊl) *n.* **1.** gelatin case for dose of medicine or drug **2.** any small enclosed area or container **3.** seed vessel of plant —**ˈcapsulize** *or* **-ise** *vt.* **1.** state in highly condensed form **2.** enclose in capsule

Capt. Captain

captain (ˈkæptɪn) *n.* **1.** commander of vessel or company of soldiers **2.** leader, chief —*vt.* **3.** be captain of

caption (ˈkæpʃən) *n.* heading, title of article, picture *etc.*

captious (ˈkæpʃəs) *a.* **1.** ready to find fault **2.** critical **3.** peevish —**ˈcaptiously** *adv.* —**ˈcaptiousness** *n.*

captive (ˈkæptɪv) *n.* **1.** prisoner —*a.* **2.** taken, imprisoned **3.** unable to avoid speeches *etc.* —**ˈcaptivate** *vt.* fascinate —**ˈcaptivating** *a.* delightful —**capˈtivity** *n.*

capture (ˈkæptʃə) *vt.* **1.** seize, make prisoner —*n.* **2.** seizure, taking —**ˈcaptor** *n.*

Capuchin (ˈkæpjʊtʃɪn, -ʃɪn) *n.* friar belonging to branch of Franciscan Order

capybara (kæpɪˈbɑːrə) *n.* largest rodent, found in S Amer.

car (kɑː) *n.* **1.** self-propelled road vehicle **2.** passenger compartment, as in cable car **3.** railway carriage of specified type —**car park** area, building where vehicles may be left for a time —**ˈcarport** *n.* shelter for car usu. consisting of roof supported by posts

carabineer *or* **carabinier** (kærəbɪˈnɪə) *n. see* **carbineer** *at* CARBINE

caracal (ˈkærəkæl) *n.* **1.** lynxlike feline mammal inhabiting deserts of N Afr. and S Asia, having smooth coat of reddish fur **2.** this fur

caracole (ˈkærəkəʊl) *or* **caracol** (ˈkærəkɒl) *Dressage n.* **1.** half turn to right or left —*vi.* **2.** execute half turn

caracul (ˈkærəkʌl) *n.* **1.** black, loosely curled fur from skins of newly born lambs of caracul sheep (*also* **Persian lamb**) **2.** sheep of Central Asia with coarse dark hair (*also* **ˈkarakul**)

carafe (kəˈræf, -ˈrɑːf) *n.* glass water bottle for table, decanter

caramel (ˈkærəməl) *n.* **1.** burnt sugar for cooking **2.** type of confectionery

carapace (ˈkærəpeɪs) *n.* thick hard shield that covers part of body of tortoise *etc.*

carat (ˈkærət) *n.* **1.** small weight used for gold, diamonds *etc.* **2.** proportional measure of twenty-fourths used to state fineness of gold

caravan (ˈkærəvæn) *n.* **1.** large enclosed vehicle for living in, pulled as trailer by car *etc.* **2.** company of merchants travelling together for safety in the East

---

THESAURUS

principal, prominent, vital **2.** excellent, fine, first, first-rate, prime, splendid, superb ~*n.* **3.** assets, cash, finance, finances, financing, funds, investment(s), means, money, principal, property, resources, stock, wealth, wherewithal

capitalism free enterprise, *laissez faire*, private enterprise, private ownership

capitulate come to terms, give in, give up, relent, submit, succumb, surrender, yield

capitulation accedence, submission, surrender, yielding

caprice changeableness, fad, fancy, fickleness, fitfulness, freak, humour, impulse, inconstancy, notion, quirk, vagary, whim, whimsy

capricious changeful, crotchety (*Inf.*), erratic, fanciful, fickle, fitful, freakish, impulsive, inconstant, mercurial, odd, queer, quirky, unpredictable, variable, wayward, whimsical

capsize invert, keel over, overturn, tip over, turn over, turn turtle, upset

capsule **1.** bolus, lozenge, pill, tablet, troche (*Medical*) **2.** case, pericarp (*Bot.*), pod, receptacle, seed vessel, sheath, shell, vessel

captain boss, chief, chieftain, commander, head, leader, master, number one (*Inf.*), officer, (senior) pilot, skipper

captivate allure, attract, beguile, bewitch, charm, dazzle, enamour, enchant, enrapture, enslave, ensnare, enthral, entrance, fascinate, hypnotize, infatuate, lure, mesmerize, seduce, win

captive **1.** *n.* convict, detainee, hostage, internee, prisoner, prisoner of war **2.** *adj.* caged, confined, ensnared, imprisoned, incarcerated, locked up, penned, restricted

captivity bondage, confinement, custody, detention, durance (*Archaic*), duress, enthralment, imprisonment, incarceration, internment, restraint, servitude, slavery, thraldom, vassalage

capture **1.** *v.* apprehend, arrest, bag, catch, collar (*Inf.*), lift (*Sl.*), nab (*Inf.*), secure, seize, take, take into custody, take prisoner **2.** *n.* apprehension, arrest, catch, imprisonment, seizure, taking, taking captive, trapping

car **1.** auto (*U.S.*), automobile, jalopy (*Inf.*), machine, motor, motorcar, vehicle **2.** buffet car, cable car, coach, dining car, (railway) carriage, sleeping car, van

—**caravanserai** (kærəˈvænsəraɪ) *or* **caravansary** (kærəˈvænsərɪ) *n.* in some Eastern countries, large inn enclosing courtyard, providing accommodation for caravans

caravel (ˈkærəvɛl) *or* **carvel** *n.* two- or three-masted sailing ship in 15th and 16th centuries

caraway (ˈkærəweɪ) *n.* plant of which the seeds are used as spice in cakes *etc.*

carbide (ˈkɑːbaɪd) *n.* compound of carbon with an element, *esp.* calcium carbide

carbine (ˈkɑːbaɪn) *n.* short rifle —**carbineer** (kɑːbɪˈnɪə), **carabiˈneer** *or* **carabiˈnier** *n.* formerly, soldier equipped with carbine

carbo- *or before vowel* **carb-** (*comb. form*) carbon, as in *carbohydrate, carbonate*

carbohydrate (kɑːbəʊˈhaɪdreɪt) *n.* any of large group of compounds containing carbon, hydrogen and oxygen, *esp.* sugars and starches as components of food

carbolic acid (kɑːˈbɒlɪk) disinfectant derived from coal tar —ˈ**carbolated** *a.* containing carbolic acid

carbon (ˈkɑːbᵊn) *n.* nonmetallic element, substance of pure charcoal, found in all organic matter —**carboˈnaceous** *a.* of, resembling or containing carbon —ˈ**carbonate** *n.* salt of carbonic acid —**carˈbonic** *a.* —**carboˈniferous** *a.* —ˈ**carbonize** *or* **-ise** *v.* —**carbon black** finely divided carbon produced by incomplete combustion of natural gas or petroleum: used in pigments and ink —**carbon dating** technique for determining age of wood *etc.*, based on its content of radioisotope ^{14}C acquired from atmosphere when it formed part of living plant —**carbon dioxide** colourless gas exhaled in respiration of animals —**carbonic acid 1.** carbon dioxide **2.** compound formed by carbon dioxide and water —**carbon monoxide** colourless, odourless poisonous gas formed when carbon compounds burn in insufficient air —**carbon paper** paper coated with a dark, waxy pigment, used for duplicating written or typed matter, producing **carbon copy** —**carbon tetrachloride** colourless volatile nonflammable liquid made from chlorine and used as solvent *etc.*

Carboniferous (kɑːbəˈnɪfərəs) *a.* **1.** of fifth period of Palaeozoic era during which coal measures were formed —*n.* **2.** Carboniferous period or rock system divided into **Upper Carboniferous** and **Lower Carboniferous** periods

Carborundum (kɑːbəˈrʌndəm) *n.* **R** artificial silicate of carbon

carboy (ˈkɑːbɔɪ) *n.* large glass jar protected by wicker casing

carbuncle (ˈkɑːbʌŋkᵊl) *n.* **1.** inflamed ulcer, boil or tumour **2.** fiery-red precious stone

carburettor, carburetter (kɑːbjʊˈrɛtə, ˈkɑːbjʊrɛtə), *or U.S.* **carburetor** (ˈkɑːbjʊreɪtə) *n.* device for vaporizing and mixing petrol with air in internal-combustion engine

carcass *or* **carcase** (ˈkɑːkəs) *n.* **1.** dead animal body **2.** skeleton **3.** *inf.* person's body

carcinoma (kɑːsɪˈnəʊmə) *n.* a cancer —**carˈcinogen** *n.* substance producing cancer

card[1] (kɑːd) *n.* **1.** thick, stiff paper **2.** piece of this giving identification *etc.* **3.** illustrated card sending greetings *etc.* **4.** one of the 52 playing cards making up a pack **5.** *inf.* a character, eccentric —*pl.* **6.** any card game **7.** employee's tax and national insurance documents or information held by employer —ˈ**cardboard** *n.* thin, stiff board made of paper pulp —**card index** index in which each entry is made on separate card —ˈ**cardsharp** *or* ˈ**cardsharper** *n.* professional card player who cheats —**card vote UK** vote by delegates, *esp.* at trade union conference, in which each delegate's vote counts as vote by all his constituents

card[2] (kɑːd) *n.* **1.** instrument for combing wool *etc.* —*vt.* **2.** comb —ˈ**carder** *n.*

cardamom *or* **cardamum** (ˈkɑːdəməm) *n.* **1.** tropical Asian plant with large hairy leaves **2.** seeds of this plant, used *esp.* as spice or condiment

cardiac (ˈkɑːdɪæk) *a.* **1.** pert. to the heart —*n.* **2.** person with heart disorder —ˈ**cardiogram** *n.* tracing made by cardiograph —ˈ**cardiograph** *n.* instrument which records movements of the heart —ˈ**cardioid** *a.* heart-shaped —**cardiˈologist** *n.* —**cardiˈology** *n.* branch of medical science concerned with heart and its diseases

cardigan (ˈkɑːdɪgən) *n.* knitted jacket

cardinal (ˈkɑːdɪnᵊl) *a.* **1.** chief, principal —*n.* **2.** highest rank, next to the Pope in R.C. Church **3.** bright red N Amer. bunting (*also* ˈ**redbird**) —ˈ**cardinalate** *n.* —**cardinal numbers** 1, 2, 3, *etc.* —**cardinal points** north, south, east and west

cardio- *or before vowel* **cardi-** (*comb. form*) heart, as in *cardiogram*

care (kɛə) *vi.* **1.** be anxious —*n.* **2.** attention **3.** pains, heed **4.** charge, protection **5.** anxiety **6.** caution —ˈ**carefree** *a.* —ˈ**careful** *a.* —ˈ**carefully** *adv.* —ˈ**carefulness** *n.* —ˈ**careless** *a.* —ˈ**carelessness** *n.* —ˈ**caretaker** *n.* **1.** person in charge of premises —*a.* **2.** temporary, interim —ˈ**careworn** *a.* showing signs of care, stress *etc.* —**care for 1.** have regard or liking for **2.** look after **3.** be disposed to

careen (kəˈriːn) *vt.* **1.** lay (ship) over on her side for cleaning and repair —*vi.* **2.** keel over **3.** sway dangerously

career (kəˈrɪə) *n.* **1.** course through life **2.** profession **3.** rapid motion —*vi.* **4.** run or move at full speed —**caˈreerist** *n.* person who seeks to advance his career by any possible means

THESAURUS

carcass body, cadaver (*Medical*), corpse, corse (*Archaic*), dead body, framework, hulk, remains, shell, skeleton

cardinal capital, central, chief, essential, first, foremost, fundamental, greatest, highest, important, key, leading, main, paramount, pre-eminent, primary, prime, principal

care 1. affliction, anxiety, burden, concern, disquiet, hardship, interest, perplexity, pressure, responsibility, solicitude, stress, tribulation, trouble, vexation, woe, worry **2.** attention, carefulness, caution, circumspection, consideration, direction, forethought, heed, management, meticulousness, pains, prudence, regard, vigilance, watchfulness **3.** charge, control, custody, guardianship, keeping, management, ministration, protection, supervision, ward

career 1. *n.* calling, employment, life work, livelihood, occupation, pursuit, vocation **2.** *v.* bolt, dash, hurtle, race, rush, speed, tear

care for 1. be fond of, desire, enjoy, find congenial, like, love, prize, take to, want **2.** attend, foster, look

caress (kəˈrɛs) *vt.* 1. fondle, embrace, treat with affection —*n.* 2. act or expression of affection

caret (ˈkærɪt) *n.* mark (‸) showing where to insert something omitted

cargo (ˈkɑːgəʊ) *n.* load, freight, carried by ship, plane *etc.* (*pl.* **-es**)

Carib (ˈkærɪb) *n.* 1. member of group of Amer. Indian peoples of NE South Amer. and Lesser Antilles (*pl.* **-s, ˈCarib**) 2. family of languages spoken by these peoples

caribou (ˈkærɪbuː) *n.* N Amer. reindeer

caricature (ˈkærɪkətjʊə) *n.* 1. likeness exaggerated or distorted to appear ridiculous —*vt.* 2. portray in this way

caries (ˈkɛəriiːz) *n.* decay of tooth or bone —**ˈcarious** *a.* (of teeth or bone) affected with caries; decayed

carillon (kəˈrɪljən) *n.* 1. set of bells *usu.* hung in tower and played by set of keys, pedals *etc.* 2. tune so played

cariole (ˈkærɪəʊl) *n. see* CARRIOLE

carl *or* **carle** (kɑːl) *n. obs., Scot.* churl

Carlovingian (kɑːləʊˈvɪndʒɪən) *Hist. see* CAROLINGIAN

Carmelite (ˈkɑːməlaɪt) *n. R.C.Ch.* 1. member of order of mendicant friars 2. member of corresponding order of nuns

carminative (ˈkɑːmɪnətɪv) *n.* 1. medicine to remedy flatulence —*a.* 2. acting as this

carmine (ˈkɑːmaɪn) *n.* 1. brilliant red colour (prepared from cochineal) —*a.* 2. of this colour

carnage (ˈkɑːnɪdʒ) *n.* slaughter

carnal (ˈkɑːnᵊl) *a.* 1. fleshly, sensual 2. worldly —**ˈcarnalism** *n.* —**carˈnality** *n.* —**ˈcarnally** *adv.* —**carnal knowledge** *chiefly law* sexual intercourse

carnation (kɑːˈneɪʃən) *n.* 1. cultivated flower 2. flesh colour

carnelian (kɑːˈniːljən) *n.* reddish-yellow translucent chalcedony, used as gemstone

carnival (ˈkɑːnɪvᵊl) *n.* 1. festive occasion 2. travelling fair 3. show or display for amusement

carnivorous (kɑːˈnɪvərəs) *a.* flesh-eating —**ˈcarnivore** *n.*

carob (ˈkærəb) *n.* 1. evergreen Mediterranean tree with edible pods 2. long blackish sugary pod of this tree, used for fodder and sometimes human food

carol (ˈkærəl) *n.* 1. song or hymn of joy or praise (*esp.* Christmas carol) —*vi.* 2. sing carols (**-ll-**)

Caroline (ˈkærəlaɪn) *or* **Carolean** (kærəˈliːən) *a.* of Charles I or Charles II (kings of England, Scotland and Ireland), society over which they ruled or their government (*also* **CaroˈIinian**)

Carolingian (kærəˈlɪndʒɪən) *Hist. a.* 1. of Frankish dynasty founded by Pepin the Short —*n.* 2. member of dynasty of Carolingian Franks (*also* **CarloˈvingIan, CaroˈIinian**)

carotid (kəˈrɒtɪd) *n.* 1. either of two principal arteries that supply blood to head and neck —*a.* 2. of either of these arteries

carouse (kəˈraʊz) *vi.* 1. have merry drinking spree —*n.* 2. merry drinking party (*also* **caˈrousal**) —**caˈrouser** *n.*

carousel (kærəˈsɛl, -ˈzɛl) *n.* US merry-go-round

carp[1] (kɑːp) *n.* freshwater fish

carp[2] (kɑːp) *vi.* 1. complain about small faults or errors 2. nag —**ˈcarper** *n.* —**ˈcarping** *a.* —**ˈcarpingly** *adv.*

carpal (ˈkɑːpᵊl) *n.* any bone of wrist

carpel (ˈkɑːpᵊl) *n.* female reproductive organ of flowering plants, consisting of ovary, style and stigma

carpenter (ˈkɑːpɪntə) *n.* worker in timber as in building *etc.* —**ˈcarpentry** *n.* art of carpenter

carpet (ˈkɑːpɪt) *n.* 1. heavy fabric for covering floor —*vt.* 2. cover (floor) with carpet 3. *inf.* call up for censure —**ˈcarpetbag** *n.* travelling bag —**ˈcarpetbagger** *n.* political adventurer —**carpet slipper** slipper orig. made with woollen upper resembling carpeting

carpus (ˈkɑːpəs) *n.* 1. wrist 2. eight small bones of human wrist (*pl.* **carpi** (ˈkɑːpaɪ))

carrageen, carragheen, *or* **carageen**

THESAURUS

after, mind, minister to, nurse, protect, provide for, tend, watch over

carefree airy, blithe, breezy, buoyant, careless, cheerful, cheery, easy-going, happy, happy-go-lucky, insouciant, jaunty, light-hearted, lightsome (*Archaic*), radiant, sunny, untroubled

careful 1. accurate, attentive, cautious, chary, circumspect, conscientious, discreet, fastidious, heedful, painstaking, precise, prudent, punctilious, scrupulous, thoughtful, thrifty 2. alert, concerned, judicious, mindful, particular, protective, solicitous, vigilant, wary, watchful

careless 1. absent-minded, cursory, forgetful, hasty, heedless, incautious, inconsiderate, indiscreet, negligent, perfunctory, regardless, remiss, thoughtless, unconcerned, unguarded, unmindful, unthinking 2. inaccurate, irresponsible, lackadaisical, neglectful, offhand, slapdash, slipshod, sloppy (*Inf.*)

carelessness inaccuracy, inattention, inconsiderateness, indiscretion, irresponsibility, neglect, negligence, omission, remissness, slackness, sloppiness (*Inf.*), thoughtlessness

caress 1. *v.* cuddle, embrace, fondle, hug, kiss, nuzzle, pet, stroke 2. *n.* cuddle, embrace, fondling, hug, kiss, pat, stroke

caretaker 1. *n.* concierge, curator, custodian, janitor, keeper, porter, superintendent, warden, watchman 2. *adj.* holding, interim, short-term, temporary

cargo baggage, consignment, contents, freight, goods, lading, load, merchandise, shipment, tonnage, ware

caricature 1. *n.* burlesque, cartoon, distortion, farce, lampoon, mimicry, parody, pasquinade, satire, send-up (*Brit. inf.*), takeoff (*Inf.*), travesty 2. *v.* burlesque, distort, lampoon, mimic, mock, parody, ridicule, satirize, send up (*Brit. inf.*), take off (*Inf.*)

carnage blood bath, bloodshed, butchery, havoc, holocaust, massacre, mass murder, murder, shambles, slaughter

carnival celebration, fair, festival, fête, fiesta, gala, holiday, jamboree, jubilee, Mardi Gras, merrymaking, revelry

carol canticle, canzonet, chorus, ditty, hymn, lay, noel, song, strain

carp cavil, censure, complain, criticize, find fault, hypercriticize, knock (*Inf.*), nag, pick holes (*Inf.*), quibble, reproach

carpenter cabinet-maker, joiner, woodworker

(ˈkærəgiːn) *n.* edible red seaweed of N Amer. and N Europe, used to make jelly *etc.* (*also* **Irish moss**)

carriage (ˈkærɪdʒ) *n.* **1.** railway coach **2.** bearing, conduct **3.** horse-drawn vehicle **4.** act, cost, of carrying —**carriage clock** portable clock, usu. in rectangular case, orig. used by travellers —**carriage forward** charge for conveying, to be paid by receiver —**carriage paid** charge for conveying, to be paid by sender —ˈ**carriageway** *n.* part of road along which traffic passes in single line

carriole *or* **cariole** (ˈkærɪəʊl) *n.* small open carriage for one

carrion (ˈkærɪən) *n.* rotting dead flesh —**carrion crow** scavenging European crow

carrot (ˈkærət) *n.* **1.** plant with orange-red edible root **2.** inducement —ˈ**carroty** *a.* red, reddish

carry (ˈkærɪ) *vt.* **1.** convey, transport **2.** capture, win **3.** effect **4.** conduct (oneself) in specified manner —*vi.* **5.** (of projectile, sound) reach or penetrate to distance (ˈ**carried**, ˈ**carrying**) —*n.* **6.** range —ˈ**carrier** *n.* **1.** one that carries goods **2.** one who, himself immune, communicates a disease to others **3.** aircraft carrier —**carrier bag** UK large paper or plastic bag for shopping *etc.* —**carrier pigeon** homing pigeon, *esp.* for carrying messages —**carrier wave** *Rad.* wave of fixed amplitude and frequency, modulated to carry signal in radio transmission *etc.* (*also* ˈ**carrier**) —ˈ**carrycot** *n.* light cot with handles, similar to but smaller than body of pram —**carry-out** *n. chiefly Scot.* **1.** alcohol bought at off-licence *etc.* for consumption elsewhere **2.** shop which sells hot cooked food for consumption away from premises —**carry on 1.** continue **2.** *inf.* fuss unnecessarily **3.** *inf.* have an affair —**carry out 1.** perform; cause to be implemented **2.** accomplish

cart (kɑːt) *n.* **1.** open (two-wheeled) vehicle, *esp.* pulled by horse —*vt.* **2.** convey in cart **3.** carry with effort —ˈ**cartage** *n.* —ˈ**carter** *n.* —ˈ**carthorse** *n.* —ˈ**cartwheel** *n.* **1.** large, spoked wheel **2.** sideways somersault —ˈ**cartwright** *n.* maker of carts

carte blanche (ˈkɑːt ˈblɑːntʃ) *Fr.* complete discretion or authority

cartel (kɑːˈtɛl) *n.* **1.** industrial combination for the purpose of fixing prices, output *etc.* **2.** alliance of political parties *etc.* to further common aims

Cartesian (kɑːˈtiːzɪən) *a.* **1.** pert. to French philosopher René Descartes (1596–1650) or his system of coordinates —*n.* **2.** adherent of his philosophy —**Cartesian coordinates** system of coordinates that defines location of point in terms of perpendicular distance from each of set of mutually perpendicular axes

Carthusian (kɑːˈθjuːzɪən) *n. R.C.Ch.* member of monastic order founded by Saint Bruno

cartilage (ˈkɑːtɪlɪdʒ) *n.* **1.** firm elastic tissue in the body **2.** gristle —**cartilaginous** (kɑːtɪˈlædʒɪnəs) *a.*

cartogram (ˈkɑːtəgræm) *n.* map showing statistical information in diagrammatic form

cartography (kɑːˈtɒgrəfɪ) *n.* mapmaking —**carˈtographer** *n.* —**cartoˈgraphic(al)** *a.*

carton (ˈkɑːtᵊn) *n.* cardboard or plastic container

cartoon (kɑːˈtuːn) *n.* **1.** drawing, *esp.* humorous or satirical **2.** sequence of drawings telling story **3.** preliminary design for painting —**carˈtoonist** *n.*

cartouche *or* **cartouch** (kɑːˈtuːʃ) *n.* **1.** carved or cast ornamental tablet or panel in form of scroll **2.** oblong figure enclosing characters expressing royal or divine names in Egyptian hieroglyphics

cartridge (ˈkɑːtrɪdʒ) *n.* **1.** case containing charge for gun **2.** container for film, magnetic tape *etc.* **3.** unit in head of gramophone pick-up —**cartridge paper** strong, thick paper

carve (kɑːv) *vt.* **1.** cut **2.** hew **3.** sculpture **4.** engrave **5.** cut (meat) in pieces or slices —ˈ**carver** *n.* —ˈ**carving** *n.*

carvel (ˈkɑːvᵊl) *n. see* CARAVEL

caryatid (kærɪˈætɪd) *n.* supporting column in shape of female figure

Casanova (kæsəˈnəʊvə) *n.* any man noted for amorous adventures

casbah (ˈkæzbɑː) *n.* (*sometimes* C-) **1.** citadel of various N Afr. cities **2.** quarter where casbah is located (*also* ˈ**kasbah**)

cascade (kæsˈkeɪd) *n.* **1.** waterfall **2.** anything resembling this —*vi.* **3.** fall in cascades

cascara (kæsˈkɑːrə) *n.* **1.** dried bark of cascara buckthorn, used as laxative and stimulant (*also* **cascara sagrada**) **2.** shrub or small tree of NW North Amer. (*also* **cascara buckthorn**)

case[1] (keɪs) *n.* **1.** instance **2.** event, circumstance **3.** question at issue **4.** state of affairs, condition **5.** arguments supporting particular action *etc.* **6.** *Med.* patient under treatment **7.** lawsuit **8.** grounds for suit **9.** grammatical relation of words in sentence —**case history** record of person's background, medical history *etc.* —**case law** law established by following judicial decisions given in earlier cases

THESAURUS

carriage 1. carrying, conveyance, conveying, delivery, freight, transport, transportation **2.** cab, coach, conveyance, vehicle **3.** *Fig.* air, bearing, behaviour, comportment, conduct, demeanour, deportment, gait, manner, mien, posture, presence

carry 1. bear, bring, conduct, convey, fetch, haul, lift, lug, move, relay, take, transfer, transmit, transport **2.** accomplish, capture, effect, gain, secure, win **3.** broadcast, communicate, display, disseminate, give, offer, publish, release, stock

carry on 1. continue, endure, keep going, last, maintain, perpetuate, persevere, persist **2.** *Inf.* create (*Sl.*), make a fuss, misbehave

carry out accomplish, achieve, carry through, consummate, discharge, effect, execute, fulfil, implement, perform, realize

carton box, case, container, pack, package, packet

cartoon animated cartoon, animated film, animation, caricature, comic strip, lampoon, parody, satire, sketch, takeoff

cartridge 1. capsule, case, cassette, container, cylinder, magazine **2.** charge, round, shell

carve chip, chisel, cut, divide, engrave, etch, fashion, form, grave, hack, hew, incise, indent, mould, sculpt, sculpture, slash, slice, whittle

cascade 1. *n.* avalanche, cataract, deluge, falls, flood, fountain, outpouring, shower, torrent, waterfall **2.** *v.* descend, flood, gush, overflow, pitch, plunge, pour, spill, surge, tumble

case[1] **1.** circumstance(s), condition, context, contingency, dilemma, event, plight, position, predicament, situation, state **2.** example, illustration, instance, occasion, occurrence, specimen **3.** *Law* ac-

case[2] (keɪs) *n.* **1.** box, sheath, covering **2.** receptacle **3.** box and contents —*vt.* **4.** put in a case —**ˈcasing** *n.* **1.** protective cover **2.** material for cover **3.** frame containing door or window (*also* **case**) —**case-harden** *vt.* **1.** harden by carbonizing the surface of (*esp.* iron) by converting into steel **2.** make hard, callous

casein (ˈkeɪsɪɪn, -siːn) *n.* protein in milk and its products —**ˈcaseous** *a.* like cheese

casement (ˈkeɪsmənt) *n.* window opening on hinges

cash (kæʃ) *n.* **1.** money, banknotes and coins —*vt.* **2.** turn into or exchange for money —**caˈshier** *n.* one in charge of receiving and paying of money —**cash-and-carry** *a./adv.* sold on basis of cash payment for merchandise that is not delivered —**ˈcashbook** *n.* —**cash crop** crop grown for sale rather than subsistence —**cash dispenser** computerized device outside bank that supplies cash when user inserts card and keys in number —**cash flow** movement of money into and out of a business —**cash register** till that records amount of money put in —**cash on delivery** service entailing cash payment to carrier on delivery of merchandise

cashew (ˈkæʃuː, kæˈʃuː) *n.* **1.** tropical tree bearing kidney-shaped nuts **2.** nut of this tree, edible only when roasted (*also* **cashew nut**)

cashier (kæˈʃɪə) *vt.* dismiss from office or service

cashmere (ˈkæʃmɪə) *n.* **1.** fine soft fabric **2.** shawl made from goat's wool

casino (kəˈsiːnəʊ) *n.* building, institution for gambling (*pl.* **-s**)

cask (kɑːsk) *n.* **1.** barrel **2.** container for wine

casket (ˈkɑːskɪt) *n.* **1.** small case for jewels *etc.* **2.** US coffin

casque (kæsk) *n. Zool.* helmet or helmetlike structure, as on bill of most hornbills

Cassandra (kəˈsændrə) *n.* **1.** *Gr. myth.* daughter of Priam and Hecuba, endowed with gift of prophecy but fated never to be believed **2.** anyone whose prophecies of doom are unheeded

cassata (kəˈsɑːtə) *n.* ice cream, *esp.* containing fruit and nuts

cassava (kəˈsɑːvə) *n.* **1.** any of various tropical plants, *esp.* Amer. species (**bitter cassava, sweet cassava**) (*also* **ˈmanioc**) **2.** starch derived from root of this plant: source of tapioca

casserole (ˈkæsərəʊl) *n.* **1.** fireproof cooking and serving dish **2.** kind of stew cooked in this dish —*v.* **3.** cook or be cooked in casserole

cassette (kæˈsɛt) *n.* plastic container for film, magnetic tape *etc.*

cassia (ˈkæsɪə) *n.* **1.** tropical plant whose pods yield **cassia pulp,** mild laxative (*see also* SENNA) **2.** lauraceous tree of tropical Asia —**cassia bark** cinnamonlike bark of this tree, used as spice

cassis (kɑːˈsiːs) *n.* blackcurrant cordial

cassock (ˈkæsək) *n.* long tunic worn by clergymen

cassowary (ˈkæsəwɛərɪ) *n.* large flightless bird of NE Aust., New Guinea and adjacent islands

cast (kɑːst) *v.* **1.** throw, fling **2.** shed **3.** throw down **4.** deposit (a vote) **5.** allot, as parts in play **6.** mould, as metal (**cast** *pt./pp.*) —*n.* **7.** throw **8.** distance thrown **9.** squint **10.** mould **11.** that which is shed or ejected **12.** set of actors **13.** type, quality —**ˈcasting** *n.* —**ˈcastaway** *n./a.* shipwrecked (person) —**casting vote** decisive vote —**cast iron** iron containing so much carbon that it must be cast into shape —**cast-iron** *a.* **1.** made of cast iron **2.** rigid, unyielding —**cast-off** *a.* abandoned —**ˈcastoff** *n.* **1.** person or thing discarded or abandoned **2.** *Print.* estimate of amount of space a piece of copy will occupy —**cast steel** steel containing varying amounts of carbon *etc.*, that is cast into shape —**cast off 1.** remove (mooring lines) that hold (vessel) to dock **2.** knot (row of stitches, *esp.* final row) in finishing off knitted or woven material **3.** *Print.* estimate amount of space that will be taken up by (book *etc.*)

castanets (kæstəˈnɛts) *pl.n.* in Spanish dancing, two small curved pieces of wood *etc.* clicked together in hand

caste (kɑːst) *n.* **1.** section of society in India **2.** social rank

castellated (ˈkæstɪleɪtɪd) *a.* **1.** having turrets and battlements, like castle **2.** having indentations similar to battlements —**castelˈlation** *n.*

caster (ˈkɑːstə) *n. see* CASTOR

caster sugar (ˈkɑːstə) finely powdered sugar (*also* **castor sugar**)

castigate (ˈkæstɪgeɪt) *vt.* **1.** punish, rebuke severely, correct **2.** chastise —**castiˈgation** *n.* —**ˈcastigator** *n.* —**castiˈgatory** *a.*

castle (ˈkɑːsᵊl) *n.* **1.** fortress **2.** country mansion **3.** chess piece —**castle in the air** *or* **in Spain** hope or desire unlikely to be realized; daydream

THESAURUS

tion, cause, dispute, lawsuit, proceedings, process, suit, trial

case[2] **1.** box, cabinet, canister, capsule, carton, cartridge, casket, chest, compact, container, crate, holder, receptacle, shell, suitcase, tray, trunk **2.** capsule, casing, cover, covering, envelope, folder, integument, jacket, sheath, wrapper, wrapping

cash banknotes, bread (*Sl.*), bullion, change, coin, coinage, currency, dough (*Sl.*), funds, money, notes, payment, ready (*Inf.*), ready money, resources, specie, wherewithal

cashier 1. *n.* accountant, bank clerk, banker, bursar, clerk, purser, teller, treasurer **2.** *v.* break, cast off, discard, discharge, dismiss, drum out, expel

casket box, case, chest, coffer, jewel box, kist (*Scot.*)

cast *v.* **1.** chuck, drive, drop, fling, hurl, impel, launch, lob, pitch, project, shed, shy, sling, throw, thrust, toss **2.** bestow, deposit, diffuse, distribute, emit, give, radiate, scatter, shed, spread **3.** allot, appoint, assign, choose, name, pick, select **4.** form, found, model, mould, set, shape ~*n.* **5.** fling, lob, throw, thrust, toss **6.** air, appearance, complexion, demeanour, look, manner, mien, semblance, shade, stamp, style, tinge, tone, turn **7.** actors, characters, company, dramatis personae, players, troupe

caste class, estate, grade, lineage, order, race, rank, social order, species, station, status, stratum

castigate beat, berate, cane, censure, chasten, chastise, correct, criticize, discipline, dress down (*Inf.*), flail, flay, flog, haul over the coals (*Inf.*), lash, rebuke, reprimand, scold, scourge, whip

castle chateau, citadel, donjon, fastness, fortress, keep, mansion, palace, peel, stronghold, tower

castor (ˈkɑːstə) *n.* **1.** bottle with perforated top **2.** small swivelled wheel on table leg *etc.*

castor oil vegetable medicinal oil

castrate (kæˈstreɪt) *vt.* **1.** remove testicles of, deprive of power of generation **2.** deprive of vigour, masculinity *etc.* —**casˈtration** *n.*

casual (ˈkæʒjʊəl) *a.* **1.** accidental **2.** unforeseen **3.** occasional **4.** unconcerned **5.** informal —**ˈcasually** *adv.* —**ˈcasualty** *n.* **1.** person killed or injured in accident, war *etc.* **2.** thing lost, destroyed, in accident *etc.*

casuarina (kæsjʊəˈraɪnə) *n.* tree of Aust. and E Indies, having jointed leafless branches

casuist (ˈkæzjʊɪst) *n.* **1.** one who studies and solves moral problems **2.** quibbler —**casuˈistical** *a.* —**ˈcasuistry** *n.*

cat (kæt) *n.* any of various feline animals, including small domesticated furred animal, and lions, tigers *etc.* —**ˈcatkin** *n.* drooping flower spike —**ˈcatty** *a.* spiteful —**cat burglar** burglar who enters buildings by climbing through upper windows *etc.* —**ˈcatcall** *n.* derisive cry —**ˈcatfish** *n.* mainly freshwater fish with catlike whiskers —**ˈcatgut** *n.* strong cord made from dried intestines of sheep *etc.*, used for stringing musical instruments and sports rackets —**ˈcatmint** *n.* scented plant —**ˈcatnap** *vi./n.* doze —**cat-o'-nine-tails** *n.* whip consisting of nine knotted thongs, used formerly to flog prisoners (*pl.* **-tails**) (*also* **cat**) —**cat's cradle** game played by making patterns with loop of string between fingers —**Catsˈeye** *n.* **R** glass reflector set in road to indicate traffic lanes —**cat's-paw** *n.* **1.** person used by another as tool; dupe **2.** pattern of ripples on surface of water caused by light wind —**ˈcatwalk** *n.* narrow, raised path or plank

C.A.T. UK College of Advanced Technology

catabolism *or* **katabolism** (kəˈtæbəlɪzəm) *n.* breaking down of complex molecules, destructive metabolism

cataclysm (ˈkætəklɪzəm) *n.* **1.** (disastrous) upheaval **2.** deluge —**cataˈclysmal** *a.*

catacomb (ˈkætəkəʊm) *n.* **1.** underground gallery for burial —*pl.* **2.** series of underground tunnels and caves

catafalque (ˈkætəfælk) *n.* temporary raised platform on which body lies in state before or during funeral

Catalan (ˈkætəlæn) *n.* **1.** language of Catalonia, closely related to Provençal **2.** native of Catalonia —*a.* **3.** of Catalonia

catalepsy (ˈkætəlɛpsɪ) *n.* condition of unconsciousness with rigidity of muscles —**cataˈleptic** *a.*

catalogue *or U.S.* **catalog** (ˈkætəlɒg) *n.* **1.** descriptive list —*vt.* **2.** make such list of **3.** enter in catalogue

catalyst (ˈkætəlɪst) *n.* substance causing or assisting a chemical reaction without taking part in it —**ˈcatalyse** *or U.S.* **-lyze** *vt.* —**caˈtalysis** *n.*

catamaran (kætəməˈræn) *n.* **1.** type of sailing boat with twin hulls **2.** raft of logs

cataplexy (ˈkætəplɛksɪ) *n.* **1.** sudden temporary paralysis, brought on by intense emotion *etc.* **2.** state assumed by animals shamming death —**cataˈplectic** *a.*

catapult (ˈkætəpʌlt) *n.* **1.** small forked stick with elastic sling used for throwing stones **2.** *Hist.* engine of war for hurling arrows, stones *etc.* **3.** launching device —*vt.* **4.** shoot forth (as) from catapult —*v.* **5.** move precipitately

cataract (ˈkætərækt) *n.* **1.** waterfall **2.** downpour **3.** disease of eye

catarrh (kəˈtɑː) *n.* inflammation of a mucous membrane —**caˈtarrhal** *a.*

catastrophe (kəˈtæstrəfɪ) *n.* **1.** great disaster, calamity **2.** culmination of a tragedy —**cataˈstrophic** *a.*

catatonia (kætəˈtəʊnɪə) *n.* form of schizophrenia characterized by stupor, with outbreaks of excitement —**catatonic** (kætəˈtɒnɪk) *a./n.*

catch (kætʃ) *vt.* **1.** take hold of, seize **2.** understand **3.** hear **4.** contract (disease) **5.** be in time for **6.** surprise, detect —*vi.* **7.** be contagious **8.** get entangled **9.** begin to burn (**caught** *pt./pp.*) —*n.* **10.** seizure **11.** thing that holds, stops *etc.* **12.** what is caught **13.** *inf.* snag, disadvantage **14.** form of musical composition **15.** thing, person worth catching —**ˈcatcher** *n.* —**ˈcatching** *a.* —**ˈcatchy** *a.* **1.** pleasant, memorable **2.** tricky —**catchment area 1.** area in which rainfall collects to form the supply of river *etc.* **2.** area from which people are allocated to a particular school, hospital *etc.* —**ˈcatchpenny** *a.* **1.** worthless **2.** made to sell quickly —**catch phrase** frequently used phrase, *esp.* associated with particular group *etc.* —**ˈcatchword** *n.*

THESAURUS

casual 1. accidental, chance, contingent, fortuitous, incidental, irregular, occasional, random, serendipitous, uncertain, unexpected, unforeseen, unintentional, unpremeditated **2.** apathetic, blasé, cursory, indifferent, informal, insouciant, lackadaisical, nonchalant, offhand, perfunctory, relaxed, unconcerned

casualty loss, sufferer, victim

cat feline, grimalkin, malkin (*Archaic*), moggy (*Sl.*), mouser, puss (*Inf.*), pussy (*Inf.*), tabby

catalogue 1. *n.* directory, gazetteer, index, inventory, list, record, register, roll, roster, schedule **2.** *v.* accession, alphabetize, classify, file, index, inventory, list, register

catapult 1. *n.* ballista, sling, slingshot (*U.S.*), trebuchet **2.** *v.* heave, hurl, hurtle, pitch, plunge, propel, shoot, toss

cataract 1. cascade, deluge, downpour, falls, Niagara, rapids, torrent, waterfall **2.** *Medical* opacity (*of the eye*)

catastrophe 1. adversity, affliction, blow, calamity, cataclysm, devastation, disaster, failure, fiasco, ill, mischance, misfortune, mishap, reverse, tragedy, trial, trouble **2.** conclusion, culmination, curtain, debacle, dénouement, end, finale, termination, upshot, winding-up

catcall *n.* boo, gibe, hiss, jeer, raspberry, whistle

catch *v.* **1.** apprehend, arrest, capture, clutch, ensnare, entangle, entrap, grab, grasp, grip, lay hold of, nab (*Inf.*), seize, snare, snatch, take **2.** detect, discover, expose, find out, surprise, take unawares, unmask **3.** contract, develop, go down with, incur, succumb to, suffer from **4.** apprehend, discern, feel, follow, grasp, hear, perceive, recognize, sense, take in, twig (*Inf.*) ~*n.* **5.** bolt, clasp, clip, fastener, hasp, hook, hook and eye, latch, sneck, snib (*Scot.*) **6.** disadvantage, drawback, fly in the ointment, hitch, snag, stumbling block, trap, trick

catching communicable, contagious, infectious, infective, transferable, transmittable

catchword byword, motto, password, refrain, slogan, watchword

catchy captivating, haunting, memorable, popular

popular phrase or idea —**catch 22** inescapable dilemma

catechize *or* **-ise** (ˈkætɪkaɪz) *vt.* 1. instruct by question and answer 2. question —**cateˈchetical** *a.* —**ˈcatechism** *n.* —**ˈcatechist** *n.* —**cateˈchumen** *n.* one under instruction in Christianity

catechu (ˈkætɪtʃuː), **cachou**, *or* **cutch** (kʌtʃ) *n.* astringent resinous substance obtained from certain tropical plants, and used in dyeing *etc.*

category (ˈkætɪgərɪ) *n.* class, order, division —**cateˈgorical** *a.* 1. positive 2. of category —**cateˈgorically** *adv.* —**ˈcategorize** *or* **-ise** *vt.*

catenary (kəˈtiːnərɪ) *n.* 1. curve formed by heavy flexible cord hanging from two points 2. hanging cable between pylons along railway track, from which trolley wire is suspended —*a.* 3. of catenary or suspended chain

catenation (kætɪˈneɪʃən) *n.* chain, or series as links of chain

cater (ˈkeɪtə) *vi.* provide what is required or desired, *esp.* food *etc.* —**ˈcaterer** *n.*

caterpillar (ˈkætəpɪlə) *n.* 1. hairy grub of moth or butterfly 2. type of tractor fitted with caterpillar wheels —**caterpillar wheel** articulated belt revolving round two or more wheels to propel heavy vehicle over difficult ground

caterwaul (ˈkætəwɔːl) *vi.* wail, howl

catharsis *or* **katharsis** (kəˈθɑːsɪs) *n.* 1. purging of emotions through evocation of pity and fear, as in tragedy 2. *Psychoanal.* bringing repressed ideas or experiences to consciousness, by means of free association *etc.* 3. purgation, *esp.* of bowels —**caˈthartic** *a.* 1. purgative 2. effecting catharsis —*n.* 3. purgative drug or agent

Cathay (kæˈθeɪ) *n. Lit., obs.* China

cathedral (kəˈθiːdrəl) *n.* 1. principal church of diocese —*a.* 2. pert. to, containing cathedral

Catherine wheel (ˈkæθrɪn) 1. firework which rotates, producing sparks 2. circular window having ribs radiating from centre

catheter (ˈkæθɪtə) *n. Med.* long slender flexible tube for inserting into bodily cavity for introducing or withdrawing fluid

cathode (ˈkæθəʊd) *n.* negative electrode —**cathode rays** stream of electrons —**cathode-ray tube** vacuum tube in which beam of electrons is focused on to fluorescent screen to give visible spot of light

catholic (ˈkæθəlɪk, ˈkæθlɪk) *a.* 1. universal 2. including whole body of Christians 3. (C-) relating to R.C. Church —*n.* 4. (C-) adherent of R.C. Church —**Caˈtholicism** *n.* —**cathoˈlicity** *n.* —**caˈtholicize** *or* **-cise** *v.*

cation (ˈkætaɪən) *n.* positively charged ion; ion attracted to cathode during electrolysis —**catiˈonic** *a.*

cattle (ˈkætᵊl) *pl.n.* beasts of pasture, *esp.* oxen, cows —**cattle-grid** *n.* heavy grid over ditch in road to prevent passage of livestock —**ˈcattleman** *n.*

Caucasoid (ˈkɔːkəzɔɪd) *a.* of, pert. to, light-complexioned racial group of mankind —**Cauˈcasian** *a.* 1. Caucasoid 2. of Caucasus in SW Soviet Union —*n.* 3. member of Caucasoid race; White person 4. native of Caucasus

caucus (ˈkɔːkəs) *n.* group, meeting, *esp.* of members of political party, with power to decide policy *etc.*

caudal (ˈkɔːdᵊl) *a.* 1. *Anat.* of posterior part of body 2. *Zool.* resembling or in position of tail —**ˈcaudate** *or* **ˈcaudated** *a.* having tail

caudle (ˈkɔːdᵊl) *n.* hot spiced wine drink made with gruel, formerly used medicinally

caught (kɔːt) *pt./pp. of* CATCH

caul (kɔːl) *n. Anat.* portion of amniotic sac sometimes covering child's head at birth

cauldron *or* **caldron** (ˈkɔːldrən) *n.* large pot used for boiling

cauliflower (ˈkɒlɪflaʊə) *n.* variety of cabbage with edible white flowering head —**cauliflower ear** permanent distortion of ear as result of ruptures of blood vessels: usu. caused by blows received in boxing

caulk *or* **calk** (kɔːk) *vt.* stop up (cracks) with waterproof filler —**ˈcaulker** *n.* —**ˈcaulking** *n.*

cause (kɔːz) *n.* 1. that which produces an effect 2. reason, origin 3. motive, purpose 4. charity, movement 5. lawsuit —*vt.* 6. bring about, make happen —**ˈcausal** *a.* —**cauˈsality** *n.* —**cauˈsation** *n.* —**ˈcausative** *a.* 1. *Gram.* relating to form or class of verbs that express causation 2. (*oft. with* of) producing effect —*n.* 3. causative form or class of verbs —**ˈcauseless** *a.* groundless

cause célèbre (ˈkɔːz səˈlɛbrə) *Fr.* famous case

causerie (ˈkəʊzərɪ) *n.* 1. informal talk 2. conversational piece of writing

THESAURUS

catechize cross-examine, drill, examine, grill (*Inf.*), interrogate, question

categorical absolute, direct, downright, emphatic, explicit, express, positive, unambiguous, unconditional, unequivocal, unqualified, unreserved

category class, classification, department, division, grade, grouping, head, heading, list, order, rank, section, sort, type

cater furnish, outfit, provide, provision, purvey, supply, victual

catholic all-embracing, all-inclusive, broad-minded, charitable, comprehensive, eclectic, ecumenical, general, global, liberal, tolerant, unbigoted, universal, unsectarian, whole, wide, world-wide

cattle beasts, bovines, cows, kine (*Archaic*), livestock, neat (*Archaic*), stock

catty backbiting, bitchy (*Sl.*), ill-natured, malevolent, malicious, mean, rancorous, spiteful, venomous

caucus assembly, conclave, convention, get-together (*Inf.*), meeting, parley, session

cause *n.* 1. agent, beginning, creator, genesis, mainspring, maker, origin, originator, prime mover, producer, root, source, spring 2. account, agency, aim, basis, consideration, end, grounds, incentive, inducement, motivation, motive, object, purpose, reason 3. attempt, belief, conviction, enterprise, ideal, movement, purpose, undertaking ~*v.* 4. begin, bring about, compel, create, effect, engender, generate, give rise to, incite, induce, lead to, motivate, occasion, precipitate, produce, provoke, result in

caustic 1. acrid, astringent, biting, burning, corroding, corrosive, keen, mordant 2. acrimonious, cutting, pungent, sarcastic, scathing, severe, stinging, trenchant, virulent

causeway (ˈkɔːzweɪ) *n.* **1.** raised way over marsh *etc.* **2.** paved street

caustic (ˈkɔːstɪk) *a.* **1.** burning **2.** bitter, severe —*n.* **3.** corrosive substance —**ˈcaustically** *adv.* —**caustic soda** *see* **sodium hydroxide** *at* SODIUM

cauterize *or* **-ise** (ˈkɔːtəraɪz) *vt.* burn with caustic or hot iron —**cauteriˈzation** *or* **-iˈsation** *n.* —**ˈcautery** *n.*

caution (ˈkɔːʃən) *n.* **1.** heedfulness, care **2.** warning —*vt.* **3.** warn —**ˈcautionary** *a.* containing warning or precept —**ˈcautious** *a.* —**ˈcautiously** *adv.* —**ˈcautiousness** *n.*

cavalcade (kævəlˈkeɪd) *n.* column or procession of riders

cavalier (kævəˈlɪə) *a.* **1.** careless, disdainful —*n.* **2.** courtly gentleman **3.** *obs.* horseman **4.** (**C-**) adherent of Charles I in English Civil War —**cavaˈlierly** *adv.*

cavalry (ˈkævəlrɪ) *n.* mounted troops

cave (keɪv) *n.* **1.** hollow place in the earth **2.** den —**cavern** (ˈkævᵊn) *n.* deep cave —**cavernous** (ˈkævənəs) *a.* —**cavernously** (ˈkævənəslɪ) *adv.* —**ˈcaving** *n.* sport of exploring caves —**cavity** (ˈkævɪtɪ) *n.* hollow —**ˈcaveman** *n.* prehistoric cave dweller —**cave in 1.** fall in **2.** submit **3.** give in

caveat (ˈkeɪvɪæt, ˈkæv-) *n.* **1.** *Law* formal notice requesting court not to take action without warning person lodging caveat **2.** a caution

caviar *or* **caviare** (ˈkævɪɑː, kævɪˈɑː) *n.* salted sturgeon roe

cavil (ˈkævɪl) *vi.* find fault without sufficient reason, make trifling objections (**-ll-**) —**ˈcaviller** *n.* —**ˈcavilling** *a.*

cavort (kəˈvɔːt) *vi.* prance, frisk

cavy (ˈkeɪvɪ) *n.* small S Amer. rodent

caw (kɔː) *n.* **1.** crow's cry —*vi.* **2.** cry so

cay (keɪ, kiː) *n.* low island or bank composed of sand and coral fragments

cayenne pepper (keɪˈɛn) pungent red pepper

cayman *or* **caiman** (ˈkeɪmən) *n.* tropical American crocodilian similar to alligator (*pl.* **-s**)

Cb *Chem.* columbium

CB Citizens' Band

C.B. Companion of the (Order of the) Bath

CBC Canadian Broadcasting Corporation

C.B.E. Commander of the (Order of the) British Empire

C.B.I. Confederation of British Industry

cc *or* **c.c. 1.** carbon copy or copies **2.** cubic centimetre

cc. chapters

C.C. 1. City Council **2.** County Council **3.** Cricket Club

cd candela

Cd *Chem.* cadmium

C.D. 1. Civil Defence (Corps) **2.** compact disc **3.** Corps Diplomatique (Diplomatic Corps)

Cdr. *Mil.* Commander

Ce *Chem.* cerium

cease (siːs) *v.* bring or come to an end —**ˈceaseless** *a.* —**ˈceaselessly** *adv.*

cedar (ˈsiːdə) *n.* **1.** large evergreen tree **2.** its wood

cede (siːd) *v.* yield, give up, transfer, *esp.* of territory

cedilla (sɪˈdɪlə) *n.* hooklike mark (̧) placed under a letter *c* to show the sound of *s*

Ceefax (ˈsiːfæks) *n.* **R** B.B.C. teletext service

ceilidh (ˈkeɪlɪ) *n.* informal social gathering for singing and dancing, *esp.* in Scotland

ceiling (ˈsiːlɪŋ) *n.* **1.** inner, upper surface of a room **2.** maximum price, wage *etc.* **3.** *Met.* lower level of clouds **4.** *Aviation* limit of height to which aircraft can climb —**ceil** *vt.* line (room), *esp.* with plaster

celandine (ˈsɛləndaɪn) *n.* yellow wild flower

celebrate (ˈsɛlɪbreɪt) *v.* **1.** rejoice or have festivities to mark (happy day, event *etc.*) —*vt.* **2.** observe (birthday *etc.*) **3.** perform (religious ceremony *etc.*) **4.** praise publicly —**ˈcelebrant** *n.* —**ˈcelebrated** *a.* famous —**celeˈbration** *n.* —**ceˈlebrity** *n.* **1.** famous person **2.** fame

THESAURUS

caution *n.* **1.** alertness, care, carefulness, circumspection, deliberation, discretion, forethought, heed, heedfulness, prudence, vigilance, watchfulness **2.** admonition, advice, counsel, injunction, warning ~*v.* **3.** admonish, advise, tip off, urge, warn

cautious alert, cagey (*Inf.*), careful, chary, circumspect, discreet, guarded, heedful, judicious, prudent, tentative, vigilant, wary, watchful

cavalcade array, march-past, parade, procession, spectacle, train

cavalier *n.* **1.** chevalier, equestrian, horseman, knight, royalist **2.** beau, blade (*Archaic*), escort, gallant, gentleman ~*adj.* **3.** arrogant, condescending, curt, disdainful, haughty, insolent, lofty, lordly, offhand, scornful, supercilious

cavalry horse, horsemen, mounted troops

cave cavern, cavity, den, grotto, hollow

caveat admonition, caution, warning

cavern cave, hollow, pothole

cavernous concave, deep-set, hollow, sunken, yawning

cavil carp, censure, complain, find fault, hypercriticize, object, quibble

cavity crater, dent, gap, hole, hollow, pit

cease break off, bring *or* come to an end, conclude, culminate, desist, die away, discontinue, end, fail, finish, halt, leave off, refrain, stay, stop, terminate

ceaseless constant, continual, continuous, endless, eternal, everlasting, incessant, indefatigable, interminable, never-ending, nonstop, perennial, perpetual, unending, unremitting, untiring

cede abandon, abdicate, allow, concede, convey, grant, hand over, make over, relinquish, renounce, resign, surrender, transfer, yield

celebrate bless, commemorate, commend, drink to, eulogize, exalt, extol, glorify, honour, keep, laud, observe, perform, praise, proclaim, publicize, rejoice, reverence, solemnize, toast

celebrated acclaimed, distinguished, eminent, famed, famous, glorious, illustrious, lionized, notable, outstanding, popular, pre-eminent, prominent, renowned, revered, well-known

celebration 1. carousal, festival, festivity, gala, jollification, jubilee, junketing, merrymaking, party, revelry **2.** anniversary, commemoration, honouring, observance, performance, remembrance, solemnization

celebrity 1. big name, big shot (*Sl.*), bigwig (*Sl.*), dignitary, lion (*Inf.*), luminary, name, personage,

celeriac (sɪˈlɛrɪæk) *n.* variety of celery with large turniplike root, used as vegetable

celerity (sɪˈlɛrɪtɪ) *n.* swiftness

celery (ˈsɛlərɪ) *n.* vegetable with long juicy edible stalks

celestial (sɪˈlɛstɪəl) *a.* **1.** heavenly, divine **2.** of the sky —**celestial equator** great circle lying on celestial sphere, plane of which is perpendicular to line joining north and south celestial poles (*also* **equiˈnoctial, equinoctial circle**) —**celestial sphere** imaginary sphere of infinitely large radius enclosing universe

celibacy (ˈsɛlɪbəsɪ) *n.* single life, unmarried state —**ˈcelibate** *n./a.*

cell (sɛl) *n.* **1.** small room, *esp.* in prison **2.** small cavity **3.** minute, basic unit of living matter **4.** device converting chemical energy into electrical energy **5.** small local group operating as nucleus of larger political or religious organization —**ˈcellular** *a.* —**ˈcellule** *n.* small cell

cellar (ˈsɛlə) *n.* **1.** underground room for storage **2.** stock of wine —**ˈcellarage** *n.* —**ˈcellarer** *n.* monastic official responsible for food *etc.* —**cellaˈret** *n.* cabinet for wine

cello (ˈtʃɛləʊ) *n.* stringed instrument of violin family

Cellophane (ˈsɛləfeɪn) *n.* **R** transparent wrapping

cellulite (ˈsɛljʊlaɪt) *n.* subcutaneous fat alleged to resist dieting

Celluloid (ˈsɛljʊlɔɪd) *n.* **1. R** synthetic plastic substance with wide range of uses **2.** coating of photographic film **3.** cinema film

cellulose (ˈsɛljʊləʊz, -ləʊs) *n.* **1.** substance of vegetable cell wall **2.** group of carbohydrates **3.** varnish

Celsius (ˈsɛlsɪəs) *a./n.* (of) scale of temperature from 0° (melting point of ice) to 100° (boiling point of water)

Celtic (ˈkɛltɪk, ˈsɛl-) *or* **Keltic** (ˈkɛltɪk) *n.* **1.** branch of languages including Gaelic and Welsh —*a.* **2.** of Celtic peoples or languages —**Celt** *or* **Kelt** *n.* **1.** person who speaks a Celtic language **2.** member of Indo-European people who in pre-Roman times inhabited Brit., Gaul and Spain

cement (sɪˈmɛnt) *n.* **1.** fine mortar **2.** adhesive, glue —*vt.* **3.** unite with cement **4.** join firmly

cemetery (ˈsɛmɪtrɪ) *n.* burial ground, *esp.* other than churchyard

cenobite (ˈsiːnəʊbaɪt) *n. see* COENOBITE

cenotaph (ˈsɛnətɑːf) *n.* monument to person buried elsewhere

Cenozoic (siːnəʊˈzəʊɪk) *see* CAINOZOIC

censer (ˈsɛnsə) *n.* pan in which incense is burned

censor (ˈsɛnsə) *n.* **1.** one authorized to examine films, books *etc.* and suppress all or part if considered morally or otherwise unacceptable —*vt.* **2.** ban or cut portions of (film *etc.*) **3.** act as censor of (behaviour *etc.*) —**cenˈsorial** *a.* of censor —**cenˈsorious** *a.* fault-finding —**cenˈsoriousness** *n.* —**ˈcensorship** *n.*

censure (ˈsɛnʃə) *n.* **1.** blame **2.** harsh criticism —*vt.* **3.** blame **4.** criticize harshly

census (ˈsɛnsəs) *n.* official counting of people, things *etc.*

cent (sɛnt) *n.* hundredth part of dollar *etc.*

cent. **1.** centigrade **2.** central **3.** century

centaur (ˈsɛntɔː) *n.* mythical creature, half man, half horse

centenary (sɛnˈtiːnərɪ) *n.* **1.** 100 years **2.** celebration of hundredth anniversary —*a.* **3.** pert. to a hundred —**centeˈnarian** *n.* one a hundred years old —**centennial** (sɛnˈtɛnɪəl) *a.* lasting, happening every hundred years

centi- *or before vowel* **cent-** (*comb. form*) **1.** one hundredth, as in *centimetre* **2.** *rare* hundred, as in *centipede*

centigrade (ˈsɛntɪgreɪd) *a.* **1.** Celsius **2.** having one hundred degrees

centigram *or* **centigramme** (ˈsɛntɪgræm) *n.* hundredth part of gram

centilitre *or U.S.* **centiliter** (ˈsɛntɪliːtə) *n.* hundredth part of litre

centime (ˈsɒntiːm; *Fr.* sɑ̃ˈtim) *n.* monetary unit of France *etc.*, worth one hundredth of standard unit of currency

centimetre *or U.S.* **centimeter** (ˈsɛntɪmiːtə) *n.* hundredth part of metre —**centimetre-gram-second** *n. see* CGS UNITS

centipede (ˈsɛntɪpiːd) *n.* small segmented animal with many legs

CENTO (ˈsɛntəʊ) Central Treaty Organization

centre *or U.S.* **center** (ˈsɛntə) *n.* **1.** midpoint **2.** pivot, axis **3.** point to or from which things move or are drawn **4.** place for specific organization or activity —**ˈcentral** *a.* —**cenˈtrality** *n.* —**centraliˈzation** *or* **-liˈsation** *n.* —**ˈcentralize** *or* **-lise** *vt.* **1.** bring to a centre **2.** concentrate under one control —**ˈcentrally** *adv.* —**ˈcentric** *a.* —**cenˈtrifugal** *a.* tending from centre —**ˈcentrifuge** *n.* **1.** rotating machine that separates liquids from solids or other liquids by centrifugal force

THESAURUS

personality, star, superstar, V.I.P. **2.** distinction, éclat, eminence, fame, glory, honour, notability, popularity, pre-eminence, prestige, prominence, renown, reputation, repute, stardom

celestial angelic, astral, divine, elysian, empyrean, eternal, ethereal, godlike, heavenly, immortal, seraphic, spiritual, sublime, supernatural

cell **1.** cavity, chamber, compartment, cubicle, dungeon, stall **2.** caucus, coterie, group, nucleus, unit

cement **1.** *v.* attach, bind, bond, cohere, combine, glue, gum, join, plaster, seal, solder, stick together, unite, weld **2.** *n.* adhesive, binder, glue, gum, paste, plaster, sealant

cemetery burial ground, churchyard, God's acre, graveyard, necropolis

censor blue-pencil, bowdlerize, cut, expurgate

censorious captious, carping, cavilling, condemnatory, disapproving, disparaging, fault-finding, hypercritical, severe

censure **1.** *v.* abuse, berate, blame, castigate, chide, condemn, criticize, denounce, rebuke, reprehend, reprimand, reproach, reprove, scold, upbraid **2.** *n.* blame, castigation, condemnation, criticism, disapproval, dressing down (*Inf.*), obloquy, rebuke, remonstrance, reprehension, reprimand, reproach, reproof, stricture

central chief, essential, focal, fundamental, inner, interior, key, main, mean, median, mid, middle, primary, principal

centralize amalgamate, compact, concentrate, concentre, condense, converge, incorporate, rationalize, streamline, unify

2. rotating device for subjecting human beings or animals to varying accelerations —*vt.* 3. subject to action of centrifuge —**cen'tripetal** *a.* tending towards centre —**'centrist** *n.* person holding moderate political views —**central bank** national bank that does business mainly with government and other banks —**central heating** method of heating building from one central source —**central processing unit** part of computer that performs logical and arithmetical operations on data —**central reserve** *or* **reservation UK** strip that separates two sides of motorway or dual carriageway —**'centreboard** *n.* supplementary keel for sailing vessel —**'centrefold** *or U.S.* **'centerfold** *n.* large coloured illustration folded to form central spread of magazine —**centre forward** *Soccer, hockey etc.* central forward in attack —**centre half** *Soccer* defender in middle of defence —**centre of gravity** point through which resultant of gravitational forces on body always acts —**'centrepiece** *n.* object used as centre of something, *esp.* for decoration

centuplicate (sɛn'tju:plɪkeɪt) *vt.* 1. increase 100 times —*a.* (sɛn'tju:plɪkɪt) 2. increased hundredfold —*n.* (sɛn'tju:plɪkɪt) 3. one hundredfold (*also* **'centuple**)

centurion (sɛn'tjʊərɪən) *n.* Roman commander of 100 men

century ('sɛntʃərɪ) *n.* 1. 100 years 2. any set of 100

cephalic (sɪ'fælɪk) *a.* 1. of head 2. situated in, on or near head

cephalopod ('sɛfələpɒd) *n.* any of various marine molluscs characterized by well-developed head and eyes and ring of sucker-bearing tentacles, including octopus

ceramic (sɪ'ræmɪk) *n.* 1. hard brittle material of baked clay 2. object made of this —*pl.* 3. (*with sing. v.*) art, techniques of making ceramic objects 4. such objects —*a.* 5. of ceramic or ceramics

cere (sɪə) *n.* soft waxy swelling, containing nostrils, at base of upper beak, as in parrot

cereal ('sɪərɪəl) *n.* 1. any edible grain, *eg* wheat, rice *etc.* 2. (breakfast) food made from grain —*a.* 3. of cereal

cerebellum (sɛrɪ'bɛləm) *n.* one of major divisions of vertebrate brain whose function is coordination of voluntary movements (*pl.* **-s, -la** (-lə))

cerebrum ('sɛrɪbrəm) *n.* 1. anterior portion of brain of vertebrates: dominant part of brain in man, associated with intellectual function *etc.* 2. brain as whole (*pl.* **-s, -bra** (-brə)) —**cerebral** ('sɛrɪbrəl; *U.S. also* sə'ri:brəl) *a.* pert. to brain —**'cerebrate** *vi. usu. jocular* use the mind; think; ponder; consider —**cere'bration** *n.* —**cerebro'spinal** *a.* of brain and spinal cord —**cerebro'vascular** *a.* of blood vessels and blood supply of brain —**cerebral palsy** impairment of muscular function and weakness of limbs, caused by damage to brain before or during birth

cerecloth ('sɪəklɒθ) *n.* waxed waterproof cloth formerly used for shrouds

ceremony ('sɛrɪmənɪ) *n.* 1. formal observance 2. sacred rite 3. courteous act —**cere'monial** *a./n.* —**cere'monially** *adv.* —**cere'monious** *a.* —**cere'moniously** *adv.* —**cere'moniousness** *n.*

cerise (sə'ri:z, -'ri:s) *n./a.* clear, pinkish red

cerium ('sɪərɪəm) *n.* steel-grey element of lanthanide series of metals, used in lighter flints

CERN (sɜ:n) Conseil Européen pour la Recherche Nucléaire; organization of European states with centre in Geneva, for research in high-energy particle physics

cert (sɜ:t) *n. inf.* something certain (*esp. in* **a dead cert**)

cert. 1. certificate 2. certification 3. certified

certain ('sɜ:tᵊn) *a.* 1. sure 2. settled, inevitable 3. some, one 4. of moderate (quantity, degree *etc.*) —**'certainly** *adv.* —**'certainty** *n.* —**'certitude** *n.* confidence

certes ('sɜ:tɪz) *adv. obs.* with certainty; truly

certify ('sɜ:tɪfaɪ) *vt.* 1. declare formally 2. endorse, guarantee 3. declare legally insane (**-fied, -fying**) —**certificate** (sə'tɪfɪkɪt) *n.* 1. written declaration —*vt.* (sə'tɪfɪkeɪt) 2. authorize by or present with official document —**certifi'cation** *n.* —**'certified** *a.* 1. holding or guaranteed by certificate 2. endorsed, guaranteed 3. (of person) declared legally insane —**'certifier** *n.* —**Certificate of Secondary Education UK** examination the first grade pass of which is equivalent to GCE O level

cerulean (sɪ'ru:lɪən) *a.* sky-blue

cervix ('sɜ:vɪks) *n.* neck, *esp.* of womb —**'cervical** *a.* —**cervical smear** *Med.* smear taken from neck of uterus for detection of cancer (*see also* PAP TEST)

cesium ('si:zɪəm) *n.* US caesium

cessation (sɛ'seɪʃən) *n.* ceasing, stopping; pause

cession ('sɛʃən) *n.* yielding up

cesspool ('sɛspu:l) *or* **cesspit** ('sɛspɪt) *n.* pit in which filthy water collects, receptacle for sewage

THESAURUS

centre 1. *n.* bull's-eye, core, crux, focus, heart, hub, mid, middle, midpoint, nucleus, pivot 2. *v.* cluster, concentrate, converge, focus, revolve

centrepiece cynosure, epergne, focus, highlight, hub, star

ceremonial 1. *adj.* formal, liturgical, ritual, ritualistic, solemn, stately 2. *n.* ceremony, formality, rite, ritual, solemnity

ceremonious civil, courteous, courtly, deferential, dignified, exact, formal, precise, punctilious, ritual, solemn, starchy (*Inf.*), stately, stiff

ceremony 1. commemoration, function, observance, parade, rite, ritual, service, show, solemnities 2. ceremonial, decorum, etiquette, form, formal courtesy, formality, niceties, pomp, propriety, protocol

certain 1. assured, confident, convinced, positive, satisfied, sure 2. ascertained, conclusive, incontrovertible, indubitable, irrefutable, known, plain, true, undeniable, undoubted, unequivocal, unmistakable, valid 3. bound, definite, destined, fated, ineluctable, inescapable, inevitable, inexorable, sure 4. decided, definite, established, fixed, settled 5. express, individual, particular, precise, special, specific

certainty 1. assurance, authoritativeness, certitude, confidence, conviction, faith, indubitableness, inevitability, positiveness, sureness, trust, validity 2. fact, reality, sure thing (*Inf.*), surety, truth

certificate authorization, credential(s), diploma, document, licence, testimonial, voucher, warrant

certify ascertain, assure, attest, authenticate, aver, avow, confirm, corroborate, declare, endorse, guarantee, notify, show, testify, validate, verify, vouch, witness

cestus *or* **caestus** (ˈsɛstəs) *n.* in classical Roman boxing, pugilist's gauntlet of bull's hide studded with metal (*pl.* **-tus, -es**)

cesura (sɪˈzjʊərə) *n. Prosody see* CAESURA

cetacean (sɪˈteɪʃən) *a.* **1.** of order of aquatic mammals having no hind limbs and blowhole for breathing: includes toothed and whalebone whales (*also* **ceˈtaceous**) —*n.* **2.** whale

cetane (ˈsiːteɪn) *n.* colourless liquid hydrocarbon used in determination of cetane number of diesel fuel (*also* **ˈhexadecane**) —**cetane number** measure of quality of diesel fuel expressed as percentage of cetane (*also* **cetane rating**)

Cf *Chem.* californium

cf. confer (*Lat.*, compare)

c/f carried forward

CFL Canadian Football League

cg centigram

cgs units metric system of units based on *centimetre, gram, second*

ch. **1.** chapter **2.** church

cha-cha-cha (tʃɑːtʃɑːˈtʃɑː) *or* **cha-cha** *n.* **1.** modern ballroom dance from Latin Amer. **2.** music composed for this dance —*vi.* **3.** perform this dance

chafe (tʃeɪf) *vt.* **1.** make sore or worn by rubbing **2.** make warm by rubbing **3.** vex, irritate —**chafing dish** vessel with heating apparatus beneath it, for cooking or keeping food warm at table

chafer (ˈtʃeɪfə) *n.* any of various beetles, such as cockchafer

chaff (tʃɑːf) *n.* **1.** husks of corn **2.** worthless matter **3.** banter —*vt.* **4.** tease good-naturedly

chaffer (ˈtʃæfə) *vi.* **1.** haggle, bargain —*n.* **2.** bargaining

chaffinch (ˈtʃæfɪntʃ) *n.* small songbird

chagrin (ˈʃægrɪn) *n.* **1.** vexation, disappointment —*vt.* **2.** embarrass **3.** annoy **4.** disappoint

chain (tʃeɪn) *n.* **1.** series of connected links or rings **2.** thing that binds **3.** connected series of things or events **4.** surveyor's measure —*vt.* **5.** fasten with chain **6.** confine **7.** restrain —**chain armour** —**chain gang** US group of prisoners chained together —**chain mail** —**chain reaction** —**chain smoker** one who smokes cigarettes *etc.* continuously, *esp.* lighting one from preceding one —**chain stitch** —**chain store**

chair (tʃɛə) *n.* **1.** movable seat, with back, for one person **2.** seat of authority **3.** professorship **4.** iron support for rail on railway —*vt.* **5.** preside over **6.** carry in triumph —**ˈchairlift** *n.* series of chairs fixed to cable for conveying people (*esp.* skiers) up mountain —**ˈchairman** *n.* one who presides over meeting —**ˈchairmanship** *n.*

chaise (ʃeɪz) *n.* light horse-drawn carriage —**chaise longue** (lɒŋ) sofa

chalcedony (kælˈsɛdənɪ) *n.* whitish or bluish-white variety of quartz

chalet (ˈʃæleɪ) *n.* Swiss wooden house

chalice (ˈtʃælɪs) *n.* **1.** *Poet.* cup; bowl **2.** communion cup

chalk (tʃɔːk) *n.* **1.** white substance, carbonate of lime **2.** crayon —*v.* **3.** rub, draw, mark with chalk —**ˈchalkiness** *n.* —**ˈchalky** *a.*

challenge (ˈtʃælɪndʒ) *vt.* **1.** call to fight or account **2.** dispute **3.** stimulate **4.** object to **5.** claim —*n.* **6.** call to engage in fight *etc.* **7.** questioning of statement *etc.* **8.** demanding situation *etc.* **9.** demand by sentry *etc.* for identification or password —**ˈchallenger** *n.* —**ˈchallenging** *a.* difficult but stimulating

chamber (ˈtʃeɪmbə) *n.* **1.** room for assembly **2.** assembly, body of men **3.** compartment **4.** cavity **5.** *obs.* room —*pl.* **6.** office or apartments of barrister **7.** lodgings —**chamberlain** (ˈtʃeɪmbəlɪn) *n.* official at court of a monarch having charge of domestic and ceremonial affairs —**ˈchambermaid** *n.* servant with care of bedrooms —**chamber music** music for performance by a few instruments —**chamber of commerce** organization composed mainly of local businessmen to promote and protect their interests —**chamber pot** vessel for urine

chameleon (kəˈmiːlɪən) *n.* **1.** small lizard famous for its power of changing colour **2.** changeable person

chamfer (ˈtʃæmfə) *vt.* **1.** groove **2.** bevel **3.** flute —*n.* **4.** groove

chamois (ˈʃæmwɑː) *n.* **1.** goatlike mountain antelope **2.** (ˈʃæmɪ) soft pliable leather

champ[1] (tʃæmp) *v.* **1.** munch (food) noisily, as horse **2.** be nervous, impatient

champ[2] (tʃæmp) *n. inf.* champion

champagne (ʃæmˈpeɪn) *n.* light, sparkling white wine of several varieties

champers (ˈʃæmpəz) *n. sl.* champagne

champion (ˈtʃæmpɪən) *n.* **1.** one that excels all others **2.** defender of a cause **3.** one who fights for another **4.** hero —*vt.* **5.** fight for, maintain —**ˈchampionship** *n.*

chance (tʃɑːns) *n.* **1.** unpredictable course of events **2.**

THESAURUS

chafe abrade, anger, annoy, exasperate, fret, fume, gall, grate, incense, inflame, irritate, offend, provoke, rage, rasp, rub, ruffle, scrape, scratch, vex, worry

chaff *n.* **1.** dregs, glumes, hulls, husks, refuse, remains, rubbish, trash, waste **2.** badinage, banter, joking, persiflage, raillery, teasing ~*v.* **3.** banter, deride, jeer, mock, rib (*Inf.*), ridicule, scoff, taunt, tease

chain *v.* **1.** bind, confine, enslave, fetter, gyve (*Archaic*), handcuff, manacle, restrain, shackle, tether, trammel, unite ~*n.* **2.** bond, coupling, fetter, link, manacle, shackle, union **3.** concatenation, progression, sequence, series, set, string, succession, train

chairman chairperson, chairwoman, director, master of ceremonies, president, presider, speaker, spokesman, toastmaster

challenge **1.** *v.* accost, arouse, beard, brave, call out, claim, confront, dare, defy, demand, dispute, impugn, investigate, object to, provoke, question, require, stimulate, summon, tax, test, throw down the gauntlet, try **2.** *n.* confrontation, dare, defiance, interrogation, provocation, question, summons to contest, test, trial, ultimatum

chamber **1.** apartment, bedroom, cavity, compartment, cubicle, enclosure, hall, hollow, room **2.** assembly, council, legislative body, legislature

champion **1.** *n.* backer, challenger, conqueror, defender, guardian, hero, nonpareil, patron, protector, title holder, upholder, victor, vindicator, warrior, winner **2.** *v.* advocate, back, defend, espouse, fight for, promote, support, uphold

fortune, luck **3.** opportunity **4.** possibility **5.** risk **6.** probability —*vt.* **7.** risk —*vi.* **8.** happen —*a.* **9.** casual, unexpected —**ˈchancy** *a.* risky

chancel (ˈtʃɑːnsəl) *n.* part of church where altar is

chancellor (ˈtʃɑːnsələ) *n.* **1.** high officer of state **2.** head of university —**ˈchancellorship** *n.* —**ˈchancellery** *or* **ˈchancellory** *n.* —**Chancellor of the Exchequer UK** cabinet minister responsible for finance

chancery (ˈtʃɑːnsərɪ) *n.* division of British High Court of Justice

chancre (ˈʃæŋkə) *n. Pathol.* small hard growth: first sign of syphilis —**ˈchancrous** *a.*

chandelier (ʃændɪˈlɪə) *n.* hanging frame with branches for holding lights

chandler (ˈtʃɑːndlə) *n.* dealer in ropes, ships' supplies *etc.*

change (tʃeɪndʒ) *v.* **1.** alter, make or become different **2.** put on (different clothes, fresh coverings) —*vt.* **3.** put or give for another **4.** exchange, interchange —*n.* **5.** alteration, variation **6.** variety **7.** conversion of money **8.** small money, coins **9.** balance received on payment —**changeaˈbility** *n.* —**ˈchangeable** *a.* —**ˈchangeably** *adv.* —**ˈchangeful** *a.* —**ˈchangeless** *a.* —**ˈchangeling** *n.* child believed substituted for another by fairies —**change of life** menopause

channel (ˈtʃænˀl) *n.* **1.** bed of stream **2.** strait **3.** deeper part of strait, bay, harbour **4.** groove **5.** means of passing or conveying **6.** band of radio frequencies **7.** television broadcasting station —*vt.* **8.** groove, furrow **9.** guide, convey

chant (tʃɑːnt) *n.* **1.** simple song or melody **2.** rhythmic or repetitious slogan —*vi.* **3.** sing or utter chant **4.** speak monotonously or repetitiously

chanticleer (tʃæntɪˈklɪə) *or* **chantecler** (tʃæntɪˈklɛə) *n.* cock

chantry (ˈtʃɑːntrɪ) *n. Christianity* **1.** endowment for singing of Masses for soul of founder **2.** chapel or altar so endowed

chanty (ˈʃæntɪ, ˈtʃæn-) *n. see* SHANTY[2]

chaos (ˈkeɪɒs) *n.* **1.** disorder, confusion **2.** state of universe before Creation —**chaˈotic** *a.*

chap[1] (tʃæp) *v.* (of skin) become dry, raw and cracked, *esp.* by exposure to cold and wind (**-pp-**) —**chapped** *a.*

chap[2] (tʃæp) *n. inf.* fellow, man

chapatti *or* **chapati** (tʃəˈpætɪ, -ˈpɑːtɪ) *n.* in Indian cookery, flat unleavened bread resembling pancake (*pl.* **-ti, -s, -es**)

chapel (ˈtʃæpˀl) *n.* **1.** private church **2.** subordinate place of worship **3.** division of church with its own altar **4.** Nonconformist place of worship **5.** (meeting of) members of trade union in particular newspaper office, printing house *etc.*

chaperon *or* **chaperone** (ˈʃæpərəʊn) *n.* **1.** one who attends young unmarried lady in public as protector —*vt.* **2.** attend in this way

chaplain (ˈtʃæplɪn) *n.* clergyman attached to chapel, regiment, warship, institution *etc.* —**ˈchaplaincy** *n.* his office

chaplet (ˈtʃæplɪt) *n.* **1.** ornamental wreath of flowers worn on head **2.** string of beads **3.** *R.C.Ch.* string of prayer beads constituting one third of rosary; prayers counted on this string **4.** narrow moulding in form of string of beads

chapman (ˈtʃæpmən) *n. obs.* trader, *esp.* itinerant pedlar

chappie (ˈtʃæpɪ) *n. inf. see* CHAP[2]

chaps (tʃæps, ʃæps) *pl.n.* cowboy's leggings of thick leather

chapter (ˈtʃæptə) *n.* **1.** division of book **2.** section, heading **3.** assembly of clergy, bishop's council *etc.* **4.**

THESAURUS

chance *n.* **1.** liability, likelihood, occasion, odds, opening, opportunity, possibility, probability, prospect, scope, time **2.** accident, casualty, coincidence, contingency, destiny, fate, fortuity, fortune, luck, misfortune, peril, providence **3.** gamble, hazard, jeopardy, risk, speculation, uncertainty ~*v.* **4.** befall, betide, come about, come to pass, fall out, happen, occur **5.** endanger, gamble, go out on a limb (*Inf.*), hazard, jeopardize, risk, stake, try, venture, wager ~*adj.* **6.** accidental, casual, contingent, fortuitous, inadvertent, incidental, random, serendipitous, unforeseeable, unforeseen, unintentional, unlooked-for

chancy dangerous, dicey (*Sl.*), dodgy (*Inf.*), hazardous, problematical, risky, speculative, uncertain

change *v.* **1.** alter, convert, diversify, fluctuate, metamorphose, moderate, modify, mutate, reform, remodel, reorganize, restyle, shift, transform, transmute, vacillate, vary, veer **2.** alternate, barter, convert, displace, exchange, interchange, remove, replace, substitute, swap (*Inf.*), trade, transmit ~*n.* **3.** alteration, difference, innovation, metamorphosis, modification, mutation, permutation, revolution, transformation, transition, transmutation, vicissitude **4.** conversion, exchange, interchange, substitution, trade **5.** break (*Inf.*), diversion, novelty, variation, variety

changeable capricious, changeful, chequered, erratic, fickle, fitful, fluid, inconstant, irregular, kaleidoscopic, labile (*Chem.*), mercurial, mobile, mutable, protean, shifting, uncertain, unpredictable, unreliable, unsettled, unstable, unsteady, vacillating, variable, versatile, volatile, wavering

changeless abiding, consistent, constant, everlasting, fixed, immutable, permanent, perpetual, regular, reliable, resolute, settled, stationary, steadfast, steady, unalterable, unchanging, uniform, unvarying

channel *n.* **1.** canal, chamber, conduit, duct, fluting, furrow, groove, gutter, main, passage, route, strait **2.** *Fig.* approach, artery, avenue, course, means, medium, path, route, way ~*v.* **3.** conduct, convey, direct, guide, transmit

chant **1.** *n.* carol, chorus, melody, psalm, song **2.** *v.* carol, chorus, croon, descant, intone, recite, sing, warble

chaos anarchy, bedlam, confusion, disorder, disorganization, entropy, lawlessness, pandemonium, tumult

chaotic anarchic, confused, deranged, disordered, disorganized, lawless, purposeless, rampageous, riotous, topsy-turvy, tumultuous, uncontrolled

chap bloke (*Inf.*), character, cove (*Sl.*), customer, fellow, guy (*Inf.*), individual, person, sort, type

chaperon **1.** *n.* companion, duenna, escort, governess **2.** *v.* accompany, attend, escort, protect, safeguard, shepherd, watch over

chapter clause, division, episode, part, section, topic

organized branch of society, fraternity —'**chapter-house** *n.*

char[1] (tʃɑː) *vt.* scorch, burn to charcoal (**-rr-**) —**charred** *a.*

char[2] (tʃɑː) *inf. n.* **1.** charwoman —*vi.* **2.** do cleaning as job (**-rr-**)

char[3] *or* **charr** (tʃɑː) *n.* troutlike small fish

char[4] (tʃɑː) *n. sl.* tea

charabanc ('ʃærəbæŋ) *n.* **UK** coach, *esp.* for sight-seeing

character ('kærɪktə) *n.* **1.** nature **2.** total of qualities making up individuality **3.** moral qualities **4.** reputation, *esp.* good one **5.** statement of qualities of person **6.** an eccentric **7.** personality in play or novel **8.** letter, sign or any distinctive mark **9.** essential feature —**character'istic** *n./a.* —**character'istically** *adv.* —**characteri'zation** *or* **-i'sation** *n.* —'**characterize** *or* **-ise** *vt.* **1.** mark out, distinguish **2.** describe by peculiar qualities —'**characterless** *a.*

charade (ʃə'rɑːd) *n.* **1.** absurd act **2.** travesty —*pl.* **3.** word-guessing parlour game with syllables of word acted

charcoal ('tʃɑːkəʊl) *n.* **1.** black residue of wood, bones *etc.*, produced by smothered burning **2.** charred wood —**charcoal-burner** *n.*

chard (tʃɑːd) *n.* beet with large succulent leaves and thick stalks, used as vegetable (*also* **Swiss chard**)

charge (tʃɑːdʒ) *vt.* **1.** ask as price **2.** bring accusation against **3.** lay task on **4.** command **5.** attack **6.** deliver injunction against **7.** fill with electricity **8.** fill, load —*vi.* **9.** make onrush, attack —*n.* **10.** cost, price **11.** accusation **12.** attack, onrush **13.** command, exhortation **14.** accumulation of electricity —*pl.* **15.** expenses —'**chargeable** *a.* —'**charger** *n.* **1.** strong, fast battle horse **2.** that which charges, *esp.* electrically

chargé d'affaires ('ʃɑːʒeɪ dæ'fɛə) **1.** temporary head of diplomatic mission in absence of ambassador or minister **2.** head of diplomatic mission of lowest level (*pl.* **chargés d'affaires** ('ʃɑːʒeɪ, -ʒeɪz))

chariot ('tʃærɪət) *n.* **1.** two-wheeled car used in ancient fighting **2.** state carriage —**chario'teer** *n.*

charisma (kə'rɪzmə) *or* **charism** ('kærɪzəm) *n.* special power of individual to inspire fascination, loyalty *etc.* —**charis'matic** *a.*

charity ('tʃærɪtɪ) *n.* **1.** the giving of help, money *etc.* to those in need **2.** organization for doing this **3.** the money *etc.* given **4.** love, kindness **5.** disposition to think kindly of others —'**charitable** *a.* —'**charitably** *adv.*

charlatan ('ʃɑːlət'n) *n.* quack, impostor —'**charlatanry** *n.*

Charles's Wain ('tʃɑːlzɪz weɪn) the Plough

charleston ('tʃɑːlstən) *n.* fast, rhythmic dance of 1920s

charlie ('tʃɑːlɪ) *n. inf.* fool

charlock ('tʃɑːlɒk) *n.* weedy Eurasian plant with yellow flowers (*also* **wild mustard**)

charlotte ('ʃɑːlət) *n.* **1.** dessert made with fruit and bread or cake crumbs, sponge cake *etc.* **2.** cold dessert made with sponge fingers, cream *etc.* (*also* **charlotte russe**)

charm (tʃɑːm) *n.* **1.** attractiveness **2.** anything that fascinates **3.** amulet **4.** magic spell —*vt.* **5.** bewitch **6.** delight, attract —**charmed** *a.* —'**charmer** *n.* —'**charming** *a.*

charnel house ('tʃɑːn'l) *esp.* formerly, vault for bones of the dead

chart (tʃɑːt) *n.* **1.** map of sea **2.** diagram or tabulated statement —*vt.* **3.** map **4.** represent on chart —**the charts** *inf.* lists produced weekly of best-selling pop records

THESAURUS

char carbonize, cauterize, scorch, sear, singe

character 1. attributes, bent, calibre, cast, complexion, constitution, disposition, individuality, kidney, make-up, marked traits, nature, personality, quality, reputation, temper, temperament, type 2. honour, integrity, rectitude, strength, uprightness 3. card (*Inf.*), eccentric, oddball (*Inf.*), oddity, original, queer fish (*Inf.*) 4. cipher, device, emblem, figure, hieroglyph, letter, logo, mark, rune, sign, symbol, type 5. part, persona, portrayal, role

characteristic 1. *adj.* distinctive, distinguishing, idiosyncratic, individual, peculiar, representative, singular, special, specific, symbolic, symptomatic, typical 2. *n.* attribute, faculty, feature, idiosyncrasy, mark, peculiarity, property, quality, trait

characterize brand, distinguish, identify, indicate, inform, mark, represent, stamp, typify

charade fake, farce, pantomime, parody, pretence, travesty

charge *v.* 1. accuse, arraign, blame, impeach, incriminate, indict, involve ~*n.* 2. accusation, allegation, imputation, indictment ~*v.* 3. assail, assault, attack, rush, storm ~*n.* 4. assault, attack, onset, onslaught, rush, sortie ~*v.* 5. afflict, burden, commit, entrust, tax ~*n.* 6. amount, cost, damage (*Inf.*), expenditure, expense, outlay, payment, price, rate ~*v.* 7. fill, instil, lade, load, suffuse 8. bid, command, enjoin, exhort, instruct, order, require ~*n.* 9. command, dictate, direction, exhortation, injunction, instruction, mandate, order, precept

charitable 1. beneficent, benevolent, bountiful, eleemosynary, generous, kind, lavish, liberal, philanthropic 2. broad-minded, considerate, favourable, forgiving, gracious, humane, indulgent, kindly, lenient, magnanimous, sympathetic, tolerant, understanding

charity 1. alms-giving, assistance, benefaction, contributions, donations, endowment, fund, gift, hand-out, philanthropy, relief 2. affection, agape, altruism, benevolence, benignity, bountifulness, bounty, compassion, fellow feeling, generosity, goodness, good will, humanity, indulgence, love, tender-heartedness

charlatan cheat, con man (*Inf.*), fake, fraud, impostor, mountebank, phoney (*Sl.*), pretender, quack, sham, swindler

charm *v.* 1. allure, attract, beguile, bewitch, cajole, captivate, delight, enamour, enchant, enrapture, entrance, fascinate, mesmerize, please, win, win over ~*n.* 2. allure, allurement, appeal, attraction, desirability, enchantment, fascination, magic, magnetism, sorcery, spell 3. amulet, fetish, good-luck piece, lucky piece, periapt (*Rare*), talisman, trinket

charming appealing, attractive, bewitching, captivating, delectable, delightful, engaging, eye-catching, fetching, irresistible, lovely, pleasant, pleasing, seductive, winning, winsome

charter (ˈtʃɑːtə) *n.* **1.** document granting privileges *etc.* **2.** patent —*vt.* **3.** let or hire **4.** establish by charter

Chartism (ˈtʃɑːtɪzəm) *n. English hist.* movement to achieve certain political reforms, demand for which was embodied in charters presented to Parliament —ˈ**Chartist** *n./a.*

chartreuse (ʃɑːˈtrɜːz; *Fr.* ʃarˈtrøːz) *n.* **1.** either of two liqueurs, green or yellow, made from herbs **2.** yellowish-green colour

charwoman (ˈtʃɑːwʊmən) *n.* woman paid to clean office, house *etc.*

chary (ˈtʃɛərɪ) *a.* cautious, sparing —ˈ**charily** *adv.* —ˈ**chariness** *n.* caution

Charybdis (kəˈrɪbdɪs) *n.* ship-devouring monster in classical mythology, identified with whirlpool off coast of Sicily

chase[1] (tʃeɪs) *vt.* **1.** hunt, pursue **2.** drive (from, away, into *etc.*) —*n.* **3.** pursuit, hunting **4.** the hunted **5.** hunting ground —ˈ**chaser** *n.* drink of beer, soda *etc.* taken after spirit

chase[2] (tʃeɪs) *vt.* engrave —ˈ**chaser** *n.* —ˈ**chasing** *n.*

chase[3] (tʃeɪs) *n.* **1.** *Letterpress print.* rectangular steel frame into which metal type and blocks are locked for printing **2.** part of cannon enclosing bore **3.** groove or channel, *esp.* to take pipe *etc.* —*vt.* **4.** cut groove, furrow or flute in (surface *etc.*) (*also* ˈ**chamfer**)

chasm (ˈkæzəm) *n.* **1.** deep cleft, fissure **2.** abyss

chassé (ˈʃæseɪ) *n.* **1.** rapid gliding step used in dancing —*vi.* **2.** perform the step

chassis (ˈʃæsɪ) *n.* **1.** framework, wheels and machinery of motor vehicle excluding body and coachwork **2.** underframe of aircraft (*pl.* **-sis** (-sɪz))

chaste (tʃeɪst) *a.* **1.** virginal **2.** pure **3.** modest **4.** virtuous —ˈ**chastely** *adv.* —**chastity** (ˈtʃæstɪtɪ) *n.*

chasten (ˈtʃeɪsᵊn) *vt.* **1.** correct by punishment **2.** restrain, subdue —ˈ**chastened** *a.* —**chastise** (tʃæsˈtaɪz) *vt.* inflict punishment on —**chastisement** (tʃæsˈtaɪzmənt) *n.*

chasuble (ˈtʃæzjʊbᵊl) *n.* priest's long sleeveless outer vestment

chat[1] (tʃæt) *vi.* **1.** talk idly or familiarly (**-tt-**) —*n.* **2.** familiar idle talk —ˈ**chattily** *adv.* —ˈ**chatty** *a.*

chat[2] (tʃæt) *n.* any of various European songbirds, Amer. warblers, Aust. wrens

chateau *or* **château** (ˈʃætəʊ) *n. esp.* in France, castle, country house (*pl.* **-teaux** (-təʊ, -təʊz), **-s**)

chatelaine (ˈʃætəleɪn; *Fr.* ʃatˈlɛn) *n.* **1.** *esp.* formerly, mistress of castle or large household **2.** chain or clasp worn at waist by women in 16th to 19th century, with handkerchief *etc.* attached

chattel (ˈtʃætᵊl) *n.* (*usu. pl.*) any movable property

chatter (ˈtʃætə) *vi.* **1.** talk idly or rapidly **2.** rattle teeth —*n.* **3.** idle talk —ˈ**chatterer** *n.* —ˈ**chattering** *n.* —ˈ**chatterbox** *n.* one who chatters incessantly

chauffeur (ˈʃəʊfə, ʃəʊˈfɜː) *n.* paid driver of motorcar (**chaufˈfeuse** *fem.*)

chauvinism (ˈʃəʊvɪnɪzəm) *n.* **1.** aggressive patriotism **2.** smug sense of superiority

cheap (tʃiːp) *a.* **1.** low in price **2.** inexpensive **3.** easily obtained **4.** of little value or estimation **5.** mean, inferior —ˈ**cheapen** *vt.* —ˈ**cheaply** *adv.* —ˈ**cheapness** *n.* —**cheap-jack** *inf. n.* **1.** person who sells cheap and shoddy goods —*a.* **2.** shoddy, inferior —ˈ**cheapskate** *n. inf.* miserly person

cheat (tʃiːt) *vt.* **1.** deceive, defraud, swindle, impose upon —*vi.* **2.** practise deceit to gain advantage —*n.* **3.** fraud

check (tʃɛk) *vt.* **1.** stop **2.** restrain **3.** hinder **4.** repress **5.** control **6.** examine for accuracy, quality *etc.* —*n.* **7.** repulse **8.** stoppage **9.** restraint **10.** brief examination for correctness or accuracy **11.** pattern of squares on fabric **12.** threat to king at chess —ˈ**checkmate** *n.* **1.** *Chess* final winning move **2.** any overthrow, defeat —*vt.* **3.** *Chess* place (opponent's king) in checkmate **4.** defeat —ˈ**checkout** *n.* counter in supermarket where customers pay —ˈ**checkup** *n.* examination (*esp.* medical) to see if all is in order

THESAURUS

chart 1. *n.* blueprint, diagram, graph, map, plan, table, tabulation **2.** *v.* delineate, draft, graph, map out, outline, plot, shape, sketch

charter 1. *n.* bond, concession, contract, deed, document, franchise, indenture, licence, permit, prerogative, privilege, right **2.** *v.* authorize, commission, employ, hire, lease, rent, sanction

chase 1. *v.* course, drive, drive away, expel, follow, hound, hunt, pursue, put to flight, run after, track **2.** *n.* hunt, hunting, pursuit, race, venery (*Archaic*)

chassis anatomy, bodywork, frame, framework, fuselage, skeleton, substructure

chaste austere, decent, decorous, elegant, immaculate, incorrupt, innocent, modest, moral, neat, pure, quiet, refined, restrained, simple, unaffected, uncontaminated, undefiled, unsullied, vestal, virginal, virtuous, wholesome

chasten afflict, castigate, chastise, correct, cow, curb, discipline, humble, humiliate, repress, soften, subdue, tame

chastise beat, berate, castigate, censure, correct, discipline, flog, lash, punish, scold, scourge, upbraid, whip

chastity celibacy, continence, innocence, maidenhood, modesty, purity, virginity, virtue

chat 1. *n.* chatter, chinwag (*Brit. inf.*), confab (*Inf.*), gossip, heart-to-heart, natter, talk, tête-à-tête **2.** *v.* chatter, chew the rag *or* fat (*Sl.*), gossip, jaw (*Sl.*), natter, rabbit (on) (*Brit. sl.*), talk

chatter *n./v.* babble, blather, chat, gab (*Inf.*), gossip, jabber, natter, prate, prattle, tattle, twaddle

chatty familiar, friendly, gossipy, informal, newsy (*Inf.*), talkative

cheap 1. bargain, cut-price, economical, economy, inexpensive, keen, low-cost, low-priced, reasonable, reduced, sale **2.** common, inferior, paltry, poor, second-rate, shoddy, tatty, tawdry, worthless **3.** base, contemptible, despicable, low, mean, scurvy, sordid, vulgar

cheapen belittle, debase, degrade, demean, denigrate, depreciate, derogate, devalue, discredit, disparage, lower

cheat *v.* **1.** bamboozle (*Inf.*), beguile, bilk, con (*Sl.*), deceive, defraud, diddle (*Inf.*), do (*Sl.*), double-cross (*Inf.*), dupe, finagle (*Inf.*), fleece, fool, gull (*Archaic*), hoax, hoodwink, mislead, rip off (*Sl.*), swindle, take for a ride (*Inf.*), take in (*Inf.*), thwart, trick, victimize ~*n.* **2.** artifice, deceit, deception, fraud, imposture, rip-off (*Sl.*), swindle, trickery **3.** charlatan, cheater, con man (*Inf.*), deceiver, dodger, double-crosser

checked (tʃɛkt) *a.* having pattern of small squares

checker (ˈtʃɛkə) *see* CHEQUER

Cheddar (ˈtʃɛdə) *n.* (*sometimes* **c-**) smooth hard orange or whitish cheese

cheek (tʃiːk) *n.* **1.** side of face below eye **2.** *inf.* impudence —*vt.* **3.** *inf.* address impudently —ˈ**cheeky** *a.*

cheep (tʃiːp) *vi./n.* (utter) high-pitched cry, as of young bird

cheer (tʃɪə) *vt.* **1.** comfort **2.** gladden **3.** encourage by shouts —*vi.* **4.** shout applause —*n.* **5.** shout of approval **6.** happiness, good spirits **7.** mood **8.** *obs.* rich food —ˈ**cheerful** *a.* —ˈ**cheerfully** *adv.* —ˈ**cheerfulness** *n.* —ˈ**cheerily** *adv.* —ˈ**cheerless** *a.* —ˈ**cheerlessness** *n.* —**cheers** *interj. inf., chiefly* UK **1.** drinking toast **2.** goodbye, cheerio **3.** thanks —ˈ**cheery** *a.* —**three cheers** three shouts of hurrah in unison to honour someone or celebrate something

cheerio (tʃɪərɪˈəʊ) *inf. interj.* **1.** *chiefly* **UK** farewell greeting **2.** *chiefly* **UK** drinking toast —*n.* **3. NZ** small sausage

cheese (tʃiːz) *n.* curd of milk coagulated, separated from whey and pressed —ˈ**cheesiness** *n.* —ˈ**cheesy** *a.* —ˈ**cheeseburger** *n.* hamburger cooked with cheese on top —ˈ**cheesecake** *n.* **1.** tart filled with cheese, *esp.* cream cheese, cream, sugar *etc.* **2.** *sl.* women displayed for their sex appeal, as in photographs or films —ˈ**cheesecloth** *n.* loosely woven cotton cloth —ˈ**cheeseparing** *a.* mean —**cheesed off UK** *sl.* bored; disgusted; angry

cheetah *or* **chetah** (ˈtʃiːtə) *n.* large, swift, spotted feline animal

chef (ʃɛf) *n.* head cook, *esp.* in restaurant

chef-d'œuvre (ʃɛˈdœːvr) *Fr.* masterpiece

chem. **1.** chemical **2.** chemistry

chemin de fer (ʃəˈmæn də ˈfɛə) gambling game, variation of baccarat

chemise (ʃəˈmiːz) *n.* loose-fitting dress hanging straight from shoulders; loose shirtlike undergarment (*also* **shift**)

chemistry (ˈkɛmɪstrɪ) *n.* science concerned with properties of substances and their combinations and reactions —ˈ**chemical** *n./a.* —ˈ**chemically** *adv.* —ˈ**chemist** *n.* **1.** qualified dispenser of prescribed medicines **2.** shop that sells medicines *etc.* **3.** one trained in chemistry —**chemical engineer** —**chemical engineering** engineering concerned with design and manufacture of plant used in industrial chemical processes —**chemical warfare** warfare using asphyxiating gases, poisons *etc.*

chemotherapy (kɛməʊˈθɛrəpɪ) *n.* treatment of disease by chemical means

chemurgy (ˈkɛmɜːdʒɪ) *n.* branch of applied chemistry devoted to the development of agricultural products —**cheˈmurgic(al)** *a.*

chenille (ʃəˈniːl) *n.* soft cord, fabric of silk or worsted

cheongsam (ˈtʃɔːŋˈsæm) *n.* (Chinese) straight dress with slit in one side of skirt

cheque *or U.S.* **check** (tʃɛk) *n.* **1.** written order to banker to pay money from one's account **2.** printed slip of paper used for this —ˈ**chequebook** *or U.S.* ˈ**checkbook** *n.* book of cheques —**cheque card** banker's card

chequer *or U.S.* **checker** (ˈtʃɛkə) *n.* **1.** marking as on chessboard **2.** marble, peg *etc.* used in games, *eg* Chinese chequers —*pl.* **3.** squares like those of chessboard **4.** (*with sing. v.*) draughts —*vt.* **5.** mark in squares **6.** variegate —ˈ**chequered** *or esp. U.S.* ˈ**checkered** *a.* **1.** marked in squares **2.** uneven, varied

cherish (ˈtʃɛrɪʃ) *vt.* **1.** treat with affection **2.** protect **3.** foster

cheroot (ʃəˈruːt) *n.* cigar with both ends open

cherry (ˈtʃɛrɪ) *n.* **1.** small red fruit with stone **2.** tree bearing it —*a.* **3.** ruddy, bright red

cherub (ˈtʃɛrəb) *n.* **1.** winged creature with human face **2.** angel (*pl.* ˈ**cherubim, -s**) —**cheˈrubic** *a.*

chervil (ˈtʃɜːvɪl) *n.* a herb

Ches. Cheshire

chess (tʃɛs) *n.* game of skill played by two with 32 pieces on chequered board of 64 squares —ˈ**chessboard** *n.* —ˈ**chessmen** *pl.n.* pieces used in chess

chest (tʃɛst) *n.* **1.** upper part of trunk of body **2.** large,

THESAURUS

(*Inf.*), impostor, knave (*Archaic*), rogue, shark, sharper, swindler, trickster

check *v.* **1.** compare, confirm, enquire into, examine, inspect, investigate, look at, look over, make sure, monitor, note, probe, scrutinize, study, test, tick, verify **2.** arrest, bar, bridle, control, curb, delay, halt, hinder, impede, inhibit, limit, nip in the bud, obstruct, pause, repress, restrain, retard, stop, thwart ~*n.* **3.** examination, inspection, investigation, research, scrutiny, test **4.** constraint, control, curb, damper, hindrance, impediment, inhibition, limitation, obstruction, restraint, stoppage

cheek audacity, brass neck (*Inf.*), brazenness, disrespect, effrontery, gall (*Inf.*), impertinence, impudence, insolence, lip (*Sl.*), nerve, sauce (*Inf.*), temerity

cheeky audacious, disrespectful, forward, impertinent, impudent, insolent, insulting, pert, saucy

cheer *v.* **1.** animate, brighten, buoy up, cheer up, comfort, console, elate, elevate, encourage, enliven, exhilarate, gladden, hearten, incite, inspirit, solace, uplift, warm **2.** acclaim, applaud, clap, hail, hurrah ~*n.* **3.** animation, buoyancy, cheerfulness, comfort, gaiety, gladness, glee, hopefulness, joy, liveliness, merriment, merry-making, mirth, optimism, solace **4.** acclamation, applause, ovation, plaudits

cheerful animated, blithe, bright, bucked (*Inf.*), buoyant, cheery, contented, enlivening, enthusiastic, gay, glad, gladsome, happy, hearty, jaunty, jolly, joyful, light-hearted, lightsome (*Archaic*), merry, optimistic, pleasant, sparkling, sprightly, sunny

cheerfulness buoyancy, exuberance, gaiety, geniality, gladness, good cheer, good humour, high spirits, jauntiness, joyousness, light-heartedness

cheerless bleak, comfortless, dark, dejected, depressed, desolate, despondent, disconsolate, dismal, dolorous, drab, dreary, dull, forlorn, gloomy, grim, joyless, melancholy, miserable, mournful, sad, sombre, sorrowful, sullen, unhappy, woebegone, woeful

cheery breezy, carefree, cheerful, good-humoured, happy, jovial, lively, pleasant, sunny

chemical compound, drug, potion, synthetic

cherish care for, cleave to, cling to, comfort, cosset, encourage, entertain, foster, harbour, hold dear, nourish, nurse, nurture, prize, shelter, support, sustain, treasure strong box —**chest of drawers** piece of furniture containing drawers

chesterfield (ˈtʃɛstəfiːld) *n.* padded sofa

chestnut (ˈtʃɛsnʌt) *n.* **1.** large reddish-brown nut growing in prickly husk **2.** tree bearing it **3.** *inf.* old joke **4.** horse of golden-brown colour —*a.* **5.** reddish-brown

cheval glass (ʃəˈvæl) full-length mirror mounted to swivel within frame

chevalier (ʃɛvəˈlɪə) *n.* **1.** member of order of merit, such as French Legion of Honour **2.** lowest title of rank in old French nobility **3.** *obs.* knight **4.** chivalrous man; gallant

Cheviot (ˈtʃiːvɪət, ˈtʃɛv-) *n.* **1.** Brit. sheep reared for its wool **2.** (*oft.* **c-**) rough woollen fabric

chevron (ˈʃɛvrən) *n.* *Mil.* V-shaped band of braid worn on sleeve to designate rank

chew (tʃuː) *v.* **1.** grind with teeth —*n.* **2.** act of chewing **3.** something that is chewed —**ˈchewy** *a.* firm, sticky when chewed —**chewing gum** —**chew the fat** *sl.* **1.** argue over a point **2.** talk idly; gossip

chi (kaɪ) *n.* 22nd letter in Gr. alphabet (χ, X)

chianti (kɪˈæntɪ) *n.* It. wine

chiaroscuro (kɪɑːrəˈskʊərəʊ) *n.* **1.** artistic distribution of light and dark masses in picture **2.** monochrome painting using light and dark only (*pl.* **-s**)

chic (ʃiːk, ʃɪk) *a.* **1.** stylish, elegant —*n.* **2.** stylishness, *esp.* in dress

chicane (ʃɪˈkeɪn) *n.* **1.** bridge or whist hand without trumps **2.** *Motor racing* barrier placed before dangerous corner to reduce speeds **3.** *rare* chicanery —*vt.* **4.** deceive or trick by chicanery —*vi.* **5.** use chicanery —**chiˈcanery** *n.* **1.** quibbling **2.** trick, artifice

chick (tʃɪk) *n.* **1.** young of birds, *esp.* of hen **2.** *sl.* girl, young woman —**ˈchicken** *n.* **1.** domestic fowl bred for flesh or eggs **2.** its flesh as food **3.** *sl.* cowardly person —*a.* **4.** *sl.* easily scared; cowardly; timid —**chicken feed** trifling amount (of money) —**chicken-hearted** *a.* timid, cowardly —**ˈchickenpox** *n.* infectious disease, *esp.* of children —**ˈchickpea** *n.* dwarf pea —**ˈchickweed** *n.* weed with small white flowers

chicle (ˈtʃɪkᵊl) *n.* substance obtained from sapodilla; main ingredient of chewing gum

chicory (ˈtʃɪkərɪ) *n.* salad plant of which the root is ground and used with, or instead of, coffee

chide (tʃaɪd) *vt.* scold, reprove, censure (**chid** *pt.*, **ˈchidden, chid** *pp.*, **ˈchiding** *pr.p.*)

chief (tʃiːf) *n.* **1.** head or principal person —*a.* **2.** principal, foremost, leading —**ˈchiefly** *adv.* —**chieftain** (ˈtʃiːftən, -tɪn) *n.* leader, chief of clan or tribe —**chief petty officer** senior naval rank for personnel without commissioned or warrant rank —**chief technician** noncommissioned officer in Royal Air Force, junior to flight sergeant

chiffchaff (ˈtʃɪftʃæf) *n.* common European warbler

chiffon (ʃɪˈfɒn, ˈʃɪfɒn) *n.* thin gauzy material —**chiffoˈnier** *n.* ornamental cupboard

chignon (ˈʃiːnjɒn) *n.* roll, knot of hair worn at back of head

chigoe (ˈtʃɪgəʊ) *n.* tropical flea, female of which burrows into skin of man *etc.* (*also* **ˈchigger**)

Chihuahua (tʃɪˈwɑːwɑː, -wə) *n.* breed of tiny dog, *orig.* from Mexico

chilblain (ˈtʃɪlbleɪn) *n.* inflamed sore on hands, legs *etc.*, due to cold

child (tʃaɪld) *n.* **1.** young human being **2.** offspring (*pl.* **children** (ˈtʃɪldrən)) —**ˈchildhood** *n.* period between birth and puberty —**ˈchildish** *a.* **1.** of or like a child **2.** silly **3.** trifling —**ˈchildishly** *adv.* —**ˈchildless** *a.* —**ˈchildlike** *a.* **1.** of or like a child **2.** innocent **3.** frank **4.** docile —**ˈchildbed** *n.* state of giving birth to child —**child benefit UK** regular government payment to parents of children up to a certain age —**ˈchildbirth** *n.* —**child minder** person who looks after children, *esp.* those whose parents are working —**child's play** very easy task

chiliad (ˈkɪlɪæd) *n.* **1.** group of one thousand **2.** thousand years

chill (tʃɪl) *n.* **1.** coldness **2.** cold with shivering **3.** anything that damps, discourages —*v.* **4.** make, become cold (*esp.* food, drink) —**chilled** *a.* —**ˈchilliness** *n.* —**ˈchilly** *a.*

chilli (ˈtʃɪlɪ) *n.* **1.** small red hot-tasting seed pod **2.** plant producing it

Chiltern Hundreds (ˈtʃɪltən) **UK** Stewardship of

THESAURUS

chest box, case, casket, coffer, crate, strongbox, trunk

chew *v.* bite, champ, crunch, gnaw, grind, masticate, munch

chic elegant, fashionable, modish, smart, stylish, trendy (*Brit. inf.*)

chide admonish, berate, blame, censure, check, criticize, find fault, give (someone) a row (*Inf.*), lecture, rebuke, reprehend, reprimand, reproach, reprove, scold, tell off (*Inf.*), upbraid

chief **1.** *adj.* capital, cardinal, central, especial, essential, foremost, grand, highest, key, leading, main, most important, outstanding, paramount, predominant, pre-eminent, premier, prevailing, primary, prime, principal, superior, supreme, uppermost, vital **2.** *n.* boss (*Inf.*), captain, chieftain, commander, director, governor, head, leader, lord, manager, master, principal, ringleader, ruler, superintendent, suzerain

chiefly above all, especially, essentially, in general, in the main, mainly, mostly, on the whole, predominantly, primarily, principally, usually

child babe, baby, bairn (*Scot.*), brat, chit, descendant, infant, issue, juvenile, kid (*Inf.*), little one, minor, nipper (*Inf.*), nursling, offspring, progeny, suckling, toddler, tot, wean (*Scot.*), youngster (*Inf.*)

childbirth accouchement, child-bearing, confinement, delivery, labour, lying-in, parturition, travail

childhood boyhood, girlhood, immaturity, infancy, minority, schooldays, youth

childish boyish, foolish, frivolous, girlish, immature, infantile, juvenile, puerile, silly, simple, trifling, weak, young

childlike artless, credulous, guileless, ingenuous, innocent, naive, simple, trustful, trusting, unfeigned

chill **1.** *v.* congeal, cool, freeze, refrigerate **2.** *n.* bite, cold, coldness, coolness, crispness, frigidity, nip, rawness, sharpness

chilly **1.** blowy, breezy, brisk, cool, crisp, draughty, fresh, nippy, penetrating, sharp **2.** frigid, hostile, unfriendly, unresponsive, unsympathetic, unwelcoming

the Chiltern Hundreds; nominal office that MP applies for to resign seat

chime (tʃaɪm) *n.* **1.** sound of bell **2.** harmonious, ringing sound —*vi.* **3.** ring harmoniously **4.** agree —*vt.* **5.** strike (bells) —**chime in** come into conversation with agreement

chimera *or* **chimaera** (kaɪˈmɪərə, kɪ-) *n.* **1.** fabled monster, made up of parts of various animals **2.** wild fancy —**chimeric(al)** (kaɪˈmɛrɪk(ᵊl), kɪ-) *a.* fanciful

chimney (ˈtʃɪmnɪ) *n.* **1.** a passage for smoke **2.** narrow vertical cleft in rock (*pl.* -s)

chimp (tʃɪmp) *n. inf.* chimpanzee

chimpanzee (tʃɪmpænˈziː) *n.* gregarious, intelligent ape of Afr.

chin (tʃɪn) *n.* part of face below mouth —**chinless wonder** UK *inf.* person, *esp.* upper-class, lacking strength of character —ˈ**chinwag** *n.* UK *inf.* chat

china (ˈtʃaɪnə) *n.* **1.** fine earthenware, porcelain **2.** cups, saucers *etc.* collectively —**china clay** *see* KAOLIN

chincherinchee (tʃɪntʃərɪnˈtʃiː, -ˈrɪntʃɪ) *n.* S Afr. plant with white or yellow flower spikes

chinchilla (tʃɪnˈtʃɪlə) *n.* S Amer. rodent with soft, grey fur

chine (tʃaɪn) *n.* **1.** backbone **2.** joint of meat **3.** ridge or crest of land

Chinese (tʃaɪˈniːz) *a.* **1.** of China, its people or their languages —*n.* **2.** native of China or descendant of one (*pl.* -ese) **3.** any of languages of China —**Chinese lantern** Asian plant cultivated for its orange-red inflated calyx

chink[1] (tʃɪŋk) *n.* cleft, crack

chink[2] (tʃɪŋk) *n.* **1.** light metallic sound —*v.* **2.** (cause to) make this sound

chinoiserie (ʃiːnwɑːzəˈriː, -ˈwɑːzərɪ) *n.* **1.** style of decorative art based on imitations of Chinese motifs **2.** object or objects in this style

chinook (tʃɪˈnuːk, -ˈnʊk) *n.* **1.** warm dry wind blowing down eastern slopes of Rocky Mountains **2.** warm moist wind blowing on to Washington and Oregon coasts

chintz (tʃɪnts) *n.* cotton cloth printed in coloured designs

chip (tʃɪp) *n.* **1.** splinter **2.** place where piece has been broken off **3.** thin strip of potato, fried **4.** tiny wafer of silicon forming integrated circuit in computer *etc.* —*vt.* **5.** chop into small pieces **6.** break small pieces from **7.** shape by cutting off pieces —*vi.* **8.** break off (-pp-) —**chip-based** *a.* using microchips in electronic equipment —ˈ**chipboard** *n.* thin rigid sheet made of compressed wood particles —**chip in 1.** interrupt **2.** contribute

chipmunk (ˈtʃɪpmʌŋk) *n.* small, striped N Amer. squirrel

chipolata (tʃɪpəˈlɑːtə) *n.* small sausage

Chippendale (ˈtʃɪpᵊndeɪl) *a.* (of furniture) in style of Thomas Chippendale, characterized by use of Chinese and Gothic motifs *etc.*

chirography (kaɪˈrɒgrəfɪ) *n.* calligraphy

chiromancy (ˈkaɪrəmænsɪ) *n.* palmistry —ˈ**chiromancer** *n.*

chiropodist (kɪˈrɒpədɪst) *n.* one who treats disorders of feet —**chiˈropody** *n.*

chiropractor (ˈkaɪrəpræktə) *n.* one skilled in treating bodily disorders by manipulation, massage *etc.* —**chiroˈpractic** *n.*

chirp (tʃɜːp) *n.* **1.** short, sharp cry of bird —*vi.* **2.** make this sound —ˈ**chirpy** *a. inf.* happy

chisel (ˈtʃɪzᵊl) *n.* **1.** cutting tool, usu. bar of steel with edge across main axis —*vt.* **2.** cut, carve with chisel **3.** *sl.* cheat (-ll-)

chit[1] (tʃɪt) *n.* informal note, memorandum

chit[2] (tʃɪt) *n.* child, young girl

chitchat (ˈtʃɪttʃæt) *n.* **1.** gossip —*vi.* **2.** gossip

chitin (ˈkaɪtɪn) *n.* polysaccharide that is principal component of outer coverings of arthropods *etc.* —ˈ**chitinous** *a.*

chivalry (ˈʃɪvəlrɪ) *n.* **1.** bravery and courtesy **2.** medieval system of knighthood —ˈ**chivalrous** *a.* —ˈ**chivalrously** *adv.*

chive (tʃaɪv) *n.* herb with mild onion flavour

chivy, chivvy (ˈtʃɪvɪ), *or* **chevy** (ˈtʃɛvɪ) UK *vt.* **1.** harass; nag **2.** hunt —*vi.* **3.** run about (ˈ**chivied,** ˈ**chivying,** ˈ**chivvied,** ˈ**chivvying** *or* ˈ**chevied,** ˈ**chevying**) —*n.* **4.** hunt **5.** *obs.* hunting cry

chloral hydrate (ˈklɔːrəl) colourless crystalline soluble solid produced by reaction of chloral with water and used as sedative

chlorine (ˈklɔːriːn) *or* **chlorin** (ˈklɔːrɪn) *n.* nonmetallic element, yellowish-green poison gas —ˈ**chlorate** *n.* salt of chloric acid —ˈ**chloric** *a.* —ˈ**chloride** *n.* **1.** compound of chlorine **2.** bleaching agent —ˈ**chlorinate** *vt.* **1.** disinfect **2.** purify with chlorine

chloroform (ˈklɔːrəfɔːm) *n.* **1.** volatile liquid formerly used as anaesthetic —*vt.* **2.** render insensible with it

chlorophyll *or U.S.* **chlorophyl** (ˈklɔːrəfɪl) *n.* green colouring matter in plants: used to colour food

chock (tʃɒk) *n.* block or wedge to prevent heavy object rolling or sliding —**chock-full** *or* **chock-a-block** *a.* packed full

chocolate (ˈtʃɒkəlɪt, ˈtʃɒklɪt, -lət) *n.* **1.** paste from ground cacao seeds **2.** confectionery, drink made from this —*a.* **3.** dark brown —**choc-ice** *n.* chocolate-covered slice of ice cream —**chocolate-box** *a. inf.* sentimentally pretty or appealing

choice (tʃɔɪs) *n.* **1.** act or power of choosing **2.** alternative **3.** thing or person chosen —*a.* **4.** select, fine, worthy of being chosen —ˈ**choicely** *adv.*

THESAURUS

chime boom, clang, dong, jingle, peal, ring, sound, strike, tinkle, tintinnabulate, toll

china ceramics, crockery, porcelain, pottery, service, tableware, ware

chink aperture, cleft, crack, cranny, crevice, cut, fissure, flaw, gap, opening, rift

chip 1. *n.* dent, flake, flaw, fragment, nick, notch, paring, scrap, scratch, shard, shaving, sliver, wafer **2.** *v.* chisel, damage, gash, nick, whittle

chip in 1. interpose, interrupt **2.** contribute, donate, go Dutch (*Inf.*), pay, subscribe

chivalrous bold, brave, courageous, courteous, courtly, gallant, gentlemanly, heroic, high-minded, honourable, intrepid, knightly, magnanimous, true, valiant

chivalry courage, courtesy, courtliness, gallantry, gentlemanliness, knight-errantry, knighthood, politeness

choir (kwaɪə) *n.* **1.** band of singers, *esp.* in church **2.** part of church set aside for them

choke (tʃəʊk) *vt.* **1.** hinder, stop the breathing of **2.** smother, stifle **3.** obstruct —*vi.* **4.** suffer choking —*n.* **5.** act, noise of choking **6.** device in carburettor to increase richness of petrol-air mixture —**choked** *a.* —ˈ**choker** *n.* **1.** woman's high collar **2.** neckband or necklace worn tightly around throat **3.** high clerical collar; stock **4.** person or thing that chokes —ˈ**chokebore** *n.* gun with bore narrowed towards muzzle —ˈ**chokedamp** *n.* carbon dioxide gas in coal mines

choler (ˈkɒlə) *n.* bile, anger —ˈ**choleric** *a.* bad-tempered

cholera (ˈkɒlərə) *n.* deadly infectious disease marked by vomiting and diarrhoea

cholesterol (kəˈlɛstərɒl) *or* **cholesterin** (kəˈlɛstərɪn) *n.* substance found in animal tissue and fat

chomp (tʃɒmp) *or* **chump** (tʃʌmp) *v.* chew noisily

choose (tʃuːz) *vt.* **1.** pick out, select **2.** take by preference —*vi.* **3.** decide, think fit (**chose, ˈchosen, ˈchoosing**) —ˈ**chooser** *n.* —ˈ**choosy** *a.* fussy

chop[1] (tʃɒp) *vt.* **1.** cut with blow **2.** hack (**-pp-**) —*n.* **3.** hewing blow **4.** slice of meat containing rib or other bone —ˈ**chopper** *n.* **1.** short axe **2.** *inf.* helicopter **3.** *inf.* large motorbike —ˈ**choppy** *a.* (of sea) having short, broken waves

chop[2] (tʃɒp) *vt.* exchange, bandy (*esp. in* **chop logic, chop and change**) (**-pp-**)

chops (tʃɒps) *pl.n. inf.* jaws, cheeks

chopsticks (ˈtʃɒpstɪks) *pl.n.* implements used by Chinese for eating food

chop suey (ˈsuːɪ) a kind of rich Chinese stew with rice

choral (ˈkɔːrəl) *a.* of, for, sung by, a choir

chorale *or* **choral** (kɒˈrɑːl) *n.* slow, stately hymn tune

chord (kɔːd) *n.* **1.** emotional response, *esp.* of sympathy **2.** simultaneous sounding of musical notes **3.** straight line joining ends of arc

chore (tʃɔː) *n.* **1.** (unpleasant) task **2.** odd job

chorea (kɒˈrɪə) *n.* disorder of central nervous system characterized by uncontrollable jerky movements (*also* **Saint Vitus's dance**)

choreography (kɒrɪˈɒgrəfɪ) *or* **choregraphy** (kɒˈrɛgrəfɪ) *n.* **1.** art of arranging dances, *esp.* ballet **2.** art, notation of ballet dancing —**choreˈographer** *or* **choˈregrapher** *n.* —**choreoˈgraphic** *or* **choreˈgraphic** *a.*

chorography *n.* art of describing and making maps of particular regions —**choroˈgraphic** *a.*

choroid (ˈkɔːrɔɪd) *or* **chorioid** (ˈkɔːrɪɔɪd) *n.* vascular membrane of eyeball between sclera and retina

chorology (kəˈrɒlədʒɪ) *n.* science of geographical distribution of plants and animals —**choˈrologist** *n.*

chortle (ˈtʃɔːtᵊl) *vi.* **1.** chuckle happily —*n.* **2.** gleeful chuckle

chorus (ˈkɔːrəs) *n.* **1.** band of singers **2.** combination of voices singing together **3.** refrain —*vt.* **4.** sing or say together —**choric** (ˈkɒrɪk) *a.* —**chorister** (ˈkɒrɪstə) *n.*

chose (tʃəʊz) *pt. of* CHOOSE —ˈ**chosen** *pp. of* CHOOSE

chough (tʃʌf) *n.* black passerine bird of Europe, Asia and Afr., with red bill

choux pastry (ʃuː) very light pastry made with eggs

chow (tʃaʊ) *n. inf.* food

chow-chow *n.* thick-coated dog with curled tail, *orig.* from China (*also* **chow**)

chowder (ˈtʃaʊdə) *n. chiefly* **US** thick soup or stew containing clams or fish

chow mein (meɪn) Chinese-American dish, consisting of mushrooms, meat, shrimps *etc.*

chrism *or* **chrisom** (ˈkrɪzəm) *n.* mixture of olive oil and balsam used for sacramental anointing

Christ (kraɪst) *n.* **1.** Jesus of Nazareth, regarded by Christians as fulfilling Old Testament prophecies of Messiah **2.** Messiah as subject of Old Testament prophecies **3.** image of Christ —*interj.* **4.** *offens. sl.* oath expressing annoyance *etc.* (*see also* JESUS)

Christian (ˈkrɪstʃən) *n.* **1.** follower of Christ —*a.* **2.** following Christ **3.** relating to Christ or his religion **4.** exhibiting kindness or goodness —**christen** (ˈkrɪsᵊn) *vt.* baptise, give name to —**Christendom** (ˈkrɪsᵊndəm) *n.* all the Christian world —**Christiˈanity** *n.* religion of Christ —ˈ**christianize** *or* **-ise** *vt.* —**Christian name** name given at baptism —**Christian Science** religious system founded by Mrs. Eddy in U.S.A.

Christmas (ˈkrɪsməs) *n.* festival of birth of Christ —ˈ**Christmassy** *a.* —**Christmas box** tip, present given at Christmas —**Christmas card** —**Christmas rose** evergreen plant of S Europe and W Asia, with white or pinkish winter-blooming flowers (*also* ˈ**hellebore, winter rose**) —**Christmas tree**

Christy *or* **Christie** (ˈkrɪstɪ) *n. Skiing* turn in which body is swung sharply round with skis parallel

chromatic (krəˈmætɪk) *a.* **1.** of colour **2.** *Mus.* of scale proceeding by semitones

chromatin (ˈkrəʊmətɪn) *n.* part of protoplasmic sub-

THESAURUS

chivvy annoy, badger, harass, hassle (*Inf.*), hound, nag, pester, plague, pressure (*Inf.*), prod, torment

choice **1.** *n.* alternative, discrimination, election, option, pick, preference, say, selection, variety **2.** *adj.* best, dainty, elect, elite, excellent, exclusive, exquisite, hand-picked, nice, precious, prime, prize, rare, select, special, superior, uncommon, unusual, valuable

choke asphyxiate, bar, block, clog, close, congest, constrict, dam, obstruct, occlude, overpower, smother, stifle, stop, strangle, suffocate, suppress, throttle

choleric angry, bad-tempered, fiery, hasty, hot, hot-tempered, ill-tempered, irascible, irritable, passionate, petulant, quick-tempered, testy, touchy

choose adopt, cull, designate, desire, elect, espouse, fix on, opt for, pick, predestine, prefer, see fit, select, settle upon, single out, take, wish

choosy discriminating, exacting, faddy, fastidious, finicky, fussy, particular, selective

chop *v.* axe, cleave, cut, fell, hack, hew, lop, sever, shear, slash, truncate

choppy blustery, broken, rough, ruffled, squally, tempestuous

chore burden, duty, errand, fag (*Inf.*), job, task

chortle cackle, chuckle, crow, guffaw

chorus **1.** choir, choristers, ensemble, singers, vocalists **2.** burden, refrain, response, strain

christen baptize, call, designate, dub, name, style, term, title

stance in nucleus of cells which takes colour in staining tests

chromatography (krəʊmə'tɒgrəfɪ) *n.* technique of separating and analysing components of mixture by selective adsorption in column of powder or on strip of paper

chrome (krəʊm) *n.* metal used in alloys and for plating

chromosome ('krəʊməsəʊm) *n.* microscopic gene-carrying body in tissue of a cell

chromosphere ('krəʊməsfɪə) *n.* layer of incandescent gas surrounding the sun

Chron. *Bible* Chronicles

chronic ('krɒnɪk) *a.* **1.** lasting a long time **2.** habitual **3.** *inf.* serious **4.** *inf.* of bad quality

chronicle ('krɒnɪk°l) *n.* **1.** record of events in order of time **2.** account —*vt.* **3.** record —'**chronicler** *n.*

chronology (krə'nɒlədʒɪ) *n.* **1.** determination of sequence of past events **2.** arrangement in order of occurrence —**chrono'logical** *a.* arranged in order of time —**chrono'logically** *adv.* —**chro'nologist** *n.*

chronometer (krə'nɒmɪtə) *n.* **1.** instrument for measuring time exactly **2.** watch —**chrono'metrical** *a.* —**chro'nometry** *n.*

chrysalis ('krɪsəlɪs) *n.* **1.** resting state of insect between grub and butterfly *etc.* **2.** case enclosing it (*pl.* **-es, chrysalides** (krɪ'sælɪdiːz))

chrysanthemum (krɪ'sænθəməm) *n.* garden flower of various colours

chub (tʃʌb) *n.* **1.** European freshwater fish **2.** any of various N Amer. fishes, *esp.* whitefishes and minnows

chubby ('tʃʌbɪ) *a.* plump

chuck[1] (tʃʌk) *vt.* **1.** *inf.* throw **2.** pat affectionately (under chin) **3.** *inf.* give up, reject

chuck[2] (tʃʌk) *n.* **1.** cut of beef **2.** device for gripping, adjusting bit in power drill *etc.*

chuckle ('tʃʌk°l) *vi.* **1.** laugh softly —*n.* **2.** such laugh —'**chucklehead** *n. inf.* stupid person; blockhead; dolt

chuff[1] (tʃʌf) *n.* **1.** puffing sound as of steam engine —*vi.* **2.** move while emitting such sounds

chuff[2] (tʃʌf) *vt.* (*usu. as pp./a.* **chuffed**) **UK** *sl.* please, delight

chug (tʃʌg) *n.* **1.** short dull sound, such as that made by engine —*vi.* **2.** (of engine *etc.*) operate while making such sounds (**-gg-**)

chukker *or* **chukka** ('tʃʌkə) *n.* period of play in game of polo

chum (tʃʌm) *n. inf.* close friend —'**chummy** *a.*

chump (tʃʌmp) *n.* **1.** *inf.* stupid person **2.** heavy block of wood **3.** thick blunt end of anything, *esp.* meat **4. UK** *sl.* head (*esp. in* **off one's chump**)

chunk (tʃʌŋk) *n.* thick, solid piece —'**chunky** *a.*

church (tʃɜːtʃ) *n.* **1.** building for Christian worship **2.** (**C-**) whole body or sect of Christians **3.** clergy —'**churchman** *n.* —**Church of England** reformed state Church in England, with Sovereign as temporal head —**church'warden** *n.* **1.** officer who represents interests of parish **2.** long clay pipe —'**churchyard** *n.*

churl (tʃɜːl) *n.* **1.** rustic **2.** ill-bred fellow —'**churlish** *a.* —'**churlishly** *adv.* —'**churlishness** *n.*

churn (tʃɜːn) *n.* **1.** large container for milk **2.** vessel for making butter —*v.* **3.** shake up, stir (liquid) violently

chute (ʃuːt) *n.* **1.** slide for sending down parcels, coal *etc.* **2.** channel **3.** slide into swimming pool **4.** narrow passageway, *eg* for spraying, counting cattle, sheep *etc.* **5.** *inf.* parachute

chutney ('tʃʌtnɪ) *n.* pickle of fruit, spices *etc.*

chyle (kaɪl) *n.* milky fluid composed of lymph and emulsified fat globules, formed in small intestine during digestion

chyme (kaɪm) *n.* thick fluid mass of partially digested food that leaves stomach

C.I.A. **US** Central Intelligence Agency

cicada (sɪ'kɑːdə) *or* **cicala** *n.* cricketlike insect

cicatrix ('sɪkətrɪks) *n.* scar of healed wound —**cicatri'zation** *or* **-i'sation** *n.* —'**cicatrize** *or* **-ise** *v.* heal

cicely ('sɪsəlɪ) *n.* perennial plant similar to chervil, used as herb (*also* **sweet cicely**)

cicerone (sɪsə'rəʊnɪ, tʃɪtʃ-) *n.* person who conducts and informs sightseers (*pl.* **-s, -ni** (-nɪ))

C.I.D. Criminal Investigation Department

-cide (*n. comb. form*) **1.** person or thing that kills, as in *insecticide* **2.** killing; murder, as in *homicide* —**-cidal** (*a. comb. form*)

cider *or* **cyder** ('saɪdə) *n.* fermented drink made from apples

c.i.f. *or* **C.I.F.** cost, insurance and freight (included in price quoted)

cigar (sɪ'gɑː) *n.* roll of tobacco leaves for smoking —**ciga'rette** *n.* finely-cut tobacco rolled in paper for smoking —**cigarette card** small picture card, formerly given away with cigarettes, now collected as hobby

cilium ('sɪlɪəm) *n.* **1.** short thread projecting from

THESAURUS

chronic **1.** confirmed, deep-rooted, deep-seated, habitual, incessant, incurable, ineradicable, ingrained, inveterate, persistent **2.** *Inf.* appalling, atrocious, awful, dreadful

chronicle **1.** *n.* account, annals, diary, history, journal, narrative, record, register, story **2.** *v.* enter, narrate, put on record, record, recount, register, relate, report, set down, tell

chronicler annalist, diarist, historian, historiographer, narrator, recorder, reporter, scribe

chronological consecutive, historical, in sequence, ordered, progressive, sequential

chubby buxom, flabby, fleshy, plump, podgy, portly, rotund, round, stout, tubby

chuck cast, discard, fling, heave, hurl, pitch, shy, sling, throw, toss

chuckle chortle, crow, exult, giggle, laugh, snigger, titter

chum companion, comrade, crony, friend, mate (*Inf.*), pal (*Inf.*)

chunk block, dollop (*Inf.*), hunk, lump, mass, piece, portion, slab, wad, wodge (*Inf.*)

churlish boorish, brusque, crabbed, harsh, ill-tempered, impolite, loutish, morose, oafish, rude, sullen, surly, uncivil, unmannerly, vulgar

churlishness boorishness, crassness, crudeness, loutishness, oafishness, rudeness, surliness, uncouthness

churn agitate, beat, boil, convulse, foam, froth, seethe, stir up, swirl, toss

cigarette cancer stick (*Sl.*), ciggy (*Inf.*), coffin nail (*Sl.*), fag (*Sl.*), gasper (*Sl.*), smoke

surface of cell *etc.*, whose rhythmic beating causes movement **2.** eyelash (*pl.* **cilia** (ˈsɪlɪə)) —**ˈciliary** *a.* of cilia —**ˈciliate** *or* **ˈciliated** *a.* —**ciliary body** part of eye that joins choroid to iris

C in C *or* **C.-in-C.** Commander-in-Chief

cinch (sɪntʃ) *n. inf.* easy task, certainty

cinchona (sɪŋˈkəʊnə) *n.* **1.** tree or shrub of S Amer. having medicinal bark **2.** dried bark of this tree, which yields quinine **3.** any of drugs derived from cinchona bark

cincture (ˈsɪŋktʃə) *n.* something that encircles, *esp.* belt or girdle

cinder (ˈsɪndə) *n.* remains of burned coal

Cinderella (sɪndəˈrɛlə) *n.* **1.** girl who achieves fame after being obscure **2.** poor, neglected or unsuccessful person or thing

cine camera (ˈsɪnɪ) camera for taking moving pictures —**cine film**

cinema (ˈsɪnɪmə) *n.* **1.** building used for showing of films **2.** films generally or collectively —**cineˈmatograph** *n.* combined camera, printer and projector —**cinemaˈtography** *n.*

cineraria (sɪnəˈrɛərɪə) *n.* garden plant with daisylike flowers

cinerarium (sɪnəˈrɛərɪəm) *n.* place for keeping ashes of dead after cremation (*pl.* **-ria** (-rɪə))

cinerary (ˈsɪnərərɪ) *a.* pert. to ashes

cinnabar (ˈsɪnəbɑː) *n.* **1.** heavy red mineral consisting of mercuric sulphide: chief ore of mercury **2.** red form of mercuric sulphide, *esp.* when used as pigment **3.** bright red; vermilion **4.** large red-and-black European moth

cinnamon (ˈsɪnəmən) *n.* **1.** spice got from bark of Asian tree **2.** the tree —*a.* **3.** light-brown colour

cinque (sɪŋk) *n.* number five in cards, dice *etc.* —**ˈcinquefoil** *n.* plant with five-lobed leaves

cipher *or* **cypher** (ˈsaɪfə) *n.* **1.** secret writing **2.** arithmetical symbol **3.** person of no importance **4.** monogram —*vt.* **5.** write in cipher

circa (ˈsɜːkə) *Lat.* about, approximately

circadian (sɜːˈkeɪdɪən) *a.* of biological processes that occur at 24-hour intervals

circle (ˈsɜːkᵊl) *n.* **1.** perfectly round figure **2.** ring **3.** *Theat.* section of seats above main level of auditorium **4.** group, society with common interest **5.** spiritualist seance **6.** class of society —*vt.* **7.** surround —*vi.* **8.** move round —**ˈcircular** *a.* **1.** round **2.** moving round —*n.* **3.** letter sent to several persons —**circulariˈzation** *or* **-iˈsation** *n.* —**ˈcircularize** *or* **-ise** *vt.* **1.** distribute circulars to **2.** canvass or petition, as for votes *etc.* by distributing letters *etc.* **3.** make circular —**ˈcirculate** *vi.* **1.** move round **2.** pass from hand to hand or place to place —*vt.* **3.** send round —**circuˈlation** *n.* **1.** flow of blood from, and back to, heart **2.** act of moving round **3.** extent of sale of newspaper *etc.* —**ˈcirculatory** *a.* —**circular saw** saw in which circular disc with toothed edge is rotated at high speed —**circulating library 1.** *esp.* **US** lending library **2.** small library circulated in turn to group of institutions

circuit (ˈsɜːkɪt) *n.* **1.** complete round or course **2.** area **3.** path of electric current **4.** round of visitation, *esp.* of judges **5.** series of sporting events **6.** district —**circuitous** (səˈkjuːɪtəs) *a.* round about, indirect —**circuitously** (səˈkjuːɪtəslɪ) *adv.* —**ˈcircuitry** *n.* electrical circuit(s) —**circuit breaker** device that under abnormal conditions stops flow of current in electrical circuit

circum- (*comb. form*) around; surrounding; on all sides, as in *circumlocution, circumpolar.* Such compounds are not given here where the meaning may easily be found from the simple word

circumambient (sɜːkəmˈæmbɪənt) *a.* surrounding

circumcise (ˈsɜːkəmsaɪz) *vt.* cut off foreskin of —**circumˈcision** *n.*

circumference (səˈkʌmfərəns) *n.* boundary line, *esp.* of circle

circumflex (ˈsɜːkəmflɛks) *n.* **1.** mark (ˆ) placed over vowel to show it is pronounced with rising and falling pitch or as long vowel —*a.* **2.** (of nerves *etc.*) bending or curving around

circumlocution (sɜːkəmləˈkjuːʃən) *n.* roundabout speech

circumnavigate (sɜːkəmˈnævɪgeɪt) *vt.* sail or fly right round —**circumnaviˈgation** *n.* —**circumˈnavigator** *n.*

circumscribe (sɜːkəmˈskraɪb, ˈsɜːkəmskraɪb) *vt.* confine, bound, limit, hamper

circumspect (ˈsɜːkəmspɛkt) *a.* watchful, cautious, prudent —**circumˈspection** *n.* —**ˈcircumspectly** *adv.*

circumstance (ˈsɜːkəmstəns) *n.* **1.** detail **2.** event **3.** matter of fact —*pl.* **4.** state of affairs **5.** condition in life, *esp.* financial **6.** surroundings or things accompanying an action —**circumˈstantial** *a.* **1.** depending on detail or circumstances **2.** detailed, minute **3.** inciden-

THESAURUS

cinema big screen (*Inf.*), films, flicks (*Sl.*), motion pictures, movies, pictures

cipher 1. nobody, nonentity **2.** character, digit, figure, number, numeral, symbol **3.** code, cryptograph **4.** device, logo, mark, monogram

circle *n.* **1.** band, circumference, coil, cordon, cycle, disc, globe, lap, loop, orb, perimeter, periphery, revolution, ring, round, sphere, turn **2.** assembly, class, clique, club, company, coterie, crowd, fellowship, fraternity, group, school, set, society ~*v.* **3.** belt, circumnavigate, circumscribe, coil, compass, curve, encircle, enclose, encompass, envelop, gird, hem in, pivot, revolve, ring, rotate, surround, tour, whirl

circuit 1. area, compass, course, journey, orbit, perambulation, revolution, round, route, tour, track **2.** boundary, bounding line, bounds, circumference, compass, district, limit, range, region, tract

circuitous ambagious (*Archaic*), devious, indirect, labyrinthine, meandering, oblique, rambling, roundabout, tortuous, winding

circulate broadcast, diffuse, disseminate, distribute, issue, make known, promulgate, propagate, publicize, publish, spread

circulation 1. currency, dissemination, distribution, spread, transmission, vogue **2.** circling, flow, motion

circumference border, boundary, bounds, circuit, edge, extremity, fringe, limits, outline, perimeter, periphery, rim, verge

circumscribe bound, confine, define, delimit, delineate, demarcate, encircle, enclose, encompass, environ, hem in, limit, mark off, restrain, restrict, surround

circumspect attentive, canny, careful, cautious, deliberate, discreet, discriminating, guarded, heedful, judicious, observant, politic, prudent, sagacious, sage, vigilant, wary, watchful

tal —**circumstanti'ality** *n.* —**circum'stantially** *adv.* —**circum'stantiate** *vt.* **1.** prove by details **2.** describe exactly —**circumstantial evidence** indirect evidence that tends to establish conclusion by inference

circumvent (sɜːkəmˈvɛnt) *vt.* outwit, evade, get round —**circum'vention** *n.*

circus (ˈsɜːkəs) *n.* **1.** (performance of) travelling group of acrobats, clowns, performing animals *etc.* **2.** circular structure for public shows **3.** circular space in town where roads converge

cirque (sɜːk) *n.* steep-sided semicircular depression found in mountainous regions

cirrhosis (sɪˈrəʊsɪs) *n.* any of various chronic progressive diseases of liver —**cirrhotic** (sɪˈrɒtɪk) *a.*

cirrus (ˈsɪrəs) *n.* high wispy cloud (*pl.* **cirri** (ˈsɪraɪ)) —**cirro'cumulus** *n.* high cloud of ice crystals grouped into small separate globular masses (*pl.* **-li** (-laɪ)) —**cirro'stratus** *n.* uniform layer of cloud above about 6000 metres (*pl.* **-tai** (-taɪ))

cisalpine (sɪsˈælpaɪn) *a.* on this (southern) side of Alps, as viewed from Rome

cisco (ˈsɪskəʊ) *n.* N Amer. whitefish (*pl.* **-s, -es**)

cist (sɪst) *or* **kist** (kɪst) *n.* box-shaped burial chamber made from stone slabs or hollowed tree-trunk

Cistercian (sɪˈstɜːʃən) *n.* member of Christian order of monks and nuns, which follows strict form of Benedictine rule (*also* **White Monk**)

cistern (ˈsɪstən) *n.* water tank

cistus (ˈsɪstəs) *n.* any of various shrubs or herbaceous plants cultivated for yellow-white or reddish roselike flowers (*also* **'rockrose**)

citadel (ˈsɪtədˀl, -dɛl) *n.* fortress in, near or commanding a city

cite (saɪt) *vt.* **1.** quote **2.** bring forward as proof **3.** commend (soldier *etc.*) for outstanding bravery *etc.* **4.** summon to appear before court of law —**ci'tation** *n.* **1.** quoting **2.** commendation for bravery *etc.*

cithara (ˈsɪθərə) *or* **kithara** (ˈkɪθərə) *n.* stringed musical instrument of ancient Greece, similar to lyre

citizen (ˈsɪtɪzˀn) *n.* **1.** native, naturalized member of state, nation *etc.* **2.** inhabitant of city —**'citizenry** *n.* citizens collectively —**'citizenship** *n.* —**Citizens' Band** range of radio frequencies assigned officially for use by public for private communication

citron (ˈsɪtrən) *n.* **1.** fruit like a lemon **2.** the tree —**'citric** *a.* of the acid of lemon or citron —**citrus fruit** citrons, lemons, limes, oranges *etc.*

citronella (sɪtrəˈnɛlə) *n.* **1.** tropical Asian grass with bluish-green lemon-scented leaves **2.** aromatic oil obtained from this grass, used in perfumes *etc.* (*also* **citronella oil**)

cittern (ˈsɪtɜːn), **cither** (ˈsɪθə), *or* **cithern** (ˈsɪθən) *n.* medieval stringed instrument resembling lute but having wire strings and flat back

city (ˈsɪtɪ) *n.* large town —**city editor** (on newspaper) **1. UK** editor in charge of financial and commercial news **2. US** editor in charge of local news —**city father** person who is prominent in public affairs of city —**the City 1.** area in central London where United Kingdom's major financial business is transacted **2.** financial institutions located in this area

civet (ˈsɪvɪt) *n.* strong, musky perfume —**civet-cat** *n.* catlike animal producing it

civic (ˈsɪvɪk) *a.* pert. to city or citizen —**'civics** *pl.n.* (*with sing. v.*) study of the rights and responsibilities of citizenship —**civic centre UK** public buildings of town, including recreational facilities and offices of local administration

civil (ˈsɪvˀl) *a.* **1.** relating to citizens of state **2.** not military **3.** refined, polite **4.** *Law* not criminal —**ci'vilian** *n.* nonmilitary person —**ci'vility** *n.* —**'civilly** *adv.* —**civil defence** organizing of civilians to deal with enemy attacks —**civil disobedience** refusal to obey laws, pay taxes *etc.*: nonviolent means of protesting —**civil engineer** person qualified to design and construct roads, bridges *etc.* —**civil engineering** —**civil law 1.** law of state relating to private affairs **2.** body of law in ancient Rome, *esp.* as applicable to private citizens **3.** law based on Roman system —**civil liberty** right of individual to freedom of speech and action —**civil marriage** *Law* marriage performed by official other than clergyman —**civil rights** *pl.n.* **1.** personal rights of individual citizen —*a.* **2.** of equality in social, economic and political rights —**civil service** service responsible for public administration of government of a country —**civil war** war between factions within same nation

civilize *or* **-ise** (ˈsɪvɪlaɪz) *vt.* **1.** bring out of barbarism **2.** refine —**civili'zation** *or* **-i'sation** *n.* —**'civilized** *or* **-ised** *a.*

THESAURUS

circumstance condition, contingency, detail, element, event, fact, factor, happening, incident, item, occurrence, particular, position, respect, situation

circumstances life style, means, position, resources, situation, state, state of affairs, station, status, times

circumstantial conjectural, contingent, detailed, founded on circumstances, hearsay, incidental, indirect, inferential, particular, presumptive, provisional, specific

cistern basin, reservoir, sink, tank, vat

citadel bastion, fastness, fortification, fortress, keep, stronghold, tower

citation 1. excerpt, illustration, passage, quotation, quote, reference, source **2.** award, commendation, mention

cite 1. adduce, advance, allude to, enumerate, evidence, extract, mention, name, quote, specify **2.** *Law* call, subpoena, summon

citizen burgess, burgher, denizen, dweller, freeman, inhabitant, ratepayer, resident, subject, townsman

city conurbation, megalopolis, metropolis, municipality

civic borough, communal, community, local, municipal, public

civil 1. civic, domestic, home, interior, municipal, political **2.** accommodating, affable, civilized, complaisant, courteous, courtly, obliging, polished, polite, refined, urbane, well-bred, well-mannered

civilization advancement, cultivation, culture, development, education, enlightenment, progress, refinement, sophistication

civilize cultivate, educate, enlighten, humanize, improve, polish, refine, sophisticate, tame

civilized cultured, educated, enlightened, humane, polite, sophisticated, tolerant, urbane

civvy (ˈsɪvɪ) *sl. n.* **1.** civilian —*pl.* **2.** civilian clothing —**civvy street** civilian life

cl centilitre

Cl *Chem.* chlorine

clack (klæk) *n.* **1.** sound, as of two pieces of wood striking together —*v.* **2.** make such sound **3.** jabber

clad (klæd) *pt./pp. of* **clothe** (*see* CLOTH)

cladding (ˈklædɪŋ) *n.* material used for outside facing of building *etc.*

claim (kleɪm) *vt.* **1.** demand as right **2.** assert **3.** call for —*n.* **4.** demand for thing supposed due **5.** right **6.** thing claimed **7.** plot of mining land marked out by stakes as required by law —ˈ**claimant** *n.*

clairvoyance (klɛəˈvɔɪəns) *n.* power of seeing things not present to senses, second sight —**clairˈvoyant** *n./a.*

clam (klæm) *n.* edible mollusc

clamber (ˈklæmbə) *vi.* climb with difficulty or awkwardly

clammy (ˈklæmɪ) *a.* moist and sticky —ˈ**clamminess** *n.*

clamour *or U.S.* **clamor** (ˈklæmə) *n.* **1.** loud shouting, outcry, noise —*vi.* **2.** shout, call noisily —ˈ**clamorous** *a.* —ˈ**clamorously** *adv.*

clamp[1] (klæmp) *n.* **1.** tool for holding or compressing —*vt.* **2.** fasten, strengthen with or as with clamp

clamp[2] (klæmp) *n.* **1.** mound of harvested root crop, covered with straw and earth to protect it from winter weather —*vt.* **2.** enclose in mound

clan (klæn) *n.* **1.** tribe or collection of families under chief and of common ancestry **2.** faction, group —ˈ**clannish** *a.* —ˈ**clannishly** *adv.* —ˈ**clannishness** *n.*

clandestine (klænˈdɛstɪn) *a.* **1.** secret **2.** sly

clang (klæŋ) *v.* **1.** (cause to) make loud ringing sound —*n.* **2.** loud ringing sound —ˈ**clanger** *n.* **1.** *inf.* conspicuous mistake **2.** that which clangs

clangor *or* **clangour** (ˈklæŋgə, ˈklæŋə) *n.* **1.** loud resonant noise **2.** uproar —*vi.* **3.** make loud resonant noise —ˈ**clangorous** *or* ˈ**clangourous** *a.*

clank (klæŋk) *n.* **1.** short sound as of pieces of metal struck together —*v.* **2.** cause, move with, such sound

clap[1] (klæp) *v.* **1.** (cause to) strike with noise **2.** strike (hands) together **3.** applaud —*vt.* **4.** pat **5.** place or put quickly (-pp-) —*n.* **6.** hard, explosive sound **7.** slap —ˈ**clapper** *n.* —ˈ**clapping** *n.* —ˈ**claptrap** *n. inf.* empty words

clap[2] (klæp) *n. sl.* gonorrhoea

claque (klæk) *n.* **1.** group of people hired to applaud **2.** group of fawning admirers

claret (ˈklærət) *n.* a dry dark red wine of Bordeaux

clarify (ˈklærɪfaɪ) *v.* make or become clear, pure or more easily understood (**-fied, -fying**) —**clarifiˈcation** *n.* —ˈ**clarity** *n.* clearness

clarinet (klærɪˈnɛt) *n.* woodwind musical instrument

clarion (ˈklærɪən) *n.* **1.** clear-sounding trumpet **2.** rousing sound

clary (ˈklɛərɪ) *n.* herb

clash (klæʃ) *n.* **1.** loud noise, as of weapons striking **2.** conflict, collision —*vi.* **3.** make clash **4.** come into conflict **5.** (of events) coincide **6.** (of colours) look ugly together —*vt.* **7.** strike together to make clash

clasp (klɑːsp) *n.* **1.** hook or other means of fastening **2.** embrace —*vt.* **3.** fasten **4.** embrace, grasp —**clasp knife**

class (klɑːs) *n.* **1.** any division, order, kind, sort **2.** rank **3.** group of school pupils *etc.* taught together **4.** division by merit **5.** quality **6.** *inf.* excellence; elegance —*vt.* **7.** assign to proper division —**classifiˈcation** *n.* —ˈ**classified** *a.* **1.** arranged in classes **2.** secret **3.** (of advertisements) arranged under headings in newspapers —ˈ**classify** *vt.* arrange methodically in classes (**-fied, -fying**) —ˈ**classy** *a. inf.* stylish, elegant —**class-conscious** *a.* aware of belonging to particular social rank —**class-consciousness** *n.*

classic (ˈklæsɪk) *a.* **1.** of first rank **2.** of highest rank generally, but *esp.* of art **3.** refined **4.** typical **5.** famous —*n.* **6.** (literary) work of recognized excellence —*pl.* **7.** ancient Latin and Greek literature —ˈ**classical** *a.* **1.** of Greek and Roman literature, art, culture **2.** of classic

THESAURUS

claim 1. *v.* allege, ask, assert, call for, challenge, collect, demand, exact, hold, insist, maintain, need, pick up, profess, require, take, uphold **2.** *n.* affirmation, allegation, application, assertion, call, demand, petition, pretension, privilege, protestation, request, requirement, right, title

clamber claw, climb, scale, scrabble, scramble, shin

clamour agitation, babel, blare, brouhaha, commotion, din, exclamation, hubbub, hullabaloo, noise, outcry, racket, shout, shouting, uproar, vociferation

clamp 1. *n.* bracket, fastener, grip, press, vice **2.** *v.* brace, clinch, fasten, fix, impose, make fast, secure

clan band, brotherhood, clique, coterie, faction, family, fraternity, gens, group, house, race, sect, sept, set, society, sodality, tribe

clang 1. *v.* bong, chime, clank, clash, jangle, resound, reverberate, ring, toll **2.** *n.* clangour, ding-dong, knell, reverberation

clap 1. acclaim, applaud, cheer **2.** bang, pat, slap, strike gently, thrust, thwack, wallop (*Inf.*), whack

claptrap affectation, blarney, bombast, bunk (*Inf.*), drivel, flannel (*Inf.*), guff (*Sl.*), hot air (*Inf.*), humbug, insincerity, nonsense, rodomontade, rubbish

clarification elucidation, explanation, exposition, illumination, interpretation, simplification

clarify 1. clear up, elucidate, explain, illuminate, make plain, resolve, simplify, throw *or* shed light on **2.** cleanse, purify, refine

clarity clearness, comprehensibility, definition, explicitness, intelligibility, limpidity, lucidity, obviousness, precision, simplicity, transparency

clash *v.* **1.** bang, clang, clank, clatter, crash, jangle, jar, rattle **2.** conflict, cross swords, feud, grapple, quarrel, war, wrangle ~*n.* **3.** brush, collision, conflict, confrontation, difference of opinion, disagreement, fight, showdown (*Inf.*)

clasp *v.* **1.** clutch, concatenate, connect, embrace, enfold, fasten, grapple, grasp, grip, hold, hug, press, seize, squeeze ~*n.* **2.** brooch, buckle, catch, clip, fastener, fastening, grip, hasp, hook, pin, snap **3.** embrace, grasp, grip, hold, hug

class 1. *n.* caste, category, classification, collection, denomination, department, division, genre, genus, grade, group, grouping, kind, league, order, rank, set, sort, species, sphere, status, type, value **2.** *v.* brand, categorize, classify, codify, designate, grade, group, rank, rate quality **3.** *Mus.* of established standards of form, complexity *etc.* —ˈ**classically** *adv.* —ˈ**classicism** *n.* —ˈ**classicist** *n.*

clatter (ˈklætə) *n.* **1.** rattling noise **2.** noisy conversation —*v.* **3.** (cause to) make clatter

clause (klɔːz) *n.* **1.** part of sentence, containing verb **2.** article in formal document as treaty, contract *etc.*

claustrophobia (klɔːstrəˈfəʊbɪə, klɒs-) *n.* abnormal fear of confined spaces

clavichord (ˈklævɪkɔːd) *n.* musical instrument with keyboard, forerunner of piano

clavicle (ˈklævɪkəl) *n.* collarbone —**claˈvicular** *a.* pert. to this

clavier (kləˈvɪə, ˈklævɪə) *n.* keyboard instrument; keyboard

claw (klɔː) *n.* **1.** sharp hooked nail of bird or beast **2.** foot of bird of prey **3.** clawlike article —*vt.* **4.** tear with claws **5.** grip

clay (kleɪ) *n.* **1.** fine-grained earth, plastic when wet, hardening when baked **2.** earth —ˈ**clayey** *a.* —**clay pigeon** disc of baked clay hurled into air as target to be shot at

claymore (ˈkleɪmɔː) *n.* ancient Highland two-edged sword

CLC Canadian Labour Congress

clean (kliːn) *a.* **1.** free from dirt, stain or defilement **2.** pure **3.** guiltless **4.** trim, shapely —*adv.* **5.** so as to leave no dirt **6.** entirely —*vt.* **7.** free from dirt —ˈ**cleaner** *n.* —**cleanliness** (ˈklɛnlɪnɪs) *n.* —**cleanly** (ˈkliːnlɪ) *adv.* **1.** in a clean manner —*a.* (ˈklɛnlɪ) **2.** clean —ˈ**cleanness** *n.* —**cleanse** (klɛnz) *vt.* make clean —**clean-cut** *a.* **1.** clearly outlined; neat **2.** definite —**come clean** *inf.* confess

clear (klɪə) *a.* **1.** pure, undimmed, bright **2.** free from cloud **3.** transparent **4.** plain, distinct **5.** without defect or drawback **6.** unimpeded —*adv.* **7.** brightly **8.** wholly, quite —*vt.* **9.** make clear **10.** acquit **11.** pass over or through **12.** make as profit **13.** free from obstruction, difficulty **14.** free by payment of dues —*vi.* **15.** become clear, bright, free, transparent —ˈ**clearance** *n.* **1.** making clear **2.** removal of obstructions, surplus stock *etc.* **3.** certificate that ship has been cleared at custom house **4.** space for moving part, vehicle, to pass within, through or past something —ˈ**clearing** *n.* land cleared of trees —ˈ**clearly** *adv.* —ˈ**clearness** *n.* —**clear-cut** *a.* **1.** definite; not vague **2.** clearly outlined —**clearing bank UK** bank that makes use of central clearing house in London —**clearing house 1.** *Banking* institution where cheques *etc.* drawn on member banks are cancelled against each other **2.** central agency for collection and distribution of information —**clear-sighted** *a.* discerning —ˈ**clearway** *n.* stretch of road on which motorists may stop only in an emergency

clearstory (ˈklɪəstɔːrɪ) *n.* *see* CLERESTORY

cleat (kliːt) *n.* **1.** wedge **2.** piece of wood or iron with two projecting ends round which ropes are made fast

cleave[1] (kliːv) *vt.* **1.** split asunder —*vi.* **2.** crack, part asunder (**clove, cleft** *pt.*, ˈ**cloven, cleft** *pp.*, ˈ**cleaving** *pr.p.*) —ˈ**cleavage** *n.* —ˈ**cleaver** *n.* short chopper

cleave[2] (kliːv) *vi.* **1.** stick, adhere **2.** be loyal (**cleaved,** ˈ**cleaving**)

THESAURUS

classic *adj.* **1.** best, consummate, finest, first-rate, masterly **2.** archetypal, definitive, exemplary, ideal, master, model, paradigmatic, quintessential, standard **3.** characteristic, regular, standard, time-honoured, typical, usual ~*n.* **4.** exemplar, masterpiece, masterwork, model, paradigm, prototype, standard

classical 1. elegant, harmonious, pure, refined, restrained, symmetrical, understated, well-proportioned **2.** Attic, Augustan, Grecian, Greek, Hellenic, Latin, Roman

classification analysis, arrangement, cataloguing, categorization, codification, grading, sorting, taxonomy

classify arrange, catalogue, categorize, codify, dispose, distribute, file, grade, pigeonhole, rank, sort, systematize, tabulate

clause 1. article, chapter, condition, paragraph, part, passage, section **2.** heading, item, point, provision, proviso, specification, stipulation

claw 1. *n.* nail, nipper, pincer, talon, tentacle, unguis **2.** *v.* dig, graze, lacerate, mangle, maul, rip, scrabble, scrape, scratch, tear

clean *adj.* **1.** faultless, flawless, fresh, hygienic, immaculate, laundered, pure, sanitary, spotless, unblemished, unsoiled, unspotted, unstained, unsullied, washed **2.** antiseptic, clarified, decontaminated, natural, purified, sterile, sterilized, unadulterated, uncontaminated, unpolluted **3.** chaste, decent, exemplary, good, honourable, innocent, moral, pure, respectable, undefiled, upright, virtuous **4.** delicate, elegant, graceful, neat, simple, tidy, trim, uncluttered ~*v.* **5.** bath, cleanse, deodorize, disinfect, do up, dust, launder, lave, mop, purge, purify, rinse, sanitize, scour, scrub, sponge, swab, sweep, vacuum, wash, wipe

clean-cut chiselled, clear, definite, etched, neat, outlined, sharp, trim, well-defined

cleanse absolve, clean, clear, lustrate, purge, purify, rinse, scour, scrub, wash

clear *adj.* **1.** bright, cloudless, fair, fine, halcyon, light, luminous, shining, sunny, unclouded, undimmed **2.** apparent, audible, coherent, comprehensible, conspicuous, definite, distinct, evident, explicit, express, incontrovertible, intelligible, lucid, manifest, obvious, palpable, patent, perceptible, plain, pronounced, recognizable, unambiguous, unequivocal, unmistakable, unquestionable **3.** empty, free, open, smooth, unhampered, unhindered, unimpeded, unlimited, unobstructed **4.** crystalline, glassy, limpid, pellucid, see-through, transparent ~*v.* **5.** clean, cleanse, erase, purify, refine, sweep away, tidy (up), wipe **6.** break up, brighten, clarify, lighten **7.** absolve, acquit, excuse, exonerate, justify, vindicate **8.** emancipate, free, liberate, set free **9.** disengage, disentangle, extricate, free, loosen, open, rid, unblock, unclog, unload, unpack **10.** jump, leap, miss, pass over, vault **11.** acquire, earn, gain, make, reap, secure

clearance allowance, gap, headroom, margin

clear-cut definite, explicit, plain, precise, specific, straightforward, unambiguous, unequivocal

clearly beyond doubt, distinctly, evidently, incontestably, incontrovertibly, markedly, obviously, openly, seemingly, undeniably, undoubtedly

cleave crack, dissever, disunite, divide, hew, open, part, rend, rive, sever, slice, split, sunder, tear asunder

clef (klɛf) *n. Mus.* mark to show pitch of stave

cleft (klɛft) *n.* **1.** crack, fissure, chasm **2.** opening made by cleaving —*v.* **3.** *pt./pp. of* CLEAVE[1] —**cleft palate** congenital fissure in midline of hard palate, oft. associated with harelip —**cleft stick** situation involving choice between two equally unsatisfactory alternatives

cleg (klɛg) *n.* horsefly

clematis (ˈklɛmətɪs) *n.* flowering climbing perennial plant

clement (ˈklɛmənt) *a.* **1.** merciful **2.** gentle **3.** mild —ˈ**clemency** *n.* —ˈ**clemently** *adv.*

clench (klɛntʃ) *vt.* **1.** set firmly together **2.** grasp, close (fist)

clerestory *or* **clearstory** (ˈklɪəstɔːrɪ) *n.* **1.** row of windows in upper part of wall of church that divides nave from aisle **2.** part of wall in which these windows are set —ˈ**clerestoried** *or* ˈ**clearstoried** *a.*

clergy (ˈklɜːdʒɪ) *n.* body of appointed ministers of Christian Church —ˈ**clergyman** *n.*

clerical (ˈklɛrɪkˀl) *a.* **1.** of clergy **2.** of, connected with, office work —ˈ**cleric** *n.* clergyman —ˈ**clericalism** *n.*

clerk (klɑːk; *U.S.* klɜːrk) *n.* **1.** subordinate who keeps files *etc.* in an office **2.** officer in charge of records, correspondence *etc.*, of department or corporation **3.** US shop assistant —ˈ**clerkly** *a.* —ˈ**clerkship** *n.* —**clerk of the works** employee who supervises building work

clever (ˈklɛvə) *a.* **1.** intelligent **2.** able, skilful, adroit —ˈ**cleverly** *adv.* —ˈ**cleverness** *n.*

clew (kluː) *n.* **1.** ball of thread or yarn **2.** *Naut.* lower corner of sail —*vt.* **3.** coil into ball

cliché (ˈkliːʃeɪ) *n.* stereotyped hackneyed phrase

click[1] (klɪk) *n.* **1.** short, sharp sound, as of latch in door **2.** catch —*v.* **3.** (cause to) make short, sharp sound

click[2] (klɪk) *vi.* **1.** *sl.* be a success **2.** *inf.* become clear **3.** *inf.* strike up friendship

client (ˈklaɪənt) *n.* **1.** customer **2.** one who employs professional person —**clientele** (kliːɒnˈtɛl) *n.* body of clients

cliff (klɪf) *n.* steep rock face —ˈ**cliffhanger** *n.* tense situation, *esp.* in film *etc.*

climacteric (klaɪˈmæktərɪk, klaɪmækˈtɛrɪk) *n.* **1.** critical event or period **2.** *see* MENOPAUSE **3.** period in life of man corresponding to menopause, characterized by diminished sexual activity —*a.* (*also* **climacˈterical**) **4.** involving crucial event or period

climate (ˈklaɪmɪt) *n.* **1.** condition of country with regard to weather **2.** prevailing feeling, atmosphere —**cliˈmatic** *a.* of climate

climax (ˈklaɪmæks) *n.* **1.** highest point, culmination **2.** point of greatest excitement, tension in story *etc.* —**cliˈmactic** *a.*

climb (klaɪm) *v.* **1.** go up or ascend **2.** progress with difficulty **3.** creep up, mount **4.** slope upwards —ˈ**climber** *n.* —ˈ**climbing** *n.*

clime (klaɪm) *n.* **1.** region, country **2.** climate

clinch (klɪntʃ) *vt.* **1.** *see* CLENCH **2.** settle, conclude (an agreement) —ˈ**clincher** *n. inf.* something decisive

cling (klɪŋ) *vi.* **1.** adhere **2.** be firmly attached **3.** be dependent (on) (**clung** *pt./pp.*)

Clingfilm (ˈklɪŋfɪlm) *n.* **R** thin polythene material having power to adhere closely: used for wrapping food

clinic (ˈklɪnɪk) *n.* place for medical examination, advice or treatment —ˈ**clinical** *a.* **1.** relating to clinic, care of sick *etc.* **2.** objective, unemotional **3.** bare, plain —ˈ**clinically** *adv.* —**clinical thermometer** thermometer used for taking body temperature

clink[1] (klɪŋk) *n.* **1.** sharp metallic sound —*v.* **2.** (cause to) make this sound

clink[2] (klɪŋk) *n. sl.* prison

clinker (ˈklɪŋkə) *n.* **1.** fused coal residues from fire or furnace **2.** hard brick

clinker-built *or* **clincher-built** *a.* (of boat) with outer boards or plates overlapping

THESAURUS

clergy churchmen, clergymen, clerics, ecclesiastics, first estate, holy orders, ministry, priesthood, the cloth

clergyman chaplain, cleric, curate, divine, father, man of God, man of the cloth, minister, padre, parson, pastor, priest, rabbi, rector, reverend (*Inf.*), vicar

clerical **1.** ecclesiastical, pastoral, priestly, sacerdotal **2.** book-keeping, clerkish, clerkly, office, secretarial, stenographic

clever able, adroit, apt, astute, brainy (*Inf.*), bright, canny, capable, cunning, deep, dexterous, discerning, expert, gifted, ingenious, intelligent, inventive, keen, knowing, knowledgeable, quick, quick-witted, rational, resourceful, sagacious, sensible, shrewd, skilful, smart, talented, witty

cleverness ability, adroitness, astuteness, brains, brightness, canniness, dexterity, flair, gift, gumption (*Inf.*), ingenuity, intelligence, nous (*Sl.*), quickness, quick wits, resourcefulness, sagacity, sense, sharpness, shrewdness, smartness, talent, wit

cliché banality, bromide, chestnut (*Inf.*), commonplace, hackneyed phrase, old saw, platitude, stereotype, truism

click *n./v.* **1.** beat, clack, snap, tick ~*v.* **2.** *Inf.* become clear, come home (to), fall into place, make sense **3.** *Sl.* be compatible, be on the same wavelength, feel a rapport, get on, go over (*Inf.*), hit it off (*Inf.*), make a hit, succeed, take to each other

client applicant, buyer, consumer, customer, dependant, habitué, patient, protégé, shopper

clientele business, clients, customers, following, market, patronage, regulars, trade

cliff bluff, crag, escarpment, face, overhang, precipice, rock face, scar, scarp

climactic climactical, critical, crucial, decisive, paramount, peak

climate **1.** clime, country, region, temperature, weather **2.** ambience, disposition, feeling, mood, temper, tendency, trend

climax acme, apogee, culmination, head, height, highlight, high spot (*Inf.*), *ne plus ultra*, pay-off (*Inf.*), peak, summit, top, zenith

climb ascend, clamber, mount, rise, scale, shin up, soar, top

clinch **1.** assure, cap, conclude, confirm, decide, determine, seal, secure, set the seal on, settle, sew up (*Inf.*), verify **2.** bolt, clamp, fasten, fix, make fast, nail, rivet, secure

cling adhere, attach to, be true to, clasp, cleave to, clutch, embrace, fasten, grasp, grip, hug, stick, twine round

clip[1] (klɪp) *vt.* **1.** cut with scissors **2.** cut short (**-pp-**) —*n.* **3.** *inf.* sharp blow —**ˈclipper** *n.* —**ˈclipping** *n.* something cut out, *esp.* article from newspaper; cutting —**clip joint** *sl.* nightclub *etc.* in which customers are overcharged

clip[2] (klɪp) *n.* device for gripping or holding together, *esp.* hair, clothing *etc.* —**ˈclipboard** *n.* portable writing board with clip at top for holding paper

clipper (ˈklɪpə) *n.* fast sailing ship

clippie (ˈklɪpɪ) *n.* **UK** *inf.* bus conductress

clique (kliːk, klɪk) *n.* **1.** small exclusive set **2.** faction, group of people —**ˈcliquish** *a.*

clitoris (ˈklɪtərɪs, ˈklaɪ-) *n.* small erectile part of female genitals

cloak (kləʊk) *n.* **1.** loose outer garment **2.** disguise, pretext —*vt.* **3.** cover with cloak **4.** disguise, conceal —**cloak-and-dagger** *a.* concerned with intrigue and espionage —**ˈcloakroom** *n.* place for keeping coats, hats, luggage

clobber (ˈklɒbə) *inf. vt.* **1.** beat, batter **2.** defeat utterly —*n.* **3.** belongings

cloche (klɒʃ) *n.* **1.** cover to protect young plants **2.** woman's close-fitting hat

clock (klɒk) *n.* **1.** instrument for measuring time **2.** device with dial for recording or measuring —**ˈclockwise** *adv./a.* in the direction that the hands of a clock rotate —**ˈclockwork** *n.* mechanism similar to that of a clock, as in a wind-up toy —**clock in** *or* **on, out** *or* **off** record arrival or departure on automatic time recorder

clod (klɒd) *n.* **1.** lump of earth **2.** blockhead —**ˈcloddish** *a.* —**ˈclodhopper** *n. inf.* **1.** clumsy person; lout **2.** (*usu. pl.*) large heavy shoe

clog (klɒg) *vt.* **1.** hamper, impede, choke up (**-gg-**) —*n.* **2.** obstruction, impediment **3.** wooden-soled shoe —**clog dance**

cloisonné (klwɑːˈzɒneɪ) *n.* **1.** enamel decoration in compartments formed by small fillets of metal —*a.* **2.** of cloisonné

cloister (ˈklɔɪstə) *n.* **1.** covered pillared arcade **2.** monastery or convent —**ˈcloistered** *a.* confined, secluded, sheltered

clomp (klɒmp) *n. see* CLUMP[2]

clone (kləʊn) *n.* **1.** group of organisms, cells of same genetic constitution as another, derived by asexual reproduction, as graft of plant *etc.* —*v.* **2.** (cause to) produce clone

clop (klɒp) *vi.* move, sound, as horse's hooves (**-pp-**)

close[1] (kləʊs) *a.* **1.** adjacent, near **2.** compact **3.** crowded **4.** affectionate, intimate **5.** almost equal **6.** careful, searching **7.** confined **8.** secret **9.** unventilated, stifling **10.** reticent **11.** niggardly **12.** strict, restricted —*adv.* **13.** nearly **14.** tightly —*n.* **15.** shut-in place **16.** precinct of cathedral —**ˈclosely** *adv.* —**ˈcloseness** *n.* —**close-fisted** *a.* **1.** mean **2.** avaricious —**close harmony** singing in which all parts except bass lie close together —**close quarters** cramped space or position —**close season** time when it is illegal to kill certain kinds of game and fish —**close shave** *inf.* narrow escape —**ˈcloseup** *n.* close view, *esp.* portion of cinema film —**at close quarters** engaged in hand-to-hand combat; in close proximity; very near together

close[2] (kləʊz) *vt.* **1.** shut **2.** stop up **3.** prevent access to **4.** finish —*vi.* **5.** come together **6.** grapple —*n.* **7.** end —**closed circuit** complete electrical circuit through which current can flow —**closed shop** place of work in which all workers must belong to a trade union

closet (ˈklɒzɪt) *n.* **1.** **US** cupboard **2.** small private room **3.** water closet, lavatory —*a.* **4.** **US** private, secret —*vt.* **5.** shut up in private room, *esp.* for conference **6.** conceal

closure (ˈkləʊʒə) *n.* **1.** act of closing **2.** ending of debate by majority vote or other authority

clot (klɒt) *n.* **1.** mass or lump **2.** *inf.* fool **3.** *Med.* coagulated mass of blood —*vt.* **4.** form into lumps —*vi.* **5.** coagulate (**-tt-**)

cloth (klɒθ) *n.* woven fabric —**clothe** (kləʊð) *vt.* put clothes on (**clothed** *or* **clad** *pt./pp.*) —**clothes** (kləʊðz) *pl.n.* **1.** dress **2.** bed coverings —**clothier** (ˈkləʊðɪə) *n.* —**clothing** (ˈkləʊðɪŋ) *n.* —**clotheshorse** (ˈkləʊðzhɔːs) *n.* **1.** frame on which to hang laundry for drying or airing **2.** *inf.* excessively fashionable person

THESAURUS

clip **1.** *v.* crop, curtail, cut, cut short, pare, prune, shear, shorten, snip, trim **2.** *n. Inf.* blow, box, clout (*Inf.*), cuff, knock, punch, skelp (*Dialect*), smack, thump, wallop (*Inf.*), whack

clique circle, clan, coterie, crew (*Inf.*), crowd, faction, gang, group, mob, pack, set

cloak **1.** *v.* camouflage, conceal, cover, disguise, hide, mask, obscure, screen, veil **2.** *n.* blind, cape, coat, cover, front, mantle, mask, pretext, shield, wrap

clog **1.** *v.* block, burden, congest, dam up, hamper, hinder, impede, jam, obstruct, occlude, shackle, stop up **2.** *n.* burden, dead weight, drag, encumbrance, hindrance, impediment, obstruction

cloistered cloistral, confined, hermitic, insulated, reclusive, restricted, secluded, sequestered, sheltered, shielded, shut off, withdrawn

close[1] *adj.* **1.** adjacent, adjoining, approaching, at hand, handy, hard by, imminent, impending, near, nearby, neighbouring, nigh **2.** compact, congested, cramped, cropped, crowded, dense, impenetrable, jam-packed, packed, short, solid, thick, tight **3.** accurate, conscientious, exact, faithful, literal, precise, strict **4.** alert, assiduous, attentive, careful, concentrated, detailed, dogged, earnest, fixed, intense, intent, keen, minute, painstaking, rigorous, searching, thorough **5.** attached, confidential, dear, devoted, familiar, inseparable, intimate, loving **6.** airless, confined, frowsty, fuggy, heavy, humid, muggy, oppressive, stale, stifling, stuffy, suffocating, sweltering, thick, unventilated **7.** hidden, private, reticent, retired, secluded, secret, secretive, taciturn, uncommunicative, unforthcoming **8.** illiberal, mean, mingy (*Inf.*), miserly, near, niggardly, parsimonious, penurious, stingy, tight-fisted, ungenerous

close[2] *v.* **1.** bar, block, choke, clog, confine, cork, fill, lock, obstruct, plug, seal, secure, shut, shut up, stop up **2.** cease, complete, conclude, culminate, discontinue, end, finish, mothball, shut down, terminate, wind up (*Inf.*) **3.** come together, connect, couple, fuse, grapple, join, unite ~*n.* **4.** cessation, completion, conclusion, culmination, denouement, end, ending, finale, finish, termination

cloth dry goods, fabric, material, stuff, textiles

clothe accoutre, apparel, array, attire, bedizen (*Archaic*), caparison, cover, deck, doll up (*Sl.*), drape,

cloud (klaʊd) *n.* **1.** condensed water vapour floating in air **2.** state of gloom **3.** multitude —*vt.* **4.** overshadow, dim, darken —*vi.* **5.** become cloudy —**'cloudless** *a.* —**'cloudy** *a.* —**'cloudburst** *n.* heavy downpour

clout (klaʊt) *n.* **1.** *inf.* blow **2.** short, flat-headed nail **3.** influence, power —*vt.* **4.** *inf.* strike

clove[1] (kləʊv) *n.* **1.** dried flower bud of tropical tree, used as spice **2.** one of small bulbs making up compound bulb

clove[2] (kləʊv) *pt. of* CLEAVE[1] —**'cloven** *pp. of* CLEAVE[1] —**cloven hoof** *or* **foot 1.** divided hoof of cow, deer *etc.* **2.** symbol of Satan

clove hitch knot for securing rope to spar, post or larger rope

clover ('kləʊvə) *n.* low-growing forage plant, trefoil —**'cloverleaf** *n.* **1.** arrangement of connecting roads, resembling four-leaf clover, that joins two intersecting main roads —*a.* **2.** in shape of leaf of clover —**be in clover** be in luxury

clown (klaʊn) *n.* **1.** comic entertainer in circus **2.** jester, fool —*vi.* **3.** play jokes or tricks **4.** act foolishly —**'clownish** *a.*

cloy (klɔɪ) *vt.* weary by sweetness, sameness *etc.*

club (klʌb) *n.* **1.** thick stick **2.** bat, stick used in some games **3.** association for pursuance of common interest **4.** building used by such association **5.** one of the suits at cards —*vt.* **6.** strike with club —*vi.* **7.** join for a common object **(-bb-)** —**club foot** deformed foot —**club root** fungal disease of cabbages *etc.*, in which roots become thickened and distorted

cluck (klʌk) *vi./n.* (make) noise of hen

clue (kluː) *n.* **1.** indication, *esp.* of solution of mystery or puzzle —*vt.* **2.** (*usu. with* up) provide with helpful information —**'clueless** *a. sl.* helpless; stupid —**not have a clue** be ignorant or incompetent

clump[1] (klʌmp) *n.* **1.** cluster of trees or plants **2.** compact mass

clump[2] (klʌmp) *vi.* **1.** walk, tread heavily —*n.* **2.** dull, heavy tread or similar sound

clumsy ('klʌmzɪ) *a.* **1.** awkward, unwieldy, ungainly **2.** badly made or arranged —**'clumsily** *adv.* —**'clumsiness** *n.*

clung (klʌŋ) *pt./pp. of* CLING

clunk (klʌŋk) *n.* (sound of) blow or something falling

cluster ('klʌstə) *n.* **1.** group, bunch —*v.* **2.** gather, grow in cluster

clutch[1] (klʌtʃ) *v.* **1.** grasp eagerly **2.** snatch (at) —*n.* **3.** grasp, tight grip **4.** device enabling two revolving shafts to be connected and disconnected at will

clutch[2] (klʌtʃ) *n.* **1.** set of eggs hatched at one time **2.** brood of chickens

clutter ('klʌtə) *v.* **1.** strew **2.** crowd together in disorder —*n.* **3.** disordered, obstructive mass of objects

Clydesdale ('klaɪdzdeɪl) *n.* heavy powerful carthorse, orig. from Scotland

cm *or* **cm.** centimetre

Cm *Chem.* curium

Cmdr. *Mil.* Commander

C.N.D. UK Campaign for Nuclear Disarmament

Co *Chem.* cobalt

CO Colorado

Co. *or* **co.** Company

Co. County

C.O. Commanding Officer

co- (*comb. form*) **1.** together, as in *coproduction* **2.** partnership or equality, as in *costar, copilot* **3.** to similar degree, as in *coextend* **4.** *Maths., astron.* of complement of angle, as in *cosecant*

c/o 1. care of **2.** carried over

coach (kəʊtʃ) *n.* **1.** long-distance or touring bus **2.** large four-wheeled carriage **3.** railway carriage **4.** tutor, instructor —*vt.* **5.** instruct —**coach-builder** *n.* —**'coachman** *n.* —**'coachwork** *n.* **1.** design and manufacture of car bodies **2.** body of car

coadjutor (kəʊ'ædʒʊtə) *n.* **1.** bishop appointed as assistant to diocesan bishop **2.** *rare* assistant

THESAURUS

dress, endow, enwrap, equip, fit out, garb, habit, invest, outfit, rig, robe, swathe

clothes, clothing apparel, attire, clobber (*Brit. sl.*), costume, dress, duds (*Inf.*), ensemble, garb, garments, gear (*Inf.*), get-up (*Inf.*), habits, outfit, raiment, rigout (*Inf.*), togs (*Inf.*), vestments, vesture, wardrobe, wear

cloud *n.* **1.** billow, darkness, fog, gloom, haze, mist, murk, nebula, nebulosity, obscurity, vapour **2.** crowd, dense mass, flock, horde, host, multitude, shower, swarm, throng ~*v.* **3.** becloud, darken, dim, eclipse, obfuscate, obscure, overcast, overshadow, shade, shadow, veil

cloudy blurred, dark, dim, dismal, dull, dusky, emulsified, gloomy, hazy, indistinct, leaden, lowering, muddy, murky, nebulous, obscure, opaque, overcast, sombre, sullen, sunless

clown 1. *n.* buffoon, comedian, dolt, fool, harlequin, jester, joker, merry-andrew, mountebank, pierrot, prankster, punchinello **2.** *v.* act the fool, act the goat, jest, mess about

club 1. *n.* bat, bludgeon, cosh, cudgel, stick, truncheon **2.** *v.* bash, baste, batter, beat, bludgeon, clobber (*Sl.*), clout (*Inf.*), cosh, hammer, pommel (*Rare*), pummel, strike **3.** *n.* association, circle, clique, company, fraternity, group, guild, lodge, order, set, society, sodality, union

clue evidence, hint, indication, inkling, intimation, lead, pointer, sign, suggestion, suspicion, tip, tip-off, trace

clump[1] *n.* bunch, bundle, cluster, mass, shock

clump[2] *v.* bumble, clomp, lumber, plod, stamp, stomp, stump, thud, thump, tramp

clumsy awkward, blundering, bumbling, bungling, cack-handed (*Inf.*), gauche, gawky, ham-fisted (*Inf.*), ham-handed (*Inf.*), heavy, ill-shaped, inept, inexpert, lumbering, maladroit, ponderous, uncoordinated, uncouth, ungainly, unhandy, unskilful, unwieldy

cluster 1. *n.* assemblage, batch, bunch, clump, collection, gathering, group, knot **2.** *v.* assemble, bunch, collect, flock, gather, group

clutch catch, clasp, cling to, embrace, fasten, grab, grapple, grasp, grip, seize, snatch

clutter 1. *n.* confusion, disarray, disorder, hotchpotch, jumble, litter, mess, muddle, untidiness **2.** *v.* litter, scatter, strew

coach *n.* **1.** bus, car, carriage, charabanc, vehicle **2.** instructor, teacher, trainer, tutor ~*v.* **3.** cram, drill, instruct, prepare, train, tutor

coagulate (kəʊˈægjʊleɪt) *v.* **1.** curdle, clot, form into a mass **2.** congeal, solidify —**coaguˈlation** *n.*

coal (kəʊl) *n.* **1.** mineral consisting of carbonized vegetable matter, used as fuel **2.** glowing ember —*v.* **3.** supply with or take in coal —**ˈcoalface** *n.* exposed seam of coal in mine —**ˈcoalfield** *n.* district in which coal is found —**coal gas** mixture of gases produced by distillation of bituminous coal and used for heating and lighting —**coal tar** black tar, produced by distillation of bituminous coal, that can be further distilled to yield benzene *etc.* —**coal tit** small songbird having black head with white patch on nape

coalesce (kəʊəˈlɛs) *vi.* unite, merge —**coaˈlescence** *n.*

coalfish (ˈkəʊlfɪʃ) *n.* food fish with dark-coloured skin

coalition (kəʊəˈlɪʃən) *n.* alliance, *esp.* of political parties

coaming (ˈkəʊmɪŋ) *n.* raised frame round ship's hatchway for keeping out water

coarse (kɔːs) *a.* **1.** rough, harsh **2.** unrefined **3.** indecent —**ˈcoarsely** *adv.* —**ˈcoarsen** *v.* make or become coarse —**ˈcoarseness** *n.* —**coarse fish** freshwater fish not of salmon family —**coarse fishing**

coast (kəʊst) *n.* **1.** sea shore —*v.* **2.** move under momentum **3.** sail along (coast) —*vi.* **4.** proceed without making much effort —**ˈcoaster** *n.* **1.** small ship **2.** that which, one who, coasts **3.** small table mat for glasses *etc.* —**ˈcoastguard** *n.* **1.** maritime force which aids shipping, prevents smuggling *etc.* **2.** member of such force (*also* **ˈcoastguardsman**)

coat (kəʊt) *n.* **1.** sleeved outer garment **2.** animal's fur or feathers **3.** covering layer —*vt.* **4.** cover with layer **5.** clothe —**coat of arms** armorial bearings

coax (kəʊks) *vt.* wheedle, cajole, persuade, force gently

coaxial (kəʊˈæksɪəl) *or* **coaxal** (kəʊˈæksəl) *a.* having the same axis —**coaxial cable** high-frequency cable with outer conductor tube surrounding insulated central conductor

cob (kɒb) *n.* **1.** short-legged stout horse **2.** male swan **3.** head of corn **4.** round loaf of bread

cobalt (ˈkəʊbɔːlt) *n.* **1.** metallic element **2.** blue pigment from it —**cobalt bomb 1.** cobalt-60 device used in radiotherapy **2.** nuclear weapon consisting of hydrogen bomb encased in cobalt

cobber (ˈkɒbə) *n.* **A** *obs.*, **NZ** friend; mate: used as term of address to males

cobble (ˈkɒbəl) *vt.* **1.** patch roughly **2.** mend (shoes) —*n.* **3.** round stone —**ˈcobbler** *n.* shoe mender —**ˈcobblestone** *n.* rounded stone used for paving (*also* **ˈcobble**)

cobbler (ˈkɒblə) *n.* **1.** sweetened iced drink, usu. made from fruit and wine **2.** *chiefly* **US** hot dessert of fruit covered with cakelike crust

cobblers (ˈkɒbləz) *pl.n.* **UK** *vulg. sl.* testicles —**(a load of old) cobblers** rubbish; nonsense

COBOL (ˈkəʊbɒl) computer programming language for general commercial use

cobra (ˈkəʊbrə) *n.* venomous, hooded snake of Asia and Afr.

cobweb (ˈkɒbwɛb) *n.* spider's web

coca (ˈkəʊkə) *n.* either of two shrubs, native to Andes, whose dried leaves contain cocaine

Coca-Cola (kəʊkəˈkəʊlə) *n.* **R** carbonated soft drink

cocaine *or* **cocain** (kəˈkeɪn) *n.* addictive narcotic drug used medicinally as anaesthetic

coccus (ˈkɒkəs) *n.* spherical or nearly spherical bacterium, such as staphylococcus (*pl.* **-ci** (-saɪ))

coccyx (ˈkɒksɪks) *n.* small triangular bone at end of spinal column (*pl.* **coccyges** (kɒkˈsaɪdʒiːz))

cochineal (kɒtʃɪˈniːl, ˈkɒtʃɪniːl) *n.* scarlet dye from Mexican insect

cochlea (ˈkɒklɪə) *n.* spiral tube that forms part of internal ear, converting sound vibrations into nerve impulses (*pl.* **-leae** (-lɪiː))

cock (kɒk) *n.* **1.** male bird, *esp.* of domestic fowl **2.** tap for liquids **3.** hammer of gun **4.** its position drawn back —*vt.* **5.** draw back (gun hammer) to firing position **6.** raise, turn in alert or jaunty manner —**ˈcockerel** *n.* young cock —**cock-a-hoop** *a.* **1.** in very high spirits **2.** boastful **3.** askew; confused —**cock-a-leekie** *or* **cocky-leeky** *n.* soup made from fowl boiled with leeks *etc.* —**cock-and-bull story** *inf.* obviously improbable story, *esp.* one used as excuse —**ˈcockcrow** *or* **ˈcockcrowing** *n.* daybreak —**cocked hat** hat with brims turned up and caught together to give two or three points —**ˈcockeyed** *a.* **1.** crosseyed **2.** with a squint **3.** askew —**ˈcockfight** *n.* staged fight between roosters —**ˈcockscomb** *or* **ˈcoxcomb** *n.* **1.** comb of domestic cock **2.** garden plant with flowers in broad spike resembling comb of cock **3.** *inf.* conceited dandy —**ˈcockshy** *n.* **UK 1.** target in throwing games **2.** throw itself (*also* **shy**) —**cockˈsure** *a.* overconfident; arrogant —**knock into a cocked hat** *sl.* outdo, defeat

cockade (kɒˈkeɪd) *n.* rosette, badge for hat

THESAURUS

coalesce amalgamate, blend, cohere, combine, come together, commingle, commix, consolidate, fraternize, fuse, incorporate, integrate, merge, mix, unite

coalition affiliation, alliance, amalgam, amalgamation, association, bloc, combination, compact, confederacy, confederation, conjunction, fusion, integration, league, merger, union

coarse **1.** boorish, brutish, coarse-grained, foul-mouthed, gruff, loutish, rough, rude, uncivil **2.** bawdy, earthy, immodest, impolite, improper, impure, indelicate, inelegant, mean, offensive, ribald, rude, smutty, vulgar **3.** coarse-grained, crude, homespun, impure, rough-hewn, unfinished, unpolished, unprocessed, unpurified, unrefined

coarsen anaesthetize, blunt, callous, deaden, desensitize, dull, harden, indurate, roughen

coarseness bawdiness, boorishness, crudity, earthiness, indelicacy, offensiveness, poor taste, ribaldry, roughness, smut, smuttiness, uncouthness, unevenness

coast **1.** *n.* beach, border, coastline, littoral, seaboard, seaside, shore, strand **2.** *v.* cruise, drift, freewheel, get by, glide, sail, taxi

coat *n.* **1.** fleece, fur, hair, hide, pelt, skin, wool **2.** coating, covering, layer, overlay ~*v.* **3.** apply, cover, plaster, smear, spread

coax allure, beguile, cajole, decoy, entice, flatter, inveigle, persuade, prevail upon, soft-soap (*Inf.*), soothe, talk into, wheedle

cock **1.** *n.* chanticleer, cockerel, rooster **2.** *v.* perk up, prick, raise, stand up

cockatoo (kɒkəˈtuː, ˈkɒkətuː) *n.* Aust., New Guinea, crested parrot

cockatrice (ˈkɒkətrɪs, -traɪs) *n.* fabulous animal similar to basilisk

cockchafer (ˈkɒktʃeɪfə) *n.* large, flying beetle

cocker spaniel (ˈkɒkə) small compact spaniel

cockle[1] (ˈkɒkᵊl) *n.* shellfish —ˈ**cockleshell** *n.* **1.** shell of cockle **2.** shell of certain other molluscs **3.** small light boat

cockle[2] (ˈkɒkᵊl) *v.* **1.** wrinkle **2.** pucker

cockney (ˈkɒknɪ) *n.* (*oft.* **C-**) native of London, *esp.* of East End (*pl.* **-s**)

cockpit (ˈkɒkpɪt) *n.* **1.** pilot's seat, compartment in small aircraft **2.** driver's seat in racing car **3.** orig. enclosure for cockfighting

cockroach (ˈkɒkrəʊtʃ) *n.* kind of insect, household pest

cocktail (ˈkɒkteɪl) *n.* **1.** short drink of spirits with flavourings *etc.* **2.** appetizer

cocky (ˈkɒkɪ) *a.* conceited, pert

cocoa (ˈkəʊkəʊ) *or* **cacao** *n.* **1.** powder made from seed of cacao (tropical) tree **2.** drink made from the powder

coconut *or* **cocoanut** (ˈkəʊkənʌt) *n.* **1.** tropical palm **2.** very large, hard nut from this palm —**coconut matting** coarse matting made from fibrous husk of coconut

cocoon (kəˈkuːn) *n.* **1.** sheath of insect in chrysalis stage **2.** any protective covering

cocopan (ˈkəʊkəʊpæn) *n.* **SA** small truck on rails used *esp.* in mines

cocotte (kəʊˈkɒt, kə-) *n.* **1.** small fireproof dish in which individual portions of food are cooked and served **2.** prostitute; promiscuous woman

cod (kɒd) *n.* large sea fish of northern hemisphere —**cod-liver oil** oil extracted from livers of cod and related fish, rich in vitamins A and D

C.O.D. cash on delivery

coda (ˈkəʊdə) *n. Mus.* final part of musical composition

coddle (ˈkɒdᵊl) *vt.* overprotect, pamper

code (kəʊd) *n.* **1.** system of letters, symbols and rules for their association to transmit messages secretly or briefly **2.** scheme of conduct **3.** collection of laws —**codifiˈcation** *n.* —ˈ**codify** *vt.*

codeine (ˈkəʊdiːn) *n.* alkaline sedative, analgesic drug

codex (ˈkəʊdɛks) *n.* ancient manuscript volume, *esp.* of Bible *etc.* (*pl.* **codices** (ˈkəʊdɪsiːz, ˈkɒdɪ-))

codger (ˈkɒdʒə) *n. inf.* old man

codicil (ˈkɒdɪsɪl) *n.* addition to will —**codiˈcillary** *a.*

codpiece (ˈkɒdpiːs) *n.* bag covering male genitals, attached to breeches: worn in 15th and 16th centuries

coeducation (kəʊɛdjʊˈkeɪʃən) *n.* instruction in schools *etc.* attended by both sexes —**co-ed** *n.* **1.** coeducational school *etc.* —*a.* **2.** coeducational —**coeduˈcational** *a.* of education of boys and girls together in mixed classes

coefficient (kəʊɪˈfɪʃənt) *n. Maths.* numerical or constant factor

coelenterate (sɪˈlɛntəreɪt, -rɪt) *n.* any of various invertebrates having saclike body with single opening (mouth), such as jellyfishes

coeliac *or U.S.* **celiac** (ˈsiːlɪæk) *a.* pert. to belly —**coeliac disease** intestinal disorder caused by inadequate absorption of fats

coenobite *or* **cenobite** (ˈsiːnəʊbaɪt) *n.* member of religious order following communal rule of life —**coenobitic(al)** *or* **cenobitic(al)** (siːnəʊˈbɪtɪk(ᵊl)) *a.*

coequal (kəʊˈiːkwəl) *a.* **1.** of same size, rank *etc.* —*n.* **2.** person or thing equal with another —**coeˈquality** *n.*

coerce (kəʊˈɜːs) *vt.* compel, force —**coˈercion** *n.* forcible compulsion or restraint —**coˈercive** *or* **coˈercible** *a.*

coeval (kəʊˈiːvᵊl) *a.* of same age or generation

coexist (kəʊɪgˈzɪst) *vi.* exist together —**coexˈistence** *n.* —**coexˈistent** *a.*

coextend (kəʊɪkˈstɛnd) *v.* extend or cause to extend equally in space or time —**coexˈtension** *n.* —**coexˈtensive** *a.*

C. of E. Church of England

coffee (ˈkɒfɪ) *n.* **1.** seeds of tropical shrub **2.** drink made from roasting and grinding these —**coffee bar** café; snack bar —**coffee mill** machine for grinding roasted coffee beans —**coffee table** low table on which coffee may be served

coffer (ˈkɒfə) *n.* **1.** chest for valuables **2.** treasury, funds

cofferdam (ˈkɒfədæm) *n.* watertight structure enabling construction work to be done under water

coffin (ˈkɒfɪn) *n.* box in which corpse is buried or cremated

C. of S. Church of Scotland

cog (kɒg) *n.* **1.** one of series of teeth on rim of wheel **2.** person, thing forming small part of big process, organization *etc.* —ˈ**cogwheel** *n.*

cogent (ˈkəʊdʒənt) *a.* convincing, compelling, persuasive —ˈ**cogency** *n.* —ˈ**cogently** *adv.*

cogitate (ˈkɒdʒɪteɪt) *vi.* think, reflect, ponder —**cogiˈtation** *n.* —ˈ**cogitative** *a.*

Cognac (ˈkɒnjæk) *n.* French brandy

cognate (ˈkɒgneɪt) *a.* of same stock, related, kindred —**cogˈnation** *n.*

THESAURUS

cockeyed askew, asymmetrical, awry, crooked, lopsided, skewwhiff (*Brit. inf.*), squint (*Inf.*)

cocky arrogant, brash, cocksure, conceited, egotistical, lordly, swaggering, swollen-headed, vain

code 1. cipher, cryptograph **2.** canon, convention, custom, ethics, etiquette, manners, maxim, regulations, rules, system

cogent compelling, conclusive, convincing, effective, forceful, forcible, influential, irresistible, potent, powerful, strong, urgent, weighty

cogitate consider, contemplate, deliberate, meditate, mull over, muse, ponder, reflect, ruminate, think

cogitation consideration, contemplation, deliberation, meditation, reflection, rumination, thought

cognate affiliated, akin, alike, allied, analogous, associated, connected, kindred, related, similar

cognition apprehension, awareness, comprehension, discernment, insight, intelligence, perception, reasoning, understanding

cognition (kɒgˈnɪʃən) *n.* act or faculty of knowing —**cogˈnitional** *a.*

cognizance *or* **cognisance** (ˈkɒgnɪzəns, ˈkɒnɪ-) *n.* knowledge, perception —**ˈcognizable** *or* **ˈcognisable** *a.* —**ˈcognizant** *or* **ˈcognisant** *a.*

cognomen (kɒgˈnəʊmɛn) *n.* surname, nickname (*pl.* **-s, -nomina** (-ˈnɒmɪnə, -ˈnəʊ-))

cognoscenti (kɒnjəʊˈʃɛntɪ, kɒgnə-) *or* **conoscenti** (kɒnəʊˈʃɛntɪ) *pl.n.* people with knowledge in particular field, *esp.* arts (*sing.* **-te** (-tiː))

cohabit (kəʊˈhæbɪt) *vi.* live together as husband and wife

coheir (kəʊˈɛə) *n.* a joint heir (**coˈheiress** *fem.*)

cohere (kəʊˈhɪə) *vi.* stick together, be consistent —**coˈherence** *n.* —**coˈherent** *a.* **1.** capable of logical speech, thought **2.** connected, making sense **3.** sticking together —**coˈherently** *adv.* —**coˈhesion** *n.* cohering —**coˈhesive** *a.*

cohort (ˈkəʊhɔːt) *n.* **1.** troop **2.** associate

COHSE (ˈkəʊzɪ) Confederation of Health Service Employees

C.O.I. UK Central Office of Information

coif (kɔɪf) *n.* **1.** close-fitting cap worn under veil in Middle Ages **2.** leather cap worn under chainmail hood **3.** (kwɑːf) *rare* coiffure —*vt.* **4.** cover with or as if with coif **5.** (kwɑːf) arrange (hair) (**-ff-**)

coiffure (kwɑːˈfjʊə) *n.* hairstyle —**coiffeur** (kwɑːˈfɜː) *n.* hairdresser

coign of vantage (kɔɪn) advantageous position for observation or action

coil (kɔɪl) *vt.* **1.** lay in rings **2.** twist into winding shape —*vi.* **3.** twist, take up a winding shape or spiral —*n.* **4.** series of rings **5.** device in vehicle *etc.* to transform low-tension current to higher voltage for ignition purposes **6.** contraceptive device inserted in womb

coin (kɔɪn) *n.* **1.** piece of money **2.** money —*vt.* **3.** make into money, stamp **4.** invent —**ˈcoinage** *n.* **1.** coining **2.** coins collectively —**ˈcoiner** *n.* maker of counterfeit money

coincide (kəʊɪnˈsaɪd) *vi.* **1.** happen together **2.** agree exactly —**coˈincidence** *n.* —**coˈincident** *a.* coinciding —**coinciˈdental** *a.*

Cointreau (ˈkwɑːntrəʊ) *n.* **R** colourless liqueur with orange flavouring

coir (ˈkɔɪə) *n.* fibre of coconut husk

coitus (ˈkəʊɪtəs) *or* **coition** (kəʊˈɪʃən) *n.* sexual intercourse

coke[1] (kəʊk) *n.* residue left from distillation of coal, used as fuel

coke[2] (kəʊk) *n. sl.* cocaine

Coke (kəʊk) *n.* **R** *short for* COCA-COLA

col (kɒl) *n.* high mountain pass

Col. **1.** Colonel **2.** Colossians

cola *or* **kola** (ˈkəʊlə) *n.* **1.** tropical tree **2.** its nut, used to flavour drink

colander (ˈkɒləndə, ˈkʌl-) *or* **cullender** *n.* culinary strainer perforated with small holes

cold (kəʊld) *a.* **1.** lacking heat **2.** indifferent, unmoved, apathetic **3.** dispiriting **4.** reserved or unfriendly **5.** (of colours) giving an impression of coldness —*n.* **6.** lack of heat **7.** illness, marked by runny nose *etc.* —**ˈcoldly** *adv.* —**ˈcoldness** *n.* —**cold-blooded** *a.* **1.** lacking pity, mercy **2.** having body temperature that varies with that of the surroundings —**cold chisel** toughened steel chisel —**cold cream** emulsion of water and fat for softening and cleansing skin —**cold feet** *sl.* loss of confidence —**cold frame** unheated wooden frame with glass top, used to protect young plants —**cold front** *Met.* boundary line between warm air mass and cold air pushing it —**cold-hearted** *a.* lacking in feeling or warmth; unkind —**cold-heartedness** *n.* —**cold shoulder** *inf.* show of indifference; slight —**cold-shoulder** *vt. inf.* treat with indifference —**cold sore** cluster of blisters at margin of lips, caused by viral infection (*also* **herpes labialis**) —**cold storage** **1.** method of preserving perishable foods *etc.* by keeping them at artificially reduced temperature **2.** *inf.* state of temporary suspension —**cold sweat** *inf.* bodily reaction to fear or nervousness, characterized by chill and moist skin —**cold war** economic, diplomatic but nonmilitary hostility —**(out) in the cold** *inf.* neglected; ignored

cole (kəʊl) *n.* any of various plants such as cabbage and rape (*also* **ˈcolewort**)

coleopteran (kɒlɪˈɒptərən) *n.* **1.** any of order of insects, including beetles, in which forewings form shell-like protective elytra (*also* **coleˈopteron**) —*a.* **2.** of this order (*also* **coleˈopterous**)

coleslaw (ˈkəʊlslɔː) *n.* salad dish based on shredded cabbage

THESAURUS

coherent articulate, comprehensible, consistent, intelligible, logical, lucid, meaningful, orderly, organized, rational, reasoned, systematic

coil convolute, curl, entwine, loop, snake, spiral, twine, twist, wind, wreathe, writhe

coin **1.** *v.* conceive, create, fabricate, forge, formulate, frame, invent, make up, mint, mould, originate, think up **2.** *n.* cash, change, copper, money, silver, specie

coincide **1.** be concurrent, coexist, occur simultaneously, synchronize **2.** accord, harmonize, match, quadrate, square, tally **3.** acquiesce, agree, concur, correspond

coincidence **1.** accident, chance, eventuality, fluke, fortuity, luck, stroke of luck **2.** concomitance, concurrence, conjunction, correlation, correspondence, synchronism

coincidental **1.** accidental, casual, chance, fluky (*Inf.*), fortuitous, unintentional, unplanned **2.** coincident, concomitant, concurrent, simultaneous, synchronous

cold *adj.* **1.** arctic, biting, bitter, bleak, brumal, chill, chilly, cool, freezing, frigid, frosty, frozen, gelid, icy, inclement, raw, wintry **2.** benumbed, chilled, chilly, freezing, frozen to the marrow, numbed, shivery **3.** aloof, apathetic, cold-blooded, dead, distant, frigid, glacial, indifferent, inhospitable, lukewarm, passionless, phlegmatic, reserved, spiritless, standoffish, stony, undemonstrative, unfeeling, unmoved, unresponsive, unsympathetic ~*n.* **4.** chill, chilliness, coldness, frigidity, frostiness, iciness, inclemency

cold-blooded barbarous, brutal, callous, cruel, dispassionate, heartless, inhuman, merciless, pitiless, ruthless, savage, steely, stony-hearted, unemotional, unfeeling, unmoved

cold-hearted callous, detached, frigid, heartless, indifferent, inhuman, insensitive, stony-hearted, uncaring, unfeeling, unkind, unsympathetic

coletit ('kəultɪt) *n. see* **coal tit** *at* COAL

coleus ('kəulɪəs) *n.* plant cultivated for its variegated leaves

coley ('kəulɪ, 'kɒlɪ) *n.* **UK** any of various edible fishes, *esp.* coalfish

colic ('kɒlɪk) *n.* severe pains in the intestines —**co'litis** *n.* inflammation of the colon

coliseum (kɒlɪ'sɪəm) *or* **colosseum** (kɒlə'sɪəm) *n.* large building, such as stadium, used for entertainments *etc.*

collaborate (kə'læbəreɪt) *vi.* work with another on a project —**collabo'ration** *n.* —**col'laborator** *n.* one who works with another, *esp.* one who aids an enemy in occupation of his own country

collage (kə'lɑːʒ, kɒ-) *n.* (artistic) composition of bits and pieces stuck together on background

collagen ('kɒlədʒən) *n.* fibrous protein of connective tissue and bones that yields gelatin on boiling

collapse (kə'læps) *vi.* **1.** fall **2.** give way **3.** lose strength, fail —*n.* **4.** act of collapsing **5.** breakdown —**col'lapsible** *or* **col'lapsable** *a.*

collar ('kɒlə) *n.* **1.** band, part of garment, worn round neck —*vt.* **2.** seize by collar **3.** *inf.* capture, seize —**'collarbone** *n.* bone from shoulder to breastbone

collate (kɒ'leɪt, kə-) *vt.* **1.** compare carefully **2.** place in order (as printed sheets for binding) —**col'lation** *n.* **1.** collating **2.** light meal

collateral (kɒ'lætərəl, kə-) *n.* **1.** security pledged for repayment of loan —*a.* **2.** accompanying **3.** side by side **4.** of same stock but different line **5.** subordinate

colleague ('kɒliːg) *n.* associate, companion in office or employment, fellow worker

collect[1] (kə'lɛkt) *vt.* **1.** gather, bring together —*vi.* **2.** come together **3.** *inf.* receive money —*adv./a.* **4. US** (of telephone calls *etc.*) on transferred-charge basis —**col'lected** *a.* **1.** calm **2.** gathered —**col'lection** *n.* —**col'lective** *n.* **1.** factory, farm *etc.*, run on principles of collectivism —*a.* **2.** formed or assembled by collection **3.** forming whole or aggregate **4.** of individuals acting in cooperation —**col'lectively** *adv.* —**col'lectivism** *n.* theory that the state should own all means of production —**col'lector** *n.* —**collective bargaining** negotiation between trade union and employer or employers' organization on incomes and working conditions of employees —**collector's item** any rare or beautiful object thought worthy of collection

collect[2] ('kɒlɛkt) *n.* short prayer

colleen ('kɒliːn, kɒ'liːn) *n. Irish name for* girl

college ('kɒlɪdʒ) *n.* **1.** place of higher education **2.** society of scholars **3.** association —**col'legian** *n.* student —**col'legiate** *a.*

collide (kə'laɪd) *vi.* **1.** strike or dash together **2.** come into conflict —**collision** (kə'lɪʒən) *n.* colliding

collie ('kɒlɪ) *n.* any of several breeds of dog orig. bred to herd sheep

collier ('kɒlɪə) *n.* **1.** coal miner **2.** coal ship —**'colliery** *n.* coal mine

collimate ('kɒlɪmeɪt) *vt.* **1.** adjust line of sight of (optical instrument) **2.** make parallel or bring into line —**colli'mation** *n.*

collocate ('kɒləkeɪt) *vt.* group, place together —**collo'cation** *n.*

collodion (kə'ləudɪən) *or* **collodium** (kə'ləudɪəm) *n.* chemical solution used in photography and medicine

colloid ('kɒlɔɪd) *n.* suspension of particles in a solution

collop ('kɒləp) *n. dial.* **1.** slice of meat **2.** small piece of anything

colloquial (kə'ləukwɪəl) *a.* pert. to, or used in, informal conversation —**col'loquialism** *n.* —**'colloquy** *n.* **1.** conversation **2.** dialogue

colloquium (kə'ləukwɪəm) *n.* **1.** gathering for discussion **2.** academic seminar (*pl.* **-s, -quia** (-kwɪə))

collusion (kə'luːʒən) *n.* secret agreement for a fraudulent purpose, *esp.* in legal proceedings —**col'lusive** *a.*

collywobbles ('kɒlɪwɒbᵊlz) *pl.n. sl.* **1.** upset stomach **2.** intense feeling of nervousness

cologne (kə'ləun) *n.* perfumed liquid (*also* **eau de cologne**)

colon[1] ('kəulən) *n.* mark (:) indicating break in sentence

colon[2] ('kəulən) *n.* part of large intestine from caecum to rectum

colonel ('kɜːnᵊl) *n.* commander of regiment or battalion —**'colonelcy** *n.*

THESAURUS

collaborate cooperate, coproduce, join forces, participate, team up, work together

collaboration alliance, association, concert, cooperation, partnership, teamwork

collaborator **1.** associate, colleague, confederate, coworker, partner, team-mate **2.** collaborationist, fraternizer, quisling, traitor, turncoat

collapse **1.** *v.* break down, cave in, come to nothing, crack up (*Inf.*), crumple, fail, faint, fall, fold, founder, give way, subside **2.** *n.* breakdown, cave-in, disintegration, downfall, exhaustion, failure, faint, flop (*Sl.*), prostration, subsidence

collar *v.* apprehend, appropriate, capture, catch, grab, lay hands on, seize

colleague aider, ally, assistant, associate, auxiliary, coadjutor (*Rare*), collaborator, companion, comrade, confederate, confrère, fellow worker, helper, partner, team-mate, workmate

collect **1.** accumulate, aggregate, amass, assemble, gather, heap, hoard, save, stockpile **2.** assemble, cluster, congregate, convene, converge, flock together, rally **3.** acquire, muster, obtain, raise, secure, solicit

collected calm, composed, confident, cool, placid, poised, self-possessed, serene, together (*Sl.*), unperturbable, unperturbed, unruffled

collection **1.** accumulation, anthology, compilation, congeries, heap, hoard, mass, pile, set, stockpile, store **2.** assemblage, assembly, assortment, cluster, company, congregation, convocation, crowd, gathering, group **3.** alms, contribution, offering, offertory

collide clash, come into collision, conflict, crash, meet head-on

collision **1.** accident, bump, crash, impact, pile-up, prang (*Inf.*), smash **2.** clash, clashing, conflict, confrontation, encounter, opposition, skirmish

colloquial conversational, demotic, everyday, familiar, idiomatic, informal, vernacular

collusion cahoots (*Inf.*), complicity, connivance, con-

colonnade (kɒlə'neɪd) *n.* row of columns

colony ('kɒlənɪ) *n.* **1.** body of people who settle in new country but remain subject to parent state **2.** country so settled **3.** distinctive group living together —**co'lonial** *a.* of colony —**co'lonialism** *n.* policy and practice of extending control over weaker peoples or areas (*also* **im'perialism**) —**co'lonialist** *n./a.* —**'colonist** *n.* —**coloni'zation** *or* **-i'sation** *n.* —**'colonize** *or* **-ise** *v.*

colophon ('kɒləfɒn, -fən) *n.* publisher's imprint or device

Colorado beetle (kɒlə'rɑːdəʊ) black-and-yellow beetle that is serious pest of potatoes

coloratura (kɒlərə'tʊərə) *n. Mus.* **1.** florid virtuoso passage **2.** soprano who specializes in such music (*also* **coloratura soprano**)

colossus (kə'lɒsəs) *n.* **1.** huge statue **2.** something, somebody very large (*pl.* **colossi** (kə'lɒsaɪ), **-es**) —**co'lossal** *a.* huge, gigantic

colostomy (kə'lɒstəmɪ) *n.* surgical formation of opening from colon on to surface of body, which functions as anus

colostrum (kə'lɒstrəm) *n.* thin milky secretion from nipples that precedes and follows true lactation

colour *or U.S.* **color** ('kʌlə) *n.* **1.** hue, tint **2.** complexion **3.** paint **4.** pigment **5.** *fig.* semblance, pretext **6.** *fig.* timbre, quality **7.** *fig.* mood —*pl.* **8.** flag **9.** *Sport* distinguishing badge, symbol —*vt.* **10.** stain, dye, paint, give colour to **11.** *fig.* disguise **12.** *fig.* influence or distort —*vi.* **13.** become coloured **14.** blush —**colo'ration** *n.* —**'colourable** *a.* **1.** capable of being coloured **2.** appearing to be true; plausible **3.** pretended; feigned —**'coloured** *a.* **1.** possessing colour **2.** having strong element of fiction or fantasy; distorted (*esp. in* **highly coloured**) —**'Coloured** *a.* **1.** non-White **2.** in S Afr., of mixed descent —**'colourful** *a.* **1.** with bright or varied colours **2.** distinctive —**'colouring** *n.* **1.** process or art of applying colour **2.** anything used to give colour, such as paint **3.** appearance with regard to shade and colour **4.** arrangements of colours, as in markings of birds **5.** colour of complexion **6.** false appearance —**'colourless** *a.* **1.** without colour **2.** lacking interest **3.** grey; pallid **4.** without prejudice; neutral —**colour bar** discrimination against people of different race, *esp.* as practised by Whites against Blacks —**colour sergeant** sergeant who carries regimental, battalion or national colours

colt (kəʊlt) *n.* young male horse —**'coltish** *a.* **1.** inexperienced; unruly **2.** playful and lively

coltsfoot ('kəʊltsfʊt) *n.* wild plant with heart-shaped leaves and yellow flowers (*pl.* **-s**)

columbine ('kɒləmbaɪn) *n.* flower with five spurred petals

column ('kɒləm) *n.* **1.** long vertical cylinder, pillar **2.** support **3.** division of page **4.** *Journalism* regular feature in paper **5.** line of troops *etc.* —**columnar** (kə'lʌmnə) *a.* —**'columnist** *n.* journalist writing regular feature for newspaper

com- *or* **con-** (*comb. form*) together; with; jointly, as in *commingle*

coma ('kəʊmə) *n.* state of unconsciousness —**'comatose** *a.*

comb (kəʊm) *n.* **1.** toothed instrument for tidying, arranging, ornamenting hair **2.** cock's crest **3.** mass of honey cells —*vt.* **4.** use comb on **5.** search with great care —**'comber** *n.* **1.** person, tool or machine that combs wool, flax *etc.* **2.** long curling wave; roller

combat ('kɒmbæt, -bət, 'kʌm-) *vt./n.* fight, contest —**'combatant** *n.* —**'combative** *a.* —**combat fatigue** *see* **battle fatigue** *at* BATTLE

combe *or* **comb** (kuːm) *n. see* COOMB

THESAURUS

spiracy, craft, deceit, fraudulent artifice, intrigue, secret understanding

colonist colonial, colonizer, frontiersman, homesteader (*U.S.*), immigrant, pioneer, planter, settler

colonize open up, people, pioneer, populate, settle

colony community, dependency, dominion, outpost, possession, province, satellite state, settlement, territory

colossal Brobdingnagian, elephantine, enormous, gargantuan, gigantic, herculean, huge, immense, mammoth, massive, monstrous, monumental, mountainous, prodigious, titanic, vast

colour *n.* **1.** colorant, coloration, complexion, dye, hue, paint, pigment, pigmentation, shade, tincture, tinge, tint **2.** *Fig.* appearance, disguise, excuse, façade, false show, guise, plea, pretence, pretext, semblance ~*v.* **3.** colourwash, dye, paint, stain, tinge, tint **4.** *Fig.* disguise, distort, embroider, exaggerate, falsify, garble, gloss over, misrepresent, pervert, prejudice, slant, taint **5.** blush, burn, crimson, flush, go crimson, redden

colourful 1. bright, brilliant, intense, jazzy (*Sl.*), kaleidoscopic, motley, multicoloured, psychedelic, rich, variegated, vibrant, vivid **2.** characterful, distinctive, graphic, interesting, lively, picturesque, rich, stimulating, unusual, vivid

colourless 1. achromatic, achromic, anaemic, ashen, bleached, drab, faded, neutral, sickly, wan, washed out **2.** characterless, dreary, insipid, lacklustre, tame, uninteresting, unmemorable, vacuous, vapid

colours banner, emblem, ensign, flag, standard

column 1. cavalcade, file, line, list, procession, queue, rank, row, string, train **2.** caryatid, obelisk, pilaster, pillar, post, shaft, support, upright

columnist correspondent, critic, editor, gossip columnist, reporter, reviewer

coma drowsiness, insensibility, lethargy, oblivion, somnolence, stupor, torpor, trance, unconsciousness

comatose drowsy, drugged, insensible, lethargic, sleepy, sluggish, somnolent, soporose (*Medical*), stupefied, torpid, unconscious

comb *v.* **1.** arrange, curry, dress, groom, untangle **2.** *Fig.* go through with a fine-tooth comb, hunt, rake, ransack, rummage, scour, screen, search, sift, sweep

combat 1. *n.* action, battle, conflict, contest, encounter, engagement, fight, skirmish, struggle, war, warfare **2.** *v.* battle, contend, contest, cope, defy, do battle with, engage, fight, oppose, resist, strive, struggle, withstand

combatant adversary, antagonist, belligerent, contender, enemy, fighter, fighting man, opponent, serviceman, soldier, warrior

combination 1. amalgam, amalgamation, blend, coalescence, composite, connection, mix, mixture **2.** alliance, association, cabal, cartel, coalition, combine, compound, confederacy, confederation, consortium, conspiracy, federation, merger, syndicate, unification, union

combine (kəmˈbaɪn) *v.* **1.** join together **2.** ally —*n.* (ˈkɒmbaɪn) **3.** trust, syndicate, *esp.* of businesses, trade organizations *etc.* —**combination** (kɒmbɪˈneɪʃən) *n.* —**combinative** (ˈkɒmbɪneɪtɪv) *a.* —**combination lock** lock that can only be opened when set of dials is turned to show specific sequence of numbers —**combine harvester** machine to harvest and thresh grain in one operation —**combining form** linguistic element that occurs only as part of compound word, such as *anthropo-* in *anthropology*

combo (ˈkɒmbəʊ) *n.* **1.** small group of jazz musicians **2.** *inf.* any combination (*pl.* **-s**)

combustion (kəmˈbʌstʃən) *n.* process of burning —**combustiˈbility** *n.* —**comˈbustible** *a.*

come (kʌm) *vi.* **1.** approach, arrive, move towards something or someone nearer **2.** reach **3.** happen as a result **4.** occur **5.** be available **6.** originate **7.** become, turn out to be (**came, come, ˈcoming**) —**ˈcoming** *a.* **1.** (of time *etc.*) approaching; next **2.** promising (*esp. in* **up and coming**) —*n.* **3.** arrival; approach —**ˈcomeback** *n. inf.* **1.** return to active life after retirement **2.** retort —**ˈcomedown** *n.* **1.** setback **2.** descent in social status —**come-hither** *a. inf.* alluring; seductive —**come-on** *n. inf.* anything that serves as lure —**comeˈuppance** *n. sl.* just retribution —**come on 1.** (of power *etc.*) start functioning **2.** progress **3.** advance, *esp.* in battle **4.** begin **5.** make entrance on stage —**come on strong** make forceful or exaggerated impression —**have it coming to one** *inf.* deserve what one is about to suffer

Comecon (ˈkɒmɪkɒn) *n.* association of Soviet-oriented Communist nations, founded in 1949 to coordinate economic development *etc.*

comedy (ˈkɒmɪdɪ) *n.* **1.** dramatic or other work of light, amusing character **2.** humour **3.** *Class. lit.* play in which main characters triumph over adversity —**coˈmedian** *n.* **1.** entertainer who tells jokes *etc.* **2.** actor in comedy (**comediˈenne** *fem.*)

comely (ˈkʌmlɪ) *a.* fair, pretty, good-looking —**ˈcomeliness** *n.*

comestible (kəˈmɛstɪbəl) *n.* (*usu. pl.*) food

comet (ˈkɒmɪt) *n.* luminous heavenly body consisting of diffuse head, nucleus and long tail —**ˈcometary** *a.*

comfit (ˈkʌmfɪt, ˈkɒm-) *n.* sweet

comfort (ˈkʌmfət) *n.* **1.** wellbeing **2.** ease **3.** consolation **4.** means of consolation or satisfaction —*vt.* **5.** soothe **6.** cheer, gladden, console —**comfortable** (ˈkʌmftəbəl) *a.* **1.** free from pain *etc.* **2.** *inf.* well-off financially —**comfortably** (ˈkʌmftəblɪ) *adv.* —**ˈcomforter** *n.* **1.** a person who comforts **2.** baby's dummy **3.** woollen scarf —**ˈcomfy** *a. inf.* comfortable

comfrey (ˈkʌmfrɪ) *n.* wild plant with hairy leaves

comic (ˈkɒmɪk) *a.* **1.** relating to comedy **2.** funny, laughable —*n.* **3.** comedian **4.** magazine consisting of strip cartoons —**ˈcomical** *a.* —**ˈcomically** *adv.* —**comic strip** sequence of drawings in newspaper *etc.*, relating comic or adventurous situation

comity (ˈkɒmɪtɪ) *n.* **1.** mutual civility; courtesy **2.** friendly recognition accorded by nation to laws and usages of another (*also* **comity of nations**)

comm. **1.** commonwealth **2.** communist

comma (ˈkɒmə) *n.* punctuation mark (,) separating parts of sentence

command (kəˈmɑːnd) *vt.* **1.** order **2.** rule **3.** compel **4.** have in one's power **5.** overlook, dominate **6.** receive as due —*vi.* **7.** exercise rule —*n.* **8.** order **9.** power of controlling, ruling, dominating, overlooking **10.** knowledge, mastery **11.** post of one commanding **12.** district commanded, jurisdiction —**ˈcommandant** *n.* —**commanˈdeer** *vt.* seize for military use, appropriate —**comˈmander** *n.* —**comˈmanding** *a.* **1.** in command **2.** with air of authority —**comˈmandment** *n.*

THESAURUS

combine amalgamate, associate, bind, blend, bond, compound, connect, cooperate, fuse, incorporate, integrate, join (together), link, marry, merge, mix, pool, put together, synthesize, unify, unite

come 1. advance, appear, approach, arrive, become, draw near, enter, happen, materialize, move, move towards, near, occur, originate, show up (*Inf.*), turn out, turn up (*Inf.*) **2.** appear, arrive, attain, enter, materialize, reach, show up (*Inf.*), turn up (*Inf.*) **3.** fall, happen, occur, take place **4.** arise, emanate, emerge, end up, flow, issue, originate, result, turn out **5.** extend, reach **6.** be available (made, offered, on offer, produced)

comeback 1. rally, rebound, recovery, resurgence, return, revival, triumph **2.** rejoinder, reply, response, retaliation, retort, riposte

comedian card (*Inf.*), clown, comic, funny man, humorist, jester, joker, laugh (*Inf.*), wag, wit

comedown anticlimax, blow, decline, deflation, demotion, disappointment, humiliation, letdown, reverse

comedy chaffing, drollery, facetiousness, farce, fun, hilarity, humour, jesting, joking, light entertainment, sitcom (*Inf.*), slapstick, wisecracking, witticisms

comeuppance chastening, deserts, due reward, dues, merit, punishment, recompense, requital, retribution

comfort *v.* **1.** alleviate, assuage, cheer, commiserate with, compassionate (*Archaic*), console, ease, encourage, enliven, gladden, hearten, inspirit, invigorate, reassure, refresh, relieve, solace, soothe, strengthen ~*n.* **2.** aid, alleviation, cheer, compensation, consolation, ease, encouragement, enjoyment, help, relief, satisfaction, succour, support **3.** cosiness, creature comforts, ease, luxury, opulence, snugness, wellbeing

comfortable 1. adequate, agreeable, ample, commodious, convenient, cosy, delightful, easy, enjoyable, homely, loose, loose-fitting, pleasant, relaxing, restful, roomy, snug **2.** at ease, contented, gratified, happy, relaxed, serene **3.** affluent, prosperous, well-off, well-to-do

comic 1. *adj.* amusing, comical, droll, facetious, farcical, funny, humorous, jocular, joking, light, rich, waggish, witty **2.** *n.* buffoon, clown, comedian, funny man, humorist, jester, wag, wit

comical absurd, amusing, comic, diverting, droll, entertaining, farcical, funny, hilarious, humorous, laughable, ludicrous, priceless, ridiculous, risible, side-splitting, silly, whimsical

coming *adj.* **1.** approaching, at hand, due, en route, forthcoming, future, imminent, impending, in store, in the wind, near, next, nigh **2.** aspiring, future, promising, up-and-coming ~*n.* **3.** accession, advent, approach, arrival

commando (kəˈmɑːndəʊ) *n.* (member of) special military unit trained for airborne, amphibious attack (*pl.* **-s**)

commedia dell'arte (kɔmˈmɛdja delˈlarte) *It.* form of improvised comedy in Italy in 16th to 18th cent., with stock characters such as Punchinello, Harlequin *etc.*

commemorate (kəˈmɛməreɪt) *vt.* **1.** celebrate, keep in memory by ceremony **2.** be a memorial of —**commemoˈration** *n.* —**comˈmemorative** *a.*

commence (kəˈmɛns) *v.* begin —**comˈmencement** *n.*

commend (kəˈmɛnd) *vt.* **1.** praise **2.** commit, entrust —**comˈmendable** *a.* —**comˈmendably** *adv.* —**commenˈdation** *n.* —**comˈmendatory** *a.*

commensurate (kəˈmɛnsərɪt, -ʃə-) *a.* **1.** equal in size or length of time **2.** in proportion, adequate —**comˈmensurable** *a.* **1.** *Maths.* having common factor; having units of same dimensions and being related by whole numbers **2.** proportionate

comment (ˈkɒmɛnt) *n.* **1.** remark, criticism **2.** gossip **3.** note, explanation —*vi.* **4.** remark, note **5.** write notes explaining or criticizing a text —**ˈcommentary** *n.* **1.** explanatory notes or comments **2.** spoken accompaniment to film *etc.* —**ˈcommentate** *vi.* —**ˈcommentator** *n.* author, speaker of commentary

commerce (ˈkɒmɜːs) *n.* **1.** buying and selling **2.** dealings **3.** trade —**comˈmercial** *a.* **1.** of, concerning, business, trade, profit *etc.* —*n.* **2.** advertisement, *esp.* on radio or television —**comˈmercialize** *or* **-lise** *vt.* **1.** make commercial **2.** exploit for profit, *esp.* at expense of quality —**commercial traveller** travelling salesman

commie *or* **commy** (ˈkɒmɪ) *n./a. inf., offens.* communist

commination (kɒmɪˈneɪʃən) *n.* act of threatening punishment or vengeance —**comminatory** (ˈkɒmɪnətərɪ) *a.*

commingle (kɒˈmɪŋgᵊl) *v.* mix or be mixed

comminute (ˈkɒmɪnjuːt) *vt.* **1.** break (bone) into small fragments **2.** divide (property) into small lots —**commiˈnution** *n.*

commis (ˈkɒmɪs, ˈkɒmɪ) *n.* **1.** agent or deputy **2.** apprentice waiter or chef (*pl.* **-mis**)

commiserate (kəˈmɪzəreɪt) *vi.* (*usu. with* with) pity, condole, sympathize —**commiserˈation** *n.*

commissar (ˈkɒmɪsɑː, kɒmɪˈsɑː) *n.* official of Communist Party responsible for political education

commissariat (kɒmɪˈsɛərɪət) *n.* military department of food supplies and transport

commissary (ˈkɒmɪsərɪ) *n.* **1.** US shop supplying food or equipment, as in military camp **2.** US army officer responsible for supplies **3.** US restaurant in film studio **4.** representative or deputy, *esp.* of bishop

commission (kəˈmɪʃən) *n.* **1.** something entrusted to be done **2.** delegated authority **3.** body entrusted with some special duty **4.** payment by percentage for doing something **5.** warrant, *esp.* royal warrant, giving authority **6.** document appointing soldier, sailor or airman to officer's rank **7.** doing, committing —*vt.* **8.** charge with duty or task **9.** *Mil.* confer a rank on **10.** give order for —**comˈmissioner** *n.* **1.** one empowered to act by commission or warrant **2.** member of commission or government board —**commissioned officer** military officer holding commission, such as Second Lieutenant in British Army, Acting Sub-Lieutenant in Royal Navy, Pilot Officer in Royal Air Force, and officers of all ranks senior to these —**commissioner for oaths** solicitor authorized to authenticate oaths on sworn statements

THESAURUS

command *v.* **1.** bid, charge, compel, demand, direct, enjoin, order, require **2.** control, dominate, govern, head, lead, manage, reign over, rule, supervise, sway ~*n.* **3.** behest, bidding, commandment, decree, direction, directive, edict, fiat, injunction, instruction, mandate, order, precept, requirement, ultimatum **4.** authority, charge, control, domination, dominion, government, grasp, management, mastery, power, rule, supervision, sway, upper hand

commandeer appropriate, confiscate, expropriate, hijack, requisition, seize, sequester, sequestrate, usurp

commander boss, captain, chief, C in C, C.O., commander-in-chief, commanding officer, director, head, leader, officer, ruler

commanding **1.** advantageous, controlling, decisive, dominant, dominating, superior **2.** assertive, authoritative, autocratic, compelling, forceful, imposing, impressive, peremptory

commemorate celebrate, honour, immortalize, keep, memorialize, observe, pay tribute to, remember, salute, solemnize

commemoration ceremony, honouring, memorial service, observance, remembrance, tribute

commemorative celebratory, dedicatory, in honour, in memory, in remembrance, memorial

commence begin, embark on, enter upon, inaugurate, initiate, open, originate, start

commend **1.** acclaim, applaud, approve, compliment, eulogize, extol, praise, recommend, speak highly of **2.** commit, confide, consign, deliver, entrust, hand over, yield

commendable admirable, creditable, deserving, estimable, exemplary, laudable, meritorious, praiseworthy, worthy

commendation acclaim, acclamation, approbation, approval, credit, encomium, encouragement, good opinion, panegyric, praise, recommendation

commensurate adequate, appropriate, coextensive, comparable, compatible, consistent, corresponding, due, equivalent, fit, fitting, in accord, proportionate, sufficient

comment *v.* **1.** animadvert, interpose, mention, note, observe, opine, point out, remark, say **2.** annotate, criticize, elucidate, explain, interpret ~*n.* **3.** animadversion, observation, remark, statement **4.** annotation, commentary, criticism, elucidation, explanation, exposition, illustration, note

commentary analysis, critique, description, exegesis, explanation, narration, notes, review, treatise, voice-over

commentator **1.** commenter, reporter, special correspondent, sportscaster **2.** annotator, critic, expositor, interpreter, scholiast

commerce **1.** business, dealing, exchange, merchandising, trade, traffic **2.** communication, dealings, intercourse, relations, socializing

commissionaire (kəmɪʃəˈnɛə) *n.* messenger, porter, doorkeeper (*usu.* uniformed)

commit (kəˈmɪt) *vt.* **1.** entrust, give in charge **2.** perpetrate, be guilty of **3.** pledge, promise **4.** compromise, entangle **5.** send for trial (-tt-) —**comˈmitment** *n.* —**comˈmittal** *n.*

committee (kəˈmɪtɪ) *n.* body appointed, elected for special business usu. from larger body

commode (kəˈməʊd) *n.* **1.** chest of drawers **2.** stool containing chamber pot

commodious (kəˈməʊdɪəs) *a.* roomy

commodity (kəˈmɒdɪtɪ) *n.* **1.** article of trade **2.** anything useful

commodore (ˈkɒmədɔː) *n.* **1.** naval officer, senior to captain **2.** president of yacht club **3.** senior captain in convoy of merchant ships

common (ˈkɒmən) *a.* **1.** shared by or belonging to all, or to several **2.** public, general **3.** ordinary, usual, frequent **4.** inferior **5.** vulgar —*n.* **6.** land belonging to community —*pl.* **7.** ordinary people **8.** (C-) lower House of British Parliament, House of Commons —**commoˈnality** *n.* **1.** fact of being common **2.** commonalty —**ˈcommonalty** *n.* general body of people —**ˈcommoner** *n.* one of the common people, *ie* not of the nobility —**ˈcommonly** *adv.* —**common fraction** *see* **simple fraction** *at* SIMPLE —**common law** body of law based on judicial decisions and custom —**common-law marriage** state of marriage deemed to exist between man and woman after years of cohabitation —**Common Market** European Economic Community —**ˈcommonplace** *a.* **1.** ordinary, everyday —*n.* **2.** trite remark **3.** anything occurring frequently —**common room** *chiefly* **UK** sitting room in schools *etc.* —**common sense** sound, practical understanding —**common time** *Mus.* time signature indicating four crotchet beats to bar; four-four time —**ˈcommonwealth** *n.* **1.** republic **2.** (C-) federation of self-governing states

commotion (kəˈməʊʃən) *n.* stir, disturbance, tumult

commune[1] (kəˈmjuːn) *vi.* converse together intimately —**comˈmunion** *n.* **1.** sharing of thoughts, feelings *etc.* **2.** fellowship **3.** body with common faith **4.** (C-) participation in sacrament of the Lord's Supper **5.** (C-) that sacrament, Eucharist

commune[2] (ˈkɒmjuːn) *n.* group of families, individuals living together and sharing property, responsibility *etc.* —**ˈcommunal** *a.* for common use

communicate (kəˈmjuːnɪkeɪt) *vt.* **1.** impart, convey **2.** reveal —*vi.* **3.** give or exchange information **4.** have connecting passage, door **5.** receive Communion —**comˈmunicable** *a.* —**comˈmunicant** *n.* one who receives Communion —**communiˈcation** *n.* **1.** act of giving, *esp.* information **2.** information, message **3.** (*usu. pl.*) passage (road, railway *etc.*) or means of exchanging messages (radio, post *etc.*) between places —*pl.* **4.** connections between military base and front —**comˈmunicative** *a.* free with information —**communication cord UK** cord or chain which may be pulled by passenger to stop train in emergency

communiqué (kəˈmjuːnɪkeɪ) *n.* official announcement

communism (ˈkɒmjʊnɪzəm) *n.* doctrine that all goods, means of production *etc.* should be property of community —**ˈcommunist** *n./a.* —**commuˈnistic** *a.*

THESAURUS

commercial business, mercantile, profit-making, sales, trade, trading

commission *n.* **1.** appointment, authority, charge, duty, employment, errand, function, mandate, mission, task, trust, warrant **2.** allowance, brokerage, compensation, cut, fee, percentage, rake-off (*Sl.*) **3.** board, body of commissioners, commissioners, committee, delegation, deputation, representative ~*v.* **4.** appoint, authorize, contract, delegate, depute, empower, engage, nominate, order, select, send

commit **1.** carry out, do, enact, execute, perform, perpetrate **2.** commend, confide, consign, deliver, deposit, engage, entrust, give, hand over **3.** align, bind, compromise, endanger, make liable, obligate, pledge, rank **4.** confine, imprison, put in custody

commitment **1.** duty, engagement, liability, obligation, responsibility, tie **2.** assurance, guarantee, pledge, promise, undertaking, vow, word

common **1.** average, commonplace, conventional, customary, daily, everyday, familiar, frequent, general, habitual, humdrum, obscure, ordinary, plain, regular, routine, run-of-the-mill, simple, standard, stock, usual, workaday **2.** accepted, general, popular, prevailing, prevalent, universal, widespread **3.** collective, communal, community, popular, public, social **4.** coarse, hackneyed, inferior, low, pedestrian, plebeian, stale, trite, undistinguished, vulgar

commonplace **1.** *adj.* common, customary, everyday, humdrum, obvious, ordinary, pedestrian, stale, threadbare, trite, uninteresting, widespread, worn out **2.** *n.* banality, cliché, platitude, truism

common sense good sense, gumption (*Inf.*), horse sense, level-headedness, mother wit, native intelligence, nous (*Sl.*), practicality, prudence, reasonableness, sound judgment, soundness, wit

commotion ado, agitation, brouhaha, bustle, disorder, disturbance, excitement, ferment, furore, fuss, hubbub, hullabaloo, hurly-burly, perturbation, racket, riot, rumpus, to-do, tumult, turmoil, uproar

communal collective, communistic, community, general, joint, neighbourhood, public, shared

commune[1] *v.* communicate, confer, confide in, converse, discourse, discuss, parley

commune[2] *n.* collective, community, cooperative, kibbutz

communicate acquaint, announce, be in contact, be in touch, connect, convey, correspond, declare, disclose, disseminate, divulge, impart, inform, make known, pass on, phone, proclaim, publish, report, reveal, ring up, signify, spread, transmit, unfold

communication **1.** connection, contact, conversation, correspondence, dissemination, intercourse, link, transmission **2.** announcement, disclosure, dispatch, information, intelligence, message, news, report, statement, word

communications **1.** routes, transport, travel **2.** information technology, media, publicity, public relations, telecommunications

communicative candid, chatty, conversable, expansive, forthcoming, frank, informative, loquacious, open, outgoing, talkative, unreserved, voluble

communion **1.** accord, affinity, agreement, closeness, communing, concord, converse, fellowship, harmony, intercourse, participation, rapport, sympathy, togetherness, unity **2.** *Church* Eucharist, Lord's Supper, Mass, Sacrament

community (kə'mju:nɪtɪ) *n.* **1.** body of people with something in common, *eg* district of residence, religion *etc.* **2.** society, the public **3.** joint ownership **4.** similarity, agreement —**community centre** building for communal activities

commute (kə'mju:t) *vi.* **1.** travel daily some distance to work —*vt.* **2.** exchange **3.** change (punishment *etc.*) into something less severe **4.** change (duty *etc.*) for money payment —**commu'tation** *n.* —**com'mutative** *a.* relating to or involving substitution —**'commutator** *n.*

compact[1] (kəm'pækt) *a.* **1.** neatly arranged or packed **2.** solid, concentrated **3.** terse —*v.* **4.** make, become compact —*vt.* **5.** compress —**com'pactly** *adv.* —**com'pactness** *n.* —**compact disc** ('kɒmpækt) small audio disc on which sound is recorded as series of metallic pits enclosed in PVC and read by optical laser system

compact[2] ('kɒmpækt) *n.* small case to hold face powder, powder puff and mirror

compact[3] ('kɒmpækt) *n.* agreement, covenant, treaty, contract

companion[1] (kəm'pænjən) *n.* **1.** mate, fellow, comrade, associate **2.** person employed to live with another —**com'panionable** *a.* —**com'panionship** *n.*

companion[2] (kəm'pænjən) *n.* **1.** raised cover over staircase from deck to cabin of ship **2.** deck skylight —**com'panionway** *n.* staircase from deck to cabin

company ('kʌmpənɪ) *n.* **1.** gathering of persons **2.** companionship, fellowship **3.** guests **4.** business firm **5.** division of regiment under captain **6.** crew of ship **7.** actors in play —**company sergeant-major** *Mil.* senior noncommissioned officer in company

compare (kəm'pɛə) *vt.* **1.** notice or point out likenesses and differences of **2.** liken **3.** make comparative and superlative of (adjective or adverb) —*vi.* **4.** compete —**comparability** (kɒmpərə'bɪlɪtɪ) *n.* —**comparable** ('kɒmpərəb'l) *a.* —**comparative** (kəm'pærətɪv) *a.* **1.** that may be compared **2.** not absolute **3.** relative, partial **4.** *Gram.* denoting form of adjective, adverb, indicating 'more' —*n.* **5.** comparative form of adjective or adverb —**comparatively** (kəm'pærətɪvlɪ) *adv.* —**comparison** (kəm'pærɪs'n) *n.* act of comparing —**compare with** be like

compartment (kəm'pɑ:tmənt) *n.* **1.** division or part divided off, *eg* in railway carriage **2.** section —**com-part'mentalize** *or* **-lise** *vt.* put into categories *etc.*, *esp.* to excessive degree

compass ('kʌmpəs) *n.* **1.** instrument for showing the north **2.** (*usu. pl.*) instrument for drawing circles **3.** circumference, measurement round **4.** space, area **5.** scope, reach —*vt.* **6.** surround **7.** comprehend **8.** attain, accomplish

compassion (kəm'pæʃən) *n.* pity, sympathy —**com'passionate** *a.* —**com'passionately** *adv.*

THESAURUS

communiqué announcement, bulletin, dispatch, news flash, official communication, report

communism Bolshevism, collectivism, Marxism, socialism, state socialism

communist Bolshevik, collectivist, Marxist, Red (*Inf.*), socialist

community **1.** association, body politic, brotherhood, commonwealth, company, district, general public, locality, people, populace, population, public, residents, society, state **2.** affinity, agreement, identity, likeness, sameness, similarity

commute **1.** barter, exchange, interchange, substitute, switch, trade **2.** *Law: of penalties, etc.* alleviate, curtail, mitigate, modify, reduce, remit, shorten, soften

compact[1] *adj.* **1.** close, compressed, condensed, dense, firm, impenetrable, impermeable, pressed together, solid, thick **2.** brief, compendious, concise, epigrammatic, laconic, pithy, pointed, succinct, terse, to the point ~*v.* **3.** compress, condense, cram, pack down, stuff, tamp

compact[2] *n.* agreement, alliance, arrangement, bargain, bond, concordat, contract, covenant, deal, entente, pact, stipulation, treaty, understanding

companion **1.** accomplice, ally, associate, buddy (*Inf.*), colleague, comrade, confederate, consort, crony, friend, mate (*Inf.*), partner **2.** aide, assistant, attendant, chaperon, duenna, escort, squire

companionable affable, congenial, conversable, convivial, cordial, familiar, friendly, genial, gregarious, neighbourly, outgoing, sociable

companionship amity, camaraderie, company, comradeship, conviviality, esprit de corps, fellowship, fraternity, friendship, rapport, togetherness

company **1.** assemblage, assembly, band, body, circle, collection, community, concourse, convention, coterie, crew, crowd, ensemble, gathering, group, league, party, set, throng, troop, troupe, turnout **2.** association, business, concern, corporation, establishment, firm, house, partnership, syndicate **3.** callers, companionship, fellowship, guests, party, presence, society, visitors

comparable **1.** a match for, as good as, commensurate, equal, equivalent, in a class with, on a par, proportionate, tantamount **2.** akin, alike, analogous, cognate, corresponding, related, similar

comparative approximate, by comparison, qualified, relative

compare **1.** *With* **with** balance, collate, contrast, juxtapose, set against, weigh **2.** *With* **to** correlate, equate, identify with, liken, parallel, resemble **3.** *Be the equal of* approach, approximate to, bear comparison, be in the same class as, be on a par with, come up to, compete with, equal, hold a candle to, match, vie

comparison collation, contrast, distinction, juxtaposition

compartment **1.** alcove, bay, berth, booth, carrel, carriage, cell, chamber, cubbyhole, cubicle, locker, niche, pigeonhole, section **2.** area, category, department, division, section, subdivision

compass *n.* **1.** area, bound, boundary, circle, circuit, circumference, enclosure, extent, field, limit, range, reach, realm, round, scope, sphere, stretch, zone ~*v.* **2.** beset, besiege, blockade, circumscribe, encircle, enclose, encompass, environ, hem in, invest (*Rare*), surround **3.** accomplish, achieve, attain, bring about, effect, execute, fulfil, perform, procure, realize

compassion charity, clemency, commiseration, compunction, condolence, fellow feeling, heart, humanity, kindness, mercy, ruth (*Archaic*), soft-heartedness, sorrow, sympathy, tender-heartedness, tenderness

compatible (kəmˈpætəbᵊl) *a.* 1. capable of harmonious existence 2. consistent, agreeing —**compatiˈbility** *n.* —**comˈpatibly** *adv.*

compatriot (kəmˈpætrɪət) *n.* fellow countryman

compeer (ˈkɒmpɪə) *n.* equal, associate, companion

compel (kəmˈpɛl) *vt.* 1. force, oblige 2. bring about by force (-ll-)

compendium (kəmˈpɛndɪəm) *n.* 1. collection of different games 2. abridgment, summary (*pl.* -s, -ia (-ɪə)) —**comˈpendious** *a.* brief but inclusive —**comˈpendiously** *adv.*

compensate (ˈkɒmpɛnseɪt) *vt.* 1. make up for 2. recompense suitably 3. reward —*vi.* 4. (*with* for) supply an equivalent —**compenˈsation** *n.*

compere (ˈkɒmpɛə) *n.* 1. one who presents artists in cabaret, television shows *etc.* —*v.* 2. act as compere (for)

compete (kəmˈpiːt) *vi.* (*oft. with* with) strive in rivalry, contend, vie —**competition** (kɒmpɪˈtɪʃən) *n.* —**competitive** (kəmˈpɛtɪtɪv) *a.* —**competitor** (kəmˈpɛtɪtə) *n.*

competent (ˈkɒmpɪtənt) *a.* 1. able, skilful 2. properly qualified 3. proper, due, legitimate 4. suitable, sufficient —ˈ**competence** *n.* efficiency —ˈ**competently** *adv.*

compile (kəmˈpaɪl) *vt.* 1. make up (*eg* book) from various sources or materials 2. gather, put together —**compilation** (kɒmpɪˈleɪʃən) *n.* —**comˈpiler** *n.*

complacent (kəmˈpleɪsᵊnt) *a.* 1. self-satisfied 2. pleased, gratified —**comˈplacence** *or* **comˈplacency** *n.* —**comˈplacently** *adv.*

complain (kəmˈpleɪn) *vi.* 1. grumble 2. bring charge, make known a grievance 3. (*with* of) make known that one is suffering from —**comˈplainant** *n.* —**comˈplaint** *n.* 1. statement of a wrong, grievance 2. ailment, illness

complaisant (kəmˈpleɪzᵊnt) *a.* obliging, willing to please, compliant —**comˈplaisance** *n.* 1. act of pleasing 2. affability

complement (ˈkɒmplɪmənt) *n.* 1. person or thing that completes something 2. full allowance, equipment *etc.* —*vt.* (ˈkɒmplɪmɛnt) 3. add to, make complete —**compleˈmentary** *a.*

complete (kəmˈpliːt) *a.* 1. full, perfect 2. finished, ended 3. entire 4. thorough —*vt.* 5. make whole, perfect 6. finish —**comˈpletely** *adv.* —**comˈpleteness** *n.* —**comˈpletion** *n.*

THESAURUS

compassionate benevolent, charitable, humane, humanitarian, indulgent, kind-hearted, kindly, lenient, merciful, pitying, sympathetic, tender, tender-hearted, understanding

compatibility affinity, agreement, amity, congeniality, empathy, harmony, like-mindedness, rapport, single-mindedness, sympathy

compatible accordant, adaptable, agreeable, congenial, congruent, congruous, consistent, consonant, harmonious, in harmony, in keeping, like-minded, reconcilable, suitable

compel bulldoze (*Inf.*), coerce, constrain, dragoon, drive, enforce, exact, force, hustle (*Sl.*), impel, make, necessitate, oblige, restrain, squeeze, urge

compensate 1. atone, indemnify, make good, make restitution, recompense, refund, reimburse, remunerate, repay, requite, reward, satisfy 2. balance, cancel (out), counteract, counterbalance, countervail, make amends, make up for, offset, redress

compensation amends, atonement, damages, indemnification, indemnity, payment, recompense, reimbursement, remuneration, reparation, requital, restitution, reward, satisfaction

compete be in the running, challenge, contend, contest, emulate, fight, pit oneself against, rival, strive, struggle, vie

competence ability, adequacy, appropriateness, capability, capacity, competency, expertise, fitness, proficiency, skill, suitability

competent able, adapted, adequate, appropriate, capable, clever, endowed, equal, fit, pertinent, proficient, qualified, sufficient, suitable

competition 1. contention, contest, emulation, one-upmanship (*Inf.*), opposition, rivalry, strife, struggle 2. championship, contest, event, puzzle, quiz, tournament

competitive aggressive, ambitious, antagonistic, at odds, combative, cutthroat, dog-eat-dog, emulous, opposing, rival, vying

competitor adversary, antagonist, challenger, competition, contestant, emulator, opponent, opposition, rival

compile accumulate, amass, anthologize, collect, cull, garner, gather, marshal, organize, put together

complacency contentment, gratification, pleasure, satisfaction, self-satisfaction, smugness

complacent contented, gratified, pleased, pleased with oneself, satisfied, self-assured, self-contented, self-righteous, self-satisfied, serene, smug, unconcerned

complain beef (*Sl.*), bellyache (*Sl.*), bemoan, bewail, bitch (*Sl.*), carp, deplore, find fault, fuss, grieve, gripe (*Inf.*), groan, grouse, growl, grumble, kick up a fuss (*Inf.*), lament, moan, whine

complaint 1. accusation, annoyance, beef (*Sl.*), bitch (*Sl.*), charge, criticism, dissatisfaction, fault-finding, grievance, gripe (*Inf.*), grouse, grumble, lament, moan, plaint, remonstrance, trouble, wail 2. affliction, ailment, disease, disorder, illness, indisposition, malady, sickness, upset

complement *n.* 1. companion, completion, consummation, correlative, counterpart, finishing touch, rounding-off, supplement 2. aggregate, capacity, entirety, quota, total, totality, wholeness ~*v.* 3. cap (*Inf.*), complete, crown, round off, set off

complementary companion, completing, correlative, corresponding, fellow, interdependent, interrelating, matched, reciprocal

complete *adj.* 1. all, entire, faultless, full, intact, integral, plenary, unabridged, unbroken, undivided, unimpaired, whole 2. accomplished, achieved, concluded, ended, finished 3. absolute, consummate, dyed-in-the-wool, perfect, thorough, thoroughgoing, total, utter ~*v.* 4. accomplish, achieve, cap, close, conclude, crown, discharge, do, end, execute, fill in, finalize, finish, fulfil, perfect, perform, realize, round off, settle, terminate, wrap up (*Inf.*)

completely absolutely, altogether, down to the ground, en masse, entirely, from A to Z, from beginning to end, fully, heart and soul, hook, line and

complex (ˈkɒmplɛks) *a.* **1.** intricate, compound, involved —*n.* **2.** complicated whole **3.** group of related buildings **4.** psychological abnormality, obsession —**comˈplexity** *n.* —**complex fraction** *Maths.* fraction in which numerator or denominator or both contain fractions (*also* **compound fraction**) —**complex number** number of form $a + bi$, where a and b are real numbers and $i = \sqrt{-1}$

complexion (kəmˈplɛkʃən) *n.* **1.** look, colour, of skin, *esp.* of face, appearance **2.** aspect, character **3.** disposition

compliant (kəmˈplaɪənt) *a. see* COMPLY

complicate (ˈkɒmplɪkeɪt) *vt.* make intricate, involved, difficult, mix up —**compliˈcation** *n.*

complicity (kəmˈplɪsɪtɪ) *n.* partnership in wrongdoing

compliment (ˈkɒmplɪmənt) *n.* **1.** expression of regard, praise **2.** flattering speech —*pl.* **3.** expression of courtesy, formal greetings —*vt.* (ˈkɒmplɪmɛnt) **4.** praise, congratulate —**compliˈmentary** *a.* **1.** expressing praise **2.** free of charge

compline (ˈkɒmplɪn, -plaɪn) *or* **complin** (ˈkɒmplɪn) *n.* last service of day in R.C. Church

comply (kəmˈplaɪ) *vi.* consent, yield, do as asked (**comˈplied, comˈplying**) —**comˈpliance** *n.* —**comˈpliant** *a.*

component (kəmˈpəʊnənt) *n.* **1.** part, element, constituent of whole —*a.* **2.** composing, making up

comport (kəmˈpɔːt) *vi.* **1.** agree —*vt.* **2.** behave

compose (kəmˈpəʊz) *vt.* **1.** arrange, put in order **2.** write, invent **3.** make up **4.** calm **5.** settle, adjust —**comˈposed** *a.* calm —**comˈposer** *n.* one who composes, *esp.* music —**ˈcomposite** *a.* made up of distinct parts —**compoˈsition** *n.* —**compositor** (kəmˈpɒzɪtə) *n.* typesetter, one who arranges type for printing —**comˈposure** *n.* calmness —**composite school** C one offering both academic and nonacademic courses

compos mentis (ˈkɒmpəs ˈmɛntɪs) *Lat.* of sound mind

compost (ˈkɒmpɒst) *n.* fertilizing mixture of decayed vegetable matter for soil

compote (ˈkɒmpəʊt) *n.* fruit stewed or preserved in syrup

compound[1] (ˈkɒmpaʊnd) *n.* **1.** mixture, joining **2.** substance, word, made up of parts —*a.* **3.** not simple **4.** composite, mixed —*vt.* (kəmˈpaʊnd) **5.** mix, make up, put together **6.** intensify, make worse **7.** *Law* agree not to prosecute in return for a consideration —*v.* **8.** compromise, settle (debt) by partial payment —**compound eye** convex eye of insects and some crusta-

THESAURUS

sinker, in full, *in toto*, perfectly, quite, root and branch, solidly, thoroughly, totally, utterly, wholly

completion accomplishment, attainment, close, conclusion, consummation, culmination, end, expiration, finalization, fruition, fulfilment, realization

complex *adj.* **1.** circuitous, complicated, convoluted, Daedalian (*Literary*), intricate, involved, knotty, labyrinthine, mingled, mixed, tangled, tortuous **2.** composite, compound, compounded, heterogeneous, manifold, multifarious, multiple ~*n.* **3.** aggregate, composite, network, organization, scheme, structure, synthesis, system **4.** fixation, fixed idea, *idée fixe*, obsession, phobia, preoccupation

complexion **1.** colour, colouring, hue, pigmentation, skin, skin tone **2.** appearance, aspect, cast, character, countenance, disposition, guise, light, look, make-up, nature, stamp

complexity complication, convolution, elaboration, entanglement, intricacy, involvement, multiplicity, ramification

compliance acquiescence, agreement, assent, complaisance, concession, concurrence, conformity, consent, deference, obedience, observance, passivity, submission, submissiveness, yielding

complicate confuse, entangle, interweave, involve, make intricate, muddle, snarl up

complication **1.** combination, complexity, confusion, entanglement, intricacy, mixture, web **2.** aggravation, difficulty, drawback, embarrassment, factor, obstacle, problem, snag

complicity abetment, collaboration, collusion, concurrence, connivance

compliment **1.** *n.* admiration, bouquet, commendation, congratulations, courtesy, eulogy, favour, flattery, honour, praise, tribute **2.** *v.* commend, congratulate, extol, felicitate, flatter, laud, pay tribute to, praise, salute, sing the praises of, speak highly of, wish joy to

complimentary **1.** appreciative, approving, commendatory, congratulatory, eulogistic, flattering, laudatory, panegyrical **2.** courtesy, donated, free, free of charge, gratis, gratuitous, honorary, on the house

compliments good wishes, greetings, regards, remembrances, respects, salutation

comply abide by, accede, accord, acquiesce, adhere to, agree to, conform to, consent to, defer, discharge, follow, fulfil, obey, observe, perform, respect, satisfy, submit, yield

component **1.** *n.* constituent, element, ingredient, item, part, piece, unit **2.** *adj.* composing, constituent, inherent, intrinsic

compose **1.** build, compound, comprise, constitute, construct, fashion, form, make, make up, put together **2.** contrive, create, devise, frame, imagine, indite, invent, produce, write **3.** adjust, arrange, reconcile, regulate, resolve, settle **4.** appease, assuage, calm, collect, control, pacify, placate, quell, quiet, soothe, still, tranquillize

composed at ease, calm, collected, confident, cool, imperturbable, level-headed, poised, relaxed, self-possessed, serene, together (*Sl.*), tranquil, unflappable, unruffled, unworried

composite blended, combined, complex, compound, conglomerate, mixed, synthesized

composition **1.** arrangement, configuration, constitution, design, form, formation, layout, make-up, organization, structure **2.** compilation, creation, fashioning, formation, formulation, invention, making, mixture, production **3.** arrangement, balance, concord, consonance, harmony, placing, proportion, symmetry

compost humus, mulch, organic fertilizer

composure aplomb, calm, calmness, collectedness, cool (*Sl.*), coolness, dignity, ease, equanimity, imperturbability, placidity, poise, sang-froid, sedateness, self-assurance, self-possession, serenity, tranquillity

ceans, consisting of numerous separate units —**compound fracture** fracture in which broken bone pierces skin —**compound interest** interest calculated on both principal and its accrued interest —**compound sentence** sentence containing at least two coordinate clauses —**compound time** *Mus.* time in which number of beats per bar is multiple of three

compound[2] (ˈkɒmpaʊnd) *n.* (fenced or walled) enclosure containing houses *etc.*

comprehend (kɒmprɪˈhɛnd) *vt.* **1.** understand, take in **2.** include, comprise —**compreˈhensible** *a.* —**compreˈhension** *n.* —**compreˈhensive** *a.* **1.** wide, full **2.** taking in much —**compreˈhensively** *adv.* —**compreˈhensiveness** *n.* —**comprehensive school** secondary school for children of all abilities

compress (kəmˈprɛs) *vt.* **1.** squeeze together **2.** make smaller in size, bulk —*n.* (ˈkɒmprɛs) **3.** pad of lint applied to wound, inflamed part *etc.* —**comˈpressible** *a.* —**comˈpression** *n.* in internal-combustion engine, squeezing of explosive charge before ignition, to give additional force —**comˈpressor** *n. esp.* machine to compress air, gas

comprise (kəmˈpraɪz) *vt.* include, contain —**comˈprisable** *a.*

compromise (ˈkɒmprəmaɪz) *n.* **1.** meeting halfway, coming to terms by giving up part of claim **2.** middle course —*v.* **3.** settle (dispute) by making concessions —*vt.* **4.** expose to risk or suspicion

Comptometer (kɒmpˈtɒmɪtə) *n.* **R** calculating machine

comptroller (kənˈtrəʊlə) *n.* controller (in some titles)

compulsion (kəmˈpʌlʃən) *n.* **1.** act of compelling **2.** irresistible impulse —**comˈpulsive** *a.* —**comˈpulsorily** *adv.* —**comˈpulsory** *a.* not optional

compunction (kəmˈpʌŋkʃən) *n.* regret for wrongdoing

compute (kəmˈpjuːt) *v.* reckon, calculate, *esp.* using computer —**compuˈtation** *n.* reckoning, estimate —**comˈputer** *n.* electronic machine for storing, retrieving information and performing calculations —**comˈputerize** *or* **-ise** *v.* equip with, perform by computer

comrade (ˈkɒmreɪd, -rɪd) *n.* mate, companion, friend —**ˈcomradeship** *n.*

con[1] (kɒn) *inf. n.* **1.** confidence trick —*vt.* **2.** swindle, defraud

con[2] (kɒn) *n.* contra, against —**pros and cons** (arguments) for and against

con[3] *or* (*esp. U.S.*) **conn** (kɒn) *vt.* direct steering of (ship) —**ˈconner** *n.*

concatenate (kɒnˈkætɪneɪt) *vt.* link together —**concateˈnation** *n.* connected chain (as of circumstances)

concave (ˈkɒnkeɪv, kɒnˈkeɪv) *a.* hollow, rounded inwards —**concavity** (kɒnˈkævɪtɪ) *n.*

conceal (kənˈsiːl) *vt.* hide, keep secret —**conˈcealment** *n.*

concede (kənˈsiːd) *vt.* **1.** admit, admit truth of **2.** grant, allow —*vi.* **3.** yield

conceit (kənˈsiːt) *n.* **1.** vanity, overweening opinion of oneself **2.** far-fetched comparison —**conˈceited** *a.*

THESAURUS

compound *v.* **1.** amalgamate, blend, coalesce, combine, concoct, fuse, intermingle, mingle, mix, synthesize, unite **2.** add to, aggravate, augment, complicate, exacerbate, heighten, intensify, magnify, worsen ~*n.* **3.** alloy, amalgam, blend, combination, composite, composition, conglomerate, fusion, medley, mixture, synthesis ~*adj.* **4.** complex, composite, conglomerate, intricate, multiple, not simple

comprehend 1. apprehend, assimilate, conceive, discern, fathom, grasp, know, make out, perceive, see, take in, understand **2.** comprise, contain, embody, embrace, enclose, encompass, include, involve, take in

comprehensible clear, coherent, conceivable, explicit, graspable, intelligible, plain, understandable

comprehension 1. conception, discernment, grasp, intelligence, judgment, knowledge, perception, realization, sense, understanding **2.** compass, domain, field, limits, province, range, reach, scope

comprehensive all-embracing, all-inclusive, blanket, broad, catholic, complete, encyclopedic, exhaustive, extensive, full, inclusive, sweeping, thorough, umbrella, wide

compress abbreviate, compact, concentrate, condense, constrict, contract, cram, crowd, crush, press, shorten, squash, squeeze, summarize, wedge

comprise be composed of, comprehend, consist of, contain, embrace, encompass, include, take in

compromise *v.* **1.** adjust, agree, arbitrate, compose, compound, concede, give and take, go fifty-fifty (*Inf.*), meet halfway, settle, strike a balance ~*n.* **2.** accommodation, accord, adjustment, agreement, concession, give-and-take, half measures, middle ground, settlement, trade-off ~*v.* **3.** discredit, dishonour, embarrass, expose, hazard, imperil, implicate, jeopardize, prejudice, weaken

compulsion 1. coercion, constraint, demand, duress, force, obligation, pressure **2.** drive, necessity, need, obsession, preoccupation, urge

compulsive besetting, compelling, driving, irresistible, obsessive, overwhelming, uncontrollable, urgent

compulsory binding, *de rigueur*, forced, imperative, mandatory, obligatory, required, requisite

compute add up, calculate, cast up, cipher, count, enumerate, estimate, figure, figure out, measure, rate, reckon, sum, tally, total

comrade ally, associate, buddy (*Inf.*), colleague, companion, compatriot, compeer, confederate, co-worker, crony, fellow, friend, mate (*Inf.*), pal (*Inf.*), partner

concave cupped, depressed, excavated, hollow, hollowed, incurved, indented, scooped, sunken

conceal bury, camouflage, cover, disguise, dissemble, hide, keep dark, keep secret, mask, obscure, screen, secrete, shelter

concealment camouflage, cover, disguise, hideaway, hide-out, hiding, secrecy

concede 1. accept, acknowledge, admit, allow, confess, grant, own **2.** cede, give up, hand over, relinquish, surrender, yield

conceit amour-propre, arrogance, complacency, egotism, narcissism, pride, self-importance, self-love, swagger, vainglory, vanity

conceited arrogant, bigheaded (*Inf.*), cocky, egotisti-

conceive (kənˈsiːv) *vt.* **1.** believe **2.** form conception of **3.** become pregnant with —*vi.* **4.** become pregnant —**conˈceivable** *a.* —**conˈceivably** *adv.* —**conceive of** have an idea of; imagine; think of

concentrate (ˈkɒnsəntreɪt) *vt.* **1.** focus (one's efforts *etc.*) **2.** increase in strength **3.** reduce to small space —*vi.* **4.** devote all attention **5.** come together —*n.* **6.** concentrated material or solution —**concenˈtration** *n.* —**concentration camp** prison camp, *esp.* one in Nazi Germany

concentric (kənˈsɛntrɪk) *a.* having the same centre

concept (ˈkɒnsɛpt) *n.* **1.** abstract idea **2.** mental expression —**conˈceptual** *a.* —**conˈceptualize** *or* **-lise** *v.*

conception (kənˈsɛpʃən) *n.* **1.** idea, notion **2.** act of conceiving

concern (kənˈsɜːn) *vt.* **1.** relate or apply to **2.** interest, affect, trouble **3.** (*with* in *or* with) involve (oneself) —*n.* **4.** affair **5.** regard, worry **6.** importance **7.** business enterprise —**conˈcerned** *a.* **1.** connected **2.** interested **3.** worried **4.** involved —**conˈcerning** *prep.* respecting, about

concert (ˈkɒnsɜːt) *n.* **1.** musical entertainment **2.** harmony, agreement —*v.* (kənˈsɜːt) **3.** arrange, plan together —**conˈcerted** *a.* **1.** mutually arranged, planned **2.** determined —**concerˈtina** *n.* **1.** musical instrument with bellows and keys —*vi.* **2.** fold, collapse, as bellows —**concerto** (kənˈtʃɛətəʊ) *n.* musical composition for solo instrument and orchestra (*pl.* **-s**) —**concert pitch 1.** frequency of 440 hertz assigned to A above middle C **2.** *inf.* state of extreme readiness

concession (kənˈsɛʃən) *n.* **1.** act of conceding **2.** thing conceded **3.** grant **4.** special privilege **5.** C land division in township survey —**concessioˈnaire, conˈcessioner** *or* **conˈcessionary** *n.* someone who holds or operates concession —**conˈcessive** *a.*

conch (kɒŋk, kɒntʃ) *n.* seashell —**conchology** (kɒŋˈkɒlədʒɪ) *n.* study, collection of shells and shellfish

concierge (kɒnsɪˈɛəʒ) *n.* in France, caretaker, doorkeeper

conciliate (kənˈsɪlɪeɪt) *vt.* pacify, win over from hostility —**conciliˈation** *n.* —**conˈciliator** *n.* —**conˈciliatory** *a.*

concise (kənˈsaɪs) *a.* brief, terse —**conˈcisely** *adv.* —**conˈciseness** *n.* —**concision** (kənˈsɪʒən) *n.*

conclave (ˈkɒnkleɪv) *n.* **1.** private meeting **2.** assembly for election of Pope

conclude (kənˈkluːd) *vt.* **1.** end, finish **2.** deduce **3.** settle **4.** decide —*vi.* **5.** come to an end —**conˈclusion** *n.* —**conˈclusive** *a.* decisive, convincing —**conˈclusively** *adv.*

THESAURUS

cal, immodest, narcissistic, overweening, puffed up, self-important, stuck up (*Inf.*), swollen-headed, vain, vainglorious

conceivable believable, credible, imaginable, possible, thinkable

conceive 1. appreciate, apprehend, believe, comprehend, envisage, fancy, grasp, imagine, realize, suppose, understand **2.** contrive, create, design, develop, devise, form, formulate, produce, project, purpose, think up **3.** become impregnated, become pregnant

concentrate 1. be engrossed in, consider closely, focus attention on, give all one's attention to, put one's mind to, rack one's brains **2.** bring to bear, centre, cluster, converge, focus **3.** accumulate, cluster, collect, congregate, gather, huddle

concentration 1. absorption, application, heed, single-mindedness **2.** bringing to bear, centralization, centring, combination, compression, consolidation, convergence, focusing, intensification **3.** accumulation, aggregation, cluster, collection, convergence, horde, mass

concept abstraction, conception, conceptualization, hypothesis, idea, image, impression, notion, theory, view

conception 1. concept, design, idea, image, notion, plan **2.** fertilization, germination, impregnation, insemination

concern *v.* **1.** affect, apply to, bear on, be relevant to, interest, involve, pertain to, regard, touch ~*n.* **2.** affair, business, charge, department, field, interest, involvement, job, matter, mission, occupation, responsibility, task, transaction **3.** bearing, importance, interest, reference, relation, relevance ~*v.* **4.** bother, disquiet, distress, disturb, make anxious, make uneasy, perturb, trouble, worry ~*n.* **5.** anxiety, apprehension, attention, burden, care, consideration, disquiet, disquietude, distress, heed, responsibility, solicitude, worry **6.** business, company, corporation, enterprise, establishment, firm, house, organization

concerned 1. active, implicated, interested, involved, mixed up, privy to **2.** anxious, bothered, distressed, disturbed, exercised, troubled, uneasy, upset, worried **3.** attentive, caring, interested, solicitous

concerning about, anent (*Scot.*), apropos of, as regards, as to, in the matter of, on the subject of, re, regarding, relating to, respecting, touching, with reference to

concert *n.* accord, agreement, concord, concordance, harmony, unanimity, union, unison

concerted agreed upon, collaborative, combined, coordinated, joint, planned, prearranged, united

concession 1. acknowledgment, admission, assent, confession, surrender, yielding **2.** adjustment, allowance, boon, compromise, grant, indulgence, permit, privilege

conciliate appease, disarm, mediate, mollify, pacify, placate, propitiate, reconcile, restore harmony, soothe, win over

conciliation appeasement, disarming, mollification, pacification, placation, propitiation, reconciliation, soothing

conciliatory appeasing, disarming, irenic, mollifying, pacific, peaceable, placatory, propitiative

concise brief, compact, compendious, compressed, condensed, epigrammatic, laconic, pithy, short, succinct, summary, synoptic, terse, to the point

conclude 1. bring down the curtain, cease, close, come to an end, complete, draw to a close, end, finish, round off, terminate, wind up (*Inf.*) **2.** assume, decide, deduce, gather, infer, judge, reckon (*Inf.*), sum up, suppose, surmise **3.** accomplish, bring about, carry out, clinch (*Inf.*), decide, determine, effect, establish, fix, pull off, resolve, settle, work out

concoct (kənˈkɒkt) *vt.* **1.** make (mixture), with various ingredients **2.** make up **3.** contrive, plan **—conˈcoction** *n.*

concomitant (kənˈkɒmɪtənt) *a.* accompanying **—conˈcomitance** *n.* existence

concord (ˈkɒnkɔːd) *n.* **1.** agreement **2.** harmony **—conˈcordance** *n.* **1.** agreement **2.** index to words of book (*esp.* Bible) **—conˈcordant** *a.* **—conˈcordat** *n.* pact or treaty, *esp.* between Vatican and another state concerning interests of religion in that state

concourse (ˈkɒnkɔːs) *n.* **1.** crowd **2.** large, open place in public area

concrete (ˈkɒnkriːt) *n.* **1.** mixture of sand, cement *etc.*, used in building *—a.* **2.** made of concrete **3.** particular, specific **4.** perceptible, actual **5.** solid **—ˈconcretely** *adv.* **—conˈcretion** *n.* **1.** mass of compressed particles **2.** stonelike growth in body

concubine (ˈkɒŋkjʊbaɪn, ˈkɒn-) *n.* **1.** woman living with man as his wife, but not married to him **2.** 'secondary' wife of inferior legal status **—concubinage** (kɒnˈkjuːbɪnɪdʒ) *n.*

concupiscence (kənˈkjuːpɪsəns) *n.* lust

concur (kənˈkɜː) *vi.* **1.** agree, express agreement **2.** happen together **3.** coincide (**-rr-**) **—conˈcurrence** *n.* **—conˈcurrent** *a.* **—conˈcurrently** *adv.* at the same time

concuss (kənˈkʌs) *vt.* injure (brain) by blow, fall *etc.* **—conˈcussion** *n.* **1.** brain injury **2.** physical shock

condemn (kənˈdɛm) *vt.* **1.** blame **2.** find guilty **3.** doom **4.** find, declare unfit for use **—condemnation** (kɒndɛmˈneɪʃən) *n.* **—condemnatory** (kɒndɛmˈneɪtərɪ) *a.*

condense (kənˈdɛns) *vt.* **1.** concentrate, make more solid **2.** turn from gas into liquid **3.** pack into few words *—vi.* **4.** turn from gas to liquid **—condenˈsation** *n.* **—conˈdenser** *n.* **1.** *Elec.* apparatus for storing electrical energy, a capacitor **2.** apparatus for reducing vapours to liquid form **3.** a lens or mirror for focusing light **—condensed milk** milk reduced by evaporation to thick concentration, with sugar added

condescend (kɒndɪˈsɛnd) *vi.* **1.** treat graciously one regarded as inferior **2.** do something below one's dignity **—condeˈscending** *a.* **—condeˈscension** *n.*

condign (kənˈdaɪn) *a.* (*esp.* of punishment) fitting; deserved

condiment (ˈkɒndɪmənt) *n.* relish, seasoning for food

condition (kənˈdɪʃən) *n.* **1.** state or circumstances of anything **2.** thing on which statement or happening or existing depends **3.** stipulation, prerequisite **4.** health, physical fitness **5.** rank *—vt.* **6.** accustom **7.** regulate **8.** make fit, healthy **9.** be essential to happening or existence of **—conˈditional** *a.* **1.** dependent on circumstances or events *—n.* **2.** *Gram.* conditional verb form, clause *etc.* **—conditioned reflex** in psychology and physiology, automatic response induced by stimulus repeatedly applied

condole (kənˈdəʊl) *vi.* **1.** grieve (with), offer sympathy **2.** commiserate (with) **—conˈdolence** *n.*

condom (ˈkɒndəm) *n.* sheathlike rubber contraceptive device worn by man

---

THESAURUS

conclusion **1.** close, completion, end, finale, finish, result, termination **2.** agreement, conviction, decision, deduction, inference, judgment, opinion, resolution, settlement, verdict

conclusive clinching, convincing, decisive, definite, definitive, final, irrefutable, ultimate, unanswerable, unarguable

concoct brew, contrive, cook up (*Inf.*), design, devise, fabricate, formulate, hatch, invent, make up, mature, plot, prepare, project, think up

concoction blend, brew, combination, compound, contrivance, creation, mixture, preparation

concrete *adj.* **1.** actual, definite, explicit, factual, material, real, sensible, specific, substantial, tangible **2.** calcified, compact, compressed, conglomerated, consolidated, firm, petrified, solid, solidified *~n.* **3.** cement (*Not in technical usage*), concretion

concubine courtesan, kept woman, leman (*Archaic*), mistress, odalisque, paramour

concur accede, accord, acquiesce, agree, approve, assent, coincide, combine, consent, cooperate, harmonize, join

concurrent **1.** coexisting, coincident, concerted, concomitant, contemporaneous, simultaneous, synchronous **2.** agreeing, at one, compatible, consentient, consistent, cooperating, harmonious, in agreement, in rapport, like-minded, of the same mind

concussion clash, collision, crash, impact, jarring, jolt, jolting, shaking, shock

condemn **1.** blame, censure, damn, denounce, disapprove, reprehend, reproach, reprobate, reprove, upbraid **2.** convict, damn, doom, pass sentence on, proscribe, sentence

condemnation **1.** blame, censure, denouncement, denunciation, disapproval, reproach, reprobation, reproof, stricture **2.** conviction, damnation, doom, judgment, proscription, sentence

condensation **1.** abridgment, contraction, digest, précis, synopsis **2.** condensate, deliquescence, distillation, liquefaction, precipitate, precipitation **3.** compression, concentration, consolidation, crystallization, curtailment, reduction

condense **1.** abbreviate, abridge, compact, compress, concentrate, contract, curtail, encapsulate, epitomize, précis, shorten, summarize **2.** boil down, coagulate, concentrate, decoct, precipitate (*Chem.*), reduce, solidify, thicken

condescend **1.** be courteous, bend, come down off one's high horse (*Inf.*), deign, humble *or* demean oneself, lower oneself, see fit, stoop, submit, unbend (*Inf.*), vouchsafe **2.** patronize, talk down to

condescending disdainful, lofty, lordly, patronizing, snobbish, snooty (*Inf.*), supercilious, superior, toffee-nosed (*Sl.*)

condition *n.* **1.** case, circumstances, plight, position, predicament, shape, situation, state, state of affairs, *status quo* **2.** arrangement, article, demand, limitation, modification, prerequisite, provision, proviso, qualification, requirement, requisite, restriction, rule, stipulation, terms **3.** fettle, fitness, health, kilter, order, shape, state of health, trim **4.** caste, class, estate, grade, order, position, rank, status, stratum *~v.* **5.** accustom, adapt, educate, equip, habituate, inure, make ready, prepare, ready, tone up, train, work out

conditional contingent, dependent, limited, provisional, qualified, subject to, with reservations

condominium (kɒndəˈmɪnɪəm) *n.* joint rule by two or more states

condone (kənˈdəʊn) *vt.* overlook, forgive, treat as not existing

condor (ˈkɒndɔː) *n.* iarge vulture found in the Andes

conduce (kənˈdjuːs) *vi.* (*with* to) **1.** help, promote **2.** tend (towards) —**conˈducive** *a.*

conduct (ˈkɒndʌkt) *n.* **1.** behaviour **2.** management —*vt.* (kənˈdʌkt) **3.** escort, guide **4.** lead, direct **5.** manage **6.** transmit (heat, electricity) —**conˈductance** *n.* ability of system to conduct electricity —**conˈduction** *n.* —**conˈductive** *a.* —**conducˈtivity** *n.* —**conˈductor** *n.* **1.** person in charge of bus *etc.*, who collects fares **2.** director of orchestra **3.** one who leads, guides **4.** substance capable of transmitting heat, electricity *etc.* **5.** US official in charge of passenger train

conduit (ˈkɒndɪt, -djʊɪt) *n.* channel or pipe for conveying water, electric cables *etc.*

cone (kəʊn) *n.* **1.** solid figure with circular base, tapering to a point **2.** fruit of pine, fir *etc.* —**ˈconic(al)** *a.* of or like cone —**conic section** one of group of curves formed by intersection of plane and right circular cone

confabulate (kənˈfæbjʊleɪt) *vi.* chat —**ˈconfab** *n. inf.* shortened form of **confabuˈlation** *n.* confidential conversation

confection (kənˈfɛkʃən) *n.* prepared delicacy, *esp.* something sweet —**conˈfectioner** *n.* dealer in fancy cakes, pastries, sweets *etc.* —**conˈfectionery** *n.* sweets, cakes *etc.*

confederate (kənˈfɛdərɪt) *n.* **1.** ally **2.** accomplice —*v.* (kənˈfɛdəreɪt) **3.** unite —**conˈfederacy** *n.* —**confedeˈration** *n.* alliance of political units

confer (kənˈfɜː) *vt.* **1.** grant, give **2.** bestow **3.** award —*vi.* **4.** consult together (-rr-) —**ˈconference** *n.* meeting for consultation or deliberation —**conˈferment** *n.*

confess (kənˈfɛs) *vt.* **1.** admit, own **2.** (of priest) hear sins of —*vi.* **3.** acknowledge **4.** declare one's sins orally to priest —**conˈfession** *n.* —**conˈfessional** *n.* confessor's stall or box —**conˈfessor** *n.* priest who hears confessions

confetti (kənˈfɛtɪ) *n.* small bits of coloured paper for throwing at weddings

confide (kənˈfaɪd) *vi.* **1.** (*with* in) tell secrets, trust —*vt.* **2.** entrust —**confidant** (kɒnfɪˈdænt, ˈkɒnfɪdænt) *n.* one entrusted with secrets (-e *fem.*) —**confidence** (ˈkɒnfɪdəns) *n.* **1.** trust **2.** boldness, assurance **3.** intimacy **4.** something confided, secret —**confident** (ˈkɒnfɪdənt) *a.* **1.** having or showing certainty; sure **2.** sure of oneself **3.** presumptuous —**confidential** (kɒnfɪˈdɛnʃəl) *a.* **1.** private **2.** secret **3.** entrusted with another's confidences —**confidentially** (kɒnfɪˈdɛnʃəlɪ) *adv.* —**confidently** (ˈkɒnfɪdəntlɪ) *adv.* —**conˈfiding** *a.* unsuspicious; trustful —**confidence trick** swindle in which victim entrusts money *etc.*, to thief, believing him honest

configuration (kənfɪgjʊˈreɪʃən) *n.* shape, aspect, conformation, arrangement

confine (kənˈfaɪn) *vt.* **1.** keep within bounds **2.** keep in house, bed *etc.* **3.** shut up, imprison —**conˈfinement** *n.* **1.** act of confining or state of being confined **2.** period of birth of child —**ˈconfines** *pl.n.* boundaries, limits

confirm (kənˈfɜːm) *vt.* **1.** make certain of, verify **2.** strengthen, settle **3.** make valid, ratify **4.** administer confirmation to —**confirˈmation** *n.* **1.** making strong, certain **2.** rite administered by bishop to confirm vows made at baptism —**conˈfirmative** *or* **conˈfirmatory** *a.* **1.** tending to confirm or establish **2.** corroborative —**conˈfirmed** *a.* (of habit *etc.*) long-established

THESAURUS

condone disregard, excuse, forgive, let pass, look the other way, make allowance for, overlook, pardon, turn a blind eye to, wink at

conduct *n.* **1.** administration, control, direction, guidance, leadership, management, organization, running, supervision ~*v.* **2.** administer, carry on, control, direct, govern, handle, lead, manage, organize, preside over, regulate, run, supervise **3.** accompany, attend, chair, convey, escort, guide, pilot, preside over, steer, usher ~*n.* **4.** attitude, bearing, behaviour, carriage, comportment, demeanour, deportment, manners, mien (*Literary*), ways

confederacy alliance, bund, coalition, compact, confederation, conspiracy, covenant, federation, league, union

confederate **1.** *n.* abettor, accessory, accomplice, ally, associate, colleague, partner **2.** *v.* ally, amalgamate, associate, band together, combine, federate, merge, unite

confer **1.** accord, award, bestow, give, grant, present, vouchsafe **2.** consult, converse, deliberate, discourse, parley, talk

conference colloquium, congress, consultation, convention, convocation, discussion, forum, meeting, seminar, symposium, teach-in

confess acknowledge, admit, allow, blurt out, come clean (*Inf.*), concede, confide, disclose, divulge, grant, make a clean breast of, own, own up, recognize

confession acknowledgment, admission, disclosure, divulgence, exposure, revelation, unbosoming

confidant, confidante alter ego, bosom friend, close friend, crony, familiar, intimate

confide **1.** admit, breathe, confess, disclose, divulge, impart, reveal, whisper **2.** commend, commit, consign, entrust

confidence **1.** belief, credence, dependence, faith, reliance, trust **2.** aplomb, assurance, boldness, courage, firmness, nerve, self-possession, self-reliance

confident **1.** certain, convinced, counting on, positive, satisfied, secure, sure **2.** assured, bold, dauntless, fearless, self-assured, self-reliant

confidential **1.** classified, hush-hush (*Inf.*), intimate, off the record, private, privy, secret **2.** faithful, familiar, trusted, trustworthy, trusty

confidentially behind closed doors, between ourselves, in camera, in confidence, in secret, personally, privately, sub rosa

confine bind, bound, cage, circumscribe, enclose, hem in, hold back, immure, imprison, incarcerate, intern, keep, limit, repress, restrain, restrict, shut up

confinement **1.** custody, detention, imprisonment, incarceration, internment **2.** *accouchement*, childbed, childbirth, labour, lying-in, parturition, time, travail

confines boundaries, bounds, circumference, edge, limits, precincts

confirm **1.** assure, buttress, clinch, establish, fix, fortify, reinforce, settle, strengthen **2.** approve, authenticate, bear out, corroborate, endorse, ratify, sanction, substantiate, validate, verify

confiscate (ˈkɒnfɪskeɪt) *vt.* seize by authority —**conˈfisˈcation** *n.* —**conˈfiscatory** *a.*

conflagration (kɒnfləˈgreɪʃən) *n.* great destructive fire

conflate (kənˈfleɪt) *vt.* combine, blend to form whole

conflict (ˈkɒnflɪkt) *n.* **1.** struggle, trial of strength **2.** disagreement —*vi.* (kənˈflɪkt) **3.** be at odds (with), be inconsistent (with) **4.** clash

confluence (ˈkɒnfluəns) *or* **conflux** (ˈkɒnflʌks) *n.* **1.** union of streams **2.** meeting place —**ˈconfluent** *a.*

conform (kənˈfɔːm) *vi.* **1.** comply with accepted standards, conventions *etc.* —*v.* **2.** adapt to rule, pattern, custom *etc.* —**conˈformable** *a.* —**conˈformably** *adv.* —**conforˈmation** *n.* structure, adaptation —**conˈformist** *n.* one who conforms, *esp.* excessively —**conˈformity** *n.* compliance

confound (kənˈfaʊnd) *vt.* **1.** baffle, perplex **2.** confuse **3.** defeat —**conˈfounded** *a. esp. inf.* damned

confrère (ˈkɒnfrɛə) *n.* fellow member of profession *etc.*

confront (kənˈfrʌnt) *vt.* **1.** face **2.** bring face to face (with) —**confronˈtation** *n.*

Confucianism (kənˈfjuːʃənɪzəm) *n.* ethical system of Confucius, Chinese philosopher, emphasizing devotion to family, peace and justice

confuse (kənˈfjuːz) *vt.* **1.** bewilder **2.** jumble **3.** make unclear **4.** mistake (one thing) for another **5.** disconcert —**conˈfusion** *n.*

confute (kənˈfjuːt) *vt.* **1.** prove wrong **2.** disprove —**confuˈtation** *n.*

conga (ˈkɒŋgə) *n.* Latin American dance performed by number of people in single file

congé (ˈkɒnʒeɪ) *n.* **1.** permission to depart or dismissal, *esp.* when formal **2.** farewell

congeal (kənˈdʒiːl) *v.* solidify by cooling or freezing —**congeˈlation** *n.*

congener (kənˈdʒiːnə, ˈkɒndʒɪnə) *n.* member of class, group *etc. esp.* any animal of specified genus

congenial (kənˈdʒiːnjəl) *a.* **1.** pleasant, to one's liking **2.** of similar disposition, tastes *etc.* —**congeniˈality** *n.* —**conˈgenially** *adv.*

congenital (kənˈdʒɛnɪtᵊl) *a.* **1.** existing at birth **2.** dating from birth

conger (ˈkɒŋgə) *n.* variety of large, voracious, sea eel

congeries (kɒnˈdʒɪəriːz) *n. sing. and pl.* collection or mass of small bodies, conglomeration

congest (kənˈdʒɛst) *v.* overcrowd or clog —**conˈgested** *a.* —**conˈgestion** *n.* abnormal accumulation, overcrowding

conglomerate (kənˈglɒmərɪt) *n.* **1.** thing, substance (*esp.* rock) composed of mixture of other, smaller elements or pieces **2.** business organization comprising many companies —*v.* (kənˈglɒməreɪt) **3.** gather

THESAURUS

confirmation **1.** authentication, corroboration, evidence, proof, substantiation, testimony, validation, verification **2.** acceptance, agreement, approval, assent, endorsement, ratification, sanction

confirmed chronic, dyed-in-the-wool, habitual, hardened, ingrained, inured, inveterate, long-established, rooted, seasoned

confiscate appropriate, commandeer, expropriate, impound, seize, sequester, sequestrate

confiscation appropriation, expropriation, forfeiture, impounding, seizure, sequestration, takeover

conflict *n.* **1.** battle, clash, collision, combat, contention, contest, encounter, engagement, fight, fracas, set-to (*Inf.*), strife, war, warfare **2.** antagonism, bad blood, difference, disagreement, discord, dissension, divided loyalties, friction, hostility, interference, opposition, strife, variance ~*v.* **3.** be at variance, clash, collide, combat, contend, contest, differ, disagree, fight, interfere, strive, struggle

conform **1.** adapt, adjust, comply, fall in with, follow, follow the crowd, obey, run with the pack, yield **2.** accord, agree, assimilate, correspond, harmonize, match, square, suit, tally

conformation anatomy, arrangement, build, configuration, form, framework, outline, shape, structure

conformist *n.* Babbitt (*U.S.*), conventionalist, stick-in-the-mud (*Inf.*), traditionalist, yes man

conformity allegiance, Babbittry (*U.S.*), compliance, conventionality, observance, orthodoxy

confound **1.** amaze, astonish, astound, baffle, bewilder, confuse, dumbfound, flabbergast (*Inf.*), mix up, mystify, nonplus, perplex, startle, surprise **2.** annihilate, contradict, demolish, destroy, explode, overthrow, overwhelm, refute, ruin

confront accost, beard, brave, bring face to face with, challenge, defy, encounter, face, face up to, oppose, stand up to

confrontation conflict, contest, crisis, encounter, set-to (*Inf.*), showdown (*Inf.*)

confuse **1.** baffle, bemuse, bewilder, darken, mystify, obscure, perplex, puzzle **2.** blend, confound, disarrange, disorder, intermingle, involve, jumble, mingle, mistake, mix up, muddle, snarl up (*Inf.*), tangle **3.** abash, addle, demoralize, discomfit, discompose, disconcert, discountenance, disorient, embarrass, fluster, mortify, nonplus, rattle (*Inf.*), shame, throw off balance, upset

confusion **1.** befuddlement, bemusement, bewilderment, disorientation, mystification, perplexity, puzzlement **2.** bustle, chaos, clutter, commotion, disarrangement, disorder, disorganization, hotchpotch, jumble, mess, muddle, shambles, tangle, turmoil, untidiness, upheaval **3.** abashment, chagrin, demoralization, discomfiture, distraction, embarrassment, fluster, perturbation

congenial adapted, agreeable, companionable, compatible, complaisant, favourable, fit, friendly, genial, kindly, kindred, like-minded, pleasant, pleasing, suitable, sympathetic, well-suited

congenital constitutional, inborn, inbred, inherent, innate, natural

congested blocked-up, clogged, crammed, crowded, jammed, overcrowded, overfilled, overflowing, packed, stuffed, stuffed-up, teeming

congestion bottleneck, clogging, crowding, jam, mass, overcrowding, snarl-up (*Inf.*), surfeit

conglomerate **1.** *adj.* amassed, clustered, composite, heterogeneous, massed **2.** *v.* accumulate, agglomerate, aggregate, cluster, coalesce, snowball **3.** *n.* agglomerate, aggregate, multinational

conglomeration accumulation, aggregation, assortment, combination, composite, hotchpotch, mass, medley, miscellany, mishmash, potpourri

together —*a.* **4.** made up of heterogeneous elements **5.** (of sedimentary rocks) consisting of rounded fragments within finer matrix —**conglomer'ation** *n.*

congratulate (kən'grætjuleɪt) *vt.* express pleasure at good fortune, success *etc.* —**congratu'lations** *pl. n.* —**con'gratulatory** *a.*

congregate ('kɒŋgrɪgeɪt) *v.* **1.** assemble **2.** collect, flock together —**congre'gation** *n.* assembly, *esp.* for worship —**congre'gational** *a.* —**Congre'gationalism** *n.* system in which each separate church is self-governing —**Congre'gationalist** *n.*

congress ('kɒŋgrɛs) *n.* **1.** meeting **2.** formal assembly for discussion **3.** legislative body —**con'gressional** *a.* —**'congressman** *n.* a member of the U.S. Congress

congruent ('kɒŋgrʊənt) *a.* **1.** suitable, accordant **2.** fitting together, *esp.* triangles —**'congruence** *n.* —**con'gruity** *n.* —**'congruous** *a.*

conic(al) ('kɒnɪk(ᵊl)) *a. see* CONE

conifer ('kəʊnɪfə, 'kɒn-) *n.* cone-bearing tree, as fir, pine *etc.* —**co'niferous** *a.*

conjecture (kən'dʒɛktʃə) *n.* **1.** guess, guesswork —*v.* **2.** guess, surmise —**con'jectural** *a.*

conjoin (kən'dʒɔɪn) *vt.* **1.** combine —*vi.* **2.** come, or act, together —**con'joint** *a.* concerted, united —**con'jointly** *adv.*

conjugal ('kɒndʒʊgᵊl) *a.* **1.** relating to marriage **2.** between married persons —**conju'gality** *n.*

conjugate ('kɒndʒʊgeɪt) *vt.* inflect verb in its various forms (past, present *etc.*) —**conju'gation** *n.*

conjunction (kən'dʒʌŋkʃən) *n.* **1.** union **2.** simultaneous happening **3.** part of speech joining words, phrases *etc.* —**con'junctive** *a.* —**con'juncture** *n.*

conjunctiva (kɒndʒʌŋk'taɪvə) *n.* mucous membrane lining eyelid —**conjuncti'vitis** *n.* inflammation of this

conjure ('kʌndʒə) *vi.* **1.** produce magic effects **2.** perform tricks by jugglery *etc.* **3.** invoke devils —*vt.* (kən'dʒʊə) **4.** implore earnestly —**conju'ration** *n.* —**'conjurer** *or* **'conjuror** *n.* —**conjure up 1.** present to the mind **2.** call up (spirit or devil) by incantation

conk (kɒŋk) *inf. vt.* **1.** strike (*esp.* on head) —*n.* **2.** nose —**conk out** *inf.* **1.** break down **2.** tire suddenly; collapse

conker ('kɒŋkə) *n. inf.* horse chestnut

connect (kə'nɛkt) *v.* **1.** join together, unite —*vt.* **2.** associate in the mind —**con'nection** *or* **con'nexion** *n.* **1.** association **2.** train *etc.* timed to enable passengers to transfer from another **3.** family relation —**con'nective** *a.* —**connecting rod** that part of engine which transfers motion from piston to crankshaft

conning tower ('kɒnɪŋ) armoured control position in submarine, battleship *etc.* (*see also* CON[3])

connive (kə'naɪv) *vi.* **1.** plot, conspire **2.** assent, refrain from preventing or forbidding —**con'nivance** *n.*

connoisseur (kɒnɪ'sɜː) *n.* **1.** critical expert in matters of taste, *esp.* fine arts **2.** competent judge

connote (kɒ'nəʊt) *vt.* imply, mean in addition to primary meaning —**conno'tation** *n.*

connubial (kə'njuːbɪəl) *a.* of marriage

conquer ('kɒŋkə) *vt.* **1.** win by force of arms, overcome **2.** defeat —*vi.* **3.** be victorious —**'conqueror** *n.* —**'conquest** *n.*

conquistador (kɒn'kwɪstədɔː) *n.* adventurer or conqueror, *esp.* one of Sp. conquerors of New World in 16th cent. (*pl.* **-s, -dores** (-dɔːrɛs))

Cons. Conservative

THESAURUS

congratulate compliment, felicitate, wish joy to

congratulations best wishes, compliments, felicitations, good wishes, greetings

congregate assemble, collect, come together, concentrate, convene, converge, convoke, flock, forgather, gather, mass, meet, muster, rally, rendezvous, throng

congregation assembly, brethren, crowd, fellowship, flock, host, laity, multitude, parish, parishioners, throng

congress assembly, chamber of deputies, conclave, conference, convention, convocation, council, delegates, diet, legislative assembly, legislature, meeting, parliament, representatives

conjecture 1. *v.* assume, fancy, guess, hypothesize, imagine, infer, suppose, surmise, suspect, theorize **2.** *n.* assumption, conclusion, fancy, guess, guesstimate (*Inf.*), guesswork, hypothesis, inference, notion, presumption, shot in the dark, speculation, supposition, surmise, theorizing, theory

conjugal bridal, connubial, hymeneal, marital, married, matrimonial, nuptial, spousal, wedded

conjunction association, coincidence, combination, concurrence, juxtaposition, union

conjure 1. juggle, play tricks **2.** bewitch, call upon, cast a spell, charm, enchant, fascinate, invoke, raise, rouse, summon up **3.** adjure, appeal to, beg, beseech, crave, entreat, implore, importune, pray, supplicate

conjurer, conjuror magician, miracle-worker, sorcerer, thaumaturge (*Rare*), wizard

conjure up bring to mind, contrive, create, evoke, produce as by magic, recall, recollect

connect affix, ally, associate, cohere, combine, couple, fasten, join, link, relate, unite

connection 1. alliance, association, attachment, coupling, fastening, junction, link, tie, union **2.** affinity, association, bond, commerce, communication, correlation, correspondence, intercourse, interrelation, link, marriage, relation, relationship, relevance, tie-in **3.** kin, kindred, kinsman, kith, relation, relative

connivance abetment, abetting, collusion, complicity, conspiring, tacit consent

connive 1. cabal, collude, conspire, cook up (*Inf.*), intrigue, plot, scheme **2.** *With* **at** abet, aid, be an accessory to, be a party to, be in collusion with, blink at, disregard, lend oneself to, let pass, look the other way, overlook, pass by, shut one's eyes to, turn a blind eye to, wink at

connoisseur aficionado, appreciator, arbiter, authority, buff (*Inf.*), cognoscente, devotee, expert, judge, savant, specialist

conquer 1. beat, checkmate, crush, defeat, discomfit, get the better of, humble, master, overcome, overpower, overthrow, prevail, quell, rout, subdue, subjugate, succeed, surmount, triumph, vanquish **2.** acquire, annex, obtain, occupy, overrun, seize, win

conqueror champion, conquistador, defeater, hero, lord, master, subjugator, vanquisher, victor, winner

conquest 1. defeat, discomfiture, mastery, overthrow, rout, triumph, vanquishment, victory **2.** acquisition, annexation, appropriation, coup, invasion, occupation, subjection, subjugation, takeover

consanguinity (kɒnsæŋˈgwɪnɪtɪ) *n.* kinship —**conˈsanˈguineous** *a.*

conscience (ˈkɒnʃəns) *n.* sense of right or wrong governing person's words and actions —**consciˈentious** *a.* **1.** scrupulous **2.** obedient to the dictates of conscience —**consciˈentiously** *adv.* —**conscience money** money paid voluntarily to compensate for dishonesty, *esp.* for taxes formerly evaded —**conscience-stricken** *a.* feeling anxious or guilty (*also* **conscience-smitten**) —**conscientious objector** one who refuses military service on moral or religious grounds

conscious (ˈkɒnʃəs) *a.* **1.** aware **2.** awake to one's surroundings and identity **3.** deliberate, intentional —ˈ**consciously** *adv.* —ˈ**consciousness** *n.* being conscious

conscript (ˈkɒnskrɪpt) *n.* **1.** one compulsorily enlisted for military service —*vt.* (kənˈskrɪpt) **2.** enrol for compulsory military service —**conˈscription** *n.*

consecrate (ˈkɒnsɪkreɪt) *vt.* make sacred —**conseˈcration** *n.*

consecutive (kənˈsɛkjʊtɪv) *a.* in unbroken succession —**conˈsecutively** *adv.*

consensus (kənˈsɛnsəs) *n.* widespread agreement, unanimity

consent (kənˈsɛnt) *vi.* **1.** agree, comply —*n.* **2.** acquiescence **3.** permission **4.** agreement —**conˈsentient** *a.*

consequence (ˈkɒnsɪkwəns) *n.* **1.** result, effect, outcome **2.** that which naturally follows **3.** significance, importance —ˈ**consequent** *a.* —**conseˈquential** *a.* important —ˈ**consequently** *adv.* therefore, as a result

conservatoire (kənˈsɜːvətwɑː) *n.* school for teaching music

conserve (kənˈsɜːv) *vt.* **1.** keep from change or decay **2.** preserve **3.** maintain —*n.* (ˈkɒnsɜːv, kənˈsɜːv) **4.** jam, preserved fruit *etc.* —**conˈservancy** *n.* **1. UK** court or commission with jurisdiction over river, port *etc.* **2.** conservation —**conserˈvation** *n.* protection, careful management of natural resources and environment —**conserˈvationist** *n./a.* —**conˈservatism** *n.* —**conˈservative** *a.* **1.** tending, or wishing to conserve **2.** moderate —*n.* **3.** *Pol.* one who desires to preserve institutions of his country against change and innovation **4.** one opposed to hasty changes or innovations —**conˈservatory** *n.* greenhouse —**conservation of energy** principle that total energy of isolated system is constant and independent of changes occurring within system —**conservation of mass** principle that total mass of isolated system is constant and independent of chemical and physical changes taking place within system

consider (kənˈsɪdə) *vt.* **1.** think over **2.** examine **3.** make allowance for **4.** have as opinion **5.** discuss —**conˈsiderable** *a.* **1.** important **2.** somewhat large —**conˈsiderably** *adv.* —**conˈsiderate** *a.* thoughtful for others' feelings, careful —**conˈsiderately** *adv.* —**consideˈration** *n.* **1.** deliberation **2.** point of importance **3.** thoughtfulness **4.** bribe, recompense —**conˈsidered** *a.* **1.** presented or thought out with care **2.** esteemed —**conˈsidering** *prep.* **1.** in view of —*adv.* **2.** *inf.* all in all; taking circumstances into account —*conj.* **3.** in view of the fact (that)

THESAURUS

conscience moral sense, principles, scruples, sense of right and wrong, still small voice

conscience-stricken ashamed, compunctious, contrite, disturbed, guilty, penitent, remorseful, repentant, sorry, troubled

conscientious 1. careful, diligent, exact, faithful, meticulous, painstaking, particular, punctilious, thorough **2.** high-minded, high-principled, honest, honourable, incorruptible, just, moral, responsible, scrupulous, straightforward, strict, upright

conscious 1. alert, alive to, awake, aware, cognizant, percipient, responsive, sensible, sentient, wise to (*Sl.*) **2.** calculated, deliberate, intentional, knowing, premeditated, rational, reasoning, responsible, self-conscious, studied, wilful

consciousness apprehension, awareness, knowledge, realization, recognition, sensibility

consecrate dedicate, devote, exalt, hallow, ordain, sanctify, set apart, venerate

consecutive chronological, following, in sequence, in turn, running, sequential, seriatim, succeeding, successive, uninterrupted

consensus agreement, common consent, concord, concurrence, general agreement, harmony, unanimity, unity

consent 1. *v.* accede, acquiesce, agree, allow, approve, assent, comply, concede, concur, permit, yield **2.** *n.* acquiescence, agreement, approval, assent, compliance, concession, concurrence, go-ahead (*Inf.*), O.K. (*Inf.*), permission, sanction

consequence 1. effect, end, event, issue, outcome, repercussion, result, upshot **2.** account, concern, import, importance, interest, moment, note, portent, significance, value, weight **3.** distinction, eminence, notability, rank, repute, standing, status

consequent ensuing, following, resultant, resulting, sequential, subsequent, successive

consequently accordingly, ergo, hence, necessarily, subsequently, therefore, thus

conservation custody, economy, guardianship, husbandry, maintenance, preservation, protection, safeguarding, safekeeping, saving, upkeep

conservative 1. *adj.* cautious, conventional, die-hard, guarded, hidebound, middle-of-the-road, moderate, quiet, reactionary, right-wing, sober, tory, traditional **2.** *n.* middle-of-the-roader, moderate, reactionary, right-winger, stick-in-the-mud (*Inf.*), tory, traditionalist

conservatory glasshouse, greenhouse, hothouse

conserve go easy on (*Inf.*), hoard, husband, keep, nurse, preserve, protect, save, store up, take care of, use sparingly

consider 1. chew over, cogitate, consult, contemplate, deliberate, discuss, examine, meditate, mull over, muse, ponder, reflect, revolve, ruminate, study, turn over in one's mind, weigh **2.** believe, deem, hold to be, judge, rate, regard as, think **3.** bear in mind, care for, keep in view, make allowance for, reckon with, regard, remember, respect, take into account

considerable 1. abundant, ample, appreciable, comfortable, goodly, great, large, lavish, marked, much, noticeable, plentiful, reasonable, sizable, substantial, tidy, tolerable **2.** distinguished, important, influential, noteworthy, renowned, significant, venerable

considerably appreciably, greatly, markedly, notice-

consign (kən'saɪn) *vt.* **1.** commit, hand over **2.** entrust to carrier —**consign'ee** *n.* —**con'signment** *n.* goods consigned —**con'signor** *n.*

consist (kən'sɪst) *vi.* **1.** be composed (of) **2.** (*with* in) have as basis **3.** agree (with), be compatible (with) —**con'sistency** *or* **con'sistence** *n.* **1.** agreement **2.** harmony **3.** degree of firmness —**con'sistent** *a.* **1.** unchanging, constant **2.** agreeing (with) —**con'sistently** *adv.*

consistory (kən'sɪstərɪ) *n.* ecclesiastical court or council, *esp.* of Pope and Cardinals

console[1] (kən'səʊl) *vt.* comfort, cheer in distress —**conso'lation** *n.* —**consolatory** (kən'sɒlətərɪ) *a.*

console[2] ('kɒnsəʊl) *n.* **1.** bracket supporting shelf **2.** keyboard, stops *etc.*, of organ **3.** cabinet for television, radio *etc.*

consolidate (kən'sɒlɪdeɪt) *vt.* **1.** combine into connected whole **2.** make firm, secure —**consoli'dation** *n.*

consols ('kɒnsɒlz, kən'sɒlz) *pl.n.* Brit. government securities

consommé (kən'sɒmeɪ) *n.* clear meat soup

consonant ('kɒnsənənt) *n.* **1.** sound making a syllable only with vowel **2.** non-vowel —*a.* **3.** agreeing, in accord —'**consonance** *n.*

consort (kən'sɔːt) *vi.* **1.** associate, keep company —*n.* ('kɒnsɔːt) **2.** husband, wife, *esp.* of ruler **3.** ship sailing with another —**con'sortium** *n.* association of banks, companies *etc.*

conspectus (kən'spɛktəs) *n.* **1.** a comprehensive view or survey of subject **2.** synopsis

conspicuous (kən'spɪkjʊəs) *a.* **1.** striking, noticeable, outstanding **2.** prominent **3.** eminent —**con'spicuously** *adv.*

conspire (kən'spaɪə) *vi.* **1.** combine for evil purpose **2.** plot, devise —**conspiracy** (kən'spɪrəsɪ) *n.* —**conspirator** (kən'spɪrətə) *n.* —**conspiratorial** (kənspɪrə'tɔːrɪəl) *a.*

constable ('kʌnstəbᵊl, 'kɒn-) *n.* **1.** policeman of the lowest rank **2.** *Hist.* officer of the peace —**con'stabulary** *n.* police force

constant ('kɒnstənt) *a.* **1.** fixed, unchanging **2.** steadfast **3.** always duly happening or continuing —*n.* **4.** quantity that does not vary —'**constancy** *n.* **1.** steadfastness **2.** loyalty —'**constantly** *adv.*

constellation (kɒnstɪ'leɪʃən) *n.* group of stars

consternation (kɒnstə'neɪʃən) *n.* alarm, dismay, panic —'**consternate** *vt.*

constipation (kɒnstɪ'peɪʃən) *n.* difficulty in emptying bowels —'**constipate** *vt.* affect with this disorder

constituent (kən'stɪtjʊənt) *a.* **1.** going towards making up whole **2.** having power to make, alter constitution of state **3.** electing representative —*n.* **4.** component part **5.** element **6.** elector —**con'stituency** *n.* **1.** body of electors **2.** parliamentary division

THESAURUS

ably, remarkably, significantly, substantially, very much

considerate attentive, charitable, circumspect, concerned, discreet, forbearing, kind, kindly, mindful, obliging, patient, tactful, thoughtful, unselfish

consideration **1.** analysis, attention, cogitation, contemplation, deliberation, discussion, examination, reflection, regard, review, scrutiny, study, thought **2.** concern, factor, issue, point **3.** concern, considerateness, friendliness, kindliness, kindness, respect, solicitude, tact, thoughtfulness **4.** fee, payment, perquisite, recompense, remuneration, reward, tip

considering all in all, all things considered, insomuch as, in the light of, in view of

consignment batch, delivery, goods, shipment

consist *With* **of** be composed of, be made up of, amount to, comprise, contain, embody, include, incorporate, involve

consistent **1.** constant, dependable, persistent, regular, steady, true to type, unchanging, undeviating **2.** accordant, agreeing, all of a piece, coherent, compatible, congruous, consonant, harmonious, logical

consolation alleviation, assuagement, cheer, comfort, ease, easement, encouragement, help, relief, solace, succour, support

console assuage, calm, cheer, comfort, encourage, express sympathy for, relieve, solace, soothe

consolidate **1.** amalgamate, cement, combine, compact, condense, conjoin, federate, fuse, harden, join, solidify, thicken, unite **2.** fortify, reinforce, secure, stabilize, strengthen

consolidation alliance, amalgamation, association, compression, condensation, federation, fortification, fusion, reinforcement, strengthening

consort **1.** *n.* associate, companion, fellow, husband, partner, spouse (*of a reigning monarch*), wife **2.** *v.* associate, fraternize, go around with, hang about *or* around with, keep company, mingle, mix

conspicuous **1.** apparent, clear, discernible, easily seen, evident, manifest, noticeable, obvious, patent, perceptible, visible **2.** celebrated, distinguished, eminent, famous, illustrious, notable, outstanding, prominent, remarkable, signal, striking **3.** blatant, flagrant, flashy, garish, glaring, showy

conspiracy cabal, collusion, confederacy, frame-up (*Sl.*), intrigue, league, machination, plot, scheme, treason

conspirator cabalist, conspirer, intriguer, plotter, schemer, traitor

conspire **1.** cabal, confederate, contrive, devise, hatch treason, intrigue, machinate, manoeuvre, plot, scheme **2.** combine, concur, conduce, contribute, cooperate, tend, work together

constancy decision, determination, devotion, fidelity, firmness, fixedness, permanence, perseverance, regularity, resolution, stability, steadfastness, steadiness, tenacity, uniformity

constant **1.** continual, even, firm, fixed, habitual, immutable, invariable, permanent, perpetual, regular, stable, steadfast, steady, unalterable, unbroken, uniform, unvarying **2.** ceaseless, continual, continuous, endless, eternal, everlasting, incessant, interminable, never-ending, nonstop, perpetual, persistent, relentless, sustained, uninterrupted, unrelenting, unremitting **3.** attached, dependable, devoted, faithful, loyal, staunch, tried-and-true, true, trustworthy, trusty, unfailing

constantly all the time, always, continually, continuously, endlessly, everlastingly, incessantly, interminably, invariably, morning, noon and night, night and day, nonstop, perpetually, relentlessly

consternation alarm, amazement, anxiety, awe, be-

constitute (ˈkɒnstɪtjuːt) *vt.* 1. compose, set up, establish, form 2. make into, found, give form to —**constiˈtution** *n.* 1. structure, composition 2. health 3. character, disposition 4. principles on which state is governed —**constiˈtutional** *a.* 1. pert. to constitution 2. in harmony with political constitution —*n.* 3. walk taken for health's sake —**constiˈtutionally** *adv.* —**ˈconstitutive** *a.* 1. having power to enact or establish 2. *see* CONSTITUENT (sense 1)

constrain (kənˈstreɪn) *vt.* force, compel —**conˈstraint** *n.* 1. compulsion 2. restraint 3. embarrassment, tension

constriction (kənˈstrɪkʃən) *n.* compression, squeezing together —**conˈstrict** *vt.* —**conˈstrictive** *a.* —**conˈstrictor** *n.* that which constricts (*see also* BOA (sense 1))

construct (kənˈstrʌkt) *vt.* 1. make, build, form 2. put together 3. compose —*n.* (ˈkɒnstrʌkt) 4. something formulated systematically —**conˈstruction** *n.* —**conˈstructive** *a.* 1. serving to improve 2. positive —**conˈstructively** *adv.*

construe (kənˈstruː) *vt.* 1. interpret 2. deduce 3. analyse grammatically

consul (ˈkɒnsəl) *n.* 1. officer appointed by a government to represent it in a foreign country 2. in ancient Rome, one of the chief magistrates —**consular** (ˈkɒnsjʊlə) *a.* —**consulate** (ˈkɒnsjʊlɪt) *n.* —**ˈconsulship** *n.*

consult (kənˈsʌlt) *vt.* seek counsel, advice, information from —**conˈsultant** *n.* 1. specialist, expert 2. senior hospital physician or surgeon —**consulˈtation** *n.* 1. consulting 2. appointment to seek professional advice, *esp.* of doctor, lawyer —**conˈsultative** *a.* 1. having privilege of consulting, but not of voting 2. advisory

consume (kənˈsjuːm) *vt.* 1. eat or drink 2. engross, possess 3. use up 4. destroy —**conˈsumer** *n.* 1. buyer or user of commodity 2. one who consumes —**conˈsumerism** *n.* 1. protection of interests of consumers 2. advocacy of high rate of consumption as basis for sound economy —**consumption** (kənˈsʌmpʃən) *n.* 1. using up 2. destruction 3. wasting disease, *esp.* tuberculosis of the lungs —**consumptive** (kənˈsʌmptɪv) *a./n.* —**consumptiveness** (kənˈsʌmptɪvnɪs) *n.*

consummate (ˈkɒnsəmeɪt) *vt.* 1. perfect 2. fulfil 3. complete (*esp.* marriage by sexual intercourse) —*a.* (kənˈsʌmɪt, ˈkɒnsəmɪt) 4. of greatest perfection or completeness —**conˈsummately** *adv.* —**consumˈmation** *n.*

cont. continued

contact (ˈkɒntækt) *n.* 1. touching 2. being in touch 3. junction of two or more electrical conductors 4. useful acquaintance —*vt.* (ˈkɒntækt, kənˈtækt) 5. put, come or be in touch (with) —**contact lens** lens fitting over eyeball to correct defect of vision

contagion (kənˈteɪdʒən) *n.* 1. passing on of disease by touch, contact 2. contagious disease 3. harmful physical or moral influence —**conˈtagious** *a.* communicable by contact, catching

contain (kənˈteɪn) *vt.* 1. hold 2. have room for 3. include, comprise 4. restrain —**conˈtainer** *n.* 1. box *etc.* for holding 2. large cargo-carrying standard-sized

THESAURUS

wilderment, confusion, dismay, distress, dread, fear, fright, horror, panic, shock, terror, trepidation

constituent *adj.* 1. basic, component, elemental, essential, integral ~*n.* 2. component, element, essential, factor, ingredient, part, principle, unit 3. elector, voter

constitute compose, comprise, create, enact, establish, fix, form, found, make, make up, set up

constitution build, character, composition, disposition, form, habit, health, make-up, nature, physique, structure, temper, temperament

constitutional *adj.* 1. congenital, inborn, inherent, intrinsic, organic 2. chartered, statutory, vested ~*n.* 3. airing, stroll, turn, walk

constrain bind, coerce, compel, drive, force, impel, necessitate, oblige, pressure, pressurize, urge

constraint 1. coercion, compulsion, force, necessity, pressure 2. bashfulness, diffidence, embarrassment, inhibition, repression, reservation, restraint, timidity 3. check, curb, damper, deterrent, hindrance, limitation, restraint, restriction

construct assemble, build, compose, create, design, elevate, engineer, erect, establish, fabricate, fashion, form, formulate, found, frame, make, manufacture, organize, put up, raise, set up, shape

construction assembly, building, composition, creation, edifice, erection, fabric, fabrication, figure, form, formation, shape, structure

constructive helpful, positive, practical, productive, useful, valuable

consult ask, ask advice of, commune, compare notes, confer, consider, debate, deliberate, interrogate, question, refer to, take counsel, turn to

consultant adviser, authority, specialist

consultation appointment, conference, council, deliberation, dialogue, discussion, examination, hearing, interview, meeting, session

consume 1. absorb, deplete, dissipate, drain, eat up, employ, exhaust, expend, finish up, fritter away, lavish, lessen, spend, squander, use, use up, utilize, vanish, waste, wear out 2. devour, eat, eat up, gobble (up), guzzle, polish off (*Inf.*), put away, swallow 3. annihilate, decay, demolish, destroy, devastate, lay waste, ravage 4. *Often passive* absorb, devour, dominate, eat up, engross, monopolize, obsess, preoccupy

consumer buyer, customer, purchaser, shopper, user

consummate 1. *v.* accomplish, achieve, carry out, compass, complete, conclude, crown, effectuate, end, finish, perfect, perform 2. *adj.* absolute, accomplished, complete, conspicuous, finished, matchless, perfect, polished, practised, skilled, superb, supreme, total, transcendent, ultimate, unqualified, utter

consumption 1. consuming, decay, decrease, depletion, destruction, diminution, dissipation, exhaustion, expenditure, loss, use, using up, utilization, waste 2. *Medical* atrophy, emaciation, phthisis, T.B., tuberculosis

contact *n.* 1. association, communication, connection 2. approximation, contiguity, junction, juxtaposition, touch, union 3. acquaintance, connection ~*v.* 4. approach, call, communicate with, get *or* be in touch with, get hold of, phone, reach, ring (up), speak to, write to

contagious catching, communicable, epidemic, epizootic (*Veterinary medicine*), infectious, pestiferous, pestilential, spreading, taking (*Inf.*), transmissible

receptacle for different modes of transport —**containeri'zation** *or* **-i'sation** *n.* —**con'tainerize** *or* **-ise** *vt.* **1.** convey in standard-sized containers **2.** adapt to use of standard-sized containers —**con'tainment** *n.* act of containing, *esp.* of restraining power of hostile country or operations of hostile military force

contaminate (kən'tæmɪneɪt) *vt.* **1.** stain, pollute, infect **2.** make radioactive —**contami'nation** *n.* pollution

contemn (kən'tɛm) *vt.* regard with contempt; scorn

contemplate ('kɒntɛmpleɪt) *vt.* **1.** reflect, meditate on **2.** gaze upon **3.** intend —**contem'plation** *n.* **1.** thoughtful consideration **2.** spiritual meditation —'**contemplative** *a./n.* (one) given to contemplation

contemporary (kən'tɛmprərɪ) *a.* **1.** existing or lasting at same time **2.** of same age **3.** present-day —*n.* **4.** one existing at same time as another —**contempo'raneous** *a.*

contempt (kən'tɛmpt) *n.* **1.** feeling that something is worthless, despicable *etc.* **2.** expression of this feeling **3.** state of being despised, disregarded **4.** wilful disrespect of authority

contend (kən'tɛnd) *vi.* **1.** strive, fight —*v.* **2.** dispute —*vt.* **3.** maintain —**con'tention** *n.* **1.** strife **2.** debate **3.** subject matter of dispute —**con'tentious** *a.* **1.** quarrelsome **2.** causing dispute —**con'tentiously** *adv.*

content[1] ('kɒntɛnt) *n.* **1.** that contained **2.** holding capacity —*pl.* **3.** that contained **4.** index of topics in book

content[2] (kən'tɛnt) *a.* **1.** satisfied **2.** willing —*vt.* **3.** satisfy —*n.* **4.** satisfaction —**con'tented** *a.* —**con'tentment** *n.*

conterminous (kən'tɜːmɪnəs) *or* **coterminous** (kəʊ'tɜːmɪnəs) *a.* **1.** of the same extent (in time *etc.*) **2.** meeting along a common boundary **3.** meeting end to end

contest ('kɒntɛst) *n.* **1.** competition **2.** conflict —*vt.* (kən'tɛst) **3.** dispute, debate **4.** fight or compete for —**con'testable** *a.* —**con'testant** *n.* —**contes'tation** *n.*

context ('kɒntɛkst) *n.* **1.** words coming before, after a word or passage **2.** conditions and circumstances of event, fact *etc.* —**con'textual** *a.*

contiguous (kən'tɪgjʊəs) *a.* touching, near —**conti'guity** *n.*

continent[1] ('kɒntɪnənt) *n.* large continuous mass of land —**conti'nental** *a.* —**continental breakfast** light breakfast of coffee and rolls —**continental drift** *Geol.* theory that earth's continents move gradually over surface of planet on substratum of magma —**conti-**

THESAURUS

contain **1.** accommodate, enclose, have capacity for, hold, incorporate, seat **2.** comprehend, comprise, embody, embrace, include, involve **3.** control, curb, hold back, hold in, repress, restrain, stifle

container holder, receptacle, repository, vessel

contaminate adulterate, befoul, corrupt, defile, deprave, infect, pollute, radioactivate, soil, stain, sully, taint, tarnish, vitiate

contamination adulteration, contagion, corruption, decay, defilement, dirtying, filth, foulness, impurity, infection, poisoning, pollution, radioactivation, rottenness, taint

contemplate **1.** brood over, consider, deliberate, meditate, meditate on, mull over, muse over, observe, ponder, reflect upon, revolve *or* turn over in one's mind, ruminate (upon), study **2.** behold, examine, eye, gaze at, inspect, regard, scrutinize, stare at, survey, view **3.** aspire to, consider, design, envisage, expect, foresee, have in view *or* in mind, intend, mean, plan, propose, think of

contemplation **1.** cogitation, consideration, deliberation, meditation, musing, pondering, reflection, reverie, rumination, thought **2.** examination, gazing at, inspection, looking at, observation, scrutiny, survey, viewing

contemplative deep *or* lost in thought, in a brown study, intent, introspective, meditative, musing, pensive, rapt, reflective, ruminative, thoughtful

contemporary *adj.* **1.** coetaneous (*Rare*), coeval, coexistent, coexisting, concurrent, contemporaneous, synchronous **2.** à la mode, current, in fashion, latest, modern, newfangled, present, present-day, recent, ultramodern, up-to-date, up-to-the-minute, with it (*Inf.*) ~*n.* **3.** compeer, fellow, peer

contempt **1.** condescension, contumely, derision, despite (*Archaic*), disdain, disregard, disrespect, mockery, neglect, scorn, slight **2.** *A state of contempt* disgrace, dishonour, humiliation, shame

contend **1.** clash, compete, contest, cope, emulate, grapple, jostle, litigate, skirmish, strive, struggle, vie **2.** affirm, allege, argue, assert, aver, avow, debate, dispute, hold, maintain

content[1] **1.** burden, essence, gist, ideas, matter, meaning, significance, substance, text, thoughts **2.** capacity, load, measure, size, volume

content[2] **1.** *v.* appease, delight, gladden, gratify, humour, indulge, mollify, placate, please, reconcile, satisfy, suffice **2.** *n.* comfort, contentment, ease, gratification, peace, peace of mind, pleasure, satisfaction **3.** *adj.* agreeable, at ease, comfortable, contented, fulfilled, satisfied, willing to accept

contented at ease, at peace, cheerful, comfortable, complacent, content, glad, gratified, happy, pleased, satisfied, serene, thankful

contention competition, contest, discord, dispute, dissension, enmity, feuding, hostility, rivalry, strife, struggle, wrangling

contentious argumentative, bickering, captious, cavilling, combative, controversial, cross, disputatious, factious, litigious, peevish, perverse, pugnacious, quarrelsome, querulous, wrangling

contentment comfort, complacency, content, contentedness, ease, equanimity, fulfilment, gladness, gratification, happiness, peace, pleasure, repletion, satisfaction, serenity

contents **1.** constituents, elements, ingredients, load **2.** chapters, divisions, subject matter, subjects, themes, topics

contest *n.* **1.** competition, game, match, tournament, trial **2.** affray, altercation, battle, combat, conflict, controversy, debate, discord, dispute, encounter, fight, shock, struggle ~*v.* **3.** compete, contend, fight, fight over, strive, vie **4.** argue, call in *or* into question, challenge, debate, dispute, doubt, litigate, object to, oppose, question

contestant aspirant, candidate, competitor, contender, entrant, participant, player

context **1.** background, connection, frame of reference, framework, relation **2.** ambience, circumstances, conditions, situation

nental quilt UK quilt, stuffed with down, used as bed cover in place of top sheet and blankets (*also* **'duvet**) —**continental shelf** sea bed surrounding continent at depths of up to about 200 metres

continent[2] ('kɒntɪnənt) *a.* **1.** able to control one's urination and defecation **2.** sexually chaste —**'continence** *n.*

contingent (kən'tɪndʒənt) *a.* **1.** depending **2.** possible **3.** accidental —*n.* **4.** group (of troops, sportsmen *etc.*) part of or representative of a larger group —**con'tingency** *n.* —**con'tingently** *adv.*

continue (kən'tɪnju:) *v.* **1.** remain, keep in existence **2.** carry on, last, go on **3.** resume **4.** prolong —**con'tinual** *a.* recurring frequently, *esp.* at regular intervals —**con'tinually** *adv.* —**con'tinuance** *n.* **1.** act of continuing **2.** duration of action *etc.* **3.** US adjournment of legal proceeding —**continu'ation** *n.* **1.** extension, extra part **2.** resumption **3.** constant succession, prolongation —**conti'nuity** *n.* **1.** logical sequence **2.** state of being continuous —**con'tinuo** *n.* **1.** *Mus.* bass part underlying piece of concerted music (*also* **basso continuo, thorough bass**) **2.** thorough-bass part as played on keyboard instrument (*pl.* **-s**) —**con'tinuous** *a.* unceasing —**con'tinuously** *adv.* —**con'tinuum** *n.* continuous series or whole with no part perceptibly different from adjacent parts (*pl.* **-'tinua, -s**)

contort (kən'tɔ:t) *vt.* twist out of normal shape —**con'tortion** *n.* —**con'tortionist** *n.* one who contorts his body to entertain

contour ('kɒntʊə) *n.* outline, shape, *esp.* mountains, coast *etc.* —**contour line** line on map drawn through places of same height —**contour map**

contra- (*comb. form*) against, as in *contraposition.* Such words are omitted where the meaning may easily be inferred from the simple word

contraband ('kɒntrəbænd) *n.* **1.** smuggled goods **2.** illegal traffic in such goods —*a.* **3.** prohibited by law

contraception (kɒntrə'sɛpʃən) *n.* prevention of conception usu. by artificial means, birth control —**contra'ceptive** *a./n.*

contract (kən'trækt) *v.* **1.** make or become smaller, shorter —*vi.* ('kɒntrækt) **2.** make a contract —*vt.* **3.** become affected by **4.** incur **5.** undertake by contract —*n.* ('kɒntrækt) **6.** bargain, agreement **7.** formal document recording agreement **8.** agreement enforceable by law —**con'tracted** *a.* drawn together —**con'tractile** *a.* tending to contract —**con'traction** *n.* —**con'tractor** *n.* one making contract, *esp.* builder —**con'tractual** *a.*

contradict (kɒntrə'dɪkt) *vt.* **1.** deny **2.** be at variance or inconsistent with —**contra'diction** *n.* —**contra'dictious** *a.* —**contra'dictor** *n.* —**contra'dictory** *a.*

contradistinction (kɒntrədɪ'stɪŋkʃən) *n.* distinction made by contrasting different qualities

contralto (kən'træltəʊ) *n.* lowest of three female voices (*pl.* **-s**)

contraption (kən'træpʃən) *n.* **1.** gadget **2.** device **3.** construction, device oft. overelaborate or eccentric

contrapuntal (kɒntrə'pʌnt'l) *a.* *Mus.* pert. to counterpoint

contrary ('kɒntrərɪ) *a.* **1.** opposed **2.** opposite, other **3.** (kən'trɛərɪ) perverse, obstinate —*n.* **4.** something the exact opposite of another —*adv.* **5.** in opposition —**contra'riety** *n.* —**con'trarily** *adv.* —**'contrariwise** *adv.* conversely

THESAURUS

continent *adj.* abstemious, abstinent, ascetic, austere, celibate, chaste, self-restrained, sober

contingent *adj.* **1.** *With* **on** *or* **upon** conditional, controlled by, dependent, subject to **2.** accidental, casual, fortuitous, haphazard, random, uncertain ~*n.* **3.** batch, body, bunch (*Inf.*), deputation, detachment, group, mission, quota, section, set

continual constant, continuous, endless, eternal, everlasting, frequent, incessant, interminable, oft-repeated, perpetual, recurrent, regular, repeated, repetitive, unceasing, uninterrupted, unremitting

continually all the time, always, constantly, endlessly, eternally, everlastingly, forever, incessantly, interminably, nonstop, persistently, repeatedly

continuation **1.** addition, extension, furtherance, postscript, sequel, supplement **2.** maintenance, perpetuation, prolongation, resumption

continue **1.** abide, carry on, endure, last, live on, persist, remain, rest, stay, stay on, survive **2.** go on, keep at, keep on, keep the ball rolling, keep up, maintain, persevere, persist in, prolong, pursue, stick at, stick to, sustain **3.** draw out, extend, lengthen, project, prolong, reach **4.** carry on, pick up where one left off, proceed, recommence, resume, return to, take up

continuity cohesion, connection, flow, interrelationship, progression, sequence, succession, whole

continuous connected, constant, continued, extended, prolonged, unbroken, unceasing, undivided, uninterrupted

contour curve, figure, form, lines, outline, profile, relief, shape, silhouette

contraband **1.** *n.* black-marketing, bootlegging, moonshine (*U.S.*), rum-running, smuggling, trafficking **2.** *adj.* banned, black-market, bootleg, bootlegged, forbidden, hot (*Inf.*), illegal, illicit, interdicted, prohibited, smuggled, unlawful

contract *v.* **1.** abbreviate, abridge, compress, condense, confine, constrict, curtail, dwindle, epitomize, lessen, narrow, purse, reduce, shrink, shrivel, tighten, wither, wrinkle **2.** agree, arrange, bargain, clinch, close, come to terms, commit oneself, covenant, engage, enter into, negotiate, pledge, stipulate **3.** acquire, be afflicted with, catch, develop, go down with (*Inf.*), incur ~*n.* **4.** agreement, arrangement, bargain, bond, commission, commitment, compact, concordat, convention, covenant, deal (*Inf.*), engagement, pact, settlement, stipulation, treaty, understanding

contraction abbreviation, compression, constriction, diminution, drawing in, elision, narrowing, reduction, shortening, shrinkage, shrivelling, tensing, tightening

contradict be at variance with, belie, challenge, contravene, controvert, counter, counteract, deny, dispute, gainsay (*Archaic*), impugn, negate, oppose

contradiction conflict, confutation, contravention, denial, incongruity, inconsistency, negation, opposite

contradictory antagonistic, antithetical, conflicting, contrary, discrepant, incompatible, inconsistent, irreconcilable, opposed, opposite, paradoxical, repugnant

contrast (kənˈtrɑːst) *vt.* **1.** distinguish by comparison of unlike or opposite qualities —*vi.* **2.** show great difference —*n.* (ˈkɒntrɑːst) **3.** striking difference **4.** *T.V.* sharpness of image

contravene (kɒntrəˈviːn) *vt.* **1.** transgress, infringe **2.** conflict with **3.** contradict —**contraˈvention** *n.*

contretemps (ˈkɒntrətɑːn) *n.* unexpected and embarrassing situation or mishap

contribute (kənˈtrɪbjuːt) *v.* **1.** give, pay to common fund **2.** write (articles *etc.*) for the press —*vi.* **3.** help to occur —**contriˈbution** *n.* —**conˈtributive** *a.* —**conˈtributor** *n.* **1.** one who writes articles for newspapers *etc.* **2.** one who donates —**conˈtributory** *a.* **1.** partly responsible **2.** giving to pension fund *etc.*

contrite (kənˈtraɪt, ˈkɒntraɪt) *a.* remorseful for wrongdoing, penitent —**conˈtritely** *adv.* —**contrition** (kənˈtrɪʃən) *n.*

contrive (kənˈtraɪv) *vt.* **1.** manage **2.** devise, invent, design —*v.* **3.** plot, scheme —**conˈtrivance** *n.* artifice or device —**conˈtrived** *a.* obviously planned, artificial —**conˈtriver** *n.*

control (kənˈtrəʊl) *vt.* **1.** command, dominate **2.** regulate **3.** direct, check, test (**-ll-**) —*n.* **4.** power to direct or determine **5.** curb, check **6.** standard of comparison in experiment —*pl.* **7.** system of instruments to control car, aircraft *etc.* —**conˈtrollable** *a.* —**conˈtroller** *n.* **1.** one who controls **2.** official controlling expenditure —**control tower** tower in airfield from which take-offs and landings are directed

controversy (ˈkɒntrəvɜːsɪ, kənˈtrɒv-) *n.* dispute, debate, *esp.* over public issues —**controˈversial** *a.* —**controˈversialist** *n.* —**ˈcontrovert** *vt.* **1.** deny **2.** argue about —**controˈvertible** *a.*

contumacy (ˈkɒntjʊməsɪ) *n.* stubborn disobedience —**contuˈmacious** *a.*

contumely (ˈkɒntjʊmɪlɪ) *n.* insulting language or treatment —**contumelious** (kɒntjʊˈmiːlɪəs) *a.* abusive, insolent

contusion (kənˈtjuːʒən) *n.* bruise —**conˈtuse** *vt.* bruise

conundrum (kəˈnʌndrəm) *n.* riddle, *esp.* with punning answer

conurbation (kɒnɜːˈbeɪʃən) *n.* densely populated urban sprawl formed by spreading of towns

convalesce (kɒnvəˈlɛs) *vi.* recover health after illness, operation *etc.* —**convaˈlescence** *n.* —**convaˈlescent** *a./n.*

convection (kənˈvɛkʃən) *n.* transmission, *esp.* of heat, by currents in liquids or gases —**conˈvector** *n.*

convene (kənˈviːn) *vt.* call together, assemble, convoke —**convention** (kənˈvɛnʃən) *n.* **1.** assembly **2.** treaty, agreement **3.** rule **4.** practice based on agreement **5.** accepted usage —**conventional** (kənˈvɛnʃənᵊl) *a.* **1.** (slavishly) observing customs of society **2.** customary **3.** (of weapons, war *etc.*) not nuclear —**conventionality** (kənvɛnʃəˈnælɪtɪ) *n.* —**conventionally** (kənˈvɛnʃənəlɪ) *adv.*

convenient (kənˈviːnɪənt) *a.* **1.** handy **2.** favourable to needs, comfort **3.** well-adapted to one's purpose —**con-**

THESAURUS

contraption apparatus, contrivance, device, gadget, mechanism, rig

contrary *adj.* **1.** adverse, antagonistic, clashing, contradictory, counter, discordant, hostile, inconsistent, inimical, opposed, opposite, paradoxical **2.** awkward, balky, cantankerous, cussed (*Inf.*), difficult, disobliging, froward, intractable, obstinate, perverse, stroppy (*Brit. sl.*), thrawn (*Northern dialect*), unaccommodating, wayward, wilful ~*n.* **3.** antithesis, converse, opposite, reverse

contrast **1.** *n.* comparison, contrariety, difference, differentiation, disparity, dissimilarity, distinction, divergence, foil, opposition **2.** *v.* compare, differ, differentiate, distinguish, oppose, set in opposition, set off

contribute **1.** add, afford, bestow, chip in, donate, furnish, give, provide, subscribe, supply **2.** be conducive, be instrumental, be partly responsible for, conduce, help, lead, tend

contribution addition, bestowal, donation, gift, grant, input, offering, subscription

contributor **1.** backer, bestower, conferrer, donor, giver, patron, subscriber, supporter **2.** correspondent, freelance, freelancer, journalist, reporter

contrite chastened, conscience-stricken, humble, in sackcloth and ashes, penitent, regretful, remorseful, repentant, sorrowful, sorry

contrivance **1.** artifice, design, dodge, expedient, fabrication, formation, intrigue, inventiveness, machination, measure, plan, plot, project, ruse, scheme, stratagem, trick **2.** apparatus, appliance, contraption, device, equipment, gadget, gear, implement, invention, machine, mechanism

contrive **1.** concoct, construct, create, design, devise, engineer, fabricate, frame, improvise, invent, wangle (*Inf.*) **2.** arrange, bring about, effect, hit upon, manage, manoeuvre, plan, plot, scheme, succeed

contrived artificial, elaborate, forced, laboured, overdone, planned, recherché, strained, unnatural

control *v.* **1.** boss (*Inf.*), call the tune, command, conduct, direct, dominate, govern, have charge of, hold the purse strings, lead, manage, manipulate, oversee, pilot, reign over, rule, steer, superintend, supervise **2.** *Used of a machine, an experiment, etc.* counteract, determine, monitor, regulate, verify ~*n.* **3.** authority, charge, command, direction, discipline, government, guidance, jurisdiction, management, mastery, oversight, rule, superintendence, supervision, supremacy **4.** brake, check, curb, limitation, regulation, restraint

controls console, control panel, dashboard, dials, instruments

controversial at issue, contended, contentious, controvertible, debatable, disputable, disputed, open to question, under discussion

controversy altercation, argument, contention, debate, discussion, dispute, dissension, polemic, quarrel, squabble, strife, wrangle, wrangling

convalescence improvement, recovery, recuperation, rehabilitation, return to health

convalescent *adj.* getting better, improving, mending, on the mend, recovering, recuperating

convene assemble, bring together, call, come together, congregate, convoke, gather, meet, muster, rally, summon

convenience **1.** accessibility, appropriateness, availability, fitness, handiness, opportuneness, serviceability, suitability, usefulness, utility **2.** accommodation, advantage, benefit, comfort, ease, enjoyment, satisfaction, service, use

ˈvenience *n.* **1.** ease, comfort, suitability **2.** (public) lavatory —*a.* **3.** (of food) quick to prepare —**conˈveniently** *adv.*

convent (ˈkɒnvənt) *n.* **1.** religious community, *esp.* of nuns **2.** their building **3.** school in which teachers are nuns (*also* **convent school**) —**conˈventual** *a.*

conventicle (kənˈvɛntɪkᵊl) *n.* **1.** secret or unauthorized assembly for worship **2.** small meeting house or chapel, *esp.* of Dissenters

converge (kənˈvɜːdʒ) *vi.* **1.** move towards same point **2.** meet, join **3.** *Maths.* (of infinite series) approach finite limit as number of terms increases —**conˈvergence** *or* **conˈvergency** *n.* —**conˈvergent** *a.*

conversant (kənˈvɜːsᵊnt) *a.* acquainted, familiar, versed (in)

converse[1] (kənˈvɜːs) *vi.* **1.** talk —*n.* (ˈkɒnvɜːs) **2.** talk —**converˈsation** *n.* —**converˈsational** *a.* —**converˈsationalist** *n.*

converse[2] (ˈkɒnvɜːs) *a.* **1.** opposite, turned round, reversed —*n.* **2.** the opposite, contrary

convert (kənˈvɜːt) *vt.* **1.** apply to another purpose **2.** change **3.** transform **4.** cause to adopt (another) religion, opinion —*vi.* **5.** *Rugby* make a conversion —*n.* (ˈkɒnvɜːt) **6.** converted person —**conˈversion** *n.* **1.** change of state **2.** unauthorized appropriation **3.** change of opinion, religion or party **4.** *Rugby* score made after a try by kicking ball over crossbar —**conˈverter** *n.* **1.** one who, that which converts **2.** electrical machine for changing alternating current into direct current **3.** vessel in which molten metal is refined —**conˈvertible** *n.* **1.** car with folding roof —*a.* **2.** capable of being converted **3.** (of car) having folding or removable roof

convex (ˈkɒnvɛks, kɒnˈvɛks) *a.* **1.** curved outwards **2.** of a rounded form —**conˈvexity** *n.*

convey (kənˈveɪ) *vt.* **1.** carry, transport **2.** impart, communicate **3.** *Law* make over, transfer —**conˈveyance** *n.* **1.** carrying **2.** vehicle **3.** act by which title to property is transferred —**conˈveyancer** *n.* one skilled in legal forms of transferring property —**conˈveyancing** *n.* this work —**conveyor belt** continuous moving belt for transporting things, *esp.* in factory

convict (kənˈvɪkt) *vt.* **1.** prove or declare guilty —*n.* (ˈkɒnvɪkt) **2.** person found guilty of crime **3.** criminal serving prison sentence —**conˈviction** *n.* **1.** verdict of guilty **2.** being convinced, firm belief, state of being sure

convince (kənˈvɪns) *vt.* firmly persuade, satisfy by evidence or argument —**conˈvincing** *a.* capable of compelling belief, effective

convivial (kənˈvɪvɪəl) *a.* sociable, festive, jovial —**conviviˈality** *n.*

convoke (kənˈvəʊk) *vt.* call together —**convoˈcation** *n.* calling together, assembly, *esp.* of clergy, university graduates *etc.*

convolute (ˈkɒnvəluːt) *vt.* twist, coil, tangle —**ˈconvoluted** *a.* —**convoˈlution** *n.*

convolvulus (kənˈvɒlvjʊləs) *n.* genus of plants with twining stems

THESAURUS

convenient **1.** adapted, appropriate, beneficial, commodious, fit, fitted, handy, helpful, labour-saving, opportune, seasonable, serviceable, suitable, suited, timely, useful, well-timed **2.** accessible, at hand, available, close at hand, handy, just round the corner, nearby, within reach

convent convent school, nunnery, religious community

convention **1.** assembly, conference, congress, convocation, council, delegates, meeting, representatives **2.** code, custom, etiquette, formality, practice, propriety, protocol, tradition, usage **3.** agreement, bargain, compact, concordat, contract, pact, protocol, stipulation, treaty

conventional **1.** accepted, common, correct, customary, decorous, expected, formal, habitual, normal, ordinary, orthodox, prevailing, prevalent, proper, regular, ritual, standard, traditional, usual, wonted **2.** bourgeois, commonplace, hackneyed, hidebound, pedestrian, prosaic, routine, run-of-the-mill, stereotyped, unoriginal

converge coincide, combine, come together, concentrate, focus, gather, join, meet, merge, mingle

conversant *Usually with* **with** acquainted, *au fait*, experienced, familiar, knowledgeable, practised, proficient, skilled, versed, well-informed, well up in (*Inf.*)

conversation chat, chinwag (*Brit. inf.*), colloquy, communication, communion, confab (*Inf.*), confabulation, conference, converse, dialogue, discourse, discussion, exchange, gossip, intercourse, powwow, talk, tête-à-tête

converse **1.** *n.* antithesis, contrary, obverse, opposite, other side of the coin, reverse **2.** *adj.* contrary, counter, opposite, reverse, reversed, transposed

conversion **1.** change, metamorphosis, transfiguration, transformation, transmogrification (*Jocular*), transmutation **2.** change of heart, proselytization, rebirth, reformation, regeneration

convert *v.* **1.** alter, change, interchange, metamorphose, transform, transmogrify (*Jocular*), transmute, transpose, turn **2.** adapt, apply, appropriate, modify, remodel, reorganize, restyle, revise **3.** baptize, bring to God, convince, proselytize, reform, regenerate, save ~*n.* **4.** catechumen, disciple, neophyte, proselyte

convex bulging, gibbous, outcurved, protuberant, rounded

convey **1.** bear, bring, carry, conduct, fetch, forward, grant, guide, move, send, support, transmit, transport **2.** communicate, disclose, impart, make known, relate, reveal, tell **3.** *Law* bequeath, cede, deliver, demise, devolve, grant, lease, transfer, will

conveyance **1.** carriage, movement, transfer, transference, transmission, transport, transportation **2.** transport, vehicle

convict **1.** *v.* condemn, find guilty, imprison, pronounce guilty, sentence **2.** *n.* con (*Sl.*), criminal, culprit, felon, jailbird, malefactor, old lag (*Sl.*), prisoner

conviction **1.** assurance, certainty, certitude, confidence, earnestness, fervour, firmness, reliance **2.** belief, creed, faith, opinion, persuasion, principle, tenet, view

convince assure, bring round, gain the confidence of, persuade, prevail upon, prove to, satisfy, sway, win over

convincing cogent, conclusive, credible, impressive, incontrovertible, likely, persuasive, plausible, powerful, probable, telling

convoy (ˈkɒnvɔɪ) *n.* **1.** party of ships, troops, lorries *etc.* travelling together for protection —*vt.* **2.** escort for protection

convulse (kənˈvʌls) *vt.* **1.** shake violently **2.** affect with violent involuntary contractions of muscles —**conˈvulsion** *n.* **1.** violent upheaval —*pl.* **2.** spasms **3.** fits of laughter or hysteria —**conˈvulsive** *a.* —**conˈvulsively** *adv.*

cony *or* **coney** (ˈkəunɪ) *n.* rabbit

coo (ku:) *n.* **1.** cry of doves —*vi.* **2.** make such cry (**cooed, ˈcooing**)

cooee *or* **cooey** (ˈku:i:) *interj.* **1.** call to attract attention —*n.* **2.** A, NZ *inf.* calling distance (*esp. in* **within (a) cooee (of)**) —*vi.* **3.** utter this call (**ˈcooeeing, ˈcooeed** *or* **ˈcooeying, ˈcooeyed**)

cook (kuk) *vt.* **1.** prepare (food) for table, *esp.* by heat **2.** *inf.* falsify (accounts *etc.*) —*vi.* **3.** undergo cooking **4.** act as cook —*n.* **5.** one who prepares food for table —**ˈcooker** *n.* **1.** cooking apparatus **2.** cooking apple —**ˈcookery** *n.* —**ˈcookie** *n. esp.* US biscuit —**cook up 1.** *inf.* invent, plan **2.** prepare (meal)

cool (ku:l) *a.* **1.** moderately cold **2.** unexcited, calm **3.** lacking friendliness or interest **4.** *inf.* calmly insolent **5.** *inf.* sophisticated, elegant —*v.* **6.** make, become cool —*n.* **7.** cool time, place *etc.* **8.** *inf.* calmness, composure —**ˈcoolant** *n.* fluid used for cooling tool, machinery *etc.* —**ˈcooler** *n.* **1.** vessel in which liquids are cooled **2.** *sl.* prison —**ˈcoolly** *adv.* —**cooling tower** structure, designed to permit free passage of air, inside which hot water trickles down, becoming cool as it does so

coolie *or* **cooly** (ˈku:lɪ) *n. oft. offens.* cheaply hired oriental unskilled labourer

coomb, combe, coombe, *or* **comb** (ku:m) *n.* valley

coon (ku:n) *n. sl. offens.* coloured person

coop[1] (ku:p) *n.* **1.** cage or pen for fowls —*vt.* (*oft. with* up) **2.** shut up in a coop **3.** confine

coop[2] *or* **co-op** (ˈkəuɒp) *n.* cooperative society or shop run by one

cooper (ˈku:pə) *n.* one who makes casks

cooperate *or* **co-operate** (kəuˈɒpəreɪt) *vi.* work together —**coopeˈration** *or* **co-operation** *n.* —**coˈoperative** *or* **co-operative** *a.* **1.** willing to cooperate **2.** (of an enterprise) owned collectively and managed for joint economic benefit —*n.* **3.** cooperative organization, such as farm —**coˈoperator** *or* **co-operator** *n.*

coopt *or* **co-opt** (kəuˈɒpt) *vt.* bring on (committee *etc.*) as member, colleague, without election by larger body choosing first members

coordinate *or* **co-ordinate** (kəuˈɔ:dɪneɪt) *vt.* **1.** bring into order as parts of whole **2.** place in same rank **3.** put into harmony —*n.* (kəuˈɔ:dɪnɪt) **4.** *Maths.* any of set of numbers defining location of point —*pl.* **5.** clothes of matching or harmonious colours and design, suitable for wearing together —*a.* (kəuˈɔ:dɪnɪt) **6.** equal in degree, status *etc.* —**coordiˈnation** *or* **co-ordination** *n.* —**coˈordinative** *or* **co-ordinative** *a.*

coot (ku:t) *n.* **1.** small black water fowl **2.** *sl.* silly (old) person

cop (kɒp) *sl. vt.* **1.** catch **2.** (*usu. with* it) be punished —*n.* **3.** policeman **4.** a capture —**cop-out** *n. sl.* act of copping out —**cop out** *sl.* fail to assume responsibility, fail to perform

copal (ˈkəupəl, -pæl) *n.* resin used in varnishes

copartner (kəuˈpɑ:tnə) *n.* joint partner —**coˈpartnership** *n.*

cope[1] (kəup) *vi.* manage successfully

cope[2] (kəup) *n.* ecclesiastical vestment like long cloak

Copernican (kəˈpɜ:nɪkən) *a.* pert. to Copernicus, Polish astronomer (1473–1543), or to his system —**Copernican system** theory published by Copernicus, which stated that earth and planets rotated around sun

copestone (ˈkəupstəun) *n.* **1.** stone used to form coping (*also* **coping stone**) **2.** stone at top of wall *etc.*

copier (ˈkɒpɪə) *n. see* COPY

copilot (ˈkəupaɪlət) *n.* second or relief pilot of aircraft

coping (ˈkəupɪŋ) *n.* top course of wall, usu. sloping to throw off rain

THESAURUS

convoy 1. *n.* armed guard, attendance, attendant, escort, guard, protection **2.** *v.* accompany, attend, escort, guard, pilot, protect, shepherd, usher

convulse agitate, churn up, derange, disorder, disturb, shake, shatter, twist, work

convulsion 1. agitation, commotion, disturbance, furore, shaking, tumult, turbulence, upheaval **2.** contortion, contraction, cramp, fit, paroxysm, seizure, spasm, throe (*Rare*), tremor

cool *adj.* **1.** chilled, chilling, chilly, coldish, nippy, refreshing **2.** calm, collected, composed, deliberate, dispassionate, imperturbable, level-headed, placid, quiet, relaxed, self-controlled, self-possessed, serene, together (*Sl.*), unemotional, unexcited, unruffled **3.** aloof, apathetic, distant, frigid, incurious, indifferent, lukewarm, offhand, reserved, standoffish, uncommunicative, unconcerned, unenthusiastic, unfriendly, uninterested, unresponsive, unwelcoming **4.** audacious, bold, brazen, cheeky, impertinent, impudent, presumptuous, shameless **5.** *Inf.* cosmopolitan, elegant, sophisticated, urbane ~*v.* **6.** chill, cool off, freeze, lose heat, refrigerate **7.** abate, allay, assuage, calm (down), dampen, lessen, moderate, quiet, temper ~*n.* **8.** *Sl.* calmness, composure, control, poise, self-control, self-discipline, self-possession, temper

coop 1. *n.* box, cage, enclosure, hutch, pen **2.** *v.* cage, confine, immure, imprison, pen, shut up

cooperate abet, aid, assist, collaborate, combine, concur, conduce, conspire, contribute, coordinate, go along with, help, join forces, pitch in, play ball (*Inf.*), pool resources, pull together, work together

cooperation assistance, collaboration, combined effort, concert, concurrence, esprit de corps, give-and-take, helpfulness, participation, responsiveness, teamwork, unity

cooperative 1. accommodating, helpful, obliging, responsive, supportive **2.** coactive, collective, combined, concerted, coordinated, joint, shared, unified, united

coordinate 1. *v.* correlate, harmonize, integrate, match, mesh, organize, relate, synchronize, systematize **2.** *adj.* coequal, correlative, correspondent, equal, equivalent, parallel, tantamount

cope carry on, get by (*Inf.*), hold one's own, make out (*Inf.*), make the grade, manage, rise to the occasion, struggle through, survive

coping saw handsaw with U-shaped frame for cutting curves in material too thick for fret saw

copious (ˈkəʊpɪəs) *a.* 1. abundant 2. plentiful 3. full, ample —**ˈcopiously** *adv.* —**ˈcopiousness** *n.*

copper[1] (ˈkɒpə) *n.* 1. reddish-brown malleable ductile metal 2. bronze money, coin 3. large washing vessel —*vt.* 4. cover with copper —**copper-bottomed** *a.* reliable, *esp.* financially —**ˈcopperplate** *n.* 1. plate of copper for engraving, etching 2. print from this 3. copybook writing 4. fine handwriting based upon that used on copperplate engravings —**ˈcoppersmith** *n.* one who works with copper

copper[2] (ˈkɒpə) *n. sl.* policeman

coppice (ˈkɒpɪs) *n.* wood of small trees

copra (ˈkɒprə) *n.* dried coconut kernels

Copt (kɒpt) *n.* 1. member of Coptic Church 2. Egyptian descended from ancient Egyptians —**ˈCoptic** *n.* 1. Afro-Asiatic language, written in Greek alphabet but descended from ancient Egyptian —*a.* 2. of this language 3. of Copts

copula (ˈkɒpjʊlə) *n.* 1. word, *esp.* verb acting as connecting link in sentence 2. connection, tie

copulate (ˈkɒpjʊleɪt) *vi.* unite sexually —**copuˈlation** *n.* —**ˈcopulative** *a.*

copy (ˈkɒpɪ) *n.* 1. imitation 2. single specimen of book 3. matter for printing 4. *Journalism inf.* suitable material for an article —*vt.* 5. make copy of, imitate 6. transcribe 7. follow example of (**ˈcopied, ˈcopying**) —**ˈcopier** *n.* person or device that copies —**ˈcopyist** *n.* —**ˈcopybook** *n.* 1. book of specimens, *esp.* of penmanship, for imitation 2. *chiefly* US book for or containing documents —*a.* 3. trite, unoriginal —**ˈcopycat** *n. inf.* person, *esp.* child, who imitates another —**ˈcopyhold** *n.* *Law* formerly, tenure less than freehold of land in England evidenced by copy of Court roll —**ˈcopyright** *n.* 1. legal exclusive right to print and publish book, article, work of art *etc.* —*vt.* 2. protect by copyright —**ˈcopywriter** *n.* one who composes advertisements —**blot one's copybook** *inf.* sully one's reputation

coquette (kəʊˈkɛt, kɒˈkɛt) *n.* woman who flirts —**ˈcoquetry** *n.* —**coˈquettish** *a.*

coracle (ˈkɒrəkᵊl) *n.* boat of wicker covered with skins

coral (ˈkɒrəl) *n.* 1. hard substánce made by sea polyps and forming growths, islands, reefs 2. ornament of coral —*a.* 3. made of coral 4. of deep pink colour —**ˈcoralline** *a.*

cor anglais (ˈkɔːr ˈɑːŋgleɪ) oboe set a fifth lower than ordinary oboe

corbel (ˈkɔːbᵊl) *n.* stone or timber projection from wall to support something

corbie (ˈkɔːbɪ) *n. Scot.* 1. raven 2. crow

cord (kɔːd) *n.* 1. thin rope or thick string 2. rib on cloth 3. ribbed fabric —*vt.* 4. fasten with cord —**ˈcordage** *n.*

cordate (ˈkɔːdeɪt) *a.* heart-shaped

cordial (ˈkɔːdɪəl) *a.* 1. hearty, sincere, warm —*n.* 2. sweet, fruit-flavoured drink —**cordiˈality** *n.* —**ˈcordially** *adv.*

cordite (ˈkɔːdaɪt) *n.* explosive compound

cordon (ˈkɔːdᵊn) *n.* 1. chain of troops or police 2. fruit tree grown as single stem —*vt.* 3. (*oft. with* off) form cordon around

cordon bleu (*Fr.* kɔrdɔ̃ ˈblø) (*esp.* of food preparation) of highest standard

cordovan (ˈkɔːdəvᵊn) *n.* fine leather now made principally from horsehide

corduroy (ˈkɔːdərɔɪ, kɔːdəˈrɔɪ) *n.* cotton fabric with velvety, ribbed surface

cordwainer (ˈkɔːdweɪnə) *n. obs.* shoemaker or worker in leather

core (kɔː) *n.* 1. horny seed case of apple and other fruits 2. central or innermost part of anything —*vt.* 3. take out the core of

co-respondent (kəʊrɪˈspɒndənt) *n.* one cited in divorce case, alleged to have committed adultery with the respondent

corgi (ˈkɔːgɪ) *n.* a small Welsh dog

coriaceous (kɒrɪˈeɪʃəs) *a.* of, like leather

coriander (kɒrɪˈændə) *n.* herb

Corinthian (kəˈrɪnθɪən) *a.* 1. of Corinth 2. of Corinthian order of architecture, ornate Greek

cork (kɔːk) *n.* 1. bark of an evergreen Mediterranean oak tree 2. piece of it or other material, *esp.* used as stopper for bottle *etc.* —*vt.* 3. stop up with cork —**ˈcorkage** *n.* charge for opening wine bottles in restaurant —**corked** *a.* tainted through having cork containing excess tannin —**ˈcorker** *n. sl.* something, someone outstanding —**ˈcorkscrew** *n.* tool for pulling out corks

corm (kɔːm) *n.* underground stem like a bulb, but more solid

cormorant (ˈkɔːmərənt) *n.* large voracious sea bird

corn[1] (kɔːn) *n.* 1. grain, fruit of cereals 2. grain of all kinds 3. US maize 4. oversentimental, trite quality in play, film *etc.* —*vt.* 5. preserve (meat) with salt —**ˈcorny** *a. inf.* trite, oversentimental, hackneyed —**ˈcorncrake** *n.* brown bird with harsh call, land rail —**ˈcornflakes** *pl.n.* breakfast cereal —**ˈcornflour** *n.* finely ground maize —**ˈcornflower** *n.* blue flower growing in cornfields

corn[2] (kɔːn) *n.* painful horny growth on foot or toe

THESAURUS

copious abundant, ample, bounteous, bountiful, extensive, exuberant, full, generous, lavish, liberal, luxuriant, overflowing, plenteous, plentiful, profuse, rich, superabundant

copy *n.* 1. archetype, carbon copy, counterfeit, duplicate, facsimile, forgery, image, imitation, likeness, model, pattern, photocopy, Photostat (*Trademark*), print, replica, replication, representation, reproduction, transcription, Xerox (*Trademark*) ~*v.* 2. counterfeit, duplicate, photocopy, Photostat (*Trademark*), replicate, reproduce, transcribe, Xerox (*Trademark*) 3. ape, echo, emulate, follow, follow suit, follow the example of, imitate, mimic, mirror, parrot, repeat, simulate

cordial affable, affectionate, agreeable, cheerful, earnest, friendly, genial, heartfelt, hearty, invigorating, sociable, warm, warm-hearted, welcoming, wholehearted

cordiality affability, amiability, friendliness, geniality, heartiness, sincerity, warmth, wholeheartedness

cordon 1. *n.* barrier, chain, line, ring 2. *v.* **cordon off** close off, encircle, enclose, fence off, isolate, picket, separate, surround

core centre, crux, essence, gist, heart, kernel, nub, nucleus, pith

cornea (ˈkɔːnɪə) *n.* transparent membrane covering front of eye

cornel (ˈkɔːnᵊl) *n.* any small tree with very hard wood, as the dogwood *etc.*

cornelian (kɔːˈniːlɪən) *n.* precious stone, kind of chalcedony

corner (ˈkɔːnə) *n.* **1.** part of room where two sides meet **2.** remote or humble place **3.** point where two walls, streets *etc.* meet **4.** angle, projection **5.** *Business* buying up of whole existing stock of commodity **6.** *Sport* free kick or shot from corner of field —*vt.* **7.** drive into position of difficulty, or leaving no escape **8.** acquire enough of (commodity) to attain control of the market **9.** attain control of (market) in such a manner (*also* **enˈgross**) —*vi.* **10.** move round corner —**ˈcornered** *a.* —**ˈcornerstone** *n.* indispensable part, basis

cornet (ˈkɔːnɪt) *n.* **1.** trumpet with valves **2.** cone-shaped ice-cream wafer

cornice (ˈkɔːnɪs) *n.* **1.** projection near top of wall **2.** ornamental, carved moulding below ceiling

Cornish (ˈkɔːnɪʃ) *a.* **1.** of Cornwall or its inhabitants —*n.* **2.** formerly, language of Cornwall: extinct by 1800 —*pl.* **3.** natives of Cornwall —**ˈCornishman** *n.* —**Cornish pasty** (ˈpæstɪ) *Cookery* pastry case with filling of meat and vegetables

cornucopia (kɔːnjuˈkəʊpɪə) *n.* symbol of plenty, consisting of goat's horn, overflowing with fruit and flowers

corolla (kəˈrɒlə) *n.* flower's inner envelope of petals

corollary (kəˈrɒlərɪ) *n.* **1.** inference from a preceding statement **2.** deduction **3.** result

corona (kəˈrəʊnə) *n.* **1.** halo around heavenly body **2.** flat projecting part of cornice **3.** top or crown (*pl.* **-s, -nae** (-niː)) —**coˈronal** *a.*

coronary (ˈkɒrənərɪ) *a.* **1.** of blood vessels surrounding heart —*n.* **2.** coronary thrombosis —**coronary thrombosis** formation of obstructing clot in coronary artery

coronation (kɒrəˈneɪʃən) *n.* ceremony of crowning a sovereign

coroner (ˈkɒrənə) *n.* officer who holds inquests on bodies of persons supposed killed by violence, accident *etc.* —**ˈcoronership** *n.*

coronet (ˈkɒrənɪt) *n.* small crown

corporal[1] (ˈkɔːpərəl) *a.* **1.** of the body **2.** material, not spiritual —**corporal punishment** punishment (flogging *etc.*) of physical nature

corporal[2] (ˈkɔːpərəl, ˈkɔːprəl) *n.* **1.** noncommissioned officer below sergeant **2.** *Navy* petty officer under a master-at-arms —**Corporal of Horse** noncommissioned rank in British army, above that of sergeant and below that of staff sergeant

corporation (kɔːpəˈreɪʃən) *n.* **1.** association, body of persons legally authorized to act as an individual **2.** authorities of town or city —**ˈcorporate** *a.*

corporeal (kɔːˈpɔːrɪəl) *a.* **1.** of the body, material **2.** tangible

corps (kɔː) *n.* **1.** military force, body of troops **2.** any organized body of persons (*pl.* **corps** (kɔːz)) —**corps de ballet** members of ballet company who dance together in group —**corps diplomatique** (dɪpləʊmæˈtiːk) body of diplomats accredited to state (*also* **diplomatic corps**)

corpse (kɔːps) *n.* dead body

corpulent (ˈkɔːpjʊlənt) *a.* fat —**ˈcorpulence** *n.*

corpus (ˈkɔːpəs) *n.* **1.** collection or body of works, *esp.* by single author **2.** main part or body of something (*pl.* **-pora** (-pərə))

corpuscle (ˈkɔːpʌsᵊl) *n.* minute organism or particle, *esp.* red and white corpuscles of blood

corral (kɒˈrɑːl) *n.* **US** enclosure for cattle, or for defence

correct (kəˈrɛkt) *vt.* **1.** set right **2.** indicate errors in **3.** rebuke, punish **4.** counteract, rectify —*a.* **5.** right, exact, accurate **6.** in accordance with facts or standards —**corˈrection** *n.* —**corˈrective** *n./a.* —**corˈrectly** *adv.* —**corˈrectness** *n.*

correlate (ˈkɒrɪleɪt) *vt.* **1.** bring into reciprocal relation —*n.* **2.** either of two things or words necessarily

THESAURUS

corner *n.* **1.** angle, bend, crook, joint **2.** cavity, cranny, hideaway, hide-out, hidey-hole (*Inf.*), hole, niche, nook, recess, retreat ~*v.* **3.** bring to bay, run to earth, trap **4.** *As in* **corner the market** engross, hog (*Sl.*), monopolize

cornerstone basis, bedrock, key, premise, starting point

corny banal, commonplace, dull, feeble, hackneyed, maudlin, mawkish, old-fashioned, old hat, sentimental, stale, stereotyped, trite

corporal *adj.* anatomical, bodily, carnal, corporeal (*Archaic*), fleshly, material, physical, somatic

corporation 1. association, corporate body, society **2.** civic authorities, council, municipal authorities, town council

corps band, body, company, contingent, crew, detachment, division, regiment, squad, squadron, team, troop, unit

corpse body, cadaver, carcass, remains, stiff (*Sl.*)

corpulent beefy (*Inf.*), bulky, burly, fat, fattish, fleshy, large, lusty, obese, overweight, plump, portly, roly-poly, rotund, stout, tubby, well-padded

correct *v.* **1.** adjust, amend, cure, emend, improve, rectify, redress, reform, regulate, remedy, right **2.** admonish, chasten, chastise, chide, discipline, punish, reprimand, reprove ~*adj.* **3.** accurate, equitable, exact, faultless, flawless, just, O.K. (*Inf.*), precise, regular, right, strict, true **4.** acceptable, appropriate, diplomatic, fitting, O.K. (*Inf.*), proper, seemly, standard

correction 1. adjustment, alteration, amendment, improvement, modification, rectification, righting **2.** admonition, castigation, chastisement, discipline, punishment, reformation, reproof

corrective *adj.* **1.** palliative, rehabilitative, remedial, restorative, therapeutic **2.** disciplinary, penal, punitive, reformatory

correctly accurately, aright, perfectly, precisely, properly, right, rightly

correctness 1. accuracy, exactitude, exactness, faultlessness, fidelity, preciseness, precision, regularity, truth **2.** *bon ton*, civility, decorum, good breeding, propriety, seemliness

correlate associate, compare, connect, coordinate, correspond, equate, interact, parallel, tie in

correlation alternation, correspondence, equivalence, interaction, interchange, interdependence, interrelationship, reciprocity

implying the other —**corre'lation** *n.* —**cor'relative** *a./n.*

correspond (kɒrɪ'spɒnd) *vi.* **1.** be in agreement, be consistent (with) **2.** be similar (to) **3.** exchange letters —**corre'spondence** *n.* **1.** agreement, corresponding **2.** similarity **3.** exchange of letters **4.** letters received —**corre'spondent** *n.* **1.** writer of letters **2.** one employed by newspaper *etc.* to report on particular topic, country *etc.* —**correspondence school** educational institution that offers tuition by post

corridor ('kɒrɪdɔː) *n.* **1.** passage in building, railway train *etc.* **2.** strip of territory (or air route) not under control of state through which it passes —**corridors of power** higher echelons of government considered as location of power and influence

corrie ('kɒrɪ) *n.* **1.** *Scot.* circular hollow on hillside **2.** *Geol. see* CIRQUE

corrigendum (kɒrɪ'dʒɛndəm) *n.* thing to be corrected (*pl.* **-da** (-də))

corrigible ('kɒrɪdʒɪb'l) *a.* **1.** capable of being corrected **2.** submissive

corroborate (kə'rɒbəreɪt) *vt.* confirm, support (statement *etc.*) —**corrobo'ration** *n.* —**cor'roborative** *a.*

corroboree (kə'rɒbərɪ) *n.* **A 1.** native assembly of sacred, festive or warlike character **2.** any noisy gathering

corrode (kə'rəʊd) *vt.* eat, wear away, eat into (by chemical action, disease *etc.*) —**cor'rosion** *n.* —**cor'rosive** *a.*

corrugate ('kɒrʊgeɪt) *v.* wrinkle, bend into wavy ridges —'**corrugated** *a.* —**corru'gation** *n.*

corrupt (kə'rʌpt) *a.* **1.** lacking integrity **2.** open to, or involving, bribery **3.** wicked **4.** spoilt by mistakes, altered for the worse (of words, literary passages *etc.*) —*vt.* **5.** make evil, pervert **6.** bribe **7.** make rotten —**corrupti'bility** *n.* —**cor'ruptible** *a.* —**cor'ruption** *n.* —**cor'ruptly** *adv.*

corsage (kɔː'sɑːʒ) *n.* (flower, spray, worn on) bodice of woman's dress

corsair ('kɔːsɛə) *n.* pirate

corselet ('kɔːslɪt) *n.* **1.** piece of armour to cover the trunk **2.** one-piece foundation garment

corset ('kɔːsɪt) *n.* close-fitting undergarment stiffened to give support or shape to the body

cortege *or* **cortège** (kɔː'teɪʒ) *n.* formal (funeral) procession

cortex ('kɔːtɛks) *n.* **1.** *Anat.* outer layer **2.** bark **3.** sheath (*pl.* **cortices** ('kɔːtɪsiːz)) —'**cortical** *a.*

cortisone ('kɔːtɪzəʊn) *n.* synthetic hormone used in the treatment of a variety of diseases

corundum (kə'rʌndəm) *n.* native crystalline aluminium oxide, used as abrasive

coruscate ('kɒrəskeɪt) *vi.* emit flashes of light; sparkle —**corus'cation** *n.*

corvette (kɔː'vɛt) *n.* lightly armed warship for escort and antisubmarine duties

corymb ('kɒrɪmb, -rɪm) *n.* inflorescence in form of flat-topped flower cluster with oldest flowers at periphery

coryza (kə'raɪzə) *n.* acute inflammation of mucous membrane of nose, with discharge of mucus; head cold

cos[1] *or* **cos lettuce** (kɒs) *n.* lettuce with long slender head and crisp leaves

cos[2] (kɒz) cosine

cosec ('kəʊsɛk) cosecant

cosecant (kəʊ'siːkənt) *n.* (of angle) trigonometric function that in right-angled triangle is ratio of length of hypotenuse to that of opposite side

cosh (kɒʃ) *n.* **1.** blunt weapon —*vt.* **2.** strike with one

cosignatory (kəʊ'sɪgnətərɪ, -trɪ) *n.* **1.** person, country *etc.* that signs document jointly with others —*a.* **2.** signing jointly

cosine ('kəʊsaɪn) *n.* in a right-angled triangle, the ratio of a side adjacent to a given angle and the hypotenuse

cosmetic (kɒz'mɛtɪk) *n.* **1.** preparation to beautify or improve skin, hair *etc.* —*a.* **2.** designed to improve appearance only

cosmic ('kɒzmɪk) *a.* **1.** relating to the universe **2.** of

THESAURUS

correspond 1. accord, agree, be consistent, coincide, complement, conform, correlate, dovetail, fit, harmonize, match, square, tally **2.** communicate, exchange letters, keep in touch, write

correspondence 1. agreement, analogy, coincidence, comparability, comparison, concurrence, conformity, congruity, correlation, fitness, harmony, match, relation, similarity **2.** communication, letters, mail, post, writing

correspondent 1. letter writer, pen friend *or* pal **2.** contributor, gazetteer (*Archaic*), journalist, reporter, special correspondent

corridor aisle, hallway, passage, passageway

corroborate authenticate, back up, bear out, confirm, document, endorse, establish, ratify, substantiate, support, sustain, validate

corrode canker, consume, corrupt, deteriorate, eat away, erode, gnaw, impair, oxidize, rust, waste, wear away

corrosive acrid, biting, caustic, consuming, corroding, erosive, virulent, wasting, wearing

corrugated channelled, creased, crinkled, fluted, furrowed, grooved, puckered, ridged, rumpled, wrinkled

corrupt *adj.* **1.** bent (*Sl.*), bribable, crooked (*Inf.*), dishonest, fraudulent, rotten, shady (*Inf.*), unethical, unprincipled, unscrupulous, venal **2.** abandoned, debased, defiled, degenerate, demoralized, depraved, dishonoured, dissolute, profligate, vicious ~*v.* **3.** bribe, debauch, demoralize, deprave, entice, fix (*Inf.*), grease (someone's) palm (*Sl.*), lure, pervert, square (*Inf.*), suborn, subvert ~*adj.* **4.** altered, distorted, doctored, falsified ~*v.* **5.** contaminate, infect, putrefy, spoil, taint

corruption 1. breach of trust, bribery, bribing, crookedness (*Inf.*), demoralization, dishonesty, extortion, fiddling (*Inf.*), fraud, fraudulency, graft, jobbery, profiteering, shadiness, shady dealings (*Inf.*), unscrupulousness, venality **2.** baseness, decadence, degeneration, degradation, depravity, evil, immorality, impurity, iniquity, perversion, profligacy, sinfulness, turpitude, vice, viciousness, wickedness **3.** decay, distortion, doctoring, falsification, infection, pollution, putrefaction, putrescence, rot, rottenness

corset belt, bodice, corselet, foundation garment, girdle, panty girdle, stays (*Rare*)

cosmetic *adj.* beautifying, nonessential, superficial, surface, touching-up

the vastness of the universe —**cosmic rays** high-energy electromagnetic rays from space

cosmo- *or before vowel* **cosm-** (*comb. form*) world; universe, as in *cosmology, cosmonaut*

cosmopolitan (kɒzməˈpɒlɪtᵊn) *n.* **1.** person who has lived and travelled in many countries —*a.* **2.** familiar with many countries **3.** sophisticated **4.** free from national prejudice —**cosmoˈpolitanism** *n.* —**cosˈmopolite** *n.*

cosmos[1] (ˈkɒzmɒs) *n.* the world or universe considered as an ordered system —**cosˈmogony** *n.* study of origin and development of universe or system in universe —**cosˈmographer** *n.* —**cosmoˈgraphic** *a.* —**cosˈmography** *n.* description or mapping of the universe —**cosmoˈlogical** *a.* —**cosˈmology** *n.* the science or study of the universe —**cosmonaut** (ˈkɒzmənɔːt) *n.* Soviet astronaut

cosmos[2] (ˈkɒzmɒs) *n.* plant cultivated for brightly coloured flowers (*pl.* **-mos, -es**)

Cossack (ˈkɒsæk) *n.* member of tribe in SE Russia

cosset (ˈkɒsɪt) *vt.* pamper, pet

cost (kɒst) *n.* **1.** price **2.** expenditure of time, labour *etc.* —*pl.* **3.** expenses of lawsuit —*vt.* **4.** have as price **5.** entail payment, loss or sacrifice of (**cost** *pt./pp.*) —**ˈcosting** *n.* system of calculating cost of production —**ˈcostliness** *n.* —**ˈcostly** *a.* **1.** valuable **2.** expensive —**cost of living** basic cost of food, clothing and shelter necessary to maintain life —**cost price** price at which article is bought by one intending to resell it

costal (ˈkɒstᵊl) *a.* pert. to side of body or ribs —**ˈcostate** *a.* ribbed

costermonger (ˈkɒstəmʌŋgə) *or* **coster** *n.* **UK,** *rare* person who sells fruit *etc.* from barrow

costive (ˈkɒstɪv) *a.* **1.** constipated **2.** niggardly

costume (ˈkɒstjuːm) *n.* **1.** style of dress of particular place or time, or for particular activity **2.** theatrical clothes —**cosˈtumier** *n.* dealer in costumes —**costume jewellery** artificial jewellery

cosy *or U.S.* **cozy** (ˈkəʊzɪ) *a.* **1.** snug, comfortable, sheltered —*n.* **2.** covering to keep teapot *etc.* hot —**ˈcosily** *or U.S.* **ˈcozily** *adv.*

cot[1] (kɒt) *n.* **1.** child's bed usu. with barred sides **2.** swinging bed on ship —**cot death** unexplained death of baby while asleep

cot[2] (kɒt) *n.* **1.** *Lit., obs.* small cottage **2.** small shelter, *esp.* for pigeons, sheep *etc.* (*also* **cote**)

cot[3] (kɒt) cotangent

cotangent (kəʊˈtændʒənt) *n.* (of angle) trigonometric function that in right-angled triangle is ratio of length of adjacent side to that of opposite side

cote (kəʊt) *or* **cot** *n.* shelter, shed for animals or birds, *eg* dovecot(e)

coterie (ˈkəʊtərɪ) *n.* **1.** exclusive group of people with common interests **2.** social clique

cotillion *or* **cotillon** (kəˈtɪljən, kəʊ-) *n. Hist.* lively dance

cotoneaster (kətəʊnɪˈæstə) *n.* garden shrub with red berries

cottage (ˈkɒtɪdʒ) *n.* small house —**cottage cheese** mild, soft cheese —**cottage industry** industry in which workers work in their own homes —**cottage pie UK** *see* **shepherd's pie** *at* SHEPHERD

cotter (ˈkɒtə) *n.* pin, wedge *etc.* to prevent relative motion of two parts of machine *etc.*

cotton (ˈkɒtᵊn) *n.* **1.** plant **2.** white downy fibrous covering of its seeds **3.** thread or cloth made of this —**cotton wool 1.** *chiefly* **UK** bleached sterilized cotton from which impurities have been removed **2.** cotton in natural state **3. UK** *inf.* state of pampered comfort and protection —**cotton to** *or* **on to** understand (idea *etc.*)

cotyledon (kɒtɪˈliːdᵊn) *n.* primary leaf of plant embryos

couch (kaʊtʃ) *n.* **1.** piece of furniture for reclining on by day, sofa —*vt.* **2.** express in a particular style of language **3.** cause to lie down —**ˈcouchant** *a. Her.* lying down

couch grass (kaʊtʃ, kuːtʃ) type of creeping grass

cougar (ˈkuːgə) *n.* puma

cough (kɒf) *vi.* **1.** expel air from lungs with sudden effort and noise, oft. to remove obstruction —*n.* **2.** act of coughing —**cough drop** lozenge to relieve cough —**cough mixture** medicine that relieves coughing

could (kʊd) *pt. of* CAN[1]

coulomb (ˈkuːlɒm) *n.* unit of quantity of electricity

coulter (ˈkəʊltə) *n.* sharp blade or disc at front of plough

council (ˈkaʊnsəl) *n.* **1.** deliberative or administrative body **2.** one of its meetings **3.** local governing authority of town *etc.* —**ˈcouncillor** *or U.S.* **ˈcouncilor** *n.* member of council

counsel (ˈkaʊnsəl) *n.* **1.** advice, deliberation, debate **2.** barrister; barristers **3.** plan, policy —*vt.* **4.** advise, recommend (**-ll-**) —**ˈcounsellor** *or U.S.* **ˈcounselor** *n.* adviser —**keep one's counsel** keep a secret

THESAURUS

cosmic grandiose, huge, immense, infinite, limitless, measureless, universal, vast

cosmopolitan 1. *adj.* catholic, sophisticated, universal, urbane, well-travelled, worldly, worldly-wise **2.** *n.* cosmopolite, jetsetter, man *or* woman of the world, sophisticate

cost *n.* **1.** amount, charge, damage (*Inf.*), expenditure, expense, figure, outlay, payment, price, rate, worth ~*v.* **2.** come to, command a price of, sell at, set (someone) back (*Inf.*) **3.** *Fig.* do disservice to, harm, hurt, injure, lose, necessitate

costly 1. dear, excessive, exorbitant, expensive, extortionate, highly-priced, steep (*Inf.*), valuable **2.** gorgeous, lavish, luxurious, opulent, precious, priceless, rich, splendid, sumptuous

costs budget, expenses, outgoings

costume apparel, attire, clothing, dress, ensemble, garb, get-up (*Inf.*), livery, national dress, outfit, robes, uniform

cosy comfortable, comfy (*Inf.*), cuddled up, homely, intimate, secure, sheltered, snug, snuggled down, tucked up, warm

cottage but-and-ben (*Scot.*), cabin, chalet, cot, hut, lodge, shack

cough 1. *n.* bark, frog *or* tickle in one's throat, hack **2.** *v.* bark, clear one's throat, hack, hawk, hem

council assembly, board, cabinet, chamber, committee, conclave, conference, congress, convention, convocation, diet, governing body, ministry, panel, parliament, synod

counsel *n.* **1.** admonition, advice, caution, consideration, consultation, deliberation, direction, fore-

count[1] (kaʊnt) *vt.* **1.** reckon, calculate, number **2.** include **3.** consider to be —*vi.* **4.** depend (on) **5.** be of importance —*n.* **6.** reckoning **7.** total number reached by counting **8.** item in list of charges or indictment **9.** act of counting —**ˈcountless** *a.* too many to be counted —**ˈcountdown** *n.* act of counting backwards to time critical operation exactly, such as launching of rocket —**counting house** room or building for book-keeping —**count down** count backwards to time critical operation exactly —**count out** **1.** *inf.* leave out; exclude **2.** (of boxing referee) judge (floored boxer) to have failed to recover within specified time

count[2] (kaʊnt) *n.* nobleman corresponding to British earl —**ˈcountess** *n.* wife or widow of count or earl

countenance (ˈkaʊntɪnəns) *n.* **1.** face or its expression **2.** support, approval **3.** composure; self-control —*vt.* **4.** give support to, approve

counter[1] (ˈkaʊntə) *n.* **1.** horizontal surface in bank, shop *etc.*, over which business is transacted **2.** disc, token used for counting or scoring, *esp.* in board games

counter[2] (ˈkaʊntə) *adv.* **1.** in opposite direction **2.** contrary —*vt.* **3.** oppose, contradict **4.** *Fencing* parry —*n.* **5.** parry

counter- (*comb. form*) reversed, opposite, rival, as in *counterclaim, counterclockwise, counterirritant, countermarch, countermeasure, countermine, counter-revolution.* Such words are not given here where the meaning may be inferred from the simple word

counteract (kaʊntərˈækt) *vt.* neutralize, hinder —**counterˈaction** *n.*

counterattack (ˈkaʊntərətæk) *v./n.* attack after enemy's advance

counterbalance (ˈkaʊntəbæləns) *n.* weight balancing or neutralizing another

counterfeit (ˈkaʊntəfɪt) *a.* **1.** sham, forged —*n.* **2.** imitation, forgery —*vt.* **3.** imitate with intent to deceive **4.** forge —**ˈcounterfeiter** *n.* —**ˈcounterfeitly** *adv.*

counterfoil (ˈkaʊntəfɔɪl) *n.* part of cheque, receipt, postal order, kept as record

counterintelligence (kaʊntərɪnˈtɛlɪdʒəns) *n.* activities designed to frustrate enemy espionage

countermand (kaʊntəˈmɑːnd) *vt.* cancel (previous order)

counterpane (ˈkaʊntəpeɪn) *n.* top cover for bed

counterpart (ˈkaʊntəpɑːt) *n.* **1.** thing so like another as to be mistaken for it **2.** something complementary to or correlative of another

counterpoint (ˈkaʊntəpɔɪnt) *n.* **1.** melody added as accompaniment to given melody **2.** art of so adding melodies

counterpoise (ˈkaʊntəpɔɪz) *n.* **1.** force, influence *etc.* that counterbalances another **2.** state of balance; equilibrium **3.** weight that balances another —*vt.* **4.** oppose with something of equal effect, weight or force; offset **5.** bring into equilibrium

counterproductive (kaʊntəprəˈdʌktɪv) *a.* tending to hinder achievement of aim; having effects contrary to those intended

Counter-Reformation (kaʊntərɛfəˈmeɪʃən) *n.* reform movement in Catholic Church in 16th and early 17th centuries

countersign (ˈkaʊntəsaɪn, kaʊntəˈsaɪn) *vt.* **1.** sign document already signed by another **2.** ratify

countersink (ˈkaʊntəsɪŋk) *vt.* enlarge (upper part of hole drilled in timber *etc.*) to take head of screw, bolt *etc.* below surface

countertenor (kaʊntəˈtɛnə) *n.* **1.** adult male voice with alto range **2.** singer with such voice

countervail (kaʊntəˈveɪl, ˈkaʊntəveɪl) *v.* **1.** act or act against with equal power or force —*vt.* **2.** make up for; compensate; offset

counterweight (ˈkaʊntəweɪt) *n.* counterbalancing weight, influence or force

countess (ˈkaʊntɪs) *n.* *see* COUNT[2]

country (ˈkʌntrɪ) *n.* **1.** region, district **2.** territory of nation **3.** land of birth, residence *etc.* **4.** rural districts

THESAURUS

thought, guidance, information, recommendation, suggestion, warning **2.** advocate, attorney, barrister, lawyer, legal adviser, solicitor ~*v.* **3.** admonish, advise, advocate, caution, exhort, instruct, recommend, urge, warn

count *v.* **1.** add (up), calculate, cast up, check, compute, enumerate, estimate, number, reckon, score, tally, tot up **2.** consider, deem, esteem, impute, judge, look upon, rate, regard, think **3.** carry weight, cut any ice (*Inf.*), enter into consideration, matter, rate, signify, tell, weigh **4.** include, number among, take into account *or* consideration ~*n.* **5.** calculation, computation, enumeration, numbering, poll, reckoning, sum, tally

countenance *n.* **1.** appearance, aspect, expression, face, features, look, mien, physiognomy, visage **2.** aid, approval, assistance, backing, endorsement, favour, sanction, support ~*v.* **3.** abet, aid, approve, back, champion, condone, encourage, endorse, help, sanction, support **4.** brook, endure, put up with (*Inf.*), stand for (*Inf.*), tolerate

counter **1.** *adv.* against, at variance with, contrarily, contrariwise, conversely, in defiance of, versus **2.** *v.* answer, hit back, meet, offset, parry, resist, respond, retaliate, return, ward off

counteract annul, check, contravene, counterbalance, countervail, cross, defeat, foil, frustrate, hinder, invalidate, negate, neutralize, offset, oppose, resist, thwart

counterfeit **1.** *v.* copy, fabricate, fake, feign, forge, imitate, impersonate, pretend, sham, simulate **2.** *adj.* bogus, copied, ersatz, faked, false, feigned, forged, fraudulent, imitation, phoney (*Sl.*), pseud (*Inf.*), pseudo (*Inf.*), sham, simulated, spurious, suppositious **3.** *n.* copy, fake, forgery, fraud, imitation, phoney (*Sl.*), reproduction, sham

countermand annul, cancel, override, repeal, rescind, retract, reverse, revoke

counterpart complement, copy, correlative, duplicate, equal, fellow, match, mate, opposite number, supplement, tally, twin

countless endless, immeasurable, incalculable, infinite, innumerable, legion, limitless, measureless, multitudinous, myriad, numberless, uncounted, untold

count out disregard, except, exclude, leave out, leave out of account, pass over

as opposed to town **5.** nation —ˈ**countrified** *a.* rural in manner or appearance —**country-and-western** *n.* urban 20th-century White folk music of SE Amer. —**country club** club in the country, having sporting and social facilities —**country dance** folk dance in which couples face one another in line —ˈ**countryman** *n.* **1.** rustic **2.** compatriot —ˈ**countryside** *n.* **1.** rural district **2.** its inhabitants

county (ˈkauntɪ) *n.* **1.** division of country **2.** shire —*a.* **3.** UK *inf.* upper-class; of or like landed gentry —**county town** town in which county's affairs are or were administered

coup (ku:) *n.* **1.** successful stroke, move or gamble **2.** (*short for* **coup d'état**) sudden, violent seizure of government

coup de grâce (ku də ˈgrɑs) *Fr.* **1.** mortal or finishing blow, *esp.* delivered as act of mercy to sufferer **2.** final or decisive stroke (*pl.* ***coups de grâce*** (ku də ˈgrɑs))

coupé (ˈku:peɪ) *n.* sporty style of motor car, *usu.* with two doors

couple (ˈkʌpᵊl) *n.* **1.** two, pair **2.** indefinite small number **3.** two people who regularly associate with each other or live together **4.** any two persons —*vt.* **5.** connect, fasten together **6.** associate, connect in the mind —*vi.* **7.** join —ˈ**coupler** *n.* —ˈ**couplet** *n.* two lines of verse, *esp.* rhyming and of equal length —ˈ**coupling** *n.* connection, *esp.* chain between railway wagons

coupon (ˈku:pɒn) *n.* **1.** ticket or voucher entitling holder to discount, gift *etc.* **2.** detachable slip used as order form **3.** (in betting *etc.*) printed form on which to forecast results

courage (ˈkʌrɪdʒ) *n.* bravery, boldness —**couˈrageous** *a.* —**couˈrageously** *adv.*

courgette (kuəˈʒɛt) *n.* type of small vegetable marrow

courier (ˈkuərɪə) *n.* **1.** express messenger **2.** person who looks after, guides travellers

course (kɔ:s) *n.* **1.** movement in space or time **2.** direction of movement **3.** successive development, sequence **4.** line of conduct or action **5.** series of lectures, exercises *etc.* **6.** any of successive parts of meal **7.** continuous line of masonry at particular level in building **8.** area where golf is played **9.** track or ground on which a race is run —*vt.* **10.** hunt —*vi.* **11.** run swiftly, gallop about **12.** (of blood) circulate —ˈ**courser** *n. Poet.* swift horse —ˈ**coursing** *n.* **1.** (of hounds or dogs) hunting by sight **2.** sport in which hounds are matched against one another in pairs for hunting of hares by sight

court (kɔ:t) *n.* **1.** space enclosed by buildings, yard **2.** area marked off or enclosed for playing various games **3.** retinue and establishment of sovereign **4.** body with judicial powers, place where it meets, one of its sittings **5.** attention, homage, flattery —*vt.* **6.** woo, try to win or attract **7.** seek, invite —ˈ**courtier** *n.* one who frequents royal court —ˈ**courtliness** *n.* —ˈ**courtly** *a.* **1.** ceremoniously polite **2.** characteristic of a court —ˈ**courtship** *n.* wooing —**court card** king, queen or jack at cards —ˈ**courthouse** *n.* public building in which courts of law are held —**court martial** court of naval or military officers for trying naval or military offences (*pl.* **court martials, courts martial**) —**court plaster** plaster, composed of isinglass on silk, formerly used to cover superficial wounds —**court shoe** low-cut shoe for women, without laces or straps —ˈ**courtyard** *n.* paved space enclosed by buildings or walls

THESAURUS

country *n.* **1.** commonwealth, kingdom, nation, people, realm, sovereign state, state **2.** fatherland, homeland, motherland, nationality, native land, *patria* **3.** land, part, region, terrain, territory **4.** citizenry, citizens, community, electors, grass roots, inhabitants, nation, people, populace, public, society, voters **5.** backwoods, boondocks (*U.S. sl.*), countryside, farmland, green belt, outback (*Australian & New Zealand*), outdoors, provinces, rural areas, sticks (*Inf.*), the back of beyond, the middle of nowhere, wide open spaces (*Inf.*)

countryman **1.** bumpkin, country dweller, farmer, hayseed (*U.S. inf.*), hind, husbandman, peasant, provincial, rustic, swain, yokel **2.** compatriot, fellow citizen

countryside country, farmland, green belt, outback (*Australian & New Zealand*), outdoors, panorama, sticks (*Inf.*), view, wide open spaces (*Inf.*)

county **1.** *n.* province, shire **2.** *adj.* huntin', shootin', and fishin' (*Inf.*), plummy (*Inf.*), tweedy, upper-class, upper-crust (*Inf.*)

coup accomplishment, action, deed, exploit, feat, manoeuvre, masterstroke, stratagem, stroke, stroke of genius, stunt, *tour de force*

couple **1.** *n.* brace, duo, pair, span (*of horses or oxen*), twain (*Archaic*), twosome **2.** *v.* buckle, clasp, conjoin, connect, hitch, join, link, marry, pair, unite, wed, yoke

coupon card, certificate, detachable portion, slip, ticket, token, voucher

courage boldness, bottle (*Sl.*), bravery, daring, dauntlessness, fearlessness, firmness, fortitude, gallantry, grit, guts (*Inf.*), hardihood, heroism, intrepidity, lion-heartedness, mettle, nerve, pluck, resolution, spunk (*Inf.*), valour

courageous audacious, bold, brave, daring, dauntless, fearless, gallant, hardy, heroic, indomitable, intrepid, lion-hearted, plucky, resolute, stout-hearted, valiant, valorous

course *n.* **1.** advance, advancement, continuity, development, flow, furtherance, march, movement, order, progress, progression, sequence, succession, unfolding **2.** channel, direction, line, orbit, passage, path, road, route, tack, track, trail, trajectory, way **3.** duration, lapse, passage, passing, sweep, term, time **4.** behaviour, conduct, manner, method, mode, plan, policy, procedure, programme, regimen **5.** cinder track, circuit, lap, race, racecourse, round **6.** classes, course of study, curriculum, lectures, programme, schedule, studies ~*v.* **7.** dash, flow, gush, move apace, race, run, scud, scurry, speed, stream, surge, tumble **8.** chase, follow, hunt, pursue

court *n.* **1.** cloister, courtyard, piazza, plaza, quad (*Inf.*), quadrangle, square, yard **2.** hall, manor, palace **3.** attendants, cortege, entourage, retinue, royal household, suite, train **4.** bar, bench, court of justice, lawcourt, seat of judgment, tribunal **5.** addresses, attention, homage, respects, suit ~*v.* **6.** chase, date, go (out) with, go steady with (*Inf.*), keep company with, make love to, pay court to, pay one's addresses to, pursue, run after, serenade, set one's cap at, sue (*Archaic*), take out, walk out with, woo **7.** cultivate, curry favour with, fawn upon, flatter, pan-

courtesan *or* **courtezan** (kɔːtɪˈzæn) *n. obs.* **1.** court mistress **2.** high-class prostitute

courtesy (ˈkɜːtɪsɪ) *n.* **1.** politeness, good manners **2.** act of civility —ˈ**courteous** *a.* polite —ˈ**courteously** *adv.* —**courtesy title** title accorded by usage to which one has no valid claim

cousin (ˈkʌzᵊn) *n.* **1.** son or daughter of uncle or aunt **2.** formerly, any kinsman —ˈ**cousinly** *a.*

couture (kuːˈtʊə) *n.* high-fashion designing and dressmaking —**couturier** (kuːˈtʊərɪeɪ) *n.* person who designs, makes and sells fashion clothes for women (**couturière** (kuːtuːrɪˈɛə) *fem.*)

cove[1] (kəʊv) *n.* small inlet of coast, sheltered bay

cove[2] (kəʊv) *n. sl.* fellow, chap

coven (ˈkʌvᵊn) *n.* gathering of witches

covenant (ˈkʌvənənt) *n.* **1.** contract, mutual agreement **2.** compact —*v.* **3.** agree to a covenant (concerning) —ˈ**Covenanter** *n. Scot. hist.* person upholding either of two 17th-cent. Presbyterian covenants

Coventry (ˈkɒvəntrɪ) *n.* —**send to Coventry** ostracize; ignore

cover (ˈkʌvə) *vt.* **1.** place or spread over **2.** extend over, spread over **3.** bring upon (oneself) **4.** screen, protect **5.** travel over **6.** include **7.** be sufficient to meet **8.** *Journalism* report on **9.** point a gun at —*n.* **10.** lid, wrapper, envelope, binding, screen, anything which covers —ˈ**coverage** *n.* amount, extent covered —ˈ**coverlet** *n.* top covering of bed —**cover charge** fixed charge added to cost of food in restaurant *etc.* —**covering letter** accompanying letter sent as explanation, introduction or record —**cover point** *Cricket* fielding position in covers; fielder in this position —**cover-up** *n.* concealment or attempted concealment of crime *etc.* —**cover up 1.** cover completely **2.** attempt to conceal (mistake or crime)

covert (ˈkʌvət) *a.* **1.** secret, veiled, concealed, sly —*n.* **2.** thicket, place sheltering game —ˈ**covertly** *adv.*

covet (ˈkʌvɪt) *vt.* long to possess, *esp.* what belongs to another —ˈ**covetous** *a.* avaricious —ˈ**covetousness** *n.*

covey (ˈkʌvɪ) *n.* brood of partridges or quail (*pl.* **-s**)

cow[1] (kaʊ) *n.* **1.** the female of the bovine and of certain other animals, *eg* elephant, whale **2.** *inf.* disagreeable woman —ˈ**cowboy** *n.* **1.** herdsman in charge of cattle on western plains of U.S. **2.** *inf.* ruthless or unscrupulous operator in business *etc.* —**cow parsley** Eurasian umbelliferous hedgerow plant —ˈ**cowpox** *n.* disease of cows, source of vaccine

cow[2] (kaʊ) *vt.* frighten into submission, overawe, subdue

coward (ˈkaʊəd) *n.* one who lacks courage, shrinks from danger —ˈ**cowardice** *n.* —ˈ**cowardly** *a.*

cower (ˈkaʊə) *vi.* crouch, shrink in fear

THESAURUS

der to, seek, solicit **8.** attract, bring about, incite, invite, prompt, provoke, seek

courteous affable, attentive, ceremonious, civil, courtly, elegant, gallant, gracious, mannerly, polished, polite, refined, respectful, urbane, well-bred, well-mannered

courtesy 1. affability, civility, courteousness, courtliness, elegance, gallantness, gallantry, good breeding, good manners, graciousness, polish, politeness, urbanity **2.** benevolence, consideration, favour, generosity, indulgence, kindness

courtier attendant, follower, henchman, liegeman, pursuivant (*Historical*), squire, train-bearer

courtly affable, aristocratic, ceremonious, chivalrous, civil, decorous, dignified, elegant, flattering, formal, gallant, highbred, lordly, obliging, polished, refined, stately, urbane

courtship courting, engagement, keeping company, pursuit, romance, suit, wooing

courtyard area, enclosure, peristyle, playground, quad, quadrangle, yard

cove anchorage, bay, creek, firth *or* frith (*Scot.*), inlet, sound

covenant *n.* **1.** arrangement, bargain, commitment, compact, concordat, contract, convention, pact, promise, stipulation, treaty, trust **2.** bond, deed ~*v.* **3.** agree, bargain, contract, engage, pledge, stipulate, undertake

cover *v.* **1.** camouflage, cloak, conceal, cover up, curtain, disguise, eclipse, enshroud, hide, hood, house, mask, obscure, screen, secrete, shade, shroud, veil ~*n.* **2.** cloak, cover-up, disguise, façade, front, mask, pretence, screen, smoke screen, veil, window-dressing ~*v.* **3.** defend, guard, protect, reinforce, shelter, shield, watch over ~*n.* **4.** camouflage, concealment, defence, guard, hiding place, protection, refuge, sanctuary, shelter, shield, undergrowth, woods ~*v.* **5.** canopy, clothe, coat, daub, dress, encase, envelop, invest, layer, mantle, overlay, overspread, put on, wrap ~*n.* **6.** binding, canopy, cap, case, clothing, coating, covering, dress, envelope, jacket, lid, sheath, top, wrapper ~*v.* **7.** comprehend, comprise, consider, contain, deal with, embody, embrace, encompass, examine, include, incorporate, involve, provide for, refer to, survey, take account of **8.** describe, detail, investigate, narrate, recount, relate, report, tell of, write up **9.** balance, compensate, counterbalance, insure, make good, make up for, offset **10.** cross, pass through *or* over, range, travel over, traverse

cover-up complicity, concealment, conspiracy, front, smoke screen, whitewash (*Inf.*)

cover up 1. conceal, cover one's tracks, feign ignorance, hide, hush up, keep dark, keep secret, keep silent about, keep under one's hat (*Inf.*), repress, stonewall, suppress, whitewash (*Inf.*) **2.** coat, cover, encrust, envelop, hide, plaster, slather (*U.S. sl.*), swathe

covet aspire to, begrudge, crave, desire, envy, fancy (*Inf.*), hanker after, have one's eye on, long for, lust after, thirst for, yearn for

covetous acquisitive, avaricious, close-fisted, envious, grasping, greedy, jealous, mercenary, rapacious, yearning

coward caitiff (*Archaic*), craven, dastard (*Archaic*), faint-heart, funk (*Inf.*), poltroon, recreant (*Archaic*), renegade, scaredy-cat (*Inf.*), skulker, sneak, yellow-belly (*Sl.*)

cowardly base, caitiff (*Archaic*), chicken (*Sl.*), chicken-hearted, craven, dastardly, faint-hearted, fearful, gutless (*Inf.*), lily-livered, pusillanimous, recreant (*Archaic*), scared, shrinking, soft, spineless, timorous, weak, weak-kneed (*Inf.*), white-livered, yellow (*Inf.*)

cowboy broncobuster (*U.S.*), cattleman, cowhand, cowpuncher (*U.S. inf.*), drover, gaucho (*S American*),

cowl (kaʊl) *n.* **1.** monk's hooded cloak **2.** its hood **3.** hooded top for chimney, ship's funnel *etc.*

cowling (ˈkaʊlɪŋ) *n.* covering for aircraft engine

co-worker *n.* fellow worker; associate

cowry *or* **cowrie** (ˈkaʊrɪ) *n.* brightly-marked sea shell

cowslip (ˈkaʊslɪp) *n.* wild species of primrose

coxcomb (ˈkɒkskəʊm) *n. obs.* one given to showing off

coxswain (ˈkɒksən, -sweɪn) *n.* steersman of boat —**cox** *n.* **1.** coxswain —*v.* **2.** command or steer

coy (kɔɪ) *a.* (pretending to be) shy, modest —**ˈcoyly** *adv.* —**ˈcoyness** *n.*

coyote (ˈkɔɪəʊt, kɔɪˈəʊtɪ; *esp. U.S.* ˈkaɪəʊt, kaɪˈəʊtɪ) *n.* N Amer. prairie wolf

coypu (ˈkɔɪpuː) *n.* aquatic rodent, orig. from S Amer., yielding nutria fur

cozen (ˈkʌzᵊn) *vt.* flatter in order to cheat, beguile

cp. compare

C.P. **1.** Canadian Pacific **2.** Cape Province **3.** Communist Party

cpd. compound

Cpl. Corporal

C.P.U. central processing unit

CQ symbol transmitted by amateur radio operator requesting communication with any other amateur radio operator

Cr *Chem.* chromium

crab[1] (kræb) *n.* **1.** edible crustacean with ten legs, noted for sidelong and backward walk **2.** type of louse —*vi.* **3.** catch crabs **4.** move sideways —**crabbed** (ˈkræbɪd) *a.* (of handwriting) hard to read —**ˈcrabby** *a.* bad-tempered —**crab louse** parasitic louse that infests pubic region in man —**catch a crab** *Rowing* dig oar too deeply for clean retrieval

crab[2] (kræb) *inf. vi.* **1.** find fault; grumble (**-bb-**) —*n.* **2.** irritable person

crab apple wild sour apple

crack (kræk) *vt.* **1.** break, split partially **2.** break with sharp noise **3.** cause to make sharp noise, as of whip, rifle *etc.* **4.** yield **5.** *inf.* tell (joke) **6.** solve, decipher —*vi.* **7.** make sharp noise **8.** split, fissure **9.** (of the voice) lose clearness when changing from boy's to man's —*n.* **10.** sharp explosive noise **11.** split, fissure **12.** flaw **13.** *inf.* joke, *esp.* sarcastic **14.** *dial.* chat **15.** *sl.* concentrated, highly addictive form of cocaine —*a.* **16.** *inf.* special, smart, of great reputation for skill —**cracked** *a.* **1.** damaged by cracking **2.** *sl.* crazy —**ˈcracker** *n.* **1.** decorated paper tube, pulled apart with a bang, containing paper hat, motto, toy *etc.* **2.** explosive firework **3.** thin dry biscuit —**ˈcrackers** *a. sl.* unbalanced, crazy —**ˈcracking** *a.* **1.** *inf.* fast; vigorous (*esp. in* **a cracking pace**) —*adv./a.* **2.** **UK** *inf.* first-class; excellent —*n.* **3.** process of breaking down hydrocarbons by heat and pressure, as in producing petrol —**ˈcrackle** *n.* **1.** sound of repeated small cracks —*vi.* **2.** make this sound —**ˈcrackling** *n.* **1.** crackle **2.** crisp skin of roast pork —**ˈcrackbrained** *a.* insane, idiotic, crazy —**ˈcrackpot** *inf. n.* **1.** eccentric person; crank —*a.* **2.** eccentric; crazy —**ˈcracksman** *n.* burglar, *esp.* safe-breaker —**get cracking** *inf.* start doing something quickly or with increased speed

cradle (ˈkreɪdᵊl) *n.* **1.** infant's bed (on rockers) **2.** *fig.* earliest resting-place or home **3.** supporting framework —*vt.* **4.** hold or rock as in a cradle **5.** cherish —**ˈcradling** *n.*

craft[1] (krɑːft) *n.* **1.** skill, ability, *esp.* manual ability **2.** cunning **3.** skilled trade **4.** members of a trade —**ˈcraftily** *adv.* —**ˈcraftsman** *n.* —**ˈcraftsmanship** *n.* —**ˈcrafty** *a.* cunning, shrewd

craft[2] (krɑːft) *n.* **1.** vessel **2.** ship (*pl.* **craft**)

crag (kræg) *n.* steep rugged rock —**ˈcraggy** *a.* rugged

crake (kreɪk) *n.* any of various birds of rail family

cram (kræm) *vt.* **1.** fill quite full **2.** stuff, force **3.** pack tightly **4.** feed to excess **5.** prepare quickly for examination —*vi.* **6.** study, *esp.* for examination, by hastily memorizing (**-mm-**) —*n.* **7.** act or condition of cramming **8.** crush

THESAURUS

herder, herdsman, rancher, ranchero (*U.S.*), stockman, wrangler (*U.S.*)

cower cringe, crouch, draw back, fawn, flinch, grovel, quail, shrink, skulk, sneak, tremble, truckle

coy arch, backward, bashful, coquettish, demure, evasive, flirtatious, kittenish, modest, overmodest, prudish, reserved, retiring, self-effacing, shrinking, shy, skittish, timid

crack *v.* **1.** break, burst, chip, chop, cleave, crackle, craze, fracture, rive, snap, splinter, split ~*n.* **2.** breach, break, chink, chip, cleft, cranny, crevice, fissure, fracture, gap, interstice, rift ~*v.* **3.** burst, crash, detonate, explode, pop, ring, snap ~*n.* **4.** burst, clap, crash, explosion, pop, report, snap ~*v.* **5.** break down, collapse, give way, go to pieces, lose control, succumb, yield **6.** decipher, fathom, get the answer to, solve, work out ~*n.* **7.** *Sl.* dig, funny remark, gag, insult, jibe, joke, quip, smart-alecky remark, wisecrack, witticism ~*adj.* **8.** *Sl.* ace, choice, elite, excellent, first-class, first-rate, hand-picked, superior

cracked **1.** broken, chipped, crazed, damaged, defective, faulty, fissured, flawed, imperfect, split **2.** *Sl.* bats (*Sl.*), batty (*Sl.*), crackbrained, crackpot (*Inf.*), crazy (*Inf.*), daft (*Sl.*), eccentric, insane, loony (*Sl.*), nuts (*Sl.*), nutty (*Sl.*), off one's head *or* nut (*Sl.*), out of one's mind, round the bend (*Sl.*), touched

cradle *n.* **1.** bassinet, cot, crib, Moses basket **2.** *Fig.* beginning, birthplace, fount, fountainhead, origin, source, spring, wellspring ~*v.* **3.** hold, lull, nestle, nurse, rock, support **4.** nourish, nurture, tend, watch over

craft[1] **1.** ability, aptitude, art, artistry, cleverness, dexterity, expertise, expertness, ingenuity, knack, know-how (*Inf.*), skill, technique, workmanship **2.** artfulness, artifice, contrivance, craftiness, cunning, deceit, duplicity, guile, ruse, scheme, shrewdness, stratagem, subterfuge, subtlety, trickery, wiles **3.** business, calling, employment, handicraft, handiwork, line, occupation, pursuit, trade, vocation, work

craft[2] aircraft, barque, boat, plane, ship, spacecraft, vessel

craftsman artificer, artisan, maker, master, skilled worker, smith, technician, wright

craftsmanship artistry, expertise, mastery, technique, workmanship

crafty artful, astute, calculating, canny, cunning, deceitful, designing, devious, duplicitous, foxy, fraudulent, guileful, insidious, knowing, scheming, sharp, shrewd, sly, subtle, tricksy, tricky, wily

cramp (kræmp) *n.* **1.** painful muscular contraction **2.** clamp for holding masonry, timber *etc.* together —*vt.* **3.** restrict, hamper **4.** hem in, keep within too narrow limits

crampon (ˈkræmpən) *or* **crampoon** (kræmˈpuːn) *n.* spike in shoe for mountain climbing, *esp.* on ice

cranberry (ˈkrænbərɪ, -brɪ) *n.* edible red berry of dwarf evergreen shrub

crane (kreɪn) *n.* **1.** wading bird with long legs, neck, and bill **2.** machine for moving heavy weights —*v.* **3.** stretch (neck) to see

crane fly insect with long spindly legs (*also* **daddy-longlegs**)

cranesbill (ˈkreɪnzbɪl) *n.* plant with pink or purple flowers and beaked fruits

craniometry (kreɪnɪˈɒmɪtrɪ) *n.* the study of the measurements of the human head

cranium (ˈkreɪnɪəm) *n.* skull (*pl.* **-s, -nia** (-nɪə)) —**ˈcranial** *a.* —**cranioˈlogical** *a.* —**craniˈologist** *n.* —**craniˈology** *n.* branch of science concerned with shape and size of human skull

crank (kræŋk) *n.* **1.** arm at right angles to axis, for turning main shaft, changing reciprocal into rotary motion *etc.* **2.** *inf.* eccentric person, faddist —*v.* **3.** start (engine) by turning crank —**ˈcranky** *a.* **1.** eccentric **2.** bad-tempered **3.** shaky —**ˈcrankpin** *n.* short cylindrical surface fitted between two arms of crank parallel to main shaft of crankshaft —**ˈcrankshaft** *n.* principal shaft of engine

cranny (ˈkrænɪ) *n.* small opening, chink —**ˈcrannied** *a.*

crap (kræp) *n.* gambling game played with two dice (*also* **craps**)

crape (kreɪp) *n.* crepe, *esp.* when used for mourning clothes

crapulent (ˈkræpjʊlənt) *or* **crapulous** (ˈkræpjʊləs) *a.* **1.** given to or resulting from intemperance **2.** suffering from intemperance; drunken —**ˈcrapulence** *n.*

crash (kræʃ) *v.* **1.** (cause to) make loud noise **2.** (cause to) fall with crash **3.** cause (aircraft) to hit land or water or (of aircraft) land in this way **4.** (cause to) collide (with another car *etc.*) **5.** move noisily or violently —*vi.* **6.** break, smash **7.** collapse, fail, *esp.* financially —*n.* **8.** loud, violent fall or impact **9.** collision, *esp.* between vehicles **10.** sudden, uncontrolled descent of aircraft to land **11.** sudden collapse or downfall **12.** bankruptcy —*a.* **13.** requiring, using, great effort to achieve results quickly —**ˈcrashing** *a. inf.* thorough (*esp. in* **crashing bore**) —**crash helmet** helmet worn by motorcyclists *etc.* to protect head —**crash-land** *v.* land (aircraft) in emergency, *esp.* with damage to craft

crass (kræs) *a.* grossly stupid —**ˈcrassly** *adv.* —**ˈcrassness** *n.*

crate (kreɪt) *n.* large (*usu.* wooden) container for packing goods

crater (ˈkreɪtə) *n.* **1.** mouth of volcano **2.** bowl-shaped cavity, *esp.* one made by explosion of large shell, bomb, mine *etc.*

cravat (krəˈvæt) *n.* man's neckcloth

crave (kreɪv) *v.* **1.** have very strong desire (for), long (for) —*vt.* **2.** ask humbly **3.** beg —**ˈcraving** *n.*

craven (ˈkreɪvᵊn) *a.* **1.** cowardly, abject, spineless —*n.* **2.** coward

craw (krɔː) *n.* **1.** bird's or animal's stomach **2.** bird's crop

crawfish (ˈkrɔːfɪʃ) *n. see* CRAYFISH

crawl (krɔːl) *vi.* **1.** move on belly or on hands and knees **2.** move very slowly **3.** ingratiate oneself, cringe **4.** swim with crawl-stroke **5.** be overrun (with) —*n.* **6.** crawling motion **7.** very slow pace or motion **8.** racing stroke at swimming —**ˈcrawler** *n.*

crayfish (ˈkreɪfɪʃ) *or esp. U.S.* **crawfish** *n.* edible freshwater crustacean like lobster

THESAURUS

crag aiguille, bluff, peak, pinnacle, rock, tor

cram **1.** compact, compress, crowd, crush, fill to overflowing, force, jam, overcrowd, overfill, pack, pack in, press, ram, shove, squeeze, stuff **2.** glut, gorge, gormandize, guzzle, overeat, overfeed, put *or* pack away, satiate, stuff **3.** *Inf.* con, grind, mug up (*Sl.*), revise, study, swot, swot up

cramp **1.** *v.* check, circumscribe, clog, confine, constrain, encumber, hamper, hamstring, handicap, hinder, impede, inhibit, obstruct, restrict, shackle, stymie, thwart **2.** *n.* ache, contraction, convulsion, crick, pain, pang, shooting pain, spasm, stiffness, stitch, twinge

cranky bizarre, capricious, eccentric, erratic, freakish, freaky (*Sl.*), funny (*Inf.*), idiosyncratic, odd, peculiar, queer, quirky, strange, wacky (*Sl.*)

cranny breach, chink, cleft, crack, crevice, fissure, gap, hole, interstice, nook, opening

crash *n.* **1.** bang, boom, clang, clash, clatter, clattering, din, racket, smash, smashing, thunder ~*v.* **2.** break, break up, dash to pieces, disintegrate, fracture, fragment, shatter, shiver, smash, splinter **3.** come a cropper (*Inf.*), dash, fall, fall headlong, give way, hurtle, lurch, overbalance, pitch, plunge, precipitate oneself, sprawl, topple **4.** bang, bump (into), collide, crash-land (*an aircraft*), drive into, have an accident, hit, hurtle into, plough into, run together, wreck ~*n.* **5.** accident, bump, collision, jar, jolt, pile-up (*Inf.*), prang (*Inf.*), smash, smash-up, thud, thump, wreck **6.** bankruptcy, collapse, debacle, depression, downfall, failure, ruin, smash ~*v.* **7.** be ruined, collapse, fail, fold, fold up, go broke (*Inf.*), go bust (*Inf.*), go under, smash ~*adj.* **8.** *Of a course of studies, etc.* emergency, intensive, immediate, round-the-clock, speeded-up, telescoped, urgent

crass asinine, blundering, boorish, bovine, coarse, dense, doltish, gross, indelicate, insensitive, lumpish, oafish, obtuse, stupid, unrefined, witless

crate box, case, container, packing case, tea chest

crater depression, dip, hollow, shell hole

crave **1.** be dying for, cry out for (*Inf.*), desire, fancy (*Inf.*), hanker after, hunger after, long for, lust after, need, pant for, pine for, require, sigh for, thirst for, want, yearn for **2.** ask, beg, beseech, entreat, implore, petition, plead for, pray for, seek, solicit, supplicate

craving appetite, cacoethes, desire, hankering, hunger, longing, lust, thirst, urge, yearning, yen (*Inf.*)

crawl **1.** advance slowly, creep, drag, go on all fours, inch, move at a snail's pace, move on hands and knees, pull *or* drag oneself along, slither, worm one's way, wriggle, writhe **2.** be overrun (alive, full of, lousy), swarm, teem **3.** abase oneself, cringe, fawn, grovel, humble oneself, toady, truckle

crayon (ˈkreɪən, -ɒn) *n.* stick or pencil of coloured chalk, wax *etc.*

craze (kreɪz) *n.* **1.** short-lived current fashion **2.** strong desire or passion, mania **3.** madness —**crazed** *a.* **1.** demented **2.** (of porcelain) having fine cracks —ˈ**crazy** *a.* **1.** insane **2.** very foolish **3.** (*with* about *or* over) madly eager (for) —**crazy paving** paving made with flat irregularly shaped slabs of stone

creak (kriːk) *n.* **1.** harsh grating noise —*vi.* **2.** make creaking sound

cream (kriːm) *n.* **1.** fatty part of milk **2.** various foods, dishes, resembling cream **3.** cosmetic *etc.* with cream-like consistency **4.** yellowish-white colour **5.** best part of anything —*vt.* **6.** take cream from **7.** take best part from **8.** beat to creamy consistency —ˈ**creamer** *n.* **1.** vessel or device for separating cream from milk **2.** powdered milk substitute for coffee —ˈ**creamery** *n.* **1.** establishment where milk and cream are made into butter and cheese **2.** place where dairy products are sold —ˈ**creamy** *a.* —**cream cheese** soft white cheese made from soured cream or milk —**cream of tartar** potassium hydrogen tartrate, *esp.* when used in baking powders

crease (kriːs) *n.* **1.** line made by folding **2.** wrinkle **3.** *Cricket* line defining bowler's and batsman's positions **4.** superficial bullet wound —*v.* **5.** make, develop creases

create (kriːˈeɪt) *vt.* **1.** bring into being **2.** give rise to **3.** make —*vi.* **4.** *inf.* make a fuss —**creˈation** *n.* —**creˈative** *a.* —**creˈator** *n.*

creature (ˈkriːtʃə) *n.* **1.** living being **2.** thing created **3.** dependant —**creature comforts** bodily comforts

crèche (krɛʃ, kreɪʃ) *n.* day nursery for very young children

credence (ˈkriːdᵊns) *n.* **1.** belief, credit **2.** side-table for elements of the Eucharist before consecration

credentials (krɪˈdɛnʃəlz) *pl.n.* **1.** testimonials **2.** letters of introduction, *esp.* those given to ambassador

credible (ˈkrɛdɪbᵊl) *a.* **1.** worthy of belief **2.** trustworthy —**crediˈbility** *n.* —ˈ**credibly** *adv.* —**credibility gap** disparity between claims or statements and facts

credit (ˈkrɛdɪt) *n.* **1.** commendation, approval **2.** source, cause, of honour **3.** belief, trust **4.** good name **5.** influence, honour or power based on trust of others **6.** system of allowing customers to take goods for later payment **7.** money at one's disposal in bank *etc.* **8.** side of book on which such sums are entered **9.** reputation for financial reliability —*pl.* **10.** list of those responsible for production of film —*vt.* **11.** (*with* with) attribute **12.** believe **13.** put on credit side of account —ˈ**creditable** *a.* bringing honour —ˈ**creditably** *adv.* —ˈ**creditor** *n.* one to whom debt is due —**credit card** card issued by banks *etc.* enabling holder to obtain goods and services on credit

THESAURUS

craze enthusiasm, fad, fashion, infatuation, mania, mode, novelty, passion, preoccupation, rage, the latest (*Inf.*), thing, trend, vogue

crazy 1. *Inf.* a bit lacking upstairs (*Inf.*), barmy (*Sl.*), batty (*Sl.*), berserk, bonkers (*Sl.*), cracked (*Sl.*), crazed, cuckoo (*Inf.*), daft (*Sl.*), delirious, demented, deranged, idiotic, insane, lunatic (*Inf. or archaic*), mad, mad as a hatter, mad as a March hare, maniacal, mental (*Sl.*), not all there (*Inf.*), nuts (*Sl.*), nutty (*Sl.*), nutty as a fruitcake (*Inf.*), off one's head (*Sl.*), of unsound mind, potty (*Inf.*), round the bend (*Sl.*), touched, unbalanced, unhinged **2.** absurd, bird-brained (*Inf.*), cockeyed (*Inf.*), derisory, fatuous, foolhardy, foolish, half-baked (*Inf.*), idiotic, ill-conceived, impracticable, imprudent, inane, inappropriate, irresponsible, ludicrous, nonsensical, potty (*Inf.*), preposterous, puerile, quixotic, senseless, short-sighted, unrealistic, unwise, unworkable, wild **3.** *Inf.* ardent, beside oneself, devoted, eager, enamoured, enthusiastic, fanatical, hysterical, infatuated, mad, passionate, smitten, very keen, wild (*Inf.*), zealous

creak *v.* grate, grind, groan, rasp, scrape, scratch, screech, squeak, squeal

cream *n.* **1.** cosmetic, emulsion, essence, liniment, lotion, oil, ointment, paste, salve, unguent **2.** best, *crème de la crème,* elite, flower, pick, prime

creamy buttery, creamed, lush, milky, oily, rich, smooth, soft, velvety

crease 1. *v.* corrugate, crimp, crinkle, crumple, double up, fold, pucker, ridge, ruck up, rumple, screw up, wrinkle **2.** *n.* bulge, corrugation, fold, groove, line, overlap, pucker, ridge, ruck, tuck, wrinkle

create 1. beget, bring into being *or* existence, coin, compose, concoct, design, develop, devise, dream up (*Inf.*), form, formulate, generate, give birth to, give life to, hatch, initiate, invent, make, originate, produce, spawn **2.** appoint, constitute, establish, found, install, invest, make, set up **3.** bring about, cause, lead to, occasion

creation 1. conception, formation, generation, genesis, making, procreation, siring **2.** constitution, development, establishment, formation, foundation, inception, institution, laying down, origination, production, setting up

creator architect, author, begetter, designer, father, framer, God, initiator, inventor, maker, originator, prime mover

creature 1. animal, beast, being, brute, critter (*U.S. dialect*), dumb animal, living thing, lower animal, quadruped **2.** body, character, fellow, human being, individual, man, mortal, person, soul, wight (*Archaic*), woman **3.** dependant, hanger-on, hireling, instrument (*Inf.*), lackey, minion, puppet, retainer, tool, wretch

credentials attestation, authorization, card, certificate, deed, diploma, docket, letter of recommendation *or* introduction, letters of credence, licence, missive, passport, recommendation, reference(s), testament, testimonial, title, voucher, warrant

credibility believability, believableness, integrity, plausibility, reliability, tenability, trustworthiness

credible 1. believable, conceivable, imaginable, likely, plausible, possible, probable, reasonable, supposable, tenable, thinkable **2.** dependable, honest, reliable, sincere, trustworthy, trusty

credit *n.* **1.** acclaim, acknowledgment, approval, commendation, fame, glory, honour, kudos, merit, praise, recognition, thanks, tribute **2.** character, clout (*Inf.*), esteem, estimation, good name, influence, position, prestige, regard, reputation, repute, standing, status **3.** belief, confidence, credence, faith, reliance, trust **4.** *As in* **be a credit to** feather in one's cap, honour, source of satisfaction *or* pride

credo (ˈkriːdəʊ, ˈkreɪ-) *n.* formal statement of beliefs, principles or opinions (*pl.* **-s**)

credulous (ˈkrɛdjʊləs) *a.* too easy of belief, easily deceived or imposed on, gullible —**creˈdulity** *n.* —**ˈcredulousness** *n.*

creed (kriːd) *n.* **1.** formal statement of Christian beliefs **2.** statement, system of beliefs or principles

creek (kriːk) *n.* narrow inlet on seacoast

creel (kriːl) *n.* angler's fishing basket

creep (kriːp) *vi.* **1.** make way along ground, as snake **2.** move with stealthy, slow movements **3.** crawl **4.** act in servile way **5.** (of skin or flesh) feel shrinking, shivering sensation, due to fear or repugnance (**crept** *pt./pp.*) —*n.* **6.** creeping **7.** *sl.* repulsive person —*pl.* **8.** *sl.* feeling of fear or repugnance —**ˈcreeper** *n.* creeping or climbing plant, *eg* ivy —**ˈcreepy** *a. inf.* **1.** uncanny, unpleasant **2.** causing flesh to creep —**creepy-crawly UK** *inf. n.* **1.** small crawling creature (*pl.* **-crawlies**) —*a.* **2.** feeling or causing sensation as of creatures crawling on skin

cremation (krɪˈmeɪʃən) *n.* burning as means of disposing of corpses —**creˈmate** *vt.* —**cremaˈtorium** *n.* place for cremation

crème de la crème (krɛm də la ˈkrɛm) *n. Fr.* the very best

crème de menthe (ˈkrɛm də ˈmɛnθ, ˈmɪnt, ˈkriːm, ˈkreɪm) liqueur flavoured with peppermint

crenate (ˈkriːneɪt) *or* **crenated** *a.* having scalloped margin, as certain leaves —**ˈcrenation** *n.*

crenellated *or U.S.* **crenelated** (ˈkrɛnɪleɪtɪd) *a.* having battlements

creole (ˈkriːəʊl) *n.* **1.** hybrid language **2.** (**C-**) native-born W Indian, Latin American, of European descent

creosote (ˈkrɪəsəʊt) *n.* **1.** oily antiseptic liquid distilled from coal or wood tar, used for preserving wood —*vt.* **2.** coat or impregnate with creosote

crepe *or* **crape** (kreɪp) *n.* **1.** fabric with crimped surface **2.** very thin pancake, oft. folded round filling —**crepe de Chine** (də ˈʃiːn) very thin crepe of silk or similar light fabric —**crepe paper** thin crinkled paper resembling crepe —**crepe rubber** rough-surfaced rubber used for soles of shoes

crepitate (ˈkrɛpɪteɪt) *vi.* make rattling or crackling sound

crepitus (ˈkrɛpɪtəs) *n.* **1.** crackling chest sound heard in pneumonia *etc.* **2.** grating sound of two ends of broken bone rubbing together

crept (krɛpt) *pt./pp. of* CREEP

crepuscular (krɪˈpʌskjʊlə) *a.* **1.** of or like twilight; dim **2.** (of creatures) active at twilight

Cres. Crescent

crescendo (krɪˈʃɛndəʊ) *n.* **1.** gradual increase of loudness, *esp.* in music —*adv.* **2.** with a crescendo

crescent (ˈkrɛsˀnt, -zˀnt) *n.* **1.** (shape of) moon as seen in first or last quarter **2.** any figure of this shape **3.** row of houses built on curve

cress (krɛs) *n.* any of various plants with edible pungent leaves

crest (krɛst) *n.* **1.** comb or tuft on bird's or animal's head **2.** plume on top of helmet **3.** top of mountain, ridge, wave *etc.* **4.** badge above shield of coat of arms, also used separately on seal, plate *etc.* —*vt.* **5.** crown **6.** reach top of —**ˈcrestfallen** *a.* cast down by failure, dejected

cretaceous (krɪˈteɪʃəs) *a.* chalky

Cretaceous (krɪˈteɪʃəs) *a.* **1.** of last period of Mesozoic era, during which chalk deposits were formed —*n.* **2.** Cretaceous period or rock system

cretin (ˈkrɛtɪn) *n.* **1.** person afflicted with cretinism **2.** *inf.* stupid person —**ˈcretinism** *n.* deficiency in thyroid gland causing physical and mental retardation

cretonne (krɛˈtɒn, ˈkrɛtɒn) *n.* unglazed cotton cloth printed in coloured patterns

crevasse (krɪˈvæs) *n.* deep open chasm, *esp.* in glacier

crevice (ˈkrɛvɪs) *n.* cleft, fissure, chink

crew (kruː) *n.* **1.** ship's, boat's or aircraft's company, excluding passengers **2.** *inf.* gang, set —*v.* **3.** serve as crew (on) —**crew cut** man's closely cropped haircut

THESAURUS

~*v.* **5.** *With* **with** accredit, ascribe to, assign to, attribute to, chalk up to (*Inf.*), impute to, refer to **6.** accept, bank on, believe, buy (*Inf.*), depend on, fall for, have faith in, rely on, swallow (*Inf.*), trust

creditable admirable, commendable, deserving, estimable, exemplary, honourable, laudable, meritorious, praiseworthy, reputable, respectable, worthy

credulity blind faith, credulousness, gullibility, naiveté, silliness, simplicity, stupidity

credulous born yesterday (*Inf.*), dupable, green, gullible, naive, overtrusting, trustful, uncritical, unsuspecting, unsuspicious

creed articles of faith, belief, canon, catechism, confession, credo, doctrine, dogma, persuasion, principles, profession (*of faith*), tenet

creek bay, bight, cove, firth *or* frith (*Scot.*), inlet

creep *v.* **1.** crawl, crawl on all fours, glide, insinuate, slither, squirm, worm, wriggle, writhe **2.** approach unnoticed, skulk, slink, sneak, steal, tiptoe **3.** crawl, dawdle, drag, edge, inch, proceed at a snail's pace **4.** bootlick (*Inf.*), cower, cringe, fawn, grovel, kowtow, scrape, suck up to (*Inf.*), toady, truckle

creeper climber, climbing plant, rambler, runner, trailing plant, vine (*Chiefly U.S.*)

creepy awful, direful, disgusting, disturbing, eerie, frightening, ghoulish, goose-pimply (*Inf.*), gruesome, hair-raising, horrible, macabre, menacing, nightmarish, ominous, scary (*Inf.*), sinister, terrifying, threatening, unpleasant, weird

crescent half-moon, meniscus, new moon, old moon, sickle, sickle-shape

crest **1.** apex, crown, head, height, highest point, peak, pinnacle, ridge, summit, top **2.** aigrette, caruncle (*Zoology*), cockscomb, comb, crown, mane, panache, plume, tassel, topknot, tuft **3.** *Heraldry* badge, bearings, charge, device, emblem, insignia, symbol

crestfallen chapfallen, dejected, depressed, despondent, disappointed, disconsolate, discouraged, disheartened, downcast, downhearted

crevice chink, cleft, crack, cranny, fissure, fracture, gap, hole, interstice, opening, rent, rift, slit, split

crew **1.** hands, (ship's) company, (ship's) complement **2.** company, corps, gang, party, posse, squad, team, working party **3.** *Inf.* assemblage, band, bunch (*Inf.*), company, crowd, gang, herd, horde, lot, mob, pack, set, swarm, troop

crewel (ˈkruːɪl) *n.* fine worsted yarn, used in fancy work and embroidery

crib (krɪb) *n.* **1.** child's cot **2.** barred rack used for fodder **3.** plagiarism **4.** translation used by students, sometimes illicitly *—vt.* **5.** confine in small space **6.** copy unfairly (**-bb-**)

cribbage (ˈkrɪbɪdʒ) *n.* card game for two, three or four players

crick (krɪk) *n.* spasm or cramp in muscles, *esp.* in neck

cricket[1] (ˈkrɪkɪt) *n.* chirping insect

cricket[2] (ˈkrɪkɪt) *n.* outdoor game played with bats, ball and wickets by teams of eleven a side **—ˈcricketer** *n.*

cri de coeur (kri də ˈkœːr) *Fr.* heartfelt or impassioned appeal (*pl.* **cris de coeur** (kri də ˈkœːr))

cried (kraɪd) *pt./pp. of* CRY

crier (ˈkraɪə) *n.* **1.** person or animal that cries **2.** formerly, official who made public announcements, *esp.* in town or court

crime (kraɪm) *n.* **1.** violation of law (usu. a serious offence) **2.** wicked or forbidden act **3.** *inf.* something to be regretted **—criminal** (ˈkrɪmɪnᵊl) *a./n.* **—criminality** (krɪmɪˈnælɪtɪ) *n.* **—criminally** (ˈkrɪmɪnəlɪ) *adv.* **—criminology** (krɪmɪˈnɒlədʒɪ) *n.* study of crime and criminals

crimp (krɪmp) *vt.* **1.** pinch into tiny parallel pleats **2.** wrinkle

Crimplene (ˈkrɪmpliːn) *n.* **R** crease-resistant synthetic material, similar to Terylene

crimson (ˈkrɪmzən) *a./n.* **1.** (of) rich deep red *—v.* **2.** turn crimson

cringe (krɪndʒ) *vi.* **1.** shrink, cower **2.** behave obsequiously

crinkle (ˈkrɪŋkᵊl) *v./n.* wrinkle

crinoline (ˈkrɪnᵊlɪn) *n.* hooped petticoat or skirt

cripple (ˈkrɪpᵊl) *n.* **1.** one not having normal use of limbs, disabled or deformed person *—vt.* **2.** maim, disable, impair **3.** weaken, lessen efficiency of

crisis (ˈkraɪsɪs) *n.* **1.** turning point or decisive moment, *esp.* in illness **2.** time of acute danger or difficulty (*pl.* **crises** (ˈkraɪsiːz))

crisp (krɪsp) *a.* **1.** brittle but firm **2.** brisk, decided **3.** clear-cut **4.** fresh, invigorating **5.** (of hair) curly *—n.* **6.** very thin, fried slice of potato, eaten cold **—ˈcrisper** *n.* refrigerator compartment for storing salads *etc.* **—ˈcrispy** *a.* **—ˈcrispbread** *n.* thin, dry biscuit

crisscross (ˈkrɪskrɒs) *v.* **1.** (cause to) move in crosswise pattern **2.** mark with or consist of pattern of crossing lines *—a.* **3.** (*esp.* of lines) crossing one another in different directions *—n.* **4.** pattern made of crossing lines *—adv.* **5.** in crosswise manner or pattern

criterion (kraɪˈtɪərɪən) *n.* standard of judgment (*pl.* **-ria** (-rɪə))

critical (ˈkrɪtɪkᵊl) *a.* **1.** fault-finding **2.** discerning **3.** skilled in or given to judging **4.** of great importance, crucial, decisive **—ˈcritic** *n.* **1.** one who passes judgment **2.** writer expert in judging works of literature, art *etc.* **—ˈcritically** *adv.* **—ˈcriticism** *n.* **—ˈcriticize** *or* **-ise** *v.* **—critique** (krɪˈtiːk) *n.* critical essay, carefully written criticism **—critical path analysis** technique for planning projects with reference to critical path, which is sequence of stages requiring longest time

THESAURUS

crib *n.* **1.** bassinet, bed, cot **2.** bin, box, bunker, manger, rack, stall **3.** *Inf.* key, translation, trot (*U.S. sl.*) *~v.* **4.** *Inf.* cheat, pass off as one's own work, pilfer, pirate, plagiarize, purloin, steal **5.** box up, cage, confine, coop, coop up, enclose, fence, imprison, limit, pen, rail, restrict, shut in

crime **1.** atrocity, fault, felony, malfeasance, misdeed, misdemeanour, offence, outrage, transgression, trespass, unlawful act, violation, wrong **2.** corruption, delinquency, guilt, illegality, iniquity, lawbreaking, malefaction, misconduct, sin, unrighteousness, vice, villainy, wickedness, wrong, wrongdoing

criminal *n.* **1.** con (*Sl.*), convict, crook (*Inf.*), culprit, delinquent, evildoer, felon, jailbird, lawbreaker, malefactor, offender, sinner, transgressor *~adj.* **2.** bent (*Sl.*), corrupt, crooked (*Inf.*), culpable, felonious, illegal, illicit, immoral, indictable, iniquitous, lawless, nefarious, peccant (*Rare*), unlawful, unrighteous, vicious, villainous, wicked, wrong **3.** *Inf.* deplorable, foolish, preposterous, ridiculous, scandalous, senseless

cringe **1.** blench, cower, dodge, draw back, duck, flinch, quail, quiver, recoil, shrink, shy, start, tremble, wince **2.** bend, bootlick (*Inf.*), bow, crawl, creep, crouch, fawn, grovel, kneel, kowtow, sneak, stoop, toady, truckle

cripple *v.* **1.** debilitate, disable, enfeeble, hamstring, incapacitate, lame, maim, mutilate, paralyse, weaken **2.** bring to a standstill, cramp, damage, destroy, halt, impair, put out of action, ruin, spoil, vitiate

crisis **1.** climacteric, climax, confrontation, critical point, crunch (*Inf.*), crux, culmination, height, moment of truth, point of no return, turning point **2.** catastrophe, critical situation, dilemma, dire straits, disaster, emergency, exigency, extremity, mess, plight, predicament, quandary, strait, trouble

crisp **1.** brittle, crispy, crumbly, crunchy, firm, fresh, unwilted **2.** bracing, brisk, fresh, invigorating, refreshing **3.** brief, brusque, clear, incisive, pithy, short, succinct, tart, terse

criterion bench mark, canon, gauge, measure, norm, principle, proof, rule, standard, test, touchstone, yardstick

critic **1.** analyst, arbiter, authority, commentator, connoisseur, expert, expositor, judge, pundit, reviewer **2.** attacker, carper, caviller, censor, censurer, detractor, fault-finder, knocker (*Inf.*), Momus, reviler, vilifier

critical **1.** captious, carping, cavilling, censorious, derogatory, disapproving, disparaging, fault-finding, nagging, niggling, nit-picking (*Inf.*) **2.** accurate, analytical, diagnostic, discerning, discriminating, fastidious, judicious, penetrating, perceptive, precise **3.** all-important, crucial, dangerous, deciding, decisive, grave, hairy (*Sl.*), high-priority, momentous, perilous, pivotal, precarious, pressing, psychological, risky, serious, urgent, vital

criticism **1.** animadversion, bad press, brickbats (*Inf.*), censure, critical remarks, disapproval, disparagement, fault-finding, flak (*Inf.*), knocking (*Inf.*), panning (*Inf.*), slam (*Sl.*), slating (*Inf.*), stricture **2.** analysis, appraisal, appreciation, assessment, com-

croak (krəʊk) *vi.* **1.** utter deep hoarse cry, as raven, frog **2.** talk dismally **3.** *sl.* die —*n.* **4.** deep hoarse cry —ˈ**croaker** *n.* —ˈ**croaky** *a.* hoarse

Croatian (krəʊˈeɪʃən) *a.* **1.** of Croatia, its people or their dialect of Serbo-Croatian —*n.* **2.** dialect of Croatia **3.** native or inhabitant of Croatia

crochet (ˈkrəʊʃeɪ, -ʃɪ) *n.* **1.** kind of handicraft like knitting, done with small hooked needle —*vi.* **2.** do such work —*vt.* **3.** make (garment *etc.*) by such work

crock (krɒk) *n.* **1.** earthenware jar or pot **2.** broken piece of earthenware **3.** *inf.* old broken-down thing or person **4.** *inf.* cripple —ˈ**crockery** *n.* earthenware dishes, utensils *etc.*

crocodile (ˈkrɒkədaɪl) *n.* **1.** large amphibious reptile **2.** line of children walking two by two —**crocodilian** (krɒkəˈdɪlɪən) *n.* **1.** large predatory reptile, such as crocodile, alligator *etc.* —*a.* **2.** of crocodiles or crocodilians —**crocodile tears** insincere grief

crocus (ˈkrəʊkəs) *n.* small bulbous plant with yellow, white or purple flowers

Croesus (ˈkriːsəs) *n.* very rich man

croft (krɒft) *n.* *Scot.* small piece of arable land, smallholding —ˈ**crofter** *n.* one who works croft

croissant (ˈkrwʌsɒŋ) *n.* crescent-shaped roll of yeast dough like pastry

Cro-Magnon man (ˈkrəʊˈmænjɒn) early type of modern man who lived in Europe during late Palaeolithic times

cromlech (ˈkrɒmlɛx) *n.* prehistoric structure, monument of flat stone resting on two upright ones

crone (krəʊn) *n.* witchlike old woman

crony (ˈkrəʊnɪ) *n.* intimate friend

crook (krʊk) *n.* **1.** hooked staff **2.** any hook, bend, sharp turn **3.** *inf.* swindler, criminal —**crooked** (ˈkrʊkɪd) *a.* **1.** bent, twisted **2.** deformed **3.** *inf.* dishonest

croon (kruːn) *v.* hum, sing in soft, low tone —ˈ**crooner** *n.*

crop (krɒp) *n.* **1.** produce of cultivation of any plant or plants **2.** harvest (*lit. or fig.*) **3.** pouch in bird's gullet **4.** stock of whip **5.** hunting whip **6.** short haircut —*vt.* **7.** cut short **8.** poll, clip **9.** (of animals) bite, eat down —*vi.* **10.** raise, produce or occupy land with crop (**-pp-**) —ˈ**cropper** *n.* *inf.* **1.** heavy fall **2.** disastrous failure —**crop-dusting** *n.* spreading fungicide *etc.* on crops from aircraft —**crop up** *inf.* happen unexpectedly

croquet (ˈkrəʊkeɪ, -kɪ) *n.* lawn game played with balls, wooden mallets and hoops

croquette (krəʊˈkɛt, krɒ-) *n.* fried ball of minced meat, fish *etc.* in breadcrumbs

crosier *or* **crozier** (ˈkrəʊʒə) *n.* bishop's or abbot's staff

cross (krɒs) *n.* **1.** structure or symbol of two intersecting lines or pieces (at right angles) **2.** such a structure of wood as means of execution by tying or nailing victim to it **3.** symbol of Christian faith **4.** any thing or mark in the shape of cross **5.** misfortune, annoyance, affliction **6.** intermixture of breeds, hybrid —*v.* **7.** move or go across (something) **8.** intersect —*vi.* **9.** meet and pass —*vt.* **10.** mark with lines across **11.** (*with* out) delete **12.** place or put in form of cross **13.** make sign of cross on or over **14.** modify breed of animals or plants by intermixture **15.** thwart **16.** oppose —*a.* **17.** out of temper, angry **18.** peevish, perverse **19.** transverse **20.** intersecting **21.** contrary **22.** adverse —ˈ**crossing** *n.* **1.** intersection of roads, rails *etc.* **2.** part of street where pedestrians are expected to cross —ˈ**crossly** *adv.* —ˈ**crosswise** *adv./a.* —ˈ**crossbar** *n.* **1.** horizontal bar, line, stripe *etc.* **2.** horizontal beam across pair of goal posts **3.** horizontal bar on man's bicycle —**cross-bench** *n.* (*usu. pl.*) **UK** seat in Parliament occupied by neutral or independent member —**cross-bencher** *n.* —ˈ**crossbill** *n.* bird whose mandibles cross when closed —ˈ**crossbow** *n.* bow fixed across wooden shoulder stock —ˈ**crossbreed** *n.* breed produced from parents of different breeds —**cross-ˈcheck** *v.* **1.** verify (report *etc.*) by consulting other sources —*n.* **2.** act of crosschecking —**cross-country** *n.* long race held over open ground —**cross-examination** *n.* —**cross-examine** *vt.* examine (witness already examined by other side) —**cross-eyed** *a.* having eye(s) turning inward —**cross-fertilization** *n.* fertilization of one plant by pollen of another —ˈ**crossfire** *n.* **1.** *Mil.* converging fire from one or more positions **2.** lively exchange of ideas, opinions *etc.* —**cross-grained** *a.* perverse —ˈ**crosspatch** *n.* *inf.* bad-tempered person —**cross-ply** *a.* (of tyre) having fabric cords in outer casing running diagonally —**cross-purpose** *n.* contrary aim or purpose —**cross-question** *vt.* **1.** cross-examine —*n.* **2.** question asked in cross-examination —**cross-refer** *v.* refer from one part to another —**cross-reference** *n.* reference within text to another part of text —ˈ**crossroads** *n.* —**cross section 1.** transverse section **2.** group of people fully representative of

THESAURUS

ment, commentary, critique, elucidation, evaluation, judgment, notice, review

criticize 1. animadvert on *or* upon, carp, censure, condemn, disapprove of, disparage, excoriate, find fault with, give (someone *or* something) a bad press, knock (*Inf.*), nag at, pan (*Inf.*), pass strictures upon, pick to pieces, slam (*Sl.*), slate (*Inf.*) **2.** analyse, appraise, assess, comment upon, evaluate, give an opinion, judge, pass judgment on, review

critique analysis, appraisal, assessment, commentary, essay, examination, review

croak *v.* **1.** caw, gasp, grunt, squawk, utter *or* speak harshly (huskily, throatily), wheeze **2.** *Sl.* die, expire, hop the twig (*Inf.*), kick the bucket (*Inf.*), pass away, perish

crook *Inf.* cheat, criminal, knave (*Archaic*), racketeer, robber, rogue, shark, swindler, thief, villain

crooked 1. anfractuous, bent, bowed, crippled, curved, deformed, deviating, disfigured, distorted, hooked, irregular, meandering, misshapen, out of shape, tortuous, twisted, twisting, warped, winding, zigzag **2.** angled, askew, asymmetric, at an angle, awry, lopsided, off-centre, slanted, slanting, squint, tilted, to one side, uneven, unsymmetrical **3.** *Inf.* bent (*Sl.*), corrupt, crafty, criminal, deceitful, dishonest, dishonourable, dubious, fraudulent, illegal, knavish, nefarious, questionable, shady (*Inf.*), shifty, treacherous, underhand, unlawful, unprincipled, unscrupulous

croon breathe, hum, purr, sing, warble

crop *n.* **1.** fruits, gathering, harvest, produce, reaping, season's growth, vintage, yield ~*v.* **2.** clip, curtail, cut, lop, mow, pare, prune, reduce, shear, shorten, snip, top, trim **3.** browse, graze, nibble

crop up appear, arise, emerge, happen, occur, spring up, turn up

a nation, community *etc.* —**cross-stitch** *n.* **1.** embroidery stitch made by two stitches forming cross —*v.* **2.** embroider (piece of needlework) with cross-stitch —**crosstalk** *n.* **1.** *Rad., telephony* unwanted sounds picked up on receiving channel **2.** **UK** rapid or witty talk —**crossword (puzzle)** puzzle built up of intersecting words, of which some letters are common, the words being indicated by clues —**at cross-purposes** conflicting; opposed; disagreeing —**the Cross** **1.** cross on which Jesus Christ was executed **2.** model or picture of this

crosse (krɒs) *n.* light staff with triangular frame to which network is attached, used in playing lacrosse

crotch (krɒtʃ) *n.* **1.** angle between legs, genital area **2.** fork

crotchet (ˈkrɒtʃɪt) *n.* musical note, equal to half the length of a minim

crotchety (ˈkrɒtʃɪtɪ) *a.* **1.** peevish **2.** irritable

croton (ˈkrəʊtᵊn) *n.* any chiefly tropical shrub or tree, seeds of which yield croton oil, formerly used as purgative

crouch (krautʃ) *vi.* **1.** bend low **2.** huddle down close to ground **3.** stoop servilely, cringe —*n.* **4.** act of stooping or bending

croup[1] (kru:p) *n.* throat disease of children, with cough

croup[2] (kru:p) *n.* **1.** hindquarters of horse **2.** place behind saddle

croupier (ˈkru:pɪə) *n.* person dealing cards, collecting money *etc.* at gambling table

crouton (ˈkru:tɒn) *n.* small piece of fried or toasted bread, usu. served in soup

crow[1] (krəʊ) *n.* large black carrion-eating bird —ˈ**crowfoot** *n.* any of several plants that have yellow or white flowers and leaves resembling foot of crow (*pl.* **-s**) —**crow's-foot** *n.* wrinkle at corner of eye —**crow's-nest** *n.* lookout platform high on ship's mast

crow[2] (krəʊ) *vi.* **1.** utter cock's cry **2.** boast one's happiness or superiority —*n.* **3.** cock's cry

crowbar (ˈkrəʊbɑ:) *n.* iron bar, usu. beaked, for levering

crowd (kraʊd) *n.* **1.** throng, mass —*vi.* **2.** flock together —*vt.* **3.** cram, force, thrust, pack **4.** fill with people —**crowd out** exclude by excess already in

crown (kraʊn) *n.* **1.** monarch's headdress **2.** wreath for head **3.** monarch **4.** monarchy **5.** royal power **6.** formerly, British coin of five shillings **7.** various foreign coins **8.** top of head **9.** summit, top **10.** completion or perfection of thing —*vt.* **11.** put crown on **12.** confer title upon **13.** occur as culmination of series of events **14.** *inf.* hit on head —**crown court** *English law* court of criminal jurisdiction holding sessions throughout England and Wales —**crown green** bowling green in which sides are lower than middle —**crown jewels** jewellery, including regalia, used by sovereign on state occasion —**crown land** public land —**crown prince** heir to throne

crozier (ˈkrəʊʒə) *n. see* CROSIER

CRT cathode-ray tube

crucial (ˈkru:ʃəl) *a.* **1.** decisive, critical **2.** *inf.* very important

cruciate (ˈkru:ʃɪɪt, -eɪt) *a.* cross-shaped

crucible (ˈkru:sɪbᵊl) *n.* small melting pot

crucify (ˈkru:sɪfaɪ) *vt.* **1.** put to death on cross **2.** treat cruelly **3.** *inf.* ridicule (ˈ**crucified,** ˈ**crucifying**) —ˈ**crucifix** *n.* **1.** cross **2.** image of (Christ on the) Cross —**cruci**ˈ**fixion** *n.* —ˈ**cruciform** *a.*

crude (kru:d) *a.* **1.** lacking taste, vulgar **2.** in natural or raw state, unrefined **3.** rough, unfinished —ˈ**crudely** *adv.* —ˈ**crudity** *n.*

THESAURUS

cross *adj.* **1.** angry, annoyed, cantankerous, captious, churlish, crotchety (*Inf.*), crusty, disagreeable, fractious, fretful, grouchy (*Inf.*), grumpy, ill-humoured, ill-tempered, impatient, in a bad mood, irascible, irritable, out of humour, peeved (*Inf.*), peevish, pettish, petulant, put out, querulous, shirty (*Sl.*), short, snappish, snappy, splenetic, sullen, surly, testy, vexed, waspish ~*v.* **2.** bridge, cut across, extend over, ford, meet, pass over, ply, span, traverse, zigzag **3.** crisscross, intersect, intertwine, lace, lie athwart of **4.** blend, crossbreed, cross-fertilize, cross-pollinate, hybridize, interbreed, intercross, mix, mongrelize **5.** block, deny, foil, frustrate, hinder, impede, interfere, obstruct, oppose, resist, thwart ~*n.* **6.** affliction, burden, grief, load, misery, misfortune, trial, tribulation, trouble, woe, worry **7.** crucifix, rood **8.** amalgam, blend, combination, crossbreed, cur, hybrid, hybridization, mixture, mongrel, mutt (*Sl.*) ~*adj.* **9.** crosswise, intersecting, oblique, transverse **10.** adverse, contrary, opposed, opposing, unfavourable

cross-examine catechize, grill (*Inf.*), interrogate, pump, question, quiz

crotch crutch, groin

crotchety awkward, bad-tempered, cantankerous, contrary, crabby, cross, crusty, curmudgeonly, difficult, disagreeable, fractious, grumpy, irritable, obstreperous, peevish, surly, testy

crouch **1.** bend down, bow, duck, hunch, kneel, squat, stoop **2.** abase oneself, cower, cringe, fawn, grovel, truckle

crow *v.* bluster, boast, brag, exult, flourish, gloat, glory in, strut, swagger, triumph, vaunt

crowd *n.* **1.** army, assembly, company, concourse, flock, herd, horde, host, mass, mob, multitude, pack, press, rabble, swarm, throng, troupe ~*v.* **2.** cluster, congregate, cram, flock, forgather, gather, huddle, mass, muster, press, push, stream, surge, swarm, throng **3.** bundle, congest, cram, pack, pile, squeeze

crown *n.* **1.** chaplet, circlet, coronal (*Poetic*), coronet, diadem, tiara **2.** bays, distinction, garland, honour, kudos, laurels, laurel wreath, prize, trophy **3.** emperor, empress, king, monarch, monarchy, queen, *rex*, royalty, ruler, sovereign, sovereignty **4.** acme, apex, crest, head, perfection, pinnacle, summit, tip, top, ultimate, zenith ~*v.* **5.** adorn, dignify, festoon, honour, invest, reward **6.** be the climax *or* culmination of, cap, complete, consummate, finish, fulfil, perfect, put the finishing touch to, round off, surmount, terminate, top **7.** *Sl.* biff (*Sl.*), box, cuff, hit over the head, punch

crucial **1.** central, critical, decisive, pivotal, psychological, searching, testing, trying **2.** *Inf.* essential, high-priority, important, momentous, pressing, urgent, vital

crucify **1.** execute, harrow, persecute, rack, torment, torture **2.** *Sl.* lampoon, pan (*Inf.*), ridicule, tear to pieces, wipe the floor with (*Inf.*)

crude **1.** boorish, coarse, crass, dirty, gross, indecent,

cruel (ˈkruːəl) *a.* **1.** delighting in others' pain **2.** causing pain or suffering —**ˈcruelly** *adv.* —**ˈcruelty** *n.*

cruet (ˈkruːɪt) *n.* **1.** small container for salt, pepper, vinegar, oil *etc.* **2.** stand holding such containers

cruise (kruːz) *vi.* **1.** travel about in a ship for pleasure *etc.* **2.** (of vehicle, aircraft) travel at safe, average speed —*n.* **3.** cruising voyage, *esp.* organized for holiday purposes —**ˈcruiser** *n.* **1.** ship that cruises **2.** warship lighter and faster than battleship —**ˈcruiserweight** *n. Boxing* light-heavyweight

crumb (krʌm) *n.* **1.** small particle, fragment, *esp.* of bread —*vt.* **2.** reduce to, break into, cover with crumbs —**ˈcrumby** *a.*

crumble (ˈkrʌmbᵊl) *v.* **1.** break into small fragments, disintegrate, crush **2.** perish, decay —*vi.* **3.** fall apart or away —*n.* **4.** pudding covered with crumbly mixture —**ˈcrumbly** *a.*

crummy (ˈkrʌmɪ) *a. sl.* inferior, contemptible

crump (krʌmp) *vi.* **1.** thud, explode with dull sound —*n.* **2.** crunching sound **3.** *inf.* shell, bomb

crumpet (ˈkrʌmpɪt) *n.* **1.** flat, soft cake eaten with butter **2.** *sl.* sexually desirable woman or women

crumple (ˈkrʌmpᵊl) *v.* **1.** (cause to) collapse **2.** make or become crushed, wrinkled, creased —**ˈcrumpled** *a.*

crunch (krʌntʃ) *n.* **1.** sound made by chewing crisp food, treading on gravel, hard snow *etc.* **2.** *inf.* critical moment or situation —*v.* **3.** (cause to) make crunching sound

crupper (ˈkrʌpə) *n.* **1.** strap holding back saddle in place by passing round horse's tail **2.** horse's hindquarters

crusade (kruːˈseɪd) *n.* **1.** medieval Christian war to recover Holy Land **2.** campaign against something believed to be evil **3.** concerted action to further a cause —*vi.* **4.** campaign vigorously for something **5.** go on crusade —**cruˈsader** *n.*

cruse (kruːz) *n.* small earthenware jug or pot

crush[1] (krʌʃ) *vt.* **1.** compress so as to break, bruise, crumple **2.** break to small pieces **3.** defeat utterly, overthrow —*n.* **4.** act of crushing **5.** crowd of people *etc.* **6.** drink prepared by or as if by crushing fruit

crush[2] (krʌʃ) *n. inf.* infatuation

crust (krʌst) *n.* **1.** hard outer part of bread **2.** similar hard outer casing on anything —*v.* **3.** cover with, form, crust —**ˈcrustily** *adv.* —**ˈcrusty** *a.* **1.** having, or like, crust **2.** short-tempered

crustacean (krʌˈsteɪʃən) *n.* hard-shelled animal, *eg* crab, lobster —**crusˈtaceous** *a.*

crutch (krʌtʃ) *n.* **1.** staff with crosspiece to go under armpit of lame person **2.** support **3.** groin, crotch

crux (krʌks) *n.* **1.** that on which a decision turns **2.** anything that puzzles very much (*pl.* **-es, cruces** (ˈkruːsiːz))

cry (kraɪ) *vi.* **1.** weep **2.** wail **3.** utter call **4.** shout **5.** clamour or beg (for) —*vt.* **6.** utter loudly, proclaim (**cried, ˈcrying**) —*n.* **7.** loud utterance **8.** scream, wail, shout **9.** call of animal **10.** fit of weeping **11.** watchword —**ˈcrying** *a.* notorious; lamentable (*esp. in* **crying shame**)

THESAURUS

lewd, obscene, smutty, tactless, tasteless, uncouth, vulgar **2.** natural, raw, unmilled, unpolished, unprepared, unprocessed, unrefined **3.** clumsy, makeshift, outline, primitive, rough, rough-hewn, rude, rudimentary, sketchy, undeveloped, unfinished, unformed, unpolished

crudely bluntly, clumsily, coarsely, impolitely, indecently, pulling no punches (*Inf.*), roughly, rudely, sketchily, tastelessly, vulgarly

crudity 1. coarseness, crudeness, impropriety, indecency, indelicacy, lewdness, loudness, lowness, obscenity, obtrusiveness, smuttiness, vulgarity **2.** clumsiness, crudeness, primitiveness, roughness, rudeness

cruel atrocious, barbarous, bitter, bloodthirsty, brutal, brutish, callous, cold-blooded, depraved, excruciating, fell (*Archaic*), ferocious, fierce, flinty, grim, hard, hard-hearted, harsh, heartless, hellish, implacable, inclement, inexorable, inhuman, inhumane, malevolent, painful, poignant, ravening, raw, relentless, remorseless, sadistic, sanguinary, savage, severe, spiteful, stony-hearted, unfeeling, unkind, unnatural, vengeful, vicious

cruelly 1. barbarously, brutally, brutishly, callously, ferociously, fiercely, heartlessly, in cold blood, mercilessly, pitilessly, sadistically, savagely, spitefully, unmercifully, viciously **2.** bitterly, deeply, fearfully, grievously, monstrously, mortally, severely

cruelty barbarity, bestiality, bloodthirstiness, brutality, brutishness, callousness, depravity, ferocity, fiendishness, hardheartedness, harshness, heartlessness, inhumanity, mercilessness, murderousness, ruthlessness, sadism, savagery, severity, spite, spitefulness, venom, viciousness

cruise *v.* **1.** coast, sail, voyage **2.** coast, drift, keep a steady pace, travel along ~*n.* **3.** boat trip, sail, sea trip, voyage

crumb atom, bit, grain, mite, morsel, particle, scrap, shred, sliver, snippet, *soupçon*, speck

crumble 1. bruise, crumb, crush, fragment, granulate, grind, pound, powder, pulverize, triturate **2.** break up, collapse, come to dust, decay, decompose, degenerate, deteriorate, disintegrate, fall apart, go to pieces (*Inf.*), go to rack and ruin, moulder, perish, tumble down

crumple 1. crease, crush, pucker, rumple, screw up, wrinkle **2.** break down, cave in, collapse, fall, give way, go to pieces

crunch 1. *v.* champ, chew noisily, chomp, grind, masticate, munch **2.** *n. Inf.* crisis, critical point, crux, emergency, hour of decision, moment of truth, test

crusade campaign, cause, drive, holy war, jihad, movement, push

crusader advocate, campaigner, champion, reformer

crush *v.* **1.** bray, break, bruise, comminute, compress, contuse, crease, crumble, crumple, crunch, mash, pound, pulverize, rumple, smash, squeeze, wrinkle **2.** conquer, extinguish, overcome, overpower, overwhelm, put down, quell, stamp out, subdue, vanquish ~*n.* **3.** crowd, huddle, jam, party

crust caking, coat, coating, concretion, covering, film, incrustation, layer, outside, scab, shell, skin, surface

crusty 1. brittle, crisp, crispy, friable, hard, short, well-baked, well-done **2.** brusque, cantankerous, captious, choleric, crabby, cross, curt, gruff, ill-humoured, irritable, peevish, prickly, short, short-tempered, snappish, snarling, splenetic, surly, testy, touchy

cryogenics (kraɪəˈdʒɛnɪks) *n.* branch of physics concerned with phenomena at very low temperatures —**cryoˈgenic** *a.*

crypt (krɪpt) *n.* vault, *esp.* under church —**ˈcryptic** *a.* secret, mysterious —**ˈcryptically** *adv.* —**ˈcryptogram** *n.* piece of writing in code —**crypˈtography** *n.* art of writing, decoding ciphers

cryptogam (ˈkrɪptəʊgæm) *n.* nonflowering plant, *eg* fern, moss *etc.*

crystal (ˈkrɪstᵊl) *n.* **1.** clear transparent mineral **2.** very clear glass **3.** cut-glass ware **4.** characteristic form assumed by many substances, with definite internal structure and external shape of symmetrically arranged plane surfaces —**ˈcrystalline** *or* **ˈcrystalloid** *a.* —**crystalliˈzation** *or* **-iˈsation** *n.* —**ˈcrystallize** *or* **-ise** *v.* **1.** (cause to) form into crystals **2.** (cause to) become definite —**crystalˈlographer** *n.* —**crystalˈlography** *n.* science of the structure, forms and properties of crystals —**crystal gazer** —**crystal gazing 1.** act of staring into crystal ball supposedly to arouse visual perceptions of future *etc.* **2.** act of trying to foresee or predict

Cs *Chem.* caesium

CSE Certificate of Secondary Education

CS gas gas causing tears, salivation and painful breathing, used in chemical warfare and civil disturbances

CST US, C Central Standard Time

CT Connecticut

ct. 1. cent **2.** carat **3.** court

ctenophore (ˈtenəfɔː, ˈtiːnə-) *n.* marine invertebrate whose body bears eight rows of fused cilia for locomotion

CTV Canadian Television (Network Ltd.)

cu *or* **cu.** cubic

Cu *Chem.* copper

cub (kʌb) *n.* **1.** young of fox and other animals **2.** (**C-**) Cub Scout —*v.* **3.** give birth to (cubs) (**-bb-**) —**Cub Scout** member of junior branch of the Scout Association

cubbyhole (ˈkʌbɪhəʊl) *n.* small, enclosed space or room

cube (kjuːb) *n.* **1.** regular solid figure contained by six equal square sides **2.** cube-shaped block **3.** product obtained by multiplying number by itself twice —*vt.* **4.** multiply thus —**ˈcubic(al)** *a.* —**ˈcubism** *n.* style of art in which objects are presented as assemblage of geometrical shapes —**ˈcubist** *n./a.* —**cube root** number or quantity whose cube is a given number or quantity —**cubic measure** system of units for measurement of volumes

cubicle (ˈkjuːbɪkᵊl) *n.* partially or totally enclosed section of room, as in dormitory

cubit (ˈkjuːbɪt) *n.* old measure of length, about 18 inches

cuckold (ˈkʌkəld) *n.* **1.** man whose wife has committed adultery —*vt.* **2.** make cuckold of

cuckoo (ˈkʊkuː) *n.* **1.** migratory bird which deposits its eggs in nests of other birds **2.** its call —*a.* **3.** *sl.* crazy —**ˈcuckoopint** *n.* European plant with arrow-shaped leaves, pale purple spadix and scarlet berries (*also* **lords-and-ladies**) —**cuckoo spit** white frothy mass on plants, produced by froghopper larvae

cucumber (ˈkjuːkʌmbə) *n.* **1.** plant with long fleshy green fruit **2.** the fruit, used in salad

cud (kʌd) *n.* food which ruminant animal brings back into mouth to chew again —**chew the cud** reflect, meditate

cuddle (ˈkʌdᵊl) *vt.* **1.** hug —*vi.* **2.** lie close and snug, nestle —*n.* **3.** close embrace, *esp.* when prolonged

cuddy (ˈkʌdɪ) *n.* small cabin in boat

cudgel (ˈkʌdʒəl) *n.* **1.** short thick stick —*vt.* **2.** beat with cudgel (**-ll-**)

cue[1] (kjuː) *n.* **1.** last words of actor's speech *etc.* as signal to another to act or speak **2.** signal, hint, example for action

cue[2] (kjuː) *n.* **1.** long tapering rod used in billiards **2.** pigtail

cuff[1] (kʌf) *n.* **1.** ending of sleeve **2.** wristband —**cuff link** one pair of linked buttons to join buttonholes on shirt cuffs —**off the cuff** *inf.* without preparation

cuff[2] (kʌf) *vt.* **1.** strike with open hand —*n.* **2.** blow of this kind

cuirass (kwɪˈræs) *n.* metal or leather armour of breastplate and backplate

Cuisenaire rod (kwɪzəˈnɛə) **R** one of set of rods of various colours and lengths representing different numbers, used to teach arithmetic to young children

cuisine (kwɪˈziːn) *n.* **1.** style of cooking **2.** menu, food offered by restaurant *etc.*

cul-de-sac (ˈkʌldəsæk, ˈkʊl-) *n.* **1.** street, lane open only at one end **2.** blind alley (*pl.* **culs-de-sac**)

THESAURUS

cry *v.* **1.** bawl, bewail, blubber, boohoo, greet (*Scot.*), howl one's eyes out, keen, lament, mewl, pule, shed tears, snivel, sob, wail, weep, whimper, whine, whinge (*Inf.*), yowl ~*n.* **2.** bawling, blubbering, crying, greet (*Scot.*), howl, keening, lament, lamentation, plaint (*Archaic*), snivel, snivelling, sob, sobbing, sorrowing, wailing, weep, weeping ~*v.* **3.** bawl, bellow, call, call out, ejaculate, exclaim, hail, halloo, holler (*Inf.*), howl, roar, scream, screech, shout, shriek, sing out, vociferate, whoop, yell ~*n.* **4.** bawl, bellow, call, ejaculation, exclamation, holler (*Inf.*), hoot, howl, outcry, roar, scream, screech, shriek, squawk, whoop, yell, yelp, yoo-hoo ~*v.* **5.** advertise, announce, bark (*Inf.*), broadcast, bruit, hawk, noise, proclaim, promulgate, publish, trumpet ~*n.* **6.** announcement, barking (*Inf.*), noising, proclamation, publication ~*v.* **7.** beg, beseech, clamour, entreat, implore, plead, pray

crypt catacomb, tomb, undercroft, vault

cub offspring, whelp, young

cuddle canoodle (*Sl.*), clasp, cosset, embrace, fondle, hug, nestle, pet, snuggle

cudgel 1. *n.* bastinado, baton, bludgeon, club, cosh, shillelagh, stick, truncheon **2.** *v.* bang, baste, batter, beat, bludgeon, cane, cosh, drub, maul, pound, pummel, thrash, thump, thwack

cue catchword, hint, key, nod, prompting, reminder, sign, signal, suggestion

cuff off the cuff ad lib, extempore, impromptu, improvised, offhand, off the top of one's head, on the spur of the moment, spontaneous, spontaneously, unrehearsed

cul-de-sac blind alley, dead end

culinary (ˈkʌlɪnərɪ) *a.* of, for, suitable for, cooking or kitchen

cull (kʌl) *vt.* **1.** gather, select **2.** take out (selected animals) from herd —*n.* **3.** act of culling

culminate (ˈkʌlmɪneɪt) *vi.* **1.** reach highest point **2.** come to climax, to a head —**culmiˈnation** *n.*

culottes (kjuːˈlɒts) *pl.n.* flared trousers (*esp.* for women) cut to look like skirt

culpable (ˈkʌlpəbᵊl) *a.* blameworthy —**culpaˈbility** *n.* —**ˈculpably** *adv.*

culprit (ˈkʌlprɪt) *n.* one guilty of usu. minor offence

cult (kʌlt) *n.* **1.** system of religious worship **2.** pursuit of, devotion to, some person, thing, or activity

cultivate (ˈkʌltɪveɪt) *vt.* **1.** till and prepare (ground) to raise crops **2.** develop, improve, refine **3.** devote attention to, cherish **4.** practise **5.** foster —**ˈcultivable** *or* **ˈcultivatable** *a.* (of land) capable of being cultivated —**cultiˈvation** *n.* —**ˈcultivator** *n.*

culture (ˈkʌltʃə) *n.* **1.** state of manners, taste and intellectual development at a time or place **2.** cultivating **3.** artificial rearing **4.** set of bacteria so reared —**ˈcultural** *a.* —**ˈcultured** *a.* refined, showing culture —**cultured pearl** pearl artificially induced to grow in oyster shell

culvert (ˈkʌlvət) *n.* tunnelled drain for passage of water under road, railway *etc.*

cum (kʌm) *Lat.* with

cumbersome (ˈkʌmbəsəm) *or* **cumbrous** (ˈkʌmbrəs) *a.* awkward, unwieldy —**ˈcumber** *vt.* **1.** obstruct; hinder **2.** *obs.* inconvenience —**ˈcumbrance** *n.* **1.** burden; obstacle; hindrance **2.** trouble; bother

Cumbrian (ˈkʌmbrɪən) *a./n.* (native or inhabitant) of Cumbria, county of NW England

cumin *or* **cummin** (ˈkʌmɪn) *n.* herb

cummerbund *or* **kummerbund** (ˈkʌməbʌnd) *n.* broad sash worn round waist

cumquat (ˈkʌmkwɒt) *n. see* KUMQUAT

cumulative (ˈkjuːmjʊlətɪv) *a.* **1.** becoming greater by successive additions **2.** representing the sum of many items

cumulus (ˈkjuːmjʊləs) *n.* cloud shaped in rounded white woolly masses (*pl.* **cumuli** (ˈkuːmjʊlaɪ))

cuneiform (ˈkjuːnɪfɔːm) *a.* wedge-shaped, *esp.* of ancient Babylonian writing

cunning (ˈkʌnɪŋ) *a.* **1.** crafty, sly **2.** ingenious —*n.* **3.** skill in deceit or evasion **4.** skill, ingenuity —**ˈcunningly** *adv.*

cup (kʌp) *n.* **1.** small drinking vessel with handle at one side **2.** any small drinking vessel **3.** contents of cup **4.** various cup-shaped formations, cavities, sockets *etc.* **5.** cup-shaped trophy as prize **6.** portion, lot **7.** iced drink of wine and other ingredients **8.** either of two cup-shaped parts of brassiere *etc.* —*vt.* **9.** shape as cup (hands *etc.*) —**ˈcupful** *n.* (*pl.* **ˈcupfuls**) —**ˈcupping** *n. Med.* formerly, use of evacuated glass cup to draw blood to surface of skin for bloodletting —**cupboard** (ˈkʌbəd) *n.* piece of furniture, recess in room, with door, for storage —**cupboard love** show of love inspired by selfish or greedy motive —**Cup Final 1.** annual final of F.A. Cup soccer competition **2.** final of any cup competition —**cup tie** *Sport* eliminating match between two teams in cup competition

THESAURUS

culminate climax, close, come to a climax, come to a head, conclude, end, end up, finish, rise to a crescendo, terminate, wind up (*Inf.*)

culmination acme, apex, apogee, climax, completion, conclusion, consummation, crown, crowning touch, finale, height, *ne plus ultra*, peak, perfection, pinnacle, punch line, summit, top, zenith

culpable answerable, at fault, blamable, blameworthy, censurable, found wanting, guilty, in the wrong, liable, reprehensible, sinful, to blame, wrong

culprit criminal, delinquent, evildoer, felon, guilty party, malefactor, miscreant, offender, person responsible, rascal, sinner, transgressor, wrongdoer

cult 1. body, church faction, clique, denomination, faith, following, party, religion, school, sect **2.** admiration, craze, devotion, idolization, reverence, veneration, worship

cultivate 1. bring under cultivation, farm, fertilize, harvest, plant, plough, prepare, tend, till, work **2.** ameliorate, better, bring on, cherish, civilize, develop, discipline, elevate, enrich, foster, improve, polish, promote, refine, train **3.** aid, devote oneself to, encourage, forward, foster, further, help, patronize, promote, pursue, support **4.** associate with, butter up, consort with, court, dance attendance upon, run after, seek out, seek someone's company *or* friendship, take trouble *or* pains with

cultivation 1. agronomy, farming, gardening, husbandry, planting, ploughing, tillage, tilling, working **2.** advancement, advocacy, development, encouragement, enhancement, fostering, furtherance, help, nurture, patronage, promotion, support **3.** devotion to, pursuit, study

culture 1. civilization, customs, life style, mores, society, stage of development, the arts, way of life **2.** accomplishment, breeding, education, elevation, enlightenment, erudition, gentility, good taste, improvement, polish, politeness, refinement, urbanity **3.** agriculture, agronomy, cultivation, farming, husbandry

cultured accomplished, advanced, educated, enlightened, erudite, genteel, highbrow, knowledgeable, polished, refined, scholarly, urbane, versed, well-bred, well-informed, well-read

culvert channel, conduit, drain, gutter, watercourse

cumbersome awkward, bulky, burdensome, clumsy, cumbrous, embarrassing, heavy, hefty (*Inf.*), incommodious, inconvenient, oppressive, unmanageable, unwieldy, weighty

cumulative accruing, accumulative, aggregate, amassed, collective, heaped, increasing, snowballing

cunning *adj.* **1.** artful, astute, canny, crafty, devious, foxy, guileful, knowing, Machiavellian, sharp, shifty, shrewd, sly, subtle, tricky, wily ~*n.* **2.** artfulness, astuteness, craftiness, deceitfulness, deviousness, foxiness, guile, shrewdness, slyness, trickery, wiliness ~*adj.* **3.** adroit, deft, dexterous, imaginative, ingenious, skilful ~*n.* **4.** ability, adroitness, art, artifice, cleverness, deftness, dexterity, finesse, ingenuity, skill, subtlety

cup beaker, cannikin, chalice, cupful, demitasse, draught, drink, goblet, potion, teacup, trophy

cupboard ambry (*Obsolete*), cabinet, closet, locker, press

cupel (ˈkjuːpᵊl, kjʊˈpɛl) *n.* small vessel used in refining metals

Cupid (ˈkjuːpɪd) *n.* god of love

cupidity (kjuːˈpɪdɪtɪ) *n.* **1.** greed for possessions **2.** covetousness

cupola (ˈkjuːpələ) *n.* dome

cupreous (ˈkjuːprɪəs) *a.* of, containing, copper

cupronickel (kjuːprəʊˈnɪkᵊl) *n.* copper alloy containing up to 40 per cent nickel

cur (kɜː) *n.* **1.** dog of mixed breed **2.** surly, contemptible or mean person

curaçao (kjʊərəˈsəʊ) *n.* liqueur flavoured with bitter orange peel

curare *or* **curari** (kjʊˈrɑːrɪ) *n.* poisonous resin of S Amer. tree, now used as muscle relaxant in medicine

curate (ˈkjʊərɪt) *n.* parish priest's appointed assistant **—ˈcuracy** *n.* his office

curative (ˈkjʊərətɪv) *a.* **1.** tending to cure disease *—n.* **2.** anything able to heal or cure

curator (kjʊəˈreɪtə) *n.* custodian, *esp.* of museum, library *etc.* **—curaˈtorial** *a.* **—cuˈratorship** *n.*

curb (kɜːb) *n.* **1.** check, restraint **2.** chain or strap passing under horse's lower jaw and giving powerful control with reins *—vt.* **3.** restrain **4.** apply curb to

curd (kɜːd) *n.* coagulated milk **—ˈcurdle** *v.* turn into curd, coagulate **—ˈcurdy** *a.*

cure (kjʊə) *vt.* **1.** heal, restore to health **2.** remedy **3.** preserve (fish, skins *etc.*) *—n.* **4.** remedy **5.** course of medical treatment **6.** successful treatment, restoration to health **—curaˈbility** *n.* **—ˈcurable** *a.* **—cure of souls** care of parish or congregation

curet *or* **curette** (kjʊəˈrɛt) *n.* surgical instrument for removing dead tissue *etc.* from some body cavities **—curettage** (kjʊərɪˈtɑːʒ, kjʊəˈrɛtɪdʒ) *n.*

curfew (ˈkɜːfjuː) *n.* **1.** official regulation restricting or prohibiting movement of people, *esp.* at night **2.** time set as deadline by such regulation

curia (ˈkjʊərɪə) *n.* **1.** papal court and government of Roman Catholic Church **2.** (in Middle Ages) court held in king's name (*pl.* **curiae** (ˈkjʊərɪiː))

curie (ˈkjʊərɪ, -riː) *n.* standard unit of radium emanation

curio (ˈkjʊərɪəʊ) *n.* rare or curious thing of the kind sought for collections (*pl.* **-s**)

curious (ˈkjʊərɪəs) *a.* **1.** eager to know, inquisitive **2.** prying **3.** puzzling, strange, odd **—curiˈosity** *n.* **1.** eagerness to know **2.** inquisitiveness **3.** strange or rare thing **—ˈcuriously** *adv.*

curium (ˈkjʊərɪəm) *n.* element produced from plutonium

curl (kɜːl) *vi.* **1.** take spiral or curved shape or path *—vt.* **2.** bend into spiral or curved shape *—n.* **3.** spiral lock of hair **4.** spiral, curved state, form or motion **—ˈcurler** *n.* **1.** pin, clasp or roller for curling hair **2.** person or thing that curls **3.** person who plays curling **—ˈcurling** *n.* game like bowls, played with large rounded stones on ice **—ˈcurly** *a.* **—curling tongs** heated, metal, scissor-like device for curling hair

curlew (ˈkɜːljuː) *n.* large long-billed wading bird

curlicue *or* **curlycue** (ˈkɜːlɪkjuː) *n.* intricate ornamental curl or twist

curmudgeon (kɜːˈmʌdʒən) *n.* surly or miserly person

currach *or* **curragh** (ˈkʌrəx, ˈkʌrə) *n. Scot., Irish* coracle

currant (ˈkʌrənt) *n.* **1.** dried type of grape **2.** fruit of various plants allied to gooseberry **3.** any of these plants

current (ˈkʌrənt) *a.* **1.** of immediate present, going on **2.** up-to-date, not yet superseded **3.** in circulation or general use *—n.* **4.** body of water or air in motion **5.** tendency, drift **6.** transmission of electricity through conductor **—ˈcurrency** *n.* **1.** money in use **2.** state of being in use **3.** time during which thing is current **—ˈcurrently** *adv.* **—current account** bank account against which cheques may be drawn at any time

curricle (ˈkʌrɪkᵊl) *n.* two-wheeled open carriage drawn by two horses side by side

curriculum (kəˈrɪkjʊləm) *n.* specified course of study (*pl.* **-s, -la** (-lə)) **—curriculum vitae** (ˈviːtaɪ, ˈvaɪtiː)

THESAURUS

curb 1. *v.* bite back, bridle, check, constrain, contain, control, hinder, impede, inhibit, moderate, muzzle, repress, restrain, restrict, retard, subdue, suppress **2.** *n.* brake, bridle, check, control, deterrent, limitation, rein, restraint

curdle clot, coagulate, condense, congeal, curd, thicken, turn sour

cure *v.* **1.** alleviate, correct, ease, heal, help, make better, mend, rehabilitate, relieve, remedy, restore, restore to health *~n.* **2.** alleviation, antidote, corrective, healing, medicine, panacea, recovery, remedy, restorative, specific, treatment *~v.* **3.** dry, kipper, pickle, preserve, salt, smoke

curiosity 1. inquisitiveness, interest, nosiness (*Inf.*), prying, snooping (*Inf.*) **2.** celebrity, freak, marvel, novelty, oddity, phenomenon, rarity, sight, spectacle, wonder **3.** bibelot, bygone, curio, knickknack, *objet d'art,* trinket

curious 1. inquiring, inquisitive, interested, puzzled, questioning, searching **2.** inquisitive, meddling, nosy (*Inf.*), peeping, peering, prying, snoopy (*Inf.*) **3.** bizarre, exotic, extraordinary, marvellous, mysterious, novel, odd, peculiar, puzzling, quaint, queer, rare, singular, strange, unconventional, unexpected, unique, unorthodox, unusual, wonderful

curl 1. *v.* bend, coil, convolute, corkscrew, crimp, crinkle, crisp, curve, entwine, frizz, loop, meander, ripple, spiral, turn, twine, twirl, twist, wind, wreathe, writhe **2.** *n.* coil, curlicue, kink, ringlet, spiral, twist, whorl

curly corkscrew, crimped, crimpy, crinkly, crisp, curled, curling, frizzy, fuzzy, kinky, permed, spiralled, waved, wavy, winding

currency 1. bills, coinage, coins, medium of exchange, money, notes **2.** acceptance, circulation, exposure, popularity, prevalence, publicity, transmission, vogue

current *adj.* **1.** accepted, circulating, common, common knowledge, customary, general, going around, in circulation, in progress, in the air, in the news, ongoing, popular, present, prevailing, prevalent, rife, widespread **2.** contemporary, fashionable, in, in fashion, in vogue, now (*Inf.*), present-day, trendy (*Inf.*), up-to-date, up-to-the-minute *~n.* **3.** course, draught, flow, jet, progression, river, stream, tide **4.** atmosphere, drift, feeling, inclination, mood, tendency, trend, undercurrent

outline of person's educational and professional history, usu. for job applications (*pl.* **curricula vitae**)

curry[1] (ˈkʌrɪ) *n.* **1.** highly-flavoured, pungent condiment, preparation of turmeric **2.** dish flavoured with it —*vt.* **3.** prepare, flavour dish with curry (**ˈcurried, ˈcurrying**)

curry[2] (ˈkʌrɪ) *vt.* **1.** groom (horse) with comb **2.** dress (leather) (**ˈcurried, ˈcurrying**) —**curry comb** metal comb for grooming horse —**curry favour** try to win favour unworthily, ingratiate oneself

curse (kɜːs) *n.* **1.** profane or obscene expression of anger *etc.* **2.** utterance expressing extreme ill will towards some person or thing **3.** affliction, misfortune, scourge —*v.* **4.** utter curse, swear (at) —*vt.* **5.** afflict —**cursed** (ˈkɜːsɪd, kɜːst) *a.* **1.** hateful **2.** wicked **3.** deserving of, or under, a curse —**cursedly** (ˈkɜːsɪdlɪ) *adv.* —**cursedness** (ˈkɜːsɪdnɪs) *n.*

cursive (ˈkɜːsɪv) *a.* written in running script, with letters joined

cursor (ˈkɜːsə) *n.* **1.** sliding part of measuring instrument, *esp.* on slide rule **2.** movable point of light *etc.* that identifies specific position on visual display unit

cursory (ˈkɜːsərɪ) *a.* rapid, hasty, not detailed, superficial —**ˈcursorily** *adv.*

curt (kɜːt) *a.* short, rudely brief, abrupt —**ˈcurtly** *adv.* —**ˈcurtness** *n.*

curtail (kɜːˈteɪl) *vt.* cut short, diminish —**curˈtailment** *n.*

curtain (ˈkɜːtᵊn) *n.* **1.** hanging drapery at window *etc.* **2.** cloth hung as screen **3.** screen separating audience and stage in theatre **4.** end to act or scene *etc.* —*pl.* **5.** *inf.* death or ruin: the end —*vt.* **6.** provide, cover with curtain —**curtain call** return to stage by performers to acknowledge applause —**curtain-raiser** *n.* **1.** short play coming before main one **2.** any preliminary event

curtsy *or* **curtsey** (ˈkɜːtsɪ) *n.* **1.** woman's bow or respectful gesture made by bending knees and lowering body —*vi.* **2.** make a curtsy

curve (kɜːv) *n.* **1.** line of which no part is straight **2.** bent line or part —*v.* **3.** bend into curve —**curˈvaceous** *a. inf.* shapely —**ˈcurvature** *n.* **1.** a bending **2.** bent shape —**curviˈlinear** *a.* of bent lines

curvet (kɜːˈvɛt) *n.* **1.** *Dressage* low leap with all four feet off the ground —*vi.* **2.** prance or frisk about

cushion (ˈkʊʃən) *n.* **1.** bag filled with soft stuffing or air, to support or ease body **2.** any soft pad or support **3.** resilient rim of billiard table —*vt.* **4.** provide, protect with cushion **5.** lessen effects of

cushy (ˈkʊʃɪ) *a. inf.* soft, comfortable, pleasant, light, well-paid

cusp (kʌsp) *n.* pointed end, *esp.* of tooth —**ˈcuspid** *n.* pointed tooth —**ˈcuspidal** *a.* **1.** ending in point **2.** of, or like, cusp

cuspidor (ˈkʌspɪdɔː) *n.* spittoon

cuss (kʌs) *inf. n.* **1.** curse; oath **2.** person or animal, *esp.* annoying one —*v.* **3.** *see* CURSE (sense 4) —**cussed** (ˈkʌsɪd) *a. inf.* **1.** *see* **cursed** *at* CURSE **2.** obstinate **3.** annoying —**ˈcussedness** *n.*

custard (ˈkʌstəd) *n.* **1.** dish made of eggs and milk **2.** sweet sauce of milk and cornflour

custody (ˈkʌstədɪ) *n.* safekeeping, guardianship, imprisonment —**cusˈtodian** *n.* keeper, caretaker, curator

custom (ˈkʌstəm) *n.* **1.** habit **2.** practice **3.** fashion, usage **4.** business patronage **5.** toll, tax —*pl.* **6.** duties levied on imports **7.** government department which collects these **8.** area in airport *etc.* where customs officials examine baggage for dutiable goods —**ˈcustomarily** *adv.* —**ˈcustomary** *a.* usual, habitual —**ˈcustomer** *n.* **1.** one who enters shop to buy, *esp.* regularly **2.** purchaser —**custom-built** *a. chiefly* US (of cars, houses *etc.*) made to specifications of buyer —**custom-made** *a. chiefly* US (of suits *etc.*) made to specifications of buyer —**customs duties** taxes laid on imported or exported goods —**customs house** building where customs are collected

THESAURUS

curse *n.* **1.** blasphemy, expletive, oath, obscenity, swearing, swearword **2.** anathema, ban, denunciation, evil eye, excommunication, execration, imprecation, jinx, malediction, malison (*Archaic*) **3.** affliction, bane, burden, calamity, cross, disaster, evil, misfortune, ordeal, plague, scourge, torment, tribulation, trouble, vexation ~*v.* **4.** be foul-mouthed, blaspheme, cuss (*Inf.*), swear, take the Lord's name in vain, turn the air blue (*Inf.*), use bad language **5.** accurse, anathematize, damn, excommunicate, execrate, fulminate, imprecate **6.** afflict, blight, burden, destroy, doom, plague, scourge, torment, trouble, vex

cursed **1.** accursed, bedevilled, blighted, cast out, confounded, damned, doomed, excommunicate, execrable, fey (*Scot.*), foredoomed, ill-fated, star-crossed, unholy, unsanctified, villainous **2.** abominable, damnable, detestable, devilish, fell (*Archaic*), fiendish, hateful, infamous, infernal, loathsome, odious, pernicious, pestilential, vile

curt abrupt, blunt, brief, brusque, concise, gruff, offhand, pithy, rude, sharp, short, snappish, succinct, summary, tart, terse, unceremonious, uncivil, ungracious

curtail abbreviate, abridge, contract, cut, cut back, cut short, decrease, dock, lessen, lop, pare down, reduce, retrench, shorten, trim, truncate

curtailment abbreviation, abridgment, contraction, cutback, cutting, cutting short, docking, retrenchment, truncation

curtain **1.** *n.* drape (*Chiefly U.S.*), hanging **2.** *v.* conceal, drape, hide, screen, shroud, shut off, shutter, veil

curve **1.** *v.* arc, arch, bend, bow, coil, hook, inflect, spiral, swerve, turn, twist, wind **2.** *n.* arc, bend, camber, curvature, half-moon, loop, trajectory, turn

cushion **1.** *n.* beanbag, bolster, hassock, headrest, pad, pillow, scatter cushion, squab **2.** *v.* bolster, buttress, cradle, dampen, deaden, muffle, pillow, protect, soften, stifle, support, suppress

custody **1.** aegis, auspices, care, charge, custodianship, guardianship, keeping, observation, preservation, protection, safekeeping, supervision, trusteeship, tutelage, ward, watch **2.** arrest, confinement, detention, durance (*Archaic*), duress, imprisonment, incarceration

custom **1.** habit, habitude (*Rare*), manner, mode, procedure, routine, way, wont **2.** convention, etiquette, fashion, form, formality, matter of course, observance, observation, policy, practice, praxis, ritual, rule, style, unwritten law, usage, use **3.** customers, patronage, trade

customarily as a rule, commonly, generally, habitu-

cut (kʌt) *vt.* **1.** sever, penetrate, wound, divide, or separate with pressure of edge or edged instrument **2.** pare, detach, trim, or shape by cutting **3.** divide **4.** intersect **5.** reduce, decrease **6.** abridge **7.** *inf.* ignore (person) **8.** strike (with whip *etc.*) **9.** hit (cricket ball) to point's left **10.** *inf.* stay deliberately away from —*vi. Cine.* **11.** call a halt to shooting sequence **12.** (*with* to) move quickly to another scene (**cut, ˈcutting**) —*n.* **13.** act of cutting **14.** stroke **15.** blow, wound (of knife, whip *etc.*) **16.** reduction, decrease **17.** fashion, shape **18.** incision **19.** engraving **20.** piece cut off **21.** division **22.** *inf.* share, *esp.* of profits —**ˈcutter** *n.* **1.** one who, that which, cuts **2.** warship's rowing and sailing boat **3.** small sloop-rigged vessel with straight running bowsprit —**ˈcutting** *n.* **1.** act of cutting, thing cut off or out, *esp.* excavation (for road, canal *etc.*) through high ground **2.** shoot, twig of plant **3.** piece cut from newspaper *etc.* —*a.* **4.** sarcastic, unkind —**ˈcutaway** *n.* **1.** man's coat cut diagonally from front waist to back of knees **2.** drawing or model of machine *etc.* in which part of casing is omitted to reveal workings —**ˈcutback** *n.* decrease; reduction —**cut glass** glass, *esp.* vases *etc.*, decorated by facet-cutting or grinding —**cut-price** *or esp. U.S.* **cut-rate** *a.* **1.** available at prices or rates below standard price or rate **2.** offering goods or services at prices below standard price —**ˈcutthroat** *a.* **1.** merciless —*n.* **2.** murderer **3.** **UK** razor with long blade that usu. folds into handle (*also* **cutthroat razor**) —**cut back 1.** shorten by cutting off end; prune **2.** reduce or make reduction (in) —**cut dead** refuse to recognize an acquaintance —**cut in 1.** drive in front of another's vehicle so as to affect his driving **2.** interrupt (in conversation) **3.** intrude

cutaneous (kjuːˈteɪnɪəs) *a.* of skin

cute (kjuːt) *a.* appealing, attractive, pretty

cuticle (ˈkjuːtɪkᵊl) *n.* dead skin, *esp.* at base of fingernail

cutis (ˈkjuːtɪs) *n. Anat.* skin (*pl.* **-tes** (-tiːz), **-es**)

cutlass (ˈkʌtləs) *n.* short broad-bladed sword

cutlery (ˈkʌtlərɪ) *n.* knives, forks, spoons *etc.* —**ˈcutler** *n.* one who makes, repairs, deals in knives and cutting implements

cutlet (ˈkʌtlɪt) *n.* small piece of meat grilled or fried

cuttlefish (ˈkʌtᵊlfɪʃ) *n.* sea mollusc like squid (*also* **ˈcuttle**) —**ˈcuttlebone** *n.* internal shell of cuttlefish, used as mineral supplement to diet of cagebirds and as polishing agent

Cwlth. Commonwealth

cwm (kuːm) *n.* **1.** in Wales, valley **2.** *Geol. see* CIRQUE

c.w.o. *or* **C.W.O.** cash with order

cwt. hundredweight

-cy (*comb. form*) **1.** state, quality, condition, as in *plutocracy, lunacy* **2.** rank, office, as in *captaincy*

cyan (ˈsaɪæn, ˈsaɪən) *n.* **1.** green-blue colour —*a.* **2.** of this colour

cyanide (ˈsaɪənaɪd) *or* **cyanid** (ˈsaɪənɪd) *n.* extremely poisonous chemical compound —**cyˈanogen** *n.* poisonous gas composed of nitrogen and carbon

cyanosis (saɪəˈnəʊsɪs) *n.* blueness of the skin

cybernetics (saɪbəˈnɛtɪks) *pl.n.* (*with sing. v.*) comparative study of control mechanisms of electronic and biological systems

cyclamate (ˈsaɪkləmeɪt, ˈsɪkləmeɪt) *n.* compound formerly used as food additive and sugar substitute

cyclamen (ˈsɪkləmən, -mɛn) *n.* plant with flowers having turned-back petals

cycle (ˈsaɪkᵊl) *n.* **1.** recurrent series or period **2.** rotation of events **3.** complete series or period **4.** development following course of stages **5.** series of poems *etc.* **6.** bicycle —*vi.* **7.** move in cycles **8.** ride bicycle —**ˈcyclic(al)** *a.* —**ˈcyclist** *n.* bicycle rider —**cyˈclometer** *n.* instrument for measuring circles or recording distance travelled by wheel, *esp.* of bicycle

cyclo- *or before vowel* **cycl-** (*comb. form*) **1.** indicating circle or ring, as in *cyclotron* **2.** denoting cyclic compound, as in *cyclopropane*

cyclone (ˈsaɪkləʊn) *n.* **1.** system of winds moving round centre of low pressure **2.** circular storm —**cyclonic** (saɪˈklɒnɪk) *a.*

THESAURUS

ally, in the ordinary way, normally, ordinarily, regularly, traditionally, usually

customary accepted, accustomed, acknowledged, common, confirmed, conventional, established, everyday, familiar, fashionable, general, habitual, normal, ordinary, popular, regular, routine, traditional, usual, wonted

customer buyer, client, consumer, habitué, patron, prospect, purchaser, regular (*Inf.*), shopper

customs duty, import charges, tariff, taxes, toll

cut *v.* **1.** chop, cleave, divide, gash, incise, lacerate, nick, notch, penetrate, pierce, score, sever, slash, slice, slit, wound **2.** carve, chip, chisel, chop, engrave, fashion, form, saw, sculpt, sculpture, shape, whittle **3.** clip, dock, fell, gather, hack, harvest, hew, lop, mow, pare, prune, reap, saw down, shave, trim **4.** contract, cut back, decrease, ease up on, lower, rationalize, reduce, slash, slim (down) **5.** abbreviate, abridge, condense, curtail, delete, edit out, excise, precis, shorten **6.** *Often with* **through, off,** *or* **across** bisect, carve, cleave, cross, dissect, divide, interrupt, intersect, part, segment, sever, slice, split, sunder **7.** avoid, cold-shoulder, freeze (someone) out (*Inf., chiefly U.S.*), grieve, hurt, ignore, insult, look straight through (someone), pain, send to Coventry, slight, snub, spurn, sting, turn one's back on, wound ~*n.* **8.** gash, graze, groove, incision, laceration, nick, rent, rip, slash, slit, stroke, wound **9.** cutback, decrease, decrement, diminution, economy, fall, lowering, reduction, saving **10.** *Inf.* chop (*Sl.*), division, kickback (*Chiefly U.S.*), percentage, piece, portion, rake-off (*Sl.*), section, share, slice **11.** configuration, fashion, form, look, mode, shape, style

cutback cut, decrease, economy, lessening, reduction, retrenchment

cut in break in, butt in, interpose, interrupt, intervene, intrude, move in

cut-price bargain, cheap, cut-rate (*Chiefly U.S.*), reduced, sale

cutthroat 1. *n.* assassin, bravo, butcher, executioner, hit man (*Sl.*), homicide, killer, liquidator, murderer, slayer (*Archaic*), thug **2.** *adj.* barbarous, bloodthirsty, bloody, cruel, death-dealing, ferocious, homicidal, merciless, murderous, savage, thuggish, violent

cutting *adj.* acid, acrimonious, barbed, bitter, caustic, hurtful, malicious, pointed, sarcastic, sardonic, scathing, severe, trenchant, wounding

cycle aeon, age, circle, era, period, phase, revolution, rotation, round (*of years*)

cyclopedia *or* **cyclopaedia** (saɪkləʊˈpiːdɪə) *n. see* ENCYCLOPEDIA

cyclopropane (saɪkləʊˈprəʊpeɪn) *n.* colourless gaseous hydrocarbon, used as anaesthetic

Cyclops (ˈsaɪklɒps) *n. Class. myth.* one of race of giants having single eye in middle of forehead (*pl.* **Cyclopes** (saɪˈkləʊpiːz), **-es**)

cyclorama (saɪkləʊˈrɑːmə) *n.* **1.** picture on interior wall of cylindrical room, designed to appear in natural perspective to spectator **2.** *Theat.* curtain or wall curving along back of stage —**cycloramic** (saɪkləʊˈræmɪk) *a.*

cyclostyle (ˈsaɪkləstaɪl) *vt.* **1.** produce (pamphlets *etc.*) in large numbers for distribution —*a./n.* **2.** (of) machine, method for doing this

cyclotron (ˈsaɪklətrɒn) *n.* powerful apparatus which accelerates the circular movement of subatomic particles in a magnetic field, used for work in nuclear disintegration *etc.*

cygnet (ˈsɪgnɪt) *n.* young swan

cylinder (ˈsɪlɪndə) *n.* **1.** roller-shaped solid or hollow body, of uniform diameter **2.** piston chamber of engine —**cyˈlindrical** *a.* —**ˈcylindroid** *a.*

cymbal (ˈsɪmbᵊl) *n.* one of pair of two brass plates struck together to produce ringing or clashing sound in music

cyme (saɪm) *n.* inflorescence in which first flower is terminal bud of main stem and subsequent flowers develop as terminal buds of lateral stems —**cyˈmiferous** *a.*

Cymric *or* **Kymric** (ˈkɪmrɪk) *a.* Welsh

cynic (ˈsɪnɪk) *n.* one who expects, believes, the worst about people, their motives, or outcome of events —**ˈcynical** *a.* —**ˈcynicism** *n.* being cynical

cynosure (ˈsɪnəzjʊə, -ʃʊə) *n.* centre of attraction

cypher (ˈsaɪfə) *see* CIPHER

cypress (ˈsaɪprəs) *n.* coniferous tree with very dark foliage

Cypriot (ˈsɪprɪət) *or* **Cypriote** (ˈsɪprɪəʊt) *n.* **1.** native of Cyprus **2.** dialect of Greek spoken in Cyprus —*a.* **3.** relating to Cyprus

Cyrillic (sɪˈrɪlɪk) *a.* **1.** relating to alphabet devised supposedly by Saint Cyril, for Slavonic languages —*n.* **2.** this alphabet

cyst (sɪst) *n.* sac containing liquid secretion or pus —**ˈcystic** *a.* **1.** of cysts **2.** of the bladder —**cysˈtitis** *n.* inflammation of bladder —**cystic fibrosis** congenital disease, usu. affecting children, characterized by chronic infection of respiratory tract and pancreatic insufficiency

cytology (saɪˈtɒlədʒɪ) *n.* study of plant and animal cells

cytoplasm (ˈsaɪtəʊplæzəm) *n.* protoplasm of cell excluding nucleus

czar (zɑː) *n. see* TSAR

czardas (ˈtʃɑːdæʃ) *n.* **1.** Hungarian national dance of alternating slow and fast sections **2.** music for this dance

Czech (tʃɛk) *n.* member of western branch of Slavs —**Czechoslovak** (tʃɛkəʊˈsləʊvæk) *or* **Czechoslovakian** (tʃɛkəʊsləʊˈvækɪən) *a.* **1.** of Czechoslovakia, its peoples or languages —*n.* **2.** (loosely) either of two languages of Czechoslovakia: Czech or Slovak

THESAURUS

cynic doubter, misanthrope, misanthropist, pessimist, sceptic, scoffer

cynical contemptuous, derisive, distrustful, ironic, misanthropic, misanthropical, mocking, pessimistic, sarcastic, sardonic, sceptical, scoffing, scornful, sneering, unbelieving

cynicism disbelief, doubt, misanthropy, pessimism, sarcasm, sardonicism, scepticism

D

d *or* **D** (diː) *n.* **1.** fourth letter of English alphabet **2.** speech sound represented by this letter (*pl.* **d's, D's** *or* **Ds**)

d *Phys.* density

D 1. *Mus.* second note of scale of C major; major or minor key having this note as its tonic **2.** *Chem.* deuterium **3.** Roman numeral, 500

d. 1. day **2.** denarius (*Lat.*, penny) **3.** departs **4.** diameter **5.** died

D. Democratic

dab[1] (dæb) *vt.* **1.** apply with momentary pressure (*esp.* anything wet and soft) **2.** strike feebly (**-bb-**) —*n.* **3.** smear **4.** slight blow or tap **5.** small mass —**ˈdabchick** *n.* small grebe —**dab hand** *inf.* someone good at something

dab[2] (dæb) *n.* small flatfish

dabble (ˈdæbᵊl) *vi.* **1.** splash about **2.** be desultory student or amateur —**ˈdabbler** *n.*

da capo (dɑː ˈkɑːpəʊ) *Mus.* repeat from beginning

dace (deɪs) *n.* small freshwater fish (*pl.* **dace, -s**)

dachshund (ˈdækshʊnd) *n.* short-legged long-bodied dog

Dacron (ˈdeɪkrɒn, ˈdæk-) *n.* **US R** Terylene

dactyl (ˈdæktɪl) *n.* metrical foot of one long followed by two short syllables

dad (dæd) *or* **daddy** (ˈdædɪ) *n. inf.* father —**daddy-longlegs** *n. inf.* crane fly

Dada (ˈdɑːdɑː) *or* **Dadaism** (ˈdɑːdɑːɪzəm) *n.* artistic movement of early 20th century, founded on principles of incongruity and irreverence towards accepted aesthetic criteria —**ˈDadaist** *n./a.*

dado (ˈdeɪdəʊ) *n.* lower part of room wall when lined or painted separately (*pl.* **-es, -s**)

daemon (ˈdiːmən) *or* **daimon** (ˈdaɪmɒn) *n.* **1.** demigod **2.** guardian spirit of place or person

daff (dæf) *inf.* daffodil

daffodil (ˈdæfədɪl) *n.* spring flower, yellow narcissus (*also* **Lent lily**)

daft (dɑːft) *a.* foolish, crazy

dag (dæg) *n.* **1.** daglock **2. A, NZ** *sl.* eccentric character —**ˈdaglock** *n.* dung-caked locks of wool around hindquarters of sheep

dagga (ˈdaxə, ˈdɑːgə) *n.* **SA** hemp, smoked as narcotic

dagger (ˈdægə) *n.* short, edged stabbing weapon

dago (ˈdeɪgəʊ) *n. offens.* Spaniard or other Latin (*pl.* **-s, -es**)

daguerreotype (dəˈgɛrəʊtaɪp) *n.* **1.** early photographic process **2.** photograph formed by this process

dahlia (ˈdeɪljə) *n.* garden plant of various colours

Dáil Éireann (ˈdɔɪl ˈɛərən) *or* **Dáil** *n.* lower chamber of parliament in the Irish Republic

daily (ˈdeɪlɪ) *a.* **1.** done, occurring, published every day —*adv.* **2.** every day —*n.* **3.** daily newspaper **4.** charwoman

dainty (ˈdeɪntɪ) *a.* **1.** delicate **2.** elegant, choice **3.** pretty and neat **4.** fastidious —*n.* **5.** delicacy —**ˈdaintily** *adv.* —**ˈdaintiness** *n.*

daiquiri (ˈdaɪkɪrɪ, ˈdæk-) *n.* iced drink containing rum, lime juice and sugar (*pl.* **-s**)

dairy (ˈdɛərɪ) *n.* place for processing milk and its products —**ˈdairying** *n.* —**dairy cattle** cows raised mainly for milk —**dairy farm** farm specializing in producing milk —**ˈdairymaid** *n.* —**ˈdairyman** *n.* —**dairy products** milk, cheese, butter *etc.*

dais (ˈdeɪɪs, deɪs) *n.* raised platform, usu. at end of hall

daisy (ˈdeɪzɪ) *n.* flower with yellow centre and white petals —**daisy-wheel** *n.* flat, wheel-shaped device with printing characters at end of spokes

Dalai Lama (ˈdælaɪ ˈlɑːmə) head of Buddhist hierarchy in Tibet

dale (deɪl) *n.* valley —**ˈdalesman** *n.* native of dale, *esp.* of N England

dalles (dælz) *pl.n.* **C** river rapids flowing between high rock walls

dally (ˈdælɪ) *vi.* **1.** trifle, spend time in idleness or amusement **2.** loiter (**ˈdallied, ˈdallying**) —**ˈdalliance** *n.*

Dalmatian (dælˈmeɪʃən) *n.* large dog, white with black spots

dal segno (ˈdæl ˈsɛnjəʊ) *Mus.* repeat from point marked with sign to word *fine*

dam[1] (dæm) *n.* **1.** barrier to hold back flow of waters **2.** water so collected —*vt.* **3.** hold with or as with dam (**-mm-**)

dam[2] (dæm) *n.* female parent (used of animals)

damage (ˈdæmɪdʒ) *n.* **1.** injury, harm, loss —*pl.* **2.**

THESAURUS

dabble 1. dip, guddle (*Scot.*), moisten, paddle, spatter, splash, sprinkle, wet **2.** dally, dip into, play at, potter, tinker, trifle (with)

dabbler amateur, dilettante, potterer, tinkerer, trifler

dab hand ace (*Inf.*), adept, dabster (*Dialect*), expert, past master, wizard

dagger bayonet, dirk, poniard, skean, stiletto

daily 1. *adj.* circadian, diurnal, everyday, quotidian **2.** *adv.* constantly, day after day, day by day, every day, often, once a day, per diem, regularly

dainty *adj.* **1.** charming, delicate, elegant, exquisite, fine, graceful, neat, petite, pretty **2.** choice, delectable, delicious, palatable, savoury, tasty, tender, toothsome **3.** choosy, fastidious, finical, finicky, fussy, mincing, nice, particular, refined, scrupulous ~*n.* **4.** *bonne bouche,* delicacy, fancy, sweetmeat, titbit

dale bottom, coomb, dell, dingle, glen, strath (*Scot.*), vale, valley

dam 1. *n.* barrage, barrier, embankment, hindrance, obstruction, wall **2.** *v.* barricade, block, block up, check, choke, confine, hold back, hold in, obstruct, restrict

damage *n.* **1.** destruction, detriment, devastation, harm, hurt, impairment, injury, loss, mischief, mutilation, suffering **2.** *Plural* compensation, fine, indemnity, reimbursement, reparation, satisfaction ~*v.* **3.** deface, harm, hurt, impair, incapacitate, injure, mar, mutilate, ruin, spoil, tamper with, weaken, wreck

sum claimed or adjudged in compensation for injury —*vt.* **3.** harm

damask (ˈdæməsk) *n.* **1.** figured woven material of silk or linen, *esp.* white table linen with design shown up by light **2.** colour of damask rose, velvety red —**damascene** (ˈdæməsiːn) *vt.* decorate (steel *etc.*) with inlaid gold or silver —**damask rose** fragrant rose used to make the perfume attar

dame (deɪm) *n.* **1.** *obs.* lady **2.** (D-) title of lady in Order of the British Empire **3.** *sl. chiefly* US woman

damn (dæm) *vt.* **1.** condemn to hell **2.** be the ruin of **3.** give hostile reception to —*vi.* **4.** curse (**damned, ˈdamning**) —*interj.* **5.** expression of annoyance, impatience *etc.* —**damnable** (ˈdæmnəbˀl) *a.* **1.** deserving damnation **2.** hateful, annoying —**damˈnation** *n.* —**damnatory** (ˈdæmnətərɪ) *a.*

damp (dæmp) *a.* **1.** moist **2.** slightly moist —*n.* **3.** diffused moisture **4.** in coal mines, dangerous gas —*vt.* **5.** make damp **6.** (*oft. with* down) deaden, discourage —**ˈdampen** *v.* **1.** make, become damp —*vt.* **2.** stifle, deaden —**ˈdamper** *n.* **1.** anything that discourages or depresses **2.** plate in flue to control draught —**ˈdamp-course** *n.* layer of impervious material in wall, to stop moisture rising (*also* **damp-proof course**)

damsel (ˈdæmzˀl) *n. obs.* girl

damson (ˈdæmzən) *n.* **1.** small dark purple plum **2.** tree bearing it **3.** its colour

dan (dæn) *n. Judo* **1.** any one of 12 black-belt grades of proficiency **2.** competitor entitled to dan grading

Dan. *Bible* Daniel

dance (dɑːns) *vi.* **1.** move with measured rhythmic steps, usu. to music **2.** be in lively movement **3.** bob up and down —*vt.* **4.** perform (dance) **5.** cause to dance —*n.* **6.** lively, rhythmical movement **7.** arrangement of such movements **8.** tune for them **9.** social gathering for the purpose of dancing —**ˈdancer** *n.*

D and C dilation and curettage (of womb)

dandelion (ˈdændɪlaɪən) *n.* yellow-flowered wild plant

dander (ˈdændə) *n. inf.* temper, fighting spirit

dandle (ˈdændˀl) *vt.* **1.** move (young child) up and down (on knee or in arms) **2.** pet; fondle

dandruff (ˈdændrəf) *or* **dandriff** (ˈdændrɪf) *n.* dead skin in small scales among the hair

dandy (ˈdændɪ) *n.* **1.** man excessively concerned with smartness of dress —*a.* **2.** *inf.* excellent —**ˈdandify** *vt.* dress like or cause to resemble a dandy —**ˈdandyism** *n.*

Dane (deɪn) *n.* **1.** native of Denmark **2.** Viking who invaded England from late 8th to 11th cent. A.D. —**ˈDanish** *a.* **1.** of Denmark —*n.* **2.** official language of Denmark **3.** people of Denmark collectively

danger (ˈdeɪndʒə) *n.* **1.** liability or exposure to harm **2.** risk, peril —**ˈdangerous** *a.* —**ˈdangerously** *adv.* —**danger money** extra money paid to compensate for risks involved in certain dangerous jobs

dangle (ˈdæŋgˀl) *vi.* **1.** hang loosely and swaying —*vt.* **2.** hold suspended **3.** tempt with

dank (dæŋk) *a.* unpleasantly damp and chilly —**ˈdankness** *n.*

danseuse (dɑ̃ˈsœːz) *n.* female dancer

daphne (ˈdæfnɪ) *n.* ornamental shrub with bell-shaped flowers

dapper (ˈdæpə) *a.* neat and precise, *esp.* in dress, spruce

dapple (ˈdæpˀl) *v.* mark or become marked with spots —**ˈdappled** *a.* **1.** spotted **2.** mottled **3.** variegated —**dapple-grey** *a.* (of horse) grey marked with darker spots

Darby and Joan (ˈdɑːbɪ, dʒəʊn) elderly married couple living in domestic harmony —**Darby and Joan Club** club for elderly people

dare (dɛə) *v.* **1.** venture, have courage (to) —*vt.* **2.**

THESAURUS

dame baroness, dowager, *grande dame,* lady, matron (*Archaic*), noblewoman, peeress

damn *v.* **1.** blast, castigate, censure, condemn, criticize, denounce, denunciate, excoriate, inveigle against, pan (*Inf.*), slam (*Sl.*), slate (*Inf.*) **2.** abuse, anathematize, blaspheme, curse, execrate, imprecate, revile, swear **3.** condemn, doom, sentence

damnable abominable, accursed, atrocious, culpable, cursed, despicable, detestable, execrable, hateful, horrible, offensive, wicked

damnation anathema, ban, condemnation, consigning to perdition, damning, denunciation, doom, excommunication, objurgation, proscription, sending to hell

damned 1. accursed, anathematized, condemned, doomed, infernal, lost, reprobate, unhappy **2.** *Sl.* confounded, despicable, detestable, hateful, infamous, infernal, loathsome, revolting

damning accusatorial, condemnatory, damnatory, dooming, implicating, implicative, incriminating

damp *n.* **1.** clamminess, dampness, dankness, dew, drizzle, fog, humidity, mist, moisture, mugginess, vapour ~*adj.* **2.** clammy, dank, dewy, dripping, drizzly, humid, misty, moist, muggy, sodden, soggy, sopping, vaporous, wet ~*v.* **3.** dampen, moisten, wet **4.** *Fig.* allay, check, chill, cool, curb, dash, deaden, deject, depress, diminish, discourage, dispirit, dull, inhibit, moderate, restrain, stifle

damper chill, cloud, cold water, curb, discouragement, gloom, hindrance, kill-joy, pall, restraint, wet blanket

dance 1. *v.* bob up and down, caper, frolic, gambol, hop, jig, prance, rock, skip, spin, sway, swing, whirl **2.** *n.* ball, dancing party, hop (*Inf.*), social

danger endangerment, hazard, insecurity, jeopardy, menace, peril, precariousness, risk, threat, venture, vulnerability

dangerous alarming, breakneck, chancy (*Inf.*), exposed, hairy (*Sl.*), hazardous, insecure, menacing, nasty, parlous (*Archaic*), perilous, precarious, risky, threatening, treacherous, ugly, unchancy (*Scot.*), unsafe, vulnerable

dangerously 1. alarmingly, carelessly, daringly, desperately, harmfully, hazardously, perilously, precariously, recklessly, riskily, unsafely, unsecurely **2.** critically, gravely, seriously, severely

dangle *v.* **1.** depend, flap, hang, hang down, sway, swing, trail **2.** brandish, entice, flaunt, flourish, lure, tantalize, tempt, wave

dapper active, brisk, chic, dainty, natty (*Inf.*), neat, nice, nimble, smart, spruce, spry, stylish, trig (*Archaic*), trim, well-groomed, well turned out

dappled brindled, checkered, flecked, freckled, mottled, piebald, pied, speckled, spotted, stippled, variegated

challenge —*n.* **3.** challenge —ˈ**daring** *a.* **1.** bold —*n.* **2.** adventurous courage —ˈ**daredevil** *a./n.* reckless (person)

dark (dɑːk) *a.* **1.** without light **2.** gloomy **3.** deep in tint **4.** secret **5.** unenlightened **6.** wicked —*n.* **7.** absence of light, colour or knowledge —ˈ**darken** *v.* —ˈ**darkly** *adv.* —ˈ**darkness** *n.* —**Dark Ages** *Hist.* period from about late 5th cent. A.D. to about 1000 A.D. —**Dark Continent** Africa when relatively unexplored —**dark horse** somebody, *esp.* competitor in race, about whom little is known —ˈ**darkroom** *n.* darkened room for processing film

darling (ˈdɑːlɪŋ) *a./n.* much loved or very lovable (person)

darn[1] (dɑːn) *vt.* **1.** mend by filling (hole) with interwoven yarn —*n.* **2.** place so mended —ˈ**darning** *n.*

darn[2] (dɑːn) *interj.* mild expletive

darnel (ˈdɑːnᵊl) *n.* grass that grows as weed in grain fields

dart (dɑːt) *n.* **1.** small light pointed missile **2.** darting motion **3.** small seam or intake in garment —*pl.* **4.** indoor game played with numbered target and miniature darts —*vt.* **5.** cast, throw rapidly (glance *etc.*) —*vi.* **6.** go rapidly or abruptly —ˈ**dartboard** *n.* circular piece of wood *etc.* used as target in darts

Darwinian (dɑːˈwɪnɪən) *a.* pert. to Charles Darwin or his theory of evolution

dash (dæʃ) *vt.* **1.** smash, throw, thrust, send with violence **2.** cast down **3.** tinge, flavour, mix —*vi.* **4.** move, go with great speed or violence —*n.* **5.** rush **6.** vigour **7.** smartness **8.** small quantity, tinge **9.** stroke (-) between words —ˈ**dasher** *n.* **C** ledge along top of boards at ice-hockey rink —ˈ**dashing** *a.* spirited, showy —ˈ**dashboard** *n.* in car *etc.*, instrument panel in front of driver

dassie (ˈdæsɪ) *n.* **SA** hyrax

dastard (ˈdæstəd) *n. obs.* contemptible, sneaking coward —ˈ**dastardly** *a.*

dasyure (ˈdæsɪjʊə) *n.* **1.** small carnivorous marsupial of Aust., New Guinea and adjacent islands **2.** ursine dasyure (*see* TASMANIAN DEVIL)

data (ˈdeɪtə, ˈdɑːtə) *pl.n.* (*oft. with sing. v.*) **1.** series of observations, measurements or facts **2.** information —**data bank** *or* **base** store of information, *esp.* in form that can be handled by computer —**data processing** sequence of operations performed on data, *esp.* by computer, to extract information *etc.*

date[1] (deɪt) *n.* **1.** day of the month **2.** statement on document of its time of writing **3.** time of occurrence **4.** period of work of art *etc.* **5.** engagement, appointment —*vt.* **6.** mark with date **7.** refer to date of **8.** reveal age of **9.** *inf.* accompany on social outing —*vi.* **10.** exist (from) **11.** betray time or period of origin, become old-fashioned —ˈ**dateless** *a.* **1.** without date **2.** immemorial —**date line** (*oft.* **D- L-**) line (approx. 180° meridian) E of which is one day earlier than W of it —ˈ**dateline** *n. Journalism* date and location of story, placed at top of article —**date stamp 1.** adjustable rubber stamp for recording date **2.** inked impression made by this

THESAURUS

dare *v.* **1.** challenge, defy, goad, provoke, taunt, throw down the gauntlet **2.** adventure, brave, endanger, gamble, hazard, make bold, presume, risk, stake, venture ~*n.* **3.** challenge, defiance, provocation, taunt

daredevil 1. *n.* adventurer, desperado, exhibitionist, madcap, show-off (*Inf.*), stunt man **2.** *adj.* adventurous, audacious, bold, daring, death-defying, madcap, reckless

daring 1. *adj.* adventurous, audacious, bold, brave, fearless, game (*Inf.*), impulsive, intrepid, plucky, rash, reckless, valiant, venturesome **2.** *n.* audacity, boldness, bottle (*Sl.*), bravery, courage, derring-do (*Archaic*), fearlessness, grit, guts (*Inf.*), intrepidity, nerve (*Inf.*), pluck, rashness, spirit, spunk (*Inf.*), temerity

dark *adj.* **1.** black, brunette, dark-skinned, dusky, ebony, sable, swarthy **2.** cloudy, darksome (*Literary*), dim, dingy, indistinct, murky, overcast, pitch-black, pitchy, shadowy, shady, sunless, unlit **3.** abstruse, arcane, concealed, cryptic, deep, enigmatic, hidden, mysterious, mystic, obscure, occult, puzzling, recondite, secret **4.** bleak, cheerless, dismal, doleful, drab, gloomy, grim, joyless, morbid, morose, mournful, sombre **5.** benighted, ignorant, uncultivated, unenlightened, unlettered **6.** atrocious, damnable, evil, foul, hellish, horrible, infamous, infernal, nefarious, satanic, sinful, sinister, vile, wicked ~*n.* **7.** darkness, dimness, dusk, gloom, murk, murkiness, obscurity, semi-darkness **8.** evening, night, nightfall, night-time, twilight **9.** *Fig.* concealment, ignorance, secrecy

darken 1. becloud, blacken, cloud up *or* over, deepen, dim, eclipse, make dark, make darker, make dim, obscure, overshadow, shade, shadow **2.** become gloomy, blacken, cast a pall over, cloud, deject, depress, dispirit, grow troubled, look black, sadden

darkness 1. blackness, dark, dimness, dusk, duskiness, gloom, murk, murkiness, nightfall, obscurity, shade, shadiness, shadows **2.** *Fig.* blindness, concealment, ignorance, mystery, privacy, secrecy, unawareness

darling *n.* **1.** beloved, dear, dearest, love, sweetheart, truelove **2.** apple of one's eye, blue-eyed boy, fair-haired boy (*U.S.*), favourite, pet, spoiled child ~*adj.* **3.** adored, beloved, cherished, dear, precious, treasured **4.** adorable, attractive, captivating, charming, enchanting, lovely, sweet

darn 1. *v.* cobble up, mend, patch, repair, sew up, stitch **2.** *n.* invisible repair, mend, patch, reinforcement

dart 1. bound, dash, flash, flit, fly, race, run, rush, scoot, shoot, spring, sprint, start, tear, whistle (*Inf.*), whiz **2.** cast, fling, hurl, launch, propel, send, shoot, sling, throw

dash *v.* **1.** break, crash, destroy, shatter, shiver, smash, splinter **2.** cast, fling, hurl, slam, sling, throw **3.** bolt, bound, dart, fly, haste, hasten, hurry, race, run, rush, speed, spring, sprint, tear ~*n.* **4.** bolt, dart, haste, onset, race, run, rush, sortie, sprint, spurt **5.** brio, élan, flair, flourish, panache, spirit, style, verve, vigour, vivacity **6.** bit, drop, flavour, hint, little, pinch, smack, *soupçon*, sprinkling, suggestion, tinge, touch

dashing 1. bold, daring, debonair, exuberant, gallant, lively, plucky, spirited, swashbuckling **2.** dapper, dazzling, elegant, flamboyant, jaunty, showy, smart, sporty, stylish, swish (*Inf.*)

data details, documents, facts, figures, information, input, materials, statistics

date[2] (deɪt) *n.* **1.** sweet, single-stone fruit of palm **2.** the palm

dative (ˈdeɪtɪv) *n.* noun case indicating indirect object *etc.*

datum (ˈdeɪtəm, ˈdɑːtəm) *n.* thing given, known, or assumed as basis for reckoning, reasoning *etc.* (*pl.* **ˈdata**)

daub (dɔːb) *vt.* **1.** coat, plaster, paint coarsely or roughly —*n.* **2.** rough picture **3.** smear —**ˈdauber** *n.*

daughter (ˈdɔːtə) *n.* one's female child —**ˈdaughterly** *a.* —**daughter-in-law** *n.* son's wife

daunt (dɔːnt) *vt.* frighten, *esp.* into giving up purpose —**ˈdauntless** *a.* intrepid, fearless

dauphin (ˈdɔːfɪn; *Fr.* doˈfɛ̃) *n.* formerly, eldest son of French king

davenport (ˈdævənpɔːt) *n.* **1.** small writing table with drawers **2.** US large couch or settee

davit (ˈdævɪt, ˈdeɪ-) *n.* crane, usu. one of pair, at ship's side for lowering and hoisting boats

Davy Jones's locker (ˈdeɪvɪ ˈdʒəʊnzɪz) sea, considered as sailors' grave

Davy lamp miner's safety lamp

daw (dɔː) *n. obs.* jackdaw

dawdle (ˈdɔːdᵊl) *vi.* idle, waste time, loiter —**ˈdawdler** *n.*

dawn (dɔːn) *n.* **1.** first light, daybreak **2.** first gleam or beginning of anything —*vi.* **3.** begin to grow light **4.** appear, begin **5.** (begin to) be understood —**ˈdawning** *n.* —**dawn chorus** singing of birds at dawn

day (deɪ) *n.* **1.** period of 24 hours **2.** time when sun is above horizon **3.** point or unit of time **4.** daylight **5.** part of day occupied by certain activity, time period **6.** special or designated day —**day bed** couch intended for use as seat and as bed —**ˈdaybook** *n. Book-keeping* book in which day's sales *etc.* are entered for later transfer to ledger —**ˈdayboy** *n.* **UK** boy who attends boarding school daily, but returns home each evening (**ˈdaygirl** *fem.*) —**ˈdaybreak** *n.* dawn —**day centre** place providing meals *etc.* where the elderly, handicapped *etc.* may spend the day —**ˈdaydream** *n.* **1.** idle fancy —*vi.* **2.** indulge in idle fantasy —**ˈdaylight** *n.* **1.** natural light **2.** dawn —*pl.* **3.** consciousness, wits —**daylight robbery** *inf.* blatant overcharging —**daylight saving** in summer, time set one hour ahead of local standard time, giving extra daylight in evenings —**day release UK** system of releasing employees for part-time education —**day room** communal living room in residential institution —**ˈdayspring** *n.* dawn —**ˈdaystar** *n.* morning star —**ˈdaytime** *n.* time between sunrise and sunset —**day-to-day** *a.* routine; everyday

Dayak (ˈdaɪæk) *n. see* DYAK

daze (deɪz) *vt.* **1.** stupefy, stun, bewilder —*n.* **2.** stupefied or bewildered state —**dazed** *a.*

dazzle (ˈdæzᵊl) *vt.* **1.** blind, confuse or overpower with brightness, light, brilliant display or prospects —*n.* **2.** brightness that dazzles the vision —**ˈdazzlement** *n.*

dB *or* **db** decibel(s)

D.B.E. Dame Commander of the British Empire

DBS Direct Broadcasting by Satellite

DC direct current

D.C. District of Columbia

D.C.B. Dame Commander of the Order of the Bath

D.C.M. Distinguished Conduct Medal

THESAURUS

date *n.* **1.** age, epoch, era, period, stage, time **2.** appointment, assignation, engagement, meeting, rendezvous, tryst ~*v.* **3.** assign a date to, determine the date of, fix the period of, put a date on **4.** bear a date, belong to, come from, exist from, originate in **5.** become obsolete, be dated, obsolesce, show one's age

daub *v.* **1.** coat, cover, paint, plaster, slap on (*Inf.*), smear **2.** bedaub, begrime, besmear, blur, deface, dirty, grime, smirch, smudge, spatter, splatter, stain, sully ~*n.* **3.** blot, blotch, smear, splodge, splotch, spot, stain

daunt 1. alarm, appal, cow, dismay, frighten, frighten off, intimidate, overawe, scare, subdue, terrify **2.** deter, discourage, dishearten, dispirit, put off, shake

dauntless bold, brave, courageous, daring, doughty, fearless, gallant, heroic, indomitable, intrepid, lion-hearted, resolute, stouthearted, undaunted, unflinching, valiant, valorous

dawdle dally, delay, dilly-dally (*Inf.*), fritter away, hang about, idle, lag, loaf, loiter, potter, trail, waste time

dawn *n.* **1.** aurora (*Literary*), cockcrow, crack of dawn, dawning, daybreak, daylight, dayspring (*Poetic*), morning, sunrise, sunup ~*v.* **2.** break, brighten, gleam, glimmer, grow light, lighten ~*n.* **3.** advent, beginning, birth, dawning, emergence, genesis, inception, onset, origin, outset, rise, start, unfolding ~*v.* **4.** appear, begin, develop, emerge, initiate, open, originate, rise, unfold **5.** come into one's head, come to mind, cross one's mind, flash across one's mind, hit, occur, register (*Inf.*), strike

day 1. daylight, daylight hours, daytime, twenty-four hours, working day **2.** age, ascendancy, cycle, epoch, era, generation, height, heyday, period, prime, time, zenith **3.** date, particular day, point in time, set time, time

daybreak break of day, cockcrow, crack of dawn, dawn, dayspring (*Poetic*), first light, morning, sunrise, sunup

daydream *n.* **1.** dream, imagining, musing, reverie, stargazing, vision, woolgathering **2.** castle in the air *or* in Spain, dream, fancy, fantasy, figment of the imagination, fond hope, pipe dream, wish ~*v.* **3.** dream, envision, fancy, fantasize, hallucinate, imagine, muse, stargaze

daylight 1. light of day, sunlight, sunshine **2.** broad day, daylight hours, daytime

daze *v.* **1.** benumb, numb, paralyse, shock, stun, stupefy **2.** amaze, astonish, astound, befog, bewilder, blind, confuse, dazzle, dumbfound, flabbergast (*Inf.*), perplex, stagger, startle, surprise ~*n.* **3.** bewilderment, confusion, distraction, shock, stupor, trance, trancelike state

dazed baffled, bemused, bewildered, confused, disorientated, dizzy, dopey (*Sl.*), flabbergasted (*Inf.*), fuddled, groggy (*Inf.*), light-headed, muddled, nonplussed, numbed, perplexed, punch-drunk, shocked, staggered, stunned, stupefied, woozy (*Inf.*)

dazzle *v.* **1.** bedazzle, blind, blur, confuse, daze **2.** amaze, astonish, awe, bowl over (*Inf.*), fascinate, hypnotize, impress, overawe, overpower, overwhelm, strike dumb, stupefy ~*n.* **3.** brilliance, flash, glitter, magnificence, razzle-dazzle (*Sl.*), razzmatazz (*Sl.*), sparkle, splendour

DD Doctor of Divinity

D-day *n.* day selected for start of something, *esp.* Allied invasion of Europe in 1944

DDT dichlorodiphenyltrichloroethane, hydrocarbon compound used as an insecticide

DE Delaware

de- (*comb. form*) removal of, from, reversal of, as in *delouse, desegregate.* Such words are not given here where the meaning may be inferred from the simple word

deacon (ˈdiːkən) *n.* **1.** one in lowest degree of holy orders **2.** one who superintends secular affairs of presbyterian church (ˈ**deaconess** *fem.*)

deactivate (diːˈæktɪveɪt) *vt.* **1.** make (bomb *etc.*) harmless or inoperative **2.** make less radioactive

dead (dɛd) *a.* **1.** no longer alive **2.** obsolete **3.** numb, without sensation **4.** no longer functioning, extinguished **5.** lacking lustre, movement or vigour **6.** sure, complete —*n.* **7.** dead person or persons (*oft. in pl.,* **the dead**) —*adv.* **8.** utterly —ˈ**deaden** *vt.* —ˈ**deadly** *a.* **1.** fatal **2.** deathlike —*adv.* **3.** as if dead —**dead-and-alive** *a.* dull —ˈ**deadbeat** *a./n. inf.* lazy, useless (person) —**dead duck** *sl.* person or thing doomed to death, failure *etc., esp.* because of mistake —**dead end 1.** cul-de-sac **2.** situation in which further progress is impossible —ˈ**deadhead** *n.* **US, C** log sticking out of water as hindrance to navigation —**dead heat** race in which competitors finish exactly even —**dead letter 1.** law no longer observed **2.** letter which post office cannot deliver —ˈ**deadline** *n.* limit of time allowed —ˈ**deadlock** *n.* standstill —**dead loss 1.** complete loss for which no compensation is paid **2.** *inf.* useless person or thing —**deadly nightshade** plant with poisonous black berries —**dead man's handle** *or* **pedal** safety switch on piece of machinery that allows operation only while depressed by operator —**dead march** solemn funeral music to accompany procession —ˈ**deadpan** *a.* expressionless —**dead reckoning** calculation of ship's position from log and compass, when observations cannot be taken —**dead set** *adv.* **1.** absolutely —*n.* **2.** resolute attack —**dead weight 1.** heavy weight or load **2.** oppressive burden **3.** difference between loaded and unloaded weights of ship **4.** intrinsic invariable weight of structure —ˈ**deadwood** *n.* **1.** dead trees or branches **2.** *inf.* useless person; encumbrance —**dead of night** time of greatest stillness and darkness

deaf (dɛf) *a.* **1.** wholly or partly without hearing **2.** unwilling to listen —ˈ**deafen** *vt.* make deaf —ˈ**deafness** *n.* —**deaf aid** hearing aid —**deaf-and-dumb** *a.* **1.** unable to hear or speak **2.** for use of deaf-mutes —**deaf-mute** *n.* **1.** person unable to hear or speak —*a.* **2.** unable to hear or speak

deal[1] (diːl) *vt.* **1.** distribute, give out **2.** inflict —*vi.* **3.** act **4.** treat **5.** do business (with, in) (**dealt** *pt./pp.*) —*n.* **6.** agreement **7.** treatment **8.** share **9.** business transaction —ˈ**dealer** *n.* **1.** one who deals (*esp.* cards) **2.** trader —ˈ**dealings** *pl.n.* transactions or relations with others —**deal with** handle, act towards

deal[2] (diːl) *n.* (plank of) fir or pine wood

dealt (dɛlt) *pt./pp. of* DEAL[1]

dean[1] (diːn) *n.* **1.** university or college official **2.** head of cathedral chapter —ˈ**deanery** *n.* cathedral dean's house or appointment

dean[2] (diːn) *n. see* DENE

dear (dɪə) *a.* **1.** beloved **2.** precious **3.** costly, expensive —*n.* **4.** beloved one —*adv.* **5.** at a high price —ˈ**dearly** *adv.* —ˈ**dearness** *n.*

dearth (dɜːθ) *n.* scarcity

death (dɛθ) *n.* **1.** dying **2.** end of life **3.** end, extinction **4.** annihilation **5.** (**D-**) personification of death, as skeleton —ˈ**deathless** *a.* immortal —ˈ**deathly** *a./adv.* like death —ˈ**deathbed** *n.* bed in which person is about

THESAURUS

dead *adj.* **1.** deceased, defunct, departed, extinct, gone, inanimate, late, lifeless, passed away, perished **2.** apathetic, callous, cold, dull, frigid, glassy, glazed, indifferent, inert, lukewarm, numb, paralysed, spiritless, torpid, unresponsive, wooden **3.** barren, inactive, inoperative, not working, obsolete, stagnant, sterile, still, unemployed, unprofitable, useless **4.** boring, dead-and-alive, dull, flat, insipid, stale, tasteless, uninteresting, vapid **5.** *Fig.* absolute, complete, downright, entire, outright, thorough, total, unqualified, utter **6.** *Inf.* dead beat (*Inf.*), exhausted, spent, tired, worn out ~*adv.* **7.** absolutely, completely, directly, entirely, exactly, totally

deaden abate, alleviate, anaesthetize, benumb, blunt, check, cushion, damp, dampen, diminish, dull, hush, impair, lessen, muffle, mute, numb, paralyse, quieten, reduce, smother, stifle, suppress, weaken

deadlock cessation, dead heat, draw, full stop, halt, impasse, stalemate, standoff, standstill, tie

deadly 1. baleful, baneful, dangerous, death-dealing, deathly, destructive, fatal, lethal, malignant, mortal, noxious, pernicious, poisonous, venomous **2.** cruel, grim, implacable, mortal, ruthless, savage, unrelenting **3.** ashen, deathlike, deathly, ghastly, ghostly, pallid, wan, white

deaf *adj.* **1.** hard of hearing, stone deaf, without hearing **2.** indifferent, oblivious, unconcerned, unhearing, unmoved

deafen din, drown out, make deaf, split *or* burst the eardrums

deal *v.* **1.** *With* **with** attend to, cope with, handle, manage, oversee, see to, take care of, treat **2.** *With* **with** concern, consider, treat (of) **3.** *With* **with** act, behave, conduct oneself **4.** bargain, buy and sell, do business, negotiate, sell, stock, trade, traffic, treat (with) ~*n.* **5.** *Inf.* agreement, arrangement, bargain, buy (*Inf.*), contract, pact, transaction, understanding ~*v.* **6.** allot, apportion, assign, bestow, dispense, distribute, divide, dole out, give, mete out, reward, share ~*n.* **7.** amount, degree, distribution, extent, portion, quantity, share, transaction

dealer chandler, marketer, merchandiser, merchant, trader, tradesman, wholesaler

dealings business, business relations, commerce, trade, traffic, transactions, truck

dear *adj.* **1.** beloved, cherished, close, darling, esteemed, familiar, favourite, intimate, precious, prized, respected, treasured **2.** at a premium, costly, expensive, high-priced, overpriced, pricey (*Inf.*) ~*n.* **3.** angel, beloved, darling, loved one, precious, treasure ~*adv.* **4.** at a heavy cost, at a high price, at great cost, dearly

dearly 1. extremely, greatly, profoundly, very much **2.** affectionately, devotedly, fondly, lovingly, tenderly **3.** at a heavy cost, at a high price, at great cost, dear

to die —ˈ**deathblow** *n.* thing or event that destroys life or hope, *esp.* suddenly —**death certificate** legal document issued by doctor, certifying death of person and stating cause if known —**death duty** tax on property left at death —**death mask** cast of person's face taken after death —**death penalty** capital punishment —**death rate** ratio of deaths in specified area *etc.* to population of that area *etc.* (*also* **mortality rate**) —**death's-head** *n.* human skull or representation of one —ˈ**deathtrap** *n.* building *etc.* considered unsafe —**death warrant** official authorization for carrying out sentence of death —**deathwatch beetle** beetle that bores into wood —**sign one's (own) death warrant** cause one's own destruction

debacle (deɪˈbɑːkᵊl, dɪ-) *n.* utter collapse, rout, disaster

debar (dɪˈbɑː) *vt.* **1.** shut out **2.** stop **3.** prohibit **4.** preclude (**-rr-**)

debark (dɪˈbɑːk) *v.* disembark

debase (dɪˈbeɪs) *vt.* **1.** lower in value, quality or character **2.** adulterate —**deˈbasement** *n.*

debate (dɪˈbeɪt) *v.* **1.** argue, discuss, *esp.* in a formal assembly **2.** consider (something) —*n.* **3.** discussion **4.** controversy —**deˈbatable** *a.* —**deˈbater** *n.*

debauch (dɪˈbɔːtʃ) *vt.* **1.** lead into a life of depraved self-indulgence —*n.* **2.** bout of sensual indulgence —**debauˈchee** *n.* dissipated person —**deˈbauchery** *n.*

debenture (dɪˈbɛntʃə) *n.* bond of company or corporation —**debenture stock** shares issued by company, which guarantee fixed return at regular intervals

debility (dɪˈbɪlɪtɪ) *n.* **1.** feebleness, *esp.* of health **2.** languor —**deˈbilitate** *vt.* weaken, enervate

debit (ˈdɛbɪt) *Accounting n.* **1.** entry in account of sum owed **2.** side of book in which such sums are entered —*vt.* **3.** charge, enter as due

debonair *or* **debonnaire** (dɛbəˈnɛə) *a.* **1.** suave **2.** genial **3.** affable

debouch (dɪˈbaʊtʃ) *vi.* move out from narrow place to wider one —**deˈbouchment** *n.*

debrief (diːˈbriːf) *v.* (of soldier *etc.*) report to superior on result of mission

debris *or* **débris** (ˈdeɪbrɪ, ˈdɛbrɪ) *n.* fragments, rubbish

debt (dɛt) *n.* **1.** what is owed **2.** state of owing —ˈ**debtor** *n.* —**debt of honour** debt that is morally but not legally binding

debug (diːˈbʌg) *vt. inf.* **1.** remove concealed microphones from (room *etc.*) **2.** remove defects in (device *etc.*) **3.** remove insects from (**-gg-**)

debunk (diːˈbʌŋk) *vt.* expose falseness, pretentiousness of, *esp.* by ridicule

debut (ˈdeɪbjuː, ˈdɛbjuː) *n.* first appearance in public —**debutante** (ˈdɛbjʊtɑːnt, -tænt) *n.* girl making official debut into society

Dec. December

deca-, deka- *or before vowel* **dec-, dek-** (*comb. form*) ten, as in *decalitre*

decade (ˈdɛkeɪd, dɪˈkeɪd) *n.* **1.** period of ten years **2.** set of ten

decadent (ˈdɛkədənt) *a.* **1.** declining, deteriorating **2.** morally corrupt —ˈ**decadence** *or* ˈ**decadency** *n.*

decaffeinated (dɪˈkæfɪneɪtɪd) *a.* (of coffee) with caffeine removed

decagon (ˈdɛkəgɒn) *n.* figure of 10 angles —**deˈcagonal** *a.*

THESAURUS

death 1. bereavement, cessation, curtains (*Inf.*), decease, demise, departure, dissolution, dying, end, exit, expiration, loss, passing, quietus, release **2.** annihilation, destruction, downfall, eradication, extermination, extinction, finish, grave, obliteration, ruin, ruination, undoing

deathless eternal, everlasting, immortal, imperishable, incorruptible, timeless, undying

deathly 1. cadaverous, deathlike, gaunt, ghastly, grim, haggard, pale, pallid, wan **2.** deadly, extreme, fatal, intense, mortal, terrible

debacle catastrophe, collapse, defeat, devastation, disaster, downfall, fiasco, havoc, overthrow, reversal, rout, ruin, ruination

debase 1. abase, cheapen, degrade, demean, devalue, disgrace, dishonour, drag down, humble, humiliate, lower, reduce, shame **2.** adulterate, bastardize, contaminate, corrupt, defile, depreciate, impair, pollute, taint, vitiate

debasement 1. adulteration, contamination, depreciation, devaluation, pollution, reduction **2.** abasement, baseness, corruption, degradation, depravation, perversion

debatable arguable, borderline, controversial, disputable, doubtful, dubious, in dispute, moot, open to question, problematical, questionable, uncertain, undecided, unsettled

debate *v.* **1.** argue, contend, contest, controvert, discuss, dispute, question, wrangle ~*n.* **2.** altercation, argument, contention, controversy, discussion, disputation, dispute, polemic ~*v.* **3.** cogitate, consider, deliberate, meditate upon, mull over, ponder, reflect, revolve, ruminate, weigh ~*n.* **4.** cogitation, consideration, deliberation, meditation, reflection

debilitate devitalize, enervate, enfeeble, exhaust, incapacitate, prostrate, relax, sap, undermine, weaken, wear out

debility decrepitude, enervation, enfeeblement, exhaustion, faintness, feebleness, frailty, incapacity, infirmity, languor, malaise, sickliness, weakness

debonair affable, buoyant, charming, cheerful, courteous, dashing, elegant, jaunty, light-hearted, refined, smooth (*Inf.*), sprightly, suave, urbane, well-bred

debris bits, brash, detritus, dross, fragments, litter, pieces, remains, rubbish, rubble, ruins, waste, wreck, wreckage

debt arrears, bill, claim, commitment, debit, due, duty, liability, obligation, score

debtor borrower, defaulter, insolvent, mortgagor

debunk cut down to size, deflate, disparage, expose, lampoon, mock, puncture, ridicule, show up

debut beginning, bow, coming out, entrance, first appearance, inauguration, initiation, introduction, launching, presentation

decadence corruption, debasement, decay, decline, degeneration, deterioration, dissipation, dissolution, fall, perversion, retrogression

decadent corrupt, debased, debauched, decaying, declining, degenerate, degraded, depraved, dissolute, immoral, self-indulgent

decagram *or* **decagramme** (ˈdɛkəgræm) *n.* measure of weight equal to 10 litres

decahedron (dɛkəˈhiːdrən) *n.* solid of 10 faces —**decaˈhedral** *a.*

decalcify (diːˈkælsɪfaɪ) *vt.* deprive of lime, as bones or teeth of their calcareous matter (**-fied, -fying**)

decalitre *or U.S.* **decaliter** (ˈdɛkəliːtə) *n.* 10 litres

Decalogue (ˈdɛkəlɒg) *n.* the Ten Commandments

decametre *or U.S.* **decameter** (ˈdɛkəmiːtə) *n.* 10 metres

decamp (dɪˈkæmp) *vi.* **1.** make off **2.** break camp **3.** abscond

decanal (dɪˈkeɪnᵊl) *a.* of dean, deanery

decant (dɪˈkænt) *vt.* pour off (liquid, as wine) without disturbing sediment —**deˈcanter** *n.* stoppered bottle for wine or spirits

decapitate (dɪˈkæpɪteɪt) *vt.* behead —**decapiˈtation** *n.* —**deˈcapitator** *n.*

decapod (ˈdɛkəpɒd) *n.* **1.** crustacean having five pairs of walking limbs, as crab *etc.* **2.** cephalopod mollusc having eight short tentacles and two longer ones, as squid *etc.*

decarbonize *or* **-ise** (diːˈkɑːbənaɪz) *vt.* remove deposit of carbon, as from motor cylinder —**decarboniˈzation** *or* **-iˈsation** *n.*

decasyllable (ˈdɛkəsɪləbᵊl) *n.* ten-syllabled line —**decasylˈlabic** *a.*

decathlon (dɪˈkæθlɒn) *n.* athletic contest with ten events

decay (dɪˈkeɪ) *v.* **1.** rot, decompose **2.** (cause to) fall off, decline —*n.* **3.** rotting **4.** a falling away, break up

decease (dɪˈsiːs) *n.* **1.** death —*vi.* **2.** die —**deˈceased** *n./a.*

deceive (dɪˈsiːv) *vt.* **1.** mislead **2.** delude **3.** cheat —**deˈceit** *n.* **1.** fraud **2.** duplicity —**deˈceitful** *a.* —**deˈceiver** *n.*

decelerate (diːˈsɛləreɪt) *vi.* slow down

December (dɪˈsɛmbə) *n.* twelfth and last month of year

decennial (dɪˈsɛnɪəl) *a.* of period of ten years —**deˈcennially** *adv.*

decent (ˈdiːsᵊnt) *a.* **1.** respectable **2.** fitting, seemly **3.** not obscene **4.** adequate **5.** *inf.* kind —**ˈdecency** *n.* —**ˈdecently** *adv.*

decentralize *or* **-ise** (diːˈsɛntrəlaɪz) *vt.* divide (government, organization) among local centres

deception (dɪˈsɛpʃən) *n.* **1.** deceiving **2.** illusion **3.** fraud **4.** trick —**deˈceptive** *a.* **1.** misleading **2.** apt to mislead

deci- (*comb. form*) one tenth, as in *decimetre*

decibel (ˈdɛsɪbɛl) *n.* unit for measuring intensity of a sound

decide (dɪˈsaɪd) *vt.* **1.** settle, determine, bring to resolution **2.** give judgment on —*vi.* **3.** come to a decision, conclusion —**deˈcided** *a.* **1.** unmistakable **2.** settled **3.** resolute —**deˈcidedly** *adv.* certainly, undoubtedly —**decision** (dɪˈsɪʒən) *n.* —**deˈcisive** *a.* —**deˈcisively** *adv.*

THESAURUS

decapitate behead, execute, guillotine

decay *v.* **1.** atrophy, crumble, decline, degenerate, deteriorate, disintegrate, dissolve, dwindle, moulder, shrivel, sink, spoil, wane, waste away, wear away, wither **2.** corrode, decompose, mortify, perish, putrefy, rot ~*n.* **3.** atrophy, collapse, decadence, decline, degeneracy, degeneration, deterioration, dying, fading, failing, wasting, withering **4.** caries, cariosity, decomposition, gangrene, mortification, perishing, putrefaction, putrescence, putridity, rot, rotting

decease **1.** *n.* death, demise, departure, dissolution, dying, release **2.** *v.* cease, die, expire, pass away *or* on *or* over, perish

deceased *adj.* dead, defunct, departed, expired, finished, former, gone, late, lifeless, lost

deceit **1.** artifice, cheating, chicanery, craftiness, cunning, deceitfulness, deception, dissimulation, double-dealing, duplicity, fraud, fraudulence, guile, hypocrisy, imposition, pretence, slyness, treachery, trickery, underhandedness **2.** artifice, blind, cheat, chicanery, deception, duplicity, fake, feint, fraud, imposture, misrepresentation, pretence, ruse, sham, shift, stratagem, subterfuge, swindle, trick, wile

deceitful counterfeit, crafty, deceiving, deceptive, designing, dishonest, disingenuous, double-dealing, duplicitous, fallacious, false, fraudulent, guileful, hypocritical, illusory, insincere, knavish (*Archaic*), sneaky, treacherous, tricky, two-faced, underhand, untrustworthy

deceive bamboozle (*Inf.*), beguile, betray, cheat, con (*Sl.*), cozen, delude, disappoint, double-cross (*Inf.*), dupe, ensnare, entrap, fool, hoax, hoodwink, impose upon, lead (someone) on (*Inf.*), mislead, outwit, pull a fast one (*Sl.*), pull the wool over (someone's) eyes, swindle, take for a ride (*Inf.*), take in (*Inf.*), trick

decency appropriateness, civility, correctness, courtesy, decorum, etiquette, fitness, good form, good manners, modesty, propriety, respectability, seemliness

decent **1.** appropriate, becoming, befitting, chaste, comely, *comme il faut*, decorous, delicate, fit, fitting, modest, nice, polite, presentable, proper, pure, respectable, seemly, suitable **2.** acceptable, adequate, ample, average, competent, fair, passable, reasonable, satisfactory, sufficient, tolerable **3.** accommodating, courteous, friendly, generous, gracious, helpful, kind, obliging, thoughtful

deception **1.** craftiness, cunning, deceit, deceitfulness, deceptiveness, dissimulation, duplicity, fraud, fraudulence, guile, hypocrisy, imposition, insincerity, legerdemain, treachery, trickery **2.** artifice, bluff, cheat, decoy, feint, fraud, hoax, illusion, imposture, leg-pull (*Brit. inf.*), lie, ruse, sham, snare, stratagem, subterfuge, trick, wile

deceptive ambiguous, deceitful, delusive, dishonest, fake, fallacious, false, fraudulent, illusory, misleading, mock, specious, spurious, unreliable

decide adjudge, adjudicate, choose, come to a conclusion, commit oneself, conclude, decree, determine, elect, end, make a decision, make up one's mind, purpose, reach *or* come to a decision, resolve, settle

decided **1.** absolute, categorical, certain, clear-cut, definite, distinct, express, indisputable, positive, pronounced, unambiguous, undeniable, undisputed, unequivocal, unquestionable **2.** assertive, decisive, deliberate, determined, emphatic, firm, resolute, strong-willed, unfaltering, unhesitating

decidedly absolutely, certainly, clearly, decisively, distinctly, downright, positively, unequivocally, unmistakably

deciduous (dɪˈsɪdjʊəs) *a.* **1.** (of trees) losing leaves annually **2.** (of antlers, teeth *etc.*) being shed at the end of a period of growth

decigram (ˈdɛsɪɡræm) *n.* tenth of gram

decilitre *or U.S.* **deciliter** (ˈdɛsɪliːtə) *n.* tenth of litre

decimal (ˈdɛsɪməl) *a.* **1.** relating to tenths **2.** proceeding by tens —*n.* **3.** decimal fraction —**decimaliˈzation** *or* **-iˈsation** *n.* —**ˈdecimalize** *or* **-ise** *vt.* convert into decimal fractions or system —**decimal system** system of weights and measures or coinage, in which value of each denomination is ten times the one below it

decimate (ˈdɛsɪmeɪt) *vt.* kill a tenth or large proportion of —**deciˈmation** *n.* —**ˈdecimator** *n.*

decimetre *or U.S.* **decimeter** (ˈdɛsɪmiːtə) *n.* tenth of metre

decipher (dɪˈsaɪfə) *vt.* **1.** make out meaning of **2.** decode —**deˈcipherable** *a.*

deck (dɛk) *n.* **1.** platform or floor, *esp.* one covering whole or part of ship's hull **2.** turntable of record-player **3.** part of tape recorder supporting tapes —*vt.* **4.** array, decorate —**deck chair** folding chair made of canvas suspended in wooden frame —**deck hand 1.** seaman assigned duties on deck of ship **2. UK** seaman who has seen sea duty for at least one year **3.** helper aboard yacht

deckle edge (ˈdɛkᵊl) **1.** rough edge of paper oft. left as ornamentation **2.** imitation of this

declaim (dɪˈkleɪm) *vi.* **1.** speak dramatically, rhetorically or passionately **2.** protest loudly —**declamation** (dɛkləˈmeɪʃən) *n.* —**declamatory** (dɪˈklæmətərɪ) *a.*

declare (dɪˈklɛə) *vt.* **1.** announce formally **2.** state emphatically **3.** show **4.** name (as liable to customs duty) —*vi.* **5.** take sides (for) **6.** *Cricket* bring innings to an end before last wicket has fallen —**declaration** (dɛkləˈreɪʃən) *n.* —**declarative** (dɪˈklærətɪv) *or* **declaratory** (dɪˈklærətərɪ) *a.* —**deˈclarer** *n. Bridge* person who names trumps or calls 'No trumps'

declassify (diːˈklæsɪfaɪ) *vt.* release (document *etc.*) from security list (**-fying, -fied**) —**declassifiˈcation** *n.*

decline (dɪˈklaɪn) *v.* **1.** refuse **2.** list case endings of (nouns) —*vi.* **3.** slope, bend or sink downwards **4.** deteriorate gradually **5.** grow smaller, diminish —*n.* **6.** gradual deterioration **7.** movement downwards **8.** diminution **9.** downward slope —**declension** (dɪˈklɛnʃən) *n.* **1.** group of nouns **2.** falling off **3.** declining —**deˈclinable** *a.* —**decliˈnation** (dɛklɪˈneɪʃən) *n.* **1.** sloping away, deviation **2.** angle

declivity (dɪˈklɪvɪtɪ) *n.* downward slope

declutch (dɪˈklʌtʃ) *vi.* disengage clutch of car *etc.*

decoction (dɪˈkɒkʃən) *n.* **1.** extraction of essence by boiling down **2.** such essence —**deˈcoct** *vt.* boil down

decode (diːˈkəʊd) *vt.* convert from code into intelligible language

decoke (diːˈkəʊk) *vt. see* DECARBONIZE

décolleté (deɪˈkɒlteɪ) *a.* (of women's garment) having a low-cut neckline —**décolletage** (deɪkɒlˈtɑːʒ) *n.* low-cut dress or neckline

decommission (diːkəˈmɪʃən) *vt.* dismantle (industrial plant or nuclear reactor) to an extent such that it can be safely abandoned

decompose (diːkəmˈpəʊz) *v.* **1.** rot **2.** separate into elements —**decompoˈsition** *n.* decay

decompress (diːkəmˈprɛs) *vt.* **1.** free from pressure **2.** return to condition of normal atmospheric pressure —**decomˈpression** *n.* —**decompression sickness** *or* **illness** disorder characterized by severe pain *etc.*, caused by sudden change in atmospheric pressure

decongestant (diːkənˈdʒɛstənt) *a./n.* (drug) relieving (*esp.* nasal) congestion

decontaminate (diːkənˈtæmɪneɪt) *vt.* free from contamination, *eg* from poisons, radioactive substances *etc.* —**decontamiˈnation** *n.*

decontrol (diːkənˈtrəʊl) *vt.* release from state control (**-ll-**)

décor *or* **decor** (ˈdeɪkɔː) *n.* **1.** decorative scheme of room *etc.* **2.** stage decoration, scenery

THESAURUS

decipher construe, crack, decode, deduce, explain, figure out (*Inf.*), interpret, make out, read, reveal, solve, understand, unfold, unravel

decision 1. arbitration, conclusion, finding, judgment, outcome, resolution, result, ruling, sentence, settlement, verdict **2.** decisiveness, determination, firmness, purpose, purposefulness, resoluteness, resolution, resolve, strength of mind *or* will

decisive 1. absolute, conclusive, critical, crucial, definite, definitive, fateful, final, influential, momentous, positive, significant **2.** decided, determined, firm, forceful, incisive, resolute, strong-minded, trenchant

deck *v.* adorn, apparel (*Archaic*), array, attire, beautify, bedeck, bedight (*Archaic*), bedizen (*Archaic*), clothe, decorate, dress, embellish, festoon, garland, grace, ornament, trim

declaim harangue, hold forth, lecture, orate, perorate, proclaim, rant, recite, speak, spiel (*Inf.*)

declamation address, harangue, lecture, oration, rant, recitation, speech, tirade

declaration 1. acknowledgment, affirmation, assertion, attestation, averment, avowal, deposition, disclosure, protestation, revelation, statement, testimony **2.** announcement, edict, manifesto, notification, proclamation, profession, promulgation, pronouncement, pronunciamento

declarative, declaratory affirmative, definite, demonstrative, enunciatory, explanatory, expository, expressive, positive

declare 1. affirm, announce, assert, attest, aver, avow, certify, claim, confirm, maintain, proclaim, profess, pronounce, state, swear, testify, validate **2.** confess, convey, disclose, make known, manifest, reveal, show

decline *v.* **1.** avoid, deny, forgo, refuse, reject, say 'no', send one's regrets, turn down **2.** decrease, diminish, dwindle, ebb, fade, fail, fall, fall off, flag, lessen, shrink, sink, wane ~*n.* **3.** abatement, diminution, downturn, dwindling, falling off, lessening, recession, slump ~*v.* **4.** decay, degenerate, deteriorate, droop, languish, pine, weaken, worsen ~*n.* **5.** decay, decrepitude, degeneration, deterioration, enfeeblement, failing, senility, weakening, worsening ~*v.* **6.** descend, dip, sink, slant, slope ~*n.* **7.** declivity, hill, incline, slope

decompose 1. break up, crumble, decay, fall apart, fester, putrefy, rot, spoil **2.** analyse, atomize, break down, break up, decompound, disintegrate, dissect, dissolve, distil, separate

decomposition breakdown, corruption, decay, disin-

decorate ('dɛkəreɪt) *vt.* **1.** beautify by additions **2.** paint or wallpaper room *etc.* **3.** invest (with an order, medal *etc.*) —**deco'ration** *n.* —**'decorative** *a.* —**'decorator** *n.* —**Decorated style** 14th-century style of English architecture characterized by geometrical tracery *etc.*

decorum (dɪ'kɔːrəm) *n.* seemly behaviour, propriety, decency —**'decorous** *a.* —**'decorously** *adv.*

decoy ('diːkɔɪ, dɪ'kɔɪ) *n.* **1.** something used to entrap others or to distract their attention **2.** bait, lure —*v.* (dɪ'kɔɪ) **3.** lure, be lured as with decoy

decrease (dɪ'kriːs) *v.* **1.** diminish, lessen —*n.* ('diːkriːs, dɪ'kriːs) **2.** lessening

decree (dɪ'kriː) *n.* **1.** order having the force of law **2.** edict —*vt.* **3.** determine judicially **4.** order —**decree absolute** final decree in divorce proceedings, which leaves parties free to remarry —**decree nisi** decree coming into effect within a certain time, unless cause is shown for rescinding it (*esp.* in divorce cases)

decrement ('dɛkrɪmənt) *n.* **1.** act or state of decreasing **2.** quantity lost by decrease

decrepit (dɪ'krɛpɪt) *a.* **1.** old and feeble **2.** broken down, worn out —**de'crepitude** *n.*

decrescendo (diːkrɪ'ʃɛndəʊ) *a.* diminuendo

decretal (dɪ'kriːtᵊl) *n.* **1.** *R.C.Ch.* papal decree; edict on doctrine or church law —*a.* **2.** of decree

decry (dɪ'kraɪ) *vt.* disparage (**de'cried, de'crying**)

dedicate ('dɛdɪkeɪt) *vt.* **1.** commit wholly to special purpose or cause **2.** inscribe or address (book *etc.*) **3.** devote to God's service —**'dedicated** *a.* **1.** devoted to particular purpose or cause **2.** *Comp.* designed to fulfil one function **3.** manufactured for specific purpose —**dedi'cation** *n.* —**'dedicator** *n.* —**'dedicatory** *a.*

deduce (dɪ'djuːs) *vt.* draw as conclusion from facts —**de'duct** *vt.* take away, subtract —**de'ductible** *a.* **1.** capable of being deducted **2.** **US** tax-deductible —**de'duction** *n.* **1.** deducting **2.** amount subtracted **3.** conclusion deduced **4.** inference from general to particular —**de'ductive** *a.* —**de'ductively** *adv.*

deed (diːd) *n.* **1.** action **2.** exploit **3.** legal document —**deed box** strong box in which deeds and other documents are kept —**deed poll** *Law* deed made by one party only, *esp.* one by which person changes his name

deejay ('diːdʒeɪ) *inf.* disc jockey

deem (diːm) *vt.* judge, consider, regard —**'deemster** *n.* title of either of two justices in Isle of Man (*also* **'dempster**)

deep (diːp) *a.* **1.** extending far down, in or back **2.** at,

THESAURUS

tegration, dissolution, putrefaction, putrescence, putridity, rot

décor colour scheme, decoration, furnishing style, ornamentation

decorate 1. adorn, beautify, bedeck, deck, embellish, enrich, grace, ornament, trim 2. colour, do up (*Inf.*), furbish, paint, paper, renovate, wallpaper 3. cite, honour, pin a medal on

decoration 1. adornment, beautification, elaboration, embellishment, enrichment, garnishing, ornamentation, trimming 2. arabesque, bauble, curlicue, falderal, flounce, flourish, frill, furbelow, garnish, ornament, scroll, spangle, trimmings, trinket 3. award, badge, colours, emblem, garter, medal, order, ribbon, star

decorative adorning, arty-crafty, beautifying, enhancing, fancy, nonfunctional, ornamental, pretty

decorous appropriate, becoming, befitting, comely, *comme il faut*, correct, decent, dignified, fit, mannerly, polite, proper, refined, sedate, seemly, staid, suitable, well-behaved

decorum behaviour, breeding, courtliness, decency, deportment, dignity, etiquette, gentility, good grace, good manners, gravity, politeness, politesse, propriety, protocol, punctilio, respectability, seemliness

decoy 1. *n.* attraction, bait, ensnarement, enticement, inducement, lure, pretence, trap 2. *v.* allure, bait, deceive, ensnare, entice, entrap, inveigle, lure, seduce, tempt

decrease 1. *v.* abate, contract, curtail, cut down, decline, diminish, drop, dwindle, ease, fall off, lessen, lower, peter out, reduce, shrink, slacken, subside, wane 2. *n.* abatement, contraction, cutback, decline, diminution, downturn, dwindling, ebb, falling off, lessening, loss, reduction, shrinkage, subsidence

decree 1. *n.* act, command, dictum, edict, enactment, law, mandate, order, ordinance, precept, proclamation, regulation, ruling, statute 2. *v.* command, decide, determine, dictate, enact, lay down, ordain, order, prescribe, proclaim, pronounce, rule

decrepit 1. aged, crippled, debilitated, doddering, effete, feeble, frail, incapacitated, infirm, superannuated, wasted, weak 2. antiquated, battered, broken-down, deteriorated, dilapidated, ramshackle, rickety, run-down, tumble-down, weather-beaten, worn-out

decry abuse, belittle, blame, censure, condemn, criticize, cry down, denounce, depreciate, derogate, detract, devalue, discredit, disparage, rail against, run down, traduce, underestimate, underrate, undervalue

dedicate 1. commit, devote, give over to, pledge, surrender 2. address, assign, inscribe, offer 3. bless, consecrate, hallow, sanctify, set apart

dedicated committed, devoted, enthusiastic, given over to, purposeful, single-minded, sworn, wholehearted, zealous

dedication 1. adherence, allegiance, commitment, devotedness, devotion, faithfulness, loyalty, single-mindedness, wholeheartedness 2. address, inscription, message 3. consecration, hallowing, sanctification

deduce conclude, derive, draw, gather, glean, infer, reason, take to mean, understand

deduct decrease by, knock off (*Inf.*), reduce by, remove, subtract, take away, take from, take off, take out, withdraw

deduction 1. assumption, conclusion, consequence, corollary, finding, inference, reasoning, result 2. abatement, allowance, decrease, diminution, discount, reduction, subtraction, withdrawal

deed 1. achievement, act, action, exploit, fact, feat, performance, reality, truth 2. *Law* contract, document, indenture, instrument, title, title deed, transaction

deem account, believe, conceive, consider, esteem, estimate, hold, imagine, judge, reckon, regard, suppose, think

of given depth **3.** profound **4.** heartfelt **5.** hard to fathom **6.** cunning **7.** engrossed, immersed **8.** (of colour) dark and rich **9.** (of sound) low and full *—n.* **10.** deep place **11.** the sea *—adv.* **12.** far down *etc.* **—'deepen** *v.* **—'deeply** *adv.* **—deep field** *Cricket* position behind bowler, near boundary **—deep'freeze** *n.* refrigerator storing frozen food **—deep-laid** *a.* (of plot or plan) carefully worked out and kept secret **—deep-rooted** *or* **deep-seated** *a.* (of ideas *etc.*) firmly fixed or held; ingrained

deer (dɪə) *n.* family of ruminant animals typically with antlers in male (*pl.* **deer, -s**) **—'deerhound** *n.* large rough-coated dog **—'deerskin** *n.* hide of deer **—'deerstalker** *n.* **1.** one who stalks deer **2.** kind of cloth hat with peaks

def (dɛf) *a. sl.* (*esp.* of hip-hop) very good

deface (dɪ'feɪs) *vt.* **1.** spoil or mar surface of **2.** disfigure **—de'facement** *n.*

de facto (deɪ 'fæktəʊ) *Lat.* existing in fact, whether legally recognized or not

defalcate ('diːfælkeɪt) *vi. Law* misuse or misappropriate property or funds entrusted to one

defame (dɪ'feɪm) *vt.* speak ill of, dishonour by slander or rumour **—defamation** (dɛfə'meɪʃən) *n.* **—defamatory** (dɪ'fæmətərɪ) *a.*

default (dɪ'fɔːlt) *n.* **1.** failure to act, appear or pay *—vi.* **2.** fail (to pay) **—de'faulter** *n. esp.* soldier guilty of military offence **—in default of** in the absence of

defeat (dɪ'fiːt) *vt.* **1.** overcome, vanquish **2.** thwart *—n.* **3.** overthrow **4.** lost battle or encounter **5.** frustration **—de'featism** *n.* attitude tending to accept defeat **—de'featist** *n./a.*

defecate ('dɛfɪkeɪt) *vi.* **1.** empty the bowels *—vt.* **2.** clear of impurities **—defe'cation** *n.*

defect (dɪ'fɛkt, 'diːfɛkt) *n.* **1.** blemish, failing 2. lack *—vi.* (dɪ'fɛkt) **3.** desert one's country, cause *etc., esp.* to join opponents **—de'fection** *n.* abandonment of duty or allegiance **—de'fective** *a.* **1.** incomplete **2.** faulty

defend (dɪ'fɛnd) *vt.* **1.** protect **2.** support by argument, evidence **3.** (try to) maintain (title *etc.*) against challenger **—de'fence** *or U.S.* **de'fense** *n.* **—de'fendant** *n.* person accused in court **—de'fender** *n.* **—defensi'bility** *n.* **—de'fensible** *a.* **—de'fensive** *a.* **1.** serving for defence *—n.* **2.** position or attitude of defence

THESAURUS

deep *adj.* **1.** abyssal, bottomless, broad, far, profound, unfathomable, wide, yawning **2.** abstract, abstruse, arcane, esoteric, hidden, mysterious, obscure, recondite, secret **3.** artful, astute, canny, cunning, designing, devious, insidious, knowing, scheming, shrewd **4.** extreme, grave, great, intense, profound **5.** absorbed, engrossed, immersed, lost, preoccupied, rapt **6.** *Of a colour* dark, intense, rich, strong, vivid **7.** *Of a sound* bass, booming, full-toned, low, low-pitched, resonant, sonorous *~n.* **8.** *Usually preceded by* **the** briny (*Inf.*), high seas, main, ocean, sea *~adv.* **9.** deeply, far down, far into, late

deepen 1. dig out, dredge, excavate, hollow, scoop out, scrape out **2.** grow, increase, intensify, magnify, reinforce, strengthen

deeply 1. completely, gravely, profoundly, seriously, severely, thoroughly, to the heart, to the quick **2.** acutely, affectingly, distressingly, feelingly, intensely, mournfully, movingly, passionately, sadly

deep-rooted *or* **deep-seated** confirmed, entrenched, fixed, ineradicable, ingrained, inveterate, rooted, settled, subconscious, unconscious

deface blemish, deform, destroy, disfigure, impair, injure, mar, mutilate, obliterate, spoil, sully, tarnish, vandalize

defacement blemish, damage, destruction, disfigurement, distortion, impairment, injury, mutilation, vandalism

de facto actual, existing, real

defamation aspersion, calumny, character assassination, denigration, disparagement, libel, obloquy, opprobrium, scandal, slander, slur, smear, traducement, vilification

defamatory abusive, calumnious, contumelious, denigrating, derogatory, disparaging, injurious, insulting, libellous, slanderous, vilifying, vituperative

defame asperse, belie, besmirch, blacken, calumniate, cast a slur on, cast aspersions on, denigrate, detract, discredit, disgrace, dishonour, disparage, libel, malign, slander, smear, speak evil of, stigmatize, traduce, vilify, vituperate

default 1. *n.* absence, defect, deficiency, dereliction, failure, fault, lack, lapse, neglect, nonpayment, omission, want **2.** *v.* bilk, defraud, dodge, evade, fail, levant (*Brit.*), neglect, rat, swindle, welsh (*Sl.*)

defaulter delinquent, embezzler, levanter (*Brit.*), nonpayer, offender, peculator, welsher (*Sl.*)

defeat *v.* **1.** beat, conquer, crush, overpower, overthrow, overwhelm, quell, repulse, rout, subdue, subjugate, vanquish **2.** baffle, balk, confound, disappoint, discomfit, foil, frustrate, get the better of, ruin, thwart *~n.* **3.** beating, conquest, debacle, overthrow, repulse, rout, trouncing, vanquishment **4.** disappointment, discomfiture, failure, frustration, rebuff, repulse, reverse, setback, thwarting

defeatist 1. *n.* pessimist, prophet of doom, quitter, submitter, yielder **2.** *adj.* pessimistic

defect *n.* **1.** blemish, blotch, error, failing, fault, flaw, foible, imperfection, mistake, spot, taint, want **2.** absence, default, deficiency, frailty, inadequacy, lack, shortcoming, weakness *~v.* **3.** abandon, apostatize, break faith, change sides, desert, go over, rebel, revolt, tergiversate, walk out on (*Inf.*)

defection abandonment, apostasy, backsliding, dereliction, desertion, rebellion, revolt

defective broken, deficient, faulty, flawed, imperfect, inadequate, incomplete, insufficient, not working, out of order, scant, short

defence 1. armament, cover, deterrence, guard, immunity, protection, resistance, safeguard, security, shelter **2.** barricade, bastion, buckler, bulwark, buttress, fastness, fortification, rampart, shield **3.** apologia, apology, argument, excuse, exoneration, explanation, extenuation, justification, plea, vindication **4.** *Law* alibi, case, declaration, denial, plea, pleading, rebuttal, testimony

defend 1. cover, fortify, guard, keep safe, preserve, protect, safeguard, screen, secure, shelter, shield, ward off, watch over **2.** assert, champion, endorse, espouse, justify, maintain, plead, speak up for, stand by, stand up for, support, sustain, uphold, vindicate

defendant appellant, defence, litigant, offender, prisoner at the bar, respondent, the accused

defer[1] (dɪˈfɜː) *vt.* put off, postpone (-rr-) —**deˈferment** *n.*

defer[2] (dɪˈfɜː) *vi.* submit to opinion or judgment of another (-rr-) —**deference** (ˈdɛfərəns) *n.* respect for another inclining one to accept his views *etc.* —**deferential** (dɛfəˈrɛnʃəl) *a.* —**deferentially** (dɛfəˈrɛnʃəlɪ) *adv.*

defiance (dɪˈfaɪəns) *n. see* DEFY

deficient (dɪˈfɪʃənt) *a.* lacking or falling short in something, insufficient —**deˈficiency** *n.* —**deficit** (ˈdɛfɪsɪt, dɪˈfɪsɪt) *n.* amount by which sum of money is too small —**deficiency disease** any condition, such as pellagra, produced by lack of vitamins *etc.*

defile[1] (dɪˈfaɪl) *vt.* **1.** make dirty, pollute, soil **2.** sully **3.** desecrate —**deˈfilement** *n.*

defile[2] (ˈdiːfaɪl, dɪˈfaɪl) *n.* **1.** narrow pass or valley —*vi.* **2.** march in file

define (dɪˈfaɪn) *vt.* **1.** state contents or meaning of **2.** show clearly the form or outline of **3.** lay down clearly, fix **4.** mark out —**deˈfinable** *a.* —**definite** (ˈdɛfɪnɪt) *a.* **1.** exact, defined **2.** clear, specific **3.** certain, sure —**definitely** (ˈdɛfɪnɪtlɪ) *adv.* —**definition** (dɛfɪˈnɪʃən) *n.* —**definitive** (dɪˈfɪnɪtɪv) *a.* conclusive, to be looked on as final —**definitively** (dɪˈfɪnɪtɪvlɪ) *adv.*

deflate (diːˈfleɪt) *v.* **1.** (cause to) collapse by release of gas **2.** *Econ.* cause deflation of (an economy *etc.*) —*vt.* **3.** take away self-esteem from —**deˈflation** *n.* **1.** deflating **2.** *Econ.* reduction of economic and industrial activity —**deˈflationary** *a.*

deflect (dɪˈflɛkt) *v.* (cause to) turn from straight course —**deˈflection** *or* **deˈflexion** *n.*

deflower (diːˈflaʊə) *vt.* deprive of virginity, innocence *etc.* —**defloration** (diːflɔːˈreɪʃən) *n.*

defoliate (diːˈfəʊlɪeɪt) *v.* (cause to) lose leaves, *esp.* by action of chemicals —**deˈfoliant** *n.* —**defoliˈation** *n.*

deforest (diːˈfɒrɪst) *vt.* clear of trees —**deforestˈation** *n.*

deform (dɪˈfɔːm) *vt.* **1.** spoil shape of **2.** make ugly **3.** disfigure —**deforˈmation** *n.* —**deˈformed** *a.* —**deˈformity** *n.*

defraud (dɪˈfrɔːd) *vt.* cheat, swindle

THESAURUS

defender **1.** bodyguard, escort, guard, protector **2.** advocate, champion, patron, sponsor, supporter, vindicator

defensible **1.** holdable, impregnable, safe, secure, unassailable **2.** justifiable, pardonable, permissible, plausible, tenable, valid, vindicable

defensive averting, defending, on the defensive, opposing, protective, safeguarding, uptight (*Sl.*), watchful, withstanding

defer[1] adjourn, delay, hold over, postpone, procrastinate, prorogue, protract, put off, put on ice, set aside, shelve, suspend, table

defer[2] accede, bow, capitulate, comply, give in, give way to, respect, submit, yield

deference **1.** acquiescence, capitulation, complaisance, compliance, obedience, obeisance, submission, yielding **2.** attention, civility, consideration, courtesy, esteem, homage, honour, obeisance, politeness, regard, respect, reverence, thoughtfulness, veneration

deferential civil, complaisant, considerate, courteous, dutiful, ingratiating, obedient, obeisant, obsequious, polite, regardful, respectful, reverential, submissive

deferment adjournment, delay, moratorium, postponement, putting off, stay, suspension

defiance challenge, confrontation, contempt, contumacy, disobedience, disregard, insolence, insubordination, opposition, provocation, rebelliousness, recalcitrance, spite

defiant aggressive, audacious, bold, challenging, contumacious, daring, disobedient, insolent, insubordinate, mutinous, provocative, rebellious, recalcitrant, refractory, truculent

deficiency **1.** defect, demerit, failing, fault, flaw, frailty, imperfection, shortcoming, weakness **2.** absence, dearth, deficit, inadequacy, insufficiency, lack, scantiness, scarcity, shortage

deficient **1.** defective, faulty, flawed, impaired, imperfect, incomplete, inferior, unsatisfactory, weak **2.** exiguous, inadequate, insufficient, lacking, meagre, scanty, scarce, short, skimpy, wanting

deficit arrears, default, deficiency, loss, shortage, shortfall

define **1.** characterize, describe, designate, detail, determine, explain, expound, interpret, specify, spell out **2.** bound, circumscribe, delimit, delineate, demarcate, limit, mark out, outline

definite **1.** clear, clear-cut, clearly defined, determined, exact, explicit, express, fixed, marked, obvious, particular, precise, specific **2.** assured, certain, decided, guaranteed, positive, settled, sure

definitely absolutely, beyond any doubt, categorically, certainly, clearly, decidedly, easily, far and away, finally, indubitably, obviously, plainly, positively, surely, undeniably, unequivocally, unmistakably, unquestionably, without doubt, without fail, without question

definition **1.** clarification, description, elucidation, explanation, exposition, statement of meaning **2.** delimitation, delineation, demarcation, determination, fixing, outlining, settling **3.** clarity, contrast, distinctness, focus, precision, sharpness

definitive absolute, authoritative, complete, conclusive, decisive, exhaustive, final, perfect, reliable, ultimate

deflate **1.** collapse, contract, empty, exhaust, flatten, puncture, shrink, void **2.** chasten, dash, debunk (*Inf.*), disconcert, dispirit, humble, humiliate, mortify, put down (*Sl.*), squash, take the wind out of (someone's) sails **3.** *Economics* decrease, depreciate, depress, devalue, diminish, reduce

deflect bend, deviate, diverge, glance off, ricochet, shy, sidetrack, slew, swerve, turn, turn aside, twist, veer, wind

deflection aberration, bend, declination, deviation, divergence, drift, refraction, swerve, veer

deform **1.** buckle, contort, distort, gnarl, malform, mangle, misshape, twist, warp **2.** cripple, deface, disfigure, injure, maim, mar, mutilate, ruin, spoil

deformed bent, blemished, crippled, crooked, disfigured, distorted, maimed, malformed, mangled, marred, misbegotten, misshapen

deformity abnormality, defect, disfigurement, distor-

defray (dɪˈfreɪ) *vt.* provide money for (expenses *etc.*)

defrock (diːˈfrɒk) *vt.* deprive (priest, minister) of ecclesiastical status

defrost (diːˈfrɒst) *v.* **1.** make, become free of frost, ice **2.** thaw

deft (dɛft) *a.* skilful, adroit —ˈ**deftly** *adv.* —ˈ**deftness** *n.*

defunct (dɪˈfʌŋkt) *a.* **1.** dead **2.** obsolete

defuse *or U.S. (sometimes)* **defuze** (diːˈfjuːz) *vt.* **1.** remove fuse of (bomb *etc.*) **2.** remove tension from (situation *etc.*)

defy (dɪˈfaɪ) *vt.* **1.** challenge, resist successfully **2.** disregard (**deˈfied, deˈfying**) —**deˈfiance** *n.* resistance —**deˈfiant** *a.* **1.** openly and aggressively hostile **2.** insolent —**deˈfiantly** *adv.*

degauss (diːˈgaʊs) *vt.* equip (ship) with apparatus which prevents it detonating magnetic mines

degenerate (dɪˈdʒɛnəreɪt) *vi.* **1.** deteriorate to lower mental, moral or physical level —*a.* (dɪˈdʒɛnərɪt) **2.** fallen away in quality —*n.* (dɪˈdʒɛnərɪt) **3.** degenerate person —**deˈgeneracy** *n.* —**degeneˈration** *n.* —**deˈgenerative** *a.*

degrade (dɪˈgreɪd) *vt.* **1.** dishonour **2.** debase **3.** reduce to lower rank —*vi.* **4.** decompose chemically —**deˈgradable** *a.* capable of chemical, biological decomposition —**degradation** (dɛgrəˈdeɪʃən) *n.* —**deˈgraded** *a.* shamed, humiliated

degree (dɪˈgriː) *n.* **1.** step, stage in process, scale, relative rank, order, condition, manner, way **2.** university rank **3.** unit of measurement of temperature or angle —**third degree** severe, lengthy examination, *esp.* of accused person by police, to extract information, confession

dehiscent (dɪˈhɪsˀnt) *a.* opening, as capsule of plant —**deˈhisce** *vi.* burst open —**deˈhiscence** *n.*

dehumanize *or* **-ise** (diːˈhjuːmənaɪz) *vt.* **1.** deprive of human qualities **2.** render mechanical, artificial or routine

dehumidify (diːhjuːˈmɪdɪfaɪ) *vt.* extract moisture from

dehydrate (diːˈhaɪdreɪt) *vt.* remove moisture from —**dehyˈdration** *n.*

de-ice (diːˈaɪs) *vt.* dislodge ice from (*eg* windscreen) or prevent its forming

deify (ˈdiːɪfaɪ, ˈdeɪ-) *vt.* make god of, treat, worship as god (ˈ**deified,** ˈ**deifying**) —**deifiˈcation** *n.* —ˈ**deiform** *a.* godlike in form

deign (deɪn) *vi.* **1.** condescend, stoop **2.** think fit

deism (ˈdiːɪzəm, ˈdeɪ-) *n.* belief in god but not in revelation —ˈ**deist** *n.* —**deˈistic** *a.* —ˈ**deity** *n.* **1.** divine status or attributes **2.** a god

déjà vu (ˈdeɪʒæ ˈvuː) *Fr.* experience of perceiving new situation as if it had occurred before

deject (dɪˈdʒɛkt) *vt.* dishearten, cast down, depress —**deˈjected** *a.* —**deˈjection** *n.*

de jure (deɪ ˈdʒʊəreɪ) *Lat.* in law, by right

dekko (ˈdɛkəʊ) *n. sl.* look

delay (dɪˈleɪ) *vt.* **1.** postpone, hold back —*vi.* **2.** be tardy, linger (**deˈlayed, deˈlaying**) —*n.* **3.** act or instance of delaying **4.** interval of time between events

THESAURUS

tion, irregularity, malformation, misproportion, misshapenness, ugliness

defraud beguile, bilk, cheat, con (*Sl.*), cozen, delude, diddle (*Inf.*), do (*Sl.*), dupe, embezzle, fleece, gull (*Archaic*), gyp (*Sl.*), outwit, pilfer, pull a fast one on (*Inf.*), rip off (*Sl.*), rob, rook (*Sl.*), swindle, trick

deft able, adept, adroit, agile, clever, dexterous, expert, handy, neat, nimble, proficient, skilful

defunct **1.** dead, deceased, departed, extinct, gone **2.** a dead letter, bygone, expired, inoperative, invalid, nonexistent, not functioning, obsolete, out of commission

defy **1.** beard, brave, challenge, confront, contemn, dare, despise, disregard, face, flout, hurl defiance at, provoke, scorn, slight, spurn **2.** baffle, defeat, elude, foil, frustrate, repel, repulse, resist, thwart, withstand

degenerate **1.** *adj.* base, corrupt, debased, debauched, decadent, degenerated, degraded, depraved, deteriorated, dissolute, fallen, immoral, low, mean, perverted **2.** *v.* decay, decline, decrease, deteriorate, fall off, lapse, regress, retrogress, rot, sink, slip, worsen

degeneration debasement, decline, degeneracy, descent, deterioration, dissipation, dissolution, regression

degradation **1.** abasement, debasement, decadence, decline, degeneracy, degeneration, demotion, derogation, deterioration, downgrading, perversion **2.** discredit, disgrace, dishonour, humiliation, ignominy, mortification, shame

degrade **1.** cheapen, corrupt, debase, demean, deteriorate, discredit, disgrace, dishonour, humble, humiliate, impair, injure, pervert, shame, vitiate **2.** break, cashier, demote, depose, downgrade, lower, reduce to inferior rank

degraded abandoned, base, corrupt, debased, debauched, decadent, depraved, despicable, disgraced, disreputable, dissolute, low, mean, profligate, sordid, vicious, vile

degree **1.** class, grade, level, order, position, rank, standing, station, status **2.** division, extent, gradation, grade, interval, limit, mark, measure, notch, point, rung, scale, stage, step, unit **3.** calibre, extent, intensity, level, measure, proportion, quality, quantity, range, rate, ratio, scale, scope, severity, standard

deign condescend, consent, deem worthy, lower oneself, see fit, stoop, think fit

deity celestial being, divine being, divinity, god, goddess, godhead, idol, immortal, supreme being

dejected blue, cast down, crestfallen, depressed, despondent, disconsolate, disheartened, dismal, doleful, down, downcast, downhearted, gloomy, glum, low, low-spirited, melancholy, miserable, morose, sad, woebegone, wretched

dejection blues, depression, despair, despondency, doldrums, downheartedness, dumps (*Inf.*), gloom, gloominess, heavy-heartedness, low spirits, melancholy, sadness, sorrow, unhappiness

de jure according to the law, by right, legally, rightfully

delay *v.* **1.** defer, hold over, postpone, procrastinate, prolong, protract, put off, shelve, stall, suspend, table, temporize ~*n.* **2.** deferment, postponement, procrastination, stay, suspension ~*v.* **3.** arrest, bog down, check, detain, halt, hinder, hold back, hold up, impede, obstruct, retard, set back, slow up, stop

delectable (dɪˈlɛktəbᵊl) *a.* delightful —**delecˈtation** *n.* pleasure

delegate (ˈdɛlɪgeɪt, -gɪt) *n.* **1.** person chosen to represent another —*vt.* (ˈdɛlɪgeɪt) **2.** send as deputy **3.** commit (authority, business *etc.*) to a deputy —**ˈdelegacy** *n.* —**deleˈgation** *n.*

delete (dɪˈliːt) *vt.* remove, cancel, erase —**deˈletion** *n.*

deleterious (dɛlɪˈtɪərɪəs) *a.* harmful, injurious

Delft (dɛlft) *n.* **1.** town in Netherlands **2.** tin-glazed earthenware orig. from Delft, usu. with blue decoration on white ground (*also* **ˈdelftware**)

deliberate (dɪˈlɪbərɪt) *a.* **1.** intentional **2.** well-considered **3.** without haste, slow —*vt.* (dɪˈlɪbəreɪt) **4.** consider, debate —**deˈliberately** *adv.* —**delibeˈration** *n.* —**deˈliberative** *a.*

delicate (ˈdɛlɪkɪt) *a.* **1.** exquisite **2.** not robust, fragile **3.** sensitive **4.** requiring tact **5.** deft —**ˈdelicacy** *n.* —**ˈdelicately** *adv.*

delicatessen (dɛlɪkəˈtɛsᵊn) *n.* shop selling *esp.* imported or unusual foods

delicious (dɪˈlɪʃəs) *a.* delightful, pleasing to senses, *esp.* taste —**deˈliciously** *adv.*

delight (dɪˈlaɪt) *vt.* **1.** please greatly —*vi.* **2.** take great pleasure (in) —*n.* **3.** great pleasure —**deˈlightful** *a.* charming

delimitation (diːlɪmɪˈteɪʃən) *n.* assigning of boundaries —**deˈlimit** *vt.*

delineate (dɪˈlɪnɪeɪt) *vt.* portray by drawing or description —**delineˈation** *n.* —**deˈlineator** *n.*

delinquent (dɪˈlɪŋkwənt) *n.* someone, *esp.* young person, guilty of delinquency —**deˈlinquency** *n.* (minor) offence or misdeed

deliquesce (dɛlɪˈkwɛs) *vi.* become liquid —**deliˈquescence** *n.* —**deliˈquescent** *a.*

delirium (dɪˈlɪrɪəm) *n.* **1.** disorder of the mind, *esp.* in feverish illness **2.** violent excitement (*pl.* **-s, -liria** (-ˈlɪrɪə)) —**deˈlirious** *a.* **1.** raving **2.** light-headed, wildly excited —**delirium tremens** (ˈtrɛmɛnz, ˈtriː-) disordered mental state produced by advanced alcoholism (*also* **D.T.s**)

deliver (dɪˈlɪvə) *vt.* **1.** carry (goods *etc.*) to destination

THESAURUS

~*n.* **4.** check, detention, hindrance, hold-up, impediment, interruption, interval, obstruction, setback, stoppage, wait ~*v.* **5.** dawdle, dilly-dally (*Inf.*), drag, lag, linger, loiter, tarry ~*n.* **6.** dawdling, dilly-dallying (*Inf.*), lingering, loitering, tarrying

delectable adorable, agreeable, appetizing, charming, dainty, delicious, delightful, enjoyable, enticing, gratifying, inviting, luscious, lush, pleasant, pleasurable, satisfying, scrumptious (*Inf.*), tasty, toothsome, yummy (*Sl.*)

delegate *n.* **1.** agent, ambassador, commissioner, deputy, envoy, legate, representative, vicar ~*v.* **2.** accredit, appoint, authorize, commission, depute, designate, empower, mandate **3.** assign, consign, devolve, entrust, give, hand over, pass on, relegate, transfer

delegation 1. commission, contingent, deputation, embassy, envoys, legation, mission **2.** assignment, commissioning, committal, deputizing, devolution, entrustment, relegation

delete blot out, blue-pencil, cancel, cross out, cut out, dele, edit, edit out, efface, erase, expunge, obliterate, remove, rub out, strike out

deliberate *v.* **1.** cogitate, consider, consult, debate, discuss, meditate, mull over, ponder, reflect, think, weigh ~*adj.* **2.** calculated, conscious, considered, designed, intentional, planned, prearranged, premeditated, purposeful, studied, thoughtful, wilful **3.** careful, cautious, circumspect, heedful, measured, methodical, ponderous, prudent, slow, thoughtful, unhurried, wary

deliberately by design, calculatingly, consciously, determinedly, emphatically, in cold blood, intentionally, knowingly, on purpose, pointedly, resolutely, studiously, wilfully, wittingly

deliberation 1. calculation, care, carefulness, caution, circumspection, cogitation, consideration, coolness, forethought, meditation, prudence, purpose, reflection, speculation, study, thought, wariness **2.** conference, consultation, debate, discussion

delicacy 1. accuracy, daintiness, elegance, exquisiteness, fineness, lightness, nicety, precision, subtlety **2.** debility, flimsiness, fragility, frailness, frailty, infirmity, slenderness, tenderness, weakness **3.** discrimination, fastidiousness, finesse, purity, refinement, sensibility, sensitiveness, sensitivity, tact, taste

delicate 1. ailing, debilitated, flimsy, fragile, frail, sickly, slender, slight, tender, weak **2.** choice, dainty, delicious, elegant, exquisite, fine, graceful, savoury, tender **3.** accurate, deft, detailed, minute, precise, skilled **4.** considerate, diplomatic, discreet, sensitive, tactful **5.** critical, difficult, precarious, sensitive, sticky (*Inf.*), ticklish, touchy **6.** careful, critical, discriminating, fastidious, prudish, pure, refined, scrupulous, squeamish

delicately carefully, daintily, deftly, elegantly, exquisitely, fastidiously, finely, gracefully, lightly, precisely, sensitively, skilfully, softly, subtly, tactfully

delicious 1. ambrosial, appetizing, choice, dainty, delectable, luscious, mouthwatering, nectareous, palatable, savoury, scrumptious (*Inf.*), tasty, toothsome, yummy (*Sl.*) **2.** agreeable, charming, delightful, enjoyable, entertaining, exquisite, pleasant, pleasing

delight *n.* **1.** ecstasy, enjoyment, felicity, gladness, gratification, happiness, joy, pleasure, rapture, transport ~*v.* **2.** amuse, charm, cheer, divert, enchant, gratify, please, ravish, rejoice, satisfy, thrill **3.** *With* **in** appreciate, enjoy, feast on, glory in, indulge in, like, love, luxuriate in, relish, revel in, savour

delightful agreeable, amusing, captivating, charming, congenial, delectable, enchanting, engaging, enjoyable, entertaining, fascinating, gratifying, heavenly, pleasant, pleasing, pleasurable, rapturous, ravishing, thrilling

delinquency crime, fault, misbehaviour, misconduct, misdeed, misdemeanour, offence, wrongdoing

delinquent criminal, culprit, defaulter, juvenile delinquent, lawbreaker, malefactor, miscreant, offender, wrongdoer, young offender

delirious 1. crazy, demented, deranged, incoherent, insane, light-headed, mad, raving, unhinged **2.** beside oneself, carried away, corybantic, ecstatic, excited, frantic, frenzied, hysterical, wild

delirium 1. aberration, derangement, hallucination, insanity, lunacy, madness, raving **2.** ecstasy, fever, frenzy, fury, hysteria, passion, rage

2. hand over 3. release 4. give birth (to) or assist in birth (of) 5. utter or present (speech *etc.*) —**de'liverance** *n.* rescue —**de'liverer** *n.* —**de'livery** *n.*

dell (dɛl) *n.* wooded hollow

Delphic ('dɛlfɪk) *or* **Delphian** *a.* pert. to Delphi or to the oracle of Apollo

delphinium (dɛl'fɪnɪəm) *n.* garden plant with tall spikes of usu. blue flowers (*pl.* **-s, -ia** (-ɪə))

delta ('dɛltə) *n.* 1. alluvial tract where river at mouth breaks into several streams 2. fourth letter in Gr. alphabet (Δ or δ) 3. shape of this letter —**delta wing** triangular swept-back aircraft wing

delude (dɪ'lu:d) *vt.* 1. deceive 2. mislead —**de'lusion** *n.* —**de'lusive** *a.*

deluge ('dɛlju:dʒ) *n.* 1. flood, great flow 2. rush 3. downpour, cloudburst —*vt.* 4. flood 5. overwhelm

de luxe (də 'lʌks, 'lʊks) 1. rich, sumptuous 2. superior in quality

delve (dɛlv) *v.* 1. (*with* into) search intensively 2. dig

demagnetize *or* **-ise** (di:'mægnətaɪz) *vt.* deprive of magnetic polarity

demagogue *or U.S.* (*sometimes*) **demagog** ('dɛməgɒg) *n.* mob leader or agitator —**demagogic** (dɛmə'gɒgɪk) *a.* —**demagogy** ('dɛməgɒgɪ) *n.*

deman (di:'mæn) *vt.* **UK** reduce the manpower of (plant, industry *etc.*)

demand (dɪ'mɑ:nd) *vt.* 1. ask as giving an order 2. ask as by right 3. call for as due, right or necessary —*n.* 4. urgent request, claim, requirement 5. call (for specific commodity) —**de'manding** *a.* requiring great skill, patience *etc.*

demarcate ('di:mɑ:keɪt) *vt.* mark boundaries or limits of —**demar'cation** *or* **demar'kation** *n.*

demean (dɪ'mi:n) *vt.* degrade, lower, humiliate

demeanour *or U.S.* **demeanor** (dɪ'mi:nə) *n.* 1. conduct, behaviour 2. bearing

demented (dɪ'mɛntɪd) *a.* 1. mad, crazy 2. beside oneself —**dementia** (dɪ'mɛnʃə, -ʃɪə) *n.* form of insanity

demerara (dɛmə'rɛərə, -'rɑ:rə) *n.* kind of brown cane sugar

demerge (dɪ'mɜ:dʒ) *v.* 1. split (business concern) into two or more independent companies —*vi.* 2. (of companies) be so split 3. undo previous merger —**de'merger** *n.*

demerit (di:'mɛrɪt) *n.* 1. bad point 2. undesirable quality

demesne (dɪ'meɪn, -'mi:n) *n.* 1. estate, territory 2. sphere of action —**hold in demesne** have unrestricted possession of

demi- (*comb. form*) half, as in *demigod.* Such words are not given here where the meaning may be inferred from the simple word

demijohn ('dɛmɪdʒɒn) *n.* large wicker-cased bottle

demilitarize *or* **-ise** (di:'mɪlɪtəraɪz) *vt.* prohibit military presence or function in (an area) —**demilitari'zation** *or* **-i'sation** *n.*

demimonde (dɛmɪ'mɒnd) *n.* class of women of doubtful reputation

demise (dɪ'maɪz) *n.* 1. death 2. conveyance by will or lease 3. transfer of sovereignty on death or abdication —*vt.* 4. convey to another by will 5. lease

demisemiquaver ('dɛmɪsɛmɪkweɪvə) *n. Mus.* note having time value of one thirty-second of semibreve

THESAURUS

deliver 1. bear, bring, carry, cart, convey, distribute, transport 2. cede, commit, give up, grant, hand over, make over, relinquish, resign, surrender, transfer, turn over, yield 3. acquit, discharge, emancipate, free, liberate, loose, ransom, redeem, release, rescue, save 4. announce, declare, give, give forth, present, proclaim, pronounce, publish, read, utter

deliverance emancipation, escape, liberation, ransom, redemption, release, rescue, salvation

delivery 1. consignment, conveyance, dispatch, distribution, handing over, surrender, transfer, transmission, transmittal 2. articulation, elocution, enunciation, intonation, speech, utterance 3. *Medical* childbirth, confinement, labour, parturition 4. deliverance, escape, liberation, release, rescue

delude bamboozle (*Inf.*), beguile, cheat, con (*Sl.*), cozen, deceive, dupe, fool, gull (*Archaic*), hoax, hoodwink, impose on, lead up the garden path (*Inf.*), misguide, mislead, take in (*Inf.*), trick

deluge *n.* 1. cataclysm, downpour, flood, inundation, overflowing, spate, torrent 2. *Fig.* avalanche, barrage, flood, rush, spate, torrent ~*v.* 3. douse, drench, drown, flood, inundate, soak, submerge, swamp 4. *Fig.* engulf, inundate, overload, overrun, overwhelm, swamp

delusion deception, error, fallacy, false impression, fancy, hallucination, illusion, misapprehension, misbelief, misconception, mistake, phantasm, self-deception

de luxe choice, costly, elegant, exclusive, expensive, grand, luxurious, opulent, palatial, plush (*Inf.*), rich, select, special, splendid, sumptuous, superior

delve burrow, dig into, examine, explore, ferret out, investigate, look into, probe, ransack, research, rummage, search, unearth

demagogue agitator, firebrand, haranguer, rabble-rouser, soapbox orator

demand *v.* 1. ask, challenge, inquire, interrogate, question, request 2. call for, cry out for, involve, necessitate, need, require, take, want 3. claim, exact, expect, insist on, order ~*n.* 4. bidding, charge, inquiry, interrogation, order, question, request, requisition 5. call, claim, necessity, need, requirement, want

demanding 1. challenging, difficult, exacting, exhausting, exigent, hard, taxing, tough, trying, wearing 2. clamorous, imperious, importunate, insistent, nagging, pressing, urgent

demarcate define, delimit, determine, differentiate, distinguish between, fix, mark, separate

demarcation 1. bound, boundary, confine, enclosure, limit, margin 2. delimitation, differentiation, distinction, division, separation

demean abase, debase, degrade, descend, humble, lower, stoop

demeanour air, bearing, behaviour, carriage, comportment, conduct, deportment, manner, mien

demented crackbrained, crazed, crazy, daft (*Sl.*), deranged, distraught, dotty (*Sl.*), foolish, frenzied, idiotic, insane, lunatic, mad, maniacal, manic, *non compos mentis,* unbalanced, unhinged

demist (diːˈmɪst) *v.* free or become free of condensation **—deˈmister** *n.*

demiurge (ˈdɛmɪɜːdʒ) *n.* name given in some philosophies (*esp.* Platonic) to the creator of the world and man

demo (ˈdɛməʊ) *inf.* demonstration

demob (diːˈmɒb) *vt. inf.* demobilize (**-bb-**)

demobilize *or* **-ise** (diːˈməʊbɪlaɪz) *vt.* **1.** disband (troops) **2.** discharge (soldier) **—demobiliˈzation** *or* **-iˈsation** *n.*

democracy (dɪˈmɒkrəsɪ) *n.* **1.** government by the people or their elected representatives **2.** state so governed **—ˈdemocrat** *n.* advocate of democracy **—demoˈcratic** *a.* **1.** connected with democracy **2.** favouring popular rights **—demoˈcratically** *adv.* **—democratiˈzation** *or* **-iˈsation** *n.* **—deˈmocratize** *or* **-ise** *vt.*

demodulation (diːmɒdjʊˈleɪʃən) *n. Electron.* process by which output wave or signal is obtained having characteristics of original modulating wave or signal

demography (dɪˈmɒgrəfɪ) *n.* study of population statistics, as births, deaths, diseases **—deˈmographer** *n.* **—demoˈgraphic** *a.*

demolish (dɪˈmɒlɪʃ) *vt.* **1.** knock down (buildings *etc.*) **2.** destroy utterly **3.** overthrow **—demoˈlition** *n.*

demon (ˈdiːmən) *n.* **1.** devil, evil spirit **2.** very cruel or malignant person **3.** person very good at or devoted to a given activity **—demoniac** (dɪˈməʊnɪæk) *n.* one possessed with a devil **—demoˈniacal** *a.* **—deˈmonic** *a.* of the nature of a devil **—demoˈnology** *n.* study of demons

demonetize *or* **-ise** (diːˈmʌnɪtaɪz) *vt.* **1.** deprive (metal) of its capacity as monetary standard **2.** withdraw from use as currency **—demonetiˈzation** *or* **-iˈsation** *n.*

demonstrate (ˈdɛmənstreɪt) *vt.* **1.** show by reasoning, prove **2.** describe, explain by specimens or experiments *—vi.* **3.** make exhibition of support, protest *etc.* by public parade, rally **4.** make show of armed force **—deˈmonstrable** *a.* **—deˈmonstrably** *adv.* **—demonˈstration** *n.* **1.** making clear, proving by evidence **2.** exhibition and description **3.** organized expression of public opinion **4.** display of armed force **—deˈmonstrative** *a.* **1.** expressing feelings, emotions easily and unreservedly **2.** pointing out **3.** conclusive **—ˈdemonstrator** *n.* **1.** one who demonstrates equipment, products *etc.* **2.** one who takes part in a public demonstration **3.** professor's assistant in laboratory *etc.*

demoralize *or* **-ise** (dɪˈmɒrəlaɪz) *vt.* **1.** deprive of courage and discipline **2.** undermine morally **—demoraliˈzation** *or* **-iˈsation** *n.*

demote (dɪˈməʊt) *vt.* reduce in status or rank **—deˈmotion** *n.*

demotic (dɪˈmɒtɪk) *a.* **1.** of common people; popular **2.** of simplified form of hieroglyphics used in ancient Egypt *—n.* **3.** demotic script of ancient Egypt

demur (dɪˈmɜː) *vi.* **1.** make difficulties, object (**-rr-**) *—n.* **2.** raising of objection **3.** objection raised **—deˈmurrer** *n. Law* exception taken to opponent's point

demure (dɪˈmjʊə) *a.* reserved, quiet **—deˈmurely** *adv.*

demurrage (dɪˈmʌrɪdʒ) *n.* charge for keeping ship *etc.* beyond time agreed for unloading

demystify (diːˈmɪstɪfaɪ) *vt.* remove mystery from; make clear **—demystifiˈcation** *n.*

den (dɛn) *n.* **1.** cave or hole of wild beast **2.** lair **3.** small room, *esp.* study **4.** site, haunt

denarius (dɪˈnɛərɪəs) *n.* **1.** ancient Roman silver coin, oft. called penny in translation **2.** gold coin worth 25 silver denarii (*pl.* **-narii** (-ˈnɛərɪaɪ))

denary (ˈdiːnərɪ) *a.* **1.** calculated by tens; decimal **2.** containing ten parts; tenfold

denationalize *or* **-ise** (diːˈnæʃənəˈlaɪz) *vt.* return (an industry) from public to private ownership **—denationaliˈzation** *or* **-iˈsation** *n.*

denature (diːˈneɪtʃə) *or* **denaturize, -ise** (diː-

THESAURUS

democracy commonwealth, government by the people, representative government, republic

democratic autonomous, egalitarian, popular, populist, representative, republican, self-governing

demolish **1.** bulldoze, destroy, dismantle, flatten, knock down, level, overthrow, pulverize, raze, ruin, tear down **2.** *Fig.* annihilate, defeat, destroy, overthrow, overturn, undo, wreck

demolition bulldozing, destruction, explosion, knocking down, levelling, razing, wrecking

demon **1.** devil, evil spirit, fiend, goblin, malignant spirit **2.** *Fig.* devil, fiend, monster, rogue, villain **3.** ace (*Inf.*), addict, fanatic, fiend, go-getter (*Inf.*), master, wizard

demonic, demoniacal **1.** devilish, diabolic, diabolical, fiendish, hellish, infernal, satanic **2.** crazed, frantic, frenetic, frenzied, furious, hectic, like one possessed, mad, maniacal, manic

demonstrable attestable, axiomatic, certain, evident, evincible, incontrovertible, indubitable, irrefutable, obvious, palpable, positive, provable, self-evident, undeniable, unmistakable, verifiable

demonstrate **1.** display, establish, evidence, evince, exhibit, indicate, manifest, prove, show, testify to **2.** describe, explain, illustrate, make clear, show how, teach **3.** march, parade, picket, protest, rally

demonstration **1.** affirmation, confirmation, display, evidence, exhibition, expression, illustration, manifestation, proof, substantiation, testimony, validation **2.** description, explanation, exposition, presentation, test, trial **3.** march, mass lobby, parade, picket, protest, rally, sit-in

demonstrative **1.** affectionate, effusive, emotional, expansive, expressive, gushing, loving, open, unreserved, unrestrained **2.** evincive, explanatory, expository, illustrative, indicative, symptomatic

demoralize **1.** cripple, daunt, deject, depress, disconcert, discourage, dishearten, dispirit, enfeeble, rattle (*Inf.*), sap, shake, undermine, unnerve, weaken **2.** corrupt, debase, debauch, deprave, lower, pervert, vitiate

demur **1.** *v.* balk, cavil, disagree, dispute, doubt, hesitate, object, pause, protest, refuse, take exception, waver **2.** *n.* compunction, demurral, demurrer, dissent, hesitation, misgiving, objection, protest, qualm, scruple

demure decorous, diffident, grave, modest, reserved, reticent, retiring, sedate, shy, sober, staid, unassuming

den **1.** cave, cavern, haunt, hide-out, hole, lair, shelter **2.** cloister, cubbyhole, hideaway, retreat, sanctuary, sanctum, snuggery, study

ˈneɪtʃəraɪz) *vt.* deprive of essential qualities, adulterate —**denatured alcohol** spirit made undrinkable

dendrology (dɛnˈdrɒlədʒɪ) *n.* natural history of trees

dene *or* **dean** (diːn) *n.* valley

dengue (ˈdɛŋgɪ) *or* **dandy** *n.* infectious tropical fever

denial (dɪˈnaɪəl) *n. see* DENY

denier (ˈdɛnɪeɪ, ˈdɛnjə) *n.* unit of weight of silk, rayon and nylon yarn

denigrate (ˈdɛnɪgreɪt) *vt.* belittle or disparage character of

denim (ˈdɛnɪm) *n.* strong cotton drill for trousers, overalls *etc.*

denizen (ˈdɛnɪzən) *n.* inhabitant

denominate (dɪˈnɒmɪneɪt) *vt.* give name to —**denomiˈnation** *n.* **1.** distinctly named church or sect **2.** name, *esp.* of class or group —**denomiˈnational** *a.* —**deˈnominator** *n.* divisor in vulgar fraction

denote (dɪˈnəʊt) *vt.* **1.** stand for, be the name of **2.** mark, indicate, show —**denoˈtation** *n.*

denouement (deɪˈnuːmɒn) *or* **dénouement** (*Fr.* denuˈmɑ̃) *n.* **1.** unravelling of dramatic plot **2.** final solution of mystery

denounce (dɪˈnaʊns) *vt.* **1.** speak violently against **2.** accuse **3.** terminate (treaty) —**denunciˈation** *n.* denouncing —**denunciatory** (dɪˈnʌnsɪətərɪ) *a.*

dense (dɛns) *a.* **1.** thick, compact **2.** stupid —ˈ**densely** *adv.* —ˈ**density** *n.* mass per unit of volume

dent (dɛnt) *n.* **1.** hollow or mark left by blow or pressure —*vt.* **2.** make dent in **3.** mark with dent

dental (ˈdɛntᵊl) *a.* **1.** of, pert. to teeth or dentistry **2.** pronounced by applying tongue to teeth —ˈ**dentate** *a.* toothed —**dentifrice** (ˈdɛntɪfrɪs) *n.* powder, paste or wash for cleaning teeth —ˈ**dentist** *n.* surgeon who attends to teeth —ˈ**dentistry** *n.* art of dentist —**denˈtition** *n.* **1.** teething **2.** arrangement of teeth —ˈ**denture** *n.* (*usu. pl.*) set of false teeth —**dental floss** soft thread for cleaning between teeth —**dental surgeon** dentist

dentine (ˈdɛntiːn) *or* **dentin** (ˈdɛntɪn) *n.* the hard bonelike part of a tooth

denude (dɪˈnjuːd) *vt.* **1.** strip, make bare **2.** expose (rock) by erosion of plants, soil *etc.* —**denudation** (dɛnjʊˈdeɪʃən) *n.*

denumerable (dɪˈnjuːmərəbᵊl) *a. Maths.* capable of being counted by correspondence with positive integers; countable

denunciation (dɪnʌnsɪˈeɪʃən) *n. see* DENOUNCE

deny (dɪˈnaɪ) *vt.* **1.** declare untrue **2.** contradict **3.** reject, disown **4.** refuse to give **5.** refuse **6.** (*refl.*) abstain from (**deˈnied, deˈnying**) —**deˈniable** *a.* —**deˈnial** *n.*

deodar (ˈdiːəʊdɑː) *n.* **1.** Himalayan cedar with drooping branches **2.** fragrant wood of this tree

deodorize *or* **-ise** (diːˈəʊdəraɪz) *vt.* rid of smell or mask smell of —**deˈodorant** *n.* —**deodoriˈzation** *or* **-iˈsation** *n.* —**deˈodorizer** *or* **-iser** *n.*

deontology (diːɒnˈtɒlədʒɪ) *n.* science of ethics and moral obligations —**deonˈtologist** *n.*

Deo volente (ˈdeɪəʊ vɒˈlɛntɪ) *Lat.* God willing

deoxidize *or* **-ise** (diːˈɒksɪdaɪz) *vt.* deprive of oxygen —**deoxidiˈzation** *or* **-iˈsation** *n.*

dep. 1. depart(s) **2.** departure **3.** deposed **4.** deposit **5.** deputy

depart (dɪˈpɑːt) *vi.* **1.** go away **2.** start out, set forth **3.** deviate, vary **4.** die —**deˈparture** *n.*

department (dɪˈpɑːtmənt) *n.* **1.** division **2.** branch **3.** province —**departˈmental** *a.* —**departˈmentally** *adv.* —**department store** large shop selling all kinds of goods

depend (dɪˈpɛnd) *vi.* **1.** (*usu. with* on) rely entirely **2.** be contingent, await settlement or decision —**deˈpendable** *a.* reliable —**deˈpendant** *n.* one for whose maintenance another is responsible —**deˈpendence** *n.* —**deˈpendency** *n.* subject territory —**deˈpendent** *a.* depending

THESAURUS

denial adjuration, contradiction, disavowal, disclaimer, dismissal, dissent, negation, prohibition, rebuff, refusal, rejection, renunciation, repudiation, repulse, retraction, veto

denigrate belittle, besmirch, blacken, calumniate, decry, defame, disparage, impugn, malign, revile, run down, slander, vilify

denomination 1. belief, communion, creed, persuasion, religious group, school, sect **2.** grade, size, unit, value **3.** body, category, class, classification, group **4.** appellation, designation, label, name, style, term, title

denote betoken, designate, express, imply, import, indicate, mark, mean, show, signify, typify

denounce accuse, arraign, attack, brand, castigate, censure, condemn, declaim against, decry, denunciate, impugn, proscribe, revile, stigmatize, vilify

dense 1. close, close-knit, compact, compressed, condensed, heavy, impenetrable, opaque, solid, substantial, thick, thickset **2.** blockish, crass, dull, obtuse, slow, slow-witted, stolid, stupid, thick, thick-witted

density body, bulk, closeness, compactness, consistency, crowdedness, denseness, impenetrability, mass, solidity, thickness, tightness

dent 1. *n.* chip, concavity, crater, depression, dimple, dip, hollow, impression, indentation, pit **2.** *v.* depress, dint, gouge, hollow, imprint, make a dent in, make concave, press in, push in

denude bare, divest, expose, lay bare, strip, uncover

deny 1. contradict, disagree with, disprove, gainsay, oppose, rebuff, refute **2.** abjure, disavow, discard, disclaim, disown, recant, renounce, repudiate, revoke **3.** begrudge, decline, disallow, forbid, negative, refuse, reject, turn down, veto, withhold

deodorant air freshener, antiperspirant, deodorizer, disinfectant, fumigant

depart 1. absent (oneself), decamp, disappear, escape, exit, go, go away, leave, migrate, quit, remove, retire, retreat, set forth, start out, take (one's) leave, vanish, withdraw **2.** deviate, differ, digress, diverge, stray, swerve, turn aside, vary, veer

department 1. district, division, province, region, sector **2.** branch, bureau, division, office, section, station, subdivision, unit **3.** area, domain, function, line, province, realm, responsibility, speciality, sphere

departure 1. exit, exodus, going, going away, leave-taking, leaving, removal, retirement, withdrawal **2.** abandonment, branching off, deviation, digression, divergence, variation, veering **3.** branching out, change, difference, innovation, novelty, shift

depict (dɪˈpɪkt) *vt.* **1.** give picture of **2.** describe in words —**deˈpiction** *n.* —**deˈpictor** *n.*

depilatory (dɪˈpɪlətərɪ, -trɪ) *n.* **1.** substance that removes hair —*a.* **2.** serving to remove hair

deplete (dɪˈpliːt) *vt.* **1.** empty **2.** reduce **3.** exhaust —**deˈpletion** *n.*

deplore (dɪˈplɔː) *vt.* **1.** lament, regret **2.** deprecate, complain of —**deˈplorable** *a.* **1.** lamentable **2.** disgraceful

deploy (dɪˈplɔɪ) *v.* **1.** (of troops, ships) (cause to) adopt battle formation —*vt.* **2.** arrange —**deˈployment** *n.*

depolarize *or* **-ise** (diːˈpəʊləraɪz) *vt.* deprive of polarity —**depolariˈzation** *or* **-iˈsation** *n.*

deponent (dɪˈpəʊnənt) *a.* **1.** (of verb) having passive form but active meaning —*n.* **2.** deponent verb **3.** one who makes statement on oath **4.** deposition

depopulate (dɪˈpɒpjʊleɪt) *v.* (cause to) be reduced in population —**depopuˈlation** *n.*

deport (dɪˈpɔːt) *vt.* expel from a country, banish —**deporˈtation** *n.*

deportment (dɪˈpɔːtmənt) *n.* behaviour, conduct, bearing —**deˈport** *vt.* behave, carry (oneself)

depose (dɪˈpəʊz) *vt.* **1.** remove from office, *esp.* of sovereign —*vi.* **2.** make statement on oath, give evidence —**deˈposable** *a.* —**deˈposal** *n.* **1.** removal from office **2.** statement made on oath

deposit (dɪˈpɒzɪt) *vt.* **1.** set down, *esp.* carefully **2.** give into safekeeping, *esp.* in bank **3.** let fall (as sediment) —*n.* **4.** thing deposited **5.** money given in part payment or as security **6.** sediment —**deˈpositary** *n.* person with whom thing is deposited —**deposition** (dɛpəˈzɪʃən) *n.* **1.** statement written and attested **2.** act of deposing or depositing —**deˈpositor** *n.* —**deˈpository** *n.* place for safekeeping —**deposit account UK** bank account that earns interest and usu. requires notice of withdrawal

depot (ˈdɛpəʊ) *n.* **1.** storehouse **2.** building for storage and servicing of buses, railway engines *etc.* **3. US** railway station

deprave (dɪˈpreɪv) *vt.* make bad, corrupt, pervert —**depravity** (dɪˈprævɪtɪ) *n.* wickedness, viciousness

deprecate (ˈdɛprɪkeɪt) *vt.* **1.** express disapproval of **2.** advise against —**depreˈcation** *n.* —**depreˈcatory** *a.*

depreciate (dɪˈpriːʃɪeɪt) *vt.* **1.** lower price, value or purchasing power of **2.** belittle —*vi.* **3.** fall in value —**depreciˈation** *n.* —**deˈpreciator** *n.* —**deˈpreciatory** *a.*

depredation (dɛprɪˈdeɪʃən) *n.* plundering, pillage —**ˈdepredate** *vt.* plunder, despoil —**ˈdepredator** *n.*

depress (dɪˈprɛs) *vt.* **1.** affect with low spirits **2.** lower in level or activity —**deˈpressant** *n.* —**deˈpressed** *a.* **1.** low in spirits; downcast **2.** lower than surrounding surface **3.** pressed down; flattened **4.** characterized by

THESAURUS

depend 1. bank on, build upon, calculate on, confide in, count on, lean on, reckon on, rely upon, trust in, turn to **2.** be based on, be contingent on, be determined by, be subject to, be subordinate to, hang on, hinge on, rest on, revolve around

dependable faithful, reliable, responsible, steady, sure, trustworthy, trusty, unfailing

dependant *n.* child, client, hanger-on, henchman, minion, minor, protégé, relative, retainer, subordinate, vassal

dependent *adj.* **1.** counting on, defenceless, helpless, immature, reliant, relying on, vulnerable, weak **2.** conditional, contingent, depending, determined by, liable to, relative, subject to

depict 1. delineate, draw, illustrate, limn, outline, paint, picture, portray, render, reproduce, sculpt, sketch **2.** characterize, describe, detail, narrate, outline, sketch

deplete bankrupt, consume, decrease, drain, empty, evacuate, exhaust, expend, impoverish, lessen, milk, reduce, use up

depletion attenuation, consumption, decrease, deficiency, diminution, dwindling, exhaustion, expenditure, lessening, lowering, reduction, using up

deplorable 1. calamitous, dire, disastrous, distressing, grievous, heartbreaking, lamentable, melancholy, miserable, pitiable, regrettable, sad, unfortunate, wretched **2.** blameworthy, disgraceful, dishonourable, disreputable, execrable, opprobrious, reprehensible, scandalous, shameful

deplore 1. bemoan, bewail, grieve for, lament, mourn, regret, rue, sorrow over **2.** abhor, censure, condemn, denounce, deprecate, disapprove of, object to

deploy arrange, dispose, extend, position, redistribute, set out, set up, spread out, station, use, utilize

deport 1. banish, exile, expatriate, expel, extradite, oust **2.** *Used reflexively* acquit, act, bear, behave, carry, comport, conduct, hold

deportation banishment, eviction, exile, expatriation, expulsion, extradition, transportation

deportment air, appearance, aspect, bearing, behaviour, carriage, cast, comportment, conduct, demeanour, manner, mien, posture, stance

depose 1. break, cashier, degrade, demote, dethrone, dismiss, displace, downgrade, oust, remove from office **2.** *Law* avouch, declare, make a deposition, testify

deposit *v.* **1.** drop, lay, locate, place, precipitate, put, settle, sit down **2.** amass, bank, consign, entrust, hoard, lodge, save, store ~*n.* **3.** down payment, instalment, money (*in bank*), part payment, pledge, retainer, security, stake, warranty **4.** accumulation, alluvium, deposition, dregs, lees, precipitate, sediment, silt

deposition 1. dethronement, dismissal, displacement, ousting, removal **2.** *Law* affidavit, declaration, evidence, sworn statement, testimony

depository depot, repository, safe-deposit box, store, storehouse, warehouse

depot 1. depository, repository, storehouse, warehouse **2.** bus station, garage, terminus

deprave brutalize, corrupt, debase, debauch, degrade, demoralize, lead astray, pervert, seduce, subvert, vitiate

depravity baseness, contamination, corruption, criminality, debasement, debauchery, degeneracy, depravation, evil, immorality, iniquity, profligacy, sinfulness, vice, viciousness, vitiation, wickedness

depreciate 1. decrease, deflate, devaluate, devalue, lessen, lose value, lower, reduce **2.** belittle, decry, denigrate, deride, detract, disparage, look down on, ridicule, run down, scorn, sneer at, traduce, underestimate, underrate, undervalue

depreciation 1. deflation, depression, devaluation, drop, fall, slump **2.** belittlement, deprecation, derogation, detraction, disparagement, pejoration

economic hardship (*also* **dis'tressed**) **5.** lowered in force *etc.* **6.** *Bot., zool.* flattened —**de'pression** *n.* **1.** hollow **2.** low spirits, dejection, despondency **3.** low state of trade, slump —**de'pressive** *a.*

deprive (dɪ'praɪv) *vt.* strip, dispossess —**deprivation** (dɛprɪ'veɪʃən) *n.* —**de'prived** *a.* lacking adequate food, care, amenities *etc.*

dept. department

depth (dɛpθ) *n.* **1.** (degree of) deepness **2.** deep place, abyss **3.** intensity (of colour, feeling) **4.** profundity (of mind) —**depth charge** *or* **bomb** bomb for use against submarines

depute (dɪ'pju:t) *vt.* **1.** allot **2.** appoint as agent or substitute —*a./n.* ('dɛpju:t) **3.** in Scotland, assistant —**depu'tation** *n.* persons sent to speak for others —'**deputize** *or* **-ise** *vi.* **1.** act for another —*vt.* **2.** depute —'**deputy** *n.* **1.** assistant **2.** substitute, delegate

derail (dɪ'reɪl) *v.* (cause to) go off the rails, as train *etc.* —**de'railment** *n.*

derailleur (də'reɪljə) *a./n.* (of) gear-change mechanism for bicycles

derange (dɪ'reɪndʒ) *vt.* **1.** make insane **2.** upset **3.** put out of place, out of order —**de'rangement** *n.*

derby ('dɜ:bɪ) *n.* **US** bowler hat

Derby ('dɑ:bɪ; *U.S.* 'dɜ:bɪ) *n.* **1.** horserace, *esp.* famous one at Epsom, England **2.** contest between local teams

deregulate (dɪ'rɛgjʊleɪt) *v.* **1.** cancel regulations (concerning an activity or process) —*vt.* **2.** exempt (an activity) from regulations —**deregu'lation** *n.*

derelict ('dɛrɪlɪkt) *a.* **1.** abandoned, forsaken **2.** falling into ruins, dilapidated —*n.* **3.** social outcast, vagrant **4.** abandoned property, ship *etc.* —**dere'liction** *n.* **1.** neglect (of duty) **2.** abandoning

derestrict (di:rɪ'strɪkt) *vt.* render or leave free from restriction, *esp.* road from speed limits

deride (dɪ'raɪd) *vt.* speak of or treat with contempt, ridicule —**derision** (dɪ'rɪʒən) *n.* ridicule —**de'risive** *a.* —**de'risory** *a.* mocking, ridiculing

de rigueur (də ri'gœ:r) *Fr.* required by etiquette or fashion

derive (dɪ'raɪv) *vt.* **1.** deduce, get (from) **2.** show origin of —*vi.* **3.** issue, be descended (from) —**derivation** (dɛrɪ'veɪʃən) *n.* —**derivative** (dɪ'rɪvətɪv) *a./n.*

derma ('dɜ:mə) *or* **dermis** ('dɜ:mɪs) *n.* the fine skin, below the epidermis, containing blood vessels

dermatitis (dɜ:mə'taɪtɪs) *n.* inflammation of skin

THESAURUS

depress **1.** cast down, chill, damp, daunt, deject, desolate, discourage, dishearten, dispirit, make despondent, oppress, sadden, weigh down **2.** debilitate, devitalize, drain, enervate, exhaust, lower, sap, slow up, weaken **3.** cheapen, depreciate, devaluate, devalue, diminish, downgrade, impair, lessen, lower, reduce **4.** flatten, level, lower, press down, push down

depressed **1.** blue, crestfallen, dejected, despondent, discouraged, dispirited, down, downcast, downhearted, fed up, glum, low, low-spirited, melancholy, moody, morose, pessimistic, sad, unhappy **2.** concave, hollow, indented, recessed, set back, sunken **3.** *Of an area, circumstances* deprived, destitute, disadvantaged, distressed, grey, needy, poor, poverty-stricken, run-down **4.** cheapened, depreciated, devalued, impaired, weakened

depression **1.** dejection, despair, despondency, dolefulness, downheartedness, dumps (*Inf.*), gloominess, hopelessness, low spirits, melancholia, melancholy, sadness, the blues **2.** *Commerce* dullness, economic decline, hard *or* bad times, inactivity, lowness, recession, slump, stagnation **3.** bowl, cavity, concavity, dent, dimple, dip, excavation, hollow, impression, indentation, pit, sag, sink, valley

deprivation **1.** denial, deprival, dispossession, divestment, expropriation, removal, withdrawal, withholding **2.** destitution, detriment, disadvantage, distress, hardship, need, privation, want

deprive bereave, despoil, dispossess, divest, expropriate, rob, strip, wrest

deprived bereft, denuded, destitute, disadvantaged, forlorn, in need, in want, lacking, necessitous, needy, poor

depth **1.** abyss, deepness, drop, extent, measure, profoundness, profundity **2.** *Fig.* astuteness, discernment, insight, penetration, profoundness, profundity, sagacity, wisdom **3.** abstruseness, complexity, obscurity, reconditeness **4.** intensity, richness, strength **5.** *Often plural* abyss, bowels of the earth, deepest (furthest, innermost, most intense, remotest) part, middle, midst

deputation commission, delegates, delegation, deputies, embassy, envoys, legation

deputize **1.** commission, delegate, depute **2.** act for, stand in for, take the place of, understudy

deputy **1.** *n.* agent, ambassador, commissioner, delegate, legate, lieutenant, nuncio, proxy, representative, second-in-command, substitute, surrogate, vicegerent **2.** *adj.* assistant, depute (*Scot.*), subordinate

derange **1.** confound, confuse, disarrange, disarray, discompose, disconcert, disorder, displace, disturb, ruffle, unsettle, upset **2.** craze, dement (*Rare*), drive mad, madden, make insane, unbalance, unhinge

derelict **1.** *adj.* abandoned, deserted, dilapidated, discarded, forsaken, neglected, ruined **2.** *n.* down-and-out, good-for-nothing, ne'er-do-well, outcast, tramp, vagrant, wastrel

dereliction **1.** delinquency, evasion, failure, faithlessness, fault, neglect, negligence, nonperformance, remissness **2.** abandonment, abdication, desertion, forsaking, relinquishment, renunciation

deride chaff, contemn, detract, disdain, disparage, flout, gibe, insult, jeer, knock (*Inf.*), mock, pooh-pooh, ridicule, scoff, scorn, sneer, taunt

derisory contemptible, insulting, laughable, ludicrous, outrageous, preposterous, ridiculous

derivation **1.** acquiring, deriving, extraction, getting, obtaining **2.** ancestry, basis, beginning, descent, etymology, foundation, genealogy, origin, root, source

derivative **1.** *adj.* acquired, borrowed, derived, inferred, obtained, procured, transmitted **2.** *n.* by-product, derivation, descendant, off-shoot, outgrowth, spin-off

derive **1.** collect, deduce, draw, elicit, extract, follow, gain, gather, get, glean, infer, obtain, procure, receive, trace **2.** *With* **from** arise, descend, emanate, flow, issue, originate, proceed, spring from, stem from

dermato-, derma- *or before vowel* **dermat-, derm-** (*comb. form*) skin, as in *dermatitis*

dermatology (dɜːməˈtɒlədʒɪ) *n.* science of skin —**dermaˈtologist** *n.* physician specializing in skin diseases

derogate (ˈdɛrəgeɪt) *vi.* **1.** (*with* from) cause to seem inferior; detract **2.** (*with* from) deviate in standard or quality —*vt.* **3.** cause to seem inferior *etc.*; disparage —**deroˈgation** *n.*

derogatory (dɪˈrɒgətərɪ) *a.* disparaging, belittling, intentionally offensive

derrick (ˈdɛrɪk) *n.* **1.** hoisting machine **2.** framework over oil well *etc.*

derring-do (ˈdɛrɪŋˈduː) *n.* (act of) spirited bravery, boldness

derringer *or* **deringer** (ˈdɛrɪndʒə) *n.* small pistol with large bore

derv (dɜːv) *n.* diesel oil for road vehicles (*d*iesel *e*ngine *r*oad *v*ehicle)

dervish (ˈdɜːvɪʃ) *n.* member of Muslim ascetic order, noted for frenzied, whirling dance

desalination (diːsælɪˈneɪʃən) *or* **desalinization, -isation** *n.* process of removing salt, *esp.* from sea water

descant (ˈdɛskænt) *n.* **1.** *Mus.* decorative variation sung as accompaniment to basic melody —*vi.* (*with* on *or* upon) **2.** talk in detail (about) **3.** dwell (on) at length

descend (dɪˈsɛnd) *vi.* **1.** come or go down **2.** slope down **3.** stoop, condescend **4.** spring (from ancestor *etc.*) **5.** pass to heir, be transmitted **6.** swoop on, attack —*vt.* **7.** go or come down —**desˈcendant** *n.* person descended from an ancestor —**desˈcendent** *a.* **1.** descending —*n.* **2.** descendant —**desˈcent** *n.*

describe (dɪˈskraɪb) *vt.* **1.** give detailed account of **2.** pronounce, label **3.** trace out (geometrical figure *etc.*) —**description** (dɪˈskrɪpʃən) *n.* **1.** detailed account **2.** marking out **3.** kind, sort, species —**descriptive** (dɪˈskrɪptɪv) *a.*

descry (dɪˈskraɪ) *vt.* make out, catch sight of, *esp.* at a distance, espy (**deˈscried, deˈscrying**)

desecrate (ˈdɛsɪkreɪt) *vt.* **1.** violate sanctity of **2.** profane **3.** convert to evil use —**deseˈcration** *n.*

desert[1] (ˈdɛzət) *n.* **1.** uninhabited and barren region —*a.* **2.** barren, uninhabited, desolate —**desert boots** ankle-high boots with soft soles

desert[2] (dɪˈzɜːt) *vt.* **1.** abandon, forsake, leave —*vi.* **2.** (*esp.* of soldiers *etc.*) run away from service —**deˈserter** *n.* —**deˈsertion** *n.*

desert[3] (dɪˈzɜːt) *n.* **1.** (*usu. pl.*) what is due as reward or punishment **2.** merit, virtue

deserve (dɪˈzɜːv) *vt.* **1.** show oneself worthy of **2.** have by conduct a claim to —**deˈserved** *a.* rightfully earned; justified; warranted —**deservedly** (dɪˈzɜːvɪdlɪ) *adv.* —**deservedness** (dɪˈzɜːvɪdnɪs) *n.* —**deˈserving** *a.* worthy (of reward *etc.*)

deshabille (deɪzæˈbiːl) *n. see* DISHABILLE

desiccate (ˈdɛsɪkeɪt) *vt.* **1.** dry **2.** dry up —**desicˈcation** *n.*

desideratum (dɪzɪdəˈrɑːtəm) *n.* something lacked and wanted (*pl.* **-ta** (-tə))

design (dɪˈzaɪn) *vt.* **1.** make working drawings for **2.** sketch **3.** plan out **4.** intend, select for —*n.* **5.** outline sketch **6.** working plan **7.** art of making decorative patterns *etc.* **8.** project, purpose, mental plan —**designedly** (dɪˈzaɪnɪdlɪ) *adv.* on purpose —**deˈsigner** *n.* **1.** *esp.* one who draws designs for manufacturers —*a.* **2.** designed by and having label of well-known fashion designer —**deˈsigning** *a.* crafty, scheming

THESAURUS

derogatory belittling, damaging, defamatory, depreciative, detracting, discreditable, dishonouring, disparaging, injurious, offensive, slighting, uncomplimentary, unfavourable, unflattering

descend **1.** alight, dismount, drop, fall, go down, move down, plummet, plunge, sink, subside, tumble **2.** dip, gravitate, incline, slant, slope **3.** be handed down, be passed down, derive, issue, originate, proceed, spring **4.** abase oneself, condescend, degenerate, deteriorate, lower oneself, stoop **5.** *Often with* **on** arrive, assail, assault, attack, come in force, invade, pounce, raid, swoop

descent **1.** coming down, drop, fall, plunge, swoop **2.** declination, declivity, dip, drop, incline, slant, slope **3.** ancestry, extraction, family tree, genealogy, heredity, lineage, origin, parentage **4.** debasement, decadence, decline, degradation, deterioration **5.** assault, attack, foray, incursion, invasion, pounce, raid, swoop

describe **1.** characterize, define, depict, detail, explain, express, illustrate, narrate, portray, recount, relate, report, specify, tell **2.** delineate, draw, mark out, outline, trace

description **1.** account, characterization, delineation, depiction, detail, explanation, narration, narrative, portrayal, report, representation, sketch **2.** brand, breed, category, class, genre, genus, ilk, kidney, kind, order, sort, species, type, variety

descriptive circumstantial, depictive, detailed, explanatory, expressive, graphic, illustrative, pictorial, picturesque, vivid

desert[1] **1.** *n.* solitude, waste, wasteland, wilderness, wilds **2.** *adj.* arid, bare, barren, desolate, infertile, lonely, solitary, uncultivated, uninhabited, unproductive, untilled, waste, wild

desert[2] *v.* abandon, abscond, betray, decamp, defect, forsake, give up, go over the hill (*Military sl.*), jilt, leave, leave high and dry, leave (someone) in the lurch, leave stranded, maroon, quit, rat (on), relinquish, renounce, resign, run out on (*Inf.*), strand, throw over, vacate, walk out on (*Inf.*)

deserter absconder, apostate, defector, escapee, fugitive, rat (*Inf.*), renegade, runaway, traitor, truant

desertion abandonment, absconding, apostasy, betrayal, defection, departure, dereliction, escape, evasion, flight, forsaking, relinquishment, truancy

deserve be entitled to, be worthy of, earn, gain, justify, merit, procure, rate, warrant, win

deserved appropriate, condign, due, earned, fair, fitting, just, justifiable, justified, meet (*Archaic*), merited, proper, right, rightful, suitable, warranted, well-earned

deserving commendable, estimable, laudable, meritorious, praiseworthy, righteous, worthy

design *v.* **1.** delineate, describe, draft, draw, outline, plan, sketch, trace ~*n.* **2.** blueprint, delineation, draft, drawing, model, outline, plan, scheme, sketch ~*v.* **3.** conceive, create, fabricate, fashion, invent, originate, think up ~*n.* **4.** arrangement, configura-

designate (ˈdɛzɪgneɪt) *vt.* **1.** name **2.** pick out **3.** appoint to office —*a.* (ˈdɛzɪgnɪt, -neɪt) **4.** appointed but not yet installed —**desigˈnation** *n.* name, appellation

desire (dɪˈzaɪə) *vt.* **1.** wish, long for **2.** ask for, entreat —*n.* **3.** longing, craving **4.** expressed wish, request **5.** sexual appetite **6.** something wished for or requested —**desiraˈbility** *n.* —**deˈsirable** *a.* worth desiring —**deˈsirous** *a.* filled with desire

desist (dɪˈzɪst) *vi.* cease, stop

desk (dɛsk) *n.* **1.** table or other piece of furniture designed for reading or writing at **2.** counter **3.** editorial section of newspaper *etc.* covering specific subject —**desk-top** *a.* of computer system, small enough to use at desk, that can produce print-quality documents

desolate (ˈdɛsəlɪt) *a.* **1.** uninhabited **2.** neglected, barren, ruinous **3.** solitary **4.** dreary, dismal, forlorn —*vt.* (ˈdɛsəleɪt) **5.** depopulate, lay waste **6.** overwhelm with grief —**desoˈlation** *n.*

despair (dɪˈspɛə) *vi.* **1.** (*oft. with* of) lose hope —*n.* **2.** loss of all hope **3.** cause of this **4.** despondency

despatch (dɪˈspætʃ) *see* DISPATCH

desperate (ˈdɛspərɪt, -prɪt) *a.* **1.** reckless from despair **2.** difficult; dangerous **3.** frantic **4.** hopelessly bad **5.** leaving no room for hope —**desperado** (dɛspəˈrɑːdəʊ) *n.* reckless, lawless person (*pl.* **-es, -s**) —**ˈdesperately** *adv.* —**despeˈration** *n.*

despise (dɪˈspaɪz) *vt.* look down on as contemptible, inferior —**despicable** (ˈdɛspɪkəbᵊl, dɪˈspɪk-) *a.* base, contemptible, vile —**despicably** (dɪˈspɪkəblɪ) *adv.*

despite (dɪˈspaɪt) *prep.* in spite of

despoil (dɪˈspɔɪl) *vt.* plunder, rob, strip —**despoliation** (dɪspəʊlɪˈeɪʃən) *n.*

THESAURUS

tion, construction, figure, form, motif, organization, pattern, shape, style ~*v.* **5.** aim, contrive, destine, devise, intend, make, mean, plan, project, propose, purpose, scheme, tailor ~*n.* **6.** enterprise, plan, project, schema, scheme, undertaking **7.** aim, end, goal, intent, intention, meaning, object, objective, point, purport, purpose, target, view **8.** *Often plural* conspiracy, evil intentions, intrigue, machination, plot, scheme

designate 1. call, christen, dub, entitle, label, name, nominate, style, term **2.** allot, appoint, assign, choose, delegate, depute, nominate, select **3.** characterize, define, denote, describe, earmark, indicate, pinpoint, show, specify, stipulate

designation denomination, description, epithet, label, mark, name, title

designer architect, artificer, couturier, creator, deviser, inventor, originator, stylist

designing artful, astute, conniving, conspiring, crafty, crooked (*Inf.*), cunning, deceitful, devious, intriguing, Machiavellian, plotting, scheming, sharp, shrewd, sly, treacherous, tricky, unscrupulous, wily

desirability advantage, benefit, merit, profit, usefulness, value, worth

desirable 1. advantageous, advisable, agreeable, beneficial, covetable, eligible, enviable, good, pleasing, preferable, profitable, worthwhile **2.** adorable, alluring, attractive, fascinating, fetching, seductive, sexy (*Inf.*)

desire *v.* **1.** aspire to, covet, crave, desiderate, fancy, hanker after, long for, set one's heart on, want, wish for, yearn for ~*n.* **2.** appetite, aspiration, craving, hankering, longing, need, want, wish, yearning, yen (*Inf.*) ~*v.* **3.** ask, entreat, importune, petition, request, solicit ~*n.* **4.** appeal, entreaty, importunity, petition, request, solicitation, supplication **5.** appetite, concupiscence, lasciviousness, lechery, libido, lust, lustfulness, passion

desirous ambitious, anxious, aspiring, avid, craving, desiring, eager, hopeful, hoping, keen, longing, ready, willing, wishing, yearning

desist abstain, break off, cease, discontinue, end, forbear, give over (*Inf.*), give up, have done with, leave off, pause, refrain from, stop, suspend

desolate *adj.* **1.** bare, barren, bleak, desert, dreary, ruined, solitary, unfrequented, uninhabited, waste, wild ~*v.* **2.** depopulate, despoil, destroy, devastate, lay low, lay waste, pillage, plunder, ravage, ruin ~*adj.* **3.** abandoned, bereft, cheerless, comfortless, companionless, dejected, depressing, despondent, disconsolate, dismal, downcast, forlorn, forsaken, gloomy, lonely, melancholy, miserable, wretched ~*v.* **4.** daunt, deject, depress, discourage, dishearten, dismay, distress, grieve

desolation 1. destruction, devastation, havoc, ravages, ruin, ruination **2.** barrenness, bleakness, desolateness, forlornness, isolation, loneliness, solitariness, solitude, wildness **3.** anguish, dejection, despair, distress, gloom, gloominess, melancholy, misery, sadness, unhappiness, woe, wretchedness

despair *v.* **1.** despond, give up, lose heart, lose hope ~*n.* **2.** anguish, dejection, depression, desperation, despondency, disheartenment, gloom, hopelessness, melancholy, misery, wretchedness **3.** burden, cross, ordeal, pain, trial, tribulation

desperado bandit, criminal, cutthroat, gangster, gunman, hoodlum (*Chiefly U.S.*), lawbreaker, mugger, outlaw, ruffian, thug

desperate 1. audacious, dangerous, daring, death-defying, determined, foolhardy, frantic, furious, hasty, hazardous, headstrong, impetuous, madcap, precipitate, rash, reckless, risky, violent, wild **2.** acute, critical, dire, drastic, extreme, great, urgent, very grave **3.** despairing, despondent, forlorn, hopeless, inconsolable, irrecoverable, irremediable, irretrievable, wretched

desperately 1. badly, dangerously, gravely, perilously, seriously, severely **2.** appallingly, fearfully, frightfully, hopelessly, shockingly

desperation 1. defiance, foolhardiness, frenzy, heedlessness, impetuosity, madness, rashness, recklessness **2.** agony, anguish, anxiety, despair, despondency, distraction, heartache, hopelessness, misery, pain, sorrow, torture, trouble, unhappiness, worry

despicable abject, base, beyond contempt, cheap, contemptible, degrading, detestable, disgraceful, disreputable, hateful, ignominious, infamous, low, mean, pitiful, reprehensible, scurvy, shameful, sordid, vile, worthless, wretched

despise abhor, contemn, deride, detest, disdain, disregard, flout, loathe, look down on, neglect, revile, scorn, slight, spurn, undervalue

despite *prep.* against, even with, in contempt of, in defiance of, in spite of, in the face of, in the teeth of, notwithstanding, regardless of, undeterred by

despoil denude, deprive, destroy, devastate, dispos-

despondent (dɪˈspɒndənt) *a.* dejected, depressed —**deˈspond** *vi.* —**deˈspondency** *n.* —**deˈspondently** *adv.*

despot (ˈdɛspɒt) *n.* tyrant, oppressor —**desˈpotic** *a.* —**desˈpotically** *adv.* —**ˈdespotism** *n.* autocratic government, tyranny

despumate (dɪˈspjuːmeɪt, ˈdɛspjʊmeɪt) *vi.* **1.** throw off impurities **2.** form scum

desquamate (ˈdɛskwəmeɪt) *vi.* (of skin) come off in scales —**desquaˈmation** *n.*

dessert (dɪˈzɜːt) *n.* sweet course, or fruit, served at end of meal —**desˈsertspoon** *n.* spoon intermediate in size between tablespoon and teaspoon

destination (dɛstɪˈneɪʃən) *n.* **1.** place a person or thing is bound for **2.** goal **3.** purpose

destine (ˈdɛstɪn) *vt.* **1.** ordain or fix beforehand **2.** set apart, devote

destiny (ˈdɛstɪnɪ) *n.* **1.** course of events; person's fate **2.** the power which foreordains

destitute (ˈdɛstɪtjuːt) *a.* **1.** in absolute want **2.** in great need, devoid (of) **3.** penniless —**destiˈtution** *n.*

destroy (dɪˈstrɔɪ) *vt.* **1.** ruin **2.** pull to pieces **3.** undo **4.** put an end to **5.** demolish **6.** annihilate —**deˈstroyer** *n.* **1.** one who destroys **2.** small, swift, heavily armed warship —**deˈstruct** *vt.* destroy (one's own missile *etc.*) for safety —**deˈstructible** *a.* —**deˈstruction** *n.* **1.** ruin, overthrow **2.** death —**deˈstructive** *a.* **1.** destroying **2.** negative, not constructive —**deˈstructively** *adv.* —**deˈstructor** *n.* that which destroys, *esp.* incinerator

desuetude (dɪˈsjuːɪtjuːd, ˈdɛswɪtjuːd) *n.* disuse, discontinuance

desultory (ˈdɛsəltərɪ, -trɪ) *a.* **1.** passing, changing fitfully from one thing to another **2.** aimless **3.** unmethodical

detach (dɪˈtætʃ) *vt.* unfasten, disconnect, separate —**deˈtachable** *a.* —**deˈtached** *a.* **1.** standing apart, isolated **2.** impersonal, disinterested —**deˈtachment** *n.* **1.** aloofness **2.** detaching **3.** a body of troops detached for special duty

detail (ˈdiːteɪl) *n.* **1.** particular **2.** small or unimportant part **3.** treatment of anything item by item **4.** party or man assigned for duty in army —*vt.* **5.** relate in full **6.** appoint for duty

detain (dɪˈteɪn) *vt.* **1.** keep under restraint **2.** hinder **3.**

THESAURUS

sess, divest, loot, pillage, plunder, ravage, rifle, rob, strip, vandalize, wreak havoc upon, wreck

despondency dejection, depression, despair, desperation, disconsolateness, discouragement, dispiritedness, downheartedness, gloom, hopelessness, low spirits, melancholy, misery, sadness, wretchedness

despondent blue, dejected, depressed, despairing, disconsolate, discouraged, disheartened, dispirited, doleful, down, downcast, downhearted, gloomy, glum, hopeless, in despair, low, low-spirited, melancholy, miserable, morose, sad, sorrowful, woebegone, wretched

despot autocrat, dictator, monocrat, oppressor, tyrant

despotic absolute, arbitrary, arrogant, authoritarian, autocratic, dictatorial, domineering, imperious, monocratic, oppressive, tyrannical, unconstitutional

despotism absolutism, autarchy, autocracy, dictatorship, monocracy, oppression, totalitarianism, tyranny

destination 1. harbour, haven, journey's end, landing-place, resting-place, station, stop, terminus 2. aim, ambition, design, end, goal, intention, object, objective, purpose, target

destine allot, appoint, assign, consecrate, decree, design, devote, doom, earmark, fate, intend, mark out, ordain, predetermine, purpose, reserve

destiny cup, divine decree, doom, fate, fortune, karma, kismet, lot, portion

destitute 1. distressed, down and out, impecunious, impoverished, indigent, insolvent, moneyless, necessitous, needy, on one's uppers, on the breadline (*Inf.*), penniless, penurious, poor, poverty-stricken 2. bereft of, deficient in, depleted, deprived of, devoid of, drained, empty of, in need of, lacking, wanting, without

destitution beggary, dire straits, distress, impecuniousness, indigence, neediness, pauperism, pennilessness, penury, privation, utter poverty, want

destroy annihilate, blow to bits, break down, crush, demolish, desolate, devastate, dismantle, dispatch, eradicate, extinguish, extirpate, gut, kill, ravage, raze, ruin, shatter, slay, smash, torpedo, waste, wipe out, wreck

destruction annihilation, crushing, demolition, devastation, downfall, end, eradication, extermination, extinction, havoc, liquidation, massacre, overthrow, overwhelming, ruin, ruination, shattering, slaughter, undoing, wreckage, wrecking

destructive 1. baleful, baneful, calamitous, cataclysmic, catastrophic, damaging, deadly, deleterious, detrimental, devastating, fatal, harmful, hurtful, injurious, lethal, noxious, pernicious, ruinous 2. adverse, antagonistic, contrary, derogatory, discouraging, discrediting, disparaging, hostile, invalidating, negative, opposed, undermining, vicious

detach cut off, disconnect, disengage, disentangle, disjoin, disunite, divide, free, isolate, loosen, remove, segregate, separate, sever, tear off, uncouple, unfasten, unhitch

detached 1. disconnected, discrete, disjoined, divided, free, loosened, separate, severed, unconnected 2. aloof, disinterested, dispassionate, impartial, impersonal, neutral, objective, reserved, unbiased, uncommitted, uninvolved, unprejudiced

detachment 1. aloofness, coolness, indifference, remoteness, unconcern 2. disinterestedness, fairness, impartiality, neutrality, nonpartisanship, objectivity 3. disconnection, disengagement, disjoining, separation, severing 4. *Military* body, detail, force, party, patrol, squad, task force, unit

detail *n.* 1. aspect, component, count, element, fact, factor, feature, item, particular, point, respect, specific, technicality 2. *Plural* fine points, minutiae, niceties, particulars, parts, trivia, trivialities 3. *Military* assignment, body, detachment, duty, fatigue, force, party, squad ~*v.* 4. catalogue, delineate, depict, describe, enumerate, individualize, itemize, narrate, particularize, portray, recite, recount, rehearse, relate, specify 5. allocate, appoint, assign, charge, commission, delegate, detach, send

detain 1. check, delay, hinder, hold up, impede, keep, keep back, retard, slow up (*or* down), stay, stop 2. arrest, confine, hold, intern, restrain keep waiting —**de'tention** *n.* 1. confinement 2. arrest 3. detaining

detect (dɪ'tɛkt) *vt.* find out or discover existence, presence, nature or identity of —**de'tection** *n.* —**de'tective** *n.* 1. policeman or private agent employed in detecting crime —*a.* 2. employed in detection —**de'tector** *n. esp.* mechanical sensing device or device for detecting radio signals

détente (deɪ'tɑ:nt; *Fr.* de'tãt) *n.* lessening of tension in political or international affairs

detention (dɪ'tɛnʃən) *n. see* DETAIN

deter (dɪ'tɜ:) *vt.* 1. discourage, frighten 2. hinder, prevent (-rr-) —**de'terrent** *a./n.*

detergent (dɪ'tɜ:dʒənt) *n.* 1. cleansing, purifying substance —*a.* 2. having cleansing power —**de'terge** *vt.*

deteriorate (dɪ'tɪərɪəreɪt) *v.* become or make worse —**deterio'ration** *n.*

determine (dɪ'tɜ:mɪn) *vt.* 1. make up one's mind on, decide 2. fix as known 3. bring to a decision 4. be deciding factor in 5. *Law* end —*vi.* 6. come to an end 7. come to decision —**de'terminable** *a.* —**de'terminant** *a./n.* —**de'terminate** *a.* fixed in scope or nature —**determi'nation** *n.* 1. determining 2. firm or resolute conduct or purpose 3. resolve —**de'termined** *a.* resolute —**de'terminism** *n.* theory that human action is settled by forces independent of will —**de'terminist** *n./a.*

detest (dɪ'tɛst) *vt.* hate, loathe —**de'testable** *a.* —**de'testably** *adv.* —**detes'tation** *n.*

dethrone (dɪ'θrəʊn) *vt.* remove from throne, depose —**de'thronement** *n.*

detonate ('dɛtəneɪt) *vt.* 1. cause (bomb, mine *etc.*) to explode —*vi.* 2. (of bomb, mine *etc.*) explode —**deto'nation** *n.* —**'detonator** *n.* mechanical, electrical device, or small amount of explosive, used to set off main explosive charge

detour ('di:tʊə) *n.* 1. course which leaves main route to rejoin it later 2. roundabout way —*vi.* 3. make detour

detoxify (di:'tɒksɪfaɪ) *vt.* remove poison from (-**fying**, -**fied**) —**detoxifi'cation** *n.*

detract (dɪ'trækt) *v.* take away (a part) from, diminish —**de'traction** *n.* —**de'tractive** *a.* —**de'tractor** *n.*

detriment ('dɛtrɪmənt) *n.* harm done, loss, damage —**detri'mental** *a.* damaging, injurious —**detri'mentally** *adv.*

detritus (dɪ'traɪtəs) *n.* worn-down matter, such as gravel or rock debris —**de'trital** *a.* —**detrition** (dɪ'trɪʃən) *n.* wearing away from solid bodies by friction

de trop (də 'tro) *Fr.* not wanted, superfluous

detrude (dɪ'tru:d) *vt.* thrust down —**de'trusion** *n.*

detumescence (di:tju'mɛsəns) *n.* subsidence of swelling

deuce (dju:s) *n.* 1. two 2. card with two spots 3. *Tennis* forty all 4. in exclamatory phrases, the devil —**deuced** ('dju:sɪd, dju:st) *a. inf.* excessive

Deut. Deuteronomy

THESAURUS

detect 1. ascertain, catch, descry, distinguish, identify, note, notice, observe, recognize, scent, spot 2. catch, disclose, discover, expose, find, reveal, track down, uncover, unmask

detection discovery, exposé, exposure, ferreting out, revelation, tracking down, uncovering, unearthing, unmasking

detective C.I.D. man, constable, cop (*Sl.*), copper (*Sl.*), dick (*Sl., chiefly U.S.*), gumshoe (*U.S. sl.*), investigator, private eye, private investigator, sleuth (*Inf.*)

detention confinement, custody, delay, hindrance, holding back, imprisonment, incarceration, keeping in, quarantine, restraint, withholding

deter caution, check, damp, daunt, debar, discourage, dissuade, frighten, hinder, inhibit from, intimidate, prevent, prohibit, put off, restrain, stop, talk out of

detergent 1. *n.* cleaner, cleanser 2. *adj.* abstergent, cleaning, cleansing, detersive, purifying

deteriorate 1. corrupt, debase, decline, degenerate, degrade, deprave, depreciate, go downhill (*Inf.*), go to pot, go to the dogs (*Inf.*), impair, injure, lower, spoil, worsen 2. be the worse for wear (*Inf.*), crumble, decay, decline, decompose, disintegrate, ebb, fade, fall apart, lapse, weaken, wear away

deterioration atrophy, corrosion, debasement, decline, degeneration, degradation, dégringolade, depreciation, descent, dilapidation, disintegration, downturn, drop, fall, lapse, retrogression, slump, vitiation, worsening

determination 1. backbone, constancy, conviction, dedication, doggedness, drive, firmness, fortitude, indomitability, perseverance, persistence, resoluteness, resolution, resolve, single-mindedness, steadfastness, tenacity, willpower 2. conclusion, decision, judgment, purpose, resolve, result, settlement, solution, verdict

determine 1. arbitrate, conclude, decide, end, finish, fix upon, ordain, regulate, settle, terminate 2. ascertain, certify, check, detect, discover, find out, learn, verify, work out 3. choose, decide, elect, establish, fix, make up one's mind, purpose, resolve 4. affect, condition, control, decide, dictate, direct, govern, impel, impose, incline, induce, influence, lead, modify, regulate, rule, shape

determined bent on, constant, dogged, firm, fixed, intent, persevering, persistent, purposeful, resolute, set on, single-minded, steadfast, strong-minded, strong-willed, tenacious, unflinching, unwavering

deterrent *n.* check, curb, defensive measures, determent, discouragement, disincentive, hindrance, impediment, obstacle, restraint

detest abhor, abominate, despise, dislike intensely, execrate, feel aversion (disgust, hostility, repugnance) towards, hate, loathe, recoil from

detonate blast, blow up, discharge, explode, fulminate, set off, touch off

detonation bang, blast, blow-up, boom, discharge, explosion, fulmination, report

detour bypass, byway, circuitous route, deviation, diversion, indirect course, roundabout way

detract devaluate, diminish, lessen, lower, reduce, take away from

detriment damage, disadvantage, disservice, harm, hurt, impairment, injury, loss, mischief, prejudice

detrimental adverse, baleful, damaging, deleterious, destructive, disadvantageous, harmful, inimical, injurious, mischievous, pernicious, prejudicial, unfavourable

deuterium (djuːˈtɪərɪəm) *n.* form of hydrogen twice as heavy as normal gas —**ˈdeuteron** *n.* nucleus of this gas

Deutsche Mark (ˈdɔɪtʃə) *or* **Deutschmark** *n.* monetary unit of Germany

deutzia (ˈdjuːtsɪə, ˈdɔɪtsɪə) *n.* shrub with white or pink flower clusters

devalue (diːˈvæljuː) *or* **devaluate** (diːˈvæljuːeɪt) *v.* **1.** (of currency) reduce or be reduced in value —*vt.* **2.** reduce the value or worth of —**devaluˈation** *n.*

devastate (ˈdɛvəsteɪt) *vt.* **1.** lay waste **2.** ravage **3.** *inf.* overwhelm —**devasˈtation** *n.*

develop (dɪˈvɛləp) *vt.* **1.** bring to maturity **2.** elaborate **3.** bring forth, bring out **4.** evolve **5.** treat (photographic plate or film) to bring out image **6.** improve value or change use of (land) by building *etc.* —*vi.* **7.** grow to maturer state (**deˈveloped, deˈveloping**) —**deˈveloper** *n.* **1.** one who develops land **2.** chemical for developing film —**deˈvelopment** *n.* —**developing country** poor country seeking to develop its resources by industrialization —**development area UK** depressed area which is given government assistance to establish new industry

deviate (ˈdiːvɪeɪt) *vi.* leave the way, turn aside, diverge —**ˈdeviant** *n./a.* (person) deviating from normal, *esp.* in sexual practices —**deviˈation** *n.* —**ˈdeviator** *n.* —**ˈdevious** *a.* **1.** deceitful, underhand **2.** roundabout, rambling **3.** erring

device (dɪˈvaɪs) *n.* **1.** contrivance, invention **2.** apparatus **3.** stratagem **4.** scheme, plot **5.** heraldic or emblematic figure or design

devil (ˈdɛvᵊl) *n.* **1.** personified spirit of evil **2.** superhuman evil being **3.** person of great wickedness, cruelty *etc.* **4.** *inf.* fellow **5.** *inf.* something difficult or annoying **6.** energy, dash, unconquerable spirit **7.** *inf.* rogue, rascal **8.** *English law* junior barrister working without payment to gain experience —*vi.* **9.** do work that passes for employer's, as for lawyer or author —*vt.* **10.** grill with hot condiments (**-ll-**) —**ˈdevilish** *a.* **1.** like, of the devil **2.** evil —*adv.* **3.** *inf.* very, extremely —**ˈdevilment** *n.* **1.** wickedness **2.** wild and reckless mischief, revelry, high spirits —**ˈdevilry** *n.* —**devil-may-care** *a.* happy-go-lucky —**devil's advocate 1.** one who advocates opposing, unpopular view, *usu.* for sake of argument **2.** *R.C.Ch.* one appointed to state disqualifications of person whom it is proposed to make a saint

devious (ˈdiːvɪəs) *a.* *see* DEVIATE

devise (dɪˈvaɪz) *vt.* **1.** plan, contrive **2.** invent **3.** plot **4.** leave by will —**deviˈsee** *n.* —**deˈvisor** *n.*

devitrification (diːvɪtrɪfɪˈkeɪʃən) *n.* loss of glassy or vitreous condition —**deˈvitrify** *vt.* deprive of character or appearance of glass (**-fied, -fying**)

devoid (dɪˈvɔɪd) *a.* (*usu. with* of) empty, lacking, free (from)

devolve (dɪˈvɒlv) *vi.* **1.** pass or fall (to, upon) —*vt.* **2.** throw (duty *etc.*) on to another —**devoˈlution** *n.* devolving, *esp.* transfer of authority from central to regional government

---

THESAURUS

devastate 1. demolish, desolate, despoil, destroy, lay waste, level, pillage, plunder, ravage, raze, ruin, sack, spoil, waste, wreck **2.** *Inf.* chagrin, confound, discomfit, discompose, disconcert, floor (*Inf.*), nonplus, overpower, overwhelm, take aback

devastation demolition, depredation, desolation, destruction, havoc, pillage, plunder, ravages, ruin, ruination, spoliation

develop 1. advance, cultivate, evolve, flourish, foster, grow, mature, progress, promote, prosper, ripen **2.** amplify, augment, broaden, dilate upon, elaborate, enlarge, expand, unfold, work out **3.** acquire, begin, breed, commence, contract, establish, form, generate, invent, originate, pick up, start **4.** be a direct result of, break out, come about, ensue, follow, happen, result

development 1. advance, advancement, evolution, expansion, growth, improvement, increase, maturity, progress, progression, spread, unfolding, unravelling **2.** change, circumstance, event, happening, incident, issue, occurrence, outcome, phenomenon, result, situation, turn of events, upshot

deviant 1. *adj.* aberrant, abnormal, bent (*Sl.*), deviate, devious, freaky (*Sl.*), heretical, kinky (*Sl.*), perverse, perverted, queer (*Inf.*), twisted, wayward **2.** *n.* deviate, freak, misfit, odd type, pervert, queer (*Inf.*)

deviate avert, bend, deflect, depart, differ, digress, diverge, drift, err, part, stray, swerve, turn, turn aside, vary, veer, wander

deviation aberration, alteration, change, deflection, departure, digression, discrepancy, disparity, divergence, fluctuation, inconsistency, irregularity, shift, variance, variation

device 1. apparatus, appliance, contraption, contrivance, gadget, gimmick, implement, instrument, invention, tool, utensil **2.** artifice, design, dodge, expedient, gambit, improvisation, manoeuvre, plan, ploy, project, purpose, ruse, scheme, shift, stratagem, strategy, stunt, trick, wile **3.** badge, colophon, crest, design, emblem, figure, insignia, logo, motif, motto, symbol, token

devil 1. *Sometimes cap.* Apollyon, archfiend, Beelzebub, Belial, Clootie (*Scot.*), demon, fiend, Lucifer, Old Harry (*Inf.*), Old Nick (*Inf.*), Prince of Darkness, Satan **2.** beast, brute, demon, monster, ogre, rogue, savage, terror, villain **3.** imp, monkey (*Inf.*), rascal, rogue, scamp, scoundrel **4.** beggar, creature, thing, unfortunate, wretch

devilish accursed, atrocious, damnable, detestable, diabolic, diabolical, execrable, fiendish, hellish, infernal, satanic, wicked

devilry 1. devilment, knavery, mischief, mischievousness, rascality, roguery **2.** cruelty, evil, malevolence, malice, vice, viciousness, villainy, wickedness

devious 1. calculating, crooked (*Inf.*), deceitful, dishonest, double-dealing, evasive, indirect, insidious, insincere, not straightforward, scheming, sly, surreptitious, treacherous, tricky, underhand, wily **2.** circuitous, confusing, crooked, deviating, erratic, excursive, indirect, misleading, rambling, roundabout, tortuous, wandering

devise arrange, conceive, concoct, construct, contrive, design, dream up, form, formulate, frame, imagine, invent, plan, plot, prepare, project, scheme, think up, work out

devoid barren, bereft, deficient, denuded, destitute, empty, free from, lacking, sans (*Archaic*), unprovided with, vacant, void, wanting, without

devolution decentralization, delegation

devolve 1. be transferred, commission, consign, delegate, depute, entrust, fall upon *or* to, rest with, transfer **2.** *Law* alienate, be handed down, convey

Devonian (dəˈvəʊnɪən) *a.* **1.** of fourth period of Palaeozoic era, between Silurian and Carboniferous periods **2.** of Devon —*n.* **3.** Devonian period or rock system

devote (dɪˈvəʊt) *vt.* set apart, give up exclusively (to person, purpose *etc.*) —**deˈvoted** *a.* loving, attached —**devotee** (dɛvəˈtiː) *n.* **1.** ardent enthusiast **2.** zealous worshipper —**deˈvotion** *n.* **1.** deep affection, loyalty **2.** dedication **3.** religious earnestness —*pl.* **4.** prayers, religious exercises —**deˈvotional** *a.*

devour (dɪˈvaʊə) *vt.* **1.** eat greedily **2.** consume, destroy **3.** read, gaze at eagerly —**deˈvourer** *n.*

devout (dɪˈvaʊt) *a.* **1.** earnestly religious, pious **2.** sincere, heartfelt —**deˈvoutly** *adv.*

dew (djuː) *n.* **1.** moisture from air deposited as small drops on cool surface between nightfall and morning **2.** any beaded moisture —*vt.* **3.** wet with or as with dew —**ˈdewiness** *n.* —**ˈdewy** *a.* —**ˈdewclaw** *n.* partly developed inner toe of dogs —**ˈdewlap** *n.* fold of loose skin hanging from neck —**dew point** temperature at which dew begins to form —**dew pond** small natural pond —**dew-worm** *n.* C large earthworm used as bait —**dewy-eyed** *a.* naive, innocent

dewberry (ˈdjuːbərɪ, -brɪ) *n.* bramble with blue-black fruits

Dewey Decimal System (ˈdjuːɪ) system of library book classification with ten main subject classes (*also* **decimal classification**)

DEW line (djuː) distant early warning line, network of sensors situated in Arctic regions of N Amer.

dexterity (dɛkˈstɛrɪtɪ) *n.* **1.** manual skill **2.** neatness **3.** deftness **4.** adroitness —**ˈdexter** *a. Her.* on the bearer's right-hand side of a shield —**ˈdexterous** *a.* showing dexterity, skilful

dextrin (ˈdɛkstrɪn) *or* **dextrine** (ˈdɛkstrɪn, -triːn) *n.* sticky substance obtained from starch, used as thickening agent in foods and as gum

dextrose (ˈdɛkstrəʊz, -trəʊs) *n.* white, soluble, sweet-tasting crystalline solid, occurring naturally in fruit, honey, animal tissue

D.F. Defender of the Faith

D.F.C. Distinguished Flying Cross

D.F.M. Distinguished Flying Medal

dg *or* **dg.** decigram

dharma (ˈdɑːmə) *n.* **1.** *Hinduism* social custom regarded as religious and moral duty **2.** *Hinduism* essential principle of cosmos; natural law; conduct that conforms with this **3.** *Buddhism* ideal truth

dhow (daʊ) *n.* lateen-rigged Arab sailing vessel

DHSS Department of Health and Social Security

di-[1] (*comb. form*) **1.** twice; two; double, as in *dicotyledon* **2.** containing two specified atoms or groups of atoms, as in *carbon dioxide*

di-[2] (*comb. form*) *see* DIA-

dia- *or before vowel* **di-** (*comb. form*) through

diabetes (daɪəˈbiːtɪs, -tiːz) *n.* any of various disorders characterized by excretion of abnormal amount of urine, *esp.* diabetes mellitus, in which body fails to store and utilize glucose —**diabetic** (daɪəˈbɛtɪk) *n./a.*

diabolic (daɪəˈbɒlɪk) *a.* devilish —**diaˈbolical** *a. inf.* very bad —**diaˈbolically** *adv.* —**diˈabolism** *n.* devil-worship

diabolo (dɪˈæbələʊ) *n.* game in which top is spun into air from string attached to two sticks

diaconal (daɪˈækənˀl) *a.* pert. to deacon —**diˈaconate** *n.* **1.** office, rank of deacon **2.** body of deacons

diacritic (daɪəˈkrɪtɪk) *n.* **1.** sign above letter or character indicating special phonetic value *etc.* —*a.* **2.** diacritical —**diaˈcritical** *a.* **1.** of a diacritic **2.** showing a distinction (*also* **diaˈcritic**)

diadem (ˈdaɪədɛm) *n.* a crown

diaeresis *or* (*esp. U.S.*) **dieresis** (daɪˈɛrɪsɪs) *n.* mark (¨) placed over vowel to show that it is sounded separately from preceding one, as in Noël (*pl.* **-ses** (-siːz))

diagnosis (daɪəgˈnəʊsɪs) *n.* identification of disease from symptoms (*pl.* **-ses** (-siːz)) —**ˈdiagnose** *v.* —**diagˈnostic** *a.*

diagonal (daɪˈægənˀl) *a.* **1.** from corner to corner **2.** oblique —*n.* **3.** line from corner to corner —**diˈagonally** *adv.*

THESAURUS

devote allot, apply, appropriate, assign, commit, concern oneself, consecrate, dedicate, enshrine, give, occupy oneself, pledge, reserve, set apart

devoted ardent, caring, committed, concerned, constant, dedicated, devout, faithful, fond, loving, loyal, staunch, steadfast, true

devotee addict, adherent, admirer, aficionado, disciple, enthusiast, fan, fanatic, follower, supporter, votary

devotion 1. adherence, allegiance, commitment, consecration, constancy, dedication, faithfulness, fidelity, loyalty **2.** adoration, devoutness, godliness, holiness, piety, prayer, religiousness, reverence, sanctity, spirituality, worship **3.** affection, ardour, attachment, earnestness, fervour, fondness, intensity, love, passion, zeal **4.** *Plural* church service, divine office, prayers, religious observance

devour 1. bolt, consume, cram, dispatch, eat, gobble, gorge, gulp, guzzle, polish off (*Inf.*), stuff, swallow, wolf **2.** annihilate, consume, destroy, ravage, spend, waste, wipe out **3.** absorb, appreciate, be engrossed by, be preoccupied, delight in, drink in, enjoy, feast on, go through, read compulsively *or* voraciously, relish, revel in, take in

devout 1. godly, holy, orthodox, pious, prayerful, pure, religious, reverent, saintly **2.** ardent, deep, devoted, earnest, fervent, genuine, heartfelt, intense, passionate, profound, serious, sincere, zealous

devoutly fervently, heart and soul, profoundly, sincerely, with all one's heart

dexterity 1. adroitness, artistry, deftness, effortlessness, expertise, facility, finesse, handiness, knack, mastery, neatness, nimbleness, proficiency, skill, smoothness, touch **2.** ability, address, adroitness, aptitude, aptness, art, cleverness, expertness, ingenuity, readiness, skilfulness, tact

diabolical appalling, atrocious, damnable, difficult, disastrous, dreadful, excruciating, fiendish, hellish, nasty, outrageous, shocking, tricky, unpleasant, vile

diagnose analyse, determine, distinguish, identify, interpret, investigate, pinpoint, pronounce, recognize

diagnosis 1. analysis, examination, investigation,

diagram (ˈdaɪəgræm) *n.* drawing, figure in lines, to illustrate something being expounded —**diagramˈmatic** *a.* —**diagramˈmatically** *adv.*

dial (ˈdaɪəl) *n.* **1.** face of clock *etc.* **2.** plate marked with graduations on which pointer moves (as on meter, weighing machine *etc.*) **3.** numbered disc on front of telephone **4.** *sl.* face —*vt.* **5.** operate (telephone) **6.** indicate on dial (**-ll-**) —**dialling tone** *or U.S.* **dial tone** continuous purring heard over telephone indicating that number can be dialled

dialect (ˈdaɪəlɛkt) *n.* **1.** characteristic speech of district **2.** local variety of a language —**diaˈlectal** *a.*

dialectic (daɪəˈlɛktɪk) *n.* art of arguing —**diaˈlectical** *a.* —**diaˈlectically** *adv.* —**dialecˈtician** *n.* **1.** logician **2.** reasoner

dialogue *or U.S.* (*oft.*) **dialog** (ˈdaɪəlɒg) *n.* **1.** conversation between two or more (persons) **2.** representation of such conversation in drama, novel *etc.* **3.** discussion between representatives of two states, countries *etc.*

dialysis (daɪˈælɪsɪs) *n. Med.* filtering of blood through membrane to remove waste products

diamagnetism (daɪəˈmægnɪtɪzəm) *n.* phenomenon exhibited by substances that are repelled by both poles of magnet

diamanté (daɪəˈmæntɪ) *n.* (fabric covered with) glittering particles —**diaˈmantine** *a.* like diamond

diameter (daɪˈæmɪtə) *n.* **1.** (length of) straight line from side to side of figure or body (*esp.* circle) through centre **2.** thickness —**diaˈmetrical** *a.* opposite —**diaˈmetrically** *adv.*

diamond (ˈdaɪəmənd) *n.* **1.** very hard and brilliant precious stone, also used in industry as an abrasive **2.** rhomboid figure **3.** suit at cards **4.** playing field in baseball —**diamond jubilee** *or* **wedding** 60th (sometimes 75th) anniversary

dianthus (daɪˈænθəs) *n.* genus of herbaceous flowers, *eg* pinks and carnations

diapason (daɪəˈpeɪzᵊn) *n.* **1.** fundamental organ stop **2.** compass of voice or instrument

diaper (ˈdaɪəpə) *n.* **1.** US baby's napkin **2.** fabric with small diamond pattern **3.** pattern of that kind —**ˈdiapered** *a.*

diaphanous (daɪˈæfənəs) *a.* transparent

diaphoretic (daɪəfəˈrɛtɪk) *n.* **1.** diaphoretic drug —*a.* **2.** relating to or causing perspiration

diaphragm (ˈdaɪəfræm) *n.* **1.** muscular partition dividing two cavities of body, midriff **2.** plate or disc wholly or partly closing tube or opening **3.** any thin dividing or covering membrane —**diaphragmatic** (daɪəfrægˈmætɪk) *a.*

diapositive (daɪəˈpɒzɪtɪv) *n.* positive transparency; slide

diarrhoea *or esp. U.S.* **diarrhea** (daɪəˈrɪə) *n.* excessive looseness of the bowels —**diarˈrhoeal** *or esp. U.S.* **diarˈrheal** *a.*

diary (ˈdaɪərɪ) *n.* **1.** daily record of events, engagements, thoughts *etc.* **2.** book for this —**ˈdiarist** *n.* writer of diary

Diaspora (daɪˈæspərə) *n.* **1.** dispersion of Jews from Palestine after Babylonian captivity; Jewish communities that arose after this **2.** (*oft.* **d-**) dispersion, as of people orig. of one nation

diastase (ˈdaɪəsteɪs, -steɪz) *n.* enzyme that converts starch into sugar

diastole (daɪˈæstəlɪ) *n.* dilation of chambers of heart

diathermy (ˈdaɪəθɜːmɪ) *or* **diathermia** (daɪəˈθɜːmɪə) *n.* heating of body tissues with electric current for medical or surgical purposes

diatom (ˈdaɪətəm) *n.* one of order of microscopic algae —**diaˈtomic** *a.* of two atoms

diatonic (daɪəˈtɒnɪk) *a. Mus.* **1.** pert. to regular major and minor scales **2.** (of melody) composed in such a scale

diatribe (ˈdaɪətraɪb) *n.* violently bitter verbal attack, invective, denunciation

dibble (ˈdɪbᵊl) *n.* **1.** small tool used to make holes in ground for bulbs *etc.* (*also* **ˈdibber**) —*v.* **2.** make hole in (ground) with dibble **3.** plant (seeds *etc.*) with dibble

dice (daɪs) *pl.n.* **1.** (*also functions as sing., orig. sing.* **die**) cubes each with six sides marked one to six for games of chance —*vi.* **2.** gamble with dice —*vt.* **3.** cut into small cubes —**ˈdicer** *n.* —**ˈdicey** *a. inf.* dangerous, risky

dicephalous (daɪˈsɛfələs) *a.* two-headed

dichotomy (daɪˈkɒtəmɪ) *n.* division into two parts

dichroism (ˈdaɪkrəʊɪzəm) *n.* property possessed by some crystals of exhibiting different colours when viewed from different directions —**diˈchroic** *a.*

dichromatic (daɪkrəʊˈmætɪk) *a.* **1.** having two colours (*also* **diˈchroic**) **2.** (of animal species) having two different colour varieties **3.** able to perceive only two colours

dick (dɪk) *n. sl.* **1.** fellow, person **2.** detective

Dickensian (dɪˈkɛnzɪən) *a.* **1.** of Charles Dickens or his novels **2.** denoting poverty, distress and exploita-

THESAURUS

scrutiny **2.** conclusion, interpretation, opinion, pronouncement

diagonal *adj.* angled, cater-cornered (*U.S. inf.*), cornerways, cross, crossways, crosswise, oblique, slanting

diagonally aslant, at an angle, cornerwise, crosswise, obliquely, on the bias, on the cross

diagram chart, drawing, figure, layout, outline, plan, representation, sketch

dialect accent, idiom, jargon, language, lingo (*Inf.*), localism, patois, pronunciation, provincialism, speech, tongue, vernacular

dialectic *Often plural* argumentation, contention, discussion, disputation, logic, polemics, ratiocination, reasoning

dialogue 1. colloquy, communication, confabulation, conference, conversation, converse, discourse, discussion, duologue, interlocution **2.** conversation, lines, script, spoken part

diametrical antipodal, antithetical, conflicting, contrary, contrasting, counter, opposed, opposite

diametrically absolutely, completely, entirely, utterly

diary appointment book, chronicle, daily record, day-to-day account, engagement book, journal

diatribe abuse, castigation, criticism, denunciation, disputation, harangue, invective, philippic, reviling, stream of abuse, stricture, tirade, verbal onslaught, vituperation

dicey chancy (*Inf.*), dangerous, difficult, risky, ticklish, tricky

tion as depicted in Dickens's novels **3.** grotesquely comic, as some Dickens characters

dicker (ˈdɪkə) *chiefly* **US** *v.* **1.** trade (goods) by bargaining; barter —*n.* **2.** petty bargain or barter

dicky[1] *or* **dickey** (ˈdɪkɪ) *n.* detachable false shirt front (*pl.* **ˈdickies, ˈdickeys**) —**ˈdickybird** *n. inf.* child's word for small bird

dicky[2] *or* **dickey** (ˈdɪkɪ) *a. sl.* shaky, unsound

dicotyledon (daɪkɒtɪˈliːdᵊn) *n.* flowering plant having two embryonic seed leaves

Dictaphone (ˈdɪktəfəʊn) *n.* **R** tape recorder, used *esp.* for dictation

dictate (dɪkˈteɪt) *v.* **1.** say or read for another to transcribe —*vt.* **2.** prescribe, lay down —*vi.* **3.** seek to impose one's will on others —*n.* (ˈdɪkteɪt) **4.** bidding —**dicˈtation** *n.* —**dicˈtator** *n.* absolute ruler —**dictaˈtorial** *a.* **1.** despotic **2.** overbearing —**dictaˈtorially** *adv.* —**dicˈtatorship** *n.*

diction (ˈdɪkʃən) *n.* **1.** choice and use of words **2.** enunciation

dictionary (ˈdɪkʃənərɪ) *n.* **1.** book setting forth, alphabetically, words of language with meanings *etc.* **2.** reference book with items in alphabetical order

dictum (ˈdɪktəm) *n.* **1.** pronouncement **2.** saying, maxim (*pl.* **-s, -ta** (-tə))

did (dɪd) *pt. of* DO[1]

didactic (dɪˈdæktɪk) *a.* **1.** designed to instruct **2.** (of people) opinionated, dictatorial —**diˈdacticism** *n.*

diddle (ˈdɪdᵊl) *vt. inf.* cheat

didgeridoo (dɪdʒərɪˈduː) *n. Mus.* native Aust. wind instrument

die[1] (daɪ) *vi.* **1.** cease to live **2.** come to an end **3.** stop functioning **4.** *inf.* be nearly overcome (with laughter *etc.*) (**died, ˈdying**) —**ˈdiehard** *n.* one who resists (reform *etc.*) to the end —**be dying for** be looking eagerly forward to

die[2] (daɪ) *n. see* DICE

die[3] (daɪ) *n.* **1.** shaped block of hard material to form metal in forge, press *etc.* **2.** tool for cutting thread on pipe *etc.* —**die-cast** *vt.* shape or form (object) by introducing molten metal or plastic into reusable mould —**die-casting** *n.*

dieldrin (ˈdiːldrɪn) *n.* highly toxic crystalline insecticide

dielectric (daɪɪˈlɛktrɪk) *n.* **1.** substance through or across which electric induction takes place **2.** nonconductor **3.** insulator

dieresis (daɪˈɛrɪsɪs) *n. see* DIAERESIS

diesel (ˈdiːzᵊl) *a.* **1.** pert. to internal-combustion engine using oil as fuel —*n.* **2.** this engine **3.** diesel oil or fuel —**diesel-electric** *n.* **1.** locomotive fitted with diesel engine driving electric generator —*a.* **2.** of such locomotive or system —**diesel oil** *or* **fuel** fuel, distilled from petroleum, used in diesel engines

diet[1] (ˈdaɪət) *n.* **1.** restricted or regulated course of feeding **2.** kind of food lived on **3.** food —*vi.* **4.** follow a dietary regimen, as to lose weight —**ˈdietary** *a.* **1.** relating to diet —*n.* **2.** a regulated diet **3.** system of dieting —**dieˈtetic** *a.* —**dieˈtetics** *pl.n.* (*with sing. v.*) science of diet —**dieˈtitian** *or* **dieˈtician** *n.* one skilled in dietetics

diet[2] (ˈdaɪət) *n.* **1.** parliament of some countries **2.** formal assembly

differ (ˈdɪfə) *vi.* **1.** be unlike **2.** disagree —**ˈdifference** *n.* **1.** unlikeness **2.** degree or point of unlikeness **3.** disagreement **4.** remainder left after subtraction —**ˈdifferent** *a.* unlike —**ˈdifferently** *adv.*

THESAURUS

dicky *adj.* fluttery, queer, shaky, unreliable, unsound, unsteady, weak

dictate *v.* **1.** read out, say, speak, transmit, utter **2.** command, decree, direct, enjoin, impose, lay down, ordain, order, prescribe, pronounce ~*n.* **3.** behest, bidding, command, decree, direction, edict, fiat, injunction, mandate, order, ordinance, requirement, statute, ultimatum, word

dictator absolute ruler, autocrat, despot, oppressor, tyrant

dictatorial 1. absolute, arbitrary, autocratic, despotic, totalitarian, tyrannical, unlimited, unrestricted **2.** authoritarian, bossy (*Inf.*), dogmatical, domineering, imperious, iron-handed, magisterial, oppressive, overbearing

dictatorship absolute rule, absolutism, authoritarianism, autocracy, despotism, reign of terror, totalitarianism, tyranny

diction 1. expression, language, phraseology, phrasing, style, usage, vocabulary, wording **2.** articulation, delivery, elocution, enunciation, fluency, inflection, intonation, pronunciation, speech

dictionary concordance, encyclopedia, glossary, lexicon, vocabulary, wordbook

die 1. breathe one's last, decease, depart, expire, finish, give up the ghost, hop the twig (*Sl.*), kick the bucket (*Sl.*), pass away, perish, snuff it (*Sl.*) **2.** decay, decline, disappear, dwindle, ebb, end, fade, lapse, pass, sink, subside, vanish, wane, wilt, wither **3.** break down, fade out *or* away, fail, fizzle out, halt, lose power, peter out, run down, stop **4.** *Usually with* **of** be overcome, collapse, succumb to **5. be dying for** ache, be eager desire, hunger, languish, long, pine for, swoon, yearn

die-hard *n.* fanatic, intransigent, old fogy, reactionary, stick-in-the-mud (*Inf.*), ultraconservative, zealot

diet[1] *n.* **1.** abstinence, dietary, fast, regime, regimen **2.** aliment, comestibles, commons, edibles, fare, food, nourishment, nutriment, provisions, rations, subsistence, sustenance, viands, victuals ~*v.* **3.** abstain, eat sparingly, fast, lose weight, reduce, slim

diet[2] chamber, congress, convention, council, legislative assembly, legislature, meeting, parliament, sitting

differ 1. be dissimilar, be distinct, contradict, contrast, depart from, diverge, run counter to, stand apart, vary **2.** clash, contend, debate, demur, disagree, dispute, dissent, oppose, take issue

difference 1. alteration, change, contrast, deviation, differentiation, discrepancy, disparity, dissimilarity, distinction, distinctness, divergence, diversity, unlikeness, variation, variety **2.** distinction, exception, idiosyncrasy, particularity, peculiarity, singularity **3.** argument, clash, conflict, contention, contrariety, contretemps, controversy, debate, disagreement, discordance, dispute, quarrel, set-to (*Inf.*), strife, tiff, wrangle **4.** balance, remainder, rest, result

different 1. altered, at odds, at variance, changed, clashing, contrasting, deviating, discrepant, disparate, dissimilar, divergent, diverse, inconsistent, opposed, unlike **2.** another, discrete, distinct, individ-

differentia (dɪfəˈrɛnʃɪə) *n. Logic* feature by which subclasses of same class of named objects can be distinguished (*pl.* **-tiae** (-ʃiː))

differential (dɪfəˈrɛnʃəl) *a.* **1.** varying with circumstances **2.** special **3.** *Maths.* pert. to an infinitesimal change in variable quantity **4.** *Phys. etc.* relating to difference between sets of motions acting in the same direction or between pressures *etc.* —*n.* **5.** *Maths.* infinitesimal difference between two consecutive states of variable quantity **6.** differential gear **7.** difference between rates of pay for different types of labour —**differˈentially** *adv.* —**differˈentiate** *vt.* **1.** serve to distinguish between, make different —*vi.* **2.** discriminate —**differentiˈation** *n.* —**differential calculus** method of calculating relative rate of change for continuously varying quantities —**differential gear** epicyclic gear mounted in driving axle of vehicle, that permits one driving wheel to rotate faster than the other, as when cornering

difficult (ˈdɪfɪkᵊlt) *a.* **1.** requiring effort, skill *etc.* to do or understand, not easy **2.** obscure —**ˈdifficulty** *n.* **1.** being difficult **2.** difficult task, problem **3.** embarrassment **4.** hindrance **5.** obscurity **6.** trouble

diffident (ˈdɪfɪdənt) *a.* lacking confidence, timid, shy —**ˈdiffidence** *n.* shyness —**ˈdiffidently** *adv.*

diffract (dɪˈfrækt) *vi.* break up, *esp.* of rays of light, sound-waves —**difˈfraction** *n.* deflection of ray of light, electromagnetic wave caused by obstacle

diffuse (dɪˈfjuːz) *vt.* **1.** spread abroad —*a.* (dɪˈfjuːs) **2.** widely spread **3.** loose, verbose, wordy —**diffusely** (dɪˈfjuːslɪ) *adv.* **1.** loosely **2.** wordily —**difˈfusible** *a.* —**difˈfusion** *n.* —**diffusive** (dɪˈfjuːsɪv) *a.* —**diffusively** (dɪˈfjuːsɪvlɪ) *adv.*

dig (dɪg) *vi.* **1.** work with spade **2.** search, investigate —*vt.* **3.** turn up with spade **4.** hollow out, make hole in **5.** excavate **6.** thrust **7.** (*oft. with* out *or* up) discover by searching (**dug, ˈdigging**) —*n.* **8.** piece of digging **9.** archaeological excavation **10.** thrust **11.** jibe, taunt —*pl.* **12.** *inf.* lodgings —**ˈdigger** *n.* **1.** one who digs **2.** goldminer **3.** Aust. or N.Z. soldier

digest (dɪˈdʒɛst, daɪ-) *vt.* **1.** prepare (food) in stomach *etc.* for assimilation **2.** bring into handy form by sorting, tabulating, summarizing **3.** reflect on **4.** absorb —*vi.* **5.** (of food) undergo digestion —*n.* (ˈdaɪdʒɛst) **6.** methodical summary, *esp.* of laws **7.** magazine containing condensed version of articles *etc.* already published elsewhere —**diˈgestible** *a.* —**diˈgestion** *n.* digesting —**diˈgestive** *a.* **1.** relating to digestion —*n.* **2.** substance that aids digestion —**digestive biscuit** round semisweet biscuit made from wholemeal flour

digit (ˈdɪdʒɪt) *n.* **1.** finger or toe **2.** any of the numbers 0 to 9 —**ˈdigital** *a.* **1.** of, resembling digits **2.** performed with fingers **3.** displaying information (time *etc.*) by numbers rather than by pointer on dial —**ˈdigitate** *or* **ˈdigitated** *a.* having separate fingers, toes —**digital clock** *or* **watch** clock or watch in which time is indicated by digits rather than by hands on dial

THESAURUS

ual, other, separate **3.** assorted, divers (*Archaic*), diverse, manifold, many, miscellaneous, multifarious, numerous, several, some, sundry, varied, various

differential 1. *adj.* diacritical, discriminative, distinctive, distinguishing **2.** *n.* amount of difference, difference, discrepancy, disparity

differentiate 1. contrast, discern, discriminate, distinguish, make a distinction, mark off, separate, set off *or* apart, tell apart **2.** adapt, alter, change, convert, make different, modify, transform

difficult 1. arduous, burdensome, demanding, formidable, hard, laborious, no picnic (*Inf.*), onerous, painful, strenuous, toilsome, uphill, wearisome **2.** dark, full of hardship, grim, hard, straitened, tough, trying **3.** abstract, abstruse, baffling, complex, complicated, delicate, enigmatical, intricate, involved, knotty, obscure, perplexing, problematical, thorny, ticklish

difficulty 1. arduousness, awkwardness, hardship, laboriousness, labour, pain, painfulness, strain, strenuousness, tribulation **2.** deep water, dilemma, distress, embarrassment, fix (*Inf.*), hot water, jam (*Inf.*), mess, perplexity, pickle (*Inf.*), plight, predicament, quandary, spot (*Inf.*), straits, trial, trouble **3.** *Often plural* complication, hindrance, hurdle, impediment, objection, obstacle, opposition, pitfall, problem, protest

diffidence backwardness, bashfulness, constraint, doubt, fear, hesitancy, hesitation, humility, insecurity, lack of self-confidence, meekness, modesty, reluctance, reserve, self-consciousness, sheepishness, shyness, timidity, timidness, timorousness, unassertiveness

diffident backward, bashful, constrained, distrustful, doubtful, hesitant, insecure, meek, modest, reluctant, reserved, self-conscious, self-effacing, sheepish, shrinking, shy, suspicious, timid, timorous, unassertive, unassuming, unobtrusive, unsure, withdrawn

diffuse *adj.* **1.** circumlocutory, copious, diffusive, digressive, discursive, long-winded, loose, maundering, meandering, prolix, rambling, vague, verbose, waffling (*Inf.*), wordy **2.** dispersed, scattered, spread out, unconcentrated ~*v.* **3.** circulate, dispel, dispense, disperse, disseminate, dissipate, distribute, propagate, scatter, spread

diffusion 1. circulation, dispersal, dispersion, dissemination, dissipation, distribution, expansion, propaganda, propagation, scattering, spread **2.** circuitousness, diffuseness, digressiveness, discursiveness, long-windedness, prolixity, rambling, verbiage, verbosity, wandering, wordiness

dig *v.* **1.** break up, burrow, delve, excavate, gouge, grub, hoe, hollow out, mine, penetrate, pierce, quarry, scoop, till, tunnel, turn over **2.** drive, jab, poke, prod, punch, thrust **3.** delve, dig down, go into, investigate, probe, research, search **4.** *With* **out** *or* **up** bring to light, come across, come up with, discover, expose, extricate, find, retrieve, root (*Inf.*), rootle, uncover, unearth ~*n.* **5.** jab, poke, prod, punch, thrust **6.** crack (*Sl.*), cutting remark, gibe, insult, jeer, quip, sneer, taunt, wisecrack (*Inf.*)

digest *v.* **1.** absorb, assimilate, concoct, dissolve, incorporate, macerate **2.** absorb, assimilate, con, consider, contemplate, grasp, master, meditate, ponder, study, take in, understand **3.** arrange, classify, codify, dispose, methodize, systematize, tabulate **4.** abridge, compress, condense, reduce, shorten, summarize ~*n.* **5.** abridgment, abstract, compendium, condensation, epitome, précis, résumé, summary, synopsis

digestion absorption, assimilation, conversion, incorporation, ingestion, transformation

—**digital computer** electronic computer consisting of numbers, letters *etc.* that are represented internally in binary notation

digitalis (dɪdʒɪˈteɪlɪs) *n.* drug made from foxglove

dignity (ˈdɪgnɪtɪ) *n.* **1.** stateliness, gravity **2.** worthiness, excellence, repute **3.** honourable office or title —ˈ**dignified** *a.* stately, majestic —ˈ**dignify** *vt.* give dignity to (**-fied, -fying**) —ˈ**dignitary** *n.* holder of high office

digraph (ˈdaɪgrɑːf) *n.* combination of two letters used to represent single sound such as *gh* in *tough*

digress (daɪˈgrɛs) *vi.* turn from main course, *esp.* to deviate from subject in speaking or writing —**diˈgression** *n.* —**diˈgressive** *a.*

dihedral (daɪˈhiːdrəl) *a.* having two plane faces or sides

dik-dik (ˈdɪkdɪk) *n.* small Afr. antelope

dike (daɪk) *n. see* DYKE

diktat (ˈdɪktɑːt) *n.* arbitrary decree

dilapidate (dɪˈlæpɪdeɪt) *v.* (cause to) fall into ruin —**diˈlapidated** *a.* **1.** in ruins **2.** decayed —**dilapiˈdation** *n.*

dilate (daɪˈleɪt, dɪ-) *vt.* **1.** widen, expand —*vi.* **2.** expand **3.** talk or write at length (on) —**diˈlation** *or* **dilatation** (daɪləˈteɪʃən) *n.*

dilatory (ˈdɪlətərɪ) *a.* tardy, slow, belated —ˈ**dilatorily** *adv.* —ˈ**dilatoriness** *n.* delay

dilemma (dɪˈlɛmə, daɪ-) *n.* **1.** position in fact or argument offering choice only between unwelcome alternatives **2.** predicament

dilettante (dɪlɪˈtɑːntɪ) *n.* **1.** person with taste and knowledge of fine arts as pastime **2.** dabbler (*pl.* **dilettanti** (dɪlɪˈtɑːntɪ)) —*a.* **3.** amateur, desultory —**dilet'tantism** *n.*

diligent (ˈdɪlɪdʒənt) *a.* unremitting in effort, industrious, hard-working —ˈ**diligence** *n.*

dill (dɪl) *n.* yellow-flowered herb with medicinal seeds

dilly (ˈdɪlɪ) *n. sl., chiefly* **US** remarkable person or thing

dilly-dally (ˈdɪlɪdælɪ) *vi. inf.* **1.** loiter **2.** vacillate

dilute (daɪˈluːt) *vt.* **1.** reduce (liquid) in strength, *esp.* by adding water **2.** thin **3.** reduce in force, effect *etc.* —*a.* **4.** weakened thus —**diluent** (ˈdɪljuənt) *a./n.* —**diˈlution** *n.*

diluvial (daɪˈluːvɪəl, dɪ-) *or* **diluvian** *a.* of, connected with, a deluge or flood, *esp.* the Flood of the Book of Genesis

dim (dɪm) *a.* **1.** indistinct, faint, not bright **2.** mentally dull **3.** unfavourable (ˈ**dimmer** *comp.*, ˈ**dimmest** *sup.*) —*v.* **4.** make, grow dim (**-mm-**) —ˈ**dimly** *adv.* —ˈ**dimmer** *n.* device for dimming electric lights —ˈ**dimness** *n.* —ˈ**dimwit** *n. inf.* stupid or silly person —**dim-witted** *a.*

dime (daɪm) *n.* 10-cent piece, coin of U.S. and Canada.

dimension (dɪˈmɛnʃən) *n.* **1.** measurement, size **2.** aspect —**diˈmensional** *a.* —**fourth dimension** *Phys.* **1.**

THESAURUS

dignified august, decorous, distinguished, exalted, formal, grave, honourable, imposing, lofty, lordly, noble, reserved, solemn, stately, upright

dignify adorn, advance, aggrandize, distinguish, elevate, ennoble, exalt, glorify, grace, honour, promote, raise

dignitary *n.* high-up (*Inf.*), notability, notable, personage, pillar of society (the church, the state), public figure, V.I.P., worthy

dignity **1.** courtliness, decorum, grandeur, gravity, hauteur, loftiness, majesty, nobility, propriety, solemnity, stateliness **2.** elevation, eminence, excellence, glory, greatness, honour, importance, nobleness, rank, respectability, standing, station, status

digress be diffuse, depart, deviate, diverge, drift, expatiate, get off the point *or* subject, go off at a tangent, ramble, stray, turn aside, wander

digression apostrophe, aside, departure, detour, deviation, divergence, diversion, footnote, obiter dictum, parenthesis, straying, wandering

dilapidated battered, broken-down, crumbling, decayed, decaying, decrepit, fallen in, falling apart, gone to rack and ruin, in ruins, neglected, ramshackle, rickety, ruined, ruinous, run-down, shabby, shaky, tumbledown, uncared for, worn-out

dilate **1.** broaden, distend, enlarge, expand, extend, puff out, stretch, swell, widen **2.** amplify, be profuse, be prolix, descant, detail, develop, dwell on, enlarge, expand, expatiate, expound, spin out

dilatory backward, behindhand, dallying, delaying, laggard, lingering, loitering, procrastinating, putting off, slack, slow, sluggish, snail-like, tardy, tarrying, time-wasting

dilemma difficulty, embarrassment, fix (*Inf.*), jam (*Inf.*), mess, perplexity, pickle (*Inf.*), plight, predicament, problem, puzzle, quandary, spot (*Inf.*), strait, tight corner

dilettante aesthete, amateur, dabbler, nonprofessional, trifler

diligence activity, application, assiduity, assiduousness, attention, attentiveness, care, constancy, earnestness, heedfulness, industry, intentness, laboriousness, perseverance, sedulousness

diligent active, assiduous, attentive, busy, careful, conscientious, constant, earnest, hard-working, indefatigable, industrious, laborious, painstaking, persevering, persistent, sedulous, studious, tireless

dilly-dally dally, dawdle, delay, dither, falter, fluctuate, hesitate, hover, linger, loiter, potter, procrastinate, shillyshally (*Inf.*), trifle, vacillate, waver

dilute *v.* **1.** adulterate, cut, make thinner, thin (out), water down, weaken **2.** *Fig.* attenuate, decrease, diffuse, diminish, lessen, mitigate, reduce, temper, weaken

dim *adj.* **1.** caliginous (*Archaic*), cloudy, dark, darkish, dusky, grey, overcast, poorly lit, shadowy, tenebrous, unilluminated **2.** bleary, blurred, faint, fuzzy, ill-defined, indistinct, obscured, shadowy, unclear **3.** dense, doltish, dull, dumb (*Inf.*), obtuse, slow, slow on the uptake (*Inf.*), stupid, thick **4.** confused, hazy, imperfect, indistinct, intangible, obscure, remote, shadowy, vague **5.** dingy, dull, feeble, lacklustre, muted, opaque, pale, sullied, tarnished, weak **6.** dashing, depressing, discouraging, gloomy, sombre, unfavourable, unpromising ~*v.* **7.** bedim, blur, cloud, darken, dull, fade, lower, obscure, tarnish, turn down

dimension *Often plural* **1.** amplitude, bulk, capacity, extent, measurement, proportions, size, volume **2.** bigness, extent, greatness, importance, largeness, magnitude, measure, range, scale, scope

time **2.** supranatural, fictional dimension additional to those of length, breadth, thickness

diminish (dɪˈmɪnɪʃ) *v.* lessen —**dimiˈnution** *n.* —**diˈminutive** *a.* **1.** very small —*n.* **2.** derivative word, affix implying smallness —**diminished responsibility** *Law* plea under which mental derangement is submitted as demonstrating lack of criminal responsibility

diminuendo (dɪmɪnjʊˈɛndəʊ) *a. Mus.* (of sound) dying away

dimity (ˈdɪmɪtɪ) *n.* strong cotton fabric

dimple (ˈdɪmpᵊl) *n.* **1.** small hollow in surface of skin, *esp.* of cheek **2.** any small hollow —*v.* **3.** mark with, show dimples

din (dɪn) *n.* continuous roar of confused noises —**din into** instil into by constant repetition

dinar (ˈdiːnɑː) *n.* **1.** standard monetary unit of Iraq, Jordan, Libya, Yugoslavia *etc.* **2.** an Iranian monetary unit

dine (daɪn) *vi.* **1.** eat dinner —*vt.* **2.** give dinner to —**ˈdiner** *n.* **1.** one who dines **2.** *chiefly* **US** small cheap restaurant **3.** railway restaurant car —**dining car** railway coach in which meals are served (*also* **restaurant car**) —**dining room** room where meals are eaten

ding (dɪŋ) *v.* **1.** ring (*esp.* with tedious repetition) —*vi.* **2.** make (imitation of) sound of bell —*n.* **3.** this sound —**ding-dong** *n.* **1.** sound of bell **2.** imitation of sound of bell **3.** violent exchange of blows or words —*a.* **4.** sounding or ringing repeatedly

dinghy, dingy, *or* **dingey** (ˈdɪŋɪ) *n.* **1.** small open boat **2.** collapsible rubber boat

dingle (ˈdɪŋgᵊl) *n.* dell

dingo (ˈdɪŋgəʊ) *n.* Aust. wild dog

dingy (ˈdɪndʒɪ) *a.* dirty-looking, dull —**ˈdinginess** *n.*

dinkum (ˈdɪŋkəm) *a.* **A, NZ** *inf.* genuine; right —**dinkum oil** truth

dinky (ˈdɪŋkɪ) *a. inf.* **1. UK** small and neat; dainty **2. US** inconsequential; insignificant

dinner (ˈdɪnə) *n.* **1.** chief meal of the day **2.** official banquet —**dinner jacket** man's semiformal evening jacket without tails, usu. black

dinosaur (ˈdaɪnəsɔː) *n.* extinct reptile, oft. of gigantic size —**dinoˈsaurian** *a.*

dint (dɪnt) *n.* dent, mark —**by dint of** by means of

diocese (ˈdaɪəsɪs) *n.* district, jurisdiction of bishop —**diocesan** (daɪˈɒsɪsᵊn) *a.* **1.** of diocese —*n.* **2.** bishop, clergyman, people of diocese

diode (ˈdaɪəʊd)*n.* **1.** semiconductor device for converting alternating current to direct current **2.** electronic valve having two electrodes between which current can flow in only one direction

dioecious (daɪˈiːʃəs) *a.* (of plants) having male and female reproductive organs on separate plants

Dionysian (daɪəˈnɪzɪən) *a.* **1.** of Dionysus, Gr. god of wine and revelry **2.** (*oft.* **d-**) wild; orgiastic

dioptre *or U.S.* **diopter** (daɪˈɒptə) *n.* unit for measuring refractive power of lens —**diˈoptrics** *pl.n.* (*with sing. v.*) that part of the science of optics which deals with refraction of light

diorama (daɪəˈrɑːmə) *n.* miniature three-dimensional scene, *esp.* as museum exhibit

dioxide (daɪˈɒksaɪd) *n.* oxide with two parts of oxygen to one of the other constituents

dioxin (daɪˈɒksɪn) *n.* any of various by-products of manufacture of certain herbicides and bactericides

dip (dɪp) *vt.* **1.** put partly or briefly into liquid, *esp.* to coat **2.** immerse **3.** lower and raise again **4.** take up in ladle, bucket *etc.* **5.** direct (headlights of vehicle) downwards —*vi.* **6.** plunge partially or temporarily **7.** go down, sink **8.** slope downwards (**-pp-**) —*n.* **9.** act of dipping **10.** bathe **11.** liquid chemical in which livestock are immersed to treat insect pests *etc.* **12.** downward slope **13.** hollow **14.** creamy (savoury) mixture in which crisps *etc.* are dipped before being eaten **15.** lottery —**ˈdipstick** *n.* graduated rod dipped into container to indicate fluid level —**dip switch** device for dipping car headlights —**dip into 1.** glance at **2.** make inroads into for funds

Dip. A. D. Diploma in Art and Design

Dip. Ed. UK Diploma in Education

diphtheria (dɪpˈθɪərɪə) *n.* infectious disease of throat with membranous growth —**diphtheritic** (dɪpθəˈrɪtɪk) *a.*

diphthong (ˈdɪfθɒŋ) *n.* union of two vowel sounds in single compound sound

diploma (dɪˈpləʊmə) *n.* **1.** document vouching for person's proficiency **2.** title to degree, honour *etc.*

diplomacy (dɪˈpləʊməsɪ) *n.* **1.** management of international relations **2.** skill in negotiation **3.** tactful, adroit dealing —**ˈdiplomat** *n.* one engaged in official diplomacy —**diploˈmatic** *a.* —**diploˈmatically** *adv.* —**diˈplomatist** *n.* **1.** diplomat **2.** tactful person —**diplomatic immunity** immunity from local jurisdiction *etc.* afforded to diplomatic staff abroad

THESAURUS

diminish 1. abate, contract, curtail, cut, decrease, lessen, lower, reduce, retrench, shrink, weaken **2.** decline, die out, dwindle, ebb, fade away, peter out, recede, shrivel, slacken, subside, wane

diminution abatement, contraction, curtailment, cut, cutback, decay, decline, decrease, deduction, lessening, reduction, retrenchment, weakening

diminutive *adj.* bantam, Lilliputian, little, midget, mini, miniature, minute, petite, pocket(-sized), pygmy, small, tiny, undersized, wee

din 1. *n.* babel, clamour, clangour, clash, clatter, commotion, crash, hubbub, hullabaloo, noise, outcry, pandemonium, racket, row, shout, uproar **2.** *v.* *Usually with* **into** drum into, go on at, hammer into, inculcate, instil, instruct, teach

dine banquet, eat, feast, lunch, sup

dinner banquet, beanfeast (*Inf.*), blowout (*Sl.*), collation, feast, main meal, meal, refection, repast, spread

dip *v.* **1.** bathe, douse, duck, dunk, immerse, plunge, rinse, souse **2.** decline, descend, disappear, droop, drop (down), fade, fall, lower, sag, set, sink, slope, slump, subside, tilt **3.** ladle, scoop, spoon **4.** *With* **in** *or* **into** browse, dabble, glance at, peruse, play at, run over, sample, skim, try **5.** *With* **in** *or* **into** draw upon, reach into ~*n.* **6.** douche, drenching, ducking, immersion, plunge, soaking **7.** bathe, dive, plunge, swim **8.** concoction, dilution, infusion, mixture, preparation, solution, suspension **9.** basin, concavity, depression, hole, hollow, incline, slope

diplomacy 1. international negotiation, statecraft, statesmanship **2.** artfulness, craft, delicacy, discretion, finesse, savoir faire, skill, subtlety, tact

diplomat conciliator, go-between, mediator, modera-

diplopia (dɪˈpləʊpɪə) *n.* double vision

dipolar (daɪˈpəʊlə) *a.* having two poles

dipole (ˈdaɪpəʊl) *n.* type of radio and television aerial

dipper (ˈdɪpə) *n.* **1.** ladle, bucket, scoop **2.** diving bird (*also* **water ouzel**)

dipsomania (dɪpsəʊˈmeɪnɪə) *n.* uncontrollable craving for alcohol —**dipsoˈmaniac** *n.* victim of this

dipterous (ˈdɪptərəs) *a.* **1.** of order of insects having single pair of wings and sucking or piercing mouthparts (*also* **ˈdipteran**) **2.** *Bot.* having two winglike parts

diptych (ˈdɪptɪk) *n.* **1.** ancient tablet hinged in centre, folding together like a book **2.** painting, carving on two hinged panels

dire (daɪə) *a.* **1.** terrible **2.** urgent

direct (dɪˈrɛkt, daɪ-) *vt.* **1.** control, manage, order **2.** tell or show the way **3.** aim, point, turn **4.** address (letter *etc.*) **5.** supervise (actors *etc.*) in play or film —*a.* **6.** frank, straightforward **7.** straight **8.** going straight to the point **9.** immediate **10.** lineal —**diˈrection** *n.* **1.** directing **2.** aim, course of movement **3.** address, instruction —**diˈrectional** *a.* **1.** of or relating to spatial direction **2.** *Electron.* having or relating to increased sensitivity to radio waves *etc.* coming from particular direction; (of aerial) transmitting or receiving radio waves more effectively in some directions than in others **3.** *Phys., electron.* concentrated in, following or producing motion in particular direction —**diˈrective** *a./n.* —**diˈrectly** *adv.* —**diˈrectness** *n.* —**diˈrector** *n.* **1.** one who directs, *esp.* a film **2.** member of board managing company (**diˈrectress** *fem.*) —**diˈrectorate** *n.* **1.** body of directors **2.** office of director —**diˈrectorship** *n.* —**diˈrectory** *n.* **1.** alphabetical book of names, addresses, streets *etc.* **2.** (**D-**) French revolutionary government 1795–9 —**direct current** continuous electric current that flows in one direction —**direct-grant school UK** formerly, school financed by endowment, fees and state grant conditional upon admittance of percentage of nonpaying pupils —**direction finder** radio receiver that determines the direction of incoming waves —**direct object** *Gram.* noun, pronoun or noun phrase whose referent receives direct action of verb —**direct speech** *or esp. U.S.* **direct discourse** reporting of what someone has said or written by quoting exact words —**direct tax** tax paid by person or organization on which it is levied

dirge (dɜːdʒ) *n.* song of mourning

dirigible (dɪˈrɪdʒɪbᵊl) *a.* **1.** steerable —*n.* **2.** balloon; airship

dirk (dɜːk) *n.* short dagger orig. carried by Scottish clansmen

dirndl (ˈdɜːndᵊl) *n.* full, gathered skirt

dirt (dɜːt) *n.* **1.** filth **2.** soil, earth **3.** obscene or pornographic material **4.** contamination —**ˈdirtiness** *n.* —**ˈdirty** *a.* **1.** unclean, filthy **2.** obscene **3.** unfair **4.** dishonest —**dirt-cheap** *a./adv. inf.* at extremely low price —**dirt track** loose-surfaced track, *eg* for motorcycle racing

dis- (*comb. form*) negation, opposition, deprivation; in many verbs indicates undoing of the action of simple

THESAURUS

tor, negotiator, politician, public relations expert, tactician

diplomatic adept, discreet, polite, politic, prudent, sensitive, subtle, tactful

dire 1. alarming, appalling, awful, calamitous, cataclysmic, catastrophic, cruel, disastrous, horrible, horrid, ruinous, terrible, woeful **2.** dismal, dreadful, fearful, gloomy, grim, ominous, portentous **3.** critical, crucial, crying, desperate, drastic, exigent, extreme, pressing, urgent

direct *v.* **1.** administer, advise, conduct, control, dispose, govern, guide, handle, lead, manage, mastermind, oversee, preside over, regulate, rule, run, superintend, supervise **2.** bid, charge, command, dictate, enjoin, instruct, order **3.** guide, indicate, lead, point in the direction of, point the way, show **4.** address, aim, cast, fix, focus, intend, level, mean, point, train, turn **5.** address, label, mail, route, send, superscribe ~*adj.* **6.** candid, frank, honest, man-to-man, matter-of-fact, open, outspoken, plain-spoken, sincere, straight, straightforward **7.** absolute, blunt, categorical, downright, explicit, express, plain, point-blank, unambiguous, unequivocal **8.** nonstop, not crooked, shortest, straight, through, unbroken, undeviating, uninterrupted **9.** face-to-face, first-hand, head-on, immediate, personal

direction 1. administration, charge, command, control, government, guidance, leadership, management, order, oversight, superintendence, supervision **2.** aim, bearing, course, line, path, road, route, track, way **3.** bent, bias, current, drift, end, orientation, proclivity, tack, tendency, tenor, trend **4.** address, label, mark, superscription

directive *n.* charge, command, decree, dictate, edict, injunction, instruction, mandate, notice, order, ordinance, regulation, ruling

directly 1. by the shortest route, exactly, in a beeline, precisely, straight, unswervingly, without deviation **2.** as soon as possible, at once, dead, due, forthwith, immediately, in a second, instantaneously, instantly, presently, promptly, pronto (*Inf.*), quickly, right away, soon, speedily, straightaway **3.** candidly, face-to-face, honestly, in person, openly, personally, plainly, point-blank, straightforwardly, truthfully, unequivocally, without prevarication

director administrator, boss (*Inf.*), chairman, chief, controller, executive, governor, head, leader, manager, organizer, principal, producer, supervisor

dirge coronach (*Scot. & Irish*), dead march, elegy, funeral song, lament, requiem, threnody

dirt 1. dust, excrement, filth, grime, impurity, mire, muck, mud, slime, smudge, stain, tarnish **2.** clay, earth, loam, soil **3.** indecency, obscenity, pornography, smut

dirty *adj.* **1.** begrimed, filthy, foul, grimy, grubby, messy, mucky, muddy, nasty, polluted, soiled, sullied, unclean **2.** blue, indecent, obscene, off-colour, pornographic, risqué, salacious, smutty, vulgar **3.** corrupt, crooked, dishonest, fraudulent, illegal, treacherous, unfair, unscrupulous, unsporting **4.** base, beggarly, contemptible, cowardly, despicable, ignominious, low, low-down (*Inf.*), mean, nasty, scurvy, shabby, sordid, squalid, vile

disability 1. affliction, ailment, complaint, defect, disablement, disorder, handicap, impairment, infirmity, malady **2.** disqualification, impotency, inability, incapacity, incompetency, unfitness, weakness

verb. In the list below, the meaning may be inferred from the word to which *dis-* is prefixed

disable (dɪsˈeɪbˀl) *vt.* **1.** make unable **2.** cripple, maim —**disaˈbility** *n.* **1.** incapacity **2.** drawback

disabuse (dɪsəˈbjuːz) *vt.* **1.** undeceive, disillusion **2.** free from error

disadvantage (dɪsədˈvɑːntɪdʒ) *n.* **1.** drawback **2.** hindrance **3.** detriment —*vt.* **4.** handicap —**disadˈvantaged** *a.* deprived, discriminated against, underprivileged —**disadvanˈtageous** *a.*

disaffected (dɪsəˈfɛktɪd) *a.* ill-disposed, alienated, estranged —**disafˈfection** *n.*

disagree (dɪsəˈgriː) *vi.* (*oft. with* with) **1.** be at variance **2.** conflict **3.** (of food *etc.*) have bad effect (on) —**disaˈgreeable** *a.* unpleasant —**disaˈgreement** *n.* **1.** difference of opinion **2.** discord **3.** discrepancy

disallow (dɪsəˈlaʊ) *vt.* reject as untrue or invalid —**disalˈlowance** *n.*

disappear (dɪsəˈpɪə) *vi.* **1.** vanish **2.** cease to exist **3.** be lost —**disapˈpearance** *n.*

disappoint (dɪsəˈpɔɪnt) *vt.* fail to fulfil (hope), frustrate —**disapˈpointment** *n.*

disapproˈbation
disapˈproval
disapˈprove
disarˈrange
disaˈvow
disˈband
disbeˈlief
disbeˈlieve
discomˈpose
discomˈposure
disconˈnect
disconˈtent
disconˈtented
disconˈtentment
disconˈtinue
disconˈtinuous
disˈcourteous
disˈcourtesy
disemˈbark
disenˈchant
disenˈtangle
disenˈtanglement
disequiˈlibrium
disesˈtablish
disesˈtablishment
disˈfranchise
disˈharmony
disˈhearten
disˈhonest
disˈhonesty
disinˈter
disinˈterment
disˈloyal
disˈloyalty
disˈmount
disorganiˈzation
disˈorganize
disproˈportion
disproˈportionate
disreˈgard
disˈreputable
disreˈpute
disreˈspect
disreˈspectful
dissatisˈfaction
disˈsatisfy
disˈsimilar
dissimiˈlarity
disˈtrust
disˈtrustful
disuˈnite

THESAURUS

disable 1. cripple, damage, debilitate, enfeeble, hamstring, handicap, immobilize, impair, incapacitate, paralyse, prostrate, put out of action, render *hors de combat,* render inoperative, unfit, unman, weaken **2.** disenable, disqualify, invalidate, render *or* declare incapable

disadvantage 1. damage, detriment, disservice, harm, hurt, injury, loss, prejudice **2.** *Often plural* burden, drawback, flaw, fly in the ointment (*Inf.*), handicap, hardship, hindrance, impediment, inconvenience, liability, minus (*Inf.*), nuisance, privation, snag, trouble, weakness, weak point

disadvantageous adverse, damaging, deleterious, detrimental, harmful, hurtful, ill-timed, inconvenient, inexpedient, injurious, inopportune, prejudicial, unfavourable

disaffected alienated, antagonistic, discontented, disloyal, dissatisfied, estranged, hostile, mutinous, rebellious, seditious, uncompliant, unsubmissive

disaffection alienation, animosity, antagonism, antipathy, aversion, breach, disagreement, discontent, dislike, disloyalty, dissatisfaction, estrangement, hostility, ill will, repugnance, resentment, unfriendliness

disagree 1. be discordant, be dissimilar, conflict, contradict, counter, depart, deviate, differ, diverge, run counter to, vary **2.** argue, bicker, clash, contend, contest, debate, differ (in opinion), dispute, dissent, fall out (*Inf.*), have words (*Inf.*), object, oppose, quarrel, take issue with, wrangle **3.** be injurious, bother, discomfort, distress, hurt, make ill, nauseate, sicken, trouble, upset

disagreeable 1. bad-tempered, brusque, churlish, contrary, cross, difficult, disobliging, ill-natured, irritable, nasty, peevish, rude, surly, unfriendly, ungracious, unlikable, unpleasant **2.** disgusting, displeasing, distasteful, nasty, objectionable, obnoxious, offensive, repellent, repugnant, repulsive, uninviting, unpalatable, unpleasant, unsavoury

disagreement 1. difference, discrepancy, disparity, dissimilarity, dissimilitude, divergence, diversity, incompatibility, incongruity, unlikeness, variance **2.** altercation, argument, clash, conflict, debate, difference, discord, dispute, dissent, division, falling out, misunderstanding, quarrel, squabble, strife, wrangle

disallow 1. abjure, disavow, disclaim, dismiss, disown, rebuff, refuse, reject, repudiate **2.** ban, cancel, embargo, forbid, prohibit, proscribe, veto

disappear 1. be lost to view, depart, drop out of sight, ebb, escape, evanesce, fade away, flee, fly, go, pass, recede, retire, vanish from sight, wane, withdraw **2.** cease, cease to be known, die out, dissolve, end, evaporate, expire, fade, leave no trace, melt away, pass away, perish, vanish

disappearance departure, desertion, disappearing, disappearing trick, eclipse, evanescence, evaporation, fading, flight, going, loss, melting, passing, vanishing, vanishing point

disappoint 1. chagrin, dash, deceive, delude, disenchant, disgruntle, dishearten, disillusion, dismay, dissatisfy, fail, let down, sadden, vex **2.** baffle, balk, defeat, disconcert, foil, frustrate, hamper, hinder, thwart

disappointment 1. chagrin, discontent, discourage-

disarm (dɪsˈɑːm) *vt.* **1.** deprive of arms or weapons **2.** reduce war weapons of (a country) **3.** win over **—disˈarmament** *n.* **—disˈarming** *a.* removing hostility, suspicion

disarray (dɪsəˈreɪ) *vt.* **1.** throw into disorder, derange *—n.* **2.** disorderliness, *esp.* of clothing

disassociate (dɪsəˈsəʊʃɪeɪt) *v. see* DISSOCIATE

disaster (dɪˈzɑːstə) *n.* calamity, sudden or great misfortune **—disˈastrous** *a.* calamitous

disbar (dɪsˈbɑː) *vt. Law* expel from the bar

disbud (dɪsˈbʌd) *vt.* remove superfluous buds, shoots from

disburse (dɪsˈbɜːs) *vt.* pay out **—disˈbursement** *n.*

disc (dɪsk) *n.* **1.** thin, flat, circular object like a coin **2.** gramophone record **—disc brake** brake in which two pads rub against flat disc attached to wheel hub when brake is applied **—disc harrow** *or* **plough** harrow or plough which cuts soil with inclined discs **—disc jockey** announcer playing records, oft. on radio

discard (dɪsˈkɑːd) *vt.* **1.** reject **2.** give up **3.** cast off, dismiss

discern (dɪˈsɜːn) *vt.* **1.** make out **2.** distinguish **—disˈcernible** *a.* **—disˈcerning** *a.* **1.** discriminating **2.** penetrating **—disˈcernment** *n.* insight

discharge (dɪsˈtʃɑːdʒ) *vt.* **1.** release **2.** dismiss **3.** emit **4.** perform (duties), fulfil (obligations) **5.** let go **6.** fire off **7.** unload **8.** pay *—n.* (ˈdɪstʃɑːdʒ, dɪsˈtʃɑːdʒ) **9.** discharging **10.** being discharged **11.** release **12.** matter emitted **13.** document certifying release, payment *etc.*

disciple (dɪˈsaɪpᵊl) *n.* follower, one who takes another as teacher and model **—disˈcipleship** *n.*

discipline (ˈdɪsɪplɪn) *n.* **1.** training that produces orderliness, obedience, self-control **2.** result of such training in order, conduct *etc.* **3.** system of rules *etc.* *—vt.* **4.** train **5.** punish **—discipliˈnarian** *n.* one who enforces rigid discipline **—ˈdisciplinary** *a.*

THESAURUS

ment, disenchantment, disillusionment, displeasure, dissatisfaction, distress, failure, frustration, ill-success, mortification, regret, unfulfilment **2.** blow, calamity, disaster, failure, fiasco, letdown, miscarriage, misfortune, setback, washout (*Inf.*)

disapproval censure, condemnation, criticism, denunciation, deprecation, disapprobation, displeasure, dissatisfaction, objection, reproach

disapprove *Often with* **of** blame, censure, condemn, deplore, deprecate, discountenance, dislike, find unacceptable, frown on, look down one's nose at (*Inf.*), object to, reject, take exception to

disarmament arms limitation, arms reduction, de-escalation, demilitarization, demobilization

disarming charming, irresistible, likable, persuasive, winning

disarrange confuse, derange, discompose, disorder, disorganize, disturb, jumble (up), mess (up), scatter, shake (up), shuffle, unsettle, untidy

disarray 1. confusion, discomposure, disharmony, dismay, disorder, disorderliness, disorganization, disunity, indiscipline, unruliness, upset **2.** chaos, clutter, dishevelment, jumble, mess, mix-up, muddle, shambles, tangle, untidiness

disaster accident, act of God, adversity, blow, calamity, cataclysm, catastrophe, misadventure, mischance, misfortune, mishap, reverse, ruin, ruination, stroke, tragedy, trouble

disastrous adverse, calamitous, cataclysmal, cataclysmic, catastrophic, destructive, detrimental, devastating, dire, dreadful, fatal, hapless, harmful, ill-fated, ill-starred, ruinous, terrible, tragic, unfortunate, unlucky, unpropitious, untoward

disbelief distrust, doubt, dubiety, incredulity, mistrust, scepticism, unbelief

discerning acute, astute, clear-sighted, critical, discriminating, ingenious, intelligent, judicious, knowing, penetrating, perceptive, percipient, perspicacious, piercing, sagacious, sensitive, sharp, shrewd, subtle, wise

discharge *v.* **1.** absolve, acquit, allow to go, clear, exonerate, free, liberate, pardon, release, set free *~n.* **2.** acquittal, clearance, exoneration, liberation, pardon, release, remittance *~v.* **3.** cashier, discard, dismiss, eject, expel, fire (*Inf.*), give (someone) the sack (*Inf.*), oust, remove, sack (*Inf.*) *~n.* **4.** congé, demobilization, dismissal, ejection, the boot (*Sl.*), the sack (*Inf.*) *~v.* **5.** detonate, explode, fire, let off, set off, shoot *~n.* **6.** blast, burst, detonation, discharging, explosion, firing, fusillade, report, salvo, shot, volley *~v.* **7.** disembogue, dispense, emit, empty, excrete, exude, give off, gush, leak, ooze, pour forth, release, void *~n.* **8.** emission, emptying, excretion, flow, ooze, pus, secretion, seepage, suppuration, vent, voiding *~v.* **9.** disburden, off-load, remove, unburden, unload *~n.* **10.** disburdening, emptying, unburdening, unloading *~v.* **11.** accomplish, carry out, do, execute, fulfil, observe, perform *~n.* **12.** accomplishment, achievement, execution, fulfilment, observance, performance *~v.* **13.** clear, honour, meet, pay, relieve, satisfy, settle, square up *~n.* **14.** payment, satisfaction, settlement

disciple adherent, apostle, believer, catechumen, convert, devotee, follower, learner, partisan, proselyte, pupil, student, supporter, votary

disciplinarian authoritarian, despot, drill sergeant, hard master, martinet, stickler, strict teacher, taskmaster, tyrant

discipline *n.* **1.** drill, exercise, method, practice, regimen, regulation, training **2.** conduct, control, orderliness, regulation, restraint, self-control, strictness **3.** castigation, chastisement, correction, punishment *~v.* **4.** break in, bring up, check, control, drill, educate, exercise, form, govern, instruct, inure, prepare, regulate, restrain, train **5.** castigate, chasten, chastise, correct, penalize, punish, reprimand, reprove

disclaim abandon, abjure, abnegate, decline, deny, disaffirm, disallow, disavow, disown, forswear, reject, renounce, repudiate

disclose 1. broadcast, communicate, confess, divulge, impart, leak, let slip, make known, make public, publish, relate, reveal, spill the beans about (*Inf.*), tell, unveil, utter **2.** bring to light, discover, exhibit, expose, lay bare, reveal, show, uncover, unveil

disclosure acknowledgment, admission, announcement, broadcast, confession, declaration, discovery, divulgence, exposé, exposure, leak, publication, revelation, uncovering

disclaim (dɪsˈkleɪm) *vt.* deny, renounce —**disˈclaimer** *n.* repudiation, denial

disclose (dɪsˈkləʊz) *vt.* **1.** allow to be seen **2.** make known —**disˈclosure** *n.* revelation

disco (ˈdɪskəʊ) discotheque

discobolus (dɪsˈkɒbələs) *n.* discus thrower (*pl.* **-li** (-laɪ))

discolour *or U.S.* **discolor** (dɪsˈkʌlə) *vt.* alter colour of, stain —**discolorˈation** *n.*

discomfit (dɪsˈkʌmfɪt) *vt.* embarrass, disconcert, baffle —**disˈcomfiture** *n.*

discomfort (dɪsˈkʌmfət) *n.* **1.** inconvenience, distress or mild pain **2.** something that disturbs or deprives of ease —*vt.* **3.** make uncomfortable or uneasy

discommode (dɪskəˈməʊd) *vt.* **1.** put to inconvenience **2.** disturb —**discomˈmodious** *a.*

disconcert (dɪskənˈsɜːt) *vt.* **1.** ruffle, confuse **2.** upset, embarrass

disconsolate (dɪsˈkɒnsəlɪt) *a.* unhappy, downcast, forlorn

discord (ˈdɪskɔːd) *n.* **1.** strife **2.** difference, dissension **3.** disagreement of sounds —**disˈcordance** *n.* —**disˈcordant** *a.* —**disˈcordantly** *adv.*

discotheque (ˈdɪskətɛk) *n.* **1.** club *etc.* for dancing to recorded music **2.** mobile equipment for providing music for dancing

discount (dɪsˈkaʊnt, ˈdɪskaʊnt) *vt.* **1.** consider as possibility but reject as unsuitable, inappropriate *etc.* **2.** deduct (amount, percentage) from usual price **3.** sell at reduced price —*n.* (ˈdɪskaʊnt) **4.** amount deducted from cost, expressed as cash amount or percentage

discountenance (dɪsˈkaʊntɪnəns) *vt.* **1.** abash **2.** discourage **3.** frown upon

discourage (dɪsˈkʌrɪdʒ) *vt.* **1.** reduce confidence of **2.** deter **3.** show disapproval of —**disˈcouragement** *n.*

discourse (ˈdɪskɔːs, dɪsˈkɔːs) *n.* **1.** conversation **2.** speech, treatise, sermon —*vi.* (dɪsˈkɔːs) **3.** speak, converse, lecture

THESAURUS

discolour fade, mar, mark, rust, soil, stain, streak, tarnish, tinge

discomfort 1. *n.* ache, annoyance, disquiet, distress, hardship, hurt, inquietude, irritation, malaise, nuisance, pain, soreness, trouble, uneasiness, unpleasantness, vexation 2. *v.* discomfit, discompose, disquiet, distress, disturb, embarrass, make uncomfortable

discomposure agitation, anxiety, confusion, discomfiture, disquiet, disquietude, distraction, disturbance, embarrassment, fluster, inquietude, malaise, nervousness, perturbation, uneasiness

disconcert abash, agitate, baffle, bewilder, confuse, discompose, disturb, flurry, fluster, nonplus, perplex, perturb, put off, put out of countenance, rattle (*Inf.*), ruffle, shake up (*Inf.*), take aback, throw off balance, trouble, unbalance, undo, unsettle, upset, worry

disconnect cut off, detach, disengage, divide, part, separate, sever, take apart, uncouple

disconsolate crushed, dejected, desolate, despairing, forlorn, gloomy, grief-stricken, heartbroken, hopeless, inconsolable, melancholy, miserable, sad, unhappy, woeful, wretched

discontent *n.* discontentment, displeasure, dissatisfaction, envy, fretfulness, regret, restlessness, uneasiness, unhappiness, vexation

discontented brassed off (*Sl.*), cheesed off (*Brit. sl.*), complaining, disaffected, disgruntled, displeased, dissatisfied, exasperated, fed up, fretful, miserable, unhappy, vexed, with a chip on one's shoulder (*Inf.*)

discontinue abandon, break off, cease, drop, end, finish, give up, halt, interrupt, leave off, pause, put an end to, quit, refrain from, stop, suspend, terminate

discord 1. clashing, conflict, contention, difference, disagreement, discordance, dispute, dissension, disunity, division, friction, incompatibility, lack of concord, opposition, rupture, strife, variance, wrangling 2. cacophony, din, disharmony, dissonance, harshness, jangle, jarring, racket, tumult

discordant 1. at odds, clashing, conflicting, contradictory, contrary, different, disagreeing, divergent, incompatible, incongruous, inconsistent, opposite 2. cacophonous, dissonant, grating, harsh, inharmonious, jangling, jarring, shrill, strident, unmelodious

discount *v.* 1. brush off, disbelieve, disregard, ignore, leave out of account, overlook, pass over 2. deduct, lower, mark down, rebate, reduce, take off ~*n.* 3. abatement, allowance, concession, cut, cut price, deduction, drawback, percentage (*Inf.*), rebate, reduction

discourage 1. abash, awe, cast down, cow, damp, dampen, dash, daunt, deject, demoralize, depress, dishearten, dismay, dispirit, frighten, intimidate, overawe, put a damper on, scare, unman, unnerve 2. check, curb, deprecate, deter, discountenance, disfavour, dissuade, divert from, hinder, inhibit, prevent, put off, restrain, talk out of, throw cold water on (*Inf.*)

discouragement 1. cold feet (*Inf.*), dejection, depression, despair, despondency, disappointment, discomfiture, dismay, downheartedness, hopelessness, loss of confidence, low spirits, pessimism 2. constraint, curb, damper, deterrent, disincentive, hindrance, impediment, obstacle, opposition, rebuff, restraint, setback

discourse *n.* 1. chat, communication, conversation, converse, dialogue, discussion, speech, talk 2. address, disquisition, dissertation, essay, homily, lecture, oration, sermon, speech, talk, treatise ~*v.* 3. confer, converse, debate, declaim, discuss, expatiate, hold forth, speak, talk

discourteous abrupt, bad-mannered, boorish, brusque, curt, disrespectful, ill-bred, ill-mannered, impolite, insolent, offhand, rude, uncivil, uncourteous, ungentlemanly, ungracious, unmannerly

discourtesy bad manners, disrespectfulness, ill-breeding, impertinence, impoliteness, incivility, insolence, rudeness, ungraciousness, unmannerliness

discover 1. bring to light, come across, come upon, dig up, find, light upon, locate, turn up, uncover, unearth 2. ascertain, descry, detect, determine, discern, disclose, espy, find out, get wise to (*Inf.*), learn, notice, perceive, realize, recognize, reveal, see, spot, uncover

discovery ascertainment, detection, disclosure, espial, exploration, finding, introduction, locating, location, origination, revelation, uncovering

discover (dɪˈskʌvə) *vt.* **1.** (be the first to) find out, light upon **2.** make known **—disˈcoverable** *a.* **—disˈcoverer** *n.* **—disˈcovery** *n.*

discredit (dɪsˈkrɛdɪt) *vt.* **1.** damage reputation of **2.** cast doubt on **3.** reject as untrue *—n.* **4.** disgrace **5.** doubt **—disˈcreditable** *a.*

discreet (dɪˈskriːt) *a.* prudent, circumspect **—disˈcreetly** *adv.* **—disˈcreetness** *n.*

discrepancy (dɪˈskrɛpənsɪ) *n.* conflict, variation, as between figures **—disˈcrepant** *a.*

discrete (dɪsˈkriːt) *a.* separate, disunited, discontinuous

discretion (dɪˈskrɛʃən) *n.* **1.** quality of being discreet **2.** prudence **3.** freedom to act as one chooses **—disˈcretionary** *or* **disˈcretional** *a.*

discriminate (dɪˈskrɪmɪneɪt) *vi.* **1.** single out particular person, group *etc.* for special favour or disfavour **2.** distinguish (between) **3.** be discerning **—discrimiˈnation** *n.* **—disˈcriminatory** *or* **disˈcriminative** *a.* **1.** based on prejudice; biased **2.** capable of making fine distinctions

discursive (dɪˈskɜːsɪv) *a.* passing from subject to subject, rambling

discus (ˈdɪskəs) *n.* disc-shaped object thrown in athletic competition (*pl.* **-es, disci** (ˈdɪskaɪ))

discuss (dɪˈskʌs) *vt.* **1.** exchange opinions about **2.** debate **—disˈcussion** *n.*

disdain (dɪsˈdeɪn) *n.* **1.** scorn, contempt *—vt.* **2.** scorn **—disˈdainful** *a.* **—disˈdainfully** *adv.*

disease (dɪˈziːz) *n.* **1.** illness **2.** disorder of health **—disˈeased** *a.*

disembodied (dɪsɪmˈbɒdɪd) *a.* (of spirit) released from bodily form

disembowel (dɪsɪmˈbaʊəl) *vt.* take out entrails of (**-ll-**)

disenchanted (dɪsɪnˈtʃɑːntɪd) *a.* disillusioned

disengage (dɪsɪnˈgeɪdʒ) *v.* **1.** release or become released from connection *etc.* **2.** *Mil.* withdraw (forces) from close action **3.** *Fencing* move (one's blade) from one side of opponent's blade to another in circular motion **—disenˈgaged** *a.* **—disenˈgagement** *n.*

THESAURUS

discredit *v.* **1.** blame, bring into disrepute, censure, defame, degrade, detract from, disgrace, dishonour, disparage, reproach, slander, slur, smear, vilify *~n.* **2.** aspersion, censure, disgrace, dishonour, disrepute, ignominy, ill-repute, imputation, odium, reproach, scandal, shame, slur, smear, stigma *~v.* **3.** challenge, deny, disbelieve, discount, dispute, distrust, doubt, mistrust, question *~n.* **4.** distrust, doubt, mistrust, question, scepticism, suspicion

discreditable blameworthy, degrading, disgraceful, dishonourable, humiliating, ignominious, improper, infamous, reprehensible, scandalous, shameful, unprincipled, unworthy

discreet careful, cautious, circumspect, considerate, diplomatic, discerning, guarded, judicious, politic, prudent, reserved, sagacious, sensible, tactful, wary

discrepancy conflict, contrariety, difference, disagreement, discordance, disparity, dissimilarity, dissonance, divergence, incongruity, inconsistency, variance, variation

discretion 1. acumen, care, carefulness, caution, circumspection, consideration, diplomacy, discernment, good sense, heedfulness, judgment, judiciousness, maturity, prudence, sagacity, tact, wariness **2.** choice, disposition, inclination, liking, mind, option, pleasure, predilection, preference, responsibility, volition, will, wish

discretionary arbitrary (*Law*), elective, nonmandatory, open, open to choice, optional, unrestricted

discriminate 1. disfavour, favour, show bias, show prejudice, single out, treat as inferior, treat differently, victimize **2.** assess, differentiate, discern, distinguish, draw a distinction, evaluate, segregate, separate, sift, tell the difference

discrimination 1. bias, bigotry, favouritism, inequity, intolerance, prejudice, unfairness **2.** acumen, acuteness, clearness, discernment, insight, judgment, keenness, penetration, perception, refinement, sagacity, subtlety, taste

discriminatory, discriminative 1. biased, favouring, inequitable, one-sided, partial, partisan, preferential, prejudiced, prejudicial, unjust, weighted **2.** analytical, astute, differentiating, discerning, discriminating, perceptive, perspicacious

discuss argue, confer, consider, consult with, converse, debate, deliberate, examine, exchange views on, get together (*Inf.*), go into, reason about, review, sift, talk about, thrash out, ventilate, weigh up the pros and cons

discussion analysis, argument, colloquy, confabulation, conference, consideration, consultation, conversation, debate, deliberation, dialogue, discourse, examination, exchange, review, scrutiny, symposium

disdain 1. *v.* belittle, contemn, deride, despise, disregard, look down on, look down one's nose at (*Inf.*), misprize, pooh-pooh, reject, scorn, slight, sneer at, spurn, undervalue **2.** *n.* arrogance, contempt, contumely, derision, dislike, haughtiness, hauteur, indifference, scorn, sneering, snobbishness, superciliousness

disdainful aloof, arrogant, contemptuous, derisive, haughty, high and mighty (*Inf.*), hoity-toity (*Inf.*), insolent, proud, scornful, sneering, supercilious, superior

disease affliction, ailment, complaint, condition, disorder, ill health, illness, indisposition, infection, infirmity, malady, sickness, upset

diseased ailing, infected, rotten, sick, sickly, tainted, unhealthy, unsound, unwell, unwholesome

disembark alight, arrive, get off, go ashore, land, step out of

disembodied bodiless, ghostly, immaterial, incorporeal, intangible, phantom, spectral, spiritual, unbodied

disenchanted blasé, cynical, disappointed, disillusioned, indifferent, jaundiced, let down, out of love, sick of, soured, undeceived

disengage 1. disentangle, ease, extricate, free, liberate, loosen, release, set free, unloose, untie **2.** detach, disconnect, disjoin, disunite, divide, separate, undo, withdraw

disengaged apart, detached, free, loose, out of gear, released, separate, unattached, unconnected, uncoupled

disengagement detachment, disconnection, disentanglement, division, separation, withdrawal

disentangle detach, disconnect, disengage, extricate,

disfavour *or U.S.* **disfavor** (dɪsˈfeɪvə) *n.* **1.** disapproval; dislike **2.** state of being disapproved of or disliked **3.** unkind act —*vt.* **4.** treat with disapproval or dislike

disfigure (dɪsˈfɪgə) *vt.* mar appearance of —**disfiguˈration** *n.* —**disˈfigurement** *n.* blemish, defect

disgorge (dɪsˈgɔːdʒ) *vt.* **1.** vomit **2.** give up —**disˈgorgement** *n.*

disgrace (dɪsˈgreɪs) *n.* **1.** shame, loss of reputation, dishonour —*vt.* **2.** bring shame or discredit upon —**disˈgraceful** *a.* shameful —**disˈgracefully** *adv.*

disgruntled (dɪsˈgrʌntᵊld) *a.* **1.** vexed **2.** put out

disguise (dɪsˈgaɪz) *vt.* **1.** change appearance of, make unrecognizable **2.** conceal, cloak **3.** misrepresent —*n.* **4.** false appearance **5.** costume, mask *etc.* to conceal identity

disgust (dɪsˈgʌst) *n.* **1.** violent distaste, loathing, repugnance —*vt.* **2.** affect with loathing

dish (dɪʃ) *n.* **1.** shallow vessel for food **2.** portion or variety of food **3.** contents of dish **4.** *sl.* attractive person —*vt.* **5.** put in dish —**ˈdishy** *a. sl., chiefly* **UK** good-looking, attractive —**dish aerial** microwave aerial, used in satellite broadcasting *etc.*, consisting of parabolic reflector —**ˈdishcloth** *n.* cloth or rag for washing or drying dishes —**dish up 1.** serve (meal *etc.*) **2.** *inf.* prepare or present, *esp.* attractively

dishabille (dɪsæˈbiːl) *or* **deshabille** *n.* state of being partly or carelessly dressed

dishevelled (dɪˈʃɛvᵊld) *a.* **1.** with disordered hair **2.** ruffled, untidy, unkempt

dishonour *or U.S.* **dishonor** (dɪsˈɒnə) *vt.* **1.** treat with disrespect **2.** fail or refuse to pay **3.** cause disgrace of (woman) by seduction or rape —*n.* **4.** lack of honour or respect **5.** state of shame or disgrace **6.** person or thing that causes loss of honour **7.** insult; affront **8.** refusal or failure to accept or pay a commercial paper —**disˈhonourable** *or U.S.* **disˈhonorable** *a.* **1.** characterized by or causing dishonour or discredit **2.** having little or no integrity; unprincipled

disillusion (dɪsɪˈluːʒən) *vt.* **1.** destroy ideals, illusions, or false ideas of —*n.* **2.** act of disillusioning or being disillusioned (*also* **disilˈlusionment**)

disincentive (dɪsɪnˈsɛntɪv) *n.* **1.** something that acts as deterrent —*a.* **2.** acting as deterrent

THESAURUS

free, loose, separate, sever, unfold, unravel, unsnarl, untangle, untwist

disfavour 1. disapprobation, disapproval, dislike, displeasure **2.** *As in* **fall into disfavour** bad books (*Inf.*), discredit, disesteem, disgrace, doghouse (*Inf.*), shame, unpopularity **3.** bad turn, discourtesy, disservice

disfigure blemish, damage, deface, deform, disfeature, distort, injure, maim, make ugly, mar, mutilate, scar

disfigurement blemish, defacement, defect, deformity, distortion, impairment, injury, mutilation, scar, spot, stain

disgrace *n.* **1.** baseness, degradation, dishonour, disrepute, ignominy, infamy, odium, opprobrium, shame **2.** aspersion, blemish, blot, defamation, reproach, scandal, slur, stain, stigma **3.** contempt, discredit, disesteem, disfavour, obloquy ~*v.* **4.** abase, bring shame upon, defame, degrade, discredit, disfavour, dishonour, disparage, humiliate, reproach, shame, slur, stain, stigmatize, sully, taint

disgraceful blameworthy, contemptible, degrading, detestable, discreditable, dishonourable, disreputable, ignominious, infamous, low, mean, opprobrious, scandalous, shameful, shocking, unworthy

disgruntled annoyed, cheesed off (*Brit. sl.*), discontented, displeased, dissatisfied, grumpy, irritated, malcontent, peeved, peevish, petulant, put out, sulky, sullen, testy, vexed

disguise *v.* **1.** camouflage, cloak, conceal, cover, hide, mask, screen, secrete, shroud, veil **2.** deceive, dissemble, dissimulate, fake, falsify, fudge, gloss over, misrepresent ~*n.* **3.** camouflage, cloak, costume, cover, get-up (*Inf.*), mask, screen, veil **4.** deception, dissimulation, façade, front, pretence, semblance, trickery, veneer

disgust 1. *v.* cause aversion, displease, fill with loathing, nauseate, offend, outrage, put off, repel, revolt, sicken, turn one's stomach **2.** *n.* abhorrence, abomination, antipathy, aversion, detestation, dislike, distaste, hatefulness, hatred, loathing, nausea, repugnance, repulsion, revulsion

dish 1. bowl, plate, platter, salver **2.** fare, food, recipe

dishearten cast down, crush, damp, dampen, dash, daunt, deject, depress, deter, discourage, dismay, dispirit, put a damper on

dishevelled bedraggled, blowzy, disarranged, disordered, frowzy, hanging loose, messy, ruffled, rumpled, tousled, uncombed, unkempt, untidy

dishonest bent (*Sl.*), cheating, corrupt, crafty, crooked (*Inf.*), deceitful, deceiving, deceptive, designing, disreputable, double-dealing, false, fraudulent, guileful, knavish (*Archaic*), lying, mendacious, perfidious, shady (*Inf.*), swindling, treacherous, unfair, unprincipled, unscrupulous, untrustworthy, untruthful

dishonesty cheating, chicanery, corruption, craft, criminality, crookedness, deceit, duplicity, falsehood, falsity, fraud, fraudulence, graft, improbity, mendacity, perfidy, sharp practice, stealing, treachery, trickery, unscrupulousness, wiliness

dishonour *v.* **1.** abase, blacken, corrupt, debase, debauch, defame, degrade, discredit, disgrace, shame, sully **2.** defile, deflower, pollute, rape, ravish, seduce ~*n.* **3.** abasement, degradation, discredit, disfavour, disgrace, disrepute, ignominy, infamy, obloquy, odium, opprobrium, reproach, scandal, shame **4.** abuse, affront, discourtesy, indignity, insult, offence, outrage, slight

dishonourable 1. base, contemptible, despicable, discreditable, disgraceful, ignoble, ignominious, infamous, scandalous, shameful **2.** blackguardly, corrupt, disreputable, shameless, treacherous, unprincipled, unscrupulous, untrustworthy

dish up ladle, prepare, present, produce, scoop, serve, spoon

disillusion *v.* break the spell, bring down to earth, disabuse, disenchant, open the eyes of, shatter one's illusions, undeceive

disincentive damper, determent, deterrent, discouragement, dissuasion, impediment

disinclination alienation, antipathy, aversion, demur, dislike, hesitance, lack of desire, lack of enthusiasm, loathness, objection, opposition, reluctance, repugnance, resistance, unwillingness

disincline (dɪsɪnˈklaɪn) *v.* make or be unwilling, reluctant or averse —**disinclination** (dɪsɪnklɪˈneɪʃən) *n.*

disinfectant (dɪsɪnˈfɛktənt) *n.* substance that prevents or removes infection —**disinˈfect** *vt.*

disinformation (dɪsɪnfəˈmeɪʃən) *n.* deliberately leaked false information intended to mislead foreign agents

disingenuous (dɪsɪnˈdʒɛnjʊəs) *a.* not sincere or frank

disinherit (dɪsɪnˈhɛrɪt) *vt.* deprive of inheritance

disintegrate (dɪsˈɪntɪgreɪt) *vi.* break up, fall to pieces —**disinteˈgration** *n.*

disinterest (dɪsˈɪntrɪst) *n.* freedom from bias or involvement —**disˈinterested** *a.*

disjoint (dɪsˈdʒɔɪnt) *vt.* **1.** put out of joint **2.** break the natural order or logical arrangement of —**disˈjointed** *a.* **1.** (of discourse) incoherent **2.** disconnected

disjunctive (dɪsˈdʒʌŋktɪv) *a.* **1.** serving to disconnect or separate **2.** *Gram.* denoting word, *esp.* conjunction, that serves to express opposition or contrast **3.** *Logic* characterizing, containing or included in disjunction —*n.* **4.** *Gram.* disjunctive word, *esp.* conjunction **5.** *Logic* disjunctive proposition

disk (dɪsk) *n.* **1.** *see* DISC **2.** *Comp.* direct-access storage device, consisting of stack of plates coated with magnetic layer, that rotates rapidly as single unit

dislike (dɪsˈlaɪk) *vt.* **1.** consider unpleasant or disagreeable —*n.* **2.** aversion; antipathy —**disˈlikable** *or* **disˈlikeable** *a.*

dislocate (ˈdɪsləkeɪt) *vt.* **1.** put out of joint **2.** disrupt, displace —**disloˈcation** *n.*

dislodge (dɪsˈlɒdʒ) *vt.* drive out or remove from hiding place or previous position —**disˈlodgement** *or* **disˈlodgment** *n.*

dismal (ˈdɪzməl) *a.* **1.** depressing **2.** depressed **3.** cheerless, dreary, gloomy —**ˈdismally** *adv.*

dismantle (dɪsˈmæntᵊl) *vt.* take apart —**disˈmantlement** *n.*

dismay (dɪsˈmeɪ) *vt.* **1.** dishearten, daunt —*n.* **2.** consternation, horrified amazement **3.** apprehension

dismember (dɪsˈmɛmbə) *vt.* **1.** remove limbs or members of **2.** divide, partition —**disˈmemberment** *n.*

dismiss (dɪsˈmɪs) *vt.* **1.** remove, discharge from employment **2.** send away **3.** reject —**disˈmissal** *n.*

disobey (dɪsəˈbeɪ) *v.* refuse or fail to obey —**disobedience** (dɪsəˈbiːdɪəns) *n.* —**disobedient** (dɪsəˈbiːdɪənt) *a.*

THESAURUS

disinfect clean, cleanse, decontaminate, deodorize, fumigate, purify, sanitize, sterilize

disinfectant antiseptic, germicide, sanitizer, sterilizer

disinherit cut off, cut off without a penny, disown, dispossess, oust, repudiate

disintegrate break apart, break up, crumble, disunite, fall apart, fall to pieces, reduce to fragments, separate, shatter, splinter

disinterest candidness, detachment, disinterestedness, dispassionateness, equity, fairness, impartiality, justice, neutrality, unbiasedness

disinterested candid, detached, dispassionate, equitable, even-handed, free from self-interest, impartial, impersonal, neutral, outside, unbiased, uninvolved, unprejudiced, unselfish

disjointed 1. aimless, confused, disconnected, disordered, fitful, incoherent, loose, rambling, spasmodic, unconnected **2.** disconnected, dislocated, displaced, disunited, divided, separated, split

dislike 1. *n.* animosity, animus, antagonism, antipathy, aversion, detestation, disapprobation, disapproval, disgust, disinclination, displeasure, distaste, enmity, hatred, hostility, loathing, repugnance **2.** *v.* abhor, abominate, be averse to, despise, detest, disapprove, disfavour, disrelish, hate, have no taste *or* stomach for, loathe, not be able to bear *or* abide, object to, scorn, shun

dislocate 1. disorder, displace, disrupt, disturb, misplace, shift **2.** disarticulate, disconnect, disengage, disjoint, disunite, luxate (*Medical*), put out of joint, unhinge

dislocation 1. disarray, disorder, disorganization, disruption, disturbance, misplacement **2.** disarticulation, disconnection, disengagement, luxation (*Medical*), unhinging

disloyal apostate, disaffected, faithless, false, perfidious, seditious, subversive, traitorous, treacherous, treasonable, two-faced, unfaithful, unpatriotic, untrustworthy

disloyalty betrayal of trust, breach of trust, breaking of faith, deceitfulness, double-dealing, falseness, falsity, inconstancy, infidelity, perfidy, Punic faith, treachery, treason, unfaithfulness

dismal black, bleak, cheerless, dark, depressing, despondent, discouraging, dolorous, dreary, forlorn, funereal, gloomy, gruesome, lonesome, lowering, lugubrious, melancholy, sad, sombre, sorrowful

dismay *v.* **1.** affright, alarm, appal, distress, fill with consternation, frighten, horrify, paralyse, scare, terrify, unnerve **2.** daunt, disappoint, discourage, dishearten, disillusion, dispirit, put off ~*n.* **3.** agitation, alarm, anxiety, apprehension, consternation, distress, dread, fear, fright, horror, panic, terror, trepidation **4.** chagrin, disappointment, discouragement, disillusionment, upset

dismember amputate, anatomize, cut into pieces, disjoint, dislimb, dislocate, dissect, divide, mutilate, rend, sever

dismiss 1. axe (*Inf.*), cashier, discharge, fire (*Inf.*), give notice to, lay off, oust, remove, sack (*Inf.*), send packing (*Inf.*) **2.** disband, disperse, dissolve, free, let go, release, send away **3.** banish, discard, dispel, disregard, drop, lay aside, pooh-pooh, put out of one's mind, reject, relegate, repudiate, set aside, shelve, spurn

dismissal 1. adjournment, congé, end, freedom to depart, permission to go, release **2.** discharge, expulsion, marching orders (*Inf.*), notice, one's cards, removal, the boot (*Sl.*), the push (*Sl.*), the sack (*Inf.*)

disobedience indiscipline, infraction, insubordination, mutiny, noncompliance, nonobservance, recalcitrance, revolt, unruliness, waywardness

disobedient contrary, contumacious, defiant, disorderly, froward, insubordinate, intractable, mischievous, naughty, noncompliant, nonobservant, obstreperous, refractory, undisciplined, unruly, wayward, wilful

disobey contravene, defy, disregard, flout, go counter to, ignore, infringe, overstep, rebel, refuse to obey, resist, transgress, violate

disoblige (dɪsəˈblaɪdʒ) *vt.* disregard the wishes, preferences of

disorder (dɪsˈɔːdə) *n.* **1.** disarray, confusion, disturbance **2.** upset of health, ailment —*vt.* **3.** upset order of **4.** disturb health of —**disˈorderly** *a.* **1.** untidy **2.** unruly

disorientate (dɪsˈɔːrɪenteɪt) *or* **disorient** *vt.* cause (someone) to lose his bearings, confuse

disown (dɪsˈəʊn) *vt.* refuse to acknowledge

disparage (dɪˈspærɪdʒ) *vt.* **1.** speak slightingly of **2.** belittle —**disˈparagement** *n.*

disparate (ˈdɪspərɪt) *a.* essentially different, unrelated —**disˈparity** *n.* **1.** inequality **2.** incongruity

dispassionate (dɪsˈpæʃənɪt) *a.* **1.** unswayed by passion **2.** calm, impartial

dispatch *or* **despatch** (dɪˈspætʃ) *vt.* **1.** send off to destination or on an errand **2.** send off **3.** finish off, get done with speed **4.** *inf.* eat up **5.** kill —*n.* **6.** sending off **7.** efficient speed **8.** official message, report —**dispatch rider** horseman or motorcyclist who carries dispatches

dispel (dɪˈspɛl) *vt.* clear, drive away, scatter (-ll-)

dispense (dɪˈspɛns) *vt.* **1.** deal out **2.** make up (medicine) **3.** administer (justice) **4.** grant exemption from —**disˈpensable** *a.* —**disˈpensary** *n.* place where medicine is made up —**dispenˈsation** *n.* **1.** act of dispensing **2.** licence; exemption **3.** provision of nature or providence —**disˈpenser** *n.* —**dispense with 1.** do away with **2.** manage without

disperse (dɪˈspɜːs) *v.* scatter —**disˈpersal** *or* **disˈpersion** *n.* —**disˈpersed** *a.* **1.** scattered **2.** placed here and there

dispirited (dɪˈspɪrɪtɪd) *a.* dejected, disheartened —**disˈpiritedly** *adv.* —**disˈpiriting** *a.*

displace (dɪsˈpleɪs) *vt.* **1.** move from the usual place **2.** remove from office **3.** take place of —**disˈplacement** *n.* **1.** displacing **2.** weight of liquid displaced by a solid in a fluid —**displaced person** person forced from his home country, *esp.* by war *etc.*

display (dɪˈspleɪ) *vt.* **1.** spread out for show **2.** show, expose to view **3.** (of visual display unit *etc.*) represent (data) visually, as on cathode-ray tube screen —*n.* **4.** displaying **5.** parade **6.** show, exhibition **7.** ostentation **8.** *Electron.* device capable of representing data visually, as on cathode-ray tube screen

displease (dɪsˈpliːz) *v.* **1.** offend **2.** annoy —**displeasure** (dɪsˈplɛʒə) *n.* anger, vexation

THESAURUS

disorderly 1. chaotic, confused, disorganized, higgledy-piggledy (*Inf.*), indiscriminate, irregular, jumbled, messy, shambolic (*Inf.*), unsystematic, untidy **2.** boisterous, disruptive, indisciplined, lawless, obstreperous, rebellious, refractory, riotous, rowdy, stormy, tumultuous, turbulent, ungovernable, unlawful, unmanageable, unruly

disorganize break up, confuse, derange, destroy, disarrange, discompose, disorder, disrupt, disturb, jumble, make a shambles of, muddle, turn topsy-turvy, unsettle, upset

disown abandon, abnegate, cast off, deny, disallow, disavow, disclaim, refuse to acknowledge *or* recognize, reject, renounce, repudiate

disparage belittle, criticize, decry, defame, degrade, denigrate, deprecate, depreciate, deride, derogate, detract from, discredit, disdain, dismiss, malign, minimize, ridicule, run down, scorn, slander, traduce, underestimate, underrate, undervalue, vilify

disparagement aspersion, belittlement, condemnation, contempt, contumely, criticism, debasement, degradation, denunciation, depreciation, derision, derogation, detraction, discredit, disdain, impairment, lessening, prejudice, reproach, ridicule, scorn, slander, underestimation

dispassionate 1. calm, collected, composed, cool, imperturbable, moderate, quiet, serene, sober, temperate, unemotional, unexcitable, unexcited, unmoved, unruffled **2.** candid, detached, disinterested, fair, impartial, impersonal, indifferent, neutral, objective, unbiased, uninvolved, unprejudiced

dispatch, despatch *v.* **1.** accelerate, consign, dismiss, express, forward, hasten, hurry, quicken, remit, send, transmit **2.** conclude, discharge, dispose of, expedite, finish, make short work of (*Inf.*), perform, settle **3.** assassinate, bump off (*Sl.*), butcher, eliminate (*Sl.*), execute, finish off, kill, murder, put an end to, slaughter, slay ~*n.* **4.** alacrity, celerity, expedition, haste, precipitateness, promptitude, promptness, quickness, rapidity, speed, swiftness **5.** account, bulletin, communication, communiqué, document, instruction, item, letter, message, missive, news, piece, report, story

dispel allay, banish, chase away, dismiss, disperse, dissipate, drive away, eliminate, expel, resolve, rout, scatter

dispensable disposable, expendable, inessential, needless, nonessential, superfluous, unnecessary, unrequired, useless

dispensation 1. allotment, appointment, apportionment, bestowal, conferment, consignment, dealing out, disbursement, distribution, endowment, supplying **2.** exception, exemption, immunity, indulgence, licence, permission, privilege, relaxation, relief, remission, reprieve

dispense 1. allocate, allot, apportion, assign, deal out, disburse, distribute, dole out, mete out, share **2.** measure, mix, prepare, supply **3.** except, excuse, exempt, exonerate, let off (*Inf.*), release, relieve, reprieve **4.** *With* **with** abstain from, do without, forgo, give up, omit, relinquish, waive **5.** *With* **with** abolish, brush aside, cancel, dispose of, disregard, do away with, get rid of, ignore, pass over, render needless, shake off

disperse 1. broadcast, circulate, diffuse, disseminate, dissipate, distribute, scatter, spread, strew **2.** break up, disappear, disband, dismiss, dispel, dissolve, rout, scatter, send off, separate, vanish

dispirited crestfallen, dejected, depressed, despondent, discouraged, disheartened, down, downcast, gloomy, glum, in the doldrums, low, morose, sad

displace 1. derange, disarrange, disturb, misplace, move, shift, transpose **2.** cashier, depose, discard, discharge, dismiss, fire (*Inf.*), remove, sack (*Inf.*) **3.** crowd out, oust, replace, succeed, supersede, supplant, take the place of **4.** dislocate, dislodge, dispossess, eject, evict, force out, unsettle

display *v.* **1.** betray, demonstrate, disclose, evidence, evince, exhibit, expose, manifest, open, open to view, present, reveal, show, unveil **2.** expand, extend, model, open out, spread out, stretch out, unfold,

disport (dɪˈspɔːt) *v.refl.* 1. amuse oneself 2. frolic, gambol

dispose (dɪˈspəʊz) *vt.* 1. arrange 2. distribute 3. incline 4. adjust —*vi.* 5. determine —**disˈposable** *a.* designed to be thrown away after use —**disˈposal** *n.* —**disˈposed** *a.* having inclination as specified (towards something) —**dispoˈsition** *n.* 1. inclination 2. temperament 3. arrangement 4. plan —**dispose of** 1. sell, get rid of 2. have authority over 3. deal with

dispossess (dɪspəˈzɛs) *vt.* cause to give up possession (of)

disprove (dɪsˈpruːv) *vt.* to show (assertion, claim *etc.*) to be incorrect

dispute (dɪˈspjuːt) *vi.* 1. debate, discuss —*vt.* 2. call in question 3. debate, argue 4. oppose, contest —*n.* 5. argument —**disˈputable** *a.* —**disˈputant** *n.* —**dispuˈtation** *n.* —**dispuˈtatious** *a.* 1. argumentative 2. quarrelsome

disqualify (dɪsˈkwɒlɪfaɪ) *vt.* make ineligible, unfit for some special purpose

disquiet (dɪsˈkwaɪət) *n.* 1. anxiety, uneasiness —*vt.* 2. cause (someone) to feel this —**disˈquietude** *n.* feeling of anxiety

disquisition (dɪskwɪˈzɪʃən) *n.* learned or elaborate treatise, discourse or essay

disrepair (dɪsrɪˈpɛə) *n.* state of bad repair, neglect

disrobe (dɪsˈrəʊb) *v.* 1. undress —*vt.* 2. divest of robes

disrupt (dɪsˈrʌpt) *vt.* 1. interrupt 2. throw into turmoil or disorder —**disˈruption** *n.* —**disˈruptive** *a.*

THESAURUS

unfurl ~*n.* **3.** array, demonstration, exhibition, exposition, exposure, manifestation, presentation, revelation, show **4.** flourish, ostentation, pageant, parade, pomp, show, spectacle

displease aggravate (*Inf.*), anger, annoy, disgust, dissatisfy, exasperate, gall, incense, irk, irritate, nettle, offend, pique, provoke, put out, rile, upset, vex

displeasure anger, annoyance, disapprobation, disapproval, disfavour, disgruntlement, dislike, dissatisfaction, distaste, indignation, irritation, offence, pique, resentment, vexation, wrath

disposable biodegradable, compostable, decomposable, nonreturnable, paper, throwaway

disposal **1.** clearance, discarding, dumping (*Inf.*), ejection, jettisoning, parting with, relinquishment, removal, riddance, scrapping, throwing away **2.** arrangement, array, dispensation, disposition, distribution, grouping, placing, position

dispose **1.** adjust, arrange, array, determine, distribute, fix, group, marshal, order, place, put, range, rank, regulate, set, settle, stand **2.** actuate, adapt, bias, condition, incline, induce, influence, lead, motivate, move, predispose, prompt, tempt

disposed apt, given, inclined, liable, likely, minded, of a mind to, predisposed, prone, ready, subject, tending towards

dispose of **1.** deal with, decide, determine, end, finish with, settle **2.** bestow, give, make over, part with, sell, transfer **3.** destroy, discard, dump (*Inf.*), get rid of, jettison, scrap, throw out *or* away, unload

disposition **1.** character, constitution, make-up, nature, spirit, temper, temperament **2.** bent, bias, habit, inclination, leaning, predisposition, proclivity, proneness, propensity, readiness, tendency **3.** adjustment, arrangement, classification, disposal, distribution, grouping, ordering, organization, placement

disproportion asymmetry, discrepancy, disparity, imbalance, inadequacy, inequality, insufficiency, lopsidedness, unevenness, unsuitableness

disproportionate excessive, incommensurate, inordinate, out of proportion, too much, unbalanced, unequal, uneven, unreasonable

disprove confute, contradict, controvert, discredit, expose, give the lie to, invalidate, negate, prove false, rebut, refute

disputation argumentation, controversy, debate, dispute, dissension, polemics

dispute *v.* **1.** altercate, argue, brawl, clash, contend, debate, discuss, quarrel, squabble, wrangle **2.** challenge, contest, contradict, controvert, deny, doubt, impugn, question ~*n.* **3.** altercation, argument, brawl, conflict, disagreement, discord, disturbance, feud, friction, quarrel, strife, wrangle **4.** argument, contention, controversy, debate, discussion, dissension

disqualify **1.** disable, incapacitate, invalidate, unfit (*Rare*) **2.** debar, declare ineligible, disentitle, preclude, prohibit, rule out

disquiet **1.** *n.* alarm, angst, anxiety, concern, disquietude, distress, disturbance, fear, foreboding, fretfulness, nervousness, restlessness, trouble, uneasiness, unrest, worry **2.** *v.* agitate, annoy, bother, concern, discompose, distress, disturb, fret, harass, incommode, make uneasy, perturb, pester, plague, trouble, unsettle, upset, vex, worry

disregard *v.* **1.** brush aside *or* away, discount, disobey, ignore, laugh off, leave out of account, make light of, neglect, overlook, pass over, pay no attention to, pay no heed to, take no notice of, turn a blind eye to **2.** brush off (*Sl.*), cold-shoulder, contemn, despise, disdain, disparage, slight, snub ~*n.* **3.** brushoff (*Sl.*), contempt, disdain, disrespect, heedlessness, ignoring, inattention, indifference, neglect, negligence, oversight, slight, the cold shoulder

disrepair collapse, decay, deterioration, dilapidation, ruination

disreputable base, contemptible, derogatory, discreditable, disgraceful, dishonourable, disorderly, ignominious, infamous, louche, low, mean, notorious, opprobrious, scandalous, shady (*Inf.*), shameful, shocking, unprincipled, vicious, vile

disrepute discredit, disesteem, disfavour, disgrace, dishonour, ignominy, ill favour, ill repute, infamy, obloquy, shame, unpopularity

disrespect contempt, discourtesy, dishonour, disregard, impertinence, impoliteness, impudence, incivility, insolence, irreverence, lack of respect, lese-majesty, rudeness, unmannerliness

disrespectful bad-mannered, cheeky, contemptuous, discourteous, ill-bred, impertinent, impolite, impudent, insolent, insulting, irreverent, misbehaved, rude, uncivil

disrupt **1.** agitate, confuse, disorder, disorganize, disturb, spoil, throw into disorder, upset **2.** break up *or* into, interfere with, interrupt, intrude, obstruct, unsettle, upset

dissect (dɪˈsɛkt, daɪ-) *vt.* **1.** cut up (body, organism) for detailed examination **2.** examine or criticize in detail —**disˈsection** *n.* —**disˈsector** *n.* anatomist

dissemble (dɪˈsɛmbᵊl) *v.* **1.** conceal, disguise (feelings *etc.*) —*vt.* **2.** simulate —**disˈsembler** *n.*

disseminate (dɪˈsɛmɪneɪt) *vt.* spread abroad, scatter —**dissemiˈnation** *n.* —**disˈseminator** *n.*

dissent (dɪˈsɛnt) *vi.* **1.** differ in opinion **2.** express such difference **3.** disagree with doctrine *etc.* of established church —*n.* **4.** such disagreement —**disˈsension** *n.* —**disˈsenter** *n.* —**disˈsentient** *a./n.*

dissertation (dɪsəˈteɪʃən) *n.* **1.** written thesis **2.** formal discourse —ˈ**dissertate** *vi.* hold forth

disservice (dɪsˈsɜːvɪs) *n.* ill turn, wrong, injury

dissident (ˈdɪsɪdənt) *n./a.* (one) not in agreement, *esp.* with government —ˈ**dissidence** *n.* **1.** dissent **2.** disagreement

dissimulate (dɪˈsɪmjʊleɪt) *v.* dissemble, practise deceit —**dissimuˈlation** *n.* —**disˈsimulator** *n.*

dissipate (ˈdɪsɪpeɪt) *vt.* **1.** scatter **2.** waste, squander —ˈ**dissipated** *a.* **1.** indulging in pleasure without restraint, dissolute **2.** scattered, wasted —**dissiˈpation** *n.* **1.** scattering **2.** frivolous, dissolute way of life

dissociate (dɪˈsəʊʃɪeɪt, -sɪ-) *v.* **1.** separate —*vt.* **2.** disconnect, sever —**dissociˈation** *n.*

dissolute (ˈdɪsəluːt) *a.* lax in morals

dissolution (dɪsəˈluːʃən) *n.* **1.** break-up **2.** termination of parliament, meeting or legal relationship **3.** destruction **4.** death

dissolve (dɪˈzɒlv) *vt.* **1.** absorb or melt in fluid **2.** break up, put an end to, annul —*vi.* **3.** melt in fluid **4.** disappear, vanish **5.** break up, scatter —**disˈsolvable** *or* **dissoluble** (dɪˈsɒljʊbᵊl) *a.* capable of being dissolved —**disˈsolvent** *n.* thing with power to dissolve

dissonant (ˈdɪsənənt) *a.* jarring, discordant —ˈ**dissonance** *n.*

dissuade (dɪˈsweɪd) *vt.* advise to refrain, persuade not to do something —**disˈsuasion** *n.* —**disˈsuasive** *a.*

dissyllable (dɪˈsɪləbᵊl) *or* **disyllable** (ˈdaɪsɪləbᵊl) *n.*

THESAURUS

disruption confusion, disarray, disorder, disorderliness, disturbance, interference, interruption, stoppage

disruptive confusing, disorderly, distracting, disturbing, obstreperous, troublemaking, troublesome, unruly, unsettling, upsetting

dissatisfaction annoyance, chagrin, disappointment, discomfort, discontent, dislike, dismay, displeasure, distress, exasperation, frustration, irritation, regret, resentment, unhappiness

dissect **1.** anatomize, cut up *or* apart, dismember, lay open **2.** analyse, break down, explore, inspect, investigate, scrutinize, study

dissection **1.** anatomization, anatomy, autopsy, dismemberment, necropsy, postmortem (examination) **2.** analysis, breakdown, examination, inspection, investigation, scrutiny

disseminate broadcast, circulate, diffuse, disperse, dissipate, distribute, proclaim, promulgate, propagate, publicize, publish, scatter, sow, spread

dissemination broadcasting, circulation, diffusion, distribution, promulgation, propagation, publication, publishing, spread

dissension conflict, conflict of opinion, contention, difference, disagreement, discord, discordance, dispute, dissent, friction, quarrel, strife, variance

dissent **1.** *v.* decline, differ, disagree, object, protest, refuse, withhold assent *or* approval **2.** *n.* difference, disagreement, discord, dissension, dissidence, nonconformity, objection, opposition, refusal, resistance

dissenter disputant, dissident, nonconformist, objector, protestant

dissentient *adj.* conflicting, differing, disagreeing, dissenting, dissident, opposing, protesting

dissertation critique, discourse, disquisition, essay, exposition, thesis, treatise

disservice bad turn, disfavour, harm, ill turn, injury, injustice, unkindness, wrong

dissident **1.** *adj.* differing, disagreeing, discordant, dissentient, dissenting, heterodox, nonconformist, schismatic **2.** *n.* agitator, dissenter, protestor, rebel, recusant

dissimilar different, disparate, divergent, diverse, heterogeneous, mismatched, not alike, not capable of comparison, not similar, unlike, unrelated, various

dissimilarity difference, discrepancy, disparity, dissimilitude, distinction, divergence, heterogeneity, incomparability, nonuniformity, unlikeness, unrelatedness

dissipate **1.** burn up, consume, deplete, expend, fritter away, indulge oneself, lavish, misspend, run through, spend, squander, waste **2.** disappear, dispel, disperse, dissolve, drive away, evaporate, scatter, vanish

dissipated **1.** abandoned, debauched, dissolute, intemperate, profligate, rakish, self-indulgent **2.** consumed, destroyed, exhausted, scattered, squandered, wasted

dissipation **1.** abandonment, debauchery, dissoluteness, drunkenness, excess, extravagance, indulgence, intemperance, lavishness, prodigality, profligacy, squandering, wantonness, waste **2.** disappearance, disintegration, dispersion, dissemination, dissolution, scattering, vanishing

dissociate **1.** break off, disband, disrupt, part company, quit **2.** detach, disconnect, distance, divorce, isolate, segregate, separate, set apart

dissolute abandoned, corrupt, debauched, degenerate, depraved, dissipated, immoral, lax, lewd, libertine, licentious, loose, profligate, rakish, unrestrained, vicious, wanton, wild

dissolution **1.** breaking up, disintegration, division, divorce, parting, resolution, separation **2.** death, decay, decomposition, demise, destruction, dispersal, extinction, overthrow, ruin **3.** adjournment, conclusion, disbandment, discontinuation, dismissal, end, ending, finish, suspension, termination

dissolve **1.** deliquesce, flux, fuse, liquefy, melt, soften, thaw **2.** crumble, decompose, diffuse, disappear, disintegrate, disperse, dissipate, dwindle, evanesce, evaporate, fade, melt away, perish, vanish, waste away **3.** break up, destroy, discontinue, dismiss, end, overthrow, ruin, suspend, terminate, wind up **4.** break into *or* up, collapse, disorganize, disunite, divorce, loose, resolve into, separate, sever

dissuade advise against, deter, discourage, disincline, divert, expostulate, persuade not to, put off, remonstrate, talk out of, urge not to, warn

word or metrical foot having two syllables —**dissyl'labic** *or* **disyl'labic** *a.*

distaff ('dɪstɑːf) *n.* cleft stick to hold wool *etc.* for spinning —**distaff side 1.** maternal side **2.** female line of family

distance ('dɪstəns) *n.* **1.** amount of space between two things **2.** remoteness **3.** aloofness, reserve —*vt.* **4.** hold or place at distance —**'distant** *a.* **1.** far off, remote **2.** haughty, cold —**'distantly** *adv.*

distaste (dɪs'teɪst) *n.* **1.** dislike of food or drink **2.** aversion, disgust —**dis'tasteful** *a.* unpleasant, displeasing to feelings —**dis'tastefully** *adv.* —**dis'tastefulness** *n.*

distemper (dɪs'tɛmpə) *n.* **1.** disease of dogs **2.** method of painting on plaster without oil **3.** paint used for this —*vt.* **4.** paint with distemper

distend (dɪ'stɛnd) *v.* swell out by pressure from within, inflate —**dis'tensible** *a.* —**dis'tension** *n.*

distich ('dɪstɪk) *n.* couplet

distil *or U.S.* **distill** (dɪs'tɪl) *vt.* **1.** vaporize and recondense (a liquid) **2.** purify, separate, concentrate (liquids) by this method **3.** *fig.* extract quality of —*vi.* **4.** trickle down (**-ll-**) —**'distillate** *n.* distilled liquid, *esp.* as fuel for some engines —**distil'lation** *n.* **1.** distilling **2.** process of evaporating or boiling liquid and condensing its vapour **3.** purification or separation of mixture by using different evaporation rates or boiling points of their components **4.** process of obtaining essence or extract of substance, usu. by heating in solvent **5.** distillate **6.** concentrated essence —**dis'tiller** *n.* one who distils, *esp.* manufacturer of alcoholic spirits —**dis'tillery** *n.*

distinct (dɪ'stɪŋkt) *a.* **1.** clear, easily seen **2.** definite **3.** separate, different —**dis'tinction** *n.* **1.** point of difference **2.** act of distinguishing **3.** eminence, repute, high honour, high quality —**dis'tinctive** *a.* characteristic —**dis'tinctly** *adv.* —**dis'tinctness** *n.*

distingué (distɛ̃'ge) *Fr.* distinguished; noble

distinguish (dɪ'stɪŋgwɪʃ) *vt.* **1.** make difference in **2.** recognize, make out **3.** honour **4.** make prominent or honoured (*usu. refl.*) **5.** class —*vi.* **6.** (*usu. with* between *or* among) draw distinction, grasp difference —**dis'tinguishable** *a.* —**dis'tinguished** *a.* **1.** noble, dignified **2.** famous, eminent

distort (dɪ'stɔːt) *vt.* **1.** put out of shape, deform **2.** misrepresent **3.** garble, falsify —**dis'tortion** *n.*

distract (dɪ'strækt) *vt.* **1.** draw attention of (someone)

THESAURUS

distance 1. absence, extent, gap, interval, lapse, length, range, reach, remoteness, remove, separation, space, span, stretch, width **2.** aloofness, coldness, coolness, frigidity, reserve, restraint, stiffness

distant 1. abroad, afar, far, faraway, far-flung, far-off, outlying, out-of-the-way, remote, removed **2.** aloof, ceremonious, cold, cool, formal, haughty, reserved, restrained, reticent, standoffish, stiff, unapproachable, unfriendly, withdrawn

distaste abhorrence, antipathy, aversion, detestation, disfavour, disgust, disinclination, dislike, displeasure, disrelish, dissatisfaction, horror, loathing, repugnance, revulsion

distasteful abhorrent, disagreeable, displeasing, loathsome, nauseous, objectionable, obnoxious, offensive, repugnant, repulsive, undesirable, uninviting, unpalatable, unpleasant, unsavoury

distend balloon, bloat, bulge, dilate, enlarge, expand, increase, inflate, puff, stretch, swell, widen

distil condense, draw out, evaporate, express, extract, press out, purify, rectify, refine, sublimate, vaporize

distillation elixir, essence, extract, quintessence, spirit

distinct 1. apparent, clear, clear-cut, decided, definite, evident, lucid, manifest, marked, noticeable, obvious, palpable, patent, plain, recognizable, sharp, unambiguous, unmistakable, well-defined **2.** detached, different, discrete, dissimilar, individual, separate, unconnected

distinction 1. differentiation, discernment, discrimination, penetration, perception, separation **2.** contrast, difference, differential, division, separation **3.** characteristic, distinctiveness, feature, individuality, mark, particularity, peculiarity, quality **4.** account, celebrity, consequence, credit, eminence, excellence, fame, greatness, honour, importance, merit, name, note, prominence, quality, rank, renown, reputation, repute, superiority, worth

distinctive characteristic, different, distinguishing, extraordinary, idiosyncratic, individual, original, peculiar, singular, special, typical, uncommon, unique

distinctly clearly, decidedly, definitely, evidently, manifestly, markedly, noticeably, obviously, palpably, patently, plainly, precisely, sharply

distinctness 1. clarity, lucidity, obviousness, plainness, sharpness, vividness **2.** detachment, difference, discreteness, disparateness, dissimilarity, dissociation, distinctiveness, individuality, separation

distinguish 1. ascertain, decide, determine, differentiate, discriminate, judge, tell apart, tell between, tell the difference **2.** categorize, characterize, classify, individualize, make distinctive, mark, separate, set apart, single out **3.** discern, know, make out, perceive, pick out, recognize, see, tell **4.** celebrate, dignify, honour, immortalize, make famous, signalize

distinguishable clear, conspicuous, discernible, evident, manifest, noticeable, obvious, perceptible, plain, recognizable, well-marked

distinguished acclaimed, celebrated, conspicuous, eminent, famed, famous, illustrious, notable, noted, renowned, well-known

distort 1. bend, buckle, contort, deform, disfigure, misshape, twist, warp, wrench, wrest **2.** bias, colour, falsify, garble, misrepresent, pervert, slant, twist

distortion 1. bend, buckle, contortion, crookedness, deformity, malformation, twist, twistedness, warp **2.** bias, colouring, falsification, misrepresentation, perversion, slant

distract 1. divert, draw away, sidetrack, turn aside **2.** amuse, beguile, engross, entertain, occupy **3.** agitate, bewilder, confound, confuse, derange, discompose, disconcert, disturb, harass, madden, perplex, puzzle, torment, trouble

distraction 1. abstraction, agitation, bewilderment, commotion, confusion, discord, disorder, disturbance **2.** amusement, beguilement, diversion, divertissement, entertainment, pastime, recreation **3.** disturbance, diversion, interference, interruption **4.** aberration, alienation, delirium, derangement, desperation, frenzy, hallucination, incoherence, insanity, mania

away from work *etc.* **2.** divert **3.** perplex, bewilder **4.** drive mad **—dis'traction** *n.*

distraint (dɪ'streɪnt) *n.* legal seizure of goods to enforce payment **—dis'train** *vt.* **—dis'trainment** *n.*

distrait (dɪ'streɪ; *Fr.* di'strɛ) *a.* **1.** absent-minded **2.** abstracted

distraught (dɪ'strɔːt) *a.* **1.** bewildered, crazed with grief **2.** frantic, distracted

distress (dɪ'strɛs) *n.* **1.** severe trouble, mental pain **2.** severe pressure of hunger, fatigue or want **3.** *Law* distraint *—vt.* **4.** afflict, give mental pain **—dis'tressed** *a.* **1.** much troubled; upset; afflicted **2.** in financial straits; poor **3.** *Econ. see* **depressed** (sense 4) *at* DEPRESS **—dis'tressful** *a.*

distribute (dɪ'strɪbjuːt) *vt.* **1.** deal out, dispense **2.** spread, dispose at intervals **3.** classify **—distri'bution** *n.* **—dis'tributive** *a.* **—dis'tributor** *n.* rotary switch distributing electricity in car engine

district ('dɪstrɪkt) *n.* **1.** region, locality **2.** portion of territory **—district nurse UK** nurse appointed to attend patients within particular district, usu. in patients' homes

disturb (dɪ'stɜːb) *vt.* trouble, agitate, unsettle, derange **—dis'turbance** *n.* **—dis'turbed** *a. Psych.* emotionally or mentally unstable **—dis'turber** *n.*

disuse (dɪs'juːs) *n.* state of being no longer used **—disused** (dɪs'juːzd) *a.*

disyllable ('daɪsɪləbᵊl) *n. see* DISSYLLABLE

ditch (dɪtʃ) *n.* **1.** long narrow hollow dug in ground for drainage *etc. —v.* **2.** make ditch in **3.** run (car *etc.*) into ditch *—vt.* **4.** *sl.* abandon, discard

dither ('dɪðə) *vi.* **1.** be uncertain or indecisive *—n.* **2.** this state

dithyramb ('dɪθɪræm, -ræmb) *n.* ancient Gr. hymn sung in honour of Dionysus **—dithy'rambic** *a.*

dittany ('dɪtənɪ) *n.* aromatic plant native to Greece

ditto ('dɪtəʊ) *n.* **1.** the aforementioned; the above; the same: used in lists *etc.* to avoid repetition, and symbolized by two small marks („) placed under thing to be repeated **2.** *inf.* duplicate (*pl.* **-s**) *—adv.* **3.** in same way *—interj.* **4.** *inf.* used to avoid repeating or confirm agreement with preceding sentence *—vt.* **5.** copy; repeat (**-toing, -toed**)

ditty ('dɪtɪ) *n.* simple song

diuretic (daɪjʊ'rɛtɪk) *a.* **1.** increasing the discharge of urine *—n.* **2.** substance with this property

diurnal (daɪ'ɜːnᵊl) *a.* **1.** daily **2.** in or of daytime **3.** taking a day

divalent (daɪ'veɪlənt, 'daɪveɪ-) *a.* capable of combining with two atoms of hydrogen or their equivalent **—di'valency** *n.*

divan (dɪ'væn) *n.* **1.** bed, couch without back or head **2.** backless low cushioned seat

dive (daɪv) *vi.* **1.** plunge under surface of water **2.** descend suddenly **3.** disappear **4.** go deep down **5.** rush or go quickly (**dived** *or U.S.* **dove** (dəʊv), **dived, 'diving**) *—n.* **6.** act of diving **7.** *sl.* disreputable bar or club **—'diver** *n.* **1.** one who descends into deep water **2.** any of various kinds of diving bird **—dive bomber** aircraft which attacks after diving steeply **—diving bell** early diving submersible having open bottom and being supplied with compressed air **—diving board** platform or springboard from which swimmers may

THESAURUS

distress *n.* **1.** affliction, agony, anguish, anxiety, desolation, discomfort, grief, heartache, misery, pain, sadness, sorrow, suffering, torment, torture, woe, worry, wretchedness **2.** adversity, calamity, destitution, difficulties, hardship, indigence, misfortune, need, poverty, privation, straits, trial, trouble ~*v.* **3.** afflict, agonize, bother, disturb, grieve, harass, harrow, pain, perplex, sadden, torment, trouble, upset, worry, wound

distressed 1. afflicted, agitated, anxious, distracted, distraught, saddened, tormented, troubled, upset, worried, wretched **2.** destitute, indigent, needy, poor, poverty-stricken, straitened

distribute 1. administer, allocate, allot, apportion, assign, deal, dispense, dispose, divide, dole out, give, measure out, mete, share **2.** circulate, convey, deliver, hand out, pass round **3.** diffuse, disperse, disseminate, scatter, spread, strew **4.** arrange, assort, categorize, class, classify, file, group

distribution 1. allocation, allotment, apportionment, dispensation, division, dole, partition, sharing **2.** circulation, diffusion, dispersal, dispersion, dissemination, propagation, scattering, spreading **3.** arrangement, assortment, classification, disposition, grouping, location, organization, placement

district area, community, locale, locality, neighbourhood, parish, quarter, region, sector, vicinity, ward

distrust 1. *v.* be sceptical of, be suspicious of, be wary of, disbelieve, discredit, doubt, misbelieve, mistrust, question, smell a rat (*Inf.*), suspect, wonder about **2.** *n.* disbelief, doubt, lack of faith, misgiving, mistrust, qualm, question, scepticism, suspicion, wariness

disturb 1. bother, butt in on, disrupt, interfere with, interrupt, intrude on, pester, rouse, startle **2.** confuse, derange, disarrange, disorder, disorganize, muddle, unsettle **3.** agitate, alarm, annoy, confound, discompose, distract, distress, excite, fluster, harass, perturb, ruffle, shake, trouble, unsettle, upset, worry

disturbance 1. agitation, annoyance, bother, confusion, derangement, disorder, distraction, hindrance, interruption, intrusion, molestation, perturbation, upset **2.** bother (*Inf.*), brawl, commotion, disorder, fracas, fray, hubbub, riot, ruckus (*Inf.*), ruction (*Inf.*), tumult, turmoil, uproar

disturbed *Psychiatry* disordered, maladjusted, neurotic, troubled, unbalanced, upset

disuse abandonment, decay, desuetude, discontinuance, idleness, neglect, non-employment, nonuse

ditch *n.* **1.** channel, drain, dyke, furrow, gully, moat, trench, watercourse ~*v.* **2.** dig, drain, excavate, gouge, trench **3.** *Sl.* abandon, discard, dispose of, drop, dump (*Inf.*), get rid of, jettison, scrap, throw out *or* overboard

dither 1. *v.* faff about (*Brit. inf.*), falter, haver, hesitate, oscillate, shillyshally (*Inf.*), swither (*Scot.*), teeter, vacillate, waver **2.** *n.* bother, flap (*Inf.*), fluster, flutter, pother, stew (*Inf.*), tiz-woz (*Inf.*), tizzy (*Inf.*), twitter

dive *v.* **1.** descend, dip, disappear, drop, duck, fall, go underwater, jump, leap, nose-dive, pitch, plummet, plunge, submerge, swoop ~*n.* **2.** dash, header (*Inf.*), jump, leap, lunge, nose dive, plunge, spring **3.** *Sl.* honky-tonk (*U.S. sl.*), joint (*Sl.*), sleazy bar dive —**diving suit** *or* **dress** waterproof suit used by divers, having heavy detachable helmet and air supply

diverge (daɪˈvɜːdʒ) *vi.* **1.** get farther apart **2.** separate —**diˈvergence** *or* **diˈvergency** *n.* —**diˈvergent** *a.*

divers (ˈdaɪvəz) *a. obs.* some, various

diverse (daɪˈvɜːs, ˈdaɪvɜːs) *a.* different, varied —**diˈversely** *adv.* —**diversifiˈcation** *n.* —**diˈversify** *vt.* **1.** make diverse or varied **2.** give variety to (**-ified, -ifying**) —**diˈversity** *n.*

divert (daɪˈvɜːt) *vt.* **1.** turn aside, ward off **2.** amuse, entertain —**diˈversion** *n.* **1.** a diverting **2.** official detour for traffic when main route is closed **3.** amusement —**diˈverting** *a.*

divertissement (dɪˈvɜːtɪsmənt) *n.* brief entertainment or diversion, usu. between acts of play

divest (daɪˈvɛst) *vt.* **1.** unclothe, strip **2.** dispossess, deprive

divide (dɪˈvaɪd) *vt.* **1.** make into two or more parts, split up, separate **2.** distribute, share **3.** classify —*v.* **4.** diverge in opinion —*vi.* **5.** become separated **6.** part into two groups for voting —*n.* **7.** watershed —**dividend** (ˈdɪvɪdɛnd) *n.* **1.** share of profits, of money divided among creditors *etc.* **2.** number to be divided by another —**diˈviders** *pl.n.* measuring compasses

divine (dɪˈvaɪn) *a.* **1.** of, pert. to, proceeding from, God **2.** sacred **3.** heavenly —*n.* **4.** theologian **5.** clergyman —*vt.* **6.** guess **7.** predict, foresee, tell by inspiration or magic —**divination** (dɪvɪˈneɪʃən) *n.* divining —**diˈvinely** *adv.* —**diˈviner** *n.* —**divinity** (dɪˈvɪnɪtɪ) *n.* **1.** quality of being divine **2.** god **3.** theology —**divining rod** (forked) stick said to move when held over ground where water is present (*also* **dowsing rod**)

division (dɪˈvɪʒən) *n.* **1.** act of dividing **2.** part of whole **3.** barrier **4.** section **5.** political constituency **6.** difference in opinion *etc.* **7.** *Maths.* method of finding how many times one number is contained in another **8.** army unit **9.** separation, disunion —**diˈvisible** *a.* capable of division —**diˈvisional** *a.* —**divisive** (dɪˈvaɪsɪv) *a.* causing disagreement —**divisor** (dɪˈvaɪzə) *n. Maths.* number which divides dividend —**division sign** symbol ÷, placed between dividend and divisor to indicate division, as in 12 ÷ 6 = 2

divorce (dɪˈvɔːs) *n.* **1.** legal dissolution of marriage **2.** complete separation, disunion —*v.* **3.** separate or be separated by divorce —*vt.* **4.** separate **5.** sunder —**divorcée** (dɪvɔːˈsiː) *or* (*masc.*) **divorcé** (dɪˈvɔːseɪ) *n.*

divot (ˈdɪvət) *n.* piece of turf

divulge (daɪˈvʌldʒ) *vt.* reveal, let out (secret) —**diˈvulgence** *n.*

THESAURUS

diverge 1. bifurcate, branch, divaricate, divide, fork, part, radiate, separate, split, spread **2.** depart, deviate, digress, stray, turn aside, wander

divergence branching out, departure, deviation, digression, divagation, ramification, separation, deflection

divergent deviating, diverging, separate

divers different, manifold, many, multifarious, numerous, several, some, sundry, varied, various

diverse 1. assorted, diversified, miscellaneous, of every description, several, sundry, varied, various **2.** different, differing, discrete, disparate, dissimilar, distinct, divergent, separate, unlike, varying

diversify alter, assort, branch out, change, expand, mix, modify, spread out, transform, variegate, vary

diversion 1. alteration, change, deflection, departure, detour, deviation, digression, variation **2.** amusement, beguilement, delight, distraction, divertissement, enjoyment, entertainment, game, gratification, pastime, play, pleasure, recreation, relaxation, sport

diversity assortment, difference, dissimilarity, distinctiveness, divergence, diverseness, diversification, heterogeneity, medley, multiplicity, range, unlikeness, variance, variegation, variety

divert 1. avert, deflect, redirect, switch, turn aside **2.** amuse, beguile, delight, entertain, gratify, recreate, regale **3.** detract, distract, draw *or* lead away from, lead astray, sidetrack

diverting amusing, beguiling, enjoyable, entertaining, fun, humorous, pleasant

divest 1. denude, disrobe, doff, remove, strip, take off, unclothe, undress **2.** deprive, despoil, dispossess, strip

divide 1. bisect, cleave, cut (up), detach, disconnect, part, partition, segregate, separate, sever, shear, split, subdivide, sunder **2.** allocate, allot, apportion, deal out, dispense, distribute, divvy (up) (*Inf.*), dole out, measure out, portion, share **3.** alienate, break up, cause to disagree, come between, disunite, estrange, set *or* pit against one another, set at variance *or* odds, sow dissension, split **4.** arrange, categorize, classify, grade, group, put in order, separate, sort

dividend bonus, cut (*Inf.*), divvy (*Inf.*), extra, gain, plus, portion, share, surplus

divine *adj.* **1.** angelic, celestial, godlike, heavenly, holy, spiritual, superhuman, supernatural **2.** consecrated, holy, religious, sacred, sanctified, spiritual **3.** beatific, blissful, exalted, mystical, rapturous, supreme, transcendent, transcendental, transmundane ~*n.* **4.** churchman, clergyman, cleric, ecclesiastic, minister, pastor, priest, reverend ~*v.* **5.** apprehend, conjecture, deduce, discern, foretell, guess, infer, intuit, perceive, prognosticate, suppose, surmise, suspect, understand **6.** *Of water or minerals* dowse

diviner 1. astrologer, augur, oracle, prophet, seer, sibyl, soothsayer **2.** *Of water or minerals* dowser

divinity 1. deity, divine nature, godhead, godhood, godliness, holiness, sanctity **2.** daemon, deity, genius, god, goddess, guardian spirit, spirit **3.** religion, religious studies, theology

divisible dividable, fractional, separable, splittable

division 1. bisection, cutting up, detaching, dividing, partition, separation, splitting up **2.** allotment, apportionment, distribution, sharing **3.** border, boundary, demarcation, divide, divider, dividing line, partition **4.** branch, category, class, compartment, department, group, head, part, portion, section, sector, segment **5.** breach, difference of opinion, disagreement, discord, disunion, estrangement, feud, rupture, split, variance

divisive alienating, damaging, detrimental, discordant, disruptive, estranging, inharmonious, pernicious, troublesome, unsettling

divorce 1. *n.* annulment, breach, break, decree nisi, dissolution, disunion, rupture, separation, severance, split-up **2.** *v.* annul, disconnect, dissociate, dissolve (*marriage*), disunite, divide, part, separate, sever, split up, sunder

divulge betray, communicate, confess, declare, dis-

divvy ('dɪvɪ) *inf. vt.* **1.** *esp.* US (*esp. with* up) divide and share —*n.* **2.** dividend

dixie ('dɪksɪ) *n.* **1.** *inf.* (military) cooking utensil or mess tin **2.** (**D-**) southern states of U.S.A. (*also* **'Dixieland**) —**'Dixieland** *n.* **1.** jazz derived from New Orleans tradition of playing, but with more emphasis on melody, regular rhythms *etc.* **2.** Dixie

D.I.Y. *or* **d.i.y.** do-it-yourself

dizzy ('dɪzɪ) *a.* **1.** feeling dazed, unsteady, as if about to fall **2.** causing or fit to cause dizziness, as speed *etc.* **3.** *inf.* silly —*vt.* **4.** make dizzy (**'dizzied, 'dizzying**) —**'dizzily** *adv.* —**'dizziness** *n.*

D.J. *or* **d.j.** **1.** dinner jacket **2.** disc jockey

djellaba ('dʒɛləbə) *n. see* JELLABA

djinni *or* **djinny** (dʒɪ'niː, 'dʒɪnɪ) *n. see* JINNI (*pl.* **djinn** (dʒɪn))

dl decilitre

D.Litt. *or* **D.Lit.** **1.** Doctor of Letters **2.** Doctor of Literature

dm decimetre

D.Mus. *or* **DMus** Doctor of Music

DNA deoxyribonucleic acid, main constituent of the chromosomes of all organisms

D-notice *n.* UK official notice sent to newspapers *etc.* prohibiting publication of certain security information

do[1] (duː; *unstressed* dʊ, də) *vt.* **1.** perform, effect, transact, bring about, finish **2.** work at **3.** work out, solve **4.** suit **5.** cover (distance) **6.** provide, prepare **7.** *sl.* cheat, swindle **8.** frustrate —*vi.* **9.** (*oft. with* for) look after **10.** act **11.** manage **12.** work **13.** fare **14.** serve, suffice **15.** happen —*v. aux.* **16.** makes negative and interrogative sentences and expresses emphasis (**did, done, 'doing**) —*n.* **17.** *inf.* celebration, festivity —**'doer** *n.* active or energetic person —**do-gooder** *n. inf.* well-intentioned person, *esp.* naive or impractical one —**do-it-yourself** *n.* hobby of constructing and repairing things oneself —**do away with** destroy —**do up** **1.** fasten **2.** renovate —**do with** **1.** need **2.** make use of —**do without** deny oneself

do[2] (dəʊ) *n. see* DOH (*pl.* **-s**)

do. ditto (*It.*, the same)

dobbin ('dɒbɪn) *n.* name for horse, *esp.* workhorse

Doberman pinscher ('dəʊbəmən 'pɪnʃə) breed of large dog with glossy black-and-tan coat

doc (dɒk) *n. inf.* doctor

docile ('dəʊsaɪl) *a.* willing to obey, submissive —**docility** (dəʊ'sɪlɪtɪ) *n.*

dock[1] (dɒk) *n.* **1.** artificial enclosure near harbour for loading or repairing ships —*v.* **2.** (of vessel) put or go into dock **3.** (of spacecraft) link or be linked together in space —**'docker** *n.* one who works at docks, *esp.* loading *etc.* cargoes —**'dockyard** *n.* enclosure with docks, for building or repairing ships

dock[2] (dɒk) *n.* **1.** solid part of tail **2.** cut end, stump —*vt.* **3.** cut short, *esp.* tail **4.** curtail, deduct (an amount) from

dock[3] (dɒk) *n.* enclosure in criminal court for prisoner

dock[4] (dɒk) *n.* coarse weed

docket ('dɒkɪt) *n.* **1.** piece of paper sent with package *etc.* with details of contents, delivery instructions *etc.* —*vt.* **2.** fix docket to

doctor ('dɒktə) *n.* **1.** medical practitioner **2.** one holding university's highest degree in any faculty —*vt.* **3.** treat medically **4.** repair, mend **5.** falsify (accounts *etc.*) **6.** *inf.* castrate, spay —**'doctoral** *a.* —**'doctorate** *n.*

doctrine ('dɒktrɪn) *n.* **1.** what is taught **2.** teaching of church, school or person **3.** belief, opinion, dogma —**doctri'naire** *n.* **1.** person who stubbornly applies theory without regard for circumstances —*a.* **2.** adhering to a doctrine in a stubborn, dogmatic way —**doctrinal** (dɒk'traɪnᵊl) *a.*

document ('dɒkjʊmənt) *n.* **1.** piece of paper *etc.* providing information or evidence —*vt.* ('dɒkjʊmɛnt) **2.** furnish with proofs, illustrations, certificates

THESAURUS

close, exhibit, expose, impart, leak, let slip, make known, proclaim, promulgate, publish, reveal, spill (*Inf.*), tell, uncover

dizzy **1.** faint, giddy, light-headed, off balance, reeling, shaky, staggering, swimming, vertiginous, weak at the knees, wobbly, woozy (*Inf.*) **2.** befuddled, bemused, bewildered, confused, dazed, dazzled, muddled **3.** lofty, steep, vertiginous **4.** *Inf.* capricious, fickle, flighty, foolish, frivolous, giddy, light-headed, scatterbrained, silly

do *v.* **1.** accomplish, achieve, act, carry out, complete, conclude, discharge, end, execute, perform, produce, transact, undertake, work **2.** answer, be adequate, be enough, be of use, be sufficient, pass muster, satisfy, serve, suffice, suit **3.** arrange, be responsible for, fix, get ready, look after, make, make ready, organize, prepare, see to, take on **4.** decipher, decode, figure out, puzzle out, resolve, solve, work out **5.** bear oneself, behave, carry oneself, comport oneself, conduct oneself **6.** fare, get along, get on, make out, manage, proceed **7.** bring about, cause, create, effect, produce **8.** *Of a play, etc.* act, give, perform, present, produce, put on **9.** *Sl.* cheat, con (*Sl.*), cozen, deceive, defraud, dupe, fleece, hoax, swindle, take (someone) for a ride (*Inf.*), trick ~*n.* **10.** *Inf.* affair, event, function, gathering, occasion, party

do away with **1.** bump off (*Sl.*), destroy, do in (*Sl.*), exterminate, kill, liquidate, murder, slay **2.** eliminate, put an end to

docile amenable, biddable, compliant, ductile, manageable, obedient, pliant, submissive, teachable (*Rare*), tractable

docility amenability, biddableness, compliance, ductility, manageability, meekness, obedience, pliancy, submissiveness, tractability

dock *n.* **1.** harbour, pier, quay, waterfront, wharf ~*v.* **2.** anchor, berth, drop anchor, land, moor, put in, tie up **3.** *Of spacecraft* couple, hook up, join, link up, rendezvous, unite

docket **1.** *n.* bill, certificate, chit, chitty, counterfoil, label, receipt, tab, tag, tally, ticket **2.** *v.* catalogue, file, index, label, mark, register, tab, tag, ticket

doctor *n.* **1.** general practitioner, G.P., medic (*Inf.*), medical practitioner, physician ~*v.* **2.** apply medication to, give medical treatment to, treat **3.** botch, cobble, do up (*Inf.*), fix, mend, patch up, repair **4.** alter, change, disguise, falsify, fudge, misrepresent, pervert, tamper with

doctrinaire *adj.* biased, dogmatic, fanatical, inflexible, insistent, opinionated, rigid

doctrine article, article of faith, belief, canon, concept, conviction, creed, dogma, opinion, precept, principle, teaching, tenet

—**docu'mentary** *a./n. esp.* (of) type of film dealing with real life, not fiction —**documen'tation** *n.*

dodder ('dɒdə) *vi.* totter or tremble, as with age —**'dodderer** *n.* feeble or inefficient person

doddle ('dɒd'l) *n.* **UK** *sl.* something easily accomplished

dodecagon (dəʊ'dɛkəgɒn) *n.* polygon having twelve sides

dodecahedron (dəʊdɛkə'hi:drən) *n.* solid figure having twelve plane faces

dodge (dɒdʒ) *v.* **1.** avoid or attempt to avoid (blow, discovery *etc.*) as by moving quickly **2.** evade (questions) by cleverness —*n.* **3.** trick, artifice **4.** ingenious method **5.** act of dodging —**'dodger** *n.* shifty person —**'dodgy** *a. inf.* **1.** dangerous **2.** unreliable **3.** tricky

Dodgem ('dɒdʒəm) *n.* **R** car used for bumping other cars in rink at funfair

dodo ('dəʊdəʊ) *n.* large extinct bird (*pl.* **-s, -es**)

doe (dəʊ) *n.* female of deer, hare, rabbit —**'doeskin** *n.* **1.** skin of deer, lamb or sheep **2.** very supple leather made from this **3.** heavy smooth cloth

Doe (dəʊ) *n. Law* formerly, name of fictitious plaintiff in action of ejectment

D.O.E. **UK** Department of the Environment

doek (dʊk) *n.* **SA** *inf.* head cloth worn *esp.* by Afr. women

doer ('du:ə) *n. see* DO[1]

does (dʌz) *third pers. sing., pres. ind. active of* DO[1]

doff (dɒf) *vt.* **1.** take off (hat, clothing) **2.** discard, lay aside

dog (dɒg) *n.* **1.** domesticated carnivorous four-legged mammal **2.** male of wolf, fox and other animals **3.** person (in contempt, abuse or playfully) **4.** name given to various mechanical contrivances acting as holdfasts **5.** device with tooth which penetrates or grips object and detains it **6.** firedog —*vt.* **7.** follow steadily or closely (**-gg-**) —**dogged** ('dɒgɪd) *a.* persistent, resolute, tenacious —**'doggy** *a.* —**'doglike** *a.* —**'dogcart** *n.* open vehicle with crosswise back-to-back seats —**dog collar** **1.** collar for dog **2.** *inf.* clerical collar **3.** *inf.* tight-fitting necklace —**dog days** **1.** hot season of the rising of Dog Star **2.** period of inactivity —**dog-ear** *n.* **1.** turned-down corner of page in book —*vt.* **2.** turn down corners of (pages) —**dog-end** *n. inf.* **1.** cigarette end **2.** rejected piece of anything —**'dogfight** *n.* **1.** skirmish between fighter planes **2.** savage contest characterized by disregard of rules —**'dogfish** *n.* very small species of shark —**'doghouse** *n.* **1.** **US** kennel **2.** *inf.* disfavour (*esp. in* **in the doghouse**) —**'dogleg** *n.* sharp bend or angle —**dog paddle** swimming stroke in which swimmer paddles his hands in imitation of swimming dog —**dog-paddle** *vi.* swim using dog paddle —**dog rose** wild rose —**'dogsbody** *n. inf.* drudge —**Dog Star** star Sirius —**dog-tired** *a. inf.* exhausted —**dog train** **C** sleigh drawn by dog team —**'dogwatch** *n.* in ships, short half-watch, 4-6, 6-8 p.m. —**'dogwood** *n.* any of various shrubs and trees —**go to the dogs** degenerate —**the dogs** greyhound race meeting

doge (dəʊdʒ) *n.* formerly, chief magistrate in Venice

doggerel ('dɒgərəl) *or* **dogrel** ('dɒgrəl) *n.* slipshod, unpoetic or trivial verse

doggo ('dɒgəʊ) *adv.* —**lie doggo** *inf.* keep quiet, still, hidden

dogie, dogy, *or* **dogey** ('dəʊgɪ) *n.* **US, C** motherless calf (*pl.* **-gies** *or* **-geys**)

dogma ('dɒgmə) *n.* **1.** article of belief, *esp.* one laid down authoritatively by church **2.** body of beliefs (*pl.* **-s, -ata** (-ətə)) —**dog'matic(al)** *a.* **1.** asserting opinions with arrogance **2.** relating to dogma —**dog'matically** *adv.* —**'dogmatism** *n.* arrogant assertion of opinion —**'dogmatist** *n.* —**'dogmatize** *or* **-ise** *v.*

doh (dəʊ) *n. Mus.* in tonic sol-fa, first degree of any major scale (*pl.* **-s**)

doily *or* **doyley** ('dɔɪlɪ) *n.* small cloth, paper, piece of lace to place under cake, dish *etc.*

Dolby ('dɒlbɪ) *n.* **R** system used in tape recorders which reduces noise level on recorded or broadcast sound

dolce ('dɒltʃɪ) *a. Mus.* sweet

doldrums ('dɒldrəmz) *pl.n.* **1.** state of depression,

THESAURUS

document **1.** *n.* certificate, instrument, legal form, paper, record, report **2.** *v.* authenticate, back up, certify, cite, corroborate, detail, give weight to, instance, particularize, substantiate, support, validate, verify

dodge *v.* **1.** dart, duck, shift, sidestep, swerve, turn aside **2.** avoid, deceive, elude, equivocate, evade, fend off, fudge, get out of, hedge, parry, shirk, shuffle, trick ~*n.* **3.** contrivance, device, feint, machination, ploy, ruse, scheme, stratagem, subterfuge, trick, wheeze (*Sl.*), wile

dodger evader, shifty so-and-so, shirker, slacker, slippery one, slyboots, trickster

doer achiever, active person, activist, bustler, dynamo, go-getter (*Inf.*), live wire (*Sl.*), organizer, powerhouse (*Sl.*), wheeler-dealer (*Inf.*)

doff **1.** *Of a hat* lift, raise, remove, take off, tip, touch **2.** *Of clothing* cast off, discard, remove, shed, slip off, slip out of, take off, throw off, undress

dog *n.* **1.** bitch, canine, cur, hound, man's best friend, mongrel, mutt (*Sl.*), pooch (*Sl.*), pup, puppy, tyke **2.** *Inf.* beast, blackguard, cur, heel (*Sl.*), knave (*Archaic*), scoundrel, villain **3.** **go to the dogs** *Inf.* degenerate, deteriorate, go down the drain, go to pot, go to ruin ~*v.* **4.** haunt, hound, plague, pursue, shadow, tail (*Inf.*), track, trail, trouble

dogged determined, firm, indefatigable, obstinate, persevering, persistent, pertinacious, resolute, single-minded, staunch, steadfast, steady, stubborn, tenacious, unflagging, unshakable, unyielding

dogma article, article of faith, belief, credo, creed, doctrine, opinion, precept, principle, teachings, tenet

dogmatic **1.** arbitrary, arrogant, assertive, categorical, dictatorial, doctrinaire, downright, emphatic, imperious, magisterial, obdurate, opinionated, overbearing, peremptory **2.** authoritative, canonical, categorical, doctrinal, ex cathedra, oracular, positive

dogmatism arbitrariness, arrogance, dictatorialness, imperiousness, opinionatedness, peremptoriness, positiveness, presumption

dogsbody drudge, general factotum, man *or* maid of all work, menial, skivvy, slave

doldrums apathy, blues, boredom, depression, dullness, dumps (*Inf.*), ennui, gloom, inertia, lassitude, listlessness, malaise, stagnation, tedium, torpor

dumps **2.** region of light winds and calms near the equator

dole (dəʊl) *n.* **1.** charitable gift **2.** (*usu. with* the) *inf.* payment under unemployment insurance —*vt.* **3.** (*usu. with* out) deal out sparingly

doleful (ˈdəʊlfʊl) *a.* dreary, mournful —**ˈdolefully** *adv.*

doll (dɒl) *n.* **1.** child's toy image of human being **2.** *sl.* attractive girl or woman —**doll up** dress up in latest fashion or smartly

dollar (ˈdɒlə) *n.* standard monetary unit of many countries, *esp.* U.S.A. and (since 1966) Aust.

dollop (ˈdɒləp) *n. inf.* semisolid lump

dolly (ˈdɒlɪ) *n.* **1.** child's word for doll **2.** wheeled support for film, TV camera **3.** any of various metal devices used as aids in hammering, riveting —**dolly bird** *sl., chiefly* **UK** attractive, fashionable girl

dolman sleeve (ˈdɒlmən) sleeve that is wide at armhole and tapers to tight wrist

dolmen (ˈdɒlmɛn) *n.* **1.** kind of cromlech **2.** stone table

dolomite (ˈdɒləmaɪt) *n.* type of limestone

dolour *or U.S.* **dolor** (ˈdɒlə) *n.* grief, sadness, distress —**ˈdolorous** *a.* —**ˈdolorously** *adv.*

dolphin (ˈdɒlfɪn) *n.* sea mammal, smaller than whale, with beaklike snout —**dolphiˈnarium** *n.* pool or aquarium for dolphins

dolt (dəʊlt) *n.* stupid fellow —**ˈdoltish** *a.*

-dom (*comb. form*) **1.** state, condition, as in *freedom* **2.** rank, office or domain of, as in *earldom* **3.** collection of persons, as in *officialdom*

domain (dəˈmeɪn) *n.* **1.** lands held or ruled over **2.** sphere, field of influence **3.** province

dome (dəʊm) *n.* **1.** rounded vault forming a roof **2.** something of this shape

Domesday Book *or* **Doomsday Book** (ˈduːmzdeɪ) record of survey of England in 1086

domestic (dəˈmɛstɪk) *a.* **1.** of, in the home **2.** home-loving **3.** (of animals) tamed, kept by man **4.** of, in one's own country, not foreign —*n.* **5.** house servant —**doˈmesticate** *vt.* **1.** tame (animals) **2.** accustom to home life **3.** adapt to an environment —**domestiˈcation** *n.* —**domesˈticity** *n.* —**domestic science** study of cooking and other subjects concerned with household skills

domicile (ˈdɒmɪsaɪl) *or* **domicil** (ˈdɒmɪsɪl) *n.* person's regular place of abode —**ˈdomiciled** *a.* living —**domiciliary** (dɒmɪˈsɪlɪərɪ) *a.* of a dwelling place

dominate (ˈdɒmɪneɪt) *vt.* **1.** rule, control, sway **2.** (of heights) overlook —*vi.* **3.** control, be the most powerful or influential member or part of something —**ˈdominant** *a./n.* —**domiˈnation** *n.* —**domiˈneer** *vi.* act imperiously, tyrannize

dominee (ˈduːmɪnɪ, ˈdʊə-) *n.* **SA** minister of Dutch Reformed Church

Dominican (dəˈmɪnɪkən) *n.* **1.** friar or nun of the order of St. Dominic —*a.* **2.** pert. to this order

dominion (dəˈmɪnjən) *n.* **1.** sovereignty, rule **2.** territory of government

Dominion Day *see* **Canada Day** *at* CANADIAN

dominoes (ˈdɒmɪnəʊz) *pl.n.* **1.** game played with 28 oblong flat pieces marked on one side with 0 to 6 spots on each half of the face —*sing.* **2.** one of these pieces **3.** cloak with eye mask for masquerading —**domino theory** theory that event in one place, *esp.* political takeover, will influence occurrence of similar events elsewhere

don[1] (dɒn) *vt.* put on (clothes) (**-nn-**)

don[2] (dɒn) *n.* **1.** fellow or tutor of college **2.** Sp. title, Sir —**ˈdonnish** *a.* of or resembling university don, *esp.* denoting pedantry or fussiness

THESAURUS

dole **1.** *n.* allowance, alms, benefit, donation, gift, grant, gratuity, modicum, parcel, pittance, portion, quota, share **2.** *v. Usually with* **out** administer, allocate, allot, apportion, assign, deal, dispense, distribute, divide, give, hand out, mete, share

dolt ass, blockhead, booby, chump (*Inf.*), clot (*Sl.*), dimwit (*Inf.*), dope (*Sl.*), dullard, dunce, fool, idiot, ignoramus, nitwit, simpleton, thickhead

domestic *adj.* **1.** domiciliary, family, home, household, private **2.** domesticated, home-loving, homely, housewifely, stay-at-home **3.** domesticated, house, house-trained, pet, tame, trained **4.** indigenous, internal, native, not foreign ~*n.* **5.** char (*Inf.*), charwoman, daily, daily help, help, maid, servant, woman (*Inf.*)

domesticate **1.** break, gentle, house-train, tame, train **2.** acclimatize, accustom, familiarize, habituate, naturalize

dominant **1.** ascendant, assertive, authoritative, commanding, controlling, governing, leading, presiding, ruling, superior, supreme **2.** chief, influential, main, outstanding, paramount, predominant, preeminent, prevailing, prevalent, primary, principal, prominent

dominate **1.** control, direct, domineer, govern, have the upper hand over, have the whip hand over, keep under one's thumb, lead, lead by the nose (*Inf.*), master, monopolize, overbear, rule, tyrannize **2.** bestride, loom over, overlook, stand head and shoulders above, stand over, survey, tower above **3.** detract from, eclipse, outshine, overrule, overshadow, predominate, prevail over

domination **1.** ascendancy, authority, command, control, influence, mastery, power, rule, superiority, supremacy, sway **2.** despotism, dictatorship, oppression, repression, subjection, subordination, suppression, tyranny

domineer bluster, boss around *or* about (*Inf.*), browbeat, bully, hector, intimidate, lord (it) over, menace, overbear, ride roughshod over, swagger, threaten, tyrannize

dominion **1.** ascendancy, authority, command, control, domination, government, jurisdiction, mastery, power, rule, sovereignty, supremacy, sway **2.** country, domain, empire, kingdom, province, realm, region, territory

don clothe oneself in, dress in, get into, pull on, put on, slip on *or* into

donate bequeath, bestow, chip in (*Inf.*), contribute, gift, give, make a gift of, present, subscribe

donation alms, benefaction, boon, contribution, gift, grant, gratuity, largess, offering, present, subscription

Doña (ˈdɒnjə) *n.* Sp. title of address equivalent to *Mrs.* or *Madam*

donate (dəʊˈneɪt) *v.* give —**doˈnation** *n.* gift to fund —**ˈdonor** *n.*

done (dʌn) *pp. of* DO¹

dong (dɒŋ) *n.* **1.** imitation of sound of bell —*vi.* **2.** make such sound

donga (ˈdɒŋgə) *n.* **SA, A** deep gully

donjon (ˈdʌndʒən, ˈdɒn-) *n. see* DUNGEON

Don Juan (ˈdɒn ˈdʒuːən) **1.** legendary Sp. nobleman and philanderer **2.** successful seducer of women

donkey (ˈdɒŋkɪ) *n.* ass (*pl.* -**s**) —**donkey engine** auxiliary engine —**donkey jacket** short, thick jacket, oft. worn by workmen —**donkey's years** *inf.* a long time —**donkey-work** *n.* drudgery

Donna (ˈdɒnə) *n.* It. title of address equivalent to *Madam*

Don Quixote (ˈdɒn kiːˈhəʊtiː, ˈkwɪksət) impractical idealist

doodle (ˈduːdᵊl) *v.* **1.** scribble absent-mindedly —*n.* **2.** picture *etc.* drawn aimlessly —**ˈdoodlebug** *n.* **1.** *see* **V-1** **2.** diviner's rod

doom (duːm) *n.* **1.** fate, destiny **2.** ruin **3.** judicial sentence, condemnation **4.** the Last Judgment —*vt.* **5.** sentence, condemn **6.** destine to destruction or suffering —**ˈdoomsday** *or* **ˈdomesday** *n.* the day of the Last Judgment

door (dɔː) *n.* hinged or sliding barrier to close any entrance —**ˈdoorjamb** *n.* one of two vertical members forming sides of doorframe (*also* **ˈdoorpost**) —**ˈdoorman** *n.* man employed to attend doors of certain buildings —**ˈdoormat** *n.* **1.** mat at entrance for wiping shoes on **2.** *sl.* person who offers little resistance to ill-treatment —**ˈdoorstop** *n.* any device which prevents open door from moving —**ˈdoorway** *n.* entrance with or without door —**door to door 1.** (of selling *etc.*) from one house to next **2.** (of journeys *etc.*) direct

dope (dəʊp) *n.* **1.** drug, *esp.* illegal, narcotic drug **2.** *inf.* information **3.** *inf.* stupid person **4.** kind of varnish —*vt.* **5.** drug (*esp.* of racehorses) —**ˈdopey** *or* **ˈdopy** *a. inf.* **1.** foolish **2.** drugged **3.** half asleep

Doppelgänger (ˈdɒpᵊlgɛŋə) *n. Legend* ghostly duplicate of living person

Doppler effect (ˈdɒplə) change in apparent frequency of sound or light wave *etc.* as result of relative motion between observer and source (*also* **Doppler shift**)

Doric (ˈdɒrɪk) *a.* **1.** of the inhabitants of Doris, in ancient Greece, or their dialect —*n.* **2.** dialect of Dorians **3.** style of Gr. architecture **4.** rustic dialect —**Dorian** (ˈdɔːrɪən) *a./n.* (member) of early Gr. race

dormant (ˈdɔːmənt) *a.* **1.** not active, in state of suspension **2.** sleeping —**ˈdormancy** *n.*

dormer (ˈdɔːmə) *n.* upright window set in sloping roof

dormitory (ˈdɔːmɪtərɪ, -trɪ) *n.* sleeping room with many beds —**dormitory town** town whose inhabitants travel elsewhere to work

Dormobile (ˈdɔːməʊbiːl) *n.* **R** vanlike vehicle specially equipped for living in while travelling

dormouse (ˈdɔːmaʊs) *n.* small hibernating mouse-like rodent

dorp (dɔːp) *n.* **SA** small town

dorsal (ˈdɔːsᵊl) *a. Anat., zool.* of, on back

dory (ˈdɔːrɪ) *n.* deep-bodied type of fish, *esp.* John Dory

dose (dəʊs) *n.* **1.** amount (of drug *etc.*) administered at one time **2.** *inf.* instance or period of something unpleasant, *esp.* disease —*vt.* **3.** give doses to —**ˈdosage** *n.*

doss (dɒs) *inf. n.* **1.** temporary bed —*vi.* **2.** sleep in dosshouse **3.** sleep —**ˈdosshouse** *n.* cheap lodging house

dossier (ˈdɒsɪeɪ) *n.* set of papers on some particular subject or event

dot¹ (dɒt) *n.* **1.** small spot, mark —*vt.* **2.** mark with dots **3.** sprinkle **4.** *sl.* hit —**ˈdotty** *a.* **1.** *sl.* crazy **2.** *sl.* (*with* about) extremely fond (of) **3.** marked with dots

dot² (dɒt) *n.* dowry

dote (dəʊt) *vi.* **1.** (*with* on *or* upon) be passionately fond (of) **2.** be silly or weak-minded —**ˈdotage** *n.* senility —**ˈdotard** *n.* —**ˈdoting** *a.* blindly affectionate

dotterel *or* **dottrel** (ˈdɒtrəl) *n.* kind of plover

dottle (ˈdɒtᵊl) *n.* plug of tobacco left in pipe after smoking

double (ˈdʌbᵊl) *a.* **1.** of two parts, layers *etc.*, folded **2.** twice as much or as many **3.** of two kinds **4.** designed for two users **5.** ambiguous **6.** deceitful —*adv.* **7.** twice **8.** to twice the amount or extent **9.** in a pair —*n.* **10.** person or thing exactly like, or mistakable for, another **11.** quantity twice as much as another **12.** sharp turn **13.** running pace —*pl.* **14.** game between 2 pairs of players —*v.* **15.** make, become double **16.** increase twofold **17.** fold in two **18.** get round, sail round

THESAURUS

donnish bookish, erudite, formalistic, pedagogic, pedantic, precise, scholarly, scholastic

donor almsgiver, benefactor, contributor, donator, giver, grantor (*Law*), philanthropist

doom *n.* **1.** catastrophe, death, destiny, destruction, downfall, fate, fortune, lot, portion, ruin **2.** condemnation, decision, decree, judgment, sentence, verdict **3.** Armageddon, Doomsday, end of the world, Judgment Day, the Last Day, the Last Judgment, the last trump ~*v.* **4.** condemn, consign, damn, decree, destine, foreordain, judge, predestine, sentence, threaten

door doorway, egress, entrance, entry, exit, ingress, opening

dope *n.* **1.** drugs, narcotic, opiate **2.** blockhead, dimwit (*Inf.*), dolt, dunce, fool, idiot, simpleton **3.** details, facts, gen (*Inf.*), info (*Inf.*), information, inside information, lowdown (*Inf.*), news, tip ~*v.* **4.** anaesthetize, doctor, drug, inject, knock out, narcotize, sedate, stupefy

dormant asleep, comatose, fallow, hibernating, inactive, inert, inoperative, latent, quiescent, sleeping, sluggish, slumbering, suspended, torpid

dose dosage, draught, drench, measure, portion, potion, prescription, quantity

dot 1. *n.* atom, circle, dab, fleck, full stop, iota, jot, mark, mite, mote, point, speck, spot **2.** *v.* dab, dabble, fleck, spot, sprinkle, stipple, stud

dotage decrepitude, feebleness, imbecility, old age, second childhood, senility, weakness

dote on *or* **upon** admire, adore, hold dear, idolize, lavish affection on, prize, treasure

doting adoring, devoted, fond, foolish, indulgent, lovesick

(headland *etc.*) —*vi.* **19.** turn sharply —ˈ**doubly** *adv.* —**double agent** spy employed simultaneously by two opposing sides —**double-barrelled** *or U.S.* **-barreled** *a.* **1.** (of gun) having two barrels **2.** extremely forceful **3.** **UK** (of surnames) having two hyphenated parts **4.** serving two purposes; ambiguous —**double bass** largest and lowest-toned instrument in violin form —**double-breasted** *a.* (of garment) having overlapping fronts —**double-check** *v.* check again; verify —**double check 1.** second examination or verification **2.** *Chess* simultaneous check from two pieces —**double chin** fold of fat under chin —**double cream** thick cream with high fat content —**double-cross** *vt.* cheat; betray —**double-crosser** *n.* —**double dagger** character (‡) used in printing to indicate cross-reference —**double-dealing** *n.* artifice, duplicity —**double-decker** *n.* **1.** *chiefly* **UK** bus with two passenger decks **2.** *inf., chiefly* **US** thing or structure having two decks, layers *etc.* —**double Dutch** *inf.* incomprehensible talk, gibberish —**double-edged** *a.* **1.** acting in two ways **2.** (of remark *etc.*) having two possible interpretations **3.** (of knife *etc.*) having cutting edge on either side of blade —**double entry** book-keeping system in which transaction is entered as debit in one account and as credit in another —**double glazing** two panes of glass in window to insulate against cold, sound *etc.* —**double-jointed** *a.* having unusually flexible joints permitting abnormal degree of motion —**double pneumonia** pneumonia affecting both lungs —**double-quick** *a./adv.* very fast —**double standard** set of principles that allows greater freedom to one person or group than another —**double take** delayed reaction to a remark, situation *etc.* —**double talk 1.** rapid speech with mixture of nonsense syllables and real words; gibberish **2.** empty, deceptive or ambiguous talk —**double time 1.** doubled wage rate for working on public holidays *etc.* **2.** *Mus.* two beats per bar **3.** *U.S. Army* fast march; slow running pace, keeping in step

double entendre (ɑːnˈtɑːndrə) word or phrase with two meanings, one usu. indelicate

doublet (ˈdʌblɪt) *n.* **1.** close-fitting body garment formerly worn by men **2.** one of two words from same root but differing in form and usu. in meaning, as *warden* and *guardian* **3.** false gem of thin layer of gemstone fused on to base of glass *etc.*

doubloon (dʌˈbluːn) *n.* ancient Sp. gold coin

doubt (daʊt) *vt.* **1.** hesitate to believe **2.** call into question **3.** suspect —*vi.* **4.** be wavering or uncertain in belief or opinion —*n.* **5.** uncertainty, wavering in belief **6.** state of affairs giving cause for uncertainty —ˈ**doubter** *n.* —ˈ**doubtful** *a.* —ˈ**doubtfully** *adv.* —ˈ**doubtless** *adv./a.*

douche (duːʃ) *n.* **1.** jet or spray of water applied to (part of) body —*vt.* **2.** give douche to

dough (dəʊ) *n.* **1.** flour or meal kneaded with water **2.** *sl.* money —ˈ**doughy** *a.* —ˈ**doughnut** *n.* sweetened and fried ball or ring-shaped piece of dough

doughty (ˈdaʊtɪ) *a.* valiant —ˈ**doughtily** *adv.* —ˈ**doughtiness** *n.* boldness

dour (dʊə) *a.* grim, stubborn, severe

douse *or* **dowse** (daʊs) *vt.* **1.** thrust into water **2.** extinguish (light)

dove (dʌv) *n.* bird of pigeon family —**dovecot** (ˈdʌvkɒt) *or* **dovecote** (ˈdʌvkəʊt) *n.* house for doves —ˈ**dovetail** *n.* **1.** joint made with fan-shaped tenon —*v.* **2.** fit closely, neatly, firmly together

dowager (ˈdaʊədʒə) *n.* widow with title or property derived from deceased husband

dowdy (ˈdaʊdɪ) *a.* **1.** unattractively or shabbily dressed —*n.* **2.** woman so dressed

dowel (ˈdaʊəl) *n.* wooden, metal peg, *esp.* joining two adjacent parts

dower (ˈdaʊə) *n.* **1.** widow's share for life of husband's estate —*vt.* **2.** endow —ˈ**dowry** *n.* **1.** property wife brings to husband at marriage **2.** any endowment —**dower house** house for use of widow, oft. on her deceased husband's estate

THESAURUS

double *adj.* **1.** binate (*Botany*), coupled, doubled, dual, duplicate, in pairs, paired, twice, twin, twofold **2.** deceitful, dishonest, false, hypocritical, insincere, Janus-faced, knavish (*Archaic*), perfidious, treacherous, two-faced, vacillating ~*v.* **3.** duplicate, enlarge, fold, grow, increase, magnify, multiply, plait, repeat ~*n.* **4.** clone, copy, counterpart, dead ringer (*Sl.*), Doppelgänger, duplicate, fellow, impersonator, lookalike, mate, replica, ringer (*Sl.*), spitting image (*Inf.*), twin

double-cross betray, cheat, defraud, hoodwink, mislead, swindle, trick, two-time (*Inf.*)

double-dealing bad faith, betrayal, cheating, deceit, deception, dishonesty, duplicity, foul play, hypocrisy, mendacity, perfidy, treachery, trickery, two-timing (*Inf.*)

double entendre ambiguity, double meaning, innuendo, play on words, pun

doubt *v.* **1.** discredit, distrust, fear, lack confidence in, misgive, mistrust, query, question, suspect ~*n.* **2.** apprehension, disquiet, distrust, fear, incredulity, lack of faith, misgiving, mistrust, qualm, scepticism, suspicion ~*v.* **3.** be dubious, be uncertain, demur, fluctuate, hesitate, scruple, vacillate, waver ~*n.* **4.** dubiety, hesitancy, hesitation, indecision, irresolution, lack of conviction, suspense, uncertainty, vacillation **5.** ambiguity, confusion, difficulty, dilemma, perplexity, problem, quandary

doubter agnostic, disbeliever, doubting Thomas, questioner, sceptic, unbeliever

doubtful 1. ambiguous, debatable, dubious, equivocal, hazardous, inconclusive, indefinite, indeterminate, obscure, precarious, problematic, questionable, unclear, unconfirmed, unsettled, vague **2.** distrustful, hesitating, in two minds (*Inf.*), irresolute, perplexed, sceptical, suspicious, tentative, uncertain, unconvinced, undecided, unresolved, unsettled, unsure, vacillating, wavering **3.** disreputable, dubious, questionable, shady (*Inf.*), suspect, suspicious

doubtless 1. assuredly, certainly, clearly, indisputably, of course, precisely, surely, truly, undoubtedly, unquestionably, without doubt **2.** apparently, most likely, ostensibly, presumably, probably, seemingly, supposedly

dour 1. dismal, dreary, forbidding, gloomy, grim, morose, sour, sullen, unfriendly **2.** austere, hard, inflexible, obstinate, rigid, rigorous, severe, strict, uncompromising, unyielding

dovetail *v.* fit, fit together, interlock, join, link, mortise, tenon, unite

dowdy dingy, drab, frowzy, frumpish, frumpy, ill-

down[1] (daʊn) *adv.* 1. to, in, or towards, lower position 2. below the horizon 3. (of payment) on the spot, immediate —*prep.* 4. from higher to lower part of 5. at lower part of 6. along —*a.* 7. depressed, miserable —*vt.* 8. knock, pull, push down 9. *inf.* drink, *esp.* quickly —**ˈdownward** *a./adv.* —**ˈdownwards** *adv.* —**ˈdowncast** *a.* 1. dejected 2. looking down —**ˈdownfall** *n.* 1. sudden loss of health, reputation *etc.* 2. fall of rain, snow *etc., esp.* sudden heavy one —**ˈdowngrade** *vt.* 1. reduce in importance or value, *esp.* to demote (person) to poorer job 2. speak of disparagingly —*n.* 3. *chiefly* US downward slope —**downˈhearted** *a.* discouraged; dejected —**ˈdownˈhill** *a.* 1. going or sloping down —*adv.* 2. towards bottom of hill; downwards —*n.* 3. downward slope of hill; descent 4. skiing race downhill —**down payment** deposit paid on item purchased on hire-purchase *etc.* —**ˈdownpour** *n.* heavy fall of rain —**ˈdownright** *a.* 1. plain, straightforward —*adv.* 2. quite, thoroughly —**ˈdownˈstage** *a./adv.* at, to front of stage —**ˈdownˈstairs** *adv.* 1. down the stairs; to or on lower floor —*n.* 2. lower or ground floor 3. **UK** *inf.* servants of household collectively —**ˈdownˈstream** *adv./a.* in or towards lower part of stream; with current —**down time** time during which computer *etc.* is not working because incapable of production, as when under repair —**down-to-earth** *a.* sensible; practical; realistic —**ˈdowntrodden** *a.* 1. subjugated; oppressed 2. trodden down —**ˈdownˈwind** *adv./a.* in same direction towards which wind is blowing; with wind from behind —**down and out** finished, defeated —**down under** *inf.* Australia and New Zealand —**go downhill** *inf.* decline; deteriorate —**have a down on** *inf.* have grudge against —**on the downgrade** waning in importance *etc.*

down[2] (daʊn) *n.* 1. soft underfeathers, hair or fibre 2. fluff —**ˈdowny** *a.*

down[3] (daʊn) *n. obs.* hill, *esp.* sand dune (*also* **downs**) —**ˈdownland** *n.* open high land (*also* **downs**)

Downing Street (ˈdaʊnɪŋ) 1. street in London: official residences of prime minister of Great Britain and chancellor of the exchequer 2. *inf.* prime minister; British Government

Down's syndrome (daʊnz) *Pathol.* chromosomal abnormality resulting in flat face and nose, short stubby fingers, vertical fold of skin at inner edge of eye and mental retardation

dowry (ˈdaʊərɪ) *n. see* DOWER

dowse (daʊz) *vi.* use divining rod —**ˈdowser** *n.* water diviner

doxology (dɒkˈsɒlədʒɪ) *n.* short hymn of praise to God

doyen (ˈdɔɪən) *n.* senior member of a body or profession (**doyenne** (dɔɪˈɛn) *fem.*)

doyley (ˈdɔɪlɪ) *n. see* DOILY

doz. dozen

doze (dəʊz) *vi.* 1. sleep drowsily, be half-asleep —*n.* 2. nap —**ˈdozy** *a.* 1. drowsy 2. *inf.* stupid

dozen (ˈdʌzˀn) *n.* (set of) twelve

D.Phil., D.Ph., *or* **DPh** Doctor of Philosophy (*also* **Ph.D., PhD**)

DPP *or* **D.P.P.** Director of Public Prosecutions

Dr. 1. Doctor 2. Drive

drab[1] (dræb) *a.* 1. dull, monotonous 2. of a dingy brown colour —*n.* 3. mud colour

drab[2] (dræb) *obs. n.* 1. slatternly woman 2. whore —*vi.* 3. consort with prostitutes (**-bb-**)

drachm (dræm) *n.* unit of weight, 1/8 of fluid ounce, 1/16 of avoirdupois ounce (*also* **fluid dram**)

drachma (ˈdrækmə) *n.* monetary unit of Greece (*pl.* **-s, -mae** (-miː))

Draconian (dreɪˈkəʊnɪən) *or* **Draconic** (dreɪˈkɒnɪk) *a.* (*oft.* **d-**) 1. like the laws of Draco 2. very harsh, cruel

draft[1] (drɑːft) *n.* 1. design, sketch 2. rough copy of document 3. order for money 4. detachment of men, *esp.* troops, reinforcements —*vt.* 5. make sketch, plan or rough design of 6. make rough copy of (writing *etc.*) —*v.* 7. detach (military personnel) from one unit to another

THESAURUS

dressed, old-fashioned, scrubby (*Inf.*), shabby, slovenly, tacky (*U.S. inf.*), unfashionable

dower dowry, inheritance, legacy, portion, provision, share

down *adj.* **1.** blue, dejected, depressed, disheartened, downcast, low, miserable, sad, unhappy ~*v.* **2.** bring down, fell, floor, knock down, overthrow, prostrate, subdue, tackle, throw, trip **3.** *Inf.* drain, drink (down), gulp, put away, swallow, toss off **4. have a down on** *Inf.* be antagonistic *or* hostile to, bear a grudge towards, be prejudiced against, be set against, feel ill will towards, have it in for (*Sl.*)

down and out derelict, destitute, impoverished, penniless, ruined

downcast cheerless, crestfallen, daunted, dejected, depressed, despondent, disappointed, disconsolate, discouraged, disheartened, dismayed, dispirited, miserable, sad, unhappy

downfall 1. breakdown, collapse, comedown, comeuppance (*Sl.*), debacle, descent, destruction, disgrace, fall, overthrow, ruin, undoing **2.** cloudburst, deluge, downpour, rainstorm

downgrade 1. degrade, demote, humble, lower *or* reduce in rank, take down a peg (*Inf.*) **2.** decry, denigrate, detract from, disparage, run down

downhearted blue, chapfallen, crestfallen, dejected, depressed, despondent, discouraged, disheartened, dismayed, dispirited, downcast, low-spirited, sad, sorrowful, unhappy

downpour cloudburst, deluge, flood, inundation, rainstorm, torrential rain

downright 1. absolute, blatant, categorical, clear, complete, explicit, out-and-out, outright, plain, positive, simple, thoroughgoing, total, undisguised, unequivocal, unqualified, utter **2.** blunt, candid, forthright, frank, honest, open, outspoken, plain, sincere, straightforward, straight-from-the-shoulder

down-to-earth common-sense, hard-headed, matter-of-fact, mundane, no-nonsense, plain-spoken, practical, realistic, sane, sensible, unsentimental

downward *adj.* declining, descending, earthward, heading down, sliding, slipping

doze 1. *v.* catnap, drop off (*Inf.*), drowse, kip (*Sl.*), nap, nod, nod off (*Inf.*), sleep, sleep lightly, slumber, snooze (*Inf.*), zizz (*Inf.*) **2.** *n.* catnap, forty winks (*Inf.*), kip (*Sl.*), little sleep, nap, shuteye (*Sl.*), siesta, snooze (*Inf.*)

drab cheerless, colourless, dingy, dismal, dreary, dull, flat, gloomy, grey, lacklustre, shabby, sombre, uninspired, vapid

draft[2] (drɑːft) *vt.* **US** select for compulsory military service

drag (dræg) *vt.* **1.** pull along with difficulty or friction **2.** trail on ground **3.** sweep with net or grapnels **4.** protract —*vi.* **5.** lag, trail **6.** (*oft. with* on *or* out) be tediously protracted (**-gg-**) —*n.* **7.** check on progress **8.** checked motion **9.** iron shoe to check wheel **10.** type of carriage **11.** lure for hounds to hunt **12.** kind of harrow **13.** sledge, net, grapnel, rake **14.** *inf.* tedious person or thing **15.** *sl.* women's clothes worn by man (*esp. in* **in drag**) —**ˈdragnet** *n.* **1.** fishing net to be dragged along sea floor **2.** comprehensive search, *esp.* by police for criminal *etc.* —**ˈdragster** *n.* car designed, modified for drag racing —**drag race** motor car race where cars are timed over measured distance

dragée (dræˈʒeɪ) *n.* sugar-coated sweet, nut or pill

draggle (ˈdræg³l) *v.* **1.** make or become wet or dirty by trailing on ground —*vi.* **2.** lag; dawdle

dragoman (ˈdrægəʊmən) *n.* in some Middle Eastern countries, *esp.* formerly, professional interpreter or guide (*pl.* **-s, -men**)

dragon (ˈdrægən) *n.* **1.** mythical fire-breathing monster, like winged crocodile **2.** type of large lizard —**ˈdragonfly** *n.* long-bodied insect with gauzy wings

dragoon (drəˈguːn) *n.* **1.** cavalryman of certain regiments —*vt.* **2.** oppress **3.** coerce

drain (dreɪn) *vt.* **1.** draw off (liquid) by pipes, ditches *etc.* **2.** dry **3.** drink to dregs **4.** empty, exhaust —*vi.* **5.** flow off or away **6.** become rid of liquid —*n.* **7.** channel for removing liquid **8.** sewer **9.** depletion, strain —**ˈdrainage** *n.* —**draining board** sloping grooved surface at side of sink for draining washed dishes *etc.* (*also* **ˈdrainer**) —**ˈdrainpipe** *n.* pipe for carrying off rainwater *etc.* —**drainpipe trousers** *or* **ˈdrainpipes** *pl.n.* trousers with narrow legs

drake (dreɪk) *n.* male duck

dram (dræm) *n.* **1.** small draught of strong drink **2.** drachm

drama (ˈdrɑːmə) *n.* **1.** stage play **2.** art or literature of plays **3.** playlike series of events —**draˈmatic** *a.* **1.** pert. to drama **2.** suitable for stage representation **3.** with force and vividness of drama **4.** striking **5.** tense **6.** exciting —**ˈdramatist** *n.* writer of plays —**dramatiˈzation** *or* **-iˈsation** *n.* —**ˈdramatize** *or* **-ise** *vt.* adapt novel for acting

dramatis personae (ˈdrɑːmətɪs pəˈsəʊnaɪ) characters in play

dramaturgy (ˈdræmətɜːdʒɪ) *n.* technique of writing and producing plays —**dramaˈturgic(al)** *a.* —**ˈdramaturgist** *or* **ˈdramaturge** *n.* playwright

drank (dræŋk) *pt. of* DRINK

drape (dreɪp) *vt.* **1.** cover, adorn with cloth **2.** arrange in graceful folds —**ˈdraper** *n.* dealer in cloth, linen *etc.* —**ˈdrapery** *n.*

drastic (ˈdræstɪk) *a.* **1.** extreme, forceful **2.** severe

draught *or U.S.* **draft** (drɑːft) *n.* **1.** current of air between apertures in room *etc.* **2.** act or action of drawing **3.** dose of medicine **4.** act of drinking **5.** quantity drunk at once **6.** inhaling **7.** depth of ship in water **8.** the drawing in of, or fish taken in, net **9.** (*now usu.* **draft**) preliminary plan or layout for work to be executed —*pl.* **10.** game played on chessboard with flat round 'men' —*a.* **11.** for drawing **12.** drawn —*vt.* **13.** *see* DRAFT[2] —**ˈdraughty** *or U.S.* **ˈdrafty** *a.* full of air currents —**ˈdraughtboard** *n.* board with 64 squares of alternating colours, for playing draughts or chess on —**draught horse** horse for vehicles carrying heavy loads —**ˈdraughtsman** *or U.S.* **ˈdraftsman** *n.* one who makes drawings, plans *etc.* —**ˈdraughtsmanship** *or U.S.* **ˈdraftsmanship** *n.*

draw (drɔː) *vt.* **1.** pull, pull along, haul **2.** inhale **3.** entice, attract **4.** delineate, portray with pencil *etc.* **5.** frame, compose, draft, write **6.** bring (upon, out *etc.*) **7.** get by lot **8.** (of ship) require (depth of water) **9.** take from (well, barrel *etc.*) **10.** receive (money) **11.** bend (bow) —*vi.* **12.** pull, shrink **13.** make, admit current of air **14.** make pictures with pencil *etc.* **15.** finish game with equal points, goals *etc.*, tie **16.** write orders for money **17.** come, approach (near) (**drew** *pt.*, **drawn** *pp.*) —*n.* **18.** act of drawing **19.** casting of lots **20.** game or contest ending in a tie —**ˈdrawable** *a.* —**drawer** (ˈdrɔːə) *n.* **1.** one who or that which draws **2.** (drɔː) sliding box in table or chest —*pl.* (drɔːz) **3.** two-legged undergarment —**ˈdrawing** *n.* **1.** art of depicting in line **2.** sketch so done **3.** action of verb —**ˈdrawback** *n.* **1.**

THESAURUS

draft *v.* **1.** compose, delineate, design, draw, draw up, formulate, outline, plan, sketch ~*n.* **2.** abstract, delineation, outline, plan, preliminary form, rough, sketch, version **3.** bill (*of exchange*), cheque, order, postal order

drag *v.* **1.** draw, hale, haul, lug, pull, tow, trail, tug, yank **2.** dawdle, draggle, lag behind, linger, loiter, straggle, trail behind **3.** *With* **on** *or* **out** draw out, extend, keep going, lengthen, persist, prolong, protract, spin out, stretch out ~*n.* **4.** *Sl.* annoyance, bore, bother, nuisance, pain (*Inf.*), pest

dragoon *v.* browbeat, bully, coerce, compel, constrain, drive, force, impel, intimidate, strong-arm (*Inf.*)

drain *v.* **1.** bleed, draw off, dry, empty, evacuate, milk, pump off *or* out, remove, tap, withdraw **2.** consume, deplete, dissipate, empty, exhaust, sap, strain, tax, use up, weary **3.** discharge, effuse, exude, flow out, leak, ooze, seep, trickle, well out **4.** drink up, finish, gulp down, quaff, swallow ~*n.* **5.** channel, conduit, culvert, ditch, duct, outlet, pipe, sewer, sink, trench, watercourse **6.** depletion, drag, exhaustion, expenditure, reduction, sap, strain, withdrawal

drainage bilge (water), seepage, sewage, sewerage, waste

dram drop, glass, measure, shot (*Inf.*), slug, snort (*Sl.*), tot

drama 1. dramatization, play, show, stage play, stage show, theatrical piece **2.** acting, dramatic art, dramaturgy, stagecraft, theatre, Thespian art **3.** crisis, dramatics, excitement, histrionics, scene, spectacle, theatrics, turmoil

dramatic 1. dramaturgic, dramaturgical, theatrical, Thespian **2.** breathtaking, climactic, electrifying, emotional, exciting, melodramatic, sensational, startling, sudden, suspenseful, tense, thrilling **3.** affecting, effective, expressive, impressive, moving, powerful, striking, vivid

dramatist dramaturge, playwright, scriptwriter

drastic desperate, dire, extreme, forceful, harsh, radical, severe, strong

draught 1. *Of air* current, flow, influx, movement, puff **2.** dragging, drawing, haulage, pulling, traction **3.** cup, dose, drench, drink, potion, quantity

anything that takes away from satisfaction 2. snag —'**drawbridge** *n.* hinged bridge that can be raised or lowered —**drawing pin UK** short tack with broad head, for fastening papers to drawing board *etc.* —**drawing room** living room, sitting room —'**drawstring** *n.* cord *etc.* run through hem around opening, so that when it is pulled tighter, the opening closes —**draw near** approach —**draw out** lengthen —**draw up** 1. arrange 2. stop

drawl (drɔːl) *v.* 1. speak or utter (words) slowly —*n.* 2. such speech —'**drawlingly** *adv.*

drawn (drɔːn) *v.* 1. *pp. of* DRAW —*a.* 2. haggard, tired or tense in appearance

dray (dreɪ) *n.* low cart without sides for heavy loads

dread (drɛd) *vt.* 1. fear greatly —*n.* 2. awe, terror —*a.* 3. feared, awful —'**dreadful** *a.* disagreeable, shocking, bad —'**dreadnought** *n.* large battleship mounting heavy guns

dream (driːm) *n.* 1. vision during sleep 2. fancy 3. reverie 4. aspiration 5. very pleasant idea, person, thing —*vi.* 6. have dreams —*vt.* 7. see, imagine in dreams 8. think of as possible (**dreamt** (drɛmt) *or* **dreamed** *pt./pp.*) —'**dreamer** *n.* —'**dreamless** *a.* —'**dreamy** *a.* 1. given to daydreams, unpractical, vague 2. *inf.* wonderful

dreary ('drɪərɪ) *a.* dismal, dull —**drear** *a. Lit.* dreary —'**drearily** *adv.* —'**dreariness** *n.* gloom

dredge[1] (drɛdʒ) *v.* 1. bring up (mud *etc.*) from sea bottom 2. deepen (channel) by dredge —*vt.* 3. search for, produce (obscure, remote, unlikely material) —*n.* 4. form of scoop or grab —'**dredger** *n.* ship for dredging

dredge[2] (drɛdʒ) *vt.* sprinkle with flour *etc.* —'**dredger** *n.*

dregs (drɛgz) *pl.n.* 1. sediment, grounds 2. worthless part

drench (drɛntʃ) *vt.* 1. wet thoroughly, soak 2. make (animal) take dose of medicine —*n.* 3. soaking 4. dose for animal

Dresden ('drɛzdᵊn) *n.* 1. city in East Germany 2. delicate and decorative porcelain ware made near Dresden (*also* **Dresden china**) —*a.* 3. of Dresden china

dress (drɛs) *vt.* 1. clothe 2. array for show 3. trim, smooth, prepare surface of 4. prepare (food) for table 5. put dressing on (wound) 6. align (troops) —*vi.* 7. put on one's clothes 8. form in proper line —*n.* 9. one-piece garment for woman 10. clothing 11. clothing for ceremonial evening wear —'**dresser** *n.* 1. one who dresses, *esp.* actors or actresses 2. surgeon's assistant 3. kitchen sideboard —'**dressing** *n.* something applied to something else, as sauce to food, ointment to wound, manure to land *etc.* —'**dressing-'down** *n. inf.* scolding —'**dressy** *a.* 1. stylish 2. fond of dress —**dress circle** first gallery in theatre —**dress coat** cutaway coat worn by men as evening dress —**dressing gown** loose robe worn while one is resting or before dressing —**dressing room** room, *esp.* one in theatre for changing costumes and make-up —**dressing station** *Mil.* first-aid post close to combat area —**dressing table** —'**dressmaker** *n.* —**dress rehearsal** 1. last rehearsal of play *etc.* using costumes *etc.* as for first night 2. any full-scale practice —**dress suit** man's evening suit, *esp.* tails

THESAURUS

draw *v.* 1. drag, haul, pull, tow, tug 2. delineate, depict, design, map out, mark out, outline, paint, portray, sketch, trace 3. allure, attract, bring forth, call forth, elicit, engage, entice, evoke, induce, influence, invite, persuade 4. extort, extract, pull out, take out 5. breathe in, drain, inhale, inspire, puff, pull, respire, suck 6. compose, draft, formulate, frame, prepare, write 7. choose, pick, select, single out, take ~*n.* 8. *Inf.* attraction, enticement, lure, pull (*Inf.*) 9. dead heat, deadlock, stalemate, tie

drawback defect, deficiency, detriment, difficulty, disadvantage, fault, flaw, fly in the ointment (*Inf.*), handicap, hindrance, hitch, impediment, imperfection, nuisance, obstacle, snag, stumbling block, trouble

drawing cartoon, delineation, depiction, illustration, outline, picture, portrayal, representation, sketch, study

drawl *v. Of speech sounds* drag out, draw out, extend, lengthen, prolong, protract

drawn fatigued, fraught, haggard, harassed, harrowed, pinched, sapped, strained, stressed, taut, tense, tired, worn

draw out drag out, extend, lengthen, make longer, prolong, prolongate, protract, spin out, stretch, string out

draw up 1. bring to a stop, halt, pull up, run in, stop, stop short 2. compose, draft, formulate, frame, prepare, write out

dread 1. *v.* anticipate with horror, cringe at, fear, have cold feet (*Inf.*), quail, shrink from, shudder, tremble 2. *n.* affright, alarm, apprehension, aversion, awe, dismay, fear, fright, funk (*Inf.*), heebie-jeebies (*Sl.*), horror, terror, trepidation 3. *adj.* alarming, awe-inspiring, awful, dire, dreaded, dreadful, frightening, frightful, horrible, terrible, terrifying

dreadful alarming, appalling, awful, dire, distressing, fearful, formidable, frightful, ghastly, grievous, hideous, horrendous, horrible, monstrous, shocking, terrible, tragic, tremendous

dream *n.* 1. daydream, delusion, fantasy, hallucination, illusion, imagination, pipe dream, reverie, speculation, trance, vagary, vision 2. ambition, aspiration, design, desire, goal, hope, notion, wish 3. beauty, delight, gem, joy, marvel, pleasure, treasure ~*v.* 4. build castles in the air *or* in Spain, conjure up, daydream, envisage, fancy, fantasize, hallucinate, have dreams, imagine, stargaze, think, visualize

dreamer daydreamer, Don Quixote, fantasist, fantasizer, fantast, idealist, romancer, theorizer, utopian, visionary

dreamy 1. fanciful, imaginary, impractical, quixotic, speculative, vague, visionary 2. absent, abstracted, daydreaming, faraway, in a reverie, musing, pensive, preoccupied, with one's head in the clouds

dreary 1. bleak, cheerless, comfortless, depressing, dismal, doleful, downcast, drear, forlorn, gloomy, glum, joyless, lonely, lonesome, melancholy, mournful, sad, solitary, sombre, sorrowful, wretched 2. boring, colourless, drab, dull, humdrum, lifeless, monotonous, routine, tedious, uneventful, uninteresting, wearisome

dregs deposit, draff, dross, grounds, lees, residue, residuum, scourings, scum, sediment, trash, waste

drench 1. drown, duck, flood, imbrue, inundate,

dressage ('dresɑːʒ) *n.* method of training horse in special manoeuvres to show obedience

drew (druː) *pt. of* DRAW

drey *or* **dray** (dreɪ) *n.* squirrel's nest

dribble ('drɪbᵊl) *v.* **1.** (allow to) flow in drops, trickle **2.** *Football* work (ball) forward with short kicks —*vi.* **3.** run at the mouth —*n.* **4.** trickle, drop —'**driblet** *n.* small portion or instalment

dried (draɪd) *pt./pp. of* DRY

drier ('draɪə) *comp. of* DRY

driest ('draɪɪst) *sup. of* DRY

drift (drɪft) *vi.* **1.** be carried as by current of air, water **2.** move aimlessly or passively —*n.* **3.** process of being driven by current **4.** slow current or course **5.** deviation from course **6.** tendency **7.** meaning **8.** wind-heaped mass of snow, sand *etc.* **9.** material driven or carried by water —'**drifter** *n.* **1.** one who, that which drifts **2.** *inf.* aimless person with no fixed job *etc.* —'**driftwood** *n.* wood washed ashore by sea

drill[1] (drɪl) *n.* **1.** boring tool or machine **2.** exercise of soldiers or others in handling of arms and manoeuvres **3.** routine teaching —*v.* **4.** bore, pierce (hole) in (material) (as if) with drill **5.** exercise in military and other routine —*vi.* **6.** practise routine

drill[2] (drɪl) *n.* **1.** machine for sowing seed **2.** small furrow for seed **3.** row of plants —*v.* **4.** sow (seed) in drills or furrows

drill[3] (drɪl) *n.* coarsely woven twilled fabric

drill[4] (drɪl) *n.* W Afr. monkey

drink (drɪŋk) *v.* **1.** swallow (liquid) **2.** take (intoxicating liquor), *esp.* to excess —*vt.* **3.** absorb (**drank** *pt.*, **drunk** *pp.*) —*n.* **4.** liquid for drinking **5.** portion of this **6.** act of drinking **7.** intoxicating liquor or excessive consumption of it —'**drinkable** *a.* —'**drinker** *n.* —**drink to** *or* **drink the health of** express good wishes *etc.* by drinking a toast to

drip (drɪp) *v.* **1.** fall or let fall in drops (**-pp-**) —*n.* **2.** act of dripping **3.** drop **4.** *Med.* intravenous administration of solution **5.** *inf.* dull, insipid person —'**dripping** *n.* **1.** melted fat that drips from roasting meat —*a.* **2.** very wet —**drip-dry** *a.* (of fabric) drying free of creases if hung up while wet —'**dripstone** *n.* projection over window or door to stop dripping of water

drive (draɪv) *vt.* **1.** urge in some direction **2.** make move and steer (vehicle, animal *etc.*) **3.** urge, impel **4.** fix by blows, as nail **5.** chase **6.** convey in vehicle **7.** hit ball with force as in golf, tennis —*vi.* **8.** keep machine, animal going, steer it **9.** be conveyed in vehicle **10.** rush, dash, drift fast (**drove, driven** ('drɪvᵊn), '**driving**) —*n.* **11.** act, action of driving **12.** journey in vehicle **13.** private road leading to house **14.** capacity for getting things done **15.** united effort, campaign **16.** energy **17.** forceful stroke in cricket, golf, tennis —'**driver** *n.* **1.** one that drives **2.** *Golf* club used for tee shots —**drive-in** *a.* **1.** denoting public facility or service designed for use by patrons in cars —*n.* **2.** *chiefly* US cinema designed to be used in such a manner —'**driveway** *n.* path for vehicles, oft. connecting house with public road —**driving belt** belt that communicates motion to machinery —**driving licence** official document authorizing person to drive motor vehicle

drivel ('drɪvᵊl) *vi.* **1.** run at mouth or nose **2.** talk nonsense (**-ll-**) —*n.* **3.** silly or senseless talk —'**driveller** *n.*

THESAURUS

saturate, soak, souse, steep, wet **2.** *Veterinary* dose, physic, purge

dress *n.* **1.** costume, ensemble, frock, garment, get-up (*Inf.*), gown, outfit, rigout (*Inf.*), robe, suit **2.** apparel, attire, clothes, clothing, costume, garb, garments, gear (*Sl.*), guise, habiliment, raiment (*Archaic*), togs, vestment ~*v.* **3.** attire, change, clothe, don, garb, put on, robe, slip on *or* into **4.** adorn, apparel (*Archaic*), array, bedeck, deck, decorate, drape, embellish, furbish, ornament, rig, trim **5.** adjust, align, arrange, comb (out), dispose, do (up), fit, groom, prepare, set, straighten **6.** bandage, bind up, plaster, treat

dressmaker couturier, modiste, seamstress, sewing woman, tailor

dribble 1. drip, drop, fall in drops, leak, ooze, run, seep, trickle **2.** drip saliva, drivel, drool, slaver, slobber

drift *v.* **1.** be carried along, coast, float, go (aimlessly), meander, stray, waft, wander ~*n.* **2.** accumulation, bank, heap, mass, mound, pile **3.** course, current, direction, flow, impulse, movement, rush, sweep, trend **4.** *Fig.* aim, design, direction, gist, implication, import, intention, meaning, object, purport, scope, significance, tendency, tenor

drill *v.* **1.** discipline, exercise, instruct, practise, rehearse, teach, train ~*n.* **2.** discipline, exercise, instruction, practice, preparation, repetition, training ~*v.* **3.** bore, penetrate, perforate, pierce, puncture, sink in ~*n.* **4.** bit, borer, boring-tool, gimlet, rotary tool

drink *v.* **1.** absorb, drain, gulp, guzzle, imbibe, partake of, quaff, sip, suck, sup, swallow, swig, swill, toss off, wash down, wet one's whistle (*Inf.*) **2.** booze (*Inf.*), carouse, go on a binge *or* bender (*Inf.*), hit the bottle (*Inf.*), indulge, pub-crawl (*Chiefly Brit. sl.*), revel, tipple, tope, wassail ~*n.* **3.** beverage, liquid, potion, refreshment, thirst quencher **4.** alcohol, booze (*Inf.*), hooch (*Sl.*), liquor, spirits, the bottle (*Inf.*) **5.** cup, draught, glass, gulp, sip, swallow, swig (*Inf.*), taste

drinker alcoholic, bibber, boozer (*Inf.*), dipsomaniac, drunk, drunkard, guzzler, inebriate, lush (*Sl.*), soak (*Sl.*), sot, sponge (*Inf.*), tippler, toper, wino (*Sl.*)

drink to pledge, pledge the health of, salute, toast

drip *v.* **1.** dribble, drizzle, drop, exude, filter, plop, splash, sprinkle, trickle ~*n.* **2.** dribble, dripping, drop, leak, trickle **3.** *Inf.* milksop, ninny, softy (*Inf.*), weakling, weed (*Inf.*), wet (*Inf.*)

drive *v.* **1.** herd, hurl, impel, propel, push, send, urge **2.** direct, go, guide, handle, manage, motor, operate, ride, steer, travel **3.** actuate, coerce, compel, constrain, force, goad, harass, impel, motivate, oblige, overburden, overwork, press, prick, prod, rush, spur **4.** dash, dig, plunge, hammer, ram, sink, stab, thrust ~*n.* **5.** excursion, hurl (*Scot.*), jaunt, journey, outing, ride, run, spin (*Inf.*), trip, turn **6.** action, advance, appeal, campaign, crusade, effort, push (*Inf.*), surge **7.** ambition, effort, energy, enterprise, get-up-and-go (*Inf.*), initiative, motivation, pressure, push (*Inf.*), vigour, zip (*Inf.*)

drivel *v.* **1.** dribble, drool, slaver, slobber **2.** babble, blether, gab (*Inf.*), gas (*Inf.*), maunder, prate, ramble, waffle (*Inf.*) ~*n.* **3.** balderdash, blah (*Sl.*), bosh (*Inf.*), bunk (*Inf.*), bunkum, fatuity, gibberish, nonsense, poppycock (*Inf.*), prating, rot, rubbish, stuff, twaddle, waffle (*Inf.*)

drizzle (ˈdrɪzᵊl) *vi.* 1. rain in fine drops —*n.* 2. fine, light rain

drogue (drəʊg) *n.* 1. any funnel-like device, *esp.* of canvas, used as sea anchor 2. small parachute 3. wind indicator 4. windsock towed behind target aircraft 5. funnel-shaped device on end of refuelling hose of tanker aircraft to receive probe of aircraft being refuelled

droll (drəʊl) *a.* funny, odd, comical —ˈ**drollery** *n.* —ˈ**drolly** *adv.*

dromedary (ˈdrʌmədərɪ) *n.* one-humped camel bred *esp.* for racing

drone (drəʊn) *n.* 1. male of honey bee 2. lazy idler 3. deep humming 4. bass pipe of bagpipe 5. its note —*vi.* 6. hum 7. talk in monotonous tone

drongo (ˈdrɒŋgəʊ) *n.* black tropical bird

drool (druːl) *vi.* slaver, drivel

droop (druːp) *vi.* 1. hang down 2. wilt, flag —*vt.* 3. let hang down —*n.* 4. drooping condition —ˈ**droopy** *a.*

drop (drɒp) *n.* 1. globule of liquid 2. very small quantity 3. fall, descent 4. distance through which thing falls 5. thing that falls, as gallows platform —*vt.* 6. let fall 7. let fall in drops 8. utter casually 9. set down, unload 10. discontinue —*vi.* 11. fall 12. fall in drops 13. lapse 14. come or go casually (**-pp-**) —ˈ**droplet** *n.* —ˈ**dropper** *n.* 1. small tube having rubber bulb at one end for dispensing drops of liquid 2. person or thing that drops —ˈ**droppings** *pl.n.* dung of rabbits, sheep, birds *etc.* —ˈ**dropout** *n.* person who fails to complete course of study or one who rejects conventional society —**drop scone** scone made by dropping spoonful of batter on hot griddle

dropsy (ˈdrɒpsɪ) *n.* disease causing watery fluid to collect in the body —ˈ**dropsical** *a.*

droshky (ˈdrɒʃkɪ) *or* **drosky** (ˈdrɒskɪ) *n.* open four-wheeled carriage, formerly used in Russia

dross (drɒs) *n.* 1. scum of molten metal 2. impurity, refuse 3. anything of little or no value

drought (draʊt) *n.* long spell of dry weather

drove[1] (drəʊv) *pt. of* DRIVE

drove[2] (drəʊv) *n.* 1. herd, flock, crowd, *esp.* in motion —*v.* 2. drive (cattle *etc.*) *esp.* a long distance —ˈ**drover** *n.* driver of cattle

drown (draʊn) *v.* 1. die or kill by immersion in liquid —*vt.* 2. get rid of as by submerging in liquid 3. (*sometimes with* out) make (sound) inaudible by louder sound

drowsy (ˈdraʊzɪ) *a.* 1. half asleep 2. lulling 3. dull —**drowse** *v.* —ˈ**drowsily** *adv.* —ˈ**drowsiness** *n.*

drub (drʌb) *vt.* thrash, beat (**-bb-**) —ˈ**drubbing** *n.* beating

drudge (drʌdʒ) *vi.* 1. work at menial or distasteful tasks, slave —*n.* 2. one who drudges, hack —ˈ**drudgery** *n.*

drug (drʌg) *n.* 1. medical substance 2. narcotic 3. commodity which is unsaleable because of overproduction —*vt.* 4. mix drugs with 5. administer drug to, *esp.* one inducing unconsciousness (**-gg-**) —**drug addict** person abnormally dependent on narcotic drugs —ˈ**drugstore** *n.* **US** pharmacy where wide variety of goods is available

drugget (ˈdrʌgɪt) *n.* coarse woollen fabric, *esp.* used for carpeting

druid (ˈdruːɪd) *n.* (*sometimes* **D-**) 1. member of an ancient order of Celtic priests 2. Eisteddfod official —**druˈidic(al)** *a.* —ˈ**druidism** *n.*

drum (drʌm) *n.* 1. percussion instrument of skin

THESAURUS

drizzle 1. *n.* fine rain, Scotch mist 2. *v.* mizzle (*Dialect*), rain, shower, spot *or* spit with rain, spray, sprinkle

droll amusing, clownish, comic, comical, diverting, eccentric, entertaining, farcical, funny, humorous, jocular, laughable, ludicrous, odd, quaint, ridiculous, risible, waggish, whimsical

drone *n.* 1. idler, leech, loafer, lounger, parasite, scrounger (*Inf.*), sluggard, sponger (*Inf.*) ~*v.* 2. buzz, hum, purr, thrum, vibrate, whirr 3. *Often with* **on** be boring, chant, drawl, intone, prose about, speak monotonously, talk interminably ~*n.* 4. buzz, hum, murmuring, purr, thrum, vibration, whirr, whirring

droop 1. bend, dangle, drop, fall down, hang (down), sag, sink 2. decline, diminish, fade, faint, flag, languish, slump, wilt, wither

drop *n.* 1. bead, bubble, driblet, drip, droplet, globule, pearl, tear 2. dab, dash, mouthful, nip, pinch, shot (*Inf.*), sip, spot, taste, tot, trace, trickle 3. abyss, chasm, declivity, descent, fall, plunge, precipice, slope 4. cut, decline, decrease, deterioration, downturn, fall-off, lowering, reduction, slump ~*v.* 5. dribble, drip, fall in drops, trickle 6. decline, depress, descend, diminish, dive, droop, fall, lower, plummet, plunge, sink, tumble 7. abandon, cease, desert, discontinue, forsake, give up, kick (*Inf.*), leave, quit, relinquish, remit, terminate 8. *Inf. Sometimes with* **off** deposit, leave, let off, set down, unload

drought aridity, dehydration, drouth (*Archaic or Scot.*), dryness, dry spell, dry weather, parchedness

drove collection, company, crowd, flock, gathering, herd, horde, mob, multitude, press, swarm, throng

drown 1. deluge, drench, engulf, flood, go down, go under, immerse, inundate, sink, submerge, swamp 2. *Fig.* deaden, engulf, muffle, obliterate, overcome, overpower, overwhelm, stifle, swallow up, wipe out

drowse be drowsy, be lethargic, be sleepy, doze, drop off (*Inf.*), nap, nod, sleep, slumber, snooze (*Inf.*)

drowsy 1. comatose, dazed, dopey (*Sl.*), dozy, drugged, half asleep, heavy, lethargic, nodding, sleepy, somnolent, tired, torpid 2. dreamy, lulling, restful, sleepy, soothing, soporific

drubbing beating, clobbering (*Sl.*), defeat, flogging, hammering (*Inf.*), licking (*Inf.*), pounding, pummelling, thrashing, trouncing, walloping (*Inf.*), whipping

drudge 1. *n.* dogsbody (*Inf.*), factotum, hack, maid *or* man of all work, menial, plodder, scullion (*Archaic*), servant, skivvy, slave, toiler, worker 2. *v.* grind (*Inf.*), keep one's nose to the grindstone, labour, moil (*Archaic or dialect*), plod, plug away (*Inf.*), slave, toil, work

drudgery chore, donkey-work, fag (*Inf.*), grind (*Inf.*), hack work, hard work, labour, menial labour, skivvying, slavery, slog, sweat (*Inf.*), sweated labour, toil

drug *n.* 1. medicament, medication, medicine, physic, poison, remedy 2. dope (*Sl.*), narcotic, opiate ~*v.* 3. administer a drug, dope (*Sl.*), dose, medicate, treat 4. anaesthetize, deaden, knock out, numb, poison, stupefy

stretched over round hollow frame, played by beating with sticks **2.** various things shaped like drum **3.** *see* **eardrum** *at* EAR[1] —*vi.* **4.** play drum —*v.* **5.** tap, thump continuously (**-mm-**) —**'drummer** *n.* one who plays drum —**'drumfire** *n.* heavy continuous rapid artillery fire —**drumhead court-martial** summary court-martial held at war front —**drum major** leader of military band —**'drumstick** *n.* **1.** stick for beating drum **2.** lower joint of cooked fowl's leg —**drum out** expel (from club *etc.*) —**drum up** obtain (support *etc.*) by solicitation or canvassing

drunk (drʌŋk) *a.* **1.** overcome by strong drink **2.** *fig.* overwhelmed by strong emotion —*v.* **3.** *pp. of* DRINK —**'drunkard** *n.* one given to excessive drinking —**'drunken** *a.* **1.** intoxicated **2.** habitually drunk **3.** caused by, showing intoxication —**'drunkenness** *n.*

drupe (dru:p) *n.* fruit that has fleshy or fibrous part around stone that encloses seed, as peach *etc.*

dry (draɪ) *a.* **1.** without moisture **2.** rainless **3.** not yielding milk or other liquid **4.** cold, unfriendly **5.** caustically witty **6.** having prohibition of alcoholic drink **7.** uninteresting **8.** needing effort to study **9.** lacking sweetness (as wines) —*vt.* **10.** remove water, moisture —*vi.* **11.** become dry **12.** evaporate (**dried, 'drying**) —**'dryer** *or* **'drier** *n.* **1.** person or thing that dries **2.** apparatus for removing moisture —**'dryly** *or* **'drily** *adv.* —**'dryness** *n.* —**dry battery** electric battery without liquid —**dry cell** primary cell in which electrolyte is in form of paste or is treated in some way to prevent spilling —**dry-clean** *vt.* clean (clothes) with solvent other than water —**dry-cleaner** *n.* —**dry dock** dock that can be pumped dry for work on ship's bottom —**dry farming** methods of producing crops in areas of low rainfall —**dry fly** *Angling* artificial fly designed to be floated on surface of water —**dry ice** solid carbon dioxide —**dry measure** unit or system of units for measuring dry goods, such as grains *etc.* —**dry point 1.** needle for engraving without acid **2.** engraving so made —**dry rot** fungoid decay in wood —**dry run** practice, rehearsal in simulated conditions —**dry-stone** *a.* (of wall) made without mortar —**dry out 1.** make or become dry **2.** *inf.* (cause to) undergo treatment for alcoholism or drug addiction

dryad ('draɪəd, -æd) *n.* wood nymph

dryly ('draɪlɪ) *adv. see* DRY

D.Sc. Doctor of Science

D.S.C. Distinguished Service Cross

D.S.M. *Mil.* Distinguished Service Medal

D.S.O. Distinguished Service Order

D.T.'s *inf.* delirium tremens

dual ('dju:əl) *a.* **1.** twofold **2.** of two, double, forming pair —**'dualism** *n.* recognition of two independent powers or principles, *eg* good and evil, mind and matter —**du'ality** *n.* —**dual carriageway UK** road on which traffic travelling in opposite directions is separated by central strip of turf *etc.*

dub (dʌb) *vt.* **1.** confer knighthood on **2.** give title to **3.** provide (film) with soundtrack not in original language **4.** smear with grease, dubbin (**-bb-**) —**'dubbin** *or* **'dubbing** *n.* grease for making leather supple

dubious ('dju:bɪəs) *a.* **1.** causing doubt, not clear or decided **2.** of suspect character —**du'biety** *n.* uncertainty, doubt

ducal ('dju:k'l) *a.* of duke or duchy

ducat ('dʌkət) *n.* former gold coin of Italy *etc.*

duchess ('dʌtʃɪs) *n.* duke's wife or widow

duchy ('dʌtʃɪ) *n.* territory of duke, dukedom

duck[1] (dʌk) *n.* **1.** common swimming bird (**drake** *masc.*) **2.** *Cricket* batsman's score of nothing **3. UK** *inf.* dear, darling (as term of address) (*also* **ducks**) —*v.* **4.** plunge (someone) under water **5.** bob down —**'duckling** *n.* —**'ducky** *or* **'duckie** *inf. n.* **1. UK** darling, dear —*a.* **2.** delightful; fine —**duck-billed platypus** *see* PLATYPUS —**'duckweed** *n.* plant that floats on ponds *etc.*

duck[2] (dʌk) *n.* **1.** strong linen or cotton fabric —*pl.* **2.** trousers made of this fabric

duck[3] (dʌk) *n.* amphibious vehicle used in World War II

duct (dʌkt) *n.* channel, tube —**'ductile** *a.* **1.** capable of being drawn into wire **2.** flexible and tough **3.** docile —**ductility** (dʌk'tɪlɪtɪ) *n.* —**'ductless** *a.* (of glands) secreting directly certain substances essential to health

THESAURUS

drum *v.* beat, pulsate, rap, reverberate, tap, tattoo, throb

drum up attract, bid for, canvass, obtain, petition, round up, solicit

drunk *adj.* bacchic, canned (*Sl.*), drunken, fu' (*Scot.*), fuddled, half seas over (*Inf.*), inebriated, intoxicated, maudlin, merry (*Inf.*), muddled, pie-eyed (*Sl.*), plastered (*Sl.*), sloshed (*Sl.*), soaked (*Inf.*), stewed (*Sl.*), stoned (*Sl.*), tiddly (*Sl.*), tight (*Inf.*), tipsy, tired and emotional (*Euphemistic*), under the influence (*Inf.*), well-oiled (*Sl.*)

drunkard alcoholic, carouser, dipsomaniac, drinker, drunk, lush (*Sl.*), soak (*Sl.*), sot, tippler, toper, wino (*Sl.*)

drunken bibulous, boozing (*Sl.*), drunk, (gin-)sodden, inebriate, intoxicated, red-nosed, sottish, tippling, toping, under the influence (*Inf.*)

drunkenness alcoholism, bibulousness, dipsomania, inebriety, insobriety, intemperance, intoxication, sottishness, tipsiness

dry *adj.* **1.** arid, barren, dehydrated, desiccated, dried up, juiceless, moistureless, parched, sapless, thirsty, torrid, waterless **2.** *Fig.* boring, dreary, dull, monotonous, plain, tedious, tiresome, uninteresting **3.** *Fig.* cutting, deadpan, droll, keen, low-key, quietly humorous, sarcastic, sharp, sly ~*v.* **4.** dehumidify, dehydrate, desiccate, drain, make dry, parch, sear **5.** *With* **out** *or* **up** become dry, become unproductive, harden, mummify, shrivel up, wilt, wither, wizen

dryness aridity, aridness, dehumidification, dehydration, drought, thirst, thirstiness

dual binary, coupled, double, duplex, duplicate, matched, paired, twin, twofold

dub 1. bestow, confer, confer knighthood upon, entitle, knight **2.** call, christen, denominate, designate, label, name, nickname, style, term

dubious 1. doubtful, hesitant, iffy (*Inf.*), sceptical, uncertain, unconvinced, undecided, unsure, wavering **2.** ambiguous, debatable, doubtful, equivocal, indefinite, indeterminate, obscure, problematical, unclear, unsettled **3.** fishy (*Inf.*), questionable, shady (*Inf.*), suspect, suspicious, undependable, unreliable, untrustworthy

duck 1. bend, bob, bow, crouch, dodge, drop, lower,

dud (dʌd) *n.* **1.** futile, worthless person or thing **2.** shell that fails to explode —*a.* **3.** worthless

dude (dju:d) *n.* tourist, *esp.* in ranch district —**dude ranch** ranch serving as guesthouse and showplace

dudgeon (ˈdʌdʒən) *n. Archaic* anger, indignation, resentment

duds (dʌdz) *pl.n. inf.* clothes

due (dju:) *a.* **1.** owing **2.** proper to be given, inflicted *etc.* **3.** adequate, fitting **4.** under engagement to arrive, be present **5.** timed (for) —*adv.* **6.** (with points of compass) exactly —*n.* **7.** person's right **8.** (*usu. pl.*) charge, fee *etc.* —ˈ**duly** *adv.* **1.** properly **2.** fitly **3.** rightly **4.** punctually —**due to 1.** attributable to **2.** caused by

duel (ˈdju:əl) *n.* **1.** arranged fight with deadly weapons, between two persons **2.** keen two-sided contest —*vi.* **3.** fight in duel (**-ll-**) —ˈ**duellist** *n.*

duenna (dju:ˈɛnə) *n.* **1.** Sp. lady-in-waiting **2.** elderly governess, guardian, chaperon

duet (dju:ˈɛt) *n.* piece of music for two performers —**duˈettist** *n.*

duff[1] (dʌf) *n.* kind of boiled pudding

duff[2] (dʌf) *vt.* **1.** manipulate, alter (article) so as to make it look like new **2.** mishit, *esp.* at golf —*a.* **3.** *sl.* bad, useless

duffel *or* **duffle** (ˈdʌfˀl) *n.* **1.** coarse woollen cloth **2.** coat made of this —**duffel bag** large cylindrical cloth bag for clothing *etc.*

duffer (ˈdʌfə) *n.* stupid inefficient person

dug[1] (dʌg) *pt./pp. of* DIG

dug[2] (dʌg) *n.* udder, teat of animal

dugong (ˈdu:gɒŋ) *n.* whalelike mammal of tropical seas

dugout (ˈdʌgaʊt) *n.* **1.** covered excavation to provide shelter for troops *etc.* **2.** canoe of hollowed-out tree **3.** *Sport* covered enclosure where players wait when not on the field

duiker *or* **duyker** (ˈdaɪkə) *n.* small Afr. antelope (*also* ˈ**duikerbok**)

duke (dju:k) *n.* **1.** peer of rank next below prince **2.** sovereign of small state called duchy (ˈ**duchess** *fem.*) —ˈ**dukedom** *n.*

dukes (dju:ks) *pl.n. sl.* fists

dulcet (ˈdʌlsɪt) *a.* (of sounds) sweet, melodious

dulcimer (ˈdʌlsɪmə) *n.* percussion instrument consisting of set of strings stretched over sounding board, played with two hammers

dull (dʌl) *a.* **1.** stupid **2.** insensible **3.** sluggish **4.** tedious **5.** lacking liveliness or variety **6.** gloomy, overcast —*v.* **7.** make or become dull —ˈ**dullard** *n.* —ˈ**dully** *adv.*

duly (ˈdju:lɪ) *adv. see* DUE

dumb (dʌm) *a.* **1.** incapable of speech **2.** silent **3.** *inf.* stupid —ˈ**dumbly** *adv.* —ˈ**dumbness** *n.* —ˈ**dumbbell** *n.* weight for exercises —**dumbˈfound** *vt.* confound into silence —**dumb show** acting without words —ˈ**dumbwaiter** *n.* **1. UK** stand placed near dining table to hold food; revolving circular tray placed on table to hold food **2.** lift for carrying rubbish *etc.* between floors

dumdum (ˈdʌmdʌm) *n.* soft-nosed expanding bullet

dummy (ˈdʌmɪ) *n.* **1.** tailor's or dressmaker's model **2.** imitation object **3.** *Cards* hand exposed on table and played by partner **4.** *Sports* feigned move or pass **5.** baby's dummy teat **6.** prototype of book, indicating appearance of finished product; designer's layout of page —*a.* **7.** sham, bogus —**dummy run** experimental run; practice; rehearsal

dump (dʌmp) *vt.* **1.** throw down in mass **2.** deposit **3.**

THESAURUS

stoop **2.** dip, dive, douse, dunk, immerse, plunge, souse, submerge, wet

duct blood vessel, canal, channel, conduit, funnel, passage, pipe, tube

dud 1. *n.* failure, flop (*Inf.*), washout (*Inf.*) **2.** *adj.* broken, bust (*Inf.*), duff (*Sl.*), failed, inoperative, kaput (*Inf.*), not functioning, valueless, worthless

dudgeon *Archaic* indignation, ire, resentment, umbrage, wrath

due *adj.* **1.** in arrears, outstanding, owed, owing, payable, unpaid **2.** appropriate, becoming, bounden, deserved, fit, fitting, just, justified, merited, obligatory, proper, requisite, right, rightful, suitable, well-earned **3.** adequate, ample, enough, plenty of, sufficient **4.** expected, expected to arrive, scheduled ~*n.* **5.** comeuppance (*Sl.*), deserts, merits, prerogative, privilege, right(s) ~*adv.* **6.** dead, direct, directly, exactly, straight, undeviatingly

duel *n.* **1.** affair of honour, single combat **2.** clash, competition, contest, encounter, engagement, fight, rivalry ~*v.* **3.** clash, compete, contend, contest, fight, rival, struggle, vie with

dues charge, charges, contribution, fee, levy, membership fee

duffer blunderer, booby, bungler, clod, clot (*Sl.*), galoot (*Sl., chiefly U.S.*), lubber, lummox (*Inf.*), oaf

dull *adj.* **1.** dense, dim, dim-witted (*Inf.*), doltish, slow, stolid, stupid, thick, unintelligent **2.** apathetic, blank, callous, dead, empty, heavy, indifferent, insensible, insensitive, lifeless, listless, passionless, slow, sluggish, unresponsive, unsympathetic, vacuous **3.** boring, commonplace, dreary, dry, flat, humdrum, monotonous, plain, prosaic, run-of-the-mill, tedious, tiresome, unimaginative, uninteresting, vapid **4.** cloudy, dim, dismal, gloomy, leaden, opaque, overcast, turbid **5.** depressed, inactive, slack, slow, sluggish, torpid, uneventful **6.** drab, faded, feeble, indistinct, lacklustre, muffled, murky, muted, sombre, subdued, subfusc, toned-down ~*v.* **7.** dampen, deject, depress, discourage, dishearten, dispirit, sadden **8.** cloud, darken, dim, fade, obscure, stain, sully, tarnish

dullard blockhead, clod, dimwit (*Inf.*), dolt, dope (*Sl.*), dunce, nitwit, numskull, oaf

duly 1. accordingly, appropriately, befittingly, correctly, decorously, deservedly, fittingly, properly, rightfully, suitably **2.** at the proper time, on time, punctually

dumb 1. at a loss for words, inarticulate, mum, mute, silent, soundless, speechless, tongue-tied, voiceless, wordless **2.** *Inf.* dense, dim-witted (*Inf.*), dull, foolish, stupid, thick, unintelligent

dumbfound amaze, astonish, astound, bewilder, bowl over (*Inf.*), confound, confuse, flabbergast (*Inf.*), nonplus, overwhelm, stagger, startle, stun, take aback

dummy *n.* **1.** figure, form, lay figure, manikin, mannequin, model **2.** copy, counterfeit, duplicate, imitation, sham, substitute ~*adj.* **3.** artificial, bogus, fake, false, imitation, mock, phoney (*Sl.*), sham, simulated

unload **4.** send (low-priced goods) for sale abroad —*n.* **5.** rubbish heap **6.** *inf.* dirty, unpleasant place **7.** temporary depot of stores or munitions —*pl.* **8.** low spirits, dejection

dumpling (ˈdʌmplɪŋ) *n.* small round pudding of dough, oft. fruity —**ˈdumpy** *a.* short, stout —**dumpy level** surveyor's levelling instrument

dun[1] (dʌn) *vt.* **1.** persistently press (debtor) for payment of debts (**-nn-**) —*n.* **2.** one who duns

dun[2] (dʌn) *a.* **1.** of dull greyish-brown —*n.* **2.** this colour **3.** horse of this colour

dunce (dʌns) *n.* slow learner, stupid pupil

dunderhead (ˈdʌndəhɛd) *n.* blockhead —**ˈdunderheaded** *a.*

dune (dju:n) *n.* sandhill on coast or desert

dung (dʌŋ) *n.* **1.** excrement of animals **2.** manure —*vt.* **3.** manure (ground) —**ˈdunghill** *n.* **1.** heap of dung **2.** foul place, condition or person

dungarée (dʌŋgəˈri:) *n.* **1.** coarse cotton fabric —*pl.* **2.** overalls made of this material

dungeon (ˈdʌndʒən) *n.* **1.** underground cell or vault for prisoners, donjon **2.** formerly, tower or keep of castle

dunk (dʌŋk) *vt.* **1.** dip (bread *etc.*) in liquid before eating it **2.** submerge

dunlin (ˈdʌnlɪn) *n.* small sandpiper

dunnage (ˈdʌnɪdʒ) *n.* material for packing cargo

dunnock (ˈdʌnək) *n.* hedge sparrow

duo (ˈdju:əʊ) *n.* pair of performers (*pl.* **-s, dui** (ˈdju:i:))

duodecimo (dju:əʊˈdɛsɪməʊ) *n.* **1.** size of book in which each sheet is folded into 12 leaves **2.** book of this size (*pl.* **-s**) —*a.* **3.** of this size —**duoˈdecimal** *a.* **1.** computed by twelves **2.** twelfth

duodenum (dju:əʊˈdi:nəm) *n.* upper part of small intestine —**duoˈdenal** *a.*

duologue *or U.S.* (*sometimes*) **duolog** (ˈdju:əlɒg) *n.* **1.** part or all of play in which speaking roles are limited to two actors **2.** *rare* dialogue

dupe (dju:p) *n.* **1.** victim of delusion or sharp practice —*vt.* **2.** deceive for advantage, impose upon

duple (ˈdju:pᵊl) *a.* **1.** *rare* double **2.** *Mus.* (of time or music) having two beats in bar

duplex (ˈdju:plɛks) *a.* twofold

duplicate (ˈdju:plɪkeɪt) *vt.* **1.** make exact copy of **2.** double —*a.* (ˈdju:plɪkɪt) **3.** double **4.** exactly the same as something else —*n.* (ˈdju:plɪkɪt) **5.** exact copy —**dupliˈcation** *n.* —**ˈduplicator** *n.* machine for making copies —**duˈplicity** *n.* deceitfulness, double-dealing, bad faith

Dur. Durham

durable (ˈdjʊərəbᵊl) *a.* lasting, resisting wear —**duraˈbility** *n.* —**ˈdurably** *adv.* —**durable goods** goods that require infrequent replacement (*also* **ˈdurables**)

dura mater (ˈdjʊərə ˈmeɪtə) outermost and toughest of three membranes covering brain and spinal cord (*also* **ˈdura**)

durance (ˈdjʊərəns) *n. obs.* imprisonment

duration (djʊˈreɪʃən) *n.* length of time something lasts

durbar (ˈdɜ:bɑ:, dɜ:ˈbɑ:) *n.* formerly, court of native ruler or governor in India or levée at such court

duress (djʊˈrɛs, djʊə-) *n.* compulsion by use of force or threats

during (ˈdjʊərɪŋ) *prep.* throughout, in the time of, in the course of

durst (dɜ:st) *obs. pt. of* DARE

dusk (dʌsk) *n.* **1.** darker stage of twilight **2.** partial darkness —**ˈduskily** *adv.* —**ˈdusky** *a.* **1.** dark **2.** dark-coloured

dust (dʌst) *n.* **1.** fine particles, powder of earth or other matter, lying on surface or blown along by wind **2.** ashes of the dead —*vt.* **3.** sprinkle with powder **4.** rid of dust —**ˈduster** *n.* cloth for removing dust —**ˈdusty** *a.* covered with dust —**ˈdustbin** *n.* large, *usu.* cylindrical container for household rubbish —**ˈdustbowl** *n.* area in which dust storms have carried away the top soil —**ˈdustcart** *n.* road vehicle for collecting refuse —**dust cover 1.** large cloth used to protect furniture from dust (*also* **ˈdustsheet**) **2.** removable paper cover to protect bound book (*also* **dust jacket**) **3.** Perspex cover for gramophone turntable —**ˈdustman** *n.* **UK** man whose job is to collect domestic refuse —**ˈdustpan** *n.* short-handled hooded shovel into which dust is

THESAURUS

dump *v.* **1.** deposit, drop, fling down, let fall, throw down **2.** discharge, dispose of, ditch (*Sl.*), empty out, get rid of, jettison, scrap, throw away *or* out, tip, unload ~*n.* **3.** junkyard, refuse heap, rubbish heap, rubbish tip, tip **4.** *Inf.* hole (*Inf.*), hovel, joint (*Sl.*), mess, pigsty, shack, shanty, slum

dumps blues, dejection, depression, despondency, dolour, gloom, gloominess, low spirits, melancholy, mopes, sadness, unhappiness, woe

dun *v.* beset, importune, pester, plague, press, urge

dunce ass, blockhead, bonehead (*Sl.*), dimwit (*Inf.*), dolt, donkey, duffer (*Inf.*), dullard, dunderhead, goose (*Inf.*), halfwit, ignoramus, loon (*Inf.*), moron, nincompoop, numskull, simpleton, thickhead

dungeon cage, cell, donjon, lockup, oubliette, prison, vault

duplicate 1. *adj.* corresponding, identical, matched, matching, twin, twofold **2.** *n.* carbon copy, clone, copy, double, facsimile, likeness, lookalike, match, mate, photocopy, Photostat (*Trademark*), replica, reproduction, ringer (*Sl.*), twin, Xerox (*Trademark*) **3.** *v.* clone, copy, double, echo, photocopy, Photostat (*Trademark*), repeat, replicate, reproduce, Xerox (*Trademark*)

durability constancy, durableness, endurance, imperishability, lastingness, permanence, persistence

durable abiding, constant, dependable, enduring, fast, firm, fixed, hard-wearing, lasting, long-lasting, permanent, persistent, reliable, resistant, sound, stable, strong, sturdy, substantial, tough

duress coercion, compulsion, constraint, pressure, threat

dusk 1. dark, evening, eventide, gloaming, nightfall, sundown, sunset, twilight **2.** *Poetic* darkness, gloom, murk, obscurity, shade, shadowiness

dusky 1. dark, dark-complexioned, dark-hued, sable, swarthy **2.** caliginous (*Archaic*), cloudy, crepuscular, darkish, dim, gloomy, murky, obscure, overcast, shadowy, shady, tenebrous, twilight, twilit, veiled

dust 1. *n.* fine fragments, grime, grit, particles, powder, powdery dirt **2.** *v.* cover, dredge, powder, scatter, sift, spray, spread, sprinkle

dusty dirty, grubby, sooty, unclean, undusted, unswept

swept —**dust-up** *n. inf.* fight; argument —**dust up** attack

Dutch (dʌtʃ) *a.* pert. to the Netherlands, its inhabitants or its language —**Dutch barn UK** farm building consisting of steel frame and curved roof —**Dutch cap** contraceptive diaphragm (*also* **cap**) —**Dutch courage** drunken bravado —**Dutch elm disease** fungal disease of elm trees characterized by withering of foliage and stems —**Dutch oven 1.** iron or earthenware container with cover, used for stews *etc.* **2.** metal box, open in front, for cooking in front of open fire —**Dutch treat** meal *etc.* where each person pays his own share —**Dutch uncle** *inf.* person who criticizes or reproves frankly and severely

duty (ˈdjuːtɪ) *n.* **1.** moral or legal obligation **2.** that which is due **3.** tax on goods **4.** military service **5.** one's proper employment —ˈ**duteous** *a.* —ˈ**dutiable** *a.* liable to customs duty —ˈ**dutiful** *a.* showing sense of duty —**duty-bound** *a.* morally obliged —**duty-free** *a./adv.* with exemption from customs or excise duties

duvet (ˈduːveɪ) *n.* quilt filled with down or artificial fibre (*also* **continental quilt**)

dux (dʌks) *n.* head pupil of school or class, leader

D.V. *Deo volente*

dwarf (dwɔːf) *n.* **1.** very undersized person **2.** mythological, small, manlike creature (*pl.* **-s, dwarves**) —*a.* **3.** unusually small, stunted —*vt.* **4.** make seem small by contrast **5.** make stunted —ˈ**dwarfish** *a.*

dwell (dwɛl) *vi.* **1.** live, make one's abode (in) **2.** fix one's attention, write or speak at length (on) (**dwelt** *pt./pp.*) —ˈ**dweller** *n.* —ˈ**dwelling** *n.* house

dwindle (ˈdwɪndᵊl) *vi.* grow less, waste away, decline

Dy *Chem.* dysprosium

Dyak *or* **Dayak** (ˈdaɪæk) *n.* member of Malaysian people of Borneo (*pl.* **-s, -ak**)

dye (daɪ) *vt.* **1.** impregnate (cloth *etc.*) with colouring matter **2.** colour thus (**dyed,** ˈ**dyeing**) —*n.* **3.** colouring matter in solution or which may be dissolved for dyeing **4.** tinge, colour —ˈ**dyeing** *n.* process or industry of colouring yarns *etc.* —ˈ**dyer** *n.* —**dyed-in-the-wool** *a.* **1.** extreme or unchanging in opinion *etc.* **2.** (of fabric) made of dyed yarn

dying (ˈdaɪɪŋ) *v.* **1.** *pr.p. of* DIE[1] —*a.* **2.** relating to or occurring at moment of death

dyke *or esp. U.S.* **dike** (daɪk) *n.* **1.** embankment to prevent flooding **2.** ditch

dynamics (daɪˈnæmɪks) *pl.n.* **1.** (*with sing. v.*) branch of physics dealing with force as producing or affecting motion **2.** physical forces —**dy**ˈ**namic** *a.* **1.** of, relating to motive force, force in operation **2.** energetic and forceful —**dy**ˈ**namical** *a.* —**dy**ˈ**namically** *adv.* —ˈ**dynamism** *n.* **1.** *Philos.* theory that attempts to explain phenomena in terms of immanent force or energy **2.** forcefulness of energetic personality

dynamite (ˈdaɪnəmaɪt) *n.* **1.** high explosive mixture —*vt.* **2.** blow up with this —ˈ**dynamiter** *n.*

dynamo (ˈdaɪnəməʊ) *n.* **1.** machine to convert mechanical into electrical energy, generator of electricity **2.** *inf.* energetic, hard-working person (*pl.*-**s**) —**dyna**ˈ**mometer** *n.* instrument to measure energy expended

dynasty (ˈdɪnəstɪ) *n.* line, family, succession of hereditary rulers —ˈ**dynast** *n.* —**dy**ˈ**nastic** *a.* of dynasty

dyne (daɪn) *n.* cgs unit of force

dys- (*comb. form*) **1.** diseased; abnormal **2.** difficult; painful **3.** bad

dysentery (ˈdɪsᵊntrɪ) *n.* infection of intestine causing severe diarrhoea

dysfunction (dɪsˈfʌŋkʃən) *n.* abnormal, impaired functioning, *esp.* of bodily organ

dyslexia (dɪsˈlɛksɪə) *n.* impaired ability to read, caused by brain disorder —**dys**ˈ**lexic** *a.*

dysmenorrhoea *or esp. U.S.* **dysmenorrhea** (dɪsmɛnəˈrɪə) *n.* abnormally difficult or painful menstruation

dyspepsia (dɪsˈpɛpsɪə) *n.* indigestion —**dys**ˈ**peptic** *a./n.*

dysprosium (dɪsˈprəʊsɪəm) *n.* metallic element of lanthanide series

dystrophy (ˈdɪstrəfɪ) *n.* wasting of body tissues, *esp.* muscles

dz. dozen

THESAURUS

dutiful compliant, conscientious, deferential, devoted, docile, duteous (*Archaic*), filial, obedient, punctilious, respectful, reverential, submissive

duty 1. assignment, business, calling, charge, engagement, function, mission, obligation, office, onus, province, responsibility, role, service, task, work **2.** allegiance, deference, loyalty, obedience, respect, reverence **3.** customs, due, excise, impost, levy, tariff, tax, toll

dwarf *n.* **1.** bantam, homunculus, hop-o'-my-thumb, Lilliputian, manikin, midget, pygmy, Tom Thumb **2.** gnome, goblin ~*adj.* **3.** baby, diminutive, dwarfed, Lilliputian, miniature, petite, pocket, small, tiny, undersized ~*v.* **4.** dim, diminish, dominate, minimize, overshadow, tower above *or* over **5.** check, cultivate by bonsai, lower, retard, stunt

dwell abide, establish oneself, hang out (*Inf.*), inhabit, live, lodge, quarter, remain, reside, rest, settle, sojourn, stay, stop

dwelling abode, domicile, dwelling house, establishment, habitation, home, house, lodging, quarters, residence

dye 1. *n.* colorant, colour, colouring, pigment, stain, tinge, tint **2.** *v.* colour, pigment, stain, tincture, tinge, tint

dyed-in-the-wool complete, confirmed, deep-rooted, entrenched, established, inveterate, through-and-through

dying at death's door, ebbing, expiring, fading, failing, final, going, *in extremis,* moribund, mortal, passing, perishing, sinking

dynamic active, driving, electric, energetic, forceful, go-ahead, go-getting (*Inf.*), high-powered, lively, magnetic, powerful, vigorous, vital, zippy (*Inf.*)

dynasty ascendancy, dominion, empire, government, house, regime, rule, sovereignty, sway

E

e *or* **E** (iː) *n.* **1.** fifth letter of English alphabet **2.** any of several speech sounds represented by this letter, as in *he, bet* (*pl.* **e's, E's** *or* **Es**)

e 1. *Maths.* transcendental number used as base of natural logarithms **2.** electron

E 1. *Mus.* third note of scale of C major; major or minor key having this note as its tonic **2.** *Phys.* energy; electromotive force **3.** East **4.** Eastern **5.** English **6.** Egypt(ian)

e. engineer(ing)

E. Earl

ea. each

each (iːtʃ) *a./pron.* every (one) taken separately

eager (ˈiːgə) *a.* **1.** having a strong wish (for something) **2.** keen, impatient —**ˈeagerly** *adv.* —**ˈeagerness** *n.* —**eager beaver** *inf.* person who displays conspicuous diligence

eagle (ˈiːgᵊl) *n.* **1.** large bird with keen sight which preys on small birds and animals **2.** *Golf* score of two strokes under par for a hole —**ˈeaglet** *n.* young eagle —**eagle-eyed** *a.* having keen eyesight

ear[1] (ɪə) *n.* **1.** organ of hearing, *esp.* external part of it **2.** sense of hearing **3.** sensitiveness to sounds **4.** attention —**ˈearache** *n.* acute pain in ear —**ˈeardrum** *n. see* **tympanic membrane** *at* TYMPANUM —**ˈearmark** *vt.* **1.** assign, reserve for definite purpose **2.** make identification mark on ear of (sheep *etc.*) —*n.* **3.** this mark —**ˈearmuffs** *pl.n.* pads of fur *etc.* for keeping ears warm —**ˈearphone** *n.* receiver for radio *etc.* held to or put in ear —**ear-piercing** *a.* deafening —**ˈearring** *n.* ornament for lobe of ear —**ˈearshot** *n.* hearing distance —**ear trumpet** trumpet-shaped instrument formerly used as hearing aid —**ˈearwig** *n.* small insect with pincerlike tail

ear[2] (ɪə) *n.* spike, head of corn

earl (ɜːl) *n.* Brit. nobleman ranking next below marquis —**ˈearldom** *n.* his domain, title

early (ˈɜːlɪ) *a./adv.* **1.** before expected or usual time **2.** in first part, near or nearer beginning of some portion of time —**early bird** *inf.* one who arrives or rises early

earn (ɜːn) *vt.* **1.** obtain by work or merit **2.** gain —**ˈearnings** *pl.n.*

earnest[1] (ˈɜːnɪst) *a.* **1.** serious, ardent **2.** sincere —**ˈearnestly** *adv.* —**in earnest** serious, determined

earnest[2] (ˈɜːnɪst) *n.* **1.** money paid over in token to bind bargain, pledge **2.** foretaste

earth (ɜːθ) *n.* **1.** planet or world we live on **2.** ground, dry land **3.** mould, soil, mineral **4.** fox's hole **5.** wire connecting electrical apparatus to earth —*vt.* **6.** cover with earth **7.** connect electrically with earth —**ˈearthen** *a.* made of clay or earth —**ˈearthly** *a.* possible, feasible —**ˈearthy** *a.* **1.** of earth **2.** uninhibited **3.** vulgar —**earth closet** lavatory in which earth is used to cover excreta —**ˈearthenware** *n.* (vessels of) baked clay —**ˈearthnut** *n.* **1.** plant of Europe and Asia, having edible dark brown tubers **2.** any of various plants having edible root, tuber or underground pod, such as peanut —**ˈearthquake** *n.* convulsion of earth's surface —**earth science** any of various sciences, such as geology, concerned with structure *etc.* of the earth —**ˈearthwork** *n.* bank of earth in fortification —**ˈearthworm** *n.* —**come back** *or* **down to earth** return to reality from fantasy

ease (iːz) *n.* **1.** comfort **2.** freedom from constraint, annoyance, awkwardness, pain or trouble **3.** idleness —*v.* **4.** make or become less burdensome **5.** give bodily or mental ease to **6.** (cause to) move carefully or gradually —*vt.* **7.** slacken **8.** relieve of pain —**ˈeasement** *n. Law* right of way *etc.* over another's land —**ˈeasily** *adv.* —**ˈeasiness** *n.* **1.** quality or condition of being easy to accomplish *etc.* **2.** ease or relaxation of manner —**ˈeasy** *a.* **1.** not difficult **2.** free from pain, care, constraint or anxiety **3.** compliant **4.** characterized by low demand **5.** fitting loosely **6.** *inf.* having no preference for any particular course of action —**easy chair** comfortable upholstered armchair —**easy-going** *a.* **1.** not fussy **2.** indolent

THESAURUS

each 1. *adj.* every **2.** *pron.* each and every one, each one, every one, one and all

eager agog, anxious, ardent, athirst, avid, earnest, enthusiastic, fervent, fervid, greedy, hot, hungry, impatient, intent, keen, longing, raring, vehement, yearning, zealous

eagerness ardour, avidity, earnestness, enthusiasm, fervour, greediness, heartiness, hunger, impatience, impetuosity, intentness, keenness, longing, thirst, vehemence, yearning, zeal

ear *Fig.* **1.** attention, consideration, hearing, heed, notice, regard **2.** appreciation, discrimination, musical perception, sensitivity, taste

early *adj.* **1.** advanced, forward, premature, untimely **2.** primeval, primitive, primordial, undeveloped, young ~*adv.* **3.** ahead of time, beforehand, betimes (*Archaic*), in advance, in good time, prematurely, too soon

earn 1. bring in, collect, draw, gain, get, gross, make, net, obtain, procure, realize, reap, receive **2.** acquire, attain, be entitled to, be worthy of, deserve, merit, rate, warrant, win

earnest *adj.* **1.** close, constant, determined, firm, fixed, grave, intent, resolute, resolved, serious, sincere, solemn, stable, staid, steady, thoughtful **2.** ardent, devoted, eager, enthusiastic, fervent, fervid, heartfelt, impassioned, keen, passionate, purposeful, urgent, vehement, warm, zealous

earnings emolument, gain, income, pay, proceeds, profits, receipts, remuneration, return, reward, salary, stipend, takings, wages

earth 1. globe, orb, planet, sphere, terrestrial sphere, world **2.** clay, clod, dirt, ground, land, loam, mould, sod, soil, topsoil, turf

earthenware ceramics, crockery, crocks, pots, pottery, terra cotta

earthly *Inf.* conceivable, feasible, imaginable, likely, possible, practical

ease *n.* **1.** calmness, comfort, content, contentment, enjoyment, happiness, leisure, peace, peace of mind, quiet, quietude, relaxation, repose, rest, restfulness, serenity, tranquillity **2.** easiness, effortlessness, facility, readiness, simplicity **3.** flexibility, freedom, informality, liberty, naturalness, unaffectedness, unconstraint, unreservedness **4.** aplomb, composure, insouciance, nonchalance, poise, relaxedness

easel (ˈiːzəl) *n.* frame to support artist's canvas *etc.*

east (iːst) *n.* **1.** part of horizon where sun rises **2.** eastern lands, orient —*a.* **3.** on, in or near east **4.** coming from east —*adv.* **5.** from or to east —**ˈeasterly** *a./adv.* from or to east —**ˈeastern** *a.* of, dwelling in, east —**ˈeasterner** *n.* —**ˈeasting** *n.* distance eastwards of a point from a given meridian —**ˈeastward** *a./n.* —**ˈeastwards** *or* **ˈeastward** *adv.* —**Eastern Church 1.** any of Christian Churches of former Byzantine Empire **2.** any Church owing allegiance to Orthodox Church —**eastern hemisphere** (*oft.* **E- H-**) **1.** that half of the globe containing Europe, Asia, Afr. and Aust. **2.** lands in this, *esp.* Asia

Easter (ˈiːstə) *n.* movable festival of the Resurrection of Christ —**Easter egg** chocolate egg or hen's egg with its shell painted, given as gift at Easter —**ˈEastertide** *n.* Easter season

easy (ˈiːzɪ) *a. see* EASE

eat (iːt) *v.* **1.** chew and swallow **2.** gnaw —*vt.* **3.** consume, destroy **4.** wear away (**ate** *pt.*, **ˈeaten** *pp.*) —**ˈeatable** *a.* —**ˈeating** *n.* **1.** food, *esp.* in relation to quality or taste —*a.* **2.** suitable for eating —**eats** *pl.n. sl.* articles of food —**eat one's words** take back something said

eau de Cologne (əʊ də kəˈləʊn) *Fr.* light perfume

eau de vie (əʊ də ˈviː) brandy

eaves (iːvz) *pl.n.* overhanging edges of roof —**ˈeavesdrop** *vi.* listen secretly —**ˈeavesdropper** *n.* —**ˈeavesdropping** *n.*

ebb (ɛb) *vi.* **1.** flow back **2.** decay —*n.* **3.** flowing back of tide **4.** decline, decay —**ebb tide**

ebony (ˈɛbənɪ) *n.* **1.** hard black wood —*a.* **2.** made of, black as ebony —**ˈebonite** *n.* vulcanite —**ˈebonize** *or* **-ise** *vt.* make colour of ebony

ebullient (ɪˈbʌljənt, ɪˈbʊl-) *a.* **1.** exuberant **2.** boiling —**eˈbullience** *n.* —**ebullition** (ɛbəˈlɪʃən) *n.* **1.** boiling **2.** effervescence **3.** outburst

EC East Central

eccentric (ɪkˈsɛntrɪk) *a.* **1.** odd, unconventional **2.** irregular **3.** not placed, or not having axis placed, centrally **4.** not circular (in orbit) —*n.* **5.** odd, unconventional person **6.** mechanical contrivance to change circular into to-and-fro movement —**ecˈcentrically** *adv.* —**eccenˈtricity** *n.*

Eccles. *or* **Eccl.** *Bible* Ecclesiastes

ecclesiastic (ɪkliːzɪˈæstɪk) *n.* **1.** clergyman —*a.* **2.** of, relating to the Christian Church —**ecclesiˈastical** *a.* —**ecclesiˈology** *n.* science of church building and decoration

eccrinology (ɛkrɪˈnɒlədʒɪ) *n.* branch of physiology that relates to bodily secretions

E.C.G. **1.** electrocardiogram **2.** electrocardiograph

echelon (ˈɛʃəlɒn) *n.* **1.** level, grade, of responsibility or command **2.** formation of troops, planes *etc.* in

THESAURUS

~*v.* **5.** abate, allay, alleviate, appease, assuage, calm, comfort, disburden, lessen, lighten, mitigate, moderate, mollify, pacify, palliate, quiet, relax, relent, relieve, slacken, soothe, still, tranquillize **6.** aid, assist, expedite, facilitate, forward, further, lessen the labour of, make easier, simplify, smooth, speed up **7.** edge, guide, inch, manoeuvre, move carefully, slide, slip, squeeze, steer

easily comfortably, effortlessly, facilely, readily, simply, smoothly, with ease, without difficulty, without trouble

easy 1. a piece of cake (*Inf.*), a pushover (*Sl.*), child's play (*Inf.*), clear, effortless, facile, light, no bother, not difficult, no trouble, painless, simple, smooth, straightforward, uncomplicated, undemanding **2.** calm, carefree, comfortable, contented, cushy (*Sl.*), easeful, leisurely, peaceful, pleasant, quiet, relaxed, satisfied, serene, tranquil, undisturbed, untroubled, unworried, well-to-do **3.** affable, casual, easy-going, friendly, gentle, graceful, gracious, informal, mild, natural, open, pleasant, relaxed, smooth, tolerant, unaffected, unceremonious, unconstrained, undemanding, unforced, unpretentious **4.** accommodating, amenable, biddable, compliant, docile, gullible, manageable, pliant, soft, submissive, suggestible, susceptible, tractable, trusting, yielding **5.** comfortable, gentle, leisurely, light, mild, moderate, temperate, undemanding, unexacting, unhurried

easy-going amenable, calm, carefree, casual, complacent, easy, even-tempered, flexible, happy-go-lucky, indulgent, insouciant, laid-back (*Inf.*), lenient, liberal, mild, moderate, nonchalant, permissive, placid, relaxed, serene, tolerant, unconcerned, uncritical, undemanding, unhurried

eat 1. chew, consume, devour, ingest, munch, scoff (*Sl.*), swallow **2.** break bread, dine, feed, have a meal, take food, take nourishment **3.** corrode, crumble, decay, dissolve, erode, rot, waste away, wear away **4. eat one's words** abjure, recant, rescind, retract, take (statement) back

eavesdrop bug (*Inf.*), listen in, monitor, overhear, tap (*Inf.*)

ebb *v.* **1.** abate, fall away, fall back, flow back, go out, recede, retire, retreat, retrocede, sink, subside, wane, withdraw ~*n.* **2.** ebb tide, going out, low tide, low water, reflux, regression, retreat, retrocession, subsidence, wane, waning, withdrawal ~*v.* **3.** decay, decline, decrease, degenerate, deteriorate, diminish, drop, dwindle, fade away, fall away, flag, lessen, peter out, shrink, sink, slacken, weaken ~*n.* **4.** decay, decline, decrease, degeneration, deterioration, diminution, drop, dwindling, fading away, flagging, lessening, petering out, shrinkage, sinking, slackening, weakening

eccentric 1. *adj.* aberrant, abnormal, anomalous, bizarre, capricious, erratic, freakish, idiosyncratic, irregular, odd, outlandish, peculiar, queer (*Inf.*), quirky, singular, strange, uncommon, unconventional, weird, whimsical **2.** *n.* case (*Inf.*), character (*Inf.*), crank (*Inf.*), freak (*Sl.*), nonconformist, odd fish (*Inf.*), oddity, weirdie *or* weirdo (*Inf.*)

eccentricity aberration, abnormality, anomaly, bizarreness, caprice, capriciousness, foible, freakishness, idiosyncrasy, irregularity, nonconformity, oddity, oddness, outlandishness, peculiarity, queerness (*Inf.*), quirk, singularity, strangeness, unconventionality, waywardness, weirdness, whimsicality, whimsicalness

ecclesiastic 1. *n.* churchman, clergyman, cleric, divine, holy man, man of the cloth, minister, parson, priest **2.** *adj. Also* **ecclesiastical** church, churchly, clerical, divine, holy, pastoral, priestly, religious, spiritual

parallel divisions, each slightly to left or right of the one in front

echidna (ɪˈkɪdnə) *n.* spine-covered mammal of Aust. and New Guinea (*pl.* **-s, -nae** (-ni:)) (*also* **spiny anteater**)

echinoderm (ɪˈkaɪnəʊdɜ:m) *n.* marine invertebrate characterized by tube feet, calcite body-covering, and five-part symmetrical body

echo (ˈɛkəʊ) *n.* **1.** repetition of sounds by reflection **2.** close imitation (*pl.* **-es**) —*vt.* **3.** repeat as echo, send back the sound of **4.** imitate closely —*vi.* **5.** resound **6.** be repeated (**ˈechoed, ˈechoing**) —**echoic** (ɛˈkəʊɪk) *a.* **1.** characteristic of or resembling echo **2.** onomatopoeic —**echo chamber** room with walls that reflect sound, used to make acoustic measurements and in recording (*also* **reverberation chamber**) —**echoloˈcation** *n.* determination of position of object by measuring reflected sound —**echo sounder** —**echo sounding** system of ascertaining depth of water by measuring time required to receive echo from sea bottom or submerged object

éclair (eɪˈklɛə, ɪˈklɛə) *n.* finger-shaped, iced cake filled with cream

éclat (eɪˈklɑ:) *n.* **1.** splendour **2.** renown **3.** acclamation

eclectic (ɪˈklɛktɪk, ɛˈklɛk-) *a.* **1.** selecting **2.** borrowing one's philosophy from various sources **3.** catholic in views or taste —*n.* **4.** person who favours eclectic approach —**eˈclecticism** *n.*

eclipse (ɪˈklɪps) *n.* **1.** blotting out of sun, moon *etc.* by another heavenly body **2.** loss of importance or power —*vt.* **3.** obscure, hide **4.** surpass —**eˈcliptic** *a.* **1.** of eclipse —*n.* **2.** apparent path of sun

eclogue (ˈɛklɒg) *n.* short poem, *esp.* pastoral dialogue

eco- (*comb. form*) ecology; ecological, as in *ecosphere*

ecology (ɪˈkɒlədʒɪ) *n.* science of plants and animals in relation to their environment —**ecoˈlogical** *a.* —**eˈcologist** *n.* specialist in or advocate of ecological studies

econ. **1.** economical **2.** economics **3.** economy

economy (ɪˈkɒnəmɪ) *n.* **1.** careful management of resources to avoid unnecessary expenditure or waste **2.** sparing, restrained or efficient use **3.** system of interrelationship of money, industry and employment in a country —**ecoˈnomic** *a.* **1.** of economics **2.** profitable **3.** economical —**ecoˈnomical** *a.* **1.** not wasteful of money, time, effort *etc.* **2.** frugal —**ecoˈnomically** *adv.* —**ecoˈnomics** *pl.n.* **1.** (*with sing. v.*) study of economies of nations **2.** (*with pl. v.*) financial aspects —**eˈconomist** *n.* specialist in economics —**eˈconomize** *or* **-ise** *v.* limit or reduce (expense, waste *etc.*)

ecosystem (ˈi:kəʊsɪstəm, ˈɛkəʊ-) *n. Ecol.* system involving interactions between community and its non-living environment

ecru (ˈɛkru:, ˈeɪkru:) *n./a.* (of) colour of unbleached linen

ecstasy (ˈɛkstəsɪ) *n.* **1.** exalted state of feeling, mystic trance **2.** frenzy —**ecˈstatic** *a.* —**ecˈstatically** *adv.*

E.C.T. electroconvulsive therapy

ecto- (*comb. form*) outer, outside, as in *ectoplasm*

-ectomy (*comb. form*) surgical excision of part, as in *appendectomy*

ectoplasm (ˈɛktəʊplæzəm) *n.* in spiritualism, supposedly a semiluminous plastic substance which exudes from medium's body

ecumenical, oecumenical (i:kjʊˈmɛnɪkəl, ɛk-) *or* **ecumenic, oecumenic** *a.* of the Christian Church throughout the world, *esp.* with regard to its unity —**ecuˈmenicalism, ecuˈmenicism** *or* **ecuˈmenism** *n.*

eczema (ˈɛksɪmə) *n.* skin disease

ed. **1.** edited **2.** edition (*pl.* **eds.**) **3.** editor (*pl.* **eds.**) **4.** education

-ed[1] (*comb. form*) forming past tense of most English verbs

-ed[2] (*comb. form*) forming past participle of most English verbs

-ed[3] (*comb. form*) possessing or having characteristics of, as in *salaried, red-blooded*

Edam (ˈi:dæm) *n.* round yellow cheese with red outside covering

E.D.C. European Defence Community

Edda (ˈɛdə) *n.* collection of old Icelandic myths

eddy (ˈɛdɪ) *n.* **1.** small whirl in water, smoke *etc.* —*vi.* **2.** move in whirls (**ˈeddied, ˈeddying**)

edelweiss (ˈeɪdəlvaɪs) *n.* white-flowered alpine plant

Eden (ˈi:dən) *n.* **1.** garden in which Adam and Eve were placed at the Creation **2.** any delightful, happy place or state

edentate (i:ˈdɛnteɪt) *n.* **1.** any mammal of the order

THESAURUS

echo *v.* **1.** repeat, resound, reverberate **2.** ape, copy, imitate, mirror, parallel, parrot, recall, reflect, reiterate, reproduce, resemble, ring, second ~*n.* **3.** answer, repetition, reverberation **4.** copy, imitation, mirror image, parallel, reflection, reiteration, reproduction, ringing

eclipse *v.* **1.** blot out, cloud, darken, dim, extinguish, obscure, overshadow, shroud, veil **2.** exceed, excel, outdo, outshine, surpass, transcend ~*n.* **3.** darkening, dimming, extinction, obscuration, occultation, shading **4.** decline, diminution, failure, fall, loss

economic **1.** business, commercial, financial, industrial, mercantile, trade **2.** money-making, productive, profitable, profit-making, remunerative, solvent, viable **3.** bread-and-butter (*Inf.*), budgetary, financial, fiscal, material, monetary, pecuniary

economical **1.** cost-effective, efficient, money-saving, sparing, time-saving, unwasteful, work-saving **2.** careful, economizing, frugal, prudent, saving, scrimping, sparing, thrifty

economize be economical, be frugal, be sparing, cut back, husband, retrench, save, scrimp, tighten one's belt

economy frugality, husbandry, parsimony, providence, prudence, restraint, retrenchment, saving, sparingness, thrift, thriftiness

ecstasy bliss, delight, elation, enthusiasm, euphoria, exaltation, fervour, frenzy, joy, rapture, ravishment, rhapsody, seventh heaven, trance, transport

ecstatic blissful, delirious, elated, enraptured, enthusiastic, entranced, euphoric, fervent, frenzied, in exaltation, in transports of delight, joyful, joyous, on cloud nine (*Inf.*), overjoyed, rapturous, rhapsodic, transported

eddy **1.** *n.* counter-current, counterflow, swirl, vortex, whirlpool **2.** *v.* swirl, whirl

Edentata, which have few or no teeth, such as anteater —*a.* **2.** of the order *Edentata*

edge (ɛdʒ) *n.* **1.** border, boundary **2.** cutting side of blade **3.** sharpness **4.** advantage **5.** acrimony, bitterness —*vt.* **6.** give edge or border to **7.** move gradually —*vi.* **8.** advance sideways or gradually —**ˈedgeways** *or* **ˈedgewise** *adv.* —**ˈedging** *n.* —**ˈedgy** *a.* irritable, sharp or keen in temper —**on edge 1.** nervy, irritable **2.** excited

edible (ˈɛdɪbᵊl) *a.* eatable, fit for eating —**ediˈbility** *n.*

edict (ˈiːdɪkt) *n.* order proclaimed by authority, decree

edifice (ˈɛdɪfɪs) *n.* building, *esp.* big one

edify (ˈɛdɪfaɪ) *vt.* improve morally, instruct (**-fied, -fying**) —**edifiˈcation** *n.* improvement of mind or morals

edit (ˈɛdɪt) *vt.* prepare (book, film, tape *etc.*) for publication or broadcast —**eˈdition** *n.* **1.** form in which something is published **2.** number of copies of new publication printed at one time —**ˈeditor** *n.* —**ediˈtorial** *a.* **1.** of editor —*n.* **2.** article stating opinion of newspaper *etc.*

edit. 1. edited **2.** edition **3.** editor

E.D.P. electronic data processing

educate (ˈɛdjʊkeɪt) *vt.* **1.** provide schooling for **2.** teach **3.** train mentally and morally **4.** train **5.** improve, develop —**educaˈbility** *or* **educataˈbility** *n.* —**ˈeducable** *or* **ˈeducatable** *a.* capable of being trained or educated —**ˈeducated** *a.* **1.** having education, *esp.* a good one **2.** cultivated —**eduˈcation** *n.* —**eduˈcational** *a.* —**eduˈcationalist** *or* **eduˈcationist** *n.* one versed in theory and practice of education —**eduˈcationally** *adv.* —**ˈeducative** *a.* —**ˈeducator** *n.* —**educated guess** guess based on experience or information

educe (ɪˈdjuːs) *vt.* **1.** bring out, elicit, develop **2.** infer, deduce —**eˈducible** *a.* —**eduction** (ɪˈdʌkʃən) *n.*

Edwardian (ɛdˈwɔːdɪən) *a.* of reign of Edward VII, king of Great Britain and Ireland —**Edˈwardianism** *n.*

-ee (*comb. form*) **1.** recipient of action, as in *assignee* **2.** person in specified state or condition, as in *absentee*

EEC European Economic Community

EEG electroencephalogram

eel (iːl) *n.* snakelike fish

e'en (iːn) *adv./n. Poet., obs.* even, evening

-eer *or* **-ier** (*comb. form*) **1.** person who is concerned with something specified, as in *auctioneer, engineer, profiteer* **2.** be concerned with something specified, as in *electioneer*

e'er (ɛə) *adv. Poet., obs.* ever

eerie (ˈɪərɪ) *a.* **1.** weird, uncanny **2.** causing superstitious fear

efface (ɪˈfeɪs) *vt.* wipe or rub out —**efˈfaceable** *a.* —**efˈfacement** *n.*

effect (ɪˈfɛkt) *n.* **1.** result, consequence **2.** efficacy **3.** impression **4.** condition of being operative —*pl.* **5.** property **6.** lighting, sounds *etc.* to accompany film, broadcast *etc.* —*vt.* **7.** bring about, accomplish —**efˈfective** *a.* **1.** having power to produce effects **2.** in effect, operative **3.** serviceable **4.** powerful **5.** striking —**efˈfectively** *adv.* —**efˈfectual** *a.* **1.** successful in producing desired effect **2.** satisfactory **3.** efficacious —**efˈfectually** *adv.* —**efˈfectuate** *vt.*

THESAURUS

edge *n.* **1.** border, bound, boundary, brim, brink, contour, fringe, limit, line, lip, margin, outline, perimeter, periphery, rim, side, threshold, verge **2.** acuteness, animation, bite, effectiveness, force, incisiveness, interest, keenness, point, pungency, sharpness, sting, urgency, zest **3.** advantage, ascendancy, dominance, lead, superiority, upper hand **4. on edge** apprehensive, eager, edgy, excited, ill at ease, impatient, irritable, keyed up, nervous, on tenterhooks, tense, uptight (*Inf.*) ~*v.* **5.** bind, border, fringe, hem, rim, shape, trim **6.** creep, ease, inch, sidle, steal, work, worm

edgy anxious, ill at ease, irascible, irritable, keyed up, nervous, on edge, restive, tense, touchy

edible comestible (*Rare*), digestible, eatable, esculent, fit to eat, good, harmless, palatable, wholesome

edict act, command, decree, dictate, dictum, enactment, fiat, injunction, law, mandate, manifesto, order, ordinance, proclamation, pronouncement, pronunciamento, regulation, ruling, statute, ukase (*Rare*)

edifice building, construction, erection, fabric (*Rare*), habitation, house, pile, structure

edify educate, elevate, enlighten, guide, improve, inform, instruct, nurture, school, teach, uplift

edit 1. adapt, annotate, censor, check, condense, correct, emend, polish, redact, rephrase, revise, rewrite **2.** assemble, compose, put together, rearrange, reorder, select

edition copy, impression, issue, number, printing, programme (*TV, Radio*), version, volume

educate civilize, coach, cultivate, develop, discipline, drill, edify, enlighten, exercise, foster, improve, indoctrinate, inform, instruct, mature, rear, school, teach, train, tutor

educated 1. coached, informed, instructed, nurtured, schooled, taught, tutored **2.** civilized, cultivated, cultured, enlightened, experienced, informed, knowledgeable, learned, lettered, literary, polished, refined, tasteful

education breeding, civilization, coaching, cultivation, culture, development, discipline, drilling, edification, enlightenment, erudition, improvement, indoctrination, instruction, knowledge, nurture, scholarship, schooling, teaching, training, tuition, tutoring

educational cultural, didactic, edifying, educative, enlightening, heuristic, improving, informative, instructive

educative didactic, edifying, educational, enlightening, heuristic, improving, informative, instructive

eerie awesome, creepy (*Inf.*), eldritch (*Poetic*), fearful, frightening, ghostly, mysterious, scary (*Inf.*), spectral, spooky (*Inf.*), strange, uncanny, unearthly, weird

efface annihilate, blot out, cancel, cross out, delete, destroy, dim, eradicate, erase, excise, expunge, extirpate, obliterate, raze, rub out, wipe out

effect *n.* **1.** aftermath, conclusion, consequence, event, fruit, issue, outcome, result, upshot **2.** clout (*Inf.*), effectiveness, efficacy, efficiency, fact, force, influence, power, reality, strength, use, validity, vigour, weight **3.** drift, essence, impact, import, impression, meaning, purport, purpose, sense, significance, tenor **4.** action, enforcement, execution, force, implementation, operation ~*v.* **5.** accomplish, achieve,

effeminate (ɪˈfɛmɪnɪt) *a.* (of man or boy) womanish, unmanly —**efˈfeminacy** *n.*

efferent (ˈɛfərənt) *a.* conveying outward or away

effervesce (ɛfəˈvɛs) *vi.* **1.** give off bubbles **2.** be in high spirits —**efferˈvescence** *n.* —**efferˈvescent** *a.*

effete (ɪˈfiːt) *a.* worn-out, decadent, feeble

efficacious (ɛfɪˈkeɪʃəs) *a.* **1.** producing or sure to produce desired effect **2.** effective **3.** powerful **4.** adequate —**ˈefficacy** *n.* **1.** potency **2.** force **3.** efficiency

efficient (ɪˈfɪʃənt) *a.* capable, competent, producing effect —**efˈficiency** *n.* —**efˈficiently** *adv.*

effigy (ˈɛfɪdʒɪ) *n.* image, likeness

effloresce (ɛflɔːˈrɛs) *vi.* burst into flower —**effloˈrescence** *n.* —**effloˈrescent** *a.*

effluent (ˈɛfluənt) *n.* **1.** liquid discharged as waste **2.** stream flowing from larger stream, lake *etc.* —*a.* **3.** flowing out —**ˈeffluence** *or* **efflux** (ˈɛflʌks) *n.* —**efˈfluvium** *n.* something flowing out invisibly, *esp.* affecting lungs or sense of smell (*pl.* **-ia** (-ɪə))

effort (ˈɛfət) *n.* **1.** exertion **2.** endeavour, attempt **3.** something achieved —**ˈeffortless** *a.*

effrontery (ɪˈfrʌntərɪ) *n.* brazen impudence

effulgent (ɪˈfʌldʒənt) *a.* radiant, shining brightly —**efˈfulgence** *n.*

effusion (ɪˈfjuːʒən) *n.* (unrestrained) outpouring —**efˈfuse** *v.* pour out, shed —**efˈfusive** *a.* gushing, demonstrative —**efˈfusively** *adv.* —**efˈfusiveness** *n.*

eft (ɛft) *n. dial., obs.* newt

EFT electronic funds transfer

EFTA (ˈɛftə) European Free Trade Association

e.g. exempli gratia (*Lat.*, for example)

egalitarian (ɪgælɪˈtɛərɪən) *a.* **1.** believing that all people should be equal **2.** promoting this ideal —*n.* **3.** adherent of egalitarian principles —**egaliˈtarianism** *n.*

egg[1] (ɛg) *n.* oval or round object produced by female of bird *etc.*, from which young emerge, *esp.* egg of domestic hen, used as food —**egg cup** —**ˈegghead** *n. inf.* intellectual —**eggˈnog** *or* **egg-noggin** *n.* drink made of eggs, milk, sugar, spice, and brandy, rum *etc.* (*also* **egg flip**) —**ˈeggplant** *n. esp.* US aubergine —**ˈeggshell** *n.* **1.** outer layer of bird's egg —*a.* **2.** (of paint) having matt finish

egg[2] (ɛg) *vt.* —**egg on 1.** encourage, urge **2.** incite

eglantine (ˈɛgləntaɪn) *n.* sweet brier

ego (ˈiːgəʊ, ˈɛgəʊ) *n.* **1.** the self **2.** the conscious thinking subject **3.** one's image of oneself **4.** morale —**ˈegoism** *n.* **1.** systematic selfishness **2.** theory that bases morality on self-interest —**ˈegoist** *n.* —**egoˈistic(al)** *a.* —**ˈegotism** *n.* **1.** selfishness **2.** self-conceit —**ˈegotist** *n.* —**egoˈtistic(al)** *a.* —**egoˈcentric** *a.* **1.** self-centred **2.** egoistic **3.** centred in the ego —**ego trip** *inf.* something undertaken to boost person's own image or appraisal of himself

THESAURUS

actuate, bring about, carry out, cause, complete, consummate, create, effectuate, execute, fulfil, give rise to, initiate, make, perform, produce

effective 1. able, active, adequate, capable, competent, effectual, efficacious, efficient, energetic, operative, productive, serviceable, useful **2.** cogent, compelling, convincing, emphatic, forceful, forcible, impressive, moving, persuasive, potent, powerful, striking, telling **3.** active, actual, current, in effect, in execution, in force, in operation, operative, real

effects belongings, chattels, furniture, gear, goods, movables, paraphernalia, possessions, property, things, trappings

effeminacy delicacy, femininity, softness, tenderness, unmanliness, weakness, womanishness, womanliness

effeminate delicate, feminine, sissy, soft, tender, unmanly, weak, womanish, womanlike, womanly

effervesce bubble, ferment, fizz, foam, froth, sparkle

effervescence 1. bubbling, ferment, fermentation, fizz, foam, foaming, froth, frothing, sparkle **2.** animation, buoyancy, ebullience, enthusiasm, excitedness, excitement, exhilaration, exuberance, gaiety, high spirits, liveliness, vim (*Sl.*), vitality, vivacity, zing (*Inf.*)

effervescent 1. bubbling, bubbly, carbonated, fermenting, fizzing, fizzy, foaming, foamy, frothing, frothy, sparkling **2.** animated, bubbly, buoyant, ebullient, enthusiastic, excited, exhilarated, exuberant, gay, in high spirits, irrepressible, lively, merry, vital, vivacious, zingy (*Inf.*)

effete 1. corrupt, debased, decadent, decayed, decrepit, degenerate, dissipated, enervated, enfeebled, feeble, ineffectual, overrefined, spoiled, weak **2.** burnt out, drained, enervated, exhausted, played out, spent, used up, wasted, worn out

efficacious active, adequate, capable, competent, effective, effectual, efficient, energetic, operative, potent, powerful, productive, serviceable, successful, useful

efficacy ability, capability, competence, effect, effectiveness, efficaciousness, efficiency, energy, force, influence, potency, power, strength, success, use, vigour, virtue, weight

efficiency ability, adeptness, capability, competence, economy, effectiveness, efficacy, power, productivity, proficiency, readiness, skilfulness, skill

efficient able, adept, businesslike, capable, competent, economic, effective, effectual, powerful, productive, proficient, ready, skilful, well-organized, workmanlike

effigy dummy, figure, guy, icon, idol, image, likeness, picture, portrait, representation, statue

effluent 1. *n.* effluvium, pollutant, sewage, waste **2.** *adj.* discharged, emanating, emitted, outflowing

effort 1. application, endeavour, energy, exertion, force, labour, pains, power, strain, stress, stretch, striving, struggle, toil, travail (*Literary*), trouble, work **2.** attempt, endeavour, go, shot (*Inf.*), stab (*Inf.*), try **3.** accomplishment, achievement, act, creation, deed, feat, job, product, production

effortless easy, facile, painless, simple, smooth, uncomplicated, undemanding, untroublesome

effulgent beaming, blazing, bright, brilliant, dazzling, flaming, fluorescent, fulgent (*Poetic*), glowing, incandescent, lucent, luminous, lustrous, radiant, refulgent (*Literary*), resplendent, shining, splendid, vivid

effusion discharge, effluence, efflux, emission, gush, outflow, outpouring, shedding, stream

effusive demonstrative, ebullient, enthusiastic, expansive, extravagant, exuberant, free-flowing, fulsome, gushing, lavish, overflowing, profuse, talkative, unreserved, unrestrained, wordy

egregious (ɪˈgriːdʒəs, -dʒɪəs) *a.* 1. outstandingly bad, blatant 2. (*esp.* of mistake *etc.*) absurdly obvious

egress (ˈiːgrɛs) *n.* 1. way out 2. departure

egret (ˈiːgrɪt) *n.* 1. lesser white heron 2. down of dandelion

Egyptian (ɪˈdʒɪpʃən) *a.* 1. of Egypt —*n.* 2. native or inhabitant of Egypt —**Egypˈtologist** *n.* —**Egypˈtology** *n.* study of archaeology and language of ancient Egypt

eh (eɪ) *interj.* exclamation expressing surprise or inquiry, or to seek confirmation of statement or question

EHF extremely high frequency

eider *or* **eider duck** (ˈaɪdə) *n.* Arctic duck —**ˈeiderdown** *n.* 1. its breast feathers 2. quilt (stuffed with feathers)

eight (eɪt) *n.* 1. cardinal number one above seven 2. eight-oared boat 3. its crew —*a.* 4. amounting to eight —**ˈeighˈteen** *a./n.* eight more than ten —**ˈeighˈteenth** *a./n.* —**ˈeighˈteenthly** *adv.* —**eighth** *a./n.* ordinal number of eight —**ˈeighthly** *adv.* —**ˈeightieth** *a./n.* —**ˈeighty** *a./n.* ten times eight —**eightsome reel** Scottish dance for eight people —**figure of eight** 1. a skating figure 2. any figure shaped as 8

einsteinium (aɪnˈstaɪnɪəm) *n.* radioactive element artificially produced from plutonium

Eire (ˈɛərə) *n.* the Republic of Ireland

E.I.S. Educational Institute of Scotland

eisteddfod (aɪˈstɛdfəd) *n.* 1. annual congress of Welsh bards 2. local gathering for competition in music and other performing arts

either (ˈaɪðə, ˈiːðə) *a./pron.* 1. one or the other 2. one of two 3. each —*adv./conj.* 4. bringing in first of alternatives or strengthening an added negation

ejaculate (ɪˈdʒækjʊleɪt) *v.* 1. eject (semen) 2. exclaim, utter suddenly —**ejacuˈlation** *n.* —**eˈjaculatory** *a.*

eject (ɪˈdʒɛkt) *vt.* 1. throw out 2. expel, drive out —**eˈjection** *n.* —**eˈjectment** *n.* —**eˈjector** *n.* —**ejection seat** *or* **ejector seat** seat, *esp.* in military aircraft, that ejects occupant in emergency

eke out (iːk) 1. make (supply) last, *esp.* by frugal use 2. supply deficiencies of 3. make with difficulty (a living *etc.*)

elaborate (ɪˈlæbərɪt) *a.* 1. carefully worked out, detailed 2. complicated —*vi.* (ɪˈlæbəreɪt) 3. expand —*vt.* (ɪˈlæbəreɪt) 4. work out in detail 5. add details to (an account *etc.*) —**elaboˈration** *n.*

élan (eɪˈlɑːn) *n.* 1. dash 2. ardour 3. impetuosity

eland (ˈiːlənd) *n.* largest S Afr. antelope, resembling elk

elapse (ɪˈlæps) *vi.* (of time) pass

elastic (ɪˈlæstɪk) *a.* 1. resuming normal shape after distortion, springy 2. flexible —*n.* 3. tape, fabric, containing interwoven strands of flexible rubber —**eˈlasticated** *a.* —**elasˈticity** *n.* —**elastic band** *see* **rubber band** *at* RUBBER[1]

elation (ɪˈleɪʃən) *n.* 1. high spirits 2. pride —**eˈlate** *vt.* (*usu. passive*) 1. raise the spirits of 2. make happy 3. exhilarate

elbow (ˈɛlbəʊ) *n.* 1. joint between fore and upper parts of arm (*esp.* outer part of it) 2. part of sleeve covering this —*vt.* 3. shove, strike with elbow —**elbow**

THESAURUS

egg on encourage, exhort, goad, incite, prod, prompt, push, spur, urge

egocentric egoistic, egoistical, egotistic, egotistical, self-centred, selfish

egoism egocentricity, egomania, egotism, narcissism, self-absorption, self-centredness, self-importance, self-interest, selfishness, self-love, self-regard, self-seeking

egoist egomaniac, egotist, narcissist, self-seeker

egoistic, egoistical egocentric, egomaniacal, egotistic, egotistical, narcissistic, self-absorbed, self-centred, self-important, self-seeking

egotism conceitedness, egocentricity, egoism, egomania, narcissism, self-admiration, self-centredness, self-conceit, self-esteem, self-importance, self-love, self-praise, superiority, vainglory, vanity

egotist bighead (*Inf.*), blowhard (*Inf.*), boaster, braggadocio, braggart, egoist, egomaniac, self-admirer, swaggerer

egotistic, egotistical boasting, bragging, conceited, egocentric, egoistic, egoistical, egomaniacal, narcissistic, opinionated, self-admiring, self-centred, self-important, superior, vain, vainglorious

egress departure, emergence, escape, exit, exodus, issue, outlet, passage out, vent, way out, withdrawal

eject 1. cast out, discharge, disgorge, emit, expel, spew, spout, throw out, vomit 2. banish, boot out (*Inf.*), bounce (*Sl.*), deport, dispossess, drive out, evacuate, evict, exile, expel, oust, remove, throw out, turn out 3. discharge, dislodge, dismiss, fire (*Inf.*), get rid of, kick out (*Inf.*), oust, sack (*Inf.*), throw out

ejection 1. casting out, disgorgement, expulsion, spouting, throwing out 2. banishment, deportation, dispossession, evacuation, eviction, exile, expulsion, ouster (*Law*), removal 3. discharge, dislodgement, dismissal, firing (*Inf.*), sacking (*Inf.*), the boot (*Sl.*), the sack (*Inf.*)

eke out 1. be economical with, be frugal with, be sparing with, economize on, husband, stretch out 2. add to, enlarge, increase, make up (with), supplement

elaborate *adj.* 1. careful, detailed, exact, intricate, laboured, minute, painstaking, perfected, precise, skilful, studied, thorough 2. complex, complicated, decorated, detailed, extravagant, fancy, fussy, involved, ornamented, ornate, ostentatious, showy ~*v.* 3. add detail, amplify, complicate, decorate, develop, devise, embellish, enhance, enlarge, expand (upon), flesh out, garnish, improve, ornament, polish, produce, refine, work out

elapse glide by, go, go by, lapse, pass, pass by, roll by, roll on, slip away, slip by

elastic 1. ductile, flexible, plastic, pliable, pliant, resilient, rubbery, springy, stretchable, stretchy, supple, yielding 2. accommodating, adaptable, adjustable, complaisant, compliant, flexible, supple, tolerant, variable, yielding

elation bliss, delight, ecstasy, euphoria, exaltation, exhilaration, exultation, glee, high spirits, joy, joyfulness, joyousness, jubilation, rapture

elbow 1. *n.* angle, bend, corner, joint, turn 2. *v.* bump, crowd, hustle, jostle, knock, nudge, push, shoulder, shove

elbowroom freedom, latitude, leeway, play, room, scope, space

grease hard work —**'elbowroom** *n.* sufficient room to move or function

elder[1] ('ɛldə) *a. comp. of* OLD **1.** older, senior —*n.* **2.** person of greater age **3.** old person **4.** official of certain churches —**'elderly** *a.* growing old —**'eldest** *a. sup. of* OLD oldest

elder[2] ('ɛldə) *n.* white-flowered tree —**'elderberry** *n.* **1.** fruit of elder **2.** elder (tree)

El Dorado (ɛl dɒ'rɑːdəʊ) fictitious country rich in gold

eldritch *or* **eldrich** ('ɛldrɪtʃ) *a.* **1.** hideous **2.** weird **3.** uncanny **4.** haggish

elect (ɪ'lɛkt) *vt.* **1.** choose by vote **2.** choose —*a.* **3.** appointed but not yet in office **4.** chosen, select, choice —**e'lection** *n.* choosing, *esp.* by voting —**election'eer** *vi.* busy oneself in political elections —**e'lective** *a.* appointed, filled or chosen by election —**e'lector** *n.* one who elects —**e'lectoral** *a.* —**e'lectorate** *n.* body of electors —**e'lectorship** *n.*

elect. *or* **elec.** **1.** electric(al) **2.** electricity

electricity (ɪlɛk'trɪsɪtɪ, iːlɛk-) *n.* **1.** form of energy associated with stationary or moving electrons or other charged particles **2.** electric current or charge **3.** science dealing with electricity —**e'lectric** *a.* **1.** derived from, produced by, producing, transmitting or powered by electricity **2.** excited, emotionally charged —**e'lectrical** *a.* —**elec'trician** *n.* one trained in installation *etc.* of electrical devices —**electrifi'cation** *n.* —**e'lectrify** *vt.* —**electric blanket** blanket containing electric heating element —**electric chair US** chair in which criminals sentenced to death are electrocuted —**electric eel** eel-like freshwater fish of N South Amer., having electric organs in body —**electric eye** *see* PHOTOCELL —**electric fire** appliance that supplies heat by means of electrically operated metal coil —**electric organ** *Mus.* organ in which sound is produced by electric devices instead of wind —**electric shock** effect of an electric current passing through body

electro- *or sometimes before vowel* **electr-** (*comb. form*) by, caused by electricity, as in *electrotherapy.* Such words are not given here where the meaning may easily be inferred from the simple word

electrocardiograph (ɪlɛktrəʊ'kɑːdɪəʊgrɑːf, -græf) *n.* instrument for recording electrical activity of heart —**electro'cardiogram** *n.* tracing produced by this instrument

electroconvulsive therapy (ɪlɛktrəʊkən'vʌlsɪv) *see* **shock therapy** *at* SHOCK[1]

electrocute (ɪ'lɛktrəkjuːt) *vt.* execute, kill by electricity —**electro'cution** *n.*

electrode (ɪ'lɛktrəʊd) *n.* conductor by which electric current enters or leaves battery, vacuum tube *etc.*

electrodynamics (ɪlɛktrəʊdaɪ'næmɪks) *pl.n.* (*with sing. v.*) dynamics of electricity

electroencephalograph (ɪlɛktrəʊɛn'sɛfələgrɑːf, -græf) *n.* instrument for recording electrical activity of brain —**electroen'cephalogram** *n.* tracing produced by this

electrolyse *or U.S.* **-yze** (ɪ'lɛktrəʊlaɪz) *vt.* decompose by electricity —**elec'trolysis** *n.*

electrolyte (ɪ'lɛktrəʊlaɪt) *n.* solution, molten substance that conducts electricity

electromagnet (ɪlɛktrəʊ'mægnɪt) *n.* magnet containing coil of wire through which electric current is passed —**electromag'netic** *a.* —**electro'magnetism** *n.* **1.** magnetism produced by electric current **2.** branch of physics concerned with interaction of electric and magnetic fields

electromotive (ɪlɛktrəʊ'məʊtɪv) *a.* of, concerned with or producing electric current —**electromotive force** *Phys.* **1.** source of energy that can cause current to flow in electrical circuit **2.** rate at which energy is drawn from this source

electron (ɪ'lɛktrɒn) *n.* one of fundamental particles of matter identified with unit of charge of negative electricity and essential component of the atom —**elec'tronic** *a.* **1.** of electrons or electronics **2.** using devices, such as semiconductors, transistors or valves, dependent on action of electrons —**elec'tronics** *pl.n.* **1.** (*with sing. v.*) technology concerned with development of electronic devices and circuits **2.** science of behaviour and control of electrons —**electronic brain** *inf.* electronic computer —**electronic data processing** data processing largely performed by electronic equipment —**electronic music** music consisting of sounds produced by electric currents prerecorded on magnetic tape —**electronic organ** *Mus.* keyboard instrument in which sounds are produced by electronic or electrical means —**electron microscope** microscope that uses electrons and electron lenses to produce magnified image —**electron tube** electrical device, such as valve, in which flow of electrons between electrodes takes place —**electron volt** unit of energy used in nuclear physics

electroplate (ɪ'lɛktrəʊpleɪt) *vt.* **1.** coat with silver *etc.* by electrolysis —*n.* **2.** articles electroplated

electroscope (ɪ'lɛktrəʊskəʊp) *n.* instrument to show presence or kind of electricity

electroshock therapy (ɪ'lɛktrəʊʃɒk) *see* **shock therapy** *at* SHOCK[1]

electrostatics (ɪlɛktrəʊ'stætɪks) *n.* branch of physics concerned with static electricity —**electro'static** *a.*

electrotype (ɪ'lɛktrəʊtaɪp) *n.* **1.** art of producing copies of type *etc.* by electric deposition of copper upon mould **2.** copy so produced

THESAURUS

elder *adj.* **1.** ancient, earlier born, first-born, older, senior ~*n.* **2.** older person, senior **3.** *Presbyterianism* church official, office bearer, presbyter

elect **1.** *v.* appoint, choose, decide upon, designate, determine, opt for, pick, pick out, prefer, select, settle on, vote **2.** *adj.* choice, chosen, elite, hand-picked, picked, preferred, select, selected

election appointment, choice, choosing, decision, determination, judgment, preference, selection, vote, voting

elector chooser, constituent, selector, voter

electric *Fig.* charged, dynamic, exciting, rousing, stimulating, stirring, tense, thrilling

electrify *Fig.* amaze, animate, astonish, astound, excite, fire, galvanize, invigorate, jolt, rouse, shock, startle, stimulate, stir, take one's breath away, thrill

elegance **1.** beauty, courtliness, dignity, exquisiteness, gentility, grace, gracefulness, grandeur, luxury, polish, politeness, refinement, sumptuousness **2.** discernment, distinction, propriety, style, taste

electrum (ɪˈlɛktrəm) *n.* alloy of gold and silver used in jewellery *etc.*

eleemosynary (ɛliːˈmɒsɪnərɪ) *a.* **1.** charitable **2.** dependent on charity

elegant (ˈɛlɪgənt) *a.* **1.** graceful, tasteful **2.** refined —**ˈelegance** *n.*

elegy (ˈɛlɪdʒɪ) *n.* lament for the dead in poem or song —**elegiac** (ɛlɪˈdʒaɪək) *a.* **1.** suited to elegies **2.** plaintive —**elegiacs** (ɛlɪˈdʒaɪəks) *pl.n.* elegiac verses

element (ˈɛlɪmənt) *n.* **1.** substance which cannot be separated into other substances by ordinary chemical techniques **2.** component part **3.** small amount, trace **4.** heating wire in electric kettle, stove *etc.* **5.** proper abode or sphere **6.** situation in which person is happiest or most effective (*esp. in* **in** *or* **out of one's element**) —*pl.* **7.** powers of atmosphere **8.** rudiments, first principles —**eleˈmental** *a.* **1.** fundamental **2.** of powers of nature —**eleˈmentary** *a.* rudimentary, simple —**elementary particle** any of several entities, such as electrons *etc.*, that are less complex than atoms —**elementary school UK** *former name for* primary school

elephant (ˈɛlɪfənt) *n.* huge four-footed, thick-skinned animal with ivory tusks and long trunk —**elephanˈtiasis** *n.* disease with hardening of skin and enlargement of legs *etc.* —**eleˈphantine** *a.* unwieldy, clumsy, heavily big

elevate (ˈɛlɪveɪt) *vt.* raise, lift up, exalt —**eleˈvation** *n.* **1.** raising **2.** height, *esp.* above sea level **3.** angle above horizon, as of gun **4.** drawing of one side of building *etc.* —**ˈelevator** *n.* **US** lift

eleven (ɪˈlɛvᵊn) *n.* **1.** number next above 10 **2.** team of 11 persons —*a.* **3.** amounting to eleven —**eˈlevenfold** *a./adv.* —**eˈlevenses** *pl.n. inf.* light mid-morning snack —**eˈleventh** *a.* ordinal number of eleven —**eleven-plus** *n. esp.* formerly, examination taken by children aged 11 or 12, that selects suitable candidates for grammar schools —**eleventh hour** latest possible time

elf (ɛlf) *n.* **1.** fairy **2.** woodland sprite (*pl.* **elves**) —**ˈelfin, ˈelfish, ˈelvish** *or* **ˈelflike** *a.* roguish, mischievous

elicit (ɪˈlɪsɪt) *vt.* **1.** draw out, evoke **2.** bring to light

elide (ɪˈlaɪd) *v.* omit (a vowel or syllable) at beginning or end of word—**eˈlision** *n.*

eligible (ˈɛlɪdʒəbᵊl) *a.* **1.** fit or qualified to be chosen **2.** suitable, desirable —**eligiˈbility** *n.*

eliminate (ɪˈlɪmɪneɪt) *vt.* remove, get rid of, set aside —**elimiˈnation** *n.* —**eˈliminator** *n.* one who, that which, eliminates

elision (ɪˈlɪʒən) *n. see* ELIDE

elite *or* **élite** (ɪˈliːt, eɪ-) *n.* **1.** choice or select body **2.** the pick or best part of society **3.** typewriter typesize (12 letters to inch) —*a.* **4.** of or suitable for an elite —**eˈlitism** *n.* **1.** belief that society should be governed by an elite **2.** pride in being one of an elite group

elixir (ɪˈlɪksə) *n.* **1.** preparation sought by alchemists to change base metals into gold, or to prolong life **2.** sovereign remedy

Elizabethan (ɪlɪzəˈbiːθən) *a.* **1.** of reigns of Elizabeth I (queen of England, 1558-1603) or Elizabeth II (queen of Great Britain and N Ireland since 1952) **2.** of style of architecture used in England during reign of Elizabeth I —*n.* **3.** person who lived in England during reign of Elizabeth I

elk (ɛlk) *n.* large deer

ell (ɛl) *n.* obsolete unit of length, approximately 45 inches

ellipse (ɪˈlɪps) *n.* oval —**elˈlipsoid** *n.* **1.** geometric surface whose plane sections are ellipses or circles **2.** solid having this shape —**ellipˈsoidal** *a.* —**elˈliptical** *a.* **1.** relating to or having the shape of an ellipse **2.** relating to or resulting from ellipsis **3.** (of speech *etc.*) very concise, obscure; circumlocutory (*also* **elˈliptic**) —**elˈliptically** *adv.*

ellipsis (ɪˈlɪpsɪs) *n. Gram.* omission of parts of word or sentence (*pl.* **ellipses** (ɪˈlɪpsiːz))

elm (ɛlm) *n.* **1.** tree with serrated leaves **2.** its wood

elocution (ɛləˈkjuːʃən) *n.* art of public speaking, voice management —**eloˈcutionist** *n.* **1.** teacher of this **2.** specialist in verse speaking

elongate (ˈiːlɒŋgeɪt) *vt.* lengthen, extend, prolong —**elonˈgation** *n.*

THESAURUS

elegant à la mode, artistic, beautiful, chic, choice, comely, courtly, cultivated, delicate, exquisite, fashionable, fine, genteel, graceful, handsome, luxurious, modish, nice, polished, refined, stylish, sumptuous, tasteful

elegy coronach (*Scot.*, *Irish*), dirge, keen, lament, plaint (*Archaic*), requiem, threnody

element 1. basis, component, constituent, essential factor, factor, feature, hint, ingredient, member, part, section, subdivision, trace, unit 2. domain, environment, field, habitat, medium, milieu, sphere

elementary 1. clear, easy, facile, plain, rudimentary, simple, straightforward, uncomplicated 2. basic, elemental, fundamental, initial, introductory, original, primary, rudimentary

elements 1. basics, essentials, foundations, fundamentals, principles, rudiments 2. atmospheric conditions, atmospheric forces, powers of nature, weather

elevate 1. heighten, hoist, lift, lift up, raise, uplift, upraise 2. advance, aggrandize, exalt, prefer, promote, upgrade 3. animate, boost, brighten, buoy up, cheer, elate, excite, exhilarate, hearten, lift up, perk up, raise, rouse, uplift

elevation 1. altitude, height 2. advancement, aggrandizement, exaltation, preferment, promotion, upgrading

elicit bring forth, bring out, bring to light, call forth, cause, derive, draw out, educe, evoke, evolve, exact, extort, extract, give rise to, obtain, wrest

eligible acceptable, appropriate, desirable, fit, preferable, proper, qualified, suitable, suited, worthy

eliminate 1. cut out, dispose of, do away with, eradicate, exterminate, get rid of, remove, stamp out, take out 2. dispense with, disregard, drop, eject, exclude, expel, ignore, knock out, leave out, omit, put out, reject, throw out

elite 1. *n.* aristocracy, best, cream, *crème de la crème*, elect, flower, gentry, high society, nobility, pick, upper class 2. *adj.* aristocratic, best, choice, crack (*Sl.*), elect, exclusive, first-class, noble, pick, selected, upper-class

elocution articulation, declamation, delivery, diction, enunciation, oratory, pronunciation, public speak-

elope (ɪˈləʊp) *vi.* run away from home with lover —**eˈlopement** *n.*

eloquence (ˈɛləkwəns) *n.* fluent, powerful use of language —**ˈeloquent** *a.* —**ˈeloquently** *adv.*

Elsan (ˈɛlsæn) *n.* **R** type of portable chemical lavatory

else (ɛls) *adv.* **1.** besides, instead **2.** otherwise —**elseˈwhere** *adv.* in or to some other place

elucidate (ɪˈluːsɪdeɪt) *vt.* throw light upon, explain —**eluciˈdation** *n.* —**eˈlucidatory** *a.*

elude (ɪˈluːd) *vt.* **1.** escape, slip away from, dodge **2.** baffle —**eˈlusion** *n.* **1.** act of eluding **2.** evasion —**eˈlusive** *a.* difficult to catch hold of, deceptive —**eˈlusively** *adv.* —**eˈlusory** *a.*

elver (ˈɛlvə) *n.* young eel

elves (ɛlvz) *n., pl. of* ELF

Elysium (ɪˈlɪzɪəm) *n.* **1.** *Gr. myth.* dwelling place of blessed after death (*also* **Elysian fields**) **2.** state or place of perfect bliss

em (ɛm) *n. Print.* the square of any size of type

em- (*comb. form*) *see* EN-

'em (əm) *pron. inf.* them

emaciate (ɪˈmeɪsɪeɪt) *v.* make or become abnormally thin —**emaciˈation** *n.*

emanate (ˈɛməneɪt) *vi.* issue, proceed, originate —**emaˈnation** *n.* —**emanative** (ˈɛmənətɪv) *a.*

emancipate (ɪˈmænsɪpeɪt) *vt.* set free —**emanciˈpation** *n.* **1.** act of setting free, *esp.* from social, legal restraint **2.** state of being set free —**emanciˈpationist** *n.* advocate of emancipation of slaves, women *etc.* —**eˈmancipator** *n.* —**emancipatory** (ɪˈmænsɪpətərɪ, -trɪ) *a.*

emasculate (ɪˈmæskjʊleɪt) *vt.* **1.** castrate **2.** enfeeble, weaken —**emascuˈlation** *n.* —**eˈmasculative** *a.*

embalm (ɪmˈbɑːm) *vt.* preserve (corpse) from decay by use of chemicals, herbs *etc.* —**emˈbalmment** *n.*

embankment (ɪmˈbæŋkmənt) *n.* artificial mound carrying road, railway, or serving to dam water

embargo (ɛmˈbɑːgəʊ) *n.* **1.** order stopping movement of ships **2.** suspension of commerce **3.** ban (*pl.* **-es**) —*vt.* **4.** put under embargo **5.** requisition

embark (ɛmˈbɑːk) *v.* **1.** put, go, on board ship, aircraft *etc.* **2.** (*with* on *or* upon) commence (new project, venture *etc.*) —**embarˈkation** *n.*

embarrass (ɪmˈbærəs) *vt.* **1.** perplex, disconcert **2.** abash **3.** confuse **4.** encumber **5.** involve in financial difficulties —**emˈbarrassment** *n.*

embassy (ˈɛmbəsɪ) *n.* **1.** office, work or official residence of ambassador **2.** deputation

embattle (ɪmˈbætᵊl) *vt.* **1.** deploy (troops) for battle **2.** fortify (position *etc.*)

embed *or* **imbed** (ɪmˈbɛd) *vt.* fix fast in something solid

embellish (ɪmˈbɛlɪʃ) *vt.* adorn, enrich —**emˈbellishment** *n.*

THESAURUS

ing, rhetoric, speech, speechmaking, utterance, voice production

elongate draw out, extend, lengthen, make longer, prolong, protract, stretch

elope abscond, bolt, decamp, disappear, escape, leave, run away, run off, slip away, steal away

eloquence expression, expressiveness, fluency, forcefulness, oratory, persuasiveness, rhetoric, way with words

eloquent articulate, fluent, forceful, graceful, moving, persuasive, silver-tongued, stirring, well-expressed

elsewhere abroad, absent, away, hence (*Archaic*), in *or* to another place, not here, not present, somewhere else

elucidate annotate, clarify, clear up, explain, explicate, expound, gloss, illuminate, illustrate, interpret, make plain, shed *or* throw light upon, spell out, unfold

elucidation annotation, clarification, comment, commentary, explanation, explication, exposition, gloss, illumination, illustration, interpretation

elude **1.** avoid, circumvent, dodge, duck (*Inf.*), escape, evade, flee, get away from, outrun, shirk, shun **2.** baffle, be beyond (someone), confound, escape, foil, frustrate, puzzle, stump, thwart

elusive **1.** difficult to catch, shifty, slippery, tricky **2.** ambiguous, deceitful, deceptive, elusory, equivocal, evasive, fallacious, fraudulent, illusory, misleading, unspecific

emaciation atrophy, attenuation, gauntness, haggardness, leanness, meagreness, scrawniness, thinness, wasting away

emanate **1.** arise, come forth, derive, emerge, flow, issue, originate, proceed, spring, stem **2.** discharge, emit, exhale, give off, give out, issue, radiate, send forth

emanation **1.** arising, derivation, emergence, flow, origination, proceeding **2.** discharge, effluent, efflux, effusion, emission, exhalation, radiation

emancipate deliver, discharge, disencumber, disenthral, enfranchise, free, liberate, manumit, release, set free, unchain, unfetter, unshackle

emancipation deliverance, discharge, enfranchisement, freedom, liberation, liberty, manumission, release

embalm mummify, preserve

embargo **1.** *n.* ban, bar, barrier, blockage, check, hindrance, impediment, interdict, interdiction, prohibition, proscription, restraint, restriction, stoppage **2.** *v.* ban, bar, block, check, impede, interdict, prohibit, proscribe, restrict, stop

embark **1.** board ship, go aboard, put on board, take on board, take ship **2.** *With* **on** *or* **upon** begin, broach, commence, engage, enter, initiate, launch, plunge into, set about, set out, start, take up, undertake

embarrass abash, chagrin, confuse, discomfit, discompose, disconcert, discountenance, distress, fluster, mortify, put out of countenance, shame, show up (*Inf.*)

embarrassment awkwardness, bashfulness, chagrin, confusion, discomfiture, discomposure, distress, humiliation, mortification, self-consciousness, shame, showing up (*Inf.*)

embellish adorn, beautify, bedeck, deck, decorate, dress up, elaborate, embroider, enhance, enrich, exaggerate, festoon, garnish, gild, grace, ornament, varnish

embellishment adornment, decoration, elaboration, embroidery, enhancement, enrichment, exaggeration, gilding, ornament, ornamentation

ember (ˈɛmbə) *n.* **1.** glowing cinder —*pl.* **2.** red-hot ashes

Ember days days appointed by Church for fasting in each quarter

embezzle (ɪmˈbɛzˀl) *vt.* divert fraudulently, misappropriate (money in trust *etc.*) —**emˈbezzlement** *n.* —**emˈbezzler** *n.*

embitter (ɪmˈbɪtə) *vt.* make bitter —**emˈbitterment** *n.*

emblazon (ɪmˈbleɪzˀn) *vt.* adorn richly, *esp.* heraldically

emblem (ˈɛmbləm) *n.* **1.** symbol **2.** badge, device —**emblemˈatic** *a.* —**emblemˈatically** *adv.*

embody (ɪmˈbɒdɪ) *vt.* **1.** give body, concrete expression to **2.** represent, include, be expression of (**emˈbodied, emˈbodying**) —**emˈbodiment** *n.*

embolden (ɪmˈbəʊldˀn) *vt.* make bold

embolism (ˈɛmbəlɪzəm) *n. Med.* obstruction of artery by blood clot or air bubble

embolus (ˈɛmbələs) *n.* material, such as blood clot, that impedes circulation (*pl.* **-li** (-laɪ))

emboss (ɪmˈbɒs) *vt.* mould, stamp or carve in relief

embrace (ɪmˈbreɪs) *vt.* **1.** clasp in arms, hug **2.** seize, avail oneself of, accept **3.** comprise —*n.* **4.** act of embracing

embrasure (ɪmˈbreɪʒə) *n.* **1.** opening in wall for cannon **2.** bevelling of wall at sides of window

embrocation (ɛmbrəʊˈkeɪʃən) *n.* lotion for rubbing limbs *etc.* to relieve pain —**ˈembrocate** *vt.*

embroider (ɪmˈbrɔɪdə) *vt.* **1.** ornament with needlework **2.** embellish, exaggerate (story) —**emˈbroidery** *n.*

embroil (ɪmˈbrɔɪl) *vt.* **1.** bring into confusion **2.** involve in hostility —**emˈbroilment** *n.*

embryo (ˈɛmbrɪəʊ) *n.* **1.** unborn or undeveloped offspring, germ **2.** undeveloped thing (*pl.* **-s**) —**embryˈologist** *n.* —**embryˈology** *n.* —**embryˈonic** *a.*

embus (ɪmˈbʌs) *v.* (*esp.* of troops) put into, mount bus (**-ss-**)

emend (ɪˈmɛnd) *vt.* remove errors from, correct —**emenˈdation** *n.* —**ˈemendator** *n.* —**eˈmendatory** *a.*

emerald (ˈɛmərəld, ˈɛmrəld) *n.* **1.** bright green precious stone —*a.* **2.** of the colour of emerald —**Emerald Isle** *Poet.* Ireland

emerge (ɪˈmɜːdʒ) *vi.* **1.** come up, out **2.** rise to notice **3.** come into view **4.** come out on inquiry —**eˈmergence** *n.* —**eˈmergent** *a.* —**eˈmersion** *n.* **1.** act or instance of emerging **2.** *Astron.* reappearance of celestial body after eclipse or occultation

emergency (ɪˈmɜːdʒənsɪ) *n.* **1.** sudden unforeseen thing or event needing prompt action **2.** difficult situation **3.** exigency, crisis

emeritus (ɪˈmɛrɪtəs) *a.* retired, honourably discharged but retaining one's title (*eg* professor) on honorary basis

emery (ˈɛmərɪ) *n.* hard mineral used for polishing —**emery board** nailfile of cardboard or wood coated with crushed emery —**emery paper** stiff paper coated with finely powdered emery

emetic (ɪˈmɛtɪk) *n./a.* (medicine) causing vomiting

emf *or* **EMF** electromotive force

emigrate (ˈɛmɪgreɪt) *vi.* go and settle in another country —**ˈemigrant** *n.* —**emiˈgration** *n.* —**ˈemigratory** *a.*

émigré (ˈɛmɪgreɪ) *n.* emigrant, *esp.* one forced to leave his country for political reasons

THESAURUS

embezzle abstract, appropriate, defalcate (*Law*), filch, have one's hand in the till (*Inf.*), misapply, misappropriate, misuse, peculate, pilfer, purloin, steal

embezzlement abstraction, appropriation, defalcation (*Law*), filching, fraud, larceny, misapplication, misappropriation, misuse, peculation, pilferage, pilfering, purloining, stealing, theft, thieving

embitter alienate, anger, disaffect, disillusion, envenom, make bitter *or* resentful, poison, sour

emblazon adorn, blazon, colour, decorate, embellish, illuminate, ornament, paint

emblem badge, crest, device, figure, image, insignia, mark, representation, sigil (*Rare*), sign, symbol, token, type

embodiment bodying forth, example, exemplar, exemplification, expression, incarnation, incorporation, manifestation, personification, realization, reification, representation, symbol, type

embolden animate, cheer, encourage, fire, hearten, inflame, inspirit, invigorate, nerve, reassure, rouse, stimulate, stir, strengthen, vitalize

embrace *v.* **1.** clasp, cuddle, encircle, enfold, grasp, hold, hug, seize, squeeze, take *or* hold in one's arms **2.** accept, adopt, avail oneself of, espouse, grab, make use of, receive, seize, take up, welcome **3.** comprise, contain, cover, deal with, embody, enclose, encompass, include, involve, provide for, subsume, take in, take into account ~*n.* **4.** clasp, clinch (*Sl.*), cuddle, hug, squeeze

embroil complicate, compromise, confound, confuse, disorder, disturb, encumber, enmesh, ensnare, entangle, implicate, incriminate, involve, mire, mix up, muddle, perplex, trouble

embryo beginning, germ, nucleus, root, rudiment

emend amend, correct, edit, improve, rectify, redact, revise

emendation amendment, correction, editing, improvement, rectification, redaction, revision

emerge 1. appear, arise, become visible, come forth, come into view, come out, come up, emanate, issue, proceed, rise, spring up, surface **2.** become apparent, become known, come out, come to light, crop up, develop, materialize, transpire, turn up

emergence advent, appearance, arrival, coming, dawn, development, disclosure, emanation, materialization, rise

emergency crisis, danger, difficulty, exigency, extremity, necessity, pass, pinch, plight, predicament, quandary, scrape (*Inf.*), strait

emigrate migrate, move, move abroad, remove

emigration departure, exodus, migration, removal

eminence 1. celebrity, dignity, distinction, esteem, fame, greatness, illustriousness, importance, notability, note, pre-eminence, prestige, prominence, rank, renown, reputation, repute, superiority **2.** elevation, height, high ground, hill, hillock, knoll, rise, summit

éminence grise (eminɑ̃s ˈgriːz) *Fr.* person who wields power and influence unofficially (*pl.* ***éminences grises*** (eminɑ̃s ˈgriːz))

eminent (ˈɛmɪnənt) *a.* distinguished, notable —**ˈeminence** *n.* **1.** distinction **2.** height **3.** rank **4.** fame **5.** rising ground **6.** (E-) title of cardinal —**ˈeminently** *adv.*

emir (ɛˈmɪə) *n.* (in Islamic world) **1.** independent ruler or chieftain **2.** military commander or governor **3.** male descendant of Mohammed —**eˈmirate** *n.*

emissary (ˈɛmɪsərɪ, -ɪsrɪ) *n.* agent, representative (*esp.* of government) sent on mission

emit (ɪˈmɪt) *vt.* give out, put forth (-tt-) —**eˈmission** *n.* —**eˈmitter** *n.*

Emmenthal (ˈɛməntɑːl) *or* **Emmenthaler** *n.* hard Swiss cheese with many holes

emollient (ɪˈmɒljənt) *a.* **1.** softening, soothing —*n.* **2.** ointment or other softening application

emolument (ɪˈmɒljʊmənt) *n.* salary, pay, profit from work

emotion (ɪˈməʊʃən) *n.* mental agitation, excited state of feeling, as joy, fear *etc.* —**eˈmote** *vi. inf.* display exaggerated emotion, as in acting —**eˈmoter** *n.* —**eˈmotional** *a.* **1.** given to emotion **2.** appealing to the emotions —**eˈmotive** *a.* tending to arouse emotion

Emp. **1.** Emperor **2.** Empire **3.** Empress

empanel *or* **impanel** (ɪmˈpænᵊl) *vt. Law* **1.** enter on list (names of persons to be summoned for jury service) **2.** select (jury) from such list (-ll-) —**emˈpanelment** *or* **imˈpanelment** *n.*

empathy (ˈɛmpəθɪ) *n.* power of understanding, imaginatively entering into, another's feelings —**emˈpathic** *or* **empaˈthetic** *a.*

emperor (ˈɛmpərə) *n.* ruler of an empire (**ˈempress** *fem.*) —**emperor penguin** Antarctic penguin, the largest known, reaching a height of 1.3 m (4 ft.)

emphasis (ˈɛmfəsɪs) *n.* **1.** importance attached **2.** stress on words **3.** vigour of speech, expression (*pl.* **-ses** (-siːz)) —**ˈemphasize** *or* **-ise** *vt.* —**emˈphatic** *a.* **1.** forceful, decided **2.** stressed —**emˈphatically** *adv.*

empire (ˈɛmpaɪə) *n.* large territory, *esp.* aggregate of states under supreme ruler, supreme control —**empire-builder** *n. inf.* person who seeks extra power, *esp.* by increasing his staff —**empire-building** *n./a.*

empirical (ɛmˈpɪrɪkᵊl) *a.* relying on experiment or experience, not on theory —**emˈpiric** *a.* **1.** empirical —*n.* **2.** one who relies solely on experience and observation —**emˈpirically** *adv.* —**empiricism** (ɛmˈpɪrɪsɪzəm) *n.*

emplacement (ɪmˈpleɪsmənt) *n.* **1.** putting in position **2.** gun platform

emplane (ɪmˈpleɪn) *v.* board or put on board aeroplane

employ (ɪmˈplɔɪ) *vt.* **1.** provide work for (a person) in return for money, hire **2.** keep busy **3.** use (**emˈployed, emˈploying**) —**emˈployee** *n.* —**emˈployer** *n.* —**em-**

THESAURUS

eminent celebrated, conspicuous, distinguished, elevated, esteemed, exalted, famous, grand, great, high, high-ranking, illustrious, important, notable, noted, noteworthy, outstanding, paramount, pre-eminent, prestigious, prominent, renowned, signal, superior, well-known

eminently conspicuously, exceedingly, exceptionally, extremely, greatly, highly, notably, outstandingly, prominently, remarkably, signally, strikingly, surpassingly, well

emission diffusion, discharge, ejaculation, ejection, emanation, exhalation, exudation, issuance, issue, radiation, shedding, transmission, utterance, venting

emit breathe forth, cast out, diffuse, discharge, eject, emanate, exhale, exude, give off, give out, give vent to, issue, radiate, send forth, send out, shed, throw out, transmit, utter, vent

emolument benefit, compensation, earnings, fee, gain, hire, pay, payment, profits, recompense, remuneration, return, reward, salary, stipend, wages

emotion agitation, ardour, excitement, feeling, fervour, passion, perturbation, sensation, sentiment, vehemence, warmth

emotional **1.** demonstrative, excitable, feeling, hot-blooded, passionate, responsive, sensitive, sentimental, susceptible, temperamental, tender, warm **2.** affecting, emotive, exciting, heart-warming, moving, pathetic, poignant, sentimental, stirring, tear-jerking (*Inf.*), thrilling, touching

emotive **1.** controversial, delicate, sensitive, touchy **2.** affecting, emotional, exciting, heart-warming, moving, pathetic, poignant, sentimental, stirring, tear-jerking (*Inf.*), thrilling, touching

emphasis accent, accentuation, attention, decidedness, force, importance, insistence, intensity, moment, positiveness, power, pre-eminence, priority, prominence, significance, strength, stress, underscoring, weight

emphasize accent, accentuate, dwell on, give priority to, highlight, insist on, lay stress on, play up, press home, put the accent on, stress, underline, underscore, weight

emphatic absolute, categorical, certain, decided, definite, direct, distinct, earnest, energetic, forceful, forcible, important, impressive, insistent, marked, momentous, positive, powerful, pronounced, resounding, significant, striking, strong, telling, unequivocal, unmistakable, vigorous

empire commonwealth, domain, imperium (*Rare*), kingdom, realm

empirical, empiric experiential, experimental, observed, practical, pragmatic

emplacement placement, placing, positioning, putting in place, setting up, stationing

employ *v.* **1.** commission, engage, enlist, hire, retain, take on **2.** engage, fill, keep busy, make use of, occupy, spend, take up, use up **3.** apply, bring to bear, exercise, exert, make use of, ply, put to use, use, utilize

employed active, busy, engaged, in a job, in employment, in work, occupied, working

employee hand, job-holder, staff member, wage-earner, worker, workman

employer boss (*Inf.*), business, company, establishment, firm, gaffer (*Inf., chiefly Brit.*), organization, outfit (*Inf.*), owner, patron, proprietor

employment **1.** engagement, enlistment, hire, retaining, taking on **2.** application, exercise, exertion, use, utilization **3.** avocation (*Archaic*), business, calling, craft, employ, job, line, métier, occupation, profession, pursuit, service, trade, vocation, work

ˈ**ployment** *n.* 1. an employing, being employed 2. work, trade 3. occupation

emporium (ɛmˈpɔːrɪəm) *n.* 1. large general shop 2. centre of commerce (*pl.* **-s, -ria** (-rɪə))

empower (ɪmˈpauə) *vt.* 1. enable 2. authorize

empress (ˈɛmprɪs) *n. see* EMPEROR

empty (ˈɛmptɪ) *a.* 1. containing nothing 2. unoccupied 3. senseless 4. vain, foolish —*v.* 5. make, become devoid of content 6. discharge (contents) (into) (ˈ**emptied,** ˈ**emptying**) —ˈ**empties** *pl.n.* empty boxes, bottles *etc.* —ˈ**emptiness** *n.* —**empty-handed** *a.* 1. carrying nothing in hands 2. having gained nothing —**empty-headed** *a.* lacking sense

empyrean (ɛmpaɪˈriːən) *n.* 1. *obs.* in ancient cosmology, highest part of the heavens 2. *Poet.* heavens; sky —*a., also* **empyˈreal** 3. of sky 4. heavenly, sublime

EMS European Monetary System

emu (ˈiːmjuː) *n.* large Aust. flightless bird like ostrich

emulate (ˈɛmjʊleɪt) *vt.* 1. strive to equal or excel 2. imitate —**emuˈlation** *n.* 1. rivalry 2. competition —ˈ**emulative** *a.* —ˈ**emulator** *n.* —ˈ**emulous** *a.* eager to equal or surpass another or his deeds

emulsion (ɪˈmʌlʃən) *n.* 1. light-sensitive coating of film 2. milky liquid with oily or resinous particles in suspension 3. paint *etc.* in this form —**eˈmulsify** *v.* (**eˈmulsified, eˈmulsifying**) —**eˈmulsive** *a.*

en (ɛn) *n. Print.* unit of measurement, half an em

en- *or* **em-** (*comb. form*) put in, into, on, as in *enrage.* Such words are not given here where the meaning may easily be inferred from the simple word

-en[1] (*comb. form*) cause to be; become; cause to have, as in *blacken, heighten*

-en[2] (*comb. form*) of; made of; resembling, as in *ashen, wooden*

enable (ɪnˈeɪbᵊl) *vt.* make able, authorize, empower, supply with means (to do something) —**enabling act** legislative act conferring certain powers on person or organization

enact (ɪnˈækt) *vt.* 1. make law 2. represent or perform as in a play —**enˈactment** *n.*

enamel (ɪˈnæməl) *n.* 1. glasslike coating applied to metal *etc.* to preserve surface 2. coating of teeth 3. any hard outer coating —*vt.* 4. decorate with enamel 5. ornament with glossy variegated colours, as if with enamel 6. portray in enamel (**-ll-**)

enamour *or U.S.* **enamor** (ɪnˈæmə) *vt.* 1. inspire with love 2. charm 3. bewitch

en bloc (ã ˈblɔk) *Fr.* 1. in a lump or block 2. all together

enc. 1. enclosed 2. enclosure

encamp (ɪnˈkæmp) *v.* set up (in) camp —**enˈcampment** *n.* camp

encapsulate *or* **incapsulate** (ɪnˈkæpsjʊleɪt) *vt.* 1. enclose in capsule 2. put in concise or abridged form

encase *or* **incase** (ɪnˈkeɪs) *vt.* place or enclose as in case —**enˈcasement** *or* **inˈcasement** *n.*

encaustic (ɪnˈkɒstɪk) *a.* 1. with colours burnt in —*n.* 2. art of ornament by burnt-in colours

-ence *or* **-ency** (*comb. form*) action, state, condition, quality, as in *benevolence, residence, patience, fluency, permanency*

enceinte (ɒnˈsænt) *a.* pregnant

encephalitis (ɛnsɛfəˈlaɪtɪs) *n.* inflammation of brain —**encephalitic** (ɛnsɛfəˈlɪtɪk) *a.*

encephalo- *or before vowel* **encephal-** (*comb. form*) brain, as in *encephalogram, encephalitis*

encephalogram (ɛnˈsɛfələgræm) *n.* x-ray photograph of brain

enchain (ɪnˈtʃeɪn) *vt.* 1. bind with chains 2. hold fast or captivate (attention *etc.*) —**enˈchainment** *n.*

enchant (ɪnˈtʃɑːnt) *vt.* 1. bewitch 2. delight —**enˈchanter** *n.* (**-tress** *fem.*) —**enˈchantment** *n.*

THESAURUS

emporium bazaar, market, mart, shop, store

empower allow, authorize, commission, delegate, enable, entitle, license, permit, qualify, sanction, warrant

emptiness 1. bareness, blankness, desertedness, desolation, destitution, vacancy, vacuum, void, waste 2. aimlessness, banality, barrenness, frivolity, futility, hollowness, inanity, ineffectiveness, meaninglessness, purposelessness, senselessness, silliness, unreality, unsatisfactoriness, unsubstantiality, vainness, valuelessness, vanity, worthlessness

empty *adj.* 1. bare, blank, clear, deserted, desolate, destitute, hollow, unfurnished, uninhabited, unoccupied, untenanted, vacant, void, waste 2. aimless, banal, bootless, frivolous, fruitless, futile, hollow, inane, ineffective, meaningless, purposeless, senseless, silly, unreal, unsatisfactory, unsubstantial, vain, valueless, worthless ~*v.* 3. clear, consume, deplete, discharge, drain, dump, evacuate, exhaust, gut, pour out, unburden, unload, use up, vacate, void

empty-headed brainless, dizzy (*Inf.*), featherbrained, flighty, frivolous, giddy, harebrained, inane, scatterbrained, silly, skittish, vacuous

enable allow, authorize, capacitate, commission, empower, facilitate, fit, license, permit, prepare, qualify, sanction, warrant

enact 1. authorize, command, decree, establish, legislate, ordain, order, pass, proclaim, ratify, sanction 2. act, act out, appear as, depict, perform, personate, play, play the part of, portray, represent

enactment 1. authorization, command, commandment, decree, dictate, edict, law, legislation, order, ordinance, proclamation, ratification, regulation, statute 2. acting, depiction, performance, personation, play-acting, playing, portrayal, representation

enamour bewitch, captivate, charm, enchant, endear, enrapture, entrance, fascinate, infatuate

encampment base, bivouac, camp, camping ground, campsite, cantonment, quarters, tents

encapsulate, incapsulate abridge, compress, condense, digest, epitomize, précis, summarize, sum up

enchant beguile, bewitch, captivate, cast a spell on, charm, delight, enamour, enrapture, enthral, fascinate, hypnotize, mesmerize, spellbind

enchanter conjurer, magician, magus, necromancer, sorcerer, spellbinder, warlock, witch, wizard

enchantment 1. allure, allurement, beguilement, bliss, charm, delight, fascination, hypnotism, mesmerism, rapture, ravishment, transport 2. charm, conjuration, incantation, magic, necromancy, sorcery, spell, witchcraft, wizardry

enchantress 1. conjurer, lamia, magician, necromancer, sorceress, spellbinder, witch 2. charmer, *femme fatale*, seductress, siren, vamp (*Inf.*)

enchilada (ɛntʃɪˈlɑːdə) *n.* Mexican dish of tortilla filled with meat, served with chilli sauce

encircle (ɪnˈsɜːkˀl) *vt.* **1.** surround **2.** enfold **3.** go round so as to encompass —**enˈcirclement** *n.*

enclave (ˈɛnkleɪv) *n.* portion of territory entirely surrounded by foreign land

enclitic (ɪnˈklɪtɪk) *a.* **1.** pronounced as part of another word —*n.* **2.** enclitic word or form

enclose *or* **inclose** (ɪnˈkləʊz) *vt.* **1.** shut in **2.** surround **3.** envelop **4.** place in with something else (in letter *etc.*) —**enˈclosure** *or* **inˈclosure** *n.* —**enclosed order** Christian religious order whose members do not go into the outside world

encomium (ɛnˈkəʊmɪəm) *n.* **1.** formal praise **2.** eulogy —**enˈcomiast** *n.* one who composes encomiums —**encomiˈastic** *a.* —**encomiˈastically** *adv.*

encompass (ɪnˈkʌmpəs) *vt.* **1.** surround, encircle **2.** contain

encore (ˈɒŋkɔː) *interj.* **1.** again, once more —*n.* **2.** call for repetition of song *etc.* **3.** the repetition —*vt.* **4.** ask to repeat

encounter (ɪnˈkaʊntə) *vt.* **1.** meet unexpectedly **2.** meet in conflict **3.** be faced with (difficulty) —*n.* **4.** casual or unexpected meeting **5.** hostile meeting; contest —**encounter group** group of people who meet to develop self-awareness and mutual understanding by openly expressing feelings *etc.*

encourage (ɪnˈkʌrɪdʒ) *vt.* **1.** hearten, animate, inspire with hope **2.** embolden —**enˈcouragement** *n.*

encroach (ɪnˈkrəʊtʃ) *vi.* **1.** intrude (on) as usurper **2.** trespass —**enˈcroachment** *n.*

encrust *or* **incrust** (ɪnˈkrʌst) *v.* cover with or form a crust or hard covering

encumber *or* **incumber** (ɪnˈkʌmbə) *vt.* **1.** hamper **2.** burden —**enˈcumbrance** *or* **inˈcumbrance** *n.* impediment, burden

-ency (*comb. form*) *see* -ENCE

encyclical (ɛnˈsɪklɪkˀl) *a.* **1.** sent to many persons or places —*n.* **2.** circular letter, *esp.* from Pope

encyclopedia *or* **encyclopaedia** (ɛnsaɪkləʊˈpiːdɪə) *n.* book, set of books of information on all subjects, or on every branch of subject, usu. arranged alphabetically —**encycloˈpedic** *or* **encycloˈpaedic** *a.* —**encycloˈpedist** *or* **encycloˈpaedist** *n.*

end (ɛnd) *n.* **1.** limit **2.** extremity **3.** conclusion, finishing **4.** fragment **5.** latter part **6.** death **7.** event, issue **8.** purpose, aim **9.** *Sport* either of the defended areas of a playing field *etc.* —*vt.* **10.** put an end to —*vi.* **11.** come to an end, finish —**ˈending** *n.* —**ˈendless** *a.* —**ˈendmost** *a.* nearest end; most distant —**ˈendways** *adv.* —**ˈendpapers** *pl.n.* blank pages at beginning and end of book —**end product** final result of process *etc., esp.* in manufacturing —**end of steel C** (town at) point to which railway tracks have been laid —**end it all** *inf.* commit suicide

endanger (ɪnˈdeɪndʒə) *vt.* put in danger or peril —**enˈdangerment** *n.*

endear (ɪnˈdɪə) *vt.* make dear or beloved —**enˈdearing** *a.* —**enˈdearingly** *adv.* —**enˈdearment** *n.* **1.** loving word **2.** tender affection

endeavour *or U.S.* **endeavor** (ɪnˈdɛvə) *vi.* **1.** try, strive —*n.* **2.** attempt, effort

THESAURUS

enclose, inclose **1.** bound, circumscribe, cover, encase, encircle, encompass, environ, fence, hedge, hem in, pen, shut in, wall in, wrap **2.** include, insert, put in, send with

encompass **1.** circle, circumscribe, encircle, enclose, envelop, environ, girdle, hem in, ring, surround **2.** admit, comprise, contain, cover, embody, embrace, hold, include, incorporate, involve, subsume, take in

encounter *v.* **1.** bump into (*Inf.*), chance upon, come upon, confront, experience, face, happen on *or* upon, meet, run across, run into (*Inf.*) **2.** attack, clash with, combat, come into conflict with, contend, cross swords with, do battle with, engage, fight, grapple with, strive, struggle ~*n.* **3.** brush, confrontation, meeting **4.** action, battle, clash, collision, combat, conflict, contest, dispute, engagement, fight, run-in (*Inf.*), set to (*Inf.*), skirmish

encourage **1.** animate, buoy up, cheer, comfort, console, embolden, hearten, incite, inspire, inspirit, rally, reassure, rouse, stimulate **2.** abet, advance, advocate, aid, boost, egg on, favour, forward, foster, further, help, promote, spur, strengthen, succour, support, urge

encouragement advocacy, aid, boost, cheer, consolation, favour, help, incitement, inspiration, inspiritment, promotion, reassurance, stimulation, stimulus, succour, support, urging

encroach appropriate, arrogate, impinge, infringe, intrude, invade, make inroads, overstep, trench, trespass, usurp

encroachment appropriation, arrogation, impingement, incursion, infringement, inroad, intrusion, invasion, trespass, usurpation, violation

encumber burden, clog, cramp, embarrass, hamper, handicap, hinder, impede, incommode, inconvenience, make difficult, obstruct, oppress, overload, retard, saddle, slow down, trammel, weigh down

encumbrance burden, clog, difficulty, drag, embarrassment, handicap, hindrance, impediment, inconvenience, liability, load, millstone, obstacle, obstruction

end *n.* **1.** bound, boundary, edge, extent, extreme, extremity, limit, point, terminus, tip **2.** attainment, cessation, close, closure, completion, conclusion, consequence, consummation, culmination, denouement, ending, expiration, expiry, finale, finish, issue, outcome, resolution, result, stop, termination, upshot, wind-up **3.** aim, aspiration, design, drift, goal, intent, intention, object, objective, point, purpose, reason **4.** bit, fragment, leftover, remainder, remnant, scrap, stub, tag end **5.** annihilation, death, demise, destruction, dissolution, doom, extermination, extinction, ruin, ruination ~*v.* **6.** bring to an end, cease, close, complete, conclude, culminate, dissolve, expire, finish, resolve, stop, terminate, wind up **7.** abolish, annihilate, destroy, exterminate, extinguish, kill, put to death, ruin

endanger compromise, hazard, imperil, jeopardize, put at risk, put in danger, risk, threaten

endear attach, attract, bind, captivate, charm, engage, win

endearing adorable, attractive, captivating, charming, engaging, lovable, sweet, winning, winsome

endearment **1.** affectionate utterance, loving word, sweet nothing **2.** affection, attachment, fondness, love

endemic (ɛnˈdɛmɪk) *a.* **1.** regularly occurring in a country or district —*n.* **2.** endemic disease

endive (ˈɛndaɪv) *n.* curly-leaved chicory used as salad

endo- *or before vowel* **end-** (*comb. form*) within, as in *endocardium, endocrine.* Such words are not given here where the meaning may easily be inferred from the simple word

endocardium (ɛndəʊˈkɑːdɪəm) *n.* lining membrane of the heart

endocrine (ˈɛndəʊkraɪn, -krɪn) *a.* of those glands (thyroid, pituitary *etc.*) which secrete hormones directly into bloodstream

endogenous (ɛnˈdɒdʒɪnəs) *a. Biol.* developing or originating within an organism —**enˈdogeny** *n.*

endorphin (ɛnˈdɔːfɪn) *n.* chemical occurring in brain, which has similar effect to morphine

endorse *or* **indorse** (ɪnˈdɔːs) *vt.* **1.** sanction **2.** confirm **3.** write (*esp.* sign name) on back of **4.** record (conviction) on (driving licence) —**endorˈsation** *n.* C approval, support —**enˈdorsement** *or* **inˈdorsement** *n.*

endow (ɪnˈdaʊ) *vt.* **1.** provide permanent income for **2.** furnish (with) —**enˈdowment** *n.* —**endowment assurance** *or* **insurance** life insurance that provides for payment of specified sum to policyholder at designated date or to his beneficiary should he die before this date

endue *or* **indue** (ɪnˈdjuː) *vt.* invest, furnish (with quality *etc.*)

endure (ɪnˈdjʊə) *vt.* **1.** undergo **2.** tolerate, bear —*vi.* **3.** last —**enˈdurable** *a.* —**enˈdurance** *n.* act or power of enduring —**enˈduring** *a.* **1.** permanent **2.** having forbearance —**enˈduringness** *n.*

enema (ˈɛnɪmə) *n.* medicine, liquid injected into rectum

enemy (ˈɛnəmɪ) *n.* **1.** hostile person **2.** opponent **3.** armed foe **4.** hostile force

energy (ˈɛnədʒɪ) *n.* **1.** vigour, force, activity **2.** source(s) of power, as oil, coal *etc.* **3.** capacity of machine, battery *etc.* for work or output of power —**enerˈgetic** *a.* —**enerˈgetically** *adv.* —**ˈenergize** *or* **-ise** *vt.* give vigour to

enervate (ˈɛnəveɪt) *vt.* weaken, deprive of vigour —**enerˈvation** *n.* lassitude, weakness

enfant terrible (ãfã tɛˈribl) *Fr.* person given to unconventional conduct or indiscreet remarks (*pl.* ***enfants terribles*** (ãfã tɛˈribl))

enfeeble (ɪnˈfiːbᵊl) *vt.* weaken, debilitate —**enˈfeeblement** *n.*

enfilade (ɛnfɪˈleɪd) *n.* fire from artillery, sweeping line from end to end

enfold *or* **infold** (ɪnˈfəʊld) *vt.* **1.** cover by enclosing **2.** embrace —**enˈfolder** *or* **inˈfolder** *n.*

enforce (ɪnˈfɔːs) *vt.* **1.** compel obedience to **2.** impose (action) upon **3.** drive home —**enˈforceable** *a.* —**enˈforcement** *n.*

THESAURUS

endeavour 1. *n.* aim, attempt, crack (*Inf.*), effort, enterprise, essay, go, shot (*Inf.*), stab (*Inf.*), trial, try, undertaking, venture **2.** *v.* aim, aspire, attempt, do one's best, essay, have a go (crack, shot, stab), labour, make an effort, strive, struggle, take pains, try, undertake

ending cessation, close, completion, conclusion, consummation, culmination, denouement, end, finale, finish, resolution, termination, wind-up

endless 1. boundless, ceaseless, constant, continual, eternal, everlasting, immortal, incessant, infinite, interminable, limitless, measureless, perpetual, unbounded, unbroken, undying, unending, uninterrupted, unlimited **2.** interminable, monotonous, overlong

endorse, indorse 1. advocate, affirm, approve, authorize, back, champion, confirm, favour, ratify, recommend, sanction, subscribe to, support, sustain, vouch for, warrant **2.** countersign, sign, superscribe, undersign

endorsement, indorsement 1. comment, countersignature, qualification, signature, superscription **2.** advocacy, affirmation, approbation, approval, authorization, backing, championship, confirmation, favour, fiat, O.K. (*Inf.*), ratification, recommendation, sanction, seal of approval, subscription to, support, warrant

endow award, bequeath, bestow, confer, donate, endue, enrich, favour, finance, fund, furnish, give, grant, invest, leave, make over, provide, settle on, supply, will

endowment award, benefaction, bequest, bestowal, boon, donation, fund, gift, grant, income, largess, legacy, presentation, property, provision, revenue

endurable bearable, sufferable, supportable, sustainable, tolerable

endurance 1. bearing, fortitude, patience, perseverance, persistence, pertinacity, resignation, resolution, stamina, staying power, strength, submission, sufferance, tenacity, toleration **2.** continuation, continuity, durability, duration, immutability, lastingness, longevity, permanence, stability

endure 1. bear, brave, cope with, experience, go through, stand, stick it out (*Inf.*), suffer, support, sustain, take it (*Inf.*), thole (*Scot.*), undergo, weather, withstand **2.** abide, allow, bear, brook, countenance, permit, put up with, stand, stick (*Sl.*), stomach, submit to, suffer, swallow, take patiently, tolerate **3.** abide, be durable, continue, hold, last, live, live on, persist, prevail, remain, stand, stay, survive, wear well

enduring abiding, continuing, durable, eternal, firm, immortal, imperishable, lasting, living, long-lasting, perennial, permanent, persistent, persisting, prevailing, remaining, steadfast, steady, surviving, unfaltering, unwavering

enemy adversary, antagonist, competitor, foe, opponent, rival, the opposition, the other side

energetic active, animated, brisk, dynamic, forceful, forcible, high-powered, indefatigable, lively, potent, powerful, spirited, strenuous, strong, tireless, vigorous, zippy (*Inf.*)

energy activity, animation, ardour, *brio,* drive, efficiency, élan, exertion, fire, force, forcefulness, get-up-and-go (*Inf.*), go (*Inf.*), intensity, life, liveliness, pluck, power, spirit, stamina, strength, strenuousness, verve, vigour, vim (*Sl.*), vitality, vivacity, zeal, zest, zip (*Inf.*)

enfold, infold clasp, embrace, enclose, encompass, envelop, enwrap, fold, hold, hug, shroud, swathe, wrap, wrap up

enforce administer, apply, carry out, coerce, compel,

enfranchise (ɪnˈfræntʃaɪz) *vt.* **1.** give right of voting to **2.** give parliamentary representation to **3.** set free —**enˈfranchisement** *n.*

Eng. 1. England **2.** English

eng. 1. engine **2.** engineer **3.** engineering **4.** engraved **5.** engraver **6.** engraving

engage (ɪnˈgeɪdʒ) *vt.* **1.** employ **2.** reserve, hire **3.** bind by contract or promise **4.** order **5.** pledge oneself **6.** betroth **7.** undertake **8.** attract **9.** occupy **10.** bring into conflict **11.** interlock —*vi.* **12.** employ oneself (in) **13.** promise **14.** begin to fight —**enˈgaged** *a.* **1.** betrothed **2.** in use **3.** occupied, busy —**enˈgagement** *n.* —**enˈgaging** *a.* charming

engender (ɪnˈdʒɛndə) *vt.* **1.** give rise to **2.** beget **3.** rouse

engine (ˈɛndʒɪn) *n.* **1.** any machine to convert energy into mechanical work, as steam or petrol engine **2.** railway locomotive **3.** fire engine —**engiˈneer** *n.* **1.** one who is in charge of engines, machinery *etc.* or construction work (*eg* roads, bridges) or installation of plant **2.** one who originates, organizes something **3.** US driver of railway locomotive —*vt.* **4.** construct as engineer **5.** contrive —**engiˈneering** *n.*

English (ˈɪŋglɪʃ) *n.* **1.** the language of Britain, the U.S.A., most parts of the Commonwealth and certain other countries **2.** the people of England —*a.* **3.** relating to England

engorge (ɪnˈgɔːdʒ) *vt.* **1.** *Pathol.* congest with blood **2.** eat (food) greedily **3.** gorge (oneself) —**enˈgorgement** *n.*

engraft *or* **ingraft** (ɪnˈgrɑːft) *vt.* **1.** graft on **2.** plant deeply **3.** incorporate

engrain (ɪnˈgreɪn) *vt. see* INGRAIN

engrave (ɪnˈgreɪv) *vt.* **1.** cut in lines on metal for printing **2.** carve, incise **3.** impress deeply —**enˈgraver** *n.* —**enˈgraving** *n.* copy of picture printed from engraved plate

engross (ɪnˈgrəʊs) *vt.* **1.** absorb (attention) **2.** occupy wholly **3.** write out in large letters or in legal form **4.** corner —**enˈgrossment** *n.*

engulf *or* **ingulf** (ɪnˈgʌlf) *vt.* swallow up

enhance (ɪnˈhɑːns) *vt.* heighten, intensify, increase value or attractiveness of —**enˈhancement** *n.*

enigma (ɪˈnɪgmə) *n.* **1.** puzzling thing or person **2.** riddle —**enigˈmatic(al)** *a.* —**enigˈmatically** *adv.*

enjambment *or* **enjambement** (ɪnˈdʒæmmənt) *n.* in verse, continuation of sentence beyond end of line

THESAURUS

constrain, exact, execute, implement, impose, insist on, oblige, prosecute, put in force, put into effect, reinforce, require, urge

enforcement 1. administration, application, carrying out, exaction, execution, implementation, imposition, prosecution, reinforcement **2.** coercion, compulsion, constraint, insistence, obligation, pressure, requirement

enfranchise 1. give the vote to, grant suffrage to, grant the franchise to, grant voting rights to **2.** emancipate, free, liberate, manumit, release, set free

enfranchisement 1. giving the vote, granting suffrage *or* the franchise, granting voting rights **2.** emancipation, freedom, freeing, liberating, liberation, manumission, release, setting free

engage 1. appoint, commission, employ, enlist, enrol, hire, retain, take on **2.** bespeak, book, charter, hire, lease, prearrange, rent, reserve, secure **3.** absorb, busy, engross, grip, involve, occupy, preoccupy, tie up **4.** allure, arrest, attach, attract, captivate, catch, charm, draw, enamour, enchant, fascinate, fix, gain, win **5.** embark on, enter into, join, partake, participate, practise, set about, take part, undertake **6.** affiance, agree, betroth (*Archaic*), bind, commit, contract, covenant, guarantee, obligate, oblige, pledge, promise, undertake, vouch, vow **7.** *Military* assail, attack, combat, come to close quarters with, encounter, fall on, fight with, give battle to, join battle with, meet, take on **8.** dovetail, interact, interconnect, interlock, join, mesh

engaged 1. affianced, betrothed (*Archaic*), pledged, promised, spoken for **2.** absorbed, busy, committed, employed, engrossed, in use, involved, occupied, preoccupied, tied up, unavailable

engagement 1. assurance, betrothal, bond, compact, contract, oath, obligation, pact, pledge, promise, troth (*Archaic*), undertaking, vow, word **2.** appointment, arrangement, commitment, date, meeting **3.** commission, employment, gig (*Sl.*), job, post, situation, stint, work **4.** action, battle, combat, conflict, confrontation, contest, encounter, fight

engaging agreeable, appealing, attractive, captivating, charming, enchanting, fascinating, fetching (*Inf.*), likable, lovable, pleasant, pleasing, winning, winsome

engender 1. beget, breed, bring about, cause, create, excite, foment, generate, give rise to, hatch, incite, induce, instigate, lead to, make, occasion, precipitate, produce, provoke **2.** beget, breed, bring forth, father, generate, give birth to, procreate, propagate, sire, spawn

engine machine, mechanism, motor

engineer 1. *n.* architect, contriver, designer, deviser, director, inventor, manager, manipulator, originator, planner, schemer **2.** *v.* bring about, cause, concoct, contrive, control, create, devise, effect, encompass, finagle (*Inf.*), manage, manoeuvre, mastermind, originate, plan, plot, scheme, wangle (*Inf.*)

engrave 1. carve, chase, chisel, cut, enchase (*Rare*), etch, grave (*Archaic*), inscribe **2.** embed, fix, impress, imprint, infix, ingrain, lodge

engraving 1. carving, etching, inscription, plate, woodcut **2.** etching, impression, print

engross 1. absorb, arrest, engage, engulf, hold, immerse, involve, occupy, preoccupy **2.** corner, monopolize, sew up (*U.S.*)

enhance add to, augment, boost, complement, elevate, embellish, exalt, heighten, improve, increase, intensify, lift, magnify, raise, reinforce, strengthen, swell

enigma conundrum, mystery, problem, puzzle, riddle

enigmatic, enigmatical ambiguous, cryptic, Delphic, doubtful, equivocal, incomprehensible, indecipherable, inexplicable, inscrutable, mysterious, obscure, perplexing, puzzling, recondite, sphinxlike, uncertain, unfathomable, unintelligible

enjoin advise, bid, call upon, charge, command, counsel, demand, direct, instruct, order, prescribe, require, urge, warn

enjoin (ɪnˈdʒɔɪn) *vt.* **1.** command **2.** impose, prescribe

enjoy (ɪnˈdʒɔɪ) *vt.* **1.** delight in **2.** take pleasure in **3.** have use or benefit of —*v. refl.* **4.** be happy —**enˈjoyable** *a.* —**enˈjoyment** *n.*

enkindle (ɪnˈkɪndˀl) *vt.* **1.** set on fire; kindle **2.** excite to activity or ardour; arouse

enlarge (ɪnˈlɑːdʒ) *vt.* **1.** make bigger **2.** reproduce on larger scale, as photograph —*vi.* **3.** grow bigger **4.** talk, write in greater detail **5.** be capable of reproduction on larger scale —**enˈlargeable** *a.* —**enˈlargement** *n.* —**enˈlarger** *n.* optical instrument for enlarging photographs

enlighten (ɪnˈlaɪtˀn) *vt.* **1.** give information to **2.** instruct, inform **3.** *Poet.* shed light on —**enˈlightenment** *n.*

enlist (ɪnˈlɪst) *v.* (persuade to) enter armed forces —**enˈlistment** *n.*

enliven (ɪnˈlaɪvˀn) *vt.* brighten, make more lively, animate

en masse (*Fr.* ɑ̃ ˈmas) **1.** in a group, body **2.** all together

enmesh, inmesh (ɪnˈmɛʃ) *or* **immesh** (ɪˈmɛʃ) *vt.* entangle

enmity (ˈɛnmɪtɪ) *n.* ill will, hostility

ennoble (ɪˈnəʊbˀl) *vt.* make noble, elevate —**enˈnoblement** *n.*

ennui (ˈɒnwiː) *n.* boredom —**ˈennuied** *or* **ennuyé** (ˈɒnwiːjeɪ) *a.*

enormous (ɪˈnɔːməs) *a.* very big, vast —**eˈnormity** *n.* **1.** a gross offence **2.** great wickedness **3.** *inf.* great size

enough (ɪˈnʌf) *a.* **1.** as much or as many as need be **2.** sufficient —*n.* **3.** sufficient quantity —*adv.* **4.** (just) sufficiently

enounce (ɪˈnaʊns) *vt.* **1.** state **2.** enunciate, proclaim —**eˈnouncement** *n.*

en passant (ɒn pæˈsɑːnt) *Fr.* in passing, by the way

enplane (ɛnˈpleɪn) *vi.* board aircraft

enquire (ɪnˈkwaɪə) *vi. see* INQUIRE

enrapture (ɪnˈræptʃə) *vt.* **1.** delight excessively **2.** charm —**enˈrapt** *or* **enˈraptured** *a.* entranced

enrich (ɪnˈrɪtʃ) *vt.* **1.** make rich **2.** add to, improve —**enˈrichment** *n.*

enrol *or U.S.* **enroll** (ɪnˈrəʊl) *vt.* **1.** write name of on roll or list **2.** engage, enlist, take in as member **3.** enter, record —*vi.* **4.** become member (-ll-) —**enˈrolment** *or U.S.* **enˈrollment** *n.*

en route (ɒn ˈruːt) *Fr.* on the way

ensconce (ɪnˈskɒns) *vt.* **1.** place snugly **2.** establish in safety

ensemble (ɒnˈsɒmbˀl) *n.* **1.** whole **2.** all parts taken together **3.** woman's complete outfit **4.** company of actors, dancers *etc.* **5.** *Mus.* group of soloists perform-

THESAURUS

enjoy **1.** appreciate, be entertained by, be pleased with, delight in, like, rejoice in, relish, revel in, take joy in, take pleasure in *or* from **2.** be blessed *or* favoured with, experience, have, have the benefit of, have the use of, own, possess, reap the benefits of, use **3. enjoy oneself** have a ball (*Inf.*), have a good time, have fun, make merry

enjoyable agreeable, amusing, delectable, delicious, delightful, entertaining, gratifying, pleasant, pleasing, pleasurable, satisfying, to one's liking

enjoyment **1.** amusement, delectation, delight, diversion, entertainment, fun, gladness, gratification, gusto, happiness, indulgence, joy, pleasure, recreation, relish, satisfaction, zest **2.** advantage, benefit, exercise, ownership, possession, use

enlarge **1.** add to, amplify, augment, blow up (*Inf.*), broaden, diffuse, dilate, distend, elongate, expand, extend, grow, heighten, increase, inflate, lengthen, magnify, make *or* grow larger, multiply, stretch, swell, wax, widen **2.** amplify, descant, develop, dilate, elaborate, expand, expatiate, give details

enlighten advise, apprise, cause to understand, civilize, counsel, edify, educate, inform, instruct, make aware, teach

enlightenment awareness, comprehension, edification, education, information, instruction, knowledge, learning, teaching, understanding, wisdom

enlist engage, enrol, enter (into), gather, join, join up, muster, obtain, procure, recruit, register, secure, sign up, volunteer

enliven animate, brighten, buoy up, cheer, cheer up, excite, exhilarate, fire, gladden, hearten, inspire, inspirit, invigorate, pep up, perk up, quicken, rouse, spark, stimulate, vitalize, vivify, wake up

enmity acrimony, animosity, animus, antagonism, antipathy, aversion, bad blood, bitterness, hate, hatred, hostility, ill will, malevolence, malice, malignity, rancour, spite, venom

ennoble aggrandize, dignify, elevate, enhance, exalt, glorify, honour, magnify, raise

ennui boredom, dissatisfaction, lassitude, listlessness, tedium, the doldrums

enormity **1.** atrociousness, atrocity, depravity, disgrace, evilness, heinousness, monstrousness, nefariousness, outrageousness, turpitude, viciousness, vileness, villainy, wickedness **2.** abomination, atrocity, crime, disgrace, evil, horror, monstrosity, outrage, villainy **3.** *Inf.* enormousness, greatness, hugeness, immensity, magnitude, massiveness, vastness

enormous astronomic, Brobdingnagian, colossal, excessive, gargantuan, gigantic, gross, huge, immense, jumbo (*Inf.*), mammoth, massive, monstrous, mountainous, prodigious, titanic, tremendous, vast

enough **1.** *adj.* abundant, adequate, ample, plenty, sufficient **2.** *n.* abundance, adequacy, ample supply, plenty, right amount, sufficiency **3.** *adv.* adequately, fairly, moderately, passably, reasonably, satisfactorily, sufficiently, tolerably

enrich **1.** make rich, make wealthy **2.** aggrandize, ameliorate, augment, cultivate, develop, endow, enhance, improve, refine, supplement

enrol **1.** chronicle, inscribe, list, note, record **2.** accept, admit, engage, enlist, join up, matriculate, recruit, register, sign up *or* on, take on

enrolment acceptance, admission, engagement, enlistment, matriculation, recruitment, registration

en route in transit, on *or* along the way, on the road

ensemble *n.* **1.** aggregate, assemblage, collection, entirety, set, sum, total, totality, whole, whole thing **2.** costume, get-up (*Inf.*), outfit, suit **3.** band, cast, chorus, company, group, supporting cast, troupe ~*adv.* **4.** all at once, all together, as a group, as a whole, at once, at the same time, en masse, in concert

ing together **6.** *Mus.* concerted passage **7.** general effect —*adv.* **8.** all together or at once

enshrine *or* **inshrine** (ɪnˈʃraɪn) *vt.* **1.** set in shrine **2.** preserve with great care and sacred affection

enshroud (ɪnˈʃraʊd) *vt.* cover or hide as with shroud

ensign (ˈɛnsaɪn) *n.* **1.** (*also* ˈɛnsən) naval or military flag **2.** badge **3.** (in U.S. Navy) commissioned officer of lowest rank

ensilage (ˈɛnsɪlɪdʒ) *n. see* SILAGE

enslave (ɪnˈsleɪv) *vt.* make into slave —**enˈslavement** *n.* bondage —**enˈslaver** *n.*

ensnare *or* **insnare** (ɪnˈsnɛə) *vt.* **1.** capture in snare or trap **2.** trick into false position **3.** entangle

ensue (ɪnˈsjuː) *vi.* follow, happen after

en suite (ã ˈsɥɪt) forming a set or single unit

ensure (ɛnˈʃʊə, -ˈʃɔː) *or* (*esp. U.S.*) **insure** *vt.* **1.** make safe or sure **2.** make certain to happen **3.** secure

E.N.T. *Med.* ear, nose and throat

-ent (*comb. form*) causing or performing action or existing in certain condition; agent that performs action, as in *astringent, dependent*

entablature (ɛnˈtæblətʃə) *n. Archit.* part of classical temple above columns, having architrave, frieze and cornice

entail (ɪnˈteɪl) *vt.* **1.** involve as result, necessitate **2.** *Law* restrict (ownership of property) to designated line of heirs

entangle (ɪnˈtæŋgᵊl) *vt.* **1.** ensnare **2.** perplex —**enˈtanglement** *n.*

entente (*Fr.* ãˈtãːt) *n.* friendly understanding between nations —**entente cordiale** (kɔrˈdjal) **1.** friendly understanding between political powers **2.** (*oft.* **E- C-**) understanding reached by France and Britain in April 1904 over colonial disputes

enter (ˈɛntə) *vt.* **1.** go, come into **2.** penetrate **3.** join **4.** write in, register —*vi.* **5.** go, come in **6.** join a party *etc.* **7.** begin —**ˈentrance** *n.* **1.** going, coming in **2.** door, passage to enter **3.** right to enter **4.** fee paid for this —**ˈentrant** *n.* one who enters, *esp.* contest —**ˈentry** *n.* **1.** entrance **2.** entering **3.** item entered, *eg* in account, list

enteric (ɛnˈtɛrɪk) *or* **enteral** (ˈɛntərəl) *a.* of intestines —**enteˈritis** *n.* bowel inflammation

enterprise (ˈɛntəpraɪz) *n.* **1.** bold or difficult undertaking **2.** bold spirit **3.** force of character in launching out **4.** business, company —**ˈenterprising** *a.*

entertain (ɛntəˈteɪn) *vt.* **1.** amuse, divert **2.** receive as guest **3.** maintain **4.** consider favourable **5.** take into consideration —**enterˈtainer** *n.* —**enterˈtaining** *a.* serving to entertain; amusing —**enterˈtainment** *n.*

enthral *or U.S.* **enthrall** (ɪnˈθrɔːl) *vt.* captivate, thrill, hold spellbound (**-ll-**) —**enˈthralment** *or U.S.* **enˈthrallment** *n.*

enthrone (ɛnˈθrəʊn) *vt.* **1.** place on throne **2.** honour; exalt **3.** assign authority to —**enˈthronement** *n.*

enthusiasm (ɪnˈθjuːzɪæzəm) *n.* ardent eagerness, zeal —**enˈthuse** *v.* (cause to) show enthusiasm —**enˈthusiast** *n.* ardent supporter —**enthusiˈastic** *a.* —**enthusiˈastically** *adv.*

THESAURUS

enshrine apotheosize, cherish, consecrate, dedicate, embalm, exalt, hallow, preserve, revere, sanctify, treasure

enshroud cloak, cloud, conceal, cover, enclose, enfold, envelop, enwrap, hide, obscure, pall, shroud, veil, wrap

ensign badge, banner, colours, flag, jack, pennant, pennon, standard, streamer

enslave bind, dominate, enchain, enthral, reduce to slavery, subjugate, yoke

ensue arise, attend, be consequent on, befall, come after, come next, come to pass (*Archaic*), derive, flow, follow, issue, proceed, result, stem, succeed, supervene, turn out *or* up

ensure, insure 1. certify, confirm, effect, guarantee, make certain, make sure, secure, warrant **2.** guard, make safe, protect, safeguard, secure

entail bring about, call for, cause, demand, encompass, give rise to, impose, involve, lead to, necessitate, occasion, require, result in

entangle 1. catch, compromise, embroil, enmesh, ensnare, entrap, foul, implicate, involve, knot, mat, mix up, ravel, snag, snare, tangle, trammel, trap **2.** bewilder, complicate, confuse, jumble, mix up, muddle, perplex, puzzle, snarl, twist

entanglement complication, confusion, ensnarement, entrapment, imbroglio (*Obsolete*), involvement, jumble, knot, mesh, mess, mix-up, muddle, snare, snarl-up (*Inf.*), tangle, toils, trap

enter 1. arrive, come *or* go in *or* into, insert, introduce, make an entrance, pass into, penetrate, pierce **2.** become a member of, begin, commence, commit oneself to, embark upon, enlist, enrol, join, participate in, set about, set out on, sign up, start, take part in, take up **3.** inscribe, list, log, note, record, register, set down, take down

enterprise 1. adventure, effort, endeavour, essay, operation, plan, programme, project, undertaking, venture **2.** activity, adventurousness, alertness, audacity, boldness, daring, dash, drive, eagerness, energy, enthusiasm, get-up-and-go (*Inf.*), gumption (*Inf.*), initiative, push (*Inf.*), readiness, resource, resourcefulness, spirit, vigour, zeal **3.** business, company, concern, establishment, firm, operation

enterprising active, adventurous, alert, audacious, bold, daring, dashing, eager, energetic, enthusiastic, go-ahead, intrepid, keen, ready, resourceful, spirited, stirring, up-and-coming, venturesome, vigorous, zealous

entertain 1. amuse, charm, cheer, delight, divert, occupy, please, recreate (*Rare*), regale **2.** accommodate, be host to, harbour, have company, have guests *or* visitors, lodge, put up, show hospitality to, treat **3.** cherish, cogitate on, conceive, consider, contemplate, foster, harbour, hold, imagine, keep in mind, maintain, muse over, ponder, support, think about, think over

entertaining amusing, charming, cheering, delightful, diverting, funny, humorous, interesting, pleasant, pleasing, pleasurable, recreative (*Rare*), witty

entertainment amusement, cheer, distraction, diversion, enjoyment, fun, good time, leisure activity, pastime, play, pleasure, recreation, satisfaction, sport, treat

enthral beguile, captivate, charm, enchant, enrapture, entrance, fascinate, grip, hold spellbound, hypnotize, intrigue, mesmerize, rivet, spellbind

enthusiasm ardour, avidity, devotion, eagerness, ear-

entice (ɪnˈtaɪs) *vt.* allure, attract, inveigle, tempt —**enˈticement** *n.* —**enˈticing** *a.* alluring

entire (ɪnˈtaɪə) *a.* **1.** whole, complete **2.** unbroken —**enˈtirely** *adv.* —**entirety** (ɪnˈtaɪərɪtɪ) *n.*

entitle (ɪnˈtaɪtˀl) *vt.* **1.** give claim to **2.** qualify **3.** give title to **4.** style

entity (ˈɛntɪtɪ) *n.* **1.** thing's being or existence **2.** reality **3.** thing having real existence

entomb (ɪnˈtuːm) *vt.* **1.** place in or as if in tomb; bury **2.** serve as tomb for —**enˈtombment** *n.*

entomology (ɛntəˈmɒlədʒɪ) *n.* study of insects —**entomoˈlogical** *a.* —**entoˈmologist** *n.* —**entoˈmologize** *or* **-ise** *vi.*

entourage (ɒntʊˈrɑːʒ) *n.* **1.** associates, retinue **2.** surroundings

entozoon (ɛntəʊˈzəʊɒn) *n.* internal parasite (*pl.* **-zoa** (-ˈzəʊə)) —**entozoic** (ɛntəʊˈzəʊɪk) *a.*

entr'acte (ɒnˈtrækt) *n.* **1.** interval between acts of play *etc.* **2.** *esp.* formerly, entertainment during such interval

entrails (ˈɛntreɪlz) *pl.n.* **1.** bowels, intestines **2.** inner parts

entrain (ɪnˈtreɪn) *v.* board or put aboard train —**enˈtrainment** *n.*

entrance[1] (ˈɛntrəns) *n.* *see* ENTER

entrance[2] (ɪnˈtrɑːns) *vt.* **1.** delight **2.** throw into a trance

entrap (ɪnˈtræp) *vt.* **1.** catch or snare as in trap **2.** trick into difficulty *etc.* (**-pp-**) —**enˈtrapment** *n.*

entreat *or* **intreat** (ɪnˈtriːt) *vt.* **1.** ask earnestly **2.** beg, implore —**enˈtreaty** *n.* earnest request

entrecôte (*Fr.* ãtrəˈkoːt) *n.* beefsteak cut from between ribs

entrée (ˈɒntreɪ) *n.* **1.** (dish served before) main course of meal **2.** right of access, admission

entrench *or* **intrench** (ɪnˈtrɛntʃ) *vt.* **1.** establish in fortified position with trenches **2.** establish firmly —**enˈtrenchment** *or* **inˈtrenchment** *n.*

entrepreneur (ɒntrəprəˈnɜː) *n.* person who attempts to profit by risk and initiative

entropy (ˈɛntrəpɪ) *n.* **1.** unavailability of the heat energy of a system for mechanical work **2.** measurement of this

entrust *or* **intrust** (ɪnˈtrʌst) *vt.* **1.** commit, charge (with) **2.** (*oft. with* to) put into care or protection of

entwine *or* **intwine** (ɪnˈtwaɪn) *vt.* **1.** plait, interweave **2.** wreathe **3.** embrace

E number any of series of numbers with prefix E indicating specific food additive recognized by EEC

enumerate (ɪˈnjuːməreɪt) *vt.* **1.** mention one by one

THESAURUS

nestness, excitement, fervour, frenzy, interest, keenness, passion, relish, vehemence, warmth, zeal, zest

enthusiast admirer, aficionado, buff (*Inf.*), devotee, fan, fanatic, fiend (*Inf.*), follower, freak (*Sl.*), lover, supporter, zealot

enthusiastic ardent, avid, devoted, eager, earnest, ebullient, excited, exuberant, fervent, fervid, forceful, hearty, keen, lively, passionate, spirited, unqualified, unstinting, vehement, vigorous, warm, wholehearted, zealous

entice allure, attract, beguile, cajole, coax, decoy, draw, inveigle, lead on, lure, persuade, prevail on, seduce, tempt, wheedle

entire 1. complete, full, total, whole **2.** absolute, full, outright, thorough, total, undiminished, unmitigated, unreserved, unrestricted **3.** intact, perfect, sound, unbroken, undamaged, unmarked, unmarred, whole, without a scratch **4.** continuous, integrated, unbroken, undivided, unified

entirely 1. absolutely, altogether, completely, fully, in every respect, perfectly, thoroughly, totally, unreservedly, utterly, wholly, without exception, without reservation **2.** exclusively, only, solely

entirety 1. absoluteness, completeness, fullness, totality, undividedness, unity, wholeness **2.** aggregate, sum, total, unity, whole

entitle 1. accredit, allow, authorize, empower, enable, enfranchise, fit for, license, make eligible, permit, qualify for, warrant **2.** call, characterize, christen, denominate, designate, dub, label, name, style, term, title

entity 1. being, body, creature, existence, individual, object, organism, presence, quantity, substance, thing **2.** essence, essential nature, quiddity (*Philosophy*), quintessence, real nature

entourage 1. associates, attendants, companions, company, cortege, court, escort, followers, following, retainers, retinue, staff, suite, train **2.** ambience, environment, environs, milieu, surroundings

entrails bowels, guts, innards (*Inf.*), insides (*Inf.*), intestines, offal, viscera

entrance[1] *n.* **1.** access, avenue, door, doorway, entry, gate, ingress, inlet, opening, passage, portal, way in **2.** appearance, arrival, coming in, entry, ingress, introduction **3.** access, admission, admittance, entrée, entry, ingress, permission to enter

entrance[2] *v.* **1.** bewitch, captivate, charm, delight, enchant enrapture, enthral, fascinate, gladden, ravish, spellbind, transport **2.** hypnotize, mesmerize, put in a trance

entrant candidate, competitor, contestant, entry, participant, player

entreaty appeal, earnest request, exhortation, importunity, petition, plea, prayer, request, solicitation, suit, supplication

entrench, intrench 1. construct defences, dig in, dig trenches, fortify **2.** anchor, dig in, embed, ensconce, establish, fix, implant, ingrain, install, lodge, plant, root, seat, set, settle

entrust, intrust assign, authorize, charge, commend, commit, confide, consign, delegate, deliver, give custody of, hand over, invest, trust, turn over

entry 1. appearance, coming in, entering, entrance, initiation, introduction **2.** access, avenue, door, doorway, entrance, gate, ingress, inlet, opening, passage, passageway, portal, way in **3.** access, admission, entrance, entrée, free passage, permission to enter **4.** account, item, jotting, listing, memo, memorandum, minute, note, record, registration

entwine, intwine braid, embrace, encircle, entwist (*Archaic*), interlace, intertwine, interweave, knit, plait, surround, twine, twist, weave, wind

enumerate 1. cite, detail, itemize, list, mention, name, quote, recapitulate, recite, recount, rehearse, relate, specify, spell out, tell **2.** add up, calculate, compute, count, number, reckon, sum up, tally, total

2. count —**enumer'ation** *n.* —**e'numerative** *a.* —**e'numerator** *n.*

enunciate (ɪ'nʌnsɪeɪt) *vt.* **1.** state clearly **2.** proclaim **3.** pronounce —**enunci'ation** *n.* —**e'nunciative** *a.* —**e'nunciator** *n.*

enuresis (ɛnjʊ'riːsɪs) *n.* involuntary discharge of urine, *esp.* during sleep —**enuretic** (ɛnjʊ'rɛtɪk) *a.*

envelop (ɪn'vɛləp) *vt.* **1.** wrap up, enclose **2.** surround **3.** encircle —**en'velopment** *n.*

envelope ('ɛnvələʊp, 'ɒn-) *n.* **1.** folded, gummed cover of letter **2.** covering, wrapper

envenom (ɪn'vɛnəm) *vt.* **1.** put poison, venom in **2.** embitter

environ (ɪn'vaɪrən) *vt.* surround —**en'vironment** *n.* **1.** surroundings **2.** conditions of life or growth —**environ'mental** *a.* —**environ'mentalist** *n.* ecologist —**en'virons** *pl.n.* districts round town *etc.*, outskirts

envisage (ɪn'vɪzɪdʒ) *vt.* **1.** conceive of as possibility **2.** visualize

envoy[1] ('ɛnvɔɪ) *n.* **1.** messenger **2.** diplomatic minister of rank below ambassador

envoy[2] *or* **envoi** ('ɛnvɔɪ) *n.* **1.** concluding stanza, notably in ballades **2.** postscript in other forms of verse or prose

envy ('ɛnvɪ) *vt.* **1.** grudge (another's good fortune, success or qualities) **2.** feel jealous of (**'envied, 'envying**) —*n.* **3.** bitter contemplation of another's good fortune **4.** jealousy **5.** object of this feeling —**'enviable** *a.* arousing envy —**'envious** *a.* full of envy

enzyme ('ɛnzaɪm) *n.* any of group of complex proteins produced by living cells and acting as catalysts in biochemical reactions

Eocene ('iːəʊsiːn) *a.* **1.** of second epoch of Tertiary period, during which hooved mammals appeared —*n.* **2.** Eocene epoch or rock series

eolith ('iːəʊlɪθ) *n.* early flint implement —**Eo'lithic** *a.* of the period before Stone Age

-eous (*comb. form*) relating to or having nature of, as in *gaseous*

EP **1.** extended-play **2.** electroplate

epaulet *or* **epaulette** ('ɛpəlɛt, -lɪt) *n.* shoulder ornament on uniform

épée ('ɛpeɪ) *n.* sword similar to foil but with heavier blade —**'épéeist** *n.*

epergne (ɪ'pɜːn) *n.* ornamental centrepiece for table, holding flowers *etc.*

Eph. *or* **Ephes.** *Bible* Ephesians

ephedrine *or* **ephedrin** (ɪ'fɛdrɪn, 'ɛfɪdriːn, -drɪn) *n.* alkaloid used for treatment of asthma and hay fever

ephemeral (ɪ'fɛmərəl) *a.* short-lived, transient —**e'phemeron** *n.* ephemeral thing (*pl.* **-s, -ra** (-rə)) (*also* **e'phemera** (*pl.* **-s, -rae** (-riː))) —**e'phemerous** *a.*

epi-, eph-, *or before vowel* **ep-** (*comb. form*) **1.** upon; above, as in *epidermis* **2.** in addition to, as in *epiphenomenon* **3.** after, as in *epilogue* **4.** near, as in *epicalyx*

epic ('ɛpɪk) *n.* **1.** long poem or story telling of achievements of hero or heroes **2.** film *etc.* about heroic deeds —*a.* **3.** of, like, an epic **4.** impressive, grand

epicene ('ɛpɪsiːn) *a.* common to both sexes

epicentre *or U.S.* **epicenter** ('ɛpɪsɛntə) *n.* focus of earthquake —**epi'central** *a.*

epicure ('ɛpɪkjʊə) *n.* one delighting in eating and drinking —**epicu'rean** *a.* **1.** of Epicurus, who taught that pleasure, in the shape of practice of virtue, was highest good **2.** given to refined sensuous enjoyment —*n.* **3.** such person or philosopher —**epicu'reanism** *n.* —**'epicurism** *n.*

epicycle ('ɛpɪsaɪk'l) *n.* circle whose centre moves on circumference of greater circle

epidemic (ɛpɪ'dɛmɪk) *a.* **1.** (*esp.* of disease) prevalent and spreading rapidly **2.** widespread —*n.* **3.** widespread occurrence of a disease **4.** rapid development, spread or growth of something —**epi'demical** *a.* —**epidemiological** (ɛpɪdiːmɪə'lɒdʒɪk'l) *a.* —**epidemiologist** (ɛpɪdiːmɪ'ɒlədʒɪst) *n.* —**epidemiology** (ɛpɪdiːmɪ'ɒlədʒɪ) *n.* branch of medical science concerned with epidemic diseases

epidermis (ɛpɪ'dɜːmɪs) *n.* outer skin

THESAURUS

enunciate 1. articulate, enounce, pronounce, say, sound, speak, utter, vocalize, voice 2. declare, proclaim, promulgate, pronounce, propound, publish, state

envelop blanket, cloak, conceal, cover, embrace, encase, encircle, enclose, encompass, enfold, engulf, enwrap, hide, obscure, sheathe, shroud, surround, swaddle, swathe, veil, wrap

envelope case, casing, coating, cover, covering, jacket, sheath, shell, skin, wrapper, wrapping

enviable advantageous, blessed, covetable, desirable, favoured, fortunate, lucky, much to be desired, privileged

envious begrudging, covetous, green-eyed, green with envy, grudging, jaundiced, jealous, malicious, resentful, spiteful

environ beset, besiege, encircle, enclose, encompass, engird, envelop, gird, hem, invest (*Rare*), ring, surround

environment atmosphere, background, conditions, context, domain, element, habitat, locale, medium, milieu, scene, setting, situation, surroundings, territory

environs district, locality, neighbourhood, outskirts, precincts, purlieus, suburbs, surrounding area, vicinity

envisage conceive (of), conceptualize, contemplate, fancy, imagine, picture, think up, visualize

envoy agent, ambassador, courier, delegate, deputy, diplomat, emissary, intermediary, legate, messenger, minister, plenipotentiary, representative

envy 1. *n.* covetousness, enviousness, grudge, hatred, ill will, jealousy, malice, malignity, resentfulness, resentment, spite, the green-eyed monster (*Inf.*) 2. *v.* be envious (of), begrudge, be jealous (of), covet, grudge, resent

ephemeral brief, evanescent, fleeting, flitting, fugacious, fugitive, impermanent, momentary, passing, short, short-lived, temporary, transient, transitory

epicure *bon vivant*, epicurean, gastronome, gourmet

epicurean 1. *adj.* hedonistic, pleasure-seeking, sensual, sybaritic 2. *n. bon vivant*, epicure, gastronome, gourmet

epidemic 1. *adj.* general, pandemic, prevailing, prevalent, rampant, rife, sweeping, wide-ranging, widespread 2. *n.* growth, outbreak, plague, rash, spread, upsurge, wave

epidiascope (ɛpɪˈdaɪəskəʊp) *n.* optical device for projecting magnified image on to screen

epidural (ɛpɪˈdjʊərəl) *n./a.* (of) spinal anaesthetic used for relief of pain during childbirth

epiglottis (ɛpɪˈglɒtɪs) *n.* cartilage that covers opening of larynx in swallowing **—epiˈglottic** *a.*

epigram (ˈɛpɪgræm) *n.* concise, witty poem or saying **—epigramˈmatic(al)** *a.* **—epigramˈmatically** *adv.* **—epiˈgrammatist** *n.*

epigraph (ˈɛpɪgrɑːf, -græf) *n.* inscription

epilepsy (ˈɛpɪlɛpsɪ) *n.* disorder of nervous system causing fits and convulsions **—epiˈleptic** *n.* **1.** sufferer from this *—a.* **2.** of, subject to, this

epilogue (ˈɛpɪlɒg) *n.* short speech or poem at end, *esp.* of play

Epiphany (ɪˈpɪfənɪ) *n.* festival of the announcement of Christ to the Magi, celebrated Jan. 6th

Epis. **1.** Episcopal; Episcopalian (*also* **Episc.**) **2.** Epistle

episcopal (ɪˈpɪskəpˀl) *a.* **1.** of bishop **2.** ruled by bishops **—eˈpiscopacy** *n.* government by body of bishops **—Episcoˈpalian** *a.* **1.** of branch of Anglican church *—n.* **2.** member, adherent of Episcopalian church **—eˈpiscopate** *n.* **1.** bishop's office, see, or duration of office **2.** body of bishops

episode (ˈɛpɪsəʊd) *n.* **1.** incident **2.** section of (serialized) book, television programme *etc.* **—episodic(al)** (ɛpɪˈsɒdɪk(ˀl)) *a.*

epistemology (ɪpɪstɪˈmɒlədʒɪ) *n.* study of source, nature and limitations of knowledge **—epistemoˈlogical** *a.* **—episteˈmologist** *n.*

epistle (ɪˈpɪsˀl) *n.* **1.** letter, *esp.* of apostle **2.** poem in letter form **—epistolary** (ɪˈpɪstələrɪ) *a.* **—epistoler** (ɪˈpɪstˀlə) *n.*

epitaph (ˈɛpɪtɑːf, -tæf) *n.* memorial inscription on tomb

epithelium (ɛpɪˈθiːlɪəm) *n.* tissue covering external and internal surfaces of body (*pl.* **-s, -lia** (-lɪə)) **—epiˈthelial** *or* **epiˈthelioid** *a.*

epithet (ˈɛpɪθɛt) *n.* additional, descriptive word or name **—epiˈthetic(al)** *a.*

epitome (ɪˈpɪtəmɪ) *n.* **1.** typical example **2.** summary **—eˈpitomist** *n.* **—eˈpitomize** *or* **-ise** *vt.* typify

E.P.N.S. electroplated nickel silver

epoch (ˈiːpɒk) *n.* **1.** beginning of period **2.** period, era, *esp.* one of notable events **—epochal** (ˈɛpɒkˀl) *a.*

epode (ˈɛpəʊd) *n.* third, or last, part of lyric ode

eponym (ˈɛpənɪm) *n.* **1.** name, *esp.* place name, derived from name of real or mythical person **2.** name of person from which such name is derived **—eˈponymous** *a.* **—eˈponymously** *adv.* **—eˈponymy** *n.*

epoxy (ɪˈpɒksɪ) *a. Chem.* of, consisting of, or containing oxygen atom joined to two different groups that are themselves joined to other groups **—epoxy** *or* **epoxide resin** any of various thermosetting synthetic resins containing epoxy groups: used in surface coatings, adhesives *etc.*

epsilon (ˈɛpsɪlɒn) *n.* fifth letter of Gr. alphabet (E, ϵ)

Epsom salts (ˈɛpsəm) medicinal preparation of hydrated magnesium sulphate, used as purgative *etc.*

equable (ˈɛkwəbˀl) *a.* **1.** even-tempered, placid **2.** uniform **—equaˈbility** *n.* **—ˈequably** *adv.*

equal (ˈiːkwəl) *a.* **1.** the same in number, size, merit *etc.* **2.** identical **3.** fit or qualified **4.** evenly balanced *—n.* **5.** one equal to another *—vt.* **6.** be equal to (**-ll-**) **—equality** (ɪˈkwɒlɪtɪ) *n.* **1.** state of being equal **2.** uniformity **—equaliˈzation** *or* **-iˈsation** *n.* **—ˈequalize** *or* **-ise** *v.* make, become, equal **—ˈequally** *adv.*

equanimity (iːkwəˈnɪmɪtɪ, ɛkwə-) *n.* calmness, composure, steadiness

equate (ɪˈkweɪt) *vt.* **1.** make equal **2.** bring to a common standard **—equation** (ɪˈkweɪʒən, -ʃən) *n.* **1.**

THESAURUS

epigram bon mot, quip, witticism

epilogue afterword, coda, concluding speech, conclusion, postscript

episode **1.** adventure, affair, business, circumstance, event, experience, happening, incident, matter, occurrence **2.** chapter, instalment, part, passage, scene, section

epistle communication, letter, message, missive, note

epithet appellation, description, designation, name, nickname, sobriquet, tag, title

epitome **1.** archetype, embodiment, essence, exemplar, personification, quintessence, representation, type, typical example **2.** abbreviation, abridgment, abstract, compendium, condensation, conspectus, contraction, digest, précis, résumé, summary, syllabus, synopsis

epitomize embody, exemplify, illustrate, incarnate, personify, represent, symbolize, typify

epoch age, date, era, period, time

equable **1.** agreeable, calm, composed, easy-going, even-tempered, imperturbable, level-headed, placid, serene, temperate, unexcitable, unflappable (*Inf.*), unruffled **2.** consistent, constant, even, regular, smooth, stable, steady, temperate, tranquil, unchanging, uniform, unvarying

equal *adj.* **1.** alike, commensurate, equivalent, identical, like, one and the same, proportionate, tantamount, the same, uniform **2.** balanced, corresponding, even, evenly balanced, evenly matched, evenly proportioned, fifty-fifty (*Inf.*), level pegging (*Brit. inf.*), matched, regular, symmetrical, uniform, unvarying **3.** able, adequate, capable, competent, fit, good enough, ready, strong enough, suitable, up to **4.** egalitarian, equable, even-handed, fair, impartial, just, unbiased ~*n.* **5.** brother, compeer, counterpart, equivalent, fellow, match, mate, parallel, peer, rival, sister, twin ~*v.* **6.** agree with, amount to, balance, be equal to, be even with, be level with, be tantamount to, come up to, correspond to, equalize, equate, even, level, match, parallel, rival, square with, tally with, tie with

equality balance, coequality, correspondence, egalitarianism, equal opportunity, equatability, equivalence, evenness, fairness, identity, likeness, parity, sameness, similarity, uniformity

equalize balance, equal, equate, even up, level, make equal, match, regularize, smooth, square, standardize

equate agree, balance, be commensurate, compare, correspond with *or* to, equalize, liken, make *or* be equal, match, offset, pair, parallel, square, tally, think of together

equation agreement, balancing, comparison, correspondence, equality, equalization, equating, equivalence, likeness, match, pairing, parallel

equating of two mathematical expressions **2.** balancing

equator (ɪˈkweɪtə) *n.* imaginary circle round earth equidistant from the poles —**equaˈtorial** *a.*

equerry (ɪˈkwɛrɪ) *n.* **1.** officer in attendance on sovereign **2.** officer in royal household in charge of horses

equestrian (ɪˈkwɛstrɪən) *a.* **1.** of, skilled in, horseriding **2.** mounted on horse —*n.* **3.** rider

equi- (*comb. form*) equal, at equal, as in *equidistant.* Such words are not given here where the meaning can easily be inferred from the simple word

equiangular (iːkwɪˈæŋgjʊlə) *a.* having equal angles

equilateral (iːkwɪˈlætərəl) *a.* having equal sides

equilibrium (iːkwɪˈlɪbrɪəm) *n.* state of steadiness, equipoise or stability (*pl.* **-s, -ria** (-rɪə))

equine (ˈɛkwaɪn) *a.* of, like a horse

equinox (ˈiːkwɪnɒks) *n.* **1.** time when sun crosses equator and day and night are equal —*pl.* **2.** points at which sun crosses equator —**equinoctial** (iːkwɪˈnɒkʃəl) *a.*

equip (ɪˈkwɪp) *vt.* supply, fit out, array (**-pp-**) —**equipage** (ˈɛkwɪpɪdʒ) *n.* **1.** carriage, horses and attendants **2.** *obs.* outfit, requisites —**eˈquipment** *n.*

equipoise (ˈɛkwɪpɔɪz) *n.* **1.** perfect balance **2.** counterpoise **3.** equanimity —*vt.* **4.** counterbalance

equitation (ɛkwɪˈteɪʃən) *n.* study and practice of riding and horsemanship

equity (ˈɛkwɪtɪ) *n.* **1.** fairness **2.** use of principles of justice to supplement law **3.** system of law so made —**ˈequitable** *a.* fair, reasonable, just —**ˈequitably** *adv.*

equiv. equivalent

equivalent (ɪˈkwɪvələnt) *a.* **1.** equal in value **2.** having the same meaning or result **3.** tantamount **4.** corresponding —**eˈquivalence** *or* **eˈquivalency** *n.*

equivocal (ɪˈkwɪvək°l) *a.* **1.** of double or doubtful meaning **2.** questionable **3.** liable to suspicion —**equivoˈcality** *n.* —**eˈquivocate** *vi.* use equivocal words to mislead —**equivoˈcation** *n.* —**eˈquivocator** *n.*

er (ə, ɜː) *interj.* sound made when hesitating in speech

Er *Chem.* erbium

E.R. Elizabeth Regina (*Lat.*, Queen Elizabeth)

-er[1] (*comb. form*) **1.** person or thing that performs specified action, as in *reader* **2.** person engaged in profession *etc.*, as in *writer* **3.** native or inhabitant of, as in *Londoner* **4.** person or thing having certain characteristic, as in *newcomer*

-er[2] (*comb. form*) forming comparative degree of adjective or adverb, as in *deeper, faster*

era (ˈɪərə) *n.* **1.** system of time in which years are numbered from particular event **2.** time of the event **3.** memorable date, period

eradicate (ɪˈrædɪkeɪt) *vt.* **1.** wipe out, exterminate **2.** root out —**eˈradicable** *a.* —**eradiˈcation** *n.* —**eˈradicative** *a./n.* —**eˈradicator** *n.*

erase (ɪˈreɪz) *vt.* **1.** rub out **2.** remove, *eg* recording from magnetic tape —**eˈraser** *n.* —**eˈrasure** *n.*

erbium (ˈɜːbɪəm) *n.* metallic element of the lanthanide series

ere (ɛə) *prep./conj.* **1.** *Poet.* before **2.** sooner than —**ereˈlong** *adv. obs., poet.* before long; soon

erect (ɪˈrɛkt) *a.* **1.** upright —*vt.* **2.** set up **3.** build —**eˈrectile** *a.* —**eˈrection** *n.* —**eˈrector** *n.*

eremite (ˈɛrɪmaɪt) *n.* Christian hermit or recluse —**eremitic(al)** (ɛrɪˈmɪtɪk(°l)) *a.* —**ˈeremitism** *n.*

erg (ɜːg) *n.* cgs unit of work or energy

ergo (ˈɜːgəʊ) *adv.* therefore

ergonomics (ɜːgəˈnɒmɪks) *pl.n.* (*with sing. v.*) study of relationship between workers and their environment

ergot (ˈɜːgət, -gɒt) *n.* **1.** disease of grain **2.** diseased

THESAURUS

equestrian 1. *adj.* in the saddle, mounted, on horseback **2.** *n.* cavalier (*Archaic*), horseman, knight, rider

equilibrium 1. balance, counterpoise, equipoise, evenness, rest, stability, steadiness, symmetry **2.** calm, calmness, collectedness, composure, coolness, equanimity, poise, self-possession, serenity, stability, steadiness

equip accoutre, arm, array, attire, deck out, dress, endow, fit out, fit up, furnish, kit out, outfit, prepare, provide, rig, stock, supply

equipment accoutrements, apparatus, appurtenances, baggage, equipage, furnishings, furniture, gear, materiel, outfit, paraphernalia, rig, stuff, supplies, tackle, tools

equitable candid, disinterested, dispassionate, due, even-handed, fair, honest, impartial, just, nondiscriminatory, proper, proportionate, reasonable, right, rightful, unbiased, unprejudiced

equity disinterestedness, equitableness, evenhandedness, fair-mindedness, fairness, fair play, honesty, impartiality, integrity, justice, reasonableness, rectitude, righteousness, uprightness

equivalence agreement, alikeness, conformity, correspondence, equality, evenness, identity, interchangeableness, likeness, match, parallel, parity, sameness, similarity, synonymy

equivalent *adj.* alike, commensurate, comparable, correspondent, corresponding, equal, even, homologous, interchangeable, of a kind, same, similar, synonymous, tantamount

equivocal ambiguous, ambivalent, doubtful, dubious, evasive, indefinite, indeterminate, misleading, oblique, obscure, questionable, suspicious, uncertain, vague

era age, cycle, date, day *or* days, epoch, generation, period, stage, time

eradicate abolish, annihilate, deracinate, destroy, efface, eliminate, erase, expunge, exterminate, extinguish, extirpate, obliterate, remove, root out, stamp out, uproot, weed out, wipe out

eradication abolition, annihilation, deracination, destruction, effacement, elimination, erasure, expunction, extermination, extinction, extirpation, obliteration, removal

erase blot, cancel, delete, efface, expunge, obliterate, remove, rub out, scratch out, wipe out

erect *adj.* **1.** elevated, firm, perpendicular, pricked-up, raised, rigid, standing, stiff, straight, upright, vertical ~*v.* **2.** build, construct, elevate, lift, mount, pitch, put up, raise, rear, set up, stand up **3.** create, establish, form, found, initiate, institute, organize, set up

erection assembly, building, construction, creation, elevation, establishment, fabrication, manufacture

seed used as drug —ˈ**ergotism** *n.* disease caused by eating ergot-infested bread

erica (ˈɛrɪkə) *n.* genus of plants including heathers

Erin (ˈɪərɪn, ˈɛərɪn) *n. obs., poet.* Ireland

ermine (ˈɜːmɪn) *n.* **1.** stoat in northern regions, *esp.* in winter **2.** its white winter fur

erne *or* **ern** (ɜːn) *n.* fish-eating sea eagle

Ernie (ˈɜːnɪ) *n.* **UK** computer that randomly selects winning numbers of Premium Bonds (*E*lectronic *R*andom *N*umber *I*ndicator *E*quipment)

erode (ɪˈrəʊd) *v.* **1.** wear away —*vt.* **2.** eat into —**eˈrosion** *n.* —**eˈrosive** *a.*

erogenous (ɪˈrɒdʒɪnəs) *or* **erogenic** (ɛrəˈdʒɛnɪk) *a.* sensitive to sexual stimulation

erotic (ɪˈrɒtɪk) *a.* relating to, or treating of, sexual pleasure —**eˈrotica** *n.* sexual literature or art —**eˈroticism** *n.*

err (ɜː) *vi.* **1.** make mistakes **2.** be wrong **3.** sin —**erˈratic** *a.* irregular in movement, conduct *etc.* —**erˈratically** *adv.* —**erratum** (ɪˈrɑːtəm) *n.* printing mistake noted for correction (*pl.* **-ta** (-tə)) —**erˈroneous** *a.* mistaken, wrong —ˈ**error** *n.* **1.** mistake **2.** wrong opinion **3.** sin

errand (ˈɛrənd) *n.* **1.** short journey for simple business **2.** purpose of such journey **3.** the business, mission of messenger —**errand boy**

errant (ˈɛrənt) *a.* **1.** wandering in search of adventure **2.** erring —ˈ**errancy** *n.* erring state or conduct —ˈ**errantry** *n.* state or conduct of knight errant

ersatz (ˈɛəzæts, ˈɜː-) *a.* substitute, imitation

Erse (ɜːs) *n.* **1.** *see* **Gaelic** *at* GAEL —*a.* **2.** of or relating to Gaelic language

erst (ɜːst) *adv.* of old, formerly

eruct (ɪˈrʌkt) *or* **eructate** *v.* **1.** belch **2.** (of volcano) pour out (fumes or volcanic matter) —**erucˈtation** *n.*

erudite (ˈɛrʊdaɪt) *a.* learned —**erudition** (ɛrʊˈdɪʃən) *n.* learning

erupt (ɪˈrʌpt) *vi.* burst out —**eˈruption** *n.* **1.** bursting out, *esp.* volcanic outbreak **2.** rash on the skin —**eˈruptive** *a.*

-ery *or* **-ry** (*comb. form*) **1.** place of business or activity, as in *bakery, refinery* **2.** class or collection of things, as in *cutlery* **3.** qualities, actions, as in *snobbery, trickery* **4.** practice, occupation, as in *husbandry* **5.** state, condition, as in *slavery*

erysipelas (ɛrɪˈsɪpɪləs) *n.* acute skin infection

erythema (ɛrɪˈθiːmə) *n.* patchy inflammation of skin —**erythematic** (ɛrɪθɪˈmætɪk) *or* **eryˈthematous** *a.*

erythrocyte (ɪˈrɪθrəʊsaɪt) *n.* red blood cell of vertebrates that transports oxygen and carbon dioxide —**erythrocytic** (ɪrɪθrəʊˈsɪtɪk) *a.*

Es *Chem.* einsteinium

escalate (ˈɛskəleɪt) *v.* increase, be increased, in extent, intensity *etc.*

escalator (ˈɛskəleɪtə) *n.* moving staircase —**escalator clause** clause in contract stipulating adjustment in wages *etc.* in event of large rise in cost of living *etc.*

escallop (ɛˈskɒləp, ɛˈskæl-) *see* SCALLOP

escalope (ˈɛskəlɒp) *n.* thin slice of meat, usu. veal

escape (ɪˈskeɪp) *vi.* **1.** get free **2.** get off safely **3.** go unpunished **4.** find way out —*vt.* **5.** elude **6.** be forgotten by —*n.* **7.** escaping —**escapade** (ˈɛskəpeɪd, ɛskəˈpeɪd) *n.* wild (mischievous) adventure —**esˈcapement** *n.* **1.** mechanism consisting of toothed wheel and anchor, used in timepieces to provide periodic impulses to pendulum or balance **2.** any similar mechanism that regulates movement —**esˈcapism** *n.* taking refuge in fantasy to avoid facing disagreeable facts —**escapologist** (ɛskəˈpɒlədʒɪst) *n.* entertainer specializing in freeing himself from confinement —**escape road** road provided on hill for driver to drive into if his brakes fail —**escape velocity** minimum velocity necessary for a body to escape from the gravitational field of the earth *etc.*

THESAURUS

erode abrade, consume, corrode, destroy, deteriorate, disintegrate, eat away, grind down, spoil, wear down *or* away

erosion abrasion, attrition, consumption, corrasion, corrosion, destruction, deterioration, disintegration, eating away, grinding down, spoiling, wear, wearing down *or* away

erotic amatory, aphrodisiac, carnal, erogenous, rousing, seductive, sensual, sexy (*Inf.*), stimulating, suggestive, titillating, voluptuous

err 1. be inaccurate, be incorrect, be in error, blunder, go astray, go wrong, make a mistake, misapprehend, miscalculate, misjudge, mistake, slip up (*Inf.*) **2.** deviate, do wrong, fall, go astray, lapse, misbehave, offend, sin, transgress, trespass

errand charge, commission, job, message, mission, task

erratic aberrant, abnormal, capricious, changeable, desultory, eccentric, fitful, inconsistent, irregular, shifting, unpredictable, unreliable, unstable, variable, wayward

erroneous amiss, fallacious, false, faulty, flawed, inaccurate, incorrect, inexact, invalid, mistaken, spurious, unfounded, unsound, untrue, wrong

error 1. bloomer (*Inf.*), blunder, boner (*Sl.*), boob (*Sl.*), delusion, erratum, fallacy, fault, flaw, howler (*Inf.*), inaccuracy, misapprehension, miscalculation, misconception, mistake, oversight, slip, solecism **2.** delinquency, deviation, fault, lapse, misdeed, offence, sin, transgression, trespass, wrong, wrongdoing

erudite cultivated, cultured, educated, knowledgeable, learned, lettered, literate, scholarly, well-educated, well-read

erupt be ejected, belch forth, blow up, break out, burst forth, burst into, burst out, discharge, explode, flare up, gush, pour forth, spew forth *or* out, spit out, spout, throw off, vent, vomit

eruption 1. discharge, ejection, explosion, flare-up, outbreak, outburst, sally, venting **2.** *Medical* inflammation, outbreak, rash

escalate amplify, ascend, be increased, enlarge, expand, extend, grow, heighten, increase, intensify, magnify, mount, raise, rise, step up

escapade adventure, antic, caper, fling, lark (*Inf.*), mischief, prank, romp, scrape (*Inf.*), spree, stunt, trick

escape *v.* **1.** abscond, bolt, break free *or* out, decamp, do a bunk (*Sl.*), flee, fly, get away, make *or* effect one's escape, make one's getaway, run away *or* off, skip, slip away ~*n.* **2.** bolt, break, break-out, decampment, flight, getaway ~*v.* **3.** avoid, circumvent, dodge, duck, elude, evade, pass, shun, slip ~*n.* **4.**

escarp (ɪˈskɑːp) *n.* steep bank under rampart —**esˈcarpment** *n.* **1.** steep hillside **2.** escarp

-escent (*a. comb. form*) beginning to be, do, show *etc.*, as in *convalescent, luminescent* —**-escence** (*n. comb. form*)

eschatology (ɛskəˈtɒlədʒɪ) *n.* study of death, judgment and last things —**eschatoˈlogical** *a.*

escheat (ɪsˈtʃiːt) *Law n.* **1.** before 1926, reversion of property to Crown in absence of legal heirs **2.** property so reverting —*v.* **3.** take (land) by escheat or (of land) revert by escheat —**esˈcheatable** *a.* —**esˈcheatage** *n.*

eschew (ɪsˈtʃuː) *vt.* avoid, abstain from, shun

eschscholtzia (ɪsˈkɒlʃə) *n.* garden plant with bright flowers, California poppy

escort (ˈɛskɔːt) *n.* **1.** armed guard for traveller *etc.* **2.** person or persons accompanying another —*vt.* (ɪsˈkɔːt) **3.** accompany or attend as escort

escritoire (ɛskrɪˈtwɑː) *n.* type of writing desk

esculent (ˈɛskjʊlənt) *a.* edible

escutcheon (ɪˈskʌtʃən) *n.* **1.** shield with coat of arms **2.** ornamental plate round keyhole *etc.* —**blot on one's escutcheon** stain on one's honour

-ese (*comb. form*) place of origin, language, style, as in *Cantonese, Japanese, journalese*

Eskimo (ˈɛskɪməʊ) *n.* **1.** one of aboriginal race inhabiting N Amer., Greenland *etc.* (*pl.* **-s**) **2.** their language

E.S.N. educationally subnormal

esoteric (ɛsəʊˈtɛrɪk) *a.* **1.** abstruse, obscure **2.** secret **3.** restricted to initiates

E.S.P. extrasensory perception

esp. especially

espadrille (ɛspəˈdrɪl) *n.* canvas shoe, *esp.* with braided cord sole

espalier (ɪˈspæljə) *n.* **1.** shrub, (fruit) tree trained to grow flat, as against wall *etc.* **2.** trellis for this

esparto *or* **esparto grass** (ɛˈspɑːtəʊ) *n.* kind of grass yielding fibre used for making rope *etc.*

especial (ɪˈspɛʃəl) *a.* **1.** pre-eminent, more than ordinary **2.** particular —**esˈpecially** *adv.*

Esperanto (ɛspəˈræntəʊ) *n.* artificial language designed for universal use —**Espeˈrantist** *n.* one who uses Esperanto

espionage (ˈɛspɪənɑːʒ) *n.* **1.** spying **2.** use of secret agents

esplanade (ɛspləˈneɪd) *n.* level space, *esp.* one used as public promenade

espouse (ɪˈspaʊz) *vt.* **1.** support, embrace (cause *etc.*) **2.** *obs.* marry —**esˈpousal** *n.*

espresso (ɛˈsprɛsəʊ) *n.* strong coffee made by forcing steam through ground coffee beans

esprit (ɛˈspriː) *n.* **1.** spirit **2.** animation —**esprit de corps** (də ˈkɔː) attachment, loyalty to the society *etc.* one belongs to

espy (ɪˈspaɪ) *vt.* catch sight of (**esˈpied, esˈpying**) —**esˈpial** *n.* observation

Esq. Esquire

-esque (*comb. form*) specified character, manner, style or resemblance, as in *picturesque, Romanesque, statuesque*

esquire (ɪˈskwaɪə) *n.* **1.** gentleman's courtesy title used on letters **2.** formerly, squire

ESRO (ˈɛzrəʊ) European Space Research Organization

-ess (*comb. form*) female, as in *actress*

essay (ˈɛseɪ; *def. 3 also* ɛˈseɪ) *n.* **1.** prose composition **2.** short treatise **3.** attempt —*vt.* (ɛˈseɪ) **4.** try, attempt **5.** test (**esˈsayed, esˈsaying**) —**ˈessayist** *n.*

essence (ˈɛsᵊns) *n.* **1.** all that makes thing what it is **2.** existence, being **3.** entity, reality **4.** extract got by distillation —**esˈsential** *a.* **1.** necessary, indispensable **2.** inherent **3.** of, constituting essence of thing —*n.* **4.** indispensable element **5.** chief point —**essentiˈality** *n.* —**essential oil** any of various volatile oils in plants, having odour *etc.* of plant from which they are extracted

E.S.T. C, US Eastern Standard Time

est. **1.** established **2.** estimate(d)

THESAURUS

avoidance, circumvention, elusion, evasion ~*v.* **5.** baffle, be beyond (someone), be forgotten by, elude, puzzle, stump

escort *n.* **1.** bodyguard, company, convoy, cortege, entourage, guard, protection, retinue, safeguard, train **2.** attendant, beau, chaperon, companion, guide, partner, protector, squire (*Rare*) ~*v.* **3.** accompany, chaperon, conduct, convoy, guard, guide, lead, partner, protect, shepherd, squire, usher

especial **1.** chief, distinguished, exceptional, extraordinary, marked, notable, noteworthy, outstanding, principal, signal, special, uncommon, unusual **2.** exclusive, express, individual, particular, peculiar, personal, private, singular, special, specific, unique

especially **1.** chiefly, conspicuously, exceptionally, extraordinarily, mainly, markedly, notably, outstandingly, principally, remarkably, signally, specially, strikingly, supremely, uncommonly, unusually **2.** exclusively, expressly, particularly, peculiarly, singularly, specifically, uniquely

espionage counter-intelligence, intelligence, spying, undercover work

espousal **1.** adoption, advocacy, backing, championing, championship, defence, embracing, maintenance, support, taking up **2.** *Archaic* affiancing, betrothal, betrothing (*Archaic*), engagement, espousing (*Archaic*), marriage, nuptials, plighting, wedding

espouse **1.** adopt, advocate, back, champion, defend, embrace, maintain, stand up for, support, take up **2.** *Archaic* betroth (*Archaic*), marry, take as spouse, take to wife, wed

essay article, composition, discourse, disquisition, dissertation, paper, piece, tract

essence **1.** being, core, crux, entity, heart, kernel, life, lifeblood, meaning, nature, pith, principle, quiddity, quintessence, significance, soul, spirit, substance **2.** concentrate, distillate, elixir, extract, spirits, tincture

essential *adj.* **1.** crucial, important, indispensable, necessary, needed, requisite, vital **2.** basic, cardinal, constitutional, elemental, elementary, fundamental, inherent, innate, intrinsic, key, main, principal **3.** absolute, complete, ideal, perfect, quintessential **4.** concentrated, distilled, extracted, rectified, refined, volatile ~*n.* **5.** basic, fundamental, must, necessity, prerequisite, principle, requisite, rudiment, *sine qua non*, vital part

-est (*comb. form*) forming superlative degree of adjective or adverb, as in *fastest*

establish (ɪˈstæblɪʃ) *vt.* **1.** make secure **2.** set up **3.** settle **4.** prove —**esˈtablishment** *n.* **1.** permanent organized body, full number of regiment *etc.* **2.** household **3.** business **4.** public institution —**Established Church** church officially recognized as national institution —**the Establishment** group, class of people holding authority within a society

estate (ɪˈsteɪt) *n.* **1.** landed property **2.** person's property **3.** area of property development, *esp.* of houses or factories **4.** class as part of nation **5.** rank, state, condition of life —**estate agent** one who sells houses *etc.* for others —**estate car** car with rear door and luggage space behind rear seats —**estate duty** *see* **death duty** *at* DEATH

esteem (ɪˈstiːm) *vt.* **1.** think highly of **2.** consider —*n.* **3.** favourable opinion, regard, respect

ester (ˈɛstə) *n. Chem.* organic compound produced by reaction between acid and alcohol

estimate (ˈɛstɪmeɪt) *vt.* **1.** form approximate idea of (amounts, measurements *etc.*) **2.** form opinion of **3.** quote probable price for —*n.* (ˈɛstɪmɪt) **4.** approximate judgment of amounts *etc.* **5.** amount *etc.* arrived at **6.** opinion **7.** price quoted by contractor —**ˈestimable** *a.* worthy of regard —**estiˈmation** *n.* **1.** opinion, judgment **2.** esteem

estrange (ɪˈstreɪndʒ) *vt.* **1.** lose affection of **2.** alienate —**esˈtrangement** *n.*

estuary (ˈɛstjʊərɪ) *n.* tidal mouth of river, inlet —**ˈestuarine** *a.*

-et (*comb. form*) small, lesser, as in *islet, baronet*

eta (ˈiːtə) *n.* seventh letter in Gr. alphabet (H, η)

E.T.A. estimated time of arrival

et al. **1.** et alibi (*Lat.*, and elsewhere) **2.** et alii (*Lat.*, and others)

etc. et cetera

et cetera (ɪt ˈsɛtrə) *Lat.* and the rest, and others, and so on —**etˈceteras** *pl.n.* miscellaneous extras

etch (ɛtʃ) *v.* **1.** make (engraving) by eating away surface of metal plate with acids *etc.* —*vt.* **2.** imprint vividly —**ˈetcher** *n.* —**ˈetching** *n.*

eternal (ɪˈtɜːnˀl) *a.* **1.** without beginning or end **2.** everlasting **3.** changeless —**eˈternally** *adv.* —**eˈternity** *n.* —**eternal triangle** emotional relationship in which there are conflicts involving a man and two women or a woman and two men —**eternity ring** ring, *esp.* one set all around with stones to symbolize continuity

ethane (ˈiːθeɪn, ˈɛθ-) *n.* odourless flammable gaseous alkane obtained from natural gas and petroleum

ether (ˈiːθə) *n.* **1.** colourless volatile liquid used as anaesthetic **2.** intangible fluid formerly supposed to fill all space **3.** the clear sky, region above clouds —**ethereal** (ɪˈθɪərɪəl) *a.* **1.** light, airy **2.** heavenly, spiritlike —**ethereality** (ɪθɪərɪˈælɪtɪ) *n.* —**etherealiˈzation** *or* **-iˈsation** *n.* —**etherealize** *or* **-ise** (ɪˈθɪərɪəlaɪz) *vt.* **1.** make or regard as being ethereal **2.** add ether to or make into ether

ethic (ˈɛθɪk) *or* **ethical** *a.* relating to morals —**ˈethically** *adv.* —**ˈethics** *pl.n.* **1.** (*with sing. v.*) science of morals **2.** moral principles, rules of conduct

THESAURUS

establish **1.** base, constitute, create, decree, enact, ensconce, entrench, fix, form, found, ground, implant, inaugurate, install, institute, organize, plant, root, secure, settle, set up, start **2.** authenticate, certify, confirm, corroborate, demonstrate, prove, ratify, show, substantiate, validate, verify

establishment **1.** business, company, concern, corporation, enterprise, firm, house, institute, institution, organization, outfit (*Inf.*), setup (*Inf.*), structure, system **2.** abode, domicile, dwelling, home, house, household, residence **3. the Establishment** established order, institutionalized authority, ruling class, the powers that be, the system

estate **1.** area, demesne, domain, holdings, lands, manor, property **2.** *Property law* assets, belongings, effects, fortune, goods, possessions, property, wealth **3.** caste, class, order, rank **4.** condition, lot, period, place, position, quality, rank, situation, standing, state, station, status

esteem *v.* **1.** admire, be fond of, cherish, honour, like, love, prize, regard highly, respect, revere, reverence, think highly of, treasure, value, venerate **2.** *Formal* account, believe, calculate, consider, deem, estimate, hold, judge, rate, reckon, regard, think, view ~*n.* **3.** admiration, consideration, credit, estimation, good opinion, honour, regard, respect, reverence, veneration

estimate *v.* **1.** appraise, assess, calculate roughly, evaluate, gauge, guess, judge, number, reckon, value **2.** assess, believe, conjecture, consider, form an opinion, guess, judge, rank, rate, reckon, surmise, think ~*n.* **3.** appraisal, appraisement, approximate calculation, assessment, evaluation, guess, guesstimate (*Inf.*), judgment, reckoning, valuation **4.** appraisal, appraisement, assessment, belief, conjecture, educated guess, estimation, judgment, opinion, surmise, thought(s)

estimation **1.** appraisal, appreciation, assessment, belief, consideration, considered opinion, estimate, evaluation, judgment, opinion, view **2.** admiration, credit, esteem, good opinion, honour, regard, respect, reverence, veneration

estrange alienate, antagonize, disaffect, disunite, divide, drive apart, lose *or* destroy the affection of, make hostile, part, separate, set at odds, withdraw, withhold

estrangement alienation, antagonization, breach, break-up, disaffection, dissociation, disunity, division, hostility, parting, separation, split, withdrawal, withholding

estuary creek, firth, fjord, inlet, mouth

et cetera and others, and so forth, and so on, and the like, and the rest, et al.

etch carve, corrode, cut, eat into, engrave, furrow, impress, imprint, incise, ingrain, inscribe, stamp

etching carving, engraving, impression, imprint, inscription, print

eternal **1.** abiding, ceaseless, constant, deathless, endless, everlasting, immortal, infinite, interminable, never-ending, perennial, perpetual, sempiternal (*Literary*), timeless, unceasing, undying, unending, unremitting, without end **2.** deathless, enduring, everlasting, immortal, immutable, imperishable, indestructible, lasting, permanent

eternity age, ages, endlessness, for ever, immortality, infinitude, infinity, perpetuity, timelessness, time without end

Ethiopian (iːθɪˈəʊpɪən) *a.* 1. of Ethiopia (state in NE Afr.) —*n.* 2. native of Ethiopia 3. any of languages of Ethiopia, *esp.* Amharic —*n./a.* 4. *obs.* Negro

ethnic (ˈɛθnɪk) *or* **ethnical** *a.* of race or relating to classification of humans into social, cultural *etc.*, groups —**ethnoˈgraphic** *a.* —**ethˈnography** *n.* description of races of men —**ethnoˈlogical** *a.* —**ethˈnology** *n.* the study of human races

ethos (ˈiːθɒs) *n.* distinctive character, spirit *etc.* of people, culture *etc.*

ethyl (ˈiːθaɪl, ˈɛθɪl) *n.* (C_2H_5) radical of ordinary alcohol and ether —**ethylene** (ˈɛθɪliːn) *n.* poisonous gas used as anaesthetic and fuel —**ethyl alcohol** *see* ALCOHOL (sense 1)

etiolate (ˈiːtɪəʊleɪt) *v.* 1. *Bot.* whiten (green plant) through lack of sunlight 2. (cause to) become pale and weak —**etioˈlation** *n.*

etiquette (ˈɛtɪkɛt, ɛtɪˈkɛt) *n.* conventional code of conduct or behaviour

Eton collar (ˈiːtʼn) broad stiff white collar worn outside Eton jacket

Eton crop short mannish hair style worn by women in 1920s

Eton jacket waist-length jacket, open in front, formerly worn by pupils of Eton College, public school for boys in S England

Etruscan (ɪˈtrʌskən) *or* **Etrurian** (ɪˈtrʊərɪən) *n.* 1. member of ancient people of Etruria in central Italy 2. language of ancient Etruscans —*a.* 3. of Etruria, Etruscans, their culture or their language

et seq. 1. et sequens (*Lat.*, and the following) 2. (*also* **et seqq.**) et sequentia (*Lat.*, and those that follow)

-ette (*comb. form*) 1. small, as in *cigarette* 2. female, as in *majorette* 3. imitation, as in *Leatherette*

étude (ˈeɪtjuːd) *n.* short musical composition, study, intended often as technical exercise

ety., etym., *or* **etymol.** 1. etymological 2. etymology

etymology (ɛtɪˈmɒlədʒɪ) *n.* 1. tracing, account of, formation of word's origin, development 2. science of this —**etymoˈlogical** *a.* —**etymoˈlogically** *adv.* —**etyˈmologist** *n.*

Eu *Chem.* europium

eu- (*comb. form*) well, as in *eugenic, euphony*

eucalyptus (juːkəˈlɪptəs) *or* **eucalypt** (ˈjuːkəlɪpt) *n.* mostly Aust. genus of tree, the gum tree, yielding timber and oil, used medicinally from leaves

Eucharist (ˈjuːkərɪst) *n.* 1. Christian sacrament of the Lord's Supper 2. the consecrated elements —**Euchaˈristic** *a.*

Euclidean *or* **Euclidian** (juːˈklɪdɪən) *a.* denoting system of geometry based on axioms of Gr. mathematician Euclid

eugenic (juːˈdʒɛnɪk) *a.* relating to, or tending towards, production of fine offspring —**euˈgenicist** *n.* —**euˈgenics** *pl.n.* (*with sing. v.*) this science

eulogy (ˈjuːlədʒɪ) *n.* 1. speech or writing in praise of person 2. praise —**ˈeulogist** *n.* —**euloˈgistic** *a.* —**euloˈgistically** *adv.* —**ˈeulogize** *or* **-ise** *v.*

eunuch (ˈjuːnək) *n.* castrated man, *esp.* formerly one employed in harem

euphemism (ˈjuːfɪmɪzəm) *n.* 1. substitution of mild term for offensive or hurtful one 2. instance of this —**ˈeuphemist** *n.* —**eupheˈmistic** *a.* —**eupheˈmistically** *adv.* —**ˈeuphemize** *or* **-ise** *v.*

euphony (ˈjuːfənɪ) *n.* pleasantness of sound —**euphonic** (juːˈfɒnɪk) *or* **euphonious** (juːˈfəʊnɪəs) *a.* pleasing to ear —**euphonium** (juːˈfəʊnɪəm) *n.* brass musical instrument, bass-tenor tuba

euphoria (juːˈfɔːrɪə) *n.* sense of wellbeing or elation —**euphoric** (juːˈfɒrɪk) *a.*

euphuism (ˈjuːfjuːɪzəm) *n.* affected high-flown manner of writing, *esp.* in imitation of Lyly's *Euphues* (1580) —**euphuˈistic** *a.*

Eur. Europe(an)

Eurasian (jʊəˈreɪʃən, -ʒən) *a.* 1. of mixed European and Asiatic descent 2. of Europe and Asia —*n.* 3. one of this descent

Euratom (jʊəˈrætəm) *n.* European Atomic Energy Community

eureka (jʊˈriːkə) *interj.* exclamation of triumph at finding something

eurhythmics *or esp. U.S.* **eurythmics** (juːˈrɪðmɪks) *pl.n.* (*with sing. v.*) system of training through physical movement to music —**euˈrhythmy** *or* **euˈrythmy** *n.*

Euro- (ˈjʊərəʊ-) *or before vowel* **Eur-** (*comb. form*) Europe; European

Eurodollar (ˈjʊərəʊdɒlə) *n.* U.S. dollar as part of European holding

European (jʊərəˈpɪən) *n./a.* (native) of Europe —**European Atomic Energy Commission** authority established by Common Market to develop peaceful uses of nuclear energy —**European Economic Community** association of a number of European nations for trade

europium (jʊˈrəʊpɪəm) *n.* silvery-white element of the lanthanide series

eurythmics (juːˈrɪðmɪks) *n. esp.* US *see* EURHYTHMICS

Eustachian tube (juːˈsteɪʃən) passage leading from pharynx to middle ear

euthanasia (juːθəˈneɪzɪə) *n.* 1. gentle, painless death 2. putting to death in this way, *esp.* to relieve suffering

euthenics (juːˈθɛnɪks) *pl.n.* (*with sing. v.*) science of the relation of environment to human beings

eV electronvolt

evacuate (ɪˈvækjʊeɪt) *vt.* 1. empty 2. (cause to) withdraw 3. discharge —**evacuˈation** *n.* —**evacuˈee** *n.* person moved from danger area, *esp.* in time of war

THESAURUS

ethical conscientious, correct, decent, fair, fitting, good, honest, honourable, just, moral, principled, proper, right, righteous, upright, virtuous

ethics conscience, moral code, morality, moral philosophy, moral values, principles, rules of conduct, standards

ethnic cultural, indigenous, national, native, racial, traditional

etiquette civility, code, convention, courtesy, customs, decorum, formalities, good *or* proper behaviour, manners, politeness, politesse, propriety, protocol, rules, usage

eulogy acclaim, acclamation, accolade, applause, commendation, compliment, encomium, exaltation, glorification, laudation, paean, panegyric, plaudit, praise, tribute

evade (ɪˈveɪd) *vt.* **1.** avoid, escape from **2.** elude —**eˈvasion** *n.* **1.** subterfuge **2.** excuse **3.** equivocation —**eˈvasive** *a.* elusive, not straightforward —**eˈvasively** *adv.*

evaluate (ɪˈvæljʊeɪt) *vt.* find or judge value of —**evaluˈation** *n.*

evanesce (ɛvəˈnɛs) *vi.* fade away —**evaˈnescence** *n.* —**evaˈnescent** *a.* fleeting, transient

evangelical (iːvænˈdʒɛlɪkˀl) *a.* **1.** of, or according to, gospel teaching **2.** of Protestant sect which maintains salvation by faith —*n.* **3.** member of evangelical sect —**evanˈgelicalism** *n.* —**eˈvangelism** *n.* —**eˈvangelist** *n.* **1.** writer of one of the four gospels **2.** ardent, zealous preacher of the gospel **3.** revivalist —**evangeliˈzation** *or* **-iˈsation** *n.* —**eˈvangelize** *or* **-ise** *vt.* **1.** preach gospel to **2.** convert

evaporate (ɪˈvæpəreɪt) *vi.* **1.** turn into, pass off in, vapour —*vt.* **2.** turn into vapour —**evapoˈration** *n.* —**eˈvaporative** *a.* —**eˈvaporator** *n.* —**evaporated milk** thick unsweetened tinned milk from which some of the water has been evaporated

evasion (ɪˈveɪʒən) *n. see* EVADE

eve (iːv) *n.* **1.** evening before (festival *etc.*) **2.** time just before (event *etc.*) **3.** *obs.* evening

even[1] (ˈiːvˀn) *a.* **1.** flat, smooth **2.** uniform in quality, equal in amount, balanced **3.** divisible by two **4.** impartial —*vt.* **5.** make even **6.** smooth **7.** equalize —*adv.* **8.** equally **9.** simply **10.** notwithstanding —**ˈevens** *a./adv.* **1.** (of bet) winning identical sum if successful **2.** (of runner) offered at such odds —**even-handed** *a.* fair; impartial —**even-handedly** *adv.* —**evenhandedness** *n.*

even[2] (ˈiːvˀn) *n. obs.* eve; evening —**ˈevensong** *n.* evening prayer

evening (ˈiːvnɪŋ) *n.* **1.** the close of day or early part of night **2.** decline, end —**evening dress** attire for formal occasion during evening —**evening star** planet, usu. Venus, seen in west just after sunset

event (ɪˈvɛnt) *n.* **1.** happening **2.** notable occurrence **3.** issue, result **4.** any one contest in series in sporting programme —**eˈventful** *a.* full of exciting events —**eˈventing** *n. chiefly* **UK** sport of taking part in equestrian competitions, usu. involving cross-country riding, jumping and dressage —**eˈventual** *a.* **1.** resulting in the end **2.** ultimate **3.** final —**eventuˈality** *n.* possible event —**eˈventually** *adv.* —**eˈventuate** *vi.* **1.** turn out **2.** happen **3.** end —**in the event that** if it should happen that

ever (ˈɛvə) *adv.* **1.** always **2.** constantly **3.** at any time —**everˈmore** *adv.* —**ˈevergreen** *n./a.* (tree or shrub) bearing foliage throughout year —**everˈlasting** *a.* **1.** eternal **2.** lasting for an indefinitely long period —**everˈlastingly** *adv.*

THESAURUS

euphoria bliss, ecstasy, elation, exaltation, exhilaration, exultation, glee, high spirits, intoxication, joy, joyousness, jubilation, rapture, transport

evacuate **1.** abandon, clear, decamp, depart, desert, forsake, leave, move out, pull out, quit, relinquish, remove, vacate, withdraw **2.** defecate, discharge, eject, eliminate, empty, excrete, expel, void

evade avoid, circumvent, decline, dodge, duck, elude, escape, escape the clutches of, get away from, shirk, shun, sidestep, steer clear of

evaluate appraise, assay, assess, calculate, estimate, gauge, judge, rank, rate, reckon, size up (*Inf.*), value, weigh

evaluation appraisal, assessment, calculation, estimate, estimation, judgment, opinion, rating, valuation

evanescent brief, ephemeral, fading, fleeting, fugacious, fugitive, impermanent, momentary, passing, short-lived, transient, transitory, vanishing

evaporate dehydrate, desiccate, dry, dry up, vaporize

evaporation dehydration, desiccation, drying, drying up, vaporization

evasion avoidance, circumvention, cop-out (*Sl.*), cunning, dodge, elusion, equivocation, escape, evasiveness, excuse, fudging, obliqueness, pretext, prevarication, ruse, shift, shirking, shuffling, sophism, sophistry, subterfuge, trickery, waffle (*Inf.*)

evasive cagey (*Inf.*), casuistic, casuistical, cunning, deceitful, deceptive, devious, dissembling, elusive, elusory, equivocating, indirect, misleading, oblique, prevaricating, shifty, shuffling, slippery, sophistical, tricky

eve **1.** day before, night before, vigil **2.** brink, edge, point, threshold, verge

even *adj.* **1.** flat, flush, horizontal, level, parallel, plane, plumb, smooth, steady, straight, true, uniform **2.** constant, metrical, regular, smooth, steady, unbroken, uniform, uninterrupted, unvarying, unwavering **3.** coequal, commensurate, comparable, drawn, equal, equalized, equally balanced, fifty-fifty (*Inf.*), identical, level, level pegging (*Brit. inf.*), like, matching, neck and neck, on a par, parallel, similar, square, the same, tied, uniform **4.** balanced, disinterested, dispassionate, equitable, fair, fair and square, impartial, just, unbiased, unprejudiced ~*adv.* **5.** despite, disregarding, in spite of, notwithstanding ~*v.* **6.** *Often followed by* **out** *or* **up** align, balance, become level, equal, equalize, flatten, level, match, regularize, smooth, square, stabilize, steady

even-handed balanced, disinterested, equitable, fair, fair and square, impartial, just, unbiased, unprejudiced

event **1.** adventure, affair, business, circumstance, episode, experience, fact, happening, incident, matter, milestone, occasion, occurrence **2.** conclusion, consequence, effect, end, issue, outcome, result, termination, upshot **3.** bout, competition, contest, game, tournament

eventful active, busy, consequential, critical, crucial, decisive, exciting, fateful, full, historic, important, lively, memorable, momentous, notable, noteworthy, remarkable, significant

eventual concluding, consequent, ensuing, final, future, later, overall, prospective, resulting, ultimate

eventuality case, chance, contingency, event, likelihood, possibility, probability

eventually after all, at the end of the day, finally, in the course of time, in the end, in the long run, one day, some day, some time, sooner or later, ultimately, when all is said and done

ever **1.** at all, at any time (period, point), by any chance, in any case, on any occasion **2.** always, at all times, constantly, continually, endlessly, eternally, everlastingly, evermore, for ever, incessantly, perpetually, relentlessly, to the end of time, unceasingly, unendingly

every (ˈɛvrɪ) *a.* **1.** each of all **2.** all possible —**ˈeverybody** *pron.* —**ˈeveryday** *a.* usual, ordinary —**ˈEveryman** *n.* (*oft.* e-) ordinary person; common man —**ˈeveryone** *pron.* —**ˈeverything** *pron.* —**ˈeverywhere** *adv.* to or in all places

evict (ɪˈvɪkt) *vt.* expel by legal process, turn out —**eˈviction** *n.* —**eˈvictor** *n.*

evident (ˈɛvɪdənt) *a.* plain, obvious —**ˈevidence** *n.* **1.** ground of belief **2.** sign, indication **3.** testimony —*vt.* **4.** indicate, prove —**eviˈdential** *a.* —**ˈevidently** *adv.* —**in evidence** conspicuous

evil (ˈiːvᵊl) *a.* **1.** bad, harmful —*n.* **2.** what is bad or harmful **3.** sin —**ˈevilly** *adv.* —**ˈevildoer** *n.* sinner —**evil-eyed** *a.* —**the evil eye 1.** look superstitiously supposed to have power of inflicting harm *etc.* **2.** power to inflict harm *etc.* by such a look

evince (ɪˈvɪns) *vt.* show, indicate

eviscerate (ɪˈvɪsəreɪt) *vt.* **1.** remove internal organs of **2.** deprive of meaning or significance —**eviscerˈation** *n.* —**eˈviscerator** *n.*

evoke (ɪˈvəʊk) *vt.* **1.** draw forth **2.** call to mind —**evocation** (ɛvəˈkeɪʃən) *n.* —**evocative** (ɪˈvɒkətɪv) *a.*

evolve (ɪˈvɒlv) *v.* **1.** develop or cause to develop gradually —*vi.* **2.** undergo slow changes in process of growth —**evolution** (iːvəˈluːʃən) *n.* **1.** evolving **2.** development of species from earlier forms —**evolutional** (iːvəˈluːʃənᵊl) *a.* —**evolutionary** (iːvəˈluːʃənərɪ) *a.* —**evolutionist** (iːvəˈluːʃənɪst) *n.*

ewe (juː) *n.* female sheep

ewer (ˈjuːə) *n.* pitcher, water jug for washstand

ex[1] (ɛks) *prep.* **1.** *Fin.* excluding; without **2.** *Comm.* without charge to buyer until removed from —**ex cathedra** (kəˈθiːdrə) **1.** with authority **2.** (of papal pronouncements) defined as infallibly true —**ex gratia** (ˈgreɪʃə) given as favour, *esp.* where no legal obligation exists —**ex hypothesi** (haɪˈpɒθəsɪ) in accordance with hypothesis stated —**ex libris** (ˈliːbrɪs) from the library of —**ex officio** (əˈfɪʃɪəʊ, əˈfɪsɪəʊ) by right of position or office —**ex post facto** (ˈfæktəʊ) having retrospective effect

ex[2] (ɛks) *n. inf.* ex-wife, ex-husband *etc.*

ex-, e-, *or* **ef-** (*comb. form*) out from, from, out of, formerly, as in *exclaim, evade, effusive, exodus.* Such words are not given here where the meaning may easily be inferred from the simple word

Ex. Exodus

ex. 1. example **2.** except(ed) **3.** extra

exacerbate (ɪgˈzæsəbeɪt, ɪkˈsæs-) *vt.* **1.** aggravate, make worse **2.** embitter —**exacerˈbation** *n.*

exact (ɪgˈzækt) *a.* **1.** precise, accurate, strictly correct —*vt.* **2.** demand, extort **3.** insist upon **4.** enforce —**exˈacting** *a.* making rigorous or excessive demands —**exˈaction** *n.* **1.** act of exacting **2.** that which is exacted, as excessive work *etc.* **3.** oppressive demand —**exˈactitude** *n.* —**exˈactly** *adv.* —**exˈactness** *n.* **1.** accuracy **2.** precision —**exˈactor** *n.*

THESAURUS

everlasting 1. abiding, deathless, endless, eternal, immortal, imperishable, indestructible, infinite, interminable, never-ending, perpetual, timeless, undying **2.** ceaseless, constant, continual, continuous, endless, incessant, interminable, never-ending, unceasing, uninterrupted, unremitting

evermore always, eternally, ever, for ever, *in perpetuum*, to the end of time

every all, each, each one, the whole number

everybody all and sundry, each one, each person, everyone, every person, one and all, the whole world

everyday accustomed, common, common or garden (*Inf.*), commonplace, conventional, customary, dull, familiar, frequent, habitual, informal, mundane, ordinary, routine, run-of-the-mill, stock, unexceptional, unimaginative, usual, wonted, workaday

everyone all and sundry, each one, each person, everybody, every person, one and all, the whole world

everything all, each thing, the aggregate, the entirety, the lot, the sum, the total, the whole caboodle (*Inf.*), the whole lot

everywhere all around, all over, far and wide *or* near, high and low, in each place, in every place, omnipresent, the world over, to *or* in all places, ubiquitous, ubiquitously

evict boot out (*Inf.*), chuck out (*Inf.*), dislodge, dispossess, eject, expel, kick out (*Inf.*), oust, put out, remove, show the door (to), throw on to the streets, throw out, turf out (*Inf.*), turn out

evidence 1. *n.* affirmation, attestation, averment, confirmation, corroboration, data, declaration, demonstration, deposition, grounds, indication, manifestation, mark, proof, sign, substantiation, testimony, token, witness **2.** *v.* demonstrate, denote, display, evince, exhibit, indicate, manifest, prove, reveal, show, signify, testify to, witness

evident apparent, clear, conspicuous, incontestable, incontrovertible, indisputable, manifest, noticeable, obvious, palpable, patent, perceptible, plain, tangible, unmistakable, visible

evidently clearly, doubtless, doubtlessly, incontestably, incontrovertibly, indisputably, manifestly, obviously, patently, plainly, undoubtedly, unmistakably, without question

evil *adj.* **1.** bad, base, corrupt, depraved, heinous, immoral, iniquitous, maleficent, malevolent, malicious, malignant, nefarious, reprobate, sinful, vicious, vile, villainous, wicked, wrong ~*n.* **2.** badness, baseness, corruption, curse, depravity, heinousness, immorality, iniquity, maleficence, malignity, sin, sinfulness, turpitude, vice, viciousness, villainy, wickedness, wrong, wrongdoing ~*adj.* **3.** baneful (*Archaic*), calamitous, catastrophic, deleterious, destructive, detrimental, dire, disastrous, harmful, hurtful, inauspicious, injurious, mischievous, painful, pernicious, ruinous, sorrowful, unfortunate, unlucky, woeful ~*n.* **4.** affliction, calamity, catastrophe, disaster, harm, hurt, ill, injury, mischief, misery, misfortune, pain, ruin, sorrow, suffering, woe

evoke 1. arouse, awaken, call, excite, give rise to, induce, recall, rekindle, stimulate, stir up, summon up **2.** call forth, educe (*Rare*), elicit, produce, provoke

evolution development, enlargement, evolvement, expansion, growth, increase, maturation, progress, progression, unfolding, unrolling, working out

evolve develop, disclose, educe, elaborate, enlarge, expand, grow, increase, mature, open, progress, unfold, unroll, work out

exact *adj.* **1.** accurate, careful, correct, definite, ex-

exaggerate (ɪgˈzædʒəreɪt) *vt.* **1.** magnify beyond truth, overstate **2.** enlarge **3.** overestimate —**exaggerˈation** *n.* —**exˈaggerative** *a.* —**exˈaggerator** *n.*

exalt (ɪgˈzɔːlt) *vt.* **1.** raise up **2.** praise **3.** make noble, dignify —**exalˈtation** *n.* **1.** an exalting **2.** elevation in rank, dignity or position **3.** rapture

exam (ɪgˈzæm) examination

examine (ɪgˈzæmɪn) *vt.* **1.** investigate **2.** look at closely **3.** ask questions of **4.** test knowledge or proficiency of **5.** inquire into —**examiˈnation** *n.* —**examiˈnee** *n.* —**exˈaminer** *n.*

example (ɪgˈzɑːmpᵊl) *n.* **1.** thing illustrating general rule **2.** specimen **3.** model **4.** warning **5.** precedent **6.** instance

exasperate (ɪgˈzɑːspəreɪt) *vt.* **1.** irritate, enrage **2.** intensify, make worse —**exasperˈation** *n.*

excavate (ˈɛkskəveɪt) *vt.* **1.** hollow out **2.** unearth **3.** make (hole) by digging —**excaˈvation** *n.* —**ˈexcavator** *n.*

exceed (ɪkˈsiːd) *vt.* **1.** be greater than **2.** go beyond **3.** surpass —**exˈceeding** *a.* **1.** very great; exceptional; excessive —*adv.* **2.** *obs.* to a great or unusual degree —**exˈceedingly** *adv.* **1.** very **2.** greatly

excel (ɪkˈsɛl) *vt.* **1.** surpass, be better than —*vi.* **2.** be very good, pre-eminent (-**ll**-) —**ˈexcellence** *n.* —**ˈExcellency** *n.* title borne by viceroys, ambassadors —**ˈexcellent** *a.* very good

THESAURUS

plicit, express, faithful, faultless, identical, literal, methodical, orderly, particular, precise, right, specific, true, unequivocal, unerring, veracious, very **2.** careful, exacting, meticulous, painstaking, punctilious, rigorous, scrupulous, severe, strict ~*v.* **3.** call for, claim, command, compel, demand, extort, extract, force, impose, insist upon, require, squeeze, wrest, wring

exacting demanding, difficult, hard, harsh, imperious, oppressive, painstaking, rigid, rigorous, severe, stern, strict, stringent, taxing, tough, unsparing

exactly *adv.* **1.** accurately, carefully, correctly, definitely, explicitly, faithfully, faultlessly, literally, methodically, precisely, rigorously, scrupulously, severely, strictly, truly, truthfully, unequivocally, unerringly, veraciously **2.** absolutely, bang, explicitly, expressly, indeed, in every respect, just, particularly, precisely, quite, specifically

exactness accuracy, carefulness, correctness, exactitude, faithfulness, faultlessness, nicety, orderliness, painstakingness, preciseness, precision, promptitude, regularity, rigorousness, rigour, scrupulousness, strictness, truth, unequivocalness, veracity

exaggerate amplify, embellish, embroider, emphasize, enlarge, exalt, hyperbolize, inflate, lay it on thick (*Inf.*), magnify, overdo, overemphasize, overestimate, overstate

exaggeration amplification, embellishment, emphasis, enlargement, exaltation, excess, extravagance, hyperbole, inflation, magnification, overemphasis, overestimation, overstatement, pretension, pretentiousness

exalt 1. advance, aggrandize, dignify, elevate, ennoble, honour, promote, raise, upgrade **2.** acclaim, apotheosize, applaud, bless, extol, glorify, idolize, laud, magnify (*Archaic*), pay homage to, pay tribute to, praise, reverence, set on a pedestal, worship

exaltation 1. advancement, aggrandizement, dignity, elevation, eminence, ennoblement, grandeur, high rank, honour, loftiness, prestige, promotion, rise, upgrading **2.** acclaim, acclamation, apotheosis, applause, blessing, extolment, glorification, glory, homage, idolization, laudation, lionization, magnification, panegyric, plaudits, praise, reverence, tribute, worship **3.** bliss, delight, ecstasy, elation, exhilaration, exultation, joy, joyousness, jubilation, rapture, transport

examination analysis, assay, catechism, checkup, exploration, inquiry, inquisition, inspection, interrogation, investigation, observation, perusal, probe, questioning, quiz, research, review, scrutiny, search, study, survey, test, trial

examine 1. analyse, appraise, assay, check, check out, consider, explore, go over *or* through, inspect, investigate, look over, peruse, ponder, pore over, probe, review, scan, scrutinize, sift, study, survey, take stock of, test, vet, weigh **2.** catechize, cross-examine, grill (*Inf.*), inquire, interrogate, question, quiz

example 1. case, case in point, exemplification, illustration, instance, sample, specimen **2.** archetype, exemplar, ideal, illustration, model, paradigm, paragon, pattern, precedent, prototype, standard **3.** admonition, caution, lesson, warning

exasperate aggravate (*Inf.*), anger, annoy, bug (*Inf.*), embitter, enrage, exacerbate, excite, gall, get (*Inf.*), incense, inflame, infuriate, irk, irritate, madden, needle (*Inf.*), nettle, peeve (*Inf.*), pique, provoke, rankle, rile (*Inf.*), rouse, try the patience of, vex

exasperation aggravation (*Inf.*), anger, annoyance, exacerbation, fury, ire (*Literary*), irritation, passion, pique, provocation, rage, vexation, wrath

excavate burrow, cut, delve, dig, dig out, dig up, gouge, hollow, mine, quarry, scoop, trench, tunnel, uncover, unearth

excavation burrow, cavity, cut, cutting, dig, diggings, ditch, dugout, hole, hollow, mine, pit, quarry, shaft, trench, trough

exceed 1. beat, be superior to, better, cap (*Inf.*), eclipse, excel, go beyond, outdistance, outdo, outreach, outrun, outshine, outstrip, overtake, pass, surmount, surpass, top, transcend **2.** go beyond the bounds of, go over the limit of, go over the top, overstep

exceeding enormous, exceptional, excessive, extraordinary, great, huge, pre-eminent, superior, superlative, surpassing, vast

exceedingly enormously, especially, exceptionally, excessively, extraordinarily, extremely, greatly, highly, hugely, inordinately, superlatively, surpassingly, unusually, vastly, very

excel 1. beat, be superior, better, cap (*Inf.*), eclipse, exceed, go beyond, outdo, outrival, outshine, pass, surmount, surpass, top, transcend **2.** be good, be master of, be proficient, be skilful, be talented, predominate, shine, show talent, take precedence

excellence distinction, eminence, fineness, goodness, greatness, high quality, merit, perfection, pre-eminence, purity, superiority, supremacy, transcendence, virtue, worth

excellent A1 (*Inf.*), admirable, capital, champion,

except (ɪk'sɛpt) *prep.* **1.** not including **2.** but —*conj.* **3.** *obs.* unless —*vt.* **4.** leave or take out **5.** exclude —**ex'cepting** *prep.* not including —**ex'ception** *n.* thing excepted, not included in a rule —**ex'ceptionable** *a.* open to objection —**ex'ceptional** *a.* not ordinary, *esp.* much above average —**ex'ceptionally** *adv.* —**take exception** be offended.

excerpt ('ɛksɜːpt) *n.* **1.** quoted or extracted passage from book *etc.* —*vt.* (ɛk'sɜːpt) **2.** extract, quote (passage from book *etc.*) —**ex'cerption** *n.*

excess (ɪk'sɛs, 'ɛksɛs) *n.* **1.** an exceeding **2.** amount by which thing exceeds **3.** too great amount **4.** intemperance, immoderate conduct —**ex'cessive** *a.* —**ex'cessively** *adv.* —**excess luggage** *or* **baggage** luggage that is more in weight or number of items than airline *etc.* will carry free

exchange (ɪks'tʃeɪndʒ) *vt.* **1.** give (something) in return for something else **2.** barter —*n.* **3.** giving one thing and receiving another **4.** thing given for another **5.** building where merchants meet for business **6.** central telephone office where connections are made *etc.* —**exchangea'bility** *n.* —**ex'changeable** *a.* —**exchange rate** rate at which currency unit of one country may be exchanged for that of another

exchequer (ɪks'tʃɛkə) *n.* government department in charge of revenue

excise[1] ('ɛksaɪz, ɛk'saɪz) *n.* duty charged on home goods during manufacture or before sale

excise[2] (ɪk'saɪz) *vt.* cut out, cut away —**excision** (ɛk'sɪʒən) *n.*

excite (ɪk'saɪt) *vt.* **1.** arouse to strong emotion, stimulate **2.** rouse up, set in motion **3.** *Elec.* magnetize poles of —**excita'bility** *n.* —**ex'citable** *a.* —**ex'citably** *adv.* —**exci'tation** *n.* —**ex'cited** *a.* emotionally or sexually aroused —**ex'citedness** *n.* —**ex'citement** *n.* —**ex'citing** *a.* **1.** thrilling **2.** rousing to action

exclaim (ɪk'skleɪm) *vi.* **1.** speak suddenly —*v.* **2.** cry out —**exclamation** (ɛksklə'meɪʃən) *n.* —**exclamatory** (ɪks'klæmətərɪ) *a.* —**exclamation mark** *or* *U.S.* **point** punctuation mark ! used after exclamations and vehement commands

exclude (ɪk'skluːd) *vt.* **1.** shut out **2.** debar **3.** reject, not consider —**ex'clusion** *n.* —**ex'clusive** *a.* **1.** excluding **2.** inclined to keep out (from society *etc.*) **3.** sole, only **4.** select —*n.* **5.** something exclusive, *esp.* story appearing only in one newspaper —**ex'clusively** *adv.*

excommunicate (ɛkskə'mjuːnɪkeɪt) *vt.* cut off from the sacraments of the Church —**excommuni'cation** *n.*

THESAURUS

choice, distinguished, estimable, exemplary, exquisite, fine, first-class, first-rate, good, great, meritorious, notable, noted, outstanding, prime, select, sterling, superb, superior, superlative, tiptop, topnotch (*Inf.*), worthy

except 1. *prep.* apart from, bar, barring, besides, but, excepting, excluding, exclusive of, omitting, other than, save (*Archaic*), saving, with the exception of 2. *v.* ban, bar, disallow, exclude, leave out, omit, pass over, reject, rule out

exception 1. anomaly, departure, deviation, freak, inconsistency, irregularity, oddity, peculiarity, quirk, special case 2. **take exception** be offended, be resentful, demur, disagree, object, quibble, take offence, take umbrage

exceptional 1. aberrant, abnormal, anomalous, atypical, deviant, extraordinary, inconsistent, irregular, odd, peculiar, rare, singular, special, strange, uncommon, unusual 2. excellent, extraordinary, marvellous, outstanding, phenomenal, prodigious, remarkable, special, superior

excess *n.* 1. glut, leftover, overabundance, overdose, overflow, overload, plethora, remainder, superabundance, superfluity, surfeit, surplus, too much 2. debauchery, dissipation, dissoluteness, exorbitance, extravagance, immoderation, intemperance, overindulgence, prodigality, unrestraint

excessive disproportionate, enormous, exaggerated, exorbitant, extravagant, extreme, immoderate, inordinate, intemperate, needless, overdone, overmuch, prodigal, profligate, superfluous, too much, unconscionable, undue, unreasonable

exchange *v.* 1. bandy, barter, change, commute, convert into, interchange, reciprocate, swap (*Inf.*), switch, trade, truck ~*n.* 2. barter, dealing, interchange, quid pro quo, reciprocity, substitution, swap (*Inf.*), switch, tit for tat, trade, traffic, truck 3. Bourse, market

excitable edgy, emotional, hasty, highly strung, hotheaded, hot-tempered, irascible, mercurial, nervous, passionate, quick-tempered, sensitive, susceptible, temperamental, testy, touchy, violent, volatile

excite agitate, animate, arouse, awaken, discompose, disturb, electrify, elicit, evoke, fire, foment, galvanize, incite, inflame, inspire, instigate, kindle, move, provoke, quicken, rouse, stimulate, stir up, thrill, titillate, waken, whet

excited aflame, agitated, animated, aroused, awakened, discomposed, disturbed, enthusiastic, feverish, flurried, high (*Inf.*), hot and bothered (*Inf.*), moved, nervous, overwrought, roused, stimulated, stirred, thrilled, tumultuous, wild, worked up

excitement 1. action, activity, ado, adventure, agitation, animation, commotion, discomposure, elation, enthusiasm, ferment, fever, flurry, furore, heat, kicks (*Inf.*), passion, perturbation, thrill, tumult, warmth 2. impulse, incitement, instigation, motivation, motive, provocation, stimulation, stimulus, urge

exciting electrifying, exhilarating, inspiring, intoxicating, moving, provocative, rip-roaring (*Inf.*), rousing, sensational, stimulating, stirring, thrilling, titillating

exclaim call, call out, cry, cry out, declare, ejaculate, proclaim, shout, utter, vociferate, yell

exclamation call, cry, ejaculation, expletive, interjection, outcry, shout, utterance, vociferation, yell

exclude 1. ban, bar, blackball, debar, disallow, embargo, forbid, interdict, keep out, ostracize, prohibit, proscribe, refuse, shut out, veto 2. count out, eliminate, except, ignore, leave out, omit, pass over, preclude, reject, repudiate, rule out, set aside

exclusion 1. ban, bar, debarment, embargo, forbiddance, interdict, nonadmission, preclusion, prohibition, proscription, refusal, veto 2. elimination, exception, omission, rejection, repudiation

exclusive 1. absolute, complete, entire, full, only, private, single, sole, total, undivided, unique, unshared, whole 2. aristocratic, chic, choice, clannish, classy (*Sl.*), cliquish, closed, discriminative, elegant, fashionable, limited, narrow, posh (*Inf.*), private, restricted, restrictive, select, selfish, snobbish 3.

excoriate (ɪkˈskɔːrɪeɪt) *vt.* **1.** strip (skin) from (person or animal) **2.** denounce vehemently —**excoriˈation** *n.*

excrement (ˈɛkskrɪmənt) *n.* **1.** waste matter from body, *esp.* from bowels **2.** dung —**excreta** (ɪkˈskriːtə) *pl.n.* excrement —**excrete** (ɪkˈskriːt) *vt.* discharge from the system —**excretion** (ɪkˈskriːʃən) *n.* —**excretory** (ɪkˈskriːtərɪ) *a.*

excrescent (ɪkˈskrɛsᵊnt) *a.* **1.** growing out of something **2.** redundant —**exˈcrescence** *n.* unnatural outgrowth

excruciate (ɪkˈskruːʃɪeɪt) *vt.* torment acutely, torture in body or mind —**exˈcruciating** *a.* —**excruciˈation** *n.*

exculpate (ˈɛkskʌlpeɪt, ɪkˈskʌlpeɪt) *vt.* free from blame, acquit —**exculˈpation** *n.* —**exˈculpatory** *a.*

excursion (ɪkˈskɜːʃən, -ʒən) *n.* **1.** journey, ramble, trip for pleasure **2.** digression —**exˈcursive** *a.* **1.** tending to digress **2.** involving detours —**exˈcursiveness** *n.* —**exˈcursus** *n.* digression (*pl.* **-es, -sus** (*rare*))

excuse (ɪkˈskjuːz) *vt.* **1.** forgive, overlook **2.** try to clear from blame **3.** seek exemption for **4.** set free, remit —*n.* (ɪkˈskjuːs) **5.** that which serves to excuse **6.** apology —**exˈcusable** *a.*

exeat (ˈɛksɪət) *n.* **UK 1.** leave of absence from school **2.** bishop's permission for priest to leave diocese to take up appointment elsewhere

exec. **1.** executive **2.** executor

execrate (ˈɛksɪkreɪt) *vt.* **1.** loathe, detest **2.** denounce, deplore **3.** curse —**ˈexecrable** *a.* abominable, hatefully bad —**exeˈcration** *n.* —**ˈexecrative** *or* **ˈexecratory** *a.*

execute (ˈɛksɪkjuːt) *vt.* **1.** inflict capital punishment on, kill **2.** carry out, perform **3.** make, produce **4.** sign (document) —**exˈecutant** *n.* performer, *esp.* of music —**exeˈcution** *n.* —**exeˈcutioner** *n.* one employed to execute criminals —**exˈecutive** *n.* **1.** person in administrative position **2.** executive body **3.** committee carrying on business of society *etc.* —*a.* **4.** carrying into effect, *esp.* of branch of government enforcing laws —**exˈecutor** *n.* person appointed to carry out provisions of a will (**exˈecutrix** *fem.*)

exegesis (ɛksɪˈdʒiːsɪs) *n.* explanation, *esp.* of Scripture (*pl.* **-geses** (-ˈdʒiːsiːz)) —**exegetic(al)** (ɛksɪˈdʒɛtɪk(ᵊl)) *a.*

exemplar (ɪgˈzɛmplə, -plɑː) *n.* model type —**exˈemplarily** *adv.* —**exˈemplary** *a.* **1.** fit to be imitated, serving as example **2.** commendable **3.** typical —**exemplifiˈcation** *n.* —**exˈemplify** *vt.* **1.** serve as example of **2.** illustrate **3.** exhibit **4.** make attested copy of (**-fied, -fying**)

exempt (ɪgˈzɛmpt) *vt.* **1.** free **2.** excuse —*a.* **3.** freed (from), not liable (for) **4.** not affected (by) —**exˈemption** *n.*

exequies (ˈɛksɪkwɪz) *pl.n.* funeral rites or procession

exercise (ˈɛksəsaɪz) *vt.* **1.** use, employ **2.** give exercise to **3.** carry out, discharge **4.** trouble, harass —*vi.* **5.** take exercise —*n.* **6.** use of limbs for health **7.** practice for training **8.** task for training **9.** lesson **10.** employment **11.** use (of limbs, faculty *etc.*)

THESAURUS

debarring, except for, excepting, excluding, leaving aside, not counting, omitting, restricting, ruling out

excommunicate anathematize, ban, banish, cast out, denounce, eject, exclude, expel, proscribe, remove, repudiate, unchurch

excruciating acute, agonizing, burning, exquisite, extreme, harrowing, insufferable, intense, piercing, racking, searing, severe, tormenting, torturous, unbearable, unendurable, violent

excursion **1.** airing, day trip, expedition, jaunt, journey, outing, pleasure trip, ramble, tour, trip **2.** detour, deviation, digression, episode, excursus, wandering

excusable allowable, defensible, forgivable, justifiable, minor, pardonable, permissible, slight, understandable, venial, warrantable

excuse *v.* **1.** absolve, acquit, bear with, exculpate, exonerate, extenuate, forgive, indulge, make allowances for, overlook, pardon, pass over, tolerate, turn a blind eye to, wink at **2.** apologize for, condone, defend, explain, justify, mitigate, vindicate **3.** absolve, discharge, exempt, free, let off, liberate, release, relieve, spare ~*n.* **4.** apology, defence, explanation, grounds, justification, mitigation, plea, pretext, reason, vindication

execrate abhor, abominate, anathematize, condemn, curse, damn, denounce, deplore, despise, detest, excoriate, hate, imprecate, loathe, revile, vilify

execration abhorrence, abomination, anathema, condemnation, contempt, curse, damnation, detestation, excoriation, hate, hatred, imprecation, loathing, malediction, odium, vilification

execute **1.** behead, electrocute, guillotine, hang, kill, put to death, shoot **2.** accomplish, achieve, administer, bring off, carry out, complete, consummate, discharge, do, effect, enact, enforce, finish, fulfil, implement, perform, prosecute, put into effect, realize, render **3.** *Law* deliver, seal, serve, sign, validate

execution **1.** accomplishment, achievement, administration, carrying out, completion, consummation, discharge, effect, enactment, enforcement, implementation, operation, performance, prosecution, realization, rendering **2.** capital punishment, hanging, killing

executioner hangman, headsman

executive *n.* **1.** administrator, director, manager, official **2.** administration, directorate, directors, government, hierarchy, leadership, management ~*adj.* **3.** administrative, controlling, decision-making, directing, governing, managerial

exemplary **1.** admirable, commendable, correct, estimable, excellent, good, honourable, ideal, laudable, meritorious, model, praiseworthy, punctilious, sterling **2.** characteristic, illustrative, representative, typical

exemplify demonstrate, depict, display, embody, evidence, exhibit, illustrate, instance, manifest, represent, serve as an example of, show

exempt **1.** *v.* absolve, discharge, except, excuse, exonerate, free, grant immunity, let off, liberate, release, relieve, spare **2.** *adj.* absolved, clear, discharged, excepted, excused, favoured, free, immune, liberated, not liable, not subject, privileged, released, spared

exemption absolution, discharge, dispensation, exception, exoneration, freedom, immunity, privilege, release

exercise *v.* **1.** apply, bring to bear, employ, enjoy, exert, practise, put to use, use, utilize, wield **2.** discipline, drill, habituate, inure, practise, train,

exert (ɪgˈzɜːt) *vt.* **1.** apply (oneself) diligently, make effort **2.** bring to bear —**exˈertion** *n.* effort, physical activity, application

exeunt (ˈɛksɪʌnt) *Lat. Theat.* they leave the stage: stage direction —**exeunt omnes** (ˈɒmneɪz) they all go out

exfoliate (ɛksˈfəʊlɪeɪt) *v.* peel in scales, layers

exhale (ɛksˈheɪl, ɪgˈzeɪl) *v.* **1.** breathe out **2.** give, pass off as vapour

exhaust (ɪgˈzɔːst) *vt.* **1.** tire out **2.** use up **3.** empty **4.** draw off **5.** treat, discuss thoroughly —*n.* **6.** used steam or fluid from engine **7.** waste gases from internal-combustion engine **8.** passage for, or coming out of this —**exhaustiˈbility** *n.* —**exˈhaustible** *a.* —**exˈhaustion** *n.* **1.** state of extreme fatigue **2.** limit of endurance —**exˈhaustive** *a.* comprehensive

exhibit (ɪgˈzɪbɪt) *vt.* **1.** show, display **2.** manifest **3.** show publicly (oft. in competition) —*n.* **4.** thing shown, *esp.* in competition or as evidence in court —**exhiˈbition** *n.* **1.** display, act of displaying **2.** public show (of works of art *etc.*) —**exhiˈbitionism** *n.* —**exhiˈbitionist** *n.* one with compulsive desire to draw attention to himself or to expose genitals publicly —**exhibitionˈistic** *a.* —**exˈhibitor** *n.* one who exhibits, *esp.* in show —**exˈhibitory** *a.*

exhilarate (ɪgˈzɪləreɪt) *vt.* enliven, gladden —**exhilaˈration** *n.* high spirits, enlivenment

exhort (ɪgˈzɔːt) *vt.* urge, admonish earnestly —**exhorˈtation** *n.* —**exˈhorter** *n.*

exhume (ɛksˈhjuːm) *vt.* unearth (what has been buried), disinter —**exhuˈmation** *n.*

exigent (ˈɛksɪdʒənt) *a.* **1.** exacting **2.** urgent, pressing —**ˈexigence** *or* **ˈexigency** *n.* **1.** pressing need **2.** emergency —**ˈexigible** *a.* liable to be exacted or demanded

exiguous (ɪgˈzɪgjʊəs, ɪkˈsɪg-) *a.* scanty, meagre

exile (ˈɛgzaɪl, ˈɛksaɪl) *n.* **1.** banishment, expulsion from one's own country **2.** long absence abroad **3.** one banished or permanently living away from his home or country —*vt.* **4.** banish, expel

exist (ɪgˈzɪst) *vi.* be, have being, live —**exˈistence** *n.* —**exˈistent** *a.*

existential (ɛgzɪˈstɛnʃəl) *a.* **1.** of existence **2.** *Philos.* based on personal experience **3.** of existentialism —**exisˈtentialism** *n.* theory which holds that man is free and responsible for his own acts

exit (ˈɛgzɪt, ˈɛksɪt) *n.* **1.** way out, **2.** going out, departure **3.** death **4.** actor's departure from stage —*vi.* **5.** go out

exo- (*comb. form*) external, outside, or beyond, as in *exothermal*

exocrine (ˈɛksəʊkraɪn) *a.* of gland (*eg* salivary, sweat) secreting its products through ducts

Exod. *Bible* Exodus

exodus (ˈɛksədəs) *n.* **1.** departure, *esp.* of crowd **2.** (**E-**) second book of Old Testament

exonerate (ɪgˈzɒnəreɪt) *vt.* **1.** free, declare free, from blame **2.** exculpate **3.** acquit —**exonerˈation** *n.* —**exˈonerative** *a.*

THESAURUS

work out **3.** afflict, agitate, annoy, burden, distress, disturb, occupy, pain, perturb, preoccupy, trouble, try, vex, worry ~*n.* **4.** action, activity, discipline, drill, drilling, effort, labour, toil, training, work, work-out **5.** accomplishment, application, discharge, employment, enjoyment, exertion, fulfilment, implementation, practice, use, utilization **6.** drill, lesson, practice, problem, schooling, schoolwork, task, work

exert 1. bring into play, bring to bear, employ, exercise, expend, make use of, put forth, use, utilize, wield **2. exert oneself** apply oneself, do one's best, endeavour, labour, make an effort, spare no effort, strain, strive, struggle, toil, try hard, work

exertion action, application, attempt, effort, employment, endeavour, exercise, industry, labour, pains, strain, stretch, struggle, toil, travail (*Literary*), trial, use, utilization

exhaust 1. bankrupt, cripple, debilitate, disable, drain, enervate, enfeeble, fatigue, impoverish, prostrate, sap, tire, tire out, weaken, wear out **2.** consume, deplete, dissipate, expend, finish, run through, spend, squander, use up, waste **3.** drain, dry, empty, strain, void

exhibit 1. *v.* air, demonstrate, disclose, display, evidence, evince, expose, express, flaunt, indicate, make clear *or* plain, manifest, offer, parade, present, put on view, reveal, show **2.** *n.* display, exhibition, illustration, model, show

exhibition airing, demonstration, display, exhibit, expo (*Inf.*), exposition, fair, manifestation, performance, presentation, representation, show, showing, spectacle

exhort admonish, advise, beseech, bid, call upon, caution, counsel, encourage, enjoin, entreat, goad, incite, persuade, press, spur, urge, warn

exhortation admonition, advice, beseeching, bidding, caution, counsel, encouragement, enjoinder (*Rare*), entreaty, goading, incitement, lecture, persuasion, sermon, urging, warning

exhume dig up, disentomb, disinter, unbury, unearth

exigency, exigence 1. acuteness, constraint, criticalness, demandingness, difficulty, distress, emergency, imperativeness, necessity, needfulness, pressingness, pressure, stress, urgency **2.** constraint, demand, necessity, need, requirement, wont **3.** crisis, difficulty, emergency, extremity, fix (*Inf.*), hardship, jam (*Inf.*), juncture, pass, pickle (*Inf.*), pinch, plight, predicament, quandary, scrape (*Inf.*), strait

exile *n.* **1.** banishment, deportation, expatriation, expulsion, ostracism, proscription, separation **2.** deportee, émigré, expatriate, outcast, refugee ~*v.* **3.** banish, deport, drive out, eject, expatriate, expel, ostracize, oust, proscribe

exist abide, be, be extant, be living, be present, breathe, continue, endure, happen, last, live, obtain, occur, prevail, remain, stand, survive

existence actuality, animation, being, breath, continuance, continuation, duration, endurance, life, subsistence, survival

existent abiding, around, current, enduring, existing, extant, in existence, living, obtaining, present, prevailing, remaining, standing, surviving

exit *n.* **1.** door, egress, gate, outlet, passage out, vent, way out **2.** adieu, departure, evacuation, exodus, farewell, going, goodbye, leave-taking, retirement, retreat, withdrawal **3.** death, decease, demise, expiry, passing away ~*v.* **4.** bid farewell, depart, go away, go offstage (*Theatre*), go out, issue, leave, retire, retreat, say goodbye, take one's leave, withdraw

exodus departure, evacuation, exit, flight, going out, leaving, migration, retirement, retreat, withdrawal

exonerate 1. absolve, acquit, clear, discharge, dis-

exorbitant (ɪg'zɔːbɪtᵊnt) *a.* very excessive, inordinate, immoderate —**ex'orbitance** *n.* —**ex'orbitantly** *adv.*

exorcise *or* **-ize** ('ɛksɔːsaɪz) *vt.* 1. cast out (evil spirits) by invocation 2. free (person) of evil spirits —**exorcism** ('ɛksɔːsɪzəm) *n.* —**exorcist** ('ɛksɔːsɪst) *n.*

exordium (ɛk'sɔːdɪəm) *n.* introductory part of a speech or treatise (*pl.* **-s, -ia** (-ɪə)) —**ex'ordial** *a.*

exoteric (ɛksəʊ'tɛrɪk) *a.* 1. understandable by the many 2. ordinary, popular

exotic (ɪg'zɒtɪk) *a.* 1. brought in from abroad, foreign 2. rare, unusual, having strange or bizarre allure —*n.* 3. exotic plant *etc.* —**ex'otica** *pl.n.* (collection of) exotic objects —**ex'oticism** *n.* —**exotic dancer** strip-tease or belly dancer

expand (ɪk'spænd) *v.* 1. increase 2. spread out 3. dilate 4. develop —**ex'pandable** *or* **ex'pandible** *a.* —**ex'panse** *n.* 1. wide space 2. open stretch of land —**expansi'bility** *n.* —**ex'pansible** *a.* —**ex'pansion** *n.* —**ex'pansionism** *n.* practice of expanding economy or territory of country —**ex'pansionist** *n./a.* —**expansion'istic** *a.* —**ex'pansive** *a.* 1. wide 2. extensive 3. friendly, talkative

expatiate (ɪk'speɪʃɪeɪt) *vi.* 1. speak or write at great length 2. enlarge —**expati'ation** *n.*

expatriate (ɛks'pætrɪeɪt) *vt.* 1. banish, exile 2. withdraw (oneself) from one's native land —*a./n.* (ɛks'pætrɪɪt, -eɪt) 3. (person) exiled or banished from his native country —**expatri'ation** *n.*

expect (ɪk'spɛkt) *vt.* 1. regard as probable 2. look forward to 3. await 4. hope for —**ex'pectancy** *n.* 1. state or act of expecting 2. that which is expected 3. hope —**ex'pectant** *a.* looking or waiting for, *esp.* for birth of child —**ex'pectantly** *adv.* —**expec'tation** *n.* 1. act or state of expecting 2. prospect of future good 3. what is expected 4. promise 5. value of something expected —*pl.* 6. prospect of fortune or profit by will

expectorate (ɪk'spɛktəreɪt) *v.* spit out (phlegm *etc.*) —**ex'pectorant** *Med. a.* 1. promoting secretion, liquefaction or expulsion of sputum from respiratory passages —*n.* 2. expectorant drug or agent —**expecto'ration** *n.*

expedient (ɪk'spiːdɪənt) *a.* 1. fitting, advisable, politic, suitable, convenient —*n.* 2. something suitable, useful, *esp.* in emergency —**ex'pediency** *n.* —**ex'pediently** *adv.*

expedite ('ɛkspɪdaɪt) *vt.* 1. help on, hasten 2. dispatch —**expedition** (ɛkspɪ'dɪʃən) *n.* 1. journey for definite (oft. scientific or military) purpose 2. people, equipment comprising expedition 3. excursion 4. promptness —**expeditionary** (ɛkspɪ'dɪʃənərɪ) *a.* —**expeditious** (ɛkspɪ'dɪʃəs) *a.* prompt, speedy

THESAURUS

miss, exculpate, excuse, justify, pardon, vindicate **2.** discharge, dismiss, except, excuse, exempt, free, let off, liberate, release, relieve

exorbitant enormous, excessive, extortionate, extravagant, extreme, immoderate, inordinate, outrageous, preposterous, unconscionable, undue, unreasonable, unwarranted

exorcise adjure, cast out, deliver (from), drive out, expel, purify

exorcism adjuration, casting out, deliverance, driving out, expulsion, purification

exotic 1. alien, external, extraneous, extrinsic, foreign, imported, introduced, naturalized, not native **2.** bizarre, colourful, curious, different, extraordinary, fascinating, glamorous, mysterious, outlandish, peculiar, strange, striking, unfamiliar, unusual

expand 1. amplify, augment, bloat, blow up, broaden, develop, dilate, distend, enlarge, extend, fatten, fill out, grow, heighten, increase, inflate, lengthen, magnify, multiply, prolong, protract, swell, thicken, wax, widen **2.** diffuse, open (out), outspread, spread (out), stretch (out), unfold, unfurl, unravel, unroll **3.** amplify, develop, dilate, elaborate, embellish, enlarge, expatiate, expound, flesh out, go into detail

expanse area, breadth, extent, field, plain, range, space, stretch, sweep, tract

expansion amplification, augmentation, development, diffusion, dilatation, distension, enlargement, expanse, growth, increase, inflation, magnification, multiplication, opening out, spread, swelling, unfolding, unfurling

expansive 1. all-embracing, broad, comprehensive, extensive, far-reaching, inclusive, thorough, voluminous, wide, wide-ranging, widespread **2.** affable, communicative, easy, effusive, free, friendly, garrulous, genial, loquacious, open, outgoing, sociable, talkative, unreserved, warm

expatiate amplify, descant, develop, dilate, dwell on, elaborate, embellish, enlarge, expound, go into detail

expatriate 1. *adj.* banished, emigrant, émigré, exiled, refugee **2.** *n.* emigrant, émigré, exile **3.** *v.* banish, exile, expel, ostracize, proscribe

expect 1. assume, believe, calculate, conjecture, forecast, foresee, imagine, presume, reckon, suppose, surmise, think, trust **2.** anticipate, await, bargain for, contemplate, envisage, hope for, look ahead to, look for, look forward to, predict, watch for

expectancy 1. anticipation, assumption, belief, conjecture, expectation, hope, looking forward, prediction, presumption, probability, supposition, surmise, suspense, waiting **2.** likelihood, outlook, prospect

expectant 1. anticipating, anxious, apprehensive, awaiting, eager, expecting, hopeful, in suspense, ready, watchful **2.** enceinte, expecting (*Inf.*), gravid, pregnant

expectation 1. assumption, assurance, belief, calculation, confidence, conjecture, forecast, likelihood, presumption, probability, supposition, surmise, trust **2.** anticipation, apprehension, chance, expectancy, fear, hope, looking forward, outlook, possibility, prediction, promise, prospect, suspense

expediency advantageousness, advisability, appropriateness, aptness, benefit, convenience, desirability, effectiveness, fitness, helpfulness, judiciousness, meetness, practicality, pragmatism, profitability, properness, propriety, prudence, suitability, usefulness, utilitarianism, utility

expedient 1. *adj.* advantageous, advisable, appropriate, beneficial, convenient, desirable, effective, fit, helpful, judicious, meet, opportune, politic, practical, pragmatic, profitable, proper, prudent, suitable, useful, utilitarian, worthwhile **2.** *n.* contrivance, device, expediency, makeshift, manoeuvre, means, measure, method, resort, resource, scheme, shift, stopgap, stratagem, substitute

expedite accelerate, advance, assist, dispatch, facili-

expel (ɪkˈspel) *vt.* **1.** drive, cast out **2.** exclude **3.** discharge (-ll-) —**expulsion** (ɪkˈspʌlʃən) *n.* —**expulsive** (ɪkˈspʌlsɪv) *a.*

expend (ɪkˈspɛnd) *vt.* **1.** spend, pay out **2.** use up —**exˈpendable** *a.* likely, or meant, to be used up or destroyed —**exˈpenditure** *n.* —**exˈpense** *n.* **1.** cost **2.** (cause of) spending —*pl.* **3.** charges, outlay incurred —**exˈpensive** *a.* high-priced, costly, dear —**expense account 1.** arrangement by which expenses are refunded to employee by employer **2.** record of such expenses

experience (ɪkˈspɪərɪəns) *n.* **1.** observation of facts as source of knowledge **2.** being affected consciously by event **3.** the event **4.** knowledge, skill, gained from life, by contact with facts and events —*vt.* **5.** undergo, suffer, meet with —**exˈperienced** *a.* skilled, expert, capable —**experiˈential** *a.*

experiment (ɪkˈspɛrɪmənt) *n.* **1.** test, trial, something done in the hope that it may succeed, or to test theory —*vi.* (ɪkˈspɛrɪmɛnt) **2.** make experiment —**experiˈmental** *a.* —**experiˈmentalist** *n.* —**experiˈmentally** *adv.*

expert (ˈɛkspɜːt) *n.* **1.** one skilful, knowledgeable, in something **2.** authority —*a.* **3.** practised, skilful —**expertise** (ɛkspɜːˈtiːz) *n.*

expiate (ˈɛkspɪeɪt) *vt.* **1.** pay penalty for **2.** make amends for —**expiˈation** *n.* —**ˈexpiator** *n.* —**ˈexpiatory** *a.*

expire (ɪkˈspaɪə) *vi.* **1.** come to an end **2.** give out breath **3.** die —*vt.* **4.** breathe out —**expiration** (ɛkspɪˈreɪʃən) *n.* —**exˈpiratory** *a.* —**exˈpiry** *n.* end

explain (ɪkˈspleɪn) *vt.* **1.** make clear, intelligible **2.** interpret **3.** elucidate **4.** give details of **5.** account for —**explanation** (ɛkspləˈneɪʃən) *n.* —**explanatory** (ɪksˈplænətərɪ, -trɪ) *or* **explanative** (ɪksˈplænətɪv) *a.*

expletive (ɪkˈspliːtɪv) *n.* **1.** exclamation **2.** oath —*a.* **3.** serving only to fill out sentence *etc.*

explicable (ˈɛksplɪkəbˀl, ɪkˈsplɪk-) *a.* explainable —**ˈexplicate** *vt.* develop, explain —**exˈplicative** *or* **exˈplicatory** *a.*

explicit (ɪkˈsplɪsɪt) *a.* **1.** stated in detail **2.** stated, not merely implied **3.** outspoken **4.** clear, plain **5.** unequivocal

explode (ɪkˈspləʊd) *vi.* **1.** go off with bang **2.** burst violently **3.** (of population) increase rapidly —*vt.* **4.** make explode **5.** discredit, expose (a theory *etc.*) —**exˈplosion** *n.* —**exˈplosive** *a./n.*

THESAURUS

tate, forward, hasten, hurry, precipitate, press, promote, quicken, rush, speed (up), urge

expedition 1. enterprise, excursion, exploration, journey, mission, quest, safari, tour, trek, trip, undertaking, voyage **2.** company, crew, explorers, team, travellers, voyagers, wayfarers **3.** alacrity, celerity, dispatch, expeditiousness, haste, hurry, promptness, quickness, rapidity, readiness, speed, swiftness

expel 1. belch, cast out, discharge, dislodge, drive out, eject, remove, spew, throw out **2.** ban, banish, bar, blackball, discharge, dismiss, drum out, evict, exclude, exile, expatriate, oust, proscribe, send packing, throw out, turf out (*Inf.*)

expend consume, disburse, dissipate, employ, exhaust, fork out (*Sl.*), go through, lay out (*Inf.*), pay out, shell out (*Inf.*), spend, use (up)

expendable dispensable, inessential, nonessential, replaceable, unimportant

expenditure application, charge, consumption, cost, disbursement, expense, outgoings, outlay, output, payment, spending, use

expense charge, consumption, cost, disbursement, expenditure, loss, outlay, output, payment, sacrifice, spending, toll, use

expensive costly, dear, excessive, exorbitant, extravagant, high-priced, inordinate, lavish, overpriced, rich, steep (*Inf.*), stiff

experience *n.* **1.** contact, doing, evidence, exposure, familiarity, involvement, know-how (*Inf.*), knowledge, observation, participation, practice, proof, training, trial, understanding **2.** adventure, affair, encounter, episode, event, happening, incident, occurrence, ordeal, test, trial ~*v.* **3.** apprehend, become familiar with, behold, encounter, endure, face, feel, go through, have, know, live through, meet, observe, participate in, perceive, sample, sense, suffer, sustain, taste, try, undergo

experienced accomplished, adept, capable, competent, expert, familiar, knowledgeable, master, practised, professional, qualified, seasoned, skilful, tested, trained, tried, veteran, well-versed

experiment 1. *n.* assay, attempt, examination, experimentation, investigation, procedure, proof, research, test, trial, trial and error, trial run, venture **2.** *v.* assay, examine, investigate, put to the test, research, sample, test, try, verify

experimental empirical, exploratory, pilot, preliminary, probationary, provisional, speculative, tentative, test, trial, trial-and-error

expert 1. *n.* ace (*Inf.*), adept, authority, connoisseur, dab hand (*Inf.*), master, past master, pro (*Inf.*), professional, specialist, virtuoso, wizard **2.** *adj.* able, adept, adroit, apt, clever, deft, dexterous, experienced, facile, handy, knowledgeable, master, masterly, practised, professional, proficient, qualified, skilful, skilled, trained, virtuoso

expertise ableness, adroitness, aptness, cleverness, command, deftness, dexterity, expertness, facility, judgment, knack, know-how (*Inf.*), knowledge, masterliness, mastery, proficiency, skilfulness, skill

expire 1. cease, close, come to an end, conclude, end, finish, lapse, run out, stop, terminate **2.** breathe out, emit, exhale, expel **3.** decease, depart, die, kick the bucket (*Inf.*), pass away *or* on, perish

explain 1. clarify, clear up, define, demonstrate, describe, disclose, elucidate, explicate (*Formal*), expound, illustrate, interpret, make clear *or* plain, resolve, solve, teach, unfold **2.** account for, excuse, give an explanation for, give a reason for, justify

explanation 1. clarification, definition, demonstration, description, elucidation, explication, exposition, illustration, interpretation, resolution **2.** account, answer, cause, excuse, justification, meaning, mitigation, motive, reason, sense, significance, vindication

explanatory demonstrative, descriptive, elucidatory, explicative, expository, illuminative, illustrative, interpretive, justifying

explicit absolute, categorical, certain, clear, definite,

exploit (ˈɛksplɔɪt) *n.* **1.** brilliant feat, deed —*vt.* (ɪkˈsplɔɪt) **2.** turn to advantage **3.** make use of for one's own ends —**exploiˈtation** *n.* —**exˈploiter** *n.*

explore (ɪkˈsplɔː) *vt.* **1.** investigate **2.** examine **3.** scrutinize **4.** examine (country *etc.*) by going through it —**exploˈration** *n.* —**exploratory** (ɪkˈsplɒrətərɪ, -trɪ) *a.* —**exˈplorer** *n.*

explosion (ɪkˈspləʊʒən) *n. see* EXPLODE

expo (ˈɛkspəʊ) *n. inf.* exposition, large international exhibition

exponent (ɪkˈspəʊnənt) *n. see* EXPOUND

export (ɪkˈspɔːt, ˈɛkspɔːt) *vt.* **1.** send (goods) out of the country —*n./a.* (ˈɛkspɔːt) **2.** (of) goods or services sold to foreign country or countries —**exporˈtation** *n.* —**exˈporter** *n.*

expose (ɪkˈspəʊz) *vt.* **1.** exhibit **2.** disclose, reveal **3.** lay open **4.** leave unprotected **5.** subject (photographic plate or film) to light —**exˈposed** *a.* **1.** not concealed **2.** without shelter from the elements **3.** vulnerable —**exposedness** (ɪkˈspəʊzɪdnɪs) *n.* —**exˈposure** *n.* **1.** act of exposing or condition of being exposed **2.** position or outlook of building **3.** lack of shelter from weather, *esp.* cold **4.** exposed surface **5.** *Photog.* act of exposing film or plate to light *etc.*; area on film or plate that has been exposed **6.** *Photog.* intensity of light falling on film or plate multiplied by time of exposure; combination of lens aperture and shutter speed used in taking photograph **7.** appearance before public, as on TV

exposé (ɛksˈpəʊzeɪ) *n.* newspaper article *etc.* disclosing scandal, crime *etc.*

exposition (ɛkspəˈzɪʃən) *n. see* EXPOUND

expostulate (ɪkˈspɒstjʊleɪt) *vi.* **1.** remonstrate **2.** reason (in a kindly manner) —**expostuˈlation** *n.* —**exˈpostulatory** *a.*

expound (ɪkˈspaʊnd) *vt.* explain, interpret —**exponent** (ɪkˈspəʊnənt) *n.* **1.** one who expounds or promotes (idea, cause *etc.*) **2.** performer, executant **3.** *Maths.* small, raised number showing the power of a factor —**expoˈnential** *a.* —**expoˈsition** *n.* **1.** explanation, description **2.** exhibition of goods *etc.* —**expositor** (ɪkˈspɒzɪtə) *n.* one who explains, interpreter —**expository** (ɪkˈspɒzɪtərɪ, -trɪ) *a.* explanatory

express (ɪkˈsprɛs) *vt.* **1.** put into words **2.** make known or understood by words, behaviour *etc.* **3.** squeeze out —*a.* **4.** definitely stated **5.** specially designed **6.** clear **7.** positive **8.** speedy **9.** (of messenger) specially sent off **10.** (of train) fast and making few stops —*adv.* **11.** specially **12.** on purpose **13.** with speed —*n.* **14.** express train or messenger **15.** rapid parcel delivery service —**exˈpressible** *a.* —**exˈpression** *n.* **1.** expressing **2.** word, phrase **3.** look, aspect **4.** feeling **5.** utterance —**exˈpressionism** *n.* theory that art depends on expression of artist's creative self, not on mere reproduction —**exˈpressive** *a.* —**exˈpressly** *adv.* —**exˈpressway** *n. esp.* US urban motorway

THESAURUS

direct, distinct, exact, express, frank, open, outspoken, patent, plain, positive, precise, specific, stated, straightforward, unambiguous, unequivocal, unqualified, unreserved

explode 1. blow up, burst, detonate, discharge, erupt, go off, set off, shatter, shiver 2. belie, debunk, discredit, disprove, give the lie to, invalidate, refute, repudiate

exploit *n.* 1. accomplishment, achievement, adventure, attainment, deed, feat, stunt ~*v.* 2. abuse, impose upon, manipulate, milk, misuse, play on *or* upon, take advantage of 3. capitalize on, cash in on (*Sl.*), make capital out of, make use of, profit by *or* from, put to use, turn to account, use, use to advantage, utilize

exploration 1. analysis, examination, inquiry, inspection, investigation, probe, research, scrutiny, search, study 2. expedition, reconnaissance, survey, tour, travel, trip

exploratory analytic, experimental, fact-finding, investigative, probing, searching, trial

explore 1. analyse, examine, inquire into, inspect, investigate, look into, probe, prospect, research, scrutinize, search 2. have *or* take a look around, range over, reconnoitre, scout, survey, tour, travel, traverse

explosion 1. bang, blast, burst, clap, crack, detonation, discharge, outburst, report 2. eruption, fit, outbreak, outburst, paroxysm

explosive unstable, volatile

exponent 1. advocate, backer, champion, defender, promoter, propagandist, proponent, spokesman, spokeswoman, supporter, upholder 2. executant, interpreter, performer, player, presenter

expose 1. display, exhibit, manifest, present, put on view, reveal, show, uncover, unveil 2. air, betray, bring to light, denounce, detect, disclose, divulge, lay bare, let out, make known, reveal, show up, smoke out, uncover, unearth, unmask 3. endanger, hazard, imperil, jeopardize, lay open, leave open, make vulnerable, risk, subject

exposed 1. bare, exhibited, laid bare, made manifest, made public, on display, on show, on view, revealed, shown, unconcealed, uncovered, unveiled 2. open, open to the elements, unprotected, unsheltered 3. in danger, in peril, laid bare, laid open, left open, liable, open, susceptible, vulnerable

exposition 1. account, commentary, critique, description, elucidation, exegesis, explanation, explication, illustration, interpretation, presentation 2. demonstration, display, exhibition, expo (*Inf.*), fair, presentation, show

expostulate argue (with), dissuade, protest, reason (with), remonstrate (with)

exposure 1. baring, display, exhibition, manifestation, presentation, publicity, revelation, showing, uncovering, unveiling 2. airing, betrayal, denunciation, detection, disclosure, divulgence, divulging, exposé, revelation, unmasking 3. danger, hazard, jeopardy, risk, vulnerability 4. aspect, frontage, location, outlook, position, setting, view

expound describe, elucidate, explain, explicate (*Formal*), illustrate, interpret, set forth, spell out, unfold

express *v.* 1. articulate, assert, asseverate, communicate, couch, declare, enunciate, phrase, pronounce, put, put across, put into words, say, speak, state, tell, utter, verbalize, voice, word 2. bespeak, convey, denote, depict, designate, disclose, divulge, embody, evince, exhibit, indicate, intimate, make known, manifest, represent, reveal, show, signify, stand for, symbolize, testify 3. extract, force out, press out, squeeze out ~*adj.* 4. accurate, categorical, certain, clear, definite, direct, distinct, exact, explicit, outright, plain, pointed, precise, unambiguous 5. clear-

expresso (ɪkˈsprɛsəʊ) *n. see* ESPRESSO

expropriate (ɛksˈprəʊprɪeɪt) *vt.* **1.** dispossess **2.** take out of owner's hands **—exproprⁱation** *n.* **—exˈpropriator** *n.*

expulsion (ɪkˈspʌlʃən) *n. see* EXPEL

expunge (ɪkˈspʌndʒ) *vt.* strike out, erase **—exˈpunction** *n.*

expurgate (ˈɛkspəgeɪt) *vt.* remove objectionable parts from (book *etc.*), purge **—expurˈgation** *n.* **—ˈexpurgator** *n.* **—exˈpurgatory** *a.*

exquisite (ɪkˈskwɪzɪt, ˈɛkskwɪzɪt) *a.* **1.** of extreme beauty or delicacy **2.** keen, acute **3.** keenly sensitive **—exˈquisitely** *adv.*

ex-serviceman *n.* man who has served in the armed forces

extant (ɛkˈstænt, ˈɛkstənt) *a.* still existing

extempore (ɪkˈstɛmpərɪ) *a./adv.* without previous thought or preparation **—extempoˈraneous** *a.* **—exˈtemporary** *a.* **—extemporiˈzation** *or* **-iˈsation** *n.* **—exˈtemporize** *or* **-ise** *vi.* **1.** speak without preparation *—vt.* **2.** devise for the occasion

extend (ɪkˈstɛnd) *vt.* **1.** stretch out, lengthen **2.** prolong in duration **3.** widen in area, scope **4.** accord, grant *—vi.* **5.** reach **6.** cover a certain area **7.** have a certain range or scope **8.** become larger or wider **—exˈtendible, exˈtendable, exˈtensible** *or* **exˈtensile** *a.* that can be extended **—exˈtension** *n.* **1.** stretching out, prolongation, enlargement **2.** expansion **3.** continuation, additional part, as of telephone *etc.* **—exˈtensive** *a.* wide, large, comprehensive **—exˈtensor** *n.* straightening muscle **—exˈtent** *n.* **1.** space or degree to which thing is extended **2.** size **3.** compass **4.** volume **—extended family** nuclear family together with blood relatives, oft. spanning three or more generations **—extended-play** *a.* denoting gramophone record same size as a single but with longer playing time

extenuate (ɪkˈstɛnjʊeɪt) *vt.* make less blameworthy, mitigate **—extenuˈation** *n.* **—exˈtenuatory** *a.*

exterior (ɪkˈstɪərɪə) *n.* **1.** the outside **2.** outward appearance *—a.* **3.** outer, outward, external **—exterior angle 1.** angle of polygon contained between one side extended and adjacent side **2.** any of four angles made by transversal that are outside region between two intersected lines

exterminate (ɪkˈstɜːmɪneɪt) *vt.* destroy utterly, annihilate, root out, eliminate **—extermiˈnation** *n.* **—exˈterminator** *n.* destroyer

THESAURUS

cut, especial, particular, singular, special **6.** direct, fast, high-speed, nonstop, quick, rapid, speedy, swift

expression 1. announcement, assertion, asseveration, communication, declaration, enunciation, mention, pronouncement, speaking, statement, utterance, verbalization, voicing **2.** demonstration, embodiment, exhibition, indication, manifestation, representation, show, sign, symbol, token **3.** air, appearance, aspect, countenance, face, look, mien (*Literary*) **4.** idiom, locution, phrase, remark, set phrase, term, turn of phrase, word

expressive eloquent, emphatic, energetic, forcible, lively, mobile, moving, poignant, striking, strong, sympathetic, telling, vivid

expressly 1. especially, exactly, intentionally, on purpose, particularly, precisely, purposely, specially, specifically **2.** absolutely, categorically, clearly, decidedly, definitely, distinctly, explicitly, in no uncertain terms, manifestly, outright, plainly, pointedly, positively, unambiguously, unequivocally, unmistakably

expropriate appropriate, arrogate, assume, commandeer, confiscate, impound, requisition, seize, take, take over

expulsion banishment, debarment, discharge, dislodgment, dismissal, ejection, eviction, exclusion, exile, expatriation, extrusion, proscription, removal

expurgate blue-pencil, bowdlerize, censor, clean up (*Inf.*), cut, purge, purify

exquisite 1. beautiful, dainty, delicate, elegant, fine, lovely, precious **2.** attractive, beautiful, charming, comely, lovely, pleasing, striking **3.** appreciative, consummate, cultivated, discerning, discriminating, fastidious, impeccable, meticulous, polished, refined, selective, sensitive **4.** acute, excruciating, intense, keen, piercing, poignant, sharp

extempore *adv./adj.* ad lib, extemporaneous, extemporary, freely, impromptu, improvised, offhand, off the cuff (*Inf.*), off the top of one's head, on the spot, spontaneously, unplanned, unpremeditated, unprepared

extemporize ad-lib, improvise, make up, play (it) by ear

extend 1. carry on, continue, drag out, draw out, elongate, lengthen, make longer, prolong, protract, spin out, spread out, stretch, unfurl, unroll **2.** carry on, continue, go on, last, take **3.** amount to, attain, go as far as, reach, spread **4.** add to, amplify, augment, broaden, develop, dilate, enhance, enlarge, expand, increase, spread, supplement, widen **5.** advance, bestow, confer, give, grant, hold out, impart, offer, present, proffer, put forth, reach out, stretch out, yield

extension 1. amplification, augmentation, broadening, continuation, delay, development, dilatation, distension, elongation, enlargement, expansion, extent, increase, lengthening, postponement, prolongation, protraction, spread, stretching, widening **2.** addendum, addition, adjunct, annexe, appendage, appendix, branch, ell, supplement, wing

extensive all-inclusive, broad, capacious, commodious, comprehensive, expanded, extended, far-flung, far-reaching, general, great, huge, large, large-scale, lengthy, long, pervasive, prevalent, protracted, spacious, sweeping, thorough, universal, vast, voluminous, wholesale, wide, widespread

extent 1. bounds, compass, play, range, reach, scope, sphere, sweep **2.** amount, amplitude, area, breadth, bulk, degree, duration, expanse, expansion, length, magnitude, measure, quantity, size, stretch, term, time, volume, width

exterior 1. *n.* appearance, aspect, coating, covering, façade, face, finish, outside, shell, skin, surface **2.** *adj.* external, outer, outermost, outside, outward, superficial, surface

exterminate abolish, annihilate, destroy, eliminate, eradicate, extirpate

external apparent, exterior, outer, outermost, outside, outward, superficial, surface, visible

external (ɪkˈstɜːnᵊl) *a.* outside, outward —**externaliˈzation, exteriorization** *or* **-isation** (ɪkstɪərɪəraɪˈzeɪʃən) *n.* —**exˈternalize, exˈteriorize** *or* **-ise** *vt.* **1.** make external **2.** *Psychol.* attribute (one's feelings) to one's surroundings —**exˈternally** *adv.*

extinct (ɪkˈstɪŋkt) *a.* **1.** having died out or come to an end **2.** no longer existing **3.** quenched, no longer burning —**exˈtinction** *n.*

extinguish (ɪkˈstɪŋgwɪʃ) *vt.* **1.** put out, quench **2.** wipe out —**exˈtinguishable** *a.* —**exˈtinguisher** *n.* device, *esp.* spraying liquid or foam, used to put out fires

extirpate (ˈɛkstəpeɪt) *vt.* **1.** root out **2.** destroy utterly —**extirˈpation** *n.* —**ˈextirpator** *n.*

extol *or U.S.* **extoll** (ɪkˈstəʊl) *vt.* praise highly (**-ll-**)

extort (ɪkˈstɔːt) *vt.* **1.** get by force or threats **2.** wring out **3.** exact —**exˈtortion** *n.* —**exˈtortionate** *a.* (of prices *etc.*) excessive, exorbitant —**exˈtortioner** *n.*

extra (ˈɛkstrə) *a.* **1.** additional **2.** larger, better, than usual —*adv.* **3.** additionally **4.** more than usually —*n.* **5.** extra thing **6.** something charged as additional **7.** *Cricket* run not scored off bat **8.** *Cine.* actor hired for crowd scenes

extra- (*comb. form*) beyond, as in *extradition, extramural, extraterritorial.* Such words are not given here where the meaning may easily be inferred from the simple word

extract (ɪkˈstrækt) *vt.* **1.** take out, *esp.* by force **2.** obtain against person's will **3.** get by pressure, distillation *etc.* **4.** deduce **5.** derive **6.** copy out, quote —*n.* (ˈɛkstrækt) **7.** passage from book, film *etc.* **8.** matter got by distillation **9.** concentrated solution —**exˈtraction** *n.* **1.** extracting, *esp.* of tooth **2.** ancestry —**exˈtractor** *n.* —**extractor fan** device for extracting stale air, fumes *etc.*

extracurricular (ɛkstrəkəˈrɪkjʊlə) *a.* **1.** taking place outside normal school timetable **2.** beyond regular duties *etc.*

extradition (ɛkstrəˈdɪʃən) *n.* delivery, under treaty, of foreign fugitive from justice to authorities concerned —**extraditable** (ˈɛkstrədaɪtəbᵊl) *a.* —**extradite** (ˈɛkstrədaɪt) *vt.* **1.** surrender (alleged offender) for trial to foreign state **2.** procure extradition of

extramural (ɛkstrəˈmjʊərəl) *a.* **1.** connected with but outside normal courses *etc.* of university or college **2.** situated outside walls or boundaries of a place

extraneous (ɪkˈstreɪnɪəs) *a.* **1.** not essential **2.** irrelevant **3.** added from without, not belonging

extraordinary (ɪkˈstrɔːdᵊnrɪ) *a.* **1.** out of the usual course **2.** additional **3.** unusual, surprising, exceptional —**exˈtraordinarily** *adv.*

extrapolate (ɪkˈstræpəleɪt) *v.* **1.** infer (something not known) from known facts **2.** *Maths.* estimate (a value) beyond known values

extrasensory (ɛkstrəˈsɛnsərɪ) *a.* of perception apparently gained without use of known senses

extraterrestrial (ɛkstrətɪˈrɛstrɪəl) *a.* of, or from outside the earth's atmosphere

extravagant (ɪkˈstrævɪgənt) *a.* **1.** wasteful **2.** exorbitant **3.** wild, absurd —**exˈtravagance** *n.* —**exˈtravagantly** *adv.* —**extravaˈganza** *n.* elaborate, lavish, entertainment, display *etc.*

THESAURUS

extinct 1. dead, defunct, gone, lost, vanished **2.** doused, extinguished, inactive, out, quenched, snuffed out **3.** abolished, defunct, ended, obsolete, terminated, void

extinction abolition, annihilation, death, destruction, dying out, eradication, excision, extermination, extirpation, obliteration, oblivion

extinguish 1. blow out, douse, put out, quench, smother, snuff out, stifle **2.** abolish, annihilate, destroy, eliminate, end, eradicate, erase, expunge, exterminate, extirpate, kill, obscure, remove, suppress, wipe out

extol acclaim, applaud, celebrate, commend, cry up, eulogize, exalt, glorify, laud, magnify (*Archaic*), panegyrize, pay tribute to, praise, sing the praises of

extort blackmail, bleed (*Inf.*), bully, coerce, exact, extract, force, squeeze, wrest, wring

extortionate excessive, exorbitant, extravagant, immoderate, inflated, inordinate, outrageous, preposterous, sky-high, unreasonable

extra 1. *adj.* accessory, added, additional, ancillary, auxiliary, fresh, further, more, new, other, supplemental, supplementary **2.** *n.* accessory, addendum, addition, adjunct, affix, appendage, appurtenance, attachment, bonus, complement, extension, supernumerary, supplement **3.** *adv.* especially, exceptionally, extraordinarily, extremely, particularly, remarkably, uncommonly, unusually

extract *v.* **1.** draw, extirpate, pluck out, pull, pull out, remove, take out, uproot, withdraw **2.** bring out, derive, draw, elicit, evoke, exact, gather, get, glean, obtain, reap, wrest, wring **3.** deduce, derive, develop, educe, elicit, evolve **4.** distil, draw out, express, obtain, press out, separate out, squeeze, take out **5.** abstract, choose, cite, copy out, cull, cut out, quote, select ~*n.* **6.** concentrate, decoction, distillate, distillation, essence, juice **7.** abstract, citation, clipping, cutting, excerpt, passage, quotation, selection

extraction 1. drawing, extirpation, pulling, removal, taking out, uprooting, withdrawal **2.** ancestry, birth, blood, derivation, descent, family, lineage, origin, parentage, pedigree, race, stock

extraneous 1. accidental, additional, adventitious, extra, incidental, inessential, needless, nonessential, peripheral, redundant, superfluous, supplementary, unessential, unnecessary, unneeded **2.** beside the point, immaterial, impertinent, inadmissible, inapplicable, inapposite, inappropriate, inapt, irrelevant, off the subject, unconnected, unrelated **3.** adventitious, alien, exotic, external, extrinsic, foreign, out of place, strange

extraordinary amazing, bizarre, curious, exceptional, fantastic, marvellous, odd, outstanding, particular, peculiar, phenomenal, rare, remarkable, singular, special, strange, surprising, uncommon, unfamiliar, unheard-of, unique, unprecedented, unusual, unwonted, weird, wonderful

extravagance 1. improvidence, lavishness, overspending, prodigality, profligacy, profusion, squandering, waste, wastefulness **2.** absurdity, dissipation, exaggeration, excess, exorbitance, folly, immoderation, outrageousness, preposterousness, recklessness, unreasonableness, unrestraint, wildness

extravagant 1. excessive, improvident, imprudent, lavish, prodigal, profligate, spendthrift, wasteful **2.** absurd, exaggerated, excessive, exorbitant, fanciful,

extreme (ɪkˈstriːm) *a.* 1. of high or highest degree 2. severe 3. going beyond moderation 4. at the end 5. outermost —*n.* 6. utmost degree 7. thing at one end or the other, first and last of series —**exˈtremely** *adv.* —**exˈtremism** *n.* —**exˈtremist** *n.* 1. advocate of extreme measures —*a.* 2. of immoderate or excessive actions, opinions *etc.* —**extremity** (ɪkˈstrɛmɪtɪ) *n.* 1. end —*pl.* 2. hands and feet 3. utmost distress 4. extreme measures —**extreme unction** sacrament in which dying person is anointed by priest

extricate (ˈɛkstrɪkeɪt) *vt.* disentangle, unravel, set free —**ˈextricable** *a.* —**extriˈcation** *n.*

extrinsic (ɛkˈstrɪnsɪk) *a.* accessory, not belonging, not intrinsic —**exˈtrinsically** *adv.*

extrovert *or* **extravert** (ˈɛkstrəvɜːt) *n.* one who is interested in other people and things rather than his own feelings —**extroˈversion** *or* **extraˈversion** *n.*

extrude (ɪkˈstruːd) *vt.* 1. squeeze, force out 2. (*esp.* of molten metal or plastic *etc.*) shape by squeezing through suitable nozzle or die

exuberant (ɪgˈzjuːbərənt) *a.* 1. high-spirited, vivacious 2. prolific, abundant, luxurious —**exˈuberance** *n.* —**exˈuberantly** *adv.*

exude (ɪgˈzjuːd) *vi.* 1. ooze out —*vt.* 2. give off (moisture) —**exuˈdation** *n.* —**exˈudative** *a.*

exult (ɪgˈzʌlt) *vi.* 1. rejoice 2. triumph —**exˈultancy** *n.* —**exˈultant** *a.* triumphant —**exulˈtation** *n.*

eye (aɪ) *n.* 1. organ of sight 2. look, glance 3. attention 4. aperture 5. view 6. judgment 7. watch, vigilance 8. thing, mark resembling eye 9. slit in needle for thread —*vt.* 10. look at 11. observe —**ˈeyeless** *a.* —**ˈeyelet** *n.* small hole for rope *etc.* to pass through —**ˈeyeball** *n.* ball of eye —**ˈeyebrow** *n.* fringe of hair above eye —**eye-catcher** *n.* —**eye-catching** *a.* striking —**ˈeyeful** *n. inf.* 1. view, glance *etc.* 2. beautiful sight, *esp.* a woman —**ˈeyeglass** *n.* 1. glass to assist sight 2. monocle —*pl.* 3. *chiefly* US spectacles —**ˈeyehole** *n.* 1. hole through which rope *etc.* is passed 2. *inf.* cavity containing eyeball 3. peephole —**ˈeyelash** *n.* hair fringing eyelid —**ˈeyelid** *n.* either of two muscular folds of skin that can be moved to cover exposed portion of eyeball —**ˈeyeliner** *n.* cosmetic used to outline eyes —**eye-opener** *n. inf.* 1. surprising news 2. revealing statement —**ˈeyepiece** *n.* lens or lenses in optical instrument nearest eye of observer —**eye shadow** coloured cosmetic put on around the eyes —**ˈeyeshot** *n.* range of vision —**ˈeyesight** *n.* ability to see —**ˈeyesore** *n.* 1. ugly object 2. thing that annoys one to see —**ˈeyestrain** *n.* fatigue of eyes, resulting from excessive use or uncorrected defects of vision —**ˈeyetooth** *n.* canine tooth —**ˈeyewash** *n. inf.* deceptive talk *etc.*, nonsense —**ˈeyewitness** *n.* one who saw something for himself —**an eye for an eye** retributive justice; retaliation

eyrie (ˈɪərɪ, ˈɛərɪ, ˈaɪərɪ) *or* **aerie** *n.* 1. nest of bird of prey, *esp.* eagle 2. high dwelling place

THESAURUS

fantastic, foolish, immoderate, inordinate, outrageous, preposterous, reckless, unreasonable, unrestrained, wild **3.** costly, excessive, exorbitant, expensive, extortionate, inordinate, overpriced, steep (*Inf.*), unreasonable

extreme *adj.* **1.** acute, great, greatest, high, highest, intense, maximum, severe, supreme, ultimate, utmost, uttermost, worst **2.** downright, egregious, exaggerated, exceptional, excessive, extraordinary, extravagant, fanatical, immoderate, inordinate, intemperate, out-and-out, outrageous, radical, remarkable, sheer, uncommon, unconventional, unreasonable, unusual, utter, zealous **3.** dire, Draconian, drastic, harsh, radical, rigid, severe, stern, strict, unbending, uncompromising **4.** faraway, far-off, farthest, final, last, most distant, outermost, remotest, terminal, ultimate, utmost, uttermost ~*n.* **5.** acme, apex, apogee, boundary, climax, consummation, depth, edge, end, excess, extremity, height, limit, maximum, minimum, nadir, pinnacle, pole, termination, top, ultimate, zenith

extremely acutely, awfully (*Inf.*), exceedingly, exceptionally, excessively, extraordinarily, greatly, highly, inordinately, intensely, markedly, quite, severely, terribly, to *or* in the extreme, ultra, uncommonly, unusually, utterly, very

extremist die-hard, fanatic, radical, ultra, zealot

extremity **1.** acme, apex, apogee, border, bound, boundary, brim, brink, edge, end, extreme, frontier, limit, margin, maximum, minimum, nadir, pinnacle, pole, rim, terminal, termination, terminus, tip, top, ultimate, verge, zenith **2.** adversity, crisis, dire straits, disaster, emergency, exigency, hardship, pinch, plight, setback, trouble

extricate clear, deliver, disembarrass, disengage, disentangle, free, get out, get (someone) off the hook (*Sl.*), liberate, release, relieve, remove, rescue, withdraw, wriggle out of

exuberant **1.** animated, buoyant, cheerful, eager, ebullient, effervescent, elated, energetic, enthusiastic, excited, exhilarated, high-spirited, in high spirits, lively, sparkling, spirited, sprightly, vigorous, vivacious, zestful **2.** abundant, copious, lavish, lush, luxuriant, overflowing, plenteous, plentiful, profuse, rank, rich, superabundant, teeming

exult **1.** be delighted, be elated, be in high spirits, be joyful, be jubilant, be overjoyed, celebrate, jubilate, jump for joy, make merry, rejoice **2.** boast, brag, crow, gloat, glory (in), revel, take delight in, taunt, triumph, vaunt

exultant cock-a-hoop, delighted, elated, exulting, flushed, gleeful, joyful, joyous, jubilant, overjoyed, rejoicing, revelling, transported, triumphant

exultation **1.** celebration, delight, elation, glee, high spirits, joy, joyousness, jubilation, merriness, rejoicing, transport **2.** boasting, bragging, crowing, gloating, glory, glorying, revelling, triumph

eye *n.* **1.** eyeball, optic (*Inf.*), orb (*Poetic*), peeper (*Sl.*) **2.** appreciation, discernment, discrimination, judgment, perception, recognition, taste **3.** *Often plural* belief, judgment, mind, opinion, point of view, viewpoint **4. an eye for an eye** justice, reprisal, requital, retaliation, retribution, revenge, vengeance ~*v.* **5.** contemplate, gaze at, glance at, have *or* take a look at, inspect, look at, peruse, regard, scan, scrutinize, stare at, study, survey, view, watch

eyesight observation, perception, range of vision, sight, vision

eyesore atrocity, blemish, blight, blot, disfigurement, disgrace, horror, mess, monstrosity, sight (*Inf.*), ugliness

eyewitness bystander, looker-on, observer, onlooker, passer-by, spectator, viewer, watcher, witness

F

f *or* **F** (ɛf) *n.* **1.** sixth letter of English alphabet **2.** speech sound represented by this letter, as in *fat* (*pl.* **f's, F's** *or* **Fs**)

f, f/, *or* **f:** f number

f. *Mus.* forte

f. *or* **F. 1.** female **2.** *Gram.* feminine **3.** folio (*pl.* **ff.** *or* **FF.**) **4.** following (page) (*pl.* **ff.**) **5.** franc **6.** furlong

F 1. *Mus.* fourth note of scale of C major; major or minor key having this note as tonic **2.** Fahrenheit **3.** *Chem.* fluorine **4.** *Phys.* force **5.** farad **6.** *Genetics* generation of filial offspring, F_1 being first generation **7.** Fellow

fa (fɑː) *n. see* FAH

FA Football Association

Fabian (ˈfeɪbɪən) *a.* **1.** of or resembling delaying tactics of Q. Fabius Maximus, Roman general; cautious —*n.* **2.** member of Fabian Society, socialist organization advocating gradual reforms

fable (ˈfeɪbᵊl) *n.* **1.** short story with moral, *esp.* one with animals as characters **2.** tale **3.** legend **4.** fiction; lie —*v.* **5.** tell (fables) —*vi.* **6.** tell lies —*vt.* **7.** talk of in manner of fable —**fabulist** (ˈfæbjʊlɪst) *n.* writer of fables —**fabulous** (ˈfæbjʊləs) *a.* **1.** amazing **2.** *inf.* extremely good **3.** told of in fables

fabric (ˈfæbrɪk) *n.* **1.** cloth **2.** texture **3.** frame, structure —ˈ**fabricate** *vt.* **1.** build **2.** frame **3.** construct **4.** invent (lie *etc.*) **5.** forge (document) —**fabriˈcation** *n.* —ˈ**fabricator** *n.*

façade *or* **facade** (fəˈsɑːd, fæ-) *n.* **1.** front of building **2.** *fig.* outward appearance

face (feɪs) *n.* **1.** front of head **2.** distorted expression **3.** outward appearance **4.** front, upper surface or chief side of anything **5.** dial of a clock *etc.* **6.** dignity **7.** *inf.* make-up (*esp. in* **put one's face on**) **8.** *Print.* printing surface of type character; style or design of character on type (*also* ˈ**typeface**) —*vt.* **9.** look or front towards **10.** meet (boldly) **11.** give a covering surface to —*vi.* **12.** turn —ˈ**faceless** *a.* **1.** without a face **2.** anonymous —ˈ**facer** *n.* **1.** person or thing that faces **2.** **UK** *inf.* difficulty, problem —**facet** (ˈfæsɪt) *n.* **1.** one side of many-sided body, *esp.* cut gem **2.** one aspect —**facial** (ˈfeɪʃəl) *a.* **1.** pert. to face —*n.* **2.** cosmetic treatment for face —ˈ**facing** *n.* **1.** piece of material used *esp.* to conceal seam and prevent fraying **2.** (*usu. pl.*) collar, cuffs *etc.* of military uniform jacket **3.** outer layer or coat of material applied to surface of wall —**face card S** court card —**face-lift** *n.* **1.** operation to tighten skin of face to remove wrinkles **2.** improvement, renovation —**face-saving** *a.* maintaining dignity —**face value 1.** value on face of commercial paper or coin **2.** apparent value —**face up to** accept (unpleasant fact *etc.*) —**on the face of it** to all appearances

facetious (fəˈsiːʃəs) *a.* **1.** (sarcastically) witty **2.** humorous, given to jesting, *esp.* at inappropriate time

facia (ˈfeɪʃɪə) *n. see* FASCIA

-facient (*comb. form*) state; quality, as in *absorbefacient*

facile (ˈfæsaɪl) *a.* **1.** easy **2.** working easily **3.** easy-going **4.** superficial, silly —**facilitate** (fəˈsɪlɪteɪt) *vt.* make easy, help progress of —**facilitation** (fəsɪlɪˈteɪʃən) *n.* —**facility** (fəˈsɪlɪtɪ) *n.* **1.** easiness **2.** dexterity —*pl.* **3.** opportunities, good conditions **4.** means, equipment for doing something

THESAURUS

fable 1. allegory, apologue, legend, myth, parable, story, tale **2.** fabrication, fairy story (*Inf.*), falsehood, fantasy, fib, fiction, figment, invention, lie, romance, tall story (*Inf.*), untruth, white lie, yarn (*Inf.*)

fabric 1. cloth, material, stuff, textile, web **2.** constitution, construction, foundations, framework, infrastructure, make-up, organization, structure

fabricate 1. assemble, build, construct, erect, fashion, form, frame, make, manufacture, shape **2.** coin, concoct, devise, fake, falsify, feign, forge, form, invent, make up, trump up

fabrication 1. assemblage, assembly, building, construction, erection, manufacture, production **2.** cock-and-bull story (*Inf.*), concoction, fable, fairy story (*Inf.*), fake, falsehood, fiction, figment, forgery, invention, lie, myth, untruth

fabulous *n.* **1.** amazing, astounding, breathtaking, fictitious, immense, inconceivable, incredible, legendary, phenomenal, unbelievable **2.** *Inf.* fantastic (*Inf.*), marvellous, out-of-this-world (*Inf.*), spectacular, superb, wonderful **3.** apocryphal, fantastic, fictitious, imaginary, invented, legendary, made-up, mythical, unreal

façade appearance, exterior, face, front, frontage, guise, mask, pretence, semblance, show, veneer

face *n.* **1.** clock (*Sl.*), countenance, dial (*Sl.*), features, kisser (*Sl.*), lineaments, mug (*Sl.*), phiz *or* phizog (*Sl.*), physiognomy, visage **2.** appearance, aspect, expression, frown, grimace, look, *moue*, pout, scowl, smirk **3.** air, appearance, disguise, display, exterior, façade, front, mask, pretence, semblance, show **4.** authority, dignity, honour, image, prestige, reputation, self-respect, standing, status **5.** aspect, cover, exterior, facet, front, outside, right side, side, surface **6. on the face of it** apparently, at first sight, seemingly, to all appearances, to the eye ~*v.* **7.** be confronted by, brave, come up against, confront, cope with, deal with, defy, encounter, experience, meet, oppose **8.** be opposite, front onto, give towards *or* onto, look onto, overlook **9.** clad, coat, cover, dress, finish, level, line, overlay, sheathe, surface, veneer

facet angle, aspect, face, part, phase, plane, side, slant, surface

facetious amusing, comical, droll, flippant, frivolous, funny, humorous, jesting, jocose, jocular, merry, playful, pleasant, tongue in cheek, unserious, waggish, witty

face up to accept, acknowledge, come to terms with, confront, cope with, deal with, meet head-on

facile 1. adept, adroit, dexterous, easy, effortless, fluent, light, proficient, quick, ready, simple, skilful, smooth, uncomplicated **2.** cursory, glib, hasty, shallow, slick, superficial

facilitate assist the progress of, ease, expedite, forward, further, help, make easy, promote, smooth the path of, speed up

facility 1. ability, adroitness, dexterity, ease, efficiency, effortlessness, expertness, fluency, knack, proficiency, quickness, readiness, skilfulness, skill,

facsimile (fæk'sɪmɪlɪ) *n.* **1.** exact copy **2.** telegraphic system in which document is scanned by photoelectricity, signals being transmitted and reproduced photographically **3.** image produced by this means

fact (fækt) *n.* **1.** thing known to be true **2.** deed **3.** reality —**'factual** *a.* —**as a matter of fact, in (point of) fact** in reality or actuality —**fact of life** (*esp.* unpleasant) inescapable truth

faction[1] ('fækʃən) *n.* **1.** (dissenting) minority group within larger body **2.** dissension —**'factious** *a.* of or producing factions

faction[2] ('fækʃən) *n.* dramatization of factual event

factitious (fæk'tɪʃəs) *a.* **1.** artificial **2.** specially made up **3.** unreal

factor ('fæktə) *n.* **1.** something contributing to a result **2.** one of numbers which multiplied together give a given number **3.** agent, dealer —**fac'torial** *Maths. n.* **1.** product of all positive integers from one up to and including given integer —*a.* **2.** of factorials or factors —**fac'totum** *n.* man-of-all-work —**factor 8** protein that participates in clotting of blood: used in treatment of haemophilia

factory ('fæktərɪ) *n.* building where things are manufactured —**factory farm** farm where animals are intensively reared using modern industrial methods —**factory ship** vessel that processes fish supplied by fleet

faculty ('fæk'ltɪ) *n.* **1.** inherent power **2.** power of the mind **3.** ability, aptitude **4.** department of university **5.** members of profession **6.** authorization —**'facultative** *a.* **1.** optional **2.** contingent

fad (fæd) *n.* **1.** short-lived fashion **2.** whim —**'faddish** *or* **'faddy** *a.*

fade (feɪd) *vi.* **1.** lose colour, strength **2.** wither **3.** grow dim **4.** disappear gradually —*vt.* **5.** cause to fade —**'fadeless** *a.* —**'fader** *n.* —**fade-in, fade-out** *n.* **1.** *Rad.* variation in strength of signals **2.** *T.V., cine.* gradual appearance and disappearance of picture

faeces *or esp. U.S.* **feces** ('fiːsiːz) *pl.n.* excrement, waste matter —**faecal** *or esp. U.S.* **fecal** ('fiːk'l) *a.*

faerie *or* **faery** ('feɪərɪ, 'fɛərɪ) *obs., poet. n.* **1.** fairyland —*a./n.* **2.** *see* FAIRY

Faeroese *or* **Faroese** (fɛərəʊ'iːz) *a.* **1.** of Faeroes, islands in N Atlantic —*n.* **2.** language of Faeroes **3.** native of Faeroes (*pl.* **-ese**)

faff (fæf) *vi.* (*oft. with* about) **UK** *inf.* dither; fuss

fag (fæg) *n.* **1.** *inf.* boring task **2.** *sl.* cigarette **3.** **US** *sl.* male homosexual **4.** **UK** *esp.* formerly, young public school boy who performs menial chores for older boy or prefect —*v.* **5.** *inf.* (*esp. with* out) tire —*vi.* **6.** do menial tasks for a senior boy in school (**-gg-**) —**fag end** **1.** last part, inferior remnant **2.** **UK** *inf.* stub of cigarette

faggot[1] *or esp. U.S.* **fagot** ('fægət) *n.* **1.** bundle of sticks for fuel *etc.* **2.** ball of chopped liver *etc.*

faggot[2] ('fægət) *n.* **US** *sl.* male homosexual

fah *or* **fa** (fɑː) *n. Mus.* **1.** in fixed system of solmization, note F **2.** in tonic sol-fa, fourth degree of major scale

Fah. *or* **Fahr.** Fahrenheit

Fahrenheit ('færənhaɪt) *a.* measured by thermometric scale with freezing point of water 32°, boiling point 212°

faïence (faɪ'ɑːns, feɪ-) *n.* glazed earthenware or china

fail (feɪl) *vi.* **1.** be unsuccessful **2.** stop operating or working **3.** be below the required standard **4.** be insufficient **5.** run short **6.** be wanting when in need **7.** lose power **8.** die away **9.** become bankrupt —*vt.* **10.** disappoint, give no help to **11.** neglect **12.** judge (candidate) to be below required standard —**'failing** *n.* **1.** deficiency **2.** fault —*prep.* **3.** in default of —**'failure** *n.* —**fail-safe** *a.* (of device) ensuring safety or remedy of malfunction in machine, weapon *etc.* —**without fail** certainly

THESAURUS

smoothness **2.** *Often plural* advantage, aid, amenity, appliance, convenience, equipment, means, opportunity, resource

facing *n.* cladding, coating, façade, false front, front, overlay, plaster, reinforcement, revetment, stucco, surface, trimming, veneer

facsimile carbon, carbon copy, copy, duplicate, photocopy, Photostat (*Trademark*), print, replica, reproduction, transcript, Xerox (*Trademark*)

fact **1.** act, deed, event, *fait accompli*, happening, incident, occurrence, performance **2.** actuality, certainty, gospel (truth), naked truth, reality, truth **3.** **in fact** actually, indeed, in point of fact, in reality, in truth, really, truly

faction **1.** bloc, cabal, camp, caucus, clique, coalition, combination, confederacy, contingent, division, gang, ginger group, group, junta, lobby, minority, party, pressure group, section, sector, set, splinter group **2.** conflict, disagreement, discord, disharmony, dissension, disunity, division, divisiveness, friction, infighting, rebellion, sedition, strife, tumult, turbulence

factious conflicting, contentious, disputatious, dissident, divisive, insurrectionary, litigious, malcontent, mutinous, partisan, rebellious, refractory, rival, sectarian, seditious, troublemaking, tumultuous, turbulent, warring

factor **1.** aspect, cause, circumstance, component, consideration, determinant, element, influence, item, part, point, thing **2.** *Scot.* agent, deputy, estate manager, middleman, reeve, steward

factory manufactory (*Obsolete*), mill, plant, works

factotum Girl Friday, handyman, jack of all trades, Man Friday, man of all work, odd job man

factual accurate, authentic, circumstantial, close, correct, credible, exact, faithful, genuine, literal, matter-of-fact, objective, precise, real, sure, true, true-to-life, unadorned, unbiased, veritable

faculty **1.** ability, adroitness, aptitude, bent, capability, capacity, cleverness, dexterity, facility, gift, knack, power, propensity, readiness, skill, talent, turn **2.** branch of learning, department, discipline, profession, school, teaching staff (*Chiefly U.S.*) **3.** authorization, licence, prerogative, privilege, right

fad affectation, craze, fancy, fashion, mania, mode, rage, trend, vogue, whim

fade **1.** blanch, bleach, blench, dim, discolour, dull, grow dim, lose colour, lose lustre, pale, wash out **2.** decline, die away, die out, dim, disappear, disperse, dissolve, droop, dwindle, ebb, etiolate, evanesce, fail, fall, flag, languish, melt away, perish, shrivel, vanish, vanish into thin air, wane, waste away, wilt, wither

fain (feɪn) *obs. a.* **1.** glad, willing; constrained *—adv.* **2.** gladly

faint (feɪnt) *a.* **1.** feeble, dim, pale **2.** weak **3.** dizzy, about to lose consciousness *—vi.* **4.** lose consciousness temporarily **—faint-hearted** *a.* timid

fair[1] (fɛə) *a.* **1.** just, impartial **2.** according to rules, legitimate **3.** blond **4.** beautiful **5.** ample **6.** of moderate quality or amount **7.** unblemished **8.** plausible **9.** middling **10.** (of weather) favourable *—adv.* **11.** honestly **12.** absolutely; quite **—'fairing** *n. Aviation* streamlined casing, or any part so shaped that it provides streamline form **—'fairish** *a.* **—'fairly** *adv.* **1.** moderately **2.** as deserved; justly **3.** positively **—'fairness** *n.* **—Fair Isle** intricate multicoloured pattern knitted with Shetland wool **—fair play** (abidance by) established standard of decency **—'fairway** *n.* **1.** navigable channel **2.** *Golf* trimmed turf between rough **—fair-weather** *a.* **1.** suitable for use in fair weather only **2.** unreliable in difficult situations **—the fair sex** women collectively

fair[2] (fɛə) *n.* **1.** travelling entertainment with sideshows, amusements *etc.* **2.** large exhibition of commercial or industrial products **3.** periodical market often with amusements **—'fairground** *n.*

fairy ('fɛərɪ) *n.* **1.** imaginary small creature with powers of magic **2.** *sl.* male homosexual *—a.* **3.** of fairies **4.** like fairy, beautiful and delicate **—fairy godmother** benefactress, *esp.* unknown **—fairy lamp** small coloured lamp for decorations **—'fairyland** *n.* **—fairy lights** small, coloured, decorative lights, *esp.* on Christmas tree **—fairy ring** circle of darker colour in grass **—fairy tale 1.** story of imaginary beings and happenings, *esp.* as told to children **2.** highly improbable account

fait accompli (fɛ takɔ̃'pli) *Fr.* something already done that cannot be altered

faith (feɪθ) *n.* **1.** trust **2.** belief (without proof) **3.** religion **4.** promise **5.** loyalty, constancy **—'faithful** *a.* constant, true **—'faithfully** *adv.* **—'faithless** *a.* **—faith healing** method of treating illness by religious faith

fake (feɪk) *vt.* **1.** conceal defects of by artifice **2.** touch up **3.** counterfeit **4.** sham *—n.* **5.** fraudulent object, person, act *—a.* **6.** not genuine **—'faker** *n.* **1.** one who deals in fakes **2.** swindler

THESAURUS

faeces bodily waste, droppings, dung, excrement, excreta, ordure, stools

fail *~v.* **1.** be defeated, be found lacking *or* wanting, be in vain, be unsuccessful, break down, come a cropper (*Inf.*), come to grief, come to naught, come to nothing, fall, fall short, fall short of, fall through, fizzle out (*Inf.*), flop (*Inf.*), founder, go astray, go down, go up in smoke (*Inf.*), meet with disaster, miscarry, misfire, miss, not make the grade (*Inf.*), run aground, turn out badly **2.** abandon, break one's word, desert, disappoint, forget, forsake, let down, neglect, omit **3.** be on one's last legs (*Inf.*), cease, conk out (*Inf.*), cut out, decline, die, disappear, droop, dwindle, fade, give out, give up, gutter, languish, peter out, sicken, sink, stop working, wane, weaken **4.** become insolvent, close down, crash, fold (*Inf.*), go bankrupt, go broke (*Inf.*), go bust (*Inf.*), go into receivership, go out of business, go to the wall, go under, smash *~n.* **5. without fail** conscientiously, constantly, dependably, like clockwork, punctually, regularly, religiously, without exception

failing 1. *n.* blemish, blind spot, defect, deficiency, drawback, error, failure, fault, flaw, foible, frailty, imperfection, lapse, miscarriage, misfortune, shortcoming, weakness **2.** *prep.* in default of, in the absence of, lacking

failure 1. abortion, breakdown, collapse, defeat, downfall, fiasco, frustration, lack of success, miscarriage, overthrow, wreck **2.** default, deficiency, dereliction, neglect, negligence, nonobservance, nonperformance, nonsuccess, omission, remissness, shortcoming, stoppage **3.** breakdown, decay, decline, deterioration, failing, loss **4.** bankruptcy, crash, downfall, folding (*Inf.*), insolvency, ruin

faint *adj.* **1.** bleached, delicate, dim, distant, dull, faded, faltering, feeble, hazy, hushed, ill-defined, indistinct, light, low, muffled, muted, soft, subdued, thin, vague, whispered **2.** feeble, remote, slight, unenthusiastic, weak **3.** dizzy, drooping, enervated, exhausted, faltering, fatigued, giddy, languid, lethargic, light-headed, muzzy, vertiginous, weak, woozy (*Inf.*) *~v.* **4.** black out, collapse, fade, fail, flake out (*Inf.*), keel over (*Inf.*), languish, lose consciousness, pass out, swoon (*Literary*), weaken

faint-hearted diffident, half-hearted, irresolute, timid, timorous, weak

fair[1] *adj.* **1.** above board, according to the rules, clean, disinterested, dispassionate, equal, equitable, even-handed, honest, honourable, impartial, just, lawful, legitimate, objective, on the level (*Inf.*), proper, square, trustworthy, unbiased, unprejudiced, upright **2.** blond, blonde, fair-haired, flaxen-haired, light, light-complexioned, tow-haired, towheaded **3.** adequate, all right, average, decent, mediocre, middling, moderate, not bad, O.K. (*Inf.*), passable, reasonable, respectable, satisfactory, so-so (*Inf.*), tolerable **4.** beauteous, beautiful, bonny, comely, handsome, lovely, pretty, well-favoured **5.** bright, clear, clement, cloudless, dry, favourable, fine, sunny, sunshiny, unclouded

fair[2] *n.* bazaar, carnival, expo (*Inf.*), exposition, festival, fête, gala, market, show

fairly 1. adequately, moderately, pretty well, quite, rather, reasonably, somewhat, tolerably **2.** deservedly, equitably, honestly, impartially, justly, objectively, properly, without fear or favour **3.** absolutely, in a manner of speaking, positively, really, veritably

fairness decency, disinterestedness, equitableness, equity, impartiality, justice, legitimacy, rightfulness, uprightness

fairy brownie, elf, hob, leprechaun, pixie, Robin Goodfellow, sprite

fairy tale 1. folk tale, romance **2.** cock-and-bull story (*Inf.*), fabrication, fantasy, fiction, invention, lie, tall story, untruth

faith 1. assurance, confidence, conviction, credence, credit, dependence, reliance, trust **2.** belief, church, communion, creed, denomination, dogma, persuasion, religion **3.** allegiance, constancy, faithfulness, fealty, fidelity, loyalty, truth, truthfulness

faithful attached, constant, dependable, devoted, loyal, reliable, staunch, steadfast, true, true-blue, trusty, truthful, unswerving, unwavering

faithless disloyal, doubting, false, false-hearted, fick-

fakir (fəˈkɪə, ˈfeɪkə) *n.* **1.** member of Islamic religious order **2.** Hindu ascetic

Falange (ˈfælændʒ) *n.* Fascist movement in Spain —**Faˈlangist** *n./a.*

falchion (ˈfɔːltʃən, ˈfɔːlʃən) *n.* broad curved medieval sword

falcon (ˈfɔːlkən, ˈfɔːkən) *n.* small bird of prey, *esp.* trained in hawking for sport —**ˈfalconer** *n.* one who keeps, trains or hunts with falcons —**ˈfalconry** *n.* hawking

falderal (ˈfældɪræl) *or* **folderol** *n.* **1.** showy but worthless trifle **2.** nonsense **3.** nonsensical refrain in old songs

fall (fɔːl) *vi.* **1.** drop, come down freely **2.** become lower **3.** decrease **4.** hang down **5.** come to the ground, cease to stand **6.** perish **7.** collapse **8.** be captured **9.** revert **10.** lapse **11.** be uttered **12.** become **13.** happen (**fell** *pt.*, **ˈfallen** *pp.*) —*n.* **14.** falling **15.** amount that falls **16.** amount of descent **17.** decrease **18.** collapse, ruin **19.** drop **20.** (*oft. pl.*) cascade **21.** cadence **22.** yielding to temptation **23.** US autumn **24.** rope of hoisting tackle —**fall guy** *inf., chiefly* US victim of confidence trick —**falling sickness** *or* **evil** *former name for* epilepsy —**falling star** *inf.* meteor —**ˈfallout** *n.* radioactive particles spread as result of nuclear explosion —**fall for** *inf.* **1.** fall in love with **2.** be taken in by —**fall out** disagree

fallacy (ˈfæləsɪ) *n.* **1.** incorrect, misleading opinion or argument **2.** flaw in logic **3.** illusion —**fallacious** (fəˈleɪʃəs) *a.* —**falliˈbility** *n.* —**ˈfallible** *a.* liable to error —**ˈfallibly** *adv.*

fallen (ˈfɔːlən) *v.* **1.** *pp. of* FALL —*a.* **2.** having sunk in reputation or honour **3.** killed in battle with glory —**fallen arch** collapse of arch formed by instep of foot, resulting in flat feet

Fallopian tube (fəˈləupɪən) either of pair of tubes through which egg cells pass from ovary to womb

fallow[1] (ˈfæləu) *a.* **1.** ploughed and harrowed but left without crop **2.** uncultivated **3.** neglected

fallow[2] (ˈfæləu) *a.* brown or reddish-yellow —**fallow deer** deer of this colour

false (fɔːls) *a.* **1.** wrong, erroneous **2.** deceptive **3.** faithless **4.** sham, artificial —**ˈfalsehood** *n.* lie —**ˈfalsely** *adv.* —**ˈfalseness** *n.* faithlessness —**falsifiˈcation** *n.* —**ˈfalsify** *vt.* **1.** alter fraudulently **2.** misrepresent **3.** disappoint (hopes *etc.*) (**ˈfalsified, ˈfalsifying**) —**ˈfalsity** *n.* —**false pretences** misrepresentation of facts to gain advantage (*esp. in* **under false pretences**)

falsetto (fɔːlˈsɛtəu) *n.* forced voice above natural range (*pl.* **-s**)

Falstaffian (fɔːlˈstɑːfɪən) *a.* like Shakespeare's Falstaff, fat, convivial and boasting

falter (ˈfɔːltə) *vi.* **1.** hesitate **2.** waver **3.** stumble —**ˈfalteringly** *adv.*

fame (feɪm) *n.* **1.** reputation **2.** renown —**famed** *a.* —**ˈfamous** *a.* **1.** widely known **2.** *inf.* excellent

familiar (fəˈmɪlɪə) *a.* **1.** well-known **2.** frequent, customary **3.** intimate **4.** closely acquainted **5.** unceremo-

THESAURUS

le, inconstant, perfidious, recreant (*Archaic*), traitorous, treacherous, unbelieving, unfaithful, unreliable, untrue, untrustworthy, untruthful

fake 1. *v.* affect, assume, copy, counterfeit, fabricate, feign, forge, pretend, put on, sham, simulate **2.** *n.* charlatan, copy, forgery, fraud, hoax, imitation, impostor, mountebank, phoney (*Sl.*), reproduction, sham **3.** *adj.* affected, artificial, assumed, counterfeit, false, forged, imitation, mock, phoney (*Sl.*), pinchbeck, pseudo, reproduction, sham

fall *v.* **1.** be precipitated, cascade, collapse, crash, descend, dive, drop, drop down, go head over heels, keel over, nose-dive, pitch, plummet, plunge, settle, sink, stumble, subside, topple, trip, trip over, tumble **2.** abate, become lower, decline, decrease, depreciate, diminish, dwindle, ebb, fall off, flag, go down, lessen, slump, subside **3.** be overthrown, be taken, capitulate, give in *or* up, give way, go out of office, pass into enemy hands, resign, succumb, surrender, yield **4.** be a casualty, be killed, be lost, be slain, die, meet one's end, perish **5.** become, befall, chance, come about, come to pass, fall out, happen, occur, take place **6.** backslide, err, go astray, lapse, offend, sin, transgress, trespass, yield to temptation ~*n.* **7.** descent, dive, drop, nose dive, plummet, plunge, slip, spill, tumble **8.** cut, decline, decrease, diminution, dip, drop, dwindling, falling off, lessening, lowering, reduction, slump **9.** capitulation, collapse, death, defeat, destruction, downfall, failure, overthrow, resignation, ruin, surrender **10.** degradation, failure, lapse, sin, slip, transgression

fallacy casuistry, deceit, deception, delusion, error, falsehood, faultiness, flaw, illusion, inconsistency, misapprehension, misconception, mistake, sophism, sophistry, untruth

fall for 1. become infatuated with, desire, fall in love with, lose one's head over, succumb to the charms of **2.** accept, be deceived (duped, fooled, taken in) by, give credence to, swallow (*Inf.*)

fallible erring, frail, ignorant, imperfect, mortal, prone to error, uncertain, weak

fall out altercate, argue, clash, differ, disagree, fight, quarrel, squabble

fallow dormant, idle, inactive, inert, resting, uncultivated, undeveloped, unplanted, untilled, unused

false 1. concocted, erroneous, faulty, fictitious, improper, inaccurate, incorrect, inexact, invalid, mistaken, unfounded, unreal, wrong **2.** artificial, bogus, counterfeit, ersatz, fake, feigned, forged, imitation, mock, pretended, sham, simulated, spurious, synthetic **3.** deceitful, deceiving, deceptive, delusive, fallacious, fraudulent, hypocritical, misleading, trumped up **4.** dishonest, dishonourable, disloyal, double-dealing, duplicitous, faithless, false-hearted, hypocritical, perfidious, treacherous, treasonable, two-faced, unfaithful, untrustworthy

falsehood fabrication, fib, fiction, lie, misstatement, story, untruth

falsification adulteration, deceit, dissimulation, distortion, forgery, misrepresentation, perversion, tampering with

falsify alter, belie, cook (*Sl.*), counterfeit, distort, doctor, fake, forge, garble, misrepresent, misstate, pervert, tamper with

falter break, hesitate, shake, speak haltingly, stammer, stumble, stutter, totter, tremble, vacillate, waver

fame celebrity, credit, eminence, glory, honour, illustriousness, name, prominence, public esteem, renown, reputation, repute, stardom

nious **6.** impertinent, too friendly —*n.* **7.** familiar friend **8.** familiar demon —**famili'arity** *n.* —**familiari'zation** *or* **-ri'sation** *n.* —**fa'miliarize** *or* **-rise** *vt.* —**fa'miliarly** *adv.*

family ('fæmılı, 'fæmlı) *n.* **1.** group of parents and children, or near relatives **2.** person's children **3.** all descendants of common ancestor **4.** household **5.** group of allied objects —**fa'milial** *a.* —**family man** married man who has children, *esp.* one who is devoted to his family —**family name** surname, *esp.* representing family honour —**family planning** control of number of children in family, *esp.* by contraception —**family tree** chart showing relationships and lines of descent of family (*also* **genealogical tree**)

famine ('fæmın) *n.* **1.** extreme scarcity of food **2.** starvation **3.** acute shortage of anything —**'famished** *a.* very hungry

famous ('feıməs) *a. see* FAME

fan[1] (fæn) *n.* **1.** instrument for producing current of air, *esp.* for ventilating or cooling **2.** folding object of paper *etc.* used, *esp.* formerly, for cooling the face **3.** outspread feathers of a bird's tail —*vt.* **4.** blow or cool with fan —*v.* **5.** spread out like fan (**-nn-**) —**fan belt** belt that drives cooling fan in car engine —**'fanjet** *n. see* TURBOFAN —**'fanlight** *n.* (fan-shaped) window over door —**'fantail** *n.* kind of bird (*esp.* pigeon) with fan-shaped tail —**fan vaulting** *Archit.* vaulting having ribs that radiate, like those of fan, from top of capital (*also* **palm vaulting**)

fan[2] (fæn) *n. inf.* **1.** devoted admirer **2.** enthusiast, particularly for sport *etc.*

Fanagalo ('fænəgələʊ) *or* **Fanakalo** *n.* **SA** pidgin language of Zulu, English and Afrikaans

fanatic (fə'nætık) *a.* **1.** filled with abnormal enthusiasm, *esp.* in religion —*n.* **2.** fanatic person —**fa'natical** *a.* —**fa'natically** *adv.* —**fa'naticism** *n.*

fancy ('fænsı) *a.* **1.** ornamental, not plain **2.** of whimsical or arbitrary kind —*n.* **3.** whim, caprice **4.** liking, inclination **5.** imagination **6.** mental image —*vt.* **7.** imagine **8.** be inclined to believe **9.** *inf.* have a liking for (**'fancied, 'fancying**) —*interj.* **10.** exclamation of surprise (*also* **fancy that**) —**'fancier** *n.* one with liking and expert knowledge (respecting some specific thing) —**'fanciful** *a.* —**'fancifully** *adv.* —**fancy dress** costume worn at masquerades *etc.* representing historical figure *etc.* —**fancy-free** *a.* having no commitments —**fancy goods** small decorative gifts —**fancy man** *sl.* **1.** woman's lover **2.** pimp —**fancy woman** *sl.* **1.** mistress **2.** prostitute

fandango (fæn'dæŋgəʊ) *n.* **1.** lively Sp. dance with castanets **2.** music for this dance (*pl.* **-s**)

fanfare ('fænfɛə) *n.* **1.** a flourish of trumpets or bugles **2.** ostentatious display

fang (fæŋ) *n.* **1.** snake's poison tooth **2.** long, pointed tooth

THESAURUS

familiar 1. accustomed, common, common or garden (*Inf.*), conventional, customary, domestic, everyday, frequent, household, mundane, ordinary, recognizable, repeated, routine, stock, well-known 2. amicable, chummy (*Inf.*), close, confidential, cordial, easy, free, free-and-easy, friendly, hail-fellow-well-met, informal, intimate, near, open, relaxed, unceremonious, unconstrained, unreserved 3. bold, disrespectful, forward, impudent, intrusive, overfree, presuming, presumptuous

familiarity 1. acquaintance, acquaintanceship, awareness, experience, grasp, understanding 2. absence of reserve, closeness, ease, fellowship, freedom, friendliness, friendship, informality, intimacy, naturalness, openness, sociability, unceremoniousness 3. boldness, disrespect, forwardness, liberties, liberty, presumption

familiarize accustom, bring into common use, coach, get to know (about), habituate, instruct, inure, make conversant, make used to, prime, school, season, train

family 1. brood, children, descendants, folk (*Inf.*), household, issue, kin, kindred, kinsmen, kith and kin, ménage, offspring, one's nearest and dearest, one's own flesh and blood, people, progeny, relations, relatives 2. ancestors, ancestry, birth, blood, clan, descent, dynasty, extraction, forebears, forefathers, genealogy, house, line, lineage, parentage, pedigree, race, sept, stemma, stirps, strain, tribe 3. class, classification, genre, group, kind, network, subdivision, system

family tree ancestry, extraction, genealogy, line, lineage, line of descent, pedigree, stemma, stirps

famine dearth, destitution, hunger, scarcity, starvation

famous acclaimed, celebrated, conspicuous, distinguished, eminent, excellent, far-famed, glorious, honoured, illustrious, legendary, lionized, much-publicized, notable, noted, prominent, remarkable, renowned, signal, well-known

fan[1] 1. *v.* air-condition, air-cool, blow, cool, refresh, ventilate, winnow (*Rare*) 2. *n.* air conditioner, blade, blower, propeller, punkah (*In India*), vane, ventilator

fan[2] adherent, admirer, aficionado, buff (*Inf.*), devotee, enthusiast, fiend (*Inf.*), follower, freak (*Sl.*), lover, rooter (*U.S.*), supporter, zealot

fanatic *n.* activist, addict, bigot, devotee, enthusiast, extremist, militant, visionary, zealot

fanatical bigoted, burning, enthusiastic, extreme, fervent, frenzied, immoderate, mad, obsessive, overenthusiastic, passionate, rabid, visionary, wild, zealous

fanciful capricious, chimerical, curious, extravagant, fabulous, fairy-tale, fantastic, ideal, imaginary, imaginative, mythical, poetic, romantic, unreal, visionary, whimsical, wild

fancy *v.* 1. be inclined to think, believe, conceive, conjecture, guess, imagine, infer, reckon, suppose, surmise, think, think likely 2. be attracted to, crave, desire, dream of, hanker after, have a yen for, long for, relish, wish for, would like, yearn for 3. *Inf.* be attracted to, be captivated by, desire, favour, go for (*Inf.*), have an eye for, like, lust after, prefer, take a liking to, take to ~*n.* 4. caprice, desire, humour, idea, impulse, inclination, notion, thought, urge, whim 5. fondness, hankering, inclination, liking, partiality, predilection, preference, relish 6. conception, image, imagination, impression 7. chimera, daydream, delusion, dream, fantasy, nightmare, phantasm, vision ~*adj.* 8. baroque, decorated, decorative, elaborate, elegant, embellished, extravagant, fanciful, intricate, ornamental, ornamented, ornate 9. capricious, chimerical, delusive, fanciful, fantastic, far-fetched, illusory, whimsical

fantasy *or* **phantasy** (ˈfæntəsɪ) *n.* 1. power of imagination, *esp.* extravagant 2. mental image 3. fanciful invention or design —**fantasia** (fænˈteɪzɪə) *n.* fanciful musical composition —**ˈfantasize** *or* **-sise** *v.* —**fanˈtastic** *a.* 1. quaint 2. grotesque 3. extremely fanciful, wild 4. *inf.* very good 5. *inf.* very large —**fanˈtastically** *adv.*

FAO Food and Agriculture Organization (of the United Nations)

far (fɑː) *adv.* 1. at or to a great distance or advanced point 2. at or to a remote time 3. by very much —*a.* 4. distant 5. more distant (**ˈfarther, ˈfurther** *comp.*, **ˈfarthest, ˈfurthest** *sup.*) —**ˈfaraway** *a.* 1. distant 2. absent-minded —**Far East** countries of E Asia, including China, Japan *etc.* —**Far Eastern** —**far-fetched** *a.* incredible —**far-flung** *a.* 1. widely distributed 2. far distant; remote —**Far North** Arctic and sub-Arctic regions —**far-off** *a.* remote; distant —**far-out** *a. sl.* 1. bizarre, avant-garde 2. wonderful —**far-sighted** *a.* 1. possessing prudence and foresight 2. *Med.* of or suffering from hyperopia 3. long-sighted —**far and away** by a very great margin —**far out** *sl.* expression of amazement or delight

farad (ˈfærəd) *n.* unit of electrical capacity —**faradaic** (færəˈdeɪɪk) *a.*

farce (fɑːs) *n.* 1. comedy of boisterous humour 2. absurd and futile proceeding —**ˈfarcical** *a.* ludicrous —**ˈfarcically** *adv.*

fare (fɛə) *n.* 1. charge for passenger's transport 2. passenger 3. food —*vi.* 4. get on 5. happen 6. travel, progress —**fare stage** 1. section of bus journey for which set charge is made 2. bus stop marking end of such section —**fareˈwell** *interj.* 1. goodbye —*n.* 2. leave-taking

farina (fəˈriːnə) *n.* 1. flour or meal made from cereal grain 2. *chiefly* UK starch —**farinaceous** (færɪˈneɪʃəs) *a.* 1. mealy 2. starchy

farm (fɑːm) *n.* 1. tract of land for cultivation or rearing livestock 2. unit of land, water, for growing or rearing a particular crop, animal *etc.* —*v.* 3. cultivate (land) 4. rear (livestock) on farm —**ˈfarmer** *n.* —**farm hand** person hired to work on farm —**ˈfarmhouse** *n.* —**ˈfarmstead** *n.* farm or part of farm consisting of main buildings together with adjacent grounds —**ˈfarmyard** *n.* —**farm out** 1. send (work) to be done by others 2. put into care of others

faro (ˈfɛərəʊ) *n.* card game

farrago (fəˈrɑːgəʊ) *n.* medley, hotchpotch (*pl.* **-s**)

farrier (ˈfærɪə) *n.* one who shoes, cares for horses —**ˈfarriery** *n.* his art

farrow (ˈfærəʊ) *n.* 1. litter of pigs —*v.* 2. give birth to (litter)

fart (fɑːt) *vulg. n.* 1. (audible) emission of gas from anus —*vi.* 2. break wind

farther (ˈfɑːðə) *adv./a. comp. of* FAR further —**ˈfarthermost** *a.* most distant —**ˈfarthest** *adv./a. sup. of* FAR furthest

farthing (ˈfɑːðɪŋ) *n.* formerly, coin worth quarter of penny

farthingale (ˈfɑːðɪŋgeɪl) *n. Hist.* hoop worn under skirts

fasces (ˈfæsiːz) *pl.n.* 1. bundle of rods bound together round axe, forming Roman badge of authority 2. emblem of It. fascists

fascia *or* **facia** (ˈfeɪʃɪə) *n.* 1. flat surface above shop window 2. *Archit.* long flat surface between mouldings under eaves 3. face of wood or stone in a building 4. dashboard (*pl.* **-ciae** (-ʃiː))

fascinate (ˈfæsɪneɪt) *vt.* 1. attract and delight by rousing interest and curiosity 2. render motionless, as with a fixed stare —**fasciˈnation** *n.*

THESAURUS

fanfare ballyhoo, fanfaronade, flourish, trump (*Archaic*), trumpet call, tucket (*Archaic*)

fantastic 1. comical, eccentric, exotic, fanciful, freakish, grotesque, imaginative, odd, outlandish, peculiar, phantasmagorical, quaint, queer, rococo, strange, unreal, weird, whimsical 2. ambitious, chimerical, extravagant, far-fetched, grandiose, illusory, ludicrous, ridiculous, unrealistic, visionary, wild 3. absurd, capricious, implausible, incredible, irrational, mad, preposterous, unlikely 4. *Inf.* enormous, extreme, great, overwhelming, severe, tremendous 5. *Inf.* excellent, first-rate, marvellous, out of this world (*Inf.*), sensational, superb, wonderful

fantasy, phantasy 1. creativity, fancy, imagination, invention, originality 2. apparition, daydream, delusion, dream, fancy, figment of the imagination, flight of fancy, hallucination, illusion, mirage, nightmare, pipe dream, reverie, vision

far *adv.* 1. afar, a good way, a great distance, a long way, deep, miles 2. considerably, decidedly, extremely, greatly, incomparably, much, very much ~*adj.* 3. distant, faraway, far-flung, far-off, far-removed, long, outlying, out-of-the-way, remote, removed

faraway 1. beyond the horizon, distant, far, far-flung, far-off, far-removed, outlying, remote 2. absent, abstracted, distant, dreamy, lost

farce 1. broad comedy, buffoonery, burlesque, comedy, satire, slapstick 2. absurdity, joke, mockery, nonsense, parody, ridiculousness, sham, travesty

farcical absurd, amusing, comic, custard-pie, derisory, diverting, droll, funny, laughable, ludicrous, nonsensical, preposterous, ridiculous, risible, slapstick

fare *n.* 1. charge, passage money, price, ticket money, transport cost 2. passenger, pick-up (*Inf.*), traveller 3. commons, diet, eatables, food, meals, menu, provisions, rations, sustenance, table, victuals ~*v.* 4. do, get along, get on, make out, manage, prosper 5. *Used impersonally* go, happen, proceed, turn out

farewell adieu, adieux *or* adieus, departure, goodbye, leave-taking, parting, sendoff (*Inf.*), valediction

far-fetched doubtful, dubious, fantastic, hard to swallow (*Inf.*), implausible, improbable, incredible, preposterous, strained, unbelievable, unconvincing, unlikely, unnatural, unrealistic

farm 1. *n.* acreage, acres, croft (*Scot.*), farmstead, grange, holding, homestead, land, plantation, ranch (*Chiefly North American*), smallholding, station (*Aust. & New Zealand*) 2. *v.* bring under cultivation, cultivate, operate, plant, practise husbandry, till the soil, work

farmer agriculturist, agronomist, husbandman, smallholder, yeoman

far-sighted acute, canny, cautious, discerning, far-

Fascism (ˈfæʃɪzəm) *n.* **1.** authoritarian political system opposed to democracy and liberalism **2.** (*oft.* **f-**) behaviour (*esp.* by those in authority) supposedly typical of this system —ˈ**Fascist** *a./n.*

fashion (ˈfæʃən) *n.* **1.** (latest) style, *esp.* of dress *etc.* **2.** manner, mode **3.** form, type —*vt.* **4.** shape, make —ˈ**fashionable** *a.* —ˈ**fashionably** *adv.*

fast[1] (fɑːst) *a.* **1.** (capable of) moving quickly **2.** permitting, providing, rapid progress **3.** ahead of true time **4.** *obs.* dissipated **5.** firm, steady **6.** permanent —*adv.* **7.** rapidly **8.** tightly —ˈ**fastness** *n.* **1.** fast state **2.** fortress, stronghold —ˈ**fastback** *n.* car with back forming continuous slope from roof to rear —**fast-breeder reactor** nuclear reactor that uses little or no moderator and produces more fissionable material than it consumes —**fast food** food, *esp.* hamburgers *etc.*, prepared and served very quickly

fast[2] (fɑːst) *vi.* **1.** go without food, or some kinds of food —*n.* **2.** act or period of fasting —ˈ**fasting** *n.*

fasten (ˈfɑːsᵊn) *vt.* **1.** attach, fix, secure —*vi.* **2.** become joined **3.** (*usu. with* on) seize (upon) —ˈ**fastening** *n.* something that fastens, such as clasp

fastidious (fæˈstɪdɪəs) *a.* **1.** hard to please **2.** discriminating, particular

fat (fæt) *n.* **1.** oily animal substance **2.** fat part —*a.* **3.** having too much fat **4.** containing fat, greasy **5.** profitable **6.** fertile (ˈ**fatter** *comp.*, ˈ**fattest** *sup.*) —*vt.* **7.** feed (animals) for slaughter (**-tt-**) —ˈ**fatness** *n.* —ˈ**fatten** *v.* —ˈ**fatty** *a./n.* —ˈ**fathead** *n. inf.* dolt, idiot —**fat stock** livestock fattened and ready for market —**fatty acid** any of class of aliphatic carboxylic acids, such as palmitic acid

fate (feɪt) *n.* **1.** power supposed to predetermine events **2.** goddess of destiny **3.** destiny **4.** person's appointed lot or condition **5.** death; destruction —*vt.* **6.** preordain —ˈ**fatal** *a.* **1.** deadly, ending in death **2.** destructive **3.** disastrous **4.** inevitable —ˈ**fatalism** *n.* **1.** belief that everything is predetermined **2.** submission to fate —ˈ**fatalist** *n.* —**fatalˈistic** *a.* —**fatalˈistically** *adv.* —**fatality** (fəˈtælɪtɪ) *n.* **1.** accident resulting in death **2.** person killed in war, accident —ˈ**fatally** *adv.* —ˈ**fateful** *a.* **1.** fraught with destiny **2.** prophetic

father (ˈfɑːðə) *n.* **1.** male parent **2.** forefather, ancestor **3.** (**F-**) God **4.** originator, early leader **5.** priest, confessor **6.** oldest member of a society —*vt.* **7.** beget **8.** originate **9.** pass as father or author of **10.** act as father to —ˈ**fatherhood** *n.* —ˈ**fatherless** *a.* —ˈ**fatherly** *a.* —**father-in-law** *n.* husband's or wife's father —ˈ**fatherland** *n.* **1.** person's native country **2.** country of person's ancestors

fathom (ˈfæðəm) *n.* **1.** measure of six feet of water —*vt.* **2.** sound (water) **3.** get to bottom of, understand —ˈ**fathomable** *a.* —ˈ**fathomless** *a.* too deep to fathom

THESAURUS

seeing, judicious, politic, prescient, provident, prudent, sage, shrewd, wise

fascinate absorb, allure, beguile, bewitch, captivate, charm, delight, enamour, enchant, engross, enrapture, enravish, enthral, entrance, hold spellbound, hypnotize, infatuate, intrigue, mesmerize, rivet, spellbind, transfix

fascination allure, attraction, charm, enchantment, glamour, lure, magic, magnetism, pull, sorcery, spell

fashion *n.* **1.** convention, craze, custom, fad, latest, latest style, look, mode, prevailing taste, rage, style, trend, usage, vogue **2.** attitude, demeanour, manner, method, mode, style, way **3.** appearance, configuration, cut, figure, form, guise (*Archaic*), line, make, model, mould, pattern, shape **4.** description, kind, sort, type ~*v.* **5.** construct, contrive, create, design, forge, form, make, manufacture, mould, shape, work

fashionable à la mode, all the go (*Inf.*), all the rage, chic, current, customary, genteel, in (*Inf.*), in vogue, latest, modern, modish, popular, prevailing, smart, stylish, trendsetting, trendy (*Inf.*), up-to-date, up-to-the-minute, usual, with it (*Inf.*)

fast *adj.* **1.** accelerated, brisk, fleet, flying, hasty, hurried, mercurial, nippy (*Inf.*), quick, rapid, speedy, swift, winged ~*adv.* **2.** apace, hastily, hell for leather, hurriedly, in haste, like a bat out of hell (*Inf.*), like a flash, like a shot (*Inf.*), posthaste, presto, quickly, rapidly, speedily, swiftly, with all haste ~*adj.* **3.** close, constant, fastened, firm, fixed, fortified, immovable, impregnable, lasting, loyal, permanent, secure, sound, staunch, steadfast, tight, unwavering ~*adv.* **4.** deeply, firmly, fixedly, securely, soundly, tightly ~*adj.* **5.** dissipated, dissolute, extravagant, gadabout, giddy, immoral, intemperate, licentious, loose, profligate, promiscuous, rakish, reckless, self-indulgent, wanton, wild

fasten affix, anchor, attach, bind, bolt, chain, connect, fix, grip, join, lace, link, lock, make fast, make firm, seal, secure, tie, unite

fat *adj.* **1.** beefy (*Inf.*), broad in the beam (*Inf.*), corpulent, elephantine, fleshy, gross, heavy, obese, overweight, plump, podgy, portly, roly-poly, rotund, solid, stout, tubby **2.** adipose, fatty, greasy, oily, oleaginous, suety **3.** affluent, cushy (*Sl.*), fertile, flourishing, fruitful, jammy (*Sl.*), lucrative, lush, productive, profitable, prosperous, remunerative, rich, thriving ~*n.* **4.** adipose tissue, blubber, bulk, cellulite, corpulence, fatness, flab, flesh, obesity, overweight, paunch, weight problem

fatal **1.** deadly, destructive, final, incurable, killing, lethal, malignant, mortal, pernicious, terminal **2.** baleful, baneful, calamitous, catastrophic, disastrous, lethal, ruinous **3.** critical, crucial, decisive, destined, determining, doomed, fateful, final, foreordained, inevitable, predestined

fatality casualty, deadliness, death, disaster, fatal accident, lethalness, loss, mortality

fate **1.** chance, destiny, divine will, fortune, kismet, nemesis, predestination, providence, weird (*Archaic*) **2.** cup, fortune, horoscope, lot, portion, stars **3.** death, destruction, doom, downfall, end, ruin

fateful critical, crucial, decisive, important, portentous, significant

father *n.* **1.** begetter, dad (*Inf.*), daddy (*Inf.*), governor (*Inf.*), old boy (*Inf.*), old man (*Inf.*), pa (*Inf.*), pater, paterfamilias, patriarch, pop (*Inf.*), sire **2.** ancestor, forebear, forefather, predecessor, progenitor **3.** architect, author, creator, founder, inventor, maker, originator, prime mover **4.** city father, elder, leader, patriarch, patron, senator **5.** abbé, confessor, curé, padre (*Inf.*), pastor, priest ~*v.* **6.** beget, get, procreate, sire **7.** create, engender, establish, found, institute, invent, originate

fatherland homeland, land of one's birth, land of one's fathers, motherland, native land, old country

fatherly affectionate, benevolent, benign, forbearing, indulgent, kind, kindly, paternal, patriarchal, protective, supportive, tender

fatigue (fəˈtiːg) *n.* **1.** weariness **2.** toil **3.** weakness of metals *etc.* subjected to stress **4.** soldier's nonmilitary duty *—pl.* **5.** special clothing worn by military personnel to carry out such duties *—vt.* **6.** weary

fatuous (ˈfætjuəs) *a.* very silly, idiotic **—faˈtuity** *n.*

faucet (ˈfɔːsɪt) *n.* US tap

fault (fɔːlt) *n.* **1.** defect **2.** flaw **3.** misdeed **4.** blame, culpability **5.** blunder, mistake **6.** *Tennis* ball wrongly served **7.** *Geol.* break in strata *—vt.* **8.** find fault in *—v.* **9.** (cause to) undergo fault *—vi.* **10.** commit a fault **—ˈfaultily** *adv.* **—ˈfaultless** *a.* **—ˈfaultlessly** *adv.* **—ˈfaulty** *a.* **—to a fault** excessively

faun (fɔːn) *n.* mythological woodland being with tail and horns

fauna (ˈfɔːnə) *n.* animals of region or period collectively (*pl.* **-s, -ae** (-iː))

faux pas (fəʊ ˈpɑː) social blunder or indiscretion (*pl.* **faux pas** (fəʊ ˈpɑːz))

favour *or U.S.* **favor** (ˈfeɪvə) *n.* **1.** goodwill **2.** approval **3.** especial kindness **4.** partiality **5.** small gift or toy given to guest at party *etc.* **6** *Hist.* badge or knot of ribbons *—vt.* **7.** regard or treat with favour **8.** oblige **9.** treat with partiality **10.** aid **11.** support **12.** resemble **—ˈfavourable** *or U.S.* **ˈfavorable** *a.* **1.** advantageous, encouraging, promising **2.** giving consent **—ˈfavourably** *or U.S.* **ˈfavorably** *adv.* **—ˈfavoured** *or U.S.* **ˈfavored** *a.* **1.** treated with favour **2.** having appearance (as specified), as in *ill-favoured* **—favourite** *or U.S.* **favorite** (ˈfeɪvərɪt) *n.* **1.** favoured person or thing **2.** horse *etc.* expected to win race *—a.* **3.** chosen, preferred **—favouritism** *or U.S.* **favoritism** (ˈfeɪvərɪtɪzəm) *n.* practice of showing undue preference

fawn[1] (fɔːn) *n.* **1.** young deer *—a.* **2.** light yellowish-brown

fawn[2] (fɔːn) *vi.* **1.** (of person) cringe, court favour servilely **2.** (*esp.* of dog) show affection by wagging tail and grovelling

fax (fæks) *n.* **1.** *see* FACSIMILE (senses 2, 3) *—vt.* **2.** send (document) by facsimile

fay (feɪ) *n.* fairy, sprite

F.B.I. US Federal Bureau of Investigation

F.C. Football Club

THESAURUS

fathom 1. divine, estimate, gauge, measure, penetrate, plumb, probe, sound **2.** comprehend, get to the bottom of, grasp, interpret, understand

fatigue 1. *v.* drain, drain of energy, exhaust, fag (out) (*Inf.*), jade, overtire, take it out of (*Inf.*), tire, weaken, wear out, weary, whack (*Inf.*) **2.** *n.* debility, ennui, heaviness, languor, lethargy, listlessness, overtiredness, tiredness

fatten broaden, coarsen, expand, gain weight, grow fat, put on weight, spread, swell, thicken, thrive

fatuous absurd, asinine, brainless, dense, dull, foolish, idiotic, inane, ludicrous, lunatic, mindless, moronic, puerile, silly, stupid, vacuous, weak-minded, witless

fault *n.* **1.** blemish, defect, deficiency, drawback, failing, flaw, imperfection, infirmity, lack, shortcoming, snag, weakness, weak point **2.** blunder, boob (*Sl.*), error, error of judgment, inaccuracy, indiscretion, lapse, mistake, negligence, offence, omission, oversight, slip, slip-up **3.** accountability, culpability, liability, responsibility **4.** delinquency, frailty, lapse, misconduct, misdeed, misdemeanour, offence, peccadillo, sin, transgression, trespass, wrong **5. to a fault** excessively, immoderately, in the extreme, needlessly, out of all proportion, overly (*U.S.*), overmuch, preposterously, ridiculously, unduly ~*v.* **6.** blame, call to account, censure, criticize, find fault with, find lacking, hold (someone) accountable (responsible, to blame), impugn

faultless 1. accurate, classic, correct, exemplary, faithful, flawless, foolproof, impeccable, model, perfect, unblemished **2.** above reproach, blameless, guiltless, immaculate, innocent, irreproachable, pure, sinless, spotless, stainless, unblemished, unspotted, unsullied

faulty bad, blemished, broken, damaged, defective, erroneous, fallacious, flawed, impaired, imperfect, imprecise, inaccurate, incorrect, invalid, malfunctioning, not working, out of order, unsound, weak, wrong

faux pas blunder, boob (*Sl.*), breach of etiquette, clanger (*Inf.*), gaffe, gaucherie, impropriety, indiscretion, solecism

favour *n.* **1.** approbation, approval, backing, bias, championship, esteem, favouritism, friendliness, good opinion, good will, grace, kindness, kind regard, partiality, patronage, support **2.** benefit, boon, courtesy, good turn, indulgence, kindness, obligement (*Scot. or Archaic*), service **3.** gift, keepsake, love-token, memento, present, souvenir, token **4.** badge, decoration, knot, ribbons, rosette ~*v.* **5.** be partial to, esteem, have in one's good books, indulge, pamper, pull strings for (*Inf.*), reward, side with, smile upon, spoil, treat with partiality, value **6.** advocate, approve, back, be in favour of, champion, choose, commend, countenance, encourage, fancy, incline towards, like, opt for, patronize, prefer, single out, support **7.** abet, accommodate, advance, aid, assist, befriend, do a kindness to, facilitate, help, oblige, promote, succour **8.** *Inf.* be the image *or* picture of, look like, resemble, take after

favourable 1. advantageous, appropriate, auspicious, beneficial, convenient, encouraging, fair, fit, good, helpful, hopeful, opportune, promising, propitious, suitable, timely **2.** affirmative, agreeable, amicable, approving, benign, encouraging, enthusiastic, friendly, kind, positive, reassuring, sympathetic, understanding, welcoming, well-disposed

favourably 1. advantageously, auspiciously, conveniently, fortunately, opportunely, profitably, to one's advantage, well **2.** agreeably, approvingly, enthusiastically, genially, graciously, helpfully, in a kindly manner, positively, with approval (approbation, cordiality), without prejudice

favourite 1. *adj.* best-loved, choice, dearest, esteemed, preferred **2.** *n.* beloved, blue-eyed boy (*Inf.*), choice, darling, dear, idol, pet, pick, preference, teacher's pet, the apple of one's eye

favouritism bias, jobs for the boys (*Inf.*), nepotism, one-sidedness, partiality, partisanship, preference, preferential treatment

fawn[1] *adj.* beige, buff, greyish-brown, neutral

fawn[2] *v.* *Often with* **on** *or* **upon** be obsequious, be servile, bow and scrape, court, crawl, creep, cringe, curry favour, dance attendance, flatter, grovel, ingratiate oneself, kneel, kowtow, lick (someone's) boots, pay court, toady, truckle

F.D. Fidei Defensor

Fe *Chem.* iron

fealty (ˈfiːəltɪ) *n.* **1.** fidelity of vassal to his lord **2.** loyalty

fear (fɪə) *n.* **1.** dread, alarm, anxiety, unpleasant emotion caused by coming evil or danger —*vi.* **2.** have this feeling, be afraid —*vt.* **3.** regard with fear **4.** shrink from **5.** revere —**ˈfearful** *a.* **1.** afraid **2.** causing fear **3.** *inf.* very unpleasant —**ˈfearfully** *adv.* —**ˈfearless** *a.* intrepid —**ˈfearlessly** *adv.* —**ˈfearsome** *a.*

feasible (ˈfiːzəbᵊl) *a.* **1.** able to be done **2.** likely —**feasiˈbility** *n.* —**ˈfeasibly** *adv.*

feast (fiːst) *n.* **1.** banquet, lavish meal **2.** religious anniversary **3.** something very pleasant, sumptuous —*vi.* **4.** partake of banquet; fare sumptuously —*vt.* **5.** regale with feast **6.** provide delight for —**ˈfeaster** *n.*

feat (fiːt) *n.* **1.** notable deed **2.** surprising or striking trick

feather (ˈfɛðə) *n.* **1.** one of the barbed shafts which form covering of birds **2.** anything resembling this —*vt.* **3.** provide, line with feathers —*vi.* **4.** grow feathers —*v.* **5.** turn (oar) edgeways —**ˈfeathery** *a.* —**feather bed** mattress filled with feathers —**featherˈbed** *vt.* pamper, spoil —**ˈfeatherbrain** *or* **ˈfeatherhead** *n.* frivolous or forgetful person —**ˈfeatherbrained** *or* **ˈfeatherheaded** *a.* —**ˈfeatherweight** *n.* very light person or thing —**feather one's nest** enrich oneself —**the white feather** cowardice

feature (ˈfiːtʃə) *n.* **1.** (*usu. pl.*) part of face **2.** characteristic or notable part of anything **3.** main or special item —*vt.* **4.** portray **5.** *Cine.* present in leading role in a film **6.** give prominence to —*vi.* **7.** be prominent —**ˈfeatureless** *a.* without striking features

Feb. February

febrile (ˈfiːbraɪl) *a.* of fever

February (ˈfɛbrʊərɪ) *n.* second month of year (normally containing 28 days; in leap year, 29)

feckless (ˈfɛklɪs) *a.* spiritless; weak; irresponsible

feculent (ˈfɛkjʊlənt) *a.* full of sediment, turbid —**ˈfeculence** *n.*

fecund (ˈfiːkənd, ˈfɛk-) *a.* fertile, fruitful, fertilizing —**ˈfecundate** *vt.* fertilize, impregnate —**fecunˈdation** *n.* —**fecundity** (fɪˈkʌndɪtɪ) *n.*

Fed. *or* **fed.** **1.** Federal **2.** Federation **3.** Federated

fed (fɛd) *pt./pp. of* FEED —**fed up** bored, dissatisfied

federal (ˈfɛdərəl) *a.* of or like the government of states which are united but retain internal independence —**ˈfederalism** *n.* —**ˈfederalist** *n./a.* —**ˈfederate** *v.*

THESAURUS

fear *n.* **1.** alarm, apprehensiveness, awe, blue funk (*Inf.*), consternation, cravenness, dismay, dread, fright, horror, panic, qualms, terror, timidity, tremors, trepidation **2.** agitation, anxiety, apprehension, concern, disquietude, distress, doubt, foreboding(s), misgiving(s), solicitude, suspicion, unease, uneasiness, worry ~*v.* **3.** apprehend, be apprehensive (afraid, frightened, scared), be in a blue funk (*Inf.*), dare not, dread, have a horror of, have a phobia about, have butterflies in one's stomach (*Inf.*), have qualms, live in dread of, shake in one's shoes, shudder at, take fright, tremble at **4.** respect, revere, reverence, stand in awe of, venerate

fearful **1.** afraid, alarmed, anxious, apprehensive, diffident, faint-hearted, frightened, hesitant, intimidated, jittery (*Inf.*), jumpy, nervous, nervy, panicky, pusillanimous, scared, shrinking, tense, timid, timorous, uneasy **2.** appalling, atrocious, awful, dire, distressing, dreadful, frightful, ghastly, grievous, grim, gruesome, hair-raising, hideous, horrendous, horrible, horrific, monstrous, shocking, terrible, unspeakable

fearfully apprehensively, diffidently, in fear and trembling, nervously, timidly, timorously, uneasily, with many misgivings *or* forebodings, with one's heart in one's mouth

fearless bold, brave, confident, courageous, daring, dauntless, doughty, gallant, game (*Inf.*), gutsy (*Sl.*), heroic, indomitable, intrepid, lion-hearted, plucky, unabashed, unafraid, undaunted, unflinching, valiant, valorous

fearsome alarming, appalling, awe-inspiring, awesome, awful, daunting, dismaying, formidable, frightening, hair-raising, horrendous, horrifying, menacing, unnerving

feasibility expediency, practicability, usefulness, viability, workability

feasible achievable, attainable, likely, possible, practicable, realizable, reasonable, viable, workable

feast *n.* **1.** banquet, barbecue, beanfeast (*Brit. inf.*), beano (*Brit. sl.*), blowout (*Sl.*), carousal, carouse, dinner, entertainment, festive board, jollification, junket, repast, revels, slap-up meal (*Brit. inf.*), spread (*Inf.*), treat **2.** celebration, festival, fête, gala day, holiday, holy day, saint's day **3.** delight, enjoyment, gratification, pleasure, treat ~*v.* **4.** eat one's fill, eat to one's heart's content, fare sumptuously, gorge, gormandize, indulge, overindulge, stuff, stuff one's face (*Sl.*), wine and dine **5.** entertain, hold a reception for, kill the fatted calf for, regale, treat, wine and dine **6.** delight, gladden, gratify, rejoice, thrill

feat accomplishment, achievement, act, attainment, deed, exploit, performance

feathery downy, feathered, fluffy, plumate *or* plumose (*Bot. & Zool.*), plumed, plumy, wispy

feature *n.* **1.** aspect, attribute, characteristic, facet, factor, hallmark, mark, peculiarity, point, property, quality, trait **2.** attraction, crowd puller (*Inf.*), draw, highlight, innovation, main item, special, special attraction, speciality, specialty ~*v.* **3.** accentuate, call attention to, emphasize, give prominence to, give the full works (*Sl.*), headline, play up, present, promote, set off, spotlight, star

feckless aimless, feeble, futile, hopeless, incompetent, ineffectual, irresponsible, shiftless, useless, weak, worthless

federate *v.* amalgamate, associate, combine, confederate, integrate, syndicate, unify, unite

federation alliance, amalgamation, association, *Bund*, coalition, combination, confederacy, copartnership, entente, federacy, league, syndicate, union

fed up (with) annoyed, blue, bored, brassed off (*Inf.*), browned-off (*Inf.*), depressed, discontented, dismal, dissatisfied, down, gloomy, glum, sick and tired of (*Inf.*), tired of, weary of

fee account, bill, charge, compensation, emolument, hire, honorarium, pay, payment, recompense, remuneration, reward, toll

form into, become, a federation —**fede'ration** *n.* 1. league 2. federal union

fee (fiː) *n.* payment for professional and other services

feeble ('fiːb°l) *a.* 1. weak 2. lacking strength or effectiveness, insipid —**'feebly** *adv.* —**feeble-minded** *a.* 1. lacking in intelligence 2. mentally defective

feed (fiːd) *vt.* 1. give food to 2. supply, support —*vi.* 3. take food (**fed** *pt./pp.*) —*n.* 4. feeding 5. fodder, pasturage 6. allowance of fodder 7. material supplied to machine 8. part of machine taking in material —**'feeder** *n.* 1. one who or that which feeds 2. child's bib 3. tributary channel —**'feedback** *n.* 1. return of part of output of electrical circuit or loudspeakers. In **negative feedback** rise in output energy reduces input energy; in **positive feedback** increase in output energy reinforces input energy 2. information received in response to enquiry *etc.* —**'feedlot** *n.* area, building where cattle are fattened for market

feel (fiːl) *vt.* 1. perceive, examine by touch 2. experience 3. find (one's way) cautiously 4. be sensitive to 5. believe, consider —*vi.* 6. have physical or emotional sensation of (something) (**felt** *pt./pp.*) —*n.* 7. act or instance of feeling 8. quality or impression of something perceived by feeling 9. sense of touch —**'feeler** *n.* 1. special organ of touch in some animals 2. proposal put forward to test others' opinion 3. that which feels —**'feeling** *n.* 1. sense of touch 2. ability to feel 3. physical sensation 4. emotion 5. sympathy, tenderness 6. conviction or opinion not solely based on reason —*pl.* 7. susceptibilities —*a.* 8. sensitive, sympathetic, heartfelt —**feel for** show sympathy or compassion towards —**feel like** have an inclination for

feet (fiːt) *n., pl. of* FOOT

feign (feɪn) *v.* pretend, sham

feint[1] (feɪnt) *n.* 1. sham attack or blow meant to deceive opponent 2. semblance, pretence —*vi.* 3. make feint

feint[2] (feɪnt) *n. Print.* narrowest rule used in production of ruled paper

feldspar ('fɛldspɑː, 'fɛlspɑː) *or* **felspar** *n.* crystalline mineral found in granite *etc.* —**feldspathic** (fɛld'spæθɪk, fɛl'spæθ-) *or* **fel'spathic** *a.*

felicity (fɪ'lɪsɪtɪ) *n.* 1. great happiness, bliss 2. appropriate expression or style —**fe'licitate** *vt.* congratulate —**felici'tation** *n.* (*usu. in pl.*) —**fe'licitous** *a.* 1. apt, well-chosen 2. happy

feline ('fiːlaɪn) *a.* 1. of cats 2. catlike —**felinity** (fɪ'lɪnɪtɪ) *n.*

fell[1] (fɛl) *pt. of* FALL

fell[2] (fɛl) *vt.* 1. knock down 2. cut down (tree) —**'feller** *n.*

fell[3] (fɛl) *a. obs.* fierce, terrible —**one fell swoop** a single hasty action or occurrence

fell[4] (fɛl) *n.* skin or hide with hair

fell[5] (fɛl) *n.* mountain, stretch of moorland, *esp.* in N of England

fellatio (fɪ'leɪʃɪəʊ) *n.* sexual activity in which penis is stimulated by partner's mouth

felloe ('fɛləʊ) *or* **felly** *n.* outer part (or section) of wheel

fellow ('fɛləʊ) *n.* 1. man, boy 2. person 3. comrade, associate 4. counterpart, like thing 5. member (of society, college *etc.*) —*a.* 6. of the same class, associated —**'fellowship** *n.* 1. fraternity 2. friendship 3. in university *etc.*, research post; special scholarship —**fellow traveller** 1. companion on journey 2. non-Communist who sympathizes with Communism

THESAURUS

feeble 1. debilitated, delicate, doddering, effete, enervated, enfeebled, etiolated, exhausted, failing, faint, frail, infirm, languid, powerless, puny, shilpit (*Scot.*), sickly, weak, weakened 2. flat, flimsy, inadequate, incompetent, indecisive, ineffective, ineffectual, inefficient, insignificant, insufficient, lame, paltry, poor, slight, tame, thin, unconvincing, weak

feeble-minded addle-pated, bone-headed (*Sl.*), deficient, dim-witted (*Inf.*), dull, dumb (*Inf.*), half-witted, idiotic, imbecilic, lacking, moronic, retarded, simple, slow on the uptake, slow-witted, soft in the head (*Inf.*), stupid, vacant, weak-minded

feed *v.* 1. cater for, nourish, provide for, provision, supply, sustain, victual, wine and dine 2. *Sometimes with* **on** devour, eat, exist on, fare, graze, live on, nurture, partake of, pasture, subsist, take nourishment 3. augment, bolster, encourage, foster, fuel, minister to, strengthen, supply ~*n.* 4. fodder, food, forage, pasturage, provender, silage

feel *v.* 1. caress, finger, fondle, handle, manipulate, maul, paw, run one's hands over, stroke, touch 2. be aware of, be sensible of, endure, enjoy, experience, go through, have, have a sensation of, know, notice, observe, perceive, suffer, take to heart, undergo 3. explore, fumble, grope, sound, test, try 4. be convinced, feel in one's bones, have a hunch, have the impression, intuit, sense 5. believe, be of the opinion that, consider, deem, hold, judge, think 6. *With* **for** be moved by, be sorry for, bleed for, commiserate, compassionate, condole with, empathize, feel compassion for, pity, sympathize with 7. **feel like** could do with, desire, fancy, feel inclined, feel the need for, feel up to, have the inclination, want ~*n.* 8. finish, surface, texture, touch 9. air, ambience, atmosphere, feeling, impression, quality, sense, vibes (*Inf.*)

feeler 1. antenna, tentacle, whisker 2. advance, approach, probe, trial balloon

feeling 1. feel, perception, sensation, sense, sense of touch, touch 2. apprehension, consciousness, hunch, idea, impression, inkling, notion, presentiment, sense, suspicion 3. affection, ardour, emotion, fervour, fondness, heat, intensity, passion, sentiment, sentimentality, warmth 4. appreciation, compassion, concern, empathy, pity, sensibility, sensitivity, sympathy, understanding 5. inclination, instinct, opinion, point of view, view

feelings ego, emotions, self-esteem, sensitivities, susceptibilities

feline catlike, leonine

fell *v.* cut, cut down, demolish, flatten, floor, hew, knock down, level, prostrate, raze, strike down

fellow *n.* 1. bloke (*Inf.*), boy, chap (*Inf.*), character, customer (*Inf.*), guy (*Inf.*), individual, man, person 2. associate, colleague, companion, compeer, comrade, co-worker, equal, friend, member, partner, peer 3. brother, counterpart, double, duplicate, match, mate, twin ~*adj.* 4. affiliated, akin, allied, associate, associated, co-, like, related, similar

fellowship 1. amity, brotherhood, camaraderie, communion, companionability, companionship, famili-

felon (ˈfɛlən) *n.* one guilty of felony —**feˈlonious** *a.* —**ˈfelony** *n.* serious crime

felspar (ˈfɛlspɑː) *n. see* FELDSPAR

felt[1] (fɛlt) *pt./pp. of* FEEL

felt[2] (fɛlt) *n.* **1.** soft, matted fabric made by bonding fibres chemically and by pressure **2.** thing made of this —*vt.* **3.** make into, or cover with, felt —*vi.* **4.** become matted like felt —**felt-tip pen** pen whose writing point is made from pressed fibres (*also* **fibre-tip pen**)

fem. feminine

female (ˈfiːmeɪl) *a.* **1.** of sex which bears offspring **2.** relating to this sex —*n.* **3.** one of this sex

feminine (ˈfɛmɪnɪn) *a.* **1.** of women **2.** womanly **3.** denoting class or type of grammatical inflection in some languages —**femiˈninity** *n.* —**ˈfeminism** *n.* advocacy of equal rights for women —**ˈfeminist** *n./a.*

femur (ˈfiːmə) *n.* thigh-bone —**ˈfemoral** *a.* of the thigh

fen (fɛn) *n.* tract of marshy land, swamp —**ˈfenny** *a.*

fence (fɛns) *n.* **1.** structure of wire, wood *etc.* enclosing an area **2.** *Machinery* guard, guide **3.** *sl.* dealer in stolen property —*vt.* **4.** erect fence on or around **5.** (*with* in) enclose —*vi.* **6.** fight (as sport) with swords **7.** avoid question *etc.* **8.** *sl.* deal in stolen property —**ˈfencing** *n.* art of swordplay

fend (fɛnd) *vt.* **1.** (*usu. with* off) ward off, repel —*vi.* **2.** provide (for oneself *etc.*) —**ˈfender** *n.* **1.** low metal frame in front of fireplace **2.** name for various protective devices **3.** frame **4.** edge **5.** buffer **6.** US mudguard of car

fenestration (fɛnɪˈstreɪʃən) *n.* arrangement of windows in a building

Fenian (ˈfiːnɪən, ˈfiːnjən) *n.* **1.** formerly, member of Irish revolutionary organization founded in U.S.A. in 19th century to fight for independent Ireland —*a.* **2.** of Fenians

fennel (ˈfɛnᵊl) *n.* yellow-flowered fragrant herb

fenugreek (ˈfɛnjʊgriːk) *n.* heavily scented leguminous plant

feoff (fiːf) *Hist. n.* **1.** *see* FIEF —*vt.* **2.** invest with benefice or fief

-fer (*n. comb. form*) person or thing that bears something specified, as in *crucifer, conifer* —**-ferous** (*a. comb. form*) bearing, producing, as in *coniferous*

feral[1] (ˈfɪərəl) *a.* wild, uncultivated

feral[2] (ˈfɪərəl) *a. obs.* funereal, gloomy

feria (ˈfɪərɪə) *n. Eccles.* ordinary weekday, not festival or fast day

fermata (fəˈmɑːtə) *n. Mus.* pause (*pl.* **-s, -te** (-tɪ))

ferment (ˈfɜːmɛnt) *n.* **1.** leaven, substance causing thing to ferment **2.** excitement, tumult —*v.* (fəˈmɛnt) **3.** (cause to) undergo chemical change with effervescence, liberation of heat and alteration of properties, *eg* process set up in dough by yeast **4.** (cause to) become excited —**fermenˈtation** *n.*

fermium (ˈfɜːmɪəm) *n.* transuranic element artificially produced by neutron bombardment of plutonium

fern (fɜːn) *n.* plant with feathery fronds —**ˈfernery** *n.* place for growing ferns —**ˈferny** *a.* full of ferns

ferocious (fəˈrəʊʃəs) *a.* fierce, savage, cruel —**ferocity** (fəˈrɒsɪtɪ) *n.*

ferret (ˈfɛrɪt) *n.* **1.** tamed animal like weasel, used to catch rabbits, rats *etc.* —*vt.* (*usu. with* out) **2.** drive out with ferrets **3.** search out —*vi.* **4.** search about, rummage

ferric (ˈfɛrɪk) *a.* pert. to, containing, iron —**ferˈriferous** *a.* yielding iron —**ˈferrous** *a.* of or containing iron in divalent state —**ferruginous** (fɛˈruːdʒɪnəs) *a.* **1.** containing iron **2.** reddish-brown —**ferroˈconcrete** *n.* concrete strengthened by framework of metal

Ferris wheel (ˈfɛrɪs) in fairground, large, vertical wheel with seats for riding

ferro- (*comb. form*) **1.** property or presence of iron, as in *ferromagnetism* **2.** presence of iron in divalent state, as in *ferrocyanide*

ferrule (ˈfɛruːl) *n.* metal cap to strengthen end of stick *etc.*

ferry (ˈfɛrɪ) *n.* **1.** boat *etc.* for transporting people, vehicles, across body of water, *esp.* as repeated or regular service **2.** place for ferrying —*v.* **3.** carry, travel, by ferry —*vt.* **4.** convey (passengers *etc.*) (**ˈferried, ˈferrying**) —**ˈferryman** *n.*

fertile (ˈfɜːtaɪl) *a.* **1.** (capable of) producing offspring, bearing crops *etc.* **2.** fruitful, producing abundantly **3.** inventive —**fertility** (fɜːˈtɪlɪtɪ) *n.* —**fertilization** *or* **-lisation** (fɜːtɪlaɪˈzeɪʃən) *n.* —**fertilize** *or* **-lise** (ˈfɜːtɪlaɪz) *vt.* make fertile —**fertilizer** *or* **-liser** (ˈfɜːtɪlaɪzə) *n.*

THESAURUS

arity, fraternization, intercourse, intimacy, kindliness, sociability **2.** association, brotherhood, club, fraternity, guild, league, order, sisterhood, society, sodality

feminine delicate, gentle, girlish, graceful, ladylike, modest, soft, tender, womanly

fen bog, holm (*Dialect*), marsh, morass, moss (*Scot.*), quagmire, slough, swamp

fence *n.* **1.** barbed wire, barricade, barrier, defence, guard, hedge, paling, palisade, railings, rampart, shield, stockade, wall ~*v.* **2.** *Often with* **in** *or* **off** bound, circumscribe, confine, coop, defend, encircle, enclose, fortify, guard, hedge, pen, protect, restrict, secure, separate, surround **3.** beat about the bush, cavil, dodge, equivocate, evade, hedge, parry, prevaricate, quibble, shift, stonewall, tergiversate

ferment *v.* **1.** boil, brew, bubble, concoct, effervesce, foam, froth, heat, leaven, rise, seethe, work ~*n.* **2.** bacteria, barm, fermentation agent, leaven, leavening, mother, mother-of-vinegar, yeast ~*v.* **3.** *Fig.* agitate, boil, excite, fester, foment, heat, incite, inflame, provoke, rouse, seethe, smoulder, stir up ~*n.* **4.** *Fig.* agitation, brouhaha, commotion, disruption, excitement, fever, frenzy, furore, glow, heat, hubbub, imbroglio, state of unrest, stew, stir, tumult, turbulence, turmoil, unrest, uproar

ferocious 1. feral, fierce, predatory, rapacious, ravening, savage, violent, wild **2.** barbaric, barbarous, bloodthirsty, brutal, brutish, cruel, merciless, pitiless, relentless, ruthless, tigerish, vicious

ferocity barbarity, bloodthirstiness, brutality, cruelty, ferociousness, fierceness, inhumanity, rapacity, ruthlessness, savageness, savagery, viciousness, wildness

ferry 1. *n.* ferryboat, packet, packet boat **2.** *v.* carry, chauffeur, convey, run, ship, shuttle, transport

fertile abundant, fat, fecund, flowering, flowing with milk and honey, fruit-bearing, fruitful, generative, luxuriant, plenteous, plentiful, productive, prolific, rich, teeming, yielding

ferule (ˈfɛruːl) *n.* **1.** flat piece of wood, such as ruler, formerly used in some schools to cane children on hand —*vt.* **2.** punish with ferule

fervent (ˈfɜːvənt) *or* **fervid** (ˈfɜːvɪd) *a.* ardent, vehement, intense —**ˈfervency** *n.* —**ˈfervently** *or* **ˈfervidly** *adv.* —**ˈfervour** *or U.S.* **ˈfervor** *n.*

fescue (ˈfɛskjuː) *or* **fescue grass** *n.* grass used as pasture, with stiff narrow leaves

fesse *or* **fess** (fɛs) *n. Her.* horizontal band across shield

festal (ˈfɛstᵊl) *a.* **1.** of feast or holiday **2.** merry, gay —**ˈfestally** *adv.*

fester (ˈfɛstə) *v.* **1.** (cause to) form pus —*vi.* **2.** rankle **3.** become embittered

festival (ˈfɛstɪvᵊl) *n.* **1.** day, period set aside for celebration, *esp.* of religious feast **2.** organized series of events, performances *etc.*, usu. in one place —**ˈfestive** *a.* **1.** joyous, merry **2.** of feast —**fesˈtivity** *n.* **1.** gaiety, mirth **2.** rejoicing —*pl.* **3.** festive proceedings

festoon (fɛˈstuːn) *n.* **1.** chain of flowers, ribbons *etc.* hung in curve between two points —*vt.* **2.** form into, adorn with festoons

fetch[1] (fɛtʃ) *vt.* **1.** go and bring **2.** draw forth **3.** be sold for —*n.* **4.** trick —**ˈfetching** *a.* attractive —**fetch up 1.** *inf.* arrive **2.** *sl.* vomit (food *etc.*)

fetch[2] (fɛtʃ) *n.* ghost or apparition of living person

fête *or* **fete** (feɪt) *n.* **1.** gala, bazaar *etc., esp.* one held out of doors **2.** festival, holiday, celebration —*vt.* **3.** feast **4.** honour with festive entertainment

fetid *or* **foetid** (ˈfɛtɪd, ˈfiː-) *a.* stinking

fetish *or* **fetich** (ˈfɛtɪʃ, ˈfiːtɪʃ) *n.* **1.** (inanimate) object believed to have magical powers **2.** excessive attention to something **3.** object, activity, to which excessive devotion is paid

fetlock (ˈfɛtlɒk) *n.* projection behind and above horse's hoof, or tuft of hair on this

fetter (ˈfɛtə) *n.* **1.** chain or shackle for feet **2.** check, restraint —*pl.* **3.** captivity —*vt.* **4.** chain up **5.** restrain, hamper

fettle (ˈfɛtᵊl) *n.* condition, state of health

fetus (ˈfiːtəs) *n. see* FOETUS

feu (fjuː) *n.* in Scotland, tenure of land in return for fixed annual payment

feud (fjuːd) *n.* **1.** bitter, lasting, mutual hostility, *esp.* between two families or tribes **2.** vendetta —*vi.* **3.** carry on feud

feudal (ˈfjuːdᵊl) *a.* **1.** of, like, medieval social and economic system based on holding land from superior in return for service **2.** *inf.* very old-fashioned —**ˈfeudalism** *n.*

fever (ˈfiːvə) *n.* **1.** condition of illness with high body temperature **2.** intense nervous excitement —**ˈfevered** *a.* —**ˈfeverish** *a.* **1.** having fever **2.** accompanied by, caused by, fever **3.** in a state of restless excitement —**ˈfeverishly** *adv.* —**ˈfeverfew** *n.* bushy plant with white flower heads —**fever pitch 1.** very fast pace **2.** intense excitement

few (fjuː) *a.* **1.** not many —*n.* **2.** small number —**a good few, quite a few** several

fey (feɪ) *a.* **1.** clairvoyant, visionary **2.** *esp. Scot.* fated to die

fez (fɛz) *n.* red, brimless, orig. Turkish tasselled cap (*pl.* **ˈfezzes**)

ff *Mus.* fortissimo

ff. 1. folios **2.** and the following (pages *etc.*)

THESAURUS

fertility abundance, fecundity, fruitfulness, luxuriance, productiveness, richness

fertilize fecundate, fructify, impregnate, inseminate, make fruitful, make pregnant, pollinate

fertilizer compost, dressing, dung, guano, manure, marl

fervent, fervid animated, ardent, devout, eager, earnest, ecstatic, emotional, enthusiastic, excited, fiery, heartfelt, impassioned, intense, perfervid (*Literary*), vehement, warm, zealous

fervour animation, ardour, eagerness, earnestness, enthusiasm, excitement, fervency, intensity, passion, vehemence, warmth, zeal

festival 1. anniversary, commemoration, feast, fête, fiesta, holiday, holy day, saint's day **2.** carnival, celebration, entertainment, festivities, fête, field day, gala, jubilee, treat

festive back-slapping, carnival, celebratory, cheery, Christmassy, convivial, festal, gala, gay, gleeful, happy, hearty, holiday, jolly, jovial, joyful, joyous, jubilant, light-hearted, merry, mirthful, sportive

festivity 1. amusement, conviviality, fun, gaiety, jollification, joviality, joyfulness, merriment, merrymaking, mirth, pleasure, revelry, sport **2.** *Often plural* carousal, celebration, entertainment, festival, festive event, festive proceedings, fun and games, jollification, party

festoon 1. *n.* chaplet, garland, lei, swag, swathe, wreath **2.** *v.* array, bedeck, beribbon, deck, decorate, drape, garland, hang, swathe, wreathe

fetch 1. bring, carry, conduct, convey, deliver, escort, get, go for, lead, obtain, retrieve, transport **2.** draw forth, elicit, give rise to, produce **3.** bring in, earn, go for, make, realize, sell for, yield

fetching alluring, attractive, captivating, charming, cute, enchanting, enticing, fascinating, intriguing, sweet, taking, winsome

fête, fete 1. *n.* bazaar, fair, festival, gala, garden party, sale of work **2.** *v.* bring out the red carpet for (someone), entertain regally, hold a reception for (someone), honour, kill the fatted calf for (someone), lionize, make much of, treat, wine and dine

fetish 1. amulet, cult object, talisman **2.** fixation, *idée fixe*, mania, obsession, thing (*Inf.*)

feud 1. *n.* argument, bad blood, bickering, broil, conflict, contention, disagreement, discord, dissension, enmity, estrangement, faction, falling out, grudge, hostility, quarrel, rivalry, strife, vendetta **2.** *v.* be at daggers drawn, be at odds, bicker, brawl, clash, contend, dispute, duel, fall out, quarrel, row, squabble, war

fever *Fig.* agitation, delirium, ecstasy, excitement, ferment, fervour, flush, frenzy, heat, intensity, passion, restlessness, turmoil, unrest

feverish 1. burning, febrile, fevered, flushed, hectic, hot, inflamed, pyretic (*Medical*) **2.** agitated, distracted, excited, frantic, frenetic, frenzied, impatient, obsessive, overwrought, restless

few *adj.* hardly any, inconsiderable, infrequent, insufficient, meagre, negligible, not many, rare, scant, scanty, scarce, scarcely any, scattered, sparse, sporadic, thin

fiancé (fɪˈɒnseɪ) *n.* person engaged to be married (**fiˈancée** *fem.*)

fiasco (fɪˈæskəʊ) *n.* breakdown, total failure (*pl.* **-s, -es**)

fiat (ˈfaɪət) *n.* **1.** decree **2.** official permission

fib (fɪb) *n.* **1.** trivial lie, falsehood —*vi.* **2.** tell fib (**-bb-**) —**ˈfibber** *n.*

fibre *or U.S.* **fiber** (ˈfaɪbə) *n.* **1.** filament forming part of animal or plant tissue **2.** substance that can be spun (*eg* wool, cotton) —**ˈfibril** *or* **fiˈbrilla** *n.* **1.** small fibre or part of fibre **2.** *Biol.* root hair (*pl.* **-s** *or* **-brillae** (-ˈbrɪliː)) —**ˈfibroid** *a.* **1.** *Anat.* (of structures or tissues) containing or resembling fibres —*n.* **2.** benign tumour derived from fibrous connective tissue (*also* **fiˈbroma**) —**fiˈbrosis** *n.* formation of abnormal amount of fibrous tissue in organ *etc.* —**fibroˈsitis** *n.* inflammation of tissues of muscle sheaths —**ˈfibrous** *a.* made of fibre —**ˈfibreboard** *n.* building material of compressed plant fibres —**ˈfibreglass** *n.* material made of fine glass fibres —**fibre optics** use of bundles of long transparent glass fibres in transmitting light

fibrin (ˈfɪbrɪn) *n.* insoluble protein in blood, causing coagulation

fibula (ˈfɪbjʊlə) *n.* slender outer bone of lower leg (*pl.* **-lae** (-liː), **-s**) —**ˈfibular** *a.*

fickle (ˈfɪkᵊl) *a.* changeable, inconstant —**ˈfickleness** *n.*

fiction (ˈfɪkʃən) *n.* **1.** prose, literary works of the imagination **2.** invented statement or story —**ˈfictional** *a.* —**ˈfictionalize** *or* **-lise** *vt.* make into fiction —**ficˈtitious** *a.* **1.** not genuine, false **2.** imaginary **3.** assumed

fiddle (ˈfɪdᵊl) *n.* **1.** violin **2.** triviality **3.** *inf.* illegal, fraudulent arrangement —*vi.* **4.** play fiddle **5.** make idle movements, fidget, trifle —*v.* **6.** *sl.* cheat, contrive —**ˈfiddling** *a.* trivial —**ˈfiddly** *a.* small, awkward to handle —**fiddler crab** burrowing crab of Amer. coastal regions, male of which has one pincerlike claw enlarged —**ˈfiddlesticks** *interj.* nonsense

Fidei Defensor (ˈfaɪdɪaɪ dɪˈfensɔː) *Lat.* Defender of the Faith

fidelity (fɪˈdelɪtɪ) *n.* **1.** faithfulness **2.** quality of sound reproduction

fidget (ˈfɪdʒɪt) *vi.* **1.** move restlessly **2.** be uneasy —*n.* **3.** (*oft. pl.*) nervous restlessness, restless mood **4.** one who fidgets —**ˈfidgety** *a.*

fiduciary (fɪˈduːʃɪərɪ) *a.* **1.** held, given in trust **2.** relating to trustee —*n.* **3.** trustee

fie (faɪ) *interj. obs., jocular* exclamation of distaste or mock dismay

fief *or* **feoff** (fiːf) *n. Hist.* land held of a superior in return for service

field (fiːld) *n.* **1.** area of (farming) land **2.** enclosed piece of land **3.** tract of land rich in specified product (*eg goldfield*) **4.** players in a game or sport collectively **5.** all competitors but the favourite **6.** battlefield **7.** area over which electric, gravitational, magnetic force can be exerted **8.** surface of shield, coin *etc.* **9.** sphere of knowledge **10.** range, area of operation —*vt.* **11.** *Sport* stop or return (ball) **12.** send (player, team) on to sportsfield —*vi.* **13.** *Sport* (of player or team) act or take turn as fielder(s) —**ˈfielder** *n.* —**field day 1.** day of manoeuvres, outdoor activities **2.** important occasion —**field events** throwing and jumping events in athletics —**ˈfieldfare** *n.* type of thrush with pale grey head and rump —**field glasses** binoculars —**field hockey US, C** hockey played on field, as distinct from ice hockey —**field marshal** army officer of highest rank —**field officer** officer holding rank of major, lieutenant colonel or colonel —**ˈfieldsman** *n. Cricket* player in field; member of fielding side (*also* **ˈfielder**) —**field sports** outdoor sports, such as hunting or fishing —**ˈfieldwork** *n.* research, practical work, conducted away from classroom, laboratory *etc.* —**field of view** area covered in telescope, camera *etc.*

THESAURUS

fiancé, fiancée betrothed, intended, prospective spouse, wife- *or* husband-to-be

fiasco catastrophe, debacle, disaster, failure, flap (*Inf.*), mess, rout, ruin, washout (*Inf.*)

fib *n.* fiction, lie, prevarication, story, untruth, white lie, whopper (*Inf.*)

fibre fibril, filament, pile, staple, strand, texture, thread

fickle blowing hot and cold, capricious, changeable, faithless, fitful, flighty, inconstant, irresolute, mercurial, mutable, quicksilver, unfaithful, unpredictable, unstable, unsteady, vacillating, variable, volatile

fickleness capriciousness, fitfulness, flightiness, inconstancy, mutability, unfaithfulness, unpredictability, unsteadiness, volatility

fiction 1. fable, fantasy, legend, myth, novel, romance, story, storytelling, tale, work of imagination, yarn (*Inf.*) **2.** cock and bull story (*Inf.*), concoction, fabrication, falsehood, fancy, fantasy, figment of the imagination, imagination, improvisation, invention, lie, tall story, untruth

fictional imaginary, invented, legendary, made-up, nonexistent, unreal

fictitious apocryphal, artificial, assumed, bogus, counterfeit, fabricated, false, fanciful, feigned, imaginary, imagined, improvised, invented, made-up, make-believe, mythical, spurious, unreal, untrue

fiddle *v.* **1.** *Often with* **with** fidget, finger, interfere with, mess about *or* around, play, tamper with, tinker, toy, trifle **2.** *Inf.* cheat, cook the books, diddle (*Inf.*), finagle (*Inf.*), fix, gerrymander, graft, manoeuvre, racketeer, swindle, wangle (*Inf.*) ~*n.* **3.** *Inf.* fix, fraud, graft, piece of sharp practice, racket, swindle, wangle (*Inf.*)

fiddling futile, insignificant, pettifogging, petty, trifling, trivial

fidelity allegiance, constancy, dependability, devotedness, devotion, faith, faithfulness, fealty, integrity, lealty (*Archaic or Scot.*), loyalty, staunchness, trueheartedness, trustworthiness

fidget 1. *v.* be like a cat on hot bricks (*Inf.*), bustle, chafe, fiddle, fret, jiggle, jitter (*Inf.*), move restlessly, squirm, twitch, worry **2.** *n. Usually* **the fidgets** fidgetiness, jitters (*Inf.*), nervousness, restlessness, unease, uneasiness

fidgety impatient, jerky, jittery (*Inf.*), jumpy, nervous, on edge, restive, restless, twitchy, uneasy

field *n.* **1.** grassland, green, greensward (*Archaic*), lea (*Literary*), mead (*Archaic*), meadow, pasture **2.** applicants, candidates, competition, competitors, contestants, entrants, possibilities, runners **3.** area, bailiwick, bounds, confines, department, discipline,

fiend (fiːnd) *n.* **1.** demon, devil **2.** wicked person **3.** person very fond of or addicted to something, *eg fresh-air fiend, drug fiend* —ˈ**fiendish** *a.* **1.** wicked **2.** *inf.* difficult; unpleasant

fierce (fɪəs) *a.* **1.** savage, wild, violent **2.** rough **3.** severe **4.** intense —ˈ**fiercely** *adv.* —ˈ**fierceness** *n.*

fiery (ˈfaɪərɪ) *a.* **1.** consisting of fire **2.** blazing, glowing, flashing **3.** irritable **4.** spirited (ˈ**fierier** *comp.,* ˈ**fieriest** *sup.*) —ˈ**fierily** *adv.*

fiesta (fɪˈɛstə) *n.* (*esp.* in Spain and Latin America) **1.** (religious) celebration **2.** carnival

FIFA (ˈfiːfə) Fédération Internationale de Football Association

fife (faɪf) *n.* **1.** high-pitched flute —*v.* **2.** play (music) on fife —ˈ**fifer** *n.*

fifteen (ˈfɪfˈtiːn) *see* FIVE

fig (fɪg) *n.* **1.** soft, pear-shaped fruit **2.** tree bearing it **3.** something of negligible value

fig. **1.** figurative(ly) **2.** figure

fight (faɪt) *v.* **1.** contend (with) in battle or in single combat **2.** maintain (cause *etc.*) against opponent —*vt.* **3.** resolve by combat (**fought** *pt./pp.*) —*n.* **4.** battle, struggle or physical combat **5.** quarrel, dispute, contest **6.** resistance **7.** boxing match —ˈ**fighter** *n.* **1.** one who fights **2.** *Mil.* aircraft designed for destroying other aircraft —**fighting chance** chance of success dependent on struggle

figment (ˈfɪgmənt) *n.* invention, purely imaginary thing

figure (ˈfɪgə) *n.* **1.** numerical symbol **2.** amount, number **3.** form, shape **4.** bodily shape **5.** appearance, *esp.* conspicuous appearance **6.** character, personage **7.** space enclosed by lines, or surfaces **8.** diagram, illustration **9.** likeness, image **10.** pattern, movement in dancing, skating, *etc.* **11.** abnormal form of expression for effect in speech, *eg* metaphor —*vt.* **12.** calculate, estimate **13.** *inf.,* **US, NZ** consider **14.** represent by picture or diagram **15.** ornament —*vi.* **16.** (*oft.* *with* in) show, appear, be conspicuous, be included —**figuˈration** *n.* **1.** *Mus.* florid ornamentation of musical passage **2.** instance of representing figuratively, as by allegory **3.** figurative representation **4.** decorating with design —ˈ**figurative** *a.* **1.** metaphorical **2.** full of figures of speech —ˈ**figuratively** *adv.* —**figurine** (fɪgəˈriːn) *n.* statuette —ˈ**figurehead** *n.* **1.** nominal leader **2.** ornamental figure under bowsprit of ship —**figure of speech** expression of language by which literal meaning of word is not employed

figwort (ˈfɪgwɜːt) *n.* plant related to foxglove, having small greenish flowers

filament (ˈfɪləmənt) *n.* **1.** fine wire in electric light bulb and radio valve which is heated by electric current **2.** threadlike body

filbert (ˈfɪlbət) *n.* **1.** N temperate shrub with edible nuts **2.** this nut (*also* ˈ**hazelnut,** ˈ**cobnut**)

THESAURUS

domain, environment, limits, line, métier, province, purview, range, scope, speciality, specialty, sphere of influence (activity, interest, study), territory ~*v.* **4.** catch, pick up, retrieve, return, stop

fiend **1.** demon, devil, evil spirit, hellhound **2.** barbarian, beast, brute, degenerate, monster, ogre, savage **3.** *Inf.* addict, enthusiast, fanatic, freak (*Sl.*), maniac

fiendish accursed, atrocious, black-hearted, cruel, demoniac, devilish, diabolical, hellish, implacable, infernal, inhuman, malevolent, malicious, malignant, monstrous, satanic, savage, ungodly, unspeakable, wicked

fierce **1.** barbarous, brutal, cruel, dangerous, fell (*Archaic*), feral, ferocious, fiery, menacing, murderous, passionate, savage, threatening, tigerish, truculent, uncontrollable, untamed, vicious, wild **2.** blustery, boisterous, furious, howling, powerful, raging, stormy, strong, tempestuous, tumultuous, uncontrollable, violent **3.** cutthroat, intense, keen, relentless, strong

fiercely ferociously, frenziedly, furiously, in a frenzy, like cat and dog, menacingly, passionately, savagely, tempestuously, tigerishly, tooth and nail, uncontrolledly, viciously, with bared teeth, with no holds barred

fight *v.* **1.** assault, battle, bear arms against, box, brawl, carry on war, clash, close, combat, come to blows, conflict, contend, cross swords, do battle, engage, engage in hostilities, exchange blows, feud, go to war, grapple, joust, scrap (*Inf.*), spar, struggle, take the field, take up arms against, tilt, tussle, wage war, war, wrestle **2.** contest, defy, dispute, make a stand against, oppose, resist, stand up to, strive, struggle, withstand ~*n.* **3.** action, affray (*Law*), altercation, battle, bout, brawl, brush, clash, combat, conflict, contest, dispute, dissension, dogfight, duel, encounter, engagement, exchange of blows, fracas, fray, free-for-all (*Inf.*), hostilities, joust, melee, passage of arms, riot, row, rumble (*U.S. sl.*), scrap (*Inf.*), scuffle, set-to (*Inf.*), skirmish, sparring match, struggle, tussle, war **4.** *Fig.* belligerence, gameness, mettle, militancy, pluck, resistance, spirit, will to resist

fighter **1.** fighting man, man-at-arms, soldier, warrior **2.** boxer, bruiser (*Inf.*), prize fighter, pugilist **3.** antagonist, battler, belligerent, combatant, contender, contestant, disputant, militant

figure *n.* **1.** character, cipher, digit, number, numeral, symbol **2.** amount, cost, price, sum, total, value **3.** form, outline, shadow, shape, silhouette **4.** body, build, chassis (*Sl.*), frame, physique, proportions, shape, torso **5.** depiction, design, device, diagram, drawing, emblem, illustration, motif, pattern, representation, sketch **6.** celebrity, character, dignitary, force, leader, notability, notable, personage, personality, presence, somebody, worthy ~*v.* **7.** *Often with* **up** add, calculate, compute, count, reckon, sum, tally, tot up, work out **8.** *Usually with* **in** act, appear, be conspicuous, be featured, be included, be mentioned, contribute to, feature, have a place in, play a part

figurehead cipher, dummy, front man (*Inf.*), leader in name only, man of straw, mouthpiece, name, nonentity, puppet, straw man (*Chiefly U.S.*), titular *or* nominal head, token

figure of speech conceit, image, trope, turn of phrase

filament cilium (*Biol. & Zool.*), fibre, fibril, pile, staple, strand, string, thread, wire

filch abstract, crib (*Inf.*), embezzle, half-inch (*Sl.*), lift (*Inf.*), misappropriate, nick (*Sl.*), pilfer, pinch (*Inf.*), purloin, rip off (*Sl.*), snaffle (*Inf.*), steal, swipe (*Sl.*), take, thieve, walk off with

filch (fɪltʃ) *vt.* steal, pilfer

file[1] (faɪl) *n.* **1.** box, folder, clip *etc.* holding papers for reference **2.** papers so kept **3.** information about specific person, subject **4.** orderly line, as of soldiers, one behind the other —*vt.* **5.** arrange (papers *etc.*) and put them away for reference **6.** *Law* place on records of a court **7.** bring (suit) in lawcourt —*vi.* **8.** march in file —**ˈfiling** *n.* —**single** (*or* **Indian**) **file** single line of people one behind the other

file[2] (faɪl) *n.* **1.** roughened tool for smoothing or shaping —*vt.* **2.** apply file to, smooth, polish —**ˈfiling** *n.* **1.** action of using file **2.** scrap of metal removed by file

filial (ˈfɪljəl) *a.* of, befitting, son or daughter —**ˈfilially** *adv.*

filibuster (ˈfɪlɪbʌstə) **US** *n.* **1.** process of obstructing legislation by using delaying tactics —*v.* **2.** obstruct (legislation) with delaying tactics —*vi.* **3.** engage in unlawful military action

filigree (ˈfɪlɪgriː) *or* **filagree** (ˈfɪləgriː) *n.* fine tracery or openwork of metal, usu. gold or silver wire

Filipino (fɪlɪˈpiːnəʊ) *n.* **1.** native of the Philippines —*a.* **2.** of the Philippines

fill (fɪl) *vt.* **1.** make full **2.** occupy completely **3.** hold, discharge duties of **4.** stop up **5.** satisfy, fulfil —*vi.* **6.** become full —*n.* **7.** full supply **8.** as much as desired **9.** soil *etc.* to bring area of ground up to required level —**ˈfiller** *n.* **1.** person or thing that fills **2.** object or substance used to add weight *etc.* or to fill in gap **3.** paste used for filling in cracks *etc.* before painting **4.** inner portion of cigar **5.** *Journalism* space-filling item in newspaper *etc.* —**ˈfilling** *n.* —**filling station** garage selling oil, petrol *etc.* —**fill the bill** *inf.* supply all that is wanted

fillet (ˈfɪlɪt) *n.* **1.** boneless slice of meat, fish **2.** narrow strip —*vt.* **3.** cut into fillets, bone —**ˈfilleted** *a.*

fillip (ˈfɪlɪp) *n.* **1.** stimulus **2.** sudden release of finger bent against thumb **3.** snap so produced —*vt.* **4.** stimulate **5.** give fillip to

filly (ˈfɪlɪ) *n.* female horse under four years old

film (fɪlm) *n.* **1.** sequence of images projected on screen, creating illusion of movement **2.** story *etc.* presented thus, and shown in cinema or on television **3.** sensitized celluloid roll used in photography, cinematography **4.** thin skin or layer **5.** dimness on eyes **6.** slight haze —*a.* **7.** connected with cinema —*vt.* **8.** photograph with cine camera **9.** make cine film of (scene, story *etc.*) —*v.* **10.** cover, become covered, with film —**ˈfilmy** *a.* **1.** membranous **2.** gauzy —**film star** popular cinema actor or actress —**film strip** strip of film composed of images projected separately as slides

Filofax (ˈfaɪləʊfæks) *n.* **R** loose-leaf ring binder with sets of different-coloured paper, used as portable personal filing system

filter (ˈfɪltə) *n.* **1.** cloth or other material, or a device, permitting fluid to pass but retaining solid particles **2.** anything performing similar function —*v.* **3.** (*oft. with* out) remove or separate (suspended particles *etc.*) from (liquid, gas *etc.*) by action of filter —*vi.* **4.** pass slowly (as if) through filter —**ˈfiltrate** *n.* filtered gas or liquid —**filter paper** porous paper for filtering liquids —**filter tip 1.** attachment to mouth end of cigarette for trapping impurities **2.** cigarette having such attachment —**filter-tipped** *a.*

filth (fɪlθ) *n.* **1.** disgusting dirt **2.** pollution **3.** obscenity —**ˈfilthily** *adv.* —**ˈfilthiness** *n.* —**ˈfilthy** *a.* **1.** unclean **2.** foul

fin (fɪn) *n.* **1.** propelling or steering organ of fish **2.** anything like this, *eg* stabilizing plane of aeroplane

fin. **1.** finance **2.** financial

finagle (fɪˈneɪgᵊl) *inf.* *vt.* **1.** get or achieve by craftiness —*v.* **2.** use trickery on (person) —**fiˈnagler** *n.*

final (ˈfaɪnᵊl) *a.* **1.** at the end **2.** conclusive —*n.* **3.** game, heat, examination *etc.* coming at end of series —**finale** (fɪˈnɑːlɪ) *n.* **1.** closing part of musical composition, opera *etc.* **2.** termination —**ˈfinalist** *n.* contestant who has reached last stage of competition —**fiˈnality** *n.* —**ˈfinalize** *or* **-lise** *v.* —**ˈfinally** *adv.*

THESAURUS

file[1] *n.* **1.** case, data, documents, dossier, folder, information, portfolio ~*v.* **2.** document, enter, pigeonhole, put in place, record, register, slot in ~*n.* **3.** column, line, list, queue, row, string ~*v.* **4.** march, parade, troop

file[2] *v.* abrade, burnish, furbish, polish, rasp, refine, rub, rub down, scrape, shape, smooth

filibuster *Chiefly U.S., with reference to legislation* **1.** *n.* delay, hindrance, obstruction, postponement, procrastination **2.** *v.* delay, hinder, obstruct, prevent, procrastinate, put off

fill **1.** brim over, cram, crowd, furnish, glut, gorge, inflate, pack, pervade, replenish, sate, satiate, satisfy, stock, store, stuff, supply, swell **2.** charge, imbue, impregnate, overspread, pervade, saturate, suffuse **3.** block, bung, close, cork, plug, seal, stop **4.** assign, carry out, discharge, engage, execute, fulfil, hold, occupy, officiate, perform, take up

filling *n.* contents, filler, innards (*Inf.*), inside, insides, padding, stuffing, wadding

film *n.* **1.** coat, coating, covering, dusting, gauze, integument, layer, membrane, pellicle, scum, skin, tissue **2.** blur, cloud, haze, haziness, mist, mistiness, opacity, veil **3.** flick (*Sl.*), motion picture, movie (*U.S. inf.*) ~*v.* **4.** photograph, shoot, take **5.** *Often with* **over** blear, blur, cloud, dull, haze, mist, veil

filmy **1.** chiffon, cobwebby, delicate, diaphanous, fine, finespun, flimsy, floaty, fragile, gauzy, gossamer, insubstantial, seethrough, sheer, transparent **2.** bleared, bleary, blurred, blurry, cloudy, dim, hazy, membranous, milky, misty, opalescent, opaque, pearly

filter *v.* **1.** clarify, filtrate, purify, refine, screen, sieve, sift, strain, winnow **2.** *Often with* **through** *or* **out** dribble, escape, exude, leach, leak, ooze, penetrate, percolate, seep, trickle, well ~*n.* **3.** gauze, membrane, mesh, riddle, sieve, strainer

filth **1.** carrion, contamination, defilement, dirt, dung, excrement, excreta, faeces, filthiness, foul matter, foulness, garbage, grime, muck, nastiness, ordure, pollution, putrefaction, putrescence, refuse, sewage, slime, sludge, squalor, uncleanness **2.** corruption, dirty-mindedness, impurity, indecency, obscenity, pornography, smut, vileness, vulgarity

filthy **1.** dirty, faecal, feculent, foul, nasty, polluted, putrid, scummy, slimy, squalid, unclean, vile **2.** begrimed, black, blackened, grimy, grubby, miry, mucky, muddy, mud-encrusted, smoky, sooty, unwashed **3.** bawdy, coarse, corrupt, depraved, dirty-minded, foul, foul-mouthed, impure, indecent, lewd, licentious, obscene, pornographic, smutty, suggestive

finance (fɪˈnæns, ˈfaɪnæns) *n.* 1. management of money 2. (*also pl.*) money resources —*vt.* 3. find capital for —**fiˈnancial** *a.* of finance —**fiˈnancially** *adv.* —**fiˈnancier** *n.* —**financial year** UK 1. annual period at end of which firm's accounts are made up 2. annual period ending Apr. 5th, over which Budget estimates are made by British Government

finch (fɪntʃ) *n.* one of family of small singing birds

find (faɪnd) *vt.* 1. come across, light upon 2. obtain 3. realize 4. experience, discover 5. discover by searching 6. supply (as funds) 7. *Law* give a verdict (upon) (**found** *pt./pp.*) —*n.* 8. finding 9. (valuable) thing found —**ˈfinder** *n.* —**ˈfinding** *n.* judicial verdict —**find out** 1. gain knowledge of (something); learn 2. detect crime, deception *etc.* of (someone)

fine[1] (faɪn) *a.* 1. choice, of high quality, excellent 2. delicate 3. subtle 4. pure 5. in small particles 6. slender 7. handsome 8. showy 9. *inf.* healthy, at ease, comfortable 10. free from rain —*vt.* 11. make clear or pure 12. refine 13. thin —**ˈfinely** *adv.* —**ˈfineness** *n.* —**ˈfinery** *n.* showy dress —**finesse** (fɪˈnɛs) *n.* elegant, skilful management —**fine art** art produced for its aesthetic value —**fine-drawn** *a.* 1. (of distinctions *etc.*) precise; subtle 2. (of wire *etc.*) drawn out until very fine —**ˈfineˈspun** *a.* 1. spun out to fine thread 2. excessively subtle or refined —**fine-tooth comb** *or* **fine-toothed comb** comb with fine, closely set teeth —**go over** *or* **through with a fine-tooth(ed) comb** examine very thoroughly

fine[2] (faɪn) *n.* 1. sum fixed as penalty —*vt.* 2. punish by fine —**in fine** 1. in conclusion 2. in brief

fines herbes (*Fr.* fin ˈzɛrb) mixture of finely chopped herbs, used to flavour omelettes *etc.*

finger (ˈfɪŋgə) *n.* 1. one of the jointed branches of the hand 2. any of various things like this —*vt.* 3. touch or handle with fingers —**ˈfingering** *n.* 1. *Mus.* technique of using one's fingers 2. *Mus.* numerals in musical part indicating this 3. fine wool yarn for manufacture of stockings *etc.* —**ˈfingerboard** *n.* part of musical instrument on which fingers are placed —**finger bowl** small bowl filled with water for rinsing fingers at table after meal —**finger plate** ornamental plate above door handle to prevent finger marks —**ˈfingerprint** *n.* impression of tip of finger, *esp.* as used for identifying criminals —**ˈfingerstall** *n.* cover to protect finger

finial (ˈfaɪnɪəl) *n. Archit.* ornament at apex of pinnacles, gables, spires *etc.*

finicky (ˈfɪnɪkɪ) *or* **finicking** *a.* 1. fastidious, fussy 2. too fine

finis (ˈfɪnɪs) *Lat.* end, *esp.* of book

THESAURUS

final 1. closing, concluding, end, eventual, last, last-minute, latest, terminal, terminating, ultimate 2. absolute, conclusive, decided, decisive, definite, definitive, determinate, finished, incontrovertible, irrevocable, settled

finale climax, close, conclusion, crowning glory, culmination, dénouement, epilogue, finis, last act

finality certitude, conclusiveness, decidedness, decisiveness, definiteness, inevitableness, irrevocability, resolution, unavoidability

finalize agree, clinch (*Inf.*), complete, conclude, decide, settle, sew up (*Inf.*), tie up, work out, wrap up (*Inf.*)

finally 1. at last, at length, at long last, at the last, at the last moment, eventually, in the end, in the long run, lastly, ultimately, when all is said and done 2. in conclusion, in summary, to conclude 3. beyond the shadow of a doubt, completely, conclusively, convincingly, decisively, for all time, for ever, for good, inescapably, inexorably, irrevocably, once and for all, permanently

finance 1. *n.* accounts, banking, business, commerce, economics, financial affairs, investment, money, money management 2. *v.* back, bankroll (*U.S.*), float, fund, guarantee, pay for, provide security for, set up in business, subsidize, support, underwrite

finances affairs, assets, capital, cash, financial condition, funds, money, resources, wherewithal

financial budgeting, economic, fiscal, monetary, money, pecuniary

find *v.* 1. catch sight of, chance upon, come across, come up with, descry, discover, encounter, espy, expose, ferret out, hit upon, lay one's hand on, light upon, locate, meet, recognize, run to earth, spot, stumble upon, track down, turn up, uncover, unearth 2. achieve, acquire, attain, earn, gain, get, obtain, procure, win 3. get back, recover, regain, repossess, retrieve 4. arrive at, ascertain, become aware, detect, discover, experience, learn, note, notice, observe, perceive, realise, remark 5. be responsible for, bring, contribute, cough up (*Inf.*), furnish, provide, supply ~*n.* 6. acquisition, asset, bargain, catch, discovery, good buy

finding award, conclusion, decision, decree, judgment, pronouncement, recommendation, verdict

find out 1. detect, discover, learn, note, observe, perceive, realize 2. bring to light, catch, detect, disclose, expose, reveal, rumble (*Sl.*), suss out (*Sl.*), uncover, unmask

fine[1] *adj.* 1. accomplished, admirable, beautiful, choice, excellent, exceptional, exquisite, first-class, first-rate, great, magnificent, masterly, ornate, outstanding, rare, select, showy, skilful, splendid, superior, supreme 2. balmy, bright, clear, clement, cloudless, dry, fair, pleasant, sunny 3. dainty, delicate, elegant, expensive, exquisite, fragile, quality 4. abstruse, acute, critical, discriminating, fastidious, hairsplitting, intelligent, keen, minute, nice, precise, quick, refined, sensitive, sharp, subtle, tasteful, tenuous 5. delicate, diaphanous, fine-grained, flimsy, gauzy, gossamer, light, lightweight, powdered, powdery, pulverized, sheer, slender, small, thin 6. clear, pure, refined, solid, sterling, unadulterated, unalloyed, unpolluted 7. attractive, bonny, good-looking, handsome, lovely, smart, striking, stylish, well-favoured

fine[2] 1. *v.* amerce (*Archaic*), mulct, penalize, punish 2. *n.* amercement (*Archaic*), damages, forfeit, penalty, punishment

finery best bib and tucker (*Inf.*), decorations, frippery, gear (*Inf.*), gewgaws, glad rags (*Sl.*), ornaments, showiness, splendour, Sunday best, trappings, trinkets

finesse adeptness, adroitness, artfulness, cleverness, craft, delicacy, diplomacy, discretion, know-how (*Inf.*), polish, quickness, savoir-faire, skill, sophistication, subtlety, tact

finger *v.* feel, fiddle with (*Inf.*), handle, manipulate, maul, meddle with, paw (*Inf.*), play about with, touch, toy with

finish ('fɪnɪʃ) *v.* 1. bring, come to an end, conclude —*vt.* 2. complete 3. perfect 4. kill —*n.* 5. end 6. way in which thing is finished, as an *oak finish* of furniture 7. final appearance —'**finisher** *n.* —**finishing school** private school for girls, that teaches social graces

finite ('faɪnaɪt) *a.* bounded, limited

Finn (fɪn) *n.* native of Finland —'**Finnish** *a.* 1. of Finland —*n.* 2. official language of Finland

finnan haddock ('fɪnən) *or* **haddie** ('hædɪ) smoked haddock

fiord (fjɔːd) *n. see* FJORD

fipple ('fɪpᵊl) *n.* wooden plug forming flue in end of pipe —**fipple flute** end-blown flute with fipple, such as recorder

fir (fɜː) *n.* 1. kind of coniferous resinous tree 2. its wood

fire (faɪə) *n.* 1. state of burning, combustion, flame, glow 2. mass of burning fuel 3. destructive burning, conflagration 4. device for heating a room *etc.* 5. ardour, keenness, spirit 6. shooting of firearms —*vt.* 7. discharge (firearm) 8. propel from firearm 9. *inf.* dismiss from employment 10. bake 11. make burn 12. supply with fuel 13. inspire 14. explode —*vi.* 15. discharge firearm 16. begin to burn —'**firing** *n.* 1. process of baking ceramics *etc.* in kiln 2. act of stoking fire or furnace 3. discharge of firearm 4. something used as fuel —**fire alarm** device to give warning of fire —'**firearm** *n.* gun, rifle, pistol *etc.* —'**fireball** *n.* 1. ball-shaped discharge of lightning 2. region of hot ionized gas at centre of nuclear explosion 3. *Astron.* large bright meteor 4. *sl.* energetic person —'**firebomb** *n. see* INCENDIARY (sense 6) —'**firebrand** *n.* 1. burning piece of wood 2. energetic (troublesome) person —'**firebreak** *n.* strip of cleared land to arrest progress of bush or grass fire —'**firebrick** *n.* refractory brick made of fire clay, for lining furnaces *etc.* —**fire brigade** organized body of men and appliances to put out fires and rescue those in danger —'**firebug** *n. inf.* person who intentionally sets fire to buildings *etc.* —**fire clay** heat-resistant clay used in making of firebricks *etc.* —'**firecracker** *n.* small cardboard container filled with explosive powder —'**firecrest** *n.* small European warbler —'**firedamp** *n.* explosive hydrocarbon gas forming in mines —'**firedog** *n.* either of pair of metal stands used to support logs in open fire —**fire drill** rehearsal of procedures for escape from fire —**fire-eater** *n.* 1. performer who simulates swallowing of fire 2. belligerent person —**fire engine** vehicle with apparatus for extinguishing fires —**fire escape** means, *esp.* stairs, for escaping from burning buildings —'**firefly** *n.* insect giving off phosphorescent glow —'**fireguard** *or* **fire screen** *n.* protective grating in front of fire —**fire hall** C fire station —**fire irons** tongs, poker and shovel —'**firelighter** *n.* composition of highly combustible material for kindling domestic fire —'**fireman** *n.* 1. member of fire brigade 2. stoker 3. assistant to locomotive driver —'**fireplace** *n.* recess in room for fire —**fire raiser** person who deliberately sets fire to property *etc.* —**fire ship** burning vessel sent drifting against enemy ships —**fire station** building housing fire brigade —'**firetrap** *n.* building unsafe in case of fire —'**firework** *n.* 1. (*oft. pl.*) device to give spectacular effects by explosions and coloured sparks —*pl.* 2. outburst of temper, anger —**firing line** 1. *Mil.* positions from which fire is delivered 2. leading position in an activity —**firing party** *or* **squad** detachment sent to fire volleys at military funeral, or to shoot criminal

firkin ('fɜːkɪn) *n.* 1. small cask 2. UK measure of 9 gallons

firm[1] (fɜːm) *a.* 1. solid 2. fixed, stable 3. steadfast 4. resolute 5. settled —*v.* 6. make, become firm

THESAURUS

finish *v.* **1.** accomplish, achieve, bring to a close *or* conclusion, carry through, cease, close, complete, conclude, culminate, deal with, discharge, do, end, execute, finalize, fulfil, get done, get out of the way, make short work of, put the finishing touch(es) to, round off, settle, stop, terminate, wind up (*Inf.*), wrap up (*Inf.*) **2.** *Often with* **off** administer *or* give the coup de grâce, annihilate, best, bring down, defeat, destroy, dispose of, drive to the wall, exterminate, get rid of, kill, overcome, overpower, put an end to, rout, ruin, worst ~*n.* **3.** cessation, close, closing, completion, conclusion, culmination, dénouement, end, ending, finale, last stage(s), termination, winding up (*Inf.*), wind-up (*Inf., chiefly U.S.*) ~*v.* **4.** elaborate, perfect, polish, refine ~*n.* **5.** appearance, grain, lustre, patina, polish, shine, smoothness, surface, texture

finite bounded, circumscribed, conditioned, delimited, demarcated, limited, restricted, subject to limitations, terminable

fire *n.* **1.** blaze, combustion, conflagration, flames, inferno **2.** barrage, bombardment, cannonade, flak, fusillade, hail, salvo, shelling, sniping, volley **3.** *Fig.* animation, ardour, brio, burning passion, dash, eagerness, élan, enthusiasm, excitement, fervency, fervour, force, heat, impetuosity, intensity, life, light, lustre, passion, radiance, scintillation, sparkle, spirit, splendour, verve, vigour, virtuosity, vivacity ~*v.* **4.** enkindle, ignite, kindle, light, put a match to, set ablaze, set aflame, set alight, set fire to, set on fire **5.** detonate, discharge, eject, explode, hurl, launch, let off, loose, pull the trigger, set off, shell, shoot, touch off **6.** *Fig.* animate, arouse, electrify, enliven, excite, galvanize, impassion, incite, inflame, inspire, inspirit, irritate, quicken, rouse, stir **7.** *Inf.* cashier, discharge, dismiss, give marching orders, make redundant, sack (*Sl.*), show the door

firebrand *Fig.* agitator, demagogue, fomenter, incendiary, instigator, rabble-rouser, soapbox orator, tub-thumper

fireworks 1. illuminations, pyrotechnics **2.** *Fig.* fit of rage, hysterics, paroxysms, rage, rows, storm, temper, trouble, uproar

firm[1] *adj.* **1.** close-grained, compact, compressed, concentrated, congealed, dense, hard, inelastic, inflexible, jelled, jellified, rigid, set, solid, solidified, stiff, unyielding **2.** anchored, braced, cemented, embedded, fast, fastened, fixed, immovable, motionless, riveted, robust, rooted, secure, secured, stable, stationary, steady, strong, sturdy, taut, tight, unfluctuating, unmoving, unshakable **3.** adamant, constant, definite, fixed, inflexible, obdurate, resolute, resolved, set on, settled, staunch, steadfast, strict, true, unalterable, unbending, unfaltering, unflinching, unshakable, unshaken, unswerving, unwavering, unyielding

firm[2] *n.* association, business, company, concern, conglomerate, corporation, enterprise, house, organization, outfit (*Inf.*), partnership

firm[2] (fɜːm) *n.* **1.** commercial enterprise **2.** partnership

firmament (ˈfɜːməmənt) *n.* expanse of sky, heavens

first (fɜːst) *a.* **1.** earliest in time or order **2.** foremost in rank or position **3.** most excellent **4.** highest, chief —*n.* **5.** beginning **6.** first occurrence of something **7.** first-class honours degree at university —*adv.* **8.** before others in time, order *etc.* —**ˈfirstly** *adv.* —**first aid** help given to injured person before arrival of doctor —**first class** *n.* **1.** class of highest value, quality *etc.* —*a.* **2.** of highest class **3.** excellent **4.** of most comfortable class of accommodation in hotel, train *etc.* **5.** UK of letters handled faster than second-class letters —**first-class** *adv.* by first-class mail, means of transportation *etc.* —**first cousin** son or daughter of one's aunt or uncle —**first-day cover** *Philately* envelope post-marked on first day of issue of its stamps —**first finger** finger next to thumb —**first-foot** *chiefly Scot. n.* **1.** first person to enter household in New Year (*also* **first-footer**) —*v.* **2.** enter the house of (someone) as first-foot —**first-footing** *n.* —**first fruits 1.** first results or profits of undertaking **2.** fruit that ripens first —**first-hand** *a.* obtained directly from the first source —**first lady** (*oft.* **F- L-**) US wife or official hostess of state governor or president —**first mate** *or* **officer** officer of merchant vessel immediately below captain —**first offender** person convicted of criminal offence for first time —**first person** grammatical category of pronouns and verbs used by speaker to refer to himself —**first-rate** *a.* of highest class or quality —**first-strike** *a.* (of nuclear missile) intended for use in opening attack calculated to destroy enemy's nuclear weapons —**first water 1.** finest quality of precious stone **2.** best quality

firth (fɜːθ) *or* **frith** *n. esp.* in Scotland, arm of the sea, river estuary

fiscal (ˈfɪskᵊl) *a.* of government finances —**fiscal year** US financial year

fish (fɪʃ) *n.* **1.** vertebrate cold-blooded animal with gills, living in water **2.** its flesh as food (*pl.* **fish, -es**) —*vi.* **3.** (attempt to) catch fish **4.** search (for something) **5.** (*with* for) try to get information indirectly —**ˈfisher** *n.* —**ˈfishery** *n.* **1.** business of fishing **2.** fishing ground —**ˈfishy** *a.* **1.** of, like, or full of fish **2.** dubious, open to suspicion —**fish cake** fried flattened ball of flaked fish mixed with mashed potatoes —**ˈfisherman** *n.* one who catches fish for a living or for pleasure —**fish-eye lens** *Photog.* lens of small focal length, that covers almost 180° —**ˈfishˈfinger** *n.* small piece of fish covered in breadcrumbs —**fish-kettle** *n.* oval pot for cooking fish —**fish meal** ground dried fish used as fertilizer *etc.* —**ˈfishmonger** *n.* seller of fish —**fish slice 1.** fish carver **2.** flat-bladed utensil for turning or lifting food in frying —**ˈfishwife** *n.* coarse, scolding woman —**fish out** find, extract

fishplate (ˈfɪʃpleɪt) *n.* piece of metal holding rails together

fissure (ˈfɪʃə) *n.* cleft, split, cleavage —**fissile** (ˈfɪsaɪl) *a.* **1.** capable of splitting **2.** tending to split —**ˈfission** *n.* **1.** splitting **2.** reproduction by division of living cells with two parts, each of which becomes complete organism **3.** splitting of atomic nucleus with release of large amount of energy —**ˈfissionable** *a.* capable of undergoing nuclear fission —**fissiparous** (fɪˈsɪpərəs) *a.* reproducing by fission

fist (fɪst) *n.* clenched hand —**ˈfisticuffs** *pl.n.* fighting

fistula (ˈfɪstjʊlə) *n.* pipelike ulcer (*pl.* **-s, -lae** (-liː))

fit[1] (fɪt) *vt.* **1.** be suited to **2.** be properly adjusted to **3.** arrange, adjust, apply, insert **4.** supply, furnish —*vi.* **5.** be correctly adjusted or adapted **6.** be of right size (**-tt-**) —*a.* **7.** well-suited, worthy **8.** qualified **9.** proper, becoming **10.** ready **11.** in good condition or health (**ˈfitter** *comp.*, **ˈfittest** *sup.*) —*n.* **12.** way anything fits, its style **13.** adjustment —**ˈfitly** *adv.* —**ˈfitment** *n.* piece of furniture —**ˈfitness** *n.* —**ˈfitted** *a.* **1.** designed for excellent fit **2.** (of carpet) cut to cover floor completely **3.** (of furniture) built to fit particular space —**ˈfitter** *n.* **1.** one who, that which, makes fit **2.** one who supervises making and fitting of garments **3.** mechanic skilled in fitting up metalwork —**ˈfitting** *a.* **1.** appropriate, suitable, proper —*n.* **2.** fixture **3.** apparatus **4.** action of fitting —**fit in 1.** give place or time to **2.** belong or conform, *esp.* after adjustment

fit[2] (fɪt) *n.* **1.** seizure with convulsions, spasms, loss of consciousness *etc.*, of epilepsy, hysteria *etc.* **2.** sudden passing attack of illness **3.** passing state, mood —**ˈfitful** *a.* spasmodic, capricious —**ˈfitfully** *adv.* —**have** *or* **throw a fit** *inf.* become very angry

THESAURUS

first *adj.* **1.** chief, foremost, head, highest, leading, pre-eminent, prime, principal, ruling **2.** earliest, initial, introductory, maiden, opening, original, premier, primeval, primitive, primordial, pristine ~*adv.* **3.** at the beginning, at the outset, before all else, beforehand, firstly, initially, in the first place, to begin with, to start with ~*n.* **4.** *As in* **from the first** beginning, commencement, inception, introduction, outset, start, starting point, word 'go' (*Inf.*)

first-hand direct, straight from the horse's mouth

first-rate admirable, A-one (*Inf.*), crack (*Sl.*), elite, excellent, exceptional, exclusive, first class, outstanding, prime, second to none, superb, superlative, tiptop, top, topnotch (*Inf.*), tops (*Sl.*)

fish out extract, extricate, find, haul out, produce, pull out

fishy 1. *Inf.* doubtful, dubious, funny (*Inf.*), implausible, improbable, odd, queer, questionable, suspect, suspicious, unlikely **2.** fishlike, piscatorial, piscatory, piscine

fissure breach, break, chink, cleavage, cleft, crack, cranny, crevice, fault, fracture, gap, hole, interstice, opening, rent, rift, rupture, slit, split

fit[1] *adj.* **1.** able, adapted, adequate, appropriate, apt, becoming, capable, competent, convenient, correct, deserving, equipped, expedient, fitted, fitting, good enough, meet (*Archaic*), prepared, proper, qualified, ready, right, seemly, suitable, trained, well-suited, worthy **2.** able-bodied, hale, healthy, in good condition, in good shape, in good trim, robust, strapping, toned up, trim, well ~*v.* **3.** accord, agree, be consonant, belong, concur, conform, correspond, dovetail, go, interlock, join, match, meet, suit, tally **4.** *Often with* **out** *or* **up** accommodate, accoutre, arm, equip, fit out, kit out, outfit, prepare, provide, rig out **5.** adapt, adjust, alter, arrange, dispose, fashion, modify, place, position, shape

fit[2] *n.* **1.** attack, bout, convulsion, paroxysm, seizure, spasm **2.** caprice, fancy, humour, mood, whim **3.** bout, burst, outbreak, outburst, spell

fitful broken, desultory, disturbed, erratic, flickering,

five (faɪv) *a./n.* cardinal number after four —**ˈfifˈteen** *a./n.* ten plus five —**ˈfifˈteenth** *a./n.* —**fifth** (fɪfθ) *a./n.* ordinal number of five —**fifthly** (ˈfɪfθlɪ) *adv.* —**fiftieth** (ˈfɪftɪɪθ) *a./n.* —**fifty** (ˈfɪftɪ) *a./n.* five tens —**ˈfiver** *n.* **UK** *inf.* five-pound note —**fives** *pl.n.* (*with sing. v.*) ball game played with hand or bat in a court —**fifth column** organization spying for enemy within country at war —**fifty-fifty** *a./adv. inf.* in equal parts —**five-a-side** *n.* football with teams of five —**five-o'clock shadow** beard growth visible late in day on man's shaven face —**ˈfivepins** *pl.n.* bowling game played *esp.* in Canada —**Five-Year Plan** in socialist economies, government plan for economic development over five-year period

fix (fɪks) *vt.* **1.** fasten, make firm or stable **2.** set, establish **3.** appoint, assign, determine **4.** make fast **5.** repair **6.** *inf.* influence the outcome of unfairly or by deception **7.** *inf.* bribe **8.** *inf.* give (someone) his just deserts —*vi.* **9.** become firm or solidified **10.** determine —*n.* **11.** difficult situation **12.** position of ship, aircraft ascertained by radar, observation *etc.* **13.** *sl.* dose of narcotic drug —**fixˈation** *n.* **1.** act of fixing **2.** preoccupation, obsession **3.** situation of being set in some way of acting or thinking —**ˈfixative** *a.* **1.** capable of, or tending to fix —*n.* **2.** fluid sprayed over drawings to prevent smudging *etc.* **3.** substance added to liquid to make it less volatile —**fixed** *a.* **1.** attached so as to be immovable **2.** stable **3.** steadily directed **4.** established as to relative position **5.** always at same time **6.** (of ideas *etc.*) firmly maintained **7.** (of element) held in chemical combination **8.** (of substance) nonvolatile **9.** arranged **10.** *inf.* equipped; provided for **11.** *inf.* illegally arranged —**fixedly** (ˈfɪksɪdlɪ) *adv.* intently —**ˈfixity** *n.* —**ˈfixture** *n.* **1.** thing fixed in position **2.** thing attached to house **3.** date for sporting event **4.** the event —**fixed star** star whose position appears to be stationary over long period of time —**fix (someone) up** attend to (someone's) needs —**fix up** arrange

fizz (fɪz) *vi.* **1.** hiss, splutter —*n.* **2.** hissing noise **3.** effervescent liquid, such as soda water, champagne —**ˈfizzle** *vi.* **1.** splutter weakly —*n.* **2.** fizzling noise **3.** fiasco —**ˈfizzy** *a.* effervescent —**fizzle out** *inf.* come to nothing, fail

fjord *or* **fiord** (fjɔːd) *n. esp.* in Norway, long, narrow inlet of sea

FL Florida

fl. 1. floor **2.** *floruit* (*Lat.*, (he or she) flourished) **3.** fluid

flabbergast (ˈflæbəgɑːst) *vt.* overwhelm with astonishment

flabby (ˈflæbɪ) *a.* **1.** hanging loose, limp **2.** out of condition, too fat **3.** feeble **4.** yielding —**flab** *n. inf.* unsightly fat on the body —**ˈflabbiness** *n.*

flaccid (ˈflæksɪd) *a.* flabby, lacking firmness —**flacˈcidity** *n.*

flag[1] (flæg) *n.* **1.** banner, piece of bunting attached to staff or halyard as standard or signal **2.** small paper emblem sold on flag days —*vt.* **3.** decorate or mark with flag(s) **4.** send or communicate (messages *etc.*) by flag signals (**-gg-**) —**flag day** day on which small flags or emblems are sold in streets for charity —**ˈflagpole** *or* **ˈflagstaff** *n.* pole on which flag is hoisted and displayed (*pl.* **-poles** *or* **-staffs, -staves** (-steɪvz)) —**ˈflagship** *n.* **1.** admiral's ship **2.** most important ship of fleet —**flag down** warn or signal (vehicle) to stop —**flag of convenience** national flag flown by ship registered in that country to gain financial or legal advantage —**flag of truce** white flag indicating invitation to enemy to negotiate

flag[2] (flæg) *n.* water plant with sword-shaped leaves, *esp.* the iris —**ˈflaggy** *a.*

THESAURUS

fluctuating, haphazard, impulsive, intermittent, irregular, spasmodic, sporadic, unstable, variable

fitfully desultorily, erratically, in fits and starts, in snatches, intermittently, interruptedly, irregularly, off and on, spasmodically, sporadically

fitness 1. adaptation, applicability, appropriateness, aptness, competence, eligibility, pertinence, preparedness, propriety, qualifications, readiness, seemliness, suitability **2.** good condition, good health, health, robustness, strength, vigour

fitted 1. adapted, cut out for, equipped, fit, qualified, right, suitable, tailor-made **2.** built-in, permanent

fitting 1. *adj.* appropriate, becoming, *comme il faut*, correct, decent, decorous, desirable, meet (*Archaic*), proper, right, seemly, suitable **2.** *n.* accessory, attachment, component, connection, part, piece, unit

fix *v.* **1.** anchor, embed, establish, implant, install, locate, place, plant, position, root, set, settle **2.** attach, bind, cement, connect, couple, fasten, glue, link, make fast, pin, secure, stick, tie **3.** agree on, appoint, arrange, arrive at, conclude, decide, define, determine, establish, limit, name, resolve, set, settle, specify **4.** adjust, correct, mend, patch up, put to rights, regulate, repair, see to, sort **5.** congeal, consolidate, harden, rigidify, set, solidify, stiffen, thicken **6.** *Inf.* bribe, fiddle, influence, manipulate, manoeuvre, pull strings (*Inf.*), rig **7.** *Sl.* cook (someone's) goose (*Inf.*), get even with, get revenge on, pay back, settle (someone's) hash (*Inf.*), sort (someone) out (*Inf.*), take retribution on, wreak vengeance on ~*n.* **8.** *Inf.* difficult situation, difficulty, dilemma, embarrassment, hole (*Sl.*), jam (*Inf.*), mess, pickle (*Inf.*), plight, predicament, quandary, spot (*Inf.*), ticklish situation

fixation complex, hang-up (*Inf.*), *idée fixe*, infatuation, mania, obsession, preoccupation, thing (*Inf.*)

fixed 1. anchored, attached, established, immovable, made fast, permanent, rigid, rooted, secure, set **2.** intent, level, resolute, steady, unbending, unblinking, undeviating, unflinching, unwavering **3.** agreed, arranged, decided, definite, established, planned, resolved, settled **4.** *Inf.* framed, manipulated, packed, put-up, rigged

fix up agree on, arrange, fix, organize, plan, settle, sort out

fizz bubble, effervesce, fizzle, froth, hiss, sparkle, sputter

fizzle out abort, collapse, come to nothing, die away, end in disappointment, fail, fall through, fold (*Inf.*), miss the mark, peter out

fizzy bubbling, bubbly, carbonated, effervescent, gassy, sparkling

flag[1] **1.** *n.* banderole, banner, colours, ensign, gonfalon, jack, pennant, pennon, standard, streamer **2.** *v.* *Sometimes with* **down** hail, salute, signal, warn, wave

flag[2] *v.* abate, decline, die, droop, ebb, fade, fail, faint, fall, fall off, feel the pace, languish, peter out, pine, sag, sink, slump, succumb, taper off, wane, weaken, weary, wilt

flag[3] (flæg) *n.* 1. flat slab of stone —*pl.* 2. pavement of flags —*vt.* 3. furnish (floor *etc.*) with flagstones (-gg-) —ˈ**flagstone** *n.*

flag[4] (flæg) *vi.* 1. droop, fade 2. lose vigour (-gg-)

flagellate (ˈflædʒɪleɪt) *vt.* scourge, flog —ˈ**flagellant** *n.* one who scourges himself, *esp.* in religious penance —**flagelˈlation** *n.* —ˈ**flagellator** *n.*

flagellum (fləˈdʒɛləm) *n.* 1. *Biol.* whiplike outgrowth from cell that acts as organ of locomotion 2. *Bot.* long thin shoot (*pl.* -la (-lə), -s)

flageolet (flædʒəˈlɛt) *n.* small flutelike instrument

flagon (ˈflægən) *n.* large bottle of wine *etc.*

flagrant (ˈfleɪgrənt) *a.* glaring, scandalous, blatant —ˈ**flagrancy** *n.* —ˈ**flagrantly** *adv.*

flail (fleɪl) *n.* 1. instrument for threshing corn by hand —*v.* 2. beat with, move as, flail

flair (flɛə) *n.* 1. natural ability 2. elegance

flak *or* **flack** (flæk) *n.* 1. anti-aircraft fire 2. *inf.* adverse criticism

flake (fleɪk) *n.* 1. small, thin piece, *esp.* particle of snow 2. piece chipped off —*v.* 3. (cause to) peel off in flakes —ˈ**flaky** *a.* —**flake out** *inf.* collapse, sleep from exhaustion

flambé (ˈflɑːmbeɪ) *a.* (of food) served in flaming brandy *etc.*

flamboyant (flæmˈbɔɪənt) *a.* 1. florid, gorgeous, showy 2. exuberant, ostentatious

flame (fleɪm) *n.* 1. burning gas, *esp.* above fire 2. visible burning 3. passion, *esp.* love 4. *inf.* sweetheart —*vi.* 5. give out flames, blaze 6. shine 7. burst out —ˈ**flaming** *a.* 1. burning with flames 2. glowing brightly 3. ardent 4. *inf.* a common intensifier —**flamethrower** *n.* weapon that ejects stream of burning fluid

flamenco (fləˈmɛŋkəʊ) *n.* Sp. dance to guitar

flamingo (fləˈmɪŋgəʊ) *n.* large pink bird with long neck and legs (*pl.* -s, -es)

flammable (ˈflæməbᵊl) *a.* liable to catch fire

flan (flæn) *n.* open sweet or savoury tart

flange (flændʒ) *n.* 1. projecting flat rim, collar or rib —*v.* 2. provide with or take form of flange

flank (flæŋk) *n.* 1. part of side between hips and ribs 2. side of anything, *eg* body of troops —*vt.* 3. guard or strengthen on flank 4. attack flank of 5. be at, move along either side of

flannel (ˈflænᵊl) *n.* 1. soft woollen fabric for clothing, *esp.* trousers 2. small piece of cloth for washing face and hands 3. *inf.* insincere talk —*pl.* 4. trousers *etc.* made of flannel —*vt.* 5. UK *inf.* flatter (-ll-) —**flanneˈlette** *n.* cotton fabric imitating flannel —ˈ**flannelly** *a.*

flap (flæp) *v.* 1. move (wings, arms *etc.*) as bird flying 2. (cause to) sway —*vt.* 3. strike with flat object —*vi.* 4. *inf.* be agitated, flustered (-pp-) —*n.* 5. act of flapping 6. broad piece of anything hanging from hinge or loosely from one side 7. movable part of aircraft wing 8. *inf.* state of excitement or panic —ˈ**flapper** *n.* in 1920s, young woman, *esp.* one flaunting unconventional behaviour —ˈ**flapjack** *n.* 1. chewy biscuit made with rolled oats 2. *chiefly* US pancake

flare (flɛə) *vi.* 1. blaze with unsteady flame 2. *inf.* (*with* up) suddenly burst into anger 3. spread outwards, as bottom of skirt —*n.* 4. instance of flaring 5. signal light —**flare-path** *n.* area lit up to facilitate landing or takeoff of aircraft —**flare-up** *n.* 1. sudden burst of fire 2. *inf.* sudden burst of emotion —**flare up** 1. burst suddenly into fire 2. *inf.* burst into anger

flash (flæʃ) *n.* 1. sudden burst of light or flame 2. sudden short blaze 3. very short time 4. brief news item 5. ribbon; badge 6. display —*vi.* 7. break into sudden flame 8. gleam 9. burst into view 10. move very fast 11. appear suddenly 12. *sl.* expose oneself indecently —*vt.* 13. cause to gleam 14. emit (light *etc.*) suddenly —*a.* 15. showy 16. sham (*also* ˈ**flashy**) —ˈ**flasher** *n.* 1. something which flashes 2. *sl.* someone who indecently exposes himself —ˈ**flashing** *n.* weatherproof material used to cover valleys between slopes of roof *etc.* —ˈ**flashback** *n.* break in continuity of book, play or film, to introduce what has taken place previously —ˈ**flashbulb** *n.* *Photog.* small light

THESAURUS

flagrant arrant, atrocious, awful, barefaced, blatant, bold, brazen, crying, dreadful, egregious, enormous, flagitious, flaunting, glaring, heinous, immodest, infamous, notorious, open, ostentatious, out-and-out, outrageous, scandalous, shameless, undisguised

flagstone block, flag, paving stone, slab

flail *v.* beat, thrash, thresh, windmill

flair 1. ability, accomplishment, aptitude, faculty, feel, genius, gift, knack, mastery, talent 2. chic, dash, discernment, elegance, panache, style, stylishness, taste

flake 1. *n.* disk, lamina, layer, peeling, scale, shaving, sliver, squama (*Biol.*), wafer 2. *v.* blister, chip, desquamate, peel (off), scale (off)

flamboyant 1. baroque, elaborate, extravagant, florid, ornate, ostentatious, rich, rococo, showy, theatrical 2. brilliant, colourful, dashing, dazzling, exciting, glamorous, swashbuckling

flame *v.* 1. blaze, burn, flare, flash, glare, glow, shine ~*n.* 2. blaze, brightness, fire, light 3. *Fig.* affection, ardour, enthusiasm, fervency, fervour, fire, intensity, keenness, passion, warmth 4. *Inf.* beau, beloved, boyfriend, girlfriend, heart-throb (*Brit.*), ladylove, lover, sweetheart

flaming 1. ablaze, afire, blazing, brilliant, burning, fiery, glowing, ignited, in flames, raging, red, red-hot 2. angry, ardent, aroused, frenzied, hot, impassioned, intense, raging, scintillating, vehement, vivid

flank *n.* 1. ham, haunch, hip, loin, quarter, side, thigh 2. side, wing ~*v.* 3. border, bound, edge, fringe, line, screen, skirt, wall

flannel *Fig.* 1. *n.* baloney (*Inf.*), blarney, equivocation, flattery, hedging, prevarication, soft soap (*Inf.*), sweet talk (*U.S. inf.*), waffle (*Inf.*), weasel words (*Inf., chiefly U.S.*) 2. *v.* blarney, butter up, flatter, soft-soap (*Inf.*), sweet-talk (*U.S. inf.*)

flap *v.* 1. agitate, beat, flail, flutter, shake, swing, swish, thrash, thresh, vibrate, wag, wave ~*n.* 2. bang, banging, beating, flutter, shaking, swinging, swish, waving ~*v.* 3. *Inf.* dither, fuss, panic ~*n.* 4. *Inf.* agitation, commotion, fluster, panic, state (*Inf.*), stew (*Inf.*), sweat (*Inf.*), tizzy (*Inf.*), twitter 5. apron, cover, fly, fold, lapel, lappet, overlap, skirt, tab, tail

flare *v.* 1. blaze, burn up, dazzle, flicker, flutter, glare, waver 2. *Often with* **out** broaden, spread out, widen ~*n.* 3. blaze, burst, dazzle, flame, flash, flicker, glare

flare up blaze, blow one's top (*Inf.*), boil over, break out, explode, fire up, fly off the handle (*Inf.*), lose control, lose one's cool (*Inf.*), lose one's temper, throw a tantrum

bulb triggered, *usu.* electrically, to produce bright flash of light —ˈ**flashcube** *n.* boxlike camera attachment, holding four flashbulbs, that turns so that each flashbulb can be used —ˈ**flashlight** *n.* **1.** *esp.* **US** torch **2.** *Photog.* brief bright light emitted by electronic flash (*also* **flash**) —**flash point** temperature at which a vapour ignites —**flash in the pan** person *etc.* that enjoys only short-lived success

flask (flɑːsk) *n.* **1.** long-necked bottle for scientific use **2.** pocket bottle **3.** vacuum flask

flat[1] (flæt) *a.* **1.** level **2.** spread out **3.** at full length **4.** smooth **5.** downright **6.** dull, lifeless **7.** *Mus.* below true pitch **8.** (of tyre) deflated, punctured **9.** (of battery) fully discharged, dead (ˈ**flatter** *comp.*, ˈ**flattest** *sup.*) —*adv.* **10.** completely, utterly; absolutely —*n.* **11.** flat object, surface or part **12.** *Mus.* note half tone below natural pitch —ˈ**flatly** *adv.* —ˈ**flatness** *n.* —ˈ**flatten** *v.* —ˈ**flatfish** *n.* type of fish which swims along sea floor on one side of body with both eyes on uppermost side —ˈ**flatfoot** *n.* **1.** condition in which instep arch of foot is flattened **2.** *sl.* policeman (*pl.* **-s, -feet**) —ˈ**flatiron** *n.* formerly, iron for pressing clothes —**flat race** race over level ground with no jumps —**flat rate** the same rate in all cases —**flat spin 1.** aircraft spin in which longitudinal axis is more nearly horizontal than vertical **2.** *inf.* state of confusion —ˈ**flatworm** *n.* parasitic or free-living invertebrate, such as fluke or tapeworm, having flattened body —**flat out** at, with maximum speed or effort

flat[2] (flæt) *n.* suite of rooms comprising a residence entirely on one floor of building —ˈ**flatlet** *n.* small flat

flatter (ˈflætə) *vt.* **1.** fawn on **2.** praise insincerely **3.** gratify vanity of **4.** represent favourably —ˈ**flatterer** *n.* —ˈ**flattery** *n.*

flatulent (ˈflætjʊlənt) *a.* **1.** suffering from, generating (excess) gases in intestines **2.** pretentious —ˈ**flatulence** *n.* **1.** flatulent condition **2.** verbosity, emptiness

flaunt (flɔːnt) *v.* **1.** show off **2.** wave proudly

flautist (ˈflɔːtɪst) *or U.S.* **flutist** (ˈfluːtɪst) *n.* flute player

flavescent (fləˈvɛsənt) *a.* yellowish; turning yellow

flavour *or U.S.* **flavor** (ˈfleɪvə) *n.* **1.** mixed sensation of smell and taste **2.** distinctive taste, savour **3.** undefinable characteristic, quality of anything —*vt.* **4.** give flavour to **5.** season —ˈ**flavouring** *or U.S.* ˈ**flavoring** *n.*

flaw[1] (flɔː) *n.* **1.** crack **2.** defect, blemish —*vt.* **3.** make flaw in —ˈ**flawless** *a.* perfect

flaw[2] (flɔː) *n.* sudden gust of wind; squall

flax (flæks) *n.* **1.** plant grown for its textile fibre and seeds **2.** its fibres, spun into linen thread —ˈ**flaxen** *a.* **1.** of flax **2.** light yellow, straw-coloured

flay (fleɪ) *vt.* **1.** strip skin off **2.** criticize severely

flea (fliː) *n.* small, wingless, jumping, blood-sucking insect —ˈ**fleabag** *n.* unkempt person, horse *etc.* —ˈ**fleabite** *n.* **1.** insect's bite **2.** trifling injury **3.** trifle —**flea-bitten** *a.* **1.** bitten by flea **2.** mean, worthless **3.** scruffy —**flea market** market for cheap goods —ˈ**fleapit** *n. inf.* shabby cinema or theatre

fleck (flɛk) *n.* **1.** small mark, streak or particle —*vt.* **2.** mark with flecks

fled (flɛd) *pt./pp. of* FLEE

fledged (flɛdʒd) *a.* **1.** (of birds) able to fly **2.** experienced, trained —ˈ**fledgling** *or* ˈ**fledgeling** *n.* **1.** young bird **2.** inexperienced person

flee (fliː) *v.* run away (from) (**fled,** ˈ**fleeing**)

THESAURUS

flash *v.* **1.** blaze, coruscate, flare, flicker, glare, gleam, glint, glisten, glitter, light, scintillate, shimmer, sparkle, twinkle ~*n.* **2.** blaze, burst, coruscation, dazzle, flare, flicker, gleam, ray, scintillation, shaft, shimmer, spark, sparkle, streak, twinkle ~*v.* **3.** bolt, dart, dash, fly, race, shoot, speed, sprint, streak, sweep, whistle, zoom ~*n.* **4.** instant, jiffy (*Inf.*), moment, second, shake, split second, trice, twinkling, twinkling of an eye, two shakes of a lamb's tail (*Inf.*) **5.** burst, demonstration, display, manifestation, outburst, show, sign, touch ~*adj.* **6.** *Inf.* cheap, glamorous, ostentatious, tacky (*U.S. inf.*), tasteless, vulgar

flashy cheap, cheap and nasty, flamboyant, flaunting, garish, gaudy, glittery, glitzy, in poor taste, jazzy (*Inf.*), loud, meretricious, ostentatious, showy, snazzy (*Inf.*), tasteless, tawdry, tinselly

flat[1] *adj.* **1.** even, horizontal, level, levelled, low, planar, plane, smooth, unbroken **2.** laid low, lying full length, outstretched, prostrate, reclining, recumbent, supine **3.** boring, dead, dull, flavourless, insipid, jejune, lacklustre, lifeless, monotonous, pointless, prosaic, spiritless, stale, tedious, uninteresting, vapid, watery, weak **4.** absolute, categorical, direct, downright, explicit, final, fixed, out-and-out, peremptory, plain, positive, straight, unconditional, unequivocal, unmistakable, unqualified **5.** blown out, burst, collapsed, deflated, empty, punctured ~*adv.* **6.** absolutely, categorically, completely, exactly, point blank, precisely, utterly **7. flat out** all out, at full gallop, at full speed, at full tilt, for all one is worth, hell for leather, posthaste, under full steam

flat[2] apartment, rooms

flatly absolutely, categorically, completely, positively, unhesitatingly

flatness 1. evenness, horizontality, levelness, smoothness, uniformity **2.** dullness, emptiness, insipidity, monotony, staleness, tedium, vapidity

flatten 1. compress, even out, iron out, level, plaster, raze, roll, smooth off, squash, trample **2.** bowl over, crush, fell, floor, knock down, knock off one's feet, prostrate, subdue

flatter 1. blandish, butter up, cajole, compliment, court, fawn, flannel (*Inf.*), humour, inveigle, lay it on (thick) (*Sl.*), praise, puff, soft-soap (*Inf.*), sweet-talk (*U.S. inf.*), wheedle **2.** become, do something for, enhance, set off, show to advantage, suit

flattery adulation, blandishment, blarney, cajolery, false praise, fawning, flannel (*Inf.*), fulsomeness, honeyed words, obsequiousness, servility, soft-soap (*Inf.*), sweet-talk (*U.S. inf.*), sycophancy, toadyism

flavour *n.* **1.** aroma, essence, extract, flavouring, odour, piquancy, relish, savour, seasoning, smack, tang, taste, zest, zing (*Inf.*) **2.** aspect, character, essence, feel, feeling, property, quality, soupçon, stamp, style, suggestion, tinge, tone, touch ~*v.* **3.** ginger up, imbue, infuse, lace, leaven, season, spice

flavouring essence, extract, spirit, tincture, zest

flaw 1. blemish, defect, disfigurement, failing, fault, imperfection, speck, spot, weakness, weak spot **2.** breach, break, cleft, crack, crevice, fissure, fracture, rent, rift, scission, split, tear

flawless 1. faultless, impeccable, perfect, spotless,

fleece (fli:s) *n.* 1. sheep's wool —*vt.* 2. rob —ˈ**fleecy** *a.*

fleet[1] (fli:t) *n.* 1. number of warships organized as unit 2. number of ships, cars *etc.* operating together —**fleet chief petty officer** noncommissioned officer in Royal Navy comparable in rank to warrant officer in army or Royal Air Force

fleet[2] (fli:t) *a.* swift, nimble —ˈ**fleeting** *a.* passing, transient —ˈ**fleetingly** *adv.*

Fleet Street (fli:t) 1. street in London where many newspaper offices are situated 2. Brit. journalism or journalists collectively

Flemish (ˈflɛmɪʃ) *n.* 1. one of two official languages of Belgium —*a.* 2. of Flanders —ˈ**Fleming** *n.* native of Flanders, medieval principality in the Low Countries, or of Flemish-speaking Belgium —**the Flemish** Flemings collectively

flense (flɛns), **flench** (flɛntʃ), *or* **flinch** (flɪntʃ) *vt.* strip (*esp.* whale) of flesh

flesh (flɛʃ) *n.* 1. soft part, muscular substance, between skin and bone 2. in plants, pulp 3. fat 4. sensual appetites —ˈ**fleshily** *adv.* —ˈ**fleshly** *a.* 1. carnal 2. material —ˈ**fleshy** *a.* 1. plump 2. pulpy —ˈ**fleshpots** *pl.n.* (places catering for) self-indulgent living —**flesh wound** wound affecting superficial tissues —**in the flesh** in person; actually present

fleur-de-lis *or* **fleur-de-lys** (flɜ:dəˈli:) *n.* 1. heraldic lily with three petals 2. iris (*pl.* **fleurs-de-lis** *or* **fleurs-de-lys** (flɜ:dəˈli:z))

flew (flu:) *pt. of* FLY[1]

flews (flu:z) *pl.n.* fleshy hanging lip of bloodhound or similar dog

flex (flɛks) *n.* 1. flexible insulated electric cable —*v.* 2. bend, be bent —**flexiˈbility** *n.* —ˈ**flexible** *a.* 1. easily bent 2. manageable 3. adaptable —ˈ**flexibly** *adv.* —ˈ**flexion** *or* ˈ**flection** *n.* 1. bending 2. bent state —ˈ**flexitime** *n.* system permitting variation in starting and finishing times of work, providing an agreed number of hours is worked over a specified period

flibbertigibbet (ˈflɪbətɪdʒɪbɪt) *n.* flighty, gossiping person

flick (flɪk) *vt.* 1. strike lightly, jerk —*n.* 2. light blow 3. jerk —*pl.* 4. *sl.* cinema —**flick knife** knife with retractable blade that springs out when button is pressed

flicker (ˈflɪkə) *vi.* 1. burn, shine, unsteadily 2. waver, quiver —*n.* 3. unsteady light or movement

flight (flaɪt) *n.* 1. act or manner of flying through air 2. number flying together, as birds 3. journey in aircraft 4. Air Force unit of command 5. power of flying 6. swift movement or passage 7. sally 8. distance flown 9. feather *etc.* fitted to arrow or dart to give it stability in flight 10. stairs between two landings 11. running away —**flight deck** 1. crew compartment in airliner 2. upper deck of aircraft carrier where aircraft take off —**flight lieutenant** officer holding commissioned rank senior to flying officer and junior to squadron leader in Royal Air Force —**flight recorder** electronic device in aircraft storing information about its flight —**flight sergeant** noncommissioned officer in Royal Air Force, junior in rank to master aircrew

flighty (ˈflaɪtɪ) *a.* 1. frivolous 2. erratic

flimsy (ˈflɪmzɪ) *a.* 1. frail, weak 2. thin 3. easily destroyed —ˈ**flimsily** *adv.*

flinch (flɪntʃ) *vi.* shrink, draw back, wince

fling (flɪŋ) *v.* 1. throw, send, move, with force (**flung** *pt./pp.*) —*n.* 2. throw 3. hasty attempt 4. spell of indulgence 5. vigorous dance

flint (flɪnt) *n.* 1. hard steel-grey stone 2. piece of this 3. hard substance used (as flint) for striking fire —ˈ**flinti-**

THESAURUS

unblemished, unsullied **2.** intact, sound, unbroken, undamaged, whole

flee abscond, avoid, beat a hasty retreat, bolt, cut and run (*Inf.*), decamp, depart, escape, fly, get away, leave, make a quick exit, make off, make oneself scarce (*Inf.*), make one's escape, make one's getaway, run away, scarper (*Sl.*), shun, skedaddle (*Inf.*), split (*Sl.*), take flight, take off (*Inf.*), take to one's heels, vanish

fleece *Fig.* bleed (*Inf.*), cheat, con (*Sl.*), defraud, despoil, diddle (*Inf.*), mulct, overcharge, plunder, rifle, rip off (*Sl.*), rob, rook (*Sl.*), soak (*Sl., chiefly U.S.*), steal, swindle, take for a ride (*Inf.*), take to the cleaners (*Sl.*)

fleet *n.* argosy, armada, flotilla, naval force, navy, sea power, squadron, task force, vessels, warships

fleeting brief, ephemeral, evanescent, flitting, flying, fugacious, fugitive, here today, gone tomorrow, momentary, passing, short, short-lived, temporary, transient, transitory

flesh **1.** beef (*Inf.*), body, brawn, fat, fatness, food, meat, tissue, weight **2.** animality, body, carnality, flesh and blood, human nature, physicality, physical nature, sensuality

flex *v.* angle, bend, contract, crook, curve, tighten

flexibility adaptability, adjustability, complaisance, elasticity, give (*Inf.*), pliability, pliancy, resilience, springiness, tensility

flexible **1.** bendable, ductile, elastic, limber, lithe, mouldable, plastic, pliable, pliant, springy, stretchy, supple, tensile, whippy, willowy, yielding **2.** adaptable, adjustable, discretionary, open, variable **3.** amenable, biddable, complaisant, compliant, docile, gentle, manageable, responsive, tractable

flick **1.** *v.* dab, fillip, flip, hit, jab, peck, rap, strike, tap, touch **2.** *n.* fillip, flip, jab, peck, rap, tap, touch

flicker *v.* **1.** flare, flash, glimmer, gutter, shimmer, sparkle, twinkle **2.** flutter, quiver, vibrate, waver ~*n.* **3.** flare, flash, gleam, glimmer, spark

flight **1.** flying, mounting, soaring, winging **2.** *Of air travel* journey, trip, voyage **3.** aerial navigation, aeronautics, air transport, aviation, flying **4.** cloud, flock, formation, squadron, swarm, unit, wing **5.** departure, escape, exit, exodus, fleeing, getaway, retreat, running away

flimsy **1.** delicate, fragile, frail, gimcrack, insubstantial, makeshift, rickety, shaky, shallow, slight, superficial, unsubstantial **2.** chiffon, gauzy, gossamer, light, sheer, thin, transparent **3.** feeble, frivolous, implausible, inadequate, poor, thin, transparent, trivial, unconvincing, unsatisfactory, weak

flinch baulk, blench, cower, cringe, draw back, duck, flee, quail, recoil, retreat, shirk, shrink, shy away, start, swerve, wince, withdraw

fling *v.* **1.** cast, catapult, chuck (*Inf.*), heave, hurl, jerk, let fly, lob (*Inf.*), pitch, precipitate, propel, send, shy, sling, throw, toss ~*n.* **2.** cast, lob, pitch, shot, throw, toss **3.** binge, bit of fun, good time, indulgence, spree **4.** attempt, bash (*Inf.*), crack (*Inf.*), gamble, go, shot, stab, trial, try, venture, whirl (*Inf.*)

ly *adv.* —ˈ**flinty** *a.* 1. like or consisting of flint 2. hard, cruel —ˈ**flintlock** *n.* 1. gunlock in which charge is ignited by spark produced by flint in hammer 2. firearm having such lock

flip (flɪp) *vt.* 1. throw or flick lightly 2. turn over —*vi.* 3. *sl., chiefly* US fly into rage or emotional outburst (*also* **flip one's lid** *or* **top**) (**-pp-**) —*n.* 4. instance, act, of flipping 5. drink with beaten egg —*a.* 6. US *inf.* flippant; pert —ˈ**flippancy** *n.* —ˈ**flippant** *a.* treating serious things lightly —ˈ**flippantly** *adv.* —ˈ**flipper** *n.* 1. limb, fin for swimming —*pl.* 2. fin-shaped rubber devices worn on feet to help in swimming —**flip side** less important side of pop record

flirt (flɜːt) *vi.* 1. toy, play with another's affections 2. trifle, toy (with) —*n.* 3. person who flirts —**flirˈtation** *n.* —**flirˈtatious** *a.*

flit (flɪt) *vi.* 1. pass lightly and rapidly 2. dart 3. *dial.* move house 4. *inf.* go away hastily, secretly (**-tt-**)

flitch (flɪtʃ) *n.* side of bacon

flittermouse (ˈflɪtəmaʊs) *n. dial.* bat (the animal)

float (fləʊt) *vi.* 1. rest, drift on surface of liquid 2. be suspended freely 3. move aimlessly —*vt.* 4. (of liquid) support, bear alone 5. in commerce, get (company) started 6. *Fin.* allow (currency) to fluctuate against other currencies in accordance with market forces —*n.* 7. anything small that floats (*esp.* to support something else, *eg* fishing net) 8. small delivery vehicle, *esp.* powered by batteries 9. motor vehicle carrying tableau *etc.* in parade 10. sum of money used to provide change —ˈ**floating** *a.* 1. having little or no attachment 2. (of organ *etc.*) displaced and abnormally movable 3. uncommitted, unfixed 4. *Fin.* (of capital) available for current use; (of debt) short-term and unfunded; (of currency) free to fluctuate against other currencies in accordance with market forces —**floˈtation** *or* **floaˈtation** *n.* act of floating, *esp.* floating of company —**floating rib** any rib of lower two pairs of ribs, which are not attached to breastbone —**floating voter** voter of no fixed political allegiance

flocculent (ˈflɒkjʊlənt) *a.* like tufts of wool

flock[1] (flɒk) *n.* 1. number of animals of one kind together 2. body of people 3. religious congregation —*vi.* 4. gather in a crowd

flock[2] (flɒk) *n.* 1. lock, tuft of wool *etc.* 2. wool refuse for stuffing cushions *etc.* —ˈ**flocky** *a.*

floe (fləʊ) *n.* sheet of floating ice

flog (flɒg) *vt.* 1. beat with whip, stick *etc.* 2. *sl.* sell (**-gg-**) —**flog a dead horse** pursue line of attack or argument from which no results can come

flood (flʌd) *n.* 1. inundation, overflow of water 2. rising of tide 3. outpouring 4. flowing water —*vt.* 5. inundate 6. cover, fill with water —*vi.* 7. arrive, move *etc.* in great numbers —ˈ**floodgate** *n.* gate, sluice for letting water in or out —ˈ**floodlight** *n.* broad, intense beam of artificial light —ˈ**floodlit** *a.* —**flood tide** 1. the rising tide 2. *fig.* peak of prosperity

floor (flɔː) *n.* 1. lower surface of room 2. set of rooms on one level, storey 3. flat space 4. (right to speak in) legislative hall —*vt.* 5. supply with floor 6. knock down 7. confound —ˈ**flooring** *n.* material for floors —**floor plan** drawing to scale of arrangement of rooms on one floor of building —**floor show** entertainment in nightclub *etc.*

floozy, floozie, *or* **floosie** (ˈfluːzɪ) *n. sl.* disreputable woman

flop (flɒp) *vi.* 1. bend, fall, collapse loosely, carelessly 2. fall flat on floor, on water *etc.* 3. *inf.* go to sleep 4. *inf.* fail (**-pp-**) —*n.* 5. flopping movement or sound 6. *inf.* failure —ˈ**floppily** *adv.* —ˈ**floppiness** *n.* —ˈ**floppy** *a.* limp, unsteady —**floppy disk** flexible magnetic disk that stores information and can be used to store data in memory of digital computer

flora (ˈflɔːrə) *n.* 1. plants of a region 2. list of them (*pl.* **-s, -rae** (-riː)) —ˈ**floral** *a.* of flowers —**floˈrescence** *n.* state or time of flowering —ˈ**floret** *n.* small flower forming part of composite flower —**floriˈbunda** *n.* type of rose whose flowers grow in large clusters —**floriˈcultural** *a.* —ˈ**floriculture** *n.* cultivation of flowers —**floriˈculturist** *n.* —**florist** (ˈflɒrɪst) *n.* dealer in flowers

THESAURUS

flip *v./n.* cast, flick, jerk, pitch, snap, spin, throw, toss, twist

flippancy cheek (*Inf.*), cheekiness, disrespectfulness, frivolity, impertinence, irreverence, levity, pertness, sauciness

flippant cheeky, disrespectful, flip (*Inf., chiefly U.S.*), frivolous, glib, impertinent, impudent, irreverent, offhand, pert, rude, saucy, superficial

flirt *v.* **1.** chat up (*Inf.*), coquet, dally, lead on, make advances, make eyes at, philander **2.** *Usually with* **with** consider, dabble in, entertain, expose oneself to, give a thought to, play with, toy with, trifle with ~*n.* **3.** coquette, heart-breaker, philanderer, tease, trifler, wanton

flirtation coquetry, dalliance, intrigue, philandering, teasing, toying, trifling

flirtatious amorous, arch, come-hither, come-on (*Inf.*), coquettish, coy, enticing, flirty, provocative, sportive, teasing

float *v.* **1.** be *or* lie on the surface, be buoyant, displace water, hang, hover, poise, rest on water, stay afloat **2.** bob, drift, glide, move gently, sail, slide, slip along **3.** get going, launch, promote, push off, set up

floating fluctuating, free, migratory, movable, unattached, uncommitted, unfixed, variable, wandering

flock *v.* **1.** collect, congregate, converge, crowd, gather, group, herd, huddle, mass, throng, troop ~*n.* **2.** colony, drove, flight, gaggle, herd, skein **3.** assembly, bevy, collection, company, congregation, convoy, crowd, gathering, group, herd, host, mass, multitude, throng

flog beat, castigate, chastise, flagellate, flay, lash, scourge, thrash, trounce, whack, whip

flood *v.* **1.** brim over, deluge, drown, immerse, inundate, overflow, pour over, submerge, swamp **2.** engulf, flow, gush, overwhelm, rush, surge, swarm, sweep ~*n.* **3.** deluge, downpour, flash flood, freshet, inundation, overflow, spate, tide, torrent **4.** flow, outpouring, rush, stream, torrent

floor **1.** *n.* level, stage, storey, tier **2.** *v. Fig.* baffle, beat, bewilder, bowl over (*Inf.*), bring up short, confound, conquer, defeat, discomfit, disconcert, dumbfound, knock down, nonplus, overthrow, perplex, prostrate, puzzle, stump, throw (*Inf.*)

flop *v.* **1.** collapse, dangle, droop, drop, fall, hang limply, sag, slump, topple, tumble **2.** *Inf.* bomb (*U.S. sl.*), close, come to nothing, fail, fall flat, fall

Florentine (ˈflɒrəntaɪn) *a.* 1. of Florence in Italy —*n.* 2. native of Florence

florid (ˈflɒrɪd) *a.* 1. with red, flushed complexion 2. ornate

florin (ˈflɒrɪn) *n.* formerly, Brit. silver two-shilling piece

floss (flɒs) *n.* 1. mass of fine, silky fibres, *eg* of cotton, silk 2. fluff —**ˈflossy** *a.* light and downy

flotation *or* **floatation** (fləʊˈteɪʃən) *n. see* FLOAT

flotilla (fləˈtɪlə) *n.* 1. fleet of small vessels 2. group of destroyers

flotsam (ˈflɒtsəm) *n.* 1. floating wreckage 2. discarded waste objects

flounce[1] (flaʊns) *vi.* 1. go, move abruptly and impatiently —*n.* 2. fling, jerk of body or limb

flounce[2] (flaʊns) *n.* ornamental gathered strip on woman's garment

flounder[1] (ˈflaʊndə) *vi.* 1. plunge and struggle, *esp.* in water or mud 2. proceed in bungling, hesitating manner —*n.* 3. act of floundering

flounder[2] (ˈflaʊndə) *n.* flatfish

flour (flaʊə) *n.* 1. powder prepared by sifting and grinding wheat *etc.* 2. fine soft powder —*vt.* 3. sprinkle with flour —**ˈflouriness** *n.* —**ˈfloury** *a.*

flourish (ˈflʌrɪʃ) *vi.* 1. thrive 2. be in the prime —*vt.* 3. brandish, wave about 4. display —*n.* 5. ornamental curve 6. showy gesture in speech *etc.* 7. waving of hand, weapon *etc.* 8. fanfare (of trumpets)

flout (flaʊt) *vt.* 1. show contempt for, mock 2. defy

flow (fləʊ) *vi.* 1. glide along as stream 2. circulate, as the blood 3. move easily 4. move in waves 5. hang loose 6. be present in abundance —*n.* 7. act, instance of flowing 8. quantity that flows 9. rise of tide 10. ample supply —**flow chart** diagram showing sequence of operations in industrial *etc.* process

flower (ˈflaʊə) *n.* 1. coloured (not green) part of plant from which fruit is developed 2. bloom, blossom 3. ornamentation 4. choicest part, pick —*pl.* 5. chemical sublimate —*vi.* 6. produce flowers 7. bloom 8. come to prime condition —*vt.* 9. ornament with flowers —**ˈflowered** *a.* 1. having flowers 2. decorated with floral design —**ˈfloweret** *n.* small flower —**ˈflowery** *a.* 1. abounding in flowers 2. full of fine words, ornamented with figures of speech —**flower girl** girl selling flowers

flown (fləʊn) *pp. of* FLY[1]

fl. oz. fluid ounce(s)

flu (fluː) influenza

fluctuate (ˈflʌktjʊeɪt) *v.* 1. vary —*vi.* 2. rise and fall, undulate —**fluctuˈation** *n.*

flue (fluː) *n.* passage or pipe for smoke or hot air, chimney

fluent (ˈfluːənt) *a.* 1. speaking, writing a given language easily and well 2. easy, graceful

fluff (flʌf) *n.* 1. soft, feathery stuff 2. down 3. *inf.* mistake —*v.* 4. make or become soft, light 5. *inf.* make mistake (in) —**ˈfluffy** *a.*

fluid (ˈfluːɪd) *a.* 1. flowing easily 2. not solid —*n.* 3. gas or liquid —**fluˈidity** *n.* —**fluid ounce** unit of capacity 1/20 of pint

fluke[1] (fluːk) *n.* 1. flat triangular point of anchor —*pl.* 2. whale's tail

fluke[2] (fluːk) *n.* 1. stroke of luck, accident —*vt.* 2. gain, make, hit by accident or by luck —**ˈfluky** *a.* 1. uncertain 2. got by luck

fluke[3] (fluːk) *n.* 1. flatfish 2. parasitic worm

flume (fluːm) *n.* narrow (artificial) channel for water

THESAURUS

short, fold (*Inf.*), founder, misfire ~*n.* 3. *Inf.* cockup (*Brit. sl.*), debacle, disaster, failure, fiasco, loser, nonstarter, washout (*Inf.*)

floral flower-patterned, flowery

florid 1. blowzy, flushed, high-coloured, high-complexioned, rubicund, ruddy 2. baroque, busy, embellished, euphuistic, figurative, flamboyant, flowery, fussy, grandiloquent, high-flown, ornate, overelaborate

flotsam debris, detritus, jetsam, junk, odds and ends, sweepings, wreckage

flounder *v.* be in the dark, blunder, fumble, grope, muddle, plunge, struggle, stumble, thrash, toss, tumble, wallow

flourish *v.* 1. bear fruit, be in one's prime, be successful, be vigorous, bloom, blossom, boom, burgeon, develop, do well, flower, get ahead, get on, go great guns (*Sl.*), go up in the world, grow, grow fat, increase, prosper, succeed, thrive 2. brandish, display, flaunt, flutter, shake, sweep, swing, swish, twirl, vaunt, wag, wave, wield ~*n.* 3. brandishing, dash, display, fanfare, parade, shaking, show, showy gesture, twirling, wave 4. curlicue, decoration, embellishment, ornamentation, plume, sweep

flout defy, deride, gibe at, insult, jeer at, laugh in the face of, mock, outrage, ridicule, scoff at, scorn, scout (*Archaic*), show contempt for, sneer at, spurn, taunt, treat with disdain

flow *v.* 1. circulate, course, glide, gush, move, pour, purl, ripple, roll, run, rush, slide, surge, sweep, swirl, whirl 2. cascade, deluge, flood, inundate, overflow, pour, run, run out, spew, spill, spurt, squirt, stream, teem, well forth ~*n.* 3. course, current, drift, flood, flux, gush, outflow, outpouring, spate, stream, tide 4. abundance, deluge, effusion, emanation, outflow, outpouring, plenty, plethora, succession, train

flower *n.* 1. bloom, blossom, efflorescence 2. *Fig.* best, choicest part, cream, elite, freshness, greatest *or* finest point, height, pick, vigour ~*v.* 3. bloom, blossom, blow, burgeon, effloresce, flourish, mature, open, unfold

flowery baroque, embellished, euphuistic, fancy, figurative, florid, high-flown, ornate, overwrought, rhetorical

fluctuate alter, alternate, change, ebb and flow, go up and down, hesitate, oscillate, rise and fall, seesaw, shift, swing, undulate, vacillate, vary, veer, waver

fluctuation alternation, change, fickleness, inconstancy, instability, oscillation, shift, swing, unsteadiness, vacillation, variation, wavering

fluent articulate, easy, effortless, facile, flowing, glib, natural, ready, smooth, smooth-spoken, voluble, well-versed

fluff 1. *n.* down, dust, dustball, fuzz, lint, nap, oose (*Scot.*), pile 2. *v. Inf.* bungle, cock up (*Sl.*), foul up (*Inf.*), make a mess off, mess up (*Inf.*), muddle, screw up (*Inf.*), spoil

fluid 1. *adj.* aqueous, flowing, in solution, liquefied, liquid, melted, molten, running, runny, watery 2. *n.* liquid, liquor, solution

flummery (ˈflʌmərɪ) *n.* **1.** nonsense, idle talk, humbug **2.** dish of milk, flour, eggs *etc.*

flummox (ˈflʌməks) *vt.* bewilder, perplex

flung (flʌŋ) *pt./pp. of* FLING

flunk (flʌŋk) **US, NZ** *inf. v.* **1.** (cause to) fail to reach required standard (in) —*vi.* **2.** (*with* out) be dismissed from school

flunky *or* **flunkey** (ˈflʌŋkɪ) *n.* **1.** servant, *esp.* liveried manservant **2.** servile person

fluorescence (fluəˈrɛsəns) *n.* emission of light or other radiation from substance when bombarded by particles (electrons *etc.*) or other radiation, as in fluorescent lamp —**fluoˈresce** *vi.* —**fluoˈrescent** *a.* —**fluorescent lamp** lamp in which ultraviolet radiation from electrical gas discharge causes layer of phosphor on tube's inside surface to fluoresce —**ˈfluoroscope** *n.* device consisting of fluorescent screen and x-ray source that enables x-ray image of person *etc.* to be observed directly —**fluoˈroscopy** *n.* examination of person *etc.* by means of fluoroscope

fluorspar (ˈfluəspɑː), **fluor** (ˈfluːɔː), *or U.S.* **fluorite** *n.* mineral containing fluorine —**ˈfluoridate** *vt.* —**fluoriˈdation** *n.* —**ˈfluoride** *n.* salt containing fluorine, *esp.* as added to domestic water supply as protection against tooth decay —**ˈfluorinate** *vt.* treat or cause to combine with fluorine —**ˈfluorine** *n.* nonmetallic element, yellowish gas

flurry (ˈflʌrɪ) *n.* **1.** squall, gust **2.** bustle, commotion **3.** death struggle of whale **4.** fluttering (as of snowflakes) —*vt.* **5.** agitate, bewilder, fluster (**ˈflurried, ˈflurrying**)

flush[1] (flʌʃ) *vi.* **1.** blush **2.** (of skin) redden **3.** flow suddenly or violently —*vt.* **4.** cleanse (*eg* toilet) by rush of water **5.** excite —*n.* **6.** reddening, blush **7.** rush of water **8.** excitement **9.** elation **10.** glow of colour **11.** freshness, vigour —*a.* **12.** full **13.** *inf.* having plenty of money **14.** *inf.* well supplied **15.** level with surrounding surface

flush[2] (flʌʃ) *vt.* cause to leave cover and take flight

flush[3] (flʌʃ) *n.* set of cards all of one suit

fluster (ˈflʌstə) *v.* **1.** make or become nervous, agitated —*n.* **2.** state of confusion or agitation

flute (fluːt) *n.* **1.** wind instrument of tube with holes stopped by fingers or keys and blowhole in side **2.** groove, channel —*vi.* **3.** play on flute —*vt.* **4.** make grooves in —**ˈfluted** *a.* —**ˈfluting** *n.*

flutter (ˈflʌtə) *v.* **1.** flap (as wings) rapidly without flight or in short flights **2.** be or make excited, agitated —*vi.* **3.** quiver —*n.* **4.** flapping movement **5.** nervous agitation **6.** *inf.* modest wager

fluvial (ˈfluːvɪəl) *a.* of rivers

flux (flʌks) *n.* **1.** discharge **2.** constant succession of changes **3.** substance mixed with metal to clean, aid adhesion in soldering *etc.* **4.** measure of strength in magnetic field

fly[1] (flaɪ) *vi.* **1.** move through air on wings or in aircraft **2.** pass quickly **3.** rush **4.** flee, run away —*vt.* **5.** operate (aircraft) **6.** cause to fly **7.** set flying —*v.* **8.** float loosely (**flew** *pt.*, **flown** *pp.*) —*n.* **9.** (zip or buttons fastening) opening in trousers **10.** flap in garment or tent **11.** flying —**ˈflier** *or* **ˈflyer** *n.* **1.** person or thing that flies **2.** aviator, pilot **3.** *inf.* long, flying leap **4.** rectangular step in straight flight of stairs **5.** *Athletics inf.* flying start —**ˈflying** *a.* hurried, brief —**ˈflyaway** *a.* **1.** (of hair *etc.*) loose and fluttering **2.** frivolous, flighty; giddy —**fly-by-night** *inf. a.* **1.** untrustworthy, *esp.* in finance —*n.* **2.** untrustworthy person —**fly-fish** *vi.* fish with artificial fly as lure —**flying boat** aeroplane fitted with floats instead of landing wheels —**flying buttress** *Archit.* arched or slanting structure attached at only one point to a mass of masonry —**flying colours** conspicuous success —**flying doctor** (*esp.* Aust.) doctor visiting patients in outback areas by aircraft —**flying fish** fish with winglike fins used for gliding above the sea —**flying fox** large fruit-eating bat —**flying officer** officer holding commissioned rank senior to pilot officer but junior to flight lieutenant in Brit. and certain other air forces —**flying picket** (in industrial disputes) member of group of pickets organized to be able to move quickly from place to place —**flying saucer** unidentified (disc-shaped) flying object, supposedly from outer space —**flying squad** special detachment of police, soldiers *etc.*, ready to act quickly —**flying start 1.** in sprinting, start by competitor anticipating starting signal **2.** start to race in which competitor is already travelling at speed as he passes starting line **3.** any promising beginning **4.** initial advantage —**ˈflyleaf** *n.* blank leaf at beginning or end of book —**ˈflyover** *n.* road passing over another by bridge —**ˈflypaper** *n.* paper with sticky and poisonous coating, *usu.* hung from ceiling to trap flies —**fly sheet 1.** fly (in tent) **2.** short handbill —**fly spray** liquid sprayed from aerosol to destroy flies —**ˈflytrap** *n.* **1.** insectivorous plant **2.** device for catching flies —**ˈflyweight** *n.* **1.** professional boxer weighing not more than 112 lbs. (51 kg); amateur boxer weighing 106-112 lbs. (48-51 kg) **2.** in Olympic wrestling, wrestler weighing not more than 115 lbs. (52 kg) —**ˈflywheel** *n.* heavy wheel regulating speed of machine

THESAURUS

flurry *n.* **1.** *Fig.* ado, agitation, bustle, commotion, disturbance, excitement, ferment, flap, fluster, flutter, furore, fuss, hurry, stir, to-do, tumult, whirl **2.** flaw, gust, squall ~*v.* **3.** agitate, bewilder, bother, bustle, confuse, disconcert, disturb, fluster, flutter, fuss, hassle (*Inf.*), hurry, hustle, rattle (*Inf.*), ruffle, unsettle, upset

flush *v.* **1.** blush, burn, colour, colour up, crimson, flame, glow, go red, redden, suffuse ~*n.* **2.** bloom, blush, colour, freshness, glow, redness, rosiness ~*v.* **3.** cleanse, douche, drench, eject, expel, flood, hose down, rinse out, swab, syringe, wash out

fluster 1. *v.* agitate, bother, bustle, confound, confuse, disturb, excite, flurry, hassle (*Inf.*), heat, hurry, make nervous, perturb, rattle (*Inf.*), ruffle, throw off balance, upset **2.** *n.* agitation, bustle, commotion, disturbance, dither, flap (*Inf.*), flurry, flutter, furore, perturbation, ruffle, state (*Inf.*), turmoil

flutter *v.* **1.** agitate, bat, beat, flap, flicker, flit, flitter, fluctuate, hover, palpitate, quiver, ripple, ruffle, shiver, tremble, vibrate, waver ~*n.* **2.** palpitation, quiver, quivering, shiver, shudder, tremble, tremor, twitching, vibration **3.** agitation, commotion, confusion, dither, excitement, flurry, fluster, perturbation, state (*Inf.*), state of nervous excitement, tremble, tumult

fly *v.* **1.** flit, flutter, hover, mount, sail, soar, take to the air, take wing, wing **2.** aviate, be at the controls, control, manoeuvre, operate, pilot **3.** elapse, flit, glide, pass, pass swiftly, roll on, run its course, slip away **4.** be off like a shot (*Inf.*), bolt, career, dart, dash, hare (*Inf.*), hasten, hurry, race, rush, scamper,

fly[2] (flaɪ) *n.* two-winged insect, *esp.* common housefly —**'flyblown** *a.* infested with larvae of blowfly —**'flycatcher** *n.* small insect-eating songbird

fly[3] (flaɪ) *a. sl.* sharp and knowing

Fm *Chem.* fermium

FM frequency modulation

fm. 1. fathom (*also* **fm**) 2. from

F.M. Field Marshal

f-number *or* **f number** *n. Photog.* numerical value of relative aperture

fo. folio

F.O. Flying Officer

foal (fəʊl) *n.* 1. young of horse, ass *etc.* —*v.* 2. bear (foal)

foam (fəʊm) *n.* 1. collection of small bubbles on liquid 2. froth of saliva or sweat 3. light cellular solid used for insulation, packing *etc.* —*v.* 4. (cause to) produce foam —*vi.* 5. be very angry (*esp. in* **foam at the mouth**) —**'foamy** *a.* —**foam rubber** rubber treated to form firm, spongy foam

fob (fɒb) *n.* 1. short watch chain 2. small pocket in waistband of trousers or waistcoat

f.o.b. *or* **F.O.B.** *Comm.* free on board

fob off 1. ignore, dismiss (someone or something) in offhand (insulting) manner 2. dispose of (-bb-)

fo'c's'le *or* **fo'c'sle** ('fəʊks°l) *n. see* FORECASTLE

focus ('fəʊkəs) *n.* 1. point at which rays meet after being reflected or refracted (*also* **focal point**) 2. state of optical image when it is clearly defined 3. state of instrument producing such image 4. point of convergence 5. point on which interest, activity is centred (*pl.* **-es, foci** ('fəʊsaɪ)) —*vt.* 6. bring to focus, adjust 7. concentrate —*vi.* 8. come to focus 9. converge ('**focused, 'focusing**) —**'focal** *a.* of, at focus —**focal length** *or* **distance** distance from focal point of lens to reflecting surface

fodder ('fɒdə) *n.* bulk food for livestock

foe (fəʊ) *n.* enemy

foetid ('fetɪd, 'fiː-) *a. see* FETID

foetus *or* **fetus** ('fiːtəs) *n.* fully-developed young in womb or egg —**'foetal** *or* **'fetal** *a.*

fog (fɒg) *n.* 1. thick mist 2. dense watery vapour in lower atmosphere 3. cloud of anything reducing visibility —*vt.* 4. cover in fog 5. puzzle (-gg-) —**'foggy** *a.* —**'fogbound** *a.* prevented from operation by fog —**'foghorn** *n.* instrument to warn ships in fog

fogy *or* **fogey** ('fəʊgɪ) *n.* old-fashioned person

foible ('fɔɪb°l) *n.* minor weakness; idiosyncrasy

foil[1] (fɔɪl) *vt.* baffle, defeat, frustrate —**'foilable** *a.*

foil[2] (fɔɪl) *n.* 1. metal in thin sheet 2. anything which sets off another thing to advantage 3. *Archit.* small arc between cusps

foil[3] (fɔɪl) *n.* light, slender, flexible sword tipped by button

foist (fɔɪst) *vt.* (*usu. with* off *or* on) sell, pass off (inferior or unwanted thing) as valuable

fold[1] (fəʊld) *vt.* 1. double up, bend part of 2. interlace (arms) 3. wrap up 4. clasp (in arms) 5. *Cooking* mix gently —*vi.* 6. become folded 7. admit of being folded 8. *inf.* fail —*n.* 9. folding 10. coil 11. winding 12. line made by folding 13. crease 14. foldlike geological formation —**'folder** *n.* binder, file for loose papers —**'foldaway** *a.* (of bed *etc.*) able to be folded away when not in use —**folding door** door in form of hinged leaves that can be folded one against another

fold[2] (fəʊld) *n.* 1. enclosure for sheep 2. body of believers, church

-fold (*comb. form*) having so many parts; being so many times as much or as many, as in *hundredfold*

folderol ('fɒldərɒl) *n. see* FALDERAL

foliage ('fəʊlɪɪdʒ) *n.* leaves collectively, leafage —**fo-li'aceous** *a.* of or like leaf —**'foliate** *a.* leaflike, having leaves —**foli'ation** *n.* 1. *Bot.* process of producing leaves; state of being in leaf; arrangement of leaves in leaf bud 2. *Archit.* ornamentation consisting of cusps and foils 3. consecutive numbering of leaves of book 4. *Geol.* arrangement of constituents of rock in leaflike layers

folio ('fəʊlɪəʊ) *n.* 1. sheet of paper folded in half to

THESAURUS

scoot, shoot, speed, sprint, tear, whiz (*Inf.*), zoom **5.** abscond, avoid, beat a retreat, clear out (*Inf.*), cut and run (*Inf.*), decamp, disappear, escape, flee, get away, hasten away, hightail (*Inf., chiefly U.S.*), light out (*Inf.*), make a getaway, make a quick exit, make one's escape, run, run for it, run from, show a clean pair of heels, shun, take flight, take off, take to one's heels

fly-by-night *adj.* cowboy (*Inf.*), dubious, questionable, shady, undependable, unreliable, untrustworthy

flying *adj.* brief, fleeting, fugacious, hasty, hurried, rushed, short-lived, transitory

foam **1.** *n.* bubbles, froth, head, lather, spray, spume, suds **2.** *v.* boil, bubble, effervesce, fizz, froth, lather

focus **1.** *n.* bull's eye, centre, centre of activity, centre of attraction, core, cynosure, focal point, headquarters, heart, hub, meeting place, target **2.** *v.* aim, bring to bear, centre, concentrate, converge, direct, fix, join, meet, pinpoint, rivet, spotlight, zero in (*Inf.*), zoom in

foe adversary, antagonist, enemy, foeman (*Archaic*), opponent, rival

fog *n.* **1.** gloom, miasma, mist, murk, murkiness, peasouper (*Inf.*), smog ~*v.* **2.** becloud, bedim, befuddle, bewilder, blind, cloud, confuse, darken, daze, dim, muddle, obfuscate, obscure, perplex, stupefy **3.** cloud, mist over *or* up, steam up

foggy blurred, brumous (*Rare*), cloudy, dim, grey, hazy, indistinct, misty, murky, nebulous, obscure, smoggy, soupy, vaporous

foil *v.* baffle, balk, check, checkmate, circumvent, counter, defeat, disappoint, elude, frustrate, nip in the bud, nullify, outwit, put a spoke in (someone's) wheel (*Brit.*), stop, thwart

foist fob off, get rid of, impose, insert, insinuate, interpolate, introduce, palm off, pass off, put over, sneak in, unload

fold *v.* **1.** bend, crease, crumple, dog-ear, double, double over, gather, intertwine, overlap, pleat, tuck, turn under ~*n.* **2.** bend, crease, double thickness, folded portion, furrow, knife-edge, layer, overlap, pleat, turn, wrinkle ~*v.* **3.** do up, enclose, enfold, entwine, envelop, wrap, wrap up **4.** *Inf.* be ruined, close, collapse, crash, fail, go bankrupt, go bust (*Inf.*), go to the wall, go under (*Inf.*), shut down

folder binder, envelope, file, portfolio

make two leaves of book **2.** book of largest common size made up of such sheets **3.** page numbered on one side only **4.** page number (*pl.* **-s**)

folk (fəʊk) *n.* **1.** (*with pl. v.*) people in general family, relatives **2.** race of people —**'folksy** *a. inf., chiefly* US **1.** of or like ordinary people **2.** friendly; affable **3.** affectedly simple —**folk dance** —**folk etymology** gradual change in form of word through influence of more familiar word with which it becomes associated —**'folklore** *n.* tradition, customs, beliefs popularly held —**folk music 1.** music passed on from generation to generation **2.** any music composed in this idiom —**folk song 1.** song handed down among common people **2.** modern song in folk idiom

follicle ('fɒlɪk^{ə}l) *n.* **1.** small sac **2.** seed vessel —**fol'licular** *a.*

follow ('fɒləʊ) *v.* **1.** go or come after —*vt.* **2.** accompany, attend on **3.** keep to (path *etc.*) **4.** take as guide, conform to **5.** engage in **6.** have a keen interest in **7.** be consequent on **8.** grasp meaning of —*vi.* **9.** come next **10.** result —**'follower** *n.* **1.** disciple **2.** supporter —**'following** *a.* **1.** about to be mentioned —*n.* **2.** body of supporters —**follow-on** *n. Cricket* immediate second innings forced on team scoring prescribed number of runs fewer than its opponents in first innings —**follow-through** *n.* in ball games, continuation of stroke after impact with ball —**follow-up** *n.* something done to reinforce initial action —**follow on** (of team) play follow-on

folly ('fɒlɪ) *n.* **1.** foolishness **2.** foolish action, idea *etc.* **3.** useless, extravagant structure

foment (fə'mɛnt) *vt.* **1.** foster, stir up **2.** bathe with hot lotions —**fomen'tation** *n.*

fond (fɒnd) *a.* **1.** tender, loving **2.** *obs.* credulous **3.** *obs.* foolish —**'fondly** *adv.* —**'fondness** *n.* —**fond of** having liking for

fondant ('fɒndənt) *n.* **1.** soft sugar mixture for sweets **2.** sweet made of this

fondle ('fɒnd^{ə}l) *vt.* caress

fondue ('fɒndju:; *Fr.* fɔ̃'dy) *n.* Swiss dish of sauce (*esp.* cheese) into which pieces of bread *etc.* are dipped

font (fɒnt) *n.* bowl for baptismal water, usu. on pedestal

fontanelle *or* **fontanel** (fɒntə'nɛl) *n.* soft, membranous gap between bones of baby's skull

food (fu:d) *n.* **1.** solid nourishment **2.** what one eats **3.** mental or spiritual nourishment —**'foodie** *or* **'foody** *n.* person with enthusiastic interest in preparation and consumption of good food —**food poisoning** acute illness caused by food that is naturally poisonous or contaminated by bacteria —**'foodstuff** *n.* food

fool (fu:l) *n.* **1.** silly, empty-headed person **2.** dupe **3.** simpleton **4.** *Hist.* jester, clown **5.** dessert of puréed fruit mixed with cream *etc.* —*vt.* **6.** delude, dupe —*vi.* **7.** act as fool —**'foolery** *n.* **1.** habitual folly **2.** act of playing the fool **3.** absurdity —**'foolish** *a.* **1.** ill-considered, silly **2.** stupid —**'foolishly** *adv.* —**'foolhardiness** *n.* —**'foolhardy** *a.* foolishly adventurous —**'foolproof** *a.* proof against failure —**fool's cap 1.** jester's or dunce's cap **2.** this as watermark —**'foolscap** *n.* size of paper which formerly had this mark —**fool's errand** fruitless undertaking —**fool's paradise** illusory happiness

THESAURUS

folk clan, ethnic group, family, kin, kindred, people, race, tribe

follow 1. come after, come next, step into the shoes of, succeed, supersede, supplant, take the place of **2.** chase, dog, hound, hunt, pursue, run after, shadow, stalk, tail, track, trail **3.** accompany, attend, bring up the rear, come *or* go with, come after, escort, tag along, tread on the heels of **4.** act in accordance with, be guided by, comply, conform, give allegiance to, heed, mind, note, obey, observe, regard, watch **5.** appreciate, catch, catch on (*Inf.*), comprehend, fathom, get, get the picture, grasp, keep up with, realize, see, take in, understand **6.** arise, be consequent, develop, emanate, ensue, flow, issue, proceed, result, spring, supervene **7.** be a devotee *or* supporter of, be devoted to, be interested in, cultivate, keep abreast of, support

follower adherent, admirer, apostle, backer, believer, convert, devotee, disciple, fan, fancier, habitué, partisan, pupil, representative, supporter, votary, worshipper

following *n.* audience, circle, clientele, coterie, entourage, fans, patronage, public, retinue, suite, support, supporters, train

folly absurdity, daftness, fatuity, foolishness, idiocy, imbecility, imprudence, indiscretion, irrationality, lunacy, madness, nonsense, preposterousness, rashness, recklessness, silliness, stupidity

fond 1. *With* **of** addicted to, attached to, enamoured of, have a liking (fancy, taste) for, have a soft spot for, hooked on, keen on, partial to, predisposed towards **2.** adoring, affectionate, amorous, caring, devoted, doting, indulgent, loving, tender, warm **3.** absurd, credulous, deluded, delusive, delusory, empty, foolish, indiscreet, naive, overoptimistic, vain

fondle caress, cuddle, dandle, pat, pet, stroke

fondly 1. affectionately, dearly, indulgently, lovingly, possessively, tenderly, with affection **2.** credulously, foolishly, naively, stupidly, vainly

fondness 1. attachment, fancy, liking, love, partiality, penchant, predilection, preference, soft spot, susceptibility, taste, weakness **2.** affection, attachment, devotion, kindness, love, tenderness

food 1. aliment, board, bread, chow (*Inf.*), comestibles, commons, cooking, cuisine, diet, eatables (*Sl.*), eats (*Sl.*), edibles, fare, foodstuffs, grub (*Sl.*), larder, meat, menu, nosh (*Sl.*), nourishment, nutriment, nutrition, pabulum (*Rare*), provender, provisions, rations, refreshment, scoff (*Sl.*), stores, subsistence, sustenance, table, tuck (*Inf.*), viands, victuals **2.** *For cattle, etc.* feed, fodder, forage, provender

fool *n.* **1.** ass, bird-brain (*Inf.*), blockhead, bonehead (*Sl.*), chump (*Inf.*), clodpate (*Archaic*), clot (*Inf.*), dimwit (*Inf.*), dolt, dope (*Sl.*), dunce, dunderhead, fat-head (*Inf.*), goose (*Inf.*), halfwit, idiot, ignoramus, illiterate, imbecile (*Inf.*), jackass, loon, mooncalf, moron, nincompoop, ninny, nit (*Inf.*), nitwit, numskull, sap (*Sl.*), silly, simpleton, twerp (*Inf.*), twit (*Inf.*) **2.** butt, chump (*Inf.*), dupe, easy mark (*Sl.*), fall guy (*Inf., chiefly U.S.*), greenhorn (*Inf.*), gull (*Archaic*), laughing stock, mug (*Sl.*), stooge (*Sl.*), sucker (*Sl.*) **3.** buffoon, clown, comic, harlequin, jester, merry-andrew, motley, pierrot, punchinello ~*v.* **4.** bamboozle, beguile, bluff, cheat, con (*Sl.*), deceive, delude, dupe, gull (*Archaic*), have

foot (fʊt) *n.* **1.** lowest part of leg, from ankle down **2.** lowest part of anything, base, stand **3.** end of bed *etc.* **4.** infantry **5.** measure of twelve inches **6.** division of verse (*pl.* **feet**) —*v.* **7.** dance (*also* **foot it**) —*vt.* **8.** walk over (*esp. in* **foot it**) **9.** pay cost of (*esp. in* **foot the bill**) —ˈ**footage** *n.* **1.** length in feet **2.** length, extent, of film used —ˈ**footie** *or* ˈ**footy** *n. sl.* football —ˈ**footing** *n.* **1.** basis, foundation **2.** firm standing, relations, conditions —*pl.* **3.** (concrete) foundations for walls of buildings —**foot-and-mouth disease** infectious viral disease in sheep, cattle *etc.* —ˈ**football** *n.* **1.** game played with large blown-up ball **2.** the ball —ˈ**footballer** *n.* —**football pools** form of gambling on results of football matches —ˈ**footboard** *n.* **1.** treadle or foot-operated lever on machine **2.** vertical board at foot of bed —**foot brake** brake operated by pressure on foot pedal —ˈ**footbridge** *n.* narrow bridge for pedestrians —ˈ**footfall** *n.* sound of footstep —**foot fault** *Tennis* fault of overstepping baseline while serving —ˈ**foothill** *n.* (*oft. pl.*) low hill at foot of mountain —ˈ**foothold** *n.* **1.** place affording secure grip for the foot **2.** secure position from which progress may be made —ˈ**footlights** *pl.n.* lights across front of stage —ˈ**footloose** *a.* free from any ties —ˈ**footman** *n.* liveried servant —ˈ**footnote** *n.* note of reference or explanation printed at foot of page —ˈ**footpad** *n. obs.* robber, highwayman —ˈ**footpath** *n.* narrow path for pedestrians —ˈ**footplate** *n.* platform for driver and fireman of locomotive —**foot-pound** *n.* unit of measurement of work in f.p.s. system —ˈ**footprint** *n.* mark left by foot —ˈ**footrest** *n.* something that provides support for feet —ˈ**footslog** *vi.* walk, go on foot —ˈ**footslogger** *n.* —ˈ**footsore** *a.* having sore feet, *esp.* from walking —ˈ**footwear** *n.* anything worn to cover feet —ˈ**footwork** *n.* skilful use of feet, as in sports *etc.*

footle (ˈfuːtˀl) *vi. inf.* (*oft. with* around *or* about) loiter aimlessly

fop (fɒp) *n.* man excessively concerned with fashion —ˈ**foppery** *n.* —ˈ**foppish** *a.* —ˈ**foppishly** *adv.*

for (fɔː; *unstressed* fə) *prep.* **1.** intended to reach **2.** directed or belonging to **3.** because of **4.** instead of **5.** towards **6.** on account of **7.** in favour of **8.** respecting **9.** during **10.** in search of **11.** in payment of **12.** in the character of **13.** in spite of —*conj.* **14.** because —**for it** *inf.* liable for punishment or blame

for- (*comb. form*) from, away, against, as in *forswear, forbid.* Such words are not given here where the meaning may easily be inferred from the simple word

forage (ˈfɒrɪdʒ) *n.* **1.** food for cattle and horses —*vi.* **2.** collect forage **3.** make roving search —**forage cap** soldier's undress cap

foramen (fɒˈreɪmɛn) *n.* natural hole, *esp.* in bone (*pl.* **-ramina** (-ˈræmɪnə), **-s**)

forasmuch as (fərəzˈmʌtʃ) *conj.* seeing that

foray (ˈfɒreɪ) *n.* **1.** raid, inroad —*vi.* **2.** make one —ˈ**forayer** *n.*

forbear[1] (ˈfɔːbɛə) *n. see* FOREBEAR

forbear[2] (fɔːˈbɛə) *v.* **1.** (*esp. with* from) cease; refrain (from) —*vi.* **2.** be patient (**forˈbore** *pt.*, **forˈborne** *pp.*) —**forˈbearance** *n.* self-control; patience —**forˈbearing** *a.*

forbid (fəˈbɪd) *vt.* prohibit, refuse to allow (**forˈbade** (fəˈbæd, -ˈbeɪd) *pt.*, **forˈbidden** *pp.*, **forˈbidding** *pr.p.*) —**forˈbidding** *a.* **1.** uninviting **2.** threatening

force (fɔːs) *n.* **1.** strength, power **2.** compulsion **3.** that which tends to produce a change in a physical system **4.** mental or moral strength **5.** body of troops, police *etc.* **6.** group of people organized for particular task or duty **7.** effectiveness, operative state **8.** violence —*vt.* **9.** constrain, compel **10.** produce by effort, strength **11.** break open **12.** urge, strain **13.** drive **14.** hasten maturity of —**forced** *a.* **1.** accomplished by great effort **2.** compulsory **3.** unnatural **4.** strained —ˈ**forceful** *a.* **1.** powerful **2.** persuasive —ˈ**forcible** *a.* **1.** done by force **2.** efficacious, compelling, impressive **3.** strong —ˈ**forcibly** *adv.* —**force-feed** *vt.* force (person or animal) to eat or swallow (food)

THESAURUS

(someone) on, hoax, hoodwink, kid (*Inf.*), make a fool of, mislead, play a trick on, put one over on (*Inf.*), take in, trick **5.** act the fool, cut capers, feign, jest, joke, kid (*Inf.*), make believe, pretend, tease

foolery antics, capers, carry-on (*Inf.*), childishness, clowning, folly, fooling, horseplay, larks, mischief, monkey tricks (*Inf.*), nonsense, practical jokes, pranks, shenanigans (*Inf.*), silliness, tomfoolery

foolhardy adventurous, bold, hot-headed, impetuous, imprudent, incautious, irresponsible, madcap, precipitate, rash, reckless, temerarious, venturesome, venturous

foolish 1. absurd, ill-advised, ill-considered, ill-judged, imprudent, incautious, indiscreet, injudicious, nonsensical, senseless, short-sighted, silly, unintelligent, unreasonable, unwise **2.** brainless, crazy, daft (*Inf.*), doltish, fatuous, half-baked (*Inf.*), half-witted, harebrained, idiotic, imbecilic, ludicrous, mad, moronic, potty (*Brit. inf.*), ridiculous, senseless, silly, simple, stupid, weak, witless

foolishly absurdly, idiotically, ill-advisedly, imprudently, incautiously, indiscreetly, injudiciously, like a fool, mistakenly, short-sightedly, stupidly, unwisely, without due consideration

foolproof certain, guaranteed, infallible, never-failing, safe, sure-fire (*Inf.*), unassailable, unbreakable

footing 1. basis, establishment, foot-hold, foundation, ground, groundwork, installation, settlement **2.** condition, grade, position, rank, relations, relationship, standing, state, status, terms

forage 1. *n. For cattle, etc.* feed, fodder, food, foodstuffs, provender **2.** *v.* cast about, explore, hunt, look round, plunder, raid, ransack, rummage, scour, scrounge (*Inf.*), search, seek

forbear abstain, avoid, cease, decline, desist, eschew, hold back, keep from, omit, pause, refrain, resist the temptation to, restrain oneself, stop, withhold

forbearance indulgence, leniency, lenity, longanimity (*Rare*), long-suffering, mildness, moderation, patience, resignation, restraint, self-control, temperance, tolerance

forbearing clement, easy, forgiving, indulgent, lenient, long-suffering, merciful, mild, moderate, patient, tolerant

forbid ban, debar, disallow, exclude, hinder, inhibit, interdict, outlaw, preclude, prohibit, proscribe, rule out, veto

forbidden banned, outlawed, out of bounds, prohibited, proscribed, taboo, *verboten*, vetoed

forbidding daunting, foreboding, frightening, grim, hostile, menacing, ominous, sinister, threatening, unfriendly

forcemeat (ˈfɔːsmiːt) *n.* mixture of chopped ingredients used for stuffing (*also* **farce**)

forceps (ˈfɔːsɪps) *pl.n.* surgical pincers

ford (fɔːd) *n.* **1.** shallow place where river may be crossed —*vt.* **2.** cross (river *etc.*) over shallow area —ˈ**fordable** *a.*

fore[1] (fɔː) *a.* **1.** in front (ˈ**former,** ˈ**further** *comp.,* ˈ**foremost, first,** ˈ**furthest** *sup.*) —*n.* **2.** front part

fore[2] (fɔː) *interj.* golfer's warning

fore- (*comb. form*) previous, before, front

fore-and-aft *a.* placed in line from bow to stern of ship

forearm (ˈfɔːrɑːm) *n.* **1.** arm between wrist and elbow —*vt.* (fɔːrˈɑːm) **2.** arm beforehand

forebear *or* **forbear** (ˈfɔːbɛə) *n.* ancestor

forebode (fɔːˈbəʊd) *vt.* indicate in advance —**foreˈboding** *n.* anticipation of evil

forecast (ˈfɔːkɑːst) *vt.* **1.** estimate beforehand (*esp.* weather); prophesy —*n.* **2.** prediction

forecastle, fo'c's'le, *or* **fo'c'sle** (ˈfəʊksˀl) *n.* **1.** forward raised part of ship **2.** sailors' quarters

foreclose (fɔːˈkləʊz) *vt.* **1.** take away power of redeeming (mortgage) **2.** prevent **3.** shut out, bar —**foreˈclosure** *n.*

forecourt (ˈfɔːkɔːt) *n.* courtyard, open space, in front of building

forefather (ˈfɔːfɑːðə) *n.* ancestor

forefinger (ˈfɔːfɪŋgə) *n.* finger next to thumb

forefoot (ˈfɔːfʊt) *n.* either of front feet of quadruped

forefront (ˈfɔːfrʌnt) *n.* **1.** extreme front **2.** position of most prominence or action

foregather (fɔːˈgæðə) *vi. see* FORGATHER

forego[1] (fɔːˈgəʊ) *vt.* precede in time, place (-ˈ**went** *pt.,* -ˈ**gone** *pp.,* -ˈ**going** *pr.p.*) —**foreˈgoing** *a.* going before, preceding —**foreˈgone** *a.* **1.** determined beforehand **2.** preceding —**foregone conclusion** result that might have been foreseen

forego[2] (fɔːˈgəʊ) *vt. see* FORGO

foreground (ˈfɔːgraʊnd) *n.* part of view, *esp.* in picture, nearest observer

forehand (ˈfɔːhænd) *a.* (of stroke in racket games) made with inner side of wrist leading

forehead (ˈfɒrɪd) *n.* part of face above eyebrows and between temples

foreign (ˈfɒrɪn) *a.* **1.** not of, or in, one's own country **2.** relating to, or connected with other countries **3.** irrelevant **4.** coming from outside **5.** unfamiliar, strange —ˈ**foreigner** *n.* —**foreign minister** *or* **secretary** (*oft.* **F- M-** *or* **S-**) cabinet minister responsible for country's dealings with other countries —**foreign office** ministry of country or state that is concerned with dealings with other states

foreknow (fɔːˈnəʊ) *vt.* know in advance —**foreknowledge** (fɔːˈnɒlɪdʒ) *n.*

foreland (ˈfɔːlənd) *n.* **1.** headland, promontory **2.** land lying in front of something, such as water

foreleg (ˈfɔːlɛg) *n.* either of front legs of horse or other quadruped

forelimb (ˈfɔːlɪm) *n.* either of front limbs of four-limbed vertebrate

forelock (ˈfɔːlɒk) *n.* lock of hair above forehead

foreman (ˈfɔːmən) *n.* **1.** one in charge of work **2.** leader of jury

foremast (ˈfɔːmɑːst; *Naut.* ˈfɔːməst) *n.* mast nearest bow

foremost (ˈfɔːməʊst) *a./adv.* first in time, place, importance *etc.*

forenoon (ˈfɔːnuːn) *n.* morning

forensic (fəˈrɛnsɪk) *a.* of courts of law —**forensic medicine** application of medical knowledge in legal matters

THESAURUS

force *n.* **1.** dynamism, energy, impact, impulse, life, might, momentum, muscle, potency, power, pressure, stimulus, strength, stress, vigour **2.** arm-twisting (*Inf.*), coercion, compulsion, constraint, duress, enforcement, pressure, violence **3.** bite, cogency, effect, effectiveness, efficacy, influence, persuasiveness, power, punch (*Inf.*), strength, validity, weight **4.** army, battalion, body, corps, detachment, division, host, legion, patrol, regiment, squad, squadron, troop, unit ~*v.* **5.** bring pressure to bear upon, coerce, compel, constrain, drive, impel, impose, make, necessitate, obligate, oblige, overcome, press, press-gang, pressure, pressurize, put the squeeze on (*Inf.*), strong-arm (*Inf.*), urge **6.** blast, break open, prise, propel, push, thrust, use violence on, wrench, wrest

forceful cogent, compelling, convincing, dynamic, effective, persuasive, pithy, potent, powerful, telling, vigorous, weighty

forcible 1. active, cogent, compelling, effective, efficient, energetic, forceful, impressive, mighty, potent, powerful, strong, telling, valid, weighty **2.** aggressive, armed, coercive, compulsory, drastic, violent

forcibly against one's will, by force, by main force, compulsorily, under compulsion, under protest, willy-nilly

forebear ancestor, father, forefather, forerunner, predecessor, progenitor

forebode augur, betoken, foreshadow, foreshow, foretell, foretoken, forewarn, indicate, portend, predict, presage, prognosticate, promise, warn of

foreboding anxiety, apprehension, apprehensiveness, chill, dread, fear, misgiving, premonition, presentiment

forecast 1. *v.* anticipate, augur, calculate, divine, estimate, foresee, foretell, plan, predict, prognosticate, prophesy **2.** *n.* anticipation, conjecture, foresight, forethought, guess, outlook, planning, prediction, prognosis, projection, prophecy

forefather ancestor, father, forebear, forerunner, predecessor, primogenitor, procreator, progenitor

foregoing above, antecedent, anterior, former, preceding, previous, prior

foreground centre, forefront, front, limelight, prominence

foreign 1. alien, borrowed, distant, exotic, external, imported, outlandish, outside, overseas, remote, strange, unfamiliar, unknown **2.** extraneous, extrinsic, incongruous, irrelevant, unassimilable, uncharacteristic, unrelated

foreigner alien, immigrant, incomer, newcomer, outlander, stranger

foremost chief, first, front, headmost, highest, inaugural, initial, leading, paramount, pre-eminent, primary, prime, principal, supreme

foreordain (fɔːrɔːˈdeɪn) *vt.* determine (events *etc.*) in future —**foreordination** (fɔːrɔːdɪˈneɪʃən) *n.*

forepaw (ˈfɔːpɔː) *n.* either of front feet of most land mammals that do not have hooves

foreplay (ˈfɔːpleɪ) *n.* sexual stimulation before intercourse

forerunner (ˈfɔːrʌnə) *n.* one who goes before, precursor

foresail (ˈfɔːseɪl; *Naut.* ˈfɔːsᵊl) *n. Naut.* **1.** aftermost headsail of fore-and-aft rigged vessel **2.** lowest sail set on foremast of square-rigged vessel

foresee (fɔːˈsiː) *vt.* see beforehand (**-ˈsaw** *pt.*, **-ˈseen** *pp.*)

foreshadow (fɔːˈʃædəʊ) *vt.* show, suggest beforehand

foreshore (ˈfɔːʃɔː) *n.* part of shore between high and low tide marks

foreshorten (fɔːˈʃɔːtᵊn) *vt.* **1.** draw (object) so that it appears shortened **2.** make shorter

foresight (ˈfɔːsaɪt) *n.* **1.** foreseeing **2.** care for future

foreskin (ˈfɔːskɪn) *n.* skin that covers the glans penis

forest (ˈfɒrɪst) *n.* **1.** area with heavy growth of trees and plants **2.** these trees **3.** *fig.* something resembling forest —*vt.* **4.** plant, create forest in (an area) —**foresˈtation** *n.* planting of trees over wide area —**ˈforester** *n.* one skilled in forestry —**ˈforestry** *n.* study, management of forest planting and maintenance

forestall (fɔːˈstɔːl) *vt.* **1.** anticipate **2.** prevent, guard against in advance

foretaste (ˈfɔːteɪst) *n.* **1.** anticipation **2.** taste beforehand

foretell (fɔːˈtel) *vt.* prophesy (**foreˈtold** *pt./pp.*)

forethought (ˈfɔːθɔːt) *n.* thoughtful consideration of future events

foretoken (ˈfɔːtəʊkən) *n.* **1.** sign of future event —*vt.* (fɔːˈtəʊkən) **2.** foreshadow

foretop (ˈfɔːtɒp; *Naut.* ˈfɔːtəp) *n.* platform at top of foremast

for ever *or* **forever** (fɔːˈrɛvə, fə-) *adv.* **1.** always **2.** eternally **3.** *inf.* for a long time

forewarn (fɔːˈwɔːn) *vt.* warn, caution in advance

forewent (fɔːˈwent) *pt. of* FOREGO[1], FOREGO[2]

foreword (ˈfɔːwɜːd) *n.* preface

forfeit (ˈfɔːfɪt) *n.* **1.** thing lost by crime or fault **2.** penalty, fine —*a.* **3.** lost by crime or fault —*vt.* **4.** lose by penalty —**ˈforfeiture** *n.*

forgather *or* **foregather** (fɔːˈgæðə) *vi.* **1.** meet together, assemble **2.** associate

forgave (fəˈgeɪv) *pt. of* FORGIVE

forge[1] (fɔːdʒ) *n.* **1.** place where metal is worked, smithy **2.** furnace, workshop for melting or refining metal —*vt.* **3.** shape (metal) by heating in fire and hammering **4.** make, shape **5.** invent **6.** make a fraudulent imitation of, counterfeit —**ˈforger** *n.* —**ˈforgery** *n.* **1.** forged document, banknote *etc.* **2.** the making of it

forge[2] (fɔːdʒ) *vi.* advance steadily

forget (fəˈgɛt) *vt.* **1.** lose memory of **2.** neglect, overlook (**forˈgot** *pt.*, **forˈgotten** *or* (US, *obs.*) **forˈgot** *pp.*, **forˈgetting** *pr.p.*) —**forˈgetful** *a.* liable to forget —**forˈgetfully** *adv.* —**forget-me-not** *n.* plant with small blue flower

forgive (fəˈgɪv) *v.* **1.** cease to blame or hold resentment (against) —*vt.* **2.** pardon —**forˈgiveness** *n.* —**forˈgiving** *a.* willing to forgive

forgo *or* **forego** (fɔːˈgəʊ) *vt.* go without, give up (**-ˈwent** *pt.*, **-ˈgone** *pp.*, **-ˈgoing** *pr.p.*)

THESAURUS

forerunner ancestor, announcer, envoy, forebear, foregoer, harbinger, herald, precursor, predecessor, progenitor, prototype

foresee anticipate, divine, envisage, forebode, forecast, foretell, predict, prophesy

foreshadow adumbrate, augur, betoken, bode, forebode, imply, indicate, portend, predict, prefigure, presage, promise, prophesy, signal

foresight anticipation, care, caution, circumspection, far-sightedness, forethought, precaution, premeditation, preparedness, prescience, prevision (*Rare*), provision, prudence

forestry arboriculture, dendrology (*Bot.*), silviculture, woodcraft, woodmanship

foretell adumbrate, augur, bode, forebode, forecast, foreshadow, foreshow, forewarn, portend, predict, presage, prognosticate, prophesy, signify, soothsay

forethought anticipation, far-sightedness, foresight, precaution, providence, provision, prudence

forever 1. always, evermore, for all time, for good and all (*Inf.*), for keeps, in perpetuity, till Doomsday, till the cows come home (*Inf.*), till the end of time, world without end **2.** all the time, constantly, continually, endlessly, eternally, everlastingly, incessantly, interminably, perpetually, unremittingly

forewarn admonish, advise, alert, apprise, caution, dissuade, give fair warning, put on guard, put on the qui vive, tip off

foreword introduction, preamble, preface, preliminary, prolegomenon, prologue

forfeit 1. *n.* amercement (*Obsolete*), damages, fine, forfeiture, loss, mulct, penalty **2.** *v.* be deprived of, be stripped of, give up, lose, relinquish, renounce, surrender

forfeiture confiscation, giving up, loss, relinquishment, sequestration (*Law*), surrender

forge *v.* **1.** construct, contrive, create, devise, fabricate, fashion, form, frame, hammer out, invent, make, mould, shape, work **2.** coin, copy, counterfeit, fake, falsify, feign, imitate

forger coiner, counterfeiter, falsifier

forgery 1. coining, counterfeiting, falsification, fraudulence, fraudulent imitation **2.** counterfeit, fake, falsification, imitation, phoney (*Inf.*), sham

forget 1. consign to oblivion, dismiss from one's mind, let bygones be bygones, let slip from the memory **2.** leave behind, lose sight of, omit, overlook

forgetful absent-minded, apt to forget, careless, dreamy, heedless, inattentive, lax, neglectful, negligent, oblivious, unmindful

forgive absolve, accept (someone's) apology, acquit, bear no malice, condone, excuse, exonerate, let bygones be bygones, let off (*Inf.*), pardon, remit

forgiveness absolution, acquittal, amnesty, condonation, exoneration, mercy, overlooking, pardon, remission

forgiving clement, compassionate, forbearing, hu-

forgot (fəˈgɒt) *pt./(US, obs.) pp. of* FORGET

fork (fɔːk) *n.* 1. pronged instrument for eating food 2. pronged tool for digging or lifting 3. division into branches 4. point of this division 5. one of the branches —*vi.* 6. branch —*vt.* 7. dig, lift, throw with fork 8. make fork-shaped —**forked** *a.* 1. having fork or forklike parts 2. zigzag —**fork-lift truck** vehicle having two power-operated horizontal prongs that can be raised and lowered —**fork out** *inf.* pay (reluctantly)

forlorn (fəˈlɔːn) *a.* 1. forsaken 2. desperate —**forlorn hope** anything undertaken with little hope of success

form (fɔːm) *n.* 1. shape 2. visible appearance 3. visible person or animal 4. structure 5. nature 6. species, kind 7. regularly drawn up document, *esp.* printed one with blanks for particulars 8. condition, *esp.* good condition 9. class in school 10. customary way of doing things 11. set order of words 12. long seat without back, bench 13. hare's nest 14. *esp.* US *see* FORME —*vt.* 15. shape, mould 16. arrange, organize 17. train 18. shape in the mind, conceive 19. go to make up, make part of —*vi.* 20. come into existence or shape —**forˈmation** *n.* 1. forming 2. thing formed 3. structure, shape, arrangement 4. military order —**ˈformative** *a.* 1. of, relating to, development 2. serving or tending to form 3. used in forming —**ˈformless** *a.*

-form (*comb. form*) having shape or form of; resembling, as in *cruciform, vermiform*

formal (ˈfɔːməl) *a.* 1. ceremonial 2. according to rule 3. of outward form or routine 4. of, for, formal occasions 5. according to rule that does not matter 6. precise; stiff —**ˈformalism** *n.* 1. quality of being formal 2. exclusive concern for form, structure, technique in an activity, *eg* art —**ˈformalist** *n.* —**forˈmality** *n.* 1. observance required by custom or etiquette 2. condition or quality of being formal 3. conformity to custom, conventionality, mere form 4. in art, precision, stiffness, as opposed to originality —**formaliˈzation** *or* **-liˈsation** *n.* —**ˈformalize** *or* **-lise** *vt.* 1. make formal 2. make official or valid 3. give definite form to —**ˈformally** *adv.*

formaldehyde (fɔːˈmældɪhaɪd) *n.* colourless, poisonous, pungent gas, used in making antiseptics and in chemistry —**ˈformalin** *n.* solution of formaldehyde in water, used as disinfectant, preservative *etc.*

format (ˈfɔːmæt) *n.* 1. size and shape of book 2. organization of television show *etc.*

forme *or U.S.* **form** (fɔːm) *n. Print.* frame for type

former (ˈfɔːmə) *a.* 1. earlier in time 2. of past times 3. first named —*n.* 4. first named thing, person or fact —**ˈformerly** *adv.* previously

Formica (fɔːˈmaɪkə) *n.* R type of laminated sheet used to make heat-resistant surfaces

formic acid (ˈfɔːmɪk) acid found in insects (*esp.* ants) and some plants

formidable (ˈfɔːmɪdəbᵊl) *a.* 1. to be feared 2. overwhelming, terrible, redoubtable 3. likely to be difficult, serious —**ˈformidably** *adv.*

THESAURUS

mane, lenient, magnanimous, merciful, mild, softhearted, tolerant

forgo, forego abandon, abjure, cede, do without, give up, leave alone *or* out, relinquish, renounce, resign, sacrifice, surrender, waive, yield

forgotten blotted out, buried, bygone, consigned to oblivion, gone (clean) out of one's mind, left behind *or* out, lost, obliterated, omitted, past, past recall, unremembered

fork *v.* bifurcate, branch, branch off, diverge, divide, go separate ways, part, split

forked angled, bifurcate(d), branched, branching, divided, pronged, split, tined, zigzag

forlorn abandoned, bereft, cheerless, comfortless, deserted, desolate, destitute, disconsolate, forgotten, forsaken, friendless, helpless, homeless, hopeless, lonely, lost, miserable, pathetic, pitiable, pitiful, unhappy, woebegone, wretched

form *v.* 1. assemble, bring about, build, concoct, construct, contrive, create, devise, establish, fabricate, fashion, forge, found, invent, make, manufacture, model, mould, produce, put together, set up, shape ~*n.* 2. appearance, cast, configuration, construction, cut, fashion, formation, model, mould, pattern, shape, structure 3. anatomy, being, body, build, figure, frame, outline, person, physique, shape, silhouette 4. condition, fettle, fitness, good condition, good spirits, health, shape, trim ~*v.* 5. arrange, combine, design, dispose, draw up, frame, organize, pattern, plan, think up ~*n.* 6. arrangement, character, description, design, guise, kind, manifestation, manner, method, mode, order, practice, semblance, sort, species, stamp, style, system, type, variety, way 7. format, framework, harmony, order, orderliness, organization, plan, proportion, structure, symmetry ~*v.* 8. accumulate, appear, become visible, come into being, crystallize, grow, materialize, rise, settle, show up, take shape 9. compose, comprise, constitute, make, make up, serve as 10. bring up, discipline, educate, instruct, rear, school, teach, train ~*n.* 11. behaviour, ceremony, conduct, convention, custom, done thing, etiquette, formality, manners, procedure, protocol, ritual, rule 12. application, document, paper, sheet 13. class, grade, rank

formal 1. approved, ceremonial, explicit, express, fixed, lawful, legal, methodical, official, prescribed, *pro forma*, regular, rigid, ritualistic, set, solemn, strict 2. affected, aloof, ceremonious, conventional, correct, exact, precise, prim, punctilious, reserved, starched, stiff, unbending

formality 1. ceremony, convention, conventionality, custom, form, gesture, matter of form, procedure, red tape, rite, ritual 2. ceremoniousness, correctness, decorum, etiquette, politesse, protocol, punctilio

formation 1. accumulation, compilation, composition, constitution, crystallization, development, establishment, evolution, forming, generation, genesis, manufacture, organization, production 2. arrangement, configuration, design, disposition, figure, grouping, pattern, rank, structure

formative determinative, developmental, influential, moulding, shaping

former 1. antecedent, anterior, *ci-devant*, earlier, erstwhile, ex-, late, one-time, previous, prior, quondam, whilom (*Archaic*) 2. ancient, bygone, departed, long ago, long gone, of yore, old, old-time, past 3. above, aforementioned, aforesaid, first mentioned, foregoing, preceding

formula (ˈfɔːmjʊlə) *n.* **1.** set form of words setting forth principle, method or rule for doing, producing something **2.** substance so prepared **3.** specific category of car in motor racing **4.** recipe **5.** *Science, maths.* rule, fact expressed in symbols and figures (*pl.* **-ulae** (-juliː), **-s**) —**ˈformulary** *n.* collection of formulas —**ˈformulate** *vt.* **1.** reduce to, express in formula, or in definite form **2.** devise —**formuˈlation** *n.* —**ˈformulator** *n.*

fornication (fɔːnɪˈkeɪʃən) *n.* sexual intercourse outside marriage —**ˈfornicate** *vi.*

forsake (fəˈseɪk) *vt.* **1.** abandon, desert **2.** give up (**forˈsook, forˈsaken, forˈsaking**)

forsooth (fəˈsuːθ) *adv. obs.* in truth

forswear (fɔːˈswɛə) *vt.* **1.** renounce **2.** deny —*v. refl.* **3.** perjure (**-ˈswore** *pt.*, **-ˈsworn** *pp.*)

forsythia (fɔːˈsaɪθɪə) *n.* widely cultivated shrub with yellow flowers

fort (fɔːt) *n.* fortified place, stronghold —**hold the fort** *inf.* keep things going during someone's absence

forte[1] (fɔːt, ˈfɔːteɪ) *n.* one's strong point, that in which one excels

forte[2] (ˈfɔːtɪ) *adv. Mus.* loudly (**forˈtissimo** *sup.*)

forth (fɔːθ) *adv.* **1.** onwards **2.** into view —**ˈforthˈcoming** *a.* **1.** about to come **2.** ready when wanted **3.** willing to talk, communicative —**forthˈwith** *adv.* at once, immediately

forthright (ˈfɔːθraɪt) *a.* direct, outspoken

fortieth (ˈfɔːtɪɪθ) *see* FOUR

fortify (ˈfɔːtɪfaɪ) *vt.* **1.** strengthen **2.** provide with defensive works (**ˈfortified, ˈfortifying**) —**fortifiˈcation** *n.*

fortitude (ˈfɔːtɪtjuːd) *n.* courage in adversity or pain, endurance

fortnight (ˈfɔːtnaɪt) *n.* two weeks —**ˈfortnightly** *a./adv.*

FORTRAN (ˈfɔːtræn) high-level computer programming language for mathematical and scientific purposes

fortress (ˈfɔːtrɪs) *n.* fortified place, *eg* castle, stronghold

fortuitous (fɔːˈtjuːɪtəs) *a.* accidental, by chance —**forˈtuitously** *adv.* —**forˈtuity** *n.*

fortune (ˈfɔːtʃən) *n.* **1.** good luck **2.** prosperity, wealth **3.** chance, luck —**ˈfortunate** *a.* —**ˈfortunately** *adv.* —**fortune-hunter** *n.* person seeking fortune, *esp.* by marriage —**fortune-teller** *n.* one who predicts a person's future

forty (ˈfɔːtɪ) *see* FOUR —**forty winks** short sleep, nap

forum (ˈfɔːrəm) *n.* (place or medium for) meeting, assembly for open discussion or debate

THESAURUS

formerly aforetime (*Archaic*), already, at one time, before, heretofore, lately, once, previously

formidable 1. appalling, dangerous, daunting, dismaying, dreadful, fearful, frightful, horrible, intimidating, menacing, shocking, terrifying, threatening **2.** arduous, challenging, colossal, difficult, mammoth, onerous, overwhelming, staggering, toilsome **3.** awesome, great, impressive, indomitable, mighty, powerful, puissant, redoubtable, terrific, tremendous

formula 1. form of words, formulary, rite, ritual, rubric **2.** blueprint, method, modus operandi, precept, prescription, principle, procedure, recipe, rule, way

formulate 1. codify, define, detail, express, frame, give form to, particularize, set down, specify, systematize **2.** coin, develop, devise, evolve, forge, invent, map out, originate, plan, work out

forsake 1. abandon, cast off, desert, disown, jettison, jilt, leave, leave in the lurch, quit, repudiate, throw over **2.** abdicate, forgo, forswear, give up, have done with, relinquish, renounce, set aside, surrender, turn one's back on, yield

forsaken abandoned, cast off, deserted, destitute, disowned, forlorn, friendless, ignored, isolated, jilted, left behind, left in the lurch, lonely, marooned, outcast, solitary

fort 1. blockhouse, camp, castle, citadel, fastness, fortification, fortress, garrison, redoubt, station, stronghold **2. hold the fort** carry on, keep things moving, keep things on an even keel, maintain the status quo, stand in, take over the reins

forte gift, long suit (*Inf.*), métier, speciality, strength, strong point, talent

forth ahead, away, forward, into the open, onward, out, out of concealment, outward

forthcoming 1. approaching, coming, expected, future, imminent, impending, prospective **2.** accessible, at hand, available, in evidence, obtainable, on tap (*Inf.*), ready **3.** chatty, communicative, expansive, free, informative, open, sociable, talkative, unreserved

forthright above-board, blunt, candid, direct, frank, open, outspoken, plain-spoken, straightforward, straight from the shoulder (*Inf.*)

forthwith at once, directly, immediately, instantly, quickly, right away, straightaway, *tout de suite*, without delay

fortification embattlement, reinforcement, strengthening

fortify 1. brace, buttress, embattle, garrison, protect, reinforce, secure, shore up, strengthen, support **2.** brace, cheer, confirm, embolden, encourage, hearten, invigorate, reassure, stiffen, strengthen, sustain

fortitude backbone, braveness, courage, dauntlessness, determination, endurance, fearlessness, firmness, grit, guts (*Inf.*), hardihood, intrepidity, patience, perseverance, pluck, resolution, staying power, stoutheartedness, strength, strength of mind, valour

fortress castle, citadel, fastness, fort, redoubt, stronghold

fortunate 1. born with a silver spoon in one's mouth, bright, favoured, golden, happy, having a charmed life, in luck, lucky, prosperous, rosy, sitting pretty (*Inf.*), successful, well-off **2.** advantageous, auspicious, convenient, encouraging, favourable, felicitous, fortuitous, helpful, opportune, profitable, promising, propitious, providential, timely

fortunately by a happy chance, by good luck, happily, luckily, providentially

fortune 1. affluence, gold mine, opulence, possessions, property, prosperity, riches, treasure, wealth **2.** accident, chance, contingency, destiny, fate, fortuity, hap (*Archaic*), hazard, kismet, luck, providence

forward (ˈfɔːwəd) *a.* 1. lying in front of something 2. onward 3. presumptuous, impudent 4. advanced, progressive 5. relating to the future —*n.* 6. player placed in forward position in various team games, *eg* football —*adv.* 7. towards the future 8. towards the front, to the front 9. into view 10. (ˈfɔːwəd; *Naut.* ˈfɒrəd) at, in fore part of ship 11. onwards, so as to make progress —*vt.* 12. help forward 13. send, dispatch —**ˈforwardly** *adv.* pertly —**ˈforwardness** *n.* —**ˈforwards** *adv.*

forwent (fɔːˈwɛnt) *pt. of* FORGO

fosse *or* **foss** (fɒs) *n.* ditch; moat

fossil (ˈfɒsᵊl) *n.* 1. remnant or impression of animal or plant, *esp.* prehistoric one, preserved in earth 2. *inf.* person, idea *etc.* that is outdated and incapable of change —*a.* 3. of, like or forming fossil 4. dug from earth 5. *inf.* antiquated —**ˈfossilize** *or* **-ise** *v.* 1. turn into fossil —*vt.* 2. petrify

foster (ˈfɒstə) *vt.* 1. promote growth or development of 2. bring up (child) *esp.* not one's own —**foster brother, sister, father, mother, parent, child** one related by upbringing, not blood

fought (fɔːt) *pt./pp. of* FIGHT

foul (faʊl) *a.* 1. loathsome, offensive 2. stinking 3. dirty 4. unfair 5. (of weather) wet, rough 6. obscene, disgustingly abusive 7. charged with harmful matter, clogged, choked —*n.* 8. act of unfair play 9. the breaking of a rule —*adv.* 10. unfairly —*v.* 11. make, become foul 12. jam —*vt.* 13. collide with —**ˈfoully** *adv.* —**foul play** 1. unfair conduct, *esp.* with violence 2. violation of rules in game —**fall foul of** 1. get into trouble with 2. (of ships) collide with

foulard (fuːˈlɑːd) *n.* soft light fabric of silk or rayon

found[1] (faʊnd) *pt./pp. of* FIND

found[2] (faʊnd) *vt.* 1. establish, institute 2. lay base of 3. base, ground —**founˈdation** *n.* 1. basis 2. base, lowest part of building 3. founding 4. endowed institution *etc.* 5. cosmetic used as base for make-up —**ˈfounder** *n.* (**ˈfoundress** *fem.*) —**foundation garment** woman's undergarment worn to shape and support figure (*also* **founˈdation**) —**foundation stone** one of stones forming foundation of building, *esp.* stone laid with public ceremony

found[3] (faʊnd) *vt.* 1. melt and run into mould 2. cast —**ˈfounder** *n.* —**ˈfoundry** *n.* 1. place for casting 2. art of this

founder (ˈfaʊndə) *vi.* 1. collapse 2. sink 3. become stuck as in mud *etc.*

foundling (ˈfaʊndlɪŋ) *n.* deserted infant

fount (faʊnt) *n.* 1. fountain 2. assortment of printing type of one size

fountain (ˈfaʊntɪn) *n.* 1. jet of water, *esp.* ornamental one 2. spring 3. source —**ˈfountainhead** *n.* source —**fountain pen** pen with ink reservoir

four (fɔː) *n./a.* cardinal number next after three —**ˈfortieth** *a./n.* —**ˈforty** *n./a.* four tens —**ˈfourˈteen** *n./a.* four plus ten —**ˈfourˈteenth** *a.* —**fourth** *a.* ordinal number of four —**ˈfourthly** *adv.* —**four-in-hand** *n.* 1. road vehicle drawn by four horses and driven by one driver 2. four-horse team 3. US long narrow tie tied in flat slipknot with ends dangling —**four-leaf clover** *or* **four-leaved clover** clover with four leaves rather than three, supposed to bring good luck —**four-letter word** any of several short English words referring to sex or excrement: regarded generally as offensive —**four-poster** *n.* bed with four posts for curtains *etc.* —**fourˈscore** *a./n. obs.* eighty —**ˈfoursome** *n.* 1. group of four

THESAURUS

forward *adj.* 1. advanced, advancing, early, forward-looking, onward, precocious, premature, progressive, well-developed 2. advance, first, fore, foremost, front, head, leading 3. assuming, bare-faced, bold, brash, brass-necked (*Inf.*), brazen, brazen-faced, cheeky, confident, familiar, fresh (*Inf.*), impertinent, impudent, overassertive, overweening, pert, presuming, presumptuous, pushy (*Inf.*) ~*adv.* 4. *Also* **forwards** ahead, forth, on, onward 5. in to consideration, into prominence, into the open, into view, out, to light, to the fore, to the surface ~*v.* 6. advance, aid, assist, back, encourage, expedite, favour, foster, further, hasten, help, hurry, promote, speed, support 7. *Commerce* dispatch, freight, post, route, send, send on, ship, transmit

forwardness boldness, brashness, brazenness, cheek (*Inf.*), cheekiness, impertinence, impudence, overconfidence, pertness, presumption

foster 1. cultivate, encourage, feed, foment, nurture, promote, stimulate, support, uphold 2. bring up, mother, nurse, raise, rear, take care of

foul *adj.* 1. contaminated, dirty, disgusting, fetid, filthy, impure, loathsome, malodorous, mephitic, nasty, nauseating, noisome, offensive, polluted, putrid, rank, repulsive, revolting, rotten, squalid, stinking, sullied, tainted, unclean 2. abusive, blasphemous, blue, coarse, dirty, filthy, foul-mouthed, gross, indecent, lewd, low, obscene, profane, scatological, scurrilous, smutty, vulgar 3. crooked, dirty, dishonest, fraudulent, inequitable, shady (*Inf.*), underhand, unfair, unjust, unscrupulous, unsportsmanlike 4. bad, blustery, disagreeable, foggy, murky, rainy, rough, stormy, wet, wild ~*v.* 5. begrime, besmear, besmirch, contaminate, defile, dirty, pollute, smear, soil, stain, sully, taint 6. block, catch, choke, clog, ensnare, entangle, jam, snarl, twist

foul play chicanery, corruption, crime, deception, dirty work, double-dealing, duplicity, fraud, perfidy, roguery, sharp practice, skulduggery, treachery, villainy

found 1. bring into being, constitute, construct, create, endow, erect, establish, fix, inaugurate, institute, organize, originate, plant, raise, settle, set up, start 2. base, bottom, build, ground, rest, root, sustain

foundation 1. base, basis, bedrock, bottom, footing, groundwork, substructure, underpinning 2. endowment, establishment, inauguration, institution, organization, setting up, settlement

founder[1] *n.* architect, author, beginner, benefactor, builder, constructor, designer, establisher, father, framer, generator, initiator, institutor, inventor, maker, organizer, originator, patriarch

founder[2] *v.* 1. be lost, go down, go to the bottom, sink, submerge 2. *Fig.* abort, break down, collapse, come to grief, come to nothing, fail, fall through, miscarry, misfire 3. collapse, fall, go lame, lurch, sprawl, stagger, stumble, trip

foundling orphan, outcast, stray, waif

fountain 1. font, fount, jet, reservoir, spout, spray, spring, well 2. *Fig.* beginning, cause, commencement, derivation, fountainhead, genesis, origin, rise, source, wellhead, wellspring

people 2. game or dance for four people —**four'square** *a.* firm, steady —**four-stroke** *n.* internal-combustion engine firing once every four strokes of piston —**fourth estate** (*sometimes* F- E-) journalists; journalism —**on all fours** on hands and knees

fowl (faʊl) *n.* 1. domestic cock or hen 2. bird, its flesh —*vi.* 3. hunt wild birds —**'fowler** *n.* —**fowling piece** light gun

fox (fɒks) *n.* 1. red bushy-tailed animal 2. its fur 3. cunning person —*vt.* 4. perplex 5. discolour (paper) with brown spots 6. mislead —*vi.* 7. act craftily —**'foxy** *a.* 1. of or resembling fox, *esp.* in craftiness 2. of reddish-brown colour 3. (of paper *etc.*) spotted, *esp.* by mildew 4. US physically attractive —**'foxglove** *n.* tall flowering plant —**'foxhole** *n. sl.* in war, small trench giving protection —**'foxhound** *n.* dog bred for hunting foxes —**fox hunt** 1. hunting of foxes with hounds 2. instance of this 3. organization for fox-hunting within area —**fox-hunting** *n.* —**fox terrier** small dog now mainly kept as pet —**'foxtrot** *n.* 1. (music for) ballroom dance —*vi.* 2. perform this dance

foyer ('fɔɪeɪ, 'fɔɪə) *n.* entrance hall in theatres, hotels *etc.*

F.P. *or* **f.p.** 1. freezing point (*also* **fp**) 2. fully paid

F.P.A. Family Planning Association

f.p.s. 1. feet per second 2. foot-pound-second

Fr *Chem.* francium

fr. 1. fragment 2. franc 3. from

Fr. 1. Father 2. Frater (*Lat.* brother) 3. French 4. Friday

fracas ('frækɑː) *n.* noisy quarrel; uproar; brawl

fraction ('frækʃən) *n.* 1. numerical quantity not an integer 2. fragment, piece —**'fractional** *a.* 1. constituting a fraction 2. forming but a small part 3. insignificant

fractious ('frækʃəs) *a.* 1. unruly 2. irritable

fracture ('fræktʃə) *n.* 1. breakage, part broken 2. breaking of bone 3. breach, rupture —*v.* 4. break

fragile ('frædʒaɪl) *a.* 1. breakable 2. frail, delicate —**fragility** (frə'dʒɪlɪtɪ) *n.*

fragment ('frægmənt) *n.* 1. piece broken off 2. small portion 3. incomplete part —*v.* (fræg'mɛnt) 4. (cause to) break into fragments —**'fragmentary** *a.*

fragrant ('freɪgrənt) *a.* sweet-smelling —**'fragrance** *n.* scent —**'fragrantly** *adv.*

frail (freɪl) *a.* 1. fragile, delicate 2. infirm, in weak health 3. morally weak —**'frailly** *adv.* —**'frailty** *n.*

frame (freɪm) *n.* 1. that in which thing is set, as square of wood round picture *etc.* 2. structure 3. build of body 4. constitution 5. mood 6. individual exposure on strip of film 7. *Snooker etc.* wooden triangle used to set up balls, balls when set up or single game finished when all balls have been potted —*vt.* 8. put together, make 9. adapt 10. put into words 11. put into frame 12. *sl.* conspire to incriminate on false charge —**frame-up** *n. sl.* 1. plot 2. manufactured evidence —**'framework** *n.* 1. structure into which completing parts can be fitted 2. supporting work

franc (fræŋk; *Fr.* frɑ̃) *n.* monetary unit of France, Switzerland and other countries

franchise ('fræntʃaɪz) *n.* 1. right of voting 2. citizenship 3. privilege or right, *esp.* right to sell certain goods

Franciscan (fræn'sɪskən) *n.* monk or nun of the order founded by St. Francis of Assisi

francium ('frænsɪəm) *n.* radioactive element of alkali-metal group

Franco- ('fræŋkəʊ-) (*comb. form*) France; French, as in *Franco-Prussian*

francolin ('fræŋkəʊlɪn) *n.* Afr. or Asian partridge

frangipani (frændʒɪ'pɑːnɪ) *n.* tropical Amer. shrub (*pl.* **-s, -'pani**)

frank (fræŋk) *a.* 1. candid, outspoken 2. sincere —*n.* 3.

THESAURUS

foxy artful, astute, canny, crafty, cunning, devious, guileful, knowing, sharp, shrewd, sly, tricky, wily

foyer antechamber, anteroom, entrance hall, lobby, reception area, vestibule

fracas affray (*Law*), aggro (*Sl.*), brawl, disturbance, donnybrook, fight, free-for-all (*Inf.*), melee, quarrel, riot, row, rumpus, scrimmage, scuffle, trouble, uproar

fractious awkward, captious, crabby, cross, fretful, froward, grouchy (*Inf.*), irritable, peevish, pettish, petulant, querulous, recalcitrant, refractory, testy, touchy, unruly

fracture 1. *n.* breach, break, cleft, crack, fissure, gap, opening, rent, rift, rupture, schism, split 2. *v.* break, crack, rupture, splinter, split

fragile breakable, brittle, dainty, delicate, feeble, fine, flimsy, frail, frangible, infirm, slight, weak

fragment 1. *n.* bit, chip, fraction, morsel, part, particle, piece, portion, remnant, scrap, shiver, sliver 2. *v.* break, break up, come apart, come to pieces, crumble, disintegrate, disunite, divide, shatter, shiver, splinter, split, split up

fragmentary bitty, broken, disconnected, discrete, disjointed, incoherent, incomplete, partial, piecemeal, scattered, scrappy, sketchy, unsystematic

fragrance aroma, balm, bouquet, fragrancy, perfume, redolence, scent, smell, sweet odour

fragrant ambrosial, aromatic, balmy, odoriferous, odorous, perfumed, redolent, sweet-scented, sweet-smelling

frail breakable, brittle, decrepit, delicate, feeble, flimsy, fragile, frangible, infirm, insubstantial, puny, slight, tender, unsound, vulnerable, weak, wispy

frailty 1. feebleness, frailness, infirmity, puniness, susceptibility, weakness 2. blemish, defect, deficiency, failing, fault, flaw, foible, imperfection, peccadillo, shortcoming, vice, weak point

frame *v.* 1. assemble, build, constitute, construct, fabricate, fashion, forge, form, institute, invent, make, manufacture, model, mould, put together, set up 2. case, enclose, mount, surround ~*n.* 3. casing, construction, fabric, form, framework, scheme, shell, structure, system 4. anatomy, body, build, carcass, morphology, physique, skeleton 5. mount, mounting, setting

frame-up fabrication, fit-up (*Sl.*), put-up job, trumped-up charge

framework core, fabric, foundation, frame, frame of reference, groundwork, plan, schema, shell, skeleton, structure, the bare bones

franchise authorization, charter, exemption, freedom, immunity, prerogative, privilege, right, suffrage, vote

official mark on letter either cancelling stamp or ensuring delivery without stamp —*vt.* **4.** mark letter thus —**ˈfrankly** *adv.* candidly —**ˈfrankness** *n.* —**franking machine** machine that prints marks on letters *etc.* indicating that postage has been paid

Frank (fræŋk) *n.* member of group of W Germanic peoples who gradually conquered most of Gaul and Germany in late 4th century A.D.—**ˈFrankish** *n.* **1.** ancient W Germanic language of Franks —*a.* **2.** of Franks or their language

Frankenstein's monster (ˈfræŋkɪnstaɪnz) creation or monster that brings disaster and is beyond the control of its creator

frankfurter (ˈfræŋkfɜːtə) *n.* smoked sausage

frankincense (ˈfræŋkɪnsɛns) *n.* aromatic gum resin burned as incense

frantic (ˈfræntɪk) *a.* **1.** distracted with rage, grief, joy *etc.* **2.** frenzied —**ˈfrantically** *adv.*

frappé (ˈfræpeɪ) *n.* **1.** drink consisting of liqueur *etc.* poured over crushed ice —*a.* **2.** (*esp.* of drinks) chilled

fraternal (frəˈtɜːnᵊl) *a.* of brother; brotherly —**fraˈternally** *adv.* —**fraˈternity** *n.* **1.** brotherliness **2.** brotherhood **3.** US college society —**fraterniˈzation** *or* **-niˈsation** *n.* —**ˈfraternize** *or* **-nise** *vi.* associate, make friends —**fratriˈcidal** *a.* —**ˈfratricide** *n.* killing, killer of brother or sister

Frau (fraʊ) *n.* married German woman: usu. used as title equivalent to *Mrs.* (*pl.* **Frauen** (ˈfraʊən), **-s**)

fraud (frɔːd) *n.* **1.** criminal deception **2.** swindle, imposture **3.** *inf.* person who acts in false or deceitful way —**ˈfraudulence** *n.* —**ˈfraudulent** *a.*

fraught (frɔːt) *a.* —**fraught with** filled with, involving

Fräulein (*Ger.* ˈfrɔɪlaɪn) *n.* unmarried German woman: oft. used as title equivalent to *Miss* (*pl.* **-lein** *or English* **-s**)

fray[1] (freɪ) *n.* **1.** fight **2.** noisy quarrel

fray[2] (freɪ) *v.* **1.** wear through by rubbing **2.** make, become ragged at edge

frazil (ˈfreɪzɪl) *n.* C broken spikes of ice formed in turbulent water

frazzle (ˈfræzᵊl) *inf. v.* **1.** make or become exhausted **2.** make or become irritated —*n.* **3.** exhausted state

freak (friːk) *n.* **1.** abnormal person, animal, thing —*a.* **2.** oddly different from what is normal —**ˈfreakish** *or* (*inf.*) **ˈfreaky** *a.* —**freak out** *inf.* (cause to) hallucinate, be wildly excited *etc.*

freckle (ˈfrɛkᵊl) *n.* **1.** light brown spot on skin, *esp.* caused by sun **2.** any small spot —*v.* **3.** mark or become marked in freckles —**ˈfreckled** *a.*

free (friː) *a.* **1.** able to act at will, not under compulsion or restraint **2.** (*with* from) not restricted or affected by **3.** not subject to cost or tax **4.** independent **5.** not exact or literal **6.** generous **7.** not in use **8.** (of person) not occupied, having no engagement **9.** loose, not fixed —*vt.* **10.** set at liberty **11.** (*with* of *or* from) remove (obstacles, pain *etc.*), rid (of) (**freed**, **ˈfreeing**) —**ˈfreebie** *n. sl.* something provided without charge —**ˈfreedom** *n.* —**ˈfreely** *adv.* —**ˈfreeboard** *n.* space between deck of vessel and waterline —**Free Church** *chiefly* UK any Protestant Church, *esp.* Presbyterian, other than Established Church —**free enterprise** economic system in which commercial organizations compete for profit with little state control —**free flight** flight of rocket *etc.* when engine has ceased to produce thrust —**free-for-all** *n.* brawl —**ˈfreehand** *a.* drawn without guiding instruments —**ˈfreehold** *n.* **1.** tenure of land without obligation of service or rent **2.** land so held —**free house** public house not bound to sell only one brewer's products —**free kick** *Soccer* place kick awarded for foul or infringement —**ˈfreelance** *a./n.* **1.** (of) self-employed, unattached person —*vi.* **2.** work as freelance —*adv.* **3.** as freelance —**free-living** *a.* **1.** given to indulgence of appetites **2.** (of animals *etc.*) not parasitic —**free love** practice of sexual relationships without fidelity to single partner —**ˈFreemason** *n.* member of secret fraternity for mutual help —**free-range** *a.* kept, produced in natural, nonintensive conditions —**free speech** right to express opinions publicly —**freeˈstanding** *a.* not attached to or supported by another object —**ˈfreestyle** *n.* **1.** race, as in swimming, in which each participant may use style of his or her choice **2.** style of professional wrestling with no internationally agreed set of rules (*also* **all-in wrestling**)

THESAURUS

frank artless, blunt, candid, direct, downright, forthright, free, honest, ingenuous, open, outright, outspoken, plain, plain-spoken, sincere, straightforward, straight from the shoulder (*Inf.*), transparent, truthful, unconcealed, undisguised, unreserved, unrestricted

frankly 1. candidly, honestly, in truth, to be honest **2.** bluntly, directly, freely, openly, plainly, straight (*Inf.*), without reserve

frankness absence of reserve, bluntness, candour, forthrightness, ingenuousness, openness, outspokenness, plain speaking, truthfulness

frantic at one's wits' end, berserk, beside oneself, distracted, distraught, fraught (*Inf.*), frenetic, frenzied, furious, hectic, mad, overwrought, raging, raving, wild

fraternity association, brotherhood, camaraderie, circle, clan, club, companionship, company, comradeship, fellowship, guild, kinship, league, set, sodality, union

fraternize associate, concur, consort, cooperate, go around with, hang out (*Inf.*), hobnob, keep company, mingle, mix, socialize, sympathize, unite

fraud 1. artifice, cheat, chicane, chicanery, craft, deceit, deception, double-dealing, duplicity, guile, hoax, humbug, imposture, sharp practice, spuriousness, stratagems, swindling, treachery, trickery **2.** bluffer, charlatan, cheat, counterfeit, double-dealer, fake, forgery, hoax, hoaxer, impostor, mountebank, phoney (*Inf.*), pretender, quack, sham, swindler

fraudulent counterfeit, crafty, criminal, crooked (*Inf.*), deceitful, deceptive, dishonest, double-dealing, duplicitous, false, knavish, phoney (*Inf.*), sham, spurious, swindling, treacherous

fray *v.* become threadbare, chafe, fret, rub, wear, wear away, wear thin

freak 1. *n.* aberration, abnormality, abortion, anomaly, grotesque, malformation, monster, monstrosity, mutant, oddity, queer fish (*Inf.*), *rara avis*, sport, teratism, weirdo *or* weirdie (*Inf.*) **2.** *adj.* aberrant, abnormal, atypical, bizarre, erratic, exceptional, fluky (*Inf.*), fortuitous, odd, queer, unaccountable, unexpected, unforeseen, unparalleled, unpredictable, unusual

—free'thinker *n.* sceptic who forms his own opinions, *esp.* in religion —**free trade** international trade free of protective tariffs —**free verse** unrhymed verse without metrical pattern —'**freeway** *n.* **US** major road —**free'wheel** *n.* **1.** device in rear hub of bicycle wheel that permits wheel to rotate while pedals are stationary —*vi.* **2.** coast —**free will 1.** apparent human ability to make choices not externally determined **2.** doctrine that human beings have such freedom of choice **3.** ability to make choice without coercion —**free-will** *a.* voluntary; spontaneous —**free and easy** casual, tolerant; easy-going —**free on board** (of shipment of goods) delivered on board ship *etc.* without charge to buyer —**International freestyle** amateur style of wrestling with agreed set of rules —**the Free World** non-Communist countries collectively

freesia ('friːzɪə) *n.* plant with fragrant, tubular flowers

freeze (friːz) *v.* **1.** change (by reduction of temperature) from liquid to solid, as water to ice —*vt.* **2.** preserve (food *etc.*) by extreme cold, as in freezer **3.** fix (prices *etc.*) —*vi.* **4.** feel very cold **5.** become rigid as with fear **6.** stop (**froze, 'frozen, 'freezing**) —'**freezer** *n.* insulated cabinet for long-term storage of perishable foodstuffs —**frozen** ('frəʊzⁿn) *a.* (of credits *etc.*) unrealizable —**freeze-dry** *vt.* preserve (substance) by rapid freezing and subsequently drying in vacuum —**freezing point** temperature at which liquid becomes solid

freight (freɪt) *n.* **1.** commercial transport (*esp.* by railway, ship) **2.** cost of this **3.** goods so carried —*vt.* **4.** send as or by freight —'**freightage** *n.* money paid for freight —'**freighter** *n.* —'**freightliner** *n.* goods train, lorry carrying containers

French (frɛntʃ) *n.* **1.** language spoken by people of France —*a.* **2.** of France —**French bread** crisp white bread in long slender loaf —**French Canadian** Canadian citizen whose native language is French —**French-Canadian** *a.* of French Canadians —**French chalk** variety of talc used to mark cloth or remove grease stains —**French dressing** salad dressing —**French fried potatoes** chips (*also* (US) **French fries**) —**French horn** musical wind instrument —**French knickers** women's underpants with wide legs —**French leave** unauthorized leave —**French letter UK** *sl.* condom —**French polish** varnish for wood made from shellac dissolved in alcohol —**French window** window extended to floor level and used as door

frenetic (frɪ'nɛtɪk) *a.* frenzied

frenzy ('frɛnzɪ) *n.* **1.** violent mental derangement **2.** wild excitement —'**frenzied** *a.*

frequent ('friːkwənt) *a.* **1.** happening often **2.** common **3.** numerous —*vt.* (frɪ'kwɛnt) **4.** go often to —'**frequency** *n.* **1.** rate of occurrence **2.** in radio *etc.*, cycles per second of alternating current —**fre'quentative** *a.* expressing repetition —'**frequently** *adv.* —**frequency modulation** *Rad.* method of transmitting information in which frequency of carrier wave is varied

THESAURUS

free *adj.* **1.** complimentary, for free (*Inf.*), for nothing, free of charge, gratis, gratuitous, on the house, unpaid, without charge **2.** at large, at liberty, footloose, independent, liberated, loose, off the hook (*Inf.*), on the loose, uncommitted, unconstrained, unengaged, unfettered, unrestrained **3.** able, allowed, clear, disengaged, loose, open, permitted, unattached, unengaged, unhampered, unimpeded, unobstructed, unregulated, unrestricted, untrammelled **4.** autarchic, autonomous, democratic, emancipated, independent, self-governing, self-ruling, sovereign **5.** at leisure, available, empty, extra, idle, not tied down, spare, unemployed, uninhabited, unoccupied, unused, vacant **6.** big (*Inf.*), bounteous, bountiful, charitable, eager, generous, hospitable, lavish, liberal, munificent, open-handed, prodigal, unsparing, unstinting, willing **7. free and easy** casual, easy-going, informal, laid-back (*Inf.*), lax, lenient, liberal, relaxed, tolerant, unceremonious ~*v.* **8.** deliver, discharge, disenthrall, emancipate, let go, let out, liberate, loose, manumit, release, set at liberty, set free, turn loose, uncage, unchain, unfetter, unleash, untie **9.** clear, cut loose, deliver, disengage, disentangle, exempt, extricate, ransom, redeem, relieve, rescue, rid, unburden, undo, unshackle

freedom 1. autonomy, deliverance, emancipation, home rule, independence, liberty, manumission, release, self-government **2.** ability, carte blanche, discretion, elbowroom, facility, flexibility, free rein, latitude, leeway, licence, opportunity, play, power, range, scope

free-for-all affray (*Law*), brawl, donnybrook, dust-up (*Inf.*), fight, fracas, melee, riot, row, shindy (*Sl.*)

freely 1. of one's own accord, of one's own free will, spontaneously, voluntarily, willingly, without prompting **2.** as you please, unchallenged, without let or hindrance, without restraint **3.** abundantly, amply, bountifully, copiously, extravagantly, lavishly, liberally, like water, open-handedly, unstintingly, with a free hand **4.** cleanly, easily, loosely, readily, smoothly

freethinker agnostic, deist, doubter, infidel, sceptic, unbeliever

freeze 1. benumb, chill, congeal, glaciate, harden, ice over *or* up, stiffen **2.** fix, hold up, inhibit, peg, stop, suspend

freezing arctic, biting, bitter, chill, chilled, cutting, frost-bound, frosty, glacial, icy, numbing, penetrating, polar, raw, Siberian, wintry

freight *n.* **1.** carriage, conveyance, shipment, transportation **2.** bales, bulk, burden, cargo, consignment, contents, goods, haul, lading, load, merchandise, payload, tonnage

frenzied agitated, all het up (*Inf.*), convulsive, distracted, distraught, excited, feverish, frantic, frenetic, furious, hysterical, mad, maniacal, rabid, uncontrolled, wild

frenzy aberration, agitation, delirium, derangement, distraction, fury, hysteria, insanity, lunacy, madness, mania, paroxysm, passion, rage, seizure, transport, turmoil

frequency constancy, frequentness, periodicity, prevalence, recurrence, repetition

frequent 1. *adj.* common, constant, continual, customary, everyday, familiar, habitual, incessant, numerous, persistent, recurrent, recurring, reiterated, repeated, usual **2.** *v.* attend, be a regular customer of, be found at, hang out at (*Inf.*), haunt, patronize, resort, visit

frequently commonly, customarily, habitually, many a time, many times, much, not infrequently, oft

fresco (ˈfrɛskəʊ) *n.* **1.** method of painting in water-colour on plaster of wall before it dries **2.** painting done thus (*pl.* **-es, -s**)

fresh (frɛʃ) *a.* **1.** not stale **2.** new **3.** additional **4.** different **5.** recent **6.** inexperienced **7.** pure **8.** not pickled, frozen *etc.* **9.** not faded or dimmed **10.** not tired **11.** (of wind) strong **12.** *inf.* impudent **13.** *inf.* arrogant —ˈ**freshen** *v.* —ˈ**freshet** *n.* **1.** rush of water at river mouth **2.** flood of river water —ˈ**freshly** *adv.* —ˈ**freshman** *or* ˈ**fresher** *n.* first-year student —ˈ**freshness** *n.* —ˈ**freshwater** *a.* **1.** of or living in fresh water **2.** (*esp.* of sailor who has not sailed on sea) inexperienced **3. US** little known

fret[1] (frɛt) *v.* **1.** irritate or be irritated **2** worry (**-tt-**) —*n.* **3.** irritation —ˈ**fretful** *a.* irritable, (easily) upset

fret[2] (frɛt) *n.* **1.** repetitive geometrical pattern **2.** small bar on fingerboard of guitar *etc.* —*vt.* **3.** ornament with carved pattern (**-tt-**) —**fret saw** saw with narrow blade and fine teeth, used for fretwork —ˈ**fretwork** *n.* carved or open woodwork in ornamental patterns and devices

Freudian (ˈfrɔɪdɪən) *a.* pert. to Austrian psychologist Sigmund Freud, or his theories —**Freudian slip** any action, such as slip of tongue, that may reveal unconscious thought

Fri. Friday

friable (ˈfraɪəbᵊl) *a.* easily crumbled —**friaˈbility** *or* ˈ**friableness** *n.*

friar (ˈfraɪə) *n.* member of mendicant religious order —ˈ**friary** *n.* house of friars —**friar's balsam** compound containing benzoin, used as inhalant

fricassee (frɪkəˈsiː, ˈfrɪkəsɪ) *n.* **1.** dish of pieces of chicken or meat, fried or stewed and served with rich sauce —*vt.* **2.** cook thus

fricative (ˈfrɪkətɪv) *n.* **1.** consonant produced by partial occlusion of air stream, such as (f) or (z) —*a.* **2.** relating to fricative

friction (ˈfrɪkʃən) *n.* **1.** rubbing **2.** resistance met with by body moving over another **3.** clash of wills *etc.*, disagreement —ˈ**frictional** *a.*

Friday (ˈfraɪdɪ) *n.* sixth day of week —**Good Friday** the Friday before Easter

fridge (frɪdʒ) *inf.* refrigerator

fried (fraɪd) *pt./pp. of* FRY[1]

friend (frɛnd) *n.* **1.** one well known to another and regarded with affection and loyalty **2.** intimate associate **3.** supporter **4.** (**F-**) Quaker —ˈ**friendless** *a.* —ˈ**friendliness** *n.* —ˈ**friendly** *a.* **1.** having disposition of a friend, kind **2.** favourable —ˈ**friendship** *n.* —**friendly society UK** association of people who pay regular dues in return for sickness benefits *etc.* —**Friends of the Earth** organization of environmentalists and conservationists

frier (ˈfraɪə) *n. see* **fryer** *at* FRY[1]

frieze[1] (friːz) *n.* ornamental band, strip (on wall)

frieze[2] (friːz) *n.* kind of coarse woollen cloth

frigate (ˈfrɪgɪt) *n.* **1.** old (sailing) warship corresponding to modern cruiser **2.** fast destroyerlike warship

THESAURUS

(*Literary*), often, oftentimes (*Archaic*), over and over again, repeatedly, thick and fast, very often

fresh 1. different, latest, modern, modernistic, new, new-fangled, novel, original, recent, this season's, unconventional, unusual, up-to-date **2.** added, additional, auxiliary, extra, further, more, other, renewed, supplementary **3.** bracing, bright, brisk, clean, clear, cool, crisp, invigorating, pure, refreshing, spanking, sparkling, stiff, sweet, unpolluted **4.** alert, bouncing, bright, bright eyed and bushy tailed (*Inf.*), chipper (*Inf., chiefly U.S.*), energetic, full of vim and vigour (*Inf.*), invigorated, keen, like a new man, lively, refreshed, rested, restored, revived, sprightly, spry, vigorous, vital **5.** dewy, undimmed, unfaded, unwearied, unwithered, verdant, vivid, young **6.** artless, callow, green, inexperienced, natural, new, raw, uncultivated, untrained, untried, youthful **7.** crude, green, natural, raw, uncured, undried, unprocessed, unsalted **8.** *Inf.* bold, brazen, cheeky, disrespectful, familiar, flip (*Inf., chiefly U.S.*), forward, impudent, insolent, pert, presumptuous, saucy, smart-alecky (*Inf.*)

freshen enliven, freshen up, liven up, refresh, restore, revitalize, rouse, spruce up, titivate

freshness innovativeness, inventiveness, newness, novelty, originality

fret 1. affront, agonize, anguish, annoy, brood, chagrin, goad, grieve, harass, irritate, lose sleep over, provoke, ruffle, torment, upset *or* distress oneself, worry **2.** agitate, bother, distress, disturb, gall, irk, nag, nettle, peeve (*Inf.*), pique, rankle with, rile, trouble, vex

fretful captious, complaining, cross, crotchety (*Inf.*), edgy, fractious, irritable, out of sorts, peevish, petulant, querulous, short-tempered, splenetic, testy, touchy, uneasy

friction 1. abrasion, attrition, chafing, erosion, fretting, grating, irritation, rasping, resistance, rubbing scraping, wearing away **2.** animosity, antagonism bad blood, bad feeling, bickering, conflict, disagreement, discontent, discord, disharmony, dispute, dissension, hostility, incompatibility, opposition, resentment, rivalry, wrangling

friend 1. Achates, alter ego, boon companion, bosom friend, buddy (*Inf.*), china (*Sl.*), chum (*Inf.*), companion, comrade, confidant, crony, familiar, intimate, mate (*Inf.*), pal, partner, playmate, soul mat **2.** adherent, advocate, ally, associate, backer, benefactor, partisan, patron, supporter, well-wisher

friendless abandoned, alienated, all alone, alone, cu off, deserted, estranged, forlorn, forsaken, isolatec lonely, lonesome, ostracized, shunned, solitary, un attached, with no one to turn to, without a friend i the world, without ties

friendliness affability, amiability, companionabilit congeniality, conviviality, geniality, kindlines mateyness (*Brit. inf.*), neighbourliness, open arm sociability, warmth

friendly affable, affectionate, amiable, amicable, a tached, attentive, auspicious, beneficial, benevolen benign, chummy (*Inf.*), close, clubby, companion able, comradely, conciliatory, confiding, convivia cordial, familiar, favourable, fond, fraternal, genia good, helpful, intimate, kind, kindly, matey (*Br inf.*), neighbourly, on good terms, on visiting term outgoing, peaceable, propitious, receptive, sociab sympathetic, thick (*Inf.*), welcoming, well-disposed

friendship affection, affinity, alliance, amity, attac ment, benevolence, closeness, concord, familiari fondness, friendliness, good-fellowship, good wi harmony, intimacy, love, rapport, regard

equipped for escort and antisubmarine duties —**frigate bird** bird of tropical and subtropical seas, with wide wingspan

fright (fraɪt) *n.* 1. sudden fear 2. shock 3. alarm 4. grotesque or ludicrous person or thing —*vt.* 5. *obs.* frighten —**ˈfrighten** *vt.* cause fear, fright in —**ˈfrightful** *a.* 1. terrible, calamitous 2. shocking 3. *inf.* very great, very large —**ˈfrightfully** *adv. inf.* 1. terribly 2. very —**ˈfrightfulness** *n.*

frigid (ˈfrɪdʒɪd) *a.* 1. formal, dull 2. (sexually) unfeeling 3. cold —**friˈgidity** *n.* —**ˈfrigidly** *adv.* —**Frigid Zone** cold region inside Arctic or Antarctic Circle where sun's rays are very oblique

frill (frɪl) *n.* 1. fluted strip of fabric gathered at one edge 2. ruff of hair, feathers around neck of dog, bird *etc.* 3. fringe 4. (*oft. pl.*) unnecessary words, politeness; superfluous thing; adornment —*vt.* 5. make into, decorate with frill

fringe (frɪndʒ) *n.* 1. ornamental edge of hanging threads, tassels *etc.* 2. anything like this 3. hair cut in front and falling over brow 4. edge, limit —*vt.* 5. adorn with fringe 6. be fringe for —*a.* 7. (of theatre *etc.*) unofficial, unconventional, extra —**fringe benefit** benefit provided by employer to supplement employee's regular pay

frippery (ˈfrɪpərɪ) *n.* 1. finery 2. trivia

Frisbee (ˈfrɪzbiː) *n.* **R** plastic disc thrown with spinning motion for recreation

Frisian (ˈfrɪʒən) *or* **Friesian** (ˈfriːʒən) *n.* 1. language spoken in NW Netherlands and adjacent islands 2. speaker of this language —*a.* 3. of this language or its speakers

frisk (frɪsk) *vi.* 1. move, leap playfully —*vt.* 2. wave briskly 3. *inf.* search (person) for concealed weapons *etc.* —*n.* 4. playful antic or movement 5. *inf.* instance of frisking a person —**ˈfriskily** *adv.* —**ˈfrisky** *a.*

fritillary (frɪˈtɪlərɪ) *n.* plant with purple or white bell-shaped flowers

fritter[1] (ˈfrɪtə) *vt.* (*usu. with* away) waste

fritter[2] (ˈfrɪtə) *n.* piece of food fried in batter

frivolous (ˈfrɪvələs) *a.* 1. not serious, flippant 2. unimportant —**friˈvolity** *n.*

frizz (frɪz) *vt.* 1. crisp, curl into small curls —*n.* 2. frizzed hair —**ˈfrizzy** *a.* crimped

frizzle (ˈfrɪzᵊl) *v.* fry, toast or grill with sizzling sound

fro (frəʊ) *adv.* away, from (*only in* **to and fro**)

frock (frɒk) *n.* 1. woman's dress 2. various similar garments —*vt.* 3. invest with office of priest —**frock coat** man's double-breasted skirted coat, as worn in 19th century

frog[1] (frɒg) *n.* tailless amphibious animal developed from tadpole —**ˈfrogman** *n.* swimmer equipped for swimming, working underwater —**ˈfrogmarch** *n.* any method of moving person against his will

frog[2] (frɒg) *n.* 1. military-style coat fastening of button and loop 2. attachment to belt to carry sword

frolic (ˈfrɒlɪk) *n.* 1. merrymaking —*vi.* 2. behave playfully (**ˈfrolicked, ˈfrolicking**) —**ˈfrolicsome** *a.*

from (frɒm; *unstressed* frəm) *prep.* expressing point

THESAURUS

fright 1. alarm, apprehension, (blue) funk (*Inf.*), cold sweat, consternation, dismay, dread, fear, fear and trembling, horror, panic, quaking, scare, shock, terror, the shivers, trepidation 2. *Inf.* eyesore, frump, mess (*Inf.*), scarecrow, sight (*Inf.*)

frighten affright (*Archaic*), alarm, appal, cow, daunt, dismay, freeze one's blood, intimidate, make one's blood run cold, make one's hair stand on end (*Inf.*), make (someone) jump out of his skin (*Inf.*), petrify, put the wind up (someone) (*Inf.*), scare, scare (someone) stiff, scare the living daylights out of (someone) (*Inf.*), shock, startle, terrify, terrorize, throw into a fright, throw into a panic, unman, unnerve

frightful 1. alarming, appalling, awful, dire, dread, dreadful, fearful, ghastly, grim, grisly, gruesome, harrowing, hideous, horrendous, horrible, horrid, lurid, macabre, petrifying, shocking, terrible, terrifying, traumatic, unnerving, unspeakable 2. annoying, awful, disagreeable, dreadful, extreme, great, insufferable, terrible, terrific, unpleasant

frigid 1. arctic, chill, cold, cool, frost-bound, frosty, frozen, gelid, glacial, hyperboreal, icy, Siberian, wintry 2. aloof, austere, cold-hearted, forbidding, formal, icy, lifeless, passionless, passive, repellent, rigid, stiff, unapproachable, unbending, unfeeling, unloving, unresponsive

frigidity aloofness, austerity, chill, cold-heartedness, coldness, frostiness, iciness, impassivity, lack of response, lifelessness, passivity, touch-me-not attitude, unapproachability, unresponsiveness, wintriness

fringe *n.* 1. binding, border, edging, hem, tassel, trimming 2. borderline, edge, limits, march, marches, margin, outskirts, perimeter, periphery ~*adj.* 3. unconventional, unofficial, unorthodox ~*v.* 4. border, edge, enclose, skirt, surround, trim

frisk 1. bounce, caper, cavort, curvet, dance, frolic, gambol, hop, jump, play, prance, rollick, romp, skip, sport, trip 2. *Inf.* check, inspect, run over, search, shake down (*U.S. sl.*)

frisky bouncy, coltish, frolicsome, full of beans (*Inf.*), full of joie de vivre, high-spirited, in high spirits, kittenish, lively, playful, rollicking, romping, spirited, sportive

fritter (away) dally away, dissipate, fool away, idle (away), misspend, run through, spend like water, squander, waste

frivolity childishness, flightiness, flippancy, flummery, folly, frivolousness, fun, gaiety, giddiness, jest, levity, light-heartedness, lightness, nonsense, puerility, shallowness, silliness, superficiality, trifling, triviality

frivolous 1. childish, dizzy, empty-headed, flighty, flip (*Inf.*), flippant, foolish, giddy, idle, ill-considered, juvenile, light-minded, nonserious, puerile, silly, superficial 2. impractical, light, minor, niggling, paltry, peripheral, petty, pointless, shallow, trifling, trivial, unimportant

frizzle crisp, fry, hiss, roast, scorch, sizzle, sputter

frolic *v.* 1. caper, cavort, cut capers, frisk, gambol, lark, make merry, play, rollick, romp, sport ~*n.* 2. antic, escapade, gambado, gambol, game, lark, prank, revel, romp, spree 3. amusement, drollery, fun, fun and games, gaiety, high jinks, merriment, skylarking (*Inf.*), sport

frolicsome coltish, frisky, gay, kittenish, lively, merry, playful, rollicking, sportive, sprightly, wanton (*Archaic*)

of departure, source, distance, cause, change of state *etc.*

frond (frɒnd) *n.* plant organ consisting of stem and foliage, usually with fruit forms, *esp.* in ferns

front (frʌnt) *n.* 1. fore part 2. position directly before or ahead 3. seaside promenade 4. battle line or area 5. *Met.* dividing line between two air masses of different characteristics 6. outward aspect, bearing 7. *inf.* something serving as a respectable cover for another, *usu.* criminal activity 8. field of activity 9. group with common goal —*v.* 10. look, face (on to) —*vt.* 11. *inf.* be a cover for —*a.* 12. of, at the front —**ˈfrontage** *n.* 1. façade of building 2. extent of front —**ˈfrontal** *a.* —**ˈfrontier** *n.* part of country which borders on another —**front bench** 1. UK foremost bench of either Government or Opposition in House of Commons 2. leadership (**frontbenchers**) of either group, who occupy this bench 3. leadership of government or opposition in various legislative assemblies —**ˈfrontispiece** *n.* illustration facing title page of book —**ˈfrontrunner** *n. inf.* leader in race *etc.*

frost (frɒst) *n.* 1. frozen dew or mist 2. act or state of freezing 3. weather in which temperature falls below point at which water turns to ice —*v.* 4. cover, be covered with frost or something similar in appearance —*vt.* 5. give slightly roughened surface to —**ˈfrostily** *adv.* —**ˈfrosting** *n.* 1. *esp.* US icing 2. rough or matt finish on glass *etc.* —**ˈfrosty** *a.* 1. accompanied by frost 2. chilly, cold 3. unfriendly —**ˈfrostbite** *n.* destruction by cold of tissue, *esp.* of fingers, ears *etc.*

froth (frɒθ) *n.* 1. collection of small bubbles, foam 2. scum 3. idle talk —*v.* 4. (cause to) foam —**ˈfrothily** *adv.* —**ˈfrothy** *a.*

froward (ˈfrəuəd) *a.* obstinate; contrary

frown (fraun) *vi.* 1. wrinkle brows —*n.* 2. act of frowning 3. show of dislike or displeasure

frowsty (ˈfraustɪ) *a.* stale, musty

frowzy *or* **frowsy** (ˈfrauzɪ) *a.* 1. dirty 2. unkempt

froze (frəuz) *pt. of* FREEZE —**ˈfrozen** *pp. of* FREEZE

F.R.S. Fellow of the Royal Society

fructify (ˈfrʌktɪfaɪ) *v.* (cause to) bear fruit (**ˈfructified, ˈfructifying**) —**fructifiˈcation** *n.*

fructose (ˈfrʌktəus) *n.* crystalline sugar occurring in many fruits

frugal (ˈfru:gˀl) *a.* 1. sparing, thrifty, economical 2. meagre —**fruˈgality** *n.* —**ˈfrugally** *adv.*

fruit (fru:t) *n.* 1. seed and its envelope, *esp.* edible one 2. vegetable products 3. (*usu. in pl.*) result, benefit —*vi.* 4. bear fruit —**ˈfruiterer** *n.* dealer in fruit —**ˈfruitful** *a.* 1. bearing fruit in abundance 2. productive, prolific 3. producing results or profits —**fruition** (fru:ˈɪʃən) *n.* 1. enjoyment 2. realization of hopes —**ˈfruitless** *a.* 1. unproductive 2. without fruit —**ˈfruity** *a.* 1. of or resembling fruit 2. (of voice) mellow, rich 3. *inf., chiefly* UK erotically stimulating; salacious —**fruit machine** gambling machine operated by coins

frump (frʌmp) *n.* dowdy woman —**ˈfrumpish** *or* **ˈfrumpy** *a.*

frustrate (frʌˈstreɪt) *vt.* 1. thwart, balk 2. disappoint —**frusˈtration** *n.*

frustum (ˈfrʌstəm) *n. Geom.* 1. part of cone or pyramid contained between base and plane parallel to base that intersects solid 2. part of such solid contained between two parallel planes intersecting solid (*pl.* **-s, -ta** (-tə))

fry[1] (fraɪ) *vt.* 1. cook with fat —*vi.* 2. be cooked thus (**fried, ˈfrying**) —*n.* 3. fried meat 4. dish of anything

THESAURUS

front *n.* **1.** anterior, exterior, façade, face, facing, foreground, forepart, frontage, obverse **2.** beginning, fore, forefront, front line, head, lead, top, van, vanguard **3.** air, appearance, aspect, bearing, countenance, demeanour, expression, exterior, face, manner, mien, show **4.** blind, cover, cover-up, disguise, façade, mask, pretext, show ~*adj.* **5.** first, foremost, head, headmost, lead, leading, topmost ~*v.* **6.** face (onto), look over *or* onto, overlook

frontier borderland, borderline, bound, boundary, confines, edge, limit, marches, perimeter, verge

frost freeze, freeze-up, hoarfrost, Jack Frost, rime

frosty **1.** chilly, cold, frozen, hoar (*Rare*), ice-capped, icicled, icy, rimy, wintry **2.** discouraging, frigid, off-putting, standoffish, unenthusiastic, unfriendly, unwelcoming

froth **1.** *n.* bubbles, effervescence, foam, head, lather, scum, spume, suds **2.** *v.* bubble over, come to a head, effervesce, fizz, foam, lather

frothy foaming, foamy, spumescent, spumous, spumy, sudsy

frown give a dirty look, glare, glower, knit one's brows, look daggers, lower, scowl

frowsty close, fuggy, fusty, ill-smelling, musty, stale, stuffy

frozen **1.** arctic, chilled, chilled to the marrow, frigid, frosted, icebound, ice-cold, ice-covered, icy, numb **2.** fixed, pegged (*of prices*), petrified, rooted, stock-still, stopped, suspended, turned to stone

frugal abstemious, careful, cheeseparing, economical, meagre, niggardly, parsimonious, penny-wise, provident, prudent, saving, sparing, thrifty

fruit **1.** crop, harvest, produce, product, yield **2.** advantage, benefit, consequence, effect, outcome, profit, result, return, reward

fruitful **1.** fecund, fertile, fructiferous **2.** abundant, copious, flush, plenteous, plentiful, productive, profuse, prolific, rich, spawning **3.** advantageous, beneficial, effective, gainful, productive, profitable, rewarding, successful, useful, well-spent, worthwhile

fruition actualization, attainment, completion, consummation, enjoyment, fulfilment, materialization, maturation, maturity, perfection, realization, ripeness

fruitless abortive, barren, bootless, futile, idle, ineffectual, in vain, pointless, profitless, to no avail, to no effect, unavailing, unfruitful, unproductive, unprofitable, unprolific, unsuccessful, useless, vain

fruity **1.** full, mellow, resonant, rich **2.** *Inf.* bawdy, blue, hot, indecent, indelicate, juicy, near the knuckle (*Inf.*), racy, ripe, risqué, salacious, sexy, smutty, spicy (*Inf.*), suggestive, titillating, vulgar

frustrate baffle, balk, block, check, circumvent, confront, counter, defeat, disappoint, foil, forestall, inhibit, neutralize, nullify, render null and void, stymie, thwart

frustration **1.** blocking, circumvention, contravention, curbing, failure, foiling, nonfulfilment, nonsuccess, obstruction, thwarting **2.** annoyance, disappointment, dissatisfaction, grievance, irritation, resentment, vexation

fried —ˈ**fryer** *or* ˈ**frier** *n.* 1. one that fries 2. utensil for deep-frying foods —**frying pan** shallow pan for frying —**fry-up** *n.* UK *inf.* 1. act of preparing mixed fried dish 2. dish itself —**out of the frying pan into the fire** from bad situation to worse one

fry[2] (fraɪ) *n.* young fishes —**small fry** young or insignificant beings

f-stop *n.* any of settings for f-number of camera

ft. 1. feet 2. foot 3. fort

fth. *or* **fthm.** fathom

fuchsia (ˈfjuːʃə) *n.* ornamental shrub with purple-red flowers

fuddle (ˈfʌdᵊl) *v.* 1. (cause to) be intoxicated, confused —*n.* 2. this state

fuddy-duddy (ˈfʌdɪdʌdɪ) *n. inf.* (elderly) dull person

fudge[1] (fʌdʒ) *n.* soft, variously flavoured sweet

fudge[2] (fʌdʒ) *vt.* 1. make, do carelessly or dishonestly 2. fake

fuel (fjʊəl) *n.* 1. material for burning as source of heat or power 2. something which nourishes —*vt.* 3. provide with fuel —**fuel cell** cell in which chemical energy is converted directly into electrical energy —**fuel injection** system for introducing fuel directly into combustion chambers of internal-combustion engine without use of carburettor

fug (fʌg) *n.* stuffy indoor atmosphere —ˈ**fuggy** *a.*

fugitive (ˈfjuːdʒɪtɪv) *n.* 1. one who flees, *esp.* from arrest or pursuit —*a.* 2. fleeing, elusive

fugue (fjuːg) *n.* musical composition in which themes are repeated in different parts

Führer *or* ***Fuehrer*** (ˈfyːrər) *n.* leader, title of Ger. dictator, *esp.* Hitler

-ful (*comb. form*) 1. full of; characterized by, as in *painful, restful* 2. able or tending to, as in *useful* 3. as much as will fill thing specified, as in *mouthful*

fulcrum (ˈfʊlkrəm, ˈfʌl-) *n.* point on which lever is placed for support (*pl.* **-cra** (-krə))

fulfil *or U.S.* **fulfill** (fʊlˈfɪl) *vt.* 1. satisfy 2. carry out 3. obey (**-ll-**) —**fulˈfilment** *or U.S.* **fulˈfillment** *n.*

full[1] (fʊl) *a.* 1. containing as much as possible 2. abundant 3. complete 4. ample 5. plump 6. (of garment) of ample cut —*adv.* 7. very 8. quite 9. exactly —ˈ**fully** *adv.* —ˈ**fullness** *or esp. U.S.* ˈ**fulness** *n.* —ˈ**fulsome** *a.* (of praise) excessive —ˈ**fullback** *n. Soccer etc.* defensive player or position held by this player —**full-blooded** *a.* 1. (*esp.* of horses) of unmixed ancestry 2. having great vigour —**full-blown** *a.* 1. characterized by fullest or best development 2. in full bloom —**full-bodied** *a.* having full rich flavour or quality —**full house** 1. *Poker* hand with three cards of same value and another pair 2. theatre *etc.* filled to capacity 3. in bingo *etc.*, set of numbers needed to win —**full-scale** *a.* 1. (of plan *etc.*) of actual size 2. using all resources —**full stop** punctuation mark (.) at end of sentence —**full-time** *a.* for entire time appropriate to activity —**full time** *adv.* 1. on full-time basis —*n.* 2. end of match —**fully fashioned** *a.* (of stockings *etc.*) shaped so as to fit closely —**fully fledged** *or* **full-fledged** *a.* 1. (of bird) having acquired adult feathers and being able to fly 2. completely developed 3. of full rank or status

full[2] (fʊl) *v.* become or make (cloth *etc.*) more compact during manufacture through shrinking and pressing —**fuller's earth** absorbent clay used for clarifying oils and fats, fulling cloth *etc.*

fulmar (ˈfʊlmə) *n.* Arctic sea bird

fulminate (ˈfʌlmɪneɪt) *vi.* 1. (*esp. with* against) criticize harshly —*n.* 2. chemical compound exploding readily —**fulmiˈnation** *n.*

THESAURUS

fuddy-duddy *n.* back number (*Inf.*), conservative, dodo (*Inf.*), fossil, museum piece, (old) fogy, square (*Inf.*), stick-in-the-mud (*Inf.*), stuffed shirt (*Inf.*)

fudge *v.* avoid, cook (*Sl.*), dodge, equivocate, evade, fake, falsify, hedge, misrepresent, patch up, shuffle, slant, stall

fuel 1. *n. Fig.* ammunition, encouragement, fodder, food, incitement, material, means, nourishment, provocation 2. *v.* charge, fan, feed, fire, incite, inflame, nourish, stoke up, sustain

fugitive *n.* deserter, escapee, refugee, runagate (*Archaic*), runaway

fulfil accomplish, achieve, answer, bring to completion, carry out, complete, comply with, conclude, conform to, discharge, effect, execute, fill, finish, keep, meet, obey, observe, perfect, perform, realise, satisfy

fulfilment accomplishment, achievement, attainment, carrying out *or* through, completion, consummation, crowning, discharge, discharging, effecting, end, implementation, observance, perfection, realization

full 1. brimful, brimming, complete, entire, filled, gorged, intact, loaded, replete, sated, satiated, satisfied, saturated, stocked, sufficient 2. abundant, adequate, all-inclusive, ample, broad, comprehensive, copious, detailed, exhaustive, extensive, generous, maximum, plenary, plenteous, plentiful, thorough, unabridged 3. chock-a-block, chock-full, crammed, crowded, in use, jammed, occupied, packed, taken 4. baggy, balloonlike, buxom, capacious, curvaceous, large, loose, plump, puffy, rounded, voluminous, voluptuous

full-blooded gutsy (*Sl.*), hearty, lusty, mettlesome, red-blooded, vigorous, virile

full-bodied fruity, full-flavoured, heady, heavy, mellow, redolent, rich, strong, well-matured

fullness 1. abundance, adequateness, ampleness, copiousness, fill, glut, plenty, profusion, repletion, satiety, saturation, sufficiency 2. broadness, completeness, comprehensiveness, entirety, extensiveness, plenitude, totality, vastness, wealth, wholeness

full-scale all-encompassing, all-out, comprehensive, exhaustive, extensive, full-dress, in-depth, major, proper, sweeping, thorough, thoroughgoing, wide-ranging

fully 1. absolutely, altogether, completely, entirely, every inch, from first to last, heart and soul, in all respects, intimately, perfectly, positively, thoroughly, totally, utterly, wholly 2. abundantly, adequately, amply, comprehensively, enough, plentifully, satisfactorily, sufficiently

fully-fledged experienced, mature, professional, proficient, qualified, senior, time-served, trained

fulmination condemnation, denunciation, diatribe, invective, obloquy, philippic, reprobation, tirade

fulsome adulatory, cloying, excessive, extravagant, fawning, gross, immoderate, ingratiating, inordinate, insincere, nauseating, overdone, saccharine, sickening, smarmy (*Inf.*), sycophantic, unctuous

fulsome ('fulsəm) *a. see* FULL[1]

fumble ('fʌmb'l) *vi.* **1.** grope about —*vt.* **2.** handle awkwardly —*n.* **3.** awkward attempt

fume (fju:m) *vi.* **1.** be angry **2.** emit smoke or vapour —*n.* **3.** (usu. pl.) smoke, vapour —**'fumigate** *vt.* apply fumes or smoke to, *esp.* for disinfection —**fumi'gation** *n.* —**'fumigator** *n.*

fumitory ('fju:mɪtərɪ) *n.* plant with spurred flowers

fun (fʌn) *n.* anything enjoyable, amusing *etc.* —**'funnily** *adv.* —**'funny** *a.* **1.** comical **2.** odd **3.** difficult to explain —**'funfair** *n.* UK amusement park, fairground

function ('fʌŋkʃən) *n.* **1.** work a thing is designed to do **2.** (large) social event **3.** duty **4.** profession **5.** *Maths.* quantity whose value depends on varying value of another —*vi.* **6.** operate, work —**'functional** *a.* **1.** having a special purpose **2.** practical, necessary **3.** capable of operating —**'functionary** *n.* official

fund (fʌnd) *n.* **1.** stock or sum of money **2.** supply, store —*pl.* **3.** money resources —*vt.* **4.** in financial, business dealings, furnish money to in form of fund

fundamental (fʌndə'mɛnt'l) *a.* **1.** of, affecting, or serving as the base **2.** essential, primary —*n.* **3.** basic rule or fact —**'fundament** *n.* **1.** buttocks **2.** foundation —**funda'mentalism** *n.* —**funda'mentalist** *n.* one laying stress on belief in literal and verbal inspiration of Bible and other traditional creeds —**fundamental particle** *see* **elementary particle** *at* ELEMENT

funeral ('fju:nərəl) *n.* (ceremony associated with) burial or cremation of dead —**funereal** (fju:'nɪərɪəl) *a.* **1.** like a funeral **2.** dark **3.** gloomy —**funeral director** undertaker —**funeral parlour** place where dead are prepared for burial or cremation

fungus ('fʌŋgəs) *n.* plant without leaves, flowers or roots, as mushroom, mould (*pl.* **fungi** ('fʌndʒaɪ, 'fʌŋgaɪ), **-es**) —**'fungal** *or* **'fungous** *a.* —**fungicide** ('fʌndʒɪsaɪd) *n.* fungus destroyer —**'fungoid** *a.* resembling fungus

funicular (fju:'nɪkjulə) *n.* cable railway on mountainside with two counterbalanced cars

funk (fʌŋk) *n.* panic (*esp. in* **blue funk**)

funky ('fʌŋkɪ) *a. inf.* (of jazz, pop *etc.*) passionate and soulful, reminiscent of early blues

funnel ('fʌn'l) *n.* **1.** cone-shaped vessel or tube **2.** chimney of locomotive or ship **3.** ventilating shaft —*v.* **4.** (cause to) move as through funnel —*vt.* **5.** concentrate, focus (**-ll-**)

funny ('fʌnɪ) *a. see* FUN —**funny bone** area near elbow where sharp tingling sensation is experienced when struck

fur (fɜ:) *n.* **1.** soft hair of animal **2.** garment *etc.* of dressed skins with such hair **3.** furlike coating —*vt.* **4.** cover with fur (**-rr-**) —**'furrier** *n.* dealer in furs —**'furry** *a.* of, like fur

fur. furlong

furbelow ('fɜ:bɪləʊ) *n.* **1.** flounce, ruffle **2.** (*oft. pl.*) showy ornamentation —*vt.* **3.** put furbelow on (garment *etc.*)

furbish ('fɜ:bɪʃ) *vt.* clean up

furcate ('fɜ:keɪt) *a.* forked, branching

furious ('fjʊərɪəs) *a.* **1.** extremely angry **2.** violent —**'furiously** *adv.* —**'furiousness** *n.*

furl (fɜ:l) *vt.* roll up and bind (sail, umbrella *etc.*)

furlong ('fɜ:lɒŋ) *n.* eighth of mile

THESAURUS

fumble **1.** bumble, feel around, flounder, grope, paw (*Inf.*), scrabble **2.** botch, bungle, make a hash of (*Inf.*), mess up, misfield, mishandle, mismanage, muff, spoil

fume *v. Fig.* boil, chafe, champ at the bit (*Inf.*), get hot under the collar (*Inf.*), get steamed up about (*Sl.*), rage, rant, rave, seethe, smoulder, storm

fumes effluvium, exhalation, exhaust, gas, haze, miasma, pollution, reek, smog, smoke, stench, vapour

fumigate clean out *or* up, cleanse, disinfect, purify, sanitize, sterilize

fun *n.* **1.** amusement, cheer, distraction, diversion, enjoyment, entertainment, frolic, gaiety, good time, high jinks, jollification, jollity, joy, junketing, living it up, merriment, merrymaking, mirth, pleasure, recreation, romp, sport, treat, whoopee (*Inf.*) **2.** buffoonery, clowning, foolery, game, horseplay, jesting, jocularity, joking, nonsense, play, playfulness, skylarking (*Inf.*), sport, teasing, tomfoolery

function *n.* **1.** activity, business, capacity, charge, concern, duty, employment, exercise, job, mission, occupation, office, operation, part, post, province, purpose, raison d'être, responsibility, role, situation, task ~*v.* **2.** act, act the part of, behave, be in commission, be in operation *or* action, be in running order, do duty, go, officiate, operate, perform, run, serve, serve one's turn, work ~*n.* **3.** affair, do (*Inf.*), gathering, reception, social occasion

functional hard-wearing, operative, practical, serviceable, useful, utilitarian, utility, working

fund *n.* **1.** capital, endowment, foundation, kitty, pool, reserve, stock, store, supply **2.** hoard, mine, repository, reserve, reservoir, source, storehouse, treasury, vein ~*v.* **3.** capitalize, endow, finance, float, pay for, promote, stake, subsidize, support

fundamental **1.** *adj.* basic, cardinal, central, constitutional, crucial, elementary, essential, first, important, indispensable, integral, intrinsic, key, necessary, organic, primary, prime, principal, rudimentary, underlying, vital **2.** *n.* axiom, basic, cornerstone, essential, first principle, law, principle, rudiment, rule, *sine qua non*

funds bread (*Sl.*), capital, cash, dough (*Sl.*), finance, hard cash, money, ready money, resources, savings, the ready (*Inf.*), the wherewithal

funeral burial, inhumation, interment, obsequies

funnel *v.* channel, conduct, convey, direct, filter, move, pass, pour

funny **1.** absurd, amusing, a scream (card, caution) (*Inf.*), comic, comical, diverting, droll, entertaining, facetious, farcical, hilarious, humorous, jocose, jocular, jolly, killing (*Inf.*), laughable, ludicrous, rich, ridiculous, riotous, risible, side-splitting, silly, slapstick, waggish, witty **2.** curious, dubious, mysterious, odd, peculiar, perplexing, puzzling, queer, remarkable, strange, suspicious, unusual, weird

furious **1.** angry, beside oneself, boiling, enraged, frantic, frenzied, fuming, incensed, infuriated, in high dudgeon, livid (*Inf.*), mad, maddened, on the warpath (*Inf.*), raging, up in arms, wrathful, wroth (*Archaic*) **2.** agitated, boisterous, fierce, impetuous, intense, savage, stormy, tempestuous, tumultuous, turbulent, ungovernable, unrestrained, vehement, violent, wild

furlough ('fɜːləʊ) *n.* US leave of absence, *esp.* to soldier

furnace ('fɜːnɪs) *n.* 1. apparatus for applying great heat to metals 2. closed fireplace for heating boiler *etc.* 3. hot place

furnish ('fɜːnɪʃ) *vt.* 1. fit up (house) with furniture 2. equip 3. supply, yield —'**furnishings** *pl.n.* furniture, carpets *etc.* with which room is furnished —'**furniture** *n.* movable contents of a house or room

furore (fjʊ'rɔːrɪ) *or esp. U.S.* **furor** ('fjʊərɔː) *n.* 1. public outburst, *esp.* of protest 2. sudden enthusiasm

furrow ('fʌrəʊ) *n.* 1. trench as made by plough 2. groove —*vt.* 3. make furrows in

further ('fɜːðə) *adv. comp. of* FAR *and* FORE[1] 1. more 2. in addition 3. at or to a greater distance or extent —*a. comp. of* FAR *and* FORE[1] 4. more distant 5. additional —*vt.* 6. help forward, promote —'**furtherance** *n.* —'**furtherer** *n.* —'**furthermore** *adv.* besides —'**furthermost** *a.* —'**furthest** *a./adv. sup. of* FAR, FORE[1] —**further education** UK formal education beyond school other than at university or polytechnic

furtive ('fɜːtɪv) *a.* stealthy, sly, secretive —'**furtively** *adv.*

fury ('fjʊərɪ) *n.* 1. wild rage, violent anger 2. violence of storm *etc.* 3. (*usu. pl.*) snake-haired avenging deity

furze (fɜːz) *n.* prickly shrub, gorse

fuscous ('fʌskəs) *a.* dark-coloured

fuse (fjuːz) *v.* 1. blend by melting 2. melt with heat 3. amalgamate 4. (cause to) fail as a result of blown fuse —*n.* 5. soft wire, with low melting point, used as safety device in electrical systems 6. device (*orig.* combustible cord) for igniting bomb *etc.* —'**fusible** *a.* —'**fusion** *n.* 1. melting 2. state of being melted 3. union of things, as atomic nuclei, as if melted together

fuselage ('fjuːzɪlɑːʒ) *n.* body of aircraft

fusil ('fjuːzɪl) *n.* light flintlock musket —**fusi'lier** *n.* soldier of certain regiments —**fusil'lade** *n.* continuous discharge of firearms

fuss (fʌs) *n.* 1. needless bustle or concern 2. complaint, objection —*vi.* 3. make fuss —'**fussily** *adv.* —'**fussiness** *n.* —'**fussy** *a.* 1. particular 2. faddy 3. overmeticulous 4. overelaborate —'**fusspot** *n.* UK *inf.* person who fusses unnecessarily

fustian ('fʌstɪən) *n.* 1. thick cotton cloth 2. inflated language

fusty ('fʌstɪ) *a.* 1. mouldy 2. smelling of damp 3. old-fashioned —'**fustily** *adv.* —'**fustiness** *n.*

futile ('fjuːtaɪl) *a.* 1. useless, ineffectual 2. trifling —**futility** (fjuː'tɪlɪtɪ) *n.*

future ('fjuːtʃə) *n.* 1. time to come 2. what will happen 3. tense of verb indicating this 4. likelihood of development —*a.* 5. that will be 6. of, relating to, time to come —'**futurism** *n.* movement in art marked by revolt against tradition —'**futurist** *n./a.* —**futur'istic** *a.* ultramodern —**fu'turity** *n.* —**future perfect** *Gram.* *a.* 1. denoting tense of verbs describing action that will have been performed by certain time —*n.* 2. future perfect tense; verb in this tense

fuze (fjuːz) *n.* US *see* FUSE (sense 6)

fuzz (fʌz) *n.* 1. fluff 2. fluffy or frizzed hair 3. blur 4. *sl.* police(man) —'**fuzzy** *a.* 1. fluffy 2. frizzy 3. blurred, indistinct

fwd. forward

-fy (*comb. form*) make; become, as in *beautify*

THESAURUS

furnish 1. appoint, decorate, equip, fit (out, up), outfit, provide, provision, rig, stock, store, supply 2. afford, bestow, endow, give, grant, offer, present, provide, reveal, supply

furniture appliances, appointments, chattels, effects, equipment, fittings, furnishings, goods, household goods, movable property, movables, possessions, things (*Inf.*)

furore 1. commotion, disturbance, excitement, flap (*Inf.*), frenzy, fury, hullabaloo, outburst, outcry, stir, to-do, uproar 2. craze, enthusiasm, mania, rage

further 1. *adj.* additional, extra, fresh, more, new, other, supplementary 2. *adv.* additionally, also, as well as, besides, furthermore, in addition, moreover, on top of, over and above, to boot, what's more, yet 3. *v.* advance, aid, assist, champion, contribute to, encourage, expedite, facilitate, forward, foster, hasten, help, lend support to, patronize, plug (*Inf.*), promote, push, speed, succour, work for

furtherance advancement, advocacy, backing, boosting, carrying-out, championship, promotion, prosecution, pursuit

furthest extreme, farthest, furthermost, most distant, outermost, outmost, remotest, ultimate, uttermost

furtive clandestine, cloaked, conspiratorial, covert, hidden, secret, secretive, skulking, slinking, sly, sneaking, sneaky, stealthy, surreptitious, underhand, under-the-table

fury 1. anger, frenzy, impetuosity, ire, madness, passion, rage, wrath 2. ferocity, fierceness, force, intensity, power, savagery, severity, tempestuousness, turbulence, vehemence, violence

fuss *n.* 1. ado, agitation, bother, bustle, commotion, confusion, excitement, fidget, flap (*Inf.*), flurry, fluster, flutter, hurry, palaver, pother, stir, storm in a teacup (*Brit.*), to-do, upset, worry 2. altercation, argument, bother, complaint, difficulty, display, furore, hassle (*Inf.*), objection, row, squabble, trouble, unrest, upset ~*v.* 3. bustle, chafe, fidget, flap (*Inf.*), fret, fume, get in a stew (*Inf.*), get worked up, labour over, make a meal of (*Inf.*), make a thing of (*Inf.*), niggle, take pains, worry

fussy 1. choosy (*Inf.*), dainty, difficult, discriminating, exacting, faddish, faddy, fastidious, finicky, hard to please, nit-picking (*Inf.*), old-maidish, old womanish, overparticular, particular, pernickety, squeamish 2. busy, cluttered, overdecorated, overelaborate, overembellished, overworked, rococo

futile 1. abortive, barren, bootless, empty, forlorn, fruitless, hollow, ineffectual, in vain, nugatory, profitless, sterile, to no avail, unavailing, unproductive, unprofitable, unsuccessful, useless, vain, valueless, worthless 2. idle, pointless, trifling, trivial, unimportant

futility 1. bootlessness, emptiness, fruitlessness, hollowness, ineffectiveness, uselessness 2. pointlessness, triviality, unimportance, vanity

future 1. *n.* expectation, hereafter, outlook, prospect, time to come 2. *adj.* approaching, coming, destined, eventual, expected, fated, forthcoming, impending, in the offing, later, prospective, subsequent, to be, to come, ultimate, unborn

G

g *or* **G** (dʒiː) *n.* **1.** seventh letter of English alphabet **2.** speech sound represented by this letter, usu. as in *grass*, or as in *page* (*pl.* **g's, G's** *or* **Gs**)

g 1. gram(s) **2.** (acceleration due to) gravity

G 1. *Mus.* fifth note of scale of C major; major or minor key having this note as its tonic **2.** gravitational constant **3.** *Phys.* conductance **4.** German **5.** giga **6.** good **7.** *sl., chiefly* **US** grand (thousand dollars or pounds)

Ga *Chem.* gallium

GA Georgia

gabble (ˈgæbᵊl) *v.* **1.** talk, utter inarticulately or too fast (**ˈgabbled, ˈgabbling**) —*n.* **2.** such talk —**gab** *vi.* **1.** talk excessively; chatter (**-bb-**) —*n.* **2.** idle or trivial talk —**ˈgabby** *a. inf.* talkative —**gift of the gab** eloquence, loquacity

gaberdine (ˈgæbədiːn, gæbəˈdiːn) *n.* **1.** fine twill cloth like serge used *esp.* for raincoats **2.** *Hist.* loose upper garment worn by Jews

gable (ˈgeɪbᵊl) *n.* triangular upper part of wall at end of ridged roof (*also* **gable end**)

gad (gæd) *vi.* (*esp. with* about) go around in search of pleasure (**-dd-**) —**ˈgadabout** *n.* pleasure-seeker

gadfly (ˈgædflaɪ) *n.* **1.** cattle-biting fly **2.** worrying person

gadget (ˈgædʒɪt) *n.* **1.** small mechanical device **2.** object valued for its novelty or ingenuity —**ˈgadgetry** *n.*

gadoid (ˈgeɪdɔɪd) *a.* **1.** of order of marine fishes typically having pectoral and pelvic fins close together and small cycloid scales —*n.* **2.** gadoid fish

gadolinium (gædəˈlɪnɪəm) *n.* malleable ferromagnetic element of lanthanide series of metals

gadwall (ˈgædwɔːl) *n.* duck related to mallard

Gael (geɪl) *n.* one who speaks Gaelic —**Gaelic** (ˈgeɪlɪk, ˈgæ-) *n.* **1.** language of Ireland and Scottish Highlands —*a.* **2.** of Gaels, their language or customs

gaff[1] (gæf) *n.* **1.** stick with iron hook for landing fish **2.** spar for top of fore-and-aft sail —*vt.* **3.** seize (fish) with gaff

gaff[2] (gæf) *n. sl.* nonsense —**blow the gaff UK** *sl.* divulge a secret

gaffe (gæf) *n.* social blunder, *esp.* tactless remark

gaffer (ˈgæfə) *n.* **1.** old man **2.** *inf.* foreman, boss

gag[1] (gæg) *vt.* **1.** stop up (person's mouth) with cloth *etc.* —*vi.* **2.** *sl.* retch, choke (**-gg-**) —*n.* **3.** cloth *etc.* put into, tied across mouth

gag[2] (gæg) *n.* joke, funny story, gimmick

gaga (ˈgɑːgɑː) *a. sl.* **1.** senile **2.** crazy

gage[1] (geɪdʒ) *n.* **1.** pledge, thing given as security **2.** challenge, or something symbolizing one

gage[2] (geɪdʒ) *see* GAUGE

gaggle (ˈgægᵊl) *n.* **1.** flock of geese **2.** *inf.* disorderly crowd

gaiety (ˈgeɪətɪ) *n. see* GAY

gain (geɪn) *vt.* **1.** obtain, secure **2.** obtain as profit **3.** win **4.** earn **5.** reach —*v.* **6.** increase, improve —*vi.* **7.** (*usu. with* on *or* upon) get nearer **8.** (of watch, machine *etc.*) operate too fast —*n.* **9.** profit **10.** increase, improvement —**ˈgainful** *a.* profitable; lucrative —**ˈgainfully** *adv.*

gainsay (geɪnˈseɪ) *vt.* deny; contradict (**gainˈsaid, gainˈsaying**)

gait (geɪt) *n.* **1.** manner of walking **2.** pace

gaiter (ˈgeɪtə) *n.* covering of leather, cloth *etc.* for lower leg

gal *or* **gal.** gallon

Gal. *Bible* Galatians

THESAURUS

gad (about) gallivant, roam, rove, run around

gadabout gallivanter, pleasure-seeker, rover

gadget appliance, contraption (*Inf.*), contrivance, device, gimmick, gizmo (*Sl., chiefly U.S.*), invention, novelty, thing, tool

gaffe bloomer (*Inf.*), blunder, boob (*Brit. sl.*), booboo (*Inf.*), clanger (*Inf.*), faux pas, gaucherie, howler, indiscretion, mistake, slip, solecism

gaffer 1. granddad, greybeard, old boy (*Inf.*), old fellow, old man, old-timer (*U.S.*) **2.** *Inf.* boss (*Inf.*), foreman, ganger, manager, overseer, superintendent, supervisor

gag[1] *v.* **1.** curb, muffle, muzzle, quiet, silence, stifle, still, stop up, suppress **2.** *Sl.* disgorge, heave, puke (*Sl.*), retch, spew, throw up (*Inf.*), vomit **3.** *Sl.* choke, gasp, pant, struggle for breath

gag[2] crack (*Sl.*), funny (*Inf.*), hoax, jest, joke, wisecrack (*Inf.*), witticism

gaiety 1. animation, blitheness, blithesomeness (*Literary*), cheerfulness, effervescence, elation, exhilaration, glee, good humour, high spirits, hilarity, *joie de vivre*, jollity, joviality, joyousness, light-heartedness, liveliness, merriment, mirth, sprightliness, vivacity **2.** celebration, conviviality, festivity, fun, jollification, merrymaking, revelry, revels **3.** brightness, brilliance, colour, colourfulness, gaudiness, glitter, show, showiness, sparkle

gaily 1. blithely, cheerfully, gleefully, happily, joyfully, light-heartedly, merrily **2.** brightly, brilliantly, colourfully, flamboyantly, flashily, gaudily, showily

gain *v.* **1.** achieve, acquire, advance, attain, bag, build up, capture, collect, enlist, gather, get, glean, harvest, improve, increase, net, obtain, pick up, procure, profit, realize, reap, secure, win, win over **2.** acquire, bring in, clear, earn, get, make, net, obtain, produce, realize, win, yield **3.** *Usually with* **on** approach, catch up with, close with, get nearer, narrow the gap, overtake **4.** arrive at, attain, come to, get to, reach ~*n.* **5.** accretion, achievement, acquisition, advance, advancement, advantage, attainment, benefit, dividend, earnings, emolument, growth, headway, improvement, income, increase, increment, lucre, proceeds, produce, profit, progress, return, rise, winnings, yield

gainsay contradict, contravene, controvert, deny, disaffirm, disagree with, dispute

gait bearing, carriage, pace, step, stride, tread, walk

gala *n.* carnival, celebration, festival, festivity, fête, jamboree, pageant, party

gala ('gɑːlə, 'geɪlə) *n.* **1.** festive occasion **2.** show **3.** competitive sporting event

galah (gə'lɑː) *n.* Aust. grey cockatoo with reddish breast

galantine ('gæləntiːn) *n.* cold dish of meat or poultry, boned, cooked, then pressed and glazed

galaxy ('gæləksɪ) *n.* **1.** system of stars bound by gravitational forces **2.** splendid gathering, *esp.* of famous people —**ga'lactic** *a.*

gale (geɪl) *n.* **1.** strong wind **2.** *inf.* loud outburst, *esp.* of laughter

galena (gə'liːnə) *or* **galenite** (gə'liːnaɪt) *n.* bluish-grey or black mineral consisting of lead sulphide: principal ore of lead

gall[1] (gɔːl) *n.* **1.** *inf.* impudence **2.** bitterness —**gall bladder** sac attached to liver, reservoir for bile —**'gallstone** *n.* hard secretion in gall bladder or ducts leading from it

gall[2] (gɔːl) *n.* **1.** painful swelling, *esp.* on horse **2.** sore caused by chafing —*vt.* **3.** make sore by rubbing **4.** vex, irritate —**'galling** *a.* irritating, exasperating, humiliating

gall[3] (gɔːl) *n.* abnormal outgrowth on trees *etc.*

gallant ('gælənt) *a.* **1.** fine, stately, brave **2.** (gə'lænt, 'gælənt) (of man) very attentive to women; chivalrous —*n.* ('gælənt, gə'lænt) **3.** lover, suitor **4.** fashionable young man —**'gallantly** *adv.* —**'gallantry** *n.*

galleon ('gælɪən) *n.* large, high-built sailing ship of war

gallery ('gælərɪ) *n.* **1.** covered walk with side openings, colonnade **2.** platform or projecting upper floor in church, theatre *etc.* **3.** group of spectators **4.** long, narrow platform on outside of building **5.** room or rooms for special purposes, *eg* showing works of art **6.** passage in wall, open to interior of building **7.** horizontal passage, as in mine *etc.*

galley ('gælɪ) *n.* **1.** one-decked vessel with sails and oars, usu. rowed by slaves or criminals **2.** kitchen of ship or aircraft **3.** large rowing boat **4.** *Print.* tray for holding composed type —**galley proof** printer's proof in long slip form —**galley slave 1.** one condemned to row in galley **2.** drudge

galliard ('gæljəd) *n.* **1.** dance in triple time for two persons **2.** music for this dance

Gallic ('gælɪk) *a.* **1.** of ancient Gaul **2.** French —**'Gallicism** *n.* French word or idiom

gallinaceous (gælɪ'neɪʃəs) *a.* of order of birds, including domestic fowl, pheasants *etc.*, having heavy rounded body and strong legs

gallium ('gælɪəm) *n.* soft, grey metal of great fusibility

gallivant ('gælɪvænt) *vi.* gad about

Gallo- ('gæləʊ-) (*comb. form*) Gaul; France, as in *Gallo-Roman*

gallon ('gælən) *n.* liquid measure of eight pints (4.55 litres)

gallop ('gæləp) *v.* **1.** go, ride at gallop —*vi.* **2.** move fast —*n.* **3.** horse's fastest pace with all four feet off the ground at once in each stride **4.** ride at this pace —**'galloper** *n.* —**'galloping** *a.* **1.** at a gallop **2.** speedy, swift

gallows ('gæləʊz) *n.* structure, usu. of two upright beams and crossbar, *esp.* for hanging criminals

Gallup Poll ('gæləp) method of finding out public opinion by questioning a cross section of the population

galoot *or* **galloot** (gə'luːt) *n. inf.* silly, clumsy person

galore (gə'lɔː) *adv.* in plenty

galoshes *or* **goloshes** (gə'lɒʃɪz) *pl.n.* waterproof overshoes

galumph (gə'lʌmpf, -'lʌmf) *vi. inf.* leap or move about clumsily or joyfully

galvanic (gæl'vænɪk) *a.* **1.** of, producing, concerning electric current, *esp.* when produced chemically **2.** *inf.* resembling effect of electric shock; startling —**'galvanize** *or* **-ise** *vt.* **1.** stimulate to action; excite; startle **2.** cover (iron *etc.*) with protective zinc coating —**galva-**

THESAURUS

gale 1. blast, cyclone, hurricane, squall, storm, tempest, tornado, typhoon **2.** *Inf.* burst, eruption, explosion, fit, howl, outbreak, outburst, peal, shout, shriek

gall[1] **1.** *Inf.* brass (*Inf.*), brass neck (*Inf.*), brazenness, cheek (*Inf.*), effrontery, impertinence, impudence, insolence, nerve (*Inf.*), sauciness **2.** acrimony, animosity, animus, antipathy, bad blood, bile, bitterness, enmity, hostility, malevolence, malice, malignity, rancour, sourness, spite, spleen, venom

gall[2] *n.* **1.** abrasion, chafe, excoriation, raw spot, scrape, sore, sore spot, wound ~*v.* **2.** abrade, bark, chafe, excoriate, fret, graze, irritate, rub raw, scrape, skin **3.** aggravate (*Inf.*), annoy, bother, exasperate, fret, harass, irk, irritate, nag, nettle, peeve (*Inf.*), pester, plague, provoke, rankle, rile (*Inf.*), rub up the wrong way, ruffle, vex

gallant *adj.* **1.** bold, brave, courageous, daring, dashing, dauntless, doughty, fearless, game (*Inf.*), heroic, honourable, intrepid, lion-hearted, manful, manly, mettlesome, noble, plucky, valiant, valorous **2.** attentive, chivalrous, courteous, courtly, gentlemanly, gracious, magnanimous, noble, polite **3.** august, dignified, elegant, glorious, grand, imposing, lofty, magnificent, noble, splendid, stately ~*n.* **4.** admirer, beau, boyfriend, escort, lover, paramour, suitor, wooer **5.** beau, blade (*Archaic*), buck (*Inf.*), dandy, fop, ladies' man, lady-killer (*Inf.*), man about town, man of fashion

gallantry 1. boldness, bravery, courage, courageousness, daring, dauntlessness, derring-do (*Archaic*), fearlessness, heroism, intrepidity, manliness, mettle, nerve, pluck, prowess, spirit, valiance, valour **2.** attentiveness, chivalry, courteousness, courtesy, courtliness, elegance, gentlemanliness, graciousness, nobility, politeness

galling aggravating (*Inf.*), annoying, bitter, bothersome, exasperating, harassing, humiliating, irksome, irritating, nettlesome, plaguing, provoking, rankling, vexatious, vexing

gallop bolt, career, dart, dash, fly, hasten, hie (*Archaic*), hurry, race, run, rush, scud, shoot, speed, sprint, tear along, zoom

galore all over the place, aplenty, everywhere, in abundance, in great quantity, in numbers, in profusion, to spare

galvanize arouse, awaken, electrify, excite, fire, inspire, invigorate, jolt, move, provoke, quicken, shock, spur, startle, stimulate, stir, thrill, vitalize, wake

ˈnometer *n.* instrument for detecting or measuring small electric currents

gambit (ˈgæmbɪt) *n.* **1.** *Chess* opening involving offer of a pawn **2.** any opening manoeuvre, comment *etc.* intended to secure an advantage

gamble (ˈgæmbᵊl) *vi.* **1.** play games of chance to win money **2.** act on expectation of something —*n.* **3.** risky undertaking **4.** bet, wager —**ˈgambler** *n.*

gamboge (gæmˈbəʊdʒ, -ˈbuːʒ) *n.* gum resin used as yellow pigment

gambol (ˈgæmbᵊl) *vi.* **1.** skip, jump playfully (**-ll-**) —*n.* **2.** playful antic

game[1] (geɪm) *n.* **1.** diversion, pastime **2.** jest **3.** contest for amusement **4.** scheme, strategy **5.** animals or birds hunted **6.** their flesh —*a.* **7.** brave **8.** willing —*vi.* **9.** gamble —**ˈgamester** *n.* gambler —**ˈgaming** *n.* gambling —**ˈgamy** *or* **ˈgamey** *a.* **1.** having smell or flavour of game **2.** *inf.* spirited; plucky; brave —**ˈgamecock** *n.* fowl bred for fighting —**ˈgamekeeper** *n.* man employed to breed and take care of game —**game laws** laws governing hunting and preservation of game —**ˈgamesmanship** *n. inf.* art of winning games or defeating opponents by cunning practices without actually cheating

game[2] (geɪm) *a.* lame, crippled

gamete (ˈgæmiːt, gəˈmiːt) *n. Biol.* sexual cell that unites with another for reproduction or the formation of a new individual

gamin (ˈgæmɪn) *n.* street urchin

gamine (ˈgæmiːn) *n.* slim, boyish girl; elfish tomboy

gamma (ˈgæmə) *n.* third letter of Gr. alphabet (Γ, γ) —**gamma ray** very penetrative electromagnetic ray

gammon[1] (ˈgæmən) *n.* **1.** cured or smoked ham **2.** bottom piece of flitch of bacon

gammon[2] (ˈgæmən) *n.* **1.** double victory in backgammon in which player throws off all his pieces before his opponent throws any —*vt.* **2.** score such a victory over

gammy (ˈgæmɪ) *a.* UK *sl. see* GAME[2]

gamp (gæmp) *n. inf.* large umbrella, usu. clumsy or very worn

gamut (ˈgæmət) *n.* whole range or scale (*orig.* o musical notes)

gander (ˈgændə) *n.* **1.** male goose **2.** *inf.* a quick loo (*esp. in* **take** (*or* **have**) **a gander**)

gang[1] (gæŋ) *n.* **1.** (criminal) group **2.** organized grou of workmen —*vi.* **3.** (*esp. with* together) form gan —**ˈganger** *n.* foreman of a gang of labourers —**gan up on** *inf.* combine against

gang[2] (gæŋ) *n. see* GANGUE

gangling (ˈgæŋglɪŋ) *or* **gangly** *a.* lanky, awkward i movement

ganglion (ˈgæŋglɪən) *n.* nerve nucleus (*pl.* **-gli** (**-glɪə**), **-s**)

gangplank (ˈgæŋplæŋk) *or* **gangway** *n.* portabl bridge for boarding or leaving vessel

gangrene (ˈgæŋgriːn) *n.* death or decay of bod tissue as result of disease or injury —**gangrenou** (ˈgæŋgrɪnəs) *a.*

gangster (ˈgæŋstə) *n.* **1.** member of criminal gang notorious or hardened criminal

gangue *or* **gang** (gæŋ) *n.* valueless and undesirab material in ore

gangway (ˈgæŋweɪ) *n.* **1.** *see* GANGPLANK **2.** passag between row of seats —*interj.* **3.** clear a path

gannet (ˈgænɪt) *n.* predatory sea bird

ganoid (ˈgænɔɪd) *a./n.* (fish) with smooth, har enamelled, bony scales, *eg* sturgeon

gantry (ˈgæntrɪ) *or* **gauntry** *n.* **1.** structure to sup port crane, railway signals *etc.* **2.** framework besid rocket on launching pad (*also* **gantry scaffold**)

gaol (dʒeɪl) *see* JAIL

gap (gæp) *n.* **1.** breach, opening, interval **2.** cleft empty space

gape (geɪp) *vi.* **1.** stare in wonder **2.** open mouth wid as in yawning **3.** be, become wide open —*n.* **4.** act o gaping

garage (ˈgærɑːʒ, -rɪdʒ) *n.* **1.** (part of) building to hous cars **2.** refuelling and repair centre for cars —*vt.* leave (car) in garage

garb (gɑːb) *n.* **1.** dress **2.** fashion of dress —*vt.* **3.** dres clothe

THESAURUS

gamble *v.* **1.** back, bet, game, have a flutter (*Inf.*), lay *or* make a bet, play, punt, stake, try one's luck, wager **2.** back, chance, hazard, put one's faith *or* trust in, risk, speculate, stake, stick one's neck out (*Inf.*), take a chance, venture ~*n.* **3.** chance, leap in the dark, lottery, risk, speculation, uncertainty, venture **4.** bet, flutter (*Inf.*), punt, wager

gambol 1. *v.* caper, cavort, curvet, cut a caper, frisk, frolic, hop, jump, prance, rollick, skip **2.** *n.* antic, caper, frolic, gambado, hop, jump, prance, skip, spring

game *n.* **1.** amusement, distraction, diversion, entertainment, frolic, fun, jest, joke, lark, merriment, pastime, play, recreation, romp, sport **2.** competition, contest, event, match, meeting, round, tournament **3.** chase, prey, quarry, wild animals **4.** *Inf.* design, device, plan, plot, ploy, scheme, stratagem, strategy, tactic, trick ~*adj.* **5.** bold, brave, courageous, dauntless, dogged, fearless, gallant, heroic, intrepid, plucky, spirited, unflinching, valiant, valorous **6.** desirous, disposed, eager, inclined, interested, prepared, ready, willing

gamut area, catalogue, compass, field, range, scal scope, series, sweep

gang band, circle, clique, club, company, coteri crew (*Inf.*), crowd, group, herd, horde, lot, mob, pac party, ring, set, shift, squad, team, troupe

gangling, gangly angular, awkward, lanky, loos jointed, rangy, rawboned, skinny, spindly, tall

gangster bandit, brigand, crook (*Inf.*), desperad gang member, hood (*U.S. sl.*), hoodlum (*Chief U.S.*), mobster (*U.S. sl.*), racketeer, robber, ruffia thug, tough

gap blank, breach, break, chink, cleft, crack, cranny crevice, discontinuity, divide, hiatus, hole, interlud intermission, interruption, interstice, interval, lacuna, lull, opening, pause, recess, rent, rift, spac vacuity, void

gape 1. gawk, gawp (*Brit. sl.*), goggle, stare, wonde **2.** crack, open, split, yawn

garbage 1. debris, detritus, junk, litter, rubbis scraps **2.** dross, filth, muck, offal, refuse, rubbis scourings, slops, sweepings, swill, trash (*Chief U.S.*), waste

garbage ('gɑːbɪdʒ) *n.* rubbish

garble ('gɑːbᵊl) *vt.* jumble or distort (story, account *etc.*)

garçon (*Fr.* gar'sɔ̃) *n.* waiter, *esp.* French

garden ('gɑːdᵊn) *n.* **1.** ground for growing flowers, fruit, or vegetables —*vi.* **2.** cultivate garden —**'gardener** *n.* —**'gardening** *n.* —**garden centre** place selling gardening tools, plants *etc.* —**garden city UK** planned town of limited size surrounded by rural belt

gardenia (gɑː'diːnɪə) *n.* (sub)tropical shrub with fragrant white or yellow flowers

garfish ('gɑːfɪʃ) *n.* elongated bony fish

garganey ('gɑːgənɪ) *n.* small Eurasian duck related to mallard

gargantuan (gɑː'gæntjʊən) *a.* (*sometimes* **G-**) immense, enormous, huge

gargle ('gɑːgᵊl) *vi.* **1.** wash throat with liquid kept moving by the breath —*vt.* **2.** wash (throat) thus —*n.* **3.** gargling **4.** preparation for this purpose

gargoyle ('gɑːgɔɪl) *n.* carved (grotesque) face on waterspout, *esp.* on Gothic church

garish ('gɛərɪʃ) *a.* **1.** showy **2.** gaudy

garland ('gɑːlənd) *n.* **1.** wreath of flowers worn or hung as decoration —*vt.* **2.** decorate with garlands

garlic ('gɑːlɪk) *n.* (bulb of) plant with strong smell and taste, used in cooking and seasoning

garment ('gɑːmənt) *n.* **1.** article of clothing —*pl.* **2.** clothes

garner ('gɑːnə) *vt.* store up, collect, as if in granary

garnet ('gɑːnɪt) *n.* red semiprecious stone

garnish ('gɑːnɪʃ) *vt.* **1.** adorn, decorate (*esp.* food) —*n.* **2.** material for this

garret ('gærɪt) *n.* room on top floor, attic

garrison ('gærɪsᵊn) *n.* **1.** troops stationed in town, fort *etc.* **2.** fortified place —*vt.* **3.** station (troops) in (fort *etc.*)

garrotte *or* **garotte** (gə'rɒt) *n.* **1.** Spanish capital punishment by strangling **2.** apparatus for this —*vt.* **3.** execute, kill thus —**gar'rotter** *or* **ga'rotter** *n.*

garrulous ('gærʊləs) *a.* (frivolously) talkative —**gar'rulity** *n.* loquacity

garter ('gɑːtə) *n.* band worn round leg to hold up sock or stocking —**garter stitch** knitting with all rows in plain stitch

gas (gæs) *n.* **1.** air-like substance, *esp.* one that does not liquefy or solidify at ordinary temperatures **2.** fossil fuel in form of gas, used for heating or lighting **3.** gaseous anaesthetic **4.** poisonous or irritant substance dispersed through atmosphere in warfare *etc.* **5.** *inf.*, *esp.* **US** petrol **6.** *inf.* idle, boastful talk (*pl.* **-es, 'gasses**) —*vt.* **7.** project gas over **8.** poison with gas —*vi.* **9.** *inf.* talk idly, boastfully (**-ss-**) —**'gaseous** *a.* of, like gas —**'gassy** *a.* —**'gasbag** *n. sl.* person who talks idly —**gas chamber** *or* **oven** airtight room into which poison gas is introduced to kill people —**gas gangrene** gangrene resulting from infection of wound by anaerobic bacteria —**'gasholder** *n.* gasometer; vessel for storing or measuring gas —**'gasman** *n.* man employed to read household gas meters, supervise gas fittings *etc.* —**gas mask** mask with chemical filter to guard against poisoning by gas —**gas meter** apparatus for measuring amount of gas passed through it —**ga'someter** *n.* tank for storing coal gas *etc.* (*also* **'gasholder**) —**gas ring** circular assembly of gas jets used for cooking —**'gasworks** *pl.n.* (*with sing. v.*) plant where gas, *esp.* coal gas, is made

gash (gæʃ) *n.* **1.** gaping wound, slash —*vt.* **2.** cut deeply

gasket ('gæskɪt) *n.* rubber, asbestos *etc.* used as seal between metal faces, *esp.* in engines

gasoline *or* **gasolene** ('gæsəliːn) *n.* **US** petrol

gasp (gɑːsp) *vi.* **1.** catch breath with open mouth, as in exhaustion or surprise —*n.* **2.** convulsive catching of breath

gasteropod ('gæstərəpɒd) *n. see* GASTROPOD

gastric ('gæstrɪk) *a.* of stomach —**gastroente'ritis** *n.* inflammation of stomach and intestines —**'gastronome, gas'tronomer** *or* **gas'tronomist** *n.* gourmet —**gastro'nomical** *a.* —**ga'stronomy** *n.* art of good eating —**gastric juice** digestive fluid secreted by stomach, containing hydrochloric acid *etc.* —**gastric ulcer** ulcer of stomach lining

gastro- *or oft. before vowel* **gastr-** (*comb. form*) stomach, as in *gastroenteritis, gastritis*

gastropod ('gæstrəpɒd) *or* **gasteropod** *n.* mollusc, *eg* snail, with disclike organ of locomotion on ventral surface

gate (geɪt) *n.* **1.** opening in wall, fence *etc.* **2.** barrier

THESAURUS

garble **1.** confuse, jumble, mix up **2.** corrupt, distort, doctor, falsify, misinterpret, misquote, misreport, misrepresent, misstate, mistranslate, mutilate, pervert, slant, tamper with, twist

garish brassy, brummagem, cheap, flash (*Inf.*), flashy, flaunting, gaudy, glaring, glittering, loud, meretricious, raffish, showy, tasteless, tawdry, vulgar

garland **1.** *n.* chaplet, coronal, crown, festoon, wreath **2.** *v.* adorn, crown, deck, festoon, wreathe

garments apparel, array, articles of clothing, attire, clothes, clothing, costume, dress, duds (*Inf.*), garb, gear (*Sl.*), habiliment, habit, outfit, raiment (*Archaic*), robes, togs, uniform, vestments, wear

garner *v.* accumulate, amass, assemble, collect, deposit, gather, hoard, husband, lay in *or* up, put by, reserve, save, stockpile, store, stow away

garnish **1.** *v.* adorn, beautify, bedeck, deck, decorate, embellish, enhance, grace, ornament, set off, trim **2.** *n.* adornment, decoration, embellishment, enhancement, garniture, ornament, ornamentation, trim, trimming

garrison *n.* **1.** armed force, command, detachment, troops, unit **2.** base, camp, encampment, fort, fortification, fortress, post, station, stronghold ~*v.* **3.** assign, mount, position, post, put on duty, station **4.** defend, guard, man, occupy, protect, supply with troops

garrulous babbling, chattering, chatty, effusive, gabby (*Inf.*), glib, gossiping, gushing, loquacious, mouthy, prating, prattling, talkative, verbose, voluble

gash **1.** *v.* cleave, cut, gouge, incise, lacerate, rend, slash, slit, split, tear, wound **2.** *n.* cleft, cut, gouge, incision, laceration, rent, slash, slit, split, tear, wound

gasp **1.** *v.* blow, catch one's breath, choke, fight for breath, gulp, pant, puff **2.** *n.* blow, ejaculation, exclamation, gulp, pant, puff

for closing it **3.** sluice **4.** any entrance or way out **5.** (entrance money paid by) those attending sporting event —**gate-crash** *v.* enter (meeting, social function *etc.*) uninvited —**'gatehouse** *n.* house built at or over gateway —**gate-leg table** *or* **gate-legged table** table with leaves supported by hinged leg swung out from frame

gâteau ('gætəʊ) *n.* elaborate, rich cake (*pl.* **-teaux** (-təʊz))

gather ('gæðə) *v.* **1.** (cause to) assemble **2.** increase gradually **3.** draw together —*vt.* **4.** collect **5.** learn, understand **6.** draw (material) into small tucks or folds —**'gathering** *n.* assembly

GATT (gæt) General Agreement on Tariffs and Trade

gauche (gəʊʃ) *a.* tactless, blundering —**gaucherie** (gəʊʃə'riː, 'gəʊʃərɪ) *n.* awkwardness, clumsiness

gaucho ('gaʊtʃəʊ) *n.* S Amer. cowboy (*pl.* **-s**)

gaud (gɔːd) *n.* showy ornament —**'gaudily** *adv.* —**'gaudiness** *n.* —**'gaudy** *a.* showy in tasteless way

gauge *or* **gage** (geɪdʒ) *n.* **1.** standard measure, as of diameter of wire, thickness of sheet metal *etc.* **2.** distance between rails of railway **3.** capacity, extent **4.** instrument for measuring such things as wire, rainfall, height of water in boiler *etc.* —*vt.* **5.** measure **6.** estimate

Gaul (gɔːl) *n.* **1.** native of Gaul, region in Roman times stretching from N Italy to S Netherlands **2.** Frenchman

gaunt (gɔːnt) *a.* lean, haggard

gauntlet ('gɔːntlɪt) *n.* **1.** armoured glove **2.** glove covering part of arm —**run the gauntlet 1.** formerly, run as punishment between two lines of men striking at runner with sticks *etc.* **2.** be exposed to criticism or unpleasant treatment **3.** undergo ordeal —**throw down the gauntlet** offer challenge

gauntry ('gɔːntrɪ) *n. see* GANTRY

gauss (gaʊs) *n.* unit of density of magnetic field (*pl.* **gauss**)

gauze (gɔːz) *n.* thin transparent fabric of silk, wire *etc.* —**'gauzy** *a.*

gave (geɪv) *pt. of* GIVE

gavel ('gævᵊl) *n.* mallet of presiding officer or auctioneer

gavotte *or* **gavot** (gə'vɒt) *n.* **1.** lively dance **2.** music for it

gawk (gɔːk) *vi.* stare stupidly —**'gawky** *a.* clumsy, awkward

gawp *or* **gaup** (gɔːp) *vi. sl.* **1.** stare stupidly **2.** gape

gay (geɪ) *a.* **1.** merry **2.** lively **3.** cheerful **4.** bright **5.** light-hearted **6.** showy **7.** given to pleasure **8.** *inf.* homosexual —**'gaiety** *n.* **1.** state or condition of being gay **2.** festivity; merrymaking —**'gaily** *adv.*

gaze (geɪz) *vi.* **1.** look fixedly —*n.* **2.** fixed look

gazebo (gə'ziːbəʊ) *n.* summer-house, turret on roof, with extensive view (*pl.* **-s, -es**)

gazelle (gə'zɛl) *n.* small graceful antelope

gazette (gə'zɛt) *n.* **1.** official newspaper for announcements of government appointments *etc.* **2.** newspaper title —*vt.* **3.** publish in gazette —**gazetteer** (gæzɪ'tɪə) *n.* geographical dictionary

gazump (gə'zʌmp) *v.* raise (price of something, *esp.* house) after agreeing it with prospective buyer

G.B. Great Britain

G.B.E. (Knight or Dame) Grand Cross of the British Empire

g.b.h. grievous bodily harm

G.C. George Cross

G.C.B. (Knight) Grand Cross of the Bath (Brit. title)

G.C.E. *or* **GCE** General Certificate of Education

G clef *see* **treble clef** *at* TREBLE

G.C.M.G. (Knight or Dame) Grand Cross of the Order of St. Michael and St. George

G.C.V.O. *or* **GCVO** (Knight or Dame) Grand Cross of the Royal Victorian Order

Gd *Chem.* gadolinium

THESAURUS

gate access, barrier, door, doorway, egress, entrance, exit, gateway, opening, passage, port (*Scot.*), portal

gather 1. accumulate, amass, assemble, bring *or* get together, collect, congregate, convene, flock, forgather, garner, group, heap, hoard, marshal, mass, muster, pile up, round up, stack up, stockpile **2.** assume, be led to believe, conclude, deduce, draw, hear, infer, learn, make, surmise, understand **3.** build, deepen, enlarge, expand, grow, heighten, increase, intensify, rise, swell, thicken, wax **4.** fold, pleat, pucker, ruffle, shirr, tuck

gathering assemblage, assembly, company, conclave, concourse, congregation, congress, convention, convocation, crowd, flock, get-together (*Inf.*), group, knot, meeting, muster, party, rally, throng, turnout

gauche awkward, clumsy, graceless, ignorant, ill-bred, ill-mannered, inelegant, inept, insensitive, lacking in social graces, maladroit, tactless, uncultured, unpolished, unsophisticated

gaudy bright, brilliant, brummagem, flash (*Inf.*), flashy, florid, garish, gay, glaring, loud, meretricious, ostentatious, raffish, showy, tasteless, tawdry, vulgar

gauge *v.* **1.** ascertain, calculate, check, compute, count, determine, measure, weigh **2.** adjudge, appraise, assess, estimate, evaluate, guess, judge, rate, reckon, value ~*n.* **3.** basis, criterion, example, exemplar, guide, guideline, indicator, measure, meter, model, pattern, rule, sample, standard, test, touchstone, yardstick **4.** bore, capacity, degree, depth, extent, height, magnitude, measure, scope, size, span, thickness, width

gaunt angular, attenuated, bony, cadaverous, emaciated, haggard, lank, lean, meagre, pinched, rawboned, scraggy, scrawny, skeletal, skinny, spare, thin, wasted

gawky awkward, clownish, clumsy, gauche, lumbering, lumpish, maladroit, oafish, ungainly

gay 1. animated, blithe, carefree, cheerful, debonair, glad, gleeful, happy, hilarious, insouciant, jolly, jovial, joyful, joyous, light-hearted, lively, merry, sparkling, sunny, vivacious **2.** bright, brilliant, colourful, flamboyant, flashy, fresh, garish, gaudy, rich, showy, vivid **3.** convivial, festive, frivolous, frolicsome, fun-loving, gamesome, merry, playful, pleasure-seeking, rakish, rollicking, sportive, waggish

gaze 1. *v.* contemplate, gape, look, look fixedly, regard, stare, view, watch, wonder **2.** *n.* fixed look, look, stare

gazette journal, newspaper, news-sheet, organ, paper, periodical

Gdns. Gardens

G.D.P. gross domestic product

Ge *Chem.* germanium

gean (giːn) *n.* **1.** white-flowered tree with round, edible red fruit **2.** its fruit

gear (gɪə) *n.* **1.** set of wheels working together, *esp.* by engaging cogs **2.** connection by which engine, motor *etc.* is brought into work **3.** arrangement by which driving wheel of cycle, car *etc.* performs more or fewer revolutions relative to pedals, pistons *etc.* **4.** equipment **5.** clothing **6.** goods, utensils **7.** apparatus, tackle, tools **8.** rigging **9.** harness —*vt.* **10.** adapt (one thing) so as to conform with another **11.** provide with gear **12.** put in gear —**'gearing** *n.* **1.** assembly of gears for transmitting motion **2.** act or technique of providing gears to transmit motion **3.** *Acc.*, **UK** ratio of company's debt capital to its equity capital —**'gearbox** *n.* case protecting gearing of bicycle, car *etc.* —**gear lever** *or U.S.* **'gearshift** *n.* lever used to move gear wheels relative to each other in motor vehicle *etc.* —**'gearwheel** *n.* toothed wheel in system of gears (*also* **gear**) —**in gear** connected up and ready for work —**out of gear 1.** disconnected, out of working order **2.** upset

gecko ('gɛkəʊ) *n.* insectivorous lizard of warm regions (*pl.* **-s, -es**)

gee (dʒiː) *interj.* **1.** exclamation to horse *etc.* to encourage it to turn to right, go on or go faster (*also* **gee up**) —*vt.* **2.** (*usu. with* up) move (horse *etc.*) ahead; urge on

geelbek ('xiːlbɛk) *n.* edible S Afr. marine fish

geese (giːs) *n., pl. of* GOOSE

geezer ('giːzə) *n. inf.* old (eccentric) man

Geiger counter ('gaɪgə) *or* **Geiger-Müller counter** ('mʊlə) instrument for detecting radioactivity, cosmic radiation and charged atomic particles

geisha ('geɪʃə) *n.* in Japan, professional female companion for men

gel (dʒɛl) *n.* **1.** jelly-like substance —*vi.* **2.** form a gel (**-ll-**) (*also* **jell**)

gelatin ('dʒɛlətɪn) *or* **gelatine** ('dʒɛlətiːn) *n.* **1.** substance prepared from animal bones *etc.*, producing edible jelly **2.** anything resembling this —**ge'latinous** *a.* like gelatin or jelly

geld (gɛld) *vt.* castrate —**'gelding** *n.* castrated horse

gelid ('dʒɛlɪd) *a.* very cold

gelignite ('dʒɛlɪgnaɪt) *n.* powerful explosive consisting of dynamite in gelatin form

gem (dʒɛm) *n.* **1.** precious stone, *esp.* when cut and polished **2.** treasure —*vt.* **3.** adorn with gems (**-mm-**)

geminate ('dʒɛmɪneɪt) *v.* double, pair, repeat —**gemi'nation** *n.*

Gemini ('dʒɛmɪnaɪ, -niː) *n.* (twins) 3rd sign of zodiac, operative May 21st–June 20th

gemma ('dʒɛmə) *n.* asexual reproductive structure in mosses *etc.* that becomes detached from parent and develops into new individual (*pl.* **-mae** (-miː))

gemsbok *or* **gemsbuck** ('gɛmzbʌk) *n.* S Afr. oryx

gen (dʒɛn) *n. inf.* information —**gen someone up UK** *inf.* brief someone in detail

gen. 1. gender **2.** general **3.** genitive **4.** genus

Gen. 1. General **2.** *Bible* Genesis

-gen (*comb. form*) **1.** producing; that which produces, as in *hydrogen* **2.** something produced, as in *antigen*

gendarme ('ʒɒndɑːm) *n.* policeman in France

gender ('dʒɛndə) *n.* **1.** sex, male or female **2.** grammatical classification of nouns, according to sex (actual or attributed)

gene (dʒiːn) *n.* biological factor determining inherited characteristics

genealogy (dʒiːnɪ'ælədʒɪ) *n.* **1.** account of descent from ancestors **2.** pedigree **3.** study of pedigrees —**genea'logical** *a.* —**gene'alogist** *n.*

genera ('dʒɛnərə) *n., pl. of* GENUS

general ('dʒɛnərəl, 'dʒɛnrəl) *a.* **1.** common, widespread **2.** not particular or specific **3.** applicable to all or most **4.** not restricted to one department **5.** usual, prevalent **6.** miscellaneous **7.** dealing with main element only **8.** vague, indefinite —*n.* **9.** army officer of rank above colonel —**gene'rality** *n.* **1.** general principle **2.** vague statement **3.** indefiniteness —**generali'zation** *or* **-i'sation** *n.* **1.** general conclusion from particular instance **2.** inference —**'generalize** *or* **-ise** *vt.* **1.** reduce to general laws —*vi.* **2.** draw general conclusions —**'generally** *adv.* —**General Certificate of Education** public examination for which certificates are awarded at ordinary, advanced or scholarship level —**general election 1.** election in which representatives are chosen in all constituencies of a state **2. US** final election from which successful candidates are sent to legislative body **3. US, C** national, state or provincial election —**general practitioner** nonspecialist doctor with practice serving particular local area —**general-purpose** *a.* having a variety of uses —**general strike** strike by all or most of workers of country *etc.*

generalissimo (dʒɛnərə'lɪsɪməʊ, dʒɛnrə-) *n.* supreme commander of combined military, naval and air forces (*pl.* **-s**)

THESAURUS

gear *n.* **1.** cog, cogwheel, gearwheel, toothed wheel **2.** cogs, gearing, machinery, mechanism, works **3.** accessories, accoutrements, apparatus, equipment, harness, instruments, outfit, paraphernalia, rigging, supplies, tackle, tools, trappings **4.** baggage, belongings, effects, kit, luggage, stuff, things **5.** *Sl.* apparel, array, attire, clothes, clothing, costume, dress, garb, garments, habit, outfit, rigout (*Inf.*), togs, wear ~*v.* **6.** adapt, adjust, equip, fit, rig, suit, tailor

gelatinous gluey, glutinous, gummy, jelly-like, mucilaginous, sticky, viscid, viscous

gelid arctic, chilly, cold, freezing, frigid, frosty, frozen, glacial, ice-cold, icy, polar

gem 1. jewel, precious stone, semiprecious stone, stone **2.** flower, jewel, masterpiece, pearl, pick, prize, treasure

genealogy ancestry, blood line, derivation, descent, extraction, family tree, line, lineage, pedigree, progeniture, stemma, stirps, stock, strain

general 1. accepted, broad, common, extensive, popular, prevailing, prevalent, public, universal, widespread **2.** accustomed, conventional, customary, everyday, habitual, normal, ordinary, regular, typical, usual **3.** approximate, ill-defined, imprecise, inaccurate, indefinite, inexact, loose, undetailed, unspecific, vague **4.** across-the-board, all-inclusive, blanket, broad, catholic, collective, comprehensive,

generate ('dʒɛnəreɪt) *vt.* **1.** bring into being **2.** produce —**gene'ration** *n.* **1.** bringing into being **2.** all persons born about same time **3.** average time between two such generations (about 30 years) —**'generative** *a.* —**'generator** *n.* **1.** apparatus for producing steam, electricity *etc.* **2.** begetter —**generation gap** years separating one generation from next, *esp.* regarded as representing difference in outlook and lack of understanding between them

generic (dʒɪ'nɛrɪk) *a.* belonging to, characteristic of class or genus —**ge'nerically** *adv.*

generous ('dʒɛnərəs, 'dʒɛnrəs) *a.* **1.** liberal, free in giving **2.** abundant —**gene'rosity** *n.* —**'generously** *adv.*

genesis ('dʒɛnɪsɪs) *n.* **1.** origin **2.** mode of formation **3.** (G-) first book of Bible (*pl.* **-eses** (-ɪsiːz))

-genesis (*comb. form*) genesis, development, generation, as in *biogenesis, parthenogenesis*

genet ('dʒɛnɪt) *or* **genette** (dʒɪ'nɛt) *n.* catlike mammal of Afr. and S Europe

genetics (dʒɪ'nɛtɪks) *pl.n.* (*with sing. v.*) scientific study of heredity and variation in organisms —**ge'netic** *a.* —**genetic code** *Biochem.* order in which four nitrogenous bases of DNA are arranged in molecule, which determines type and amount of protein synthesized in cell —**genetic engineering** alteration of structure of chromosomes in living organisms to produce effects beneficial to man in medicine, agriculture *etc.* —**genetic fingerprinting** pattern of DNA unique to each individual, which can be analysed in sample of blood, saliva or tissue: used as means of identification

Geneva Convention (dʒɪ'niːvə) international agreement, formulated in 1864, establishing code for wartime treatment of sick or wounded: revised to cover maritime warfare and prisoners of war

genial ('dʒiːnjəl, -nɪəl) *a.* **1.** cheerful, warm in behaviour **2.** mild, conducive to growth —**geni'ality** *n.* —**'genially** *adv.*

genie ('dʒiːnɪ) *n.* in fairy tales, servant appearing by, and working, magic

genital ('dʒɛnɪtᵊl) *a.* relating to sexual organs or reproduction —**'genitals** *pl.n.* the sexual organs

genitive ('dʒɛnɪtɪv) *a./n.* possessive (case) —**genitival** (dʒɛnɪ'taɪvᵊl) *a.*

genius ('dʒiːnɪəs, -njəs) *n.* **1.** (person with) exceptional power or ability, *esp.* of mind **2.** distinctive spirit or nature (of nation *etc.*)

genocide ('dʒɛnəʊsaɪd) *n.* murder of a nationality or ethnic group

-genous (*comb. form*) **1.** yielding; generating, as in *erogenous* **2.** generated by; issuing from, as in *endogenous*

genre ('ʒɑːnrə) *n.* **1.** kind **2.** sort **3.** style **4.** painting of homely scene

gent (dʒɛnt) *inf. n.* **1.** gentleman —*pl.* **2.** men's public lavatory

genteel (dʒɛn'tiːl) *a.* **1.** well-bred **2.** stylish **3.** affectedly proper —**gen'teelly** *adv.*

gentian ('dʒɛnʃən) *n.* plant, usu. with blue flowers —**gentian violet** violet dye used as antiseptic *etc.*

Gentile ('dʒɛntaɪl) *a.* **1.** of race other than Jewish **2.** heathen —*n.* **3.** person, *esp.* Christian, who is not a Jew

gentle ('dʒɛntᵊl) *a.* **1.** mild, quiet, not rough or severe **2.** soft and soothing **3.** courteous **4.** moderate **5.** gradual **6.** noble **7.** well-born —**gen'tility** *n.* **1.** noble birth **2.**

THESAURUS

encyclopedic, generic, indiscriminate, miscellaneous, panoramic, sweeping, total, universal

generality 1. abstract principle, generalization, loose statement, sweeping statement, vague notion 2. approximateness, impreciseness, indefiniteness, inexactness, lack of detail, looseness, vagueness

generally 1. almost always, as a rule, by and large, conventionally, customarily, for the most part, habitually, in most cases, mainly, normally, on average, on the whole, ordinarily, regularly, typically, usually 2. commonly, extensively, popularly, publicly, universally, widely 3. approximately, broadly, chiefly, for the most part, in the main, largely, mainly, mostly, on the whole, predominantly, principally

generate beget, breed, bring about, cause, create, engender, form, give rise to, initiate, make, originate, procreate, produce, propagate, spawn, whip up

generation 1. begetting, breeding, creation, engenderment, formation, genesis, origination, procreation, production, propagation, reproduction 2. age group, breed, crop 3. age, day, days, epoch, era, period, time, times

generosity beneficence, benevolence, bounteousness, bounty, charity, kindness, liberality, munificence, open-handedness.

generous 1. beneficent, benevolent, bounteous, bountiful, charitable, free, hospitable, kind, lavish, liberal, munificent, open-handed, princely, ungrudging, unstinting 2. abundant, ample, copious, full, lavish, liberal, overflowing, plentiful, rich, unstinting

genesis beginning, birth, commencement, creation, dawn, engendering, formation, generation, inception, origin, outset, propagation, root, source, start

genial affable, agreeable, amiable, cheerful, cheery, congenial, convivial, cordial, easygoing, enlivening, friendly, glad, good-natured, happy, hearty, jolly, jovial, joyous, kind, kindly, merry, pleasant, sunny, warm, warm-hearted

geniality affability, agreeableness, amiability, cheerfulness, cheeriness, congenialness, conviviality, cordiality, friendliness, gladness, good cheer, good nature, happiness, heartiness, jollity, joviality, joy, joyousness, kindliness, kindness, mirth, pleasantness, sunniness, warm-heartedness, warmth

genius 1. adept, brain (*Inf.*), expert, intellect (*Inf.*), maestro, master, master-hand, mastermind, virtuoso 2. ability, aptitude, bent, brilliance, capacity, creative power, endowment, faculty, flair, gift, inclination, knack, propensity, talent, turn

genteel aristocratic, civil, courteous, courtly, cultivated, cultured, elegant, fashionable, formal, gentlemanly, ladylike, mannerly, polished, polite, refined, respectable, stylish, urbane, well-bred, well-mannered

gentility 1. civility, courtesy, courtliness, cultivation, culture, decorum, elegance, etiquette, good breeding, good manners, mannerliness, polish, politeness, propriety, refinement, respectability, urbanity 2. blue blood, gentle birth, good family, high birth, nobility, rank

respectability, politeness —ˈ**gentleness** *n.* **1.** quality of being gentle **2.** tenderness —ˈ**gently** *adv.* —ˈ**gentry** *n.* people of social standing next below nobility —ˈ**gentlefolk** *or* ˈ**gentlefolks** *pl.n.* persons regarded as being of good breeding —ˈ**gentleman** *n.* **1.** chivalrous well-bred man **2.** man of good social position **3.** man (used as a mark of politeness) —ˈ**gentlemanly** *or* ˈ**gentlemanlike** *a.* —**gentlemen's agreement** agreement binding by honour but not valid in law —ˈ**gentlewoman** *n.*

genuflect (ˈdʒɛnjʊflɛkt) *vi.* bend knee, *esp.* in worship —**genuˈflection** *or* **genuˈflexion** *n.*

genuine (ˈdʒɛnjʊɪn) *a.* **1.** real, true, not fake; authentic **2.** sincere **3.** pure

genus (ˈdʒiːnəs) *n.* class, order, group (*esp.* of insects, animals *etc.*) with common characteristics, usu. comprising several species (*pl.* **-es,** ˈ**genera**)

geo- (*comb. form*) earth, as in *geomorphology*

geocentric (dʒiːəʊˈsɛntrɪk) *a. Astron.* **1.** measured, seen from the earth **2.** having the earth as centre —**geoˈcentrically** *adv.*

geode (ˈdʒiːəʊd) *n.* **1.** cavity lined with crystals **2.** stone containing this

geodesic (dʒiːəʊˈdɛsɪk, -ˈdiː-) *a.* of geometry of curved surfaces (*also* **geoˈdetic**) —**geodesic dome** light but strong hemispherical construction formed from set of polygons

geodesy (dʒɪˈɒdɪsɪ) *n.* science of measuring the earth's surface

geog. 1. geographer **2.** geographic(al) **3.** geography

geography (dʒɪˈɒgrəfɪ) *n.* science of earth's form, physical features, climate, population *etc.* —**geˈographer** *n.* —**geoˈgraphic(al)** *a.* —**geoˈgraphically** *adv.* —**geographical mile** *see* **nautical mile** *at* NAUTICAL

geoid (ˈdʒiːɔɪd) *n.* **1.** hypothetical surface that corresponds to mean sea level, extending under continents **2.** shape of the earth

geol. 1. geologic(al) **2.** geologist **3.** geology

geology (dʒɪˈɒlədʒɪ) *n.* science of earth's crust, rocks, strata *etc.* —**geoˈlogical** *a.* —**geoˈlogically** *adv.* —**geˈologist** *n.*

geometry (dʒɪˈɒmɪtrɪ) *n.* science of properties and relations of lines, surfaces *etc.* —**geoˈmetric(al)** *a.* —**geoˈmetrically** *adv.* —**geomeˈtrician** *n.* —**geometric progression** sequence of numbers, each of which differs from succeeding one by constant ratio, as 1, 2, 4, 8 —**geometric series** such numbers written as sum

geophysics (dʒiːəʊˈfɪzɪks) *pl.n.* (*with sing. v.*) science dealing with the physics of the earth —**geoˈphysical** *a.* —**geoˈphysicist** *n.*

Geordie (ˈdʒɔːdɪ) *n.* native of Tyneside

George Cross (dʒɔːdʒ) British award for bravery

georgette *or* **georgette crepe** (dʒɔːˈdʒɛt) *n.* fine, silky, semitransparent fabric

Georgian (ˈdʒɔːdʒjən) *a.* of the times of the four Georges (1714–1830) or of George V (1910–36)

georgic (ˈdʒɔːdʒɪk) *n.* poem on rural life, *esp.* one by Virgil

geostationary (dʒiːəʊˈsteɪʃənərɪ) *a.* (of satellite) in orbit around earth so it remains over same point on surface

geotropism (dʒɪˈɒtrəpɪzəm) *n.* response of plant part to stimulus of gravity

Ger. 1. German **2.** Germany

geranium (dʒɪˈreɪnɪəm) *n.* **1.** common cultivated plant with red, pink or white flowers, pelargonium **2.** strong pink colour

gerbil *or* **gerbille** (ˈdʒɜːbɪl) *n.* burrowing desert rodent of Asia and Afr.

gerent (ˈdʒɛrənt) *n.* ruler, governor, director

gerfalcon (ˈdʒɜːfɔːlkən, -fɔːkən) *n. see* GYRFALCON

geriatrics (dʒɛrɪˈætrɪks) *pl.n.* (*with sing. v.*) branch of science dealing with old age and its diseases —**geriˈatric** *a./n.* old (person)

germ (dʒɜːm) *n.* **1.** microbe, *esp.* causing disease **2.** elementary thing **3.** rudiment of new organism, of animal or plant —**germiˈcidal** *a.* —ˈ**germicide** *n.* substance for destroying disease germs —**germ cell** sexual reproductive cell —**germ warfare** use of bacteria against enemy

german (ˈdʒɜːmən) *a.* **1.** of the same parents **2.** closely akin (*only in* **brother-, sister-, cousin-german**)

German (ˈdʒɜːmən) *n./a.* (language or native) of Germany —**Gerˈmanic** *n.* **1.** branch of Indo-European family of languages including Dutch, German *etc.* **2.** unrecorded language from which these languages developed (*also* **Proto-Germanic**) —*a.* **3.** of this group of languages **4.** of Germany, German language or any people that speaks Germanic language —**German measles** *see* RUBELLA

germander (dʒɜːˈmændə) *n.* European plant having two-lipped flowers with very small upper lip

germane (dʒɜːˈmeɪn) *a.* relevant, pertinent

germanium (dʒɜːˈmeɪnɪəm) *n.* grey element that is semiconducting metalloid

THESAURUS

gentle 1. amiable, benign, bland, compassionate, dove-like, humane, kind, kindly, lenient, meek, merciful, mild, pacific, peaceful, placid, quiet, soft, sweet-tempered, tender **2.** balmy, calm, clement, easy, light, low, mild, moderate, muted, placid, quiet, serene, slight, smooth, soft, soothing, temperate, tranquil, untroubled **3.** easy, gradual, imperceptible, light, mild, moderate, slight, slow **4.** *Archaic* aristocratic, courteous, cultured, elegant, genteel, gentlemanlike, gentlemanly, high-born, ladylike, noble, polished, polite, refined, upper-class, well-born, well-bred

gentlemanly civil, civilized, courteous, cultivated, gallant, genteel, gentlemanlike, honourable, mannerly, noble, obliging, polished, polite, refined, reputable, suave, urbane, well-bred, well-mannered

genuine 1. actual, authentic, bona fide, honest, legitimate, natural, original, pure, real, sound, sterling, true, unadulterated, unalloyed, veritable **2.** artless, candid, earnest, frank, heartfelt, honest, sincere, unaffected, unfeigned

germ 1. bacterium, bug (*Inf.*), microbe, microorganism, virus **2.** beginning, bud, cause, embryo, origin, root, rudiment, seed, source, spark **3.** bud, egg, embryo, nucleus, ovule, ovum, seed, spore, sprout

germane akin, allied, apposite, appropriate, apropos, apt, cognate, connected, fitting, kindred, material, pertinent, proper, related, relevant, suitable, to the point *or* purpose

germinate bud, develop, generate, grow, originate, pullulate, shoot, sprout, swell, vegetate

germinate (ˈdʒɜːmɪneɪt) *v.* (cause to) sprout or begin to grow —**germiˈnation** *n.* —**ˈgerminative** *a.*

gerontology (dʒɛrɒnˈtɒlədʒɪ) *n.* scientific study of ageing and problems of elderly people —**geronˈtologist** *n.*

gerrymander (ˈdʒɛrɪmændə) *vt.* **1.** divide constituencies of (voting area) so as to give one party unfair advantage **2.** manipulate or adapt to one's advantage —*n.* **3.** act or result of gerrymandering

gerund (ˈdʒɛrənd) *n.* noun formed from verb, *eg living*

gerundive (dʒɪˈrʌndɪv) *n.* **1.** in Latin grammar, adjective formed from verb, expressing desirability *etc.* of activity denoted by verb —*a.* **2.** of gerund or gerundive

gesso (ˈdʒɛsəʊ) *n.* **1.** white ground of plaster and size, used to prepare panels *etc.* for painting *etc.* **2.** any white substance, *esp.* plaster of Paris, that forms ground when mixed with water

Gestapo (gɛˈstɑːpəʊ) *n.* secret state police in Nazi Germany

gestate (ˈdʒɛsteɪt) *v.* carry (developing young) in uterus during pregnancy —**gesˈtation** *n.*

gesticulate (dʒɛˈstɪkjʊleɪt) *vi.* use expressive movements of hands and arms when speaking —**gesticuˈlation** *n.*

gesture (ˈdʒɛstʃə) *n.* **1.** movement to convey meaning **2.** indication of state of mind —*vi.* **3.** make such a movement

get (gɛt) *vt.* **1.** obtain, procure **2.** contract **3.** catch **4.** earn **5.** cause to go or come **6.** bring into position or state **7.** induce **8.** engender **9.** *inf.* understand —*vi.* **10.** succeed in coming or going **11.** (*oft. with* to) reach, attain **12.** become (**got, ˈgetting**) —**ˈgetaway** *n.* escape —**get-together** *n. inf.* small informal social gathering —**get-up** *n. inf.* **1.** costume, outfit **2.** arrangement of book *etc.* —**get-up-and-go** *n. inf.* energy, drive —**get across** (cause to) be understood —**get at 1.** gain access to **2.** mean, intend **3.** annoy **4.** criticize **5.** influence —**get by** *inf.* manage, *esp.* in spite of difficulties —**get on 1.** grow late **2.** (of person) grow old **3.** make progress, manage, fare **4.** (*oft. with* with) establish friendly relationship **5.** (*with* with) continue to do —**get (one's) goat** *sl.* make (one) angry, annoyed —**get one's own back** *inf.* obtain one's revenge —**have got** possess —**have got to** must, have to

geum (ˈdʒiːəm) *n.* garden plant with orange, yellow or white flowers

geyser (ˈgiːzə; *U.S.* ˈgaɪzər) *n.* **1.** hot spring throwing up spout of water from time to time **2.** apparatus for heating water and delivering it from a tap

ghastly (ˈgɑːstlɪ) *a.* **1.** *inf.* unpleasant **2.** deathlike, pallid **3.** *inf.* unwell **4.** horrible —*adv.* **5.** sickly

ghat (gɔːt) *n.* (in India) **1.** stairs leading down to river **2.** mountain pass

ghee (giː) *n.* clarified butter used in Indian cookery

gherkin (ˈgɜːkɪn) *n.* small cucumber used in pickling

ghetto (ˈgɛtəʊ) *n.* densely populated (*esp.* by one racial group) slum area (*pl.* **-s, -es**) —**ghetto blaster** *inf.* portable cassette recorder with built-in speakers

ghost (gəʊst) *n.* **1.** spirit, dead person appearing again **2.** spectre **3.** semblance **4.** faint trace **5.** one who writes work to appear under another's name —*v.* **6.** ghostwrite —*vt.* **7.** haunt —**ˈghostly** *a.* —**ghost town** deserted town, *esp.* one in western U.S.A. that was formerly a boom town —**ˈghostwrite** *v.* write (article *etc.*) on behalf of person who is then credited as author (*also* **ghost**) —**ˈghostwriter** *n.*

ghoul (guːl) *n.* **1.** malevolent spirit **2.** person with morbid interests **3.** fiend —**ˈghoulish** *a.* **1.** of or like ghoul **2.** horrible

G.H.Q. *Mil.* General Headquarters

ghyll (gɪl) *n. see* GILL[3]

GI (*short for* **Government Issue,** stamped on U.S. military equipment) *inf.* U.S. soldier

giant (ˈdʒaɪənt) *n.* **1.** mythical being of superhuman size **2.** very tall person, plant *etc.* —*a.* **3.** huge —**giˈgantic** *a.* enormous, huge

THESAURUS

gestation development, evolution, incubation, maturation, pregnancy, ripening

gesticulate gesture, indicate, make a sign, motion, sign, signal, wave

gesture 1. *n.* action, gesticulation, indication, motion, sign, signal **2.** *v.* gesticulate, indicate, motion, sign, signal, wave

get 1. achieve, acquire, attain, bag, bring, come by, come into possession of, earn, fall heir to, fetch, gain, glean, inherit, make, net, obtain, pick up, procure, realize, reap, receive, secure, succeed to, win **2.** be afflicted with, become infected with, be smitten by, catch, come down with, contract, fall victim to, take **3.** arrest, capture, collar (*Inf.*), grab, lay hold of, seize, take, trap **4.** become, come to be, grow, turn, wax **5.** catch, comprehend, fathom, follow, hear, notice, perceive, see, take in, understand, work out **6.** arrive, come, make it (*Inf.*), reach **7.** arrange, contrive, fix, manage, succeed, wangle (*Inf.*) **8.** coax, convince, induce, influence, persuade, prevail upon, sway, talk into, wheedle, win over

get across bring home to, communicate, convey, get (something) through to, impart, make clear *or* understood, put over, transmit

get at 1. acquire, attain, come to grips with, gain access to, get, get hold of, reach **2.** hint, imply, intend, lead up to, mean, suggest **3.** annoy, attack, blame, carp, criticize, find fault with, irritate, nag, pick on, taunt **4.** bribe, buy off, corrupt, influence, suborn, tamper with

getaway break, break-out, decampment, escape, flight

get by *Inf.* contrive, cope, exist, fare, get along, make both ends meet, manage, subsist, survive

get on 1. advance, cope, fare, get along, make out (*Inf.*), manage, progress, prosper, succeed **2.** agree, be compatible, be friendly, concur, get along, harmonize, hit it off (*Inf.*)

ghastly ashen, cadaverous, deathlike, deathly pale, dreadful, frightful, grim, grisly, gruesome, hideous, horrendous, horrible, horrid, livid, loathsome, pale, pallid, repellent, shocking, spectral, terrible, terrifying, wan

ghost 1. apparition, phantasm, phantom, revenant, shade (*Literary*), soul, spectre, spirit, spook (*Inf.*), wraith **2.** glimmer, hint, possibility, semblance, shadow, suggestion, trace

ghostly eerie, ghostlike, phantasmal, phantom, spectral, spooky (*Inf.*), supernatural, uncanny, unearthly, weird, wraithlike

giant 1. *n.* behemoth, colossus, Hercules, leviathan,

giaour (ˈdʒaʊə) *n. derogatory* non-Muslim, *esp.* Christian

gib (gɪb) *n.* **1.** metal wedge, pad or thrust bearing let into steam engine crosshead —*vt.* **2.** fasten or supply with gib (**-bb-**)

Gib (dʒɪb) *n. inf.* Gibraltar

gibber (ˈdʒɪbə) *vi.* **1.** make meaningless sounds with mouth **2.** jabber, chatter —**ˈgibberish** *n.* meaningless speech or words

gibbet (ˈdʒɪbɪt) *n.* **1.** gallows **2.** post with arm on which executed criminals were formerly hung **3.** death by hanging —*vt.* **4.** hang on gibbet **5.** hold up to scorn

gibbon (ˈgɪbᵊn) *n.* type of ape

gibbous (ˈgɪbəs) *or* **gibbose** (ˈgɪbəʊs) *a.* **1.** (of moon *etc.*) more than half illuminated **2.** hunchbacked **3.** bulging —**ˈgibbousness** *or* **gibbosity** (gɪˈbɒsɪtɪ) *n.*

gibe *or* **jibe** (dʒaɪb) *v.* **1.** utter taunts (at) **2.** mock **3.** jeer —*n.* **4.** provoking remark

giblets (ˈdʒɪblɪts) *pl.n.* internal edible parts of fowl, as liver, gizzard *etc.*

giddy (ˈgɪdɪ) *a.* **1.** dizzy, feeling as if about to fall **2.** liable to cause this feeling **3.** flighty, frivolous —**ˈgiddily** *adv.* —**ˈgiddiness** *n.*

gift (gɪft) *n.* **1.** thing given, present **2.** faculty, power —*vt.* **3.** present, endow, bestow —**ˈgifted** *a.* talented —**gift token** voucher given as present which recipient can exchange for gift

gig (gɪg) *n.* **1.** light, two-wheeled carriage **2.** *inf.* single booking of musicians to play at concert *etc.* **3.** cluster of fish-hooks

giga- (ˈgɪgə, ˈgaɪgə) (*comb. form*) 10^9, as in *gigavolt*

gigantic (dʒaɪˈgæntɪk) *a. see* GIANT

giggle (ˈgɪgᵊl) *vi.* **1.** laugh nervously, foolishly —*n.* **2.** such a laugh **3.** joke

gigolo (ˈʒɪgələʊ) *n.* **1.** man kept by (older) woman **2.** man paid to escort women

gigot (ˈdʒɪgət) *n.* **1.** leg of lamb or mutton **2.** leg-of-mutton sleeve

gild[1] (gɪld) *vt.* **1.** put thin layer of gold on **2.** make falsely attractive (**ˈgilded** *pt.*, **gilt** *or* **ˈgilded** *pp.*) —**gilt** *a.* **1.** gilded —*n.* **2.** thin layer of gold applied in gilding **3.** superficial appearance —**gilt-edged** *a.* **1.** (of securities) dated over short, medium, or long term, and characterized by minimum risk and usu. issued by Government **2.** (of books *etc.*) having gilded edges

gild[2] (gɪld) *n. see* GUILD

gill[1] (gɪl) *n.* (*usu. pl.*) breathing organ in fish

gill[2] (dʒɪl) *n.* liquid measure, quarter of pint (0.142 litres)

gill[3] *or* **ghyll** (gɪl) *n.* **UK** *dial.* **1.** narrow stream; rivulet **2.** wooded ravine

gillie, ghillie, *or* **gilly** (ˈgɪlɪ) *n.* in Scotland, attendant for hunting or fishing

gillyflower *or* **gilliflower** (ˈdʒɪlɪflaʊə) *n.* fragrant flower

gilt (gɪlt) *n.* young female pig

gimbals (ˈdʒɪmbᵊlz, ˈgɪm-) *pl.n.* pivoted rings, for keeping things, *eg* compass, horizontal at sea

gimcrack (ˈdʒɪmkræk) *a.* **1.** cheap; shoddy —*n.* **2.** cheap showy trifle

gimlet (ˈgɪmlɪt) *n.* boring tool, usu. with screw point —**gimlet-eyed** *a.* having a piercing glance

gimmick (ˈgɪmɪk) *n.* clever device, stratagem *etc.*, *esp.* designed to attract attention or publicity

gimp *or* **guimpe** (gɪmp) *n.* narrow fabric or braid used as edging or trimming

gin[1] (dʒɪn) *n.* spirit flavoured with juniper berries —**gin rummy** version of rummy in which player may go out if odd cards outside his sequences total less than ten points

gin[2] (dʒɪn) *n.* **1.** primitive engine in which vertical shaft is turned to drive horizontal beam in a circle **2.** machine for separating cotton from seeds **3.** snare, trap

ginger (ˈdʒɪndʒə) *n.* **1.** plant with hot-tasting spicy root used in cooking *etc.* **2.** the root **3.** *inf.* spirit, mettle **4.** light reddish-yellow colour —**ˈgingery** *a.* **1.** of, like ginger **2.** hot **3.** high-spirited **4.** reddish —**ginger ale** ginger-flavoured soft drink —**ginger beer** effervescing beverage made by fermenting ginger —**ˈgingerbread** *n.* cake flavoured with ginger —**ginger group** group within a party, association *etc.* that enlivens or radicalizes its parent body —**ginger snap** *or* **nut** crisp biscuit flavoured with ginger —**ginger up** stimulate

gingerly (ˈdʒɪndʒəlɪ) *adv.* **1.** cautiously, warily, reluctantly —*a.* **2.** cautious, reluctant or timid

THESAURUS

monster, titan **2.** *adj.* Brobdingnagian, colossal, elephantine, enormous, gargantuan, gigantic, huge, immense, jumbo (*Inf.*), large, mammoth, monstrous, prodigious, titanic, vast

gibberish babble, balderdash, blather, double talk, drivel, gabble, gobbledegook (*Inf.*), jabber, jargon, mumbo jumbo, nonsense, prattle, twaddle, yammer (*Inf.*)

gibe, jibe 1. *v.* deride, flout, jeer, make fun of, mock, poke fun at, ridicule, scoff, scorn, sneer, taunt, twit **2.** *n.* crack (*Sl.*), cutting remark, derision, dig, jeer, mockery, ridicule, sarcasm, scoffing, sneer, taunt

giddiness dizziness, faintness, light-headedness, vertigo

giddy 1. dizzy, dizzying, faint, light-headed, reeling, unsteady, vertiginous **2.** capricious, careless, changeable, changeful, erratic, fickle, flighty, frivolous, heedless, impulsive, inconstant, irresolute, irresponsible, reckless, scatterbrained, silly, thoughtless, unbalanced, unstable, unsteady, vacillating, volatile, wild

gift 1. benefaction, bequest, bonus, boon, bounty, contribution, donation, grant, gratuity, largess, legacy, offering, present **2.** ability, aptitude, attribute, bent, capability, capacity, endowment, faculty, flair, genius, knack, power, talent, turn

gifted able, accomplished, adroit, brilliant, capable, clever, expert, ingenious, intelligent, masterly, skilled, talented

gigantic Brobdingnagian, colossal, Cyclopean, elephantine, enormous, gargantuan, giant, herculean, huge, immense, mammoth, monstrous, prodigious, stupendous, titanic, tremendous, vast

giggle *v./n.* cackle, chortle, chuckle, laugh, snigger, te-hee, titter, twitter

gild adorn, beautify, bedeck, brighten, coat, deck, dress up, embellish, embroider, enhance, enrich, garnish, grace, ornament

gimmick contrivance, device, dodge, gadget, gambit,

gingham (ˈgɪŋəm) *n.* cotton cloth, usu. checked, woven from dyed yarn

gingivitis (dʒɪndʒɪˈvaɪtɪs) *n.* inflammation of gums

ginkgo (ˈgɪŋkgəʊ) *or* **gingko** (ˈgɪŋkəʊ) *n.* ornamental Chinese tree (*pl.* **-es**)

ginseng (ˈdʒɪnsɛŋ) *n.* **1.** plant of China or of N Amer., whose roots are used medicinally in China **2.** root of this plant or substance obtained from root

gip (dʒɪp) *vt./n.* **1.** *see* GYP[1] *—n.* **2.** *see* GYP[2]

Gipsy (ˈdʒɪpsɪ) *n. see* GYPSY

giraffe (dʒɪˈrɑːf, -ˈræf) *n.* Afr. ruminant animal, with spotted coat and very long neck and legs

gird[1] (gɜːd) *vt.* **1.** put belt round **2.** fasten (clothes) thus **3.** equip with sword **4.** prepare (oneself) **5.** encircle (**girt, ˈgirded** *pt./pp.*) —**ˈgirder** *n.* large beam, *esp.* of steel

gird[2] (gɜːd) *dial. v.* **1.** jeer (at); mock *—n.* **2.** taunt; gibe

girdle[1] (ˈgɜːdᵊl) *n.* **1.** corset **2.** waistband **3.** anything that surrounds, encircles *—vt.* **4.** surround, encircle

girdle[2] (ˈgɜːdᵊl) *n.* griddle

girl (gɜːl) *n.* **1.** female child **2.** young (unmarried) woman —**ˈgirlhood** *n.* —**ˈgirlie** *a. inf.* (of magazine) featuring nude or scantily dressed women —**ˈgirlish** *a.* —**girl Friday** female employee with wide range of secretarial and clerical duties —**ˈgirlfriend** *n.* **1.** female friend with whom male is romantically or sexually involved **2.** any female friend —**Girl Guide** *see* GUIDE (sense 5)

giro (ˈdʒaɪrəʊ) *n.* system operated by banks and post offices which provides for the transfer of money between accounts or by giro cheque (*pl.* **-s**)

girt[1] (gɜːt) *pt./pp. of* GIRD[1]

girt[2] (gɜːt) *vt.* **1.** bind; encircle; gird **2.** measure girth of

girth (gɜːθ) *n.* **1.** measurement around something **2.** leather or cloth band put around horse's belly to hold saddle *etc.* *—vt.* **3.** surround, secure with girth

gist (dʒɪst) *n.* substance, main point (of remarks *etc.*)

give (gɪv) *vt.* **1.** bestow, confer ownership of, make present of **2.** deliver **3.** impart **4.** assign **5.** yield, supply **6.** utter, emit **7.** be host of (party *etc.*) **8.** make over **9.** cause to have *—vi.* **10.** yield, give way, move (**gave, ˈgiven, ˈgiving**) *—n.* **11.** yielding, elasticity —**give-and-take** *n.* **1.** mutual concessions, shared benefits and cooperation **2.** smoothly flowing exchange of ideas and talk —**ˈgiveaway** *n.* **1.** betrayal or disclosure, *esp.* when unintentional *—a.* **2.** very cheap (*esp. in* **giveaway prices**) —**give and take** make mutual concessions —**give away 1.** donate or bestow as gift *etc.* **2.** sell very cheaply **3.** reveal, betray **4.** fail to use (opportunity) through neglect **5.** present (bride) formally to her husband in marriage ceremony —**give or take** plus or minus —**give up 1.** acknowledge defeat **2.** abandon

gizzard (ˈgɪzəd) *n.* part of bird's stomach

glabrous (ˈgleɪbrəs) *a. Biol.* without hairs or any unevenness; smooth

glacé (ˈglæsɪ) *a.* **1.** crystallized, candied, iced **2.** glossy

glacier (ˈglæsɪə, ˈgleɪs-) *n.* river of ice, slow-moving mass of ice formed by accumulated snow in mountain valleys —**glacial** (ˈgleɪsɪəl, -ʃəl) *a.* **1.** of ice, or of glaciers **2.** very cold —**glaciated** (ˈgleɪsɪeɪtɪd) *a.* —**glaciation** (gleɪsɪˈeɪʃən) *n.* —**glacial period** time when large part of earth's surface was covered by ice

glad (glæd) *a.* **1.** pleased **2.** happy, joyous **3.** giving joy —**ˈgladden** *vt.* make glad —**ˈgladly** *adv.* —**ˈgladness** *n.* —**glad eye** *inf.* inviting or seductive glance (*esp. in* **give (someone) the glad eye**) —**ˈgladrags** *pl.n. sl.* clothes for special occasions

glade (gleɪd) *n.* clear, grassy space in wood or forest

gladiator (ˈglædɪeɪtə) *n.* trained fighter in Roman arena

gladiolus (glædɪˈəʊləs) *n.* kind of iris, with sword-shaped leaves (*pl.* **-lus, -li** (-laɪ))

Gladstone bag (ˈglædstən) travelling bag

glair (glɛə) *n.* **1.** white of egg **2.** sticky substance *—vt.* **3.** smear with white of egg —**ˈglairy** *a.*

Glam. (glæm) Glamorgan

THESAURUS

gizmo (*Sl., chiefly U.S.*), ploy, scheme, stratagem, stunt, trick

gingerly 1. *adv.* carefully, cautiously, charily, circumspectly, hesitantly, reluctantly, squeamishly, suspiciously, timidly, warily **2.** *adj.* careful, cautious, chary, circumspect, hesitant, reluctant, squeamish, suspicious, timid, wary

gird 1. belt, bind, girdle **2.** blockade, encircle, enclose, encompass, enfold, engird, environ, hem in, pen, ring, surround **3.** brace, fortify, make ready, prepare, ready, steel

girdle 1. *n.* band, belt, cincture, cummerbund, fillet, sash, waistband **2.** *v.* bind, bound, encircle, enclose, encompass, engird, environ, gird, hem, ring, surround

girl bird (*Sl.*), chick (*Sl.*), colleen (*Irish*), damsel (*Archaic*), daughter, female child, lass, lassie (*Inf.*), maid (*Archaic*), maiden (*Archaic*), miss, wench

girth bulk, circumference, measure, size

gist core, drift, essence, force, idea, import, marrow, meaning, nub, pith, point, quintessence, sense, significance, substance

give 1. accord, administer, allow, award, bestow, commit, confer, consign, contribute, deliver, donate, entrust, furnish, grant, hand over *or* out, make over, permit, present, provide, supply, vouchsafe **2.** announce, be a source of, communicate, emit, impart, issue, notify, pronounce, publish, render, transmit, utter **3.** allow, cede, concede, devote, grant, hand over, lend, relinquish, surrender, yield **4.** bend, break, collapse, fall, recede, retire, sink

give away betray, disclose, divulge, expose, inform on, leak, let out, let slip, reveal, uncover

give up abandon, capitulate, cease, cede, cut out, desist, despair, forswear, hand over, leave off, quit, relinquish, renounce, resign, stop, surrender, throw in the towel, waive

glad 1. blithesome (*Literary*), cheerful, chuffed (*Sl.*), contented, delighted, gay, gleeful, gratified, happy, jocund, jovial, joyful, overjoyed, pleased, willing **2.** animated, cheerful, cheering, cheery, delightful, felicitous, gratifying, joyous, merry, pleasant, pleasing

gladden cheer, delight, elate, enliven, exhilarate, gratify, hearten, please, rejoice

gladly cheerfully, freely, gaily, gleefully, happily, jovially, joyfully, joyously, merrily, readily, willingly, with (a) good grace, with pleasure

gladness animation, blitheness, cheerfulness, delight, felicity, gaiety, glee, happiness, high spirits, hilarity, jollity, joy, joyousness, mirth, pleasure

glamour *or U.S. (sometimes)* **glamor** ('glæmə) *n.* alluring charm, fascination —'**glamorize, -ise,** *or U.S. (sometimes)* '**glamourize** *vt.* make appear glamorous —'**glamorous** *a.*

glance (glɑːns) *vi.* **1.** look rapidly or briefly **2.** allude briefly to or touch on subject **3.** (*usu. with* off) glide off (something struck) —*n.* **4.** brief look **5.** flash **6.** gleam **7.** sudden (deflected) blow

gland (glænd) *n.* one of various small organs controlling different bodily functions by chemical means —'**glanders** *n.* contagious horse disease —'**glandular** *a.* —**glandular fever** acute disease characterized by fever, swollen lymph nodes *etc.* (*also* **infectious mononucleosis**)

glare (glɛə) *vi.* **1.** look fiercely **2.** shine brightly, intensely **3.** be conspicuous —*n.* **4.** angry stare —'**glaring** *a.*

glasnost ('glæsnɒst) *n.* policy of public frankness and accountability developed in U.S.S.R. under Mikhail Gorbachov's leadership

glass (glɑːs) *n.* **1.** hard transparent substance made by fusing sand, soda, potash *etc.* **2.** things made of it **3.** tumbler **4.** its contents **5.** lens **6.** mirror **7.** telescope **8.** barometer **9.** microscope —*pl.* **10.** spectacles —'**glassily** *adv.* —'**glassiness** *n.* —'**glassy** *a.* **1.** like glass **2.** expressionless —**glass-blower** *n.* —**glass-blowing** *n.* process of shaping molten glass by blowing air into it through tube —'**glasshouse** *n.* **1.** greenhouse **2.** *inf.* army prison —**glass-paper** *n.* paper coated with pulverized glass for smoothing and polishing —**glass wool** insulating fabric

Glaswegian (glæz'wiːdʒən) *a.* **1.** of Glasgow, city in Scotland —*n.* **2.** native or inhabitant of Glasgow

glaucoma (glɔː'kəʊmə) *n.* eye disease —**glau'comatous** *a.*

glaucous ('glɔːkəs) *a.* **1.** *Bot.* covered with waxy or powdery bloom **2.** bluish-green

glaze (gleɪz) *vt.* **1.** furnish with glass **2.** cover with glassy substance —*vi.* **3.** become glassy —*n.* **4.** transparent coating **5.** substance used for this **6.** glossy surface —'**glazier** *n.* person who glazes windows

gleam (gliːm) *n.* **1.** slight or passing beam of light **2.** faint or momentary show —*vi.* **3.** give out gleams

glean (gliːn) *v.* **1.** pick up (facts *etc.*) **2.** gather (useful remnants of crop) in cornfields after harvesting —'**gleaner** *n.*

glebe (gliːb) *n.* land belonging to parish church or benefice

glee (gliː) *n.* **1.** mirth, merriment **2.** musical composition for three or more voices —'**gleeful** *a.* —'**gleefully** *adv.*

glen (glɛn) *n.* narrow valley, usu. wooded and with a stream, *esp.* in Scotland

glengarry (glɛn'gærɪ) *n.* Scottish woollen boat-shaped cap with ribbons hanging down back

glib (glɪb) *a.* **1.** fluent but insincere or superficial **2.** plausible —'**glibly** *adv.* —'**glibness** *n.*

glide (glaɪd) *vi.* **1.** pass smoothly and continuously **2.** (of aeroplane) move without use of engines —*n.* **3.** smooth, silent movement **4.** *Mus.* sounds made in passing from tone to tone —'**glider** *n.* aircraft without engine which moves in air currents —'**gliding** *n.* sport of flying gliders

glimmer ('glɪmə) *vi.* **1.** shine faintly, flicker —*n.* **2.** glow or twinkle of light —'**glimmering** *n.* **1.** faint gleam of light **2.** faint idea, notion

glimpse (glɪmps) *n.* **1.** brief or incomplete view —*vt.* **2.** catch glimpse of

glint (glɪnt) *v.* **1.** flash —*vi.* **2.** glance, glitter **3.** reflect —*n.* **4.** bright gleam; flash

THESAURUS

glamorous alluring, attractive, beautiful, bewitching, captivating, charming, dazzling, elegant, enchanting, entrancing, exciting, fascinating, glittering, glossy, lovely, prestigious, smart

glamour allure, appeal, attraction, beauty, bewitchment, charm, enchantment, fascination, magnetism, witchery

glance *v.* **1.** gaze, glimpse, look, peek, peep, scan, view **2.** bounce, brush, graze, rebound, ricochet, skim ~*n.* **3.** brief look, dekko (*Sl.*), gander (*Inf.*), glimpse, look, peek, peep, quick look, squint, view **4.** flash, gleam, glimmer, glint, reflection, sparkle, twinkle **5.** allusion, passing mention, reference

glare *v.* **1.** frown, give a dirty look, glower, look daggers, lower, scowl, stare angrily **2.** blaze, dazzle, flame, flare ~*n.* **3.** angry stare, black look, dirty look, frown, glower, lower, scowl **4.** blaze, brilliance, dazzle, flame, flare, glow

glaring 1. blatant, conspicuous, egregious, flagrant, gross, manifest, obvious, open, outrageous, outstanding, overt, patent, rank, unconcealed, visible **2.** blazing, bright, dazzling, glowing

glassy 1. clear, glossy, icy, shiny, slick, slippery, smooth, transparent **2.** blank, cold, dazed, dull, empty, expressionless, fixed, glazed, lifeless, vacant

glaze 1. *v.* burnish, coat, enamel, furbish, gloss, lacquer, polish, varnish **2.** *n.* coat, enamel, finish, gloss, lacquer, lustre, patina, polish, shine, varnish

gleam *n.* **1.** beam, flash, glimmer, glow, ray **2.** flicker, glimmer, hint, inkling, ray, suggestion, trace ~*v.* **3.** coruscate, flare, flash, glance, glimmer, glint, glisten, glitter, glow, scintillate, shimmer, shine, sparkle

glee cheerfulness, delight, elation, exhilaration, exuberance, exultation, fun, gaiety, gladness, hilarity, jocularity, jollity, joviality, joy, joyfulness, joyousness, liveliness, merriment, mirth, sprightliness, triumph, verve

gleeful cheerful, cock-a-hoop, delighted, elated, exuberant, exultant, gay, gratified, happy, jocund, jovial, joyful, joyous, jubilant, merry, mirthful, overjoyed, pleased, triumphant

glib artful, easy, fast-talking, fluent, garrulous, insincere, plausible, quick, ready, slick, slippery, smooth, smooth-tongued, suave, talkative, voluble

glide coast, drift, float, flow, fly, roll, run, sail, skate, skim, slide, slip, soar

glimmer *v.* **1.** blink, flicker, gleam, glisten, glitter, glow, shimmer, shine, sparkle, twinkle ~*n.* **2.** blink, flicker, gleam, glow, ray, shimmer, sparkle, twinkle **3.** flicker, gleam, grain, hint, inkling, ray, suggestion, trace

glimpse 1. *n.* brief view, glance, look, peek, peep, quick look, sight, sighting, squint **2.** *v.* catch sight of, descry, espy, sight, spot, spy, view

glint 1. *v.* flash, gleam, glimmer, glitter, shine, sparkle, twinkle **2.** *n.* flash, gleam, glimmer, glitter, shine, sparkle, twinkle, twinkling

glissade (glɪˈsɑːd, -ˈseɪd) *n.* **1.** gliding dance step **2.** slide, usu. on feet down slope of ice —*vi.* **3.** perform glissade

glisten (ˈglɪsᵊn) *vi.* gleam by reflecting light

glister (ˈglɪstə) *vi./n. obs.* glitter

glitch (glɪtʃ) *n.* sudden instance of malfunctioning in electronic system

glitter (ˈglɪtə) *vi.* **1.** shine with bright quivering light, sparkle **2.** be showy —*n.* **3.** lustre **4.** sparkle —**glitterati** (glɪtəˈrɑːtiː) *pl.n. inf.* leaders of society, *esp.* the rich and beautiful —**glitter ice C** ice formed from freezing rain

glitzy (ˈglɪtsɪ) *a. sl.* showily attractive; flashy; glittery

gloaming (ˈgləʊmɪŋ) *n. Scot., poet.* evening twilight

gloat (gləʊt) *vi.* regard, dwell (on) with smugness or malicious satisfaction

glob (glɒb) *n. inf.* soft lump or mass

globe (gləʊb) *n.* **1.** sphere with map of earth or stars **2.** heavenly sphere, *esp.* the earth **3.** ball, sphere —ˈ**global** *a.* —**globular** (ˈglɒbjʊlə) *a.* globe-shaped —**globule** (ˈglɒbjuːl) *n.* **1.** small round particle **2.** drop —ˈ**globe-trotter** *n.* (habitual) worldwide traveller —**the globe** the world; the earth

globulin (ˈglɒbjʊlɪn) *n.* kind of simple protein

glockenspiel (ˈglɒkənspiːl, -ʃpiːl) *n.* percussion instrument of metal bars which are struck with hammers

glomerate (ˈglɒmərɪt) *a.* **1.** gathered into rounded mass **2.** *Anat.* (*esp.* of glands) conglomerate in structure

gloom (gluːm) *n.* **1.** darkness **2.** melancholy, depression —ˈ**gloomily** *adv.* —ˈ**gloomy** *a.*

glory (ˈglɔːrɪ) *n.* **1.** renown, honourable fame **2.** splendour **3.** exalted or prosperous state **4.** heavenly bliss —*vi.* **5.** take pride (ˈ**gloried,** ˈ**glorying**) —**glorifiˈcation** *n.* —ˈ**glorify** *vt.* **1.** make glorious **2.** invest with glory (**-ified, -ifying**) —ˈ**glorious** *a.* **1.** illustrious **2.** splendid **3.** excellent **4.** delightful —ˈ**gloriously** *adv.* —**glory hole** *inf.* untidy cupboard, room or receptacle for storage

Glos. (glɒs) Gloucestershire

gloss[1] (glɒs) *n.* **1.** surface shine, lustre —*vt.* **2.** put gloss on **3.** (*esp. with* over) (try to) cover up, pass over (fault, error) —ˈ**glossiness** *n.* —ˈ**glossy** *a.* **1.** smooth, shiny —*n.* **2.** magazine printed on shiny paper

gloss[2] (glɒs) *n.* **1.** marginal interpretation of word **2.** comment, explanation —*vt.* **3.** interpret **4.** comment **5.** (*oft. with* over) explain away —ˈ**glossary** *n.* list of items peculiar to a field of knowledge with explanations

glottis (ˈglɒtɪs) *n.* human vocal apparatus, larynx (*pl.* **-es, -tides** (-tɪdiːz)) —ˈ**glottal** *or* ˈ**glottic** *a.*

glove (glʌv) *n.* **1.** (*oft. pl.*) covering for the hand —*vt.* **2.** cover with, or as with glove —**glove box** *or* **compartment** small storage area in dashboard of car —**the gloves 1.** boxing gloves **2.** boxing

glow (gləʊ) *vi.* **1.** give out light and heat without flames **2.** shine **3.** experience feeling of wellbeing or satisfaction **4.** be or look hot **5.** burn with emotion —*n.* **6.** shining heat **7.** warmth of colour **8.** feeling of wellbeing **9.** ardour —**glow-worm** *n.* female insect giving out green light

THESAURUS

glisten coruscate, flash, glance, glare, gleam, glimmer, glint, glitter, scintillate, shimmer, shine, sparkle, twinkle

glitter 1. *v.* coruscate, flare, flash, glare, gleam, glimmer, glint, glisten, scintillate, shimmer, shine, sparkle, twinkle **2.** *n.* beam, brightness, brilliance, flash, glare, gleam, lustre, radiance, scintillation, sheen, shimmer, shine, sparkle

gloat crow, exult, glory, relish, revel in, rub it in (*Inf.*), triumph, vaunt

globe ball, earth, orb, planet, round, sphere, world

globule bead, bubble, drop, droplet, particle, pearl, pellet

gloom 1. blackness, cloud, cloudiness, dark, darkness, dimness, dullness, dusk, duskiness, gloominess, murk, murkiness, obscurity, shade, shadow, twilight **2.** blues, dejection, depression, desolation, despair, despondency, downheartedness, low spirits, melancholy, misery, sadness, sorrow, unhappiness, woe

gloomy 1. black, crepuscular, dark, dim, dismal, dreary, dull, dusky, murky, obscure, overcast, shadowy, sombre, Stygian, tenebrous **2.** bad, black, cheerless, comfortless, depressing, disheartening, dispiriting, dreary, joyless, sad, saddening, sombre **3.** blue, chapfallen, cheerless, crestfallen, dejected, despondent, dismal, dispirited, down, downcast, downhearted, down in the dumps (*Inf.*), down in the mouth, glum, in low spirits, melancholy, miserable, moody, morose, pessimistic, sad, saturnine, sullen

glorify 1. add lustre to, aggrandize, augment, dignify, elevate, enhance, ennoble, immortalize, lift up, magnify, raise **2.** adore, apotheosize, beatify, bless, canonize, deify, enshrine, exalt, honour, idolize, pay homage to, revere, sanctify, venerate, worship **3.** celebrate, cry up (*Inf.*), eulogize, extol, hymn, laud, lionize, magnify, panegyrize, praise, sing *or* sound the praises of

glorious 1. celebrated, distinguished, elevated, eminent, excellent, famed, famous, grand, honoured, illustrious, magnificent, majestic, noble, noted, renowned, sublime, triumphant **2.** beautiful, bright, brilliant, dazzling, divine, effulgent, gorgeous, radiant, resplendent, shining, splendid, superb **3.** *Inf.* delightful, enjoyable, excellent, fine, great, heavenly (*Inf.*), marvellous, pleasurable, splendid, wonderful

glory *n.* **1.** celebrity, dignity, distinction, eminence, exaltation, fame, honour, illustriousness, immortality, kudos, praise, prestige, renown **2.** grandeur, greatness, magnificence, majesty, nobility, pageantry, pomp, splendour, sublimity, triumph **3.** beauty, brilliance, effulgence, gorgeousness, lustre, radiance, resplendence ~*v.* **4.** boast, crow, exult, gloat, pride oneself, relish, revel, take delight, triumph

gloss[1] *n.* **1.** brightness, brilliance, burnish, gleam, lustre polish, sheen, shine, varnish, veneer ~*v.* **2.** burnish, finish, furbish, glaze, lacquer, polish, shine, varnish, veneer **3.** camouflage, conceal, cover up, disguise, hide, mask, smooth over, veil, whitewash (*Inf.*)

gloss[2] **1.** *n.* annotation, comment, commentary, elucidation explanation, footnote, interpretation, note, scholium, translation **2.** *v.* annotate, comment, construe, elucidate, explain, interpret, translate

glossy bright, brilliant, burnished, glassy, glazed,

glower (ˈglaʊə) *vi.* **1.** scowl —*n.* **2.** sullen or angry stare

gloxinia (glɒkˈsɪnɪə) *n.* tropical plant with large bell-shaped flowers

glucose (ˈgluːkəʊz, -kəʊs) *n.* type of sugar found in fruit *etc.*

glue (gluː) *n.* **1.** any natural or synthetic adhesive **2.** any sticky substance —*vt.* **3.** fasten with glue —**ˈgluey** *a.*

glum (glʌm) *a.* sullen, moody, gloomy

glut (glʌt) *n.* **1.** surfeit, excessive amount —*vt.* **2.** feed, gratify to the full or to excess **3.** overstock (market *etc.*) with commodity (**-tt-**)

gluten (ˈgluːtᵊn) *n.* protein present in cereal grain —**ˈglutinous** *a.* sticky, gluey

glutton[1] (ˈglʌtᵊn) *n.* **1.** greedy person **2.** one with great liking or capacity for something —**ˈgluttonous** *a.* like glutton, greedy —**ˈgluttony** *n.*

glutton[2] (ˈglʌtᵊn) *n.* wolverine

glycerin (ˈglɪsərɪn), **glycerine** (ˈglɪsərɪn, glɪsəˈriːn), *or* **glycerol** (ˈglɪsərɒl) *n.* colourless sweet liquid with wide application in chemistry and industry

glycogen (ˈglaɪkəʊdʒən) *n.* polysaccharide consisting of glucose units: form in which carbohydrate is stored in animals —**glycoˈgenesis** *n.* —**glycoˈgenic** *a.*

glyptic (ˈglɪptɪk) *a.* pert. to carving, *esp.* on precious stones

gm. gram

G.M. George Medal

G-man *n.* **1.** **US** *sl.* FBI agent **2.** *Irish* political detective

GMT Greenwich Mean Time

gnarled (nɑːld) *or* **gnarly** *a.* **1.** knobby, rugged **2.** (*esp.* of hands) twisted

gnash (næʃ) *vt.* grind (teeth) together as in anger or pain

gnat (næt) *n.* small, biting, two-winged fly

gnaw (nɔː) *v.* **1.** bite or chew steadily **2.** (*esp. with* at) cause distress (to)

gneiss (naɪs) *n.* coarse-grained metamorphic rock

gnome (nəʊm) *n.* **1.** legendary creature like small old man **2.** *Facetious, derogatory* international financier

gnomic (ˈnəʊmɪk, ˈnɒm-) *a.* of or like an aphorism

gnomon (ˈnəʊmɒn) *n.* **1.** stationary arm that projects shadow on sundial **2.** geometric figure remaining after parallelogram has been removed from corner of larger parallelogram

gnostic (ˈnɒstɪk) *a.* **1.** of, relating to knowledge, *esp.* spiritual knowledge —*n.* **2.** (**G-**) adherent of Gnosticism —**ˈGnosticism** *n.* religious movement characterized by belief in intuitive spiritual knowledge: regarded as heresy by Christian Church

GNP Gross National Product

gnu (nuː) *n.* S Afr. antelope somewhat like ox (*pl.* **-s, gnu**)

go (gəʊ) *vi.* **1.** move along, make way **2.** be moving **3.** depart **4.** function **5.** make specified sound **6.** fail, give way, break down **7.** elapse **8.** be kept, put **9.** be able to be put **10.** result **11.** (*with* towards) contribute to (result) **12.** (*with* towards) tend to **13.** be accepted, have force **14.** become (**went** *pt.*, **gone** *pp.*) —*n.* **15.** going **16.** energy, vigour **17.** attempt **18.** turn —**ˈgoer** *n.* **1.** person who attends something regularly, as in *filmgoer* **2.** person or thing that goes, *esp.* very fast **3.** **A** *inf.* acceptable idea *etc.* **4.** **A, NZ** energetic person —**ˈgoing** *n.* **1.** departure; farewell **2.** condition of road surface with regard to walking *etc.* **3.** *inf.* speed, progress *etc.* —*a.* **4.** thriving (*esp. in* **a going concern**) **5.** current; accepted **6.** available —**goner** (ˈgɒnə) *n.* person beyond help or recovery, *esp.* person about to die —**go-ahead** *n.* **1.** *inf.* permission to proceed —*a.* **2.** enterprising, ambitious —**go-between** *n.* person who acts as intermediary for two people or groups —**go-by** *n. sl.* deliberate snub or slight (*esp. in* **give (a person) the go-by**) —**go-getter** *n. inf.* ambitious person —**go-go dancer** dancer, usu. scantily dressed, who performs rhythmic and oft. erotic modern dance routines in nightclubs *etc.* —**going-over** *n. inf.* **1.** check; examination; investigation **2.** castigation; thrashing (*pl.* **goings-over**) —**goings-on** *pl.n. inf.* **1.** actions or conduct, *esp.* regarded with disapproval **2.** happenings or events, *esp.* mysterious or suspicious —**go-kart** *or* **go-cart** *n.* *see* KART —**go-slow** *n.* deliberate slackening of the rate of production as form of industrial protest —**go down** **1.** move to lower place or level; sink, decline, decrease *etc.* **2.** be defeated; lose **3.** be remembered or recorded (*esp. in* **go down in history**) **4.** (*usu. with* with) **UK** fall ill; be infected

THESAURUS

lustrous, polished, sheeny, shining, shiny, silken, silky, sleek, smooth

glow *n.* **1.** burning, gleam, glimmer, incandescence, lambency, light, luminosity, phosphorescence **2.** brightness, brilliance, effulgence, radiance, splendour, vividness **3.** ardour, earnestness, enthusiasm, excitement, fervour, gusto, impetuosity, intensity, passion, vehemence, warmth **4.** bloom, blush, flush, reddening, rosiness ~*v.* **5.** brighten, burn, gleam, glimmer, redden, shine, smoulder **6.** be suffused, blush, colour, fill, flush, radiate, thrill, tingle

glower **1.** *v.* frown, give a dirty look, glare, look daggers, lower, scowl **2.** *n.* angry stare, black look, dirty look, frown, glare, lower, scowl

glue **1.** *n.* adhesive, cement, gum, mucilage, paste **2.** *v.* affix, agglutinate, cement, fix, gum, paste, seal, stick

glum chapfallen, churlish, crabbed, crestfallen, crusty, dejected, doleful, down, gloomy, gruff, grumpy, ill-humoured, low, moody, morose, pessimistic, saturnine, sour, sulky, sullen, surly

glut *n.* **1.** excess, overabundance, oversupply, saturation, superabundance, superfluity, surfeit, surplus ~*v.* **2.** cram, fill, gorge, overfeed, satiate, stuff **3.** choke, clog, deluge, flood, inundate, overload, oversupply, saturate

glutton gannet (*Sl.*), gobbler, gorger, gormandizer, gourmand, pig (*Inf.*)

gluttony gormandizing, gourmandism, greed, greediness, piggishness, rapacity, voraciousness, voracity

gnarled contorted, knotted, knotty, knurled, leathery, rough, rugged, twisted, weather-beaten, wrinkled

gnaw **1.** bite, chew, munch, nibble, worry **2.** distress, fret, harry, haunt, nag, plague, prey on one's mind, trouble, worry

go *v.* **1.** advance, decamp, depart, fare (*Archaic*), journey, leave, make for, move, move out, pass, proceed, repair, set off, travel, withdraw **2.** function,

goad (gəʊd) *n.* **1.** spiked stick for driving cattle **2.** anything that urges to action **3.** incentive —*vt.* **4.** urge on **5.** torment

goal (gəʊl) *n.* **1.** end of race **2.** object of effort **3.** posts through which ball is to be driven in football *etc.* **4.** the score so made —**ˈgoalkeeper** *n. Sport* player in goal whose duty is to prevent ball from entering it

goat (gəʊt) *n.* four-footed animal with long hair, horns and beard —**goaˈtee** *n.* pointed tuftlike beard growing on chin —**goat-herd** *n.* —**ˈgoatsucker** *n.* **US** nightjar —**get (someone's) goat** *sl.* annoy (someone)

gob (gɒb) *n.* **1.** lump **2.** *sl.* mouth —**ˈgobbet** *n.* lump (of food) —**ˈgobble** *v.* eat hastily, noisily or greedily

gobble (ˈgɒbˀl) *n.* **1.** throaty, gurgling cry of the turkey-cock —*vi.* **2.** make this sound —**ˈgobbler** *n.* male turkey

gobbledegook *or* **gobbledygook** (ˈgɒbˀldɪguːk) *n.* pretentious language, *esp.* as used by officials

goblet (ˈgɒblɪt) *n.* drinking cup

goblin (ˈgɒblɪn) *n. Folklore* small, usu. malevolent being

goby (ˈgəʊbɪ) *n.* small spiny-finned fish having ventral fins modified as sucker

god (gɒd) *n.* **1.** superhuman being worshipped as having supernatural power **2.** object of worship, idol **3.** (G-) in monotheistic religions, the Supreme Being, creator and ruler of the universe (**ˈgoddess** *fem.*) —**ˈgodlike** *a.* —**ˈgodliness** *n.* —**ˈgodly** *a.* devout, pious —**ˈgodchild** *n.* person sponsored by adults at baptism (**ˈgodson** *or* **ˈgoddaughter**) —**god-fearing** *a.* religious, good —**ˈgodforsaken** *a.* hopeless, dismal —**ˈgodhead** *n.* divine nature or deity —**ˈgodparent** *n.* sponsor at baptism (**ˈgodfather** *or* **ˈgodmother**) —**ˈgodsend** *n.* something unexpected but welcome —**ˈGodˈspeed** *interj./n.* expression of good wishes for person's success and safety

godetia (gəˈdiːʃə) *n.* annual garden plant

godwit (ˈgɒdwɪt) *n.* large shore bird of N regions

goffer (ˈgəʊfə) *vt.* **1.** press pleats into (frill) **2.** decorate (edges of book) —*n.* **3.** ornamental frill made by pressing pleats **4.** decoration formed by goffering books

gogga (ˈxɒxə) *n.* **SA** *inf.* insect, creepy-crawly

goggle (ˈgɒgˀl) *vi.* **1.** (of eyes) bulge **2.** stare —*pl.n.* **3.** protective spectacles —**ˈgogglebox** *n.* **UK** *sl.* television set

Goidelic (gɔɪˈdɛlɪk) *n.* **1.** N group of Celtic languages, consisting of Irish Gaelic, Scottish Gaelic and Manx —*a.* **2.** of or characteristic of this group of languages

goitre *or U.S.* **goiter** (ˈgɔɪtə) *n.* enlargement of thyroid gland, in some cases nearly doubling size of neck

gold (gəʊld) *n.* **1.** yellow precious metal **2.** coins made of this **3.** wealth **4.** beautiful or precious thing **5.** colour of gold —*a.* **6.** of, like gold —**ˈgolden** *a.* —**ˈgoldcrest** *n.* small bird with yellow crown —**gold-digger** *n.* woman skilful in extracting money from men —**golden age 1.** *Class. myth.* first and best age of mankind, when existence was happy, prosperous and innocent **2.** most flourishing period, *esp.* in history of art or nation —**golden eagle** large eagle of mountainous regions of N hemisphere —**Golden Fleece** *Gr. myth.* fleece of winged ram stolen by Jason and Argonauts —**golden handshake** *inf.* money given to employee on retirement or for loss of employment —**golden mean** middle course between extremes —**goldenˈrod** *n.* tall plant with golden flower spikes —**golden rule** important principle —**golden wedding** fiftieth wedding anniversary —**ˈgoldfield** *n.* place where gold deposits are known to exist —**ˈgoldfinch** *n.* bird with yellow feathers —**ˈgoldfish** *n.* any of various ornamental pond or aquarium fish —**gold plate 1.** thin coating of gold, usu. produced by electroplating **2.** vessels or utensils made of gold —**gold-plate** *vt.* —**gold rush** large-scale migration of people to territory where gold has been found —**ˈgoldsmith** *n.* **1.** dealer in articles made of gold **2.** artisan who makes such articles —**gold standard** financial arrangement whereby currencies of countries accepting it are expressed in fixed terms of gold

golf (gɒlf) *n.* **1.** outdoor game in which small hard ball is struck with clubs into a succession of holes —*vi.* **2.** play this game —**ˈgolfer** *n.* —**golf club 1.** long-shafted club with wood or metal head used to strike golf ball **2.** (premises of) association of golf players, usu. having its own course and facilities —**golf course** *or* **links** area of open land on which golf is played

Goliath (gəˈlaɪəθ) *n. Bible* Philistine giant killed by David with stone from sling

golliwog (ˈgɒlɪwɒg) *n.* black-faced doll

golly (ˈgɒlɪ) *interj.* exclamation of mild surprise

THESAURUS

move, operate, perform, run, work **3.** avail, concur, conduce, contribute, incline, lead to, serve, tend, work towards **4.** develop, eventuate, fall out, fare, happen, proceed, result, turn out, work out **5.** elapse, expire, flow, lapse, pass, slip away ~*n.* **6.** attempt, bid, crack (*Inf.*), effort, essay, shot (*Inf.*), stab, try, turn, whack (*Inf.*), whirl (*Inf.*) **7.** *Inf.* activity, animation, drive, energy, force, get-up-and-go (*Inf.*), life, oomph (*Inf.*), pep, spirit, verve, vigour, vitality, vivacity

goad 1. *n.* impetus, incentive, incitement, irritation, motivation, pressure, spur, stimulation, stimulus, urge **2.** *v.* annoy, arouse, drive, egg on, exhort, harass, hound, impel, incite, instigate, irritate, lash, prick, prod, prompt, propel, spur, stimulate, sting, urge, worry

go-ahead 1. *n. Inf.* assent, authorization, consent, green light, leave, O.K. (*Inf.*), permission **2.** *adj.* ambitious, enterprising, go-getting (*Inf.*), pioneering, progressive, up-and-coming

goal aim, ambition, design, destination, end, intention, limit, mark, object, objective, purpose, target

go-between agent, broker, dealer, factor, intermediary, liaison, mediator, medium, middleman

godforsaken bleak, dismal, dreary, forlorn, gloomy, wretched

godlike celestial, deific, deiform, divine, heavenly, superhuman, transcendent

godly devout, god-fearing, good, holy, pious, religious, righteous, saintly

go down 1. be beaten, collapse, decline, decrease, drop, fall, founder, go under, lose, set, sink, submerge, submit, suffer defeat **2.** be commemorated (recalled, recorded, remembered)

godsend blessing, boon, manna, stroke of luck, windfall

golden blond *or* blonde, flaxen, yellow

goloshes (gəˈlɒʃɪz) *pl.n. see* GALOSHES

-gon (*comb. form*) figure having specified number of angles, as in *pentagon*

gonad (ˈgɒnæd) *n.* gland producing gametes

gondola (ˈgɒndələ) *n.* Venetian canal boat **—gondoˈlier** *n.* rower of gondola

gone (gɒn) *pp. of* GO

gonfalon (ˈgɒnfələn) *n.* **1.** banner hanging from crossbar, used *esp.* by certain medieval Italian republics **2.** battle flag suspended crosswise on staff, usu. having serrated edge

gong (gɒŋ) *n.* **1.** metal plate with turned rim which resounds as bell when struck with soft mallet **2.** anything used thus

gonorrhoea *or esp. U.S.* **gonorrhea** (gɒnəˈrɪə) *n.* a venereal disease

good (gʊd) *a.* **1.** commendable **2.** right **3.** proper **4.** excellent **5.** beneficial **6.** well-behaved **7.** virtuous **8.** kind **9.** financially safe or secure **10.** adequate **11.** sound **12.** valid (ˈ**better** *comp.,* **best** *sup.*) *—n.* **13.** benefit **14.** wellbeing **15.** profit *—pl.* **16.** property **17.** wares **—ˈgoodly** *a.* large, considerable **—ˈgoodness** *n.* **—Good Book** the Bible **—good-hearted** *a.* kind and generous **—Good Samaritan 1.** *N.T.* figure in one of Christ's parables who is example of compassion towards those in distress **2.** kindly person who helps another in difficulty **—good sort** *inf.* agreeable person **—good turn** helpful, friendly act; good deed; favour **—good will 1.** kindly feeling, heartiness **2.** value of a business in reputation *etc.* over and above its tangible assets **—goody-goody** *n.* **1.** *inf.* smugly virtuous or sanctimonious person *—a.* **2.** smug and sanctimonious

goodbye (gʊdˈbaɪ) *interj./n.* form of address on parting

gooey (ˈguːɪ) *a. inf.* sticky, soft **—goo** *n. inf.* **1.** sticky substance **2.** coy or sentimental language or ideas

goof (guːf) *inf. n.* **1.** mistake **2.** stupid person *—vi.* **3.** make mistake **—ˈgoofy** *a.* silly, sloppy

googly (ˈguːglɪ) *n. Cricket* ball which changes direction unexpectedly on the bounce

goon (guːn) *n. inf.* stupid fellow

goosander (guːˈsændə) *n.* type of duck

goose (guːs) *n.* **1.** web-footed bird **2.** its flesh **3.** simpleton (*pl.* **geese**) **—goose flesh** bristling of skin due to cold, fright **—goose step** formal parade step

gooseberry (ˈgʊzbərɪ, -brɪ) *n.* **1.** thorny shrub **2.** its hairy fruit **3.** *inf.* unwelcome third party (*oft. in* **play gooseberry**)

gopher (ˈgəʊfə) *n.* various species of Amer. burrowing rodents

Gordian knot (ˈgɔːdɪən) **1.** in Greek legend, complicated knot, tied by King Gordius, that Alexander the Great cut with sword **2.** intricate problem (*esp. in* **cut the Gordian knot**)

gore[1] (gɔː) *n.* (dried) blood from wound **—ˈgorily** *adv.* **—ˈgory** *a.* **1.** horrific; bloodthirsty **2.** involving bloodshed and killing **3.** covered in gore

gore[2] (gɔː) *vt.* pierce with horns

gore[3] (gɔː) *n.* **1.** triangular piece inserted to shape garment *—vt.* **2.** shape thus

gorge (gɔːdʒ) *n.* **1.** ravine **2.** disgust, resentment *—vi.* **3.** eat greedily **—ˈgorget** *n.* armour, ornamentation or clothing for throat **—gorge oneself** stuff oneself with food

gorgeous (ˈgɔːdʒəs) *a.* **1.** splendid, showy, dazzling **2.** *inf.* extremely pleasing

Gorgon (ˈgɔːgən) *n.* terrifying or repulsive woman

Gorgonzola (gɔːgənˈzəʊlə) *n.* blue-veined Italian cheese

gorilla (gəˈrɪlə) *n.* largest anthropoid ape, found in Afr.

THESAURUS

gone 1. elapsed, ended, finished, over, past **2.** absent, astray, away, lacking, lost, missing, vanished

good *adj.* **1.** acceptable, admirable, agreeable, capital, choice, commendable, excellent, fine, first-class, first-rate, great, pleasant, pleasing, positive, precious, satisfactory, splendid, super (*Inf.*), superior, tiptop, valuable, worthy **2.** admirable, estimable, ethical, exemplary, honest, honourable, moral, praiseworthy, right, righteous, upright, virtuous, worthy **3.** able, accomplished, adept, adroit, capable, clever, competent, dexterous, efficient, expert, first-rate, proficient, reliable, satisfactory, serviceable, skilled, sound, suitable, talented, thorough, trustworthy, useful **4.** adequate, advantageous, auspicious, beneficial, convenient, favourable, fit, fitting, healthy, helpful, opportune, profitable, propitious, salubrious, salutary, suitable, useful, wholesome **5.** sound, uncorrupted, untainted, whole **6.** altruistic, approving, beneficent, benevolent, charitable, friendly, gracious, humane, kind, kind-hearted, kindly, merciful, obliging, well-disposed **7.** authentic, bona fide, dependable, genuine, honest, legitimate, proper, real, reliable, sound, true, trustworthy, valid **8.** decorous, dutiful, mannerly, obedient, orderly, polite, proper, seemly, well-behaved, well-mannered **9.** adequate, ample, sufficient ~*n.* **10.** advantage, avail, behalf, benefit, gain, interest, profit, service, use, usefulness, welfare, wellbeing, worth

goodbye adieu, farewell, leave-taking, parting

goodly ample, considerable, large, significant, sizable, substantial, tidy (*Inf.*)

goodness 1. excellence, merit, quality, superiority, value, worth **2.** beneficence, benevolence, friendliness, generosity, good will, graciousness, humaneness, kind-heartedness, kindliness, kindness, mercy, obligingness **3.** honesty, honour, integrity, merit, morality, probity, rectitude, righteousness, uprightness, virtue **4.** advantage, benefit

goods 1. appurtenances, belongings, chattels, effects, gear, movables, paraphernalia, possessions, property, things, trappings **2.** commodities, merchandise, stock, stuff, wares

good will amity, benevolence, favour, friendliness, friendship, heartiness, kindliness, zeal

gorge 1. *n.* canyon, cleft, clough (*Dialect*), defile, fissure, pass, ravine **2.** *v.* bolt, cram, devour, feed, fill, glut, gobble, gormandize, gulp, guzzle, overeat, raven, sate, satiate, stuff, surfeit, swallow, wolf

gorgeous 1. beautiful, brilliant, dazzling, elegant, glittering, grand, luxuriant, magnificent, opulent, ravishing, resplendent, showy, splendid, stunning (*Inf.*), sumptuous, superb **2.** *Inf.* attractive, bright, delightful, enjoyable, exquisite, fine, glorious, good, good-looking, lovely, pleasing

gormandize *or* **-dise** (ˈgɔːməndaɪz) *v.* eat (food) hurriedly or like a glutton

gormless (ˈgɔːmlɪs) *a. inf.* stupid

gorse (gɔːs) *n.* prickly shrub

gory (ˈgɔːrɪ) *a. see* GORE[1]

gosh (gɒʃ) *interj.* exclamation of mild surprise or wonder

goshawk (ˈgɒshɔːk) *n.* large hawk

gosling (ˈgɒzlɪŋ) *n.* young goose

gospel (ˈgɒspᵊl) *n.* **1.** unquestionable truth **2.** (**G-**) any of first four books of New Testament

gossamer (ˈgɒsəmə) *n.* **1.** filmy substance like spider's web **2.** thin gauze or silk fabric

gossip (ˈgɒsɪp) *n.* **1.** idle (malicious) talk about other persons, *esp.* regardless of facts **2.** one who talks thus (*also* **ˈgossipmonger**) —*vi.* **3.** engage in gossip **4.** chatter —**gossip column** part of newspaper devoted to gossip about well-known people

got (gɒt) *pt./pp. of* GET

Goth (gɒθ) *n.* **1.** member of East Germanic people who invaded Roman Empire from 3rd to 5th cent. **2.** rude or barbaric person —**ˈGothic** *a.* **1.** *Archit.* of the pointed arch style common in Europe from 12th–16th centuries **2.** of Goths **3.** (*sometimes* **g-**) barbarous **4.** (*sometimes* **g-**) of literary style characterized by gloom, the grotesque, and the supernatural —*n.* **5.** (of type) German black letter

gotten (ˈgɒtᵊn) **US** *pp. of* GET

gouache (gʊˈɑːʃ) *n.* **1.** painting technique using opaque watercolour in which pigments are bound with glue (*also* **body colour**) **2.** paint used in this technique **3.** painting done by this method

Gouda (ˈgaʊdə) *n.* large, flat, round Dutch cheese with mild flavour

gouge (gaʊdʒ) *vt.* (*usu. with* out) **1.** scoop out **2.** force out —*n.* **3.** chisel with curved cutting edge

goulash (ˈguːlæʃ) *n.* stew of meat and vegetables seasoned with paprika (*also* **Hungarian goulash**)

gourd (gʊəd) *n.* **1.** trailing or climbing plant **2.** its large fleshy fruit **3.** its rind as vessel

gourmand (ˈgʊəmənd) *or* **gormand** (ˈgɔːmənd) *n.* glutton

gourmet (ˈgʊəmeɪ) *n.* **1.** connoisseur of wine, food **2.** epicure

gout (gaʊt) *n.* disease characterized by inflammation, *esp.* of joints —**ˈgouty** *a.*

Gov. *or* **gov.** **1.** government **2.** governor

govern (ˈgʌvᵊn) *vt.* **1.** rule, direct, guide, control **2.** decide, determine **3.** be followed by (grammatical case *etc.*) —**ˈgovernable** *a.* —**ˈgovernance** *n.* act of governing —**ˈgoverness** *n.* woman teacher, *esp.* in private household —**ˈgovernment** *n.* **1.** exercise of political authority in directing a people, state *etc.* **2.** system by which community is ruled **3.** body of people in charge of government of state **4.** ministry **5.** executive power **6.** control **7.** direction **8.** exercise of authority —**governˈmental** *a.* —**ˈgovernor** *n.* **1.** one who governs, *esp.* one invested with supreme authority in state *etc.* **2.** chief administrator of an institution **3.** member of committee responsible for an organization or institution **4.** regulator for speed of engine —**governor general** **1.** representative of Crown in dominion of commonwealth **2.** UK governor with jurisdiction over other governors (*pl.* **governors general, governor generals**)

Govt. *or* **govt.** government

gown (gaʊn) *n.* **1.** loose flowing outer garment **2.** woman's (long) dress **3.** official robe, as in university *etc.*

goy (gɔɪ) *n. sl.* derogatory word used by Jews for non-Jew (*pl.* **goyim** (ˈgɔɪɪm), **-s**)

G.P. General Practitioner

G.P.O. General Post Office

Gr. **1.** Grecian **2.** Greece **3.** Greek

gr. **1.** grain(s) **2.** gram(me)(s) **3.** gross

grab (græb) *vt.* **1.** grasp suddenly **2.** snatch (**-bb-**) —*n.* **3.** sudden clutch **4.** quick attempt to seize **5.** device or implement for clutching

grace (greɪs) *n.* **1.** charm, elegance **2.** accomplishment **3.** good will, favour **4.** sense of propriety **5.** postponement granted **6.** short thanksgiving before or after meal **7.** title of duke or archbishop —*pl.* **8.** affectation of manner (*esp. in* **airs and graces**) —*vt.* **9.** add grace to, honour —**ˈgraceful** *a.* —**ˈgracefully** *adv.* —**ˈgraceless** *a.* shameless, depraved —**ˈgracious** *a.* **1.** favourable **2.** kind **3.** pleasing **4.** indulgent, beneficent, condescending —**ˈgraciously** *adv.* —**grace note** *Mus.* melodic ornament

THESAURUS

gory blood-soaked, bloodstained, bloodthirsty, bloody, ensanguined (*Literary*), murderous, sanguinary

gospel certainty, fact, the last word, truth, verity

gossip *n.* **1.** blether, chinwag (*Brit. inf.*), chitchat, clishmaclaver (*Scot.*), hearsay, idle talk, jaw (*Sl.*), newsmongering (*Old-fashioned*), prattle, scandal, small talk, tittle-tattle **2.** babbler, blatherskite, blether, busybody, chatterbox (*Inf.*), chatterer, flibbertigibbet, gossipmonger, newsmonger (*Old-fashioned*), prattler, quidnunc, scandalmonger, tattler, telltale ~*v.* **3.** blather, blether, chat, gabble, jaw (*Sl.*), prate, prattle, tattle

govern **1.** administer, be in power, command, conduct, control, direct, guide, hold sway, lead, manage, order, oversee, pilot, reign, rule, steer, superintend, supervise **2.** bridle, check, contain, control, curb, direct, discipline, get the better of, hold in check, inhibit, master, regulate, restrain, subdue, tame **3.** decide, determine, guide, influence, rule, sway, underlie

government **1.** administration, authority, dominion, execution, governance, law, polity, rule, sovereignty, state, statecraft **2.** administration, executive, ministry, powers-that-be, regime **3.** authority, command, control, direction, domination, guidance, management, regulation, restraint, superintendence, supervision, sway

governor administrator, boss (*Inf.*), chief, commander, comptroller, controller, director, executive, head, leader, manager, overseer, ruler, superintendent, supervisor

gown costume, dress, frock, garb, garment, habit, robe

grab bag, capture, catch, catch *or* take hold of, clutch, grasp, grip, latch on to, nab (*Inf.*), pluck, seize, snap up, snatch

grace *n.* **1.** attractiveness, beauty, charm, comeli-

Graces (ˈgreɪsɪz) *pl.n. Gr. myth.* three sister goddesses, givers of charm and beauty

grade (greɪd) *n.* **1.** step, stage **2.** degree of rank *etc.* **3.** class **4.** mark, rating **5.** slope —*vt.* **6.** arrange in classes **7.** assign grade to **8.** level (ground), move (earth) with grader —**gradation** (grəˈdeɪʃən) *n.* **1.** series of degrees or steps **2.** each of them **3.** arrangement in steps **4.** in painting, gradual passing from one shade *etc.* to another —ˈ**grader** *n.* **1.** person or thing that grades **2.** machine with wide blade used in road making —**make the grade** succeed

gradient (ˈgreɪdɪənt) *n.* (degree of) slope

gradual (ˈgrædjʊəl) *a.* **1.** taking place by degrees **2.** slow and steady **3.** not steep —ˈ**gradually** *adv.*

graduate (ˈgrædjʊeɪt) *vi.* **1.** take university degree —*vt.* **2.** divide into degrees **3.** mark, arrange according to scale —*n.* (ˈgrædjʊɪt) **4.** holder of university degree —**graduˈation** *n.* —**graduated pension UK** national pension scheme in which employees' contributions are scaled in accordance with their wage rate

Graeco- *or esp. U.S.* **Greco-** (ˈgriːkəʊ-, ˈgrɛkəʊ-) (*comb. form*) Greek, as in *Graeco-Roman*

graffiti (græˈfiːtiː) *pl.n.* (*oft.* obscene) writing, drawing on walls (*sing.* **grafˈfito**)

graft[1] (grɑːft) *n.* **1.** shoot of plant set in stalk of another **2.** the process **3.** surgical transplant of skin to an area of body in need of tissue —*vt.* **4.** insert (shoot) in another stalk **5.** transplant (living tissue in surgery)

graft[2] (grɑːft) *n.* **1.** *inf.* hard work **2.** self-advancement, profit by unfair means, *esp.* through official or political privilege **3.** bribe **4.** swindle —ˈ**grafter** *n.*

Grail (greɪl) *n. see* **Holy Grail** *at* HOLY

grain (greɪn) *n.* **1.** seed, fruit of cereal plant **2.** wheat and allied plants **3.** small hard particle **4.** unit of weight, 1/7000th of pound avoirdupois (0.0648 gram) **5.** texture **6.** arrangement of fibres **7.** any very small amount **8.** natural temperament or disposition —ˈ**grainy** *a.*

gram *or* **gramme** (græm) *n.* unit of weight in metric system, one thousandth of a kilogram

-gram (*comb. form*) drawing; something written or recorded, as in *hexagram, telegram*

gramineous (grəˈmɪnɪəs) *a.* **1.** of or belonging to grass family **2.** resembling grass; grasslike (*also* **graminaceous** (græmɪˈneɪʃəs))

graminivorous (græmɪˈnɪvərəs) *a.* (of animals) feeding on grass

grammar (ˈgræmə) *n.* **1.** science of structure and usages of language **2.** book on this **3.** correct use of words —**grammarian** (grəˈmɛərɪən) *n.* —**gramˈmatical** *a.* according to grammar —**gramˈmatically** *adv.* —**grammar school** *esp.* formerly, state-maintained secondary school providing education with strong academic bias

gramophone (ˈgræməfəʊn) *n.* instrument for reproducing sounds on discs, record-player

grampus (ˈgræmpəs) *n.* **1.** type of dolphin **2.** person who huffs, breathes heavily

gran (græn) *or* **granny** (ˈgrænɪ) *n. inf.* grandmother —**granny flat** flat in or added to house (for elderly parent) —**granny knot** *or* **granny's knot** reef knot with ends crossed wrong way

granary (ˈgrænərɪ; *U.S.* ˈgreɪnərɪ) *n.* **1.** storehouse for grain **2.** rich grain growing region

grand (grænd) *a.* **1.** imposing **2.** magnificent **3.** majestic **4.** noble **5.** splendid **6.** eminent **7.** lofty **8.** chief, of chief importance **9.** final (total) —**grandeur** (ˈgrændʒə) *n.* **1.** nobility **2.** magnificence **3.** dignity —**granˈdiloquence** *n.* —**granˈdiloquent** *a.* pompous in speech —**granˈdiloquently** *adv.* —ˈ**grandiose** *a.* **1.** imposing **2.** affectedly grand **3.** striking —**grandchild** (ˈgræntʃaɪld) *n.* child of one's child (**grandson** (ˈgrænsʌn, ˈgrænd-) *or* **granddaughter** (ˈgrændɔːtə)) —**grand duke 1.** prince or nobleman who rules territory, state or principality **2.** son or male descendant in male line of Russian tsar —**grandfather clock** long-pendulum clock in tall standing wooden case —**grand**

THESAURUS

ness, ease, elegance, finesse, gracefulness, loveliness, pleasantness, poise, polish, refinement, shapeliness, tastefulness **2.** benefaction, beneficence, benevolence, favour, generosity, goodness, good will, kindliness, kindness **3.** breeding, consideration, cultivation, decency, decorum, etiquette, mannerliness, manners, propriety, tact **4.** benediction, blessing, prayer, thanks, thanksgiving ~*v.* **5.** adorn, beautify, bedeck, deck, decorate, dignify, distinguish, elevate, embellish, enhance, enrich, favour, garnish, glorify, honour, ornament, set off

graceful agile, beautiful, becoming, charming, comely, easy, elegant, fine, flowing, gracile (*Rare*), natural, pleasing, smooth, symmetrical, tasteful

gracious accommodating, affable, amiable, beneficent, benevolent, benign, benignant, charitable, chivalrous, civil, compassionate, considerate, cordial, courteous, courtly, friendly, hospitable, indulgent, kind, kindly, lenient, merciful, obliging, pleasing, polite, well-mannered

grade *n.* **1.** brand, category, class, condition, degree, echelon, group, level, mark, notch, order, place, position, quality, rank, rung, size, stage, station, step **2.** **make the grade** *Inf.* come through with flying colours, come up to scratch (*Inf.*), measure up, measure up to expectations, pass muster, prove acceptable, succeed, win through **3.** acclivity, bank, declivity, gradient, hill, incline, rise, slope ~*v.* **4.** arrange, brand, class, classify, evaluate, group, order, range, rank, rate, sort, value

gradient acclivity, bank, declivity, grade, hill, incline, rise, slope

gradual continuous, even, gentle, graduated, moderate, piecemeal, progressive, regular, slow, steady, successive, unhurried

gradually bit by bit, by degrees, drop by drop, evenly, gently, little by little, moderately, piece by piece, piecemeal, progressively, slowly, steadily, step by step, unhurriedly

graduate *v.* **1.** calibrate, grade, mark off, measure out, proportion, regulate **2.** arrange, classify, grade, group, order, range, rank, sort

graft 1. *n.* bud, implant, scion, shoot, splice, sprout **2.** *v.* affix, implant, ingraft, insert, join, splice, transplant

grain 1. cereals, corn **2.** grist, kernel, seed **3.** atom, bit, crumb, fragment, granule, iota, jot, mite, modicum, molecule, morsel, mote, ounce, particle, piece, scintilla (*Rare*), scrap, scruple, spark, speck, suspicion, trace, whit **4.** fibre, nap, pattern, surface, texture, weave **5.** character, disposition, humour, inclination, make-up, temper

jury *Law esp.* in U.S.A., jury summoned to inquire into accusations of crime and ascertain whether evidence is adequate to found indictment —**Grand National** annual steeplechase run at Aintree, Liverpool —**grand opera** opera with serious plot and fully composed text —**grandparent** (ˈgrænpɛərənt, ˈgrænd-) *n.* parent of parent (**grandfather** (ˈgrænfɑːðə, ˈgrænd-) *or* **grandmother** (ˈgrænmʌðə, ˈgrænd-)) —**grand piano** large harp-shaped piano with horizontal strings —**grandstand** (ˈgrænstænd, ˈgrænd-) *n.* structure with tiered seats for spectators

grande dame (grɑ̃d ˈdam) *Fr.* woman regarded as most experienced or prominent member of her profession *etc.*

grandee (grænˈdiː) *n.* Spanish nobleman of highest rank

grand mal (ˈgrɒn ˈmæl) form of epilepsy characterized by convulsions and loss of consciousness

Grand Prix (*Fr.* grɑ̃ ˈpri) any of series of international formula motor races

grange (greɪndʒ) *n.* country house with farm buildings

granite (ˈgrænɪt) *n.* hard crystalline igneous rock —**graˈnitic** *a.*

granivorous (græˈnɪvərəs) *a.* feeding on grain or seeds

grant (grɑːnt) *vt.* **1.** consent to fulfil (request) **2.** permit **3.** bestow **4.** admit —*n.* **5.** sum of money provided by government for specific purpose, as education **6.** gift **7.** allowance, concession —**granˈtee** *n.* —**ˈgranter** *or (Law)* **ˈgrantor** *n.* —**grant-in-aid** *n.* money granted by central to local government for programme *etc.* (*pl.* **grants-in-aid**)

granule (ˈgrænjuːl) *n.* small grain —**ˈgranular** *a.* of or like grains —**ˈgranulate** *vt.* **1.** form into grains —*vi.* **2.** take form of grains —**granuˈlation** *n.* —**granulated sugar** coarsely ground white sugar

grape (greɪp) *n.* fruit of vine —**grape hyacinth** plant with clusters of small, rounded blue flowers —**ˈgrapeshot** *n.* bullets scattering when fired —**ˈgrapevine** *n.* **1.** grape-bearing vine **2.** *inf.* unofficial means of conveying information

grapefruit (ˈgreɪpfruːt) *n.* subtropical citrus fruit

graph (grɑːf, græf) *n.* drawing depicting relation of different numbers, quantities *etc.* (*also* **chart**)

-graph (*n. comb. form*) **1.** instrument that writes or records, as in *telegraph* **2.** writing, record; drawing, as in *autograph, lithograph* —**-grapher** (*n. comb. form*) **1.** person skilled in subject, as in *geographer, photographer* **2.** person who writes or draws in specified way, as in *stenographer, lithographer* —**-graphic(al)** (*a. comb. form*) —**-graphy** (*n. comb. form*) **1.** form of writing, representing *etc.*, as in *calligraphy, photography* **2.** art; descriptive science, as in *choreography, oceanography*

graphic (ˈgræfɪk) *or* **graphical** *a.* **1.** vividly descriptive **2.** of, in, relating to, writing, drawing, painting *etc.* —**ˈgraphically** *adv.* —**ˈgraphics** *pl.n.* **1.** (*with sing. v.*) art of drawing in accordance with mathematical principles **2.** (*with sing. v.*) study of writing systems **3.** (*with pl. v.*) drawings *etc.* in layout of magazine or book —**ˈgraphite** *n.* form of carbon (used in pencils) —**graˈphology** *n.* study of handwriting —**graphic arts** fine or applied visual arts based on drawing or use of line, *esp.* illustration and print-making —**graphic equalizer** electronic device for cutting or boosting selected frequencies, using small linear faders —**graph paper** paper with intersecting lines for drawing graphs *etc.*

grapnel (ˈgræpnᵊl) *n.* **1.** hooked iron instrument for seizing anything **2.** small anchor with several flukes

grapple (ˈgræpᵊl) *v.* **1.** come to grips, wrestle **2.** cope, contend —*n.* **3.** grappling **4.** grapnel —**grappling iron** *or* **hook** grapnel, *esp.* for securing ships

grasp (grɑːsp) *v.* **1.** (try, struggle to) seize hold (of) —*vt.* **2.** understand —*n.* **3.** act of grasping **4.** grip **5.** comprehension —**ˈgrasping** *a.* greedy, avaricious

grass (grɑːs) *n.* **1.** common type of plant with jointed stems and long narrow leaves (including cereals, bamboo *etc.*) **2.** such plants grown as lawn **3.** pasture **4.** *sl.* marijuana **5.** *sl.* informer, *esp.* criminal who betrays

THESAURUS

grand 1. august, dignified, elevated, eminent, exalted, fine, glorious, grandiose, great, haughty, illustrious, imposing, impressive, large, lofty, lordly, luxurious, magnificent, majestic, monumental, noble, opulent, palatial, princely, regal, splendid, stately, striking, sublime, sumptuous 2. admirable, excellent, fine, first-class, first-rate, great (*Inf.*), marvellous (*Inf.*), outstanding, smashing (*Inf.*), splendid, super (*Inf.*), superb, terrific (*Inf.*), very good, wonderful 3. chief, head, highest, leading, main, pre-eminent, principal, supreme

grandeur augustness, dignity, greatness, importance, loftiness, magnificence, majesty, nobility, pomp, splendour, state, stateliness, sublimity

grandiose 1. affected, ambitious, bombastic, extravagant, flamboyant, high-flown, ostentatious, pompous, pretentious, showy 2. ambitious, grand, imposing, impressive, lofty, magnificent, majestic, monumental, stately

grant 1. *v.* accede to, accord, acknowledge, admit, agree to, allocate, allot, allow, assign, award, bestow, cede, concede, confer, consent to, donate, give, impart, permit, present, vouchsafe, yield 2. *n.* admission, allocation, allotment, allowance, award, benefaction, bequest, boon, bounty, concession, donation, endowment, gift, present, subsidy

granule atom, crumb, fragment, grain, iota, jot, molecule, particle, scrap, speck

graphic clear, descriptive, detailed, explicit, expressive, forcible, illustrative, lively, lucid, picturesque, striking, telling, vivid, well-drawn

grapple 1. catch, clasp, clutch, come to grips, fasten, grab, grasp, grip, hold, hug, lay *or* take hold, make fast, seize, wrestle 2. address oneself to, attack, battle, clash, combat, confront, contend, cope, deal with, do battle, encounter, engage, face, fight, struggle, tackle, take on, tussle, wrestle

grasp *v.* 1. catch, clasp, clinch, clutch, grab, grapple, grip, hold, lay *or* take hold of, seize, snatch 2. catch *or* get the drift of, catch on, comprehend, follow, get, realize, see, take in, understand ~*n.* 3. clasp, clutches, embrace, grip, hold, possession, tenure 4. awareness, comprehension, ken, knowledge, mastery, perception, realization, understanding

grasping acquisitive, avaricious, close-fisted, covetous, greedy, mean, miserly, niggardly, penny-pinching (*Inf.*), rapacious, selfish, stingy, tightfisted, usurious, venal

others to police —*vt.* 6. cover with grass —*vi.* 7. *sl.* (*with* on) inform —**grass hockey** C hockey played on field —ˈ**grasshopper** *n.* jumping, chirping insect —**grass roots** fundamentals —ˈ**grassroots** *a.* coming from ordinary people, the rank and file —**grass widow** wife whose husband is absent

grate[1] (greɪt) *vt.* 1. rub into small bits on rough surface —*vi.* 2. rub with harsh noise 3. have irritating effect —ˈ**grater** *n.* utensil with rough surface for reducing substance to small particles

grate[2] (greɪt) *n.* framework of metal bars for holding fuel in fireplace —ˈ**grating** *n.* framework of parallel or latticed bars covering opening

grateful (ˈgreɪtful) *a.* 1. thankful 2. appreciative 3. pleasing —ˈ**gratefully** *adv.* —ˈ**gratefulness** *n.* —**gratitude** (ˈgrætɪtjuːd) *n.* sense of being thankful for favour

gratify (ˈgrætɪfaɪ) *vt.* 1. satisfy 2. please 3. indulge —**gratifiˈcation** *n.*

gratin (*Fr.* graˈtɛ̃) *n.* 1. method of cooking with covering of breadcrumbs to form light crust 2. dish so cooked

gratis (ˈgreɪtɪs, ˈgrætɪs, ˈgrɑːtɪs) *adv./a.* free, for nothing

gratuitous (grəˈtjuːɪtəs) *a.* 1. given free 2. uncalled for —**graˈtuitously** *adv.* —**graˈtuity** *n.* 1. gift of money for services rendered 2. donation

gravamen (grəˈveɪmɛn) *n.* 1. *Law* part of accusation weighing most heavily against accused 2. *Law* substance of complaint 3. *rare* grievance (*pl.* **-vamina** (-ˈvæmɪnə))

grave[1] (greɪv) *n.* 1. hole dug to bury corpse 2. *Poet.* death —ˈ**gravestone** *n.* monument on grave —ˈ**graveyard** *n.*

grave[2] (greɪv) *a.* 1. serious, weighty 2. dignified, solemn 3. plain, dark in colour 4. deep in note —ˈ**gravely** *adv.*

grave[3] (greɪv) *vt.* clean (ship's bottom) by scraping —**graving dock** dry dock

grave[4] (grɑːv) *n.* *Phonet.* accent (`) used to indicate quality of vowel, full pronunciation of syllable *etc.*

gravel (ˈgræv^əl) *n.* 1. small stones 2. coarse sand —*vt.* 3. cover with gravel (-ll-) —ˈ**gravelly** *a.*

graven (ˈgreɪv^ən) *a.* carved, engraved

Graves (grɑːv) *n.* 1. (*sometimes* **g-**) white or red wine from district around Bordeaux, France 2. dry or medium sweet white wine from any country

gravid (ˈgrævɪd) *a.* pregnant

gravimetric (grævɪˈmɛtrɪk) *a.* 1. of measurement by weight 2. *Chem.* of analysis of quantities by weight

gravitate (ˈgrævɪteɪt) *vi.* 1. move by gravity 2. tend (towards centre of attraction) 3. sink, settle down —**graviˈtation** *n.*

gravity (ˈgrævɪtɪ) *n.* 1. force of attraction of one body for another, *esp.* of objects to the earth 2. heaviness 3. importance 4. seriousness 5. staidness

gravy (ˈgreɪvɪ) *n.* 1. juices from meat in cooking 2. sauce for food made from these —**gravy boat** small boat-shaped vessel for serving gravy

gray (greɪ) *see* GREY —ˈ**grayling** *n.* fish of salmon family

graze[1] (greɪz) *v.* feed on (grass, pasture) —ˈ**grazier** *n.* one who raises cattle for market —ˈ**grazing** *n.* 1. vegetation on ranges or pastures that is available for livestock to feed upon 2. land on which this is growing

graze[2] (greɪz) *vt.* 1. touch lightly in passing, scratch, scrape —*n.* 2. grazing 3. abrasion

grease (griːs) *n.* 1. soft melted fat of animals 2. thick oil as lubricant —*vt.* (griːs, griːz) 3. apply grease to —ˈ**greaser** *n.* 1. one who greases 2. *inf.* mechanic 3. *sl.* unpleasant, dirty person —ˈ**greasily** *adv.* —ˈ**greasiness** *n.* —ˈ**greasy** *a.* —**grease gun** appliance for injecting oil or grease into machinery —**grease monkey** *inf.*

THESAURUS

grate *v.* 1. mince, pulverize, shred, triturate 2. creak, grind, rasp, rub, scrape, scratch 3. annoy, chafe, exasperate, fret, gall, get one down, get on one's nerves (*Inf.*), irk, irritate, jar, nettle, peeve, rankle, rub one up the wrong way, set one's teeth on edge, vex

grateful 1. appreciative, beholden, indebted, obliged, thankful 2. acceptable, agreeable, favourable, gratifying, nice, pleasing, refreshing, restful, satisfactory, satisfying, welcome

gratify cater to, delight, favour, fulfil, give pleasure, gladden, humour, indulge, please, recompense, requite, satisfy, thrill

gratis for nothing, free, freely, free of charge, gratuitously, on the house, unpaid

gratitude appreciation, gratefulness, indebtedness, obligation, recognition, sense of obligation, thankfulness, thanks

gratuitous 1. complimentary, free, spontaneous, unasked-for, unpaid, unrewarded, voluntary 2. assumed, baseless, causeless, groundless, irrelevant, needless, superfluous, uncalled-for, unfounded, unjustified, unmerited, unnecessary, unprovoked, unwarranted, wanton

gratuity baksheesh, benefaction, bonus, boon, bounty, donation, gift, largess, perquisite, *pourboire*, present, recompense, reward, tip

grave[1] *n.* burying place, crypt, last resting place, mausoleum pit, sepulchre, tomb, vault

grave[2] 1. dignified, dour, dull, earnest, gloomy, grim-faced, heavy, leaden, long-faced, muted, quiet, sage (*Obsolete*), sedate, serious, sober, solemn, sombre, staid, subdued, thoughtful, unsmiling 2. acute, critical, crucial, dangerous, exigent, hazardous, important, life-and-death, momentous, of great consequence, perilous, pressing, serious, severe, significant, threatening, urgent, vital, weighty

graveyard boneyard (*Inf.*), burial ground, cemetery, charnel house, churchyard, God's acre (*Literary*), necropolis

gravitate 1. *With* **to** *or* **towards** be influenced (attracted, drawn, pulled), incline, lean, move, tend 2. be precipitated, descend, drop, fall, precipitate, settle, sink

gravity 1. acuteness, consequence, exigency, hazardousness, importance, moment, momentousness, perilousness, pressingness, seriousness, severity, significance, urgency, weightiness 2. demureness, dignity, earnestness, gloom, grimness, reserve, sedateness, seriousness, sobriety, solemnity, thoughtfulness

graze *v.* 1. brush, glance off, kiss, rub, scrape, shave, skim, touch 2. abrade, bark, chafe, scrape, scratch, skin ~*n.* 3. abrasion, scrape, scratch

greasy fatty, oily, slick, slimy, slippery

mechanic —ˈ**greasepaint** *n.* theatrical make-up —**grease the palm** (*or* **hand**) **of** bribe

great (greɪt) *a.* **1.** large, big **2.** important **3.** pre-eminent, distinguished **4.** *inf.* excellent —ˈ**greatly** *adv.* —ˈ**greatness** *n.* —**Great Bear** *see* URSA MAJOR —**great circle** circular section of sphere with radius equal to that of sphere —ˈ**greatcoat** *n.* overcoat, *esp.* military —**Great Dane** breed of very large dog —**Great Russian** *n.* **1.** *Linguis.* Russian **2.** member of chief East Slavonic people of Russia —*a.* **3.** of this people or their language —**great seal** (*oft.* **G- S-**) principal seal of nation *etc.* used to authenticate documents of highest importance —**Great War** World War I

great- (*comb. form*) indicates a degree further removed in relationship, as in *great-grandfather*

greave (gri:v) *n.* (*oft. pl.*) armour for leg below knee

grebe (gri:b) *n.* aquatic bird

Grecian (ˈgri:ʃən) *a.* of (ancient) Greece —**Grecian profile** profile in which nose and forehead form almost straight line

Greco- (*comb. form*) *esp.* **US** *see* GRAECO-

greed (gri:d) *n.* excessive consumption of, desire for, food, wealth —ˈ**greedily** *adv.* —ˈ**greediness** *n.* voracity of appetite —ˈ**greedy** *a.* **1.** gluttonous **2.** eagerly desirous **3.** voracious **4.** covetous

Greek (gri:k) *n.* **1.** native language of Greece —*a.* **2.** of Greece, the Greeks or the Greek language —**Greek cross** cross with four arms of same length —**Greek Orthodox Church 1.** established Church of Greece, in which Metropolitan of Athens has primacy of honour (*also* **Greek Church**) **2.** *see* **Orthodox Church** *at* ORTHODOX

green (gri:n) *a.* **1.** of colour between blue and yellow **2.** grass-coloured **3.** emerald **4.** unripe **5.** (of bacon) unsmoked **6.** inexperienced **7.** gullible **8.** envious **9.** (*oft.* **G-**) concerned with preserving the environment —*n.* **10.** colour **11.** area of grass, *esp.* for playing bowls *etc.* **12.** (*oft.* **G-**) member of political movement whose main concern is preserving the environment —*pl.* **13.** green vegetables —ˈ**greenery** *n.* vegetation —**green bean** any bean plant, such as French bean, having narrow green edible pods —**green belt** area of farms, open country around a town —**Green Cross Code UK** code for children giving rules for road safety —**green-eyed** *a.* jealous, envious —**green-eyed monster** jealousy, envy —ˈ**greenfinch** *n.* European finch with dull green plumage in male —**green fingers** talent for gardening —ˈ**greenfly** *n.* aphid, small green garden pest —ˈ**greengage** *n.* kind of plum —ˈ**greengrocer** *n.* dealer in vegetables and fruit —ˈ**greengrocery** *n.* —ˈ**greenhorn** *n.* inexperienced person, newcomer —ˈ**greenhouse** *n.* glasshouse for rearing plants —ˈ**greenkeeper** *n.* person responsible for maintaining golf course *etc.* —**green light 1.** signal to go, *esp.* green traffic light **2.** permission to proceed with project *etc.* —**green paper** (*oft.* **G- P-**) **UK** government document containing policy proposals to be discussed, *esp.* by Parliament —**green pepper** green unripe fruit of sweet pepper, eaten raw or cooked —**green pound** unit of account used in calculating Britain's contributions to and payments from Community Agricultural Fund of EEC —ˈ**greenroom** *n.* room for actors when offstage —ˈ**greenshank** *n.* large European sandpiper —**greenstick fracture** fracture in children in which bone is partly bent and splinters only on convex side of bend —ˈ**greenstone** *n.* New Zealand jade —ˈ**greensward** *n.* turf

Greenwich Mean Time *or* **Greenwich Time** (ˈgrɪnɪdʒ) local time of 0° meridian passing through Greenwich, England: standard time for Britain and basis for calculating times throughout world

greet (gri:t) *vt.* **1.** meet with expressions of welcome **2.** accost, salute **3.** receive —ˈ**greeting** *n.*

gregarious (grɪˈgɛərɪəs) *a.* **1.** fond of company, sociable **2.** living in flocks —**greˈgariousness** *n.*

Gregorian calendar (grɪˈgɔ:rɪən) calendar introduced by Pope Gregory XIII, whereby ordinary year is made to consist of 365 days

Gregorian chant *see* PLAINSONG

THESAURUS

great 1. big, bulky, colossal, enormous, extensive, gigantic, huge, immense, large, mammoth, prodigious, stupendous, tremendous, vast, voluminous **2.** capital, chief, grand, leading, main, major, paramount, primary, principal, prominent, superior **3.** consequential, critical, crucial, grave, heavy, important, momentous, serious, significant, weighty **4.** celebrated, distinguished, eminent, exalted, excellent, famed, famous, glorious, illustrious, notable, noteworthy, outstanding, prominent, remarkable, renowned, superlative, talented **5.** august, chivalrous, dignified, distinguished, exalted, fine, glorious, grand, heroic, high-minded, idealistic, impressive, lofty, magnanimous, noble, princely, sublime **6.** *Inf.* admirable, excellent, fantastic (*Inf.*), fine, first-rate, good, marvellous (*Inf.*), terrific (*Inf.*), tremendous (*Inf.*), wonderful

greatly by much, considerably, enormously, exceedingly, extremely, highly, hugely, immensely, markedly, mightily, much, notably, powerfully, remarkably, tremendously, vastly, very much

greatness 1. bulk, enormity, hugeness, immensity, largeness, length, magnitude, mass, prodigiousness, size, vastness **2.** gravity, heaviness, import, importance, moment, momentousness, seriousness, significance, urgency, weight **3.** celebrity, distinction, eminence, fame, glory, grandeur, illustriousness, lustre, note, renown

greed, greediness 1. edacity, esurience, gluttony, gormandizing, hunger, insatiableness, ravenousness, voracity **2.** acquisitiveness, avidity, covetousness, craving, cupidity, desire, eagerness, graspingness, longing, rapacity, selfishness

greedy 1. edacious, esurient, gluttonous, gormandizing, hoggish, hungry, insatiable, piggish, ravenous, voracious **2.** acquisitive, avaricious, avid, covetous, craving, desirous, eager, grasping, hungry, impatient, rapacious, selfish

green *adj.* **1.** fresh, immature, new, raw, recent, unripe **2.** callow, credulous, gullible, ignorant, immature, inexperienced, inexpert, ingenuous, innocent, naive, new, raw, unpolished, unpractised, unskilful, unsophisticated, untrained, unversed, wet behind the ears (*Inf.*) **3.** covetous, envious, grudging, jealous, resentful *~n.* **4.** common, grassplot, lawn, sward, turf

greet accost, address, compliment, hail, meet, nod to, receive, salute, tip one's hat to, welcome

greeting address, hail, reception, salutation, salute, welcome

gregarious affable, companionable, convivial, cordial, friendly, outgoing, sociable, social

gremlin ('grɛmlɪn) *n.* imaginary being blamed for mechanical and other troubles

grenade (grɪ'neɪd) *n.* explosive shell or bomb, thrown by hand or shot from rifle —**grenadier** (grɛnə'dɪə) *n.* 1. soldier of Grenadier Guards 2. formerly, grenade thrower

grenadine (grɛnə'diːn, 'grɛnədiːn) *n.* syrup made from pomegranate juice, for sweetening and colouring drinks

grew (gruː) *pt.* of GROW

grey *or U.S.* **gray** (greɪ) *a.* 1. between black and white, as ashes or lead 2. clouded 3. dismal 4. turning white 5. aged 6. intermediate, indeterminate —*n.* 7. grey colour 8. grey or whitish horse —**Grey Friar** Franciscan friar —'**greyhen** *n.* female of black grouse —'**greyhound** *n.* swift slender dog used in coursing and racing —'**greylag** *or* **greylag goose** *n.* large grey Eurasian goose —**grey matter** 1. greyish tissue of brain and spinal cord, containing nerve cell bodies and fibres 2. *inf.* brains; intellect

grid (grɪd) *n.* 1. network of horizontal and vertical lines, bars *etc.* 2. any interconnecting system of links 3. national network of electricity supply

griddle ('grɪdᵊl) *n.* flat iron plate for cooking (*also* '**girdle**)

gridiron ('grɪdaɪən) *n.* 1. frame of metal bars for grilling 2. (field of play for) American football

grief (griːf) *n.* deep sorrow —'**grievance** *n.* real or imaginary grounds for complaint —**grieve** *vi.* 1. feel grief —*vt.* 2. cause grief to —'**grievous** *a.* 1. painful, oppressive 2. very serious —**grief-stricken** *a.* stricken with grief; sorrowful

griffin ('grɪfɪn), **griffon**, *or* **gryphon** *n.* fabulous monster with eagle's head and wings and lion's body

grill (grɪl) *n.* 1. device on cooker to radiate heat downwards 2. food cooked under grill 3. gridiron —*v.* 4. cook (food) under grill —*vt.* 5. subject to severe questioning —'**grilling** *a.* 1. very hot —*n.* 2. severe cross-examination —'**grillroom** *n.* restaurant where grilled food is served

grille *or* **grill** (grɪl) *n.* grating, crosswork of bars over opening

grilse (grɪls) *n.* salmon at stage when it returns for first time from sea (*pl.* **-s, grilse**)

grim (grɪm) *a.* 1. stern 2. of stern or forbidding aspect, relentless 3. joyless —'**grimly** *adv.*

grimace (grɪ'meɪs) *n.* 1. wry face —*vi.* 2. pull wry face

grimalkin (grɪ'mælkɪn, -'mɔːl-) *n.* 1. old cat, *esp.* female cat 2. crotchety or shrewish old woman

grime (graɪm) *n.* 1. ingrained dirt, soot —*vt.* 2. soil, dirty, blacken —'**grimy** *a.*

grin (grɪn) *vi.* 1. show teeth, as in laughter (**-nn-**) —*n.* 2. grinning smile

grind (graɪnd) *vt.* 1. crush to powder 2. oppress 3. make sharp, smooth 4. grate —*vi.* 5. perform action of grinding 6. *inf.* work, *esp.* study hard 7. grate (**ground** *pt./pp.*) —*n.* 8. *inf.* hard work 9. act of grinding —'**grinder** *n.* —'**grindstone** *n.* stone used for grinding

gringo ('grɪŋgəʊ) *n.* in Mexico, contemptuous name for foreigner, *esp.* Englishman or American (*pl.* **-s**)

grip (grɪp) *n.* 1. firm hold, grasp 2. grasping power 3. mastery 4. handle 5. suitcase or travelling bag (*also* '**handgrip**) —*vt.* 6. grasp or hold tightly 7. hold interest or attention of (**-pp-**)

gripe (graɪp) *vi.* 1. *inf.* complain (persistently) —*n.* 2. intestinal pain (*esp.* in infants) 3. *inf.* complaint

grippe *or* **grip** (grɪp) *n.* influenza

grisly ('grɪzlɪ) *a.* grim, causing terror, ghastly

grist (grɪst) *n.* corn to be ground —**grist to** (*or* **for**) **the** (*or* **one's**) **mill** something which can be turned to advantage

gristle ('grɪsᵊl) *n.* cartilage, tough flexible tissue

grit (grɪt) *n.* 1. rough particles of sand 2. coarse sandstone 3. courage —*n./a.* 4. (G-) C *inf.* Liberal —*pl.* 5. wheat *etc.* coarsely ground —*vt.* 6. clench, grind (teeth) (**-tt-**) —'**grittiness** *n.* —'**gritty** *a.*

THESAURUS

grey 1. cheerless, cloudy, dark, depressing, dim, dismal, drab, dreary dull, foggy, gloomy, misty, murky, overcast, sunless 2. anonymous, indistinct, neutral, unclear, unidentifiable 3. aged, ancient, elderly, experienced, hoary, mature, old, venerable

grief affliction, agony, anguish, bereavement, dejection, distress, grievance, heartache, heartbreak, misery, mournfulness, mourning, pain, regret, remorse, sadness, sorrow, suffering, trial, tribulation, trouble, woe

grievance affliction, beef (*Sl.*), complaint, damage, distress, grief, gripe (*Inf.*), hardship, injury, injustice, resentment, sorrow, trial, tribulation, trouble, unhappiness, wrong

grieve 1. ache, bemoan, bewail, complain, deplore, lament, mourn, regret, rue, sorrow, suffer, wail, weep 2. afflict, agonize, break the heart of, crush, distress, hurt, injure, make one's heart bleed, pain, sadden, wound

grievous 1. afflicting, calamitous, damaging, distressing, dreadful, grave, harmful, heavy, hurtful, injurious, lamentable, oppressive, painful, severe, wounding 2. agonized, grief-stricken, heart-rending, mournful, pitiful, sorrowful, tragic

grim forbidding, formidable, harsh, implacable, merciless, morose, relentless, resolute, ruthless, severe, stern, sullen, unrelenting, unyielding

grimace 1. *n.* face, frown, mouth, scowl, sneer, wry face 2. *v.* frown, make a face *or* faces, mouth, scowl, sneer

grime dirt, filth, smut, soot

grimy begrimed, besmeared, besmirched, dirty, filthy, foul, grubby, smutty, soiled, sooty, unclean

grind *v.* 1. abrade, comminute, crush, granulate, grate, kibble, mill, pound, powder, pulverize, triturate 2. file, polish, sand, sharpen, smooth, whet 3. gnash, grate, grit, scrape ~*n.* 4. *Inf.* chore, drudgery, hard work, labour, sweat (*Inf.*), task, toil

grip *n.* 1. clasp, handclasp (*U.S.*), purchase 2. clutches, comprehension, control, domination, grasp, hold, influence, keeping, mastery, perception, possession, power, tenure, understanding ~*v.* 3. clasp, clutch, grasp, hold, latch on to, seize, take hold of 4. catch up, compel, engross, enthral, entrance, fascinate, hold, involve, mesmerize, rivet, spellbind

grisly abominable, appalling, awful, dreadful, frightful, ghastly, grim, gruesome, hideous, horrible, horrid, macabre, shocking, sickening, terrible, terrifying

grizzle[1] (ˈgrɪzᵊl) *v.* make, become grey —ˈ**grizzled** *a.* —ˈ**grizzly** *a.* —**grizzly bear** large Amer. bear

grizzle[2] (ˈgrɪzᵊl) *vi. inf.* grumble, whine, complain

groan (grəʊn) *vi.* 1. make low, deep sound of grief or pain 2. be in pain or overburdened —*n.* 3. groaning sound

groat (grəʊt) *n.* formerly, silver coin worth four pennies

groats (grəʊts) *pl.n.* hulled and crushed grain of oats, wheat or certain other cereals

grocer (ˈgrəʊsə) *n.* dealer in foodstuffs —ˈ**groceries** *pl.n.* commodities sold by grocer —ˈ**grocery** *n.* trade, premises of grocer

grog (grɒg) *n.* spirit (*esp.* rum) and water —ˈ**groggy** *a. inf.* unsteady, shaky, weak

grogram (ˈgrɒgrəm) *n.* coarse fabric of silk, wool, or silk mixed with wool or mohair, formerly used for clothing

groin (grɔɪn) *n.* 1. fold where legs meet abdomen 2. euphemism for genitals 3. *Archit.* edge made by intersection of two vaults —*vt.* 4. build with groins

groom (gruːm, grʊm) *n.* 1. person caring for horses 2. *see* **bridegroom** *at* BRIDE 3. officer in royal household —*vt.* 4. tend or look after 5. brush or clean (*esp.* horse) 6. train (someone for something) —ˈ**groomsman** *n.* friend attending bridegroom —**well-groomed** *a.* neat, smart

groove (gruːv) *n.* 1. narrow channel, hollow, *esp.* cut by tool 2. rut, routine —*vt.* 3. cut groove in —ˈ**groovy** *a. sl.* fashionable, exciting

grope (grəʊp) *vi.* feel about, search blindly

groper (ˈgrəʊpə) *or* **grouper** *n.* large marine fish of warm and tropical seas

grosbeak (ˈgrəʊsbiːk, ˈgrɒs-) *n.* finch with large powerful bill

grosgrain (ˈgrəʊgreɪn) *n.* heavy ribbed silk or rayon fabric used for trimming clothes *etc.*

gros point (grəʊ) 1. needlepoint stitch covering two horizontal and two vertical threads 2. work done in this stitch

gross (grəʊs) *a.* 1. very fat 2. total, not net 3. coarse 4. indecent 5. flagrant 6. thick, rank —*n.* 7. twelve dozen —ˈ**grossly** *adv.* —**gross national product** total value of final goods and services produced annually by nation

grotesque (grəʊˈtɛsk) *a.* 1. (horribly) distorted 2. absurd —*n.* 3. 16th-cent. decorative style using distorted human, animal and plant forms 4. grotesque person, thing —**groˈtesquely** *adv.*

grotto (ˈgrɒtəʊ) *n.* cave

grotty (ˈgrɒtɪ) *a. inf.* dirty, untidy, unpleasant

grouch (graʊtʃ) *inf. n.* 1. persistent grumbler 2. discontented mood —*vi.* 3. grumble, be peevish

ground[1] (graʊnd) *n.* 1. surface of earth 2. soil, earth 3. (*oft. pl.*) reason, motive 4. coating to work on with paint 5. background, main surface worked on in painting, embroidery *etc.* 6. special area 7. bottom of sea —*pl.* 8. dregs, *esp.* from coffee 9. enclosed land round house —*vt.* 10. establish 11. instruct (in elements) 12. place on ground —*vi.* 13. run ashore —ˈ**grounded** *a.* (of aircraft) unable or not permitted to fly —ˈ**grounding** *n.* basic general knowledge of a subject —ˈ**groundless** *a.* without reason —**ground crew** group of people in charge of maintenance and repair of aircraft —**ground floor** floor of building level or almost level with ground —ˈ**groundnut** *n.* 1. earthnut 2. peanut —ˈ**groundsheet** *n.* waterproof sheet on ground under tent *etc.* —ˈ**groundsman** *n.* person employed to maintain sports ground *etc.* —ˈ**groundspeed** *n.* aircraft's speed in relation to ground —**ground swell** 1. considerable swell of sea, oft. caused by distant storm 2. rapidly developing general opinion —ˈ**groundwork** *n.* 1. preliminary work as foundation or basis 2. ground or background of painting *etc.* —**get in on the ground floor** *inf.* be in project *etc.* from its inception

ground[2] (graʊnd) *pt./pp. of* GRIND

THESAURUS

grit *n.* 1. dust, gravel, pebbles, sand 2. backbone, courage, determination, doggedness, fortitude, gameness, guts (*Inf.*), hardihood, mettle, nerve, perseverance, pluck, resolution, spirit, tenacity, toughness ~*v.* 3. clench, gnash, grate, grind

gritty 1. abrasive, dusty, grainy, granular, gravelly, rasping, rough, sandy 2. brave, courageous, determined, dogged, game, hardy, mettlesome, plucky, resolute, spirited, steadfast, tenacious, tough

groan 1. *n.* cry, moan, sigh, whine 2. *v.* cry, moan, sigh, whine

groggy dazed, dizzy, faint, muzzy, reeling, shaky, staggering, unsteady, weak, wobbly, woozy (*Inf.*)

groom *n.* 1. currier (*Rare*), hostler *or* ostler (*Archaic*), stableboy, stableman ~*v.* 2. clean, dress, get up (*Inf.*), preen, primp, smarten up, spruce up, tidy, turn out 3. brush, clean, curry, rub down, tend 4. coach, drill, educate, make ready, nurture, prepare, prime, ready, train

groove channel, cut, cutting, flute, furrow, gutter, hollow, indentation, rebate, rut, score, trench

grope cast about, feel, finger, fish, flounder, fumble, grabble, scrabble, search

gross *adj.* 1. big, bulky, corpulent, dense, fat, great, heavy, hulking, large, lumpish, massive, obese, overweight, thick 2. aggregate, before deductions, before tax, entire, total, whole 3. coarse, crude, improper, impure, indecent, indelicate, lewd, low, obscene, offensive, ribald, rude, sensual, smutty, unseemly, vulgar 4. apparent, arrant, blatant, downright, egregious, flagrant, glaring, grievous, heinous, manifest, obvious, outrageous, plain, rank, serious, shameful, sheer, shocking, unmitigated, unqualified, utter 5. boorish, callous, coarse, crass, dull, ignorant, imperceptive, insensitive, tasteless, uncultured, undiscriminating, unfeeling, unrefined, unsophisticated

grotesque absurd, bizarre, deformed, distorted, fantastic, freakish, incongruous, ludicrous, malformed, misshapen, odd, outlandish, preposterous, ridiculous, strange, unnatural, weird

ground *n.* 1. clod, dirt, dry land, dust, earth, field, land, loam, mould, sod, soil, terra firma, terrain, turf 2. *Often plural* area, country, district, domain, estate, fields, gardens, habitat, holding, land, property, realm, terrain, territory, tract 3. *Usually plural* account, argument, base, basis, call, cause, excuse, factor, foundation, inducement, justification, motive, occasion, premise, pretext, rationale, reason 4. *Usually plural* deposit, dregs, grouts, lees, sediment, settlings ~*v.* 5. base, establish, fix, found, set, settle 6. acquaint with, coach, familiarize with, inform, initiate, instruct, prepare, teach, train, tutor

groundless baseless, chimerical, empty, false, idle, illusory, imaginary, unauthorized, uncalled-for, un-

groundsel (ˈgraʊnsəl) *n.* yellow flowered plant

group (gruːp) *n.* **1.** number of persons or things considered as collective unit **2.** number of persons bound together by common interests *etc.* **3.** small musical band of players or singers **4.** class **5.** two or more figures forming one artistic design —*v.* **6.** place, fall into group —**group captain** officer holding commissioned rank senior to squadron leader but junior to air commodore in British R.A.F. and certain other air forces —**group therapy** *Psych.* simultaneous treatment of number of individuals brought together to share their problems in group discussion

grouper (ˈgruːpə) *n. see* GROPER

grouse[1] (graʊs) *n.* **1.** game bird **2.** its flesh (*pl.* **grouse**)

grouse[2] (graʊs) *vi.* **1.** grumble, complain —*n.* **2.** complaint —ˈ**grouser** *n.* grumbler

grout (graʊt) *n.* **1.** thin fluid mortar —*vt.* **2.** fill up with grout

grove (grəʊv) *n.* **1.** small group of trees **2.** road lined with trees

grovel (ˈgrɒvᵊl) *vi.* **1.** abase oneself **2.** lie face down (**-ll-**)

grow (grəʊ) *vi.* **1.** develop naturally **2.** increase in size, height *etc.* **3.** be produced **4.** become by degrees —*vt.* **5.** produce by cultivation (**grew** *pt.,* **grown** *pp.*) —**growth** *n.* **1.** growing **2.** increase **3.** what has grown or is growing —**growing pains 1.** pains in joints sometimes experienced by growing children **2.** difficulties besetting new enterprise in early stages —**grown-up** *a./n.* adult

growl (graʊl) *vi.* **1.** make low guttural sound of anger **2.** rumble **3.** murmur, complain —*n.* **4.** act or sound of growling

groyne *or esp. U.S.* **groin** (grɔɪn) *n.* wall or jetty built out from riverbank or shore to control erosion

grub (grʌb) *vt.* **1.** (*oft. with* up *or* out) dig superficially **2.** root up —*vi.* **3.** dig, rummage **4.** plod (**-bb-**) —*n.* **5.** larva of insect **6.** *sl.* food —ˈ**grubby** *a.* dirty

grudge (grʌdʒ) *vt.* **1.** be unwilling to give, allow —*n.* **2.** ill will

gruel (ˈgruːəl) *n.* food of oatmeal *etc.,* boiled in milk or water —ˈ**gruelling** *or U.S.* ˈ**grueling** *a./n.* exhausting, severe (experience)

gruesome (ˈgruːsəm) *a.* fearful, horrible, grisly —ˈ**gruesomeness** *n.*

gruff (grʌf) *a.* rough in manner or voice, surly —ˈ**gruffly** *adv.*

grumble (ˈgrʌmbᵊl) *vi.* **1.** complain **2.** rumble, murmur **3.** make growling sounds —*n.* **4.** complaint **5.** low growl —ˈ**grumbler** *n.*

grumpy (ˈgrʌmpɪ) *or* **grumpish** *a.* ill-tempered, surly —ˈ**grumpily** *or* ˈ**grumpishly** *adv.*

THESAURUS

founded, unjustified, unprovoked, unsupported, unwarranted

groundwork base, basis, cornerstone, footing, foundation, fundamentals, preliminaries, preparation, spadework, underpinnings

group *n.* **1.** aggregation, assemblage, association, band, batch, bunch, category, circle, class, clique, clump, cluster, collection, company, congregation, coterie, crowd, faction, formation, gang, gathering, organization, pack, party, set, troop ~*v.* **2.** arrange, assemble, associate, assort, bracket, class, classify, dispose, gather, marshal, order, organize, put together, range, sort **3.** associate, band together, cluster, congregate, consort, fraternize, gather, get together

grouse 1. *v.* beef (*Sl.*), bellyache (*Sl.*), bitch (*Sl.*), carp, complain, find fault, gripe (*Inf.*), grouch (*Inf.*), grumble, moan, whine **2.** *n.* beef (*Sl.*), complaint, grievance, gripe (*Inf.*), grouch (*Inf.*), grumble, moan, objection

grovel abase oneself, bootlick (*Inf.*), bow and scrape, cower, crawl, creep, cringe, crouch, demean oneself, fawn, flatter, humble oneself, kowtow, sneak, toady

grow 1. develop, enlarge, expand, extend, fill out, get bigger, get taller, heighten, increase, multiply, spread, stretch, swell, thicken, widen **2.** develop, flourish, germinate, shoot, spring up, sprout, vegetate **3.** arise, issue, originate, spring, stem **4.** advance, expand, flourish, improve, progress, prosper, succeed, thrive **5.** become, come to be, develop (into), get, turn, wax **6.** breed, cultivate, farm, nurture, produce, propagate, raise

grown-up 1. *adj.* adult, fully-grown, mature, of age **2.** *n.* adult, man, woman

growth 1. aggrandizement, augmentation, development, enlargement, evolution, expansion, extension, growing, heightening, increase, multiplication, proliferation, stretching, thickening, widening **2.** crop, cultivation, development, germination, produce, production, shooting, sprouting, vegetation **3.** advance, advancement, expansion, improvement, progress, prosperity, rise, success

grub *v.* **1.** burrow, dig up, probe, pull up, root (*Inf.*), rootle (*Brit.*), search for, uproot **2.** ferret, forage, hunt, rummage, scour, search, uncover, unearth **3.** drudge, grind (*Inf.*), labour, plod, slave, slog, sweat, toil ~*n.* **4.** caterpillar, larva, maggot **5.** *Sl.* eats (*Sl.*), food, nosh (*Sl.*), rations, sustenance, victuals

grubby besmeared, dirty, filthy, frowzy, grimy, manky (*Scot. dialect*), mean, messy, mucky, scruffy, seedy, shabby, slovenly, smutty, soiled, sordid, squalid, unkempt, untidy, unwashed

grudge 1. *n.* animosity, animus, antipathy, aversion, bitterness, dislike, enmity, grievance, hard feelings, hate, ill will, malevolence, malice, pique, rancour, resentment, spite, venom **2.** *v.* begrudge, be reluctant, complain, covet, envy, hold back, mind, resent, stint

gruelling arduous, backbreaking, brutal, crushing, demanding, difficult, exhausting, fatiguing, fierce, grinding, hard, harsh, laborious, punishing, severe, stiff, strenuous, taxing, tiring, trying

gruesome abominable, awful, fearful, ghastly, grim, grisly, hideous, horrendous, horrible, horrid, horrific, horrifying, loathsome, macabre, repugnant, repulsive, shocking, spine-chilling, terrible

gruff 1. bad-tempered, bearish, blunt, brusque, churlish, crabbed, crusty, curt, discourteous, grouchy (*Inf.*), grumpy, ill-humoured, ill-natured, impolite, rough, rude, sour, sullen, surly, uncivil, ungracious, unmannerly **2.** croaking, guttural, harsh, hoarse, husky, low, rasping, rough, throaty

grumble *v.* **1.** beef (*Sl.*), bellyache (*Sl.*), bitch (*Sl.*), carp, complain, find fault, gripe (*Inf.*), grouch (*Inf.*), grouse, moan, repine, whine **2.** growl, gurgle, murmur, mutter, roar, rumble ~*n.* **3.** beef (*Sl.*), complaint, grievance, gripe (*Inf.*), grouch (*Inf.*), grouse, moan, objection **4.** growl, gurgle, murmur, muttering, roar, rumble

grunt (grʌnt) *vi.* 1. make sound characteristic of pig —*n.* 2. deep, hoarse sound of pig 3. gruff noise

Gruyère *or* **Gruyère cheese** (ˈgruːjɛə) *n.* pale yellow whole milk cheese with holes

gryphon (ˈgrɪfən) *n. see* GRIFFIN

grysbok (ˈgraɪsbɒk) *n.* small Afr. antelope

G.S. 1. General Secretary 2. General Staff

G-string *n.* 1. very small covering for genitals 2. *Mus.* string tuned to G

G-suit *n.* close-fitting garment worn by crew of high-speed aircraft, pressurized to prevent blackout during manoeuvres

GT gran turismo (touring car, used of (sports) car capable of high speed)

guanaco (gwɑːˈnɑːkəʊ) *n.* cud-chewing S Amer. mammal closely related to domesticated llama (*pl.* **-s**)

guano (ˈgwɑːnəʊ) *n.* sea bird manure (*pl.* **-s**)

guarantee (gærənˈtiː) *n.* 1. formal assurance, *esp.* in writing, that product *etc.* will meet certain standards, last for given time *etc.* —*vt.* 2. give guarantee of, for something 3. secure (against risk *etc.*) (**guaranˈteed, guaranˈteeing**) —**guaranˈtor** *n.* one who undertakes fulfilment of another's promises —**ˈguaranty** *n.* 1. pledge of responsibility for fulfilling another person's obligations in case of default 2. thing given or taken as security for guaranty 3. act of providing security 4. guarantor —*v.* 5. guarantee

guard (gɑːd) *vt.* 1. protect, defend —*vi.* 2. be careful, take precautions —*n.* 3. person, group that protects, supervises, keeps watch 4. sentry 5. soldiers protecting anything 6. official in charge of train 7. protection 8. screen for enclosing anything dangerous 9. protector 10. posture of defence —*pl.* 11. (G-) any of certain British regiments —**ˈguarded** *a.* 1. kept under surveillance 2. prudent, restrained or noncommittal —**ˈguardedly** *adv.* —**ˈguardian** *n.* 1. keeper, protector 2. person having custody of infant *etc.* —**ˈguardianship** *n.* care —**ˈguardhouse** *or* **ˈguardroom** *n.* place for stationing those on guard or for prisoners —**ˈguardsman** *n.* soldier in Guards

guava (ˈgwɑːvə) *n.* tropical tree with fruit used to make jelly

gubernatorial (gjuːbənəˈtɔːrɪəl, guː-) *a. chiefly* US of or relating to governor

gudgeon[1] (ˈgʌdʒən) *n.* small freshwater fish

gudgeon[2] (ˈgʌdʒən) *n.* 1. pivot bearing 2. socket for rudder 3. kind of connecting pin

guelder-rose (ˈgɛldərəʊz) *n.* shrub with clusters of white flowers

guerdon (ˈgɜːdən) *n.* reward

Guernsey (ˈgɜːnzɪ) *n.* 1. breed of cattle 2. close-fitting knitted jumper

guerrilla *or* **guerilla** (gəˈrɪlə) *n.* member of irregular armed force, *esp.* fighting established force, government *etc.*

guess (gɛs) *vt.* 1. estimate without calculation 2. conjecture, suppose 3. US consider, think —*vi.* 4. form conjectures —*n.* 5. estimate —**ˈguesswork** *n.* 1. set of conclusions *etc.* arrived at by guessing 2. process of making guesses

guest (gɛst) *n.* 1. one entertained at another's house 2. one living in hotel —**ˈguesthouse** *n.* boarding house, usu. without alcoholic licence

guff (gʌf) *n. sl.* silly talk

guffaw (gʌˈfɔː) *n.* 1. burst of boisterous laughter —*vi.* 2. laugh in this way

guide (gaɪd) *n.* 1. one who shows the way 2. adviser 3. book of instruction or information 4. contrivance for directing motion 5. (*usu.* G-) member of organization for girls equivalent to Scouts —*vt.* 6. lead, act as guide to 7. arrange —**ˈguidance** *n.* —**ˈguider** *n.* adult leader of company of Guides —**guided missile** missile whose flight path is controlled by radio or preprogrammed homing mechanism —**guide dog** dog trained to lead blind person —**ˈguideline** *n.* principle put forward to determine course of action

THESAURUS

guarantee 1. *n.* assurance, bond, certainty, collateral, covenant, earnest, guaranty, pledge, promise, security, surety, undertaking, warranty, word, word of honour 2. *v.* answer for, assure, certify, ensure, insure, maintain, make certain, pledge, promise, protect, secure, stand behind, swear, vouch for, warrant

guard *v.* 1. cover, defend, escort, keep, mind, oversee, patrol, police, preserve, protect, safeguard, save, screen, secure, shelter, shield, supervise, tend, watch, watch over ~*n.* 2. custodian, defender, lookout, picket, protector, sentinel, sentry, warder, watch, watchman 3. convoy, escort, patrol 4. buffer, bulwark, bumper, defence, pad, protection, rampart, safeguard, screen, security, shield

guarded cagey (*Inf.*), careful, cautious, circumspect, discreet, noncommittal, prudent, reserved, restrained, reticent, suspicious, wary

guardian attendant, champion, curator, custodian, defender, escort, guard, keeper, preserver, protector, trustee, warden, warder

guerrilla freedom fighter, irregular, member of the underground *or* resistance, partisan, underground fighter

guess *v.* 1. conjecture, estimate, fathom, hypothesize, penetrate, predict, solve, speculate, work out 2. believe, conjecture, dare say, deem, divine, fancy, hazard, imagine, judge, reckon, suppose, surmise, suspect, think ~*n.* 3. conjecture, feeling, hypothesis, judgment, notion, prediction, reckoning, speculation, supposition, surmise, suspicion, theory

guesswork conjecture, estimation, presumption, speculation, supposition, surmise, suspicion, theory

guest boarder, caller, company, lodger, visitant, visitor

guidance advice, auspices, conduct, control, counsel, counselling, direction, government, help, instruction, intelligence, leadership, management, teaching

guide *v.* 1. accompany, attend, conduct, convoy, direct, escort, lead, pilot, shepherd, show the way, steer, usher 2. command, control, direct, handle, manage, manoeuvre, steer 3. advise, counsel, educate, govern, influence, instruct, oversee, regulate, rule, superintend, supervise, sway, teach, train ~*n.* 4. adviser, attendant, chaperon, cicerone, conductor, controller, counsellor, director, escort, leader, mentor, monitor, pilot, steersman, teacher, usher 5. beacon, clue, guiding light, key, landmark, lodestar, mark, marker, pointer, sign, signal, signpost 6. catalogue, directory, guidebook, handbook, instructions, key, manual, vade mecum

guidon (ˈgaɪdᵊn) *n.* **1.** pennant, used as marker, *esp.* by cavalry regiments **2.** man or vehicle that carries this

guild *or* **gild** (gɪld) *n.* **1.** organization, club **2.** society for mutual help, or with common object **3.** *Hist.* society of merchants or tradesmen —ˈ**guildhall** *n.* meeting place of guild or corporation

guilder (ˈgɪldə) *or* **gulden** (ˈgʊldᵊn) *n.* **1.** standard monetary unit of Netherlands (*also* ˈ**gilder**) **2.** former gold or silver coin of Germany, Austria or Netherlands (*pl.* **-s, -der** *or* **-s, -den**)

guile (gaɪl) *n.* cunning, deceit —ˈ**guileful** *a.* —ˈ**guilefully** *adv.* —ˈ**guileless** *a.*

guillemot (ˈgɪlɪmɒt) *n.* species of sea bird

guillotine (ˈgɪlətiːn) *n.* **1.** device for beheading **2.** machine for cutting paper **3.** in parliament *etc.*, method of restricting length of debate by fixing time for taking vote —*vt.* (gɪləˈtiːn) **4.** behead **5.** use guillotine on **6.** limit (debate) by guillotine

guilt (gɪlt) *n.* **1.** fact, state of having done wrong **2.** responsibility for criminal or moral offence —ˈ**guiltily** *adv.* —ˈ**guiltiness** *n.* —ˈ**guiltless** *a.* innocent —ˈ**guilty** *a.* having committed an offence

guinea (ˈgɪnɪ) *n.* formerly, gold coin worth 21 shillings —**guinea fowl** bird allied to pheasant —**guinea pig 1.** rodent originating in S Amer. **2.** *inf.* person or animal used in experiments

guipure (gɪˈpjʊə) *n.* **1.** any of many types of lace that have their pattern connected by threads, rather than supported on net mesh (*also* **guipure lace**) **2.** heavy corded trimming; gimp

guise (gaɪz) *n.* external appearance, *esp.* one assumed —ˈ**guiser** *n.* —ˈ**guising** *n.* in Scotland and N England, custom of disguising oneself in fancy dress and visiting people's houses at Hallowe'en

guitar (gɪˈtɑː) *n.* usu. 6-stringed instrument played by plucking or strumming —**guiˈtarist** *n.* player of guitar

Gulag (ˈguːlæg) *n.* central administrative department of Soviet security service, responsible for prisons, labour camps *etc.*

gulch (gʌltʃ) *n.* **1.** ravine **2.** gully

gulf (gʌlf) *n.* **1.** large inlet of the sea **2.** chasm **3.** large gap —**Gulf Stream** warm ocean current flowing from Gulf of Mexico towards NW Europe (*also* **North Atlantic Drift**) —ˈ**gulfweed** *n.* seaweed forming dense floating masses in tropical Atlantic waters, *esp.* Gulf Stream (*also* **sarˈgasso, sargasso weed**)

gull[1] (gʌl) *n.* long-winged web-footed sea bird

gull[2] (gʌl) *n.* **1.** dupe, fool —*vt.* **2.** dupe, cheat —**gulliˈbility** *n.* —ˈ**gullible** *a.* easily imposed on, credulous

gullet (ˈgʌlɪt) *n.* food passage from mouth to stomach

gully (ˈgʌlɪ) *n.* channel or ravine worn by water

gulp (gʌlp) *vt.* **1.** swallow eagerly —*vi.* **2.** gasp, choke —*n.* **3.** act of gulping

gum[1] (gʌm) *n.* firm flesh in which teeth are set —ˈ**gummy** *a.* toothless —ˈ**gumboil** *n.* abscess on gum

gum[2] (gʌm) *n.* **1.** sticky substance issuing from certain trees **2.** an adhesive **3.** chewing gum —*vt.* **4.** stick with gum (**-mm-**) —ˈ**gummy** *a.* —ˈ**gumboots** *pl.n.* boots of rubber —**gum resin** mixture of resin and gum obtained from various plants and trees —ˈ**gumtree** *n.* any species of eucalypt —**gum up the works** *inf.* impede progress —**up a gumtree** *sl.* in a difficult position

gumption (ˈgʌmpʃən) *n.* **1.** resourcefulness **2.** shrewdness, sense

gun (gʌn) *n.* **1.** weapon with metal tube from which missiles are discharged by explosion **2.** cannon, pistol *etc.* —*vt.* **3.** (*oft. with* down) shoot **4.** race (engine of car) —*vi.* **5.** hunt with gun (**-nn-**) —ˈ**gunner** *n.* —ˈ**gunnery** *n.* use or science of large guns —ˈ**gunboat** *n.* small warship —**gunboat diplomacy** diplomacy conducted by threats of military intervention —ˈ**guncotton** *n.* cellulose nitrate containing large amount of nitrogen: used as explosive —**gun dog** (breed of) dog used to find or retrieve game —ˈ**gunman** *n.* armed criminal —ˈ**gunmetal** *n.* alloy of copper and tin or zinc, formerly used for guns —ˈ**gunpoint** *n.* muzzle of gun —ˈ**gunpowder** *n.* explosive mixture of saltpetre, sulphur and charcoal —ˈ**gunroom** *n.* in warship, mess room of junior officers —ˈ**gunrunner** *n.* —ˈ**gunrunning** *n.* smuggling of guns and ammunition into country —ˈ**gunshot** *n.* **1.** shot or range of gun —*a.* **2.** caused by missile from gun —ˈ**gunstock** *n.* wooden handle or support to which is attached barrel of rifle —**gunwale** *or* **gunnel** (ˈgʌnᵊl) *n.* upper edge of ship's side —**at gunpoint** under threat of being shot

gunge (gʌndʒ) *n. inf.* any sticky, unpleasant substance

gunk (gʌŋk) *n. inf.* any dirty, oily matter

THESAURUS

guild association, brotherhood, club, company, corporation, fellowship, fraternity, league, lodge, order, organization, society, union

guile art, artfulness, artifice, cleverness, craft, craftiness, cunning, deceit, deception, duplicity, gamesmanship (*Inf.*), knavery, ruse, sharp practice, slyness, treachery, trickery, trickiness, wiliness

guilt blame, blameworthiness, criminality, culpability, delinquency, guiltiness, iniquity, misconduct, responsibility, sinfulness, wickedness, wrong, wrongdoing

guiltless blameless, clean (*Sl.*), clear, immaculate, impeccable, innocent, irreproachable, pure, sinless, spotless, unimpeachable, unsullied, untainted, untarnished

guilty at fault, blameworthy, convicted, criminal, culpable, delinquent, erring, evil, felonious, iniquitous, offending, reprehensible, responsible, sinful, to blame, wicked, wrong

gulf **1.** bay, bight, sea inlet **2.** abyss, breach, chasm, cleft, gap, opening, rent, rift, separation, split, void, whirlpool

gullibility credulity, innocence, naiveté, simplicity, trustingness

gullible born yesterday, credulous, easily taken in, foolish, green, innocent, naive, silly, simple, trusting, unsceptical, unsophisticated, unsuspecting

gully channel, ditch, gutter, watercourse

gulp *v.* **1.** bolt, devour, gobble, guzzle, knock back (*Inf.*), quaff, swallow, swig (*Inf.*), swill, toss off, wolf **2.** choke, gasp, stifle, swallow

gum **1.** *n.* adhesive, cement, exudate, glue, mucilage, paste, resin **2.** *v.* affix, cement, clog, glue, paste, stick, stiffen

gumption ability, acumen, astuteness, cleverness, common sense, discernment, enterprise, get-up-and-go (*Inf.*), horse sense, initiative, mother wit, nous

gunny (ˈgʌnɪ) *n.* strong, coarse sacking made from jute

guppy (ˈgʌpɪ) *n.* small colourful aquarium fish

gurgle (ˈgɜːgᵊl) *n.* **1.** bubbling noise —*vi.* **2.** utter, flow with gurgle

Gurkha (ˈgɜːkə) *n.* **1.** any of a warlike people in Nepal **2.** member of this people serving as soldier in British army

gurnard (ˈgɜːnəd) *or* **gurnet** (ˈgɜːnɪt) *n.* spiny armour-headed sea fish

guru (ˈgʊruː, ˈguːruː) *n.* spiritual teacher, *esp.* in India

gush (gʌʃ) *vi.* **1.** flow out suddenly and copiously, spurt **2.** act effusively —*n.* **3.** sudden and copious flow **4.** effusiveness —ˈ**gusher** *n.* **1.** gushing person **2.** something, such as oil well, that gushes

gusset (ˈgʌsɪt) *n.* triangle or diamond-shaped piece of material let into garment —ˈ**gusseted** *a.*

gust (gʌst) *n.* **1.** sudden blast of wind **2.** burst of rain, anger, passion *etc.* —ˈ**gusty** *a.*

gustation (gʌˈsteɪʃən) *n.* act of tasting or faculty of taste —ˈ**gustatory** *a.*

gusto (ˈgʌstəʊ) *n.* enjoyment, zest

gut (gʌt) *n.* **1.** (*oft. pl.*) entrails, intestines **2.** material made from guts of animals, *eg* for violin strings *etc.* —*pl.* **3.** *inf.* essential, fundamental part **4.** courage —*vt.* **5.** remove guts from (fish *etc.*) **6.** remove, destroy contents of (house) (-tt-) —ˈ**gutless** *a. inf.* lacking courage —ˈ**gutsy** *a. inf.* **1.** greedy **2.** courageous

gutta-percha (ˈgʌtəˈpɜːtʃə) *n.* (tropical tree producing) whitish rubber substance

gutter (ˈgʌtə) *n.* **1.** shallow trough for carrying off water from roof or side of street —*vt.* **2.** make channels in —*vi.* **3.** flow in streams **4.** (of candle) melt away by wax forming channels and running down —**gutter press** journalism that relies on sensationalism —ˈ**guttersnipe** *n.* **1.** neglected slum child **2.** mean vindictive person

guttural (ˈgʌtərəl) *a.* **1.** of, relating to, or produced in, the throat —*n.* **2.** guttural sound or letter

guy[1] (gaɪ) *n.* **1.** effigy of Guy Fawkes burnt on Nov. 5th **2.** *inf.* person (*usu.* male) —*vt.* **3.** make fun of, ridicule —**wise guy** *inf., usu. disparaging* clever person

guy[2] (gaɪ) *n.* **1.** rope, chain to steady, secure something (*eg* tent) —*vt.* **2.** keep in position by guy —ˈ**guyrope** *n.*

guzzle (ˈgʌzᵊl) *v.* eat or drink greedily

gybe *or* **jibe** (dʒaɪb) *vi.* **1.** (of boom of fore-and-aft sail) swing over to other side with following wind **2.** alter course thus

gym (dʒɪm) *n.* **1.** gymnasium **2.** gymnastics —**gym shoes** *see* PLIMSOLLS —ˈ**gymslip** *n.* tunic or pinafore dress worn by schoolgirls, oft. part of school uniform

gymkhana (dʒɪmˈkɑːnə) *n.* competition or display of horse riding

gymnasium (dʒɪmˈneɪzɪəm) *n.* place equipped for muscular exercises, athletic training (*pl.* **-s, -nasia** (-ˈneɪzɪə)) —ˈ**gymnast** *n.* expert in gymnastics —**gym**ˈ**nastics** *pl.n.* muscular exercises, with or without apparatus, *eg* parallel bars

gymnosperm (ˈdʒɪmnəʊspɜːm, ˈgɪm-) *n.* seed-bearing plant in which ovules are borne naked on open scales, oft. in cones; any conifer or related plant

gynaecology *or U.S.* **gynecology** (gaɪnɪˈkɒlədʒɪ) *n.* branch of medicine dealing with diseases in women —**gynaeco**ˈ**logical, gynaeco**ˈ**logic** *or U.S.* **gyneco**ˈ**logical, gyneco**ˈ**logic** *a.* —**gynae**ˈ**cologist** *or U.S.* **gyne**ˈ**cologist** *n.*

gyp[1] (dʒɪp) *sl. vt.* **1.** swindle, cheat, defraud —*n.* **2.** act of cheating **3.** person who gyps

gyp[2] (dʒɪp) *n.* **UK, NZ** *sl.* severe pain

gypsophila (dʒɪpˈsɒfɪlə) *n.* garden plant with small white or pink flowers

gypsum (ˈdʒɪpsəm) *n.* crystalline sulphate of lime: source of plaster

Gypsy *or* **Gipsy** (ˈdʒɪpsɪ) *n.* one of wandering race originally from NW India, Romany

gyrate (dʒaɪˈreɪt) *vi.* move in circle, spirally, revolve —**gy**ˈ**ration** *n.* —**gy**ˈ**rational** *a.* —**gyratory** (ˈdʒaɪrətərɪ) *a.* revolving, spinning

gyrfalcon *or* **gerfalcon** (ˈdʒɜːfɔːlkən, -fɔːkən) *n.* large, rare falcon

gyro (ˈdʒaɪrəʊ) *n.* **1.** *see* GYROCOMPASS **2.** *see* GYROSCOPE (*pl.* **-s**)

gyro- *or before vowel* **gyr-** (*comb. form*) **1.** rotating

THESAURUS

(*Brit. sl.*), resourcefulness, sagacity, savvy (*Sl.*), shrewdness, spirit, wit(s)

gunman assassin, bandit, bravo, desperado, gangster, gunslinger (*U.S. sl.*), hit man (*Sl.*), killer, mobster (*U.S. sl.*), murderer, terrorist, thug

gurgle **1.** *v.* babble, bubble, burble, crow, lap, murmur, plash, purl, ripple, splash **2.** *n.* babble, murmur, purl, ripple

guru authority, guiding light, leader, maharishi, master, mentor, sage, swami, teacher, tutor

gush *v.* **1.** burst, cascade, flood, flow, jet, pour, run, rush, spout, spurt, stream **2.** babble, blather, chatter, effervesce, effuse, enthuse, jabber, overstate, spout ~*n.* **3.** burst, cascade, flood, flow, jet, outburst, outflow, rush, spout, spurt, stream, torrent **4.** babble, blather, chatter, effusion, exuberance

gust *n.* **1.** blast, blow, breeze, flurry, gale, puff, rush, squall **2.** burst, eruption, explosion, fit, gale, outburst, paroxysm, passion, storm, surge

gusto appetite, appreciation, brio, delight, enjoyment, enthusiasm, exhilaration, fervour, liking, pleasure, relish, savour, verve, zeal, zest

gut *n.* **1.** *Often plural* belly, bowels, entrails, innards (*Inf.*), insides (*Inf.*), intestines, inwards, paunch, stomach, viscera **2.** *Plural. Inf.* audacity, backbone, boldness, bottle (*Sl.*), courage, daring, forcefulness, grit, hardihood, mettle, nerve, pluck, spirit, spunk (*Inf.*), willpower ~*v.* **3.** clean, disembowel, draw, dress, eviscerate **4.** clean out, despoil, empty, pillage, plunder, ransack, ravage, rifle, sack, strip

gutter channel, conduit, ditch, drain, duct, pipe, sluice, trench, trough, tube

guttural deep, gravelly, gruff, hoarse, husky, low, rasping, rough, thick, throaty

guy **1.** *n. Inf.* bloke (*Brit. inf.*), cat (*Sl.*), chap, fellow, lad, man, person, youth **2.** *v.* caricature, make (a) game of, make fun of, mock, poke fun at, rib (*Inf.*), ridicule, send up (*Brit inf.*), take off (*Inf.*)

guzzle bolt, carouse, cram, devour, drink, gobble, gorge, gormandize, knock back (*Inf.*), quaff, stuff (oneself), swill, tope, wolf

Gypsy, Gipsy Bohemian, nomad, rambler, roamer, Romany, rover, traveller, vagabond, vagrant, wanderer

or gyrating motion, as in *gyroscope* **2.** gyroscope, as in *gyrocompass*

gyrocompass (ˈdʒaɪrəʊkʌmpəs) *n.* compass using gyroscope to indicate true north

gyroscope (ˈdʒaɪrəskəʊp) *n.* disc or wheel so mounted as to be able to rotate about any axis, *esp.* to keep disc (with compass *etc.*) level despite movement of ship *etc.* —**gyroscopic** (dʒaɪrəˈskɒpɪk) *a.*

gyrostabilizer *or* **-liser** (dʒaɪrəʊˈsteɪbɪlaɪzə) *n.* gyroscopic device to prevent rolling of ship or aeroplane

gyve (dʒaɪv) *obs. vt.* **1.** shackle, fetter —*n.* **2.** (*usu. pl.*) fetter

H

h *or* **H** (eɪtʃ) **1.** eighth letter of English alphabet **2.** speech sound represented by this letter **3.** something shaped like an H

H **1.** (of pencils) hard **2.** *Chem.* hydrogen

ha hectare

habeas corpus (ˈheɪbɪəs ˈkɔːpəs) writ issued to produce prisoner in court

haberdasher (ˈhæbədæʃə) *n.* dealer in articles of dress, ribbons, pins, needles *etc.* **—ˈhaberdashery** *n.*

habiliments (həˈbɪlɪmənts) *pl.n.* dress

habit (ˈhæbɪt) *n.* **1.** settled tendency or practice **2.** constitution **3.** customary apparel, *esp.* of nun or monk **4.** woman's riding dress **—haˈbitual** *a.* **1.** formed or acquired by habit **2.** usual, customary **—haˈbitually** *adv.* **—haˈbituate** *vt.* accustom **—habituˈation** *n.* **—habitué** (həˈbɪtjʊeɪ) *n.* constant visitor

habitable (ˈhæbɪtəbᵊl) *a.* fit to live in **—ˈhabitant** *n.* C (descendant of) original French settler **—ˈhabitat** *n.* natural home (of animal *etc.*) **—habiˈtation** *n.* dwelling place

hachure (hæˈʃjʊə) *n.* shading of short lines drawn on relief map to indicate gradients

hacienda (hæsɪˈɛndə) *n.* ranch or large estate in Spanish Amer.

hack[1] (hæk) *vt.* **1.** cut, chop (at) violently **2.** *Sport* foul by kicking the shins *—vi.* **3.** *inf.* utter harsh, dry cough *—n.* **4.** cut or gash **5.** any tool used for shallow digging **—ˈhacker** *n.* **1.** one who hacks **2.** *sl.* computer fanatic, *esp.* one who, through personal computer, breaks into computer system of a company *etc.* **—ˈhackery** *n. inf.* practice of gaining illegal access to computer system

hack[2] (hæk) *n.* **1.** horse for ordinary riding **2.** drudge, *esp.* writer of inferior literary works **—hack work** dull, repetitive work

hackle (ˈhækᵊl) *n.* **1.** neck feathers of turkey *etc.* *—pl.* **2.** hairs on back of neck of dog and other animals, which are raised in anger

hackney (ˈhæknɪ) *n.* carriage or coach kept for hire

hackneyed (ˈhæknɪd) *a.* (of words *etc.*) stale, trite because of overuse

hacksaw (ˈhæksɔː) *n.* handsaw for cutting metal

had (hæd) *pt./pp. of* HAVE

haddock (ˈhædək) *n.* large, edible seafish

hadedah (ˈhɑːdɪdɑː) *n.* S Afr. ibis

Hades (ˈheɪdiːz) *n.* **1.** abode of the dead **2.** underworld **3.** hell

hadj (hædʒ) *n. see* HAJJ

haematite *or U.S.* **hematite** (ˈhiːmətaɪt, ˈhɛm-) *n.* ore of iron

haematology *or U.S.* **hematology** (hiːməˈtɒlədʒɪ) *n.* branch of medicine concerned with diseases of blood

haemo-, haema-, *or before vowel* **haem-** (*comb. form*) blood

haemoglobin *or U.S.* **hemoglobin** (hiːməʊˈgləʊbɪn) *n.* colouring and oxygen-bearing matter of red blood corpuscles

haemophilia *or U.S.* **hemophilia** (hiːməʊˈfɪlɪə) *n.* hereditary tendency to intensive bleeding as blood fails to clot **—haemoˈphiliac** *or U.S.* **hemoˈphiliac** *n.*

haemorrhage *or U.S.* **hemorrhage** (ˈhɛmərɪdʒ) *n.* profuse bleeding

haemorrhoids *or U.S.* **hemorrhoids** (ˈhɛmərɔɪdz) *pl.n.* swollen veins in rectum (*also* **piles**)

hafnium (ˈhæfnɪəm) *n.* metallic element found in zirconium ores

haft (hɑːft) *n.* **1.** handle (of knife *etc.*) *—vt.* **2.** provide with haft

hag (hæg) *n.* **1.** ugly old woman **2.** witch **—hag-ridden** *a.* troubled, careworn

haggard (ˈhægəd) *a.* **1.** wild-looking **2.** anxious, careworn *—n.* **3.** *Falconry* untamed hawk

haggis (ˈhægɪs) *n.* Scottish dish made from sheep's heart, lungs, liver, chopped with oatmeal, suet, onion *etc.* and boiled in stomach-bag

haggle (ˈhægᵊl) *vi.* (*oft. with* over) bargain, wrangle (over price, terms *etc.*)

hagiology (hægɪˈɒlədʒɪ) *n.* literature of the lives and

THESAURUS

habit *n.* **1.** bent, custom, disposition, manner, mannerism, practice, proclivity, propensity, quirk, tendency, way **2.** convention, custom, mode, practice, routine, rule, second nature, usage, wont **3.** constitution, disposition, frame of mind, make-up, nature **4.** apparel, dress, garb, garment, habiliment, riding dress

habitation abode, domicile, dwelling, dwelling house, home, house, living quarters, lodging, quarters, residence

habitual **1.** accustomed, common, customary, familiar, fixed, natural, normal, ordinary, regular, routine, standard, traditional, usual, wonted **2.** chronic, confirmed, constant, established, frequent, hardened, ingrained, inveterate, persistent, recurrent

habituate acclimatize, accustom, break in, condition, discipline, familiarize, harden, inure, make used to, school, season, train

habitué constant customer, frequenter, frequent visitor, regular (*Inf.*), regular patron

hack[1] *v.* **1.** chop, cut, gash, hew, kick, lacerate, mangle, mutilate, notch, slash *~n.* **2.** chop, cut, gash, notch, slash *~v.* **3.** *Inf.* bark, cough, rasp

hack[2] *n.* **1.** Grub Street writer, literary hack, penny-a-liner, scribbler **2.** drudge, plodder, slave **3.** crock, hired horse, horse, jade, nag, poor old tired horse

hackneyed banal, clichéd, common, commonplace, overworked, pedestrian, played out (*Inf.*), run-of-the-mill, stale, stereotyped, stock, threadbare, timeworn, tired, trite, unoriginal, worn-out

hag beldam (*Archaic*), crone, fury, harridan, Jezebel, shrew, termagant, virago, vixen, witch

haggard careworn, drawn, emaciated, gaunt, ghastly, hollow-eyed, pinched, shrunken, thin, wan, wasted, wrinkled

haggle **1.** bargain, barter, beat down, chaffer, dicker (*Chiefly U.S.*), higgle, palter **2.** bicker, dispute, quarrel, squabble, wrangle

legends of saints —**hagi'ographer** *n.* —**hagi'ography** *n.* writing of this

ha-ha[1] ('hɑː'hɑː) *or* **haw-haw** ('hɔː'hɔː) *interj.* **1.** representation of the sound of laughter **2.** exclamation expressing derision, mockery *etc.*

ha-ha[2] ('hɑːhɑː) *or* **haw-haw** ('hɔːhɔː) *n.* sunken fence bordering garden *etc.*, that allows uninterrupted views from within

haiku ('haɪkuː) *or* **hokku** ('hɒkuː) *n.* epigrammatic Japanese verse form in 17 syllables (*pl.* **-ku**)

hail[1] (heɪl) *n.* **1.** (shower of) pellets of ice **2.** intense shower, barrage —*v.* **3.** pour down as shower of hail —**'hailstone** *n.*

hail[2] (heɪl) *vt.* **1.** greet, *esp.* enthusiastically **2.** acclaim, acknowledge **3.** call —**hail from** come from —**Hail Mary** *see* AVE MARIA

hair (hɛə) *n.* **1.** filament growing from skin of animal, as covering of man's head **2.** such filaments collectively —**'hairiness** *n.* —**'hairy** *a.* —**'hairdo** *n.* way of dressing hair —**'hairdresser** *n.* one who attends to and cuts hair, *esp.* women's hair —**'hairgrip** *n. chiefly* **UK** tightly bent metal hair clip (*also* (*esp.* **US**) **bobby pin**) —**'hairline** *a./n.* very fine (line) —**'hairpiece** *n.* **1.** wig or toupee **2.** false hair attached to one's real hair to give it greater bulk or length —**'hairpin** *n.* pin for keeping hair in place —**hairpin bend** U-shaped turn of road —**hair-raising** *a.* terrifying —**hair's-breadth** *n.* very short margin or distance —**hair shirt** rough shirt worn as penance by religious ascetics —**hair slide** ornamental hinged clip for the hair —**'hairsplitting** *n.* making of overfine distinctions —**'hairspring** *n.* very fine, delicate spring in timepiece —**hair trigger** trigger operated by light touch

hajj *or* **hadj** (hædʒ) *n.* pilgrimage to Mecca that every Muslim is required to make (*pl.* **'hajjes** *or* **'hadjes**) —**'hajji, 'hadji,** *or* **'haji** *n.* Muslim who has made pilgrimage to Mecca (*pl.* **'hajjis, 'hadjis,** *or* **'hajis**)

hake (heɪk) *n.* edible fish of the cod family

halberd ('hælbəd) *or* **halbert** *n.* combined spear and battleaxe

halcyon ('hælsɪən) *n.* bird fabled to calm the sea and to breed on floating nest, kingfisher —**halcyon days** time of peace and happiness

hale[1] (heɪl) *a.* robust, healthy (*esp. in* **hale and hearty**)

hale[2] (heɪl) *vt.* pull; drag —**'haler** *n.*

half (hɑːf) *n.* **1.** either of two equal parts of something (*pl.* **halves**) —*a.* **2.** forming half —*adv.* **3.** to the extent of half —**half-and-half** *n.* mixture of half one thing and half another thing —**'halfback** *n. Football* man behind forwards —**half-baked** *a.* **1.** underdone **2.** *inf.* immature, silly —**half-blood** *n.* **1.** relationship between individuals having only one parent in common; individual having such relationship **2.** half-breed —**half-breed** *or* **half-caste** *n.* person with parents of different races —**half-brother, -sister** *n.* brother (sister) by one parent only —**half-cock** *n.* halfway position of firearm's hammer when trigger is locked —**half-cocked** *a.* ill-prepared —**half-crown** *n.* formerly, British coin worth 12½ (new) pence —**half-hearted** *a.* unenthusiastic —**half-hitch** *n.* knot made by passing end of piece of rope around itself and through loop thus made —**half-life** *n.* time taken for half the atoms in radioactive material to decay —**half-mast** *n.* (of flag) halfway position to which flag is lowered on mast to mourn dead —**half measures** inadequate measures or actions —**half-nelson** *n.* hold in wrestling —**halfpenny** ('heɪpnɪ) *n.* **1.** British coin worth half a new penny (*also* (*inf.*) **half**) **2.** formerly, coin worth half an old penny —**half-size** *n.* any size, *esp.* in clothing, halfway between two sizes —**half term** **UK** short holiday midway through academic term —**half-timbered** *or* **half-timber** *a.* (of building) having exposed timber framework filled with brick —**half-time** *n. Sport* rest period between two halves of game —**half-title** *n.* **1.** title of book as printed on right-hand page preceding title page **2.** title on separate page preceding section of book —**'halftone** *n.* illustration printed from relief plate, showing light and shadow by means of minute dots —**half-track** *n.* vehicle with caterpillar tracks on wheels that supply motive power only —**half-true** *a.* —**half-truth** *n.* partially true statement intended to mislead —**half volley** striking of ball the moment it bounces —**half'way** *adv./a.* at or to half distance —**halfway house** **1.** place to rest midway on journey **2.** halfway point in any progression **3.** centre or hostel to facilitate readjustment to private life of released prisoners *etc.* —**'halfwit** *n.* **1.** mentally-retarded person **2.** stupid person —**by halves** imperfectly —**go halves**

THESAURUS

hail[1] *Fig.* **1.** *n.* barrage, bombardment, pelting, rain, shower, storm, volley **2.** *v.* barrage, batter, beat down upon, bombard, pelt, rain, rain down on, shower, storm, volley

hail[2] **1.** acclaim, acknowledge, applaud, cheer, exalt, glorify greet, honour, salute, welcome **2.** accost, address, call, flag down, halloo, shout to, signal to, sing out, speak to, wave down **3.** *With* **from** be a native of, be born in, come from, originate in

hair head of hair, locks, mane, mop, shock, tresses

hair-raising alarming, bloodcurdling, breathtaking, creepy, exciting, frightening, horrifying, petrifying, scary, shocking, spine-chilling, startling, terrifying, thrilling

hair's-breadth *n.* fraction, hair, jot, narrow margin, whisker

hairy bearded, bewhiskered, bushy, fleecy, furry, hirsute, pileous (*Biol.*), pilose (*Biol.*), shaggy, stubbly, unshaven, woolly

hale able-bodied, blooming, fit, flourishing, healthy, hearty, in fine fettle, in the pink, robust, sound, strong, vigorous, well

half **1.** *n.* bisection, division, equal part, fifty per cent, fraction, hemisphere, portion, section **2.** *adj.* divided, fractional, halved, incomplete, limited, moderate, partial **3.** *adv.* after a fashion, all but, barely, inadequately, incompletely, in part, partially, partly, pretty nearly, slightly

half-baked brainless, crazy, foolish, harebrained, senseless, silly, stupid

half-hearted apathetic, cool, indifferent, lacklustre, listless, lukewarm, neutral, passive, perfunctory, spiritless, tame, unenthusiastic, uninterested

halfway **1.** *adv.* midway, to *or* in the middle, to the midpoint **2.** *adj.* central, equidistant, intermediate, mid, middle, midway

halfwit dimwit (*Inf.*), dolt, dullard, dunce, dunderhead, fool, idiot, imbecile (*Inf.*), mental defective, moron, nitwit, simpleton

share expenses *etc.* equally —**half seas over** *inf.* drunk —**meet halfway** compromise with

halibut (ˈhælɪbət) *n.* large edible flatfish

halitosis (hælɪˈtəʊsɪs) *n.* bad-smelling breath

hall (hɔːl) *n.* **1.** (entrance) passage **2.** large room or building belonging to particular group or used for particular purpose, *esp.* public assembly —ˈ**hallway** *n.* hall or corridor

hallelujah, halleluiah (hælɪˈluːjə), *or* **alleluia** (ælɪˈluːjə) *n./interj.* exclamation of praise to God

hallmark (ˈhɔːlmɑːk) *n.* **1.** mark used to indicate standard of tested gold and silver **2.** mark of excellence **3.** distinguishing feature

hallo (həˈləʊ) *interj. see* HELLO

halloo (həˈluː), **hallo,** *or* **halloa** (həˈləʊ) *n.* **1.** call to spur on hunting dogs —*vi.* **2.** shout loudly

hallow (ˈhæləʊ) *vt.* make or honour as holy —**Hallowe'en** *or* **Halloween** (hæləʊˈiːn) *n.* the evening of Oct. 31st, the day before Allhallows or All Saints' Day

hallucinate (həˈluːsɪneɪt) *vi.* suffer illusions —**halluciˈnation** *n.* illusion —**halˈlucinatory** *a.* —**halˈlucinogen** *n.* drug inducing hallucinations

halm (hɔːm) *n. see* HAULM

halo (ˈheɪləʊ) *n.* **1.** circle of light round moon, sun *etc.* **2.** disc of light round saint's head in picture **3.** aura surrounding admired person, thing *etc.* (*pl.* **-es, -s**) —*vt.* **4.** surround with halo

halogen (ˈhælədʒɛn) *n.* any of the chemical elements fluorine, chlorine, bromine, iodine, and astatine —**halogenous** (həˈlɒdʒɪnəs) *a.*

halt[1] (hɔːlt) *n.* **1.** interruption or end to progress *etc.*, *esp.* as command to stop marching **2.** minor railway station without station buildings —*v.* **3.** (cause to) stop

halt[2] (hɔːlt) *vi.* falter, fail —ˈ**halting** *a.* hesitant, lame

halter (ˈhɔːltə) *n.* **1.** rope or strap with headgear to fasten horses or cattle **2.** low-cut dress style with strap passing behind neck **3.** noose for hanging a person —*vt.* **4.** put halter on

halve (hɑːv) *vt.* **1.** cut in half **2.** reduce to half **3.** share

halyard *or* **halliard** (ˈhæljəd) *n.* rope for raising sail, signal flags *etc.*

ham (hæm) *n.* **1.** meat, *esp.* salted or smoked, from thigh of pig **2.** actor adopting exaggerated, unconvincing style **3.** amateur radio enthusiast —*v.* **4.** overact (**-mm-**) —ˈ**hammy** *a. inf.* **1.** (of actor) tending to overact **2.** (of play, performance *etc.*) overacted —**ham-fisted** *or* **ham-handed** *a.* clumsy —ˈ**hamstring** *n.* **1.** tendon at back of knee —*vt.* **2.** cripple by cutting this

hamadryad (hæməˈdraɪəd) *n. Class. myth.* nymph which inhabits tree and dies with it

hamburger (ˈhæmbɜːgə) *n.* fried cake of minced beef, *esp.* served in bread roll

Hamitic (hæˈmɪtɪk, hə-) *n.* **1.** group of N Afr. languages related to Semitic —*a.* **2.** denoting this group of languages **3.** denoting Hamites, group of peoples of N Afr., including ancient Egyptians, supposedly descended from Noah's son Ham

hamlet (ˈhæmlɪt) *n.* small village

hammer (ˈhæmə) *n.* **1.** tool usu. with heavy head at end of handle, for beating, driving nails *etc.* **2.** machine with similar function **3.** contrivance for exploding charge of gun **4.** auctioneer's mallet **5.** metal ball on wire thrown in sports —*v.* **6.** strike (blows) with, or as with, hammer —ˈ**hammerhead** *n.* shark with wide, flattened head —ˈ**hammertoe** *n.* deformed toe —**hammer and sickle** emblem on flag of Soviet Union, representing industrial workers and peasants respectively —**hammer out** solve problem by full investigation of difficulties

hammock (ˈhæmək) *n.* bed of canvas *etc.*, hung on cords

hamper[1] (ˈhæmpə) *n.* **1.** large covered basket **2.** large parcel, box *etc.* of food, wines *etc.*, *esp.* one sent as Christmas gift

hamper[2] (ˈhæmpə) *vt.* impede, obstruct movements of

hamster (ˈhæmstə) *n.* type of rodent, sometimes kept as pet

hamstrung (ˈhæmstrʌŋ) *a.* **1.** crippled **2.** thwarted

hand (hænd) *n.* **1.** extremity of arm beyond wrist **2.** side, quarter, direction **3.** style of writing **4.** cards dealt to player **5.** measure of four inches **6.** manual worker **7.** sailor **8.** help, aid **9.** pointer on dial **10.** applause —*vt.* **11.** pass **12.** deliver **13.** hold out —ˈ**handful** *n.* **1.** small quantity or number **2.** *inf.* person or thing causing problems (*pl.* **-s**) —ˈ**handily** *adv.* —ˈ**handiness** *n.* **1.** dexterity **2.** state of being near, available —ˈ**handy** *a.*

THESAURUS

hall 1. corridor, entrance hall, entry, foyer, hallway, lobby, passage, passageway, vestibule **2.** assembly room, auditorium, chamber, concert hall, meeting place

hallmark 1. authentication, device, endorsement, mark, seal, sign, stamp, symbol **2.** badge, emblem, indication, sure sign, telltale sign

hallucination aberration, apparition, delusion, dream, fantasy, figment of the imagination, illusion, mirage, phantasmagoria, vision

halo aura, aureole *or* aureola, corona, halation (*Photog.*), nimbus, radiance, ring of light

halt[1] *v.* **1.** break off, call it a day, cease, close down, come to an end, desist, draw up, pull up, rest, stand still, stop, wait **2.** arrest, block, bring to an end, check, curb, cut short, end, hold back, impede, obstruct, stem, terminate ~*n.* **3.** arrest, break, close, end, impasse, interruption, pause, stand, standstill, stop, stoppage, termination

halt[2] *v.* **1.** be defective, falter, hobble, limp, stumble **2.** be unsure, boggle, dither, haver, hesitate, pause, stammer, swither (*Scot. dialect*), think twice, waver

halting awkward, faltering, hesitant, imperfect, laboured, stammering, stumbling, stuttering

halve 1. bisect, cut in half, divide equally, reduce by fifty per cent, share equally, split in two **2. by halves** imperfectly, incompletely, scrappily, skimpily

hammer *v.* bang, beat, drive, hit, knock, strike, tap

hammer out accomplish, bring about, come to a conclusion, complete, excogitate, finish, form a resolution, make a decision, negotiate, produce, settle, sort out, thrash out, work out

hamper *v.* bind, cramp, curb, embarrass, encumber, entangle, fetter, frustrate, hamstring, handicap, hinder, hold up, impede, interfere with, obstruct, prevent, restrain, restrict, slow down, thwart, trammel

hamstrung at a loss, crippled, disabled, helpless, *hors de combat*, incapacitated, paralysed

1. convenient 2. clever with the hands —ˈ**handbag** *n.* 1. woman's bag for personal articles 2. bag for carrying in hand —ˈ**handbill** *n.* small printed notice —ˈ**handbook** *n.* small reference or instruction book —ˈ**handcuff** *n.* 1. fetter for wrist, usu. joined in pair —*vt.* 2. secure thus —ˈ**handicraft** *n.* manual occupation or skill —ˈ**handiwork** *n.* thing done by particular person —**handkerchief** (ˈhæŋkətʃɪf, -tʃiːf) *n.* 1. small square of fabric carried in pocket for wiping nose *etc.* 2. neckerchief —**hand-me-down** *n. inf.* 1. something, *esp.* outgrown garment, passed down from one person to another 2. anything already used by another —**hand-out** *n.* 1. money, food *etc.* given free 2. pamphlet giving news, information *etc.* —**hand-pick** *vt.* select with great care —**hand-picked** *a.* —ˈ**handset** *n.* telephone mouthpiece and earpiece mounted as single unit —**hands-on** *a.* involving active participation and operating experience —ˈ**handspring** *n.* gymnastic feat in which person leaps forwards or backwards into handstand and then on to his feet —ˈ**handstand** *n.* act of supporting body in upside-down position by hands alone —**hand-to-hand** *a./adv.* at close quarters —**hand-to-mouth** *a./adv.* with barely enough money or food to satisfy immediate needs —ˈ**handwriting** *n.* way person writes —ˈ**handyman** *n.* 1. man employed to do various tasks 2. man skilled in odd jobs —**hand in glove** very intimate

h & c hot and cold (water)

handicap (ˈhændɪkæp) *n.* 1. something that hampers or hinders 2. race, contest in which chances are equalized by starts, weights carried *etc.* 3. condition so imposed 4. any physical disability —*vt.* 5. hamper 6. impose handicaps on (-**pp**-) —ˈ**handicapped** *a.* physically or mentally disabled

handle (ˈhændᵊl) *n.* 1. part of utensil *etc.* which is to be held —*vt.* 2. touch, feel with hands 3. manage 4. deal with 5. trade —ˈ**handler** *n.* 1. person who trains and controls animals 2. trainer or second of boxer —ˈ**handlebars** *pl.n.* curved metal bar used to steer bicycle, motorbike *etc.*

handsome (ˈhændsəm) *a.* 1. of fine appearance 2. generous 3. ample —ˈ**handsomely** *adv.*

hanepoot (ˈhɑːnəpɔːt) *n.* **SA** type of grape

hang (hæŋ) *vt.* 1. suspend 2. kill by suspension by neck (**hanged** *pt./pp.*) 3. attach, set up (wallpaper, doors *etc.*) —*vi.* 4. be suspended (**hung** *pt./pp.*) —ˈ**hanger** *n.* frame on which clothes *etc.* can be hung —ˈ**hangdog** *a.* sullen, dejected —**hanger-on** *n.* sycophantic follower or dependant (*pl.* **hangers-on**) —**hang-glider** *n.* glider like large kite, with pilot hanging in frame below —**hang-gliding** *n.* —ˈ**hangman** *n.* executioner —ˈ**hangnail** *n.* piece of skin hanging loose at base or side of fingernail —ˈ**hangover** *n.* after-effects of too much drinking —**hang-up** *n. inf.* persistent emotional problem —**hang out** *inf.* reside, frequent

hangar (ˈhæŋə) *n.* large shed for aircraft

hank (hæŋk) *n.* coil, skein, length, *esp.* as measure of yarn

hanker (ˈhæŋkə) *vi.* (*with* for *or* after) have a yearning

THESAURUS

hand *n.* **1.** fist, mitt (*Sl.*), palm, paw (*Inf.*) **2.** aid, assistance, help, support **3.** artificer, artisan, craftsman, employee, hired man, labourer, operative, worker, workman **4.** calligraphy, chirography, handwriting, longhand, penmanship, script **5.** clap, ovation, round of applause **6. hand in glove** allied, in cahoots (*Inf.*), in league, in partnership ~*v.* **7.** deliver, hand over, pass

handbook Baedeker, guide, guidebook, instruction book, manual, vade mecum

handcuff 1. *v.* fetter, manacle, shackle **2.** *n. Plural* bracelets (*Sl.*), cuffs (*Inf.*), fetters, manacles, shackles

handicap *n.* **1.** barrier, block, disadvantage, drawback, encumbrance, hindrance, impediment, limitation, millstone, obstacle, restriction, shortcoming, stumbling block **2.** defect, disability, impairment ~*v.* **3.** burden, encumber, hamper, hamstring, hinder, hold back, impede, limit, place at a disadvantage, restrict, retard

handicraft art, artisanship, craft, craftsmanship, handiwork, skill, workmanship

handiwork 1. craft, handicraft, handwork **2.** achievement, artefact, creation, design, invention, product, production, result

handle *n.* **1.** grip, haft, handgrip, helve, hilt, knob, stock ~*v.* **2.** feel, finger, fondle, grasp, hold, maul, paw (*Inf.*), pick up, poke, touch **3.** control, direct, guide, manage, manipulate, manoeuvre, operate, steer, use, wield **4.** administer, conduct, cope with, deal with, manage, supervise, take care of, treat **5.** discourse, discuss, treat **6.** carry, deal in, market, sell, stock, trade, traffic in

hand-out 1. alms, charity, dole **2.** bulletin, circular, free sample, leaflet, literature (*Inf.*), press release

hand-picked choice, chosen, elect, elite, recherché, select, selected

handsome 1. admirable, attractive, becoming, comely, elegant, fine, good-looking, graceful, majestic, personable, stately, well-proportioned **2.** abundant, ample, bountiful, considerable, generous, gracious, large, liberal, magnanimous, plentiful, sizable

handsomely abundantly, amply, bountifully, generously, liberally, magnanimously, munificently, plentifully, richly

handwriting calligraphy, chirography, fist, hand, longhand, penmanship, scrawl, script

handy 1. accessible, at *or* on hand, available, close, convenient, near, nearby, within reach **2.** convenient, easy to use, helpful, manageable, neat, practical, serviceable, useful **3.** adept, adroit, clever, deft, dexterous, expert, nimble, proficient, ready, skilful, skilled

hang 1. be pendent, dangle, depend, droop, incline, suspend **2.** execute, gibbet, send to the gallows, string up (*Inf.*) **3.** attach, cover, deck, decorate, drape, fasten, fix, furnish **4.** be poised, drift, float, hover, remain, swing

hangdog *adj.* abject, browbeaten, cowed, cringing, defeated, downcast, furtive, guilty, shamefaced, sneaking, wretched

hanger-on dependant, follower, freeloader (*Sl., chiefly U.S.*), lackey, leech, minion, parasite, sponger (*Inf.*), sycophant

hangover aftereffects, crapulence, head (*Inf.*), morning after (*Inf.*)

hang-up block, difficulty, inhibition, obsession, preoccupation, problem, thing (*Inf.*)

hank coil, length, loop, piece, roll, skein

hanky *or* **hankie** (ˈhæŋkɪ) *n. inf.* handkerchief

hanky-panky (ˈhæŋkɪˈpæŋkɪ) *n. inf.* **1.** trickery **2.** illicit sexual relations

Hansard (ˈhænsɑːd) *n.* official printed record of speeches, debates *etc.* in Brit., Aust. and other parliaments

Hanseatic League (hænsɪˈætɪk) commercial organization of towns in N Germany formed to protect and control trade

hansom (ˈhænsəm) *n.* (*sometimes* **H-**) two-wheeled horse-drawn cab for two to ride inside with driver mounted up behind

Hants. (hænts) Hampshire

haphazard (hæpˈhæzəd) *a.* **1.** random **2.** careless

hapless (ˈhæplɪs) *a.* unlucky

happen (ˈhæpᵊn) *vi.* **1.** come about, occur **2.** chance (to do) —ˈ**happening** *n.* occurrence, event

happy (ˈhæpɪ) *a.* **1.** glad **2.** content **3.** lucky, fortunate **4.** apt —ˈ**happily** *adv.* —ˈ**happiness** *n.* —**happy-go-lucky** *a.* casual, light-hearted

harakiri (hærəˈkɪrɪ) *or* **harikari** *n.* formerly, in Japan, ritual suicide by disembowelling

harangue (həˈræŋ) *n.* **1.** vehement speech **2.** tirade —*v.* **3.** address (person or crowd) in angry, forceful or persuasive way

harass (ˈhærəs) *vt.* worry, trouble, torment —ˈ**harassment** *n.*

harbinger (ˈhɑːbɪndʒə) *n.* **1.** one who announces another's approach **2.** forerunner, herald

harbour *or U.S.* **harbor** (ˈhɑːbə) *n.* **1.** shelter for ships **2.** shelter —*vt.* **3.** give shelter or protection to **4.** maintain (secretly) (*esp.* grudge *etc.*)

hard (hɑːd) *a.* **1.** firm, resisting pressure **2.** solid **3.** difficult to understand **4.** harsh, unfeeling **5.** difficult to bear **6.** practical, shrewd **7.** heavy **8.** strenuous **9.** (of water) not making lather well with soap **10.** (of drugs) highly addictive —*adv.* **11.** vigorously **12.** with difficulty **13.** close —ˈ**harden** *v.* —ˈ**hardly** *adv.* **1.** unkindly, harshly **2.** scarcely, not quite **3.** only just —ˈ**hardness** *n.* —ˈ**hardship** *n.* **1.** ill luck **2.** severe toil, suffering **3.** instance of this —ˈ**hardback** *n.* **1.** book bound in stiff covers —*a.* **2.** of or denoting hardback or publication of hardbacks (*also* ˈ**casebound,** ˈ**hardbound,** ˈ**hardcover**) —**hard-bitten** *a. inf.* tough and realistic —ˈ**hardboard** *n.* thin stiff sheet made of compressed sawdust and woodchips —**hard-boiled** *a.* **1.** boiled so long as to be hard **2.** *inf.* (of person) experienced, unemotional, unsympathetic —**hard copy** *Comp.* output that can be read by eye —**hard core 1.** members of group who form intransigent nucleus resisting change **2.** material, such as broken stones, used to form foundation for road *etc.* —**hard-core** *a.* **1.** (of pornography) depicting sexual acts in explicit detail **2.** completely established in belief *etc.* —**hard court** tennis court made of asphalt, concrete *etc.* —**hard disk** *Comp.* inflexible disk in sealed container, usu. with storage capacity of several megabytes —**hard-headed** *a.* shrewd —**hard**ˈ**hearted** *a.* unkind or intolerant —**hard**ˈ**heartedness** *n.* —**hard labour** formerly, penalty of compulsory labour in addition to imprisonment —**hard line** uncompromising course or policy —**hard**ˈ**liner** *n.* —**hard palate** anterior bony portion of roof of mouth —**hard-pressed** *a.* **1.** in difficulties **2.** closely pursued —**hard sell** aggressive technique of selling or advertising —**hard shoulder** surfaced verge at motorway edge for emergency stops —ˈ**hardware** *n.* **1.** tools, implements **2.** necessary (parts of) machinery **3.** *Comp.* mechanical and electronic parts —ˈ**hard-**

THESAURUS

hanker *With* **for** *or* **after** covet, crave, desire, hunger, itch, long, lust, pine, thirst, want, wish, yearn, yen (*Inf.*)

haphazard 1. accidental, arbitrary, chance, fluky (*Inf.*), random **2.** aimless, careless, casual, disorderly, disorganized, hit or miss (*Inf.*), indiscriminate, slapdash, slipshod, unmethodical, unsystematic

happen 1. appear, arise, come about, come off (*Inf.*), come to pass, crop up (*Inf.*), develop, ensue, eventuate, follow, materialize, occur, present itself, result, take place, transpire (*Inf.*) **2.** become of, befall, betide **3.** chance, fall out, have the fortune to be, supervene, turn out

happening accident, adventure, affair, case, chance, episode, event, experience, incident, occasion, occurrence, phenomenon, proceeding, scene

happily 1. agreeably, contentedly, delightedly, enthusiastically, freely, gladly, heartily, willingly, with pleasure **2.** blithely, cheerfully, gaily, gleefully, joyfully, joyously, merrily **3.** auspiciously, favourably, fortunately, luckily, opportunely, propitiously, providentially, seasonably **4.** appropriately, aptly, felicitously, gracefully, successfully

happiness beatitude, blessedness, bliss, cheer, cheerfulness, cheeriness, contentment, delight, ecstasy, elation, enjoyment, exuberance, felicity, gaiety, gladness, high spirits, joy, jubilation, light-heartedness, merriment, pleasure, prosperity, satisfaction, wellbeing

happy 1. blessed, blest, blissful, blithe, cheerful, content, contented, delighted, ecstatic, elated, glad, gratified, jolly, joyful, joyous, jubilant, merry, overjoyed, over the moon (*Inf.*), pleased, sunny, thrilled, walking on air (*Inf.*) **2.** advantageous, appropriate, apt, auspicious, befitting, convenient, enviable, favourable, felicitous, fortunate, lucky, opportune, promising, propitious, satisfactory, seasonable, successful, timely, well-timed

happy-go-lucky blithe, carefree, casual, devil-may-care, easy-going, heedless, improvident, insouciant, irresponsible, light-hearted, nonchalant, unconcerned, untroubled

harangue 1. *n.* address, declamation, diatribe, exhortation, lecture, oration, philippic, screed, speech, spiel (*Inf.*), tirade **2.** *v.* address, declaim, exhort, hold forth, lecture, rant, spout (*Inf.*)

harass annoy, badger, bait, beleaguer, bother, chivvy (*Brit.*), devil (*Inf.*), disturb, exasperate, exhaust, fatigue, harry, hassle (*Inf.*), hound, perplex, persecute, pester, plague, tease, tire, torment, trouble, vex, weary, worry

harassment aggravation (*Inf.*), annoyance, badgering, bedevilment, bother, hassle (*Inf.*), irritation, molestation, nuisance, persecution, pestering, torment, trouble, vexation

harbour *n.* **1.** anchorage, destination, haven, port **2.** asylum, covert, haven, refuge, retreat, sanctuary, sanctum, security, shelter ~*v.* **3.** conceal, hide, lodge, protect, provide refuge, relieve, secrete, shelter, shield **4.** believe, brood over, cherish, cling to, entertain, foster, hold, imagine, maintain, nurse, nurture, retain

wood *n.* wood from deciduous trees —**hard of hearing** rather deaf —**hard up** very short of money

hardy (ˈhɑːdɪ) *a.* **1.** robust, vigorous **2.** bold **3.** (of plants) able to grow in the open all year round —ˈ**hardihood** *n.* extreme boldness, audacity —ˈ**hardily** *adv.* —ˈ**hardiness** *n.*

hare (hɛə) *n.* animal like large rabbit, with longer legs and ears, noted for speed —ˈ**harebell** *n.* round-leaved bell-flower —ˈ**harebrained** *a.* rash, wild —ˈ**harelip** *n.* fissure of upper lip —**hare and hounds** paper chase

harem (ˈhɛərəm, hɑːˈriːm) *or* **hareem** (hɑːˈriːm) *n.* **1.** women's part of Mohammedan dwelling **2.** one man's wives collectively

haricot (ˈhærɪkəʊ) *n.* type of French bean that can be dried and stored

harikari (hærɪˈkɑːrɪ) *n. see* HARAKIRI

hark (hɑːk) *vi.* listen —**hark back** return (to previous subject of discussion)

harlequin (ˈhɑːlɪkwɪn) *n.* stock comic character, *esp.* masked clown in diamond-patterned costume —**harlequiˈnade** *n.* **1.** scene in pantomime **2.** buffoonery

Harley Street (ˈhɑːlɪ) street in central London famous for its large number of medical specialists' consulting rooms

harlot (ˈhɑːlət) *n.* whore, prostitute —ˈ**harlotry** *n.*

harm (hɑːm) *n.* **1.** damage, injury —*vt.* **2.** cause harm to —ˈ**harmful** *a.* —ˈ**harmfully** *adv.* —ˈ**harmless** *a.* unable or unlikely to hurt —ˈ**harmlessly** *adv.*

harmony (ˈhɑːmənɪ) *n.* **1.** agreement **2.** concord **3.** peace **4.** *Mus.* combination of notes to make chords **5.** melodious sound —**harmonic** (hɑːˈmɒnɪk) *a.* **1.** of harmony —*n.* **2.** tone or note whose frequency is a

THESAURUS

hard *adj.* **1.** compact, dense, firm, impenetrable, inflexible, rigid, rocklike, solid, stiff, stony, strong, tough, unyielding **2.** arduous, backbreaking, burdensome, exacting, exhausting, fatiguing, formidable, Herculean, laborious, rigorous, strenuous, toilsome, tough, uphill, wearying **3.** baffling, complex, complicated, difficult, intricate, involved, knotty, perplexing, puzzling, tangled, thorny, unfathomable **4.** callous, cold, cruel, exacting, grim, hardhearted, harsh, implacable, obdurate, pitiless, ruthless, severe, stern, strict, stubborn, unfeeling, unjust, unkind, unrelenting, unsparing, unsympathetic **5.** calamitous, dark, disagreeable, disastrous, distressing, grievous, grim, intolerable, painful, unpleasant **6.** driving, fierce, forceful, heavy, powerful, strong, violent ~*adv.* **7.** energetically, fiercely, forcefully, forcibly, heavily, intensely, powerfully, severely, sharply, strongly, vigorously, violently, with all one's might, with might and main **8.** assiduously, determinedly, diligently, doggedly, earnestly, industriously, intently, persistently, steadily, strenuously, untiringly **9.** agonizingly, badly, distressingly, harshly, laboriously, painfully, roughly, severely, with difficulty

hard-bitten *or* **hard-boiled** case-hardened, cynical, down-to-earth, hard-headed, hard-nosed (*Sl.*), matter-of-fact, practical, realistic, shrewd, tough, unsentimental

hard-core 1. dedicated, die-hard, dyed-in-the-wool, extreme, intransigent, obstinate, rigid, staunch, steadfast **2.** explicit, obscene

harden 1. anneal, bake, cake, freeze, set, solidify, stiffen **2.** brace, buttress, fortify, gird, indurate, nerve, reinforce, steel, strengthen, toughen **3.** accustom, brutalize, case-harden, habituate, inure, season, train

hard-headed astute, cool, hard-boiled (*Inf.*), level-headed, practical, pragmatic, realistic, sensible, shrewd, tough, unsentimental

hardhearted callous, cold, cruel, hard, heartless, indifferent, inhuman, insensitive, intolerant, merciless, pitiless, stony, uncaring, unfeeling, unkind, unsympathetic

hardiness boldness, courage, fortitude, intrepidity, resilience, resolution, robustness, ruggedness, sturdiness, toughness, valour

hardly almost not, barely, by no means, faintly, infrequently, just, not at all, not quite, no way, only, only just, scarcely, with difficulty

hard-pressed harried, hotly pursued, in difficulties, pushed (*Inf.*), under attack, under pressure, up against it (*Inf.*), with one's back to the wall

hardship adversity, affliction, austerity, burden, calamity, destitution, difficulty, fatigue, grievance, labour, misery, misfortune, need, oppression, persecution, privation, suffering, toil, torment, trial, tribulation, trouble, want

hard up bankrupt, broke (*Inf.*), bust (*Inf.*), cleaned out (*Sl.*), impecunious, impoverished, in the red (*Inf.*), on one's uppers (*Inf.*), out of pocket, penniless, poor, short, short of cash *or* funds, skint (*Brit. sl.*)

hardy 1. firm, fit, hale, healthy, hearty, in fine fettle, lusty, robust, rugged, sound, stalwart, stout, strong, sturdy, tough, vigorous **2.** bold, brave, courageous, daring, heroic, intrepid, manly, plucky, resolute, stouthearted, valiant, valorous

hark back look back, recall, recollect, regress, remember, revert, think back

harlot call girl, fallen woman, hussy, loose woman, pro (*Inf.*), prostitute, scrubber (*Sl.*), streetwalker, strumpet, tart (*Inf.*), tramp (*Sl.*), whore

harm 1. *n.* abuse, damage, detriment, disservice, hurt, ill, impairment, injury, loss, mischief, misfortune **2.** *v.* abuse, blemish, damage, hurt, ill-treat, ill-use, impair, injure, maltreat, mar, molest, ruin, spoil, wound

harmful baleful, baneful, damaging, deleterious, destructive, detrimental, disadvantageous, evil, hurtful, injurious, noxious, pernicious

harmless gentle, innocent, innocuous, innoxious, inoffensive, nontoxic, not dangerous, safe, unobjectionable

harmonious 1. agreeable, compatible, concordant, congruous, consonant, coordinated, correspondent, dulcet, euphonious, harmonic, harmonizing, matching, mellifluous, melodious, musical, sweet-sounding, symphonious (*Literary*), tuneful **2.** agreeable, amicable, compatible, concordant, congenial, cordial, *en rapport*, fraternal, friendly, in accord, in harmony, in unison, of one mind, sympathetic

harmonize accord, adapt, agree, arrange, attune, be in unison, be of one mind, blend, chime with, cohere, compose, coordinate, correspond, match, reconcile, suit, tally, tone in with

multiple of its pitch —**harmonica** (hɑːˈmɒnɪkə) *n.* any of various musical instruments, *esp.* mouth organ —**harmonics** (hɑːˈmɒnɪks) *pl.n.* **1.** science of musical sounds **2.** harmonious sounds —**harˈmonious** *a.* —**harˈmoniously** *adv.* —**ˈharmonist** *n.* —**harˈmonium** *n.* small organ —**harmoniˈzation** *or* **-niˈsation** *n.* —**ˈharmonize** *or* **-nise** *vt.* **1.** bring into harmony **2.** cause to agree **3.** reconcile —*vi.* **4.** be in harmony **5.** sing in harmony, as with other singers

harness (ˈhɑːnɪs) *n.* **1.** equipment for attaching horse to cart, plough *etc.* **2.** any such equipment —*vt.* **3.** put on, in harness **4.** utilize energy or power of (waterfall *etc.*) —**in harness** in or at one's routine work

harp (hɑːp) *n.* **1.** musical instrument of strings played by hand —*vi.* **2.** play on harp **3.** (*with* on *or* upon) dwell (on) continuously —**ˈharper** *or* **ˈharpist** *n.* —**ˈharpsichord** *n.* stringed instrument like piano

harpoon (hɑːˈpuːn) *n.* **1.** barbed spear with rope attached for catching whales —*vt.* **2.** catch, kill with or as if with a harpoon —**harˈpooner** *n.* —**harpoon gun** gun for firing harpoon in whaling

harpy (ˈhɑːpɪ) *n.* **1.** monster with body of woman and wings and claws of bird **2.** cruel, grasping person

harridan (ˈhærɪdᵊn) *n.* shrewish old woman, hag

harrier (ˈhærɪə) *n.* **1.** hound used in hunting hares **2.** falcon **3.** cross-country runner

harrow (ˈhærəʊ) *n.* **1.** implement for smoothing, levelling, or stirring up soil —*vt.* **2.** draw harrow over **3.** distress greatly —**ˈharrowing** *a.* **1.** heart-rending **2.** distressful

harry (ˈhærɪ) *vt.* **1.** harass **2.** ravage (**-ried, -rying**)

harsh (hɑːʃ) *a.* **1.** rough, discordant **2.** severe **3.** unfeeling —**ˈharshly** *adv.*

hart (hɑːt) *n.* male deer —**hartshorn** (ˈhɑːtshɔːn) *n.* material made from harts' horns, formerly chief source of ammonia

hartal (hɑːˈtɑːl) *n.* in India, act of suspending work, *esp.* in political protest

hartebeest (ˈhɑːtɪbiːst) *or* **hartbeest** (ˈhɑːtbiːst) *n.* Afr. antelope

harum-scarum (ˈhɛərəmˈskɛərəm) *a.* **1.** reckless, wild **2.** giddy

harvest (ˈhɑːvɪst) *n.* **1.** (season for) gathering in grain **2.** gathering **3.** crop **4.** product of action —*v.* **5.** reap and gather in (crop) —**ˈharvester** *n.*

has (hæz) *third person sing. pres. indicative of* HAVE —**has-been** *n. inf.* person or thing that is no longer popular, successful *etc.*

hash (hæʃ) *n.* **1.** dish of hashed meat *etc.* **2.** *inf.* hashish —*vt.* **3.** cut up small, chop **4.** mix up

hashish (ˈhæʃiːʃ, -ɪʃ) *or* **hasheesh** *n.* resinous extract of Indian hemp, *esp.* used as hallucinogen

haslet (ˈhæzlɪt) *or* **harslet** (ˈhɑːzlɪt, ˈhɑːs-) *n.* loaf of cooked minced pig's offal, eaten cold

hasp (hɑːsp) *n.* **1.** clasp passing over staple for fastening door *etc.* —*vt.* **2.** fasten, secure with hasp

hassle (ˈhæsᵊl) *inf. n.* **1.** quarrel **2.** great deal of bother or trouble —*vi.* **3.** quarrel, fight —*vt.* **4.** harass (persistently)

hassock (ˈhæsək) *n.* **1.** kneeling-cushion **2.** tuft of grass

hast (hæst) *obs. second person sing. pres. indicative of* HAVE

haste (heɪst) *n.* **1.** speed, quickness, hurry —*vi.* **2.** *Poet.* hasten —**hasten** (ˈheɪsᵊn) *v.* (cause to) hurry, increase speed —**ˈhastily** *adv.* —**ˈhasty** *a.*

THESAURUS

harmony **1.** accord, agreement, amicability, amity, compatibility, concord, conformity, consensus, cooperation, friendship, good will, like-mindedness, peace, rapport, sympathy, unanimity, understanding, unity **2.** balance, compatibility, concord, congruity, consistency, consonance, coordination, correspondence, fitness, parallelism, suitability, symmetry **3.** euphony, melodiousness, melody, tune, tunefulness

harness *n.* **1.** equipment, gear, tack, tackle, trappings **2. in harness** active, at work, busy, in action, working ~*v.* **3.** couple, hitch up, put in harness, saddle, yoke **4.** apply, channel, control, employ, exploit, make productive, mobilize, render useful, turn to account, utilize

harp *With* **on** *or* **upon** dwell on, go on, labour, press, reiterate, renew, repeat

harrowing agonizing, alarming, chilling, distressing, disturbing, excruciating, frightening, heartbreaking, heart-rending, nerve-racking, painful, racking, soaring, terrifying, tormenting, traumatic

harry **1.** annoy, badger, bedevil, chivvy, disturb, fret, harass, hassle (*Inf.*), molest, persecute, pester, plague, tease, torment, trouble, vex, worry **2.** depredate (*Rare*), despoil, devastate, pillage, plunder, raid, ravage, rob, sack

harsh **1.** coarse, croaking, crude, discordant, dissonant, glaring, grating, guttural, jarring, rasping, raucous, rough, strident, unmelodious **2.** abusive, austere, bitter, bleak, brutal, comfortless, cruel, dour, Draconian, grim, hard, pitiless, punitive, relentless, ruthless, severe, sharp, Spartan, stern, stringent, unfeeling, unkind, unpleasant, unrelenting

harshly brutally, cruelly, grimly, roughly, severely, sharply, sternly, strictly

harvest *n.* **1.** harvesting, harvest-time, ingathering, reaping **2.** crop, produce, yield **3.** *Fig.* consequence, effect, fruition, product, result, return ~*v.* **4.** gather, mow, pick, pluck, reap

hassle *n.* **1.** altercation, argument, bickering, disagreement, dispute, fight, quarrel, squabble, tussle, wrangle **2.** bother, difficulty, inconvenience, problem, struggle, trial, trouble, upset ~*v.* **3.** annoy, badger, bother, bug (*Inf.*), harass, harry, hound, pester

haste **1.** alacrity, briskness, celerity, dispatch, expedition, fleetness, nimbleness, promptitude, quickness, rapidity, rapidness, speed, swiftness, urgency, velocity **2.** bustle, hastiness, helter-skelter, hurry, hustle, impetuosity, precipitateness, rashness, recklessness, rush

hasten **1.** bolt, dash, fly, haste, hurry (up), make haste, race, run, rush, scurry, scuttle, speed, sprint, step on it (*Inf.*), tear (along) **2.** accelerate, advance, dispatch, expedite, goad, hurry (up), precipitate, press, push forward, quicken, speed (up), step up (*Inf.*), urge

hastily **1.** apace, double-quick, fast, posthaste, promptly, quickly, rapidly, speedily, straightaway **2.** heedlessly, hurriedly, impetuously, impulsively, on the spur of the moment, precipitately, rashly, recklessly, too quickly

hat (hæt) *n.* head-covering, usu. with brim —**'hatter** *n.* dealer in, maker of hats —**hat trick** any three successive achievements, *esp.* in sport

hatch[1] (hætʃ) *v.* 1. (of young, *esp.* of birds) (cause to) emerge from egg —*vt.* 2. contrive, devise —**'hatchery** *n.*

hatch[2] (hætʃ) *n.* 1. hatchway 2. trapdoor over it 3. opening in wall or door, as service hatch, to facilitate service of meals *etc.* between two rooms 4. lower half of divided door —**'hatchback** *n.* car with single lifting door in rear —**'hatchway** *n.* opening in deck of ship *etc.*

hatch[3] (hætʃ) *vt.* 1. engrave or draw lines on for shading 2. shade with parallel lines

hatchet ('hætʃɪt) *n.* small axe —**hatchet job** *inf.* malicious verbal or written attack —**hatchet man** *inf.* person carrying out unpleasant assignments for another —**bury the hatchet** make peace

hate (heɪt) *vt.* 1. dislike strongly, bear malice towards —*n.* 2. intense dislike 3. that which is hated —**'hateful** *a.* detestable —**'hatefully** *adv.* —**hatred** ('heɪtrɪd) *n.* extreme dislike, active ill-will

hauberk ('hɔːbɜːk) *n.* long coat of mail

haughty ('hɔːtɪ) *a.* proud, arrogant —**'haughtily** *adv.* —**'haughtiness** *n.*

haul (hɔːl) *vt.* 1. pull, drag with effort —*vi.* 2. (of wind) shift —*n.* 3. hauling 4. something that is hauled 5. catch of fish 6. acquisition 7. distance (to be) covered —**'haulage** *n.* 1. carrying of loads 2. charge for this —**'haulier** *n.* firm, person that transports goods by road

haulm *or* **halm** (hɔːm) *n.* 1. stalks of beans, potatoes, grasses *etc.* collectively 2. single stem of such plant

haunch (hɔːntʃ) *n.* 1. human hip or fleshy hindquarter of animal 2. leg and loin of venison

haunt (hɔːnt) *vt.* 1. visit regularly 2. visit in form of ghost 3. recur to —*n.* 4. place frequently visited —**'haunted** *a.* 1. frequented by ghosts 2. worried —**'haunting** *a.* 1. (of memories) poignant or persistent 2. poignantly sentimental —**'hauntingly** *adv.*

hautboy ('əʊbɔɪ) *n.* 1. strawberry with large fruit 2. *obs.* oboe

haute couture (ot ku'tyːr) *Fr.* high fashion

hauteur (əʊ'tɜː) *n.* haughty spirit

Havana cigar (hə'vænə) fine quality of cigar (*also* **Ha'vana**)

have (hæv) *vt.* 1. hold, possess 2. be possessed, affected with 3. cheat, outwit 4. engage in 5. obtain 6. contain 7. allow 8. cause to be (done) 9. give birth to 10. as auxiliary, forms perfect and other tenses (*pres. tense:* I *have,* thou *hast,* he *has,* we, you, they *have*) (**had, 'having**) —**have to** be obliged to

haven ('heɪvᵊn) *n.* place of safety

haver ('heɪvə) *vi.* UK 1. *dial.* babble; talk nonsense 2. dither —*n.* 3. (*usu. pl.*) *Scot.* nonsense

haversack ('hævəsæk) *n.* canvas bag for provisions *etc.*, carried on back or shoulder when hiking

havoc ('hævək) *n.* 1. devastation, ruin 2. *inf.* confusion, chaos

haw (hɔː) *n.* 1. fruit of hawthorn 2. hawthorn

hawfinch ('hɔːfɪntʃ) *n.* uncommon European finch

THESAURUS

hasty 1. brisk, eager, expeditious, fast, fleet, hurried, prompt, rapid, speedy, swift, urgent 2. foolhardy, headlong, heedless, impetuous, impulsive, indiscreet, precipitate, rash, reckless, thoughtless, unduly quick

hatch 1. breed, bring forth, brood, incubate 2. *Fig.* conceive, concoct, contrive, cook up (*Inf.*), design, devise, dream up (*Inf.*), plan, plot, project, scheme, think up

hatchet man assassin, bravo, calumniator, cutthroat, debunker, defamer, destroyer, detractor, gunman, hired assassin, hit man (*Sl.*), killer, murderer, smear campaigner, thug, traducer

hate *v.* 1. abhor, abominate, be hostile to, be repelled by, be sick of, despise, detest, dislike, execrate, have an aversion to, loathe, recoil from 2. be loath, be reluctant, be sorry, be unwilling, dislike, feel disinclined, have no stomach for, shrink from ~*n.* 3. abhorrence, abomination, animosity, animus, antagonism, antipathy, aversion, detestation, dislike, enmity, execration, hatred, hostility, loathing, odium

hateful abhorrent, abominable, despicable, detestable, disgusting, execrable, forbidding, foul, heinous, horrible, loathsome, obnoxious, odious, offensive, repellent, repugnant, repulsive, revolting, vile

hatred abomination, animosity, animus, antagonism, antipathy, aversion, detestation, dislike, enmity, execration, hate, ill will, odium, repugnance, revulsion

haughty arrogant, assuming, conceited, contemptuous, disdainful, high, high and mighty (*Inf.*), hoity-toity (*Inf.*), imperious, lofty, overweening, proud, scornful, snobbish, snooty (*Inf.*), stuck-up (*Inf.*), supercilious, uppish (*Brit. inf.*)

haul *v.* 1. drag, draw, hale, heave, lug, pull, tow, trail, tug ~*n.* 2. drag, heave, pull, tug 3. booty, catch, find, gain, harvest, loot, spoils, takings, yield

haunt *v.* 1. visit, walk 2. beset, come back, obsess, plague, possess, prey on, recur, stay with, torment, trouble, weigh on 3. frequent, hang around *or* about, repair, resort, visit ~*n.* 4. den, gathering place, hangout (*Inf.*), meeting place, rendezvous, resort, stamping ground

haunted 1. cursed, eerie, ghostly, jinxed, possessed, spooky (*Inf.*) 2. obsessed, plagued, preoccupied, tormented, troubled, worried

haunting disturbing, eerie, evocative, indelible, nostalgic, persistent, poignant, recurrent, recurring, unforgettable

have 1. hold, keep, obtain, occupy, own, possess, retain 2. accept, acquire, gain, get, obtain, procure, receive, secure, take 3. comprehend, comprise, contain, embody, include, take in 4. endure, enjoy, experience, feel, meet with, suffer, sustain, undergo 5. *Sl.* cheat, deceive, dupe, fool, outwit, swindle, take in (*Inf.*), trick 6. *Usually* **have to** be bound, be compelled, be forced, be obliged, have got to, must, ought, should 7. allow, consider, entertain, permit, put up with (*Inf.*), think about, tolerate 8. bear, beget, bring forth, bring into the world, deliver, give birth to

haven asylum, refuge, retreat, sanctuary, sanctum, shelter

havoc 1. carnage, damage, desolation, despoliation, destruction, devastation, rack and ruin, ravages, ruin, slaughter, waste, wreck 2. *Inf.* chaos, confusion, disorder, disruption, mayhem, shambles

hawk[1] (hɔːk) *n.* **1.** bird of prey smaller than eagle **2.** supporter, advocate of warlike policies —*vi.* **3.** hunt with hawks **4.** soar and swoop like hawk —**hawk-eyed** *a.* **1.** having extremely keen sight **2.** vigilant or observant

hawk[2] (hɔːk) *vt.* offer (goods) for sale, as in street —ˈ**hawker** *n.*

hawk[3] (hɔːk) *vi.* clear throat noisily

hawse (hɔːz) *n.* part of ship's bows with holes for cables

hawser (ˈhɔːzə) *n.* large rope or cable

hawthorn (ˈhɔːθɔːn) *n.* thorny shrub or tree having pink or white flowers and reddish fruits (*also* **(UK) may, may tree,** ˈ**mayflower)**

hay (heɪ) *n.* grass mown and dried —ˈ**haybox** *n.* box filled with hay in which heated food is left to finish cooking —**hay fever** allergic reaction to pollen, dust *etc.* —ˈ**haymaker** *n.* **1.** person who cuts or turns hay **2.** either of two machines, one designed to crush stems of hay, the other to break and bend them, in order to cause more rapid and even drying **3.** *Boxing sl.* wild swinging punch —ˈ**haymaking** *a./n.* —ˈ**haystack** *n.* large pile of hay —ˈ**haywire** *a.* **1.** crazy **2.** disorganized

hazard (ˈhæzəd) *n.* **1.** chance **2.** risk, danger —*vt.* **3.** expose to risk **4.** run risk of —ˈ**hazardous** *a.* risky

haze (heɪz) *n.* **1.** mist, oft. due to heat **2.** obscurity —ˈ**hazy** *a.* **1.** misty **2.** obscured **3.** vague

hazel (ˈheɪzᵊl) *n.* **1.** bush bearing nuts **2.** yellowish-brown colour of the nuts —*a.* **3.** light yellowish brown

Hb haemoglobin

HB UK (on pencils) hard-black

H.B.C. Hudson's Bay Company

H-bomb hydrogen bomb

H.C.F. *or* **h.c.f.** highest common factor

he (hiː; *unstressed* iː) *pron.* **1.** (*third person masculine pronoun*) person, animal already referred to **2.** (*comb. form*) male, as in *he-goat* —**he-man** *n. inf.* strongly built muscular man

He *Chem.* helium

HE *or* **H.E. 1.** high explosive **2.** His Eminence **3.** His (*or* Her) Excellency

head (hɛd) *n.* **1.** upper part of person's or animal's body, containing mouth, sense organs and brain **2.** upper part of anything **3.** chief of organization, school *etc.* **4.** chief part **5.** aptitude, capacity **6.** culmination or crisis (*esp. in* **bring** *or* **come to a head**) **7.** leader **8.** section of chapter **9.** title **10.** headland **11.** person, animal considered as unit **12.** white froth on beer *etc.* **13.** *inf.* headache —*a.* **14.** chief, principal **15.** (of wind) contrary —*vt.* **16.** be at the top, head of **17.** lead, direct **18.** provide with head **19.** hit (ball) with head —*vi.* **20.** (*with* for) make (for) **21.** form a head —ˈ**header** *n.* **1.** *inf.* headlong fall or dive **2.** brick laid with end in face of wall **3.** action of striking ball with head —ˈ**heading** *n.* title —**heads** *adv. inf.* with obverse side (of coin) uppermost —ˈ**heady** *a.* apt to intoxicate or excite —ˈ**headache** *n.* **1.** continuous pain in head **2.** *inf.* worrying circumstance —ˈ**headboard** *n.* vertical board at head of bed —ˈ**headdress** *n.* any head covering, *esp.* ornate one —ˈ**headgear** *n.* **1.** hat, headdress *etc.* **2.** any part of horse's harness worn on head **3.** hoisting mechanism at pithead of mine —**head-hunter** *n.* —**head-hunting** *n.* **1.** practice among certain peoples of removing heads of slain enemies and preserving them as trophies **2.** (of company or corporation) recruitment of, or drive to recruit, new high-level personnel —ˈ**headland** *n.* promontory —ˈ**headlight** *n.* powerful lamp carried on front of locomotive, motor vehicle *etc.* —ˈ**headline** *n.* news summary, *usu.* in large type in newspaper —ˈ**headlong** *adv.* **1.** with head foremost **2.** with great haste —**head-on** *adv./a.* **1.** (of collision *etc.*) front foremost **2.** with directness —ˈ**headphones** *pl.n.* electrical device consisting of two earphones held in position by strap over head (*also* (*inf.*) **cans)** —ˈ**headquarters** *pl.n.* **1.** residence of commander-in-chief **2.** centre of operations —ˈ**headroom** *or* ˈ**headway** *n.* height of bridge *etc.*; clearance —ˈ**headshrinker** *n.* **1.** *sl.* psychiatrist (*also* **shrink**) **2.** head-hunter who shrinks heads of his victims —ˈ**headstall** *n.* part of bridle that fits round horse's head —**head start** initial advantage in competitive situation —ˈ**headstone** *n.* gravestone —ˈ**headstrong** *a.* self-willed —ˈ**headwaters** *pl.n.* tributary streams of river —ˈ**headway** *n.* advance, progress —ˈ**headwind** *n.* wind blowing directly against course of aircraft or ship —ˈ**headword** *n.* key word placed at beginning of line *etc.* as in dictionary entry

THESAURUS

hawk *v.* bark (*Inf.*), cry, market, peddle, sell, tout (*Inf.*), vend

hazardous 1. dangerous, dicey (*Sl., chiefly Brit.*), difficult, fraught with danger, hairy (*Sl.*), insecure, perilous, precarious, risky, unsafe **2.** chancy (*Inf.*), haphazard, precarious, uncertain, unpredictable

haze cloud, dimness, film, fog, mist, obscurity, smog, smokiness, steam, vapour

hazy 1. blurry, cloudy, dim, dull, faint, foggy, misty, nebulous, obscure, overcast, smoky, veiled **2.** *Fig.* fuzzy, ill-defined, indefinite, indistinct, loose, muddled, muzzy, nebulous, uncertain, unclear, vague

head *n.* **1.** conk (*Sl.*), cranium, crown, loaf (*Sl.*), noddle (*Inf., chiefly Brit.*), nut (*Sl.*), pate, skull **2.** boss (*Inf.*), captain, chief, chieftain, commander, director, headmaster, headmistress, head teacher, leader, manager, master, principal, superintendent, supervisor **3.** apex, crest, crown, height, peak, pitch, summit, tip, top, vertex **4.** ability, aptitude, brain, brains (*Inf.*), capacity, faculty, flair, intellect, intelligence, mentality, mind, talent, thought, understanding **5.** climax, conclusion, crisis, culmination, end, turning point **6.** *Geog.* cape, foreland, headland, point, promontory ~*adj.* **7.** arch, chief, first, foremost, front, highest, leading, main, pre-eminent, premier, prime, principal, supreme, topmost ~*v.* **8.** be *or* go first, cap, crown, lead, lead the way, precede, top **9.** be in charge of, command, control, direct, govern, guide, lead, manage, rule, run, supervise **10.** *Often with* **for** aim, go to, make a beeline for, make for, point, set off for, set out, start towards, steer, turn

headache 1. cephalalgia (*Medical*), migraine, neuralgia **2.** *Inf.* bane, bother, inconvenience, nuisance, problem, trouble, vexation, worry

heading caption, headline, name, rubric, title

headlong *adv.* **1.** headfirst, headforemost, head-on **2.** hastily, heedlessly, helter-skelter, hurriedly, pell-mell, precipitately, rashly, thoughtlessly, wildly

headstrong contrary, foolhardy, froward, heedless, imprudent, impulsive, intractable, mulish, obstinate, perverse, pig-headed, rash, reckless, self-willed, stubborn, ungovernable, unruly, wilful

heal (hiːl) *v.* make or become well —**health** (hɛlθ) *n.* **1.** soundness of body **2.** condition of body **3.** toast drunk in person's honour —**healthily** (ˈhɛlθɪlɪ) *adv.* —**healthiness** (ˈhɛlθɪnɪs) *n.* —**healthy** (ˈhɛlθɪ) *a.* **1.** of strong constitution **2.** of or producing good health, wellbeing *etc.* **3.** vigorous —**health centre** surgery and offices of group medical practice —**health visitor UK** nurse who visits and gives advice to old and sick in their homes

heap (hiːp) *n.* **1.** pile of things lying one on another **2.** great quantity —*vt.* **3.** pile **4.** load (with)

hear (hɪə) *vt.* **1.** perceive by ear **2.** listen to **3.** *Law* try (case) **4.** heed —*vi.* **5.** perceive sound **6.** (*with* of *or* about) learn (**heard** (hɜːd) *pt./pp.*) —ˈ**hearer** *n.* —ˈ**hearing** *n.* **1.** ability to hear **2.** earshot **3.** judicial examination —ˈ**hearsay** *n.* **1.** rumour —*a.* **2.** based on hearsay —**hear! hear!** exclamation of approval, agreement

hearken *or U.S.* (*sometimes*) **harken** (ˈhɑːkən) *vi.* listen

hearse (hɜːs) *n.* funeral carriage for carrying coffin to grave

heart (hɑːt) *n.* **1.** organ which makes blood circulate **2.** seat of emotions and affections **3.** mind, soul, courage **4.** central part **5.** playing card marked with symbol of heart **6.** one of these marks —ˈ**hearten** *v.* make, become cheerful —ˈ**heartily** *adv.* —ˈ**heartless** *a.* unfeeling —ˈ**hearty** *a.* **1.** friendly **2.** vigorous **3.** in good health **4.** satisfying the appetite —ˈ**heartache** *n.* intense anguish or mental suffering —**heart attack** sudden severe malfunction of heart —ˈ**heartbreak** *n.* intense and overwhelming grief or disappointment —ˈ**heartbreaking** *a.* —ˈ**heartburn** *n.* pain in higher intestine —**heart failure 1.** inability of heart to pump adequate amount of blood to tissues **2.** sudden cessation of heartbeat, resulting in death —ˈ**heartfelt** *a.* sincerely and strongly felt —ˈ**heartfree** *a.* with the affections free or disengaged —**heart-rending** *a.* **1.** overwhelming with grief **2.** agonizing —**heart-searching** *n.* examination of one's feelings or conscience —ˈ**heartsease** *n.* wild pansy —**heart-throb** *n.* *sl.* object of infatuation —**heart-to-heart** *a.* **1.** (*esp.* of conversation) concerned with personal problems —*n.* **2.** intimate conversation —**heart-warming** *a.* **1.** pleasing; gratifying **2.** emotionally moving —ˈ**heartwood** *n.* central core of dark hard wood in tree trunks —**by heart** by memory

hearth (hɑːθ) *n.* **1.** part of room where fire is made **2.** home

heat (hiːt) *n.* **1.** hotness **2.** sensation of this **3.** hot weather or climate **4.** warmth of feeling, anger *etc.* **5.**

THESAURUS

headway advance, improvement, progress, progression, way

heady 1. inebriating, intoxicating, potent, spirituous, strong **2.** exciting, exhilarating, intoxicating, overwhelming, stimulating, thrilling

heal cure, make well, mend, regenerate, remedy, restore, treat

health 1. fitness, good condition, haleness, healthiness, robustness, salubrity, soundness, strength, vigour, wellbeing **2.** condition, constitution, fettle, form, shape, state, tone

healthy 1. active, blooming, fit, flourishing, hale, hale and hearty, hardy, hearty, in fine feather, in fine fettle, in fine form, in good condition, in good shape (*Inf.*), in the pink, physically fit, robust, sound, strong, sturdy, vigorous, well **2.** beneficial, bracing, good for one, healthful, health-giving, hygienic, invigorating, nourishing, nutritious, salubrious, salutary, wholesome

heap *n.* **1.** accumulation, aggregation, collection, hoard, lot, mass, mound, mountain, pile, stack, stockpile, store **2.** *Often plural Inf.* abundance, a lot, great deal, lashings (*Brit. inf.*), load(s) (*Inf.*), lots (*Inf.*), mass, mint, ocean(s), oodles (*Inf.*), plenty, pot(s) (*Inf.*), quantities, stack(s), tons ~*v.* **3.** accumulate, amass, augment, bank, collect, gather, hoard, increase, mound, pile, stack, stockpile, store **4.** assign, bestow, burden, confer, load, shower upon

hear 1. attend, be all ears (*Inf.*), catch, eavesdrop, give attention, hark, hearken (*Archaic*), heed, listen in, listen to, overhear **2.** ascertain, be informed, be told of, discover, find out, gather, get wind of (*Inf.*), hear tell (*Dialect*), learn, pick up, understand **3.** *Law* examine, investigate, judge, try

hearing 1. audition, auditory, ear, perception **2.** auditory range, earshot, hearing distance, range, reach, sound **3.** inquiry, investigation, review, trial

hearsay buzz, gossip, grapevine (*Inf.*), idle talk, mere talk, *on dit*, report, rumour, talk, talk of the town, tittle-tattle, word of mouth

heart 1. character, disposition, emotion, feeling, inclination, nature, sentiment, soul, sympathy, temperament **2.** affection, benevolence, compassion, concern, humanity, love, pity, tenderness, understanding **3.** boldness, bravery, courage, fortitude, guts (*Inf.*), mettle, mind, nerve, pluck, purpose, resolution, spirit, spunk (*Inf.*), will **4.** central part, centre, core, crux, essence, hub, kernel, marrow, middle, nucleus, pith, quintessence, root **5. by heart** by memory, by rote, off pat, parrot-fashion (*Inf.*), pat, word for word

heartbreaking agonizing, bitter, desolating, disappointing, distressing, grievous, heart-rending, pitiful, poignant, sad, tragic

heartfelt ardent, cordial, deep, devout, earnest, fervent, genuine, hearty, honest, profound, sincere, unfeigned, warm, wholehearted

heartily 1. cordially, deeply, feelingly, genuinely, profoundly, sincerely, unfeignedly, warmly **2.** eagerly, earnestly, enthusiastically, resolutely, vigorously, zealously

heartless brutal, callous, cold, cold-blooded, cold-hearted, cruel, hard, hardhearted, harsh, inhuman, merciless, pitiless, uncaring, unfeeling, unkind

heart-rending affecting, distressing, harrowing, heartbreaking, moving, pathetic, piteous, pitiful, poignant, sad, tragic

heart-to-heart 1. *adj.* candid, intimate, open, personal, sincere, unreserved **2.** *n.* cosy chat, tête-à-tête

heart-warming 1. gratifying, pleasing, rewarding, satisfying **2.** affecting, cheering, encouraging, heartening, moving, touching, warming

hearty 1. affable, ardent, back-slapping, cordial, eager, ebullient, effusive, enthusiastic, friendly, generous, genial, jovial, unreserved, warm **2.** active, energetic, hale, hardy, healthy, robust, sound, strong, vigorous, well **3.** ample, filling, nourishing, sizable, solid, square, substantial

sexual excitement caused by readiness to mate in female animals 6. one of many races *etc.* to decide persons to compete in finals —*v.* 7. make, become hot —ˈ**heated** *a.* angry —ˈ**heatedly** *adv.* —ˈ**heater** *n.* any device for supplying heat, such as a convector —**heat pump** device for extracting heat from substance that is at slightly higher temperature than its surroundings and delivering it to factory *etc.* at much higher temperature —ˈ**heatstroke** *n.* condition resulting from prolonged exposure to intense heat, characterized by fever —**heat wave** continuous spell of abnormally hot weather

heath (hi:θ) *n.* 1. tract of wasteland 2. low-growing evergreen shrub

heathen (ˈhi:ðən) *a.* 1. not adhering to a religious system 2. pagan 3. barbarous 4. unenlightened —*n.* 5. heathen person (*pl.* -s, ˈ**heathen**) —ˈ**heathendom** *n.* —ˈ**heathenish** *a.* 1. of or like heathen 2. rough 3. barbarous —ˈ**heathenism** *n.*

heather (ˈhɛðə) *n.* shrub growing on heaths and mountains —ˈ**heathery** *a.*

Heath Robinson (hi:θ ˈrɒbɪnsən) (of mechanical device) absurdly complicated in design

heave (hi:v) *vt.* 1. lift with effort 2. throw (something heavy) 3. utter (sigh) —*vi.* 4. swell, rise 5. feel nausea —*n.* 6. act or effort of heaving

heaven (ˈhɛvən) *n.* 1. abode of God 2. place of bliss 3. (*also pl.*) sky —ˈ**heavenly** *a.* 1. lovely, delightful, divine 2. beautiful 3. of or like heaven

heavy (ˈhɛvɪ) *a.* 1. weighty, striking, falling with force 2. dense 3. sluggish 4. difficult, severe 5. sorrowful 6. serious 7. dull —ˈ**heavily** *adv.* —ˈ**heaviness** *n.* —**heavy-duty** *a.* made to withstand hard wear, bad weather *etc.* —**heavy-handed** *a.* 1. clumsy 2. harsh and oppressive —**heavy-hearted** *a.* sad; melancholy —**heavy industry** basic, large-scale industry producing metal, machinery *etc.* —**heavy-metal** *a.* of type of rock music characterized by strong beat and amplified instrumental effects —**heavy water** deuterium oxide, water in which normal hydrogen content has been replaced by deuterium

Heb. *or* **Hebr.** 1. Hebrew 2. *Bible* Hebrews

hebdomadal (hɛbˈdɒmədəl) *a.* weekly

Hebrew (ˈhi:bru:) *n.* 1. member of an ancient Semitic people 2. their language 3. its modern form, used in Israel —**Heˈbraic(al)** *a.* of or characteristic of Hebrews, their language or culture

heckle (ˈhɛkəl) *v.* interrupt or try to annoy (speaker) by questions, taunts *etc.*

hectare (ˈhɛktɑ:) *n.* one hundred ares or 10 000 square metres (2.471 acres)

hectic (ˈhɛktɪk) *a.* rushed, busy

hecto- *or before vowel* **hect-** (*comb. form*) one hundred, *esp.* in metric system, as in *hectolitre, hectometre*

hector (ˈhɛktə) *vt.* 1. bully —*vi.* 2. bluster —*n.* 3. blusterer

THESAURUS

heat *n.* **1.** calefaction, fever, fieriness, high temperature, hotness, hot spell, sultriness, swelter, torridity, warmness, warmth **2.** *Fig.* agitation, ardour, earnestness, excitement, fervour, fever, fury, impetuosity, intensity, passion, vehemence, violence, warmth, zeal ~*v.* **3.** become warm, chafe, flush, glow, grow hot, make hot, reheat, warm up

heated angry, bitter, excited, fierce, fiery, frenzied, furious, impassioned, intense, passionate, raging, stormy, tempestuous, vehement, violent

heathen *n.* **1.** idolater, idolatress, infidel, pagan, unbeliever **2.** barbarian, philistine, savage ~*adj.* **3.** godless, heathenish, idolatrous, infidel, irreligious, pagan **4.** barbaric, philistine, savage, uncivilized, unenlightened

heave 1. drag (up), elevate, haul (up), heft (*Inf.*), hoist, lever, lift, pull (up), raise, tug **2.** cast, fling, hurl, pitch, send, sling, throw, toss **3.** breathe heavily, groan, puff, sigh, sob, suspire (*Archaic*), utter wearily **4.** billow, breathe, dilate, exhale, expand, palpitate, pant, rise, surge, swell, throb **5.** gag (*Sl.*), retch, spew, throw up (*Inf.*), vomit

heaven 1. abode of God, bliss, Elysium *or* Elysian fields (*Greek myth*), happy hunting ground (*Amerind legend*), hereafter, life everlasting, life to come, next world, nirvana (*Buddhism, Hinduism*), paradise, Valhalla (*Norse myth*), Zion (*Christianity*) **2.** *Usually plural* empyrean (*Poetic*), ether, firmament, sky, welkin (*Archaic*) **3.** *Fig.* bliss, dreamland, ecstasy, enchantment, felicity, happiness, paradise, rapture, seventh heaven, sheer bliss, transport, utopia

heavenly 1. *Inf.* alluring, beautiful, blissful, delightful, divine (*Inf.*), entrancing, exquisite, glorious, lovely, rapturous, ravishing, sublime, wonderful **2.** angelic, beatific, blessed, blest, celestial, cherubic, divine, empyrean, extraterrestrial, godlike, holy, immortal, paradisaical, seraphic, superhuman, supernal (*Literary*), supernatural

heavily 1. awkwardly, clumsily, ponderously, weightily **2.** laboriously, painfully, with difficulty **3.** dejectedly, dully, gloomily, sluggishly, woodenly **4.** closely, compactly, densely, fast, hard, thick, thickly

heaviness 1. gravity, heftiness, ponderousness, weight **2.** arduousness, burdensomeness, grievousness, onerousness, oppressiveness, severity, weightiness **3.** deadness, dullness, languor, lassitude, numbness, sluggishness, torpor **4.** dejection, depression, despondency, gloom, gloominess, glumness, melancholy, sadness, seriousness

heavy 1. bulky, hefty, massive, ponderous, portly, weighty **2.** burdensome, difficult, grievous, hard, harsh, intolerable, laborious, onerous, oppressive, severe, tedious, vexatious, wearisome **3.** apathetic, drowsy, dull, inactive, indolent, inert, listless, slow, sluggish, stupid, torpid, wooden **4.** crestfallen, dejected, depressed, despondent, disconsolate, downcast, gloomy, grieving, melancholy, sad, sorrowful **5.** complex, deep, difficult, grave, profound, serious, solemn, weighty **6.** dull, gloomy, leaden, louring, lowering, overcast

heavy-handed 1. awkward, bungling, clumsy, graceless, ham-fisted (*Inf.*), ham-handed (*Inf.*), inept, inexpert, like a bull in a china shop (*Inf.*), maladroit, unhandy **2.** bungling, inconsiderate, insensitive, tactless, thoughtless **3.** autocratic, domineering, harsh, oppressive, overbearing

heckle bait, barrack (*Inf.*), disrupt, interrupt, jeer, pester, shout down, taunt

hectic animated, boisterous, chaotic, excited, fevered, feverish, flurrying, flustering, frantic, frenetic, frenzied, furious, heated, riotous, rumbustious, tumultuous, turbulent, wild

heddle (ˈhɛdᵊl) *n. Weaving* one of set of frames of vertical wires

hedge (hɛdʒ) *n.* 1. fence of bushes —*vt.* 2. surround with hedge 3. obstruct 4. hem in 5. guard against risk of loss in (bet *etc.*), *esp.* by laying bets with other bookmakers —*vi.* 6. make or trim hedges 7. be evasive 8. secure against loss —**ˈhedgehog** *n.* small animal covered with spines —**ˈhedgerow** *n.* bushes forming hedge —**hedge sparrow** small brownish songbird

hedonism (ˈhiːdᵊnɪzəm, ˈhɛd-) *n.* 1. doctrine that pleasure is the chief good 2. indulgence in sensual pleasure —**heˈdonics** *pl.n.* (*with sing. v.*) 1. branch of psychology concerned with the study of pleasant and unpleasant sensations 2. in philosophy, study of pleasures —**ˈhedonist** *n.* —**hedoˈnistic** *a.*

heed (hiːd) take notice of —**ˈheedful** *a.* —**ˈheedless** *a.* careless

heehaw (hiːˈhɔː) *interj.* imitation or representation of braying sound of donkey

heel[1] (hiːl) *n.* 1. hinder part of foot 2. part of shoe supporting this 3. *sl.* undesirable person —*vt.* 4. supply with heel 5. touch (ground, ball) with heel —**ˈheelball** *n.* mixture of beeswax and lampblack used by shoemakers and in taking rubbings, *esp.* brass rubbings

heel[2] (hiːl) *v.* 1. (of ship) (cause to) lean to one side —*n.* 2. heeling, list

hefty (ˈhɛftɪ) *a.* 1. bulky 2. weighty 3. strong

hegemony (hɪˈgɛmənɪ) *n.* leadership, political domination —**hegemonic** (hɛgəˈmɒnɪk) *a.*

Hegira *or* **Hejira** (ˈhɛdʒɪrə) *n.* 1. flight of Mohammed from Mecca to Medina in 622 A.D. 2. (*oft.* **h-**) escape or flight

heifer (ˈhɛfə) *n.* young cow

height (haɪt) *n.* 1. measure from base to top 2. quality of being high 3. elevation 4. highest degree 5. (*oft. pl.*) hilltop —**ˈheighten** *vt.* 1. make higher 2. intensify —**height of land US, C** watershed

heinous (ˈheɪnəs, ˈhiː-) *a.* atrocious, extremely wicked, detestable

heir (ɛə) *n.* person entitled to inherit property or rank (**ˈheiress** *fem.*) —**ˈheirloom** *n.* thing that has been in family for generations

held (hɛld) *pt./pp. of* HOLD[1]

helical (ˈhɛlɪkᵊl) *a.* spiral

helicopter (ˈhɛlɪkɒptə) *n.* aircraft made to rise vertically by pull of airscrew revolving horizontally —**ˈheliport** *n.* airport for helicopters

helio- *or before vowel* **heli-** (*comb. form*) sun, as in *heliocentric*

heliocentric (hiːlɪəʊˈsɛntrɪk) *a.* 1. having sun at its centre 2. measured in relation to sun —**helioˈcentrically** *adv.*

heliograph (ˈhiːlɪəʊgrɑːf) *n.* signalling apparatus employing mirror to reflect sun's rays

heliostat (ˈhiːlɪəʊstæt) *n.* astronomical instrument used to reflect light of sun in constant direction

heliotherapy (hiːlɪəʊˈθɛrəpɪ) *n.* therapeutic use of sunlight

heliotrope (ˈhiːlɪətrəʊp, ˈhɛljə-) *n.* 1. plant with purple flowers 2. bluish-violet to purple colour —**heliotropic** (hiːlɪəʊˈtrɒpɪk) *a.* growing, turning towards source of light

helium (ˈhiːlɪəm) *n.* very light nonflammable gaseous element

helix (ˈhiːlɪks) *n.* 1. spiral 2. incurving fold that forms margin of external ear (*pl.* **helices** (ˈhɛlɪsiːz), **-es**)

hell (hɛl) *n.* 1. abode of the damned 2. abode of the dead generally 3. place or state of wickedness, misery or torture —**ˈhellish** *a./adv.* —**hellˈbent** *a.* (*with* on) *inf.* strongly or rashly intent —**ˈhellfire** *n.* 1. torment of hell, envisaged as eternal fire —*a.* 2. characterizing sermons that emphasize this —**Hell's Angel** member of motorcycle gang who typically dress in leather clothing, noted for their lawless behaviour

THESAURUS

hector bluster, boast, browbeat, bully, bullyrag, harass, huff and puff, intimidate, menace, provoke, ride roughshod over, roister, threaten, worry

hedge *n.* 1. hedgerow, quickset ~*v.* 2. border, edge, enclose, fence, surround 3. block, confine, hem in (about, around), hinder, obstruct, restrict 4. beg the question, be noncommittal, dodge, duck, equivocate, evade, prevaricate, pussyfoot (*Inf.*), quibble, sidestep, temporize, waffle (*Inf.*) 5. cover, fortify, guard, insure, protect, safeguard, shield

heed attend, bear in mind, be guided by, consider, follow, give ear to, listen to, mark, mind, note, obey, observe, pay attention to, regard, take notice of, take to heart

heedful attentive, careful, cautious, chary, circumspect, mindful, observant, prudent, vigilant, wary, watchful

heedless careless, foolhardy, imprudent, inattentive, incautious, neglectful, negligent, oblivious, precipitate, rash, reckless, thoughtless, unmindful, unobservant, unthinking

heel[1] *n. Sl.* blackguard, bounder (*Brit. inf.*), cad (*Brit inf.*), rotter (*Sl., chiefly Brit.*), scoundrel, swine

heel[2] *v.* cant, careen, incline, keel over, lean over, list, tilt

hefty 1. beefy (*Inf.*), big, brawny, burly, hulking, husky (*Inf.*), massive, muscular, robust, strapping, strong 2. forceful, heavy, powerful, thumping (*Sl.*), vigorous 3. ample, awkward, bulky, colossal, cumbersome, heavy, large, massive, ponderous, substantial, tremendous, unwieldy, weighty

height 1. altitude, elevation, highness, loftiness, stature, tallness 2. apex, apogee, crest, crown, elevation, hill, mountain, peak, pinnacle, summit, top, vertex, zenith 3. acme, dignity, eminence, exaltation, grandeur, loftiness, prominence 4. climax, culmination, extremity, limit, maximum, *ne plus ultra*, ultimate, utmost degree, uttermost

heighten 1. add to, aggravate, amplify, augment, enhance, improve, increase, intensify, magnify, sharpen, strengthen 2. elevate, enhance, ennoble, exalt, magnify, raise, uplift

heir beneficiary, heiress (*Fem.*), inheritor, inheritress *or* inheritrix (*Fem.*), next in line, scion, successor

hell 1. Abaddon, abode of the damned, abyss, Acheron (*Greek myth*), bottomless pit, fire and brimstone, Gehenna (*New Testament, Judaism*), Hades (*Greek myth*), hellfire, infernal regions, inferno, lower world, nether world, Tartarus (*Greek myth*), underworld 2. affliction, agony, anguish, martyrdom, misery, nightmare, ordeal, suffering, torment, trial, wretchedness

hellebore (ˈhɛlɪbɔː) *n.* plant with white flowers that bloom in winter, Christmas rose

Hellenic (hɛˈlɛnɪk, -ˈliː-) *a.* pert. to inhabitants of Greece —**ˈHellenist** *n.*

hello, hallo, *or* **hullo** (hɛˈləʊ, hə-; ˈhɛləʊ) *interj.* expression of greeting or surprise

helm (hɛlm) *n.* tiller, wheel for turning ship's rudder

helmet (ˈhɛlmɪt) *n.* defensive or protective covering for head (*also* **helm**)

helminth (ˈhɛlmɪnθ) *n.* parasitic worm, *esp.* nematode or fluke —**helˈminthic** *or* **helminthoid** (ˈhɛlmɪnθɔɪd, hɛlˈmɪnθɔɪd) *a.*

Helot (ˈhɛlət, ˈhiː-) *n.* **1.** in ancient Sparta, member of class of serfs owned by state **2.** (*usu.* **h-**) serf or slave —**ˈHelotism** *n.* —**ˈHelotry** *n.*

help (hɛlp) *vt.* **1.** aid, assist **2.** support **3.** succour **4.** remedy, prevent —*n.* **5.** act of helping or being helped **6.** person or thing that helps —**ˈhelper** *n.* —**ˈhelpful** *a.* —**ˈhelping** *n.* single portion of food taken at meal —**ˈhelpless** *a.* **1.** useless, incompetent **2.** unaided **3.** unable to help —**ˈhelplessly** *adv.* —**ˈhelpmate** *or* **ˈhelpmeet** *n.* **1.** helpful companion **2.** husband or wife

helter-skelter (ˈhɛltəˈskɛltə) *adv./a./n.* **1.** (in) hurry and confusion —*n.* **2.** high spiral slide at fairground

helve (hɛlv) *n.* handle of hand tool such as axe or pick

hem[1] (hɛm) *n.* **1.** border of cloth, *esp.* one made by turning over edge and sewing it down —*vt.* **2.** sew thus **3.** (*usu. with* in) confine, shut in (**-mm-**) —**ˈhemstitch** *n.* **1.** ornamental stitch —*v.* **2.** decorate (hem *etc.*) with hemstitches

hem[2] (hɛm) *n./interj.* **1.** representation of sound of clearing throat, used to gain attention *etc.* —*vi.* **2.** utter this sound (**-mm-**) —**hem** (*or* **hum**) **and haw** hesitate in speaking

hemi- (*comb. form*) half, as in *hemisphere*

hemisphere (ˈhɛmɪsfɪə) *n.* **1.** half sphere **2.** half of celestial sphere **3.** half of the earth —**hemispheric(al)** (hɛmɪˈsfɛrɪk(ᵊl)) *a.*

hemistich (ˈhɛmɪstɪk) *n.* half line of verse

hemlock (ˈhɛmlɒk) *n.* **1.** poisonous plant **2.** poison extracted from it **3.** US evergreen of pine family

hemo- (*comb. form*) US *see* HAEMO-

hemp (hɛmp) *n.* **1.** Indian plant **2.** its fibre used for rope *etc.* **3.** any of several narcotic drugs made from varieties of hemp —**ˈhempen** *a.* made of hemp or rope

hen (hɛn) *n.* female of domestic fowl and others —**ˈhenpeck** *vt.* (of woman) harass (a man, *esp.* husband) by nagging

henbane (ˈhɛnbeɪn) *n.* poisonous plant with sticky hairy leaves

hence (hɛns) *adv.* **1.** from this point **2.** for this reason —**ˈhenceˈforward** *or* **ˈhenceˈforth** *adv.* from now onwards

henchman (ˈhɛntʃmən) *n.* trusty follower

henge (hɛndʒ) *n.* circular monument, oft. containing circle of stones

henna (ˈhɛnə) *n.* **1.** flowering shrub **2.** reddish dye made from it

henotheism (ˈhɛnəʊθiːɪzəm) *n.* belief in one god (of several) as special god of one's family, tribe *etc.*

henry (ˈhɛnrɪ) *n.* SI unit of electrical inductance

hepatic (hɪˈpætɪk) *a.* pert. to the liver —**hepaˈtitis** *n.* inflammation of the liver

hepta- *or before vowel* **hept-** (*comb. form*) seven, as in *heptameter*

heptagon (ˈhɛptəgən) *n.* figure with seven angles —**hepˈtagonal** *a.*

heptarchy (ˈhɛptɑːkɪ) *n.* rule by seven

her (hɜː; *unstressed* hə, ə) *a.* objective and possessive case of SHE —**hers** *pron.* of her —**herˈself** *pron.*

herald (ˈhɛrəld) *n.* **1.** messenger, envoy **2.** officer who makes royal proclamations, arranges ceremonies, regulates armorial bearings *etc.* —*vt.* **3.** announce **4.** proclaim approach of —**heˈraldic** *a.* —**ˈheraldry** *n.* study of (right to have) heraldic bearings

THESAURUS

hellish 1. damnable, damned, demoniacal, devilish, diabolical, fiendish, infernal **2.** abominable, accursed, atrocious, barbarous, cruel, detestable, execrable, inhuman, monstrous, nefarious, vicious, wicked

helm *Nautical* rudder, steering gear, tiller, wheel

help *v.* **1.** abet, aid, assist, back, befriend, cooperate, lend a hand, promote, relieve, save, second, serve, stand by, succour, support **2.** alleviate, ameliorate, cure, ease, facilitate, heal, improve, mitigate, relieve, remedy, restore **3.** abstain, avoid, control, eschew, forbear, hinder, keep from, prevent, refrain from, resist, shun, withstand ~*n.* **4.** advice, aid, assistance, avail, benefit, cooperation, guidance, helping hand, service, support, use, utility **5.** assistant, employee, hand, helper, worker **6.** balm, corrective, cure, relief, remedy, restorative, salve, succour

helper abettor, adjutant, aide, aider, ally, assistant, attendant, auxiliary, coadjutor, collaborator, colleague, deputy, helpmate, mate, partner, right-hand man, second, subsidiary, supporter

helpful 1. advantageous, beneficial, constructive, favourable, fortunate, practical, productive, profitable, serviceable, timely, useful **2.** accommodating, beneficent, benevolent, caring, considerate, cooperative, friendly, kind, neighbourly, supportive, sympathetic

helping *n.* dollop (*Inf.*), piece, plateful, portion, ration, serving

helpless 1. abandoned, defenceless, dependent, destitute, exposed, forlorn, unprotected, vulnerable **2.** debilitated, disabled, feeble, impotent, incapable, incompetent, infirm, paralysed, powerless, unfit, weak

helter-skelter 1. *adv.* carelessly, hastily, headlong, hurriedly, pell-mell, rashly, recklessly, wildly **2.** *adj.* anyhow, confused, disordered, haphazard, higgledy-piggledy (*Inf.*), hit-or-miss, jumbled, muddled, random, topsy-turvy

hem 1. *n.* border, edge, fringe, margin, trimming **2.** *v.* *Usually with* **in** beset, border, circumscribe, confine, edge, enclose, environ, hedge in, restrict, shut in, skirt, surround

hence ergo, for this reason, on that account, therefore, thus

henceforth from now on, from this day forward, hence, hereafter, hereinafter, in the future

herald *n.* **1.** bearer of tidings, crier, messenger ~*v.* **2.** advertise, announce, broadcast, proclaim, publicize, publish, trumpet **3.** foretoken, harbinger, indicate, pave the way, portend, precede, presage, promise, show, usher in

herb (hɜːb; *U.S.* ɜːrb) *n.* 1. plant with soft stem which dies down after flowering 2. plant, such as rosemary, used in cookery or medicine —**her'baceous** *a.* 1. of, like herbs 2. flowering perennially —**'herbage** *n.* 1. herbs 2. grass 3. pasture —**'herbal** *a.* 1. of herbs —*n.* 2. book on herbs —**'herbalist** *n.* 1. writer on herbs 2. dealer in medicinal herbs —**her'barium** *n.* collection of dried plants (*pl.* **-s, -ia** (-ɪə)) —**'herbicide** *n.* chemical which destroys plants —**her'bivorous** *a.* feeding on plants

Hercules ('hɜːkjuliːz) *n.* mythical hero noted for strength —**herculean** (hɜːkju'liːən) *a.* requiring great strength, courage *etc.*

herd (hɜːd) *n.* 1. company of animals, *usu.* of same species, feeding or travelling together 2. herdsman —*v.* 3. collect or be collected together —*vt.* 4. tend (livestock) —**herd instinct** *Psychol.* inborn tendency to associate with others and follow group's behaviour —**'herdsman** *n.*

here (hɪə) *adv.* 1. in this place 2. at or to this point —**here'after** *adv.* 1. in time to come —*n.* 2. future existence —**here'by** *adv.* by means of or as result of this —**hereto'fore** *adv.* before —**here'with** *adv.* together with this

heredity (hɪ'rɛdɪtɪ) *n.* tendency of organism to transmit its nature to its descendants —**here'ditament** *n.* *Law* property that can be inherited —**he'reditarily** *adv.* —**he'reditary** *a.* 1. descending by inheritance 2. holding office by inheritance 3. that can be transmitted from one generation to another

heresy ('hɛrəsɪ) *n.* opinion contrary to orthodox opinion or belief —**'heretic** *n.* one holding opinions contrary to orthodox faith —**he'retical** *a.* —**he'retically** *adv.*

heritage ('hɛrɪtɪdʒ) *n.* 1. what may be or is inherited 2. anything from past, *esp.* owned or handed down by tradition —**'heritable** *a.* that can be inherited

hermaphrodite (hɜː'mæfrədaɪt) *n.* 1. animal or flower that has both male and female reproductive organs 2. person having both male and female characteristics

hermetic (hɜː'mɛtɪk) *or* **hermetical** *a.* sealed so as to be airtight —**her'metically** *adv.*

hermit ('hɜːmɪt) *n.* one living in solitude, *esp.* from religious motives —**'hermitage** *n.* his abode —**hermit crab** soft-bodied crustacean living in and carrying about empty shells of molluscs

hernia ('hɜːnɪə) *n.* projection of (part of) organ through lining encasing it (*pl.* **-s, -iae** (-ɪiː)) —**'hernial** *a.*

hero ('hɪərəʊ) *n.* 1. one greatly regarded for achievements or qualities 2. principal character in play *etc.* 3. illustrious warrior 4. demigod (*pl.* **-es**) (**heroine** ('hɛrəʊɪn) *fem.*) —**heroic** (hɪ'rəʊɪk) *a.* 1. of, like hero 2. courageous, daring —**heroically** (hɪ'rəʊɪkəlɪ) *adv.* —**heroics** (hɪ'rəʊɪks) *pl.n.* extravagant behaviour —**heroism** ('hɛrəʊɪzəm) *n.* 1. qualities of hero 2. courage, boldness —**heroic verse** type of verse suitable for epic or heroic subjects —**hero worship** 1. admiration of heroes or of great men 2. excessive admiration of others —**hero-worship** *vt.* feel admiration or adulation for

heroin ('hɛrəʊɪn) *n.* white crystalline derivative of morphine, a highly addictive narcotic

heron ('hɛrən) *n.* long-legged wading bird —**'heronry** *n.* place where herons breed

herpes ('hɜːpiːz) *n.* any of several skin diseases, including shingles (**herpes zoster**) and cold sores (**herpes simplex**)

Herr (*German* hɛr) *n.* German man: used before name as title equivalent to *Mr* (*pl.* **Herren** ('hɛrən))

herring ('hɛrɪŋ) *n.* important food fish of northern hemisphere —**'herringbone** *n.* stitch or pattern of zigzag lines —**herring gull** common gull that has white plumage with black-tipped wings

Herts. (hɑːts) Hertfordshire

hertz (hɜːts) *n.* SI unit of frequency (*pl.* **hertz**)

hesitate ('hɛzɪteɪt) *vi.* 1. hold back 2. feel or show indecision 3. be reluctant —**'hesitancy** *or* **hesi'tation** *n.* 1. wavering 2. doubt 3. stammering —**'hesitant** *a.* undecided, pausing —**'hesitantly** *adv.*

THESAURUS

herd 1. *n.* assemblage, collection, crowd, crush, drove, flock, horde, mass, mob, multitude, press, swarm, throng 2. *v.* assemble, associate, collect, congregate, flock, gather, huddle, muster, rally

hereafter 1. *adv.* after this, from now on, hence, henceforth, henceforward, in future 2. *n.* afterlife, future life, life after death, next world, the beyond

hereditary 1. family, genetic, inborn, inbred, inheritable, transmissible 2. ancestral, bequeathed, handed down, inherited, patrimonial, traditional, transmitted, willed

heredity congenital traits, constitution, genetic make-up, genetics, inheritance

heresy apostasy, dissidence, error, heterodoxy, iconoclasm, impiety, revisionism, schism, unorthodoxy

heretic apostate, dissenter, dissident, nonconformist, renegade, revisionist, schismatic, sectarian, separatist

heretical freethinking, heterodox, iconoclastic, idolatrous, impious, revisionist, schismatic, unorthodox

heritage bequest, birthright, endowment, estate, inheritance, legacy, lot, patrimony, portion, share, tradition

hermit anchoret, anchorite, eremite, monk, recluse, solitary, stylite

hero 1. celebrity, champion, conqueror, exemplar, great man, heart-throb (*Brit.*), idol, man of the hour, popular figure, star, superstar, victor 2. lead actor, leading man, male lead, principal male character, protagonist

heroic 1. bold, brave, courageous, daring, dauntless, doughty, fearless, gallant, intrepid, lion-hearted, stouthearted, undaunted, valiant, valorous 2. classical, Homeric, legendary, mythological

heroine 1. celebrity, goddess, ideal, woman of the hour 2. diva, female lead, lead actress, leading lady, prima donna, principal female character, protagonist

heroism boldness, bravery, courage, courageousness, daring, fearlessness, fortitude, gallantry, intrepidity, prowess, spirit, valour

hero worship admiration, adoration, adulation, idealization, idolization, putting on a pedestal, veneration

hesitant diffident, doubtful, half-hearted, halting, hanging back, hesitating, irresolute, lacking confidence, reluctant, sceptical, shy, timid, uncertain, unsure, vacillating, wavering

Hesperus (ˈhɛspərəs) *n.* evening star, *esp.* Venus

hessian (ˈhɛsɪən) *n.* coarse jute cloth

hest (hɛst) *n.* behest, command

hetaera (hɪˈtɪərə) *or* **hetaira** (hɪˈtaɪrə) *n. esp.* in ancient Greece, prostitute, *esp.* educated courtesan (*pl.* **-taerae** (-ˈtɪəriː) *or* **-tairai** (-ˈtaɪraɪ))

hetero- (*comb. form*) other; different, as in *heterosexual*

heterodox (ˈhɛtərəʊdɒks) *a.* not orthodox —**ˈheterodoxy** *n.*

heterodyne (ˈhɛtərəʊdaɪn) *v.* **1.** *Electron.* mix (two alternating signals) to produce two signals having frequencies corresponding to sum and difference of original frequencies —*a.* **2.** produced by, operating by, or involved in heterodyning two signals

heterogeneous (hɛtərəʊˈdʒiːnɪəs) *a.* composed of diverse elements —**heterogeˈneity** *n.*

heteromorphic (hɛtərəʊˈmɔːfɪk) *or* **heteromorphous** *a. Biol.* **1.** differing from normal form **2.** (*esp.* of insects) having different forms at different stages of life cycle —**heteroˈmorphism** *n.*

heterosexual (hɛtərəʊˈsɛksjʊəl) *n.* person sexually attracted to members of the opposite sex —**heterosexuˈality** *n.*

het up (hɛt) *inf.* angry; excited

heuchera (ˈhɔɪkərə) *n.* plant with ornamental foliage

heuristic (hjʊəˈrɪstɪk) *a.* serving to find out or to stimulate investigation

hew (hjuː) *v.* chop, cut with axe (**hewn, hewed** *pp.*) —**ˈhewer** *n.*

hexa- *or before vowel* **hex-** (*comb. form*) six, as in *hexachord*

hexagon (ˈhɛksəgən) *n.* figure with six angles —**hexˈagonal** *a.*

hexagram (ˈhɛksəgræm) *n.* star-shaped figure formed by extending sides of regular hexagon to meet at six points

hexameter (hɛkˈsæmɪtə) *n.* line of verse of six feet

hexapod (ˈhɛksəpɒd) *n.* insect

hey (heɪ) *interj.* expression indicating surprise, dismay, discovery *etc.* —**ˈheyday** *n.* bloom, prime —**hey presto** exclamation used by conjurors to herald climax of trick

Hf *Chem.* hafnium

HF, H.F., hf, *or* **h.f.** high frequency

hf. half

Hg *Chem.* mercury

HGV UK heavy goods vehicle

H.H. 1. His (*or* Her) Highness **2.** His Holiness (title of Pope)

HI Hawaii

hiatus (haɪˈeɪtəs) *n.* break or gap where something is missing (*pl.* **-es, hiˈatus**)

hibernate (ˈhaɪbəneɪt) *vi.* pass the winter, *esp.* in a torpid state —**hiberˈnation** *n.* —**ˈhibernator** *n.*

Hibernian (haɪˈbɜːnɪən) *a./n.* Irish (person)

hibiscus (hɪˈbɪskəs) *n.* flowering (sub)tropical shrub

hiccup (ˈhɪkʌp) *n.* **1.** spasm of the breathing organs with an abrupt cough-like sound —*vi.* **2.** make a hiccup or hiccups (*also* **ˈhiccough**)

hick (hɪk) *inf. a.* **1.** rustic **2.** unsophisticated —*n.* **3.** person like this

hickory (ˈhɪkərɪ) *n.* **1.** N Amer. nut-bearing tree **2.** its tough wood

hide[1] (haɪd) *vt.* **1.** put, keep out of sight **2.** conceal, keep secret —*vi.* **3.** conceal oneself (**hid** (hɪd) *pt.*, **hidden** (ˈhɪdᵊn) *or* **hid** *pp.*, **ˈhiding** *pr.p.*) —*n.* **4.** place of concealment, *eg* for birdwatcher —**ˈhideaway** *n.* hiding place or secluded spot —**hide-out** *n.* hiding place

hide[2] (haɪd) *n.* skin of animal —**ˈhiding** *n. sl.* thrashing —**ˈhidebound** *a.* **1.** restricted, *esp.* by petty rules *etc.* **2.** narrow-minded **3.** (of tree) having bark so close that it impedes growth

hideous (ˈhɪdɪəs) *a.* repulsive, revolting —**ˈhideously** *adv.*

hie (haɪ) *v. obs.* hasten (**hied** *pt./pp.*, **ˈhying** *or* **ˈhieing** *pr.p.*)

hierarchy (ˈhaɪərɑːkɪ) *n.* system of persons or things arranged in graded order —**hierˈarchic(al)** *a.*

hieratic (haɪəˈrætɪk) *a.* **1.** of priests **2.** of cursive form

THESAURUS

hesitate 1. be uncertain, delay, dither, doubt, haver (*Brit.*), pause, shillyshally (*Inf.*), swither (*Scot. dialect*), vacillate, wait, waver **2.** balk, be reluctant, be unwilling, boggle, demur, hang back, scruple, shrink from, think twice **3.** falter, fumble, hem and haw, stammer, stumble, stutter

hesitation 1. delay, doubt, dubiety, hesitancy, indecision, irresolution, uncertainty, vacillation **2.** demurral, misgiving(s), qualm(s), reluctance, scruple(s), unwillingness **3.** faltering, fumbling, hemming and hawing, stammering, stumbling, stuttering

hew axe, chop, cut, hack, lop, split

heyday bloom, flowering, pink, prime, prime of life, salad days

hiatus aperture, blank, breach, break, chasm, discontinuity, gap, interruption, interval, lacuna, lapse, opening, rift, space

hidden abstruse, clandestine, close, concealed, covered, covert, cryptic, dark, hermetic, hermetical, masked, mysterious, mystic, mystical, obscure, occult, recondite, secret, shrouded, ulterior, unrevealed, unseen, veiled

hide[1] **1.** cache, conceal, go into hiding, go to ground, go underground, hole up, lie low, secrete, take cover **2.** blot out, bury, camouflage, cloak, conceal, cover, disguise, eclipse, mask, obscure, screen, shelter, shroud, veil **3.** hush up, keep secret, suppress, withhold

hide[2] fell, pelt, skin

hidebound brassbound, conventional, narrow, narrow-minded, rigid, set, set in one's ways, strait-laced, ultraconservative

hideous 1. ghastly, grim, grisly, grotesque, gruesome, monstrous, repulsive, revolting, ugly, unsightly **2.** abominable, appalling, awful, detestable, disgusting, dreadful, horrendous, horrible, horrid, loathsome, macabre, odious, shocking, sickening, terrible, terrifying

hide-out den, hideaway, hiding place, lair, secret place, shelter

hiding *n.* beating, caning, drubbing, flogging, larruping (*Brit. dialect*), lathering (*Inf.*), licking (*Inf.*), spanking, tanning (*Sl.*), thrashing, walloping (*Inf.*), whaling, whipping

hierarchy grading, pecking order, ranking

of hieroglyphics used by priests in ancient Egypt —*n.* **3.** hieratic script of ancient Egypt —**hier'atically** *adv.*

hieroglyphic (haɪərə'glɪfɪk) *a.* **1.** of a system of picture writing, *esp.* as used in ancient Egypt —*n.* **2.** symbol representing object, concept, or sound **3.** symbol, picture, difficult to decipher —**'hieroglyph** *n.*

hi-fi ('haɪ'faɪ) *inf. a.* **1.** *see* **high-fidelity** *at* HIGH —*n.* **2.** high-fidelity equipment

higgledy-piggledy ('hɪgᵊldɪ'pɪgᵊldɪ) *adv./a. inf.* in confusion

high (haɪ) *a.* **1.** tall, lofty **2.** far up **3.** (of roads) main **4.** (of meat) tainted **5.** (of season) well advanced **6.** (of sound) acute in pitch **7.** expensive **8.** of great importance, quality, or rank **9.** *inf.* in state of euphoria, *esp.* induced by drugs **10.** *inf.* bad-smelling —*adv.* **11.** far up **12.** strongly, to a great extent **13.** at, to a high pitch **14.** at a high rate —**'highly** *adv.* —**'highness** *n.* **1.** quality of being high **2.** (**H-**) title of prince or princess —**'highball** *n.* **US** long iced drink consisting of spirit base with soda water *etc.* —**'highbrow** *sl. n.* **1.** intellectual, *esp.* intellectual snob —*a.* **2.** intellectual **3.** difficult **4.** serious —**'highchair** *n.* long-legged chair for child, *esp.* one with table-like tray —**High Church** party within Church of England emphasizing authority of bishops and importance of sacraments, rituals and ceremonies —**high commissioner** senior diplomatic representative sent by one Commonwealth country to another —**higher education** education and training at colleges, universities *etc.* —**high explosive** extremely powerful chemical explosive —**highfa'lutin** *or* **highfa'luting** *a. inf.* pompous or pretentious —**high-fidelity** *a.* of high-quality sound-reproducing equipment —**high-flier** *or* **high-flyer** *n.* **1.** person extreme in aims, ambition *etc.* **2.** person of great ability, *esp.* in career —**high-flown** *a.* extravagant, bombastic —**high frequency** radio frequency lying between 30 and 3 megahertz —**High German** standard German language, historically developed from the form of W Germanic spoken in S Germany —**high-handed** *a.* domineering, dogmatic —**high jump** athletic event in which competitor has to jump over high bar —**Highland** ('haɪlənd) *a.* of, from the Highlands of Scotland —**highland(s)** ('haɪlənd(z)) (*pl.*)*n.* relatively high ground —**high-level language** *Comp.* programming language closer to human language or mathematical notation than to machine language —**'highlight** *n.* **1.** lightest or brightest area in painting, photograph *etc.* **2.** outstanding feature —*vt.* **3.** bring into prominence —**highly strung** excitable, nervous —**High Mass** solemn and elaborate sung Mass —**high-minded** *a.* having or characterized by high moral principles —**high-mindedness** *n.* —**high-powered** *a.* **1.** (of optical instrument or lens) having high magnification **2.** dynamic and energetic —**high-pressure** *a.* **1.** having, using, or designed to withstand pressure above normal **2.** *inf.* (of selling) persuasive in aggressive and persistent manner —**high priest** **1.** *Judaism* priest of highest rank **2.** head of cult —**high-rise** *a.* of building that has many storeys —**high school** **1.** **UK** *see* **grammar school** *at* GRAMMAR **2.** **US, NZ** secondary school —**high seas** open seas, outside jurisdiction of any one nation —**high-sounding** *a.* pompous, imposing —**high-spirited** *a.* vivacious, bold or lively —**high tea** early evening meal usu. with cooked course followed by cakes *etc.*, accompanied by tea —**high tech** **1.** high technology **2.** style of interior design using features of industrial equipment —**high-tech** *a.* —**high technology** highly sophisticated oft. electronic, techniques used in manufacturing *etc.* —**high-technology** *a.* —**high-tension** *a.* carrying or operating at relatively high voltage —**high tide** **1.** tide at its highest level **2.** culminating point —**high time** latest possible time —**high treason** act of treason directly affecting sovereign or state —**high water** **1.** high tide **2.** state of any stretch of water at its highest level —**'highway** *n.* **1.** main road **2.** ordinary route —**Highway Code** **UK** regulations and recommendations applying to all road users —**'highwayman** *n.* formerly, robber on road, *esp.* mounted —**the high jump** **UK** *inf.* severe reprimand or punishment

THESAURUS

high *adj.* **1.** elevated, lofty, soaring, steep, tall, towering **2.** arch, chief, consequential, distinguished, eminent, exalted, important, influential, leading, powerful, prominent, ruling, significant, superior **3.** capital, extreme, grave, important, serious **4.** *Inf.* delirious, euphoric, freaked out (*Inf.*), hyped up (*Sl.*), inebriated, intoxicated, on a trip (*Inf.*), spaced out (*Sl.*), stoned (*Sl.*), tripping (*Inf.*), turned on (*Sl.*) **5.** costly, dear, exorbitant, expensive, high-priced, steep (*Inf.*), stiff **6.** acute, high-pitched, penetrating, piercing, piping, sharp, shrill, soprano, strident, treble **7.** extravagant, grand, lavish, luxurious, rich **8.** gamy, niffy (*Sl.*), pongy (*Brit. sl.*), strong-flavoured, tainted, whiffy (*Inf.*) ~*adv.* **9.** aloft, at great height, far up, way up

highbrow **1.** *n.* aesthete, Brahmin (*U.S.*), brain (*Inf.*), brainbox (*Sl.*), egghead (*Inf.*), intellectual, mastermind, savant, scholar **2.** *adj.* bookish, brainy (*Inf.*), cultivated, cultured, deep, highbrowed, intellectual, sophisticated

high-flown elaborate, exaggerated, extravagant, florid, grandiose, highfalutin (*Inf.*), inflated, lofty, magniloquent, overblown, pretentious

high-handed arbitrary, autocratic, bossy (*Inf.*), despotic, dictatorial, domineering, imperious, inconsiderate, oppressive, overbearing, peremptory, self-willed, tyrannical, wilful

highland *n.* heights, hill country, hills, mountainous region, plateau, tableland, uplands

highlight **1.** *n.* best part, climax, feature, focal point, focus, high point, high spot, main feature, memorable part, peak **2.** *v.* accent, accentuate, bring to the fore, emphasize, feature, focus attention on, give prominence to, play up, set off, show up, spotlight, stress, underline

highly decidedly, eminently, exceptionally, extraordinarily, extremely, greatly, immensely, supremely, tremendously, vastly, very, very much

highly strung easily upset, edgy, excitable, irascible, irritable, nervous, nervy (*Brit. inf.*), neurotic, restless, sensitive, stressed, taut, temperamental, tense

high-minded elevated, ethical, fair, good, honourable, idealistic, magnanimous, moral, noble, principled, pure, righteous, upright, virtuous, worthy

high-powered aggressive, driving, dynamic, effective, energetic, enterprising, forceful, go-ahead, go-getting (*Inf.*), highly capable, vigorous

high-pressure *Of salesmanship* aggressive, bludgeoning, coercive, compelling, forceful, high-powered, importunate, insistent, intensive, persistent, persuasive, pushy (*Inf.*)

high-sounding affected, artificial, bombastic, extravagant, flamboyant, florid, grandiloquent, grandi-

hijack *or* **highjack** (ˈhaɪdʒæk) *vt.* **1.** divert or wrongfully take command of (vehicle or its contents) while in transit **2.** rob —**ˈhijacker** *or* **ˈhighjacker** *n.*

hike (haɪk) *vi.* **1.** walk a long way (for pleasure) in country —*vt.* **2.** pull (up), hitch —*n.* **3.** long walk —**ˈhiker** *n.*

hilarity (hɪˈlærɪtɪ) *n.* cheerfulness, gaiety —**hilarious** (hɪˈlɛərɪəs) *a.*

hill (hɪl) *n.* **1.** natural elevation, small mountain **2.** mound —**ˈhillock** *n.* little hill —**ˈhilly** *a.* —**ˈhillbilly** *n.* unsophisticated (country) person

hilt (hɪlt) *n.* handle of sword *etc.* —**to the hilt** to the full

hilum (ˈhaɪləm) *n. Bot.* scar on seed marking its point of attachment to seed stalk (*pl.* **-la** (-lə))

him (hɪm; *unstressed* ɪm) *pron.* objective case of HE —**himˈself** *pron.* emphatic form of HE

hind[1] (haɪnd) *or* **hinder** (ˈhaɪndə) *a.* at the back, posterior —**ˈhindquarter** *n.* **1.** one of two back quarters of carcass of beef *etc.* —*pl.* **2.** rear, *esp.* of four-legged animal —**ˈhindsight** *n.* **1.** ability to understand, after something has happened, what should have been done **2.** firearm's rear sight

hind[2] (haɪnd) *n.* female of deer

hinder (ˈhɪndə) *vt.* obstruct, impede, delay —**ˈhindrance** *n.*

Hindi (ˈhɪndɪ) *n.* language of N central India —**ˈHindu** *or* **ˈHindoo** *n.* person who adheres to **Hinduism,** the dominant religion of India —**Hindustani, Hindoostani** (hɪnduˈstɑːnɪ), *or* **Hindoˈstani** *n.* **1.** dialect of Hindi spoken in Delhi **2.** all spoken forms of Hindi and Urdu considered together —*a.* **3.** of or relating to these languages or Hindustan

hinge (hɪndʒ) *n.* **1.** movable joint, as that on which door hangs —*vt.* **2.** attach with, or as with, hinge —*vi.* **3.** turn, depend (on)

hinny (ˈhɪnɪ) *n.* sterile hybrid offspring of male horse and female donkey

hint (hɪnt) *n.* **1.** slight indication or suggestion —*v.* **2.** (*sometimes with* at) suggest indirectly

hinterland (ˈhɪntəlænd) *n.* district lying behind coast, or near city, port *etc.*

hip[1] (hɪp) *n.* **1.** (*oft. pl.*) either side of body below waist and above thigh **2.** angle formed where sloping sides of roof meet **3.** fruit of rose, *esp.* wild

hip[2] (hɪp) *a. sl.* **1.** aware of or following latest trends **2.** informed

hip-hop *n.* U.S. pop culture movement of 1980s comprising rap music, graffiti and break dancing

hippie *or* **hippy** (ˈhɪpɪ) *n.* (young) person whose behaviour, dress *etc.* implies rejection of conventional values

hippo (ˈhɪpəʊ) *n. inf.* hippopotamus (*pl.* **-s**)

Hippocratic oath (hɪpəʊˈkrætɪk) oath taken by doctor to observe code of medical ethics

hippodrome (ˈhɪpədrəʊm) *n.* **1.** music hall **2.** variety theatre **3.** circus

hippogriff *or* **hippogryph** (ˈhɪpəʊgrɪf) *n.* griffinlike creature with horse's body

hippopotamus (hɪpəˈpɒtəməs) *n.* large Afr. animal living in rivers (*pl.* **-es, -mi** (-maɪ))

hire (haɪə) *vt.* **1.** obtain temporary use of by payment **2.** engage for wage —*n.* **3.** hiring or being hired **4.** payment for use of something —**ˈhireling** *n.* one who serves for wages —**hire-purchase** *n.* system by which something becomes hirer's after stipulated number of payments

hirsute (ˈhɜːsjuːt) *a.* hairy

his (hɪz; *unstressed* ɪz) *pron./a.* belonging to him

Hispanic (hɪˈspænɪk) *a.* of or derived from Spain or the Spanish —**Hisˈpanicism** *n.*

THESAURUS

ose, high-flown, imposing, magniloquent, ostentatious, overblown, pompous, pretentious, stilted, strained

high-spirited animated, boisterous, bold, bouncy, daring, dashing, ebullient, effervescent, energetic, exuberant, frolicsome, full of life, fun-loving, gallant, lively, mettlesome, spirited, spunky (*Inf.*), vibrant, vital, vivacious

hijack commandeer, expropriate, seize, skyjack, take over

hike *v.* **1.** back-pack, hoof it (*Sl.*), leg it (*Inf.*), ramble, tramp, walk **2.** *Usually with* **up** hitch up, jack up, lift, pull up, raise ~*n.* **3.** journey on foot, march, ramble, tramp, trek, walk

hilarious amusing, comical, convivial, entertaining, exhilarated, funny, gay, happy, humorous, jolly, jovial, joyful, joyous, merry, mirthful, noisy, rollicking, side-splitting, uproarious

hilarity amusement, boisterousness, cheerfulness, conviviality, exhilaration, exuberance, gaiety, glee, high spirits, jollification, jollity, joviality, joyousness, laughter, levity, merriment, mirth

hill **1.** brae (*Scot.*), down (*Archaic*), elevation, eminence, fell, height, hillock, hilltop, knoll, mound, mount, prominence, tor **2.** drift, heap, hummock, mound, pile, stack **3.** acclivity, brae (*Scot.*), climb, gradient, incline, rise, slope

hillock barrow, hummock, knap (*Dialect*), knoll, monticule, mound, tump (*Western Brit. dialect*)

hilt **1.** grip, haft, handgrip, handle, helve **2.** **to the hilt** completely, entirely, fully, totally, wholly

hind after, back, caudal (*Anat.*), hinder, posterior, rear

hinder arrest, check, debar, delay, deter, encumber, frustrate, hamper, hamstring, handicap, hold up *or* back, impede, interrupt, obstruct, oppose, prevent, retard, slow down, stop, stymie, thwart, trammel

hindrance bar, barrier, check, deterrent, difficulty, drag, drawback, encumbrance, handicap, hitch, impediment, interruption, limitation, obstacle, obstruction, restraint, restriction, snag, stoppage, stumbling block, trammel

hinge *v.* be contingent, be subject to, depend, hang, pivot, rest, revolve around, turn

hint *n.* **1.** allusion, clue, implication, indication, inkling, innuendo, insinuation, intimation, mention, reminder, suggestion, tip-off, word to the wise **2.** advice, help, pointer, suggestion, tip, wrinkle (*Inf.*) ~*v.* **3.** allude, cue, imply, indicate, insinuate, intimate, let it be known, mention, prompt, suggest, tip off

hippie beatnik, bohemian, dropout, flower child

hire *v.* **1.** appoint, commission, employ, engage, sign up, take on **2.** charter, engage, lease, let, rent ~*n.* **3.** charge, cost, fee, price, rent, rental

hispid ('hɪspɪd) *a.* 1. rough with bristles or minute spines 2. bristly, shaggy —**his'pidity** *n.*

hiss (hɪs) *vi.* 1. make sharp sound of letter *s, esp.* in disapproval —*vt.* 2. express disapproval of, deride thus —*n.* 3. sound like that of prolonged *s* —**'hissing** *n.*

hist. 1. historian 2. historical 3. history

histamine ('hɪstəmiːn) *n.* substance released by body tissues, sometimes creating allergic reactions

histogeny (hɪ'stɒdʒənɪ) *n.* formation and development of organic tissues

histogram ('hɪstəgræm) *n.* graph using vertical columns to illustrate frequency distribution

histology (hɪ'stɒlədʒɪ) *n.* branch of biology concerned with the structure of organic tissues —**his'tologist** *n.*

history ('hɪstərɪ) *n.* 1. record of past events 2. study of these 3. past events 4. train of events, public or private 5. course of life or existence 6. systematic account of phenomena —**his'torian** *n.* writer of history —**historic** (hɪ'stɒrɪk) *a.* noted in history —**historical** (hɪ'stɒrɪk°l) *a.* 1. of, based on, history 2. belonging to the past —**historically** (hɪ'stɒrɪkəlɪ) *adv.* —**histo'ricity** *n.* historical authenticity —**histori'ographer** *n.* 1. official historian 2. one who studies historical method

histrionic (hɪstrɪ'ɒnɪk) *a.* excessively theatrical, insincere, artificial in manner —**histri'onics** *pl.n.* behaviour like this

hit (hɪt) *vt.* 1. strike with blow or missile 2. affect injuriously 3. reach —*vi.* 4. strike a blow 5. (*with* upon) light (upon) (**hit, 'hitting**) —*n.* 6. blow 7. *inf.* success —**'hitter** *n.* —**hit-and-run** *a.* 1. denoting motor-vehicle accident in which driver leaves scene without stopping 2. (of attack *etc.*) relying on surprise allied to rapid departure from scene of operations —**hit man** US hired assassin —**hit parade** list of currently most popular songs, ranked in order of sales per record —**hit it off** get along (with person) —**hit or miss** casual; haphazard —**hit the hay** *sl.* go to bed —**hit the trail** *or* **road** *inf.* 1. proceed on journey 2. leave

hitch (hɪtʃ) *vt.* 1. fasten with loop *etc.* 2. raise, move with jerk —*vi.* 3. be caught or fastened —*n.* 4. difficulty 5. knot, fastening 6. jerk —**'hitchhike** *or* **hitch** *vi.* travel by begging free rides

hither ('hɪðə) *adv.* 1. to or towards this place (*esp. in* **come hither**) —*a.* 2. *obs.* situated on this side —**'hither'to** *adv.* up to now or to this time

HIV human immunodeficiency virus: the virus that causes AIDS

hive (haɪv) *n.* 1. structure in which bees live or are housed 2. *fig.* place swarming with busy occupants —*v.* 3. gather, place bees, in hive —**hive away** store, keep —**hive off** 1. transfer 2. dispose of

hives (haɪvz) *pl.n.* eruptive skin disease

H.M. His (*or* Her) Majesty

H.M.C.S. His (*or* Her) Majesty's Canadian Ship

H.M.I. UK His (*or* Her) Majesty's Inspector (of schools)

H.M.S. His (*or* Her) Majesty's Service *or* Ship

H.M.S.O. UK His (*or* Her) Majesty's Stationery Office

H.N.C. UK Higher National Certificate

H.N.D. UK Higher National Diploma

ho (həʊ) *interj.* 1. imitation or representation of sound of deep laugh (*also* **ho-ho**) 2. exclamation used to attract attention *etc.*

Ho *Chem.* holmium

hoard (hɔːd) *n.* 1. stock, store, *esp.* hidden away —*vt.* 2. amass and hide away 3. store

hoarding ('hɔːdɪŋ) *n.* 1. large board for displaying advertisements 2. temporary wooden fence round building or piece of ground

hoarse (hɔːs) *a.* rough, harsh-sounding, husky —**'hoarsely** *adv.* —**'hoarseness** *n.*

hoary ('hɔːrɪ) *a.* 1. grey with age 2. greyish-white 3. of great antiquity 4. venerable —**'hoarfrost** *n.* frozen dew

hoax (həʊks) *n.* 1. practical joke 2. deceptive trick —*vt.* 3. play trick upon 4. deceive —**'hoaxer** *n.*

THESAURUS

hiss *n.* 1. buzz, hissing, sibilance, sibilation ~*v.* 2. rasp, shrill, sibilate, wheeze, whirr, whistle, whiz 3. blow a raspberry, boo, catcall, condemn, damn, decry, deride, hoot, jeer, mock, revile, ridicule

historian annalist, biographer, chronicler, historicgrapher, recorder

historic celebrated, consequential, epoch-making, extraordinary, famous, momentous, notable, outstanding, red-letter, remarkable, significant

historical actual, archival, attested, authentic, chronicled, documented, factual, real, verifiable

history 1. account, annals, autobiography, biography, chronicle, memoirs, narration, narrative, recapitulation, recital, record, relation, saga, story 2. ancient history, antiquity, bygone times, days of old, days of yore, olden days, the good old days, the old days, the past, yesterday, yesteryear

hit *v.* 1. bang, bash (*Inf.*), batter, beat, belt (*Sl.*), clip (*Sl.*), clobber (*Sl.*), clout (*Inf.*), cuff, flog, knock, lob, punch, slap, smack, smite (*Archaic*), knock, rap, shot, slap, smack, stroke, swipe (*Inf.*), wallop (*Inf.*) 2. *Inf.* sellout, sensation, smash (*Inf.*), success, triumph, winner

hitch *v.* 1. attach, connect, couple, fasten, harness, join, make fast, tether, tie, unite, yoke 2. *Often with* **up** hoick, jerk, pull, tug, yank 3. *Inf.* hitchhike, thumb a lift ~*n.* 4. catch, check, delay, difficulty, drawback, hindrance, hold-up, impediment, mishap, problem, snag, stoppage, trouble

hither close, closer, here, near, nearer, nigh (*Archaic*), over here, to this place

hitherto heretofore, previously, so far, thus far, till now, until now, up to now

hit or miss aimless, casual, cursory, disorganized, haphazard, indiscriminate, perfunctory, random, undirected, uneven

hoard 1. *n.* accumulation, cache, fund, heap, mass, pile, reserve, stockpile, store, supply, treasure-trove 2. *v.* accumulate, amass, buy up, cache, collect, deposit, garner, gather, hive, lay up, put away, put by, save, stash away (*Inf.*), stockpile, store, treasure

hoarse croaky, discordant, grating, gravelly, growling, gruff, guttural, harsh, husky, rasping, raucous, rough, throaty

hoary 1. frosty, grey, grey-haired, grizzled, hoar, silvery, white, white-haired 2. aged, ancient, antiquated, antique, old, venerable

hoax 1. *n.* cheat, con (*Sl.*), deception, fast one (*Inf.*),

hob (hɒb) *n.* **1.** flat-topped casing of fireplace **2.** top area of cooking stove —**ˈhobnail** *n.* large-headed nail for boot soles

hobble (ˈhɒbᵊl) *vi.* **1.** walk lamely —*vt.* **2.** tie legs of (horse *etc.*) together —*n.* **3.** straps or ropes put on an animal's legs to prevent it straying **4.** limping gait

hobbledehoy (hɒbᵊldɪˈhɔɪ) *n. obs.* rough, ill-mannered clumsy youth

hobby (ˈhɒbɪ) *n.* **1.** favourite occupation as pastime **2.** small falcon —**ˈhobbyhorse** *n.* **1.** toy horse **2.** favourite topic, preoccupation

hobgoblin (hɒbˈgɒblɪn) *n.* mischievous fairy

hobnob (ˈhɒbnɒb) *vi.* (*oft. with* with) **1.** be familiar **2.** *obs.* drink (**-bb-**)

hobo (ˈhəʊbəʊ) *n.* shiftless, wandering person (*pl.* **-s, -es**)

Hobson's choice (ˈhɒbsᵊnz) choice of taking what is offered or nothing at all

hock[1] (hɒk) *n.* **1.** backward-pointing joint on leg of horse *etc.*, corresponding to human ankle —*vt.* **2.** disable by cutting tendons of hock

hock[2] (hɒk) *n.* dry white wine

hock[3] (hɒk) *inf.*, *chiefly* **US** *vt.* **1.** pawn, pledge —*n.* **2.** state of being in pawn —**ˈhocker** *n.* —**in hock 1.** in prison **2.** in debt **3.** in pawn

hockey (ˈhɒkɪ) *n.* **1.** team game played on field with ball and curved sticks **2. US, C** ice hockey

hocus-pocus (ˈhəʊkəsˈpəʊkəs) *n.* **1.** trickery **2.** mystifying jargon

hod (hɒd) *n.* **1.** small trough on a staff for carrying mortar, bricks *etc.* **2.** tall, narrow coal scuttle

hoe (həʊ) *n.* **1.** tool for weeding, breaking ground *etc.* —*v.* **2.** dig, weed or till (surface soil) with hoe (**hoed, ˈhoeing**)

hog (hɒg) *n.* **1.** pig, *esp.* castrated male for fattening **2.** greedy, dirty person —*vt.* **3.** *inf.* eat, use selfishly (**-gg-**) —**ˈhogback** *n.* **1.** narrow ridge with steep sides (*also* **hog's back**) **2.** *Archaeol.* tomb with sloping sides —**ˈhogshead** *n.* **1.** large cask **2.** liquid measure, having several values, used *esp.* for alcoholic beverages —**ˈhogwash** *n.* **1.** nonsense **2.** pig food

Hogmanay (hɒgməˈneɪ) *n.* in Scotland, last day of year

hoick (hɔɪk) *vt.* raise abruptly and sharply

hoi polloi (ˈhɔɪ pəˈlɔɪ) **1.** the common mass of people **2.** the masses

hoist (hɔɪst) *vt.* raise aloft, raise with tackle *etc.*

hoity-toity (hɔɪtɪˈtɔɪtɪ) *a. inf.* arrogant, haughty

hokum (ˈhəʊkəm) *n.* **US** *sl.* **1.** claptrap; bunk **2.** obvious or hackneyed material of a sentimental nature in film *etc.*

hold[1] (həʊld) *vt.* **1.** keep fast, grasp **2.** support in or with hands *etc.* **3.** maintain in position **4.** have capacity for **5.** own, occupy **6.** carry on **7.** detain **8.** celebrate **9.** keep back **10.** believe —*vi.* **11.** cling **12.** remain fast or unbroken **13.** (*with* to) abide (by) **14.** keep **15.** remain relevant, valid or true (**held** *pt./pp.*) —*n.* **16.** grasp **17.** influence —**ˈholder** *n.* —**ˈholding** *n.* (*oft. pl.*) property, such as land or stocks and shares —**ˈholdall** *n.* valise or case for carrying clothes *etc.* —**ˈholdfast** *n.* clamp —**holding company** company with controlling shareholdings in other companies —**ˈholdup** *n.* **1.** armed robbery **2.** delay

hold[2] (həʊld) *n.* space in ship or aircraft for cargo

hole (həʊl) *n.* **1.** hollow place, cavity **2.** perforation **3.** opening **4.** *inf.* unattractive place **5.** *inf.* difficult situation —*vt.* **6.** make holes in **7.** drive into a hole —*vi.* **8.** go into a hole —**ˈholey** *a.* —**hole-and-corner** *a. inf.* furtive or secretive

holiday (ˈhɒlɪdeɪ) *n.* day or other period of rest from work *etc.*, *esp.* spent away from home

THESAURUS

fraud, imposture, joke, practical joke, prank, ruse, spoof (*Inf.*), swindle, trick **2.** *v.* bamboozle (*Inf.*), befool, bluff, con (*Sl.*), deceive, delude, dupe, fool, gammon (*Inf.*), gull, (*Archaic*), hoodwink, hornswoggle (*Sl.*), swindle, take in (*Inf.*), take (someone) for a ride (*Inf.*), trick

hobby diversion, favourite occupation, (leisure) activity, leisure pursuit, pastime, relaxation, sideline

hobnob associate, consort, fraternize, hang about, keep company, mingle, mix, socialize

hoi polloi admass, *canaille*, commonalty, riffraff, the (common) herd, the common people, the great unwashed (*Inf. and derogatory*), the lower orders, the masses, the plebs, the populace, the proles (*Derogatory sl., chiefly Brit.*), the proletariat, the rabble, the third estate

hoist *v.* elevate, erect, heave, lift, raise, rear, upraise

hold *v.* **1.** have, keep, maintain, occupy, own, possess, retain **2.** adhere, clasp, cleave, clinch, cling, clutch, cradle, embrace, enfold, grasp, grip, stick **3.** arrest, bind, check, confine, curb, detain, imprison, restrain, stay, stop, suspend **4.** assume, believe, consider, deem, entertain, esteem, judge, maintain, presume, reckon, regard, think, view **5.** continue, endure, last, persevere, persist, remain, resist, stay, wear **6.** assemble, call, carry on, celebrate, conduct, convene, have, officiate at, preside over, run, solemnize **7.** bear, brace, carry, prop, shoulder, support, sustain, take **8.** accommodate, comprise, contain, have a capacity for, seat, take **9.** apply, be in force, be the case, exist, hold good, operate, remain true, remain valid, stand up ~*n.* **10.** clasp, clutch, grasp, grip **11.** anchorage, foothold, footing, leverage, prop, purchase, stay, support, vantage **12.** ascendancy, authority, clout (*Inf.*), control, dominance, dominion, influence, mastery, pull (*Inf.*), sway

holder 1. bearer, custodian, incumbent, keeper, occupant, owner, possessor, proprietor, purchaser **2.** case, container, cover, housing, receptacle, sheath

hold-up 1. bottleneck, delay, difficulty, hitch, obstruction, setback, snag, stoppage, traffic jam, trouble, wait **2.** burglary, mugging (*Inf.*), robbery, stick-up (*Sl.*), theft

hole 1. aperture, breach, break, crack, fissure, gap, opening, orifice, outlet, perforation, puncture, rent, split, tear, vent **2.** cave, cavern, cavity, chamber, depression, excavation, hollow, pit, pocket, scoop, shaft **3.** *Inf.* dive (*Sl.*), dump (*Inf.*), hovel, joint (*Sl.*), slum **4.** *Sl.* dilemma, fix (*Inf.*), imbroglio, jam (*Inf.*), mess, predicament, quandary, scrape (*Inf.*), tangle, (tight) spot (*Inf.*)

holiday 1. break, leave, recess, time off, vacation **2.** anniversary, bank holiday, celebration, feast, festival, festivity, fête, gala, public holiday, saint's day

holier-than-thou goody-goody (*Inf.*), pietistic, pietistical, priggish, religiose, sanctimonious, self-righteous, self-satisfied, smug, unctuous

holiness blessedness, devoutness, divinity, godliness,

holland ('hɒlənd) *n.* linen fabric —**'Hollands** *n.* spirit, gin

holler ('hɒlə) *inf. v.* 1. shout or yell (something) —*n.* 2. shout; call

hollo ('hɒləʊ) *or* **holla** ('hɒlə) *n./interj.* 1. cry for attention, or of encouragement (*pl.* **-s**) —*vi.* 2. shout

hollow ('hɒləʊ) *a.* 1. having a cavity, not solid 2. empty 3. false 4. insincere 5. not full-toned —*n.* 6. cavity, hole, valley —*vt.* 7. make hollow, make hole in 8. excavate

holly ('hɒlɪ) *n.* evergreen shrub with prickly leaves and red berries

hollyhock ('hɒlɪhɒk) *n.* tall plant bearing many large flowers

holmium ('hɒlmɪəm) *n.* silver-white metallic element of lanthanide series

holm oak (həʊm) evergreen Mediterranean oak tree

holocaust ('hɒləkɔːst) *n.* great destruction of life, *esp.* by fire

holograph ('hɒləgræf, -grɑːf) *n.* document wholly written by the signer

holography (hɒ'lɒgrəfɪ) *n.* science of using lasers to produce photographic record (**hologram**) which can reproduce a three-dimensional image

holster ('həʊlstə) *n.* leather case for pistol, hung from belt *etc.*

holt (həʊlt) *n. Poet.* wood, wooded hill

holy ('həʊlɪ) *a.* 1. belonging, devoted to God 2. free from sin 3. divine 4. consecrated —**'holily** *adv.* —**'holiness** *n.* 1. sanctity 2. (**H-**) Pope's title —**holier-than-thou** *a.* offensively sanctimonious or self-righteous —**Holy Communion** service of the Eucharist —**holy day** day of religious festival —**Holy Ghost** *or* **Spirit** third person of Trinity —**Holy Grail** cup or dish used by Christ at the Last Supper —**holy orders** 1. sacrament whereby person is admitted to Christian ministry 2. grades of Christian ministry 3. status of ordained Christian minister —**Holy See** *R.C.Ch.* 1. the see of the pope as bishop of Rome 2. Roman curia —**Holy Week** week before Easter —**the Holy Land** Palestine

homage ('hɒmɪdʒ) *n.* 1. tribute, respect, reverence 2. formal acknowledgment of allegiance

homburg ('hɒmbɜːg) *n.* man's hat of soft felt with dented crown and stiff upturned brim

home (həʊm) *n.* 1. dwelling-place 2. residence 3. native place 4. institution for the elderly, infirm *etc.* —*a.* 5. of one's home, country *etc.* —*adv.* 6. to, at one's home 7. to the point —*v.* 8. direct or be directed on to a point or target —**'homeless** *a.* —**'homely** *a.* plain —**'homeward** *a./adv.* —**'homewards** *adv.* —**home-brew** *n.* alcoholic drink made at home —**Home Counties** counties surrounding London —**home economics** study of diet, budgeting and other subjects concerned with running a home —**home help UK** woman employed, *esp.* by local authority, to do housework in person's home —**Home Office UK** government department responsible for internal affairs —**home rule** 1. self-government 2. partial autonomy sometimes granted to national minority or colony —**Home Secretary UK** head of Home Office —**'homesick** *a.* depressed by absence from home —**'homesickness** *n.* —**'homespun** *a.* 1. domestic 2. simple —*n.* 3. cloth made of homespun yarn —**'homestead** *n.* 1. house with outbuildings, *esp.* on farm 2. **US, C** house and land occupied by owner and exempt from seizure and forced sale for debt —**'homesteader** *n.* —**'homework** *n.* school work to be done at home —**'homing** *a. Zool.* of ability to return home after travelling great distances —**homing pigeon** domestic pigeon developed for its homing instinct, used for racing (*also* **'homer**) —**bring home to** impress deeply upon —**home and dry** safe or successful

homeo-, homoeo-, *or* **homoio-** (*comb. form*) like, similar, as in *homeomorphism*

homeopathy *or* **homoeopathy** (həʊmɪ'ɒpəθɪ) *n.* treatment of disease by small doses of drug that produces, in healthy person, symptoms similar to those of disease being treated —**'homeopath** *or* **'homoeopath** *n.* one who believes in or practises homeopathy —**homeo'pathic** *or* **homoeo'pathic** *a.* —**homeo'pathically** *or* **homoeo'pathically** *adv.*

homicide ('hɒmɪsaɪd) *n.* 1. killing of human being 2. killer —**homi'cidal** *a.*

THESAURUS

piety, purity, religiousness, righteousness, sacredness, saintliness, sanctity, spirituality, virtuousness

hollow *adj.* **1.** empty, not solid, unfilled, vacant, void **2.** cavernous, concave, deep-set, depressed, indented, sunken **3.** deep, dull, expressionless, flat, low, muffled, muted, reverberant, rumbling, sepulchral, toneless **4.** artificial, cynical, deceitful, faithless, false, flimsy, hollow-hearted, hypocritical, insincere, treacherous, unsound, weak ~*n.* **5.** basin, bowl, cave, cavern, cavity, concavity, crater, cup, den, dent, depression, dimple, excavation, hole, indentation, pit, trough **6.** bottom, dale, dell, dingle, glen, valley ~*v.* **7.** channel, dig, dish, excavate, furrow, gouge, groove, pit, scoop

holocaust annihilation, carnage, conflagration, destruction, devastation, genocide, inferno, massacre, mass murder

holy 1. devout, divine, faithful, god-fearing, godly, hallowed, pious, pure, religious, righteous, saintly, sublime, virtuous **2.** blessed, consecrated, dedicated, hallowed, sacred, sacrosanct, sanctified, venerable, venerated

home *n.* **1.** abode, domicile, dwelling, dwelling place, habitation, house, residence **2.** birthplace, family, fireside, hearth, homestead, home town, household **3.** abode, element, environment, habitat, habitation, haunt, home ground, range, stamping ground, territory **4. bring home to** drive home, emphasize, impress upon, make clear, press home ~*adj.* **5.** central, domestic, familiar, family, household, inland, internal, local, national, native

homeless abandoned, destitute, displaced, dispossessed, down-and-out, exiled, forlorn, forsaken, outcast, unsettled

homely everyday, familiar, modest, natural, ordinary, plain, simple, unaffected, unassuming, unpretentious

homespun artless, coarse, homely, home-made, inelegant, plain, rough, rude, rustic, unpolished, unsophisticated

homicidal deadly, death-dealing, lethal, maniacal, mortal, murderous

homicide 1. bloodshed, killing, manslaughter, murder, slaying **2.** killer, murderer, slayer

homily (ˈhɒmɪlɪ) *n.* 1. sermon 2. religious discourse —**homiˈletic** *a.* —**homiˈletics** *pl.n.* (*with sing. v.*) art of preaching

hominid (ˈhɒmɪnɪd) *n.* 1. member of mammal family, extinct or living —*a.* 2. of or belonging to mammal family

hominoid (ˈhɒmɪnɔɪd) *a.* 1. manlike 2. of or belonging to primate family, which includes anthropoid apes and man —*n.* 3. hominoid animal

Homo (ˈhəʊməʊ) *n.* genus to which modern man belongs —**Homo sapiens** (ˈsæpɪɛnz) specific name of modern man

homo- (*comb. form*) same, as in *homosexual.* Such words are not given here where the meaning may easily be inferred from the simple word

homogeneous (həʊməˈdʒiːnɪəs, hɒm-) *a.* 1. formed of uniform parts 2. similar, uniform 3. of the same nature —**homogeˈneity** *n.* —**homogenize** *or* **-nise** (hɒˈmɒdʒɪnaɪz) *vt.* break up fat globules in (milk and cream) to distribute them evenly

homograph (ˈhɒməgrɑːf) *n.* one of group of words spelt in the same way but having different meanings —**homoˈgraphic** *a.*

homologous (həʊˈmɒləgəs, hɒ-), **homological** (həʊməˈlɒdʒɪkˀl, hɒm-), *or* **homologic** *a.* having the same relation, relative position *etc.* —ˈ**homologue** *n.* homologous thing

homonym (ˈhɒmənɪm) *n.* word of same form as another, but having different meaning —**homoˈnymic** *or* **hoˈmonymous** *a.*

homosexual (həʊməʊˈsɛksjʊəl, hɒm-) *n.* 1. person sexually attracted to members of the same sex —*a.* 2. of or relating to homosexuals or homosexuality —**homosexuˈality** *n.*

Hon *or* **Hon.** 1. Honourable 2. (*also* **h-**) honorary

hone (həʊn) *n.* 1. whetstone —*vt.* 2. sharpen with hone

honest (ˈɒnɪst) *a.* 1. not cheating, lying, stealing *etc.* 2. genuine 3. without pretension —ˈ**honestly** *adv.* —ˈ**honesty** *n.* 1. quality of being honest 2. plant with silvery seed pods

honey (ˈhʌnɪ) *n.* sweet fluid made by bees —ˈ**honeyed** *or* ˈ**honied** *a. Poet.* 1. flattering or soothing 2. made sweet or agreeable 3. full of honey —ˈ**honeybee** *n.* any of various social bees widely domesticated as source of honey and beeswax (*also* **hive bee**) —ˈ**honeycomb** *n.* 1. wax structure in hexagonal cells in which bees place honey, eggs *etc.* —*vt.* 2. fill with cells or perforations —ˈ**honeydew** *n.* 1. sweet sticky substance found on plants 2. type of sweet melon —ˈ**honeymoon** *n.* holiday taken by newly-wedded pair —ˈ**honeysuckle** *n.* climbing plant

honk (hɒŋk) *n.* 1. call of wild goose 2. any sound like this, *esp.* sound of motor horn —*vi.* 3. make this sound

honky-tonk (ˈhɒŋkɪtɒŋk) *n.* 1. US *sl.* cheap disreputable nightclub *etc.* 2. style of ragtime piano-playing

honour *or U.S.* **honor** (ˈɒnə) *n.* 1. personal integrity 2. renown 3. reputation 4. sense of what is right or due 5. chastity 6. high rank or position 7. source, cause of honour 8. pleasure, privilege —*pl.* 9. mark of respect 10. distinction in examination —*vt.* 11. respect highly 12. confer honour on 13. accept or pay (bill *etc.*) when due —**honoˈrarium** *n.* a fee (*pl.* **-s, -ia** (-ɪə)) —ˈ**honorary** *a.* 1. conferred for the sake of honour only 2. holding position without pay or usual requirements 3. giving services without pay —**honoˈrific** *a.* conferring honour —ˈ**honourable** *or U.S.* ˈ**honorable** *a.* —ˈ**honourably** *or U.S.* ˈ**honorably** *adv.*

hooch *or* **hootch** (huːtʃ) *n.* US *sl.* alcoholic drink, *esp.* illicitly distilled spirits

hood (hʊd) *n.* 1. covering for head and neck, oft. part of cloak or gown 2. hoodlike thing as (adjustable) top

THESAURUS

homogeneity analogousness, comparability, consistency, correspondence, identicalness, oneness, sameness, similarity, uniformity

homogeneous akin, alike, analogous, cognate, comparable, consistent, identical, kindred, similar, uniform, unvarying

homosexual *adj.* bent (*Sl.*), camp (*Inf.*), gay (*Inf.*), homoerotic, lesbian, queer (*Inf.*), sapphic

honest 1. conscientious, decent, ethical, high-minded, honourable, law-abiding, reliable, reputable, scrupulous, trustworthy, trusty, truthful, upright, veracious, virtuous 2. above board, authentic, bona fide, genuine, honest to goodness, on the level (*Inf.*), on the up and up, proper, real, straight, true 3. candid, direct, forthright, frank, ingenuous, open, outright, plain, sincere, straightforward, undisguised, unfeigned

honestly 1. by fair means, cleanly, ethically, honourably, in good faith, lawfully, legally, legitimately, on the level (*Inf.*), with clean hands 2. candidly, frankly, in all sincerity, in plain English, plainly, straight (out), to one's face, truthfully

honesty 1. faithfulness, fidelity, honour, incorruptibility, integrity, morality, probity, rectitude, reputability, scrupulousness, straightness, trustworthiness, truthfulness, uprightness, veracity, virtue 2. bluntness, candour, equity, even-handedness, fairness, frankness, genuineness, openness, outspokenness, plainness, sincerity, straightforwardness

honorary complimentary, ex officio, formal, *honoris causa,* in name *or* title only, nominal, titular, unofficial, unpaid

honour *n.* 1. credit, dignity, distinction, elevation, esteem, fame, glory, high standing, prestige, rank, renown, reputation, repute 2. acclaim, accolade, adoration, commendation, deference, homage, kudos, praise, recognition, regard, respect, reverence, tribute, veneration 3. decency, fairness, goodness, honesty, integrity, morality, principles, probity, rectitude, righteousness, trustworthiness, uprightness 4. compliment, credit, favour, pleasure, privilege, source of pride *or* satisfaction 5. chastity, innocence, modesty, purity, virginity, virtue ~*v.* 6. admire, adore, appreciate, esteem, exalt, glorify, hallow, prize, respect, revere, reverence, value, venerate, worship 7. acclaim, celebrate, commemorate, commend, compliment, decorate, dignify, exalt, glorify, laud, lionize, praise 8. accept, acknowledge, cash, clear, credit, pass, pay, take

honourable 1. ethical, fair, high-minded, honest, just, moral, principled, true, trustworthy, trusty, upright, upstanding, virtuous 2. distinguished, eminent, great, illustrious, noble, notable, noted, prestigious, renowned, venerable 3. creditable, estimable, proper, reputable, respectable, respected, right, righteous, virtuous

honours adornments, awards, decorations, dignities, distinctions, laurels, titles

of motorcar, perambulator *etc.* **3.** *esp.* US car bonnet —ˈ**hooded** *a.* covered with or shaped like hood —**hooded crow** crow that has grey body and black head, wings, and tail (*also* (*Scot.*) ˈ**hoodie, hoodie crow**) —ˈ**hoodwink** *vt.* deceive

hoodlum (ˈhuːdləm) *n.* gangster, bully —**hood** *n.* US *sl.* hoodlum

hoodoo (ˈhuːduː) *n.* cause of bad luck

hooey (ˈhuːɪ) *n./interj. sl.* nonsense

hoof (huːf) *n.* horny casing of foot of horse *etc.* (*pl.* **-s, hooves**) —**on the hoof** (of livestock) alive

hoo-ha (ˈhuːhɑː) *n.* needless fuss, bother *etc.*

hook (hʊk) *n.* **1.** bent piece of metal used to suspend, hold, or pull something **2.** something resembling hook in shape or function **3.** curved cutting tool **4.** *Boxing* blow delivered with bent elbow —*vt.* **5.** grasp, catch, hold, as with hook **6.** fasten with hook **7.** *Golf* drive (ball) widely to the left **8.** *Cricket* hit off (ball) to leg —**hooked** *a.* **1.** shaped like hook **2.** caught **3.** *sl.* addicted —ˈ**hooker** *n.* **1.** US *sl.* prostitute **2.** *Rugby* player who uses feet to get ball in scrum —**hook-up** *n.* linking of radio, television stations —ˈ**hookworm** *n.* parasitic worm infesting humans and animals

hookah *or* **hooka** (ˈhʊkə) *n.* oriental pipe in which smoke is drawn through water and long tube

hooligan (ˈhuːlɪgən) *n.* violent, irresponsible (young) person —ˈ**hooliganism** *n.*

hoop (huːp) *n.* **1.** rigid circular band of metal, wood *etc.* **2.** such a band used for binding barrel *etc.*, for use as toy, or for jumping through as in circus acts —*vt.* **3.** bind with hoops **4.** encircle —**go through the hoop(s)** *inf.* go through an ordeal or test

hoopla (ˈhuːplɑː) *n.* game played at fairgrounds *etc.*, by throwing rings at objects for prizes

hoopoe (ˈhuːpuː) *n.* bird with large crest

hooray (huːˈreɪ) *or* **hoorah** (huːˈrɑː) *interj.* **1.** *see* HURRAH **2.** (huːˈruː) **A, NZ** cheerio (*also* **hooˈroo**)

hoot (huːt) *n.* **1.** owl's cry or similar sound **2.** cry of disapproval or derision **3.** *inf.* funny person or thing —*vi.* **4.** utter hoot, *esp.* in derision **5.** sound motor horn **6.** *inf.* laugh —ˈ**hooter** *n.* **1.** device (*eg* horn) to emit hooting sound **2.** *sl.* nose

Hoover (ˈhuːvə) *n.* **1. R** vacuum cleaner —*v.* **2.** (**h-**) vacuum

hooves (huːvz) *n., pl. of* HOOF

hop[1] (hɒp) *vi.* **1.** spring on one foot **2.** *inf.* move quickly (**-pp-**) —*n.* **3.** leap, skip **4.** one stage of journey —ˈ**hopscotch** *n.* children's game of hopping in pattern drawn on ground

hop[2] (hɒp) *n.* **1.** climbing plant with bitter cones used to flavour beer *etc.* —*pl.* **2.** the cones

hope (həʊp) *n.* **1.** expectation of something desired **2.** thing that gives, or object of, this feeling —*v.* **3.** feel hope —ˈ**hopeful** *a.* —ˈ**hopefully** *adv. inf.* it is hoped —ˈ**hopeless** *a.* —**young hopeful** promising boy or girl

hopper (ˈhɒpə) *n.* **1.** one who hops **2.** device for feeding material into mill or machine, or grain into railway truck *etc.* **3.** mechanical hop-picker **4. SA** *see* COCOPAN

horal (ˈhɔːrəl) *or* **horary** (ˈhɔːrərɪ) *a. obs.* **1.** pert. to an hour **2.** hourly

horde (hɔːd) *n.* large crowd, *esp.* moving together

horehound *or* **hoarhound** (ˈhɔːhaund) *n.* plant with bitter juice formerly used medicinally

horizon (həˈraɪzᵊn) *n.* **1.** boundary of part of the earth seen from any given point **2.** line where earth and sky seem to meet **3.** boundary of mental outlook —**horizontal** (hɒrɪˈzɒntᵊl) *a.* parallel with horizon, level —**horizontally** (hɒrɪˈzɒntəlɪ) *adv.*

hormone (ˈhɔːməʊn) *n.* **1.** substance secreted by certain glands which stimulates organs of the body **2.** synthetic substance with same effect

horn (hɔːn) *n.* **1.** hard projection on heads of certain animals, *eg* cows **2.** substance of horns **3.** various things made of, or resembling it **4.** wind instrument *orig.* made of horn **5.** device, *esp.* in car, emitting sound as warning *etc.* —**horned** *a.* having horns —ˈ**horny** *a.* **1.** of, like or hard as horn **2.** having horn(s) **3.** *sl.* sexually aroused —ˈ**hornbeam** *n.* tree with smooth grey bark —ˈ**hornbill** *n.* type of bird with horny growth on large bill —ˈ**hornbook** *n.* page bearing religious text or alphabet, held in frame with thin window of horn over it —**horn of plenty** *see* CORNUCOPIA —ˈ**hornpipe** *n.* lively dance, *esp.* associated with sailors

THESAURUS

hoodwink bamboozle (*Inf.*), befool, cheat, con (*Sl.*), cozen, delude, dupe, fool, gull (*Archaic*), hoax, impose, lead up the garden path (*Inf.*), mislead, pull a fast one on (*Inf.*), rook (*Sl.*), swindle, trick

hook *n.* **1.** catch, clasp, fastener, hasp, holder, link, lock, peg ~*v.* **2.** catch, clasp, fasten, fix, hasp, secure **3.** catch, enmesh, ensnare, entrap, snare, trap

hooligan delinquent, hoodlum (*Chiefly U.S.*), rowdy, ruffian, tough, vandal, yob *or* yobbo (*Brit. sl.*)

hoop band, circlet, girdle, loop, ring, wheel

hoot *n.* **1.** call, cry, toot **2.** boo, catcall, hiss, jeer, yell **3.** *Inf.* card (*Inf.*), caution (*Inf.*), laugh (*Inf.*), scream (*Inf.*) ~*v.* **4.** boo, catcall, condemn, decry, denounce, execrate, hiss, howl down, jeer, yell at **5.** cry, scream, shout, shriek, toot, whoop, yell

hop 1. *v.* bound, caper, dance, jump, leap, skip, spring, vault **2.** *n.* bounce, bound, jump, leap, skip, spring, step, vault

hope 1. *n.* ambition, anticipation, assumption, belief, confidence, desire, dream, expectancy, expectation, faith, longing **2.** *v.* anticipate, aspire, await, believe, contemplate, count on, desire, expect, foresee, long, look forward to, rely, trust

hopeful 1. anticipating, assured, buoyant, confident, expectant, looking forward to, optimistic, sanguine **2.** auspicious, bright, cheerful, encouraging, heartening, promising, propitious, reassuring, rosy

hopefully *Inf.* all being well, conceivably, expectedly, feasibly, probably

hopeless 1. defeatist, dejected, demoralized, despairing, desperate, despondent, disconsolate, downhearted, forlorn, in despair, pessimistic, woebegone **2.** helpless, incurable, irremediable, irreparable, irreversible, lost, past remedy, remediless **3.** forlorn, futile, impossible, impracticable, pointless, unachievable, unattainable, useless, vain

horde band, crew, crowd, drove, gang, host, mob, multitude, pack, press, swarm, throng, troop

horizon 1. field of vision, skyline, vista **2.** compass, ken, perspective, prospect, purview, range, realm, scope, sphere, stretch

hornblende (ˈhɔːnblɛnd) *n.* mineral consisting of silica, with magnesia, lime, or iron

hornet (ˈhɔːnɪt) *n.* large insect of wasp family

horologe (ˈhɒrəlɒdʒ) *n. rare* any timepiece —**hoˈrology** *n.* art or science of clock-making and measuring time

horoscope (ˈhɒrəskəʊp) *n.* **1.** observation of, or scheme showing disposition of planets *etc.*, at given moment, *esp.* birth, by which character and abilities of individual are predicted **2.** telling of person's fortune by this method

horror (ˈhɒrə) *n.* **1.** terror **2.** loathing, fear **3.** its cause —**horˈrendous** *a.* horrific —**ˈhorrible** *a.* exciting horror, hideous, shocking —**ˈhorribly** *adv.* —**ˈhorrid** *a.* **1.** unpleasant, repulsive **2.** *inf.* unkind —**horˈrific** *a.* particularly horrible —**ˈhorrify** *vt.* move to horror (**-ified, -ifying**)

hors d'oeuvre (ɔː ˈdɜːvr) small dish served before main meal

horse (hɔːs) *n.* **1.** four-footed animal used for riding and draught **2.** cavalry **3.** vaulting-block **4.** frame for support *etc., esp.* for drying clothes —*vt.* **5.** provide with horse or horses —**ˈhorsy** *or* **ˈhorsey** *a.* **1.** having to do with horses **2.** devoted to horses or horse racing —**horse brass** decorative brass ornament, orig. attached to horse's harness —**horse chestnut** tree with conical clusters of white or pink flowers and large nuts —**ˈhorseflesh** *n.* **1.** horses collectively **2.** flesh of horse, *esp.* edible horse meat —**ˈhorsefly** *n.* large, bloodsucking fly —**horse laugh** harsh boisterous laugh —**ˈhorseman** *n.* rider on horse (**ˈhorsewoman** *fem.*) —**ˈhorseplay** *n.* rough or rowdy play —**ˈhorsepower** *n.* unit of power of engine *etc.* 550 foot-pounds per second —**ˈhorseradish** *n.* plant with pungent root —**horse sense** *see* **common sense** *at* COMMON —**ˈhorseshoe** *n.* **1.** protective U-shaped piece of iron nailed to horse's hoof **2.** thing so shaped —**ˈhorsetail** *n.* green flowerless plant with erect, jointed stem —**horse about** *or* **around** *inf.* play roughly, boisterously

hortatory (ˈhɔːtətərɪ) *or* **hortative** (ˈhɔːtətɪv) *a.* tending to exhort; encouraging —**horˈtation** *n.*

horticulture (ˈhɔːtɪkʌltʃə) *n.* art or science of gardening —**hortiˈcultural** *a.* —**hortiˈculturist** *n.*

Hos. *Bible* Hosea

hosanna (həʊˈzænə) *n./interj.* cry of praise, adoration

hose (həʊz) *n.* **1.** flexible tube for conveying liquid or gas **2.** stockings —*vt.* **3.** water with hose —**ˈhosier** *n.* dealer in stockings *etc.* —**ˈhosiery** *n.* stockings *etc.*

hospice (ˈhɒspɪs) *n. obs.* traveller's house of rest kept by religious order

hospital (ˈhɒspɪtᵊl) *n.* institution for care of sick —**hospitaliˈzation** *or* **-liˈsation** *n.* —**ˈhospitalize** *or* **-lise** *vt.* place for care in hospital

hospitality (hɒspɪˈtælɪtɪ) *n.* friendly and liberal reception of strangers or guests —**ˈhospitable** *a.* welcoming, kindly —**ˈhospitably** *adv.*

host[1] (həʊst) *n.* **1.** one who entertains another (**ˈhostess** *fem.*) **2.** innkeeper **3.** compere of show **4.** animal, plant on which parasite lives —*v.* **5.** be host of (party, programme *etc.*)

host[2] (həʊst) *n.* large number

Host (həʊst) *n.* consecrated bread of the Eucharist

hosta (ˈhɒstə) *n.* garden plant with large ornamental leaves

hostage (ˈhɒstɪdʒ) *n.* person taken or given as pledge or security

hostel (ˈhɒstᵊl) *n.* building providing accommodation at low cost for particular category of people, as students or the homeless —**ˈhostelry** *n. obs.* inn

hostile (ˈhɒstaɪl) *a.* **1.** opposed, antagonistic **2.** warlike **3.** of or relating to an enemy **4.** unfriendly —**hostility** (hɒˈstɪlɪtɪ) *n.* **1.** enmity —*pl.* **2.** acts of warfare

hot (hɒt) *a.* **1.** of high temperature, very warm, giving or feeling heat **2.** angry **3.** severe **4.** recent, new **5.** much favoured **6.** spicy **7.** *sl.* good, quick, smart **8.** *sl.* stolen (**ˈhotter** *comp.*, **ˈhottest** *sup.*) —**ˈhotly** *adv.* —**ˈhotness** *n.* —**hot air** *inf.* boastful, empty talk —**ˈhot-**

THESAURUS

horrible abhorrent, abominable, appalling, awful, dreadful, fearful, frightful, ghastly, grim, grisly, gruesome, heinous, hideous, horrid, loathsome, repulsive, revolting, shameful, shocking, terrible, terrifying

horrid **1.** awful, disagreeable, disgusting, dreadful, horrible, nasty, offensive, terrible, unpleasant **2.** abominable, alarming, appalling, formidable, frightening, hair-raising, harrowing, hideous, horrific, odious, repulsive, revolting, shocking, terrifying, terrorizing **3.** *Inf.* beastly (*Inf.*), cruel, mean, nasty, unkind

horrify **1.** affright, alarm, frighten, intimidate, petrify, scare, terrify, terrorize **2.** appal, disgust, dismay, outrage, shock, sicken

horror **1.** alarm, apprehension, awe, consternation, dismay, dread, fear, fright, panic, terror **2.** abhorrence, abomination, antipathy, aversion, detestation, disgust, hatred, loathing, repugnance, revulsion

horseman cavalier, cavalryman, dragoon, equestrian, horse-soldier, rider

horseplay buffoonery, clowning, fooling around, high jinks, pranks, romping, rough-and-tumble, roughhousing (*Sl.*), skylarking (*Inf.*)

hospitable amicable, bountiful, cordial, friendly, generous, genial, gracious, kind, liberal, sociable, welcoming

hospitality cheer, conviviality, cordiality, friendliness, heartiness, hospitableness, neighbourliness, sociability, warmth, welcome

host[1] *n.* **1.** entertainer, innkeeper, landlord, master of ceremonies, proprietor **2.** anchor man, compere (*Brit.*), presenter ~*v.* **3.** compere (*Brit.*), introduce, present

host[2] army, array, drove, horde, legion, multitude, myriad, swarm, throng

hostage captive, gage, pawn, pledge, prisoner, security, surety

hostile **1.** antagonistic, anti (*Inf.*), bellicose, belligerent, contrary, ill-disposed, inimical, malevolent, opposed, opposite, rancorous, unkind, warlike **2.** adverse, alien, inhospitable, unfriendly, unpropitious, unsympathetic, unwelcoming

hostilities conflict, fighting, state of war, war, warfare

hostility abhorrence, animosity, animus, antagonism, antipathy, aversion, detestation, enmity, hatred, ill will, malevolence, malice, opposition, resentment, unfriendliness

bed *n.* 1. bed of earth heated by manure and grass for young plants 2. any place encouraging growth —**hot-blooded** *a.* passionate, excitable —**hot dog** hot sausage, *esp.* frankfurter, in split bread roll —**'hotfoot** *vi./adv.* (go) quickly —**'hothead** *n.* hasty, intemperate person —**hot-headed** *a.* impetuous, rash or hot-tempered —**hot- headedness** *n.* —**'hothouse** *n.* 1. forcing house for plants 2. heated building for cultivating tropical plants in cold or temperate climates —**hot line** direct communication link between heads of government *etc.* —**hot money** capital that is transferred from one commercial centre to another seeking best opportunity for short-term gain —**'hotplate** *n.* 1. heated plate on electric cooker 2. portable device for keeping food warm —**'hotpot** *n.* UK casserole covered with layer of potatoes —**hot rod** car with engine that has been modified to produce increased power —**hot seat** 1. *inf.* difficult or dangerous position 2. US *sl.* electric chair —**hot-foot it** go quickly —**in hot water** *inf.* in trouble

hotchpotch ('hɒtʃpɒtʃ) *or esp. U.S.* **hodgepodge** ('hɒdʒpɒdʒ) *n.* 1. medley 2. dish of many ingredients

hotel (həʊ'tɛl) *n.* commercial establishment providing lodging and meals —**hotel keeper** *or* **ho'telier** *n.*

Hottentot ('hɒtᵊntɒt) *n.* member of a native S Afr. race, now nearly extinct (*pl.* **-tot, -s**)

hough (hɒx) *see* HOCK[1]

hound (haʊnd) *n.* 1. hunting dog —*vt.* 2. chase, pursue 3. urge on

hour (aʊə) *n.* 1. twenty-fourth part of day 2. sixty minutes 3. time of day 4. appointed time —*pl.* 5. fixed periods for work, prayers *etc.* 6. book of prayers —**'hourly** *adv.* 1. every hour 2. frequently —*a.* 3. frequent 4. happening every hour —**'hourglass** *n.* 1. device consisting of two transparent chambers linked by narrow channel, containing quantity of sand that takes specified time to trickle from one chamber to the other —*a.* 2. well-proportioned with small waist

houri ('hʊərɪ) *n.* beautiful nymph of the Muslim paradise (*pl.* **-s**)

house (haʊs) *n.* 1. building for human habitation 2. building for other specified purpose 3. legislative or other assembly 4. family 5. business firm 6. theatre audience —*v.* (haʊz) 7. give or receive shelter, lodging or storage —*vt.* 8. cover; contain —**housing** ('haʊzɪŋ) *n.* 1. (providing of) houses 2. part or structure designed to cover, protect, contain —**house arrest** confinement to one's own home rather than in prison —**'houseboat** *n.* boat for living in on river *etc.* —**'housebound** *a.* unable to leave one's house because of illness *etc.* —**'housebreaker** *n.* burglar —**'housecoat** *n.* woman's long loose garment for casual wear at home —**'household** *n.* inmates of house collectively —**'householder** *n.* 1. occupier of house as his dwelling 2. head of household —**household name** *or* **word** person or thing that is very well known —**'housekeeper** *n.* person managing affairs of household —**'housekeeping** *n.* (money for) running household —**'housemaid** *n.* maidservant who cleans rooms *etc.* —**housemaid's knee** inflammation and swelling of bursa in front of kneecap —**'houseman** *n.* junior doctor who is member of medical staff of hospital —**House of Commons UK, C** lower chamber of Parliament —**House of Lords UK** upper chamber of Parliament, composed of the peers of the realm —**house-proud** *a.* preoccupied with appearance of one's house —**'housetop** *n.* roof of house —**house-train** *vt.* **UK** train (pets) to urinate and defecate outdoors —**house-warming** *n.* party to celebrate entry into new house —**'housewife** *n.* woman who runs a household —**'housework** *n.* work of running home, such as cleaning *etc.* —**housey-housey** *n.* gambling game, bingo —**proclaim from the housetops** announce publicly

hove (həʊv) *chiefly Naut. pt./pp. of* HEAVE

hovel ('hɒvᵊl) *n.* mean dwelling

hover ('hɒvə) *vi.* 1. (of bird *etc.*) hang in the air 2. loiter 3. be in state of indecision —**'hovercraft** *n.* type of craft which can travel over both land and sea on a cushion of air

THESAURUS

hot 1. blistering, boiling, burning, fiery, flaming, heated, piping hot, roasting, scalding, scorching, searing, steaming, sultry, sweltering, torrid, warm 2. acrid, biting, peppery, piquant, pungent, sharp, spicy 3. *Fig.* fierce, fiery, inflamed, irascible, raging, stormy, touchy, vehement, violent 4. fresh, just out, latest, new, recent, up to the minute 5. approved, favoured, in demand, in vogue, popular, sought-after

hot air blather, blether, bombast, bosh (*Inf.*), bunkum, claptrap (*Inf.*), empty talk, gas (*Sl.*), guff (*Sl.*), rant, tall talk (*Inf.*), verbiage, wind

hotbed breeding ground, den, forcing house, nest, nursery, seedbed

hot-blooded ardent, excitable, fervent, fiery, heated, impulsive, passionate, rash, spirited, temperamental, wild

hotchpotch conglomeration, farrago, gallimaufry, hash, jumble, medley, *mélange*, mess, miscellany, mishmash, mixture, olio, olla podrida, potpourri

hotfoot hastily, helter-skelter, hurriedly, pell-mell, posthaste, quickly, speedily

hothead daredevil, desperado, hotspur, madcap, tearaway

hot-headed fiery, foolhardy, hasty, hot-tempered, impetuous, precipitate, quick-tempered, rash, reckless, unruly, volatile

hound *v.* 1. chase, drive, give chase, hunt, hunt down, pursue 2. badger, goad, harass, harry, impel, persecute, pester, prod, provoke

house *n.* 1. abode, building, domicile, dwelling, edifice, habitation, home, homestead, residence 2. family, household, ménage 3. business, company, concern, establishment, firm, organization, outfit (*Inf.*), partnership 4. Commons, legislative body, parliament ~*v.* 5. accommodate, billet, board, domicile, harbour, lodge, put up, quarter, take in 6. contain, cover, keep, protect, sheathe, shelter, store

household *n.* family, home, house, ménage

householder homeowner, occupant, resident, tenant

housekeeping home economy, homemaking (*U.S.*), housecraft, household management, housewifery

housing 1. accommodation, dwellings, homes, houses 2. case, casing, container, cover, covering, enclosure, sheath

hovel cabin, den, hole, hut, shack, shanty, shed

hover 1. be suspended, drift, float, flutter, fly, hang, poise 2. hang about, linger, wait nearby 3. alternate, dither, falter, fluctuate, haver (*Brit.*), oscillate, pause, seesaw, swither (*Scot. dialect*), vacillate, waver

how (haʊ) *adv.* 1. in what way 2. by what means 3. in what condition 4. to what degree —**howbeit** (haʊˈbiːɪt) *adv. obs.* nevertheless —**howˈever** *adv.* 1. nevertheless 2. in whatever way, degree 3. all the same

howdah (ˈhaʊdə) *n.* (canopied) seat on elephant's back

howitzer (ˈhaʊɪtsə) *n.* short gun firing shells at high elevation

howl (haʊl) *vi.* 1. utter long loud cry —*n.* 2. such cry —**ˈhowler** *n.* 1. one that howls 2. *inf.* stupid mistake —**ˈhowling** *a. inf.* great

hoyden *or* **hoiden** (ˈhɔɪdᵊn) *n.* wild, boisterous girl, tomboy —**ˈhoydenish** *or* **ˈhoidenish** *a.*

H.P. 1. high pressure 2. horsepower (*also* **hp**) 3. UK hire purchase (*also* **h.p.**)

H.Q. *or* **h.q.** headquarters

hr. *or* **hr** hour

H.R.H. His (*or* Her) Royal Highness

HT *Phys.* high tension

hub (hʌb) *n.* 1. middle part of wheel, from which spokes radiate 2. central point of activity

hubble-bubble (ˈhʌbᵊlˈbʌbᵊl) *n.* 1. *see* HOOKAH 2. turmoil 3. gargling sound

hubbub (ˈhʌbʌb) *n.* 1. confused noise of many voices 2. uproar

hubris (ˈhjuːbrɪs) *or* **hybris** (ˈhaɪbrɪs) *n.* pride or arrogance —**huˈbristic** *or* **hyˈbristic** *a.*

huckaback (ˈhʌkəbæk) *n.* coarse absorbent linen or cotton fabric used for towels *etc.* (*also* **huck**)

huckster (ˈhʌkstə) *n.* 1. person using aggressive or questionable methods of selling —*vt.* 2. sell (goods) thus

huddle (ˈhʌdᵊl) *n.* 1. crowded mass 2. *inf.* impromptu conference —*v.* 3. heap, crowd together 4. hunch (oneself)

hue (hjuː) *n.* colour, complexion

hue and cry 1. public uproar, outcry 2. formerly, loud outcry usu. in pursuit of wrongdoer

huff (hʌf) *n.* 1. passing mood of anger —*v.* 2. make or become angry, resentful —*vi.* 3. blow, puff heavily —**ˈhuffily** *adv.* —**ˈhuffy** *a.*

hug (hʌg) *vt.* 1. clasp tightly in the arms 2. cling to 3. keep close to (**-gg-**) —*n.* 4. fond embrace

huge (hjuːdʒ) *a.* very big —**ˈhugely** *adv.* very much

huggermugger (ˈhʌgəmʌgə) *n.* 1. confusion 2. *rare* secrecy —*a./adv. obs.* 3. with secrecy 4. in confusion —*vt.* 5. *obs.* keep secret —*vi.* 6. *obs.* act secretly

Huguenot (ˈhjuːgənəʊ, -nɒt) *n.* 1. French Calvinist, *esp.* of 16th or 17th century —*a.* 2. designating French Protestant Church

huh (*spelling pron.* hʌ) *interj.* exclamation of derision, bewilderment, inquiry *etc.*

hula (ˈhuːlə) *or* **hula-hula** *n.* native dance of Hawaii

Hula-Hoop *n.* R hoop of plastic *etc.* swung round body by wriggling hips

hulk (hʌlk) *n.* 1. body of abandoned vessel 2. *offens.* large, unwieldy person or thing —**ˈhulking** *a.* unwieldy, bulky

hull (hʌl) *n.* 1. frame, body of ship 2. calyx of strawberry, raspberry, or similar fruit 3. shell, husk —*vt.* 4. remove shell, hull from 5. pierce hull of (vessel *etc.*)

hullabaloo *or* **hullaballoo** (hʌləbəˈluː) *n.* uproar, clamour, row

hullo (hʌˈləʊ) *interj. see* HELLO

hum (hʌm) *vi.* 1. make low continuous sound as bee 2. *sl.* smell unpleasantly 3. *sl.* be very active —*vt.* 4. sing with closed lips (**-mm-**) —*n.* 5. humming sound 6. *sl.* smell 7. *sl.* great activity 8. in radio, disturbance affecting reception —**ˈhummingbird** *n.* very small bird whose wings make humming noise

human (ˈhjuːmən) *a.* of, relating to, or characteristic of mankind —**humane** (hjuːˈmeɪn) *a.* 1. benevolent, kind 2. merciful —**ˈhumanism** *n.* 1. belief in human effort rather than religion 2. interest in human welfare and affairs 3. classical literary culture —**ˈhumanist** *n.* —**humaniˈtarian** *n.* 1. philanthropist —*a.* 2. having the welfare of mankind at heart —**huˈmanity** *n.* 1. human nature 2. human race 3. kindliness —*pl.* 4. study of literature, philosophy, the arts —**ˈhumanize** *or* **-ise** *vt.* 1. make human 2. civilize —**ˈhumanly** *adv.* —**ˈhumanoid** *a.* 1. like human being in appearance —*n.* 2. being with human rather than anthropoid characteristics 3. in science fiction, robot or creature resembling human being —**humanˈkind** *n.* whole race of man

THESAURUS

however after all, anyhow, be that as it may, but, nevertheless, nonetheless, notwithstanding, on the other hand, still, though, yet

howl 1. *n.* bay, bellow, clamour, cry, groan, hoot, outcry, roar, scream, shriek, ululation, wail, yelp, yowl 2. *v.* bellow, cry, cry out, lament, quest (*used of hounds*), roar, scream, shout, shriek, ululate, wail, weep, yell, yelp

howler bloomer (*Brit. inf.*), blunder, boner (*Sl.*), bull (*Sl.*), clanger (*Inf.*), error, malapropism, mistake, schoolboy howler

hub centre, core, focal point, focus, heart, middle, nerve centre, pivot

huddle *n.* 1. confusion, crowd, disorder, heap, jumble, mass, mess, muddle 2. *Inf.* confab (*Inf.*), conference, discussion, meeting ~*v.* 3. cluster, converge, crowd, flock, gather, press, throng 4. crouch, cuddle, curl up, hunch up, make oneself small, nestle, snuggle

hue 1. colour, dye, shade, tincture, tinge, tint, tone 2. aspect, cast, complexion, light

hue and cry brouhaha, clamour, furore, hullabaloo, much ado, outcry, ruction (*Inf.*), rumpus, uproar

hug *v.* 1. clasp, cuddle, embrace, enfold, hold close, squeeze, take in one's arms 2. cling to, follow closely, keep close, stay near 3. cherish, cling, hold onto, nurse, retain ~*n.* 4. bear hug, clasp, clinch (*Sl.*), embrace, squeeze

huge Brobdingnagian, bulky, colossal, enormous, extensive, gargantuan, giant, gigantic, great, immense, jumbo (*Inf.*), large, mammoth, massive, monumental, mountainous, prodigious, stupendous, titanic, tremendous, vast

hulk 1. derelict, frame, hull, shell, shipwreck, wreck 2. lout, lubber, lump (*Inf.*), oaf

hull *n.* 1. body, casing, covering, frame, framework, skeleton 2. husk, peel, pod, rind, shell, shuck, skin ~*v.* 3. husk, peel, shell, shuck, skin, trim

hum 1. bombinate *or* bombilate (*Literary*), buzz,

humble (ˈhʌmbəl) *a.* **1.** lowly, modest —*vt.* **2.** bring low, abase, humiliate —**ˈhumbly** *adv.* —**humble pie** formerly, pie made from heart, entrails *etc.* of deer —**eat humble pie** be forced to behave humbly

humbug (ˈhʌmbʌg) *n.* **1.** impostor **2.** sham, nonsense, deception **3.** sweet of boiled sugar —*vt.* **4.** deceive; defraud (**-gg-**)

humdinger (ˈhʌmdɪŋə) *n. sl.* excellent person or thing

humdrum (ˈhʌmdrʌm) *a.* commonplace, dull, monotonous

humeral (ˈhjuːmərəl) *a.* of shoulder —**ˈhumerus** *n.* long bone of upper arm (*pl.* **-meri** (-məraɪ))

humid (ˈhjuːmɪd) *a.* moist, damp —**huˈmidifier** *n.* device for increasing amount of water vapour in air in room *etc.* —**huˈmidify** *vt.* —**huˈmidity** *n.*

humiliate (hjuːˈmɪlɪeɪt) *vt.* lower dignity of, abase, mortify —**humiliˈation** *n.*

humility (hjuːˈmɪlɪtɪ) *n.* **1.** state of being humble **2.** meekness

hummock (ˈhʌmək) *n.* **1.** low knoll, hillock **2.** ridge of ice

humour *or U.S.* **humor** (ˈhjuːmə) *n.* **1.** faculty of saying or perceiving what excites amusement **2.** state of mind, mood **3.** temperament **4.** *obs.* any of various fluids of body —*vt.* **5.** gratify, indulge —**ˈhumorist** *n.* person who acts, speaks, writes humorously —**ˈhumorous** *a.* **1.** funny **2.** amusing —**ˈhumorously** *adv.*

hump (hʌmp) *n.* **1.** normal or deforming lump, *esp.* on back **2.** hillock **3.** *inf.* dejection —*vt.* **4.** make hump-shaped **5.** *sl.* carry, heave —**ˈhumpback** *n.* person with hump —**ˈhumpbacked** *a.* having a hump

humph (*spelling pron.* hʌmf) *interj.* exclamation of annoyance, indecision *etc.*

humus (ˈhjuːməs) *n.* decayed vegetable and animal mould

Hun (hʌn) *n.* **1.** member of Asiatic nomadic peoples who invaded Europe in 4th and 5th centuries A.D. **2.** *inf. derog.* German **3.** *inf.* vandal —**ˈHunlike** *a.* —**ˈHunnish** *a.*

hunch (hʌntʃ) *n.* **1.** intuition or premonition **2.** hump —*vt.* **3.** thrust, bend into hump —**ˈhunchback** *n.* humpback

THESAURUS

croon, drone, mumble, murmur, purr, sing, throb, thrum, vibrate, whir **2.** be active, be busy, bustle, buzz, move, pulsate, pulse, stir, vibrate

human *adj.* anthropoid, fleshly, manlike, mortal

humane benevolent, benign, charitable, clement, compassionate, forbearing, forgiving, gentle, good, good-natured, kind, kind-hearted, kindly, lenient, merciful, mild, sympathetic, tender, understanding

humanitarian **1.** *adj.* altruistic, beneficent, benevolent, charitable, compassionate, humane, philanthropic, public-spirited **2.** *n.* altruist, benefactor, Good Samaritan, philanthropist

humanities classical studies, classics, liberal arts, literae humaniores

humanity **1.** flesh, Homo sapiens, humankind, human race, man, mankind, men, mortality, people **2.** human nature, humanness, mortality **3.** benevolence, benignity, brotherly love, charity, compassion, fellow feeling, kind-heartedness, kindness, mercy, philanthropy, sympathy, tenderness, tolerance, understanding

humanize civilize, cultivate, educate, enlighten, improve, mellow, polish, reclaim, refine, soften, tame

humble *adj.* **1.** meek, modest, self-effacing, submissive, unassuming, unostentatious, unpretentious **2.** common, commonplace, insignificant, low, low-born, lowly, mean, modest, obscure, ordinary, plebeian, poor, simple, undistinguished, unimportant, unpretentious ~*v.* **3.** abase, abash, break, bring down, chagrin, chasten, crush, debase, degrade, demean, disgrace, humiliate, lower, mortify, put down (*Sl.*), reduce, shame, sink, subdue, take down a peg (*Inf.*)

humbug *n.* **1.** bluff, cheat, deceit, deception, dodge, feint, fraud, hoax, imposition, imposture, ruse, sham, swindle, trick, trickery, wile **2.** charlatan, cheat, con man (*Sl.*), faker, fraud, impostor, phoney (*Sl.*), quack, swindler, trickster **3.** baloney (*Inf.*), cant, charlatanry, claptrap (*Inf.*), eyewash (*Inf.*), gammon (*Brit. inf.*), hypocrisy, nonsense, quackery, rubbish ~*v.* **4.** bamboozle (*Inf.*), befool, beguile, cheat, cozen, deceive, delude, dupe, fool, gull (*Archaic*), hoax, hoodwink, impose, mislead, swindle, take in (*Inf.*), trick

humdrum boring, commonplace, dreary, dull, monotonous, mundane, ordinary, repetitious, routine, tedious, tiresome, uneventful, uninteresting, unvaried, wearisome

humid clammy, damp, dank, moist, muggy, steamy, sticky, sultry, watery, wet

humidity clamminess, damp, dampness, dankness, dew, humidness, moistness, moisture, mugginess, sogginess, wetness

humiliate abase, abash, bring low, chagrin, chasten, crush, debase, degrade, discomfit, disgrace, embarrass, humble, make (someone) eat humble pie, mortify, put down (*Sl.*), shame, subdue, take down a peg (*Inf.*)

humiliation abasement, affront, chagrin, condescension, degradation, disgrace, dishonour, embarrassment, humbling, ignominy, indignity, loss of face, mortification, put-down, resignation, self-abasement, shame, submission, submissiveness

humility diffidence, humbleness, lack of pride, lowliness, meekness, modesty, self-abasement, servility, submissiveness, unpretentiousness

humorist comedian, comic, droll, eccentric, funny man, jester, joker, wag, wit

humorous amusing, comic, comical, entertaining, facetious, farcical, funny, hilarious, jocose, jocular, laughable, ludicrous, merry, playful, pleasant, side-splitting, waggish, whimsical, witty

humour *n.* **1.** amusement, comedy, drollery, facetiousness, fun, funniness, jocularity, ludicrousness, wit **2.** comedy, farce, gags (*Sl.*), jesting, jests, jokes, joking, pleasantry, wisecracks (*Inf.*), wit, witticisms, wittiness **3.** disposition, frame of mind, mood, spirits, temper ~*v.* **4.** accommodate, cosset, favour, flatter, go along with, gratify, indulge, mollify, pamper, spoil

hump *n.* **1.** bulge, bump, knob, mound, projection, protrusion, protuberance, swelling ~*v.* **2.** arch, curve, form a hump, hunch, lift, tense **3.** *Sl.* carry, heave, hoist, lug, shoulder

hunch **1.** *n.* feeling, idea, impression, inkling, intuition, premonition, presentiment, suspicion **2.** *v.*

hundred (ˈhʌndrəd) *n./a.* cardinal number, ten times ten —ˈ**hundredfold** *a./adv.* —ˈ**hundredth** *a./n.* ordinal number of a hundred —**hundreds and thousands** tiny beads of coloured sugar, used in decorating cakes *etc.* —ˈ**hundredweight** *n.* weight of 112 lbs. (50.8 kg), 20th part of ton

hung (hʌŋ) *v.* 1. *pt./pp. of* HANG —*a.* 2. (of jury *etc.*) unable to decide 3. not having majority —**hung-over** *a. inf.* suffering from aftereffects of excessive drinking —**hung parliament** parliament in which no party has absolute majority —**hung up** *inf.* 1. delayed 2. emotionally disturbed

hunger (ˈhʌŋgə) *n.* 1. discomfort, exhaustion from lack of food 2. strong desire —*vi.* 3. (*usu. with* for *or* after) have great desire (for) —ˈ**hungrily** *adv.* —ˈ**hungry** *a.* having keen appetite —**hunger strike** refusal of all food, as protest

hunk (hʌŋk) *n.* 1. thick piece 2. *sl., chiefly* US sexually attractive man

hunkers (ˈhʌŋkəz) *pl.n. dial.* haunches

hunt (hʌnt) *v.* 1. (seek out to) kill or capture for sport or food 2. search (for) —*n.* 3. chase, search 4. track of country hunted over 5. (party organized for) hunting 6. pack of hounds 7. hunting district or society —ˈ**hunter** *n.* 1. one who hunts (ˈ**huntress** *fem.*) 2. horse, dog bred for hunting —ˈ**huntsman** *n.* man in charge of pack of hounds

hurdle (ˈhɜːdˀl) *n.* 1. portable frame of bars for temporary fences or for jumping over 2. obstacle —*pl.* 3. race over hurdles —*vi.* 4. race over hurdles —ˈ**hurdler** *n.* one who races over hurdles

hurdy-gurdy (ˈhɜːdɪˈgɜːdɪ) *n.* mechanical (musical) instrument (*eg* barrel organ)

hurl (hɜːl) *vt.* throw violently —**hurly-burly** *n.* loud confusion

hurling (ˈhɜːlɪŋ) *or* **hurley** *n.* Irish game like hockey

hurrah (hʊˈrɑː), **hooray** (huːˈreɪ), *or* **hoorah** (huːˈrɑː) *interj.* exclamation of joy or applause

hurricane (ˈhʌrɪkˀn) *n.* very strong, potentially destructive wind or storm —**hurricane lamp** lamp with glass covering round flame

hurry (ˈhʌrɪ) *v.* 1. (cause to) move or act in great haste (ˈ**hurried**, ˈ**hurrying**) —*n.* 2. undue haste 3. eagerness —ˈ**hurriedly** *adv.*

hurst (hɜːst) *n. obs.* 1. wood 2. sandbank

hurt (hɜːt) *vt.* 1. injure, damage, give pain to 2. wound feelings of, distress —*vi.* 3. *inf.* feel pain (**hurt** *pt./pp.*) —*n.* 4. wound, injury, harm —ˈ**hurtful** *a.*

hurtle (ˈhɜːtˀl) *vi.* 1. move rapidly 2. rush violently 3. whirl

husband (ˈhʌzbənd) *n.* 1. married man —*v.* 2. economize, manage or use to best advantage —ˈ**husbandry** *n.* 1. farming 2. economy

hush (hʌʃ) *v.* 1. make or be silent —*n.* 2. stillness 3. quietness —**hush-hush** *a. inf.* secret —**hush up** suppress (rumours, information), make secret

husk (hʌsk) *n.* 1. dry covering of certain seeds and

THESAURUS

arch, bend, crouch, curve, draw in, huddle, hump, squat, stoop, tense

hunchback crookback (*Rare*), crouch-back (*Archaic*), humpback, kyphosis (*Pathol.*), Quasimodo

hunger *n.* **1.** appetite, emptiness, esurience, famine, hungriness, ravenousness, starvation, voracity **2.** appetence, appetite, craving, desire, greediness, itch, lust, yearning, yen (*Inf.*) ~*v.* **3.** crave, desire, hanker, itch, long, pine, starve, thirst, want, wish, yearn

hungry 1. empty, famished, famishing, hollow, peckish (*Inf., chiefly Brit.*), ravenous, sharp-set, starved, starving, voracious **2.** athirst, avid, covetous, craving, desirous, eager, greedy, keen, yearning

hunk block, chunk, gobbet, lump, mass, piece, slab, wedge, wodge (*Brit. inf.*)

hunt *v.* **1.** chase, gun for, hound, pursue, stalk, track, trail **2.** ferret about, forage, go in quest of, look, look high and low, rummage through, scour, search, seek, try to find ~*n.* **3.** chase, hunting, investigation, pursuit, quest, search

hurdle *n.* **1.** barricade, barrier, fence, hedge, wall **2.** barrier, complication, difficulty, handicap, hindrance, impediment, obstacle, obstruction, snag, stumbling block

hurl cast, chuck (*Inf.*), fire, fling, heave, launch, let fly, pitch, project, propel, send, shy, sling, throw, toss

hurly-burly bedlam, brouhaha, chaos, commotion, confusion, disorder, furore, hubbub, pandemonium, tumult, turbulence, turmoil, uproar

hurricane cyclone, gale, storm, tempest, tornado, twister (*U.S. inf.*), typhoon, willy-willy (*Aust.*), windstorm

hurried breakneck, brief, cursory, hasty, hectic, perfunctory, precipitate, quick, rushed, short, slapdash, speedy, superficial, swift

hurry *v.* **1.** dash, fly, get a move on (*Inf.*), lose no time, make haste, rush, scoot, scurry, step on it (*Inf.*) **2.** accelerate, expedite, goad, hasten, hustle, push on, quicken, speed (up), urge ~*n.* **3.** bustle, celerity, commotion, dispatch, expedition, flurry, haste, precipitation, promptitude, quickness, rush, speed, urgency

hurt *v.* **1.** bruise, damage, disable, harm, impair, injure, mar, spoil, wound **2.** ache, be sore, be tender, burn, pain, smart, sting, throb **3.** afflict, aggrieve, annoy, cut to the quick, distress, grieve, pain, sadden, sting, upset, wound ~*n.* **4.** discomfort, distress, pain, pang, soreness, suffering **5.** bruise, sore, wound **6.** damage, detriment, disadvantage, harm, injury, loss, mischief, wrong ~*adj.* **7.** bruised, cut, damaged, grazed, harmed, injured, scarred, scraped, scratched, wounded **8.** aggrieved, crushed, injured, miffed (*Inf.*), offended, pained, piqued, rueful, sad, wounded

hurtful cruel, cutting, damaging, destructive, detrimental, disadvantageous, distressing, harmful, injurious, malicious, mean, mischievous, nasty, pernicious, prejudicial, spiteful, unkind, upsetting, wounding

husband *v.* budget, conserve, economize, hoard, manage thriftily, save, store, use sparingly

husbandry 1. agriculture, agronomy, cultivation, farming, land management, tillage **2.** careful management, economy, frugality, good housekeeping, thrift

hush 1. *v.* mute, muzzle, quieten, shush, silence, still, suppress **2.** *n.* calm, peace, peacefulness, quiet, silence, still (*Poetic*), stillness, tranquillity

hush-hush classified, confidential, restricted, secret, top-secret

fruits **2.** worthless outside part —*vt.* **3.** remove husk from —**ˈhusky** *a.* **1.** rough in tone **2.** hoarse **3.** dry as husk, dry in the throat **4.** of, full of, husks **5.** *inf.* big and strong

husky (ˈhʌskɪ) *n.* **1.** Arctic sledgedog **2.** C *sl.* Inuit

hussar (hʊˈzɑː) *n.* lightly armed cavalry soldier

hussy (ˈhʌsɪ, -zɪ) *n.* cheeky girl or young woman

hustings (ˈhʌstɪŋz) *pl.n.* **1.** platform from which parliamentary candidates were nominated **2.** political campaigning

hustle (ˈhʌsᵊl) *v.* **1.** push about, jostle, hurry —*vi.* **2.** *sl.* solicit —*n.* **3.** instance of hustling —**ˈhustler** *n.*

hut (hʌt) *n.* any small house or shelter, usu. of wood or metal

hutch (hʌtʃ) *n.* box-like pen for rabbits *etc.*

hyacinth (ˈhaɪəsɪnθ) *n.* **1.** bulbous plant with bell-shaped flowers, *esp.* purple-blue **2.** this blue **3.** orange gem jacinth

hyaena (haɪˈiːnə) *n. see* HYENA

hyaline (ˈhaɪəlɪn) *a.* clear, translucent

hybrid (ˈhaɪbrɪd) *n.* **1.** offspring of two plants or animals of different species **2.** mongrel —*a.* **3.** cross-bred —**ˈhybridism** *n.* —**ˈhybridize** *or* **-ise** *v.* (cause to) produce hybrids; cross-breed

hydatid (ˈhaɪdətɪd) *a./n.* (of) watery cyst, resulting from development of tapeworm larva causing serious disease (in man)

hydra (ˈhaɪdrə) *n.* **1.** fabulous many-headed water serpent **2.** any persistent problem **3.** freshwater polyp (*pl.* **-s, -drae** (-driː)) —**hydra-headed** *a.* hard to root out

hydrangea (haɪˈdreɪndʒə) *n.* ornamental shrub with pink, blue, or white flowers

hydrant (ˈhaɪdrənt) *n.* water-pipe with nozzle for hose

hydrate (ˈhaɪdreɪt) *n.* **1.** chemical compound containing water that is chemically combined with substance —*v.* **2.** (cause to) undergo treatment or impregnation with water —**hyˈdration** *n.* —**ˈhydrator** *n.*

hydraulic (haɪˈdrɒlɪk) *a.* concerned with, operated by, pressure transmitted through liquid in pipe —**hyˈdraulics** *pl.n.* (*with sing. v.*) science of mechanical properties of liquid in motion

hydro (ˈhaɪdrəʊ) *n.* **UK** (*esp.* formerly) hotel or resort offering facilities for hydropathic treatment (*pl.* **-s**)

Hydro (ˈhaɪdrəʊ) *n.* **C** hydroelectric power company

hydro- *or before vowel* **hydr-** (*comb. form*) **1.** water, as in *hydroelectric* **2.** presence of hydrogen, as in *hydrocarbon*

hydrocarbon (haɪdrəʊˈkɑːbᵊn) *n.* compound of hydrogen and carbon

hydrocephalus (haɪdrəʊˈsɛfələs) *or* **hydrocephaly** (haɪdrəʊˈsɛfəlɪ) *n.* accumulation of cerebrospinal fluid within ventricles of brain —**hydrocephalic** (haɪdrəʊsɛˈfælɪk) *or* **hydroˈcephalous** *a.*

hydrochloric acid (haɪdrəˈklɒrɪk) strong colourless acid used in many industrial and laboratory processes

hydrocyanic acid (haɪdrəʊsaɪˈænɪk) *see* **hydrogen cyanide** *at* HYDROGEN

hydrodynamics (haɪdrəʊdaɪˈnæmɪks, -dɪ-) *pl.n.* (*with sing. v.*) science of the motions of system wholly or partly fluid

hydroelectric (haɪdrəʊɪˈlɛktrɪk) *a.* pert. to generation of electricity by use of water

hydrofoil (ˈhaɪdrəfɔɪl) *n.* fast, light vessel with hull raised out of water at speed by vanes in water

hydrogen (ˈhaɪdrɪdʒən) *n.* colourless gas which combines with oxygen to form water —**ˈhydrogenate** *v.* (cause to) undergo reaction with hydrogen —**hydrogenˈation** *n.* —**hydrogen bomb** atom bomb of enormous power in which hydrogen nuclei are converted into helium nuclei —**hydrogen cyanide** colourless poisonous liquid with faint odour of bitter almonds, used for making plastics and as war gas —**hydrogen peroxide** colourless liquid used as antiseptic and bleach

hydrography (haɪˈdrɒgrəfɪ) *n.* description of waters of the earth —**hyˈdrographer** *n.* —**hydroˈgraphic** *a.*

hydrology (haɪˈdrɒlədʒɪ) *n.* study of distribution, use *etc.* of the water of the earth and its atmosphere —**hydrologic** (haɪdrəˈlɒdʒɪk) *a.* —**hyˈdrologist** *n.*

hydrolysis (haɪˈdrɒlɪsɪs) *n.* decomposition of chemical compound reacting with water

hydrometer (haɪˈdrɒmɪtə) *n.* device for measuring relative density of liquid

hydrophilic (haɪdrəʊˈfɪlɪk) *a. Chem.* tending to dissolve in, mix with, or be wetted by water —**ˈhydrophile** *n.*

hydrophobia (haɪdrəˈfəʊbɪə) *n.* aversion to water, esp. as symptom of rabies

hydrophone (ˈhaɪdrəfəʊn) *n.* instrument for detecting sound through water

hydroplane (ˈhaɪdrəʊpleɪn) *n.* **1.** light skimming motorboat **2.** seaplane **3.** vane controlling motion of submarine *etc.*

hydroponics (haɪdrəʊˈpɒnɪks) *pl.n.* (*with sing. v.*) science of cultivating plants in water without using soil

hydrosphere (ˈhaɪdrəsfɪə) *n.* watery part of earth's surface, including oceans, lakes, water vapour in atmosphere *etc.*

hydrostatics (haɪdrəʊˈstætɪks) *pl.n.* (*with sing. v.*) branch of science concerned with mechanical properties and behaviour of fluids that are not in motion —**hydroˈstatic** *a.*

hydrotherapy (haɪdrəʊˈθɛrəpɪ) *n. Med.* treatment of disease by external application of water

hydrotropism (haɪˈdrɒtrəpɪzəm) *n.* directional growth of plants in response to water

hydrous (ˈhaɪdrəs) *a.* containing water

hydroxide (haɪˈdrɒksaɪd) *n.* **1.** base or alkali containing ion OH^- **2.** any compound containing -OH group

hydrozoan (haɪdrəʊˈzəʊən) *n.* **1.** any coelenterate of

THESAURUS

husk bark, chaff, covering, glume, hull, rind, shuck

husky 1. croaking, croaky, gruff, guttural, harsh, hoarse, rasping, raucous, rough, throaty 2. *Inf.* beefy (*Inf.*), brawny, burly, hefty, muscular, powerful, rugged, stocky, strapping, thickset

hustle bustle, crowd, elbow, force, haste, hasten, hurry, impel, jog, jostle, push, rush, shove, thrust

hut cabin, den, hovel, lean-to, refuge, shanty, shed, shelter

hybrid *n.* amalgam, composite, compound, cross, crossbreed, half-blood, half-breed, mixture, mongrel, mule

the class *Hydrozoa*, which includes hydra and Portuguese man-of-war —*a.* **2.** of *Hydrozoa*

hyena *or* **hyaena** (haɪˈiːnə) *n.* wild animal related to dog

hygiene (ˈhaɪdʒiːn) *n.* **1.** principles and practice of health and cleanliness **2.** study of these principles —**hyˈgienic** *a.* —**hyˈgienically** *adv.* —**ˈhygienist** *n.*

hygrometer (haɪˈgrɒmɪtə) *n.* instrument for measuring humidity of air

hygroscopic (haɪgrəˈskɒpɪk) *a.* readily absorbing moisture from the atmosphere

hymen (ˈhaɪmɛn) *n.* **1.** membrane partly covering vagina of virgin **2.** (**H-**) Greek god of marriage

hymenopterous (haɪmɪˈnɒptərəs) *a.* of large order of insects having two pairs of membranous wings —**hymeˈnopteran** *or* **hymeˈnopteron** *n.* any hymenopterous insect (*pl.* **-terans, -tera** (-tərə) *or* **-terons**)

hymn (hɪm) *n.* **1.** song of praise, *esp.* to God —*vt.* **2.** praise in song —**hymnal** (ˈhɪmnᵊl) *a.* **1.** of hymns —*n.* **2.** book of hymns (*also* **hymn book**) —**hymnodist** (ˈhɪmnədɪst) *n.* —**hymnody** (ˈhɪmnədɪ) *n.* singing or composition of hymns

hyoscyamine (haɪəˈsaɪəmiːn) *n.* poisonous alkaloid occurring in henbane and related plants and used in medicine

hype[1] (haɪp) *sl. n.* **1.** hypodermic syringe **2.** drug addict —*vi.* **3.** (*with* up) inject oneself with drug

hype[2] (haɪp) *sl. n.* **1.** deception; racket **2.** intensive or exaggerated publicity or sales promotion —*vt.* **3.** market or promote, using exaggerated or intensive publicity

hyper- (*comb. form*) over, above, excessively, as in *hyperactive.* Such words are not given here where the meaning may easily be inferred from the simple word

hyperbola (haɪˈpɜːbələ) *n.* curve produced when cone is cut by plane making larger angle with the base than the side makes (*pl.* **-s, -le** (-liː))

hyperbole (haɪˈpɜːbəlɪ) *n.* rhetorical exaggeration —**hyperbolic(al)** (haɪpəˈbɒlɪk(ᵊl)) *a.*

Hyperborean (haɪpəˈbɔːrɪən) *a./n.* (inhabitant) of extreme north

hypercritical (haɪpəˈkrɪtɪkᵊl) *a.* too critical —**hyperˈcriticism** *n.*

hyperglycaemia *or U.S.* **hyperglycemia** (haɪpəglaɪˈsiːmɪə) *n. Pathol.* abnormally large amount of sugar in blood —**hyperglyˈcaemic** *or U.S.* **hyperglyˈcemic** *a.*

hypermarket (ˈhaɪpəmɑːkɪt) *n.* **UK** huge self-service store

hyperon (ˈhaɪpərɒn) *n. Phys.* any baryon that is not a nucleon

hyperopia (haɪpəˈrəʊpɪə) *n.* inability to see near objects clearly because images received by eye are focused behind retina —**hyperopic** (haɪpəˈrɒpɪk) *a.*

hypersensitive (haɪpəˈsɛnsɪtɪv) *a.* unduly vulnerable emotionally or physically

hypersonic (haɪpəˈsɒnɪk) *a.* concerned with or having velocity of at least five times that of sound in same medium under the same conditions —**hyperˈsonics** *n.*

hypertension (haɪpəˈtɛnʃən) *n.* abnormally high blood pressure

hypertrophy (haɪˈpɜːtrəfɪ) *n.* **1.** enlargement of organ or part resulting from increase in size of cells —*v.* **2.** (cause to) undergo this condition

hyperventilation (haɪpəvɛntɪˈleɪʃən) *n.* increase in rate of breathing, sometimes resulting in cramp and dizziness

hyphen (ˈhaɪfᵊn) *n.* short line (-) indicating that two words or syllables are to be connected —**ˈhyphenate** *vt.* —**ˈhyphenated** *a.* joined by hyphen

hypno- *or before vowel* **hypn-** (*comb. form*) **1.** sleep, as in *hypnopaedia* **2.** hypnosis, as in *hypnotherapy*

hypnosis (hɪpˈnəʊsɪs) *n.* induced state like deep sleep in which subject acts on external suggestion (*pl.* **-ses** (-siːz)) —**hypnotic** (hɪpˈnɒtɪk) *a.* of hypnosis or of the person or thing producing it —**ˈhypnotism** *n.* —**ˈhypnotist** *n.* —**ˈhypnotize** *or* **-tise** *vt.* affect with hypnosis —**hypnoˈtherapy** *n.* use of hypnosis in treatment of physical or mental disorders

hypo (ˈhaɪpəʊ) *n.* sodium thiosulphate, used as fixer in developing photographs

hypo- *or before vowel* **hyp-** (*comb. form*) under, below, less, as in *hypocrite, hyphen.* Such words are not given here where meaning may easily be inferred from simple word

hypocaust (ˈhaɪpəkɔːst) *n.* ancient Roman underfloor heating system

hypochondria (haɪpəˈkɒndrɪə) *n.* morbid depression, without cause, about one's own health —**hypoˈchondriac** *a./n.* —**hypochondriacal** (haɪpəʊkɒnˈdraɪəkᵊl) *a.*

hypocrisy (hɪˈpɒkrəsɪ) *n.* **1.** assuming of false appearance of virtue **2.** insincerity —**ˈhypocrite** *n.* —**hypoˈcritical** *a.* —**hypoˈcritically** *adv.*

hypodermic (haɪpəˈdɜːmɪk) *a.* **1.** introduced, injected beneath the skin —*n.* **2.** hypodermic syringe or needle

hypogastric (haɪpəˈgæstrɪk) *a.* relating to, situated in, lower part of abdomen

hypostasis (haɪˈpɒstəsɪs) *n.* **1.** *Metaphys.* essential

THESAURUS

hygiene cleanliness, hygienics, sanitary measures, sanitation

hygienic aseptic, clean, disinfected, germ-free, healthy, pure, salutary, sanitary, sterile

hype ballyhoo (*Inf.*), brouhaha, build-up, plugging (*Inf.*), publicity, puffing, racket, razz-matazz (*Sl.*)

hyperbole amplification, enlargement, exaggeration, magnification, overstatement

hypercritical captious, carping, cavilling, censorious, fault-finding, finicky, fussy, hair-splitting, niggling, overcritical, overexacting, overscrupulous, pernickety (*Inf.*), strict

hypnotic mesmeric, mesmerizing, narcotic, opiate, sleep-inducing, somniferous, soothing, soporific, spellbinding

hypnotize mesmerize, put in a trance, put to sleep

hypocrisy cant, deceit, deceitfulness, deception, dissembling, duplicity, falsity, imposture, insincerity, pharisaism, phariseeism, phoneyness (*Sl.*), pretence, sanctimoniousness, speciousness, two-facedness

hypocrite charlatan, deceiver, dissembler, fraud, Holy Willie, impostor, Pecksniff, pharisee, phoney (*Sl.*), pretender, Tartuffe, whited sepulchre

hypocritical canting, deceitful, deceptive, dissembling, duplicitous, false, fraudulent, hollow, insincere, Janus-faced, pharisaical, phoney (*Sl.*), sanctimonious, specious, spurious, two-faced

nature of anything 2. *Christianity* any of the three persons of the Godhead 3. accumulation of blood in organ or part as result of poor circulation (*pl.* **-ses** (-si:z)) —**hypostatic** (haɪpəˈstætɪk) *or* **hypoˈstatical** *a.*

hypotension (haɪpəʊˈtɛnʃən) *n. Pathol.* abnormally low blood pressure —**hypoˈtensive** *a.*

hypotenuse (haɪˈpɒtɪnjuːz) *n.* side of a right-angled triangle opposite the right angle

hypothecate (haɪˈpɒθɪkeɪt) *vt. Law* pledge (personal property) as security for debt without transferring possession —**hypotheˈcation** *n.* —**hyˈpothecator** *n.*

hypothermia (haɪpəʊˈθɜːmɪə) *n.* condition of having body temperature reduced to dangerously low level

hypothesis (haɪˈpɒθɪsɪs) *n.* 1. suggested explanation of something 2. assumption as basis of reasoning (*pl.* **-eses** (-ɪsiːz)) —**hyˈpothesize** *or* **-ise** *v.* —**hypoˈthetical** *a.* —**hypoˈthetically** *adv.*

hypso- *or before vowel* **hyps-** (*comb. form*) height, as in *hypsometry*

hypsography (hɪpˈsɒgrəfɪ) *n.* branch of geography dealing with altitudes

hypsometer (hɪpˈsɒmɪtə) *n.* instrument for measuring altitudes —**hypˈsometry** *n.* science of measuring altitudes

hyrax (ˈhaɪræks) *n.* genus of hoofed but rodent-like animals (*pl.* **-es, hyraces** (ˈhaɪrəsiːz))

hyssop (ˈhɪsəp) *n.* small aromatic herb

hysterectomy (hɪstəˈrɛktəmɪ) *n.* surgical operation for removing the uterus

hysteresis (hɪstəˈriːsɪs) *n. Phys.* lag or delay in changes in variable property of a system

hysteria (hɪˈstɪərɪə) *n.* 1. mental disorder with emotional outbursts 2. any frenzied emotional state 3. fit of crying or laughing —**hysterical** (hɪˈstɛrɪkˈl) *a.* —**hysterically** (hɪˈstɛrɪkəlɪ) *adv.* —**hysterics** (hɪˈstɛrɪks) *pl.n.* fits of hysteria

Hz hertz

THESAURUS

hypothesis assumption, postulate, premise, premiss, proposition, supposition, theory, thesis

hypothetical academic, assumed, conjectural, imaginary, putative, speculative, supposed, theoretical

hysteria agitation, delirium, frenzy, hysterics, madness, panic, unreason

hysterical berserk, beside oneself, convulsive, crazed, distracted, distraught, frantic, frenzied, mad, overwrought, raving, uncontrollable

I

i *or* **I** (aɪ) *n.* **1.** ninth letter of English alphabet **2.** any of several speech sounds represented by this letter **3.** something shaped like I (*pl.* **i's, I's** *or* **Is**) **—dot one's i's and cross one's t's** pay attention to detail

I (aɪ) *pron.* the pronoun of the first person singular

I **1.** *Chem.* iodine **2.** *Phys.* current **3.** *Phys.* isospin **4.** Roman numeral, one

IA Iowa

-ia (*comb. form*) **1.** in place names, as in *Columbia* **2.** in names of diseases, as in *pneumonia* **3.** in words denoting condition or quality, as in *utopia* **4.** in names of botanical genera and zoological classes, as in *Reptilia* **5.** in collective nouns borrowed from Latin, as in *regalia*

IAEA International Atomic Energy Agency

-ial (*comb. form*) of or relating to, as in *managerial*

iamb (ˈaɪæm, ˈaɪæmb) *or* **iambus** (aɪˈæmbəs) *n.* metrical foot of short and long syllable (*pl.* **ˈiambs** *or* **-buses, -bi** (-baɪ)) **—iˈambic** *a.*

IATA (aɪˈɑːtə, iːˈɑːtə) International Air Transport Association

iatric (aɪˈætrɪk) *or* **iatrical** *a.* of medicine or physicians, *esp.* as suffix **-iatrics, -iatry,** as in *paediatrics, psychiatry*

I.B.A. Independent Broadcasting Authority

Iberian (aɪˈbɪərɪən) *a.* of Iberia, *ie* Spain and Portugal

ibex (ˈaɪbɛks) *n.* wild goat with large horns (*pl.* **-es, ibices** (ˈɪbɪsiːz, ˈaɪ-), **ˈibex**)

ibid. *or* **ib.** ibidem (*Lat.,* in the same place)

ibis (ˈaɪbɪs) *n.* storklike bird

-ible (*a. comb. form*) *see* -ABLE **—-ibility** (*n. comb. form*) **—-ibly** (*adv. comb. form*)

IBM International Business Machines Corporation

i/c **1.** in charge (of) **2.** internal combustion

-ic (*comb. form*) **1.** of, relating to or resembling, as in *periodic* (*also* **-ical**) **2.** *Chem.* indicating that element is chemically combined in higher of two possible valence states, as in *ferric*

I.C.A. **1.** UK Institute of Contemporary Arts **2.** Institute of Chartered Accountants

-ical (*a. comb. form*) *see* -IC (sense 1) **—-ically** (*adv. comb. form*)

ICBM intercontinental ballistic missile

ice (aɪs) *n.* **1.** frozen water **2.** frozen confection, ice cream **—*v.*** **3.** (*oft. with* up, over *etc.*) cover, become covered with ice **—*vt.*** **4.** cool with ice **5.** cover with icing **—ˈicicle** *n.* tapering spike of ice hanging where water has dripped **—ˈicily** *adv.* **—ˈiciness** *n.* **—ˈicing** *n.* mixture of sugar and water *etc.* used to decorate cakes **—ˈicy** *a.* **1.** covered with ice **2.** cold **3.** chilling **—ice age** *see* **glacial period** *at* GLACIER **—ˈiceberg** *n.* large floating mass of ice **—ˈicebox** *n.* **1.** compartment in refrigerator for storing or making ice **2.** insulated cabinet packed with ice for storing food **—ˈicebreaker** *n.* **1.** vessel for breaking up ice in bodies of water (*also* **ˈiceboat**) **2.** device for breaking ice into smaller pieces **—ˈicecap** *n.* mass of glacial ice that permanently covers polar regions *etc.* **—ice cream** sweetened frozen dessert made from cream, eggs *etc.* **—ice floe** sheet of floating ice **—ice hockey** team game played on ice with puck **—ice lolly** ice cream, flavoured ice on stick **—ice pack** **1.** bag *etc.* containing ice, applied to part of body to reduce swelling *etc.* **2.** *see* **pack ice** *at* PACK **—ice skate** boot having steel blade fitted to sole to enable wearer to glide over ice **—ice-skate** *vi.* glide over ice on ice skates **—ice-skater** *n.* **—on thin ice** unsafe; vulnerable

I.C.E. UK Institution of Civil Engineers

Icelandic (aɪsˈlændɪk) *a.* **1.** of Iceland **—*n.*** **2.** official language of Iceland

I.Chem.E. Institution of Chemical Engineers

ichneumon (ɪkˈnjuːmən) *n.* greyish-brown mongoose

ichor (ˈaɪkɔː) *n.* **1.** *Gr. myth.* fluid said to flow in veins of gods **2.** *Pathol.* foul-smelling watery discharge from wound or ulcer **—ˈichorous** *a.*

ichthyology (ɪkθɪˈɒlədʒɪ) *n.* scientific study of fish **—ichthyosaurus** (ɪkθɪəˈsɔːrəs) *n.* prehistoric marine animal (*pl.* **-i** (-aɪ))

I.C.I. Imperial Chemical Industries

icicle (ˈaɪsɪkᵊl) *n. see* ICE

icon *or* **ikon** (ˈaɪkɒn) *n.* image, representation, *esp.* of religious figure **—iˈconoclasm** *n.* **—iˈconoclast** *n.* **1.** one who attacks established principles *etc.* **2.** breaker of icons **—iconoˈclastic** *a.* **—icoˈnography** *n.* **1.** icons collectively **2.** study of icons

icono- *or before vowel* **icon-** (*comb. form*) image; likeness, as in *iconology*

ictus (ˈɪktəs) *n.* **1.** *Prosody* metrical or rhythmical stress in verse feet, as contrasted with stress accent on words **2.** *Med.* sudden attack or stroke (*pl.* **-es, -tus**) **—ˈictal** *a.*

id (ɪd) *n. Psychoanal.* the mind's instinctive energies

ID **1.** identification **2.** Idaho

-id (*comb. form*) member of zoological family, as in *cyprinid*

-idae (*comb. form*) name of zoological family, as in *Felidae*

idea (aɪˈdɪə) *n.* **1.** notion in the mind **2.** conception **3.** vague belief **4.** plan, aim **—iˈdeal** *n.* **1.** conception of something that is perfect **2.** perfect person or thing **—*a.*** **3.** perfect **4.** visionary **5.** existing only in idea **—iˈdealism** *n.* **1.** tendency to seek perfection in everything **2.** philosophy that mind is the only reality **—iˈdealist** *n.* **1.** one who holds doctrine of idealism **2.** one who strives after the ideal **3.** impractical person **—idealˈistic** *a.* **—idealiˈzation** *or* **-iˈsation** *n.* **—iˈdealize** *or* **-ise** *vt.* portray as ideal **—iˈdeally** *adv.*

THESAURUS

ice on thin ice at risk, in jeopardy, open to attack, out on a limb, sticking one's neck out (*Inf.*), unsafe, vulnerable

icy 1. arctic, biting, bitter, chill, chilling, chilly, cold, freezing, frost-bound, frosty, frozen over, ice-cold, raw **2.** glacial, glassy, like a sheet of glass, rimy, slippery, slippy (*Inf.*)

idea 1. abstraction, concept, conception, conclusion, fancy, impression, judgment, perception, thought, understanding **2.** belief, conviction, doctrine, interpretation, notion, opinion, teaching, view, viewpoint **3.** approximation, clue, estimate, guess, hint, impression, inkling, intimation, notion, suspicion **4.** aim, end, import, intention, meaning, object, objec-

idée fixe (ide ˈfiks) *Fr.* fixed idea; obsession (*pl.* ***idées fixes*** (ide ˈfiks))

idem (ˈaɪdɛm, ˈɪdɛm) *Lat.* the same

identity (aɪˈdɛntɪtɪ) *n.* **1.** individuality **2.** being the same, exactly alike —**iˈdentical** *a.* very same —**iˈdentically** *adv.* —**iˈdentifiable** *a.* —**identifiˈcation** *n.* (means of) identifying —**iˈdentify** *vt.* **1.** establish identity of **2.** treat as identical —*v.* **3.** associate (oneself) (**iˈdentified, iˈdentifying**) —**identification parade** group of persons assembled for purpose of discovering whether witness can identify suspect —**Iˈdentikit** *n.* **R** set of pictures of parts of faces that can be built up to form likeness of person sought by police *etc.*

ideo- (*comb. form*) idea; ideas, as in *ideology*

ideogram (ˈɪdɪəʊgræm) *or* **ideograph** (ˈɪdɪəʊgrɑːf) *n.* picture, symbol, figure *etc.* suggesting an object without naming it —**ideˈography** *n.* representation of things by ideographs

ideology (aɪdɪˈɒlədʒɪ) *n.* body of ideas, beliefs of group, nation *etc.* —**ideoˈlogical** *a.*

ides (aɪdz) *n.* the 15th of March, May, July and Oct. and the 13th of other months of the Ancient Roman calendar

id est (ɪd ɛst) *Lat.* that is

idiocy (ˈɪdɪəsɪ) *n. see* IDIOT

idiom (ˈɪdɪəm) *n.* **1.** way of expression natural or peculiar to a language or group **2.** characteristic style of expression —**idioˈmatic** *a.* **1.** using idioms **2.** colloquial

idiosyncrasy (ɪdɪəʊˈsɪŋkrəsɪ) *n.* peculiarity of mind, temper or disposition in a person

idiot (ˈɪdɪət) *n.* **1.** mentally deficient person **2.** foolish, senseless person —**ˈidiocy** *n.* **1.** state of being an idiot **2.** foolish act or remark —**idiˈotic** *a.* utterly senseless or stupid —**idiˈotically** *adv.* —**idiot board** *sl.* autocue

idle (ˈaɪdᵊl) *a.* **1.** unemployed **2.** lazy **3.** useless; vain **4.** groundless —*vi.* **5.** be idle **6.** (of engine) run slowly with gears disengaged —*vt.* **7.** (*esp. with* away) waste —**ˈidleness** *n.* —**ˈidler** *n.* —**ˈidly** *adv.*

idol (ˈaɪdᵊl) *n.* **1.** image of deity as object of worship **2.** object of excessive devotion —**iˈdolater** *n.* worshipper of idols (**iˈdolatress** *fem.*) —**iˈdolatrous** *a.* —**iˈdolatry** *n.* —**ˈidolize** *or* **-ise** *vt.* **1.** love or venerate to excess **2.** make an idol of

idyll *or U.S. (sometimes)* **idyl** (ˈɪdɪl) *n.* **1.** short de-

THESAURUS

tive, plan, purpose, *raison d'être*, reason, sense, significance

ideal *n.* **1.** archetype, criterion, epitome, example, exemplar, last word, model, nonpareil, paradigm, paragon, pattern, perfection, prototype, standard, standard of perfection ~*adj.* **2.** archetypal, classic, complete, consummate, model, optimal, perfect, quintessential, supreme **3.** abstract, conceptual, hypothetical, intellectual, mental, theoretical, transcendental **4.** fanciful, imaginary, impractical, ivory-tower, unattainable, unreal, Utopian, visionary

idealist *n.* romantic, Utopian, visionary

idealistic impracticable, optimistic, perfectionist, quixotic, romantic, starry-eyed, Utopian, visionary

ideally all things being equal, if one had one's way, in a perfect world, under the best of circumstances

identical alike, corresponding, duplicate, equal, equivalent, indistinguishable, interchangeable, like, matching, selfsame, the same, twin

identification 1. cataloguing, classifying, establishment of identity, labelling, naming, pinpointing, recognition **2.** association, connection, empathy, fellow feeling, involvement, rapport, relationship, sympathy **3.** credentials, ID, letters of introduction, papers

identify 1. catalogue, classify, diagnose, label, make out, name, pick out, pinpoint, place, put one's finger on (*Inf.*), recognize, single out, spot, tag **2.** *Often with* **with** ally, associate, empathize, feel for, put in the same category, put oneself in the place *or* shoes of, relate to, respond to, see through another's eyes, think of in connection (with)

identity 1. distinctiveness, existence, individuality, oneness, particularity, personality, self, selfhood, singularity, uniqueness **2.** accord, correspondence, empathy, rapport, sameness, unanimity, unity

idiocy abject stupidity, asininity, fatuity, fatuousness, foolishness, imbecility, inanity, insanity, lunacy, senselessness, tomfoolery

idiom 1. expression, locution, phrase, set phrase, turn of phrase **2.** jargon, language, mode of expression, parlance, style, talk, usage, vernacular

idiomatic dialectal, native, vernacular

idiosyncrasy affectation, characteristic, eccentricity, habit, mannerism, oddity, peculiarity, personal trait, quirk, singularity, trick

idiot ass, blockhead, booby, cretin, dimwit (*Inf.*), dunderhead, fool, halfwit, imbecile, mooncalf, moron, nincompoop, nitwit, simpleton

idiotic asinine, crazy, daft (*Inf.*), dumb (*Inf.*), fatuous, foolhardy, foolish, halfwitted, harebrained, imbecile, imbecilic, inane, insane, lunatic, moronic, senseless, stupid, unintelligent

idle *adj.* **1.** dead, empty, gathering dust, inactive, jobless, mothballed, out of action *or* operation, out of work, redundant, stationary, ticking over, unemployed, unoccupied, unused, vacant **2.** indolent, lackadaisical, lazy, shiftless, slothful, sluggish **3.** abortive, bootless, fruitless, futile, groundless, ineffective, of no avail, otiose, pointless, unavailing, unproductive, unsuccessful, useless, vain, worthless ~*v.* **4.** *Often followed by* **away** dally, dawdle, fool, fritter, kill time, laze, loiter, lounge, potter, waste, while **5.** coast, drift, mark time, shirk, sit back and do nothing, skive (*Brit. sl.*), slack, slow down, take it easy (*Inf.*), vegetate

idleness 1. inaction, inactivity, leisure, time on one's hands, unemployment **2.** hibernation, inertia, laziness, shiftlessness, sloth, sluggishness, torpor, vegetating **3.** dilly-dallying (*Inf.*), lazing, loafing, pottering, skiving (*Brit. sl.*), time-wasting, trifling

idol 1. deity, god, graven image, image, pagan symbol **2.** *Fig.* beloved, darling, favourite, hero, pet, pin-up (*Sl.*), superstar

idolater 1. heathen, idol-worshipper, pagan **2.** admirer, adorer, devotee, idolizer, votary, worshipper

idolatry adoration, adulation, apotheosis, deification, exaltation, glorification, hero worship, idolizing

idolize admire, adore, apotheosize, bow down before, deify, dote upon, exalt, glorify, hero-worship, look up to, love, revere, reverence, venerate, worship, worship to excess

scriptive poem of picturesque or charming scene or episode, *esp.* of rustic life **2.** charming or picturesque scene or event —**i'dyllic** *a.* **1.** of, like, idyll **2.** delightful —**i'dyllically** *adv.*

i.e. id est

I.E.E. Institution of Electrical Engineers

if (ɪf) *conj.* **1.** on condition or supposition that **2.** whether **3.** although —*n.* **4.** uncertainty, doubt (*esp. in* **ifs and buts**)

-iferous (*comb. form*) containing, yielding, as in *carboniferous*

igloo *or* **iglu** (ˈɪgluː) *n.* dome-shaped Eskimo house of snow and ice

igneous (ˈɪgnɪəs) *a.* (*esp.* of rocks) formed as molten rock cools and hardens

ignis fatuus (ˈɪgnɪs ˈfætjʊəs) will-o'-the-wisp (*pl.* **ignes fatui** (ˈɪgniːz ˈfætjʊaɪ))

ignite (ɪgˈnaɪt) *v.* (cause to) burn —**ignition** (ɪgˈnɪʃən) *n.* **1.** act of kindling or setting on fire **2.** in internal-combustion engine, means of firing explosive mixture, usu. electric spark

ignoble (ɪgˈnəʊbəl) *a.* **1.** mean, base **2.** of low birth —**ig'nobly** *adv.*

ignominy (ˈɪgnəmɪnɪ) *n.* **1.** dishonour, disgrace **2.** shameful act —**igno'minious** *a.*

ignore (ɪgˈnɔː) *vt.* disregard; leave out of account —**ignoramus** (ɪgnəˈreɪməs) *n.* ignorant person (*pl.* **-es**) —**'ignorance** *n.* lack of knowledge —**'ignorant** *a.* **1.** lacking knowledge **2.** uneducated **3.** unaware —**'ignorantly** *adv.*

iguana (ɪˈgwɑːnə) *n.* large tropical American lizard

ikebana (iːkəˈbɑːnə) *n.* Japanese decorative art of flower arrangement

ikon (ˈaɪkɒn) *n. see* ICON

il- (*comb. form*) *see* IN-¹, IN-²

ileum (ˈɪlɪəm) *n.* lower part of small intestine —**'ileac** *a.*

ilex (ˈaɪlɛks) *n.* any of genus of trees or shrubs such as holly and inkberry

ilium (ˈɪlɪəm) *n.* uppermost and widest of three sections of hipbone (*pl.* **-ia** (-ɪə)) —**'iliac** *a.*

ilk (ɪlk) *a.* same —**of that ilk 1.** of the same type or class **2.** *Scot.* of the place of the same name

ill (ɪl) *a.* **1.** not in good health **2.** bad, evil **3.** faulty **4.** unfavourable —*n.* **5.** evil, harm **6.** mild disease —*adv.* **7.** badly **8.** hardly, with difficulty —**'illness** *n.* —**ill-advised** *a.* imprudent, injudicious —**ill-bred** *a.* badly brought up; lacking good manners —**ill-considered** *a.* done without due consideration; not thought out —**ill-disposed** *a.* (*oft. with* towards) not kindly disposed —**ill fame** bad reputation —**ill-fated** *a.* unfortunate —**ill-favoured** *a.* ugly, deformed —**ill-founded** *a.* not founded on true or reliable premises; unsubstantiated —**ill-gotten** *a.* obtained dishonestly —**ill-mannered** *a.* boorish, uncivil —**ill-natured** *a.* naturally unpleasant and mean —**ill-omened** *a.* unlucky, inauspicious —**ill-starred** *a.* unlucky, ill-fated —**ill-timed** *a.* inopportune —**ill-treat** *vt.* treat cruelly —**ill-use** (ˈɪlˈjuːz) *vt.* **1.** use badly or cruelly; abuse —*n.* (ˈɪlˈjuːs), *also* **ill-usage 2.** harsh or cruel treatment; abuse —**ill will** unkind feeling, hostility —**house of ill fame** brothel

THESAURUS

if 1. *conj.* admitting, allowing, assuming, granting, in case, on condition that, on the assumption that, provided, providing, supposing, though, whenever, wherever, whether **2.** *n.* condition, doubt, hesitation, stipulation, uncertainty

ignite burn, burst into flames, catch fire, fire, flare up, inflame, kindle, light, put a match to (*Inf.*), set alight, set fire to, take fire, touch off

ignominious abject, despicable, discreditable, disgraceful, dishonourable, disreputable, humiliating, indecorous, inglorious, mortifying, scandalous, shameful, sorry, undignified

ignominy bad odour, contempt, discredit, disgrace, dishonour, disrepute, humiliation, infamy, mortification, obloquy, odium, opprobrium, reproach, shame, stigma

ignorance 1. greenness, inexperience, innocence, nescience (*Literary*), oblivion, unawareness, unconsciousness, unfamiliarity **2.** benightedness, blindness, illiteracy, lack of education, mental darkness, unenlightenment, unintelligence

ignorant 1. benighted, blind to, inexperienced, innocent, in the dark about, oblivious, unaware, unconscious, unenlightened, uninformed, uninitiated, unknowing, unschooled, unwitting **2.** green, illiterate, naive, unaware, uncultivated, uneducated, unknowledgeable, unlearned, unlettered, unread, untaught, untrained, untutored

ignore be oblivious to, bury one's head in the sand, cold-shoulder, cut (*Inf.*), disregard, give the cold shoulder to, neglect, overlook, pass over, pay no attention to, reject, send (someone) to Coventry, shut one's eyes to, take no notice of, turn a blind eye to, turn a deaf ear to, turn one's back on

ill *adj.* **1.** ailing, dicky (*Sl.*), diseased, funny (*Inf.*), indisposed, infirm, laid up (*Inf.*), not up to snuff (*Inf.*), off-colour, on the sick list (*Inf.*), out of sorts (*Inf.*), poorly (*Inf.*), queasy, queer, seedy (*Inf.*), sick, under the weather (*Inf.*), unhealthy, unwell, valetudinarian **2.** bad, damaging, deleterious, detrimental, evil, foul, harmful, iniquitous, injurious, ruinous, unfortunate, unlucky, vile, wicked, wrong **3.** disturbing, foreboding, inauspicious, ominous, sinister, threatening, unfavourable, unhealthy, unlucky, unpromising, unpropitious, unwholesome ~*n.* **4.** affliction, harm, hurt, injury, misery, misfortune, pain, trial, tribulation, trouble, unpleasantness, woe **5.** ailment, complaint, disease, disorder, illness, indisposition, infirmity, malady, malaise, sickness **6.** abuse, badness, cruelty, damage, depravity, destruction, evil, ill usage, malice, mischief, suffering, wickedness ~*adv.* **7.** badly, hard, inauspiciously, poorly, unfavourably, unfortunately, unluckily **8.** barely, by no means, hardly, insufficiently, scantily

ill-advised foolhardy, foolish, ill-considered, ill-judged, impolitic, imprudent, inappropriate, incautious, indiscreet, injudicious, misguided, overhasty, rash, reckless, short-sighted, thoughtless, unseemly, unwise, wrong-headed

ill-bred bad-mannered, boorish, churlish, coarse, crass, discourteous, ill-mannered, impolite, indelicate, rude, uncivil, uncivilized, uncouth, ungallant, ungentlemanly, unladylike, unmannerly, unrefined, vulgar

ill-disposed against, antagonistic, anti (*Inf.*), antipathetic, averse, disobliging, down on (*Inf.*), hostile, inimical, opposed, uncooperative, unfriendly, unwelcoming

illegal (ɪˈliːgᵊl) *a.* **1.** forbidden by law; unlawful; illicit **2.** unauthorized or prohibited by code of official or accepted rules —**illeˈgality** *n.* —**ilˈlegally** *adv.*

illegible (ɪˈlɛdʒɪbᵊl) *a.* unable to be read or deciphered —**illegiˈbility** *or* **ilˈlegibleness** *n.*

illegitimate (ɪlɪˈdʒɪtɪmɪt) *a.* **1.** born out of wedlock **2.** unlawful **3.** not regular —**illeˈgitimacy** *n.*

illiberal (ɪˈlɪbərəl) *a.* **1.** narrow-minded; prejudiced; intolerant **2.** not generous; mean **3.** lacking in culture or refinement —**illiberˈality** *n.*

illicit (ɪˈlɪsɪt) *a.* **1.** illegal **2.** prohibited, forbidden

illimitable (ɪˈlɪmɪtəbᵊl) *a.* that cannot be limited, boundless, unrestricted, infinite —**ilˈlimitableness** *n.*

illiterate (ɪˈlɪtərɪt) *a.* **1.** not literate, unable to read or write **2.** violating accepted standards in reading and writing **3.** uneducated, ignorant, uncultured —*n.* **4.** illiterate person —**ilˈliteracy** *n.*

illogical (ɪˈlɒdʒɪkᵊl) *a.* **1.** characterized by lack of logic; senseless; unreasonable **2.** disregarding logical principles —**illogiˈcality** *or* **ilˈlogicalness** *n.* —**ilˈlogically** *adv.*

illuminate (ɪˈluːmɪneɪt) *vt.* **1.** light up **2.** clarify **3.** decorate with lights **4.** decorate with gold and colours —**ilˈluminant** *n.* agent of lighting —**illumiˈnation** *n.* —**ilˈluminative** *a.*

illusion (ɪˈluːʒən) *n.* deceptive appearance or belief —**ilˈlusionist** *n.* conjuror —**ilˈlusory** *or* **ilˈlusive** *a.* false

illust. *or* **illus.** **1.** illustrated **2.** illustration

illustrate (ˈɪləstreɪt) *vt.* **1.** provide with pictures or examples **2.** exemplify —**illusˈtration** *n.* **1.** picture, diagram **2.** example **3.** act of illustrating —**ˈillustrative** *a.* providing explanation —**ˈillustrator** *n.*

illustrious (ɪˈlʌstrɪəs) *a.* famous, distinguished, exalted

I.L.O. International Labour Organization

THESAURUS

illegal actionable (*Law*), banned, black-market, bootleg, criminal, felonious, forbidden, illicit, lawless, outlawed, prohibited, proscribed, unauthorized, unconstitutional, under the counter, unlawful, unlicensed, unofficial, wrongful

illegality crime, criminality, felony, illegitimacy, illicitness, lawlessness, unlawfulness, wrong, wrongness

illegible crabbed, faint, hard to make out, hieroglyphic, indecipherable, obscure, scrawled, undecipherable, unreadable

illegitimate 1. illegal, illicit, improper, unauthorized, unconstitutional, unlawful, unsanctioned **2.** baseborn (*Archaic*), bastard, born on the wrong side of the blanket, born out of wedlock, fatherless, misbegotten (*Literary*), natural, spurious (*Rare*)

ill-fated blighted, doomed, hapless, ill-omened, ill-starred, luckless, star-crossed, unfortunate, unhappy, unlucky

ill-founded baseless, empty, groundless, idle, unjustified, unproven, unreliable, unsubstantiated, unsupported

illicit 1. black-market, bootleg, contraband, criminal, felonious, illegal, illegitimate, prohibited, unauthorized, unlawful, unlicensed **2.** clandestine, forbidden, furtive, guilty, immoral, improper, wrong

illiteracy benightedness, ignorance, illiterateness, lack of education

illiterate benighted, ignorant, uncultured, uneducated, unlettered, untaught, untutored

ill-mannered badly behaved, boorish, churlish, coarse, discourteous, ill-behaved, ill-bred, impolite, insolent, loutish, rude, uncivil, uncouth, unmannerly

ill-natured bad-tempered, catty (*Inf.*), churlish, crabbed, cross, cross-grained, disagreeable, disobliging, malevolent, malicious, mean, nasty, perverse, petulant, spiteful, sulky, sullen, surly, unfriendly, unkind, unpleasant

illness affliction, ailment, attack, complaint, disability, disease, disorder, ill health, indisposition, infirmity, malady, malaise, poor health, sickness

illogical absurd, fallacious, faulty, inconclusive, inconsistent, incorrect, invalid, irrational, meaningless, senseless, sophistical, specious, spurious, unreasonable, unscientific, unsound

ill-starred doomed, ill-fated, ill-omened, inauspicious, star-crossed, unfortunate, unhappy, unlucky

ill-timed awkward, inappropriate, inconvenient, inept, inopportune, unseasonable, untimely, unwelcome

ill-treat abuse, damage, handle roughly, harass, harm, harry, ill-use, injure, knock about, maltreat, mishandle, misuse, oppress, wrong

illuminate 1. brighten, illumine (*Literary*), irradiate, light, light up **2.** clarify, clear up, elucidate, enlighten, explain, give insight into, instruct, make clear, shed light on **3.** adorn, decorate, illustrate, ornament

illumination 1. beam, brightening, brightness, light, lighting, lighting up, lights, radiance, ray **2.** awareness, clarification, edification, enlightenment, insight, inspiration, instruction, perception, revelation, understanding

illusion 1. chimera, daydream, fantasy, figment of the imagination, hallucination, ignis fatuus, mirage, mockery, phantasm, semblance, will-o'-the-wisp **2.** deception, delusion, error, fallacy, false impression, fancy, misapprehension, misconception

illusory, illusive apparent, Barmecide, beguiling, chimerical, deceitful, deceptive, delusive, fallacious, false, hallucinatory, misleading, mistaken, seeming, sham, unreal, untrue

illustrate 1. bring home, clarify, demonstrate, elucidate, emphasize, exemplify, exhibit, explain, instance, interpret, make clear, make plain, point up, show **2.** adorn, decorate, depict, draw, ornament, picture, sketch

illustration 1. analogy, case, case in point, clarification, demonstration, elucidation, example, exemplification, explanation, instance, interpretation, specimen **2.** adornment, decoration, figure, picture, plate, sketch

illustrious brilliant, celebrated, distinguished, eminent, exalted, famed, famous, glorious, great, noble, notable, noted, prominent, remarkable, renowned, resplendent, signal, splendid

ill will acrimony, animosity, animus, antagonism, antipathy, aversion, bad blood, dislike, enmity, envy, grudge, hard feelings, hatred, hostility, malevolence, malice, no love lost, rancour, resentment, spite, unfriendliness, venom

I.L.P. Independent Labour Party

im- (*comb. form*) *see* IN-[1], IN-[2]

image (ˈɪmɪdʒ) *n.* **1.** representation or likeness of person or thing **2.** optical counterpart, as in mirror **3.** double, copy **4.** general impression **5.** mental picture created by words, *esp.* in literature **6.** personality presented to the public by a person —*vt. rare* **7.** make image of **8.** reflect —**ˈimagery** *n.* images collectively, *esp.* in literature

imagine (ɪˈmædʒɪn) *vt.* **1.** picture to oneself **2.** think **3.** conjecture —**iˈmaginable** *a.* —**iˈmaginary** *a.* existing only in fancy —**imagiˈnation** *n.* **1.** faculty of making mental images of things not present **2.** fancy —**imˈaginative** *a.* —**imˈaginatively** *adv.*

imago (ɪˈmeɪgəʊ) *n.* **1.** last, perfected state of insect life **2.** image (*pl.* **-s, imagines** (ɪˈmædʒəniːz))

imam (ɪˈmɑːm) *n.* Islamic minister or priest

imbalance (ɪmˈbæləns) *n.* lack of balance, proportion

imbecile (ˈɪmbɪsiːl, -saɪl) *n.* **1.** idiot —*a.* **2.** idiotic —**imbecility** (ɪmbɪˈsɪlɪtɪ) *n.*

imbed (ɪmˈbɛd) *vt. see* EMBED

imbibe (ɪmˈbaɪb) *vt.* **1.** drink in **2.** absorb —*vi.* **3.** drink

imbricate (ˈɪmbrɪkɪt, -keɪt) *a.* lying over each other in regular order, like tiles or shingles on roof (*also* **ˈimbricated**) —**imbriˈcation** *n.*

imbroglio (ɪmˈbrəʊlɪəʊ) *n.* complicated situation, plot (*pl.* **-s**)

imbue (ɪmˈbjuː) *vt.* inspire

I. Mech. E. Institution of Mechanical Engineers

IMF International Monetary Fund

imitate (ˈɪmɪteɪt) *vt.* **1.** take as model **2.** mimic, copy —**ˈimitable** *a.* —**imiˈtation** *n.* **1.** act of imitating **2.** copy of original **3.** likeness **4.** counterfeit —**ˈimitative** *a.* —**ˈimitator** *n.*

immaculate (ɪˈmækjʊlɪt) *a.* **1.** spotless **2.** pure **3.** unsullied

immanent (ˈɪmənənt) *a.* existing within, inherent —**ˈimmanence** *n.*

immaterial (ɪməˈtɪərɪəl) *a.* **1.** unimportant, trifling **2.** not consisting of matter **3.** spiritual

immaˈture
imˈmobile
imˈmoderate
imˈmodest
imˈmov(e)able
imˈpalpable
imˈpatience
imˈpatient
imˈpenetrable
imˈplausible
impoˈlite
impreˈcise
imˈprobable
imˈprudent
imˈpure

THESAURUS

image **1.** appearance, effigy, figure, icon, idol, likeness, picture, portrait, reflection, representation, statue **2.** chip off the old block (*Inf.*), counterpart, (dead) ringer (*Sl.*), Doppelgänger, double, facsimile, replica, similitude, spit (*Inf.*), spitting image *or* spit and image (*Inf.*) **3.** conceit, concept, conception, figure, idea, impression, mental picture, perception, trope

imaginable believable, comprehensible, conceivable, credible, likely, plausible, possible, supposable, thinkable, under the sun, within the bounds of possibility

imaginary assumed, chimerical, dreamlike, fancied, fanciful, fictional, fictitious, hallucinatory, hypothetical, ideal, illusive, illusory, imagined, invented, legendary, made-up, mythological, nonexistent, phantasmal, shadowy, supposed, suppositious, supposititious, unreal, unsubstantial, visionary

imagination **1.** creativity, enterprise, fancy, ingenuity, insight, inspiration, invention, inventiveness, originality, resourcefulness, vision, wit, wittiness **2.** chimera, conception, fancy, idea, ideality, illusion, image, invention, notion, supposition, unreality

imaginative clever, creative, dreamy, enterprising, fanciful, fantastic, ingenious, inspired, inventive, original, poetical, visionary, vivid, whimsical

imagine **1.** conceive, conceptualize, conjure up, create, devise, dream up (*Inf.*), envisage, fantasize, form a mental picture of, frame, invent, picture, plan, project, scheme, see in the mind's eye, think of, think up, visualize **2.** apprehend, assume, believe, conjecture, deduce, deem, fancy, gather, guess, infer, realize, suppose, surmise, suspect, take for granted, take it, think

imbecile **1.** *n.* bungler, cretin, dolt, dotard, fool, halfwit, idiot, moron, thickhead **2.** *adj.* asinine, fatuous, feeble-minded, foolish, idiotic, imbecilic, inane, ludicrous, moronic, simple, stupid, thick, witless

imbecility asininity, childishness, cretinism, fatuity, foolishness, idiocy, inanity, incompetency, stupidity

imbibe **1.** consume, drink, knock back (*Inf.*), quaff, sink (*Inf.*), suck, swallow, swig (*Inf.*) **2.** *Literary* absorb, acquire, assimilate, gain, gather, ingest, receive, take in

imitate affect, ape, burlesque, caricature, copy, counterfeit, do (*Inf.*), do an impression of, duplicate, echo, emulate, follow, follow in the footsteps of, follow suit, impersonate, mimic, mirror, mock, parody, personate, repeat, send up (*Brit. inf.*), simulate, spoof (*Inf.*), take a leaf out of (someone's) book, take off (*Inf.*), travesty

imitation **1.** aping, copy, counterfeit, counterfeiting, duplication, echoing, likeness, mimicry, resemblance, simulation **2.** fake, forgery, impersonation, impression, mockery, parody, reflection, replica, reproduction, sham, substitution, takeoff (*Inf.*), travesty

imitative copied, copycat (*Inf.*), copying, derivative, echoic, mimetic, mimicking, mock, onomatopoeic, parrotlike, plagiarized, pseudo (*Inf.*), put-on, second-hand, simulated, unoriginal

imitator aper, copier, copycat (*Inf.*), echo, epigone (*Rare*), follower, impersonator, impressionist, mimic, parrot, shadow

immaculate **1.** clean, impeccable, neat, neat as a new pin, spick-and-span, spruce, trim, unexceptionable **2.** above reproach, faultless, flawless, guiltless, incorrupt, innocent, perfect, pure, sinless, spotless, stainless, unblemished, uncontaminated, undefiled, unpolluted, unsullied, untarnished, virtuous

immaterial **1.** a matter of indifference, extraneous, impertinent, inapposite, inconsequential, inconsiderable, inessential, insignificant, irrelevant, of little

immeasurable (ɪˈmɛʒərəbᵊl) *a.* incapable of being measured, *esp.* by virtue of great size; limitless —**immeasuraˈbility** *or* **imˈmeasurableness** *n.* —**imˈmeasurably** *adv.*

immediate (ɪˈmiːdɪət) *a.* **1.** occurring at once **2.** direct, not separated by others —**imˈmediacy** *n.* —**imˈmediately** *adv.*

immemorial (ɪmɪˈmɔːrɪəl) *a.* beyond memory

immense (ɪˈmɛns) *a.* huge, vast —**imˈmensely** *adv.* —**imˈmensity** *n.* vastness

immerse (ɪˈmɜːs) *vt.* **1.** dip, plunge into liquid **2.** involve, engross —**imˈmersion** *n.* immersing —**immersion heater** *or* **imˈmerser** *n.* electric appliance for heating liquid in which it is immersed

immigrate (ˈɪmɪgreɪt) *vi.* come into country as settler —**ˈimmigrant** *n./a.* —**immiˈgration** *n.*

imminent (ˈɪmɪnənt) *a.* **1.** liable to happen soon **2.** close at hand —**ˈimminence** *n.* —**ˈimminently** *adv.*

immobilize *or* **-ise** (ɪˈməʊbɪlaɪz) *vt.* **1.** make immobile **2.** *Fin.* convert (circulating capital) into fixed capital —**immobiliˈzation** *or* **-iˈsation** *n.* —**imˈmobilizer** *or* **-iser** *n.*

immolate (ˈɪməʊleɪt) *vt.* kill, sacrifice —**immoˈlation** *n.*

immoral (ɪˈmɒrəl) *a.* **1.** corrupt **2.** promiscuous **3.** indecent **4.** unethical —**immoˈrality** *n.*

immortal (ɪˈmɔːtᵊl) *a.* **1.** deathless **2.** famed for all time —*n.* **3.** immortal being **4.** god **5.** one whose fame will last —**immorˈtality** *n.* —**imˈmortalize** *or* **-ise** *vt.*

immune (ɪˈmjuːn) *a.* **1.** proof (against a disease *etc.*) **2.** secure **3.** exempt —**imˈmunity** *n.* **1.** state of being immune **2.** freedom from prosecution, tax *etc.* —**immuniˈzation** *or* **-niˈsation** *n.* process of making immune to disease —**ˈimmunize** *or* **-nise** *vt.* make immune —**immuˈnology** *n.* branch of biology concerned with study of immunity

immure (ɪˈmjʊə) *vt.* imprison, wall up

immutable (ɪˈmjuːtəbᵊl) *a.* unchangeable

imp (ɪmp) *n.* **1.** little devil **2.** mischievous child —**ˈimpish** *a.* of or like an imp; mischievous

THESAURUS

account, of no consequence, of no importance, trifling, trivial, unimportant, unnecessary **2.** airy, disembodied, ethereal, ghostly, incorporeal, metaphysical, spiritual, unembodied, unsubstantial

immature **1.** adolescent, crude, green, imperfect, premature, raw, undeveloped, unfinished, unfledged, unformed, unripe, unseasonable, untimely, young **2.** babyish, callow, childish, inexperienced, infantile, jejune, juvenile, puerile, wet behind the ears (*Inf.*)

immeasurable bottomless, boundless, endless, illimitable, immense, incalculable, inestimable, inexhaustible, infinite, limitless, measureless, unbounded, unfathomable, unlimited, vast

immediate **1.** instant, instantaneous **2.** adjacent, close, contiguous, direct, near, nearest, next, primary, proximate, recent

immediately **1.** at once, before you could say Jack Robinson (*Inf.*), directly, forthwith, instantly, now, promptly, pronto (*Inf.*), right away, right now, straight away, this instant, this very minute, *tout de suite*, unhesitatingly, without delay, without hesitation **2.** at first hand, closely, directly, nearly

immemorial age-old, ancient, archaic, fixed, long-standing, of yore, olden (*Archaic*), rooted, time-honoured, traditional

immense Brobdingnagian, colossal, elephantine, enormous, extensive, giant, gigantic, great, huge, illimitable, immeasurable, infinite, interminable, jumbo (*Inf.*), large, mammoth, massive, monstrous, monumental, prodigious, stupendous, titanic, tremendous, vast

immensity bulk, enormity, expanse, extent, greatness, hugeness, infinity, magnitude, massiveness, scope, size, sweep, vastness

immersion **1.** baptism, bathe, dip, dipping, dousing, ducking, dunking, plunging, submerging **2.** *Fig.* absorption, concentration, involvement, preoccupation

immigrant incomer, newcomer, settler

imminent at hand, brewing, close, coming, fast-approaching, forthcoming, gathering, impending, in the air, in the offing, looming, menacing, near, nigh (*Archaic*), on the horizon, on the way, threatening

immobile at a standstill, at rest, fixed, frozen, immobilized, immotile, immovable, like a statue, motionless, rigid, riveted, rooted, stable, static, stationary, stiff, still, stock-still, stolid, unmoving

immobilize bring to a standstill, cripple, disable, freeze, halt, lay up (*Inf.*), paralyse, put out of action, render inoperative, stop, transfix

immoderate egregious, enormous, exaggerated, excessive, exorbitant, extravagant, extreme, inordinate, intemperate, over the odds (*Inf.*), profligate, steep (*Inf.*), uncalled-for, unconscionable, uncontrolled, undue, unjustified, unreasonable, unrestrained, unwarranted, wanton

immoral abandoned, bad, corrupt, debauched, degenerate, depraved, dishonest, dissolute, evil, impure, indecent, iniquitous, lewd, licentious, nefarious, obscene, of easy virtue, pornographic, profligate, reprobate, sinful, unchaste, unethical, unprincipled, vicious, vile, wicked, wrong

immorality badness, corruption, debauchery, depravity, dissoluteness, evil, iniquity, licentiousness, profligacy, sin, turpitude, vice, wickedness, wrong

immortal *adj.* **1.** abiding, constant, death-defying, deathless, endless, enduring, eternal, everlasting, imperishable, incorruptible, indestructible, lasting, perennial, perpetual, sempiternal (*Literary*), timeless, undying, unfading ~*n.* **2.** god, goddess, Olympian **3.** genius, great (*Usually plural*), hero, paragon

immortality **1.** deathlessness, endlessness, eternity, everlasting life, incorruptibility, indestructibility, perpetuity, timelessness **2.** celebrity, fame, glorification, gloriousness, glory, greatness, renown

immortalize apotheosize, celebrate, commemorate, enshrine, eternalize, eternize, exalt, glorify, memorialize, perpetuate, solemnize

immovable fast, firm, fixed, immutable, jammed, rooted, secure, set, stable, stationary, stuck, unbudgeable

immune clear, exempt, free, insusceptible, invulnerable, let off (*Inf.*), not affected, not liable, not subject, proof (against), protected, resistant, safe, unaffected

immunity **1.** amnesty, charter, exemption, exoneration, franchise, freedom, indemnity, invulnerability, liberty, licence, prerogative, privilege, release, right **2.** immunization, protection, resistance

imp. 1. imperative 2. imperfect

impact (ˈɪmpækt) *n.* 1. collision 2. profound effect —*vt.* (ɪmˈpækt) 3. drive, press —**imˈpacted** *a.* 1. (of tooth) wedged against another tooth below gum 2. (of fracture) having jagged broken ends wedged into each other

impair (ɪmˈpɛə) *vt.* weaken, damage —**imˈpairment** *n.*

impala (ɪmˈpɑːlə) *n.* antelope of S Afr.

impale *or* **empale** (ɪmˈpeɪl) *vt.* 1. pierce with sharp instrument 2. combine (two coats of arms) by placing them side by side with line between —**imˈpalement** *or* **emˈpalement** *n.*

impanel (ɪmˈpænᵊl) *vt. esp.* US *see* EMPANEL

impart (ɪmˈpɑːt) *vt.* 1. communicate (information *etc.*) 2. give

impartial (ɪmˈpɑːʃəl) *a.* 1. not biased or prejudiced 2. fair —**impartiˈality** *n.*

impassable (ɪmˈpɑːsəbᵊl) *a.* 1. not capable of being passed 2. blocked, as mountain pass

impasse (ɪmˈpɑːs, æmˈpɑːs) *n.* 1. deadlock 2. place, situation, from which there is no outlet

impassible (ɪmˈpæsəbᵊl) *a. rare* 1. not susceptible to pain or injury 2. impassive; unmoved —**impassiˈbility** *or* **imˈpassibleness** *n.*

impassioned (ɪmˈpæʃənd) *a.* deeply moved, ardent

impassive (ɪmˈpæsɪv) *a.* 1. showing no emotion 2. calm —**impasˈsivity** *n.*

impasto (ɪmˈpæstəʊ) *n.* 1. paint applied thickly, so that brush marks are evident 2. technique of painting in this way

impeach (ɪmˈpiːtʃ) *vt.* 1. charge with crime 2. call to account 3. denounce —**imˈpeachable** *a.* —**imˈpeachment** *n.*

impeccable (ɪmˈpɛkəbᵊl) *a.* without flaw or error —**impeccaˈbility** *n.*

impecunious (ɪmpɪˈkjuːnɪəs) *a.* poor —**impecuniˈosity** *n.*

impede (ɪmˈpiːd) *vt.* hinder —**imˈpedance** *n. Elec.* measure of opposition offered to flow of alternating current —**impediment** (ɪmˈpɛdɪmənt) *n.* 1. obstruction 2. defect —**impedimenta** (ɪmpɛdɪˈmɛntə) *pl.n.* 1. any objects that impede progress, *esp.* baggage and equipment carried by army 2. *Law* obstructions to making of contract, *esp.* of marriage

impel (ɪmˈpɛl) *vt.* 1. induce, incite 2. drive, force (-ll-) —**imˈpeller** *n.*

impend (ɪmˈpɛnd) *vi.* 1. threaten, be imminent 2. (*with* over) *rare* hang —**imˈpending** *a.*

THESAURUS

immunize inoculate, protect, safeguard, vaccinate

imp brat, demon, devil, gamin, minx, rascal, rogue, scamp, sprite, urchin

impact 1. bang, blow, bump, collision, concussion, contact, crash, force, jolt, knock, shock, smash, stroke, thump 2. brunt, burden, consequences, effect, full force, impression, influence, meaning, power, repercussions, significance, thrust, weight

impair blunt, damage, debilitate, decrease, deteriorate, diminish, enervate, enfeeble, harm, hinder, injure, lessen, mar, reduce, spoil, undermine, vitiate, weaken, worsen

impart 1. communicate, convey, disclose, discover, divulge, make known, pass on, relate, reveal, tell 2. accord, afford, bestow, confer, contribute, give, grant, lend, offer, yield

impartial detached, disinterested, equal, equitable, even-handed, fair, just, neutral, nondiscriminating, nonpartisan, objective, open-minded, unbiased, unprejudiced, without fear or favour

impartiality detachment, disinterest, disinterestedness, dispassion, equality, equity, even-handedness, fairness, lack of bias, neutrality, nonpartisanship, objectivity, open-mindedness

impassable blocked, closed, impenetrable, obstructed, pathless, trackless, unnavigable

impasse blind alley (*Inf.*), dead end, deadlock, stalemate, standoff, standstill

impassioned animated, ardent, blazing, excited, fervent, fervid, fiery, furious, glowing, heated, inflamed, inspired, intense, passionate, rousing, stirring, vehement, violent, vivid, warm, worked up

impatience 1. haste, hastiness, heat, impetuosity, intolerance, irritability, irritableness, quick temper, rashness, shortness, snappiness, vehemence, violence 2. agitation, anxiety, avidity, disquietude, eagerness, edginess, fretfulness, nervousness, restiveness, restlessness, uneasiness

impatient 1. abrupt, brusque, curt, demanding, edgy, hasty, hot-tempered, indignant, intolerant, irritable, quick-tempered, snappy, sudden, testy, vehement, violent 2. agog, athirst, chafing, eager, fretful, headlong, impetuous, like a cat on hot bricks (*Inf.*), restless, straining at the leash

impeach 1. accuse, arraign, blame, censure, charge, criminate (*Rare*), denounce, indict, tax 2. call into question, cast aspersions on, cast doubt on, challenge, disparage, impugn, question

impeachment accusation, arraignment, indictment

impeccable above suspicion, exact, exquisite, faultless, flawless, immaculate, incorrupt, innocent, irreproachable, perfect, precise, pure, sinless, stainless, unblemished, unerring, unimpeachable

impecunious broke (*Inf.*), cleaned out (*Sl.*), destitute, indigent, insolvent, penniless, poverty-stricken, skint (*Sl.*), stony (*Sl.*), strapped (*Sl.*)

impede bar, block, brake, check, clog, curb, delay, disrupt, hamper, hinder, hold up, obstruct, restrain, retard, slow (down), stop, throw a spanner in the works (*Inf.*), thwart

impediment bar, barrier, block, check, clog, curb, defect, difficulty, encumbrance, hindrance, obstacle, obstruction, snag, stumbling block

impedimenta accoutrements, baggage, belongings, effects, equipment, gear, junk (*Inf.*), luggage, movables, odds and ends, paraphernalia, possessions, stuff, things, trappings, traps

impel actuate, compel, constrain, drive, force, goad, incite, induce, influence, inspire, instigate, motivate, move, oblige, power, prod, prompt, propel, push, require, spur, stimulate, urge

impending approaching, brewing, coming, forthcoming, gathering, hovering, imminent, in the offing, looming, menacing, near, nearing, on the horizon, threatening

impenetrable dense, hermetic, impassable, impermeable, impervious, inviolable, solid, thick, unpierceable

impenitent (ɪmˈpɛnɪtənt) *a.* not sorry or penitent; unrepentant —**imˈpenitence** *n.*

imperative (ɪmˈpɛrətɪv) *a.* **1.** necessary **2.** peremptory **3.** expressing command —*n.* **4.** imperative mood —**imˈperatively** *adv.*

imperceptible (ɪmpəˈsɛptɪbᵊl) *a.* too slight, subtle, gradual *etc.* to be perceived —**imperceptiˈbility** *n.* —**imperˈceptibly** *adv.*

imperfect (ɪmˈpɜːfɪkt) *a.* **1.** exhibiting or characterized by faults, mistakes *etc.;* defective **2.** not complete or finished; deficient **3.** *Gram.* denoting tense of verbs usu. used to describe continuous or repeated past actions or events **4.** *Law* legally unenforceable **5.** *Mus.* proceeding to dominant from tonic, subdominant or any chord other than dominant **6.** *Mus.* of or relating to all intervals other than fourth, fifth and octave —*n.* **7.** *Gram.* (verb in) imperfect tense —**imperˈfection** *n.* **1.** condition or quality of being imperfect **2.** fault, defect

imperial (ɪmˈpɪərɪəl) *a.* **1.** of empire or emperor **2.** majestic **3.** denoting weights and measures established by law in Brit. —**imˈperialism** *n.* **1.** extension of empire **2.** belief in colonial empire —**imˈperialist** *a./n.* —**imperialˈistic** *a.*

imperil (ɪmˈpɛrɪl) *vt.* bring into peril, endanger (**-ll-**)

imperious (ɪmˈpɪərɪəs) *a.* domineering; haughty; dictatorial

impermeable (ɪmˈpɜːmɪəbᵊl) *a.* (of substance) not allowing passage of fluid through interstices —**impermeaˈbility** *n.*

impersonal (ɪmˈpɜːsənᵊl) *a.* **1.** objective, having no personal significance **2.** devoid of human warmth, personality *etc.* **3.** (of verb) without personal subject —**impersonˈality** *n.*

impersonate (ɪmˈpɜːsəneɪt) *vt.* **1.** pretend to be (another person) **2.** imitate **3.** play the part of —**impersonˈation** *n.* —**imˈpersonator** *n.*

impertinent (ɪmˈpɜːtɪnənt) *a.* insolent, rude —**imˈpertinence** *n.* —**imˈpertinently** *adv.*

imperturbable (ɪmpɜːˈtɜːbəbᵊl) *a.* calm, not excitable —**imperˈturbably** *adv.*

impervious (ɪmˈpɜːvɪəs) *or* **imperviable** *a.* **1.** not affording passage **2.** (*oft. with* to) not receptive (to feeling, argument *etc.*) —**imˈperviously** *adv.* —**imˈperviousness** *n.*

impetigo (ɪmpɪˈtaɪgəʊ) *n.* contagious skin disease

impetuous (ɪmˈpɛtjʊəs) *a.* likely to act without consideration, rash —**impetuˈosity** *n.* —**imˈpetuously** *adv.*

impetus (ˈɪmpɪtəs) *n.* **1.** force with which body moves **2.** impulse

impinge (ɪmˈpɪndʒ) *vi.* **1.** (*usu. with* on *or* upon) encroach **2.** (*usu. with* on, against *or* upon) collide (with) —**imˈpingement** *n.*

impious (ˈɪmpɪəs) *a.* irreverent, profane, wicked —**impiety** (ɪmˈpaɪɪtɪ) *n.* **1.** lack of reverence or proper respect for a god **2.** any lack of proper respect **3.** impious act

THESAURUS

imperative 1. compulsory, crucial, essential, exigent, indispensable, insistent, obligatory, pressing, urgent, vital **2.** authoritative, autocratic, commanding, dictatorial, domineering, high-handed, imperious, lordly, magisterial, peremptory

imperceptible faint, fine, gradual, impalpable, inappreciable, inaudible, indiscernible, indistinguishable, infinitesimal, insensible, invisible, microscopic, minute, shadowy, slight, small, subtle, tiny, undetectable, unnoticeable

imperceptibly by a hair's-breadth, inappreciably, indiscernibly, invisibly, little by little, slowly, subtly, unnoticeably, unobtrusively, unseen

imperfect broken, damaged, defective, deficient, faulty, flawed, immature, impaired, incomplete, inexact, limited, partial, patchy, rudimentary, sketchy, undeveloped, unfinished

imperfection blemish, defect, deficiency, failing, fallibility, fault, flaw, foible, frailty, inadequacy, incompleteness, infirmity, insufficiency, peccadillo, shortcoming, stain, taint, weakness, weak point

imperial 1. kingly, majestic, princely, queenly, regal, royal, sovereign **2.** august, exalted, grand, great, high, imperious, lofty, magnificent, noble, superior, supreme

imperil endanger, expose, hazard, jeopardize, risk

impersonal bureaucratic, businesslike, cold, detached, dispassionate, formal, inhuman, neutral, remote

impersonate act, ape, do (*Inf.*), do an impression of, enact, imitate, masquerade as, mimic, pass oneself off as, personate, pose as (*Inf.*), take off (*Inf.*)

impersonation caricature, imitation, impression, mimicry, parody, takeoff (*Inf.*)

impertinence assurance, audacity, backchat (*Inf.*), boldness, brass neck (*Sl.*), brazenness, cheek (*Inf.*), disrespect, effrontery, forwardness, impudence, incivility, insolence, nerve (*Inf.*), pertness, presumption, rudeness, sauce (*Inf.*)

impertinent bold, brazen, cheeky (*Inf.*), discourteous, disrespectful, flip (*Inf.*), forward, fresh (*Inf.*), impolite, impudent, insolent, interfering, pert, presumptuous, rude, saucy (*Inf.*), uncivil, unmannerly

imperturbable calm, collected, complacent, composed, cool, equanimous, nerveless, sedate, self-possessed, stoical, tranquil, undisturbed, unexcitable, unflappable (*Inf.*), unmoved, unruffled

impervious 1. hermetic, impassable, impenetrable, impermeable, imperviable, invulnerable, resistant, sealed **2.** closed to, immune, invulnerable, proof against, unaffected by, unmoved by, unreceptive, unswayable, untouched by

impetuosity haste, hastiness, impulsiveness, precipitancy, precipitateness, rashness, vehemence, violence

impetuous ardent, eager, fierce, furious, hasty, headlong, impassioned, impulsive, passionate, precipitate, rash, spontaneous, spur-of-the-moment, unbridled, unplanned, unpremeditated, unreflecting, unrestrained, unthinking, vehement, violent

impetuously helter-skelter, impulsively, in the heat of the moment, on the spur of the moment, passionately, rashly, recklessly, spontaneously, unthinkingly, vehemently, without thinking

impetus 1. catalyst, goad, impulse, impulsion, incentive, motivation, push, spur, stimulus **2.** energy, force, momentum, power

impiety godlessness, iniquity, irreligion, irreverence,

implacable (ɪmˈplækəbᵊl) *a.* **1.** not to be appeased **2.** unyielding —**implacaˈbility** *n.*

implant (ɪmˈplɑːnt) *vt.* **1.** insert, fix —*n.* (ˈɪmplɑːnt) **2.** anything implanted, *esp.* surgically, such as tissue graft

implement (ˈɪmplɪmənt) *n.* **1.** tool, instrument, utensil —*vt.* (ˈɪmplɪmɛnt) **2.** carry out (instructions *etc.*); put into effect

implicate (ˈɪmplɪkeɪt) *vt.* **1.** involve, include **2.** imply **3.** *rare* entangle —**impliˈcation** *n.* something implied —**imˈplicit** *a.* **1.** implied but not expressed **2.** absolute and unreserved

implode (ɪmˈpləʊd) *v.* collapse inwards

implore (ɪmˈplɔː) *vt.* entreat earnestly

imply (ɪmˈplaɪ) *vt.* **1.** indicate by hint, suggest **2.** mean **(imˈplied, imˈplying)**

impolitic (ɪmˈpɒlɪtɪk) *a.* not politic or expedient —**imˈpoliticly** *adv.*

imponderable (ɪmˈpɒndərəbᵊl, -drəbᵊl) *a.* **1.** unable to be weighed or assessed —*n.* **2.** something difficult or impossible to assess —**imponderaˈbility** *n.* —**imˈponderably** *adv.*

import (ɪmˈpɔːt, ˈɪmpɔːt) *vt.* **1.** bring in, introduce (*esp.* goods from foreign country) **2.** imply —*n.* (ˈɪmpɔːt) **3.** thing imported **4.** meaning **5.** importance **6.** C *sl.* sportsman not native to area where he plays —**imˈportable** *a.* —**imporˈtation** *n.* —**imˈporter** *n.*

important (ɪmˈpɔːtᵊnt) *a.* **1.** of great consequence **2.** momentous **3.** pompous —**imˈportance** *n.* —**imˈportantly** *adv.*

importune (ɪmˈpɔːtjuːn) *vt.* request, demand of (someone) persistently —**imˈportunate** *a.* persistent —**imˈportunately** *adv.* —**imporˈtunity** *n.*

impose (ɪmˈpəʊz) *vt.* **1.** levy (tax, duty *etc.*) —*vi.* **2.** (*usu. with* on *or* upon) take advantage (of), practise deceit (on) —**imˈposing** *a.* impressive —**impoˈsition** *n.* **1.** that which is imposed **2.** tax **3.** burden **4.** deception —ˈ**impost** *n.* duty, tax on imports

impossible (ɪmˈpɒsəbᵊl) *a.* **1.** incapable of being done or experienced **2.** absurd **3.** unreasonable —**impossiˈbility** *n.* —**imˈpossibly** *adv.*

THESAURUS

profaneness, profanity, sacrilege, sinfulness, ungodliness, unholiness, unrighteousness, wickedness

impinge 1. encroach, invade, make inroads, obtrude, trespass, violate **2.** clash, collide, dash, strike

impious blasphemous, godless, iniquitous, irreligious, irreverent, profane, sacrilegious, sinful, ungodly, unholy, unrighteous, wicked

implacability implacableness, inexorability, inflexibility, intractability, mercilessness, pitilessness, relentlessness, ruthlessness, unforgivingness, vengefulness

implacable cruel, inexorable, inflexible, intractable, merciless, pitiless, rancorous, relentless, remorseless, ruthless, unappeasable, unbending, uncompromising, unforgiving, unrelenting, unyielding

implant embed, fix, graft, ingraft, insert, place, plant, root, sow

implement 1. *n.* agent, apparatus, appliance, device, gadget, instrument, tool, utensil **2.** *v.* bring about, carry out, complete, effect, enforce, execute, fulfil, perform, put into action *or* effect, realize

implicate associate, compromise, concern, embroil, entangle, imply, include, incriminate, inculpate, involve, mire, tie up with

implication conclusion, inference, innuendo, meaning, overtone, presumption, ramification, significance, signification, suggestion

implicit 1. contained, implied, inferred, inherent, latent, tacit, taken for granted, undeclared, understood, unspoken **2.** absolute, constant, entire, firm, fixed, full, steadfast, total, unhesitating, unqualified, unreserved, unshakable, unshaken, wholehearted

implied hinted at, implicit, indirect, inherent, insinuated, suggested, tacit, undeclared, unexpressed, unspoken, unstated

implore beg, beseech, conjure, crave, entreat, go on bended knee to, importune, plead with, pray, solicit, supplicate

imply 1. connote, give (someone) to understand, hint, insinuate, intimate, signify, suggest **2.** betoken, denote, entail, evidence, import, include, indicate, involve, mean, point to, presuppose

impolite bad-mannered, boorish, churlish, discourteous, disrespectful, ill-bred, ill-mannered, indecorous, indelicate, insolent, loutish, rough, rude, uncivil, ungallant, ungentlemanly, ungracious, unladylike, unmannerly, unrefined

import *n.* **1.** bearing, drift, gist, implication, intention, meaning, message, purport, sense, significance, thrust **2.** consequence, importance, magnitude, moment, significance, substance, weight ~*v.* **3.** bring in, introduce, land

importance 1. concern, consequence, import, interest, moment, momentousness, significance, substance, value, weight **2.** distinction, eminence, esteem, influence, mark, pre-eminence, prestige, prominence, standing, status, usefulness, worth

important 1. far-reaching, grave, large, material, meaningful, momentous, of substance, primary, salient, serious, signal, significant, substantial, urgent, weighty **2.** eminent, foremost, high-level, high-ranking, influential, leading, notable, noteworthy, of note, outstanding, powerful, pre-eminent, prominent, seminal

importunate burning, clamant, clamorous, demanding, dogged, earnest, exigent, insistent, persistent, pertinacious, pressing, solicitous, troublesome, urgent

impose 1. decree, establish, exact, fix, institute, introduce, lay, levy, ordain, place, promulgate, put, set **2.** *With* **on** *or* **upon a.** abuse, exploit, play on, take advantage of, use **b.** con (*Inf.*), deceive, dupe, hoodwink, pull the wool over (somebody's) eyes, trick

imposing august, commanding, dignified, effective, grand, impressive, majestic, stately, striking

imposition 1. artifice, cheating, con (*Inf.*), deception, dissimulation, fraud, hoax, imposture, stratagem, trickery **2.** burden, charge, constraint, duty, levy, tax

impossibility hopelessness, impracticability, inability, inconceivability

impossible 1. beyond one, beyond the bounds of possibility, hopeless, impracticable, inconceivable, not to be thought of, out of the question, unachievable, unattainable, unobtainable, unthinkable **2.** absurd, inadmissible, insoluble, intolerable, ludi-

impost (ˈɪmpəʊst) *n. Archit.* member at top of column that supports arch

impostor *or* **imposter** (ɪmˈpɒstə) *n.* deceiver, one who assumes false identity —**imˈposture** *n.*

impotent (ˈɪmpətənt) *a.* **1.** powerless **2.** (of males) incapable of sexual intercourse —**ˈimpotence** *n.* —**ˈimpotently** *adv.*

impound (ɪmˈpaʊnd) *vt.* **1.** take legal possession of and, oft., place in a pound (cars, animals *etc.*) **2.** confiscate

impoverish *or* **empoverish** (ɪmˈpɒvərɪʃ) *vt.* make poor or weak —**imˈpoverishment** *or* **emˈpoverishment** *n.*

impracticable (ɪmˈpræktɪkəbᵊl) *a.* **1.** incapable of being put into practice or accomplished **2.** unsuitable for desired use —**impracticaˈbility** *n.* —**imˈpracticably** *adv.*

impractical (ɪmˈpræktɪkᵊl) *a.* **1.** not practical or workable **2.** not gifted with practical skills —**impractiˈcality** *n.* —**imˈpractically** *adv.*

imprecation (ɪmprɪˈkeɪʃən) *n.* **1.** invoking of evil **2.** curse —**ˈimprecate** *v.*

impregnable (ɪmˈprɛgnəbᵊl) *a.* **1.** proof against attack **2.** unassailable **3.** unable to be broken into —**impregnaˈbility** *n.* —**imˈpregnably** *adv.*

impregnate (ˈɪmprɛgneɪt) *vt.* **1.** saturate, infuse **2.** make pregnant —**impregˈnation** *n.*

impresario (ɪmprəˈsɑːrɪəʊ) *n.* organizer of public entertainment; manager of opera, ballet *etc.* (*pl.* **-s**)

impress[1] (ɪmˈprɛs) *vt.* **1.** affect deeply, usu. favourably **2.** imprint, stamp **3.** fix —*n.* (ˈɪmprɛs) **4.** act of impressing **5.** mark impressed —**impressiˈbility** *n.* —**imˈpressible** *a.* —**imˈpression** *n.* **1.** effect produced, *esp.* on mind **2.** notion, belief **3.** imprint **4.** a printing **5.** total of copies printed at once **6.** printed copy —**impressionaˈbility** *n.* —**imˈpressionable** *a.* susceptible to external influences —**imˈpressionism** *n.* art style that renders general effect without detail —**imˈpressionist** *n.* —**impressionˈistic** *a.* —**imˈpressive** *a.* making deep impression

impress[2] (ɪmˈprɛs) *vt.* press into service

imprest (ɪmˈprɛst) *vt.* **1.** advance on loan by government —*n.* **2.** money advanced by government

imprimatur (ɪmprɪˈmeɪtə, -ˈmɑː-) *n.* licence to print book *etc.*

imprint (ˈɪmprɪnt) *n.* **1.** mark made by pressure **2.** characteristic mark **3.** publisher's or printer's name and address in book *etc.* —*vt.* (ɪmˈprɪnt) **4.** produce (mark) on (surface) by pressure, printing or stamping **5.** fix in mind

imprison (ɪmˈprɪzən) *vt.* put in prison —**imˈprisonment** *n.*

improbity (ɪmˈprəʊbɪtɪ) *n.* dishonesty, wickedness, unscrupulousness

impromptu (ɪmˈprɒmptjuː) *adv./a.* **1.** extempore; unrehearsed —*n.* **2.** improvisation

THESAURUS

crous, outrageous, preposterous, unacceptable, unanswerable, ungovernable, unreasonable, unsuitable, unworkable

impostor charlatan, cheat, deceiver, fake, fraud, hypocrite, impersonator, knave (*Archaic*), phoney (*Sl.*), pretender, quack, rogue, sham, trickster

impotence disability, enervation, feebleness, frailty, helplessness, inability, inadequacy, incapacity, incompetence, ineffectiveness, inefficacy, inefficiency, infirmity, paralysis, powerlessness, uselessness, weakness

impotent disabled, emasculate, enervated, feeble, frail, helpless, incapable, incapacitated, incompetent, ineffective, infirm, nerveless, paralysed, powerless, unable, unmanned, weak

impoverish **1.** bankrupt, beggar, break, ruin **2.** deplete, diminish, drain, exhaust, pauperize, reduce, sap, use up, wear out

impracticability futility, hopelessness, impossibility, impracticality, unsuitableness, unworkability, uselessness

impracticable **1.** impossible, out of the question, unachievable, unattainable, unfeasible, unworkable **2.** awkward, impractical, inapplicable, inconvenient, unserviceable, unsuitable, useless

impractical impossible, impracticable, inoperable, nonviable, unrealistic, unserviceable, unworkable, visionary, wild

impracticality hopelessness, impossibility, inapplicability, unworkability

imprecise ambiguous, blurred round the edges, careless, equivocal, estimated, fluctuating, hazy, ill-defined, inaccurate, indefinite, indeterminate, inexact, inexplicit, loose, rough, sloppy (*Inf.*), vague, wide of the mark, woolly

impregnable immovable, impenetrable, indestructible, invincible, invulnerable, secure, strong, unassailable, unbeatable, unconquerable, unshakable

impregnate **1.** fill, imbrue (*Rare*), imbue, infuse, percolate, permeate, pervade, saturate, soak, steep, suffuse **2.** fecundate, fertilize, fructify, get with child, inseminate, make pregnant

impress **1.** affect, excite, grab (*Sl.*), influence, inspire, make an impression, move, stir, strike, sway, touch **2.** *Often with* **on** *or* **upon** bring home to, emphasize, fix, inculcate, instil into, stress **3.** emboss, engrave, imprint, indent, mark, print, stamp

impression **1.** effect, feeling, impact, influence, reaction, sway **2.** belief, concept, conviction, fancy, feeling, funny feeling (*Inf.*), hunch, idea, memory, notion, opinion, recollection, sense, suspicion **3.** brand, dent, hollow, impress, imprint, indentation, mark, outline, stamp, stamping **4.** edition, imprinting, issue, printing

impressionable feeling, gullible, ingenuous, open, receptive, responsive, sensitive, suggestible, susceptible, vulnerable

impressive affecting, exciting, forcible, moving, powerful, stirring, touching

imprint **1.** *n.* impression, indentation, mark, print, sign, stamp **2.** *v.* engrave, establish, etch, fix, impress, print, stamp

imprison confine, constrain, detain, immure, incarcerate, intern, jail, lock up, put away, put under lock and key, send down (*Inf.*), send to prison

imprisonment confinement, custody, detention, durance (*Archaic*), duress, incarceration, internment, porridge (*Sl.*)

improbable doubtful, dubious, fanciful, far-fetched,

improper (ɪmˈprɒpə) *a.* 1. lacking propriety; not seemly or fitting 2. unsuitable for certain use or occasion; inappropriate 3. irregular; abnormal —**impropriety** (ɪmprəˈpraɪɪtɪ) *n.* 1. lack of propriety; indecency 2. improper act or use 3. state of being improper —**improper fraction** fraction in which numerator is greater than denominator, as 7/6

improve (ɪmˈpru:v) *v.* make or become better in quality, value, health *etc.* —**imˈprovable** *a.* —**imˈprovement** *n.* —**imˈprover** *n.*

improvident (ɪmˈprɒvɪdənt) *a.* 1. thriftless; imprudent 2. negligent —**imˈprovidence** *n.*

improvise (ˈɪmprəvaɪz) *v.* 1. perform or make quickly from materials at hand 2. perform (poem, piece of music *etc.*), composing as one goes along —**improviˈsation** *n.*

impudent (ˈɪmpjʊdənt) *a.* disrespectful, impertinent —**ˈimpudence** *n.* —**ˈimpudently** *adv.*

impugn (ɪmˈpju:n) *vt.* call in question, challenge

impulse (ˈɪmpʌls) *n.* 1. sudden inclination to act 2. sudden application of force 3. motion caused by it 4. stimulation of nerve moving muscle —**imˈpulsion** *n.* impulse —**imˈpulsive** *a.* given to acting without reflection, rash

impunity (ɪmˈpju:nɪtɪ) *n.* freedom, exemption from injurious consequences or punishment

impurity (ɪmˈpjʊərɪtɪ) *n.* 1. quality of being impure 2. impure thing or element 3. *Electron.* small quantity of element added to pure semiconductor crystal to control its electrical conductivity

impute (ɪmˈpju:t) *vt.* ascribe, attribute —**imputaˈbility** *n.* —**impuˈtation** *n.* 1. that which is imputed as a charge or fault 2. reproach, censure

in (ɪn) *prep.* 1. expresses inclusion within limits of space, time, circumstance, sphere *etc.* —*adv.* 2. in or into some state, place *etc.* 3. *inf.* in vogue *etc.* —*a.* 4. *inf.* fashionable —**in for** about to be affected by —**ins and outs** intricacies, complications; details

In *Chem.* indium

IN Indiana

in. inch(es)

in-[1], **il-**, **im-**, *or* **ir-** (*comb. form*) 1. not; non-, as in *incredible, illegal, imperfect, irregular* 2. lack of, as in *inexperience.* See words listed at foot of relevant pages

THESAURUS

implausible, questionable, unbelievable, uncertain, unconvincing, unlikely, weak

impromptu 1. *adj.* ad-lib, extemporaneous, extempore, extemporized, improvised, offhand, off the cuff (*Inf.*), spontaneous, unpremeditated, unprepared, unrehearsed, unscripted, unstudied 2. *adv.* ad lib, off the cuff (*Inf.*), off the top of one's head (*Inf.*), on the spur of the moment, spontaneously, without preparation

improper 1. impolite, indecent, indecorous, indelicate, off-colour, risqué, smutty, suggestive, unbecoming, unfitting, unseemly, untoward, vulgar 2. ill-timed, inapplicable, inapposite, inappropriate, inapt, incongruous, infelicitous, inopportune, malapropos, out of place, uncalled-for, unfit, unseasonable, unsuitable, unsuited, unwarranted 3. abnormal, erroneous, false, inaccurate, incorrect, irregular, wrong

impropriety 1. bad taste, immodesty, incongruity, indecency, indecorum, unsuitability, vulgarity 2. blunder, faux pas, gaffe, gaucherie, mistake, slip, solecism

improve 1. advance, ameliorate, amend, augment, better, correct, help, mend, polish, rectify, touch up, upgrade 2. develop, enhance, gain strength, increase, look up (*Inf.*), make strides, perk up, pick up, progress, rally, reform, rise, take a turn for the better (*Inf.*), take on a new lease of life (*Inf.*) 3. convalesce, gain ground, gain strength, grow better, make progress, mend, recover, recuperate, turn the corner

improvement 1. advancement, amelioration, amendment, augmentation, betterment, correction, gain, rectification 2. advance, development, enhancement, furtherance, increase, progress, rally, recovery, reformation, rise, upswing

improvisation ad-lib, ad-libbing, expedient, extemporizing, impromptu, invention, makeshift, spontaneity

improvise 1. ad-lib, coin, extemporize, invent, play it by ear (*Inf.*), speak off the cuff (*Inf.*) 2. concoct, contrive, devise, make do, throw together

imprudent careless, foolhardy, foolish, heedless, ill-advised, ill-considered, ill-judged, impolitic, improvident, incautious, inconsiderate, indiscreet, injudicious, irresponsible, overhasty, rash, reckless, temerarious, unthinking, unwise

impudence assurance, audacity, backchat (*Inf.*), boldness, brass neck (*Sl.*), bumptiousness, cheek (*Inf.*), effrontery, face (*Inf.*), impertinence, insolence, lip (*Sl.*), nerve (*Inf.*), pertness, presumption, rudeness, sauciness, shamelessness

impudent audacious, bold, bold-faced, brazen, bumptious, cheeky (*Inf.*), cocky (*Inf.*), forward, fresh (*Inf.*), immodest, impertinent, insolent, pert, presumptuous, rude, saucy (*Inf.*), shameless

impulse 1. catalyst, force, impetus, momentum, movement, pressure, push, stimulus, surge, thrust 2. *Fig.* caprice, drive, feeling, incitement, inclination, influence, instinct, motive, notion, passion, resolve, urge, whim, wish

impulsive devil-may-care, emotional, hasty, headlong, impetuous, instinctive, intuitive, passionate, precipitate, quick, rash, spontaneous, unconsidered, unpredictable, unpremeditated

impunity dispensation, exemption, freedom, immunity, liberty, licence, nonliability, permission, security

impure 1. admixed, adulterated, alloyed, debased, mixed, unrefined 2. contaminated, defiled, dirty, filthy, foul, infected, polluted, sullied, tainted, unclean, unwholesome, vitiated 3. carnal, coarse, corrupt, gross, immodest, immoral, indecent, indelicate, lascivious, lewd, licentious, lustful, obscene, prurient, ribald, salacious, smutty, unchaste, unclean

imputation accusation, ascription, aspersion, attribution, blame, censure, charge, insinuation, reproach, slander, slur

impute accredit, ascribe, assign, attribute, credit, lay at the door of, refer, set down to

inability disability, disqualification, impotence, inadequacy, incapability, incapacity, incompetence, ineptitude, powerlessness

in-[2], **il-**, **im-**, *or* **ir-** (*comb. form*) **1.** in; into; towards; within; on, as in *infiltrate, immigrate* **2.** having intensive or causative function, as in *inflame, imperil*

in absentia (ɪn æbˈsɛntɪə) *Lat.* in absence of (someone indicated)

inadvertent (ɪnədˈvɜːtᵊnt) *a.* **1.** not attentive **2.** negligent **3.** unintentional —**inadˈvertence** *or* **inadˈvertency** *n.* —**inadˈvertently** *adv.*

inalienable (ɪnˈeɪljənəbᵊl) *a.* not able to be transferred to another —**inalienaˈbility** *n.*

inamorata (ɪnæməˈrɑːtə) *or* (*masc.*) **inamorato** (ɪnæməˈrɑːtəʊ) *n.* person with whom one is in love; lover (*pl.* **-s**)

inane (ɪˈneɪn) *a.* foolish, silly, vacant —**inanition** (ɪnəˈnɪʃən) *n.* **1.** exhaustion **2.** silliness —**inanity** (ɪˈnænɪtɪ) *n.*

inanimate (ɪnˈænɪmɪt) *a.* **1.** lacking qualities of living beings **2.** appearing dead **3.** lacking vitality

inapposite (ɪnˈæpəzɪt) *a.* not appropriate or pertinent

inapt (ɪnˈæpt) *a.* **1.** not apt or fitting **2.** lacking skill; inept —**inˈaptitude** *or* **inˈaptness** *n.*

inasmuch as (ɪnəzˈmʌtʃ) seeing that

inaˈbility
inacˈcessible
inˈaccurate
inˈadequate
inadˈmissible
inadˈvisable
inˈapplicable
inapˈpropriate
inarˈticulate
inatˈtentive
inˈaudible
inˈcapable
inˈcomparable
incomˈpatible
incomˈplete
incompreˈhensible
inconˈclusive
inconˈsiderable
inconˈsiderate
inconˈsistent
inconˈsolable
inconˈspicuous
inˈconstant
inconˈtestable
inˈcontinent
inconˈvenience
inconˈvenient
incorˈrect
incorˈruptible
inˈcurable
indeˈcipherable
indeˈcision
indeˈcisive
indeˈfinable
inˈdefinite
indeˈstructible
indisˈcernible
indisˈputable
indisˈtinct
indisˈtinguishable
inefˈficient
inˈelegant
inˈequitable
inesˈsential
inexˈact
inexˈcusable
inexˈpedient
inexˈpensive
inexˈperience
inˈexpert
inˈfertile
inferˈtility
inˈformal
inˈfrequent
inˈgratitude
inˈhospitable
injuˈdicious
inofˈfensive
inˈsanitary
inˈsensitive
inˈseparable
insigˈnificant
insinˈcere
inˈsoluble
instaˈbility
insubˈstantial
insufˈficient
insurˈmountable
inˈtangible
inˈtolerable
inˈtolerant
inˈvariable

THESAURUS

inaccessible impassable, out of reach, out of the way, remote, unapproachable, unattainable, un-get-at-able (*Inf.*), unreachable

inaccurate careless, defective, discrepant, erroneous, faulty, imprecise, incorrect, in error, inexact, mistaken, out, unfaithful, unreliable, unsound, wide of the mark, wild, wrong

inadequate 1. defective, deficient, faulty, imperfect, incommensurate, incomplete, insubstantial, insufficient, meagre, niggardly, scanty, short, sketchy, skimpy, sparse **2.** found wanting, inapt, incapable, incompetent, not up to scratch (*Inf.*), unequal, unfitted, unqualified

inadvertently 1. carelessly, heedlessly, in an unguarded moment, negligently, thoughtlessly, unguardedly, unthinkingly **2.** accidentally, by accident, by mistake, involuntarily, mistakenly, unintentionally, unwittingly

inadvisable ill-advised, impolitic, imprudent, inexpedient, injudicious, unwise

inane asinine, daft (*Inf.*), devoid of intelligence, empty, fatuous, frivolous, futile, idiotic, imbecilic, mindless, puerile, senseless, silly, stupid, trifling, unintelligent, vacuous, vain, vapid, worthless

inanimate cold, dead, defunct, extinct, inactive, inert, insensate, insentient, lifeless, quiescent, soulless, spiritless

inapplicable inapposite, inappropriate, inapt, irrelevant, unsuitable, unsuited

inappropriate disproportionate, ill-fitted, ill-suited, ill-timed, improper, incongruous, malapropos, out of place, tasteless, unbecoming, unbefitting, unfit, unfitting, unseemly, unsuitable, untimely

inapt 1. ill-fitted, ill-suited, inapposite, inappropriate, infelicitous, unsuitable, unsuited **2.** awkward, clumsy, dull, gauche, incompetent, inept, inexpert, maladroit, slow, stupid

inarticulate 1. blurred, incoherent, incomprehensible, indistinct, muffled, mumbled, unclear, unintelligible **2.** dumb, mute, silent, speechless, tongue-tied, unspoken, unuttered, unvoiced, voiceless, wordless **3.** faltering, halting, hesitant, poorly spoken

inattentive absent-minded, careless, distracted, distrait, dreamy, heedless, inadvertent, neglectful, negligent, preoccupied, regardless, remiss, thoughtless, unheeding, unmindful, unobservant, vague

inaugurate (ɪnˈɔːgjʊreɪt) *vt.* **1.** begin, initiate the use of, *esp.* with ceremony **2.** admit to office —**inˈaugural** *a.* —**inˈaugurally** *adv.* —**inauguˈration** *n.* **1.** act of inaugurating **2.** ceremony to celebrate the initiation or admittance of

inauspicious (ɪnɔːˈspɪʃəs) *a.* not auspicious; unlucky; unfavourable —**inausˈpiciously** *adv.*

inboard (ˈɪnbɔːd) *a.* inside hull or bulwarks

inborn (ˈɪnˈbɔːn) *a.* existing from birth; inherent

inbreed (ˈɪnˈbriːd) *v.* breed from union of closely related individuals (**ˈinˈbred** *pt./pp.*) —**ˈinˈbred** *a.* **1.** produced as result of inbreeding **2.** inborn, ingrained —**ˈinˈbreeding** *n.*

inc. 1. inclusive **2.** incorporated **3.** increase

incalculable (ɪnˈkælkjʊləbᵊl) *a.* beyond calculation; very great

in camera in secret or private session

incandescent (ɪnkænˈdɛsᵊnt) *a.* **1.** glowing with heat, shining **2.** (of artificial light) produced by glowing filament —**incanˈdesce** *vi.* glow —**incanˈdescence** *n.*

incantation (ɪnkænˈteɪʃən) *n.* magic spell or formula, charm

incapacitate (ɪnkəˈpæsɪteɪt) *vt.* **1.** disable; make unfit **2.** disqualify —**incaˈpacity** *n.*

incarcerate (ɪnˈkɑːsəreɪt) *vt.* imprison —**incarceˈration** *n.* —**inˈcarcerator** *n.*

incarnate (ɪnˈkɑːneɪt) *vt.* **1.** embody in flesh, *esp.* in human form —*a.* (ɪnˈkɑːnɪt, -neɪt) **2.** embodied in flesh, in human form **3.** typified —**incarˈnation** *n.*

incendiary (ɪnˈsɛndɪərɪ) *a.* **1.** of malicious setting on fire of property **2.** creating strife, violence *etc.* **3.** designed to cause fires —*n.* **4.** fire raiser **5.** agitator **6.** bomb filled with inflammatory substance —**inˈcendiarism** *n.*

incense[1] (ˈɪnsɛns) *n.* **1.** gum, spice giving perfume when burned **2.** its smoke —*vt.* **3.** burn incense to **4.** perfume with it

incense[2] (ɪnˈsɛns) *vt.* enrage

incentive (ɪnˈsɛntɪv) *n.* **1.** something that arouses to effort or action **2.** stimulus

inception (ɪnˈsɛpʃən) *n.* beginning

incessant (ɪnˈsɛsᵊnt) *a.* unceasing

incest (ˈɪnsɛst) *n.* sexual intercourse between two people too closely related to marry —**inˈcestuous** *a.*

inch[1] (ɪntʃ) *n.* **1.** one twelfth of foot, or 0.0254 metre —*v.* **2.** move very slowly

inch[2] (ɪntʃ) *n. Scot., Irish* small island

inchoate (ɪnˈkəʊeɪt, -ˈkəʊɪt) *a.* **1.** just begun **2.** undeveloped

incident (ˈɪnsɪdənt) *n.* **1.** event, occurrence —*a.* (*usu. with* to) **2.** naturally attaching (to) **3.** striking, falling (upon) —**ˈincidence** *n.* **1.** degree, extent or frequency of occurrence **2.** a falling on, or affecting —**inciˈdental** *a.* occurring as a minor part or an inevitable accompaniment or by chance —**inciˈdentally** *adv.* **1.** by chance **2.** by the way —**inciˈdentals** *pl.n.* accompanying items —**incidental music** background music for film *etc.*

THESAURUS

inaudible indistinct, low, mumbling, out of earshot, stifled, unheard

inaugural dedicatory, first, initial, introductory, maiden, opening

inaugurate 1. begin, commence, get under way, initiate, institute, introduce, kick off (*Inf.*), launch, originate, set in motion, set up, usher in **2.** induct, install, instate, invest **3.** commission, dedicate, open, ordain

inauguration 1. initiation, institution, launch, launching, opening, setting up **2.** induction, installation, investiture

inauspicious bad, black, discouraging, ill-omened, ominous, unfavourable, unfortunate, unlucky, unpromising, unpropitious, untoward

inborn congenital, connate, hereditary, inbred, ingrained, inherent, inherited, innate, instinctive, intuitive, native, natural

inbred constitutional, deep-seated, ingrained, inherent, innate, native, natural

incalculable boundless, countless, enormous, immense, incomputable, inestimable, infinite, innumerable, limitless, measureless, numberless, uncountable, untold, vast, without number

incantation abracadabra, chant, charm, conjuration, formula, hex (*U.S. dialect*), invocation, spell

incapable 1. feeble, inadequate, incompetent, ineffective, inept, inexpert, insufficient, not equal to, not up to, unfit, unfitted, unqualified, weak **2.** helpless, impotent, powerless, unable, unfit

incapacitate cripple, disable, disqualify, immobilize, lay up (*Inf.*), paralyse, prostrate, put out of action (*Inf.*), scupper (*Brit. sl.*), unfit (*Rare*)

incapacity disqualification, feebleness, impotence, inability, inadequacy, incapability, incompetency, ineffectiveness, powerlessness, unfitness, weakness

incarcerate commit, confine, coop up, detain, gaol, immure, impound, imprison, intern, jail, lock up, put under lock and key, restrain, restrict, send down (*Brit.*), throw in jail

incarnate 1. in bodily form, in human form, in the flesh, made flesh **2.** embodied, personified, typified

incarnation avatar, bodily form, embodiment, exemplification, impersonation, manifestation, personification, type

incendiary *adj.* **1.** dissentious, inflammatory, provocative, rabble-rousing, seditious, subversive ~*n.* **2.** arsonist, firebug (*Inf.*), fire raiser, pyromaniac **3.** agitator, demagogue, firebrand, insurgent, rabble-rouser, revolutionary

incense[1] *n.* aroma, balm, bouquet, fragrance, perfume, redolence, scent

incense[2] *v.* anger, enrage, exasperate, excite, get one's hackles up, inflame, infuriate, irritate, madden, make one's blood boil (*Inf.*), make one see red (*Inf.*), make one's hackles rise, provoke, raise one's hackles, rile (*Inf.*)

incentive bait, carrot (*Inf.*), encouragement, enticement, goad, impetus, impulse, inducement, lure, motivation, motive, spur, stimulant, stimulus

inception beginning, birth, commencement, dawn, inauguration, initiation, kickoff (*Inf.*), origin, outset, rise, start

incessant ceaseless, constant, continual, continuous, endless, eternal, everlasting, interminable, never-ending, nonstop, perpetual, persistent, relentless,

incinerate (ɪnˈsɪnəreɪt) *vt.* burn up completely; reduce to ashes —**incinerˈation** *n.* —**inˈcinerator** *n.* furnace or apparatus for incinerating something, *esp.* refuse

incipient (ɪnˈsɪpɪənt) *a.* beginning

incise (ɪnˈsaɪz) *vt.* produce (lines *etc.*) by cutting into surface of (something) with sharp tool —**incision** (ɪnˈsɪʒən) *n.* **1.** act of incising **2.** cut, gash, notch **3.** cut made with knife during surgical operation —**incisive** (ɪnˈsaɪsɪv) *a.* **1.** (of remark *etc.*) keen, biting **2.** sharp —**inˈcisor** *n.* cutting tooth

incite (ɪnˈsaɪt) *vt.* stir up or provoke to action —**inciˈtation** *or* **inˈcitement** *n.*

incl. **1.** including **2.** inclusive

inclement (ɪnˈklɛmənt) *a.* (of weather) stormy, severe, cold —**inˈclemency** *n.*

incline (ɪnˈklaɪn) *v.* **1.** lean, slope **2.** (cause to) be disposed —*vt.* **3.** bend or lower (head *etc.*) —*n.* (ˈɪnklaɪn, ɪnˈklaɪn) **4.** slope —**inclination** (ɪnklɪˈneɪʃən) *n.* **1.** liking, tendency, preference **2.** sloping surface **3.** degree of deviation —**inclined plane** plane whose angle to horizontal is less than right angle

inclose (ɪnˈkləʊz) *vt. see* ENCLOSE

include (ɪnˈkluːd) *vt.* **1.** have as (part of) contents **2.** comprise **3.** add in **4.** take in —**inˈclusion** *n.* —**inˈclusive** *a.* including (everything) —**inˈclusively** *adv.*

incognito (ɪnkɒgˈniːtəʊ) *or* (*fem.*) **incognita** *adv./a.* **1.** under assumed identity —*n.* **2.** assumed identity (*pl.* **-s**)

incognizant (ɪnˈkɒgnɪzənt) *a.* unaware —**inˈcognizance** *n.*

incoherent (ɪnkəʊˈhɪərənt) *a.* **1.** lacking clarity, disorganized **2.** inarticulate —**incoˈherence** *n.* —**incoˈherently** *adv.*

income (ˈɪnkʌm, ˈɪnkəm) *n.* **1.** amount of money, *esp.* annual, from salary, investments *etc.* **2.** receipts —**income tax** personal tax levied on annual income

incoming (ˈɪnkʌmɪŋ) *a.* **1.** coming in **2.** about to come into office; next **3.** (of interest *etc.*) being received; accruing

incommensurable (ɪnkəˈmɛnʃərəbᵊl) *a.* **1.** incapable of being measured comparatively **2.** incommensurate **3.** *Maths.* having no common factor other than 1 —*n.* **4.** something incommensurable —**incommensuraˈbility** *n.*

incommensurate (ɪnkəˈmɛnʃərɪt) *a.* **1.** disproportionate **2.** incommensurable

incommode (ɪnkəˈməʊd) *vt.* trouble, inconvenience, disturb —**incomˈmodious** *a.* **1.** cramped **2.** inconvenient

incommunicado (ɪnkəmjuːnɪˈkɑːdəʊ) *a./adv.* deprived (by force or by choice) of communication with others

incomparable (ɪnˈkɒmpərəbᵊl, -prəbᵊl) *a.* **1.** beyond or above comparison; matchless; unequalled **2.** lacking basis for comparison; not having qualities or features that can be compared —**incomparaˈbility** *or* **inˈcomparableness** *n.* —**inˈcomparably** *adv.*

THESAURUS

unbroken, unceasing, unending, unrelenting, unremitting

incident adventure, circumstance, episode, event, fact, happening, matter, occasion, occurrence

incidental 1. accidental, casual, chance, fortuitous, odd, random 2. ancillary, minor, nonessential, occasional, secondary, subordinate, subsidiary

incidentally 1. accidentally, by chance, casually, fortuitously 2. by the bye, by the way, in passing, parenthetically

incidentals contingencies, extras, minutiae, odds and ends

incinerate burn up, carbonize, char, consume by fire, cremate, reduce to ashes

incipient beginning, commencing, developing, embryonic, inceptive, inchoate, nascent, originating, starting

incise carve, chisel, cut (into), engrave, etch

incision cut, gash, notch, opening, slash, slit

incisive 1. acute, keen, penetrating, perspicacious, piercing, trenchant 2. acid, biting, caustic, cutting, mordant, sarcastic, sardonic, satirical, severe, sharp

incite agitate for *or* against, animate, drive, egg on, encourage, excite, foment, goad, impel, inflame, instigate, prompt, provoke, put up to, rouse, set on, spur, stimulate, stir up, urge, whip up

incitement agitation, encouragement, goad, impetus, impulse, inducement, instigation, motivation, motive, prompting, provocation, spur, stimulus

inclemency bitterness, boisterousness, rawness, rigour, roughness, severity, storminess

inclement bitter, boisterous, foul, harsh, intemperate, rigorous, rough, severe, stormy, tempestuous

inclination 1. affection, aptitude, bent, bias, desire, disposition, fancy, fondness, leaning, liking, partiality, penchant, predilection, predisposition, prejudice, proclivity, proneness, propensity, stomach, taste, tendency, turn, turn of mind, wish 2. angle, bend, bending, deviation, gradient, incline, leaning, pitch, slant, slope, tilt

incline *v.* 1. be disposed *or* predisposed, bias, influence, persuade, predispose, prejudice, sway, tend, turn 2. bend, bow, lower, nod, stoop 3. bend, bevel, cant, deviate, diverge, lean, slant, slope, tend, tilt, tip, veer ~*n.* 4. acclivity, ascent, declivity, descent, dip, grade, gradient, ramp, rise, slope

include 1. comprehend, comprise, contain, cover, embody, embrace, encompass, incorporate, involve, subsume, take in, take into account 2. add, allow for, build in, count, enter, insert, introduce, number among

inclusion addition, incorporation, insertion

inclusive across-the-board, all-embracing, all in, all together, blanket, catch-all (*Chiefly U.S.*), comprehensive, full, general, *in toto*, overall, sweeping, umbrella, without exception

incognito disguised, in disguise, under an assumed name, unknown, unrecognized

incoherence disconnectedness, disjointedness, inarticulateness, unintelligibility

incoherent confused, disconnected, disjointed, disordered, inarticulate, inconsistent, jumbled, loose, muddled, rambling, stammering, stuttering, unconnected, uncoordinated, unintelligible, wandering, wild

income earnings, gains, interest, means, pay, proceeds, profits, receipts, revenue, salary, takings, wages

incompetent (ɪnˈkɒmpɪtənt) *a.* **1.** not possessing necessary ability, skill *etc.* to do or carry out task; incapable **2.** marked by lack of ability, skill *etc.* **3.** *Law* not legally qualified —*n.* **4.** incompetent person —**inˈcompetence** *or* **inˈcompetency** *n.*

incongruous (ɪnˈkɒŋgrʊəs) *or* **incongruent** *a.* **1.** not appropriate **2.** inconsistent, absurd —**inconˈgruity** *n.* —**inˈcongruously** *adv.*

inconsequential (ɪnkɒnsɪˈkwɛnʃəl) *or* **inconsequent** (ɪnˈkɒnsɪkwənt) *a.* **1.** illogical **2.** irrelevant; trivial

incontrovertible (ɪnkɒntrəˈvɜːtəbᵊl) *a.* undeniable; indisputable

incorporate (ɪnˈkɔːpəreɪt) *v.* **1.** include **2.** unite into one body **3.** form into corporation —**incorpoˈration** *n.*

incorporeal (ɪnkɔːˈpɔːrɪəl) *a.* **1.** without material form, body or substance **2.** spiritual, metaphysical **3.** *Law* having no material existence —**incorpoˈreity** *or* **incorporeˈality** *n.*

incorrigible (ɪnˈkɒrɪdʒəbᵊl) *a.* **1.** beyond correction or reform **2.** firmly rooted —**incorrigiˈbility** *n.*

increase (ɪnˈkriːs) *v.* **1.** make or become greater in size, number *etc.* —*n.* (ˈɪnkriːs) **2.** growth, enlargement —**inˈcreasingly** *adv.* more and more

incredible (ɪnˈkrɛdəbᵊl) *a.* **1.** unbelievable **2.** *inf.* marvellous; amazing

THESAURUS

incoming approaching, arriving, entering, homeward, landing, new, returning, succeeding

incomparable beyond compare, inimitable, matchless, paramount, peerless, superlative, supreme, transcendent, unequalled, unmatched, unparalleled, unrivalled

incomparably beyond compare, by far, easily, eminently, far and away, immeasurably

incompatible antagonistic, antipathetic, conflicting, contradictory, discordant, discrepant, disparate, ill-assorted, incongruous, inconsistent, inconsonant, irreconcilable, mismatched, uncongenial, unsuitable, unsuited

incompetence inability, inadequacy, incapability, incapacity, incompetency, ineffectiveness, ineptitude, ineptness, insufficiency, skill-lessness, unfitness, uselessness

incompetent bungling, floundering, incapable, incapacitated, ineffectual, inept, inexpert, insufficient, skill-less, unable, unfit, unfitted, unskilful, useless

incomplete broken, defective, deficient, fragmentary, imperfect, insufficient, lacking, partial, short, unaccomplished, undeveloped, undone, unexecuted, unfinished, wanting

incomprehensible above one's head, all Greek to (*Inf.*), baffling, beyond comprehension, beyond one's grasp, enigmatic, impenetrable, inconceivable, inscrutable, mysterious, obscure, opaque, perplexing, puzzling, unfathomable, unimaginable, unintelligible, unthinkable

inconclusive ambiguous, indecisive, indeterminate, open, uncertain, unconvincing, undecided, unsettled, up in the air (*Inf.*), vague

incongruity conflict, discrepancy, disparity, inappropriateness, inaptness, incompatibility, inconsistency, inharmoniousness, unsuitability

incongruous absurd, conflicting, contradictory, contrary, disconsonant, discordant, extraneous, improper, inappropriate, inapt, incoherent, incompatible, inconsistent, out of keeping, out of place, unbecoming, unsuitable, unsuited

inconsiderable exiguous, inconsequential, insignificant, light, minor, negligible, petty, slight, small, small-time (*Inf.*), trifling, trivial, unimportant

inconsiderate careless, indelicate, insensitive, intolerant, rude, self-centred, selfish, tactless, thoughtless, uncharitable, ungracious, unkind, unthinking

inconsistent **1.** at odds, at variance, conflicting, contradictory, contrary, discordant, discrepant, incoherent, incompatible, in conflict, incongruous, irreconcilable, out of step **2.** capricious, changeable, erratic, fickle, inconstant, irregular, unpredictable, unstable, unsteady, vagarious (*Rare*), variable

inconsolable brokenhearted, desolate, despairing, heartbroken, heartsick, prostrate with grief, sick at heart

inconspicuous camouflaged, hidden, insignificant, modest, muted, ordinary, plain, quiet, retiring, unassuming, unnoticeable, unobtrusive, unostentatious

incontestable beyond doubt, beyond question, certain, incontrovertible, indisputable, indubitable, irrefutable, self-evident, sure, undeniable, unquestionable

incontinent debauched, lascivious, lecherous, lewd, loose, lustful, profligate, promiscuous, unchaste, wanton

incontrovertible beyond dispute, certain, established, incontestable, indisputable, indubitable, irrefutable, positive, sure, undeniable, unquestionable, unshakable

inconvenience annoyance, awkwardness, bother, difficulty, disadvantage, disruption, disturbance, drawback, fuss, hindrance, nuisance, trouble, uneasiness, upset, vexation

inconvenient annoying, awkward, bothersome, disadvantageous, disturbing, embarrassing, inopportune, tiresome, troublesome, unseasonable, unsuitable, untimely, vexatious

incorporate absorb, amalgamate, assimilate, blend, coalesce, combine, consolidate, embody, fuse, include, integrate, merge, mix, subsume, unite

incorrect erroneous, false, faulty, flawed, improper, inaccurate, inappropriate, inexact, mistaken, out, specious, unfitting, unsuitable, untrue, wide of the mark (*Inf.*), wrong

incorrigible hardened, hopeless, incurable, intractable, inveterate, irredeemable, unreformed

incorruptible **1.** above suspicion, honest, honourable, just, straight, trustworthy, unbribable, upright **2.** everlasting, imperishable, undecaying

increase **1.** *v.* add to, advance, aggrandize, amplify, augment, boost, build up, develop, dilate, enhance, enlarge, escalate, expand, extend, grow, heighten, inflate, intensify, magnify, mount, multiply, proliferate, prolong, raise, snowball, spread, step up (*Inf.*), strengthen, swell, wax **2.** *n.* addition, augmentation, boost, development, enlargement, escalation, expansion, extension, gain, growth, increment, intensification, rise, upsurge, upturn

increasingly more and more, progressively, to an increasing extent

incredulous (ɪnˈkrɛdʒʊləs) *a.* unbelieving —**increˈdulity** *n.*

increment (ˈɪnkrɪmənt) *n.* increase, *esp.* one of a series

incriminate (ɪnˈkrɪmɪneɪt) *vt.* **1.** imply guilt of **2.** charge with crime —**inˈcriminatory** *a.*

incrust (ɪnˈkrʌst) *v. see* ENCRUST

incubate (ˈɪnkjʊbeɪt) *vt.* **1.** provide (eggs, embryos, bacteria *etc.*) with heat or other favourable condition for development —*vi.* **2.** develop in this way —**incuˈbation** *n.* —**ˈincubator** *n.* apparatus for artificially hatching eggs, for rearing premature babies

incubus (ˈɪnkjʊbəs) *n.* **1.** nightmare; obsession **2.** (*orig.*) demon believed to afflict sleeping person (*pl.* **-bi** (-baɪ), **-es**)

inculcate (ˈɪnkʌlkeɪt, ɪnˈkʌlkeɪt) *vt.* impress on the mind —**inculˈcation** *n.* —**ˈinculcator** *n.*

inculpate (ˈɪnkʌlpeɪt, ɪnˈkʌlpeɪt) *vt.* incriminate; cause blame to be imputed to —**inculˈpation** *n.* —**inˈculpative** *or* **inˈculpatory** *a.*

incumbent (ɪnˈkʌmbənt) *a.* **1.** lying, resting —*n.* **2.** holder of office, *esp.* church benefice —**inˈcumbency** *n.* **1.** obligation **2.** office or tenure of incumbent —**it is incumbent on** it is the duty of

incur (ɪnˈkɜː) *vt.* **1.** fall into **2.** bring upon oneself (**-rr-**) —**inˈcursion** *n.* **1.** invasion **2.** penetration

incuse (ɪnˈkjuːz) *vt.* **1.** impress by striking or stamping —*a.* **2.** hammered —*n.* **3.** impression made by stamping

ind. **1.** independent **2.** index **3.** indicative

Ind. **1.** Independent **2.** India **3.** Indian **4.** Indies

indaba (ɪnˈdɑːbə) *n.* **SA** **1.** meeting, discussion **2.** problem

indebted (ɪnˈdɛtɪd) *a.* **1.** owing gratitude (for help, favours *etc.*) **2.** owing money —**inˈdebtedness** *n.*

indecent (ɪnˈdiːsᵊnt) *a.* **1.** offensive to standards of decency, *esp.* in sexual matters **2.** unseemly, improper (*esp. in* **indecent haste**) —**inˈdecency** *n.* **1.** state or quality of being indecent **2.** indecent act *etc.* —**indecent exposure** offence of indecently exposing one's body, *esp.* genitals, in public

indeed (ɪnˈdiːd) *adv.* **1.** in truth, really, in fact, certainly —*interj.* **2.** denoting surprise, doubt *etc.*

indefatigable (ɪndɪˈfætɪgəbᵊl) *a.* untiring —**indeˈfatigably** *adv.*

indefeasible (ɪndɪˈfiːzəbᵊl) *a.* that cannot be lost or annulled —**indefeasiˈbility** *n.*

indefensible (ɪndɪˈfɛnsəbᵊl) *a.* not justifiable or defensible —**indeˈfensibly** *adv.*

indelible (ɪnˈdɛlɪbᵊl) *a.* **1.** that cannot be blotted out, effaced or erased **2.** producing such a mark —**indeliˈbility** *n.* —**inˈdelibly** *adv.*

indelicate (ɪnˈdɛlɪkɪt) *a.* **1.** coarse **2.** embarrassing, tasteless

indemnity (ɪnˈdɛmnɪtɪ) *n.* **1.** compensation for loss **2.**

THESAURUS

incredible **1.** absurd, beyond belief, far-fetched, implausible, impossible, improbable, inconceivable, preposterous, unbelievable, unimaginable, unthinkable **2.** *Inf.* ace (*Inf.*), amazing, astonishing, astounding, awe-inspiring, extraordinary, far-out (*Sl.*), great, marvellous, prodigious, superhuman, wonderful

incredulity disbelief, distrust, doubt, scepticism, unbelief

incredulous disbelieving, distrustful, doubtful, doubting, dubious, mistrustful, sceptical, suspicious, unbelieving, unconvinced

increment accretion, accrual, accrument, addition, advancement, augmentation, enlargement, gain, increase, step (up)

incriminate accuse, arraign, blacken the name of, blame, charge, impeach, implicate, inculpate, indict, involve, point the finger at (*Inf.*), stigmatize

incur arouse, bring (upon oneself), contract, draw, earn, expose oneself to, gain, induce, lay oneself open to, meet with, provoke

incurable fatal, inoperable, irrecoverable, irremediable, remediless, terminal

indebted beholden, grateful, in debt, obligated, obliged, under an obligation

indecency bawdiness, coarseness, crudity, foulness, grossness, immodesty, impropriety, impurity, indecorum, indelicacy, lewdness, licentiousness, obscenity, outrageousness, pornography, smut, smuttiness, unseemliness, vileness, vulgarity

indecent **1.** blue, coarse, crude, dirty, filthy, foul, gross, immodest, improper, impure, indelicate, lewd, licentious, pornographic, salacious, scatological, smutty, vile **2.** ill-bred, improper, in bad taste, indecorous, offensive, outrageous, tasteless, unbecoming, unseemly, vulgar

indecipherable crabbed, illegible, indistinguishable, unintelligible, unreadable

indecision ambivalence, doubt, hesitancy, hesitation, indecisiveness, irresolution, shilly-shallying (*Inf.*), uncertainty, vacillation, wavering

indecisive **1.** doubtful, faltering, hesitating, in two minds (*Inf.*), irresolute, pussyfooting (*Inf.*), tentative, uncertain, undecided, undetermined, vacillating, wavering **2.** inconclusive, indefinite, indeterminate, unclear, undecided

indeed actually, certainly, doubtlessly, in point of fact, in truth, positively, really, strictly, to be sure, truly, undeniably, undoubtedly, verily (*Archaic*), veritably

indefensible faulty, inexcusable, insupportable, unforgivable, unjustifiable, unpardonable, untenable, unwarrantable, wrong

indefinable dim, hazy, impalpable, indescribable, indistinct, inexpressible, nameless, obscure, unrealized, vague

indefinite ambiguous, confused, doubtful, equivocal, evasive, general, ill-defined, imprecise, indeterminate, indistinct, inexact, loose, obscure, uncertain, unclear, undefined, undetermined, unfixed, unknown, unlimited, unsettled, vague

indelible enduring, indestructible, ineffaceable, ineradicable, inexpungible, inextirpable, ingrained, lasting, permanent

indelicate blue, coarse, crude, embarrassing, gross, immodest, improper, indecent, indecorous, low, near the knuckle (*Inf.*), obscene, off-colour, offensive, risqué, rude, suggestive, tasteless, unbecoming, unseemly, untoward, vulgar

indemnify **1.** endorse, guarantee, insure, protect, secure, underwrite **2.** compensate, pay, reimburse, remunerate, repair, repay, requite, satisfy

security against loss —**indemnifiˈcation** *n.* —**inˈdemnify** *vt.* **1.** give indemnity to **2.** compensate (**inˈdemnified, inˈdemnifying**)

indent (ɪnˈdɛnt) *v.* **1.** set (written matter *etc.*) in from margin *etc.* **2.** notch (edge, border *etc.*); make (something) jagged **3.** cut (document in duplicate) so that irregular lines may be matched **4.** make an order upon (someone) or for (something) —*n.* (ˈɪndɛnt) **5.** notch **6.** order, requisition —**idenˈtation** *n.* **1.** hollowed, notched or cut place, as an edge or coastline **2.** series of hollows, notches or cuts **3.** act of indenting; condition of being indented **4.** leaving of space or amount of space left between margin and start of indented line (*also* **inˈdention, ˈindent**) —**inˈdention** *n.* indentation (on page) —**inˈdenture** *n.* **1.** indented document **2.** contract, *esp.* one binding apprentice to master —*vt.* **3.** bind thus

independent (ɪndɪˈpɛndənt) *a.* **1.** not subject to others **2.** self-reliant **3.** free **4.** valid in itself **5.** politically of no party —**indeˈpendence** *or* **indeˈpendency** *n.* **1.** being independent **2.** self-reliance **3.** self-support —**indeˈpendently** *adv.* —**independent clause** *Gram.* main or coordinate clause —**independent school UK** school that is neither financed nor controlled by government or local authorities

in-depth *a.* carefully worked out, detailed, thorough

indescribable (ɪndɪˈskraɪbəbᵊl) *a.* **1.** beyond description **2.** too intense *etc.* for words —**indeˈscribably** *adv.*

indeterminate (ɪndɪˈtɜːmɪnɪt) *a.* **1.** uncertain **2.** inconclusive **3.** incalculable **4.** *Maths.* having no numerical meaning; (of an equation) having more than one variable and an unlimited number of solutions

index (ˈɪndɛks) *n.* **1.** alphabetical list of references, usu. at end of book **2.** pointer, indicator **3.** *Maths.* exponent (*pl.* **-es, ˈindices**) —*vt.* **4.** provide (book) with index **5.** insert in index —**index finger** finger next to thumb (*also* **ˈforefinger**) —**index-linked** *a.* (of wages, interest rates *etc.*) directly related to cost-of-living index and rising accordingly

Indian (ˈɪndɪən) *n.* **1.** native of India **2.** aboriginal American —*a.* **3.** of India **4.** of Amer. Indians or any of their languages —**ˈIndic** *a.* **1.** denoting, belonging to or relating to Indian branch of Indo-European languages —*n.* **2.** this group of languages (*also* **Indo-Aryan**) —**ˈIndiaman** *n.* formerly, merchant ship engaged in trade with India —**Indian club** bottle-shaped club, usu. used by gymnasts *etc.* —**Indian corn** *see* MAIZE —**Indian file** single file —**Indian hemp** cannabis —**Indian ink** very dark black (drawing) ink —**Indian list C** *inf.* list of people to whom spirits may not be sold —**Indian summer** period of unusually warm weather, *esp.* in autumn —**India paper** thin soft opaque printing paper —**India rubber** rubber, eraser

indicate (ˈɪndɪkeɪt) *vt.* **1.** point out **2.** state briefly **3.** signify —**indiˈcation** *n.* **1.** sign **2.** token **3.** explanation —**inˈdicative** *a.* **1.** (*with* of) pointing (to) **2.** *Gram.* stating fact —*n.* **3.** *Gram.* (verb in) indicative mood —**ˈindicator** *n.* **1.** one who, that which, indicates **2.** on vehicle, flashing light showing driver's intention to turn

indices (ˈɪndɪsiːz) *n., pl. of* INDEX

indict (ɪnˈdaɪt) *vt.* accuse, *esp.* by legal process —**inˈdictable** *a.* —**inˈdictment** *n.*

indifferent (ɪnˈdɪfrənt, -fərənt) *a.* **1.** uninterested **2.** unimportant **3.** neither good nor bad **4.** inferior **5.** neutral —**inˈdifference** *n.*

THESAURUS

indemnity **1.** guarantee, insurance, protection, security **2.** compensation, redress, reimbursement, remuneration, reparation, requital, restitution, satisfaction

indent *v.* **1.** ask for, order, request, requisition **2.** cut, dint, mark, nick, notch, pink, scallop, score, serrate

independence autarchy, autonomy, freedom, home rule, liberty, self-determination, self-government, self-reliance, self-rule, self-sufficiency, separation, sovereignty

independent **1.** absolute, free, liberated, separate, unconnected, unconstrained, uncontrolled, unrelated **2.** autarchic, autarchical, autonomous, decontrolled, nonaligned, self-determining, self-governing, separated, sovereign **3.** bold, individualistic, liberated, self-contained, self-reliant, self-sufficient, self-supporting, unaided, unconventional

independently alone, autonomously, by oneself, individually, on one's own, separately, solo, unaided

indescribable beggaring description, beyond description, beyond words, incommunicable, indefinable, ineffable, inexpressible, unutterable

indestructible abiding, durable, enduring, everlasting, immortal, imperishable, incorruptible, indelible, indissoluble, lasting, nonperishable, permanent, unbreakable, unfading

indeterminate imprecise, inconclusive, indefinite, inexact, uncertain, undefined, undetermined, unfixed, unspecified, unstipulated, vague

index **1.** clue, guide, indication, mark, sign, symptom, token **2.** director, forefinger, hand, indicator, needle, pointer

indicate **1.** add up to (*Inf.*), bespeak, be symptomatic of, betoken, denote, evince, imply, manifest, point to, reveal, show, signify, suggest **2.** designate, point out, point to, specify

indication clue, evidence, explanation, forewarning, hint, index, inkling, intimation, manifestation, mark, note, omen, portent, sign, signal, suggestion, symptom, warning

indicative exhibitive, indicatory, indicial, pointing to, significant, suggestive, symptomatic

indicator display, gauge, guide, index, mark, marker, meter, pointer, sign, signal, signpost, symbol

indictment accusation, allegation, charge, impeachment, prosecution, summons

indifference **1.** absence of feeling, aloofness, apathy, callousness, carelessness, coldness, coolness, detachment, disregard, heedlessness, inattention, lack of interest, negligence, stoicalness, unconcern **2.** disinterestedness, dispassion, equity, impartiality, neutrality, objectivity **3.** insignificance, irrelevance, triviality, unimportance

indifferent **1.** aloof, apathetic, callous, careless, cold, cool, detached, distant, heedless, impervious, inattentive, regardless, uncaring, unconcerned, unimpressed, uninterested, unmoved, unresponsive, unsympathetic **2.** immaterial, insignificant, of no consequence, unimportant **3.** average, fair, mediocre, middling, moderate, ordinary, passable, perfunctory, so-so (*Inf.*), undistinguished, uninspired **4.** disinterested, dispassionate, equitable, impartial, neutral, nonaligned, nonpartisan, objective, unbiased, uninvolved, unprejudiced

indigenous (ɪnˈdɪdʒɪnəs) *a.* born in or natural to a country —**indigene** (ˈɪndɪdʒiːn) *n.* **1.** aborigine **2.** native

indigent (ˈɪndɪdʒənt) *a.* poor; needy —**ˈindigence** *n.* poverty

indigestion (ɪndɪˈdʒɛstʃən) *n.* (discomfort, pain caused by) difficulty in digesting food —**indiˈgestible** *a.*

indignant (ɪnˈdɪgnənt) *a.* **1.** moved by anger and scorn **2.** angered by sense of injury or injustice —**inˈdignantly** *adv.* —**indigˈnation** *n.* —**inˈdignity** *n.* humiliation; insult, slight

indigo (ˈɪndɪgəʊ) *n.* **1.** blue dye obtained from plant **2.** the plant (*pl.* **-s, -es**) —*a.* **3.** deep blue

indirect (ɪndɪˈrɛkt) *a.* **1.** deviating from direct course or line **2.** not coming as direct effect or consequence **3.** not straightforward, open or fair —**indiˈrectly** *adv.* —**indiˈrectness** *n.* —**indirect object** *Gram.* noun, pronoun or noun phrase indicating recipient or beneficiary of action of verb and its direct object —**indirect speech** *or esp. U.S.* **indirect discourse** reporting of something said by conveying what was meant rather than repeating exact words (*also* **reported speech**) —**indirect tax** tax levied on goods or services rather than on individuals or companies

indiscreet (ɪndɪˈskriːt) *a.* not discreet; imprudent; tactless —**indiscretion** (ɪndɪˈskrɛʃən) *n.* **1.** characteristic or state of being indiscreet **2.** indiscreet act, remark *etc.*

indiscrete (ɪndɪˈskriːt) *a.* not divisible or divided into parts

indiscriminate (ɪndɪˈskrɪmɪnɪt) *a.* **1.** lacking discrimination **2.** jumbled

indispensable (ɪndɪˈspɛnsəbᵊl) *a.* necessary; essential

indisposition (ɪndɪspəˈzɪʃən) *n.* **1.** sickness **2.** disinclination —**indisˈpose** *vt.* —**indisˈposed** *a.* **1.** unwell, not fit **2.** disinclined

indissoluble (ɪndɪˈsɒljʊbᵊl) *a.* permanent

indium (ˈɪndɪəm) *n.* soft silver-white metallic element

individual (ɪndɪˈvɪdjʊəl) *a.* **1.** single **2.** characteristic of single person or thing **3.** distinctive —*n.* **4.** single person or thing, *esp.* when regarded as distinct from others —**indiˈvidualism** *n.* principle of asserting one's independence —**indiˈvidualist** *n.* —**individualˈistic** *a.*

THESAURUS

indigestion dyspepsia, dyspepsy, upset stomach

indignant angry, annoyed, disgruntled, exasperated, fuming (*Inf.*), furious, heated, huffy (*Inf.*), in a huff, incensed, in high dudgeon, irate, livid (*Inf.*), mad (*Inf.*), miffed (*Inf.*), narked (*Sl.*), peeved (*Inf.*), provoked, resentful, riled, scornful, seeing red (*Inf.*), sore (*Inf.*), up in arms (*Inf.*), wrathful

indignation anger, exasperation, fury, ire (*Literary*), pique, rage, resentment, righteous anger, scorn, umbrage, wrath

indignity abuse, affront, contumely, dishonour, disrespect, humiliation, injury, insult, obloquy, opprobrium, outrage, reproach, slap in the face (*Inf.*), slight, snub

indirect **1.** backhanded, circuitous, circumlocutory, crooked, devious, long-drawn-out, meandering, oblique, periphrastic, rambling, roundabout, tortuous, wandering, winding, zigzag **2.** ancillary, collateral, contingent, incidental, secondary, subsidiary, unintended

indirectly by implication, circumlocutorily, in a roundabout way, obliquely, periphrastically, second-hand

indiscernible hidden, impalpable, imperceptible, indistinct, indistinguishable, invisible, unapparent, undiscernible

indiscreet foolish, hasty, heedless, ill-advised, ill-considered, ill-judged, impolitic, imprudent, incautious, injudicious, naive, rash, reckless, tactless, undiplomatic, unthinking, unwise

indiscretion error, faux pas, folly, foolishness, gaffe, gaucherie, imprudence, mistake, rashness, recklessness, slip, slip of the tongue, tactlessness

indiscriminate **1.** aimless, careless, desultory, general, hit or miss (*Inf.*), random, sweeping, uncritical, undiscriminating, unmethodical, unselective, unsystematic, wholesale **2.** chaotic, confused, haphazard, higgledy-piggledy (*Inf.*), jumbled, mingled, miscellaneous, mixed, mongrel, motley, promiscuous, undistinguishable

indispensable crucial, essential, imperative, key, necessary, needed, needful, requisite, vital

indisposed **1.** ailing, confined to bed, ill, laid up (*Inf.*), on the sick list (*Inf.*), poorly (*Inf.*), sick, unwell **2.** averse, disinclined, loath, reluctant, unwilling

indisposition **1.** ailment, ill health, illness, sickness **2.** aversion, disinclination, dislike, distaste, hesitancy, reluctance, unwillingness

indisputable absolute, beyond doubt, certain, evident, incontestable, incontrovertible, indubitable, irrefutable, positive, sure, unassailable, undeniable, unquestionable

indissoluble abiding, binding, enduring, eternal, fixed, imperishable, incorruptible, indestructible, inseparable, lasting, permanent, solid, unbreakable

indistinct ambiguous, bleary, blurred, confused, dim, doubtful, faint, fuzzy, hazy, ill-defined, indefinite, indeterminate, indiscernible, indistinguishable, misty, muffled, obscure, out of focus, shadowy, unclear, undefined, unintelligible, vague, weak

indistinguishable **1.** alike, identical, like as two peas in a pod (*Inf.*), (the) same, twin **2.** imperceptible, indiscernible, invisible, obscure

individual **1.** *adj.* characteristic, discrete, distinct, distinctive, exclusive, identical, idiosyncratic, own, particular, peculiar, personal, personalized, proper, respective, separate, several, single, singular, special, specific, unique **2.** *n.* being, body (*Inf.*), character, creature, mortal, party, person, personage, soul, type, unit

individualism egocentricity, egoism, freethinking, independence, originality, self-direction, self-interest, self-reliance

individualist freethinker, independent, loner, lone wolf, maverick, nonconformist, original

individuality character, discreteness, distinction, distinctiveness, originality, peculiarity, personality, separateness, singularity, uniqueness

individually apart, independently, one at a time, one by one, personally, separately, severally, singly

—**individu'ality** *n.* 1. distinctive character 2. personality —**indi'vidualize** *or* **-lise** *vt.* make (or treat as) individual —**indi'vidually** *adv.* singly

Indo- ('ɪndəʊ-) (*comb. form*) India; Indian, as in *Indo-European*

indoctrinate (ɪn'dɒktrɪneɪt) *vt.* implant beliefs in the mind of

Indo-European *a.* 1. denoting or belonging to family of languages that includes English 2. denoting or belonging to any of the peoples speaking these languages —*n.* 3. Indo-European family of languages

indolent ('ɪndələnt) *a.* lazy —'**indolence** *n.*

indomitable (ɪn'dɒmɪtəbᵊl) *a.* unyielding

indoor ('ɪndɔː) *a.* 1. within doors 2. under cover —**in'doors** *adv.* inside or into house or other building

indorse (ɪn'dɔːs) *vt. see* ENDORSE

indubitable (ɪn'djuːbɪtəbᵊl) *a.* beyond doubt; certain —**in'dubitably** *adv.*

induce (ɪn'djuːs) *vt.* 1. persuade 2. bring on 3. cause 4. produce by induction —**in'ducement** *n.* incentive, attraction

induct (ɪn'dʌkt) *vt.* install in office —**in'ductance** *n.* —**in'duction** *n.* 1. an inducting 2. general inference from particular instances 3. production of electric or magnetic state in body by its being near (not touching) electrified or magnetized body 4. in internal combustion engine, part of the piston's action which draws gas from carburettor —**in'ductive** *a.* —**in'ductively** *adv.* —**in'ductor** *n.* —**induction coil** transformer for producing high voltage from low voltage

indue (ɪn'djuː) *vt. see* ENDUE

indulge (ɪn'dʌldʒ) *vt.* 1. gratify 2. give free course to 3. pamper 4. spoil —**in'dulgence** *n.* 1. an indulging 2. extravagance 3. something granted as a favour or privilege 4. *R.C.Ch.* remission of temporal punishment due after absolution —**in'dulgent** *a.* —**in'dulgently** *adv.*

induna (ɪn'duːnə) *n.* **SA** headman, overseer

indurate ('ɪndjʊreɪt) *v.* 1. make or become hard or callous 2. make or become hardy —*a.* ('ɪndjʊrɪt) 3. hardened, callous, or unfeeling —'**indurative** *a.*

industry ('ɪndəstrɪ) *n.* 1. manufacture, processing *etc.* of goods 2. branch of this 3. diligence, habitual hard work —**in'dustrial** *a.* of industries, trades —**in'dustrialist** *n.* person engaged in control of industrial enterprise —**in'dustrialize** *or* **-lise** *v.* —**in'dustrious** *a.* diligent —**industrial estate** **UK** area of land set aside for industry and business —**Industrial Revolution** transformation in 18th and 19th centuries of Brit. and other countries into industrial nations

-ine (*comb. form*) 1. of, relating to or belonging to, as in *saturnine* 2. consisting of; resembling, as in *crystalline* 3. indicating any of various classes of chemical compounds, as in *chlorine, nicotine, glycerine* (*also* **-in**) 4. indicating feminine form, as in *heroine*

inebriate (ɪn'iːbrɪeɪt) *vt.* 1. make drunk; intoxicate —*a.* (ɪn'iːbrɪɪt) 2. drunken —*n.* (ɪn'iːbrɪɪt) 3. habitual drunkard —**inebri'ation** *or* **inebriety** (ɪnɪ'braɪɪtɪ) *n.* drunkenness

inedible (ɪn'ɛdɪbᵊl) *a.* 1. not eatable 2. unfit for food —**inedi'bility** *n.*

ineducable (ɪn'ɛdjʊkəbᵊl) *a.* incapable of being educated, *esp.* through mental retardation

ineffable (ɪn'ɛfəbᵊl) *a.* 1. too great or sacred for words 2. unutterable —**ineffa'bility** *n.* —**in'effably** *adv.*

ineligible (ɪn'ɛlɪdʒəbəl) *a.* not fit or qualified (for something) —**ineligi'bility** *n.*

ineluctable (ɪnɪ'lʌktəbᵊl) *a.* (*esp.* of fate) incapable of being avoided; inescapable

inept (ɪn'ɛpt) *a.* 1. absurd 2. out of place 3. clumsy —**in'eptitude** *n.*

THESAURUS

indoctrinate brainwash, drill, ground, imbue, initiate, instruct, school, teach, train

indolent fainéant, idle, inactive, inert, lackadaisical, languid, lazy, lethargic, listless, lumpish, slack, slothful, slow, sluggish, torpid, workshy

indomitable invincible, resolute, staunch, steadfast, unbeatable, unconquerable, unflinching, untameable, unyielding

indubitable certain, evident, incontestable, incontrovertible, indisputable, irrefutable, obvious, sure, unarguable, undeniable, undoubted, unquestionable, veritable

induce 1. actuate, convince, draw, encourage, get, impel, incite, influence, instigate, move, persuade, press, prevail upon, prompt, talk into 2. bring about, cause, effect, engender, generate, give rise to, lead to, occasion, produce, set in motion

inducement attraction, bait, carrot (*Inf.*), cause, come-on (*Inf.*), consideration, encouragement, impulse, incentive, incitement, influence, lure, motive, reward, spur, stimulus, urge

indulge 1. cater to, give way to, gratify, pander to, regale, satiate, satisfy, treat oneself to, yield to 2. baby, coddle, cosset, favour, foster, give in to, go along with, humour, mollycoddle, pamper, pet, spoil

indulgence 1. excess, fondness, immoderation, intemperance, intemperateness, kindness, leniency, pampering, partiality, permissiveness, profligacy, profligateness, spoiling 2. appeasement, fulfilment, gratification, satiation, satisfaction 3. extravagance, favour, luxury, privilege, treat

indulgent compliant, easy-going, favourable, fond, forbearing, gentle, gratifying, kind, kindly, lenient, liberal, mild, permissive, tender, tolerant, understanding

industrialist baron, big businessman, boss, capitalist, captain of industry, financier, magnate, manufacturer, producer, tycoon

industrious active, assiduous, busy, conscientious, diligent, energetic, hard-working, laborious, persevering, persistent, productive, purposeful, sedulous, steady, tireless, zealous

industry 1. business, commerce, commercial enterprise, manufacturing, production, trade 2. activity, application, assiduity, determination, diligence, effort, labour, perseverance, persistence, tirelessness, toil, vigour, zeal

inefficient disorganized, feeble, incapable, incompetent, ineffectual, inefficacious, inept, inexpert, slipshod, sloppy, wasteful, weak

ineligible disqualified, incompetent (*Law*), objectionable, ruled out, unacceptable, undesirable, unequipped, unfit, unfitted, unqualified, unsuitable

inept 1. awkward, bumbling, bungling, cack-handed

inequality (ɪnɪˈkwɒlɪtɪ) *n.* **1.** state or quality of being unequal **2.** lack of smoothness or regularity **3.** *Maths.* statement indicating that value of one quantity or expression is not equal to another; relation of being unequal

inert (ɪnˈɜːt) *a.* **1.** without power of action or resistance **2.** slow, sluggish **3.** chemically unreactive —**inertia** (ɪnˈɜːʃə, -ʃɪə) *n.* **1.** inactivity **2.** property by which matter continues in its existing state of rest or motion in straight line, unless that state is changed by external force —**inˈertly** *adv.* —**inˈertness** *n.* —**inertia-reel seat-belt** car seat-belt in which belt is free to unwind from metal drum except when rapid deceleration occurs —**inertia selling** practice of sending unrequested goods to householders, followed by bill if goods are not returned

inescapable (ɪnɪˈskeɪpəbᵊl) *a.* incapable of being escaped or avoided

inestimable (ɪnˈɛstɪməbᵊl) *a.* too good, too great to be estimated

inevitable (ɪnˈɛvɪtəbᵊl) *a.* **1.** unavoidable **2.** sure to happen —**inevitaˈbility** *n.* —**inˈevitably** *adv.*

inexorable (ɪnˈɛksərəbᵊl) *a.* relentless —**inˈexorably** *adv.*

inexpiable (ɪnˈɛkspɪəbᵊl) *a.* **1.** incapable of being expiated **2.** *obs.* implacable

inexplicable (ɪnɪkˈsplɪkəbᵊl) *a.* impossible to explain

in extenso (ɪn ɪkˈstɛnsəʊ) *Lat.* at full length

in extremis (ɪn ɪkˈstriːmɪs) *Lat.* at the point of death

inextricable (ɪnɛksˈtrɪkəbᵊl) *a.* **1.** not able to be escaped from **2.** not able to be disentangled *etc.* **3.** extremely involved or intricate —**inextricaˈbility** *or* **inexˈtricableness** *n.* —**inexˈtricably** *adv.*

inf. **1.** infinitive **2.** informal **3.** information

infallible (ɪnˈfæləbᵊl) *a.* **1.** unerring **2.** not liable to fail **3.** certain, sure —**infalliˈbility** *n.* —**inˈfallibly** *adv.*

infamous (ˈɪnfəməs) *a.* **1.** notorious **2.** shocking —**ˈinfamously** *adv.* —**ˈinfamy** *n.*

infant (ˈɪnfənt) *n.* very young child —**ˈinfancy** *n.* —**inˈfanticide** *n.* **1.** murder of newborn child **2.** person guilty of this —**ˈinfantile** *a.* childish —**infantile paralysis** *see* POLIOMYELITIS —**infant school UK** school for children aged between 5 and 7

infante (ɪnˈfæntɪ) *n.* formerly, son of king of Spain or Portugal, *esp.* one not heir to throne —**infanta** (ɪnˈfæntə) *n.* **1.** formerly, daughter of king of Spain or Portugal **2.** wife of infante

THESAURUS

(*Inf.*), clumsy, gauche, incompetent, inexpert, maladroit, unhandy, unskilful, unworkmanlike **2.** absurd, improper, inappropriate, inapt, infelicitous, malapropos, meaningless, out of place, pointless, ridiculous, unfit, unsuitable

ineptitude **1.** clumsiness, gaucheness, incapacity, incompetence, inexpertness, unfitness, unhandiness **2.** absurdity, inappropriateness, pointlessness, uselessness

inequality bias, difference, disparity, disproportion, diversity, imparity, irregularity, lack of balance, preferentiality, prejudice, unevenness

inequitable biased, discriminatory, one-sided, partial, partisan, preferential, prejudiced, unfair, unjust

inert dead, dormant, dull, idle, immobile, inactive, inanimate, indolent, lazy, leaden, lifeless, motionless, passive, quiescent, slack, slothful, sluggish, slumberous (*Chiefly poetic*), static, still, torpid, unmoving, unreactive, unresponsive

inertia apathy, deadness, disinclination to move, drowsiness, dullness, idleness, immobility, inactivity, indolence, languor, lassitude, laziness, lethargy, listlessness, passivity, sloth, sluggishness, stillness, stupor, torpor, unresponsiveness

inescapable certain, destined, fated, ineluctable, ineludible (*Rare*), inevitable, inexorable, sure, unavoidable

inestimable beyond price, immeasurable, incalculable, invaluable, precious, priceless, prodigious

inevitable assured, certain, decreed, destined, fixed, ineluctable, inescapable, inexorable, necessary, ordained, settled, sure, unavoidable, unpreventable

inevitably as a necessary consequence, as a result, automatically, certainly, necessarily, of necessity, perforce, surely, unavoidably, willy-nilly

inexcusable indefensible, inexpiable, outrageous, unforgivable, unjustifiable, unpardonable, unwarrantable

inexorable adamant, cruel, hard, harsh, immovable, implacable, ineluctable, inescapable, inflexible, merciless, obdurate, pitiless, relentless, remorseless, severe, unappeasable, unbending, unrelenting, unyielding

inexorably implacably, inevitably, irresistibly, relentlessly, remorselessly, unrelentingly

inexpensive bargain, budget, cheap, economical, low-cost, low-priced, modest, reasonable

inexperience callowness, greenness, ignorance, newness, rawness, unexpertness, unfamiliarity

inexperienced amateur, callow, fresh, green, immature, new, raw, unaccustomed, unacquainted, unfamiliar, unfledged, unpractised, unschooled, unseasoned, unskilled, untrained, untried, unused, unversed, wet behind the ears (*Inf.*)

inexpert amateurish, awkward, bungling, cack-handed (*Inf.*), clumsy, inept, maladroit, skill-less, unhandy, unpractised, unprofessional, unskilful, unskilled, unworkmanlike

inexplicable baffling, beyond comprehension, enigmatic, incomprehensible, inscrutable, insoluble, mysterious, mystifying, strange, unaccountable, unfathomable, unintelligible

inextricably indissolubly, indistinguishably, inseparably, intricately, irretrievably, totally

infallibility **1.** faultlessness, impeccability, irrefutability, omniscience, perfection, supremacy, unerringness **2.** dependability, reliability, safety, sureness, trustworthiness

infallible **1.** faultless, impeccable, omniscient, perfect, unerring, unimpeachable **2.** certain, dependable, foolproof, reliable, sure, sure-fire (*Inf.*), trustworthy, unbeatable, unfailing

infamous abominable, atrocious, base, detestable, disgraceful, dishonourable, disreputable, egregious, flagitious, hateful, heinous, ignominious, ill-famed, iniquitous, loathsome, monstrous, nefarious, notorious, odious, opprobrious, outrageous, scandalous, scurvy, shameful, shocking, vile, villainous, wicked

infancy babyhood, early childhood

infant *n.* babe, baby, bairn (*Scot.*), child, little one,

infantry (ˈɪnfəntrɪ) *n.* foot soldiers

infatuate (ɪnˈfætjʊeɪt) *vt.* inspire with folly or foolish passion —**inˈfatuated** *a.* foolishly enamoured —**infatuˈation** *n.*

infect (ɪnˈfɛkt) *vt.* **1.** affect (with disease) **2.** contaminate —**inˈfection** *n.* —**inˈfectious** *a.* catching, spreading, pestilential —**infectious hepatitis** acute infectious viral disease characterized by inflammation of liver, fever and jaundice —**infectious mononucleosis** acute infectious disease characterized by fever, sore throat, swollen lymph nodes *etc.* (*also* **glandular fever**)

infelicitous (ɪnfɪˈlɪsɪtəs) *a.* unfortunate; unsuitable —**infeˈlicity** *n.* **1.** being infelicitous **2.** unsuitable or inapt remark *etc.*

infer (ɪnˈfɜː) *vt.* deduce, conclude (-rr-) —**ˈinference** *n.* —**inferˈential** *a.* deduced

inferior (ɪnˈfɪərɪə) *a.* **1.** of poor quality **2.** lower —*n.* **3.** one lower (in rank *etc.*) —**inferiˈority** *n.* —**inferiority complex** *Psychoanal.* repressed sense of inferiority

infernal (ɪnˈfɜːnᵊl) *a.* **1.** devilish **2.** hellish **3.** *inf.* irritating, confounded —**inˈfernally** *adv.*

inferno (ɪnˈfɜːnəʊ) *n.* **1.** region of hell **2.** conflagration (*pl.* -s)

infest (ɪnˈfɛst) *vt.* inhabit or overrun in dangerously or unpleasantly large numbers —**infesˈtation** *n.*

infidelity (ɪnfɪˈdɛlɪtɪ) *n.* **1.** unfaithfulness **2.** religious disbelief **3.** disloyalty **4.** treachery —**ˈinfidel** *n.* **1.** unbeliever —*a.* **2.** rejecting a specific religion, *esp.* Christianity or Islam **3.** of unbelievers or unbelief

infield (ˈɪnfiːld) *n.* **1.** *Cricket* area of field near pitch **2.** *Baseball* area of playing field enclosed by base lines —**ˈinfielder** *n.*

infighting (ˈɪnfaɪtɪŋ) *n.* **1.** *Boxing* combat at close quarters **2.** intense conflict, as between members of same organization —**ˈinfighter** *n.*

infiltrate (ˈɪnfɪltreɪt) *v.* **1.** trickle through —*vt.* **2.** (cause to) gain access surreptitiously **3.** cause to pass through pores —**infilˈtration** *n.*

infin. infinitive

infinite (ˈɪnfɪnɪt) *a.* boundless —**ˈinfinitely** *adv.* exceedingly —**infiniˈtesimal** *a.* extremely, infinitely small —**inˈfinitude** *n.* state or quality of being infinite —**inˈfinity** *n.* unlimited and endless extent

infinitive (ɪnˈfɪnɪtɪv) *a.* **1.** *Gram.* in mood expressing notion of verb without limitation of tense, person or number —*n.* **2.** verb in this mood **3.** the mood

infirm (ɪnˈfɜːm) *a.* **1.** physically weak **2.** mentally weak **3.** irresolute —**inˈfirmary** *n.* hospital; sick quarters —**inˈfirmity** *n.*

infix (ɪnˈfɪks, ˈɪnfɪks) *vt.* **1.** fix firmly in **2.** instil, inculcate **3.** *Gram.* insert (affix) into middle of word

THESAURUS

neonate, newborn child, suckling, toddler, tot, wean (*Scot.*)

infantile babyish, childish, immature, puerile, tender, weak, young

infatuate befool, beguile, besot, bewitch, captivate, delude, enchant, enrapture, enravish, fascinate, make a fool of, mislead, obsess, stupefy, sweep one off one's feet, turn (someone's) head

infatuated beguiled, besotted, bewitched, captivated, carried away, crazy about (*Inf.*), enamoured, enraptured, fascinated, head over heels in love with, inflamed, intoxicated, obsessed, possessed, smitten (*Inf.*), spellbound, swept off one's feet, under the spell of

infatuation crush (*Inf.*), fixation, folly, foolishness, madness, obsession, passion, thing (*Inf.*)

infect affect, blight, contaminate, corrupt, defile, influence, poison, pollute, spread to *or* among, taint, touch, vitiate

infection contagion, contamination, corruption, defilement, poison, pollution, septicity, virus

infectious catching, communicable, contagious, contaminating, corrupting, defiling, infective, pestilential, poisoning, polluting, spreading, transmittable, virulent, vitiating

infer conclude, conjecture, deduce, derive, gather, presume, read between the lines, surmise, understand

inference assumption, conclusion, conjecture, consequence, corollary, deduction, illation (*Rare*), presumption, reading, surmise

inferior *adj.* **1.** junior, lesser, lower, menial, minor, secondary, subordinate, subsidiary, under, underneath **2.** bad, imperfect, indifferent, low-grade, mean, mediocre, poor, poorer, second-class, second-rate, shoddy, substandard, worse ~*n.* **3.** junior, menial, subordinate, underling

inferiority **1.** badness, deficiency, imperfection, inadequacy, insignificance, meanness, mediocrity, shoddiness, unimportance, worthlessness **2.** abasement, inferior status *or* standing, lowliness, subordination, subservience

infernal **1.** chthonian, Hadean, hellish, lower, nether, Plutonian, Stygian, Tartarean (*Literary*), underworld **2.** accursed, damnable, damned, demonic, devilish, diabolical, fiendish, hellish, malevolent, malicious, satanic

infertile barren, infecund, nonproductive, sterile, unfruitful, unproductive

infertility barrenness, infecundity, sterility, unfruitfulness, unproductiveness

infest beset, flood, invade, overrun, penetrate, ravage, swarm, throng

infiltrate creep in, filter through, insinuate oneself, penetrate, percolate, permeate, pervade, sneak in (*Inf.*), work *or* worm one's way into

infinite absolute, all-embracing, bottomless, boundless, enormous, eternal, everlasting, illimitable, immeasurable, immense, inestimable, inexhaustible, interminable, limitless, measureless, never-ending, numberless, perpetual, stupendous, total, unbounded, uncounted, untold, vast, wide, without end, without number

infinitesimal atomic, inappreciable, insignificant, microscopic, minuscule, minute, negligible, teeny, tiny, unnoticeable, wee

infinity boundlessness, endlessness, eternity, immensity, infinitude, perpetuity, vastness

infirm **1.** ailing, debilitated, decrepit, doddering, doddery, enfeebled, failing, feeble, frail, lame, weak **2.** faltering, indecisive, insecure, irresolute, shaky, unsound, unstable, vacillating, wavering, weak, wobbly

infirmity debility, decrepitude, deficiency, feebleness, frailty, ill health, imperfection, sickliness, vulnerability, weakness

—*n.* (ˈɪnfɪks) **4.** *Gram.* affix inserted into middle of word

in flagrante delicto (ɪn fləˈgræntɪ dɪˈlɪktəʊ) while committing the offence

inflame (ɪnˈfleɪm) *vt.* **1.** rouse to anger, excitement **2.** cause inflammation in —*vi* **3.** become inflamed —**inflammability** (ɪnflæməˈbɪlɪtɪ) *n.* —**inflammable** (ɪnˈflæməbᵊl) *a.* **1.** easily set on fire **2.** excitable —**inflammation** (ɪnfləˈmeɪʃən) *n.* infection of part of the body, with pain, heat, swelling and redness —**inflammatory** (ɪnˈflæmətərɪ, -trɪ) *a.*

inflate (ɪnˈfleɪt) *v.* **1.** blow up with air, gas **2.** swell —*vt.* **3.** cause economic inflation of (prices *etc.*) —*vi.* **4.** undergo economic inflation —**inˈflatable** *a.* —**inˈflation** *n.* increase in prices and fall in value of money —**inˈflationary** *a.*

inflect (ɪnˈflɛkt) *vt.* **1.** modify (words) to show grammatical relationships **2.** bend inwards —**inˈflection** *or* **inˈflexion** *n.* **1.** modification of word **2.** modulation of voice

inflexible (ɪnˈflɛksəbᵊl) *a.* **1.** incapable of being bent **2.** stern —**inflexiˈbility** *n.*

inflict (ɪnˈflɪkt) *vt.* **1.** impose **2.** deliver forcibly —**inˈfliction** *n.* **1.** inflicting **2.** punishment

in-flight *a.* provided during flight in aircraft

inflorescence (ɪnflɔːˈrɛsəns) *n.* **1.** the unfolding of blossoms **2.** *Bot.* arrangement of flowers on stem

inflow (ˈɪnfləʊ) *n.* **1.** something, such as liquid or gas, that flows in **2.** act of flowing in; influx

influence (ˈɪnflʊəns) *n.* **1.** effect of one person or thing on another **2.** power of person or thing having an effect **3.** thing, person exercising this —*vt.* **4.** sway **5.** induce **6.** affect —**influˈential** *a.*

influenza (ɪnflʊˈɛnzə) *n.* contagious feverish catarrhal virus disease

influx (ˈɪnflʌks) *n.* **1.** a flowing in **2.** inflow

info (ˈɪnfəʊ) *n. inf.* information

infold (ɪnˈfəʊld) *vt. see* ENFOLD

inform (ɪnˈfɔːm) *vt.* **1.** tell **2.** animate —*vi.* **3.** (*oft. with* on *or* against) give information (about) —**inˈformant** *n.* one who tells —**inforˈmation** *n.* **1.** knowledge acquired through experience or study **2.** knowledge of specific and timely events or situations; news **3.** act of informing; condition of being informed **4.** office, agency *etc.* providing information **5.** charge or complaint made before justices of peace, usu. on oath, to institute summary criminal proceedings **6.** *Comp.* results derived from processing of data according to programmed instructions **7.** *Comp.* information operated on by computer program (*also* **ˈdata**) —**inforˈmational** *a.* —**inˈformative** *a.* —**inˈformed** *a.* having much knowledge or education; learned, cultured —**inˈformer** *n.* **1.** person who informs against someone, *esp.* criminal **2.** person who provides information —**information technology** technology concerned with collecting and storing information, *esp.* by computer or electronically —**information theory** collection of mathematical theories concerned with coding, transmitting, storing, retrieving and decoding information

THESAURUS

inflame agitate, anger, arouse, embitter, enrage, exasperate, excite, fire, foment, heat, ignite, impassion, incense, infuriate, intoxicate, kindle, madden, provoke, rile, rouse, stimulate

inflammable combustible, flammable, incendiary

inflammation burning, heat, painfulness, rash, redness, sore, soreness, tenderness

inflammatory anarchic, demagogic, explosive, fiery, incendiary, inflaming, instigative, insurgent, intemperate, provocative, rabble-rousing, rabid, riotous, seditious

inflate aerate, amplify, balloon, bloat, blow up, boost, dilate, distend, enlarge, escalate, expand, increase, puff up *or* out, pump up, swell

inflection **1.** accentuation, intonation, modulation **2.** *Gram.* conjugation, declension

inflexibility **1.** hardness, immovability, inelasticity, rigidity, stiffness, stringency **2.** fixity, intransigence, obduracy, obstinacy, steeliness

inflexible **1.** adamant, brassbound, dyed-in-the-wool, firm, fixed, hard and fast, immovable, immutable, implacable, inexorable, intractable, iron, obdurate, obstinate, relentless, resolute, rigorous, set, set in one's ways, steadfast, steely, strict, stringent, stubborn, unadaptable, unbending, unchangeable, uncompromising, unyielding **2.** hard, hardened, inelastic, nonflexible, rigid, stiff, taut

inflict administer, apply, deliver, exact, impose, levy, mete *or* deal out, visit, wreak

infliction **1.** administration, exaction, imposition, perpetration, wreaking **2.** affliction, penalty, punishment, trouble, visitation, worry

influence *n.* **1.** agency, ascendancy, authority, control, credit, direction, domination, effect, guidance, magnetism, mastery, power, pressure, rule, spell, sway, weight **2.** clout (*Inf.*), connections, good offices, hold, importance, leverage, power, prestige, pull (*Inf.*), weight ~*v.* **3.** act *or* work upon, affect, arouse, bias, control, count, direct, dispose, guide, impel, impress, incite, incline, induce, instigate, lead to believe, manipulate, modify, move, persuade, predispose, prompt, rouse, sway **4.** bring pressure to bear upon, carry weight with, make oneself felt, pull strings (*Inf.*)

influential authoritative, controlling, effective, efficacious, forcible, guiding, important, instrumental, leading, meaningful, momentous, moving, persuasive, potent, powerful, significant, telling, weighty

influx arrival, convergence, flow, incursion, inflow, inrush, inundation, invasion, rush

inform **1.** acquaint, advise, apprise, communicate, enlighten, give (someone) to understand, instruct, leak to, let know, make conversant (with), notify, put (someone) in the picture (*Inf.*), send word to, teach, tell, tip off **2.** *Often with* **against** *or* **on** betray, blab, blow the whistle on (*U.S. inf.*), clype (*Scot.*), denounce, grass (*Brit. sl.*), incriminate, inculpate, nark (*Brit. sl.*), peach (*Sl.*), rat, snitch (*Sl.*), squeal (*Sl.*), tell on (*Inf.*) **3.** animate, characterize, illuminate, imbue, inspire, permeate, suffuse, typify

informal casual, colloquial, easy, familiar, natural, relaxed, simple, unceremonious, unconstrained, unofficial

information advice, counsel, data, dope (*Sl.*), facts, gen (*Brit. inf.*), info (*Inf.*), inside story, instruction, intelligence, knowledge, lowdown (*Inf.*), material, message, news, notice, report, tidings, word

informative edifying, educational, enlightening, illuminating, instructive, revealing

infra (ˈɪnfrə) *adv.* 1. below 2. under 3. after —**infra dig** *inf.* beneath one's dignity —**infraˈred** *a.* denoting rays below red end of visible spectrum —**infraˈsonic** *a.* having frequency below that of sound

infraction (ɪnˈfrækʃən) *n. see* INFRINGE

infrangible (ɪnˈfrændʒɪbᵊl) *a.* 1. incapable of being broken 2. not capable of being violated or infringed —**infrangiˈbility** *or* **inˈfrangibleness** *n.*

infrastructure (ˈɪnfrəstrʌktʃə) *n.* basic structure or fixed capital items of an organization or economic system

infringe (ɪnˈfrɪndʒ) *vt.* transgress, break —**inˈfraction** *n.* breach, violation —**inˈfringement** *n.*

infuriate (ɪnˈfjʊərɪeɪt) *vt.* enrage

infuse (ɪnˈfjuːz) *v.* 1. soak to extract flavour *etc.* —*vt.* 2. instil, charge —**inˈfusible** *a.* capable of being infused —**inˈfusion** *n.* 1. an infusing 2. liquid extract obtained

infusible (ɪnˈfjuːzəbᵊl) *a.* not fusible; not easily melted; having high melting point —**infusiˈbility** *or* **inˈfusibleness** *n.*

-ing[1] (*comb. form*) 1. action of, process of, result of or something connected with verb, as in *meeting, wedding, winnings* 2. something used in, consisting of, involving *etc.*, as in *tubing, soldiering*

-ing[2] (*comb. form*) 1. forming present participle of verbs, as in *walking, believing* 2. forming participial adjectives, as in *growing boy, sinking ship* 3. forming adjectives not derived from verbs, as in *swashbuckling*

ingenious (ɪnˈdʒiːnjəs, -nɪəs) *a.* 1. clever at contriving 2. cleverly contrived —**inˈgeniously** *adv.* —**ingeˈnuity** *n.*

ingénue (ænʒeɪˈnjuː) *n.* 1. artless girl or young woman 2. actress playing such a part

ingenuous (ɪnˈdʒɛnjʊəs) *a.* 1. frank 2. naive, innocent —**inˈgenuously** *adv.*

ingest (ɪnˈdʒɛst) *vt.* take (food or liquid) into the body —**inˈgestible** *a.* —**inˈgestion** *n.*

inglenook (ˈɪŋgᵊlnʊk) *n.* corner by a fireplace

inglorious (ɪnˈglɔːrɪəs) *a.* dishonourable, shameful, disgraceful

ingot (ˈɪŋgət) *n.* brick of cast metal, *esp.* gold

ingrain *or* **engrain** (ɪnˈgreɪn) *vt.* 1. implant deeply 2. *obs.* dye, infuse deeply —**inˈgrained** *or* **enˈgrained** *a.* 1. deep-rooted 2. inveterate 3. (*esp.* of dirt) worked into or through fibre, grain, pores *etc.*

ingratiate (ɪnˈgreɪʃɪeɪt) *v. refl.* get (oneself) into favour —**inˈgratiatingly** *adv.*

ingredient (ɪnˈgriːdɪənt) *n.* component part of a mixture

ingress (ˈɪngrɛs) *n.* 1. entry 2. means or right of entrance

ingrown (ˈɪngrəʊn, ɪnˈgrəʊn) *a.* 1. (*esp.* of toenail) grown abnormally into flesh 2. grown within; native; innate

inhabit (ɪnˈhæbɪt) *vt.* dwell in —**inˈhabitable** *a.* —**inˈhabitant** *n.* —**inhabiˈtation** *n.*

inhale (ɪnˈheɪl) *v.* breathe in (air *etc.*) —**inˈhalant** *a.* 1. (*esp.* of medicinal preparation) inhaled for its therapeutic effect 2. inhaling —*n.* 3. inhalant medicinal preparation —**inhaˈlation** *n.* —**inˈhaler** *n.* device producing and assisting inhalation of therapeutic vapours

inhere (ɪnˈhɪə) *vi.* 1. (of qualities) exist 2. (of rights) be vested —**inˈherence** *or* **inˈherency** *n.* —**inˈherent** *a.* existing as an inseparable part

inherit (ɪnˈhɛrɪt) *vt.* 1. receive as heir 2. derive from parents —*vi.* 3. succeed as heir —**inheritaˈbility** *or* **inˈheritableness** *n.* —**inˈheritable** *a.* 1. capable of

THESAURUS

informed abreast, acquainted, *au courant, au fait*, briefed, conversant, enlightened, erudite, expert, familiar, genned up (*Brit. inf.*), in the know (*Inf.*), knowledgeable, learned, posted, primed, reliable, up, up to date, versed, well-read

informer accuser, betrayer, grass (*Brit. sl.*), Judas, nark (*Brit. sl.*), sneak, squealer (*Sl.*), stool pigeon

infrequent few and far between, occasional, rare, sporadic, uncommon, unusual

infringe break, contravene, disobey, transgress, violate

infringement breach, contravention, infraction, noncompliance, nonobservance, transgression, trespass, violation

infuriate anger, be like a red rag to a bull, enrage, exasperate, get one's back up (*Inf.*), get one's goat (*Sl.*), incense, irritate, madden, make one's blood boil, make one see red (*Inf.*), make one's hackles rise, provoke, raise one's hackles, rile

ingenious adroit, bright, brilliant, clever, crafty, creative, dexterous, fertile, inventive, masterly, original, ready, resourceful, shrewd, skilful, subtle

ingenuity adroitness, cleverness, faculty, flair, genius, gift, ingeniousness, inventiveness, knack, originality, resourcefulness, sharpness, shrewdness, skill, turn

ingenuous artless, candid, childlike, frank, guileless, honest, innocent, naive, open, plain, simple, sincere, trustful, trusting, unreserved, unsophisticated, unstudied

inglorious discreditable, disgraceful, dishonourable, disreputable, failed, humiliating, ignoble, ignominious, infamous, obscure, shameful, unheroic, unknown, unsuccessful, unsung

ingratiate be a yes man, blandish, crawl, curry favour, fawn, flatter, get in with (*Inf.*), get on the right side of, grovel, insinuate oneself, lick (someone's) boots, play up to, rub (someone) up the right way (*Inf.*), seek the favour (of someone), suck up to (*Inf.*), toady, worm oneself into (someone's) favour

ingratitude thanklessness, unappreciativeness, ungratefulness

ingredient component, constituent, element, part

inhabit abide, dwell, live, lodge, make one's home, occupy, people, populate, possess, reside, take up residence in, tenant

inhabitant aborigine, citizen, denizen, dweller, indigene, indweller, inmate, native, occupant, occupier, resident, tenant

inhale breathe in, draw in, gasp, respire, suck in

inherent basic, congenital, connate, essential, hereditary, inborn, inbred, inbuilt, ingrained, inherited, innate, instinctive, intrinsic, native, natural

inherit accede to, be bequeathed, be left, come into, fall heir to, succeed to

inheritance bequest, birthright, heritage, legacy, patrimony

being transmitted by heredity **2.** capable of being inherited —**in'heritance** *n.*

inhesion (ɪn'hiːʒən) *n.* inherence

inhibit (ɪn'hɪbɪt) *vt.* **1.** restrain (impulse, desire *etc.*) **2.** hinder (action) **3.** forbid —**inhibition** (ɪnɪ'bɪʃən, ɪnhɪ-) *n.* **1.** repression of emotion, instinct **2.** a stopping or retarding —**in'hibitory** *a.*

inhuman (ɪn'hjuːmən) *a.* **1.** cruel, brutal **2.** not human —**inhu'manity** *n.*

inhume (ɪn'hjuːm) *vt.* bury, inter —**inhu'mation** *n.*

inimical (ɪ'nɪmɪk°l) *a.* **1.** unfavourable **2.** unfriendly; hostile

inimitable (ɪ'nɪmɪtəb°l) *a.* defying imitation

iniquity (ɪ'nɪkwɪtɪ) *n.* **1.** gross injustice **2.** wickedness, sin —**in'iquitous** *a.* **1.** unfair, unjust **2.** sinful **3.** *inf.* outrageous

initial (ɪ'nɪʃəl) *a.* **1.** of, occurring at the beginning —*n.* **2.** initial letter, *esp.* of person's name —*vt.* **3.** mark, sign with one's initials (**-ll-**) —**in'itially** *adv.* —**initial teaching alphabet** alphabet of 44 characters for teaching beginners to read English

initiate (ɪ'nɪʃɪeɪt) *vt.* **1.** originate, begin **2.** admit into closed society **3.** instruct in elements of something —*n.* (ɪ'nɪʃɪɪt, -eɪt) **4.** initiated person —**initi'ation** *n.* —**in'itiative** *n.* **1.** first step, lead **2.** ability to act independently —*a.* **3.** originating —**in'itiatory** *a.*

inject (ɪn'dʒɛkt) *vt.* introduce (*esp.* fluid, medicine *etc.* with syringe) —**in'jection** *n.*

injunction (ɪn'dʒʌŋkʃən) *n.* **1.** judicial order to restrain **2.** authoritative order

injury ('ɪndʒərɪ) *n.* **1.** physical damage or harm **2.** wrong —**'injurable** *a.* —**'injure** *vt.* **1.** do harm or damage to **2.** offend, *esp.* by injustice —**'injured** *a.* —**in'jurious** *a.* —**in'juriously** *adv.* —**injury time** *Soccer* extra time added on to compensate for time spent attending to injured players during match

injustice (ɪn'dʒʌstɪs) *n.* **1.** want of justice **2.** wrong **3.** injury **4.** unjust act

THESAURUS

inhibit arrest, bar, bridle, check, constrain, cramp (someone's) style (*Inf.*), curb, debar, discourage, forbid, frustrate, hinder, hold back *or* in, impede, obstruct, prevent, prohibit, restrain, stop

inhibition bar, check, embargo, hang-up (*Sl.*), hindrance, interdict, mental blockage, obstacle, prohibition, reserve, restraint, restriction, reticence, self-consciousness, shyness

inhospitable 1. cool, uncongenial, unfriendly, ungenerous, unkind, unreceptive, unsociable, unwelcoming, xenophobic **2.** bare, barren, bleak, desolate, empty, forbidding, hostile, lonely, sterile, unfavourable, uninhabitable

inhuman animal, barbaric, barbarous, bestial, brutal, cold-blooded, cruel, diabolical, fiendish, heartless, merciless, pitiless, remorseless, ruthless, savage, unfeeling, vicious

inhumanity atrocity, barbarism, brutality, brutishness, cold-bloodedness, cold-heartedness, cruelty, hardheartedness, heartlessness, pitilessness, ruthlessness, unkindness, viciousness

inimical adverse, antagonistic, antipathetic, contrary, destructive, disaffected, harmful, hostile, hurtful, ill-disposed, injurious, noxious, opposed, oppugnant (*Rare*), pernicious, repugnant, unfavourable, unfriendly, unwelcoming

inimitable consummate, incomparable, matchless, nonpareil, peerless, supreme, unequalled, unexampled, unique, unmatched, unparalleled, unrivalled, unsurpassable

iniquitous abominable, accursed, atrocious, base, criminal, evil, heinous, immoral, infamous, nefarious, reprehensible, reprobate, sinful, unjust, unrighteous, vicious, wicked

iniquity abomination, baseness, crime, evil, evildoing, heinousness, infamy, injustice, misdeed, offence, sin, sinfulness, unrighteousness, wickedness, wrong, wrongdoing

initial *adj.* beginning, commencing, early, first, inaugural, inceptive, inchoate, incipient, introductory, opening, primary

initially at *or* in the beginning, at first, at the outset, at the start, first, firstly, in the early stages, originally, primarily, to begin with

initiate *v.* **1.** begin, break the ice, commence, get under way, inaugurate, institute, kick off (*Inf.*), launch, lay the foundations of, open, originate, pioneer, set going, set in motion, set the ball rolling, start **2.** coach, familiarize with, indoctrinate, induct, instate, instruct, introduce, invest, teach, train ~*n.* **3.** beginner, convert, entrant, learner, member, novice, probationer, proselyte, tyro

initiation admission, commencement, debut, enrolment, entrance, inauguration, inception, induction, installation, instatement, introduction, investiture

initiative 1. advantage, beginning, commencement, first move, first step, lead **2.** ambition, drive, dynamism, enterprise, get-up-and-go (*Inf.*), inventiveness, leadership, originality, push (*Inf.*), resource, resourcefulness

inject 1. inoculate, jab (*Inf.*), shoot (*Inf.*), vaccinate **2.** bring in, infuse, insert, instil, interject, introduce

injection 1. inoculation, jab (*Inf.*), shot (*Inf.*), vaccination, vaccine **2.** dose, infusion, insertion, interjection, introduction

injudicious foolish, hasty, ill-advised, ill-judged, ill-timed, impolitic, imprudent, incautious, inconsiderate, indiscreet, inexpedient, rash, unthinking, unwise

injunction admonition, command, dictate, exhortation, instruction, mandate, order, precept, ruling

injure abuse, blemish, blight, break, damage, deface, disable, harm, hurt, impair, maltreat, mar, ruin, spoil, tarnish, undermine, vitiate, weaken, wound, wrong

injured 1. broken, disabled, hurt, lamed, undermined, weakened, wounded **2.** cut to the quick, disgruntled, displeased, hurt, long-suffering, put out, reproachful, stung, unhappy, upset, wounded **3.** abused, blackened, blemished, defamed, ill-treated, maligned, maltreated, offended, tarnished, vilified, wronged

injury abuse, damage, detriment, disservice, evil, grievance, harm, hurt, ill, injustice, mischief, ruin, wound, wrong

injustice bias, discrimination, favouritism, inequality, inequity, iniquity, one-sidedness, oppression, partiality, partisanship, prejudice, unfairness, unjustness, unlawfulness, wrong

ink (ɪŋk) *n.* **1.** fluid used for writing or printing —*vt.* **2.** mark with ink **3.** cover, smear with ink —**ˈinker** *n.* —**ˈinky** *a.* **1.** resembling ink, *esp.* in colour; dark; black **2.** of, containing or stained with ink —**ˈinkstand** *n.* —**ˈinkwell** *n.* vessel for holding ink

inkling (ˈɪŋklɪŋ) *n.* hint, slight knowledge or suspicion

inkosi (ɪŋˈkɔːsɪ) *n.* SA chief, leader

inlaid (ˈɪnleɪd, ɪnˈleɪd) *pt./pp. of* INLAY

inland (ˈɪnlænd, -lənd) *n.* **1.** interior of country —*a.* (ˈɪnlənd) **2.** in interior of country **3.** away from the sea **4.** within a country —*adv.* **5.** in or towards the inland

in-law *n.* relative by marriage

inlay (ɪnˈleɪ) *vt.* **1.** embed **2.** decorate with inset pattern (**ˈinlaid** *pt./pp.*) —*n.* (ˈɪnleɪ) **3.** inlaid piece or pattern

inlet (ˈɪnlɛt) *n.* **1.** entrance **2.** mouth of creek **3.** piece inserted

in loco parentis (ɪn ˈləʊkəʊ pəˈrɛntɪs) *Lat.* in place of a parent

inmate (ˈɪnmeɪt) *n.* occupant, *esp.* of prison, hospital *etc.*

inmost (ˈɪnməʊst) *a. sup. of* IN most inward, deepest

inn (ɪn) *n.* **1.** public house providing food and accommodation **2.** hotel —**ˈinnkeeper** *n.* —**Inns of Court 1.** four societies admitting to English Bar **2.** their buildings

innards (ˈɪnədz) *pl.n. inf.* internal organs or working parts (*orig.* **ˈinwards**)

innate (ɪˈneɪt, ˈɪneɪt) *a.* **1.** inborn **2.** inherent

inner (ˈɪnə) *a.* **1.** lying within —*n.* **2.** ring next to bull's-eye on target —**ˈinnermost** *a.* —**inner city** sections of a large city in or near its centre —**inner man 1.** mind; soul **2.** *jocular* stomach; appetite (**inner woman** *fem.*) —**inner tube** rubber air tube of pneumatic tyre

innings (ˈɪnɪŋz) *n.* **1.** (*with sing. v.*) *Sport* player's or side's turn of batting **2.** (*sometimes with sing. v.*) spell, turn

innocent (ˈɪnəsənt) *a.* **1.** pure **2.** guiltless **3.** harmless —*n.* **4.** innocent person, *esp.* young child —**ˈinnocence** *n.* —**ˈinnocently** *adv.*

innocuous (ɪˈnɒkjʊəs) *a.* harmless

innovate (ˈɪnəveɪt) *vt.* introduce (changes, new things) —**innoˈvation** *n.* —**ˈinnovator** *n.*

innuendo (ɪnjʊˈɛndəʊ) *n.* **1.** allusive remark, hint **2.** indirect accusation (*pl.* **-es**)

innumerable (ɪˈnjuːmərəbᵊl, ɪˈnjuːmrəbᵊl) *or* **innumerous** *a.* countless; very numerous

innumerate (ɪˈnjuːmərɪt) *a.* **1.** having neither knowledge nor understanding of mathematics or science —*n.* **2.** innumerate person —**inˈnumeracy** *n.*

inoculate (ɪˈnɒkjʊleɪt) *vt.* immunize by injecting vaccine —**inocuˈlation** *n.*

inoperable (ɪnˈɒpərəbᵊl, -ˈɒprə-) *a.* **1.** unworkable **2.** *Med.* that cannot be operated on —**inˈoperative** *a.* **1.** not operative **2.** ineffective

inopportune (ɪnˈɒpətjuːn) *a.* badly timed

inordinate (ɪnˈɔːdɪnɪt) *a.* excessive

inorganic (ɪnɔːˈgænɪk) *a.* **1.** not having structure or characteristics of living organisms **2.** of substances without carbon

inpatient (ˈɪnpeɪʃənt) *n.* patient that stays in hospital

in perpetuum (ɪn pɜːˈpɛtjʊəm) *Lat.* for ever

input (ˈɪnpʊt) *n.* **1.** act of putting in **2.** that which is put

THESAURUS

inkling clue, conception, faintest *or* foggiest idea, glimmering, hint, idea, indication, intimation, notion, suggestion, suspicion, whisper

inland *adj.* domestic, interior, internal, upcountry

inlet arm (of the sea), bay, bight, cove, creek, entrance, firth *or* frith (*Scot.*), ingress, passage, sea loch (*Scot.*)

inmost basic, buried, central, deep, deepest, essential, intimate, personal, private, secret

innate congenital, connate, constitutional, essential, inborn, inbred, indigenous, ingrained, inherent, inherited, instinctive, intrinsic, intuitive, native, natural

inner central, essential, inside, interior, internal, intestinal, inward, middle

innkeeper host, hostess, hotelier, landlady, landlord, mine host, publican

innocence 1. blamelessness, chastity, clean hands, guiltlessness, incorruptibility, probity, purity, righteousness, sinlessness, stainlessness, uprightness, virginity, virtue **2.** harmlessness, innocuousness, innoxiousness, inoffensiveness

innocent *adj.* **1.** blameless, clear, faultless, guiltless, honest, in the clear, not guilty, uninvolved, unoffending **2.** chaste, immaculate, impeccable, incorrupt, pristine, pure, righteous, sinless, spotless, stainless, unblemished, unsullied, upright, virgin, virginal **3.** harmless, innocuous, inoffensive, unmalicious, unobjectionable, well-intentioned, well-meant ~*n.* **4.** babe (in arms) (*Inf.*), child, greenhorn (*Inf.*), ingénue (*fem.*)

innovation alteration, change, departure, introduction, modernism, modernization, newness, novelty, variation

innuendo aspersion, hint, implication, imputation, insinuation, intimation, overtone, suggestion, whisper

innumerable beyond number, countless, incalculable, infinite, many, multitudinous, myriad, numberless, numerous, unnumbered, untold

inoffensive harmless, humble, innocent, innocuous, innoxious, mild, neutral, nonprovocative, peaceable, quiet, retiring, unobjectionable, unobtrusive, unoffending

inoperative broken, broken-down, defective, *hors de combat*, ineffective, ineffectual, inefficacious, invalid, nonactive, null and void, out of action, out of commission, out of order, out of service, unserviceable, unworkable, useless

inopportune ill-chosen, ill-timed, inappropriate, inauspicious, inconvenient, malapropos, mistimed, unfavourable, unfortunate, unpropitious, unseasonable, unsuitable, untimely

inordinate disproportionate, excessive, exorbitant, extravagant, immoderate, intemperate, preposterous, unconscionable, undue, unreasonable, unrestrained, unwarranted

inorganic artificial, chemical, man-made, mineral

inquest inquiry, inquisition, investigation, probe

in, as resource needed for industrial production *etc.* **3.** data *etc.* fed into a computer

inquest (ˈɪnkwɛst) *n.* **1.** legal or judicial inquiry presided over by a coroner **2.** detailed inquiry or discussion

inquietude (ɪnˈkwaɪɪtjuːd) *n.* restlessness, uneasiness, anxiety —**inˈquiet** *a.*

inquire *or* **enquire** (ɪnˈkwaɪə) *vi.* seek information —**inˈquirer** *or* **enˈquirer** *n.* —**inˈquiry** *or* **enˈquiry** *n.* **1.** question **2.** investigation

inquisition (ɪnkwɪˈzɪʃən) *n.* **1.** searching investigation, official inquiry **2.** *Hist.* (**I-**) tribunal for suppression of heresy —**inˈquisitor** *n.* —**inquisiˈtorial** *a.*

inquisitive (ɪnˈkwɪzɪtɪv) *a.* **1.** curious **2.** prying

in re (ɪn ˈreɪ) in the matter of: used *esp.* in bankruptcy proceedings

inroad (ˈɪnrəʊd) *n.* incursion

inrush (ˈɪnrʌʃ) *n.* sudden, usu. overwhelming, inward flow or rush; influx

ins. **1.** inches **2.** insurance

insane (ɪnˈseɪn) *a.* **1.** mentally deranged; crazy **2.** senseless —**inˈsanely** *adv.* **1.** like a lunatic, madly **2.** excessively —**insanity** (ɪnˈsænɪtɪ) *n.*

insatiable (ɪnˈseɪʃəbəl, -ʃɪə-) *or* **insatiate** (ɪnˈseɪʃɪɪt) *a.* incapable of being satisfied

inscribe (ɪnˈskraɪb) *vt.* **1.** write, engrave (in or on something) **2.** mark **3.** dedicate **4.** trace (figure) within another —**inscription** (ɪnˈskrɪpʃən) *n.* **1.** inscribing **2.** words inscribed on monument *etc.*

inscrutable (ɪnˈskruːtəbəl) *a.* **1.** mysterious, impenetrable **2.** affording no explanation —**inscrutaˈbility** *n.* —**inˈscrutably** *adv.*

insect (ˈɪnsɛkt) *n.* small invertebrate animal with six legs, usu. segmented body and two or four wings —**inˈsecticide** *n.* preparation for killing insects —**insecˈtivorous** *a.* insect-eating

insecure (ɪnsɪˈkjʊə) *a.* **1.** not safe or firm **2.** anxious, not confident

inseminate (ɪnˈsɛmɪneɪt) *vt.* implant semen into —**artificial insemination** impregnation of the female by artificial means

insensate (ɪnˈsɛnseɪt, -sɪt) *a.* **1.** without sensation, unconscious **2.** unfeeling

insensible (ɪnˈsɛnsəbəl) *a.* **1.** unconscious **2.** without feeling **3.** not aware **4.** not perceptible —**insensiˈbility** *n.* —**inˈsensibly** *adv.* imperceptibly

insert (ɪnˈsɜːt) *vt.* **1.** introduce **2.** place or put in, into or between —*n.* (ˈɪnsɜːt) **3.** something inserted —**inˈsertion** *n.*

THESAURUS

inquire, enquire ask, query, question, request information, seek information

inquiry, enquiry 1. examination, exploration, inquest, interrogation, investigation, probe, research, scrutiny, search, study, survey 2. query, question

inquisition cross-examination, examination, grilling (*Inf.*), inquest, inquiry, investigation, question, quizzing, third degree (*Inf.*)

inquisitive curious, inquiring, intrusive, nosy (*Inf.*), nosy-parkering (*Inf.*), peering, probing, prying, questioning, scrutinizing, snooping (*Inf.*), snoopy (*Inf.*)

inroad advance, encroachment, foray, incursion, intrusion, invasion, irruption, onslaught, raid

insane 1. crazed, crazy, demented, deranged, mad, mentally disordered, mentally ill, *non compos mentis*, of unsound mind, out of one's mind, unhinged 2. barmy (*Sl.*), batty (*Sl.*), bonkers (*Sl.*), cracked (*Sl.*), crackers (*Sl.*), cuckoo (*Inf.*), loony (*Sl.*), loopy (*Inf.*), mental (*Sl.*), nuts (*Sl.*), nutty (*Sl.*), off one's chump (*Inf.*), off one's head (*Inf.*), off one's nut (*Inf.*), off one's rocker (*Inf.*), round the bend (*Inf.*), round the twist (*Inf.*), screwy (*Inf.*) 3. bizarre, daft (*Inf.*), fatuous, foolish, idiotic, impractical, irrational, irresponsible, lunatic (*Inf.*), preposterous, senseless, stupid

insanitary contaminated, dirtied, dirty, disease-ridden, feculent, filthy, impure, infected, infested, insalubrious, noxious, polluted, unclean, unhealthy, unhygienic

insanity 1. aberration, craziness, delirium, dementia, frenzy, madness, mental derangement, mental disorder, mental illness 2. folly, irresponsibility, lunacy, preposterousness, senselessness, stupidity

insatiable gluttonous, greedy, insatiate, intemperate, quenchless, rapacious, ravenous, unappeasable, unquenchable, voracious

inscribe 1. carve, cut, engrave, etch, impress, imprint 2. engross, enlist, enrol, enter, record, register, write 3. address, dedicate

inscription dedication, engraving, label, legend, lettering, saying, words

inscrutable 1. blank, deadpan, enigmatic, impenetrable, poker-faced (*Inf.*), sphinxlike, unreadable 2. hidden, incomprehensible, inexplicable, mysterious, undiscoverable, unexplainable, unfathomable, unintelligible

insecure 1. afraid, anxious, uncertain, unconfident, unsure 2. dangerous, defenceless, exposed, hazardous, ill-protected, open to attack, perilous, unguarded, unprotected, unsafe, unshielded, vulnerable 3. built upon sand, flimsy, frail, insubstantial, loose, on thin ice, precarious, rickety, rocky, shaky, unreliable, unsound, unstable, unsteady, weak, wobbly

insensibility 1. apathy, callousness, dullness, indifference, insensitivity, lethargy, thoughtlessness, torpor 2. inertness, numbness, unconsciousness

insensible 1. anaesthetized, benumbed, dull, inert, insensate, numbed, senseless, stupid, torpid 2. apathetic, callous, cold, deaf, hard-hearted, impassive, impervious, indifferent, oblivious, unaffected, unaware, unconscious, unfeeling, unmindful, unmoved, unresponsive, unsusceptible, untouched 3. imperceivable, imperceptible, minuscule, negligible, unnoticeable

insensitive callous, crass, hardened, imperceptive, indifferent, obtuse, tactless, thick-skinned, tough, uncaring, unconcerned, unfeeling, unresponsive, unsusceptible

inseparable 1. conjoined, inalienable, indissoluble, indivisible, inseverable 2. bosom, close, devoted, intimate

insert embed, enter, implant, infix, interject, interpolate, interpose, introduce, place, pop in (*Inf.*), put, set, stick in, tuck in, work in

insertion addition, implant, inclusion, insert, inset, interpolation, introduction, supplement

in-service *a.* denoting training that is given to employees during the course of employment

inset (ˈɪnsɛt) *n.* **1.** something extra inserted, *esp.* as decoration —*vt.* (ɪnˈsɛt) **2.** set or place in or within; insert

inshore (ˈɪnˈʃɔː) *adv./a.* near shore

inside (ˈɪnˈsaɪd) *n.* **1.** inner side, surface or part —*a.* (ˈɪnsaɪd) **2.** of, in, or on inside —*adv.* (ɪnˈsaɪd) **3.** in or into the inside **4.** *sl.* in prison —*prep.* (ɪnˈsaɪd) **5.** within, on inner side of

insidious (ɪnˈsɪdɪəs) *a.* **1.** stealthy, treacherous **2.** unseen but deadly —**inˈsidiously** *adv.*

insight (ˈɪnsaɪt) *n.* mental penetration, discernment

insignia (ɪnˈsɪgnɪə) *pl.n.* badges, emblems of honour or office (*sing.* **inˈsignia**)

insinuate (ɪnˈsɪnjʊeɪt) *vt.* **1.** hint **2.** work (oneself) into favour **3.** introduce gradually or subtly —**insinuˈation** *n.*

insipid (ɪnˈsɪpɪd) *a.* **1.** dull, spiritless **2.** tasteless —**insiˈpidity** *n.*

insist (ɪnˈsɪst) *vi.* (*oft. with* on *or* upon) **1.** demand persistently **2.** maintain **3.** emphasize —**inˈsistence** *n.* —**inˈsistent** *a.*

in situ (ɪn ˈsɪtjuː) *Lat.* in its original position

in so far *or U.S.* **insofar** *adv.* (*usu. with* as *or* that) to the degree or extent (that)

insole (ˈɪnsəʊl) *n.* **1.** inner sole of shoe or boot **2.** loose additional inner sole to give extra warmth or make shoe fit

insolent (ˈɪnsələnt) *a.* arrogantly impudent —**ˈinsolence** *n.* —**ˈinsolently** *adv.*

insomnia (ɪnˈsɒmnɪə) *n.* sleeplessness —**inˈsomniac** *a./n.*

insomuch (ɪnsəʊˈmʌtʃ) *adv.* to such an extent

insouciant (ɪnˈsuːsɪənt) *a.* indifferent, careless, unconcerned —**inˈsouciance** *n.*

inspan (ɪnˈspæn) *vt.* SA harness, yoke (**-nn-**)

inspect (ɪnˈspɛkt) *vt.* examine closely or officially —**inˈspection** *n.* —**inˈspector** *n.* **1.** one who inspects **2.** high-ranking police officer —**inˈspectorate** *n.* **1.** office, rank or duties of inspector **2.** body of inspectors **3.** district under inspector —**inspecˈtorial** *a.*

THESAURUS

inside **1.** *n.* contents, inner part, interior **2.** *adv.* indoors, under cover, within **3.** *adj.* inner, innermost, interior, internal, intramural, inward

insidious artful, crafty, crooked, cunning, deceitful, deceptive, designing, disingenuous, duplicitous, guileful, intriguing, Machiavellian, slick, sly, smooth, sneaking, stealthy, subtle, surreptitious, treacherous, tricky, wily

insight acumen, awareness, comprehension, discernment, intuition, intuitiveness, judgment, observation, penetration, perception, perspicacity, understanding, vision

insignia badge, crest, decoration, distinguishing mark, earmark, emblem, ensign, symbol

insignificant flimsy, immaterial, inconsequential, inconsiderable, irrelevant, meagre, meaningless, minor, negligible, nondescript, nonessential, not worth mentioning, nugatory, of no account (consequence, moment), paltry, petty, scanty, trifling, trivial, unimportant, unsubstantial

insincere deceitful, deceptive, devious, dishonest, disingenuous, dissembling, dissimulating, double-dealing, duplicitous, evasive, faithless, false, hollow, hypocritical, Janus-faced, lying, mendacious, perfidious, pretended, two-faced, unfaithful, untrue, untruthful

insinuate **1.** allude, hint, imply, indicate, intimate, suggest **2.** infiltrate, infuse, inject, instil, introduce **3.** curry favour, get in with (*Inf.*), ingratiate, worm *or* work one's way in

insinuation **1.** allusion, aspersion, hint, implication, innuendo, slur, suggestion **2.** infiltration, infusion, ingratiating, injection, instillation, introduction

insipid **1.** anaemic, banal, bland, characterless, colourless, drab, dry, dull, flat, jejune, lifeless, limp, pointless, prosaic, prosy, spiritless, stale, stupid, tame, tedious, trite, unimaginative, uninteresting, vapid, weak, wearisome, wishy-washy (*Inf.*) **2.** bland, flavourless, savourless, tasteless, unappetizing, watered down, watery, wishy-washy (*Inf.*)

insipidity **1.** banality, colourlessness, dullness, flatness, lack of imagination, pointlessness, staleness, tameness, tediousness, triteness, uninterestingness, vapidity **2.** blandness, flavourlessness, lack of flavour, tastelessness

insist **1.** be firm, brook no refusal, demand, lay down the law, not take no for an answer, persist, press (someone), require, stand firm, stand one's ground, take *or* make a stand, urge **2.** assert, asseverate, aver, claim, contend, hold, maintain, reiterate, repeat, swear, urge, vow

insistence assertion, contention, demands, emphasis, importunity, insistency, persistence, pressing, reiteration, stress, urging

insistent demanding, dogged, emphatic, exigent, forceful, importunate, incessant, peremptory, persevering, persistent, pressing, unrelenting, urgent

insolence abuse, audacity, backchat (*Inf.*), boldness, cheek (*Inf.*), chutzpah (*U.S. inf.*), contemptuousness, contumely, disrespect, effrontery, gall (*Inf.*), impertinence, impudence, incivility, insubordination, offensiveness, pertness, rudeness, sauce (*Inf.*), uncivility

insolent abusive, bold, brazen-faced, contemptuous, fresh (*Inf.*), impertinent, impudent, insubordinate, insulting, pert, rude, saucy, uncivil

insoluble baffling, impenetrable, indecipherable, inexplicable, mysterious, mystifying, obscure, unaccountable, unfathomable, unsolvable

insolvent bankrupt, broke (*Inf.*), failed, gone bust (*Inf.*), gone to the wall (*Inf.*), in queer street (*Inf.*), in receivership, in the hands of the receivers, on the rocks (*Inf.*), ruined

insomnia sleeplessness, wakefulness

inspect check, examine, give (something *or* someone) the once-over (*Inf.*), go over *or* through, investigate, look over, oversee, scan, scrutinize, search, superintend, supervise, survey, vet

inspection check, checkup, examination, investigation, look-over, once-over (*Inf.*), review, scan, scrutiny, search, superintendence, supervision, surveillance, survey

inspector censor, checker, critic, examiner, investigator, overseer, scrutineer, scrutinizer, superintendent, supervisor

inspiration **1.** arousal, awakening, encouragement,

inspire (ɪnˈspaɪə) *vt.* **1.** animate, invigorate **2.** arouse, create feeling, thought in **3.** give rise to —*vi.* **4.** breathe in, inhale —**inspiration** (ɪnspɪˈreɪʃən) *n.* **1.** good idea **2.** creative influence or stimulus

inspirit (ɪnˈspɪrɪt) *vt.* animate, put spirit into, encourage

inst. (*instant*) of the current month

install *or* **instal** (ɪnˈstɔːl) *vt.* **1.** have (apparatus) put in **2.** establish **3.** place (person in office *etc.*) with ceremony —**installation** (ɪnstəˈleɪʃən) *n.* **1.** act of installing **2.** that which is installed

instalment *or U.S.* **installment** (ɪnˈstɔːlmənt) *n.* **1.** payment of part of debt **2.** any of parts of a whole delivered in succession —**installment plan US** hire-purchase

instance (ˈɪnstəns) *n.* **1.** example, particular case **2.** request **3.** stage in proceedings —*vt.* **4.** cite —**for instance** for or as an example

instant (ˈɪnstənt) *n.* **1.** moment, point of time —*a.* **2.** immediate **3.** urgent **4.** (of foods) requiring little preparation —**instanˈtaneous** *a.* happening in an instant —**instanˈtaneously** *adv.* —**inˈstanter** *adv. Law* at once —**ˈinstantly** *adv.* at once

instead (ɪnˈstɛd) *adv.* **1.** (*with* of) in place (of) **2.** as a substitute

instep (ˈɪnstɛp) *n.* top of foot between toes and ankle

instigate (ˈɪnstɪgeɪt) *vt.* **1.** incite, urge **2.** bring about —**instiˈgation** *n.* —**ˈinstigator** *n.*

instil *or* (*esp. U.S.*) **instill** (ɪnˈstɪl) *vt.* implant; inculcate —**instilˈlation** *n.* —**inˈstilment** *n.*

instinct (ˈɪnstɪŋkt) *n.* **1.** inborn impulse or propensity **2.** unconscious skill **3.** intuition —**inˈstinctive** *a.* —**inˈstinctively** *adv.*

institute (ˈɪnstɪtjuːt) *vt.* **1.** establish, found **2.** appoint **3.** set going —*n.* **4.** society for promoting some public object, *esp.* scientific **5.** its building —**instiˈtution** *n.* **1.** an instituting **2.** establishment for care or education, hospital, college *etc.* **3.** an established custom or law or (*inf.*) figure —**instiˈtutional** *a.* **1.** of institutions **2.** routine —**instiˈtutionalize** *or* **-ise** *vt.* **1.** subject to (adverse) effects of confinement in institution **2.** place in an institution —*v.* **3.** make or become an institution —**ˈinstitutor** *or* **ˈinstituter** *n.*

THESAURUS

influence, muse, spur, stimulus **2.** afflatus, creativity, genius, illumination, insight, revelation

inspire 1. animate, be responsible for, encourage, enliven, fire *or* touch the imagination of, galvanize, hearten, imbue, influence, infuse, inspirit, instil, spark off, spur, stimulate **2.** arouse, enkindle, excite, give rise to, produce, quicken, stir

instability capriciousness, changeableness, disequilibrium, fickleness, fitfulness, fluctuation, fluidity, frailty, imbalance, impermanence, inconstancy, insecurity, irresolution, mutability, oscillation, precariousness, restlessness, shakiness, transience, unpredictability, unsteadiness, vacillation, variability, volatility, wavering, weakness

install, instal 1. fix, lay, lodge, place, position, put in, set up, station **2.** establish, inaugurate, induct, instate, institute, introduce, invest, set up **3.** ensconce, position, settle

installation 1. establishment, fitting, instalment, placing, positioning, setting up **2.** inauguration, induction, instatement, investiture **3.** equipment, machinery, plant, system

instalment chapter, division, episode, part, portion, repayment, section

instance *n.* **1.** case, case in point, example, illustration, occasion, occurrence, precedent, situation, time **2.** application, behest, demand, entreaty, importunity, impulse, incitement, insistence, instigation, pressure, prompting, request, solicitation, urging ~*v.* **3.** adduce, cite, mention, name, quote, specify

instant *n.* **1.** flash, jiffy (*Inf.*), moment, second, shake (*Inf.*), split second, tick (*Brit. inf.*), trice, twinkling, twinkling of an eye (*Inf.*), two shakes of a lamb's tail (*Inf.*) **2.** juncture, moment, occasion, point, time ~*adj.* **3.** direct, immediate, instantaneous, on-the-spot, prompt, quick, split-second, urgent **4.** convenience, fast, precooked, ready-mixed **5.** burning, exigent, imperative, importunate, pressing, urgent

instantaneous direct, immediate, instant, on-the-spot

instantaneously at once, forthwith, immediately, in a fraction of a second, instantly, in the same breath, in the twinkling of an eye (*Inf.*), like greased lightning (*Inf.*), on the instant, on the spot, promptly, quick as lightning, straight away, then and there

instantly at once, directly, forthwith, immediately, instantaneously, instanter (*Law*), now, on the spot, pronto (*Inf.*), right away, right now, straight away, there and then, this minute, *tout de suite*, without delay

instead 1. alternatively, in lieu, in preference, on second thoughts, preferably, rather **2.** *With* **of** as an alternative *or* equivalent to, in lieu of, in place of, rather than

instigate actuate, bring about, encourage, foment, impel, incite, influence, initiate, kindle, move, persuade, prompt, provoke, rouse, set on, spur, start, stimulate, stir up, urge, whip up

instigation behest, bidding, encouragement, incentive, incitement, prompting, urging

instigator agitator, firebrand, fomenter, goad, incendiary, inciter, leader, mischief-maker, motivator, prime mover, ringleader, spur, troublemaker

instil, instill engender, engraft, imbue, implant, impress, inculcate, infix, infuse, insinuate, introduce

instinct aptitude, faculty, feeling, gift, gut feeling (*Inf.*), gut reaction (*Inf.*), impulse, intuition, knack, natural inclination, predisposition, proclivity, sixth sense, talent, tendency, urge

instinctive automatic, inborn, inherent, innate, instinctual, intuitional, intuitive, involuntary, mechanical, native, natural, reflex, spontaneous, unlearned, unpremeditated, unthinking, visceral

instinctively automatically, by instinct, intuitively, involuntarily, naturally, without thinking

institute 1. *v.* appoint, begin, bring into being, commence, constitute, enact, establish, fix, found, induct, initiate, install, introduce, invest, launch, ordain, organize, originate, pioneer, put into operation, set in motion, settle, set up, start **2.** *n.* academy, association, college, conservatory, foundation, guild, institution, school, seat of learning, seminary, society

institution 1. constitution, creation, enactment, establishment, formation, foundation, initiation, introduction, investiture, investment, organization

instruct (ɪnˈstrʌkt) *vt.* **1.** teach **2.** inform **3.** order **4.** brief (solicitor, barrister) —**inˈstruction** *n.* **1.** teaching **2.** order —*pl.* **3.** directions —**inˈstructive** *a.* **1.** informative **2.** useful —**inˈstructively** *adv.* —**inˈstructor** *n.* (**inˈstructress** *fem.*)

instrument (ˈɪnstrəmənt) *n.* **1.** tool, implement, means, person, thing used to make, do, measure *etc.* **2.** mechanism for producing musical sound **3.** legal document —**instruˈmental** *a.* **1.** acting as instrument or means **2.** helpful **3.** belonging to, produced by musical instruments —**instruˈmentalist** *n.* player of musical instrument —**instrumenˈtality** *n.* agency, means —**instruˈmentally** *adv.* —**instrumenˈtation** *n.* arrangement of music for instruments

insubordinate (ɪnsəˈbɔːdɪnɪt) *a.* **1.** not submissive **2.** mutinous, rebellious —**insubordiˈnation** *n.*

insufferable (ɪnˈsʌfərəbᵊl) *a.* intolerable; unendurable —**inˈsufferably** *adv.*

insular (ˈɪnsjʊlə) *a.* **1.** of an island **2.** remote, detached **3.** narrow-minded; prejudiced —**insuˈlarity** *n.*

insulate (ˈɪnsjʊleɪt) *vt.* **1.** prevent or reduce transfer of electricity, heat, sound *etc.* to or from (body or device) by surrounding with nonconducting material **2.** isolate, detach —**insuˈlation** *n.* —ˈ**insulator** *n.*

insulin (ˈɪnsjʊlɪn) *n.* pancreatic hormone used in treating diabetes

insult (ɪnˈsʌlt) *vt.* **1.** behave rudely to **2.** offend —*n.* (ˈɪnsʌlt) **3.** offensive remark **4.** affront —**inˈsulting** *a.* —**inˈsultingly** *adv.*

insuperable (ɪnˈsuːpərəbᵊl, -prəbᵊl, -ˈsjuː-) *a.* **1.** that cannot be got over or surmounted **2.** unconquerable —**insuperaˈbility** *n.* —**inˈsuperably** *adv.*

insupportable (ɪnsəˈpɔːtəbᵊl) *a.* **1.** incapable of being endured; intolerable; insufferable **2.** incapable of being supported or justified; indefensible

insure (ɪnˈʃʊə, -ˈʃɔː) *vi.* **1.** contract for payment in event of loss, death *etc.* by payment of premiums —*vt.* **2.** make such contract about **3.** (*with* against) make safe (against) —**inˈsurable** *a.* —**inˈsurance** *n.* —**inˈsurer** *n.* —**insurance policy** contract of insurance

insurgent (ɪnˈsɜːdʒənt) *a.* **1.** in revolt —*n.* **2.** rebel —**inˈsurgence** *or* **insurˈrection** *n.* revolt

THESAURUS

2. academy, college, establishment, foundation, hospital, institute, school, seminary, society, university **3.** convention, custom, fixture, law, practice, ritual, rule, tradition

institutional 1. accepted, bureaucratic, conventional, established, establishment (*Inf.*), formal, organized, orthodox, societal **2.** cheerless, clinical, cold, drab, dreary, dull, forbidding, formal, impersonal, monotonous, regimented, routine, uniform, unwelcoming

instruct 1. bid, charge, command, direct, enjoin, order, tell **2.** coach, discipline, drill, educate, enlighten, ground, guide, inform, school, teach, train, tutor **3.** acquaint, advise, apprise, brief, counsel, inform, notify, tell

instruction 1. apprenticeship, coaching, discipline, drilling, education, enlightenment, grounding, guidance, information, lesson(s), preparation, schooling, teaching, training, tuition, tutelage **2.** briefing, command, direction, directive, injunction, mandate, order, ruling

instructions advice, directions, guidance, information, key, orders, recommendations, rules

instructive cautionary, didactic, edifying, educational, enlightening, helpful, illuminating, informative, instructional, revealing, useful

instructor adviser, coach, demonstrator, exponent, guide, master, mentor, mistress, pedagogue, preceptor (*Rare*), schoolmaster, schoolmistress, teacher, trainer, tutor

instrument 1. apparatus, appliance, contraption (*Inf.*), contrivance, device, gadget, implement, mechanism, tool, utensil **2.** agency, agent, channel, factor, force, means, mechanism, medium, organ, vehicle

instrumental active, assisting, auxiliary, conducive, contributory, helpful, helping, influential, involved, of help *or* service, subsidiary, useful

insubordinate contumacious, defiant, disobedient, disorderly, fractious, insurgent, mutinous, rebellious, recalcitrant, refractory, riotous, seditious, turbulent, undisciplined, ungovernable, unruly

insubordination defiance, disobedience, indiscipline, insurrection, mutinousness, mutiny, rebellion, recalcitrance, revolt, riotousness, sedition, ungovernability

insufferable detestable, dreadful, enough to test the patience of a saint, enough to try the patience of Job, impossible, insupportable, intolerable, more than flesh and blood can stand, outrageous, past bearing, too much, unbearable, unendurable, unspeakable

insufficient deficient, inadequate, incapable, incommensurate, incompetent, lacking, short, unfitted, unqualified

insular *Fig.* blinkered, circumscribed, closed, contracted, cut off, illiberal, inward-looking, isolated, limited, narrow, narrow-minded, parish-pump, parochial, petty, prejudiced, provincial

insulate *Fig.* close off, cocoon, cushion, cut off, isolate, protect, sequester, shield, wrap up in cotton wool

insult 1. *n.* abuse, affront, aspersion, contumely, indignity, insolence, offence, outrage, rudeness, slap in the face (*Inf.*), slight, snub **2.** *v.* abuse, affront, call names, give offence to, injure, miscall (*Dialect*), offend, outrage, revile, slag (*Sl.*), slander, slight, snub

insulting abusive, affronting, contemptuous, degrading, disparaging, insolent, offensive, rude, scurrilous, slighting

insuperable impassable, insurmountable, invincible, unconquerable

insupportable 1. insufferable, intolerable, past bearing, unbearable, unendurable **2.** indefensible, unjustifiable, untenable

insurance assurance, cover, coverage, guarantee, indemnification, indemnity, protection, provision, safeguard, security, something to fall back on (*Inf.*), warranty

insure assure, cover, guarantee, indemnify, underwrite, warrant

insurgent 1. *n.* insurrectionist, mutineer, rebel, resister, revolter, revolutionary, revolutionist, rioter **2.** *adj.* disobedient, insubordinate, insurrectionary, mutinous, rebellious, revolting, revolutionary, riotous, seditious

insurmountable hopeless, impassable, impossible,

int. 1. interest 2. interior 3. internal 4. international

intact (ɪnˈtækt) *a.* 1. untouched 2. uninjured

intaglio (ɪnˈtɑːlɪəʊ) *n.* 1. engraved design 2. gem so cut (*pl.* **-s, -gli** (-ljiː)) —**inˈtagliated** *a.*

intake (ˈɪnteɪk) *n.* 1. what is taken in 2. quantity taken in 3. opening for taking in 4. in car, air passage into carburettor

integer (ˈɪntɪdʒə) *n.* 1. whole number 2. whole of anything

integral (ˈɪntɪgrəl) *a.* constituting an essential part of a whole —**ˈintegrate** *v.* 1. combine into one whole 2. unify diverse elements (of community *etc.*) —**inteˈgration** *n.* —**integral calculus** branch of mathematics of changing quantities, which calculates total effects of the change —**integrated circuit** tiny electronic circuit, usu. on silicon chip

integrity (ɪnˈtɛgrɪtɪ) *n.* 1. honesty 2. original perfect state

integument (ɪnˈtɛgjʊmənt) *n.* natural covering, skin, rind, husk

intellect (ˈɪntɪlɛkt) *n.* power of thinking and reasoning —**intelˈlectual** *a.* 1. of, appealing to intellect 2. having good intellect —*n.* 3. one endowed with intellect and attracted to intellectual things —**intellectuˈality** *n.*

intelligent (ɪnˈtɛlɪdʒənt) *a.* 1. having, showing good intellect 2. quick at understanding 3. informed 4. of or employing advanced technology, *esp.* involving computers —**inˈtelligence** *n.* 1. quickness of understanding 2. mental power or ability 3. intellect 4. information, news, *esp.* military information —**inˈtelligently** *adv.* —**intelliˈgentsia** *n.* intellectual or cultured classes —**intelligiˈbility** *n.* —**inˈtelligible** *a.* understandable —**inˈtelligibly** *adv.* —**intelligence quotient** measure of intelligence of individual, derived by dividing individual's mental age by his actual age and multiplying result by 100

intemperate (ɪnˈtɛmpərɪt, -prɪt) *a.* 1. drinking alcohol to excess 2. immoderate 3. unrestrained —**inˈtemperance** *n.*

intend (ɪnˈtɛnd) *v.* propose, mean (to do, say *etc.*) —**inˈtended** *a.* 1. planned, future —*n.* 2. *inf.* proposed spouse

intense (ɪnˈtɛns) *a.* 1. very strong or acute 2. emotional —**intensifiˈcation** *n.* —**inˈtensify** *v.* 1. make or become stronger 2. increase (**inˈtensified, inˈtensifying**) —**inˈtensity** *n.* 1. intense quality 2. strength —**inˈtensive** *a.* characterized by intensity or emphasis on specified factor —**inˈtensively** *adv.*

intent (ɪnˈtɛnt) *n.* 1. purpose —*a.* 2. concentrating 3. resolved, bent 4. preoccupied, absorbed —**inˈtention** *n.* purpose, aim —**inˈtentional** *a.* —**inˈtently** *adv.* —**inˈtentness** *n.*

THESAURUS

insuperable, invincible, overwhelming, unconquerable

insurrection coup, insurgency, mutiny, putsch, rebellion, revolt, revolution, riot, rising, sedition, uprising

intact all in one piece, complete, entire, perfect, scatheless, sound, together, unbroken, undamaged, undefiled, unharmed, unhurt, unimpaired, uninjured, unscathed, untouched, unviolated, virgin, whole

integral basic, component, constituent, elemental, essential, fundamental, indispensable, intrinsic, necessary, requisite

integrate accommodate, amalgamate, assimilate, blend, coalesce, combine, fuse, harmonize, incorporate, intermix, join, knit, merge, mesh, unite

integration amalgamation, assimilation, blending, combining, commingling, fusing, harmony, incorporation, mixing, unification

integrity 1. candour, goodness, honesty, honour, incorruptibility, principle, probity, purity, rectitude, righteousness, uprightness, virtue 2. coherence, cohesion, completeness, soundness, unity, wholeness

intellect brains (*Inf.*), intelligence, judgment, mind, reason, sense, understanding

intellectual 1. *adj.* bookish, cerebral, highbrow, intelligent, mental, rational, scholarly, studious, thoughtful 2. *n.* academic, egghead (*Inf.*), highbrow, thinker

intelligence 1. acumen, alertness, aptitude, brain power, brains (*Inf.*), brightness, capacity, cleverness, comprehension, discernment, grey matter (*Inf.*), intellect, mind, nous (*Brit. sl.*), penetration, perception, quickness, reason, understanding 2. advice, data, disclosure, facts, findings, gen (*Inf.*), information, knowledge, low-down (*Inf.*), news, notice, notification, report, rumour, tidings, tip-off, word

intelligent acute, alert, apt, brainy (*Inf.*), bright, clever, discerning, enlightened, instructed, knowing, penetrating, perspicacious, quick, quick-witted, rational, sharp, smart, thinking, well-informed

intelligentsia eggheads (*Inf.*), highbrows, illuminati, intellectuals, literati, masterminds, the learned

intelligibility clarity, clearness, comprehensibility, distinctness, explicitness, lucidity, plainness, precision, simplicity

intelligible clear, comprehensible, distinct, lucid, open, plain, understandable

intemperate excessive, extravagant, extreme, immoderate, incontinent, inordinate, intoxicated, passionate, prodigal, profligate, self-indulgent, severe, tempestuous, unbridled, uncontrollable, ungovernable, unrestrained, violent, wild

intend aim, be resolved *or* determined, contemplate, determine, have in mind *or* view, mean, meditate, plan, propose, purpose, scheme

intense 1. acute, agonizing, close, concentrated, deep, excessive, exquisite, extreme, fierce, forceful, great, harsh, intensive, powerful, profound, protracted, severe, strained 2. ardent, burning, consuming, eager, earnest, energetic, fanatical, fervent, fervid, fierce, forcible, heightened, impassioned, keen, passionate, speaking, vehement

intensify add fuel to the flames (*Inf.*), add to, aggravate, boost, concentrate, deepen, emphasize, enhance, escalate, exacerbate, heighten, increase, magnify, quicken, redouble, reinforce, set off, sharpen, step up (*Inf.*), strengthen, whet

intensity ardour, concentration, depth, earnestness, emotion, energy, excess, extremity, fanaticism, fervency, fervour, fierceness, fire, force, intenseness, keenness, passion, potency, power, severity, strain, strength, tension, vehemence, vigour

intensive all-out, comprehensive, concentrated, demanding, exhaustive, in-depth, thorough, thorough-going

intent *adj.* 1. absorbed, alert, attentive, committed,

inter (ɪnˈtɜː) *vt.* bury (-rr-) —**inˈterment** *n.*

inter- (*comb. form*) between, among, mutually, as in *interglacial, interrelation.* Such words are not given here where the meaning may easily be inferred from the simple word

interact (ɪntərˈækt) *vi.* act on each other —**interˈaction** *n.*

inter alia (ˈɪntər ˈeɪlɪə) *Lat.* among other things

interbreed (ɪntəˈbriːd) *v.* breed within a related group

intercede (ɪntəˈsiːd) *vi.* plead (in favour of), mediate —**intercession** (ɪntəˈsɛʃən) *n.* —**intercessor** (ɪntəˈsɛsə) *n.*

intercept (ɪntəˈsɛpt) *vt.* **1.** cut off **2.** seize, stop in transit —**interˈception** *n.* —**interˈceptor** *or* **interˈcepter** *n.* **1.** one who, that which intercepts **2.** fast fighter plane, missile *etc.*

interchange (ɪntəˈtʃeɪndʒ) *v.* **1.** (cause to) exchange places —*n.* (ˈɪntətʃeɪndʒ) **2.** motorway junction —**interˈchangeable** *a.* able to be exchanged in position or use

intercity (ɪntəˈsɪtɪ) *a.* linking cities directly

intercom (ˈɪntəkɒm) *n.* internal telephonic system

intercommunion (ɪntəkəˈmjuːnjən) *n.* association between Churches, involving *esp.* mutual reception of Holy Communion

intercontinental (ɪntəkɒntɪˈnɛntˀl) *a.* **1.** connecting continents **2.** (of missile) able to reach one continent from another

intercourse (ˈɪntəkɔːs) *n.* **1.** mutual dealings; communication **2.** sexual joining of two people; copulation

interdict (ˈɪntədɪkt) *n.* **1.** decree of Pope restraining clergy from performing divine service **2.** formal prohibition —*vt.* (ɪntəˈdɪkt) **3.** prohibit, forbid **4.** restrain —**interˈdiction** *n.*

interdisciplinary (ɪntəˈdɪsɪplɪnərɪ) *a.* involving two or more academic disciplines

interest (ˈɪntrɪst, -tərɪst) *n.* **1.** concern, curiosity **2.** thing exciting this **3.** sum paid for use of borrowed money **4.** (*oft. pl.*) benefit, advantage **5.** (*oft. pl.*) right, share —*vt.* **6.** excite curiosity or concern of **7.** cause to become involved in something; concern —**ˈinterested** *a.* **1.** showing or having interest **2.** personally involved or implicated —**ˈinteresting** *a.* —**ˈinterestingly** *adv.*

interface (ˈɪntəfeɪs) *n.* area, surface, boundary linking two systems

interfere (ɪntəˈfɪə) *vi.* **1.** meddle, intervene **2.** hinder **3.**

intercolˈlegiate
intercomˈmunicate
interˈcompany
interconˈnect
interconˈnection
interdenomiˈnational
interdepartˈmental
interdeˈpend
interdeˈpendence
interˈflow
intergaˈlactic
interˈknit
interˈmesh
interˈmingle
interˈmix
interˈracial
interˈwar
interˈweave

THESAURUS

concentrated, determined, eager, earnest, engrossed, fixed, industrious, intense, occupied, piercing, preoccupied, rapt, resolute, resolved, steadfast, steady, watchful, wrapped up **2.** bent, hellbent (*Inf.*), set ~*n.* **3.** aim, design, end, goal, intention, meaning, object, objective, plan, purpose

intention aim, design, end, end in view, goal, idea, intent, meaning, object, objective, point, purpose, scope, target, view

intentional calculated, deliberate, designed, done on purpose, intended, meant, planned, prearranged, preconcerted, premeditated, purposed, studied, wilful

intently attentively, closely, fixedly, hard, keenly, searchingly, steadily, watchfully

inter bury, entomb, inhume, inurn, lay to rest, sepulchre

intercede advocate, arbitrate, interpose, intervene, mediate, plead, speak

intercept arrest, block, catch, check, cut off, deflect, head off, interrupt, obstruct, seize, stop, take

intercession advocacy, entreaty, good offices, intervention, mediation, plea, pleading, prayer, solicitation, supplication

interchange *v.* alternate, bandy, barter, exchange, reciprocate, swap (*Inf.*), switch, trade

interchangeable commutable, equivalent, exchangeable, identical, reciprocal, synonymous, the same, transposable

intercourse 1. association, commerce, communication, communion, connection, contact, converse, correspondence, dealings, intercommunication, trade, traffic, truck **2.** carnal knowledge, coition, coitus, congress, copulation, intimacy, sex (*Inf.*), sexual act, sexual intercourse, sexual relations

interest *n.* **1.** affection, attention, attentiveness, attraction, concern, curiosity, notice, regard, suspicion, sympathy **2.** advantage, benefit, gain, good, profit **3.** authority, claim, commitment, influence, investment, involvement, participation, portion, right, share, stake ~*v.* **4.** amuse, arouse one's curiosity, attract, divert, engross, fascinate, hold the attention of, intrigue, move, touch **5.** affect, concern, engage, involve

interested 1. affected, attentive, attracted, curious, drawn, excited, fascinated, intent, keen, moved, responsive, stimulated **2.** biased, concerned, implicated, involved, partial, partisan, predisposed, prejudiced

interesting absorbing, amusing, appealing, attractive, compelling, curious, engaging, engrossing, entertaining, gripping, intriguing, pleasing, provocative, stimulating, suspicious, thought-provoking, unusual

interfere 1. butt in, get involved, intermeddle, intervene, intrude, meddle, poke one's nose in (*Inf.*), stick one's oar in (*Inf.*), tamper **2.** *Often with* **with** be a drag upon (*Sl.*), block, clash, collide, conflict, cramp, frustrate, get in the way of, hamper, handicap, hinder, impede, inhibit, obstruct, trammel

interference 1. intermeddling, intervention, intrusion, meddlesomeness, meddling, prying **2.** clashing, collision, conflict, impedance, obstruction, opposition (*with* with) *euphemistic* assault sexually **—inter'ference** *n.* **1.** act of interfering **2.** *Rad.* interruption of reception by atmospherics or by unwanted signals

interferon (ɪntəˈfɪərɒn) *n.* a cellular protein that stops the development of an invading virus

interim (ˈɪntərɪm) *n.* **1.** meantime *—a.* **2.** temporary, intervening

interior (ɪnˈtɪərɪə) *a.* **1.** inner **2.** inland **3.** indoors *—n.* **4.** inside **5.** inland region **—interior angle** angle of polygon contained between two adjacent sides **—interior decoration** colours, furniture *etc.* of interior of house *etc.*

interject (ɪntəˈdʒɛkt) *vt.* interpose (remark *etc.*) **—inter'jection** *n.* **1.** exclamation **2.** interjected remark

interlace (ɪntəˈleɪs) *vt.* unite, as by lacing together **—inter'lacement** *n.*

interlard (ɪntəˈlɑːd) *vt.* intersperse

interleave (ɪntəˈliːv) *vt.* insert, as blank leaves in book, between other leaves **—'interleaf** *n.* extra leaf

interlining (ˈɪntəlaɪnɪŋ) *n.* material used to interline parts of garments

interlock (ɪntəˈlɒk) *v.* **1.** lock together firmly *—a.* (ˈɪntəlɒk) **2.** knitted with close, small stitches

interlocutor (ɪntəˈlɒkjʊtə) *n.* one who takes part in conversation **—interlo'cution** *n.* dialogue **—inter'locutory** *a.*

interloper (ˈɪntələʊpə) *n.* one intruding in another's affairs

interlude (ˈɪntəluːd) *n.* **1.** interval (in play *etc.*) **2.** something filling an interval

intermarry (ɪntəˈmærɪ) *vi.* **1.** (of families, races, religions) become linked by marriage **2.** marry within one's family **—inter'marriage** *n.*

intermediate (ɪntəˈmiːdɪɪt) *a.* coming between; interposed **—inter'mediary** *n./a.*

intermezzo (ɪntəˈmɛtsəʊ) *n.* short performance between acts of play or opera (*pl.* **-s, -mezzi** (-ˈmɛtsiː))

interminable (ɪnˈtɜːmɪnəbᵊl) *a.* endless

intermit (ɪntəˈmɪt) *v.* stop for a time (-tt-) **—inter'mission** *n.* **1.** interval, as between parts of film *etc.* **2.** period between events or activities; pause **3.** act of intermitting; state of being intermitted **—inter'mittent** *a.* occurring at intervals

intern (ɪnˈtɜːn) *vt.* **1.** confine to special area or camp *—n.* (ˈɪntɜːn) **2.** internee **3.** US houseman (*also* **'interne**) **—inter'nee** *n.* person who is interned, *esp.* enemy citizen in wartime or terrorism suspect **—in'ternment** *n.*

internal (ɪnˈtɜːnᵊl) *a.* **1.** inward **2.** interior **3.** of a nation's domestic as opposed to foreign affairs *—n.* **4.** *euphemistic* medical examination of vagina or uterus **—in'ternally** *adv.* **—internal combustion** process of exploding mixture of air and fuel in piston-fitted cylinder

international (ɪntəˈnæʃənᵊl) *a.* **1.** of relations between nations *—n.* **2.** game or match between teams of different countries **—inter'nationalism** *n.* ideal or practice of cooperation and understanding between nations **—inter'nationalist** *n.* **—inter'nationally** *adv.* **—International Phonetic Alphabet** series of signs and letters for representation of human speech sounds

Internationale (ɛ̃tɛrnasjɔˈnal) *Fr.* socialistic hymn

internecine (ɪntəˈniːsaɪn) *a.* **1.** mutually destructive **2.** deadly

interpellate (ɪnˈtɜːpɛleɪt) *vt.* interrupt business of the day to demand explanation from (minister) **—interpel'lation** *n.*

interplanetary (ɪntəˈplænɪtərɪ, -trɪ) *a.* of, linking planets

interplay (ˈɪntəpleɪ) *n.* **1.** action and reaction of two things, sides *etc.* upon each other **2.** interaction **3.** reciprocation

Interpol (ˈɪntəpɒl) International Criminal Police Organization

interpolate (ɪnˈtɜːpəleɪt) *vt.* **1.** insert (new, *esp.* misleading matter) in (book *etc.*) **2.** interject (remark) **3.** *Maths.* estimate (a value) between known values **—interpo'lation** *n.*

interpose (ɪntəˈpəʊz) *vt.* **1.** insert **2.** say as interruption **3.** put in the way *—vi.* **4.** intervene **—interpo'sition** *n.*

THESAURUS

interim 1. *adj.* acting, caretaker, improvised, intervening, makeshift, pro tem, provisional, stopgap, temporary **2.** *n.* interregnum, interval, meantime, meanwhile

interior *adj.* **1.** inner, inside, internal, inward **2.** *Geog.* central, inland, remote, upcountry *~n.* **3.** bosom, centre, contents, core, heart, innards (*Inf.*), inside **4.** *Geog.* centre, heartland, upcountry

interjection cry, ejaculation, exclamation, interpolation, interposition

interloper gate-crasher (*Inf.*), intermeddler, intruder, meddler, trespasser, uninvited guest, unwanted visitor

interlude break, breathing space, delay, episode, halt, hiatus, intermission, interval, pause, respite, rest, spell, stop, stoppage, wait

intermediate halfway, in-between (*Inf.*), intermediary, interposed, intervening, mean, mid, middle, midway, transitional

interment burial, burying, funeral, inhumation, sepulture

interminable boundless, ceaseless, dragging, endless, everlasting, immeasurable, infinite, limitless, long, long-drawn-out, long-winded, never-ending, perpetual, protracted, unbounded, unlimited, wearisome

intermingle amalgamate, blend, combine, commingle, commix, fuse, interlace, intermix, interweave, merge, mix

intermission break, cessation, entr'acte, interlude, interruption, interval, let-up (*Inf.*), lull, pause, recess, respite, rest, stop, stoppage, suspense, suspension

intermittent broken, discontinuous, fitful, irregular, occasional, periodic, punctuated, recurrent, recurring, spasmodic, sporadic, stop-go (*Inf.*)

intern confine, detain, hold, hold in custody

internal 1. inner, inside, interior, intimate, private, subjective **2.** civic, domestic, home, in-house, intramural

international cosmopolitan, ecumenical (*Rare*), global, intercontinental, universal, worldwide

interpolate add, insert, intercalate, introduce

interpolation addition, aside, insert, insertion, intercalation, interjection, introduction

interpose 1. come *or* place between, intercede, interfere, intermediate, intervene, intrude, step in **2.**

interpret (ɪnˈtɜːprɪt) *vt.* **1.** explain **2.** *Art* render, represent —*vi.* **3.** translate, *esp.* orally —**interpreˈtation** *n.* —**inˈterpreter** *n.*

interregnum (ɪntəˈrɛgnəm) *n.* **1.** interval between reigns **2.** gap in continuity (*pl.* **-na** (-nə), **-s**)

interrelate (ɪntərɪˈleɪt) *v.* place in or come into mutual or reciprocal relationship —**interreˈlation** *n.*

interrogate (ɪnˈtɛrəgeɪt) *vt.* question, *esp.* closely or officially —**interroˈgation** *n.* —**interˈrogative** *a.* **1.** questioning —*n.* **2.** word used in asking question —**inˈterrogator** *n.* —**interˈrogatory** *a.* **1.** of inquiry —*n.* **2.** question, set of questions —**interrogation mark** *see* **question mark** *at* QUESTION

interrupt (ɪntəˈrʌpt) *v.* **1.** break in (upon) —*vt.* **2.** stop the course of **3.** block —**interˈruption** *n.*

interscholastic (ɪntəskəˈlæstɪk) *a.* **1.** (of sports events, competitions *etc.*) occurring between two or more schools **2.** representative of various schools

intersect (ɪntəˈsɛkt) *vt.* **1.** divide by passing across or through —*vi.* **2.** meet and cross —**interˈsection** *n.* point where lines, roads cross

interspace (ɪntəˈspeɪs) *vt.* **1.** make or occupy space between —*n.* (ˈɪntəspeɪs) **2.** space between or among things —**interspatial** (ɪntəˈspeɪʃəl) *a.*

intersperse (ɪntəˈspɜːs) *vt.* sprinkle (something) with or (something) among or in —**interˈspersion** *n.*

interstate (ˈɪntəsteɪt) *a.* **US** between, involving two or more states

interstellar (ɪntəˈstɛlə) *a.* (of the space) between stars

interstice (ɪnˈtɜːstɪs) *n.* chink, gap, crevice —**interˈstitial** *a.*

intertwine (ɪntəˈtwaɪn) *v.* twist together, entwine

interval (ˈɪntəvəl) *n.* **1.** intervening time or space **2.** pause, break **3.** short period between parts of play, concert *etc.* **4.** difference (of pitch)

intervene (ɪntəˈviːn) *vi.* **1.** come into a situation in order to change it **2.** (*with* on *or* between) be, come (between or among) **3.** occur in meantime **4.** interpose —**intervention** (ɪntəˈvɛnʃən) *n.*

interview (ˈɪntəvjuː) *n.* **1.** meeting, *esp.* formally arranged and involving questioning of a person —*vt.* **2.** have interview with —**interviewˈee** *n.* —**ˈinterviewer** *n.*

intestate (ɪnˈtɛsteɪt, -tɪt) *a.* **1.** not having made a will —*n.* **2.** person dying intestate —**inˈtestacy** *n.*

intestine (ɪnˈtɛstɪn) *n.* (*usu. pl.*) lower part of alimentary canal between stomach and anus —**inˈtestinal** *a.* of bowels

intimate[1] (ˈɪntɪmɪt) *a.* **1.** closely acquainted, familiar **2.** private **3.** extensive **4.** having sexual relations —*n.* **5.** intimate friend —**ˈintimacy** *n.*

intimate[2] (ˈɪntɪmeɪt) *vt.* **1.** announce **2.** imply —**intiˈmation** *n.* notice

THESAURUS

insert, interject, interrupt (with), introduce, put forth

interpret adapt, clarify, construe, decipher, decode, define, elucidate, explain, explicate, expound, make sense of, paraphrase, read, render, solve, spell out, take, throw light on, translate, understand

interpretation analysis, clarification, construction, diagnosis, elucidation, exegesis, explanation, explication, exposition, meaning, performance, portrayal, reading, rendering, rendition, sense, signification, translation, understanding, version

interpreter annotator, commentator, exponent, scholiast, translator

interrogate ask, catechize, cross-examine, cross-question, enquire, examine, give (someone) the third degree (*Inf.*), grill (*Inf.*), inquire, investigate, pump, put the screws on (*Inf.*), question, quiz

interrogation cross-examination, cross-questioning, enquiry, examination, grilling (*Inf.*), inquiry, inquisition, probing, questioning, third degree (*Inf.*)

interrogative curious, inquiring, inquisitive, inquisitorial, questioning, quizzical

interrupt barge in (*Inf.*), break, break in, break off, break (someone's) train of thought, butt in, check, cut, cut off, cut short, delay, disconnect, discontinue, disjoin, disturb, disunite, divide, heckle, hinder, hold up, interfere (with), intrude, lay aside, obstruct, punctuate, separate, sever, stay, stop, suspend

interruption break, cessation, disconnection, discontinuance, disruption, dissolution, disturbance, disuniting, division, halt, hiatus, hindrance, hitch, impediment, intrusion, obstacle, obstruction, pause, separation, severance, stop, stoppage, suspension

intersect bisect, crisscross, cross, cut, cut across, divide, meet

intersection crossing, crossroads, interchange, junction

interval break, delay, distance, gap, hiatus, interim, interlude, intermission, meantime, meanwhile, opening, pause, period, playtime, rest, season, space, spell, term, time, wait

intervene 1. arbitrate, intercede, interfere, interpose oneself, intrude, involve oneself, mediate, step in (*Inf.*), take a hand (*Inf.*) **2.** befall, come to pass, ensue, happen, occur, succeed, supervene, take place

intervention agency, intercession, interference, interposition, intrusion, mediation

interview 1. *n.* audience, conference, consultation, dialogue, evaluation, meeting, oral (examination), press conference, talk **2.** *v.* examine, interrogate, question, sound out, talk to

interviewer examiner, interlocutor, interrogator, investigator, questioner, reporter

intestinal abdominal, coeliac, duodenal, gut (*Inf.*), inner, stomachic, visceral

intestines bowels, entrails, guts, innards (*Inf.*), insides (*Inf.*), internal organs, viscera, vitals

intimacy closeness, confidence, confidentiality, familiarity, fraternization, understanding

intimate[1] *adj.* **1.** bosom, cherished, close, confidential, dear, friendly, near, nearest and dearest, thick (*Inf.*), warm **2.** confidential, personal, private, privy, secret **3.** deep, detailed, exhaustive, experienced, first-hand, immediate, in-depth, penetrating, personal, profound, thorough ~*n.* **4.** bosom friend, buddy (*Inf.*), china (*Brit. sl.*), chum (*Inf.*), close friend, comrade, confidant, confidante, (constant) companion, crony, familiar, friend, mate (*Inf.*), mucker (*Brit. sl.*), pal

intimate[2] *v.* allude, announce, communicate, declare, drop a hint, give (someone) to understand, hint,

intimidate (ɪnˈtɪmɪdeɪt) *vt.* **1.** frighten into submission **2.** deter by threats —**intimiˈdation** *n.* —**inˈtimidator** *n.*

into (ˈɪntuː; *unstressed* ˈɪntə) *prep.* **1.** expresses motion to a point within **2.** indicates change of state **3.** indicates coming up against, encountering **4.** indicates arithmetical division

intone (ɪnˈtəʊn) *or* **intonate** *vt.* **1.** chant **2.** recite in monotone —**intoˈnation** *n.* **1.** modulation of voice **2.** intoning **3.** accent

in toto (ɪn ˈtəʊtəʊ) *Lat.* totally, entirely, completely

intoxicate (ɪnˈtɒksɪkeɪt) *vt.* **1.** make drunk **2.** excite to excess —**inˈtoxicant** *a./n.* (anything) causing intoxication —**intoxiˈcation** *n.*

intr. intransitive

intra- (*comb. form*) within, as in *intrastate*

intractable (ɪnˈtræktəbᵊl) *a.* **1.** difficult to influence **2.** hard to control

intramural (ɪntrəˈmjʊərəl) *a. chiefly* **US** *Education* operating within or involving those in single establishment

intransigent (ɪnˈtrænsɪdʒənt) *a.* uncompromising, obstinate

intransitive (ɪnˈtrænsɪtɪv) *a.* denoting a verb that does not require direct object —**intransiˈtivity** *or* **inˈtransitiveness** *n.*

intrauterine (ɪntrəˈjuːtəraɪn) *a.* within the womb (*see also* IUD)

intravenous (ɪntrəˈviːnəs) *a.* into a vein

in-tray *n.* tray for incoming papers *etc.* requiring attention

intrepid (ɪnˈtrɛpɪd) *a.* fearless, undaunted —**intreˈpidity** *n.*

intricate (ˈɪntrɪkɪt) *a.* involved, puzzlingly entangled —**ˈintricacy** *n.* —**ˈintricately** *adv.*

intrigue (ɪnˈtriːg, ˈɪntriːg) *n.* **1.** underhand plot **2.** secret love affair —*vi.* (ɪnˈtriːg) **3.** carry on intrigue —*vt.* (ɪnˈtriːg) **4.** interest, puzzle

intrinsic (ɪnˈtrɪnsɪk) *or* **intrinsical** *a.* inherent; essential —**inˈtrinsically** *adv.*

intro. *or* **introd. 1.** introduction **2.** introductory

intro- (*comb. form*) into, within, as in *introduce, introvert*

introduce (ɪntrəˈdjuːs) *vt.* **1.** make acquainted **2.** present **3.** bring in **4.** bring forward **5.** bring into practice **6.** insert —**introˈduction** *n.* **1.** an introducing **2.** presentation of one person to another **3.** preliminary section or treatment **4.** *Mus.* opening passage in movement or composition, that precedes main material —**introˈductory** *a.* preliminary

introit (ˈɪntrɔɪt) *n. Eccles.* anthem sung as priest approaches altar

introspection (ɪntrəˈspɛkʃən) *n.* examination of one's own thoughts —**introˈspective** *a.*

THESAURUS

impart, imply, indicate, insinuate, let it be known, make known, remind, state, suggest, tip (someone) the wink (*Brit. inf.*), warn

intimation announcement, communication, declaration, notice

intimidate affright (*Archaic*), alarm, appal, browbeat, bully, coerce, cow, daunt, dishearten, dismay, dispirit, frighten, lean on (*Inf.*), overawe, scare, scare off (*Inf.*), subdue, terrify, terrorize, threaten, twist someone's arm (*Inf.*)

intimidation arm-twisting (*Inf.*), browbeating, bullying, coercion, fear, menaces, pressure, terror, terrorization, threat(s)

intolerable beyond bearing, excruciating, impossible, insufferable, insupportable, more than flesh and blood can stand, not to be borne, painful, unbearable, unendurable

intolerant bigoted, chauvinistic, dictatorial, dogmatic, fanatical, illiberal, impatient, narrow, narrow-minded, one-sided, prejudiced, racialist, racist, small-minded, uncharitable, xenophobic

intone chant, croon, intonate, recite, sing

intoxicate 1. addle, befuddle, fuddle, go to one's head, inebriate, put (someone) under the table (*Inf.*), stupefy **2.** *Fig.* elate, excite, exhilarate, inflame, make one's head spin, stimulate

intoxication 1. drunkenness, inebriation, inebriety, insobriety, tipsiness **2.** *Fig.* delirium, elation, euphoria, exaltation, excitement, exhilaration, infatuation

intransigent hardline, immovable, intractable, obdurate, obstinate, stubborn, tenacious, tough, unbending, unbudgeable, uncompromising, unyielding

intrepid audacious, bold, brave, courageous, daring, dauntless, doughty, fearless, gallant, game (*Inf.*), heroic, lion-hearted, nerveless, plucky, resolute, stalwart, stouthearted, unafraid, undaunted, unflinching, valiant, valorous

intricacy complexity, complication, convolutions, elaborateness, entanglement, intricateness, involution, involvement, knottiness, obscurity

intricate baroque, Byzantine, complex, complicated, convoluted, daedal (*Literary*), difficult, elaborate, fancy, involved, knotty, labyrinthine, obscure, perplexing, rococo, sophisticated, tangled, tortuous

intrigue *v.* **1.** arouse the curiosity of, attract, charm, fascinate, interest, pique, rivet, tickle one's fancy, titillate **2.** connive, conspire, machinate, manoeuvre, plot, scheme ~*n.* **3.** cabal, chicanery, collusion, conspiracy, double-dealing, knavery, machination, manipulation, manoeuvre, plot, ruse, scheme, sharp practice, stratagem, trickery, wile **4.** affair, amour, intimacy, liaison, romance

intrinsic basic, built-in, central, congenital, constitutional, elemental, essential, fundamental, genuine, inborn, inbred, inherent, native, natural, real, true, underlying

introduce 1. acquaint, do the honours, familiarize, make known, make the introduction, present **2.** begin, bring in, commence, establish, found, inaugurate, initiate, institute, launch, organize, pioneer, set up, start, usher in **3.** announce, lead into, lead off, open, preface **4.** add, inject, insert, interpolate, interpose, put in, throw in (*Inf.*)

introduction 1. baptism, debut, establishment, first acquaintance, inauguration, induction, initiation, institution, launch, pioneering, presentation **2.** commencement, exordium, foreword, intro (*Inf.*), lead-in, opening, opening passage, opening remarks, overture, preamble, preface, preliminaries, prelude, proem, prolegomena, prolegomenon, prologue **3.** addition, insertion, interpolation

introvert ('ɪntrəvɜːt) *n. Psychoanal.* one who looks inwards rather than at the external world —**intro'versible** *a.* —**intro'version** *n.* —**intro'versive** *a.* —**'introverted** *a.*

intrude (ɪn'truːd) *v.* thrust (oneself) in uninvited —**in'truder** *n.* —**in'trusion** *n.* —**in'trusive** *a.*

intrust (ɪn'trʌst) *vt. see* ENTRUST

intuition (ɪntjʊ'ɪʃən) *n.* **1.** immediate mental apprehension without reasoning **2.** immediate insight —**in'tuit** *vt.* —**in'tuitive** *a.*

Inuit ('ɪnjuːɪt) *n.* **C** Eskimo of N Amer. or Greenland

inundate ('ɪnʌndeɪt) *vt.* **1.** flood **2.** overwhelm —**inun'dation** *n.*

inure *or* **enure** (ɪ'njʊə) *vt.* accustom, *esp.* to hardship, danger *etc.*

in vacuo (ɪn 'vækjʊəʊ) *Lat.* in vacuum

invade (ɪn'veɪd) *v.* **1.** enter (a country *etc.*) by force with hostile intent —*vt.* **2.** overrun **3.** pervade —**in'vader** *n.* —**in'vasion** *n.* **1.** act of invading with armed forces **2.** any encroachment or intrusion **3.** onset of something harmful, *esp.* disease

invalid[1] ('ɪnvəliːd, -lɪd) *n.* **1.** one suffering from chronic ill health —*a.* **2.** ill, suffering from sickness or injury —*vt.* **3.** cause to become an invalid **4.** (*usu. with* out) *chiefly* **UK** require (member of armed forces) to retire from active service because of illness *etc.*

invalid[2] (ɪn'vælɪd) *a.* **1.** not valid; having no cogency or legal force **2.** *Logic* having conclusion that does not necessarily follow from its premises; not valid —**in'validate** *vt.* **1.** render weak or ineffective, as argument **2.** take away legal force or effectiveness of; annul —**invali'dation** *n.* —**in'validator** *n.*

invaluable (ɪn'væljʊəbᵊl) *a.* priceless

Invar (ɪn'vɑː) *n.* **R** steel containing 30 per cent nickel, with low coefficient of expansion

invasion (ɪn'veɪʒən) *n. see* INVADE

inveigh (ɪn'veɪ) *vi.* speak violently —**invective** (ɪn'vɛktɪv) *n.* abusive speech or writing, vituperation

inveigle (ɪn'viːgᵊl, -'veɪ-) *vt.* entice, seduce, wheedle —**in'veiglement** *n.*

invent (ɪn'vɛnt) *vt.* **1.** devise, originate **2.** fabricate (falsehoods *etc.*) —**in'vention** *n.* **1.** that which is invented **2.** ability to invent **3.** contrivance **4.** deceit; lie —**in'ventive** *a.* resourceful; creative —**in'ventively** *adv.* —**in'ventor** *n.*

inventory ('ɪnvəntərɪ, -trɪ) *n.* **1.** detailed list of goods *etc.* —*vt.* **2.** make list of

THESAURUS

introductory early, elementary, first, inaugural, initial, initiatory, opening, precursory, prefatory, preliminary, preparatory, starting

introspective brooding, contemplative, inner-directed, introverted, inward-looking, meditative, pensive, subjective

introverted indrawn, inner-directed, introspective, inward-looking, self-centred, self-contained, withdrawn

intrude butt in, encroach, infringe, interfere, interrupt, meddle, obtrude, push in, thrust oneself in *or* forward, trespass, violate

intruder burglar, gate-crasher (*Inf.*), infiltrator, interloper, invader, prowler, raider, snooper (*Inf.*), squatter, thief, trespasser

intrusion encroachment, infringement, interference, interruption, invasion, trespass, violation

intrusive disturbing, forward, impertinent, importunate, interfering, invasive, meddlesome, nosy (*Inf.*), officious, presumptuous, pushy (*Inf.*), uncalled-for, unwanted

intuition discernment, hunch, insight, instinct, perception, presentiment, sixth sense

intuitive innate, instinctive, instinctual, involuntary, spontaneous, unreflecting, untaught

inundate deluge, drown, engulf, flood, glut, immerse, overflow, overrun, overwhelm, submerge, swamp

invade 1. assail, assault, attack, burst in, descend upon, encroach, infringe, make inroads, occupy, raid, violate **2.** infect, infest, overrun, overspread, penetrate, permeate, pervade, swarm over

invader aggressor, alien, attacker, looter, plunderer, raider, trespasser

invalid[1] **1.** *adj.* ailing, bedridden, disabled, feeble, frail, ill, infirm, poorly (*Inf.*), sick, sickly, valetudinarian, weak **2.** *n.* convalescent, patient, valetudinarian

invalid[2] *adj.* baseless, fallacious, false, ill-founded, illogical, inoperative, irrational, not binding, nugatory, null, null and void, unfounded, unscientific, unsound, untrue, void, worthless

invalidate abrogate, annul, cancel, nullify, overrule, overthrow, quash, render null and void, rescind, undermine, undo, weaken

invaluable beyond price, costly, inestimable, precious, priceless, valuable

invariable changeless, consistent, constant, fixed, immutable, inflexible, regular, rigid, set, unalterable, unchangeable, unchanging, unfailing, uniform, unvarying, unwavering

invasion 1. aggression, assault, attack, foray, incursion, inroad, irruption, offensive, onslaught, raid **2.** breach, encroachment, infiltration, infraction, infringement, intrusion, overstepping, usurpation, violation

invective abuse, berating, billingsgate, castigation, censure, contumely, denunciation, diatribe, obloquy, philippic(s), reproach, revilement, sarcasm, tirade, tongue-lashing, vilification, vituperation

invent 1. coin, come up with (*Inf.*), conceive, contrive, create, design, devise, discover, dream up (*Inf.*), formulate, imagine, improvise, originate, think up **2.** concoct, cook up (*Inf.*), fabricate, feign, forge, make up, trump up

invention 1. brainchild (*Inf.*), contraption, contrivance, creation, design, development, device, discovery, gadget **2.** coinage, creativeness, creativity, genius, imagination, ingenuity, inspiration, inventiveness, originality, resourcefulness **3.** deceit, fabrication, fake, falsehood, fantasy, fib (*Inf.*), fiction, figment *or* product of (someone's) imagination, forgery, lie, prevarication, sham, story, tall story (*Inf.*), untruth, yarn

inventive creative, fertile, gifted, imaginative, ingenious, innovative, inspired, original, resourceful

inventor architect, author, coiner, creator, designer, father, framer, maker, originator

inventory *n.* account, catalogue, file, list, record, register, roll, roster, schedule, stock book

invert (ɪnˈvɜːt) *vt.* **1.** turn upside down **2.** reverse position, relations of —**inverse** (ɪnˈvɜːs, ˈɪnvɜːs) *a.* **1.** inverted **2.** opposite —**inˈversely** *adv.* —**inˈversion** *n.* —**inverted comma** *or* **turned comma** *see* **quotation mark** *at* QUOTE

invertebrate (ɪnˈvɜːtɪbrɪt, -breɪt) *n.* **1.** animal having no vertebral column —*a.* **2.** spineless

invest (ɪnˈvɛst) *vt.* **1.** lay out (money, time, effort *etc.*) for profit or advantage **2.** install **3.** endow **4.** *obs.* clothe **5.** *Poet.* cover, as with garment —**inˈvestiture** *n.* formal installation of person in office or rank —**inˈvestment** *n.* **1.** investing **2.** money invested **3.** stocks and shares bought —**inˈvestor** *n.* —**investment trust** financial enterprise that invests its subscribed capital in securities for its investors' benefit

investigate (ɪnˈvɛstɪgeɪt) *vt.* inquire into; examine —**investiˈgation** *n.* —**inˈvestigator** *n.*

inveterate (ɪnˈvɛtərɪt) *a.* **1.** deep-rooted; long-established **2.** confirmed —**inˈveteracy** *n.*

invidious (ɪnˈvɪdɪəs) *a.* likely to cause ill will or envy —**inˈvidiously** *adv.*

invigilate (ɪnˈvɪdʒɪleɪt) *vi.* supervise examination candidates —**inˈvigilator** *n.*

invigorate (ɪnˈvɪgəreɪt) *vt.* give vigour to, strengthen

invincible (ɪnˈvɪnsəbˀl) *a.* unconquerable —**invinciˈbility** *n.*

inviolable (ɪnˈvaɪələbˀl) *a.* **1.** not to be profaned; sacred **2.** unalterable —**inˈviolate** *a.* **1.** unhurt **2.** unprofaned **3.** unbroken

invisible (ɪnˈvɪzəbˀl) *a.* **1.** not visible; not able to be perceived by eye **2.** concealed from sight; hidden **3.** not easily seen or noticed **4.** kept hidden from public view; secret; clandestine **5.** *Econ.* of services, such as insurance and freight, rather than goods —*n.* **6.** *Econ.* invisible item of trade; service —**invisiˈbility** *or* **inˈvisibleness** *n.* —**inˈvisibly** *adv.*

invite (ɪnˈvaɪt) *vt.* **1.** request the company of **2.** ask courteously **3.** ask for **4.** attract, call forth —*n.* (ˈɪnvaɪt) **5.** *inf.* invitation —**invitation** (ɪnvɪˈteɪʃən) *n.* —**inˈviting** *a.* tempting; alluring; attractive

invoice (ˈɪnvɔɪs) *n.* **1.** a list of goods or services sold, with prices —*vt.* **2.** present with an invoice **3.** make an invoice of

invoke (ɪnˈvəʊk) *vt.* **1.** call on **2.** appeal to **3.** ask earnestly for **4.** summon —**invoˈcation** *n.*

involuntary (ɪnˈvɒləntərɪ, -trɪ) *a.* **1.** not done voluntarily **2.** unintentional **3.** instinctive

involute (ˈɪnvəluːt) *a.* **1.** complex **2.** coiled spirally **3.**

THESAURUS

inverse *adj.* contrary, converse, inverted, opposite, reverse, reversed, transposed

inversion antipode, antithesis, contraposition, contrariety, contrary, opposite, reversal, transposal, transposition

invert capsize, introvert, intussuscept (*Pathol.*), invaginate (*Pathol.*), overset, overturn, reverse, transpose, turn inside out, turn turtle, turn upside down, upset, upturn

invest **1.** advance, devote, lay out, put in, sink, spend **2.** endow, endue, provide, supply **3.** adopt, consecrate, enthrone, establish, inaugurate, induct, install, ordain **4.** *Archaic* array, bedeck, bedizen (*Archaic*), clothe, deck, drape, dress, robe

investigate consider, enquire into, examine, explore, go into, inquire into, inspect, look into, make enquiries, probe, put to the test, scrutinize, search, sift, study

investigation analysis, enquiry, examination, exploration, fact finding, hearing, inquest, inquiry, inspection, probe, research, review, scrutiny, search, study, survey

investigator dick (*Sl.*), examiner, gumshoe (*U.S. sl.*), inquirer, (private) detective, private eye (*Inf.*), researcher, reviewer, sleuth *or* sleuthhound (*Inf.*)

investiture admission, enthronement, inauguration, induction, installation, instatement, investing, investment, ordination

investment **1.** asset, investing, speculation, transaction, venture **2.** ante (*Inf.*), contribution, stake

inveterate chronic, confirmed, deep-dyed, deep-rooted, deep-seated, dyed-in-the-wool, entrenched, established, habitual, hard-core, hardened, incorrigible, incurable, ineradicable, ingrained, long-standing, obstinate

invidious discriminatory, envious (*Obsolete*), hateful, obnoxious, odious, offensive, repugnant, slighting, undesirable

invigorate animate, brace, buck up (*Inf.*), energize, enliven, exhilarate, fortify, freshen (up), galvanize, harden, liven up, nerve, pep up, perk up, put new heart into, quicken, refresh, rejuvenate, revitalize, stimulate, strengthen

invincible impregnable, indestructible, indomitable, inseparable, insuperable, invulnerable, unassailable, unbeatable, unconquerable, unsurmountable, unyielding

inviolable hallowed, holy, inalienable, sacred, sacrosanct, unalterable

inviolate entire, intact, pure, sacred, stainless, unbroken, undefiled, undisturbed, unhurt, unpolluted, unstained, unsullied, untouched, virgin, whole

invisible **1.** imperceptible, indiscernible, out of sight, unperceivable, unseen **2.** concealed, disguised, hidden, inappreciable, inconspicuous, infinitesimal, microscopic

invitation **1.** asking, begging, bidding, call, invite (*Inf.*), request, solicitation, summons, supplication **2.** allurement, challenge, come-on (*Inf.*), coquetry, enticement, glad eye (*Inf.*), incitement, inducement, open door, overture, provocation, temptation

invite **1.** ask, beg, bid, call, request, request the pleasure of (someone's) company, solicit, summon **2.** allure, ask for (*Inf.*), attract, bring on, court, draw, encourage, entice, lead, leave the door open to, provoke, solicit, tempt, welcome

inviting alluring, appealing, attractive, beguiling, captivating, delightful, engaging, enticing, fascinating, intriguing, magnetic, mouthwatering, pleasing, seductive, tempting, warm, welcoming, winning

invocation appeal, beseeching, entreaty, petition, prayer, supplication

invoke **1.** adjure, appeal to, beg, beseech, call upon, conjure, entreat, implore, petition, pray, solicit, supplicate **2.** apply, call in, have recourse to, implement, initiate, put into effect, resort to, use

involuntary **1.** compulsory, forced, obligatory, reluctant, unwilling **2.** automatic, blind, conditioned, instinctive, instinctual, reflex, spontaneous, unconscious, uncontrolled, unintentional, unthinking

rolled inwards (*also* **invo'luted**) —*n.* 4. *Maths.* a type of curve —**invo'lution** *n.*

involve (ɪn'vɒlv) *vt.* 1. include 2. entail 3. implicate (person) 4. concern 5. entangle —**in'volved** *a.* 1. complicated 2. concerned —**in'volvement** *n.*

inward ('ɪnwəd) *a.* 1. internal 2. situated within 3. spiritual, mental —*adv.* 4. towards the inside 5. into the mind (*also* **'inwards**) —*pl.n.* 6. *see* INNARDS —**'inwardly** *adv.* 1. in the mind 2. internally

iodine ('aɪədiːn) *n.* nonmetallic element found in seaweed and used in antiseptic tincture, photography and dyeing —**iodide** ('aɪədaɪd) *n.* 1. salt of hydriodic acid, containing the iodide ion 2. compound containing an iodine atom —**'iodize** *or* **-dise** *vt.* treat with iodine or iodide —**iodoform** (aɪ'ɒdəfɔːm) *n.* antiseptic

I.O.M. Isle of Man

ion ('aɪən, -ɒn) *n.* electrically charged atom or group of atoms —**i'onic** *a.* —**ioni'zation** *or* **-i'sation** *n.* —**'ionize** *or* **-ise** *v.* change or become changed into ions —**i'onosphere** *n.* region of atmosphere 60 to 100 km above earth's surface

-ion (*comb. form*) action, process, state, as in *creation, objection*

Ionic (aɪ'ɒnɪk) *a. Archit.* distinguished by scroll-like decoration on columns

iota (aɪ'əʊtə) *n.* 1. ninth letter in Gr. alphabet (Ι, ι) 2. (*usu. with* not one *or* an) very small amount

IOU *n.* signed paper acknowledging debt

-ious (*comb. form*) characterized by; full of, as in *ambitious, suspicious*

I.O.W. Isle of Wight

IPA International Phonetic Alphabet

ipecac ('ɪpɪkæk) *or* **ipecacuanha** (ɪpɪkækju'ænə) *n.* S Amer. plant yielding an emetic

ipso facto ('ɪpsəʊ 'fæktəʊ) *Lat.* by that very fact

I.Q. intelligence quotient

Ir *Chem.* iridium

Ir. 1. Ireland 2. Irish

ir- (*comb. form*) *see* IN-

I.R.A. Irish Republican Army

Iranian (ɪ'reɪnɪən) *n.* 1. native or inhabitant of Iran —*a.* 2. of Iran

irascible (ɪ'ræsɪbᵊl) *a.* hot-tempered —**irasci'bility** *n.* —**i'rascibly** *adv.*

ire (aɪə) *n.* anger, wrath —**i'rate** *a.* angry

iridaceous (ɪrɪ'deɪʃəs, aɪ-) *a.* belonging to iris family

iridescent (ɪrɪ'desᵊnt) *a.* exhibiting changing colours like those of the rainbow —**iri'descence** *n.*

iridium (aɪ'rɪdɪəm, ɪ'rɪd-) *n.* very hard, corrosion-resistant metal

iris ('aɪrɪs) *n.* 1. circular membrane of eye containing pupil 2. plant with sword-shaped leaves and showy flowers (*pl.* **-es, irides** ('aɪrɪdiːz, 'ɪrɪ-))

Irish ('aɪrɪʃ) *a.* 1. of Ireland, its people or their language —*n.* 2. Irish Gaelic —**Irish coffee** coffee mixed with whiskey and topped with cream —**Irish Gaelic** Goidelic language of the Celts of Ireland; official language of the Republic of Ireland since 1921 —**Irish stew** stew made of mutton, potatoes, onions *etc.*

irk (ɜːk) *vt.* irritate, vex —**'irksome** *a.* tiresome

iron ('aɪən) *n.* 1. metallic element, much used for tools *etc.*, and the raw material of steel 2. tool *etc.* of this metal 3. appliance used, when heated, to smooth cloth 4. metal-headed golf club 5. splintlike support for malformed leg 6. great hardness, strength or resolve —*pl.* 7. fetters —*a.* 8. of, like iron 9. inflexible, unyielding 10. robust —*v.* 11. smooth, cover, fetter *etc.* with iron or an iron —**'irony** *a.* of, resembling, or containing iron —**Iron Age** era of iron implements —**iron'clad** *a.* protected with or as with iron —**Iron Curtain** 1. guarded border between countries of Soviet bloc and the rest of Europe 2. (i- c-) any barrier that separates communities or ideologies —**iron hand** harsh or rigorous control —**ironing board** board, usu. on legs, with suitable covering on which to iron clothes —**iron lung** apparatus for administering artificial respiration —**iron maiden** medieval instrument of torture, consisting of enclosed space lined with iron spikes —**'ironmaster** *n.* **UK** manufacturer of iron —**'ironmonger** *n.* dealer in hardware —**'ironmongery** *n.* his wares —**iron pyrites** *see* PYRITES —**iron rations** emergency food supplies, *esp.* for military personnel in action —**'ironstone** *n.* 1. any rock consisting mainly of iron-bearing ore 2. tough durable earthenware —**'ironwood** *n.* various S Afr. trees —**'ironwork** *n.* work done in iron, *esp.* decorative work —**'ironworks** *pl.n.* (*sometimes with sing. v.*) building in which iron is smelted, cast or wrought

irony ('aɪrənɪ) *n.* 1. (*usu.* humorous or mildly sarcastic) use of words to mean the opposite of what is said 2.

THESAURUS

involve 1. entail, imply, mean, necessitate, presuppose, require 2. affect, associate, compromise, concern, connect, draw in, implicate, incriminate, inculpate, mix up (*Inf.*), touch 3. comprehend, comprise, contain, cover, embrace, include, incorporate, number among, take in 4. complicate, embroil, enmesh, entangle, link, mire, mix up, snarl up, tangle

involved 1. Byzantine, complex, complicated, confusing, convoluted, difficult, elaborate, intricate, knotty, labyrinthine, sophisticated, tangled, tortuous 2. caught (up), concerned, implicated, in on (*Inf.*), mixed up in *or* with, occupied, participating, taking part

involvement 1. association, commitment, concern, connection, dedication, interest, participation, responsibility 2. complexity, complication, difficulty, embarrassment, entanglement, imbroglio, intricacy, problem, ramification

inward *adj.* confidential, hidden, inmost, inner, innermost, inside, interior, internal, personal, private, privy, secret

inwardly at heart, deep down, in one's head, in one's inmost heart, inside, privately, secretly, to oneself, within

Irish Hibernian

irksome annoying, boring, bothersome, burdensome, disagreeable, exasperating, irritating, tedious, tiresome, troublesome, uninteresting, unwelcome, vexatious, vexing, wearisome

iron *adj.* 1. chalybeate, ferric, ferrous, irony 2. *Fig.* adamant, cruel, hard, heavy, immovable, implacable, indomitable, inflexible, obdurate, rigid, robust, steel, steely, strong, tough, unbending, unyielding

ironic, ironical 1. double-edged, mocking, sarcastic, sardonic, satirical, scoffing, sneering, wry 2. incongruous, paradoxical

irons bonds, chains, fetters, gyves (*Archaic*), manacles, shackles

event, situation opposite of that expected —**iˈronic(al)** *a.* of, using irony

irradiate (ɪˈreɪdɪeɪt) *vt.* **1.** treat by irradiation **2.** shine upon, throw light upon, light up —**irradiˈation** *n.* impregnation by x-rays, light rays

irrational (ɪˈræʃənˀl) *a.* **1.** inconsistent with reason or logic **2.** incapable of reasoning **3.** *Maths.* (of equation *etc.*) containing one or more variables in irreducible radical form or raised to fractional power —**irrationˈality** *n.*

irreconcilable (ɪˈrɛkˀnsaɪləbˀl, ɪrɛkˀnˈsaɪ-) *a.* **1.** not able to be reconciled; incompatible —*n.* **2.** person or thing that is implacably hostile **3.** (*usu. pl.*) one of various principles *etc.* that are incapable of being brought into agreement —**irreconcilaˈbility** *n.* —**irˈreconcilably** *adv.*

irrecoverable (ɪrɪˈkʌvərəbˀl, -ˈkʌvrə-) *a.* **1.** not able to be recovered or regained **2.** not able to be remedied or rectified

irredeemable (ɪrɪˈdiːməbˀl) *a.* **1.** (of bonds *etc.*) without date of redemption of capital; incapable of being bought back directly or paid off **2.** (of paper money) not convertible into specie **3.** (of loss) not able to be recovered; irretrievable **4.** not able to be improved or rectified; irreparable —**irreˈdeemably** *adv.*

irredentist (ɪrɪˈdɛntɪst) *n.* **1.** (*sometimes* **I-**) person, *esp.* member of 19th-century It. association, who favoured acquisition of territory that had once been part of his country —*a.* **2.** of irredentism —**irreˈdentism** *n.*

irreducible (ɪrɪˈdjuːsɪbˀl) *a.* **1.** not able to be reduced or lessened **2.** not able to be brought to simpler or reduced form **3.** *Maths.* (of polynomial) unable to be factorized into polynomials of lower degree —**irreduciˈbility** *n.*

irrefutable (ɪˈrɛfjʊtəbˀl, ɪrɪˈfjuːtəbˀl) *a.* that cannot be refuted, disproved

irreg. irregular(ly)

irregular (ɪˈrɛgjʊlə) *a.* **1.** lacking uniformity or symmetry; uneven in shape, arrangement *etc.* **2.** not occurring at expected or equal intervals **3.** differing from normal or accepted practice or routine **4.** (of formation, inflections or derivations of word) not following usual pattern of formation in language **5.** (of troops) not belonging to regular forces —*n.* **6.** soldier not in regular army —**irreguˈlarity** *n.*

irrelevant (ɪˈrɛləvənt) *a.* not relating or pertinent to matter at hand; not important —**irˈrelevance** *or* **irˈrelevancy** *n.*

irreparable (ɪˈrɛpərəbˀl, ɪˈrɛprəbˀl) *a.* not able to be repaired or remedied

irreplaceable (ɪrɪˈpleɪsəbˀl) *a.* not able to be replaced

irrepressible (ɪrɪˈprɛsəbˀl) *a.* not capable of being repressed, controlled or restrained —**irrepressiˈbility** *n.* —**irreˈpressibly** *adv.*

irreproachable (ɪrɪˈprəʊtʃəbˀl) *a.* not deserving reproach; blameless

irresistible (ɪrɪˈzɪstəbˀl) *a.* **1.** not able to be resisted or refused; overpowering **2.** very fascinating or alluring —**irreˈsistibly** *adv.*

THESAURUS

irony **1.** mockery, sarcasm, satire **2.** contrariness, incongruity, paradox

irrational **1.** absurd, crazy, foolish, illogical, injudicious, nonsensical, preposterous, silly, unreasonable, unreasoning, unsound, unthinking, unwise **2.** aberrant, brainless, crazy, demented, insane, mindless, muddle-headed, raving, senseless, unstable, wild

irrationality absurdity, brainlessness, illogicality, insanity, lack of judgment, lunacy, madness, preposterousness, senselessness, unreasonableness, unsoundness

irreconcilable clashing, conflicting, diametrically opposed, incompatible, incongruous, inconsistent, opposed

irrecoverable gone for ever, irreclaimable, irredeemable, irremediable, irreparable, irretrievable, lost, unregainable, unsalvageable, unsavable

irrefutable apodeictic, apodictic, beyond question, certain, incontestable, incontrovertible, indisputable, indubitable, invincible, irrefragable, irresistible, sure, unanswerable, unassailable, undeniable, unquestionable

irregular *adj.* **1.** desultory, disconnected, eccentric, erratic, fitful, fluctuating, fragmentary, haphazard, intermittent, nonuniform, occasional, out of order, patchy, random, shifting, spasmodic, sporadic, uncertain, unmethodical, unpunctual, unsteady, unsystematic, variable, wavering **2.** abnormal, anomalous, capricious, disorderly, eccentric, exceptional, extraordinary, immoderate, improper, inappropriate, inordinate, odd, peculiar, queer, quirky, unconventional, unofficial, unorthodox, unsuitable, unusual **3.** asymmetrical, broken, bumpy, craggy, crooked, elliptic, elliptical, holey, jagged, lopsided, lumpy, pitted, ragged, rough, serrated, unequal, uneven, unsymmetrical ~*n.* **4.** guerrilla, partisan, volunteer

irregularity **1.** asymmetry, bumpiness, crookedness, jaggedness, lack of symmetry, lopsidedness, lumpiness, patchiness, raggedness, roughness, unevenness **2.** aberration, abnormality, anomaly, breach, deviation, eccentricity, freak, malfunction, malpractice, oddity, peculiarity, singularity, unconventionality, unorthodoxy **3.** confusion, desultoriness, disorderliness, disorganization, haphazardness, lack of method, randomness, uncertainty, unpunctuality, unsteadiness

irrelevance, irrelevancy inappositeness, inappropriateness, inaptness, inconsequence, non sequitur

irrelevant beside the point, extraneous, immaterial, impertinent, inapplicable, inapposite, inappropriate, inapt, inconsequent, neither here nor there, unconnected, unrelated

irreparable beyond repair, incurable, irrecoverable, irremediable, irreplaceable, irretrievable, irreversible

irreplaceable indispensable, invaluable, priceless, unique, vital

irrepressible boisterous, bubbling over, buoyant, ebullient, effervescent, insuppressible, uncontainable, uncontrollable, unmanageable, unquenchable, unrestrainable, unstoppable

irreproachable beyond reproach, blameless, faultless, guiltless, impeccable, inculpable, innocent, irreprehensible, irreprovable, perfect, pure, unblemished, unimpeachable

irresistible **1.** compelling, imperative, overmastering, overpowering, overwhelming, potent, urgent **2.** alluring, beckoning, enchanting, fascinating, ravishing, seductive, tempting

irresolute (ɪˈrɛzəluːt) *a.* lacking resolution; wavering; hesitating —**irˈresolutely** *adv.* —**irˈresoluteness** *or* **irresoˈlution** *n.*

irrespective (ɪrɪˈspɛktɪv) *a.* —**irrespective of** without taking account of

irresponsible (ɪrɪˈspɒnsəbᵊl) *a.* **1.** not showing or done with due care for consequences of one's actions or attitudes; reckless **2.** not capable of bearing responsibility —**irresponsiˈbility** *or* **irreˈsponsibleness** *n.* —**irreˈsponsibly** *adv.*

irretrievable (ɪrɪˈtriːvəbᵊl) *a.* not able to be retrieved, recovered or repaired —**irretrievaˈbility** *n.* —**irreˈtrievably** *adv.*

irreverence (ɪˈrɛvərəns, ɪˈrɛvrəns) *n.* **1.** lack of due respect or veneration **2.** disrespectful remark or act —**irˈreverent** *a.*

irreversible (ɪrɪˈvɜːsəbᵊl) *a.* **1.** not able to be reversed **2.** not able to be revoked or repealed **3.** *Chem., phys.* capable of changing or producing change in one direction only —**irreversiˈbility** *n.* —**irreˈversibly** *adv.*

irrevocable (ɪˈrɛvəkəbᵊl) *a.* not able to be changed, undone, altered

irrigate (ˈɪrɪgeɪt) *vt.* water by artificial channels, pipes *etc.* —**irriˈgation** *n.* —**ˈirrigator** *n.*

irritate (ˈɪrɪteɪt) *vt.* **1.** annoy **2.** inflame **3.** stimulate —**ˈirritable** *a.* easily annoyed —**ˈirritably** *adv.* —**ˈirritant** *a./n.* (person or thing) causing irritation —**irriˈtation** *n.*

irrupt (ɪˈrʌpt) *vi.* **1.** enter forcibly **2.** increase suddenly —**irˈruption** *n.*

is (ɪz) third person singular, *present indicative of* BE

Is. **1.** *Bible* Isaiah (*also* **Isa.**) **2.** Island(s); Isle(s)

I.S.B.N. *or* **ISBN** International Standard Book Number

-ise (*comb. form*) *see* -IZE

isinglass (ˈaɪzɪŋglɑːs) *n.* kind of gelatine obtained from some freshwater fish

Islam (ˈɪzlɑːm) *n.* Mohammedan faith or world —**Isˈlamic** *a.*

island (ˈaɪlənd) *n.* **1.** piece of land surrounded by water **2.** anything like this, as raised piece for pedestrians in middle of road —**ˈislander** *n.* inhabitant of island

isle (aɪl) *n.* island —**ˈislet** *n.* little island

ism (ˈɪzəm) *n. inf., oft. derogatory* unspecified doctrine, system or practice

-ism (*comb. form*) **1.** action, process, result, as in *criticism* **2.** state; condition, as in *paganism* **3.** doctrine, system, body of principles and practices, as in *Leninism, spiritualism* **4.** behaviour; characteristic quality, as in *heroism* **5.** characteristic usage, *esp.* of language, as in *Scotticism*

isobar (ˈaɪsəʊbɑː) *n.* line on map connecting places of equal mean barometric pressure —**isoˈbaric** *a.*

isochronal (aɪˈsɒkrənᵊl) *or* **isochronous** *a.* **1.** having same duration; equal in time **2.** occurring at equal time intervals; having uniform period of vibration —**iˈsochronism** *n.*

isolate (ˈaɪsəleɪt) *vt.* place apart or alone —**isoˈlation** *n.* —**isoˈlationism** *n.* policy of not participating in international affairs —**isoˈlationist** *n./a.*

isomer (ˈaɪsəmə) *n.* substance with same molecules as another but different atomic arrangement —**isoˈmeric** *a.* —**iˈsomerism** *n.*

isometric (aɪsəʊˈmɛtrɪk) *a.* **1.** having equal dimensions **2.** relating to muscular contraction without movement —**isoˈmetrics** *pl.n.* (*with sing. v.*) system of isometric exercises

isomorphism (aɪsəʊˈmɔːfɪzəm) *n.* **1.** *Biol.* similarity of form **2.** *Chem.* existence of two or more substances of different composition in similar crystalline form **3.** *Maths.* one-to-one correspondence between elements of two or more sets —**isoˈmorphic** *or* **isoˈmorphous** *a.*

THESAURUS

irresolute doubtful, fickle, half-hearted, hesitant, hesitating, indecisive, infirm, in two minds, tentative, undecided, undetermined, unsettled, unstable, unsteady, vacillating, wavering, weak

irrespective of apart from, despite, discounting, in spite of, notwithstanding, regardless of, without reference to, without regard to

irresponsible careless, featherbrained, flighty, giddy, harebrained, harum-scarum, ill-considered, immature, reckless, scatter-brained, shiftless, thoughtless, undependable, unreliable, untrustworthy, wild

irreverence cheek (*Inf.*), cheekiness (*Inf.*), derision, disrespect, flippancy, impertinence, impudence, lack of respect, mockery, sauce (*Inf.*)

irreverent cheeky (*Inf.*), contemptuous, derisive, disrespectful, flip (*Inf.*), flippant, iconoclastic, impertinent, impious, impudent, mocking, saucy, tongue-in-cheek

irreversible final, incurable, irreparable, irrevocable, unalterable

irrevocable changeless, fated, fixed, immutable, invariable, irremediable, irretrievable, irreversible, predestined, predetermined, settled, unalterable, unchangeable, unreversible

irrigate flood, inundate, moisten, water, wet

irritable bad-tempered, cantankerous, choleric, crabbed, crabby, cross, crotchety (*Inf.*), dyspeptic, exasperated, fiery, fretful, hasty, hot, ill-humoured, ill-tempered, irascible, narky (*Inf.*), out of humour, oversensitive, peevish, petulant, prickly, snappish, snappy, snarling, tense, testy, touchy

irritate **1.** aggravate (*Inf.*), anger, annoy, bother, drive one up the wall (*Inf.*), enrage, exasperate, fret, get in one's hair (*Inf.*), get one's back up (*Inf.*), get one's hackles up, get on one's nerves (*Inf.*), harass, incense, inflame, infuriate, needle (*Inf.*), nettle, offend, pester, provoke, raise one's hackles, rankle with, rub up the wrong way (*Inf.*), ruffle, try one's patience, vex **2.** aggravate, chafe, fret, inflame, intensify, pain, rub

irritation **1.** anger, annoyance, crossness, displeasure, exasperation, ill humour, ill temper, impatience, indignation, irritability, resentment, shortness, snappiness, testiness, vexation, wrath **2.** aggravation (*Inf.*), annoyance, goad, irritant, nuisance, pain (*Inf.*), pain in the neck (*Inf.*), pest, provocation, tease, thorn in one's flesh

isolate cut off, detach, disconnect, divorce, insulate, quarantine, segregate, separate, sequester, set apart

isolation aloofness, detachment, disconnection, exile, insularity, insulation, loneliness, quarantine, remoteness, retirement, seclusion, segregation, self-sufficiency, separation, solitude, withdrawal

isosceles (aɪˈsɒsɪliːz) *a.* (of triangle) having two sides equal

isotherm (ˈaɪsəʊθɜːm) *n.* line on map connecting points of equal mean temperature

isotope (ˈaɪsətəʊp) *n.* atom of element having a different nuclear mass and atomic weight from other atoms in same element —**isotopic** (aɪsəˈtɒpɪk) *a.*

isotropic (aɪsəʊˈtrɒpɪk) *or* **isotropous** (aɪˈsɒtrəpəs) *a.* **1.** having uniform physical properties in all directions **2.** *Biol.* not having predetermined axes —**iˈsotropy** *n.*

Israel (ˈɪzreɪəl, -rɪəl) *n.* **1.** republic in SW Asia, established as modern state of Israel **2.** ancient kingdom of Jews in this region —**ˈIsraelite** *n.* *Bible* member of ethnic group claiming descent from Jacob; Hebrew —**Children of Israel** the Jewish people or nation

issue (ˈɪʃjuː) *n.* **1.** sending or giving out officially or publicly **2.** number or amount so given out **3.** discharge **4.** offspring, children **5.** topic of discussion **6.** question, dispute **7.** outcome, result —*vi.* **8.** go out **9.** result (in) **10.** arise (from) —*vt.* **11.** emit, give out, send out **12.** distribute **13.** publish —**take issue** disagree

-ist (*comb. form*) **1.** person who performs certain action or is concerned with something specified, as in *motorist, soloist* **2.** person who practises in specific field, as in *physicist* **3.** person who advocates particular doctrine, system *etc.;* of doctrine advocated, as in *socialist* **4.** person characterized by specified trait, tendency *etc.;* of such a trait, as in *purist* —**-istic** (*a. comb. form*)

isthmus (ˈɪsməs) *n.* neck of land between two seas

it (ɪt) *pron.* neuter pronoun of the third person —**its** *a.* belonging to it —**itˈself** *pron.* emphatic form of IT

i.t.a. *or* **I.T.A.** initial teaching alphabet

ital italic (type)

Italian (ɪˈtæljən) *n.* **1.** language of Italy **2.** native of Italy —*a.* **3.** of Italy —**Iˈtalianate** *or* **Italiaˈnesque** *a.* Italian in style or character

italic (ɪˈtælɪk) *a.* (of type) sloping —**iˈtalicize** *or* **-ise** *vt.* put in italics —**iˈtalics** *pl.n.* italic type, now used for emphasis *etc.*

itch (ɪtʃ) *n.* **1.** irritation in the skin **2.** restless desire —*vi.* **3.** feel or produce irritating or tickling sensation **4.** have a restless desire (to do something) —**ˈitchy** *a.*

item (ˈaɪtəm) *n.* **1.** single thing in list, collection *etc.* **2.** piece of information **3.** entry in account *etc.* —*adv.* (ˈaɪtɛm) **4.** also —**ˈitemize** *or* **-ise** *vt.*

iterate (ˈɪtəreɪt) *vt.* repeat —**iterˈation** *n.* —**iterative** (ˈɪtərətɪv) *a.*

itinerant (ɪˈtɪnərənt, aɪ-) *a.* **1.** travelling from place to place **2.** working for a short time in various places **3.** travelling on circuit —**iˈtineracy** *n.* —**iˈtinerary** *n.* **1.** record, line of travel **2.** route **3.** guidebook

-itis (*comb. form*) inflammation of specified part, as in *tonsillitis*

ITV Independent Television

IUD intrauterine device (for contraception)

IVF in-vitro fertilization: fertilization made to occur outside of body, *esp.* in test tube

ivory (ˈaɪvərɪ, -vrɪ) *n.* **1.** hard white substance of the tusks of elephants *etc.* **2.** yellowish-white colour; cream —*a.* **3.** yellowish-white; cream —**ˈivories** *pl.n.* *sl.* **1.** piano keys **2.** billiard balls **3.** teeth **4.** dice —**ivory tower** seclusion, remoteness

ivy (ˈaɪvɪ) *n.* climbing evergreen plant —**ˈivied** *a.* covered with ivy

-ize *or* **-ise** (*comb. form*) **1.** cause to become, resemble or agree with, as in *legalize* **2.** become; change into, as in *crystallize* **3.** affect in specified way; subject to, as in *hypnotize* **4.** act according to some principle, policy *etc.*, as in *economize*

THESAURUS

issue *n.* **1.** affair, argument, concern, controversy, matter, matter of contention, point, point in question, problem, question, subject, topic **2. take issue** challenge, disagree, dispute, object, oppose, raise an objection, take exception **3.** conclusion, consequence, culmination, effect, end, finale, outcome, pay-off (*Inf.*), result, termination, upshot **4.** copy, edition, impression, instalment, number, printing **5.** circulation, delivery, dispersion, dissemination, distribution, granting, issuance, issuing, publication, sending out, supply, supplying **6.** children, descendants, heirs, offspring, progeny, scions, seed (*Biblical*) ~*v.* **7.** announce, broadcast, circulate, deliver, distribute, emit, give out, promulgate, publish, put in circulation, put out, release **8.** arise, be a consequence of, come forth, emanate, emerge, flow, originate, proceed, rise, spring, stem

itch *v.* **1.** crawl, irritate, prickle, tickle, tingle **2.** ache, burn, crave, hanker, hunger, long, lust, pant, pine, yearn ~*n.* **3.** irritation, itchiness, prickling, tingling **4.** craving, desire, hankering, hunger, longing, lust, passion, restlessness, yearning, yen (*Inf.*)

item **1.** article, aspect, component, consideration, detail, entry, matter, particular, point, thing **2.** account, article, bulletin, dispatch, feature, note, notice, paragraph, piece, report

itinerant *adj.* ambulatory, Gypsy, journeying, migratory, nomadic, peripatetic, roaming, roving, travelling, unsettled, vagabond, vagrant, wandering, wayfaring

itinerary **1.** circuit, journey, line, programme, route, schedule, tour **2.** Baedeker, guide, guidebook

ivory tower cloister, refuge, remoteness, retreat, sanctum, seclusion, splendid isolation, unreality, world of one's own

J

j *or* **J** (dʒeɪ) *n.* **1.** tenth letter of English alphabet **2.** speech sound represented by this letter (*pl.* **j's, J's** *or* **Js**)

jab (dʒæb) *vt.* **1.** poke roughly **2.** thrust, stab abruptly (**-bb-**) —*n.* **3.** poke **4.** *inf.* injection

jabber (ˈdʒæbə) *vi.* **1.** chatter **2.** talk rapidly, incoherently —ˈ**jabberwocky** *n.* nonsense, *esp.* in verse

jabot (ˈʒæbəʊ) *n.* frill, ruffle at throat or breast of garment

jacaranda (dʒækəˈrændə) *n.* S Amer. tree with fern-like leaves and pale purple flowers

jacinth (ˈdʒæsɪnθ) *n.* reddish-orange precious stone

jack (dʒæk) *n.* **1.** fellow, man **2.** *inf.* sailor **3.** male of some animals **4.** device for lifting heavy weight, *esp.* motor car **5.** various mechanical appliances **6.** lowest court card, with picture of pageboy **7.** *Bowls* ball aimed at **8.** socket and plug connection in electronic equipment **9.** small flag, *esp.* national, at sea —*vt.* **10.** (*usu. with* up) lift (an object) with a jack —**Jack Frost** personification of frost —**jack-in-office** *n.* self-important petty official —**jack-in-the-box** *n.* toy consisting of figure on tight spring in box, which springs out when lid is opened (*pl.* **jack-in-the-boxes, jacks-in-the-box**) —**jack of all trades** person who undertakes many kinds of work (*pl.* **jacks of all trades**) —**jack-o'-lantern** *n.* **1.** lantern made from hollowed pumpkin, cut to represent human face **2.** will-o'-the-wisp —**Jack Tar** *chiefly lit.* sailor

jackal (ˈdʒækɔːl) *n.* wild, gregarious animal of Asia and Afr. closely allied to dog

jackanapes (ˈdʒækəneɪps) *n.* **1.** conceited impertinent person **2.** mischievous child **3.** *obs.* monkey

jackass (ˈdʒækæs) *n.* **1.** the male of the ass **2.** blockhead —**laughing jackass** the Aust. kookaburra

jackboot (ˈdʒækbuːt) *n.* large riding boot coming above knee

jackdaw (ˈdʒækdɔː) *n.* small kind of crow

jacket (ˈdʒækɪt) *n.* **1.** outer garment, short coat **2.** outer casing, cover —ˈ**jacketed** *a.*

jackhammer (ˈdʒækhæmə) *n.* hand-held hammer drill

jackknife (ˈdʒæknaɪf) *n.* **1.** clasp knife **2.** dive with sharp bend at waist in midair —*vi.* **3.** (of articulated lorry) go out of control in such a way that trailer forms right angle to tractor

jackpot (ˈdʒækpɒt) *n.* large prize, accumulated stake, as pool in poker —**hit the jackpot** win a jackpot; achieve great success, *esp.* through luck

jack rabbit US hare

jacks (dʒæks) *pl.n.* game in which bone or metal pieces (**jackstones**) are thrown and picked up between bounces of small ball

Jacobean (dʒækəˈbɪən) *a.* of the reign of James I

Jacobite (ˈdʒækəbaɪt) *n.* adherent of Stuarts after overthrow of James II

Jacquard (ˈdʒækɑːd, dʒəˈkɑːd) *n.* fabric in which design is incorporated into the weave

Jacuzzi (dʒəˈkuːzɪ) *n.* **R 1.** device which swirls water in bath **2.** bath containing such a device

jade[1] (dʒeɪd) *n.* **1.** ornamental semiprecious stone, usu. dark green **2.** this colour

jade[2] (dʒeɪd) *n.* **1.** old worn-out horse **2.** *obs., offens.* woman considered to be disreputable —ˈ**jaded** *a.* **1.** tired **2.** off colour

Jaffa (ˈdʒæfə, ˈdʒɑː-) *n.* **1.** port in W Israel **2.** large orange with thick skin

jag[1] (dʒæg) *n.* sharp or ragged projection —**jagged** (ˈdʒægɪd) *a.*

jag[2] (dʒæg) *n. sl.* **1.** intoxication from drugs or alcohol **2.** bout of drinking or drug taking

jaguar (ˈdʒægjʊə) *n.* large S Amer. spotted animal of cat family

jail *or* **gaol** (dʒeɪl) *n.* **1.** building for confinement of criminals or suspects —*vt.* **2.** send to, confine in prison —ˈ**jailer,** ˈ**jailor** *or* ˈ**gaoler** *n.* —ˈ**jailbird** *or* ˈ**gaolbird** *n.* hardened criminal

jalopy *or* **jaloppy** (dʒəˈlɒpɪ) *n. inf.* old car

jalousie (ˈʒæluziː) *n.* **1.** blind or shutter constructed from angled slats of wood *etc.* **2.** window made of angled slats of glass

jam (dʒæm) *vt.* **1.** pack together **2.** (*oft. with* on) apply fiercely **3.** squeeze **4.** *Rad.* block (another station) with impulses of equal wavelength —*v.* **5.** (cause to) stick together and become unworkable —*vi.* **6.** *sl.* play in jam session (**-mm-**) —*n.* **7.** fruit preserved by boiling with sugar **8.** crush **9.** hold-up of traffic **10.** awkward situation —**jam-packed** *a.* filled to capacity —**jam session** (improvised) jazz or pop music session

jamb *or* **jambe** (dʒæm) *n.* side post of door, window *etc.*

jamboree (dʒæmbəˈriː) *n.* **1.** large gathering or rally of Scouts **2.** spree, celebration

THESAURUS

jab *v./n.* dig, lunge, nudge, poke, prod, punch, stab, tap, thrust

jacket case, casing, coat, covering, envelope, folder, sheath, skin, wrapper, wrapping

jackpot award, bonanza, kitty, pool, pot, prize, reward, winnings

jade harridan, hussy, nag, shrew, slattern, slut, trollop, vixen, wench

jaded exhausted, fagged (out) (*Inf.*), fatigued, spent, tired, tired-out, weary

jagged barbed, broken, cleft, craggy, denticulate, indented, notched, pointed, ragged, ridged, rough, serrated, snaggy, spiked, toothed, uneven

jail, gaol 1. *n.* borstal, brig (*Chiefly U.S.*), clink (*Sl.*), cooler (*Sl.*), inside (*Sl.*), jailhouse (*Southern U.S.*), jug (*Sl.*), lockup, nick (*Sl.*), penitentiary (*U.S.*), prison, quod (*Sl.*), reformatory, stir (*Sl.*) **2.** *v.* confine, detain, immure, impound, imprison, incarcerate, lock up, send down

jailer, gaoler captor, guard, keeper, screw (*Sl.*), turnkey (*Archaic*), warden, warder

jam *v.* **1.** cram, crowd, crush, force, pack, press, ram, squeeze, stuff, throng, wedge ~*n.* **2.** crowd, crush, horde, mass, mob, multitude, pack, press, swarm, throng **3.** bind, dilemma, fix (*Inf.*), hole (*Sl.*), pickle (*Inf.*), plight, predicament, quandary, scrape (*Inf.*), spot (*Inf.*), strait, trouble

jamboree carnival, carouse, celebration, festival, fes-

jammy ('dʒæmɪ) *a.* **UK** *sl.* **1.** pleasant; desirable **2.** lucky

Jan. January

jangle ('dʒæŋg'l) *v.* **1.** (cause to) sound harshly, as bell —*vt.* **2.** produce jarring effect on —*n.* **3.** harsh sound

janitor ('dʒænɪtə) *n.* **1.** caretaker **2.** doorkeeper (**'janitress** *fem.*)

January ('dʒænjʊərɪ) *n.* first month

japan (dʒə'pæn) *n.* **1.** very hard, *usu.* black varnish —*vt.* **2.** cover with this (**-nn-**)

Japanese (dʒæpə'ni:z) *a.* **1.** of Japan —*n.* **2.** native of Japan (*pl.* **-nese**) **3.** official language of Japan

jape (dʒeɪp) *n./vi.* joke

japonica (dʒə'pɒnɪkə) *n.* shrub with red flowers (*also* **Japanese quince**)

jar[1] (dʒɑ:) *n.* **1.** usu. round vessel of glass, earthenware *etc.* **2.** *inf.* glass of beer

jar[2] (dʒɑ:) *v.* **1.** (cause to) vibrate suddenly, violently —*vt.* **2.** have disturbing, painful effect on (**-rr-**) —*n.* **3.** jarring sound **4.** shock *etc.*

jardinière (ʒɑ:dɪ'njɛə) *n.* ornamental pot for growing plants

jargon ('dʒɑ:gən) *n.* **1.** specialized language concerned with particular subject **2.** pretentious or nonsensical language

Jas. James

jasmine ('dʒæsmɪn, 'dʒæz-) *n.* flowering shrub

jasper ('dʒæspə) *n.* red, yellow, dark green or brown quartz

jaundice ('dʒɔ:ndɪs) *n.* **1.** disease marked by yellowness of skin (*also* **'icterus**) **2.** bitterness, ill humour **3.** prejudice —*vt.* **4.** make prejudiced, bitter *etc.*

jaunt (dʒɔ:nt) *n.* **1.** short pleasurable excursion —*vi.* **2.** go on such an excursion —**jaunting car** formerly, light, two-wheeled, one-horse car used in Ireland

jaunty ('dʒɔ:ntɪ) *a.* **1.** sprightly **2.** brisk **3.** smart, trim —**'jauntily** *adv.*

Javanese (dʒɑ:və'ni:z) *a.* **1.** of island of Java, in Indonesia —*n.* **2.** native or inhabitant of Java (*pl.* **-ese**) **3.** Malayan language of Java

javelin ('dʒævlɪn) *n.* spear, *esp.* for throwing in sporting events

jaw (dʒɔ:) *n.* **1.** one of bones in which teeth are set —*pl.* **2.** mouth **3.** gripping part of vice *etc.* **4.** *fig.* narrow opening of gorge or valley —*vi.* **5.** *sl.* talk lengthily

jay (dʒeɪ) *n.* noisy bird with brilliant plumage —**'jaywalk** *vi.* walk in or across street carelessly or illegally —**'jaywalker** *n.*

jazz (dʒæz) *n.* syncopated music and dance —**'jazzy** *a.* flashy, showy —**jazz up 1.** play as jazz **2.** make more lively, appealing

jealous ('dʒɛləs) *a.* **1.** distrustful of the faithfulness (of) **2.** envious **3.** suspiciously watchful —**'jealously** *adv.* —**'jealousy** *n.*

jeans (dʒi:nz) *pl.n.* casual trousers, *esp.* made of denim

Jeep (dʒi:p) *n.* **R** light four-wheel drive motor utility vehicle

jeer (dʒɪə) *v.* **1.** scoff —*n.* **2.** scoff, taunt, gibe

Jehovah (dʒɪ'həʊvə) *n.* *O.T.* God —**Jehovah's Witness** member of Christian sect who believes end of world is near

jejune (dʒɪ'dʒu:n) *a.* **1.** simple, naive **2.** meagre

Jekyll and Hyde ('dʒɛk'l; haɪd) person with two distinct personalities, one good, the other evil

jell *or* **gel** (dʒɛl) *v.* **1.** congeal —*vi.* **2.** *inf.* assume definite form

jellaba *or* **jellabah** ('dʒɛləbə) *n.* loose cloak with hood, worn *esp.* in N Afr.

jelly ('dʒɛlɪ) *n.* **1.** semitransparent food made with gelatine, becoming softly stiff as it cools **2.** anything of the consistency of this —**'jellyfish** *n.* jellylike small sea animal

jemmy ('dʒɛmɪ) *or* *U.S.* **jimmy** ('dʒɪmɪ) *n.* short steel crowbar, pinchbar

jenny ('dʒɛnɪ) *n.* **1.** female ass **2.** female wren

jeopardy ('dʒɛpədɪ) *n.* (*usu. with* in) danger —**'jeopardize** *or* **-ise** *vt.* endanger

Jer. *Bible* Jeremiah

THESAURUS

tivity, fête, frolic, jubilee, merriment, party, revelry, spree

jangle 1. *v.* chime, clank, clash, clatter, jingle, rattle, vibrate **2.** *n.* cacophony, clang, clangour, clash, din, dissonance, jar, racket, rattle, reverberation

janitor caretaker, concierge, custodian, doorkeeper, porter

jar[1] amphora, carafe, container, crock, flagon, jug, pitcher, pot, receptacle, urn, vase, vessel

jar[2] *v.* **1.** agitate, convulse, disturb, grate, irritate, jolt, offend, rasp, rattle (*Inf.*), rock, shake, vibrate **2.** annoy, clash, discompose, grate, grind, irk, irritate, nettle

jargon 1. argot, cant, dialect, idiom, lingo (*Inf.*), parlance, patois, slang, tongue, usage **2.** balderdash, bunkum (*Inf.*), drivel, gabble, gibberish, gobbledegook, mumbo jumbo, nonsense, palaver, rigmarole, twaddle

jaunt airing, excursion, expedition, outing, promenade, ramble, stroll, tour, trip

jaunty airy, breezy, buoyant, carefree, dapper, gay, high-spirited, lively, perky, self-confident, showy, smart, sprightly, spruce, trim

jaw *v.* babble, chat, chatter, gossip, lecture, talk

jaws abyss, aperture, entrance, gates, ingress, maw, mouth, opening, orifice

jazz up animate, enhance, enliven, heighten, improve

jealous 1. covetous, desirous, emulous, envious, green, green-eyed, grudging, intolerant, invidious, resentful, rival **2.** anxious, apprehensive, attentive, guarded, mistrustful, protective, solicitous, suspicious, vigilant, wary, watchful, zealous

jealousy covetousness, distrust, envy, heart-burning, ill-will, mistrust, possessiveness, resentment, spite, suspicion

jeer 1. *v.* banter, barrack, cock a snook at (*Brit.*), contemn, deride, flout, gibe, heckle, hector, knock (*Sl.*), mock, ridicule, scoff, sneer, taunt **2.** *n.* abuse, aspersion, catcall, derision, gibe, hiss, hoot, obloquy, ridicule, scoff, sneer, taunt

jeopardize chance, endanger, expose, gamble, hazard, imperil, risk, stake, venture

jeopardy danger, endangerment, exposure, hazard, insecurity, liability, peril, precariousness, risk, venture, vulnerability

jerboa (dʒɜːˈbəʊə) *n.* **1.** small Afr. burrowing rodent resembling a mouse **2.** desert rat

jeremiad (dʒɛrɪˈmaɪəd) *n.* lamentation; complaint

jerk[1] (dʒɜːk) *n.* **1.** sharp, abruptly stopped movement **2.** twitch **3.** sharp pull **4.** *sl.* stupid person —*v.* **5.** move or throw with a jerk —**ˈjerkily** *adv.* —**ˈjerkiness** *n.* —**ˈjerky** *a.* uneven, spasmodic

jerk[2] (dʒɜːk) *vt.* **1.** preserve (beef *etc.*) by cutting into strips and drying in sun —*n.* **2.** jerked meat (*also* **ˈjerky**)

jerkin (ˈdʒɜːkɪn) *n.* sleeveless jacket, *esp.* of leather

Jerry (ˈdʒɛrɪ) *n.* **UK** *sl.* **1.** German, *esp.* German soldier **2.** Germans collectively

jerry-built (ˈdʒɛrɪ) *a.* of flimsy construction with cheap materials —**jerry-builder** *n.*

jerry can flat-sided can for storing or transporting motor fuel *etc.*

jersey (ˈdʒɜːzɪ) *n.* **1.** knitted jumper **2.** machine-knitted fabric **3.** (**J-**) breed of cow

jessamine (ˈdʒɛsəmɪn) *n. see* JASMINE

jest (dʒɛst) *n./vi.* joke —**ˈjester** *n.* joker, *esp.* employed by medieval ruler

Jesuit (ˈdʒɛzjʊɪt) *n.* member of Society of Jesus, order founded by Ignatius Loyola in 1534 —**Jesuˈitical** *a.* of Jesuits

Jesus (ˈdʒiːzəs) *n.* **1.** ?4 B.C.-?29 A.D., founder of Christianity, believed by Christians to be the Son of God (*also* **Jesus Christ, Jesus of Nazareth**) —*interj. taboo slang* **2.** used to express intense surprise, dismay *etc.* (*also* **Jesus wept**)

jet[1] (dʒɛt) *n.* **1.** stream of liquid, gas *etc.*, *esp.* shot from small hole **2.** the small hole **3.** spout, nozzle **4.** aircraft driven by jet propulsion —*vt.* **5.** throw out —*vi.* **6.** shoot forth —*v.* **7.** transport or be transported by jet (**-tt-**) —**jet lag** fatigue caused by crossing time zones in jet aircraft —**jet-propelled** *a.* driven by jet propulsion —**jet propulsion** propulsion by thrust provided by jet of gas or liquid —**jet set** rich, fashionable social set, members of which travel widely for pleasure —**ˈjet-setter** *n.*

jet[2] (dʒɛt) *n.* hard black mineral capable of brilliant polish —**jet-black** *a.* glossy black

jetsam (ˈdʒɛtsəm) *n.* cargo thrown overboard to lighten ship and later washed ashore —**ˈjettison** *vt.* **1.** abandon **2.** throw overboard

jetty (ˈdʒɛtɪ) *n.* small pier, wharf

Jew (dʒuː) *n.* person of Hebrew religion or ancestry —**ˈJewish** *a.* —**ˈJewry** *n.* Jews collectively —**jew's-harp** *n.* small musical instrument held between teeth and played by finger

jewel (ˈdʒuːəl) *n.* **1.** precious stone **2.** ornament containing one **3.** precious thing —**ˈjeweller** *or U.S.* **ˈjeweler** *n.* dealer in jewels —**jewellery** *or U.S.* **jewelry** (ˈdʒuːəlrɪ) *n.*

jewfish (ˈdʒuːfɪʃ) *n.* large fish of tropical and temperate waters

Jezebel (ˈdʒɛzəbɛl) *n.* **1.** *O.T.* wife of Ahab, king of Israel **2.** (*sometimes* **j-**) shameless or scheming woman

jib (dʒɪb) *n.* **1.** triangular sail set forward of mast **2.** projecting arm of crane or derrick —*vi.* **3.** object to proceeding **4.** (of horse, person) stop and refuse to go on (**-bb-**) —**ˈjibber** *n.* —**jib boom** spar from end of bowsprit

jibe[1] (dʒaɪb) *or* **jib** (dʒɪb) *see* GYBE, GIBE

jibe[2] (dʒaɪb) *vi. inf.* agree; accord; harmonize

jiffy (ˈdʒɪfɪ) *or* **jiff** *n. inf.* very short period of time

Jiffy bag (ˈdʒɪfɪ) **R** large padded envelope

jig (dʒɪg) *n.* **1.** lively dance **2.** music for it **3.** small mechanical device **4.** mechanical device used as guide for cutting *etc.* **5.** *Angling* any of various lures —*vi.* **6.** dance jig **7.** make jerky up-and-down movements (**-gg-**) —**ˈjigger** *n.* —**ˈjigsaw** *n.* machine fretsaw —**jigsaw (puzzle)** picture stuck on board and cut into interlocking pieces with jigsaw

jigger (ˈdʒɪgə) *n.* small glass for spirits

jiggery-pokery (ˈdʒɪgərɪˈpəʊkərɪ) *n. inf.* trickery, nonsense

jiggle (ˈdʒɪgᵊl) *v.* move (up and down *etc.*) with short jerky movements

jilt (dʒɪlt) *vt.* cast off (lover)

jim crow (ˈdʒɪm ˈkrəʊ) (*oft.* **J- C-**) **US** **1.** policy or practice of segregating Negroes **2.** *derogatory* Negro **3.** implement for bending iron bars or rails

jimjams (ˈdʒɪmdʒæmz) *pl.n.* **1.** *sl.* delirium tremens **2.** state of nervous tension or anxiety

jingle (ˈdʒɪŋgᵊl) *n.* **1.** mixed metallic noise, as of shaken chain **2.** catchy, rhythmic verse, song *etc.* —*v.* **3.** (cause to) make jingling sound

THESAURUS

jeremiad complaint, groan, keen, lament, lamentation, moan, plaint, wail

jerk *v./n.* jolt, lurch, pull, throw, thrust, tug, tweak, twitch, wrench, yank

jerky bouncy, bumpy, convulsive, fitful, jolting, jumpy, rough, shaky, spasmodic, tremulous, twitchy, uncontrolled

jerry-built cheap, defective, faulty, flimsy, ramshackle, rickety, shabby, slipshod, thrown together, unsubstantial

jest 1. *n.* banter, bon mot, crack (*Sl.*), fun, gag (*Sl.*), hoax, jape, joke, play, pleasantry, prank, quip, sally, sport, wisecrack (*Inf.*), witticism **2.** *v.* banter, chaff, deride, gibe, jeer, joke, kid (*Inf.*), mock, quip, scoff, sneer, tease

jester 1. comedian, comic, humorist, joker, quipster, wag, wit **2.** buffoon, clown, fool, harlequin, madcap, mummer, pantaloon, prankster, zany

jet *n.* **1.** flow, fountain, gush, spout, spray, spring, stream **2.** atomizer, nose, nozzle, rose, spout, sprayer, sprinkler ~*v.* **3.** flow, gush, issue, rush, shoot, spew, spout, squirt, stream, surge **4.** fly, soar, zoom

jettison abandon, discard, dump, eject, expel, heave, scrap, throw overboard, unload

jetty breakwater, dock, groyne, mole, pier, quay, wharf

jewel 1. brilliant, gemstone, ornament, precious stone, rock (*Sl.*), sparkler (*Inf.*), trinket **2.** charm, find, gem, humdinger (*Sl.*), masterpiece, paragon, pearl, prize, rarity, treasure (*Fig.*), wonder

jewellery finery, gems, jewels, ornaments, precious stones, regalia, treasure, trinkets

Jezebel harlot, harridan, hussy, jade, virago, wanton, witch

jib balk, recoil, refuse, retreat, shrink, stop short

jingo (ˈdʒɪŋgəʊ) *n.* **1.** loud, bellicose patriot **2.** jingoism (*pl.* -es) —**ˈjingoism** *n.* chauvinism —**jingoˈistic** *a.* —**by jingo** exclamation of surprise

jinks (dʒɪŋks) *pl.n.* boisterous merrymaking (*esp. in* **high jinks**)

jinni, jinnee *or* **djinni** (dʒɪˈniː) *n.* spirit in Muslim mythology who could assume human or animal form (*pl.* **jinn** *or* **djinn** (dʒɪn))

jinx (dʒɪŋks) *n.* **1.** force, person, thing bringing bad luck —*vt.* **2.** be or put a jinx on

jitters (ˈdʒɪtəz) *pl.n.* worried nervousness, anxiety —**ˈjittery** *a.* nervous —**ˈjitterbug** *n.* **1.** fast jerky Amer. dance popular in 1940s **2.** person who dances jitterbug —*vi.* **3.** perform such dance

jiujitsu *or* **jiujutsu** (dʒuːˈdʒɪtsuː) *n. see* JUJITSU

jive (dʒaɪv) *n.* **1.** (dance performed to) rock and roll music, *esp.* of 1950s —*vi.* **2.** dance the jive

job (dʒɒb) *n.* **1.** piece of work, task **2.** post, office **3.** *inf.* difficult task **4.** *inf.* crime, *esp.* robbery —**ˈjobber** *n.* stockjobber —**ˈjobbing** *a.* doing single, particular jobs for payment —**ˈjobless** *a./pl.n.* unemployed (people) —**job centre** government office in town centre providing information about vacant jobs —**job lot 1.** assortment sold together **2.** miscellaneous collection

Job's comforter (dʒəʊbz) person who adds to distress while purporting to give sympathy

jockey (ˈdʒɒkɪ) *n.* **1.** professional rider in horse races (*pl.* -s) —*v.* **2.** (*esp. with* for) manoeuvre (**ˈjockeyed, ˈjockeying**)

jockstrap (ˈdʒɒkstræp) *n.* piece of elasticated material worn by men, *esp.* athletes, to support genitals (*also* **athletic support**)

jocose (dʒəˈkəʊs) *a.* waggish, humorous —**joˈcosely** *adv.* —**jocosity** (dʒəˈkɒsɪtɪ) *n.* —**jocular** (ˈdʒɒkjʊlə) *a.* **1.** joking **2.** given to joking —**jocularity** (dʒɒkjʊˈlærɪtɪ) *n.*

jocund (ˈdʒɒkənd) *a.* merry, cheerful —**joˈcundity** *n.*

jodhpurs (ˈdʒɒdpəz) *pl.n.* tight-legged riding breeches

jog (dʒɒg) *vi.* **1.** run slowly or move at a trot, *esp.* for physical exercise —*vt.* **2.** jar, nudge **3.** remind, stimulate (-gg-) —*n.* **4.** jogging —**ˈjogger** *n.* —**ˈjogging** *n.* —**jog trot** slow regular trot

joggle (ˈdʒɒgᵊl) *v.* **1.** move to and fro in jerks **2.** shake —*n.* **3.** act of joggling

john (dʒɒn) *n.* **US** *sl.* lavatory

John Bull typical Englishman

joie de vivre (ʒwad ˈvivr) *Fr.* enjoyment of life, ebullience

join (dʒɔɪn) *vt.* **1.** put together, fasten, unite **2.** become member of —*vi.* **3.** become united, connected **4.** (*with* up) enlist **5.** (*usu. with* in) take part —*n.* **6.** joining **7.** place of joining —**ˈjoiner** *n.* **1.** maker of finished woodwork **2.** one who joins —**ˈjoinery** *n.* joiner's work

joint (dʒɔɪnt) *n.* **1.** arrangement by which two things fit together, rigidly or loosely **2.** place of this **3.** meat for roasting, oft. with bone **4.** *inf.* house, place *etc.* **5.** *sl.* disreputable bar or nightclub **6.** *sl.* marijuana cigarette —*a.* **7.** common **8.** shared by two or more —*vt.* **9.** connect by joints **10.** divide at the joints —**ˈjointly** *adv.* —**joint-stock company 1.** UK business enterprise characterized by sharing of ownership between shareholders, whose liability is limited **2.** US business enterprise whose owners are issued shares of transferable stock but do not enjoy limited liability —**out of joint 1.** dislocated **2.** disorganized

jointure (ˈdʒɔɪntʃə) *n. Law* property settled on wife for her use after husband's death

joist (dʒɔɪst) *n.* one of the parallel beams stretched from wall to wall on which to fix floor or ceiling —**ˈjoisted** *a.*

joke (dʒəʊk) *n.* **1.** thing said or done to cause laughter **2.** something said or done merely in fun **3.** ridiculous or humorous circumstance —*vi.* **4.** make jokes —**ˈjoker** *n.* **1.** one who jokes **2.** *sl.* fellow **3.** extra card in pack, counting as highest card in some games

THESAURUS

jig *v.* bob, bounce, caper, jiggle, jounce, prance, shake, skip, twitch, wiggle, wobble

jingle *v.* **1.** chime, clatter, clink, jangle, rattle, ring, tinkle, tintinnabulate ~*n.* **2.** clang, clangour, clink, rattle, reverberation, ringing, tinkle **3.** chorus, ditty, doggerel, limerick, melody, song, tune

jinx 1. *n.* black magic, curse, evil eye, hex (*U.S.*), nemesis, plague, voodoo **2.** *v.* bewitch, curse, hex (*U.S.*)

jitters anxiety, fidgets, nerves, nervousness, tenseness, the shakes (*Inf.*), the willies (*Inf.*)

jittery agitated, anxious, fidgety, jumpy, nervous, quivering, shaky, trembling

job 1. affair, assignment, charge, chore, concern, contribution, duty, enterprise, errand, function, pursuit, responsibility, role, stint, task, undertaking, venture, work **2.** activity, business, calling, capacity, career, craft, employment, function, livelihood, métier, occupation, office, position, post, profession, situation, trade, vocation

jobless idle, inactive, out of work, unemployed, unoccupied

jockey cajole, engineer, finagle (*Inf.*), ingratiate, insinuate, manage, manipulate, manoeuvre, negotiate, trim, wheedle

jocular amusing, comical, droll, facetious, frolicsome, funny, humorous, jesting, jocose, jocund, joking, jolly, jovial, playful, roguish, sportive, teasing, waggish, whimsical, witty

jog 1. activate, arouse, nudge, prod, prompt, push, remind, shake, stimulate, stir, suggest **2.** bounce, jar, jerk, jiggle, joggle, jolt, jostle, jounce, rock, shake **3.** canter, dogtrot, lope, run, trot

joie de vivre ebullience, enjoyment, enthusiasm, gaiety, gusto, joy, joyfulness, pleasure, relish, zest

join 1. accompany, add, adhere, annex, append, attach, cement, combine, connect, couple, fasten, knit, link, marry, splice, tie, unite, yoke **2.** affiliate with, associate with, enlist, enrol, enter, sign up

joint *n.* **1.** articulation, connection, hinge, intersection, junction, juncture, knot, nexus, node, seam, union ~*adj.* **2.** collective, combined, communal, concerted, consolidated, cooperative, joined, mutual, shared, united ~*v.* **3.** connect, couple, fasten, fit, join, unite **4.** carve, cut up, dismember, dissect, divide, segment, sever, sunder

jointly as one, collectively, in common, in conjunction, in league, in partnership, mutually, together, unitedly

joke 1. *n.* frolic, fun, gag (*Sl.*), jape, jest, lark, play,

jolly (ˈdʒɒlɪ) *a.* **1.** jovial **2.** festive, merry —*vt.* **3.** (*esp. with* along) (try to) make (person, occasion *etc.*) happier (**ˈjollied, ˈjollying**) —**jollifiˈcation** *n.* merrymaking —**ˈjollity** *n.*

Jolly Roger pirates' flag with white skull and crossbones on black field

jolt (dʒəʊlt) *n.* **1.** sudden jerk **2.** bump **3.** shock —*v.* **4.** move, shake with jolts —**ˈjolty** *a.*

Jonah (ˈdʒəʊnə) *or* **Jonas** (ˈdʒəʊnəs) *n.* **1.** *O.T.* Hebrew prophet who was swallowed by whale **2.** person believed to bring bad luck to those around him

jonquil (ˈdʒɒŋkwɪl) *n.* **1.** fragrant yellow or white narcissus —*a.* **2.** pale yellow

Josh. *Bible* Joshua

joss (dʒɒs) *n.* Chinese idol —**joss house** Chinese temple —**joss stick** stick of Chinese incense

jostle (ˈdʒɒsᵊl) *or* **justle** (ˈdʒʌsᵊl) *v.* knock or push against (someone)

jot (dʒɒt) *n.* **1.** small amount, whit —*vt.* **2.** write briefly; make note of (**-tt-**) —**ˈjotter** *n.* notebook

joule (dʒuːl) *n. Elec.* unit of work or energy

journal (ˈdʒɜːnᵊl) *n.* **1.** daily newspaper or other periodical **2.** daily record **3.** logbook **4.** part of axle or shaft resting on the bearings —**journaˈlese** *n.* **1.** journalists' jargon **2.** high-flown style, full of clichés —**ˈjournalism** *n.* editing, writing in periodicals —**ˈjournalist** *n.* —**journaˈlistic** *a.*

journey (ˈdʒɜːnɪ) *n.* **1.** travelling from one place to another; excursion **2.** distance travelled —*vi.* **3.** travel

journeyman (ˈdʒɜːnɪmən) *n.* craftsman or artisan employed by another

joust (dʒaʊst) *Hist. n.* **1.** encounter with lances between two mounted knights —*vi.* **2.** engage in joust

Jove (dʒəʊv) *n. see* JUPITER (sense 1) —**ˈJovian** *a.* —**by Jove** exclamation of surprise

jovial (ˈdʒəʊvɪəl) *a.* convivial, merry, gay

jowl (dʒaʊl) *n.* **1.** cheek, jaw **2.** outside of throat when prominent

joy (dʒɔɪ) *n.* **1.** gladness, pleasure, delight **2.** cause of this —**ˈjoyful** *a.* —**ˈjoyless** *a.* —**ˈjoyous** *a.* **1.** having happy nature or mood **2.** joyful —**ˈjoyously** *adv.* —**joy ride** trip, *esp.* in stolen car —**ˈjoystick** *n. inf.* control column of aircraft

J.P. Justice of the Peace

Jr. *or* **jr.** Junior

jubilate (ˈdʒuːbɪleɪt) *vi.* rejoice —**ˈjubilant** *a.* exultant —**ˈjubilantly** *adv.* —**jubiˈlation** *n.*

jubilee (ˈdʒuːbɪliː) *n.* time of rejoicing, *esp.* 25th or 50th anniversary

Jud. *Bible* Judges

Judaic (dʒuːˈdeɪɪk) *a.* of the Jews or Judaism —**ˈJudaism** *n.* **1.** religion of the Jews **2.** religious and cultural traditions of the Jews **3.** the Jews collectively —**ˈJudaize** *or* **-ise** *vt.* **1.** make Jewish —*v.* **2.** conform or bring into conformity with Judaism

Judas (ˈdʒuːdəs) *n.* **1.** *N.T.* apostle who betrayed Jesus to his enemies for 30 pieces of silver **2.** person who betrays a friend; traitor

judder (ˈdʒʌdə) *inf. vi.* **1.** shake, vibrate —*n.* **2.** a vibrating motion

judge (dʒʌdʒ) *n.* **1.** officer appointed to try cases in court of law **2.** one who decides in dispute, contest *etc.* **3.** one able to form reliable opinion, arbiter **4.** umpire **5.** in Jewish history, ruler —*vi.* **6.** act as judge —*vt.* **7.** act as judge of **8.** try, estimate **9.** decide —**ˈjudgment** *or* **ˈjudgement** *n.* **1.** faculty of judging **2.** sentence of court **3.** opinion **4.** misfortune regarded as sign of divine displeasure —**Judgment Day** occasion of Last Judgment by God at end of world

THESAURUS

pun, quip, quirk, sally, sport, whimsy, wisecrack (*Inf.*), witticism, yarn **2.** *v.* banter, chaff, deride, frolic, gambol, jest, kid (*Inf.*), mock, quip, ridicule, taunt, tease

joker buffoon, clown, comedian, comic, humorist, jester, kidder (*Inf.*), prankster, trickster, wag, wit

jolly blithesome, carefree, cheerful, convivial, festive, frolicsome, funny, gay, gladsome, hilarious, jocund, jovial, joyful, joyous, jubilant, merry, mirthful, playful, sportive, sprightly

jolt *v.* **1.** jar, jerk, jog, jostle, knock, push, shake, shove ~*n.* **2.** bump, jar, jerk, jog, jump, lurch, quiver, shake, start **3.** blow, bolt from the blue, bombshell, reversal, setback, shock, surprise, thunderbolt

jostle bump, butt, crowd, elbow, hustle, jog, joggle, jolt, press, push, scramble, shake, shove, squeeze, throng, thrust

journal 1. chronicle, daily, gazette, magazine, monthly, newspaper, paper, periodical, record, register, review, tabloid, weekly **2.** chronicle, commonplace book, daybook, diary, log, record

journalist broadcaster, columnist, commentator, contributor, correspondent, hack, newsman, newspaperman, pressman, reporter, scribe (*Inf.*), stringer

journey 1. *n.* excursion, expedition, jaunt, odyssey, outing, passage, peregrination, pilgrimage, progress, ramble, tour, travel, trek, trip, voyage **2.** *v.* fare, fly, go, peregrinate, proceed, ramble, range, roam, rove, tour, travel, traverse, trek, voyage, wander, wend

jovial airy, animated, blithe, buoyant, cheery, convivial, cordial, gay, glad, happy, hilarious, jocose, jocund, jolly, jubilant, merry, mirthful

joy 1. bliss, delight, ecstasy, elation, exaltation, exultation, felicity, festivity, gaiety, gladness, glee, hilarity, pleasure, rapture, ravishment, satisfaction, transport **2.** charm, delight, gem, jewel, pride, prize, treasure, treat, wonder

joyful blithesome, delighted, elated, enraptured, glad, gladsome, gratified, happy, jocund, jolly, jovial, jubilant, light-hearted, merry, pleased, satisfied

joyless cheerless, dejected, depressed, dismal, dispirited, downcast, dreary, gloomy, miserable, sad, unhappy

joyous cheerful, festive, heartening, joyful, merry, rapturous

jubilant elated, enraptured, euphoric, excited, exuberant, exultant, glad, joyous, overjoyed, rejoicing, rhapsodic, thrilled, triumphal, triumphant

jubilation celebration, ecstasy, elation, excitement, exultation, festivity, jamboree, joy, jubilee. triumph

jubilee carnival, celebration, festival, festivity, fête, gala, holiday

judge *n.* **1.** adjudicator, arbiter, arbitrator, moderator, referee, umpire **2.** appraiser, arbiter, assessor, authority, connoisseur, critic, evaluator, expert **3.**

judicature (ˈdʒuːdɪkətʃə) *n.* **1.** administration of justice **2.** body of judges —**juˈdicial** *a.* **1.** of, or by, a court or judge **2.** having qualities proper to a judge **3.** discriminating —**juˈdicially** *adv.* —**juˈdiciary** *n.* system of courts and judges —**juˈdicious** *a.* well-judged, sensible, prudent

judo (ˈdʒuːdəʊ) *n.* modern sport derived from jujitsu

jug (dʒʌg) *n.* **1.** vessel for liquids, with handle and small spout **2.** its contents **3.** *sl.* prison —*vt.* **4.** stew (*esp.* hare) in jug (**-gg-**)

juggernaut (ˈdʒʌgənɔːt) *n.* **1.** large heavy lorry **2.** any irresistible, destructive force

juggle (ˈdʒʌgᵊl) *v.* **1.** throw and catch (several objects) so most are in the air simultaneously **2.** manage, manipulate (accounts *etc.*) to deceive —*n.* **3.** act of juggling —ˈ**juggler** *n.*

jugular vein (ˈdʒʌgjʊlə) one of three large veins of the neck returning blood from the head

juice (dʒuːs) *n.* **1.** liquid part of vegetable, fruit or meat **2.** *inf.* electric current **3.** *inf.* petrol **4.** vigour, vitality —ˈ**juicy** *a.* succulent

jujitsu, jujutsu, *or* **jiujutsu** (dʒuːˈdʒɪtsuː) *n.* the Japanese art of wrestling and self-defence

juju (ˈdʒuːdʒuː) *n.* **1.** object superstitiously revered by certain W Afr. peoples and used as charm or fetish **2.** power associated with juju

jujube (ˈdʒuːdʒuːb) *n.* **1.** any of several spiny trees that have yellowish flowers and dark red edible fruits **2.** fruit of any of these trees **3.** lozenge of gelatine, sugar *etc.*

jukebox (ˈdʒuːkbɒks) *n.* automatic, coin-operated record-player

Jul. July

julep (ˈdʒuːlɪp) *n.* **1.** sweet drink **2.** medicated drink

Julian (ˈdʒuːljən) *a.* of Julius Caesar —**Julian calendar** calendar as adjusted by Julius Caesar in 46 B.C., in which the year was made to consist of 365 days, 6 hours, instead of 365 days

julienne (dʒuːlɪˈɛn) *n.* kind of clear soup

July (dʒuːˈlaɪ) *n.* seventh month

jumble (ˈdʒʌmbᵊl) *v.* **1.** mingle, mix in confusion **2.** remember in confused form —*n.* **3.** confused heap, muddle **4.** articles for jumble sale —**jumble sale** sale of miscellaneous, usu. second-hand, items

jumbo (ˈdʒʌmbəʊ) *n. inf.* **1.** elephant **2.** anything very large (*pl.* **-s**) —**jumbo jet** *inf.* large jet-propelled airliner

jump (dʒʌmp) *v.* **1.** (cause to) spring, leap (over) **2.** pass or skip (over) —*vi.* **3.** move hastily **4.** rise steeply **5.** parachute from aircraft **6.** start, jerk (with astonishment *etc.*) **7.** (of faulty film *etc.*) make abrupt movements —*vt.* **8.** come off (tracks, rails *etc.*) **9.** *inf.* attack without warning —*n.* **10.** act of jumping **11.** obstacle to be jumped **12.** distance, height jumped **13.** sudden nervous jerk or start **14.** sudden rise in prices *etc.* —ˈ**jumper** *n.* **1.** one who, that which jumps **2.** sweater, pullover —ˈ**jumpy** *a.* nervous —**jumped-up** *a. inf.* suddenly risen in significance, *esp.* when appearing arrogant —**jump jet** *inf.* fixed-wing jet aircraft that can land and take off vertically —**jump leads** electric cables to connect discharged car battery to external battery to aid starting of engine —**jump suit** one-piece garment of trousers and top

Jun. **1.** June **2.** junior (*also* **jun.**)

junction (ˈdʒʌŋkʃən) *n.* **1.** railway station *etc.* where lines, routes join **2.** place of joining **3.** joining

juncture (ˈdʒʌŋktʃə) *n.* state of affairs

June (dʒuːn) *n.* sixth month

jungle (ˈdʒʌŋgᵊl) *n.* **1.** tangled vegetation of equatorial

THESAURUS

beak (*Brit. sl.*), justice, magistrate ~*v.* **4.** adjudge, adjudicate, arbitrate, ascertain, conclude, decide, determine, discern, distinguish, mediate, referee, umpire **5.** appraise, appreciate, assess, consider, criticize, esteem, estimate, evaluate, examine, rate, review, value **6.** adjudge, condemn, decree, doom, find, pass sentence, pronounce sentence, rule, sentence, sit, try

judgment **1.** acumen, common sense, discernment, discrimination, intelligence, penetration, percipience, perspicacity, prudence, sagacity, sense, shrewdness, taste, understanding, wisdom **2.** arbitration, award, conclusion, decision, decree, determination, finding, order, result, ruling, sentence, verdict **3.** appraisal, assessment, belief, conviction, deduction, diagnosis, estimate, finding, opinion, valuation, view **4.** damnation, doom, fate, misfortune, punishment, retribution

judicial **1.** judiciary, juridical, legal, official **2.** discriminating, distinguished, impartial, judgelike, magisterial, magistral

judicious acute, astute, careful, cautious, circumspect, considered, diplomatic, discerning, discreet, discriminating, enlightened, expedient, informed, politic, prudent, rational, reasonable, sagacious, sage, sane, sapient, sensible, shrewd, skilful, sober, sound, thoughtful, well-advised, well-judged, wise

jug carafe, container, crock, ewer, jar, pitcher, urn, vessel

juggle alter, change, disguise, doctor (*Inf.*), falsify, fix (*Inf.*), manipulate, manoeuvre, misrepresent, modify, tamper with

juice extract, fluid, liquid, liquor, nectar, sap, secretion, serum

juicy lush, moist, sappy, succulent, watery

jumble **1.** *v.* confound, confuse, disarrange, dishevel, disorder, disorganize, entangle, mistake, mix, muddle, shuffle, tangle **2.** *n.* chaos, clutter, confusion, disarrangement, disarray, disorder, farrago, gallimaufry, hodgepodge, hotchpotch, litter, medley, *mélange*, mess, miscellany, mishmash, mixture, muddle

jump *v.* **1.** bounce, bound, caper, clear, gambol, hop, hurdle, leap, skip, spring, vault **2.** flinch, jerk, recoil, start, wince **3.** avoid, digress, evade, miss, omit, overshoot, skip, switch **4.** advance, ascend, boost, escalate, gain, hike, increase, mount, rise, surge ~*n.* **5.** bound, buck, caper, hop, leap, skip, spring, vault **6.** barricade, barrier, fence, hurdle, impediment, obstacle, rail **7.** advance, augmentation, boost, increase, increment, rise, upsurge, upturn **8.** jar, jerk, jolt, lurch, shock, start, swerve, twitch, wrench

jumper pullover, sweater, woolly

jumpy agitated, anxious, apprehensive, fidgety, jittery, nervous, on edge, restless, shaky, tense, timorous

junction alliance, combination, connection, coupling, joint, juncture, linking, seam, union

forest **2.** land covered with it **3.** tangled mass **4.** condition of intense competition, struggle for survival —**ˈjungly** *a.*

junior (ˈdʒuːnjə) *a.* **1.** younger **2.** of lower standing —*n.* **3.** junior person —**junior school** UK school for children aged between 7 and 11 —**junior technician** rank in Royal Air Force comparable to that of private in army

juniper (ˈdʒuːnɪpə) *n.* evergreen shrub with berries yielding oil of juniper, used for medicine and gin making

junk[1] (dʒʌŋk) *n.* **1.** discarded, useless objects **2.** *inf.* nonsense **3.** *sl.* narcotic drug —**ˈjunkie** *or* **ˈjunky** *n. sl.* drug addict —**junk food** food eaten in addition to or instead of regular meals, oft. with low nutritional value

junk[2] (dʒʌŋk) *n.* Chinese sailing vessel

junket (ˈdʒʌŋkɪt) *n.* **1.** curdled milk flavoured and sweetened —*vi.* **2.** feast, picnic

junta (ˈdʒʊntə) *n.* group of military officers holding power in a country

Jupiter (ˈdʒuːpɪtə) *n.* **1.** Roman chief of gods **2.** largest of the planets

Jurassic (dʒʊˈræsɪk) *a.* **1.** of second period of Mesozoic era —*n.* **2.** Jurassic period or rock system

juridical (dʒʊˈrɪdɪkˀl) *a.* of law or administration of justice; legal

jurisdiction (dʒʊərɪsˈdɪkʃən) *n.* **1.** administration of justice **2.** authority **3.** territory covered by it —**jurisˈprudence** *n.* science of, skill in, law —**ˈjurist** *n.* one skilled in law —**juˈristic(al)** *a.*

jury (ˈdʒʊərɪ) *n.* **1.** body of persons sworn to render verdict in court of law **2.** body of judges of competition —**ˈjuror** *or* **ˈjuryman** *n.* one of jury —**jury box** enclosure in court where jury sit

jury- (*comb. form*) *chiefly naut.* makeshift, as in *jury-rigged*

just (dʒʌst) *a.* **1.** fair **2.** upright, honest **3.** proper, right, equitable —*adv.* **4.** exactly **5.** barely **6.** at this instant **7.** merely, only **8.** really —**ˈjustice** *n.* **1.** quality of being just **2.** fairness **3.** judicial proceedings **4.** judge, magistrate —**jusˈticiary** *a.* **1.** of administration of justice —*n.* **2.** officer or administrator of justice; judge —**ˈjustifiable** *a.* —**ˈjustifiably** *adv.* —**justifiˈcation** *n.* —**ˈjustify** *vt.* **1.** prove right, true or innocent **2.** vindicate **3.** excuse (**-ified, -ifying**) —**ˈjustly** *adv.* —**justice of the peace** lay magistrate whose function is to preserve peace in his area and try summarily minor cases

jut (dʒʌt) *vi.* **1.** (*oft. with* out) project, stick out (**-tt-**) —*n.* **2.** projection

jute (dʒuːt) *n.* fibre of certain plants, used for rope, canvas *etc.*

juvenile (ˈdʒuːvɪnaɪl) *a.* **1.** young **2.** of, for young children **3.** immature —*n.* **4.** young person, child —**juveˈnescence** *n.* —**juveˈnescent** *a.* becoming young —**juvenilia** (dʒuːvɪˈnɪlɪə) *pl.n.* works produced in author's youth —**juvenility** (dʒuːvɪˈnɪlɪtɪ) *n.* —**juvenile court** court dealing with young offenders or children in need of care —**juvenile delinquent** young person guilty of some offence, antisocial behaviour *etc.*

juxtapose (dʒʌkstəˈpəʊz) *vt.* put side by side —**juxtaˈpoˈsition** *n.* contiguity, being side by side

THESAURUS

junior inferior, lesser, lower, minor, secondary, subordinate, younger

junk clutter, debris, leavings, litter, oddments, odds and ends, refuse, rubbish, rummage, scrap, trash, waste

jurisdiction **1.** authority, command, control, dominion, influence, power, prerogative, rule, say, sway **2.** area, bounds, circuit, compass, district, dominion, field, orbit, province, range, scope, sphere, zone

just *adj.* **1.** blameless, conscientious, decent, equitable, fair, fairminded, good, honest, honourable, impartial, lawful, pure, right, righteous, unbiased, upright, virtuous **2.** appropriate, apt, condign, deserved, due, fitting, justified, legitimate, merited, proper, reasonable, rightful, suitable, well-deserved ~*adv.* **3.** absolutely, completely, entirely, exactly, perfectly, precisely **4.** hardly, lately, only now, recently, scarcely **5.** at most, but, merely, no more than, nothing but, only, simply, solely

justice **1.** equity, fairness, honesty, impartiality, integrity, justness, law, legality, legitimacy, reasonableness, rectitude, right **2.** judge, magistrate

justifiable acceptable, defensible, excusable, fit, lawful, legitimate, proper, reasonable, right, sound, tenable, understandable, valid, vindicable, warrantable, well-founded

justification **1.** absolution, apology, approval, defence, exculpation, excuse, exoneration, explanation, extenuation, plea, rationalization, vindication **2.** basis, defence, grounds, plea, reason, warrant

justify absolve, acquit, approve, confirm, defend, establish, exculpate, excuse, exonerate, explain, legalize, legitimize, maintain, substantiate, support, sustain, uphold, validate, vindicate, warrant

justly accurately, correctly, equally, equitably, fairly, honestly, impartially, lawfully, properly

jut bulge, extend, impend, overhang, poke, project, protrude, stick out

juvenile **1.** *n.* adolescent, boy, child, girl, infant, minor, youth **2.** *adj.* babyish, boyish, callow, childish, girlish, immature, inexperienced, infantile, jejune, puerile, undeveloped, unsophisticated, young, youthful

juxtaposition adjacency, closeness, contact, contiguity, nearness, propinquity, proximity, vicinity

K

k *or* **K** (keɪ) *n.* **1.** 11th letter of English alphabet **2.** speech sound represented by this letter, as in *kitten* (*pl.* **k's, K's** *or* **Ks**)

k 1. kilo **2.** *Maths.* unit vector along *z*-axis **3.** knit

K 1. kelvin **2.** *Chess* king **3.** *Chem.* potassium **4.** *Phys.* kaon **5.** one thousand **6.** *Comp.* unit of 1024 words, bytes or bits

Kaffir *or* **Kafir** (ˈkæfə) *n.* **SA** *obs., offens.* any black African —**kaffirboom** (ˈkæfəbʊəm) *n.* S Afr. flowering tree —**kaffir corn** S Afr. variety of sorghum

kaftan *or* **caftan** (ˈkæftæn) *n.* **1.** long coatlike Eastern garment **2.** imitation of it, *esp.* as woman's long, loose dress with sleeves

Kaiser (ˈkaɪzə) *n.* (*sometimes* **k-**) *Hist.* **1.** any of three German emperors **2.** any Austro-Hungarian emperor

kale *or* **kail** (keɪl) *n.* type of cabbage

kaleidoscope (kəˈlaɪdəskəʊp) *n.* **1.** optical toy for producing changing symmetrical patterns by multiple reflections of coloured glass chips *etc.*, in inclined mirrors enclosed in tube **2.** any complex, frequently changing pattern —**kaleidoscopic** (kəlaɪdəˈskɒpɪk) *a.* swiftly changing

Kamasutra (kɑːməˈsuːtrə) *n.* ancient Hindu text on erotic pleasure

kamikaze (kæmɪˈkɑːzɪ) *n.* (*oft.* **K-**) suicidal attack, *esp.* as in World War II, by Japanese pilots

kangaroo (kæŋgəˈruː) *n.* **1.** Aust. marsupial with very strongly developed hind legs for jumping —*vi.* **2.** *inf.* (of car) move forward with sudden jerks —**kangaroo court** irregular, illegal court

kaolin (ˈkeɪəlɪn) *n.* fine white clay used for porcelain and medicinally

kaon (ˈkeɪɒn) *n.* meson that has rest mass of about 996 or 964 electron masses (*also* **K-meson**)

kapok (ˈkeɪpɒk) *n.* **1.** tropical tree **2.** fibre from its seed pods used to stuff cushions *etc.*

kappa (ˈkæpə) *n.* tenth letter in Gr. alphabet (K, κ)

kaput (kæˈpʊt) *a. inf.* ruined, broken, no good

karakul *or* **caracul** (ˈkærəkᵊl) *n.* **1.** breed of sheep of central Asia having coarse black, grey or brown hair: lambs have soft curled hair **2.** fur prepared from these lambs

karate (kəˈrɑːtɪ) *n.* Japanese system of unarmed combat using feet, hands, elbows *etc.* as weapons in a variety of ways

karoo *or* **karroo** (kəˈruː) *n.* **SA** high, arid plateau

kaross (kəˈrɒs) *n.* **SA** cloak made of skins

kart (kɑːt) *n.* light low-framed vehicle with small wheels and engine for recreational racing (**karting**) (*also* **go-cart, go-kart**)

katabolism (kəˈtæbəlɪzəm) *n. see* CATABOLISM

katydid (ˈkeɪtɪdɪd) *n.* green long-horned grasshopper living in trees in N Amer.

kauri (ˈkaʊrɪ) *n.* large N.Z. pine giving valuable timber (*pl.* **-s**)

kava (ˈkɑːvə) *n.* **1.** Polynesian shrub **2.** beverage prepared from the aromatic roots of this shrub

kayak *or* **kaiak** (ˈkaɪæk) *n.* **1.** Eskimo canoe made of sealskins stretched over frame **2.** any canoe of this design

kazoo (kəˈzuː) *n.* cigar-shaped musical instrument producing nasal sound

K.B. Knight of the Bath

kc kilocycle

K.C. King's Counsel

kcal kilocalorie

kea (ˈkeɪə) *n.* large New Zealand parrot with brownish-green plumage

kebab (kəˈbæb) *n.* dish of small pieces of meat, tomatoes *etc.* grilled on skewers (*also* **shish kebab**)

kedge (kɛdʒ) *n.* **1.** small anchor —*vt.* **2.** move (ship) by cable attached to kedge

kedgeree (kɛdʒəˈriː) *n.* dish of fish cooked with rice, eggs *etc.*

keek (kiːk) *n./vi. Scot.* peep

keel (kiːl) *n.* lowest longitudinal support on which ship is built —**ˈkeelhaul** *vt.* **1.** formerly, punish by hauling under keel of ship **2.** rebuke severely —**keelson** (ˈkɛlsən, ˈkiːl-) *or* **kelson** (ˈkɛlsən) *n.* line of timbers or plates bolted to keel —**keel over 1.** turn upside down **2.** *inf.* collapse suddenly —**on an even keel** well-balanced; steady

keen[1] (kiːn) *a.* **1.** sharp **2.** acute **3.** eager **4.** shrewd **5.** strong **6.** (of price) competitive —**ˈkeenly** *adv.* —**ˈkeenness** *n.*

keen[2] (kiːn) *n.* **1.** funeral lament —*vi.* **2.** wail over the dead

keep (kiːp) *vt.* **1.** retain possession of, not lose **2.** store **3.** cause to continue **4.** take charge of **5.** maintain **6.** detain **7.** provide upkeep of **8.** reserve —*vi.* **9.** remain good **10.** remain **11.** continue (**kept** *pt./pp.*) —*n.* **12.** living or support **13.** charge or care **14.** central tower of castle, stronghold —**ˈkeeper** *n.* —**ˈkeeping** *n.* **1.** harmony, agreement **2.** care, charge, possession —**ˈkeepsake** *n.* gift that evokes memories of person or event

THESAURUS

keen 1. ardent, avid, devoted to, eager, earnest, ebullient, enthusiastic, fervid, fierce, fond of, impassioned, intense, zealous **2.** acid, acute, biting, caustic, cutting, edged, finely honed, incisive, penetrating, piercing, pointed, razorlike, sardonic, satirical, sharp, tart, trenchant **3.** astute, brilliant, canny, clever, discerning, discriminating, perceptive, perspicacious, quick, sagacious, sapient, sensitive, shrewd, wise

keenness 1. ardour, avidity, avidness, diligence, eagerness, earnestness, ebullience, enthusiasm, fervour, impatience, intensity, passion, zeal, zest **2.** acerbity, harshness, incisiveness, mordancy, penetration, pungency, rigour, severity, sharpness, sternness, trenchancy, unkindness, virulence **3.** astuteness, canniness, cleverness, discernment, insight, sagacity, sapience, sensitivity, shrewdness, wisdom

keep *v.* **1.** conserve, control, hold, maintain, possess, preserve, retain **2.** accumulate, amass, carry, deal in, deposit, furnish, garner, heap, hold, pile, place, stack, stock, store, trade in **3.** care for, defend, guard, look after, maintain, manage, mind, operate, protect, safeguard, shelter, shield, tend, watch over **4.** board,

keg (kɛg) *n.* **1.** small barrel **2.** metal container for beer

kelp (kɛlp) *n.* **1.** large seaweed **2.** its ashes, yielding iodine

kelt (kɛlt) *n.* salmon that has recently spawned

kelvin (ˈkɛlvɪn) *a.* **1.** of thermometric scale starting at absolute zero (-273.15° Celsius) *—n.* **2.** SI unit of temperature

ken (kɛn) *n.* **1.** range of knowledge *—v.* **2.** in Scotland, know (**kenned** *or* **kent** *pt./pp.*)

kendo (ˈkɛndəʊ) *n.* Japanese form of fencing using wooden staves

kennel (ˈkɛnᵊl) *n.* **1.** house, shelter for dog *—pl.* **2.** place for breeding, boarding dogs *—vt.* **3.** put into kennel (**-ll-**)

kentledge (ˈkɛntlɪdʒ) *n. Naut.* scrap metal used as ballast

kepi (ˈkeɪpiː) *n.* military cap with circular top and horizontal peak (*pl.* **-s**)

kept (kɛpt) *pt./pp. of* KEEP

kerb *or U.S.* **curb** (kɜːb) *n.* stone edging to footpath **—kerb crawler —kerb crawling** driving slowly beside pavement and seeking to entice someone into car for sexual purposes

kerchief (ˈkɜːtʃɪf) *n.* **1.** head-cloth **2.** handkerchief

kerfuffle (kəˈfʌfᵊl) *n. inf.* commotion, disorder

kermes (ˈkɜːmɪz) *n.* insect used for red dyestuff

kernel (ˈkɜːnᵊl) *n.* **1.** inner seed of nut or fruit stone **2.** central, essential part

kerosene *or* **kerosine** (ˈkɛrəsiːn) *n.* paraffin oil distilled from petroleum or coal and shale

kestrel (ˈkɛstrəl) *n.* small falcon

ketch (kɛtʃ) *n.* two-masted sailing vessel

ketchup (ˈkɛtʃəp), **catchup** (ˈkætʃəp, ˈkɛtʃ-), *or* **catsup** (ˈkætsəp) *n.* sauce of vinegar, tomatoes *etc.*

ketone (ˈkiːtəʊn) *n.* chemical compound with general formula R′COR, where R and R′ are usu. alkyl or aryl groups **—ketonic** (kɪˈtɒnɪk) *a.*

kettle (ˈkɛtᵊl) *n.* metal vessel with spout and handle, *esp.* for boiling water **—ˈkettledrum** *n.* musical instrument made of membrane stretched over copper hemisphere **—a fine kettle of fish** awkward situation, mess

key[1] (kiː) *n.* **1.** instrument for operating lock, winding clock *etc.* **2.** something providing control, explanation, means of achieving an end *etc.* **3.** *Mus.* set of related notes **4.** operating lever of typewriter, piano, organ *etc.* **5.** spanner **6.** mode of thought *—vt.* **7.** provide symbols on (map *etc.*) to assist identification of positions on it **8.** scratch (plaster surface) to provide bond for plaster or paint **9.** insert (copy, information) by keystroke *—a.* **10.** vital **11.** most important **—ˈkeyboard** *n.* set of keys on piano *etc.* **—ˈkeyhole** *n.* aperture in lock case into which key is inserted **—key money** fee, payment required from new tenant of house *etc.* before he moves in **—ˈkeynote** *n.* **1.** dominant idea **2.** basic note of musical key **—key punch** device having keyboard operated manually to transfer data onto punched cards *etc.* (*also* **card punch**) **—keypunch** *vt.* transfer (data) by key punch **—key signature** *Mus.* sharps or flats at beginning of each stave line to indicate key **—ˈkeystone** *n.* **1.** central stone of arch **2.** something necessary to connect other related things **—ˈkeystroke** *n.* depression of single key on keyboard of typewriter, computer *etc.* **—key in** enter (information or instructions) in computer *etc.* by means of keyboard *etc.*

key[2] (kiː) *n. see* CAY

kg *or* **kg.** kilogram

K.G. Knight of the Order of the Garter

K.G.B. Soviet secret police

khaki (ˈkɑːkɪ) *a.* **1.** dull yellowish-brown *—n.* **2.** dull yellowish-brown colour **3.** hard-wearing fabric of this colour, used *esp.* for military uniforms (*pl.* **-s**)

khan (kɑːn) *n.* **1.** formerly, (title borne by) medieval Chinese emperors and Mongol and Turkic rulers **2.** title of respect borne by important personages in Afghanistan and central Asia

Khmer (kmɛə) *n.* member of a people of Kampuchea

kHz kilohertz

kibble (ˈkɪbᵊl) *vt.* grind into small pieces

kibbutz (kɪˈbʊts) *n.* Jewish communal agricultural settlement in Israel (*pl.* **kibbutzim** (kɪbʊtˈsiːm))

kibosh (ˈkaɪbɒʃ) *n. sl.* **—put the kibosh on 1.** silence **2.** get rid of **3.** defeat

kick (kɪk) *vi.* **1.** strike out with foot **2.** (*sometimes with* against) be recalcitrant **3.** recoil *—vt.* **4.** strike or hit with foot **5.** score (goal) with a kick **6.** *inf.* free oneself of (habit *etc.*) *—n.* **7.** foot blow **8.** recoil **9.** excitement, thrill **—ˈkickback** *n.* **1.** strong reaction **2.** money paid illegally for favours done *etc.* **—ˈkickoff** *n.* **1.** place kick from centre of field in football **2.** time at which first such kick is due to take place **—ˈkickstand** *n.* short metal bar which when kicked into vertical position holds stationary cycle upright **—kick-start** *vt.* start (motorcycle engine) by pedal that is kicked downwards **—kick-starter** *n.* this pedal **—kick off 1.** start game of football **2.** *inf.* begin (discussion *etc.*)

THESAURUS

feed, foster, maintain, nourish, nurture, provide for, provision, subsidize, support, sustain, victual **5.** arrest, block, check, constrain, control, curb, delay, detain, deter, hamper, hamstring, hinder, hold, hold back, impede, inhibit, keep back, limit, obstruct, prevent, restrain, retard, shackle, stall, withhold *~n.* **6.** board, food, livelihood, living, maintenance, means, nourishment, subsistence, support **7.** castle, citadel, donjon, dungeon, fastness, stronghold, tower

keeper attendant, caretaker, curator, custodian, defender, gaoler, governor, guard, guardian, jailer, overseer, preserver, steward, superintendent, warden, warder

keeping 1. aegis, auspices, care, charge, custody, guardianship, keep, maintenance, patronage, possession, protection, safekeeping, trust **2.** accord, agreement, balance, compliance, conformity, congruity, consistency, correspondence, harmony, observance, proportion

keepsake emblem, favour, memento, relic, remembrance, reminder, souvenir, symbol, token

keg barrel, cask, drum, firkin, hogshead, tun, vat

kernel core, essence, germ, gist, grain, marrow, nub, pith, seed, substance

key *n.* **1.** latchkey, opener **2.** *Fig.* answer, clue, cue, explanation, guide, indicator, interpretation, lead, means, pointer, sign, solution, translation *~adj.* **3.** basic, chief, crucial, decisive, essential, fundamental, important, leading, main, major, pivotal, principal

keynote centre, core, essence, gist, heart, kernel, marrow, pith, substance, theme

kid (kɪd) *n.* **1.** young goat **2.** leather of its skin **3.** *inf.* child —*vt.* **4.** tease; deceive —*vi.* **5.** behave, speak in fun (**-dd-**) —**kid glove** glove made of kidskin —**kid'glove** *a.* **1.** overdelicate **2.** diplomatic; tactful —**handle with kid gloves** treat with great tact or caution

kidnap (ˈkɪdnæp) *vt.* seize and hold to ransom (**-pp-**) —**ˈkidnapper** *n.*

kidney (ˈkɪdnɪ) *n.* **1.** either of the pair of organs which secrete urine **2.** animal kidney used as food **3.** nature, kind (*esp. in* **of the same** *or* **a different kidney**) (*pl.* **-s**) —**kidney bean 1.** dwarf French bean **2.** scarlet runner —**kidney machine** machine carrying out functions of kidney

kill (kɪl) *vt.* **1.** deprive of life **2.** destroy **3.** neutralize **4.** pass (time) **5.** weaken; dilute **6.** *inf.* exhaust **7.** *inf.* cause to suffer pain **8.** *inf.* quash, defeat, veto —*n.* **9.** act or time of killing **10.** animals *etc.* killed in hunt —**ˈkiller** *n.* one who, that which, kills —**ˈkilling** *inf. a.* **1.** very tiring **2.** very funny —*n.* **3.** sudden success, *esp.* on stock market —**killer whale** ferocious toothed whale most common in cold seas —**kill-joy** *n.* person who spoils other people's pleasure

kiln (kɪln) *n.* furnace, oven

kilo (ˈkiːləʊ) *n.* kilogram (*pl.* **-s**)

kilo- (*comb. form*) one thousand, as in *kilolitre, kilometre*

kilocycle (ˈkɪləʊsaɪkˀl) *n. short for* kilocycle per second: former unit of frequency equal to 1 kilohertz

kilogram *or* **kilogramme** (ˈkɪləʊgræm) *n.* weight of 1000 grams

kilohertz (ˈkɪləʊhɜːts) *n.* one thousand cycles per second

kiloton (ˈkɪləʊtʌn) *n.* **1.** one thousand tons **2.** explosive power, *esp.* of nuclear weapon, equal to power of 1000 tons of TNT

kilowatt (ˈkɪləʊwɒt) *n. Elec.* one thousand watts —**kilowatt-hour** *n.* unit of energy equal to work done by power of 1000 watts in one hour

kilt (kɪlt) *n. usu.* tartan knee-length skirt, deeply pleated, worn orig. by Scottish Highlanders

kimono (kɪˈməʊnəʊ) *n.* **1.** loose, wide-sleeved Japanese robe, fastened with sash **2.** European garment like this (*pl.* **-s**)

kin (kɪn) *n.* **1.** family, relatives —*a.* **2.** related by blood —**kindred** (ˈkɪndrɪd) *n.* **1.** relationship by blood **2.** relatives collectively —*a.* **3.** similar **4.** related —**ˈkinsfolk** *pl.n.* —**ˈkinship** *n.*

-kin (*comb. form*) small, as in *lambkin*

kind (kaɪnd) *n.* **1.** genus, sort, class —*a.* **2.** sympathetic, considerate **3.** good, benevolent **4.** gentle —**ˈkindliness** *n.* —**ˈkindly** *a.* **1.** kind, genial —*adv.* **2.** in a considerate or humane way —**ˈkindness** *n.* —**kind-hearted** *a.* kindly, readily sympathetic —**in kind 1.** (of payment) in goods rather than money **2.** with something similar

kindergarten (ˈkɪndəgɑːtˀn) *n.* class, school for children of about four to six years old

kindle (ˈkɪndˀl) *vt.* **1.** set on fire **2.** inspire, excite —*vi.* **3.** catch fire —**ˈkindling** *n.* wood, straw *etc.* to kindle fire

THESAURUS

kick *v.* **1.** boot, punt **2.** *Fig.* complain, gripe (*Inf.*), grumble, object, oppose, protest, rebel, resist, spurn **3.** *Inf.* abandon, desist from, give up, leave off, quit, stop ~*n.* **4.** buzz (*Sl.*), enjoyment, excitement, fun, gratification, pleasure, stimulation, thrill

kick off *v.* begin, commence, get under way, initiate, open, start

kid 1. *n.* baby, bairn, boy, child, girl, infant, lad, little one, stripling, teenager, tot, youngster, youth **2.** *v.* bamboozle, beguile, cozen, delude, fool, gull (*Archaic*), hoax, hoodwink, jest, joke, mock, plague, pretend, rag (*Sl.*), ridicule, tease, trick

kidnap abduct, capture, hijack, hold to ransom, remove, seize, skyjack, steal

kill 1. annihilate, assassinate, bump off (*Sl.*), butcher, destroy, dispatch, do away with, do in (*Sl.*), eradicate, execute, exterminate, extirpate, knock off (*Sl.*), liquidate, massacre, murder, neutralize, obliterate, slaughter, slay, take (someone's) life, waste (*Sl.*) **2.** *Fig.* cancel, cease, deaden, defeat, extinguish, halt, quash, quell, ruin, scotch, smother, stifle, still, stop, suppress, veto

killer assassin, butcher, cutthroat, destroyer, executioner, exterminator, gunman, hit man (*Sl.*), liquidator, murderer, slaughterer, slayer

killing *n.* **1.** *Inf.* bomb (*Sl.*), bonanza, cleanup (*Inf.*), coup, gain, profit, success, windfall ~*adj.* **2.** *Inf.* debilitating, enervating, exhausting, fatiguing, punishing, tiring **3.** *Inf.* absurd, amusing, comical, hilarious, ludicrous, uproarious

kill-joy dampener, damper, spoilsport, wet blanket (*Inf.*)

kin 1. *n.* connections, family, kindred, kinsfolk, kinsmen, kith, people, relations, relatives **2.** *adj.* akin, allied, close, cognate, consanguine, consanguineous, kindred, near, related

kind 1. *n.* brand, breed, class, family, genus, ilk, race, set, sort, species, variety **2.** *adj.* affectionate, amiable, amicable, beneficent, benevolent, benign, bounteous, charitable, clement, compassionate, congenial, considerate, cordial, courteous, friendly, generous, gentle, good, gracious, humane, indulgent, kind-hearted, kindly, lenient, loving, mild, neighbourly, obliging, philanthropic, propitious, sympathetic, tender-hearted, thoughtful, understanding

kind-hearted altruistic, amicable, compassionate, considerate, generous, good-natured, gracious, helpful, humane, kind, sympathetic, tender-hearted

kindle 1. fire, ignite, inflame, light, set fire to **2.** *Fig.* agitate, animate, arouse, awaken, bestir, enkindle, exasperate, excite, foment, incite, induce, inflame, inspire, provoke, rouse, sharpen, stimulate, stir, thrill

kindliness amiability, beneficence, benevolence, benignity, charity, compassion, friendliness, gentleness, humanity, kind-heartedness, kindness, sympathy

kindly 1. *adj.* beneficial, benevolent, benign, compassionate, cordial, favourable, genial, gentle, good-natured, hearty, helpful, kind, mild, pleasant, polite, sympathetic, warm **2.** *adv.* agreeably, cordially, graciously, politely, tenderly, thoughtfully

kindness affection, amiability, beneficence, benevolence, charity, clemency, compassion, decency, fellow-feeling, generosity, gentleness, goodness, good will, grace, hospitality, humanity, indulgence, kind-

kinematic (kɪnɪˈmætɪk) *a.* of motion without reference to mass or force —**kineˈmatics** *pl.n.* (*with sing. v.*) science of this —**kineˈmatograph** *n. see* **cinematograph** *at* CINEMA

kinetic (kɪˈnɛtɪk) *a.* of motion in relation to force —**kiˈnetics** *pl.n.* (*with sing. v.*) science of this —**kinetic art** art, *esp.* sculpture, that moves or has moving parts

king (kɪŋ) *n.* **1.** male sovereign ruler of independent state, monarch **2.** piece in game of chess **3.** highest court card, with picture of a king **4.** *Draughts* two pieces on top of one another, allowed freedom of movement —**ˈkingdom** *n.* **1.** state ruled by king **2.** realm **3.** sphere —**ˈkingly** *a.* **1.** royal **2.** appropriate to a king —**ˈkingship** *n.* —**King Charles spaniel** toy breed of spaniel with very long ears —**ˈkingcup** *n.* **UK** any of several yellow-flowered plants, *esp.* marsh marigold —**ˈkingfisher** *n.* small bird with bright plumage, which dives for fish —**ˈkingpin** *n.* **1.** swivel pin **2.** central or front pin in bowling **3.** *inf.* chief person or thing —**king post** beam in roof framework rising from tie beam to the ridge —**King's Bench** (when sovereign is male) *another name for* **Queen's Bench** (*see* QUEEN) —**King's Counsel** (when sovereign is male) *another name for* **Queen's Counsel** (*see* QUEEN) —**King's English** (*esp.* when British sovereign is male) standard Southern British English —**king's evidence** (when sovereign is male) *another name for* **queen's evidence** (*see* QUEEN) —**king's highway** (in Britain, *esp.* when sovereign is male) public road or right of way —**king-size** *or* **king-sized** *a.* **1.** large **2.** larger than standard size

kingklip (ˈkɪŋklɪp) *n.* S Afr. marine fish

kink (kɪŋk) *n.* **1.** tight twist in rope, wire, hair *etc.* **2.** crick, as of neck **3.** *inf.* eccentricity —*v.* **4.** make, become kinked —**ˈkinky** *a.* **1.** full of kinks **2.** *inf.* eccentric, *esp.* given to deviant (sexual) practices

kiosk (ˈkiːɒsk) *n.* **1.** small, sometimes movable booth selling drinks, cigarettes, newspapers *etc.* **2.** public telephone box

kipper (ˈkɪpə) *vt.* **1.** cure (fish) by splitting open, rubbing with salt and drying or smoking —*n.* **2.** kippered fish

kirk (kɜːk) *n.* in Scotland, church

Kirsch (kɪəʃ) *or* **Kirschwasser** (ˈkɪəʃvɑːsə) *n.* brandy made from cherries

kismet (ˈkɪzmɛt, ˈkɪs-) *n.* fate, destiny

kiss (kɪs) *n.* **1.** touch or caress with lips **2.** light touch —*vt.* **3.** touch with the lips as an expression of love, greeting *etc.* —*vi.* **4.** join lips with another person in act of love or desire —**ˈkisser** *n.* **1.** one who kisses **2.** *sl.* mouth; face —**kiss curl UK** circular curl of hair pressed flat against cheek or forehead —**kiss of life** mouth-to-mouth resuscitation

kist (kɪst) *n.* large wooden chest

kit (kɪt) *n.* **1.** outfit, equipment **2.** personal effects, *esp.* of traveller **3.** set of pieces of equipment sold ready to be assembled —**ˈkitbag** *n.* bag for holding soldier's or traveller's kit —**kit out** *or* **up** *chiefly* **UK** provide with kit of personal effects and necessities

kitchen (ˈkɪtʃɪn) *n.* room used for preparing and cooking food —**kitchenˈette** *n.* small room (or part of larger room) used for cooking —**kitchen garden** garden for raising vegetables, herbs *etc.* —**kitchen sink** *n.* **1.** sink in kitchen —*a.* **2.** sordidly domestic

kite (kaɪt) *n.* **1.** light papered frame flown in wind **2.** *sl.* aeroplane **3.** large hawk —**Kite mark** official mark on articles approved by British Standards Institution

kith (kɪθ) *n.* acquaintance, kindred (*only in* **kith and kin**)

kitsch (kɪtʃ) *n.* vulgarized, pretentious art, literature *etc.*, usu. with popular, sentimental appeal

kitten (ˈkɪtᵊn) *n.* young cat —**ˈkittenish** *a.* **1.** like kitten; lively **2.** (of woman) flirtatious, *esp.* coyly

kittiwake (ˈkɪtɪweɪk) *n.* type of seagull

kitty (ˈkɪtɪ) *n.* **1.** kitten or cat **2.** in some gambling games, pool **3.** communal fund

kiwi (ˈkiːwɪ) *n.* **1.** N.Z. flightless bird having long beak, stout legs and weakly barbed feathers **2.** *inf.* New Zealander (*pl.* **-s**)

kl. kilolitre

klaxon (ˈklæksᵊn) *n.* formerly, powerful electric motor horn

kleptomania (klɛptəʊˈmeɪnɪə) *n.* compulsive tendency to steal *esp.* when there is no obvious motivation —**kleptoˈmaniac** *n.*

klipspringer (ˈklɪpsprɪŋə) *n.* small agile Afr. antelope

kloof (kluːf) *n.* **SA** mountain pass

km *or* **km.** kilometre

knack (næk) *n.* **1.** acquired facility or dexterity **2.** trick **3.** habit

THESAURUS

liness, magnanimity, patience, philanthropy, tenderness, tolerance, understanding

kindred *n.* **1.** affinity, consanguinity, relationship **2.** connections, family, flesh, kin, kinsfolk, kinsmen, lineage, relations, relatives *~adj.* **3.** affiliated, akin, allied, cognate, congenial, corresponding, kin, like, matching, related, similar

king crowned head, emperor, majesty, monarch, overlord, prince, ruler, sovereign

kingdom **1.** dominion, dynasty, empire, monarchy, realm, reign, sovereignty **2.** commonwealth, county, division, nation, province, state, territory, tract **3.** area, domain, field, province, sphere, territory

kink **1.** bend, coil, corkscrew, crimp, entanglement, frizz, knot, tangle, twist, wrinkle **2.** cramp, crick, pang, pinch, spasm, stab, tweak, twinge **3.** crotchet, eccentricity, fetish, foible, idiosyncrasy, quirk, singularity, vagary, whim

kinky **1.** bizarre, eccentric, odd, outlandish, peculiar, queer, quirky, strange, unconventional, weird **2.** degenerated, depraved, deviant, licentious, perverted, unnatural, warped **3.** coiled, crimped, curled, curly, frizzled, frizzy, tangled, twisted

kinship blood relationship, consanguinity, kin, relation, ties of blood

kiosk bookstall, booth, counter, newsstand, stall, stand

kiss **1.** *v.* buss (*Archaic*), canoodle (*Inf.*), greet, neck (*Inf.*), osculate, peck (*Inf.*), salute, smooch (*Inf.*) **2.** *n.* buss (*Archaic*), osculation, peck (*Inf.*), smacker (*Sl.*)

kit accoutrements, apparatus, effects, equipment, gear, impedimenta, implements, instruments, outfit, paraphernalia, provisions, rig, supplies, tackle, tools, trappings, utensils

kitchen cookhouse, galley, kitchenette

knacker ('nækə) *n.* buyer of worn-out horses *etc.*, for killing —'**knackered** *a. sl.* exhausted

knapsack ('næpsæk) *n.* soldier's or traveller's bag to strap to the back, rucksack

knapweed ('næpwi:d) *n.* plant having purplish thistlelike flowers

knave (neɪv) *n.* **1.** jack at cards **2.** *obs.* rogue —'**knavery** *n.* villainy —'**knavish** *a.*

knead (ni:d) *vt.* **1.** work (flour) into dough **2.** work, massage —'**kneader** *n.*

knee (ni:) *n.* **1.** joint between thigh and lower leg **2.** part of garment covering knee **3.** lap —*vt.* **4.** strike, push with knee —'**kneecap** *n.* bone in front of knee —**knees-up** *n. inf.* party, oft. with dancing

kneel (ni:l) *vi.* fall, rest on knees (**knelt** *pt./pp.*)

knell (nɛl) *n.* **1.** sound of a bell, *esp.* at funeral or death **2.** portent of doom

knelt (nɛlt) *pt./pp. of* KNEEL

knew (nju:) *pt. of* KNOW

knickerbockers ('nɪkəbɒkəz) *pl.n.* loose-fitting breeches gathered at knees

knickers ('nɪkəz) *pl.n.* woman's undergarment for lower half of body

knick-knack ('nɪknæk) *n.* trifle, trinket

knife (naɪf) *n.* **1.** cutting blade, *esp.* one in handle, used as implement or weapon (*pl.* **knives**) —*vt.* **2.** cut or stab with knife —**knife edge** critical, possibly dangerous situation

knight (naɪt) *n.* **1.** man of rank below baronet, having right to prefix *Sir* to his name **2.** member of medieval order of chivalry **3.** champion **4.** piece in chess —*vt.* **5.** confer knighthood on —'**knighthood** *n.* —'**knightly** *a.*

knit (nɪt) *v.* **1.** form (garment *etc.*) by putting together series of loops in wool or other yarn **2.** draw together **3.** unite ('**knitted, knit** *pt./pp.*, '**knitting** *pr.p.*) —'**knitter** *n.* —'**knitting** *n.* **1.** knitted work **2.** act of knitting —'**knitwear** *n.* knitted clothes, *esp.* sweaters

knives (naɪvz) *n., pl. of* KNIFE

knob (nɒb) *n.* rounded lump, *esp.* at end or on surface of anything —'**knobby** *or* '**knobbly** *a.*

knock (nɒk) *vt.* **1.** strike, hit **2.** *inf.* disparage —*vi.* **3.** rap audibly **4.** (of engine) make metallic noise, pink —*n.* **5.** blow, rap —'**knocker** *n.* **1.** metal appliance for knocking on door **2.** person or thing that knocks —**knocking copy** publicity material designed to denigrate competing product —**knock-kneed** *a.* having incurved legs —'**knockout** *n.* **1.** blow *etc.* that renders unconscious **2.** *inf.* person or thing overwhelmingly attractive —**knock down 1.** strike to ground with blow, as in boxing **2.** in auctions, declare (article) sold **3.** demolish **4.** dismantle for ease of transport **5.** *inf.* reduce (price *etc.*) —**knocked up** *inf.* exhausted, tired, worn out —**knock off** *inf.* **1.** cease work **2.** make hurriedly **3.** kill **4.** steal —**knock out 1.** render unconscious **2.** *inf.* overwhelm, amaze

knoll (nəʊl) *n.* small rounded hill, mound

knot[1] (nɒt) *n.* **1.** fastening of strands by looping and pulling tight **2.** cockade, cluster **3.** small closely knit group **4.** tie, bond **5.** hard lump, *esp.* of wood where branch joins or has joined **6.** unit of speed of one nautical mile (1852m) per hour **7.** difficulty —*vt.* **8.** tie with knot, in knots (-tt-) —'**knotty** *a.* **1.** full of knots **2.** puzzling, difficult —'**knothole** *n.* hole in wood where knot has been

knot[2] (nɒt) *n.* small northern sandpiper with grey plumage

know (nəʊ) *vt.* **1.** be aware of **2.** have information about **3.** be acquainted with **4.** recognize **5.** have experience of, understand —*vi.* **6.** have information or understanding (**knew** *pt.*, **known** *pp.*) —'**knowable** *a.* —'**knowing** *a.* cunning, shrewd —'**knowingly** *adv.* **1.** shrewdly **2.** deliberately —**knowledge** ('nɒlɪdʒ) *n.* **1.** knowing **2.** what one knows **3.** learning —**knowledgeable** *or* **knowledgable** ('nɒlɪdʒəbᵊl) *a.* well-informed —**known** *a.* identified —**know-how** *n. inf.* practical knowledge, experience, aptitude —**in the know** *inf.* informed

THESAURUS

knack ability, adroitness, aptitude, bent, capacity, dexterity, expertise, expertness, facility, flair, forte, genius, gift, handiness, ingenuity, propensity, quickness, skilfulness, skill, talent, trick

knave blackguard, bounder (*Inf.*), cheat, rapscallion, rascal, reprobate, rogue, rotter (*Sl.*), scallywag (*Inf.*), scamp, scapegrace, scoundrel, swindler, varlet (*Archaic*), villain

knavery chicanery, corruption, deceit, deception, dishonesty, double-dealing, duplicity, fraud, imposture, rascality, roguery, trickery, villainy

knead blend, form, manipulate, massage, mould, press, rub, shape, squeeze, stroke, work

knell *n.* chime, peal, ringing, sound, toll

knickers bloomers, briefs, drawers, panties, smalls, underwear

knick-knack bagatelle, bauble, bibelot, bric-a-brac, gewgaw, gimcrack, kickshaw, plaything, trifle, trinket

knife 1. *n.* blade, cutter, cutting tool **2.** *v.* cut, impale, lacerate, pierce, slash, stab, wound

knit affix, ally, bind, connect, contract, fasten, heal, interlace, intertwine, join, link, loop, mend, secure, tie, unite, weave

knob boss, bulk, bump, bunch, door-handle, knot, knurl, lump, nub, projection, protrusion, protuberance, snag, stud, swell, swelling, tumour

knock *v.* **1.** buffet, clap, cuff, hit, punch, rap, slap, smack, smite (*Archaic*), strike, thump, thwack ~*n.* **2.** blow, box, clip, clout, cuff, hammering, rap, slap, smack, thump ~*v.* **3.** *Inf.* abuse, belittle, carp, cavil, censure, condemn, criticize, deprecate, disparage, find fault, lambaste, run down, slam (*Sl.*)

knock down batter, clout (*Inf.*), demolish, destroy, fell, floor, level, pound, raze, smash, wallop (*Inf.*), wreck

knock off 1. clock off, clock out, complete, conclude, finish, stop work, terminate **2.** filch, nick (*Sl.*), pilfer, pinch, purloin, rob, steal, thieve **3.** assassinate, bump off (*Sl.*), do away with, do in (*Sl.*), kill, liquidate, murder, slay, waste (*Sl.*)

knockout 1. *coup de grâce*, kayo (*Sl.*), K.O. (*Sl.*) **2.** hit, sensation, smash, smash-hit, stunner (*Inf.*), success, triumph, winner

knot *v.* **1.** bind, complicate, entangle, knit, loop, secure, tether, tie, weave ~*n.* **2.** bond, bow, braid, connection, joint, ligature, loop, rosette, tie **3.** aggregation, bunch, clump, cluster, collection, heap, mass, pile, tuft **4.** assemblage, band, circle, clique, company, crew (*Inf.*), crowd, gang, group, mob, pack, set, squad

knuckle ('nʌkᵊl) *n.* **1.** bone at finger joint **2.** knee joint of calf or pig —*vt.* **3.** strike with knuckles —**knuckle-duster** *n.* metal appliance worn on knuckles to add force to blow —**knuckle down** *inf.* get down (to work) —**knuckle under** yield, submit —**near the knuckle** *inf.* approaching indecency

knur, knurr (nɜː), *or* **knar** (nɑː) *n.* **1.** knot in wood **2.** hard lump

knurl *or* **nurl** (nɜːl) *vt.* **1.** impress with series of fine ridges or serrations —*n.* **2.** small ridge, *esp.* one of series —**knurled** *or* **nurled** *a.* **1.** serrated **2.** gnarled

koala *or* **koala bear** (kəʊ'ɑːlə) *n.* marsupial Aust. animal, native bear

kohl (kəʊl) *n.* powdered antimony used *esp.* in Eastern countries for darkening the eyelids

kohlrabi (kəʊl'rɑːbɪ) *n.* type of cabbage with edible stem (*also* **turnip cabbage**)

kokanee (kəʊ'kænɪ) *n.* salmon of N Amer. lakes

kola ('kəʊlə) *n. see* COLA

kolinsky (kə'lɪnskɪ) *n.* **1.** any of various Asian minks **2.** rich tawny fur of this animal

komatik ('kəʊmætɪk) *n.* **C** Eskimo sledge with wooden runners

kook (kuːk) *n.* **US** *inf.* eccentric or foolish person —'**kooky** *or* '**kookie** *a.*

kookaburra ('kʊkəbʌrə) *n.* large Aust. kingfisher with cackling cry (*also* **laughing jackass**)

kopeck *or* **copeck** ('kəʊpɛk) *n.* Soviet monetary unit, one hundredth of rouble

koppie *or* **kopje** ('kɒpɪ) *n.* **SA** small hill

Koran (kɔː'rɑːn) *n.* sacred book of Muslims

kosher ('kəʊʃə) *a.* **1.** permitted, clean, good, as of food *etc.*, conforming to the Jewish dietary law **2.** *inf.* legitimate, authentic —*n.* **3.** kosher food

kowtow ('kaʊtaʊ) *n.* **1.** former Chinese custom of touching ground with head in respect **2.** submission —*vi.* (*esp. with* to) **3.** prostrate oneself **4.** be obsequious, fawn (on)

Kr *Chem.* krypton

kraal (krɑːl) *n.* **SA** **1.** hut village, *esp.* one surrounded by fence **2.** corral

kraken ('krɑːkən) *n.* mythical Norwegian sea monster

krans (krɑːns) *n.* **SA** cliff

Kraut (kraʊt) *a./n. sl., offens.* German

Kremlin ('krɛmlɪn) *n.* central government of Soviet Union

krill (krɪl) *n.* small shrimplike marine animal

kris (krɪs) *n.* Malayan and Indonesian knife with scalloped edge (*also* **crease, creese**)

krona ('krəʊnə) *n.* standard monetary unit of Sweden (*pl.* **-nor** (-nə))

krone ('krəʊnə) *n.* standard monetary unit of Norway and Denmark (*pl.* **-ner** (-nə))

krypton ('krɪptɒn) *n.* rare gaseous element present in atmosphere

KS Kansas

Kt *Chess* knight (*also* **N**)

kudos ('kjuːdɒs) *n.* **1.** fame **2.** credit

kudu *or* **koodoo** ('kuːduː) *n.* Afr. antelope with spiral horns

Ku Klux Klan ('kuː 'klʌks 'klæn) **1.** secret organization of White Southerners formed after U.S. Civil War to fight Black emancipation **2.** secret organization of White Protestant Americans, mainly in South, who use violence against Blacks, Jews *etc.*

kukri ('kʊkrɪ) *n.* heavy, curved Gurkha knife

kulak ('kuːlæk) *n.* independent well-to-do Russian peasant

kumara *or* **kumera** ('kuːmərə) *n.* **NZ** sweet potato

kümmel ('kʊməl) *n.* cumin-flavoured German liqueur

kumquat *or* **cumquat** ('kʌmkwɒt) *n.* **1.** small Chinese tree **2.** its round orange fruit

kung fu ('kʌŋ 'fuː) Chinese martial art combining techniques of judo and karate

kW *or* **kw** kilowatt

kwashiorkor (kwæʃɪ'ɔːkə) *n.* severe malnutrition of young children, resulting from dietary deficiency of protein

kWh, kwh, *or* **kw-h** kilowatt-hour

KWIC (kwɪk) key word in context (*esp. in* **KWIC index**)

KWOC (kwɒk) key word out of context

KY Kentucky

kyle (kaɪl) *n. Scot.* narrow strait or channel

kymograph ('kaɪməgrɑːf) *n.* instrument for recording on graph pressure, oscillations, sound waves

THESAURUS

know 1. apprehend, comprehend, experience, fathom, feel certain, ken (*Scot.*), learn, notice, perceive, realize, recognize, see, undergo, understand **2.** associate with, be acquainted with, be familiar with, fraternize with, have dealings with, have knowledge of, recognize **3.** differentiate, discern, distinguish, identify, make out, perceive, recognize, see, tell

know-how ability, adroitness, aptitude, capability, dexterity, experience, expertise, faculty, flair, ingenuity, knack, knowledge, proficiency, savoir-faire, skill, talent

knowing acute, cunning, eloquent, expressive, meaningful, perceptive, sagacious, shrewd, significant

knowingly consciously, deliberately, intentionally, on purpose, purposely, wilfully, wittingly

knowledge 1. education, enlightenment, erudition, instruction, intelligence, learning, scholarship, schooling, science, tuition, wisdom **2.** ability, apprehension, cognition, comprehension, consciousness, discernment, grasp, judgment, recognition, understanding **3.** acquaintance, cognizance, familiarity, information, intimacy, notice

knowledgeable acquainted, *au courant*, *au fait*, aware, cognizant, conscious, conversant, experienced, familiar, in the know (*Inf.*), understanding, well-informed

known acknowledged, admitted, avowed, celebrated, common, confessed, familiar, famous, manifest, noted, obvious, patent, plain, popular, published, recognized, well-known

knuckle under *v.* accede, acquiesce, capitulate, give in, give way, submit, succumb, surrender, yield

L

l *or* **L** (ɛl) *n.* **1.** 12th letter of English alphabet **2.** speech sound represented by this letter **3.** something shaped like L (*pl.* **l's, L's** *or* **Ls**)

L **1.** lambert **2.** large **3.** Latin **4.** (on Brit. motor vehicles) learner driver **5.** *Phys.* length **6.** pound (*usually written:* £) **7.** longitude **8.** *Electron.* inductor (in circuit diagrams) **9.** *Phys.* latent heat **10.** *Phys.* self-inductance **11.** Roman numeral, 50

L. *or* **l.** **1.** lake **2.** left **3.** line (*pl.* **LL.** *or* **ll.**) **4.** litre

la (lɑː) *n. Mus. see* LAH

La *Chem.* lanthanum

LA Louisiana

laager (ˈlɑːgə) *n.* **SA** encampment surrounded by wagons

lab (læb) *inf.* laboratory

Lab. **1.** *Pol.* Labour **2.** Labrador

label (ˈleɪbᵊl) *n.* **1.** slip of paper, metal *etc.*, fixed to object to give information about it **2.** brief, descriptive phrase or term —*vt.* **3.** fasten label to **4.** mark with label **5** describe or classify in a word or phrase (**-ll-**)

labiate (ˈleɪbɪeɪt, -ɪt) *n.* **1.** plant of family *Labiatae*, having square stems, aromatic leaves and two-lipped corolla —*a.* **2.** of family *Labiatae*

labium (ˈleɪbɪəm) *n.* **1.** lip; liplike structure **2.** any of four lip-shaped folds of vulva, comprising outer pair (**labia majora**) and inner pair (**labia minora**) (*pl.* **-bia** (-bɪə)) —ˈ**labial** *a.* **1.** of the lips **2.** pronounced with the lips —*n.* **3.** speech sound pronounced thus

laboratory (ləˈbɒrətərɪ, -trɪ; *U.S.* ˈlæbrətɔːrɪ) *n.* place for scientific investigations or for manufacture of chemicals

labour *or U.S.* **labor** (ˈleɪbə) *n.* **1.** exertion of body or mind **2.** task **3.** workers collectively **4.** effort, pain of childbirth or time taken for this —*vi.* **5.** work hard **6.** strive **7.** maintain normal motion with difficulty **8.** (*esp.* of ship) be tossed heavily —*vt.* **9.** stress to excess —**laˈborious** *a* tedious —**laˈboriously** *adv.* —ˈ**laboured** *or U.S.* ˈ**labored** *a.* uttered, done, with difficulty —ˈ**labourer** *or U.S.* ˈ**laborer** *n.* one who labours, *esp.* man doing manual work for wages —**labour exchange UK** *old name for* Employment Service Agency —**Labour Party** **1.** Brit. political party, generally supporting interests of organized labour **2.** similar party in various other countries —**labour-saving** *a.* eliminating or lessening physical labour

Labrador (ˈlæbrədɔː) *n.* breed of large, smooth-coated retriever dog (*also* **Labrador retriever**)

laburnum (ləˈbɜːnəm) *n.* tree with yellow hanging flowers

labyrinth (ˈlæbərɪnθ) *n.* **1.** network of tortuous passages, maze **2.** inexplicable difficulty **3.** perplexity —**labyˈrinthine** *a.*

lac[1] (læk) *n.* resinous substance secreted by some insects

lac[2] (lɑːk) *n.* one hundred thousand (of rupees)

lace (leɪs) *n.* **1.** fine patterned openwork fabric **2.** cord, usu. one of pair, to draw edges together, *eg* to tighten shoes *etc.* **3.** ornamental braid —*vt.* **4.** fasten with laces **5.** flavour with spirit —ˈ**lacy** *a.* fine, like lace

lacerate (ˈlæsəreɪt) *vt.* **1.** tear, mangle **2.** distress —ˈ**lacerable** *a.* —**lacerˈation** *n.*

lachrymal, lacrimal, *or* **lacrymal** (ˈlækrɪməl) *a.* of tears —ˈ**lachrymatory,** ˈ**lacrimatory,** *or* ˈ**lacrymatory** *a.* causing tears or inflammation of eyes —ˈ**lachrymose** *a.* tearful

lack (læk) *n.* **1.** deficiency, need —*vt.* **2.** need, be short of —ˈ**lacklustre** *or U.S.* ˈ**lackluster** *a.* lacking brilliance or vitality

lackadaisical (lækəˈdeɪzɪkᵊl) *a.* **1.** languid, listless **2.** lazy, careless

lackey (ˈlækɪ) *n.* **1.** servile follower **2.** footman (*pl.* **-s**) —*vi.* **3.** be or play, the lackey **4.** (*with* for) wait (upon)

THESAURUS

label *n.* **1.** docket (*Chiefly Brit.*), marker, sticker, tag, tally, ticket **2.** characterization, classification, description, epithet ~*v.* **3.** docket (*Chiefly Brit.*), mark, stamp, sticker, tag, tally **4.** brand, call, characterize, class, classify, define, describe, designate, identify, name

labour *n.* **1.** industry, toil, work **2.** employees, hands, labourers, workers, work force, workmen **3.** donkey-work, drudgery, effort, exertion, grind (*Inf.*), industry, pains, painstaking, sweat (*Inf.*), toil, travail **4.** chore, job, task, undertaking **5.** childbirth, contractions, delivery, labour pains, pains, parturition, throes, travail ~*v.* **6.** drudge, endeavour, grind (*Inf.*), peg along *or* away (*Chiefly Brit.*), plod, plug along *or* away (*Inf.*), slave, strive, struggle, sweat (*Inf.*), toil, travail, work **7.** dwell on, elaborate, overdo, overemphasize, strain **8.** *Of a ship* heave, pitch, roll, toss

laboured awkward, difficult, forced, heavy, stiff, strained

labourer blue-collar worker, drudge, hand, labouring man, manual worker, navvy (*Brit. inf.*), unskilled worker, worker, working man, workman

labyrinth coil, complexity, complication, convolution, entanglement, intricacy, jungle, knotty problem, maze, perplexity, puzzle, riddle, snarl, tangle, windings

lace *n.* **1.** filigree, netting, openwork, tatting **2.** bootlace, cord, shoelace, string, thong, tie ~*v.* **3.** attach, bind, close, do up, fasten, intertwine, interweave, thread, tie, twine **4.** add to, fortify, mix in, spike

lacerate **1.** claw, cut, gash, jag, maim, mangle, rend, rip, slash, tear, wound **2.** *Fig.* afflict, distress, harrow, rend, torment, torture, wound

lachrymose crying, dolorous, lugubrious, mournful, sad, tearful, weeping, weepy (*Inf.*), woeful

lack **1.** *n.* absence, dearth, deficiency, deprivation, destitution, insufficiency, need, privation, scantiness, scarcity, shortage, shortcoming, shortness, want **2.** *v.* be deficient in, be short of, be without, miss, need, require, want

lackadaisical **1.** apathetic, dull, enervated, half-hearted, indifferent, languid, languorous, lethargic, limp, listless, spiritless **2.** abstracted, dreamy, idle, indolent, inert, lazy

lackey **1.** creature, fawner, flatterer, flunky, hanger-on, instrument, menial, minion, parasite, pawn, sycophant, toady, tool, yes man **2.** attendant, flunky, footman, manservant, valet

lacklustre boring, dim, drab, dry, dull, flat, leaden, lifeless, lustreless, muted, prosaic, sombre, unimagi-

laconic (ləˈkɒnɪk) *a.* **1.** using, expressed in few words **2.** brief, terse **3.** offhand, not caring —**laˈconically** *adv.* —**laˈconicism** *n.*

lacquer (ˈlækə) *n.* **1.** hard varnish —*vt.* **2.** coat with this

lacrimal (ˈlækrɪməl) *a. see* LACHRYMAL

lacrosse (ləˈkrɒs) *n.* ball game played with long-handled racket or crosse

lacrymal (ˈlækrɪməl) *a. see* LACHRYMAL

lactic (ˈlæktɪk) *a.* of milk —**ˈlactate** *vi.* secrete milk —**lacˈtation** *n.* —**lacˈtometer** *n.* instrument for measuring purity and density of milk —**ˈlactose** *n.* white crystalline substance occurring in milk —**lactic acid** colourless syrupy acid found in sour milk *etc.*

lacuna (ləˈkjuːnə) *n.* gap, missing part, *esp.* in document or series (*pl.* **-nae** (-niː), **-s**)

lad (læd) *n.* boy, young fellow

ladder (ˈlædə) *n.* **1.** frame of two poles connected by rungs, used for climbing **2.** flaw in stockings, jumpers *etc.*, caused by running of torn stitch —**ladder back** type of chair in which back is constructed of horizontal slats between two uprights

lade (leɪd) *vt.* **1.** load **2.** ship **3.** burden, weigh down (**ˈladen** *pp.*) —**ˈlading** *n.* cargo, freight

la-di-da, lah-di-dah, *or* **la-de-da** (lɑːdiːˈdɑː) *a. inf.* affecting exaggeratedly genteel manners or speech

ladle (ˈleɪdᵊl) *n.* **1.** spoon with long handle and large bowl —*vt.* **2.** (*oft. with* out) serve out (as) with ladle

lady (ˈleɪdɪ) *n.* **1.** female counterpart of gentleman **2.** *polite term for* a woman **3.** title of some women of rank —**ˈladies** *or* **ladies' room** *n. inf.* women's public lavatory —**ˈladyship** *n.* title of a lady —**ˈladybird** *n.* small beetle, usu. red with black spots —**Lady Day** Feast of the Annunciation, 25th March —**lady-in-waiting** *n.* lady who attends queen or princess (*pl.* **ladies-in-waiting**) —**lady-killer** *n. inf.* man who believes he is irresistible to women —**ˈladylike** *a.* **1.** gracious **2.** well-mannered —**lady's finger** species of small banana —**lady's-slipper** *n.* orchid with reddish or purple flowers —**Our Lady** the Virgin Mary

lag[1] (læg) *vi.* **1.** (*oft. with* behind) go too slowly, fall behind (**-gg-**) —*n.* **2.** lagging, interval of time between events —**ˈlaggard** *n.* one who lags —**ˈlagging** *a.* loitering, slow

lag[2] (læg) *vt.* wrap (boiler, pipes *etc.*) with insulating material (**-gg-**) —**ˈlagging** *n.* this material

lag[3] (læg) *n. sl.* convict (*esp. in* **old lag**)

lager (ˈlɑːgə) *n.* light-bodied type of beer

lagoon (ləˈguːn) *n.* saltwater lake, enclosed by atoll, or separated by sandbank from sea

lah *or* **la** (lɑː) *n. Mus.* in tonic solfa, sixth note of any major scale; submediant

laic (ˈleɪɪk) *a.* secular, lay —**laiciˈzation** *or* **-ciˈsation** *n.* —**ˈlaicize** *or* **-cise** *vt.* render secular or lay

laid (leɪd) *pt./pp. of* LAY[2] —**laid-back** *a.* relaxed in style or character; easy-going and unhurried —**laid paper** paper with regular mesh impressed upon it

lain (leɪn) *pp. of* LIE[1]

lair (lɛə) *n.* resting place, den of animal

laird (lɛəd) *n.* Scottish landowner —**ˈlairdship** *n.* estate

laissez faire *or* ***laisser faire*** (lɛseɪ ˈfɛə) *Fr.* **1.** principle of nonintervention, *esp.* by government in commercial affairs **2.** indifference

laity (ˈleɪɪtɪ) *n.* laymen, the people as opposed to clergy

lake[1] (leɪk) *n.* expanse of inland water —**ˈlakelet** *n.*

lake[2] (leɪk) *n.* red pigment

lam[1] (læm) *vt. sl.* beat, hit (**-mm-**) —**ˈlamming** *n.* beating, thrashing

lam[2] (læm) *n.* **US** *sl.* —**on the lam** making an escape

Lam. *Bible* Lamentations

lama (ˈlɑːmə) *n.* Buddhist priest in Tibet or Mongolia —**ˈLamaism** *n.* form of Buddhism of Tibet and Mongolia —**ˈLamaist** *n./a.* —**ˈlamasery** *n.* monastery of lamas

lamb (læm) *n.* **1.** young of the sheep **2.** its meat **3.** innocent or helpless creature —*vi.* **4.** (of sheep) give birth —**ˈlambkin** *n.* **1.** small lamb **2.** term of affection for child —**ˈlamblike** *a.* meek, gentle —**ˈlambskin** *n.* **1.** skin of lamb, *esp.* with wool still on **2.** material or garment prepared from this —**lamb's tails** pendulous catkins of hazel tree —**lamb's wool** soft, fine wool (*also* **ˈlambswool**)

lambaste *or* **lambast** (læmˈbeɪst) *vt.* **1.** beat **2.** reprimand

lambda (ˈlæmdə) *n.* 11th letter in Gr. alphabet (Λ, λ)

lambent (ˈlæmbənt) *a.* **1.** (of flame) flickering softly **2.** glowing

lambert (ˈlæmbət) *n.* cgs unit of illumination

lame (leɪm) *a.* **1.** crippled in a limb, *esp.* leg **2.** limping **3.** (of excuse *etc.*) unconvincing —*vt.* **4.** cripple —**lame duck** disabled, weak person or thing

THESAURUS

native, uninspired, vapid

laconic brief, compact, concise, crisp, curt, pithy, sententious, short, succinct, terse, to the point

lad boy, chap (*Inf.*), fellow, guy (*Inf.*), juvenile, kid, laddie (*Scot.*), schoolboy, shaver (*Inf.*), stripling, youngster, youth

laden burdened, charged, encumbered, fraught, full, hampered, loaded, oppressed, taxed, weighed down, weighted

lady-killer Casanova, Don Juan, heartbreaker, ladies' man, libertine, Lothario, philanderer, rake, roué, wolf (*Inf.*), womanizer

ladylike courtly, cultured, decorous, elegant, genteel, modest, polite, proper, refined, respectable, well-bred

lag be behind, dawdle, delay, drag (behind), drag one's feet, hang back, idle, linger, loiter, saunter, straggle, tarry, trail

laggard dawdler, idler, lingerer, loafer, loiterer, lounger, saunterer, slowcoach (*Brit. inf.*), sluggard, snail, straggler

laid-back at ease, casual, easy-going, free and easy, relaxed, unflappable (*Inf.*), unhurried

lair burrow, den, earth, form, hole, nest, resting place

laissez faire *n.* free enterprise, free trade, individualism, live and let live, nonintervention

lame **1.** crippled, defective, disabled, game, halt (*Archaic*), handicapped, hobbling, limping **2.** *Fig.* feeble, flimsy, inadequate, insufficient, poor, thin, unconvincing, unsatisfactory, weak

lamé ('lɑːmeɪ) *n./a.* (fabric) interwoven with gold or silver thread

lamella (lə'mɛlə) *n.* thin plate or scale (*pl.* **-lae** (-liː), **-s**) —**la'mellar** *or* **lamellate** ('læmɪleɪt, -lɪt) *a.*

lament (lə'mɛnt) *v.* **1.** feel, express sorrow (for) —*n.* **2.** passionate expression of grief **3.** song of grief —**'lamentable** *a.* deplorable —**lamen'tation** *n.*

lamina ('læmɪnə) *n.* thin plate, scale, flake (*pl.* **-nae** (-niː), **-s**) —**laminate** ('læmɪneɪt) —*vt.* **1.** make (sheet of material) by bonding together two or more thin sheets **2.** split, beat, form into thin sheets **3.** cover with thin sheet of material —*n.* ('læmɪneɪt, -nɪt) **4.** laminated sheet —**lami'nation** *n.*

Lammas ('læməs) *n.* Aug. 1st, formerly a harvest festival

lammergeier *or* **lammergeyer** ('læməgaɪə) *n.* type of rare vulture

lamp (læmp) *n.* **1.** any of various appliances (*esp.* electrical) that produce light, heat, radiation *etc.* **2.** formerly, vessel holding oil burned by wick for lighting —**'lampblack** *n.* pigment made from soot —**'lamplight** *n.* —**'lamppost** *n.* post supporting lamp in street —**'lampshade** *n.*

lampoon (læm'puːn) *n.* **1.** satire ridiculing person, literary work *etc.* —*vt.* **2.** satirize, ridicule —**lam'pooner** *or* **lam'poonist** *n.*

lamprey ('læmprɪ) *n.* fish like an eel with a sucker mouth

lance (lɑːns) *n.* **1.** horseman's spear —*vt.* **2.** pierce with lance or lancet —**lanceolate** ('lɑːnsɪəleɪt, -lɪt) *a.* lance-shaped, tapering —**'lancer** *n.* formerly, cavalry soldier armed with lance —**'lancers** *pl.n.* (*with sing. v.*) **1.** quadrille for eight or sixteen couples **2.** music for this dance —**'lancet** *n.* pointed two-edged surgical knife —**lance corporal** *or* **sergeant** noncommissioned officer in army

Lancs. (læŋks) Lancashire

land (lænd) *n.* **1.** solid part of earth's surface **2.** ground, soil **3.** country **4.** property consisting of land —*pl.* **5.** estates —*vi.* **6.** come to land, disembark **7.** bring an aircraft or (of aircraft) come from air to land or water **8.** alight, step down **9.** arrive on ground **10. C** be legally admitted as immigrant —*vt.* **11.** bring to land **12.** bring to some point or condition **13.** *inf.* obtain **14.** catch **15.** *inf.* strike —**'landed** *a.* possessing, consisting of lands —**'landing** *n.* **1.** act of landing **2.** platform between flights of stairs **3.** a landing stage —**'landward** *a./adv.* —**'landwards** *adv.* —**land agent 1.** person who administers landed estate and its tenancies **2.** person who acts as agent for sale of land —**'landfall** *n.* ship's approach to land at end of voyage —**'landgrave** *n.* *German hist.* **1.** (from 13th century to 1806) count who ruled over specified territory **2.** (after 1806) title of various sovereign princes —**landing gear US** undercarriage —**landing stage** platform for embarkation and disembarkation —**'landlocked** *a.* enclosed by land —**'landlord** *or* **'landlady** *n.* **1.** person who lets land, houses *etc.* **2.** master or mistress of inn, boarding house *etc.* —**'landlubber** *n.* person ignorant of the sea and ships —**'landmark** *n.* **1.** boundary mark, conspicuous object, as guide for direction *etc.* **2.** event, decision *etc.* considered as important stage in development of something —**'landmass** *n.* large continuous area of land —**land mine** *Mil.* explosive charge placed in ground, usu. detonated by stepping or driving on it —**'landowner** *n.* person who owns land —**'landscape** *n.* **1.** piece of inland scenery **2.** picture of it **3.** prospect —*v.* **4.** create, arrange, (garden, park *etc.*) —**landscape gardening** —**landscape painter** —**'landslide** *or* **'landslip** *n.* **1.** falling of soil, rock *etc.* down mountainside **2.** overwhelming electoral victory —**land of milk and honey 1.** land of natural fertility promised to Israelites by God **2.** any fertile land *etc.*

landau ('lændɔː) *n.* four-wheeled carriage with folding top

lane (leɪn) *n.* **1.** narrow road or street **2.** specified route followed by shipping or aircraft **3.** area of road for one stream of traffic

lang. language

language ('læŋgwɪdʒ) *n.* **1.** system of sounds, symbols *etc.* for communicating thought **2.** specialized vocabulary used by a particular group **3.** style of speech or expression —**language laboratory** room equipped with tape recorders *etc.* for learning foreign languages

languish ('læŋgwɪʃ) *vi.* **1.** be or become weak or faint

THESAURUS

lament *v.* **1.** bemoan, bewail, complain, deplore, grieve, mourn, regret, sorrow, wail, weep ~*n.* **2.** complaint, keening, lamentation, moan, moaning, plaint, ululation, wail, wailing **3.** coronach (*Scot., Irish*), dirge, elegy, monody, requiem, threnody

lamentable deplorable, distressing, grievous, mournful, regrettable, sorrowful, tragic, unfortunate, woeful

lamentation dirge, grief, grieving, keening, lament, moan, mourning, plaint, sobbing, sorrow, ululation, wailing, weeping

lampoon 1. *n.* burlesque, caricature, parody, pasquinade, satire, send-up (*Brit. inf.*), skit, squib, takeoff (*Inf.*) **2.** *v.* burlesque, caricature, make fun of, mock, parody, pasquinade, ridicule, satirize, send up (*Brit. inf.*), squib, take off (*Inf.*)

land *n.* **1.** dry land, earth, ground, terra firma **2.** dirt, ground, loam, soil **3.** countryside, farming, farmland, rural districts **4.** acres, estate, grounds, property, real property, realty **5.** country, district, fatherland, motherland, nation, province, region, territory, tract ~*v.* **6.** alight, arrive, berth, come to rest, debark, disembark, dock, touch down **7.** *Inf.* acquire, gain, get, obtain, secure, win

landlord 1. host, hotelier, hotel-keeper, innkeeper **2.** freeholder, lessor, owner, proprietor

landmark 1. feature, monument **2.** crisis, milestone, turning point, watershed **3.** benchmark, boundary, cairn, milepost, signpost

landscape countryside, outlook, panorama, prospect, scene, scenery, view, vista

landslide *n.* avalanche, landslip, rockfall

language 1. communication, conversation, discourse, expression, interchange, parlance, speech, talk, utterance, verbalization, vocalization **2.** argot, cant, dialect, idiom, jargon, lingo (*Inf.*), lingua franca, patois, speech, terminology, tongue, vernacular, vocabulary **3.** diction, expression, phraseology, phrasing, style, wording

languid 1. drooping, faint, feeble, languorous, limp, pining, sickly, weak, weary **2.** indifferent, lackadaisical, languorous, lazy, listless, spiritless, unenthusiastic, uninterested **3.** dull, heavy, inactive, inert, lethargic, sluggish, torpid

2. be in depressing or painful conditions 3. droop, pine —ˈ**languid** *a.* 1. lacking energy, interest 2. spiritless, dull —ˈ**languidly** *adv.* —**languor** (ˈlæŋgə) *n.* 1. want of energy or interest 2. faintness 3. tender mood 4. softness of atmosphere —**languorous** (ˈlæŋgərəs) *a.*

lank (læŋk) *a.* 1. lean and tall 2. greasy and limp —ˈ**lanky** *a.* tall, thin and ungainly

lanolin (ˈlænəlɪn) *or* **lanoline** (ˈlænəlɪn, -liːn) *n.* grease from wool used in ointments *etc.*

lantern (ˈlæntən) *n.* 1. transparent case for lamp or candle 2. erection on dome or roof to admit light —**lantern jaw** long hollow jaw that gives face drawn appearance —**lantern-jawed** *a.* —ˈ**lanthorn** *n. obs.* lantern

lanthanum (ˈlænθənəm) *n.* silvery-white ductile metallic element —**lanthanide series** class of 15 chemically related elements **(lanthanides)** with atomic numbers from 57 (lanthanum) to 71 (lutetium)

lanyard *or* **laniard** (ˈlænjəd) *n.* 1. short cord for securing knife or whistle 2. short nautical rope 3. cord for firing cannon

lap[1] (læp) *n.* 1. the part between waist and knees of a person when sitting 2. *fig.* place where anything lies securely 3. single circuit of racecourse, track 4. stage or part of journey 5. single turn of wound thread *etc.* —*vt.* 6. enfold, wrap round 7. overtake (opponent) to be one or more circuits ahead (**-pp-**) —ˈ**lappet** *n.* flap, fold —ˈ**lapdog** *n.* small pet dog —**lap joint** joint made by placing one member over another and fastening together (*also* **lapped joint**) —**lap of honour** ceremonial circuit of racing track *etc.* by winner of race

lap[2] (læp) *v.* 1. (*oft. with* up) drink by scooping up with tongue 2. (of waves *etc.*) beat softly (**-pp-**)

lapel (ləˈpɛl) *n.* part of front of coat *etc.* folded back towards shoulders

lapidary (ˈlæpɪdərɪ) *a.* 1. of stones 2. engraved on stone —*n.* 3. cutter, engraver of stones

lapis lazuli (ˈlæpɪs ˈlæzjulaɪ) bright blue stone or pigment

lapse (læps) *n.* 1. fall (in standard, condition, virtue *etc.*) 2. slip 3. mistake 4. passing (of time *etc.*) —*vi.* 5. fall away 6. end, *esp.* through disuse

lapwing (ˈlæpwɪŋ) *n.* type of plover

larboard (ˈlɑːbəd) *n./a. obs.* port (side of ship)

larceny (ˈlɑːsɪnɪ) *n.* theft

larch (lɑːtʃ) *n.* deciduous coniferous tree

lard (lɑːd) *n.* 1. prepared pig's fat —*vt.* 2. insert strips of bacon in (meat) 3. intersperse, decorate (speech) (with strange words *etc.*) —ˈ**lardy** *a.* —**lardy cake UK** rich sweet cake made of bread dough, lard, sugar and dried fruit

larder (ˈlɑːdə) *n.* storeroom or cupboard for food

large (lɑːdʒ) *a.* 1. broad in range or area 2. great in size, number *etc.* 3. liberal 4. generous —*adv.* 5. in a big way —ˈ**largely** *adv.* —**larˈgess** *or* **larˈgesse** *n.* 1. bounty 2. gift 3. donation —ˈ**largish** *a.* fairly large —**large-scale** *a.* 1. wide-ranging, extensive 2. (of maps and models) constructed or drawn to big scale —**at large** 1. free, not confined 2. in general 3. fully

largo (ˈlɑːgəʊ) *a./adv. Mus.* to be performed moderately slowly

lariat (ˈlærɪət) *n.* lasso

lark[1] (lɑːk) *n.* small, brown singing bird, skylark —ˈ**larkspur** *n.* plant with spikes of blue, pink or white flowers

lark[2] (lɑːk) *n.* 1. frolic, spree —*vi.* 2. indulge in lark —ˈ**larky** *a.*

larrigan (ˈlærɪgən) *n.* knee-high moccasin boot worn by trappers *etc.*

larva (ˈlɑːvə) *n.* insect in immature but active stage (*pl.* **-ae** (-iː)) —ˈ**larval** *a.* —ˈ**larviform** *a.*

larynx (ˈlærɪŋks) *n.* part of throat containing vocal cords (*pl.* **larynges** (ləˈrɪndʒiːz), **-es**) —**larynˈgeal** *or* **laˈryngal** *a.* 1. of larynx 2. *Phonet.* articulated at larynx; glottal —**larynˈgitis** *n.* inflammation of larynx

lasagne *or* **lasagna** (ləˈzænjə, -ˈsæn-) *n.* pasta formed in wide, flat sheets

lascar (ˈlæskə) *n.* E Indian seaman

lascivious (ləˈsɪvɪəs) *a.* lustful

laser (ˈleɪzə) *n.* device for concentrating electromagnetic radiation or light of mixed frequencies into an intense, narrow, concentrated beam

lash[1] (læʃ) *n.* 1. stroke with whip 2. flexible part of

THESAURUS

languish 1. decline, droop, fade, fail, faint, flag, sicken, waste, weaken, wilt, wither 2. *Often with* **for** desire, hanker, hunger, long, pine, sigh, want, yearn 3. brood, despond, grieve, repine, sorrow

lank 1. dull, lifeless, limp, long, lustreless, straggling 2. attenuated, emaciated, gaunt, lanky, lean, rawboned, scraggy, scrawny, skinny, slender, slim, spare, thin

lanky angular, bony, gangling, gaunt, loose-jointed, rangy, rawboned, scraggy, scrawny, spare, tall, thin, weedy (*Inf.*)

lap[1] 1. *n.* circle, circuit, course, distance, loop, orbit round, tour 2. *v.* cover, enfold, envelop, fold, swaddle, swathe, turn, twist, wrap

lap[2] 1. gurgle, plash, purl, ripple, slap, splash, swish, was 2. drink, lick, sip, sup

lapse *n.* 1. error, failing, fault, indiscretion, mistake, negligence, omission, oversight, slip 2. backsliding, decline, descent, deterioration, drop, fall, relapse ~*v.* 3. decline, degenerate, deteriorate, drop, fail, fall, sink, slide, slip 4. become obsolete, become void, end, expire, run out, stop, terminate

large 1. big, bulky, colossal, considerable, enormous, giant, gigantic, goodly, great, huge, immense, jumbo (*Inf.*), king-size, man-size, massive, monumental, sizable, substantial, tidy (*Inf.*), vast 2. abundant, ample, broad, capacious, comprehensive, copious, extensive, full, generous, grand, grandiose, liberal, plentiful, roomy, spacious, sweeping, wide 3. **at large a.** at liberty, free, on the loose, on the run, roaming, unconfined **b.** as a whole, chiefly, generally, in general, in the main, mainly **c.** at length, considerably, exhaustively, greatly, in full detail

large-scale broad, extensive, far-reaching, global, sweeping, vast, wholesale, wide, wide-ranging

largess 1. alms-giving, benefaction, bounty, charity, generosity, liberality, munificence, open-handedness, philanthropy 2. bequest, bounty, donation, endowment, gift, grant, present

lark 1. *n.* antic, caper, escapade, fling, frolic, fun, gambol, game, jape, mischief, prank, revel, rollick, romp, skylark, spree 2. *v.* caper, cavort, cut capers, frolic, gambol, have fun, make mischief, play, rollick, romp, sport

whip **3.** eyelash —*vt.* **4.** strike with whip, thong *etc.* **5.** dash against (as waves) **6.** attack verbally, ridicule **7.** flick, wave sharply to and fro —**ˈlashing** *n.* **1.** whipping, flogging **2.** scolding —*pl.* **3.** (*usu. with* of) **UK** *inf.* large amounts; lots —**lash out 1.** burst into or resort to verbal or physical attack **2.** *inf.* be extravagant, as in spending

lash² (læʃ) *vt.* fasten or bind tightly with cord *etc.* —**ˈlashing** *n.* rope *etc.* used for binding or securing —**lash-up** *n.* temporary connection of equipment for experimental or emergency use

lass (læs) *n.* girl —**ˈlassie** *n. inf.* little lass; girl

Lassa fever (ˈlæsə) serious viral disease of Central W Afr., characterized by high fever *etc.*

lassitude (ˈlæsɪtjuːd) *n.* weariness

lasso (læˈsuː, ˈlæsəʊ) *n.* **1.** rope with noose for catching cattle *etc.* (*pl.* **-s, -es**) —*vt.* **2.** catch (as) with lasso (**lasˈsoed, lasˈsoing**)

last¹ (lɑːst) *a./adv.* **1.** after all others, coming at the end **2.** most recent(ly) —*a.* **3.** *sup. of* LATE **4.** only remaining —*n.* **5.** last person or thing —**ˈlastly** *adv.* finally —**last-ditch** *a.* made or done as last desperate effort in face of opposition —**last name** *see* SURNAME —**last rites** *Christianity* religious rites prescribed for those close to death —**the Last Judgment** occasion, after resurrection of dead at end of world, when, according to Bible, God will decree final destinies of all men according to good and evil in earthly lives (*also* **the Last Day, ˈDoomsday, Judgment Day**) —**the last straw** final irritation or problem that stretches one's endurance or patience beyond limit

last² (lɑːst) *vi.* continue, hold out, remain alive or unexhausted, endure —**ˈlasting** *a.* permanent; enduring —**ˈlastingly** *adv.*

last³ (lɑːst) *n.* model of foot on which shoes are made, repaired

lat. latitude

latch (lætʃ) *n.* **1.** fastening for door, consisting of bar, catch for it, and lever to lift it **2.** small lock with spring action —*vt.* **3.** fasten with latch —**latchkey child** child who has to let himself in at home after school as his parents are out at work

late (leɪt) *a.* **1.** coming after the appointed time **2.** delayed **3.** that was recently but now is not **4.** recently dead **5.** recent in date **6.** of late stage of development (**ˈlater** *comp.*, **ˈlatest, last** *sup.*) —*adv.* **7.** after proper time **8.** recently **9.** at, till late hour —**ˈlately** *adv.* not long since —**ˈlatish** *a.* rather late —**Late Greek** Greek language from about 3rd to 8th century A.D. —**Late Latin** form of written Latin used from 3rd to 7th century A.D.

lateen sail (ləˈtiːn) triangular sail on long yard hoisted to head of mast

latent (ˈleɪtᵊnt) *a.* **1.** existing but not developed **2.** hidden

lateral (ˈlætərəl) *a.* of, at, from the side —**ˈlaterally** *adv.* —**lateral thinking** way of solving problems by employing unorthodox means

laterite (ˈlætəraɪt) *n.* brick-coloured rock or clay formed by weathering of rock in tropical regions

latex (ˈleɪtɛks) *n.* sap or fluid of plants, *esp.* of rubber tree (*pl.* **-es, latices** (ˈlætɪsiːz)) —**laticiferous** (lætɪˈsɪfərəs) *a.* bearing or containing latex or sap

lath (lɑːθ) *n.* thin strip of wood (*pl.* **laths** (lɑːðz, lɑːθs)) —**ˈlathing** *n.* —**ˈlathy** *a.* **1.** like a lath **2.** tall and thin

lathe (leɪð) *n.* machine for turning object while it is being shaped

lather (ˈlɑːðə) *n.* **1.** froth of soap and water **2.** frothy sweat —*vi.* **3.** form lather —*vt.* **4.** *inf.* beat

Latin (ˈlætɪn) *n.* **1.** language of ancient Romans —*a.* **2.** of ancient Romans **3.** of, in their language **4.** speaking a language descended from Latin —**ˈLatinism** *n.* word, idiom imitating Latin —**LaˈtInity** *n.* **1.** manner of writing Latin **2.** Latin style —**Latin America** those areas of Amer. whose official languages are Spanish and Portuguese, derived from Latin: S Amer., Central Amer., Mexico and certain islands in the Caribbean —**Latin American** *n./a.*

latitude (ˈlætɪtjuːd) *n.* **1.** angular distance on meridian reckoned N or S from equator **2.** deviation from a

THESAURUS

lash¹ *n.* **1.** blow, hit, stripe, stroke, swipe (*Inf.*) ~*v.* **2.** beat, birch, chastise, flagellate, flog, horsewhip, lam (*Sl.*), scourge, thrash, whip **3.** beat, buffet, dash, drum, hammer, hit, knock, larrup (*Dialect*), pound, smack, strike **4.** attack, belabour, berate, castigate, censure, criticize, flay, lambaste, lampoon, ridicule, satirize, scold, tear into (*Inf.*), upbraid

lash² bind, fasten, join, make fast, rope, secure, strap, tie

lass bird (*Sl.*), chick (*Sl.*), colleen (*Irish*), damsel, girl, lassie (*Scot.*), maid, maiden, miss, schoolgirl, young woman

last¹ *adj.* **1.** aftermost, at the end, hindmost, rearmost **2.** latest, most recent **3.** closing, concluding, extreme, final, furthest, remotest, terminal, ultimate, utmost ~*adv.* **4.** after, behind, bringing up the rear, in *or* at the end, in the rear ~*n.* **5.** close, completion, conclusion, end, ending, finale, finish, termination

last² *v.* abide, carry on, continue, endure, hold on, hold out keep, keep on, persist, remain, stand up, survive, wear

last-ditch all-out (*Inf.*), desperate, final, frantic, heroic, straining, struggling

lasting abiding, continuing, deep-rooted, durable, enduring, indelible, lifelong, long-standing, long-term, perennial, permanent, perpetual, unceasing, undying, unending

lastly after all, all in all, at last, finally, in conclusion, in the end, to conclude, to sum up, ultimately

latch 1. *n.* bar, bolt, catch, clamp, fastening, hasp, hook, lock, sneck (*Dialect*) **2.** *v.* bar, bolt, fasten, lock, make fast, secure, sneck (*Dialect*)

late *adj.* **1.** behind, behindhand, belated, delayed, last-minute, overdue, slow, tardy, unpunctual **2.** advanced, fresh, modern, new, recent **3.** dead, deceased, defunct, departed, ex-, former, old, past, preceding, previous ~*adv.* **4.** at the last minute, behindhand, behind time, belatedly, dilatorily, slowly, tardily, unpunctually

lately in recent times, just now, latterly, not long ago, of late, recently

lateral edgeways, flanking, side, sideward, sideways

latest *adj.* current, fashionable, in, modern, most recent, newest, now, up-to-date, up-to-the-minute, with it (*Inf.*)

lather *n.* **1.** bubbles, foam, froth, soap, soapsuds, suds ~*v.* **2.** foam, froth, soap **3.** *Inf.* beat, cane, drub, flog, lambaste, strike, thrash, whip

standard **3.** freedom from restriction **4.** scope —*pl.* **5.** regions —**lati'tudinal** *a.* —**latitudi'narian** *a.* claiming, showing latitude of thought, *esp.* in religion —**latitudi'narianism** *n.*

latrine (lə'triːn) *n.* in army *etc.*, lavatory

latter ('lætə) *a.* **1.** second of two **2.** later **3.** more recent —*n.* **4.** second or last-mentioned person or thing —**'latterly** *adv.*

lattice ('lætɪs) *n.* **1.** structure of strips of wood, metal *etc.* crossing with spaces between **2.** window so made —**'latticed** *a.*

laud (lɔːd) *Lit. n.* **1.** praise, song of praise —*vt.* **2.** praise, glorify —**lauda'bility** *n.* —**'laudable** *a.* praiseworthy —**'laudably** *adv.* —**lau'dation** *n.* **1.** praise **2.** honour paid —**'laudatory** *a.* expressing, containing praise

laudanum ('lɔːdᵊnəm) *n.* tincture of opium

laugh (lɑːf) *vi.* **1.** make sounds instinctively expressing amusement, merriment or scorn —*n.* **2.** such sound —**'laughable** *a.* ludicrous —**'laughably** *adv.* —**'laughter** *n.* —**laughing gas** nitrous oxide as anaesthetic —**laughing hyena** spotted hyena, so called from its cry —**laughing jackass** *see* KOOKABURRA —**laughing stock** object of general derision

launch[1] (lɔːntʃ) *vt.* **1.** set afloat **2.** set in motion **3.** begin **4.** propel (missile, spacecraft) into space **5.** hurl, send —*vi.* **6.** enter on course —**'launcher** *n.* installation, vehicle, device for launching rockets, missiles *etc.* —**launching pad** *or* **launch pad** platform from which spacecraft *etc.* is launched

launch[2] (lɔːntʃ) *n.* large power-driven boat

laundry ('lɔːndrɪ) *n.* **1.** place for washing clothes, *esp.* as a business **2.** clothes *etc.* for washing —**'launder** *vt.* wash and iron —**Launder'ette** *n.* R shop with coin-operated washing, drying machines

laureate ('lɔːrɪɪt) *a.* crowned with laurels —**'laureateship** *n.* post of poet laureate —**poet laureate** poet with appointment to Royal Household, nominally to compose verses on occasions of national importance

laurel ('lɒrəl) *n.* **1.** glossy-leaved shrub, bay tree —*pl.* **2.** its leaves, emblem of victory or merit

lava ('lɑːvə) *n.* molten matter thrown out by volcanoes, solidifying as it cools

lavatory ('lævətərɪ, -trɪ) *n.* toilet, water closet

lave (leɪv) *vt. obs.* wash, bathe

lavender ('lævəndə) *n.* **1.** shrub with fragrant flowers **2.** colour of the flowers, pale lilac —**lavender water** perfume or toilet water made from flowers of lavender plant

lavish ('lævɪʃ) *a.* **1.** giving or spending profusely **2.** very, too abundant —*vt.* **3.** spend, bestow profusely

law (lɔː) *n.* **1.** rule binding on community **2.** system of such rules **3.** legal science **4.** knowledge, administration of it **5.** *inf.* (member of) police force **6.** general principle deduced from facts **7.** invariable sequence of events in nature —**'lawful** *a.* allowed by law —**'lawfully** *adv.* —**'lawless** *a.* **1.** ignoring laws **2.** violent —**'lawlessly** *adv.* —**'lawyer** *n.* professional expert in law —**law-abiding** *a.* **1.** obedient to laws **2.** well-behaved —**law agent** in Scotland, solicitor entitled to appear for client in any Sheriff Court —**'lawgiver** *n.* one who makes laws —**Law Lord** member of House of Lords who sits as highest court of appeal —**'lawsuit** *n.* prosecution of claim in court

lawn[1] (lɔːn) *n.* stretch of carefully tended turf in garden *etc.* —**lawn mower** hand- or power-operated

THESAURUS

latitude 1. breadth, compass, extent, range, reach, room, scope, space, span, spread, sweep, width **2.** elbowroom, freedom, indulgence, laxity, leeway, liberty, licence, play, unrestrictedness

latter closing, concluding, last, last-mentioned, later, latest, modern, recent, second

latterly hitherto, lately, of late, recently

lattice fretwork, grating, grid, grille, latticework, mesh, network, openwork, reticulation, tracery, trellis, web

laudable admirable, commendable, creditable, estimable, excellent, meritorious, of note, praiseworthy, worthy

laudatory acclamatory, adulatory, approbatory, approving, commendatory, complimentary, eulogistic, panegyrical

laugh 1. *v.* be convulsed (*Inf.*), be in stitches, chortle, chuckle, crease up (*Inf.*), giggle, guffaw, roar with laughter, snigger, split one's sides, titter **2.** *n.* belly laugh (*Inf.*), chortle, chuckle, giggle, guffaw, roar *or* shriek of laughter, snigger, titter

laughable absurd, derisive, derisory, ludicrous, nonsensical, preposterous, ridiculous, worthy of scorn

laughing stock Aunt Sally (*Brit.*), butt, everybody's fool, fair game, figure of fun, target, victim

laughter cachinnation, chortling, chuckling, giggling, guffawing, laughing, tittering

launch 1. cast, discharge, dispatch, fire, project, propel, send off, set afloat, set in motion, throw **2.** begin, commence, embark upon, inaugurate, initiate, instigate, introduce, open, start

laurels acclaim, awards, bays, commendation, credit, distinction, fame, glory, honour, kudos, praise, prestige, recognition, renown, reward

lavatory bathroom, bog (*Brit. sl.*), can (*U.S. sl.*), cloakroom (*Brit.*), Gents, head(s) (*Nautical sl.*), john (*U.S. sl.*), Ladies, latrine, loo (*Brit. inf.*), powder room, (public) convenience, toilet, washroom, water closet, W.C.

lavish *adj.* **1.** abundant, copious, exuberant, lush, luxuriant, opulent, plentiful, profuse, prolific, sumptuous **2.** bountiful, effusive, free, generous, liberal, munificent, open-handed, unstinting **3.** exaggerated, excessive, extravagant, immoderate, improvident, intemperate, prodigal, thriftless, unreasonable, unrestrained, wasteful, wild ~*v.* **4.** deluge, dissipate, expend, heap, pour, shower, spend, squander, waste

law 1. charter, code, constitution, jurisprudence **2.** act, code, command, commandment, covenant, decree, edict, enactment, order, ordinance, rule, statute **3.** axiom, canon, criterion, formula, precept, principle, regulation, standard

law-abiding compliant, dutiful, good, honest, honourable, lawful, obedient, orderly, peaceable, peaceful

lawful allowable, authorized, constitutional, just, legal, legalized, legitimate, licit, permissible, proper, rightful, valid, warranted

lawless anarchic, chaotic, disorderly, insubordinate, insurgent, mutinous, rebellious, reckless, riotous, seditious, ungoverned, unrestrained, unruly, wild

machine for cutting grass —**lawn tennis** tennis played on grass court

lawn[2] (lɔːn) *n.* fine linen

lawrencium (lɒˈrɛnsɪəm) *n.* element artificially produced from californium

lawyer (ˈlɔːjə, ˈlɔɪə) *n. see* LAW

lax (læks) *a.* 1. not strict 2. lacking precision 3. loose, slack —ˈ**laxative** *a.* 1. having loosening effect on bowels —*n.* 2. agent stimulating evacuation of faeces —ˈ**laxity** *or* ˈ**laxness** *n.* 1. slackness 2. looseness of (moral) standards —ˈ**laxly** *adv.*

lay[1] (leɪ) *pt. of* LIE[1] —ˈ**layabout** *n.* lazy person

lay[2] (leɪ) *vt.* 1. deposit, set, cause to lie 2. *taboo sl.* have sexual intercourse with (**laid**, ˈ**laying**) —*n. taboo sl.* 3. act of sexual intercourse 4. sexual partner —ˈ**layer** *n.* 1. single thickness of some substance, as stratum or coating on surface 2. laying hen 3. shoot of plant pegged down or partly covered with earth to encourage root growth —*vt.* 4. propagate (plants) by making layers —**lay-by** *n.* stopping place for traffic beside road —**lay-off** *n.* —ˈ**layout** *n.* arrangement, *esp.* of matter for printing —**lay off** dismiss (staff) during slack period —**lay on** 1. provide, supply 2. apply 3. strike —**lay out** 1. display 2. expend 3. prepare for burial 4. *sl.* knock out —**lay waste** devastate

lay[3] (leɪ) *n.* minstrel's song

lay[4] (leɪ) *a.* 1. not clerical or professional 2. of or done by persons not clergymen —**Lay Lord** peer in House of Lords other than a Law Lord —ˈ**layman** *n.* ordinary person —**lay reader** 1. *Ch. of England* person licensed by bishop to conduct religious services other than Eucharist 2. *R.C.Ch.* layman chosen to read epistle at Mass

layette (leɪˈɛt) *n.* clothes, accessories *etc.* for newborn child

lay figure 1. jointed figure of the body used by artists 2. nonentity

lazy (ˈleɪzɪ) *a.* averse to work, indolent —**laze** *vi.* indulge in laziness —ˈ**lazily** *adv.* —ˈ**laziness** *n.*

lb *or* **lb.** pound

l.b.w. leg before wicket

l.c. 1. left centre (of stage *etc.*) 2. loco citato 3. *Print.* lower case

l.c.d., lcd, L.C.D., *or* **LCD** lowest common denominator

LCD liquid crystal display

L.C.J. UK Lord Chief Justice

l.c.m. *or* **L.C.M.** lowest common multiple

L/Cpl. lance corporal

L.D.S. 1. Latter-day Saints 2. laus Deo semper (*Lat.*, praise be to God for ever) 3. UK Licentiate in Dental Surgery (*also* **LDS**)

lea (liː) *n. Poet.* piece of meadow or open ground

leach (liːtʃ) *v.* 1. remove or be removed from substance by percolating liquid 2. (cause to) lose soluble substances by action of percolating liquid —*n.* 3. act or process of leaching 4. substance that is leached or constituents removed by leaching 5. porous vessel for leaching

lead[1] (liːd) *vt.* 1. guide, conduct 2. persuade 3. direct 4. control —*vi.* 5. be, go, play first 6. (*with* to) result (in) 7. give access (**led** (lɛd), ˈ**leading**) —*n.* 8. leading 9. that which leads or is used to lead 10. example 11. front or principal place, role *etc.* 12. cable bringing current to electric instrument —ˈ**leader** *n.* 1. one who leads 2. article in newspaper expressing editorial views (*also* **leading article**) —ˈ**leadership** *n.* —**leading aircraftman** *Brit. Air Force* rank above aircraftman (**leading aircraftwoman** *fem.*) —**leading case** legal decision used as precedent —**leading light** *inf.* important or outstanding person, *esp.* in organization —**leading note** *Mus.* 1. seventh degree of major or minor scale (*also* **subˈtonic**) 2. *esp.* in cadences, note that tends most naturally to resolve to note lying one semitone above —**leading question** question worded to prompt answer desired —**leading rating** rank in Royal Navy comparable but junior to that of corporal in army —**lead time** time between design of product and its production

THESAURUS

lawsuit action, argument, case, cause, contest, dispute, litigation, proceedings, prosecution, suit, trial

lawyer advocate, attorney, barrister, counsel, counsellor, legal adviser, solicitor

lax 1. careless, casual, easy-going, lenient, neglectful, negligent, overindulgent, remiss, slack, slipshod 2. broad, general, imprecise, inaccurate, indefinite, inexact, nonspecific, shapeless, vague 3. flabby, flaccid, loose, slack, soft, yielding

lay[1] 1. deposit, establish, leave, place, plant, posit, put, set, set down, settle, spread 2. arrange, dispose, locate, organize, position, set out 3. bear, deposit, produce

lay[2] 1. laic, laical, nonclerical, secular 2. amateur, inexpert, nonprofessional, nonspecialist

layabout beachcomber, good-for-nothing, idler, laggard, loafer, lounger, ne'er-do-well, shirker, skiver (*Brit. sl.*), slubberdegullion (*Archaic*), vagrant, wastrel

layer 1. bed, ply, row, seam, stratum, thickness, tier 2. blanket, coat, coating, cover, covering, film, mantle, sheet

layman amateur, lay person, nonprofessional, outsider

lay off discharge, dismiss, drop, let go, make redundant, oust, pay off

lay on cater (for), furnish, give, provide, supply

layout arrangement, design, draft, formation, geography, outline, plan

lay out 1. arrange, design, display, exhibit, plan, spread out 2. *Inf.* disburse, expend, fork out (*Sl.*), invest, pay, shell out (*Inf.*), spend 3. *Inf.* kayo (*Sl.*), knock for six (*Inf.*), knock out, knock unconscious, KO (*Sl.*)

laziness dilatoriness, do-nothingness, faineance, faineancy, idleness, inactivity, indolence, lackadaisicalness, slackness, sloth, slothfulness, slowness, sluggishness, tardiness

lazy idle, inactive, indolent, inert, remiss, shiftless, slack, slothful, slow, workshy

leach drain, extract, filter, filtrate, lixiviate (*Chem.*), percolate, seep, strain

lead *v.* 1. conduct, escort, guide, pilot, precede, show the way, steer, usher 2. cause, dispose, draw, incline, induce, influence, persuade, prevail, prompt 3. command, direct, govern, head, manage, preside over, supervise 4. be ahead (of), blaze a trail, come first, exceed, excel, outdo, outstrip, surpass, transcend 5.

lead[2] (lɛd) *n.* **1.** soft heavy grey metal **2.** plummet, used for sounding depths of water **3.** graphite —*pl.* **4.** lead-covered piece of roof **5.** strips of lead used to widen spaces in printing *etc.* —*vt.* **6.** cover, weight or space with lead (**ˈleaded, ˈleading**) —**ˈleaden** *a.* **1.** of, like lead **2.** heavy **3.** dull —**leaded windows** windows made of small panes framed in lead —**lead poisoning 1.** acute or chronic poisoning by lead, characterized by abdominal pain *etc.* **2.** **US** *sl.* death or injury resulting from being shot with bullets —**ˈleadsman** *n.* sailor who heaves the lead

leaf (li:f) *n.* **1.** organ of photosynthesis in plants, consisting of a flat, usu. green blade on stem **2.** two pages of book *etc.* **3.** thin sheet **4.** flap, movable part of table *etc.* (*pl.* **leaves** (li:vz)) —*v.* **5.** (*oft. with* through) turn through (pages *etc.*) cursorily —**ˈleafless** *a.* —**ˈleaflet** *n.* **1.** small leaf **2.** single sheet, often folded, of printed matter for distribution, handbill —**ˈleafy** *a.*

league[1] (li:g) *n.* **1.** agreement for mutual help **2.** parties to it **3.** federation of clubs *etc.* **4.** *inf.* class, level —*vi.* **5.** form an alliance; combine in an association —**ˈleaguer** *n.* member of league —**league football 1.** *chiefly* **A** rugby league football (*also* **league**) **2.** **A** Australian Rules competition conducted within league

league[2] (li:g) *n. obs.* measure of distance, about three miles

leak (li:k) *n.* **1.** hole, defect, that allows escape or entrance of liquid, gas, radiation *etc.* **2.** disclosure **3.** *sl.* act of urinating —*vi.* **4.** let fluid *etc.* in or out **5.** (of fluid *etc.*) find its way through leak —*vt.* **6.** let escape —*v.* **7.** (*oft. with* out) (allow to) become known little by little —**ˈleakage** *n.* **1.** leaking **2.** gradual escape or loss —**ˈleaky** *a.*

lean[1] (li:n) *a.* **1.** lacking fat **2.** thin **3.** meagre **4.** (of mixture of fuel and air) with too little fuel —*n.* **5.** lean part of meat, mainly muscular tissue

lean[2] (li:n) *v.* **1.** rest (against) **2.** bend, incline —*vi.* **3.** (*with* to *or* towards) tend (towards) **4.** (*with* on *or* upon) depend, rely (on) (**leaned** *or* **leant** (lɛnt) *pt./pp.*) —**ˈleaning** *n.* tendency —**lean-to** *n.* room, shed built against existing wall

leap (li:p) *vi.* **1.** spring, jump —*vt.* **2.** spring over (**leaped** *or* **leapt** (lɛpt) *pt./pp.*) —*n.* **3.** jump —**ˈleapfrog** *n.* **1.** game in which player vaults over another bending down —*v.* **2.** (cause to) advance by jumps or stages (**-gg-**) —**leap year** year with Feb. 29th as extra day, occurring every fourth year

learn (lɜ:n) *vt.* **1.** gain knowledge of or acquire skill in (something) by study, practice or teaching —*vi.* **2.** gain knowledge **3.** be taught **4.** (*oft. with* of *or* about) find out (**learnt** *or* **learned** *pt./pp.*) —**learned** (ˈlɜ:nɪd) *a.* **1.** erudite, deeply read **2.** showing much learning —**learnedly** (ˈlɜ:nɪdlɪ) *adv.* —**ˈlearner** *n.* —**ˈlearning** *n.* knowledge got by study

lease (li:s) *n.* **1.** contract by which land or property is rented for stated time by owner to tenant —*vt.* **2.** let, rent by, take on lease —**ˈleasehold** *a.* held on lease

THESAURUS

bring on, cause, conduce, contribute, produce, result in, serve, tend ~*n.* **6.** advance, advantage, edge, first place, margin, precedence, primacy, priority, start, supremacy, van, vanguard **7.** direction, example, guidance, leadership, model **8.** clue, guide, hint, indication, suggestion, tip, trace **9.** leading role, principal, protagonist, star part, title role

leader bellwether, boss (*Inf.*), captain, chief, chieftain, commander, conductor, counsellor, director, guide, head, number one, principal, ringleader, ruler, superior

leadership 1. administration, direction, directorship, domination, guidance, management, running, superintendency **2.** authority, command, control, influence, initiative, pre-eminence, supremacy, sway

leading chief, dominant, first, foremost, governing, greatest, highest, main, number one, outstanding, pre-eminent, primary, principal, ruling, superior

leaf *n.* **1.** blade, bract, flag, foliole, frond, needle, pad **2.** folio, page, sheet ~*v.* **3.** browse, flip, glance, riffle, skim, thumb (through)

leaflet advert (*Brit. inf.*), bill, booklet, brochure, circular, handbill, pamphlet

league *n.* **1.** alliance, association, band, coalition, combination, combine, compact, confederacy, confederation, consortium, federation, fellowship, fraternity, group, guild, partnership, union **2.** ability group, category, class, level ~*v.* **3.** ally, amalgamate, associate, band, collaborate, combine, confederate, join forces, unite

leak *n.* **1.** aperture, chink, crack, crevice, fissure, hole, opening, puncture **2.** disclosure, divulgence ~*v.* **3.** discharge, drip, escape, exude, ooze, pass, percolate, seep, spill, trickle **4.** disclose, divulge, give away, let slip, let the cat out of the bag, make known, make public, pass on, reveal, spill the beans (*Inf.*), tell

leaky cracked, holey, leaking, not watertight, perforated, porous, punctured, split, waterlogged

lean[1] *adj.* **1.** angular, bony, emaciated, gaunt, lank, rangy, scraggy, scrawny, skinny, slender, slim, spare, thin, unfatty, wiry **2.** bare, inadequate, meagre, pitiful, poor, scanty, sparse

lean[2] *v.* **1.** be supported, prop, recline, repose, rest **2.** bend, incline, slant, slope, tilt, tip **3.** be disposed to, be prone to, favour, gravitate towards, have a propensity, prefer, tend **4.** confide, count on, depend, have faith in, rely, trust

leaning aptitude, bent, bias, disposition, inclination, liking, partiality, penchant, predilection, proclivity, proneness, propensity, taste, tendency

leap *v.* **1.** bounce, bound, caper, cavort, frisk, gambol, hop, jump, skip, spring **2.** clear, jump (over), vault **3.** advance, become prominent, escalate, gain attention, increase, rocket, soar, surge ~*n.* **4.** bound, caper, frisk, hop, jump, skip, spring, vault **5.** escalation, increase, rise, surge, upsurge, upswing

learn 1. acquire, attain, become able, grasp, imbibe, master, pick up **2.** ascertain, detect, determine, discern, discover, find out, gain, gather, hear, understand

learned academic, cultured, erudite, experienced, expert, highbrow, intellectual, lettered, literate, scholarly, skilled, versed, well-informed, well-read

learner apprentice, beginner, disciple, neophyte, novice, pupil, scholar, student, trainee, tyro

learning acquirements, attainments, culture, education, erudition, information, knowledge, letters, literature, lore, research, scholarship, schooling, study, tuition, wisdom

lease *v.* charter, hire, let, loan, rent

leash 1. *n.* lead, rein, tether **2.** *v.* fasten, secure, tether, tie up

leash (liːʃ) *n.* **1.** thong for holding a dog **2.** set of three animals held in leash —*vt.* **3.** hold in, secure by leash

least (liːst) *sup. of* LITTLE *a.* **1.** smallest —*n.* **2.** smallest one —*adv.* **3.** in smallest degree

leather (ˈlɛðə) *n.* prepared skin of animal —**ˈleathery** *a.* like leather, tough —**ˈleatherjacket** *n.* crane fly grub —**ˈleatherwood** *n.* N Amer. tree with tough, leathery bark

leave[1] (liːv) *vt.* **1.** go away from **2.** deposit **3.** allow to remain **4.** entrust **5.** bequeath —*vi.* **6.** go away, set out (**left, ˈleaving**)

leave[2] (liːv) *n.* **1.** permission **2.** permission to be absent from work, duty **3.** period of such absence **4.** formal parting —**leave of absence 1.** leave from work or duty, *esp.* for a long time **2.** this period of time —**leave-taking** *n.* act of departing; farewell —**by** *or* **with your leave** with your permission

leave[3] (liːv) *vi.* produce or grow leaves (**leaved, ˈleaving**)

leaven (ˈlɛvᵊn) *n.* **1.** yeast **2.** *fig.* transforming influence —*vt.* **3.** raise with leaven **4.** taint; modify

lecher (ˈlɛtʃə) *n.* man given to lewdness —**lech** *vi. inf.* (*usu. with* after) behave lecherously (towards) —**ˈlecherous** *a.* **1.** lewd **2.** provoking lust **3.** lascivious —**ˈlecherously** *adv.* —**ˈlecherousness** *n.* —**ˈlechery** *n.*

lectern (ˈlɛktən) *n.* reading desk, *esp.* in church

lection (ˈlɛkʃən) *n.* **1.** difference in copies of manuscript or book **2.** reading —**ˈlectionary** *n.* book, list of scripture lessons for particular days —**ˈlector** *n.* reader

lecture (ˈlɛktʃə) *n.* **1.** instructive discourse **2.** speech of reproof —*vi.* **3.** deliver discourse —*vt.* **4.** reprove —**ˈlecturer** *n.* —**ˈlectureship** *n.* appointment as lecturer

LED light-emitting diode

ledge (lɛdʒ) *n.* **1.** narrow shelf sticking out from wall, cliff *etc.* **2.** ridge, rock below surface of sea

ledger (ˈlɛdʒə) *n.* **1.** book of debit and credit accounts, chief account book of firm **2.** flat stone —**ledger line** *Mus.* short line, above or below stave

lee (liː) *n.* **1.** shelter **2.** side of anything, *esp.* ship, away from wind —**ˈleeward** *a./n.* **1.** (on) lee side —*adv.* **2.** towards this side —**lee shore** shore towards which wind is blowing —**ˈleeway** *n.* **1.** leeward drift of ship **2.** room for free movement within limits **3.** loss of progress

leech[1] (liːtʃ) *n.* **1.** species of bloodsucking worm **2.** *Hist.* physician —**ˈleechcraft** *n.*

leech[2] (liːtʃ) *n.* edge of a sail

leek (liːk) *n.* **1.** plant like onion with long bulb and thick stem **2.** this as Welsh emblem

leer (lɪə) *vi.* **1.** glance with malign, sly or lascivious expression —*n.* **2.** such glance —**ˈleery** *a.* **1.** *chiefly dial.* knowing, sly **2.** *sl.* (*with* of) suspicious, wary

lees (liːz) *pl.n.* **1.** sediment of wine *etc.* **2.** dregs of liquor

leet (liːt) *n.* in Scotland, selected list of candidates for office

left[1] (lɛft) *a.* **1.** denotes the side that faces west when the front faces north **2.** opposite to the right —*n.* **3.** the left hand or part **4.** *Pol.* reforming or radical party (*also* **left wing**) —*adv.* **5.** on or towards the left —**ˈleftist** *n./a.* (person) of the political left —**left-handed** *a.* **1.** using left hand with greater ease than right **2.** performed with left hand **3.** designed for use by left hand **4.** awkward, clumsy **5.** ironically ambiguous **6.** turning from right to left; anticlockwise —*adv.* **7.** with left hand —**left-hander** *n.*

left[2] (lɛft) *pt./pp. of* LEAVE[1]

leg (lɛg) *n.* **1.** one of limbs on which person or animal walks, runs, stands **2.** part of garment covering leg **3.** anything which supports, as leg of table **4.** stage of journey **5.** *Cricket* part of field away from the striker's bat —**ˈleggings** *pl.n.* covering of leather or other

THESAURUS

least feeblest, fewest, last, lowest, meanest, minimum, minutest, poorest, slightest, smallest, tiniest

leathery coriaceous, durable, hard, hardened, leatherlike, leathern (*Archaic*), rough, rugged, tough, wrinkled

leave[1] *v.* **1.** abandon, decamp, depart, desert, disappear, do a bunk (*Brit. sl.*), exit, flit (*Inf.*), forsake, go, go away, move, pull out, quit, relinquish, retire, set out, take off (*Inf.*), withdraw **2.** cause, deposit, generate, produce, result in **3.** allot, assign, cede, commit, consign, entrust, give over, refer **4.** bequeath, demise, devise (*Law*), hand down, transmit, will

leave[2] *n.* **1.** allowance, authorization, concession, consent, dispensation, freedom, liberty, permission, sanction **2.** furlough, holiday, leave of absence, sabbatical, time off, vacation **3.** adieu, departure, farewell, goodbye, leave-taking, parting, retirement, withdrawal

leaven *n.* **1.** barm, ferment, leavening, yeast **2.** *Fig.* catalyst, influence, inspiration ~*v.* **3.** ferment, lighten, raise, work

lecherous carnal, concupiscent, goatish (*Archaic*), lascivious, lewd, libidinous, licentious, lubricous, lustful, prurient, randy (*Sl., chiefly Brit.*), raunchy (*U.S. Sl.*), ruttish, salacious, unchaste, wanton

lechery carnality, concupiscence, debauchery, lasciviousness, lecherousness, leching (*Inf.*), lewdness, libertinism, libidinousness, licentiousness, lubricity, lust, lustfulness, profligacy, prurience, rakishness, randiness (*Sl., chiefly Brit.*), salaciousness, sensuality, wantonness, womanizing

lecture *n.* **1.** address, discourse, disquisition, harangue, instruction, lesson, speech, talk ~*v.* **2.** address, discourse, expound, give a talk, harangue, hold forth, speak, talk, teach ~*n.* **3.** castigation, censure, chiding, dressing-down (*Inf.*), going-over (*Inf.*), rebuke, reprimand, reproof, scolding, talking-to (*Inf.*), telling off (*Inf.*), wigging (*Brit. sl.*) ~*v.* **4.** admonish, berate, carpet (*Inf.*), castigate, censure, chide, rate, reprimand, reprove, scold, tell off (*Inf.*)

ledge mantle, projection, ridge, shelf, sill, step

leer *n./v.* eye, gloat, goggle, grin, ogle, smirk, squint, stare, wink

lees deposit, dregs, grounds, precipitate, refuse, sediment, settlings

leeway elbowroom, latitude, margin, play, room, scope, space

left *adj.* larboard (*Nautical*), left-hand, port, sinistral

left-handed 1. awkward, cack-handed (*Inf.*), careless, clumsy, fumbling, gauche, maladroit **2.** ambiguous, backhanded, double-edged, enigmatic, equivocal, indirect, ironic, sardonic

material for legs —ˈ**leggy** *a.* **1.** long-legged **2.** (of plants) straggling —ˈ**legless** *a.* **1.** without legs **2.** *inf.* very drunk —**leg-pull** *n.* **UK** *inf.* practical joke, mild deception —ˈ**legroom** *n.* room to move legs comfortably, as in car —**leg before wicket** *Cricket* manner of dismissal on grounds that batsman has been struck on leg by bowled ball that otherwise would have hit wicket

legacy (ˈlɛɡəsɪ) *n.* **1.** anything left by will, bequest **2.** thing handed down to successor —**legaˈtee** *n.* recipient of legacy

legal (ˈliːɡ³l) *a.* of, appointed or permitted by, or based on, law —**legalˈese** *n.* conventional language in which legal documents are written —ˈ**legalism** *n.* strict adherence to law, *esp.* letter of law rather than its spirit —**legalˈistic** *a.* —**leˈgality** *n.* —**legaliˈzation** *or* **-iˈsation** *n.* —ˈ**legalize** *or* **-ise** *vt.* make legal —ˈ**legally** *adv.* —**legal aid** financial assistance available to persons unable to meet full cost of legal proceedings —**legal tender** currency that creditor must by law accept in redemption of debt

legate (ˈlɛɡɪt) *n.* ambassador, *esp.* papal —ˈ**legateship** *n.* —**leˈgation** *n.* **1.** diplomatic minister and his staff **2.** his residence

legato (lɪˈɡɑːtəʊ) *adv. Mus.* smoothly

legend (ˈlɛdʒənd) *n.* **1.** traditional story or myth **2.** traditional literature **3.** famous, renowned, person or event **4.** inscription —ˈ**legendary** *a.*

legerdemain (lɛdʒədəˈmeɪn) *n.* **1.** juggling, conjuring, sleight of hand **2.** trickery

leger line (ˈlɛdʒə) *see* **ledger line** *at* LEDGER

leghorn (ˈlɛɡhɔːn) *n.* **1.** kind of straw **2.** hat made of it **3.** (**L-**) (lɛˈɡɔːn) breed of fowls

legible (ˈlɛdʒəb³l) *a.* easily read —**legiˈbility** *n.* —ˈ**legibly** *adv.*

legion (ˈliːdʒən) *n.* **1.** body of infantry in Roman army **2.** various modern military bodies **3.** association of veterans **4.** large number —*a.* **5.** very numerous —ˈ**legionary** *a./n.* —**legionˈnaire** *n.* (*oft.* **L-**) member of military force or association —**Legionnaire's disease** sometimes fatal bacterial infection which has symptoms similar to those of pneumonia

legislator (ˈlɛdʒɪsleɪtə) *n.* maker of laws —ˈ**legislate** *vi.* make laws —**legisˈlation** *n.* **1.** act of legislating **2.** laws which are made —ˈ**legislative** *a.* —ˈ**legislature** *n.* body that makes laws of a state —**legislative assembly** (*oft.* **L- A-**) single-chamber legislature in most Canad. provinces

legitimate (lɪˈdʒɪtɪmɪt) *a.* **1.** born in wedlock **2.** lawful, regular **3.** fairly deduced —*vt.* (lɪˈdʒɪtɪmeɪt) **4.** make legitimate —**leˈgitimacy** *n.* —**leˈgitimateness** *n.* —**legitiˈmation** *n.* —**leˈgitimism** *n.* —**leˈgitimist** *n.* supporter of hereditary title to monarchy —**leˈgitimize** *or* **-mise** *vt.* legitimate

leguan (ˈlɛɡuɑːn) *n.* large S Afr. lizard

legume (ˈlɛɡjuːm, lɪˈɡjuːm) *n.* **1.** long dry fruit produced by leguminous plants; pod **2.** any of various table vegetables, *esp.* beans or peas **3.** any leguminous plant —**leˈguminous** *a.* (of plants) pod-bearing

lei (leɪ) *n.* garland of flowers

Leics. (ˈlɛstəʃə) Leicestershire

leisure (ˈlɛʒə) *n.* **1.** freedom from occupation **2.** spare time —ˈ**leisured** *a.* with plenty of spare time —ˈ**leisurely** *a.* **1.** deliberate, unhurried —*adv.* **2.** slowly —**leisure centre** a building that provides facilities for a range of leisure pursuits, such as library, sports hall, café *etc.*

THESAURUS

leg **1.** limb, lower limb, member, pin (*Inf.*), stump (*Inf.*) **2.** brace, prop, support, upright **3.** lap, part, portion, section, segment, stage, stretch

legacy **1.** bequest, devise (*Law*), estate, gift, heirloom, inheritance **2.** birthright, endowment, heritage, inheritance, patrimony, throwback, tradition

legal **1.** allowable, allowed, authorized, constitutional, lawful, legalized, legitimate, licit, permissible, proper, rightful, sanctioned, valid **2.** forensic, judicial, juridical

legality accordance with the law, admissibleness, lawfulness, legitimacy, permissibility, rightfulness, validity

legalize allow, approve, authorize, decriminalize, legitimate, legitimatize, license, permit, sanction, validate

legation consulate, delegation, diplomatic mission, embassy, envoys, ministry, representation

legend **1.** fable, fiction, folk tale, myth, narrative, saga, story, tale **2.** celebrity, luminary, marvel, phenomenon, prodigy, spectacle, wonder **3.** caption, device, inscription, motto

legendary **1.** apocryphal, fabled, fabulous, fanciful, fictitious, mythical, romantic, storied, traditional **2.** celebrated, famed, famous, illustrious, immortal, renowned, well-known

legibility clarity, decipherability, ease of reading, legibleness, neatness, plainness, readability, readableness

legible clear, decipherable, distinct, easily read, easy to read, neat, plain, readable

legion *n.* **1.** army, brigade, company, division, force, troop **2.** drove, horde, host, mass, multitude, myriad, number, throng ~*adj.* **3.** countless, multitudinous, myriad, numberless, numerous, very many

legislate codify, constitute, enact, establish, make laws, ordain, pass laws, prescribe, put in force

legislation **1.** codification, enactment, lawmaking, prescription, regulation **2.** act, bill, charter, law, measure, regulation, ruling, statute

legislative *adj.* congressional, judicial, juridical, jurisdictive, lawgiving, lawmaking, ordaining, parliamentary

legislator lawgiver, lawmaker, parliamentarian

legislature assembly, chamber, congress, diet, house, lawmaking body, parliament, senate

legitimate *adj.* **1.** acknowledged, authentic, authorized, genuine, lawful, legal, legit (*Sl.*), licit, proper, real, rightful, sanctioned, statutory, true **2.** admissible, correct, just, justifiable, logical, reasonable, sensible, valid, warranted, well-founded ~*v.* **3.** authorize, legalize, legitimatize, legitimize, permit, pronounce lawful, sanction

legitimize authorize, legalize, legitimate, permit, pronounce lawful, sanction

leisure breathing space, ease, freedom, free time, holiday, liberty, opportunity, pause, quiet, recreation, relaxation, respite, rest, retirement, spare moments, spare time, time off, vacation

leitmotiv *or* **leitmotif** (ˈlaɪtməʊtiːf) *n. Mus.* recurring theme associated with some person, situation, thought

L.E.M. (lɛm) lunar excursion module

lemming (ˈlɛmɪŋ) *n.* rodent of arctic regions

lemon (ˈlɛmən) *n.* **1.** pale yellow acid fruit **2.** tree bearing it **3.** its colour **4.** *sl.* useless or defective person or thing —**lemonˈade** *n.* drink made from lemon juice —**lemon curd** creamy spread made of lemons, butter *etc.* —**lemon sole** European flatfish highly valued as food

lemur (ˈliːmə) *n.* nocturnal animal like monkey

lend (lɛnd) *vt.* **1.** give temporary use of **2.** let out for hire or interest **3.** give, bestow (**lent, ˈlending**) —**ˈlender** *n.* —**lends itself to** is suitable for

length (lɛŋkθ, lɛŋθ) *n.* **1.** quality of being long **2.** measurement from end to end **3.** duration **4.** extent **5.** piece of a certain length —**ˈlengthen** *v.* **1.** make, become longer **2.** draw out —**ˈlengthily** *adv.* —**ˈlengthways** *or U.S.* **ˈlengthwise** *adv./a.* in direction of length —**ˈlengthy** *a.* (over)long —**at length 1.** in full detail **2.** at last

lenient (ˈliːnɪənt) *a.* mild, tolerant, not strict —**ˈlenience** *or* **ˈleniency** *n.* —**ˈleniently** *adv.*

lenity (ˈlɛnɪtɪ) *n.* **1.** mercy **2.** clemency

lens (lɛnz) *n.* piece of glass or similar material with one or both sides curved, used to converge or diverge light rays in cameras, spectacles, telescopes *etc.* (*pl.* **-es**)

lent (lɛnt) *pt./pp. of* LEND

Lent (lɛnt) *n.* period of fasting from Ash Wednesday to Easter Eve —**ˈLenten** *a.* of, in or suitable to Lent

lentil (ˈlɛntɪl) *n.* edible seed of leguminous plant —**lenˈticular** *a.* like lentil

lento (ˈlɛntəʊ) *adv. Mus.* slowly

Leo (ˈliːəʊ) *n.* (lion) 5th sign of zodiac, operative *c.* Jul. 22nd–Aug. 21st

leonine (ˈliːənaɪn) *a.* like a lion

leopard (ˈlɛpəd) *n.* large, spotted, carnivorous animal of cat family, like panther (**ˈleopardess** *fem.*)

leotard (ˈlɪətɑːd) *n.* tight-fitting garment covering most of body, worn by acrobats, dancers *etc.*

leper (ˈlɛpə) *n.* **1.** one suffering from leprosy **2.** person ignored or despised —**ˈleprosy** *n.* disease forming silvery scales on the skin and eating away the parts affected —**ˈleprous** *a.*

Lepidoptera (lɛpɪˈdɒptərə) *pl.n.* order of insects with four wings covered with fine gossamer scales, as moths, butterflies —**lepiˈdopterist** *n.* person who studies or collects moths and butterflies —**lepiˈdopterous** *a.*

leprechaun (ˈlɛprəkɔːn) *n.* mischievous elf of Irish folklore

lepton (ˈlɛptɒn) *n. Phys.* any of group of elementary particles and their antiparticles, that participate in weak interactions

lesbian (ˈlɛzbɪən) *n.* homosexual woman —**ˈlesbianism** *n.*

lese-majesty (ˈliːzˈmædʒɪstɪ) *n.* **1.** treason **2.** taking of liberties

lesion (ˈliːʒən) *n.* **1.** injury **2.** injurious change in texture or action of an organ of the body

less (lɛs) *comp. of* LITTLE *a.* **1.** not so much —*n.* **2.** smaller part, quantity **3.** a lesser amount —*adv.* **4.** to a smaller extent or degree —*prep.* **5.** after deducting, minus —**ˈlessen** *v.* diminish, reduce —**ˈlesser** *a.* **1.** less **2.** smaller **3.** minor

-less (*comb. form*) **1.** without; lacking, as in *speechless* **2.** not able to (do something) or not able to be (done, performed *etc.*), as in *countless*

lessee (lɛˈsiː) *n.* one to whom lease is granted

lesson (ˈlɛsᵊn) *n.* **1.** instalment of course of instruction **2.** content of this **3.** experience that teaches **4.** portion of Scripture read in church

lessor (ˈlɛsɔː, lɛˈsɔː) *n.* grantor of a lease

lest (lɛst) *conj.* **1.** in order that not **2.** for fear that

let[1] (lɛt) *vt.* **1.** allow, enable, cause to **2.** allow to escape

THESAURUS

leisurely 1. *adj.* comfortable, easy, gentle, laid-back (*Inf.*), lazy, relaxed, restful, slow, unhurried **2.** *adv.* at one's convenience, at one's leisure, comfortably, deliberately, easily, indolently, lazily, lingeringly, slowly, unhurriedly, without haste

lend 1. accommodate one with, advance, loan **2.** add, afford, bestow, confer, contribute, furnish, give, grant, impart, present, provide, supply **3. lend itself to** be adaptable, be appropriate, be serviceable, fit, present opportunities of, suit

length 1. *Of linear extent* distance, extent, longitude, measure, reach, span **2.** *Of time* duration, period, space, span, stretch, term **3.** measure, piece, portion, section, segment **4.** elongation, extensiveness, lengthiness, protractedness **5. at length a.** completely, fully, in depth, in detail, thoroughly, to the full **b.** at last, at long last, eventually, finally, in the end

lengthen continue, draw out, elongate, expand, extend, increase, make longer, prolong, protract, spin out, stretch

lengthy diffuse, drawn-out, extended, interminable, lengthened, long, long-drawn-out, long-winded, overlong, prolix, prolonged, protracted, tedious, verbose, very long

leniency, lenience clemency, compassion, forbearance, gentleness, indulgence, lenity, mercy, mildness, moderation, tenderness, tolerance

lenient clement, compassionate, forbearing, forgiving, gentle, indulgent, kind, merciful, mild, sparing, tender, tolerant

lesbian *n.* butch (*Sl.*), dyke (*Sl.*), sapphist, tribade

less 1. *adj.* shorter, slighter, smaller **2.** *adv.* barely, little, meagrely, to a smaller extent **3.** *prep.* excepting, lacking, minus, subtracting, without

lessen abate, abridge, contract, curtail, decrease, de-escalate, degrade, die down, diminish, dwindle, ease, erode, grow less, impair, lighten, lower, minimize, moderate, narrow, reduce, shrink, slacken, slow down, weaken, wind down

lesser inferior, less important, lower, minor, secondary, slighter, subordinate, under-

lesson 1. class, coaching, instruction, period, schooling, teaching, tutoring **2.** assignment, drill, exercise, homework, lecture, practice, reading, recitation, task **3.** deterrent, example, exemplar, message, model, moral, precept

3. grant use of for rent, lease —*vi.* 4. be leased —*v. aux.* 5. used to express a proposal, command, threat, assumption (**let, 'letting**) —**'letdown** *n.* disappointment —**let-up** *n. inf.* lessening, abatement —**let down** 1. lower 2. disappoint 3. undo, shorten and resew (hem) 4. untie (long hair that is bound up) and allow to fall loose 5. deflate —**let off** 1. allow to disembark or leave 2. explode or fire (bomb *etc.*) 3. excuse from (work *etc*) 4. *inf.* allow to get away without expected punishment *etc.* —**let's** let us: used to express suggestion *etc.* by speaker to himself and hearers

let[2] (lɛt) *n.* 1. hindrance 2. in some games, minor infringement or obstruction of ball requiring replaying of point

lethal (ˈliːθəl) *a.* deadly

lethargy (ˈlɛθədʒɪ) *n.* 1. apathy, want of energy or interest 2. unnatural drowsiness —**leˈthargic** *a.* —**leˈthargically** *adv.*

letter (ˈlɛtə) *n.* 1. alphabetical symbol 2. written message 3. strict meaning, interpretation —*pl.* 4. literature 5. knowledge of books —*vt.* 6. mark with, in, letters —**'lettered** *a.* learned —**letter bomb** explosive device in envelope, detonated when envelope is opened —**'letterhead** *n.* sheet of writing paper printed with one's address, name *etc.* —**'letterpress** *n.* printed matter as distinct from illustrations *etc.* —**letter of credit** letter issued by bank entitling bearer to draw funds from that bank or its agencies —**letters patent** document under seal of state, granting exclusive right, privilege

lettuce (ˈlɛtɪs) *n.* plant grown for use in salad

leucocyte *or esp. U.S.* **leukocyte** (ˈluːkəsaɪt) *n.* one of white blood corpuscles

leucoma (luːˈkəʊmə) *n.* disorder of the eye, characterized by opacity of the cornea

leukaemia *or esp. U.S.* **leukemia** (luːˈkiːmɪə) *n.* a progressive blood disease

Lev. *Bible* Leviticus

Levant (lɪˈvænt) *n. old name for* area of E Mediterranean now occupied by Lebanon, Syria and Israel —**leˈvanter** *n.* (*sometimes* **L-**) 1. easterly wind in W Mediterranean area 2. inhabitant of the Levant —**Levantine** (ˈlɛvəntaɪn) *a./n.*

levee[1] (ˈlɛvɪ, ˈlɛveɪ) *n.* 1. Brit. sovereign's reception for men only 2. *Hist.* reception held by sovereign on rising

levee[2] (ˈlɛvɪ) *n.* 1. natural or artificial river embankment 2. landing place

level (ˈlɛvᵊl) *a.* 1. horizontal 2. even in surface 3. consistent in style, quality *etc.* —*n.* 4. horizontal line or surface 5. instrument for showing, testing horizontal plane 6. position on scale 7. standard, grade 8. horizontal passage in mine —*vt.* 9. make level 10. bring to same level 11. knock down 12. aim (gun or accusation *etc.*) —*vi.* 13. *inf.* (*esp. with* with) be honest, frank (**-ll-**) —**'leveller** *or U.S.* **'leveler** *n.* advocate of social equality —**level crossing** point where railway line and road intersect —**level-headed** *a.* not apt to be carried away by emotion

lever (ˈliːvə) *n.* 1. rigid bar pivoted about a fulcrum to transfer a force with mechanical advantage 2. handle pressed, pulled *etc.* to operate something —*vt.* 3. prise, move with lever —**'leverage** *n.* 1. action, power of lever 2. influence 3. power to accomplish something 4. advantage

leveret (ˈlɛvərɪt, -vrɪt) *n.* young hare

leviathan (lɪˈvaɪəθən) *n.* 1. sea monster 2. anything huge or formidable

levitation (lɛvɪˈteɪʃən) *n.* the power of raising a solid body into the air supernaturally —**'levitate** *v.* (cause to) do this

levity (ˈlɛvɪtɪ) *n.* 1. inclination to make a joke of serious matters, frivolity 2. facetiousness

THESAURUS

let[1] *v.* 1. allow, authorize, give leave, give permission, give the go-ahead (green light, O.K.) (*Inf.*), grant, permit, sanction, suffer (*Archaic*), tolerate, warrant 2. hire, lease, rent 3. allow, cause, enable, grant, make, permit

let[2] *n.* constraint, hindrance, impediment, interference, obstacle, obstruction, prohibition, restriction

letdown anticlimax, bitter pill, blow, comedown (*Inf.*), disappointment, disgruntlement, disillusionment, frustration, setback, washout (*Inf.*)

let down disappoint, disenchant, disillusion, dissatisfy, fail, fall short, leave in the lurch, leave stranded

lethal baleful, dangerous, deadly, deathly, destructive, devastating, fatal, mortal, murderous, noxious, pernicious, poisonous, virulent

lethargic apathetic, comatose, debilitated, drowsy, dull, enervated, heavy, inactive, indifferent, inert, languid, lazy, listless, sleepy, slothful, slow, sluggish, somnolent, stupefied, torpid

lethargy apathy, drowsiness, dullness, hebetude (*Rare*), inaction, indifference, inertia, languor, lassitude, listlessness, sleepiness, sloth, slowness, sluggishness, stupor, torpidity, torpor

let off 1. detonate, discharge, emit, explode, exude, fire, give off, leak, release 2. absolve, discharge, dispense, excuse, exempt, exonerate, forgive, pardon, release, spare

letter 1. character, sign, symbol 2. acknowledgment, answer, billet (*Archaic*), communication, dispatch, epistle, line, message, missive, note, reply

letters belles-lettres, culture, erudition, humanities, learning, literature, scholarship

let-up abatement, break, cessation, interval, lessening, lull, pause, recess, remission, respite, slackening

level *adj.* 1. consistent, even, flat, horizontal, plain, plane, smooth, uniform 2. aligned, balanced, commensurate, comparable, equivalent, even, flush, in line, neck and neck, on a line, on a par, proportionate ~*v.* 3. even off *or* out, flatten, make flat, plane, smooth 4. bulldoze, demolish, destroy, devastate, equalize, flatten, knock down, lay low, pull down, raze, smooth, tear down, wreck 5. aim, beam, direct, focus, point, train 6. *Inf.* be above board, be frank, be honest, be open, be straightforward, be up front (*Sl.*), come clean (*Inf.*), keep nothing back ~*n.* 7. achievement, degree, grade, position, rank, stage, standard, standing, status 8. flat surface, horizontal, plain, plane

level-headed balanced, calm, collected, composed, cool, dependable, even-tempered, reasonable, sane, self-possessed, sensible, steady, together (*Sl., chiefly U.S.*), unflappable (*Inf.*)

lever 1. *n.* bar, crowbar, handle, handspike, jemmy 2. *v.* force, jemmy, move, prise, pry (*U.S.*), purchase, raise

levy (ˈlɛvɪ) *vt.* 1. impose (tax) 2. raise (troops) (**ˈlevied, ˈlevying**) —*n.* 3. imposition or collection of taxes 4. enrolling of troops 5. amount, number levied

lewd (lu:d) *a.* 1. lustful 2. indecent —**ˈlewdly** *adv.* —**ˈlewdness** *n.*

lexicon (ˈlɛksɪkən) *n.* dictionary —**ˈlexical** *a.* —**lexiˈcographer** *n.* writer of dictionaries —**lexiˈcography** *n.*

ley (leɪ, li:) *n.* 1. arable land temporarily under grass 2. line joining two prominent points in landscape, thought to be line of prehistoric track (*also* **ley line**)

Leyden jar (ˈlaɪdᵊn) *Phys.* early type of capacitor consisting of glass jar with lower part of inside and outside coated with tinfoil

L.F. *Rad.* low frequency

LG *or* **L.G.** Low German

Li *Chem.* lithium

liable (ˈlaɪəbᵊl) *a.* 1. answerable 2. exposed 3. subject 4. likely —**liaˈbility** *n.* 1. state of being liable, obligation 2. hindrance, disadvantage —*pl.* 3. debts

liaison (lɪˈeɪzɒn) *n.* 1. union 2. connection 3. intimacy, *esp.* secret —**liˈaise** *vi.* communicate and maintain contact —**liaison officer** officer who keeps units of troops in touch

liana (lɪˈɑ:nə) *or* **liane** (lɪˈɑ:n) *n.* climbing plant of tropical forests

liar (ˈlaɪə) *n.* one who tells lies

lib (lɪb) *inf.* liberation

lib. 1. liber (*Lat.*, book) 2. librarian 3. library

Lib. Liberal

libation (laɪˈbeɪʃən) *n.* drink poured as offering to the gods

libel (ˈlaɪbᵊl) *n.* 1. published statement falsely damaging person's reputation —*vt.* 2. defame falsely (-ll-) —**ˈlibellous** *or* **ˈlibelous** *a.* defamatory

liberal (ˈlɪbərəl, ˈlɪbrəl) *a.* 1. (*also* **L-**) of political party favouring democratic reforms or favouring individual freedom 2. generous 3. tolerant 4. abundant 5. (of education) designed to develop general cultural interests —*n.* 6. one who has liberal ideas or opinions —**ˈliberalism** *n.* principles of Liberal Party —**libeˈrality** *n.* munificence —**ˈliberalize** *or* **-ise** *v.* —**ˈliberally** *adv.*

liberate (ˈlɪbəreɪt) *vt.* set free —**libeˈration** *n.* —**ˈliberator** *n.*

libertarian (lɪbəˈtɛərɪən) *n.* 1. believer in freedom of thought *etc.*, or in free will —*a.* 2. of, like a libertarian —**liberˈtarianism** *n.*

libertine (ˈlɪbəti:n, -taɪn) *n.* 1. morally dissolute person —*a.* 2. dissolute —**ˈlibertinism** *n.*

liberty (ˈlɪbətɪ) *n.* 1. freedom —*pl.* 2. rights, privileges —**at liberty** 1. free 2. having the right —**take liberties** be presumptuous

THESAURUS

leverage ascendancy, authority, clout (*Inf.*), influence, pull (*Inf.*), purchasing power, rank, weight

levity facetiousness, fickleness, flightiness, flippancy, frivolity, giddiness, light-heartedness, light-mindedness, silliness, skittishness, triviality

levy *v.* 1. charge, collect, demand, exact, gather, impose, tax 2. call, call up, conscript, mobilize, muster, press, raise, summon ~*n.* 3. assessment, collection, exaction, gathering, imposition 4. assessment, duty, excise, fee, imposition, impost, tariff, tax, toll

lewd bawdy, blue, dirty, impure, indecent, lascivious, libidinous, licentious, loose, lustful, obscene, pornographic, profligate, salacious, smutty, unchaste, vile, vulgar, wanton, wicked

lewdness bawdiness, carnality, crudity, debauchery, depravity, impurity, indecency, lasciviousness, lechery, licentiousness, lubricity, obscenity, pornography, profligacy, salaciousness, smut, smuttiness, unchastity, vulgarity, wantonness

liability 1. accountability, answerability, culpability, duty, obligation, onus, responsibility 2. burden, disadvantage, drag, drawback, encumbrance, handicap, hindrance, impediment, inconvenience, millstone, minus (*Inf.*), nuisance 3. likelihood, probability, proneness, susceptibility, tendency

liable 1. accountable, amenable, answerable, bound, chargeable, obligated, responsible 2. exposed, open, subject, susceptible, vulnerable 3. apt, disposed, inclined, likely, prone, tending

liaison 1. communication, connection, contact, go-between, hook-up, interchange, intermediary 2. affair, amour, entanglement, illicit romance, intrigue, love affair, romance

liar fabricator, falsifier, fibber, perjurer, prevaricator, storyteller (*Inf.*)

libel 1. *n.* aspersion, calumny, defamation, denigration, obloquy, slander, smear, vituperation 2. *v.* blacken, calumniate, defame, derogate, drag (someone's) name through the mud, malign, revile, slander, slur, smear, traduce, vilify

libellous aspersive, calumniatory, calumnious, defamatory, derogatory, false, injurious, malicious, maligning, scurrilous, slanderous, traducing, untrue, vilifying, vituperative

liberal 1. advanced, humanistic, latitudinarian, libertarian, progressive, radical, reformist 2. beneficent, bounteous, bountiful, charitable, free-handed, generous, kind, open-handed, open-hearted, unstinting 3. advanced, broad-minded, catholic, enlightened, high-minded, humanitarian, indulgent, magnanimous, permissive, tolerant, unbiased, unbigoted, unprejudiced 4. abundant, ample, bountiful, copious, handsome, lavish, munificent, plentiful, profuse, rich

liberality beneficence, benevolence, bounty, charity, free-handedness, generosity, kindness, largess, munificence, open-handedness, philanthropy

liberate deliver, discharge, disenthral, emancipate, free, let loose, let out, manumit, redeem, release, rescue, set free

liberation deliverance, emancipation, enfranchisement, freedom, freeing, liberating, liberty, manumission, redemption, release, unfettering, unshackling

liberator deliverer, emancipator, freer, manumitter, redeemer, rescuer, saviour

libertine 1. *n.* debauchee, lecher, loose liver, profligate, rake, reprobate, roué, seducer, sensualist, voluptuary, womanizer 2. *adj.* abandoned, corrupt, debauched, decadent, degenerate, depraved, dissolute, immoral, licentious, profligate, rakish, reprobate, voluptuous, wanton

liberty 1. autonomy, emancipation, freedom, immunity, independence, liberation, release, self-determination, sovereignty 2. authorization, carte blanche, dispensation, exemption, franchise, free-

libido (lɪˈbiːdəʊ) *n.* **1.** life force **2.** emotional craving, *esp.* of sexual origin (*pl.* **-s**) **—libidinous** (lɪˈbɪdɪnəs) *a.* lustful

Libra (ˈliːbrə) *n.* **1.** (balance) 7th sign of zodiac, operative *c.* Sept. 22nd–Oct. 22nd **2.** (ˈlaɪbrə) (**l-**) *Hist.* a pound weight (*pl.* **-brae** (-briː))

library (ˈlaɪbrərɪ) *n.* **1.** room, building where books are kept **2.** collection of books, gramophone records *etc.* **3.** reading, writing room in house **—liˈbrarian** *n.* keeper of library **—liˈbrarianship** *n.*

libretto (lɪˈbrɛtəʊ) *n.* words of an opera (*pl.* **-s, -ti** (-tiː)) **—liˈbrettist** *n.*

lice (laɪs) *n., pl. of* LOUSE

licence *or U.S.* **license** (ˈlaɪsəns) *n.* **1.** (document, certificate giving) leave, permission **2.** excessive liberty **3.** dissoluteness **4.** writer's, artist's transgression of rules of his art (*oft.* **poetic licence**) **—ˈlicense** *vt.* grant licence to **—licenˈsee** *n.* holder of licence **—liˈcentiate** *n.* one licensed to practise art, profession

licentious (laɪˈsɛnʃəs) *a.* **1.** dissolute **2.** sexually immoral **—liˈcentiously** *adv.*

lichee (laɪˈtʃiː) *n. see* LITCHI

lichen (ˈlaɪkən, ˈlɪtʃən) *n.* small flowerless plants forming crust on rocks, trees *etc.* **—ˈlichened** *a.* **—licheˈnology** *n.*

lich gate *or* **lych gate** (lɪtʃ) roofed gate of churchyard

licit (ˈlɪsɪt) *a. rare* lawful

lick (lɪk) *vt.* **1.** pass the tongue over **2.** touch lightly **3.** *sl.* defeat **4.** *sl.* flog, beat *—n.* **5.** act of licking **6.** small amount (*esp.* of paint *etc.*) **7.** block or natural deposit of salt or other chemical licked by cattle *etc.* **8.** *inf.* speed **—ˈlicking** *n. sl.* beating

licorice (ˈlɪkərɪs) *n. see* LIQUORICE

lid (lɪd) *n.* **1.** movable cover **2.** cover of the eye **3.** *sl.* hat

lido (ˈliːdəʊ) *n.* pleasure centre with swimming and boating (*pl.* **-s**)

lie[1] (laɪ) *vi.* **1.** be horizontal, at rest **2.** be situated **3.** remain, be in certain state or position **4.** exist, be found **5.** recline (**lay, lain, ˈlying**) *—n.* **6.** state (of affairs *etc.*) **7.** direction

lie[2] (laɪ) *vi.* **1.** make false statement (**lied, ˈlying**) *—n.* **2.** deliberate falsehood **—ˈliar** *n.* person who tells lies **—white lie** untruth said without evil intent **—give the lie to** disprove

lief (liːf) *adv.* **1.** *rare* gladly, willingly *—a. obs.* **2.** ready; glad **3.** dear, beloved

liege (liːdʒ) *a.* **1.** bound to render or receive feudal service **2.** faithful *—n.* **3.** lord **4.** vassal, subject

lien (lɪən, ˈliːən) *n.* right to hold another's property until claim is met

lieu (ljuː, luː) *n.* place **—in lieu (of)** instead (of)

lieutenant (lɛfˈtɛnənt; *in Navy,* ləˈtɛnənt; *U.S.* luːˈtɛnənt) *n.* **1.** deputy **2.** *Army* rank below captain **3.** *Navy* rank below commander **4.** US police officer **—lieutenant colonel** officer holding commissioned rank immediately junior to colonel in certain armies, air forces and marine corps **—lieutenant commander** officer holding commissioned rank immediately junior to commander in certain navies **—lieutenant general** officer holding commissioned rank immediately junior to general in certain armies, air forces and marine corps **—lieutenant governor 1.** deputy governor **2.** US elected official who acts as deputy to state governor **3.** C representative of Crown in province: appointed by federal government

life (laɪf) *n.* **1.** active principle of existence of animals and plants, animate existence **2.** time of its lasting **3.** history of such existence **4.** way of living **5.** vigour, vivacity (*pl.* **lives**) **—ˈlifeless** *a.* **1.** dead.**2.** inert **3.** dull **—life assurance** insurance providing for payment of specified sum to named beneficiary on death of policyholder (*also* **life insurance**) **—life belt** buoyant device to keep afloat person in danger of drowning **—ˈlifeblood** *n.* **1.** blood, considered as vital to life **2.** essential or animating force **—life buoy** buoyant device for keeping people afloat in emergency **—ˈlifeguard** *n.* person at beach or pool to guard people against risk of drowning **—life jacket** inflatable sleeveless jacket worn to keep person afloat when in danger of drowning **—ˈlifelike** *a.* closely resembling life **—ˈlifeline** *n.* **1.** line thrown or fired aboard vessel for hauling in hawser for breeches buoy **2.** line by which deep-sea diver is raised or lowered **3.** vital line

THESAURUS

dom, leave, licence, permission, prerogative, privilege, right, sanction **3. at liberty** free, not confined, on the loose, unlimited, unoccupied, unrestricted

libidinous carnal, concupiscent, debauched, impure, incontinent, lascivious, lecherous, lickerish (*Archaic*), loose, lustful, prurient, randy (*Sl., chiefly Brit.*), ruttish, salacious, sensual, unchaste, wanton, wicked

licence *n.* **1.** authority, authorization, carte blanche, certificate, charter, dispensation, entitlement, exemption, immunity, leave, liberty, permission, permit, privilege, right, warrant **2.** freedom, independence, latitude, liberty, self-determination **3.** abandon, anarchy, disorder, excess, immoderation, impropriety, indulgence, irresponsibility, lawlessness, laxity, profligacy, unruliness

license *v.* accredit, allow, authorize, certify, commission, empower, permit, sanction, warrant

licentious abandoned, debauched, disorderly, dissolute, immoral, impure, lascivious, lax, lewd, libertine, libidinous, lubricous, lustful, profligate, promiscuous, sensual, uncontrollable, uncontrolled, uncurbed, unruly, wanton

lick *v.* **1.** brush, lap, taste, tongue, touch, wash **2.** *Inf.* **a.** defeat, overcome, rout, trounce, vanquish, wipe the floor with (*Inf.*) **b.** beat, flog, slap, spank, strike, thrash, wallop (*Inf.*) **c.** beat, best, excel, outdo, outstrip, surpass, top *~n.* **3.** bit, brush, dab, little, sample, speck, stroke, taste, touch

licking 1. beating, drubbing, flogging, hiding (*Inf.*), spanking, tanning (*Sl.*), thrashing, whipping **2.** beating, defeat, drubbing, trouncing

lie[1] *v.* **1.** be prone, be prostrate, be recumbent, be supine, couch, loll, lounge, recline, repose, rest, sprawl, stretch out **2.** be, be buried, be found, be interred, be located, belong, be placed, be situated, exist, extend, remain **3.** *Usually with* **in** be present, consist, dwell, exist, inhere, pertain

lie[2] **1.** *v.* dissimulate, equivocate, fabricate, falsify, fib, forswear oneself, invent, misrepresent, perjure, prevaricate, tell a lie, tell untruths **2.** *n.* deceit, fabrication, falsehood, falsification, falsity, fib, fiction, invention, mendacity, prevarication, untruth, white lie

of access or communication —ˈ**lifelong** *a.* lasting a lifetime —**life preserver 1.** UK club kept for self-defence **2.** US life belt; life jacket —**life-size** *or* **life-sized** *a.* representing actual size —**life style** particular attitudes, habits *etc.* of person or group —ˈ**lifetime** *n.* length of time person, animal or object lives or functions

lift (lɪft) *vt.* **1.** raise in position, status, mood, volume *etc.* **2.** take up and remove **3.** exalt spiritually **4.** *inf.* steal —*vi.* **5.** rise —*n.* **6.** raising apparatus **7.** cage raised and lowered in vertical shaft to transport people or goods **8.** act of lifting **9.** ride in car *etc.* as passenger **10.** air force acting at right angles on aircraft wing, so lifting it **11.** *inf.* feeling of cheerfulness, uplift —ˈ**liftoff** *n.* **1.** initial movement of rocket from launching pad **2.** instant at which this occurs —**lift off** (of rocket) leave launching pad

ligament (ˈlɪgəmənt) *n.* band of tissue joining bones —ˈ**ligature** *n.* **1.** anything which binds **2.** thread for tying up artery **3.** *Print.* character of two or more joined letters

light[1] (laɪt) *a.* **1.** of, or bearing little weight **2.** not severe **3.** gentle **4.** easy, requiring little effort **5.** trivial **6.** (of industry) producing small, usu. consumer goods, using light machinery —*adv.* **7.** in light manner —*vi.* **8.** alight (from vehicle *etc.*) **9.** (*with* on *or* upon) come by chance (upon) (ˈ**lighted, lit** *pt./pp.*) —ˈ**lighten** *vt.* reduce, remove (load *etc.*) —ˈ**lightly** *adv.* —ˈ**lightness** *n.* —**lights** *pl.n.* lungs of animals —**light-fingered** *a.* having nimble fingers, *esp.* for thieving or picking pockets —**light flyweight** amateur boxer weighing not more than 48 kg (106 lbs) —**light-headed** *a.* **1.** dizzy, inclined to faint **2.** delirious —**light-hearted** *a.* carefree —**light heavyweight 1.** professional boxer weighing 72.5–79.5 kg (160–175 lbs) **2.** amateur boxer weighing 75–81 kg (165–179 lbs) (*also* (**UK**) ˈ**cruiserweight**) **3.** wrestler weighing usu. 87–97 kg (192–214 lbs) —**light middleweight** amateur boxer weighing 67–71 kg (148–157 lbs) —**light-minded** *a.* frivolous —ˈ**lightweight** *n./a.* (person) of little weight or importance —**light welterweight** amateur boxer weighing 60–63.5 kg (132–140 lbs)

light[2] (laɪt) *n.* **1.** electromagnetic radiation by which things are visible **2.** source of this, lamp **3.** window **4.** mental vision **5.** light part of anything **6.** means or act of setting fire to something **7.** understanding —*pl.* **8.** traffic lights —*a.* **9.** bright **10.** pale, not dark —*vt.* **11.** set burning **12.** give light to —*vi.* **13.** take fire **14.** brighten (ˈ**lighted, lit** *pt./pp.*) —ˈ**lighten** *vt.* give light to —ˈ**lighting** *n.* apparatus for supplying artificial light —ˈ**lightning** *n.* visible discharge of electricity in atmosphere —ˈ**lighthouse** *n.* tower with a light to guide ships —**light year** *Astron.* distance light travels in one year, about six million million miles

lighter (ˈlaɪtə) *n.* **1.** device for lighting cigarettes *etc.* **2.** flat-bottomed boat for unloading ships

THESAURUS

life 1. animation, being, breath, entity, growth, sentience, viability, vitality **2.** being, career, continuance, course, duration, existence, lifetime, span, time **3.** autobiography, biography, career, confessions, history, life story, memoirs, story **4.** behaviour, conduct, life style, way of life **5.** activity, animation, brio, energy, get-up-and-go (*Inf.*), go (*Inf.*), high spirits, liveliness, oomph (*Inf.*), sparkle, spirit, verve, vigour, vitality, vivacity, zest **6.** creatures, living beings, living things, organisms, wildlife

lifeless 1. cold, dead, deceased, defunct, extinct, inanimate, inert **2.** cold, colourless, dull, flat, heavy, hollow, lacklustre, lethargic, listless, passive, pointless, slow, sluggish, spent, spiritless, static, stiff, torpid, wooden **3.** comatose, dead to the world, in a faint, inert, insensate, insensible, out cold, out for six, unconscious

lifelike authentic, exact, faithful, graphic, natural, photographic, real, realistic, true-to-life, undistorted, vivid

lifelong constant, enduring, for all one's life, for life, lasting, lifetime, long-lasting, long-standing, perennial, permanent, persistent

lifetime all one's born days, career, course, day(s), existence, life span, one's natural life, period, span, time

lift *v.* **1.** bear aloft, buoy up, draw up, elevate, heft (*Inf.*), hoist, pick up, raise, raise high, rear, upheave, uplift, upraise **2.** advance, ameliorate, boost, dignify, elevate, enhance, exalt, improve, promote, raise, upgrade **3.** ascend, climb, mount, rise **4.** *Inf.* appropriate, copy, crib (*Inf.*), half-inch (*Brit. sl.*), nick (*Sl., chiefly Brit.*), pilfer, pinch (*Inf.*), pirate, plagiarize, pocket, purloin, steal, take, thieve ~*n.* **5.** car ride, drive, ride, run, transport **6.** boost, encouragement, fillip, pick-me-up, reassurance, shot in the arm (*Inf.*), uplift **7.** elevator (*Chiefly U.S.*)

light[1] *adj.* **1.** airy, buoyant, delicate, easy, flimsy, imponderous, insubstantial, lightsome, lightweight, portable, slight, underweight **2.** faint, gentle, indistinct, mild, moderate, slight, soft, weak **3.** inconsequential, inconsiderable, insignificant, minute, scanty, slight, small, thin, tiny, trifling, trivial, unsubstantial, wee **4.** cushy (*Sl.*), easy, effortless, manageable, moderate, simple, undemanding, unexacting, untaxing ~*v.* **5.** alight, land, perch, settle **6.** *With* **on** *or* **upon** chance, come across, discover, encounter, find, happen upon, hit upon, stumble on

light[2] *n.* **1.** blaze, brightness, brilliance, effulgence, flash, glare, gleam, glint, glow, illumination, incandescence, lambency, luminescence, luminosity, lustre, phosphorescence, radiance, ray, refulgence, scintillation, shine, sparkle **2.** beacon, bulb, candle, flare, lamp, lantern, lighthouse, star, taper, torch, windowpane **3.** awareness, comprehension, elucidation, explanation, illustration, information, insight, knowledge, understanding **4.** flame, lighter, match ~*adj.* **5.** aglow, bright, brilliant, glowing, illuminated, luminous, lustrous, shining, sunny, well-lighted, well-lit **6.** bleached, blond, faded, fair, light-hued, light-toned, pale, pastel ~*v.* **7.** fire, ignite, inflame, kindle, set a match to **8.** brighten, clarify, floodlight, flood with light, illuminate, illumine, irradiate, lighten, light up, put on, switch on, turn on **9.** animate, brighten, cheer, irradiate, lighten

lighten[1] **1.** disburden, ease, make lighter, reduce in weight, unload **2.** alleviate, ameliorate, assuage, ease, facilitate, lessen, mitigate, reduce, relieve

lighten[2] become light, brighten, flash, gleam, illuminate, irradiate, light up, make bright, shine

light-fingered crafty, crooked (*Inf.*), dishonest, furtive, pilfering, pinching (*Inf.*), shifty, sly, stealing, thieving, underhand

light-headed delirious, dizzy, faint, giddy, hazy, vertiginous, woozy (*Inf.*)

light-hearted blithe, blithesome (*Literary*), bright,

ligneous (ˈlɪgnɪəs) *a.* of, or of the nature of, wood —**ˈlignite** *n.* woody or brown coal

lignin (ˈlɪgnɪn) *n.* organic substance which forms characteristic part of all woody fibres

lignum vitae (ˈlɪgnəm ˈvaɪtɪ) *Lat.* **1.** tropical tree **2.** its extremely hard wood

like[1] (laɪk) *a.* **1.** resembling **2.** similar to **3.** characteristic of —*adv.* **4.** in the manner of —*n.* **5.** similar thing —**ˈlikelihood** *n.* probability —**ˈlikely** *a.* **1.** probable **2.** hopeful, promising —*adv.* **3.** probably —**ˈliken** *vt.* compare —**ˈlikeness** *n.* **1.** resemblance **2.** portrait —**ˈlikewise** *adv.* **1.** in addition; moreover; also **2.** in like manner

like[2] (laɪk) *vt.* find agreeable, enjoy, love —**ˈlikable** *or* **ˈlikeable** *a.* —**ˈliking** *n.* **1.** fondness **2.** inclination, taste

-like (*comb. form*) **1.** resembling, similar to, as in *lifelike* **2.** having characteristics of, as in *childlike*

lilac (ˈlaɪlək) *n.* **1.** shrub bearing pale mauve or white flowers **2.** pale mauve colour —*a.* **3.** of lilac colour

Lilliputian (lɪlɪˈpjuːʃɪən) *a.* **1.** diminutive —*n.* **2.** midget, pygmy

Lilo (ˈlaɪləʊ) *n.* **R** inflatable rubber mattress (*pl.* **-s**)

lilt (lɪlt) *vi.* **1.** (of melody) have a lilt **2.** move lightly —*n.* **3.** rhythmical effect in music, swing —**ˈlilting** *a.*

lily (ˈlɪlɪ) *n.* bulbous flowering plant —**lily-livered** *a.* cowardly; timid —**lily-white** *a.* **1.** of a pure white **2.** *inf.* pure; irreproachable —**lily of the valley** small garden plant with fragrant, white bell-like flowers

limb[1] (lɪm) *n.* **1.** arm or leg **2.** wing **3.** branch of tree —**limbed** *a.* **1.** having limbs **2.** having specified number or kind of limbs

limb[2] (lɪm) *n.* **1.** edge of sun or moon **2.** edge of sextant

limber[1] (ˈlɪmbə) *n.* detachable front of gun carriage

limber[2] (ˈlɪmbə) *a.* pliant, lithe —**limber up** loosen stiff muscles by exercises

limbo[1] (ˈlɪmbəʊ) *n.* **1.** (*oft.* **L-**) supposed region intermediate between Heaven and Hell for the unbaptised **2.** intermediate, indeterminate place or state (*pl.* **-s**)

limbo[2] (ˈlɪmbəʊ) *n.* W Indian dance in which dancers pass under a bar (*pl.* **-s**)

lime[1] (laɪm) *n.* **1.** any of certain calcium compounds used in making fertilizer, cement —*vt.* **2.** treat (land) with lime —**ˈlimy** *a.* of, like or smeared with birdlime —**ˈlimekiln** *n.* kiln in which calcium carbonate is calcined to produce quicklime —**ˈlimelight** *n.* **1.** formerly, intense white light obtained by heating lime **2.** glare of publicity —**ˈlimestone** *n.* sedimentary rock used in building

lime[2] (laɪm) *n.* small acid fruit like lemon —**ˈlimy** *a.* —**lime juice** juice of lime prepared as drink

lime[3] (laɪm) *n.* tree, the linden

limerick (ˈlɪmərɪk) *n.* self-contained, nonsensical, humorous verse of five lines

limey (ˈlaɪmɪ) *n.* **US** *sl.* British person

limit (ˈlɪmɪt) *n.* **1.** utmost extent or duration **2.** boundary —*vt.* **3.** restrict, restrain, bound —**ˈlimitable** *a.* —**limiˈtation** *n.* —**ˈlimited** *a.* **1.** restricted; confined **2.** without scope; narrow **3.** (of governing powers *etc.*) restricted or checked, by or as if by constitution, laws or assembly **4.** *chiefly* **UK** (of business enterprise) owned by shareholders whose liability for enterprise's debts is restricted —**ˈlimitless** *a.* —**limited company** —**limited liability** principle whereby liability of shareholder is in proportion to amount of his stock

THESAURUS

carefree, cheerful, effervescent, frolicsome, gay, glad, gleeful, happy-go-lucky, insouciant, jocund, jolly, jovial, joyful, joyous, merry, playful, sunny, untroubled, upbeat (*Inf.*)

lightly **1.** airily, delicately, faintly, gently, gingerly, slightly, softly, timidly **2.** easily, effortlessly, readily, simply

lightweight *adj.* inconsequential, insignificant, of no account, paltry, petty, slight, trifling, trivial, unimportant, worthless

likable, likeable agreeable, amiable, appealing, attractive, charming, engaging, friendly, genial, nice, pleasant, pleasing, sympathetic, winning, winsome

like[1] **1.** *adj.* akin, alike, allied, analogous, approximating, cognate, corresponding, equivalent, identical, parallel, relating, resembling, same, similar **2.** *n.* counterpart, equal, fellow, match, parallel, twin

like[2] *v.* **1.** adore (*Inf.*), be fond of, be keen on, be partial to, delight in, dig (*Sl.*), enjoy, go for (*Sl.*), love, relish, revel in **2.** admire, appreciate, approve, cherish, esteem, hold dear, prize, take a shine to (*Inf.*), take to **3.** care to, choose, choose to, desire, fancy, feel inclined, prefer, select, want, wish

likelihood chance, good chance, liability, likeliness, possibility, probability, prospect, reasonableness, strong possibility

likely *adj.* **1.** anticipated, apt, disposed, expected, in a fair way, inclined, liable, on the cards, possible, probable, prone, tending, to be expected **2.** fair, favourite, hopeful, odds-on, promising, up-and-coming ~*adv.* **3.** doubtlessly, in all probability, like as not (*Inf.*), like enough (*Inf.*), no doubt, presumably, probably

liken compare, equate, juxtapose, match, parallel, relate, set beside

likeness **1.** affinity, correspondence, resemblance, similarity, similitude **2.** copy, counterpart, delineation, depiction, effigy, facsimile, image, model, photograph, picture, portrait, replica, representation, reproduction, study

liking affection, affinity, appreciation, attraction, bent, bias, desire, fondness, inclination, love, partiality, penchant, predilection, preference, proneness, propensity, soft spot, stomach, taste, tendency, weakness

limb **1.** appendage, arm, extension, extremity, leg, member, part, wing **2.** bough, branch, offshoot, projection, spur

limelight attention, celebrity, fame, glare of publicity, prominence, public eye, publicity, public notice, recognition, stardom, the spotlight

limit *n.* **1.** bound, breaking point, cutoff point, deadline, end, end point, furthest bound, greatest extent, termination, the bitter end, ultimate, utmost **2.** *Often plural* border, boundary, confines, edge, end, extent, frontier, perimeter, periphery, precinct ~*v.* **3.** bound, check, circumscribe, confine, curb, delimit, demarcate, fix, hem in, hinder, ration, restrain, restrict, specify

limitation block, check, condition, constraint, control, curb, disadvantage, drawback, impediment, obstruction, qualification, reservation, restraint, restriction, snag

limn (lɪm) *vt.* paint; depict; draw —**limner** (ˈlɪmnə) *n.*

limousine (ˈlɪməziːn, lɪməˈziːn) *n.* large, luxurious car

limp[1] (lɪmp) *a.* without firmness or stiffness —**ˈlimply** *adv.*

limp[2] (lɪmp) *vi.* **1.** walk lamely —*n.* **2.** limping gait

limpet (ˈlɪmpɪt) *n.* shellfish which sticks tightly to rocks

limpid (ˈlɪmpɪd) *a.* **1.** clear **2.** translucent —**limˈpidity** *n.* —**ˈlimpidly** *adv.*

linchpin (ˈlɪntʃpɪn) *n.* **1.** pin to hold wheel on its axle **2.** essential person or thing

Lincs. (lɪŋks) Lincolnshire

linctus (ˈlɪŋktəs) *n.* syrupy cough medicine

linden (ˈlɪndən) *n.* deciduous tree with fragrant flowers, the lime

line (laɪn) *n.* **1.** long narrow mark **2.** stroke made with pen *etc.* **3.** continuous length without breadth **4.** row **5.** series, course **6.** telephone connection **7.** progeny **8.** province of activity **9.** shipping company **10.** railway track **11.** any class of goods **12.** cord **13.** string **14.** wire **15.** advice, guidance **16.** *inf.* medical certificate —*vt.* **17.** cover inside of **18.** mark with lines **19.** bring into line **20.** be, form border, edge of —**ˈlinage** *n.* **1.** number of lines in piece of written or printed matter **2.** payment for written material according to number of lines —**lineage** (ˈlɪnɪɪdʒ) *n.* descent from, descendants of an ancestor —**lineal** (ˈlɪnɪəl) *a.* **1.** of lines **2.** in direct line of descent —**lineament** (ˈlɪnɪəmənt) *n.* (*oft.pl.*) feature —**linear** (ˈlɪnɪə) *a.* of, in lines —**lineation** (lɪnɪˈeɪʃən) *n.* **1.** marking with lines **2.** arrangement of or division into lines —**ˈliner** *n.* large ship or aircraft of passenger line —**ˈlining** *n.* covering for inside of garment *etc.* —**linear measure** system of units for measurement of length —**line drawing** drawing made with lines only —**line printer** electromechanical device that prints a line of characters at a time —**ˈlinesman** *n.* in some sports, official who helps referee, umpire —**line-up** *n.* **1.** row or arrangement of people or things assembled for particular purpose **2.** members of such row or arrangement —**get a line on** obtain all relevant information about —**line of fire** flight path of missile discharged from firearm —**line up 1.** form, put into or organize line-up **2.** produce, organize and assemble **3.** align

linen (ˈlɪnɪn) *a.* **1.** made of flax —*n.* **2.** cloth made of flax **3.** linen articles collectively **4.** sheets, tablecloths *etc.;* shirts (orig. made of linen)

ling[1] (lɪŋ) *n.* slender food fish

ling[2] (lɪŋ) *n.* heather

-ling (*comb. form*) **1.** *oft. disparaging* person or thing associated with group, activity or quality specified, as in *nestling, underling* **2.** diminutive, as in *duckling*

linger (ˈlɪŋgə) *vi.* delay, loiter, remain long

lingerie (ˈlænʒərɪ) *n.* women's underwear or nightwear

lingo (ˈlɪŋgəʊ) *n. inf.* language, speech, *esp.* applied to dialects (*pl.* **-es**)

lingua franca (ˈlɪŋgwə ˈfræŋkə) *It.* language used for communication between people of different mother tongues (*pl.* **lingua francas, linguae francae** (ˈlɪŋgwiː ˈfrænsiː))

lingual (ˈlɪŋgwəl) *a.* **1.** of the tongue or language —*n.* **2.** sound made by the tongue, as *d, l, t* —**ˈlinguist** *n.* one skilled in languages or language study —**linˈguistic** *a.* of languages or their study —**linˈguistics** *pl.n.* (*with sing. v.*) study, science of language

liniment (ˈlɪnɪmənt) *n.* embrocation

link (lɪŋk) *n.* **1.** ring of a chain **2.** connection **3.** measure, 1-100th part of chain —*vt.* **4.** join with, as with, link **5.** intertwine —*vi.* **6.** be so joined —**ˈlinkage** *n.* —**ˈlinkman** *n.* presenter of television or radio programme consisting of number of outside broadcasts from different locations

links (lɪŋks) *pl.n.* golf course

linnet (ˈlɪnɪt) *n.* songbird of finch family

lino (ˈlaɪnəʊ) linoleum

linocut (ˈlaɪnəʊkʌt) *n.* **1.** design cut in relief on block of linoleum **2.** print from this

linoleum (lɪˈnəʊlɪəm) *n.* floor covering of hessian with smooth, hard, decorative coating of powdered cork, linseed oil *etc.*

THESAURUS

limited 1. bounded, checked, circumscribed, confined, constrained, controlled, curbed, defined, finite, fixed, hampered, hemmed in, restricted **2.** cramped, diminished, inadequate, insufficient, minimal, narrow, reduced, restricted, short, unsatisfactory

limitless boundless, countless, endless, illimitable, immeasurable, immense, inexhaustible, infinite, measureless, never-ending, numberless, unbounded, uncalculable, undefined, unending, unlimited, untold, vast

limp[1] drooping, flabby, flaccid, flexible, floppy, lax, limber, loose, pliable, relaxed, slack, soft

limp[2] **1.** *v.* falter, halt (*Archaic*), hobble, hop, shamble, shuffle **2.** *n.* hobble, lameness

line *n.* **1.** band, bar, channel, dash, groove, mark, rule, score, scratch, streak, stripe, stroke, underline **2.** crease, crow's foot, furrow, mark, wrinkle **3.** cable, cord, filament, rope, strand, string, thread, wire **4.** axis, course, direction, path, route, track, trajectory **5.** activity, area, business, calling, department, employment, field, forte, interest, job, occupation, profession, province, pursuit, specialization, trade, vocation **6.** column, crocodile (*Brit.*), file, procession, queue, rank, row, sequence, series **7.** ancestry, breed, family, lineage, race, stock, strain, succession ~*v.* **8.** crease, cut, draw, furrow, inscribe, mark, rule, score, trace, underline **9.** border, bound, edge, fringe, rank, rim, skirt, verge **10.** ceil, cover, face, fill, interline

lineaments configuration, countenance, face, features, line, outline, phiz *or* phizog (*Sl., chiefly Brit.*), physiognomy, trait, visage

line-up arrangement, array, row, selection, team

line up 1. fall in, form ranks, queue up **2.** assemble, come up with, lay on, obtain, organize, prepare, procure, produce, secure **3.** align, arrange, array, marshal, order, range, regiment, straighten

linger 1. hang around, loiter, remain, stay, stop, tarry, wait **2.** dally, dawdle, delay, idle, lag, procrastinate, take one's time **3.** abide, continue, endure, persist, remain, stay

link *n.* **1.** association, attachment, bond, connection, joint, knot, relationship, tie, tie-up, vinculum ~*v.* **2.** attach, bind, connect, couple, fasten, join, tie, unite, yoke **3.** associate, bracket, connect, identify, relate

linseed (ˈlɪnsiːd) *n.* seed of flax plant —**linseed oil** yellow oil extracted from it

linsey-woolsey (ˈlɪnzɪˈwʊlzɪ) *n.* rough fabric of linen warp and coarse wool or cotton filling

lint (lɪnt) *n.* soft material for dressing wounds

lintel (ˈlɪntᵊl) *n.* top piece of door or window

lion (ˈlaɪən) *n.* large animal of cat family (**ˈlioness** *fem.*) —**ˈlionize** *or* **-ise** *vt.* treat as celebrity —**lion-hearted** *a.* brave —**the lion's share** largest portion

lip (lɪp) *n.* **1.** either edge of the mouth **2.** edge or margin **3.** *sl.* impudence —**lip-reading** *n.* method of understanding spoken words by interpreting movements of speaker's lips —**lip salve** ointment for the lips —**lip service** insincere tribute or respect —**ˈlipstick** *n.* cosmetic preparation in stick form, for colouring lips

liqueur (lɪˈkjʊə; *Fr.* liˈkœːr) *n.* alcoholic liquor flavoured and sweetened

liquid (ˈlɪkwɪd) *a.* **1.** fluid, not solid or gaseous **2.** flowing smoothly **3.** (of assets) in form of money or easily converted into money —*n.* **4.** substance in liquid form —**liqueˈfaction** *or* **liquiˈfaction** *n.* —**ˈliquefy** *or* **ˈliquify** *v.* make or become liquid —**liˈquescence** *n.* —**liˈquescent** *a.* tending to become liquid —**ˈliquidize** *or* **-dise** *v.* —**ˈliquidizer** *or* **-diser** *n.* kitchen appliance with blades for puréeing vegetables, blending liquids *etc.* (*also* **ˈblender**) —**liquid air** *or* **gas** air or gas reduced to liquid state on application of increased pressure at low temperature —**liquid crystal display** display of numbers, *esp.* in electronic calculator, using cells containing a liquid with crystalline properties, that change their reflectivity when an electric field is applied to them —**liquid fuel** petrol, paraffin oil *etc.*, carried in liquid form and vaporized for combustion —**liquid measure** system of units for measuring volumes of liquids or their containers

liquidate (ˈlɪkwɪdeɪt) *vt.* **1.** pay (debt) **2.** arrange affairs of and dissolve (company) **3.** wipe out, kill —**liquiˈdation** *n.* **1.** process of clearing up financial affairs **2.** state of being bankrupt —**ˈliquidator** *n.* official appointed to liquidate business —**liˈquidity** *n.* state of being able to meet financial obligations

liquor (ˈlɪkə) *n.* liquid, *esp.* an alcoholic one

liquorice *or U.S.* **licorice** (ˈlɪkərɪs, -ərɪʃ) *n.* **1.** black substance used in medicine and as a sweet **2.** plant or its root from which liquorice is obtained

lira (ˈlɪərə; *It.* ˈliːra) *n.* monetary unit of Italy and Turkey (*pl.* **lire** (ˈlɪərɪ; *It.* ˈliːre), **-s**)

lisle (laɪl) *n.* fine hand-twisted cotton thread

lisp (lɪsp) *vi.* **1.** speak with faulty pronunciation of 's' and 'z' **2.** speak falteringly —*n.* **3.** such pronunciation or speech

lissom *or* **lissome** (ˈlɪsəm) *a.* **1.** supple **2.** agile

list[1] (lɪst) *n.* **1.** inventory, register **2.** catalogue **3.** edge of cloth —*pl.* **4.** field for combat —*vt.* **5.** place on list —**listed building** UK building officially recognized as having historical or architectural interest and therefore protected from demolition or alteration —**list price** selling price of merchandise as quoted in catalogue or advertisement

list[2] (lɪst) *vi.* **1.** (of ship) lean to one side —*n.* **2.** inclination of ship

listen (ˈlɪsᵊn) *vi.* try to hear, attend (to) —**ˈlistener** *n.*

listless (ˈlɪstlɪs) *a.* indifferent, languid —**ˈlistlessly** *adv.*

lit (lɪt) *pt./pp. of* LIGHT[1], LIGHT[2]

litany (ˈlɪtənɪ) *n.* prayer with responses from congregation

litchi, lichee, *or* **lychee** (laɪˈtʃiː) *n.* **1.** Chinese tree with red edible fruits **2.** fruit of this tree, which has whitish juicy pulp and is usu. eaten dried or as preserve —**litchi nut** dried fruit of this tree

literal (ˈlɪtərəl) *a.* **1.** according to sense of actual words, not figurative **2.** exact in wording **3.** of letters —**ˈliteralism** *n.* **1.** disposition to take words and statements in literal sense **2.** literal or realistic portrayal in art or literature —**ˈliterally** *adv.*

literate (ˈlɪtərɪt) *a.* **1.** able to read and write **2.**

THESAURUS

lip 1. brim, brink, edge, margin, rim **2.** *Sl.* backchat (*Inf.*), cheek (*Inf.*), effrontery, impertinence, insolence, rudeness, sauce (*Inf.*)

liquid *n.* **1.** fluid, juice, liquor, solution *~adj.* **2.** aqueous, flowing, fluid, liquefied, melted, molten, running, runny, thawed, wet **3.** *Of assets* convertible, negotiable

liquidate 1. clear, discharge, honour, pay, pay off, settle, square **2.** abolish, annul, cancel, dissolve, terminate **3.** annihilate, bump off (*Sl.*), destroy, dispatch, do away with, do in (*Sl.*), eliminate, exterminate, finish off, get rid of, kill, murder, remove, rub out (*U.S. sl.*), silence, wipe out (*Inf.*)

liquor 1. alcohol, booze (*Inf.*), drink, grog, hard stuff (*Inf.*), hooch (*Sl., chiefly U.S.*), intoxicant, juice (*Inf.*), spirits, strong drink **2.** broth, extract, gravy, infusion, juice, liquid, stock

list[1] **1.** *n.* catalogue, directory, file, index, inventory, invoice, leet (*Scot.*), listing, record, register, roll, schedule, series, syllabus, tabulation, tally **2.** *v.* bill, book, catalogue, enrol, enter, enumerate, file, index, itemize, note, record, register, schedule, set down, tabulate, write down

list[2] **1.** *v.* cant, careen, heel, heel over, incline, lean, tilt, tip **2.** *n.* cant, leaning, slant, tilt

listen 1. attend, be all ears, be attentive, give ear, hang on (someone's) words, hark, hear, hearken (*Archaic*), keep one's ears open, lend an ear, pin back one's ears (*Inf.*), prick up one's ears **2.** concentrate, do as one is told, give heed to, heed, mind, obey, observe, pay attention, take notice

listless apathetic, enervated, heavy, impassive, inattentive, indifferent, indolent, inert, languid, languishing, lethargic, lifeless, limp, lymphatic, mopish, sluggish, spiritless, supine, torpid, vacant

literacy ability, articulacy, articulateness, cultivation, education, knowledge, learning, proficiency, scholarship

literal accurate, close, exact, faithful, strict, verbatim, word for word

literally actually, exactly, faithfully, plainly, precisely, really, simply, strictly, to the letter, truly, verbatim, word for word

literary bookish, erudite, learned, lettered, literate, scholarly, well-read

literate cultivated, cultured, educated, erudite, informed, knowledgeable, learned, lettered, scholarly, well-informed, well-read

educated —*n.* 3. literate person —'**literacy** *n.* —**literati** (lɪtə'rɑːtiː) *pl.n.* scholarly, literary people

literature ('lɪtərɪtʃə, 'lɪtrɪ-) *n.* 1. books and writings, *esp.* of particular country, period or subject 2. *inf.* printed material —'**literarily** *adv.* —'**literary** *a.* of or learned in literature

lithe (laɪð) *a.* supple, pliant —'**lithesome** *a.* lissom, supple

lithium ('lɪθɪəm) *n.* one of the lightest alkaline metals

litho ('laɪθəʊ) *n.* 1. lithography 2. lithograph (*pl.* -**s**) —*a.* 3. lithographic —*adv.* 4. lithographically

litho- *or before vowel* **lith-** (*comb. form*) stone, as in *lithograph*

lithography (lɪ'θɒgrəfɪ) *n.* method of printing from metal or stone block using the antipathy of grease and water —'**lithograph** *n.* 1. print so produced —*vt.* 2. print thus —**li'thographer** *n.* —**litho'graphic** *a.*

litigate ('lɪtɪgeɪt) *vt.* 1. contest in law —*vi.* 2. carry on a lawsuit —'**litigant** *n./a.* (person) conducting a lawsuit —**liti'gation** *n.* lawsuit —**litigious** (lɪ'tɪdʒəs) *a.* 1. given to engaging in lawsuits 2. disputatious

litmus ('lɪtməs) *n.* blue dye turned red by acids and restored to blue by alkali —**litmus paper**

litotes ('laɪtəʊtiːz) *n.* ironical understatement for rhetorical effect (*pl.* -**tes**)

litre *or U.S.* **liter** ('liːtə) *n.* measure of volume of fluid, one cubic decimetre, about 1.75 pints

Litt.D. *or* **Lit.D.** 1. Doctor of Letters 2. Doctor of Literature

litter ('lɪtə) *n.* 1. untidy refuse 2. odds and ends 3. young of animal produced at one birth 4. straw *etc.* as bedding for animals 5. portable couch 6. kind of stretcher for wounded —*v.* 7. strew (with) litter 8. give birth to (young) —**litter lout** *or U.S.* '**litterbug** *n. sl.* person who drops refuse in public places

little ('lɪt'l) *a.* 1. small, not much (**less, least**) —*n.* 2. small quantity —*adv.* 3. to a small extent 4. not much or often 5. not at all (**less, least**) —**little people** *Folklore* small supernatural beings, such as leprechauns —**the Little Bear** Ursa Minor

littoral ('lɪtərəl) *a.* 1. pert. to the seashore —*n.* 2. coastal district

liturgy ('lɪtədʒɪ) *n.* prescribed form of public worship —**li'turgical** *a.*

live[1] (lɪv) *v.* 1. have life 2. pass one's life 3. continue in life 4. continue, last 5. dwell 6. feed —'**livable** *or* '**liveable** *a.* 1. suitable for living in 2. tolerable —'**liver** *n.* person who lives in specified way —'**living** *n.* 1. action of being in life 2. people now alive 3. way of life 4. means of living 5. church benefice —**living room** room in house used for relaxation and entertainment —**living wage** wage adequate to maintain person and his family in reasonable comfort

live[2] (laɪv) *a.* 1. living, alive 2. active, vital 3. flaming 4. (of rail *etc.*) carrying electric current 5. (of broadcast) transmitted during the actual performance —'**liveliness** *n.* —'**lively** *a.* brisk, active, vivid —'**liven** *vt.* (*esp. with* up) make (more) lively —'**livestock** *n.* domestic animals —**live wire** 1. wire carrying electric current 2. able, very energetic person

livelihood ('laɪvlɪhʊd) *n.* 1. means of living 2. subsistence, support

livelong ('lɪvlɒŋ) *a.* lasting throughout the whole day

liver ('lɪvə) *n.* 1. organ secreting bile 2. animal liver as

THESAURUS

literature 1. belles-lettres, letters, lore, writings, written works 2. brochure, information, leaflet, pamphlet

lithe flexible, limber, lissom, loose-jointed, loose-limbed, pliable, pliant, supple

litigant claimant, contestant, disputant, litigator, party, plaintiff

litigate contest at law, file a suit, go to court, go to law, institute legal proceedings, press charges, prosecute, sue

litigation action, case, contending, disputing, lawsuit, process, prosecution

litigious argumentative, belligerent, contentious, disputatious, quarrelsome

litter *n.* 1. debris, detritus, fragments, muck, refuse, rubbish, shreds 2. brood, family, offspring, progeny, young 3. bedding, couch, floor cover, mulch, straw-bed 4. palanquin, stretcher ~*v.* 5. clutter, derange, disarrange, disorder, mess up, scatter, strew

little *adj.* 1. diminutive, dwarf, elfin, infinitesimal, Lilliputian, mini, miniature, minute, petite, pygmy, short, slender, small, tiny, wee 2. hardly any, insufficient, meagre, scant, skimpy, small, sparse ~*adv.* 3. barely, hardly, not much, not quite, only just 4. hardly ever, not often, rarely, scarcely, seldom ~*n.* 5. bit, dab, dash, fragment, hint, modicum, particle, pinch, small amount, snippet, speck, spot, taste, touch, trace, trifle

live[1] *v.* 1. be, be alive, breathe, draw breath, exist, have life 2. be permanent, be remembered, last, persist, prevail, remain alive 3. *Sometimes with* **in** abide, dwell, hang out (*Inf.*), inhabit, lodge, occupy, reside, settle, stay (*Chiefly Scot.*) 4. abide, continue, earn a living, endure, fare, feed, get along, lead, make ends meet, pass, remain, subsist, support oneself, survive

live[2] *adj.* 1. alive, animate, breathing, existent, living, quick (*Archaic*), vital 2. active, burning, controversial, current, hot, pertinent, pressing, prevalent, topical, unsettled, vital 3. *Inf.* active, alert, brisk, dynamic, earnest, energetic, lively, vigorous, vivid, wide-awake 4. active, alight, blazing, burning, connected, glowing, hot, ignited, smouldering, switched on

livelihood employment, job, living, maintenance, means, (means of) support, occupation, (source of) income, subsistence, sustenance, work

liveliness activity, animation, boisterousness, briskness, dynamism, energy, gaiety, quickness, smartness, spirit, sprightliness, vitality, vivacity

lively 1. active, agile, alert, brisk, chipper (*Inf.*), chirpy, energetic, full of pep (*Inf.*), keen, nimble, perky, quick, sprightly, spry, vigorous 2. astir, bustling, busy, buzzing, crowded, eventful, moving, stirring 3. bright, colourful, exciting, forceful, invigorating, racy, refreshing, stimulating, vivid

liven animate, brighten, buck up (*Inf.*), enliven, hot up (*Inf.*), pep up, perk up, put life into, rouse, stir, vitalize, vivify

liverish 1. bilious, queasy, sick 2. crotchety (*Inf.*), crusty, disagreeable, fratchy (*Inf.*), grumpy, ill-humoured, irascible, irritable, peevish, snappy, splenetic

food —**ˈliverish** *a.* 1. unwell, as from liver upset 2. cross, touchy, irritable

liverwort (ˈlɪvəwɜːt) *n.* plant growing in wet places and resembling green seaweed or leafy moss

livery (ˈlɪvərɪ) *n.* 1. distinctive dress of person or group, *esp.* servant(s) 2. allowance of food for horses 3. US a livery stable —**ˈliveried** *a.* (*esp.* of servants *etc.*) wearing livery —**ˈliveryman** *n.* member of a London guild —**livery stable** stable where horses are kept at a charge or hired out

lives (laɪvz) *n., pl. of* LIFE

livid (ˈlɪvɪd) *a.* 1. of a bluish pale colour 2. discoloured, as by bruising 3. *inf.* angry, furious

lizard (ˈlɪzəd) *n.* four-footed reptile

L.J. Lord Justice

L.L. 1. Late Latin 2. Low Latin 3. Lord Lieutenant

llama (ˈlɑːmə) *n.* woolly animal used as beast of burden in S Amer.

LL.B. Bachelor of Laws

LL.D. Doctor of Laws

Lloyd's (lɔɪdz) *n.* association of London underwriters originally concerned with marine insurance and shipping information and now subscribing a variety of insurance policies and publishing daily list (**Lloyd's List**) of shipping data and news

loach (ləʊtʃ) *n.* carplike freshwater fish

load (ləʊd) *n.* 1. burden 2. amount usu. carried at once 3. actual load carried by vehicle 4. resistance against which engine has to work 5. amount of electrical energy drawn from a source —*vt.* 6. put load on or into 7. charge (gun) 8. weigh down —**ˈloaded** *a.* 1. carrying a load 2. (of dice) dishonestly weighted 3. biased 4. (of question) containing hidden trap or implication 5. *sl.* wealthy 6. *sl.* drunk

loadstar (ˈləʊdstɑː) *n. see* **lodestar** *at* LODE

loaf[1] (ləʊf) *n.* 1. mass of bread as baked 2. shaped mass of food (*pl.* **loaves**)

loaf[2] (ləʊf) *vi.* idle, loiter —**ˈloafer** *n.* idler

loam (ləʊm) *n.* fertile soil

loan (ləʊn) *n.* 1. act of lending 2. thing lent 3. money borrowed at interest 4. permission to use —*vt.* 5. lend, grant loan of

loath *or* **loth** (ləʊθ) *a.* unwilling, reluctant —**loathe** (ləʊð) *vt.* hate, abhor —**loathing** (ˈləʊðɪŋ) *n.* 1. disgust 2. repulsion —**loathsome** (ˈləʊðsəm) *a.* disgusting

loaves (ləʊvz) *n., pl. of* LOAF[1]

lob (lɒb) *n.* 1. in tennis *etc.*, shot pitched high in air —*v.* 2. throw, pitch (shot) thus (**-bb-**)

lobby (ˈlɒbɪ) *n.* 1. corridor into which rooms open 2. passage or room in legislative building, *esp.* houses of parliament of Britain and Aust., to which the public has access 3. group which tries to influence members of lawmaking assembly —**ˈlobbying** *n.* frequenting lobby to collect news or influence members —**ˈlobbyist** *n. chiefly* US person employed by particular interest to lobby —**lobby correspondent** reporter who frequents the lobby (in House of Commons) to gain parliamentary news

lobe (ləʊb) *n.* 1. any rounded projection 2. subdivision of body organ 3. soft, hanging part of ear —**ˈlobar** *a.* of lobe —**ˈlobate** *a.* 1. having or resembling lobes 2. (of birds) having separate toes each fringed with weblike lobe —**lobed** *a.* —**loˈbotomy** *n.* surgical incision into lobe of organ, *esp.* brain

lobelia (ləʊˈbiːlɪə) *n.* garden plant with blue, red or white flowers

lobster (ˈlɒbstə) *n.* shellfish with long tail and claws, turning red when boiled

lobworm (ˈlɒbwɜːm) *n.* lugworm

local (ˈləʊkᵊl) *a.* 1. of, existing in particular place 2. confined to a definite spot, district or part of the body 3. of place —*n.* 4. person belonging to a district 5. *inf.* (nearby) pub —**locale** (ləʊˈkɑːl) *n.* scene of event —**loˈcality** *n.* 1. place, situation 2. district —**ˈlocalize** *or* **-ise** *vt.* assign, restrict to definite place —**ˈlocally** *adv.* —**local anaesthetic** anaesthetic which produces insensibility in one part of body —**local authority** UK governing body of county *etc.* —**local colour** behaviour *etc.* characteristic of a certain region or time, introduced into novel *etc.* to supply realism

THESAURUS

livery attire, clothing, costume, dress, garb, raiment (*Poetic*), regalia, suit, uniform, vestments

live wire ball of fire (*Inf.*), dynamo, go-getter (*Inf.*), hustler (*U.S.*), life and soul of the party, self-starter

livid 1. angry, black-and-blue, bruised, contused, discoloured, purple 2. ashen, blanched, bloodless, doughy, greyish, leaden, pale, pallid, pasty, wan, waxen 3. *Inf.* angry, beside oneself, boiling, enraged, exasperated, fuming, furious, incensed, indignant, infuriated, mad (*Inf.*), outraged

living *n.* 1. animation, being, existence, existing, life, subsistence 2. life style, mode of living, way of life 3. job, livelihood, maintenance, (means of) support, occupation, (source of) income, subsistence, sustenance, work 4. *Church of England* benefice

load *n.* 1. bale, cargo, consignment, freight, lading, shipment 2. affliction, burden, encumbrance, incubus, millstone, onus, oppression, pressure, trouble, weight, worry ~*v.* 3. cram, fill, freight, heap, lade, pack, pile, stack, stuff 4. burden, encumber, hamper, oppress, saddle with, trouble, weigh down, worry 5. *Of firearms* charge, make ready, prepare to fire, prime

loaded 1. burdened, charged, freighted, full, laden, weighted 2. biased, distorted, weighted 3. *Sl.* affluent, flush (*Inf.*), moneyed, rich, rolling (*Sl.*), wealthy, well-heeled (*Sl.*), well off, well-to-do

loaf block, cake, cube, lump, slab

loan 1. *n.* accommodation, advance, allowance, credit, mortgage, touch (*Sl.*) 2. *v.* accommodate, advance, allow, credit, lend, let out

loath, loth against, averse, backward, counter, disinclined, indisposed, opposed, reluctant, resisting, unwilling

loathing abhorrence, abomination, antipathy, aversion, detestation, disgust, execration, hatred, horror, odium, repugnance, repulsion, revulsion

loathsome abhorrent, abominable, detestable, disgusting, execrable, hateful, horrible, nasty, nauseating, obnoxious, odious, offensive, repugnant, repulsive, revolting, vile

lobby *n.* 1. corridor, entrance hall, foyer, hall, hallway, passage, passageway, porch, vestibule 2. pressure group

local *adj.* 1. community, district, neighbourhood, parish, provincial, regional 2. confined, limited, nar-

locate (ləʊˈkeɪt) *vt.* **1.** attribute to a place **2.** find the place of **3.** situate —**loˈcation** *n.* **1.** placing **2.** situation **3.** site of film production away from studio **4. SA** black Afr. or coloured township —**locative** (ˈlɒkətɪv) *a./n.* (of) grammatical case denoting 'place where'

loch (lɒx) *n.* Scottish lake or long narrow bay

loci (ˈləʊsaɪ) *n., pl. of* LOCUS

lock[1] (lɒk) *n.* **1.** appliance for fastening door, lid *etc.* **2.** mechanism for firing gun **3.** enclosure in river or canal for moving boats from one level to another **4.** extent to which vehicle's front wheels will turn **5.** appliance to check the revolution of a wheel **6.** interlocking **7.** block, jam —*vt.* **8.** fasten, make secure with lock **9.** join firmly **10.** cause to become immovable **11.** embrace closely —*vi.* **12.** become fixed or united **13.** become immovable —**ˈlocker** *n.* small cupboard with lock —**ˈlockjaw** *n.* tetanus —**ˈlocknut** *n.* second nut used on top of first on bolt to prevent it shaking loose —**ˈlockout** *n.* exclusion of workmen by employers as means of coercion —**ˈlocksmith** *n.* one who makes and mends locks —**ˈlockup** *n.* **1.** prison **2.** garage, storage area away from main premises

lock[2] (lɒk) *n.* tress of hair

locket (ˈlɒkɪt) *n.* small hinged pendant for portrait *etc.*

loco[1] (ˈləʊkəʊ) *inf.* locomotive

loco[2] (ˈləʊkəʊ) *a.* **1.** *sl., chiefly* **US** insane —*vt.* **2. US** *sl.* make insane

locomotive (ləʊkəˈməʊtɪv) *n.* **1.** engine for pulling carriages on railway tracks —*a.* **2.** having power of moving from place to place —**locoˈmotion** *n.* action, power of moving

locum tenens (ˈləʊkəm ˈtiːnɛnz) *Lat.* substitute, *esp.* for doctor or clergyman during absence (*pl.* **locum tenentes** (təˈnɛntiːz)) (*also* **ˈlocum**) —**locum tenency**

locus (ˈləʊkəs) *n.* **1.** exact place or locality **2.** curve made by all points satisfying certain mathematical condition, or by point, line or surface moving under such condition (*pl.* **ˈloci**)

locust (ˈləʊkəst) *n.* destructive winged insect —**locust bean** bean-shaped fruit of locust tree —**locust tree 1.** N. Amer. leguminous tree having prickly branches, white flowers and reddish-brown seed pods **2.** the carob

locution (ləʊˈkjuːʃən) *n.* **1.** a phrase **2.** speech **3.** mode or style of speaking

lode (ləʊd) *n.* a vein of ore —**ˈlodestar** *or* **ˈloadstar** *n.* Pole Star —**ˈlodestone** *or* **ˈloadstone** *n.* magnetic iron ore

lodge (lɒdʒ) *n.* **1.** house, cabin used seasonally or occasionally, *eg* for hunting, skiing **2.** gatekeeper's house **3.** meeting place of branch of Freemasons *etc.* **4.** the branch —*vt.* **5.** house **6.** deposit **7.** bring (a charge *etc.*) against someone —*vi.* **8.** live in another's house at fixed charge **9.** come to rest —**ˈlodger** *n.* —**ˈlodgings** *pl.n.* rented room(s) in another person's house —**ˈlodgment** *or* **ˈlodgement** *n.* lodging, being lodged

loft (lɒft) *n.* **1.** space between top storey and roof **2.** gallery in church *etc.* —*vt.* **3.** send (golf ball *etc.*) high —**ˈloftily** *adv.* haughtily —**ˈloftiness** *n.* —**ˈlofty** *a.* **1.** of great height **2.** elevated **3.** haughty

log[1] (lɒg) *n.* **1.** portion of felled tree stripped of branches **2.** detailed record of voyages, time travelled *etc.* of ship, aircraft *etc.* **3.** apparatus used formerly for measuring ship's speed —*vt.* **4.** keep a record of **5.** travel (specified distance, time) (**-gg-**) —**ˈlogger** *n.* lumberjack —**ˈlogging** *n.* **US** cutting and transporting logs to river —**ˈlogbook** *n.*

log[2] (lɒg) *n.* logarithm

logan (ˈləʊgən) *n.* **C** *see* BOGAN

loganberry (ˈləʊgənbərɪ, -brɪ) *n.* **1.** trailing prickly plant, cross between raspberry and blackberry **2.** its purplish-red fruit

logarithm (ˈlɒgərɪðəm) *n.* one of series of arithmetical functions tabulated for use in calculation —**logaˈrithmic** *a.*

loggerhead (ˈlɒgəhɛd) *n.* —**at loggerheads** quarrelling, disputing

THESAURUS

row, parish, parochial, provincial, pump, restricted, small-town ~*n.* **3.** character (*Inf.*), inhabitant, local yokel (*Disparaging*), native, resident

locality 1. area, district, neck of the woods (*Inf.*), neighbourhood, region, vicinity **2.** locale, location, place, position, scene, setting, site, spot

localize 1. circumscribe, concentrate, confine, contain, delimit, delimitate, limit, restrain, restrict **2.** ascribe, assign, narrow down, pinpoint, specify

locate 1. come across, detect, discover, find, lay one's hands on, pin down, pinpoint, run to earth, track down, unearth **2.** establish, fix, place, put, seat, set, settle, situate

location bearings, locale, locus, place, point, position, site, situation, spot, venue, whereabouts

lock[1] *n.* **1.** bolt, clasp, fastening, padlock ~*v.* **2.** bolt, close, fasten, latch, seal, secure, shut, sneck (*Dialect*) **3.** clench, engage, entangle, entwine, join, link, mesh, unite **4.** clasp, clutch, embrace, encircle, enclose, grapple, grasp, hug, press

lock[2] curl, ringlet, strand, tress, tuft

lockup cell, cooler (*Sl.*), gaol, jail, jug (*Sl.*), police cell

lodge *n.* **1.** cabin, chalet, cottage, gatehouse, house, hunting lodge, hut, shelter **2.** assemblage, association, branch, chapter, club, group, society ~*v.* **3.** accommodate, billet, board, entertain, harbour, put up, quarter, room, shelter, sojourn, stay, stop **4.** become fixed, catch, come to rest, imbed, implant, stick **5.** deposit, file, lay, place, put, put on record, register, set, submit

lodger boarder, guest, paying guest, P.G., resident, roomer, tenant

lodging *Often plural* abode, accommodation, apartments, boarding, digs (*Brit. inf.*), dwelling, habitation, quarters, residence, rooms, shelter

lofty 1. elevated, high, raised, sky-high, soaring, tall, towering **2.** dignified, distinguished, elevated, exalted, grand, illustrious, imposing, majestic, noble, renowned, stately, sublime, superior **3.** arrogant, condescending, disdainful, haughty, high and mighty (*Inf.*), lordly, patronizing, proud, snooty (*Inf.*), supercilious, toffee-nosed (*Brit. sl.*)

log *n.* **1.** block, bole, chunk, piece of timber, stump, trunk **2.** account, chart, daybook, journal, listing, logbook, record, tally ~*v.* **3.** book, chart, make a note of, note, record, register, report, set down, tally

loggerhead at loggerheads at daggers drawn, at each other's throats, at enmity, at odds, estranged, feuding, in dispute, opposed, quarrelling

loggia (ˈlɒdʒə, ˈlɒdʒɪə) *n.* covered, arcaded gallery (*pl.* **-s, loggie** (ˈlɒdʒɛ))

logic (ˈlɒdʒɪk) *n.* **1.** art or philosophy of reasoning **2.** reasoned thought or argument **3.** coherence of various facts, events *etc.* —**ˈlogical** *a.* **1.** of logic **2.** according to reason **3.** reasonable **4.** apt to reason correctly —**ˈlogically** *adv.* —**loˈgician** *n.*

logistics (lɒˈdʒɪstɪks) *pl.n.* (*with sing. or pl. v.*) **1.** the transport, housing and feeding of troops **2.** organization of any project, operation —**loˈgistical** *a.*

logo (ˈləugəu, ˈlɒg-) *n.* company emblem or similar device (*pl.* **-s**)

Logos (ˈlɒgɒs) *n.* the Divine Word incarnate, Christ

-logue *or U.S.* **-log** (*comb. form*) speech or discourse of particular kind, as in *travelogue, monologue*

-logy (*n. comb. form*) **1.** science or study of, as in *musicology* **2.** writing, discourse or body of writings, as in *trilogy, phraseology, martyrology* —**-logical** *or* **-logic** (*a. comb. form*) —**-logist** (*n. comb. form*)

loin (lɔɪn) *n.* **1.** part of body between ribs and hip **2.** cut of meat from this —*pl.* **3.** hips and lower abdomen —**ˈloincloth** *n.* garment covering loins only

loiter (ˈlɔɪtə) *vi.* **1.** dawdle, hang about **2.** idle —**ˈloiterer** *n.*

loll (lɒl) *vi.* **1.** sit, lie lazily **2.** (*esp.* of the tongue) hang out —*vt.* **3.** hang out (tongue)

lollipop (ˈlɒlɪpɒp) *n.* boiled sweet *etc.* on small wooden stick —**lollipop man UK** *inf.* person holding circular sign on pole who stops traffic so children may cross road (**lollipop lady** *fem.*)

lollop (ˈlɒləp) *vi. chiefly* **UK 1.** walk or run with clumsy or relaxed bouncing movement **2.** lounge

lolly (ˈlɒlɪ) *n.* **1.** *inf.* lollipop; ice lolly **2.** *sl.* money

London pride (ˈlʌndən) saxifrage with pinkish-white flowers

lone (ləun) *a.* solitary —**ˈloneliness** *n.* —**ˈlonely** *a.* **1.** sad because alone **2.** unfrequented **3.** solitary, alone —**ˈloner** *n. inf.* one who prefers to be alone —**ˈlonesome** *a. chiefly* **US** lonely

long[1] (lɒŋ) *a.* **1.** having length, *esp.* great length, in space or time **2.** extensive **3.** protracted —*adv.* **4.** for a long time —**ˈlongways** *or U.S.* **ˈlongwise** *adv. see* **lengthways** *at* LENGTH —**ˈlongbow** *n. esp.* in medieval England, large powerful hand-drawn bow —**long division** process of dividing one number by another and putting steps down in full —**long-drawn-out** *a.* overprolonged, extended —**ˈlonghair** *a. inf.* of intellectuals or their tastes, *esp.* preferring classical music to jazz *etc.* (*also* **long-haired**) —**ˈlonghand** *n.* writing of words, letters *etc.* in full —**long-headed** *a.* astute; shrewd; sagacious —**long johns** *inf.* underpants with long legs —**long jump** athletic contest in which competitors try to cover farthest distance possible with running jump from fixed board or mark —**long off** *Cricket* fielding position near boundary behind bowler on offside of pitch —**long on** *Cricket* fielding position near boundary behind bowler on leg side of pitch —**long-playing** *a.* (of record) lasting for 10 to 30 minutes because of its fine grooves —**long-range** *a.* **1.** of the future **2.** able to travel long distances without refuelling **3.** (of weapons) designed to hit distant target —**long shot** competitor, undertaking, bet *etc.* with small chance of success —**long-standing** *a.* existing for a long time —**long-term** *a.* **1.** lasting or extending over a long time **2.** *Fin.* maturing after a long period —**long ton** the imperial ton (2240 lbs) —**long wave** radio wave with wavelength greater than 1000 metres —**long-winded** *a.* tediously loquacious

long[2] (lɒŋ) *vi.* have keen desire, yearn —**ˈlonging** *n.* yearning

long. longitude

longeron (ˈlɒndʒərən) *n.* long spar running fore and aft in body of aircraft

longevity (lɒnˈdʒɛvɪtɪ) *n.* long existence or life

longitude (ˈlɒndʒɪtjuːd) *n.* distance east or west from standard meridian —**longiˈtudinal** *a.* **1.** of length or longitude **2.** lengthwise

longshoreman (ˈlɒŋʃɔːmən) *n.* **US** wharf labourer

loo (luː) *n. inf.* lavatory

loofah (ˈluːfə) *n.* **1.** pod of plant used as sponge **2.** the plant

look (luk) *vi.* **1.** direct, use eyes **2.** face **3.** seem **4.** (*with* for) search **5.** (*with* for) hope **6.** (*with* after) take care (of) —*n.* **7.** looking **8.** view **9.** search **10.** (*oft. pl.*) appearance —**looker-on** *n.* spectator —**looking glass**

THESAURUS

logic 1. argumentation, deduction, dialectics, ratiocination, science of reasoning, syllogistic reasoning **2.** good reason, good sense, reason, sense, sound judgment **3.** chain of thought, coherence, connection, link, rationale, relationship

logical 1. clear, cogent, coherent, consistent, deducible, pertinent, rational, reasonable, relevant, sound, valid, well-organized **2.** judicious, most likely, necessary, obvious, plausible, reasonable, sensible, wise

loiter dally, dawdle, delay, dilly-dally (*Inf.*), hang about *or* around, idle, lag, linger, loaf, loll, saunter, skulk, stroll

loll 1. flop, lean, loaf, lounge, recline, relax, slouch, slump, sprawl **2.** dangle, droop, drop, flap, flop, hang, hang loosely, sag

lone by oneself, deserted, isolated, lonesome, one, only, separate, separated, single, sole, solitary, unaccompanied

loneliness aloneness, desertedness, desolation, dreariness, forlornness, isolation, lonesomeness, seclusion, solitariness, solitude

lonely 1. abandoned, destitute, estranged, forlorn, forsaken, friendless, lonesome, outcast **2.** alone, apart, by oneself, companionless, isolated, lone, single, solitary, withdrawn **3.** deserted, desolate, isolated, off the beaten track (*Inf.*), out-of-the-way, remote, secluded, sequestered, solitary, unfrequented, uninhabited

long[1] *adj.* **1.** elongated, expanded, extended, extensive, far-reaching, lengthy, spread out, stretched **2.** dragging, interminable, late, lengthy, lingering, long-drawn-out, prolonged, protracted, slow, sustained, tardy

long[2] *v.* covet, crave, desire, dream of, hanker, hunger, itch lust, pine, want, wish, yearn

longing ambition, aspiration, coveting, craving, desire, hankering, hungering, itch, thirst, urge, wish, yearning, yen (*Inf.*)

long-standing abiding, enduring, established, fixed, hallowed by time, long-established, long-lasting, long-lived, time-honoured

long-winded diffuse, discursive, garrulous, lengthy, long-drawn-out, overlong, prolix, prolonged, rambling, repetitious, tedious, verbose, wordy

mirror —ˈ**lookout** *n.* **1.** guard **2.** place for watching **3.** prospect **4.** watchman **5.** *inf.* worry, concern —**good looks** beauty —**look after** tend —**look down on** despise

loom[1] (lu:m) *n.* **1.** machine for weaving **2.** middle part of oar

loom[2] (lu:m) *vi.* **1.** appear dimly **2.** seem ominously close **3.** assume great importance

loon (lu:n) *n. inf.* stupid, foolish person —ˈ**loony** *a./n.* —**loony bin** *inf.* mental hospital

loop (lu:p) *n.* **1.** figure made by curved line crossing itself **2.** similar rounded shape in cord, rope *etc.* crossed on itself **3.** contraceptive coil **4.** aerial manoeuvre in which aircraft describes complete circle **5.** *Figure skating* curve crossing itself made on single edge —*vt.* **6.** make loop in or of —**loop line** railway line which leaves, then rejoins, main line

loophole (ˈlu:phəul) *n.* **1.** means of escape, of evading rule without infringing it **2.** vertical slit in wall, *esp.* for defence

loose (lu:s) *a.* **1.** not tight, fastened, fixed or tense **2.** slack **3.** vague **4.** dissolute —*vt.* **5.** free **6.** unfasten **7.** slacken —*vi.* **8.** (*with* off) shoot, let fly (bullet *etc.*) —ˈ**loosely** *adv.* —ˈ**loosen** *v.* make or become loose —ˈ**looseness** *n.* —**loose-jointed** *a.* **1.** supple and easy in movement **2.** loosely built; with ill-fitting joints —**loose-leaf** *a.* (of binder *etc.*) capable of being opened to allow removal and addition of pages —**on the loose 1.** free **2.** *inf.* on a spree

loot (lu:t) *n./v.* plunder

lop[1] (lɒp) *vt.* (*usu. with* off) **1.** cut away (twigs and branches) from tree **2.** chop (off) (**-pp-**)

lop[2] (lɒp) *vi.* hang limply (**-pp-**) —**lop-eared** *a.* having drooping ears —**lopˈsided** *a.* with one side lower than the other, badly balanced

lope (ləup) *vi.* run with long, easy strides

loquacious (lɒˈkweɪʃəs) *a.* talkative —**loquacity** (lɒˈkwæsɪtɪ) *n.*

loquat (ˈləukwɒt, -kwət) *n.* **1.** Japanese plum tree **2.** its fruit

lor (lɔ:) *interj. nonstandard* exclamation of surprise or dismay

loran (ˈlɔ:rən) *n.* radio navigation system operating over long distances

lord (lɔ:d) *n.* **1.** British nobleman, peer of the realm **2.** feudal superior **3.** one ruling others **4.** owner **5.** God —*v.* **6.** be domineering (*esp. in* **lord it over someone**) —ˈ**lordliness** *n.* —ˈ**lordly** *a.* **1.** imperious, proud **2.** fit for a lord —ˈ**lordship** *n.* **1.** rule, ownership **2.** domain **3.** title of some noblemen —**Lord Chief Justice** judge second only to Lord Chancellor; president of one division of High Court of Justice —**Lord (High) Chancellor** *Brit. government* cabinet minister who is head of judiciary in England and Wales, and Speaker of the House of Lords —**Lord Lieutenant 1. UK** representative of Crown in county **2.** formerly, British viceroy in Ireland —**Lord Mayor** mayor in City of London and certain other boroughs —**Lord President of the Council UK** cabinet minister who presides at meetings of Privy Council —**Lord Privy Seal UK** senior cabinet minister without official duties —**the Lord's Day** Christian Sabbath; Sunday —**the Lord's Prayer** prayer taught by Jesus Christ to his disciples (*also* **Our Father, Paterˈnoster**) —**the Lord's Supper** *see* **Holy Communion** *at* HOLY —**the Lords Temporal UK** peers other than bishops in their capacity as members of House of Lords

THESAURUS

look *v.* **1.** behold (*Archaic*), consider, contemplate, examine, eye, feast one's eyes upon, gaze, glance, inspect, observe, peep, regard, scan, scrutinize, see, study, survey, take a gander at (*Inf.*), view, watch **2.** appear, display, evidence, exhibit, look like, make clear, manifest, present, seem, seem to be, show, strike one as **3.** face, front, front on, give onto, overlook **4.** anticipate, await, expect, hope, reckon on **5.** forage, hunt, search, seek ~*n.* **6.** examination, eyeful (*Inf.*), gaze, glance, glimpse, inspection, look-see (*Sl.*), observation, once-over (*Inf.*), peek, review, sight, squint (*Inf.*), survey, view **7.** air, appearance, aspect, bearing, cast, complexion, countenance, demeanour, effect, expression, face, fashion, guise, manner, mien (*Literary*), semblance

look after attend to, care for, guard, keep an eye on, mind, nurse, protect, sit with, supervise, take care of, take charge of, tend, watch

look down on contemn, despise, disdain, hold in contempt, look down one's nose at (*Inf.*), misprize, scorn, sneer, spurn, treat with contempt, turn one's nose up (at) (*Inf.*)

lookout 1. guard, qui vive, readiness, vigil, watch **2.** guard, sentinel, sentry, vedette (*Military*), watchman **3.** beacon, citadel, observation post, post, tower, watchtower **4.** *Inf.* business, concern, funeral (*Inf.*), pigeon (*Brit. inf.*), worry **5.** chances, future, likelihood, outlook, prospect, view

loom appear, become visible, be imminent, bulk, emerge, hover, impend, menace, take shape, threaten

loop 1. *n.* bend, circle, coil, convolution, curl, curve, eyelet, hoop, kink, loophole, noose, ring, spiral, twirl, twist, whorl **2.** *v.* bend, braid, circle, coil, connect, curl, curve round, encircle, fold, join, knot, roll, spiral, turn, twist, wind round

loophole 1. aperture, knothole, opening, slot **2.** *Fig.* avoidance, escape, evasion, excuse, let-out, means of escape, plea, pretence, pretext, subterfuge

loose *adj.* **1.** floating, free, insecure, movable, released, unattached, unbound, unconfined, unfastened, unfettered, unrestricted, unsecured, untied, wobbly **2.** baggy, easy, hanging, loosened, not fitting, not tight, relaxed, slack, slackened, sloppy **3.** diffuse, disconnected, disordered, ill-defined, imprecise, inaccurate, indefinite, indistinct, inexact, rambling, random, vague **4.** abandoned, debauched, disreputable, dissipated, dissolute, fast, immoral, lewd, libertine, licentious, profligate, promiscuous, unchaste, wanton ~*v.* **5.** detach, disconnect, disengage, ease, free, let go, liberate, loosen, release, set free, slacken, unbind, undo, unfasten, unleash, unloose, untie

loosen detach, let out, separate, slacken, unbind, undo, unloose, unstick, untie, work free, work loose

loot 1. *n.* booty, goods, haul, plunder, prize, spoils, swag (*Sl.*) **2.** *v.* despoil, pillage, plunder, raid, ransack, ravage, rifle, rob, sack

lopsided askew, asymmetrical, awry, cockeyed, crooked, disproportionate, off balance, one-sided, out of shape, out of true, squint, tilting, unbalanced, unequal, uneven, warped

lord 1. commander, governor, king, leader, liege, mas-

lore (lɔː) *n.* 1. learning 2. body of facts and traditions

lorgnette (lɔːˈnjɛt) *n.* pair of spectacles mounted on long handle

lorikeet (ˈlɒrɪkiːt, lɒrɪˈkiːt) *n.* small parrot

loris (ˈlɔːrɪs) *n.* tree-dwelling, nocturnal Asian animal (*pl.* **-ris**)

lorn (lɔːn) *a. poet.* 1. abandoned 2. desolate

lorry (ˈlɒrɪ) *n.* motor vehicle for transporting loads by road, truck

lory (ˈlɔːrɪ), **lowry** *or* **lowrie** (ˈlaʊrɪ) *n.* small, brightly coloured parrot of Aust. and Indonesia

lose (luːz) *vt.* 1. be deprived of, fail to retain or use 2. let slip 3. fail to get 4. (of clock *etc.*) run slow by (specified amount) 5. be defeated in —*vi.* 6. suffer loss (**lost** *pt./pp.*, **ˈlosing** *pr.p.*) —**ˈloser** *n.* 1. person or thing that loses 2. *inf.* person or thing that seems destined to fail *etc.* —**loss** (lɒs) *n.* 1. a losing 2. what is lost 3. harm or damage resulting from losing —**lost** (lɒst) *a.* 1. unable to be found 2. unable to find one's way 3. bewildered 4. not won 5. not utilized

lot (lɒt) *pron.* 1. great number —*n.* 2. collection 3. large quantity 4. share 5. fate 6. destiny 7. item at auction 8. one of a set of objects used to decide something by chance (*esp. in* **to cast lots**) 9. area of land —*pl.* 10. *inf.* great numbers or quantity —*adv.* 11. *inf.* a great deal

loth (ləʊθ) *a. see* LOATH

lotion (ˈləʊʃən) *n.* liquid for washing wounds, improving skin *etc.*

lottery (ˈlɒtərɪ) *n.* 1. method of raising funds by selling tickets and prizes by chance 2. gamble

lotto (ˈlɒtəʊ) *n.* game of chance like bingo

lotus *or* **lotos** (ˈləʊtəs) *n.* 1. legendary plant whose fruits induce forgetfulness when eaten 2. Egyptian water lily —**lotus-eater** *n. Gk myth.* one of people encountered by Odysseus in N Afr. who lived in indolent forgetfulness, drugged by fruit of legendary lotus —**lotus position** seated cross-legged position used in yoga *etc.*

loud (laʊd) *a.* 1. strongly audible 2. noisy 3. obtrusive —**ˈloudly** *adv.* —**ˈloudmouth** *n. inf.* person who brags or talks too loudly —**ˈloudmouthed** *a.* —**loudˈspeaker** *n.* instrument for converting electrical signals into sound audible at a distance

lough (lɒx) *n.* in Ireland, loch

lounge (laʊndʒ) *vi.* 1. sit, lie, walk or stand in a relaxed manner —*n.* 2. living room of house 3. general waiting, relaxing area in airport, hotel *etc.* —**ˈlounger** *n.* loafer —**lounge suit** man's suit for daytime wear

lour (laʊə) *see* LOWER

lourie (ˈlaʊrɪ) *n.* S Afr. bird with bright plumage

louse (laʊs) *n.* parasitic insect (*pl.* **lice**) —**lousy** (ˈlaʊzɪ) *a.* 1. *sl.* nasty, unpleasant 2. (*with* with) *sl.* (too) generously provided, thickly populated (with) 3. *sl.* bad, poor 4. having lice

lout (laʊt) *n.* crude, oafish person —**ˈloutish** *a.*

louvre *or U.S.* **louver** (ˈluːvə) *n.* 1. one of a set of boards or slats set parallel and slanted to admit air but not rain 2. ventilating structure of these

THESAURUS

ter, monarch, overlord, potentate, prince, ruler, seigneur, sovereign, superior 2. earl, noble, nobleman, peer, viscount 3. **lord it over** act big (*Sl.*), be overbearing, boss around (*Inf.*), domineer, order around, play the lord, pull rank, put on airs, swagger

lordly 1. arrogant, condescending, despotic, dictatorial, disdainful, domineering, haughty, high and mighty (*Inf.*), high-handed, hoity-toity (*Inf.*), imperious, lofty, overbearing, patronizing, proud, stuck-up (*Inf.*), supercilious, toffee-nosed (*Sl., chiefly Brit.*), tyrannical 2. aristocratic, dignified, exalted, gracious, grand, imperial, lofty, majestic, noble, princely, regal, stately

lore 1. beliefs, doctrine, experience, folk-wisdom, mythos, saws, sayings, teaching, traditional wisdom, traditions, wisdom 2. erudition, knowhow (*Inf.*), knowledge, learning, letters, scholarship

lose 1. be deprived of, displace, drop, fail to keep, forget, mislay, misplace, miss, suffer loss 2. capitulate, default, fail, fall short, forfeit, lose out on (*Inf.*), miss, pass up (*Inf.*), yield 3. be defeated, be the loser, be worsted, come a cropper (*Inf.*), come to grief, get the worst of, lose out, suffer defeat, take a licking (*Inf.*)

loser also-ran, dud (*Inf.*), failure, flop (*Inf.*), lemon (*Sl.*), no-hoper (*Austral. sl.*), underdog, washout (*Inf.*)

loss 1. bereavement, deprivation, disappearance, failure, forfeiture, losing, misfortune, mislaying, privation 2. cost, damage, defeat, destruction, detriment, disadvantage, harm, hurt, impairment, injury, ruin

lot 1. assortment, batch, bunch (*Inf.*), collection, consignment, crowd, group, quantity, set 2. accident, chance, destiny, doom, fate, fortune, hazard, plight, portion 3. allowance, cut (*Inf.*), parcel, part, percentage, piece, portion, quota, ration, share 4. **a lot** *or* **lots** abundance, a great deal, heap(s), large amount, load(s) (*Inf.*), masses (*Inf.*), numbers, ocean(s), oodles (*Inf.*), piles, plenty, quantities, reams (*Inf.*), scores, stack(s)

lotion balm, cream, embrocation, liniment, salve, solution

lottery 1. draw, raffle, sweepstake 2. chance, gamble, hazard, risk, toss-up (*Inf.*), venture

loud 1. blaring, blatant, boisterous, booming, clamorous, deafening, ear-piercing, ear-splitting, forte (*Music*), high-sounding, noisy, obstreperous, piercing, resounding, rowdy, sonorous, stentorian, strident, strong, thundering, tumultuous, turbulent, vehement, vociferous 2. *Fig.* brassy, flamboyant, flashy, garish, gaudy, glaring, lurid, ostentatious, showy, tasteless, tawdry, vulgar 3. brash, brazen, coarse, crass, crude, loud-mouthed (*Inf.*), offensive, raucous, vulgar

loudly at full volume, at the top of one's voice, clamorously, deafeningly, fortissimo (*Music*), lustily, noisily, shrilly, uproariously, vehemently, vigorously, vociferously

lounge *v.* laze, lie about, loaf, loiter, loll, recline, relax, saunter, sprawl, take it easy (*Inf.*)

lout bear, boor, churl, oaf, yahoo, yob *or* yobbo (*Brit. sl.*)

lovable adorable, amiable, attractive, captivating, charming, cuddly, delightful, enchanting, endearing, engaging, fetching (*Inf.*), likable, lovely, pleasing, sweet, winning, winsome

lovage (ˈlʌvɪdʒ) *n.* European umbelliferous plant used for flavouring food

love (lʌv) *n.* **1.** warm affection **2.** benevolence **3.** charity **4.** sexual passion **5.** sweetheart **6.** *Tennis etc.* score of nothing —*vt.* **7.** admire passionately **8.** delight in —*vi.* **9.** be in love —ˈ**lovable** *or* ˈ**loveable** *a.* —ˈ**loveless** *a.* —ˈ**loveliness** *n.* —ˈ**lovely** *a.* beautiful, delightful —ˈ**lover** *n.* —ˈ**loving** *a.* **1.** affectionate **2.** tender —ˈ**lovingly** *adv.* —ˈ**lovebird** *n.* **1.** small parrot **2.** budgerigar **3.** *inf.* lover —**love child** *euphemistic* illegitimate child, bastard —**love-in-a-mist** *n.* plant with pale-blue flowers —**love letter** —**love-lies-bleeding** *n.* plant with long, drooping red flowers —ˈ**lovelorn** *a.* forsaken by, pining for a lover —ˈ**lovesick** *a.* pining or languishing because of love —ˈ**lovesickness** *n.* —**lovey-dovey** *a.* making excessive or ostentatious display of affection —**loving cup** bowl formerly passed round at banquet —**make love (to)** have sexual intercourse (with)

low[1] (ləʊ) *a.* **1.** not tall, high or elevated **2.** humble **3.** coarse, vulgar **4.** dejected **5.** ill **6.** not loud **7.** moderate **8.** cheap —ˈ**lower** *vt.* **1.** cause, allow to descend **2.** move down **3.** degrade —*vi.* **4.** diminish —*a.* **5.** below in position or rank **6.** at an early stage, period of development —ˈ**lowliness** *n.* —ˈ**lowly** *a.* modest, humble —**low**ˈ**born** *or* **low**ˈ**bred** *a. rare* of ignoble or common parentage —ˈ**lowbrow** *n./a.* (one) having no intellectual or cultural interests —**Low Church** section of Anglican Church stressing evangelical beliefs and practices —ˈ**lowdown** *n. inf.* inside information —**low-down** *a. inf.* mean, shabby, dishonourable —**lower case** bottom half of compositor's type case, in which small letters are kept —**lower-case** *a.* **1.** of small letters —*vt.* **2.** print with lower-case letters —**lower class** social stratum having lowest position in social hierarchy —**lower-class** *a.* **1.** of lower class **2.** inferior; vulgar —**lower house** one of houses of bicameral legislature, usu. the larger and more representative (*also* **lower chamber**) —**low frequency 1.** in electricity, any frequency of alternating current from about 30 to 10,000 cycles **2.** frequency within audible range —**Low German** language of N Germany, spoken *esp.* in rural areas (*also* ˈ**Plattdeutsch**) —**low-grade** *a.* of inferior quality —**low-key** *a.* subdued, restrained, not intense —**lowland** (ˈləʊlənd) *n.* low-lying country —**Lowlander** (ˈləʊləndə) *n.* —**Lowlands** (ˈləʊləndz) *n.* less mountainous parts of Scotland —**Low Latin** any form of Latin other than classical, such as Medieval Latin —**Low Mass** Mass that has simplified ceremonial form and is spoken rather than sung —**low-minded** *a.* having vulgar or crude mind and character —**low profile** position or attitude characterized by deliberate avoidance of prominence or publicity —**low-tension** *a.* carrying, operating at low voltage —**low tide 1.** tide at lowest level or time at which it reaches this **2.** lowest point —**low water 1.** low tide **2.** state of any stretch of water at its lowest level

low[2] (ləʊ) *n.* **1.** cry of cattle, bellow —*vi.* **2.** (of cattle) utter their cry, bellow

lower (ˈlaʊə) *or* **lour** *vi.* **1.** look gloomy or threatening, as sky **2.** scowl —*n.* **3.** scowl, frown

lox[1] (lɒks) *n.* kind of smoked salmon

lox[2] (lɒks) *n. short for* liquid oxygen, *esp.* when used as oxidizer for rocket fuels

loyal (ˈlɔɪəl) *a.* faithful, true to allegiance —ˈ**loyalist** *n.* —ˈ**Loyalist** *n.* C United Empire Loyalist —ˈ**loyally** *adv.* —ˈ**loyalty** *n.* —**loyal toast** toast drunk in pledging allegiance to sovereign, usu. after meal

THESAURUS

love *v.* **1.** adore, adulate, be attached to, be in love with, cherish, dote on, have affection for, hold dear, idolize, prize, think the world of, treasure, worship **2.** appreciate, delight in, desire, enjoy, fancy, have a weakness for, like, relish, savour, take pleasure in ~*n.* **3.** adoration, adulation, affection, amity, ardour, attachment, devotion, fondness, friendship, infatuation, liking, passion, rapture, regard, tenderness, warmth **4.** angel, beloved, darling, dear, dearest, dear one, inamorata, inamorato, loved one, lover, sweet, sweetheart, truelove

lovely 1. admirable, adorable, amiable, attractive, beautiful, charming, comely, exquisite, graceful, handsome, pretty, sweet, winning **2.** agreeable, captivating, delightful, enchanting, engaging, enjoyable, gratifying, nice, pleasant, pleasing

lover admirer, beau, beloved, boyfriend, fancy man (*Sl.*), fancy woman (Sl.), fiancé, fiancée, flame (*Inf.*), girlfriend, inamorata, inamorato, mistress, paramour, suitor, swain (*Archaic*), sweetheart

loving affectionate, amorous, ardent, cordial, dear, demonstrative, devoted, doting, fond, friendly, kind, solicitous, tender, warm, warm-hearted

low 1. little, short, small, squat, stunted **2.** coarse, common, crude, disgraceful, dishonourable, disreputable, gross, ill-bred, obscene, rough, rude, unbecoming, undignified, unrefined, vulgar **3.** humble, lowborn, lowly, meek, obscure, plain, plebeian, poor, simple, unpretentious **4.** blue, brassed off (*Inf.*), dejected, depressed, despondent, disheartened, down, downcast, down in the dumps (*Inf.*), fed up, forlorn, gloomy, glum, miserable, morose, sad, unhappy **5.** debilitated, dying, exhausted, feeble, frail, ill, prostrate, reduced, sinking, stricken, weak **6.** gentle, hushed, muffled, muted, quiet, soft, subdued, whispered **7.** cheap, economical, inexpensive, moderate, modest, reasonable **8.** abject, base, contemptible, dastardly, degraded, depraved, despicable, ignoble, mean, menial, nasty, scurvy, servile, sordid, unworthy, vile, vulgar

lowdown dope (*Sl.*), gen (*Brit. inf.*), info (*Inf.*), information, inside story, intelligence

lower[1] *adj.* **1.** inferior, junior, lesser, low-level, minor, secondary, second-class, smaller, subordinate, under ~*v.* **2.** depress, drop, fall, let down, make lower, sink, submerge, take down **3.** abase, belittle, condescend, debase, degrade, deign, demean, devalue, disgrace, downgrade, humble, humiliate, stoop **4.** abate, curtail, cut, decrease, diminish, lessen, minimize, moderate, prune, reduce, slash

lower[2], **lour 1.** blacken, cloud up *or* over, darken, loom, menace, threaten **2.** frown, give a dirty look, glare, glower, look daggers, look sullen, scowl

low-grade bad, inferior, not good enough, not up to snuff (*Inf.*), poor, second-rate, substandard

low-key low-pitched, muffled, muted, played down, quiet, restrained, subdued, toned down, understated

lowly 1. docile, dutiful, gentle, humble, meek, mild, modest, submissive, unassuming **2.** average, common, homespun, modest, ordinary, plain, poor, simple, unpretentious

loyal attached, constant, dependable, devoted, dutiful, faithful, patriotic, staunch, steadfast, tried and

lozenge (ˈlɒzɪndʒ) *n.* **1.** small sweet or tablet of medicine **2.** rhombus, diamond figure

LP long-playing (record)

LPG *or* **LP gas** liquefied petroleum gas

L-plate *n.* sign on car driven by learner driver

Lr *Chem.* lawrencium

LSD **1.** lysergic acid diethylamide (hallucinogenic drug) **2.** librae, solidi, denarii (*Lat.*, pounds, shillings, pence)

L.S.E. London School of Economics

Lt. Lieutenant

Ltd. *or* **ltd.** Limited (Liability)

Lu *Chem.* lutetium

lubber (ˈlʌbə) *n.* **1.** clumsy fellow **2.** unskilled seaman

lubricate (ˈlu:brɪkeɪt) *vt.* **1.** oil, grease **2.** make slippery —**ˈlubricant** *n.* substance used for this —**lubriˈcation** *n.* —**ˈlubricator** *n.* —**luˈbricity** *n.* **1.** slipperiness, smoothness **2.** lewdness

lucent (ˈlu:sᵊnt) *a.* bright, shining

lucerne (lu:ˈsɜ:n) *n.* fodder plant like clover, alfalfa

lucid (ˈlu:sɪd) *a.* **1.** clear **2.** easily understood **3.** sane —**luˈcidity** *or* **ˈlucidness** *n.* —**ˈlucidly** *adv.*

luck (lʌk) *n.* **1.** fortune, good or bad **2.** good fortune **3.** chance —**ˈluckily** *adv.* fortunately —**ˈluckless** *a.* having bad luck —**ˈlucky** *a.* having good luck —**lucky dip** UK **1.** box containing small prizes for which children search **2.** *inf.* undertaking of uncertain outcome

lucre (ˈlu:kə) *n. usu. facetious* money, wealth —**ˈlucrative** *a.* very profitable —**filthy lucre** *inf.* money

ludicrous (ˈlu:dɪkrəs) *a.* absurd, laughable, ridiculous

ludo (ˈlu:dəʊ) *n.* game played with dice and counters on board

luff (lʌf) *n.* **1.** the part of fore-and-aft sail nearest mast —*v.* **2.** sail (ship) into wind so that sails flap —*vi.* **3.** (of sails) flap

lug[1] (lʌg) *v.* drag (something heavy) with effort (**-gg-**)

lug[2] (lʌg) *n.* **1.** projection, tag serving as handle or support **2.** *inf.* ear

luggage (ˈlʌgɪdʒ) *n.* traveller's trunks and other baggage

lugger (ˈlʌgə) *n.* working boat (*eg* fishing, prawning lugger) orig. fitted with lugsail

lugsail (ˈlʌgsəl) *n.* oblong sail fixed on yard which hangs slanting on mast

lugubrious (luˈgu:brɪəs) *a.* mournful, doleful, gloomy —**luˈgubriously** *adv.*

lugworm (ˈlʌgwɜ:m) *n.* large worm used as bait, lobworm

lukewarm (lu:kˈwɔ:m) *a.* **1.** moderately warm, tepid **2.** unenthusiastic

lull (lʌl) *vt.* **1.** soothe, sing (to sleep) **2.** make quiet —*vi.* **3.** become quiet, subside —*n.* **4.** brief time of quiet in storm *etc.* —**lullaby** (ˈlʌləbaɪ) *n.* lulling song, *esp.* for children

lumbar (ˈlʌmbə) *a.* relating to body between lower ribs and hips —**lumbago** (lʌmˈbeɪgəʊ) *n.* rheumatism in the lower part of the back

lumber (ˈlʌmbə) *n.* **1.** disused articles, useless rubbish **2.** sawn timber —*vi.* **3.** move heavily —*vt.* **4.** *inf.* burden with something unpleasant —**ˈlumberjack** *n.* US, C man who fells trees and prepares logs for transport to mill

lumen (ˈlu:mɪn) *n.* SI unit of luminous flux (*pl.* **-s**, **-mina** (-mɪnə))

luminous (ˈlu:mɪnəs) *a.* **1.** bright **2.** shedding light **3.** glowing **4.** lucid —**ˈluminary** *n.* **1.** learned person **2.** heavenly body giving light —**lumiˈnescence** *n.* emission of light at low temperatures by process (*eg* chemical) not involving burning —**lumiˈnosity** *n.*

THESAURUS

true, true, true-blue, true-hearted, trustworthy, trusty, unswerving, unwavering

loyalty allegiance, constancy, dependability, devotion, faithfulness, fealty, fidelity, patriotism, reliability, staunchness, steadfastness, true-heartedness, trueness, trustiness, trustworthiness

lubricate grease, make slippery, make smooth, oil, smear

lucid **1.** clear, clear-cut, comprehensible, crystal clear, distinct, evident, explicit, intelligible, limpid, obvious, pellucid, plain, transparent **2.** clear, crystalline, diaphanous, glassy, limpid, pellucid, pure, translucent, transparent **3.** all there, clear-headed, *compos mentis*, in one's right mind, rational, reasonable, sane, sensible, sober, sound

luck **1.** accident, chance, destiny, fate, fortuity, fortune, hap (*Archaic*), hazard **2.** advantage, blessing, break (*Inf.*), fluke, godsend, good fortune, good luck, prosperity, serendipity, stroke, success, windfall

luckily favourably, fortunately, happily, opportunely, propitiously, providentially

luckless calamitous, cursed, disastrous, doomed, hapless, hopeless, ill-fated, ill-starred, jinxed, star-crossed, unfortunate, unhappy, unlucky, unpropitious, unsuccessful

lucky advantageous, blessed, charmed, favoured, fortunate, prosperous, serendipitous, successful

lucrative advantageous, fat, fruitful, gainful, high-income, money-making, paying, productive, profitable, remunerative, well-paid

lucre gain, mammon, money, pelf, profit, riches, spoils, wealth

ludicrous absurd, burlesque, comic, comical, crazy, droll, farcical, funny, incongruous, laughable, nonsensical, odd, outlandish, preposterous, ridiculous, silly, zany

luggage baggage, bags, cases, gear, impedimenta, paraphernalia, suitcases, things, trunks

lugubrious dirgelike, dismal, doleful, dreary, funereal, gloomy, melancholy, morose, mournful, sad, serious, sombre, sorrowful, woebegone, woeful

lukewarm **1.** blood-warm, tepid, warm **2.** *Fig.* apathetic, cold, cool, half-hearted, indifferent, laodicean, phlegmatic, unconcerned, unenthusiastic, uninterested, unresponsive

lull *v.* **1.** allay, calm, compose, hush, lullaby, pacify, quell, quiet, rock to sleep, soothe, still, subdue, tranquillize **2.** abate, cease, decrease, diminish, dwindle, ease off, let up, moderate, quieten down, slacken, subside, wane ~*n.* **3.** calm, calmness, hush, let-up (*Inf.*), pause, quiet, respite, silence, stillness, tranquillity

lullaby berceuse, cradlesong

lumber *n.* **1.** castoffs, clutter, discards, jumble, junk, refuse, rubbish, trash, trumpery, white elephants ~*v.* **2.** *Brit. sl.* burden, encumber, impose upon,

lump (lʌmp) *n.* **1.** shapeless piece or mass **2.** swelling **3.** large sum —*vt.* **4.** (*oft. with* together) throw (together) in one mass or sum —*vi.* **5.** move heavily —**ˈlumpish** *a.* **1.** clumsy **2.** stupid —**ˈlumpy** *a.* **1.** full of lumps **2.** uneven —**lump sum** relatively large sum of money, paid at one time —**lump it** *inf.* put up with something

lunar (ˈluːnə) *a.* relating to the moon —**lunar module** module used to carry astronauts from spacecraft to surface of moon and back

lunatic (ˈluːnətɪk) *a.* **1.** insane —*n.* **2.** insane person —**ˈlunacy** *n.* —**lunatic asylum** *old name for* institution for mentally ill —**lunatic fringe** extreme, radical section of group *etc.*

lunch (lʌntʃ) *n.* **1.** meal taken in the middle of the day —*v.* **2.** eat, entertain to lunch —**luncheon** (ˈlʌntʃən) *n.* a lunch —**luncheon voucher** voucher worth specified amount issued to employees and redeemable at restaurant for food

lung (lʌŋ) *n.* one of the two organs of respiration in vertebrates —**ˈlungfish** *n.* type of fish with air-breathing lung —**ˈlungworm** *n.* parasitic worm infesting lungs of some animals —**ˈlungwort** *n.* flowering plant

lunge (lʌndʒ) *vi.* **1.** thrust with sword *etc.* —*n.* **2.** such thrust **3.** sudden movement of body, plunge

lupin *or U.S.* **lupine** (ˈluːpɪn) *n.* leguminous plant with tall spikes of flowers

lupine (ˈluːpaɪn) *a.* like a wolf

lupus (ˈluːpəs) *n.* skin disease

lurch (lɜːtʃ) *n.* **1.** sudden roll to one side —*vi.* **2.** stagger —**leave in the lurch** leave in difficulties

lurcher (ˈlɜːtʃə) *n.* crossbred dog trained to hunt silently

lure (lʊə) *n.* **1.** something which entices **2.** bait **3.** power to attract —*vt.* **4.** entice **5.** attract

lurid (ˈlʊərɪd) *a.* **1.** vivid in shocking detail, sensational **2.** pale, wan **3.** lit with unnatural glare —**ˈluridly** *adv.*

lurk (lɜːk) *vi.* lie hidden —**ˈlurking** *a.* (of suspicion) not definite

luscious (ˈlʌʃəs) *a.* **1.** sweet, juicy **2.** extremely pleasurable or attractive

lush[1] (lʌʃ) *a.* (of grass *etc.*) luxuriant and juicy, fresh

lush[2] (lʌʃ) *n.* **US** *sl.* **1.** heavy drinker **2.** alcoholic —**ˈlushy** *a.*

lust (lʌst) *n.* **1.** strong desire for sexual gratification **2.** any strong desire —*vi.* **3.** have passionate desire —**ˈlustful** *a.* —**ˈlustily** *adv.* —**ˈlusty** *a.* vigorous, healthy

lustration (lʌsˈtreɪʃən) *n.* purification by sacrifice —**ˈlustral** *a.* used in lustration —**ˈlustrate** *vt.*

lustre *or U.S.* **luster** (ˈlʌstə) *n.* **1.** gloss, sheen **2.** splendour **3.** renown **4.** glory **5.** glossy material **6.** metallic pottery glaze —**ˈlustrous** *a.* shining, luminous

lute[1] (luːt) *n.* old stringed musical instrument played with the fingers —**ˈlutenist** *or* **ˈlutist** *n.*

lute[2] (luːt) *n.* **1.** composition to make joints airtight —*vt.* **2.** close with lute

lutetium *or* **lutecium** (luˈtiːʃɪəm) *n.* silvery-white metallic element of lanthanide series

Lutheran (ˈluːθərən) *n.* **1.** follower of Luther, German leader of Protestant Reformation, or member of Lu-

---

THESAURUS

land, load, saddle **3.** clump, lump along, plod, shamble, shuffle, stump, trudge, trundle, waddle

luminous 1. bright, brilliant, glowing, illuminated, lighted, lit, luminescent, lustrous, radiant, resplendent, shining, vivid **2.** clear, evident, intelligible, lucid, obvious, perspicuous, plain, transparent

lump *n.* **1.** ball, bunch, cake, chunk, clod, cluster, dab, gob, gobbet, group, hunk, mass, nugget, piece, spot, wedge **2.** bulge, bump, growth, protrusion, protuberance, swelling, tumescence, tumour ~*v.* **3.** agglutinate, aggregate, batch, bunch, coalesce, collect, combine, conglomerate, consolidate, group, mass, pool, unite

lunacy 1. dementia, derangement, idiocy, insanity, madness, mania, psychosis **2.** aberration, absurdity, craziness, folly, foolhardiness, foolishness, idiocy, imbecility, madness, senselessness, stupidity, tomfoolery

lunatic 1. *adj.* barmy (*Sl.*), bonkers (*Sl.*), crackbrained, crazy, daft, demented, deranged, insane, irrational, mad, maniacal, nuts (*Sl.*), psychotic, unhinged **2.** *n.* loony (*Sl.*), madman, maniac, nut (*Sl.*), nutcase (*Sl.*), nutter (*Sl.*), psychopath

lunge 1. *n.* charge, cut, jab, pass, pounce, spring, stab, swing, swipe, thrust **2.** *v.* bound, charge, cut, dash, dive, fall upon, hit at, jab, leap, pitch into, plunge, poke, pounce, set upon, stab, strike at, thrust

lure 1. *v.* allure, attract, beckon, decoy, draw, ensnare, entice, inveigle, invite, lead on, seduce, tempt **2.** *n.* allurement, attraction, bait, carrot (*Inf.*), come-on (*Inf.*), decoy, enticement, inducement, magnet, siren song, temptation

lurid 1. exaggerated, graphic, melodramatic, sensational, shocking, startling, unrestrained, vivid, yellow (*Of journalism*) **2.** ashen, ghastly, pale, pallid, sallow, wan **3.** bloody, fiery, flaming, glaring, glowering, intense, livid, overbright, sanguine

lurk conceal oneself, crouch, go furtively, hide, lie in wait, move with stealth, prowl, skulk, slink, sneak, snoop

luscious appetizing, delectable, delicious, honeyed, juicy, mouth-watering, palatable, rich, savoury, scrumptious (*Inf.*), succulent, sweet, toothsome, yummy (*Sl.*)

lush 1. abundant, dense, flourishing, green, lavish, overgrown, prolific, rank, teeming, verdant **2.** fresh, juicy, ripe, succulent, tender

lust *n.* **1.** carnality, concupiscence, lasciviousness, lechery, lewdness, libido, licentiousness, pruriency, randiness (*Sl., chiefly Brit.*), salaciousness, sensuality, wantonness **2.** appetence, appetite, avidity, covetousness, craving, cupidity, desire, greed, longing, passion, thirst ~*v.* **3.** be consumed with desire for, covet, crave, desire, hunger for *or* after, lech after (*Inf.*), need, slaver over, want, yearn

lustre 1. burnish, gleam, glint, glitter, gloss, glow, sheen, shimmer, shine, sparkle **2.** brightness, brilliance, dazzle, lambency, luminousness, radiance, resplendence **3.** distinction, fame, glory, honour, illustriousness, prestige, renown

lusty brawny, energetic, hale, healthy, hearty, in fine fettle, powerful, red-blooded (*Inf.*), robust, rugged, stalwart, stout, strapping, strong, sturdy, vigorous, virile theran Church —*a.* **2.** of Luther or his doctrines **3.** of Lutheran Church —**'Lutheranism** *n.*

lutz (luts) *n. Ice-skating* jump from one skate with complete turn in air and return to other skate

lux (lʌks) *n.* SI unit of illumination (*pl.* **lux**)

luxe (lʌks, luks; *Fr.* lyks) *n. see* DE LUXE

luxury ('lʌkʃərɪ), *n.* **1.** possession and use of costly, choice things for enjoyment **2.** enjoyable but not necessary thing **3.** comfortable surroundings —**luxuriance** (lʌg'zjʊərɪəns) *n.* abundance, proliferation —**luxuriant** (lʌg'zjʊərɪənt) *a.* **1.** growing thickly **2.** abundant —**luxuriantly** (lʌg'zjʊərɪəntlɪ) *adv.* —**luxuriate** (lʌg'zjʊərɪeɪt) *vi.* **1.** indulge in luxury **2.** flourish profusely **3.** take delight —**luxurious** (lʌg'zjʊərɪəs) *a.* **1.** fond of luxury **2.** self-indulgent **3.** sumptuous —**luxuriously** (lʌg'zjʊərɪəslɪ) *adv.*

LV luncheon voucher

lyceum (laɪ'sɪəm) *n.* public building for concerts *etc.*

lychee (laɪ'tʃiː) *n. see* LITCHI

lych gate (lɪtʃ) *see* LICH GATE

lyddite ('lɪdaɪt) *n.* powerful explosive used in shells

lye (laɪ) *n.* water made alkaline with wood ashes *etc.* for use as cleansing agent

lying ('laɪɪŋ) *pr.p. of* LIE[1], LIE[2] —**lying-in** *n.* confinement in childbirth (*pl.* **lyings-in**)

lymph (lɪmf) *n.* colourless bodily fluid, mainly of white blood cells —**lym'phatic** *a.* **1.** of lymph **2.** flabby, sluggish —*n.* **3.** vessel in the body conveying lymph —**lymph node** any of numerous bean-shaped masses of tissue, situated along course of lymphatic vessels

lynch (lɪntʃ) *vt.* put to death without trial —**lynch law** procedure of self-appointed court trying and executing accused

lynx (lɪŋks) *n.* animal of cat family —**lynx-eyed** *a.* having keen sight

lyre (laɪə) *n* instrument like harp —**lyric** ('lɪrɪk) *n.* **1.** lyric poem —*pl.* **2.** words of popular song —**lyric(al)** ('lɪrɪk(ᵊl)) *a.* **1.** of short personal poems expressing emotion **2.** of lyre **3.** meant to be sung —**lyricist** ('lɪrɪsɪst) *n.* —**lyrist** ('lɪrɪst) *n.* **1.** lyric poet **2.** ('laɪərɪst) player on lyre —**'lyrebird** *n.* Aust. bird, the male of which displays tail shaped like a lyre —**wax lyrical** express great enthusiasm

-lyte (*n. comb. form*) substance that can be decomposed or broken down, as in *electrolyte* —**-lytic** (*a. comb. form*) loosening, dissolving, as in *paralytic*

THESAURUS

luxurious 1. comfortable, costly, de luxe, expensive, lavish, magnificent, opulent, plush (*Inf.*), rich, ritzy (*Sl.*), splendid, sumptuous, well-appointed **2.** epicurean, pampered, pleasure-loving, self-indulgent, sensual, sybaritic, voluptuous

luxury 1. affluence, hedonism, opulence, richness, splendour, sumptuousness, voluptuousness **2.** bliss, comfort, delight, enjoyment, gratification, indulgence, pleasure, satisfaction, wellbeing **3.** extra, extravagance, frill, indulgence, nonessential, treat

lying *adj.* deceitful, dishonest, dissembling, double-dealing, false, guileful, mendacious, perfidious, treacherous, two-faced, untruthful

lyric 1. *adj. Of poetry* expressive, lyrical, melodic, musical, songlike **2.** *n. Plural* book, libretto, text, the words, words of a song

M

m *or* **M** (ɛm) *n.* **1.** 13th letter of English alphabet **2.** speech sound represented by this letter (*pl.* **m's, M's** *or* **Ms**)

m metre(s)

M **1.** Mach **2.** mega- **3.** *Currency* mark(s) **4.** million **5.** UK motorway **6.** Roman numeral, 1000

m. **1.** male **2.** married **3.** masculine **4.** mile **5.** minute

M. **1.** Medieval **2.** Monsieur

ma (mɑː) *n. inf.* mother

MA Massachusetts

M.A. Master of Arts

ma'am (mæm, mɑːm; *unstressed* məm) *n.* madam

mac *or* **mack** (mæk) *n.* UK *inf.* mackintosh

Mac-, Mc- *or* **M'-** (*comb. form*) in surnames of Gaelic origin, son of, as in *MacDonald*

macabre (məˈkɑːbə, -brə) *a.* gruesome, ghastly

macadam (məˈkædəm) *n.* road surface made of pressed layers of small broken stones —**maˈcadamize** *or* **-ise** *vt.* pave (road) with this

macaroni *or* **maccaroni** (mækəˈrəʊnɪ) *n.* pasta in long, thin tubes (*pl.* **-s, -es**)

macaroon (mækəˈruːn) *n.* small cake, biscuit containing almonds

macaw (məˈkɔː) *n.* kind of parrot

mace[1] (meɪs) *n.* **1.** staff with metal head **2.** staff of office

mace[2] (meɪs) *n.* spice made of the husk of the nutmeg

macerate (ˈmæsəreɪt) *v.* **1.** soften by soaking **2.** (cause to) waste away —**maceˈration** *n.*

machete (məˈʃɛtɪ, -ˈtʃeɪ-) *n.* broad, heavy knife used for cutting or as a weapon

Machiavellian (mækɪəˈvelɪən) *a.* politically unprincipled, crafty, perfidious, subtle, deep-laid

machination (mækɪˈneɪʃən) *n.* (*usu. pl.*) plotting, intrigue —**ˈmachinate** *v.* lay or devise (plots)

machine (məˈʃiːn) *n.* **1.** apparatus combining action of several parts to apply mechanical force **2.** controlling organization **3.** mechanical appliance **4.** vehicle —*vt.* **5.** sew, print, shape *etc.* with machine —**maˈchinery** *n.* **1.** parts of machine collectively **2.** machines —**maˈchinist** *n.* one who makes or works machines —**machine gun** gun firing repeatedly and continuously with an automatic loading and firing mechanism —**machine-readable** *a.* (of data) in a form that can be directly fed into a computer —**machine shop** workshop in which machine tools are operated —**machine tool** power-driven machine, such as lathe, for cutting or shaping metals *etc.*

machismo (mæˈkɪzməʊ, -ˈtʃɪz-) *n.* strong or exaggerated masculine pride or masculinity (*oft.* **macho** (ˈmætʃəʊ))

Mach (number) (mæx) *n.* the ratio of the air speed of an aircraft to the velocity of sound under given conditions

mack (mæk) *n.* UK *inf. see* MAC

mackerel (ˈmækrəl) *n.* edible sea fish with blue and silver stripes

mackintosh *or* **macintosh** (ˈmækɪntɒʃ) *n.* **1.** waterproof raincoat of rubberized cloth **2.** any raincoat

macramé (məˈkrɑːmɪ) *n.* ornamental work of knotted cord

macro- *or before vowel* **macr-** (*comb. form*) **1.** large, long, or great in size or duration, as in *macroscopic* **2.** *Pathol.* abnormal enlargement, as in *macrocephaly*

macrobiotics (mækrəʊbaɪˈɒtɪks) *pl.n.* (*with sing. v.*) dietary system advocating whole grain and vegetables grown without chemical additives

macrocosm (ˈmækrəkɒzəm) *n.* **1.** the universe **2.** any large, complete system

macron (ˈmækrɒn) *n.* diacritical mark (¯) placed over letter to represent long vowel

macroscopic (mækrəʊˈskɒpɪk) *a.* **1.** visible to the naked eye **2.** concerned with large units —**macroˈscopically** *adv.*

mad (mæd) *a.* **1.** suffering from mental disease, insane **2.** wildly foolish **3.** very enthusiastic **4.** excited **5.** *inf.* furious, angry —**ˈmadden** *vt.* make mad —**ˈmadly** *adv.* —**ˈmadness** *n.* **1.** insanity **2.** folly —**ˈmadhouse** *n. inf.* **1.** mental hospital or asylum **2.** state of uproar or confusion —**ˈmadman** *n.*

madam (ˈmædəm) *n.* **1.** polite form of address to a woman **2.** *inf.* precocious or conceited girl

madame (ˈmædəm) *n.* married Frenchwoman

madcap (ˈmædkæp) *n.* **1.** reckless person —*a.* **2.** reckless

THESAURUS

macabre cadaverous, deathlike, deathly, dreadful, eerie, frightening, frightful, ghastly, ghostly, ghoulish, grim, grisly, gruesome, hideous, horrid

machine **1.** apparatus, appliance, contraption, contrivance, device, engine, instrument, mechanism, tool **2.** agency, machinery, organization, party, setup (*Inf.*), structure, system

machinery apparatus, equipment, gear, instruments, mechanism, tackle, tools, works

mad **1.** aberrant, bananas (*Sl.*), barmy (*Sl.*), batty (*Sl.*), bonkers (*Sl.*), crackers (*Sl.*), crazed, crazy (*Inf.*), cuckoo (*Inf.*), delirious, demented, deranged, distracted, frantic, frenzied, insane, loony (*Sl.*), loopy (*Inf.*), lunatic, mental (*Sl.*), *non compos mentis*, nuts (*Sl.*), nutty (*Sl.*), off one's chump (*Sl.*), off one's head, off one's nut (*Sl.*), off one's rocker (*Sl.*), off one's trolley (*Sl.*), of unsound mind, out of one's mind, psychotic, rabid, raving, round the bend (*Brit. sl.*), round the twist (*Brit. sl.*), screwy (*Inf.*), unbalanced, unhinged, unstable **2.** absurd, daft (*Inf.*), foolhardy, foolish, imprudent, irrational, ludicrous, nonsensical, preposterous, senseless, unreasonable, unsafe, unsound, wild **3.** *Inf.* angry, berserk, enraged, exasperated, fuming, furious, in a wax (*Inf.*), incensed, infuriated, irate, irritated, livid (*Inf.*), raging, resentful, seeing red (*Inf.*), wild, wrathful **4.** ardent, avid, crazy, daft (*Inf.*), devoted, dotty (*Brit. sl.*), enamoured, enthusiastic, fanatical, fond, hooked (*Sl.*), impassioned, infatuated, in love with, keen, nuts (*Sl.*), wild, zealous **5.** abandoned, agitated, boisterous, ebullient, energetic, excited, frenetic, frenzied, gay, riotous, uncontrolled, unrestrained, wild

madden annoy, craze, derange, drive one crazy (off

madder (ˈmædə) *n.* **1.** climbing plant **2.** its root **3.** red dye made from this

made (meɪd) *pt./pp. of* MAKE —**made-up** *a.* **1.** invented **2.** wearing make-up **3.** put together

Madeira (məˈdɪərə) *n.* rich sherry wine —**Madeira cake** rich sponge cake

mademoiselle (mædmwəˈzɛl) *n.* **1.** young unmarried French girl or woman **2.** French teacher or governess

Madonna (məˈdɒnə) *n.* **1.** the Virgin Mary **2.** picture or statue of her

madrepore (mædrɪˈpɔː) *n.* kind of coral

madrigal (ˈmædrɪgᵊl) *n.* **1.** unaccompanied part song **2.** short love poem or song

maelstrom (ˈmeɪlstrəʊm) *n.* **1.** great whirlpool **2.** turmoil

maenad (ˈmiːnæd) *n. Class. lit.* frenzied female worshipper of Dionysus

maestoso (maɪˈstəʊsəʊ) *adv. Mus.* grandly, in majestic manner

maestro (ˈmaɪstrəʊ) *n.* **1.** outstanding musician, conductor **2.** man regarded as master of any art (*pl.* **-tri** (trɪ), **-s**)

mae west (meɪ) *sl.* inflatable life jacket

Mafia (ˈmæfɪə) *n.* international secret criminal organization, *orig.* Italian

magazine (mægəˈziːn) *n.* **1.** periodical publication with stories and articles by different writers **2.** appliance for supplying cartridges automatically to gun **3.** storehouse for explosives or arms

magenta (məˈdʒɛntə) *a./n.* (of) deep purplish-red colour

maggot (ˈmægət) *n.* grub, larva —ˈ**maggoty** *a.* infested with maggots

magi (ˈmeɪdʒaɪ) *pl.n.* **1.** priests of ancient Persia **2.** the wise men from the East at the Nativity (*sing.* **-gus** (-gəs))

magic (ˈmædʒɪk) *n.* **1.** art of supposedly invoking supernatural powers to influence events *etc.* **2.** any mysterious agency or power **3.** witchcraft, conjuring —*a.* **4.** magical, enchanting —ˈ**magical** *a.* —ˈ**magically** *adv.* —**maˈgician** *n.* one skilled in magic, wizard, conjurer, enchanter —**magic lantern** early form of projector using slides

magistrate (ˈmædʒɪstreɪt, -strɪt) *n.* **1.** civil officer administering law **2.** justice of the peace —**magisˈterial** *a.* **1.** of, referring to magistrate **2.** dictatorial —ˈ**magistracy** *n.* **1.** office of magistrate **2.** magistrates collectively

magma (ˈmægmə) *n.* **1.** paste or suspension consisting of finely divided solid dispersed in liquid **2.** molten rock inside earth's crust

magnanimous (mægˈnænɪməs) *a.* noble, generous, not petty —**magnaˈnimity** *n.*

magnate (ˈmægneɪt, -nɪt) *n.* influential or wealthy person

magnesium (mægˈniːzɪəm) *n.* metallic element —**magˈnesia** *n.* white powder compound of this, used in medicine

magnet (ˈmægnɪt) *n.* **1.** piece of iron, steel having properties of attracting iron, steel and pointing north and south when suspended **2.** lodestone —**magˈnetic** *a.* **1.** with properties of magnet **2.** exerting powerful attraction —**magˈnetically** *adv.* —ˈ**magnetism** *n.* **1.** magnetic phenomena **2.** science of magnetic phenom-

THESAURUS

one's head, out of one's mind, round the bend (*Brit. sl.*), round the twist (*Brit. sl.*), to distraction), enrage, exasperate, get one's hackles up, incense, inflame, infuriate, irritate, make one's blood boil, make one see red (*Inf.*), make one's hackles rise, provoke, raise one's hackles, unhinge, upset, vex

made-up fabricated, false, fictional, imaginary, invented, make-believe, mythical, specious, trumped-up, unreal, untrue

madly 1. crazily, deliriously, dementedly, distractedly, frantically, frenziedly, hysterically, insanely, rabidly **2.** absurdly, foolishly, irrationally, ludicrously, nonsensically, senselessly, unreasonably, wildly **3.** energetically, excitedly, furiously, hastily, hurriedly, like mad, quickly, rapidly, recklessly, speedily, violently, wildly **4.** *Inf.* desperately, devotedly, exceedingly, excessively, extremely, intensely, passionately, to distraction

madman loony (*Sl.*), lunatic, maniac, mental case (*Sl.*), nut (*Sl.*), nutcase (*Sl.*), nutter (*Sl.*), psycho (*Sl.*), psychopath, psychotic

madness 1. aberration, craziness, delusion, dementia, derangement, distraction, insanity, lunacy, mania, mental illness, psychopathy, psychosis **2.** absurdity, daftness (*Inf.*), folly, foolhardiness, foolishness, nonsense, preposterousness, wildness

magazine 1. journal, pamphlet, paper, periodical **2.** ammunition dump, arsenal, depot, powder-room (*Obsolete*), store, storehouse, warehouse

magic *n.* **1.** black art, enchantment, necromancy, occultism, sorcery, sortilege, spell, theurgy, witchcraft, wizardry **2.** conjuring, hocus-pocus, illusion, jiggery-pokery (*Inf., chiefly Brit.*), jugglery, legerdemain, prestidigitation, sleight of hand, trickery **3.** allurement, charm, enchantment, fascination, glamour, magnetism, power ~*adj.* **4.** *Also* **magical** bewitching, charismatic, charming, enchanting, entrancing, fascinating, magnetic, marvellous, miraculous, sorcerous, spellbinding

magician archimage (*Rare*), conjurer, conjuror, enchanter, enchantress, illusionist, necromancer, sorcerer, thaumaturge (*Rare*), theurgist, warlock, witch, wizard

magisterial arrogant, assertive, authoritative, bossy (*Inf.*), commanding, dictatorial, domineering, high-handed, imperious, lordly, masterful, overbearing, peremptory

magistrate bailie (*Scot.*), J.P., judge, justice, justice of the peace, provost (*Scot.*)

magnanimity altruism, beneficence, big-heartedness, bountifulness, charitableness, generosity, high-mindedness, largess, munificence, nobility, open-handedness, selflessness, unselfishness

magnanimous beneficent, big, big-hearted, bountiful, charitable, free, generous, great-hearted, handsome, high-minded, kind, kindly, munificent, noble, open-handed, selfless, ungrudging, unselfish, unstinting

magnate 1. baron, big cheese (*Sl.*), big noise (*Sl.*), big shot (*Sl.*), big wheel (*Sl.*), bigwig (*Sl.*), captain of industry, chief, fat cat (*Sl.*), leader, mogul, Mr. Big (*Sl.*), nabob (*Inf.*), notable, plutocrat, tycoon, V.I.P. **2.** aristocrat, baron, bashaw, grandee, magnifico, merchant, noble, notable, personage, prince

ena 3. personal charm or power of attracting others —ˈ**magnetite** *n.* black magnetizable mineral that is important source of iron —**magnetiˈzation** *or* **-iˈsation** *n.* —ˈ**magnetize** *or* **-ise** *vt.* 1. make into a magnet 2. attract as if by magnet 3. fascinate —**magneto** (mægˈniːtəʊ) *n.* apparatus for ignition in internal-combustion engine (*pl.* **-s**) —**magneˈtometer** *n.* instrument used to measure magnetic force —ˈ**magnetron** *n.* two-electrode electronic valve used with applied magnetic field to generate high-power microwave oscillations —**magnetic field** field of force surrounding permanent magnet or moving charged particle —**magnetic mine** mine designed to activate when magnetic field is detected —**magnetic needle** magnetized rod used in certain instruments for indicating direction of magnetic field —**magnetic north** direction in which compass needle points, usu. at angle of true north —**magnetic pole** 1. either of two regions in magnet where magnetic induction is concentrated 2. either of two variable points on earth's surface towards which magnetic needle points —**magnetic storm** sudden severe disturbance of earth's magnetic field —**magnetic tape** long coated plastic strip for recording sound or video signals

Magnificat (mægˈnɪfɪkæt) *n.* hymn of Virgin Mary in *Luke* 1. 46–55, used as canticle

magnificent (mægˈnɪfɪsᵊnt) *a.* 1. splendid 2. stately, imposing 3. excellent —**magˈnificence** *n.* —**magˈnificently** *adv.*

magnify (ˈmægnɪfaɪ) *vt.* 1. increase apparent size of, as with lens 2. exaggerate 3. make greater (**-fied, -fying**) —**magnifiˈcation** *n.*

magniloquent (mægˈnɪləkwənt) *a.* 1. speaking pompously 2. grandiose —**magˈniloquence** *n.*

magnitude (ˈmægnɪtjuːd) *n.* 1. importance 2. greatness, size

magnolia (mægˈnəʊlɪə) *n.* shrub or tree with large white, sweet-scented flowers

magnox (ˈmægnɒks) *n.* alloy of mostly magnesium with small amounts of aluminium used in fuel elements of nuclear reactor —**magnox reactor**

magnum (ˈmægnəm) *n.* large wine bottle (approx. 52 fluid ounces)

magnum opus great work of art or literature

magpie (ˈmægpaɪ) *n.* black-and-white bird

Magyar (ˈmægjɑː) *n.* 1. member of prevailing race in Hungary 2. native speech of Hungary —*a.* 3. pert. to Magyars 4. *Dressmaking* cut with sleeves and bodice of garment in one piece

maharajah *or* **maharaja** (mɑːhəˈrɑːdʒə) *n.* former title of some Indian princes

maharani *or* **maharanee** (mɑːhəˈrɑːniː) *n.* 1. wife of maharajah 2. woman holding rank of maharajah

maharishi (mɑːhɑːˈriːʃɪ, məˈhɑːriːʃɪ) *n.* Hindu religious teacher or mystic

mahatma (məˈhɑːtmə) *n.* 1. *Hinduism* man of saintly life with supernatural powers 2. one endowed with great wisdom and power

mahjong *or* **mah-jongg** (mɑːˈdʒɒŋ) *n.* Chinese table game for four, played with pieces called tiles

mahogany (məˈhɒgənɪ) *n.* tree yielding reddish-brown wood

mahout (məˈhaʊt) *n.* in India and E Indies, elephant driver or keeper

maiden (ˈmeɪdᵊn) *n.* 1. *Lit.* young unmarried woman —*a.* 2. unmarried 3. of, suited to maiden 4. first 5. having blank record —**maid** *n.* 1. *Lit.* young unmarried woman 2. woman servant —ˈ**maidenhood** *n.* —ˈ**maidenly** *a.* modest —ˈ**maidenhair** *n.* fern with delicate stalks and fronds —ˈ**maidenhead** *n.* 1. hymen 2. virginity —**maiden name** woman's surname before marriage —**maid of honour** 1. UK small tart with almond-flavoured filling 2. unmarried lady attending queen or princess 3. US principal unmarried attendant of bride —**maiden over** *Cricket* over in which no runs are scored

mail[1] (meɪl) *n.* 1. letters *etc.* transported and delivered by the post office 2. letters *etc.* conveyed at one time 3. the postal system 4. train, ship *etc.* carrying mail —*vt.* 5. send by post —**mail order** 1. order for merchandise sent by post 2. system of buying and selling merchandise through post

THESAURUS

magnetic alluring, attractive, captivating, charismatic, charming, enchanting, entrancing, fascinating, hypnotic, irresistible, mesmerizing, seductive

magnetism allure, appeal, attraction, attractiveness, captivatingness, charisma, charm, draw, drawing power, enchantment, fascination, hypnotism, magic, mesmerism, power, pull, seductiveness, spell

magnification aggrandizement, amplification, augmentation, blow-up (*Inf.*), boost, build-up, deepening, dilation, enhancement, enlargement, exaggeration, expansion, heightening, increase, inflation, intensification

magnificence brilliance, glory, gorgeousness, grandeur, luxuriousness, luxury, majesty, nobility, opulence, pomp, resplendence, splendour, stateliness, sublimity, sumptuousness

magnificent august, brilliant, elegant, elevated, exalted, excellent, fine, glorious, gorgeous, grand, grandiose, imposing, impressive, lavish, luxurious, majestic, noble, opulent, outstanding, princely, regal, resplendent, rich, splendid, stately, sublime, sumptuous, superb, superior, transcendent

magnify 1. aggrandize, amplify, augment, blow up (*Inf.*), boost, build up, deepen, dilate, enlarge, expand, heighten, increase, intensify 2. aggravate, blow up, blow up out of all proportion, dramatize, enhance, exaggerate, inflate, make a mountain out of a molehill, overdo, overemphasize, overestimate, overplay, overrate, overstate

magnitude 1. consequence, eminence, grandeur, greatness, importance, mark, moment, note, significance, weight 2. amount, amplitude, bigness, bulk, capacity, dimensions, enormity, expanse, extent, hugeness, immensity, intensity, largeness, mass, measure, proportions, quantity, size, space, strength, vastness, volume

maid 1. damsel, girl, lass, lassie (*Inf.*), maiden, miss, nymph (*Poetic*), wench 2. abigail (*Archaic*), handmaiden (*Archaic*), housemaid, maid-servant, servant, serving-maid

maiden *n.* 1. damsel, girl, lass, lassie (*Inf.*), maid, miss, nymph, virgin, wench ~*adj.* 2. chaste, intact, pure, undefiled, unmarried, unwed, virgin, virginal 3. first, inaugural, initial, initiatory, introductory 4. fresh, new, unbroached, untapped, untried, unused

maidenly chaste, decent, decorous, demure, gentle,

mail[2] (meɪl) *n.* armour of interlaced rings or overlapping plates —**mailed** *a.* covered with mail

maim (meɪm) *vt.* cripple, mutilate

main (meɪn) *a.* **1.** chief, principal, leading —*n.* **2.** principal pipe, line carrying water, electricity *etc.* **3.** chief part **4.** strength, power **5.** *obs.* open sea —**ˈmainly** *adv.* for the most part, chiefly —**main chance** one's own interests (*usu. in* **have an eye to the main chance**) —**main clause** *Gram.* clause that can stand alone as sentence —**main force** physical strength —**mainland** (ˈmeɪnlənd) *n.* stretch of land which forms main part of a country —**main line 1.** *Railways* trunk route between two points **2.** *sl.* main vein into which narcotic drug can be injected —**ˈmainline** *vi. sl.* inject drug thus —**ˈmainmast** *n.* chief mast in ship —**mainsail** (ˈmeɪnseɪl; *Naut.* ˈmeɪnsᵊl) *n.* lowest sail of mainmast —**ˈmainspring** *n.* **1.** chief spring of watch or clock **2.** chief cause or motive —**ˈmainstay** *n.* **1.** rope from mainmast **2.** chief support —**ˈmainstream** *n.* **1.** main current (of river, cultural trend *etc.*) —*a.* **2.** of style of jazz that lies between traditional and modern

maintain (meɪnˈteɪn) *vt.* **1.** carry on **2.** preserve **3.** support **4.** sustain **5.** keep up **6.** keep supplied **7.** affirm **8.** support by argument **9.** defend —**mainˈtainable** *a.* —**ˈmaintenance** *n.* **1.** maintaining **2.** means of support **3.** upkeep of buildings *etc.* **4.** provision of money for separated or divorced spouse

maisonette *or* **maisonnette** (meɪzəˈnɛt) *n.* part of house, usu. on two floors, fitted as self-contained dwelling

maître d'hôtel (mɛtrə dəʊˈtɛl) *Fr.* restaurant manager

maize (meɪz) *n.* type of corn

Maj. Major

majesty (ˈmædʒɪstɪ) *n.* **1.** stateliness **2.** sovereignty **3.** grandeur —**maˈjestic** *a.* **1.** splendid **2.** regal —**maˈjestically** *adv.*

majolica (məˈdʒɒlɪkə, məˈjɒl-) *or* **maiolica** (məˈjɒlɪkə) *n.* type of ornamented Italian pottery

major (ˈmeɪdʒə) *n.* **1.** army officer ranking next above captain **2.** major scale in music **3.** **US, A, NZ** principal field of study at university *etc.* **4.** person of legal majority —*a.* **5.** greater in number, quality, extent **6.** significant, serious —*vi.* **7.** (*usu. with* in) **US, A, NZ** do one's principal study (in particular subject) —**maˈjority** *n.* **1.** greater number **2.** larger party voting together **3.** excess of the vote on one side **4.** coming of age **5.** rank of major —**major-domo** (ˈdəʊməʊ) *n.* house steward (*pl.* **-s**) —**major general** *Mil.* officer immediately junior to lieutenant general —**major scale** *Mus.* scale with semitones instead of whole tones after third and seventh notes

make (meɪk) *vt.* **1.** construct **2.** produce **3.** create **4.** establish **5.** appoint **6.** amount to **7.** cause to (do something) **8.** accomplish **9.** reach **10.** earn —*vi.* **11.** tend (**made, ˈmaking**) —*n.* **12.** brand, type, style —**ˈMaker** *n.* title given to God (as Creator) —**ˈmaking** *n.* **1.** creation —*pl.* **2.** necessary requirements or qualities —**make-believe** *n.* fantasy or pretence —**ˈmakeshift** *n.* temporary expedient —**make-up** *n.* **1.** cosmetics **2.** characteristics **3.** layout —**ˈmakeweight** *n.* trifle added to make something stronger or better —**(go to) meet one's Maker** die —**make believe** pretend; enact fantasy —**make up 1.** compose **2.** compile **3.** complete **4.** compensate **5.** apply cosmetics **6.** invent —**on the make** *sl.* **1.** intent on gain **2.** in search of sexual partner

THESAURUS

girlish, modest, pure, reserved, undefiled, unsullied, vestal, virginal, virtuous

mail *n.* **1.** correspondence, letters, packages, parcels, post **2.** post, postal service, postal system ~*v.* **3.** dispatch, forward, post, send, send by mail *or* post

maim cripple, disable, hamstring, hurt, impair, incapacitate, injure, lame, mangle, mar, mutilate, put out of action, wound

main *adj.* **1.** capital, cardinal, central, chief, critical, crucial, essential, foremost, head, leading, necessary, outstanding, paramount, particular, predominant, pre-eminent, premier, primary, prime, principal, special, supreme, vital ~*n.* **2.** cable, channel, conduit, duct, line, pipe **3.** effort, force, might, potency, power, puissance, strength

mainly above all, chiefly, first and foremost, for the most part, generally, in general, in the main, largely, mostly, most of all, on the whole, overall, predominantly, primarily, principally, substantially, to the greatest extent, usually

mainstay anchor, backbone, bulwark, buttress, chief support, linchpin, pillar, prop

maintain **1.** care for, carry on, conserve, continue, finance, keep, keep up, prolong, look after, nurture, perpetuate, preserve, provide, retain, supply, support, sustain, take care of, uphold **2.** affirm, allege, assert, asseverate, aver, avow, claim, contend, declare, hold, insist, profess, state **3.** advocate, argue for, back, champion, defend, fight for, justify, plead for, stand by, take up the cudgels for, uphold, vindicate

maintenance **1.** care, carrying-on, conservation, continuance, continuation, keeping, nurture, perpetuation, preservation, prolongation, provision, repairs, retainment, supply, support, sustainment, sustention, upkeep **2.** aliment, alimony, allowance, food, keep, livelihood, living, subsistence, support, sustenance, upkeep

majestic august, awesome, dignified, elevated, exalted, grand, grandiose, imperial, imposing, impressive, kingly, lofty, magnificent, monumental, noble, pompous, princely, regal, royal, splendid, stately, sublime, superb

majesty augustness, awesomeness, dignity, exaltedness, glory, grandeur, imposingness, impressiveness, kingliness, loftiness, magnificence, nobility, pomp, queenliness, royalty, splendour, state, stateliness, sublimity

major **1.** better, bigger, chief, elder, greater, higher, larger, leading, main, most, senior, superior, supreme, uppermost **2.** critical, crucial, grave, great, important, notable, outstanding, pre-eminent, radical, serious, significant, vital, weighty

majority **1.** best part, bulk, greater number, mass, more, most, plurality, preponderance, superiority **2.** adulthood, manhood, maturity, seniority, womanhood

make *v.* **1.** assemble, build, compose, constitute, construct, create, fabricate, fashion, forge, form, frame, manufacture, mould, originate, produce, put together, shape, synthesize **2.** accomplish, beget, bring about, cause, create, effect, engender, generate,

mako (ˈmɑːkəʊ) *n.* type of shark (*pl.* -s)

mal- (*comb. form*) ill, badly, as in *malformation, malfunction*

malacca *or* **malacca cane** (məˈlækə) *n.* brown cane used for walking stick

malachite (ˈmæləkaɪt) *n.* green mineral

maladjusted (mæləˈdʒʌstɪd) *a.* **1.** *Psychol.* unable to meet the demands of society **2.** badly adjusted **—malˈadˈjustment** *n.*

maladministration (mælədmɪnɪsˈtreɪʃən) *n.* inefficient or dishonest administration

maladroit (mæləˈdrɔɪt) *a.* clumsy, awkward

malady (ˈmælədɪ) *n.* disease

malaise (mæˈleɪz) *n.* vague, unlocated feeling of discomfort

malapropism (ˈmæləprɒpɪzəm) *or* **malaprop** *n.* ludicrous misuse of word

malapropos (mælæprəˈpəʊ) *a./adv.* inappropriate(ly)

malaria (məˈlɛərɪə) *n.* infectious disease caused by bite of some mosquitoes **—maˈlarial** *a.*

Malathion (mæləˈθaɪɒn) *n.* **R** insecticide consisting of organic phosphate

Malay (məˈleɪ) *n.* **1.** native of Malaysia or Indonesia **2.** language of this people **—Maˈlayan** *a./n.*

malcontent (ˈmælkəntɛnt) *a.* **1.** actively discontented **—*n.* 2.** malcontent person

male (meɪl) *a.* **1.** of sex producing gametes which fertilize female gametes **2.** of men or male animals **—*n.* 3.** male person or animal

malediction (mælɪˈdɪkʃən) *n.* curse

malefactor (ˈmælɪfæktə) *n.* criminal

maleficent (məˈlɛfɪsənt) *a.* harmful, hurtful **—maˈleficence** *n.*

malevolent (məˈlɛvələnt) *a.* full of ill will **—maˈlevolence** *n.*

malice (ˈmælɪs) *n.* **1.** ill will **2.** spite **—maˈlicious** *a.* **1.** intending evil or unkindness **2.** spiteful **3.** moved by hatred **—maˈliciously** *adv.*

malign (məˈlaɪn) *a.* **1.** evil in influence or effect **—*vt.* 2.** slander, misrepresent **—malignancy** (məˈlɪgnənsɪ) *n.* **—malignant** (məˈlɪgnənt) *a.* **1.** feeling extreme ill

THESAURUS

give rise to, lead to, occasion, produce **3.** cause, coerce, compel, constrain, dragoon, drive, force, impel, induce, oblige, press, pressurize, prevail upon, require **4.** appoint, assign, create, designate, elect, install, invest, nominate, ordain **5.** draw up, enact, establish, fix, form, frame, pass **6.** add up to, amount to, compose, constitute, embody, form, represent **7.** acquire, clear, earn, gain, get, net, obtain, realize, secure, take in, win **8.** arrive at, arrive in time for, attain, catch, get to, meet, reach *~n.* **9.** brand, build, character, composition, constitution, construction, cut, designation, form, kind, make-up, mark, model, shape, sort, structure, style, type, variety

make-believe charade, dream, fantasy, imagination, play-acting, pretence, unreality

make believe act as if *or* though, dream, enact, fantasize, imagine, play, play-act, pretend

Maker Creator, God

makeshift expedient, shift, stopgap, substitute

make-up 1. cosmetics, face (*Inf.*), greasepaint (*Theatre*), *maquillage*, paint (*Inf.*), powder, war paint (*Inf., humorous*) **2.** arrangement, assembly, composition, configuration, constitution, construction, form, format, formation, organization, structure **3.** build, cast of mind, character, constitution, disposition, figure, frame of mind, make, nature, stamp, temper, temperament

make up 1. compose, comprise, constitute, form **2.** coin, compose, concoct, construct, cook up (*Inf.*), create, devise, dream up, fabricate, formulate, frame, hatch, invent, originate, trump up, write **3.** complete, fill, meet, supply **4.** *With* **for** atone, balance, compensate, make amends, offset, recompense, redeem, redress, requite

makings beginnings, capability, capacity, ingredients, materials, potentiality, potential(s), qualities

maladjusted alienated, disturbed, estranged, hung-up (*Sl.*), neurotic, unstable

maladministration blundering, bungling, corruption, dishonesty, incompetence, inefficiency, malfeasance (*Law*), malpractice, misgovernment, mismanagement, misrule

malady affliction, ailment, complaint, disease, disorder, ill, illness, indisposition, infirmity, sickness

malcontent 1. *adj.* disaffected, discontented, disgruntled, disgusted, dissatisfied, dissentious, factious, ill-disposed, rebellious, resentful, restive, unhappy, unsatisfied **2.** *n.* agitator, complainer, fault-finder, grouch (*Inf.*), grouser, grumbler, mischief-maker, rebel, troublemaker

malefactor convict, criminal, crook (*Inf.*), culprit, delinquent, evildoer, felon, lawbreaker, miscreant, offender, outlaw, transgressor, villain, wrongdoer

malevolence hate, hatred, ill will, malice, maliciousness, malignity, rancour, spite, spitefulness, vengefulness, vindictiveness

malevolent baleful, evil-minded, hateful (*Archaic*), hostile, ill-natured, malicious, malign, malignant, pernicious, rancorous, spiteful, vengeful, vicious, vindictive

malice animosity, animus, bad blood, bitterness, enmity, evil intent, hate, hatred, ill will, malevolence, maliciousness, malignity, rancour, spite, spitefulness, spleen, vengefulness, venom, vindictiveness

malicious baleful, bitchy (*Sl.*), bitter, catty (*Inf.*), evil-minded, hateful, ill-disposed, ill-natured, injurious, malevolent, malignant, mischievous, pernicious, rancorous, resentful, spiteful, vengeful, vicious

malign 1. *adj.* bad, baleful, baneful, deleterious, destructive, evil, harmful, hostile, hurtful, injurious, malevolent, malignant, pernicious, vicious, wicked **2.** *v.* abuse, blacken (someone's name), calumniate, defame, denigrate, derogate, disparage, do a hatchet job on (*Inf.*), harm, injure, libel, revile, run down, slander, smear, speak ill of, traduce, vilify

malignant 1. baleful, bitter, destructive, harmful, hostile, hurtful, inimical, injurious, malevolent, malicious, malign, of evil intent, pernicious, spiteful, vicious **2.** *Medical* cancerous, dangerous, deadly, evil, fatal, irremediable, metastatic, uncontrollable, virulent

will **2.** (of disease) resistant to therapy —**malignantly** (məˈlɪgnəntlɪ) *adv.* —**malignity** (məˈlɪgnɪtɪ) *n.* malignant disposition

malinger (məˈlɪŋgə) *vi.* feign illness to escape duty —**maˈlingerer** *n.*

mall (mɔːl, mæl) *n.* **1.** level, shaded walk **2.** street, shopping area closed to vehicles

mallard (ˈmælɑːd) *n.* wild duck

malleable (ˈmælɪəbˀl) *a.* **1.** capable of being hammered into shape **2.** adaptable —**malleaˈbility** *n.*

mallet (ˈmælɪt) *n.* **1.** (wooden) hammer **2.** croquet or polo stick

mallow (ˈmæləʊ) *n.* wild plant with purple flowers

malmsey (ˈmɑːmzɪ) *n.* strong sweet wine

malnutrition (mælnjuːˈtrɪʃən) *n.* inadequate nutrition

malodorous (mælˈəʊdərəs) *a.* evil-smelling

malpractice (mælˈpræktɪs) *n.* immoral, illegal or unethical conduct

malt (mɔːlt) *n.* **1.** grain used for brewing —*v.* **2.** make into or become malt —**ˈmaltster** *n.* maker of malt

Maltese (mɔːlˈtiːz) *a.* **1.** of or relating to Malta, its inhabitants, or their language —*n.* **2.** native or inhabitant of Malta (*pl.* **-tese**) **3.** official language of Malta —**Maltese cross** cross with triangular arms that taper towards centre

maltreat (mælˈtriːt) *vt.* treat badly, handle roughly —**malˈtreatment** *n.*

mama *or chiefly U.S.* **mamma** (məˈmɑː) *n. old-fashioned* mother

mamba (ˈmæmbə) *n.* deadly S Afr. snake

mambo (ˈmæmbəʊ) *n.* Latin Amer. dance like rumba (*pl.* **-s**)

mamilla *or U.S.* **mammilla** (mæˈmɪlə) *n.* **1.** nipple or teat **2.** any nipple-shaped prominence (*pl.* **-lae** (-liː)) —**ˈmamillary** *or U.S.* **ˈmammillary** *a.*

mamma (ˈmæmə) *n.* milk-secreting organ of female mammals: breast in women, udder in cows *etc.* (*pl.* **-mae** (-miː)) —**ˈmammary** *a.*

mammal (ˈmæməl) *n.* animal of type that suckles its young —**mammalian** (mæˈmeɪlɪən) *a.*

mammon (ˈmæmən) *n.* **1.** wealth regarded as source of evil **2.** (**M-**) false god of covetousness —**ˈmammonism** *n.* —**ˈmammonist** *n.*

mammoth (ˈmæməθ) *n.* **1.** extinct animal like an elephant —*a.* **2.** colossal

man (mæn) *n.* **1.** human being **2.** person **3.** human race **4.** adult male **5.** **SA** *sl.* any person **6.** manservant **7.** piece used in chess *etc.* (*pl.* **men**) —*vt.* **8.** supply (ship *etc.*) with necessary men **9.** fortify (-nn-) —**ˈmanful** *a.* brave, vigorous —**ˈmanfully** *adv.* —**ˈmanhood** *n.* —**ˈmanikin, ˈmanakin** *or* **ˈmannikin** *n.* **1.** little man **2.** model of human body **3.** lay figure —**ˈmanlike** *a.* —**ˈmanliness** *n.* —**ˈmanly** *a.* —**ˈmannish** *a.* like a man —**man Friday 1.** loyal male servant or assistant **2.** any factotum, *esp.* in office (*also* **Girl Friday, Person Friday**) —**ˈmanhandle** *vt.* treat roughly —**ˈmanhole** *n.* opening through which man may pass to a drain, sewer *etc.* —**man-hour** *n.* unit of work in industry, equal to work done by one man in one hour —**ˈmanhunt** *n.* organized search for fugitive —**manˈkind** *n.* human beings in general —**man-of-war** *or* **man o' war** *n.* **1.** warship **2.** *see* **Portuguese man-of-war** *at* PORTUGUESE —**ˈmanpower** *n.* **1.** power of human effort **2.** available number of workers —**ˈmanslaughter** *n.* culpable homicide without malice aforethought —**man in the street** typical person —**man of letters 1.** writer **2.** scholar —**man of the world** man of wide experience

manacle (ˈmænəkˀl) *n.* **1.** fetter, handcuff —*vt.* **2.** shackle

manage (ˈmænɪdʒ) *v.* **1.** be in charge (of), administer **2.** succeed in (doing) —*vt.* **3.** control **4.** handle, cope with **5.** conduct, carry on —**ˈmanageable** *a.* —**ˈmanagement** *n.* **1.** those who manage, as board of directors *etc.* **2.** administration **3.** skilful use of means **4.** conduct —**ˈmanager** *n.* **1.** one in charge of business, institution, actor *etc.* (**manageˈress** *fem.*) **2.** one who manages efficiently —**manaˈgerial** *a.* —**ˈmanaging** *a.* having administrative control

mañana (məˈnjɑːnə) *Sp.* **1.** tomorrow **2.** some other and later time

THESAURUS

malpractice 1. abuse, dereliction, misbehaviour, misconduct, mismanagement, negligence **2.** abuse, misdeed, offence, transgression

maltreat abuse, bully, damage, handle roughly, harm, hurt, ill-treat, injure, mistreat

mammoth Brobdingnagian, colossal, enormous, gargantuan, giant, gigantic, huge, immense, jumbo (*Inf.*), massive, mighty, monumental, mountainous, prodigious, stupendous, titanic, vast

man *n.* **1.** bloke (*Brit. inf.*), chap (*Inf.*), gentleman, guy (*Inf.*), male **2.** adult, being, body, human, human being, individual, one, person, personage, somebody, soul **3.** Homo sapiens, humanity, humankind, human race, mankind, mortals, people **4.** attendant, employee, follower, hand, hireling, manservant, retainer, servant, soldier, subject, subordinate, valet, vassal, worker, workman ~*v.* **5.** crew, fill, furnish with men, garrison, occupy, people, staff

manacle 1. *n.* bond, chain, fetter, gyve (*Archaic*), handcuff, iron, shackle, tie **2.** *v.* bind, chain, check, clap *or* put in irons, confine, constrain, curb, fetter, hamper, handcuff, inhibit, put in chains, restrain, shackle, tie one's hands

manage 1. administer, be in charge (of), command, concert, conduct, direct, govern, manipulate, oversee, preside over, rule, run, superintend, supervise **2.** accomplish, arrange, bring about *or* off, contrive, cope with, deal with, effect, engineer, succeed **3.** control, dominate, govern, guide, handle, influence, manipulate, operate, pilot, ply, steer, train, use, wield **4.** carry on, cope, fare, get along, get by, get on, make do, make out, muddle through, shift, survive

manageable amenable, compliant, controllable, convenient, docile, easy, governable, handy, submissive, tamable, tractable, wieldy

management 1. administration, board, bosses (*Inf.*), directorate, directors, employers, executive(s) **2.** administration, care, charge, command, conduct, control, governance, government, guidance, handling, manipulation, operation, rule, running, superintendence, supervision

manager administrator, boss (*Inf.*), comptroller, conductor, controller, director, executive, gaffer (*Inf.*), governor, head, organizer, overseer, proprietor, superintendent, supervisor

manatee (mænə'ti:) *n.* large, plant-eating aquatic mammal

Manchu (mæn'tʃu:) *n.* **1.** member of Mongoloid people of Manchuria (*pl.* **-s, -'chu**) **2.** language of this people

Mancunian (mæŋ'kju:nɪən) *n.* **1.** native or inhabitant of Manchester —*a.* **2.** of Manchester

mandala ('mændələ, mæn'dɑ:lə) *n.* any of various designs, usu. circular, symbolizing the universe

mandarin ('mændərɪn) *n.* **1.** *Hist.* Chinese high-ranking bureaucrat **2.** *fig.* any high government official **3.** Chinese variety of orange —**mandarin duck** Asian duck, the male of which has brightly coloured patterned plumage and crest

mandate ('mændeɪt, -dɪt) *n.* **1.** command of, or commission to act for, another **2.** commission from United Nations to govern a territory **3.** instruction from electorate to representative or government —**'mandated** *a.* committed to a mandate —**mandatory** ('mændətərɪ, -trɪ) *n.* **1.** holder of a mandate —*a., also* **'mandatary 2.** compulsory

mandible ('mændɪbᵊl) *n.* **1.** lower jawbone **2.** either part of bird's beak —**man'dibular** *a.* of, like mandible

mandolin *or* **mandoline** (mændə'lɪn) *n.* stringed musical instrument

mandrake ('mændreɪk) *or* **mandragora** (mæn'drægərə) *n.* narcotic plant

mandrel *or* **mandril** ('mændrəl) *n.* **1.** axis on which material is supported in a lathe **2.** rod round which metal is cast or forged

mandrill ('mændrɪl) *n.* large blue-faced baboon

mane (meɪn) *n.* long hair on neck of horse, lion *etc.* —**maned** *a.*

manganese (mæŋgə'ni:z) *n.* **1.** metallic element **2.** black oxide of this

mange (meɪndʒ) *n.* skin disease of dogs *etc.* —**'mangy** *or* **'mangey** *a.* scruffy, shabby

mangelwurzel ('mæŋgᵊlwɜ:zᵊl) *or* **mangoldwurzel** ('mæŋgəʊldwɜ:zᵊl) *n.* variety of beet used as cattle food

manger ('meɪndʒə) *n.* eating trough in stable

mangle[1] ('mæŋgᵊl) *n.* **1.** machine for rolling clothes *etc.* to remove water —*vt.* **2.** press in mangle

mangle[2] ('mæŋgᵊl) *vt.* mutilate, spoil, hack

mango ('mæŋgəʊ) *n.* **1.** tropical fruit **2.** tree bearing it (*pl.* **-s, -es**)

mangrove ('mæŋgrəʊv, 'mæn-) *n.* tropical tree which grows on muddy banks of estuaries

mania ('meɪnɪə) *n.* **1.** madness **2.** prevailing craze —**'maniac, maniacal** (mə'naɪəkᵊl) *or* **manic** ('mænɪk) *a.* affected by mania —**'maniac** *n. inf.* **1.** mad person **2.** crazy enthusiast —**manic-depressive** *a. Psych.* **1.** pert. to mental disorder characterized by alternation between extreme confidence and deep depression —*n.* **2.** person afflicted with this disorder

manicure ('mænɪkjʊə) *n.* **1.** treatment and care of fingernails and hands —*vt.* **2.** apply such treatment to —**'manicurist** *n.* one doing this professionally

manifest ('mænɪfɛst) *a.* **1.** clearly revealed, visible, undoubted —*vt.* **2.** make manifest —*n.* **3.** list of cargo for customs —**manifes'tation** *n.* —**'manifestly** *adv.* clearly —**mani'festo** *n.* declaration of policy by political party, government, or movement (*pl.* **-s, -es**)

manifold ('mænɪfəʊld) *a.* **1.** numerous and varied —*n.* **2.** in internal-combustion engine, pipe with several outlets —*vt.* **3.** make copies of (document)

manikin, manakin, *or* **mannikin** ('mænɪkɪn) *n.* *see* MAN

Manila (mə'nɪlə) *n.* **1.** fibre used for ropes **2.** tough paper

manipulate (mə'nɪpjʊleɪt) *vt.* **1.** handle **2.** deal with skilfully **3.** manage **4.** falsify —**manipu'lation** *n.* **1.** act of manipulating, working by hand **2.** skilled use of hands —**ma'nipulative** *a.* —**ma'nipulator** *n.*

THESAURUS

mandate authority, authorization, bidding, charge, command, commission, decree, directive, edict, fiat, injunction, instruction, order, precept, sanction, warrant

mandatory binding, compulsory, obligatory, required, requisite

manful bold, brave, courageous, daring, determined, gallant, hardy, heroic, indomitable, intrepid, manly, noble, powerful, resolute, stalwart, stout, stout-hearted, strong, valiant, vigorous

manfully boldly, bravely, courageously, desperately, determinedly, gallantly, hard, heroically, intrepidly, like a Trojan, like one possessed, like the devil, nobly, powerfully, resolutely, stalwartly, stoutly, strongly, to the best of one's ability, valiantly, vigorously, with might and main

mangle butcher, cripple, crush, cut, deform, destroy, disfigure, distort, hack, lacerate, maim, mar, maul, mutilate, rend, ruin, spoil, tear, wreck

mangy dirty, mean, moth-eaten, scabby (*Inf.*), scruffy, seedy, shabby, shoddy, squalid

manhandle handle roughly, knock about, maul, paw (*Inf.*), pull, push, rough up

manhood manfulness, manliness, masculinity, virility

mania 1. aberration, craziness, delirium, dementia, derangement, disorder, frenzy, insanity, lunacy, madness **2.** cacoethes, craving, craze, desire, enthusiasm, fad (*Inf.*), fetish, fixation, obsession, partiality, passion, preoccupation, rage, thing (*Inf.*)

maniac 1. loony (*Sl.*), lunatic, madman, madwoman, nutcase (*Sl.*), nutter (*Brit. sl.*), psycho (*Sl.*), psychopath **2.** enthusiast, fan, fanatic, fiend (*Inf.*), freak (*Sl.*)

manifest 1. *adj.* apparent, clear, conspicuous, distinct, evident, glaring, noticeable, obvious, open, palpable, patent, plain, unmistakable, visible **2.** *v.* declare, demonstrate, display, establish, evince, exhibit, expose, express, make plain, prove, reveal, set forth, show

manifestation appearance, demonstration, disclosure, display, exhibition, exposure, expression, indication, instance, mark, materialization, revelation, show, sign, symptom, token

manifold abundant, assorted, copious, diverse, diversified, many, multifarious, multifold, multiple, multiplied, multitudinous, numerous, varied, various

manipulate 1. employ, handle, operate, ply, use, wield, work **2.** conduct, control, direct, engineer, guide, influence, manoeuvre, negotiate, steer

mankind Homo sapiens, humanity, humankind, human race, man, people

manliness manfulness, manhood, masculinity, virility

manna (ˈmænə) *n.* **1.** food of Israelites in the wilderness **2.** any spiritual or divine nourishment

mannequin (ˈmænɪkɪn) *n.* woman who models clothes, *esp.* at fashion shows

manner (ˈmænə) *n.* **1.** way thing happens or is done **2.** sort, kind **3.** custom **4.** style *—pl.* **5.** (correct) social behaviour —**ˈmannered** *a.* having idiosyncrasies or mannerisms; affected —**ˈmannerism** *n.* person's distinctive habit, trait —**ˈmannerly** *a.* polite

manoeuvre *or U.S.* **maneuver** (məˈnuːvə) *n.* **1.** contrived, complicated, perhaps deceptive plan or action **2.** skilful management *—vt.* **3.** contrive or accomplish with skill or cunning *—vi.* **4.** manipulate situations *etc.* in order to gain some end *—v.* **5.** (cause to) perform manoeuvres

manor (ˈmænə) *n.* **1.** *Hist.* land belonging to a lord **2.** feudal unit of land —**maˈnorial** *a.* —**manor house** residence of lord of manor

manqué (ˈmɒŋkeɪ) *Fr.* unfulfilled; would-be

mansard roof (ˈmænsɑːd, -səd) roof with break in its slope, lower part being steeper than upper

manse (mæns) *n.* house of minister in some religious denominations

mansion (ˈmænʃən) *n.* large house

mantel *or* **mantle** (ˈmæntᵊl) *n.* structure round fireplace —**mantel shelf** *or* **ˈmantelpiece** *n.* shelf at top of mantel

mantilla (mænˈtɪlə) *n.* in Spain, (lace) scarf worn as headdress

mantis (ˈmæntɪs) *n.* genus of insects including the stick insects and leaf insects (*pl.* **mantes** (ˈmæntiːz))

mantissa (mænˈtɪsə) *n.* fractional part of common logarithm

mantle (ˈmæntᵊl) *n.* **1.** loose cloak **2.** covering **3.** incandescent gauze round gas jet *—vt.* **4.** cover **5.** conceal

mantra (ˈmæntrə, ˈmʌn-) *n.* *Hinduism* any of those parts of the sacred literature which consist of metrical psalms of praise

manual (ˈmænjʊəl) *a.* **1.** of, or done with, the hands **2.** by human labour, not automatic *—n.* **3.** handbook **4.** textbook **5.** organ keyboard

manufacture (mænjʊˈfæktʃə) *vt.* **1.** process, make (materials) into finished articles **2.** produce (articles) **3.** invent, concoct *—n.* **4.** making of articles, materials, *esp.* in large quantities **5.** anything produced from raw materials —**manuˈfacturer** *n.* owner of factory

manumit (mænjʊˈmɪt) *vt.* free from slavery (**-tt-**) —**manuˈmission** *n.*

manure (məˈnjʊə) *vt.* **1.** enrich (land) *—n.* **2.** dung or chemical fertilizer used to enrich land

manuscript (ˈmænjʊskrɪpt) *n.* **1.** book, document, written by hand **2.** copy for printing *—a.* **3.** handwritten

Manx (mæŋks) *a.* **1.** of Isle of Man *—n.* **2.** Manx language —**Manx cat** tailless breed of cat —**ˈManxman** *n.*

many (ˈmɛnɪ) *a.* **1.** numerous (**more** *comp.*, **most** *sup.*) *—n.* **2.** large number

Maoism (ˈmaʊɪzəm) *n.* form of Marxism advanced by Mao Tse-Tung in China —**ˈMaoist** *n./a.*

Maori (ˈmaʊrɪ, ˈmɑːrɪ) *n.* **1.** member of New Zealand native race (*pl.* **-s, -ri**) **2.** their language

map (mæp) *n.* **1.** flat representation of the earth or some part of it, or of the heavens *—vt.* **2.** make a map of **3.** (*with* out) plan (**-pp-**)

maple (ˈmeɪpᵊl) *n.* tree of the sycamore family, a variety of which yields sugar —**maple leaf** leaf of maple tree, national emblem of Canada —**maple syrup** *chiefly* **US** sweet syrup made from sap of sugar maple

maquis (mɑːˈkiː) *n.* **1.** scrubby undergrowth of Mediterranean countries **2.** (*oft.* **M-**) name adopted by French underground resistance movement in WWII

mar (mɑː) *vt.* spoil, impair (**-rr-**)

THESAURUS

manly male, manful, masculine, virile

manner 1. approach, custom, fashion, form, genre, habit, line, means, method, mode, practice, procedure, process, routine, style, tack, tenor, usage, way, wont **2.** brand, breed, category, form, kind, nature, sort, type, variety

mannered affected, artificial, posed, pretentious, pseudo (*Inf.*), put-on, stilted

mannerism characteristic, foible, habit, idiosyncrasy, peculiarity, quirk, trait, trick

mannerly civil, civilized, courteous, decorous, genteel, gentlemanly, gracious, ladylike, polished, polite, refined, respectful, well-behaved, well-bred, well-mannered

manners 1. bearing, behaviour, breeding, carriage, comportment, conduct, demeanour, deportment **2.** ceremony, courtesy, decorum, etiquette, formalities, good form, polish, politeness, politesse, proprieties, protocol, refinement, social graces, the done thing

manoeuvre *n.* **1.** action, artifice, dodge, intrigue, machination, move, movement, plan, plot, ploy, ruse, scheme, stratagem, subterfuge, tactic, trick **2.** deployment, evolution, exercise, movement, operation ~*v.* **3.** contrive, devise, engineer, intrigue, machinate, manage, manipulate, plan, plot, pull strings, scheme, wangle (*Inf.*) **4.** deploy, exercise, move **5.** direct, drive, guide, handle, navigate, negotiate, pilot, steer

mansion abode, dwelling, habitation, hall, manor, residence, seat, villa

mantle *n.* **1.** *Archaic* cape, cloak, hood, shawl, wrap **2.** blanket, canopy, cloud, cover, covering, curtain, envelope, pall, screen, shroud, veil ~*v.* **3.** blanket, cloak, cloud, cover, disguise, envelop, hide, mask, overspread, screen, shroud, veil, wrap

manual 1. *adj.* done by hand, hand-operated, human, physical **2.** *n.* bible, enchiridion (*Rare*), guide, guidebook, handbook, instructions, workbook

manufacture *v.* **1.** assemble, build, compose, construct, create, fabricate, forge, form, make, mass-produce, mould, process, produce, put together, shape, turn out **2.** concoct, cook up (*Inf.*), devise, fabricate, hatch, invent, make up, think up, trump up ~*n.* **3.** assembly, construction, creation, fabrication, making, mass-production, produce, production

manure compost, droppings, dung, muck, ordure

many 1. *adj.* abundant, copious, countless, divers (*Archaic*), frequent, innumerable, manifold, multifarious, multifold, multitudinous, myriad, numerous, profuse, sundry, umpteen (*Inf.*), varied, various **2.** *n.* a horde, a lot, a mass, a multitude, a thousand

Mar. March

marabou (ˈmærəbuː) *n.* **1.** kind of stork **2.** its soft white lower tail feathers, used to trim hats *etc.* **3.** kind of silk

maraca (məˈrækə) *n.* percussion instrument of gourd containing dried seeds *etc.*

maraschino (mærəˈskiːnəʊ) *n.* liqueur made from cherries

marathon (ˈmærəθən) *n.* **1.** long-distance race **2.** endurance contest

maraud (məˈrɔːd) *vi.* **1.** make raid for plunder —*v.* **2.** pillage —**maˈrauder** *n.*

marble (ˈmɑːbᵊl) *n.* **1.** kind of limestone capable of taking polish **2.** slab of, sculpture in this **3.** small ball used in children's game —**ˈmarbled** *a.* having mottled appearance, like marble —**ˈmarbly** *a.*

marc (mɑːk) *n.* **1.** remains of grapes *etc.* that have been pressed for wine-making **2.** brandy distilled from these

marcasite (ˈmɑːkəsaɪt) *n.* **1.** pale yellow crystallized iron pyrites **2.** polished form of steel or white metal used for making jewellery

march[1] (mɑːtʃ) *vi.* **1.** walk with military step **2.** go, progress —*vt.* **3.** cause to march —*n.* **4.** action of marching **5.** distance marched in day **6.** tune to accompany marching —**marching orders 1.** *Mil.* instructions about march, its destination *etc.* **2.** *inf.* any notice of dismissal, *esp.* from employment —**march-past** *n.* review of troops as they march past a saluting point

march[2] (mɑːtʃ) *n.* **1.** border or frontier —*vi.* **2.** (*oft. with* upon *or* with) share a common border (with)

March (mɑːtʃ) *n.* third month —**March hare** hare during its breeding season, noted for its excitable behaviour

marchioness (ˈmɑːʃənɪs, mɑːʃəˈnɛs) *n.* wife, widow of marquis

Mardi Gras (ˈmɑːdɪ ˈgrɑː) **1.** festival of Shrove Tuesday **2.** revelry celebrating this

mare[1] (mɛə) *n.* female horse —**mare's nest** supposed discovery which proves worthless

mare[2] (ˈmɑːreɪ, -rɪ) *n.* (**M-** *when part of name*) huge dry plain on surface of moon (*pl.* **maria** (ˈmɑːrɪə))

margarine (mɑːdʒəˈriːn, mɑːg-) *or* **margarin** (ˈmɑːdʒərɪn, ˈmɑːg-, mɑːdʒəˈriːn, mɑːg-) *n.* butter substitute made from vegetable fats

marge (mɑːdʒ) *n. inf.* margarine

margin (ˈmɑːdʒɪn) *n.* **1.** border, edge **2.** space round printed page **3.** amount allowed beyond what is necessary —**ˈmarginal** *a.* —**marginal seat** *Pol.* constituency in which political party cannot be certain of retaining majority

marguerite (mɑːgəˈriːt) *n.* large daisy

marigold (ˈmærɪgəʊld) *n.* plant with yellow flowers

marijuana (mærɪjuˈɑːnə) *or* **marihuana** (mærɪˈhwɑːnə) *n.* dried flowers and leaves of hemp plant, used as narcotic

marimba (məˈrɪmbə) *n.* Latin Amer. percussion instrument resembling a xylophone

marina (məˈriːnə) *n.* mooring facility for yachts and pleasure boats

marinade (mærɪˈneɪd) *n.* seasoned, flavoured liquid used to soak fish, meat *etc.* before cooking —**ˈmarinate** *v.*

marine (məˈriːn) *a.* **1.** of the sea or shipping **2.** used at, found in sea —*n.* **3.** shipping, fleet **4.** soldier trained for land or sea combat —**mariner** (ˈmærɪnə) *n.* sailor

marionette (mærɪəˈnɛt) *n.* puppet worked with strings

marital (ˈmærɪtᵊl) *a.* relating to a husband or to marriage

maritime (ˈmærɪtaɪm) *a.* **1.** connected with seafaring, naval **2.** bordering on the sea **3.** (of climate) having small temperature differences between summer and winter —**Maritime Provinces** certain of the Canadian provinces with coasts facing the Gulf of St. Lawrence or Atlantic (*also* **ˈMaritimes**)

marjoram (ˈmɑːdʒərəm) *n.* aromatic herb

mark[1] (mɑːk) *n.* **1.** line, dot, scar *etc.* **2.** sign, token **3.** inscription **4.** letter, number showing evaluation of schoolwork *etc.* **5.** indication **6.** target —*vt.* **7.** make a mark on **8.** be distinguishing mark of **9.** indicate **10.** notice **11.** watch **12.** assess, *eg* examination paper **13.** stay close to (sporting opponent) to hamper his play —**marked** *a.* **1.** obvious, evident, or noticeable **2.** singled out, *esp.* as target of attack **3.** *Linguis.* distinguished by specific feature, as in phonology —**markedly** (ˈmɑːkɪdlɪ) *adv.* —**ˈmarker** *n.* **1.** one who, that which keeps score at games **2.** counter used at card playing *etc.* —**ˈmarksman** *n.* skilled shot

THESAURUS

and one, heaps (*Inf.*), large numbers, lots (*Inf.*), piles (*Inf.*), plenty, scores, tons (*Inf.*), umpteen (*Inf.*)

mar blemish, blight, blot, damage, deface, detract from, disfigure, harm, hurt, impair, injure, maim, mangle, mutilate, ruin, scar, spoil, stain, sully, taint, tarnish, vitiate

maraud despoil, forage, foray, harry, loot, pillage, plunder, raid, ransack, ravage, reive (*Dialect*), sack

marauder bandit, brigand, buccaneer, cateran (*Scot.*), corsair, freebooter, mosstrooper, outlaw, pillager, pirate, plunderer, raider, ravager, reiver (*Dialect*), robber

march *v.* **1.** file, footslog, pace, parade, stalk, stride, strut, tramp, tread, walk ~*n.* **2.** hike, routemarch, tramp, trek, walk **3.** gait, pace, step, stride

margin 1. border, bound, boundary, brim, brink, confine, edge, limit, perimeter, periphery, rim, side, verge **2.** allowance, compass, elbowroom, extra, latitude, leeway, play, room, scope, space, surplus

marginal bordering, borderline, on the edge, peripheral

marijuana bhang, cannabis, charas, dope (*Sl.*), ganja, grass (*Sl.*), hash (*Sl.*), hashish, hemp, kif, leaf (*Sl.*), mary jane (*U.S. sl.*), pot (*Sl.*), smoke (*Inf.*), stuff (*Sl.*), tea (*U.S. sl.*), weed (*Sl.*)

marine maritime, nautical, naval, ocean-going, oceanic, pelagic, saltwater, sea, seafaring, seagoing, thalassic

mariner bluejacket, gob (*Inf.*), hand, Jack Tar, matelot (*Brit. sl.*), navigator, sailor, salt, sea dog, seafarer, seafaring man, seaman, tar

marital conjugal, connubial, married, matrimonial, nuptial, spousal, wedded

maritime 1. marine, nautical, naval, oceanic, sea, seafaring **2.** coastal, littoral, seaside

mark[2] (mɑːk) *n.* German coin

market (ˈmɑːkɪt) *n.* **1.** assembly, place for buying and selling **2.** demand for goods **3.** centre for trade —*vt.* **4.** offer or produce for sale —**ˈmarketable** *a.* —**ˈmarketing** *n.* business of selling goods, including advertising, packaging *etc.* —**market garden** *chiefly* **UK** establishment where fruit and vegetables are grown for sale —**market research** analysis of data relating to demand for product

marl (mɑːl) *n.* **1.** clayey soil used as fertilizer —*vt.* **2.** fertilize with it

marline, marlin (ˈmɑːlɪn), *or* **marling** (ˈmɑːlɪŋ) *n.* two-strand cord —**ˈmarlinespike, ˈmarlinspike** *or* **ˈmarlingspike** *n.* pointed tool, *esp.* for unravelling rope to be spliced

marmalade (ˈmɑːməleɪd) *n.* preserve usu. made of oranges, lemons *etc.*

marmoreal (mɑːˈmɔːrɪəl) *or* **marmorean** *a.* of or like marble

marmoset (ˈmɑːməzɛt) *n.* small bushy-tailed monkey

marmot (ˈmɑːmət) *n.* burrowing rodent

maroon[1] (məˈruːn) *n.* **1.** brownish-crimson **2.** firework —*a.* **3.** of the colour

maroon[2] (məˈruːn) *vt.* **1.** leave (person) on deserted island or coast **2.** isolate, cut off by any means

marquee (mɑːˈkiː) *n.* large tent

marquetry *or* **marqueterie** (ˈmɑːkɪtrɪ) *n.* inlaid work, wood mosaic

marquis (ˈmɑːkwɪs, mɑːˈkiː) *n.* nobleman of rank below duke —**marquisate** (ˈmɑːkwɪzɪt) *n.*

marquise (mɑːˈkiːz) *n.* **1.** in various countries, marchioness **2.** gemstone cut in pointed oval shape

marrow (ˈmærəʊ) *n.* **1.** fatty substance inside bones **2.** vital part **3.** vegetable marrow —**ˈmarrowy** *a.* —**ˈmarrowfat** *n.* large pea

marry (ˈmærɪ) *v.* **1.** take (someone as husband or wife) in marriage **2.** unite closely —*vt.* **3.** join as husband and wife (**ˈmarried, ˈmarrying**) —**marriage** (ˈmærɪdʒ) *n.* **1.** state of being married **2.** wedding —**marriageable** (ˈmærɪdʒəbᵊl) *a.* —**marriage bureau** business concern set up to introduce people wishing to get married —**marriage guidance** advice given to couples who have problems in their married life —**marriage lines** certificate stating that marriage has taken place

Mars (mɑːz) *n.* **1.** Roman god of war **2.** planet nearest but one to earth —**Martian** (ˈmɑːʃən) *n.* **1.** supposed inhabitant of Mars —*a.* **2.** of Mars

Marseillaise (mɑːsəˈleɪz) *n.* the French national anthem

marsh (mɑːʃ) *n.* low-lying wet land —**ˈmarshy** *a.* —**marsh gas** gas composed of methane produced when vegetation decomposes under water —**marshˈmallow** *n.* spongy sweet orig. made from root of **marsh mallow,** shrubby plant growing near marshes

marshal (ˈmɑːʃəl) *n.* **1.** high officer of state **2.** **US** law enforcement officer —*vt.* **3.** arrange in due order **4.** conduct with ceremony (**-ll-**) —**field marshal** military officer of the highest rank —**marshalling yard** railway depot for goods trains —**Marshal of the Royal Air Force** rank in Royal Air Force comparable to that of field marshal in army

marsupial (mɑːˈsjuːpɪəl, -ˈsuː-) *n.* **1.** animal that carries its young in pouch, *eg* kangaroo —*a.* **2.** of marsupials —**marˈsupium** *n.* external pouch in most female marsupials (*pl.* **-pia** (-pɪə))

mart (mɑːt) *n.* **1.** place of trade **2.** market

Martello tower (mɑːˈtɛləʊ) round fort, for coast defence

marten (ˈmɑːtɪn) *n.* **1.** weasel-like animal **2.** its fur

martial (ˈmɑːʃəl) *a.* **1.** relating to war **2.** warlike, brave —**court martial** *see* COURT —**martial law** law

THESAURUS

mark *n.* **1.** blemish, blot, blotch, bruise, dent, impression, line, nick, pock, scar, scratch, smudge, splotch, spot, stain, streak **2.** badge, blaze, brand, characteristic, device, earmark, emblem, evidence, feature, hallmark, impression, incision, index, indication, label, note, print, proof, seal, sign, stamp, symbol, symptom, token **3.** aim, end, goal, object, objective, purpose, target ~*v.* **4.** blemish, blot, blotch, brand, bruise, dent, impress, imprint, nick, scar, scratch, smudge, splotch, stain, streak **5.** brand, characterize, identify, label, stamp **6.** betoken, denote, distinguish, evince, exemplify, illustrate, show **7.** attend, hearken (*Archaic*), mind, note, notice, observe, pay attention, pay heed, regard, remark, watch **8.** appraise, assess, correct, evaluate, grade

marked apparent, clear, considerable, conspicuous, decided, distinct, evident, manifest, notable, noted, noticeable, obvious, outstanding, patent, prominent, pronounced, remarkable, salient, signal, striking

markedly clearly, considerably, conspicuously, decidedly, distinctly, evidently, greatly, manifestly, notably, noticeably, obviously, outstandingly, patently, remarkably, signally, strikingly, to a great extent

market **1.** *n.* bazaar, fair, mart **2.** *v.* offer for sale, retail, sell, vend

marketable in demand, merchantable, salable, sought after, vendible, wanted

marksman crack shot (*Inf.*), deadeye (*Inf., chiefly U.S.*), dead shot (*Inf.*), good shot, sharpshooter

maroon abandon, cast ashore, cast away, desert, leave, leave high and dry (*Inf.*), strand

marriage espousal, match, matrimony, nuptial rites, nuptials, wedding, wedding ceremony, wedlock

married hitched (*Inf.*), joined, one, spliced (*Inf.*), united, wed, wedded

marrow core, cream, essence, gist, heart, kernel, pith, quick, quintessence, soul, spirit, substance

marry **1.** become man and wife, espouse, get hitched (*Inf.*), get spliced (*Inf.*), take the plunge (*Inf.*), take to wife, tie the knot (*Inf.*), walk down the aisle (*Inf.*), wed, wive (*Archaic*) **2.** ally, bond, join, knit, link, match, merge, splice, tie, unify, unite, yoke

marsh bog, fen, morass, moss (*Scot., & northern English dialect*), quagmire, slough, swamp

marshal **1.** align, arrange, array, assemble, collect, deploy, dispose, draw up, gather, group, line up, muster, order, organize, rank **2.** conduct, escort, guide, lead, shepherd, usher

marshy boggy, fenny, miry, quaggy, spongy, swampy, waterlogged, wet

martial bellicose, belligerent, brave, heroic, military, soldierly, warlike

enforced by military authorities in times of danger or emergency

martin ('mɑːtɪn) *n.* species of swallow

martinet (mɑːtɪ'nɛt) *n.* strict disciplinarian

martingale ('mɑːtɪŋgeɪl) *n.* strap to prevent horse from throwing up its head

martini (mɑː'tiːnɪ) *n.* **1.** cocktail containing *esp.* vermouth, gin, bitters **2.** (**M-**) **R** Italian vermouth (*pl.* **-s**)

Martinmas ('mɑːtɪnməs) *n.* feast of St. Martin, Nov. 11th

martlet ('mɑːtlɪt) *n. Her.* bird without feet

martyr ('mɑːtə) *n.* **1.** one put to death for his beliefs **2.** one who suffers in some cause **3.** one in constant suffering —*vt.* **4.** make martyr of —'**martyrdom** *n.* —**martyr'ology** *n.* list, history of Christian martyrs

marvel ('mɑːv^ə^l) *vi.* **1.** wonder (**-ll-**) —*n.* **2.** wonderful thing —'**marvellous** *or U.S.* '**marvelous** *a.* **1.** amazing **2.** wonderful

Marxism ('mɑːksɪzəm) *n.* state socialism as conceived by Karl Marx —'**Marxian** *a.* —'**Marxist** *n./a.*

marzipan ('mɑːzɪpæn) *n.* paste of almonds, sugar *etc.* used in sweets, cakes *etc.*

Masai ('mɑːsaɪ, mɑː'saɪ) *n.* **1.** member of Negroid pastoral people living chiefly in Kenya and Tanzania (*pl.* **-s, -sai**) **2.** language of this people

masc. masculine

mascara (mæ'skɑːrə) *n.* cosmetic for darkening eyelashes

mascot ('mæskət) *n.* thing supposed to bring luck

masculine ('mæskjʊlɪn) *a.* **1.** relating to males **2.** manly **3.** of the grammatical gender to which names of males belong

maser ('meɪzə) *n.* device for amplifying microwaves

mash (mæʃ) *n.* **1.** meal mixed with warm water **2.** warm food for horses *etc.* **3.** *inf.* mashed potatoes —*vt.* **4.** make into a mash **5.** crush into soft mass or pulp

mashie *or* **mashy** ('mæʃɪ) *n. Golf* iron club with deep sloping blade for lob shots

mask (mɑːsk) *n.* **1.** covering for face **2.** *Surg.* covering for nose and mouth **3.** disguise, pretence —*vt.* **4.** cover with mask **5.** hide, disguise —**masking tape** adhesive tape used to protect surfaces surrounding an area to be painted

masochism ('mæsəkɪzəm) *n.* abnormal condition where pleasure (*esp.* sexual) is derived from pain, humiliation *etc.* —'**masochist** *n.* —**maso'chistic** *a.*

mason ('meɪs^ə^n) *n.* **1.** worker in stone **2.** (**M-**) Freemason —**Masonic** (mə'sɒnɪk) *a.* of Freemasonry —'**masonry** *n.* **1.** stonework **2.** (**M-**) Freemasonry

masque *or* **mask** (mɑːsk) *n. Hist.* form of theatrical performance —**masquerade** (mæskə'reɪd) *n.* **1.** masked ball —*vi.* **2.** appear in disguise

mass (mæs) *n.* **1.** quantity of matter **2.** dense collection of this **3.** large quantity or number —*v.* **4.** form into a mass —'**massive** *a.* large and heavy —'**massy** *a.* solid, weighty —**mass market** market for mass-produced goods —**mass-market** *a.* of mass market —**mass media** means of communication to large numbers of people, such as television, newspapers *etc.* —**mass-produce** *vt.* produce (standardized articles) in large quantities —**mass production** —**mass spectrometer** instrument in which ions are separated by electric or magnetic fields according to their ratios of charge to mass (*also* '**spectroscope**) —**the masses** the populace

Mass (mæs, mɑːs) *n.* service of the Eucharist, *esp.* in R.C. Church

massacre ('mæsəkə) *n.* **1.** indiscriminate, large-scale killing, *esp.* of unresisting people —*vt.* **2.** kill indiscriminately

massage ('mæsɑːʒ, -sɑːdʒ) *n.* **1.** rubbing and kneading of muscles *etc.* as curative treatment —*vt.* **2.** apply this treatment to **3.** manipulate (figures *etc.*) in order to deceive —**masseur** (mæ'sɜː) *n.* one who practises massage (**masseuse** (mæ'sɜːz) *fem.*)

massé *or* **massé shot** ('mæsɪ) *n. Billiards* stroke with cue upright

massif ('mæsiːf) *n.* compact group of mountains

mast[1] (mɑːst) *n.* **1.** pole for supporting ship's sails **2.** tall upright support for aerial *etc.* —'**masthead** *n.* **1.** *Naut.* head of mast **2.** name of newspaper, its proprietors, staff *etc.*, printed at top of front page —*vt.* **3.** raise (sail) to masthead

THESAURUS

martinet disciplinarian, drillmaster, stickler

martyrdom agony, anguish, ordeal, persecution, suffering, torment, torture

marvel **1.** *v.* be amazed, be awed, be filled with surprise, gape, gaze, goggle, wonder **2.** *n.* genius, miracle, phenomenon, portent, prodigy, whiz (*Inf.*), wonder

marvellous **1.** amazing, astonishing, astounding, breathtaking, extraordinary, miraculous, phenomenal, prodigious, remarkable, singular, spectacular, stupendous, wondrous **2.** *Inf.* colossal, excellent, fabulous (*Inf.*), fantastic (*Inf.*), glorious, great (*Inf.*), magnificent, sensational, smashing (*Inf.*), splendid, stupendous, super (*Inf.*), superb, terrific (*Inf.*), wonderful

masculine male, manful, manlike, manly, mannish, virile

mask *n.* **1.** domino, false face, visor, vizard (*Archaic*) **2.** blind, camouflage, cloak, concealment, cover, cover-up, disguise, façade, front, guise, screen, semblance, show, veil, veneer ~*v.* **3.** camouflage, cloak, conceal, cover, disguise, hide, obscure, screen, veil

mass *n.* **1.** block, chunk, concretion, hunk, lump, piece **2.** accumulation, aggregation, assemblage, batch, bunch, collection, combination, conglomeration, heap, load, lot, pile, quantity, stack **3.** assemblage, band, body, bunch (*Inf.*), crowd, group, horde, host, lot, mob, number, throng, troop **4.** bulk, dimension, greatness, magnitude, size ~*v.* **5.** accumulate, amass, assemble, collect, congregate, forgather, gather, mob, muster, rally, swarm, throng

massacre **1.** *n.* annihilation, blood bath, butchery, carnage, extermination, killing, mass slaughter, murder, slaughter **2.** *v.* annihilate, butcher, cut to pieces, exterminate, kill, mow down, murder, slaughter, slay, wipe out

massage **1.** *n.* kneading, manipulation, rubbing, rub-down **2.** *v.* knead, manipulate, rub, rub down

massive big, bulky, colossal, enormous, extensive, gargantuan, gigantic, great, heavy, hefty, huge, hulking, immense, imposing, impressive, mammoth, monster, monumental, ponderous, solid, substantial, titanic, vast, weighty, whacking (*Inf.*), whopping (*Inf.*)

mast[2] (mɑːst) *n.* fruit of beech, oak *etc.* used as pig fodder

mastectomy (mæˈstɛktəmɪ) *n.* surgical removal of a breast

master (ˈmɑːstə) *n.* **1.** one in control **2.** employer **3.** head of household **4.** owner **5.** document *etc.* from which copies are made **6.** captain of merchant ship **7.** expert **8.** great artist **9.** teacher —*vt.* **10.** overcome **11.** acquire knowledge of or skill in —**ˈmasterful** *a.* imperious, domineering —**ˈmasterly** *a.* showing great competence —**ˈmastery** *n.* **1.** full understanding **2.** expertise **3.** authority **4.** victory —**master aircrew** warrant officer rank in Royal Air Force —**master key** key that opens many different locks —**ˈmastermind** *vt.* **1.** plan, direct —*n.* **2.** very intelligent person, *esp.* one who directs an undertaking —**ˈmasterpiece** *n.* outstanding work —**ˈmasterstroke** *n.* outstanding piece of strategy *etc.* —**Master of Arts** (*or* **Science** *etc.*) **1.** degree given by university usu. to postgraduate **2.** person who has this degree —**master of ceremonies** person who presides over public ceremony *etc.*, introducing events *etc.*

mastic (ˈmæstɪk) *n.* **1.** gum got from certain trees **2.** puttylike substance

masticate (ˈmæstɪkeɪt) *v.* chew —**mastiˈcation** *n.* —**ˈmasticatory** *a.*

mastiff (ˈmæstɪf) *n.* large dog

mastitis (mæˈstaɪtɪs) *n.* inflammation of breast or udder

mastodon (ˈmæstədɒn) *n.* extinct elephantlike mammal

mastoid (ˈmæstɔɪd) *a.* **1.** nipple-shaped —*n.* **2.** prominence on bone behind human ear —**mastoiˈditis** *n.* inflammation of this area

masturbate (ˈmæstəbeɪt) *v.* stimulate (one's own or one's partner's) genital organs —**masturˈbation** *n.*

mat[1] (mæt) *n.* **1.** small rug **2.** piece of fabric to protect another surface or to wipe feet on *etc.* **3.** thick tangled mass —*v.* **4.** form into such mass (**-tt-**) —**on the mat** *inf.* called up for reprimand

mat[2] *or* **matt** (mæt) *a.* dull, lustreless, not shiny

matador (ˈmætədɔː) *n.* man who slays bull in bullfights

match[1] (mætʃ) *n.* **1.** contest, game **2.** equal **3.** person, thing exactly corresponding to another **4.** marriage **5.** person regarded as eligible for marriage —*vt.* **6.** get something corresponding to (colour, pattern *etc.*) **7.** oppose, put in competition with **8.** join (in marriage) —*vi.* **9.** correspond —**ˈmatchless** *a.* unequalled —**ˈmatchboard** *n.* long, flimsy board tongued and grooved for lining work —**ˈmatchmaker** *n.* one who schemes to bring about a marriage —**match play** *Golf* scoring according to number of holes won and lost

match[2] (mætʃ) *n.* **1.** small stick with head which ignites when rubbed **2.** fuse —**ˈmatchbox** *n.* —**ˈmatchlock** *n.* early musket fired by fuse —**ˈmatchwood** *n.* small splinters

mate[1] (meɪt) *n.* **1.** comrade **2.** husband, wife **3.** one of pair **4.** officer in merchant ship **5.** *inf.* common Brit. and Aust. term of address, *esp.* between males —*v.* **6.** marry or join in marriage **7.** pair —**ˈmatey** *a. inf.* friendly, sociable

mate[2] (meɪt) *n./vt. Chess* checkmate

mater (ˈmeɪtə) *n. sl.* **UK** mother

material (məˈtɪərɪəl) *n.* **1.** substance from which thing is made **2.** cloth, fabric —*a.* **3.** of matter or body **4.** affecting physical wellbeing **5.** unspiritual **6.** important, essential —**maˈterialism** *n.* **1.** excessive interest in, desire for money and possessions **2.** doctrine that

THESAURUS

master *n.* **1.** boss (*Inf.*), captain, chief, commander, controller, director, employer, governor, head, lord, manager, overlord, overseer, owner, principal, ruler, skipper (*Inf.*), superintendent **2.** ace (*Inf.*), adept, dab hand (*Brit. inf.*), doyen, expert, genius, maestro, past master, pro (*Inf.*), virtuoso, wizard **3.** guide, guru, instructor, pedagogue, preceptor, schoolmaster, spiritual leader, swami, teacher, tutor ~*v.* **4.** acquire, become proficient in, get the hang of (*Inf.*), grasp, learn **5.** bridle, check, conquer, curb, defeat, overcome, overpower, quash, quell, subdue, subjugate, suppress, tame, triumph over, vanquish

masterful arrogant, authoritative, bossy (*Inf.*), despotic, dictatorial, domineering, high-handed, imperious, magisterial, overbearing, overweening, peremptory, self-willed, tyrannical

masterly adept, adroit, clever, consummate, crack (*Inf.*), dexterous, excellent, expert, exquisite, fine, finished, first-rate, masterful, skilful, skilled, superior, superlative, supreme

mastermind **1.** *v.* be the brains behind (*Inf.*), conceive, devise, direct, manage, organize, plan **2.** *n.* architect, authority, brain(s) (*Inf.*), director, engineer, genius, intellect, manager, organizer, planner, virtuoso

masterpiece *chef d'oeuvre*, classic, jewel, magnum opus, master work, *pièce de résistance*, *tour de force*

mastery **1.** command, comprehension, familiarity, grasp, knowledge, understanding **2.** ability, acquirement, attainment, cleverness, deftness, dexterity, expertise, finesse, know-how (*Inf.*), proficiency, prowess, skill, virtuosity **3.** ascendancy, authority, command, conquest, control, domination, dominion, pre-eminence, rule, superiority, supremacy, sway, triumph, upper hand, victory, whip hand

match *n.* **1.** bout, competition, contest, game, test, trial **2.** competitor, counterpart, equal, equivalent, peer, rival **3.** companion, complement, counterpart, equal, equivalent, fellow, mate, tally **4.** copy, dead ringer (*Sl.*), double, duplicate, equal, lookalike, replica, ringer (*Sl.*), spit (*Inf.*), spit and image (*Inf.*), spitting image (*Inf.*), twin **5.** affiliation, alliance, combination, couple, duet, marriage, pair, pairing, partnership, union ~*v.* **6.** ally, combine, couple, join, link, marry, mate, pair, unite, yoke **7.** accompany, accord, adapt, agree, blend, coordinate, correspond, fit, go with, harmonize, suit, tally, tone with **8.** compare, compete, contend, emulate, equal, measure up to, oppose, pit against, rival, vie

matchless consummate, exquisite, incomparable, inimitable, peerless, perfect, superlative, supreme, unequalled, unique, unmatched, unparalleled, unrivalled

mate *n.* **1.** better half (*Humorous*), husband, partner, spouse, wife **2.** *Inf.* buddy (*Inf.*), china (*Brit. sl.*), chum (*Inf.*), comrade, crony, friend, pal (*Inf.*) **3.** companion, double, fellow, match, twin ~*v.* **4.** breed, copulate, couple, pair **5.** marry, match, wed **6.** couple, join, match, pair, yoke

nothing but matter exists, denying independent existence of spirit **—ma'terialist** *a./n.* **—material'istic** *a.* **—ma'terialize** *or* **-ise** *vi.* **1.** come into existence or view *—vt.* **2.** make material **—ma'terially** *adv.* appreciably

materiel *or* **matériel** (mətɪərɪ'ɛl) *n.* equipment of organization, *esp.* of military force

maternal (mə'tɜːnᵊl) *a.* of, related through mother **—ma'ternity** *n.* motherhood

mathematics (mæθə'mætɪks) *pl.n.* (*with sing. v.*) science of number, quantity, shape and space **—mathe'matical** *a.* **—mathe'matically** *adv.* **—mathema'tician** *n.*

maths (mæθs) *n. inf.* mathematics

matinée ('mætɪneɪ) *n.* afternoon performance in theatre **—matinée coat** short coat for baby

matins *or* **mattins** ('mætɪnz) *pl.n.* morning prayers

matriarch ('meɪtrɪɑːk) *n.* mother as head and ruler of family **—'matriarchal** *a.* **—'matriarchy** *n.* society with matriarchal government and descent reckoned in female line

matricide ('mætrɪsaɪd, 'meɪ-) *n.* **1.** the crime of killing one's mother **2.** one who does this

matriculate (mə'trɪkjʊleɪt) *v.* enrol, be enrolled in a college or university **—matricu'lation** *n.*

matrimony ('mætrɪmənɪ) *n.* marriage **—matri'monial** *a.*

matrix ('meɪtrɪks, 'mæ-) *n.* **1.** substance, situation in which something originates, takes form, or is enclosed **2.** mould for casting **3.** *Maths.* rectangular array of elements set out in rows and columns (*pl.* **matrices** ('meɪtrɪsiːz, 'mæ-))

matron ('meɪtrən) *n.* **1.** married woman **2.** *former name for* nursing officer **3.** woman who superintends domestic arrangements of public institution, boarding school *etc.* **—'matronly** *a.* sedate **—matron of honour** married woman serving as chief attendant to bride

matt (mæt) *a. see* MAT[2]

Matt. *Bible* Matthew

matter ('mætə) *n.* **1.** substance of which thing is made **2.** physical or bodily substance **3.** affair, business **4.** cause of trouble **5.** substance of book *etc.* **6.** pus *—vi.* **7.** be of importance, signify **—matter-of-fact** *a.* unimaginative or emotionless **—matter of fact** fact that is undeniably true **—as a matter of fact** actually; in fact

mattock ('mætək) *n.* tool like pick with ends of blades flattened for cutting, hoeing

mattress ('mætrɪs) *n.* **1.** stuffed flat case, often with springs, or foam rubber pad, used as part of bed **2.** underlay

mature (mə'tjʊə, -'tʃʊə) *a.* **1.** ripe, completely developed **2.** grown-up *—v.* **3.** bring, come to maturity *—vi.* **4.** (of bill) fall due **—matu'ration** *n.* process of maturing **—ma'turity** *n.* full development

matutinal (mætjʊ'taɪnᵊl) *a.* of, occurring in, or during morning

maudlin ('mɔːdlɪn) *a.* weakly or tearfully sentimental

maul (mɔːl) *vt.* **1.** handle roughly **2.** beat; bruise *—n.* **3.** heavy wooden hammer **4.** *Rugby* loose scrum

maulstick ('mɔːlstɪk) *or* **mahlstick** *n.* light stick with ball at one end, held in left hand to support right hand while painting

maunder ('mɔːndə) *vi.* talk, act aimlessly, dreamily

maundy ('mɔːndɪ) *n.* **1.** foot-washing ceremony on Thursday before Easter **2.** royal alms given on that day

mausoleum (mɔːsə'lɪəm) *n.* stately building as a tomb (*pl.* **-s, -lea** (-'lɪə))

mauve (məʊv) *a./n.* (of) pale purple colour

maverick ('mævərɪk) *n.* **1.** US unbranded steer, stray cow **2.** independent, unorthodox person

maw (mɔː) *n.* stomach, crop

mawkish ('mɔːkɪʃ) *a.* **1.** weakly sentimental, maudlin **2.** sickly

THESAURUS

material *n.* **1.** body, constituents, element, matter, stuff, substance *~adj.* **2.** bodily, concrete, corporeal, fleshly, nonspiritual, palpable, physical, substantial, tangible, worldly **3.** consequential, essential, grave, important, indispensable, key, meaningful, momentous, serious, significant, vital, weighty

materialize appear, come about, come into being, come to pass, happen, occur, take place, take shape, turn up

materially considerably, essentially, gravely, greatly, much, seriously, significantly, substantially

matrimonial conjugal, connubial, hymeneal, marital, married, nuptial, spousal, wedded, wedding

matrimony marital rites, marriage, nuptials, wedding ceremony, wedlock

matrix forge, mould, origin, source, womb

matter *n.* **1.** body, material, stuff, substance **2.** affair, business, concern, episode, event, incident, issue, occurrence, proceeding, question, situation, subject, thing, topic, transaction **3.** argument, context, purport, sense, subject, substance, text, thesis **4.** complication, difficulty, distress, problem, trouble, upset, worry **5.** *Medical* discharge, purulence, pus, secretion *~v.* **6.** be important, be of consequence, carry weight, count, have influence, make a difference, mean something, signify

matter-of-fact deadpan, down-to-earth, dry, dull, emotionless, flat, lifeless, mundane, plain, prosaic, sober, unembellished, unimaginative, unsentimental, unvarnished

mature 1. *adj.* adult, complete, fit, full-blown, fully fledged, full-grown, grown, grown-up, matured, mellow, of age, perfect, prepared, ready, ripe, ripened, seasoned **2.** *v.* age, become adult, bloom, come of age, develop, grow up, maturate, mellow, perfect, reach adulthood, ripen, season

maturity adulthood, completion, experience, full bloom, full growth, fullness, majority, manhood, maturation, matureness, perfection, ripeness, wisdom, womanhood

maudlin lachrymose, mawkish, mushy (*Inf.*), overemotional, sentimental, slushy (*Inf.*), soppy (*Brit. inf.*), tearful, weepy (*Inf.*)

maul 1. abuse, handle roughly, ill-treat, manhandle, molest, paw **2.** batter, beat, beat up (*Inf.*), claw, knock about, lacerate, mangle, pummel, rough up, thrash

maunder 1. dawdle, dilly-dally (*Inf.*), drift, idle, loaf, meander, mooch (*Sl.*), potter, ramble, straggle, stray, traipse (*Inf.*) **2.** babble, blather, blether, chatter, gabble, prattle, rabbit (*Brit. sl.*), ramble, rattle on, witter (*Inf.*)

max. maximum

maxi (ˈmæksɪ) *a.* **1.** (of garment) reaching ankle **2.** large, considerable

maxilla (mækˈsɪlə) *n.* jawbone (*pl.* **-lae** (-liː)) —**maxˈillary** *a.* of the jaw

maxim (ˈmæksɪm) *n.* **1.** general truth, proverb **2.** rule of conduct, principle

maximum (ˈmæksɪməm) *n.* **1.** greatest size or number **2.** highest point (*pl.* **-s, -ma** (-mə)) —*a.* **3.** greatest —**ˈmaximize** *or* **-ise** *vt.*

maxwell (ˈmækswəl) *n.* cgs unit of magnetic flux

may (meɪ) *v. aux.* expresses possibility, permission, opportunity *etc.* (**might** *pt.*) —**maybe** (ˈmeɪbiː) *adv.* **1.** perhaps **2.** possibly

May (meɪ) *n.* **1.** fifth month **2.** (**m-**) hawthorn or its flowers —**ˈmayfly** *n.* short-lived flying insect, found near water —**ˈmaypole** *n.* pole set up for dancing round on **May Day**, first day of May —**May queen** girl chosen to preside over May-Day celebrations

Maya (ˈmaɪə) *n.* **1.** member of Amer. Indian people of Yucatan, Belize and N Guatemala (*pl.* **-ya, -s**) **2.** language of this people

Mayday (ˈmeɪdeɪ) *n.* international radiotelephone distress signal

mayhap (ˈmeɪhæp) *adv. obs.* perhaps

mayhem *or* **maihem** (ˈmeɪhɛm) *n.* **1.** depriving person by violence of limb, member or organ, or causing mutilation of body **2.** any violent destruction **3.** confusion

mayonnaise (meɪəˈneɪz) *n.* creamy sauce of egg yolks, oil *etc.*, *esp.* for salads

mayor (mɛə) *n.* head of municipality —**ˈmayoral** *a.* —**ˈmayoralty** *n.* (time of) office of mayor —**ˈmayoress** *n.* **1.** mayor's wife **2.** lady mayor

maze (meɪz) *n.* **1.** labyrinth **2.** network of paths, lines **3.** state of confusion

mazurka *or* **mazourka** (məˈzɜːkə) *n.* **1.** lively Polish dance like polka **2.** music for it

MB Manitoba

M.B. Bachelor of Medicine

M.B.E. Member of the Order of the British Empire

M.C. **1.** Master of Ceremonies **2.** Military Cross

M.C.C. Marylebone Cricket Club

M.Ch. Master of Surgery

Md *Chem.* mendelevium

MD Maryland

M.D. Doctor of Medicine

me[1] (miː; *unstressed* mɪ) *pron.* objective case of pronoun I

me[2] (miː) *n. Mus. see* MI

ME Maine

ME *or* **M.E.** Middle English

M.E. **1.** Marine Engineer **2.** Mechanical Engineer **3.** Methodist Episcopal **4.** Mining Engineer **5.** in titles, Most Excellent

mea culpa (ˈmeɪɑː ˈkʊlpɑː) *Lat.* my fault

mead[1] (miːd) *n.* alcoholic drink made from honey

mead[2] (miːd) *n. obs., poet.* meadow

meadow (ˈmɛdəʊ) *n.* piece of grassland —**ˈmeadowsweet** *n.* plant with dense heads of small fragrant flowers

meagre *or U.S.* **meager** (ˈmiːgə) *a.* **1.** lean, thin **2.** scanty, insufficient

meal[1] (miːl) *n.* **1.** occasion when food is served and eaten **2.** the food —**meals-on-wheels** *n.* **UK** service taking hot meals to elderly, infirm *etc.* —**meal ticket** **1.** **US** luncheon voucher **2.** *sl.* person, situation *etc.* providing source of livelihood or income

meal[2] (miːl) *n.* grain ground to powder —**ˈmealy** *a.* —**mealy-mouthed** *a.* euphemistic, insincere in what one says

mealie (ˈmiːlɪ) *n.* **SA** maize

mean[1] (miːn) *vt.* **1.** intend **2.** signify —*vi.* **3.** have the intention of behaving (**meant** *pt./pp.*, **ˈmeaning** *pr.p.*) —**ˈmeaning** *n.* **1.** sense, significance —*a.* **2.** expressive —**ˈmeaningful** *a.* of great meaning or significance —**ˈmeaningless** *a.*

mean[2] (miːn) *a.* **1.** ungenerous, petty **2.** miserly, nig-

THESAURUS

mawkish emotional, feeble, gushy (*Inf.*), maudlin, mushy (*Inf.*), schmaltzy (*Sl.*), sentimental, slushy (*Inf.*), soppy (*Brit. inf.*)

maxim adage, aphorism, apophthegm, axiom, byword, gnome, motto, proverb, rule, saw, saying

maximum **1.** *n.* apogee, ceiling, crest, extremity, height, most, peak, pinnacle, summit, top, upper limit, utmost, uttermost, zenith **2.** *adj.* greatest, highest, maximal, most, paramount, supreme, topmost, utmost

maybe it could be, mayhap (*Archaic*), peradventure (*Archaic*), perchance (*Archaic*), perhaps, possibly

mayhem chaos, commotion, confusion, destruction, disorder, fracas, havoc, trouble, violence

maze **1.** convolutions, intricacy, labyrinth, meander **2.** *Fig.* bewilderment, confusion, imbroglio, mesh, perplexity, puzzle, snarl, tangle, uncertainty, web

meadow field, grassland, lea (*Poetic*), ley, pasture

meagre **1.** deficient, exiguous, inadequate, insubstantial, little, paltry, poor, puny, scanty, scrimpy, short, skimpy, slender, slight, small, spare, sparse **2.** bony, emaciated, gaunt, hungry, lank, lean, scraggy, scrawny, skinny, starved, thin, underfed

mean[1] *v.* **1.** betoken, connote, convey, denote, drive at, express, hint at, imply, indicate, purport, represent, say, signify, spell, stand for, suggest, symbolize **2.** aim, aspire, contemplate, design, desire, have in mind, intend, plan, propose, purpose, set out, want, wish **3.** adumbrate, augur, betoken, foreshadow, foretell, herald, portend, presage, promise

mean[2] *adj.* **1.** beggarly, close, mercenary, mingy (*Brit. inf.*), miserly, near (*Inf.*), niggardly, parsimonious, penny-pinching, penurious, selfish, stingy, tight, tight-fisted, ungenerous **2.** bad-tempered, cantankerous, churlish, disagreeable, hostile, ill-tempered, malicious, nasty, rude, sour, unfriendly, unpleasant **3.** abject, base, callous, contemptible, degenerate, degraded, despicable, disgraceful, dishonourable, hard-hearted, ignoble, low-minded, narrow-minded, petty, scurvy, shabby, shameful, sordid, vile, wretched **4.** beggarly, contemptible, down-at-heel, insignificant, miserable, paltry, petty, poor, run-down, scruffy, seedy, shabby, sordid, squalid, tawdry, wretched

gardly **3.** unpleasant **4.** callous **5.** shabby **6.** ashamed —**ˈmeanly** *adv.* —**ˈmeanness** *n.*

mean[3] (miːn) *n.* **1.** thing which is intermediate **2.** middle point —*pl.* **3.** that by which thing is done **4.** money **5.** resources —*a.* **6.** intermediate in time, quality *etc.* **7.** average —**means test** enquiry into person's means to decide eligibility for pension, grant *etc.* —**ˈmeantime** *or* **ˈmeanwhile** *adv./n.* (during) time between one happening and another —**by all means** certainly —**by no means** not at all

meander (mɪˈændə) *vi.* **1.** flow windingly **2.** wander aimlessly

meant (mɛnt) *pt./pp. of* MEAN[1]

measles (ˈmiːzəlz) *n.* infectious disease producing rash of red spots —**ˈmeasly** *a.* **1.** *inf.* poor, wretched, stingy **2.** of measles

measure (ˈmɛʒə) *n.* **1.** size, quantity **2.** vessel, rod, line *etc.* for ascertaining size or quantity **3.** unit of size or quantity **4.** course, plan of action **5.** law **6.** poetical rhythm **7.** musical time **8.** *Poet.* tune **9.** *obs.* dance —*vt.* **10.** ascertain size, quantity of **11.** indicate measurement of **12.** estimate **13.** bring into competition against —*vi.* **14.** make measurement(s) **15.** be (so much) in size or quantity —**ˈmeasurable** *a.* —**ˈmeasured** *a.* **1.** determined by measure **2.** steady **3.** rhythmical **4.** carefully considered —**ˈmeasurement** *n.* **1.** measuring **2.** size —*pl.* **3.** dimensions

meat (miːt) *n.* **1.** animal flesh as food **2.** food —**ˈmeaty** *a.* **1.** (tasting) of, like meat **2.** brawny **3.** full of import or interest

Mecca (ˈmɛkə) *n.* **1.** holy city of Islam **2.** place that attracts visitors

mech. **1.** mechanical **2.** mechanics **3.** mechanism

mechanic (mɪˈkænɪk) *n.* **1.** one employed in working with machinery **2.** skilled workman —*pl.* **3.** scientific theory of motion —**meˈchanical** *a.* **1.** concerned with machines or operation of them **2.** worked, produced (as though) by machine **3.** acting without thought —**meˈchanically** *adv.* —**mechaˈnician** *n.* —**mechanical drawing** *see* **technical drawing** *at* TECHNICAL

mechanism (ˈmɛkənɪzəm) *n.* **1.** structure of machine **2.** piece of machinery —**mechaniˈzation** *or* **-iˈsation** *n.* —**ˈmechanize** *or* **-ise** *vt.* **1.** equip with machinery **2.** make mechanical, automatic **3.** *Mil.*

THESAURUS

mean[3] **1.** *n.* average, balance, compromise, happy medium, median, middle, middle course *or* way, mid-point, norm **2.** *adj.* average, intermediate, medial, median, medium, middle, middling, normal, standard

meander **1.** *v.* ramble, snake, stravaig (*Scot.*), stray, stroll, turn, wander, wind, zigzag **2.** *n.* bend, coil, curve, loop, turn, twist, zigzag

meaning **1.** *n.* connotation, denotation, drift, explanation, gist, implication, import, interpretation, message, purport, sense, significance, signification, substance, upshot, value **2.** *adj.* eloquent, expressive, meaningful, pointed, pregnant, speaking, suggestive

meaningful **1.** important, material, purposeful, relevant, serious, significant, useful, valid, worthwhile **2.** eloquent, expressive, meaning, pointed, pregnant, speaking, suggestive

meaningless aimless, empty, futile, hollow, inane, inconsequential, insignificant, insubstantial, nonsensical, nugatory, pointless, purposeless, senseless, trifling, trivial, useless, vain, valueless, worthless

meanness **1.** minginess (*Brit. inf.*), miserliness, niggardliness, parsimony, penuriousness, selfishness, stinginess, tight-fistedness **2.** bad temper, cantankerousness, churlishness, disagreeableness, hostility, ill temper, malice, maliciousness, nastiness, rudeness, sourness, unfriendliness, unpleasantness **3.** abjectness, baseness, degeneracy, degradation, despicableness, disgracefulness, dishonourableness, low-mindedness, narrow-mindedness, pettiness, scurviness, shabbiness, shamefulness, sordidness, vileness, wretchedness **4.** beggarliness, contemptibleness, insignificance, paltriness, pettiness, poorness, scruffiness, seediness, shabbiness, sordidness, squalor, tawdriness, wretchedness

means **1.** agency, avenue, channel, course, expedient, instrument, measure, medium, method, mode, process, way **2.** affluence, capital, estate, fortune, funds, income, money, property, resources, riches, substance, wealth, wherewithal **3. by all means** absolutely, certainly, definitely, doubtlessly, of course, positively, surely **4. by no means** absolutely not, definitely not, in no way, not at all, not in the least, not in the slightest, not the least bit, on no account

meantime at the same time, concurrently, for now, for the duration, for the moment, for then, in the interim, in the interval, in the intervening time, in the meantime, in the meanwhile, simultaneously

meanwhile at the same time, concurrently, for now, for the duration, for the moment, for then, in the interim, in the interval, in the intervening time, in the meantime, in the meanwhile, simultaneously

measurable assessable, computable, determinable, gaugeable, mensurable, quantifiable, quantitative

measure *n.* **1.** amount, amplitude, capacity, degree, extent, magnitude, portion, proportion, quantity, quota, range, ration, reach, scope, share, size **2.** gauge, metre, rule, scale, yardstick **3.** act, action, course, deed, expedient, manoeuvre, means, procedure, proceeding, step **4.** act, bill, enactment, law, resolution, statute **5.** beat, cadence, foot, metre, rhythm, verse ~*v.* **6.** appraise, assess, calculate, calibrate, compute, determine, estimate, evaluate, gauge, judge, mark out, quantify, rate, size, sound, survey, value, weigh

measurement **1.** appraisal, assessment, calculation, calibration, computation, estimation, evaluation, judgment, mensuration, metage, survey, valuation **2.** amount, amplitude, area, capacity, depth, dimension, extent, height, length, magnitude, size, volume, weight, width

meat aliment, cheer, chow (*Inf.*), comestibles, eats (*Sl.*), fare, flesh, food, grub (*Inf.*), nourishment, nutriment, provender, provisions, rations, subsistence, sustenance, viands, victuals

mechanical **1.** automated, automatic, machine-driven **2.** automatic, cold, cursory, dead, emotionless, habitual, impersonal, instinctive, involuntary, lacklustre, lifeless, machine-like, matter-of-fact, perfunctory, routine, spiritless, unconscious, unfeeling, unthinking

mechanism **1.** apparatus, appliance, contrivance, device, instrument, machine, structure, system, tool **2.** action, components, gears, innards (*Inf.*), machinery, motor, workings, works

equip with armoured vehicles —ˈ**mechanized** *or* **-ised** *a.*

med. 1. medical 2. medicine 3. medieval 4. medium

Med (mɛd) *n. inf.* Mediterranean region

M.Ed. Master of Education

medal (ˈmɛdᵊl) *n.* piece of metal with inscription *etc.* used as reward or memento —**meˈdallion** *n.* 1. large medal 2. any of various things like this in decorative work —ˈ**medallist** *or U.S.* ˈ**medalist** *n.* 1. winner of a medal 2. maker of medals

meddle (ˈmɛdᵊl) *vi.* interfere, busy oneself unnecessarily —ˈ**meddlesome** *a.*

media (ˈmi:dɪə) *n., pl. of* MEDIUM, used *esp.* of the mass media, radio, television *etc.* —**media event** event staged for or exploited by the mass media

mediaeval (mɛdɪˈi:vᵊl) *a. see* MEDIEVAL

medial (ˈmi:dɪəl) *a.* 1. in the middle 2. pert. to a mean or average —ˈ**median** *a./n.* middle (point or line)

mediate (ˈmi:dɪeɪt) *vi.* 1. intervene to reconcile —*vt.* 2. bring about by mediation —*a.* (ˈmi:dɪɪt) 3. depending on mediation —**mediˈation** *n.* 1. intervention on behalf of another 2. act of going between —ˈ**mediator** *n.*

medicine (ˈmɛdɪsɪn, ˈmɛdsɪn) *n.* 1. drug or remedy for treating disease 2. science of preventing, diagnosing, alleviating, or curing disease —ˈ**medic** *n. inf.* 1. doctor 2. medical orderly 3. medical student —ˈ**medical** *a.* —ˈ**medically** *adv.* —**meˈdicament** *n.* remedy —ˈ**medicate** *vt.* impregnate with medicinal substances —**mediˈcation** *n.* —ˈ**medicative** *a.* healing —**meˈdicinal** *a.* curative —ˈ**medico** *n. inf.* 1. doctor 2. medical student (*pl.* **-s**) —**medical certificate** doctor's certificate giving evidence of person's fitness or unfitness for work *etc.* —**medicine ball** heavy ball for physical training —**medicine man** witch doctor

medieval *or* **mediaeval** (mɛdɪˈi:vᵊl) *a.* of Middle Ages —**mediˈevalism** *or* **mediˈaevalism** *n.* 1. spirit of Middle Ages 2. cult of medieval ideals —**mediˈevalist** *or* **mediˈaevalist** *n.* student of the Middle Ages —**Medieval Greek** Greek language from 7th cent. A.D.–1204 —**Medieval Latin** Latin language as used throughout Europe in Middle Ages

mediocre (mi:dɪˈəʊkə) *a.* 1. neither bad nor good, ordinary, middling 2. second-rate —**mediocrity** (mi:dɪˈɒkrɪtɪ, mɛd-) *n.*

meditate (ˈmɛdɪteɪt) *vi.* 1. be occupied in thought 2. reflect deeply on spiritual matters —**mediˈtation** *n.* 1. thought 2. absorption in thought 3. religious contemplation —ˈ**meditative** *a.* 1. thoughtful 2. reflective —ˈ**meditatively** *adv.*

Mediterranean (mɛdɪtəˈreɪnɪən) *n.* 1. *short for* **Mediterranean Sea,** sea between S Europe, N Afr., and SW Asia 2. native or inhabitant of Mediterranean country —*a.* 3. of Mediterranean Sea

medium (ˈmi:dɪəm) *a.* 1. between two qualities, degrees *etc.*, average —*n.* 2. middle quality, degree 3. intermediate substance conveying force 4. means, agency of communicating news *etc.* to public, as radio, newspapers *etc.* 5. person through whom communication can supposedly be held with spirit world 6. surroundings, environment (*pl.* **-s,** ˈ**media**) —**medium waves** *Rad.* waves between 100 and 1000 metres

medlar (ˈmɛdlə) *n.* 1. tree with fruit like small apple 2. the fruit, eaten when decayed

medley (ˈmɛdlɪ) *n.* miscellaneous mixture (*pl.* **-s**)

medulla (mɪˈdʌlə) *n.* 1. marrow 2. pith 3. inner tissue —**meˈdullary** *a.*

Medusa (mɪˈdju:zə) *n.* 1. *Myth.* Gorgon whose head turned beholders into stone 2. (**m-**) jellyfish (*pl.* **-sae** (-zi:))

meek (mi:k) *a.* submissive, humble —ˈ**meekly** *adv.* —ˈ**meekness** *n.*

meerkat (ˈmɪəkæt) *n.* S Afr. mongoose

meerschaum (ˈmɪəʃəm) *n.* 1. white substance like clay 2. tobacco pipe bowl made of this

THESAURUS

meddle butt in, interfere, intermeddle, interpose, intervene, intrude, pry, put one's oar in, stick one's nose in (*Inf.*), tamper

mediate act as middleman, arbitrate, bring to an agreement, bring to terms, conciliate, intercede, interpose, intervene, make peace between, moderate, reconcile, referee, resolve, restore harmony, settle, step in (*Inf.*), umpire

mediator advocate, arbiter, arbitrator, go-between, honest broker, interceder, intermediary, judge, middleman, moderator, negotiator, peacemaker, referee, umpire

medicinal analeptic, curative, healing, medical, remedial, restorative, roborant, sanatory, therapeutic

medicine cure, drug, medicament, medication, physic, remedy

mediocre average, commonplace, fair to middling (*Inf.*), indifferent, inferior, insignificant, mean, medium, middling, ordinary, passable, pedestrian, run-of-the-mill, second-rate, so-só (*Inf.*), tolerable, undistinguished, uninspired

mediocrity commonplaceness, indifference, inferiority, insignificance, ordinariness, poorness, unimportance

meditate be in a brown study, cogitate, consider, contemplate, deliberate, muse, ponder, reflect, ruminate, study, think

meditation brown study, cerebration, cogitation, concentration, contemplation, musing, pondering, reflection, reverie, ruminating, rumination, study, thought

medium *adj.* 1. average, fair, intermediate, mean, medial, median, mediocre, middle, middling, midway ~*n.* 2. average, centre, compromise, mean, middle, middle course (ground, path, way), midpoint 3. agency, avenue, channel, form, instrument, instrumentality, means, mode, organ, vehicle, way 4. atmosphere, conditions, element, environment, habitat, influences, milieu, setting, surroundings 5. spiritist, spiritualist

medley assortment, confusion, farrago, gallimaufry, hodgepodge, hotchpotch, jumble, *mélange*, miscellany, mishmash, mixed bag (*Inf.*), mixture, olio, omnium-gatherum, pastiche, patchwork, potpourri, salmagundi

meek deferential, docile, forbearing, gentle, humble, long-suffering, mild, modest, patient, peaceful, soft, submissive, unassuming, unpretentious, yielding

meekness deference, docility, forbearance, gentleness, humbleness, humility, long-suffering, lowliness, mildness, modesty, patience, peacefulness, resignation, softness, submission, submissiveness

meet[1] (miːt) *vt.* 1. come face to face with, encounter 2. satisfy 3. pay —*vi.* 4. come face to face 5. converge at specified point 6. assemble 7. come into contact (**met** *pt./pp.*) —*n.* 8. meeting, *esp.* for sports —**'meeting** *n.* 1. assembly 2. encounter

meet[2] (miːt) *a. obs.* fit, suitable

mega- (*comb. form*) 1. denoting 10^6, as in *megawatt* 2. in computer technology, denoting 2^{20} (1 048 576), as in *megabyte* 3. large, great, as in *megalith*

megadeath (ˈmɛgədɛθ) *n.* death of a million people, *esp.* in nuclear war

megahertz (ˈmɛgəhɜːts) *n.* one million hertz (*pl.* **ˈmegahertz**)

megalith (ˈmɛgəlɪθ) *n.* great stone —**megaˈlithic** *a.*

megalomania (mɛgələʊˈmeɪnɪə) *n.* desire for, delusions of grandeur, power *etc.* —**megaloˈmaniac** *a./n.*

megalopolis (mɛgəˈlɒpəlɪs) *n.* urban complex, usu. comprising several towns —**megalopolitan** (mɛgələˈpɒlɪtˀn) *a./n.*

megaphone (ˈmɛgəfəʊn) *n.* cone-shaped instrument to amplify voice

megaton (ˈmɛgətʌn) *n.* 1. one million tons 2. explosive power of 1 000 000 tons of TNT

megohm (ˈmɛgəʊm) *n. Elec.* one million ohms

meiosis (maɪˈəʊsɪs) *n.* type of cell division in which nucleus divides into four daughter nuclei, each containing half chromosome number of parent nucleus (*pl.* **-ses** (-siːz)) —**meiotic** (maɪˈɒtɪk) *a.*

melamine (ˈmɛləmiːn) *n.* colourless crystalline compound used in making synthetic resins —**melamine resin** resilient kind of plastic

melancholy (ˈmɛlənkəlɪ) *n.* 1. sadness, dejection, gloom —*a.* 2. gloomy, dejected —**melancholia** (mɛlənˈkəʊlɪə) *n.* mental disease accompanied by depression —**melancholic** (ˈmɛlənkɒlɪk) *n./a.*

Melanesian (mɛləˈniːzɪən) *a.* 1. of Melanesia, its people, or their languages —*n.* 2. native or inhabitant of Melanesia 3. group or branch of languages spoken in Melanesia

mélange (meˈlɑ̃ːʒ) *Fr.* mixture

melanin (ˈmɛlənɪn) *n.* dark pigment found in hair, skin *etc.* of man

Melba toast (ˈmɛlbə) very thin crisp toast

melee *or* **mêlée** (ˈmɛleɪ) *n.* confused, noisy fight or crowd

meliorate (ˈmiːlɪəreɪt) *v.* improve —**melioˈration** *n.* —**ˈmeliorism** *n.* doctrine that the world may be improved by human effort —**ˈmeliorist** *n.*

mellifluous (mɪˈlɪfluəs) *or* **mellifluent** *a.* (of sound) smooth, sweet —**melˈlifluence** *n.*

mellow (ˈmɛləʊ) *a.* 1. ripe 2. softened by age, experience 3. soft, not harsh 4. genial, gay —*v.* 5. make, become mellow

melodeon *or* **melodion** (mɪˈləʊdɪən) *n. Mus.* 1. small accordion 2. keyboard instrument similar to harmonium

melodrama (ˈmɛlədrɑːmə) *n.* 1. play full of sensational and startling situations, often highly emotional 2. overdramatic behaviour, emotion —**melodraˈmatic** *a.*

melody (ˈmɛlədɪ) *n.* 1. series of musical notes which make tune 2. sweet sound —**melodic** (mɪˈlɒdɪk) *a.* 1. of or relating to melody 2. of or relating to part in piece of music —**meˈlodious** *a.* 1. pleasing to the ear 2. tuneful —**ˈmelodist** *n.* 1. singer 2. composer

melon (ˈmɛlən) *n.* large, fleshy, juicy fruit

melt (mɛlt) *v.* 1. (cause to) become liquid by heat 2. dissolve 3. soften 4. (cause to) waste away 5. blend —*vi.* 6. disappear (**ˈmelted** *pt./pp.*, **ˈmolten** *pp.*) —**ˈmelting** *a.* 1. softening 2. languishing 3. tender —**ˈmeltdown** *n.* (in nuclear reactor) melting of fuel rods as result of defect in cooling system, with possible escape of radiation —**melting point** temperature at which solid turns into liquid —**ˈmeltwater** *n.* melted snow or ice

mem. 1. member 2. memoir 3. memorandum 4. memorial

member (ˈmɛmbə) *n.* 1. any of individuals making up body or society 2. limb 3. any part of complex whole

THESAURUS

meet 1. bump into, chance on, come across, confront, contact, encounter, find, happen on, run across, run into 2. abut, adjoin, come together, connect, converge, cross, intersect, join, link up, touch, unite 3. answer, carry out, come up to, comply, cope with, discharge, equal, fulfil, gratify, handle, match, measure up, perform, satisfy 4. assemble, collect, come together, congregate, convene, forgather, gather, muster, rally

meeting 1. assignation, confrontation, encounter, engagement, introduction, rendezvous, tryst (*Archaic*) 2. assembly, audience, company, conclave, conference, congregation, convention, convocation, gathering, get-together (*Inf.*), meet, rally, reunion, session

melancholy 1. *n.* blues, dejection, depression, despondency, gloom, gloominess, low spirits, pensiveness, sadness, sorrow, unhappiness, woe 2. *adj.* blue, dejected, depressed, despondent, disconsolate, dismal, dispirited, doleful, down, downcast, downhearted, down in the dumps (*Inf.*), down in the mouth, gloomy, glum, heavy-hearted, joyless, low, low-spirited, lugubrious, melancholic, miserable, moody, mournful, pensive, sad, sombre, sorrowful, unhappy, woebegone, woeful

mellow *adj.* 1. delicate, full-flavoured, juicy, mature, perfect, rich, ripe, soft, sweet, well-matured 2. cheerful, cordial, elevated, expansive, genial, half-tipsy, happy, jolly, jovial, merry (*Brit. inf.*), relaxed ~*v.* 3. develop, improve, mature, perfect, ripen, season, soften, sweeten

melodious concordant, dulcet, euphonious, harmonious, melodic, musical, silvery, sweet-sounding, sweet-toned, tuneful

melodramatic blood-and-thunder, extravagant, hammy (*Inf.*), histrionic, overdramatic, overemotional, sensational, stagy, theatrical

melody 1. air, descant, music, refrain, song, strain, theme, tune 2. euphony, harmony, melodiousness, music, musicality, tunefulness

melt 1. deliquesce, diffuse, dissolve, flux, fuse, liquefy, soften, thaw 2. *Often with* **away** disappear, disperse, dissolve, evanesce, evaporate, fade, vanish

member 1. associate, fellow, representative 2. appendage, arm, component, constituent, element, extremity, leg, limb, organ, part, portion

membership 1. associates, body, fellows, members 2. belonging, enrolment, fellowship, participation

—ˈ**membership** *n.* —**Member of Parliament** member of House of Commons or similar legislative body

membrane (ˈmɛmbreɪn) *n.* thin flexible tissue in plant or animal body

memento (mɪˈmɛntəʊ) *n.* thing serving to remind, souvenir (*pl.* **-s, -es**) —**memento mori** (ˈmɔːriː) object intended to remind people of death

memo (ˈmɛməʊ, ˈmiːməʊ) memorandum

memoir (ˈmɛmwɑː) *n.* **1.** autobiography, personal history or biography **2.** record of events

memory (ˈmɛmərɪ) *n.* **1.** faculty of recollecting, recalling to mind **2.** recollection **3.** thing remembered **4.** length of time one can remember **5.** commemoration **6.** part or faculty of computer which stores information —**memorabilia** (mɛmərəˈbɪlɪə) *pl.n.* memorable events or things (*sing.* **-rabile** (-ˈræbɪlɪ)) —ˈ**memorable** *a.* worthy of remembrance, noteworthy —ˈ**memorably** *adv.* —**memoˈrandum** *n.* **1.** note to help the memory *etc.* **2.** informal letter **3.** note of contract (*pl.* **-s, -da** (-də)) —**meˈmorial** *a.* **1.** of, preserving memory —*n.* **2.** thing, *esp.* a monument, which serves to keep in memory —**meˈmorialist** *n.* —**meˈmorialize** *or* **-ise** *vt.* commemorate —ˈ**memorize** *or* **-ise** *vt.* commit to memory

memsahib (ˈmɛmsɑːɪb, -hɪb) *n.* formerly in India, term of respect used of European married woman

men (mɛn) *n., pl. of* MAN

menace (ˈmɛnɪs) *n.* **1.** threat —*v.* **2.** threaten

ménage (meɪˈnɑːʒ) *n.* persons of a household —***ménage à trois*** (menaːʒ a ˈtrwa) *Fr.* sexual arrangement involving married couple and lover of one of them (*pl.* ***ménages à trois*** (menaːʒ a ˈtrwa))

menagerie (mɪˈnædʒərɪ) *n.* exhibition, collection of wild animals

mend (mɛnd) *vt.* **1.** repair, patch **2.** reform, correct, put right —*vi.* **3.** improve, *esp.* in health —*n.* **4.** repaired breakage, hole —**on the mend** regaining health

mendacious (mɛnˈdeɪʃəs) *a.* untruthful —**mendacity** (mɛnˈdæsɪtɪ) *n.* (tendency to) untruthfulness

mendelevium (mɛndɪˈliːvɪəm) *n.* transuranic element artificially produced by bombardment of einsteinium

mendicant (ˈmɛndɪkənt) *a.* **1.** begging —*n.* **2.** beggar —ˈ**mendicancy** *or* **menˈdicity** *n.* begging

menhir (ˈmɛnhɪə) *n.* single, upright monumental stone, monolith

menial (ˈmiːnɪəl) *a.* **1.** of work requiring little skill **2.** of household duties or servants **3.** servile —*n.* **4.** servant **5.** servile person

meninges (mɪˈnɪndʒiːz) *pl.n.* three membranes that envelop brain and spinal cord (*sing.* **meninx** (ˈmiːnɪŋks)) —**meˈningeal** *a.* —**meninˈgitis** *n.* inflammation of the membranes of the brain

meniscus (mɪˈnɪskəs) *n.* **1.** curved surface of liquid **2.** curved lens

menopause (ˈmɛnəʊpɔːz) *n.* final cessation of menstruation

menorah (mɪˈnɔːrə) *n. Judaism* seven-branched candelabrum used in ceremonies

menses (ˈmɛnsiːz) *n.* **1.** menstruation **2.** period of time during which one menstruation occurs **3.** matter discharged during menstruation (*pl.* ˈ**menses**)

menstruation (mɛnstruˈeɪʃən) *n.* approximately monthly discharge of blood and cellular debris from womb of nonpregnant woman —ˈ**menstrual** *a.* —ˈ**menstruate** *vi.*

mensuration (mɛnʃəˈreɪʃən) *n.* measuring, *esp.* of areas

-ment (*comb. form*) **1.** state; condition; quality, as in *enjoyment* **2.** result or product of action, as in *embankment* **3.** process; action, as in *management*

mental (ˈmentˀl) *a.* **1.** of, done by the mind **2.** *inf.* feeble-minded, mad —**menˈtality** *n.* state or quality of mind —ˈ**mentally** *adv.*

THESAURUS

memoir account, biography, essay, journal, life, monograph, narrative, record, register

memorable catchy, celebrated, distinguished, extraordinary, famous, historic, illustrious, important, impressive, momentous, notable, noteworthy, remarkable, signal, significant, striking, unforgettable

memorial **1.** *adj.* commemorative, monumental **2.** *n.* cairn, memento, monument, plaque, record, remembrance, souvenir

memorize commit to memory, con (*Archaic*), get by heart, learn, learn by heart, learn by rote, remember

memory **1.** recall, recollection, remembrance, reminiscence, retention **2.** commemoration, honour, remembrance

menace *v.* **1.** alarm, bode ill, browbeat, bully, frighten, impend, intimidate, loom, lour, lower, terrorize, threaten, utter threats to ~*n.* **2.** commination, intimidation, scare, threat, warning **3.** danger, hazard, jeopardy, peril

mend *v.* **1.** cure, darn, fix, heal, patch, rectify, refit, reform, remedy, renew, renovate, repair, restore, retouch **2.** ameliorate, amend, better, correct, emend, improve, rectify, reform, revise **3.** convalesce, get better, heal, recover, recuperate ~*n.* **4.** darn, patch, repair, stitch **5. on the mend** convalescent, convalescing, getting better, improving, recovering, recuperating

mendacious deceitful, deceptive, dishonest, duplicitous, fallacious, false, fraudulent, insincere, lying, perfidious, perjured, untrue, untruthful

menial *adj.* **1.** boring, dull, humdrum, low-status, routine, unskilled **2.** abject, base, degrading, demeaning, fawning, grovelling, humble, ignoble, ignominious, low, lowly, mean, obsequious, servile, slavish, sorry, subservient, sycophantic ~*n.* **3.** attendant, dogsbody (*Inf.*), domestic, drudge, flunky, labourer, lackey, serf, servant, skivvy (*Brit.*), slave, underling

menstruation catamenia (*Physiology*), courses (*Physiology*), flow (*Inf.*), menses, menstrual cycle, monthly (*Inf.*), period, the curse (*Inf.*)

mental **1.** cerebral, intellectual **2.** deranged, disturbed, insane, lunatic, mad, mentally ill, psychiatric, psychotic, unbalanced, unstable

mentality **1.** brainpower, brains, comprehension, grey matter (*Inf.*), intellect, intelligence quotient, I.Q., mental age, mind, rationality, understanding, wit **2.** attitude, cast of mind, character, disposition, frame of mind, make-up, outlook, personality, psychology, turn of mind, way of thinking

mentally in one's head, intellectually, in the mind, inwardly, psychologically, rationally, subjectively

menthol (ˈmɛnθɒl) *n.* organic compound found in peppermint, used medicinally

mention (ˈmɛnʃən) *vt.* **1.** refer to briefly, speak of —*n.* **2.** acknowledgment **3.** reference to or remark about person or thing —**ˈmentionable** *a.* fit or suitable to be mentioned

mentor (ˈmɛntɔː) *n.* wise, trusted adviser, guide

menu (ˈmɛnjuː) *n.* list of dishes to be served, or from which to order

meow, miaou, miaow (mɪˈaʊ, mjaʊ), *or* **miaul** (mɪˈaʊl, mjaʊl) *vi.* **1.** (of cat) make characteristic crying sound —*interj.* **2.** imitation of this sound

M.E.P. Member of European Parliament

mercantile (ˈmɜːkəntaɪl) *a.* of, engaged in trade, commerce

mercenary (ˈmɜːsɪnərɪ, -sɪnrɪ) *a.* **1.** influenced by greed **2.** working merely for reward —*n.* **3.** hired soldier

mercer (ˈmɜːsə) *n. esp.* formerly, dealer in fabrics —**ˈmercery** *n.* his trade, goods

mercerize *or* **-ise** (ˈmɜːsəraɪz) *vt.* give lustre to (cotton fabrics) by treating with chemicals —**ˈmercerized** *or* **-ised** *a.*

merchant (ˈmɜːtʃənt) *n.* **1.** one engaged in trade **2.** wholesale trader —**merchandise** (ˈmɜːtʃəndaɪs, -daɪz) *n.* his wares —**merchant bank UK** financial institution engaged in accepting foreign bills and underwriting new security issues —**ˈmerchantman** *n.* trading ship —**merchant navy** ships engaged in a nation's commerce

mercury (ˈmɜːkjʊrɪ) *n.* **1.** silvery metal, liquid at ordinary temperature, quicksilver **2.** **(M-)** *Roman myth.* messenger of the gods **3.** **(M-)** planet nearest to sun —**merˈcurial** *a.* **1.** relating to, containing mercury **2.** lively, changeable

mercy (ˈmɜːsɪ) *n.* refraining from infliction of suffering by one who has right, power to inflict it, compassion —**ˈmerciful** *a.* —**ˈmerciless** *a.* —**mercy killing** *see* EUTHANASIA

mere[1] (mɪə) *a.* **1.** only **2.** not more than **3.** nothing but —**ˈmerely** *adv.*

mere[2] (mɪə) *n. obs.* lake

meretricious (mɛrɪˈtrɪʃəs) *a.* **1.** superficially or garishly attractive **2.** insincere

merganser (mɜːˈgænsə) *n.* large, crested diving duck

merge (mɜːdʒ) *v.* (cause to) lose identity or be absorbed —**ˈmerger** *n.* **1.** combination of business firms into one **2.** absorption into something greater

meridian (məˈrɪdɪən) *n.* **1.** circle of the earth passing through poles **2.** imaginary circle in sky passing through celestial poles **3.** highest point reached by star *etc.* **4.** period of greatest splendour —*a.* **5.** of meridian **6.** at peak of something

meringue (məˈræŋ) *n.* **1.** baked mixture of white of eggs and sugar **2.** cake of this

merino (məˈriːnəʊ) *n.* **1.** breed of sheep originating in Spain (*pl.* **-s**) **2.** long, fine wool of this sheep **3.** yarn or cloth made from this wool

merit (ˈmɛrɪt) *n.* **1.** excellence, worth **2.** quality of deserving reward —*pl.* **3.** excellence —*vt.* **4.** deserve —**meriˈtocracy** *n.* **1.** rule by persons chosen for their superior talents or intellect **2.** persons constituting such group —**meriˈtorious** *a.* deserving praise

merlin (ˈmɜːlɪn) *n.* small falcon

mermaid (ˈmɜːmeɪd) *n.* imaginary sea creature with upper part of woman and lower part of fish

merry (ˈmɛrɪ) *a.* joyous, cheerful —**ˈmerrily** *adv.* —**ˈmerriment** *n.* —**merry-go-round** *n.* roundabout

THESAURUS

mention *v.* **1.** acknowledge, adduce, allude to, bring up, broach, call attention to, cite, communicate, declare, disclose, divulge, hint at, impart, intimate, make known, name, point out, recount, refer to, report, reveal, speak about *or* of, state, tell, touch upon ~*n.* **2.** acknowledgment, citation, recognition, tribute **3.** allusion, announcement, indication, notification, observation, reference, remark

mentor adviser, coach, counsellor, guide, guru, instructor, teacher, tutor

menu bill of fare, carte du jour, tariff (*Chiefly Brit.*)

mercantile commercial, marketable, trade, trading

mercenary *adj.* **1.** acquisitive, avaricious, bribable, covetous, grasping, greedy, money-grubbing (*Inf.*), sordid, venal **2.** bought, hired, paid, venal ~*n.* **3.** condottiere (*Hist.*), free companion (*Hist.*), freelance (*Hist.*), hireling, soldier of fortune

merchandise commodities, goods, produce, products, staples, stock, stock in trade, truck, vendibles, wares

merchant broker, dealer, retailer, salesman, seller, shopkeeper, trader, tradesman, trafficker, vendor, wholesaler

merciful beneficent, benignant, clement, compassionate, forbearing, forgiving, generous, gracious, humane, kind, lenient, liberal, mild, pitying, soft, sparing, sympathetic, tender-hearted

merciless barbarous, callous, cruel, fell (*Archaic*), hard, hard-hearted, harsh, heartless, implacable, inexorable, inhumane, pitiless, relentless, ruthless, severe, unappeasable, unfeeling, unforgiving, unmerciful, unpitying, unsparing, unsympathetic

mercy benevolence, charity, clemency, compassion, favour, forbearance, forgiveness, grace, kindness, leniency, pity, quarter

mere *adj.* absolute, bare, common, complete, entire, nothing more than, plain, pure, pure and simple, sheer, simple, stark, unadulterated, unmitigated, unmixed, utter

merge amalgamate, be swallowed up by, become lost in, blend, coalesce, combine, consolidate, converge, fuse, incorporate, intermix, join, meet, meld, melt into, mingle, mix, tone with, unite

merger amalgamation, coalition, combination, consolidation, fusion, incorporation, union

merit *n.* **1.** advantage, asset, excellence, good, goodness, integrity, quality, strong point, talent, value, virtue, worth, worthiness **2.** claim, credit, desert, due, right ~*v.* **3.** be entitled to, be worthy of, deserve, earn, have a claim to, have a right to, have coming to one, incur, rate, warrant

meritorious admirable, commendable, creditable, deserving, excellent, exemplary, good, honourable, laudable, praiseworthy, right, righteous, virtuous, worthy

merriment amusement, conviviality, festivity, frolic, fun, gaiety, glee, hilarity, jocularity, jollity, joviality, laughter, levity, liveliness, merry-making, mirth, revelry, sport

mésalliance (meˈzælɪəns) *n.* marriage with person of lower social status

mescaline *or* **mescalin** (ˈmɛskəliːn, -lɪn) *n.* hallucinogenic drug derived from **mescal buttons**, button-like tubercles of the mescal cactus of Mexico

mesdames (ˈmeɪdæm) *n., pl. of* MADAME

mesdemoiselles (meɪdmwəˈzɛl) *n., pl. of* MADEMOISELLE

mesembryanthemum (mɪzɛmbrɪˈænθɪməm) *n.* low-growing plant with daisylike flowers of various colours

mesh (mɛʃ) *n.* **1.** (one of the open spaces of, or wires *etc.* forming) network, net —*v.* **2.** entangle, become entangled **3.** (of gears) engage —*vi.* **4.** coordinate

mesmerism (ˈmɛzmərɪzəm) *n. former term for* HYPNOTISM —**mesˈmeric** *a.* —**ˈmesmerist** *n.* —**ˈmesmerize** *or* **-ise** *vt.* **1.** hypnotize **2.** fascinate, hold spellbound

meso- *or before vowel* **mes-** (*comb. form*) middle or intermediate, as in *mesomorph*

Mesolithic (mɛsəʊˈlɪθɪk) *n.* **1.** period between Palaeolithic and Neolithic —*a.* **2.** of or relating to Mesolithic

meson (ˈmiːzɒn) *n.* elementary atomic particle

Mesozoic (mɛsəʊˈzəʊɪk) *a.* of, denoting, or relating to era of geological time that began 225 000 000 years ago and lasted about 155 000 000 years

mess (mɛs) *n.* **1.** untidy confusion **2.** trouble, difficulty **3.** group in armed services who regularly eat together **4.** place where they eat —*vi.* **5.** make mess **6.** *Mil.* eat in a mess —*vt.* **7.** muddle —**ˈmessy** *a.* —**mess about** *or* **around** potter about

message (ˈmɛsɪdʒ) *n.* **1.** communication sent **2.** meaning, moral **3.** errand —**ˈmessenger** *n.* bearer of message

Messiah (mɪˈsaɪə) *n.* **1.** Jews' promised deliverer **2.** Christ —**Messianic** (mɛsɪˈænɪk) *a.*

messieurs (ˈmɛsəz) *n., pl. of* MONSIEUR

Messrs. (ˈmɛsəz) *n., pl. of* MR.

met (mɛt) *pt./pp. of* MEET[1]

Met (mɛt) *a./n. inf.* Meteorological (Office in London)

met. **1.** meteorological **2.** meteorology **3.** metropolitan

meta- *or sometimes before vowel* **met-** (*comb. form*) change, as in *metamorphose, metathesis*

metabolism (mɪˈtæbəlɪzəm) *n.* chemical process of living body —**metaˈbolic** *a.* —**meˈtabolize** *or* **-ise** *v.*

metacarpus (mɛtəˈkɑːpəs) *n.* **1.** skeleton of hand between wrist and fingers **2.** corresponding bones in other vertebrates (*pl.* **-pi** (-paɪ)) —**metaˈcarpal** *a./n.*

metal (ˈmɛtᵊl) *n.* **1.** mineral substance, opaque, fusible and malleable, capable of conducting heat and electricity **2.** broken stone for macadamized roads —**meˈtallic** *a.* —**ˈmetalloid** *n.* **1.** nonmetallic element that has some of properties of metal —*a.* (*also* **metalˈloidal**) **2.** of or being metalloid **3.** resembling metal —**metalˈlurgic** *or* **metalˈlurgical** *a.* —**meˈtallurgist** *n.* —**meˈtallurgy** *n.* scientific study of extracting, refining metals, and their structure and properties

metal. *or* **metall.** **1.** metallurgical **2.** metallurgy

metamorphosis (mɛtəˈmɔːfəsɪs) *n.* change of shape, character *etc.* (*pl.* **-phoses** (-fəsiːz)) —**metaˈmorphic** *a.* (*esp.* of rocks) changed in texture, structure by heat, pressure *etc.* —**metaˈmorphose** *v.* transform

metaphor (ˈmɛtəfə, -fɔː) *n.* **1.** figure of speech in which term is transferred to something it does not literally apply to **2.** instance of this —**metaˈphorical** *a.* figurative —**metaˈphorically** *adv.*

metaphysics (mɛtəˈfɪzɪks) *pl.n.* (*with sing. v.*) branch of philosophy concerned with being and knowing —**metaˈphysical** *a.* —**metaphyˈsician** *n.*

metastasis (mɪˈtæstəsɪs) *n. Pathol.* spreading of disease, *esp.* cancer cells, from one part of body to another (*pl.* **-ses** (-siːz)) —**metastatic** (mɛtəˈstætɪk) *a.*

metatarsus (mɛtəˈtɑːsəs) *n.* **1.** skeleton of foot between toes and ankle **2.** corresponding bones in other vertebrates (*pl.* **-si** (-saɪ)) —**metaˈtarsal** *a./n.*

metathesis (mɪˈtæθəsɪs) *n.* transposition, *esp.* of letters in word, *eg* Old English *bridd* gives modern *bird* (*pl.* **-eses** (-əsiːz))

metazoan (mɛtəˈzəʊən) *n.* **1.** any animal having a

THESAURUS

merry blithe, blithesome, carefree, cheerful, convivial, festive, frolicsome, fun-loving, gay, glad, gleeful, happy, jocund, jolly, joyful, joyous, light-hearted, mirthful, rollicking, sportive, vivacious

mesh *n.* **1.** net, netting, network, plexus, reticulation, tracery, web ~*v.* **2.** catch, enmesh, ensnare, entangle, net, snare, tangle, trap **3.** combine, come together, connect, coordinate, dovetail, engage, fit together, harmonize, interlock, knit

mesmerize captivate, enthral, entrance, fascinate, grip, hold spellbound, hypnotize, magnetize, spellbind

mess *n.* **1.** botch, chaos, clutter, confusion, dirtiness, disarray, disorder, disorganization, hash (*Inf.*), jumble, litter, mishmash, shambles, turmoil, untidiness **2.** difficulty, dilemma, fine kettle of fish (*Inf.*), fix (*Inf.*), imbroglio, jam (*Inf.*), mix-up, muddle, perplexity, pickle (*Inf.*), plight, predicament, stew (*Inf.*) ~*v.* **3.** *Often with* **up** befoul, besmirch, botch, bungle, clutter, dirty, disarrange, dishevel, foul, litter, make a hash of (*Inf.*), muck up (*Brit. sl.*), muddle, pollute, scramble

mess about *or* **around** amuse oneself, dabble, footle (*Inf.*), muck about (*Inf.*), play about *or* around, potter, trifle

message **1.** bulletin, communication, communiqué, dispatch, intimation, letter, memorandum, missive, note, notice, tidings, word **2.** idea, import, meaning, moral, point, purport, theme **3.** commission, errand, job, mission, task

messenger agent, bearer, carrier, courier, delivery boy, emissary, envoy, errand-boy, go-between, harbinger, herald, runner

messy chaotic, cluttered, confused, dirty, dishevelled, disordered, disorganized, grubby, littered, muddled, shambolic (*Inf.*), sloppy (*Inf.*), slovenly, unkempt, untidy

metaphor allegory, analogy, emblem, figure of speech, image, symbol, trope

metaphorical allegorical, emblematic, emblematical, figurative, symbolic, tropical (*Rhetoric*)

mete *v.* administer, allot, apportion, assign, deal, dispense, distribute, divide, dole, measure, parcel, portion, ration, share

body composed of many cells —*a.* (*also* **meta'zoic**) **2.** of or relating to metazoans

mete (mi:t) *vt.* measure —**mete out 1.** distribute **2.** allot as punishment

metempsychosis (mɛtəmsaɪ'kəʊsɪs) *n.* migration of soul from one body to another (*pl.* **-ses** (-si:z)) —**metempsy'chosist** *n.*

meteor ('mi:tɪə) *n.* small, fast-moving celestial body, visible as streak of incandescence if it enters earth's atmosphere —**mete'oric** *a.* **1.** of, like meteor **2.** brilliant but short-lived —**'meteorite** *n.* fallen meteor —**'meteoroid** *n.* any of small celestial bodies that are thought to orbit sun —**meteor'oidal** *a.*

meteorology (mi:tɪə'rɒlədʒɪ) *n.* study of earth's atmosphere, *esp.* for weather forecasting —**meteoro'logical** *a.* —**meteor'ologist** *n.*

meter ('mi:tə) *n.* **1.** that which measures **2.** instrument for recording consumption of gas, electricity *etc.*

Meth. Methodist

methane ('mi:θeɪn) *n.* inflammable gas, compound of carbon and hydrogen

methanol ('mɛθənɒl) *n.* colourless, poisonous liquid used as solvent and fuel (*also* **methyl alcohol**)

methinks (mɪ'θɪŋks) *v. impers. obs.* it seems to me (**me'thought** *pt.*)

method ('mɛθəd) *n.* **1.** way, manner **2.** technique **3.** orderliness, system —**me'thodical** *a.* orderly —**'methodize** *or* **-ise** *vt.* reduce to order —**metho'dology** *n.* particular method or procedure

Methodist ('mɛθədɪst) *n.* **1.** member of any of the churches originated by John Wesley and his followers —*a.* **2.** of or relating to Methodism or the Methodist Church —**'Methodism** *n.*

meths (mɛθs) *n. inf.* methylated spirits

methyl ('mi:θaɪl, 'mɛθɪl) *n.* (compound containing) a saturated hydrocarbon group of atoms —**'methylate** *vt.* **1.** combine with methyl **2.** mix with methanol —**methylated spirits** alcoholic mixture denatured with methanol

meticulous (mɪ'tɪkjʊləs) *a.* (over)particular about details

métier ('metɪeɪ) *n.* **1.** profession, vocation **2.** forte

Métis (mɛ'ti:s) *n.* C person of mixed parentage

metonymy (mɪ'tɒnɪmɪ) *n.* figure of speech in which thing is replaced by another associated with it, *eg the Crown* for *the king* —**meto'nymical** *a.*

metre *or U.S.* **meter** ('mi:tə) *n.* **1.** unit of length in decimal system **2.** SI unit of length **3.** rhythm of poem —**metric** ('mɛtrɪk) *a.* of system of weights and measures in which metre is a unit —**metrical** ('mɛtrɪk'l) *a.* of measurement of poetic metre —**metricate** ('mɛtrɪkeɪt) *v.* convert (measuring system *etc.*) from nonmetric to metric units —**metri'cation** *n.* —**metric ton** *see* TONNE

Metro ('mɛtrəʊ) *n.* C metropolitan city administration

metronome ('mɛtrənəʊm) *n.* instrument which marks musical time by means of ticking pendulum

metropolis (mɪ'trɒpəlɪs) *n.* chief city of a country, region —**metro'politan** *a.* **1.** of metropolis —*n.* **2.** bishop with authority over other bishops of a province

-metry (*n. comb. form*) process or science of measuring, as in *geometry* —**-metric** (*a. comb. form*)

mettle ('mɛt'l) *n.* courage, spirit —**'mettlesome** *a.* high-spirited

mew[1] (mju:) *n.* **1.** cry of cat, gull —*vi.* **2.** utter this cry

mew[2] (mju:) *n.* any sea gull, *esp.* common gull

mews (mju:z) *pl.n.* (*sing. v.*) yard, street, orig. of stables, now oft. converted to houses

Mex. 1. Mexican **2.** Mexico

mezzanine ('mɛzəni:n, 'mɛtsəni:n) *n.* intermediate storey, balcony between two main storeys, *esp.* between first and second floors

mezzo ('mɛtsəʊ) *adv. Mus.* moderately; quite —**mezzo-soprano** *n.* voice, singer between soprano and contralto (*pl.* **-s**)

mezzotint ('mɛtsəʊtɪnt) *n.* **1.** method of engraving by scraping roughened surface **2.** print so made

mf *Mus.* mezzo forte

MF 1. *Rad.* medium frequency. **2.** Middle French

mfr. 1. manufacture **2.** manufacturer

mg *or* **mg.** milligram(s)

Mg *Chem.* magnesium

M. Glam. Mid Glamorgan

Mgr. 1. manager **2.** Monseigneur **3.** Monsignor

MHG Middle High German

MHz megahertz

mi *or* **me** (mi:) *n. Mus.* in tonic sol-fa, third degree of any major scale

MI 1. Military Intelligence **2.** Michigan

MI5 Military Intelligence, section five

miaou *or* **miaow** (mɪ'aʊ, mjaʊ) *see* MEOW

miasma (mɪ'æzmə) *n.* unwholesome or foreboding atmosphere (*pl.* **-mata** (-mətə), **-s**) —**miasmatic** (mi:əz'mætɪk) *a.*

mica ('maɪkə) *n.* mineral found as glittering scales, plates

mice (maɪs) *n., pl. of* MOUSE

Michaelmas ('mɪk'lməs) *n.* feast of Archangel St. Michael, 29th September —**Michaelmas daisy** common garden flower of aster family

mickey *or* **micky** ('mɪkɪ) *n. inf.* —**take the mickey** *or* **micky out of** tease

Mickey Finn (fɪn) *sl.* drink containing drug to make drinker unconscious

THESAURUS

meteoric brief, brilliant, dazzling, ephemeral, fast, flashing, fleeting, momentary, overnight, rapid, spectacular, speedy, sudden, swift, transient

method 1. approach, arrangement, course, fashion, form, manner, mode, modus operandi, plan, practice, procedure, process, programme, routine, rule, scheme, style, system, technique, way **2.** design, form, order, orderliness, organization, pattern, planning, purpose, regularity, structure, system

methodical businesslike, deliberate, disciplined, efficient, meticulous, neat, ordered, orderly, organized, painstaking, planned, precise, regular, structured, systematic, tidy, well-regulated

meticulous detailed, exact, fastidious, fussy, microscopic, painstaking, particular, perfectionist, precise, punctilious, scrupulous, strict, thorough

métier 1. calling, craft, line, occupation, profession, pursuit, trade, vocation **2.** forte, long suit (*Inf.*), speciality, specialty, strong point, strong suit

metropolis capital, city

micro (ˈmaɪkrəʊ) *n. inf.* 1. microcomputer 2. microprocessor (*pl.* -s)

micro- *or before vowel* **micr-** (*comb. form*) 1. small or minute, as in *microdot* 2. magnification or amplification, as in *microscope, microphone* 3. involving use of microscope, as in *microscopy*

microbe (ˈmaɪkrəʊb) *n.* 1. minute organism 2. disease germ —**miˈcrobial** *a.*

microbiology (maɪkrəʊbaɪˈɒlədʒɪ) *n.* branch of biology involving study of microorganisms —**microbioˈlogic(al)** *a.*

microchemistry (maɪkrəʊˈkɛmɪstrɪ) *n.* chemical experimentation with minute quantities of material —**microˈchemical** *a.*

microchip (ˈmaɪkrəʊtʃɪp) *n.* small wafer of silicon *etc.* containing electronic circuits (*also* **chip**)

microcircuit (ˈmaɪkrəʊsɜːkɪt) *n.* miniature electronic circuit, *esp.* integrated circuit —**microˈcircuitry** *n.*

microcomputer (maɪkrəʊkəmˈpjuːtə) *n.* computer in which central processing unit is contained in one or more silicon chips

microcopy (ˈmaɪkrəʊkɒpɪ) *n.* minute photographic replica useful for storage because of its small size

microcosm (ˈmaɪkrəʊkɒzəm) *or* **microcosmos** (maɪkrəʊˈkɒzmɒs) *n.* 1. miniature representation, model *etc.* of some larger system 2. man as epitome of universe —**microˈcosmic** *a.*

microdot (ˈmaɪkrəʊdɒt) *n.* extremely small microcopy

microelectronics (maɪkrəʊɪlɛkˈtrɒnɪks) *pl.n.* (*with sing. v.*) branch of electronics concerned with microcircuits

microfiche (ˈmaɪkrəʊfiːʃ) *n.* microfilm in sheet form

microfilm (ˈmaɪkrəʊfɪlm) *n.* miniaturized recording of manuscript, book on roll of film

microgroove (ˈmaɪkrəʊgruːv) *n.* 1. narrow groove of long-playing gramophone record —*a.* 2. (of a record) having such grooves

micrometer (maɪˈkrɒmɪtə) *n.* instrument for measuring very small distances or angles

microminiaturization *or* **-isation** (maɪkrəʊmɪnɪtʃəraɪˈzeɪʃən) *n.* production of small components and circuits and equipment in which they are used

micron (ˈmaɪkrɒn) *n.* unit of length, one millionth of a metre

microorganism (maɪkrəʊˈɔːgənɪzəm) *n.* organism of microscopic size

microphone (ˈmaɪkrəfəʊn) *n.* instrument for amplifying, transmitting sounds

microprint (ˈmaɪkrəʊprɪnt) *n.* greatly reduced photographic copy of print, read by magnifying device

microprocessor (maɪkrəʊˈprəʊsɛsə) *n.* integrated circuit acting as central processing unit in small computer

microscope (ˈmaɪkrəskəʊp) *n.* instrument by which very small body is magnified and made visible —**microscopic** (maɪkrəˈskɒpɪk) *a.* 1. of microscope 2. very small —**microscopy** (maɪˈkrɒskəpɪ) *n.* use of microscope

microstructure (ˈmaɪkrəʊstrʌktʃə) *n.* structure on microscopic scale, *esp.* of alloy as observed by etching, polishing *etc.* under microscope

microsurgery (maɪkrəʊˈsɜːdʒərɪ) *n.* minute surgical dissection or manipulation of individual cells under a microscope

microwave (ˈmaɪkrəʊweɪv) *n.* electromagnetic wave with wavelength of a few centimetres, used in radar, cooking *etc.*

micturate (ˈmɪktjʊreɪt) *vi.* urinate —**micturition** (mɪktjʊˈrɪʃən) *n.*

mid (mɪd) *a.* intermediate, in the middle of —**ˈmidˈday** *n.* noon —**midland** (ˈmɪdlənd) *n.* 1. middle part of country —*pl.* 2. central England —**ˈmidnight** *n.* twelve o'clock at night —**midnight sun** sun visible at midnight during summer inside Arctic and Antarctic circles —**mid-off** *n. Cricket* fielding position on off side closest to bowler —**mid-on** *n. Cricket* fielding position on on side closest to bowler —**ˈmidshipman** *n.* naval officer of lowest commissioned rank —**ˈmidˈsummer** *n.* 1. summer solstice 2. middle of summer —**ˈmidway** *a./adv.* halfway —**mid-wicket** *n. Cricket* fielding position on on side, midway between square leg and mid-on —**ˈmidˈwinter** *n.*

midden (ˈmɪdᵊn) *n.* 1. dunghill 2. rubbish heap

middle (ˈmɪdᵊl) *a.* 1. equidistant from two extremes 2. medium, intermediate —*n.* 3. middle point or part —**ˈmiddling** *a.* 1. mediocre 2. moderate —*adv.* 3. *inf.* moderately —**middle age** period of life between youth and old age, usu. considered to be between ages of 40 and 60 —**middle-aged** *a.* —**Middle Ages** period from end of Roman Empire to Renaissance, roughly A.D. 500–1500 —**middle C** *Mus.* note written on first ledger line below treble staff or first ledger line above bass staff —**middle class** social class of businessmen, professional people *etc.* —**middle-class** *a.* —**middle ear** sound-conducting part of ear —**Middle East** (loosely) area around E Mediterranean, *esp.* Israel and Arab countries from Turkey to N Afr. and eastwards to Iran —**Middle Eastern** —**Middle English** English language from about 1100 to about 1450 —**Middle High German** High German from about 1200 to about 1500 —**Middle Low German** Low German from about 1200 to about 1500 —**ˈmiddleman** *n.* trader between producer and consumer —**middle-of-the-road** *a.* not extreme; moderate —**middle school** UK school for children aged between 8 or 9 and 12 or 13 —**ˈmiddleweight** *n.* 1. professional boxer weighing 154–160 lbs. (70–72.5 kg); amateur boxer weighing 157–165 lbs. (71–75 kg) 2. wrestler weighing usu. 172–192 lbs. (78–87 kg)

midge (mɪdʒ) *n.* gnat or similar insect

midget (ˈmɪdʒɪt) *n.* very small person or thing

THESAURUS

microbe bacillus, bacterium, bug (*Inf.*), germ, microorganism, virus

microscopic imperceptible, infinitesimal, invisible, minuscule, minute, negligible, tiny

midday noon, noonday, noontide, noontime, twelve noon, twelve o'clock

middle 1. *adj.* central, halfway, intermediate, intervening, mean, medial, median, medium, mid 2. *n.* centre, focus, halfway point, heart, inside, mean, midpoint, midsection, midst, thick

middleman broker, distributor, entrepreneur, go-between, intermediary

middling adequate, all right, average, fair, indifferent, mediocre, medium, moderate, modest, O.K. (*Inf.*), okay (*Inf.*), ordinary, passable, run-of-the-

midi (ˈmɪdɪ) *a.* (of skirt *etc.*) reaching to below knee or midcalf

midriff (ˈmɪdrɪf) *n.* middle part of body

midst (mɪdst) *prep.* **1.** in the middle of —*n.* **2.** middle —**in the midst of** surrounded by, among

midwife (ˈmɪdwaɪf) *n.* trained person who assists at childbirth —**midwifery** (ˈmɪdwɪfərɪ) *n.* art, practice of this

mien (miːn) *n.* person's bearing, demeanour or appearance

might[1] (maɪt) *pt. of* MAY

might[2] (maɪt) *n.* power, strength —ˈ**mightily** *adv.* **1.** strongly **2.** powerfully —ˈ**mighty** *a.* **1.** of great power **2.** strong **3.** valiant **4.** important —*adv.* **5.** *inf.* very

mignonette (mɪnjəˈnɛt) *n.* grey-green plant with sweet-smelling flowers

migraine (ˈmiːgreɪn, ˈmaɪ-) *n.* severe headache, often with nausea and other symptoms

migrate (maɪˈgreɪt) *vi.* move from one place to another —ˈ**migrant** *n./a.* —**miˈgration** *n.* **1.** act of passing from one place, condition to another **2.** number migrating together —ˈ**migratory** *a.* **1.** of, capable of migration **2.** (of animals) changing from one place to another according to season

mikado (mɪˈkɑːdəʊ) *n.* (*oft.* **M-**) *obs.* Japanese emperor

mike (maɪk) *n. inf.* microphone

milady *or* **miladi** (mɪˈleɪdɪ) *n.* formerly, continental title used for English gentlewoman

milch (mɪltʃ) *a.* giving, kept for milk

mild (maɪld) *a.* **1.** not strongly flavoured **2.** gentle, merciful **3.** calm or temperate —ˈ**mildly** *adv.* —ˈ**mildness** *n.* —**mild steel** any strong tough steel that contains low quantity of carbon

mildew (ˈmɪldjuː) *n.* **1.** destructive fungus on plants or things exposed to damp —*v.* **2.** become tainted, affect with mildew

mile (maɪl) *n.* measure of length, 1760 yards, 1.609 km —ˈ**mileage** *or* ˈ**milage** *n.* **1.** distance in miles **2.** travelling expenses per mile **3.** miles travelled (per gallon of petrol) **4.** *inf.* advantage, profit, use —**mileˈometer** *or* **miˈlometer** *n.* device that records number of miles vehicle has travelled —ˈ**milestone** *n.* **1.** stone marker showing distance **2.** significant event, achievement

milfoil (ˈmɪlfɔɪl) *n.* yarrow

milieu (ˈmiːljɜː) *n.* environment, condition in life

military (ˈmɪlɪtərɪ, -trɪ) *a.* **1.** of, for, soldiers, armies or war —*n.* **2.** armed services —ˈ**militancy** *n.* —ˈ**militant** *a.* **1.** aggressive, vigorous in support of cause **2.** prepared, willing to fight —ˈ**militarism** *n.* enthusiasm for military force and methods —ˈ**militarist** *n.* —ˈ**militarize** *or* **-ise** *vt.* convert to military use —**militia** (mɪˈlɪʃə) *n.* military force of citizens for home service

militate (ˈmɪlɪteɪt) *vi.* (*esp. with* against) have strong influence, effect (on)

milk (mɪlk) *n.* **1.** white fluid with which mammals feed their young **2.** fluid in some plants —*vt.* **3.** draw milk from —ˈ**milky** *a.* **1.** containing, like milk **2.** (of liquids) opaque, clouded —**milk-and-water** *a.* weak, feeble, or insipid —**milk bar** snack bar specializing in milk drinks —**milk float UK** small motor vehicle used to deliver milk to houses —ˈ**milkmaid** *n. esp.* formerly, woman working with cows or in dairy —**milk run** *inf. Aeron.* routine and uneventful flight —**milk shake** frothy drink made of milk, flavouring, and *usu.* ice cream —ˈ**milksop** *n.* effeminate fellow —**milk teeth** first set of teeth in young mammals —**Milky Way** luminous band of stars *etc.* stretching across sky, the galaxy —**milk of magnesia** suspension of magnesium hydroxide in water, used as laxative

mill (mɪl) *n.* **1.** factory **2.** machine for grinding, pulverizing corn, paper *etc.* —*vt.* **3.** put through mill **4.** cut fine grooves across edges of (*eg* coins) —*vi.* **5.** move in

THESAURUS

mill, so-so (*Inf.*), tolerable, unexceptional, unremarkable

midget dwarf, gnome, homuncule, homunculus, manikin, pygmy, shrimp (*Inf.*), Tom Thumb

midnight dead of night, middle of the night, the witching hour, twelve o'clock (at night)

midst **1.** bosom, centre, core, depths, heart, hub, interior, middle, thick **2.** **in the midst of** among, during, enveloped by, in the middle of, in the thick of, surrounded by

midway betwixt and between, halfway, in the middle

might ability, capability, capacity, clout (*Sl.*), efficacy, efficiency, energy, force, potency, power, prowess, puissance, strength, sway, vigour

mighty doughty, forceful, hardy, indomitable, lusty, manful, potent, powerful, puissant, robust, stalwart, stout, strapping, strong, sturdy, vigorous

migrant **1.** *n.* drifter, emigrant, gypsy, immigrant, itinerant, nomad, rover, tinker, transient, vagrant, wanderer **2.** *adj.* drifting, gypsy, immigrant, itinerant, migratory, nomadic, roving, shifting, transient, travelling, vagrant, wandering

migrate drift, emigrate, journey, move, roam, rove, shift, travel, trek, voyage, wander

migration emigration, journey, movement, roving, shift, travel, trek, voyage, wandering

migratory gypsy, itinerant, migrant, nomadic, peripatetic, roving, shifting, transient, travelling, unsettled, vagrant, wandering

mild amiable, balmy, bland, calm, clement, compassionate, docile, easy, easy-going, equable, forbearing, forgiving, gentle, indulgent, kind, meek, mellow, merciful, moderate, pacific, peaceable, placid, pleasant, serene, smooth, soft, temperate, tender, tranquil, warm

mildness blandness, calmness, clemency, docility, forbearance, gentleness, indulgence, kindness, leniency, lenity, meekness, mellowness, moderation, placidity, smoothness, softness, temperateness, tenderness, tranquillity, warmth

milieu background, element, environment, locale, location, *mise en scène*, scene, setting, sphere, surroundings

militant *adj.* **1.** active, aggressive, assertive, combative, vigorous **2.** belligerent, combating, contending, embattled, fighting, in arms, warring

military **1.** *adj.* armed, martial, soldierlike, soldierly, warlike **2.** *n.* armed forces, army, forces, services

militia fencibles (*History*), National Guard (*U.S.*), reserve(s), Territorial Army (*Brit.*), trainband (*History*), yeomanry (*History*)

milk-and-water feeble, innocuous, insipid, jejune, vapid, weak, wishy-washy (*Inf.*)

confused manner, as cattle or crowds of people —ˈ**miller** *n.* —ˈ**millpond** *n.* pool formed by damming stream to provide water to turn mill wheel —ˈ**millrace** *n.* current of water driving mill wheel —ˈ**millstone** *n.* flat circular stone for grinding

millennium (mɪˈlɛnɪəm) *n.* **1.** period of a thousand years during which some claim Christ is to reign on earth **2.** period of a thousand years **3.** period of peace, happiness (*pl.* **-s, -ia** (-ɪə))

millepede (ˈmɪlɪpiːd) *or* **milleped** (ˈmɪlɪpɛd) *n.* small animal with jointed body and many pairs of legs

miller's thumb (ˈmɪləz) any of several small freshwater European fishes having flattened body

millet (ˈmɪlɪt) *n.* a cereal grass

milli- (*comb. form*) thousandth, as in *millilitre*

milliard (ˈmɪlɪɑːd, ˈmɪljɑːd) *n.* **UK** thousand million

millibar (ˈmɪlɪbɑː) *n.* unit of atmospheric pressure

milligram *or* **milligramme** (ˈmɪlɪgræm) *n.* thousandth part of a gram

millimetre *or U.S.* **millimeter** (ˈmɪlɪmiːtə) *n.* thousandth part of a metre

milliner (ˈmɪlɪnə) *n.* maker of, dealer in women's hats, ribbons *etc.* —ˈ**millinery** *n.* his goods or work

million (ˈmɪljən) *n.* 1000 thousands —**millionˈaire** *n.* **1.** owner of a million pounds, dollars *etc.* **2.** very rich man —ˈ**millionth** *a./n.*

milometer (maɪˈlɒmɪtə) *n. see* **mileometer** *at* MILE

milt (mɪlt) *n.* spawn of male fish

mime (maɪm) *n.* **1.** acting without the use of words —*v.* **2.** act in mime

mimic (ˈmɪmɪk) *vt.* **1.** imitate (person, manner *etc.*), *esp.* for satirical effect (ˈ**mimicked,** ˈ**mimicking**) —*n.* **2.** one who, or animal which does this, or is adept at it —*a.* **3.** imitative, simulated —**miˈmetic** *a.* **1.** of, resembling, or relating to imitation **2.** *Biol.* of or exhibiting protective resemblance to another species —ˈ**mimicry** *n.* mimicking

mimosa (mɪˈməʊsə, -zə) *n.* genus of plants with fluffy, yellow flowers and sensitive leaves

min. **1.** minim **2.** minimum **3.** minute

Min. **1.** Minister **2.** Ministry

mina (ˈmaɪnə) *n. see* MYNA

minaret (mɪnəˈrɛt, ˈmɪnərɛt) *n.* tall slender tower of mosque

minatory (ˈmɪnətərɪ, -trɪ) *or* **minatorial** *a.* threatening or menacing

mince (mɪns) *vt.* **1.** cut, chop small **2.** soften or moderate (words *etc.*) —*vi.* **3.** walk, speak in affected manner —*n.* **4.** minced meat —ˈ**mincer** *n.* —ˈ**mincing** *a.* affected in manner —ˈ**mincemeat** *n.* mixture of currants, spices, suet *etc.* —**mince pie** pie containing mincemeat or mince

mind (maɪnd) *n.* **1.** thinking faculties as distinguished from the body, intellectual faculties **2.** memory, attention **3.** intention **4.** opinion **5.** sanity —*vt.* **6.** take offence at **7.** care for **8.** attend to **9.** be cautious, careful about **10.** be concerned, troubled about —*vi.* **11.** be careful —ˈ**minder** *n.* **1.** one who looks after someone or something **2.** *see* **child minder** *at* CHILD **3.** *sl.* aide to someone in public life, who keeps control of press and public relations **4.** *sl.* bodyguard or assistant, *esp.* in criminal underworld —ˈ**mindful** *a.* **1.** heedful **2.** keeping in memory —ˈ**mindless** *a.* stupid, careless —**mind-reader** *n.* person seemingly able to discern thoughts of another —**mind's eye** visual memory or imagination

mine[1] (maɪn) *pron.* belonging to me

mine[2] (maɪn) *n.* **1.** deep hole for digging out coal, metals *etc.* **2.** in war, hidden deposit of explosive to blow up ship *etc.* **3.** profitable source —*vt.* **4.** dig from mine **5.** make mine in or under **6.** place explosive mines in, on —*vi.* **7.** make, work in mine —ˈ**miner** *n.* one who works in a mine —ˈ**minefield** *n.* area of land or sea containing mines —ˈ**minelayer** *n.* ship for laying mines —ˈ**minesweeper** *n.* ship for clearing away mines

THESAURUS

mill *n.* **1.** factory, foundry, plant, shop, works **2.** crusher, grinder ~*v.* **3.** comminute, crush, granulate, grate, grind, pound, powder, press, pulverize **4.** crowd, seethe, swarm, throng

mime **1.** *n.* dumb show, gesture, mummery, pantomime **2.** *v.* act out, gesture, pantomime, represent, simulate

mimic **1.** *v.* ape, caricature, imitate, impersonate, parody, take off (*Inf.*) **2.** *n.* caricaturist, copycat (*Inf.*), imitator, impersonator, impressionist, parodist, parrot **3.** *adj.* echoic, imitation, imitative, make-believe, mimetic, mock, sham, simulated

mince **1.** chop, crumble, cut, grind, hash **2.** diminish, euphemize, extenuate, hold back, moderate, palliate, soften, spare, tone down, weaken **3.** attitudinize, give oneself airs, ponce (*Sl.*), pose, posture

mincing affected, dainty, effeminate, foppish, lah-di-dah (*Inf.*), nice, niminy-piminy, poncy (*Sl.*), precious, pretentious, sissy

mind *n.* **1.** brain(s) (*Inf.*), grey matter (*Inf.*), intellect, intelligence, mentality, ratiocination, reason, sense, spirit, understanding, wits **2.** memory, recollection, remembrance **3.** brain, head, imagination, psyche **4.** attitude, belief, feeling, judgment, opinion, outlook, point of view, sentiment, thoughts, view, way of thinking **5.** bent, desire, disposition, fancy, inclination, intention, leaning, notion, purpose, tendency, urge, will, wish **6.** attention, concentration, thinking, thoughts **7.** judgment, marbles (*Inf.*), mental balance, rationality, reason, sanity, senses, wits ~*v.* **8.** be affronted, be bothered, care, disapprove, dislike, look askance at, object, resent, take offence **9.** adhere to, attend, comply with, follow, heed, listen to, mark, note, notice, obey, observe, pay attention, pay heed to, regard, respect, take heed, watch **10.** attend to, guard, have charge of, keep an eye on, look after, take care of, tend, watch **11.** be careful, be cautious, be on (one's) guard, be wary, take care, watch

mindful alert, alive to, attentive, aware, careful, chary, cognizant, conscious, heedful, regardful, respectful, sensible, thoughtful, wary, watchful

mindless asinine, brutish, careless, foolish, forgetful, gratuitous, heedless, idiotic, imbecilic, inattentive, moronic, neglectful, negligent, oblivious, obtuse, stupid, thoughtless, unintelligent, unmindful, unthinking, witless

mine *n.* **1.** coalfield, colliery, deposit, excavation, lode, pit, shaft, vein **2.** abundance, fund, hoard, reserve, source, stock, store, supply, treasury, wealth ~*v.* **3.** delve, dig for, dig up, excavate, extract, hew, quarry, unearth **4.** lay mines in *or* under, sow with mines

miner coalminer, collier (*Brit.*), pitman (*Brit.*)

mineral (ˈmɪnərəl, ˈmɪnrəl) *n.* 1. naturally occurring inorganic substance, *esp.* as obtained by mining —*a.* 2. of, containing minerals —**ˈmineralist** *n.* —**mineraˈlogical** *a.* —**minerˈalogy** *n.* science of minerals —**mineral water** water containing some mineral, *esp.* natural or artificial kinds for drinking

minestrone (mɪnɪˈstrəʊnɪ) *n.* type of soup containing pasta

mingle (ˈmɪŋgᵊl) *v.* mix, blend, unite, merge

mingy (ˈmɪndʒɪ) *a.* UK *inf.* miserly, stingy, or niggardly

mini (ˈmɪnɪ) *n.* something small or miniature —**ˈminiskirt** *n.* very short skirt, one at least four inches above knee

mini- (*comb. form*) smaller or shorter than standard size

miniature (ˈmɪnɪtʃə) *n.* 1. small painted portrait 2. anything on small scale —*a.* 3. small-scale, minute —**ˈminiaturist** *n.* —**ˈminiaturize** *or* **-ise** *vt.* make or construct on a very small scale

minibus (ˈmɪnɪbʌs) *n.* small bus for about ten passengers

minim (ˈmɪnɪm) *n.* 1. unit of fluid measure, one sixtieth of a drachm 2. *Mus.* note half the length of semibreve

minimize *or* **-ise** (ˈmɪnɪmaɪz) *vt.* bring to, estimate at smallest possible amount —**ˈminimal** *a.* —**ˈminimum** *n.* 1. lowest size or quantity (*pl.* **-s, -ma** (-mə)) —*a.* 2. least possible —**minimum lending rate** formerly, minimum rate of interest at which the Bank of England lent money —**minimum wage** lowest wage that employer is permitted to pay by law or union contract

minion (ˈmɪnjən) *n.* 1. favourite 2. servile dependant

minister (ˈmɪnɪstə) *n.* 1. person in charge of department of State 2. diplomatic representative 3. clergyman —*vi.* 4. (*oft. with* to) attend to needs (of), take care (of) —**minisˈterial** *a.* —**minisˈterialist** *n.* supporter of government —**ˈministrant** *a./n.* —**minisˈtration** *n.* rendering help, *esp.* to sick —**ˈministry** *n.* 1. office of clergyman 2. body of ministers forming government 3. act of ministering —**minister of state** UK minister, usu. below cabinet rank, appointed to assist senior minister —**Minister of the Crown** UK any Government minister of cabinet rank

miniver (ˈmɪnɪvə) *n.* a white fur used in ceremonial costumes

mink (mɪŋk) *n.* 1. variety of weasel 2. its (brown) fur

minnow (ˈmɪnəʊ) *n.* small freshwater fish

Minoan (mɪˈnəʊən) *a.* 1. of Bronze Age culture of Crete from about 3000 B.C. to about 1100 B.C. —*n.* 2. Cretan belonging to Minoan culture

minor (ˈmaɪnə) *a.* 1. lesser 2. under age —*n.* 3. person below age of legal majority 4. minor scale in music —**miˈnority** *n.* 1. lesser number 2. smaller party voting together 3. ethical or religious group in a minority in any state 4. state of being a minor —**minor scale** *Mus.* scale with semitones instead of whole tones after second and seventh notes

Minotaur (ˈmɪnətɔː) *n.* fabled monster, half bull, half man

minster (ˈmɪnstə) *n.* 1. *Hist.* monastery church 2. cathedral, large church

minstrel (ˈmɪnstrəl) *n.* 1. medieval singer, musician, poet —*pl.* 2. performers of negro songs —**ˈminstrelsy** *n.* 1. art, body of minstrels 2. collection of songs

mint[1] (mɪnt) *n.* 1. place where money is coined —*vt.* 2. coin, invent

mint[2] (mɪnt) *n.* aromatic plant

minuet (mɪnjuˈɛt) *n.* 1. stately dance 2. music for it

minus (ˈmaɪnəs) *prep.* 1. less, with the deduction of, deprived of —*a.* 2. lacking 3. negative —*n.* 4. the sign of subtraction (-)

minuscule (ˈmɪnəskjuːl) *n.* 1. lower-case letter 2. writing using such letters —*a.* 3. relating to, printed in, or written in small letters 4. very small —**minuscular** (mɪˈnʌskjʊlə) *a.*

minute[1] (maɪˈnjuːt) *a.* 1. very small 2. precise —**miˈnutely** *adv.* —**minutiae** (mɪˈnjuːʃɪiː) *pl.n.* trifles, precise details

minute[2] (ˈmɪnɪt) *n.* 1. 60th part of hour or degree 2. moment 3. memorandum —*pl.* 4. record of proceedings of meeting *etc.* —*vt.* 5. make minute of 6. record in minutes —**minute steak** small steak that can be cooked quickly

THESAURUS

mingle alloy, blend, coalesce, combine, commingle, compound, intermingle, intermix, interweave, join, marry, merge, mix, unite

miniature *adj.* baby, diminutive, dwarf, Lilliputian, little, midget, mini, minuscule, minute, pocket, pygmy, reduced, scaled-down, small, tiny, toy, wee

minimal least, least possible, littlest, minimum, nominal, slightest, smallest, token

minimize 1. abbreviate, attenuate, curtail, decrease, diminish, miniaturize, prune, reduce, shrink 2. belittle, decry, deprecate, depreciate, discount, disparage, make light *or* little of, play down, underestimate, underrate

minimum 1. *n.* bottom, depth, least, lowest, nadir, slightest 2. *adj.* least, least possible, littlest, lowest, minimal, slightest, smallest

minion bootlicker (*Inf.*), creature, darling, dependant, favourite, flatterer, flunky, follower, hanger-on, henchman, hireling, lackey, lickspittle, myrmidon, parasite, pet, sycophant, toady, underling, yes man

minister *n.* 1. churchman, clergyman, cleric, divine, ecclesiastic, parson, pastor, preacher, priest, vicar 2. administrator, ambassador, cabinet member, delegate, diplomat, envoy, executive, office-holder, official, plenipotentiary ~*v.* 3. accommodate, administer, answer, attend, be solicitous of, cater to, pander to, serve, take care of, tend

ministry 1. holy orders, the church, the priesthood, the pulpit 2. bureau, department, office

minor inconsequential, inconsiderable, inferior, insignificant, junior, lesser, light, negligible, paltry, petty, secondary, slight, small, smaller, subordinate, trifling, trivial, unimportant, younger

minstrel bard, harper, jongleur, musician, singer, troubadour

mint coin, construct, devise, fabricate, fashion, forge, invent, make up, produce, think up

minute[1] *adj.* 1. diminutive, fine, infinitesimal, Lilliputian, little, microscopic, miniature, minuscule, slender, small, tiny 2. close, critical, detailed, exact, exhaustive, meticulous, painstaking, precise, punctilious

minx (mɪŋks) *n.* bold, flirtatious woman

Miocene (ˈmaɪəsiːn) *a.* **1.** of or denoting fourth epoch of Tertiary period —*n.* **2.** this epoch or rock system

miracle (ˈmɪrək²l) *n.* **1.** supernatural event **2.** marvel —**miˈraculous** *a.* —**miˈraculously** *adv.* —**miracle play** drama (*esp.* medieval) based on sacred subject

mirage (ˈmɪrɑːʒ) *n.* deceptive image in atmosphere, *eg* of lake in desert

mire (maɪə) *n.* **1.** swampy ground, mud —*vt.* **2.** stick in, dirty with mud

mirror (ˈmɪrə) *n.* **1.** glass or polished surface reflecting images —*vt.* **2.** reflect —**mirror image 1.** image as observed in mirror **2.** object that corresponds to another in reverse as does image in mirror

mirth (mɜːθ) *n.* merriment, gaiety —**ˈmirthful** *a.* —**ˈmirthless** *a.*

mis- (*comb. form*) wrong(ly), bad(ly). See the list below

misadventure (mɪsədˈvɛntʃə) *n.* unlucky chance

misalliance (mɪsəˈlaɪəns) *n.* unsuitable alliance or marriage —**misalˈly** *v.*

misanthrope (ˈmɪzənθrəʊp) *or* **misanthropist** (mɪˈzænθrəpɪst) *n.* hater of mankind —**misanthropic** (mɪzənˈθrɒpɪk) *a.* —**miˈsanthropy** *n.*

misappropriate (mɪsəˈprəʊprɪeɪt) *vt.* **1.** put to dishonest use **2.** embezzle —**misappropriˈation** *n.*

misbegotten (mɪsbɪˈgɒt²n) *a.* **1.** unlawfully obtained **2.** badly conceived or designed **3.** *Lit., dial.* illegitimate; bastard

miscarry (mɪsˈkærɪ) *vi.* **1.** bring forth young prematurely **2.** go wrong, fail —**misˈcarriage** *n.*

miscast (mɪsˈkɑːst) *v.* **1.** distribute (acting parts) wrongly —*vt.* **2.** assign to unsuitable role

miscegenation (mɪsɪdʒɪˈneɪʃən) *n.* interbreeding of races

miscellaneous (mɪsəˈleɪnɪəs) *a.* mixed, assorted

misadˈdress
misadminisˈtration
misaˈlignment
misapˈply
misbeˈhave
misˈcalculate
misconˈceive
misˈconduct
misˈcount
misˈdeed
misˈfortune
misˈgovern
misˈgovernment
misˈhandle
misˈhear
misˈjudge
misˈmanage
misˈmanagement
misperˈception
misˈread
misˈstate
misˈstatement
misˈtime
misˈtreat
misˈtype
misunderˈstand
misˈuse

THESAURUS

minute² *n.* **1.** sixtieth of an hour, sixty seconds **2.** flash, instant, jiffy (*Inf.*), moment, second, shake (*Inf.*), tick (*Inf.*), trice

minutely closely, critically, exactly, exhaustively, in detail, meticulously, painstakingly, precisely, with a fine-tooth comb

minutes memorandum, notes, proceedings, record(s), transactions, transcript

minutiae details, finer points, niceties, particulars, subtleties, trifles, trivia

minx baggage (*Inf.*), coquette, flirt, hoyden, hussy, jade, tomboy, wanton

miracle marvel, phenomenon, prodigy, thaumaturgy, wonder

miraculous amazing, astonishing, astounding, extraordinary, incredible, inexplicable, magical, marvellous, phenomenal, preternatural, prodigious, superhuman, supernatural, thaumaturgic, unaccountable, unbelievable, wonderful, wondrous

mirage hallucination, illusion, optical illusion, phantasm

mire *n.* **1.** bog, marsh, morass, quagmire, swamp **2.** dirt, muck, mud, ooze, slime ~*v.* **3.** bog down, flounder, sink, stick in the mud **4.** begrime, besmirch, bespatter, cake, dirty, muddy, soil

mirror 1. *n.* glass, looking-glass, reflector, speculum **2.** *v.* copy, depict, echo, emulate, follow, reflect, represent, show

mirth amusement, cheerfulness, festivity, frolic, fun, gaiety, gladness, glee, hilarity, jocularity, jollity, joviality, joyousness, laughter, levity, merriment, merrymaking, pleasure, rejoicing, revelry, sport

mirthful amused, amusing, blithe, cheerful, cheery, festive, frolicsome, funny, gay, glad, gladsome (*Archaic*), happy, hilarious, jocund, jolly, jovial, laughable, light-hearted, merry, playful, sportive, uproarious, vivacious

misadventure accident, bad break (*Inf.*), bad luck, calamity, catastrophe, debacle, disaster, failure, ill fortune, ill luck, mischance, misfortune, mishap, reverse, setback

misanthrope cynic, egoist, egotist, mankind-hater, misanthropist

misappropriate defalcate (*Law*), embezzle, misapply, misspend, misuse, peculate, pocket, steal, swindle

misbehave act up (*Inf.*), be bad, be insubordinate, be naughty, carry on (*Inf.*), get up to mischief, muck about (*Brit. sl.*)

miscalculate blunder, calculate wrongly, err, get (it) wrong (*Inf.*), go wrong, make a mistake, misjudge, overestimate, overrate, slip up, underestimate, underrate

miscarriage 1. miss (*Inf.*), spontaneous abortion **2.** botch (*Inf.*), breakdown, error, failure, misadventure, mischance, misfire, mishap, mismanagement, nonsuccess, perversion, thwarting, undoing

miscarry 1. abort **2.** come to grief, come to nothing, fail, fall through, gang agley (*Scot.*), go amiss, go astray, go awry, go wrong, misfire

miscellaneous assorted, confused, diverse, diversified, farraginous, heterogeneous, indiscriminate, jumbled, many, mingled, mixed, motley, multifarious, multiform, promiscuous, sundry, varied, various

miscellany anthology, assortment, collection, diversity, farrago, gallimaufry, hotchpotch, jumble, medley, *mélange*, mixed bag, mixture, omnium-gatherum, potpourri, salmagundi, variety

—**mis'cellany** *n.* 1. collection of assorted writings in one book 2. medley

mischance (mɪsˈtʃɑːns) *n.* unlucky event

mischief (ˈmɪstʃɪf) *n.* 1. annoying behaviour 2. inclination to tease, disturb 3. harm 4. source of harm or annoyance —**ˈmischievous** *a.* 1. (of a child) full of pranks 2. disposed to mischief 3. having harmful effect

miscible (ˈmɪsɪbᵊl) *a.* capable of mixing

misconception (mɪskənˈsɛpʃən) *n.* wrong idea, belief

miscreant (ˈmɪskrɪənt) *n.* wicked person, evildoer, villain

misdemeanour *or U.S.* **misdemeanor** (mɪsdɪˈmiːnə) *n.* 1. formerly, offence less grave than a felony 2. minor offence

misdoubt (mɪsˈdaut) *v. obs.* doubt or suspect

mise en scène (miz ā ˈsɛn) *Fr.* 1. arrangement of scenery *etc.* in play; stage setting 2. environment of event

miser (ˈmaɪzə) *n.* 1. hoarder of money 2. stingy person —**ˈmiserliness** *n.* —**ˈmiserly** *a.* 1. avaricious 2. niggardly

miserable (ˈmɪzərəbᵊl) *a.* 1. very unhappy, wretched 2. causing misery 3. worthless 4. squalid —**ˈmisery** *n.* 1. great unhappiness 2. distress 3. poverty 4. UK *inf.* habitually depressed, discontented person

misericord *or* **misericorde** (mɪˈzɛrɪkɔːd) *n.* ledge projecting from underside of hinged seat of choir stall in church, on which occupant can support himself while standing

misfire (mɪsˈfaɪə) *vi.* fail to fire, start, function successfully

misfit (ˈmɪsfɪt) *n. esp.* person not suited to his environment or work

misgiving (mɪsˈgɪvɪŋ) *n.* (*oft. pl.*) feeling of fear, doubt *etc.*

misguided (mɪsˈgaɪdɪd) *a.* foolish, unreasonable

mishap (ˈmɪshæp) *n.* minor accident

mishmash (ˈmɪʃmæʃ) *n.* confused collection or mixture

THESAURUS

mischance accident, bad break (*Inf.*), bad luck, calamity, contretemps, disaster, ill chance, ill fortune, ill luck, infelicity, misadventure, misfortune, mishap

mischief 1. devilment, impishness, misbehaviour, monkey business (*Inf.*), naughtiness, pranks, roguery, roguishness, shenanigans (*Inf.*), trouble, waywardness 2. damage, detriment, disadvantage, disruption, evil, harm, hurt, injury, misfortune, trouble

mischievous 1. arch, bad, badly behaved, exasperating, frolicsome, impish, naughty, playful, puckish, rascally, roguish, sportive, teasing, troublesome, vexatious, wayward 2. bad, damaging, deleterious, destructive, detrimental, evil, harmful, hurtful, injurious, malicious, malignant, pernicious, sinful, spiteful, troublesome, vicious, wicked

misconception delusion, error, fallacy, misapprehension, misconstruction, mistaken belief, misunderstanding, wrong end of the stick (*Inf.*), wrong idea

misconduct delinquency, dereliction, immorality, impropriety, malfeasance (*Law*), malpractice, malversation (*Rare*), misbehaviour, misdemeanour, mismanagement, naughtiness, rudeness, transgression, unethical behaviour, wrongdoing

misdemeanour fault, infringement, misbehaviour, misconduct, misdeed, offence, peccadillo, transgression, trespass

miser cheapskate (*Inf.*), churl, curmudgeon, hunks (*Rare*), niggard, penny-pincher (*Inf.*), screw (*Sl.*), Scrooge, skinflint, tightwad (*U.S. sl.*)

miserable 1. afflicted, broken-hearted, crestfallen, dejected, depressed, desolate, despondent, disconsolate, distressed, doleful, down, downcast, down in the mouth (*Inf.*), forlorn, gloomy, heartbroken, melancholy, mournful, sorrowful, unhappy, woebegone, wretched 2. destitute, impoverished, indigent, meagre, needy, penniless, poor, poverty-stricken, scanty 3. abject, bad, contemptible, deplorable, despicable, detestable, disgraceful, lamentable, low, mean, pathetic, piteous, pitiable, scurvy, shabby, shameful, sordid, sorry, squalid, vile, worthless, wretched

miserly avaricious, beggarly, close, close-fisted, covetous, grasping, illiberal, mean, mingy (*Brit. inf.*), near, niggardly, parsimonious, penny-pinching (*Inf.*), penurious, sordid, stingy, tightfisted, ungenerous

misery 1. agony, anguish, depression, desolation, despair, discomfort, distress, gloom, grief, hardship, melancholy, sadness, sorrow, suffering, torment, torture, unhappiness, woe, wretchedness 2. destitution, indigence, need, penury, poverty, privation, sordidness, squalor, want, wretchedness 3. *Brit. inf.* grouch (*Inf.*), killjoy, moaner, pessimist, prophet of doom, sourpuss (*Inf.*), spoilsport, wet blanket (*Inf.*)

misfire fail, fail to go off, fall through, go phut (*Inf.*), go wrong, miscarry

misfit eccentric, fish out of water (*Inf.*), nonconformist, square peg (in a round hole) (*Inf.*)

misfortune 1. bad luck, evil fortune, hard luck, ill luck, infelicity 2. accident, adversity, affliction, blow, calamity, disaster, evil chance, failure, hardship, harm, loss, misadventure, mischance, misery, mishap, reverse, setback, stroke of bad luck, tragedy, trial, tribulation, trouble

misgiving anxiety, apprehension, distrust, doubt, hesitation, qualm, reservation, scruple, suspicion, uncertainty, unease, worry

misguided deluded, erroneous, foolish, ill-advised, imprudent, injudicious, labouring under a delusion *or* misapprehension, misled, misplaced, mistaken, uncalled-for, unreasonable, unwarranted, unwise

mishandle botch, bungle, make a hash of (*Inf.*), make a mess of, mess up (*Inf.*), mismanage, muff, screw (up) (*Inf.*)

mishap accident, adversity, bad luck, calamity, contretemps, disaster, evil chance, evil fortune, hard luck, ill fortune, ill luck, infelicity, misadventure, mischance, misfortune

misjudge be wrong about, get the wrong idea about, miscalculate, overestimate, overrate, underestimate, underrate

mislay be unable to find, be unable to put *or* lay one's hand on, forget the whereabouts of, lose, lose track of, misplace, miss

mislay (mɪsˈleɪ) *vt.* put in place which cannot later be remembered

mislead (mɪsˈliːd) *vt.* **1.** give false information to **2.** lead astray (**misˈled** *pt./pp.*) —**misˈleading** *a.* deceptive

misnomer (mɪsˈnəʊmə) *n.* **1.** wrong name or term **2.** use of this

misogamy (mɪˈsɒgəmɪ, maɪ-) *n.* hatred of marriage —**miˈsogamist** *n.*

misogyny (mɪˈsɒdʒɪnɪ, maɪ-) *n.* hatred of women —**miˈsogynist** *n.*

misrepresent (mɪsrɛprɪˈzɛnt) *vt.* portray in wrong or misleading light

misrule (mɪsˈruːl) *vt.* **1.** govern inefficiently or without justice —*n.* **2.** inefficient or unjust government **3.** disorder

miss (mɪs) *vt.* **1.** fail to hit, reach, find, catch, or notice **2.** not be in time for **3.** omit **4.** notice or regret absence of **5.** avoid —*vi.* **6.** (of engine) misfire —*n.* **7.** fact, instance of missing —**ˈmissing** *a.* **1.** lost **2.** absent —**missing link 1.** hypothetical extinct animal intermediate between anthropoid apes and man **2.** any missing section or part in series

Miss (mɪs) *n.* **1.** title of unmarried woman **2.** (**m-**) girl

missal (ˈmɪsˀl) *n.* book containing prayers *etc.* of the Mass

missile (ˈmɪsaɪl) *n.* that which may be thrown, shot, homed to damage, destroy —**guided missile** *see* GUIDE

mission (ˈmɪʃən) *n.* **1.** specific task or duty **2.** calling in life **3.** delegation **4.** sending or being sent on some service **5.** those sent —**ˈmissionary** *n.* **1.** one sent to a place, society to spread religion —*a.* **2.** of, like missionary or religious mission

missis *or* **missus** (ˈmɪsɪz, -ɪs) *n.* (*usu. with* the) *inf.* one's wife or wife of person addressed or referred to

missive (ˈmɪsɪv) *n.* letter

misspend (mɪsˈspɛnd) *v.* spend thoughtlessly or wastefully (**-ˈspending, -ˈspent**)

mist (mɪst) *n.* water vapour in fine drops —**ˈmistily** *adv.* —**ˈmisty** *a.* **1.** full of mist **2.** dim **3.** obscure

mistake (mɪˈsteɪk) *n.* **1.** error, blunder —*vt.* **2.** fail to understand **3.** form wrong opinion about **4.** take (person or thing) for another —**misˈtaken** *a.* **1.** wrong in opinion *etc.* **2.** arising from error in judgment *etc.*

mister (ˈmɪstə) *n.* title of courtesy to man

mistle thrush *or* **missel thrush** (ˈmɪsˀl) European thrush with brown back and spotted breast

mistletoe (ˈmɪsˀltəʊ) *n.* evergreen parasitic plant with white berries, which grows on trees

mistook (mɪˈstʊk) *pt. of* MISTAKE

mistral (ˈmɪstrəl, mɪˈstrɑːl) *n.* strong, dry, N wind in France

mistress (ˈmɪstrɪs) *n.* **1.** object of man's illicit love **2.** woman with mastery or control **3.** woman owner **4.** woman teacher **5.** *obs.* title given to married woman

mistrial (mɪsˈtraɪəl) *n. Law* trial made void because of some error

mistrust (mɪsˈtrʌst) *vt.* **1.** have doubts or suspicions about —*n.* **2.** distrust —**misˈtrustful** *a.*

THESAURUS

mislead beguile, bluff, deceive, delude, fool, give (someone) a bum steer (*Sl.*), hoodwink, lead astray, misdirect, misguide, misinform, pull the wool over (someone's) eyes (*Inf.*), take in (*Inf.*)

misleading ambiguous, casuistical, confusing, deceitful, deceptive, delusive, delusory, disingenuous, evasive, false, sophistical, specious, spurious, tricky (*Inf.*), unstraightforward

mismanage be incompetent, be inefficient, botch, bungle, make a hash of (*Inf.*), make a mess of, maladminister, mess up, misconduct, misdirect, misgovern, mishandle

misrepresent belie, disguise, distort, falsify, garble, misinterpret, misstate, pervert, twist

misrule 1. bad government, maladministration, misgovernment, mismanagement **2.** anarchy, chaos, confusion, disorder, lawlessness, tumult, turmoil

miss[1] *v.* **1.** avoid, be late for, blunder, err, escape, evade, fail, fail to grasp, fail to notice, forego, lack, leave out, let go, let slip, lose, miscarry, mistake, omit, overlook, pass over, pass up, skip **2.** feel the loss of, long for, need, pine for, want, wish, yearn for ~*n.* **3.** blunder, error, failure, fault, loss, mistake, omission, oversight, want

miss[2] damsel, girl, lass, lassie (*Inf.*), maid, maiden, schoolgirl, spinster, young lady

missile projectile, rocket, weapon

missing absent, astray, gone, lacking, left behind, left out, lost, mislaid, misplaced, not present, nowhere to be found, unaccounted-for, wanting

mission 1. aim, assignment, business, calling, charge, commission, duty, errand, goal, job, office, operation, purpose, pursuit, quest, task, trust, undertaking, vocation, work **2.** commission, delegation, deputation, embassy, legation, ministry, task force

missionary apostle, converter, evangelist, preacher, propagandist, proselytizer

missive communication, dispatch, epistle, letter, memorandum, message, note, report

misspent dissipated, idle, imprudent, misapplied, prodigal, profitless, squandered, thrown away, wasted

mist cloud, condensation, dew, drizzle, film, fog, haar (*Eastern Brit.*), haze, smog, smur *or* smir (*Scot.*), spray, steam, vapour

mistake *n.* **1.** bloomer (*Brit. inf.*), blunder, boob (*Brit. sl.*), boo-boo (*Inf.*), clanger (*Inf.*), erratum, error, error of judgment, false move, fault, faux pas, gaffe, goof (*Inf.*), howler (*Inf.*), inaccuracy, miscalculation, misconception, misstep, misunderstanding, oversight, slip, slip-up (*Inf.*), solecism ~*v.* **2.** get wrong, misapprehend, misconceive, misconstrue, misinterpret, misjudge, misread, misunderstand **3.** accept as, confound, confuse with, misinterpret as, mix up with, take for **4.** be wide of *or* be off the mark, be wrong, err, miscalculate, misjudge

mistaken barking up the wrong tree (*Inf.*), erroneous, fallacious, false, faulty, inaccurate, inappropriate, incorrect, in the wrong, labouring under a misapprehension, misguided, misinformed, mislead, off target, off the mark, unfounded, unsound, wide of the mark, wrong

mistreat abuse, brutalize, handle roughly, harm, ill-treat, ill-use, injure, knock about (*Inf.*), maltreat, manhandle, maul, misuse, molest, rough up, wrong

misunderstanding (mɪsʌndəˈstændɪŋ) *n.* 1. failure to understand properly 2. disagreement —**misunderˈstood** *a.* not properly or sympathetically understood

mite (maɪt) *n.* 1. very small insect 2. anything very small 3. small but well-meant contribution

mitigate (ˈmɪtɪgeɪt) *vt.* make less severe —**mitiˈgation** *n.* —**mitigating circumstances** circumstances which lessen the culpability of an offender

mitosis (maɪˈtəʊsɪs, mɪ-) *n.* cell division in which nucleus divides into daughter nuclei, each containing same number of chromosomes as parent nucleus —**mitotic** (maɪˈtɒtɪk, mɪ-) *a.*

mitre *or U.S.* **miter** (ˈmaɪtə) *n.* 1. bishop's headdress 2. joint between two pieces of wood *etc.* meeting at right angles —*vt.* 3. join with, shape for a mitre joint 4. put mitre on

mitt (mɪt) *n.* 1. glove leaving fingers bare 2. baseball catcher's glove 3. *sl.* hand

mitten (ˈmɪtᵊn) *n.* glove with two compartments, one for thumb and one for fingers

mix (mɪks) *vt.* 1. put together, combine, blend, mingle —*vi.* 2. be mixed 3. associate —**mixed** *a.* composed of different elements, races, sexes *etc.* —**ˈmixer** *n.* one who, that which mixes —**ˈmixture** *n.* —**mixed bag** *inf.* something composed of diverse elements, people *etc.* —**mixed blessing** situation *etc.* having advantages and disadvantages —**mixed doubles** *Tennis* game with man and woman as partners on each side —**mixed grill** dish of grilled chops, sausages, bacon *etc.* —**mixed marriage** marriage between persons of different races or religions —**mixed-up** *a. inf.* confused —**mix-up** *n.* confused situation

mizzen *or* **mizen** (ˈmɪzᵊn) *n.* lowest fore-and-aft sail on aftermost mast of ship —**mizzenmast** *or* **mizenmast** (ˈmɪzᵊnmɑːst; *Naut.* ˈmɪzᵊnməst) *n.* aftermost mast on full-rigged ship

mks units metric system of units based on the metre, kilogram and second

ml millilitre(s)

M.L. Medieval Latin

M.L.A. C Member of the Legislative Assembly

M.Litt. UK Master of Letters

Mlle *or* **Mlle.** Mademoiselle (*pl.* **Mlles, Mlles.**)

MLR minimum lending rate

mm millimetre(s)

M.M. Military Medal

Mme *or* **Mme.** Madame (*pl.* **Mmes, Mmes.**)

M.Mus. Master of Music

Mn *Chem.* manganese

MN Minnesota

MNA *or* **M.N.A.** C Member of the National Assembly

mnemonic (nɪˈmɒnɪk) *a.* 1. helping the memory —*n.* 2. something intended to help the memory

mo (məʊ) *n. inf.* moment

Mo *Chem.* molybdenum

MO Missouri

M.O. Medical Officer

THESAURUS

mistress concubine, doxy (*Archaic*), fancy woman (*Sl.*), girlfriend, inamorata, kept woman, ladylove (*Rare*), lover, paramour

mistrust 1. *v.* apprehend, beware, be wary of, distrust, doubt, fear, have doubts about, suspect 2. *n.* apprehension, distrust, doubt, dubiety, fear, misgiving, scepticism, suspicion, uncertainty, wariness

mistrustful apprehensive, cautious, chary, cynical, distrustful, doubtful, dubious, fearful, hesitant, leery (*Sl.*), sceptical, suspicious, uncertain, wary

misty bleary, blurred, cloudy, dark, dim, foggy, fuzzy, hazy, indistinct, murky, nebulous, obscure, opaque, overcast, unclear, vague

misunderstand get (it) wrong, get the wrong end of the stick (*Inf.*), get the wrong idea (about), misapprehend, misconceive, misconstrue, mishear, misinterpret, misjudge, misread, miss the point (of), mistake

misunderstanding 1. error, false impression, misapprehension, misconception, misconstruction, misinterpretation, misjudgment, misreading, mistake, mix-up, wrong idea 2. argument, breach, conflict, difference, difficulty, disagreement, discord, dissension, falling-out (*Inf.*), quarrel, rift, rupture, squabble, variance

misunderstood misconstrued, misheard, misinterpreted, misjudged, misread, unappreciated, unrecognized

misuse 1. *n.* abuse, barbarism, catachresis, corruption, desecration, dissipation, malapropism, misapplication, misemployment, misusage, perversion, profanation, solecism, squandering, waste 2. *v.* abuse, corrupt, desecrate, dissipate, misapply, misemploy, pervert, profane, prostitute, squander, waste

mitigate abate, allay, appease, assuage, blunt, calm, check, diminish, dull, ease, extenuate, lessen, lighten, moderate, modify, mollify, pacify, palliate, placate, quiet, reduce the force of, remit, soften, soothe, subdue, take the edge off, temper, tone down, tranquillize, weaken

mitigation abatement, allaying, alleviation, assuagement, diminution, easement, extenuation, moderation, mollification, palliation, relief, remission

mix *v.* 1. alloy, amalgamate, associate, blend, coalesce, combine, commingle, commix, compound, cross, fuse, incorporate, intermingle, interweave, join, jumble, merge, mingle, put together, unite 2. associate, come together, consort, fraternize, hang out (*Inf.*), hobnob, join, mingle, socialize

mixed 1. alloyed, amalgamated, blended, combined, composite, compound, fused, incorporated, joint, mingled, united 2. assorted, cosmopolitan, diverse, diversified, heterogeneous, miscellaneous, motley, varied 3. crossbred, hybrid, interbred, interdenominational, mongrel

mixed-up bewildered, confused, distraught, disturbed, maladjusted, muddled, perplexed, puzzled, upset

mixture admixture, alloy, amalgam, amalgamation, association, assortment, blend, brew, combine, composite, compound, concoction, conglomeration, cross, fusion, hotchpotch, jumble, medley, *mélange*, miscellany, mix, potpourri, salmagundi, union, variety

mix-up confusion, disorder, fankle (*Scot.*), jumble, mess, mistake, misunderstanding, muddle, snarl-up (*Brit. inf.*), tangle

-mo (*comb. form*) in bookbinding, indicating book size by specifying number of leaves formed by folding one sheet of paper, as in *sixteenmo*

moa (ˈməʊə) *n.* any of various extinct flightless birds of New Zealand

moan (məʊn) *n.* **1.** low murmur, usually of pain —*v.* **2.** utter (words *etc.*) with moan —*vi.* **3.** lament

moat (məʊt) *n.* **1.** deep wide ditch, *esp.* round castle —*vt.* **2.** surround with moat

mob (mɒb) *n.* **1.** disorderly crowd of people **2.** mixed assembly —*vt.* **3.** attack in mob, hustle or ill-treat (**-bb-**) —ˈ**mobster** *n.* **US** *sl.* gangster

mobcap (ˈmɒbkæp) *n.* formerly, woman's large cotton cap with pouched crown

mobile (ˈməʊbaɪl) *a.* **1.** capable of movement **2.** easily moved or changed —*n.* **3.** hanging structure of card, plastic *etc.*, designed to move in air currents —**mobility** (məʊˈbɪlɪtɪ) *n.*

mobilize *or* **-ise** (ˈməʊbɪlaɪz) *vi.* **1.** (of armed services) prepare for military service —*vt.* **2.** organize for a purpose —**mobiliˈzation** *or* **-iˈsation** *n.* in war time, calling up of men and women for active service

moccasin (ˈmɒkəsɪn) *n.* Amer. Indian soft shoe, usu. of deerskin

mocha (ˈmɒkə) *n.* **1.** type of strong, dark coffee **2.** this flavour

mock (mɒk) *vt.* **1.** make fun of, ridicule **2.** mimic —*vi.* **3.** scoff —*n.* **4.** act of mocking **5.** laughing stock —*a.* **6.** sham, imitation —ˈ**mocker** *n.* —ˈ**mockery** *n.* **1.** derision **2.** travesty —**mocking bird** N Amer. bird which imitates songs of others —**mock orange** shrub with white fragrant flowers —**mock turtle soup** imitation turtle soup made from calf's head —**mock-up** *n.* scale model —**put the mockers on** *inf.* ruin chances of success of

mod[1] (mɒd) **UK** *a.* **1.** of any fashion in dress regarded as stylish, *esp.* that of early 1960s —*n.* **2.** member of group of teenagers, orig. in mid-1960s, noted for their clothes-consciousness

mod[2] (mɒd) *n.* annual Highland Gaelic meeting with musical and literary competitions

mod. **1.** moderate **2.** modern

mod cons (kɒnz) *inf.* modern conveniences

mode (məʊd) *n.* **1.** method, manner **2.** prevailing fashion **3.** *Mus.* any of various scales of notes within one octave —ˈ**modal** *a.* **1.** of or relating to mode or manner **2.** *Gram.* expressing distinction of mood **3.** *Metaphys.* of or relating to form of thing as opposed to its substance *etc.* **4.** *Mus.* of or relating to mode —**moˈdality** *n.* —ˈ**modish** *a.* in the fashion —**modiste** (məʊˈdiːst) *n.* fashionable dressmaker or milliner

model (ˈmɒdᵊl) *n.* **1.** miniature representation **2.** pattern **3.** person or thing worthy of imitation **4.** person employed by artist to pose, or by dress designer to display clothing —*vt.* **5.** make model of **6.** mould —*v.* **7.** display (clothing) for dress designer (**-ll-**)

moderate (ˈmɒdərɪt) *a.* **1.** not going to extremes, temperate, medium —*n.* **2.** person of moderate views —*v.* (ˈmɒdəreɪt) **3.** make, become less violent or excessive **4.** preside (over) —**modeˈration** *n.* —ˈ**moderator** *n.* **1.** mediator **2.** president of Presbyterian body **3.** arbitrator

moderato (mɒdəˈrɑːtəʊ) *adv.* *Mus.* **1.** at moderate tempo **2.** direction indicating that tempo specified be used with restraint

modern (ˈmɒdən) *a.* **1.** of present or recent times **2.** in, of current fashion —*n.* **3.** person living in modern times —ˈ**modernism** *n.* (support of) modern tendencies, thoughts *etc.* —ˈ**modernist** *n.* —**moˈdernity** *n.* —**moderniˈzation** *or* **-iˈsation** *n.* —ˈ**modernize** *or* **-ise**

THESAURUS

moan **1.** *n.* groan, lament, lamentation, sigh, sob, sough, wail, whine **2.** *v.* bemoan, bewail, deplore, grieve, groan, keen, lament, mourn, sigh, sob, sough, whine

mob *n.* **1.** assemblage, body, collection, crowd, drove, flock, gang, gathering, herd, horde, host, mass, multitude, pack, press, swarm, throng **2.** class, company, crew (*Inf.*), gang, group, lot, set, troop ~*v.* **3.** crowd around, jostle, overrun, set upon, surround, swarm around

mobile ambulatory, itinerant, locomotive, migrant, motile, movable, moving, peripatetic, portable, travelling, wandering

mobilize activate, animate, call to arms, call up, get *or* make ready, marshal, muster, organize, prepare, put in motion, rally, ready

mock *v.* **1.** chaff, deride, flout, insult, jeer, laugh at, laugh to scorn, make fun of, poke fun at, ridicule, scoff, scorn, show contempt for, sneer, take the mickey (out of) (*Inf.*), taunt, tease **2.** ape, burlesque, caricature, counterfeit, imitate, lampoon, mimic, parody, satirize, send up (*Brit. inf.*), take off (*Inf.*), travesty ~*n.* **3.** banter, derision, gibe, jeering, mockery, ridicule, scorn, sneer, sneering **4.** Aunt Sally (*Brit.*), butt, dupe, fool, jest, laughing stock, sport, travesty ~*adj.* **5.** artificial, bogus, counterfeit, dummy, ersatz, fake, faked, false, feigned, forged, fraudulent, imitation, phoney (*Sl.*), pretended, pseudo (*Inf.*), sham, spurious

mockery **1.** contempt, contumely, derision, disdain, disrespect, gibes, insults, jeering, ridicule, scoffing, scorn **2.** burlesque, caricature, deception, farce, imitation, lampoon, laughing stock, mimicry, parody, pretence, send-up (*Brit. sl.*), sham, spoof (*Inf.*), take-off (*Inf.*), travesty

model *n.* **1.** copy, dummy, facsimile, image, imitation, miniature, mock-up, replica, representation **2.** archetype, design, epitome, example, exemplar, gauge, ideal, lodestar, mould, original, paradigm, paragon, pattern, prototype, standard, type **3.** poser, sitter, subject **4.** mannequin ~*v.* **5.** base, carve, cast, design, fashion, form, mould, pattern, plan, sculpt, shape **6.** display, show off, sport (*Inf.*), wear

moderate *adj.* **1.** calm, controlled, cool, deliberate, equable, gentle, judicious, limited, middle-of-the-road, mild, modest, peaceable, reasonable, restrained, sober, steady, temperate **2.** average, fair, fairish, fair to middling (*Inf.*), indifferent, mediocre, medium, middling, ordinary, passable, so-so (*Inf.*), unexceptional ~*v.* **3.** abate, allay, appease, assuage, calm, control, curb, decrease, diminish, lessen, mitigate, modulate, pacify, play down, quiet, regulate, repress, restrain, soften, soft pedal (*Inf.*), subdue, tame, temper, tone down **4.** arbitrate, chair, judge, mediate, preside, referee, take the chair

moderation calmness, composure, coolness, equanimity, fairness, judiciousness, justice, justness, mildness, moderateness, reasonableness, restraint, sedateness, temperance

vt. bring up to date —**Modern English** English language since about 1450 —**modern languages** current European languages as subject of study

modest (ˈmɒdɪst) *a.* 1. not overrating one's qualities or achievements 2. shy 3. moderate, not excessive 4. decorous, decent —ˈ**modestly** *adv.* —ˈ**modesty** *n.*

modicum (ˈmɒdɪkəm) *n.* small quantity

modify (ˈmɒdɪfaɪ) *vt.* 1. change slightly 2. tone down (-**fied**, -**fying**) —**modifiˈcation** *n.* —ˈ**modifier** *n. esp.* word qualifying another

modulate (ˈmɒdjʊleɪt) *vt.* 1. regulate 2. vary in tone —*vi.* 3. change key of music —**moduˈlation** *n.* 1. modulating 2. *Electron.* superimposing signals on to high-frequency carrier —ˈ**modulator** *n.*

module (ˈmɒdjuːl) *n.* (detachable) unit, section, component with specific function —ˈ**modular** *a.* of, consisting of, or resembling module or modulus

modulus (ˈmɒdjʊləs) *n.* 1. *Phys.* coefficient expressing specified property of specified substance 2. *Maths.* number by which logarithm to one base is multiplied to give the corresponding logarithm to another base 3. *Maths.* integer that can be divided exactly into the difference between two other integers (*pl.* -**li** (-laɪ))

modus operandi (ˈməʊdəs ɒpəˈrændiː) *Lat.* method of operating, tackling task (*pl.* ***modi operandi*** (ˈməʊdiː))

modus vivendi (vɪˈvendiː) *Lat.* working arrangement between conflicting interests (*pl.* ***modi vivendi*** (ˈməʊdiː))

mog (mɒg) *or* **moggy** *n.* **UK** *sl.* cat

mogul (ˈməʊgʌl, məʊˈgʌl) *n.* important or powerful person

M.O.H. Medical Officer of Health

mohair (ˈməʊhɛə) *n.* 1. fine cloth of goat's hair 2. hair of Angora goat

Mohammed (məʊˈhæmɪd) *n.* prophet and founder of Islam —**Moˈhammedan** *a./n.* Muslim —**Moˈhammedanism** *n.* another word (not in Muslim use) for ISLAM

moiety (ˈmɔɪɪtɪ) *n.* a half

moire (mwɑː) *n.* fabric, usu. silk, having watered effect —**moiré** (ˈmwɑːreɪ) *a.* 1. having watered or wavelike pattern —*n.* 2. such pattern, impressed on fabrics by means of engraved rollers 3. any fabric having such pattern, moire

moist (mɔɪst) *a.* damp, slightly wet —**moisten** (ˈmɔɪsᵊn) *v.* —ˈ**moisture** *n.* liquid, *esp.* diffused or in drops —ˈ**moisturize** *or* -**ise** *vt.* add, restore moisture to (skin *etc.*)

moke (məʊk) *n. sl.* donkey

mol *Chem.* mole

molar (ˈməʊlə) *a.* 1. (of teeth) for grinding —*n.* 2. molar tooth

molasses (məˈlæsɪz) *n.* syrup, by-product of process of sugar refining

mole[1] (məʊl) *n.* small dark protuberant spot on the skin

mole[2] (məʊl) *n.* 1. small burrowing animal 2. spy, informer —ˈ**molehill** *n.* small mound of earth thrown up by burrowing mole —**make a mountain out of a molehill** exaggerate unimportant matter out of all proportion

mole[3] (məʊl) *n.* 1. pier or breakwater 2. causeway 3. harbour within this

mole[4] (məʊl) *n.* SI unit of amount of substance

molecule (ˈmɒlɪkjuːl) *n.* 1. simplest freely existing chemical unit, composed of two or more atoms 2. very small particle —**moˈlecular** *a.* of, inherent in molecules —**molecular weight** sum of all atomic weights of atoms in a molecule

molest (məˈlɛst) *vt.* pester, interfere with so as to annoy or injure —**molestation** (məʊlɛˈsteɪʃən) *n.*

moll (mɒl) *n. sl.* 1. gangster's female accomplice 2. prostitute

mollify (ˈmɒlɪfaɪ) *vt.* calm down, placate, soften (-**fied**, -**fying**) —**mollifiˈcation** *n.*

mollusc *or U.S.* **mollusk** (ˈmɒləsk) *n.* soft-bodied, usu. hard-shelled animal, *eg* snail, oyster

mollycoddle (ˈmɒlɪkɒdᵊl) *vt.* pamper

Molotov cocktail (ˈmɒlətɒf) incendiary petrol bomb

THESAURUS

modern contemporary, current, fresh, late, latest, neoteric (*Rare*), new, newfangled, novel, present, present-day, recent, twentieth-century, up-to-date, up-to-the-minute, with-it (*Inf.*)

modernize bring into the twentieth century, bring up to date, rejuvenate, remake, remodel, renew, renovate, revamp, update

modest 1. bashful, blushing, coy, demure, diffident, discreet, humble, meek, quiet, reserved, reticent, retiring, self-conscious, self-effacing, shy, simple, unassuming, unpretentious 2. fair, limited, middling, moderate, ordinary, small, unexceptional

modesty bashfulness, coyness, decency, demureness, diffidence, discreetness, humbleness, humility, lack of pretension, meekness, propriety, quietness, reserve, reticence, self-effacement, shyness, simplicity, timidity, unobtrusiveness, unpretentiousness

modification adjustment, alteration, change, modulation, mutation, qualification, refinement, reformation, restriction, revision, variation

modify 1. adapt, adjust, alter, change, convert, recast, redo, refashion, reform, remodel, reorganize, reshape, revise, rework, transform, vary 2. abate, lessen, limit, lower, moderate, qualify, reduce, restrain, restrict, soften, temper, tone down

mogul baron, bashaw, big cheese (*Sl.*), big gun (*Sl.*), big noise (*Brit. sl.*), big shot (*Sl.*), big wheel (*Sl.*), lord, magnate, nabob (*Inf.*), notable, personage, potentate, tycoon, V.I.P.

moist clammy, damp, dampish, dank, dewy, dripping, drizzly, humid, not dry, rainy, soggy, wet, wettish

moisten bedew, damp, dampen, humidify, lick, moisturize, soak, water, wet

moisture damp, dampness, dankness, dew, humidity, liquid, perspiration, sweat, water, wateriness, wetness

molecule atom, iota, jot, mite, mote, particle, speck

molest 1. abuse, afflict, annoy, badger, beset, bother, bug (*Inf.*), disturb, harass, harry, hector, irritate, persecute, pester, plague, tease, torment, upset, vex, worry 2. abuse, accost, assail, attack, harm, hurt, illtreat, injure, interfere with, maltreat, manhandle

molten (ˈmәʊltәn) *a.* **1.** liquefied; melted **2.** made by having been melted —*v.* **3.** *pp. of* MELT

molto (ˈmɒltәʊ) *adv. Mus.* very

molybdenum (mɒˈlɪbdɪnәm) *n.* silver-white metallic element

moment (ˈmәʊmәnt) *n.* **1.** very short space of time **2.** (present) point in time —**ˈmomentarily** *adv.* —**ˈmomentary** *a.* lasting only a moment —**moment of truth** moment when person or thing is put to test

momentous (mәʊˈmɛntәs) *a.* of great importance

momentum (mәʊˈmɛntәm) *n.* **1.** force of a moving body **2.** impetus gained from motion (*pl.* **-ta** (-tә), **-s**)

mon. monetary

Mon. Monday

monad (ˈmɒnæd, ˈmәʊ-) *n.* **1.** *Philos.* any fundamental singular metaphysical entity (*pl.* **-s, -ades** (-әdiːz)) **2.** single-celled organism **3.** atom, ion, or radical with valency of one —**monadic** (mɒˈnædɪk) *a.*

monandrous (mɒˈnændrәs) *a.* **1.** having only one male sexual partner over a period of time **2.** (of plants) having flowers with only one stamen —**moˈnandry** *n.*

monarch (ˈmɒnәk) *n.* sovereign ruler of a state —**monˈarchic** *a.* —**ˈmonarchist** *n.* supporter of monarchy —**ˈmonarchy** *n.* **1.** state ruled by sovereign **2.** his rule

monastery (ˈmɒnәstәrɪ) *n.* house occupied by a religious order —**moˈnastic** *a.* **1.** relating to monks, nuns, or monasteries —*n.* **2.** monk, recluse —**moˈnasticism** *n.*

monaural (mɒˈnɔːrәl) *a.* relating to, having, or hearing with only one ear

Monday (ˈmʌndɪ) *n.* second day of the week, or first of working week

money (ˈmʌnɪ) *n.* banknotes, coin *etc.*, used as medium of exchange (*pl.* **-s, -ies**) —**ˈmonetarism** *n.* theory that inflation is caused by increase in money supply —**ˈmonetarist** *n./a.* —**ˈmonetary** *a.* —**monetiˈzation** *or* **-iˈsation** *n.* —**ˈmonetize** *or* **-ise** *vt.* make into, recognize as money —**ˈmoneyed** *or* **ˈmonied** *a.* rich —**ˈmoneybags** *n. sl.* very rich person —**money-grubbing** *a. inf.* seeking greedily to obtain money —**ˈmoneylender** *n.* person who lends money at interest as a living —**money-spinner** *n. inf.* enterprise, idea *etc.* that is source of wealth

mongolism (ˈmɒŋgәlɪzәm) *n.* Down's syndrome —**ˈmongol** *n./a.* (one) afflicted with this —**ˈmongoloid** *a.* relating to or characterized by mongolism

Mongoloid (ˈmɒŋgәlɔɪd) *a.* of major racial group of mankind, including most of peoples of Asia, Eskimos, and N Amer. Indians

mongoose (ˈmɒŋguːs) *n.* small animal of Asia and Afr. noted for killing snakes (*pl.* **-s**)

mongrel (ˈmʌŋgrәl) *n.* **1.** animal, *esp.* dog, of mixed breed, hybrid —*a.* **2.** of mixed breed

monitor (ˈmɒnɪtә) *n.* **1.** person or device which checks, controls, warns or keeps record of something **2.** pupil assisting teacher with odd jobs in school **3.** television set used in a studio for checking programme being transmitted **4.** type of large lizard —*vt.* **5.** watch, check on —**moˈnition** *n.* warning —**ˈmonitory** *a.*

monk (mʌŋk) *n.* one of a religious community of men bound by vows of poverty *etc.* —**ˈmonkish** *a.* —**ˈmonkshood** *n.* poisonous plant with hooded flowers

monkey (ˈmʌŋkɪ) *n.* **1.** long-tailed primate **2.** mischievous child —*vi.* **3.** meddle, fool —**monkey business** *inf.* mischievous or dishonest behaviour or acts —**monkey nut UK** peanut —**monkey puzzle** coniferous tree with sharp stiff leaves —**monkey wrench** spanner with movable jaws

mono (ˈmɒnәʊ) *a.* **1.** monophonic —*n.* **2.** monophonic sound

mono- *or before vowel* **mon-** (*comb. form*) single, as in *monosyllabic*

THESAURUS

moment **1.** flash, instant, jiffy (*Inf.*), minute, no time, second, shake (*Inf.*), split second, tick (*Brit. inf.*), trice, twinkling, two shakes (*Inf.*), two shakes of a lamb's tail (*Inf.*) **2.** hour, instant, juncture, point, point in time, stage, time

momentarily briefly, for a moment (little while, minute, second, short time, short while), for an instant, temporarily

momentary brief, ephemeral, evanescent, fleeting, flying, fugitive, hasty, passing, quick, short, short-lived, temporary, transitory

momentous consequential, critical, crucial, decisive, earth-shaking (*Inf.*), fateful, grave, historic, important, of moment, pivotal, serious, significant, vital, weighty

momentum drive, energy, force, impetus, power, propulsion, push, strength, thrust

monarch crowned head, emperor, empress, king, potentate, prince, princess, queen, ruler, sovereign

monarchy **1.** absolutism, autocracy, despotism, kingship, monocracy, royalism, sovereignty **2.** empire, kingdom, principality, realm

monastery abbey, cloister, convent, friary, house, nunnery, priory, religious community

monastic ascetic, austere, celibate, cenobitic, cloistered, cloistral, coenobitic, contemplative, conventual, eremitic, hermit-like, monachal, monkish, recluse, reclusive, secluded, sequestered, withdrawn

monetary budgetary, capital, cash, financial, fiscal, pecuniary

money banknotes, bread (*Sl.*), capital, cash, coin, currency, dough (*Sl.*), filthy lucre (*Facetious*), funds, gelt (*Sl.*), green (*Sl.*), hard cash, legal tender, lolly (*Brit. sl.*), loot (*Inf.*), mazuma (*Sl., chiefly U.S.*), moolah (*Sl.*), pelf (*Contemptuous*), readies (*Inf.*), riches, specie, spondulix (*Sl.*), the ready (*Inf.*), the wherewithal, wealth

mongrel **1.** *n.* bigener (*Biol.*), cross, crossbreed, half-breed, hybrid, mixed breed **2.** *adj.* bastard, cross-bred, half-breed, hybrid, of mixed breed

monitor **1.** *n.* guide, invigilator, overseer, prefect (*Brit.*), supervisor, watchdog **2.** *v.* check, follow, keep an eye on, keep track of, observe, oversee, record, scan, supervise, survey, watch

monk brother, friar (*loosely*), monastic, religious

monkey *n.* **1.** primate, simian **2.** devil, imp, mischief maker, rascal, rogue, scamp ~*v.* **3.** fiddle, fool, interfere, meddle, mess, play, tamper, tinker, trifle

monkey business **1.** carry-on (*Inf.*), clowning, mischief, monkey tricks, pranks, shenanigans (*Inf.*), skylarking (*Inf.*), tomfoolery **2.** chicanery, dishonesty, funny business, hanky-panky (*Inf.*), skulduggery (*Inf.*), trickery

monochrome ('mɒnəkrəʊm) *n.* **1.** representation in one colour —*a.* **2.** of one colour —**monochro'matic** *a.*

monocle ('mɒnək³l) *n.* single eyeglass

monocotyledon (mɒnəʊkɒtɪ'li:d³n) *n.* any of various flowering plants having single embryonic seed leaf and leaves with parallel veins —**monocoty'ledonous** *a.*

monocular (mɒ'nɒkjʊlə) *a.* one-eyed

monogamy (mɒ'nɒgəmɪ) *n.* custom of being married to one person at a time

monogram ('mɒnəgræm) *n.* design of letters interwoven

monograph ('mɒnəgrɑ:f) *n.* short book on single subject

monogyny (mɒ'nɒdʒɪnɪ) *n.* having only one female sexual partner over a period of time —**mo'nogynous** *a.*

monolith ('mɒnəlɪθ) *n.* monument consisting of single standing stone

monologue ('mɒnəlɒg) *n.* **1.** dramatic composition with only one speaker **2.** long speech by one person

monomania (mɒnəʊ'meɪnɪə) *n.* excessive preoccupation with one thing

monomial (mɒ'nəʊmɪəl) *n.* **1.** *Maths.* expression consisting of single term —*a.* **2.** consisting of single algebraic term

mononucleosis (mɒnəʊnju:klɪ'əʊsɪs) *n.* **1.** *Pathol.* presence of large number of monocytes in blood **2.** *see* **infectious mononucleosis** *at* INFECT

monophonic (mɒnəʊ'fɒnɪk) *a.* **1.** (of reproduction of sound) using only one channel between source and loudspeaker (*also* **mo'naural**) **2.** *Mus.* of style of musical composition consisting of single melodic line

monoplane ('mɒnəʊpleɪn) *n.* aeroplane with one pair of wings

monopoly (mə'nɒpəlɪ) *n.* **1.** exclusive possession of trade, privilege *etc.* **2.** **(M-)** **R** board game for two to six players —**mo'nopolist** *n.* —**mo'nopolize** *or* **-lise** *vt.* claim, take exclusive possession of

monorail ('mɒnəʊreɪl) *n.* railway with cars running on or suspended from single rail

monosodium glutamate (mɒnəʊ'səʊdɪəm 'glu:təmeɪt) white crystalline substance used as food additive

monosyllable ('mɒnəsɪləb³l) *n.* word of one syllable

monotheism ('mɒnəʊθi:ɪzəm) *n.* belief in only one God —**'monotheist** *n.*

monotone ('mɒnətəʊn) *n.* continuing on one note —**mo'notonous** *a.* lacking in variety, dull, wearisome —**mo'notony** *n.*

monovalent (mɒnəʊ'veɪlənt) *a.* *Chem.* **1.** having valency of one **2.** having only one valency (*also* **uni'valent**) —**mono'valence** *or* **mono'valency** *n.*

monoxide (mɒ'nɒksaɪd) *n.* oxide that contains one oxygen atom per molecule

Monseigneur (mɔ̃sɛ'ɲœ:r) *Fr.* title given to French bishops, prelates, and princes (*pl.* ***Messeigneurs*** (mesɛ'ɲœ:r))

monsieur (məs'jɜ:) *n.* French title of address equivalent to *sir* when used alone or *Mr.* before name

Monsignor (mɒn'si:njə) *n.* *R.C.Ch.* ecclesiastical title attached to certain offices

monsoon (mɒn'su:n) *n.* **1.** seasonal wind of SE Asia **2.** very heavy rainfall season

monster ('mɒnstə) *n.* **1.** fantastic imaginary beast **2.** misshapen animal or plant **3.** very wicked person **4.** huge person, animal or thing —*a.* **5.** huge —**mon'strosity** *n.* **1.** monstrous being **2.** deformity **3.** distortion —**'monstrous** *a.* **1.** of, like monster **2.** unnatural **3.** enormous **4.** horrible —**'monstrously** *adv.*

monstrance ('mɒnstrəns) *n.* *R.C.Ch.* vessel in which consecrated Host is exposed for adoration

montage (mɒn'tɑ:ʒ) *n.* **1.** elements of two or more pictures imposed upon a single background to give a unified effect **2.** method of editing a film

montbretia (mɒn'bri:ʃə) *n.* plant with orange flowers on long stems

month (mʌnθ) *n.* **1.** one of twelve periods into which the year is divided **2.** period of moon's revolution —**'monthly** *a.* **1.** happening or payable once a month —*adv.* **2.** once a month —*n.* **3.** magazine published every month

monument ('mɒnjʊmənt) *n.* anything that commemorates, *esp.* a building or statue —**monu'mental** *a.* **1.** vast, lasting **2.** of or serving as monument —**monumental mason** maker and engraver of tombstones

THESAURUS

monologue harangue, lecture, sermon, soliloquy, speech

monopolize control, corner, corner the market in, dominate, engross, exercise *or* have a monopoly of, hog (*Sl.*), keep to oneself, take over, take up

monotonous all the same, boring, colourless, droning, dull, flat, humdrum, plodding, repetitious, repetitive, samey (*Inf.*), soporific, tedious, tiresome, toneless, unchanging, uniform, uninflected, unvaried, wearisome

monotony boredom, colourlessness, dullness, flatness, humdrumness, monotonousness, repetitiveness, repetitiousness, routine, sameness, tediousness, tedium, tiresomeness, uniformity, wearisomeness

monster *n.* **1.** barbarian, beast, bogeyman, brute, demon, devil, fiend, ogre, savage, villain **2.** abortion, freak, lusus naturae, miscreation, monstrosity, mutant, teratism **3.** behemoth, Brobdingnagian, colossus, giant, leviathan, mammoth, titan ~*adj.* **4.** Brobdingnagian, colossal, enormous, gargantuan, giant, gigantic, huge, immense, jumbo (*Inf.*), mammoth, massive, monstrous, stupendous, titanic, tremendous

monstrosity abortion, eyesore, freak, horror, lusus naturae, miscreation, monster, mutant, ogre, teratism

monstrous **1.** abnormal, dreadful, enormous, fiendish, freakish, frightful, grotesque, gruesome, hellish, hideous, horrendous, horrible, miscreated, obscene, teratoid, terrible, unnatural **2.** colossal, elephantine, enormous, gargantuan, giant, gigantic, great, huge, immense, mammoth, massive, prodigious, stupendous, titanic, towering, tremendous, vast

month four weeks, moon, thirty days

monument **1.** cairn, cenotaph, commemoration, gravestone, headstone, marker, mausoleum, memorial, obelisk, pillar, shrine, statue, tombstone **2.** memento, record, remembrance, reminder, testament, token, witness

moo (muː) *n.* 1. cry of cow —*vi.* 2. make this noise, low

mooch (muːtʃ) *vi. sl.* loaf, slouch

mood[1] (muːd) *n.* state of mind and feelings —**ˈmoody** *a.* 1. gloomy, pensive 2. changeable in mood

mood[2] (muːd) *n. Gram.* form indicating function of verb

Moog synthesizer (muːg, məʊg) R electrophonic instrument operated by keyboard and pedals

moon (muːn) *n.* 1. satellite which takes lunar month to revolve round earth 2. any secondary planet —*vi.* 3. (*oft. with* around) go about dreamily —**ˈmoony** *a.* 1. *inf.* dreamy or listless 2. of or like moon —**ˈmooncalf** *n.* 1. born fool; dolt 2. person who idles time away (*pl.* **-calves**) —**ˈmoonlight** *n.* 1. light of moon —*vi.* 2. hold two paid occupations —**moonlight flit** hurried departure by night to escape from one's creditors —**ˈmoonscape** *n.* general surface of moon or representation of it —**ˈmoonshine** *n.* 1. whisky illicitly distilled 2. nonsense —**ˈmoonshot** *n.* launching of spacecraft *etc.* to moon —**ˈmoonstone** *n.* transparent semiprecious stone —**ˈmoonstruck** *a.* deranged

moor[1] (mʊə, mɔː) *n.* tract of open uncultivated land, often hilly and heather-clad —**ˈmoorhen** *n.* water bird

moor[2] (mʊə, mɔː) *v.* secure (ship) with chains or ropes —**ˈmoorage** *n.* place, charge for mooring —**ˈmoorings** *pl.n.* 1. ropes *etc.* for mooring 2. something providing stability, security

Moor (mʊə, mɔː) *n.* member of race in Morocco and adjoining parts of N Afr.

moose (muːs) *n.* N Amer. deer, like elk

moot (muːt) *a.* 1. that is open to argument, debatable —*vt.* 2. bring for discussion —*n.* 3. meeting

mop (mɒp) *n.* 1. bundle of yarn, cloth *etc.* on end of stick, used for cleaning 2. tangle (of hair *etc.*) —*vt.* 3. clean, wipe with mop or other absorbent stuff (**-pp-**)

mope (məʊp) *vi.* be gloomy, apathetic

moped (ˈməʊpɛd) *n.* light motorized bicycle

moquette (mɒˈkɛt) *n.* thick fabric used for upholstery *etc.*

moraine (mɒˈreɪn) *n.* accumulated mass of debris, earth, stones *etc.*, deposited by glacier

moral (ˈmɒrəl) *a.* 1. pert. to right and wrong conduct 2. of good conduct —*n.* 3. practical lesson, *eg* of fable —*pl.* 4. habits with respect to right and wrong, *esp.* in matters of sex —**ˈmoralist** *n.* teacher of morality —**moˈrality** *n.* 1. good moral conduct 2. moral goodness or badness 3. kind of medieval drama, containing moral lesson —**ˈmoralize** *or* **-lise** *vi.* 1. write, talk about moral aspect of things —*vt.* 2. interpret morally —**ˈmorally** *adv.* —**moral philosophy** branch of philosophy dealing with ethics —**moral victory** triumph that is psychological rather than practical

morale (mɒˈrɑːl) *n.* degree of confidence, hope of person or group

morass (məˈræs) *n.* 1. marsh 2. mess

moratorium (mɒrəˈtɔːrɪəm) *n.* 1. act authorizing postponement of payments *etc.* 2. delay (*pl.* **-ria** (-rɪə))

moray (mɒˈreɪ) *n.* large, voracious eel

morbid (ˈmɔːbɪd) *a.* 1. unduly interested in death 2. gruesome 3. diseased

mordant (ˈmɔːdᵊnt) *a.* 1. biting 2. corrosive 3. scathing —*n.* 4. substance that fixes dyes

more (mɔː) *comp. of* MANY *and* MUCH *a.* 1. greater in quantity or number —*adv.* 2. to a greater extent 3. in addition —*pron.* 4. greater or additional amount or number —**moreˈover** *adv.* besides, further

---

THESAURUS

monumental 1. awe-inspiring, awesome, classic, enduring, enormous, epoch-making, historic, immortal, important, lasting, majestic, memorable, outstanding, prodigious, significant, stupendous, unforgettable 2. commemorative, cyclopean, funerary, memorial, monolithic, statuary 3. *Inf.* colossal, gigantic, great, immense, massive, tremendous, whopping (*Inf.*)

mood disposition, frame of mind, humour, spirit, state of mind, temper, tenor, vein

moody 1. angry, broody, cantankerous, crabbed, crabby, crestfallen, cross, crotchety (*Inf.*), crusty, curt, dismal, doleful, dour, downcast, down in the dumps (*Inf.*), down in the mouth (*Inf.*), frowning, gloomy, glum, huffish, huffy, ill-humoured, ill-tempered, in a huff, in the doldrums, introspective, irascible, irritable, lugubrious, melancholy, miserable, mopish, mopy, morose, offended, out of sorts (*Inf.*), pensive, petulant, piqued, sad, saturnine, short-tempered, splenetic, sulky, sullen, temperamental, testy, touchy, waspish, wounded 2. capricious, changeable, erratic, faddish, fickle, fitful, flighty, impulsive, inconstant, mercurial, temperamental, unpredictable, unstable, unsteady, volatile

moon *v.* daydream, idle, languish, mooch (*Sl.*), mope, waste time

moor[1] fell (*Brit.*), heath, moorland, muir (*Scot.*)

moor[2] anchor, berth, dock, fasten, fix, lash, make fast, secure tie up

moot 1. *adj.* arguable, at issue, contestable, controversial, debatable, disputable, doubtful, open, open to debate, undecided, unresolved, unsettled 2. *v.* bring up, broach, introduce, propose, put forward, suggest, ventilate

mop *n.* 1. sponge, squeegee, swab 2. mane, shock, tangle, thatch ~*v.* 3. clean, soak up, sponge, swab, wash, wipe

moral *adj.* 1. ethical 2. blameless, chaste, decent, ethical, good, high-minded, honest, honourable, incorruptible, innocent, just, meritorious, noble, principled, proper, pure, right, righteous, upright, upstanding, virtuous ~*n.* 3. lesson, meaning, message, point, significance

morale confidence, esprit de corps, heart, mettle, self-esteem, spirit, temper

morality 1. chastity, decency, ethicality, ethicalness, goodness, honesty, integrity, justice, principle, rectitude, righteousness, rightness, uprightness, virtue 2. conduct, ethics, habits, ideals, manners, moral code, morals, mores, philosophy, principles, standards

morals behaviour, conduct, ethics, habits, integrity, manners, morality, mores, principles, scruples, standards

moratorium freeze, halt, postponement, respite, standstill, stay, suspension

morbid 1. brooding, ghoulish, gloomy, grim, melancholy, pessimistic, sick, sombre, unhealthy, unwholesome 2. dreadful, ghastly, grisly, gruesome, hideous, horrid, macabre 3. ailing, deadly, diseased, infected, malignant, pathological, sick, sickly, unhealthy, unsound

more 1. *adj.* added, additional, extra, fresh, further,

morel (mɒˈrɛl) *n.* edible fungus in which mushroom has pitted cap

morello (məˈrɛləʊ) *n.* variety of small dark sour cherry (*pl.* **-s**)

mores (ˈmɔːreɪz) *pl.n.* customs and conventions embodying fundamental values of society *etc.*

morganatic marriage (mɔːgəˈnætɪk) marriage of king or prince in which wife does not share husband's rank or possessions and children do not inherit from father

morgen (ˈmɔːgən) *n.* **SA** land unit, approx. two acres (0.8 hectare)

morgue (mɔːg) *n.* mortuary

moribund (ˈmɒrɪbʌnd) *a.* **1.** dying **2.** stagnant

Mormon (ˈmɔːmən) *n.* member of religious sect founded in U.S.A. —**ˈMormonism** *n.*

mornay (ˈmɔːneɪ) *a.* denoting cheese sauce used in various dishes

morning (ˈmɔːnɪŋ) *n.* early part of day until noon —**morn** *n. Poet.* morning —**morning dress** formal day dress for men, comprising cutaway frock coat, usu. with grey trousers and top hat —**morning-glory** *n.* plant with trumpet-shaped flowers which close in late afternoon —**morning sickness** *inf.* nausea occurring shortly after rising during early months of pregnancy —**morning star** planet, usu. Venus, seen just before sunrise —**the morning after** *inf.* aftereffects of excess, *esp.* hangover

morocco (məˈrɒkəʊ) *n.* goatskin leather

moron (ˈmɔːrɒn) *n.* **1.** mentally deficient person **2.** *inf.* fool —**moˈronic** *a.*

morose (məˈrəʊs) *a.* sullen, moody

morphine (ˈmɔːfiːn) *or* **morphia** (ˈmɔːfɪə) *n.* narcotic extract of opium, drug used to induce sleep and relieve pain

morphology (mɔːˈfɒlədʒɪ) *n.* **1.** science of structure of organisms **2.** form and structure of words of a language —**morphoˈlogical** *a.*

morris dance (ˈmɒrɪs) English folk dance

morrow (ˈmɒrəʊ) *n. Poet.* next day

Morse (mɔːs) *n.* system of telegraphic signalling in which letters of alphabet are represented by combinations of dots and dashes, or short and long flashes

morsel (ˈmɔːsᵊl) *n.* fragment, small piece

mortal (ˈmɔːtᵊl) *a.* **1.** subject to death **2.** causing death —*n.* **3.** mortal creature —**morˈtality** *n.* **1.** state of being mortal **2.** great loss of life **3.** death rate —**ˈmortally** *adv.* **1.** fatally **2.** deeply, intensely —**mortal sin** *R.C.Ch.* sin meriting damnation

mortar (ˈmɔːtə) *n.* **1.** mixture of lime, sand and water for holding bricks and stones together **2.** small cannon firing over short range **3.** vessel in which substances are pounded —**ˈmortarboard** *n.* square academic cap

mortgage (ˈmɔːgɪdʒ) *n.* **1.** conveyance of property as security for debt with provision that property be reconveyed on payment within agreed time —*vt.* **2.** convey by mortgage **3.** pledge as security —**mortgaˈgee** *n.* —**mortgagor** (mɔːgɪˈdʒɔː) *or* **mortgaˈger** *n.*

mortify (ˈmɔːtɪfaɪ) *vt.* **1.** humiliate **2.** subdue by self-denial —*vi.* **3.** (of flesh) be affected with gangrene (**-fied, -fying**) —**mortifiˈcation** *n.*

mortise *or* **mortice** (ˈmɔːtɪs) *n.* **1.** hole in piece of wood *etc.* to receive the tongue (tenon) and end of another piece —*vt.* **2.** make mortise in **3.** fasten by mortise and tenon —**mortise lock** lock embedded in door

THESAURUS

new, other, spare, supplementary **2.** *adv.* better, further, longer, to a greater extent

moreover additionally, also, as well, besides, further, furthermore, in addition, into the bargain, likewise, to boot, too, what is more, withal (*Literary*)

moribund 1. at death's door, breathing one's last, doomed, dying, fading fast, failing, (having) one foot in the grave, *in extremis*, near death, near the end, on one's deathbed, on one's last legs **2.** at a standstill, declining, forceless, obsolescent, on its last legs, on the way out, stagnant, stagnating, standing still, waning, weak

morning a.m., break of day, dawn, daybreak, forenoon, morn (*Poetic*), morrow (*Archaic*), sunrise

moron ass, blockhead, bonehead (*Sl.*), cretin, dimwit (*Inf.*), dolt, dope (*Sl.*), dummy (*Sl.*), dunce, dunderhead, fool, halfwit, idiot, imbecile, mental defective, muttonhead (*Sl.*), numskull, simpleton, thickhead

morose blue, churlish, crabbed, crabby, cross, crusty, depressed, dour, down, down in the dumps (*Inf.*), gloomy, glum, grouchy (*Inf.*), gruff, ill-humoured, ill-natured, ill-tempered, in a bad mood, low, melancholy, moody, mournful, perverse, pessimistic, saturnine, sour, sulky, sullen, surly, taciturn

morsel bit, bite, crumb, fraction, fragment, grain, mouthful, nibble, part, piece, scrap, segment, slice, snack, soupçon, taste, titbit

mortal *adj.* **1.** corporeal, earthly, ephemeral, human, impermanent, passing, sublunary, temporal, transient, worldly **2.** deadly, death-dealing, destructive, fatal, killing, lethal, murderous, terminal ~*n.* **3.** being, body, earthling, human, human being, individual, man, person, woman

mortality 1. ephemerality, humanity, impermanence, temporality, transience **2.** bloodshed, carnage, death, destruction, fatality, killing, loss of life

mortification 1. abasement, annoyance, chagrin, discomfiture, dissatisfaction, embarrassment, humiliation, loss of face, shame, vexation **2.** abasement, chastening, control, denial, discipline, subjugation **3.** *Medical* corruption, festering, gangrene, necrosis, putrescence

mortified 1. abashed, affronted, annoyed, ashamed, chagrined, chastened, confounded, crushed, deflated, discomfited, displeased, embarrassed, given a showing up (*Inf.*), humbled, humiliated, made to eat humble pie (*Inf.*), put down, put out (*Inf.*), put to shame, rendered speechless, shamed, vexed **2.** abased, chastened, conquered, controlled, crushed, disciplined, subdued **3.** *Of flesh* decayed, gangrenous, necrotic, rotted

mortify 1. abase, abash, affront, annoy, chagrin, chasten, confound, crush, deflate, disappoint, discomfit, displease, embarrass, humble, humiliate, make (someone) eat humble pie (*Inf.*), put down, put to shame, shame, take (someone) down a peg (*Inf.*), vex **2.** abase, chasten, control, deny, discipline, subdue **3.** *Of flesh* become gangrenous, corrupt, deaden, die, fester, gangrene, necrose, putrefy

mortuary funeral parlour, morgue

mortuary (ˈmɔːtʃʊərɪ) *n.* **1.** building where corpses are kept before burial —*a.* **2.** of, for burial

mosaic (məˈzeɪɪk) *n.* **1.** picture or pattern of small bits of coloured stone, glass *etc.* **2.** this process of decoration

Mosaic (məʊˈzeɪɪk) *a.* of Moses

Moselle (məʊˈzɛl) *n.* light white wine

Moslem (ˈmɒzləm) *n. see* MUSLIM

mosque (mɒsk) *n.* Muslim temple

mosquito (məˈskiːtəʊ) *n.* various kinds of flying, biting insects (*pl.* **-es**)

moss (mɒs) *n.* **1.** small plant growing in masses on moist surfaces **2.** peat bog, swamp —ˈ**mossy** *a.* covered with moss —**moss agate** agate with mosslike markings —**moss stitch** knitting stitch made up of alternate plain and purl stitches

mossie (ˈmɒsɪ) *n.* **SA** Cape sparrow

most (məʊst) *sup. of* MUCH *and* MANY *a.* **1.** greatest in size, number, or degree —*n.* **2.** greatest number, amount, or degree —*adv.* **3.** in the greatest degree **4.** **US** almost —ˈ**mostly** *adv.* for the most part, generally, on the whole —**Most Reverend** courtesy title applied to archbishops

M.O.T. Ministry of Transport —**M.O.T. (test)** compulsory annual test of the roadworthiness of vehicles over a certain age

mote (məʊt) *n.* tiny speck

motel (məʊˈtɛl) *n.* roadside hotel with accommodation for motorists and vehicles

motet (məʊˈtɛt) *n.* short sacred vocal composition

moth (mɒθ) *n.* **1.** usu. nocturnal insect like butterfly **2.** its grub —ˈ**mothy** *a.* infested with moths —ˈ**mothball** *n.* **1.** small ball of camphor or naphthalene to repel moths from stored clothing *etc.* —*vt.* **2.** put in mothballs **3.** store, postpone *etc.* —ˈ**motheaten** *a.* **1.** eaten, damaged by grub of moth **2.** decayed, scruffy

mother (ˈmʌðə) *n.* **1.** female parent **2.** head of religious community of women —*a.* **3.** natural, native, inborn —*vt.* **4.** act as mother to —ˈ**motherhood** *n.* —ˈ**motherly** *a.* —**Mother Carey's chicken** (ˈkɛərɪz) *see* **stormy petrel** *at* STORM —**mother country 1.** original country of colonists or settlers **2.** person's native country —**mother earth 1.** earth as a mother, particularly in its fertility **2.** soil; ground —**mother-in-law** *n.* mother of one's husband or wife —**mother of pearl** iridescent lining of certain shells —**mother tongue 1.** language first learned by child **2.** language from which another has evolved

motif (məʊˈtiːf) *n.* **1.** dominating theme **2.** recurring design

motion (ˈməʊʃən) *n.* **1.** process or action or way of moving **2.** proposal in meeting **3.** application to judge **4.** evacuation of bowels —*v.* **5.** signal or direct by sign —ˈ**motionless** *a.* still, immobile

motive (ˈməʊtɪv) *n.* **1.** that which makes person act in particular way **2.** inner impulse —*a.* **3.** causing motion —ˈ**motivate** *vt.* **1.** instigate **2.** incite —**motiˈvation** *n.* —ˈ**motivative** *a.* —**motive power 1.** any source of energy used to produce motion **2.** means of supplying power to engine, vehicle *etc.*

mot juste (mo ˈʒyst) *Fr.* appropriate word or expression (*pl.* ***mots justes*** (mo ˈʒyst))

motley (ˈmɒtlɪ) *a.* **1.** miscellaneous, varied **2.** multicoloured —*n.* **3.** motley colour or mixture **4.** jester's particoloured dress

motocross (ˈməʊtəkrɒs) *n.* motorcycle race over rough course

motor (ˈməʊtə) *n.* **1.** that which imparts movement **2.** machine to supply motive power **3.** motorcar —*vi.* **4.** travel by car —ˈ**motoring** *n.* —ˈ**motorist** *n.* user of motorcar —ˈ**motorize** *or* **-ise** *vt.* **1.** equip with motor **2.** provide with motor transport —ˈ**motorbike,** ˈ**motorboat,** ˈ**motorcar,** ˈ**motorcycle, motor scooter** *n.* vehicles driven by motor —**motorcade** (ˈməʊtəkeɪd) *n.* parade of cars —**motor nerve** nerve which controls muscular movement —ˈ**motorway** *n.* main road for fast-moving traffic, with limited access

mottle (ˈmɒtᵊl) *vt.* **1.** mark with blotches, variegate —*n.* **2.** arrangement of blotches **3.** blotch on surface

motto (ˈmɒtəʊ) *n.* **1.** saying adopted as rule of conduct **2.** short inscribed sentence **3.** word or sentence on heraldic crest (*pl.* **-s, -es**)

moue (mu) *Fr.* pouting look

moufflon (ˈmuːflɒn) *n.* wild mountain sheep

THESAURUS

mostly above all, almost entirely, as a rule, chiefly, customarily, for the most part, generally, largely, mainly, most often, on the whole, particularly, predominantly, principally, usually

motheaten antiquated, decayed, decrepit, dilapidated, obsolete, outdated, outworn, ragged, seedy, shabby, stale, tattered, threadbare, worn-out

mother 1. *n.* dam, ma (*Inf.*), mater, mom (*U.S. inf.*), mum (*Brit. inf.*), mummy (*Brit. inf.*), old lady (*Inf.*), old woman (*Inf.*) **2.** *adj.* connate, inborn, innate, native, natural **3.** *v.* care for, cherish, nurse, nurture, protect, raise, rear, tend

motion *n.* **1.** action, change, flow, kinesics, locomotion, mobility, motility, move, movement, passage, passing, progress, travel **2.** proposal, proposition, recommendation, submission, suggestion ~*v.* **3.** beckon, direct, gesticulate, gesture, nod, signal, wave

motionless at a standstill, at rest, calm, fixed, frozen, halted, immobile, inanimate, inert, lifeless, paralysed, standing, static, stationary, still, stock-still, transfixed, unmoved, unmoving

motivate actuate, arouse, bring, cause, draw, drive, give incentive to, impel, induce, inspire, inspirit, instigate, lead, move, persuade, prompt, provoke, set on, stimulate, stir, trigger

motivation 1. ambition, desire, drive, hunger, inspiration, interest, wish **2.** impulse, incentive, incitement, inducement, inspiration, instigation, motive, persuasion, reason, spur, stimulus

motive 1. *n.* cause, design, ground(s), incentive, incitement, inducement, influence, inspiration, intention, mainspring, motivation, object, occasion, purpose, rationale, reason, spur, stimulus, thinking **2.** *adj.* activating, driving, impelling, motivating, moving, operative, prompting

motley 1. assorted, disparate, dissimilar, diversified, heterogeneous, mingled, miscellaneous, mixed, unlike, varied **2.** chequered, multicoloured, particoloured, polychromatic, polychrome, polychromous, rainbow, variegated

motto adage, byword, cry, formula, gnome, maxim, precept, proverb, rule, saw, saying, slogan, watchword

mould[1] *or U.S.* **mold** (məʊld) *n.* **1.** hollow object in which metal *etc.* is cast **2.** pattern for shaping **3.** character **4.** shape, form —*vt.* **5.** shape or pattern —ˈ**moulding** *or U.S.* ˈ**molding** *n.* **1.** moulded object **2.** ornamental edging **3.** decoration —ˈ**mouldboard** *or U.S.* ˈ**moldboard** *n.* curved blade of plough

mould[2] *or U.S.* **mold** (məʊld) *n.* fungoid growth caused by dampness —ˈ**mouldy** *or U.S.* ˈ**moldy** *a.* stale, musty

mould[3] *or U.S.* **mold** (məʊld) *n.* loose or surface earth —ˈ**moulder** *or U.S.* ˈ**molder** *vi.* decay into dust

moult *or U.S.* **molt** (məʊlt) *v.* **1.** cast or shed (fur, feathers *etc.*) —*n.* **2.** moulting

mound (maʊnd) *n.* **1.** heap of earth or stones **2.** small hill

mount (maʊnt) *vi.* **1.** rise **2.** increase **3.** get on horseback —*vt.* **4.** get up on **5.** frame (picture) **6.** fix, set up **7.** provide with horse —*n.* **8.** that on which thing is supported or fitted **9.** horse **10.** hill

mountain (ˈmaʊntɪn) *n.* **1.** hill of great size **2.** surplus —**mountainˈeer** *n.* one who lives among or climbs mountains —**mountainˈeering** *n.* —ˈ**mountainous** *a.* very high, rugged —**mountain lion** puma

mountebank (ˈmaʊntɪbæŋk) *n.* charlatan, fake

Mountie *or* **Mounty** (ˈmaʊntɪ) *n. inf.* member of Royal Canadian Mounted Police

mourn (mɔːn) *v.* feel, show sorrow (for) —ˈ**mourner** *n.* —ˈ**mournful** *a.* **1.** sad **2.** dismal —ˈ**mournfully** *adv.* —ˈ**mourning** *n.* **1.** grieving **2.** conventional signs of grief for death **3.** clothes of mourner —**mourning band** piece of black material, *esp.* armband, worn to indicate mourning

mouse (maʊs) *n.* **1.** small rodent (*pl.* **mice**) —*vi.* (maʊz) **2.** catch, hunt mice **3.** prowl —ˈ**mouser** *n.* cat used for catching mice —ˈ**mousy** *or* ˈ**mousey** *a.* **1.** like mouse, *esp.* in colour **2.** meek, shy —ˈ**mousetrap** *n.* **1.** any trap for catching mice **2.** **UK** *inf.* cheese of indifferent quality

mousse (muːs) *n.* sweet dish of flavoured cream whipped and chilled

moustache *or U.S.* **mustache** (məˈstɑːʃ) *n.* hair on the upper lip —**moustache cup** cup with partial cover to protect drinker's moustache

mouth (maʊθ) *n.* **1.** opening in head for eating, speaking *etc.* **2.** opening into anything hollow **3.** outfall of river **4.** entrance to harbour *etc.* —*vt.* (maʊð) **5.** declaim, *esp.* in public **6.** form (words) with lips without speaking **7.** take, move in mouth —ˈ**mouthful** *n.* **1.** as much as is held in mouth at one time **2.** small quantity, as of food **3.** word *etc.* difficult to say —**mouth organ** harmonica —ˈ**mouthpiece** *n.* **1.** end of anything placed between lips, *eg* pipe **2.** spokesman —ˈ**mouthwash** *n.* medicated solution for cleansing mouth

move (muːv) *vt.* **1.** change position of **2.** stir emotions of **3.** incite **4.** propose for consideration —*vi.* **5.** change places **6.** change one's dwelling *etc.* **7.** take action —*n.* **8.** a moving **9.** motion towards some goal —ˈ**movable** *or* ˈ**moveable** *a./n.* —ˈ**movement** *n.* **1.** process, action of moving **2.** moving parts of machine **3.** division of piece of music

THESAURUS

mould[1] *n.* **1.** cast, die, form, matrix, pattern, shape **2.** brand, build, configuration, construction, cut, design, fashion, form, format, frame, kind, line, make, pattern, shape, structure, style **3.** calibre, character, ilk, kidney, kind, nature, quality, sort, stamp, type ~*v.* **4.** carve, cast, construct, create, fashion, forge, form, make, model, sculpt, shape, stamp, work

mould[2] blight, fungus, mildew, mouldiness, mustiness

mouldy bad, blighted, decaying, fusty, mildewed, musty, rotten, rotting, spoiled, stale

mound **1.** bing (*Scot.*), drift, heap, pile, stack **2.** bank, dune, embankment, hill, hillock, knoll, rise

mount *v.* **1.** bestride, climb onto, climb up on, get astride, get (up) on, jump on **2.** arise, ascend, rise, soar, tower **3.** accumulate, build, escalate, grow, increase, intensify, multiply, pile up, swell **4.** display, frame, set, set off **5.** emplace, fit, install, place, position, put in place, set up ~*n.* **6.** backing, base, fixture, foil, frame, mounting, setting, stand, support **7.** horse, steed (*Literary*)

mountain **1.** alp, ben (*Scot.*), elevation, eminence, fell (*Brit.*), height, mount, peak **2.** abundance, heap, mass, mound, pile, stack, ton

mountainous alpine, high, highland, rocky, soaring, steep, towering, upland

mourn bemoan, bewail, deplore, grieve, keen, lament, miss, rue, sorrow, wail, wear black, weep

mournful **1.** afflicting, calamitous, deplorable, distressing, grievous, lamentable, melancholy, painful, piteous, plaintive, sad, sorrowful, tragic, unhappy, woeful **2.** brokenhearted, cheerless, desolate, disconsolate, downcast, funereal, gloomy, grief-stricken, grieving, heartbroken, heavy, heavy-hearted, joyless, lugubrious, melancholy, rueful, sad, sombre, unhappy, woeful

mourning **1.** bereavement, grief, grieving, keening, lamentation, weeping, woe **2.** black, sackcloth and ashes, weeds, widow's weeds

mouth *n.* **1.** chops (*Sl.*), gob (*Sl.*), jaws, lips, maw, trap (*Sl.*), yap (*Sl.*) **2.** aperture, cavity, crevice, door, entrance, gateway, inlet, lips, opening, orifice, rim

mouthful bit, bite, drop, forkful, little, morsel, sample, sip, spoonful, sup, swallow, taste

mouthpiece agent, delegate, representative, spokesman, spokeswoman

movable detachable, mobile, not fixed, portable, portative, transferable, transportable

move *v.* **1.** advance, budge, change position, drift, go, march, proceed, progress, shift, stir, walk **2.** carry, change, shift, switch, transfer, transport, transpose **3.** change residence, flit (*Scot., & northern English dialect*), go away, leave, migrate, move house, quit, relocate, remove **4.** actuate, affect, agitate, cause, excite, give rise to, impel, impress, incite, induce, influence, inspire, instigate, lead, make an impression on, motivate, persuade, prompt, rouse, stimulate, touch, urge **5.** advocate, propose, put forward, recommend, suggest, urge ~*n.* **6.** act, action, deed, manoeuvre, measure, motion, movement, ploy, shift, step, stratagem, stroke, turn **7.** change of address, flit (*Scot., & northern English dialect*), flitting (*Scot., & northern English dialect*), migration, relocation, removal, shift, transfer

movement **1.** act, action, activity, advance, agitation, change, development, displacement, exercise, flow, manoeuvre, motion, move, moving, operation, progress, progression, shift, steps, stir, stirring,

movie (ˈmu:vɪ) US *inf. n.* **1.** film *—pl.* **2.** cinema
mow (məʊ) *v.* cut (grass *etc.*) (**mown** *pp.*) —ˈ**mower** *n.* man or machine that mows
mp *or* **m.p.** *Mus.* mezzo piano
M.P. **1.** Member of Parliament **2.** Military Police **3.** Mounted Police
m.p.g. miles per gallon
m.p.h. miles per hour
M.Phil. *or* **M.Ph.** Master of Philosophy
Mr. (ˈmɪstə) mister
Mrs. (ˈmɪsɪz) title of married woman —**Mrs. Mopp** charwoman
MS Mississippi
Ms. (mɪz, məs) title used instead of Miss or Mrs.
MS. *or* **ms.** manuscript (*pl.* **MSS.** *or* **mss.**)
M.Sc. Master of Science
M.S.C. Manpower Services Commission
M.S.T. US, C Mountain Standard Time
MT Montana
Mt. *or* **mt.** Mount
M.Tech. Master of Technology
mu (mju:) *n.* 12th letter in Gr. alphabet (M, μ)
much (mʌtʃ) *a.* **1.** existing in quantity *—n.* **2.** large amount **3.** a great deal **4.** important matter *—adv.* **5.** in a great degree **6.** nearly (**more** *comp.*, **most** *sup.*)
mucilage (ˈmju:sɪlɪdʒ) *n.* gum, glue
muck (mʌk) *n.* **1.** cattle dung **2.** unclean refuse —ˈ**mucky** *a.* **1.** dirty **2.** messy **3.** unpleasant —ˈ**muckrake** *vi.* seek out and expose scandal, *esp.* concerning public figures —ˈ**muckraking** *n.* —ˈ**mucksweat** *n.* UK *inf.* profuse sweat or state of profuse sweating —**muck about** UK *sl.* **1.** waste time; misbehave **2.** annoy, interfere (with) —**muck up** UK *sl.* ruin, spoil
mucus (ˈmju:kəs) *n.* viscid fluid secreted by mucous membrane —**mu**ˈ**cosity** *n.* —ˈ**mucous** *a.* **1.** resembling mucus **2.** secreting mucus **3.** slimy —**mucous membrane** lining of canals and cavities of the body
mud (mʌd) *n.* **1.** wet and soft earth **2.** *inf.* slander —ˈ**muddy** *a.* —ˈ**mudguard** *n.* cover over wheel to prevent mud, water *etc.* being splashed —ˈ**mudlark** *n.* **1.** formerly, one who made a living by picking up odds and ends in the mud of tidal rivers **2.** *sl., rare* street urchin —ˈ**mudpack** *n.* cosmetic paste to improve complexion —ˈ**mudslinger** *n.* —ˈ**mudslinging** *n.* casting malicious slurs on an opponent, *esp.* in politics
muddle (ˈmʌdᵊl) *vt.* **1.** (*esp. with* up) confuse **2.** bewilder **3.** mismanage *—n.* **4.** confusion **5.** tangle
muesli (ˈmju:zlɪ) *n.* mixture of grain, dried fruit *etc.* eaten with milk
muezzin (mu:ˈɛzɪn) *n.* crier who summons Muslims to prayer
muff[1] (mʌf) *n.* tube-shaped covering to keep the hands warm
muff[2] (mʌf) *vt.* miss, bungle, fail in
muffin (ˈmʌfɪn) *n.* round, spongy, flat scone
muffle (ˈmʌfᵊl) *vt.* wrap up, *esp.* to deaden sound —ˈ**muffler** *n.* scarf
mufti (ˈmʌftɪ) *n.* plain clothes as distinguished from uniform, *eg* of soldier
mug[1] (mʌg) *n.* drinking cup
mug[2] (mʌg) *n. sl.* **1.** face **2.** fool, simpleton, one easily imposed upon *—vt.* **3.** *inf.* rob violently (**-gg-**) —ˈ**mugger** *n.*
mug[3] (mʌg) *vi. inf.* (*esp. with* up) study hard (**-gg-**)
muggins (ˈmʌgɪnz) *n. inf.* fool, simpleton
muggy (ˈmʌgɪ) *a.* damp and stifling
mukluk (ˈmʌklʌk) *n.* C Eskimo's soft (sealskin) boot
mulatto (mju:ˈlætəʊ) *n.* child of one White and one Negro parent (*pl.* **-s, -es**)
mulberry (ˈmʌlbərɪ, -brɪ) *n.* **1.** tree whose leaves are used to feed silkworms **2.** its purplish fruit
mulch (mʌltʃ) *n.* **1.** straw, leaves *etc.*, spread as protection for roots of plants *—vt.* **2.** protect thus
mulct (mʌlkt) *vt.* **1.** defraud **2.** fine
mule[1] (mju:l) *n.* **1.** animal which is cross between horse and ass **2.** hybrid **3.** spinning machine —**muleteer** (mju:lɪˈtɪə) *n.* mule driver —ˈ**mulish** *a.* obstinate
mule[2] (mju:l) *n.* backless shoe or slipper
mull[1] (mʌl) *vt.* heat (wine) with sugar and spices —**mull over** think over, ponder
mull[2] (mʌl) *n.* light muslin fabric of soft texture
mullah *or* **mulla** (ˈmʌlə, ˈmulə) *n.* Muslim theologian

THESAURUS

transfer **2.** action, innards (*Inf.*), machinery, mechanism, workings, works **3.** *Music* division, part, passage, section
mow crop, cut, scythe, shear, trim
much 1. *adj.* abundant, a lot of, ample, considerable, copious, great, plenteous, plenty of, sizeable, substantial **2.** *adv.* a great deal, a lot, considerably, decidedly, exceedingly, frequently, greatly, indeed, often, regularly **3.** *n.* a good deal, a great deal, a lot, an appreciable amount, heaps (*Inf.*), loads (*Inf.*), lots (*Inf.*), plenty
muck 1. dung, manure, ordure **2.** dirt, filth, gunge (*Inf.*), gunk (*Inf.*), mire, mud, ooze, scum, sewage, slime, sludge
muck up botch, bungle, make a mess of, make a muck of (*Sl.*), mar, mess up, muff, ruin, screw up (*Inf.*), spoil
mud clay, dirt, mire, ooze, silt, sludge
muddle *v.* **1.** confuse, disarrange, disorder, disorganize, jumble, make a mess of, mess, mix up, scramble, spoil, tangle **2.** befuddle, bewilder, confound, confuse, daze, disorient, perplex, stupefy ~*n.* **3.** chaos, clutter, confusion, daze, disarray, disorder, disorganization, fankle (*Scot.*), jumble, mess, mix-up, perplexity, plight, predicament, tangle
muddy bespattered, boggy, clarty (*Scot., & northern English dialect*), dirty, grimy, marshy, miry, mucky, mud-caked, quaggy, soiled, swampy
muffle 1. cloak, conceal, cover, disguise, envelop, hood, mask, shroud, swaddle, swathe, wrap up **2.** deaden, dull, gag, hush, muzzle, quieten, silence, soften, stifle, suppress
mug[1] beaker, cup, flagon, jug, pot, tankard, toby jug
mug[2] chump (*Inf.*), gull (*Archaic*), easy *or* soft touch (*Sl.*), fool, innocent, mark (*Sl.*), muggins (*Brit. sl.*), simpleton, sucker (*Sl.*)
muggy clammy, close, damp, humid, moist, oppressive, sticky, stuffy, sultry
mull over consider, contemplate, deliberate, examine, meditate, muse on, ponder, reflect on, review, ruminate, study, think about, think over, turn over in one's mind, weigh

mullein ('mʌlɪn) *n.* plant with tall spikes of yellow flowers

mullet ('mʌlɪt) *n.* edible sea fish

mulligatawny (mʌlɪgə'tɔ:nɪ) *n.* soup made with curry powder

mullion ('mʌlɪən) *n.* upright dividing bar in window —**'mullioned** *a.*

multangular (mʌl'tæŋgjʊlə) *or* **multiangular** *a.* having many angles

multi- (*comb. form*) many, as in *multiracial, multistorey.* Such words are omitted where the meaning may easily be found from the simple word

multifarious (mʌltɪ'fɛərɪəs) *a.* of various kinds or parts —**multi'fariously** *adv.*

multilateral (mʌltɪ'lætərəl, -'lætrəl) *a.* **1.** of or involving more than two nations or parties **2.** having many sides

multinational (mʌltɪ'næʃən'l) *a.* (of large business company) operating in several countries

multiple ('mʌltɪp'l) *a.* **1.** having many parts —*n.* **2.** quantity which contains another an exact number of times —**multipli'cand** *n. Maths.* number to be multiplied —**multipli'cation** *n.* —**multi'plicity** *n.* variety, greatness in number —**'multiplier** *n.* **1.** person or thing that multiplies **2.** number by which multiplicand is multiplied **3.** *Phys.* any instrument, as photomultiplier, for increasing effect —**'multiply** *vt.* **1.** increase in number **2.** add (a number) to itself a given number of times —*vi.* **3.** increase in number or amount (**-plied, -plying**) —**multiple-choice** *a.* having a number of possible given answers out of which the correct one must be chosen —**multiple sclerosis** chronic disease of central nervous system, resulting in speech disorder, partial paralysis *etc.* —**multiplication table** one of group of tables giving results of multiplying two numbers together

multiplex ('mʌltɪplɛks) *a. Telecomm.* capable of transmitting numerous messages over same wire or channel

multitude ('mʌltɪtju:d) *n.* **1.** great number **2.** great crowd **3.** populace —**multi'tudinous** *a.* very numerous

mum (mʌm) *n. inf.* mother

mumble ('mʌmb'l) *vi.* **1.** speak indistinctly —*v.* **2.** mutter

mumbo jumbo ('mʌmbəʊ) **1.** foolish religious reverence or incantation **2.** meaningless or unnecessarily complicated language

mummer ('mʌmə) *n.* actor in dumb show —**mum** *a.* **1.** silent —*v.* **2.** act in mime (**-mm-**) —**'mummery** *n.* dumb-show acting

mummy ('mʌmɪ) *n.* embalmed body —**'mummify** *v.* (**-fied, -fying**)

mumps (mʌmps) *pl.n.* infectious disease marked by swelling in the glands of the neck

mun. municipal

munch (mʌntʃ) *v.* **1.** chew noisily and vigorously **2.** crunch

mundane ('mʌndeɪn, mʌn'deɪn) *a.* **1.** ordinary, everyday **2.** belonging to this world, earthly

municipal (mju:'nɪsɪp'l) *a.* belonging to affairs of city or town —**munici'pality** *n.* **1.** city or town with local self-government **2.** its governing body

munificent (mju:'nɪfɪsənt) *a.* very generous —**mu'nificence** *n.* bounty

muniments ('mju:nɪmənts) *pl.n.* title deeds, documents verifying ownership

munition (mju:'nɪʃən) *n.* (*usu. pl.*) military stores

muon ('mju:ɒn) *n.* positive or negative elementary particle with mass 207 times that of electron

mural ('mjʊərəl) *n.* **1.** painting on a wall —*a.* **2.** of or on a wall

murder ('mɜ:də) *n.* **1.** unlawful premeditated killing of human being —*vt.* **2.** kill thus —**'murderer** *n.* (**'murderess** *fem.*) —**'murderous** *a.*

murk *or* **mirk** (mɜ:k) *n.* thick darkness —**'murky** *or* **'mirky** *a.* gloomy

murmur ('mɜ:mə) *n.* **1.** low, indistinct sound —*vi.* **2.** make such a sound **3.** complain —*vt.* **4.** utter in a low voice

THESAURUS

multifarious different, diverse, diversified, legion, manifold, many, miscellaneous, multiform, multiple, multitudinous, numerous, sundry, varied, variegated

multiple collective, manifold, many, multitudinous, numerous, several, sundry, various

multiply accumulate, augment, breed, build up, expand, extend, increase, proliferate, propagate, reproduce, spread

multitude 1. army, assemblage, assembly, collection, concourse, congregation, crowd, great number, horde, host, legion, lot, lots (*Inf.*), mass, mob, myriad, sea, swarm, throng 2. commonalty, common people, herd, hoi polloi, mob, populace, proletariat, public, rabble

munch champ, chew, chomp, crunch, masticate, scrunch

mundane 1. banal, commonplace, day-to-day, everyday, humdrum, ordinary, prosaic, routine, workaday 2. earthly, fleshly, human, material, mortal, secular, sublunary, temporal, terrestrial, worldly

municipal borough, city, civic, community, public, town, urban

municipality borough, burgh (*Scot.*), city, district, town, township, urban community

munificence beneficence, benevolence, bigheartedness, bounteousness, bounty, generosity, generousness, largess, liberality, magnanimousness, open-handedness, philanthropy

munificent beneficent, benevolent, big-hearted, bounteous, bountiful, free-handed, generous, lavish, liberal, magnanimous, open-handed, philanthropical, princely, rich, unstinting

murder 1. *n.* assassination, bloodshed, butchery, carnage, homicide, killing, manslaughter, massacre, slaying 2. *v.* assassinate, bump off (*Inf.*), butcher, destroy, dispatch, do in (*Inf.*), do to death, eliminate (*Sl.*), hit (*U.S. sl.*), kill, massacre, rub out (*U.S. sl.*), slaughter, slay, take the life of, waste (*U.S. sl.*)

murderer assassin, butcher, cutthroat, hit man (*Sl.*), homicide, killer, slaughterer, slayer

murderous barbarous, bloodthirsty, bloody, brutal, cruel, deadly, death-dealing, destructive, devastating, fatal, fell (*Archaic*), ferocious, internecine, lethal, sanguinary, savage, slaughterous, withering

murky cheerless, cloudy, dark, dim, dismal, dreary,

murrain (ˈmʌrɪn) *n.* cattle plague

mus. 1. museum 2. music(al)

Mus.B. *or* **Mus.Bac.** Bachelor of Music

muscat (ˈmʌskət, -kæt) *n.* 1. musk-flavoured grape 2. raisin —**muscaˈtel** *n.* 1. muscat 2. strong wine made from it

muscle (ˈmʌsˀl) *n.* 1. part of body which produces movement by contracting 2. system of muscles —**muscular** (ˈmʌskjulə) *a.* 1. with well-developed muscles 2. strong 3. of, like muscle —**musculature** (ˈmʌskjulətʃə) *n.* 1. arrangement of muscles in organ or part 2. total muscular system of organism —**muscle-bound** *a.* with muscles stiff through over-development —ˈ**muscleman** *n.* 1. man with highly developed muscles 2. henchman employed by gangster *etc.* to intimidate or use violence upon victims —**muscular dystrophy** disease with wasting of muscles —**muscle in** *inf.* force one's way in

Muscovy duck (ˈmʌskəvɪ) *or* **musk duck** large crested widely domesticated S Amer. duck

Mus.D. *or* **Mus.Doc.** Doctor of Music

muse (mju:z) *vi.* 1. ponder 2. consider meditatively 3. be lost in thought —*n.* 4. state of musing or abstraction 5. reverie

Muse (mju:z) *n.* one of the nine goddesses inspiring learning and the arts

museum (mju:ˈzɪəm) *n.* (place housing) collection of natural, artistic, historical or scientific objects —**museum piece** 1. object fit to be kept in museum 2. *inf.* person or thing regarded as antiquated

mush (mʌʃ) *n.* 1. soft pulpy mass 2. *inf.* cloying sentimentality —ˈ**mushy** *a.*

mushroom (ˈmʌʃru:m, -rum) *n.* 1. fungoid growth, typically with stem and cap structure, some species edible —*vi.* 2. shoot up rapidly 3. expand —**mushroom cloud** mushroom-shaped cloud produced by nuclear explosion

music (ˈmju:zɪk) *n.* 1. art form using melodious and harmonious combination of notes 2. laws of this 3. composition in this art —ˈ**musical** *a.* 1. of, like music 2. interested in, or with instinct for, music 3. pleasant to ear —*n.* 4. show, film in which music plays essential part —ˈ**musically** *adv.* —**muˈsician** *n.* —**musiˈcologist** *n.* —**musiˈcology** *n.* scientific study of music —**musical chairs** party game in which players walk around chairs to music, there being one fewer chairs than players: when music stops, player without a chair is eliminated —**musical comedy** light dramatic entertainment with songs, dances *etc.* —**music box** *or* **musical box** mechanical instrument that plays tunes by means of pins on revolving cylinder striking tuned teeth of comblike metal plate —**music centre** single hi-fi unit containing turntable, amplifier, radio and cassette player —**music hall** variety theatre

musk (mʌsk) *n.* 1. scent obtained from gland of **musk deer** 2. any of various plants with similar scent —ˈ**musky** *a.* —ˈ**muskmelon** *n.* any of several varieties of melon, such as cantaloupe, having ribbed or warty rind and musky aroma —**musk ox** ox of Arctic Amer. —ˈ**muskrat** *n.* 1. N Amer. rodent found near water 2. its fur —**musk rose** rose cultivated for its white musk-scented flowers

muskeg (ˈmʌskɛg) *n.* C boggy hollow

muskellunge (ˈmʌskəlʌndʒ) *or* **maskinonge** (ˈmæskənɒndʒ) *n.* N Amer. freshwater game fish

musket (ˈmʌskɪt) *n. Hist.* infantryman's gun —**muskeˈteer** *n.* —ˈ**musketry** *n.* (use of) small firearms

Muslim (ˈmuzlɪm, ˈmʌz-) *or* **Moslem** *n.* 1. follower of religion of Islam —*a.* 2. of religion, culture *etc.* of Islam

muslin (ˈmʌzlɪn) *n.* fine cotton fabric —ˈ**muslined** *a.*

musquash (ˈmʌskwɒʃ) *n.* muskrat

mussel (ˈmʌsˀl) *n.* bivalve shellfish

must[1] (mʌst; *unstressed* məst, məs) *v. aux.* 1. be obliged to, or certain to —*n.* 2. something one must do

must[2] (mʌst) *n.* 1. newly-pressed grape juice 2. unfermented wine

mustang (ˈmʌstæŋ) *n.* wild horse

mustard (ˈmʌstəd) *n.* 1. powder made from the seeds of a plant, used in paste as a condiment 2. the plant —**mustard gas** poisonous gas causing blistering

muster (ˈmʌstə) *v.* 1. assemble —*n.* 2. assembly, *esp.* for exercise, inspection

musty (ˈmʌstɪ) *a.* mouldy, stale —**must** *or* ˈ**mustiness** *n.*

mutate (mju:ˈteɪt) *v.* (cause to) undergo mutation —ˈ**mutable** *a.* liable to change —ˈ**mutant** *n.* mutated animal, plant *etc.* —**muˈtation** *n.* change, *esp.* genetic change causing divergence from kind or racial type

mute (mju:t) *a.* 1. dumb 2. silent —*n.* 3. dumb person 4. *Mus.* contrivance to soften tone of instruments —ˈ**muted** *a.* 1. (of sound) muffled 2. (of light) subdued —ˈ**mutely** *adv.*

THESAURUS

dull, dusky, foggy, gloomy, grey, impenetrable, misty, nebulous, obscure, overcast

murmur *n.* 1. babble, buzzing, drone, humming, mumble, muttering, purr, rumble, susurrus (*Literary*), undertone, whisper, whispering ~*v.* 2. babble, buzz, drone, hum, mumble, mutter, purr, rumble, speak in an undertone, whisper 3. beef (*Sl.*), carp, cavil, complain, gripe (*Inf.*), grouse, grumble, moan (*Inf.*)

muscle 1. *n.* muscle tissue, sinew, tendon, thew 2. *v.* **muscle in** *Inf.* butt in, elbow one's way in, force one's way in, impose oneself

muscular athletic, beefy (*Inf.*), brawny, husky (*Inf.*), lusty, powerful, powerfully built, robust, sinewy, stalwart, strapping, strong, sturdy, vigorous, well-knit

muse be in a brown study, be lost in thought, brood, cogitate, consider, contemplate, deliberate, dream, meditate, mull over, ponder, reflect, ruminate, speculate, think, think over, weigh

mushroom *v.* boom, burgeon, expand, flourish, grow rapidly, increase, luxuriate, proliferate, shoot up, spread, spring up, sprout

musical dulcet, euphonious, harmonious, lilting, lyrical, melodic, melodious, sweet-sounding, tuneful

must *n.* duty, essential, fundamental, imperative, necessary thing, necessity, obligation, prerequisite, requirement, requisite, *sine qua non*

muster 1. *v.* assemble, call together, call up, collect, come together, congregate, convene, convoke, enrol, gather, group, marshal, meet, mobilize, rally, round up, summon 2. *n.* assemblage, assembly, collection, concourse, congregation, convention, convocation, gathering, meeting, mobilization, rally, roundup

muti (ˈmuːtɪ) *n.* **SA** (herbal) medicine

mutilate (ˈmjuːtɪleɪt) *vt.* **1.** deprive of a limb or other part **2.** damage, deface —**mutiˈlation** *n.* —**ˈmutilator** *n.*

mutiny (ˈmjuːtɪnɪ) *n.* **1.** rebellion against authority, esp. against officers of disciplined body —*vi.* **2.** commit mutiny (**ˈmutinied, ˈmutinying**) —**mutiˈneer** *n.* —**ˈmutinous** *a.* rebellious

mutt (mʌt) *n. inf.* **1.** stupid person **2.** dog

mutter (ˈmʌtə) *vi.* **1.** speak with mouth nearly closed, indistinctly **2.** grumble —*vt.* **3.** utter in such tones —*n.* **4.** act, sound of muttering

mutton (ˈmʌtᵊn) *n.* flesh of sheep used as food —**ˈmuttonchops** *pl.n.* side whiskers trimmed in shape of chops —**ˈmuttonhead** *n. sl.* fool

mutual (ˈmjuːtʃʊəl) *a.* **1.** done, possessed *etc.* by each of two with respect to the other **2.** reciprocal **3.** *inf.* common to both or all —**ˈmutually** *adv.*

Muzak (ˈmjuːzæk) *n.* **R** recorded light music played in shops *etc.*

muzzle (ˈmʌzᵊl) *n.* **1.** mouth and nose of animal **2.** cover for these to prevent biting **3.** open end of gun —*vt.* **4.** put muzzle on **5.** silence, gag

muzzy (ˈmʌzɪ) *a.* indistinct, confused, muddled

mW milliwatt(s)

MW megawatt(s)

Mx *Phys.* maxwell

my (maɪ) *a.* belonging to me —**myˈself** *pron.* emphatic or reflexive form of I

myalgia (maɪˈældʒɪə) *n.* pain in a muscle

mycelium (maɪˈsiːlɪəm) *n.* vegetative body of fungi (*pl.* **-lia** (-lɪə)) —**myˈcelial** *a.*

Mycenaean (maɪsɪˈniːən) *a.* **1.** of ancient Mycenae or its inhabitants **2.** of Aegean civilization of Mycenae (1400 to 1100 B.C.)

mycology (maɪˈkɒlədʒɪ) *n.* science of fungi

myna, mynah, *or* **mina** (ˈmaɪnə) *n.* Indian bird related to starling

myopia (maɪˈəʊpɪə) *n.* short-sightedness —**myopic** (maɪˈɒpɪk) *a.*

myosotis (maɪəˈsəʊtɪs) *n.* any of various kinds of small plant with blue, pink or white flowers, *eg* forget-me-not

myriad (ˈmɪrɪəd) *a.* **1.** innumerable —*n.* **2.** large indefinite number

myriapod (ˈmɪrɪəpɒd) *n.* **1.** any of group of terrestrial arthropods having long segmented body, such as the centipede —*a.* **2.** of or belonging to this group

myrmidon (ˈmɜːmɪdɒn, -dᵊn) *n.* follower or henchman

myrrh (mɜː) *n.* aromatic gum, formerly used as incense

myrtle (ˈmɜːtᵊl) *n.* flowering evergreen shrub

myself (maɪˈsɛlf) *pron. see* MY

mystery (ˈmɪstərɪ, -trɪ) *n.* **1.** obscure or secret thing **2.** anything strange or inexplicable **3.** religious rite **4.** in Middle Ages, biblical play —**mysˈterious** *a.* —**mysˈteriously** *adv.*

mystic (ˈmɪstɪk) *n.* **1.** one who seeks divine, spiritual knowledge, *esp.* by prayer, contemplation *etc.* —*a.* **2.** of hidden meaning, *esp.* in religious sense —**ˈmystical** *a.* —**ˈmysticism** *n.*

mystify (ˈmɪstɪfaɪ) *vt.* bewilder, puzzle (**-fied, -fying**) —**mystifiˈcation** *n.*

mystique (mɪˈstiːk) *n.* aura of mystery, power *etc.*

myth (mɪθ) *n.* **1.** tale with supernatural characters or events **2.** invented story **3.** imaginary person or object —**ˈmythical** *a.* —**mythoˈlogical** *a.* —**myˈthologist** *n.* —**myˈthology** *n.* **1.** myths collectively **2.** study of them

myxomatosis (mɪksəməˈtəʊsɪs) *n.* contagious, fatal disease of rabbits caused by a virus

THESAURUS

musty airless, dank, decayed, frowsty, fusty, mildewed, mildewy, mouldy, old, smelly, stale, stuffy

mute aphasiac, aphasic, aphonic, dumb, mum, silent, speechless, unexpressed, unspeaking, unspoken, voiceless, wordless

mutilate 1. amputate, butcher, cripple, cut to pieces, cut up, damage, disable, disfigure, dismember, hack, injure, lacerate, lame, maim, mangle **2.** adulterate, bowdlerize, butcher, censor, cut, damage, distort, expurgate, hack, mar, spoil

mutinous bolshie (*Brit. inf.*), contumacious, disobedient, insubordinate, insurgent, rebellious, refractory, revolutionary, riotous, seditious, subversive, ungovernable, unmanageable, unruly

mutiny 1. *n.* defiance, disobedience, insubordination, insurrection, rebellion, refusal to obey orders, resistance, revolt, revolution, riot, rising, strike, uprising **2.** *v.* be insubordinate, defy authority, disobey, rebel, refuse to obey orders, resist, revolt, rise up, strike

mutter complain, grouch, grouse, grumble, mumble, murmur, rumble

mutual common, communal, correlative, interactive, interchangeable, interchanged, joint, reciprocal, reciprocated, requited, returned, shared

mysterious abstruse, arcane, baffling, concealed, covert, cryptic, curious, dark, enigmatic, furtive, hidden, impenetrable, incomprehensible, inexplicable, inscrutable, insoluble, mystical, mystifying, obscure, perplexing, puzzling, recondite, secret, secretive, sphinxlike, strange, uncanny, unfathomable, unknown, veiled, weird

mystery conundrum, enigma, problem, puzzle, question, riddle, secrecy, secret

mystic, mystical abstruse, arcane, cabalistic, cryptic, enigmatical, esoteric, hidden, inscrutable, metaphysical, mysterious, nonrational, occult, otherworldly, paranormal, preternatural, supernatural, transcendental

mystify baffle, bamboozle (*Inf.*), beat (*Sl.*), befog, bewilder, confound, confuse, elude, escape, perplex, puzzle, stump

myth allegory, fable, fairy story, fiction, folk tale, legend, parable, saga, story, tradition

mythical 1. allegorical, chimerical, fabled, fabulous, fairy-tale, legendary, mythological, storied **2.** fabricated, fanciful, fantasy, fictitious, imaginary, invented, made-up, make-believe, nonexistent, pretended, unreal, untrue

mythology folklore, folk tales, legend, lore, mythos, myths, stories, tradition

N

n *or* **N** (ɛn) *n.* **1.** 14th letter of English alphabet **2.** speech sound represented by this letter (*pl.* **n's, N's** *or* **Ns**)

n (ɛn) *a.* indefinite number (of) —**nth** (ɛnθ) *a.* **1.** *Maths.* of unspecified ordinal number, usu. greatest in series **2.** *inf.* being last or most extreme of long series —**to the nth degree** *inf.* to the utmost extreme

N **1.** *Chess* knight **2.** *Chem.* nitrogen **3.** *Phys.* newton **4.** north(ern)

n. **1.** neuter **2.** noun **3.** number

Na *Chem.* sodium

NAAFI (ˈnæfɪ) *n.* organization providing canteens *etc.* for the services (*N*avy, *A*rmy and *A*ir *F*orce *I*nstitutes)

naartjie (ˈnɑːtʃɪ) *n.* **SA** tangerine

nab (næb) *vt. inf.* **1.** arrest criminal **2.** catch suddenly (**-bb-**)

nacre (ˈneɪkə) *n.* **1.** mother-of-pearl **2.** shellfish

nadir (ˈneɪdɪə, ˈnæ-) *n.* **1.** point opposite the zenith **2.** lowest point

nae (neɪ) *Scots word for* no (sense 1)

naff (næf) *a.* **UK** *sl.* inferior, useless —**naff off UK** *sl.* forceful expression of dismissal or contempt

nag[1] (næg) *v.* **1.** scold or annoy constantly **2.** cause pain to constantly (**-gg-**) —*n.* **3.** nagging **4.** one who nags

nag[2] (næg) *n.* **1.** *inf.* horse **2.** small horse for riding

naiad (ˈnaɪæd) *n.* water nymph (*pl.* **-s, -ades** (-ədiːz))

naïf (nɑːˈiːf) *a. see* NAIVE

nail (neɪl) *n.* **1.** horny shield at ends of fingers, toes **2.** claw **3.** small metal spike for fixing wood *etc.* —*vt.* **4.** fix, stud with nails **5.** *inf.* catch —ˈ**nailfile** *n.* small file used to trim nails —**nail set** punch for driving head of nail below or flush with surrounding surface

naive, naïve (nɑːˈiːv, naɪˈiːv), *or* **naïf** *a.* simple, unaffected, ingenuous —**naiveté, naïveté** (nɑːiːvˈteɪ) *or* **naivety** (naɪˈiːvtɪ) *n.*

naked (ˈneɪkɪd) *a.* **1.** without clothes **2.** exposed, bare **3.** undisguised —ˈ**nakedly** *adv.* —ˈ**nakedness** *n.* —**naked eye** the eye unassisted by any optical instrument

NALGO (ˈnælgəʊ) National and Local Government Officers' Association

namby-pamby (næmbɪˈpæmbɪ) *a.* **1.** weakly **2.** sentimental **3.** insipid —*n.* **4.** namby-pamby person

name (neɪm) *n.* **1.** word by which person, thing *etc.* is denoted **2.** reputation **3.** title **4.** credit **5.** family **6.** famous person —*vt.* **7.** give name to **8.** call by name **9.** entitle **10.** appoint **11.** mention **12.** specify —ˈ**nameless** *a.* **1.** without a name **2.** indescribable **3.** too dreadful to be mentioned **4.** obscure —ˈ**namely** *adv.* that is to say —**name day** **1.** *R.C.Ch.* feast day of saint whose name one bears **2.** *St. Ex.* day before setting day, when stockbrokers are given names of purchasers (*also* **ticket day**) —**name-dropper** *n.* —**name-dropping** *n. inf.* referring frequently to famous people, *esp.* as though they were intimate friends, in order to impress others —ˈ**nameplate** *n.* small panel on door bearing occupant's name —ˈ**namesake** *n.* person with same name as another

nancy *or* **nancy boy** (ˈnænsɪ) *n.* effeminate or homosexual boy or man

nankeen (næŋˈkiːn) *or* **nankin** (ˈnænkɪn) *n.* **1.** buff-coloured cotton fabric **2.** pale greyish-yellow colour

nanny (ˈnænɪ) *n.* child's nurse —**nanny goat** she-goat

nano- (*comb. form*) 10^{-9}, as in *nanosecond*

nap[1] (næp) *vi.* **1.** take short sleep, *esp.* in daytime (**-pp-**) —*n.* **2.** short sleep

nap[2] (næp) *n.* downy surface on cloth made by projecting fibres

nap[3] (næp) *n.* card game similar to whist

THESAURUS

nadir bottom, depths, lowest point, minimum, rock bottom, zero

nag[1] **1.** *v.* annoy, badger, berate, chivvy, goad, harass, harry, henpeck, irritate, pester, plague, provoke, scold, torment, upbraid, vex, worry **2.** *n.* harpy, scold, shrew, tartar, termagant, virago

nag[2] hack, horse, jade, plug (*U.S.*)

nail *v.* attach, fasten, fix, hammer, join, pin, secure, tack

naive artless, candid, childlike, confiding, frank, guileless, ingenuous, innocent, jejune, natural, open, simple, trusting, unaffected, unpretentious, unsophisticated, unworldly

naiveté artlessness, candour, frankness, guilelessness, inexperience, ingenuousness, innocence, naturalness, openness, simplicity

naked **1.** bare, denuded, disrobed, divested, exposed, in one's birthday suit (*Inf.*), in the altogether (*Inf.*), in the buff (*Inf.*), nude, starkers (*Inf.*), stripped, unclothed, unconcealed, uncovered, undraped, undressed **2.** blatant, evident, manifest, open, overt, patent, plain, simple, stark, unadorned, undisguised, unexaggerated, unmistakable, unqualified, unvarnished

nakedness **1.** baldness, bareness, nudity, undress **2.** openness, plainness, simplicity, starkness

namby-pamby anaemic, colourless, feeble, insipid, mawkish, prim, prissy (*Inf.*), sentimental, spineless, vapid, weak, wishy-washy (*Inf.*)

name *n.* **1.** appellation, cognomen, denomination, designation, epithet, handle (*Sl.*), moniker (*Inf.*), nickname, sobriquet, term, title **2.** character, credit, reputation ~*v.* **3.** baptize, call, christen, denominate, dub, entitle, label, style, term **4.** appoint, choose, cite, classify, commission, designate, identify, mention, nominate, select, specify

nameless **1.** anonymous, innominate, undesignated, unnamed, untitled **2.** incognito, obscure, undistinguished, unheard-of, unknown, unsung **3.** abominable, horrible, indescribable, ineffable, inexpressible, unmentionable, unspeakable, unutterable

namely i.e., specifically, that is to say, to wit, viz.

nap[1] **1.** *v.* catnap, doze, drop off (*Inf.*), drowse, nod nod off (*Inf.*), rest, sleep, snooze (*Inf.*) **2.** *n.* catnap, forty winks (*Inf.*), rest, shuteye (*Sl.*), siesta, sleep

nap[2] down, fibre, grain, pile, shag, weave

napalm ('neɪpɑːm, 'næ-) *n.* jellied petrol, highly inflammable, used in bombs *etc.*

nape (neɪp) *n.* back of neck

naphtha ('næfθə, 'næp-) *n.* inflammable oil distilled from coal *etc.* —**'naphthalene** *n.* white crystalline product distilled from coal tar, used in disinfectants, mothballs *etc.*

napkin ('næpkɪn) *n.* **1.** cloth, paper for wiping fingers or lips at table, serviette **2.** small towel **3.** nappy

nappy ('næpɪ) *n.* towelling cloth or other material placed around waist, between legs, of baby to absorb its excrement

narcissus (nɑː'sɪsəs) *n.* genus of bulbous plants including daffodil, jonquil, *esp.* one with white flowers (*pl.* **-cissi** (-'sɪsaɪ)) —**'narcissism** *n.* abnormal love and admiration of oneself —**'narcissist** *n.*

narcotic (nɑː'kɒtɪk) *n.* **1.** any of a group of drugs, including morphine and opium, producing numbness and stupor, used medicinally but addictive —*a.* **2.** of narcotics or narcosis —**narcosis** (nɑː'kəʊsɪs) *n.* effect of narcotic

nard (nɑːd) *n.* **1.** *see* **spikenard** *at* SPIKE **2.** plant whose aromatic roots were formerly used in medicine

nark (nɑːk) *vt. sl.* annoy, irritate

narrate (nə'reɪt) *vt.* relate, recount, tell (story) —**nar'ration** *n.* —**'narrative** *n.* **1.** account, story —*a.* **2.** relating —**nar'rator** *n.*

narrow ('nærəʊ) *a.* **1.** of little breadth, *esp.* in comparison to length **2.** limited **3.** barely adequate or successful —*v.* **4.** make, become narrow —**'narrowly** *adv.* —**'narrowness** *n.* —**'narrows** *pl.n.* narrow part of straits —**narrow boat** long narrow bargelike boat used on canals —**narrow gauge** smaller distance between lines of railway than standard gauge of 56½ inches —**narrow-gauge** *a.* of railway with narrow gauge —**narrow-minded** *a.* **1.** illiberal **2.** bigoted —**narrow-mindedness** *n.* prejudice, bigotry

narwhal, narwal ('nɑːwəl), *or* **narwhale** ('nɑːweɪl) *n.* arctic whale with tusk developed from teeth

NASA ('næsə) National Aeronautics and Space Administration

nasal ('neɪzᵊl) *a.* **1.** of nose —*n.* **2.** sound partly produced in nose —**'nasalize** *or* **-lise** *vt.* make nasal in sound —**'nasally** *adv.*

nascent ('næsᵊnt, 'neɪ-) *a.* **1.** just coming into existence **2.** springing up

nasturtium (nə'stɜːʃəm) *n.* **1.** genus of plants which includes the watercress **2.** trailing garden plant with red or orange flowers

nasty ('nɑːstɪ) *a.* foul, disagreeable, unpleasant —**'nastily** *adv.* —**'nastiness** *n.*

NAS/UWT National Association of Schoolmasters/Union of Women Teachers

nat. 1. national **2.** native **3.** natural

natal ('neɪtᵊl) *a.* of birth

natatory (nə'teɪtərɪ) *or* **natatorial** (nætə'tɔːrɪəl) *a.* of swimming —**na'tation** *n.*

nation ('neɪʃən) *n.* people or race organized as a state —**national** ('næʃənᵊl) *a.* **1.** belonging or pert. to a nation **2.** public, general —*n.* **3.** member of a nation —**nationalism** ('næʃənəlɪzəm) *n.* **1.** loyalty, devotion to one's country **2.** movement for independence of state, people, ruled by another —**nationalist** ('næʃənəlɪst) *n./a.* —**nationality** (næʃə'nælɪtɪ) *n.* **1.** national quality or feeling **2.** fact of belonging to particular nation —**nationalization** *or* **-lisation** (næʃənəlaɪ'zeɪʃən) *n.* acquisition and management of industries by the State —**nationalize** *or* **-lise** ('næʃənəlaɪz) *vt.* convert (private industry, resources *etc.*) to state control —**nationally** ('næʃənəlɪ) *adv.* —**national assistance** *old name for* supplementary benefit —**national debt** total financial obligations incurred by nation's central government —**National Front** political organization opposing immigration and advocating extreme nationalism —**national grid** UK **1.** network of high-voltage electric power lines linking major electric power stations **2.** metric coordinate system used in Ordnance Survey maps —**National Health Service** system of medical services financed mainly by taxation —**national insurance** state insurance scheme providing payments to the unemployed, sick *etc.* —**national park** area of land controlled by the state to preserve its natural beauty *etc.* —**National Trust** organization concerned with preservation of historic buildings and areas of countryside of great beauty

THESAURUS

narcissism egotism, self-admiration, self-love, vanity

narcotic 1. *n.* anaesthetic, analgesic, anodyne, drug, opiate, painkiller, sedative, tranquillizer **2.** *adj.* analgesic, calming, dulling, hypnotic, Lethean, numbing, painkilling, sedative, somnolent, soporific, stupefacient, stupefactive, stupefying

narrate chronicle, describe, detail, recite, recount, rehearse, relate, repeat, report, set forth, tell, unfold

narration description, explanation, reading, recital, rehearsal, relation, storytelling, telling, voice-over (*in film*)

narrative account, chronicle, detail, history, report, statement, story, tale

narrator annalist, author, bard, chronicler, commentator, raconteur, reciter, relater, reporter, storyteller, writer

narrow *adj.* **1.** circumscribed, close, confined, constricted, contracted, cramped, incapacious, limited, meagre, near, pinched, restricted, scanty, straitened, tight **2.** attenuated, fine, slender, slim, spare, tapering, thin ~*v.* **3.** circumscribe, constrict, diminish, limit, reduce, simplify, straiten, tighten

narrowly barely, by a whisker *or* hair's-breadth, just, only just, scarcely

narrow-minded biased, bigoted, conservative, hidebound, illiberal, insular, intolerant, opinionated, parochial, petty, prejudiced, provincial, reactionary, short-sighted, small-minded, strait-laced

narrows channel, gulf, passage, sound, straits

nastiness 1. defilement, dirtiness, filth, filthiness, foulness, impurity, pollution, squalor, uncleanliness **2.** disagreeableness, malice, meanness, offensiveness, spitefulness, unpleasantness

nasty 1. dirty, disagreeable, disgusting, filthy, foul, horrible, loathsome, malodorous, mephitic, nauseating, noisome, objectionable, obnoxious, odious, offensive, polluted, repellent, repugnant, sickening, unappetizing, unpleasant, vile **2.** abusive, annoying, bad-tempered, despicable, disagreeable, distasteful, malicious, mean, spiteful, unpleasant, vicious, vile

native (ˈneɪtɪv) *a.* **1.** inborn **2.** born in particular place **3.** found in pure state **4.** that was place of one's birth *—n.* **5.** one born in a place **6.** member of indigenous race of a country **7.** species of plant, animal *etc.* originating in a place

nativity (nəˈtɪvɪtɪ) *n.* **1.** birth **2.** time, circumstances of birth **3.** (N-) birth of Christ

NATO (ˈneɪtəʊ) North Atlantic Treaty Organization

NATSOPA (nætˈsəʊpə) National Society of Operative Printers and Assistants

natter (ˈnætə) *vi. inf.* talk idly

natty (ˈnætɪ) *a.* neat and smart; spruce —ˈ**nattily** *adv.*

nature (ˈneɪtʃə) *n.* **1.** innate or essential qualities of person or thing **2.** class, sort **3.** life force **4.** (*oft.* **N-**) power underlying all phenomena in material world **5.** material world as a whole **6.** natural unspoilt scenery or countryside, and plants and animals in it **7.** disposition, temperament —**natural** (ˈnætʃrəl) *a.* **1.** of, according to, occurring in, provided by, nature **2.** inborn **3.** normal **4.** unaffected **5.** illegitimate *—n.* **6.** something, somebody well suited for something **7.** *Mus.* character (♮) used to remove effect of sharp or flat preceding it —**naturalism** (ˈnætʃrəlɪzəm) *n.* **1.** movement, *esp.* in art and literature, advocating realism **2.** belief that all religious truth is based on study of natural causes and processes **3.** *Philos.* rational account of world in terms of natural forces **4.** action or thought caused by natural instincts —**naturalist** (ˈnætʃrəlɪst) *n.* student of natural history —**naturalistic** (nætʃrəˈlɪstɪk) *a.* of or imitating nature in effect or characteristics —**naturalization** *or* **-lisation** (nætʃrəlaɪˈzeɪʃən) *n.* —**naturalize** *or* **-lise** (ˈnætʃrəlaɪz) *vt.* **1.** admit to citizenship **2.** accustom to new climate —**naturally** (ˈnætʃrəlɪ) *adv.* **1.** of or according to nature **2.** by nature **3.** of course —ˈ**naturism** *n.* **1.** nature-worship **2.** nudism —ˈ**naturist** *n.* nudist —**natural gas** gaseous mixture, consisting mainly of methane, trapped below ground; used extensively as fuel —**natural history** study of animals and plants —**natural number** any of positive integers 1, 2, 3, 4,... —**natural philosophy** physical science, *esp.* physics —**natural resources** naturally occurring materials such as coal *etc.* —**natural science** any of sciences that are involved in study of physical world, including biology, physics *etc.* —**natural selection** process resulting in survival of those individuals from population of animals *etc.* that are best adapted to prevailing environmental conditions —**nature trail** path through countryside of particular interest to naturalists

naught (nɔːt) *n.* **1.** *obs.* nothing **2.** cipher 0 —**set at naught** defy, disregard

naughty (ˈnɔːtɪ) *a.* **1.** disobedient, not behaving well **2.** *inf.* mildly indecent —ˈ**naughtily** *adv.*

nausea (ˈnɔːzɪə, -sɪə) *n.* feeling that precedes vomiting —ˈ**nauseate** *vt.* sicken —ˈ**nauseous** *a.* **1.** disgusting **2.** causing nausea

nautical (ˈnɔːtɪkəl) *a.* **1.** of seamen or ships **2.** marine —**nautical mile** 1852 metres

nautilus (ˈnɔːtɪləs) *n.* univalvular shellfish (*pl.* **-es, -tili** (-tɪlaɪ))

naval (ˈneɪvəl) *a. see* NAVY

nave[1] (neɪv) *n.* main part of church

nave[2] (neɪv) *n.* hub of wheel

navel (ˈneɪvəl) *n.* small scar, depression in middle of abdomen where umbilical cord was attached (*also* **umˈbilicus**)

navigate (ˈnævɪgeɪt) *v.* **1.** plan, direct, plot path or position of (ship *etc.*) **2.** travel —ˈ**navigable** *a.* —**naviˈgation** *n.* **1.** science of directing course of seagoing

THESAURUS

nation commonwealth, community, country, people, population, race, realm, society, state, tribe

national **1.** *adj.* civil, countrywide, governmental, nationwide, public, state, widespread **2.** *n.* citizen, inhabitant, native, resident, subject

nationalism allegiance, chauvinism, fealty, jingoism, loyalty, nationality, patriotism

native **1.** *adj.* built-in, congenital, endemic, hereditary, inborn, inbred, indigenous, ingrained, inherent, inherited, innate, instinctive, intrinsic, inveterate, natal, natural **2.** *n.* aborigine, autochthon, citizen, countryman, dweller, inhabitant, national, resident

natter *v.* blather, blether, chatter, gabble, gossip, jabber, jaw (*Sl.*), palaver, prate, prattle, talk, talk idly, witter (*Inf.*)

natty chic, dapper, elegant, fashionable, neat, smart, snazzy (*Inf.*), spruce, stylish, trim, well-dressed, well-turned-out

natural **1.** common, everyday, legitimate, logical, normal, ordinary, regular, typical, usual **2.** characteristic, congenital, essential, inborn, indigenous, inherent, innate, instinctive, intuitive, natal, native **3.** artless, candid, frank, genuine, ingenuous, open, real, simple, spontaneous, unaffected, unpretentious, unsophisticated, unstudied

naturalism factualism, realism, verisimilitude

naturalist biologist, botanist, ecologist, zoologist

naturalize acclimate, acclimatize, acculturate, accustom, adapt, adopt, domesticate, enfranchise, familiarize, grant citizenship, habituate

nature **1.** attributes, character, complexion, constitution, essence, features, make-up, quality, traits **2.** category, description, kind, sort, species, style, type, variety **3.** cosmos, creation, earth, environment, universe, world **4.** disposition, humour, mood, outlook, temper, temperament **5.** country, countryside, landscape, natural history, scenery

naughty **1.** annoying, bad, disobedient, exasperating, fractious, impish, misbehaved, mischievous, perverse, playful, refractory, roguish, sinful, teasing, wayward, wicked, worthless **2.** bawdy, blue, improper, lewd, obscene, off-colour, ribald, risqué, smutty, vulgar

nausea biliousness, qualm(s), queasiness, retching, sickness, squeamishness, vomiting

nauseate disgust, horrify, offend, repel, repulse, revolt, sicken

nautical marine, maritime, naval, oceanic, seafaring, seagoing, yachting

naval marine, maritime, nautical, oceanic

navel bellybutton (*Inf.*), omphalos (*Literary*), umbilicus

navigate con (*Nautical*), cross, cruise, direct, drive, guide, handle, journey, manoeuvre, pilot, plan, plot, sail, skipper, steer, voyage

navigation cruising, helmsmanship, pilotage, sailing, seamanship, steering, voyaging

navigator mariner, pilot, seaman

vessel, or of aircraft in flight 2. shipping —ˈ**navigator** *n.* one who navigates

navvy (ˈnævɪ) *n.* labourer employed on roads, railways *etc.*

navy (ˈneɪvɪ) *n.* 1. fleet 2. warships of country with their crews and organization —*a.* 3. navy-blue —ˈ**naval** *a.* of the navy —**navy-blue** *a.* very dark blue

Nazi (ˈnɑːtsɪ) *n.* 1. member of the National Socialist political party in Germany, 1919-45 2. one who thinks, acts like a Nazi (*pl.* **-s**) —*a.* 3. of Nazis —ˈ**Nazism** *or* ˈ**Naziism** *n.* Nazi doctrine

Nb *Chem.* niobium

NB New Brunswick

NB, N.B., *or* **n.b.** nota bene

NC North Carolina

N.C.B. National Coal Board

N.C.O. noncommissioned officer

Nd *Chem.* neodymium

ND North Dakota

N.D.P. C New Democratic Party

Ne *Chem.* neon

NE 1. northeast(ern) 2. Nebraska

Neanderthal (nɪˈændətɑːl) *a.* of a type of primitive man

neap (niːp) *a.* low —**neap tide** the low tide at the first and third quarters of the moon

Neapolitan (nɪəˈpɒlɪtᵊn) *n.* 1. native of Naples —*a.* 2. of Naples

near (nɪə) *prep.* 1. close to —*adv.* 2. at or to a short distance —*a.* 3. close at hand 4. closely related 5. narrow, so as barely to escape 6. stingy 7. (of vehicles, horses *etc.*) left —*v.* 8. approach —ˈ**nearly** *adv.* 1. closely 2. almost —ˈ**nearness** *n.* —ˈ**nearby** *a.* adjacent —**Near East** 1. *see* **Middle East** *at* MIDDLE 2. formerly, Balkan States and area of Ottoman Empire —**near-sighted** *a.* relating to or suffering from myopia

neat (niːt) *a.* 1. tidy, orderly 2. efficient 3. precise, deft 4. cleverly worded 5. undiluted 6. simple and elegant 7. *sl., chiefly* US pleasing; admirable; excellent —ˈ**neaten** *vt.* make neat; tidy —ˈ**neatly** *adv.* —ˈ**neatness** *n.*

neath *or* **'neath** (niːθ) *prep. obs.* beneath

N.E.B. 1. New English Bible 2. National Enterprise Board

nebula (ˈnɛbjʊlə) *n. Astron.* diffuse cloud of particles, gases (*pl.* **-s, -ulae** (-jʊliː)) —ˈ**nebulous** *a.* 1. cloudy 2. vague, indistinct

necessary (ˈnɛsɪsərɪ) *a.* 1. needful, requisite, that must be done 2. unavoidable, inevitable —ˈ**necessarily** *adv.* —**neˈcessitate** *vt.* make necessary —**neˈcessitous** *a.* poor, needy, destitute —**neˈcessity** *n.* 1. something needed, requisite 2. constraining power or state of affairs 3. compulsion 4. poverty

neck (nɛk) *n.* 1. part of body joining head to shoulders 2. narrower part of a bottle *etc.* 3. narrow piece of anything between wider parts —*vi.* 4. *sl.* embrace, cuddle —ˈ**neckerchief** *n.* kerchief for the neck —ˈ**necklet** *n.* neck ornament, piece of fur *etc.* —**necklace** (ˈnɛklɪs) *n.* ornament round the neck —ˈ**necktie** *n.* US *see* TIE (sense 6)

necro- *or before vowel* **necr-** (*comb. form*) death, dead body, dead tissue, as in *necrosis*

necromancy (ˈnɛkrəʊmænsɪ) *n.* magic, *esp.* by communication with dead —ˈ**necromancer** *n.* wizard

necrophilia (nɛkrəʊˈfɪlɪə) *n.* sexual attraction for or intercourse with dead bodies (*also* **necroˈmania, neˈcrophilism**)

THESAURUS

navy argosy (*Archaic*), armada, fleet, flotilla, warships

near *adj.* 1. adjacent, adjoining, alongside, at close quarters, beside, bordering, close, close by, contiguous, nearby, neighbouring, nigh, touching 2. approaching, forthcoming, imminent, impending, in the offing, looming, near-at-hand, next, on the cards (*Inf.*) 3. akin, allied, attached, connected, dear, familiar, intimate, related 4. *Inf.* close-fisted, mean, miserly, niggardly, parsimonious, stingy, tightfisted, ungenerous

nearby *adj.* adjacent, adjoining, convenient, handy, neighbouring

nearly *adv.* about, all but, almost, approaching, approximately, as good as, closely, just about, not quite, practically, roughly, virtually, well-nigh

near-sighted myopic, short-sighted

neat 1. accurate, dainty, fastidious, methodical, nice, orderly, shipshape, smart, spick-and-span, spruce, straight, systematic, tidy, trim, uncluttered 2. adept, adroit, agile, apt, clever, deft, dexterous, efficient, effortless, elegant, expert, graceful, handy, nimble, practised, precise, skilful, stylish, well-judged 3. *Of alcoholic drinks* pure, straight, undiluted, unmixed

neatly 1. accurately, daintily, fastidiously, methodically, nicely, smartly, sprucely, systematically, tidily 2. adeptly, adroitly, agilely, aptly, cleverly, deftly, dexterously, efficiently, effortlessly, elegantly, expertly, gracefully, handily, nimbly, precisely, skilfully, stylishly

neatness 1. accuracy, daintiness, fastidiousness, methodicalness, niceness, nicety, orderliness, smartness, spruceness, straightness, tidiness, trimness 2. adeptness, adroitness, agility, aptness, cleverness, deftness, dexterity, efficiency, effortlessness, elegance, expertness, grace, gracefulness, handiness, nimbleness, preciseness, precision, skilfulness, skill, style, stylishness

nebulous ambiguous, amorphous, cloudy, confused, dim, hazy, imprecise, indefinite, indeterminate, indistinct, misty, murky, obscure, shadowy, shapeless, uncertain, unclear, unformed, vague

necessarily accordingly, automatically, axiomatically, by definition, certainly, compulsorily, consequently, incontrovertibly, ineluctably, inevitably, inexorably, irresistibly, naturally, *nolens volens*, of course, of necessity, perforce, undoubtedly, willy-nilly

necessary 1. compulsory, *de rigueur*, essential, imperative, indispensable, mandatory, needed, needful, obligatory, required, requisite, vital 2. certain, fated, inescapable, inevitable, inexorable, unavoidable

necessitate call for, coerce, compel, constrain, demand, force, impel, make necessary, oblige, require

necessity 1. demand, exigency, indispensability, need, needfulness, requirement 2. desideratum, essential, fundamental, necessary, need, prerequisite, requirement, requisite, *sine qua non*, want 3. destitution, extremity, indigence, need, penury, poverty, privation 4. compulsion, destiny, fate, inevitability, inexorableness, obligation

necropolis (nɛˈkrɒpəlɪs) *n.* cemetery (*pl.* **-es, -oleis** (-əleɪs))

nectar (ˈnɛktə) *n.* **1.** honey of flowers **2.** drink of the gods —ˈ**nectary** *n.* honey gland of flower

nectarine (ˈnɛktərɪn) *n.* variety of peach

N.E.D.C. National Economic Development Council

née *or* **nee** (neɪ) *a.* indicating maiden name of married woman

need (niːd) *vt.* **1.** want, require —*n.* **2.** (state, instance of) want **3.** requirement **4.** necessity **5.** poverty —ˈ**needful** *a.* necessary, requisite —ˈ**needless** *a.* unnecessary —**needs** *adv.* of necessity (*esp. in* **needs must** *or* **must needs**) —ˈ**needy** *a.* poor, in want

needle (ˈniːdᵊl) *n.* **1.** pointed pin with an eye and no head, for sewing **2.** long, pointed pin for knitting **3.** pointer of gauge, dial **4.** magnetized bar of compass **5.** stylus for record player **6.** leaf of fir or pine **7.** obelisk **8.** *inf.* hypodermic syringe —*vt.* **9.** *inf.* goad, provoke —ˈ**needlecord** *n.* corduroy fabric with narrow ribs —ˈ**needlepoint** *n.* **1.** embroidery done on canvas with various stitches so as to resemble tapestry **2.** point lace —**needle time** *chiefly* **UK** time allocated by radio channel to broadcasting of recorded music —ˈ**needlework** *n.* embroidery, sewing

ne'er (nɛə) *adv. Lit.* never —**ne'er-do-well** *n.* worthless person

nefarious (nɪˈfɛərɪəs) *a.* wicked

neg. negative(ly)

negate (nɪˈgeɪt) *vt.* deny, nullify —**neˈgation** *n.* contradiction, denial

negative (ˈnɛgətɪv) *a.* **1.** expressing denial or refusal **2.** lacking enthusiasm, energy, interest **3.** not positive **4.** (of electrical charge) having the same polarity as the charge of an electron —*n.* **5.** negative word or statement **6.** *Photog.* picture made by action of light on chemicals in which lights and shades are reversed —*vt.* **7.** disprove, reject —**negative feedback** *see* **feedback** *at* FEED

neglect (nɪˈglɛkt) *vt.* **1.** disregard, take no care of **2.** omit through carelessness —*vi.* **3.** fail (to do) —*n.* **4.** fact of neglecting or being neglected —**neˈglectful** *a.*

negligee, negligée, *or* **negligé** (ˈnɛglɪʒeɪ) *n.* woman's light, gauzy nightdress or dressing gown

negligence (ˈnɛglɪdʒəns) *n.* **1.** neglect **2.** carelessness —ˈ**negligent** *a.* —ˈ**negligible** *a.* **1.** able to be disregarded **2.** very small or unimportant

negotiate (nɪˈgəʊʃɪeɪt) *vi.* **1.** discuss with view to mutual settlement —*vt.* **2.** arrange by conference **3.** transfer (bill, cheque *etc.*) **4.** get over, past, around (obstacle) —**neˈgotiable** *a.* —**negotiˈation** *n.* **1.** treating with another on business **2.** discussion **3.** transference (of bill, cheque *etc.*) —**neˈgotiator** *n.*

Negro (ˈniːgrəʊ) *n.* member of Black orig. Afr. race (*pl.* **-es**) (ˈ**Negress** *fem.*) —ˈ**negritude** *n.* **1.** fact of being a Negro **2.** awareness and cultivation of Negro culture *etc.* —ˈ**Negroid** *a.* of or like a Negro

negus (ˈniːgəs) *n.* hot drink of port and lemon juice

THESAURUS

need *v.* **1.** call for, demand, have occasion to *or* for, lack, miss, necessitate, require, want ~*n.* **2.** longing, requisite, want, wish **3.** deprivation, destitution, distress, extremity, impecuniousness, inadequacy, indigence, insufficiency, lack, neediness, paucity, penury, poverty, privation, shortage **4.** emergency, exigency, necessity, obligation, urgency, want **5.** demand, desideratum, essential, requirement, requisite

needful essential, indispensable, necessary, needed, required, requisite, stipulated, vital

needle *v.* aggravate (*Inf.*), annoy, bait, goad, harass, irk, irritate, nag, nettle, pester, prick, prod, provoke, rile, ruffle, spur, sting, taunt

needless causeless, dispensable, excessive, expendable, gratuitous, groundless, nonessential, pointless, redundant, superfluous, uncalled-for, undesired, unnecessary, unwanted, useless

needlework embroidery, fancywork, needlecraft, sewing, stitching, tailoring

needy deprived, destitute, disadvantaged, impecunious, impoverished, indigent, on the breadline (*Inf.*), penniless, poor, poverty-stricken, underprivileged

nefarious abominable, atrocious, base, criminal, depraved, detestable, dreadful, evil, execrable, foul, heinous, horrible, infamous, infernal, iniquitous, monstrous, odious, opprobrious, shameful, sinful, vicious, vile, villainous, wicked

negate **1.** abrogate, annul, cancel, countermand, invalidate, neutralize, nullify, repeal, rescind, retract, reverse, revoke, void, wipe out **2.** contradict, deny, disallow, disprove, gainsay, oppose, refute

negation antithesis, antonym, contradiction, contrary, converse, counterpart, denial, disavowal, disclaimer, inverse, opposite, rejection, renunciation, reverse

negative *adj.* **1.** contradictory, contrary, denying, dissenting, opposing, recusant, refusing, rejecting, resisting **2.** colourless, cynical, gloomy, jaundiced, neutral, pessimistic, uncooperative, unenthusiastic, uninterested, unwilling, weak ~*n.* **3.** contradiction, denial, refusal

neglect *v.* **1.** contemn, disdain, disregard, ignore, leave alone, overlook, pass by, rebuff, scorn, slight, spurn **2.** be remiss, evade, forget, let slide, omit, pass over, procrastinate, shirk, skimp ~*n.* **3.** disdain, disregard, disrespect, heedlessness, inattention, indifference, slight, unconcern **4.** carelessness, default, dereliction, failure, forgetfulness, laxity, laxness, neglectfulness, negligence, oversight, remissness, slackness, slovenliness

negligence carelessness, default, dereliction, disregard, failure, forgetfulness, heedlessness, inadvertence, inattention, inattentiveness, indifference, laxity, laxness, neglect, omission, oversight, remissness, shortcoming, slackness, thoughtlessness

negligent careless, cursory, disregardful, forgetful, heedless, inadvertent, inattentive, indifferent, neglectful, nonchalant, offhand, regardless, remiss, slack, thoughtless, unmindful, unthinking

negligible imperceptible, inconsequential, insignificant, minor, minute, petty, small, trifling, trivial, unimportant

negotiable debatable, discussable, discussible, transactional, transferable

negotiate **1.** adjudicate, arbitrate, arrange, bargain, conciliate, confer, consult, contract, deal, debate, discuss, handle, manage, mediate, parley, settle, transact, work out **2.** clear, cross, get over, get past, get round, pass, pass through, surmount

negotiation arbitration, bargaining, debate, diplomacy, discussion, mediation, transaction

neigh (neɪ) *n.* 1. cry of horse —*vi.* 2. utter this cry

neighbour *or U.S.* **neighbor** (ˈneɪbə) *n.* one who lives near another —**ˈneighbourhood** *or U.S.* **ˈneighborhood** *n.* 1. district 2. people of a district 3. region round about —**ˈneighbouring** *or U.S.* **ˈneighboring** *a.* situated nearby —**ˈneighbourly** *or U.S.* **ˈneighborly** *a.* 1. as or befitting a good or friendly neighbour 2. friendly 3. sociable 4. helpful

neither (ˈnaɪðə, ˈniːðə) *a./pron.* 1. not the one or the other —*adv.* 2. not on the one hand 3. not either —*conj.* 4. not

nelson (ˈnɛlsən) *n.* wrestling hold in which wrestler places his arm(s) under his opponent's arm(s) from behind and exerts pressure with his palms on back of opponent's neck

nematode (ˈnɛmətəʊd) *n.* any of class of unsegmented worms having tough outer cuticle, including hookworm and filaria (*also* **nematode worm, ˈroundworm**)

nemesia (nɪˈmiːʒə) *n.* garden plant with flowers of various colours

Nemesis (ˈnɛmɪsɪs) *n.* 1. retribution 2. the goddess of vengeance (*pl.* **-ses** (-siːz))

neo- *or sometimes before vowel* **ne-** (*comb. form*) new, later, revived in modified form, based upon

neodymium (niːəʊˈdɪmɪəm) *n.* silvery-white metallic element of lanthanide series

Neolithic (niːəˈlɪθɪk) *a.* of the later Stone Age

neologism (nɪˈɒlədʒɪzəm) *or* **neology** *n.* new-coined word or phrase —**neˈologize** *or* **-gise** *vi.*

neon (ˈniːɒn) *n.* one of the inert constituent gases of the atmosphere, used in illuminated signs and lights —**neon lamp** tube containing neon, that gives red glow when voltage is applied

neophyte (ˈniːəʊfaɪt) *n.* 1. new convert 2. beginner, novice

nephew (ˈnɛvjuː, ˈnɛf-) *n.* brother's or sister's son

nephritis (nɪˈfraɪtɪs) *n.* inflammation of a kidney

nepotism (ˈnɛpətɪzəm) *n.* undue favouritism towards one's relations

Neptune (ˈnɛptjuːn) *n.* 1. god of the sea 2. planet second farthest from sun

neptunium (nɛpˈtjuːnɪəm) *n.* synthetic metallic element

nerve (nɜːv) *n.* 1. sinew, tendon 2. fibre or bundle of fibres conveying feeling, impulses to motion *etc.* to and from brain and other parts of body 3. assurance 4. bravery, coolness in danger 5. audacity —*pl.* 6. irritability, unusual sensitiveness to fear, annoyance *etc.* —*vt.* 7. give courage or strength to —**ˈnerveless** *a.* 1. without nerves 2. useless 3. weak 4. paralysed —**ˈnervous** *a.* 1. excitable, timid 2. apprehensive, worried 3. of the nerves —**ˈnervously** *adv.* —**ˈnervousness** *n.* —**ˈnervy** *a.* 1. nervous 2. jumpy 3. irritable 4. on edge —**nerve cell** *see* NEURON —**nerve centre** 1. group of nerve cells associated with specific function 2. principal source of control over any complex activity —**nerve gas** poisonous gas that has paralysing effect on central nervous system that can be fatal —**nerve-racking** *or* **nerve-wracking** *a.* very distressing, exhausting or harrowing —**nervous breakdown** condition of mental, emotional disturbance, disability —**nervous system** sensory and control apparatus of animals, consisting of network of nerve cells (*see also* NEURON)

ness (nɛs) *n.* headland, cape

nest (nɛst) *n.* 1. place in which bird lays and hatches its eggs 2. animal's breeding place 3. snug retreat —*vi.* 4. make, have a nest —**nest egg** (fund of) money in reserve

nestle (ˈnɛsᵊl) *vi.* settle comfortably, usu. pressing in or close to something

nestling (ˈnɛstlɪŋ, ˈnɛslɪŋ) *n.* bird too young to leave nest

net[1] (nɛt) *n.* 1. openwork fabric of meshes of cord *etc.* 2. piece of it used to catch fish *etc.* —*vt.* 3. cover with, or catch in, net (-tt-) —**ˈnetting** *n.* string or wire net —**ˈnetball** *n.* game in which ball has to be thrown through elevated horizontal ring, from which hangs short piece of netting

net[2] *or* **nett** (nɛt) *a.* 1. left after all deductions 2. free from deduction —*vt.* 3. gain, yield as clear profit —**net profit** gross profit minus all operating costs not included in calculation of gross profit

nether (ˈnɛðə) *a.* lower —**ˈnethermost** *a.* farthest down; lowest —**nether world** 1. underworld 2. hell (*also* **nether regions**)

THESAURUS

neighbourhood community, confines, district, environs, locale, locality, precincts, proximity, purlieus, quarter, region, surroundings, vicinity

neighbouring abutting, adjacent, adjoining, bordering, connecting, contiguous, near, nearby, nearest, next, surrounding

nerve *n.* 1. bottle (*Brit. sl.*), bravery, coolness, courage, daring, determination, endurance, energy, fearlessness, firmness, force, fortitude, gameness, grit (*Inf.*), guts (*Inf.*), hardihood, intrepidity, mettle, might, pluck, resolution, spirit, spunk (*Inf.*), steadfastness, vigour, will 2. *Inf.* audacity, boldness, brass (*Inf.*), brazenness, cheek (*Inf.*), effrontery, gall, impertinence, impudence, insolence, sauce (*Inf.*), temerity ~*v.* 3. brace, embolden, encourage, fortify, hearten, invigorate, steel, strengthen

nerve-racking annoying, difficult, distressing, frightening, harassing, harrowing, maddening, stressful, tense, trying, worrying

nerves anxiety, fretfulness, imbalance, nervousness, strain, stress, tension

nervous agitated, anxious, apprehensive, edgy, excitable, fearful, fidgety, flustered, hesitant, highly strung, hysterical, jittery (*Inf.*), jumpy, nervy (*Inf.*), neurotic, on edge, ruffled, shaky, tense, timid, timorous, uneasy, uptight (*Inf.*), weak, worried

nervous breakdown breakdown, collapse, crack-up (*Inf.*), nervous disorder, neurasthenia (*Obsolete*)

nervousness agitation, anxiety, disquiet, excitability, fluster, perturbation, tension, timidity, touchiness, tremulousness, worry

nest den, haunt, hideaway, refuge, resort, retreat, snuggery

nest egg cache, deposit, fund(s), reserve, savings, store

nestle cuddle, curl up, huddle, nuzzle, snuggle

nestling chick, fledgling

net[1] 1. *n.* lacework, lattice, mesh, netting, network, openwork, reticulum, tracery, web 2. *v.* bag, capture, catch, enmesh, ensnare, entangle, nab (*Inf.*), trap

net[2], **nett** 1. *adj.* after taxes, clear, final, take-home

netsuke (ˈnɛtsʊkɪ) *n.* carved wooden or ivory toggle or button worn in Japan

nettle (ˈnɛtᵊl) *n.* **1.** plant with stinging hairs on the leaves —*vt.* **2.** irritate, provoke —**nettle rash** urticaria

network (ˈnɛtwɜːk) *n.* **1.** system of intersecting lines, roads *etc.* **2.** interconnecting group of people or things **3.** in broadcasting, group of stations connected to transmit same programmes simultaneously

neural (ˈnjʊərəl) *a.* of the nerves

neuralgia (njʊˈrældʒə) *n.* pain in, along nerves, *esp.* of face and head —**neuˈralgic** *a.*

neuritis (njʊˈraɪtɪs) *n.* inflammation of nerves

neuro- *or before vowel* **neur-** (*comb. form*) nerve; nervous system, as in *neurology*

neurology (njʊˈrɒlədʒɪ) *n.* science, study of nerves —**neuˈrologist** *n.*

neuron (ˈnjʊərɒn) *or* **neurone** (ˈnjʊərəʊn) *n.* cell specialized to conduct nerve impulses (*also* **nerve cell**) —**neuˈronic** *a.*

neurosis (njʊˈrəʊsɪs) *n.* relatively mild mental disorder (*pl.* **-ses** (-siːz)) —**neurotic** (njʊˈrɒtɪk) *a.* **1.** suffering from nervous disorder **2.** abnormally sensitive —*n.* **3.** neurotic person

neurosurgery (njʊərəʊˈsɜːdʒərɪ) *n.* branch of surgery concerned with nervous system —**neuroˈsurgical** *a.*

neuter (ˈnjuːtə) *a.* **1.** neither masculine nor feminine —*n.* **2.** neuter word **3.** neuter gender —*vt.* **4.** castrate, spay (domestic animal)

neutral (ˈnjuːtrəl) *a.* **1.** taking neither side in war, dispute *etc.* **2.** without marked qualities **3.** belonging to neither of two classes —*n.* **4.** neutral nation or a subject of one **5.** neutral gear —**neuˈtrality** *n.* —**ˈneutralize** *or* **-ise** *vt.* **1.** make ineffective **2.** counterbalance —**neutral gear** in vehicle, position of gears that leaves transmission disengaged

neutrino (njuːˈtriːnəʊ) *n. Phys.* stable elementary particle with zero rest mass (*pl.* **-s**)

neutron (ˈnjuːtrɒn) *n.* electrically neutral particle of the nucleus of an atom —**neutron bomb** nuclear bomb designed to destroy people but not buildings

never (ˈnɛvə) *adv.* at no time —**neverˈmore** *adv. Lit.* never again —**never-never** *n. inf.* hire-purchase system of buying —**nevertheˈless** *adv.* for all that, notwithstanding

new (njuː) *a.* **1.** not existing before, fresh **2.** that has lately come into some state or existence **3.** unfamiliar, strange —*adv.* **4.** recently, fresh (*usu.* **ˈnewly**) —**ˈnewly** *adv.* —**ˈnewness** *n.* —**ˈnewcomer** *n.* recent arrival —**newˈfangled** *a.* of new fashion —**new maths** approach to mathematics in which basic principles of set theory are introduced at elementary level —**new moon** moon when it appears as narrow waxing crescent —**ˈnewspeak** *n.* language of bureaucrats and politicians, regarded as deliberately ambiguous and misleading —**New Testament** collection of writings composed soon after Christ's death and added to Jewish writings of Old Testament to make up Christian Bible —**new town UK** town planned as complete unit and built with government sponsorship, *esp.* to accommodate overspill population —**New Year** first day or days of year —**the New World** the Americas; western hemisphere

newel (ˈnjuːəl) *n.* **1.** central pillar of winding staircase **2.** post at top or bottom of staircase rail

news (njuːz) *n.* **1.** report of recent happenings, tidings **2.** interesting fact not previously known —**ˈnewsy** *a.* full of news —**news agency** organization that collects news reports for newspapers *etc.* (*also* **press agency**) —**ˈnewsagent** *n.* shopkeeper who sells and distributes newspapers —**news bulletin** the latest news, *esp.* as broadcast by radio and television —**ˈnewscast** *n.* news broadcast —**ˈnewscaster** *n.* —**ˈnewsflash** *n.* brief item of important news, oft. interrupting radio or television programme —**ˈnewsletter** *n.* **1.** printed periodical bulletin circulated to members of group (*also* **newssheet**) **2.** *Hist.* written or printed account of news —**ˈnewspaper** *n.* periodical publication containing news —**ˈnewsprint** *n.* paper of the kind used for

THESAURUS

2. *v.* accumulate, bring in, clear, earn, gain, make, realize, reap

nether basal, below, beneath, bottom, inferior, lower, under

nether world Avernus, Hades, hell, infernal regions, nether regions, underworld

nettle annoy, chafe, exasperate, fret, goad, harass, incense, irritate, pique, provoke, ruffle, sting, tease, vex

network arrangement, channels, circuitry, complex, convolution, grid, grill, interconnections, labyrinth, maze, mesh, net, nexus, organization, plexus, structure, system, tracks, web

neurosis abnormality, affliction, derangement, deviation, instability, maladjustment, mental disturbance, mental illness, obsession, phobia, psychological *or* emotional disorder

neurotic abnormal, anxious, compulsive, deviant, disordered, distraught, disturbed, maladjusted, manic, nervous, obsessive, overwrought, unhealthy, unstable

neuter *v.* castrate, doctor (*Inf.*), dress, emasculate, fix (*Inf.*), geld, spay

neutral 1. disinterested, dispassionate, even-handed, impartial, indifferent, nonaligned, nonbelligerent, noncombatant, noncommittal, nonpartisan, sitting on the fence, unaligned, unbiased, uncommitted, undecided, uninvolved, unprejudiced **2.** achromatic, colourless, dull, expressionless, indeterminate, indistinct, indistinguishable, intermediate, toneless, undefined

neutrality detachment, disinterestedness, impartiality, nonalignment, noninterference, noninterventionism, noninvolvement, nonpartisanship

neutralize cancel, compensate for, counteract, counterbalance, frustrate, invalidate, negate, nullify, offset, undo

nevertheless but, even so, however, nonetheless, notwithstanding, regardless, still, yet

new advanced, contemporary, current, different, fresh, latest, modern, modernistic, modish, newfangled, novel, original, recent, topical, ultramodern, unfamiliar, unknown, unused, unusual, up-to-date, virgin

newcomer alien, arrival, beginner, foreigner, immigrant, incomer, novice, outsider, settler, stranger

newfangled contemporary, fashionable, modern, new, new-fashioned, novel, recent

newly anew, freshly, just, lately, latterly, recently

newspapers *etc.* —ˈ**newsreel** *n.* cinema or television film giving news —ˈ**newsstand** *n.* stand from which newspapers are sold —ˈ**newsworthy** *a.* sufficiently interesting or important to be reported as news

newt (njuːt) *n.* small, tailed amphibious creature

newton (ˈnjuːtᵊn) *n.* SI unit of force

next (nɛkst) *a./adv.* **1.** nearest **2.** immediately following —**next door** at or to adjacent house, flat *etc.* —**next-of-kin** *n.* nearest relative

nexus (ˈnɛksəs) *n.* tie, connection, link (*pl.* ˈ**nexus**)

NF Newfoundland

N.F.U. National Farmers' Union

N.G.A. National Graphical Association

NH New Hampshire

N.H.S. National Health Service

Ni *Chem.* nickel

N.I. **1.** UK National Insurance **2.** Northern Ireland

nib (nɪb) *n.* **1.** (split) pen point **2.** bird's beak —*pl.* **3.** crushed cocoa beans

nibble (ˈnɪbᵊl) *v.* **1.** take little bites (of) —*n.* **2.** little bite

nibs (nɪbz) *n.* mock title of respect, as in *his nibs*

nice (naɪs) *a.* **1.** pleasant **2.** friendly, kind **3.** attractive **4.** subtle, fine **5.** careful, exact **6.** difficult to decide —ˈ**nicely** *adv.* —**nicety** (ˈnaɪsɪtɪ) *n.* **1.** minute distinction or detail **2.** subtlety **3.** precision

niche (nɪtʃ, niːʃ) *n.* **1.** recess in wall **2.** suitable place in life, public estimation *etc.*

nick (nɪk) *vt.* **1.** make notch in, indent **2.** *sl.* steal —*n.* **3.** notch **4.** exact point of time **5.** *sl.* prison —**in good nick** *inf.* in good condition

nickel (ˈnɪkᵊl) *n.* **1.** silver-white metal much used in alloys and plating **2.** US, C five-cent piece —**nickel silver** white alloy containing copper, zinc and nickel (*also* **German silver**)

nicker[1] (ˈnɪkə) *vi.* **1.** (of horse) neigh softly **2.** snigger

nicker[2] (ˈnɪkə) *n.* UK *sl.* pound sterling (*pl.* ˈ**nicker**)

nicknack (ˈnɪkˌnæk) *n. see* KNICK-KNACK

nickname (ˈnɪkneɪm) *n.* familiar name added to or replacing an ordinary name

nicotine (ˈnɪkətiːn) *n.* poisonous oily liquid in tobacco —ˈ**nicotinism** *n.* tobacco poisoning

nictitate (ˈnɪktɪteɪt) *or* **nictate** (ˈnɪkteɪt) *v.* blink —**nictiˈtation** *or* **nicˈtation** *n.*

niece (niːs) *n.* brother's or sister's daughter

nifty (ˈnɪftɪ) *a. inf.* **1.** neat, smart **2.** quick

niggard (ˈnɪgəd) *n.* mean, stingy person —ˈ**niggardly** *a./adv.*

nigger (ˈnɪgə) *n. offens.* Negro

niggle (ˈnɪgᵊl) *vi.* **1.** find fault continually —*vt.* **2.** annoy —ˈ**niggling** *a.* **1.** petty **2.** irritating and persistent

nigh (naɪ) *a./adv./prep. obs., poet.* near

night (naɪt) *n.* **1.** time of darkness between sunset and sunrise **2.** end of daylight **3.** dark —ˈ**nightie** *or* ˈ**nighty** *n.* woman's nightdress —ˈ**nightly** *a.* **1.** happening, done every night **2.** of the night —*adv.* **3.** every night **4.** by night —**nights** *adv. inf.* at night, *esp.* regularly —**night blindness** *Pathol.* inability to see normally in dim light (*also* **nyctaˈlopia**) —ˈ**nightcap** *n.* **1.** cap worn in bed **2.** late-night (alcoholic) drink —ˈ**nightclub** *n.* establishment for dancing, music *etc.* opening late at night —ˈ**nightdress** *n.* woman's loose robe worn in bed —ˈ**nightfall** *n.* approach of darkness; dusk —ˈ**nightingale** *n.* small bird which sings *usu.* at night —ˈ**nightjar** *n.* nocturnal bird with harsh cry —ˈ**nightmare** *n.* **1.** very bad dream **2.** terrifying experience —**night safe** safe built into outside wall of bank, in which customers deposit money when bank is closed —**night school** educational institution that holds classes in evening —ˈ**nightshade** *n.* any of various plants of potato family, some of them with very poisonous berries —ˈ**nightspot** *n. inf.* nightclub —**night-time** *n.* —**night watch** **1.** guard kept at night, *esp.* for security **2.** period of time watch is kept **3.** night watchman

THESAURUS

news account, advice, bulletin, communiqué, disclosure, dispatch, exposé, gossip, hearsay, information, intelligence, leak, news flash, release, report, revelation, rumour, scandal, statement, story, tidings, word

next *adj.* **1.** consequent, ensuing, following, later, subsequent, succeeding **2.** adjacent, adjoining, closest, nearest, neighbouring ~*adv.* **3.** afterwards, closely, following, later, subsequently, thereafter

nibble **1.** *n.* bite, crumb, morsel, peck, taste **2.** *v.* bite, eat, gnaw, munch, nip, peck, pick at

nice **1.** agreeable, amiable, attractive, charming, commendable, courteous, delightful, friendly, good, kind, likable, pleasant, pleasurable, polite, prepossessing, refined, well-mannered **2.** accurate, careful, critical, delicate, discriminating, exact, exacting, fastidious, fine, meticulous, precise, rigorous, scrupulous, strict, subtle

nicely **1.** acceptably, agreeably, amiably, attractively, charmingly, commendably, courteously, delightfully, kindly, likably, pleasantly, pleasingly, pleasurably, politely, prepossessingly, well **2.** accurately, carefully, critically, delicately, exactingly, exactly, fastidiously, finely, meticulously, precisely, rigorously, scrupulously, strictly, subtly

nicety **1.** accuracy, exactness, fastidiousness, finesse, meticulousness, minuteness, precision **2.** delicacy, discrimination, distinction, nuance, refinement, subtlety

niche **1.** alcove, corner, hollow, nook, opening, recess **2.** calling, pigeonhole (*Inf.*), place, position, slot (*Inf.*), vocation

nick chip, cut, dent, mark, notch, scar, score, scratch, snick

nickname diminutive, epithet, familiar name, handle (*Sl.*), label, pet name, moniker (*Inf.*), sobriquet

niggard cheapskate (*Inf.*), cheeseparer, churl, miser, penny-pincher (*Inf.*), screw (*Sl.*), Scrooge, skinflint

niggardly avaricious, close, covetous, frugal, grudging, mean, mercenary, miserly, near (*Inf.*), parsimonious, penurious, Scroogelike, sordid, sparing, stinging, stingy, tightfisted, ungenerous

niggle **1.** carp, cavil, criticize, find fault, fuss **2.** annoy, irritate, rankle, worry

niggling **1.** cavilling, finicky, fussy, insignificant, minor, nit-picking (*Inf.*), pettifogging, petty, piddling (*Inf.*), quibbling, trifling, unimportant **2.** gnawing, irritating, persistent, troubling, worrying

night dark, darkness, dead of night, hours of darkness, night-time, night watches

nightfall crepuscule, dusk, eve (*Archaic*), evening,

nihilism ('naɪlɪzəm) *n.* **1.** rejection of all religious and moral principles **2.** opposition to all constituted authority or government —'**nihilist** *n.* —**nihil'istic** *a.*

nil (nɪl) *n.* nothing, zero

nimble ('nɪmb°l) *a.* agile, active, quick, dexterous —'**nimbly** *adv.*

nimbus ('nɪmbəs) *n.* **1.** rain or storm cloud **2.** cloud of glory, halo (*pl.* **-bi** (-baɪ), **-es**)

nincompoop ('nɪnkəmpu:p, 'nɪŋ-) *n.* fool, simpleton

nine (naɪn) *a./n.* cardinal number next above eight —'**nine'teen** *a./n.* nine more than ten —'**nine'teenth** *a.* —'**ninetieth** *a.* —'**ninety** *a./n.* nine tens —**ninth** (naɪnθ) *a.* —**ninthly** ('naɪnθlɪ) *adv.* —**nine-days wonder** something that arouses great interest but only for short period —'**ninepins** *pl.n.* (*with sing. v.*) game where wooden pins are set up to be knocked down by rolling ball, skittles —**nineteenth hole** *Golf sl.* bar in golf clubhouse

niobium (naɪ'əʊbɪəm) *n.* white superconductive metallic element that occurs principally in black mineral columbite and tantalite

nip (nɪp) *vt.* **1.** pinch sharply **2.** detach by pinching, bite **3.** check growth of (plants) thus **4.** *sl.* steal —*vi.* **5.** *inf.* hurry (**-pp-**) —*n.* **6.** pinch **7.** check to growth **8.** sharp coldness of weather **9.** short drink —'**nipper** *n.* **1.** thing (*eg* crab's claw) that nips **2.** *inf.* small child —*pl.* **3.** pincers —'**nippy** *a. inf.* **1.** cold **2.** quick

nipple ('nɪp°l) *n.* **1.** point of a breast, teat **2.** anything like this

Nippon ('nɪpɒn) *n.* Japan

nisi ('naɪsaɪ) *a. see* **decree nisi** *at* DECREE

Nissen hut ('nɪs°n) temporary military building of corrugated sheet steel

nit (nɪt) *n.* **1.** egg of louse or other parasite **2.** *inf.* nitwit —**nit-picking** *a. inf.* overconcerned with detail, *esp.* to find fault —**nitty-gritty** *n. inf.* basic facts, details —'**nitwit** *n. inf.* fool

nitre *or U.S.* **niter** ('naɪtə) *n.* **1.** potassium nitrate **2.** sodium nitrate

nitrogen ('naɪtrədʒən) *n.* one of the gases making up the air —'**nitrate** *n.* compound of nitric acid and an alkali —'**nitric** *or* '**nitrous** *a.* —'**nitrify** *vt.* **1.** treat or cause to react with nitrogen **2.** treat (soil) with nitrates **3.** (of nitrobacteria) convert (ammonium compounds) into nitrates by oxidation —**ni'trogenous** *a.* of, containing nitrogen —**nitric acid** colourless corrosive liquid —**nitrobac'teria** *pl.n.* soil bacteria involved in nitrification —**nitrogen cycle** natural circulation of nitrogen by living organisms —**nitroglycerin** (naɪtrəʊ'glɪsərɪn) *or* **nitroglycerine** (naɪtrəʊ'glɪsəri:n) *n.* explosive liquid —**nitrous oxide** colourless gas with sweet smell, used as anaesthetic in dentistry (*also* **laughing gas**)

nix (nɪks) *n. sl.* nothing

NJ New Jersey

NM New Mexico

NNE north-northeast

NNW north-northwest

no (nəʊ) *a.* **1.** not any, not a **2.** not at all —*adv.* **3.** expresses negative reply to question or request —*n.* **4.** refusal **5.** denial **6.** negative vote or voter (*pl.* **-es**) —**no-ball** *n.* **1.** *Cricket* illegal ball for which batting side scores run **2.** *Rounders* illegal ball, *esp.* one bowled too high or too low —*interj.* **3.** *Cricket, rounders* call by umpire indicating no-ball —**no-claim bonus** reduction on insurance premium, *esp.* one covering motor vehicle, if no claims have been made within specified period (*also* **no-claims bonus**) —**no-go** *a. sl.* **1.** not functioning properly **2.** hopeless —**no-go area** district barricaded off, which police, army can only enter by force —**no-man's-land** *n.* **1.** waste or unclaimed land **2.** contested land between two opposing forces —**no-one** *or* **no one** nobody —**no-trump** *Cards n.* **1.** bid or contract to play without trumps (*also* **no-trumps**) —*a.* **2.** (of hand) of balanced distribution suitable for playing without trumps (*also* **no-trumper**) —'**noway** *adv. sl.* not at all

No *Chem.* nobelium

No. number (*pl.* **Nos.**)

n.o. *Cricket* not out

nob (nɒb) *n. sl.* **1.** member of upper classes **2.** head

nobble ('nɒb°l) *vt. sl.* **1.** disable (*esp.* racehorse with drugs) **2.** secure dishonestly **3.** catch (criminal) **4.** cheat, swindle

THESAURUS

eventide, gloaming, sundown, sunset, twilight, vespers

nightly *adv./adj.* **1.** each night, every night, night after night, nights (*Inf.*) ~*adv.* **2.** after dark, at night, by night, in the night, nights (*Inf.*), nocturnally ~*adj.* **3.** night-time, nocturnal

nightmare **1.** bad dream, hallucination, incubus, succubus **2.** horror, ordeal, torment, trial, tribulation

nil duck, love, naught, *nihil,* none, nothing, zero

nimble active, agile, alert, brisk, deft, dexterous, lively, nippy (*Brit. inf.*), proficient, prompt, quick, quick-witted, ready, smart, sprightly, spry, swift

nimbly actively, acutely, agilely, alertly, briskly, deftly, dexterously, easily, fast, fleetly, proficiently, promptly, quickly, quick-wittedly, readily, sharply, smartly, speedily, spryly, swiftly

nimbus aura, aureole, cloud, corona, glow, halo, irradiation

nincompoop blockhead, dimwit (*Inf.*), dolt, dunce, fool, idiot, ninny, nitwit, noodle, numskull, simpleton

nip **1.** *v.* bite, catch, clip, compress, grip, nibble, pinch, snag, snap, snip, squeeze, tweak, twitch **2.** *n.* dram, draught, drop, finger, mouthful, peg (*Brit.*), portion, shot (*Inf.*), sip, snifter (*Inf.*), *soupçon,* sup, swallow, taste

nipper **1.** claw, pincer **2.** *Inf.* baby, boy, child, girl, infant, kid (*Inf.*), little one, tot

nipple breast, dug, mamilla, pap, papilla, teat, tit, udder

nippy **1.** biting, chilly, nipping, sharp, stinging **2.** *Brit. inf.* active, agile, fast, nimble, quick, spry

nit-picking captious, carping, cavilling, finicky, fussy, hairsplitting, pedantic, pettifogging, quibbling

nitty-gritty basics, brass tacks (*Inf.*), core, crux, essence, essentials, facts, fundamentals, gist, heart of the matter, reality, substance

nitwit dimwit (*Inf.*), dummy (*Sl.*), fool, halfwit, nincompoop, ninny, simpleton

nob big shot (*Sl.*), bigwig (*Sl.*), fat cat (*U.S. sl.*), nabob (*Inf.*), toff (*Brit. sl.*)

nobelium (nəʊˈbiːlɪəm) *n.* synthetic element produced from curium

noble (ˈnəʊbᵊl) *a.* **1.** of the nobility **2.** showing, having high moral qualities **3.** impressive, excellent —*n.* **4.** member of the nobility —**noˈbility** *n.* **1.** class holding special rank, usu. hereditary, in state **2.** quality of being noble —**ˈnobly** *adv.* —**ˈnobleman** *n.*

noblesse oblige (nəʊˈblɛs əʊˈbliːʒ) *oft. ironic* supposed obligation of nobility to be honourable and generous

nobody (ˈnəʊbədɪ) *n.* **1.** no person **2.** person of no importance

nocturnal (nɒkˈtɜːnᵊl) *a.* **1.** of, in, by, night **2.** active by night

nocturne (ˈnɒktɜːn) *n.* **1.** dreamy piece of music **2.** night scene

nod (nɒd) *v.* **1.** bow (head) slightly and quickly in assent, command *etc.* —*vi.* **2.** let head droop with sleep (**-dd-**) —*n.* **3.** act of nodding —**nodding acquaintance** slight knowledge of person or subject —**nod off** *inf.* fall asleep

noddle (ˈnɒdᵊl) *n. inf.* head

node (nəʊd) *n.* **1.** knot or knob **2.** point at which curve crosses itself —**ˈnodal** *a.* —**ˈnodical** *a.*

nodule (ˈnɒdjuːl) *n.* **1.** little knot **2.** rounded irregular mineral mass

Noel *or* **Noël** (nəʊˈɛl) *n.* **1.** Christmas **2.** Christmas carol

noggin (ˈnɒgɪn) *n.* **1.** small amount of liquor **2.** small mug **3.** *inf.* head

noise (nɔɪz) *n.* **1.** any sound, *esp.* disturbing one **2.** clamour, din **3.** loud outcry **4.** talk; interest —*vt.* **5.** (*usu. with* abroad *or* about) spread (gossip *etc.*) —**ˈnoiseless** *a.* without noise, quiet, silent —**ˈnoisily** *adv.* —**ˈnoisy** *a.* **1.** making much noise **2.** clamorous

noisome (ˈnɔɪsəm) *a.* **1.** (*esp.* of smells) offensive **2.** harmful, noxious

nom. nominative

nomad (ˈnəʊmæd) *n.* **1.** member of tribe with no fixed dwelling place **2.** wanderer —**noˈmadic** *a.*

nom de plume (ˈnɒm də ˈpluːm) *Fr.* writer's assumed name, pen name, pseudonym (*pl.* **noms de plume**)

nomenclature (nəʊˈmɛnklətʃə; *U.S.* ˈnəʊmənkleɪtʃər) *n.* terminology of particular science *etc.*

nominal (ˈnɒmɪnᵊl) *a.* **1.** in name only **2.** (of fee *etc.*) small, insignificant **3.** of a name or names —**ˈnominalism** *n.* philosophical theory that general word, such as *dog,* is merely name and does not denote real object, the general idea 'dog' —**ˈnominalist** *n.* —**ˈnominally** *adv.* **1.** in name only **2.** not really

nominate (ˈnɒmɪneɪt) *vt.* **1.** propose as candidate **2.** appoint to office —**nomiˈnation** *n.* —**ˈnominative** *a./n.* (of) case of nouns, pronouns when subject of verb —**ˈnominator** *n.* —**nomiˈnee** *n.* candidate

non- (*comb. form*) negatives the idea of the simple word. See the list below

nonage (ˈnəʊnɪdʒ) *n.* **1.** *Law* state of being under any of various ages at which person may legally enter into certain transactions **2.** any period of immaturity

nonagenarian (nəʊnədʒɪˈnɛərɪən) *a.* **1.** aged between ninety and ninety-nine —*n.* **2.** person of such age

nonaligned (nɒnəˈlaɪnd) *a.* (of states *etc.*) not part of a major alliance or power bloc

nonce (nɒns) *n.* —**nonce word** word coined for single occasion —**for the nonce 1.** for the occasion only **2.** for the present

THESAURUS

nobble 1. disable, handicap, incapacitate, weaken **2.** filch, knock off (*Sl.*), nick (*Sl.*), pilfer, pinch (*Inf.*), purloin, snitch (*Sl.*), steal, swipe (*Sl.*) **3.** get hold of, grab, take

nobility 1. aristocracy, elite, high society, lords, nobles, patricians, peerage, ruling class, upper class **2.** dignity, eminence, excellence, grandeur, greatness, illustriousness, loftiness, magnificence, majesty, nobleness, stateliness, sublimity, superiority, worthiness **3.** honour, incorruptibility, integrity, uprightness, virtue

noble *n.* **1.** aristocrat, lord, nobleman, peer ~*adj.* **2.** aristocratic, blue-blooded, gentle (*Archaic*), highborn, lordly, patrician, titled **3.** august, dignified, distinguished, elevated, eminent, excellent, grand, great, imposing, impressive, lofty, splendid, stately **4.** honourable, upright, virtuous, worthy

nobody 1. no-one **2.** cipher, lightweight (*Inf.*), menial, nonentity, nothing (*Inf.*)

nocturnal night, nightly, night-time, of the night

nod *v.* **1.** agree, assent, concur, show agreement **2.** be sleepy, doze, droop, drowse, nap, sleep, slump ~*n.* **3.** acknowledgment, beck, gesture, greeting, indication, salute, sign, signal

no go futile, hopeless, impossible, not on (*Inf.*), vain

noise 1. *n.* babble, blare, clamour, clatter, commotion, cry, din, fracas, hubbub, outcry, pandemonium, racket, row, sound, talk, tumult, uproar **2.** *v.* advertise, bruit (*Archaic*), circulate, gossip, publicize, repeat, report, rumour

noiseless hushed, inaudible, mute, muted, quiet, silent, soundless, still

noisy boisterous, cacophonous, chattering, clamorous, deafening, ear-splitting, loud, obstreperous, piercing, riotous, strident, tumultuous, turbulent, uproarious, vociferous

nomad drifter, itinerant, migrant, rambler, rover, vagabond, wanderer

nomadic itinerant, migrant, migratory, pastoral, peripatetic, roaming, roving, travelling, vagrant, wandering

nom de plume alias, assumed name, nom de guerre, pen name, pseudonym

nomenclature classification, codification, locution, phraseology, taxonomy, terminology, vocabulary

nominal 1. ostensible, pretended, professed, puppet, purported, self-styled, so-called, *soi-disant,* supposed, theoretical, titular **2.** inconsiderable, insignificant, minimal, small, symbolic, token, trifling, trivial

nominate appoint, assign, choose, commission, designate, elect, elevate, empower, name, present, propose, recommend, select, submit, suggest, term

nomination appointment, choice, designation, election, proposal, recommendation, selection, suggestion

nonchalant (ˈnɒnʃələnt) *a.* casually unconcerned, indifferent, cool —**ˈnonchalance** *n.*

noncombatant (nɒnˈkɒmbətənt) *n.* **1.** civilian during war **2.** member of army who does not fight, *eg* doctor, chaplain

noncommissioned officer (nɒnkəˈmɪʃənd) *Mil.* subordinate officer, risen from the ranks

noncommittal (nɒnkəˈmɪtᵊl) *a.* avoiding definite preference or pledge

non compos mentis (ˈnɒn ˈkɒmpəs ˈmɛntɪs) *Lat.* of unsound mind

nonconformist (nɒnkənˈfɔːmɪst) *n.* dissenter, *esp.* from Established Church —**nonconˈformity** *n.*

nondescript (ˈnɒndɪskrɪpt) *a.* lacking distinctive characteristics, indeterminate

none (nʌn) *pron.* **1.** no-one, not any —*a.* **2.** no —*adv.* **3.** in no way —**nonesuch** *or* **nonsuch** (ˈnʌnsʌtʃ) *n. obs.* matchless person or thing; nonpareil —**nonetheˈless** *adv.* despite that, however

nonentity (nɒnˈɛntɪtɪ) *n.* **1.** insignificant person, thing **2.** nonexistent thing

nonevent (nɒnɪˈvɛnt) *n.* disappointing or insignificant occurrence, *esp.* one predicted to be important

nonferrous (nɒnˈfɛrəs) *a.* **1.** denoting metal other than iron **2.** not containing iron

nonflammable (nɒnˈflæməbᵊl) *a.* **1.** incapable of burning **2.** not easily set on fire

nonintervention (nɒnɪntəˈvɛnʃən) *n.* refusal to intervene, *esp.* abstention by state from intervening in affairs of other states

noniron (nɒnˈaɪən) *a.* not requiring ironing

nonnuclear (nɒnˈnjuːklɪə) *a.* not operated by or using nuclear energy

nonpareil (ˈnɒnpərəl, nɒnpəˈreɪl) *a.* **1.** unequalled, matchless —*n.* **2.** person or thing unequalled or unrivalled

nonpartisan *or* **nonpartizan** (nɒnpɑːtɪˈzæn) *a.* not supporting any single political party

nonplus (nɒnˈplʌs) *vt.* disconcert, confound or bewilder completely (**-ss-**)

nonproliferation (nɒnprəlɪfərˈeɪʃən) *n.* limitation of production *esp. of* nuclear weapons

nonacˈceptance
nonagˈgression
nonalcoˈholic
nonapˈpearance
nonbeˈliever
nonbelˈligerent
non-Catholic
noncomˈbustible
nonˈcommunist
noncomˈpetitive
noncomˈpliance
nonconˈsecutive
nonconˈtagious
nonconˈtributory
noncontroˈversial
noncooperˈation
nondeˈlivery
nondenomiˈnational
nonˈdrinker
nonˈdriver
nonesˈsential
nonexˈistent
nonˈfiction
noninˈfectious
noninˈflammable
nonmagˈnetic
nonmaˈlignant
nonˈmember
nonˈmetal
nonˈmilitant
non-negotiable
nonobˈservance
nonoperˈational
nonˈpayment
nonˈpoisonous
nonˈporous
non-profit-making
nonˈracial
nonˈreader
nonˈregistered
nonrepreˈsentative
nonˈresident
nonreˈsistant
nonreˈturnable
nonseˈlective
nonˈshrink(able)
nonˈslip
nonˈsmoker
nonˈstandard
nonˈstick
nonˈstop
nonˈswimmer
nonˈtaxable
nonˈtechnical
nonˈtoxic
nontransˈferable
nonˈvenomous
nonˈverbal
nonˈviolent
nonˈvoter

THESAURUS

nominee aspirant, candidate, contestant, entrant, favourite, protégé, runner

nonaligned impartial, neutral, uncommitted, undecided

nonchalance calm, composure, cool (*Sl.*), equanimity, imperturbability, indifference, sang-froid, self-possession, unconcern

nonchalant airy, apathetic, blasé, calm, careless, casual, collected, cool, detached, dispassionate, indifferent, insouciant, offhand, unconcerned, unemotional, unperturbed

noncommittal ambiguous, careful, cautious, circumspect, discreet, equivocal, evasive, guarded, indefinite, neutral, politic, reserved, tactful, temporizing, tentative, unrevealing, vague, wary

non compos mentis crazy, deranged, insane, mentally ill, of unsound mind

nonconformist dissenter, dissentient, heretic, iconoclast, individualist, maverick, protester, radical, rebel

nondescript characterless, common or garden (*Inf.*), commonplace, dull, featureless, indeterminate, mousy, ordinary, unclassifiable, unclassified, undistinguished, unexceptional, uninspiring, uninteresting, unmemorable, unremarkable

none nil, nobody, no-one, no part, not a bit, not any, nothing, not one, zero

nonentity cipher, lightweight (*Inf.*), mediocrity, nobody, small fry, unimportant person

nonessential dispensable, excessive, expendable, extraneous, inessential, peripheral, superfluous, unimportant, unnecessary

nonetheless despite that, even so, however, in spite of that, nevertheless, yet

nonexistent chimerical, fancied, fictional, hallucinatory, hypothetical, illusory, imaginary, imagined, insubstantial, legendary, missing, mythical, unreal

nonrepresentational (nɒnrɛprɪzɛnˈteɪʃənˀl) *a. Art* abstract

nonsectarian (nɒnsɛkˈtɛərɪən) *a.* not sectarian; not confined to any specific religion

nonsense (ˈnɒnsəns) *n.* **1.** lack of sense **2.** absurd language **3.** absurdity **4.** silly conduct —**nonˈsensical** *a.* **1.** ridiculous **2.** meaningless **3.** without sense

non sequitur (ˈnɒn ˈsɛkwɪtə) *Lat.* statement with little or no relation to what preceded it

nonstarter (nɒnˈstɑːtə) *n.* **1.** horse that fails to run in race for which it has been entered **2.** person or thing that has little chance of success

non-U *a.* UK *inf.* (*esp.* of language) not characteristic of upper class

noodle[1] (ˈnuːdˀl) *n.* strip of pasta served in soup *etc.*

noodle[2] (ˈnuːdˀl) *n.* simpleton, fool

nook (nʊk) *n.* sheltered corner, retreat —**ˈnooky** *a.*

noon (nuːn) *n.* midday, twelve o'clock —**ˈnoonday** *n.* noon —**ˈnoontide** *n.* the time about noon

noose (nuːs) *n.* **1.** running loop **2.** snare —*vt.* **3.** catch, ensnare in noose, lasso

nor (nɔː; *unstressed* nə) *conj.* and not

nor' *or* **nor** (nɔː) north (*esp.* in compounds)

Nor. **1.** Norman **2.** north **3.** Norway **4.** Norwegian

Nordic (ˈnɔːdɪk) *a.* pert. to peoples of Germanic stock

norm (nɔːm) *n.* **1.** average level of achievement **2.** rule or authoritative standard **3.** model **4.** standard type or pattern —**ˈnormal** *a.* **1.** ordinary **2.** usual **3.** conforming to type —*n.* **4.** *Geom.* perpendicular —**norˈmality** *n.* —**normaliˈzation** *or* **-iˈsation** *n.* —**ˈnormalize** *or* **-ise** *vt.* **1.** bring or make into normal state **2.** bring into conformity with standard **3.** heat (steel) above critical temperature and allow it to cool in air to relieve internal stresses; anneal —**ˈnormally** *adv.* —**ˈnormative** *a.* creating or prescribing norm or standard

Norman (ˈnɔːmən) *n.* **1.** in Middle Ages, member of people of Normandy in N France, descended from 10th-century Scandinavian conquerors of the country and native French **2.** native of Normandy **3.** medieval Norman and English dialect of Old French (*also* **Norman French**) —*a.* **4.** of Normans or their dialect of French **5.** of Normandy **6.** denoting Romanesque architecture used in Britain from Norman Conquest until 12th century, characterized by massive masonry walls *etc.*

Norse (nɔːs) *a.* **1.** of ancient and medieval Scandinavia **2.** of Norway —*n.* **3.** N group of Germanic languages, spoken in Scandinavia **4.** any of these languages, *esp.* in ancient or medieval forms —**ˈNorseman** *n. see* VIKING —**the Norse 1.** Norwegians **2.** Vikings

north (nɔːθ) *n.* **1.** direction to the right of person facing the sunset **2.** part of the world, of country *etc.* towards this point —*adv.* **3.** towards or in the north —*a.* **4.** to, from or in the north —**northerly** (ˈnɔːðəlɪ) *a.* **1.** of or situated in north —*n.* **2.** wind from the north —**northern** (ˈnɔːðən) *a.* —**northerner** (ˈnɔːðənə) *n.* person from the north —**northward** (ˈnɔːθwəd; *Naut.* ˈnɔːðəd) *a./n./adv.* —**northwards** (ˈnɔːθwədz) *adv.* —**northeast** (nɔːθˈiːst; *Naut.* nɔːrˈiːst) *n.* **1.** direction midway between north and east **2.** (*oft.* **N-**) area lying in or towards this direction —*a.* **3.** (*sometimes* **N-**) of northeastern part of specified country *etc.* **4.** in, towards or facing northeast **5.** (*esp.* of wind) from northeast (*also* **northˈeastern**) —*adv.* **6.** in, to, towards or (*esp.* of wind) from northeast —**Northˈeast** *n.* northeastern part of England, *esp.* Northumberland and Durham —**northeaster** (nɔːθˈiːstə; *Naut.* nɔːrˈiːstə) *n.* strong wind or storm from northeast —**northern hemisphere** (*oft.* **N- H-**) half of globe lying north of equator —**northern lights** aurora borealis —**north-northeast** *n.* **1.** direction midway between north and northeast —*a./adv.* **2.** in, from or towards this direction —**north-northwest** *n.* **1.** direction midway between northwest and north —*a./adv.* **2.** in, from or towards this direction —**North Pole 1.** northernmost point on earth's axis **2.** *Astron.* point of intersection of earth's extended axis and northern half of celestial sphere (*also* **north celestial pole**) —**North-Sea gas** UK natural gas obtained from deposits below North Sea —**northwest** (nɔːθˈwɛst; *Naut.* nɔːˈwɛst) *n.* **1.** direction midway between north and west **2.** (*oft.* **N-**) area lying in or towards this direction —*a.* **3.** (*sometimes* **N-**) of northwestern part of specified country *etc.* (*also* **northˈwestern**) —*a./adv.* **4.** in, to, towards or (*esp.* of wind) from northwest —**northwester** (nɔːθˈwɛstə; *Naut.* nɔːˈwɛstə) *n.* strong wind or storm from northwest —**the North Star** *see* **the Pole Star** *at* POLE[2]

Northants. (nɔːˈθænts) Northamptonshire

Northd. Northumberland

Northum. Northumbria

Norw. **1.** Norway **2.** Norwegian

Norwegian (nɔːˈwiːdʒən) *a.* **1.** of Norway —*n.* **2.** any of various North Germanic languages of Norway **3.** native of Norway

Nos. numbers

THESAURUS

nonsense absurdity, balderdash, blather, bombast, bunk (*Inf.*), claptrap (*Inf.*), double Dutch (*Brit. inf.*), drivel, fatuity, folly, foolishness, gibberish, inanity, jest, ludicrousness, ridiculousness, rot, rubbish, senselessness, silliness, stuff, stupidity, trash, twaddle, waffle (*Brit. inf.*)

nonstop **1.** *adj.* ceaseless, constant, continuous, direct, endless, incessant, interminable, relentless, steady, unbroken, unending, unfaltering, uninterrupted, unremitting **2.** *adv.* ceaselessly, constantly, continuously, directly, endlessly, incessantly, interminably, relentlessly, steadily, unbrokenly, unendingly, unfalteringly, uninterruptedly, unremittingly, without stopping

nook alcove, cavity, corner, cranny, crevice, cubbyhole, hide-out, inglenook (*Brit.*), niche, opening, recess, retreat

noon high noon, midday, noonday, noontide, noontime, twelve noon

norm average, benchmark, criterion, mean, measure, model, pattern, rule, standard, type, yardstick

normal accustomed, acknowledged, average, common, conventional, habitual, natural, ordinary, popular, regular, routine, run-of-the-mill, standard, typical, usual

normality accustomedness, averageness, commonness, commonplaceness, conventionality, habitualness, naturalness, ordinariness, popularity, regularity, routineness, typicality, usualness

normally as a rule, commonly, habitually, ordinarily, regularly, typically, usually

north **1.** *adj.* Arctic, boreal, northerly, northern, polar **2.** *adv.* northerly, northward(s)

nose (nəʊz) *n.* **1.** organ of smell, used also in breathing **2.** any projection resembling a nose, as prow of ship, aircraft *etc.* —*v.* **3.** (cause to) move forward slowly and carefully —*vt.* **4.** touch with nose **5.** smell, sniff —*vi.* **6.** smell **7.** (*with* into, around, about *etc.*) pry —ˈ**nosy** *or* ˈ**nosey** *a. inf.* inquisitive —ˈ**nosebag** *n.* bag fastened around head of horse in which feed is placed —ˈ**noseband** *n.* detachable part of horse's bridle that goes around nose —**nose dive** downward sweep of aircraft —ˈ**nosegay** *n.* bunch of flowers —**nosy parker** *inf., chiefly* UK prying person

nosh (nɒʃ) *sl. n.* **1.** food —*v.* **2.** eat —**nosh-up** *n.* **UK** *sl.* large and satisfying meal

nostalgia (nɒˈstældʒə, -dʒɪə) *n.* **1.** longing for return of past events **2.** homesickness —**nosˈtalgic** *a.*

nostril (ˈnɒstrɪl) *n.* one of the two external openings of the nose

nostrum (ˈnɒstrəm) *n.* **1.** quack medicine **2.** secret remedy

not (nɒt) *adv.* expressing negation, refusal, denial —**not proven** (ˈprəʊvᵊn) a third verdict available to Scottish courts, returned when there is insufficient evidence to convict

nota bene (ˈnəʊtə ˈbiːnɪ) *Lat.* note well

notable (ˈnəʊtəbᵊl) *a.* **1.** worthy of note, remarkable —*n.* **2.** person of distinction —**notaˈbility** *n.* an eminent person —ˈ**notably** *adv.*

notary (ˈnəʊtərɪ) *n.* person authorized to draw up deeds, contracts

notation (nəʊˈteɪʃən) *n.* **1.** representation of numbers, quantities, by symbols **2.** set of such symbols **3.** C footnote, memorandum

notch (nɒtʃ) *n.* **1.** V-shaped cut or indentation **2.** *inf.* step, grade —*vt.* **3.** make notches in

note (nəʊt) *n.* **1.** brief comment or record **2.** short letter **3.** banknote **4.** symbol for musical sound **5.** single tone **6.** sign **7.** indication, hint **8.** fame **9.** notice **10.** regard —*pl.* **11.** brief jottings written down for future reference —*vt.* **12.** observe, record **13.** heed —ˈ**noted** *a.* well-known —ˈ**notelet** *n.* folded card with printed design on front, for writing short letter —ˈ**notebook** *n.* small book with blank pages for writing —ˈ**notepaper** *n.* paper for writing letters; writing paper —ˈ**noteworthy** *a.* **1.** worth noting **2.** remarkable

nothing (ˈnʌθɪŋ) *n.* **1.** no thing **2.** not anything, nought —*adv.* **3.** not at all, in no way —ˈ**nothingness** *n.*

notice (ˈnəʊtɪs) *n.* **1.** observation **2.** attention, consideration **3.** warning, intimation, announcement **4.** advance notification of intention to end a contract *etc.*, as of employment **5.** review —*vt.* **6.** observe, mention **7.** give attention to —ˈ**noticeable** *a.* **1.** conspicuous **2.** attracting attention **3.** appreciable

notify (ˈnəʊtɪfaɪ) *vt.* **1.** report **2.** give notice of or to (**-fied, -fying**) —ˈ**notifiable** *a.* —**notifiˈcation** *n.*

notion (ˈnəʊʃən) *n.* **1.** concept **2.** opinion **3.** whim —ˈ**notional** *a.* speculative, imaginary, abstract

THESAURUS

nose *v.* **1.** detect, scent, search (for), smell, sniff **2.** ease forward, nudge, nuzzle, push, shove **3.** meddle, pry, snoop (*Inf.*)

nose dive dive, drop, plummet, plunge

nosegay bouquet, posy

nostalgia homesickness, longing, pining, regret, regretfulness, remembrance, reminiscence, wistfulness, yearning

nostalgic homesick, longing, regretful, sentimental, wistful

nostrum cure, cure-all, drug, elixir, medicine, panacea, patent medicine, potion, quack medicine, remedy, sovereign cure, specific, treatment

nosy, nosey curious, eavesdropping, inquisitive, interfering, intrusive, meddlesome, prying, snooping (*Inf.*)

notability celebrity, dignitary, notable, personage, V.I.P., worthy

notable 1. *adj.* celebrated, conspicuous, distinguished, eminent, evident, extraordinary, famous, manifest, marked, memorable, noteworthy, noticeable, notorious, outstanding, pre-eminent, pronounced, rare, remarkable, renowned, striking, uncommon, unusual, well-known **2.** *n.* celebrity, dignitary, notability, personage, V.I.P., worthy

notably conspicuously, distinctly, especially, markedly, noticeably, outstandingly, particularly, remarkably, signally, strikingly, uncommonly

notation characters, code, script, signs, symbols, system

notch *n.* **1.** cleft, cut, incision, indentation, mark, nick, score **2.** *Inf.* cut (*Inf.*), degree, grade, level, step ~*v.* **3.** cut, indent, mark, nick, score, scratch

note *n.* **1.** annotation, comment, communication, epistle, gloss, jotting, letter, memo, memorandum, message, minute, record, remark, reminder **2.** indication, mark, sign, symbol, token **3.** heed, notice, observation, regard **4.** celebrity, character, consequence, distinction, eminence, fame, prestige, renown, reputation ~*v.* **5.** denote, designate, indicate, mark, mention, notice, observe, perceive, record, register, remark, see

notebook commonplace book, diary, exercise book, jotter, journal, memorandum book, notepad, record book

noted acclaimed, celebrated, conspicuous, distinguished, eminent, famous, illustrious, notable, notorious, prominent, recognized, renowned, well-known

notes impressions, jottings, outline, record, report, sketch

noteworthy exceptional, extraordinary, important, notable, outstanding, remarkable, significant, unusual

nothing bagatelle, cipher, emptiness, naught, nonexistence, nothingness, nought, nullity, trifle, void, zero

notice *v.* **1.** detect, discern, distinguish, heed, mark, mind, note, observe, perceive, remark, see, spot ~*n.* **2.** cognizance, consideration, heed, note, observation, regard **3.** advice, announcement, communication, instruction, intelligence, intimation, news, notification, order, warning **4.** advertisement, comment, criticism, poster, review, sign **5.** attention, civility, respect

noticeable appreciable, clear, conspicuous, distinct, evident, manifest, observable, obvious, perceptible, plain, striking, unmistakable

notification advice, alert, announcement, declaration, information, intelligence, message, notice, notifying, publication, statement, telling, warning

notorious (nəʊˈtɔːrɪəs) *a.* **1.** known for something bad **2.** well-known —**notoriety** (nəʊtəˈraɪɪtɪ) *n.* discreditable publicity

Notts. (nɒts) Nottinghamshire

notwithstanding (nɒtwɪθˈstændɪŋ) *prep.* **1.** in spite of —*adv.* **2.** all the same —*conj.* **3.** although

nougat (ˈnuːgɑː) *n.* chewy sweet containing nuts, fruit *etc.*

nought (nɔːt) *n.* **1.** nothing **2.** cipher 0

noun (naʊn) *n.* word used as name of person, idea, or thing, substantive

nourish (ˈnʌrɪʃ) *vt.* **1.** feed **2.** nurture **3.** tend **4.** encourage —**ˈnourishment** *n.*

nous (naʊs) *n.* **1.** mind, intellect **2.** common sense

nouveau riche (nuvo ˈriʃ) *Fr.* person who has acquired wealth recently and is regarded as vulgarly ostentatious (*pl.* ***nouveaux riches*** (nuvo ˈriʃ))

nouvelle cuisine (ˈnuːvɛl kwiːˈziːn) style of preparing food, *oft.* raw or only lightly cooked, with unusual combinations of flavours

Nov. November

nova (ˈnəʊvə) *n.* star that suddenly becomes brighter then loses brightness through months or years (*pl.* **-vae** (-viː), **-s**)

novel[1] (ˈnɒvəl) *n.* fictitious tale in book form —**noveˈlette** *n.* **1.** short novel **2.** trite, oversentimental novel —**ˈnovelist** *n.* writer of novels

novel[2] (ˈnɒvəl) *a.* **1.** new, recent **2.** strange —**ˈnovelty** *n.* **1.** newness **2.** something new or unusual **3.** small ornament, trinket

novella (nəʊˈvɛlə) *n.* **1.** short narrative tale, *esp.* one having satirical point **2.** short novel (*pl.* **-s, -le** (-leɪ))

November (nəʊˈvɛmbə) *n.* eleventh month

novena (nəʊˈviːnə) *n.* *R.C.Ch.* prayers, services, lasting nine consecutive days (*pl.* **-nae** (-niː))

novice (ˈnɒvɪs) *n.* **1.** one new to anything **2.** beginner **3.** candidate for admission to religious order —**novitiate** *or* **noviciate** (nəʊˈvɪʃɪɪt, -eɪt) *n.* **1.** probationary period **2.** part of religious house for novices **3.** novice

now (naʊ) *adv.* **1.** at the present time **2.** immediately **3.** recently (*oft. with* just) —*conj.* **4.** seeing that, since —**ˈnowadays** *adv.* in these times, at present

Nowel *or* **Nowell** (nəʊˈɛl) *n.* *see* NOEL

nowhere (ˈnəʊwɛə) *adv.* not in any place or state

noxious (ˈnɒkʃəs) *a.* poisonous, harmful

nozzle (ˈnɒzəl) *n.* pointed spout, *esp.* at end of hose

Np *Chem.* neptunium

NS Nova Scotia

N.S.B. National Savings Bank

N.S.P.C.C. National Society for the Prevention of Cruelty to Children

N.S.T. Newfoundland Standard Time

N.S.W. New South Wales

N.T. **1.** National Trust **2.** New Testament **3.** Northern Territory **4.** no trumps

nt. wt. *or* **nt wt** net weight

nu (njuː) *n.* 13th letter in Gr. alphabet (N, ν)

nuance (njuːˈɑːns, ˈnjuːɑːns) *n.* delicate shade of difference, in colour, tone of voice *etc.*

nub (nʌb) *n.* **1.** small lump **2.** main point (of story *etc.*)

nubile (ˈnjuːbaɪl) *a.* marriageable

nucleus (ˈnjuːklɪəs) *n.* **1.** centre, kernel **2.** beginning meant to receive additions **3.** core of the atom (*pl.* **-lei** (-lɪaɪ)) —**ˈnuclear** *a.* of, pert. to atomic nucleus —**nucleˈonics** *pl.n.* (*with sing. v.*) branch of physics dealing with applications of nuclear energy —**nuclear bomb** bomb whose force is due to uncontrolled nuclear fusion or nuclear fission —**nuclear disarmament** elimination of nuclear weapons from country's armament —**nuclear energy** energy released by nuclear fission —**nuclear family** *Sociol., anthropol.* primary social unit consisting of parents and their offspring —**nuclear fission** disintegration of the atom —**nuclear fusion** reaction in which two nuclei combine to form nucleus with release of energy (*also* **ˈfusion**) —**nuclear physics** branch of physics concerned with structure of nucleus and particles of which it consists —**nuclear reaction** change in structure and energy content of atomic nucleus by interaction with another nucleus, particle —**nuclear reactor** *see* **reactor** *at* REACT —**nuclear winter** period of low temperatures and little light that has been suggested would occur after nuclear war —**nucleic acid** (njuːˈkliːɪk, -ˈkleɪ-) *Biochem.* any of group of complex compounds with high molecular weight that are vital constituents of all living cells

THESAURUS

notify acquaint, advise, alert, announce, apprise, declare, inform, publish, tell, warn

notion **1.** apprehension, belief, concept, conception, idea, impression, inkling, judgment, knowledge, opinion, sentiment, understanding, view **2.** caprice, desire, fancy, impulse, inclination, whim, wish

notional abstract, conceptual, fanciful, hypothetical, ideal, imaginary, speculative, theoretical, unreal, visionary

notoriety dishonour, disrepute, infamy, obloquy, opprobrium, scandal

notorious **1.** dishonourable, disreputable, infamous, opprobrious, scandalous **2.** blatant, flagrant, glaring, obvious, open, overt, patent, undisputed

notwithstanding although, despite, however, nevertheless, nonetheless, though, yet

nought naught, nil, nothing, nothingness, zero

nourish **1.** attend, feed, furnish, nurse, nurture, supply, sustain, tend **2.** comfort, cultivate, encourage, foster, maintain, promote, support

nourishment aliment, diet, food, nutriment, nutrition, sustenance, viands, victuals

nouveau riche arriviste, new-rich, parvenu, upstart

novel **1.** *adj.* different, fresh, innovative, new, original, rare, singular, strange, uncommon, unfamiliar, unusual **2.** *n.* fiction, narrative, romance, story, tale

novelty **1.** freshness, innovation, newness, oddity, originality, strangeness, surprise, unfamiliarity, uniqueness **2.** bagatelle, bauble, curiosity, gadget, gewgaw, gimcrack, gimmick, knick-knack, memento, souvenir, trifle, trinket

novice amateur, apprentice, beginner, convert, learner, neophyte, newcomer, novitiate, probationer, proselyte, pupil, tyro

now **1.** at once, immediately, instanter (*Law*), instantly, presently (*Scot. & U.S.*), promptly, straightaway **2.** any more, at the moment, nowadays, these days

nowadays any more, at the moment, in this day and age, now, these days, today

nude (nju:d) *n.* **1.** state of being naked **2.** (picture, statue *etc.* of) naked person —*a.* **3.** naked —ˈ**nudism** *n.* practice of nudity —ˈ**nudist** *n.* —ˈ**nudity** *n.*

nudge (nʌdʒ) *vt.* **1.** touch slightly with elbow —*n.* **2.** such touch

nugatory (ˈnju:gətərɪ, -trɪ) *a.* trifling, futile

nugget (ˈnʌgɪt) *n.* rough lump of native gold

nuisance (ˈnju:səns) *n.* something or someone harmful, offensive, annoying or disagreeable

N.U.J. National Union of Journalists

null (nʌl) *a.* of no effect, void —ˈ**nullify** *vt.* **1.** cancel **2.** make useless or ineffective (**-fied, -fying**) —ˈ**nullity** *n.* state of being null and void —**null set** *Maths.* set having no members (*also* **empty set**)

num. **1.** number **2.** numeral

Num. Numbers

N.U.M. National Union of Mineworkers

numb (nʌm) *a.* **1.** deprived of feeling, *esp.* by cold —*vt.* **2.** make numb **3.** deaden —ˈ**numbskull** *n. see* NUMSKULL

number (ˈnʌmbə) *n.* **1.** sum, aggregate **2.** word or symbol saying how many **3.** single issue of a paper *etc.* issued in regular series **4.** classification as to singular or plural **5.** song, piece of music **6.** performance **7.** company, collection **8.** identifying number, as of particular house, telephone *etc.* **9.** *sl.* measure, correct estimation —*vt.* **10.** count **11.** class, reckon **12.** give a number to **13.** amount to —ˈ**numberless** *a.* countless —**number crunching** the performing of complicated calculations involving large numbers, *esp.* at high speed by computer —**number one** *n.* **1.** *inf.* oneself —*a.* **2.** first in importance, urgency *etc.* —ˈ**numberplate** *n.* plate mounted on front and back of motor vehicle bearing registration number —**Number Ten** 10 Downing Street, British prime minister's official London residence

numeral (ˈnju:mərəl) *n.* sign or word denoting a number —ˈ**numerable** *a.* able to be numbered or counted —ˈ**numeracy** *n.* —**numerate** (ˈnju:mərɪt) *a.* **1.** able to use numbers in calculations —*vt.* (ˈnju:məreɪt) **2.** count —**numeˈration** *n.* —ˈ**numerator** *n.* top part of fraction, figure showing how many of the fractional units are taken —**nuˈmerical** *a.* of, in respect of, number or numbers —**numeˈrology** *n.* study of numbers, and of their supposed influence on human affairs —ˈ**numerous** *a.* many

numismatic (nju:mɪzˈmætɪk) *a.* of coins —**numisˈmatics** *pl.n.* (*with sing. v.*) the study of coins —**nuˈmismatist** *n.*

numskull *or* **numbskull** (ˈnʌmskʌl) *n.* dolt, dunce

nun (nʌn) *n.* woman living (in convent) under religious vows —ˈ**nunnery** *n.* convent of nuns

nuncio (ˈnʌnʃɪəʊ, -sɪ-) *n.* ambassador of the Pope (*pl.* **-s**)

nunny bag (ˈnʌnɪ) *C* small sealskin haversack

NUPE (ˈnju:pɪ) National Union of Public Employees

nuptial (ˈnʌpʃəl, -tʃəl) *a.* of, relating to marriage —ˈ**nuptials** *pl.n.* (*sometimes with sing. v.*) **1.** marriage **2.** wedding ceremony

N.U.R. National Union of Railwaymen

nurse (nɜ:s) *n.* **1.** person trained for care of sick or injured **2.** woman tending another's child —*vt.* **3.** act as nurse to **4.** suckle **5.** pay special attention to **6.** harbour (grudge *etc.*) —ˈ**nursery** *n.* **1.** room for children **2.** rearing place for plants —ˈ**nursemaid** *or* ˈ**nurserymaid** *n.* woman employed to look after children (*also* **nurse**) —ˈ**nurseryman** *n.* one who raises plants for sale —**nursery rhyme** short traditional verse or song for children —**nursery school** school for young children —**nursery slope** gentle slope for beginners in skiing —**nursing home** private hospital or residence for aged or infirm persons —**nursing officer** administrative head of nursing staff of hospital

nurture (ˈnɜ:tʃə) *n.* **1.** bringing up **2.** education **3.** rearing **4.** nourishment —*vt.* **5.** bring up **6.** educate

THESAURUS

nucleus basis, centre, core, focus, heart, kernel, nub, pivot

nude *au naturel*, bare, disrobed, exposed, in one's birthday suit (*Inf.*), in the altogether (*Inf.*), in the buff (*Inf.*), naked, starkers (*Inf.*), stark-naked, stripped, unclad, unclothed, uncovered, undraped, undressed

nudge *v.* bump, dig, elbow, jog, poke, prod, push, shove, touch

nudity bareness, nakedness, undress

nugget chunk, clump, hunk, lump, mass, piece

nuisance annoyance, bore, bother, inconvenience, infliction, irritation, offence, pest, plague, problem, trouble, vexation

null characterless, ineffectual, inoperative, invalid, nonexistent, null and void, powerless, useless, vain, valueless, void, worthless

nullify abolish, abrogate, annul, bring to naught, cancel, counteract, countervail, invalidate, negate, neutralize, quash, render null and void, repeal, rescind, revoke, veto, void

nullity ineffectualness, invalidity, nonexistence, powerlessness, uselessness, valuelessness, voidness, worthlessness

numb **1.** *adj.* benumbed, dead, deadened, frozen, immobilized, insensible, insensitive, paralysed, stupefied, torpid, unfeeling **2.** *v.* benumb, deaden, dull, freeze, immobilize, paralyse, stun, stupefy

number *n.* **1.** character, count, digit, figure, integer, numeral, sum, total, unit **2.** aggregate, amount, collection, company, crowd, horde, many, multitude, quantity, throng **3.** copy, edition, imprint, issue, printing ~*v.* **4.** account, add, calculate, compute, count, enumerate, include, reckon, tell, total

numberless countless, endless, infinite, innumerable, multitudinous, myriad, unnumbered, untold

numeral character, cipher, digit, figure, integer, number, symbol

numerous abundant, copious, many, plentiful, profuse, several

nunnery abbey, cloister, convent, house, monastery

nuptials espousal (*Archaic*), marriage, matrimony, wedding

nurse *v.* **1.** care for, look after, minister to, tend, treat **2.** breast-feed, feed, nourish, nurture, suckle, wet-nurse **3.** *Fig.* cherish, cultivate, encourage, foster, harbour, keep alive, preserve, promote, succour, support

nurture *n.* **1.** diet, food, nourishment **2.** development, discipline, education, instruction, rearing, training, upbringing ~*v.* **3.** bring up, cultivate, develop, discipline, educate, instruct, rear, school, train

N.U.S. 1. National Union of Seamen 2. National Union of Students

nut (nʌt) *n.* 1. fruit consisting of hard shell and kernel 2. hollow metal collar into which a screw fits 3. *inf.* head 4. *inf.* eccentric or crazy person (*also* **ˈnutter**) —*vi.* 5. gather nuts (**-tt-**) —**ˈnutty** *a.* 1. of, like nut 2. pleasant to taste and bite 3. *sl.* insane, crazy (*also* **nuts**) —**ˈnutcase** *n. sl.* insane or foolish person —**ˈnutcracker** *n.* 1. (*oft. pl.*) device for cracking shells of nuts 2. Old World or North American bird having speckled plumage and feeding on nuts *etc.* —**ˈnuthatch** *n.* small songbird —**ˈnutmeg** *n.* aromatic seed of Indian tree —**ˈnutshell** *n.* shell around kernel of nut —**in a nutshell** in essence; briefly —**nuts and bolts** *inf.* essential or practical details

N.U.T. National Union of Teachers

nutria (ˈnjuːtrɪə) *n.* fur of coypu

nutrient (ˈnjuːtrɪənt) *a.* 1. nourishing —*n.* 2. something nutritious

nutriment (ˈnjuːtrɪmənt) *n.* nourishing food —**nuˈtrition** *n.* 1. receiving foods 2. act of nourishing —**nuˈtritious** *or* **ˈnutritive** *a.* 1. nourishing 2. promoting growth

nux vomica (ˈnʌks ˈvɒmɪkə) seed of tree which yields strychnine

nuzzle (ˈnʌzˀl) *v.* 1. burrow, press with nose —*vi.* 2. nestle

NV Nevada

NW northwest(ern)

N.W.T. Northwest Territories (of Canada)

NY New York

nylon (ˈnaɪlɒn) *n.* 1. synthetic material used for fabrics, bristles, ropes *etc.* —*pl.* 2. stockings made of this

nymph (nɪmf) *n.* legendary semidivine maiden of sea, woods, mountains *etc.*

nymphomania (nɪmfəˈmeɪnɪə) *n.* abnormally intense sexual desire in women —**nymphoˈmaniac** *n.*

N.Z. *or* **N. Zeal.** New Zealand

THESAURUS

nut 1. kernel, seed, stone 2. *Sl.* brain, head, mind, reason, senses 3. *Sl.* crackpot (*Inf.*), crank (*Inf.*), eccentric, loony (*Sl.*), lunatic, madman, maniac, nutcase (*Sl.*)

nutritious alimental, alimentative, beneficial, healthful, health-giving, invigorating, nourishing, nutritive, strengthening, wholesome

nuts bananas (*Brit. sl.*), batty (*Sl.*), crazy (*Inf.*), demented, deranged, eccentric, insane, irrational, loony (*Sl.*), loopy (*Inf.*), mad, nutty (*Sl.*)

O

o *or* **O** (əʊ) *n.* **1.** 15th letter of English alphabet **2.** any of several speech sounds represented by this letter, as in *code, pot, cow* or *form* **3.** *see* NOUGHT (*pl.* **o's, O's** *or* **Os**)

O[1] **1.** *Chem.* oxygen **2.** human blood type of ABO group **3.** Old

O[2] (əʊ) *interj.* **1.** *see* OH **2.** exclamation introducing invocation, entreaty, wish *etc.*

o' (ə) *prep. inf.* of

O'- (*comb. form*) in surnames of Irish Gaelic origin, descendant of, as in *O'Corrigan*

oaf (əʊf) *n.* **1.** lout **2.** dolt

oak (əʊk) *n.* **1.** common, deciduous forest tree —*pl.* **2.** (**O-**) horse race for fillies held annually at Epsom —**ˈoaken** *a.* of oak —**oak apple** *or* **gall** round gall on oak trees

oakum (ˈəʊkəm) *n.* loose fibre got by unravelling old rope

O. & M. organization and method (in studies of working methods)

O.A.P. old age pensioner

oar (ɔː) *n.* **1.** wooden lever with broad blade worked by the hands to propel boat **2.** oarsman —*v.* **3.** row —**ˈoarsman** *n.* —**ˈoarsmanship** *n.* skill in rowing

OAS **1.** Organization of American States **2.** *Organisation de l'Armée Secrète;* organization which opposed Algerian independence by acts of terrorism

oasis (əʊˈeɪsɪs) *n.* fertile spot in desert (*pl.* **oases** (əʊˈeɪsiːz))

oast (əʊst) *n.* kiln for drying hops

oat (əʊt) *n.* **1.** (*usu. pl.*) grain of cereal plant **2.** the plant —**ˈoaten** *a.* —**ˈoatmeal** *n.*

oath (əʊθ) *n.* **1.** confirmation of truth of statement by naming something sacred **2.** curse (*pl.* **oaths** (əʊðz))

OAU Organization of African Unity

ob. **1.** (on tombstones *etc.*) obiit (*Lat.*, he or she died) **2.** obiter (*Lat.*, incidentally, in passing) **3.** oboe

ob- (*comb. form*) inverse; inversely, as in *obovate*

obbligato *or* **obligato** (ɒblɪˈgɑːtəʊ) *Mus. a.* **1.** not to be omitted —*n.* **2.** essential part in score (*pl.* **-s, -ti** (-tiː))

obdurate (ˈɒbdjʊrɪt) *a.* stubborn, unyielding —**ˈobduracy** *or* **ˈobdurateness** *n.*

O.B.E. Officer of the Order of the British Empire

obedience (əˈbiːdɪəns) *n.* submission to authority —**oˈbedient** *a.* **1.** willing to obey **2.** compliant **3.** dutiful —**oˈbediently** *adv.*

obeisance (əʊˈbeɪsəns, əʊˈbiː-) *n.* bow; curtsy

obelisk (ˈɒbɪlɪsk) *n.* tapering rectangular stone column with pyramidal apex

obese (əʊˈbiːs) *a.* very fat, corpulent —**oˈbesity** *n.*

obey (əˈbeɪ) *vt.* **1.** do the bidding of **2.** act in accordance with —*vi.* **3.** do as ordered **4.** submit to authority

obfuscate (ˈɒbfʌskeɪt) *vt.* **1.** perplex **2.** darken

obituary (əˈbɪtjʊərɪ) *n.* **1.** notice, record of death **2.** biographical sketch of deceased person, *esp.* in newspaper (*also* (*inf.*) **ˈobit**)

obj. **1.** object **2.** objective

object[1] (ˈɒbdʒɪkt) *n.* **1.** material thing **2.** that to which feeling or action is directed **3.** end, aim **4.** *Gram.* word dependent on verb or preposition —**object lesson** lesson with practical and concrete illustration —**no object** not an obstacle or hindrance

object[2] (əbˈdʒɛkt) *vt.* **1.** state in opposition —*vi.* **2.** feel dislike or reluctance (to something) —**obˈjection** *n.* —**obˈjectionable** *a.* **1.** disagreeable **2.** justly liable to objection —**obˈjector** *n.*

THESAURUS

oaf blockhead, bonehead (*Sl.*), booby, brute, clod, dolt, dullard, dummy (*Sl.*), dunce, fool, galoot (*Sl.*), gawk, goon, gorilla (*Inf.*), halfwit, idiot, imbecile, lout, lummox (*Inf.*), moron, nincompoop, sap (*Sl.*), simpleton

oath **1.** affirmation, avowal, bond, pledge, promise, sworn statement, vow, word **2.** blasphemy, curse, cuss (*Inf.*), expletive, imprecation, malediction, profanity, strong language, swearword

obdurate adamant, callous, dogged, firm, fixed, hard, hard-hearted, harsh, immovable, implacable, indurate (*Rare*), inexorable, inflexible, iron, mulish, obstinate, perverse, pig-headed, proof against persuasion, relentless, stiff-necked, stubborn, unbending, unfeeling, unimpressible, unrelenting, unshakable, unyielding

obedience accordance, acquiescence, agreement, compliance, conformability, deference, docility, dutifulness, duty, observance, respect, reverence, submission, submissiveness, subservience, tractability

obedient acquiescent, amenable, biddable, compliant, deferential, docile, duteous, dutiful, law-abiding, observant, regardful, respectful, submissive, subservient, tractable, under control, well-trained, yielding

obelisk column, monolith, monument, needle, pillar, shaft

obese corpulent, Falstaffian, fat, fleshy, gross, heavy, outsize, overweight, paunchy, plump, podgy, portly, roly-poly, rotund, stout, tubby, well-upholstered (*Inf.*)

obesity bulk, corpulence, *embonpoint*, fatness, fleshiness, grossness, overweight, portliness, stoutness, tubbiness, weight problem

obey **1.** abide by, act upon, adhere to, be ruled by, carry out, comply, conform, discharge, do what is expected, embrace, execute, follow, fulfil, heed, keep, mind, observe, perform, respond, serve **2.** bow to, come to heel, do what one is told, get into line, give in, give way, knuckle under (*Inf.*), submit, surrender (to), take orders from, toe the line, yield

object[1] *n.* **1.** article, body, entity, fact, item, phenomenon, reality, thing **2.** aim, butt, focus, recipient, target, victim **3.** design, end, end in view, end purpose, goal, idea, intent, intention, motive, objective, point, purpose, reason

object[2] *v.* argue against, demur, expostulate, oppose, protest raise objections, take exception

objection cavil, censure, counter-argument, demur, doubt, exception, niggle (*Inf.*), opposition, protest, remonstrance, scruple

objectionable abhorrent, deplorable, disagreeable, dislikable, displeasing, distasteful, exceptionable,

objective (əbˈdʒɛktɪv) *a.* **1.** external to the mind **2.** impartial —*n.* **3.** thing or place aimed at —**objecˈtivity** *n.*

objet d'art (ɔbʒɛ ˈdaːr) *Fr.* small object considered to be of artistic worth (*pl.* ***objets d'art*** (ɔbʒɛ ˈdaːr))

oblate[1] (ˈɒbleɪt) *a.* (of sphere) flattened at the poles

oblate[2] (ˈɒbleɪt) *n.* person dedicated to religious work

oblation (ɒˈbleɪʃən) *n.* offering —**obˈlational** *a.*

obligato (ɒblɪˈgɑːtəʊ) *see* OBBLIGATO

oblige (əˈblaɪdʒ) *vt.* **1.** bind morally or legally to do service to **2.** compel —**obligate** (ˈɒblɪgeɪt) *vt.* **1.** bind, *esp.* by legal contract **2.** put under obligation —**obligation** (ɒblɪˈgeɪʃən) *n.* **1.** binding duty, promise **2.** debt of gratitude —**obligatory** (ɒˈblɪgətərɪ, -trɪ) *a.* **1.** required **2.** binding —**oˈbliging** *a.* ready to serve others, civil, helpful, courteous

oblique (əˈbliːk) *a.* **1.** slanting **2.** indirect —**oˈbliquely** *adv.* —**obliquity** (əˈblɪkwɪtɪ) *n.* **1.** slant **2.** dishonesty —**oblique angle** angle not a right angle

obliterate (əˈblɪtəreɪt) *vt.* blot out, efface, destroy completely —**obliteˈration** *n.*

oblivion (əˈblɪvɪən) *n.* forgetting or being forgotten —**obˈlivious** *a.* **1.** forgetful **2.** unaware

oblong (ˈɒblɒŋ) *a.* **1.** rectangular, with adjacent sides unequal —*n.* **2.** oblong figure

obloquy (ˈɒbləkwɪ) *n.* **1.** reproach, abuse **2.** disgrace **3.** detraction

obnoxious (əbˈnɒkʃəs) *a.* offensive, disliked, odious

oboe (ˈəʊbəʊ) *n.* woodwind instrument, hautboy —ˈ**oboist** *n.*

obs. **1.** observation **2.** obsolete

obscene (əbˈsiːn) *a.* **1.** indecent, lewd **2.** repulsive —**obscenity** (əbˈsɛnɪtɪ) *n.*

obscure (əbˈskjʊə) *a.* **1.** unclear, indistinct **2.** unexplained **3.** dark, dim **4.** humble —*vt.* **5.** make unintelligible **6.** dim **7.** conceal —**obˈscurant** *n.* one who opposes enlightenment or reform —**obscuˈrantism** *n.* —**obˈscurity** *n.* **1.** indistinctness **2.** lack of intelligibility **3.** darkness **4.** obscure, *esp.* unrecognized, place or position **5.** retirement

THESAURUS

indecorous, insufferable, intolerable, noxious, obnoxious, offensive, regrettable, repugnant, unacceptable, undesirable, unpleasant, unseemly, unsociable

objective **1.** *adj.* detached, disinterested, dispassionate, equitable, even-handed, fair, impartial, impersonal, judicial, just, open-minded, unbiased, uncoloured, unemotional, uninvolved, unprejudiced **2.** *n.* aim, ambition, aspiration, design, end, end in view, goal, intention, mark, object, purpose, target

objectivity detachment, disinterest, disinterestedness, dispassion, equitableness, impartiality, impersonality

obligation **1.** accountability, accountableness, burden, charge, compulsion, duty, liability, must, onus, requirement, responsibility, trust **2.** agreement, bond, commitment, contract, debt, engagement, promise, understanding

obligatory binding, coercive, compulsory, *de rigueur*, enforced, essential, imperative, mandatory, necessary, required, requisite, unavoidable

oblige bind, coerce, compel, constrain, force, impel, make, necessitate, obligate, require

obliging accommodating, agreeable, amiable, civil, complaisant, considerate, cooperative, courteous, eager to please, friendly, good-natured, helpful, kind, polite, willing

oblique **1.** angled, aslant, at an angle, inclined, slanted, slanting, sloped, sloping, tilted **2.** backhanded, circuitous, circumlocutory, evasive, implied, indirect, roundabout, sidelong

obliquely **1.** aslant, aslope, at an angle, diagonally, slantwise **2.** circuitously, evasively, in a roundabout manner *or* way, indirectly, not in so many words

obliterate annihilate, blot out, cancel, delete, destroy, destroy root and branch, efface, eradicate, erase, expunge, extirpate, root out, wipe off the face of the earth, wipe out

obliteration annihilation, deletion, effacement, elimination, eradication, erasure, expunction, extirpation, wiping (blotting, rooting, sponging) out

oblivion abeyance, disregard, forgetfulness, insensibility, neglect, obliviousness, unawareness, unconsciousness, (waters of) Lethe

oblivious blind, careless, deaf, disregardful, forgetful, heedless, ignorant, inattentive, insensible, neglectful, negligent, regardless, unaware, unconcerned, unconscious, unmindful, unobservant

obnoxious abhorrent, abominable, detestable, disagreeable, disgusting, dislikable, foul, hateable, hateful, horrid, insufferable, loathsome, nasty, nauseating, objectionable, odious, offensive, repellent, reprehensible, repugnant, repulsive, revolting, sickening, unpleasant

obscene **1.** bawdy, blue, coarse, dirty, disgusting, Fescennine (*Rare*), filthy, foul, gross, immodest, immoral, improper, impure, indecent, lewd, licentious, loose, offensive, pornographic, prurient, ribald, salacious, scabrous, shameless, smutty, suggestive, unchaste, unwholesome **2.** *Fig.* atrocious, evil, heinous, loathsome, outrageous, shocking, sickening, vile, wicked

obscenity **1.** bawdiness, blueness, coarseness, dirtiness, filthiness, foulness, grossness, immodesty, impurity, lewdness, licentiousness, pornography, prurience, salacity, smuttiness, suggestiveness, vileness **2.** abomination, affront, atrocity, blight, evil, offence, outrage, vileness, wrong

obscure *adj.* **1.** abstruse, ambiguous, arcane, concealed, confusing, cryptic, deep, doubtful, enigmatic, esoteric, hazy, hidden, incomprehensible, indefinite, intricate, involved, mysterious, occult, opaque, recondite, unclear, vague **2.** blurred, clouded, cloudy, dark, dim, dusky, faint, gloomy, indistinct, murky, obfuscated, shadowy, shady, sombre, tenebrous, unlit, veiled **3.** humble, inconspicuous, inglorious, little-known, lowly, minor, nameless, out-of-the-way, remote, undistinguished, unheard-of, unhonoured, unimportant, unknown, unnoted, unseen, unsung ~*v.* **4.** conceal, cover, disguise, hide, muddy, obfuscate, screen, throw a veil over, veil **5.** adumbrate, bedim, befog, block, block out, blur, cloak, cloud, darken, dim, dull, eclipse, mask, overshadow, shade, shroud

obscurity **1.** abstruseness, ambiguity, complexity, impenetrableness, incomprehensibility, intricacy,

obsequies (ˈɒbsɪkwɪz) *pl.n.* funeral rites

obsequious (əbˈsiːkwɪəs) *a.* servile, fawning

observe (əbˈzɜːv) *vt.* **1.** notice, remark **2.** watch **3.** note systematically **4.** keep, follow *—vi.* **5.** make a remark **—obˈservable** *a.* **—obˈservably** *adv.* **—obˈservance** *n.* **1.** paying attention **2.** keeping **—obˈservant** *a.* quick to notice **—obserˈvation** *n.* **1.** action, habit of observing **2.** noticing **3.** remark **—obˈservatory** *n.* place for watching stars *etc.* **—obˈserver** *n.*

obsess (əbˈsɛs) *vt.* haunt, fill the mind of **—obˈsession** *n.* **1.** fixed idea **2.** domination of the mind by one idea **—obˈsessive** *a.*

obsidian (ɒbˈsɪdɪən) *n.* fused volcanic rock, forming hard, dark, natural glass

obsolete (ˈɒbsəliːt, ɒbsəˈliːt) *a.* disused, out of date **—obsoˈlescent** *a.* going out of use

obstacle (ˈɒbstəkˀl) *n.* **1.** hindrance **2.** impediment, barrier, obstruction

obstetrics (ɒbˈstɛtrɪks) *pl.n.* (*with sing. v.*) branch of medicine concerned with childbirth and care of women before and after childbirth **—obˈstetric(al)** *a.* **—obsteˈtrician** *n.*

obstinate (ˈɒbstɪnɪt) *a.* **1.** stubborn **2.** self-willed **3.** unyielding **4.** hard to overcome or cure **—ˈobstinacy** *n.* **—ˈobstinately** *adv.*

obstreperous (əbˈstrɛpərəs) *a.* unruly, noisy, boisterous

obstruct (əbˈstrʌkt) *vt.* **1.** block up **2.** hinder, impede **—obˈstruction** *n.* **—obˈstructionist** *n.* one who deliberately opposes transaction of business **—obˈstructive** *a.*

obtain (əbˈteɪn) *vt.* **1.** get **2.** acquire **3.** procure by effort *—vi.* **4.** be customary **—obˈtainable** *a.* procurable

obtrude (əbˈtruːd) *v.* thrust forward unduly **—obˈtrusion** *n.* **—obˈtrusive** *a.* forward, pushing **—obˈtrusively** *adv.*

THESAURUS

reconditeness, vagueness **2.** darkness, dimness, dusk, duskiness, gloom, haze, haziness, indistinctness, murkiness, shadowiness, shadows **3.** inconspicuousness, ingloriousness, insignificance, lowliness, namelessness, nonrecognition, unimportance

observable apparent, appreciable, clear, detectable, discernible, evident, noticeable, obvious, open, patent, perceivable, perceptible, recognizable, visible

observance adherence to, attention, carrying out, celebration, compliance, discharge, fulfilment, heeding, honouring, notice, observation, performance

observant alert, attentive, eagle-eyed, heedful, mindful, obedient, perceptive, quick, sharp-eyed, submissive, vigilant, watchful, wide-awake

observation 1. attention, cognition, consideration, examination, experience, information, inspection, knowledge, monitoring, notice, review, scrutiny, study, surveillance, watching **2.** annotation, comment, finding, note, obiter dictum, opinion, pronouncement, reflection, remark, thought, utterance

observe 1. detect, discern, discover, espy, note, notice, perceive, see, spot, witness **2.** contemplate, keep an eye on (*Inf.*), keep under observation, look at, monitor, pay attention to, regard, scrutinize, study, survey, view, watch **3.** animadvert, comment, declare, mention, note, opine, remark, say, state **4.** abide by, adhere to, comply, conform to, follow, fulfil, heed, honour, keep, mind, obey, perform, respect **5.** celebrate, commemorate, keep, remember, solemnize

observer beholder, bystander, commentator, eyewitness, looker-on, onlooker, spectator, spotter, viewer, watcher, witness

obsess bedevil, be on one's mind, be uppermost in one's thoughts, consume, dominate, engross, grip, haunt, monopolize, plague, possess, preoccupy, prey on one's mind, rule, torment

obsession bee in one's bonnet (*Inf.*), complex, enthusiasm, fetish, fixation, hang-up (*Inf.*), *idée fixe*, infatuation, mania, phobia, preoccupation, ruling passion, thing (*Inf.*)

obsessive besetting, compulsive, consuming, fixed, gripping, haunting, tormenting, unforgettable

obsolescent declining, dying out, on the decline, on the wane, on the way out, past its prime, waning

obsolete anachronistic, ancient, antediluvian, antiquated, antique, archaic, bygone, dated, *démodé*, discarded, disused, extinct, musty, old, old-fashioned, old hat, out, outmoded, out of date, out of fashion, out of the ark (*Inf.*), outworn, passé, superannuated, *vieux jeu*

obstacle bar, barrier, check, difficulty, hindrance, hitch, hurdle, impediment, interference, interruption, obstruction, snag, stumbling block

obstinacy doggedness, firmness, inflexibility, intransigence, mulishness, obduracy, perseverance, persistence, pertinacity, pig-headedness, resoluteness, stubbornness, tenacity, wilfulness

obstinate contumacious, determined, dogged, firm, headstrong, immovable, inflexible, intractable, intransigent, mulish, opinionated, persistent, pertinacious, perverse, pig-headed, recalcitrant, refractory, self-willed, steadfast, strong-minded, stubborn, tenacious, unyielding, wilful

obstreperous boisterous, clamorous, disorderly, loud, noisy, out of control, out of hand, rackety, rambunctious (*Inf.*), rampaging, raucous, restive, riotous, rip-roaring (*Inf.*), roistering, roisterous, rough, rowdy, stroppy (*Brit. sl.*), tempestuous, tumultuous, turbulent, uncontrolled, undisciplined, unmanageable, unruly, uproarious, vociferous, wild

obstruct arrest, bar, barricade, block, bring to a standstill, check, choke, clog, cumber, curb, cut off, frustrate, get in the way of, hamper, hamstring, hide, hinder, hold up, impede, inhibit, interfere with, interrupt, mask, obscure, prevent, restrict, retard, shield, shut off, slow down, stop, thwart, trammel

obstruction bar, barricade, barrier, blockage, check, difficulty, hindrance, impediment, snag, stop, stoppage, trammel

obstructive awkward, blocking, delaying, hindering, inhibiting, preventative, restrictive, stalling, uncooperative, unhelpful

obtain 1. achieve, acquire, attain, come by, earn, gain, get, get hold of, get one's hands on, procure, secure **2.** be in force, be prevalent, be the case, exist, hold, prevail, stand

obtainable achievable, at hand, attainable, available, on tap (*Inf.*), procurable, ready, realizable, to be had

obtrusive forward, importunate, interfering, intrusive, meddling, nosy, officious, prying, pushy (*Inf.*)

obtuse (əbˈtjuːs) *a.* **1.** dull of perception **2.** stupid **3.** (of angle) greater than right angle **4.** not pointed —**obˈtusely** *adv.*

obverse (ˈɒbvɜːs) *n.* **1.** fact, idea *etc.* which is the complement of another **2.** side of coin, medal *etc.* that has the principal design —*a.* **3.** facing the observer **4.** complementary, opposite

obviate (ˈɒbvɪeɪt) *vt.* remove, make unnecessary

obvious (ˈɒbvɪəs) *a.* **1.** clear, evident **2.** wanting in subtlety

O.C. Officer Commanding

occasion (əˈkeɪʒən) *n.* **1.** time when thing happens **2.** reason, need **3.** opportunity **4.** special event —*vt.* **5.** cause —**ocˈcasional** *a.* **1.** happening, found now and then **2.** produced for some special event, as *occasional music* —**ocˈcasionally** *adv.* sometimes, now and then

Occident (ˈɒksɪdənt) *n.* the West —**Occiˈdental** *a.*

occlude (əˈkluːd) *vt.* shut in or out —**ocˈclusion** *n.* —**ocˈclusive** *a.* serving to occlude —**occluded front** *Met.* line occurring where cold front of depression has overtaken warm front, raising warm sector from ground level (*also* **ocˈclusion**)

occult (ɒˈkʌlt, ˈɒkʌlt) *a.* **1.** secret, mysterious **2.** supernatural —*n.* **3.** esoteric knowledge —*vt.* (ɒˈkʌlt) **4.** hide from view —**occulˈtation** *n.* eclipse —**ˈoccultism** *n.* study of supernatural —**ocˈcultness** *n.* mystery

occupy (ˈɒkjʊpaɪ) *vt.* **1.** inhabit, fill **2.** employ **3.** take possession of (**-pied, -pying**) —**ˈoccupancy** *n.* **1.** fact of occupying **2.** residing —**ˈoccupant** *n.* —**occuˈpation** *n.* **1.** employment **2.** pursuit **3.** fact of occupying **4.** seizure —**occuˈpational** *a.* **1.** pert. to occupation, *esp.* of diseases arising from a particular occupation **2.** pert. to use of occupations, *eg* craft, hobbies *etc.* as means of rehabilitation —**ˈoccupier** *n.* tenant —**occupational therapy** *Med.* therapeutic use of crafts, hobbies *etc.*, esp. in rehabilitation of emotionally disturbed patients

occur (əˈkɜː) *vi.* **1.** happen **2.** come to mind (**-rr-**) —**ocˈcurrence** *n.* happening

ocean (ˈəʊʃən) *n.* **1.** great body of water **2.** large division of this **3.** the sea —**oceanic** (əʊʃɪˈænɪk) *a.* —**oceanˈographer** *n.* —**oceanˈography** *n.* study of physical and biological features of the sea —**oceanˈology** *n.* study of the sea, *esp.* of its economic geography —**ocean-going** *a.* (of ship, boat *etc.*) suited for travel on ocean

ocelot (ˈɒsɪlɒt, ˈəʊ-) *n.* Amer. leopard

oche (ˈɒkɪ) *n.* *Darts* mark on floor behind which player must stand to throw

ochre *or U.S.* **ocher** (ˈəʊkə) *n.* various earths used as yellow or brown pigments —**ochreous** (ˈəʊkrɪəs, ˈəʊkərəs), **ochrous** (ˈəʊkrəs), **ochry** (ˈəʊkərɪ, ˈəʊkrɪ) *or U.S.* **ˈocherous, ˈochery** *a.*

o'clock (əˈklɒk) *adv.* by the clock

OCR optical character reader *or* recognition

Oct. October

oct- (*comb. form*) eight

octagon (ˈɒktəgən) *n.* plane figure with eight angles —**ocˈtagonal** *a.*

octahedron (ɒktəˈhiːdrən) *n.* solid figure with eight sides (*pl.* **-s, -dra** (-drə))

octane (ˈɒkteɪn) *n.* ingredient of motor fuel —**octane rating** measure of quality or type of petrol

octave (ˈɒktɪv) *n.* **1.** *Mus.* eighth note above or below given note **2.** this space **3.** eight lines of verse

octavo (ɒkˈteɪvəʊ) *n.* book in which each sheet is folded three times forming eight leaves (*pl.* **-s**)

octennial (ɒkˈtɛnɪəl) *a.* lasting, happening every eight years

octet (ɒkˈtɛt) *n.* **1.** group of eight **2.** music for eight instruments or singers

October (ɒkˈtəʊbə) *n.* tenth month

THESAURUS

obvious apparent, clear, clear as a bell, conspicuous, distinct, evident, indisputable, manifest, much in evidence, noticeable, open, overt, palpable, patent, perceptible, plain, plain as the nose on your face (*Inf.*), pronounced, recognizable, right under one's nose (*Inf.*), self-evident, self-explanatory, staring one in the face (*Inf.*), sticking out a mile (*Inf.*), straightforward, transparent, unconcealed, undeniable, undisguised, unmistakable, unsubtle, visible

occasion *n.* **1.** chance, convenience, incident, moment, occurrence, opening, opportunity, time **2.** affair, celebration, event, experience, occurrence **3.** call, cause, excuse, ground(s), inducement, influence, justification, motive, prompting, provocation, reason ~*v.* **4.** bring about, cause, create, effect, elicit, engender, evoke, generate, give rise to, induce, influence, inspire, lead to, move, originate, persuade, produce, prompt, provoke

occasional casual, desultory, incidental, infrequent, intermittent, irregular, odd, rare, sporadic, uncommon

occasionally at intervals, at times, (every) now and then, every so often, from time to time, irregularly, now and again, off and on, on and off, once in a while, on occasion, periodically, sometimes

occupant addressee, denizen, holder, incumbent, indweller, inhabitant, inmate, lessee, occupier, resident, tenant, user

occupation **1.** activity, business, calling, craft, employment, job, line (of work), post, profession, pursuit, trade, vocation, walk of life, work **2.** control, holding, occupancy, possession, residence, tenancy, tenure, use **3.** conquest, foreign rule, invasion, seizure, subjugation

occupied **1.** busy, employed, engaged, hard at it (*Inf.*), tied up (*Inf.*), working **2.** engaged, full, in use, taken, unavailable **3.** full, inhabited, lived-in, peopled, settled, tenanted

occupy **1.** *Often passive* absorb, amuse, busy, divert, employ, engage, engross, entertain, hold the attention of, immerse, interest, involve, keep busy *or* occupied, monopolize, preoccupy, take up, tie up **2.** be established in, be in residence in, dwell in, ensconce oneself in, establish oneself in, inhabit, live in, own, possess, reside in, stay in (*Scot.*), tenant **3.** cover, fill, hold, permeate, pervade, take up, use, utilize **4.** capture, garrison, hold, invade, keep, overrun, seize, take over, take possession of

occur **1.** arise, befall, betide, chance, come about, come off (*Inf.*), come to pass (*Archaic*), crop up (*Inf.*), eventuate, happen, materialize, result, take place, turn up (*Inf.*) **2.** *With* **to** come to mind, come to one, cross one's mind, dawn on, enter one's head, spring to mind, strike one, suggest (offer, present) itself

occurrence adventure, affair, circumstance, episode, event, happening, incident, instance, proceeding, transaction

octogenarian (ɒktəʊdʒɪˈnɛərɪən) *or* **octogenary** (ɒkˈtɒdʒɪnərɪ) *n.* **1.** person aged between eighty and ninety —*a.* **2.** of an octogenarian

octopus (ˈɒktəpəs) *n.* mollusc with eight arms covered with suckers —**ˈoctopod** *n./a.* (mollusc) with eight feet

octosyllable (ˈɒktəsɪləbˀl) *n.* word, line of verse of eight syllables

OCTU (ˈɒktuː) UK Officer Cadets' Training Unit

ocular (ˈɒkjʊlə) *a.* of eye or sight —**ˈocularly** *adv.*

oculist (ˈɒkjʊlɪst) *n. Med. obs.* ophthalmologist

O.D. *Med.* overdose

odd (ɒd) *a.* **1.** strange, queer **2.** incidental, random **3.** that is one in addition when the rest have been divided into equal groups **4.** not even **5.** not part of a set —**ˈoddity** *n.* **1.** odd person or thing **2.** quality of being odd —**ˈoddment** *n.* (oft. *pl.*) **1.** remnant **2.** trifle —**odds** *pl.n.* (*with* on *or* against) **1.** advantage conceded in betting **2.** likelihood —**odd-jobman** *or* **odd-jobber** *n.* person who does casual work, *esp.* domestic repairs —**odds-on** *a.* **1.** (of chance, horse *etc.*) rated at even money or less to win **2.** regarded as more or most likely to win, happen *etc.* —**odds and ends** odd fragments or scraps

ode (əʊd) *n.* lyric poem on particular subject

odium (ˈəʊdɪəm) *n.* hatred, widespread dislike —**ˈodious** *a.* hateful, repulsive, obnoxious

odometer (ɒˈdɒmɪtə, əʊ-) *n.* **US** mileometer

odour *or U.S.* **odor** (ˈəʊdə) *n.* smell —**odoˈriferous** *a.* spreading an odour —**ˈodorous** *a.* **1.** fragrant **2.** scented —**ˈodourless** *or U.S.* **ˈodorless** *a.*

Odyssey (ˈɒdɪsɪ) *n.* **1.** Homer's epic describing Odysseus' return from Troy **2.** any long adventurous journey

OE, O.E., *or* **OE.** Old English (language)

O.E.C.D. Organization for Economic Cooperation and Development

oedema *or* **edema** (ɪˈdiːmə) *n.* swelling in body tissues, due to accumulation of fluid (*pl.* **-mata** (-mətə))

Oedipus complex (ˈiːdɪpəs) *Psychoanal.* usu. unconscious desire of child to possess sexually parent of opposite sex —**ˈoedipal** *or* **oediˈpean** *a.*

o'er (ɔː, əʊə) *prep./adv. Poet.* over

oesophagus *or U.S.* **esophagus** (iːˈsɒfəgəs) *n.* canal from mouth to stomach, gullet (*pl.* **-gi** (-gaɪ)) —**oesophageal** *or U.S.* **esophageal** (iːsɒfəˈdʒiːəl) *a.*

oestrogen (ˈiːstrədʒən, ˈɛstrə-) *or U.S.* **estrogen** *n.* hormone in females *esp.* controlling changes, cycles in reproductive organs

of (ɒv; *unstressed* əv) *prep.* denotes removal, separation, ownership, attribute, material, quality

off (ɒf) *adv.* **1.** away —*prep.* **2.** away from —*a.* **3.** not operative **4.** cancelled or postponed **5.** bad, sour *etc.* **6.** distant **7.** (of horses, vehicles *etc.*) right **8.** *Cricket* to bowler's left —**ˈoffing** *n.* part of sea visible to observer on ship or shore —**ˈoffbeat** *n.* **1.** *Mus.* any of normally unaccented beats in bar —*a.* **2.** unusual, unconventional or eccentric —**off chance** slight possibility —**off colour** slightly ill —**off cut** piece of paper, wood *etc.* remaining after main pieces have been cut; remnant —**offˈhand** *a.* **1.** without previous thought **2.** curt (*also* **offˈhanded**) —**off key 1.** *Mus.* not in correct key; out of tune **2.** out of keeping; discordant —**off-licence** *n.* place where alcoholic drinks are sold for consumption elsewhere —**off line 1.** of or concerned with part of computer system not connected to central processing unit but controlled by computer storage device **2.** disconnected from computer —**off-load** *vt.* get rid of (something unpleasant or burdensome), as by delegation to another —**off-peak** *a.* of or relating to services as used outside periods of intensive use —**off-putting** *a.* **UK** *inf.* disconcerting or disturbing —**offset** (ˈɒfsɛt) *n.* **1.** that which counterbalances, compensates **2.** method of printing —*vt.* (ɒfˈsɛt) **3.** counterbalance, compensate for **4.** print (text *etc.*) using offset process —**ˈoffshoot** *n.* **1.** shoot or branch growing from main stem of plant **2.** something that develops from principal source —**ˈoffˈside** *a./adv. Sport* illegally forward —**ˈoffspring** *n.* children, issue —**off-the-peg** *a.* (of clothing) ready to wear; not produced especially for person buying —**in the offing** likely to happen soon —**on the off chance** with hope

off. **1.** office **2.** officer **3.** official

offal (ˈɒfˀl) *n.* **1.** edible entrails of animal **2.** refuse

THESAURUS

odd **1.** abnormal, atypical, bizarre, curious, deviant, different, eccentric, exceptional, extraordinary, fantastic, freak, freakish, freaky (*Sl.*), funny, irregular, kinky (*Sl.*), outlandish, out of the ordinary, peculiar, quaint, queer, rare, remarkable, singular, strange, uncanny, uncommon, unconventional, unusual, weird, whimsical **2.** casual, fragmentary, incidental, irregular, miscellaneous, occasional, periodic, random, seasonal, sundry, varied, various **3.** leftover, lone, remaining, single, solitary, spare, surplus, unconsumed, uneven, unmatched, unpaired

oddity **1.** abnormality, anomaly, eccentricity, freak, idiosyncrasy, irregularity, kink (*Sl.*), peculiarity, phenomenon, quirk, rarity **2.** card (*Inf.*), crank (*Inf.*), fish out of water, maverick, misfit, oddball (*Inf., chiefly U.S.*), odd bird (*Inf.*), odd fish (*Brit. inf.*), rara avis, screwball (*U.S. sl.*), weirdie *or* weirdo (*Inf.*) **3.** abnormality, bizarreness, eccentricity, extraordinariness, freakishness, incongruity, oddness, outlandishness, peculiarity, queerness, singularity, strangeness, unconventionality, unnaturalness

odds **1.** advantage, allowance, edge, lead, superiority **2.** balance, chances, likelihood, probability

odds and ends bits, bits and pieces, debris, leavings, litter, oddments, remnants, rubbish, scraps, sundry *or* miscellaneous items

odious abhorrent, abominable, detestable, disgusting, execrable, foul, hateful, horrible, horrid, loathsome, obnoxious, offensive, repellent, repugnant, repulsive, revolting, unpleasant, vile

odour aroma, bouquet, essence, fragrance, perfume, redolence, scent, smell, stench, stink

off *adj.* **1.** absent, cancelled, finished, gone, inoperative, postponed, unavailable **2.** bad, decomposed, high, mouldy, rancid, rotten, sour, turned ~*adv.* **3.** apart, aside, away, elsewhere, out

offbeat bizarre, Bohemian, eccentric, far-out (*Sl.*), freaky (*Sl.*), idiosyncratic, kinky (*Sl.*), novel, oddball (*Chiefly U.S. inf.*), *outré*, strange, uncommon, unconventional, unorthodox, unusual, way-out (*Inf.*), weird

off colour ill, not up to par, off form, out of sorts,

offend (əˈfɛnd) *vt.* **1.** hurt feelings of, displease —*vi.* **2.** do wrong —**ofˈfence** *or U.S.* **ofˈfense** *n.* **1.** wrong **2.** crime **3.** insult —**ofˈfender** *n.* —**ofˈfensive** *a.* **1.** causing displeasure **2.** aggressive —*n.* **3.** position or movement of attack

offer (ˈɒfə) *vt.* **1.** present for acceptance or refusal **2.** tender **3.** propose **4.** attempt —*vi.* **5.** present itself —*n.* **6.** offering, bid —**ˈofferer** *or* **ˈofferor** *n.* —**ˈoffering** *n.* **1.** something that is offered **2.** contribution **3.** sacrifice, as of animal, to deity —**ˈoffertory** *n.* **1.** offering of the bread and wine at the Eucharist **2.** collection in church service

office (ˈɒfɪs) *n.* **1.** room(s), building, in which business, clerical work *etc.* is done **2.** commercial or professional organization **3.** official position **4.** service **5.** duty **6.** form of worship —*pl.* **7.** task **8.** service —**ˈofficer** *n.* **1.** one in command in army, navy, ship *etc.* **2.** official

official (əˈfɪʃəl) *a.* **1.** with, by, authority —*n.* **2.** one holding office, *esp.* in public body —**ofˈficialdom** *n.* officials collectively, or their attitudes, work, usu. in contemptuous sense —**officiaˈlese** *n.* language characteristic of official documents, *esp.* when verbose —**Official Receiver** officer who manages estate of bankrupt

officiate (əˈfɪʃɪeɪt) *vi.* **1.** perform duties of office **2.** perform ceremony

officious (əˈfɪʃəs) *a.* **1.** importunate in offering service **2.** interfering

oft (ɒft) *adv.* often (*obs., poet.* except in combinations such as *oft-repeated*

often (ˈɒfᵊn) *adv.* many times, frequently

ogee arch (ˈəʊdʒiː) pointed arch with S-shaped curve on both sides

ogle (ˈəʊgᵊl) *v.* **1.** stare, look (at) amorously —*n.* **2.** this look —**ˈogler** *n.*

ogre (ˈəʊgə) *n.* **1.** *Folklore* man-eating giant **2.** monster (**ˈogress** *fem.*)

oh (əʊ) *interj.* exclamation of surprise, pain *etc.*

OH Ohio

ohm (əʊm) *n.* unit of electrical resistance —**ˈohmic** *a.* —**ˈohmmeter** *n.*

O.H.M.S. On His (*or* Her) Majesty's Service

-oid (*comb. form*) likeness, resemblance, similarity, as in *anthropoid*

oil (ɔɪl) *n.* **1.** any of a number of viscous liquids with smooth, sticky feel and wide variety of uses **2.** petro-

THESAURUS

peaky, poorly (*Inf.*), queasy, run down, sick, under the weather (*Inf.*), unwell, washed out

offence 1. breach of conduct, crime, delinquency, fault, lapse, misdeed, misdemeanour, peccadillo, sin, transgression, trespass, wrong, wrongdoing 2. affront, displeasure, harm, hurt, indignity, injury, injustice, insult, outrage, put-down (*Sl.*), slight, snub

offend affront, annoy, disgruntle, displease, fret, gall, give offence, hurt (someone's) feelings, insult, irritate, miff (*Inf.*), outrage, pain, pique, provoke, put (someone's) back up (*Inf.*), rile, slight, snub, tread on (someone's) toes (*Inf.*), upset, vex, wound

offender criminal, culprit, delinquent, lawbreaker, malefactor, miscreant, sinner, transgressor, wrongdoer

offensive *adj.* 1. abusive, annoying, detestable, discourteous, displeasing, disrespectful, embarrassing, impertinent, insolent, insulting, irritating, objectionable, rude, uncivil, unmannerly 2. aggressive, attacking, invading ~*n.* 3. attack, drive, onslaught, push (*Inf.*)

offer *v.* 1. bid, extend, give, hold out, proffer, put on the market, put under the hammer, put up for sale, tender 2. afford, furnish, make available, place at (someone's) disposal, present, provide, show 3. advance, extend, move, propose, put forth, put forward, submit, suggest 4. be at (someone's) service, come forward, offer one's services, volunteer ~*n.* 5. attempt, bid, endeavour, essay, overture, proposal, proposition, submission, suggestion, tender

offering contribution, donation, gift, oblation (*in religious contexts*), present, sacrifice, subscription, widow's mite

offhand abrupt, aloof, brusque, careless, casual, cavalier, couldn't-care-less, curt, glib, informal, offhanded, perfunctory, take-it-or-leave-it (*Inf.*), unceremonious, unconcerned, uninterested

office 1. appointment, business, capacity, charge, commission, duty, employment, function, obligation, occupation, place, post, responsibility, role, service, situation, station, trust, work 2. *Plural* advocacy, aegis, aid, auspices, backing, favour, help, intercession, intervention, mediation, patronage, recommendation, referral, support, word

officer agent, appointee, bureaucrat, dignitary, executive, functionary, office-holder, official, public servant, representative

official 1. *adj.* accredited, authentic, authoritative, authorized, bona fide, certified, endorsed, ex cathedra, ex officio, formal, legitimate, licensed, proper, sanctioned, straight from the horse's mouth (*Inf.*) 2. *n.* agent, bureaucrat, executive, functionary, office bearer, officer, representative

officiate chair, conduct, emcee (*Inf.*), manage, oversee, preside, serve, superintend

officious bustling, dictatorial, forward, impertinent, inquisitive, interfering, intrusive, meddlesome, meddling, mischievous, obtrusive, opinionated, overbusy, overzealous, pragmatical (*Rare*), pushy (*Inf.*), self-important

off-load disburden, discharge, dump, get rid of, jettison, shift, take off, transfer, unburden, unload, unship

off-putting daunting, discomfiting, disconcerting, discouraging, dismaying, dispiriting, disturbing, formidable, frustrating, intimidating, unnerving, unsettling, upsetting

offset 1. *v.* balance out, cancel out, compensate for, counteract, counterbalance, counterpoise, countervail, make up for, neutralize 2. *n.* balance, compensation, counterbalance, counterweight, equipoise

offshoot adjunct, appendage, branch, by-product, development, limb, outgrowth, spin-off, sprout

offspring child, children, descendant, descendants, family, fry, heir, heirs, issue, kids (*Inf.*), progeny, scion, seed, spawn, successor, successors, young

often again and again, frequently, generally, many a time, much, oft (*Poetic*), oftentimes (*Archaic*), ofttimes (*Archaic*), over and over again, repeatedly, time after time, time and again

ogre bogey, bogeyman, bugbear, demon, devil, giant, monster, spectre

leum **3.** any of variety of petroleum derivatives, *esp.* as fuel or lubricant —*vt.* **4.** lubricate with oil **5.** apply oil to —**ˈoily** *a.* **1.** soaked in or smeared with oil or grease **2.** consisting of, containing or resembling oil **3.** flatteringly servile or obsequious —**oil cake** stock feed consisting of compressed linseed —**ˈoilcloth** *n.* waterproof material made by treating cotton fabric with drying oil or synthetic resin —**ˈoilfield** *n.* area containing reserves of petroleum —**ˈoilfired** *a.* (of central heating *etc.*) using oil as fuel —**oil painting 1.** picture painted with oil paints **2.** art of painting with oil paints **3.** *inf.* person or thing regarded as good-looking (*esp. in* **she's no oil painting**) —**oil rig** *see* RIG (sense 6) —**ˈoilskin** *n.* cloth treated with oil to make it waterproof —**oil slick** mass of floating oil covering area of water —**oil well** boring into earth or sea bed for extraction of petroleum —**well oiled** *sl.* drunk

ointment (ˈɔɪntmənt) *n.* greasy preparation for healing or beautifying the skin

OK Oklahoma

O.K. *inf. a./adv.* **1.** all right —*n.* **2.** approval —*vt.* **3.** approve (**O.K.ing** (əʊˈkeɪɪŋ), **O.K.ed** (əʊˈkeɪd))

okapi (əʊˈkɑːpɪ) *n.* Afr. animal like short-necked giraffe (*pl.* **-s, -pi**)

okra (ˈəʊkrə) *n.* **1.** annual plant with yellow-and-red flowers and edible pods **2.** pod of this plant, eaten in soups, stews *etc.*

old (əʊld) *a.* **1.** aged, having lived or existed long **2.** belonging to earlier period (**ˈolder, ˈelder** *comp.*, **ˈoldest, ˈeldest** *sup.*) —**ˈolden** *a.* old —**ˈoldie** *n. inf.* old song, film, person *etc.* —**ˈoldish** *a.* —**old age pension** *see* PENSION[1] —**Old Bailey** Central Criminal Court of England —**old boy 1.** (*sometimes* **O- B-**) **UK** male ex-pupil of school **2.** *inf., chiefly* **UK** familiar name used to refer to man; old man —**old country** country of origin of immigrant or immigrant's ancestors —**Old English** English language from time of earliest Saxon settlements in fifth century A.D. to about 1100 (*also* **Anglo-Saxon**) —**old-fashioned** *a.* **1.** in style of earlier period, out of date **2.** fond of old ways —*n.* **3.** cocktail containing spirit, bitters, fruit *etc.* —**old guard 1.** group that works for long-established principles *etc.* **2.** conservative element in political party or other groups —**old hat** old-fashioned; trite —**old maid** elderly spinster —**old man 1.** *inf.* father; husband **2.** (*sometimes* **O-M-**) *inf.* man in command, such as employer, foreman *etc.* **3.** *jocular* affectionate term used in addressing man —**old master 1.** one of great European painters before 19th cent. **2.** painting by one of these —**Old Nick** *inf., jocular* Satan —**old school 1.** *chiefly* **UK** one's former school **2.** group of people favouring traditional ideas *etc.* —**old school tie 1. UK** distinctive tie that indicates which school wearer attended **2.** attitudes, values *etc.* associated with British public schools —**Old Testament** collection of books comprising sacred Scriptures of Hebrews; first part of Christian Bible —**old wives' tale** belief passed on as piece of traditional wisdom —**Old World** eastern hemisphere —**old-world** *a.* of former times, *esp.* quaint or traditional

oleaginous (əʊlɪˈædʒɪnəs) *a.* **1.** oily, producing oil **2.** unctuous, fawning —**oleˈaginousness** *n.*

oleander (əʊlɪˈændə) *n.* poisonous evergreen flowering shrub

oleo- (*comb. form*) oil, as in *oleomargarine*

O level UK 1. basic level of General Certificate of Education **2.** pass in subject at O level

olfactory (ɒlˈfæktərɪ, -trɪ) *a.* of smelling

oligarchy (ˈɒlɪgɑːkɪ) *n.* government by a few —**ˈoligarch** *n.* —**oliˈgarchic(al)** *a.*

Oligocene (ˈɒlɪgəʊsiːn, ɒˈlɪg-) *a.* **1.** of third epoch of Tertiary period —*n.* **2.** Oligocene epoch or rock series

olive (ˈɒlɪv) *n.* **1.** evergreen tree **2.** its oil-yielding fruit **3.** its wood —*a.* **4.** greyish-green —**olive branch** any offering of peace or conciliation —**olive oil** pale yellow oil extracted from olives, used in medicines *etc.*

Olympian (əˈlɪmpɪən) *a.* **1.** of Mount Olympus or classical Greek gods **2.** majestic in manner or bearing **3.** of ancient Olympia or its inhabitants —*n.* **4.** god of Mount Olympus **5.** inhabitant of ancient Olympia

Olympic (əˈlɪmpɪk) *a.* **1.** of Olympic Games **2.** of ancient Olympia —**Olympic Games 1.** Panhellenic festival, held every fourth year in honour of Zeus at ancient Olympia **2.** modern revival of these games

O.M. Order of Merit

ombudsman (ˈɒmbʊdzmən) *n.* official who investigates citizens' complaints against government *etc.*

THESAURUS

oil *v.* grease, lubricate

ointment balm, cerate, cream, embrocation, emollient, liniment, lotion, salve, unguent

O.K., okay 1. *adj.* acceptable, accurate, adequate, all right, approved, convenient, correct, fair, fine, good, in order, middling, not bad (*Inf.*), passable, permitted, satisfactory, so-so (*Inf.*), tolerable **2.** *n.* agreement, approbation, approval, assent, authorization, consent, endorsement, go-ahead (*Inf.*), green light, permission, sanction, say-so (*Inf.*), seal of approval **3.** *v.* agree to, approve, authorize, consent to, endorse, give one's consent to, give the go-ahead to (*Inf.*), give the green light to, give the thumbs up to, pass, rubber-stamp (*Inf.*), sanction, say yes to

old 1. advanced in years, aged, ancient, decrepit, elderly, full of years, getting on (*Inf.*), grey, grey-haired, grizzled, hoary, mature, over the hill (*Inf.*), past one's prime, patriarchal, senescent, senile, venerable **2.** antediluvian, antiquated, antique, cast-off, crumbling, dated, decayed, done, hackneyed, obsolete, old-fashioned, outdated, outmoded, out of date, passé, stale, superannuated, timeworn, unfashionable, unoriginal, worn-out **3.** aboriginal, antique, archaic, bygone, early, immemorial, of old, of yore, olden (*Archaic*), original, primeval, primitive, primordial, pristine, remote **4.** earlier, erstwhile, ex-, former, one-time, previous, quondam

old-fashioned ancient, antiquated, archaic, behind the times, corny (*Sl.*), dated, dead, *démodé*, fusty, musty, not with it (*Inf.*), obsolescent, obsolete, old-fangled, (old-)fogyish, old hat, old-time, outdated, outmoded, out of date, out of style, out of the ark (*Inf.*), passé, past, square (*Inf.*), superannuated, unfashionable

old man elder, elder statesman, father, gaffer, grandfather, greybeard, O.A.P. (*Brit.*), old codger (*Inf.*), old stager, oldster (*Inf.*), old-timer (*U.S.*), patriarch, senior citizen

old-world archaic, ceremonious, chivalrous, courtly, gallant, old-fashioned, picturesque, quaint, traditional

omega (ˈəʊmɪgə) *n.* **1.** last letter in Gr. alphabet (Ω, ω) **2.** end

omelette *or esp. U.S.* **omelet** (ˈɒmlɪt) *n.* dish of eggs beaten up and fried with seasoning

omen (ˈəʊmən) *n.* prophetic object or happening —**ominous** (ˈɒmɪnəs) *a.* boding evil, threatening

omicron (əʊˈmaɪkrɒn, ˈɒmɪkrɒn) *n.* 15th letter in Gr. alphabet (O, *o*)

omit (əʊˈmɪt) *vt.* **1.** leave out, neglect **2.** leave undone (-tt-) —**oˈmission** *n.* —**oˈmissive** *a.*

omni- (*comb. form*) all

omnibus (ˈɒmnɪbʌs, -bəs) *n.* **1.** large road vehicle travelling on set route and taking passengers at any stage (*also* **bus**) **2.** book containing several works —*a.* **3.** serving, containing several objects

omnidirectional (ɒmnɪdɪˈrɛkʃənˀl, -daɪ-) *a.* in radio, denotes transmission, reception in all directions

omnipotent (ɒmˈnɪpətənt) *a.* all-powerful —**omˈnipotence** *n.*

omnipresent (ɒmnɪˈprɛzˀnt) *a.* present everywhere —**omniˈpresence** *n.*

omniscient (ɒmˈnɪsɪənt) *a.* knowing everything —**omˈniscience** *n.*

omnivorous (ɒmˈnɪvərəs) *a.* **1.** devouring all foods **2.** not fastidious

on (ɒn) *prep.* **1.** above and touching, at, near, towards *etc.* **2.** attached to **3.** concerning **4.** performed upon **5.** during **6.** taking regularly —*a.* **7.** operating **8.** taking place **9.** *Cricket* denoting part of field to left of right-handed batter, and to right of bowler —*adv.* **10.** so as to be on **11.** forwards **12.** continuously *etc.* **13.** in progress —**ˈoncoming** *a.* **1.** coming nearer in space or time; approaching —*n.* **2.** approach; onset —**ˈongoing** *a.* **1.** actually in progress **2.** continually moving forward —**on line** of or concerned with peripheral device that is directly connected to and controlled by central processing unit of computer —**ˈonrush** *n.* forceful forward rush or flow —**ˈonset** *n.* **1.** violent attack **2.** assault **3.** beginning —**ˈonslaught** *n.* attack —**on stream** (of manufacturing process, equipment *etc.*) in or about to go into operation or production —**ˈonward** *a.* **1.** advanced or advancing —*adv.* **2.** in advance, ahead, forward —**ˈonwards** *adv.*

ON Ontario

on- (*comb. form*) on, as in *onlooker*

onager (ˈɒnədʒə) *n.* wild ass (*pl.* **-gri** (-graɪ), **-s**)

onanism (ˈəʊnənɪzəm) *n.* masturbation

O.N.C. UK Ordinary National Certificate

once (wʌns) *adv.* **1.** one time **2.** formerly **3.** ever —**once-over** *n. inf.* quick examination —**at once** immediately; simultaneously

oncost (ˈɒnkɒst) *n.* UK (*sometimes pl.*) *see* **overheads** *at* OVERHEAD

O.N.D. UK Ordinary National Diploma

one (wʌn) *a.* **1.** lowest cardinal number **2.** single **3.** united **4.** only, without others **5.** identical —*n.* **6.** number or figure 1 **7.** unity **8.** single specimen —*pron.* **9.** particular but not stated person **10.** any person —**ˈoneness** *n.* **1.** unity **2.** uniformity **3.** singleness —**oneˈself** *pron.* —**one-armed bandit** *inf.* fruit machine operated by pulling down lever at one side —**one-horse** *a. inf.* small; obscure —**one-night stand 1.** performance given only once at any one place **2.** *inf.* sexual encounter lasting only one night —**one-off** *n.* UK something that is carried out or made only once (*also* **one-shot**) —**one-sided** *a.* **1.** partial **2.** uneven —**one-track** *a.* **1.** *inf.* obsessed with one idea, subject *etc.* **2.** having or consisting of single track —**one-way** *a.* denotes system of traffic circulation in one direction only

onerous (ˈɒnərəs, ˈəʊ-) *a.* burdensome

onion (ˈʌnjən) *n.* edible bulb of pungent flavour

only (ˈəʊnlɪ) *a.* **1.** being the one specimen —*adv.* **2.** solely, merely, exclusively —*conj.* **3.** but then, excepting that

o.n.o. or near(est) offer

onomatopoeia (ɒnəmætəˈpiːə) *n.* formation of a word by using sounds that resemble or suggest the object or action to be named —**onomatoˈpoeic** *or* **onomatopoetic** (ɒnəmætəpəʊˈɛtɪk) *a.*

onto *or* **on to** (ˈɒntʊ; *unstressed* ˈɒntə) *prep.* **1.** on top of **2.** aware of

ontology (ɒnˈtɒlədʒɪ) *n.* science of being or reality —**ontoˈlogical** *a.* —**onˈtologist** *n.*

onus (ˈəʊnəs) *n.* responsibility, burden

THESAURUS

omen augury, foreboding, foretoken, indication, portent, premonition, presage, prognostic, prognostication, sign, straw in the wind, warning, writing on the wall

ominous baleful, dark, fateful, foreboding, inauspicious, menacing, minatory, portentous, premonitory, sinister, threatening, unpromising, unpropitious

omission default, exclusion, failure, forgetfulness, gap, lack, leaving out, neglect, noninclusion, oversight

omit disregard, drop, eliminate, exclude, fail, forget, give (something) a miss (*Inf.*), leave out, leave (something) undone, let (something) slide, miss (out), neglect, overlook, pass over, skip

omnipotence divine right, invincibility, mastery, sovereignty, supremacy, supreme power, undisputed sway

omnipotent all-powerful, almighty, supreme

once 1. at one time, formerly, in the old days, in the past, in times gone by, in times past, long ago, once upon a time, previously **2. at once a.** directly, forthwith, immediately, instantly, now, right away, straight away, straightway (*Archaic*), this (very) minute, without delay, without hesitation **b.** at *or* in one go (*Inf.*), at the same time, simultaneously, together

one-horse backwoods, inferior, minor, obscure, petty, quiet, sleepy, slow, small, small-time (*Inf.*), tinpot (*Brit. inf.*), unimportant

onerous backbreaking, burdensome, crushing, demanding, difficult, exacting, exhausting, exigent, formidable, grave, hard, heavy, laborious, oppressive, responsible, taxing, weighty

one-sided biased, coloured, discriminatory, inequitable, lopsided, partial, partisan, prejudiced, unequal, unfair, unjust

only 1. *adv.* at most, barely, exclusively, just, merely, purely, simply **2.** *adj.* exclusive, individual, lone, one and only, single, sole, solitary, unique

onomatopoeic echoic, imitative, onomatopoetic

onslaught assault, attack, blitz, charge, offensive, onrush, onset

onyx ('ɒnɪks) *n.* variety of chalcedony

oodles ('u:dᵊlz) *pl.n. inf.* abundance

oolite ('əʊəlaɪt) *n.* any sedimentary rock, *esp.* limestone, consisting of tiny spherical grains within fine matrix —**oolitic** (əʊə'lɪtɪk) *a.*

ooze (u:z) *vi.* **1.** pass slowly out —*v.* **2.** exude (moisture *etc.*) —*n.* **3.** sluggish flow **4.** wet mud, slime —**'oozy** *a.*

op. 1. opera **2.** operation **3.** opus

o.p. *or* **O.P.** out of print

opal ('əʊpᵊl) *n.* glassy gemstone displaying variegated colours —**opa'lescent** *a.*

opaque (əʊ'peɪk) *a.* not allowing the passage of light, not transparent —**opacity** (əʊ'pæsɪtɪ) *n.*

op. cit. opere citato (*Lat.,* in the work cited)

OPEC ('əʊpɛk) Organization of Petroleum Exporting Countries

open ('əʊpᵊn) *a.* **1.** not shut or blocked up **2.** without lid or door **3.** bare **4.** undisguised **5.** not enclosed, covered or exclusive **6.** spread out, accessible **7.** frank, sincere —*vt.* **8.** set open, uncover, give access to **9.** disclose, lay bare **10.** begin **11.** make a hole in —*vi.* **12.** become open **13.** begin —*n.* **14.** clear space, unenclosed country **15.** *Sport* competition in which all may enter —**'opening** *n.* **1.** hole, gap **2.** beginning **3.** opportunity —*a.* **4.** first **5.** initial —**'openly** *adv.* without concealment —**open-and-shut** *a.* easily decided or solved —**'opencast** *a.* (of coal) mined from the surface, not underground —**open-ended** *a.* without definite limits, as of duration or amount —**open-handed** *a.* generous —**open-hearted** *a.* frank, magnanimous —**open-heart surgery** surgical repair of heart during which blood circulation is oft. maintained mechanically —**open-minded** *a.* unprejudiced —**open-plan** *a.* having no or few dividing walls between areas —**open prison** prison without restraints to prevent absconding —**open secret** something that is supposed to be secret but is widely known —**Open University UK** university for mature students studying by television and radio lectures, correspondence courses *etc.* —**open verdict** coroner's verdict not stating cause (of death) —**'openwork** *n.* pattern with interstices

opera ('ɒpərə, 'ɒprə) *n.* musical drama —**oper'atic** *a.* of opera —**ope'retta** *n.* light, comic opera —**opera glasses** small binoculars used by audiences in theatres *etc.*

operation (ɒpə'reɪʃən) *n.* **1.** working, way things work **2.** scope **3.** act of surgery **4.** military action —**opera'bility** *n.* —**'operable** *a.* **1.** capable of being treated by surgical operation **2.** capable of being put into practice —**'operate** *vt.* **1.** cause to function **2.** control functioning of —*vi.* **3.** work **4.** produce an effect **5.** perform act of surgery **6.** exert power —**ope'rational** *a.* **1.** of operation(s) **2.** working —**'operative** *a.* **1.** working —*n.* **2.** worker, *esp.* with a special skill —**'operator** *n.* —**operating theatre** room in which surgical operations are performed —**operations re-**

THESAURUS

onus burden, liability, load, obligation, responsibility, task

ooze 1. *v.* bleed, discharge, drain, dribble, drip, drop, emit, escape, exude, filter, leach, leak, overflow with, percolate, seep, strain, sweat, weep **2.** *n.* alluvium, mire, muck, mud, silt, slime, sludge

opaque clouded, cloudy, dim, dull, filmy, hazy, impenetrable, lustreless, muddied, muddy, murky, obfuscated, turbid

open *adj.* **1.** agape, ajar, expanded, extended, gaping, revealed, spread out, unbarred, unclosed, uncovered, unfastened, unfolded, unfurled, unlocked, unobstructed, unsealed, yawning **2.** airy, bare, clear, exposed, extensive, free, navigable, not built-up, passable, rolling, spacious, sweeping, uncluttered, uncrowded, unenclosed, unfenced, unsheltered, wide, wide-open **3.** accessible, available, free, general, nondiscriminatory, public, unconditional, unengaged, unoccupied, unqualified, unrestricted, vacant **4.** apparent, avowed, barefaced, blatant, clear, conspicuous, downright, evident, flagrant, frank, manifest, noticeable, obvious, overt, plain, unconcealed, undisguised, visible **5.** artless, candid, fair, frank, guileless, honest, ingenuous, innocent, natural, sincere, transparent, unreserved ~*v.* **6.** begin, begin business, commence, get *or* start the ball rolling, inaugurate, initiate, kick off (*Inf.*), launch, put up one's plate, set in motion, set up shop, start **7.** clear, crack, throw wide, unbar, unblock, unclose, uncork, uncover, undo, unfasten, unlock, unseal, untie, unwrap **8.** disclose, divulge, exhibit, explain, lay bare, pour out, show, uncover

open-handed bountiful, free, generous, lavish, liberal, munificent, unstinting

opening *n.* **1.** aperture, breach, break, chink, cleft, crack, fissure, gap, hole, interstice, orifice, perforation, rent, rupture, slot, space, split, vent **2.** break (*Inf.*), chance, look-in (*Inf.*), occasion, opportunity, place, vacancy **3.** beginning, birth, commencement, dawn, inauguration, inception, initiation, kickoff (*Inf.*), launch, launching, onset, outset, start ~*adj.* **4.** beginning, commencing, early, first, inaugural, initial, initiatory, introductory, maiden, primary

openly 1. candidly, face to face, forthrightly, frankly, plainly, straight from the shoulder (*Inf.*), unhesitatingly, unreservedly **2.** blatantly, brazenly, flagrantly, in full view, in public, publicly, shamelessly, unabashedly, unashamedly, wantonly, without pretence

open-minded broad, broad-minded, catholic, dispassionate, enlightened, free, impartial, liberal, reasonable, receptive, tolerant, unbiased, undogmatic, unprejudiced

operate 1. act, be in action, function, go, perform, run, work **2.** be in charge of, handle, manage, manoeuvre, use, work

operation 1. action, affair, course, exercise, motion, movement, performance, procedure, process, use, working **2.** assault, campaign, exercise, manoeuvre

operational functional, going, in working order, operative, prepared, ready, usable, viable, workable, working

operative 1. *adj.* active, current, effective, efficient, functional, functioning, in force, in operation, operational, serviceable, standing, workable **2.** *n.* artisan, employee, hand, labourer, machinist, mechanic, worker

operator 1. conductor, driver, handler, mechanic, operative, practitioner, skilled employee, technician, worker **2.** administrator, contractor, dealer, director, manager, speculator, trader

search analysis of problems in business involving quantitative techniques

operculum (əʊˈpɜːkjʊləm) *n.* lid; cover (*pl.* **-s, -la** (-lə))

ophidian (əʊˈfɪdɪən) *a.* **1.** snakelike **2.** of suborder of reptiles which comprises snakes —*n.* **3.** any reptile of this suborder

ophthalmic (ɒfˈθælmɪk) *a.* of eyes —**ophˈthalmia** *n.* inflammation of eye —**ophthalˈmologist** *n.* —**ophthalˈmology** *n.* study of eye and its diseases —**ophˈthalmoscope** *n.* instrument for examining interior of eye —**ophthalmic optician** optician qualified to prescribe spectacles *etc.*

opiate (ˈəʊpɪɪt) *see* OPIUM

opinion (əˈpɪnjən) *n.* **1.** what one thinks about something **2.** belief, judgment —**opine** (əʊˈpaɪn) *vt.* **1.** think —*vi.* **2.** utter opinion —**oˈpinionated** *a.* **1.** stubborn in one's opinions **2.** dogmatic

opium (ˈəʊpɪəm) *n.* addictive narcotic drug made from poppy —**ˈopiate** *n.* **1.** drug containing opium **2.** narcotic —*a.* **3.** inducing sleep **4.** soothing

opossum (əˈpɒsəm) *or* **possum** *n.* small Amer. and Aust. marsupial animal

opp. **1.** opposed **2.** opposite

opponent (əˈpəʊnənt) *n.* adversary, antagonist

opportune (ˈɒpətjuːn) *a.* seasonable, well-timed —**opporˈtunism** *n.* policy of doing what is expedient at the time regardless of principle —**opporˈtunist** *n./a.* —**opporˈtunity** *n.* **1.** favourable time or condition **2.** good chance

oppose (əˈpəʊz) *vt.* **1.** resist, withstand **2.** contrast **3.** set against —**opˈposer** *n.* —**ˈopposite** *a.* **1.** contrary **2.** facing **3.** diametrically different **4.** adverse —*n.* **5.** the contrary —*prep./adv.* **6.** facing **7.** on the other side —**oppoˈsition** *n.* **1.** antithesis **2.** resistance **3.** obstruction **4.** hostility **5.** group opposing another **6.** party opposing that in power —**opposite number** person holding corresponding position on another side or situation

oppress (əˈprɛs) *vt.* **1.** govern with tyranny **2.** weigh down —**opˈpression** *n.* **1.** act of oppressing **2.** severity **3.** misery —**opˈpressive** *a.* **1.** tyrannical **2.** hard to bear **3.** heavy **4.** (of weather) hot and tiring —**opˈpressively** *adv.* —**opˈpressor** *n.*

opprobrium (əˈprəʊbrɪəm) *n.* disgrace —**opˈprobrious** *a.* **1.** reproachful **2.** shameful **3.** abusive

oppugn (əˈpjuːn) *vt.* call into question, dispute

opt (ɒpt) *vi.* make a choice —**ˈoptative** *a.* **1.** expressing wish or desire —*n.* **2.** mood of verb expressing wish

opt. **1.** optical **2.** optional

optic (ˈɒptɪk) *a.* **1.** of eye or sight —*n.* **2.** eye —*pl.* **3.** (*with sing. v.*) science of sight and light —**ˈoptical** *a.* —**opˈtician** *n.* maker of, dealer in spectacles, optical instruments —**optical character reader** computer device enabling characters, usu. printed on paper, to be optically scanned and input to storage device

optimism (ˈɒptɪmɪzəm) *n.* **1.** disposition to look on the bright side **2.** doctrine that good must prevail in

THESAURUS

opinion assessment, belief, conception, conjecture, estimation, feeling, idea, impression, judgment, mind, notion, persuasion, point of view, sentiment, theory, view

opinionated adamant, biased, bigoted, bull-headed, cocksure, dictatorial, doctrinaire, dogmatic, inflexible, obdurate, obstinate, overbearing, pig-headed, prejudiced, self-assertive, single-minded, stubborn, uncompromising

opponent adversary, antagonist, challenger, competitor, contestant, disputant, dissentient, enemy, foe, opposer, rival, the opposition

opportune advantageous, appropriate, apt, auspicious, convenient, favourable, felicitous, fit, fitting, fortunate, happy, lucky, proper, propitious, seasonable, suitable, timely, well-timed

opportunism expediency, exploitation, Machiavellianism, making hay while the sun shines (*Inf.*), pragmatism, realism, *Realpolitik*, striking while the iron is hot (*Inf.*), trimming, unscrupulousness

opportunity break (*Inf.*), chance, convenience, hour, look-in (*Inf.*), moment, occasion, opening, scope, time

oppose **1.** bar, check, combat, confront, contradict, counter, counterattack, defy, face, fight, fly in the face of, hinder, obstruct, prevent, resist, speak against, stand up to, take a stand against, take issue with, take on, thwart, withstand **2.** compare, contrast, counterbalance, match, pit *or* set against, play off

opposite *adj.* **1.** corresponding, facing, fronting **2.** adverse, antagonistic, antithetical, conflicting, contradictory, contrary, contrasted, diametrically opposed, different, differing, diverse, hostile, inconsistent, inimical, irreconcilable, opposed, reverse, unlike ~*n.* **3.** antithesis, contradiction, contrary, converse, inverse, reverse, the other extreme, the other side of the coin (*Inf.*)

opposition **1.** antagonism, competition, contrariety, counteraction, disapproval, hostility, obstruction, obstructiveness, prevention, resistance, unfriendliness **2.** antagonist, competition, foe, opponent, other side, rival

oppress **1.** afflict, burden, depress, dispirit, harass, lie *or* weigh heavy upon, sadden, take the heart out of, torment, vex **2.** abuse, crush, harry, maltreat, overpower, overwhelm, persecute, rule with an iron hand, subdue, subjugate, suppress, trample underfoot, tyrannize over, wrong

oppression abuse, brutality, calamity, cruelty, hardship, harshness, injury, injustice, iron hand, maltreatment, misery, persecution, severity, subjection, suffering, tyranny

oppressive **1.** brutal, burdensome, cruel, despotic, grinding, harsh, heavy, inhuman, onerous, overbearing, overwhelming, repressive, severe, tyrannical, unjust **2.** airless, close, heavy, muggy, overpowering, stifling, stuffy, suffocating, sultry, torrid

oppressor autocrat, bully, despot, harrier, intimidator, iron hand, persecutor, scourge, slave-driver, taskmaster, tormentor, tyrant

opt (for) choose, decide (on), elect, exercise one's discretion (in favour of), go for (*Inf.*), make a selection, plump for, prefer

optimistic **1.** disposed to take a favourable view, idealistic, seen through rose-coloured spectacles, Utopian **2.** assured, bright, buoyant, buoyed up, cheerful, confident, encouraged, expectant, hopeful, positive, sanguine

the end **3.** belief that the world is the best possible world —**ˈoptimist** *n.* —**optiˈmistic** *a.* —**optiˈmistically** *adv.*

optimum (ˈɒptɪməm) *a./n.* the best, the most favourable (*pl.* **-s, -ma** (-mə))

option (ˈɒpʃən) *n.* **1.** choice **2.** preference **3.** thing chosen **4.** in business, purchased privilege of either buying or selling things at specified price within specified time —**ˈoptional** *a.* leaving to choice

optometrist (ɒpˈtɒmɪtrɪst) *n.* person *usu.* not medically qualified, testing eyesight, prescribing corrective lenses *etc.* —**opˈtometry** *n.*

opulent (ˈɒpjʊlənt) *a.* **1.** rich **2.** copious —**ˈopulence** *or* **ˈopulency** *n.* riches, wealth

opus (ˈəʊpəs) *n.* **1.** work **2.** musical composition (*pl.* **opera** (ˈɒpərə), **-es**)

or (ɔː; *unstressed* ə) *conj.* **1.** introduces alternatives **2.** if not

OR Oregon

-or[1] (*comb. form*) person or thing that does what is expressed by verb, as in *actor, sailor*

-or[2] (*comb. form*) **1.** state, condition, activity, as in *terror, error* **2. US** *see* -OUR

O.R. **1.** Official Receiver **2.** operational research

oracle (ˈɒrəkˀl) *n.* **1.** divine utterance, prophecy, *oft.* ambiguous, given at shrine of god **2.** the shrine **3.** wise or mysterious adviser **4.** **(O-)** **R** ITV teletext service —**oˈracular** *a.* **1.** of oracle **2.** prophetic **3.** authoritative **4.** ambiguous

oral (ˈɔːrəl, ˈɒrəl) *a.* **1.** spoken **2.** by mouth —*n.* **3.** spoken examination —**ˈorally** *adv.*

orange (ˈɒrɪndʒ) *n.* **1.** bright reddish-yellow round fruit **2.** tree bearing it **3.** fruit's colour —**orangeˈade** *n.* effervescent orange-flavoured drink —**ˈorangery** *n.* building, such as greenhouse, in which orange trees are grown

Orangeman (ˈɒrɪndʒmən) *n.* member of society founded as secret order in Ireland to uphold Protestantism

orang-utan (ɔːræŋuːˈtæn, ɔːræŋˈuːtæn) *or* **orang-outang** (ɔːræŋuːˈtæŋ, ɔːræŋˈuːtæŋ) *n.* large Indonesian ape

orator (ˈɒrətə) *n.* **1.** maker of speech **2.** skilful speaker —**oˈration** *n.* formal speech —**oraˈtorical** *a.* of orator or oration —**ˈoratory** *n.* **1.** speeches **2.** eloquence **3.** small private chapel

oratorio (ɒrəˈtɔːrɪəʊ) *n.* semi-dramatic composition of sacred music (*pl.* **-s**)

orb (ɔːb) *n.* globe, sphere —**orˈbicular** *a.*

orbit (ˈɔːbɪt) *n.* **1.** track of planet, satellite, comet *etc.*, around another heavenly body **2.** field of influence, sphere **3.** eye socket —*v.* **4.** move in, or put into, an orbit

Orcadian (ɔːˈkeɪdɪən) *n.* **1.** native or inhabitant of the Orkneys —*a.* **2.** of or relating to the Orkneys

orchard (ˈɔːtʃəd) *n.* **1.** area for cultivation of fruit trees **2.** the trees

orchestra (ˈɔːkɪstrə) *n.* **1.** band of musicians **2.** place for such a band in theatre *etc.* (*also* **orchestra pit**) —**orˈchestral** *a.* —**ˈorchestrate** *vt.* **1.** compose or arrange (music) for orchestra **2.** organize, arrange

orchid (ˈɔːkɪd) *n.* genus of various flowering plants

ordain (ɔːˈdeɪn) *vt.* **1.** admit to Christian ministry **2.** confer holy orders upon **3.** decree, enact **4.** destine —**ordiˈnation** *n.*

ordeal (ɔːˈdiːl) *n.* **1.** severe, trying experience **2.** *Hist.* form of trial by which accused underwent severe physical test

order (ˈɔːdə) *n.* **1.** regular or proper arrangement or condition **2.** sequence **3.** peaceful condition of society **4.** rank, class **5.** group **6.** command **7.** request for something to be supplied **8.** mode of procedure **9.** instruction **10.** monastic society —*vt.* **11.** command **12.** request (something) to be supplied or made **13.** arrange —**ˈorderliness** *n.* —**ˈorderly** *a.* **1.** tidy **2.** methodical **3.** well-behaved —*n.* **4.** hospital attendant **5.** soldier following officer to carry orders —**ˈordinal** *a.* **1.** showing position in a series —*n.* **2.** ordinal number

THESAURUS

optimum *adj.* A1 (*Inf.*), best, choicest, flawless, highest, ideal, most favourable *or* advantageous, optimal, peak, perfect, superlative

option alternative, choice, election, preference, selection

optional discretionary, elective, extra, noncompulsory, open, possible, up to the individual, voluntary

opulence affluence, easy circumstances, easy street (*Inf.*), fortune, lavishness, luxuriance, luxury, plenty, prosperity, riches, richness, sumptuousness, wealth

opulent **1.** affluent, lavish, luxurious, moneyed, prosperous, rich, sumptuous, wealthy, well-heeled (*Sl.*), well-off, well-to-do **2.** abundant, copious, lavish, luxuriant, plentiful, profuse, prolific

oracle **1.** augur, Cassandra, prophet, seer, sibyl, soothsayer **2.** answer, augury, divination, divine utterance, prediction, prognostication, prophecy, revelation, vision **3.** adviser, authority, guru, high priest, horse's mouth, mastermind, mentor, pundit, source, wizard

oral spoken, verbal, viva voce, vocal

oration address, declamation, discourse, harangue, homily, lecture, speech, spiel (*Inf.*)

orator Cicero, declaimer, lecturer, public speaker, rhetorician, speaker, spellbinder, spieler (*Inf.*)

oratorical bombastic, Ciceronian, declamatory, eloquent, grandiloquent, high-flown, magniloquent, rhetorical, silver-tongued, sonorous

oratory declamation, elocution, eloquence, grandiloquence, public speaking, rhetoric, speechifying, speech-making, spieling (*Inf.*)

orb ball, circle, globe, ring, round, sphere

orbit *n.* **1.** circle, circumgyration, course, cycle, ellipse, path, revolution, rotation, track, trajectory **2.** *Fig.* ambit, compass, course, domain, influence, range, reach, scope, sphere, sphere of influence, sweep ~*v.* **3.** circle, circumnavigate, encircle, revolve around

orchestrate **1.** arrange, score **2.** arrange, concert, coordinate, integrate, organize, present, put together, set up, stage-manage

ordain **1.** anoint, appoint, call, consecrate, destine, elect, frock, invest, nominate **2.** fate, foreordain, intend, predestine, predetermine **3.** decree, dictate, enact, enjoin, fix, lay down, legislate, order, prescribe, pronounce, rule, set, will

ordeal affliction, agony, anguish, nightmare, suffering, test, torture, trial, tribulation(s), trouble(s)

—ordinal number number denoting order, quality or degree in group, such as *first, second, third* **—Order of Merit UK** order conferred on civilians and servicemen for eminence in any field

ordinance (ˈɔːdɪnəns) *n.* **1.** decree, rule **2.** rite, ceremony

ordinary (ˈɔːdᵊnrɪ) *a.* **1.** usual, normal **2.** common **3.** plain **4.** commonplace *—n.* **5.** bishop in his province **—ˈordinarily** *adv.* **—Ordinary level UK** *formal name for* O LEVEL **—ordinary rating** rank in Royal Navy comparable to that of private in army

ordinate (ˈɔːdɪnɪt) *n.* vertical or *y*-coordinate of point in two-dimensional system of Cartesian coordinates

ordnance (ˈɔːdnəns) *n.* **1.** big guns, artillery **2.** military stores **—Ordnance Survey** official geographical survey of Britain

Ordovician (ɔːdəʊˈvɪʃɪən) *a.* **1.** of, denoting or formed in second period of Palaeozoic era *—n.* **2** Ordovician period or rock system

ordure (ˈɔːdjʊə) *n.* **1.** dung **2.** filth

ore (ɔː) *n.* naturally occurring mineral which yields metal

oregano (ɒrɪˈgɑːnəʊ) *n.* herb, variety of marjoram

organ (ˈɔːgən) *n.* **1.** musical wind instrument of pipes and stops, played by keys **2.** member of animal or plant carrying out particular function **3.** means of action **4.** medium of information, *esp.* newspaper **—orˈganic** *a.* **1.** of, derived from, living organisms **2.** of bodily organs **3.** affecting bodily organs **4.** having vital organs **5.** *Chem.* of compounds formed from carbon **6.** grown with fertilizers derived from animal or vegetable matter **7.** organized, systematic **—orˈganically** *adv.* **—ˈorganist** *n.* organ player **—organ loft** gallery in church *etc.* for an organ

organdie *or esp. U.S.* **organdy** (ˈɔːgəndɪ) *n.* light, transparent muslin

organize *or* **-ise** (ˈɔːgənaɪz) *vt.* **1.** give definite structure to **2.** get up, arrange **3.** put into working order **4.** unite in a society **—ˈorganism** *n.* **1.** organized body or system **2.** plant, animal **—organiˈzation** *or* **-iˈsation** *n.* **1.** act of organizing **2.** body of people **3.** society **—ˈorganizer** *or* **-iser** *n.*

orgasm (ˈɔːgæzəm) *n.* sexual climax

orgy (ˈɔːdʒɪ) *n.* **1.** drunken or licentious revel, debauch **2.** act of immoderation, overindulgence

oriel (ˈɔːrɪəl) *n.* **1.** projecting part of an upper room with a window **2.** the window

orient (ˈɔːrɪənt) *n.* **1.** (**O-**) the East **2.** lustre of best pearls *—a.* **3.** rising **4.** (**O-**) Eastern *—vt.* (ˈɔːrɪɛnt) **5.** place so as to face East **6.** adjust or align (oneself *etc.*) according to surroundings or circumstances **7.** position or set (map *etc.*) with reference to compass *etc.* **—oriˈental** *a./n.* **—oriˈentalist** *n.* expert in Eastern languages and history **—ˈorientate** *vt.* orient **—orienˈtation** *n.* **—orienˈteering** *n.* competitive sport involving compass and map-reading skills

THESAURUS

order *n.* **1.** arrangement, harmony, method, neatness, orderliness, organization, pattern, plan, propriety, regularity, symmetry, system, tidiness **2.** arrangement, array, categorization, classification, codification, disposal, disposition, grouping, layout, line, line-up, ordering, placement, progression, sequence, series, setup (*inf.*), structure, succession **3.** calm, control, discipline, law, law and order, peace, quiet, tranquillity **4.** caste, class, degree, grade, hierarchy, pecking order (*Inf.*), position, rank, status **5.** breed, cast, class, family, genre, genus, ilk, kind, sort, species, subclass, taxonomic group, tribe, type **6.** behest, command, decree, dictate, direction, directive, injunction, instruction, law, mandate, ordinance, precept, regulation, rule, say-so (*Inf.*), stipulation **7.** application, booking, commission, request, requisition, reservation **8.** association, brotherhood, community, company, fraternity, guild, league, lodge, organization, sect, sisterhood, society, sodality, union ~*v.* **9.** adjure, bid, charge, command, decree, direct, enact, enjoin, instruct, ordain, prescribe, require **10.** apply for, authorize, book, call for, contract for, engage, prescribe, request, reserve, send away for **11.** adjust, align, arrange, catalogue, class, classify, conduct, control, dispose, group, lay out, manage, marshal, neaten, organize, put to rights, regulate, set in order, sort out, systematize, tabulate, tidy

orderly *adj.* **1.** businesslike, in apple-pie order (*Inf.*), in order, methodical, neat, regular, scientific, shipshape, systematic, systematized, tidy, trim, well-organized, well-regulated **2.** controlled, decorous, disciplined, law-abiding, nonviolent, peaceable, quiet, restrained, well-behaved

ordinarily as a rule, commonly, customarily, generally, habitually, in general, in the general run (of things), in the usual way, normally, usually

ordinary **1.** accustomed, common, customary, established, everyday, habitual, humdrum, normal, prevailing, quotidian, regular, routine, settled, standard, stock, typical, usual, wonted **2.** common or garden (*Inf.*), conventional, familiar, homespun, household, humble, modest, plain, prosaic, run-of-the-mill, simple, unmemorable, unpretentious, unremarkable, workaday **3.** average, commonplace, fair, indifferent, inferior, mean, mediocre, pedestrian, second-rate, stereotyped, undistinguished, unexceptional, uninspired, unremarkable

organ **1.** device, implement, instrument, tool **2.** element, member, part, process, structure, unit **3.** agency, channel, forum, journal, means, medium, mouthpiece, newspaper, paper, periodical, publication, vehicle, voice

organism animal, being, body, creature, entity, living thing, structure

organization **1.** assembling, assembly, construction, coordination, disposal, formation, forming, formulation, making, management, methodology, organizing, planning, regulation, running, standardization, structuring **2.** association, body, combine, company, concern, confederation, consortium, corporation, federation, group, institution, league, outfit (*Inf.*), syndicate

organize arrange, be responsible for, catalogue, classify, codify, constitute, construct, coordinate, dispose, establish, form, frame, get going (*Inf.*), get together (*Sl.*), group, lay the foundations of, lick into shape, look after, marshal, pigeonhole, put in order, put together, run, see to (*Inf.*), set up, shape, straighten out, systematize, tabulate, take care of

orgy **1.** bacchanal, bacchanalia, debauch, revel, revelry, Saturnalia **2.** binge (*Inf.*), bout, excess, indulgence, overindulgence, splurge, spree, surfeit

orientation **1.** bearings, coordination, direction, loca-

orifice (ˈɒrɪfɪs) *n.* opening, mouth of a cavity, *eg* pipe

orig. 1. origin 2. original(ly)

origami (ɒrɪˈgɑːmɪ) *n.* Japanese art of paper folding

origin (ˈɒrɪdʒɪn) *n.* 1. beginning 2. source 3. parentage

original (əˈrɪdʒɪnˀl) *a.* 1. primitive, earliest 2. new, not copied or derived 3. thinking or acting for oneself 4. eccentric —*n.* 5. pattern, thing from which another is copied 6. unconventional or strange person —**origiˈnality** *n.* power of producing something individual to oneself —**oˈriginally** *adv.* 1. at first 2. in the beginning —**original sin** *Theol.* state of sin held to be innate in mankind as descendants of Adam

originate (əˈrɪdʒɪneɪt) *v.* come or bring into existence, begin —**origiˈnation** *n.* —**oˈriginator** *n.*

oriole (ˈɔːrɪəul) *n.* tropical thrushlike bird

orison (ˈɒrɪzˀn) *n.* prayer

Orlon (ˈɔːlɒn) *n.* R crease-resistant acrylic fabric used for clothing *etc.*

ormolu (ˈɔːməluː) *n.* 1. gilded bronze 2. gold-coloured alloy 3. articles of these

ornament (ˈɔːnəmənt) *n.* 1. any object used to adorn or decorate 2. decoration —*vt.* (ˈɔːnəmɛnt) 3. adorn —**ornaˈmental** *a.*

ornate (ɔːˈneɪt) *a.* highly decorated or elaborate

ornery (ˈɔːnərɪ) *a.* US *dial., inf.* 1. stubborn; vile-tempered 2. low; treacherous 3. ordinary

ornithology (ɔːnɪˈθɒlədʒɪ) *n.* science of birds —**ornithoˈlogical** *a.* —**orniˈthologist** *n.*

orotund (ˈɒrəutʌnd) *a.* 1. full, clear and musical 2. pompous

orphan (ˈɔːfən) *n.* child bereaved of one or both parents —**ˈorphanage** *n.* institution for care of orphans —**ˈorphanhood** *n.*

orrery (ˈɒrərɪ) *n.* mechanical model of solar system to show revolutions, planets *etc.*

orris *or* **orrice** (ˈɒrɪs) *n.* any of various kinds of iris

ortho- *or before vowel* **orth-** (*comb. form*) right, correct

orthodontics (ɔːθəuˈdɒntɪks) *or* **orthodontia** (ɔːθəuˈdɒntɪə) *n.* branch of dentistry concerned with correcting irregularities of teeth —**orthoˈdontic** *a.* —**orthoˈdontist** *n.*

orthodox (ˈɔːθədɒks) *a.* 1. holding accepted views 2. conventional —**ˈorthodoxy** *n.* —**Orthodox Church** 1. collective body of Eastern Churches that were separated from western Church in 11th century and are in communion with Gr. patriarch of Constantinople 2. any of these Churches

orthography (ɔːˈθɒgrəfɪ) *n.* correct spelling

orthopaedics *or U.S.* **orthopedics** (ɔːθəˈpiːdɪks) *pl.n.* (*with sing. v.*) branch of surgery concerned with disorders of spine and joints and repair of deformities of these parts —**orthoˈpaedic** *or U.S.* **orthoˈpedic** *a.*

orthopterous (ɔːˈθɒptərəs) *a.* of large order of insects, including crickets, locusts and grasshoppers, having leathery forewings and membranous hind wings

ortolan (ˈɔːtələn) *n.* a small bird, *esp.* as table delicacy

-ory[1] (*comb. form*) 1. place for, as in *observatory* 2. something having specified use, as in *directory*

THESAURUS

tion, position, sense of direction **2.** acclimatization, adaptation, adjustment, assimilation, breaking in, familiarization, introduction, settling in

orifice aperture, cleft, hole, mouth, opening, perforation, pore, rent, vent

origin **1.** base, basis, cause, derivation, *fons et origo*, font (*Poetic*), fountain, fountainhead, occasion, provenance, root, roots, source, spring, wellspring **2.** beginning, birth, commencement, creation, dawning, early stages, emergence, foundation, genesis, inauguration, inception, launch, origination, outset, start **3.** ancestry, beginnings, birth, descent, extraction, family, heritage, lineage, parentage, pedigree, stirps, stock

original *adj.* **1.** aboriginal, autochthonous, commencing, earliest, early, embryonic, first, infant, initial, introductory, opening, primary, primitive, primordial, pristine, rudimentary, starting **2.** creative, fertile, fresh, imaginative, ingenious, innovative, innovatory, inventive, new, novel, resourceful, seminal, unconventional, unprecedented, untried, unusual **3.** archetypal, authentic, first, first-hand, genuine, master, primary, prototypical ~*n.* **4.** archetype, master, model, paradigm, pattern, precedent, prototype, standard, type **5.** anomaly, card (*Inf.*), case (*Inf.*), character, eccentric, nonconformist, oddity, queer fish (*Brit. inf.*), weirdo (*Inf.*)

originality boldness, break with tradition, cleverness, creativeness, creative spirit, creativity, daring, freshness, imagination, imaginativeness, individuality, ingenuity, innovation, innovativeness, inventiveness, new ideas, newness, novelty, resourcefulness, unconventionality, unorthodoxy

originally at first, at the outset, at the start, by origin (birth, derivation), first, initially, in the beginning, in the first place, to begin with

originate **1.** arise, be born, begin, come, derive, emanate, emerge, flow, issue, proceed, result, rise, spring, start, stem **2.** bring about, conceive, create, develop, discover, evolve, form, formulate, generate, give birth to, inaugurate, initiate, institute, introduce, invent, launch, pioneer, produce, set in motion, set up

originator architect, author, creator, father, founder, generator, innovator, inventor, maker, mother, pioneer, prime mover

ornament **1.** *n.* accessory, adornment, bauble, decoration, embellishment, frill, furbelow, garnish, gewgaw, knick-knack, trimming, trinket **2.** *v.* adorn, beautify, bedizen (*Archaic*), brighten, deck, decorate, dress up, embellish, festoon, garnish, gild, grace, prettify, prink, trim

ornamental attractive, beautifying, decorative, embellishing, for show, showy

ornate aureate, baroque, beautiful, bedecked, busy, convoluted, decorated, elaborate, elegant, fancy, florid, flowery, fussy, high-wrought, ornamented, overelaborate, rococo

orthodox accepted, approved, conformist, conventional, correct, customary, doctrinal, established, official, received, sound, traditional, true, well-established

orthodoxy authoritativeness, authority, conformism, conformity, conventionality, devotion, devoutness, faithfulness, inflexibility, received wisdom, soundness, traditionalism

-ory[2] (*comb. form*) of, relating to; characterized by; having effect of, as in *contributory*

oryx (ˈɒrɪks) *n.* large Afr. antelope (*pl.* **-es, -yx**)

Os *Chem.* osmium

O.S. **1.** Old Style **2.** Ordinary Seaman **3. UK** Ordnance Survey **4.** outsize **5.** (*also* **OS**) Old Saxon (language)

Oscar (ˈɒskə) *n.* any of several small gold statuettes awarded annually in U.S.A. for outstanding achievements in films

oscillate (ˈɒsɪleɪt) *vi.* **1.** swing to and fro **2.** waver **3.** fluctuate (regularly) **—oscilˈlation** *n.* **—ˈoscillator** *n.* **—ˈoscillatory** *a.* **—osˈcilloscope** *n.* electronic instrument producing visible representation of rapidly changing quantity

osculate (ˈɒskjʊleɪt) *v. jocular* kiss **—ˈoscular** *a.* **—oscuˈlation** *n.* **—ˈosculatory** *a.*

osier (ˈəʊzɪə) *n.* species of willow used for basketwork

-osis (*comb. form*) **1.** process; state, as in *metamorphosis* **2.** diseased condition, as in *tuberculosis* **3.** formation or development of something, as in *fibrosis*

osmium (ˈɒzmɪəm) *n.* heaviest known of metallic elements

osmosis (ɒzˈməʊsɪs, ɒs-) *n.* percolation of fluids through porous partitions **—osmotic** (ɒzˈmɒtɪk, ɒs-) *a.*

osprey (ˈɒsprɪ, -preɪ) *n.* **1.** fishing hawk **2.** plume

osseous (ˈɒsɪəs) *a.* **1.** of, like bone **2.** bony **—ossifiˈcation** *n.* **—ˈossify** *v.* **1.** turn into bone *—vi.* **2.** grow rigid (**-fied, -fying**)

ostensible (ɒˈstɛnsɪbᵊl) *a.* **1.** apparent **2.** professed **—osˈtensibly** *adv.*

ostentation (ɒstɛnˈteɪʃən) *n.* show, pretentious display **—ostenˈtatious** *a.* **1.** given to display **2.** showing off **—ostenˈtatiously** *adv.*

osteo- *or before vowel* **oste-** (*comb. form*) bone(s)

osteomyelitis (ɒstɪəʊmaɪɪˈlaɪtɪs) *n.* inflammation of bone marrow

osteopathy (ɒstɪˈɒpəθɪ) *n.* art of treating disease by removing structural derangement by manipulation, *esp.* of spine **—ˈosteopath** *n.* one skilled in this art

ostler (ˈɒslə) *or* **hostler** *n. Hist.* stableman at an inn

ostracize *or* **-ise** (ˈɒstrəsaɪz) *vt.* exclude, banish from society, exile **—ˈostracism** *n.* social boycotting

ostrich (ˈɒstrɪtʃ) *n.* large swift-running flightless Afr. bird

O.T. **1.** occupational therapy **2.** Old Testament **3.** overtime

O.T.C. UK Officers' Training Corps

other (ˈʌðə) *a.* **1.** not this **2.** not the same **3.** alternative, different *—pron.* **4.** other person or thing **—ˈotherwise** *adv.* **1.** differently **2.** in another way *—conj.* **3.** or else, if not **—otherˈworldly** *a.* **1.** of or relating to spiritual or imaginative world **2.** impractical, unworldly

otiose (ˈəʊtɪəʊs, -əʊz) *a.* **1.** superfluous **2.** useless

otitis (əʊˈtaɪtɪs) *n.* inflammation of ear

otter (ˈɒtə) *n.* furry aquatic fish-eating animal

Ottoman (ˈɒtəmən) *or* **Othman** (ˈɒθmən) *a.* **1.** Turkish *—n.* **2.** Turk **3.** (**o-**) cushioned, backless seat, storage box (*pl.* **-s**)

ou (əʊ) *n.* **SA** *sl.* man **—oubaas** (ˈəʊbɑːs) *n.* man in authority

oubliette (uːblɪˈɛt) *n.* dungeon entered by trapdoor

ouch (aʊtʃ) *interj.* exclamation of sudden pain

ought (ɔːt) *v. aux.* **1.** expressing duty, obligation or advisability **2.** be bound

Ouija (ˈwiːdʒə) *n.* **R** board with letters and symbols used to obtain messages at seances

ouma (ˈəʊmɑː) *n.* **SA** **1.** grandmother **2.** elderly woman

ounce (aʊns) *n.* a weight, sixteenth of avoirdupois pound (28.4 grams), twelfth of troy pound (31.1 grams)

oupa (ˈəʊpɑː) *n.* **SA** **1.** grandfather **2.** elderly man

our (aʊə) *a.* belonging to us **—ours** *pron.* **—ourˈself** *pron.* myself, used in regal or formal style **—ourˈselves** *pl. pron.* emphatic or reflexive form of WE

-our (*comb. form*) state, condition, activity, as in *behaviour, labour*

-ous (*comb. form*) **1.** having; full of, as in *dangerous, spacious* **2.** *Chem.* indicating that element is chemically combined in lower of two possible valency states, as in *ferrous*

ousel (ˈuːzᵊl) *n. see* OUZEL

oust (aʊst) *vt.* put out, expel

out (aʊt) *adv.* **1.** from within, away **2.** wrong **3.** on strike *—a.* **4.** not worth considering **5.** not allowed **6.** unfashionable **7.** unconscious **8.** not in use, operation *etc.* **9.** at an end **10.** not burning **11.** *Sport* dismissed **—ˈouter** *a.* away from the inside **—ˈoutermost** *or* **ˈoutmost** *a.* on extreme outside **—ˈouting** *n.* pleasure excursion **—ˈoutward** *a./adv.* **—ˈoutwardly** *adv.* **—ˈoutwards** *adv.* **—out-and-out** *a.* thoroughgoing; complete **—outer space** any region of space beyond atmosphere of earth **—out-of-the-way** *a.* **1.** distant from more populous areas **2.** uncommon or unusual

THESAURUS

oscillate fluctuate, seesaw, sway, swing, vacillate, vary, vibrate, waver

oscillation fluctuation, instability, seesawing, swing, vacillation, variation, wavering

ossify fossilize, freeze, harden, indurate (*Rare*), petrify, solidify, stiffen

ostensible alleged, apparent, avowed, exhibited, manifest, outward, plausible, pretended, professed, purported, seeming, so-called, specious, superficial, supposed

ostensibly apparently, for the ostensible purpose of, on the face of it, on the surface, professedly, seemingly, supposedly, to all intents and purposes

ostentation affectation, boasting, display, exhibitionism, flamboyance, flashiness, flaunting, flourish, pageantry, parade, pomp, pretension, pretentiousness, show, showiness, showing off (*Inf.*), swank (*Inf.*), vaunting, window-dressing

ostentatious boastful, conspicuous, crass, dashing, extravagant, flamboyant, flash (*Inf.*), flashy, flaunted, gaudy, loud, obtrusive, pompous, pretentious, showy, swanky (*Inf.*), vain, vulgar

ostracize avoid, banish, blackball, blacklist, boycott, cast out, cold-shoulder, exclude, excommunicate, exile, expatriate, expel, give (someone) the cold shoulder, reject, send to Coventry, shun

other *adj.* **1.** added, additional, alternative, auxiliary, extra, further, more, spare, supplementary **2.** contrasting, different, dissimilar, distinct, diverse, remaining, separate, unrelated, variant

otherwise **1.** *conj.* if not, or else, or then **2.** *adv.* any other way, contrarily, differently

—out of date no longer valid, current, or fashionable **—out of pocket 1.** having lost money, as in a commercial enterprise **2.** without money to spend **3.** (of expenses) unbudgeted and paid for in cash

out- (*comb. form*) **1.** beyond, in excess, as in *outclass, outdistance, outsize* **2.** so as to surpass or defeat, as in *outfox, outmanoeuvre* **3.** outside, away from, as in *outpatient, outgrowth.* See the list below

outback (ˈaʊtbæk) *n.* A remote, sparsely populated country

outbalance (aʊtˈbæləns) *vt.* **1.** outweigh **2.** exceed in weight

outboard (ˈaʊtbɔːd) *a.* (of boat's engine) mounted outside stern

outbreak (ˈaʊtbreɪk) *n.* sudden occurrence, *esp.* of disease or strife

outburst (ˈaʊtbɜːst) *n.* bursting out, *esp.* of violent emotion

outcast (ˈaʊtkɑːst) *n.* **1.** someone rejected *—a.* **2.** rejected, cast out

outclass (aʊtˈklɑːs) *vt.* excel, surpass

outcome (ˈaʊtkʌm) *n.* result

outcrop (ˈaʊtkrɒp) *n. Geol.* **1.** rock coming out of stratum to the surface *—vi.* (aʊtˈkrɒp) **2.** come out to the surface (**-pp-**)

outcry (ˈaʊtkraɪ) *n.* **1.** widespread or vehement protest *—vt.* (aʊtˈkraɪ) **2.** cry louder or make more noise than

outdo (aʊtˈduː) *vt.* surpass or exceed in performance (**-ˈdoing, -ˈdid, -ˈdone**)

outdoors (aʊtˈdɔːz) *adv.* in the open air **—ˈoutdoor** *a.*

outfall (ˈaʊtfɔːl) *n.* mouth of river

outfit (ˈaʊtfɪt) *n.* **1.** equipment **2.** clothes and accessories **3.** *inf.* group or association regarded as a unit **—ˈoutfitter** *n.* one who deals in outfits

outflank (aʊtˈflæŋk) *vt.* **1.** get beyond the flank of (enemy army) **2.** circumvent

outgoing (ˈaʊtgəʊɪŋ) *a.* **1.** departing **2.** friendly, sociable

outgrow (aʊtˈgrəʊ) *vt.* **1.** become too large or too old for **2.** surpass in growth (**-ˈgrew, -ˈgrown, -ˈgrowing**)

outhouse (ˈaʊthaʊs) *n.* shed *etc.* near main building

outlandish (aʊtˈlændɪʃ) *a.* queer, extravagantly strange

outlaw (ˈaʊtlɔː) *n.* **1.** one beyond protection of the law **2.** exile, bandit *—vt.* **3.** make (someone) an outlaw **4.** ban **—ˈoutlawry** *n.*

outˈbid
outˈdistance
ˈoutflow
outˈfox
ˈoutgrowth
outˈlast
outˈlive
outmaˈnoeuvre
outˈmatch
outˈnumber
ˈoutpatient
outˈplay
ˈoutpost
outˈrank
outˈreach
outˈrival
outˈrun
outˈshine
ˈoutsize
outˈsmart
ˈoutˈspread
outˈstare
ˈoutstation
outˈstretch
outˈvalue
outˈvote
outˈweigh

THESAURUS

out *adj.* **1.** impossible, not allowed, not on (*Inf.*), ruled out, unacceptable **2.** antiquated, behind the times, dated, dead, *démodé,* old-fashioned, old hat, passé, square (*Inf.*), unfashionable **3.** at an end, cold, dead, doused, ended, exhausted, expired, extinguished, finished, used up

out-and-out absolute, complete, consummate, downright, dyed-in-the-wool, outright, perfect, thoroughgoing, total, unmitigated, unqualified, utter

outbreak burst, epidemic, eruption, explosion, flare-up, flash, outburst, rash, spasm, upsurge

outburst access, attack, discharge, eruption, explosion, fit of temper, flare-up, gush, outbreak, outpouring, paroxysm, spasm, storm, surge

outcast *n.* castaway, derelict, displaced person, exile, leper, pariah, *persona non grata,* refugee, reprobate, untouchable, vagabond, wretch

outclass be a cut above (*Inf.*), beat, eclipse, exceed, excel, leave *or* put in the shade, leave standing (*Inf.*), outdistance, outdo, outrank, outshine, outstrip, overshadow, surpass

outcome aftereffect, aftermath, conclusion, consequence, end, end result, issue, payoff (*Inf.*), result, upshot

outcry clamour, commotion, complaint, cry, exclamation, howl, hue and cry, hullaballoo, noise, outburst, protest, scream, screech, uproar, yell

outdistance leave behind, leave standing (*Inf.*), lose, outrun, outstrip, shake off

outdo beat, be one up on, best, eclipse, exceed, excel, get the better of, go one better than (*Inf.*), outclass, outdistance, outfox, outjockey, outmanoeuvre, outshine, outsmart (*Inf.*), overcome, surpass, top, transcend

outdoor alfresco, open-air, out-of-door(s), outside

outer exposed, exterior, external, outlying, outside, outward, peripheral, remote, superficial, surface

outfit *n.* **1.** accoutrements, clothes, costume, ensemble, equipment, garb, gear, get-up (*Inf.*), kit, rigout (*Inf.*), suit, togs (*Inf.*), trappings **2.** *Inf.* clique, company, corps, coterie, crew, firm, *galère,* group, organization, set, setup (*Inf.*), squad, team, unit

outfitter clothier, costumier, couturier, dressmaker, haberdasher (*U.S.*), modiste, tailor

outflow discharge, drainage, ebb, effluence, efflux, effusion, emanation, emergence, gush, jet, outfall, outpouring, rush, spout

outgoing 1. departing, ex-, former, last, leaving, past, retiring, withdrawing **2.** approachable, communicative, cordial, demonstrative, easy, expansive, extrovert, friendly, genial, gregarious, informal, open, sociable, sympathetic, unreserved, warm

outing excursion, expedition, jaunt, pleasure trip, spin (*Inf.*), trip

outlandish alien, barbarous, bizarre, eccentric, exotic,

outlay (ˈaʊtleɪ) *n.* expenditure

outlet (ˈaʊtlɛt, -lɪt) *n.* **1.** opening, vent **2.** means of release or escape **3.** market for product or service

outline (ˈaʊtlaɪn) *n.* **1.** rough sketch **2.** general plan **3.** lines enclosing visible figure —*vt.* **4.** sketch **5.** summarize

outlook (ˈaʊtlʊk) *n.* **1.** point of view **2.** probable outcome **3.** view

outlying (ˈaʊtlaɪɪŋ) *a.* distant, remote

outmoded (aʊtˈməʊdɪd) *a.* no longer fashionable or accepted

output (ˈaʊtpʊt) *n.* **1.** quantity produced **2.** *Comp.* information produced

outrage (ˈaʊtreɪdʒ) *n.* **1.** violation of others' rights **2.** gross or violent offence or indignity **3.** anger arising from this —*vt.* **4.** offend grossly **5.** insult **6.** injure, violate —**outˈrageous** *a.*

outré (uˈtre) *a.* **1.** extravagantly odd **2.** bizarre

outrigger (ˈaʊtrɪgə) *n.* **1.** frame, *esp.* with float attached, outside boat's gunwale **2.** frame on rowing boat's side with rowlock **3.** boat equipped with such a framework

outright (ˈaʊtraɪt) *a.* **1.** undisputed **2.** downright **3.** positive —*adv.* **4.** completely **5.** instantly **6.** openly

outset (ˈaʊtsɛt) *n.* beginning

outside (ˈaʊtˈsaɪd) *n.* **1.** exterior **2.** **C** settled parts of Canada —*adv.* (aʊtˈsaɪd) **3.** not inside **4.** in the open air —*a.* (ˈaʊtsaɪd) **5.** on exterior **6.** remote, unlikely **7.** greatest possible, probable —**outˈsider** *n.* **1.** person outside specific group **2.** contestant thought unlikely to win —**outside broadcast** *T.V., rad.* broadcast not made from studio

outskirts (ˈaʊtskɜːts) *pl.n.* outer areas, districts, *esp.* of city

outspan (ˈaʊtspæn) *n.* **SA** **1.** unyoking of oxen **2.** area for rest

outspoken (aʊtˈspəʊkən) *a.* frank, candid

THESAURUS

fantastic, far-out (*Sl.*), foreign, freakish, grotesque, *outré*, preposterous, queer, strange, unheard-of, weird

outlaw **1.** *n.* bandit, brigand, desperado, exile, fugitive, highwayman, marauder, outcast, pariah, robber **2.** *v.* ban, banish, bar, condemn, disallow, embargo, exclude, forbid, interdict, make illegal, prohibit, proscribe, put a price on (someone's) head

outlay *n.* cost, disbursement, expenditure, expenses, investment, outgoings, spending

outlet **1.** avenue, channel, duct, egress, exit, means of expression, opening, orifice, release, safety valve, vent, way out **2.** market, shop, store

outline *n.* **1.** draft, drawing, frame, framework, layout, lineament(s), plan, rough, skeleton, sketch, tracing **2.** bare facts, main features, recapitulation, résumé, rough idea, rundown, summary, synopsis, thumbnail sketch **3.** configuration, contour, delineation, figure, form, profile, shape, silhouette ~*v.* **4.** adumbrate, delineate, draft, plan, rough out, sketch (in), summarize, trace

outlive come through, endure beyond, live through, outlast, survive

outlook **1.** angle, attitude, frame of mind, perspective, point of view, slant, standpoint, viewpoint, views **2.** expectations, forecast, future, prospect **3.** aspect, panorama, prospect, scene, view, vista

outlying backwoods, distant, far-flung, outer, out-of-the-way, peripheral, provincial, remote

outmoded anachronistic, antediluvian, antiquated, antique, archaic, behind the times (*Inf.*), bygone, dated, *démodé*, fossilized, obsolescent, obsolete, olden (*Archaic*), oldfangled, old-fashioned, old-time, out, out of date, out of style, outworn, passé, square (*Inf.*), superannuated, superseded, unfashionable, unusable

out of date antiquated, archaic, dated, discarded, elapsed, expired, extinct, invalid, lapsed, obsolete, old-fashioned, outmoded, outworn, passé, stale, superannuated, superseded, unfashionable

out-of-the-way **1.** distant, far-flung, inaccessible, isolated, lonely, obscure, off the beaten track, outlying, remote, secluded, unfrequented **2.** abnormal, curious, exceptional, extraordinary, odd, outlandish, out of the ordinary, peculiar, strange, uncommon, unusual

output achievement, manufacture, outturn (*Rare*), product, production, productivity, yield

outrage *n.* **1.** atrocity, barbarism, enormity, evil, inhumanity **2.** abuse, affront, desecration, indignity, injury, insult, offence, profanation, rape, ravishing, shock, violation, violence **3.** anger, fury, hurt, indignation, resentment, shock, wrath ~*v.* **4.** affront, incense, infuriate, madden, make one's blood boil, offend, scandalize, shock **5.** abuse, defile, desecrate, injure, insult, maltreat, rape, ravage, ravish, violate

outrageous **1.** abominable, atrocious, barbaric, beastly, egregious, flagrant, heinous, horrible, infamous, inhuman, iniquitous, nefarious, scandalous, shocking, unspeakable, villainous, violent, wicked **2.** disgraceful, excessive, exorbitant, extravagant, immoderate, offensive, preposterous, scandalous, shocking, steep (*Inf.*), unreasonable

outright *adj.* **1.** absolute, arrant, complete, consummate, downright, out-and-out, perfect, positive, pure, thorough, thoroughgoing, total, unconditional, undeniable, unmitigated, unqualified, utter, wholesale **2.** definite, direct, flat, straightforward, undisputed, unequivocal, unqualified ~*adv.* **3.** absolutely, completely, explicitly, openly, overtly, straightforwardly, thoroughly, to the full, without hesitation, without restraint **4.** at once, cleanly, immediately, instantaneously, instantly, on the spot, straight away, there and then, without more ado

outset beginning, commencement, early days, inauguration, inception, kickoff (*Inf.*), onset, opening, start, starting point

outshine be head and shoulders above, be superior to, eclipse, leave *or* put in the shade, outclass, outdo, outstrip, overshadow, surpass, top, transcend, upstage

outside *adj.* **1.** exterior, external, extramural, extraneous, extreme, out, outdoor, outer, outermost, outward, surface **2.** distant, faint, marginal, negligible, remote, slight, slim, small, unlikely ~*n.* **3.** exterior, façade, face, front, skin, surface, topside

outsider alien, foreigner, incomer, interloper, intruder, newcomer, nonmember, odd man out, outlander, stranger

outstanding (aʊtˈstændɪŋ) *a.* **1.** excellent **2.** remarkable **3.** unsettled, unpaid

outstrip (aʊtˈstrɪp) *vt.* outrun, surpass

outwit (aʊtˈwɪt) *vt.* get the better of by cunning

outwork (ˈaʊtwɜːk) *n.* part of fortress outside main wall

ouzel *or* **ousel** (ˈuːzᵊl) *n.* **1.** type of thrush **2.** kind of diving bird

ouzo (ˈuːzəʊ) *n.* strong aniseed-flavoured spirit from Greece

ova (ˈəʊvə) *n., pl. of* OVUM

oval (ˈəʊvᵊl) *a.* **1.** egg-shaped, elliptical *—n.* **2.** something of this shape

ovary (ˈəʊvərɪ) *n.* female egg-producing organ —**oˈvarian** *a.*

ovation (əʊˈveɪʃən) *n.* enthusiastic burst of applause

oven (ˈʌvᵊn) *n.* heated chamber for baking in

over (ˈəʊvə) *adv.* **1.** above, above and beyond, going beyond, in excess, too much, past, finished, in repetition, across, downwards *etc.* *—prep.* **2.** above **3.** on, upon **4.** more than, in excess of, along *etc.* *—a.* **5.** upper, outer *—n.* **6.** *Cricket* set of six balls bowled by bowler from same end of pitch

over- (*comb. form*) too, too much, in excess, above, to a prostrate position. See the list below

overall (ˈəʊvərɔːl) *n.* **1.** (*also pl.*) loose garment worn as protection against dirt *etc.* *—a.* **2.** total

overbalance (əʊvəˈbæləns) *v.* **1.** lose or cause to lose balance *—n.* (ˈəʊvəbæləns) **2.** excess of weight, value *etc.*

overbearing (əʊvəˈbɛərɪŋ) *a.* domineering

overblown (əʊvəˈbləʊn) *a.* excessive, bombastic

overboard (ˈəʊvəbɔːd) *adv.* from a vessel into the water

overcast (ˈəʊvəkɑːst) *a.* covered over, *esp.* by clouds

overcoat (ˈəʊvəkəʊt) *n.* warm coat worn over outer clothes

overcome (əʊvəˈkʌm) *vt.* **1.** conquer **2.** surmount **3.** make incapable or powerless *—vi.* **4.** be victorious

overaˈbundance
overˈact
overamˈbitious
overˈanxious
overˈawe
overˈbook
overˈburden
overˈcautious
overˈcharge
ˈovercoat
overˈcompensate
overˈconfident
overˈcook
overˈcrowd
overdeˈpendent
overdeˈvelop
overˈdo
ˈoverdose
overˈdue
overˈeager
overˈeat
overˈemphasize
overˈestimate
overexˈcite
overexˈert
overexˈpand
overˈfill

THESAURUS

outskirts borders, boundary, edge, environs, faubourgs, periphery, purlieus, suburbia, suburbs, vicinity

outspoken abrupt, blunt, candid, direct, explicit, forthright, frank, free, free-spoken, open, plain-spoken, round, unceremonious, undissembling, unequivocal, unreserved

outstanding 1. celebrated, distinguished, eminent, excellent, exceptional, great, important, impressive, meritorious, pre-eminent, special, superior, superlative, well-known **2.** arresting, conspicuous, eye-catching, marked, memorable, notable, noteworthy, prominent, remarkable, salient, signal, striking **3.** due, ongoing, open, owing, payable, pending, remaining, uncollected, unpaid, unresolved, unsettled

outward *adj.* apparent, evident, exterior, external, noticeable, observable, obvious, ostensible, outer, outside, perceptible, superficial, surface, visible

outwardly apparently, as far as one can see, externally, officially, on the face of it, on the surface, ostensibly, professedly, seemingly, superficially, to all appearances, to all intents and purposes, to the eye

outweigh cancel (out), compensate for, eclipse, make up for, outbalance, overcome, override, predominate, preponderate, prevail over, take precedence over, tip the scales

outwit cheat, circumvent, deceive, defraud, dupe, get the better of, gull (*Archaic*), make a fool *or* monkey of, outfox, outjockey, outmanoeuvre, outsmart (*Inf.*), outthink, put one over on (*Inf.*), run rings round (*Inf.*), swindle, take in (*Inf.*)

oval *adj.* egg-shaped, ellipsoidal, elliptical, ovate, oviform, ovoid

ovation acclaim, acclamation, applause, cheering, cheers, clapping, laudation, plaudits, tribute

over *adv.* **1.** accomplished, ancient history (*Inf.*), at an end, by, bygone, closed, completed, concluded, done (with), ended, finished, gone, past, settled, up (*Inf.*) **2.** beyond, extra, in addition, in excess, left over, remaining, superfluous, surplus, unused *~prep.* **3.** above, on, on top of, superior to, upon **4.** above, exceeding, in excess of, more than *~adv.* **5.** above, aloft, on high, overhead

overact exaggerate, ham *or* ham up (*Inf.*), overdo, overplay

overall all-embracing, blanket, complete, comprehensive, general, global, inclusive, long-range, long-term, total, umbrella

overawe abash, alarm, browbeat, cow, daunt, frighten, intimidate, scare, terrify

overbalance capsize, keel over, lose one's balance, lose one's footing, overset, overturn, slip, take a tumble, tip over, topple over, tumble, turn turtle, upset

overbearing arrogant, autocratic, bossy (*Inf.*), cavalier, despotic, dictatorial, dogmatic, domineering, haughty, high-handed, imperious, lordly, magisterial, officious, oppressive, overweening, peremptory, supercilious, superior, tyrannical

overcast clouded, clouded over, cloudy, darkened, dismal, dreary, dull, grey, hazy, leaden, lowering, murky, sombre, sunless, threatening

overcharge cheat, clip (*Sl.*), diddle (*Inf.*), do (*Sl.*), fleece, rip off (*Sl.*), rook (*Sl.*), short-change, sting (*Inf.*), surcharge

overdraft ('əʊvədrɑːft) *n.* withdrawal of money in excess of credit balance on bank account

overdrive ('əʊvədraɪv) *n.* **1.** very high gear in motor vehicle used at high speeds to reduce wear —*vt.* (əʊvə'draɪv) **2.** drive too hard or too far; overwork (-'**driving,** -'**drove,** -'**driven**)

overhaul (əʊvə'hɔːl) *vt.* **1.** examine and set in order, repair **2.** overtake —*n.* ('əʊvəhɔːl) **3.** thorough examination, *esp.* for repairs

overhead ('əʊvəhɛd) *a.* **1.** over one's head, above —*adv.* (əʊvə'hɛd) **2.** aloft, above —'**overheads** *pl.n.* expenses of running a business, over and above cost of manufacturing and of raw materials

overhear (əʊvə'hɪə) *vt.* hear (person, remark *etc.*) without knowledge of speaker (-'**hearing,** -'**heard**)

overkill ('əʊvəkɪl) *n.* capacity, advantage greater than required

overland ('əʊvəlænd) *a./adv.* by land

overlap (əʊvə'læp) *v.* **1.** (of two things) extend or lie partly over (each other) **2.** cover and extend beyond (something) —*vi.* **3.** coincide partly in time, subject *etc.* (**-pp-**) —*n.* ('əʊvəlæp) **4.** part that overlaps or is overlapped **5.** amount, length *etc.* overlapping

overleaf ('əʊvəliːf) *adv.* on other side of page

overlook (əʊvə'lʊk) *vt.* **1.** fail to notice **2.** disregard **3.** look over

overpower (əʊvə'paʊə) *vt.* **1.** conquer by superior force **2.** have such strong effect on as to make ineffective **3.** supply with more power than necessary —**over'powering** *a.*

override (əʊvə'raɪd) *vt.* **1.** set aside, disregard **2.** cancel **3.** trample down

over'flow *v.*
'overflow *n.*
over'grow
over'hang
over'hasty
overin'dulge
overin'dulgence
overin'sistent
over'joy
'overlay
over'lie
over'load *v.*
'overload *n.*
'overlord
over'many
over'modest
over'much
over'night
'overpass
over'pay
overpopu'lation
over'price
overpro'duce
overpro'duction
over'rate
over'reach
overre'act

THESAURUS

overcome beat, best, be victorious, come out on top (*Inf.*), conquer, crush, defeat, get the better of, lick (*Inf.*), master, overpower, overthrow, overwhelm, prevail, render incapable (helpless, powerless), rise above, subdue, subjugate, surmount, survive, triumph over, vanquish, weather, worst

overconfident brash, cocksure, foolhardy, hubristic, overweening, presumptuous, riding for a fall (*Inf.*), uppish (*Brit. inf.*)

overdo be intemperate, belabour, carry too far, do to death (*Inf.*), exaggerate, gild the lily, go overboard (*Inf.*), go to extremes, lay it on thick (*Inf.*), not know when to stop, overindulge, overplay, overreach, overstate, overuse, overwork, run riot

overdue behindhand, behind schedule, behind time, belated, late, long delayed, not before time (*Inf.*), owing, tardy, unpunctual

overeat binge (*Inf.*), eat like a horse (*Inf.*), gorge, gormandize, guzzle, make a pig of oneself (*Inf.*), overindulge, pack away (*Sl.*), pig away (*Sl.*), stuff, stuff oneself

overemphasize belabour, blow up out of all proportion, lay too much stress on, make a big thing of (*Inf.*), make a mountain out of a molehill (*Inf.*), make something out of nothing, make too much of, overdramatize, overstress

overflow *v.* **1.** bubble (brim, fall, pour, run, slop, well) over, discharge, pour out, run with, shower, spill, spray, surge **2.** cover, deluge, drown, flood, inundate, soak, submerge, swamp ~*n.* **3.** discharge, flash flood, flood, flooding, inundation, overabundance, spill, spilling over, surplus

overhang *v.* beetle, bulge, cast a shadow, extend, jut, loom, project, protrude, stick out

overhaul *v.* **1.** check, do up (*Inf.*), examine, inspect, recondition, re-examine, repair, restore, service, survey ~*n.* **2.** check, checkup, examination, going-over (*Inf.*), inspection, reconditioning, service ~*v.* **3.** catch up with, draw level with, get ahead of, overtake, pass

overhead **1.** *adv.* above, aloft, atop, in the sky, on high, skyward, up above, upward **2.** *adj.* aerial, overhanging, roof, upper

overheads burden, oncosts, operating cost(s), running cost(s)

overindulge be immoderate *or* intemperate, drink *or* eat too much, have a binge (*Inf.*), live it up (*Inf.*), make a pig of oneself (*Inf.*), overdo it

overindulgence excess, immoderation, intemperance, overeating, surfeit

overload burden, encumber, oppress, overburden, overcharge, overtax, saddle (with), strain, weigh down

overlook **1.** disregard, fail to notice, forget, ignore, leave out of consideration, leave undone, miss, neglect, omit, pass, slight, slip up on **2.** blink at, condone, disregard, excuse, forgive, let bygones be bygones, let one off with, let pass, let ride, make allowances for, pardon, turn a blind eye to, wink at **3.** afford a view of, command a view of, front on to, give upon, have a view of, look over *or* out on

overpower beat, conquer, crush, defeat, get the upper hand over, immobilize, knock out, master, overcome, overthrow, overwhelm, quell, subdue, subjugate, vanquish

overpowering compelling, extreme, forceful, invincible, irrefutable, irresistible, nauseating, overwhelming, powerful, sickening, strong, suffocating, telling, unbearable, uncontrollable

overrate assess too highly, exaggerate, make too much of, overestimate, overpraise, overprize, over-

overrule (əʊvə'ru:l) *vt.* **1.** disallow arguments of (person) by use of authority **2.** rule or decide against (decision *etc.*) **3.** prevail over; influence **4.** exercise rule over

overseas ('əʊvə'si:z) *a.* **1.** foreign **2.** from or to a place over the sea (*also* **over'sea**) *—adv.* (əʊvə'si:z) **3.** beyond the sea; abroad

overseer ('əʊvəsi:ə) *n.* supervisor **—over'see** *vt.* supervise

oversight ('əʊvəsaɪt) *n.* **1.** failure to notice **2.** mistake

overt ('əʊvɜ:t) *a.* open, unconcealed

overtake (əʊvə'teɪk) *vt.* **1.** move past (vehicle, person) travelling in same direction **2.** come up with in pursuit **3.** catch up

overthrow (əʊvə'θrəʊ) *vt.* **1.** upset, overturn **2.** defeat (-'**threw**, -'**thrown**, -'**throwing**) *—n.* ('əʊvəθrəʊ) **3.** ruin **4.** defeat **5.** fall

overtime ('əʊvətaɪm) *n.* **1.** time at work, outside normal working hours **2.** payment for this time

overtone ('əʊvətəʊn) *n.* additional meaning, nuance

overture ('əʊvətjʊə) *n.* **1.** *Mus.* orchestral introduction **2.** opening of negotiations **3.** formal offer

overweening (əʊvə'wi:nɪŋ) *a.* thinking too much of oneself

overwhelm (əʊvə'wɛlm) *vt.* **1.** crush **2.** submerge, engulf **—over'whelming** *a.* **1.** decisive **2.** irresistible **—over'whelmingly** *adv.*

overwrought (əʊvə'rɔ:t) *a.* **1.** overexcited **2.** too elaborate

ovi- *or* **ovo-** (*comb. form*) egg; ovum, as in *oviform*

over'ripe
over'run
over'sensitive
over'shadow
'overshoe
over'shoot
oversimplifi'cation
over'simplify
over'sleep
over'specialize
over'spend
over'spill *v.*
'overspill *n.*
over'stay
over'steer *v.*
'oversteer *n.*
over'step
over'stock *v.*
over'stretch
over'tire
'overtop
over'turn
over'use
over'weight
over'work *v.*
'overwork *n.*
over'zealous

THESAURUS

sell, overvalue, rate too highly, think *or* expect too much of, think too highly of

override annul, cancel, countermand, disregard, ignore, nullify, outweigh, overrule, quash, reverse, ride roughshod over, set aside, supersede, take no account of, trample underfoot, upset, vanquish

overrule **1.** alter, annul, cancel, countermand, disallow, invalidate, make null and void, outvote, override, overturn, recall, repeal, rescind, reverse, revoke, rule against, set aside, veto **2.** bend to one's will, control, direct, dominate, govern, influence, prevail over, sway

overseer boss (*Inf.*), chief, foreman, gaffer (*Inf.*), manager, master, super (*Inf.*), superintendent, superior, supervisor

oversight blunder, carelessness, delinquency, error, fault, inattention, lapse, laxity, mistake, neglect, omission, slip

overt apparent, manifest, observable, obvious, open, patent, plain, public, unconcealed, undisguised, visible

overtake catch up with, do better than, draw level with, get past, leave behind, outdistance, outdo, outstrip, overhaul, pass

overthrow *v.* **1.** abolish, beat, bring down, conquer, crush, defeat, depose, dethrone, do away with, master, oust, overcome, overpower, overwhelm, subdue, subjugate, topple, unseat, vanquish **2.** bring to ruin, demolish, destroy, knock down, level, overturn, put an end to, raze, ruin, subvert, upend, upset *~n.* **3.** defeat, deposition, destruction, dethronement, discomfiture, disestablishment, displacement, dispossession, downfall, end, fall, ousting, prostration, rout, ruin, subjugation, subversion, suppression, undoing, unseating

overtone association, connotation, flavour, hint, implication, innuendo, intimation, nuance, sense, suggestion, undercurrent

overture **1.** *Often plural* advance, approach, conciliatory move, invitation, offer, opening move, proposal, proposition, signal, tender **2.** *Music* introduction, opening, prelude

overturn capsize, keel over, knock over *or* down, overbalance, reverse, spill, tip over, topple, tumble, upend, upset, upturn

overweening arrogant, cavalier, cocksure, cocky, conceited, egotistical, haughty, high and mighty (*Inf.*), high-handed, insolent, lordly, opinionated, pompous, presumptuous, proud, self-confident, supercilious, uppish (*Brit. inf.*), vain, vainglorious

overweight *adj.* ample, bulky, chubby, chunky, corpulent, fat, fleshy, gross, heavy, hefty, huge, massive, obese, on the plump side, outsize, plump, podgy, portly, stout, tubby (*Inf.*), well-padded (*Inf.*), well-upholstered (*Inf.*)

overwhelm **1.** bury, crush, deluge, engulf, flood, inundate, snow under, submerge, swamp **2.** crush, cut to pieces, destroy, massacre, overpower, overrun, rout

overwhelming breathtaking, crushing, devastating, invincible, irresistible, overpowering, shattering, stunning, towering, uncontrollable, vast, vastly superior

overwork be a slave-driver *or* hard taskmaster to, burden, burn the midnight oil, drive into the ground, exhaust, exploit, fatigue, oppress, overstrain, overtax, overuse, prostrate, strain, sweat (*Inf.*), wear out, weary, work one's fingers to the bone

overwrought **1.** agitated, beside oneself, distracted, excited, frantic, in a state (tizzy, twitter) (*Inf.*), keyed up, on edge, overexcited, overworked, stirred, strung up (*Inf.*), tense, uptight (*Inf.*), worked up (*Inf.*), wound up (*Inf.*) **2.** baroque, busy, contrived, florid, flowery, fussy, overdone, overelaborate, overembellished, overornate, rococo

oviduct ('ɒvɪdʌkt, 'əʊ-) *n.* tube through which ova are conveyed from ovary (*also* (in mammals) **Fallopian tube**) —**oviducal** (ɒvɪ'djuːk°l, əʊ-) *or* **ovi'ductal** *a.*

oviform ('əʊvɪfɔːm) *a.* egg-shaped

ovine ('əʊvaɪn) *a.* of, like, sheep

oviparous (əʊ'vɪpərəs) *a.* laying eggs

ovoid ('əʊvɔɪd) *a.* egg-shaped

ovoviviparous (əʊvəʊvaɪ'vɪpərəs) *a.* (of certain reptiles, fishes *etc.*) producing eggs that hatch within body of mother —**ovovivi'parity** *n.*

ovule ('ɒvjuːl) *n.* unfertilized seed —**'ovulate** *vi.* produce, discharge egg from ovary —**ovu'lation** *n.*

ovum ('əʊvəm) *n.* female egg cell, in which development of foetus takes place (*pl.* **'ova**)

owe (əʊ) *vt.* be bound to repay, be indebted for —**'owing** *a.* owed, due —**owing to** caused by, as a result of

owl (aʊl) *n.* night bird of prey —**'owlet** *n.* young owl —**'owlish** *a.* solemn and dull

own (əʊn) *a.* **1.** emphasizes possession —*vt.* **2.** possess **3.** acknowledge —*vi.* **4.** confess —**'owner** *n.* —**'ownership** *n.* possession

ox (ɒks) *n.* **1.** large cloven-footed and usu. horned farm animal **2.** bull or cow (*pl.* **'oxen**) —**'oxbow** *n.* **1.** U-shaped harness collar of ox **2.** lake formed from deep bend of river —**'oxeye** *n.* daisylike plant —**'oxtail** *n.* skinned tail of ox, used *esp.* in soups and stews —**'oxtongue** *n.* **1.** any of various plants having bristly tongue-shaped leaves **2.** tongue of ox, braised or boiled as food

oxalis ('ɒksəlɪs, ɒk'sælɪs) *n.* genus of plants —**oxalic acid** (ɒk'sælɪk) poisonous acid derived from oxalis

Oxbridge ('ɒksbrɪdʒ) *n.* Brit. universities of Oxford and Cambridge, *esp.* considered as prestigious academic institutions

oxen ('ɒksən) *n., pl. of* ox

Oxfam ('ɒksfæm) Oxford Committee for Famine Relief

oxide ('ɒksaɪd) *n.* compound of oxygen and one other element —**oxidate** ('ɒksɪdeɪt) *v.* —**oxidation** (ɒksɪ'deɪʃən) *n.* act or process of oxidizing —**oxidization** *or* **-isation** (ɒksɪdaɪ'zeɪʃən) *n.* —**oxidize** *or* **-ise** ('ɒksɪdaɪz) *v.* (cause to) combine with oxide, rust

Oxon. ('ɒksən) Oxfordshire

oxygen ('ɒksɪdʒən) *n.* gas in atmosphere essential to life, combustion *etc.* —**'oxygenate, 'oxygenize** *or* **-ise** *vt.* combine or treat with oxygen —**oxya'cetylene** *a.* denoting flame used for welding produced by mixture of oxygen and acetylene —**oxygen tent** *Med.* transparent enclosure covering patient, into which oxygen is released to help maintain respiration

oxymoron (ɒksɪ'mɔːrɒn) *n.* figure of speech in which two ideas of opposite meaning are combined to form an expressive phrase or epithet, as in *cruel kindness* (*pl.* **-mora** (-'mɔːrə))

oyez *or* **oyes** ('əʊjɛs, -jɛz) *n.* call, uttered three times by public crier or court official

oyster ('ɔɪstə) *n.* edible bivalve mollusc or shellfish —**'oystercatcher** *n.* shore bird

oz *or* **oz.** ounce

ozone ('əʊzəʊn, əʊ'zəʊn) *n.* form of oxygen with pungent odour —**'ozonize** *or* **-ise** *vt.*

THESAURUS

owe be beholden to, be in arrears, be in debt, be obligated *or* indebted, be under an obligation to

owing *adj.* due, outstanding, overdue, owed, payable, unpaid, unsettled

owing to *prep.* as a result of, because of, caused by, on account of

own *adj.* **1.** individual, particular, personal, private ~*v.* **2.** be in possession of, be responsible for, enjoy, have, hold, keep, possess, retain **3.** acknowledge, admit, allow, allow to be valid, avow, concede, confess, disclose, go along with (*Inf.*), grant, recognize

owner holder, landlord, lord, master, mistress, possessor, proprietor, proprietress, proprietrix

ownership dominion, possession, proprietary rights, proprietorship, right of possession, title

P

p *or* **P** (piː) *n.* **1.** 16th letter of English alphabet **2.** speech sound represented by this letter (*pl.* **p's, P's** *or* **Ps**) —**mind one's p's and q's** be careful to use polite language

p 1. page **2.** pence **3.** penny **4.** *Mus.* piano (softly)

P 1. (car) park **2.** *Chess* pawn **3.** *Chem.* phosphorus **4.** pressure

Pa *Chem.* protactinium

PA Pennsylvania

P.A. 1. personal assistant **2.** *Mil.* Post Adjutant **3.** power of attorney **4.** press agent **5.** Press Association **6.** private account **7.** public-address system **8.** publicity agent **9.** Publishers Association **10.** purchasing agent

p.a. per annum

PABX UK private automatic branch exchange (*see also* PBX)

pace[1] (peɪs) *n.* **1.** step **2.** its length **3.** rate of movement **4.** walk, gait —*vi.* **5.** step —*vt.* **6.** set speed for **7.** cross, measure with steps —ˈ**pacer** *n.* one who sets the pace for another —ˈ**pacemaker** *n. esp.* electronic device surgically implanted in those with heart disease

pace[2] (ˈpeɪsɪ; *Lat.* ˈpɑːkɛ) *prep.* with due deference to: used to acknowledge politely someone who disagrees

pachyderm (ˈpækɪdɜːm) *n.* thick-skinned animal, *eg* elephant —**pachyˈdermatous** *a.* thick-skinned, stolid

pacify (ˈpæsɪfaɪ) *vt.* **1.** calm **2.** restore to peace (**-ified, -ifying**) —**paˈcific** *a.* **1.** peaceable **2.** calm, tranquil —**pacifiˈcation** *n.* —**pacifiˈcatory** *a.* tending to make peace —ˈ**pacifier** *n.* **1.** person or thing that pacifies **2.** US baby's dummy or teething ring —ˈ**pacifism** *n.* —ˈ**pacifist** *n.* **1.** advocate of abolition of war **2.** one who refuses to participate in war

pack (pæk) *n.* **1.** bundle **2.** band of animals **3.** large set of people or things **4.** set of, container for, retail commodities **5.** set of playing cards **6.** mass of floating ice —*v.* **7.** put (articles) together in suitcase *etc.* **8.** press tightly together, cram —*vt.* **9.** make into a bundle **10.** fill with things **11.** fill (meeting *etc.*) with one's own supporters **12.** (*oft. with* off *or* away) order off —ˈ**package** *n.* **1.** parcel **2.** set of items offered together —*vt.* **3.** wrap in or put into package —ˈ**packet** *n.* **1.** small parcel **2.** small container (and contents) **3.** *sl.* large sum of money —**package holiday** holiday with fixed itinerary and at price inclusive of travel and lodging —**packet (boat)** *n.* mail-boat —ˈ**packhorse** *n.* horse for carrying goods —**pack ice** loose floating ice which has been compacted together —**pack saddle** saddle for carrying goods

pact (pækt) *n.* covenant, agreement, compact

pad[1] (pæd) *n.* **1.** piece of soft stuff used as a cushion, protection *etc.* **2.** block of sheets of paper **3.** foot or sole of various animals **4.** place for launching rockets **5.** *sl.* residence —*vt.* **6.** make soft, fill in, protect *etc.* with pad or padding (**-dd-**) —ˈ**padding** *n.* **1.** material used for stuffing **2.** literary matter put in simply to increase quantity —**padded cell** room, *esp.* in mental hospital, with padded surfaces, in which violent inmates are placed

pad[2] (pæd) *vi.* **1.** walk with soft step **2.** travel slowly (**-dd-**) —*n.* **3.** sound of soft footstep

paddle[1] (ˈpædᵊl) *n.* **1.** short oar with broad blade at one or each end —*v.* **2.** move by, as with, paddles **3.** row gently —**paddle wheel** wheel with crosswise blades striking water successively to propel ship

paddle[2] (ˈpædᵊl) *vi.* **1.** walk with bare feet in shallow water —*n.* **2.** act of paddling

paddock (ˈpædək) *n.* small grass field or enclosure

paddy[1] (ˈpædɪ) *n.* rice growing or in the husk —**paddy field** field where rice is grown

THESAURUS

pace *n.* **1.** gait, measure, step, stride, tread, walk **2.** clip (*Inf.*), lick (*Inf.*), momentum, motion, movement, progress, rate, speed, tempo, time, velocity ~*v.* **3.** march, patrol, pound, stride, walk back and forth, walk up and down **4.** count, determine, mark out, measure, step

pacific 1. appeasing, conciliatory, diplomatic, irenic, pacificatory, peacemaking, placatory, propitiatory **2.** dovelike, dovish, friendly, gentle, mild, nonbelligerent, nonviolent, pacifist, peaceable, peace-loving **3.** at peace, calm, halcyon, peaceful, placid, quiet, serene, smooth, still, tranquil, unruffled

pacifist conchie (*Inf.*), conscientious objector, dove, passive resister, peace lover, peacemonger, peacenik (*Inf.*), satyagrahi

pack *n.* **1.** back pack, bale, bundle, burden, fardel (*Archaic*), kit, kitbag, knapsack, load, package, packet, parcel, rucksack, truss **2.** assemblage, band, bunch, collection, company, crew, crowd, deck, drove, flock, gang, group, herd, lot, mob, set, troop ~*v.* **3.** batch, bundle, burden, load, package, packet, store, stow **4.** charge, compact, compress, cram, crowd, fill, jam, mob, press, ram, stuff, tamp, throng, wedge **5.** *With* **off** bundle out, dismiss, hustle out, send away, send packing (*Inf.*), send someone about his business

package *n.* **1.** box, carton, container, packet, parcel **2.** amalgamation, combination, entity, unit, whole ~*v.* **3.** batch, box, pack, packet, parcel (up), wrap, wrap up

packet 1. bag, carton, container, package, parcel, poke (*Dialect*), wrapper, wrapping **2.** *Sl.* a bob or two (*Brit. inf.*), bomb (*Brit. sl.*), bundle (*Sl.*), fortune, king's ransom (*Inf.*), lot(s), mint, pile (*Inf.*), pot(s) (*Inf.*), pretty penny (*Inf.*), tidy sum (*Inf.*)

pact agreement, alliance, arrangement, bargain, bond, compact, concord, concordat, contract, convention, covenant, deal, league, protocol, treaty, understanding

pad *n.* **1.** buffer, cushion, protection, stiffening, stuffing, wad **2.** block, jotter, notepad, tablet, writing pad **3.** foot, paw, sole **4.** *Sl.* apartment, flat, hang-out (*Inf.*), home, place, quarters, room ~*v.* **5.** cushion, fill, line, pack, protect, shape, stuff

padding 1. filling, packing, stuffing, wadding **2.** hot air (*Inf.*), prolixity, verbiage, verbosity, waffle (*Inf.*), wordiness

paddle[1] **1.** *n.* oar, scull, sweep **2.** *v.* oar, propel pull, row, scull

paddle[2] dabble, plash, slop, splash (about), stir, wade

paddy[2] (ˈpædɪ) *n. inf.* temper

padlock (ˈpædlɒk) *n.* **1.** detachable lock with hinged hoop to go through staple or ring —*vt.* **2.** fasten thus

padre (ˈpɑːdrɪ) *n.* chaplain with the armed forces

paean *or U.S. (sometimes)* **pean** (ˈpiːən) *n.* song of triumph or thanksgiving

paederast (ˈpɛdəræst) *n. see* PEDERAST

paediatrics *or U.S.* **pediatrics** (piːdɪˈætrɪks) *n.* branch of medicine dealing with diseases and disorders of children —**paediaˈtrician** *or U.S.* **pediaˈtrician** *n.*

paedo-, pedo- *or before vowel* **paed-, ped-** (*comb. form*) child, children, as in *paedophilia*

paedophilia (piːdəʊˈfɪlɪə) *n.* condition of being sexually attracted to children —**paedophile** (ˈpiːdəʊfaɪl) *or* **paedoˈphiliac** *n./a.*

paella (paɪˈɛlə) *n.* **1.** Sp. dish of rice, shellfish *etc.* **2.** pan in which paella is cooked

pagan (ˈpeɪgən) *a./n.* heathen —**ˈpaganism** *n.*

page[1] (peɪdʒ) *n.* one side of leaf of book *etc.*

page[2] (peɪdʒ) *n.* **1.** boy servant or attendant —*vt.* **2.** summon by loudspeaker announcement —**ˈpageboy** *n.* medium-length hairstyle with ends of hair curled under

pageant (ˈpædʒənt) *n.* **1.** show of persons in costume in procession, dramatic scenes *etc.*, usu. illustrating history **2.** brilliant show —**ˈpageantry** *n.*

paginate (ˈpædʒɪneɪt) *vt.* number pages of —**pagiˈnation** *n.*

pagoda (pəˈgəʊdə) *n.* pyramidal temple or tower of Chinese or Indian type

paid (peɪd) *pt./pp. of* PAY —**put paid to** *inf.* end, destroy

pail (peɪl) *n.* bucket —**ˈpailful** *n.*

paillasse (ˈpælɪæs, pælɪˈæs) *n. see* PALLIASSE

pain (peɪn) *n.* **1.** bodily or mental suffering **2.** penalty or punishment —*pl.* **3.** trouble, exertion —*vt.* **4.** inflict pain upon —**pained** *a.* having or expressing pain or distress, *esp.* mental or emotional —**ˈpainful** *a.* —**ˈpainfully** *adv.* —**ˈpainless** *a.* —**ˈpainlessly** *adv.* —**ˈpainkiller** *n.* drug, as aspirin, that reduces pain —**ˈpainstaking** *a.* diligent, careful

paint (peɪnt) *n.* **1.** colouring matter spread on a surface with brushes, roller, spray gun *etc.* —*vt.* **2.** portray, colour, coat, or make picture of, with paint **3.** apply make-up to **4.** describe —**ˈpainter** *n.* —**ˈpainting** *n.* picture in paint

painter (ˈpeɪntə) *n.* line at bow of boat for tying it up

pair (pɛə) *n.* **1.** set of two, *esp.* existing or generally used together —*v.* **2.** (*oft. with* off) group or be grouped in twos

paisley (ˈpeɪzlɪ) *n.* pattern of small curving shapes

pajamas (pəˈdʒɑːməz) *pl.n.* US *see* PYJAMAS

Pakistani (pɑːkɪˈstɑːnɪ) *a.* **1.** of Pakistan, country in Indian subcontinent —*n.* **2.** native or inhabitant of Pakistan

pal (pæl) *n. inf.* friend —**ˈpally** *a. inf.* on friendly terms

palace (ˈpælɪs) *n.* **1.** residence of king, bishop *etc.* **2.** stately mansion —**paˈlatial** *a.* **1.** like a palace **2.** magnificent —**ˈpalatine** *a.* with royal privileges

paladin (ˈpælədɪn) *n. Hist.* knight errant

palaeo-, *before vowel* **palae-** *or esp. U.S.* **paleo-, pale-** (*comb. form*) old, ancient, prehistoric, as in *palaeography*

Palaeocene (ˈpælɪəʊsiːn) *a.* **1.** of first epoch of Tertiary period —*n.* **2.** Palaeocene epoch or rock series

Palaeolithic (pælɪəʊˈlɪθɪk) *a.* of the old Stone Age

palaeontology (pælɪɒnˈtɒlədʒɪ) *n.* study of past geological periods and fossils —**palaeontoˈlogical** *a.*

Palaeozoic (pælɪəʊˈzəʊɪk) *a.* **1.** of geological time

THESAURUS

pagan **1.** *n.* Gentile, heathen, idolater, infidel, polytheist, unbeliever **2.** *adj.* Gentile, heathen, heathenish, idolatrous, infidel, irreligious, polytheistic

page[1] *n.* folio, leaf, sheet, side

page[2] **1.** *n.* attendant, bellboy (*U.S.*), footboy, pageboy, servant, squire **2.** *v.* announce, call, call out, preconize, seek, send for, summon

pageant display, extravaganza, parade, procession, ritual, show, spectacle, tableau

pageantry display, drama, extravagance, glamour, glitter, grandeur, magnificence, parade, pomp, show, showiness, spectacle, splash (*Inf.*), splendour, state, theatricality

pain *n.* **1.** ache, cramp, discomfort, hurt, irritation, pang, smarting, soreness, spasm, suffering, tenderness, throb, throe (*Rare*), trouble, twinge **2.** affliction, agony, anguish, bitterness, distress, grief, heartache, misery, suffering, torment, torture, tribulation, woe, wretchedness ~*v.* **3.** ail, chafe, discomfort, harm, hurt, inflame, injure, smart, sting, throb **4.** afflict, aggrieve, agonize, cut to the quick, disquiet, distress, grieve, hurt, sadden, torment, torture, vex, worry, wound

pained aggrieved, anguished, distressed, hurt, injured, miffed (*Inf.*), offended, reproachful, stung, unhappy, upset, worried, wounded

painful **1.** afflictive, disagreeable, distasteful, distressing, grievous, saddening, unpleasant **2.** aching, agonizing, excruciating, harrowing, hurting, inflamed, raw, smarting, sore, tender, throbbing

painfully alarmingly, clearly, deplorably, distressingly, dreadfully, excessively, markedly, sadly, unfortunately, woefully

painkiller anaesthetic, analgesic, anodyne, drug, palliative, remedy, sedative

painless easy, effortless, fast, no trouble, pain-free, quick, simple, trouble-free

pains assiduousness, bother, care, diligence, effort, industry, labour, special attention, trouble

painstaking assiduous, careful, conscientious, diligent, earnest, exacting, hard-working, industrious, meticulous, persevering, punctilious, scrupulous, sedulous, strenuous, thorough, thoroughgoing

paint *n.* **1.** colour, colouring, dye, emulsion, pigment, stain, tint ~*v.* **2.** catch a likeness, delineate, depict, draw, figure, picture, portray, represent, sketch **3.** apply, coat, colour, cover, daub, decorate, slap on (*Inf.*) **4.** bring to life, capture, conjure up a vision, depict, describe, evoke, make one see, portray, put graphically, recount, tell vividly

pair **1.** *n.* brace, combination, couple, doublet, duo, match, matched set, span, twins, two of a kind, twosome, yoke **2.** *v.* bracket, couple, join, marry, match, match up, mate, pair off, put together, team, twin, wed, yoke

that began with Cambrian period and lasted until end of Permian period —*n.* **2.** Palaeozoic era

palanquin *or* **palankeen** (pælənˈkiːn) *n.* covered litter, formerly used in Orient, carried on shoulders of four men

palate (ˈpælɪt) *n.* **1.** roof of mouth **2.** sense of taste —**ˈpalatable** *a.* agreeable to eat —**ˈpalatal** *or* **ˈpalatine** *a.* **1.** of the palate **2.** made by placing tongue against palate —*n.* **3.** palatal sound

palatial (pəˈleɪʃəl) *a. see* PALACE

palaver (pəˈlɑːvə) *n.* **1.** fuss **2.** conference, discussion

pale[1] (peɪl) *a.* **1.** wan, dim, whitish —*vi.* **2.** whiten **3.** lose superiority or importance —**ˈpaleface** *n.* derogatory term for White person, said to have been used by N Amer. Indians

pale[2] (peɪl) *n.* stake, boundary —**ˈpaling** *n.* upright plank making up fence

paleo- *or before vowel* **pale-** (*comb. form*) *esp.* **US** *see* PALAEO-

Palestinian (pælɪˈstɪnɪən) *a.* **1.** of Palestine, former country in Middle East —*n.* **2.** native or inhabitant of this area **3.** descendant of inhabitant of this area, displaced when Israel became state

palette *or* **pallet** (ˈpælɪt) *n.* artist's flat board for mixing colours on —**palette knife** spatula with thin flexible blade, used in painting *etc.*

palimony (ˈpælɪmənɪ) *n U.S.* alimony awarded to nonmarried partner after break-up of long relationship

palindrome (ˈpælɪndrəʊm) *n.* word, verse or sentence that is the same when read backwards or forwards

palisade (pælɪˈseɪd) *n.* **1.** fence of stakes —*vt.* **2.** enclose or protect with one

pall[1] (pɔːl) *n.* **1.** cloth spread over a coffin **2.** depressing, oppressive atmosphere —**ˈpallbearer** *n.* one carrying, attending coffin at funeral

pall[2] (pɔːl) *vi.* **1.** become tasteless or tiresome **2.** cloy

palladium (pəˈleɪdɪəm) *n.* silvery-white element of platinum metal group, used in jewellery *etc.*

pallet[1] (ˈpælɪt) *n.* **1.** straw mattress **2.** small bed

pallet[2] (ˈpælɪt) *n.* portable platform for storing and moving goods

palliasse *or* **paillasse** (ˈpælɪæs, pælɪˈæs) *n.* straw mattress

palliate (ˈpælɪeɪt) *vt.* **1.** relieve without curing **2.** excuse —**palliˈation** *n.* —**palliative** (ˈpælɪətɪv) *a.* **1.** giving temporary or partial relief —*n.* **2.** that which excuses, mitigates or alleviates

pallid (ˈpælɪd) *a.* pale, wan, colourless —**ˈpallor** *n.* paleness

palm (pɑːm) *n.* **1.** inner surface of hand **2.** tropical tree **3.** leaf of the tree as symbol of victory —*vt.* **4.** conceal in palm of hand **5.** pass off by trickery —**palmate** (ˈpælmeɪt, -mɪt) *or* **ˈpalmated** *a.* **1.** shaped like open hand **2.** *Bot.* having five lobes that spread out from common point **3.** (of water birds) having three toes connected by web —**ˈpalmist** *n.* —**ˈpalmistry** *n.* fortune-telling from lines on palm of hand —**ˈpalmy** *a.* flourishing, successful —**palm oil** oil obtained from fruit of certain palms —**Palm Sunday** Sunday before Easter —**palm off** (*oft. with* on) **1.** offer, sell or spend fraudulently **2.** divert in order to be rid of

palomino (pæləˈmiːnəʊ) *n.* golden horse with white mane and tail (*pl.* **-s**)

palpable (ˈpælpəbᵊl) *a.* **1.** obvious **2.** certain **3.** that may be touched or felt —**ˈpalpably** *adv.*

palpate (ˈpælpeɪt) *vt. Med.* examine by touch

palpitate (ˈpælpɪteɪt) *vi.* **1.** throb **2.** pulsate violently —**palpiˈtation** *n.* **1.** throbbing **2.** violent, irregular beating of heart

palsy (ˈpɔːlzɪ) *n.* paralysis

paltry (ˈpɔːltrɪ) *a.* worthless, contemptible, trifling

pampas (ˈpæmpəz) *n.* (*oft. with pl. v.*) vast grassy treeless plains in S Amer.

pamper (ˈpæmpə) *vt.* overindulge, spoil by coddling

pamphlet (ˈpæmflɪt) *n.* thin unbound book usu. on some topical subject

pan[1] (pæn) *n.* **1.** broad, shallow vessel **2.** bowl of lavatory **3.** depression in ground, *esp.* where salt forms

THESAURUS

palatable appetizing, delectable, delicious, luscious, mouthwatering, savoury, tasty, toothsome

palate appetite, heart, stomach, taste

palatial de luxe, grand, grandiose, illustrious, imposing, luxurious, magnificent, majestic, opulent, plush (*Inf.*), regal, spacious, splendid, stately, sumptuous

pale *adj.* **1.** anaemic, ashen, ashy, bleached, bloodless, colourless, faded, light, pallid, pasty, sallow, wan, washed-out, white, whitish **2.** dim, faint, feeble, inadequate, poor, thin, weak ~*v.* **3.** become pale, blanch, go white, lose colour, whiten **4.** decrease, diminish, fade, lessen

pall *v.* become dull *or* tedious, bore, cloy, glut, jade, satiate, sicken, surfeit, tire, weary

palm **1.** hand, mitt (*Sl.*), paw (*Inf.*) **2.** *Fig.* bays, crown, fame, glory, honour, laurels, merit, prize, success, triumph, trophy, victory

palm off **1.** *With* **on** *or* **with** fob off, foist off, pass off **2.** *With* **on** foist on, force upon, impose upon, take advantage of, thrust upon, unload upon

palmy flourishing, fortunate, glorious, golden, halcyon, happy, joyous, luxurious, prosperous, thriving, triumphant

palpable **1.** apparent, blatant, clear, conspicuous, evident, manifest, obvious, open, patent, plain, unmistakable, visible **2.** concrete, material, real, solid, substantial, tangible, touchable

palpitate beat, flutter, pitapat, pitter-patter, pound, pulsate, pulse, quiver, shiver, throb, tremble, vibrate

paltry base, beggarly, contemptible, derisory, despicable, inconsiderable, insignificant, low, meagre, mean, Mickey Mouse (*Sl.*), minor, miserable, petty, picayune (*U.S.*), piddling (*Inf.*), pitiful, poor, puny, slight, small, sorry, trifling, trivial, twopenny-halfpenny (*Brit. inf.*), unimportant, worthless, wretched

pamper baby, cater to one's every whim, coddle, cosset, fondle, gratify, humour, indulge, mollycoddle, pet, spoil

pamphlet booklet, brochure, circular, folder, leaflet, tract

pan[1] **1.** *n.* container, pot, saucepan, vessel **2.** *v. Inf.* censure, criticize, flay, hammer (*Brit.*), knock (*Inf.*), roast (*Inf.*), rubbish (*Inf.*), slam (*Sl.*), slate (*Inf.*), throw brickbats at (*Inf.*)

—*vt.* **4.** wash (gold ore) in pan **5.** *inf.* criticize harshly (**-nn-**) —ˈ**pantile** *n.* curved roofing tile —**pan out** result

pan[2] (pæn) *v.* move (film camera) slowly while filming to cover scene, follow moving object *etc.* (**-nn-**)

pan- (*comb. form*) all, as in *panacea, pantomime.* Such words are not given here where the meaning may easily be inferred from simple word

panacea (pænəˈsɪə) *n.* universal remedy, cure for all ills

panache (pəˈnæʃ, -ˈnɑːʃ) *n.* dashing style

Panama hat (pænəˈmɑː) straw hat

Pan-American *a.* of North, South and Central Amer. collectively

pancake (ˈpænkeɪk) *n.* **1.** thin cake of batter fried in pan **2.** flat cake or stick of compressed make-up —*vi.* **3.** *Aviation* make flat landing by dropping in a level position —**Pancake Day** *see* **Shrove Tuesday** *at* SHROVETIDE

panchromatic (pænkrəʊˈmætɪk) *a. Photog.* sensitive to light of all colours

pancreas (ˈpæŋkrɪəs) *n.* digestive gland behind stomach —**pancreˈatic** *a.*

panda (ˈpændə) *n.* large black and white bearlike mammal of China —**panda car** police patrol car

pandemic (pænˈdɛmɪk) *a.* (of disease) occurring over wide area

pandemonium (pændɪˈməʊnɪəm) *n.* scene of din and uproar

pander (ˈpændə) *v.* **1.** (*esp. with* to) give gratification (to weakness or desires) —*n.* **2.** pimp

pandit (ˈpʌndɪt; *spelling pron.* ˈpændɪt) *n. see* PUNDIT (sense 2)

P. & L. profit and loss

p. & p. UK postage and packing

pane (peɪn) *n.* single piece of glass in window or door

panegyric (pænɪˈdʒɪrɪk) *n.* speech of praise —**paneˈgyrical** *a.* laudatory —**paneˈgyrist** *n.*

panel (ˈpænᵊl) *n.* **1.** compartment of surface, usu. raised or sunk, *eg* in door **2.** any distinct section of something, *eg* of car body **3.** strip of material inserted in garment **4.** group of persons as team in quiz game *etc.* **5.** list of jurors, doctors *etc.* **6.** thin board with picture on it —*vt.* **7.** adorn with panels (**-ll-**) —ˈ**panelling** *or U.S.* ˈ**paneling** *n.* panelled work —ˈ**panellist** *or U.S.* ˈ**panelist** *n.* member of panel —**panel beater** one who repairs damage to car body —**panel game** quiz *etc.* played by group of people, *esp.* on TV

pang (pæŋ) *n.* **1.** sudden pain, sharp twinge **2.** compunction

pangolin (pæŋˈgəʊlɪn) *n.* mammal with scaly body and long snout for feeding on ants *etc.* (*also* **scaly anteater**)

panic (ˈpænɪk) *n.* **1.** sudden and infectious fear **2.** extreme fright **3.** unreasoning terror —*a.* **4.** of fear *etc.* —*v.* **5.** feel or cause to feel panic (**-icked, -icking**) —ˈ**panicky** *a.* **1.** inclined to panic **2.** nervous —ˈ**panicmonger** *n.* one who starts panic —**panic-stricken** *or* **panic-struck** *a.*

panicle (ˈpænɪkᵊl) *n.* compound raceme, as in oat

panjandrum (pænˈdʒændrəm) *n.* pompous self-important man

pannier (ˈpænɪə) *n.* basket carried by beast of burden, bicycle, or on person's shoulders

panoply (ˈpænəplɪ) *n.* complete, magnificent array —ˈ**panoplied** *a.*

panorama (pænəˈrɑːmə) *n.* **1.** wide or complete view **2.** picture arranged round spectator or unrolled before him —**panoˈramic** *a.*

panpipes (ˈpænpaɪps) *pl.n.* (*oft. sing., oft.* **P-**) number of reeds or whistles of graduated lengths bound together to form musical wind instrument (*also* **pipes of Pan, ˈsyrinx**)

pansy (ˈpænzɪ) *n.* **1.** flower, species of violet **2.** *inf.* effeminate man

pant (pænt) *vi.* **1.** gasp for breath **2.** yearn, long **3.** throb —*n.* **4.** gasp

pantaloon (pæntəˈluːn) *n.* **1.** in pantomime, foolish old man who is the butt of clown —*pl.* **2.** *inf.* baggy trousers

pantechnicon (pænˈtɛknɪkən) *n.* large van, *esp.* for carrying furniture

pantheism (ˈpænθɪɪzəm) *n.* identification of God with

THESAURUS

pan[2] *v.* follow, move, scan, sweep, swing, track, traverse

panacea catholicon, cure-all, elixir, nostrum, sovereign remedy, universal cure

panache a flourish, *brio*, dash, élan, flair, flamboyance, spirit, style, swagger, verve

pandemonium babel, bedlam, chaos, clamour, commotion, confusion, din, hubbub, hue and cry, hullabaloo, racket, ruckus (*Inf.*), ruction (*Inf.*), rumpus, tumult, turmoil, uproar

pang ache, agony, anguish, discomfort, distress, gripe, pain, prick, spasm, stab, sting, stitch, throe (*Rare*), twinge, wrench

panic *n.* **1.** agitation, alarm, consternation, dismay, fear, fright, horror, hysteria, scare, terror ~*v.* **2.** become hysterical, be terror-stricken, go to pieces (*Inf.*), lose one's bottle (*Sl.*), lose one's nerve, overreact **3.** alarm, put the wind up (someone) (*Inf.*), scare, startle, terrify, unnerve

panicky afraid, agitated, distressed, fearful, frantic, frenzied, frightened, hysterical, in a flap (*Inf.*), in a tizzy (*Inf.*), jittery (*Inf.*), nervous, windy (*Sl.*), worked up, worried

panic-stricken *or* **panic-struck** aghast, agitated, alarmed, appalled, fearful, frenzied, frightened, frightened out of one's wits, frightened to death, horrified, horror-stricken, hysterical, in a cold sweat (*Inf.*), panicky, petrified, scared, scared stiff, startled, terrified, terror-stricken, unnerved

panoply array, attire, dress, garb, get-up (*Inf.*), insignia, raiment (*Archaic*), regalia, show, trappings, turnout

panorama **1.** bird's-eye view, prospect, scenery, scenic view, view, vista **2.** overall picture, overview, perspective, survey

panoramic all-embracing, bird's-eye, comprehensive, extensive, far-reaching, general, inclusive, overall, scenic, sweeping, wide

pant *v.* **1.** blow, breathe, gasp, heave, huff, palpitate, puff, throb, wheeze **2.** *Fig.* ache, covet, crave, desire, hanker after, hunger, long, pine, set one's heart on, sigh, thirst, want, yearn ~*n.* **3.** gasp, huff, puff, wheeze

the universe —ˈ**pantheist** *n.* —**pantheˈistic** *a.* —ˈ**pantheon** *n.* temple of all gods

panther (ˈpænθə) *n.* variety of leopard

panties (ˈpæntɪz) *pl.n.* women's undergarment

pantihose (ˈpæntɪhəʊz) *n.* tights

panto (ˈpæntəʊ) *n.* **UK** *inf.* pantomime (*pl.* **-s**)

pantograph (ˈpæntəgrɑːf) *n.* instrument for copying maps *etc.* to any scale

pantomime (ˈpæntəmaɪm) *n.* **1.** theatrical show, usu. produced at Christmastime, oft. founded on fairy tale **2.** dramatic entertainment in dumbshow

pantry (ˈpæntrɪ) *n.* room for storing food or utensils

pants (pænts) *pl.n.* **1.** undergarment for lower trunk **2.** **US** trousers

panzer (ˈpænzə; *Ger.* ˈpantsər) *a.* **1.** of fast mechanized armoured units employed by German army in World War II —*n.* **2.** vehicle belonging to panzer unit, *esp.* tank —*pl.* **3.** armoured troops

pap[1] (pæp) *n.* **1.** soft food for infants, invalids *etc.* **2.** pulp, mash **3.** **SA** maize porridge

pap[2] (pæp) *n.* **1.** breast **2.** nipple

papa (pəˈpɑː) *n. inf.* father

papacy (ˈpeɪpəsɪ) *n.* **1.** office of Pope **2.** papal system —ˈ**papal** *a.* of, relating to, the Pope

paparazzo (pæpəˈrætsəʊ) *n.* freelance photographer who takes candid-camera shots of famous people (*pl.* **-razzi** (-ˈrætsiː))

papaw *or* **pawpaw** (ˈpɔːpɔː) *n.* **1.** tree bearing melon-shaped fruit **2.** its fruit (*also* **papaya** (pəˈpaɪə))

paper (ˈpeɪpə) *n.* **1.** material made by pressing pulp of rags, straw, wood *etc.* into thin, flat sheets **2.** printed sheet of paper **3.** newspaper **4.** article, essay **5.** set of examination questions —*pl.* **6.** documents *etc.* —*vt.* **7.** cover, decorate with paper —ˈ**paperback** *n.* book with flexible covers —ˈ**paperboy** *n.* boy employed to deliver newspapers (ˈ**papergirl** *fem.*) —**paper chase** cross-country run in which runner lays trail of paper for others to follow —ˈ**paperclip** *n.* clip for holding sheets of paper together, *esp.* one of bent wire —ˈ**paperhanger** *n.* person who hangs wallpaper as occupation —ˈ**paperknife** *n.* knife with comparatively blunt blade for opening sealed envelopes *etc.* —**paper money** paper currency issued by government or central bank as legal tender —ˈ**paperweight** *n.* small heavy object to prevent loose papers from scattering —ˈ**paperwork** *n.* clerical work, such as writing of reports or letters

papier-mâché (pæpjeɪˈmæʃeɪ) *n.* pulp from rags or paper mixed with size, shaped by moulding and dried hard

papilla (pəˈpɪlə) *n.* **1.** small projection of tissue at base of hair *etc.* **2.** any similar protuberance (*pl.* **-lae** (-liː)) —**paˈpillary,** ˈ**papillate** *or* ˈ**papillose** *a.*

papoose (pəˈpuːs) *n.* N Amer. Indian child

paprika (ˈpæprɪkə, pæˈpriː-) *n.* (powdered seasoning prepared from) type of red pepper

Pap test *or* **smear** (pæp) *Med.* examination of stained cells in smear taken of bodily secretions, *esp.* from uterus, for detection of cancer

papyrus (pəˈpaɪrəs) *n.* **1.** species of reed **2.** (manuscript written on) kind of paper made from this plant (*pl.* **-ri** (-raɪ), **-es**)

par (pɑː) *n.* **1.** equality of value or standing **2.** face value (of stocks and shares) **3.** *Golf* estimated standard score —ˈ**parity** *n.* **1.** equality **2.** analogy —**par value** value imprinted on face of share certificate or bond and used to assess dividend *etc.*

par. **1.** paragraph **2.** parallel **3.** parenthesis

para- *or before vowel* **par-** (*comb. form*) beside, beyond, as in *paradigm, parallel, parody*

parable (ˈpærəbᵊl) *n.* allegory, story with a moral lesson —**paraˈbolic(al)** *a.* of parable

parabola (pəˈræbələ) *n.* section of cone cut by plane parallel to the cone's side —**paraˈbolic** *a.* of parabola

paracetamol (pærəˈsiːtəmɒl, -ˈsɛtə-) *n.* mild drug used as alternative to aspirin

parachute (ˈpærəʃuːt) *n.* **1.** apparatus extending like umbrella used to retard the descent of a falling body —*v.* **2.** land or cause to land by parachute —ˈ**parachutist** *n.*

parade (pəˈreɪd) *n.* **1.** display **2.** muster of troops **3.** parade ground **4.** public walk —*vi.* **5.** march —*vt.* **6.** display

paradigm (ˈpærədaɪm) *n.* example, model —**paradigmatic** (pærədɪgˈmætɪk) *a.*

paradise (ˈpærədaɪs) *n.* **1.** Heaven **2.** state of bliss **3.** Garden of Eden

paradox (ˈpærədɒks) *n.* statement that seems absurd or self-contradictory but may be true —**paraˈdoxical** *a.*

paraffin (ˈpærəfɪn) *n.* waxlike or liquid hydrocarbon mixture used as fuel, solvent, in candles *etc.*

paragon (ˈpærəgən) *n.* pattern or model of excellence

THESAURUS

pants **1.** *Brit.* boxer shorts, briefs, drawers, knickers, panties, underpants, Y-fronts **2.** *U.S.* slacks, trousers

pap baby food, mash, mush, pulp

paper *n.* **1.** *Often plural* certificate, deed, documents, instrument, record **2.** *Plural* archive, diaries, documents, dossier, file, letters, records **3.** daily, gazette, journal, news, newspaper, organ, rag (*Inf.*) **4.** analysis, article, assignment, composition, critique, dissertation, essay, examination, monograph, report, script, study, thesis, treatise ~*v.* **5.** cover with paper, hang, line, paste up, wallpaper

par *n.* **1.** average, level, mean, median, norm, standard, usual **2.** balance, equal footing, equality, equilibrium, equivalence, parity

parable allegory, exemplum, fable, lesson, moral tale, story

parade *n.* **1.** array, cavalcade, ceremony, column, march, pageant, procession, review, spectacle, train **2.** array, display, exhibition, flaunting, ostentation, pomp, show, spectacle, vaunting ~*v.* **3.** defile, march, process **4.** air, brandish, display, exhibit, flaunt, make a show of, show, show off (*Inf.*), strut, swagger, vaunt

paradise **1.** City of God, divine abode, Elysian fields, garden of delights (*Islam*), heaven, heavenly kingdom, Olympus (*Poetic*), Promised Land, Zion **2.** Eden, Garden of Eden **3.** bliss, delight, felicity, heaven, seventh heaven, utopia

paradox absurdity, ambiguity, anomaly, contradiction, enigma, inconsistency, mystery, oddity, puzzle

paradoxical absurd, ambiguous, baffling, confounding, contradictory, enigmatic, equivocal, illogical,

paragraph (ˈpærəgrɑːf, -græf) *n.* **1.** section of chapter or book **2.** short notice, as in newspaper —*vt.* **3.** arrange in paragraphs

parakeet *or* **parrakeet** (ˈpærəkiːt) *n.* small kind of parrot

parallax (ˈpærəlæks) *n.* apparent difference in object's position or direction as viewed from different points

parallel (ˈpærəlɛl) *a.* **1.** continuously at equal distances **2.** precisely corresponding —*n.* **3.** line equidistant from another at all points **4.** thing exactly like another **5.** comparison **6.** line of latitude —*vt.* **7.** represent as similar, compare —**ˈparallelism** *n.* —**paralˈlelogram** *n.* four-sided plane figure with opposite sides parallel —**parallel bars** *Gymnastics* pair of wooden bars on uprights used for exercises

paralysis (pəˈrælɪsɪs) *n.* incapacity to move or feel, due to damage to nervous system (*pl.* **-yses** (-ɪsiːz)) —**ˈparalyse** *or U.S.* **-lyze** *vt.* **1.** afflict with paralysis **2.** cripple **3.** make useless or ineffectual —**paraˈlytic** *a./n.* (person) afflicted with paralysis —**infantile paralysis** poliomyelitis

paramedical (pærəˈmɛdɪkᵊl) *a.* of persons working in various capacities in support of medical profession

parameter (pəˈræmɪtə) *n.* any constant limiting factor

paramilitary (pærəˈmɪlɪtərɪ, -trɪ) *a.* of civilian group organized on military lines or in support of the military

paramount (ˈpærəmaʊnt) *a.* supreme, eminent, pre-eminent, chief

paramour (ˈpærəmʊə) *n. esp.* formerly, illicit lover, mistress

parang (ˈpɑːræŋ) *n.* heavy Malay knife

paranoia (pærəˈnɔɪə) *n.* mental disease with delusions of fame, grandeur, persecution —**paranoiac** (pærəˈnɔɪɪk) *a./n.* —**ˈparanoid** *a.* **1.** of paranoia **2.** *inf.* exhibiting fear of persecution *etc.* —*n.* **3.** person afflicted with paranoia

parapet (ˈpærəpɪt, -pɛt) *n.* low wall, railing along edge of balcony, bridge *etc.*

paraphernalia (pærəfəˈneɪlɪə) *pl.n.* (*sometimes with sing. v.*) **1.** personal belongings **2.** odds and ends of equipment

paraphrase (ˈpærəfreɪz) *n.* **1.** expression of meaning of passage in other words **2.** free translation —*vt.* **3.** put into other words

paraplegia (pærəˈpliːdʒə) *n.* paralysis of lower half of body —**paraˈplegic** *n./a.*

parapsychology (pærəsaɪˈkɒlədʒɪ) *n.* study of subjects pert. to extrasensory perception, *eg* telepathy

Paraquat (ˈpærəkwɒt) *n.* **R** very poisonous weedkiller

parasite (ˈpærəsaɪt) *n.* **1.** animal or plant living in or on another **2.** self-interested hanger-on —**parasitic** (pærəˈsɪtɪk) *a.* of the nature of, living as, parasite —**ˈparasitism** *n.*

parasol (ˈpærəsɒl) *n.* sunshade

parataxis (pærəˈtæksɪs) *n.* arrangement of sentences which omits connecting words

parathion (pærəˈθaɪɒn) *n.* toxic oil used as insecticide

paratroops (ˈpærətruːps) *pl.n.* troops trained to descend by parachute

paratyphoid fever (pærəˈtaɪfɔɪd) infectious disease similar to but distinct from typhoid fever

parboil (ˈpɑːbɔɪl) *vt.* boil until partly cooked

parcel (ˈpɑːsᵊl) *n.* **1.** packet of goods, *esp.* one enclosed in paper **2.** quantity dealt with at one time **3.** piece of land —*vt.* **4.** wrap up **5.** divide into parts (**-ll-**)

parch (pɑːtʃ) *v.* **1.** dry by heating **2.** make, become hot and dry **3.** scorch **4.** roast slightly

parchment (ˈpɑːtʃmənt) *n.* **1.** sheep, goat, calf skin prepared for writing **2.** manuscript of this

pardon (ˈpɑːdᵊn) *vt.* **1.** forgive, excuse —*n.* **2.** forgiveness **3.** release from punishment —**ˈpardonable** *a.* —**ˈpardonably** *adv.*

THESAURUS

impossible, improbable, inconsistent, puzzling, riddling

paragon apotheosis, archetype, criterion, cynosure, epitome, exemplar, ideal, jewel, masterpiece, model, nonesuch (*Archaic*), nonpareil, paradigm, pattern, prototype, quintessence, standard

paragraph clause, item, notice, part, passage, portion, section, subdivision

parallel *adj.* **1.** aligned, alongside, coextensive, equidistant, side by side **2.** akin, analogous, complementary, correspondent, corresponding, like, matching, resembling, similar, uniform ~*n.* **3.** analogue, complement, corollary, counterpart, duplicate, equal, equivalent, likeness, match, twin **4.** analogy, comparison, correlation, correspondence, likeness, parallelism, resemblance, similarity ~*v.* **5.** agree, be alike, chime with, compare, complement, conform, correlate, correspond, equal, keep pace (with), match

paralyse cripple, debilitate, disable, incapacitate, lame

paralysis immobility, palsy, paresis (*Pathol.*)

paralytic *adj.* crippled, disabled, immobile, immobilized, incapacitated, lame, numb, palsied, paralysed

parameter constant, criterion, framework, guideline, limit, limitation, restriction, specification

paramount capital, cardinal, chief, dominant, eminent, first, foremost, main, outstanding, predominant, pre-eminent, primary, prime, principal, superior, supreme

paraphernalia accoutrements, apparatus, appurtenances, baggage, belongings, clobber (*Brit. sl.*), effects, equipage, equipment, gear, impedimenta, material, stuff, tackle, things, trappings

paraphrase 1. *n.* interpretation, rehash, rendering, rendition, rephrasing, restatement, rewording, translation, version **2.** *v.* express in other words *or* one's own words, interpret, rehash, render, rephrase, restate, reword

parasite bloodsucker (*Inf.*), cadger, drone (*Brit.*), hanger-on, leech, scrounger (*Inf.*), sponge (*Inf.*), sponger (*Inf.*)

parasitic bloodsucking (*Inf.*), cadging, leechlike, scrounging (*Inf.*), sponging (*Inf.*)

parcel *n.* **1.** bundle, carton, pack, package, packet **2.** piece of land, plot, property, tract ~*v.* **3.** *Often with* **up** do up, pack, package, tie up, wrap **4.** *Often with* **out** allocate, allot, apportion, carve up, deal out, dispense, distribute, divide, dole out, mete out, portion, share out, split up

pare (pɛə) *vt.* **1.** trim, cut edge or surface of **2.** decrease bit by bit —**ˈparing** *n.* piece pared off, rind

parent (ˈpɛərənt) *n.* father or mother —**ˈparentage** *n.* descent, extraction —**paˈrental** *a.* —**ˈparenthood** *n.* —**parent teacher association** group of parents of children at school and their teachers formed in order to foster better understanding between them *etc.*

parenthesis (pəˈrɛnθɪsɪs) *n.* word or sentence inserted in passage independently of grammatical sequence and usu. marked off by brackets, dashes, or commas —**paˈrentheses** *pl.n.* round brackets, ( ), used for this —**paˈrenthesize** *or* **-sise** *vt.* **1.** place in parentheses **2.** insert as parenthesis **3.** intersperse with parentheses —**parenˈthetical** *a.*

par excellence (par ɛkseˈlɑ̃:s; *English* pɑ:r ˈɛksələns) *Fr.* to degree of excellence; beyond comparison

pariah (pəˈraɪə, ˈpærɪə) *n.* social outcast

parietal (pəˈraɪɪtˀl) *a.* of the walls of bodily cavities, *eg* skull

pari-mutuel (pærɪˈmju:tjʊəl) *n.* system of betting in which those who have bet on winners of race share in total amount wagered less percentage for management (*pl.* **pari-mutuels, paris-mutuels** (pærɪˈmju:tjʊəlz))

parish (ˈpærɪʃ) *n.* **1.** district under one clergyman **2.** subdivision of county —**paˈrishioner** *n.* inhabitant of parish —**parish clerk** person designated to assist in various church duties —**parish register** book in which births, baptisms, marriages, and deaths in parish are recorded

parity (ˈpærɪtɪ) *n. see* PAR

park (pɑ:k) *n.* **1.** large area of land in natural state preserved for recreational use **2.** large enclosed piece of ground, usu. with grass or woodland, attached to country house or for public use **3.** area designed to accommodate a number of related enterprises **4.** space in camp for military supplies —*vt.* **5.** leave for a short time **6.** manoeuvre (car) into a suitable space **7.** arrange or leave in a park —**parking meter** timing device, usu. coin-operated, that indicates how long vehicle may be left parked —**parking ticket** summons served for parking offence —**ˈparkland** *n.* grassland with scattered trees

parka (ˈpɑ:kə) *n.* warm waterproof coat, oft. with hood

parkin (ˈpɑ:kɪn) *n.* **UK** moist spicy ginger cake

Parkinson's disease (ˈpɑ:kɪnsənz) progressive chronic disorder of central nervous system characterized by impaired muscular coordination and tremor (*also* **ˈparkinsonism**)

Parkinson's law notion, expressed facetiously as law of economics, that work expands to fill time available

Parl. 1. Parliament **2.** parliamentary (*also* **parl.**)

parlance (ˈpɑ:ləns) *n.* **1.** way of speaking, conversation **2.** idiom

parley (ˈpɑ:lɪ) *n.* **1.** meeting between leaders or representatives of opposing forces to discuss terms —*vi.* **2.** hold discussion about terms

parliament (ˈpɑ:ləmənt) *n.* **1.** (**P-**) the legislature of the United Kingdom **2.** any similar legislative assembly —**parliamenˈtarian** *n.* member of parliament —**parliaˈmentary** *a.* —**parliamentary private secretary UK** backbencher in Parliament who assists minister

parlour *or U.S.* **parlor** (ˈpɑ:lə) *n.* **1.** sitting room, room for receiving company in small house **2.** place for milking cows **3. US** room or shop as business premises, *esp.* hairdresser *etc.*

Parmesan cheese (pɑ:mɪˈzæn) hard dry cheese used grated, *esp.* on pasta dishes *etc.*

parochial (pəˈrəʊkɪəl) *a.* **1.** narrow, provincial **2.** of a parish —**paˈrochialism** *n.*

parody (ˈpærədɪ) *n.* **1.** composition in which author's style is made fun of by imitation **2.** travesty —*vt.* **3.** write parody of (**-odied, -odying**) —**ˈparodist** *n.*

parole (pəˈrəʊl) *n.* **1.** early freeing of prisoner on

THESAURUS

parch blister, burn, dehydrate, desiccate, dry up, evaporate, make thirsty, scorch, sear, shrivel, wither

pardon 1. *v.* absolve, acquit, amnesty, condone, exculpate, excuse, exonerate, forgive, free, let off (*Inf.*), liberate, overlook, release, remit, reprieve **2.** *n.* absolution, acquittal, allowance, amnesty, condonation, discharge, excuse, exoneration, forgiveness, grace, indulgence, mercy, release, remission, reprieve

pardonable allowable, condonable, excusable, forgivable, minor, not serious, permissible, understandable, venial

parent begetter, father, guardian, mother, procreator, progenitor, sire

parentage ancestry, birth, derivation, descent, extraction, family, line, lineage, origin, paternity, pedigree, race, stirps, stock

pariah exile, leper, outcast, outlaw, undesirable, unperson, untouchable

parish church, churchgoers, community, congregation, flock, fold, parishioners

parity 1. consistency, equality, equal terms, equivalence, par, parallelism, quits (*Inf.*), uniformity, unity **2.** affinity, agreement, analogy, conformity, congruity, correspondence, likeness, resemblance, sameness, similarity, similitude

park 1. *n.* estate, garden, grounds, parkland, pleasure garden, recreation ground, woodland **2.** *v.* leave, manoeuvre, position, station

parley 1. *n.* colloquy, confab (*Inf.*), conference, council, dialogue, discussion, meeting, palaver, powwow, talk(s) **2.** *v.* confabulate, confer, deliberate, discuss, negotiate, palaver, powwow, speak, talk

parliament 1. assembly, congress, convocation, council, diet, legislature, senate, talking shop (*Inf.*) **2. Parliament** Houses of Parliament, Mother of Parliaments, the House, the House of Commons and the House of Lords, Westminster

parliamentary congressional, deliberative, governmental, lawgiving, lawmaking, legislative

parlour best room, drawing room, front room, lounge, reception room, sitting room

parochial insular, inward-looking, limited, narrow, narrow-minded, parish-pump, petty, provincial, restricted, small-minded

parody *n.* **1.** burlesque, caricature, imitation, lampoon, satire, send-up (*Brit. inf.*), skit, spoof (*Inf.*), takeoff (*Inf.*) **2.** apology, caricature, farce, mockery, travesty ~*v.* **3.** burlesque, caricature, do a takeoff of (*Inf.*), lampoon, mimic, poke fun at, satirize, send up (*Brit. inf.*), spoof (*Inf.*), take off (*Inf.*), travesty .

condition he is of good behaviour 2. word of honour —*vt.* 3. place on parole

parotid (pəˈrɒtɪd) *a.* 1. relating to or situated near parotid gland —*n.* 2. parotid gland —**parotid gland** large salivary gland in front of and below each ear

-parous (*comb. form*) giving birth to, as in *oviparous*

paroxysm (ˈpærəksɪzəm) *n.* sudden violent attack of pain, rage, laughter

parquet (ˈpɑːkeɪ, -kɪ) *n.* 1. flooring of wooden blocks arranged in pattern —*vt.* 2. cover (floor) with parquet —**parquetry** (ˈpɑːkɪtrɪ) *n.*

parr (pɑː) *n.* salmon up to two years of age (*pl.* **-s, parr**)

parrakeet (ˈpærəkiːt) *n. see* PARAKEET

parricide (ˈpærɪsaɪd) *n.* murder or murderer of a parent

parrot (ˈpærət) *n.* 1. any of several related birds with short hooked beak, some varieties of which can imitate speaking 2. unintelligent imitator —**parrot fever** *or* **disease** *see* **psittacosis** *at* PSITTACINE

parry (ˈpærɪ) *vt.* 1. ward off, turn aside (**ˈparried, ˈparrying**) —*n.* 2. act of parrying, *esp.* in fencing

parse (pɑːz) *vt.* 1. describe (word) 2. analyse (sentence) in terms of grammar —**ˈparser** *n. Comp.* program that interprets ordinary language typed into computer by recognizing key words or analysing sentence structure and translating into machine language

parsec (ˈpɑːsɛk) *n.* unit of length used in expressing distance of stars

parsimony (ˈpɑːsɪmənɪ) *n.* 1. stinginess 2. undue economy —**parsiˈmonious** *a.* sparing

parsley (ˈpɑːslɪ) *n.* herb used for seasoning, garnish *etc.*

parsnip (ˈpɑːsnɪp) *n.* edible yellow root vegetable

parson (ˈpɑːsᵊn) *n.* 1. clergyman of parish or church 2. clergyman —**ˈparsonage** *n.* parson's house —**parson's nose** fatty extreme end portion of tail of fowl when cooked

part (pɑːt) *n.* 1. portion, section, share 2. division 3. actor's role 4. duty 5. (*oft. pl.*) region 6. interest —*v.* 7. divide 8. separate —**ˈparting** *n.* 1. division between sections of hair on head 2. separation 3. leave-taking —**ˈpartly** *adv.* in part —**part exchange** transaction in which used goods are taken as partial payment —**part of speech** class of words sharing important syntactic or semantic features; group of words in language that may occur in similar positions or fulfil similar functions in sentence —**part song** song for several voices singing in harmony —**part-time** *a.* 1. for less than entire time appropriate to activity —*adv.* 2. on part-time basis —**part-timer** *n.*

part. 1. participle 2. particular

partake (pɑːˈteɪk) *vi.* 1. (*with* of) take or have share (in) 2. take food or drink (**-ˈtook, -ˈtaken, -ˈtaking**)

parterre (pɑːˈtɛə) *n.* 1. ornamental arrangement of beds in a flower garden 2. the pit of a theatre

parthenogenesis (pɑːθɪnəʊˈdʒɛnɪsɪs) *n.* type of reproduction, occurring in some insects and flowers, in which unfertilized ovum develops directly into new individual —**parthenogeˈnetic** *a.*

Parthian shot (ˈpɑːθɪən) hostile remark or gesture delivered while departing

partial (ˈpɑːʃəl) *a.* 1. not general or complete 2. prejudiced 3. (*with* to) fond (of) —**partiˈality** *n.* 1. favouritism 2. fondness —**ˈpartially** *adv.* partly

participate (pɑːˈtɪsɪpeɪt) *v.* (*with* in) 1. share (in) 2. take part (in) —**parˈticipant** *n.* —**particiˈpation** *n.* —**parˈticipator** *n.*

THESAURUS

paroxysm attack, convulsion, eruption, fit, flare-up (*Inf.*), outburst, seizure, spasm

parrot *n. Fig.* copycat (*Inf.*), imitator, (little) echo, mimic

parry 1. block, deflect, fend off, hold at bay, rebuff, repel, repulse, stave off, ward off 2. avoid, circumvent, dodge, duck (*Inf.*), evade, fence, fight shy of, shun, sidestep

parsimonious cheeseparing, close, close-fisted, frugal, grasping, mean, mingy (*Brit. inf.*), miserable, miserly, near (*Inf.*), niggardly, penny-pinching (*Inf.*), penurious, saving, scrimpy, skinflinty, sparing, stingy, stinting, tightfisted

parsimony frugality, meanness, minginess (*Brit. inf.*), miserliness, nearness (*Inf.*), niggardliness, penny-pinching (*Inf.*), stinginess, tightness

parson churchman, clergyman, cleric, divine, ecclesiastic, incumbent, man of God, man of the cloth, minister, pastor, preacher, priest, rector, reverend (*Inf.*), vicar

part *n.* 1. bit, fraction, fragment, lot, particle, piece, portion, scrap, section, sector, segment, share, slice 2. branch, component, constituent, department, division, element, ingredient, limb, member, module, organ, piece, unit 3. behalf, cause, concern, faction, interest, party, side 4. bit, business, capacity, charge, duty, function, involvement, office, place, responsibility, role, say, share, task, work 5. *Theat.* character, lines, role 6. *Often plural* airt (*Scot.*), area, district, neck of the woods (*Inf.*), neighbourhood, quarter, region, territory, vicinity ~*v.* 7. break, cleave, come apart, detach, disconnect, disjoin, dismantle, disunite, divide, rend, separate, sever, split, tear 8. break up, depart, go, go away, go (their) separate ways, leave, part company, quit, say goodbye, separate, split up, take one's leave, withdraw

partake 1. *With* **in** engage, enter into, participate, share, take part 2. *With* **of** consume, eat, receive, share, take

partial 1. fragmentary, imperfect, incomplete, limited, uncompleted, unfinished 2. biased, discriminatory, influenced, interested, one-sided, partisan, predisposed, prejudiced, tendentious, unfair, unjust 3. **be partial to** be fond of, be keen on, be taken with, care for, have a liking (soft spot, weakness) for

partiality 1. bias, favouritism, partisanship, predisposition, preference, prejudice 2. affinity, fondness, inclination, liking, love, penchant, predilection, predisposition, preference, proclivity, taste, weakness

partially fractionally, halfway, incompletely, in part, moderately, not wholly, partly, piecemeal, somewhat, to a certain extent *or* degree

participant associate, contributor, member, partaker, participator, party, shareholder

participate be a participant, be a party to, engage in, enter into, get in on the act, have a hand in, join in, partake, perform, share, take part

participation assistance, contribution, involvement, joining in, partaking, partnership, sharing in, taking part

participle (ˈpɑːtɪsɪpᵊl) *n.* adjective made by inflection from verb and keeping verb's relation to dependent words —**partiˈcipial** *a.*

particle (ˈpɑːtɪkᵊl) *n.* **1.** minute portion of matter **2.** least possible amount **3.** minor part of speech in grammar, prefix, suffix

parti-coloured (ˈpɑːtɪkʌləd) *a.* differently coloured in different parts, variegated

particular (pəˈtɪkjʊlə) *a.* **1.** relating to one, not general **2.** distinct **3.** minute **4.** very exact **5.** fastidious —*n.* **6.** detail, item —*pl.* **7.** detailed account **8.** items of information —**particuˈlarity** *n.* —**parˈticularize** *or* **-ise** *vt.* mention in detail —**parˈticularly** *adv.*

partisan *or* **partizan** (pɑːtɪˈzæn, ˈpɑːtɪzæn) *n.* **1.** adherent of a party **2.** guerrilla, member of resistance movement —*a.* **3.** adhering to faction **4.** prejudiced

partition (pɑːˈtɪʃən) *n.* **1.** division **2.** interior dividing wall —*vt.* **3.** divide, cut into sections

partitive (ˈpɑːtɪtɪv) *a.* **1.** *Gram.* indicating that noun involved in construction refers only to part of what it otherwise refers to **2.** serving to separate or divide into parts —*n.* **3.** *Gram.* partitive linguistic element or feature

partner (ˈpɑːtnə) *n.* **1.** ally or companion **2.** a member of a partnership **3.** one that dances with another **4.** a husband or wife **5.** *Golf, Tennis etc.* one who plays with another against opponents —*vt.* **6.** (cause to) be a partner (of) —**ˈpartnership** *n.* association of persons for business *etc.*

partridge (ˈpɑːtrɪdʒ) *n.* any of various game birds of the grouse family

parturition (pɑːtjʊˈrɪʃən) *n.* **1.** act of bringing forth young **2.** childbirth —**parˈturient** *a.* **1.** of childbirth **2.** giving birth **3.** producing new idea *etc.*

party (ˈpɑːtɪ) *n.* **1.** social assembly **2.** group of persons travelling or working together **3.** group of persons united in opinion **4.** side **5.** person —*a.* **6.** of, belonging to, a party or faction —**party line 1.** telephone line serving two or more subscribers **2.** policies of political party —**party wall** common wall separating adjoining premises

parvenu *or* (*fem.*) **parvenue** (ˈpɑːvənjuː) *n.* **1.** one newly risen into position of notice, power, wealth **2.** upstart

pas (pɑː) *n.* dance step or movement, *esp.* in ballet (*pl.* **pas**)

pascal (ˈpæskᵊl) *n.* SI unit of pressure

Paschal (ˈpɑːskᵊl, ˈpæskᵊl) *a.* of the Passover or Easter

pasha *or* **pacha** (ˈpɑːʃə, ˈpæʃə) *n.* formerly, high official of Ottoman Empire or modern Egyptian kingdom: placed after name when used as title

pasqueflower (ˈpɑːskflaʊə) *n.* **1.** small purple-flowered plant of N and Central Europe and W Asia **2.** any of several related N Amer. plants

pass (pɑːs) *vt.* **1.** go by, beyond, through *etc.* **2.** exceed **3.** be accepted by **4.** undergo successfully **5.** spend **6.** transfer **7.** exchange **8.** disregard **9.** undergo (examination) successfully **10.** bring into force, sanction (a parliamentary bill *etc.*) —*vi.* **11.** go **12.** be transferred from one state or person to another **13.** elapse —*n.* **14.** way, *esp.* a narrow and difficult way **15.** permit, licence, authorization **16.** successful result from test **17.** condition **18.** *Sport* transfer of ball —**ˈpassable** *a.* (just) acceptable —**ˈpassing** *a.* **1.** transitory **2.** cursory, casual —**ˈpassbook** *n.* **1.** book for keeping record of withdrawals from and payments into building society **2.** bankbook **3.** SA official document to identify bearer, his race, residence and employment —**passer-by** *n.* person that is passing by, *esp.* on foot (*pl.* **passers-by**) —**ˈpasskey** *n.* **1.** any of various keys, *esp.* latchkey **2.** master key **3.** skeleton key —**pass up** ignore, neglect; reject

THESAURUS

particle atom, bit, crumb, grain, iota, jot, mite, molecule, mote, piece, scrap, shred, speck, tittle, whit

particular *adj.* **1.** distinct, exact, express, peculiar, precise, special, specific **2.** blow-by-blow, circumstantial, detailed, itemized, minute, painstaking, precise, selective, thorough **3.** choosy (*Inf.*), critical, dainty, demanding, discriminating, exacting, fastidious, finicky, fussy, meticulous, nice (*Rare*), overnice, pernickety (*Inf.*), picky (*Inf.*) ~*n.* **4.** *Usually plural* circumstance, detail, fact, feature, item, specification

particularly distinctly, especially, explicitly, expressly, in particular, specifically

parting *n.* **1.** adieu, departure, farewell, going, goodbye, leave-taking, valediction **2.** breaking, detachment, divergence, division, partition, rift, rupture, separation, split

partisan *n.* **1.** adherent, backer, champion, devotee, disciple, follower, stalwart, supporter, upholder, votary ~*adj.* **2.** biased, factional, interested, one-sided, partial, prejudiced, sectarian, tendentious ~*n.* **3.** guerrilla, irregular, resistance fighter, underground fighter

partition *n.* **1.** dividing, division, segregation, separation, severance, splitting **2.** barrier, divider, room divider, screen, wall ~*v.* **3.** apportion, cut up, divide, parcel out, portion, section, segment, separate, share, split up, subdivide

partly halfway, incompletely, in part, in some measure, not fully, partially, relatively, slightly, somewhat, to a certain degree *or* extent, up to a certain point

partner 1. accomplice, ally, associate, bedfellow, collaborator, colleague, companion, comrade, confederate, copartner, helper, mate, participant, team-mate **2.** bedfellow, consort, helpmate, husband, mate, spouse, wife

partnership alliance, association, combine, company, conglomerate, cooperative, corporation, firm, house, society, union

party 1. at-home, bash (*Inf.*), celebration, do (*Inf.*), festivity, function, gathering, get-together (*Inf.*), knees-up (*Brit. inf.*), rave-up (*Brit. sl.*), reception, shindig (*Sl.*), social, social gathering, soirée **2.** band, body, bunch (*Inf.*), company, crew, detachment (*Military*), gang, gathering, group, squad, team, unit **3.** alliance, association, cabal, clique, coalition, combination, confederacy, coterie, faction, grouping, league, set, side **4.** individual, person, somebody, someone

pass *v.* **1.** depart, elapse, flow, go, go by *or* past, lapse, leave, move, move onwards, proceed, roll, run **2.** beat, exceed, excel, go beyond, outdistance, outdo, outstrip, surmount, surpass, transcend **3.** answer, come up to scratch (*Inf.*), do, get through, graduate, pass muster, qualify, succeed, suffice, suit **4.** be-

passage (ˈpæsɪdʒ) *n.* **1.** channel, opening **2.** way through, corridor **3.** part of book *etc.* **4.** journey, voyage, fare **5.** enactment of law by parliament *etc.* **6.** *rare* conversation; dispute —**ˈpassageway** *n.* way, *esp.* one in or between buildings; passage

passé (ˈpɑːseɪ, ˈpæseɪ) *a.* **1.** out of date **2.** past the prime

passenger (ˈpæsɪndʒə) *n.* **1.** traveller, *esp.* by public conveyance **2.** one of a team who does not pull his weight

passerine (ˈpæsəraɪn, -riːn) *a.* of the order of perching birds

passim (ˈpæsɪm) *Lat.* everywhere, throughout

passion (ˈpæʃən) *n.* **1.** ardent desire, *esp.* sexual **2.** any strongly felt emotion **3.** suffering (*esp.* that of Christ) —**ˈpassionate** *a.* (easily) moved by strong emotions —**ˈpassionflower** *n.* tropical Amer. plant —**passion fruit** edible fruit of passionflower —**Passion play** play depicting Passion of Christ

passive (ˈpæsɪv) *a.* **1.** unresisting **2.** submissive **3.** inactive **4.** denoting grammatical mood of verb in which the action is suffered by the subject —**pasˈsivity** *n.* —**passive resistance** resistance to government *etc.* without violence, as by fasting, demonstrating or refusing to cooperate —**passive smoking** inhalation of smoke from other people's cigarettes by nonsmoker

Passover (ˈpɑːsəʊvə) *n.* Jewish spring festival

passport (ˈpɑːspɔːt) *n.* official document granting permission to pass, travel abroad *etc.*

password (ˈpɑːswɜːd) *n.* **1.** word, phrase, to distinguish friend from enemy **2.** countersign

past (pɑːst) *a.* **1.** ended **2.** gone by **3.** elapsed —*n.* **4.** bygone times —*adv.* **5.** by **6.** along —*prep.* **7.** beyond **8.** after —**past master 1.** person with talent for, or experience in a particular activity **2.** person who has held office of master in guild *etc.* —**past participle** participial form of verbs used to modify noun that is logically object of verb, also used in certain compound tenses and passive forms of verb —**past perfect** *Gram. a.* **1.** denoting tense of verbs used in relating past events where action had already occurred at time of action of main verb that is itself in past tense —*n.* **2.** past perfect tense **3.** verb in this tense

pasta (ˈpæstə) *n.* any of several variously shaped edible preparations of dough, *eg* spaghetti

paste (peɪst) *n.* **1.** soft composition, as toothpaste **2.** soft plastic mixture or adhesive **3.** fine glass to imitate gems —*vt.* **4.** fasten with paste —**ˈpasty** *a.* **1.** like paste **2.** white **3.** sickly —**ˈpasteboard** *n.* stiff thick paper

pastel (ˈpæstᵊl, pæˈstɛl) *n.* **1.** coloured crayon **2.** art of drawing with crayons **3.** pale, delicate colour —*a.* **4.** delicately tinted

pastern (ˈpæstən) *n.* part of horse's foot between fetlock and hoof

pasteurize *or* **-ise** (ˈpæstəraɪz, -stjə-, ˈpɑː-) *vt.* sterilize by heat —**pasteuriˈzation** *or* **-iˈsation** *n.*

pastiche (pæˈstiːʃ) *or* **pasticcio** (pæˈstɪtʃəʊ) *n.* **1.** literary, musical, artistic work composed of parts borrowed from other works and loosely connected together **2.** work imitating another's style

pastille *or* **pastil** (ˈpæstɪl) *n.* **1.** lozenge **2.** aromatic substance burnt as fumigator

pastime (ˈpɑːstaɪm) *n.* **1.** that which makes time pass agreeably **2.** recreation

THESAURUS

guile, devote, employ, experience, fill, occupy, spend, suffer, undergo, while away **5.** convey, deliver, exchange, give, hand, kick, let have, reach, send, throw, transfer, transmit **6.** accept, adopt, approve, authorize, decree, enact, establish, legislate, ordain, ratify, sanction, validate **7.** disregard, ignore, miss, neglect, not heed, omit, overlook, skip (*Inf.*) ~*n.* **8.** canyon, col, defile, gap, gorge, ravine **9.** authorization, identification, licence, passport, permission, permit, safe-conduct, ticket, warrant **10.** condition, juncture, pinch, plight, predicament, situation, stage, state, state of affairs, straits

passable acceptable, adequate, admissible, allowable, all right, average, fair, fair enough, mediocre, middling, moderate, not too bad, ordinary, presentable, so-so (*Inf.*), tolerable, unexceptional

passage 1. avenue, channel, course, lane, opening, path, road, route, thoroughfare, way **2.** corridor, doorway, entrance, entrance hall, exit, hall, hallway, lobby, passageway, vestibule **3.** clause, excerpt, extract, paragraph, piece, quotation, reading, section, sentence, text, verse **4.** crossing, journey, tour, trek, trip, voyage **5.** acceptance, enactment, establishment, legalization, legislation, passing, ratification

passenger fare, hitchhiker, pillion rider, rider, traveller

passer-by bystander, onlooker, witness

passing *adj.* **1.** brief, ephemeral, fleeting, momentary, short, short-lived, temporary, transient, transitory **2.** casual, cursory, glancing, hasty, quick, shallow, short, slight, superficial

passion 1. animation, ardour, eagerness, emotion, excitement, feeling, fervour, fire, heat, intensity, joy, rapture, spirit, transport, warmth, zeal, zest **2.** adoration, affection, ardour, attachment, concupiscence, desire, fondness, infatuation, itch, keenness, love, lust

passionate animated, ardent, eager, emotional, enthusiastic, excited, fervent, fervid, fierce, frenzied, heartfelt, impassioned, impetuous, impulsive, intense, strong, vehement, warm, wild, zealous

passive acquiescent, compliant, docile, enduring, inactive, inert, lifeless, long-suffering, nonviolent, patient, quiescent, receptive, resigned, submissive, unassertive, uninvolved, unresisting

pass up decline, forgo, give (something) a miss (*Inf.*), ignore, let go, let slip, miss, neglect, refuse, reject

password countersign, key word, open sesame, signal, watchword

past *adj.* **1.** accomplished, completed, done, elapsed, ended, extinct, finished, forgotten, gone, over, over and done with, spent **2.** ancient, bygone, early, erstwhile, foregoing, former, late, long-ago, olden, preceding, previous, prior, quondam, recent ~*n.* **3.** antiquity, days gone by, days of yore, former times, good old days, history, long ago, olden days, old times, times past, yesteryear (*Literary*) ~*adv.* **4.** across, beyond, by, on, over ~*prep.* **5.** after, beyond, farther than, later than, outside, over, subsequent to

paste 1. *n.* adhesive, cement, glue, gum, mucilage **2.** *v.* cement, fasten, fix, glue, gum, stick

pastel *adj.* delicate, light, muted, pale, soft, soft-hued

pastiche blend, farrago, gallimaufry, hotchpotch, medley, *mélange*, miscellany, mixture, motley

pastime activity, amusement, distraction, diversion,

pastor (ˈpɑːstə) *n.* clergyman in charge of a congregation —**ˈpastoral** *a.* **1.** of, or like, shepherd's or rural life **2.** of office of pastor —*n.* **3.** poem describing rural life —**pastorale** (pæstəˈrɑːl) *n. Mus.* **1.** composition evocative of rural life **2.** musical play based on rustic story (*pl.* **-s, -rali** (*It.* -ˈraːli)) —**ˈpastorate** *n.* office, jurisdiction of pastor

pastry (ˈpeɪstrɪ) *n.* article of food made chiefly of flour, fat and water

pasture (ˈpɑːstʃə) *n.* **1.** grass for food of cattle **2.** ground on which cattle graze —*v.* **3.** (cause to) graze —**ˈpasturage** *n.* (right to) pasture

pasty (ˈpæstɪ) *n.* small pie of meat and crust, baked without a dish

pat[1] (pæt) *vt.* **1.** tap (**-tt-**) —*n.* **2.** light, quick blow **3.** small mass, as of butter, beaten into shape

pat[2] (pæt) *adv.* **1.** exactly **2.** fluently **3.** opportunely —*a.* **4.** glib **5.** exactly right

pat. patent(ed)

patch (pætʃ) *n.* **1.** piece of cloth sewed on garment **2.** spot **3.** plot of ground **4.** protecting pad for the eye **5.** small contrasting area **6.** short period —*vt.* **7.** mend **8.** repair clumsily —**ˈpatchy** *a.* **1.** of uneven quality **2.** full of patches —**ˈpatchwork** *n.* **1.** work composed of pieces sewn together **2.** jumble

patchouli *or* **patchouly** (ˈpætʃʊlɪ, pəˈtʃuːlɪ) *n.* **1.** Indian herb **2.** perfume made from it

pate (peɪt) *n.* **1.** head **2.** top of head

pâté (ˈpæteɪ) *n.* spread of finely minced liver *etc.* —**pâté de foie gras** (*Fr.* pɑte də fwa ˈgrɑ) smooth rich paste made from liver of specially fattened goose (*pl.* **pâtés de foie gras** (*Fr.* pɑte))

patella (pəˈtɛlə) *n.* kneecap (*pl.* **patellae** (pəˈtɛliː)) —**paˈtellar** *a.*

paten (ˈpætᵊn) *n.* plate for bread in the Eucharist

patent (ˈpeɪtᵊnt, ˈpætᵊnt) *n.* **1.** deed securing to person exclusive right to invention —*a.* **2.** open **3.** (ˈpeɪtᵊnt) evident; manifest **4.** open to public perusal, as in *letters patent* —*vt.* **5.** secure a patent for —**patenˈtee** *n.* one that has a patent —**patently** (ˈpeɪtᵊntlɪ) *adv.* obviously —**patent leather** (ˈpeɪtᵊnt) (imitation) leather processed to give hard, glossy surface —**patent medicine** (ˈpeɪtᵊnt) medicine with patent, available without prescription —**Patent Office** government department that issues patents

pater (ˈpeɪtə) *n.* **UK** *sl.* father

paterfamilias (peɪtəfəˈmɪlɪæs) *n.* father of a family (*pl.* **patresfamilias** (pɑːtreɪzfəˈmɪlɪæs))

paternal (pəˈtɜːnᵊl) *a.* **1.** fatherly **2.** of a father —**paˈternalism** *n.* authority exercised in a way that limits individual responsibility —**paternalˈistic** *a.* —**paˈternity** *n.* **1.** relation of a father to his offspring **2.** fatherhood

paternoster (pætəˈnɒstə) *n.* **1.** Lord's Prayer **2.** beads of rosary **3.** type of lift

path (pɑːθ) *n.* **1.** way or track **2.** course of action —**ˈpathway** *n.* **1.** path **2.** *Biochem.* chain of reactions associated with particular metabolic process

-path (*comb. form*) **1.** person suffering from specified disease or disorder, as in *neuropath* **2.** practitioner of particular method of treatment, as in *osteopath*

pathetic (pəˈθɛtɪk) *a.* **1.** affecting or moving tender emotions **2.** distressingly inadequate —**paˈthetically** *adv.* —**pathetic fallacy** *Lit.* presentation of nature *etc.* as possessing human feelings

pathogenic (pæθəˈdʒɛnɪk) *a.* producing disease —**paˈthogeny** *n.* mode of development of disease

pathology (pəˈθɒlədʒɪ) *n.* science of diseases —**pathoˈlogical** *a.* **1.** of the science of disease **2.** due to disease **3.** *inf.* compulsively motivated

pathos (ˈpeɪθɒs) *n.* power of exciting tender emotions

-pathy (*n. comb. form*) **1.** feeling, perception, as in *telepathy* **2.** disease, as in *psychopathy* **3.** method of treating disease, as in *osteopathy* —**-pathic** (*a. comb. form*)

patient (ˈpeɪʃənt) *a.* **1.** bearing trials calmly —*n.* **2.** person under medical treatment —**ˈpatience** *n.* **1.** quality of enduring **2.** card game for one

THESAURUS

entertainment, game, hobby, leisure, play, recreation, relaxation, sport

past master ace (*Inf.*), artist, dab hand (*Brit. inf.*), expert, old hand, virtuoso, wizard

pastor churchman, clergyman, divine, ecclesiastic, minister, parson, priest, rector, vicar

pastoral *adj.* **1.** Arcadian, bucolic, country, georgic (*Literary*), idyllic, rural, rustic, simple **2.** clerical, ecclesiastical, ministerial, priestly

pasture grass, grassland, grazing, grazing land, lea (*Poetic*), meadow, pasturage, shieling (*Scot.*)

pat *v.* **1.** caress, dab, fondle, pet, slap, stroke, tap, touch ~*n.* **2.** clap, dab, light blow, slap, stroke, tap **3.** cake, dab, lump, portion, small piece

patch *n.* **1.** piece of material, reinforcement **2.** bit, scrap, shred, small piece, spot, stretch **3.** area, ground, land, plot, tract ~*v.* **4.** cover, fix, mend, reinforce, repair, sew up

patchwork confusion, hash, hotchpotch, jumble, medley, mishmash, mixture, pastiche

patchy bitty, erratic, fitful, irregular, random, sketchy, spotty, uneven, variable, varying

patent 1. *adj.* apparent, blatant, clear, conspicuous, downright, evident, flagrant, glaring, indisputable, manifest, obvious, open, palpable, transparent, unconcealed, unequivocal, unmistakable **2.** *n.* copyright, invention, licence

paternal 1. benevolent, concerned, fatherlike, fatherly, protective, solicitous, vigilant **2.** patrilineal, patrimonial

paternity fatherhood, fathership

path 1. footpath, footway, pathway, towpath, track, trail, walkway (*Chiefly U.S.*) **2.** avenue, course, direction, passage, procedure, road, route, track, walk, way

pathetic 1. affecting, distressing, heartbreaking, heart-rending, melting, moving, pitiable, plaintive, poignant, sad, tender, touching **2.** deplorable, feeble, inadequate, lamentable, meagre, miserable, paltry, petty, pitiful, poor, puny, sorry, wet (*Brit. inf.*), woeful

pathos pitiableness, pitifulness, plaintiveness, poignancy, sadness

patience constancy, diligence, endurance, fortitude, long-suffering, perseverance, persistence, resignation, stoicism, submission

patient 1. *adj.* enduring, long-suffering, persevering, persistent, philosophical, quiet, resigned, self-possessed, serene, stoical, submissive, uncomplaining, untiring **2** *n.* case, invalid, sick person, sufferer

patina (ˈpætɪnə) *n.* **1.** fine layer on a surface **2.** sheen of age on woodwork

patio (ˈpætɪəʊ) *n.* paved area adjoining house (*pl.* **-s**)

patois (ˈpætwɑː; *Fr.* paˈtwa) *n.* regional dialect (*pl.* **patois** (ˈpætwɑːz; *Fr.* paˈtwa)

pat. pend. patent pending

patriarch (ˈpeɪtrɪɑːk) *n.* father and ruler of family, *esp.* Biblical —**patriˈarchal** *a.* venerable —**ˈpatriarchy** *n.* **1.** form of social organization in which male is head of family and descent, kinship and title are traced through male line **2.** society governed by such system

patrician (pəˈtrɪʃən) *n.* **1.** noble of ancient Rome **2.** one of noble birth —*a.* **3.** of noble birth

patricide (ˈpætrɪsaɪd) *n.* murder or murderer of father

patriot (ˈpeɪtrɪət, ˈpæt-) *n.* one that loves his country and maintains its interests —**patriotic** (pætrɪˈɒtɪk) *a.* inspired by love of one's country —**patriotism** (ˈpætrɪətɪzəm) *n.*

patrol (pəˈtrəʊl) *n.* **1.** regular circuit by guard **2.** person, small group patrolling **3.** unit of Scouts or Guides —*v.* **4.** go round on guard or reconnoitring (**-ll-**)

patron (ˈpeɪtrən) *n.* **1.** one who sponsors or aids artists, charities *etc.* **2.** protector **3.** regular customer **4.** guardian saint **5.** one that has disposition of church living *etc.* —**patronage** (ˈpætrənɪdʒ) *n.* support given by, or position of, a patron —**patronize** *or* **-ise** (ˈpætrənaɪz) *vt.* **1.** assume air of superiority towards **2.** frequent as customer **3.** encourage —**ˈpatronizing** *or* **-ising** *a.* condescending

patronymic (pætrəˈnɪmɪk) *n.* name derived from that of parent or an ancestor

patter (ˈpætə) *vi.* **1.** make noise, as sound of quick, short steps **2.** tap in quick succession **3.** pray, talk rapidly —*n.* **4.** quick succession of taps **5.** *inf.* glib, rapid speech

pattern (ˈpætᵊn) *n.* **1.** arrangement of repeated parts **2.** design **3.** shape to direct cutting of cloth *etc.* **4.** model **5.** specimen —*vt.* **6.** (*with* on, after) model **7.** decorate with pattern

paucity (ˈpɔːsɪtɪ) *n.* **1.** scarcity **2.** smallness of quantity **3.** fewness

paunch (pɔːntʃ) *n.* belly

pauper (ˈpɔːpə) *n.* poor person, *esp.,* formerly, one supported by the public —**ˈpauperism** *n.* **1.** destitution **2.** extreme poverty

pause (pɔːz) *vi.* **1.** cease for a time —*n.* **2.** stop or rest

pavane *or* **pavan** (pəˈvɑːn, ˈpævᵊn) *n.* **1.** slow, stately dance of 16th and 17th centuries **2.** music for this dance

pave (peɪv) *vt.* **1.** form surface on with stone or brick **2.** prepare, make easier (*esp. in* **pave the way**) —**ˈpavement** *n.* **1.** paved floor, footpath **2.** material for paving

pavilion (pəˈvɪljən) *n.* **1.** clubhouse on playing field *etc.* **2.** building for housing exhibition *etc.* **3.** large ornate tent

pavlova (pævˈləʊvə) *n.* meringue cake with whipped cream and fruit

paw (pɔː) *n.* **1.** foot of animal —*v.* **2.** scrape with forefoot —*vt.* **3.** handle roughly **4.** stroke with the hands

THESAURUS

patriot chauvinist, flag-waver (*Inf.*), jingo, lover of one's country, loyalist, nationalist

patriotic chauvinistic, flag-waving (*Inf.*), jingoistic, loyal, nationalistic

patriotism flag-waving (*Inf.*), jingoism, love of one's country, loyalty, nationalism

patrol *n.* **1.** guarding, policing, protecting, rounds, safeguarding, vigilance, watching **2.** garrison, guard, patrolman, sentinel, watch, watchman ~*v.* **3.** guard, inspect, keep guard, keep watch, make the rounds, police, pound, range, safeguard, walk the beat

patron 1. advocate, angel (*Inf.*), backer, benefactor, champion, defender, friend, guardian, helper, philanthropist, protector, sponsor, supporter **2.** buyer, client, customer, frequenter, habitué, shopper

patronage aid, assistance, backing, benefaction, championship, encouragement, help, promotion, sponsorship, support

patronize 1. be lofty with, look down on, talk down to, treat as inferior, treat condescendingly, treat like a child **2.** assist, back, befriend, foster, fund, help, maintain, promote, sponsor, subscribe to, support **3.** be a customer *or* client of, buy from, deal with, do business with, frequent, shop at, trade with

patronizing condescending, contemptuous, disdainful, gracious, haughty, lofty, snobbish, stooping, supercilious, superior, toffee-nosed (*Sl.*)

patter *v.* **1.** scurry, scuttle, skip, tiptoe, trip, walk lightly **2.** beat, pat, pelt, pitapat, pitter-patter, rat-a-tat, spatter, tap ~*n.* **3.** pattering, pitapat, pitter-patter, tapping ~*v.* **4.** babble, blab, chatter, hold forth, jabber, prate, rattle off, rattle on, spiel (*Inf.*), spout (*Inf.*), tattle ~*n.* **5.** line, monologue, pitch, spiel (*Inf.*)

pattern *n.* **1.** arrangement, decoration, decorative design, design, device, figure, motif, ornament **2.** arrangement, method, order, orderliness, plan, sequence, system **3.** design, diagram, guide, instructions, original, plan, stencil, template **4.** archetype, criterion, cynosure, example, exemplar, guide, model, norm, original, paradigm, paragon, prototype, sample, specimen, standard ~*v.* **5.** copy, emulate, follow, form, imitate, model, mould, order, shape, style **6.** decorate, design, trim

paucity dearth, deficiency, fewness, insufficiency, lack, meagreness, paltriness, poverty, rarity, scantiness, scarcity, shortage, slenderness, slightness, smallness, sparseness, sparsity

paunch abdomen, beer-belly (*Sl.*), belly, corporation (*Brit. inf.*), pot, potbelly

pauper bankrupt, beggar, down-and-out, have-not, indigent, insolvent, mendicant, poor person

pause 1. *v.* break, cease, delay, deliberate, desist, discontinue, halt, have a breather (*Inf.*), hesitate, interrupt, rest, stop briefly, take a break, wait, waver **2.** *n.* break, breather (*Inf.*), caesura, cessation, delay, discontinuance, gap, halt, hesitation, interlude, intermission, interruption, interval, let-up (*Inf.*), lull, respite, rest, stay, stoppage, wait

pave asphalt, concrete, cover, flag, floor, macadamize, surface, tar, tile

paw *v.* grab, handle roughly, manhandle, maul, molest

pawl (pɔːl) *n.* pivoted lever shaped to engage with ratchet wheel to prevent motion in particular direction

pawn[1] (pɔːn) *vt.* **1.** deposit (article) as security for money borrowed —*n.* **2.** article deposited —**ˈpawnbroker** *n.* lender of money on goods pledged

pawn[2] (pɔːn) *n.* **1.** piece in chess **2.** *fig.* person used as mere tool

pawpaw (ˈpɔːpɔː) *n. see* PAPAW

pax (pæks) *n. chiefly R.C.Ch.* **1.** kiss of peace **2.** small plate formerly used to convey kiss of peace from celebrant at Mass to those attending it —*interj.* **3.** **UK** *school sl.* call signalling end to hostilities or claiming immunity from rules of game

P.A.X. **UK** private automatic exchange

pay (peɪ) *vt.* **1.** give (money *etc.*) for goods or services rendered **2.** compensate **3.** give, bestow **4.** be profitable to **5.** (*with* out) release bit by bit, as rope **6.** (*with* out) spend —*vi.* **7.** be remunerative or profitable (**paid, ˈpaying**) —*n.* **8.** wages **9.** paid employment —**ˈpayable** *a.* **1.** justly due **2.** profitable —**payˈee** *n.* person to whom money is paid or due —**ˈpayment** *n.* discharge of debt —**payˈola** *n. inf.* **1.** bribe given to secure special treatment, *esp.* to disc jockey to promote commercial product **2.** practice of paying or receiving such bribes —**pay bed** bed in hospital for which user has paid as private patient —**paying guest** boarder, lodger, *esp.* in private house —**ˈpayload** *n.* **1.** part of cargo earning revenue **2.** explosive power of missile *etc.* —**ˈpaymaster** *n.* official of government *etc.*, responsible for payment of wages and salaries —**ˈpayoff** *n.* **1.** final settlement, *esp.* in retribution **2.** *inf.* climax, consequence or outcome of events *etc.* **3.** final payment of debt *etc.* **4.** time of such payment **5.** *inf.* bribe —**pay packet 1.** envelope containing employee's wages **2.** the wages —**ˈpayroll** *n.* **1.** list of employees, specifying salary or wage of each **2.** total of these amounts or actual money equivalent —**pay as you earn UK, NZ** system by which income tax is paid by employers directly to government —**pay off 1.** pay all that is due in wages *etc.* and discharge from employment **2.** pay complete amount of (debt *etc.*) **3.** turn out to be profitable **4.** take revenge on (person) or for (wrong done) **5.** *inf.* give bribe to

P.A.Y.E. pay as you earn

Pb *Chem.* lead

PBX **UK** private branch exchange; telephone system that handles internal and external calls of building *etc.*

P.C. **1.** Police Constable **2.** Privy Councillor **3.** C Progressive Conservative

p.c. **1.** per cent **2.** personal computer **3.** postcard

Pd *Chem.* palladium

pd. paid

P.D.S.A. **UK** People's Dispensary for Sick Animals

PE Prince Edward Island

P.E. physical education

pea (piː) *n.* **1.** fruit, growing in pods, of climbing plant **2.** the plant —**pea-green** *a.* of shade of green like colour of green peas —**pea jacket** *or* **ˈpeacoat** *n.* sailor's short heavy woollen overcoat —**peaˈsouper** *n. inf.* thick fog

peace (piːs) *n.* **1.** freedom from war **2.** harmony **3.** quietness of mind **4.** calm **5.** repose —**ˈpeaceable** *a.* disposed to peace —**ˈpeaceably** *adv.* —**ˈpeaceful** *a.* **1.** free from war, tumult **2.** mild **3.** undisturbed —**ˈpeacefully** *adv.* —**ˈpeacemaker** *n.* person who establishes peace, *esp.* between others —**peace offering 1.** something given to adversary in hope of procuring or maintaining peace **2.** *Judaism* sacrificial meal shared between offerer and Jehovah —**peace pipe** pipe smoked by N Amer. Indians, *esp.* as token of peace (*also* **ˈcalumet**)

peach[1] (piːtʃ) *n.* **1.** stone fruit of delicate flavour **2.** *inf.* anything very pleasant **3.** pinkish-yellow colour —**ˈpeachy** *a.* **1.** like peach **2.** *inf.* fine, excellent

peach[2] (piːtʃ) *vi. sl.* become informer

peacock (ˈpiːkɒk) *n.* **1.** male of bird (**ˈpeafowl**) with fanlike tail, brilliantly coloured (**ˈpeahen** *fem.*) —*vi.* **2.** strut about or pose, like a peacock

THESAURUS

pawn[1] **1.** *v.* deposit, gage (*Archaic*), hazard, hock (*Inf., chiefly U.S.*), mortgage, pledge, pop (*Inf.*), stake, wager **2.** *n.* assurance, bond, collateral, gage, guarantee, guaranty, pledge, security

pawn[2] *n.* cat's-paw, creature, dupe, instrument, plaything, puppet, stooge (*Sl.*), tool, toy

pay *v.* **1.** clear, compensate, cough up (*Inf.*), discharge, foot, give, honour, liquidate, meet, offer, recompense, reimburse, remit, remunerate, render, requite, reward, settle, square up **2.** be advantageous, benefit, be worthwhile, repay, serve **3.** bestow, extend, give, grant, present, proffer, render **4.** *Often with* **for** answer for, atone, be punished, compensate, get one's deserts, make amends, suffer, suffer the consequences **5.** be profitable, be remunerative, make a return, make money, provide a living ~*n.* **6.** allowance, compensation, earnings, emoluments, fee, hire, income, payment, recompense, reimbursement, remuneration, reward, salary, stipend, takings, wages

payable due, mature, obligatory, outstanding, owed, owing, receivable, to be paid

payment defrayal, discharge, outlay, paying, remittance, settlement

pay off 1. discharge, dismiss, fire, lay off, let go, sack (*Inf.*) **2.** clear, discharge, liquidate, pay in full, settle, square **3.** be effective (profitable, successful), succeed, work **4.** get even with (*Inf.*), pay back, retaliate, settle a score **5.** *Inf.* bribe, buy off, corrupt, get at, grease the palm of (*Sl.*), oil (*Inf.*), suborn

peace 1. accord, agreement, amity, concord, harmony **2.** armistice, cessation of hostilities, conciliation, pacification, treaty, truce **3.** calm, composure, contentment, placidity, relaxation, repose, serenity **4.** calm, calmness, hush, peacefulness, quiet, quietude, repose, rest, silence, stillness, tranquillity

peaceable 1. amiable, amicable, conciliatory, dovish, friendly, gentle, inoffensive, mild, nonbelligerent, pacific, peaceful, peace-loving, placid, unwarlike **2.** balmy, calm, peaceful, quiet, restful, serene, still, tranquil, undisturbed

peaceful 1. amicable, at peace, free from strife, friendly, harmonious, nonviolent, on friendly *or* good terms, without hostility **2.** calm, gentle, placid, quiet, restful, serene, still, tranquil, undisturbed, unruffled, untroubled **3.** conciliatory, irenic, pacific, peaceable, peace-loving, placatory, unwarlike

peacemaker appeaser, arbitrator, conciliator, mediator, pacifier, peacemonger

peak (pi:k) *n.* **1.** pointed end of anything, *esp.* hill's sharp top **2.** point of greatest development *etc.* **3.** sharp increase **4.** projecting piece on front of cap —*v.* **5.** (cause to) form, reach peaks —**peaked** *or* **ˈpeaky** *a.* **1.** like, having a peak **2.** sickly, wan, drawn —**peak hour** time at which maximum occurs, either in amount of traffic or demand for gas *etc.* —**peak load** maximum load on electrical power-supply system

peal (pi:l) *n.* **1.** loud sound or succession of loud sounds **2.** changes rung on set of bells **3.** chime —*v.* **4.** sound loudly

peanut (ˈpi:nʌt) *n.* **1.** pea-shaped nut that ripens underground —*pl.* **2.** *inf.* trifling amount of money

pear (pɛə) *n.* **1.** tree yielding sweet, juicy fruit **2.** the fruit —**pear-shaped** *a.* shaped like a pear, heavier at the bottom than the top

pearl (pɜ:l) *n.* hard, lustrous structure found in several molluscs, *esp.* pearl oyster and used as jewel —**ˈpearly** *a.* like pearls —**pearl barley** barley with skin ground off —**pearl diver** *or* **fisher** person who dives for pearl-bearing molluscs

peasant (ˈpɛzᵊnt) *n.* member of low social class, *esp.* in rural district —**ˈpeasantry** *n.* peasants collectively

pease (pi:z) *n. obs., dial.* pea (*pl.* **pease**) —**pease pudding** *chiefly* **UK** dish of boiled split peas

peat (pi:t) *n.* **1.** decomposed vegetable substance found in bogs **2.** turf of it used for fuel —**peat moss** any of various mosses, *esp.* sphagnum, that grow in wet places and decay to form peat (*see also* SPHAGNUM)

pebble (ˈpɛbᵊl) *n.* **1.** small roundish stone **2.** pale, transparent rock crystal **3.** grainy, irregular surface —*vt.* **4.** pave, cover with pebbles —**pebble dash** finish for exterior walls with small stones in plaster

pecan (pɪˈkæn, ˈpi:kən) *n.* **1.** N Amer. tree, species of hickory, allied to walnut **2.** its edible nut

peccadillo (pɛkəˈdɪləʊ) *n.* **1.** slight offence **2.** petty crime (*pl.* **-es, -s**)

peccary (ˈpɛkərɪ) *n.* vicious Amer. animal allied to pig

peck[1] (pɛk) *n.* **1.** fourth part of bushel, 2 gallons **2.** great deal

peck[2] (pɛk) *v.* **1.** pick, strike with or as with beak **2.** nibble —*vt.* **3.** *inf.* kiss quickly —*n.* **4.** act, instance of pecking —**ˈpeckish** *a. inf.* hungry

pecker (ˈpɛkə) *n.* **UK** *sl.* good spirits (*esp. in* **keep one's pecker up**)

pectin (ˈpɛktɪn) *n.* gelatinizing substance obtained from ripe fruits —**ˈpectic** *a.* **1.** congealing **2.** denoting pectin

pectoral (ˈpɛktərəl) *a.* **1.** of the breast —*n.* **2.** chest medicine **3.** breastplate —**pectoral fin** either of pair of fins, situated just behind head in fishes

peculate (ˈpɛkjʊleɪt) *v.* **1.** embezzle **2.** steal —**pecuˈlation** *n.* —**ˈpeculator** *n.*

peculiar (pɪˈkju:lɪə) *a.* **1.** strange **2.** particular **3.** (*with* to) belonging (to) —**peculiˈarity** *n.* **1.** oddity **2.** characteristic **3.** distinguishing feature

pecuniary (pɪˈkju:nɪərɪ) *a.* relating to, or consisting of, money

-ped *or* **-pede** (*comb. form*) foot or feet, as in *quadruped, centipede*

pedagogue *or U.S.* (*sometimes*) **pedagog** (ˈpɛdəgɒg) *n.* **1.** schoolmaster **2.** pedant —**pedaˈgogic** *a.* —**pedagogy** (ˈpɛdəgɒgɪ, -gɒdʒɪ, -gəʊdʒɪ) *n.* principles, practice or profession of teaching

pedal (ˈpɛdᵊl) *n.* **1.** something to transmit motion from foot **2.** foot lever to modify tone or swell of musical instrument **3.** *Mus.* note, usu. bass, held through successive harmonies —*a.* (ˈpi:dᵊl) **4.** of a foot —*v.* **5.** propel (bicycle) by using pedals —*vi.* **6.** use pedals (**-ll-**)

pedalo (ˈpɛdələʊ) *n.* small watercraft with paddle wheel propelled by foot pedals

pedant (ˈpɛdᵊnt) *n.* one who overvalues, or insists on, petty details of book-learning, grammatical rules *etc.* —**peˈdantic** *a.*

peddle (ˈpɛdᵊl) *v.* go round selling (goods) —**ˈpeddler** *n.* one who sells narcotic drugs

pederast *or* **paederast** (ˈpɛdəræst) *n.* man who has homosexual relations with boy —**ˈpederasty** *or* **ˈpaederasty** *n.*

pedestal (ˈpɛdɪstᵊl) *n.* base of column, pillar

pedestrian (pɪˈdɛstrɪən) *n.* **1.** one who walks on foot —*a.* **2.** going on foot **3.** commonplace; dull, uninspiring

THESAURUS

peak *n.* 1. aiguille, apex, brow, crest, pinnacle, point, summit, tip, top 2. acme, apogee, climax, crown, culmination, high point, maximum point, *ne plus ultra*, zenith ~*v.* 3. be at its height, climax, come to a head, culminate, reach its highest point, reach the zenith

peal 1. *n.* blast, carillon, chime, clamour, clang, clap, crash, resounding, reverberation, ring, ringing, roar, rumble, sound, tintinnabulation 2. *v.* chime, crack, crash, resonate, resound, reverberate, ring, roar, roll, rumble, sound, tintinnabulate, toll

peasant churl (*Archaic*), countryman, hind (*Archaic*), rustic, son of the soil, swain (*Archaic*)

peccadillo error, indiscretion, infraction, lapse, misdeed, misdemeanour, petty offence, slip, trifling fault

peck *v./n.* bite, dig, hit, jab, kiss, nibble, pick, poke, prick, strike, tap

peculiar 1. abnormal, bizarre, curious, eccentric, exceptional, extraordinary, far-out (*Sl.*), freakish, funny, odd, offbeat, outlandish, out-of-the-way, quaint, queer, singular, strange, uncommon, unconventional, unusual, weird 2. appropriate, characteristic, distinct, distinctive, distinguishing, endemic, idiosyncratic, individual, local, particular, personal, private, restricted, special, specific, unique

peculiarity 1. abnormality, bizarreness, eccentricity, foible, freakishness, idiosyncrasy, mannerism, oddity, odd trait, queerness, quirk 2. attribute, characteristic, distinctiveness, feature, mark, particularity, property, quality, singularity, speciality, trait

pedagogue dogmatist, dominie (*Scot.*), educator, instructor, master, mistress, pedant, schoolmaster, schoolmistress, teacher

pedantic abstruse, academic, bookish, didactic, donnish, erudite, formal, fussy, hairsplitting, nitpicking (*Inf.*), overnice, particular, pedagogic, pompous, precise, priggish, punctilious, scholastic, schoolmasterly, sententious, stilted

peddle flog (*Sl.*), hawk, huckster, market, push (*Inf.*), sell, sell door to door, trade, vend

pedestal base, dado (*Architect.*), foot, foundation, mounting, pier, plinth, socle, stand, support

—**pe'destrianism** *n.* the practice of walking —**pe'destrianize** *or* **-ise** *vt.* convert into area for use of pedestrians only —**pedestrian crossing** place marked where pedestrians may cross road —**pedestrian precinct** area for pedestrians only to shop *etc.*

pedi- (*comb. form*) foot, as in *pedicure*

pediatrics (pi:dɪ'ætrɪks) *n. see* PAEDIATRICS

pedicure ('pɛdɪkjʊə) *n.* medical or cosmetic treatment of feet

pedigree ('pɛdɪgri:) *n.* **1.** register of ancestors **2.** genealogy

pediment ('pɛdɪmənt) *n.* triangular part over Greek portico *etc.* —**pedi'mental** *a.*

pedlar *or esp. U.S.* **peddler** ('pɛdlə) *n.* **1.** one who sells **2.** hawker

pedo- *or before vowel* **ped-** (*comb. form*) **US** *see* PAEDO-

peduncle (pɪ'dʌŋk³l) *n.* **1.** flower stalk **2.** stalklike structure

peek (pi:k) *vi./n.* peep, glance

peel[1] (pi:l) *vt.* **1.** strip off skin, rind or any form of covering from —*vi.* **2.** come off, as skin, rind —*n.* **3.** rind, skin —**peeled** *a. inf.* (of eyes) watchful

peel[2] (pi:l) *n.* **UK** fortified tower of 16th cent. on borders of Scotland

peen (pi:n) *n.* **1.** end of hammer head opposite striking face, oft. rounded or wedge-shaped —*vt.* **2.** strike with peen of hammer or stream of metal shot

peep[1] (pi:p) *vi.* **1.** look slyly or quickly —*n.* **2.** such a look —'**peeper** *n.* **1.** person who peeps **2.** (*oft. pl.*) *sl.* eye —**Peeping Tom** man who furtively observes women undressing; voyeur —'**peepshow** *n.* box with peephole through which series of pictures can be seen

peep[2] (pi:p) *vi.* **1.** cry, as chick **2.** chirp —*n.* **3.** such a cry

peer[1] (pɪə) *n.* **1.** nobleman **2.** one of the same rank ('**peeress** *fem.*) —'**peerage** *n.* **1.** body of peers **2.** rank of peer —'**peerless** *a.* without match or equal —**peer group** social group composed of individuals of approximately same age

peer[2] (pɪə) *vi.* look closely and intently

peevish ('pi:vɪʃ) *a.* **1.** fretful **2.** irritable —**peeved** *a. inf.* sulky, irritated —'**peevishly** *adv.* —'**peevishness** *n.* annoyance

peewit *or* **pewit** ('pi:wɪt) *n. see* LAPWING

peg (pɛg) *n.* **1.** nail or pin for joining, fastening, marking *etc.* **2.** (mark of) level, standard *etc.* —*vt.* **3.** fasten with pegs **4.** stabilize (prices) **5.** *inf.* throw —*vi.* **6.** (*with* away) persevere (**-gg-**) —'**pegboard** *n.* **1.** board having pattern of holes into which small pegs can be fitted, used for playing certain games or keeping score **2.** *see* **solitaire** (sense 1) *at* SOLITARY **3.** hardboard perforated by pattern of holes in which articles may be hung, as for display —**peg leg** *inf.* **1.** artificial leg, *esp.* one made of wood **2.** person with artificial leg —**peg out** *sl.* die

peignoir ('peɪnwɑ:) *n.* lady's dressing gown, jacket, wrapper

pejorative (pɪ'dʒɒrətɪv, 'pi:dʒər-) *a.* (of words *etc.*) with unpleasant, disparaging connotation

Pekingese (pi:kɪŋ'i:z) *or* **Pekinese** (pi:kə'ni:z) *n.* small Chinese dog (*also* **peke**) —**Peking man** (pi:'kɪŋ) early type of man, remains of which were found in cave near Peking

pelargonium (pɛlə'gəʊnɪəm) *n.* plant with red, white or pink flowers

pelf (pɛlf) *n. contemptuous* money; wealth

pelican ('pɛlɪkən) *n.* large, fish-eating waterfowl with large pouch beneath its bill —**pelican crossing** road crossing with pedestrian-operated traffic-light system

pelisse (pɛ'li:s) *n.* **1.** fur-trimmed cloak **2.** loose coat, usu. fur-trimmed, worn *esp.* by women in early 19th cent.

pellagra (pə'leɪgrə, -'læ-) *n. Pathol.* disease caused by dietary deficiency of niacin, characterized by scaling of skin *etc.*

pellet ('pɛlɪt) *n.* little ball, pill

pellicle ('pɛlɪk³l) *n.* thin skin, film

pell-mell ('pɛl'mɛl) *adv.* in utter confusion, headlong

pellucid (pɛ'lu:sɪd) *a.* **1.** translucent **2.** clear —**pellu'cidity** *n.*

pelmet ('pɛlmɪt) *n.* ornamental drapery or board, concealing curtain rail

pelt[1] (pɛlt) *vt.* **1.** strike with missiles —*vi.* **2.** throw missiles **3.** rush **4.** fall persistently, as rain

THESAURUS

pedestrian 1. *n.* footslogger, foot-traveller, walker **2.** *adj.* banal, boring, commonplace, dull, flat, humdrum, mediocre, mundane, ordinary, plodding, prosaic, run-of-the-mill, unimaginative, uninspired, uninteresting

pedigree ancestry, blood, breed, derivation, descent, extraction, family, family tree, genealogy, heritage, line, lineage, race, stemma, stirps, stock

peek 1. *v.* glance, keek (*Scot.*), look, peep, peer, snatch a glimpse, sneak a look, spy, squinny, take *or* have a gander (*Inf.*), take a look **2.** *n.* blink, gander (*Inf.*), glance, glim (*Scot.*), glimpse, keek (*Scot.*), look, look-see (*Sl.*), peep

peel 1. *v.* decorticate, desquamate, flake off, pare, scale, skin, strip off **2.** *n.* epicarp, exocarp, peeling, rind, skin

peep 1. *v.* keek (*Scot.*), look from hiding, look surreptitiously, peek, peer, sneak a look, spy, steal a look **2.** *n.* gander (*Inf.*), glim (*Scot.*), glimpse, keek (*Scot.*), look, look-see (*Sl.*), peek

peer[1] *n.* **1.** aristocrat, baron, count, duke, earl, lord, marquess, marquis, noble, nobleman, viscount **2.** coequal, compeer, equal, fellow, like, match

peer[2] *v.* gaze, inspect, peep, scan, scrutinize, snoop, spy, squinny, squint

peerage aristocracy, lords and ladies, nobility, peers, titled classes

peerless beyond compare, excellent, incomparable, matchless, nonpareil, outstanding, second to none, superlative, unequalled, unique, unmatched, unparalleled, unrivalled, unsurpassed

peevish acrimonious, cantankerous, captious, childish, churlish, crabbed, cross, crotchety (*Inf.*), crusty, fractious, fretful, grumpy, ill-natured, ill-tempered, irritable, pettish, petulant, querulous, ratty (*Brit. sl.*), short-tempered, snappy, splenetic, sulky, sullen, surly, testy, touchy, waspish, whingeing (*Inf.*)

peg *v.* **1.** attach, fasten, fix, join, make fast, secure **2.** *With* **away** apply oneself to, beaver away (*Brit. inf.*), keep at it, keep going, keep on, persist, plod along, plug away at (*Inf.*), stick to it, work at, work away **3.** *Of prices, etc.* control, fix, freeze, limit, set

pelt[2] (pɛlt) *n.* raw hide or skin

pelvis (ˈpɛlvɪs) *n.* bony cavity at base of human trunk (*pl.* **-es, -ves** (-viːz)) —ˈ**pelvic** *a.* pert. to pelvis

Pemb. Pembrokeshire

pen[1] (pɛn) *n.* **1.** instrument for writing —*vt.* **2.** compose **3.** write (**-nn-**) —**pen friend** pen pal —ˈ**penknife** *n.* small knife with one or more blades that fold into handle; pocketknife —ˈ**penmanship** *n.* style or technique of writing by hand —**pen name** author's pseudonym —**pen pal** person with whom one exchanges letters, oft. person in another country whom one has not met (*also* **pen friend**) —ˈ**penpusher** *n.* clerk involved with boring paperwork

pen[2] (pɛn) *n.* **1.** small enclosure, as for sheep —*vt.* **2.** put, keep in enclosure (**-nn-**)

pen[3] (pɛn) *n.* female swan

Pen. Peninsula

penal (ˈpiːnᵊl) *a.* of, incurring, inflicting, punishment —ˈ**penalize** *or* **-ise** *vt.* **1.** impose penalty on **2.** handicap —**penalty** (ˈpɛnᵊltɪ) *n.* **1.** punishment for crime or offence **2.** forfeit **3.** *Sport* handicap or disadvantage imposed for infringement of rule *etc.* —**penal code** codified body of laws that relate to crime and punishment

penance (ˈpɛnəns) *n.* **1.** suffering submitted to as expression of penitence **2.** repentance

pence (pɛns) *n., pl. of* PENNY

penchant (ˈpɛntʃənt; *Fr.* pɑ̃ˈʃɑ̃) *n.* inclination, decided taste

pencil (ˈpɛnsᵊl) *n.* **1.** instrument as of graphite, for writing *etc.* **2.** *Optics* narrow beam of light —*vt.* **3.** paint or draw **4.** mark with pencil (**-ll-**)

pendant (ˈpɛndənt) *n.* hanging ornament —ˈ**pendent** *a.* **1.** suspended, hanging **2.** projecting

pending (ˈpɛndɪŋ) *prep.* **1.** during, until —*a.* **2.** awaiting settlement **3.** undecided **4.** imminent

pendulous (ˈpɛndjʊləs) *a.* hanging, swinging —ˈ**pendulum** *n.* suspended weight swinging to and fro, *esp.* as regulator for clock

penetrate (ˈpɛnɪtreɪt) *vt.* **1.** enter into **2.** pierce **3.** arrive at the meaning of —**penetraˈbility** *n.* quality of being penetrable —ˈ**penetrable** *a.* capable of being entered or pierced —ˈ**penetrating** *a.* **1.** sharp **2.** easily heard **3.** subtle **4.** quick to understand —**peneˈtration** *n.* insight, acuteness —ˈ**penetrative** *a.* **1.** piercing **2.** discerning —ˈ**penetrator** *n.*

penguin (ˈpɛŋgwɪn) *n.* flightless, short-legged swimming bird

penicillin (pɛnɪˈsɪlɪn) *n.* antibiotic drug effective against a wide range of diseases, infections

peninsula (pɪˈnɪnsjʊlə) *n.* portion of land nearly surrounded by water —**peˈninsular** *a.*

penis (ˈpiːnɪs) *n.* male organ of copulation (and of urination) in man and many mammals (*pl.* **-es, penes** (ˈpiːniːz))

penitent (ˈpɛnɪtənt) *a.* **1.** affected by sense of guilt —*n.* **2.** one that repents of sin —ˈ**penitence** *n.* **1.** sorrow for sin **2.** repentance —**peniˈtential** *a.* of, or expressing, penitence —**peniˈtentiary** *a.* **1.** relating to penance, or to the rules of penance —*n.* **2.** US prison

pennant (ˈpɛnənt) *n.* long narrow flag

pennon (ˈpɛnən) *n.* small pointed or swallow-tailed flag

penny (ˈpɛnɪ) *n.* Brit. bronze coin, now 100th part of pound (*pl.* **pence,** ˈ**pennies**) —ˈ**penniless** *a.* **1.** having no money **2.** poor —**Penny Black** first postage stamp, issued in Brit. in 1840 —**penny-dreadful** *n.* **UK** *inf.* cheap, oft. lurid book or magazine (*pl.* **-s**) —**penny-farthing** *n.* **UK** early type of bicycle with large front

THESAURUS

pelt *v.* **1.** assail, batter, beat, belabour, bombard, cast, hurl, pepper, pummel, shower, sling, strike, thrash, throw, wallop (*Inf.*) **2.** belt (*Sl.*), career, charge, dash, hurry, run fast, rush, shoot, speed, tear, whiz (*Inf.*) **3.** bucket down (*Inf.*), pour, rain cats and dogs (*Inf.*), rain hard, teem

pen[1] *v.* commit to paper, compose, draft, draw up, jot down, write

pen[2] **1.** *n.* cage, coop, enclosure, fold, hutch, sty **2.** *v.* cage, confine, coop up, enclose, fence in, hedge, hem in, hurdle, mew (up), shut up *or* in

penal corrective, disciplinary, penalizing, punitive, retributive

penalize award a penalty against (*Sport*), correct, discipline, handicap, impose a penalty on, inflict a handicap on, punish, put at a disadvantage

penalty disadvantage, fine, forfeit, forfeiture, handicap, mulct, price, punishment, retribution

penance atonement, mortification, penalty, punishment, reparation, sackcloth and ashes

penchant affinity, bent, bias, disposition, fondness, inclination, leaning, liking, partiality, predilection, predisposition, proclivity, proneness, propensity, taste, tendency, turn

pending awaiting, forthcoming, hanging fire, imminent, impending, in the balance, in the offing, undecided, undetermined, unsettled, up in the air

penetrate 1. bore, enter, go through, perforate, pierce, prick, probe, stab **2.** diffuse, enter, get in, infiltrate, permeate, pervade, seep, suffuse **3.** *Fig.* comprehend, decipher, discern, fathom, figure out (*Inf.*), get to the bottom of, grasp, understand, unravel, work out

penetrating 1. biting, carrying, harsh, intrusive, pervasive, piercing, pungent, sharp, shrill, stinging, strong **2.** *Fig.* acute, astute, critical, discerning, discriminating, incisive, intelligent, keen, perceptive, perspicacious, profound, quick, sagacious, searching, sharp, sharp-witted, shrewd

penetration acuteness, astuteness, discernment, insight, keenness, perception, perspicacity, sharpness, shrewdness, wit

penitence compunction, contrition, regret, remorse, repentance, ruefulness, self-reproach, shame, sorrow

penitent *adj.* abject, apologetic, atoning, conscience-stricken, contrite, regretful, remorseful, repentant, rueful, sorrowful, sorry

penmanship calligraphy, chirography, fist (*Inf.*), hand, handwriting, longhand, script, writing

pen name allonym, nom de plume, pseudonym

pennant banderole, banner, burgee (*Nautical*), ensign, flag, jack, pennon, streamer

penniless bankrupt, broke (*Inf.*), cleaned out (*Sl.*), destitute, impecunious, impoverished, indigent, moneyless, necessitous, needy, on one's uppers, penurious, poor, poverty-stricken, ruined, skint (*Brit. sl.*), stony-broke (*Brit. sl.*), strapped (*U.S. sl.*), without a penny to one's name

wheel and small rear wheel —**penny-pincher** *n. inf.* person who is excessively careful with money —**penny-pinching** *n./a.* —**penny-wise** *a.* greatly concerned with saving small sums of money —**'pennyworth** *n.* **1.** amount that can be bought for a penny **2.** small amount —**penny-wise and pound-foolish** careful about trifles but wasteful in large ventures

penology (pi:ˈnɒlədʒɪ) *n.* study of punishment and prevention of crime

pension[1] (ˈpɛnʃən) *n.* **1.** regular payment to old people, retired public officials, soldiers *etc.* —*vt.* **2.** grant pension to —**ˈpensioner** *n.*

pension[2] (pãˈsjɔ̃) *Fr.* **1.** continental boarding house **2.** (full) board

pensive (ˈpɛnsɪv) *a.* **1.** thoughtful with sadness **2.** wistful

penstemon (pɛnˈsti:mən) *n. see* PENTSTEMON

pent (pɛnt) *a.* shut up, kept in —**pent-up** *a.* not released, repressed

penta- (*comb. form*) five, as in *pentagon, pentameter*

pentacle (ˈpɛntəkᵊl) *n.* **1.** star-shaped figure with five points **2.** such figure used by Pythagoreans, black magicians *etc.* (*also* **ˈpentagram, ˈpentangle**)

pentagon (ˈpɛntəgɒn) *n.* plane figure having five angles —**penˈtagonal** *a.*

Pentagon (ˈpɛntəgɒn) *n.* military headquarters in U.S.A.

pentameter (pɛnˈtæmɪtə) *n.* verse of five metrical feet

Pentateuch (ˈpɛntətju:x) *n.* first five books of Old Testament

pentathlon (pɛnˈtæθlən) *n.* athletic contest of five events

pentatonic scale (pɛntəˈtɒnɪk) *Mus.* scale consisting of five notes

Pentecost (ˈpɛntɪkɒst) *n.* **1.** Whitsuntide **2.** Jewish harvest festival on 50th day after Passover —**Penteˈcostal** *a.* **1.** of any of various Christian groups that emphasize charismatic aspects of Christianity **2.** of Pentecost or influence of Holy Ghost —*n.* **3.** member of a Pentecostal Church —**Penteˈcostalist** *n./a.*

penthouse (ˈpɛnthaʊs) *n.* apartment, flat or other structure on top, or top floor, of building

pentode (ˈpɛntəʊd) *n. Electron.* five-electrode thermionic valve, having anode, cathode and three grids

pentstemon (pɛntˈsti:mən) *or* **penstemon** *n.* bright-flowered garden plant

penult (ˈpɛnʌlt, pɪˈnʌlt) *n.* last syllable but one of word —**peˈnultimate** *a.* next before the last

penumbra (pɪˈnʌmbrə) *n.* **1.** imperfect shadow **2.** in an eclipse, the partially shadowed region which surrounds the full shadow

penury (ˈpɛnjʊrɪ) *n.* **1.** extreme poverty **2.** extreme scarcity —**peˈnurious** *a.* **1.** niggardly, stingy **2.** poor, scanty

peony (ˈpi:ənɪ) *n.* any of genus of N Amer. plants with showy red, pink or white flowers

people (ˈpi:pᵊl) *pl.n.* **1.** persons generally **2.** community, nation **3.** family —*n.* **4.** race —*vt.* **5.** stock with inhabitants, populate

pep (pɛp) *n.* **1.** vigour **2.** energy **3.** enthusiasm —*vt.* (*usu. with* up) **4.** impart energy to **5.** speed up (**-pp-**) —**pep pill** *inf.* tablet containing stimulant —**pep talk** *inf.* enthusiastic talk designed to increase confidence, production *etc.*

pepper (ˈpɛpə) *n.* **1.** fruit of climbing plant, which yields pungent aromatic spice **2.** various slightly pungent vegetables, *eg* capsicum —*vt.* **3.** season with pepper **4.** sprinkle, dot **5.** pelt with missiles —**ˈpeppery** *a.* **1.** having the qualities of pepper **2.** irritable —**pepper-and-salt** *a.* **1.** (of cloth *etc.*) marked with fine mixture of black and white **2.** (of hair) streaked with grey —**ˈpeppercorn** *n.* **1.** dried pepper berry **2.** something trifling —**pepper mill** hand mill used to grind peppercorns —**ˈpeppermint** *n.* **1.** plant noted for aromatic pungent liquor distilled from it **2.** a sweet flavoured with this

pepsin (ˈpɛpsɪn) *n.* enzyme produced in stomach, which, when activated by acid, breaks down proteins

peptic (ˈpɛptɪk) *a.* relating to digestion or digestive juices

per (pɜ:; *unstressed* pə) *prep.* **1.** for each **2.** by **3.** in manner of

per- (*comb. form*) through, thoroughly, as in *perfect, perspicacious*

peradventure (pərədˈvɛntʃə, pɜ:r-) *obs. adv.* **1.** by chance; perhaps —*n.* **2.** chance; doubt

perambulate (pəˈræmbjʊleɪt) *vt.* **1.** walk through or over **2.** traverse —*vi.* **3.** walk about —**perˈambulator** *n.* pram

per annum (ˈænəm) *Lat.* by the year

per capita (ˈkæpɪtə) of or for each person

perceive (pəˈsi:v) *vt.* **1.** obtain knowledge of through senses **2.** observe **3.** understand —**perˈceivable** *a.* —**perceptiˈbility** *n.* —**perˈceptible** *a.* discernible, recognizable —**perˈception** *n.* **1.** faculty of perceiving **2.** intuitive judgment —**perˈceptive** *a.*

THESAURUS

pension allowance, annuity, benefit, superannuation

pensioner O.A.P., retired person, senior citizen

pensive blue (*Inf.*), cogitative, contemplative, dreamy, grave, in a brown study (*Inf.*), meditative, melancholy, mournful, musing, preoccupied, reflective, ruminative, sad, serious, sober, solemn, sorrowful, thoughtful, wistful

pent-up bottled up, bridled, checked, constrained, curbed, held back, inhibited, repressed, smothered, stifled, suppressed

penury **1.** beggary, destitution, indigence, need, pauperism, poverty, privation, straitened circumstances, want **2.** dearth, deficiency, lack, paucity, scantiness, scarcity, shortage, sparseness

people *n.* **1.** human beings, humanity, humans, mankind, men and women, mortals, persons **2.** citizens, clan, community, family, folk, inhabitants, nation, population, public, race, tribe ~*v.* **3.** colonize, inhabit, occupy, populate, settle

pepper *v.* **1.** flavour, season, spice **2.** bespeckle, dot, fleck, spatter, speck, sprinkle, stipple, stud **3.** bombard, pelt, riddle, scatter, shower

peppery **1.** fiery, highly seasoned, hot, piquant, pungent, spicy **2.** choleric, hot-tempered, irascible, irritable, quick-tempered, snappish, testy, touchy, waspish

perceive **1.** be aware of, behold, descry, discern, discover, distinguish, espy, make out, note, notice, observe, recognize, remark, see, spot **2.** appreciate,

percentage (pəˈsɛntɪdʒ) *n.* proportion or rate per hundred —**per cent** in each hundred —**perˈcentile** *n.* one of 99 actual or notional values of a variable dividing its distribution into 100 groups with equal frequencies (*also* (**US**) **ˈcentile**)

perception (pəˈsɛpʃən) *n. see* PERCEIVE

perch[1] (pɜːtʃ) *n.* any of a family of freshwater fishes

perch[2] (pɜːtʃ) *n.* **1.** resting place, as for bird **2.** formerly, measure of 5½ yards —*vt.* **3.** place, as on perch —*vi.* **4.** alight, settle on fixed body **5.** roost **6.** balance

perchance (pəˈtʃɑːns) *adv. Poet.* perhaps

percipient (pəˈsɪpɪənt) *a.* **1.** having faculty of perception **2.** perceiving —*n.* **3.** one who perceives

percolate (ˈpɜːkəleɪt) *v.* **1.** pass through fine mesh as liquor **2.** permeate **3.** filter —**percoˈlation** *n.* —**ˈpercolator** *n.* coffeepot with filter

percussion (pəˈkʌʃən) *n.* **1.** collision **2.** impact **3.** vibratory shock —**perˈcussionist** *n. Mus.* person who plays percussion instrument —**perˈcussive** *a.* —**percussion cap** detonator consisting of paper or thin metal cap containing material that explodes when struck —**percussion instrument** one played by being struck, *eg* drum, cymbals *etc.*

perdition (pəˈdɪʃən) *n.* spiritual ruin

peregrinate (ˈpɛrɪgrɪneɪt) *vi.* travel about, roam —**peregriˈnation** *n.*

peregrine (ˈpɛrɪgrɪn) *n.* type of falcon

peremptory (pəˈrɛmptərɪ) *a.* **1.** authoritative, imperious **2.** forbidding debate **3.** decisive

perennial (pəˈrɛnɪəl) *a.* **1.** lasting through the years **2.** perpetual, unfailing —*n.* **3.** plant lasting more than two years —**peˈrennially** *adv.*

perfect (ˈpɜːfɪkt) *a.* **1.** complete **2.** finished **3.** whole **4.** unspoilt **5.** faultless **6.** correct, precise **7.** excellent **8.** of highest quality —*n.* **9.** tense denoting a complete act —*vt.* (pəˈfɛkt) **10.** improve **11.** finish **12.** make skilful —**perˈfectable** *a.* capable of becoming perfect —**perˈfection** *n.* **1.** state of being perfect **2.** faultlessness —**perˈfectionism** *n.* **1.** *Philos.* doctrine that man can attain perfection in this life **2.** demand for highest standard of excellence —**perˈfectionist** *n.* —**ˈperfectly** *adv.* —**perfect participle** past participle

perfidy (ˈpɜːfɪdɪ) *n.* treachery, disloyalty —**perˈfidious** *a.*

perforate (ˈpɜːfəreɪt) *vt.* make holes in, penetrate —**perfoˈration** *n.*

perforce (pəˈfɔːs) *adv.* of necessity

perform (pəˈfɔːm) *vt.* **1.** bring to completion **2.** accomplish; fulfil **3.** represent on stage —*vi.* **4.** function **5.** act part **6.** play, as on musical instrument —**perˈformance** *n.* —**perˈformer** *n.*

THESAURUS

apprehend, comprehend, conclude, deduce, feel, gather, get (*Inf.*), grasp, know, learn, realize, see, sense, understand

perceptible apparent, appreciable, clear, conspicuous, detectable, discernible, distinct, evident, noticeable, observable, obvious, palpable, perceivable, recognizable, tangible, visible

perception apprehension, awareness, conception, consciousness, discernment, feeling, grasp, idea, impression, insight, notion, observation, recognition, sensation, sense, taste, understanding

perceptive acute, alert, astute, aware, discerning, insightful, intuitive, observant, penetrating, percipient, perspicacious, quick, responsive, sensitive, sharp

perch 1. *n.* branch, pole, post, resting place, roost **2.** *v.* alight, balance, land, rest, roost, settle, sit on

perchance by chance, for all one knows, haply (*Archaic*), maybe, mayhap (*Archaic*), peradventure (*Archaic*), perhaps, possibly, probably

percipient alert, alive, astute, aware, discerning, discriminating, intelligent, penetrating, perceptive, perspicacious, quick-witted, sharp, wide-awake

percolate drain, drip, exude, filter, filtrate, leach, ooze, penetrate, perk (*of coffee, inf.*), permeate, pervade, seep, strain, transfuse

percussion blow, brunt, bump, clash, collision, concussion, crash, impact, jolt, knock, shock, smash, thump

peremptory 1. absolute, binding, categorical, commanding, compelling, decisive, final, imperative, incontrovertible, irrefutable, obligatory, undeniable **2.** arbitrary, assertive, authoritative, autocratic, bossy (*Inf.*), dictatorial, dogmatic, domineering, high-handed, imperious, intolerant, overbearing

perennial 1. abiding, chronic, constant, continual, continuing, enduring, incessant, inveterate, lasting, lifelong, persistent, recurrent, unchanging **2.** ceaseless, deathless, eternal, everlasting, immortal, imperishable, never-ending, permanent, perpetual, unceasing, undying, unfailing, uninterrupted

perfect *adj.* **1.** absolute, complete, completed, consummate, entire, finished, full, out-and-out, sheer, unadulterated, unalloyed, unmitigated, utter, whole **2.** blameless, excellent, faultless, flawless, ideal, immaculate, impeccable, pure, splendid, spotless, sublime, superb, superlative, supreme, unblemished, unmarred, untarnished **3.** accurate, close, correct, exact, faithful, precise, right, spot-on (*Brit. inf.*), strict, true, unerring **4.** accomplished, adept, experienced, expert, finished, masterly, polished, practised, skilful, skilled ~*v.* **5.** accomplish, achieve, carry out, complete, consummate, effect, finish, fulfil, perform, realize **6.** ameliorate, cultivate, develop, elaborate, hone, improve, polish, refine

perfection completeness, exactness, excellence, exquisiteness, faultlessness, integrity, maturity, perfectness, precision, purity, sublimity, superiority, wholeness

perfectionist formalist, precisian, precisionist, purist, stickler

perfectly 1. absolutely, altogether, completely, consummately, entirely, fully, quite, thoroughly, totally, utterly, wholly **2.** admirably, exquisitely, faultlessly, flawlessly, ideally, impeccably, superbly, superlatively, supremely, to perfection, wonderfully

perfidious corrupt, deceitful, dishonest, disloyal, double-dealing, double-faced, faithless, false, recreant (*Archaic*), traitorous, treacherous, treasonous, two-faced, unfaithful, untrustworthy

perfidy betrayal, deceit, disloyalty, double-dealing, duplicity, faithlessness, falsity, infidelity, perfidiousness, treachery, treason

perforate bore, drill, hole, honeycomb, penetrate, pierce, punch, puncture

perfume (ˈpɜːfjuːm) *n.* **1.** agreeable scent **2.** fragrance —*vt.* (pəˈfjuːm) **3.** imbue with an agreeable odour, scent —**perˈfumer** *n.* —**perˈfumery** *n.* perfumes in general

perfunctory (pəˈfʌŋktərɪ) *a.* **1.** superficial **2.** hasty **3.** done indifferently

pergola (ˈpɜːgələ) *n.* **1.** area covered by plants growing on trellis **2.** the trellis

perhaps (pəˈhæps; *inf.* præps) *adv.* possibly

peri- (*comb. form*) round, as in *perimeter, period, periphrasis*

perianth (ˈpɛrɪænθ) *n.* outer part of flower, consisting of calyx and corolla

pericardium (pɛrɪˈkɑːdɪəm) *n.* membrane enclosing the heart (*pl.* **-dia** (-dɪə)) —**periˈcardiac** *or* **periˈcardial** *a.* —**pericarˈditis** *n.* inflammation of this

perigee (ˈpɛrɪdʒiː) *n.* point in its orbit around earth when moon or satellite is nearest earth

perihelion (pɛrɪˈhiːlɪən) *n.* point in orbit of planet or comet when nearest to sun (*pl.* **-lia** (-lɪə))

peril (ˈpɛrɪl) *n.* **1.** danger **2.** exposure to injury —ˈ**perilous** *a.* full of peril, hazardous

perimeter (pəˈrɪmɪtə) *n.* **1.** *Maths.* outer boundary of an area; length of this **2.** medical instrument for measuring the field of vision

perineum (pɛrɪˈniːəm) *n.* **1.** region of body between anus and genital organs **2.** surface of human trunk between thighs (*pl.* **-nea** (-ˈniːə))

period (ˈpɪərɪəd) *n.* **1.** particular portion of time **2.** a series of years **3.** single occurrence of menstruation **4.** cycle **5.** conclusion **6.** full stop (.) at end of sentence **7.** complete sentence —*a.* **8.** (of furniture, dress, play *etc.*) belonging to particular time in history —**periˈodic** *a.* recurring at regular intervals —**periˈodical** *a./n.* **1.** (of) publication issued at regular intervals —*a.* **2.** of a period **3.** periodic —**perioˈdicity** *n.* —**periodic law** principle that chemical properties of elements are periodic functions of their atomic weights or, more accurately, of their atomic numbers —**periodic table** table of elements, arranged in order of increasing atomic number, based on periodic law

peripatetic (pɛrɪpəˈtɛtɪk) *a.* itinerant, walking, travelling about

periphery (pəˈrɪfərɪ) *n.* **1.** circumference **2.** surface, outside —**peˈripheral** *a.* **1.** minor, unimportant **2.** of periphery

periphrasis (pəˈrɪfrəsɪs) *n.* **1.** roundabout speech or phrase **2.** circumlocution (*pl.* **-rases** (-rəsiːz)) —**periˈphrastic** *a.*

periscope (ˈpɛrɪskəʊp) *n.* instrument, used *esp.* in submarines, for giving view of objects on different level —**periscopic** (pɛrɪˈskɒpɪk) *a.*

perish (ˈpɛrɪʃ) *vi.* **1.** die, waste away **2.** decay, rot —**perishaˈbility** *n.* —ˈ**perishable** *a.* **1.** that will not last long —*pl.n.* **2.** perishable food —ˈ**perishing** *a.* **1.** *inf.* (of weather *etc.*) extremely cold **2.** *sl.* confounded

peristalsis (pɛrɪˈstælsɪs) *n. Physiol.* succession of waves of involuntary muscular contraction of various bodily tubes, *esp.* of alimentary tract (*pl.* **-ses** (-siːz))

peristyle (ˈpɛrɪstaɪl) *n.* **1.** range of pillars surrounding building, square *etc.* **2.** court within this

peritoneum (pɛrɪtəˈniːəm) *n.* membrane lining internal surface of abdomen (*pl.* **-s, -nea** (-ˈniːə)) —**peritoˈnitis** *n.* inflammation of peritoneum

periwig (ˈpɛrɪwɪg) *n. Hist.* wig

periwinkle (ˈpɛrɪwɪŋkᵊl) *n.* **1.** flowering plant **2.** small edible shellfish (*also* ˈ**winkle**)

perjure (ˈpɜːdʒə) *vt.* render (oneself) guilty of perjury —ˈ**perjury** *n.* **1.** crime of false testimony on oath **2.** false swearing

perk[1] (pɜːk) *n. inf.* perquisite

perk[2] (pɜːk) *vi. inf.* (of coffee) percolate

perky (ˈpɜːkɪ) *a.* lively, cheerful, jaunty, gay —**perk up** make, become cheerful

THESAURUS

perform 1. accomplish, achieve, act, bring about, carry out, complete, comply with, discharge, do, effect, execute, fulfil, function, observe, pull off, satisfy, transact, work **2.** act, appear as, depict, enact, play, present, produce, put on, render, represent, stage

performance 1. accomplishment, achievement, act, carrying out, completion, conduct, consummation, discharge, execution, exploit, feat, fulfilment, work **2.** acting, appearance, exhibition, gig (*Inf.*), interpretation, play, portrayal, presentation, production, representation, show **3.** action, conduct, efficiency, functioning, operation, practice, running, working

performer actor, actress, artiste, play-actor, player, Thespian, trouper

perfume aroma, attar, balminess, bouquet, cologne, essence, fragrance, incense, odour, redolence, scent, smell, sweetness

perfunctory automatic, careless, cursory, heedless, inattentive, indifferent, mechanical, negligent, offhand, routine, sketchy, slipshod, slovenly, stereotyped, superficial, unconcerned, unthinking, wooden

perhaps as the case may be, conceivably, feasibly, for all one knows, it may be, maybe, perchance (*Archaic*), possibly

peril danger, exposure, hazard, insecurity, jeopardy, menace, pitfall, risk, uncertainty, vulnerability

perilous chancy (*Inf.*), dangerous, exposed, fraught with danger, hairy (*Sl.*), hazardous, parlous (*Archaic*), precarious, risky, threatening, unsafe, unsure, vulnerable

perimeter ambit, border, borderline, boundary, bounds, circumference, confines, edge, limit, margin, periphery

period 1. interval, season, space, span, spell, stretch, term, time, while **2.** aeon, age, course, cycle, date, days, epoch, era, generation, season, stage, term, time, years

periodical *n.* journal, magazine, monthly, organ, paper, publication, quarterly, review, serial, weekly

perish 1. be killed, be lost, decease, die, expire, lose one's life, pass away **2.** decay, decompose, disintegrate, moulder, rot, waste, wither

perishable decaying, decomposable, destructible, easily spoilt, liable to rot, short-lived, unstable

perjure (oneself) bear false witness, commit perjury, forswear, give false testimony, lie under oath, swear falsely

perjury bearing false witness, false oath, false statement, false swearing, forswearing, giving false testimony, lying under oath, oath breaking, violation of an oath, wilful falsehood

perm (pɜːm) *n. inf. see* **permutation** (sense 3) *at* PERMUTE

permafrost (ˈpɜːməfrɒst) *n.* permanently frozen ground

permanent (ˈpɜːmənənt) *a.* **1.** continuing in same state **2.** lasting —**ˈpermanence** *or* **ˈpermanency** *n.* fixedness —**permanent wave** (treatment of hair producing) long-lasting style (*also* **perm**) —**permanent way** *chiefly* **UK** track of railway, including sleepers, rails *etc.*

permanganate (pəˈmæŋgəneɪt, -nɪt) *n.* salt of an acid of manganese

permeate (ˈpɜːmɪeɪt) *vt.* **1.** pervade, saturate **2.** pass through pores of —**ˈpermeable** *a.* admitting of passage of fluids

Permian (ˈpɜːmɪən) *a.* **1.** of last period of Palaeozoic era, between Carboniferous and Triassic periods —*n.* **2.** Permian period or rock system

permit (pəˈmɪt) *vt.* **1.** allow **2.** give leave to (-tt-) —*n.* (ˈpɜːmɪt) **3.** warrant or licence to do something **4.** written permission —**perˈmissible** *a.* allowable —**perˈmission** *n.* authorization, leave, liberty —**perˈmissive** *a.* (too) tolerant, lenient, *esp.* sexually

permute (pəˈmjuːt) *vt.* change sequence of —**permuˈtation** *n.* **1.** mutual transference **2.** *Maths.* arrangement of a number of quantities in every possible order **3.** fixed combinations for selections of results on football pools

pernicious (pəˈnɪʃəs) *a.* **1.** wicked or mischievous **2.** extremely hurtful **3.** having quality of destroying or injuring —**pernicious anaemia** form of anaemia characterized by lesions of spinal cord, weakness, diarrhoea *etc.*

pernickety (pəˈnɪkɪtɪ) *a. inf.* fussy, fastidious about trifles

peroration (pɛrəˈreɪʃən) *n.* concluding part of oration —**ˈperorate** *vi.*

peroxide (pəˈrɒksaɪd) *n.* **1.** oxide of a given base containing greatest quantity of oxygen **2.** *see* **hydrogen peroxide** *at* HYDROGEN

perpendicular (pɜːpənˈdɪkjʊlə) *a.* **1.** at right angles to the plane of the horizon **2.** at right angles to given line or surface **3.** exactly upright —*n.* **4.** line falling at right angles on another line or plane

perpetrate (ˈpɜːpɪtreɪt) *vt.* perform or be responsible for (deception, crime *etc.*) —**perpeˈtration** *n.* —**ˈperpetrator** *n.*

perpetual (pəˈpɛtjʊəl) *a.* **1.** continuous **2.** lasting for ever —**perˈpetually** *adv.* —**perˈpetuate** *vt.* **1.** make perpetual **2.** not to allow to be forgotten —**perpetuˈation** *n.* —**perpeˈtuity** *n.* —**perpetual motion** motion of hypothetical mechanism that continues indefinitely without any external source of energy

perplex (pəˈplɛks) *vt.* **1.** puzzle, bewilder **2.** make difficult to understand —**perˈplexity** *n.* puzzled or tangled state

perquisite (ˈpɜːkwɪzɪt) *n.* **1.** any incidental benefit from a certain type of employment **2.** casual payment in addition to salary

THESAURUS

permanence constancy, continuance, continuity, dependability, durability, duration, endurance, finality, fixedness, fixity, immortality, indestructibility, lastingness, perdurability (*Rare*), permanency, perpetuity, stability, survival

permanent abiding, constant, durable, enduring, everlasting, fixed, immutable, imperishable, indestructible, invariable, lasting, long-lasting, perennial, perpetual, persistent, stable, steadfast, unchanging, unfading

permeate charge, diffuse throughout, fill, filter through, imbue, impregnate, infiltrate, pass through, penetrate, percolate, pervade, saturate, seep through, soak through, spread throughout

permissible acceptable, admissible, allowable, all right, authorized, kosher (*Inf.*), lawful, legal, legit (*Sl.*), legitimate, licit, O.K. (*Inf.*), permitted, proper, sanctioned

permission allowance, approval, assent, authorization, consent, dispensation, freedom, go-ahead (*Inf.*), green light, leave, liberty, licence, permit, sanction, sufferance, tolerance

permissive acquiescent, easy-going, forbearing, free, indulgent, latitudinarian, lax, lenient, liberal, open-minded, tolerant

permit **1.** *v.* admit, agree, allow, authorize, consent, empower, enable, endorse, endure, give leave *or* permission, grant, let, license, sanction, suffer, tolerate, warrant **2.** *n.* authorization, liberty, licence, pass, passport, permission, sanction, warrant

permutation alteration, change, shift, transformation, transmutation, transposition

pernicious bad, baleful, baneful (*Archaic*), damaging, dangerous, deadly, deleterious, destructive, detrimental, evil, fatal, harmful, hurtful, injurious, maleficent, malevolent, malicious, malign, malignant, noisome, noxious, offensive, pestilent, poisonous, ruinous, venomous, wicked

pernickety careful, carping, difficult to please, exacting, fastidious, finicky, fussy, hairsplitting, nice, nitpicking (*Inf.*), overprecise, painstaking, particular, punctilious

peroration closing remarks, conclusion, recapitulation, recapping (*Inf.*), reiteration, summing-up

perpendicular at right angles to, on end, plumb, straight, upright, vertical

perpetrate be responsible for, bring about, carry out, commit, do, effect, enact, execute, inflict, perform, wreak

perpetual **1.** abiding, endless, enduring, eternal, everlasting, immortal, infinite, lasting, never-ending, perennial, permanent, sempiternal (*Literary*), unchanging, undying, unending **2.** ceaseless, constant, continual, continuous, endless, incessant, interminable, never-ending, perennial, persistent, recurrent, repeated, unceasing, unfailing, uninterrupted, unremitting

perpetuate continue, eternalize, immortalize, keep alive, keep going, keep up, maintain, preserve, sustain

perplex **1.** baffle, befuddle, beset, bewilder, confound, confuse, dumbfound, mix up, muddle, mystify, nonplus, puzzle, stump **2.** complicate, encumber, entangle, involve, jumble, mix up, snarl up, tangle, thicken

perplexity bafflement, bewilderment, confusion, incomprehension, mystification, puzzlement, stupefaction

perquisite benefit, bonus, dividend, extra, fringe benefit, perk (*Inf.*), plus

perry (ˈpɛrɪ) *n.* fermented drink made from pears

per se (seɪ) *Lat.* by or in itself

persecute (ˈpɜːsɪkjuːt) *vt.* 1. oppress because of race, religion *etc.* 2. subject to persistent ill-treatment —**perseˈcution** *n.* —**ˈpersecutor** *n.*

persevere (pɜːsɪˈvɪə) *vi.* (*oft. with* in) persist, maintain effort —**perseˈverance** *n.* persistence

Persian (ˈpɜːʃən) *a.* 1. of ancient Persia or modern Iran —*n.* 2. native or inhabitant of modern Iran; Iranian 3. language of Iran or Persia in any of ancient or modern forms —**Persian cat** long-haired domestic cat —**Persian lamb** 1. black loosely curled fur from karakul lamb 2. karakul lamb

persimmon (pɜːˈsɪmən) *n.* 1. any of several tropical trees typically having hard wood 2. its fruit

persist (pəˈsɪst) *vi.* (*oft. with* in) continue in spite of obstacles or objections —**perˈsistence** *or* **perˈsistency** *n.* —**perˈsistent** *a.* 1. persisting 2. steady 3. persevering 4. lasting

person (ˈpɜːsᵊn) *n.* 1. individual (human) being 2. body of human being 3. *Gram.* classification, or one of the classes, of pronouns and verb forms according to the person speaking, spoken to, or spoken of —**perˈsona** *n.* assumed character (*pl.* **-nae** (-niː)) —**ˈpersonable** *a.* good-looking —**ˈpersonage** *n.* notable person —**ˈpersonal** *a.* 1. individual, private, or one's own 2. of, relating to grammatical person —**persoˈnality** *n.* 1. distinctive character 2. a celebrity —**ˈpersonalize** *or* **-ise** *vt.* 1. endow with personal or individual qualities 2. mark with person's initials, name *etc.* 3. take personally 4. personify —**ˈpersonally** *adv.* in person —**ˈpersonalty** *n.* personal property —**ˈpersonate** *vt.* pass oneself off as —**persoˈnation** *n.* —**personal column** newspaper column containing personal messages *etc.* —**personal computer** small inexpensive computer used in word processing *etc.* —**personal property** *Law* all property except land and interests in land that pass to heir —**in person** actually present

persona non grata (pɜːˈsəʊnə nɒn ˈgrɑːtə) *Lat.* 1. unacceptable or unwelcome person 2. diplomat who is not acceptable to government to whom he is accredited (*pl.* ***personae non gratae*** (pɜːˈsəʊniː nɒn ˈgrɑːtiː))

personify (pɜːˈsɒnɪfaɪ) *vt.* 1. represent as person 2. typify (**-ified, -ifying**) —**personifiˈcation** *n.*

personnel (pɜːsəˈnɛl) *n.* 1. staff employed in a service or institution 2. department that interviews or keeps records of employees

perspective (pəˈspɛktɪv) *n.* 1. mental view 2. art of drawing on flat surface to give effect of solidity and relative distances and sizes 3. drawing in perspective

Perspex (ˈpɜːspɛks) *n.* **R** transparent acrylic substitute for glass

perspicacious (pɜːspɪˈkeɪʃəs) *a.* having quick mental insight —**perspicacity** (pɜːspɪˈkæsɪtɪ) *n.*

perspicuous (pəˈspɪkjʊəs) *a.* 1. clearly expressed 2. lucid 3. plain 4. obvious —**perspiˈcuity** *n.*

perspire (pəˈspaɪə) *vi.* sweat —**perspiration** (pɜːspəˈreɪʃən) *n.* sweating

THESAURUS

persecute 1. afflict, distress, dragoon, harass, hound, hunt, ill-treat, injure, maltreat, martyr, molest, oppress, pursue, torment, torture, victimize 2. annoy, badger, bait, bother, pester, tease, vex, worry

perseverance constancy, dedication, determination, diligence, doggedness, endurance, indefatigability, persistence, pertinacity, purposefulness, resolution, sedulity, stamina, steadfastness, tenacity

persevere be determined *or* resolved, carry on, continue, endure, go on, hang on, hold fast, hold on (*Inf.*), keep going, keep on *or* at, maintain, persist, plug away (*Inf.*), pursue, remain, stand firm, stick at *or* to

persist 1. be resolute, continue, hold on (*Inf.*), insist, persevere, stand firm 2. abide, carry on, continue, endure, keep up, last, linger, remain

persistence constancy, determination, diligence, doggedness, endurance, grit, indefatigability, perseverance, pertinacity, pluck, resolution, stamina, steadfastness, tenacity, tirelessness

persistent 1. assiduous, determined, dogged, enduring, fixed, immovable, indefatigable, obdurate, obstinate, persevering, pertinacious, resolute, steadfast, steady, stubborn, tenacious, tireless, unflagging 2. constant, continual, continuous, endless, incessant, interminable, never-ending, perpetual, relentless, repeated, unrelenting, unremitting

person 1. being, body, human, human being, individual, living soul, soul 2. **in person** bodily, in the flesh, oneself, personally

personable affable, agreeable, amiable, attractive, charming, good-looking, handsome, likable, nice, pleasant, pleasing, presentable, winning

personage big noise (*Brit. sl.*), big shot (*Sl.*), celebrity, dignitary, luminary, notable, personality, public figure, somebody, V.I.P., well-known person, worthy

personal exclusive, individual, intimate, own, particular, peculiar, private, privy, special

personality 1. character, disposition, identity, individuality, make-up, nature, psyche, temper, temperament, traits 2. celebrity, famous name, household name, notable, personage, star, well-known face, well-known person

personally in person, in the flesh

personate act, depict, do (*Inf.*), enact, feign, imitate, impersonate, play-act, portray, represent

personification embodiment, image, incarnation, likeness, portrayal, recreation, representation, semblance

personify body forth, embody, epitomize, exemplify, express, image (*Rare*), incarnate, mirror, represent, symbolize, typify

personnel employees, helpers, human resources, liveware, members, men and women, people, staff, workers, work force

perspective angle, attitude, broad view, context, frame of reference, objectivity, outlook, overview, proportion, relation, relative importance, relativity, way of looking

perspicacious acute, alert, astute, aware, clear-sighted, clever, discerning, keen, observant, penetrating, perceptive, percipient, sagacious, sharp, sharp-witted, shrewd

perspicacity acumen, acuteness, discernment, discrimination, insight, keenness, penetration, perceptiveness, percipience, perspicaciousness, perspicuity, sagaciousness, sagacity, sharpness, shrewdness, wit

perspiration exudation, moisture, sweat, wetness

persuade (pəˈsweɪd) *vt.* **1.** bring (one to do something) by argument, charm *etc.* **2.** convince —**perˈsuasion** *n.* **1.** art, act of persuading **2.** way of thinking or belief —**perˈsuasive** *a.*

pert (pɜːt) *a.* forward, saucy

pertain (pəˈteɪn) *vi.* (*oft. with* to) **1.** belong, relate, have reference (to) **2.** concern

pertinacious (pɜːtɪˈneɪʃəs) *a.* obstinate, persistent —**pertinacity** (pɜːtɪˈnæsɪtɪ) *or* **pertiˈnaciousness** *n.* doggedness, resolution

pertinent (ˈpɜːtɪnənt) *a.* relating to the matter at hand —**ˈpertinence** *or* **ˈpertinency** *n.* relevance

perturb (pəˈtɜːb) *vt.* **1.** disturb greatly **2.** alarm —**perˈturbable** *a.* —**perturˈbation** *n.* agitation of mind

peruke (pəˈruːk) *n. Hist.* wig

peruse (pəˈruːz) *vt.* read, *esp.* in slow and careful, or leisurely, manner —**peˈrusal** *n.*

pervade (pɜːˈveɪd) *vt.* **1.** spread through **2.** be rife among —**perˈvasion** *n.* —**perˈvasive** *a.*

pervert (pəˈvɜːt) *vt.* **1.** turn to wrong use **2.** lead astray —*n.* (ˈpɜːvɜːt) **3.** one who shows unhealthy abnormality, *esp.* in sexual matters —**perˈverse** *a.* **1.** obstinately or unreasonably wrong **2.** self-willed **3.** headstrong **4.** wayward —**perˈversely** *adv.* —**perˈversion** *n.*

pervious (ˈpɜːvɪəs) *a.* **1.** permeable **2.** penetrable, giving passage

peseta (pəˈseɪtə; *Sp.* peˈseta) *n.* Sp. monetary unit

peso (ˈpeɪsəʊ; *Sp.* ˈpeso) *n.* standard monetary unit of Argentina, Mexico *etc.* (*pl.* **pesos** (ˈpeɪsəʊz; *Sp.* ˈpesos))

pessary (ˈpɛsərɪ) *n.* **1.** instrument used to support mouth and neck of uterus **2.** appliance to prevent conception **3.** medicated suppository

pessimism (ˈpɛsɪmɪzəm) *n.* **1.** tendency to see the worst side of things **2.** theory that everything turns to evil —**ˈpessimist** *n.* —**pessiˈmistic** *a.*

pest (pɛst) *n.* **1.** troublesome or harmful thing, person or insect **2.** *rare* plague —**ˈpesticide** *n.* chemical for killing pests, *esp.* insects —**pesˈtiferous** *a.* **1.** troublesome **2.** bringing plague

pester (ˈpɛstə) *vt.* trouble or vex persistently, harass

pestilence (ˈpɛstɪləns) *n.* epidemic disease, *esp.* bubonic plague —**ˈpestilent** *a.* **1.** troublesome **2.** deadly —**pestiˈlential** *a.*

THESAURUS

perspire be damp, be wet, drip, exude, glow, pour with sweat, secrete, sweat, swelter

persuade 1. actuate, advise, allure, bring round (*Inf.*), coax, counsel, entice, impel, incite, induce, influence, inveigle, prevail upon, prompt, sway, talk into, urge, win over 2. cause to believe, convert, convince, satisfy

persuasion 1. blandishment, cajolery, conversion, enticement, exhortation, inducement, influencing, inveiglement, wheedling 2. cogency, force, persuasiveness, potency, power, pull (*Inf.*) 3. belief, certitude, conviction, credo, creed, faith, firm belief, fixed opinion, opinion, tenet, views

persuasive cogent, compelling, convincing, credible, effective, eloquent, forceful, impelling, impressive, inducing, influential, logical, moving, plausible, sound, telling, touching, valid, weighty, winning

pertain appertain, apply, be appropriate, bear on, befit, belong, be part of, be relevant, concern, refer, regard, relate

pertinacious bull-headed, determined, dogged, headstrong, inflexible, intractable, mulish, obdurate, obstinate, persevering, persistent, perverse, pigheaded, relentless, resolute, self-willed, strongwilled, stubborn, tenacious, unyielding, wilful

pertinent admissible, *ad rem*, applicable, apposite, appropriate, apropos, apt, fit, fitting, germane, material, pat, proper, relevant, suitable, to the point, to the purpose

perturb 1. agitate, alarm, bother, discompose, disconcert, discountenance, disquiet, disturb, fluster, ruffle, trouble, unsettle, upset, vex, worry 2. confuse, disarrange, disorder, muddle, unsettle

perusal browse, check, examination, inspection, look through, read, scrutiny, study

peruse browse, check, examine, inspect, look through, read, run one's eye over, scan, scrutinize, study

pervade affect, charge, diffuse, extend, fill, imbue, infuse, overspread, penetrate, percolate, permeate, spread through, suffuse

pervasive common, extensive, general, inescapable, omnipresent, permeating, pervading, prevalent, rife, ubiquitous, universal, widespread

perverse 1. abnormal, contradictory, contrary, delinquent, depraved, deviant, disobedient, froward, improper, incorrect, miscreant, rebellious, refractory, troublesome, unhealthy, unmanageable, unreasonable 2. contrary, contumacious, cross-grained, dogged, headstrong, intractable, intransigent, obdurate, wilful, wrong-headed 3. contrary, mulish, obstinate, pig-headed, stubborn, unyielding, wayward

perversion 1. aberration, abnormality, debauchery, depravity, deviation, immorality, kink (*Brit. sl.*), kinkiness (*Sl.*), unnaturalness, vice, vitiation, wickedness 2. corruption, distortion, falsification, misinterpretation, misrepresentation, misuse, twisting

pervert *v.* 1. abuse, distort, falsify, garble, misconstrue, misinterpret, misrepresent, misuse, twist, warp 2. corrupt, debase, debauch, degrade, deprave, desecrate, initiate, lead astray, subvert ~*n.* 3. debauchee, degenerate, deviant, weirdo (*Sl.*)

pessimism cynicism, dejection, depression, despair, despondency, distrust, gloom, gloominess, gloomy outlook, glumness, hopelessness, melancholy

pessimist cynic, defeatist, doomster, gloom merchant (*Inf.*), kill-joy, melancholic, misanthrope, prophet of doom, wet blanket (*Inf.*), worrier

pessimistic bleak, cynical, dark, dejected, depressed, despairing, despondent, distrustful, downhearted, fatalistic, foreboding, gloomy, glum, hopeless, melancholy, misanthropic, morose, resigned, sad

pest 1. annoyance, bane, bore, bother, irritation, nuisance, pain (*Inf.*), pain in the neck (*Inf.*), thorn in one's flesh, trial, vexation 2. bane, blight, bug, curse, epidemic, infection, pestilence, plague, scourge

pester annoy, badger, bedevil, bother, bug (*Inf.*), chivvy, disturb, drive one up the wall (*Sl.*), fret, get at, get on someone's nerves, harass, harry, hassle (*Inf.*), irk, nag, pick on, plague, ride (*Inf.*), torment, worry

pestilence Black Death, epidemic, pandemic, plague, visitation

pestilential 1. annoying, dangerous, deleterious, de-

pestle (ˈpɛsᵊl) *n.* **1.** instrument with which things are pounded in a mortar —*v.* **2.** pound with pestle

pet[1] (pɛt) *n.* **1.** animal kept for companionship *etc.* **2.** person regarded with affection —*vt.* **3.** make pet of —*v.* **4.** *inf.* hug, embrace, fondle (-tt-)

pet[2] (pɛt) *n.* fit of sulkiness, *esp.* at what is felt to be a slight; pique —ˈ**pettish** *a.* peevish, petulant

Pet. *Bible* Peter

petal (ˈpɛtᵊl) *n.* white or coloured leaflike part of flower —ˈ**petalled** *a.*

petard (pɪˈtɑːd) *n.* formerly, an explosive device

peter (ˈpiːtə) *vi.* —**peter out** *inf.* disappear, lose power gradually

Peter Pan youthful or immature man

petersham (ˈpiːtəʃəm) *n.* thick corded ribbon used to stiffen belts *etc.*

pethidine (ˈpɛθɪdiːn) *n.* water-soluble drug used as analgesic (*also* **meˈperidine**)

petiole (ˈpɛtɪəʊl) *n.* **1.** stalk by which leaf is attached to plant **2.** *Zool.* slender stalk or stem, as between thorax and abdomen of ants —ˈ**petiolate** *a.*

petit (ˈpɛtɪ) *a. Law* small, petty —**petit bourgeois** *n.* **1.** section of middle class with lowest social status, as shopkeepers *etc.* **2.** member of this stratum (*pl.* **petits bourgeois** (ˈpɛtɪ ˈbʊəʒwɑːz)) (*also* **petite bourgeoisie, petty bourgeoisie**) —*a.* **3.** of petit bourgeois, *esp.* indicating sense of self-righteousness *etc.* —**petit four** any of various small fancy cakes and biscuits (*pl.* **petits fours** (ˈpɛtɪ ˈfɔːz)) —**petit jury** jury of 12 persons empanelled to determine facts of case and decide issue pursuant to direction of court on points of law (*also* **petty jury**) —**petit mal** (mæl) mild form of epilepsy characterized by periods of impairment or loss of consciousness for up to 30 seconds —**petit point** (pɔɪnt, pwɔɪ) **1.** small diagonal needlepoint stitch used for fine detail **2.** work done with such stitches

petite (pəˈtiːt) *a.* (of women) small, dainty

petition (pɪˈtɪʃən) *n.* **1.** entreaty, request, *esp.* one presented to sovereign or parliament —*vt.* **2.** present petition to —**peˈtitionary** *a.*

petrel (ˈpɛtrəl) *n.* any of a family of sea birds

petrify (ˈpɛtrɪfaɪ) *vt.* **1.** turn to stone **2.** *fig.* make motionless with fear **3.** make dumb with amazement (**-ified, -ifying**) —**petriˈfaction** *or* **petrifiˈcation** *n.*

petrochemical (pɛtrəʊˈkɛmɪkᵊl) *n.* **1.** any substance, such as acetone or ethanol, obtained from petroleum —*a.* **2.** of petrochemicals; related to petrochemistry —**petroˈchemistry** *n.*

petrocurrency (ˈpɛtrəʊˈkʌrənsɪ) *n.* currency oil-producing countries acquire as profit from oil sales to other countries

petrodollar (ˈpɛtrəʊdɒlə) *n.* money earned by country by exporting of petroleum

petrolatum (pɛtrəˈleɪtəm) *n.* translucent gelatinous substance obtained from petroleum

petroleum (pəˈtrəʊlɪəm) *n.* mineral oil —ˈ**petrol** *n.* refined petroleum used in motorcars *etc.* —**petroleum jelly** *see* PETROLATUM —**petrol station UK** filling station

petrology (pɛˈtrɒlədʒɪ) *n.* study of rocks and their structure

petticoat (ˈpɛtɪkəʊt) *n.* women's undergarment worn under skirts, dresses *etc.*

pettifogger (ˈpɛtɪfɒgə) *n.* **1.** low-class lawyer **2.** one given to mean dealing in small matters

petty (ˈpɛtɪ) *a.* **1.** unimportant, trivial **2.** small-minded, mean **3.** on a small scale —**petty cash** cash kept by firm to pay minor incidental expenses —**petty jury** *see* **petit jury** *at* PETIT —**petty officer** noncommissioned officer in Navy

petulant (ˈpɛtjʊlənt) *a.* given to small fits of temper, peevish —ˈ**petulance** *or* ˈ**petulancy** *n.*

petunia (pɪˈtjuːnɪə) *n.* any plant of tropical Amer. genus with funnel-shaped purple or white flowers

pew (pjuː) *n.* **1.** fixed seat in church **2.** *inf.* chair, seat

pewit *or* **peewit** (ˈpiːwɪt) *n. see* LAPWING

pewter (ˈpjuːtə) *n.* **1.** alloy of tin and lead **2.** ware made of this

pH potential of hydrogen; measure of acidity or alkalinity of solution

phalanx (ˈfælæŋks) *n.* body of men formed in close array (*pl.* **-es, phalanges** (fæˈlændʒiːz))

phalarope (ˈfælərəʊp) *n.* any of a family of small wading birds

THESAURUS

structive, detrimental, evil, foul, harmful, hazardous, injurious, pernicious, ruinous, troublesome **2.** catching, contagious, contaminated, deadly, disease-ridden, infectious, malignant, noxious, pestiferous, poisonous, venomous

pet[1] *n.* **1.** apple of one's eye, blue-eyed boy (*Inf.*), darling, favourite, idol, jewel, treasure ~*v.* **2.** baby, coddle, cosset, mollycoddle, pamper, spoil **3.** caress, fondle, pat, stroke **4.** *Inf.* canoodle (*Sl.*), cuddle, kiss, neck (*Inf.*), smooch (*Sl.*), snog (*Brit. sl.*)

pet[2] bad mood, huff, ill temper, miff (*Inf.*), paddy (*Brit inf.*), paddywhack (*Brit. inf.*), pique, pout, sulk, sulks, tantrum, temper

peter out come to nothing, die out, dwindle, ebb, evaporate, fade, fail, give out, run dry, run out, stop, taper off, wane

petition 1. *n.* address, appeal, application, entreaty, invocation, memorial, plea, prayer, request, round robin, solicitation, suit, supplication **2.** *v.* adjure, appeal, ask, beg, beseech, call upon, crave, entreat, plead, pray, press, solicit, sue, supplicate, urge

petrified 1. fossilized, ossified, rocklike **2.** aghast, appalled, dazed, dumbfounded, frozen, horrified, numb, scared stiff, shocked, speechless, stunned, stupefied, terrified, terror-stricken

petrify 1. calcify, fossilize, harden, set, solidify, turn to stone **2.** amaze, appal, astonish, astound, confound, dumbfound, horrify, immobilize, paralyse, stun, stupefy, terrify, transfix

petty 1. contemptible, inconsiderable, inessential, inferior, insignificant, little, measly (*Inf.*), negligible, paltry, piddling (*Inf.*), slight, small, trifling, trivial, unimportant **2.** cheap, grudging, mean, mean-minded, shabby, small-minded, spiteful, stingy, ungenerous

petulance bad temper, crabbiness, ill humour, irritability, peevishness, pettishness, pique, pouts, querulousness, spleen, sulkiness, sullenness, waspishness

petulant bad-tempered, captious, cavilling, crabbed, cross, crusty, fault-finding, fretful, ill-humoured, impatient, irritable, moody, peevish, perverse, pouting, querulous, snappish, sour, sulky, sullen, ungracious, waspish

phallus ('fæləs) *n.* 1. penis 2. symbol of it used in primitive rites (*pl.* **-es, -li** (-laɪ)) —**'phallic** *a.* —**'phallicism** *n.*

phantasm ('fæntæzəm) *n.* 1. vision of absent person 2. illusion —**phantasma'goria** *or* **phan'tasmagory** *n.* 1. crowd of dim or unreal figures 2. exhibition of illusions —**phan'tasmal** *a.* —**'phantasy** *n. see* FANTASY

phantom ('fæntəm) *n.* 1. apparition, spectre, ghost 2. fancied vision

Pharaoh ('fɛərəʊ) *n.* title of ancient Egyptian kings

Pharisee ('færɪsi:) *n.* 1. sanctimonious person 2. hypocrite —**phari'saic(al)** *a.*

pharmaceutical (fɑ:mə'sju:tɪk'l) *or* **pharmaceutic** *a.* of pharmacy —**pharma'ceutics** *pl.n.* (*with sing. v.*) science of pharmacy —**'pharmacist** *n.* person qualified to dispense drugs —**pharma'cology** *n.* study of drugs —**pharmacopoeia** *or U.S.* (*sometimes*) **pharmacopeia** (fɑ:məkə'pi:ə) *n.* official book with list and directions for use of drugs —**'pharmacy** *n.* 1. preparation and dispensing of drugs 2. dispensary

pharos ('fɛərɒs) *n.* marine lighthouse or beacon

pharynx ('færɪŋks) *n.* cavity forming back part of mouth and terminating in gullet (*pl.* **pharynges** (fæ'rɪndʒi:z)) —**pharyn'geal** *or* **pha'ryngal** *a.* —**pharyn'gitis** *n.* inflammation of pharynx

phase (feɪz) *n.* 1. any distinct or characteristic period or stage in a development or chain of events —*vt.* 2. arrange, execute in stages or to coincide with something else

Ph.D. Doctor of Philosophy (*also* **D.Phil.**)

pheasant ('fɛz'nt) *n.* any of various game birds with bright plumage

pheno- *or before vowel* **phen-** (*comb. form*) 1. showing, manifesting, as in *phenotype* 2. indicating that molecule contains benzene rings, as in *phenobarbitone*

phenobarbitone (fi:nəʊ'bɑ:bɪtəʊn) *or* **phenobarbital** (fi:nəʊ'bɑ:bɪt'l) *n.* drug inducing sleep

phenol ('fi:nɒl) *n.* carbolic acid

phenomenon (fɪ'nɒmɪnən) *n.* 1. anything appearing or observed 2. remarkable person or thing (*pl.* **phenomena** (fɪ'nɒmɪnə)) —**phe'nomenal** *a.* 1. relating to phenomena 2. remarkable 3. recognizable or evidenced by senses —**phe'nomenalism** *n.* 1. theory that only phenomena are real and can be known 2. tendency to think about things as phenomena only —**phe'nomenalist** *n./a.*

phenyl ('fi:naɪl, 'fɛnɪl) *a.* of, containing or consisting of monovalent group C_6H_5, derived from benzene

phew (fju:) *interj.* exclamation of relief, surprise *etc.*

phi (faɪ) *n.* 21st letter in Gr. alphabet (Φ, φ) (*pl.* **-s**)

phial ('faɪəl) *n.* small bottle for medicine *etc.*

Phil. 1. *Bible* Philippians 2. Philippines 3. Philadelphia

philander (fɪ'lændə) *vi.* (of man) flirt with women

philanthropy (fɪ'lænθrəpɪ) *n.* 1. practice of doing good to one's fellow men 2. love of mankind —**philan'thropic** *a.* loving mankind, benevolent —**phi'lanthropist** *or* **'philanthrope** *n.*

philately (fɪ'lætəlɪ) *n.* stamp collecting —**phila'telic** *a.* —**phi'latelist** *n.*

-phile *or* **-phil** (*comb. form*) person or thing having fondness for something specified, as in *bibliophile*

philharmonic (fɪlhɑ:'mɒnɪk, fɪlə-) *a.* 1. fond of music 2. (**P-** *when part of name*) denoting orchestra, choir *etc.* devoted to music

philhellene (fɪl'hɛli:n) *n.* 1. lover of Greece and Greek culture 2. *European hist.* supporter of cause of Greek national independence —**philhel'lenic** *a.*

philippic (fɪ'lɪpɪk) *n.* bitter or impassioned speech of denunciation; invective

Philistine ('fɪlɪstaɪn) *n.* 1. ignorant, smug person 2. member of non-Semitic people who inhabited ancient Philistia —*a.* 3. (*sometimes* **p-**) boorishly uncultured 4. of the ancient Philistines —**philistinism** ('fɪlɪstɪnɪzəm) *n.*

Phillips ('fɪlɪps) *n.* screwdriver that can be used on screw (**Phillips screw**) that has two slots crossing at centre of head

philo- *or before vowel* **phil-** (*comb. form*) love of, as in *philology, philanthropic*

philology (fɪ'lɒlədʒɪ) *n.* science of structure and development of languages —**philo'logical** *a.* —**phi'lologist** *or* **phi'lologer** *n.*

philos. 1. philosopher 2. philosophical

philosophy (fɪ'lɒsəfɪ) *n.* 1. pursuit of wisdom 2. study of realities and general principles 3. system of theories on nature of things or on conduct 4. calmness of mind —**phi'losopher** *n.* one who studies, possesses or originates philosophy —**philo'sophic(al)** *a.* 1. of, like

THESAURUS

phantom 1. apparition, eidolon, ghost, phantasm, revenant, shade (*Literary*), spectre, spirit, spook (*Inf.*), wraith 2. chimera, figment, figment of the imagination, hallucination, illusion, vision

pharisee canter, dissembler, dissimulator, fraud, humbug, hypocrite, phoney (*Sl.*), pietist, whited sepulchre

phase aspect, chapter, condition, development, juncture, period, point, position, stage, state, step, time

phenomenon 1. circumstance, episode, event, fact, happening, incident, occurrence 2. exception, marvel, miracle, nonpareil, prodigy, rarity, sensation, sight, spectacle, wonder

philander coquet, court, dally, flirt, fool around (*Inf.*), toy, trifle, womanize (*Inf.*)

philanthropic alms-giving, altruistic, beneficent, benevolent, benignant, charitable, eleemosynary, gracious, humane, humanitarian, kind, kind-hearted, munificent, public-spirited

philanthropist alms-giver, altruist, benefactor, contributor, donor, giver, humanitarian, patron

philanthropy alms-giving, altruism, beneficence, benevolence, benignity, bounty, brotherly love, charitableness, charity, generosity, humanitarianism, kind-heartedness, liberality, munificence, openhandedness, patronage, public-spiritedness

philistine 1. *n.* barbarian, boor, bourgeois, Goth, ignoramus, lout, lowbrow, vulgarian, yahoo 2. *adj.* anti-intellectual, boorish, bourgeois, crass, ignorant, lowbrow, tasteless, uncultivated, uncultured, uneducated, unrefined

philosopher dialectician, logician, metaphysician, sage, seeker after truth, theorist, thinker, wise man

philosophical, philosophic 1. abstract, erudite, learned, logical, rational, sagacious, theoretical, thoughtful, wise 2. calm, collected, composed, cool, impassive, imperturbable, patient, resigned, serene, stoical, tranquil, unruffled

philosophy **2.** wise, learned **3.** calm, stoical **—phi'losophize** *or* **-phise** *vi.* **1.** reason like philosopher **2.** theorize **3.** moralize

philtre *or U.S.* **philter** ('fɪltə) *n.* love potion

phlebitis (flɪ'baɪtɪs) *n.* inflammation of a vein

phlegm (flɛm) *n.* **1.** viscid substance formed by mucous membrane and ejected by coughing *etc.* **2.** calmness, sluggishness **—phlegmatic(al)** (flɛg'mætɪk(ᵊl)) *a.* **1.** not easily agitated **2.** composed

phloem ('fləʊɛm) *n.* tissue in higher plants that conducts synthesized food substances to all parts of plant

phlogiston (flɒ'dʒɪstɒn, -tən) *n. Chem.* hypothetical substance formerly thought to be present in all combustible materials

phlox (flɒks) *n.* any of chiefly N Amer. genus of flowering plants (*pl.* **phlox, -es**)

phobia ('fəʊbɪə) *n.* **1.** fear, aversion **2.** unreasoning dislike

-phobia (*n. comb. form*) extreme abnormal fear of or aversion to, as in *acrophobia, claustrophobia* **—-phobe** (*n. comb. form*) one that fears or hates, as in *xenophobe* **—-phobic** (*a. comb. form*)

Phoenician (fə'nɪʃɪən, -'ni:ʃən) *n.* **1.** member of ancient Semitic people of NW Syria **2.** extinct language of this people *—a.* **3.** of Phoenicia, Phoenicians or their language

phoenix *or U.S.* **phenix** ('fi:nɪks) *n.* **1.** legendary bird **2.** unique thing

phone (fəʊn) *n./v. inf.* telephone **—'phonecard** *n.* **1.** public telephone operated by special card instead of coins **2.** the card used **—phone-in** *n. Rad., T.V.* programme in which listeners' or viewers' questions, comments *etc.* are telephoned to studio and broadcast live as part of discussion

-phone (*n. comb. form*) **1.** device giving off sound, as in *telephone* —(*a. comb. form*) **2.** speaking a particular language, as in *Francophone* **—-phonic** (*a. comb. form*)

phoneme ('fəʊni:m) *n. Linguis.* one of set of speech sounds in a language, that serve to distinguish one word from another **—pho'nemic** *a.* **—pho'nemics** *pl. n.* (*with sing. v.*) aspect of linguistics concerned with classification and analysis of phonemes of a language

phonetic (fə'nɛtɪk) *a.* of vocal sounds **—phone'tician** *or* **'phonetist** *n.* **—pho'netics** *pl.n.* (*with sing. v.*) science of vocal sounds

phoney *or* **phony** ('fəʊnɪ) *a. inf.* **1.** counterfeit, sham, fraudulent **2.** suspect

phono- *or before vowel* **phon-** (*comb. form*) sounds, as in *phonology*

phonograph ('fəʊnəgrɑ:f, -græf) *n.* instrument recording and reproducing sounds **—phono'graphic** *a.*

phonology (fə'nɒlədʒɪ) *n.* **1.** study of speech sounds and their development **2.** system of sounds in a language **—phono'logic(al)** *a.* **—pho'nologist** *n.*

phosphorus ('fɒsfərəs) *n.* toxic, flammable, nonmetallic element which appears luminous in the dark **—'phosphate, 'phosphide, 'phosphite** *n.* compounds of phosphorus **—'phosphor** *n.* substance capable of emitting light when irradiated with particles of electromagnetic radiation **—phospho'resce** *vi.* exhibit phosphorescence **—phospho'rescence** *n.* faint glow in the dark **—phos'phoric** *a.* of or containing phosphorus with valence of five **—'phosphorous** *a.* of or containing phosphorus in trivalent state

photo ('fəʊtəʊ) *n. inf.* photograph (*pl.* **-s**) **—photo finish** photo taken at end of race to show placing of contestants

photo- (*comb. form*) light, as in *photometer, photosynthesis*

photocell ('fəʊtəʊsel) *n.* device in which photoelectric or photovoltaic effect or photoconductivity is used to produce current or voltage when exposed to light or other electromagnetic radiation (*also* **photoelectric cell, electric eye**)

photochemistry (fəʊtəʊ'kɛmɪstrɪ) *n.* study of chemical action of light

photoconductivity (fəʊtəʊkɒndʌk'tɪvɪtɪ) *n.* change in electrical conductivity of certain substances as a result of absorption of electromagnetic radiation

photocopy ('fəʊtəʊkɒpɪ) *n.* **1.** photographic reproduction *—vt.* **2.** make photocopy of **—'photocopier** *n.* instrument using light-sensitive photographic materials to reproduce written, printed or graphic work

photoelectricity (fəʊtəʊɪlɛk'trɪsɪtɪ) *n.* electricity produced or affected by action of light **—photoe'lectric** *a.* of electric or electronic effects caused by light or other electromagnetic radiation **—photoelectric cell** *see* PHOTOCELL

photoelectron (fəʊtəʊɪ'lɛktrɒn) *n.* electron liberated from metallic surface by action of beam of light

Photofit ('fəʊtəʊfɪt) *n.* **R** method of combining photographs of facial features, hair *etc.* into composite picture of face: used by police to trace suspects, criminals *etc.*

photoflood ('fəʊtəʊflʌd) *n.* highly incandescent tungsten lamp used for indoor photography, television *etc.*

photogenic (fəʊtə'dʒɛnɪk) *a.* (*esp.* of person) capable of being photographed attractively

photograph ('fəʊtəgrɑ:f, -græf) *n.* **1.** picture made by chemical action of light on sensitive film *—vt.* **2.** take photograph of **—pho'tographer** *n.* **—photo'graphic** *a.* **—pho'tography** *n.*

THESAURUS

philosophy 1. aesthetics, knowledge, logic, metaphysics, rationalism, reason, reasoning, thinking, thought, wisdom 2. attitude to life, basic idea, beliefs, convictions, doctrine, ideology, principle, tenets, thinking, values, viewpoint, *Weltanschauung*, world-view 3. composure, coolness, dispassion, equanimity, resignation, restraint, self-possession, serenity, stoicism

phlegmatic apathetic, bovine, cold, dull, frigid, heavy, impassive, indifferent, lethargic, listless, lymphatic, matter-of-fact, placid, sluggish, stoical, stolid, undemonstrative, unemotional, unfeeling

phobia aversion, detestation, dislike, distaste, dread, fear, hatred, horror, irrational fear, loathing, obsession, overwhelming anxiety, repulsion, revulsion, terror, thing (*Inf.*)

phone 1. *n.* blower (*Inf.*), telephone 2. *v.* buzz (*Inf.*), call, get on the blower (*Inf.*), give someone a bell (*Brit. sl.*), give someone a buzz (*Inf.*), give someone a call, give someone a ring, give someone a tinkle (*Brit. inf.*), make a call, ring, ring up, telephone

photogravure (fəʊtəʊɡrəˈvjʊə) *n.* **1.** process of etching, product of photography **2.** picture so reproduced

photolithography (fəʊtəʊlɪˈθɒɡrəfɪ) *n.* art of printing from photographs transferred to stone or metal plate **—photolithoˈgraphic** *a.*

photometer (fəʊˈtɒmɪtə) *n.* instrument for measuring intensity of light **—phoˈtometry** *n.*

photomontage (fəʊtəʊmɒnˈtɑːʒ) *n.* **1.** technique of producing composite picture by combining several photographs **2.** composite picture so produced

photon (ˈfəʊtɒn) *n.* quantum of electromagnetic radiation energy, as of light *etc.* having both particle and wave behaviour

photosensitive (fəʊtəʊˈsɛnsɪtɪv) *a.* sensitive to electromagnetic radiation, *esp.* light **—photosensiˈtivity** *n.* **—photoˈsensitize** *or* **-tise** *vt.*

Photostat (ˈfəʊtəʊstæt) *n.* **1. R** apparatus for obtaining direct, facsimile, photographic reproductions of documents, manuscripts, drawings *etc.*, without printing from negatives —*vt.* **2.** take Photostat copy of

photosynthesis (fəʊtəʊˈsɪnθɪsɪs) *n.* process by which green plant uses sun's energy to build up carbohydrate reserves

phototropism (fəʊtəʊˈtrəʊpɪzəm) *n.* growth response of plant parts to stimulus of light

photovoltaic effect (fəʊtəʊvɒlˈteɪɪk) effect when electromagnetic radiation falls on thin film of one solid deposited on surface of dissimilar solid producing a difference in potential between the two materials

phrase (freɪz) *n.* **1.** group of words **2.** pithy expression **3.** mode of expression —*vt.* **4.** express in words **—phraseology** (freɪzɪˈɒlədʒɪ) *n.* manner of expression, choice of words **—phrasal verb** phrase consisting of verb and preposition, oft. with meaning different to the parts (*eg* take in)

phrenology (frɪˈnɒlədʒɪ) *n.* **1.** formerly, study of skull's shape **2.** theory that character and mental powers are indicated by shape of skull **—phrenoˈlogical** *a.* **—phreˈnologist** *n.*

phut (fʌt) *n. inf.* dull, heavy sound **—go phut** collapse

phylactery (fɪˈlæktərɪ) *n.* leather case containing religious texts worn by Jewish men

phylum (ˈfaɪləm) *n.* **1.** major taxonomic division of animals and plants that contain one or more classes **2.** group of related language families or linguistic stocks (*pl.* **-la** (-lə))

phys. 1. physical **2.** physician **3.** physics **4.** physiological **5.** physiology

physic (ˈfɪzɪk) *n.* **1.** *rare* medicine, *esp.* cathartic —*pl.* **2.** (*with sing. v.*) science of properties of matter and energy **—ˈphysical** *a.* **1.** bodily, as opposed to mental or moral **2.** material **3.** of physics of body **—ˈphysically** *adv.* **—phyˈsician** *n.* qualified medical practitioner **—ˈphysicist** *n.* one skilled in, or student of physics **—physical chemistry** chemistry concerned with way in which physical properties of substances depend on their chemical structure, properties and reactions **—physical education** training and practice in sports, gymnastics *etc.* **—physical geography** branch of geography that deals with natural features of earth's surface **—physical jerks** *sl.* physical exercises **—physical science** any science concerned with nonliving matter, such as physics, chemistry *etc.* **—physical training** method of keeping fit by following course of bodily exercises

physiognomy (fɪzɪˈɒnəmɪ) *n.* **1.** judging character by face **2.** face **3.** outward appearance of something

physiography (fɪzɪˈɒɡrəfɪ) *n.* science of the earth's surface **—physiˈographer** *n.*

physiology (fɪzɪˈɒlədʒɪ) *n.* science of normal function of living things **—physiˈologist** *n.*

physiotherapy (fɪzɪəʊˈθɛrəpɪ) *n.* therapeutic use of physical means, as massage *etc.* **—physioˈtherapist** *n.*

physique (fɪˈziːk) *n.* bodily structure, constitution and development

pi[1] (paɪ) *n.* **1.** 16th letter in Gr. alphabet (Π, π) **2.** *Maths.* ratio of circumference of circle to its diameter (*pl.* **-s**)

pi[2] *or* **pie** (paɪ) *n.* **1.** jumbled pile of printer's type **2.** jumbled mixture (*pl.* **pies**) —*vt.* **3.** spill and mix (set type) indiscriminately **4.** mix up (**pied** *pt./pp.*, **ˈpiing, ˈpieing** *pr.p.*)

pia mater (ˈpaɪə ˈmeɪtə) innermost of three membranes that cover brain and spinal cord

piano (pɪˈænəʊ) *n.* **1.** (*orig.* **pianoforte** (pɪænəʊˈfɔːtɪ)) musical instrument with strings which are struck by hammers worked by keyboard (*pl.* **-s**) —*a./adv.* (ˈpjɑːnəʊ) **2.** *Mus.* to be performed softly **—piaˈnissimo** *a./adv. Mus.* to be performed very quietly **—ˈpianist** *n.* performer on piano **—Piaˈnola** *n.* **R** mechanically played piano **—piano accordion** accordion in which right hand plays pianolike keyboard (*also* **acˈcordion**) **—piano accordionist**

piazza (pɪˈætsə; *It.* ˈpjattsa) *n.* square, marketplace

pibroch (ˈpiːbrɒx) *n.* form of bagpipe music

pica (ˈpaɪkə) *n.* **1.** printing type of 6 lines to the inch (*also* **em, pica em**) **2.** formerly, size of type equal to 12 point **3.** typewriter type size (10 letters to inch)

THESAURUS

phoney affected, assumed, bogus, counterfeit, fake, false, forged, imitation, pseudo (*Inf.*), put-on, sham, spurious, trick

photograph 1. *n.* image, likeness, photo (*Inf.*), picture, print, shot, slide, snap (*Inf.*), snapshot, transparency **2.** *v.* capture on film, film, get a shot of, record, shoot, snap (*Inf.*), take, take a picture of, take (someone's) picture

photographic accurate, cinematic, detailed, exact, faithful, filmic, graphic, lifelike, minute, natural, pictorial, precise, realistic, retentive, visual, vivid

phrase 1. *n.* expression, group of words, idiom, locution, motto, remark, saying, tag, utterance, way of speaking **2.** *v.* couch, express, formulate, frame, present, put, put into words, say, term, utter, voice, word

phraseology choice of words, diction, expression, idiom, language, parlance, phrase, phrasing, speech, style, syntax, wording

physical 1. bodily, carnal, corporal, corporeal, earthly, fleshly, incarnate, mortal, somatic, unspiritual **2.** material, natural, palpable, real, sensible, solid, substantial, tangible, visible

physician doc (*Inf.*), doctor, doctor of medicine, general practitioner, G.P., healer, M.D., medic (*Inf.*), medical practitioner, medico (*Inf.*), sawbones (*Sl.*), specialist

physique body, build, constitution, figure, form, frame, make-up, shape, structure

picador (ˈpɪkədɔː) *n.* mounted bullfighter with lance

picaresque (pɪkəˈrɛsk) *a.* (of fiction) episodic and dealing with adventures of rogues

piccalilli (ˈpɪkəlɪlɪ) *n.* pickle of mixed vegetables in mustard sauce

piccaninny *or* **pickaninny** (pɪkəˈnɪnɪ) *n. offens.* small Negro child —ˈ**piccanin** *n.* **SA** male Afr. child

piccolo (ˈpɪkələʊ) *n.* small flute (*pl.* **-s**)

pick[1] (pɪk) *vt.* **1.** choose, select carefully **2.** pluck, gather **3.** peck at **4.** pierce with something pointed **5.** find occasion for —*n.* **6.** act of picking **7.** choicest part —**picked** *a.* selected with care —ˈ**pickings** *pl.n.* **1.** gleanings **2.** odds and ends of profit —ˈ**picky** *a. inf.* fussy; finicky —ˈ**picklock** *n.* instrument for opening locks —**pick-me-up** *n. inf.* **1.** tonic **2.** stimulating drink —ˈ**pickpocket** *n.* one who steals from another's pocket —**pick-up** *n.* **1.** device for conversion of mechanical energy into electric signals, as in record player *etc.* **2.** small truck —**pick on** find fault with —**pick up 1.** raise, lift **2.** collect **3.** improve, get better **4.** accelerate

pick[2] (pɪk) *n.* tool with curved iron crossbar and wooden shaft, used for breaking up hard ground or masonry —ˈ**pickaxe** *n.* pick

pickaback (ˈpɪkəbæk) *n. see* PIGGYBACK

picket (ˈpɪkɪt) *n.* **1.** prong, pointed stake **2.** party of trade unionists posted to deter would-be workers during strike —*vt.* **3.** post as picket **4.** beset with pickets **5.** tether to peg —**picket fence** fence of pickets —**picket line** line of people acting as pickets

pickle (ˈpɪkᵊl) *n.* **1.** food preserved in brine, vinegar *etc.* **2.** liquid used for preserving **3.** awkward situation **4.** mischievous child —*pl.* **5.** pickled vegetables —*vt.* **6.** preserve in pickle —ˈ**pickled** *a. inf.* drunk

picnic (ˈpɪknɪk) *n.* **1.** pleasure excursion during which food is consumed outdoors —*vi.* **2.** take part in picnic (ˈ**picnicked,** ˈ**picnicking**)

picot (ˈpiːkəʊ) *n.* any of pattern of small loops, as on lace

picric acid (ˈpɪkrɪk) powerful acid used in dyeing, medicine and as ingredient in certain explosives

Pict (pɪkt) *n.* member of ancient race of NE Scotland —ˈ**Pictish** *a.*

pictograph (ˈpɪktəgrɑːf) *n.* **1.** picture or symbol standing for word or group of words, as in written Chinese **2.** chart on which symbols are used to represent values (*also* ˈ**pictogram**)

picture (ˈpɪktʃə) *n.* **1.** drawing or painting **2.** mental image **3.** beautiful or picturesque object —*pl.* **4.** cinema —*vt.* **5.** represent in, or as in, a picture —**picˈtorial** *a.* **1.** of, in, with, painting or pictures **2.** graphic —*n.* **3.** newspaper with pictures —**picˈtorially** *adv.* —**picturesque** (pɪktʃəˈrɛsk) *a.* **1.** such as would be effective in picture **2.** striking, vivid —**picture card** *see* **court card** *at* COURT —**picture moulding 1.** edge around framed picture **2.** moulding or rail near top of wall from which pictures are hung (*also* **picture rail**) —**picture postcard** postcard with picture on one side —**picture window** large window having single pane of glass, usu. facing view

piddling (ˈpɪdlɪŋ) *a. inf.* petty; trifling

pidgin (ˈpɪdʒɪn) *n.* language made up of elements of two or more other languages

pie (paɪ) *n.* **1.** baked dish of meat or fruit *etc.*, usu. with pastry crust **2.** *obs.* magpie —**pie chart** circular graph divided into sectors proportional to magnitudes of quantities represented —**pie in the sky** *inf.* illusory hope of some future good

piebald (ˈpaɪbɔːld) *a.* **1.** irregularly marked with black and white **2.** motley —*n.* **3.** piebald horse or other animal —**pied** *a.* **1.** piebald **2.** variegated

piece (piːs) *n.* **1.** bit, part, fragment **2.** single object **3.** literary or musical composition *etc.* **4.** *sl.* young woman **5.** small object used in draughts, chess *etc.* —*vt.* **6.** (*with* together) mend, put together —**piece goods** goods, *esp.* fabrics, made in standard widths and lengths —ˈ**piecemeal** *adv.* by, in, or into pieces, a bit at a time —ˈ**piecework** *n.* work paid for according to quantity produced

THESAURUS

pick *v.* **1.** choose, decide upon, elect, fix upon, handpick, mark out, opt for, select, settle upon, sift out, single out, sort out **2.** collect, cull, cut, gather, harvest, pluck, pull **3.** have no appetite, nibble, peck at, play *or* toy with, push the food round the plate **4.** foment, incite, instigate, provoke, start **5.** break into, break open, crack, force, jemmy, open, prise open ~*n.* **6.** choice, choosing, decision, option, preference, selection **7.** choicest, *crème de la crème*, elect, elite, flower, pride, prize, the best, the cream, the tops (*Sl.*)

picket *n.* **1.** pale, paling, palisade, peg, post, stake, stanchion, upright **2.** demonstrator, picketer, protester ~*v.* **3.** blockade, boycott, demonstrate

pickle *n.* **1.** *Inf.* bind (*Inf.*), difficulty, dilemma, fix (*Inf.*), hot water (*Inf.*), jam (*Inf.*), predicament, quandary, scrape (*Inf.*), spot (*Inf.*), tight spot **2.** *Brit. inf.* little horror, mischief, mischief maker, monkey, naughty child, rascal ~*v.* **3.** cure, keep, marinade, preserve, steep

pick-me-up bracer (*Inf.*), drink, pick-up (*Sl.*), refreshment, restorative, roborant, shot in the arm (*Inf.*), stimulant, tonic

pick on badger, bait, blame, bully, goad, hector, tease, torment

pick up *v.* **1.** gather, grasp, hoist, lift, raise, take up, uplift **2.** gain, gain ground, get better, improve, make a comeback (*Inf.*), mend, perk up, rally, recover, take a turn for the better **3.** call for, collect, get, give someone a lift, go to get, uplift (*Scot.*)

picnic excursion, *fête champêtre*, outdoor meal, outing

pictorial expressive, graphic, illustrated, picturesque, representational, scenic, striking, vivid

picture *n.* **1.** delineation, drawing, effigy, engraving, illustration, image, likeness, painting, photograph, portrait, portrayal, print, representation, similitude, sketch ~*v.* **2.** conceive of, envision, image, see, see in the mind's eye, visualize **3.** delineate, depict, describe, draw, illustrate, paint, photograph, portray, render, represent, show, sketch

picturesque attractive, beautiful, charming, colourful, graphic, pretty, quaint, scenic, striking, vivid

piddling derisory, fiddling, insignificant, little, measly (*Inf.*), Mickey Mouse (*Sl.*), paltry, petty, piffling, puny, trifling, trivial, unimportant, useless, worthless

pièce de résistance (pjɛs də rezisˈtɑ̃:s) *Fr.* principal item

pied-à-terre (pjetaˈtɛ:r) *Fr.* flat or other lodging for occasional use (*pl.* ***pieds-à-terre*** (pjetaˈtɛ:r))

pier (pɪə) *n.* **1.** structure running into sea as landing stage **2.** piece of solid upright masonry, *esp.* supporting bridge —**pier glass** tall narrow mirror designed to hang on wall between windows

pierce (pɪəs) *vt.* **1.** make hole in **2.** make a way through —ˈ**piercing** *a.* keen, penetrating

Pierrot (ˈpɪərəʊ; *Fr.* pjɛˈro) *n.* pantomime character, clown

piety (ˈpaɪɪtɪ) *n.* **1.** godliness **2.** devoutness, goodness **3.** dutifulness —ˈ**pietism** *n.* exaggerated or affected piety

piezoelectric effect (paɪi:zəʊɪˈlɛktrɪk) *or* **piezoelectricity** (paɪi:zəʊɪlɛkˈtrɪsɪtɪ) *n. Phys.* **1.** production of electricity or electric polarity by applying mechanical stress to certain crystals **2.** converse effect in which stress is produced in crystal as result of applied potential difference

piffle (ˈpɪfˀl) *n. inf.* rubbish, twaddle, nonsense

pig (pɪg) *n.* **1.** wild or domesticated mammal killed for pork, ham, bacon **2.** *inf.* greedy, dirty person **3.** *sl.* policeman **4.** oblong mass of smelted metal —*vi.* **5.** (of sow) produce litter (**-gg-**) —ˈ**piggery** *n.* **1.** place for keeping, breeding pigs **2.** greediness —ˈ**piggish** *a.* **1.** dirty **2.** greedy **3.** stubborn —ˈ**piggy** *n.* child's word for a pig —ˈ**piglet** *n.* young pig —**piggy bank** child's bank shaped like pig with slot for coins —**pig-headed** *a.* obstinate —**pig iron** crude iron produced in blast furnace and poured into moulds —ˈ**pigskin** *n.* **1.** skin of domestic pig **2.** leather made of this skin **3.** US *inf.* football —*a.* **4.** made of pigskin —ˈ**pigsty** *or U.S.* ˈ**pigpen** *n.* **1.** pen for pigs; sty **2.** UK untidy place —ˈ**pigswill** *n.* waste food *etc.* fed to pigs (*also* **pig's wash**) —ˈ**pigtail** *n.* plait of hair hanging from back or either side of head

pigeon (ˈpɪdʒɪn) *n.* **1.** bird of many wild and domesticated varieties, oft. trained to carry messages **2.** *inf.* concern, responsibility (*oft. in* **it's his, her** *etc.*, **pigeon**) —ˈ**pigeonhole** *n.* **1.** compartment for papers in desk *etc.* —*vt.* **2.** defer **3.** classify —**pigeon-toed** *a.* with feet, toes turned inwards

piggyback (ˈpɪgɪbæk) *or* **pickaback** *n.* ride on back of man or animal, given to child

pigment (ˈpɪgmənt) *n.* colouring matter, paint or dye —**pigmenˈtation** *n.* **1.** coloration in plants, animals or man caused by presence of pigments **2.** deposition of pigment in animals, plants or man

pigmy (ˈpɪgmɪ) *see* PYGMY

pike[1] (paɪk) *n.* any of various types of large, predatory freshwater fishes

pike[2] (paɪk) *n.* spear formerly used by infantry

pilaster (pɪˈlæstə) *n.* square column, usu. set in wall

pilau (pɪˈlaʊ), **pilaf, pilaff** (ˈpɪlæf), *or* **pilaw** (pɪˈlɔ:) *n.* Oriental dish of meat or fowl boiled with rice, spices *etc.*

pilchard (ˈpɪltʃəd) *n.* small sea fish like the herring

pile[1] (paɪl) *n.* **1.** heap **2.** great mass of building —*vt.* **3.** heap (up), stack (load) —*vi.* **4.** (*with* in, out, off *etc.*) move in a group —**pile-up** *n. inf.* multiple collision of vehicles —**atomic pile** nuclear reactor —**pile up 1.** gather or be gathered in pile **2.** *inf.* (cause to) crash

pile[2] (paɪl) *n.* beam driven into the ground, *esp.* as foundation for building in water or wet ground —ˈ**piledriver** *n.* machine for driving down piles

pile[3] (paɪl) *n.* **1.** nap of cloth, *esp.* of velvet, carpet *etc.* **2.** down

piles (paɪlz) *pl.n.* tumours of veins of rectum, haemorrhoids

pilfer (ˈpɪlfə) *v.* steal in small quantities

THESAURUS

piebald black and white, brindled, dappled, flecked, mottled, pied, speckled, spotted

piece *n.* **1.** allotment, bit, chunk, division, fraction, fragment, length, morsel, mouthful, part, portion, quantity, scrap, section, segment, share, shred, slice **2.** article, bit (*Sl.*), composition, creation, item, production, study, work, work of art ~*v.* **3.** *With* **together** assemble, compose, fix, join, mend, patch, repair, restore, unite

pièce de résistance *chef-d'oeuvre*, jewel, masterpiece, masterwork, showpiece

piecemeal *adv.* at intervals, bit by bit, by degrees, by fits and starts, fitfully, intermittently, little by little, partially, slowly

pier *n.* **1.** jetty, landing place, promenade, quay, wharf **2.** buttress, column, pile, piling, pillar, post, support, upright

pierce bore, drill, enter, penetrate, perforate, prick, probe, puncture, run through, spike, stab, stick into, transfix

piercing 1. *Usually of sound* ear-splitting, high-pitched, loud, penetrating, sharp, shattering, shrill **2.** alert, aware, keen, penetrating, perceptive, perspicacious, probing, quick-witted, searching, sharp, shrewd

piety devotion, devoutness, dutifulness, duty, faith, godliness, grace, holiness, piousness, religion, reverence, sanctity, veneration

pig 1. boar, grunter, hog, piggy, piglet, porker, shoat, sow, swine **2.** *Inf.* animal, beast, boor, brute, glutton, greedy guts (*Sl.*), guzzler, hog (*Inf.*), slob (*Sl.*), sloven, swine

pigeon 1. bird, culver (*Archaic*), cushat, dove, squab **2.** *Brit. inf.* baby (*Sl.*), business, concern, lookout (*Inf.*), responsibility, worry

pigeonhole *n.* **1.** compartment, cubbyhole, cubicle, locker, niche, place, section ~*v.* **2.** defer, file, postpone, put off, shelve **3.** catalogue, characterize, classify, codify, compartmentalize, label, slot (*Inf.*), sort

pig-headed bull-headed, contrary, cross-grained, dense, froward, inflexible, mulish, obstinate, perverse, self-willed, stiff-necked, stubborn, stupid, unyielding, wilful, wrong-headed

pigment colorant, colour, colouring, colouring matter, dye, dyestuff, paint, stain, tincture, tint

pile[1] *n.* **1.** accumulation, assemblage, assortment, collection, heap, hoard, mass, mound, mountain, stack, stockpile **2.** building, edifice, erection, structure ~*v.* **3.** accumulate, amass, assemble, collect, gather, heap, hoard, load up, mass, stack, store **4.** charge, crowd, crush, flock, flood, jam, pack, rush, stream

pile[2] beam, column, foundation, pier, piling, pillar, post, support, upright

pile[3] down, fibre, filament, fur, hair, nap, plush, shag, surface

pilgrim ('pɪlgrɪm) *n.* **1.** one who journeys to sacred place **2.** wanderer, wayfarer —'**pilgrimage** *n.* —**the Pilgrim Fathers** *or* **Pilgrims** English Puritans who founded Plymouth Colony in Massachusetts

pill (pɪl) *n.* **1.** small ball of medicine swallowed whole **2.** anything disagreeable which has to be endured —'**pillbox** *n.* **1.** small box for pills **2.** small round hat —**the pill** oral contraceptive

pillage ('pɪlɪdʒ) *v.* **1.** plunder, ravage, sack —*n.* **2.** seizure of goods, *esp.* in war **3.** plunder

pillar ('pɪlə) *n.* **1.** slender, upright structure, column **2.** prominent supporter —**pillar box UK** red pillar-shaped public letter box situated on pavement

pillion ('pɪljən) *n.* seat, cushion, for passenger behind rider of motorcycle or horse

pillory ('pɪlərɪ) *n.* **1.** frame with holes for head and hands in which offender was formerly confined and exposed to public abuse and ridicule —*vt.* **2.** expose to ridicule and abuse **3.** set in pillory ('**pilloried,** '**pillorying**)

pillow ('pɪləʊ) *n.* **1.** cushion for the head, *esp.* in bed —*vt.* **2.** lay on, or as on, pillow —'**pillowcase** *or* '**pillowslip** *n.* removable washable cover of cotton *etc.* for pillow

pilot ('paɪlət) *n.* **1.** person qualified to fly an aircraft or spacecraft **2.** one qualified to take charge of ship entering or leaving harbour **3.** steersman **4.** guide —*a.* **5.** experimental and preliminary —*vt.* **6.** act as pilot to **7.** steer —'**pilotage** *n.* **1.** act of piloting ship or aircraft **2.** pilot's fee —**pilot fish** small fish of tropical and subtropical seas which oft. accompanies sharks —**pilot house** *Naut.* enclosed structure on bridge of vessel from which it can be navigated; wheelhouse —**pilot lamp** small light in electric circuit that lights when current is on —**pilot light 1.** small auxiliary flame lighting main burner in gas appliance *etc.* **2.** small electric light as indicator —**pilot officer** most junior commissioned rank in British Royal Air Force and in certain other air forces

pilule ('pɪlju:l) *n.* small pill

pimento (pɪ'mɛntəʊ) *n.* **1.** allspice **2.** sweet red pepper (*pl.* **-s**) (*also* **pimiento** (pɪ'mjɛntəʊ, -'mɛn-))

pimp (pɪmp) *n.* **1.** one who solicits for prostitute —*vi.* **2.** act as pimp

pimpernel ('pɪmpənɛl, -nᵊl) *n.* any of several plants with small scarlet, blue or white flowers closing in dull weather

pimple ('pɪmpᵊl) *n.* small pus-filled spot on skin

pin (pɪn) *n.* **1.** short thin piece of stiff wire with point and head, for fastening **2.** wooden or metal peg or rivet —*vt.* **3.** fasten with pin **4.** seize and hold fast (**-nn-**) —'**pinball** *n.* electrically operated table game, where small ball is shot through various hazards —'**pincushion** *n.* small cushion in which pins are stuck ready for use —'**pinhead** *n.* **1.** head of pin **2.** something very small **3.** *sl.* stupid person —**pin money** trivial sum —'**pinpoint** *vt.* mark exactly —'**pinprick** *n.* **1.** slight puncture made (as if) by pin **2.** small irritation —*vt.* **3.** puncture (as if) with pin —'**pinstripe** *n.* in textiles, very narrow stripe in fabric or fabric itself —**pin tuck** narrow, ornamental fold, *esp.* on shirt fronts *etc.* —'**pinwheel** *n.* *see* CATHERINE WHEEL (sense 1) —**on pins and needles** in a state of anxious suspense —**pins and needles** *inf.* tingling sensation in fingers *etc.* caused by return of normal blood circulation after its temporary impairment

pinafore ('pɪnəfɔ:) *n.* **1.** apron **2.** dress with a bib top (*also* **pinafore dress**)

pince-nez ('pænsneɪ, 'pɪns-; *Fr.* pɛ̃s'ne) *n.* eyeglasses kept on nose by spring (*pl.* **pince-nez**)

pincers ('pɪnsəz) *pl.n.* **1.** tool for gripping, composed of two limbs crossed and pivoted **2.** claws of lobster *etc.*

pinch (pɪntʃ) *vt.* **1.** nip, squeeze **2.** stint **3.** *inf.* steal **4.** *inf.* arrest —*n.* **5.** nip **6.** as much as can be taken up between finger and thumb **7.** stress **8.** emergency —'**pinchbar** *n.* jemmy

THESAURUS

pile-up accident, collision, crash, multiple collision, smash, smash-up (*Inf.*)

pilfer appropriate, embezzle, filch, knock off (*Sl.*), lift (*Inf.*), nick (*Brit. sl.*), pinch (*Inf.*), purloin, rifle, rob, snaffle (*Brit. inf.*), snitch (*Sl.*), steal, swipe (*Sl.*), take, thieve, walk off with

pilgrim crusader, hajji, palmer, traveller, wanderer, wayfarer

pilgrimage crusade, excursion, expedition, hajj, journey, mission, tour, trip

pill 1. bolus, capsule, pellet, pilule, tablet **2. the pill** oral contraceptive **3.** *Sl.* bore, drag (*Sl.*), nuisance, pain (*Inf.*), pain in the neck (*Inf.*), pest, trial

pillage *v.* **1.** depredate (*Rare*), despoil, freeboot, loot, maraud, plunder, raid, ransack, ravage, reive (*Dialect*), rifle, rob, sack, spoil (*Archaic*), spoliate, strip ~*n.* **2.** depredation, devastation, marauding, plunder, rapine, robbery, sack, spoliation **3.** booty, loot, plunder, spoils

pillar 1. column, pier, pilaster, piling, post, prop, shaft, stanchion, support, upright **2.** leader, leading light (*Inf.*), mainstay, rock, supporter, tower of strength, upholder, worthy

pillory *v.* brand, cast a slur on, denounce, expose to ridicule, heap *or* pour scorn on, hold up to shame, lash, show up, stigmatize

pilot 1. *n.* airman, aviator, captain, conductor, coxswain, director, flier, guide, helmsman, leader, navigator, steersman **2.** *v.* conduct, control, direct, drive, fly, guide, handle, lead, manage, navigate, operate, shepherd, steer **3.** *adj.* experimental, model, test, trial

pimple boil, papule (*Pathol.*), plook (*Scot.*), pustule, spot, swelling

pin *v.* **1.** affix, attach, fasten, fix, join, secure **2.** fix, hold down, hold fast, immobilize, pinion, press, restrain

pinch *v.* **1.** compress, grasp, nip, press, squeeze, tweak **2.** afflict, be stingy, distress, economize, oppress, pinch pennies, press, scrimp, skimp, spare, stint **3.** *Inf.* filch, knock off (*Sl.*), lift (*Inf.*), nick (*Brit. sl.*), pilfer, purloin, rob, snaffle (*Brit. inf.*), snatch, snitch (*Sl.*), steal, swipe (*Sl.*) **4.** *Inf.* apprehend, arrest, bust (*Inf.*), collar (*Inf.*), do (*Sl.*), nab (*Inf.*), nick (*Brit. sl.*), pick up (*Sl.*), pull in (*Brit. sl.*), run in (*Sl.*), take into custody ~*n.* **5.** nip, squeeze, tweak **6.** bit, dash, jot, mite, small quantity, *soupçon*, speck, taste **7.** crisis, difficulty, emergency, exigency, hardship, necessity, oppression, pass, plight, predicament, pressure, strait, stress

pinchbeck (ˈpɪntʃbɛk) *n.* **1.** zinc and copper alloy —*a.* **2.** counterfeit, flashy

pine[1] (paɪn) *n.* **1.** any of a genus of evergreen coniferous trees **2.** its wood —**pine cone** seed-producing structure of pine tree

pine[2] (paɪn) *vi.* **1.** yearn **2.** waste away with grief

pineal (ˈpɪnɪəl) *a.* shaped like pine cone —**pineal gland** small cone-shaped gland situated at base of brain

pineapple (ˈpaɪnæpᵊl) *n.* **1.** tropical plant with spiny leaves bearing large edible fruit **2.** the fruit

ping (pɪŋ) *n.* **1.** short high-pitched resonant sound, as of bullet striking metal or sonar echo —*vi.* **2.** make such noise

Ping-Pong (ˈpɪŋpɒŋ) *n.* **R** table tennis

pinion[1] (ˈpɪnjən) *n.* **1.** bird's wing —*vt.* **2.** disable or confine by binding wings, arms *etc.*

pinion[2] (ˈpɪnjən) *n.* small cogwheel

pink (pɪŋk) *n.* **1.** pale reddish colour **2.** garden plant **3.** best condition, fitness —*a.* **4.** of colour pink —*vt.* **5.** pierce **6.** ornament with perforations or scalloped, indented edge —*vi.* **7.** (of engine) knock

pinkie *or* **pinky** (ˈpɪŋkɪ) *n.* **US,** *Scot.* little finger

pinnace (ˈpɪnɪs) *n.* ship's tender

pinnacle (ˈpɪnəkᵊl) *n.* **1.** highest pitch or point **2.** mountain peak **3.** pointed turret on buttress or roof

pinnate (ˈpɪneɪt, ˈpɪnɪt) *a.* **1.** like feather **2.** (of compound leaves) having leaflets growing opposite each other in pairs on either side of stem

pinny (ˈpɪnɪ) *n. inf.* pinafore

pint (paɪnt) *n.* liquid measure, half a quart, 1/8 gallon (.568 litre) —**pint-size** *or* **pint-sized** *a. inf.* very small

pintle (ˈpɪntᵊl) *n.* pivot pin

pinto (ˈpɪntəʊ) **US** *a.* **1.** marked with patches of white; piebald —*n.* **2.** pinto horse (*pl.* **-s**)

pin-up *n. inf.* picture of sexually attractive person, *esp.* (partly) naked

pion (ˈpaɪɒn) *or* **pi meson** *n. Phys.* meson having positive or negative charge and rest mass 273 times that of electron, or no charge and rest mass 264 times that of electron

pioneer (paɪəˈnɪə) *n.* **1.** explorer **2.** early settler **3.** originator **4.** one of advance party preparing road for troops —*vi.* **5.** act as pioneer or leader

pious (ˈpaɪəs) *a.* **1.** devout **2.** righteous

pip[1] (pɪp) *n.* seed in fruit

pip[2] (pɪp) *n.* **1.** high-pitched sound used as time signal on radio **2.** spot on playing cards, dice or dominoes **3.** *inf.* star on junior officer's shoulder showing rank

pip[3] (pɪp) *n.* disease of fowl —**give someone the pip** *sl.* annoy someone

pip[4] (pɪp) *vt.* **UK** *sl.* **1.** wound, *esp.* with gun **2.** defeat (person), *esp.* when his success seems certain (*oft.* *in* **pip at the post**) **3.** blackball, ostracize (**-pp-**)

pipe (paɪp) *n.* **1.** tube of metal or other material **2.** tube with small bowl at end for smoking tobacco **3.** musical instrument, whistle **4.** wine cask —*pl.* **5.** bagpipes —*v.* **6.** play on pipe **7.** utter (something) shrilly —*vt.* **8.** convey by pipe **9.** ornament with a piping or fancy edging —**ˈpiper** *n.* player of pipe or bagpipes —**ˈpiping** *n.* **1.** system of pipes **2.** decoration of icing on cake **3.** fancy edging or trimming on clothes **4.** act or art of playing pipe, *esp.* bagpipes —**ˈpipeclay** *n.* **1.** white clay used in manufacture of tobacco pipes *etc.* and for whitening leather *etc.* —*vt.* **2.** whiten with pipeclay —**pipe cleaner** short length of thin wires twisted so as to hold tiny tufts of yarn: used to clean stem of tobacco pipe —**pipe dream** fanciful, impossible plan *etc.* —**ˈpipeline** *n.* **1.** long pipe for transporting oil, water *etc.* **2.** means of communication —**pipe down** *sl.* stop talking, making noise *etc.* —**pipe up 1.** commence singing or playing musical instrument **2.** speak up, *esp.* in shrill voice —**in the pipeline 1.** yet to come **2.** in process of completion *etc.*

pipette (pɪˈpɛt) *n.* slender glass tube to transfer fluids from one vessel to another

pipit (ˈpɪpɪt) *n.* any of various songbirds, *esp.* meadow pipit

pippin (ˈpɪpɪn) *n.* any of several kinds of apple

THESAURUS

pine 1. *Often with* **for** ache, carry a torch for, covet, crave, desire, hanker, hunger for, long, lust after, sigh, thirst for, wish, yearn **2.** decay, decline, droop, dwindle, fade, flag, languish, peak, sicken, sink, waste, weaken, wilt, wither

pinion *v.* bind, chain, confine, fasten, fetter, immobilize, manacle, pin down, shackle, tie

pink 1. *n.* acme, best, height, peak, perfection, summit **2.** *adj.* flesh, flushed, reddish, rose, roseate, rosy, salmon

pinnacle 1. acme, apex, apogee, crest, crown, eminence, height, meridian, peak, summit, top, vertex, zenith **2.** belfry, cone, needle, obelisk, pyramid, spire, steeple

pinpoint define, distinguish, get a fix on, home in on, identify, locate, spot

pioneer *n.* **1.** colonist, colonizer, explorer, frontiersman, settler **2.** developer, founder, founding father, innovator, leader, trailblazer ~*v.* **3.** create, develop, discover, establish, initiate, instigate, institute, invent, launch, lay the groundwork, map out, open up, originate, prepare, show the way, start, take the lead

pious 1. dedicated, devoted, devout, God-fearing, godly, holy, religious, reverent, righteous, saintly, spiritual **2.** goody-goody, holier-than-thou, hypocritical, pietistic, religiose, sanctimonious, self-righteous, unctuous

pipe *n.* **1.** conduit, conveyor, duct, hose, line, main, passage, pipeline, tube **2.** briar, clay, meerschaum **3.** fife, horn, tooter, whistle, wind instrument ~*v.* **4.** cheep, peep, play, sing, sound, tootle, trill, tweet, twitter, warble, whistle **5.** bring in, channel, conduct, convey, siphon, supply, transmit

pipe down belt up (*Sl.*), be quiet, hold one's tongue, hush, quieten down, shush, shut one's mouth, shut up (*Inf.*), silence

pipeline 1. conduit, conveyor, duct, line, passage, pipe, tube **2. in the pipeline** brewing, coming, getting ready, in process, in production, on the way, under way

piquant 1. biting, highly-seasoned, peppery, pungent, savoury, sharp, spicy, stinging, tangy, tart, with a kick (*Inf.*), zesty **2.** interesting, lively, provocative, racy, salty, scintillating, sparkling, spirited, stimulating

pipsqueak (ˈpɪpskwiːk) *n. inf.* insignificant or contemptible person or thing

piquant (ˈpiːkənt, -kɑːnt) *a.* **1.** pungent **2.** stimulating —**ˈpiquancy** *or* **ˈpiquantness** *n.*

pique (piːk) *n.* **1.** feeling of injury, baffled curiosity or resentment —*vt.* **2.** hurt pride of **3.** irritate **4.** stimulate

piranha *or* **piraña** (pɪˈrɑːnjə) *n.* any of various small voracious freshwater fishes of tropical Amer.

pirate (ˈpaɪrɪt) *n.* **1.** sea robber **2.** publisher *etc.* who infringes copyright —*n./a.* **3.** (person) broadcasting illegally —*vt.* **4.** use or reproduce (artistic work *etc.*) illicitly —**ˈpiracy** *n.* —**piˈratic(al)** *a.* —**piˈratically** *adv.*

pirouette (pɪrʊˈɛt) *n.* **1.** spinning round on the toe —*vi.* **2.** perform pirouette

Pisces (ˈpaɪsiːz, ˈpɪ-) *pl.n.* (fishes) 12th sign of zodiac, operative *c.* Feb. 19th-Mar. 20th —**piscatorial** (pɪskəˈtɔːrɪəl) *or* **piscatory** (ˈpɪskətərɪ) *a.* of fishing or fishes —**piscine** (ˈpɪsaɪn) *a.* of fish

pistachio (pɪˈstɑːʃɪəʊ) *n.* **1.** small hard-shelled, sweet-tasting nut **2.** tree producing it (*pl.* **-s**)

pistil (ˈpɪstɪl) *n.* seed-bearing organ of flower —**ˈpistillate** *a.* (of plants) **1.** having pistils but no anthers **2.** producing pistils

pistol (ˈpɪstᵊl) *n.* **1.** small firearm for one hand —*vt.* **2.** shoot with pistol (**-ll-**)

piston (ˈpɪstən) *n.* in internal-combustion engine, steam engine *etc.*, cylindrical part propelled to and fro in hollow cylinder by pressure of gas *etc.* to convert reciprocating motion to rotation

pit[1] (pɪt) *n.* **1.** deep hole in ground **2.** mine or its shaft **3.** depression **4.** part of theatre occupied by orchestra (*also* **orchestra pit**) **5.** enclosure where animals were set to fight **6.** servicing, refuelling area on motor-racing track —*vt.* **7.** set to fight, match **8.** mark with small dents or scars (**-tt-**) —**ˈpitfall** *n.* **1.** any hidden danger **2.** covered pit for catching animals or men —**ˈpithead** *n.* top of mine shaft and buildings *etc.* around it

pit[2] (pɪt) *chiefly* **US** *n.* **1.** stone of cherry *etc.* —*vt.* **2.** extract stone from (fruit) (**-tt-**)

pitapat (ˈpɪtəpæt) *adv.* **1.** with quick light taps —*vi.* **2.** make quick light taps (**-tt-**) —*n.* **3.** such taps

pitch[1] (pɪtʃ) *vt.* **1.** cast or throw **2.** set up **3.** set the key of (a tune) —*vi.* **4.** fall headlong **5.** (of ship) plunge lengthwise —*n.* **6.** act of pitching **7.** degree, height, intensity **8.** slope **9.** distance airscrew advances during one revolution **10.** distance between threads of screw, teeth of saw *etc.* **11.** acuteness of tone **12.** part of ground where wickets are set up **13.** *Sport* field of play **14.** station of street vendor *etc.* **15.** *inf.* persuasive sales talk —**ˈpitcher** *n.* **US** *Baseball* player who delivers ball to batter —**pitched battle 1.** battle ensuing from deliberate choice of time and place **2.** any fierce encounter, *esp.* one with large numbers —**ˈpitchfork** *n.* **1.** fork for lifting hay *etc.* —*vt.* **2.** throw with, as with, pitchfork —**pitch pipe** small pipe that sounds note or notes of standard frequency, used for establishing correct starting note for unaccompanied singing —**pitch in 1.** cooperate; contribute **2.** begin energetically —**pitch into 1.** assail physically or verbally **2.** get on with doing (something)

pitch[2] (pɪtʃ) *n.* **1.** dark sticky substance obtained from tar or turpentine —*vt.* **2.** coat with this —**ˈpitchy** *a.* **1.** covered with pitch **2.** black as pitch —**pitch-black** *or* **pitch-dark** *a.* very dark —**pitch pine** any of various kinds of resinous pine

pitchblende (ˈpɪtʃblɛnd) *n.* mineral composed largely of uranium oxide, yielding radium

pitcher (ˈpɪtʃə) *n.* large jug —**pitcher plant** insectivorous plant with leaves modified to form pitcherlike organs that attract and trap insects

pith (pɪθ) *n.* **1.** tissue in stems and branches of certain plants **2.** essential substance, most important part —**ˈpithily** *adv.* —**ˈpithless** *a.* —**ˈpithy** *a.* **1.** terse, cogent, concise **2.** consisting of pith —**pith helmet** lightweight hat made of pith that protects wearer from sun (*also* **ˈtopee, ˈtopi**)

THESAURUS

pique *n.* **1.** annoyance, displeasure, grudge, huff, hurt feelings, irritation, miff (*Inf.*), offence, resentment, umbrage, vexation, wounded pride ~*v.* **2.** affront, annoy, displease, gall, get (*Inf.*), incense, irk, irritate, miff (*Inf.*), mortify, nettle, offend, peeve (*Inf.*), provoke, put out, put someone's nose out of joint (*Inf.*), rile, sting, vex, wound **3.** arouse, excite, galvanize, goad, kindle, provoke, rouse, spur, stimulate, stir, whet

piracy buccaneering, freebooting, hijacking, infringement, plagiarism, rapine, robbery at sea, stealing, theft

pirate *n.* **1.** buccaneer, corsair, filibuster, freebooter, marauder, raider, rover, sea robber, sea rover, sea wolf **2.** cribber (*Inf.*), infringer, plagiarist, plagiarizer ~*v.* **3.** appropriate, borrow, copy, crib (*Inf.*), lift (*Inf.*), plagiarize, poach, reproduce, steal

pit *n.* **1.** abyss, cavity, chasm, coal mine, crater, dent, depression, dimple, excavation, gulf, hole, hollow, indentation, mine, pockmark, pothole, trench ~*v.* **2.** *Often with* **against** match, oppose, put in opposition, set against **3.** dent, dint, gouge, hole, indent, mark, nick, notch, pockmark, scar

pitch *v.* **1.** bung (*Brit. sl.*), cast, chuck (*Inf.*), fling, heave, hurl, launch, lob (*Inf.*), sling, throw, toss **2.** erect, fix, locate, place, plant, put up, raise, settle, set up, station **3.** flounder, lurch, make heavy weather, plunge, roll, toss, wallow, welter **4.** dive, drop, fall headlong, stagger, topple, tumble ~*n.* **5.** angle, cant, dip, gradient, incline, slope, steepness, tilt **6.** degree, height, highest point, level, point, summit **7.** harmonic, modulation, sound, timbre, tone **8.** line, patter, sales talk, spiel (*Inf.*) **9.** field of play, ground, park (*Brit. inf.*), sports field

pitch-black dark, ebony, inky, jet, jet-black, pitch-dark, raven, sable, unlit

pitch in 1. chip in (*Inf.*), contribute, cooperate, do one's bit, help, join in, lend a hand, participate **2.** begin, fall to, get busy, get cracking (*Inf.*), plunge into, set about, set to, tackle

piteous affecting, deplorable, distressing, doleful, grievous, heartbreaking, heart-rending, lamentable, miserable, mournful, moving, pathetic, pitiable, pitiful, plaintive, poignant, sad, sorrowful, woeful, wretched

pitfall 1. catch, danger, difficulty, drawback, hazard, peril, snag, trap **2.** deadfall, downfall, pit, snare, trap

pith core, crux, essence, gist, heart, heart of the matter, kernel, marrow, meat, nub, point, quintessence, salient point, the long and the short of it

pithy brief, cogent, compact, concise, epigrammatic,

piton (ˈpiːtɒn) *n. Mountaineering* metal spike that may be driven into crevice and used to secure rope *etc.*

pittance (ˈpɪtᵊns) *n.* **1.** small allowance **2.** inadequate wages

pitter-patter (ˈpɪtəpætə) *n.* **1.** sound of light rapid taps or pats, as of raindrops —*vi.* **2.** make such sound —*adv.* **3.** with such sound

pituitary (pɪˈtjuːɪtərɪ) *a.* of, pert. to, endocrine gland at base of brain

pity (ˈpɪtɪ) *n.* **1.** sympathy, sorrow for others' suffering **2.** regrettable fact —*vt.* **3.** feel pity for (**ˈpitied, ˈpitying**) —**ˈpiteous** *a.* **1.** deserving pity **2.** sad, wretched —**ˈpitiable** *a.* —**ˈpitiably** *adv.* —**ˈpitiful** *a.* **1.** woeful **2.** contemptible —**ˈpitiless** *a.* feeling no pity, hard, merciless

più (pjuː) *adv. Mus.* more (quickly *etc.*)

pivot (ˈpɪvət) *n.* **1.** shaft or pin on which thing turns —*vt.* **2.** furnish with pivot —*vi.* **3.** hinge on pivot —**ˈpivotal** *a.* **1.** of, acting as, pivot **2.** of crucial importance

pixie *or* **pixy** (ˈpɪksɪ) *n.* fairy

pizza (ˈpiːtsə) *n.* dish, *orig.* It., of baked disc of dough covered with wide variety of savoury toppings —**pizzeria** (piːtsəˈriːə) *n.* place selling pizzas

pizzicato (pɪtsɪˈkɑːtəʊ) *a./n. Mus.* (note, passage) played by plucking string of violin *etc.* with finger

pl. 1. place 2. plate 3. plural

plaas (plɑːs) *n.* **SA** farm

placard (ˈplækɑːd) *n.* **1.** paper or card with notice on one side for posting up or carrying; poster —*vt.* **2.** post placards on **3.** advertise, display on placards

placate (pləˈkeɪt) *vt.* conciliate, pacify, appease —**plaˈcatory** *a.*

place (pleɪs) *n.* **1.** locality, spot **2.** position **3.** stead **4.** duty **5.** town, village, residence, buildings **6.** office, employment **7.** seat, space —*vt.* **8.** put in particular place **9.** set **10.** identify **11.** make (order, bet *etc.*) —**ˈplacement** *n.* **1.** act of placing or state of being placed **2.** arrangement, position **3.** process of finding employment —**place kick** *Football* kick in which ball is placed in position before it is kicked —**place-kick** *v.* kick (ball) in this way —**place mat** small mat serving as individual table cover for person at meal —**place setting** cutlery, crockery and glassware laid for one person at dining table

placebo (pləˈsiːbəʊ) *n.* sugar pill *etc.* given to unsuspecting patient as active drug (*pl.* **-s, -es**)

placenta (pləˈsɛntə) *n.* **1.** organ formed in uterus during pregnancy, providing nutrients for foetus **2.** afterbirth (*pl.* **-s, -tae** (-tiː)) —**plaˈcental** *a.*

placer (ˈplæsə) *n.* surface sediment containing particles of gold or some other valuable mineral

placid (ˈplæsɪd) *a.* **1.** calm **2.** equable —**plaˈcidity** *n.* mildness, quiet

placket (ˈplækɪt) *n.* opening at top of skirt *etc.* fastened with buttons, zip *etc.*

plagiarism (ˈpleɪdʒərɪzəm) *n.* act of taking ideas, passages *etc.* from an author and presenting them as one's own —**ˈplagiarize** *or* **-ise** *v.*

plague (pleɪg) *n.* **1.** highly contagious disease, *esp.* bubonic plague **2.** *inf.* nuisance **3.** affliction —*vt.* **4.** trouble, annoy

plaice (pleɪs) *n.* European flatfish

THESAURUS

expressive, finely honed, forceful, laconic, meaningful, pointed, short, succinct, terse, to the point, trenchant

pitiful **1.** deplorable, distressing, grievous, heartbreaking, heart-rending, lamentable, miserable, pathetic, piteous, pitiable, sad, woeful, wretched **2.** abject, base, beggarly, contemptible, despicable, inadequate, insignificant, low, mean, miserable, paltry, scurvy, shabby, sorry, vile, worthless

pitiless brutal, callous, cold-blooded, cold-hearted, cruel, hardhearted, harsh, heartless, implacable, inexorable, inhuman, merciless, relentless, ruthless, uncaring, unfeeling, unmerciful, unsympathetic

pittance allowance, chicken feed (*Sl.*), drop, mite, modicum, peanuts (*Sl.*), portion, ration, slave wages, trifle

pity *n.* **1.** charity, clemency, commiseration, compassion, condolence, fellow feeling, forbearance, kindness, mercy, sympathy, tenderness, understanding **2.** crime (*Inf.*), crying shame, misfortune, regret, sad thing, shame, sin ~*v.* **3.** bleed for, commiserate with, condole with, feel for, feel sorry for, grieve for, have compassion for, sympathize with, weep for

pivot **1.** *n.* axis, axle, fulcrum, spindle, swivel **2.** *v.* be contingent, depend, hang, hinge, rely, revolve round, turn

pixie brownie, elf, fairy, sprite

placard advertisement, *affiche*, bill, poster, public notice, sticker

placate appease, assuage, calm, conciliate, humour, mollify, pacify, propitiate, satisfy, soothe, win over

place *n.* **1.** area, location, locus, point, position, site, situation, spot, station, venue, whereabouts **2.** city, district, hamlet, locale, locality, neighbourhood, quarter, region, town, vicinity, village **3.** grade, position, rank, station, status **4.** appointment, berth (*Inf.*), billet (*Inf.*), employment, job, position, post **5.** abode, apartment, domicile, dwelling, flat, home, house, manor, mansion, pad (*Sl.*), property, residence, seat **6.** accommodation, room, space, stead **7.** affair, charge, concern, duty, function, prerogative, responsibility, right, role ~*v.* **8.** bung (*Inf.*), deposit, dispose, establish, fix, install, lay, locate, plant, position, put, rest, set, settle, situate, stand, station, stick (*Inf.*) **9.** arrange, class, classify, grade, group, order, rank, sort **10.** associate, identify, know, put one's finger on, recognize, remember, set in context

placid calm, collected, composed, cool, equable, even, even-tempered, gentle, halcyon, imperturbable, mild, peaceful, quiet, self-possessed, serene, still, tranquil, undisturbed, unexcitable, unmoved, unruffled, untroubled

plagiarize appropriate, borrow, crib (*Inf.*), infringe, lift (*Inf.*), pirate, steal, thieve

plague *n.* **1.** contagion, disease, epidemic, infection, pandemic, pestilence **2.** *Fig.* affliction, bane, blight, calamity, cancer, curse, evil, scourge, torment, trial **3.** *Inf.* aggravation (*Inf.*), annoyance, bother, irritant, nuisance, pain (*Inf.*), pest, problem, thorn in one's flesh, vexation ~*v.* **4.** afflict, annoy, badger, bedevil, bother, disturb, fret, harass, harry, hassle (*Inf.*), haunt, molest, pain, persecute, pester, tease, torment, torture, trouble, vex

plaid (plæd) *n.* **1.** long Highland cloak or shawl **2.** checked or tartan pattern

Plaid Cymru (plaɪd ˈkʌmrɪ) Welsh nationalist party

plain (pleɪn) *a.* **1.** flat, level **2.** unobstructed, not intricate **3.** clear, obvious **4.** easily understood **5.** simple **6.** ordinary **7.** without decoration **8.** not beautiful —*n.* **9.** tract of level country —*adv.* **10.** clearly —ˈ**plainly** *adv.* —ˈ**plainness** *n.* —**plain chocolate** chocolate with slightly bitter flavour and dark colour —**plain clothes** civilian dress, as opposed to uniform —**plain flour** flour to which no raising agent has been added —**plain sailing** unobstructed course of action —**plain speaking** frankness, candour

plainsong (ˈpleɪnsɒŋ) *n.* style of unison unaccompanied vocal music used in medieval Church

plaint (pleɪnt) *n.* **1.** *Law* statement of complaint **2.** *obs.* lament —ˈ**plaintiff** *n.* *Law* one who sues in court —ˈ**plaintive** *a.* sad, mournful

plait (plæt) *n.* **1.** braid of hair, straw *etc.* —*vt.* **2.** form or weave into plaits

plan (plæn) *n.* **1.** scheme **2.** way of proceeding **3.** project, design **4.** drawing of horizontal section **5.** diagram, map —*vt.* **6.** make plan of **7.** arrange beforehand (**-nn-**)

planchette (plɑːnˈʃɛt) *n.* small board used in spiritualism

plane[1] (pleɪn) *n.* **1.** smooth surface **2.** a level **3.** carpenter's tool for smoothing wood —*vt.* **4.** make smooth with plane —*a.* **5.** perfectly flat or level —ˈ**planar** *a.* **1.** of plane **2.** lying in one plane; flat —ˈ**planer** *n.* planing machine

plane[2] (pleɪn) *vi.* **1.** (of aeroplane) glide **2.** (of boat) rise and partly skim over water —*n.* **3.** wing of aeroplane **4.** aeroplane

plane[3] (pleɪn) *n.* tree with broad leaves

planet (ˈplænɪt) *n.* heavenly body revolving round the sun —ˈ**planetary** *a.* of planets

planetarium (plænɪˈtɛərɪəm) *n.* **1.** an apparatus that shows the movement of sun, moon, stars and planets by projecting lights on the inside of a dome **2.** building in which the apparatus is housed (*pl.* **-s, -ia** (-ɪə))

plangent (ˈplændʒənt) *a.* resounding

plank (plæŋk) *n.* **1.** long flat piece of sawn timber —*vt.* **2.** cover with planks

plankton (ˈplæŋktən) *n.* minute animal and vegetable organisms floating in ocean

plant (plɑːnt) *n.* **1.** any living organism feeding on inorganic substances and without power of locomotion **2.** such an organism that is smaller than tree or shrub **3.** equipment or machinery needed for manufacture **4.** building and equipment for manufacturing purposes **5.** heavy vehicles used for road building *etc.* —*vt.* **6.** set in ground to grow **7.** support, establish **8.** stock with plants **9.** *sl.* hide, *esp.* to deceive or observe —ˈ**planter** *n.* **1.** one who plants **2.** ornamental pot or stand for house plants

plantain[1] (ˈplæntɪn) *n.* any of various low-growing herbs with broad leaves

plantain[2] (ˈplæntɪn) *n.* **1.** tropical plant like banana **2.** its fruit

plantation (plænˈteɪʃən) *n.* **1.** estate for cultivation of tea, tobacco *etc.* **2.** wood of planted trees **3.** formerly, colony

plaque (plæk, plɑːk) *n.* **1.** ornamental plate, tablet **2.** plate of clasp or brooch **3.** filmy deposit on surfaces of teeth, conducive to decay

-plasm (*n. comb. form*) *Biol.* material forming cells, as in *protoplasm* —**-plasmic** (*a. comb. form*)

plasma (ˈplæzmə) *or* **plasm** (ˈplæzəm) *n.* clear yellowish fluid portion of blood —ˈ**plasmic** *a.*

plaster (ˈplɑːstə) *n.* **1.** mixture of lime, sand *etc.* for coating walls *etc.* **2.** piece of fabric spread with medicinal or adhesive substance —*vt.* **3.** apply plaster to **4.** apply like plaster —ˈ**plastered** *a.* *sl.* intoxicated; drunk —ˈ**plasterer** *n.* —ˈ**plasterboard** *n.* thin board in form of layer of plaster compressed between two layers of fibreboard, used to form or cover walls *etc.* —**plaster of Paris** (ˈpærɪs) **1.** white powder that sets to hard solid when mixed with water, used for sculptures and casts *etc.* **2.** hard plaster produced when this powder is mixed with water

plastic (ˈplæstɪk) *n.* **1.** any of a group of synthetic products derived from casein, cellulose *etc.*, which can be readily moulded into any form and are extremely durable —*a.* **2.** made of plastic **3.** easily

THESAURUS

plain *adj.* **1.** apparent, clear, comprehensible, distinct, evident, legible, lucid, manifest, obvious, patent, transparent, unambiguous, understandable, unmistakable, visible **2.** common, commonplace, everyday, frugal, homely, lowly, modest, ordinary, simple, unaffected, unpretentious, workaday **3.** austere, bare, basic, discreet, modest, muted, pure, restrained, severe, simple, Spartan, stark, unadorned, unembellished, unornamented, unpatterned, unvarnished **4.** ill-favoured, not beautiful, not striking, ordinary, ugly, unalluring, unattractive, unlovely, unprepossessing **5.** even, flat, level, plane, smooth ~*n.* **6.** flatland, grassland, lowland, open country, plateau, prairie, steppe, tableland

plaintive disconsolate, doleful, grief-stricken, grievous, heart-rending, melancholy, mournful, pathetic, piteous, pitiful, rueful, sad, sorrowful, wistful, woebegone, woeful

plan *n.* **1.** contrivance, design, device, idea, method, plot, procedure, programme, project, proposal, proposition, scenario, scheme, strategy, suggestion, system **2.** blueprint, chart, delineation, diagram, drawing, illustration, layout, map, representation, scale drawing, sketch ~*v.* **3.** arrange, concoct, contrive, design, devise, draft, formulate, frame, invent, organize, outline, plot, prepare, represent, scheme, think out

plane[1] *n.* **1.** flat surface, level surface **2.** condition, degree, footing, level, position, stratum ~*adj.* **3.** even, flat, flush, horizontal, level, plain, regular, smooth, uniform

plane[2] *v.* glide, sail, skate, skim, volplane

plant *n.* **1.** bush, flower, herb, shrub, vegetable, weed **2.** factory, foundry, mill, shop, works, yard **3.** apparatus, equipment, gear, machinery ~*v.* **4.** implant, put in the ground, scatter, seed, set out, sow, transplant **5.** establish, fix, found, imbed, insert, institute, lodge, root, set, settle

plaque badge, brooch, cartouche, medal, medallion, panel, plate, slab, tablet

plaster *n.* **1.** gypsum, mortar, plaster of Paris, stucco **2.** adhesive plaster, bandage, dressing, Elastoplast (*Trademark*), sticking plaster ~*v.* **3.** bedaub, besmear, coat, cover, daub, overlay, smear, spread

moulded, pliant **4.** capable of being moulded **5.** produced by moulding **6.** *sl.* superficially attractive yet unoriginal or artificial —**plasticity** (plæˈstɪsɪtɪ) *n.* ability to be moulded —ˈ**plasticizer** *or* **-ciser** *n.* any of number of substances added to materials to soften and improve flexibility *etc.* —**plastic bomb** bomb consisting of adhesive jellylike explosive fitted around detonator —**plastic bullet** bullet consisting of cylinder of plastic about four inches long, usu. causing less severe injuries than ordinary bullet, and used *esp.* for riot control (*also* **baton round**) —**plastic surgery** repair or reconstruction of missing or malformed parts of the body for medical or cosmetic reasons

Plasticine (ˈplæstɪsiːn) *n.* R modelling material like clay

plate (pleɪt) *n.* **1.** shallow round dish **2.** flat thin sheet of metal, glass *etc.* **3.** utensils of gold or silver **4.** device for printing **5.** illustration in book **6.** device used by dentists to straighten children's teeth **7.** *inf.* set of false teeth —*vt.* **8.** cover with thin coating of gold, silver or other metal —ˈ**plateful** *n.* —ˈ**plater** *n.* —**plate glass** kind of thick glass used for mirrors, windows *etc.*

plateau (ˈplætəʊ) *n.* **1.** tract of level high land, tableland **2.** period of stability (*pl.* **-s, -eaux** (-əʊz))

platelet (ˈpleɪtlɪt) *n.* minute particle occurring in blood of vertebrates and involved in clotting of blood

platen (ˈplætᵊn) *n.* **1.** *Printing* plate by which paper is pressed against type **2.** roller in typewriter

platform (ˈplætfɔːm) *n.* **1.** raised level surface or floor, stage **2.** raised area in station from which passengers board trains **3.** political programme —**platform ticket** ticket for admission to railway platforms but not for travel

platinum (ˈplætɪnəm) *n.* white heavy malleable metal —**platinum-blond** *or* **platinum-blonde** *a.* **1.** (of hair) of pale silver-blond colour **2.** having hair of this colour

platitude (ˈplætɪtjuːd) *n.* commonplace remark —**platiˈtudinous** *a.*

Platonic (pləˈtɒnɪk) *a.* **1.** of Plato or his philosophy **2.** (*oft.* **p-**) (of love) purely spiritual, friendly —**Platonism** (ˈpleɪtənɪzəm) *n.* **1.** teachings of Plato, Gr. philosopher, and his followers **2.** philosophical theory that meanings of general words are real entities (forms) and describe particular objects *etc.* by virtue of some relationship of these to form —**Platonist** (ˈpleɪtənɪst) *n.*

platoon (pləˈtuːn) *n.* body of soldiers employed as unit

platteland (ˈplatəlant) *n.* **SA** rural district

platter (ˈplætə) *n.* flat dish

platypus (ˈplætɪpəs) *n.* small Aust. egg-laying amphibious mammal, with dense fur, webbed feet and ducklike bill (*also* **duck-billed platypus**)

plaudit (ˈplɔːdɪt) *n.* act of applause, hand-clapping

plausible (ˈplɔːzəbᵊl) *a.* **1.** apparently fair or reasonable **2.** fair-spoken —**plausiˈbility** *n.*

play (pleɪ) *vi.* **1.** amuse oneself **2.** take part in game **3.** behave carelessly; trifle **4.** act a part on the stage **5.** perform on musical instrument **6.** move with light or irregular motion, flicker *etc.* —*vt.* **7.** contend with in game **8.** take part in (game) **9.** act the part of **10.** perform (music) **11.** perform on (instrument) **12.** use, work (instrument) —*n.* **13.** dramatic piece or performance **14.** sport **15.** amusement **16.** manner of action or conduct **17.** activity **18.** brisk or free movement **19.** gambling —ˈ**player** *n.* —ˈ**playful** *a.* lively —ˈ**playback** *n.* **1.** act or process of reproducing recording, *esp.* on magnetic tape **2.** part of tape recorder serving to or used for reproducing recorded material —ˈ**playbill** *n.* **1.** poster or bill advertising play **2.** programme of play —ˈ**playboy** *n.* man, *esp.* of private means, who devotes himself to the pleasures of nightclubs, female company *etc.* —ˈ**playground** *n.* **1.** outdoor area for children's play, *esp.* one having swings *etc.* or adjoining school **2.** place popular as sports or holiday resort —ˈ**playgroup** *n.* group of young children playing regularly under adult supervision —ˈ**playhouse** *n.* theatre —**playing card** one of set of 52 cards used in card games —**playing fields** extensive piece of ground for open-air games —ˈ**playmate** *or* ˈ**playfellow** *n.* friend or partner in play or recreation —**play-off** *n.* **1.** *Sport* extra contest to decide winner when competitors are tied **2.** *chiefly* **US** contest or series of games to determine championship —ˈ**playpen** *n.* small enclosure, usu. portable, in which young child can be left to play in safety —ˈ**plaything** *n.* toy —ˈ**playtime** *n.* time for play or recreation, *esp.* school break —ˈ**playwright** *n.* author of plays —**play back** reproduce (recorded material) on (magnetic tape) by means of tape recorder —**play off 1.** (*usu. with* against) manipulate as if playing game **2.** take part in play-off —**play on words** pun

THESAURUS

plastic *adj.* **1.** compliant, docile, easily influenced, impressionable, malleable, manageable, pliable, receptive, responsive, tractable **2.** ductile, fictile, flexible, mouldable, pliable, pliant, soft, supple **3.** *Sl.* artificial, false, meretricious, phoney (*Inf.*), pseudo (*Inf.*), sham, specious, spurious, superficial, synthetic

plate *n.* **1.** dish, platter, trencher (*Archaic*) **2.** layer, panel, sheet, slab **3.** illustration, lithograph, print ~*v.* **4.** anodize, coat, cover, electroplate, face, gild, laminate, nickel, overlay, platinize, silver

plateau 1. highland, mesa, table, tableland, upland **2.** level, levelling off, stability, stage

platform 1. dais, podium, rostrum, stage, stand **2.** manifesto, objective(s), party line, policy, principle, programme, tenet(s)

platitude banality, bromide, cliché, commonplace, hackneyed saying, inanity, stereotype, trite remark, truism

platitudinous banal, clichéd, commonplace, corny (*Sl.*), hack, hackneyed, overworked, set, stale, stereotyped, stock, tired, trite, truistic, vapid, well-worn

platoon company, group, outfit (*Inf.*), patrol, squad, squadron, team

platter charger, dish, plate, salver, tray, trencher (*Archaic*)

plausible believable, colourable, conceivable, credible, fair-spoken, glib, likely, persuasive, possible, probable, reasonable, smooth, smooth-talking, smooth-tongued, specious, tenable

play *v.* **1.** amuse oneself, caper, engage in games, entertain oneself, frisk, frolic, gambol, have fun, revel, romp, sport, trifle **2.** be in a team, challenge, compete, contend against, participate, rival, take on, take part, vie with **3.** act, act the part of, execute, impersonate, perform, personate, portray, represent, take the part of ~*n.* **4.** comedy, drama, dramatic piece, entertainment, farce, masque, performance,

plaza (ˈplɑːzə) *n.* **1.** open space or square **2.** complex of shops *etc.*

PLC Public Limited Company

plea (pliː) *n.* **1.** entreaty **2.** statement of prisoner or defendant **3.** excuse **—plead** *vi.* **1.** make earnest appeal **2.** address court of law *—vt.* **3.** bring forward as excuse or plea (**ˈpleaded** *or* (US, *Scot.*) **pled** (plɛd), **ˈpleading**) **—ˈpleadings** *pl.n. Law* formal written statements presented alternately by plaintiff and defendant in lawsuit

please (pliːz) *vt.* **1.** be agreeable to **2.** gratify **3.** delight *—vi.* **4.** like, be willing *—adv.* **5.** word of request **—pleasance** (ˈplɛzəns) *n.* secluded part of garden **—pleasant** (ˈplɛzᵊnt) *a.* pleasing, agreeable **—pleasantly** (ˈplɛzᵊntlɪ) *adv.* **—pleasantry** (ˈplɛzᵊntrɪ) *n.* joke, humour **—pleasurable** (ˈplɛʒərəbᵊl) *a.* giving pleasure **—pleasure** (ˈplɛʒə) *n.* **1.** enjoyment, satisfaction **2.** will, choice

pleat (pliːt) *n.* **1.** any of various types of fold made by doubling material back on itself *—vt.* **2.** make, gather into pleats

plebeian (pləˈbiːən) *a.* **1.** belonging to the common people **2.** low or rough *—n.* **3.** one of the common people (*also* (*offens. sl.*) **pleb** (plɛb))

plebiscite (ˈplɛbɪsaɪt, -sɪt) *n.* decision by direct voting of the electorate

plectrum (ˈplɛktrəm) *or* **plectron** (ˈplɛktrən) *n.* small implement for plucking strings of guitar *etc.* (*pl.* **-tra** (-trə), **-trums** *or* **-tra, -trons**)

pledge (plɛdʒ) *n.* **1.** promise **2.** thing given over as security **3.** toast *—vt.* **4.** promise formally **5.** bind or secure by pledge **6.** give over as security

Pleiocene (ˈplaɪəʊsiːn) *n. see* PLIOCENE

Pleistocene (ˈplaɪstəsiːn) *a.* **1.** of glacial period of formation *—n.* **2.** Pleistocene epoch or rock series

plenary (ˈpliːnərɪ, ˈplɛn-) *a.* **1.** complete, without limitations, absolute **2.** (of meeting *etc.*) with all members present

plenipotentiary (plɛnɪpəˈtɛnʃərɪ) *a./n.* (envoy) having full powers

plenitude (ˈplɛnɪtjuːd) *n.* **1.** completeness, entirety **2.** abundance

plenty (ˈplɛntɪ) *n.* **1.** abundance **2.** quite enough **—ˈplenteous** *a.* **1.** ample **2.** rich **3.** copious **—ˈplentiful** *a.* abundant

plenum (ˈpliːnəm) *n.* **1.** space as considered to be full of matter (opposed to vacuum) **2.** condition of fullness (*pl.* **-s, -na** (-nə))

THESAURUS

piece, radio play, show, stage show, television drama, tragedy **5.** amusement, caper, diversion, entertainment, frolic, fun, gambol, game, jest, pastime, prank, recreation, romp, sport **6.** gambling, gaming **7.** action, activity, elbowroom, exercise, give (*Inf.*), latitude, leeway, margin, motion, movement, operation, range, room, scope, space, sweep, swing **8.** action, activity, employment, function, operation, transaction, working **9.** foolery, fun, humour, jest, joking, lark (*Inf.*), prank, sport, teasing

playboy gay dog, ladies' man, lady-killer (*Inf.*), lover boy (*Sl.*), man about town, philanderer, pleasure seeker, rake, roué, socialite, womanizer

player 1. competitor, contestant, participant, sportsman, sportswoman, team member **2.** actor, actress, entertainer, performer, Thespian, trouper **3.** artist, instrumentalist, musician, music maker, performer, virtuoso

playful cheerful, coltish, frisky, frolicsome, gay, impish, joyous, kittenish, larkish (*Inf.*), lively, merry, mischievous, puckish, rollicking, spirited, sportive, sprightly, vivacious

playmate chum (*Inf.*), companion, comrade, friend, neighbour, pal (*Inf.*), playfellow

plaything amusement, bauble, game, gewgaw, gimcrack, pastime, toy, trifle, trinket

playwright dramatist, dramaturge, dramaturgist

plea 1. appeal, begging, entreaty, intercession, overture, petition, prayer, request, suit, supplication **2.** *Law* action, allegation, cause, suit **3.** apology, claim, defence, excuse, explanation, extenuation, justification, pretext, vindication

plead 1. appeal (to), ask, beg, beseech, crave, entreat, implore, importune, petition, request, solicit, supplicate **2.** adduce, allege, argue, assert, maintain, put forward, use as an excuse

pleasant 1. acceptable, agreeable, amusing, delectable, delightful, enjoyable, fine, gratifying, lovely, nice, pleasing, pleasurable, refreshing, satisfying, welcome **2.** affable, agreeable, amiable, charming, cheerful, cheery, congenial, engaging, friendly, genial, good-humoured, likable, nice

pleasantry badinage, banter, bon mot, good-natured remark, jest, joke, quip, sally, witticism

please 1. amuse, charm, cheer, content, delight, entertain, give pleasure to, gladden, gratify, humour, indulge, rejoice, satisfy, suit, tickle, tickle pink **2.** be inclined, choose, desire, like, opt, prefer, see fit, want, will, wish

pleasure 1. amusement, bliss, comfort, contentment, delectation, delight, diversion, ease, enjoyment, gladness, gratification, happiness, joy, recreation, satisfaction, solace **2.** choice, command, desire, inclination, mind, option, preference, purpose, will, wish

plebeian 1. *adj.* base, coarse, common, ignoble, low, lowborn, lower-class, mean, non-U (*Brit. inf.*), proletarian, uncultivated, unrefined, vulgar, working-class **2.** *n.* commoner, common man, man in the street, peasant, pleb (*Brit. sl.*), prole (*Sl.*), proletarian

pledge *n.* **1.** assurance, covenant, oath, promise, undertaking, vow, warrant, word, word of honour **2.** bail, bond, collateral, deposit, earnest, gage, guarantee, pawn, security, surety **3.** health, toast *~v.* **4.** contract, engage, give one's oath (word, word of honour), promise, swear, undertake, vouch, vow **5.** bind, engage, gage (*Archaic*), guarantee, mortgage, plight

plentiful abundant, ample, bounteous (*Literary*), bountiful, complete, copious, generous, inexhaustible, infinite, lavish, liberal, overflowing, plenteous, profuse

plenty abundance, enough, fund, good deal, great deal, heap(s) (*Inf.*), lots (*Inf.*), mass, masses, mine, mountain(s), oodles (*Inf.*), pile(s) (*Inf.*), plethora quantities, quantity, stack(s), store, sufficiency, volume

plethora excess, glut, overabundance, profusion superabundance, superfluity, surfeit, surplus

plethora (ˈplɛθərə) *n.* oversupply

pleura (ˈplʊərə) *n.* membrane lining the chest and covering the lungs (*pl.* **pleurae** (ˈplʊəriː)) —ˈ**pleurisy** *n.* inflammation of the pleura

pliable (ˈplaɪəbˀl) *a.* easily bent or influenced —**pliaˈbility** *n.* —ˈ**pliancy** *n.* —ˈ**pliant** *a.* pliable

pliers (ˈplaɪəz) *pl.n.* tool with hinged arms and jaws for gripping

plight[1] (plaɪt) *n.* **1.** distressing state **2.** predicament

plight[2] (plaɪt) *vt.* promise —**plight one's troth** make a promise, *esp.* of marriage

Plimsoll line (ˈplɪmsəl) mark on ships indicating maximum draught permitted when loaded

plimsolls *or* **plimsoles** (ˈplɪmsəlz) *pl.n.* rubber-soled canvas shoes

plinth (plɪnθ) *n.* slab as base of column *etc.*

Pliocene *or* **Pleiocene** (ˈplaɪəʊsiːn) *a.* **1.** of the most recent tertiary deposits —*n.* **2.** Pliocene epoch or rock series

plissé (ˈpliːseɪ, ˈplɪs-) *n.* **1.** fabric with wrinkled finish, achieved by treatment involving caustic soda **2.** such finish on fabric

P.L.O. Palestine Liberation Organization

plod (plɒd) *vi.* walk or work doggedly (**-dd-**)

plonk[1] (plɒŋk) *v.* **1.** drop, fall suddenly and heavily —*n.* **2.** act or sound of this

plonk[2] (plɒŋk) *n. inf.* alcoholic drink, *esp.* (cheap) wine

plop (plɒp) *n.* **1.** sound of object falling into water without splash —*v.* **2.** (cause to) fall with such sound (**-pp-**)

plosion (ˈpləʊʒən) *n. Phonet.* sound of abrupt break or closure, *esp.* audible release of stop (*also* **exˈplosion**) —ˈ**plosive** *Phonet. a.* **1.** accompanied by plosion —*n.* **2.** plosive consonant; stop

plot[1] (plɒt) *n.* **1.** secret plan, conspiracy **2.** essence of story, play *etc.* —*vt.* **3.** devise secretly **4.** mark position of **5.** make map of —*vi.* **6.** conspire (**-tt-**)

plot[2] (plɒt) *n.* small piece of land

plough *or esp. U.S.* **plow** (plaʊ) *n.* **1.** implement for turning up soil **2.** similar implement for clearing snow *etc.* —*vt.* **3.** turn up with plough, furrow —*vi.* **4.** (*with* through) work (at) slowly —ˈ**ploughman** *or esp. U.S.* ˈ**plowman** *n.* —**ploughman's lunch** meal of cheese, bread and oft. beer —ˈ**ploughshare** *or esp. U.S.* ˈ**plowshare** *n.* blade of plough —**the Plough** group of seven brightest stars in constellation Ursa Major (*also* **Charles's Wain**)

plover (ˈplʌvə) *n.* any of various shore birds, typically with round head, straight bill and long pointed wings

plow (plaʊ) US *see* PLOUGH

ploy (plɔɪ) *n.* **1.** stratagem **2.** occupation **3.** prank

P.L.R. Public Lending Right

pluck (plʌk) *vt.* **1.** pull, pick off **2.** strip **3.** sound strings of (guitar *etc.*) with fingers, plectrum —*n.* **4.** courage **5.** sudden pull or tug —ˈ**pluckily** *adv.* —ˈ**plucky** *a.* courageous

plug (plʌg) *n.* **1.** thing fitting into and filling a hole **2.** *Elec.* device connecting appliance to electricity supply **3.** tobacco pressed hard **4.** *inf.* recommendation, advertisement —*vt.* **5.** stop with plug **6.** *inf.* advertise (product, show *etc.*) by constant repetition, as on television **7.** *sl.* punch **8.** *sl.* shoot —*vi.* **9.** *inf.* (*with* away) work hard (**-gg-**) —**plug in** connect (electrical appliance) with power source by means of plug

plum (plʌm) *n.* **1.** stone fruit **2.** tree bearing it **3.** choicest part, piece, position *etc.* —*a.* **4.** choice **5.** dark reddish-purple colour —ˈ**plummy** *a.* **1.** of plums **2.** UK *inf.* (of speech) deep, refined and somewhat drawling **3.** UK *inf.* choice; desirable

plumage (ˈpluːmɪdʒ) *n. see* PLUME

plumb (plʌm) *n.* **1.** ball of lead (**plumb bob**) attached to string used for sounding, finding the perpendicular *etc.* —*a.* **2.** perpendicular —*adv.* **3.** perpendicularly **4.**

THESAURUS

pliable **1.** bendable, bendy, ductile, flexible, limber, lithe, malleable, plastic, pliant, supple **2.** adaptable, compliant, docile, easily led, impressionable, influenceable, manageable, persuadable, pliant, receptive, responsive, susceptible, tractable, yielding

pliant **1.** bendable, bendy, ductile, flexible, lithe, plastic, pliable, supple **2.** adaptable, biddable, compliant, easily led, impressionable, influenceable, manageable, persuadable, pliable, susceptible, tractable, yielding

plight *n.* case, circumstances, condition, difficulty, dilemma, extremity, hole (*Sl.*), jam (*Inf.*), perplexity, pickle (*Inf.*), predicament, scrape (*Inf.*), situation, spot (*Inf.*), state, straits, trouble

plod **1.** clump, drag, lumber, slog, stomp (*Inf.*), tramp, tread, trudge **2.** drudge, grind (*Inf.*), grub, labour, peg away, persevere, plough through, plug away (*Inf.*), slog, soldier on, toil

plot[1] *n.* **1.** cabal, conspiracy, covin (*Law*), intrigue, machination, plan, scheme, stratagem **2.** action, narrative, outline, scenario, story, story line, subject, theme, thread ~*v.* **3.** cabal, collude, conspire, contrive, hatch, intrigue, machinate, manoeuvre, plan, scheme **4.** calculate, chart, compute, draft, draw, locate, map, mark, outline **5.** brew, conceive, concoct, contrive, cook up (*Inf.*), design, devise, frame, hatch, imagine, lay, project

plot[2] *n.* allotment, area, ground, lot, parcel, patch, tract

plough *v.* break ground, cultivate, dig, furrow, ridge, till, turn over

pluck *n.* **1.** backbone, boldness, bottle (*Brit. sl.*), bravery, courage, determination, grit, guts (*Inf.*), hardihood, heart, intrepidity, mettle, nerve, resolution, spirit, spunk (*Inf.*) ~*v.* **2.** collect, draw, gather, harvest, pick, pull out *or* off **3.** catch, clutch, jerk, pull at, snatch, tug, tweak, yank **4.** finger, pick, plunk, strum, thrum, twang

plucky bold, brave, courageous, daring, doughty, game, gritty, gutsy (*Sl.*), hardy, heroic, intrepid, mettlesome, spirited, spunky (*Inf.*), undaunted, unflinching, valiant

plug *n.* **1.** bung, cork, spigot, stopper, stopple **2.** cake, chew, pigtail, quid, twist, wad **3.** *Inf.* advert (*Brit. inf.*), advertisement, good word, hype (*Sl.*), mention, publicity, puff, push ~*v.* **4.** block, bung, choke, close, cork, cover, fill, pack, seal, stop, stopper, stopple, stop up, stuff **5.** *Inf.* advertise, build up, hype (*Sl.*), mention, promote, publicize, puff, push, write up **6.** *Sl.* gun down, pick off, pop, pot, put a bullet in, shoot **7.** *With* **away** *Inf.* drudge, grind (*Inf.*), labour, peg away, plod, slog, toil

plum *Fig.* **1.** *n.* bonus, cream, find, pick, prize, treasure **2.** *adj.* best, choice, first-class, prize

exactly 5. US *inf.* downright 6. honestly 7. exactly —*vt.* 8. set exactly upright 9. find depth of 10. reach, undergo 11. equip with, connect to plumbing system —**ˈplumber** *n.* worker who attends to water and sewage systems —**ˈplumbing** *n.* 1. trade of plumber 2. system of water and sewage pipes —**ˈplumbline** *n.* cord with plumb attached

plume (pluːm) *n.* 1. feather 2. ornament of feathers or horsehair —*vt.* 3. furnish with plumes 4. pride (oneself) —**ˈplumage** *n.* bird's feathers collectively

plummet (ˈplʌmɪt) *vi.* 1. plunge headlong —*n.* 2. plumbline

plump[1] (plʌmp) *a.* 1. of rounded form, moderately fat, chubby —*v.* 2. (*oft. with* up *or* out) make, become plump

plump[2] (plʌmp) *vi.* 1. sit, fall abruptly —*vt.* 2. drop, throw abruptly —*adv.* 3. suddenly 4. heavily 5. directly —**plump for** choose, vote only for

plunder (ˈplʌndə) *vt.* 1. take by force 2. rob systematically —*vi.* 3. rob —*n.* 4. pillage 5. booty, spoils

plunge (plʌndʒ) *vt.* 1. put forcibly —*vi.* 2. throw oneself 3. enter, rush with violence 4. descend very suddenly —*n.* 5. dive —**ˈplunger** *n.* 1. rubber suction cap to unblock drains 2. pump piston —**take the plunge** *inf.* 1. embark on risky enterprise 2. get married

plunk (plʌŋk) *v.* 1. pluck (string of banjo *etc.*) 2. drop suddenly

pluperfect (pluːˈpɜːfɪkt) *a./n.* (tense) expressing action completed before past point of time

plural (ˈplʊərəl) *a.* 1. of, denoting more than one person or thing —*n.* 2. word in its plural form —**ˈpluralism** *n.* 1. holding of more than one appointment, vote *etc.* 2. coexistence of different social groups *etc.* in one society —**ˈpluralist** *n./a.* —**pluˈrality** *n.* majority of votes *etc.*

plus (plʌs) *prep.* 1. with addition of (*usu.* indicated by the sign +) —*a.* 2. to be added 3. positive —**plus fours** men's baggy knickerbockers reaching below knee, now only worn for golf *etc.*

plush (plʌʃ) *n.* 1. fabric with long nap, long-piled velvet —*a.* 2. luxurious

Pluto[1] (ˈpluːtəʊ) *n. Gr. myth.* god of underworld; Hades —**Pluˈtonian** *a.* pert. to Pluto or the infernal regions, dark —**plutonic** (pluːˈtɒnɪk) *a.* (of igneous rocks) derived from magma that has cooled and solidified below surface of earth

Pluto[2] (ˈpluːtəʊ) *n.* second smallest planet and farthest known from sun

plutocracy (pluːˈtɒkrəsɪ) *n.* 1. government by the rich 2. state ruled thus 3. wealthy class —**ˈplutocrat** *n.* wealthy man —**plutoˈcratic** *a.*

plutonium (pluːˈtəʊnɪəm) *n.* radioactive metallic element used *esp.* in nuclear reactors and weapons

pluvial (ˈpluːvɪəl) *a.* of, caused by the action of rain

ply[1] (plaɪ) *vt.* 1. wield 2. work at 3. supply pressingly 4. urge 5. keep busy —*vi.* 6. go to and fro, run regularly (**plied, ˈplying**)

ply[2] (plaɪ) *n.* 1. fold or thickness 2. strand of yarn —**ˈplywood** *n.* board of thin layers of wood glued together with grains at right angles

Plymouth Brethren (ˈplɪməθ) strongly Puritanical religious sect having no organized ministry

Pm *Chem.* promethium

p.m. *or* **P.M.** 1. post meridiem (*Lat.*, after noon) 2. post-mortem

P.M. 1. Paymaster 2. Postmaster 3. Prime Minister

P.M.G. 1. Paymaster General 2. Postmaster General

PMS premenstrual syndrome

PMT premenstrual tension

pneumatic (njʊˈmætɪk) *a.* of, worked by, inflated with wind or air —**pneuˈmatics** *pl.n.* (*with sing. v.*) branch of physics concerned with mechanical properties of gases, *esp.* air

pneumonia (njuːˈməʊnɪə) *n.* inflammation of the lungs

po (pəʊ) *n.* **UK** *inf.* chamber pot (*pl.* **-s**)

Po *Chem.* polonium

P.O. 1. Petty Officer 2. postal order (*also* **p.o.**) 3. Post Office

poach[1] (pəʊtʃ) *vt.* 1. catch (game) illegally 2. trample, make swampy or soft —*vi.* 3. trespass for purpose of poaching 4. encroach

poach[2] (pəʊtʃ) *vt.* simmer (eggs, fish *etc.*) gently in water *etc.* —**ˈpoacher** *n.*

pock (pɒk) *n.* pustule, as in smallpox *etc.*

pocket (ˈpɒkɪt) *n.* 1. small bag inserted in garment 2. cavity filled with ore *etc.* 3. socket, cavity, pouch or hollow 4. mass of water or air differing from that surrounding it 5. isolated group or area 6. **SA** bag of vegetables or fruit —*vt.* 7. put into one's pocket 8. appropriate, steal —*a.* 9. small —**ˈpocketbook** *n. chief-*

THESAURUS

plumb *n.* 1. lead, plumb bob, plummet, weight ~*adv.* 2. perpendicularly, up and down, vertically 3. bang, exactly, precisely, slap, spot-on (*Brit. inf.*) ~*v.* 4. delve, explore, fathom, gauge, go into, measure, penetrate, probe, search, sound

plume 1. *n.* aigrette, crest, feather, pinion, quill 2. *v. With* **on** *or* **upon** congratulate oneself, pat oneself on the back, pique oneself, preen oneself, pride oneself

plump *adj.* beefy (*Inf.*), burly, buxom, chubby, corpulent, dumpy, fat, fleshy, full, obese, podgy, portly, roly-poly, rotund, round, stout, tubby, well-covered, well-upholstered (*Inf.*)

plunder 1. *v.* despoil, devastate, loot, pillage, raid, ransack, ravage, rifle, rob, sack, spoil, steal, strip 2. *n.* booty, ill-gotten gains, loot, pillage, prey, prize, rapine, spoils, swag (*Sl.*)

plunge *v.* 1. cast, descend, dip, dive, douse, drop, fall, go down, immerse, jump, nose-dive, pitch, plummet, sink, submerge, swoop, throw, tumble 2. career, charge, dash, hurtle, lurch, rush, tear ~*n.* 3. descent, dive, drop, fall, immersion, jump, submersion, swoop

plus 1. *prep.* added to, and, coupled with, with, with the addition of 2. *adj.* added, additional, extra, positive, supplementary

plutocrat capitalist, Croesus, Dives, fat cat (*Sl.*), magnate, millionaire, moneybags (*Sl.*), rich man, tycoon

ply 1. carry on, exercise, follow, practise, pursue, work at 2. employ, handle, manipulate, swing, utilize, wield 3. assail, beset, besiege, bombard, harass, importune, press, urge

poach appropriate, encroach, hunt *or* fish illegally, infringe, intrude, plunder, rob, steal, steal game, trespass

ly **US** small bag or case for money, papers *etc.* —**'pocketknife** *n.* small knife with one or more blades that fold into handle; penknife —**pocket money 1.** small, regular allowance given to children by parents **2.** allowance for small, occasional expenses

poco ('pəukəu; *It.* 'pɔːko) *or* **un poco** *a./adv. Mus.* little; to a small degree

pod (pɒd) *n.* **1.** long seed vessel, as of peas, beans *etc.* —*vi.* **2.** form pods —*vt.* **3.** shell (**-dd-**)

-pod *or* **-pode** (*comb. form*) indicating certain type or number of feet, as in *arthropod, tripod*

podgy ('pɒdʒɪ) *a.* short and fat

podium ('pəudɪəm) *n.* small raised platform (*pl.* **-s, -dia** (-dɪə))

poem ('pəuɪm) *n.* imaginative composition in rhythmic lines —**poesy** ('pəuɪzɪ) *n.* poetry —**'poet** *n.* writer of poems (**'poetess** *fem.*) —**poetaster** (pəuɪ'tæstə, -'teɪ-) *n.* would-be or inferior poet —**po'etic(al)** *a.* —**po'etically** *adv.* —**'poetry** *n.* art or work of poet, verse —**poetic justice** fitting retribution —**poetic licence** justifiable departure from conventional rules of form, fact *etc.*, as in poetry

po-faced *a.* wearing disapproving stern expression

pogey *or* **pogy** ('pəugɪ) *n.* **C** *sl.* **1.** unemployment insurance **2.** dole

pogo stick ('pəugəu) stout pole with handle at top, steps for feet and spring at bottom, so that user can spring up, down and along on it

pogrom ('pɒgrəm) *n.* organized persecution and massacre, *esp.* of Jews in Russia

poignant ('pɔɪnjənt, -nənt) *a.* **1.** moving **2.** biting, stinging **3.** vivid **4.** pungent —**'poignancy** *or* **'poignance** *n.*

poinciana (pɔɪnsɪ'ɑːnə) *n.* tropical tree with scarlet flowers

poinsettia (pɔɪn'sɛtɪə) *n. orig.* Amer. shrub, widely cultivated for its clusters of scarlet leaves, resembling petals

point (pɔɪnt) *n.* **1.** dot, mark **2.** punctuation mark **3.** item, detail **4.** unit of value **5.** position, degree, stage **6.** moment **7.** gist of an argument **8.** purpose **9.** striking or effective part or quality **10.** essential object or thing **11.** sharp end **12.** single unit in scoring **13.** headland **14.** one of direction marks of compass **15.** movable rail changing train to other rails **16.** fine kind of lace **17.** act of pointing **18.** power point **19.** printing unit, one twelfth of a pica —*pl.* **20.** electrical contacts in distributor of engine —*vi.* **21.** show direction or position by extending finger **22.** direct attention **23.** (of dog) indicate position of game by standing facing it —*vt.* **24.** aim, direct **25.** sharpen **26.** fill up joints of (brickwork *etc.*) with mortar **27.** give value to (words *etc.*) —**'pointed** *a.* **1.** sharp **2.** direct, telling —**'pointedly** *adv.* —**'pointer** *n.* **1.** index **2.** indicating rod *etc.* used for pointing **3.** indication **4.** dog trained to point —**'pointless** *a.* **1.** blunt **2.** futile, irrelevant —**point-blank** *a.* **1.** aimed horizontally **2.** plain, blunt —*adv.* **3.** with level aim (there being no necessity to elevate for distance) **4.** at short range —**point duty** police regulation of traffic —**point-to-point** *n.* steeplechase usu. for amateur riders only —**point of no return 1.** point at which irreversible commitment must be made to action *etc.* **2.** point in journey at which, if one continues, supplies will be insufficient for return to starting place —**point of order** question raised in meeting as to whether rules governing procedures are being breached (*pl.* **points of order**) —**point of sale** (in retail distribution) place and time when sale is made —**point of view 1.** position from which someone or something is observed **2.** mental viewpoint or attitude (*pl.* **points of view**)

pointillism ('pwæntɪlɪzəm) *n.* technique of painting elaborated from impressionism, in which dots of unmixed colour are juxtaposed on white ground so that from distance they fuse in viewer's eye into appropriate intermediate tones —**'pointillist** *n./a.*

THESAURUS

pocket 1. *n.* bag, compartment, hollow, pouch, receptacle, sack **2.** *adj.* abridged, compact, concise, little, miniature, pint-size(d) (*Inf.*), portable, potted (*Inf.*), small **3.** *v.* appropriate, filch, help oneself to, lift (*Inf.*), pilfer, purloin, snaffle (*Brit. inf.*), steal, take

pod *n./v.* hull, husk, shell, shuck

podgy chubby, chunky, dumpy, fat, fleshy, plump, roly-poly, rotund, short and fat, squat, stout, stubby, stumpy, tubby

podium dais, platform, rostrum, stage

poem lyric, ode, rhyme, song, sonnet, verse

poet bard, lyricist, maker (*Archaic*), rhymer, versifier

poetic elegiac, lyric, lyrical, metrical, rhythmical, songlike

poetry metrical composition, poems, poesy (*Archaic*), rhyme, rhyming, verse

poignancy 1. emotion, emotionalism, evocativeness, feeling, pathos, piteousness, plaintiveness, sadness, sentiment, tenderness **2.** bitterness, intensity, keenness, piquancy, pungency, sharpness

poignant 1. affecting, agonizing, bitter, distressing, heartbreaking, heart-rending, intense, moving, painful, pathetic, sad, touching, upsetting **2.** acute, biting, caustic, keen, penetrating, piercing, pointed, sarcastic, severe **3.** acrid, piquant, pungent, sharp, stinging, tangy

point *n.* **1.** dot, full stop, mark, period, speck, stop **2.** location, place, position, site, spot, stage, station **3.** apex, end, nib, prong, sharp end, spike, spur, summit, tine, tip, top **4.** bill, cape, foreland, head, headland, ness (*Archaic*), promontory **5.** circumstance, condition, degree, extent, position, stage **6.** instant, juncture, moment, time, very minute **7.** aim, design, end, goal, intent, intention, motive, object, objective, purpose, reason, use, usefulness, utility **8.** burden, core, crux, drift, essence, gist, heart, import, main idea, marrow, matter, meaning, nub, pith, proposition, question, subject, text, theme, thrust **9.** aspect, detail, facet, feature, instance, item, nicety, particular **10.** aspect, attribute, characteristic, peculiarity, property, quality, respect, side, trait **11.** score, tally, unit ~*v.* **12.** bespeak, call attention to, denote, designate, direct, indicate, show, signify **13.** aim, bring to bear, direct, level, train **14.** barb, edge, sharpen, taper, whet

point-blank *adj.* abrupt, blunt, categorical, direct, downright, explicit, express, plain, straight-from-the-shoulder, unreserved

pointed 1. acicular, acuminate, acute, barbed, cuspidate, edged, mucronate, sharp **2.** accurate, acute, biting, cutting, incisive, keen, penetrating, pertinent, sharp, telling, trenchant

pointless absurd, aimless, fruitless, futile, inane,

poise (pɔɪz) *n.* **1.** composure **2.** self-possession **3.** balance, equilibrium, carriage (of body *etc.*) —*v.* **4.** (cause to) be balanced or suspended —*vt.* **5.** hold in readiness

poison (ˈpɔɪzᵊn) *n.* **1.** substance which kills or injures when introduced into living organism —*vt.* **2.** give poison to **3.** infect **4.** pervert, spoil —ˈ**poisoner** *n.* —ˈ**poisonous** *a.* —**poison ivy** N Amer. shrub or climbing plant that causes itching rash on contact —**poison-pen letter** malicious anonymous letter

poke[1] (pəʊk) *vt.* **1.** push, thrust with finger, stick *etc.* **2.** thrust —*vi.* **3.** make thrusts **4.** pry —*n.* **5.** act of poking —ˈ**poker** *n.* metal rod for poking fire —ˈ**poky** *or* ˈ**pokey** *a.* small, confined, cramped

poke[2] (pəʊk) —**pig in a poke** something bought *etc.* without previous inspection

poker (ˈpəʊkə) *n.* card game —**poker face** *inf.* face without expression, as of poker player concealing value of his cards —**poker-faced** *a.*

pol. **1.** political **2.** politics

Pol. **1.** Poland **2.** Polish

polar (ˈpəʊlə) *a. see* POLE[2]

Polaris (pəˈlɑːrɪs) *n.* **1.** brightest star in constellation Ursa Minor, situated slightly less than 1° from north celestial pole (*also* **Pole Star, North Star**) **2.** type of Amer. ballistic missile, usu. fired by submarine

Polaroid (ˈpəʊlərɔɪd) *n.* **R** **1.** type of plastic which polarizes light **2.** camera that develops print very quickly inside itself

polder (ˈpəʊldə, ˈpɒl-) *n.* land reclaimed from the sea

pole[1] (pəʊl) *n.* **1.** long rounded piece of wood *etc.* —*vt.* **2.** propel with pole —**pole-vault** *vi.* perform or compete in the pole vault —**pole-vaulter** *n.* —**the pole vault** field event in which competitors attempt to clear high bar with aid of long flexible pole —**up the pole** *inf.* **1.** slightly mad **2.** in error, confused

pole[2] (pəʊl) *n.* **1.** either of the ends of axis of earth or celestial sphere **2.** either of opposite ends of magnet, electric cell *etc.* —ˈ**polar** *a.* **1.** pert. to the N and S pole, or to magnetic poles **2.** directly opposite in tendency, character *etc.* —**poˈlarity** *n.* —**polariˈzation** *or* **-iˈsation** *n.* —ˈ**polarize** *or* **-ise** *vt.* give polarity to —**polar bear** white Arctic bear —**polar circle** either Arctic Circle or Antarctic Circle —**the Pole Star** star closest to N celestial pole at any particular time, at present Polaris

poleaxe *or U.S.* **poleax** (ˈpəʊlæks) *n.* **1.** battle-axe —*vt.* **2.** hit, fell as with poleaxe

polecat (ˈpəʊlkæt) *n.* small animal of weasel family

polemic (pəˈlɛmɪk) *a.* **1.** controversial (*also* **poˈlemical**) —*n.* **2.** war of words, argument —**poˈlemics** *pl.n.* (*with sing. v.*) art or practice of dispute or argument

police (pəˈliːs) *n.* **1.** the civil force which maintains public order —*vt.* **2.** keep in order —**police dog** dog trained to help police —**poˈliceman** *n.* member of police force (**poˈlicewoman** *fem.*) —**police state** state or country in which repressive government maintains control through police —**police station** office or headquarters of police force of district

policy[1] (ˈpɒlɪsɪ) *n.* **1.** course of action adopted, *esp.* in state affairs **2.** prudence

policy[2] (ˈpɒlɪsɪ) *n.* insurance contract

poliomyelitis (pəʊlɪəʊmaɪəˈlaɪtɪs) *n.* disease of spinal cord characterized by fever and sometimes paralysis (*also* **infantile paralysis**)

polish (ˈpɒlɪʃ) *vt.* **1.** make smooth and glossy **2.** refine —*n.* **3.** shine **4.** polishing **5.** substance for polishing **6.** refinement

Polish (ˈpəʊlɪʃ) *a.* **1.** of Poland —*n.* **2.** official language of Poland

Politburo (ˈpɒlɪtbjʊərəʊ) *n.* **1.** executive committee of a Communist Party **2.** supreme policy-making authority in most Communist countries

polite (pəˈlaɪt) *a.* **1.** showing regard for others in manners, speech *etc.* **2.** refined, cultured —**poˈlitely** *adv.* —**poˈliteness** *n.* courtesy

THESAURUS

ineffectual, irrelevant, meaningless, nonsensical, senseless, silly, stupid, unavailing, unproductive, unprofitable, useless, vague, vain, worthless

poise **1.** *n.* aplomb, assurance, calmness, composure, cool (*Sl.*), coolness, dignity, elegance, equanimity, equilibrium, grace, presence, presence of mind, sang-froid, savoir-faire, self-possession, serenity **2.** *v.* balance, float, hang, hang in midair, hang suspended, hold, hover, position, support, suspend

poison *n.* **1.** bane, toxin, venom ~*v.* **2.** adulterate, contaminate, envenom, give (someone) poison, infect, kill, murder, pollute **3.** corrupt, defile, deprave, pervert, subvert, taint, undermine, vitiate, warp

poisonous **1.** baneful (*Archaic*), deadly, fatal, lethal, mephitic, mortal, noxious, toxic, venomous, virulent **2.** baleful, baneful (*Archaic*), corruptive, evil, malicious, noxious, pernicious, pestiferous, pestilential, vicious

poke *v.* **1.** butt, dig, elbow, hit, jab, nudge, prod, punch, push, shove, stab, stick, thrust **2.** butt in, interfere, intrude, meddle, nose, peek, poke one's nose into (*Inf.*), pry, snoop (*Inf.*), tamper ~*n.* **3.** butt, dig, hit, jab, nudge, prod, punch, thrust

poky confined, cramped, incommodious, narrow, small, tiny

polar **1.** Antarctic, Arctic, cold, extreme, freezing, frozen, furthest, glacial, icy, terminal **2.** antagonistic, antipodal, antithetical, contradictory, contrary, diametric, opposed, opposite

pole[1] bar, mast, post, rod, shaft, spar, staff, standard, stick

pole[2] antipode, extremity, limit, terminus

police *n.* **1.** boys in blue (*Inf.*), constabulary, fuzz (*Sl.*), law enforcement agency, police force, the law (*Inf.*), the Old Bill (*Sl.*) ~*v.* **2.** control, guard, keep in order, keep the peace, patrol, protect, regulate, watch **3.** *Fig.* check, monitor, observe, oversee, supervise

policeman bobby (*Inf.*), bogey (*Sl.*), constable, cop (*Sl.*), copper (*Sl.*), fuzz (*Sl.*), gendarme (*Sl.*), officer, peeler (*Obsolete Brit. sl.*), pig (*Sl.*), rozzer (*Sl.*)

policy **1.** action, approach, code, course, custom, guideline, line, plan, practice, procedure, programme, protocol, rule, scheme, stratagem, theory **2.** discretion, good sense, prudence, sagacity, shrewdness, wisdom

polish *v.* **1.** brighten, buff, burnish, clean, furbish, rub, shine, smooth, wax **2.** brush up, correct, cultivate, emend, enhance, finish, improve, perfect, refine, touch up ~*n.* **3.** brightness, brilliance, finish, glaze, gloss, lustre, sheen, smoothness, sparkle, veneer **4.** varnish, wax **5.** *Fig.* class (*Inf.*), elegance,

politic (ˈpɒlɪtɪk) *a.* **1.** wise **2.** shrewd **3.** expedient **4.** cunning —**poˈlitical** *a.* of the state or its affairs —**poliˈtician** *n.* one engaged in politics —**ˈpolitics** *pl.n.* **1.** (*with sing. v.*) art of government **2.** political affairs or life —**ˈpolity** *n.* **1.** form of government **2.** organized state **3.** civil government —**political asylum** refuge given to someone for political reasons —**political economy** *former name for* economics —**political prisoner** someone imprisoned for holding or expressing particular political beliefs —**political science** study of state, government and politics —**political scientist**

polka (ˈpɒlkə) *n.* **1.** lively dance in 2/4 time **2.** music for it —**polka dot** one of pattern of bold spots on fabric *etc.*

poll (pəʊl) *n.* **1.** voting **2.** counting of votes **3.** number of votes recorded **4.** canvassing of sample of population to determine general opinion **5.** (top of) head —*vt.* **6.** receive (votes) **7.** take votes of **8.** lop, shear **9.** cut horns from (animals) —*vi.* **10.** vote —**ˈpollster** *n.* one who conducts polls —**polling booth** voting place at election —**polling station** place to which voters go during election to cast votes —**poll tax** tax levied per head of adult population (*also* **community charge**)

pollard (ˈpɒləd) *n.* **1.** hornless animal of normally horned variety **2.** tree on which a close head of young branches has been made by polling —*vt.* **3.** make a pollard of

pollen (ˈpɒlən) *n.* fertilizing dust of flower —**ˈpollinate** *vt.* —**pollen count** measure of pollen present in air over 24-hour period

pollute (pəˈluːt) *vt.* **1.** make foul **2.** corrupt **3.** desecrate —**polˈlutant** *n.* —**polˈlution** *n.*

polo (ˈpəʊləʊ) *n.* game like hockey played by teams of 4 players on horseback —**polo neck 1.** collar on garment, worn rolled over to fit closely round neck **2.** sweater with such collar

polonaise (pɒləˈneɪz) *n.* **1.** Polish dance **2.** music for it

polonium (pəˈləʊnɪəm) *n.* radioactive element that occurs in trace amounts in uranium ores

poltergeist (ˈpɒltəgaɪst) *n.* noisy mischievous spirit

poltroon (pɒlˈtruːn) *n.* abject coward

poly (ˈpɒlɪ) *n. inf.* polytechnic

poly- (*comb. form*) many, as in *polysyllabic*

polyamide (pɒlɪˈæmaɪd) *n.* any of a class of synthetic polymeric materials

polyandry (ˈpɒlɪændrɪ) *n.* polygamy in which woman has more than one husband

polyanthus (pɒlɪˈænθəs) *n.* cultivated primrose

polychrome (ˈpɒlɪkrəʊm) *a.* **1.** having various colours —*n.* **2.** work of art in many colours —**polychroˈmatic** *a.*

polyester (pɒlɪˈɛstə) *n.* any of large class of synthetic materials used as plastics, textile fibres *etc.*

polygamy (pəˈlɪgəmɪ) *n.* custom of being married to several persons at same time —**poˈlygamist** *n.*

polyglot (ˈpɒlɪglɒt) *a.* speaking, writing in several languages

polygon (ˈpɒlɪgɒn) *n.* figure with many angles or sides —**poˈlygonal** *a.*

polygraph (ˈpɒlɪgrɑːf, -græf) *n.* **1.** instrument for recording pulse rate and perspiration, used *esp.* as lie detector **2.** device for producing copies of written matter

polygyny (pəˈlɪdʒənɪ) *n.* polygamy in which man has more than one wife

polyhedron (pɒlɪˈhiːdrən) *n.* solid figure contained by many faces (*pl.* **-s, -dra** (-drə))

polymath (ˈpɒlɪmæθ) *n.* person of great and varied learning

polymer (ˈpɒlɪmə) *n.* compound, as polystyrene, that has large molecules formed from repeated units —**polyˈmeric** *a.* of polymer —**polymeriˈzation** *or* **-iˈsation** *n.* —**ˈpolymerize** *or* **-ise** *v.*

polymorphous (pɒlɪˈmɔːfəs) *or* **polymorphic** *a.* **1.** having, taking or passing through many different forms or stages **2.** exhibiting or undergoing polymorphism

Polynesian (pɒlɪˈniːʒən, -ʒɪən) *a.* **1.** of Polynesia, group of Pacific islands, its people or any of their languages —*n.* **2.** member of people of Polynesia, generally of Caucasoid features with light skin and wavy hair **3.** branch of Malayo-Polynesian family of languages, including Maori and Hawaiian

polynomial (pɒlɪˈnəʊmɪəl) *a.* **1.** of two or more names or terms —*n.* **2.** mathematical expression consisting of sum of terms each of which is product of constant and one or more variables raised to positive or zero integral power **3.** mathematical expression consisting of sum of a number of terms (*also* **multiˈnomial**)

polyp (ˈpɒlɪp) *n.* **1.** sea anemone or allied animal **2.** tumour with branched roots (*also* **ˈpolypus**)

polyphase (ˈpɒlɪfeɪz) *a.* (of alternating current of electricity) possessing number of regular sets of alternations

THESAURUS

finesse, finish, grace, politesse, refinement, style, suavity, urbanity

polite 1. affable, civil, complaisant, courteous, deferential, gracious, mannerly, obliging, respectful, well-behaved, well-mannered **2.** civilized, courtly, cultured, elegant, genteel, polished, refined, urbane, well-bred

politic 1. artful, astute, canny, crafty, cunning, designing, ingenious, intriguing, Machiavellian, scheming, shrewd, sly, subtle, unscrupulous **2.** advisable, diplomatic, discreet, expedient, in one's best interests, judicious, prudent, sagacious, sensible, tactful, wise

politician legislator, Member of Parliament, M.P., office bearer, politico (*Inf., chiefly U.S.*), public servant, statesman

politics affairs of state, civics, government, government policy, political science, polity, statecraft, statesmanship

poll *n.* **1.** figures, returns, tally, vote, voting **2.** ballot, canvass, census, count, Gallup Poll, (public) opinion poll, sampling, survey ~*v.* **3.** register, tally **4.** ballot, canvass, interview, question, sample, survey

pollute 1. adulterate, befoul, contaminate, dirty, foul, infect, make filthy, mar, poison, soil, spoil, stain, taint **2.** besmirch, corrupt, debase, debauch, defile, deprave, desecrate, dishonour, profane, sully, violate

pollution adulteration, contamination, corruption, defilement, dirtying, foulness, impurity, taint, uncleanness, vitiation

polyphony (pəˈlɪfənɪ) *n.* polyphonic style of composition or piece of music utilizing it **—polyˈphonic** *a.* **1.** *Mus.* composed of relatively independent parts; contrapuntal **2.** many-voiced

polystyrene (pɒlɪˈstaɪriːn) *n.* synthetic material used *esp.* as white rigid foam for packing *etc.*

polytechnic (pɒlɪˈtɛknɪk) *n.* **1.** college dealing mainly with various arts and crafts *—a.* **2.** of or relating to technical instruction

polytheism (ˈpɒlɪθiːɪzəm, pɒlɪˈθiːɪzəm) *n.* belief in many gods **—ˈpolytheist** *n.*

polythene (ˈpɒlɪθiːn) *n.* tough thermoplastic material

polyunsaturated (pɒlɪʌnˈsætʃʊreɪtɪd) *a.* of group of fats that do not form cholesterol in blood

polyurethane (pɒlɪˈjʊərəθeɪn) *n.* class of synthetic materials, oft. in foam or flexible form

polyvalent (pɒlɪˈveɪlənt, pəˈlɪvələnt) *a.* having more than one valency

pomace (ˈpʌmɪs) *n.* **1.** pulpy residue of apples or similar fruit after crushing and pressing, as in cider-making **2.** any pulpy substance left after crushing *etc.*

pomade (pəˈmɑːd) *n.* **1.** perfumed oil or ointment applied to hair, to make it smooth and shiny *—vt.* **2.** put pomade on

pomander (pəʊˈmændə) *n.* (container for) mixture of sweet-smelling herbs *etc.*

pomegranate (ˈpɒmɪgrænɪt, ˈpɒmgrænɪt) *n.* **1.** tree cultivated for its edible fruit **2.** its fruit with thick rind containing many seeds in red pulp

Pomeranian (pɒməˈreɪnɪən) *n.* breed of small dog

pomfret *or* **pomfret-cake** (ˈpʌmfrɪt, ˈpɒm-) *n.* small black rounded confection of liquorice (*also* **Pontefract cake**)

pommel (ˈpʌməl, ˈpɒm-) *n.* **1.** front of saddle **2.** knob of sword hilt *—vt.* **3.** *see* PUMMEL

pommy (ˈpɒmɪ) *n.* (*sometimes* **P-**) **A, NZ** *sl.* British person (*also* **pom**)

pomp (pɒmp) *n.* splendid display or ceremony

pompon (ˈpɒmpɒn) *or* **pompom** (ˈpɒmpɒm) *n.* tuft of ribbon, wool, feathers *etc.* decorating hat, shoe *etc.*

pompous (ˈpɒmpəs) *a.* **1.** self-important **2.** ostentatious **3.** (of language) inflated, stilted **—pomˈposity** *n.*

ponce (pɒns) *n. sl.* **1.** effeminate man **2.** pimp

poncho (ˈpɒntʃəʊ) *n.* loose circular cloak with hole for head (*pl.* **-s**)

pond (pɒnd) *n.* small body, pool or lake of still water

ponder (ˈpɒndə) *v.* **1.** muse, meditate, think over **2.** consider, deliberate (on)

ponderous (ˈpɒndərəs) *a.* **1.** heavy, unwieldy **2.** boring

pong (pɒŋ) *inf. n.* **1.** strong (unpleasant) smell *—vi.* **2.** stink

pontiff (ˈpɒntɪf) *n.* **1.** Pope **2.** high priest **3.** bishop **—ponˈtifical** *a.* **—pontificate** (pɒnˈtɪfɪkɪt) *n.* **1.** dignity or office of pontiff *—vi.* (pɒnˈtɪfɪkeɪt) **2.** speak bombastically (*also* **ˈpontify**) **3.** act as pontiff

pontoon[1] (pɒnˈtuːn) *n.* flat-bottomed boat or metal drum for use in supporting temporary bridge

pontoon[2] (pɒnˈtuːn) *n.* gambling card game (*also* **twenty-one**)

pony (ˈpəʊnɪ) *n.* **1.** horse of small breed **2.** very small glass, *esp.* for liqueurs **—ˈponytail** *n.* long hair tied in one bunch at back of head **—pony trekking** act of riding ponies cross-country, *esp.* as pastime

poodle (ˈpuːdᵊl) *n.* pet dog with long curly hair oft. clipped fancifully

poof (pʊf, puːf) *or* **poove** (puːv) *n. sl.* homosexual man

pooh (puː) *interj.* exclamation of disdain, contempt or disgust **—pooh-pooh** *vt.* express disdain or scorn for; dismiss, belittle

Pooh-Bah (ˈpuːˈbɑː) *n.* pompous official

pool[1] (puːl) *n.* **1.** small body of still water **2.** deep place in river or stream **3.** puddle **4.** swimming pool

pool[2] (puːl) *n.* **1.** common fund or resources **2.** group of people, *eg* typists, any of whom can work for any of several employers **3.** collective stakes in various games **4.** cartel **5.** variety of billiards *—pl.* **6.** *see* **football pools** *at* FOOT *—vt.* **7.** put in common fund

poop (puːp) *n.* ship's stern

poor (pʊə, pɔː) *a.* **1.** having little money **2.** unproductive **3.** inadequate, insignificant **4.** needy **5.** miserable, pitiable **6.** feeble **7.** not fertile **—ˈpoorly** *adv.* **1.** badly *—a.* **2.** *inf.* not in good health **—ˈpoorness** *n.* **—poor box** box, *esp.* in church, used for collection of alms or money for poor **—ˈpoorhouse** *n.* formerly, publicly maintained institution offering accommodation to the poor

THESAURUS

pomp ceremony, flourish, grandeur, magnificence, pageant, pageantry, parade, solemnity, splendour, state

pompous **1.** affected, arrogant, bloated, grandiose, imperious, magisterial, ostentatious, overbearing, pontifical, portentous, pretentious, puffed up, self-important, showy, supercilious, vainglorious **2.** boastful, bombastic, flatulent, fustian, grandiloquent, high-flown, inflated, magniloquent, orotund, overblown, turgid, windy

pond dew pond, duck pond, fish pond, lochan (*Scot.*), millpond, pool, small lake, tarn

ponder brood, cerebrate, cogitate, consider, contemplate, deliberate, examine, excogitate, give thought to, meditate, mull over, muse, puzzle over, reflect, ruminate, study, think, weigh

ponderous **1.** bulky, cumbersome, cumbrous, heavy, hefty, huge, massive, unwieldy, weighty **2.** dreary, dull, heavy, laboured, lifeless, long-winded, pedantic, pedestrian, plodding, prolix, stilted, stodgy, tedious, verbose

pontificate declaim, dogmatize, expound, hold forth, lay down the law, pontify, preach, pronounce, sound off

pooh-pooh belittle, brush aside, deride, disdain, dismiss, disregard, make little of, play down, scoff, scorn, slight, sneer, sniff at, spurn, turn up one's nose at (*Inf.*)

pool[1] **1.** lake, mere, pond, puddle, splash, tarn **2.** swimming bath, swimming pool

pool[2] *n.* **1.** collective, combine, consortium, group, syndicate, team, trust **2.** bank, funds, jackpot, kitty, pot, stakes ~*v.* **3.** amalgamate, combine, join forces, league, merge, put together, share

poor **1.** badly off, broke (*Inf.*), destitute, hard up (*Inf.*), impecunious, impoverished, indigent, in need, in want, necessitous, needy, on one's beam-ends, on one's uppers, on the rocks, penniless, penurious,

poort (pʊət) *n.* **SA** narrow mountain pass

pop[1] (pɒp) *vi.* **1.** make small explosive sound **2.** *inf.* go or come unexpectedly or suddenly —*vt.* **3.** cause to make small explosive sound **4.** put or place suddenly (**-pp-**) —*n.* **5.** small explosive sound **6.** *inf.* nonalcoholic fizzy drink —ˈ**popper** *n.* **1.** person or thing that pops **2.** **UK** *inf.* press stud **3.** *chiefly* **US** container for cooking popcorn in —ˈ**popcorn** *n.* **1.** any kind of maize that puffs up when roasted **2.** the roasted product —ˈ**popgun** *n.* toy gun that fires pellet or cork by means of compressed air

pop[2] (pɒp) *n. inf.* **1.** father **2.** old man

pop[3] (pɒp) *n.* **1.** music of general appeal, *esp.* to young people —*a. inf.* **2.** popular

pop. **1.** popular **2.** population

P.O.P. Post Office Preferred (size of envelopes *etc.*)

pope (pəʊp) *n.* (*oft.* **P-**) bishop of Rome and head of R.C. Church —ˈ**popery** *n. offens.* papal system, doctrines —ˈ**popish** *a. derogatory* belonging to or characteristic of Roman Catholicism

popeyed (ˈpɒpaɪd) *a.* **1.** having bulging, prominent eyes **2.** staring in astonishment

popinjay (ˈpɒpɪndʒeɪ) *n.* **1.** conceited or talkative person **2.** *obs.* parrot

poplar (ˈpɒplə) *n.* tree noted for its slender tallness

poplin (ˈpɒplɪn) *n.* corded fabric *usu.* of cotton

poppadom *or* **poppadum** (ˈpɒpədəm) *n.* thin, round, crisp Indian bread

poppet (ˈpɒpɪt) *n.* **1.** term of affection for small child or sweetheart **2.** mushroom-shaped valve lifted from seating by applying axial force to stem (*also* **poppet valve**) **3.** *Naut.* temporary supporting brace for vessel hauled on land

poppy (ˈpɒpɪ) *n.* bright-flowered plant yielding opium —**Poppy Day** *inf.* Remembrance Sunday

poppycock (ˈpɒpɪkɒk) *n. inf.* nonsense

popsy (ˈpɒpsɪ) *n. old-fashioned* **UK** *sl.* attractive young woman

populace (ˈpɒpjʊləs) *n.* (*sometimes with pl. v.*) the common people, the masses

popular (ˈpɒpjʊlə) *a.* **1.** finding general favour **2.** of, by the people —**popuˈlarity** *n.* state or quality of being generally liked —**populariˈzation** *or* **-iˈsation** *n.* —ˈ**popularize** *or* **-ise** *vt.* make popular —ˈ**popularly** *adv.* —**popular front** (*oft.* **P- F-**) left-wing group or party that opposes spread of fascism

populate (ˈpɒpjʊleɪt) *vt.* fill with inhabitants —**popuˈlation** *n.* **1.** inhabitants **2.** the number of such inhabitants —ˈ**populous** *a.* thickly populated or inhabited

porbeagle (ˈpɔːbiːgᵊl) *n.* any of several sharks of northern seas (*also* **mackerel shark**)

porcelain (ˈpɔːslɪn) *n.* fine earthenware, china —**porcelain clay** kaolin

porch (pɔːtʃ) *n.* covered approach to entrance of building

porcine (ˈpɔːsaɪn) *a.* of, like pigs

porcupine (ˈpɔːkjʊpaɪn) *n.* any of various rodents covered with long, pointed quills

pore[1] (pɔː) *vi.* **1.** fix eye or mind **2.** (*with* over) study closely

pore[2] (pɔː) *n.* minute opening, *esp.* in skin —**poˈrosity** *n.* —ˈ**porous** *a.* **1.** allowing liquid to soak through **2.** full of pores

pork (pɔːk) *n.* pig's flesh used as food —ˈ**porker** *n.* pig raised for food —ˈ**porky** *a.* fleshy, fat —**porkpie hat** hat with round flat crown and brim that can be turned up or down

THESAURUS

poverty-stricken, skint (*Brit. sl.*), stony-broke (*Brit. sl.*) **2.** deficient, exiguous, inadequate, incomplete, insufficient, lacking, meagre, miserable, niggardly, pitiable, reduced, scanty, skimpy, slight, sparse, straitened **3.** below par, faulty, feeble, inferior, low-grade, mediocre, rotten (*Inf.*), rubbishy, second-rate, shabby, shoddy, sorry, substandard, unsatisfactory, valueless, weak, worthless **4.** bad, bare, barren, depleted, exhausted, fruitless, impoverished, infertile, sterile, unfruitful, unproductive **5.** hapless, ill-fated, luckless, miserable, pathetic, pitiable, unfortunate, unhappy, unlucky, wretched

poorly **1.** *adv.* badly, crudely, inadequately, incompetently, inexpertly, inferiorly, insufficiently, meanly, shabbily, unsatisfactorily, unsuccessfully **2.** *adj. Inf.* ailing, below par, ill, indisposed, off colour, out of sorts, rotten (*Inf.*), seedy (*Inf.*), sick, under the weather (*Inf.*), unwell

pop *v.* **1.** bang, burst, crack, explode, go off, report, snap **2.** *Often with* **in, out,** *etc. Inf.* appear, call, come *or* go suddenly, drop in (*Inf.*), leave quickly, nip in (*Brit. inf.*), nip out (*Brit. inf.*), visit **3.** insert, push, put, shove, slip, stick, thrust, tuck ~*n.* **4.** bang, burst, crack, explosion, noise, report **5.** *Inf.* fizzy drink, lemonade, soda water, soft drink

pope Bishop of Rome, Holy Father, pontiff, Vicar of Christ

populace commonalty, crowd, general public, hoi polloi, inhabitants, masses, mob, multitude, people, rabble, throng

popular **1.** accepted, approved, celebrated, famous, fashionable, favoured, favourite, in, in demand, in favour, liked, sought-after, well-liked **2.** common, conventional, current, general, prevailing, prevalent, public, standard, stock, ubiquitous, universal, widespread

popularity acceptance, acclaim, adoration, approval, celebrity, currency, esteem, fame, favour, idolization, lionization, recognition, regard, renown, reputation, repute, vogue

popularize disseminate, familiarize, give currency to, give mass appeal, make available to all, simplify, spread, universalize

popularly commonly, conventionally, customarily, generally, ordinarily, regularly, traditionally, universally, usually, widely

populate colonize, inhabit, live in, occupy, people, settle

population citizenry, community, denizens, folk, inhabitants, natives, people, populace, residents, society

populous crowded, heavily populated, overpopulated, packed, populated, swarming, teeming, thronged

pore[1] *v.* brood, contemplate, dwell on, examine, go over, peruse, ponder, read, scrutinize, study

pore[2] *n.* hole, opening, orifice, outlet, stoma

pornographic blue, dirty, filthy, indecent, lewd, obscene, offensive, prurient, salacious, smutty

porn (pɔːn) *or* **porno** *n. inf.* pornography

pornography (pɔːˈnɒgrəfɪ) *n.* indecent literature, films *etc.* —**porˈnographer** *n.* —**pornoˈgraphic** *a.* —**pornoˈgraphically** *adv.*

porphyry (ˈpɔːfɪrɪ) *n.* reddish stone with embedded crystals

porpoise (ˈpɔːpəs) *n.* blunt-nosed sea mammal like dolphin (*pl.* **-poise, -s**)

porridge (ˈpɒrɪdʒ) *n.* **1.** soft food of oatmeal *etc.* boiled in water **2.** *sl.* imprisonment

porringer (ˈpɒrɪndʒə) *n.* small dish, oft. with handle, for soup, porridge *etc.*

port[1] (pɔːt) *n.* **1.** harbour, haven **2.** town with harbour

port[2] (pɔːt) *n.* **1.** left side of ship or aircraft (*also* (*formerly*) **ˈlarboard**) —*v.* **2.** turn to left side of ship

port[3] (pɔːt) *n.* strong red wine

port[4] (pɔːt) *n.* opening in side of ship —**ˈporthole** *n.* small opening or window in side of ship

port[5] (pɔːt) *Mil. vt.* **1.** carry (rifle *etc.*) diagonally across body —*n.* **2.** this position

Port. **1.** Portugal **2.** Portuguese

portable (ˈpɔːtəbᵊl) *n./a.* (something) easily carried

portage (ˈpɔːtɪdʒ) *n.* (cost of) transport

portal (ˈpɔːtᵊl) *n.* large doorway or imposing gate

portcullis (pɔːtˈkʌlɪs) *n.* defence grating to raise or lower in front of castle gateway

portend (pɔːˈtɛnd) *vt.* foretell, be an omen of —**ˈportent** *n.* **1.** omen, warning **2.** marvel —**porˈtentous** *a.* **1.** ominous, threatening **2.** pompous

porter[1] (ˈpɔːtə) *n.* **1.** person employed to carry burden, *eg* on railway **2.** doorkeeper —**ˈporterage** *n.* (charge for) carrying of supplies

porter[2] (ˈpɔːtə) *n.* **UK** dark sweet ale brewed from black malt —**ˈporterhouse** *n.* thick choice steak of beef cut from middle ribs or sirloin (*also* **porterhouse steak**)

portfolio (pɔːtˈfəʊlɪəʊ) *n.* **1.** flat portable case for loose papers **2.** office of minister of state (*pl.* **-s**)

portico (ˈpɔːtɪkəʊ) *n.* **1.** colonnade **2.** covered walk (*pl.* **-es, -s**)

portière (pɔːtɪˈɛə; *Fr.* pɔrˈtjɛːr) *n.* curtain hung in doorway

portion (ˈpɔːʃən) *n.* **1.** part **2.** share **3.** helping **4.** destiny, lot —*vt.* **5.** divide into shares —**ˈportionless** *a.*

portly (ˈpɔːtlɪ) *a.* bulky, stout

portmanteau (pɔːtˈmæntəʊ) *n.* leather suitcase, *esp.* one opening into two compartments (*pl.* **-s, -teaux** (-təʊz)) —**portmanteau word** word formed by joining together beginning and end of two other words (*also* **blend**)

portray (pɔːˈtreɪ) *vt.* make pictures of, describe —**portrait** (ˈpɔːtrɪt, -treɪt) *n.* likeness of (face of) individual —**portraiture** (ˈpɔːtrɪtʃə) *n.* —**porˈtrayal** *n.* act of portraying

Portuguese (pɔːtjʊˈgiːz) *a.* pert. to Portugal or its inhabitants —**Portuguese man-of-war** kind of jellyfish

pose (pəʊz) *vt.* **1.** place in attitude **2.** put forward —*vi.* **3.** assume attitude, affect or pretend to be a certain character —*n.* **4.** attitude, *esp.* one assumed for effect —**ˈposer** *n.* one who poses —**poseur** (pəʊˈzɜː) *n.* one who assumes affected attitude to create impression

poser (ˈpəʊzə) *n.* puzzling question

posh (pɒʃ) *a. inf.* **1.** smart, elegant, stylish **2.** upper-class or genteel

posit (ˈpɒzɪt) *vt.* lay down as principle

position (pəˈzɪʃən) *n.* **1.** place **2.** situation **3.** location, attitude **4.** status **5.** state of affairs **6.** employment **7.** strategic point **8.** *Mus.* vertical spacing or layout of written notes in chord —*vt.* **9.** place in position

THESAURUS

pornography dirt, erotica, filth, indecency, obscenity, porn (*Inf.*), porno (*Inf.*), smut

porous absorbent, absorptive, penetrable, permeable, pervious, spongy

port *Nautical* anchorage, harbour, haven, roads, roadstead, seaport

portable compact, convenient, easily carried, handy, light, lightweight, manageable, movable, portative

portend adumbrate, augur, bespeak, betoken, bode, foreshadow, foretell, foretoken, forewarn, harbinger, herald, indicate, omen, point to, predict, presage, prognosticate, promise, threaten, warn of

portent augury, foreboding, foreshadowing, forewarning, harbinger, indication, omen, premonition, presage, presentiment, prognostic, prognostication, sign, threat, warning

portentous **1.** alarming, crucial, fateful, important, menacing, minatory, momentous, ominous, significant, sinister, threatening **2.** bloated, elephantine, heavy, pompous, ponderous, pontifical, self-important, solemn

porter **1.** baggage attendant, bearer, carrier **2.** caretaker, concierge, doorkeeper, doorman, gatekeeper, janitor

portion *n.* **1.** bit, fraction, fragment, morsel, part, piece, scrap, section, segment **2.** allocation, allotment, allowance, division, lot, measure, parcel, quantity, quota, ration, share **3.** helping, piece, serving **4.** cup, destiny, fate, fortune, lot, luck ~*v.* **5.** allocate, allot, apportion, assign, deal, distribute, divide, divvy up (*Inf.*), dole out, parcel out, partition, share out

portrait image, likeness, painting, photograph, picture, portraiture, representation, sketch

portray **1.** delineate, depict, draw, figure, illustrate, limn, paint, picture, render, represent, sketch **2.** characterize, depict, describe, paint a mental picture of, put in words

portrayal characterization, delineation, depiction, description, interpretation, picture, rendering, representation

pose *v.* **1.** arrange, model, position, sit, sit for **2.** *Often with* **as** feign, impersonate, masquerade as, pass oneself off as, pretend to be, profess to be, sham **3.** affect, attitudinize, posture, put on airs, show off (*Inf.*), strike an attitude **4.** advance, posit, present, propound, put, put forward, set, state, submit ~*n.* **5.** attitude, bearing, mien (*Literary*), position, posture, stance **6.** act, affectation, air, attitudinizing, façade, front, mannerism, masquerade, posturing, pretence, role

poser brain-teaser (*Inf.*), conundrum, enigma, knotty point, problem, puzzle, question, riddle, tough one, vexed question

position *n.* **1.** area, bearings, locale, locality, location, place, point, post, reference, site, situation, spot, station, whereabouts **2.** arrangement, attitude, disposition, pose, posture, stance **3.** angle, attitude,

positive (ˈpɒzɪtɪv) *a.* **1.** certain, sure **2.** definite, absolute, unquestionable **3.** utter, downright **4.** confident **5.** not negative **6.** greater than zero **7.** *Elec.* having deficiency of electrons —*n.* **8.** something positive **9.** *Photog.* print in which lights and shadows are not reversed —**ˈpositively** *adv.* —**ˈpositivism** *n.* philosophy recognizing only matters of fact and experience —**ˈpositivist** *a./n.* (one) believing in this —**positive discrimination** provision of special opportunities for disadvantaged group —**positive feedback** *see* **feedback** (sense 1) *at* FEED

positron (ˈpɒzɪtrɒn) *n.* positive electron

poss. 1. possession 2. possessive 3. possible 4. possibly

posse (ˈpɒsɪ) *n.* **1.** US body of men, *esp.* for maintaining law and order **2.** C group of trained horsemen who perform at rodeos

possess (pəˈzɛs) *vt.* **1.** own **2.** (of evil spirit *etc.*) have mastery of —**posˈsession** *n.* **1.** act of possessing **2.** thing possessed **3.** ownership —**posˈsessive** *a.* **1.** of, indicating possession **2.** with excessive desire to possess, control —*n.* **3.** possessive case in grammar

possible (ˈpɒsɪbˀl) *a.* **1.** that can, or may, be, exist, happen or be done **2.** worthy of consideration —*n.* **3.** possible candidate —**possiˈbility** *n.* —**ˈpossibly** *adv.* perhaps

possum (ˈpɒsəm) *n. see* OPOSSUM —**play possum** pretend to be dead, asleep *etc.* to deceive opponent

post[1] (pəʊst) *n.* **1.** upright pole of timber or metal fixed firmly, usu. to support or mark something —*vt.* **2.** display **3.** put up (notice *etc.*) on wall *etc.* —**ˈposter** *n.* **1.** large advertising bill **2.** one who posts bills —**poster paints** *or* **colours** lustreless paints used for writing posters *etc.*

post[2] (pəʊst) *n.* **1.** official carrying of letters or parcels **2.** collection or delivery of these **3.** office **4.** situation **5.** point, station, place of duty **6.** place where soldier is stationed **7.** place held by body of troops **8.** fort —*vt.* **9.** put into official box for carriage by post **10.** supply with latest information **11.** station (soldiers *etc.*) in particular spot **12.** transfer (entries) to ledger —*adv.* **13.** in haste —**ˈpostage** *n.* charge for delivering letters or parcels —**ˈpostal** *a.* —**postage stamp 1.** printed paper label with gummed back for attaching to mail as official indication that required postage has been paid **2.** mark printed on envelope *etc.* serving same function —**postal order** written order, available at post office, for payment of sum of money —**ˈpostbag** *n.* **1.** *chiefly* UK mailbag **2.** mail received by magazine, radio programme *etc.* —**ˈpostbox** *n. chiefly* UK box into which mail is put for collection —**ˈpostcard** *n.* stamped card sent by post —**ˈpostcode** *or* **postal code** *n.* system of letters and numbers used to aid sorting of mail —**post-free** *adv./a.* **1.** UK with postage prepaid; postpaid **2.** free of postal charge —**ˈpostman** *n.* man who collects or delivers post —**postman's knock** parlour game involving exchange of kisses —**ˈpostmark** *n.* official mark with name of office *etc.* stamped on letters —**ˈpostmaster** *or* **ˈpostmistress** *n.* official in charge of post office —**postmaster general** executive head of postal service in certain countries (*pl.* **postmasters general**) —**post office** place where postal business is conducted —**ˈpostˈpaid** *adv./a.* with postage prepaid

post- (*comb. form*) after, behind, later than, as in *postwar.* Such compounds are not given here where the meaning can easily be found from the simple word

postdate (pəʊstˈdeɪt) *vt.* assign date to (event *etc.*) that is later than actual date

THESAURUS

belief, opinion, outlook, point of view, slant, stance, stand, standpoint, view, viewpoint **4.** circumstances, condition, pass, plight, predicament, situation, state, state of affairs, strait(s) **5.** caste, class, consequence, importance, place, prestige, rank, reputation, standing, station, stature, status **6.** berth (*Inf.*), billet (*Inf.*), capacity, duty, employment, function, job, occupation, office, place, post, role, situation ~*v.* **7.** arrange, array, dispose, fix, lay out, locate, place, put, set, settle, stand, stick (*Inf.*)

positive 1. absolute, actual, affirmative, categorical, certain, clear, clear-cut, conclusive, concrete, decisive, definite, direct, explicit, express, firm, incontrovertible, indisputable, real, unequivocal, unmistakable, unquestionable **2.** assured, certain, confident, convinced, sure **3.** assertive, cocksure, confident, decided, dogmatic, emphatic, firm, forceful, opinionated, peremptory, resolute, stubborn **4.** beneficial, constructive, effective, efficacious, forward-looking, helpful, practical, productive, progressive, useful **5.** *Inf.* absolute, complete, consummate, out-and-out, perfect, rank, thorough, thoroughgoing, unmitigated, utter

positively absolutely, assuredly, categorically, certainly, definitely, emphatically, firmly, surely, undeniably, unequivocally, unmistakably, unquestionably, with certainty, without qualification

possess 1. be blessed with, be born with, be endowed with, enjoy, have, have to one's name, hold, own **2.** acquire, control, dominate, hold, occupy, seize, take over, take possession of **3.** bewitch, consume, control, dominate, enchant, fixate, influence, mesmerize, obsess, put under a spell

possession 1. control, custody, hold, occupancy, occupation, ownership, proprietorship, tenure, title **2.** *Plural* assets, belongings, chattels, effects, estate, goods and chattels, property, things, wealth

possessive acquisitive, controlling, covetous, dominating, domineering, grasping, jealous, overprotective, selfish

possibility 1. feasibility, likelihood, plausibility, potentiality, practicability, workableness **2.** chance, hazard, hope, liability, likelihood, odds, probability, prospect, risk

possible 1. conceivable, credible, hypothetical, imaginable, likely, potential **2.** attainable, doable, feasible, on (*Inf.*), practicable, realizable, viable, within reach, workable

possibly God willing, haply (*Archaic*), maybe, mayhap (*Archaic*), peradventure (*Archaic*), perchance (*Archaic*), perhaps

post[1] **1.** *n.* column, newel, pale, palisade, picket, pillar pole, shaft, stake, standard, stock, support, upright **2.** *v.* advertise, affix, announce, display, make known, pin up, proclaim, promulgate, publicize, publish, put up, stick up

post[2] *n.* **1.** appointment, assignment, berth (*Inf.*), billet (*Inf.*), employment, job, office, place, position, situation **2.** beat, place, position, station ~*v.* **3.** assign, establish, locate, place, position, put, situate, station ~*n.* **4.** collection, delivery, mail, postal ser-

poste restante (ˈpəʊst rɪˈstænt) *Fr.* department of post office where travellers' letters are kept till called for

posterior (pɒˈstɪərɪə) *a.* **1.** later **2.** hinder —*n.* **3.** the buttocks

posterity (pɒˈstɛrɪtɪ) *n.* **1.** later generations **2.** descendants

postern (ˈpɒstən) *n.* **1.** private entrance **2.** small door, gate

postgraduate (pəʊstˈgrædjʊɪt) *a.* **1.** carried on after graduation —*n.* **2.** student taking course of study after graduation

posthaste (ˈpəʊstˈheɪst) *adv.* **1.** with great haste —*n.* **2.** *obs.* great haste

posthumous (ˈpɒstjʊməs) *a.* **1.** occurring after death **2.** born after father's death **3.** (of book etc.) published after author's death —**ˈposthumously** *adv.*

posthypnotic suggestion (pəʊsthɪpˈnɒtɪk) suggestion made to subject while in hypnotic trance, to be acted upon some time after emerging from trance

postilion *or* **postillion** (pɒˈstɪljən) *n. Hist.* man riding one of pair of horses drawing a carriage

postimpressionism (pəʊstɪmˈprɛʃənɪzəm) *n.* movement in painting at end of 19th cent. which rejected naturalism and momentary effects of impressionism but adapted its use of pure colour to paint subjects with greater subjective emotion —**postimˈpressionist** *n./a.*

post meridiem (məˈrɪdɪəm) *see* P.M.

postmortem (pəʊstˈmɔːtəm) *n.* **1.** analysis of recent event —*a.* **2.** taking place after death —**postmortem examination** medical examination of dead body

postnatal (pəʊstˈneɪtˀl) *a.* after birth

post-obit (pəʊstˈəʊbɪt, -ˈɒbɪt) *a.* taking effect after death

postoperative (pəʊstˈɒpərətɪv) *a.* of period following surgical operation

postpone (pəʊstˈpəʊn, pəˈspəʊn) *vt.* put off to later time, defer —**postˈponement** *n.*

postprandial (pəʊstˈprændɪəl) *a.* after-dinner

postscript (ˈpəʊsskrɪpt) *n.* **1.** note added at end of letter, after signature **2.** supplement added to book, document *etc.*

postulant (ˈpɒstjʊlənt) *n.* candidate for admission to religious order

postulate (ˈpɒstjʊleɪt) *vt.* **1.** take for granted **2.** lay down as self-evident **3.** stipulate —*n.* (ˈpɒstjʊlɪt) **4.** proposition assumed without proof **5.** prerequisite —**postuˈlation** *n.*

posture (ˈpɒstʃə) *n.* **1.** attitude, position of body —*vi.* **2.** pose

posy (ˈpəʊzɪ) *n.* bunch of flowers

pot (pɒt) *n.* **1.** round vessel **2.** cooking vessel **3.** trap, *esp.* for crabs, lobsters **4.** *sl.* cannabis —*pl.* **5.** *inf.* a lot —*vt.* **6.** put into, preserve in pot (-tt-) —**ˈpotted** *a.* **1.** preserved in a pot **2.** *inf.* abridged —**ˈpotbellied** *a.* —**ˈpotbelly** *n.* **1.** protruding belly **2.** one having such a belly —**ˈpotboiler** *n. inf.* artistic work of little merit produced quickly to make money —**pot-bound** *a.* (of pot plant) having grown to fill all available root space and lacking room for continued growth —**ˈpotherb** *n.* any plant having leaves, stems *etc.* that are used in cooking —**ˈpothole** *n.* **1.** pitlike cavity in rocks, usu. limestone, produced by faulting and water action **2.** hole worn in road —**ˈpotholer** *n.* —**ˈpotholing** *n.* **UK** sport in which participants explore underground caves —**ˈpothook** *n.* **1.** S-shaped hook for suspending pot over fire **2.** long hook for lifting hot pots *etc.* **3.** S-shaped mark, oft. made by children when learning to write —**ˈpothunter** *n.* **1.** person who hunts for profit without regard to rules of sport **2.** *inf.* person who enters competitions for sole purpose of winning prizes —**ˈpotˈluck** *n.* **1.** whatever food is available without special preparation **2.** choice dictated by lack of alternative (*esp. in* **take potluck**) —**pot plant** plant grown in flowerpot —**pot roast** meat cooked slowly in covered pot with little water —**ˈpotsherd** *n.* broken fragment of pottery —**pot shot** easy or random shot —**potter's wheel** device with horizontal rotating disc, on which clay is moulded by hand —**potting shed** building in which plants are grown in flowerpots before being planted outside —**the Potteries** region of W central England in which china industries are concentrated

potable (ˈpəʊtəbˀl) *a.* drinkable

potage (pɔˈtaːʒ; *English* pəʊˈtɑːʒ) *Fr.* thick soup

potash (ˈpɒtæʃ) *n.* **1.** alkali used in soap *etc.* **2.** crude potassium carbonate

potassium (pəˈtæsɪəm) *n.* white metallic element —**potassium nitrate** crystalline compound used in gunpowders, fertilizers and as preservative (*also* **saltˈpetre, ˈnitre**)

potato (pəˈteɪtəʊ) *n.* plant with tubers grown for food (*pl.* **-es**) —**potato crisp** *see* CRISP (sense 6) —**sweet potato 1.** trailing plant **2.** its edible sweetish tubers

poteen (pɒˈtiːn) *n.* in Ireland, illicitly distilled alcoholic liquor

THESAURUS

vice ~*v.* **5.** dispatch, mail, send, transmit **6.** advise, brief, fill in on, inform, notify, report to

poster advertisement, *affiche*, announcement, bill, notice, placard, public notice, sticker

posterity 1. children, descendants, family, heirs, issue, offspring, progeny, scions, seed **2.** future, future generations, succeeding generations

postmortem *n.* analysis, autopsy, dissection, examination, necropsy

postpone adjourn, defer, delay, hold over, put back, put off, shelve, suspend, table

postponement adjournment, deferment, deferral, delay, moratorium, respite, stay, suspension

postscript addition, afterthought, afterword, appendix, P.S., supplement

postulate advance, assume, hypothesize, posit, predicate, presuppose, propose, put forward, suppose, take for granted, theorize

posture *n.* **1.** attitude, bearing, carriage, disposition, mien (*Literary*), pose, position, set, stance **2.** attitude, disposition, feeling, frame of mind, inclination, mood, outlook, point of view, stance, standpoint ~*v.* **3.** affect, attitudinize, do for effect, make a show, pose, put on airs, show off (*Inf.*), try to attract attention

potent 1. efficacious, forceful, mighty, powerful, puissant, strong, vigorous **2.** authoritative, commanding, dominant, dynamic, influential, powerful

potent (ˈpəʊtᵊnt) *a.* **1.** powerful, influential **2.** (of male) capable of sexual intercourse —ˈ**potency** *n.* **1.** physical or moral power **2.** efficacy

potentate (ˈpəʊtᵊnteɪt) *n.* ruler

potential (pəˈtɛnʃəl) *a.* **1.** latent, that may or might but does not now exist or act —*n.* **2.** possibility **3.** amount of potential energy **4.** *Elec.* level of electric pressure —**potentiˈality** *n.* —**potential difference** difference in electric potential between two points in electric field

pother (ˈpɒðə) *n.* **1.** commotion, fuss **2.** choking cloud of smoke *etc.*

potion (ˈpəʊʃən) *n.* dose of medicine or poison

potpourri (pəʊˈpʊərɪ) *n.* **1.** mixture of rose petals, spices *etc.* **2.** musical, literary medley (*pl.* **-s**)

pottage (ˈpɒtɪdʒ) *n.* thick soup containing vegetables and meat

potter[1] (ˈpɒtə) *n.* maker of earthenware vessels —ˈ**pottery** *n.* **1.** earthenware **2.** place where it is made **3.** art of making it

potter[2] (ˈpɒtə) *or esp. U.S.* **putter** (ˈpʌtə) *vi.* work, act in feeble, unsystematic way

potty (ˈpɒtɪ) *a. inf.* **1.** (of person) mad **2.** (of thing) silly, trivial

pouch (paʊtʃ) *n.* **1.** small bag **2.** *Anat.* any sac, pocket or pouchlike cavity —*vt.* **3.** put into pouch

pouf *or* **pouffe** (pu:f) *n.* large solid cushion

poultice (ˈpəʊltɪs) *n.* soft composition of mustard, kaolin *etc.*, applied hot to sore or inflamed parts of body

poultry (ˈpəʊltrɪ) *n.* domestic fowls collectively —ˈ**poulterer** *n.* dealer in poultry

pounce (paʊns) *vi.* **1.** spring suddenly, swoop —*n.* **2.** swoop or sudden descent

pound[1] (paʊnd) *vt.* **1.** beat, thump **2.** crush to pieces or powder —*vi.* **3.** walk, run heavily

pound[2] (paʊnd) *n.* **1.** unit of troy weight **2.** unit of avoirdupois weight equal to 0.454 kg **3.** monetary unit in U.K. —ˈ**poundage** *n.* **1.** charge of so much per pound of weight **2.** charge of so much per pound sterling **3.** weight expressed in pounds —**pound note** banknote valued at one pound sterling

pound[3] (paʊnd) *n.* **1.** enclosure for stray animals or officially removed vehicles **2.** confined space

poundal (ˈpaʊndᵊl) *n.* unit of force in the foot-pound-second system

pour (pɔ:) *vi.* **1.** come out in a stream, crowd *etc.* **2.** flow freely **3.** rain heavily —*vt.* **4.** give out thus **5.** cause to run out

pourboire (purˈbwa:r) *Fr.* tip; gratuity

pout[1] (paʊt) *v.* **1.** thrust out (lips) —*vi.* **2.** look sulky —*n.* **3.** act of pouting —ˈ**pouter** *n.* pigeon with power of inflating its crop

pout[2] (paʊt) *n.* type of food fish (*pl.* **pout, -s**)

poverty (ˈpɒvətɪ) *n.* **1.** state of being poor **2.** poorness **3.** lack of means **4.** scarcity —**poverty-stricken** *a.* suffering from extreme poverty —**poverty trap** situation of being unable to raise one's living standard because one is dependent on state benefits which are reduced if one gains any extra income

P.O.W. prisoner of war

powder (ˈpaʊdə) *n.* **1.** solid matter in fine dry particles **2.** medicine in this form **3.** gunpowder **4.** face powder *etc.* —*vt.* **5.** apply powder to **6.** reduce to powder; pulverize —ˈ**powdery** *a.* —**powder keg 1.** small barrel to hold gunpowder **2.** potential source of violence *etc.* —**powder puff** soft pad for applying cosmetic powder —**powder room** ladies' cloakroom

power (ˈpaʊə) *n.* **1.** ability to do or act **2.** strength **3.** authority **4.** control **5.** person or thing having authority **6.** mechanical energy **7.** electricity supply **8.** rate of doing work **9.** product from continuous multiplication of number by itself —ˈ**powered** *a.* having or operated by mechanical or electrical power —ˈ**powerful** *a.* —ˈ**powerless** *a.* —ˈ**powerhouse** *or* **power station** *n.* installation for generating and distributing electric power —**power point** socket on wall for plugging in electrical appliance —**power of attorney 1.** legal authority to act for another person in certain specified matters **2.** document conferring such authority

THESAURUS

potential 1. *adj.* budding, dormant, embryonic, future, hidden, inherent, latent, likely, possible, promising, undeveloped, unrealized **2.** *n.* ability, aptitude, capability, capacity, possibility, potentiality, power, the makings, what it takes (*Inf.*), wherewithal

potion brew, concoction, cup, dose, draught, elixir, mixture, philtre, tonic

potter dabble, fiddle (*Inf.*), footle (*Inf.*), fribble, fritter, mess about, poke along, tinker

pottery ceramics, earthenware, stoneware, terra cotta

pouch bag, container, pocket, poke (*Dialect*), purse, sack

pounce 1. *v.* ambush, attack, bound onto, dash at, drop, fall upon, jump, leap at, snatch, spring, strike, swoop, take by surprise, take unawares **2.** *n.* assault, attack, bound, jump, leap, spring, swoop

pound[1] **1.** batter, beat, belabour, clobber (*Sl.*), hammer, pelt, pummel, strike, thrash, thump **2.** bray (*Dialect*), bruise, comminute, crush, powder, pulverize, triturate **3.** clomp, march, stomp (*Inf.*), thunder, tramp **4.** beat, palpitate, pitapat, pulsate, pulse, throb

pound[2] *n.* compound, enclosure, pen, yard

pour 1. decant, let flow, spill, splash **2.** course, emit, flow, gush, run, rush, spew, spout, stream **3.** bucket down (*Inf.*), come down in torrents, rain, rain cats and dogs (*Inf.*), rain hard *or* heavily, sheet, teem **4.** crowd, stream, swarm, teem, throng

pout 1. *v.* glower, look petulant, look sullen, lower, make a *moue*, mope, pull a long face, purse one's lips, sulk, turn down the corners of one's mouth **2.** *n.* glower, long face, *moue*, sullen look

poverty 1. beggary, destitution, distress, hand-to-mouth existence, hardship, indigence, insolvency, necessitousness, necessity, need, pauperism, pennilessness, penury, privation, want **2.** dearth, deficiency, insufficiency, lack, paucity, scarcity, shortage **3.** aridity, bareness, barrenness, deficiency, infertility, meagreness, poorness, sterility, unfruitfulness

poverty-stricken bankrupt, beggared, broke (*Inf.*), destitute, distressed, impecunious, impoverished, indigent, needy, on one's beam-ends, on one's uppers, penniless, penurious, poor, skint (*Brit. sl.*), stony-broke (*Brit. sl.*)

powder *n.* **1.** dust, fine grains, loose particles, pounce, talc ~*v.* **2.** crush, granulate, grind, pestle,

powwow (ˈpaʊwaʊ) *n.* **1.** conference *—vi.* **2.** confer

pox (pɒks) *n.* **1.** one of several diseases marked by pustular eruptions of skin **2.** *inf.* syphilis

pp *or* **pp.** **1.** per procurationem (*Lat.*, by proxy; for and on behalf of) **2.** pianissimo

pp. pages

p.p. **1.** parcel post **2.** past participle **3.** prepaid **4.** post paid **5.** by delegation to **6.** on prescriptions, after meal

ppd. **1.** postpaid **2.** prepaid

P.P.S. **1.** parliamentary private secretary **2.** post postscriptum (*also* **p.p.s.**)

PQ Quebec

Pr *Chem.* praseodymium

pr. **1.** pair (*pl.* **prs.**) **2.** present **3.** price **4.** pronoun

P.R. **1.** proportional representation **2.** public relations

practical (ˈpræktɪkˀl) *a.* **1.** given to action rather than theory **2.** relating to action or real existence **3.** useful **4.** in effect though not in name **5.** virtual **—practicaˈbility** *n.* **—ˈpracticable** *a.* that can be done, used *etc.* **—ˈpractically** *adv.* **—pracˈtitioner** *n.* one engaged in a profession **—practical joke** trick usu. intended to make victim appear foolish

practice (ˈpræktɪs) *n.* **1.** habit **2.** mastery, skill **3.** exercise of art or profession **4.** action, not theory *—v.* **5.** US *see* PRACTISE

practise *or U.S.* **practice** (ˈpræktɪs) *vt.* **1.** do repeatedly, work at to gain skill **2.** do habitually **3.** put into action *—vi.* **4.** exercise oneself **5.** exercise profession

praetor *or* **pretor** (ˈpriːtə, -tɔː) *n.* in ancient Rome, senior magistrate ranking just below consul

pragmatic (prægˈmætɪk) *a.* **1.** concerned with practical consequence **2.** of the affairs of state **—pragˈmatical** *a.* **—ˈpragmatism** *n.*

prairie (ˈprɛərɪ) *n.* large treeless tract of grassland of Central U.S.A. and Canad. **—prairie dog** small Amer. rodent allied to marmot **—prairie oyster** drink consisting of raw egg, vinegar, salt and pepper: supposed cure for hangover

praise (preɪz) *n.* **1.** commendation **2.** fact, state of being praised *—vt.* **3.** express approval, admiration of **4.** speak well of **5.** glorify **—ˈpraiseworthy** *a.*

praline (ˈprɑːliːn) *n.* sweet composed of nuts and sugar

pram (præm) *n.* carriage for baby

prance (prɑːns) *vi.* **1.** swagger **2.** caper **3.** walk with bounds *—n.* **4.** prancing

prandial (ˈprændɪəl) *a.* of dinner

prang (præŋ) *inf. v.* **1.** crash or damage (car, aircraft *etc.*) **2.** damage (town *etc.*) by bombing *—n.* **3.** crash in a car, aircraft *etc.*

prank (præŋk) *n.* mischievous trick or escapade, frolic

prase (preɪz) *n.* light green translucent chalcedony

praseodymium (preɪzɪəʊˈdɪmɪəm) *n.* malleable element of lanthanide series of metals

THESAURUS

pound, pulverize **3.** cover, dredge, dust, scatter, sprinkle, strew

power **1.** ability, capability, capacity, competence, competency, faculty, potential **2.** brawn, energy, force, forcefulness, intensity, might, muscle, potency, strength, vigour, weight **3.** ascendancy, authority, command, control, dominance, domination, dominion, influence, mastery, rule, sovereignty, supremacy, sway **4.** authority, authorization, licence, prerogative, privilege, right, warrant

powerful **1.** energetic, mighty, potent, robust, stalwart, strapping, strong, sturdy, vigorous **2.** authoritative, commanding, controlling, dominant, influential, prevailing, puissant, sovereign, supreme

powerless **1.** debilitated, disabled, etiolated, feeble, frail, helpless, impotent, incapable, incapacitated, ineffectual, infirm, paralysed, prostrate, weak **2.** defenceless, dependent, disenfranchised, disfranchised, ineffective, subject, tied, unarmed, vulnerable

practicability advantage, feasibility, operability, possibility, practicality, use, usefulness, value, viability, workability

practicable achievable, attainable, doable, feasible, performable, possible, viable, within the realm of possibility, workable

practical **1.** applied, efficient, empirical, experimental, factual, functional, pragmatic, realistic, utilitarian **2.** businesslike, down-to-earth, everyday, hard-headed, matter-of-fact, mundane, ordinary, realistic, sensible, workaday **3.** doable, feasible, practicable, serviceable, sound, useful, workable

practically **1.** all but, almost, basically, close to, essentially, fundamentally, in effect, just about, nearly, to all intents and purposes, very nearly, virtually, well-nigh **2.** clearly, matter-of-factly, rationally, realistically, reasonably, sensibly, unsentimentally, with common sense

practice **1.** custom, habit, method, mode, praxis, routine, rule, system, tradition, usage, use, usual procedure, way, wont **2.** action, application, effect, exercise, experience, operation, use **3.** business, career, profession, vocation, work

practise **1.** discipline, drill, exercise, go over, go through, polish, prepare, rehearse, repeat, study, train, warm up, work out **2.** apply, carry out, do, follow, live up to, observe, perform, put into practice **3.** carry on, engage in, ply, pursue, specialize in, undertake, work at

pragmatic businesslike, down-to-earth, efficient, hard-headed, matter-of-fact, practical, realistic, sensible, utilitarian

praise *n.* **1.** acclaim, acclamation, accolade, applause, approbation, approval, cheering, commendation, compliment, congratulation, encomium, eulogy, good word, kudos, laudation, ovation, panegyric, plaudit, tribute **2.** adoration, devotion, glory, homage, thanks, worship *~v.* **3.** acclaim, admire, applaud, approve, cheer, compliment, congratulate, cry up, eulogize, extol, honour, laud, pay tribute to, sing the praises of **4.** adore, bless, exalt, give thanks to, glorify, magnify (*Archaic*), pay homage to, worship

praiseworthy admirable, commendable, creditable, estimable, excellent, exemplary, fine, honourable, laudable, meritorious, worthy

prance **1.** bound, caper, cavort, dance, frisk, gambol, jump, leap, romp, skip, spring **2.** parade, show off (*Inf.*), stalk, strut, swagger, swank (*Inf.*)

prank antic, caper, escapade, frolic, jape, lark (*Inf.*), practical joke, skylarking (*Inf.*), trick

prate (preɪt) *vi.* **1.** talk idly, chatter —*n.* **2.** idle or trivial talk

prattle (ˈpræt°l) *vi.* **1.** talk like child —*n.* **2.** trifling, childish talk —ˈ**prattler** *n.* babbler

prawn (prɔːn) *n.* edible sea crustacean like shrimp but larger

praxis (ˈpræksɪs) *n.* practice, *esp.* as opposed to theory (*pl.* **-es, praxes** (ˈpræksiːz))

pray (preɪ) *vt.* **1.** ask earnestly, entreat —*vi.* **2.** offer prayers, *esp.* to God —**prayer** (prɛə) *n.* **1.** action, practice of praying to God **2.** earnest entreaty —**prayer rug** small carpet on which Muslim kneels while saying prayers (*also* **prayer mat**) —**prayer wheel** *Buddhism esp.* in Tibet, wheel or cylinder inscribed with prayers, each revolution of which is counted as uttered prayer —**praying mantis** *or* **mantid** *see* MANTIS

pre- (*comb. form*) before, beforehand, as in *prenatal, prerecord, preshrunk.* Such compounds are not given here where the meaning can easily be found from the simple word

preach (priːtʃ) *vi.* **1.** deliver sermon **2.** give moral, religious advice —*vt.* **3.** set forth in religious discourse **4.** advocate —ˈ**preacher** *n.*

preamble (priːˈæmb°l) *n.* introductory part of story *etc.*

prebend (ˈprɛbənd) *n.* stipend of canon or member of cathedral chapter —ˈ**prebendary** *n.* holder of this

Precambrian *or* **Pre-Cambrian** (priːˈkæmbrɪən) *a.* **1.** of earliest geological era, which lasted for about 4000 000 000 years before Cambrian period —*n.* **2.** Precambrian era

precarious (prɪˈkɛərɪəs) *a.* insecure, unstable, perilous

precaution (prɪˈkɔːʃən) *n.* **1.** previous care to prevent evil or secure good **2.** preventative measure —**preˈcautionary** *a.*

precede (prɪˈsiːd) *vt.* go, come before in rank, order, time *etc.* —**precedence** (ˈprɛsɪdəns) *n.* priority in position, rank, time *etc.* —**precedent** (ˈprɛsɪdənt) *n.* previous example or occurrence taken as rule

precentor (prɪˈsɛntə) *n.* leader of singing choir or congregation

precept (ˈpriːsɛpt) *n.* rule for conduct, maxim —**preˈceptor** *n.* instructor —**precepˈtorial** *a.*

precinct (ˈpriːsɪŋkt) *n.* **1.** enclosed, limited area **2.** area in town, oft. closed to traffic, reserved for particular activity **3. US** administrative area of city —*pl.* **4.** environs

precious (ˈprɛʃəs) *a.* **1.** beloved, cherished **2.** of great value, highly valued **3.** rare —**preciˈosity** *n.* overrefinement in art or literature —ˈ**preciously** *adv.* —ˈ**preciousness** *n.* —**precious metal** gold, silver or platinum —**precious stone** rare mineral, such as diamond, ruby *etc.*, highly valued as gemstone

precipice (ˈprɛsɪpɪs) *n.* very steep cliff or rockface —**precipitous** (prɪˈsɪpɪtəs) *a.* sheer

precipitant (prɪˈsɪpɪtənt) *a.* **1.** hasty, rash **2.** abrupt —**preˈcipitance** *or* **preˈcipitancy** *n.*

precipitate (prɪˈsɪpɪteɪt) *vt.* **1.** hasten happening of **2.** throw headlong **3.** *Chem.* cause to be deposited in solid form from solution —*a.* (prɪˈsɪpɪtɪt) **4.** too sudden **5.** rash, impetuous —*n.* (prɪˈsɪpɪtɪt) **6.** substance chemi-

THESAURUS

prattle babble, blather, blether, chatter, clack, drivel, gabble, jabber, patter, rattle on, run on, twitter, witter (*Inf.*)

pray 1. offer a prayer, recite the rosary, say one's prayers **2.** adjure, ask, beg, beseech, call upon, crave, cry for, entreat, implore, importune, invoke, petition, plead, request, solicit, sue, supplicate, urge

prayer 1. communion, devotion, invocation, litany, orison, supplication **2.** appeal, entreaty, petition, plea, request, suit, supplication

preach 1. address, deliver a sermon, evangelize, exhort, orate **2.** admonish, advocate, exhort, harangue, lecture, moralize, sermonize, urge

preacher clergyman, evangelist, minister, missionary, parson, revivalist

preamble exordium, foreword, introduction, opening statement *or* remarks, overture, preface, prelude, proem, prolegomenon

precarious chancy (*Inf.*), dangerous, dicey (*Sl.*), dodgy (*Brit. inf.*), doubtful, dubious, hairy (*Sl.*), hazardous, insecure, perilous, risky, shaky, slippery, touch and go, tricky, uncertain, unreliable, unsafe, unsettled, unstable, unsteady, unsure

precaution 1. insurance, preventative measure, protection, provision, safeguard, safety measure **2.** anticipation, care, caution, circumspection, foresight, forethought, providence, prudence, wariness

precede antecede, antedate, come first, forerun, go ahead of, go before, head, herald, introduce, lead, pave the way, preface, take precedence, usher

precedence antecedence, lead, pre-eminence, preference, primacy, priority, rank, seniority, superiority, supremacy

precedent *n.* antecedent, authority, criterion, example, exemplar, instance, model, paradigm, pattern, previous example, prototype, standard

precept 1. behest, canon, command, commandment, decree, direction, instruction, law, mandate, order, ordinance, principle, regulation, rule, statute **2.** axiom, byword, guideline, maxim, motto, principle, rule, saying

precinct 1. bound, boundary, confine, enclosure, limit **2.** area, district, quarter, section, sector, zone

precincts borders, bounds, confines, district, environs, limits, milieu, neighbourhood, purlieus, region, surrounding area

precious 1. adored, beloved, cherished, darling, dear, dearest, favourite, idolized, loved, prized, treasured, valued **2.** choice, costly, dear, expensive, exquisite, fine, high-priced, inestimable, invaluable, priceless, prized, rare, recherché, valuable

precipice bluff, brink, cliff, cliff face, crag, height, rockface, sheer drop, steep

precipitate *v.* **1.** accelerate, advance, bring on, dispatch, expedite, further, hasten, hurry, press, push forward, quicken, speed up, trigger **2.** cast, discharge, fling, hurl, launch, let fly, send forth, throw ~*adj.* **3.** frantic, harum-scarum, hasty, heedless, hurried, ill-advised, impetuous, impulsive, indiscreet, madcap, precipitous, rash, reckless **4.** abrupt, brief, quick, sudden, unexpected, without warning

precipitous abrupt, dizzy, falling sharply, high, perpendicular, sheer, steep

cally precipitated —**pre'cipitately** *adv.* —**precipi'tation** *n.* rain, snow, sleet *etc.*

precis *or* **précis** ('preɪsi:) *n.* abstract, summary (*pl.* **precis** *or* **précis** ('preɪsi:z))

precise (prɪ'saɪs) *a.* **1.** definite **2.** particular **3.** exact, strictly worded **4.** careful in observance **5.** punctilious, formal —**pre'cisely** *adv.* —**precision** (prɪ'sɪʒən) *n.* accuracy

preclude (prɪ'klu:d) *vt.* **1.** prevent from happening **2.** shut out

precocious (prɪ'kəʊʃəs) *a.* developed, matured early or too soon —**precocity** (prɪ'kɒsɪtɪ) *or* **pre'cociousness** *n.*

precognition (pri:kɒg'nɪʃən) *n. Psychol.* alleged ability to foresee future events —**pre'cognitive** *a.*

preconceive (pri:kən'si:v) *vt.* form an idea of beforehand —**precon'ception** *n.*

precondition (pri:kən'dɪʃən) *n.* necessary or required condition

precursor (prɪ'kɜ:sə) *n.* forerunner —**pre'cursive** *or* **pre'cursory** *a.*

pred. predicate

predate (pri:'deɪt) *vt.* **1.** affix date to (document *etc.*) that is earlier than actual date **2.** assign date to (event *etc.*) that is earlier than actual or previously assigned date of occurrence **3.** be or occur at earlier date than; precede in time

predatory ('prɛdətərɪ) *a.* **1.** hunting, killing other animals *etc.* for food **2.** plundering —'**predator** *n.* predatory animal

predecease (pri:dɪ'si:s) *vt.* die before (some other person)

predecessor ('pri:dɪsɛsə) *n.* **1.** one who precedes another in an office or position **2.** ancestor

predestine (pri:'dɛstɪn) *or* **predestinate** (pri:'dɛstɪneɪt) *vt.* decree beforehand, foreordain —**predesti'nation** *n.*

predetermine (pri:dɪ'tɜ:mɪn) *vt.* **1.** determine beforehand **2.** influence, bias —**predetermi'nation** *n.*

predicament (prɪ'dɪkəmənt) *n.* perplexing, embarrassing or difficult situation

predicant ('prɛdɪkənt) *a.* **1.** of preaching —*n.* **2.** member of religious order founded for preaching, *esp.* Dominican

predicate ('prɛdɪkeɪt) *vt.* **1.** affirm, assert **2.** (*with* on *or* upon) *chiefly* US base (argument *etc.*) —*n.* ('prɛdɪkɪt) **3.** that which is predicated **4.** *Gram.* statement made about a subject —'**predicable** *a.* **1.** capable of being predicated —*n.* **2.** quality that can be predicated **3.** *Logic* any of five general forms of attribution, namely genus, species, differentia, property and accident —**predi'cation** *n.* —**pre'dicative** *a.*

predict (prɪ'dɪkt) *vt.* foretell, prophesy —**pre'dictable** *a.* —**pre'diction** *n.*

predikant (prɛdɪ'kænt) *n.* in S Afr., minister in Dutch Reformed Church

predilection (pri:dɪ'lɛkʃən) *n.* preference, liking, partiality

predispose (pri:dɪ'spəʊz) *vt.* **1.** incline, influence **2.** make susceptible

THESAURUS

precise 1. absolute, accurate, actual, clear-cut, correct, definite, exact, explicit, express, fixed, literal, particular, specific, strict, unequivocal **2.** careful, ceremonious, exact, fastidious, finicky, formal, inflexible, meticulous, nice, particular, prim, punctilious, puritanical, rigid, scrupulous, stiff, strict

precisely absolutely, accurately, bang, correctly, exactly, just, just so, literally, neither more nor less, plumb (*Inf.*), slap (*Inf.*), smack (*Inf.*), square, squarely, strictly

precision accuracy, care, correctness, definiteness, exactitude, exactness, fidelity, meticulousness, nicety, particularity, preciseness

preclude check, debar, exclude, forestall, hinder, inhibit, make impossible, make impracticable, obviate, prevent, prohibit, put a stop to, restrain, rule out, stop

precocious advanced, ahead, bright, developed, forward, quick, smart

preconception bias, notion, preconceived idea *or* notion, predisposition, prejudice, prepossession, presumption, presupposition

precondition essential, must, necessity, prerequisite, requirement, *sine qua non*

precursor 1. forerunner, harbinger, herald, messenger, usher, vanguard **2.** antecedent, forebear, forerunner, originator, pioneer, predecessor

precursory antecedent, introductory, preceding, prefatory, preliminary, preparatory, previous, prior

predatory 1. carnivorous, hunting, predacious, rapacious, raptorial, ravening **2.** despoiling, greedy, marauding, pillaging, plundering, rapacious, ravaging, thieving, voracious, vulturine, vulturous

predecessor 1. antecedent, forerunner, precursor, previous (former, prior) job holder **2.** ancestor, antecedent, forebear, forefather

predestination destiny, doom, election (*Theology*), fate, foreordainment, foreordination, lot, necessity, predetermination

predestine doom, fate, foreordain, mean, predestinate, predetermine, pre-elect, preordain

predicament corner, dilemma, emergency, fix (*Inf.*), hole (*Sl.*), jam (*Inf.*), mess, pickle (*Inf.*), pinch, plight, quandary, scrape (*Inf.*), situation, spot (*Inf.*), state

predicate 1. affirm, assert, aver, avouch, avow, contend, declare, maintain, proclaim, state **2.** *With* **on** *or* **upon** base, build, establish, found, ground, postulate, rest

predict augur, divine, forebode, forecast, foresee, foretell, portend, presage, prognosticate, prophesy, soothsay

predictable anticipated, calculable, certain, expected, foreseeable, foreseen, likely, reliable, sure, surefire (*Inf.*)

prediction augury, divination, forecast, prognosis, prognostication, prophecy, soothsaying

predilection bias, fancy, fondness, inclination, leaning, liking, love, partiality, penchant, predisposition, preference, proclivity, proneness, propensity, taste, tendency, weakness

predispose affect, bias, dispose, incline, induce, influence, lead, make (one) of a mind to, prejudice, prepare, prime, prompt, sway

predominance ascendancy, control, dominance, dominion, edge, greater number, hold, leadership, mastery, paramountcy, preponderance, supremacy, sway, upper hand, weight

predominate (prɪˈdɒmɪneɪt) *vi.* be main or controlling element —**preˈdominance** *n.* —**preˈdominant** *a.* chief

pre-eminent (prɪˈɛmɪnənt) *a.* excelling all others, outstanding —**pre-eminence** *n.* —**pre-eminently** *adv.*

pre-empt (prɪˈɛmpt) *vt.* acquire in advance of or to exclusion of others —**pre-emption** *n.* —**pre-emptive** *a.*

preen (priːn) *vt.* **1.** (of birds) trim (feathers) with beak, plume **2.** smarten (oneself)

pref. **1.** preface **2.** preference **3.** prefix

prefabricate (priːˈfæbrɪkeɪt) *vt.* manufacture (buildings *etc.*) in shaped sections, for rapid assembly on site —**ˈprefab** *n.* prefabricated building, *esp.* house

preface (ˈprɛfɪs) *n.* **1.** introduction to book *etc.* —*vt.* **2.** introduce —**ˈprefatory** *a.*

prefect (ˈpriːfɛkt) *n.* **1.** person put in authority **2.** schoolchild in position of limited power over others —**ˈprefecture** *n.* office, residence, district of a prefect

prefer (prɪˈfɜː) *vt.* **1.** like better **2.** promote (**-rr-**) —**preferable** (ˈprɛfərəbˀl) *a.* more desirable —**preferably** (ˈprɛfərəblɪ) *adv.* —**preference** (ˈprɛfərəns, ˈprɛfrəns) *n.* —**preferential** (prɛfəˈrɛnʃəl) *a.* giving, receiving preference —**preˈferment** *n.* promotion, advancement

prefigure (priːˈfɪgə) *vt.* exhibit, suggest by previous types, foreshadow —**preˈfigurative** *a.*

prefix (ˈpriːfɪks) *n.* **1.** preposition or particle put at beginning of word or title —*vt.* (priːˈfɪks, ˈpriːfɪks) **2.** put as introduction **3.** put before word to make compound

pregnant (ˈprɛgnənt) *a.* **1.** carrying foetus in womb **2.** full of meaning, significance **3.** inventive —**ˈpregnancy** *n.*

prehensile (prɪˈhɛnsaɪl) *a.* capable of grasping —**prehensility** (priːhɛnˈsɪlɪtɪ) *n.*

prehistoric (priːhɪˈstɒrɪk) *or* **prehistorical** *a.* before period in which written history begins —**preˈhistory** *n.*

prejudge (priːˈdʒʌdʒ) *vt.* judge beforehand, *esp.* without sufficient evidence

prejudice (ˈprɛdʒʊdɪs) *n.* **1.** preconceived opinion **2.** bias, partiality **3.** injury likely to happen to person or his rights as result of others' action or judgment —*vt.* **4.** influence **5.** bias **6.** injure —**prejuˈdicial** *a.* **1.** injurious **2.** disadvantageous

prelate (ˈprɛlɪt) *n.* bishop or other church dignitary of equal or higher rank —**ˈprelacy** *n.* his office —**prelatical** (prɪˈlætɪkˀl) *a.*

preliminary (prɪˈlɪmɪnərɪ) *a.* **1.** preparatory, introductory —*n.* **2.** introductory, preparatory statement, action **3.** eliminating contest held before main competition

THESAURUS

predominant ascendant, capital, chief, controlling, dominant, important, leading, main, paramount, preponderant, prevailing, prevalent, primary, prime, principal, prominent, ruling, sovereign, superior, supreme

predominate be most noticeable, carry weight, get the upper hand, hold sway, outweigh, overrule, overshadow, preponderate, prevail, reign, rule, tell

pre-eminence distinction, excellence, paramountcy, predominance, prestige, prominence, renown, superiority, supremacy, transcendence

pre-eminent chief, consummate, distinguished, excellent, foremost, incomparable, matchless, outstanding, paramount, peerless, predominant, renowned, superior, supreme, transcendent, unequalled, unrivalled, unsurpassed

pre-eminently above all, by far, conspicuously, eminently, emphatically, exceptionally, far and away, incomparably, inimitably, matchlessly, notably, *par excellence*, particularly, second to none, signally, singularly, strikingly, superlatively, supremely

pre-empt acquire, anticipate, appropriate, arrogate, assume, seize, take over, usurp

preen **1.** *Of birds* clean, plume **2.** array, deck out, doll up (*Sl.*), dress up, prettify, primp, prink, spruce up, titivate, trim

preface **1.** *n.* exordium, foreword, introduction, preamble, preliminary, prelude, proem, prolegomenon, prologue **2.** *v.* begin, introduce, launch, lead up to, open, precede, prefix

prefer **1.** adopt, be partial to, choose, desire, elect, fancy, favour, go for, incline towards, like better, opt for, pick, plump for, select, single out, wish, would rather, would sooner **2.** advance, aggrandize, elevate, move up, promote, raise, upgrade

preferable best, better, choice, chosen, favoured, more desirable, more eligible, superior, worthier

preferably as a matter of choice, by choice, first, in *or* for preference, much rather, much sooner, rather, sooner, willingly

preference **1.** choice, desire, election, favourite, first choice, option, partiality, pick, predilection, selection, top of the list **2.** advantage, favoured treatment, favouritism, first place, precedence, pride of place, priority

preferential advantageous, better, favoured, partial, partisan, privileged, special, superior

preferment advancement, dignity, elevation, exaltation, promotion, rise, upgrading

pregnancy gestation, gravidity

pregnant **1.** big *or* heavy with child, enceinte, expectant, expecting (*Inf.*), gravid, in the club (*Brit. sl.*), in the family way (*Inf.*), in the pudding club (*Sl.*), preggers (*Brit. inf.*), with child **2.** charged, eloquent, expressive, loaded, meaningful, pointed, significant, suggestive, telling, weighty **3.** creative, imaginative, inventive, original, seminal

prehistoric earliest, early, primeval, primitive, primordial

prejudge anticipate, forejudge, jump to conclusions, make a hasty assessment, presume, presuppose

prejudice *n.* **1.** bias, jaundiced eye, partiality, preconceived notion, preconception, prejudgment, warp **2.** bigotry, chauvinism, discrimination, injustice, intolerance, narrow-mindedness, racism, sexism, unfairness **3.** damage, detriment, disadvantage, harm, hurt, impairment, loss, mischief ~*v.* **4.** bias, colour, distort, influence, jaundice, poison, predispose, prepossess, slant, sway, warp **5.** damage, harm, hinder, hurt, impair, injure, mar, spoil, undermine

prejudicial counterproductive, damaging, deleterious, detrimental, disadvantageous, harmful, hurtful, inimical, injurious, undermining, unfavourable

preliminary **1.** *adj.* exploratory, first, initial, initiatory, introductory, opening, pilot, precursory, prefatory, preparatory, prior, qualifying, test, trial **2.** *n.*

prelims (ˈpriːlɪmz, prəˈlɪmz) *pl.n.* **1.** pages of book, such as title page *etc.* before main text (*also* **front matter**) **2.** first public examinations taken for bachelor's degree in some universities **3.** in Scotland, school examinations taken before public examinations

prelude (ˈprɛljuːd) *n.* **1.** *Mus.* introductory movement **2.** performance, event *etc.* serving as introduction —*v.* **3.** serve as prelude to (something) —*vt.* **4.** introduce

premarital (priːˈmærɪtᵊl) *a.* occurring before marriage

premature (prɛməˈtjʊə, ˈprɛmətjʊə) *a.* **1.** happening, done before proper time **2.** impulsive, hasty **3.** (of infant) born before end of full period of gestation

premeditate (prɪˈmɛdɪteɪt) *vt.* consider, plan beforehand —**premediˈtation** *n.*

premenstrual (priːˈmɛnstrʊəl) *a.* of period in menstrual cycle just before menstruation

premier (ˈprɛmjə) *n.* **1.** prime minister **2.** head of government of Aust. state —*a.* **3.** chief, foremost **4.** first —**ˈpremiership** *n.*

premiere (ˈprɛmɪɛə, ˈprɛmɪə) *n.* first public performance of a play, film *etc.*

premise (ˈprɛmɪs) *n.* **1.** *Logic* proposition from which inference is drawn (*also* **ˈpremiss**) —*pl.* **2.** house, building with its belongings **3.** *Law* beginning of deed —*vt.* (prɪˈmaɪz, ˈprɛmɪs) **4.** state by way of introduction

premium (ˈpriːmɪəm) *n.* **1.** bonus **2.** sum paid for insurance **3.** excess over nominal value **4.** great value or regard —**Premium Savings Bond** bond issued by government on which no interest is paid but cash prizes can be won

premonition (prɛməˈnɪʃən) *n.* presentiment, foreboding

preoccupy (priːˈɒkjʊpaɪ) *vt.* occupy to the exclusion of other things (**-pying, -pied**) —**preoccuˈpation** *n.* mental concentration or absorption

preordain (priːɔːˈdeɪn) *vt.* ordain or decree beforehand

prep (prɛp) *n. inf.* **1.** preparation for schoolwork **2.** *chiefly* **US** preparatory school

prep. **1.** preparation **2.** preparatory **3.** preposition

prepare (prɪˈpɛə) *vt.* **1.** make ready **2.** make —*vi.* **3.** get ready —**preparation** (prɛpəˈreɪʃən) *n.* **1.** making ready beforehand **2.** something that is prepared, as a medicine **3.** at school, (time spent) preparing work for lesson —**preparatory** (prɪˈpærətərɪ) *a.* **1.** serving to prepare **2.** introductory —**preparedness** (prɪˈpɛərɪdnɪs) *n.* state of being prepared —**preparatory school 1. UK** private school for children between ages of 6 and 13, generally preparing pupils for public school **2.** in Amer., private secondary school preparing pupils for college (*also* **prep school**)

prepay (priːˈpeɪ) *vt.* pay in advance

prepense (prɪˈpɛns) *a.* usu. in legal contexts, premeditated (*esp. in* **malice prepense**)

preponderate (prɪˈpɒndəreɪt) *vi.* be of greater weight or power —**preˈponderance** *n.* superiority of power, numbers *etc.*

preposition (prɛpəˈzɪʃən) *n.* word marking relation

THESAURUS

beginning, first round, foundation, groundwork, initiation, introduction, opening, preamble, preface, prelims, prelude, preparation, start

prelude beginning, commencement, curtain-raiser, exordium, foreword, intro (*Inf.*), introduction, overture, preamble, preface, preliminary, preparation, proem, prolegomenon, prologue, start

premature 1. abortive, early, embryonic, forward, green, immature, incomplete, predeveloped, raw, undeveloped, unfledged, unripe, unseasonable, untimely **2.** *Fig.* hasty, ill-considered, ill-timed, impulsive, inopportune, overhasty, precipitate, previous (*Inf.*), rash, too soon, untimely

premeditation deliberation, design, determination, forethought, intention, malice aforethought, planning, plotting, prearrangement, predetermination, purpose

premier *n.* **1.** chancellor, head of government, P.M., prime minister ~*adj.* **2.** arch, chief, first, foremost, head, highest, leading, main, primary, prime, principal, top **3.** earliest, first, inaugural, initial, original

premiere debut, first night, first performance, first showing, opening

premise, premiss argument, assertion, assumption, ground, hypothesis, postulate, postulation, presupposition, proposition, supposition, thesis

premises building, establishment, place, property, site

premium 1. bonus, boon, bounty, fee, percentage (*Inf.*), perk (*Brit. inf.*), perquisite, prize, recompense, remuneration, reward **2.** appreciation, regard, stock, store, value

premonition apprehension, feeling, feeling in one's bones, foreboding, forewarning, funny feeling (*Inf.*), hunch, idea, intuition, misgiving, omen, portent, presage, presentiment, sign, suspicion, warning

preoccupation absence of mind, absent-mindedness, absorption, abstraction, brown study, daydreaming, engrossment, immersion, inattentiveness, musing, oblivion, pensiveness, prepossession, reverie, woolgathering

preoccupied absent-minded, absorbed, abstracted, caught up in, distracted, distrait, engrossed, faraway, heedless, immersed, in a brown study, intent, lost in, lost in thought, oblivious, rapt, taken up, unaware, wrapped up

preparation 1. development, getting ready, groundwork, preparing, putting in order **2.** *Often plural* arrangement, measure, plan, provision **3.** composition, compound, concoction, medicine, mixture, tincture **4.** homework, prep (*Inf.*), revision, schoolwork, study, swotting (*Inf.*)

preparatory basic, elementary, introductory, opening, prefatory, preliminary, preparative, primary

prepare 1. adapt, adjust, anticipate, arrange, coach, dispose, form, groom, make provision, make ready, plan, practise, prime, put in order, train, warm up **2.** brace, fortify, gird, ready, steel, strengthen **3.** assemble, concoct, construct, contrive, draw up, fashion, fix up, get up (*Inf.*), make, produce, put together, turn out

preparedness alertness, fitness, order, preparation, readiness

preponderance ascendancy, bulk, dominance, domination, dominion, extensiveness, greater numbers, greater part, lion's share, mass, power, predominance, prevalence, superiority, supremacy, sway, weight

between noun or pronoun and other words —**prepo'sitional** *a.*

prepossess (pri:pə'zɛs) *vt.* 1. preoccupy or engross mentally 2. impress, *esp.* favourably, beforehand —**prepos'sessing** *a.* inviting favourable opinion, attractive, winning —**prepos'session** *n.*

preposterous (prɪ'pɒstərəs) *a.* utterly absurd, foolish

prepuce ('pri:pju:s) *n.* 1. retractable fold of skin covering tip of penis; foreskin 2. similar fold of skin covering tip of clitoris

Pre-Raphaelite (pri:'ræfəlaɪt) *n.* 1. member of **Pre-Raphaelite Brotherhood,** association of painters and writers founded in 1848 to revive qualities of It. painting before Raphael —*a.* 2. of Pre-Raphaelite painting and painters

prerequisite (pri:'rɛkwɪzɪt) *n./a.* (something) required as prior condition

prerogative (prɪ'rɒgətɪv) *n.* 1. peculiar power or right, *esp.* as vested in sovereign —*a.* 2. privileged

pres. 1. present (time) 2. presidential

Pres. President

presage ('prɛsɪdʒ) *n.* 1. omen, indication of something to come —*vt.* ('prɛsɪdʒ, prɪ'seɪdʒ) 2. foretell

presbyopia (prɛzbɪ'əupɪə) *n.* progressively diminishing ability of the eye to focus, *esp.* on near objects; long-sightedness

presbyter ('prɛzbɪtə) *n.* 1. elder in early Christian church 2. priest 3. member of a presbytery —**Presby'terian** *a./n.* (member) of Protestant church governed by lay elders —**Presby'terianism** *n.* —**'presbytery** *n.* 1. church court composed of all ministers within a certain district and one ruling elder from each church 2. *R.C.Ch.* priest's house

prescience ('prɛsɪəns) *n.* foreknowledge —**'prescient** *a.*

prescribe (prɪ'skraɪb) *v.* 1. set out rules (for) 2. order 3. ordain 4. order use of (medicine) —**prescription** (prɪ'skrɪpʃən) *n.* 1. prescribing 2. thing prescribed 3. written statement of it —**prescriptive** (prɪ'skrɪptɪv) *a.*

present[1] ('prɛzᵊnt) *a.* 1. that is here 2. now existing or happening —*n.* 3. present time or tense —**'presence** *n.* 1. being present 2. appearance, bearing —**'presently** *adv.* 1. soon 2. US at present —**presence of mind** ability to remain calm and act constructively during crises —**present-day** *a.* of modern day; current —**present participle** participial form of verbs used adjectivally when action it describes is contemporaneous with that of main verb of sentence and also used in formation of certain compound tenses —**present perfect** *Gram. see* PERFECT (sense 9)

present[2] (prɪ'zent) *vt.* 1. introduce formally 2. show 3. give 4. offer 5. point, aim —*n.* ('prɛzᵊnt) 6. gift —**pre'sentable** *a.* fit to be seen —**presentation** (prɛzən'teɪʃən) *n.*

presentiment (prɪ'zɛntɪmənt) *n.* sense of something (*esp.* evil) about to happen

preserve (prɪ'zɜ:v) *vt.* 1. keep from harm, injury or decay 2. maintain 3. pickle —*n.* 4. special area 5. that

THESAURUS

prepossessing alluring, amiable, appealing, attractive, beautiful, bewitching, captivating, charming, engaging, fair, fascinating, fetching, good-looking, handsome, inviting, likable, lovable, magnetic, pleasing, striking, taking, winning

preposterous absurd, asinine, bizarre, crazy, excessive, exorbitant, extravagant, extreme, foolish, impossible, incredible, insane, irrational, laughable, ludicrous, monstrous, nonsensical, out of the question, outrageous, ridiculous, senseless, shocking, unreasonable, unthinkable

prerequisite 1. *adj.* called for, essential, imperative, indispensable, mandatory, necessary, needful, obligatory, of the essence, required, requisite, vital 2. *n.* condition, essential, imperative, must, necessity, precondition, qualification, requirement, requisite, *sine qua non*

prerogative advantage, authority, birthright, choice, claim, droit, due, exemption, immunity, liberty, perquisite, privilege, right, sanction, title

prescribe appoint, assign, command, decree, define, dictate, direct, enjoin, fix, impose, lay down, ordain, order, require, rule, set, specify, stipulate

prescription 1. direction, formula, instruction, recipe 2. drug, medicine, mixture, preparation, remedy

presence 1. attendance, being, companionship, company, existence, habitation, inhabitance, occupancy, residence 2. air, appearance, aspect, aura, bearing, carriage, comportment, demeanour, ease, mien (*Literary*), personality, poise, self-assurance

presence of mind alertness, aplomb, calmness, composure, cool (*Sl.*), coolness, imperturbability, levelheadedness, phlegm, quickness, sang-froid, self-assurance, self-command, self-possession, wits

present[1] *adj.* 1. contemporary, current, existent, existing, extant, immediate, instant, present-day 2. accounted for, at hand, available, here, in attendance, near, nearby, ready, there, to hand ~*n.* 3. here and now, now, present moment, the time being, this day and age, today

present[2] *v.* 1. acquaint with, introduce, make known 2. demonstrate, display, exhibit, give, mount, put before the public, put on, show, stage 3. adduce, advance, declare, expound, extend, hold out, introduce, offer, pose, produce, proffer, put forward, raise, recount, relate, state, submit, suggest, tender 4. award, bestow, confer, donate, entrust, furnish, give, grant, hand over, offer, proffer, put at (someone's) disposal ~*n.* 5. benefaction, boon, bounty, donation, endowment, favour, gift, grant, gratuity, largess, offering, prezzie (*Inf.*)

presentable acceptable, becoming, decent, fit to be seen, good enough, not bad (*Inf.*), O.K. (*Inf.*), passable, proper, respectable, satisfactory, suitable, tolerable

presentation 1. award, bestowal, conferral, donation, giving, investiture, offering 2. demonstration, display, exhibition, performance, production, representation, show 3. coming out, debut, introduction, launch, launching, reception

presentiment anticipation, apprehension, expectation, fear, feeling, foreboding, forecast, forethought, hunch, intuition, misgiving, premonition, presage

presently anon (*Archaic*), before long, by and by, in a minute, in a moment, in a short while, pretty soon (*Inf.*), shortly, soon

preservation conservation, defence, keeping, maintenance, perpetuation, protection, safeguarding, safekeeping, safety, salvation, security, storage, support, upholding

which is preserved, as fruit *etc.* **6.** place where game is kept for private fishing, shooting —**preservation** (prɛzəˈveɪʃən) *n.* —**preˈservative** *n.* **1.** chemical added to perishable foods, drinks *etc.* to prevent them from rotting —*a.* **2.** tending to preserve **3.** having quality of preserving

preside (prɪˈzaɪd) *vi.* **1.** be chairman **2.** (*with* over) superintend —**presidency** (ˈprɛzɪdənsɪ) *n.* —**president** (ˈprɛzɪdənt) *n.* head of society, company, republic *etc.* —**presidential** (prɛzɪˈdɛnʃəl) *a.*

presidium (prɪˈsɪdɪəm) *n.* **1.** (*oft.* **P-**) in Communist countries, permanent committee of larger body, such as legislature, that acts for it when it is in recess **2.** collective presidency

press[1] (prɛs) *vt.* **1.** subject to push or squeeze **2.** smooth by pressure or heat **3.** urge steadily, earnestly —*vi.* **4.** bring weight to bear **5.** throng **6.** hasten —*n.* **7.** a pressing **8.** machine for pressing, *esp.* printing machine **9.** printing house **10.** art or process of printing **11.** newspapers collectively **12.** crowd **13.** stress **14.** large cupboard —**ˈpressing** *a.* **1.** urgent **2.** persistent —**press agent** person employed to advertise and secure press publicity for any person, enterprise *etc.* —**press conference** interview for press reporters given by politician *etc.* —**press gallery** area for newspaper reporters, *esp.* in legislative assembly —**ˈpressman** *n.* **1.** printer who attends to the press **2.** journalist —**press stud** fastening device, one part with projecting knob that snaps into hole on another part —**press-up** *n.* exercise in which body is alternately raised and lowered by arms only, trunk being kept straight (*also* (US) **push-up**)

press[2] (prɛs) *vt.* force to serve in navy or army —**press gang** formerly, body of men employed to press men into naval service —**press-gang** *vt.* force (someone) to do something

pressure (ˈprɛʃə) *n.* **1.** act of pressing **2.** influence **3.** authority **4.** difficulties **5.** *Phys.* thrust per unit area —**pressuriˈzation** *or* **-iˈsation** *n.* in aircraft, maintenance of normal atmospheric pressure at high altitudes —**ˈpressurize** *or* **-ise** *vt.* —**pressure cooker** vessel like saucepan which cooks food rapidly by steam under pressure —**pressure group** organized group which exerts influence on policies, public opinion *etc.*

Prestel (ˈprɛstɛl) *n.* **R** Post Office viewdata service

prestidigitation (prɛstɪdɪdʒɪˈteɪʃən) *n. see* **sleight of hand** *at* SLEIGHT —**prestiˈdigitator** *n.*

prestige (prɛˈstiːʒ) *n.* **1.** reputation based on high achievement, character, wealth *etc.* **2.** power to impress or influence —**prestigious** (prɛˈstɪdʒəs) *a.*

presto (ˈprɛstəʊ) *adv.* **1.** *Mus.* quickly **2.** immediately (*esp. in* **hey presto**)

prestressed (priːˈstrɛst) *a.* (of concrete) containing stretched steel cables for strengthening

presume (prɪˈzjuːm) *vt.* **1.** take for granted —*vi.* **2.** take liberties —**preˈsumably** *adv.* **1.** probably **2.** doubtlessly —**presumption** (prɪˈzʌmpʃən) *n.* **1.** forward, arrogant opinion or conduct **2.** strong probability —**presumptive** (prɪˈzʌmptɪv) *a.* that may be assumed as true or valid until contrary is proved —**presumptuous** (prɪˈzʌmptjʊəs) *a.* forward, impudent, taking liberties —**presumptuously** (prɪˈzʌmptjʊəslɪ) *adv.* —**heir presumptive** heir whose right may be defeated by birth of nearer relative

presuppose (priːsəˈpəʊz) *vt.* assume or take for granted beforehand —**presuppoˈsition** *n.*

THESAURUS

preserve *v.* **1.** care for, conserve, defend, guard, keep, protect, safeguard, save, secure, shelter, shield **2.** continue, keep, keep up, maintain, perpetuate, retain, sustain, uphold ~*n.* **3.** area, domain, field, realm, specialism, sphere **4.** *Often plural* confection, confiture, conserve, jam, jelly, marmalade, sweetmeat **5.** game reserve, reservation, reserve, sanctuary

preside administer, be at the head of, be in authority, chair, conduct, control, direct, govern, head, lead, manage, officiate, run, superintend, supervise

press *v.* **1.** bear down on, compress, condense, crush, depress, force down, jam, mash, push, reduce, squeeze, stuff **2.** calender, finish, flatten, iron, mangle, put the creases in, smooth, steam **3.** clasp, crush, embrace, encircle, enfold, fold in one's arms, hold close, hug, squeeze **4.** beg, entreat, exhort, implore, importune, petition, plead, pressurize, sue, supplicate, urge **5.** cluster, crowd, flock, gather, hasten, herd, hurry, mill, push, rush, seethe, surge, swarm, throng ~*n.* **6. the press** Fleet Street, fourth estate, journalism, news media, newspapers, the papers **7.** bunch, crowd, crush, flock, herd, horde, host, mob, multitude, pack, push (*Inf.*), swarm, throng **8.** bustle, demand, hassle (*Inf.*), hurry, pressure, strain, stress, urgency

pressing burning, constraining, crucial, exigent, high-priority, imperative, important, importunate, serious, urgent, vital

pressure 1. compressing, compression, crushing, force, heaviness, squeezing, weight **2.** coercion, compulsion, constraint, force, influence, obligation, power, sway **3.** adversity, affliction, burden, demands, difficulty, distress, exigency, hassle (*Inf.*), heat, hurry, load, press, strain, stress, urgency

prestige authority, cachet, celebrity, credit, distinction, eminence, esteem, fame, honour, importance, influence, kudos, regard, renown, reputation, standing, stature, status, weight

presumably apparently, doubtless, doubtlessly, in all likelihood, in all probability, it would seem, likely, most likely, on the face of it, probably, seemingly

presume 1. assume, believe, conjecture, infer, posit, postulate, presuppose, suppose, surmise, take for granted, take it, think **2.** dare, go so far, have the audacity, make bold, make so bold, take the liberty, undertake, venture

presumption 1. assurance, audacity, boldness, brass (*Inf.*), brass neck (*Inf.*), cheek (*Inf.*), effrontery, forwardness, gall (*Inf.*), impudence, insolence, nerve (*Inf.*), presumptuousness, temerity **2.** basis, chance, grounds, likelihood, plausibility, probability, reason

presumptuous arrogant, audacious, bigheaded (*Inf.*), bold, conceited, foolhardy, forward, impudent, insolent, overconfident, overfamiliar, overweening, presuming, pushy (*Inf.*), rash, too big for one's boots, uppish (*Brit. inf.*)

presuppose accept, assume, consider, imply, posit, postulate, presume, suppose, take as read, take for granted, take it

presupposition assumption, belief, hypothesis, preconceived idea, preconception, premise, presumption, supposition, theory

pretend (prɪˈtɛnd) *vt.* **1.** claim or allege (something untrue) **2.** make believe, as in play —*vi.* **3.** lay claim (to) —**preˈtence** *or U.S.* **preˈtense** *n.* **1.** simulation **2.** pretext —**preˈtender** *n.* claimant (to throne) —**preˈtension** *n.* —**preˈtentious** *a.* **1.** making claim to special merit or importance **2.** given to outward show

preter- (*comb. form*) beyond, more than

preterite *or esp. U.S.* **preterit** (ˈprɛtərɪt) *a.* **1.** past **2.** expressing past state or action —*n.* **3.** past tense

preternatural (priːtəˈnætʃrəl) *a.* **1.** out of ordinary way of nature **2.** abnormal, supernatural

pretext (ˈpriːtɛkst) *n.* **1.** excuse **2.** pretence

pretty (ˈprɪtɪ) *a.* **1.** having beauty that is attractive rather than imposing **2.** charming —*adv.* **3.** fairly, moderately —**ˈprettify** *vt.* make pretty, *esp.* in trivial way; embellish —**ˈprettily** *adv.* —**ˈprettiness** *n.* —**pretty-pretty** *a. inf.* excessively or ostentatiously pretty

pretzel (ˈprɛtsəl) *n.* small, brittle, savoury biscuit

prevail (prɪˈveɪl) *vi.* **1.** gain mastery **2.** triumph **3.** be in fashion, generally established —**preˈvailing** *a.* **1.** widespread **2.** predominant —**prevalence** (ˈprɛvələns) *n.* —**prevalent** (ˈprɛvələnt) *a.* extensively existing, rife

prevaricate (prɪˈværɪkeɪt) *vi.* **1.** make evasive or misleading statements **2.** quibble —**prevariˈcation** *n.* —**preˈvaricator** *n.*

prevent (prɪˈvɛnt) *vt.* stop, hinder —**preˈventable** *a.* —**preˈventative** *a.* preventing, or serving to prevent, *esp.* disease (*also* **preˈventive**) —**preˈvention** *n.* —**preˈventive** *a./n.*

preview (ˈpriːvjuː) *n.* **1.** advance showing **2.** showing of scenes from forthcoming film

previous (ˈpriːvɪəs) *a.* **1.** earlier **2.** preceding **3.** *inf.* hasty —**ˈpreviously** *adv.* before

prey (preɪ) *n.* **1.** animal hunted and killed by another carnivorous animal **2.** victim —*vi.* (*oft. with* (up)on) **3.** seize for food **4.** treat as prey **5.** afflict, obsess

price (praɪs) *n.* **1.** that for which thing is bought or sold

THESAURUS

pretence 1. acting, charade, deceit, deception, fabrication, fakery, faking, falsehood, feigning, invention, make-believe, sham, simulation, subterfuge, trickery **2.** claim, cloak, colour, cover, excuse, façade, garb, guise, mask, masquerade, pretext, ruse, semblance, show, veil, wile

pretend 1. affect, allege, assume, counterfeit, dissemble, dissimulate, fake, falsify, feign, impersonate, make out, pass oneself off as, profess, put on, sham, simulate **2.** act, imagine, make believe, make up, play, play the part of, suppose **3.** allege, aspire, claim, lay claim, profess, purport

pretender aspirant, claimant, claimer

pretension 1. aspiration, assertion, assumption, claim, demand, pretence, profession **2.** affectation, airs, conceit, hypocrisy, ostentation, pomposity, pretentiousness, self-importance, show, showiness, snobbery, snobbishness, vainglory, vanity

pretentious affected, assuming, bombastic, conceited, exaggerated, extravagant, flaunting, grandiloquent, grandiose, highfalutin (*Inf.*), high-flown, high-sounding, hollow, inflated, magniloquent, mannered, ostentatious, overambitious, pompous, puffed up, showy, snobbish, specious, vainglorious

pretext affectation, alleged reason, appearance, cloak, cover, device, excuse, guise, mask, ploy, pretence, red herring, ruse, semblance, show, simulation, veil

pretty 1. *adj.* appealing, attractive, beautiful, bonny, charming, comely, cute, fair, good-looking, graceful, lovely, personable **2.** *adv. Inf.* fairly, kind of (*Inf.*), moderately, quite, rather, reasonably, somewhat

prevail 1. be victorious, carry the day, gain mastery, overcome, overrule, prove superior, succeed, triumph, win **2.** abound, be current (prevalent, widespread), exist generally, obtain, predominate, preponderate

prevailing 1. common, current, customary, established, fashionable, general, in style, in vogue, ordinary, popular, prevalent, set, usual, widespread **2.** dominant, influential, main, operative, predominant, predominating, preponderating, principal, ruling

prevalence 1. acceptance, commonness, common occurrence, currency, frequency, pervasiveness, popularity, profusion, regularity, ubiquity, universality **2.** ascendancy, hold, mastery, predominance, preponderance, primacy, rule, sway

prevalent accepted, common, commonplace, current, customary, established, everyday, extensive, frequent, general, habitual, popular, rampant, rife, ubiquitous, universal, usual, widespread

prevaricate beat about the bush, beg the question, cavil, deceive, dodge, equivocate, evade, give a false colour to, hedge, lie, palter, quibble, shift, shuffle, stretch the truth, tergiversate

prevarication cavilling, deceit, deception, equivocation, evasion, falsehood, falsification, lie, misrepresentation, pretence, quibbling, tergiversation, untruth

prevent anticipate, avert, avoid, balk, bar, block, check, counteract, defend against, foil, forestall, frustrate, hamper, head off, hinder, impede, inhibit, intercept, nip in the bud, obstruct, obviate, preclude, restrain, stave off, stop, thwart, ward off

preventative, preventive *adj.* **1.** hampering, hindering, impeding, obstructive **2.** counteractive, deterrent, inhibitory, precautionary, prophylactic, protective, shielding ~*n.* **3.** block, hindrance, impediment, obstacle, obstruction **4.** deterrent, neutralizer, prevention, prophylactic, protection, protective, remedy, safeguard, shield

prevention 1. anticipation, avoidance, deterrence, elimination, forestalling, obviation, precaution, preclusion, prophylaxis, safeguard, thwarting **2.** bar, check, deterrence, frustration, hindrance, impediment, interruption, obstacle, obstruction, stoppage

previous 1. antecedent, anterior, earlier, erstwhile, ex-, foregoing, former, one-time, past, preceding, prior, quondam, sometime **2.** *Inf.* ahead of oneself, precipitate, premature, too early, too soon, untimely

previously at one time, a while ago, before, beforehand, earlier, formerly, heretofore, hitherto, in advance, in anticipation, in days *or* years gone by, in the past, once, then, until now

prey *n.* **1.** game, kill, quarry **2.** dupe, fall guy (*Inf.*), mark, mug (*Sl.*), target, victim ~*v.* **3.** devour, eat, feed upon, hunt, live off, seize **4.** blackmail, bleed (*Inf.*), bully, exploit, intimidate, take advantage of, terrorize, victimize **5.** afflict, burden, distress, hang over, haunt, obsess, oppress, trouble, weigh down, weigh heavily, worry

2. cost 3. value 4. reward 5. odds in betting —*vt.* 6. fix, ask price for —ˈ**priceless** *a.* 1. invaluable 2. *inf.* very funny —ˈ**pricey** *or* ˈ**pricy** *a. inf.* expensive —**price control** establishment of maximum price levels for basic goods and services by government —**at any price** whatever the price or cost

prick (prɪk) *vt.* 1. pierce slightly with sharp point 2. cause to feel mental pain 3. mark by prick —*v.* 4. (*usu. with* up) erect (ears) —*n.* 5. slight hole made by pricking 6. pricking or being pricked 7. sting 8. remorse 9. that which pricks 10. sharp point —ˈ**prickle** *n.* 1. thorn, spike —*vi.* 2. feel tingling or pricking sensation —ˈ**prickly** *a.* —**prickly heat** inflammation of skin with stinging pains —**prickly pear** 1. tropical cactus having flattened or cylindrical spiny joints and oval fruit 2. fruit of prickly pear

pride (praɪd) *n.* 1. too high an opinion of oneself, inordinate self-esteem 2. worthy self-esteem 3. feeling of elation or great satisfaction 4. something causing this 5. group (of lions) —*v.refl.* 6. take pride

prie-dieu (priːˈdjɜː) *n.* piece of furniture consisting of low surface for kneeling upon and narrow front surmounted by rest, for use when praying

priest (priːst) *or* (*fem.*) **priestess** *n.* official minister of religion, clergyman —ˈ**priesthood** *n.* —ˈ**priestly** *a.*

prig (prɪg) *n.* self-righteous person who professes superior culture, morality *etc.* —ˈ**priggery** *n.* —ˈ**priggish** *a.*

prim (prɪm) *a.* very restrained, formally prudish

prima (ˈpriːmə) *a.* first —**prima ballerina** leading female ballet dancer —**prima donna** (ˈdɒnə) 1. principal female singer in opera 2. *inf.* temperamental person (*pl.* -**s**)

primacy (ˈpraɪməsɪ) *n.* 1. state of being first in rank, grade *etc.* 2. office of archbishop

prima facie (ˈpraɪmə ˈfeɪʃɪ) *Lat.* at first sight

primal (ˈpraɪməl) *a.* 1. of earliest age 2. first, original —ˈ**primarily** *adv.* —ˈ**primary** *a.* 1. chief 2. of the first stage, decision *etc.* 3. elementary —**primary accent** *or* **stress** *Linguis.* strongest accent in word or breath group —**primary school** 1. in England and Wales, school for children below age of 11 2. in Scotland, school for children below age of 12 3. in U.S., school equivalent to first three or four grades of elementary school

primate[1] (ˈpraɪmeɪt) *n.* one of order of mammals including monkeys and man

primate[2] (ˈpraɪmeɪt) *n.* archbishop

prime[1] (praɪm) *a.* 1. fundamental 2. original 3. chief 4. best —*n.* 5. first, best part of anything 6. youth 7. full health and vigour —*vt.* 8. prepare (gun, engine, pump *etc.*) for use 9. fill up, *eg* with information, liquor —ˈ**priming** *n.* powder mixture used for priming gun —**prime meridian** the 0° meridian from which other meridians are calculated, usu. taken to pass through Greenwich —**Prime Minister** leader of government —**prime number** integer that cannot be divided into other integers but is only divisible by itself or 1

THESAURUS

price *n.* 1. amount, asking price, assessment, bill, charge, cost, damage (*Inf.*), estimate, expenditure, expense, face value, fee, figure, outlay, payment, rate, valuation, value, worth 2. consequences, cost, penalty, sacrifice, toll 3. bounty, compensation, premium, recompense, reward 4. **at any price** anyhow, cost what it may, expense no object, no matter what the cost, regardless, whatever the cost ~*v.* 5. assess, cost, estimate, evaluate, put a price on, rate, value

priceless 1. beyond price, cherished, costly, dear, expensive, incalculable, incomparable, inestimable, invaluable, irreplaceable, precious, prized, rare, rich, treasured, worth a king's ransom 2. *Inf.* absurd, a hoot (*Brit. inf.*), amusing, a scream (*Inf.*), comic, droll, funny, hilarious, killing (*Inf.*), rib-tickling, ridiculous, riotous, side-splitting

prick *v.* 1. bore, jab, lance, perforate, pierce, pink, punch, puncture, stab 2. bite, itch, prickle, smart, sting, tingle 3. cut, distress, grieve, move, pain, stab, touch, trouble, wound 4. *Usually with* **up** point, raise, rise, stand erect ~*n.* 5. cut, gash, hole, perforation, pinhole, puncture, wound 6. gnawing, pang, prickle, smart, spasm, sting, twinge

prickle 1. *n.* barb, needle, point, spike, spine, spur, thorn 2. *v.* itch, smart, sting, tingle, twitch

prickly 1. barbed, brambly, briery, bristly, spiny, thorny 2. crawling, itchy, pricking, prickling, scratchy, sharp, smarting, stinging, tingling

pride *n.* 1. *amour-propre*, dignity, honour, self-esteem, self-respect, self-worth 2. arrogance, bigheadedness (*Inf.*), conceit, egotism, haughtiness, hauteur, hubris, loftiness, *morgue*, presumption, pretension, pretentiousness, self-importance, self-love, smugness, snobbery, superciliousness, vainglory, vanity 3. boast, gem, jewel, pride and joy, prize, treasure 4. delight, gratification, joy, pleasure, satisfaction ~*v.* 5. be proud of, boast, brag, congratulate oneself, crow, exult, flatter oneself, glory in, pique, plume, preen, revel in, take pride, vaunt

priest churchman, clergyman, cleric, curate, divine, ecclesiastic, father, father confessor, holy man, man of God, man of the cloth, minister, padre (*Inf.*), vicar

priestly canonical, clerical, ecclesiastic, hieratic, pastoral, priestlike, sacerdotal

prig goody-goody (*Inf.*), Holy Joe (*Inf.*), Holy Willie (*Inf.*), Mrs Grundy, old maid (*Inf.*), pedant, prude, puritan, stuffed shirt (*Inf.*)

priggish goody-goody (*Inf.*), holier-than-thou, narrow-minded, pedantic, prim, prudish, puritanical, self-righteous, self-satisfied, smug, starchy (*Inf.*), stiff, stuffy

prim demure, fastidious, formal, fussy, old-maidish (*Inf.*), particular, precise, priggish, prissy (*Inf.*), proper, prudish, puritanical, schoolmarmish (*Brit. inf.*), starchy (*Inf.*), stiff, strait-laced

prima donna diva, leading lady, star

primarily 1. above all, basically, chiefly, especially, essentially, for the most part, fundamentally, generally, mainly, mostly, on the whole, principally 2. at first, at *or* from the start, first and foremost, initially, in the beginning, in the first place, originally

primary 1. best, capital, cardinal, chief, dominant, first, greatest, highest, leading, main, paramount, prime, principal, top 2. aboriginal, earliest, initial, original, primal, primeval, primitive, primordial, pristine 3. basic, beginning, elemental, essential, fundamental, radical, ultimate, underlying 4. elementary, introductory, rudimentary, simple

prime *adj.* 1. best, capital, choice, excellent, first-class, first-rate, grade A, highest, quality, select,

prime² (praɪm) *vt.* prepare for paint with preliminary coating of oil, size *etc.* **—ˈprimer** *n.* paint *etc.* for priming

primer (ˈpraɪmə) *n.* elementary school book or manual

primeval *or* **primaeval** (praɪˈmiːvᵊl) *a.* of the earliest age of the world

primitive (ˈprɪmɪtɪv) *a.* **1.** of an early undeveloped kind, ancient **2.** crude, rough

primogeniture (praɪməʊˈdʒɛnɪtʃə) *n.* rule by which real estate passes to the first-born son **—primoˈgenital** *a.* **—primoˈgenitor** *n.* **1.** forefather; ancestor **2.** earliest parent or ancestor, as of race

primordial (praɪˈmɔːdɪəl) *a.* existing at or from the beginning

primp (prɪmp) *v.* dress (oneself), *esp.* in fine clothes; prink

primrose (ˈprɪmrəʊz) *n.* **1.** any of various pale-yellow spring flowers of the genus *Primula* **2.** this colour *—a.* **3.** of this colour **—primrose path** pleasurable way of life

primula (ˈprɪmjʊlə) *n.* any of a genus of plants including primrose, oxlip *etc.*

Primus (ˈpraɪməs) *n.* **R** portable cooking stove, used *esp.* by campers

prince (prɪns) *n.* **1.** son or in Brit. grandson of king or queen **2.** ruler, chief (**prinˈcess** *fem.*) **—ˈprincely** *a.* **1.** generous, lavish **2.** stately **3.** magnificent **—princess royal** eldest daughter of Brit. or, formerly, Prussian sovereign **—Prince of Wales** eldest son and heir apparent of Brit. sovereign

principal (ˈprɪnsɪpᵊl) *a.* **1.** chief in importance *—n.* **2.** person for whom another is agent **3.** head of institution, *esp.* school or college **4.** sum of money lent and yielding interest **5.** chief actor *etc.* **—princiˈpality** *n.* territory, dignity of prince **—principal boy** leading male role in pantomime, played by woman **—principal parts** *Gram.* main inflected forms of verb, from which all other inflections may be deduced

principle (ˈprɪnsɪpᵊl) *n.* **1.** moral rule **2.** settled reason of action **3.** uprightness **4.** fundamental truth or element **—ˈprincipled** *a.* having high moral principles

prink (prɪŋk) *v.* **1.** dress (oneself *etc.*) finely; deck out *—vi.* **2.** preen oneself

print (prɪnt) *vt.* **1.** reproduce (words, pictures *etc.*) by pressing inked types on blocks to paper *etc.* **2.** produce thus **3.** write in imitation of this **4.** impress **5.** *Photog.* produce (pictures) from negatives **6.** stamp (fabric) with coloured design *—n.* **7.** printed matter **8.** printed lettering **9.** written imitation of printed type **10.** photograph **11.** impression, mark left on surface by thing that has pressed against it **12.** printed cotton fabric **—ˈprinter** *n.* one engaged in printing **—ˈprinting** *n.* **1.** business or art of producing printed matter **2.** printed text **3.** copies of book *etc.* printed at one time (*also* **imˈpression**) **4.** form of writing in which letters resemble printed letters **—printed circuit** electronic circuit with wiring printed on an insulating base **—printer's devil** apprentice or errand boy in printing establishment **—printing press** machine for printing **—print-out** *n.* printed information from computer, teleprinter *etc.* **—out of print** no longer available from publisher

prior (ˈpraɪə) *a.* **1.** earlier *—n.* **2.** chief of religious house or order (**-ess** *fem.*) **—priˈority** *n.* **1.** precedence **2.** something given special attention **—ˈpriory** *n.* monastery, nunnery under prior, prioress

prise *or* **prize** (praɪz) *vt.* **1.** force open by levering **2.** obtain (information *etc.*) with difficulty

prism (ˈprɪzəm) *n.* transparent solid usu. with triangular ends and rectangular sides, used to disperse light into spectrum or refract it in optical instruments *etc.* **—prisˈmatic** *a.* **1.** of prism shape **2.** (of colour) such as is produced by refraction through prism, rainbowlike, brilliant

THESAURUS

selected, superior, top **2.** basic, earliest, fundamental, original, primary, underlying **3.** chief, leading, main, predominant, pre-eminent, primary, principal, ruling, senior *~n.* **4.** best days, bloom, flower, full flowering, height, heyday, maturity, peak, perfection, zenith **5.** beginning, morning, opening, spring, start *~v.* **6.** break in, coach, fit, get ready, groom, make ready, prepare, train **7.** brief, clue up, fill in (*Inf.*), gen up (*Brit. inf.*), give someone the lowdown (*Inf.*), inform, notify, tell

primeval, primaeval ancient, earliest, early, first, old, original, prehistoric, primal, primitive, primordial, pristine

primitive 1. earliest, early, elementary, first, original, primary, primeval, primordial, pristine **2.** barbarian, barbaric, crude, rough, rude, rudimentary, savage, simple, uncivilized, uncultivated, undeveloped, unrefined **3.** childlike, naive, simple, undeveloped, unsophisticated, untrained, untutored

prince lord, monarch, potentate, ruler, sovereign

princely 1. bounteous, bountiful, generous, gracious, lavish, liberal, magnanimous, munificent, open-handed, rich **2.** august, dignified, grand, high-born, imperial, imposing, lofty, magnificent, majestic, noble, regal, royal, sovereign, stately

principal *adj.* **1.** capital, cardinal, chief, controlling, dominant, essential, first, foremost, highest, key, leading, main, most important, paramount, pre-eminent, primary, prime, strongest *~n.* **2.** boss (*Inf.*), chief, director, head, leader, master, ruler, superintendent **3.** dean, director, head (*Inf.*), headmaster, headmistress, head teacher, master, rector **4.** assets, capital, capital funds, money **5.** first violin, lead, leader, star

principle 1. assumption, axiom, canon, criterion, dictum, doctrine, dogma, ethic, formula, fundamental, golden rule, law, maxim, moral law, precept, proposition, rule, standard, truth, verity **2.** attitude, belief, code, credo, ethic, morality, opinion, tenet **3.** conscience, integrity, morals, probity, rectitude, scruples, sense of duty, sense of honour, uprightness

print *v.* **1.** engrave, go to press, impress, imprint, issue, mark, publish, put to bed (*Inf.*), run off, stamp *~n.* **2.** book, magazine, newspaper, newsprint, periodical, printed matter, publication, typescript **3. out of print** no longer published, o.p., unavailable, unobtainable **4.** copy, engraving, photo (*Inf.*), photograph, picture, reproduction **5.** characters, face, font (*Chiefly U.S.*), fount, lettering, letters, type, typeface

priority first concern, greater importance, precedence, pre-eminence, preference, prerogative, rank, right of way, seniority, superiority, supremacy, the lead

priory abbey, cloister, convent, monastery, nunnery, religious house

prison (ˈprɪzᵊn) *n.* jail —ˈ**prisoner** *n.* 1. one kept in prison 2. captive —**prisoner of war** person, *esp.* serviceman, captured by enemy in time of war

prissy (ˈprɪsɪ) *a. inf.* fussy, prim

pristine (ˈprɪstaɪn, -tiːn) *a.* 1. original 2. primitive 3. unspoiled, good

private (ˈpraɪvɪt) *a.* 1. secret, not public 2. reserved for, or belonging to, or concerning, an individual only 3. personal 4. secluded 5. denoting soldier of lowest rank 6. not part of National Health Service 7. not controlled by State —*n.* 8. private soldier —**privacy** (ˈpraɪvəsɪ, ˈprɪvəsɪ) *n.* —ˈ**privately** *adv.* —**privatiˈzation** *or* **-iˈsation** *n.* —ˈ**privatize** *or* **-ise** *vt.* take into or return to private ownership (a company or concern previously owned by the State) —**private bill** bill presented to Parliament or Congress on behalf of individual, corporation *etc.* —**private company** limited company that does not issue shares for public subscription —**private eye** *inf.* private detective —**private member's bill** parliamentary bill sponsored by Member of Parliament who is not government minister —**private parts** *or* ˈ**privates** *pl.n.* genitals —**private school** school accepting mostly fee-paying pupils

privateer (praɪvəˈtɪə) *n. Hist.* 1. privately owned armed vessel authorized by government to take part in war 2. captain of such ship

privation (praɪˈveɪʃən) *n.* 1. loss or lack of comforts or necessities 2. hardship 3. act of depriving —**privative** (ˈprɪvətɪv) *a.*

privet (ˈprɪvɪt) *n.* bushy evergreen shrub used for hedges

privilege (ˈprɪvɪlɪdʒ) *n.* 1. advantage or favour that only a few obtain 2. right, advantage belonging to person or class —ˈ**privileged** *a.* enjoying special right or immunity

privy (ˈprɪvɪ) *a.* 1. admitted to knowledge of secret —*n.* 2. lavatory, *esp.* outhouse 3. *Law* person having interest in an action —ˈ**privily** *adv.* —**privy council** council of state of monarch —**privy purse** (*oft.* **P- P-**) 1. allowance voted by Parliament for private expenses of monarch 2. official responsible for dealing with monarch's private expenses (*also* **Keeper of the Privy Purse**) —**privy seal** (*oft.* **P- S-**) UK seal affixed to documents issued by royal authority: of less importance than great seal

prize[1] (praɪz) *n.* 1. reward given for success in competition 2. thing striven for 3. thing won, *eg* in lottery *etc.* —*a.* 4. winning or likely to win a prize —*vt.* 5. value highly —ˈ**prizefight** *n.* boxing match for money —ˈ**prizefighter** *n.*

prize[2] (praɪz) *n.* ship, property captured in (naval) warfare

pro[1] (prəʊ) *adv./prep.* in favour (of)

pro[2] (prəʊ) *n.* 1. professional 2. prostitute (*pl.* **-s**) —*a.* 3. professional

P.R.O. 1. Public Records Office 2. public relations officer

pro- (*comb. form*) for, instead of, before, in front, as in *proconsul, pronoun, project.* Such compounds are not given here where the meaning may easily be found from the simple word

probable (ˈprɒbəbᵊl) *a.* likely —**probaˈbility** *n.* 1. likelihood 2. anything that has appearance of truth —ˈ**probably** *adv.*

probate (ˈprəʊbɪt, -beɪt) *n.* 1. proving of authenticity of will 2. certificate of this

probation (prəˈbeɪʃən) *n.* 1. system of dealing with lawbreakers, *esp.* juvenile ones, by placing them under supervision of probation officer for stated period 2. testing of candidate before admission to full membership —**proˈbationer** *n.* person on probation —**probation officer** officer of court who supervises offenders placed on probation

probe (prəʊb) *vt.* 1. search into, examine, question closely —*n.* 2. that which probes, or is used to probe 3. thorough inquiry

probity (ˈprəʊbɪtɪ) *n.* honesty, uprightness, integrity

THESAURUS

prison can (*Sl.*), choky (*Sl.*), clink (*Sl.*), confinement, cooler (*Sl.*), dungeon, gaol, glasshouse (*Military inf.*), jail, jug (*Sl.*), lockup, penal institution, penitentiary (*U.S.*), quod (*Sl.*), stir (*Sl.*)

prisoner 1. con (*Sl.*), convict, jailbird, lag (*Sl.*) 2. captive, detainee, hostage, internee

privacy 1. isolation, privateness, retirement, retreat, seclusion, separateness, sequestration, solitude 2. clandestineness, concealment, confidentiality, secrecy

private *adj.* 1. clandestine, closet, confidential, hush-hush (*Inf.*), in camera, inside, off the record, privy (*Archaic*), secret, unofficial 2. exclusive, individual, intimate, own, particular, personal, reserved, special 3. independent, nonpublic 4. concealed, isolated, not overlooked, retired, secluded, secret, separate, sequestered, solitary, withdrawn ~*n.* 5. enlisted man (*U.S.*), private soldier, squaddy (*Inf.*), tommy (*Brit. inf.*), Tommy Atkins (*Brit. inf.*)

privilege advantage, benefit, birthright, claim, concession, due, entitlement, franchise, freedom, immunity, liberty, prerogative, right, sanction

privileged 1. advantaged, elite, entitled, favoured, honoured, indulged, powerful, ruling, special 2. allowed, empowered, exempt, free, granted, licensed, sanctioned, vested

prize[1] *n.* 1. accolade, award, honour, premium, reward, trophy 2. haul, jackpot, purse, stakes, windfall, winnings 3. aim, ambition, conquest, desire, gain, goal, hope ~*adj.* 4. award-winning, best, champion, first-rate, outstanding, top, topnotch (*Inf.*), winning

prize[2] *v.* appreciate, cherish, esteem, hold dear, regard highly, set store by, treasure, value

probability chance(s), expectation, liability, likelihood, likeliness, odds, presumption, prospect

probable apparent, credible, feasible, likely, most likely, odds-on, on the cards, ostensible, plausible, possible, presumable, presumed, reasonable, seeming

probably as likely as not, doubtless, in all likelihood, in all probability, likely, maybe, most likely, perchance (*Archaic*), perhaps, possibly, presumably

probation apprenticeship, examination, initiation, novitiate, test, trial, trial period

probe *v.* 1. examine, explore, go into, investigate, look into, query, scrutinize, search, sift, sound, test, verify 2. explore, feel around, poke, prod ~*n.* 3. detection, examination, exploration, inquest, inquiry, investigation, research, scrutiny, study

problem (ˈprɒbləm) *n.* 1. matter *etc.* difficult to deal with or solve 2. question set for solution 3. puzzle —**probleˈmatic(al)** *a.* 1. questionable; uncertain 2. disputable

proboscis (prəʊˈbɒsɪs) *n.* trunk or long snout, *eg* of elephant (*pl.* **-es, proboscides** (prəʊˈbɒsɪdiːz))

proceed (prəˈsiːd) *vi.* 1. go forward, continue 2. be carried on 3. go to law —**proˈcedural** *a.* —**proˈcedure** *n.* 1. act, manner of proceeding 2. conduct —**proˈceeding** *n.* 1. act or course of action 2. transaction —*pl.* 3. minutes of meeting 4. methods of prosecuting charge, claim *etc.* —**ˈproceeds** *pl.n.* price or profit

process (ˈprəʊsɛs) *n.* 1. series of actions or changes 2. method of operation 3. state of going on 4. action of law 5. outgrowth —*vt.* 6. handle, treat, prepare by special method of manufacture *etc.* —**proˈcession** *n.* 1. regular, orderly progress 2. train of persons in formal order

proclaim (prəˈkleɪm) *vt.* announce publicly, declare —**proclamation** (prɒkləˈmeɪʃən) *n.*

proclivity (prəˈklɪvɪtɪ) *n.* inclination, tendency

proconsul (prəʊˈkɒnsᵊl) *n. Hist.* governor of province

procrastinate (prəʊˈkræstɪneɪt, prə-) *vi.* put off (an action) until later, delay —**procrastiˈnation** *n.* —**proˈcrastinator** *n.*

procreate (ˈprəʊkrɪeɪt) *v.* produce (offspring) —**procreˈation** *n.*

Procrustean (prəʊˈkrʌstɪən) *a.* compelling uniformity by violence

proctor (ˈprɒktə) *n.* university official with disciplinary powers

procure (prəˈkjʊə) *vt.* 1. obtain, acquire 2. provide 3. bring about —*vi.* 4. act as pimp —**proˈcurable** *a.* —**procuration** (prɒkjʊˈreɪʃən) *n.* —**procurator** (ˈprɒkjʊreɪtə) *n.* one who manages another's affairs —**proˈcurement** *n.* —**proˈcurer** *n.* 1. one who procures 2. pimp —**procurator fiscal** in Scotland, legal officer who performs functions of public prosecutor and coroner

prod (prɒd) *vt.* 1. poke with something pointed (**-dd-**) —*n.* 2. prodding 3. goad 4. pointed instrument

prodigal (ˈprɒdɪgᵊl) *a.* 1. wasteful 2. extravagant —*n.* 3. spendthrift —**prodiˈgality** *n.* reckless extravagance

prodigy (ˈprɒdɪdʒɪ) *n.* 1. person with some marvellous gift 2. thing causing wonder —**proˈdigious** *a.* 1. very great, immense 2. extraordinary —**proˈdigiously** *adv.*

produce (prəˈdjuːs) *vt.* 1. bring into existence 2. yield 3. make 4. bring forward 5. manufacture 6. exhibit 7. present on stage, film, television 8. *Geom.* extend in length —*n.* (ˈprɒdjuːs) 9. that which is yielded or made —**proˈducer** *n.* person who produces, *esp.* play, film *etc.* —**product** (ˈprɒdʌkt) *n.* 1. result of process of

THESAURUS

problem *n.* 1. can of worms (*Inf.*), complication, difficulty, dilemma, disagreement, dispute, disputed point, doubt, hard nut to crack (*Inf.*), point at issue, predicament, quandary, trouble 2. brain-teaser (*Inf.*), conundrum, enigma, poser, puzzle, question, riddle

problematic chancy (*Inf.*), debatable, doubtful, dubious, enigmatic, moot, open to doubt, problematical, puzzling, questionable, tricky, uncertain, unsettled

procedure action, conduct, course, custom, form, formula, method, modus operandi, operation, performance, plan of action, policy, practice, process, routine, scheme, step, strategy, system, transaction

proceed advance, carry on, continue, get going, get on with, get under way with, go ahead, go on, make a start, move on, press on, progress, set in motion

proceeding 1. act, action, course of action, deed, measure, move, occurrence, procedure, process, step, undertaking, venture 2. *Plural* account, affairs, annals, archives, business, dealings, doings, matters, minutes, records, report, transactions

proceeds earnings, gain, income, price, produce, products, profit, receipts, returns, revenue, takings, yield

process *n.* 1. action, course, course of action, manner, means, measure, method, mode, operation, performance, practice, procedure, proceeding, system, transaction 2. advance, course, development, evolution, formation, growth, movement, progress, progression, stage, step, unfolding 3. *Law* action, case, suit, trial ~*v.* 4. deal with, dispose of, fulfil, handle, take care of 5. alter, convert, prepare, refine, transform, treat

procession 1. cavalcade, column, cortege, file, march, motorcade, parade, train 2. course, cycle, run, sequence, series, string, succession, train

proclaim advertise, affirm, announce, blaze (abroad), blazon (abroad), circulate, declare, enunciate, give out, herald, indicate, make known, profess, promulgate, publish, shout from the housetops (*Inf.*), show, trumpet

proclamation announcement, declaration, decree, edict, manifesto, notice, notification, promulgation, pronouncement, pronunciamento, publication

procrastinate adjourn, be dilatory, dally, defer, delay, drag one's feet (*Inf.*), gain time, play a waiting game, play for time, postpone, prolong, protract, put off, retard, stall, temporize

procure acquire, appropriate, buy, come by, earn, effect, find, gain, get, get hold of, lay hands on, manage to get, obtain, pick up, purchase, secure, win

prod *v.* 1. dig, drive, elbow, jab, nudge, poke, prick, propel, push, shove ~*n.* 2. boost, dig, elbow, jab, nudge, poke, push, shove 3. goad, poker, spur, stick

prodigal 1. *adj.* excessive, extravagant, immoderate, improvident, intemperate, profligate, reckless, spendthrift, squandering, wanton, wasteful 2. *n.* big spender, profligate, spendthrift, squanderer, wastrel

prodigality abandon, dissipation, excess, extravagance, immoderation, intemperance, profligacy, recklessness, squandering, wantonness, waste, wastefulness

prodigious 1. colossal, enormous, giant, gigantic, huge, immeasurable, immense, inordinate, mammoth, massive, monstrous, monumental, stupendous, tremendous, vast 2. abnormal, amazing, astounding, exceptional, extraordinary, fabulous, fantastic (*Inf.*), flabbergasting (*Inf.*), impressive, marvellous, miraculous, phenomenal, remarkable, staggering, startling, striking, stupendous, unusual, wonderful

prodigy 1. child genius, genius, mastermind, talent, whiz (*Inf.*), whiz kid (*Inf.*), wizard, wonder child, wunderkind 2. marvel, miracle, one in a million, phenomenon, rare bird (*Inf.*), sensation, wonder

manufacture **2.** number resulting from multiplication —**pro'duction** *n.* **1.** producing **2.** things produced —**pro'ductive** *a.* **1.** fertile **2.** creative **3.** efficient —**productivity** (prɒdʌk'tɪvɪtɪ) *n.*

proem ('prəʊɛm) *n.* introduction or preface, such as to work of literature

Prof. Professor

profane (prə'feɪn) *a.* **1.** irreverent, blasphemous **2.** not sacred —*vt.* **3.** pollute, desecrate —**profanation** (prɒfə'neɪʃən) *n.* —**profanity** (prə'fænɪtɪ) *n.* profane talk or behaviour, blasphemy

profess (prə'fɛs) *vt.* **1.** affirm, acknowledge **2.** confess publicly **3.** assert **4.** claim, pretend —**professedly** (prə'fɛsɪdlɪ) *adv.* avowedly —**pro'fession** *n.* **1.** calling or occupation, *esp.* learned, scientific or artistic **2.** a professing **3.** vow of religious faith on entering religious order —**pro'fessional** *a.* **1.** engaged in a profession **2.** engaged in a game or sport for money —*n.* **3.** paid player —**pro'fessor** *n.* teacher of highest rank in university —**professorial** (prɒfɪ'sɔːrɪəl) *a.* —**professoriate** (prɒfɪ'sɔːrɪɪt) *n.* body of university professors —**pro'fessorship** *n.*

proffer ('prɒfə) *vt./n.* offer

proficient (prə'fɪʃənt) *a.* skilled; expert —**pro'ficiency** *n.*

profile ('prəʊfaɪl) *n.* **1.** outline, *esp.* of face, as seen from side **2.** brief biographical sketch

profit ('prɒfɪt) *n.* **1.** (*oft. pl.*) money gained **2.** benefit obtained —*v.* **3.** benefit —**'profitable** *a.* yielding profit —**profi'teer** *n.* **1.** one who makes excessive profits at the expense of the public —*vi.* **2.** make excessive profits —**'profitless** *a.* —**profit-sharing** *n.* system in which portion of net profit of business is distributed to employees, usu. in proportion to wages or length of service

profligate ('prɒflɪgɪt) *a.* **1.** dissolute **2.** reckless, wasteful —*n.* **3.** dissolute person —**'profligacy** *n.*

THESAURUS

produce *v.* **1.** compose, construct, create, develop, fabricate, invent, make, manufacture, originate, put together, turn out **2.** afford, bear, beget, breed, bring forth, deliver, engender, furnish, give, render, supply, yield **3.** advance, bring forward, bring to light, demonstrate, exhibit, offer, present, put forward, set forth, show **4.** direct, do, exhibit, mount, present, put before the public, put on, show, stage **5.** *Geometry* extend, lengthen, prolong, protract ~*n.* **6.** crop, fruit and vegetables, greengrocery, harvest, product, yield

producer **1.** director, impresario, *régisseur* **2.** farmer, grower, maker, manufacturer

product artefact, commodity, concoction, creation, goods, invention, merchandise, produce, production, work

production **1.** assembly, construction, creation, fabrication, formation, making, manufacture, manufacturing, origination, preparation, producing **2.** direction, management, presentation, staging

productive **1.** creative, dynamic, energetic, fecund, fertile, fruitful, generative, inventive, plentiful, producing, prolific, rich, teeming, vigorous **2.** advantageous, beneficial, constructive, effective, efficient, fruitful, gainful, gratifying, profitable, rewarding, useful, valuable, worthwhile

productivity abundance, mass production, output, production, productive capacity, productiveness, work rate, yield

profane *adj.* **1.** disrespectful, godless, heathen, idolatrous, impious, impure, irreligious, irreverent, pagan, sacrilegious, sinful, ungodly, wicked **2.** lay, secular, temporal, unconsecrated, unhallowed, unholy, unsanctified, worldly **3.** abusive, blasphemous, coarse, crude, filthy, foul, obscene, vulgar ~*v.* **4.** abuse, commit sacrilege, contaminate, debase, defile, desecrate, misuse, pervert, pollute, prostitute, violate, vitiate

profanity abuse, blasphemy, curse, cursing, execration, foul language, four-letter word, impiety, imprecation, irreverence, malediction, obscenity, profaneness, sacrilege, swearing, swearword

profess **1.** acknowledge, admit, affirm, announce, assert, asseverate, aver, avow, certify, confess, confirm, declare, maintain, own, proclaim, state, vouch **2.** act as if, allege, call oneself, claim, dissemble, fake, feign, let on, make out, pretend, purport, sham

professedly admittedly, avowedly, by open declaration, confessedly

profession **1.** business, calling, career, employment, line, line of work, métier, occupation, office, position, sphere, vocation, walk of life **2.** acknowledgment, affirmation, assertion, attestation, avowal, claim, confession, declaration, statement, testimony, vow

professor don (*Brit.*), fellow (*Brit.*), head of faculty, prof (*Inf.*)

proficiency ability, accomplishment, aptitude, competence, dexterity, expertise, expertness, facility, knack, know-how (*Inf.*), mastery, skilfulness, skill, talent

proficient able, accomplished, adept, apt, capable, clever, competent, conversant, efficient, experienced, expert, gifted, masterly, qualified, skilful, skilled, talented, trained, versed

profile *n.* **1.** contour, drawing, figure, form, outline, portrait, shape, side view, silhouette, sketch **2.** biography, characterization, character sketch, sketch, thumbnail sketch, vignette

profit *n.* **1.** *Often plural* bottom line, earnings, emoluments, gain, percentage (*Inf.*), proceeds, receipts, return, revenue, surplus, takings, winnings, yield **2.** advancement, advantage, avail, benefit, gain, good, interest, use, value ~*v.* **3.** aid, avail, benefit, be of advantage to, better, contribute, gain, help, improve, promote, serve, stand in good stead **4.** capitalize on, cash in on (*Sl.*), exploit, learn from, make capital of, make good use of, make the most of, put to good use, reap the benefit of, take advantage of, turn to advantage *or* account, use, utilize

profitable **1.** commercial, cost-effective, fruitful, gainful, lucrative, money-making, paying, remunerative, rewarding, worthwhile **2.** advantageous, beneficial, fruitful, productive, rewarding, serviceable, useful, valuable, worthwhile

profiteer **1.** *n.* exploiter, racketeer **2.** *v.* exploit, fleece, make a quick buck (*Sl.*), make someone pay through the nose, overcharge, racketeer, sting (*Inf.*)

profligate *adj.* **1.** abandoned, corrupt, debauched, degenerate, depraved, dissipated, dissolute, immor-

pro forma (ˈprəʊ ˈfɔːmə) *Lat.* prescribing a set form

profound (prəˈfaʊnd) *a.* **1.** very learned **2.** deep —**profundity** (prəˈfʌndɪtɪ) *n.*

profuse (prəˈfjuːs) *a.* abundant, prodigal —**proˈfusion** *n.*

progeny (ˈprɒdʒɪnɪ) *n.* children —**progenitor** (prəʊˈdʒɛnɪtə) *n.* ancestor

progesterone (prəʊˈdʒɛstərəʊn) *n.* hormone which prepares uterus for pregnancy and prevents further ovulation

prognathous (prɒgˈneɪθəs) *or* **prognathic** (prɒgˈnæθɪk) *a.* with projecting lower jaw

prognosis (prɒgˈnəʊsɪs) *n.* **1.** art of foretelling course of disease by symptoms **2.** forecast (*pl.* **-noses** (-ˈnəʊsiːz)) —**prognostic** (prɒgˈnɒstɪk) *a.* **1.** of, serving as prognosis —*n.* **2.** *Med.* any symptom used in making prognosis **3.** sign of some future occurrence —**prognosticate** (prɒgˈnɒstɪkeɪt) *vt.* foretell —**prognostication** (prɒgnɒstɪˈkeɪʃən) *n.*

programme *or U.S.* **program** (ˈprəʊgræm) *n.* **1.** plan, detailed notes of intended proceedings **2.** broadcast on radio or television **3.** syllabus or curriculum —ˈ**program** *n.* **1.** detailed instructions for computer —*vt.* **2.** feed program into (computer) **3.** arrange detailed instructions for (computer) (**-mm-**) —ˈ**programmer** *n.* person who writes program

progress (ˈprəʊgrɛs) *n.* **1.** onward movement **2.** development —*vi.* (prəˈgrɛs) **3.** go forward **4.** improve —**proˈgression** *n.* **1.** moving forward **2.** advance, improvement **3.** increase or decrease of numbers or magnitudes according to fixed law **4.** *Mus.* regular succession of chords —**proˈgressive** *a.* **1.** progressing by degrees **2.** favouring political or social reform

prohibit (prəˈhɪbɪt) *vt.* forbid —**prohibition** (prəʊɪˈbɪʃən) *n.* **1.** act of forbidding **2.** interdict **3.** interdiction of supply and consumption of alcoholic drinks —**proˈhibitive** *a.* **1.** tending to forbid or exclude **2.** (of prices) very high —**proˈhibitory** *a.*

project (ˈprɒdʒɛkt) *n.* **1.** plan, scheme **2.** design —*vt.* (prəˈdʒɛkt) **3.** plan **4.** throw **5.** cause to appear on distant background —*vi.* (prəˈdʒɛkt) **6.** stick out, protrude —**projectile** (prəˈdʒɛktaɪl) *n.* **1.** heavy missile, *esp.* shell or ball —*a.* **2.** designed for throwing —**projection** (prəˈdʒɛkʃən) *n.* —**projectionist** (prəˈdʒɛkʃənɪst) *n.* operator of film projector —**projector** (prəˈdʒɛktə) *n.* **1.** apparatus for projecting photographic images, films, slides on screen **2.** one that forms scheme or design

prolapse (ˈprəʊlæps, prəʊˈlæps) *n.* falling, slipping down of part of body from normal position (*also* **proˈlapsus**)

prolate (ˈprəʊleɪt) *a.* having polar diameter greater than the equatorial diameter

prole (prəʊl) *n. derogatory sl., chiefly* UK proletarian

prolegomena (prəʊlɛˈgɒmɪnə) *pl.n.* introductory remarks prefixed to book; preface

THESAURUS

al, iniquitous, libertine, licentious, loose, promiscuous, shameless, unprincipled, vicious, vitiated, wanton, wicked, wild **2.** extravagant, immoderate, improvident, prodigal, reckless, spendthrift, squandering, wasteful ~*n.* **3.** debauchee, degenerate, dissipater, libertine, rake, reprobate, roué

profound **1.** abstruse, deep, discerning, erudite, learned, penetrating, philosophical, recondite, sagacious, sage, serious, skilled, subtle, thoughtful, weighty, wise **2.** abysmal, bottomless, cavernous, deep, fathomless, yawning **3.** abject, acute, deep, deeply felt, extreme, great, heartfelt, heartrending, hearty, intense, keen, sincere

profuse **1.** abundant, ample, bountiful, copious, luxuriant, overflowing, plentiful, prolific, teeming **2.** excessive, extravagant, exuberant, fulsome, generous, immoderate, lavish, liberal, open-handed, prodigal, unstinting

profusion abundance, bounty, copiousness, cornucopia, excess, extravagance, exuberance, glut, lavishness, luxuriance, multitude, oversupply, plenitude, plethora, prodigality, quantity, riot, superabundance, superfluity, surplus, wealth

progeny breed, children, descendants, family, issue, lineage, offspring, posterity, race, scions, seed, stock, young

programme *n.* **1.** agenda, curriculum, line-up, list, listing, list of players, order of events, order of the day, plan, schedule, syllabus **2.** broadcast, performance, presentation, production, show **3.** design, order of the day, plan, plan of action, procedure, project, scheme

progress *n.* **1.** advance, course, movement, onward course, passage, progression, way **2.** advance, advancement, amelioration, betterment, breakthrough, development, gain, gaining ground, growth, headway, improvement, increase, progression, promotion, step forward ~*v.* **3.** advance, come on, continue, cover ground, forge ahead, gain ground, gather way, get on, go forward, make headway, make one's way, make strides, move on, proceed, travel **4.** advance, ameliorate, better, blossom, develop, gain, grow, improve, increase, mature

progression advance, advancement, furtherance, gain, headway, movement forward, progress

progressive **1.** accelerating, advancing, continuing, continuous, developing, escalating, growing, increasing, intensifying, ongoing **2.** advanced, avant-garde, dynamic, enlightened, enterprising, forward-looking, go-ahead, liberal, modern, radical, reformist, revolutionary, up-and-coming

prohibit **1.** ban, debar, disallow, forbid, interdict, outlaw, proscribe, veto **2.** constrain, hamper, hinder, impede, make impossible, obstruct, preclude, prevent, restrict, rule out, stop

prohibition **1.** constraint, exclusion, forbiddance, interdiction, negation, obstruction, prevention, restriction **2.** ban, bar, disallowance, embargo, injunction, interdict, proscription, veto

prohibitive **1.** forbidding, prohibiting, proscriptive, repressive, restraining, restrictive, suppressive **2.** *Esp. of prices* beyond one's means, excessive, exorbitant, extortionate, high-priced, preposterous, sky-high, steep (*Inf.*)

project *n.* **1.** activity, assignment, design, enterprise, job, occupation, plan, programme, proposal, scheme, task, undertaking, venture, work ~*v.* **2.** contemplate, contrive, design, devise, draft, frame, map out, outline, plan, propose, purpose, scheme **3.** cast, discharge, fling, hurl, launch, make carry, propel, shoot, throw, transmit **4.** beetle, bulge, extend, jut, overhang, protrude, stand out, stick out

projectile bullet, missile, rocket, shell

proletariat (prəʊlɪˈtɛərɪət) *n.* **1.** all wage earners collectively **2.** lowest class of community, working class —**proleˈtarian** *a./n.*

proliferate (prəˈlɪfəreɪt) *v.* grow or reproduce rapidly —**proliferˈation** *n.*

prolific (prəˈlɪfɪk) *a.* **1.** producing fruit, offspring *etc.* in abundance **2.** producing constant or successful results **3.** fruitful

prolix (ˈprəʊlɪks, prəʊˈlɪks) *a.* (of speech *etc.*) wordy, long-winded —**proˈlixity** *n.*

prologue *or U.S.* (*oft.*) **prolog** (ˈprəʊlɒg) *n.* preface, *esp.* speech before play

prolong (prəˈlɒŋ) *vt.* lengthen, protract —**prolongation** (prəʊlɒŋˈgeɪʃən) *n.*

prom (prɒm) *n.* promenade (concert)

promenade (prɒməˈnɑːd) *n.* **1.** leisurely walk **2.** place made or used for this —*vi.* **3.** take leisurely walk **4.** go up and down —**promenade concert** concert at which audience stands

promethium (prəˈmiːθɪəm) *n.* radioactive element of lanthanide series artificially produced by fission of uranium

prominent (ˈprɒmɪnənt) *a.* **1.** sticking out **2.** conspicuous **3.** distinguished —**ˈprominence** *n.*

promiscuous (prəˈmɪskjʊəs) *a.* **1.** indiscriminate, *esp.* in sexual relations **2.** mixed without distinction —**promiscuity** (prɒmɪˈskjuːɪtɪ) *n.*

promise (ˈprɒmɪs) *v.* **1.** give undertaking or assurance (of) —*vi.* **2.** be likely —*n.* **3.** undertaking to do or not to do something **4.** potential —**ˈpromising** *a.* **1.** showing good signs, hopeful **2.** showing potential —**ˈpromissory** *a.* containing promise —**Promised Land 1.** *O.T.* land of Canaan, promised by God to Abraham and his descendants as their heritage **2.** *Christianity* heaven **3.** place where one expects to find greater happiness —**promissory note** written promise to pay sum to person named, at specified time

promontory (ˈprɒməntərɪ, -trɪ) *n.* point of high land jutting out into the sea, headland

promote (prəˈməʊt) *vt.* **1.** help forward **2.** move up to higher rank or position **3.** work for **4.** encourage sale of —**proˈmoter** *n.* —**proˈmotion** *n.* **1.** advancement **2.** preferment

prompt (prɒmpt) *a.* **1.** done at once **2.** acting with alacrity **3.** punctual **4.** ready —*vt.* **5.** urge, suggest —*v.* **6.** help out (actor or speaker) by reading or suggesting next words —**ˈprompter** *n.* —**ˈpromptitude** *or* **ˈpromptness** *n.* —**ˈpromptly** *adv.*

THESAURUS

projection bulge, eaves, jut, ledge, overhang, protrusion, protuberance, ridge, shelf, sill

proletarian **1.** *adj.* cloth-cap (*Inf.*), common, plebeian, working-class **2.** *n.* commoner, Joe Bloggs (*Brit. inf.*), man of the people, pleb (*Sl.*), plebeian, prole (*Sl.*), worker

proletariat commonalty, commoners, hoi polloi, labouring classes, lower classes, lower orders, plebs, proles (*Sl.*), the common people, the great unwashed (*Derogatory*), the herd, the masses, the rabble, wage-earners, working class

prolific abundant, bountiful, copious, fecund, fertile, fruitful, generative, luxuriant, productive, profuse, rank, rich, teeming

prologue exordium, foreword, introduction, preamble, preface, preliminary, prelude, proem

prolong carry on, continue, delay, drag out, draw out, extend, lengthen, make longer, perpetuate, protract, spin out, stretch

promenade *n.* **1.** boulevard, esplanade, parade, prom, public walk, walkway **2.** airing, constitutional, saunter, stroll, turn, walk ~*v.* **3.** perambulate, saunter, stretch one's legs, stroll, take a walk, walk

prominence **1.** bulge, jutting, projection, protrusion, protuberance, swelling **2.** conspicuousness, markedness, outstandingness, precedence, salience, specialness, top billing, weight **3.** celebrity, distinction, eminence, fame, greatness, importance, name, notability, pre-eminence, prestige, rank, reputation, standing

prominent **1.** bulging, jutting, projecting, protruding, protrusive, protuberant, standing out **2.** conspicuous, easily seen, eye-catching, in the foreground, noticeable, obtrusive, obvious, outstanding, pronounced, remarkable, salient, striking, to the fore, unmistakable **3.** celebrated, chief, distinguished, eminent, famous, foremost, important, leading, main, noted, outstanding, popular, pre-eminent, renowned, respected, top, well-known, well-thought-of

promiscuous **1.** abandoned, debauched, dissipated, dissolute, fast, immoral, lax, libertine, licentious, loose, of easy virtue, profligate, unbridled, unchaste, wanton, wild **2.** chaotic, confused, disordered, diverse, heterogeneous, ill-assorted, indiscriminate, intermingled, intermixed, jumbled, mingled, miscellaneous, mixed, motley **3.** careless, casual, haphazard, heedless, indifferent, indiscriminate, irregular, irresponsible, random, slovenly, uncontrolled, uncritical, undiscriminating, unfastidious, unselective

promise *v.* **1.** assure, contract, cross one's heart, engage, give an undertaking, give one's word, guarantee, pledge, plight, stipulate, swear, take an oath, undertake, vouch, vow, warrant **2.** augur, bespeak, betoken, bid fair, denote, give hope of, hint at, hold a probability, hold out hopes of, indicate, lead one to expect, look like, seem likely to, show signs of, suggest ~*n.* **3.** assurance, bond, commitment, compact, covenant, engagement, guarantee, oath, pledge, undertaking, vow, word, word of honour **4.** ability, aptitude, capability, capacity, flair, potential, talent

promising **1.** auspicious, bright, encouraging, favourable, full of promise, hopeful, likely, propitious, reassuring, rosy **2.** able, gifted, likely, rising, talented, up-and-coming

promote **1.** advance, aid, assist, back, boost, contribute to, develop, encourage, forward, foster, further, help, nurture, stimulate, support **2.** aggrandize, dignify, elevate, exalt, honour, kick upstairs (*Inf.*), prefer, raise, upgrade **3.** advocate, call attention to, champion, endorse, espouse, popularize, push for, recommend, speak for, sponsor, support, urge, work for **4.** advertise, beat the drum for (*Inf.*), hype (*Sl.*), plug (*Inf.*), publicize, puff, push, sell

promotion **1.** advancement, aggrandizement, elevation, ennoblement, exaltation, honour, move up, preferment, rise, upgrading **2.** advancement, advocacy, backing, boosting, cultivation, development, encouragement, espousal, furtherance, progress, support

prompt *adj.* **1.** early, immediate, instant, instantaneous, on time, punctual, quick, rapid, speedy, swift, timely, unhesitating **2.** alert, brisk, eager, efficient,

promulgate (ˈprɒməlgeɪt) *vt.* proclaim, publish —**promulˈgation** *n.* —**ˈpromulgator** *n.*

pron. 1. pronoun 2. pronunciation

prone (prəʊn) *a.* 1. lying face or front downwards 2. inclined —**ˈproneness** *n.*

prong (prɒŋ) *n.* single spike of fork or similar instrument

pronghorn (ˈprɒŋhɔːn) *n.* Amer. antelope

pronoun (ˈprəʊnaʊn) *n.* word used to replace noun —**proˈnominal** *a.* pert. to, like pronoun

pronounce (prəˈnaʊns) *vt.* 1. utter formally 2. form with organs of speech 3. say distinctly 4. declare —*vi.* 5. give opinion or decision —**proˈnounceable** *a.* —**proˈnounced** *a.* strongly marked, decided —**proˈnouncement** *n.* declaration —**pronunciˈation** *n.* 1. manner in which word *etc.* is pronounced 2. articulation 3. phonetic transcription of a word

pronto (ˈprɒntəʊ) *adv. inf.* at once, immediately, quickly

proof (pruːf) *n.* 1. evidence 2. thing which proves 3. test, demonstration 4. trial impression from type or engraved plate 5. *Photog.* print from a negative 6. standard of strength of alcoholic drink —*a.* 7. giving impenetrable defence 8. of proved strength —**ˈproofread** *v.* read and correct (proofs) —**ˈproofreader** *n.* —**ˈproofreading** *n.* —**proof spirit UK** mixture of alcohol and water or alcoholic beverage that contains 49.28 per cent of alcohol by weight, 57.1 per cent by volume at 60°F (15.6°C): used as standard of alcoholic liquids

-proof (*comb. form*) impervious to; resisting effects of, as in *waterproof*

prop[1] (prɒp) *vt.* 1. support, sustain, hold up (**-pp-**) —*n.* 2. pole, beam *etc.* used as support

prop[2] (prɒp) *n.* propeller —**ˈpropjet** *n. see* TURBOPROP

prop[3] (prɒp) *n.* (theatrical) property

prop. 1. proper(ly) 2. property 3. proposition 4. proprietor

propaganda (prɒpəˈgændə) *n.* organized dissemination of information to assist or damage political cause *etc.* —**propaˈgandist** *a./n.*

propagate (ˈprɒpəgeɪt) *vt.* 1. reproduce, breed, spread by sowing, breeding *etc.* 2. transmit —*vi.* 3. breed, multiply —**propaˈgation** *n.* —**ˈpropagative** *a.*

propane (ˈprəʊpeɪn) *n.* colourless, flammable gas from petroleum

propel (prəˈpɛl) *vt.* cause to move forward (**-ll-**) —**proˈpellant** *or* **proˈpellent** *n.* something causing propulsion, *eg* rocket fuel —**proˈpeller** *n.* revolving shaft with blades for driving ship or aircraft —**proˈpulsion** *n.* act of driving forward —**proˈpulsive** *or* **proˈpulsory** *a.* 1. tending, having power to propel 2. urging on

propene (ˈprəʊpiːn) *n.* colourless gaseous alkene obtained by cracking petroleum (*also* **ˈpropylene**)

propensity (prəˈpɛnsɪtɪ) *n.* 1. inclination or bent 2. tendency 3. disposition

THESAURUS

expeditious, quick, ready, responsive, smart, willing ~*v.* 3. cause, impel, incite, induce, inspire, instigate, motivate, move, provoke, spur, stimulate, urge 4. assist, cue, help out, jog the memory, prod, refresh the memory, remind 5. call forth, cause, elicit, evoke, give rise to, occasion, provoke, suggest

prompter 1. autocue, idiot board (*Sl.*), Teleprompter (*Trademark*) 2. agitator, catalyst, gadfly, inspirer, instigator, moving spirit, prime mover

promptly at once, by return, directly, immediately, instantly, on the dot, on time, pronto (*Inf.*), punctually, quickly, speedily, swiftly, unhesitatingly

promptness alacrity, alertness, briskness, dispatch, eagerness, haste, promptitude, punctuality, quickness, readiness, speed, swiftness, willingness

promulgate advertise, announce, broadcast, circulate, communicate, declare, decree, disseminate, issue, make known, make public, notify, proclaim, promote, publish, spread

prone 1. face down, flat, horizontal, lying down, procumbent, prostrate, recumbent, supine 2. apt, bent, disposed, given, inclined, liable, likely, predisposed, subject, susceptible, tending

prong point, projection, spike, tine, tip

pronounce 1. accent, articulate, enunciate, say, sound, speak, stress, utter, vocalize, voice 2. affirm, announce, assert, declare, decree, deliver, judge, proclaim

pronounced broad, clear, conspicuous, decided, definite, distinct, evident, marked, noticeable, obvious, striking, strong, unmistakable

pronouncement announcement, declaration, decree, dictum, edict, judgment, manifesto, notification, proclamation, promulgation, pronunciamento, statement

pronunciation accent, accentuation, articulation, diction, elocution, enunciation, inflection, intonation, speech, stress

proof *n.* 1. attestation, authentication, certification, confirmation, corroboration, demonstration, evidence, substantiation, testimony, verification 2. *As in* **put to the proof** assay, examination, experiment, ordeal, scrutiny, test, trial 3. *Printing* galley, galley proof, page proof, pull, slip, trial impression, trial print ~*adj.* 4. impenetrable, impervious, repellent, resistant, strong, tight, treated

prop 1. *v.* bolster, brace, buttress, hold up, maintain, shore, stay, support, sustain, truss, uphold 2. *n.* brace, buttress, mainstay, stanchion, stay, support, truss

propaganda advertising, agitprop, ballyhoo (*Inf.*), brainwashing, disinformation, hype (*Sl.*), information, newspeak, promotion, publicity

propagate 1. beget, breed, engender, generate, increase, multiply, procreate, produce, proliferate, reproduce 2. broadcast, circulate, diffuse, disseminate, make known, proclaim, promote, promulgate, publicize, publish, spread, transmit

propagation 1. breeding, generation, increase, multiplication, procreation, proliferation, reproduction 2. circulation, communication, diffusion, dissemination, distribution, promotion, promulgation, spread, spreading, transmission

propel drive, force, impel, launch, push, send, set in motion, shoot, shove, start, thrust

propensity aptness, bent, bias, disposition, inclination, leaning, liability, penchant, predisposition, proclivity, proneness, susceptibility, tendency, weakness

proper (ˈprɒpə) *a.* **1.** appropriate **2.** correct **3.** conforming to etiquette, decorous **4.** strict **5.** (of noun) denoting individual person or place —**ˈproperly** *adv.* —**proper fraction** fraction in which numerator has lower absolute value than denominator

property (ˈprɒpətɪ) *n.* **1.** that which is owned **2.** estate whether in lands, goods or money **3.** quality, attribute of something **4.** article used on stage in play *etc.*

prophet (ˈprɒfɪt) *n.* **1.** inspired teacher or revealer of Divine Will **2.** foreteller of future (**-ess** *fem.*) —**prophecy** (ˈprɒfɪsɪ) *n.* prediction, prophetic utterance —**prophesy** (ˈprɒfɪsaɪ) *v.* foretell —**prophetic** (prəˈfetɪk) *a.*

prophylactic (prɒfɪˈlæktɪk) *n./a.* **1.** (something) done or used to ward off disease —*n.* **2.** US condom —**prophyˈlaxis** *n.*

propinquity (prəˈpɪŋkwɪtɪ) *n.* nearness, proximity, close kinship

propitiate (prəˈpɪʃieɪt) *vt.* appease, gain favour of —**propitiˈation** *n.* —**proˈpitiatory** *a.* —**proˈpitious** *a.* favourable, auspicious

proponent (prəˈpəʊnənt) *n.* one who advocates something

proportion (prəˈpɔːʃən) *n.* **1.** relative size or number **2.** comparison **3.** due relation between connected things or parts **4.** share **5.** relation —*pl.* **6.** dimensions —*vt.* **7.** arrange proportions of —**proˈportionable** *a.* —**proˈportional** *or* **proˈportionate** *a.* **1.** having a due proportion **2.** corresponding in size, number *etc.* —**proˈportionally** *adv.* —**proportional representation** representation of parties in elective body in proportion to votes they win

propose (prəˈpəʊz) *vt.* **1.** put forward for consideration **2.** nominate **3.** intend —*vi.* **4.** offer marriage —**proˈposal** *n.* —**proˈposer** *n.* —**proposition** (prɒpəˈzɪʃən) *n.* **1.** offer **2.** statement, assertion **3.** theorem **4.** suggestion of terms **5.** *inf.* thing to be dealt with

propound (prəˈpaʊnd) *vt.* put forward for consideration or solution

proprietor (prəˈpraɪətə) *n.* owner (**-tress, -trix** *fem.*) —**proˈprietary** *a.* **1.** belonging to owner **2.** made by firm with exclusive rights of manufacture

propriety (prəˈpraɪətɪ) *n.* properness, correct conduct, fitness

propulsion (prəˈpʌlʃən) *n. see* PROPEL

propylene (ˈprəʊpɪliːn) *n. see* PROPENE

pro rata (ˈrɑːtə) *Lat.* in proportion

prorogue (prəˈrəʊg) *vt.* dismiss (parliament) at end of session without dissolution

prosaic (prəʊˈzeɪɪk) *a.* commonplace, unromantic

pros and cons various arguments in favour of and against motion, course of action *etc.*

THESAURUS

proper 1. appropriate, apt, becoming, befitting, fit, fitting, legitimate, meet (*Archaic*), right, suitable, suited **2.** *comme il faut*, decent, decorous, *de rigueur*, genteel, gentlemanly, ladylike, mannerly, polite, punctilious, refined, respectable, seemly **3.** accepted, accurate, conventional, correct, established, exact, formal, orthodox, precise, right

property 1. assets, belongings, building(s), capital, chattels, effects, estate, goods, holdings, house(s), means, possessions, resources, riches, wealth **2.** acres, estate, freehold, holding, land, real estate, real property, realty, title **3.** ability, attribute, characteristic, feature, hallmark, idiosyncrasy, mark, peculiarity, quality, trait, virtue

prophecy augury, divination, forecast, foretelling, prediction, prognosis, prognostication, revelation, second sight, soothsaying, vaticination (*Rare*)

prophesy augur, divine, forecast, foresee, foretell, forewarn, predict, presage, prognosticate, soothsay, vaticinate (*Rare*)

prophet augur, Cassandra, clairvoyant, diviner, forecaster, oracle, prognosticator, prophesier, seer, sibyl, soothsayer

prophetic augural, divinatory, fatidic (*Rare*), foreshadowing, mantic, oracular, predictive, presaging, prescient, prognostic, sibylline, vatic (*Rare*)

propitious advantageous, auspicious, bright, encouraging, favourable, fortunate, full of promise, happy, lucky, opportune, promising, prosperous, rosy, timely

proportion 1. distribution, ratio, relationship, relative amount **2.** agreement, balance, congruity, correspondence, harmony, symmetry **3.** amount, cut (*Inf.*), division, fraction, measure, part, percentage, quota, segment, share **4.** *Plural* amplitude, breadth, bulk, capacity, dimensions, expanse, extent, magnitude, measurements, range, scope, size, volume

proportional, proportionate balanced, commensurate, comparable, compatible, consistent, correspondent, corresponding, equitable, equivalent, even, in proportion, just

proposal bid, design, motion, offer, overture, plan, presentation, proffer, programme, project, proposition, recommendation, scheme, suggestion, tender, terms

propose 1. advance, come up with, present, proffer, propound, put forward, submit, suggest, tender **2.** introduce, invite, name, nominate, present, put up, recommend **3.** aim, design, have every intention, have in mind, intend, mean, plan, purpose, scheme **4.** ask for someone's hand (in marriage), offer marriage, pay suit, pop the question (*Inf.*)

proposition *n.* motion, plan, programme, project, proposal, recommendation, scheme, suggestion

propound advance, advocate, contend, lay down, postulate, present, propose, put forward, set forth, submit, suggest

proprietor, proprietress, proprietrix deed holder, freeholder, landlady, landlord, landowner, owner, possessor, titleholder

propriety 1. appropriateness, aptness, becomingness, correctness, fitness, properness, rightness, seemliness, suitableness **2.** breeding, courtesy, decency, decorum, delicacy, etiquette, good form, good manners, manners, modesty, politeness, protocol, punctilio, rectitude, refinement, respectability, seemliness

propulsion drive, impetus, impulse, impulsion, momentum, motive power, power, pressure, propelling force, push, thrust

prosaic banal, boring, commonplace, dry, dull, everyday, flat, hackneyed, humdrum, matter-of-fact, mundane, ordinary, pedestrian, routine, stale, tame, trite, unimaginative, uninspiring, unromantic, vapid, workaday

proscenium (prəˈsiːnɪəm) *n.* arch or opening framing stage (*pl.* **-nia** (-nɪə))

proscribe (prəʊˈskraɪb) *vt.* outlaw, condemn **—proscription** (prəʊˈskrɪpʃən) *n.*

prose (prəʊz) *n.* speech or writing without rhyme or metre **—ˈprosily** *adv.* **—ˈprosiness** *n.* **—ˈprosy** *a.* tedious, dull

prosecute (ˈprɒsɪkjuːt) *vt.* carry on, bring legal proceedings against **—proseˈcution** *n.* **—ˈprosecutor** *n.* (**-trix** *fem.*)

proselyte (ˈprɒsɪlaɪt) *n.* convert **—proselytism** (ˈprɒsɪlɪtɪzəm) *n.* **—proselytize** *or* **-ise** (ˈprɒsɪlɪtaɪz) *v.*

prosody (ˈprɒsədɪ) *n.* system, study of versification **—ˈprosodist** *n.*

prospect (ˈprɒspɛkt) *n.* **1.** (*sometimes pl.*) expectation, chance for success **2.** view, outlook **3.** likely customer or subscriber **4.** mental view **—***v.* (prəˈspɛkt) **5.** explore, *esp.* for gold **—proˈspective** *a.* **1.** anticipated **2.** future **—proˈspectively** *adv.* **—proˈspector** *n.* **—proˈspectus** *n.* circular describing company, school *etc.*

prosper (ˈprɒspə) *v.* (cause to) do well **—prosˈperity** *n.* good fortune, wellbeing **—ˈprosperous** *a.* **1.** doing well, successful **2.** flourishing, rich, well-off **—ˈprosperously** *adv.*

prostate (ˈprɒsteɪt) *n.* gland accessory to male generative organs

prosthesis (ˈprɒsθɪsɪs) *n.* (replacement of part of body with) artificial substitute (*pl.* **-ses** (-siːz))

prostitute (ˈprɒstɪtjuːt) *n.* **1.** one who offers sexual intercourse in return for payment **—***vt.* **2.** make a prostitute of **3.** put to unworthy use **—prostiˈtution** *n.*

prostrate (ˈprɒstreɪt) *a.* **1.** lying flat **2.** crushed, submissive, overcome **—***vt.* (prɒˈstreɪt) **3.** throw flat on ground **4.** reduce to exhaustion **—prosˈtration** *n.*

Prot. **1.** Protestant **2.** Protectorate

protactinium (prəʊtækˈtɪnɪəm) *n.* toxic radioactive element that occurs in uranium ores and is produced by neutron irradiation of thorium

protagonist (prəʊˈtægənɪst) *n.* **1.** leading character **2.** principal actor **3.** champion of a cause

protasis (ˈprɒtəsɪs) *n.* introductory clause of conditional sentence (*pl.* **-ses** (-siːz))

protean (prəʊˈtiːən, ˈprəʊtɪən) *a.* **1.** variable **2.** versatile

protect (prəˈtɛkt) *vt.* defend, guard, keep from harm **—proˈtection** *n.* **—proˈtectionist** *n.* one who advocates protecting industries by taxing competing imports **—proˈtective** *a.* **—proˈtector** *n.* **1.** one who protects **2.** regent **—proˈtectorate** *n.* **1.** relation of state to territory it protects and controls **2.** such territory **3.** office, period of protector of a state

THESAURUS

proscribe **1.** ban, boycott, censure, condemn, damn, denounce, doom, embargo, forbid, interdict, prohibit, reject **2.** attaint (*Archaic*), banish, blackball, deport, exclude, excommunicate, exile, expatriate, expel, ostracize, outlaw

prosecute **1.** *Law* arraign, bring action against, bring suit against, bring to trial, do (*Sl.*), indict, litigate, prefer charges, put in the dock, put on trial, seek redress, sue, summon, take to court, try **2.** carry on, conduct, direct, discharge, engage in, manage, perform, practise, work at

prospect *n.* **1.** anticipation, calculation, contemplation, expectation, future, hope, odds, opening, outlook, plan, presumption, probability, promise, proposal, thought **2.** landscape, outlook, panorama, perspective, scene, sight, spectacle, view, vision, vista **3.** *Sometimes plural* chance, likelihood, possibility ~*v.* **4.** explore, go after, look for, search, seek, survey

prospective about to be, anticipated, approaching, awaited, coming, destined, eventual, expected, forthcoming, future, hoped-for, imminent, intended, likely, looked-for, possible, potential, soon-to-be, -to-be, to come

prospectus announcement, catalogue, conspectus, list, outline, plan, programme, scheme, syllabus, synopsis

prosper advance, be fortunate, bloom, do well, fare well, flourish, flower, get on, grow rich, make good, make it (*Inf.*), progress, succeed, thrive

prosperity affluence, boom, ease, fortune, good fortune, good times, life of luxury, life of Riley (*Inf.*), luxury, plenty, prosperousness, riches, success, the good life, wealth, wellbeing

prosperous **1.** blooming, booming, doing well, flourishing, fortunate, lucky, on the up and up (*Brit.*), palmy, prospering, successful, thriving **2.** affluent, in clover (*Inf.*), in the money (*Inf.*), moneyed, opulent, rich, wealthy, well-heeled (*Sl.*), well-off, well-to-do

prostitute **1.** *n.* bawd (*Archaic*), brass (*Sl.*), call girl, camp follower, cocotte, courtesan, fallen woman, *fille de joie*, harlot, hooker (*U.S. sl.*), hustler (*Sl.*), loose woman, moll (*Sl.*), pro (*Sl.*), streetwalker, strumpet, tart (*Inf.*), trollop, white slave, whore **2.** *v.* cheapen, debase, degrade, demean, devalue, misapply, pervert, profane

prostitution harlotry, harlot's trade, Mrs. Warren's profession, streetwalking, the game (*Sl.*), the oldest profession, vice, whoredom

prostrate *adj.* **1.** abject, bowed low, flat, horizontal, kowtowing, procumbent, prone **2.** brought to one's knees, crushed, defenceless, disarmed, helpless, impotent, overcome, overwhelmed, paralysed, powerless, reduced, submissive ~*v.* **3.** *Of oneself* abase, bend the knee to, bow before, bow down to, cast oneself before, cringe, fall at (someone's) feet, fall on one's knees before, grovel, kneel, kowtow, submit **4.** drain, exhaust, fag out (*Inf.*), fatigue, sap, tire, wear out, weary

protagonist **1.** central character, hero, heroine, lead, leading character, principal **2.** advocate, champion, exponent, leader, mainstay, moving spirit, prime mover, standard-bearer, supporter

protean changeable, ever-changing, many-sided, mercurial, multiform, mutable, polymorphous, variable, versatile, volatile

protect care for, chaperon, cover, cover up for, defend, foster, give sanctuary, guard, harbour, keep, keep safe, look after, mount *or* stand guard over, preserve, safeguard, save, screen, secure, shelter, shield, support, take under one's wing, watch over

protection **1.** aegis, care, charge, custody, defence, guardianship, guarding, preservation, protecting, safeguard, safekeeping, safety, security **2.** armour,

protégé *or* (*fem.*) **protégée** (ˈprəʊtɪʒeɪ) *n.* one under another's care, protection or patronage

protein (ˈprəʊtiːn) *n.* any of various kinds of organic compound which form most essential part of food of living creatures

pro tempore (ˈprəʊ ˈtɛmpərɪ) *Lat.* for the time being (*also* **pro tem**)

protest (ˈprəʊtɛst) *n.* **1.** declaration or demonstration of objection —*vi.* (prəˈtɛst) **2.** object —*v.* **3.** make declaration (against) **4.** assert formally —**protesˈtation** *n.* strong declaration

Protestant (ˈprɒtɪstənt) *a.* **1.** belonging to any branch of the Western Church outside the Roman Catholic Church —*n.* **2.** member of such a church —ˈ**Protestantism** *n.*

protium (ˈprəʊtɪəm) *n.* most common isotope of hydrogen

proto- *or sometimes before vowel* **prot-** (*comb. form*) first, as in *prototype*

protocol (ˈprəʊtəkɒl) *n.* **1.** diplomatic etiquette **2.** draft of terms signed by parties as basis of formal treaty

proton (ˈprəʊtɒn) *n.* positively charged particle in nucleus of atom

protoplasm (ˈprəʊtəplæzəm) *n.* substance that is living matter of all animal and plant cells —**protoˈplasmic** *a.*

prototype (ˈprəʊtətaɪp) *n.* **1.** original or model after which thing is copied **2.** pattern

protozoan (prəʊtəˈzəʊən) *n.* minute animal of lowest and simplest class (*pl.* **-zoa** (-ˈzəʊə))

protract (prəˈtrækt) *vt.* **1.** lengthen **2.** prolong **3.** delay **4.** draw to scale —**proˈtracted** *a.* **1.** long-drawn-out **2.** tedious —**proˈtraction** *n.* —**proˈtractor** *n.* instrument for measuring angles on paper

protrude (prəˈtruːd) *v.* stick out, (cause to) project —**proˈtrusile** *a. Zool.* capable of being thrust forward —**proˈtrusion** *n.* —**proˈtrusive** *a.* thrusting forward —**proˈtrusively** *adv.*

protuberant (prəˈtjuːbərənt) *a.* bulging out —**proˈtuberance** *or* **proˈtuberancy** *n.* bulge, swelling

proud (praʊd) *a.* **1.** feeling or displaying pride **2.** arrogant **3.** gratified **4.** noble **5.** self-respecting **6.** stately —ˈ**proudly** *adv.* —**proud flesh** flesh growing around healing wound

Prov. **1.** Provençal **2.** *Bible* Proverbs **3.** Province **4.** Provost

prove (pruːv) *vt.* **1.** establish validity of **2.** demonstrate, test —*vi.* **3.** turn out (to be *etc.*) **4.** (of dough) rise in warm place before baking (**proved,** ˈ**proven** *pp.*) —**proven** (ˈpruːvᵊn, ˈprəʊ-) *a.* proved —**proving ground** place for testing new equipment *etc.*

provenance (ˈprɒvɪnəns) *n.* place of origin, source

Provençal (prɒvɒnˈsɑːl; *Fr.* prɔvɑ̃ˈsal) *a.* **1.** of Provence, former province of SE France, its dialect of French or its Romance language —*n.* **2.** language of Provence, closely related to French and Italian, belonging to Romance group of Indo-European family **3.** native or inhabitant of Provence

provender (ˈprɒvɪndə) *n.* fodder

proverb (ˈprɒvɜːb) *n.* short, pithy, traditional saying in common use —**proˈverbial** *a.*

THESAURUS

barrier, buffer, bulwark, cover, guard, refuge, safeguard, screen, shelter, shield

protective careful, covering, defensive, fatherly, insulating, jealous, maternal, motherly, paternal, possessive, protecting, safeguarding, sheltering, shielding, vigilant, warm, watchful

protector advocate, benefactor, bodyguard, champion, counsel, defender, guard, guardian, guardian angel, knight in shining armour, patron, safeguard, tower of strength

protégé, protégée charge, dependant, discovery, pupil, student, ward

protest *n.* **1.** complaint, declaration, demur, demurral, disapproval, dissent, formal complaint, objection, outcry, protestation, remonstrance ~*v.* **2.** complain, cry out, demonstrate, demur, disagree, disapprove, expostulate, express disapproval, kick (against) (*Inf.*), object, oppose, remonstrate, say no to, take exception **3.** affirm, argue, assert, asseverate, attest, avow, contend, declare, insist, maintain, profess, testify, vow

protestation affirmation, asseveration, avowal, declaration, oath, pledge, profession, vow

protocol **1.** code of behaviour, conventions, courtesies, customs, decorum, etiquette, formalities, good form, manners, politesse, propriety, rules of conduct **2.** agreement, compact, concordat, contract, convention, covenant, pact, treaty

prototype archetype, example, first, mock-up, model, norm, original, paradigm, pattern, precedent, standard, type

protract continue, drag on *or* out, draw out, extend, keep going, lengthen, prolong, spin out, stretch out

protracted dragged out, drawn-out, extended, interminable, lengthy, long, long-drawn-out, neverending, overlong, prolonged, spun out, time-consuming

protrude bulge, come through, extend, jut, obtrude, point, pop (*of eyes*), project, shoot out, stand out, start (from), stick out

protrusion bulge, bump, jut, lump, outgrowth, projection, protuberance, swelling

protuberance bulge, bump, excrescence, knob, lump, outgrowth, process, projection, prominence, protrusion, swelling, tumour

proud **1.** appreciative, content, contented, glad, gratified, honoured, pleased, satisfied, self-respecting, well-pleased **2.** arrogant, boastful, conceited, disdainful, egotistical, haughty, high and mighty (*Inf.*), imperious, lordly, narcissistic, orgulous (*Archaic*), overbearing, presumptuous, self-important, self-satisfied, snobbish, snooty (*Inf.*), stuck-up (*Inf.*), supercilious, toffee-nosed (*Sl.*), vain **3.** august, distinguished, eminent, grand, great, illustrious, imposing, magnificent, majestic, noble, splendid, stately

prove **1.** ascertain, attest, authenticate, bear out, confirm, corroborate, demonstrate, determine, establish, evidence, evince, justify, show, show clearly, substantiate, verify **2.** analyse, assay, check, examine, experiment, put to the test, put to trial, test, try **3.** be found to be, come out, end up, result, turn out

proverb adage, aphorism, apophthegm, byword, dictum, gnome, maxim, saw, saying

proverbial accepted, acknowledged, archetypal, axiomatic, conventional, current, customary, famed, fa-

provide (prəˈvaɪd) *vi.* 1. make preparation —*vt.* 2. supply, equip, prepare, furnish, give —**proˈvider** *n.* —**proˈviding** *or* **proˈvided** *conj.* (*sometimes with* that) on condition or understanding (that)

provident (ˈprɒvɪdənt) *a.* 1. thrifty 2. showing foresight —**ˈprovidence** *n.* 1. kindly care of God or nature 2. foresight 3. economy —**proviˈdential** *a.* strikingly fortunate, lucky —**proviˈdentially** *adv.*

province (ˈprɒvɪns) *n.* 1. division of a country, district 2. sphere of action —*pl.* 3. any part of country outside capital —**proˈvincial** *a.* 1. of a province 2. unsophisticated 3. narrow in outlook —*n.* 4. unsophisticated person 5. inhabitant of province —**proˈvincialism** *n.* 1. narrowness of outlook 2. lack of refinement 3. idiom peculiar to province

provision (prəˈvɪʒən) *n.* 1. a providing, *esp.* for the future 2. thing provided —*pl.* 3. food 4. *Law* articles of instrument or statute —*vt.* 5. supply with food —**proˈvisional** *a.* 1. temporary 2. conditional

proviso (prəˈvaɪzəʊ) *n.* condition (*pl.* -s, -es)

provoke (prəˈvəʊk) *vt.* 1. irritate 2. incense 3. arouse 4. excite 5. cause —**provocation** (prɒvəˈkeɪʃən) *n.* —**provocative** (prəˈvɒkətɪv) *a.*

provost (ˈprɒvəst) *n.* 1. one who superintends or presides 2. head of certain colleges 3. administrative head of Scottish burgh

prow (praʊ) *n.* bow of vessel

prowess (ˈpraʊɪs) *n.* 1. bravery, fighting capacity 2. skill

prowl (praʊl) *vi.* 1. roam stealthily, *esp.* in search of prey or booty —*n.* 2. act of prowling —**ˈprowler** *n.* —**on the prowl** 1. moving about stealthily 2. pursuing members of opposite sex

prox. proximo

proximate (ˈprɒksɪmɪt) *a.* nearest, next, immediate —**proxˈimity** *n.* —**ˈproximo** *adv.* in the next month

proxy (ˈprɒksɪ) *n.* 1. authorized agent or substitute 2. writing authorizing one to act as this

prude (pruːd) *n.* one who affects excessive modesty or propriety —**ˈprudery** *n.* —**ˈprudish** *a.*

THESAURUS

mous, legendary, notorious, self-evident, time-honoured, traditional, typical, unquestioned, well-known

provide 1. accommodate, cater, contribute, equip, furnish, outfit, provision, stock up, supply 2. add, afford, bring, give, impart, lend, present, produce, render, serve, yield 3. *With* **for** *or* **against** anticipate, arrange for, forearm, get ready, make arrangements, make plans, plan ahead, plan for, prepare for, take measures, take precautions

providence 1. destiny, divine intervention, fate, fortune, God's will, predestination 2. care, caution, discretion, far-sightedness, foresight, forethought, perspicacity, presence of mind, prudence

provident canny, careful, cautious, discreet, economical, equipped, far-seeing, far-sighted, forearmed, foresighted, frugal, prudent, sagacious, shrewd, thrifty, vigilant, well-prepared, wise

providential fortuitous, fortunate, happy, heaven-sent, lucky, opportune, timely, welcome

provider benefactor, donor, giver, source, supplier

providing, provided *conj.* as long as, contingent upon, given, if and only if, in case, in the event, on condition, on the assumption, subject to, upon these terms, with the proviso, with the understanding

province 1. colony, county, department, dependency, district, division, domain, region, section, territory, tract, zone 2. *Fig.* area, business, capacity, charge, concern, duty, employment, field, function, line, orbit, part, pigeon (*Brit. inf.*), post, responsibility, role, sphere

provincial *adj.* 1. country, home-grown, homespun, local, rural, rustic 2. insular, inward-looking, limited, narrow, narrow-minded, parish-pump, parochial, small-minded, small-town (*U.S.*), uninformed, unsophisticated, upcountry ~*n.* 3. country cousin, rustic, yokel

provision 1. accoutrement, catering, equipping, fitting out, furnishing, providing, supplying, victualling 2. arrangement, plan, prearrangement, precaution, preparation

provisional conditional, contingent, interim, limited, pro tem, provisory, qualified, stopgap, temporary, tentative, transitional

provisions comestibles, eatables, eats (*Sl.*), edibles, fare, food, foodstuff, groceries, grub (*Sl.*), provender, rations, stores, supplies, sustenance, viands, victuals

proviso clause, condition, limitation, provision, qualification, requirement, reservation, restriction, rider, stipulation, strings

provocation 1. *casus belli*, cause, grounds, incitement, inducement, instigation, justification, motivation, reason, stimulus 2. affront, annoyance, challenge, dare, grievance, indignity, injury, insult, offence, red rag, taunt, vexation

provocative 1. aggravating (*Inf.*), annoying, challenging, disturbing, galling, goading, incensing, insulting, offensive, outrageous, provoking, stimulating 2. alluring, arousing, erotic, exciting, inviting, seductive, sexy (*Inf.*), stimulating, suggestive, tantalizing, tempting

provoke 1. affront, aggravate (*Inf.*), anger, annoy, chafe, enrage, exasperate, gall, get on one's nerves, incense, infuriate, insult, irk, irritate, madden, make one's blood boil, offend, pique, put out, rile, try one's patience, vex 2. bring about, bring on *or* down, call forth, cause, draw forth, elicit, evoke, excite, fire, generate, give rise to, incite, induce, inflame, inspire, instigate, kindle, lead to, motivate, move, occasion, precipitate, produce, promote, prompt, rouse, stimulate, stir

prow bow(s), fore, forepart, front, head, nose, sharp end (*Jocular*), stem

prowess 1. ability, accomplishment, adeptness, adroitness, aptitude, attainment, command, dexterity, excellence, expertise, expertness, facility, genius, mastery, skill, talent 2. boldness, bravery, courage, daring, dauntlessness, doughtiness, fearlessness, gallantry, hardihood, heroism, intrepidity, mettle, valiance, valour

prowl cruise, hunt, lurk, move stealthily, nose around, patrol, range, roam, rove, scavenge, skulk, slink, sneak, stalk, steal

proximity adjacency, closeness, contiguity, juxtaposition, nearness, neighbourhood, propinquity, vicinity

proxy agent, attorney, delegate, deputy, factor, representative, substitute, surrogate

prudent (ˈpruːdᵊnt) *a.* **1.** careful, discreet **2.** sensible —**ˈprudence** *n.* **1.** habit of acting with careful deliberation **2.** wisdom applied to practice —**pruˈdential** *a.*

prune[1] (pruːn) *n.* dried plum

prune[2] (pruːn) *vt.* **1.** cut out (dead parts, excessive branches *etc.*) from **2.** shorten, reduce —**pruning hook** tool with curved blade terminating in hook, used for pruning

prurient (ˈprʊərɪənt) *a.* **1.** given to, springing from lewd thoughts **2.** having unhealthy curiosity or desire —**ˈprurience** *or* **ˈpruriency** *n.*

pruritus (prʊəˈraɪtəs) *n. Pathol.* intense itching —**pruritic** (prʊəˈrɪtɪk) *a.*

prussic acid (ˈprʌsɪk) extremely poisonous aqueous solution of hydrogen cyanide

pry (praɪ) *vi.* **1.** make furtive or impertinent inquiries **2.** look curiously —*vt.* **3.** US force open (**pried, ˈprying**)

P.S. postscript (*also* **p.s.**)

Ps. *or* **Psa.** *Bible* Psalm(s)

psalm (sɑːm) *n.* **1.** sacred song **2.** (**P-**) any of the sacred songs making up the Book of Psalms in the Bible —**ˈpsalmist** *n.* writer of psalms —**psalmody** (ˈsɑːmədɪ, ˈsæl-) *n.* art, act of singing sacred music —**Psalter** (ˈsɔːltə) *n.* **1.** book of psalms **2.** copy of the Psalms as separate book —**psaltery** (ˈsɔːltərɪ) *n.* obsolete stringed instrument like lyre

PSBR public sector borrowing requirement

psephology (sɛˈfɒlədʒɪ) *n.* statistical study of elections

pseud (sjuːd) *inf. n.* **1.** false or pretentious person —*a.* **2.** sham, fake (*also* **ˈpseudo**)

pseudo- *or sometimes before vowel* **pseud-** (*comb. form*) sham, as in *pseudo-Gothic, pseudomodern.* Such compounds are not given here where the meaning may easily be inferred from the simple word

pseudonym (ˈsjuːdənɪm) *n.* **1.** false, fictitious name **2.** pen name —**pseudonymous** (sjuːˈdɒnɪməs) *a.*

pshaw (pʃɔː) *interj. rare* exclamation of disgust, impatience, disbelief *etc.*

psi (psaɪ) *n.* 23rd letter in Gr. alphabet (Ψ, ψ), transliterated as *ps*

psittacine (ˈsɪtəsaɪn, -sɪn) *a.* pert. to, like parrots —**psittaˈcosis** *n.* dangerous infectious disease, germ of which is carried by parrots

psoriasis (səˈraɪəsɪs) *n.* skin disease characterized by formation of reddish spots and patches covered with silvery scales

psst (pst) *interj.* exclamation of beckoning, *esp.* made surreptitiously

P.S.T. US, C Pacific Standard Time

P.S.V. public service vehicle

psyche (ˈsaɪkɪ) *n.* human mind or soul

psychedelic (saɪkɪˈdɛlɪk) *a.* **1.** of or causing hallucinations **2.** like intense colours *etc.* experienced during hallucinations

psychic (ˈsaɪkɪk) *a.* **1.** sensitive to phenomena lying outside range of normal experience **2.** of soul or mind **3.** that appears to be outside region of physical law —**psyˈchiatry** *n.* medical treatment of mental diseases —**ˈpsychical** *a.* psychic —**psychoˈanalyse** *or esp. U.S.* **psychoˈanalyze** *vt.* treat by psychoanalysis —**psychoaˈnalysis** *n.* method of studying and treating mental disorders —**psychoˈanalyst** *n.* —**psychogenic** (saɪkəʊˈdʒɛnɪk) *a. Psychol.* (*esp.* of disorders or symptoms) of mental, rather than organic origin —**psychokiˈnesis** *n.* (in parapsychology) alteration of state of object supposedly by mental influence alone —**psychoˈlogical** *a.* **1.** of psychology **2.** of the mind —**psyˈchologist** *n.* —**psyˈchology** *n.* **1.** study of mind **2.** *inf.* person's mental make-up —**psyˈchometry** *n.* **1.** measurement, testing of psychological processes **2.** supposed ability to divine unknown person's qualities by handling object used or worn by him —**ˈpsychopath** *n.* person afflicted with severe mental disorder causing him to commit antisocial, oft. violent acts —**psychoˈpathic** *a.* —**psyˈchosis** *n.* severe mental disorder in which person's contact with reality becomes distorted (*pl.* **-choses** (-ˈkəʊsiːz)) —**psychosoˈmatic** *a.* of physical disorders thought to have psychological causes —**psychoˈtherapy** *n.* treatment of disease by psychological, rather than by physical, means —**psychological moment** most appropriate time for producing desired effect —**psychological warfare** military application of psychology, *esp.* to manipulation of morale in time of war

psycho (ˈsaɪkəʊ) *sl. n.* **1.** psychopath (*pl.* **-s**) —*a.* **2.** psychopathic

THESAURUS

prude Grundy, old maid (*Inf.*), prig, puritan, schoolmarm (*Brit. inf.*)

prudence canniness, care, caution, circumspection, common sense, discretion, good sense, heedfulness, judgment, judiciousness, sagacity, vigilance, wariness, wisdom

prudent canny, careful, cautious, circumspect, discerning, discreet, judicious, politic, sagacious, sage, sensible, shrewd, vigilant, wary, wise

prudery Grundyism, old-maidishness (*Inf.*), overmodesty, priggishness, primness, prudishness, puritanicalness, squeamishness, starchiness (*Inf.*), strictness, stuffiness

prudish demure, narrow-minded, old-maidish (*Inf.*), overmodest, overnice, priggish, prim, prissy (*Inf.*), proper, puritanical, schoolmarmish (*Brit. inf.*), squeamish, starchy (*Inf.*), strait-laced, stuffy, Victorian

prune clip, cut, cut back, dock, lop, pare down, reduce, shape, shorten, snip, trim

pry be a busybody, be inquisitive, be nosy (*Inf.*), ferret about, interfere, intrude, meddle, nose into, peep, peer, poke, poke one's nose in *or* into (*Inf.*), snoop (*Inf.*)

prying curious, eavesdropping, impertinent, inquisitive, interfering, intrusive, meddlesome, meddling, nosy (*Inf.*), snooping (*Inf.*), snoopy (*Inf.*), spying

psalm chant, hymn, paean, song of praise

pseudo *adj.* artificial, bogus, counterfeit, ersatz, fake, false, imitation, mock, not genuine, phoney (*Sl.*), pretended, quasi-, sham, spurious

pseudonym alias, assumed name, false name, incognito, nom de guerre, nom de plume, pen name, professional name, stage name

psyche anima, essential nature, individuality, inner man, innermost self, mind, personality, pneuma (*Philos.*), self, soul, spirit, subconscious, true being

psychic **1.** clairvoyant, extrasensory, mystic, occult, preternatural, supernatural, telekinetic, telepathic **2.** mental, psychogenic, psychological, spiritual

psycho- *or sometimes before vowel* **psych-** (*comb. form*) mind, psychological or mental processes, as in *psychology, psychosomatic*

Pt *Chem.* platinum

pt. 1. part 2. pint 3. point

Pt. 1. Point 2. Port

p.t. 1. past tense 2. pro tempore

P.T. 1. physical therapy 2. physical training

P.T.A. parent teacher association

ptarmigan (ˈtɑːmɪgən) *n.* bird of grouse family which turns white in winter (*pl.* **-s, -gan**)

Pte. Private (soldier)

ptero- (*comb. form*) wing, as in *pterodactyl*

pterodactyl (tɛrəˈdæktɪl) *n.* extinct flying reptile with batlike wings

P.T.O. *or* **p.t.o.** please turn over

ptomaine *or* **ptomain** (ˈtəʊmeɪn) *n.* any of group of poisonous alkaloids found in decaying matter

Pu *Chem.* plutonium

pub (pʌb) *n.* public house, building with bar(s) and licence to sell alcoholic drinks —**pub-crawl** *sl., chiefly* UK *n.* 1. drinking tour of number of pubs or bars —*vi.* 2. make such tour

pub. 1. public 2. publication 3. published 4. publisher 5. publishing

puberty (ˈpjuːbətɪ) *n.* sexual maturity —ˈ**pubertal** *a.*

pubes (ˈpjuːbiːz) *n.* 1. region above external genital organs, covered with hair from time of puberty 2. pubic hair (*pl.* ˈ**pubes**) 3. *pl. of* PUBIS

pubescent (pjuːˈbɛsᵊnt) *a.* 1. arriving or arrived at puberty 2. (of certain plants and animals or their parts) covered with fine short hairs or down —**puˈbescence** *n.*

pubic (ˈpjuːbɪk) *a.* of the lower abdomen

pubis (ˈpjuːbɪs) *n.* one of three sections of hipbone that forms part of pelvis (*pl.* **-bes** (-biːz))

public (ˈpʌblɪk) *a.* 1. of or concerning the public as a whole 2. not private 3. open to general observation or knowledge 4. accessible to all 5. serving the people —*n.* 6. the community or its members —ˈ**publican** *n.* keeper of public house —ˈ**publicly** *adv.* —**public-address system** system of microphones, amplifiers and loudspeakers for increasing sound level, used in auditoriums *etc.* (*also* **P.A. system**) —**public company** limited company whose shares may be purchased by the public —**public convenience** public lavatory —**public enemy** notorious person, such as criminal, regarded as menace to public —**public house** pub —**public lending right** right of authors to receive payment when books are borrowed from public libraries —**public relations** promotion of good relations of an organization or authority with the general public —**public school** 1. in England and Wales, private independent fee-paying school 2. in some Canad. provinces, a local elementary school —**public servant** 1. elected or appointed holder of public office 2. A, NZ civil servant —**public service** government employment —**public spirit** interest in and devotion to welfare of community —**public-spirited** *a.* having or showing active interest in good of community —**public transport** trains, buses *etc.* that have fixed routes and are available to general public —**public utility** enterprise concerned with provision to public of essentials, such as electricity *etc.*

publicist (ˈpʌblɪsɪst) *n.* 1. writer on public concerns 2. journalist —**pubˈlicity** *n.* 1. process of attracting public attention 2. attention thus gained —*a.* 3. pert. to advertisement —ˈ**publicize** *or* **-ise** *vt.* advertise

publish (ˈpʌblɪʃ) *vt.* 1. prepare and issue for sale (books, music *etc.*) 2. make generally known 3. proclaim —**publiˈcation** *n.* —ˈ**publisher** *n.*

puce (pjuːs) *a./n.* purplish-brown (colour)

puck[1] (pʌk) *n.* rubber disc used instead of ball in ice hockey

puck[2] (pʌk) *n.* mischievous sprite —ˈ**puckish** *a.*

pucker (ˈpʌkə) *v.* 1. gather into wrinkles —*n.* 2. crease, fold

pudding (ˈpʊdɪŋ) *n.* 1. sweet, usu. cooked dessert, oft.

THESAURUS

psychological 1. cerebral, cognitive, intellectual, mental 2. all in the mind, emotional, imaginary, irrational, psychosomatic, subconscious, subjective, unconscious, unreal

psychology 1. behaviourism, science of mind, study of personality 2. *Inf.* attitude, mental make-up, mental processes, thought processes, way of thinking, what makes one tick

psychopath insane person, lunatic, madman, maniac, mental case, nutcase (*Sl.*), nutter (*Brit. sl.*), psychotic, sociopath

pub, public house alehouse (*Archaic*), bar, boozer (*Inf.*), inn, local (*Brit. inf.*), roadhouse, tavern

puberty adolescence, awkward age, juvenescence, pubescence, teenage, teens, young adulthood

public *adj.* 1. civic, civil, common, general, national, popular, social, state, universal, widespread 2. accessible, communal, community, free to all, not private, open, open to the public, unrestricted 3. acknowledged, exposed, in circulation, known, notorious, obvious, open, overt, patent, plain, published, recognized ~*n.* 4. citizens, commonalty, community, country, electorate, everyone, hoi polloi, masses, multitude, nation, people, populace, population, society, voters

publication 1. advertisement, airing, announcement, appearance, broadcasting, declaration, disclosure, dissemination, notification, proclamation, promulgation, publishing, reporting 2. book, booklet, brochure, handbill, issue, leaflet, magazine, newspaper, pamphlet, periodical

publicity advertising, attention, ballyhoo (*Sl.*), boost, build-up, hype (*Sl.*), plug (*Inf.*), press, promotion, public notice, puff, puffery (*Inf.*)

publicize advertise, beat the drum for (*Inf.*), bring to public notice, broadcast, give publicity to, hype (*Sl.*), make known, play up, plug (*Inf.*), promote, puff, push, spotlight, spread about, write up

public-spirited altruistic, charitable, community-minded, generous, humanitarian, philanthropic, unselfish

publish 1. bring out, issue, print, produce, put out 2. advertise, announce, broadcast, circulate, communicate, declare, disclose, distribute, divulge, impart, leak, proclaim, promulgate, publicize, reveal, spread

pudding afters (*Brit. inf.*), dessert, last course, pud (*Inf.*), second course, sweet

made from suet, flour *etc.* **2.** sweet course of meal **3.** soft savoury dish with pastry or batter **4.** kind of sausage

puddle (ˈpʌdˀl) *n.* **1.** small muddy pool **2.** rough cement for lining ponds *etc.* —*vt.* **3.** line with puddle **4.** make muddy

pudendum (pjuːˈdɛndəm) *n.* (*oft. pl.*) human external genital organs, *esp.* of female (*pl.* **-da** (-də)) —**puˈdendal** *or* **ˈpudic** *a.*

pudgy (ˈpʌdʒɪ) *a. esp.* **US** *see* PODGY

puerile (ˈpjʊəraɪl) *a.* **1.** childish **2.** foolish **3.** trivial

puerperium (pjʊəˈpɪərɪəm) *n.* period of about six weeks after childbirth —**puerperal** (pjuːˈɜːpərəl) *a.* —**puerperal fever** formerly, blood poisoning caused by infection during childbirth

puff (pʌf) *n.* **1.** short blast of breath, wind *etc.* **2.** its sound **3.** type of pastry **4.** laudatory notice or advertisement —*vi.* **5.** blow abruptly **6.** breathe hard —*vt.* **7.** send out in a puff **8.** blow out, inflate **9.** advertise **10.** smoke hard —**puffed** *a.* **1.** breathless; winded **2.** swollen; puffy —**ˈpuffy** *a.* **1.** short-winded **2.** swollen —**puff adder 1.** large venomous Afr. viper that inflates its body when alarmed **2.** N Amer. nonvenomous snake that inflates its body when alarmed (*also* **hognose snake**) —**ˈpuffball** *n.* **1.** ball-shaped fungus **2.** skirt that puffs out wide and is nipped into narrow hem —**puff pastry** *or U.S.* **puff paste** dough for making a rich flaky pastry

puffin (ˈpʌfɪn) *n.* any of various sea birds with large brightly-coloured beaks

pug (pʌg) *n.* **1.** small snub-nosed dog **2.** *sl.* boxer —**pug nose** snub nose

pugilism (ˈpjuːdʒɪlɪzəm) *n.* art, practice or profession of fighting with fists; boxing —**ˈpugilist** *n.* —**pugiˈlistic** *a.*

pugnacious (pʌgˈneɪʃəs) *a.* given to fighting —**pugnacity** (pʌgˈnæsɪtɪ) *n.*

puissant (ˈpjuːɪsˀnt) *a. Poet.* powerful, mighty —**puissance** (ˈpjuːɪsˀns, ˈpwiːsɑːns) *n.* showjumping competition over very high fences

puke (pjuːk) *sl. vi.* **1.** vomit —*n.* **2.** act of vomiting

pukka *or* **pucka** (ˈpʌkə) *a. Anglo-Indian* properly or perfectly done, constructed *etc.*; good; genuine

pulchritude (ˈpʌlkrɪtjuːd) *n. Lit.* beauty

pule (pjuːl) *vi.* whine; whimper

pull (pʊl) *vt.* **1.** exert force on (object) to move it towards source of force **2.** strain, stretch **3.** tear **4.** propel by rowing —*n.* **5.** act of pulling **6.** force exerted by it **7.** draught of liquor **8.** *inf.* power, influence —**pull in 1.** (of train) arrive **2.** (of car *etc.*) draw in to side of road, stop **3.** attract **4.** *sl.* arrest —**pull off** *inf.* carry through to successful issue —**pull out 1.** withdraw **2.** extract **3.** (of train) depart **4.** (of car *etc.*) move away from side of road; move out to overtake —**pull (someone's) leg** *inf.* make fun of (someone) —**pull up 1.** tear up **2.** recover lost ground **3.** improve **4.** come to a stop **5.** halt **6.** reprimand

pullet (ˈpʊlɪt) *n.* young hen

pulley (ˈpʊlɪ) *n.* wheel with groove in rim for cord, used to raise weights by downward pull

Pullman (ˈpʊlmən) *n.* railway saloon car (*pl.* **-s**) (*also* **Pullman car**)

pullover (ˈpʊləʊvə) *n.* jersey, sweater without fastening, to be pulled over head

pulmonary (ˈpʌlmənərɪ, ˈpʊl-) *a.* **1.** of lungs **2.** having lungs or lunglike organs

pulp (pʌlp) *n.* **1.** soft, moist, vegetable or animal matter **2.** flesh of fruit **3.** any soft soggy mass —*vt.* **4.** reduce to pulp

pulpit (ˈpʊlpɪt) *n.* raised (enclosed) platform for preacher

pulsar (ˈpʌlsɑː) *n.* small dense star emitting radio waves

pulse[1] (pʌls) *n.* **1.** movement of blood in arteries corresponding to heartbeat, discernible to touch, *eg* in wrist **2.** any regular beat or vibration —**pulˈsate** *vi.* throb, quiver —**pulˈsation** *n.*

pulse[2] (pʌls) *n.* edible seeds of pod-bearing plants, *eg* beans

pulverize *or* **-ise** (ˈpʌlvəraɪz) *vt.* **1.** reduce to powder **2.** smash, demolish —**pulveriˈzation** *or* **-iˈsation** *n.*

puma (ˈpjuːmə) *n.* large Amer. feline carnivore, cougar

THESAURUS

puerile babyish, childish, foolish, immature, inane, infantile, irresponsible, jejune, juvenile, naive, petty, ridiculous, silly, trivial, weak

puff *n.* **1.** blast, breath, draught, emanation, flurry, gust, whiff **2.** advertisement, commendation, favourable mention, good word, plug (*Inf.*), sales talk ~*v.* **3.** blow, breathe, exhale, gasp, gulp, pant, wheeze **4.** drag (*Sl.*), draw, inhale, pull at *or* on, smoke, suck **5.** *Usually with* **up** bloat, dilate, distend, expand, inflate, swell **6.** hype (*Sl.*), overpraise, plug (*Inf.*), praise, promote, publicize, push

puffed breathless, done in (*Inf.*), exhausted, gasping, out of breath, panting, short of breath, spent, winded

puffy bloated, distended, enlarged, inflamed, inflated, puffed up, swollen

pugilist boxer, bruiser (*Inf.*), fighter, prizefighter, pug (*Sl.*)

pugnacious aggressive, antagonistic, argumentative, bellicose, belligerent, choleric, combative, contentious, disputatious, hot-tempered, irascible, irritable, petulant, quarrelsome

pull *v.* **1.** drag, draw, haul, jerk, tow, trail, tug, yank **2.** dislocate, rend, rip, sprain, strain, stretch, tear, wrench **3. pull someone's leg** *Inf.* chaff, have (someone) on, joke, make fun of, poke fun at, rag, rib (*Inf.*), tease, twit ~*n.* **4.** jerk, tug, twitch, yank **5.** attraction, drawing power, effort, exertion, force, forcefulness, influence, lure, magnetism, power **6.** *Inf.* advantage, clout (*Inf.*), influence, leverage, muscle, weight

pull off accomplish, bring off, carry out, manage, score a success, secure one's object, succeed

pull out abandon, depart, evacuate, leave, quit, rat on, retreat, stop participating, withdraw

pull up 1. dig out, lift, raise, tear up, uproot **2.** brake, come to a halt, halt, reach a standstill, stop **3.** admonish, carpet (*Inf.*), castigate, dress down (*Inf.*), rebuke, reprimand, reprove, take to task, tell off (*Inf.*), tick off (*Inf.*)

pulp *n.* **1.** flesh, marrow, soft part **2.** mash, mush, pap, paste, pomace, semiliquid, semisolid, triturate ~*v.* **3.** crush, mash, pulverize, squash, triturate

pulse *n.* beat, beating, oscillation, pulsation, rhythm, stroke, throb, throbbing, vibration

pumice ('pʌmɪs) *n.* light porous variety of volcanic rock used to scour, smooth and polish (*also* **pumice stone**)

pummel ('pʌməl) *vt.* strike repeatedly (-ll-)

pump[1] (pʌmp) *n.* **1.** appliance in which piston and handle are used for raising water, or putting in or taking out air, liquid *etc.* —*vt.* **2.** raise, put in, take out *etc.* with pump **3.** empty by means of pump **4.** extract information from —*vi.* **5.** work pump **6.** work like pump —**pump iron** *sl.* lift weights

pump[2] (pʌmp) *n.* light shoe

pumpernickel ('pʌmpənɪk'l) *n.* sour black bread made of coarse rye flour

pumpkin ('pʌmpkɪn) *n.* any of several varieties of gourd, eaten *esp.* as vegetable

pun (pʌn) *n.* **1.** humorous use of words that have the same sound, but have different meanings —*vi.* **2.** make pun (-nn-) —'**punster** *n.*

punch[1] (pʌntʃ) *n.* **1.** tool for perforating or stamping **2.** blow with fist **3.** *inf.* vigour —*vt.* **4.** stamp, perforate with punch **5.** strike with fist —'**punchball** *n.* **1.** stuffed or inflated ball or bag, either suspended or supported by flexible rod, that is punched for exercise, *esp.* boxing training **2.** US game resembling baseball —**punch-drunk** *or* (*inf.*) '**punchy** *a.* dazed, as by repeated blows —**punched card** *or esp. U.S.* **punch card** card on which data can be coded in form of punched holes —**punched tape** *or U.S.* **perforated tape** strip of paper used in computers *etc.* for recording information in form of punched holes (*also* **paper tape**) —**punch line** culminating part of joke *etc.*, that gives it its point —**punch-up** *n.* UK *sl.* fight, brawl

punch[2] (pʌntʃ) *n.* drink of spirits or wine with fruit juice, spice *etc.*

punctilious (pʌŋk'tɪlɪəs) *a.* **1.** making much of details of etiquette **2.** very exact, particular

punctual ('pʌŋktjuəl) *a.* in good time, not late, prompt —**punctu'ality** *n.* —'**punctually** *adv.*

punctuate ('pʌŋktjueɪt) *vt.* **1.** insert punctuation marks into **2.** interrupt at intervals —**punctu'ation** *n.* marks, *eg* commas, colons *etc.*, put in writing to assist in making sense clear

puncture ('pʌŋktʃə) *n.* **1.** small hole made by sharp object, *esp.* in tyre **2.** act of puncturing —*vt.* **3.** prick hole in, perforate

pundit *or* **pandit** ('pʌndɪt) *n.* **1.** self-appointed expert **2.** Brahman learned in Sanskrit and, *esp.* in Hindu religion, philosophy or law

pungent ('pʌndʒənt) *a.* **1.** biting **2.** irritant **3.** piercing **4.** tart **5.** caustic —'**pungency** *n.*

punish ('pʌnɪʃ) *vt.* **1.** cause (someone) to suffer for offence **2.** inflict penalty on **3.** use or treat roughly —'**punishable** *a.* —'**punishment** *n.* —**punitive** ('pju:nɪtɪv) *a.* inflicting or intending to inflict punishment

punk[1] (pʌŋk) *a./n.* **1.** inferior, rotten, worthless (person or thing) **2.** petty (hoodlum) **3.** (of) style of rock music

punk[2] (pʌŋk) *n.* dried decayed wood or other substance that smoulders when ignited: used as tinder

punka *or* **punkah** ('pʌŋkə) *n.* **1.** fan made of palm leaf or leaves **2.** large fan made of palm leaves *etc.* worked mechanically to cool room

punnet ('pʌnɪt) *n.* small basket for fruit

punt[1] (pʌnt) *n.* **1.** flat-bottomed, square-ended boat, propelled by pushing with pole —*vt.* **2.** propel thus

punt[2] (pʌnt) *Sport vt.* **1.** kick (ball) before it touches ground, when let fall from hands —*n.* **2.** such a kick

punt[3] (pʌnt) *vi.* gamble, bet —'**punter** *n.* **1.** one who punts **2.** professional gambler **3.** *inf.* customer or client, *esp.* prostitute's client

THESAURUS

pump *v.* **1.** *With* **out** bail out, drain, draw off, drive out, empty, force out, siphon **2.** cross-examine, give (someone) the third degree, grill (*Inf.*), interrogate, probe, question closely, quiz, worm out of

pun double entendre, equivoque, paronomasia (*Rhetoric*), play on words, quip, witticism

punch *v.* **1.** bash (*Inf.*), biff (*Sl.*), bop (*Inf.*), box, clout (*Inf.*), hit, plug (*Sl.*), pummel, slam, slug, smash, sock (*Sl.*), strike, wallop (*Inf.*) ~*n.* **2.** bash (*Inf.*), biff (*Sl.*), blow, bop (*Inf.*), clout (*Inf.*), hit, jab, knock, plug (*Sl.*), sock (*Sl.*), thump, wallop (*Inf.*) **3.** *Inf.* bite, drive, effectiveness, force, forcefulness, impact, point, verve, vigour ~*v.* **4.** bore, cut, drill, perforate, pierce, pink, prick, puncture, stamp

punch-drunk befuddled, confused, dazed, groggy (*Inf.*), in a daze, knocked silly, punchy (*Inf.*), reeling, slaphappy (*Inf.*), staggering, stupefied, unsteady, woozy (*Inf.*)

punctilious careful, ceremonious, conscientious, exact, finicky, formal, fussy, meticulous, nice, particular, precise, proper, scrupulous, strict

punctual early, exact, in good time, on the dot, on time, precise, prompt, punctilious, seasonable, strict, timely

punctuality promptitude, promptness, readiness, regularity

punctuate break, interject, interrupt, intersperse, pepper, sprinkle

puncture **1.** *n.* break, cut, damage, hole, leak, nick, opening, perforation, rupture, slit **2.** *v.* bore, cut, nick, penetrate, perforate, pierce, prick, rupture

pundit buff (*Inf.*), maestro, one of the cognoscenti, (self-appointed) authority *or* expert

pungent **1.** acid, acrid, aromatic, bitter, highly flavoured, hot, peppery, piquant, seasoned, sharp, sour, spicy, stinging, strong, tangy, tart **2.** acrimonious, acute, barbed, biting, caustic, cutting, incisive, keen, mordant, penetrating, piercing, poignant, pointed, sarcastic, scathing, sharp, stinging, stringent, telling, trenchant

punish **1.** beat, castigate, chasten, chastise, correct, discipline, flog, give a lesson to, give (someone) the works (*Sl.*), lash, penalize, rap someone's knuckles, scourge, sentence, slap someone's wrist, whip **2.** abuse, batter, give (someone) a going over (*Inf.*), harm, hurt, injure, knock about, maltreat, manhandle, misuse, oppress, rough up

punishable blameworthy, chargeable, convictable, criminal, culpable, indictable

punishment **1.** chastening, chastisement, comeuppance (*Sl.*), correction, discipline, just deserts, penalty, penance, punitive measures, retribution, sanction, what for (*Inf.*) **2.** *Inf.* abuse, beating, hard work, maltreatment, manhandling, pain, rough treatment, slave labour, torture, victimization

punitive in reprisal, in retaliation, retaliative, retaliatory, revengeful, vindictive

puny (ˈpjuːnɪ) *a.* small and feeble

pup (pʌp) *n.* young of certain animals, *eg* dog

pupa (ˈpjuːpə) *n.* stage between larva and adult in metamorphosis of insect, chrysalis (*pl.* **pupae** (ˈpjuːpiː)) —ˈ**pupal** *a.*

pupil (ˈpjuːpᵊl) *n.* **1.** person being taught **2.** opening in iris of eye

puppet (ˈpʌpɪt) *n.* small doll or figure of person *etc.* controlled by operator's hand —**puppeˈteer** *n.* —ˈ**puppetry** *n.* —**puppet show** show with puppets worked by hidden showman —**puppet state** state that appears independent but is controlled by another

puppy (ˈpʌpɪ) *n.* young dog —**puppy fat** fatty tissue in child or adolescent, usu. disappearing with age

purblind (ˈpɜːblaɪnd) *a.* **1.** partly or nearly blind **2.** lacking in insight or understanding

purchase (ˈpɜːtʃɪs) *vt.* **1.** buy —*n.* **2.** act of buying **3.** what is bought **4.** leverage, grip

purdah (ˈpɜːdə) *n.* **1.** Muslim, Hindu custom of keeping women in seclusion **2.** screen, veil to achieve this

pure (pjʊə) *a.* **1.** unmixed, untainted **2.** simple **3.** spotless **4.** faultless **5.** innocent **6.** concerned with theory only —ˈ**purely** *adv.* —**purifiˈcation** *n.* —ˈ**purificatory** *a.* —ˈ**purify** *v.* make, become pure, clear or clean (**-ified, -ifying**) —ˈ**purism** *n.* excessive insistence on correctness of language —ˈ**purist** *n.* —ˈ**purity** *n.* state of being pure —**purebred** (ˈpjʊəˈbrɛd) *a.* **1.** denoting pure strain obtained through many generations of controlled breeding —*n.* (ˈpjʊəbrɛd) **2.** purebred animal

purée (ˈpjʊəreɪ) *n.* **1.** pulp of cooked fruit or vegetables —*vt.* **2.** make (cooked foods) into purée

purgatory (ˈpɜːgətərɪ) *n.* place or state of torment, pain or distress, *esp.* temporary —**purgaˈtorial** *a.*

purge (pɜːdʒ) *vt.* **1.** make clean, purify **2.** remove, get rid of **3.** clear out —*n.* **4.** act, process of purging **5.** removal of undesirable members from political party, army *etc.* —**purgation** (pɜːˈgeɪʃən) *n.* —**purgative** (ˈpɜːgətɪv) *a./n.*

Puritan (ˈpjʊərɪtᵊn) *n.* **1.** *Hist.* member of extreme Protestant party **2.** (**p-**) person of extreme strictness in morals or religion —**puriˈtanic(al)** *a.* **1.** strict in the observance of religious and moral duties **2.** overscrupulous —ˈ**puritanism** *n.*

purl[1] (pɜːl) *n.* **1.** stitch that forms ridge in knitting —*v.* **2.** knit in purl stitch

purl[2] (pɜːl) *vi.* flow with burbling sound, swirl, babble

purlieus (ˈpɜːljuːz) *pl.n.* outlying parts, outskirts

purlin *or* **purline** (ˈpɜːlɪn) *n.* horizontal beam that provides support for rafters of roof

purloin (pɜːˈlɔɪn) *vt.* **1.** steal **2.** pilfer

purple (ˈpɜːpᵊl) *n./a.* (of) colour between crimson and violet —**Purple Heart** decoration awarded to members of U.S. Armed Forces for wound received in action

purport (pɜːˈpɔːt) *vt.* **1.** claim to be (true *etc.*) **2.** signify, imply —*n.* (ˈpɜːpɔːt) **3.** meaning **4.** apparent meaning **5.** significance

purpose (ˈpɜːpəs) *n.* **1.** reason, object **2.** design **3.** aim, intention —*vt.* **4.** intend —ˈ**purposely** *adv.* —**purpose-**

THESAURUS

punt *v.* back, bet, gamble, lay, stake, wager

punter *n.* **1.** backer, better, gambler **2.** *Inf.* client, customer

puny diminutive, dwarfish, feeble, frail, little, pint-sized (*Inf.*), pygmy, sickly, stunted, tiny, underfed, undersized, undeveloped, weak, weakly

pupil beginner, catechumen, disciple, learner, neophyte, novice, scholar, schoolboy, schoolgirl, student, tyro

purchase *v.* **1.** acquire, buy, come by, gain, get, get hold of, invest in, make a purchase, obtain, pay for, pick up, procure, secure, shop for ~*n.* **2.** acquisition, asset, buy, gain, investment, possession, property **3.** advantage, edge, foothold, footing, grasp, grip, hold, influence, lever, leverage, support, toehold

pure **1.** authentic, clear, flawless, genuine, natural, neat, perfect, real, simple, straight, true, unalloyed, unmixed **2.** clean, disinfected, germ-free, immaculate, pasteurized, sanitary, spotless, sterile, sterilized, unadulterated, unblemished, uncontaminated, unpolluted, untainted, wholesome **3.** blameless, chaste, faultless, guileless, honest, immaculate, innocent, maidenly, modest, true, uncorrupted, undefiled, unspotted, unstained, unsullied, upright, virgin, virginal, virtuous **4.** absolute, complete, mere, sheer, simple, thorough, unmitigated, unqualified, utter **5.** abstract, academic, philosophical, speculative, theoretical

purely absolutely, completely, entirely, exclusively, just, merely, only, plainly, simply, solely, totally, wholly

purge *v.* **1.** clean out, dismiss, do away with, eject, eradicate, expel, exterminate, get rid of, kill, liquidate, oust, remove, rid of, rout out, sweep out, wipe out **2.** absolve, cleanse, clear, exonerate, expiate, forgive, pardon, purify, wash ~*n.* **3.** cleanup, crushing, ejection, elimination, eradication, expulsion, liquidation, reign of terror, removal, suppression, witch hunt

purify **1.** clarify, clean, cleanse, decontaminate, disinfect, filter, fumigate, refine, sanitize, wash **2.** absolve, cleanse, exculpate, exonerate, lustrate, redeem, sanctify, shrive

purist classicist, formalist, pedant, precisian, stickler

puritan **1.** *n.* fanatic, moralist, pietist, prude, rigorist, zealot **2.** *adj.* ascetic, austere, hidebound, intolerant, moralistic, narrow, narrow-minded, prudish, puritanical, severe, strait-laced, strict

puritanical ascetic, austere, bigoted, disapproving, fanatical, forbidding, narrow, narrow-minded, prim, proper, prudish, puritan, rigid, severe, stiff, strait-laced, strict, stuffy

purpose *n.* **1.** aim, design, function, idea, intention, object, point, principle, reason **2.** aim, ambition, aspiration, design, desire, end, goal, hope, intention, object, objective, plan, project, scheme, target, view, wish **3.** **on purpose** by design, deliberately, designedly, intentionally, knowingly, purposely, wilfully, wittingly ~*v.* **4.** aim, aspire, commit oneself, contemplate, decide, design, determine, have a mind to, intend, make up one's mind, mean, meditate, plan, propose, resolve, set one's sights on, think to, work towards

purposely by design, calculatedly, consciously, deliberately, designedly, expressly, intentionally, knowingly, on purpose, wilfully, with intent

built *a.* made to serve specific purpose —**on purpose** intentionally

purr (pɜː) *n.* 1. (*esp.* of cats) make low vibrant sound, usu. considered as expressing pleasure *etc.* —*vi.* 2. utter this sound

purse (pɜːs) *n.* 1. small bag for money 2. resources 3. money as prize —*vt.* 4. pucker (mouth, lips *etc.*) in wrinkles —*vi.* 5. become wrinkled and drawn in —**ˈpurser** *n.* ship's officer who keeps accounts —**purse strings** control of expenditure (*esp. in* **hold** *or* **control the purse strings**)

purslane (ˈpɜːslɪn) *n.* plant used (*esp.* formerly) in salads and as potherb

pursue (pəˈsjuː) *vt.* 1. run after 2. chase 3. aim at 4. engage in 5. continue 6. follow —*vi.* 7. go in pursuit 8. continue —**purˈsuance** *n.* carrying out —**purˈsuant** *adj. chiefly law* in agreement or conformity —**purˈsuer** *n.* —**purˈsuit** *n.* 1. running after, attempt to catch 2. occupation

pursuivant (ˈpɜːsɪvənt) *n.* officer of College of Arms below herald

purulent (ˈpjʊərʊlənt) *a. see* PUS

purvey (pəˈveɪ) *vt.* supply (provisions) —**purˈveyance** *n.* —**purˈveyor** *n.*

purview (ˈpɜːvjuː) *n.* scope, range

pus (pʌs) *n.* yellowish matter produced by suppuration —**purulence** (ˈpjʊərʊləns) *n.* —**ˈpurulent** *a.* 1. forming, discharging pus 2. septic

push (pʊʃ) *vt.* 1. move, try to move away by pressure 2. drive, impel 3. *inf.* sell (*esp.* narcotic drugs) illegally —*vi.* 4. make thrust 5. advance with steady effort —*n.* 6. thrust 7. persevering self-assertion 8. big military advance 9. *sl.* dismissal —**ˈpusher** *n.* —**ˈpushing** *or inf.* **ˈpushy** *a.* given to pushing oneself —**push-bike** *n.* UK *inf.* bicycle —**push button** electrical switch operated by pressing button, which closes or opens circuit —**push-button** *a.* 1. operated by push button 2. initiated as simply as by pressing button —**ˈpushchair** *n.* (collapsible) chair-shaped carriage for baby —**ˈpushover** *n. sl.* 1. something easily achieved 2. person *etc.* easily taken advantage of or defeated —**push-start** *vt.* 1. start (motor vehicle) by pushing while in gear, thus turning engine —*n.* 2. this process

pusillanimous (pjuːsɪˈlænɪməs) *a.* cowardly —**pusillaˈnimity** *n.*

puss (pʊs) *n.* cat (*also* **ˈpussy**) —**pussy willow** willow tree with silvery silky catkins

pussyfoot (ˈpʊsɪfʊt) *vi. inf.* 1. move stealthily 2. act indecisively, procrastinate

pustule (ˈpʌstjuːl) *n.* pimple containing pus —**ˈpustular** *a.* —**pustulate** (ˈpʌstjʊleɪt) *v.* 1. (cause to) form into pustules —*a.* (ˈpʌstjʊlɪt) 2. covered with pustules

put (pʊt) *vt.* 1. place 2. set 3. express 4. throw (*esp.* shot) (**put, ˈputting**) —*n.* 5. throw —**put across** express successfully —**put-down** *n.* cruelly critical remark —**put-up** *a.* dishonestly or craftily prearranged (*esp. in* **put-up job**) —**put down** 1. make written record of 2. repress 3. consider 4. attribute 5. put (animal) to death because of old age or illness 6. table on agenda 7. *sl.* reject, humiliate —**put off** 1. postpone 2. disconcert 3. repel —**put up** 1. erect 2. accommodate 3. nominate

putative (ˈpjuːtətɪv) *a.* reputed, supposed —**ˈputatively** *adv.*

THESAURUS

purse *n.* **1.** money-bag, pouch, wallet **2.** coffers, exchequer, funds, means, money, resources, treasury, wealth, wherewithal **3.** award, gift, present, prize, reward ~*v.* **4.** close, contract, press together, pucker, tighten, wrinkle

pursue 1. accompany, attend, chase, dog, follow, give chase to, go after, harass, harry, haunt, hound, hunt, hunt down, plague, run after, shadow, stalk, tail, track **2.** aim for, aspire to, desire, have as one's goal, purpose, seek, strive for, try for, work towards **3.** adhere to, carry on, continue, cultivate, hold to, keep on, maintain, persevere in, persist in, proceed, see through **4.** apply oneself, carry on, conduct, engage in, perform, ply, practise, prosecute, tackle, wage, work at

pursuit 1. chase, hunt, hunting, inquiry, quest, search, seeking, tracking, trail, trailing **2.** activity, hobby, interest, line, occupation, pastime, pleasure, vocation

purview ambit, compass, confines, extent, field, limit, orbit, province, range, reach, scope, sphere

push *v.* **1.** depress, drive, poke, press, propel, ram, shove, thrust **2.** elbow, jostle, make *or* force one's way, move, shoulder, shove, squeeze, thrust **3.** egg on, encourage, expedite, hurry, impel, incite, persuade, press, prod, speed (up), spur, urge ~*n.* **4.** butt, jolt, nudge, poke, prod, shove, thrust **5.** *Inf.* ambition, determination, drive, dynamism, energy, enterprise, get-up-and-go (*Inf.*), go (*Inf.*), gumption (*Inf.*), initiative, vigour, vitality **6.** *Inf.* advance, assault, attack, charge, effort, offensive, onset, thrust **7. the push** *Sl.* discharge, dismissal, marching orders (*Inf.*), one's books (*Inf.*), one's cards, the boot (*Sl.*), the sack (*Inf.*)

pushing 1. ambitious, determined, driving, dynamic, enterprising, go-ahead, on the go, purposeful, resourceful **2.** assertive, bold, brash, bumptious, forward, impertinent, intrusive, presumptuous, pushy (*Inf.*), self-assertive

pushover 1. child's play (*Inf.*), cinch (*Sl.*), doddle (*Brit. sl.*), picnic (*Inf.*), piece of cake (*Brit. inf.*), walkover (*Inf.*) **2.** chump (*Inf.*), easy *or* soft mark, easy game (*Inf.*), mug (*Sl.*), soft touch (*Inf.*), stooge (*Sl.*), sucker (*Sl.*), walkover (*Inf.*)

pussyfoot 1. creep, prowl, slink, steal, tip-toe, tread warily **2.** beat about the bush, be noncommittal, equivocate, hedge, hum and haw, prevaricate, sit on the fence, tergiversate

pustule abscess, blister, boil, fester, gathering, pimple, ulcer

put 1. bring, deposit, establish, fix, lay, place, position, rest, set, settle, situate **2.** assign, constrain, employ, force, induce, make, oblige, require, set, subject to **3.** express, phrase, pose, set, state, utter, word **4.** cast, fling, heave, hurl, lob, pitch, throw, toss

put across communicate, convey, explain, get across, get through, make clear, make oneself understood, spell out

putative alleged, assumed, commonly believed, imputed, presumed, presumptive, reported, reputed, supposed

put down 1. enter, inscribe, log, record, set down, take down, transcribe, write down **2.** crush, quash,

putrid (ˈpjuːtrɪd) *a.* **1.** decomposed **2.** rotten —**ˈputrefy** *v.* make or become rotten (**-efied, -efying**) —**putreˈfaction** *n.* —**puˈtrescence** *n.* —**puˈtrescent** *a.* becoming rotten —**puˈtridity** *n.*

Putsch (putʃ) *n.* surprise attempt to overthrow the existing power, political revolt

putt (pʌt) *vt.* strike (golf ball) along ground in direction of hole —**ˈputter** *n.* golf club for putting —**putting green 1.** on golf course, area of closely mown grass at end of fairway where hole is **2.** area of smooth grass with several holes for putting games

puttee *or* **putty** (ˈpʌtɪ) *n.* strip of cloth wound round leg like bandage, serving as gaiter

putty (ˈpʌtɪ) *n.* **1.** paste of whiting and oil as used by glaziers **2.** jeweller's polishing powder —*vt.* **3.** fix, fill with putty (**-ied, -ying**)

puzzle (ˈpʌzᵊl) *v.* **1.** perplex or be perplexed —*n.* **2.** bewildering, perplexing question, problem or toy —**ˈpuzzlement** *n.*

PVC polyvinyl chloride (synthetic thermoplastic material used in insulation, shoes *etc.*)

pyaemia *or* **pyemia** (paɪˈiːmɪə) *n.* form of blood poisoning —**pyˈaemic** *or* **pyˈemic** *a.*

pye-dog *or* **pie-dog** (ˈpaɪdɒg) *n.* ownerless half-wild Asian dog

pygmy *or* **pigmy** (ˈpɪgmɪ) *n.* **1.** abnormally undersized person **2.** (**P-**) member of one of dwarf peoples of Equatorial Afr. —*a.* **3.** undersized

pyjamas *or U.S.* **pajamas** (pəˈdʒɑːməz) *pl.n.* sleeping suit of trousers and jacket

pylon (ˈpaɪlən) *n.* towerlike erection, *esp.* to carry electric cables

pyo- *or before vowel* **py-** (*comb. form*) pus, as in *pyosis*

pyorrhoea *or esp. U.S.* **pyorrhea** (paɪəˈrɪə) *n.* inflammation of the gums with discharge of pus and loosening of teeth

pyramid (ˈpɪrəmɪd) *n.* **1.** solid figure with sloping sides meeting at apex **2.** structure of this shape, *esp.* ancient Egyptian **3.** group of persons or things highest in the middle —**pyˈramidal** *a.* —**pyramid selling** practice adopted by some manufacturers of advertising for distributors and selling them batches of goods. The first distributors then advertise for more distributors who are sold subdivisions of original batches at increased price. This process continues until final distributors are left with stock that is unsaleable except at loss

pyre (paɪə) *n.* pile of wood for burning a dead body

pyrethrum (paɪˈriːθrəm) *n.* **1.** any of several types of cultivated chrysanthemums **2.** insecticide made from it

pyretic (paɪˈrɛtɪk) *a. Pathol.* of fever

Pyrex (ˈpaɪrɛks) *n.* **R** glassware resistant to heat

pyrite (ˈpaɪraɪt) *n.* yellow mineral consisting of iron sulphide in cubic crystalline form

pyrites (paɪˈraɪtiːz) *n.* **1.** *see* PYRITE **2.** any of a number of other disulphides of metals, *esp.* of copper and tin (*pl.* **pyˈrites**)

pyro- *or before vowel* **pyr-** (*comb. form*) **1.** fire or heat, as in *pyromania, pyrometer* **2.** *Chem.* new substance obtained by heating another, as in *pyroboric acid* **3.** *Min.* having property that changes upon application of heat; having flame-coloured appearance, as in *pyroxylin*

pyrogenic (paɪrəʊˈdʒɛnɪk) *or* **pyrogenous** (paɪˈrɒdʒɪnəs) *a.* **1.** produced by or producing heat **2.** causing or resulting from fever

pyrography (paɪˈrɒgrəfɪ) *n.* **1.** art of burning designs on wood or leather with heated tools **2.** design made by this process

pyromania (paɪrəʊˈmeɪnɪə) *n. Psych.* uncontrollable impulse and practice of setting things on fire —**pyroˈmaniac** *n.*

pyrometer (paɪˈrɒmɪtə) *n.* instrument for measuring very high temperature —**pyˈrometry** *n.*

pyrotechnics (paɪrəʊˈtɛknɪks) *pl.n.* **1.** (*with sing. v.*) manufacture of fireworks **2.** (*with sing. or pl. v.*) firework display —**pyroˈtechnist** *n.*

Pyrrhic victory (ˈpɪrɪk) victory won at high cost

Pythagoras' theorem (paɪˈθægərəs) theorem that in right-angled triangle square of length of hypotenuse equals sum of squares of other two sides

python (ˈpaɪθən) *n.* large nonpoisonous snake that crushes its prey —**ˈpythoness** *n.* woman, such as Apollo's priestess at Delphi, believed to be possessed by oracular spirit —**pythonic** (paɪˈθɒnɪk) *a.*

pyx *or* **pix** (pɪks) *n.* **1.** box in Brit. Royal Mint holding specimen coins kept to be tested for weight (*also* **pyx chest**) **2.** vessel in which consecrated Host is preserved

THESAURUS

quell, repress, silence, stamp out, suppress **3.** *With* **to** ascribe, attribute, impute, set down **4.** destroy, do away with, put away, put out of its misery, put to sleep **5.** *Sl.* condemn, crush, deflate, dismiss, disparage, humiliate, mortify, reject, shame, slight, snub

put off 1. defer, delay, hold over, postpone, put back, reschedule **2.** abash, confuse, discomfit, disconcert, dismay, distress, nonplus, perturb, rattle (*Inf.*), throw (*Inf.*), unsettle

putrid bad, contaminated, corrupt, decayed, decomposed, fetid, foul, off, putrefied, rancid, rank, reeking, rotten, rotting, spoiled, stinking, tainted

put up 1. build, construct, erect, fabricate, raise **2.** accommodate, board, entertain, give one lodging, house, lodge, take in **3.** float, nominate, offer, present, propose, put forward, recommend, submit

puzzle *v.* **1.** baffle, beat (*Sl.*), bewilder, confound, confuse, flummox, mystify, nonplus, perplex, stump **2.** ask oneself, brood, cudgel *or* rack one's brains, mull over, muse, ponder, study, think about, think hard, wonder ~*n.* **3.** brain-teaser (*Inf.*), conundrum, enigma, labyrinth, maze, mystery, paradox, poser, problem, question, question mark, riddle **4.** bafflement, bewilderment, confusion, difficulty, dilemma, perplexity, quandary, uncertainty

puzzlement bafflement, bewilderment, confusion, disorientation, doubt, doubtfulness, mystification, perplexity, surprise, uncertainty, wonder

q *or* **Q** (kju:) *n.* 1. 17th letter of English alphabet 2. speech sound represented by this letter (*pl.* **q's, Q's** *or* **Qs**)

Q 1. *Chess* Queen 2. Question

q. 1. quart 2. quarter 3. quarto (*pl.* **qq., Qq.**) (*also* **Q.**) 4. question

Q.C. Queen's Counsel

Q.E.D. quod erat demonstrandum (*Lat.*, which was to be proved)

Qld. Queensland

Q.M. Quartermaster

qr. 1. quarter 2. quire (*pl.* **qrs.**)

qt. 1. quart (*pl.* **qt., qts.**) 2. quantity

q.t. *inf.* quiet —**on the q.t.** secretly

qua (kweɪ, kwɑ:) *prep.* in the capacity of

quack (kwæk) *n.* 1. harsh cry of duck 2. pretender to medical or other skill —*vi.* 3. (of duck) utter cry

quad (kwɒd) 1. quadrangle 2. quadrant 3. quadraphonic 4. quadruplet

quadrangle (ˈkwɒdræŋgᵊl) *n.* 1. four-sided figure 2. four-sided courtyard in a building —**quadˈrangular** *a.*

quadrant (ˈkwɒdrənt) *n.* 1. quarter of circle 2. instrument for taking angular measurements —**quadˈrate** *vt.* make square —**quadratic** (kwɒˈdrætɪk) *a.* (of equation) involving square of unknown quantity

quadraphonic *or* **quadrophonic** (kwɒdrəˈfɒnɪk) *a.* (of a sound system) using four independent speakers

quadrennial (kwɒˈdrɛnɪəl) *a.* 1. occurring every four years 2. lasting four years —*n.* 3. period of four years

quadri- *or before vowel* **quadr-** (*comb. form*) four

quadrilateral (kwɒdrɪˈlætərəl) *a.* 1. four-sided —*n.* 2. four-sided figure

quadrille (kwɒˈdrɪl, kwə-) *n.* 1. square dance 2. music played for it 3. old card game

quadrillion (kwɒˈdrɪljən) *n.* 1. in Brit. and Germany, number represented as one followed by 24 zeros (10^{24}) 2. in Amer. and France, number represented as one followed by 15 zeros (10^{15}) (*pl.* **-s, quadˈrillion**) —**quadˈrillionth** *a.*

quadriplegia (kwɒdrɪˈpli:dʒɪə) *n.* paralysis of all four limbs (*also* **tetraˈplegia**) —**quadriˈplegic** *a.*

quadrivalent (kwɒdrɪˈveɪlənt) *a.* *Chem.* having four valencies (*also* **tetraˈvalent**) —**quadriˈvalency** *or* **quadriˈvalence** *n.*

quadruped (ˈkwɒdrupɛd) *n.* four-footed animal —**quadˈrupedal** *a.*

quadruple (ˈkwɒdrupᵊl, kwɒˈdru:pᵊl) *a.* 1. fourfold —*v.* 2. make, become four times as much —**quadˈruplicate** *a.* fourfold

quadruplet (ˈkwɒdruplɪt, kwɒˈdru:plɪt) *n.* one of four offspring born at one birth

quaff (kwɒf) *v.* drink heartily or in one draught

quag (kwæg) *n.* bog, swamp

quagga (ˈkwægə) *n.* recently extinct member of horse family

quail¹ (kweɪl) *n.* small bird of partridge family

quail² (kweɪl) *vi.* flinch; cower

quaint (kweɪnt) *a.* 1. interestingly old-fashioned or odd 2. curious 3. whimsical —**ˈquaintly** *adv.* —**ˈquaintness** *n.*

quake (kweɪk) *vi.* shake, tremble

Quaker (ˈkweɪkə) *n.* member of Christian sect, the **Society of Friends** (**ˈQuakeress** *fem.*)

qualify (ˈkwɒlɪfaɪ) *vi.* 1. make oneself competent —*vt.* 2. moderate 3. limit 4. make competent 5. ascribe quality to 6. describe (**-fied, -fying**) —**qualifiˈcation** *n.* 1. thing that qualifies, attribute 2. restriction 3. qualifying

quality (ˈkwɒlɪtɪ) *n.* 1. attribute, characteristic, property 2. degree of excellence 3. rank —**ˈqualitative** *a.* depending on quality —**qualitative analysis** *Chem.* decomposition of substance to determine kinds of constituents present; result obtained by such determination —**quality control** control of relative quality of manufactured product, usu. by statistical sampling techniques

qualm (kwɑ:m) *n.* 1. misgiving 2. sudden feeling of sickness —**ˈqualmish** *a.*

THESAURUS

quack *n.* charlatan, fake, fraud, humbug, impostor, mountebank, phoney (*Sl.*), pretender, quacksalver (*Archaic*)

quail blanch, blench, cower, cringe, droop, faint, falter, flinch, have cold feet (*Inf.*), quake, recoil, shake, shrink, shudder, tremble

quaint 1. bizarre, curious, droll, eccentric, fanciful, fantastic, odd, old-fashioned, original, peculiar, queer, singular, strange, unusual, whimsical 2. antiquated, antique, artful, charming, gothic, ingenious, old-fashioned, old-world, picturesque

quake convulse, move, pulsate, quail, quiver, rock, shake, shiver, shudder, throb, totter, tremble, vibrate, waver, wobble

qualification 1. ability, accomplishment, aptitude, attribute, capability, capacity, eligibility, endowment(s), fitness, quality, skill, suitability, suitableness 2. allowance, caveat, condition, criterion, exception, exemption, limitation, modification, objection, prerequisite, proviso, requirement, reservation, restriction, stipulation

qualified 1. able, accomplished, adept, capable, certificated, competent, efficient, equipped, experienced, expert, fit, knowledgeable, licensed, practised, proficient, skilful, talented, trained 2. bounded, circumscribed, conditional, confined, contingent, equivocal, guarded, limited, modified, provisional, reserved, restricted

qualify 1. capacitate, certify, commission, condition, empower, endow, equip, fit, ground, permit, prepare, ready, sanction, train 2. abate, adapt, assuage, circumscribe, diminish, ease, lessen, limit, mitigate, moderate, modify, modulate, reduce, regulate, restrain, restrict, soften, temper, vary 3. characterize, describe, designate, distinguish, modify, name

quality 1. aspect, attribute, characteristic, condition, feature, mark, peculiarity, property, trait 2. calibre, distinction, excellence, grade, merit, position, preeminence, rank, standing, status, superiority, value, worth

qualm 1. anxiety, apprehension, compunction, dis-

quandary (ˈkwɒndrɪ) *n.* state of perplexity; puzzling situation; dilemma

quango (ˈkwæŋgəʊ) *n.* quasi-autonomous national government (*or* nongovernmental) organization (*pl.* **-s**)

quantity (ˈkwɒntɪtɪ) *n.* **1.** size, number, amount **2.** specified or considerable amount —**ˈquantify** *vt.* discover, express quantity of —**ˈquantitative** *a.* **1.** involving considerations of amount or size **2.** capable of being measured **3.** *Prosody* of metrical system based on length of syllables —**ˈquantum** *n.* desired or required amount (*pl.* **-ta**) —**quantitative analysis** *Chem.* decomposition of substance to determine amount of each constituent; result obtained by such determination —**quantity surveyor** one who estimates cost of materials, labour for building job —**quantum theory** theory that in radiation, energy of electrons is discharged not continuously but in discrete units or quanta

quarantine (ˈkwɒrəntiːn) *n.* **1.** isolation to prevent spreading of infection —*vt.* **2.** put, keep in quarantine

quark (kwɑːk) *n. Phys.* any of several hypothetical particles thought to be fundamental units of matter

quarrel[1] (ˈkwɒrəl) *n.* **1.** angry dispute **2.** argument —*vi.* **3.** argue **4.** find fault (**-ll-**) —**ˈquarrelsome** *a.*

quarrel[2] (ˈkwɒrəl) *n.* **1.** crossbow arrow **2.** diamond-shaped pane

quarry[1] (ˈkwɒrɪ) *n.* **1.** object of hunt or pursuit **2.** prey

quarry[2] (ˈkwɒrɪ) *n.* **1.** excavation where stone *etc.* is got from ground for building *etc.* —*v.* **2.** get (stone *etc.*) from quarry (**ˈquarried, ˈquarrying**)

quart (kwɔːt) *n.* liquid measure equal to quarter of gallon or 2 pints (1.1 litres)

quarter (ˈkwɔːtə) *n.* **1.** fourth part **2. US, C** 25 cents **3.** unit of weight, 28 lbs. **4.** region, district **5.** mercy —*pl.* **6.** lodgings —*vt.* **7.** divide into quarters —*v.* **8.** billet or be billeted in lodgings —**ˈquarterly** *a.* **1.** happening, due *etc.* each quarter of year —*n.* **2.** quarterly periodical —**quarˈtet** *or* **quarˈtette** *n.* **1.** group of four musicians **2.** music for four performers —**ˈquarto** *n.* **1.** size of book in which sheets are folded into four leaves (*pl.* **-s**) —*a.* **2.** of this size —**quarter day** any of four days in the year when certain payments become due —**ˈquarterdeck** *n.* after part of upper deck used *esp.* for official, ceremonial purposes —**quarterˈfinal** *n.* round before semifinal in competition —**quarter horse** small, powerful breed of horse —**ˈquarterlight** *n.* **UK** small pivoted window in door of car —**ˈquartermaster** *n.* **1.** officer responsible for stores **2.** rating in navy, usu. petty officer, with particular responsibility for navigational duties —**ˈquarterstaff** *n.* long staff for fighting (*pl.* **-staves**)

quartz (kwɔːts) *n.* stone of pure crystalline silica —**ˈquartzite** *n.* quartz rock

quasar (ˈkweɪzɑː, -sɑː) *n.* extremely distant starlike object emitting powerful radio waves

quash (kwɒʃ) *vt.* **1.** annul **2.** reject **3.** subdue forcibly

quasi- (*comb. form*) seemingly, resembling but not actually being, as in *quasi-scientific*

quassia (ˈkwɒʃə) *n.* tropical Amer. tree

quaternary (kwəˈtɜːnərɪ) *a.* **1.** of the number four **2.** having four parts **3.** (**Q-**) *Geol.* of most recent period, after Tertiary —*n.* **4.** (**Q-**) Quaternary period or rock system

quatrain (ˈkwɒtreɪn) *n.* four-line stanza, *esp.* rhymed alternately

quatrefoil (ˈkætrəfɔɪl) *n.* **1.** leaf composed of four leaflets **2.** *Archit.* carved ornament having four arcs arranged about common centre

quaver (ˈkweɪvə) *vt.* **1.** say or sing in quavering tones —*vi.* **2.** tremble, shake, vibrate —*n.* **3.** musical note half length of crotchet **4.** quavering trill

quay (kiː) *n.* **1.** solid, fixed landing stage **2.** wharf

queasy (ˈkwiːzɪ) *a.* inclined to, or causing, sickness

queen (kwiːn) *n.* **1.** king's wife **2.** female sovereign **3.** piece in chess **4.** fertile female bee, wasp *etc.* **5.** court card with picture of a queen, ranking between king

THESAURUS

quiet, doubt, hesitation, misgiving, regret, reluctance, remorse, scruple, twinge *or* pang of conscience, uncertainty, uneasiness **2.** agony, attack, nausea, pang, queasiness, sickness, spasm, throe (*Rare*), twinge

quandary bewilderment, cleft stick, delicate situation, difficulty, dilemma, doubt, embarrassment, impasse, perplexity, plight, predicament, puzzle, strait, uncertainty

quantity 1. aggregate, allotment, amount, lot, number, part, portion, quota, sum, total **2.** bulk, capacity, expanse, extent, greatness, length, magnitude, mass, measure, size, volume

quarrel *n.* **1.** affray, altercation, argument, brawl, breach, broil, commotion, contention, controversy, difference (of opinion), disagreement, discord, disputation, dispute, dissension, dissidence, disturbance, feud, fight, fracas, fray, misunderstanding, row, scrap (*Inf.*), spat, squabble, strife, tiff, tumult, vendetta, wrangle ~*v.* **2.** altercate, argue, bicker, brawl, clash, differ, disagree, dispute, fall out (*Inf.*), fight, row, spar, squabble, wrangle **3.** carp, cavil, complain, decry, disapprove, find fault, object to, take exception to

quarrelsome argumentative, belligerent, cat-and-dog (*Inf.*), choleric, combative, contentious, cross, disputatious, fractious, ill-tempered, irascible, irritable, peevish, petulant, pugnacious, querulous

quarry aim, game, goal, objective, prey, prize, victim

quarter *n.* **1.** area, direction, district, locality, location, neighbourhood, part, place, point, position, province, region, side, spot, station, territory, zone **2.** clemency, compassion, favour, forgiveness, leniency, mercy, pity ~*v.* **3.** accommodate, billet, board, house, install, lodge, place, post, put up, station

quarters abode, accommodation, barracks, billet, cantonment (*Military*), chambers, digs (*Inf.*), domicile, dwelling, habitation, lodging, lodgings, post, residence, rooms, shelter, station

quash 1. beat, crush, destroy, extinguish, extirpate, overthrow, put down, quell, quench, repress, squash, subdue, suppress **2.** annul, cancel, declare null and void, invalidate, nullify, overrule, overthrow, rescind, reverse, revoke, set aside, void

quasi- 1. almost, apparently, partly, seemingly, supposedly **2.** apparent, fake, mock, near, nominal, pretended, pseudo-, seeming, semi-, sham, so-called, synthetic, virtual, would-be

quaver 1. *v.* flicker, flutter, oscillate, pulsate, quake, quiver, shake, shudder, thrill, tremble, trill, twitter, vibrate, waver **2.** *n.* break, quiver, shake, sob, throb, tremble, trembling, tremor, trill, vibration, warble

and jack 6. *inf.* male homosexual —ˈ**queenly** *a./adv.* —**Queen-Anne** (æn) *n.* 1. style of furniture popular in early 18th century, characterized by use of curves, cabriole leg *etc.* —*a.* 2. in or of this style 3. of style of architecture popular in early 18th-century England, characterized by red-brick construction with classical ornamentation —**queen consort** wife of reigning king —**queen dowager** widow of king —**queen mother** widow of former king who is also mother of reigning sovereign —**Queen's Bench** one of the divisions of the High Court in England —**Queen's Counsel** 1. in England when sovereign is female, barrister appointed Counsel to Crown on recommendation of Lord Chancellor 2. in Canad., honorary title which may be bestowed by government on lawyers with long experience —**Queen's English** when Brit. sovereign is female, standard S Brit. English —**queen's evidence** evidence given by criminal against his accomplice(s) —**queen's highway** 1. in Brit. when sovereign is female, any public road or right of way 2. in Canad., main road maintained by provincial government

Queensberry rules (ˈkwi:nzbərɪ) 1. code of rules followed in modern boxing 2. *inf.* gentlemanly conduct, *esp.* in dispute

queer (kwɪə) *a.* 1. odd, strange 2. *inf.* homosexual —*n.* 3. *inf.* homosexual —*vt. inf.* 4. spoil 5. interfere with

quell (kwɛl) *vt.* 1. crush, put down 2. allay 3. pacify

quench (kwɛntʃ) *vt.* 1. slake 2. extinguish, put out 3. suppress

quern (kwɜ:n) *n.* stone hand mill

querulous (ˈkwɛruləs, ˈkwɛrjʊ-) *a.* 1. fretful 2. peevish, whining

query (ˈkwɪərɪ) *n.* 1. question 2. mark of interrogation —*vt.* 3. question (ˈ**queried**, ˈ**querying**)

quest (kwɛst) *n./vi.* search

question (ˈkwɛstʃən) *n.* 1. sentence seeking for answer 2. that which is asked 3. interrogation 4. inquiry 5. problem 6. point for debate 7. debate, strife —*vt.* 8. ask questions of, interrogate 9. dispute 10. doubt —ˈ**questionable** *a.* doubtful, *esp.* not clearly true or honest —**questionnaire** (kwɛstʃəˈnɛə, kɛs-) *n.* list of questions drawn up for formal answer —**question mark** 1. punctuation mark ?, used at end of questions *etc.* where doubt or ignorance is implied 2. this mark used for any other purpose, as to draw attention to possible mistake (*also* **interrogation mark**) —**question time** in parliamentary bodies of British type, time set aside each day for questions to government ministers

queue (kju:) *n.* 1. line of waiting persons, vehicles —*vi.* 2. (*with* up) wait in queue

quibble (ˈkwɪbᵊl) *n.* 1. trivial objection —*vi.* 2. make this

quiche (ki:ʃ) *n.* open savoury tart

quick (kwɪk) *a.* 1. rapid, swift 2. keen 3. brisk 4. hasty —*n.* 5. sensitive flesh 6. innermost feelings (*esp. in* **cut to the quick**) —*adv.* 7. *inf.* rapidly —ˈ**quicken** *v.* make, become faster or more lively —ˈ**quickie** *n. inf.* a quick one —ˈ**quickly** *adv.* —ˈ**quicklime** *n.* calcium oxide —ˈ**quicksand** *n.* loose wet sand easily yielding to pressure and engulfing persons, animals *etc.* —ˈ**quickset** *chiefly* UK *n.* 1. plant or cutting, *esp.* of hawthorn, set so as to form hedge; such plants or cuttings collectively 2. hedge composed of such plants —*a.* 3. composed of such plants —ˈ**quicksilver** *n.* mercury —ˈ**quickstep** *n.* 1. ballroom dance —*vi.* 2. perform this dance —**quick-tempered** *a.* irascible —**quick-witted** *a.* having keenly alert mind —**quick-wittedness** *n.* —**the quick** *obs.* living people

THESAURUS

queen consort, monarch, ruler, sovereign

queer 1. *adj.* abnormal, anomalous, atypical, curious, disquieting, droll, eerie, erratic, extraordinary, funny, odd, outlandish, *outré*, peculiar, remarkable, singular, strange, uncanny, uncommon, unconventional, unnatural, unorthodox, unusual, weird 2. *v.* botch, endanger, harm, impair, imperil, injure, jeopardize, mar, ruin, spoil, thwart, wreck

quell 1. conquer, crush, defeat, extinguish, overcome, overpower, put down, quash, squelch, stamp out, stifle, subdue, suppress, vanquish 2. allay, alleviate, appease, assuage, calm, compose, deaden, dull, mitigate, moderate, mollify, pacify, quiet, silence, soothe

quench 1. check, crush, destroy, douse, end, extinguish, put out, smother, snuff out, squelch, stifle, suppress 2. allay, appease, cool, sate, satiate, satisfy, slake

querulous cantankerous, captious, carping, censorious, complaining, critical, cross, discontented, dissatisfied, fault-finding, fretful, grouchy (*Inf.*), grumbling, hard to please, irascible, irritable, murmuring, peevish, petulant, plaintive, sour, testy, touchy, waspish, whining

query *v.* 1. ask, enquire, question 2. challenge, disbelieve, dispute, distrust, doubt, mistrust, suspect ~*n.* 3. demand, doubt, hesitation, inquiry, objection, problem, question, reservation, scepticism, suspicion

quest *n.* adventure, crusade, enterprise, expedition, exploration, hunt, journey, mission, pilgrimage, pursuit, search, voyage

question *v.* 1. ask, catechize, cross-examine, enquire, examine, grill (*Inf.*), interrogate, interview, investigate, probe, pump (*Inf.*), quiz, sound out 2. call into question, cast doubt upon, challenge, controvert, disbelieve, dispute, distrust, doubt, impugn, mistrust, oppose, query, suspect ~*n.* 3. examination, inquiry, interrogation, investigation 4. argument, confusion, contention, controversy, debate, difficulty, dispute, doubt, dubiety, misgiving, problem, query, uncertainty 5. issue, motion, point, point at issue, proposal, proposition, subject, theme, topic

questionable arguable, controversial, controvertible, debatable, disputable, doubtful, dubious, dubitable, equivocal, fishy (*Inf.*), moot, paradoxical, problematical, shady (*Inf.*), suspect, suspicious, uncertain, unproven, unreliable

queue chain, concatenation, file, line, order, progression, sequence, series, string, succession, train

quibble 1. *v.* carp, cavil, equivocate, evade, pretend, prevaricate, shift, split hairs 2. *n.* artifice, cavil, complaint, criticism, duplicity, equivocation, evasion, nicety, niggle, objection, pretence, prevarication, protest, quirk, shift, sophism, subterfuge, subtlety

quick 1. active, brief, brisk, cursory, expeditious, express, fast, fleet, hasty, headlong, hurried, perfunctory, prompt, rapid, speedy, sudden, swift 2.

quid[1] (kwɪd) *n.* piece of tobacco suitable for chewing

quid[2] (kwɪd) *n. inf.* pound (sterling) (*pl.* **quid**)

quiddity (ˈkwɪdɪtɪ) *n.* **1.** essential nature **2.** petty or trifling distinction; quibble

quid pro quo (ˈkwɪd prəʊ ˈkwəʊ) *Lat.* something given in exchange

quiescent (kwɪˈɛsᵊnt) *a.* **1.** at rest, inactive, inert **2.** silent —**quiˈescence** *or* **quiˈescency** *n.*

quiet (ˈkwaɪət) *a.* **1.** with little or no motion or noise **2.** undisturbed **3.** not showy or obtrusive —*n.* **4.** state of peacefulness, absence of noise or disturbance —*v.* **5.** make, become quiet —**ˈquieten** *v.* make, become quiet —**ˈquietly** *adv.* —**ˈquietness** *or* **ˈquietude** *n.*

quietism (ˈkwaɪətɪzəm) *n.* passive attitude to life, *esp.* as form of religion —**ˈquietist** *n.*

quietus (kwaɪˈiːtəs, -ˈeɪtəs) *n.* **1.** anything that serves to quash, eliminate or kill **2.** release from life; death **3.** discharge or settlement of debts, duties *etc.*

quiff (kwɪf) *n.* **UK** tuft of hair brushed up above forehead

quill (kwɪl) *n.* **1.** large feather **2.** hollow stem of this **3.** pen, plectrum made from feather **4.** spine of porcupine

quilt (kwɪlt) *n.* **1.** padded coverlet —*vt.* **2.** stitch (two pieces of cloth) with pad between

quin (kwɪn) quintuplet

quince (kwɪns) *n.* **1.** acid pear-shaped fruit **2.** tree bearing it

quincunx (ˈkwɪnkʌŋks) *n.* group of five objects arranged in shape of rectangle with one at each corner and fifth in centre

quinine (kwɪˈniːn; *U.S.* ˈkwaɪnaɪn) *n.* bitter drug made from bark of tree, used to treat fever, and as tonic

Quinquagesima (kwɪŋkwəˈdʒɛsɪmə) *n.* Sunday 50 days before Easter

quinquennial (kwɪnˈkwɛnɪəl) *a.* occurring once in, or lasting, five years

quinquereme (ˈkwɪŋkwɪriːm) *n.* ancient Roman galley with five banks of oars

quinsy (ˈkwɪnzɪ) *n.* inflammation of throat or tonsils

quintessence (kwɪnˈtɛsəns) *n.* **1.** purest form, essential feature **2.** embodiment —**quintesˈsential** *a.*

quintet *or* **quintette** (kwɪnˈtɛt) *n.* **1.** set of five singers or players **2.** composition for five voices or instruments

quintillion (kwɪnˈtɪljən) *n.* **1.** in Brit. and Germany, number represented as one followed by 30 zeros (10^{30}) **2.** in Amer. and France, number represented as one followed by 18 zeros (10^{18}) (*pl.* **-s, quinˈtillion**) —**quinˈtillionth** *a.*

quintuple (ˈkwɪntjʊpᵊl, kwɪnˈtjuːpᵊl) *vt.* **1.** multiply by five —*a.* **2.** five times as much or as many; fivefold **3.** consisting of five parts —*n.* **4.** quantity or number five times as great as another

quintuplet (ˈkwɪntjʊplɪt, kwɪnˈtjuːplɪt) *n.* one of five offspring born at one birth

quip (kwɪp) *n.* **1.** witty saying —*vi.* **2.** make quip (**-pp-**)

quire (kwaɪə) *n.* 24 sheets of writing paper

quirk (kwɜːk) *n.* **1.** individual peculiarity of character **2.** unexpected twist or turn

quisling (ˈkwɪzlɪŋ) *n.* traitor who aids occupying enemy force

quit (kwɪt) *vi.* **1.** stop doing a thing **2.** depart —*vt.* **3.** leave, go away from **4.** cease from (**quit** *or* **ˈquitted** *pt./pp.*) —*a.* **5.** free, rid —**quits** *a.* on equal or even terms by repayment *etc.* —**ˈquittance** *n.* **1.** discharge **2.** receipt —**ˈquitter** *n.* one lacking perseverance

THESAURUS

agile, alert, animated, energetic, flying, keen, lively, nimble, spirited, sprightly, spry, vivacious, winged

quicken **1.** accelerate, dispatch, expedite, hasten, hurry, impel, precipitate, speed **2.** activate, animate, arouse, energize, excite, galvanize, incite, inspire, invigorate, kindle, refresh, reinvigorate, resuscitate, revitalize, revive, rouse, stimulate, strengthen, vitalize, vivify

quickly abruptly, at a rate of knots (*Inf.*), at *or* on the double, at speed, briskly, expeditiously, fast, hastily, hell for leather, hurriedly, immediately, instantly, posthaste, promptly, quick, rapidly, soon, speedily, swiftly, with all speed

quick-tempered choleric, excitable, fiery, hot-tempered, impatient, impulsive, irascible, irritable, petulant, quarrelsome, shrewish, splenetic, testy, waspish

quick-witted alert, astute, clever, keen, perceptive, sharp, shrewd, smart

quiescent calm, dormant, in abeyance, inactive, latent, motionless, peaceful, placid, quiet, resting, serene, silent, smooth, still, tranquil, unagitated, undisturbed, unmoving, unruffled

quiet *adj.* **1.** dumb, hushed, inaudible, low, low-pitched, noiseless, peaceful, silent, soft, soundless **2.** calm, contented, gentle, mild, motionless, pacific, peaceful, placid, restful, serene, smooth, tranquil, untroubled **3.** isolated, private, retired, secluded, secret, sequestered, undisturbed, unfrequented **4.** conservative, modest, plain, restrained, simple, sober, subdued, unassuming, unobtrusive, unpretentious ~*n.* **5.** calmness, ease, peace, quietness, repose, rest, serenity, silence, stillness, tranquillity

quieten *v.* allay, alleviate, appease, assuage, blunt, calm, compose, deaden, dull, hush, lull, mitigate, mollify, muffle, mute, palliate, quell, quiet, shush (*Inf.*), silence, soothe, stifle, still, stop, subdue, tranquillize

quietly **1.** confidentially, dumbly, in a low voice *or* whisper, in an undertone, inaudibly, in hushed tones, in silence, mutely, noiselessly, privately, secretly, silently, softly, without talking **2.** calmly, contentedly, dispassionately, meekly, mildly, patiently, placidly, serenely, undemonstratively **3.** coyly, demurely, diffidently, humbly, modestly, unassumingly, unobtrusively, unostentatiously, unpretentiously

quietness calm, calmness, hush, peace, placidity, quiescence, quiet, quietude, repose, rest, serenity, silence, still, stillness, tranquillity

quilt bedspread, comforter (*U.S.*), counterpane, coverlet, duvet, eiderdown

quip *n.* badinage, *bon mot*, gibe, jest, joke, pleasantry, repartee, retort, riposte, sally, wisecrack (*Inf.*), witticism

quirk aberration, caprice, characteristic, eccentricity, fancy, fetish, foible, habit, *idée fixe*, idiosyncrasy, kink, mannerism, oddity, peculiarity, singularity, trait, vagary, whim

quitch grass (kwɪtʃ) *see* COUCH GRASS

quite (kwaɪt) *adv.* 1. wholly, completely 2. very considerably 3. somewhat, rather —*interj.* 4. exactly, just so

quiver[1] (ˈkwɪvə) *vi.* 1. shake, tremble —*n.* 2. quivering 3. vibration

quiver[2] (ˈkwɪvə) *n.* carrying case for arrows

quixotic (kwɪkˈsɒtɪk) *a.* unrealistically and impractically optimistic, idealistic, chivalrous

quiz (kwɪz) *n.* 1. entertainment in which general or specific knowledge of players is tested by questions 2. examination, interrogation —*vt.* 3. question, interrogate (-zz-) —ˈ**quizzical** *a.* 1. questioning 2. mocking

quod (kwɒd) *n. sl.* prison

quoin (kɔɪn, kwɔɪn) *n.* 1. external corner of building 2. small wedge for locking printing type into forme

quoit (kɔɪt) *n.* 1. ring for throwing at peg as a game —*pl.* 2. (*with sing. v.*) the game

quondam (ˈkwɒndæm) *a.* of an earlier time; former

quorum (ˈkwɔːrəm) *n.* least number that must be present in meeting to make its transactions valid

quota (ˈkwəʊtə) *n.* 1. share to be contributed or received 2. specified number, quantity, which may be imported or admitted

quote (kwəʊt) *vt.* 1. copy or repeat passages from 2. refer to, *esp.* to confirm view 3. state price for —ˈ**quotable** *a.* —**quoˈtation** *n.* —**quotation mark** either of punctuation marks used to begin or end quotation, respectively " and " or ' and '

quoth (kwəʊθ) *v. obs.* said

quotidian (kwəʊˈtɪdɪən) *a.* 1. daily 2. everyday, commonplace

quotient (ˈkwəʊʃənt) *n.* number resulting from dividing one number by another

q.v. quod vide (*Lat.*, which see)

qwerty *or* **QWERTY** (ˈkwɜːtɪ) *n. inf.* standard typewriter keyboard

THESAURUS

quisling betrayer, collaborator, fifth columnist, Judas, renegade, traitor, turncoat

quit *v.* **1.** abandon, abdicate, decamp, depart, desert, exit, forsake, go, leave, pull out, relinquish, renounce, resign, retire, surrender, take off (*Inf.*), withdraw **2.** abandon, cease, conclude, discontinue, drop, end, give up, halt, stop, suspend ~*adj.* **3.** absolved, acquitted, clear, discharged, exculpated, exempt, exonerated, free, released, rid of

quite 1. absolutely, completely, considerably, entirely, fully, in all respects, largely, perfectly, precisely, totally, wholly, without reservation **2.** fairly, moderately, rather, reasonably, relatively, somewhat, to a certain extent, to some degree

quiver 1. *v.* agitate, convulse, oscillate, palpitate, pulsate, quake, quaver, shake, shiver, shudder, tremble, vibrate **2.** *n.* convulsion, oscillation, palpitation, pulsation, shake, shiver, shudder, spasm, throb, tic, tremble, tremor, vibration

quiz 1. *n.* examination, investigation, questioning, test **2.** *v.* ask, catechize, examine, grill (*Inf.*), interrogate, investigate, pump (*Inf.*), question

quota allocation, allowance, assignment, cut (*Inf.*), part, portion, proportion, ration, share, slice, whack (*Inf.*)

quotation 1. citation, cutting, excerpt, extract, passage, quote (*Inf.*), reference, selection **2.** *Commerce* bid price, charge, cost, estimate, figure, price, quote (*Inf.*), rate, tender

quote adduce, attest, cite, detail, extract, instance, name, paraphrase, proclaim, recall, recite, recollect, refer to, repeat, retell

R

r *or* **R** (ɑː) *n.* **1.** 18th letter of English alphabet **2.** speech sound represented by this letter (*pl.* **r's, R's** *or* **Rs**) —**the three Rs** three skills regarded as fundamentals of education: reading, writing and arithmetic

R **1.** *Chem.* radical **2.** rand **3.** rupee **4.** Réaumur (scale) **5.** *Phys., electron.* resistance **6.** roentgen *or* röntgen **7.** *Chess* rook **8.** Royal **9.** *Chem.* gas constant **10.** radius

R. **1.** Regina (*Lat.,* Queen) **2.** Rex (*Lat.,* King) **3.** River

Ra *Chem.* radium

R.A. **1.** Rear Admiral **2.** Royal Academy **3.** Royal Artillery

R.A.A.F. Royal Australian Air Force

rabbet (ˈræbɪt) *see* REBATE[2]

rabbi (ˈræbaɪ) *n.* Jewish learned man, spiritual leader (*pl.* **-s**) —**rabbinical** (rəˈbɪnɪkᵊl) *or* **rabˈbinic** *a.*

rabbit (ˈræbɪt) *n.* **1.** small burrowing rodent like hare —*vi.* **2.** hunt rabbits —**rabbit punch** sharp blow to back of neck

rabble (ˈræbᵊl) *n.* **1.** crowd of vulgar, noisy people **2.** mob —**rabble-rouser** *n.* person who manipulates passions of mob; demagogue

Rabelaisian (ræbəˈleɪzɪən, -ʒən) *a.* **1.** of or resembling work of François Rabelais, Fr. writer, characterized by broad, oft. bawdy humour and sharp satire —*n.* **2.** student or admirer of Rabelais

rabid (ˈræbɪd, ˈreɪ-) *a.* **1.** relating to or having rabies **2.** furious **3.** mad **4.** fanatical —**ˈrabidly** *adv.* —**ˈrabidness** *n.*

rabies (ˈreɪbiːz) *n. Pathol.* acute infectious viral disease transmitted by dogs *etc.*

R.A.C. **1.** Royal Automobile Club **2.** Royal Armoured Corps

raccoon *or* **racoon** (rəˈkuːn) *n.* small N Amer. mammal

race[1] (reɪs) *n.* **1.** contest of speed, as in running, swimming *etc.* **2.** contest, rivalry **3.** strong current of water, *esp.* leading to water wheel —*pl.* **4.** meeting for horse racing —*vt.* **5.** cause to run rapidly —*vi.* **6.** run swiftly **7.** (of engine, pedal *etc.*) move rapidly and erratically, *esp.* on removal of resistance —**ˈracer** *n.* person, vehicle, animal that races —**ˈracecourse** *n.* long broad track, over which horses are raced (*also* (*esp.* **US**) **ˈracetrack**) —**race meeting** prearranged fixture for racing horses *etc.* over set course —**ˈracetrack** *n.* **1.** circuit for motor racing *etc.* **2.** *esp.* **US** racecourse

race[2] (reɪs) *n.* **1.** group of people of common ancestry with distinguishing physical features, skin colour *etc.* **2.** species **3.** type —**ˈracial** *a.* —**ˈracialism** *or* **ˈracism** *n.* **1.** belief in innate superiority of particular race **2.** antagonism towards members of different race based on this belief —**ˈracialist** *or* **ˈracist** *a./n.* —**race relations** **1.** (*with pl. v.*) relations between members of two or more human races, *esp.* within single community **2.** (*with sing. v.*) branch of sociology concerned with such relations —**race riot** riot among members of different races in same community

raceme (rəˈsiːm) *n.* cluster of flowers along a central stem, as in foxglove

rack[1] (ræk) *n.* **1.** framework for displaying or holding baggage, books, hats, bottles *etc.* **2.** *Mech.* straight bar with teeth on its edge, to work with pinion **3.** instrument of torture by stretching —*vt.* **4.** stretch on rack or wheel **5.** torture **6.** stretch, strain —**ˈracking** *a.* agonizing —**rack-and-pinion** *n.* **1.** device for converting rotary into linear motion and vice versa, in which gearwheel (pinion) engages with flat toothed bar (rack) —*a.* **2.** (of type of steering gear in motor vehicles) having track rod with rack along part of its length that engages with pinion attached to steering column —**rack railway** mountain railway having middle rail fitted with rack that engages pinion on locomotive (*also* **cog railway**) —**rack-rent** *n.* **1.** high rent that annually equals value of property upon which it is charged **2.** any extortionate rent —*vt.* **3.** charge extortionate rent for

rack[2] (ræk) *n.* destruction (*esp. in* **rack and ruin**)

rack[3] *or* **wrack** (ræk) *n.* broken mass of clouds blown by wind

rack[4] (ræk) *vt.* clear (wine, beer *etc.*) by drawing it off from dregs

rack[5] (ræk) *n.* neck or rib section of mutton, lamb or pork

racket[1] (ˈrækɪt) *n.* **1.** loud noise, uproar **2.** occupation by which money is made illegally —**racketˈeer** *n.* one making illegal profits —**racketˈeering** *n.* —**ˈrackety** *a.* noisy

racket[2] *or* **racquet** (ˈrækɪt) *n.* **1.** bat used in tennis *etc.* —*pl.n.* **2.** (*with sing. v.*) ball game played in paved, walled court

THESAURUS

rabble **1.** *canaille*, crowd, herd, horde, mob, swarm, throng **2.** *Derogatory canaille*, commonalty, commoners, common people, crowd, dregs, hoi polloi, lower classes, masses, peasantry, populace, proletariat, riffraff, scum, the great unwashed (*Inf.*), trash

rabid **1.** hydrophobic, mad **2.** berserk, crazed, frantic, frenzied, furious, infuriated, mad, maniacal, raging, violent, wild **3.** bigoted, extreme, fanatical, fervent, intemperate, intolerant, irrational, narrow-minded, zealous

race[1] **1.** *n.* chase, competition, contention, contest, dash, pursuit, rivalry **2.** *v.* career, compete, contest, dart, dash, fly, gallop, hare (*Brit. inf.*), hasten, hurry, run, run like mad (*Inf.*), speed, tear, zoom

race[2] blood, breed, clan, ethnic group, family, folk, house, issue, kin, kindred, line, lineage, nation, offspring, people, progeny, seed (*Archaic*), stock, tribe, type

racial ethnic, ethnological, folk, genealogical, genetic, national, tribal

rack *n.* **1.** frame, framework, stand, structure ~*v.* **2.** afflict, agonize, crucify, distress, excruciate, harass, harrow, oppress, pain, torment, torture **3.** force, pull, shake, strain, stress, stretch, tear, wrench

racket **1.** babel, ballyhoo (*Inf.*), clamour, commotion, din, disturbance, fuss, hubbub, hullabaloo, noise, outcry, pandemonium, row, shouting, tumult, uproar **2.** criminal activity, fraud, illegal enterprise, scheme

raconteur (rækɒnˈtɜː) *n.* skilled storyteller

racy (ˈreɪsɪ) *a.* 1. spirited 2. lively 3. having strong flavour 4. spicy 5. piquant —**ˈracily** *adv.* —**ˈraciness** *n.*

RADA (ˈrɑːdə) UK Royal Academy of Dramatic Art

radar (ˈreɪdɑː) *n.* device for finding range and direction by ultrahigh-frequency point-to-point radio waves, which reflect back to their source and reveal position and nature of objects sought —**radar trap** device using radar to detect motorists exceeding speed limit

raddled (ˈrædᵊld) *a.* (*esp.* of person) unkempt or rundown in appearance

radial (ˈreɪdɪəl) *a. see* RADIUS

radiate (ˈreɪdɪeɪt) *v.* 1. emit, be emitted in rays —*vi.* 2. spread out from centre —**ˈradiance** *n.* 1. brightness 2. splendour —**ˈradiant** *a.* 1. beaming 2. shining 3. emitting rays —*n.* 4. point or object that emits radiation, *esp.* part of heater that gives out heat 5. *Astron.* the point in space from which a meteor shower appears to emanate —**radiˈation** *n.* 1. transmission of heat, light *etc.* from one body to another 2. particles, rays, emitted in nuclear decay 3. act of radiating —**ˈradiator** *n.* 1. that which radiates, *esp.* heating apparatus for rooms 2. cooling apparatus of car engine —**radiant energy** energy emitted or propagated in form of particles or electromagnetic radiation —**radiation sickness** *Pathol.* illness caused by overexposure of body to ionizing radiations from radioactive material *etc.*

radical (ˈrædɪkᵊl) *a.* 1. fundamental, thorough 2. extreme 3. *Maths.* of roots of numbers or quantities —*n.* 4. person of extreme (political) views 5. radicle 6. *Maths.* number expressed as root of another 7. group of atoms of several elements which remain unchanged in a series of chemical compounds —**ˈradicalism** *n.* —**radical sign** symbol $\sqrt{}$ placed before number or quantity to indicate extraction of root, *esp.* square root

radicle (ˈrædɪkᵊl) *n. Bot.* root

radio (ˈreɪdɪəʊ) *n.* 1. use of electromagnetic waves for broadcasting, communication *etc.* 2. device for receiving, amplifying radio signals 3. broadcasting, content of radio programmes —*vt.* 4. transmit (message *etc.*) by radio —**radioˈactive** *a.* emitting invisible rays that penetrate matter —**radioacˈtivity** *n.* —**radio astronomy** astronomy in which radio telescope is used to detect and analyse radio signals received on earth from radio sources in space —**radiocarbon dating** technique for determining age of organic materials based on their content of radioisotope ^{14}C acquired from atmosphere when they formed part of living plant (*see also* **carbon dating** *at* CARBON) —**radioˈchemical** *a.* —**radioˈchemist** *n.* —**radioˈchemistry** *n.* chemistry of radioactive elements and their compounds —**radio frequency** 1. any frequency that lies in range 10 kilohertz to 300 000 megahertz and can be used for broadcasting 2. frequency transmitted by particular radio station —**ˈradiogram** *n.* 1. UK unit comprising radio and gramophone 2. message transmitted by radiotelegraphy 3. radiograph —**ˈradiograph** *n.* image produced on sensitized film or plate by radiation —**radiˈographer** *n.* —**radiˈography** *n.* production of image on film or plate by radiation —**radioˈisotope** *n.* radioactive isotope —**radiˈologist** *n.* —**radiˈology** *n.* science of use of rays in medicine —**radioscopic** (reɪdɪəʊˈskɒpɪk) *a.* —**radiˈoscopy** *n. see* **fluoroscopy** *at* FLUORESCENCE —**radiosonde** (ˈreɪdɪəʊsɒnd) *n.* airborne instrument to send meteorological information back to earth by radio —**radioˈtelegraph** *v./n.* —**radioteˈlegraphy** *n.* telegraphy in which messages (usu. in Morse code) are transmitted by radio waves —**radioˈtelephone** *n.* 1. device for communications by means of radio waves —*v.* 2. telephone (person) by radiotelephone —**radioteˈlephony** *n.* —**radio telescope** instrument used in radio astronomy to pick up and analyse radio waves from space and to transmit radio waves —**radioˈtherapy** *n.* diagnosis and treatment of disease by x-rays

radio- (*comb. form*) 1. denoting radio, broadcasting or radio frequency, as in *radiogram* 2. indicating radioactivity or radiation, as in *radiochemistry*

radish (ˈrædɪʃ) *n.* pungent root vegetable

radium (ˈreɪdɪəm) *n.* radioactive metallic element

radius (ˈreɪdɪəs) *n.* 1. straight line from centre to circumference of circle 2. outer of two bones in forearm (*pl.* **radii** (ˈreɪdɪaɪ), **-es**) —**ˈradial** *a.* 1. arranged like radii of circle 2. of ray or rays 3. of radius —**ˈradian** *n.* SI unit of plane angle; angle between two radii of circle that cut off on circumference arc equal in length to radius —**radial-ply** *a.* (of motor tyre) having fabric cords in outer casing running radially, enabling sidewalls to be flexible

radon (ˈreɪdɒn) *n.* radioactive gaseous element

RAF (*nonstandard* ræf) *or* **R.A.F.** Royal Air Force

raffia *or* **raphia** (ˈræfɪə) *n.* prepared palm fibre for making mats *etc.*

raffish (ˈræfɪʃ) *a.* disreputable

raffle (ˈræfᵊl) *n.* 1. lottery in which an article is assigned by lot to one of those buying tickets —*vt.* 2. dispose of by raffle

raft (rɑːft) *n.* floating structure of logs, planks *etc.*

rafter (ˈrɑːftə) *n.* one of main beams of roof

rag[1] (ræg) *n.* 1. fragment of cloth 2. torn piece 3. *inf.* newspaper *etc.*, *esp.* one considered worthless 4. piece of ragtime music —*pl.* 5. tattered clothing —**ragged** (ˈrægɪd) *a.* 1. shaggy 2. torn 3. clothed in torn clothes 4. lacking smoothness —**rag-and-bone man** UK man

THESAURUS

racy 1. animated, buoyant, energetic, entertaining, exciting, exhilarating, heady, lively, sparkling, spirited, stimulating, vigorous, zestful 2. distinctive, piquant, pungent, rich, sharp, spicy, strong, tangy, tart, tasty

radiance brightness, brilliance, effulgence, glare, gleam, glitter, glow, incandescence, light, luminosity, lustre, resplendence, shine

radiant beaming, bright, brilliant, effulgent, gleaming, glittering, glorious, glowing, incandescent, luminous, lustrous, resplendent, shining, sparkling, sunny

radiate 1. diffuse, disseminate, emanate, emit, give off *or* out, gleam, glitter, pour, scatter, send out, shed, shine, spread 2. branch out, diverge, issue, spread out

radiation emanation, emission, rays

radical *adj.* 1. basic, constitutional, deep-seated, essential, fundamental, innate, native, natural, organic, profound, thoroughgoing 2. complete, entire, excessive, extreme, extremist, fanatical, revolutionary, severe, sweeping, thorough, violent ~*n.* 3. extremist, fanatic, militant, revolutionary

raffle draw, lottery, sweep, sweepstake

who buys and sells discarded clothing *etc.* —ˈ**ragbag** *n.* confused assortment —ˈ**ragtag** *n. derogatory* common people; rabble (*esp. in* **ragtag and bobtail**) —ˈ**ragtime** *n.* style of jazz piano music —**rag trade** *inf.* clothing industry, trade —ˈ**ragwort** *n.* European plant with yellow daisylike flowers (*see also* GROUNDSEL)

rag[2] (ræg) *vt.* **1.** tease **2.** torment **3.** play practical jokes on (**-gg-**) —*n.* **4. a.** period of carnival with procession *etc.* organized by students to raise money for charities **b.** (*as modifier*): *rag day*

ragamuffin (ˈrægəmʌfɪn) *n.* ragged, dirty person

rage (reɪdʒ) *n.* **1.** violent anger or passion **2.** fury —*vi.* **3.** speak, act with fury **4.** proceed violently and without check (as storm, battle *etc.*) **5.** be widely and violently prevalent —**all the rage** very popular

raglan (ˈræglən) *a.* of sleeves that continue to the neck so that there are no shoulder seams

ragout (ræˈguː) *n.* highly seasoned stew of meat and vegetables

raid (reɪd) *n.* **1.** rush, attack **2.** foray —*vt.* **3.** make raid on —ˈ**raider** *n.*

rail[1] (reɪl) *n.* horizontal bar, *esp.* as part of fence, track *etc.* —ˈ**railing** *n.* fence, barrier made of rails supported by posts —ˈ**railhead** *n.* farthest point to which railway line extends —ˈ**railway** *or U.S.* ˈ**railroad** *n.* **1.** track of iron rails on which trains run **2.** company operating railway —**off the rails** *inf.* **1.** astray **2.** on wrong track **3.** in error **4.** leading reckless, dissipated life

rail[2] (reɪl) *vi.* (*with* at *or* against) **1.** utter abuse **2.** scoff **3.** scold **4.** reproach —ˈ**raillery** *n.* banter

rail[3] (reɪl) *n.* any of various kinds of marsh bird

raiment (ˈreɪmənt) *n. obs.* clothing

rain (reɪn) *n.* **1.** moisture falling in drops from clouds **2.** fall of such drops —*vi.* **3.** fall as rain —*vt.* **4.** pour down like rain —ˈ**rainy** *a.* —ˈ**rainbow** *n.* arch of prismatic colours in sky —ˈ**raincoat** *n.* light water-resistant overcoat —ˈ**rainfall** *n.* **1.** precipitation in form of raindrops **2.** *Met.* amount of precipitation in specified place and time —ˈ**rainforest** *n.* dense forest found in tropical areas of heavy rainfall —**rain gauge** instrument for measuring rainfall —**rain shadow** relatively dry area on leeward side of high ground in path of rain-bearing winds —**rainy day** future time of need, *esp.* financial —**take a rain check** *Inf.* accept postponement of offer

raise (reɪz) *vt.* **1.** lift up **2.** set up **3.** build **4.** increase **5.** elevate **6.** promote **7.** heighten, as pitch of voice **8.** breed into existence **9.** levy, collect **10.** end (siege etc.)

raisin (ˈreɪzᵊn) *n.* dried grape

raison d'être (rɛzɔ̃ ˈdɛtr) *Fr.* reason or justification for existence (*pl.* ***raisons d'être*** (rɛzɔ̃ ˈdɛtr))

raj (rɑːdʒ) *n.* rule, sway, *esp.* in India —ˈ**rajah** *or* ˈ**raja** *n.* (formerly) Indian prince or ruler

rake[1] (reɪk) *n.* **1.** tool with long handle and crosspiece with teeth for gathering hay, leaves *etc.* —*vt.* **2.** gather, smooth with rake **3.** sweep, search over **4.** sweep with shot —**rake-off** *n. inf.* monetary commission, *esp.* illegal

rake[2] (reɪk) *n.* dissolute or dissipated man —ˈ**rakish** *a.* dissolute; profligate

rake[3] (reɪk) *n.* **1.** slope, *esp.* backwards, of ship's funnel *etc.* —*v.* **2.** incline from perpendicular —ˈ**rakish** *a.* appearing dashing or speedy

rally[1] (ˈrælɪ) *vt.* **1.** bring together, *esp.* what has been scattered, as routed army or dispersed troops —*vi.* **2.** come together **3.** regain health or strength, revive (ˈ**rallied**, ˈ**rallying**) —*n.* **4.** act of rallying **5.** assembly, *esp.* outdoor, of any organization **6.** *Tennis* lively exchange of strokes

THESAURUS

ragbag confusion, hotchpotch, jumble, medley, miscellany, mixture, omnium-gatherum, potpourri

rage *n.* **1.** agitation, anger, frenzy, fury, high dudgeon, ire, madness, mania, obsession, passion, rampage, raving, vehemence, violence, wrath ~*v.* **2.** be beside oneself, be furious, blow one's top, blow up (*Inf.*), chafe, foam at the mouth, fret, fume, rant and rave, rave, seethe, storm, throw a fit (*Inf.*) **3.** be at its height, be uncontrollable, rampage, storm, surge

ragged 1. contemptible, down at heel, frayed, in holes, in rags, in tatters, mean, poor, rent, scraggy, shabby, shaggy, tattered, tatty, threadbare, torn, unkempt, worn-out **2.** crude, jagged, notched, poor, rough, rugged, serrated, uneven, unfinished

rags castoffs, old clothes, tattered clothing, tatters

raid 1. *n.* attack, break-in, descent, foray, hit-and-run attack, incursion, inroad, invasion, irruption, onset, sally, seizure, sortie, surprise attack **2.** *v.* assault, attack, break into, descend on, fall upon, forage (*Military*), foray, invade, pillage, plunder, reive (*Dialect*), rifle, sack, sally forth, swoop down upon

raider attacker, forager (*Military*), invader, marauder, plunderer, reiver (*Dialect*), robber, thief

railing balustrade, barrier, fence, paling, rails

rain *n.* **1.** cloudburst, deluge, downpour, drizzle, fall, precipitation, raindrops, rainfall, showers ~*v.* **2.** bucket down (*Inf.*), come down in buckets (*Inf.*), drizzle, fall, pour, rain cats and dogs (*Inf.*), shower, teem **3.** deposit, drop, fall, shower, sprinkle

rainy damp, drizzly, showery, wet

raise 1. build, construct, elevate, erect, exalt, heave, hoist, lift, move up, promote, put up, rear, set upright, uplift **2.** advance, aggravate, amplify, augment, boost, enhance, enlarge, escalate, exaggerate, heighten, hike (up) (*Inf.*), increase, inflate, intensify, jack up, magnify, put up, reinforce, strengthen **3.** advance, aggrandize, elevate, exalt, prefer, promote, upgrade **4.** activate, arouse, awaken, cause, evoke, excite, foment, foster, incite, instigate, kindle, motivate, provoke, set on foot, stir up, summon up, whip up **5.** bring about, cause, create, engender, give rise to, occasion, originate, produce, provoke, start **6.** assemble, collect, form, gather, get, levy, mass, mobilize, muster, obtain, rally, recruit **7.** breed, bring up, cultivate, develop, grow, nurture, produce, propagate, rear **8.** abandon, end, give up, lift, relieve, relinquish, remove, terminate

rake[1] *v.* **1.** collect, gather, remove, scrape up **2.** break up, harrow, hoe, scour, scrape, scratch **3.** comb, examine, hunt, ransack, scan, scour, scrutinize, search **4.** enfilade, pepper, sweep

rake[2] *n.* debauchee, dissolute man, lecher, libertine, playboy profligate, rakehell (*Archaic*), roué, sensualist, voluptuary

rally *v.* **1.** bring *or* come to order, reassemble, re-form, regroup, reorganize, unite ~*n.* **2.** regrouping, reorganization, reunion, stand ~*v.* **3.** assemble, bond together, bring *or* come together, collect, convene, gather, get together, marshal, mobilize, muster, or-

rally[2] ('rælɪ) *v.* mock or ridicule (someone) in good-natured way; chaff; tease

ram (ræm) *n.* **1.** male sheep **2.** hydraulic machine **3.** battering engine —*vt.* **4.** force, drive **5.** strike against with force **6.** stuff **7.** strike with ram (**-mm-**) —**'ramrod** *n.* **1.** rod for cleaning barrel of rifle *etc.* **2.** rod for ramming in charge of muzzle-loading firearm

RAM (ræm) *Comp.* random access memory

R.A.M. Royal Academy of Music

Ramadan, Rhamadhan (ræmə'dɑːn) *or* **Ramazan** (ræmə'zɑːn) *n.* **1.** 9th Mohammedan month **2.** strict fasting observed during this time

ramble ('ræmb'l) *vi.* **1.** walk without definite route **2.** wander **3.** talk incoherently **4.** spread in random fashion —*n.* **5.** rambling walk —**'rambler** *n.* **1.** climbing rose **2.** one who rambles

rambutan (ræm'buːt'n) *n.* **1.** SE Asian tree **2.** its bright red edible fruit

R.A.M.C. Royal Army Medical Corps

ramekin *or* **ramequin** ('ræmɪkɪn) *n.* **1.** small fireproof dish **2.** savoury food baked in it

ramify ('ræmɪfaɪ) *v.* **1.** spread in branches, subdivide —*vi.* **2.** become complex (**-ified, -ifying**) —**ramifi'cation** *n.* **1.** branch, subdivision **2.** process of branching out **3.** consequence

ramp (ræmp) *n.* gradual slope joining two level surfaces

rampage (ræm'peɪdʒ) *vi.* **1.** dash about violently —*n.* ('ræmpeɪdʒ, ræm'peɪdʒ) **2.** angry or destructive behaviour —**ram'pageous** *a.* —**on the rampage** behaving violently or destructively

rampant ('ræmpənt) *a.* **1.** violent **2.** rife **3.** rearing

rampart ('ræmpɑːt) *n.* **1.** mound, wall for defence —*vt.* **2.** defend with rampart

rampike ('ræmpaɪk) *n.* C tall tree, burnt or bare of branches

ramshackle ('ræmʃæk'l) *a.* tumbledown, rickety, makeshift

ran (ræn) *pt. of* RUN

ranch (rɑːntʃ) *n.* **1.** Amer. cattle farm —*vi.* **2.** manage a ranch —**'rancher** *n.*

rancherie ('rɑːntʃərɪ) *n.* C Indian reservation

rancid ('rænsɪd) *a.* (of food) having unpleasant smell or taste —**ran'cidity** *n.*

rancour *or U.S.* **rancor** ('ræŋkə) *n.* bitter, inveterate hate —**'rancorous** *a.* **1.** malignant **2.** virulent

rand (rænd, rɒnt) *n.* monetary unit of S Afr.

R & B rhythm-and-blues

R & D research and development

random ('rændəm) *a.* made or done by chance, without plan —**at random** haphazard(ly)

randy ('rændɪ) *a. sl.* sexually aroused

rang (ræŋ) *pt. of* RING[2]

range (reɪndʒ) *n.* **1.** limits **2.** row **3.** scope, sphere **4.** distance missile can travel **5.** distance of mark shot at **6.** place for shooting practice or rocket testing **7.** series **8.** kitchen stove —*vt.* **9.** set in row **10.** classify **11.** roam —*vi.* **12.** extend **13.** roam **14.** pass from one point to another **15.** fluctuate (as prices) —**'ranger** *n.* **1.** official in charge of or patrolling park *etc.* **2.** (**R-**) member of senior branch of Guides —**'rangy** *a.* **1.** with long, slender limbs **2.** spacious —**'rangefinder** *n.* instrument for finding distance away of given object

THESAURUS

ganize, round up, summon, unite ~*n.* **4.** assembly, conference, congregation, convention, convocation, gathering, mass meeting, meeting, muster ~*v.* **5.** come round, get better, get one's second wind, improve, perk up, pick up, pull through, recover, recuperate, regain one's strength, revive, take a turn for the better ~*n.* **6.** comeback (*Inf.*), improvement, recovery, recuperation, renewal, resurgence, revival, turn for the better

ram *v.* **1.** butt, collide with, crash, dash, drive, force, hit, impact, run into, slam, smash, strike **2.** beat, cram, crowd, drum, force, hammer, jam, pack, pound, stuff, tamp, thrust

ramble *v.* **1.** amble, drift, perambulate, peregrinate, range, roam, rove, saunter, straggle, stravaig (*Scot.*), stray, stroll, traipse (*Inf.*), walk, wander **2.** meander, snake, twist and turn, wind, zigzag **3.** babble, chatter, digress, expatiate, maunder, rabbit on (*Brit. sl.*), rattle on, wander, witter on (*Inf.*) ~*n.* **4.** excursion, hike, perambulation, peregrination, roaming, roving, saunter, stroll, tour, traipse (*Inf.*), trip, walk

rambler drifter, hiker, roamer, rover, stroller, walker, wanderer, wayfarer

ramification **1.** branch, development, divarication, division, excrescence, extension, forking, offshoot, outgrowth, subdivision **2.** complication, consequence, development, result, sequel, upshot

ramp grade, gradient, incline, inclined plane, rise, slope

rampage *v.* **1.** go berserk, rage, run amuck, run riot, run wild, storm, tear ~*n.* **2.** destruction, frenzy, fury, rage, storm, tempest, tumult, uproar, violence **3. on the rampage** amuck, berserk, destructive, out of control, raging, rampant, riotous, violent, wild

rampant **1.** aggressive, dominant, excessive, flagrant, on the rampage, out of control, out of hand, outrageous, raging, rampaging, riotous, unbridled, uncontrollable, ungovernable, unrestrained, vehement, violent, wanton, wild **2.** epidemic, exuberant, luxuriant, prevalent, profuse, rank, rife, spreading like wildfire, unchecked, uncontrolled, unrestrained, widespread **3.** *Heraldry* erect, rearing, standing, upright

rampart barricade, bastion, breastwork, bulwark, defence, earthwork, embankment, fence, fort, fortification, guard, parapet, security, stronghold, wall

ramshackle broken-down, crumbling, decrepit, derelict, dilapidated, flimsy, jerry-built, rickety, shaky, tottering, tumbledown, unsafe, unsteady

rancid bad, fetid, foul, frowsty, fusty, musty, off, putrid, rank, rotten, sour, stale, strong-smelling, tainted

random **1.** accidental, adventitious, aimless, arbitrary, casual, chance, desultory, fortuitous, haphazard, hit or miss, incidental, indiscriminate, purposeless, spot, stray, unplanned, unpremeditated **2. at random** accidentally, adventitiously, aimlessly, arbitrarily, by chance, casually, haphazardly, indiscriminately, irregularly, purposelessly, randomly, unsystematically, willy-nilly

range *n.* **1.** amplitude, area, bounds, compass, confines, distance, domain, extent, field, latitude, limits, orbit, parameters (*Inf.*), province, purview, radius, reach, scope, span, sphere, sweep **2.** chain, file,

rani *or* **ranee** (ˈrɑːnɪ) *n.* queen or princess; wife of rajah

rank[1] (ræŋk) *n.* **1.** row, line **2.** place where taxis wait **3.** order **4.** social class **5.** status **6.** relative place or position —*pl.* **7.** common soldiers **8.** great mass or majority of people (*also* **rank and file**) —*vt.* **9.** draw up in rank, classify —*vi.* **10.** have rank, place **11.** have certain distinctions

rank[2] (ræŋk) *a.* **1.** growing too thickly, coarse **2.** offensively strong **3.** rancid **4.** vile **5.** flagrant —ˈ**rankly** *adv.*

rankle (ˈræŋkəl) *vi.* fester, continue to cause anger, resentment or bitterness

ransack (ˈrænsæk) *vt.* **1.** search thoroughly **2.** pillage, plunder

ransom (ˈrænsəm) *n.* **1.** release from captivity by payment **2.** amount paid —*vt.* **3.** pay ransom for —ˈ**ransomer** *n.*

rant (rænt) *vi.* **1.** rave in violent, high-sounding language —*n.* **2.** noisy, boisterous speech **3.** wild gaiety —ˈ**ranter** *n.*

ranunculus (rəˈnʌŋkjʊləs) *n.* any of a genus of plants that includes buttercup, crowfoot and spearwort

rap[1] (ræp) *n.* **1.** smart slight blow **2.** fast, rhythmic monologue over musical backing —*vt.* **3.** give rap to (**-pp-**) —**rap music** —**take the rap** *sl.* suffer punishment, whether guilty or not

rap[2] (ræp) *n.* the least amount (*esp. in* **not to care a rap**)

rapacious (rəˈpeɪʃəs) *a.* **1.** greedy **2.** grasping —**rapacity** (rəˈpæsɪtɪ) *n.*

rape[1] (reɪp) *vt.* **1.** force (woman) to submit unwillingly to sexual intercourse —*n.* **2.** act of raping **3.** any violation or abuse

rape[2] (reɪp) *n.* plant with oil-yielding seeds, also used as fodder (*also* ˈ**colza, cole**)

rapid (ˈræpɪd) *a.* **1.** quick, swift —*pl.n.* **2.** part of river with fast, turbulent current —**raˈpidity** *or* ˈ**rapidness** *n.* —ˈ**rapidly** *adv.* —**rapid eye movement** movement of eyeballs during sleep, while sleeper is dreaming

rapier (ˈreɪpɪə) *n.* fine-bladed sword used as thrusting weapon

rapine (ˈræpaɪn) *n.* plunder

rapport (ræˈpɔː) *n.* harmony, agreement

rapprochement (raprɔʃˈmɑ̃) *Fr.* re-establishment of friendly relations between nations

rapscallion (ræpˈskæljən) *n.* rascal, rogue

rapt (ræpt) *a.* engrossed, spellbound —ˈ**rapture** *n.* ecstasy —ˈ**rapturous** *a.*

raptorial (ræpˈtɔːrɪəl) *a.* **1.** predatory **2.** of the order of birds of prey

THESAURUS

line, rank, row, sequence, series, string, tier **3.** assortment, class, collection, gamut, kind, lot, order, selection, series, sort, variety ~*v.* **4.** align, arrange, array, dispose, draw up, line up, order **5.** arrange, bracket, catalogue, categorize, class, classify, file, grade, group, pigeonhole, rank **6.** cruise, explore, ramble, roam, rove, straggle, stray, stroll, sweep, traverse, wander **7.** extend, fluctuate, go, reach, run, stretch, vary between

rank[1] *n.* **1.** caste, class, classification, degree, dignity division, echelon, grade, level, nobility, order, position, quality, sort, standing, station, status, stratum, type **2.** column, file, formation, group, line, range, row, series, tier ~*v.* **3.** align, arrange, array, class, classify, dispose, grade, line up, locate, marshal, order, position, range, sort

rank[2] **1.** abundant, dense, exuberant, flourishing, lush, luxuriant, productive, profuse, strong-growing, vigorous **2.** bad, disagreeable, disgusting, fetid, foul, fusty, gamy, mephitic, musty, noisome, noxious, off, offensive, pungent, putrid, rancid, revolting, stale, stinking, strong-smelling **3.** absolute, arrant, blatant, complete, downright, egregious, excessive, extravagant, flagrant, glaring, gross, rampant, sheer, thorough, total, undisguised, unmitigated, utter **4.** abusive, atrocious, coarse, crass, filthy, foul, gross, indecent, nasty, obscene, outrageous, scurrilous, shocking, vile, vulgar

rank and file body, general public, majority, mass, masses

rankle anger, annoy, chafe, embitter, fester, gall, get one's goat (*Inf.*), irk, irritate, rile

ransack 1. comb, explore, go through, rake, rummage, scour, search, turn inside out **2.** despoil, gut, loot, pillage, plunder, raid, ravage, rifle, sack, strip

ransom *n.* **1.** deliverance, liberation, redemption, release, rescue **2.** money, payment, payoff, price ~*v.* **3.** buy (someone) out (*Inf.*), buy the freedom of, deliver, liberate, obtain *or* pay for the release of, redeem, release, rescue, set free

rant 1. *v.* bellow, bluster, cry, declaim, rave, roar, shout, spout (*Inf.*), vociferate, yell **2.** *n.* bluster, bombast, diatribe, fanfaronade (*Rare*), harangue, philippic, rhetoric, tirade, vociferation

rapacious avaricious, extortionate, grasping, greedy, insatiable, marauding, plundering, predatory, preying, ravenous, usurious, voracious, wolfish

rapacity avarice, avidity, cupidity, graspingness, greed, greediness, insatiableness, predatoriness, rapaciousness, ravenousness, usury, voraciousness, voracity, wolfishness

rape *n.* **1.** outrage, ravishment, sexual assault, violation **2.** abuse, defilement, desecration, maltreatment, perversion, violation ~*v.* **3.** outrage, ravish, sexually assault, violate

rapid brisk, expeditious, express, fast, fleet, flying, hasty, hurried, precipitate, prompt, quick, speedy, swift

rapidity alacrity, briskness, celerity, dispatch, expedition, fleetness, haste, hurry, precipitateness, promptitude, promptness, quickness, rush, speed, speediness, swiftness, velocity

rapidly at speed, briskly, expeditiously, fast, hastily, hurriedly, in a hurry, in a rush, in haste, like a shot, precipitately, promptly, quickly, speedily, swiftly, with dispatch

rapport affinity, bond, empathy, harmony, interrelationship, link, relationship, sympathy, understanding

rapt 1. absorbed, carried away, engrossed, enthralled, entranced, fascinated, gripped, held, intent, preoccupied, spellbound **2.** bewitched, blissful, captivated, charmed, delighted, ecstatic, enchanted, enraptured, rapturous, ravished, transported

rapture beatitude, bliss, cloud nine (*Inf.*), delecta-

rare[1] (rɛə) *a.* 1. uncommon 2. infrequent 3. of uncommon quality 4. (of atmosphere) having low density, thin —ˈ**rarely** *adv.* seldom —ˈ**rarity** *n.* 1. anything rare 2. rareness —**rare earth** 1. any oxide of lanthanide 2. any element of lanthanide series (*also* **rare-earth element**)

rare[2] (rɛə) *a.* (of meat) lightly cooked

rarebit (ˈrɛəbɪt) *n.* savoury cheese dish (*also* **Welsh rabbit**)

rarefy (ˈrɛərɪfaɪ) *v.* 1. make, become thin, rare or less dense —*vt.* 2. refine (**-fied, -fying**) —**rareˈfaction** *or* **rarefiˈcation** *n.*

raring (ˈrɛərɪŋ) *a.* enthusiastically willing, ready

rascal (ˈrɑːskəl) *n.* 1. rogue 2. naughty (young) person —**rasˈcality** *n.* roguery, baseness —ˈ**rascally** *a./adv.*

rase (reɪz) *vt. see* RAZE

rash[1] (ræʃ) *a.* hasty, reckless, incautious —ˈ**rashly** *adv.*

rash[2] (ræʃ) *n.* 1. skin eruption 2. outbreak, series of (unpleasant) occurrences

rasher (ˈræʃə) *n.* thin slice of bacon or ham

rasp (rɑːsp) *n.* 1. harsh, grating noise 2. coarse file —*vt.* 3. scrape with rasp —*vi.* 4. grate upon 5. irritate 6. make scraping noise 7. speak in grating voice

raspberry (ˈrɑːzbərɪ, -brɪ) *n.* 1. red, juicy, edible berry 2. plant which bears it 3. *inf.* spluttering noise with tongue and lips to show contempt

Rastafarian (ræstəˈfɛərɪən) *n.* 1. member of Jamaican cult that regards Ras Tafari, former emperor of Ethiopia, Haile Selassie, as God —*a.* 2. of Rastafarians —ˈ**Rasta** *a./n.*

rat (ræt) *n.* 1. small rodent 2. *inf.* contemptible person, *esp.* deserter, informer *etc.* —*vi.* 3. inform 4. (*with* on) betray 5. (*with* on) desert, abandon 6. hunt rats (**-tt-**) —ˈ**ratter** *n.* 1. dog or cat that catches and kills rats 2. *inf.* worker who works during strike; blackleg; scab (*also* **rat**) —ˈ**ratty** *a. sl.* 1. mean, ill-tempered, irritable 2. (of hair) straggly, unkempt, greasy —**rat-catcher** *n.* one whose job is to drive away or destroy vermin, *esp.* rats —**rat race** continual hectic competitive activity —ˈ**ratsbane** *n.* rat poison, *esp.* arsenic oxide —**smell a rat** have suspicions of some treacherous practice

ratchet (ˈrætʃɪt) *n.* set of teeth on bar or wheel allowing motion in one direction only

rate[1] (reɪt) *n.* 1. proportion between two things 2. charge 3. degree of speed *etc.* —*pl.* 4. local tax on property —*vt.* 5. value 6. estimate value of 7. assess for local taxation —ˈ**ratable** *or* ˈ**rateable** *a.* 1. that can be rated 2. liable to pay rates —**ratable value** *or* **rateable value UK** fixed value assigned to property by local authority, on basis of which variable annual rates are charged —**rate-cap** *vt.* **UK** impose on (local authority) upper limit on rates it may levy —**rate-capping** *n.* —ˈ**ratepayer** *n.*

rate[2] (reɪt) *vt.* scold, chide

rather (ˈrɑːðə) *adv.* 1. to some extent 2. preferably 3. more willingly

ratify (ˈrætɪfaɪ) *vt.* confirm (**-ified, -ifying**) —**ratifiˈcation** *n.*

rating (ˈreɪtɪŋ) *n.* 1. valuing or assessing 2. fixing a rate 3. classification, *esp.* of ship 4. rank or grade as of naval personnel 5. angry rebuke

ratio (ˈreɪʃɪəʊ) *n.* 1. proportion 2. quantitative relation

ratiocinate (rætɪˈɒsɪneɪt) *vi.* reason —**ratiociˈnation** *n.*

ration (ˈræʃən) *n.* 1. fixed allowance of food *etc.* —*vt.* 2. supply with, limit to certain amount

rational (ˈræʃənəl) *a.* 1. reasonable, sensible 2. capable

THESAURUS

tion, delight, ecstasy, enthusiasm, euphoria, exaltation, felicity, happiness, joy, ravishment, rhapsody, seventh heaven, spell, transport

rapturous blissful, delighted, ecstatic, enthusiastic, euphoric, exalted, happy, in seventh heaven, joyful, joyous, on cloud nine (*Inf.*), overjoyed, over the moon (*Inf.*), ravished, rhapsodic, transported

rare 1. exceptional, few, infrequent, out of the ordinary, recherché, scarce, singular, sparse, sporadic, strange, thin on the ground, uncommon, unusual 2. admirable, choice, excellent, exquisite, extreme, fine, great, incomparable, peerless, superb, superlative

rarely almost never, hardly, hardly ever, infrequently, little, once in a blue moon, once in a while, only now and then, on rare occasions, scarcely ever, seldom

rarity 1. curio, curiosity, find, gem, one-off, pearl, treasure 2. infrequency, scarcity, shortage, singularity, sparseness, strangeness, uncommonness, unusualness 3. choiceness, excellence, exquisiteness, fineness, incomparability, incomparableness, peerlessness, quality, superbness

rascal blackguard, caitiff (*Archaic*), devil, disgrace, good-for-nothing, imp, knave (*Archaic*), miscreant, ne'er-do-well, rake, rapscallion, reprobate, rogue, scallywag (*Inf.*), scamp, scoundrel, varmint (*Inf.*), villain, wastrel, wretch

rash[1] adventurous, audacious, brash, careless, foolhardy, harebrained, harum-scarum, hasty, headlong, headstrong, heedless, helter-skelter, hot-headed, ill-advised, ill-considered, impetuous, imprudent, impulsive, incautious, indiscreet, injudicious, madcap, precipitate, premature, reckless, thoughtless, unguarded, unthinking, unwary, venturesome

rash[2] 1. eruption, outbreak 2. epidemic, flood, outbreak, plague, series, spate, succession, wave

rate *n.* 1. degree, percentage, proportion, ratio, relation, scale, standard 2. charge, cost, dues, duty, fee, figure, hire, price, tariff, tax, toll 3. gait, measure, pace, speed, tempo, time, velocity ~*v.* 4. adjudge, appraise, assess, class, classify, consider, count, esteem, estimate, evaluate, grade, measure, rank, reckon, regard, value, weigh 5. *Sl.* admire, esteem, respect, think highly of, value

rather 1. a bit, a little, fairly, kind of (*Inf.*), moderately, pretty (*Inf.*), quite, relatively, slightly, somewhat, sort of (*Inf.*), to some degree, to some extent 2. instead, more readily, more willingly, preferably, sooner

ratify affirm, approve, authenticate, authorize, bear out, bind, certify, confirm, consent to, corroborate, endorse, establish, sanction, sign, uphold, validate

rating class, classification, degree, designation, estimate, evaluation, grade, order, placing, position, rank, rate, standing, status

ratio arrangement, correlation, correspondence, equation, fraction, percentage, proportion, rate, relation, relationship

ration *n.* 1. allotment, allowance, dole, helping, measure, part, portion, provision, quota, share ~*v.* 2. *With* **out** allocate, allot, apportion, deal, distribute, dole, give out, issue, measure out, mete, parcel out 3. budget, conserve, control, limit, restrict, save

of thinking, reasoning —**rationale** (ræʃəˈnɑːl) *n.* reasons given for actions *etc.* —ˈ**rationalism** *n.* philosophy which regards reason as only guide or authority —ˈ**rationalist** *n.* —**ratioˈnality** *n.* —**rationaliˈzation** *or* **-iˈsation** *n.* —ˈ**rationalize** *or* **-ise** *vt.* **1.** justify by plausible reasoning **2.** reorganize to improve efficiency *etc.* —ˈ**rationally** *adv.*

ratline *or* **ratlin** (ˈrætlɪn) *n. Naut.* any of light lines tied across shrouds of sailing vessel for climbing aloft

rattan *or* **ratan** (ræˈtæn) *n.* **1.** climbing palm with jointed stems **2.** cane made of this

rattle (ˈrætᵊl) *vi.* **1.** give out succession of short sharp sounds **2.** clatter —*vt.* **3.** shake briskly causing a sharp clatter of sounds **4.** *inf.* confuse, fluster —*n.* **5.** succession of short sharp sounds **6.** baby's toy filled with small pellets for making this sound **7.** set of horny rings in rattlesnake's tail —ˈ**rattling** *adv. inf.* very —ˈ**rattlesnake** *n.* poisonous snake —ˈ**rattletrap** *n. inf.* broken-down old vehicle, *esp.* car

raucous (ˈrɔːkəs) *a.* **1.** hoarse **2.** harsh

raunchy (ˈrɔːntʃɪ) *a.* **US** *sl.* **1.** lecherous, smutty **2.** slovenly; dirty

ravage (ˈrævɪdʒ) *vt.* **1.** lay waste, plunder —*n.* **2.** destruction

rave (reɪv) *vi.* **1.** talk wildly, as in delirium **2.** write or speak (about) enthusiastically —*n.* **3.** enthusiastic or extravagant praise —ˈ**raving** *a.* **1.** delirious; frenzied **2.** *inf.* exciting admiration —*adv.* **3.** so as to cause raving —**rave-up** *n. sl.* party

ravel (ˈrævᵊl) *vt.* **1.** entangle **2.** fray out **3.** disentangle (**-ll-**)

raven[1] (ˈreɪvᵊn) *n.* **1.** black bird like crow —*a.* **2.** jet-black

raven[2] (ˈrævᵊn) *v.* seek (prey, plunder) —ˈ**ravening** *a.* (of animals) voracious; predatory —ˈ**ravenous** *a.* very hungry

ravine (rəˈviːn) *n.* narrow steep-sided valley worn by stream, gorge

ravioli (rævɪˈəʊlɪ) *n.* small, thin pieces of dough filled with highly seasoned, chopped meat and cooked

ravish (ˈrævɪʃ) *vt.* **1.** enrapture **2.** commit rape upon —ˈ**ravishing** *a.* lovely, entrancing

raw (rɔː) *a.* **1.** uncooked **2.** not manufactured or refined **3.** skinned **4.** inexperienced, unpractised, as recruits **5.** sensitive **6.** chilly —ˈ**rawˈboned** *a.* having lean bony physique —**raw deal** unfair or dishonest treatment —ˈ**rawhide** *n.* **1.** untanned hide **2.** whip made of this —**in the raw 1.** *inf.* without clothes; naked **2.** in natural or unmodified state

ray[1] (reɪ) *n.* **1.** single line or narrow beam of light, heat *etc.* **2.** any of set of radiating lines —*vi.* **3.** come out in rays **4.** radiate

ray[2] (reɪ) *n.* marine fish, oft. very large, with winglike pectoral fins and whiplike tail

ray[3] (reɪ) *n. Mus.* in tonic solfa, second degree of any major scale; supertonic

rayon (ˈreɪɒn) *n.* (fabric made of) synthetic fibre

raze *or* **rase** (reɪz) *vt.* **1.** destroy completely **2.** wipe out, delete **3.** level

razor (ˈreɪzə) *n.* sharp instrument for shaving or for cutting hair —ˈ**razorbill** *n.* N Atlantic auk

razzle-dazzle (ˈræzᵊlˈdæzᵊl) *or* **razzmatazz** (ˈræzməˈtæz) *n. sl.* **1.** noisy or showy fuss or activity **2.** spree; frolic

Rb *Chem.* rubidium

R.C. **1.** Red Cross **2.** Roman Catholic

R.C.A. **1.** Radio Corporation of America **2.** Royal College of Art

R.C.A.F. Royal Canadian Air Force

R.C.M. Royal College of Music

R.C.M.P. Royal Canadian Mounted Police

THESAURUS

rational 1. enlightened, intelligent, judicious, logical, lucid, realistic, reasonable, sagacious, sane, sensible, sound, wise **2.** cerebral, cognitive, ratiocinative, reasoning, thinking **3.** all there (*Inf.*), balanced, *compos mentis*, in one's right mind, lucid, normal, of sound mind, sane

rationale exposition, grounds, logic, motivation, philosophy, principle, *raison d'être*, reasons, theory

rationalize 1. account for, excuse, explain away, extenuate, justify, make allowance for, make excuses for, vindicate **2.** make cuts, make more efficient, streamline, trim

rattle *v.* **1.** bang, clatter, jangle **2.** bounce, jar, jiggle, jolt, jounce, shake, vibrate **3.** *Inf.* discomfit, discompose, disconcert, discountenance, disturb, faze (*U.S. inf.*), frighten, perturb, put (someone) off his stride, put (someone) out of countenance, scare, shake, upset

raucous grating, harsh, hoarse, husky, loud, noisy, rasping, rough, strident

ravage 1. *v.* demolish, desolate, despoil, destroy, devastate, gut, lay waste, leave in ruins, loot, pillage, plunder, ransack, raze, ruin, sack, shatter, spoil, wreak havoc on, wreck **2.** *n. Often plural* damage, demolition, depredation, desolation, destruction, devastation, havoc, pillage, plunder, rapine, ruin, ruination, spoliation, waste

rave *v.* **1.** babble, be delirious, fume, go mad, rage, rant, roar, run amuck, splutter, storm, talk wildly, thunder **2.** *With* **about** *Inf.* be delighted by, be mad about (*Inf.*), be wild about (*Inf.*), cry up, enthuse, gush, praise, rhapsodize ~*n.* **3.** *Inf.* acclaim, applause, encomium, praise

ravenous famished, starved, starving, very hungry

ravine canyon, clough (*Dialect*), defile, flume, gap (*U.S.*), gorge, gulch (*U.S.*), gully, linn (*Scot.*), pass

raving berserk, crazed, crazy, delirious, frantic, frenzied, furious, hysterical, insane, irrational, mad, out of one's mind, rabid, raging, wild

raw 1. bloody (*of meat*), fresh, natural, uncooked, undressed, unprepared **2.** basic, coarse, crude, green, natural, organic, rough, unfinished, unprocessed, unrefined, unripe, untreated **3.** abraded, chafed, grazed, open, scratched, sensitive, skinned, sore, tender **4.** callow, green, ignorant, immature, inexperienced, new, undisciplined, unpractised, unseasoned, unskilled, untrained, untried **5.** biting, bitter, bleak, chill, chilly, cold, damp, freezing, harsh, piercing, unpleasant, wet

ray bar, beam, flash, gleam, shaft

raze 1. bulldoze, demolish, destroy, flatten, knock down, level, pull down, remove, ruin, tear down, throw down **2.** delete, efface, erase, expunge, extinguish, extirpate, obliterate, rub out, scratch out, strike out, wipe out

R.C.N. 1. Royal Canadian Navy 2. Royal College of Nursing

Rd. Road

re[1] (reɪ, riː) *n. Mus. see* RAY[3]

re[2] (riː) *prep.* with reference to, concerning

Re *Chem.* rhenium

R.E. 1. Royal Engineers 2. religious education

re- (*comb. form*) again. See the list below, where the meaning may be inferred from the word to which *re-* is prefixed

reach (riːtʃ) *vt.* 1. arrive at 2. extend as far as 3. succeed in touching 4. attain to —*vi.* 5. stretch out hand 6. extend —*n.* 7. act of reaching 8. power of touching 9. grasp, scope 10. range 11. stretch of river between two bends —**ˈreachable** *a.* —**reach-me-down** *n.* 1. *see* **hand-me-down** *at* HAND 2. ready-made garment

react (rɪˈækt) *vi.* act in return, opposition or towards former state —**reˈactance** *n. Elec.* resistance in coil, apart from ohmic resistance, due to current reacting on itself —**reˈaction** *n.* 1. any action resisting another 2. counter or backward tendency 3. mental depression following overexertion 4. *inf.* response 5. chemical or nuclear change, combination or decomposition —**reˈactionary** *n./a.* (person) opposed to change, *esp.* in politics *etc.* —**reˈactive** *a.* chemically active —**nuclear reactor** apparatus in which nuclear reaction is maintained and controlled to produce nuclear energy

reˈactivate
readˈdress
readˈjust
readˈmission
readˈmit
reafˈfirm
reaffirˈmation
reaˈlign
reaˈlignment
reˈallocate
reapˈpear
reapˈpearance
reapˈpraisal
reapˈpraise
rearˈrange
rearˈrangement
reasˈsemble
reasˈsert
reasˈsertion
reasˈsess
reasˈsessment
reaˈwaken
reˈborn
reˈbuild
reˈcapture
reˈcast
reˈcharge
recomˈmence
reconˈnect
reconˈnection
reconˈsider
reconˈstruct
reconˈstruction
reconˈvene
re-cover
re-create
reˈdecorate
redeˈploy
redeˈsign
redeˈvelop
redeˈvelopment
rediˈrect
rediˈrection
redisˈcover
redisˈtribute
redistriˈbution
reˈdo
reˈdraft
reˈdraw
re-echo
re-educate
re-elect
re-election
re-emerge
re-emergence
re-emphasize
re-employ
re-enact
re-enactment
re-enforce
re-enforcement
re-enter
re-equip
re-examine
reˈfill *v.*
ˈrefill *n.*
reˈforest
re-ˈform
reˈfuel
reˈfurnish
reˈgain
reˈgrow
reˈharden
reˈheat
reˈhouse
reimˈpose
reinˈterpret
reinterpreˈtation
reintroˈduce
reintroˈduction
reˈkindle
reˈlay *v.*
ˈrelay *n.*
reˈlight
reˈload
reloˈcate
reloˈcation
reˈmarriage
reˈmarry
reˈmatch *v.*
ˈrematch *n.*
reˈmodel
reˈnumber
reˈoccupy
reˈopen
reˈorder
reorganiˈzation
reˈorganize
reˈpack
reˈpaint
reˈpaper
reˈphrase
reˈplant
reˈprint *v.*
ˈreprint *n.*
reˈroute
reˈset
reˈsettle
reˈshuffle
reˈspray *v.*
ˈrespray *n.*
reˈstart
reˈstock
reˈsurface
reˈthink *v.*
ˈrethink *n.*
reˈtrial
reˈtry
reˈtype
reuˈnite
reˈuse
reˈvisit
reˈwind

THESAURUS

reach *v.* **1.** arrive at, attain, get as far as, get to, land at, make **2.** contact, extend to, get (a) hold of, go as far as, grasp, stretch to, touch **3.** amount to, arrive at, attain, climb to, come to, drop, fall, move, rise, sink ~*n.* **4.** ambit, capacity, command, compass, distance, extension, extent, grasp, influence, juris-

read (ri:d) *vt.* **1.** look at and understand (written or printed matter) **2.** learn by reading **3.** interpret mentally **4.** read and utter **5.** interpret **6.** study **7.** understand (any indicating instrument) **8.** (of instrument) register —*vi.* **9.** be occupied in reading **10.** find mentioned in reading (**read** (rɛd) *pt./pp.*) —**reada'bility** *n.* —**'readable** *a.* that can be read, or read with pleasure —**'reader** *n.* **1.** one who reads **2.** university lecturer **3.** school textbook **4.** one who reads manuscripts submitted to publisher **5.** one who reads printer's proofs —**'readership** *n.* all readers of particular publication or author —**'reading** *n.* —**read-out** *n.* **1.** retrieving of information from computer memory or storage device **2.** information retrieved —**read between the lines** *inf.* deduce a meaning that is implied —**read out** **1.** read aloud **2.** US expel from political party *etc.* **3.** retrieve information from computer memory or storage device

ready ('rɛdɪ) *a.* **1.** prepared for use or action **2.** willing, prompt —**'readily** *adv.* **1.** promptly **2.** willingly —**'readiness** *n.* —**ready-made** *a.* **1.** made for purchase and immediate use by customer **2.** extremely convenient; ideally suited **3.** unoriginal, conventional —*n.* **4.** ready-made article, *esp.* garment —**ready reckoner** table of numbers used to facilitate simple calculations, *esp.* for working out interest *etc.*

reagent (ri:'eɪdʒənt) *n.* chemical substance that reacts with another and is used to detect presence of the other —**re'agency** *n.*

real (rɪəl) *a.* **1.** existing in fact **2.** happening **3.** actual **4.** genuine **5.** (of property) consisting of land and houses —**'realism** *n.* **1.** regarding things as they are **2.** artistic treatment with this outlook —**'realist** *n.* —**rea'listic** *a.* —**reality** (rɪ'ælɪtɪ) *n.* real existence —**'really** *adv.* —**'realty** *n.* real estate —**real estate** landed property —**real tennis** ancient form of tennis played in four-walled indoor court

realize *or* **-ise** ('rɪəlaɪz) *vt.* **1.** apprehend, grasp significance of **2.** accomplish, make real **3.** convert into money —**reali'zation** *or* **-i'sation** *n.*

realm (rɛlm) *n.* **1.** kingdom, domain **2.** province, sphere

ream[1] (ri:m) *n.* **1.** twenty quires of paper, generally 480 sheets —*pl.* **2.** *inf.* large quantity of written matter

ream[2] (ri:m) *vt.* enlarge, bevel out, as hole in metal —**'reamer** *n.* tool for this

reap (ri:p) *v.* **1.** cut and gather (harvest) —*vt.* **2.** receive as fruit of previous activity —**'reaper** *n.*

rear[1] (rɪə) *n.* **1.** back part **2.** part of army, procession *etc.* behind others —**'rearmost** *a.* —**rear admiral** lowest flag rank in certain navies —**'rearguard** *n.* troops protecting rear of army —**rear light** *or* **lamp** red light attached to rear of motor vehicle —**rear-view mirror** mirror on motor vehicle enabling driver to see traffic behind —**'rearward** *a.* **1.** towards or in rear —*adv.* **2.** towards or in rear (*also* **'rearwards**) —*n.* **3.** position in rear, *esp.* rear division of military formation

THESAURUS

diction, mastery, power, range, scope, spread, stretch, sweep

react acknowledge, answer, reply, respond

reaction 1. acknowledgment, answer, feedback, reply, response **2.** compensation, counteraction, counterbalance, counterpoise, recoil **3.** conservatism, counter-revolution, obscurantism, the right

reactionary 1. *adj.* blimpish, conservative, counter-revolutionary, obscurantist, rightist **2.** *n.* Colonel Blimp, conservative, counter-revolutionary, die-hard, obscurantist, rightist, right-winger

read 1. glance at, look at, peruse, pore over, refer to, run one's eye over, scan, study **2.** announce, declaim, deliver, recite, speak, utter **3.** comprehend, construe, decipher, discover, interpret, perceive the meaning of, see, understand **4.** display, indicate, record, register, show

readily 1. cheerfully, eagerly, freely, gladly, promptly, quickly, voluntarily, willingly, with good grace, with pleasure **2.** at once, easily, effortlessly, in no time, quickly, right away, smoothly, speedily, straight away, unhesitatingly, without delay, without demur, without difficulty, without hesitation

readiness 1. fitness, maturity, preparation, preparedness, ripeness **2.** aptness, eagerness, gameness (*Inf.*), inclination, keenness, willingness **3.** promptitude, promptness, quickness, rapidity

reading 1. examination, inspection, perusal, review, scrutiny, study **2.** homily, lecture, lesson, performance, recital, rendering, rendition, sermon **3.** conception, construction, grasp, impression, interpretation, treatment, understanding, version

ready *adj.* **1.** all set, arranged, completed, fit, in readiness, organized, prepared, primed, ripe, set **2.** agreeable, apt, disposed, eager, game (*Inf.*), glad, happy, inclined, keen, minded, predisposed, prone, willing **3.** prompt, quick, rapid, smart

real absolute, actual, authentic, bona fide, certain, essential, existent, factual, genuine, heartfelt, honest, intrinsic, legitimate, positive, right, rightful, sincere, true, unaffected, unfeigned, valid, veritable

realistic 1. businesslike, common-sense, down-to-earth, hard-headed, level-headed, matter-of-fact, practical, pragmatic, rational, real, sensible, sober, unromantic, unsentimental **2.** authentic, faithful, genuine, graphic, lifelike, natural, naturalistic, representational, true, true to life, truthful

reality actuality, authenticity, certainty, corporeality, fact, genuineness, materiality, realism, truth, validity, verisimilitude, verity

realization 1. appreciation, apprehension, awareness, cognizance, comprehension, conception, consciousness, grasp, imagination, perception, recognition, understanding **2.** accomplishment, achievement, carrying-out, completion, consummation, effectuation, fulfilment

realize 1. appreciate, apprehend, be cognizant of, become aware of, become conscious of, catch on (*Inf.*), comprehend, conceive, grasp, imagine, recognize, take in, twig (*Brit. inf.*), understand **2.** accomplish, actualize, bring about, bring off, bring to fruition, carry out *or* through, complete, consummate, do, effect, effectuate, fulfil, make concrete, make happen, perform, reify **3.** acquire, bring *or* take in, clear, earn, gain, get, go for, make, net, obtain, produce, sell for

really absolutely, actually, assuredly, categorically, certainly, genuinely, in actuality, indeed, in fact, in reality, positively, surely, truly, undoubtedly, verily, without a doubt

rear[2] (rɪə) *vt.* 1. care for and educate (children) 2. breed 3. erect —*vi.* 4. rise, *esp.* on hind feet

reason (ˈriːzᵊn) *n.* 1. ground, motive 2. faculty of thinking 3. sanity 4. sensible or logical thought or view —*vi.* 5. think logically in forming conclusions 6. (*usu. with* with) persuade by logical argument into doing *etc.* —ˈ**reasonable** *a.* 1. sensible, not excessive 2. suitable 3. logical —ˈ**reasoning** *n.* 1. drawing of conclusions from facts *etc.* 2. arguments, proofs *etc.* so adduced

reassure (riːəˈʃʊə) *vt.* restore confidence to

rebate[1] (ˈriːbeɪt) *n.* 1. discount, refund —*vt.* (rɪˈbeɪt) 2. deduct

rebate[2] (ˈriːbeɪt, ˈræbɪt) *or* **rabbet** *n.* 1. recess, groove cut into piece of timber to join with matching piece —*vt.* 2. cut rebate in

rebel (rɪˈbɛl) *vi.* 1. revolt, resist lawful authority, take arms against ruling power (-**ll**-) —*n.* (ˈrɛbᵊl) 2. one who rebels 3. insurgent —*a.* (ˈrɛbᵊl) 4. in rebellion —**re**ˈ**bellion** *n.* organized open resistance to authority, revolt —**re**ˈ**bellious** *a.* —**re**ˈ**belliously** *adv.*

rebirth (riːˈbɜːθ) *n.* 1. revival, renaissance 2. second or new birth

rebore (ˈriːbɔː) *n.* boring of cylinder to regain true shape

rebound (rɪˈbaʊnd) *vi.* 1. spring back 2. misfire, *esp.* so as to hurt perpetrator (of plan, deed *etc.*) —*n.* (ˈriːbaʊnd) 3. act of springing back or recoiling 4. return —**re**ˈ**bounder** *n.* small trampoline, used *esp.* at home, for aerobic exercising

rebuff (rɪˈbʌf) *n.* 1. blunt refusal 2. check —*vt.* 3. repulse, snub

rebuke (rɪˈbjuːk) *vt.* 1. reprove, reprimand, find fault with —*n.* 2. reprimand, scolding

rebus (ˈriːbəs) *n.* riddle in which names of things *etc.* are represented by pictures standing for syllables *etc.* (*pl.* -**es**)

rebut (rɪˈbʌt) *vt.* refute, disprove (-**tt**-) —**re**ˈ**buttal** *n.*

rec. 1. receipt 2. recipe 3. record

recalcitrant (rɪˈkælsɪtrənt) *a./n.* wilfully disobedient (person) —**re**ˈ**calcitrance** *n.*

recall (rɪˈkɔːl) *vt.* 1. recollect, remember 2. call, summon, order back 3. annul, cancel 4. revive, restore —*n.* 5. annulment, summons to return 6. ability to remember

THESAURUS

reap acquire, bring in, collect, cut, derive, gain, garner, gather, get, harvest, obtain, win

rear[1] *n.* back, back end, end, rearguard, stern, tail, tail end

rear[2] *v.* **1.** breed, bring up, care for, cultivate, educate, foster, grow, nurse, nurture, raise, train **2.** build, construct, erect, fabricate, put up **3.** loom, rise, soar, tower

reason *n.* **1.** apprehension, brains, comprehension, intellect, judgment, logic, mentality, mind, ratiocination, rationality, reasoning, sanity, sense(s), sound mind, soundness, understanding **2.** aim, basis, cause, design, end, goal, grounds, impetus, incentive, inducement, intention, motive, object, occasion, purpose, target, warrant, why and wherefore (*Inf.*) **3.** apologia, apology, argument, case, defence, excuse, explanation, exposition, ground, justification, rationale, vindication **4.** bounds, limits, moderation, propriety, reasonableness, sense, sensibleness, wisdom ~*v.* **5.** conclude, deduce, draw conclusions, infer, make out, ratiocinate, resolve, solve, syllogize, think, work out **6.** *With* **with** argue, bring round (*Inf.*), debate, dispute, dissuade, expostulate, move, persuade, prevail upon, remonstrate, show (someone) the error of his ways, talk into *or* out of, urge, win over

reasonable **1.** advisable, arguable, believable, credible, intelligent, judicious, justifiable, logical, plausible, practical, rational, reasoned, sane, sensible, sober, sound, tenable, well-advised, well thought-out, wise **2.** acceptable, average, equitable, fair, fit, honest, inexpensive, just, moderate, modest, O.K. (*Inf.*), proper, right, tolerable, within reason

reasoning **1.** analysis, cogitation, deduction, logic, ratiocination, reason, thinking, thought **2.** argument, case, exposition, hypothesis, interpretation, proof, train of thought

reassure bolster, buoy up, cheer up, comfort, encourage, hearten, inspirit, put *or* set one's mind at rest, relieve (someone) of anxiety, restore confidence to

rebel *v.* **1.** man the barricades, mutiny, resist, revolt, rise up, take to the streets, take up arms **2.** come out against, defy, disobey, dissent, refuse to obey ~*n.* **3.** insurgent, insurrectionary, mutineer, resistance fighter, revolutionary, revolutionist, secessionist **4.** apostate, dissenter, heretic, nonconformist, schismatic ~*adj.* **5.** insubordinate, insurgent, insurrectionary, mutinous, rebellious, revolutionary

rebellion **1.** insurgence, insurgency, insurrection, mutiny, resistance, revolt, revolution, rising, uprising **2.** apostasy, defiance, disobedience, dissent, heresy, insubordination, nonconformity, schism

rebellious contumacious, defiant, disaffected, disloyal, disobedient, disorderly, insubordinate, insurgent, insurrectionary, intractable, mutinous, rebel, recalcitrant, revolutionary, seditious, turbulent, ungovernable, unruly

rebirth new beginning, regeneration, reincarnation, renaissance, renascence, renewal, restoration, resurgence, resurrection, revitalization, revival

rebound *v.* **1.** bounce, recoil, resound, return, ricochet, spring back **2.** backfire, boomerang, misfire, recoil ~*n.* **3.** bounce, comeback, kickback, repercussion, return, ricochet

rebuff **1.** *v.* brush off (*Sl.*), check, cold-shoulder, cut, decline, deny, discourage, put off, refuse, reject, repulse, resist, slight, snub, spurn, turn down **2.** *n.* brushoff (*Sl.*), check, cold shoulder, defeat, denial, discouragement, opposition, refusal, rejection, repulse, slight, snub, thumbs down

rebuke **1.** *v.* admonish, bawl out (*Inf.*), berate, blame, carpet (*Inf.*), castigate, censure, chide, dress down (*Inf.*), haul (someone) over the coals (*Inf.*), lecture, reprehend, reprimand, reproach, reprove, scold, take to task, tear (someone) off a strip (*Inf.*), tell off (*Inf.*), tick off (*Inf.*), upbraid **2.** *n.* admonition, blame, castigation, censure, dressing down (*Inf.*), lecture, reprimand, reproach, reproof, reproval, row, telling-off (*Inf.*), ticking-off (*Inf.*), tongue-lashing, wigging (*Brit. sl.*)

recalcitrant contrary, contumacious, defiant, disobedient, insubordinate, intractable, obstinate, refractory, stubborn, uncontrollable, ungovernable, unmanageable, unruly, unwilling, wayward, wilful

recant (rɪˈkænt) *v.* withdraw (statement, opinion *etc.*) —**recanˈtation** *n.*

recap (ˈriːkæp, riːˈkæp) *v.* 1. recapitulate (-pp-) —*n.* (ˈriːkæp) 2. recapitulation

recapitulate (riːkəˈpɪtjuleɪt) *vt.* 1. state again briefly 2. repeat —**recapituˈlation** *n.*

recce (ˈrɛkɪ) *sl.* *n.* 1. reconnaissance —*v.* 2. reconnoitre

recd. *or* **rec'd.** received

recede (rɪˈsiːd) *vi.* 1. go back 2. become distant 3. slope backwards 4. start balding

receipt (rɪˈsiːt) *n.* 1. written acknowledgment of money received 2. receiving or being received —*vt.* 3. acknowledge payment of in writing

receive (rɪˈsiːv) *vt.* 1. take, accept, get 2. experience 3. greet (guests) —**reˈceivable** *a.* —**reˈceiver** *n.* 1. officer appointed to take public money 2. one who takes stolen goods knowing them to have been stolen 3. equipment in telephone, radio or television that converts electrical signals into sound and light

recent (ˈriːsᵊnt) *a.* 1. that has lately happened 2. new 3. (R-) of second and most recent epoch of Quaternary period, which began 10 000 years ago (*also* **ˈHolocene**) —*n.* 4. (R-) the Recent epoch or rock series (*also* **ˈHolocene**) —**ˈrecently** *adv.*

receptacle (rɪˈsɛptəkᵊl) *n.* vessel, place or space to contain anything

reception (rɪˈsɛpʃən) *n.* 1. receiving 2. manner of receiving 3. welcome 4. formal party 5. area for receiving guests, clients *etc.* 6. in broadcasting, quality of signals received —**reˈceptionist** *n.* person who receives guests, clients *etc.* —**reception room** 1. room in house suitable for entertaining guests 2. room in hotel suitable for receptions *etc.*

receptive (rɪˈsɛptɪv) *a.* able, quick, willing to receive new ideas, suggestions *etc.* —**receptivity** (riːsɛpˈtɪvɪtɪ) *or* **reˈceptiveness** *n.*

recess (rɪˈsɛs, ˈriːsɛs) *n.* 1. niche, alcove 2. hollow 3. secret, hidden place 4. remission or suspension of business 5. vacation, holiday

recession (rɪˈsɛʃən) *n.* 1. period of reduction in trade 2. act of receding —**reˈcessive** *a.* receding

recessional (rɪˈsɛʃənᵊl) *n.* hymn sung while clergy retire

recherché (rəˈʃɛəʃeɪ) *a.* 1. of studied elegance 2. exquisite 3. choice

recidivism (rɪˈsɪdɪvɪzəm) *n.* habitual relapse into crime —**reˈcidivist** *n./a.*

recipe (ˈrɛsɪpɪ) *n.* 1. directions for cooking a dish 2. prescription 3. expedient

recipient (rɪˈsɪpɪənt) *a.* 1. that can or does receive —*n.* 2. one who, that which receives —**reˈcipience** *or* **reˈcipiency** *n.*

reciprocal (rɪˈsɪprəkᵊl) *a.* 1. complementary 2. mutual 3. moving backwards and forwards 4. alternating —**reˈciprocally** *adv.* —**reˈciprocate** *vt.* 1. give and receive mutually 2. return —*vi.* 3. move backwards and forwards —**reciproˈcation** *n.* —**reciprocity** (rɛsɪˈprɒsɪtɪ) *n.*

recite (rɪˈsaɪt) *vt.* repeat aloud, *esp.* to audience —**reˈcital** *n.* 1. musical performance, usu. by one person 2. act of reciting 3. narration of facts *etc.* 4. story 5. public entertainment of recitations *etc.* —**recitation** (rɛsɪˈteɪʃən) *n.* 1. recital, usu. from memory, of poetry or prose 2. recountal —**recitative** (rɛsɪtəˈtiːv) *n.* musical declamation —**reˈciter** *n.*

THESAURUS

recall *v.* 1. bring *or* call to mind, call *or* summon up, evoke, look *or* think back to, mind (*Dialect*), recollect, remember, reminisce about 2. abjure, annul, call back, call in, cancel, countermand, nullify, repeal, rescind, retract, revoke, take back, withdraw ~*n.* 3. annulment, cancellation, nullification, recision, repeal, rescindment, rescission, retraction, revocation, withdrawal 4. memory, recollection, remembrance

recant abjure, apostatize, deny, disavow, disclaim, disown, forswear, recall, renounce, repudiate, retract, revoke, take back, unsay, withdraw

recapitulate epitomize, go over again, outline, recap (*Inf.*), recount, reiterate, repeat, restate, review, run over, run through again, summarize, sum up

recede abate, draw back, ebb, fall back, go back, regress, retire, retreat, retrogress, return, subside, withdraw

receipt 1. acknowledgment, counterfoil, proof of purchase, sales slip, stub, voucher 2. acceptance, delivery, receiving, reception, recipience

receive 1. accept, accept delivery of, acquire, be given, be in receipt of, collect, derive, get, obtain, pick up, take 2. bear, be subjected to, encounter, experience, go through, meet with, suffer, sustain, undergo 3. accommodate, admit, be at home to, entertain, greet, meet, take in, welcome

recent contemporary, current, fresh, late, latter, latter-day, modern, new, novel, present-day, up-to-date, young

recently currently, freshly, lately, newly, not long ago, of late

receptacle container, holder, repository

reception 1. acceptance, admission, receipt, receiving, recipience 2. acknowledgment, greeting, reaction, recognition, response, treatment, welcome 3. do (*Inf.*), entertainment, function, levee, party, soirée

receptive 1. alert, bright, perceptive, quick on the uptake (*Inf.*), responsive, sensitive 2. accessible, amenable, approachable, favourable, friendly, hospitable, interested, open, open-minded, open to suggestions, susceptible, sympathetic, welcoming

recess 1. alcove, bay, cavity, corner, depression, hollow, indentation, niche, nook, oriel 2. break, cessation of business, closure, holiday, intermission, interval, respite, rest, vacation

recession decline, depression, downturn, slump

recipe 1. directions, ingredients, instructions 2. formula, method, modus operandi, prescription, procedure, process, programme, technique

reciprocal alternate, complementary, correlative, corresponding, equivalent, exchanged, give-and-take, interchangeable, interdependent, mutual, reciprocative, reciprocatory

reciprocate barter, exchange, feel in return, interchange, reply, requite, respond, return, return the compliment, swap, trade

recital account, description, detailing, enumeration, narration, narrative, performance, reading, recapitu-

reckless (ˈrɛklɪs) *a.* heedless, incautious —**ˈrecklessness** *n.*

reckon (ˈrɛkən) *v.* **1.** count —*vt.* **2.** include **3.** consider **4.** think, deem —*vi.* **5.** make calculations —**ˈreckoner** *n.* —**ˈreckoning** *n.* **1.** counting, calculating **2.** settlement of account *etc.* **3.** bill, account **4.** retribution for one's actions (*esp. in* **day of reckoning**) **5.** *Navigation see* **dead reckoning** *at* DEAD

reclaim (rɪˈkleɪm) *vt.* **1.** make fit for cultivation **2.** bring back **3.** reform **4.** demand the return of —**reˈclaimable** *a.*

recline (rɪˈklaɪn) *vi.* sit, lie back or on one's side

recluse (rɪˈkluːs) *n.* **1.** hermit —*a.* **2.** living in complete retirement —**reˈclusion** *n.* —**reˈclusive** *a.*

recognize *or* **-ise** (ˈrɛkəgnaɪz) *vt.* **1.** know again **2.** treat as valid **3.** notice, show appreciation of —**recognition** (rɛkəgˈnɪʃən) *n.* —**ˈrecognizable** *or* **-isable** *a.* —**recognizance** *or* **recognisance** (rɪˈkɒgnɪzəns) *n.* **1.** avowal **2.** bond by which person undertakes before court to observe some condition **3.** *obs.* recognition

recoil (rɪˈkɔɪl) *vi.* **1.** draw back in horror *etc.* **2.** go wrong so as to hurt the perpetrator **3.** (*esp.* of gun when fired) rebound —*n.* (rɪˈkɔɪl, ˈriːkɔɪl) **4.** backward spring **5.** retreat **6.** recoiling

recollect (rɛkəˈlɛkt) *vt.* call back to mind, remember —**recolˈlection** *n.*

recommend (rɛkəˈmɛnd) *vt.* **1.** advise, counsel **2.** praise, commend **3.** make acceptable —**recommenˈdation** *n.*

recompense (ˈrɛkəmpɛns) *vt.* **1.** reward **2.** compensate, make up for —*n.* **3.** compensation **4.** reward **5.** requital

reconcile (ˈrɛkənsaɪl) *vt.* **1.** bring back into friendship **2.** adjust, settle, harmonize —**ˈreconcilable** *a.* —**ˈreconcilement** *n.* —**reconciliation** (rɛkənsɪlɪˈeɪʃən) *n.*

recondite (rɪˈkɒndaɪt, ˈrɛkəndaɪt) *a.* obscure, abstruse, little known

recondition (riːkənˈdɪʃən) *vt.* restore to good condition or working order

reconnoitre *or U.S.* **reconnoiter** (rɛkəˈnɔɪtə) *vt.* **1.** make preliminary survey of **2.** survey position of (enemy) —*vi.* **3.** make reconnaissance —**reconnaissance** (rɪˈkɒnɪsəns) *n.* **1.** an examination or survey for military or engineering purposes **2.** scouting

THESAURUS

lation, recitation, rehearsal, relation, rendering, repetition, statement, story, tale, telling

recitation lecture, narration, passage, performance, piece, reading, recital, rendering, telling

recite declaim, deliver, describe, detail, do one's party piece (*Inf.*), enumerate, itemize, narrate, perform, recapitulate, recount, rehearse, relate, repeat, speak, tell

reckless careless, daredevil, devil-may-care, foolhardy, harebrained, harum-scarum, hasty, headlong, heedless, ill-advised, imprudent, inattentive, incautious, indiscreet, irresponsible, madcap, mindless, negligent, overventuresome, precipitate, rash, regardless, thoughtless, wild

reckon **1.** add up, calculate, compute, count, enumerate, figure, number, tally, total **2.** account, appraise, consider, count, deem, esteem, estimate, evaluate, gauge, hold, judge, look upon, rate, regard, think of **3.** assume, believe, be of the opinion, conjecture, expect, fancy, guess (*Inf.*), imagine, suppose, surmise, think

reckoning **1.** adding, addition, calculation, computation, count, counting, estimate, summation, working **2.** account, bill, charge, due, score, settlement **3.** doom, judgment, last judgment, retribution

reclaim get *or* take back, recapture, recover, redeem, reform, regain, regenerate, reinstate, rescue, restore, retrieve, salvage

recline be recumbent, lay (something) down, lean, lie (down), loll, lounge, repose, rest, sprawl, stretch out

recluse **1.** *n.* anchoress, anchorite, ascetic, eremite, hermit, monk, solitary **2.** *adj.* cloistered, isolated, reclusive, retiring, secluded, sequestered, solitary, withdrawn

recognition **1.** detection, discovery, identification, recall, recollection, remembrance **2.** acceptance, acknowledgment, admission, allowance, appreciation, avowal, awareness, cognizance, concession, confession, notice, perception, realization, respect, understanding **3.** acknowledgment, appreciation, approval, gratitude, greeting, honour, salute

recognize **1.** identify, know, know again, make out, notice, place, recall, recollect, remember, spot **2.** accept, acknowledge, admit, allow, appreciate, avow, be aware of, concede, confess, grant, own, perceive, realize, respect, see, understand **3.** acknowledge, appreciate, approve, greet, honour, salute

recoil *v.* **1.** jerk back, kick, react, rebound, resile, spring back **2.** balk at, draw back, falter, flinch, quail, shrink, shy away **3.** backfire, boomerang, go wrong, misfire, rebound ~*n.* **4.** backlash, kick, reaction, rebound, repercussion

recollect call to mind, mind (*Dialect*), place, recall, remember, reminisce, summon up

recollection impression, memory, mental image, recall, remembrance, reminiscence

recommend **1.** advance, advise, advocate, counsel, enjoin, exhort, propose, put forward, suggest, urge **2.** approve, commend, endorse, praise, put in a good word for, speak well of, vouch for **3.** make attractive (acceptable, appealing, interesting)

recommendation **1.** advice, counsel, proposal, suggestion, urging **2.** advocacy, approbation, approval, blessing, commendation, endorsement, favourable mention, good word, plug (*Inf.*), praise, reference, sanction, testimonial

reconcile **1.** appease, bring to terms, conciliate, make peace between, pacify, placate, propitiate, re-establish friendly relations between, restore harmony between, reunite **2.** adjust, compose, harmonize, patch up, put to rights, rectify, resolve, settle, square

reconciliation **1.** appeasement, conciliation, détente, pacification, propitiation, *rapprochement,* reconcilement, reunion, understanding **2.** accommodation, adjustment, compromise, harmony, rectification, settlement

recondite abstruse, arcane, cabbalistic, concealed, dark, deep, difficult, esoteric, hidden, involved, mysterious, mystical, obscure, occult, profound, secret

recondition do up (*Inf.*), fix up (*Inf., chiefly U.S.*), overhaul, remodel, renew, renovate, repair, restore, revamp

reconnaissance exploration, inspection, investigation, observation, patrol, recce (*Sl.*), reconnoitring, scan, scouting, scrutiny, survey

reconstitute (riːˈkɒnstɪtjuːt) *vt.* restore (food) to former state, *esp.* by addition of water to a concentrate

record (ˈrɛkɔːd) *n.* **1.** document or other thing that records **2.** disc with indentations which gramophone transforms into sound **3.** best recorded achievement **4.** known facts about person's past —*vt.* (rɪˈkɔːd) **5.** put in writing **6.** register —*v.* (rɪˈkɔːd) **7.** preserve (sound, TV programmes *etc.*) on plastic disc, magnetic tape *etc.* for reproduction on playback device —**reˈcorder** *n.* **1.** one who, that which records **2.** type of flute **3.** judge in certain courts —**reˈcording** *n.* **1.** process of making records from sound **2.** something recorded, *eg* radio or TV programme —**recorded delivery** Post Office service by which official record of posting and delivery is obtained for letter or package —**Record Office** institution in which official records are stored and kept (*also* **Public Record Office**) —**record-player** *n.* machine for playing gramophone records —**for the record** for the sake of strict factual accuracy —**off the record** confidential or confidentially

recount (rɪˈkaʊnt) *vt.* tell in detail

re-count (riːˈkaʊnt) *v.* **1.** count (votes *etc.*) again —*n.* (ˈriːkaʊnt) **2.** second or further count, *esp.* of votes

recoup (rɪˈkuːp) *vt.* **1.** recompense, compensate **2.** recover (what has been expended or lost)

recourse (rɪˈkɔːs) *n.* **1.** (resorting to) source of help **2.** *Law* right of action or appeal

recover (rɪˈkʌvə) *vt.* **1.** regain, get back —*vi.* **2.** get back health —**reˈcoverable** *a.* —**reˈcovery** *n.*

recreant (ˈrɛkrɪənt) *a.* **1.** cowardly, disloyal —*n.* **2.** recreant person **3.** renegade —**ˈrecreance** *or* **ˈrecreancy** *n.*

recreation (rɛkrɪˈeɪʃən) *n.* agreeable or refreshing occupation, relaxation, amusement —**ˈrecreative** *a.*

recriminate (rɪˈkrɪmɪneɪt) *vi.* make countercharge or mutual accusation —**recrimiˈnation** *n.* mutual abuse and blame —**reˈcriminative** *or* **reˈcriminatory** *a.*

recrudesce (riːkruːˈdɛs) *vi.* break out again —**recruˈdescence** *n.* —**recruˈdescent** *a.*

recruit (rɪˈkruːt) *n.* **1.** newly-enlisted soldier **2.** one newly joining society *etc.* —*vt.* **3.** enlist (fresh soldiers *etc.*) —**reˈcruitment** *n.*

rectangle (ˈrɛktæŋgˈl) *n.* oblong four-sided figure with four right angles —**recˈtangular** *a.* shaped thus

rectify (ˈrɛktɪfaɪ) *vt.* **1.** put right, correct, remedy **2.** purify (**-fied, -fying**) —**rectifiˈcation** *n.* **1.** act of setting right **2.** refining by repeated distillation **3.** *Elec.* conversion of alternating current into direct current —**ˈrectifier** *n.* thing that rectifies

rectilinear (rɛktɪˈlɪnɪə) *or* **rectilineal** *a.* **1.** in straight line **2.** characterized by straight lines

rectitude (ˈrɛktɪtjuːd) *n.* **1.** moral uprightness **2.** honesty of purpose

THESAURUS

reconnoitre explore, get the lie of the land, inspect, investigate, make a reconnaissance (of), observe, patrol, recce (*Sl.*), scan, scout, scrutinize, see how the land lies, spy out, survey

reconsider change one's mind, have second thoughts, reassess, re-evaluate, re-examine, rethink, review, revise, take another look at, think again, think better of, think over, think twice

reconstruct reassemble, rebuild, recreate, re-establish, reform, regenerate, remake, remodel, renovate, reorganize, restore

record *n.* **1.** account, annals, archives, chronicle, diary, document, entry, file, journal, log, memoir, memorandum, memorial, minute, register, report **2.** documentation, evidence, memorial, remembrance, testimony, trace, witness **3.** background, career, curriculum vitae, history, performance, track record (*Inf.*) **4.** album, disc, EP, forty-five, gramophone record, LP, platter (*U.S. sl.*), recording, release, single **5. off the record** confidential, confidentially, in confidence, in private, not for publication, private, sub rosa, under the rose, unofficial, unofficially ~*v.* **6.** chalk up (*Inf.*), chronicle, document, enrol, enter, inscribe, log, minute, note, preserve, put down, put on file, put on record, register, report, set down, take down, transcribe, write down **7.** contain, give evidence of, indicate, read, register, say, show **8.** cut, lay down (*Sl.*), make a recording of, put on wax (*Inf.*), tape, tape-record, video, video-tape, wax (*Inf.*)

recorder annalist, archivist, chronicler, clerk, diarist, historian, registrar, scorekeeper, scorer, scribe

recording cut (*Inf.*), disc, gramophone record, record, tape, video

recount delineate, depict, describe, detail, enumerate, give an account of, narrate, portray, recite, rehearse, relate, repeat, report, tell, tell the story of

recover 1. find again, get back, make good, recapture, reclaim, recoup, redeem, regain, repair, repossess, restore, retake, retrieve, take back, win back **2.** bounce back, come round, convalesce, feel oneself again, get back on one's feet, get better, get well, heal, improve, mend, pick up, pull through, rally, recuperate, regain one's health *or* strength, revive, take a turn for the better

recovery 1. convalescence, healing, improvement, mending, rally, recuperation, return to health, revival, turn for the better **2.** recapture, reclamation, redemption, repair, repossession, restoration, retrieval

recreation amusement, distraction, diversion, enjoyment, entertainment, exercise, fun, hobby, leisure activity, pastime, play, pleasure, refreshment, relaxation, relief, sport

recrimination bickering, counterattack, countercharge, mutual accusation, name-calling, quarrel, retaliation, retort, squabbling

recruit *v.* **1.** draft, enlist, enrol, impress, levy, mobilize, muster, raise, strengthen **2.** engage, enrol, gather, obtain, procure, proselytize, round up, take on, win (over) ~*n.* **3.** apprentice, beginner, convert, greenhorn (*Inf.*), helper, initiate, learner, neophyte, novice, proselyte, rookie (*Inf.*), trainee, tyro

rectify 1. adjust, amend, correct, emend, fix, improve, make good, mend, put right, redress, reform, remedy, repair, right, square **2.** *Chem.* distil, purify, refine, separate

rectitude correctness, decency, equity, goodness, honesty, honour, incorruptibility, integrity, justice, morality, principle, probity, righteousness, scrupulousness, uprightness, virtue

recto (ˈrɛktəʊ) *n.* right-hand page of book, front of leaf (*pl.* **-s**)

rector (ˈrɛktə) *n.* **1.** clergyman with care of parish **2.** head of certain institutions, chiefly academic —ˈ**rectorship** *n.* —ˈ**rectory** *n.* rector's house

rectum (ˈrɛktəm) *n.* final section of large intestine (*pl.* **-s, -ta** (-tə)) —ˈ**rectal** *a.*

recumbent (rɪˈkʌmbənt) *a.* lying down —**reˈcumbence** *or* **reˈcumbency** *n.*

recuperate (rɪˈku:pəreɪt, -ˈkju:-) *vi.* **1.** recover from illness, convalesce —*v.* **2.** restore, be restored from losses *etc.* —**recuperˈation** *n.*

recur (rɪˈkɜ:) *vi.* **1.** happen again **2.** return again and again **3.** go or come back in mind (**-rr-**) —**reˈcurrence** *n.* repetition —**reˈcurrent** *a.*

recusant (ˈrɛkjʊzənt) *n.* **1.** one who refused to conform to rites of Established Anglican Church —*a.* **2.** obstinate in refusal

recycle (ri:ˈsaɪkˀl) *vt.* **1.** reprocess (manufactured substance) for use again **2.** reuse

red (rɛd) *a.* **1.** of colour varying from crimson to orange and seen in blood, rubies, glowing fire *etc.* —*n.* **2.** the colour **3.** *inf.* communist —ˈ**redden** *vt.* **1.** make red —*vi.* **2.** become red **3.** flush —ˈ**reddish** *a.* —**red blood cell** *see* ERYTHROCYTE —**red-blooded** *a.* **1.** vigorous **2.** virile —ˈ**redbreast** *n.* robin —ˈ**redbrick** *a.* of provincial and relatively new university —**red carpet** **1.** strip of red carpeting laid for important dignitaries to walk on **2.** deferential treatment accorded to person of importance —ˈ**redcoat** *n.* **1.** *obs.* soldier **2.** C *inf.* Mountie —**Red Crescent** emblem of Red Cross Society in Muslim country —**Red Cross** international humanitarian organization providing medical care for war casualties, famine relief *etc.* —**red deer** large deer formerly widely distributed in woodlands of Europe and Asia —**Red Ensign** ensign of British Merchant Navy, having Union Jack on red background at upper corner; also national flag of Canad. until 1965 —ˈ**redfish** *n.* any of various types of fish —**red flag** **1.** emblem of communist party **2.** (**R- F-**) their song **3.** danger signal —**red-handed** *a. inf.* (caught) in the act —**red hat** broad-brimmed crimson hat given to cardinals as symbol of rank —ˈ**redhead** *n.* person with red hair —ˈ**redheaded** *a.* —**red herring** topic introduced to divert attention from main issue —**red-hot** *a.* **1.** (*esp.* of metal) heated to temperature at which it glows red **2.** extremely hot **3.** keen, excited, eager **4.** furious; violent **5.** very recent or topical —**red-hot poker** garden plant with tall spikes of red or orange flowers —**Red Indian** N Amer. Indian —**red lead** red poisonous insoluble oxide of lead —**red-letter day** memorably important or happy occasion —**red light** **1.** signal to stop, *esp.* traffic signal **2.** danger signal **3.** red lamp hanging outside house indicating it is a brothel —**red-light district** district containing many brothels —**red pepper** **1.** pepper plant cultivated for its hot pungent red podlike fruits **2.** this fruit **3.** ripe red fruit of sweet pepper **4.** *see* CAYENNE PEPPER —**red rag** provocation; something that infuriates —ˈ**redshank** *n.* large European sandpiper —**red shift** shift in spectral lines of stellar spectrum towards red end of visible region relative to wavelength of these lines in terrestrial spectrum —ˈ**redskin** *n. inf.* Amer. Indian —ˈ**redstart** *n.* **1.** European songbird of thrush family **2.** N Amer. warbler —**red tape** excessive adherence to official rules —ˈ**redwing** *n.* small European thrush having speckled breast and reddish flanks —ˈ**redwood** *n.* giant coniferous tree of California —**in the red** *inf.* in debt —**see red** *inf.* be angry

redeem (rɪˈdi:m) *vt.* **1.** buy back **2.** set free **3.** free from sin **4.** make up for —**reˈdeemable** *a.* —**redemption** (rɪˈdɛmpʃən) *n.* —**The Redeemer** Jesus Christ

redeploy (ri:dɪˈplɔɪ) *v.* assign new positions or tasks to (labour *etc.*) —**redeˈployment** *n.*

redolent (ˈrɛdəʊlənt) *a.* **1.** smelling strongly, fragrant **2.** reminiscent —ˈ**redolence** *n.*

redouble (rɪˈdʌbˀl) *v.* **1.** increase, multiply, intensify **2.** *Bridge* double a second time

redoubt (rɪˈdaʊt) *n.* detached outwork in fortifications

redoubtable (rɪˈdaʊtəbˀl) *a.* dreaded, formidable

redound (rɪˈdaʊnd) *vi.* **1.** contribute **2.** recoil

redress (rɪˈdrɛs) *vt.* **1.** set right **2.** make amends for —*n.* **3.** compensation, amends

reduce (rɪˈdju:s) *vt.* **1.** bring down, lower **2.** lessen, weaken **3.** bring by force or necessity to some state or action **4.** slim **5.** simplify **6.** dilute —*vi.* **7.** *Chem.* separate substance from others with which it is combined —**reˈducible** *a.* —**reduction** (rɪˈdʌkʃən) *n.* —**reducing agent** substance used to deoxidize or lessen density of another substance

THESAURUS

recuperate convalesce, get back on one's feet, get better, improve, mend, pick up, recover, regain one's health

recur **1.** come again, come and go, come back, happen again, persist, reappear, repeat, return, revert **2.** be remembered, come back, haunt one's thoughts, return to mind, run through one's mind

recurrent continued, cyclical, frequent, habitual, periodic, recurring, regular, repeated, repetitive

recycle reclaim, reprocess, reuse, salvage, save

red *n.* **1. in the red** *Inf.* bankrupt, in arrears, in debit, in debt, in deficit, insolvent, on the rocks, overdrawn, owing money, showing a loss **2. see red** *Inf.* be *or* get very angry, be beside oneself with rage (*Inf.*), become enraged, blow one's top, boil, go mad (*Inf.*), go off one's head (*Sl.*), lose one's rag (*Sl.*), lose one's temper, seethe

redden blush, colour (up), crimson, flush, go red, suffuse

redeem **1.** buy back, reclaim, recover, recover possession of, regain, repossess, repurchase, retrieve, win back **2.** atone for, compensate for, defray, make amends for, make good, make up for, offset, outweigh, redress, save **3.** buy the freedom of, deliver, emancipate, extricate, free, liberate, pay the ransom of, ransom, rescue, save, set free

redemption **1.** reclamation, recovery, repossession, repurchase, retrieval **2.** amends, atonement, compensation, expiation, reparation **3.** deliverance, emancipation, liberation, ransom, release, rescue, salvation

redress *v.* **1.** compensate for, make amends (reparation, restitution) for, make up for, pay for, put right, recompense for **2.** adjust, amend, balance, correct, ease, even up, mend, put right, rectify, reform, regu-

redundant (rɪˈdʌndənt) *a.* **1.** superfluous **2.** (of worker) deprived of job because it is no longer needed —**reˈdundancy** *n.* —**redundancy payment** sum of money given to worker made redundant by employer

reduplicate (rɪˈdjuːplɪkeɪt) *v.* **1.** make or become double; repeat **2.** repeat (sound or syllable) in word or (of sound or syllable) be repeated —*a.* (rɪˈdjuːplɪkɪt) **3.** doubled; repeated **4.** (of petals or sepals) having margins curving outwards —**redupliˈcation** *n.*

reed (riːd) *n.* **1.** any of various marsh or water plants **2.** tall straight stem of one **3.** *Mus.* vibrating cane or metal strip of certain wind instruments —ˈ**reedy** *a.* **1.** full of reeds **2.** like reed instrument **3.** harsh and thin in tone —ˈ**reedbuck** *n.* S Afr. antelope with buff coat —**reed bunting** common European bunting that has brown streaked plumage

reef (riːf) *n.* **1.** ridge of rock or coral near surface of sea **2.** vein of ore **3.** part of sail which can be rolled up to reduce area —*vt.* **4.** take in a reef of —ˈ**reefer** *n.* **1.** sailor's jacket **2.** *sl.* hand-rolled cigarette, *esp.* containing cannabis —**reef knot** knot consisting of two overhand knots turned opposite ways (*also* **square knot**)

reek (riːk) *n.* **1.** strong (unpleasant) smell —*vi.* **2.** emit fumes **3.** smell

reel (riːl, rɪəl) *n.* **1.** spool on which film is wound **2.** *Cine.* portion of film **3.** winding apparatus **4.** bobbin **5.** thread wound on this **6.** lively dance **7.** music for it **8.** act of staggering —*vt.* **9.** wind on to reel **10.** draw (in) by means of reel —*vi.* **11.** stagger, sway, rock —**reel off** recite, write fluently, quickly

re-entry (riːˈɛntrɪ) *n.* **1.** retaking possession of land *etc.* **2.** return of spacecraft into earth's atmosphere

reeve[1] (riːv) *n.* **1.** *Hist.* manorial steward or official **2.** C president of local (rural) council

reeve[2] (riːv) *vt.* pass (rope) through hole, in block *etc.*

reeve[3] (riːv) *n.* female of ruff (bird)

ref. **1.** referee **2.** reference **3.** reformed

refectory (rɪˈfɛktərɪ, -trɪ) *n.* room for meals in college *etc.* —**reˈfection** *n.* meal —**refectory table** long narrow dining table supported by two trestles

refer (rɪˈfɜː) *vi.* **1.** relate, allude —*vt.* **2.** send or go for information **3.** trace, ascribe **4.** submit for decision (-rr-) —**referable** (ˈrɛfərəbˀl) *or* **reˈferrable** *a.* —**referee** (rɛfəˈriː) *n.* **1.** arbitrator **2.** person willing to testify to someone's character *etc.* **3.** umpire —*v.* **4.** act as referee (in) —**reference** (ˈrɛfərəns, ˈrɛfrəns) *n.* **1.** act of referring **2.** citation or direction in book **3.** appeal to judgment of another **4.** testimonial **5.** one to whom inquiries as to character *etc.* may be made —**referendum** (rɛfəˈrɛndəm) *n.* submitting of question to electorate (*pl.* **-s, -da** (-də)) —**reˈferral** *n.* act, instance of referring —**reference library** library where books may be consulted but not taken away by readers

refine (rɪˈfaɪn) *vt.* purify —**reˈfined** *a.* **1.** not coarse or vulgar; genteel, elegant, polite **2.** freed from impurities; purified —**reˈfinement** *n.* **1.** subtlety **2.** improvement, elaboration **3.** fineness of feeling, taste or manners —**reˈfiner** *n.* —**reˈfinery** *n.* place where sugar, oil *etc.* is refined

refit (riːˈfɪt) *v.* **1.** make or be made ready for use again by repairing *etc.* (-tt-) —*n.* (ˈriːfɪt) **2.** repair or re-equipping, as of ship, for further use

reflation (riːˈfleɪʃən) *n.* (steps taken to produce) increase in economic activity of country *etc.*

reflect (rɪˈflɛkt) *vt.* **1.** throw back, *esp.* rays of light **2.** cast (discredit *etc.*) upon —*vi.* **3.** meditate —**reˈflection** *or* **reˈflexion** *n.* **1.** act of reflecting **2.** return of rays of heat, light or waves of sound from surface **3.** image of object given back by mirror *etc.* **4.** conscious thought **5.** meditation **6.** expression of thought —**reˈflective** *a.* **1.** meditative, quiet, contemplative **2.** throwing back images —**reˈflector** *n.* polished surface for reflecting light *etc.*

THESAURUS

late, relieve, remedy, repair, restore the balance, square ~*n.* **3.** amends, atonement, compensation, payment, quittance, recompense, reparation, requital, restitution

reduce 1. abate, abridge, contract, curtail, cut down, debase, decrease, depress, dilute, diminish, impair, lessen, lower, moderate, shorten, slow down, tone down, truncate, turn down, weaken, wind down **2.** be *or* go on a diet, diet, lose weight, shed weight, slenderize (*Chiefly U.S.*), slim, trim **3.** bring down the price of, cheapen, cut, discount, lower, mark down, slash

redundant *de trop*, excessive, extra, inessential, inordinate, supererogatory, superfluous, supernumerary, surplus, unnecessary, unwanted

reek *v.* **1.** hum (*Sl.*), pong (*Brit. inf.*), smell, smell to high heaven, stink **2.** *Dialect* fume, give off smoke *or* fumes, smoke, steam ~*n.* **3.** effluvium, fetor, mephitis, odour, pong (*Brit. inf.*), smell, stench, stink

reel falter, lurch, pitch, rock, roll, stagger, stumble, sway, totter, waver, wobble

refer 1. advert, allude, bring up, cite, hint, invoke, make mention of, make reference, mention, speak of, touch on **2.** direct, guide, point, recommend, send **3.** apply, consult, go, have recourse to, look up, seek information from, turn to **4.** apply, be directed to, belong, be relevant to, concern, pertain, relate **5.** accredit, ascribe, assign, attribute, credit, impute, put down to **6.** commit, consign, deliver, hand over, pass on, submit, transfer, turn over

referee 1. *n.* adjudicator, arbiter, arbitrator, judge, ref (*Inf.*), umpire **2.** *v.* adjudicate, arbitrate, judge, umpire

reference 1. allusion, citation, mention, note, quotation, remark **2.** certification, character, credentials, endorsement, good word, recommendation, testimonial

referendum plebiscite, popular vote, public vote

refine clarify, cleanse, distil, filter, process, purify, rarefy

refined 1. civil, civilized, courtly, cultivated, cultured, elegant, genteel, gentlemanly, gracious, ladylike, polished, polite, sophisticated, urbane, well-bred, well-mannered **2.** cultured, delicate, discerning, discriminating, exact, fastidious, fine, nice, precise, punctilious, sensitive, sublime, subtle **3.** clarified, clean, distilled, filtered, processed, pure, purified

refinement 1. fine point, fine tuning, nicety, nuance, subtlety **2.** civility, civilization, courtesy, courtliness, cultivation, culture, delicacy, discrimination, elegance, fastidiousness, fineness, finesse, finish, gentility, good breeding, good manners, grace, graciousness, polish, politeness, politesse, precision, sophistication, style, taste, urbanity

reflex ('ri:flɛks) *n.* **1.** reflex action **2.** reflected image **3.** reflected light, colour *etc.* —*a.* **4.** (of muscular action) involuntary **5.** reflected **6.** bent back —**re'flexive** *a. Gram.* denoting agent's action on himself —**reflex action** involuntary response to (nerve) stimulation

reflux ('ri:flʌks) *n.* flowing back, ebb —**refluence** ('rɛfluəns) *n.* —**refluent** ('rɛfluənt) *a.* returning, ebbing

reform (rɪ'fɔ:m) *vt.* **1.** improve **2.** reconstruct —*vi.* **3.** abandon evil practices —*n.* **4.** improvement —**reformation** (rɛfə'meɪʃən) *n.* —**re'formatory** *n.* **1.** institution for reforming juvenile offenders —*a.* **2.** reforming —**re'former** *n.*

refract (rɪ'frækt) *vt.* change course of (light *etc.*) passing from one medium to another —**re'fraction** *n.* —**re'fractive** *a.*

refractory (rɪ'fræktərɪ) *a.* **1.** unmanageable **2.** difficult to treat or work **3.** *Med.* resistant to treatment **4.** resistant to heat

refrain[1] (rɪ'freɪn) *vi.* abstain

refrain[2] (rɪ'freɪn) *n.* chorus

refresh (rɪ'frɛʃ) *vt.* **1.** give freshness to **2.** revive **3.** renew **4.** brighten **5.** provide with refreshment —**re'fresher** *n.* that which refreshes —**re'freshment** *n.* **1.** that which refreshes, *esp.* food, drink **2.** restorative

refrigerate (rɪ'frɪdʒəreɪt) *vt.* **1.** freeze **2.** cool —**re'frigerant** *n.* **1.** refrigerating substance —*a.* **2.** causing cooling or freezing —**refriger'ation** *n.* —**re'frigerator** *n.* apparatus in which foods, drinks are kept cool

refuge ('rɛfju:dʒ) *n.* shelter, protection, retreat, sanctuary —**refu'gee** *n.* one who seeks refuge, *esp.* in foreign country

refulgent (rɪ'fʌldʒənt) *a.* shining, radiant —**re'fulgence** *n.* —**re'fulgency** *n.* splendour

refund (rɪ'fʌnd) *vt.* **1.** pay back —*n.* ('ri:fʌnd) **2.** return of money to purchaser or amount so returned

refurbish (ri:'fɜ:bɪʃ) *vt.* furbish, furnish or polish anew

refuse[1] (rɪ'fju:z) *v.* decline, deny, reject —**re'fusal** *n.* **1.** denial of anything demanded or offered **2.** option

refuse[2] ('rɛfju:s) *n.* rubbish, useless matter

refute (rɪ'fju:t) *vt.* disprove —**refutable** ('rɛfjʊtəbᵊl, rɪ'fju:-) *a.* —**refutation** (rɛfjʊ'teɪʃən) *n.*

regal ('ri:gᵊl) *a.* of, like a king —**regalia** (rɪ'geɪlɪə) *pl.n.* (*sometimes with sing. v.*) **1.** insignia of royalty, as used at coronation *etc.* **2.** emblems of high office, an order *etc.* —**re'gality** *n.* —**'regally** *adv.*

regale (rɪ'geɪl) *vt.* **1.** give pleasure to **2.** feast —**re'galement** *n.*

regard (rɪ'gɑ:d) *vt.* **1.** look at **2.** consider **3.** relate to **4.** heed —*n.* **5.** look **6.** attention **7.** particular respect **8.** esteem —*pl.* **9.** expression of good will —**re'gardful** *a.* heedful, careful —**re'garding** *prep.* in respect of; on

THESAURUS

reflect 1. echo, give back, imitate, mirror, reproduce, return, throw back **2.** cogitate, consider, contemplate, deliberate, meditate, mull over, muse, ponder, ruminate, think, wonder

reflection 1. counterpart, echo, image, mirror image **2.** cerebration, cogitation, consideration, contemplation, deliberation, idea, impression, meditation, musing, observation, opinion, pondering, rumination, study, thinking, thought, view

reform *v.* **1.** ameliorate, amend, better, correct, emend, improve, mend, rebuild, reclaim, reconstitute, reconstruct, rectify, regenerate, rehabilitate, remodel, renovate, reorganize, repair, restore, revolutionize **2.** get back on the straight and narrow (*Inf.*), go straight (*Inf.*), mend one's ways, turn over a new leaf ~*n.* **3.** amelioration, amendment, betterment, correction, improvement, rectification, rehabilitation, renovation

refrain *v.* abstain, avoid, cease, desist, do without, eschew, forbear, give up, leave off, renounce, stop

refresh 1. brace, breathe new life into, cheer, cool, enliven, freshen, inspirit, reanimate, reinvigorate, rejuvenate, revitalize, revive, revivify, stimulate **2.** brush up (*Inf.*), jog, prod, prompt, renew, stimulate **3.** renew, renovate, repair, replenish, restore, top up

refrigerate chill, cool, freeze, keep cold

refuge asylum, bolt hole, harbour, haven, hide-out, protection, resort, retreat, sanctuary, security, shelter

refugee displaced person, émigré, escapee, exile, fugitive, runaway

refund 1. *v.* give back, make good, pay back, reimburse, repay, restore, return **2.** *n.* reimbursement, repayment, return

refurbish clean up, do up (*Inf.*), fix up (*Inf., chiefly U.S.*), mend, overhaul, re-equip, refit, remodel, renovate, repair, restore, revamp, set to rights, spruce up

refusal 1. defiance, denial, knockback (*Sl.*), negation, no, rebuff, rejection, repudiation, thumbs down **2.** choice, consideration, opportunity, option

refuse *v.* decline, deny, reject, repel, repudiate, say no, spurn, turn down, withhold

refute confute, counter, discredit, disprove, give the lie to, negate, overthrow, prove false, rebut, silence

regain get back, recapture, recoup, recover, redeem, repossess, retake, retrieve, take back, win back

regard *v.* **1.** behold, eye, gaze at, look closely at, mark, notice, observe, remark, scrutinize, view, watch **2.** account, adjudge, believe, consider, deem, esteem, estimate, hold, imagine, judge, look upon, rate, see, suppose, think, treat, value, view **3.** apply to, be relevant to, concern, have a bearing on, have to do with, interest, pertain to, relate to **4.** attend, heed, listen to, mind, note, pay attention to, respect, take into consideration, take notice of ~*n.* **5.** attention, heed, mind, notice **6.** account, affection, attachment, care, concern, consideration, deference, esteem, honour, love, note, reputation, repute, respect, store, sympathy, thought **7.** aspect, detail, feature, item, matter, particular, point, respect **8.** gaze, glance, look, scrutiny, stare **9.** *Plural* best wishes, compliments, devoirs, good wishes, greetings, respects, salutations

regarding about, apropos, as regards, as to, concerning, in *or* with regard to, in re, in respect of, in the matter of, on the subject of, re, respecting, with reference to

regardless 1. *adj.* disregarding, heedless, inattentive, inconsiderate, indifferent, neglectful, negligent, rash, reckless, remiss, unconcerned, unmindful **2.** *adv.* anyway, come what may, despite everything, for all that, in any case, in spite of everything, nevertheless, no matter what, nonetheless

the subject of —**re'gardless** *a.* 1. heedless —*adv.* 2. in spite of everything

regatta (rɪ'gætə) *n.* meeting for yacht or boat races

regenerate (rɪ'dʒɛnəreɪt) *v.* 1. (cause to) undergo spiritual rebirth 2. reform morally 3. reproduce, re-create 4. reorganize —*a.* (rɪ'dʒɛnərɪt) 5. born anew —**regener'ation** *n.* —**re'generative** *a.* —**re'generator** *n.*

regent ('riːdʒənt) *n.* 1. ruler of kingdom during absence, minority *etc.*, of its monarch —*a.* 2. ruling —**'regency** *n.* status of, (period of) office of regent

reggae ('rɛgeɪ) *n.* style of popular West Indian music with strong beat

regicide ('rɛdʒɪsaɪd) *n.* 1. one who kills a king 2. this crime

regime *or* **régime** (reɪ'ʒiːm) *n.* 1. system of government, administration 2. *see* REGIMEN (sense 1)

regimen ('rɛdʒɪmɛn) *n.* 1. prescribed system of diet *etc.* (*also* **re'gime**) 2. rule

regiment ('rɛdʒɪmənt) *n.* 1. organized body of troops as unit of army —*vt.* ('rɛdʒɪmɛnt) 2. discipline, organize rigidly or too strictly —**regi'mental** *a.* of regiment —**regi'mentals** *pl.n.* uniform

region ('riːdʒən) *n.* 1. area, district 2. stretch of country 3. part of the body 4. sphere, realm 5. (*oft.* **R-**) administrative division of a country —**'regional** *a.*

register ('rɛdʒɪstə) *n.* 1. list 2. catalogue 3. roll 4. device for registering 5. written record 6. range of voice or instrument —*v.* 7. show, be shown on meter, face *etc.* —*vt.* 8. enter in register 9. record 10. show 11. set down in writing 12. *Print., photog.* cause to correspond precisely —**regis'trar** *n.* 1. keeper of a register 2. senior hospital doctor, junior to consultant —**regis'tration** *n.* —**'registry** *n.* 1. registering 2. place where registers are kept, *esp.* of births, marriages, deaths —**registered post** 1. Post Office service by which compensation is paid for loss of or damage to mail for which registration fee has been paid 2. mail sent by this service —**registration number** sequence of numbers and letters displayed on motor vehicle to identify it

regorge (rɪ'gɔːdʒ) *vt.* vomit up

regress (rɪ'grɛs) *vi.* 1. return, revert to former place, condition *etc.* —*n.* ('riːgrɛs) 2. movement in backward direction —**re'gression** *n.* 1. act of returning 2. retrogression —**re'gressive** *a.* falling back —**re'gressively** *adv.*

regret (rɪ'grɛt) *vt.* 1. feel sorry, distressed for loss of or on account of (-tt-) —*n.* 2. sorrow, distress for thing done or left undone or lost —**re'gretful** *a.* —**re'grettable** *a.*

regular ('rɛgjʊlə) *a.* 1. normal 2. habitual 3. done, occurring, according to rule 4. periodical 5. straight, level 6. living under rule 7. belonging to standing army —*n.* 8. regular soldier 9. *inf.* regular customer —**regu'larity** *n.* —**'regularize** *or* **-ise** *v.*

regulate ('rɛgjʊleɪt) *vt.* 1. adjust 2. arrange 3. direct 4. govern 5. put under rule —**regu'lation** *n.* 1. regulating 2. rule —**'regulator** *n.* contrivance to produce uniformity of motion, as fly wheel, governor valve *etc.*

regurgitate (rɪ'gɜːdʒɪteɪt) *v.* 1. vomit 2. bring back (swallowed food) into mouth —**regurgi'tation** *n.*

rehabilitate (riːə'bɪlɪteɪt) *vt.* 1. help (person) to readjust to society after period of illness, imprisonment *etc.* 2. restore to reputation or former position 3. make fit again 4. reinstate —**rehabili'tation** *n.*

rehash (riː'hæʃ) *vt.* 1. rework, reuse —*n.* 2. old materials presented in new form

THESAURUS

regenerate breathe new life into, change, inspirit, invigorate, reawaken, reconstruct, re-establish, reinvigorate, rejuvenate, renew, renovate, reproduce, restore, revive, revivify, uplift

regime administration, establishment, government, leadership, management, reign, rule, system

regiment *v.* bully, control, discipline, order, organize, regulate, systematize

region 1. area, country, district, division, expanse, land, locality, part, place, province, quarter, section, sector, territory, tract, zone 2. domain, field, province, realm, sphere, world 3. area, locality, neighbourhood, range, scope, vicinity

regional district, local, parochial, provincial, sectional, zonal

register *n.* 1. annals, archives, catalogue, chronicle, diary, file, ledger, list, log, memorandum, record, roll, roster, schedule ~*v.* 2. catalogue, check in, chronicle, enlist, enrol, enter, inscribe, list, note, record, set down, sign on *or* up, take down 3. be shown, bespeak, betray, display, exhibit, express, indicate, manifest, mark, read, record, reflect, reveal, say, show

regress backslide, degenerate, deteriorate, ebb, fall away *or* off, fall back, go back, lapse, lose ground, recede, relapse, retreat, retrogress, return, revert, wane

regret 1. *v.* bemoan, be upset, bewail, deplore, feel remorse for, feel sorry for, grieve, lament, miss, mourn, repent, rue, weep over 2. *n.* bitterness, compunction, contrition, disappointment, grief, lamentation, pang of conscience, penitence, remorse, repentance, ruefulness, self-reproach, sorrow

regrettable deplorable, disappointing, distressing, ill-advised, lamentable, pitiable, sad, shameful, unfortunate, unhappy, woeful, wrong

regular 1. common, commonplace, customary, daily, everyday, habitual, normal, ordinary, routine, typical, unvarying, usual 2. consistent, constant, established, even, fixed, ordered, periodic, rhythmic, set, stated, steady, systematic, uniform 3. dependable, efficient, formal, methodical, orderly, standardized, steady, systematic 4. balanced, even, flat, level, smooth, straight, symmetrical, uniform 5. approved, bona fide, classic, correct, established, formal, official, orthodox, prevailing, proper, sanctioned, standard, time-honoured, traditional

regulate adjust, administer, arrange, balance, conduct, control, direct, fit, govern, guide, handle, manage, moderate, modulate, monitor, order, organize, oversee, rule, run, settle, superintend, supervise, systematize, tune

regulation *n.* 1. adjustment, administration, arrangement, control, direction, governance, government, management, modulation, supervision, tuning 2. commandment, decree, dictate, direction, edict, law, order, ordinance, precept, procedure, requirement, rule, standing order, statute

rehabilitate 1. adjust, redeem, reform, reintegrate, save 2. clear, convert, fix up, make good, mend, rebuild, recondition, reconstitute, reconstruct, re-

rehearse (rɪˈhɜːs) *vt.* **1.** practise (play *etc.*) **2.** repeat aloud **3.** say over again **4.** train, drill —**reˈhearsal** *n.*

Reich (raɪx) *n.* **1.** Holy Roman Empire (962-1806) (**First Reich**) **2.** Hohenzollern empire in Germany from 1871 to 1918 (**Second Reich**) **3.** Nazi dictatorship in Germany from 1933-45 (**Third Reich**)

reign (reɪn) *n.* **1.** period of sovereign's rule —*vi.* **2.** be sovereign **3.** be supreme

reimburse (riːɪmˈbɜːs) *vt.* **1.** refund **2.** pay back —**reimˈbursement** *n.*

rein (reɪn) *n.* **1.** (*oft. pl.*) narrow strap attached to bit to guide horse **2.** instrument for governing —*vt.* **3.** check, manage with reins **4.** control —**give (a) free rein** remove restraints

reincarnation (riːɪnkɑːˈneɪʃən) *n.* **1.** rebirth of soul in successive bodies **2.** one of series of such transmigrations —**reˈincarnate** *vt.*

reindeer (ˈreɪndɪə) *n.* deer of cold regions, *eg* Lapland (*pl.* **-deer, -s**)

reinforce (riːɪnˈfɔːs) *vt.* **1.** strengthen with new support, material, force **2.** strengthen with additional troops, ships *etc.* —**reinˈforcement** *n.* —**reinforced concrete 1.** concrete strengthened internally by steel bars **2.** ferroconcrete

reinstate (riːɪnˈsteɪt) *vt.* replace, restore, re-establish —**reinˈstatement** *n.*

reiterate (riːˈɪtəreɪt) *vt.* repeat again and again —**re-iterˈation** *n.* repetition

reject (rɪˈdʒɛkt) *vt.* **1.** refuse to accept **2.** put aside **3.** discard **4.** renounce —*n.* (ˈriːdʒɛkt) **5.** person or thing rejected as not up to standard —**reˈjection** *n.* refusal

rejig (riːˈdʒɪg) *vt.* **1.** re-equip (factory, plant) **2.** *inf.* rearrange (**-gg-**)

rejoice (rɪˈdʒɔɪs) *v.* **1.** make or be joyful, merry —*vt.* **2.** exult **3.** gladden

rejoin (rɪˈdʒɔɪn) *vt.* **1.** reply **2.** (riːˈdʒɔɪn) join again —**reˈjoinder** *n.* answer, retort

rejuvenate (rɪˈdʒuːvɪneɪt) *vt.* restore to youth —**rejuveˈnation** *n.* —**rejuveˈnescence** *n.* process of growing young again

relapse (rɪˈlæps) *vi.* **1.** fall back (into evil, illness *etc.*) —*n.* **2.** act or instance of relapsing

relate (rɪˈleɪt) *vt.* **1.** narrate, recount **2.** establish relation between —*vi.* (*with* to) **3.** have reference or relation **4.** form sympathetic relationship —**reˈlated** *a.* **1.** connected; associated **2.** connected by kinship or marriage

relation (rɪˈleɪʃən) *n.* **1.** relative quality or condition **2.** connection by blood or marriage **3.** connection (between things) **4.** act of relating **5.** narrative —**reˈlationship** *n.* —**relative** (ˈrɛlətɪv) *a.* **1.** dependent on relation to something else, not absolute **2.** having reference or relation —*n.* **3.** one connected by blood or marriage **4.** relative word or thing —**relatively** (ˈrɛlətɪvlɪ) *adv.* —**relativity** (rɛləˈtɪvɪtɪ) *n.* **1.** state of being relative **2.** subject of two theories of Albert Einstein, dealing with relationships of space, time and motion and acceleration and gravity

THESAURUS

establish, reinstate, reinvigorate, renew, renovate, restore

rehearsal 1. drill, going-over, practice, practice session, preparation, reading, rehearsing, run-through **2.** account, catalogue, description, enumeration, list, narration, recital, recounting, relation, telling

rehearse 1. act, drill, go over, practise, prepare, ready, recite, repeat, run through, study, train, try out **2.** delineate, depict, describe, detail, enumerate, go over, list, narrate, recite, recount, relate, review, run through, spell out, tell, trot out (*Inf.*)

reign *n.* **1.** ascendancy, command, control, dominion, empire, hegemony, influence, monarchy, power, rule, sovereignty, supremacy, sway ~*v.* **2.** administer, be in power, command, govern, hold sway, influence, occupy *or* sit on the throne, rule, wear the crown, wield the sceptre **3.** be rampant, be rife, be supreme, hold sway, obtain, predominate, prevail

rein *n.* **1.** brake, bridle, check, control, curb, harness, hold, restraint, restriction **2. give (a) free rein (to)** free, give a free hand, give carte blanche, give (someone) his head, give way to, indulge, let go, remove restraints ~*v.* **3.** bridle, check, control, curb, halt, hold, hold back, limit, restrain, restrict, slow down

reincarnation metempsychosis, rebirth, transmigration of souls

reinforce augment, bolster, buttress, emphasize, fortify, harden, increase, prop, shore up, stiffen, strengthen, stress, supplement, support, toughen, underline

reinforcement 1. addition, amplification, augmentation, enlargement, fortification, increase, strengthening, supplement **2.** brace, buttress, prop, shore, stay, support

reinstate bring back, recall, re-establish, rehabilitate, replace, restore, return

reject 1. *v.* cast aside, decline, deny, despise, disallow, discard, eliminate, exclude, jettison, jilt, rebuff, refuse, renounce, repel, repudiate, repulse, say no to, scrap, spurn, throw away *or* out, turn down, veto **2.** *n.* castoff, discard, failure, flotsam, second

rejection brushoff (*Sl.*), denial, dismissal, elimination, exclusion, rebuff, refusal, renunciation, repudiation, thumbs down, veto

rejoice be glad (happy, overjoyed), celebrate, delight, exult, glory, joy, jump for joy, make merry, revel, triumph

relapse *v.* **1.** backslide, degenerate, fail, fall back, lapse, regress, retrogress, revert, slip back, weaken **2.** deteriorate, fade, fail, sicken, sink, weaken, worsen ~*n.* **3.** backsliding, fall from grace, lapse, recidivism, regression, retrogression, reversion **4.** deterioration, recurrence, setback, turn for the worse, weakening, worsening

relate 1. chronicle, describe, detail, give an account of, impart, narrate, present, recite, recount, rehearse, report, set forth, tell **2.** ally, associate, connect, coordinate, correlate, couple, join, link **3.** appertain, apply, bear upon, be relevant to, concern, have reference to, have to do with, pertain, refer

related 1. accompanying, affiliated, agnate, akin, allied, associated, cognate, concomitant, connected, correlated, interconnected, joint, linked **2.** agnate, akin, cognate, consanguineous, kin, kindred

relation 1. affiliation, affinity, consanguinity, kindred, kinship, propinquity, relationship **2.** application, bearing, bond, comparison, connection, correlation, interdependence, link, pertinence, reference, regard, similarity, tie-in **3.** account, description,

relax (rɪˈlæks) *vt.* **1.** make loose or slack —*vi.* **2.** become loosened or slack **3.** ease up from effort or attention **4.** become more friendly, less strict —**relaxˈation** *n.* **1.** relaxing recreation **2.** alleviation **3.** abatement

relay (ˈriːleɪ) *n.* **1.** fresh set of people or animals relieving others **2.** *Elec.* device for making or breaking local circuit **3.** *Rad., T.V.* broadcasting station receiving programmes from another station —*vt.* (rɪˈleɪ) **4.** pass on, as message (**reˈlayed, reˈlaying**) —**relay race** race between teams of which each runner races part of distance

release (rɪˈliːs) *vt.* **1.** give up, surrender, set free **2.** permit public showing of (film *etc.*) —*n.* **3.** setting free **4.** releasing **5.** written discharge **6.** permission to show publicly **7.** film, record *etc.* newly issued

relegate (ˈrɛlɪgeɪt) *vt.* **1.** banish, consign **2.** demote —**releˈgation** *n.*

relent (rɪˈlɛnt) *vi.* give up harsh intention, become less severe —**reˈlentless** *a.* **1.** pitiless **2.** merciless

relevant (ˈrɛlɪvənt) *a.* having to do with the matter in hand, to the point —**ˈrelevance** *n.*

reliable (rɪˈlaɪəbᵊl) *a. see* RELY

relic (ˈrɛlɪk) *n.* **1.** thing remaining, *esp.* as memorial of saint **2.** memento —*pl.* **3.** remains, traces **4.** *obs.* dead body —**ˈrelict** *n. obs.* widow

relief (rɪˈliːf) *n.* **1.** alleviation, end of pain, distress *etc.* **2.** money, food given to victims of disaster, poverty *etc.* **3.** release from duty **4.** one who relieves another from work or duty **5.** bus, plane *etc.* that carries passengers when a scheduled service is full **6.** freeing of besieged city *etc.* **7.** projection of carved design from surface **8.** distinctness, prominence —**reˈlieve** *vt.* bring or give relief to —**relief map** map showing elevations and depressions of country in relief

religion (rɪˈlɪdʒən) *n.* system of belief in, worship of a supernatural power or god —**religiose** (rɪˈlɪdʒɪəʊs) *a.* affectedly or extremely pious; sanctimoniously religious —**religiosity** (rɪlɪdʒɪˈɒsɪtɪ) *n.* —**reˈligious** *a.* **1.** pert. to religion **2.** pious **3.** conscientious —**reˈligiously** *adv.* **1.** in religious manner **2.** scrupulously **3.** conscientiously

relinquish (rɪˈlɪŋkwɪʃ) *vt.* **1.** give up, abandon **2.** surrender or renounce (claim, right *etc.*) —**reˈlinquishment** *n.*

reliquary (ˈrɛlɪkwərɪ) *n.* case or shrine for holy relics

relish (ˈrɛlɪʃ) *vt.* **1.** enjoy, like —*n.* **2.** liking, gusto **3.** savoury taste **4.** taste, flavour

THESAURUS

narration, narrative, recital, recountal, report, story, tale

relationship affair, association, bond, communications, conjunction, connection, correlation, exchange, kinship, liaison, link, parallel, proportion, rapport, ratio, similarity, tie-up

relative *adj.* **1.** allied, associated, comparative, connected, contingent, corresponding, dependent, proportionate, reciprocal, related, respective **2.** applicable, apposite, appropriate, appurtenant, apropos, germane, pertinent, relevant **3.** *With* **to** corresponding to, in proportion to, proportional to ~*n.* **4.** connection, kinsman, kinswoman, member of one's *or* the family, relation

relatively comparatively, in *or* by comparison, rather, somewhat, to some extent

relax 1. abate, diminish, ease, ebb, lessen, let up, loosen, lower, mitigate, moderate, reduce, relieve, slacken, weaken **2.** be *or* feel at ease, calm, laze, let oneself go (*Inf.*), let one's hair down (*Inf.*), loosen up, put one's feet up, rest, soften, take it easy (*Inf.*), take one's ease, tranquillize, unbend, unwind

relaxation 1. amusement, enjoyment, entertainment, fun, leisure, pleasure, recreation, refreshment, rest **2.** abatement, diminution, easing, lessening, let-up (*Inf.*), moderation, reduction, slackening, weakening

relay 1. *n.* relief, shift, turn **2.** *v.* broadcast, carry, communicate, hand on, pass on, send, spread, transmit

release *v.* **1.** deliver, discharge, disengage, drop, emancipate, extricate, free, let go, let out, liberate, loose, manumit, set free, turn loose, unchain, undo, unfasten, unfetter, unloose, unshackle, untie **2.** break, circulate, disseminate, distribute, issue, launch, make known, make public, present, publish, put out, unveil ~*n.* **3.** acquittal, deliverance, delivery, discharge, emancipation, freedom, liberation, liberty, manumission, relief **4.** announcement, issue, offering, proclamation, publication

relent 1. acquiesce, be merciful, capitulate, change one's mind, come round, forbear, give in, give quarter, give way, have pity, melt, show mercy, soften, unbend, yield **2.** die down, drop, ease, fall, let up, relax, slacken, slow, weaken

relentless cruel, fierce, grim, hard, harsh, implacable, inexorable, inflexible, merciless, pitiless, remorseless, ruthless, uncompromising, undeviating, unforgiving, unrelenting, unstoppable, unyielding

relevant admissible, *ad rem*, applicable, apposite, appropriate, appurtenant, apt, fitting, germane, material, pertinent, proper, related, relative, significant, suited, to the point, to the purpose

reliable certain, dependable, faithful, honest, predictable, regular, responsible, safe, sound, stable, sure, tried and true, true, trustworthy, trusty, unfailing, upright

relic fragment, keepsake, memento, remembrance, remnant, scrap, souvenir, survival, token, trace, vestige

relief 1. abatement, alleviation, assuagement, balm, comfort, cure, deliverance, ease, easement, mitigation, palliation, release, remedy, solace **2.** aid, assistance, help, succour, support, sustenance **3.** break, breather (*Inf.*), diversion, let-up (*Inf.*), refreshment, relaxation, remission, respite, rest

relieve 1. abate, alleviate, appease, assuage, calm, comfort, console, cure, diminish, dull, ease, mitigate, mollify, palliate, relax, salve, soften, solace, soothe **2.** aid, assist, bring aid to, help, succour, support, sustain **3.** give (someone) a break *or* rest, stand in for, substitute for, take over from, take the place of **4.** deliver, discharge, disembarrass, disencumber, exempt, free, release, unburden

religious 1. churchgoing, devotional, devout, divine, doctrinal, faithful, god-fearing, godly, holy, pious, pure, reverent, righteous, sacred, scriptural, sectarian, spiritual, theological **2.** conscientious, exact, faithful, fastidious, meticulous, punctilious, rigid, rigorous, scrupulous, unerring, unswerving

relish *v.* **1.** appreciate, delight in, enjoy, fancy, like, look forward to, luxuriate in, prefer, revel in, savour, taste ~*n.* **2.** appetite, appreciation, enjoyment, fan-

relive (riːˈlɪv) *vt.* experience (sensation *etc.*) again, *esp.* in imagination —**reˈlivable** *a.*

reluctant (rɪˈlʌktənt) *a.* unwilling, loath, disinclined —**reˈluctance** *n.*

rely (rɪˈlaɪ) *vi.* **1.** depend **2.** (*with* on) trust (**reˈlied, reˈlying**) —**reliaˈbility** *n.* —**reˈliable** *a.* trustworthy, dependable —**reˈliance** *n.* **1.** trust **2.** confidence **3.** dependence —**reˈliant** *a.* confident

REM rapid eye movement

remain (rɪˈmeɪn) *vi.* **1.** stay, be left behind **2.** continue **3.** abide **4.** last —**reˈmainder** *n.* **1.** rest, what is left after subtraction —*vt.* **2.** offer (end of consignment of goods, material *etc.*) at reduced prices —**reˈmains** *pl.n.* **1.** relics, *esp.* of ancient buildings **2.** dead body

remand (rɪˈmɑːnd) *vt.* send back, *esp.* into custody —**remand home** *or* **centre** place of detention for young delinquents

remark (rɪˈmɑːk) *vi.* **1.** make casual comment —*vt.* **2.** comment, observe **3.** say **4.** take notice of —*n.* **5.** observation, comment —**reˈmarkable** *a.* noteworthy, unusual —**reˈmarkably** *adv.* **1.** exceedingly **2.** unusually

REME (ˈriːmiː) Royal Electrical and Mechanical Engineers

remedy (ˈrɛmɪdɪ) *n.* **1.** means of curing, counteracting or relieving disease, trouble *etc.* —*vt.* **2.** put right (**-edied, -edying**) —**remediable** (rɪˈmiːdɪəbᵊl) *a.* —**remedial** (rɪˈmiːdɪəl) *a.* designed, intended to correct specific disability, handicap *etc.*

remember (rɪˈmɛmbə) *vt.* **1.** retain in, recall to memory **2.** have in mind —**reˈmembrance** *n.* **1.** memory **2.** token **3.** souvenir **4.** reminiscence —**Remembrance Day 1. UK** Sunday closest to Nov. 11th, on which the dead of both World Wars are commemorated (*also* **Remembrance Sunday**) **2. C** statutory holiday observed on Nov. 11th in memory of the dead of both World Wars

remind (rɪˈmaɪnd) *vt.* **1.** cause to remember **2.** put in mind —**reˈminder** *n.*

reminisce (rɛmɪˈnɪs) *vi.* talk, write of past times, experiences *etc.* —**remiˈniscence** *n.* **1.** remembering **2.** thing recollected —*pl.* **3.** memoirs —**remiˈniscent** *a.* reminding, suggestive

remiss (rɪˈmɪs) *a.* negligent, careless —**reˈmissly** *adv.*

remit (rɪˈmɪt) *v.* **1.** send (money) for goods, services *etc., esp.* by post **2.** refrain from exacting (penalty) —*vt.* **3.** give up **4.** restore, return **5.** slacken **6.** *obs.* forgive (**-tt-**) —*n.* (ˈriːmɪt, rɪˈmɪt) **7.** area of competence, authority —**reˈmissible** *a.* —**reˈmission** *n.* **1.** abatement **2.** reduction in length of prison term **3.** pardon, forgiveness —**reˈmittance** *n.* **1.** sending of

THESAURUS

cy, fondness, gusto, liking, love, partiality, penchant, predilection, stomach, taste, zest **3.** flavour, piquancy, savour, smack, spice, tang, taste, trace

reluctance aversion, backwardness, disinclination, dislike, disrelish, distaste, hesitancy, indisposition, loathing, repugnance, unwillingness

reluctant averse, backward, disinclined, grudging, hesitant, indisposed, loath, recalcitrant, slow, unenthusiastic, unwilling

rely bank, be confident of, be sure of, bet, count, depend, have confidence in, lean, reckon, repose trust in, swear by, trust

remain abide, be left, cling, continue, delay, dwell, endure, go on, last, linger, persist, prevail, rest, stand, stay, stay behind, stay put (*Inf.*), survive, tarry, wait

remainder balance, dregs, excess, leavings, relic, remains, remnant, residue, residuum, rest, surplus, trace, vestige(s)

remains 1. balance, crumbs, debris, detritus, dregs, fragments, leavings, leftovers, oddments, odds and ends, pieces, relics, remainder, remnants, residue, rest, scraps, traces, vestiges **2.** body, cadaver, carcass, corpse

remark *v.* **1.** animadvert, comment, declare, mention, observe, pass comment, reflect, say, state **2.** espy, heed, make out, mark, note, notice, observe, perceive, regard, see, take note *or* notice of ~*n.* **3.** assertion, comment, declaration, observation, opinion, reflection, statement, thought, utterance, word **4.** acknowledgment, attention, comment, consideration, heed, mention, notice, observation, recognition, regard, thought

remarkable conspicuous, distinguished, extraordinary, famous, impressive, miraculous, notable, noteworthy, odd, outstanding, phenomenal, pre-eminent, prominent, rare, signal, singular, strange, striking, surprising, uncommon, unusual, wonderful

remedy *n.* **1.** antidote, counteractive, cure, medicament, medicine, nostrum, panacea, physic (*Rare*), relief, restorative, specific, therapy, treatment **2.** antidote, corrective, countermeasure, panacea, redress, relief, solution ~*v.* **3.** ameliorate, correct, fix, put right, rectify, redress, reform, relieve, repair, set to rights, solve

remember bear in mind, call to mind, call up, commemorate, keep in mind, look back (on), recall, recognize, recollect, reminisce, retain, summon up, think back

remind awaken memories of, bring back to, bring to mind, call to mind, call up, jog one's memory, make (someone) remember, prompt, put in mind, refresh one's memory

reminiscence anecdote, memoir, memory, recall, recollection, reflection, remembrance, retrospection, review

reminiscent evocative, redolent, remindful, similar, suggestive

remiss careless, culpable, delinquent, derelict, dilatory, forgetful, heedless, inattentive, indifferent, lackadaisical, lax, neglectful, negligent, regardless, slack, slipshod, sloppy (*Inf.*), slothful, slow, tardy, thoughtless, unmindful

remission 1. absolution, acquittal, amnesty, discharge, excuse, exemption, exoneration, forgiveness, indulgence, pardon, release, reprieve **2.** abatement, abeyance, alleviation, amelioration, decrease, diminution, ebb, lessening, let-up (*Inf.*), lull, moderation, reduction, relaxation, respite, suspension

remit *v.* **1.** dispatch, forward, mail, post, send, transmit **2.** cancel, desist, forbear, halt, repeal, rescind, stop **3.** abate, alleviate, decrease, diminish, dwindle, ease up, fall away, mitigate, moderate, reduce, relax, sink, slacken, soften, wane, weaken ~*n.* **4.** authorization, brief, guidelines, instructions, orders, terms of reference

remittance allowance, consideration, fee, payment

money **2.** money sent **—re'mittence** *n.* **—re'mittent** *a.* (of symptoms of disease) characterized by periods of diminished severity **—re'mittently** *adv.*

remix (riː'mɪks) *v.* **1.** change balance and separation of (a recording) *—n.* ('riːmɪks) **2.** remixed version of a recording

remnant ('rɛmnənt) *n.* **1.** (*oft. pl.*) fragment or small piece remaining **2.** oddment

remonstrate ('rɛmənstreɪt) *vi.* protest, reason, argue **—re'monstrance** *n.*

remorse (rɪ'mɔːs) *n.* regret and repentance **—re'morseful** *a.* **—re'morsefully** *adv.* **—re'morseless** *a.* pitiless

remote (rɪ'məʊt) *a.* **1.** far away, distant **2.** aloof **3.** slight **—re'motely** *adv.* **—remote control** control of apparatus from a distance by electrical device

remould (riː'məʊld) *see* RETREAD

remove (rɪ'muːv) *vt.* **1.** take away or off **2.** transfer **3.** withdraw *—vi.* **4.** go away, change residence *—n.* **5.** degree of difference **—re'movable** *a.* **—re'moval** *n.*

remunerate (rɪ'mjuːnəreɪt) *vt.* reward, pay **—remuner'ation** *n.* **—re'munerative** *a.*

renaissance (rə'neɪsəns; *U.S. also* 'rɛnəsɒns) *or* **renascence** (rɪ'næsəns, -'neɪ-) *n.* revival, rebirth, *esp.* (**R-**) revival of learning in 14th-16th centuries

renal ('riːn'l) *a.* of the kidneys

renascent (rɪ'næs'nt, -'neɪ-) *a.* springing up again into being

rend (rɛnd) *v.* **1.** tear, wrench apart **2.** burst, break, split (**rent, 'rending**)

render ('rɛndə) *vt.* **1.** submit, present **2.** give in return, deliver up **3.** cause to become **4.** portray, represent **5.** melt down **6.** cover with plaster

rendezvous ('rɒndɪvuː) *n.* **1.** meeting place **2.** appointment **3.** haunt **4.** assignation (*pl.* **-vous** (-vuːz)) *—vi.* **5.** meet, come together

rendition (rɛn'dɪʃən) *n.* **1.** performance **2.** translation

renegade ('rɛnɪgeɪd) *n.* **1.** deserter **2.** outlaw **3.** rebel

renege *or* **renegue** (rɪ'niːg, -'neɪg) *vi.* go back (on promise *etc.*)

renew (rɪ'njuː) *vt.* **1.** begin again **2.** reaffirm **3.** make valid again **4.** make new **5.** revive **6.** restore to former state **7.** replenish *—vi.* **8.** be made new **9.** grow again **—renewa'bility** *n.* quality of being renewable **—re'newable** *a.* **—re'newal** *n.* **1.** revival, restoration **2.** regeneration

rennet ('rɛnɪt) *n.* preparation for curdling milk

renounce (rɪ'naʊns) *vt.* **1.** give up, cast off, disown **2.** abjure **3.** resign, as title or claim **—renunci'ation** *n.* **1.** act or instance of renouncing **2.** formal declaration renouncing something

renovate ('rɛnəveɪt) *vt.* restore, repair, renew, do up **—reno'vation** *n.*

THESAURUS

remnant bit, end, fragment, hangover, leftovers, piece, remainder, remains, residue, residuum, rest, rump, scrap, shred, survival, trace, vestige

remonstrate argue, challenge, complain, dispute, dissent, expostulate, object, protest, take exception, take issue

remorse anguish, bad *or* guilty conscience, compassion, compunction, contrition, grief, guilt, pangs of conscience, penitence, pity, regret, repentance, ruefulness, self-reproach, shame, sorrow

remorseful apologetic, ashamed, chastened, conscience-stricken, contrite, guilt-ridden, guilty, penitent, regretful, repentant, rueful, sad, self-reproachful, sorrowful, sorry

remorseless callous, cruel, hard, hardhearted, harsh, implacable, inhumane, merciless, pitiless, ruthless, savage, uncompassionate, unforgiving, unmerciful

remote 1. backwoods, distant, far, faraway, far-off, godforsaken, inaccessible, isolated, lonely, off the beaten track, outlying, out-of-the-way, secluded **2.** doubtful, dubious, faint, implausible, inconsiderable, meagre, negligible, outside, poor, slender, slight, slim, small, unlikely **3.** abstracted, aloof, cold, detached, distant, faraway, indifferent, introspective, introverted, removed, reserved, standoffish, unapproachable, uncommunicative, uninterested, uninvolved, withdrawn

removal 1. abstraction, dislodgment, dismissal, displacement, dispossession, ejection, elimination, eradication, erasure, expulsion, expunction, extraction, purging, stripping, subtraction, taking off, uprooting, withdrawal **2.** departure, flitting (*Scot., & northern English dialect*), move, relocation, transfer

remove 1. abolish, abstract, amputate, carry off *or* away, delete, depose, detach, dethrone, discharge, dislodge, dismiss, displace, do away with, doff, efface, eject, eliminate, erase, expel, expunge, extract, get rid of, move, oust, purge, relegate, shed, strike out, take away, take off, take out, throw out, transfer, transport, unseat, wipe out, withdraw **2.** depart, flit (*Scot., & northern English dialect*), move, move away, quit, relocate, shift, transfer, transport, vacate

remuneration compensation, earnings, emolument, fee, income, indemnity, pay, payment, profit, recompense, reimbursement, reparation, repayment, retainer, return, reward, salary, stipend, wages

remunerative gainful, lucrative, moneymaking, paying, profitable, recompensing, rewarding, rich, worthwhile

renaissance, renascence awakening, new birth, new dawn, reappearance, reawakening, rebirth, reemergence, regeneration, renewal, restoration, resurgence, resurrection, revival

render 1. contribute, deliver, furnish, give, make available, pay, present, provide, show, submit, supply, tender, turn over, yield **2.** exchange, give, return, swap, trade **3.** cause to become, leave, make **4.** act, depict, do, give, interpret, perform, play, portray, present, represent **5.** cede, deliver, give, give up, hand over, relinquish, surrender, turn over, yield **6.** give back, make restitution, pay back, repay, restore, return

renew begin again, breathe new life into, bring up to date, continue, extend, fix up (*Inf., chiefly U.S.*), mend, modernize, overhaul, prolong, reaffirm, recommence, recreate, re-establish, refit, refresh, refurbish, regenerate, rejuvenate, renovate, reopen, repair, repeat, replace, replenish, restate, restock, restore, resume, revitalize, transform

renounce abandon, abdicate, abjure, abnegate, abstain from, cast off, decline, deny, discard, disclaim, disown, eschew, forgo, forsake, forswear, give up, leave off, quit, recant, reject, relinquish, repudiate, resign, spurn, swear off, throw off, waive, wash one's hands of

renown (rɪˈnaʊn) *n.* fame

rent[1] (rɛnt) *n.* **1.** payment for use of land, buildings, machines *etc.* —*vt.* **2.** hold by lease **3.** hire **4.** let —ˈ**rental** *n.* sum payable as rent —**rent boy** young male prostitute

rent[2] (rɛnt) *n.* **1.** tear **2.** fissure —*v.* **3.** *pt./pp. of* REND

renunciation (rɪnʌnsɪˈeɪʃən) *n. see* RENOUNCE

rep[1] *or* **repp** (rɛp) *n.* fabric with corded surface for upholstery *etc.*

rep[2] (rɛp) *a./n.* repertory (company, theatre, group)

rep[3] (rɛp) *n.* representative, travelling salesman

repaid (rɪˈpeɪd) *pt./pp. of* REPAY

repair[1] (rɪˈpɛə) *vt.* **1.** make whole, sound again **2.** mend **3.** patch **4.** restore —*n.* **5.** act or process of repairing —**reˈpairable** *a.* —**reparation** (rɛpəˈreɪʃən) *n.* **1.** repairing **2.** amends, compensation

repair[2] (rɪˈpɛə) *vi.* (*usu. with* to) resort, go

repartee (rɛpɑːˈtiː) *n.* **1.** witty retort **2.** interchange of witty retorts

repast (rɪˈpɑːst) *n.* meal

repatriate (riːˈpætrɪeɪt) *vt.* send (someone) back to his own country —**repatriˈation** *n.*

repay (rɪˈpeɪ) *vt.* **1.** pay back, refund **2.** make return for (**reˈpaid, reˈpaying**) —**reˈpayable** *a.* —**reˈpayment** *n.*

repeal (rɪˈpiːl) *vt.* **1.** revoke, annul, cancel —*n.* **2.** act of repealing

repeat (rɪˈpiːt) *vt.* **1.** say, do again **2.** reproduce —*vi.* **3.** recur —*n.* **4.** act, instance of repeating, *esp.* TV show broadcast again —**reˈpeatedly** *adv.* **1.** again and again **2.** frequently —**reˈpeater** *n.* **1.** firearm that may be discharged many times without reloading **2.** timepiece that strikes hours —**repeˈtition** *n.* **1.** act of repeating **2.** thing repeated **3.** piece learnt by heart and repeated —**repetitious** (rɛpɪˈtɪʃəs) *a.* repeated unnecessarily —**repetitive** (rɪˈpɛtɪtɪv) *a.* repeated

repel (rɪˈpɛl) *vt.* **1.** drive back, ward off, refuse **2.** be repulsive to (**-ll-**) —**reˈpellent** *a.* **1.** distasteful **2.** resisting (water *etc.*) —*n.* **3.** that which repels, *esp.* chemical to repel insects

repent (rɪˈpɛnt) *vi.* **1.** wish one had not done something **2.** feel regret for deed or omission —*vt.* **3.** feel regret for —**reˈpentance** *n.* contrition —**reˈpentant** *a.*

repercussion (riːpəˈkʌʃən) *n.* **1.** (*oft. pl.*) indirect effect, oft. unpleasant **2.** recoil **3.** echo

repertory (ˈrɛpətərɪ, -trɪ) *n.* **1.** repertoire, collection **2.** store —**repertoire** (ˈrɛpətwɑː) *n.* stock of plays, songs *etc.* that player or company can give —**repertory company, theatre** *or* **group** (theatre *etc.* with) permanent company producing succession of plays

repetition (rɛpɪˈtɪʃən) *n. see* REPEAT

THESAURUS

renovate do up (*Inf.*), fix up (*Inf., chiefly U.S.*), modernize, overhaul, recondition, reconstitute, recreate, refit, reform, refurbish, rehabilitate, remodel, renew, repair, restore, revamp

rent[1] **1.** *n.* fee, hire, lease, payment, rental, tariff **2** *v.* charter, hire, lease, let

rent[2] breach, break, chink, crack, flaw, gash, hole, opening, perforation, rip, slash, slit, split, tear

renunciation abandonment, abdication, abjuration, abnegation, abstention, denial, disavowal, disclaimer, eschewal, forswearing, giving up, rejection, relinquishment, repudiation, resignation, spurning, surrender, waiver

repair[1] **1.** *v.* fix, heal, make good, mend, patch, patch up, put back together, put right, recover, rectify, redress, renew, renovate, restore, restore to working order, retrieve, square **2.** *n.* adjustment, darn, mend, overhaul, patch, restoration

repair[2] **1.** betake oneself, go, head for, leave for, move, remove, retire, set off for, withdraw **2.** have recourse, resort, turn

reparation amends, atonement, compensation, damages, indemnity, propitiation, recompense, redress, renewal, repair, requital, restitution, satisfaction

repartee badinage, banter, bon mot, persiflage, pleasantry, raillery, riposte, sally, wit, witticism, wittiness, wordplay

repay 1. compensate, make restitution, pay back, recompense, refund, reimburse, remunerate, requite, restore, return, reward, settle up with, square **2.** avenge, even *or* settle the score with, get back at (*Inf.*), get even with (*Inf.*), get one's own back on (*Inf.*), make reprisal, reciprocate, retaliate, return the compliment, revenge

repeal 1. *v.* abolish, abrogate, annul, cancel, countermand, declare null and void, invalidate, nullify, recall, rescind, reverse, revoke, set aside, withdraw **2.** *n.* abolition, abrogation, annulment, cancellation, invalidation, nullification, rescinding, rescindment, rescission, revocation, withdrawal

repeat 1. *v.* duplicate, echo, iterate, quote, recapitulate, recite, redo, rehearse, reiterate, relate, renew, replay, reproduce, rerun, reshow, restate, retell **2.** *n.* duplicate, echo, recapitulation, reiteration, repetition, replay, reproduction, rerun, reshowing

repeatedly again and again, frequently, many a time and oft, many times, often, over and over, time after time, time and (time) again

repel 1. beat off, check, confront, decline, drive off, fight, hold off, keep at arm's length, oppose, parry, put to flight, rebuff, refuse, reject, repulse, resist, ward off **2.** disgust, give one the creeps (*Inf.*), make one shudder, make one sick, nauseate, offend, put one off, revolt, sicken, turn one off (*Inf.*), turn one's stomach

repellent 1. abhorrent, abominable, discouraging, disgusting, distasteful, hateful, horrid, loathsome, nauseating, noxious, obnoxious, odious, offensive, off-putting (*Brit. inf.*), repugnant, repulsive, revolting, sickening **2.** impermeable, proof, repelling, resistant

repent atone, be ashamed, be contrite, be sorry, deplore, feel remorse, lament, regret, relent, reproach oneself, rue, see the error of one's ways, show penitence, sorrow

repentance compunction, contrition, grief, guilt, penitence, regret, remorse, sackcloth and ashes, self-reproach, sorriness, sorrow

repentant apologetic, ashamed, chastened, contrite, penitent, regretful, remorseful, rueful, self-reproachful, sorry

repercussion backlash, consequence, echo, rebound, recoil, result, reverberation, side effect

repetition duplication, echo, iteration, reappearance, recapitulation, recital, recurrence, redundancy, rehearsal, reiteration, relation, renewal, repeat, repetitiousness, replication, restatement, return, tautology

repine (rɪˈpaɪn) *vi.* fret, complain

replace (rɪˈpleɪs) *vt.* **1.** substitute for **2.** put back —**reˈplacement** *n.*

replay (ˈriːpleɪ) *n.* **1.** immediate reshowing on TV of incident in sport, *esp.* in slow motion (*also* **action replay**) **2.** replaying of a match —*vt.* (riːˈpleɪ) **3.** play again

replenish (rɪˈplɛnɪʃ) *vt.* fill up again —**reˈplenishment** *n.*

replete (rɪˈpliːt) *a.* filled, gorged —**reˈpletion** *n.* complete fullness

replica (ˈrɛplɪkə) *n.* **1.** exact copy **2.** facsimile, duplicate —**ˈreplicate** *vt.* make, be a copy of

reply (rɪˈplaɪ) *v.* **1.** answer (**reˈplied, reˈplying**) —*n.* **2.** an answer; response

report (rɪˈpɔːt) *n.* **1.** account, statement **2.** written statement of child's progress at school **3.** rumour **4.** repute **5.** bang —*vt.* **6.** announce, relate **7.** make, give account of **8.** take down in writing **9.** complain about —*vi.* **10.** make report **11.** act as reporter **12.** present oneself (to) —**reˈporter** *n.* one who reports, *esp.* for newspaper —**reported speech** *see* **indirect speech** *at* INDIRECT

repose (rɪˈpəʊz) *n.* **1.** peace **2.** composure **3.** sleep —*vi.* **4.** rest —*vt.* **5.** lay at rest **6.** place **7.** rely, lean (on) —**repository** (rɪˈpɒzɪtərɪ, -trɪ) *n.* **1.** place where valuables are deposited for safekeeping **2.** store

repossess (riːpəˈzɛs) *vt.* take back possession of (property), *esp.* for nonpayment of money due under hire-purchase agreement —**reposˈsession** *n.*

repoussé (rəˈpuːseɪ) *a.* **1.** embossed **2.** hammered into relief from reverse side —*n.* **3.** metal work so produced

reprehend (rɛprɪˈhɛnd) *vt.* find fault with —**repreˈhensible** *a.* **1.** deserving censure **2.** unworthy —**repreˈhension** *n.* censure

represent (rɛprɪˈzɛnt) *vt.* **1.** stand for **2.** deputize for **3.** act, play **4.** symbolize **5.** make out to be **6.** call up by description or portrait —**representˈtation** *n.* —**repreˈsentative** *n.* **1.** one chosen to stand for group **2.** travelling salesman —*a.* **3.** typical

THESAURUS

repetitive boring, dull, mechanical, monotonous, recurrent, samey (*Inf.*), tedious, unchanging, unvaried

repine brood, complain, fret, grieve, grumble, lament, languish, moan, mope, murmur, sulk

replace follow, oust, put back, re-establish, reinstate, restore, stand in lieu of, substitute, succeed, supersede, supplant, supply, take over from, take the place of

replacement double, fill-in, proxy, stand-in, substitute, successor, surrogate, understudy

replenish fill, furnish, make up, provide, refill, reload, renew, replace, restock, restore, stock, supply, top up

replete abounding, brimful, brimming, charged, chock-full, crammed, filled, full, full to bursting, full up, glutted, gorged, jammed, jam-packed, sated, satiated, stuffed, teeming, well-provided, well-stocked

reply 1. *v.* acknowledge, answer, come back, counter, echo, make answer, react, reciprocate, rejoin, respond, retaliate, retort, return, riposte, write back 2. *n.* acknowledgment, answer, comeback (*Inf.*), counter, echo, reaction, reciprocation, rejoinder, response, retaliation, retort, return, riposte

report *n.* 1. account, announcement, article, communication, communiqué, declaration, description, detail, dispatch, information, message, narrative, news, note, paper, piece, recital, record, relation, statement, story, summary, tale, tidings, version, word, write-up 2. gossip, hearsay, rumour, talk 3. character, esteem, fame, regard, reputation, repute 4. bang, blast, boom, crack, crash, detonation, discharge, explosion, noise, reverberation, sound ~*v.* 5. air, announce, bring word, broadcast, circulate, communicate, cover, declare, describe, detail, document, give an account of, inform of, mention, narrate, note, notify, pass on, proclaim, publish, recite, record, recount, relate, relay, state, tell, write up 6. appear, arrive, be present, clock in *or* on, come, present oneself, show up (*Inf.*), turn up

reporter announcer, correspondent, hack (*Derogatory*), journalist, newscaster, newshound (*Inf.*), newspaperman, newspaperwoman, pressman, writer

repose *n.* 1. ease, inactivity, peace, quiet, quietness, quietude, relaxation, respite, rest, restfulness, sleep, slumber, stillness, tranquillity 2. aplomb, calmness, composure, dignity, equanimity, peace of mind, poise, self-possession, serenity, tranquillity ~*v.* 3. lay down, lie, lie down, lie upon, recline, relax, rest, rest upon, sleep, slumber, take it easy (*Inf.*), take one's ease

reprehensible bad, blameworthy, censurable, condemnable, culpable, delinquent, discreditable, disgraceful, errant, erring, ignoble, objectionable, opprobrious, remiss, shameful, unworthy

represent 1. act for, be, betoken, correspond to, equal, equate with, express, mean, serve as, speak for, stand for, substitute for, symbolize 2. embody, epitomize, exemplify, personify, symbolize, typify 3. delineate, denote, depict, describe, designate, evoke, express, illustrate, outline, picture, portray, render, reproduce, show, sketch 4. describe as, make out to be, pass off as, pose as, pretend to be 5. act, appear as, assume the role of, enact, exhibit, perform, play the part of, produce, put on, show, stage

representation account, delineation, depiction, description, illustration, image, likeness, model, narration, narrative, picture, portrait, portrayal, relation, resemblance, sketch

representative *n.* 1. agent, commercial traveller, rep, salesman, traveller 2. archetype, embodiment, epitome, exemplar, personification, type, typical example 3. agent, commissioner, councillor, delegate, depute (*Scot.*), deputy, member, member of parliament, M.P., proxy, spokesman, spokeswoman ~*adj.* 4. archetypal, characteristic, emblematic, evocative, exemplary, illustrative, symbolic, typical

repress bottle up, chasten, check, control, crush, curb, hold back, hold in, inhibit, keep in check, master, muffle, overcome, overpower, quash, quell, restrain, silence, smother, stifle, subdue, subjugate, suppress, swallow

repression authoritarianism, censorship, coercion, constraint, control, despotism, domination, inhibition, restraint, subjugation, suppression, tyranny

repressive absolute, authoritarian, coercive, despotic, dictatorial, harsh, oppressive, severe, tough, tyrannical

repress (rɪˈprɛs) *vt.* keep down or under, quell, check —**reˈpression** *n.* restraint —**reˈpressive** *a.*

reprieve (rɪˈpriːv) *vt.* **1.** suspend execution of (condemned person) **2.** give temporary relief to —*n.* **3.** postponement or cancellation of punishment **4.** respite **5.** last-minute intervention

reprimand (ˈrɛprɪmɑːnd) *n.* **1.** sharp rebuke —*vt.* **2.** rebuke sharply

reprisal (rɪˈpraɪzˀl) *n.* retaliation

reproach (rɪˈprəʊtʃ) *vt.* **1.** blame, rebuke —*n.* **2.** scolding, upbraiding **3.** expression of this **4.** thing bringing discredit —**reˈproachful** *a.*

reprobate (ˈrɛprəʊbeɪt) *a.* **1.** depraved **2.** cast off by God —*n.* **3.** depraved or disreputable person —*vt.* **4.** disapprove of, reject —**reproˈbation** *n.*

reproduce (riːprəˈdjuːs) *vt.* **1.** produce copy of **2.** bring (new individuals) into existence **3.** re-create, produce anew —*vi.* **4.** propagate **5.** generate —**reproˈducible** *a.* —**reproˈduction** *n.* **1.** process of reproducing **2.** that which is reproduced **3.** facsimile, as of painting *etc.* —**reproˈductive** *a.*

reprove (rɪˈpruːv) *vt.* censure, rebuke —**reˈproof** *n.*

reptile (ˈrɛptaɪl) *n.* cold-blooded, air-breathing vertebrate with horny scales or plates, as snake, tortoise *etc.* —**reptilian** (rɛpˈtɪlɪən) *a.*

republic (rɪˈpʌblɪk) *n.* state without monarch in which supremacy of people or their elected representatives is formally acknowledged —**reˈpublican** *a./n.* —**reˈpublicanism** *n.*

repudiate (rɪˈpjuːdɪeɪt) *vt.* **1.** reject authority or validity of **2.** cast off, disown

repugnant (rɪˈpʌgnənt) *a.* **1.** offensive **2.** distasteful **3.** contrary —**reˈpugnance** *n.* **1.** dislike, aversion **2.** incompatibility

repulse (rɪˈpʌls) *vt.* **1.** drive back **2.** rebuff **3.** repel —*n.* **4.** driving back, rejection, rebuff —**reˈpulsion** *n.* **1.** distaste, aversion **2.** *Phys.* force separating two objects —**reˈpulsive** *a.* loathsome, disgusting

repute (rɪˈpjuːt) *vt.* **1.** reckon, consider —*n.* **2.** reputation, credit —**reputable** (ˈrɛpjʊtəbˀl) *a.* **1.** of good repute **2.** respectable —**reputation** (rɛpjʊˈteɪʃən) *n.* **1.** estimation in which person is held **2.** character **3.** good name —**reˈputed** *a.* generally reckoned or considered; supposed —**reˈputedly** *adv.*

request (rɪˈkwɛst) *n.* **1.** asking **2.** thing asked for —*vt.* **3.** ask

THESAURUS

reprieve *v.* **1.** grant a stay of execution to, let off the hook (*Sl.*), pardon, postpone *or* remit the punishment of **2.** abate, allay, alleviate, mitigate, palliate, relieve, respite ~*n.* **3.** abeyance, amnesty, deferment, pardon, postponement, remission, stay of execution, suspension **4.** abatement, alleviation, let-up (*Inf.*), mitigation, palliation, relief, respite

reprimand **1.** *n.* admonition, blame, castigation, censure, dressing-down (*Inf.*), flea in one's ear (*Inf.*), lecture, rebuke, reprehension, reproach, reproof, row, talking-to (*Inf.*), telling-off (*Inf.*), ticking-off (*Inf.*), tongue-lashing, wigging (*Brit. sl.*) **2.** *v.* admonish, blame, castigate, censure, check, chide, dress down (*Inf.*), give (someone) a row (*Inf.*), haul over the coals (*Inf.*), lecture, rap over the knuckles (*Inf.*), rebuke, reprehend, reproach, reprove, scold, send one away with a flea in one's ear (*Inf.*), take to task, tell off (*Inf.*), tick off (*Inf.*), tongue-lash, upbraid

reprisal an eye for an eye, counterstroke, requital, retaliation, retribution, revenge, vengeance

reproach **1.** *v.* abuse, blame, censure, chide, condemn, criticize, defame, discredit, disparage, find fault with, rebuke, reprehend, reprimand, reprove, scold, take to task, upbraid **2.** *n.* abuse, blame, blemish, censure, condemnation, contempt, disapproval, discredit, disgrace, dishonour, disrepute, ignominy, indignity, obloquy, odium, opprobrium, scorn, shame, slight, slur, stain, stigma

reproachful abusive, admonitory, castigatory, censorious, condemnatory, contemptuous, critical, disappointed, disapproving, fault-finding, reproving, scolding, upbraiding

reproduce **1.** copy, duplicate, echo, emulate, imitate, match, mirror, parallel, print, recreate, repeat, replicate, represent, transcribe **2.** breed, generate, multiply, procreate, produce young, proliferate, propagate, spawn

reproduction **1.** breeding, generation, increase, multiplication, procreation, proliferation, propagation **2.** copy, duplicate, facsimile, imitation, picture, print, replica

reproof admonition, blame, castigation, censure, chiding, condemnation, criticism, dressing-down (*Inf.*), rebuke, reprehension, reprimand, reproach, reproval, scolding, ticking-off (*Inf.*), tongue-lashing, upbraiding

reprove abuse, admonish, berate, blame, censure, check, chide, condemn, rebuke, reprehend, reprimand, scold, take to task, tell off (*Inf.*), tick off (*Inf.*), upbraid

repudiate abandon, abjure, cast off, cut off, deny, desert, disavow, discard, disclaim, disown, forsake, reject, renounce, rescind, retract, reverse, revoke, turn one's back on, wash one's hands of

repugnant **1.** abhorrent, abominable, disgusting, distasteful, foul, hateful, horrid, loathsome, nauseating, objectionable, obnoxious, odious, offensive, repellent, revolting, sickening, vile **2.** adverse, antagonistic, antipathetic, averse, contradictory, contrary, hostile, incompatible, inconsistent, inimical, opposed

repulsive abhorrent, abominable, disagreeable, disgusting, distasteful, forbidding, foul, hateful, hideous, horrid, loathsome, nauseating, objectionable, obnoxious, odious, offensive, repellent, revolting, sickening, ugly, unpleasant, vile

reputable creditable, estimable, excellent, good, honourable, honoured, legitimate, of good repute, reliable, respectable, trustworthy, upright, well-thought-of, worthy

reputation character, credit, distinction, esteem, estimation, fame, honour, name, opinion, renown, repute, standing, stature

repute celebrity, distinction, esteem, estimation, fame, name, renown, reputation, standing, stature

reputed accounted, alleged, believed, considered, deemed, estimated, held, ostensible, putative, reckoned, regarded, rumoured, said, seeming, supposed, thought

reputedly allegedly, apparently, ostensibly, seemingly, supposedly

request **1.** *v.* appeal for, apply for, ask (for), beg, beseech, call for, demand, desire, entreat, petition,

Requiem (ˈrɛkwɪɛm) *n.* **1.** Mass for the dead **2.** music for this

requiescat in pace (rɛkwɪˈɛskæt ɪn ˈpɑːkɛ) *Lat.* may he (or she) rest in peace

require (rɪˈkwaɪə) *vt.* **1.** want, need **2.** demand —**reˈquirement** *n.* **1.** essential condition **2.** specific need **3.** want

requisite (ˈrɛkwɪzɪt) *a.* **1.** necessary **2.** essential —*n.* **3.** something indispensable; necessity

requisition (rɛkwɪˈzɪʃən) *n.* **1.** formal demand, *eg* for materials or supplies —*vt.* **2.** demand (supplies) **3.** press into service

requite (rɪˈkwaɪt) *vt.* repay —**reˈquital** *n.*

reredos (ˈrɪədɒs) *n.* ornamental screen behind altar

rerun (riːˈrʌn) *vt.* **1.** broadcast or put on (film *etc.*) again **2.** run (race *etc.*) again —*n.* (ˈriːrʌn) **3.** film *etc.* that is broadcast again; repeat **4.** race that is run again

resale price maintenance (ˈriːseɪl) practice by which manufacturer establishes fixed or minimum price for resale of brand product by retailers or other distributors

rescind (rɪˈsɪnd) *vt.* cancel, annul —**resˈcindment** *or* **rescission** (rɪˈsɪʒən) *n.*

rescue (ˈrɛskjuː) *vt.* **1.** save, deliver, extricate (**-cuing, -cued**) —*n.* **2.** act or instance of rescuing —**ˈrescuer** *n.* —**ˈrescuing** *n.*

research (rɪˈsɜːtʃ) *n.* **1.** investigation, *esp.* scientific study to discover facts —*v.* **2.** carry out investigations (on, into) —**reˈsearcher** *n.*

resemble (rɪˈzɛmbˀl) *vt.* **1.** be like **2.** look like —**reˈsemblance** *n.*

resent (rɪˈzɛnt) *vt.* **1.** show, feel indignation at **2.** retain bitterness about —**reˈsentful** *a.* —**reˈsentment** *n.*

reserve (rɪˈzɜːv) *vt.* **1.** hold back, set aside, keep for future use —*n.* **2.** (*also pl.*) something, *esp.* money, troops *etc.*, kept for emergencies **3.** area of land reserved for particular purpose or for use by particular group of people *etc.* (*also* **reserˈvation**) **4.** reticence, concealment of feelings or friendliness —**reservation** (rɛzəˈveɪʃən) *n.* **1.** reserving **2.** thing reserved **3.** doubt **4.** exception; limitation —**reˈserved** *a.* not showing feelings, lacking cordiality —**reˈservist** *n.* one serving in reserve —**reserve price UK** minimum price acceptable to owner of property being auctioned

reservoir (ˈrɛzəvwɑː) *n.* **1.** enclosed area for storage of water, *esp.* for community supplies **2.** receptacle for liquid, gas *etc.* **3.** place where anything is kept in store

reside (rɪˈzaɪd) *vi.* dwell permanently —**residence**

THESAURUS

pray, put in for, requisition, seek, solicit, sue for, supplicate **2.** *n.* appeal, application, asking, begging, call, demand, desire, entreaty, petition, prayer, requisition, solicitation, suit, supplication

require 1. crave, depend upon, desire, have need of, lack, miss, need, stand in need of, want, wish **2.** ask, beg, beseech, bid, call upon, command, compel, constrain, demand, direct, enjoin, exact, insist upon, instruct, oblige, order, request **3.** call for, demand, involve, necessitate, take

requirement demand, desideratum, essential, lack, must, necessity, need, precondition, prerequisite, qualification, requisite, *sine qua non*, specification, stipulation, want

requisite 1. *adj.* called for, essential, indispensable, mandatory, necessary, needed, needful, obligatory, prerequisite, required, vital **2.** *n.* condition, desideratum, essential, must, necessity, need, precondition, prerequisite, requirement, *sine qua non*

requisition *n.* **1.** application, call, demand, request, summons ~*v.* **2.** apply for, call for, demand, put in for, request **3.** appropriate, commandeer, occupy, seize, take over, take possession of

rescue 1. *v.* deliver, extricate, free, get out, liberate, recover, redeem, release, salvage, save, save the life of, set free **2.** *n.* deliverance, extrication, liberation, recovery, redemption, release, relief, salvage, salvation, saving

research 1. *n.* analysis, delving, examination, experimentation, exploration, fact-finding, groundwork, inquiry, investigation, probe, scrutiny, study **2.** *v.* analyse, consult the archives, do tests, examine, experiment, explore, investigate, look into, make inquiries, probe, scrutinize, study

resemblance affinity, analogy, closeness, comparability, comparison, conformity, correspondence, counterpart, facsimile, image, kinship, likeness, parallel, parity, sameness, semblance, similarity, similitude

resemble bear a resemblance to, be like, be similar to, duplicate, echo, favour (*Inf.*), look like, mirror, parallel, put one in mind of, remind one of, take after

resent be angry about, bear a grudge about, begrudge, be in a huff about, be offended by, dislike, feel bitter about, grudge, harbour a grudge against, have hard feelings about, object to, take amiss, take as an insult, take exception to, take offence at, take umbrage at

resentful aggrieved, angry, bitter, embittered, exasperated, grudging, huffish, huffy, hurt, in a huff, incensed, indignant, in high dudgeon, irate, jealous, miffed (*Inf.*), offended, peeved (*Inf.*), piqued, put out, revengeful, unforgiving, wounded

resentment anger, animosity, bitterness, displeasure, fury, grudge, huff, hurt, ill feeling, ill will, indignation, ire, irritation, malice, pique, rage, rancour, umbrage, vexation, wrath

reservation 1. condition, demur, doubt, hesitancy, proviso, qualification, scepticism, scruple, stipulation **2.** enclave, homeland, preserve, reserve, sanctuary, territory, tract

reserve *v.* **1.** conserve, hang on to, hoard, hold, husband, keep, keep back, lay up, preserve, put by, retain, save, set aside, stockpile, store, withhold **2.** bespeak, book, engage, prearrange, pre-engage, retain, secure ~*n.* **3.** backlog, cache, capital, fund, hoard, reservoir, savings, stock, stockpile, store, supply **4.** park, preserve, reservation, sanctuary, tract **5.** aloofness, constraint, coolness, formality, modesty, reluctance, reservation, restraint, reticence, secretiveness, shyness, silence, taciturnity

reserved aloof, cautious, close-mouthed, cold, cool, demure, formal, modest, prim, restrained, reticent, retiring, secretive, shy, silent, standoffish, taciturn, unapproachable, uncommunicative, undemonstrative, unforthcoming, unresponsive, unsociable

reservoir 1. basin, lake, pond, tank **2.** container, holder, receptacle, repository, store, tank

(ˈrɛzɪdəns) *n.* 1. home 2. house —**residency** (ˈrɛzɪdənsɪ) *n.* official dwelling, *esp.*, formerly, of Brit. government agent —**resident** (ˈrɛzɪdənt) *a./n.* —**residential** (rɛzɪˈdɛnʃəl) *a.* 1. (of part of town) consisting mainly of residences 2. of, connected with residence 3. providing living accommodation

residue (ˈrɛzɪdjuː) *n.* what is left, remainder —**residual** (rɪˈzɪdjuəl) *a.* —**residuary** (rɪˈzɪdjuərɪ) *a.* —**reˈsiduum** *n. formal* residue (*pl.* **-ua** (-juə))

resign (rɪˈzaɪn) *vt.* 1. give up 2. reconcile (oneself) —*vi.* 3. give up office, employment *etc.* —**resignation** (rɛzɪgˈneɪʃən) *n.* 1. resigning 2. being resigned, submission —**reˈsigned** *a.* content to endure

resilient (rɪˈzɪlɪənt) *a.* 1. (of an object) capable of returning to normal after stretching *etc.*; elastic 2. (of a person) recovering quickly from shock *etc.* —**reˈsilience** *or* **reˈsiliency** *n.*

resin (ˈrɛzɪn) *n.* sticky substance formed in and oozing from plants, *esp.* firs and pines (*also* **ˈrosin**) —**ˈresinous** *a.* of, like resin

resist (rɪˈzɪst) *v.* 1. refrain from 2. oppose —**reˈsistance** *n.* 1. act of resisting 2. opposition 3. hindrance 4. *Elec.* opposition offered by circuit to passage of current through it —**reˈsistant** *a.* —**reˈsistible** *a.* —**resisˈtivity** *n.* measure of electrical resistance —**reˈsistor** *n.* component of electrical circuit producing resistance

resit (riːˈsɪt) *vt.* 1. sit (examination) again —*n.* (ˈriːsɪt) 2. examination one must sit again

resolute (ˈrɛzəluːt) *a.* determined —**ˈresolutely** *adv.* —**resoˈlution** *n.* 1. resolving 2. firmness 3. purpose or thing resolved upon 4. decision of court or vote of assembly

resolve (rɪˈzɒlv) *vi.* 1. make up one's mind 2. decide with effort of will —*vt.* 3. form by resolution of vote 4. separate component parts of 5. make clear —*n.* 6. resolution 7. fixed purpose —**resoluˈbility, resolvaˈbility** *or* **reˈsolubleness, reˈsolvableness** *n.* —**resoluble** (rɪˈzɒljubˀl, ˈrɛzəl-) *or* **reˈsolvable** *a.* able to be resolved or analysed —**reˈsolved** *a.* fixed in purpose or intention; determined —**resolvedly** (rɪˈzɒlvɪdlɪ) *adv.* —**reˈsolvent** *a./n.* —**reˈsolver** *n.*

resonance (ˈrɛzənəns) *n.* 1. echoing, *esp.* in deep tone 2. sound produced by body vibrating in sympathy with neighbouring source of sound —**ˈresonant** *a.* —**ˈresonate** *v.* —**ˈresonator** *n.*

resort (rɪˈzɔːt) *vi.* 1. have recourse 2. (*with* to) frequent —*n.* 3. place of recreation, *eg* beach 4. recourse 5. frequented place 6. haunt

resound (rɪˈzaʊnd) *vi.* echo, ring, go on sounding —**reˈsounding** *a.* 1. echoing 2. thorough

THESAURUS

reside abide, dwell, hang out (*Inf.*), have one's home, inhabit, live, lodge, remain, settle, sojourn, stay

residence 1. abode, domicile, dwelling, habitation, home, house, household, lodging, pad (*Sl.*), place, quarters 2. hall, manor, mansion, palace, seat, villa

resident 1. *n.* citizen, denizen, indweller, inhabitant, local, lodger, occupant, tenant 2. *adj.* dwelling, inhabiting, living, local, neighbourhood, settled

residue balance, dregs, excess, extra, leftovers, remainder, remains, remnant, residuum, rest, surplus

resign 1. abandon, abdicate, cede, forgo, forsake, give in one's notice, give up, hand over, leave, quit, relinquish, renounce, surrender, turn over, vacate, yield 2. **resign oneself** accept, acquiesce, bow, give in, give up, reconcile, submit, yield

resignation 1. abandonment, abdication, departure, leaving, notice, relinquishment, renunciation, retirement, surrender 2. acceptance, acquiescence, compliance, endurance, forbearing, fortitude, nonresistance, passivity, patience, submission, sufferance

resigned acquiescent, compliant, long-suffering, patient, stoical, subdued, submissive, unprotesting, unresisting

resilient 1. bouncy, elastic, flexible, plastic, pliable, rubbery, springy, supple, whippy 2. bouncy, buoyant, hardy, irrepressible, quick to recover, strong, tough

resist 1. battle, be proof against, check, combat, confront, contend with, counteract, countervail, curb, defy, dispute, fight back, hinder, hold out against, oppose, put up a fight (against), refuse, repel, stand up to, struggle against, thwart, weather, withstand 2. abstain from, avoid, forbear, forgo, keep from, leave alone, prevent oneself from, refrain from, refuse, turn down

resistance battle, combat, contention, counteraction, defiance, fight, fighting, hindrance, impediment, intransigence, obstruction, opposition, refusal, struggle

resistant 1. hard, impervious, insusceptible, proof against, strong, tough, unaffected by, unyielding 2. antagonistic, combative, defiant, dissident, hostile, intractable, intransigent, opposed, recalcitrant, unwilling

resolute bold, constant, determined, dogged, firm, fixed, inflexible, obstinate, persevering, purposeful, relentless, set, staunch, steadfast, strong-willed, stubborn, tenacious, unbending, undaunted, unflinching, unshakable, unshaken, unwavering

resolution 1. boldness, constancy, courage, dedication, determination, doggedness, earnestness, energy, firmness, fortitude, obstinacy, perseverance, purpose, relentlessness, resoluteness, resolve, sincerity, staunchness, staying power, steadfastness, stubbornness, tenacity, willpower 2. aim, decision, declaration, determination, intent, intention, judgment, motion, purpose, resolve, verdict 3. answer, end, finding, outcome, settlement, solution, solving, sorting out, unravelling, upshot, working out

resolve *v.* 1. agree, conclude, decide, design, determine, fix, intend, make up one's mind, purpose, settle, undertake 2. answer, clear up, crack, elucidate, fathom, find the solution to, work out 3. banish, clear up, dispel, explain, remove 4. analyse, anatomize, break down, clear, disentangle, disintegrate, dissect, dissolve, liquefy, melt, reduce, separate, solve, split up, unravel ~*n.* 5. conclusion, decision, design, intention, objective, project, purpose, resolution, undertaking 6. boldness, courage, determination, earnestness, firmness, resoluteness, resolution, steadfastness, willpower

resort *v.* 1. avail oneself of, bring into play, employ, exercise, fall back on, have recourse to, look to, make use of, turn to, use, utilize 2. frequent, go, haunt, head for, repair, visit ~*n.* 3. haunt, holiday centre, refuge, retreat, spot, tourist centre, watering place

resource (rɪˈzɔːs, -ˈsɔːs) *n.* **1.** capability, ingenuity **2.** that to which one resorts for support **3.** expedient —*pl.* **4.** source of economic wealth **5.** stock that can be drawn on **6.** means of support, funds —**reˈsourceful** *a.* —**reˈsourcefully** *adv.* —**reˈsourcefulness** *n.*

respect (rɪˈspɛkt) *n.* **1.** deference, esteem **2.** point, aspect **3.** reference, relation —*vt.* **4.** treat with esteem **5.** show consideration for —**respectaˈbility** *n.* —**reˈspectable** *a.* **1.** worthy of respect, decent **2.** fairly good —**reˈspecter** *n.* —**reˈspectful** *a.* —**reˈspecting** *prep.* concerning —**reˈspective** *a.* **1.** relating separately to each of those in question **2.** several, separate —**reˈspectively** *adv.*

respire (rɪˈspaɪə) *v.* breathe —**respirable** (ˈrɛspɪrəbᵊl) *a.* —**respiration** (rɛspəˈreɪʃən) *n.* —**respirator** (ˈrɛspəreɪtə) *n.* apparatus worn over mouth and breathed through as protection against dust, poison gas *etc.* or to provide artificial respiration —**respiratory** (ˈrɛspərətərɪ, -trɪ) *a.*

respite (ˈrɛspɪt, -paɪt) *n.* **1.** pause **2.** interval **3.** suspension of labour **4.** delay **5.** reprieve

resplendent (rɪˈsplɛndənt) *a.* **1.** brilliant, splendid **2.** shining —**reˈsplendence** *or* **reˈsplendency** *n.*

respond (rɪˈspɒnd) *vi.* **1.** answer **2.** act in answer to any stimulus **3.** react —**reˈspondent** *a.* **1.** replying —*n.* **2.** one who answers **3.** defendant —**reˈsponse** *n.* answer —**reˈsponsive** *a.* readily reacting to some influence —**reˈsponsiveness** *n.*

responsible (rɪˈspɒnsəbᵊl) *a.* **1.** liable to answer (for) **2.** accountable **3.** dependable **4.** involving responsibility **5.** of good credit or position —**responsiˈbility** *n.* **1.** state of being responsible **2.** duty **3.** charge **4.** obligation

rest[1] (rɛst) *n.* **1.** repose **2.** freedom from exertion *etc.* **3.** that on which anything rests or leans **4.** pause, *esp.* in music **5.** support —*vi.* **6.** take rest **7.** be supported —*vt.* **8.** give rest to **9.** place on support —**ˈrestful** *a.* —**ˈrestless** *a.*

THESAURUS

(*Brit.*) **4.** alternative, chance, course, expedient, hope, possibility, recourse, reference

resound echo, fill the air, re-echo, resonate, reverberate, ring

resounding booming, echoing, full, powerful, resonant, reverberating, rich, ringing, sonorous, sounding, vibrant

resource 1. ability, capability, cleverness, ingenuity, initiative, inventiveness, quick-wittedness, resourcefulness, talent **2.** appliance, contrivance, course, device, expedient, means, resort

resourceful able, bright, capable, clever, creative, imaginative, ingenious, inventive, quick-witted, sharp, talented

resources assets, capital, funds, holdings, materials, means, money, property, reserves, riches, supplies, wealth, wherewithal

respect *n.* **1.** admiration, appreciation, approbation, consideration, deference, esteem, estimation, honour, recognition, regard, reverence, veneration **2.** aspect, characteristic, detail, facet, feature, matter, particular, point, sense, way **3.** bearing, connection, reference, regard, relation ~*v.* **4.** admire, adore, appreciate, defer to, esteem, have a good *or* high opinion of, honour, look up to, recognize, regard, revere, reverence, set store by, show consideration for, think highly of, value, venerate **5.** abide by, adhere to, attend, comply with, follow, heed, honour, notice, obey, observe, pay attention to, regard, show consideration for

respectable 1. admirable, decent, decorous, dignified, estimable, good, honest, honourable, proper, reputable, respected, upright, venerable, worthy **2.** ample, appreciable, considerable, decent, fair, fairly good, goodly, presentable, reasonable, sizable, substantial, tidy (*Inf.*), tolerable

respective corresponding, individual, own, particular, personal, relevant, separate, several, specific, various

respite 1. break, breather (*Inf.*), breathing space, cessation, halt, hiatus, intermission, interruption, interval, let-up (*Inf.*), lull, pause, recess, relaxation, relief, rest **2.** adjournment, delay, moratorium, postponement, reprieve, stay, suspension

respond acknowledge, act in response, answer, come back, counter, react, reciprocate, rejoin, reply, retort, return

response acknowledgment, answer, comeback (*Inf.*), counterblast, feedback, reaction, rejoinder, reply, retort, return, riposte

responsibility 1. accountability, amenability, answerability, care, charge, duty, liability, obligation, onus, trust **2.** blame, burden, culpability, fault, guilt **3.** conscientiousness, dependability, levelheadedness, maturity, rationality, reliability, sensibleness, soberness, stability, trustworthiness

responsible 1. at the helm, carrying the can (*Inf.*), in authority, in charge, in control **2.** accountable, amenable, answerable, bound, chargeable, duty-bound, liable, subject, under obligation **3.** authoritative, decision-making, executive, high, important **4.** at fault, culpable, guilty, to blame **5.** adult, conscientious, dependable, level-headed, mature, rational, reliable, sensible, sober, sound, stable, trustworthy

responsive alive, awake, aware, forthcoming, impressionable, open, perceptive, quick to react, reactive, receptive, sensitive, sharp, susceptible, sympathetic

rest[1] *n.* **1.** calm, doze, forty winks (*Inf.*), idleness, inactivity, leisure, lie-down, motionlessness, nap, refreshment, relaxation, relief, repose, siesta, sleep, slumber, snooze (*Inf.*), somnolence, standstill, stillness, tranquillity **2.** break, breather (*Inf.*), breathing space, cessation, halt, holiday, interlude, intermission, interval, lull, pause, stop, time off, vacation **3.** base, holder, prop, shelf, stand, support, trestle ~*v.* **4.** be at ease, be calm, doze, have a snooze (*Inf.*), have forty winks (*Inf.*), idle, laze, lie down, lie still, nap, put one's feet up, refresh oneself, relax, sit down, sleep, slumber, snooze (*Inf.*), take a nap, take it easy (*Inf.*), take one's ease **5.** be supported, lay, lean, lie, prop, recline, repose, sit, stand, stretch out **6.** break off, cease, come to a standstill, desist, discontinue, halt, have a break, knock off (*Inf.*), stay, stop, take a breather (*Inf.*) **7.** base, be based, be founded, depend, found, hang, hinge, lie, rely, reside, turn

rest[2] **1.** *n.* balance, excess, leftovers, others, remainder remains, remnants, residue, residuum, rump, surplus **2.** *v.* be left, continue being, go on being, keep, remain, stay

rest[2] (rɛst) *n.* 1. remainder 2. others —*vi.* 3. remain 4. continue to be

restaurant (ˈrɛstərɒŋ, ˈrɛstrɒŋ) *n.* commercial establishment serving food —**restaurateur** (rɛstərəˈtɜː) *n.* keeper of restaurant —**restaurant car UK** railway coach in which meals are served (*also* **dining car**)

restitution (rɛstɪˈtjuːʃən) *n.* 1. giving back or making up 2. reparation, compensation

restive (ˈrɛstɪv) *a.* 1. restless 2. resisting control, impatient

restore (rɪˈstɔː) *vt.* 1. build up again, repair, renew 2. re-establish 3. give back —**restoration** (rɛstəˈreɪʃən) *n.* —**restorative** (rɪˈstɒrətɪv) *a.* 1. restoring —*n.* 2. medicine to strengthen *etc.* —**reˈstorer** *n.*

restrain (rɪˈstreɪn) *vt.* 1. check, hold back 2. prevent 3. confine —**reˈstraint** *n.* restraining, control, *esp.* self-control

restrict (rɪˈstrɪkt) *vt.* limit, bound —**reˈstriction** *n.* 1. limitation 2. restraint 3. rule —**reˈstrictive** *a.* —**restricted area** area in which speed limit for vehicles applies —**restrictive practice UK** trading agreement against public interest

result (rɪˈzʌlt) *vi.* 1. follow as consequence 2. happen 3. (*with* in) end —*n.* 4. effect, outcome —**reˈsultant** *a.* arising as result

resume (rɪˈzjuːm) *v.* begin again —**résumé** (ˈrɛzjʊmeɪ) *n.* summary, abstract —**resumption** (rɪˈzʌmpʃən) *n.* 1. resuming 2. fresh start —**resumptive** (rɪˈzʌmptɪv) *a.*

resurgence (rɪˈsɜːdʒəns) *n.* rising again —**reˈsurgent** *a.*

resurrect (rɛzəˈrɛkt) *vt.* 1. restore to life, resuscitate 2. use once more (something discarded *etc.*) —**resurˈrection** *n.* 1. rising again (*esp.* from dead) 2. revival

resuscitate (rɪˈsʌsɪteɪt) *vt.* revive to life, consciousness —**resusciˈtation** *n.*

retail (ˈriːteɪl) *n.* 1. sale of goods in small quantities —*adv.* 2. by retail —*v.* 3. sell, be sold, retail 4. (rɪˈteɪl) recount —**ˈretailer** *n.*

retain (rɪˈteɪn) *vt.* 1. keep 2. engage services of —**reˈtainer** *n.* 1. fee to retain professional adviser, *esp.* barrister 2. *Hist.* follower of nobleman *etc.* —**retention** (rɪˈtɛnʃən) *n.* —**retentive** (rɪˈtɛntɪv) *a.* capable of retaining, remembering —**retaining wall** wall constructed to hold back earth *etc.* (*also* **reˈvetment**)

retake (riːˈteɪk) *vt.* 1. take back, capture again 2. *Cine.*

THESAURUS

restful calm, calming, comfortable, languid, pacific, peaceful, placid, quiet, relaxed, relaxing, serene, sleepy, soothing, tranquil, tranquillizing, undisturbed, unhurried

restive agitated, edgy, fidgety, fractious, fretful, ill at ease, impatient, jittery (*Inf.*), jumpy, nervous, on edge, recalcitrant, refractory, restless, uneasy, unquiet, unruly

restless 1. active, bustling, changeable, footloose, hurried, inconstant, irresolute, moving, nomadic, roving, transient, turbulent, unsettled, unstable, unsteady, wandering 2. agitated, anxious, disturbed, edgy, fidgeting, fidgety, fitful, fretful, ill at ease, jumpy, nervous, on edge, restive, sleepless, tossing and turning, troubled, uneasy, unquiet, unruly, unsettled, worried

restoration 1. reconstruction, recovery, refreshment, refurbishing, rehabilitation, rejuvenation, renewal, renovation, repair, revitalization, revival 2. recovery, re-establishment, reinstallation, reinstatement, replacement, restitution, return

restore 1. fix, mend, rebuild, recondition, reconstruct, recover, refurbish, rehabilitate, renew, renovate, repair, retouch, set to rights, touch up 2. bring back to health, build up, reanimate, refresh, rejuvenate, revitalize, revive, revivify, strengthen 3. bring back, give back, hand back, recover, re-establish, reinstate, replace, return, send back 4. reconstitute, re-enforce, reimpose, reinstate, reintroduce

restrain 1. bridle, check, confine, constrain, contain, control, curb, curtail, debar, govern, hamper, handicap, harness, hinder, hold, hold back, inhibit, keep, keep under control, limit, muzzle, prevent, repress, restrict, subdue, suppress 2. arrest, bind, chain, confine, detain, fetter, hold, imprison, jail, lock up, manacle, pinion, tie up

restraint 1. coercion, command, compulsion, confines, constraint, control, curtailment, grip, hindrance, hold, inhibition, limitation, moderation, prevention, restriction, self-control, self-discipline, self-possession, self-restraint, suppression 2. ban, bridle, check, curb, embargo, interdict, limit, limitation, rein, taboo

restrict bound, circumscribe, confine, contain, cramp, demarcate, hamper, handicap, hem in, impede, inhibit, keep within bounds *or* limits, limit, regulate, restrain

restriction check, condition, confinement, constraint, containment, control, curb, demarcation, handicap, inhibition, limitation, regulation, restraint, rule, stipulation

result *n.* 1. conclusion, consequence, decision, development, effect, end, event, fruit, issue, outcome, product, reaction, sequel, termination, upshot ~*v.* 2. appear, arise, derive, develop, emanate, ensue, eventuate, flow, follow, happen, issue, spring, stem, turn out 3. *With* **in** culminate, end, finish, terminate, wind up (*Inf.*)

resume begin again, carry on, continue, go on, proceed, recommence, reinstitute, reopen, restart, take up *or* pick up where one left off

resumption carrying on, continuation, fresh outbreak, new beginning, re-establishment, renewal, reopening, restart, resurgence

resurrect breathe new life into, bring back, raise from the dead, reintroduce, renew, restore to life, revive

resurrection comeback (*Inf.*), raising *or* rising from the dead, reappearance, rebirth, renaissance, renascence, renewal, restoration, resurgence, resuscitation, return, return from the dead, revival

resuscitate breathe new life into, bring round, bring to life, give artificial respiration to, give the kiss of life (*Inf.*), quicken, reanimate, renew, rescue, restore, resurrect, revitalize, revive, revivify, save

retain 1. absorb, contain, detain, grasp, grip, hang *or* hold onto, hold, hold back, hold fast, keep, keep possession of, maintain, preserve, reserve, restrain, save 2. commission, employ, engage, hire, pay, reserve

retainer 1. attendant, dependant, domestic, flunky, footman, lackey, servant, supporter, valet, vassal 2. advance, deposit, fee

shoot (scene) again **3.** tape (recording) again *—n.* (ˈriːteɪk) **4.** *Cine.* rephotographed scene **5.** retaped recording

retaliate (rɪˈtælɪeɪt) *vi.* **1.** repay someone in kind **2.** revenge oneself **—retaliˈation** *n.* **—reˈtaliative** *or* **reˈtaliatory** *a.*

retard (rɪˈtɑːd) *vt.* **1.** make slow or late **2.** keep back **3.** impede development of **—retarˈdation** *n.* **—reˈtarded** *a.* underdeveloped, *esp.* mentally

retch (rɛtʃ, riːtʃ) *vi.* try to vomit

reticent (ˈrɛtɪsənt) *a.* **1.** reserved in speech **2.** uncommunicative **—ˈreticence** *n.*

reticulate (rɪˈtɪkjʊlɪt) *a.* **1.** made or arranged like a net (*also* **reˈticular**) *—v.* (rɪˈtɪkjʊleɪt) **2.** make, be like net **—reticuˈlation** *n.*

retina (ˈrɛtɪnə) *n.* light-sensitive membrane at back of eye (*pl.* **-s, -nae** (-niː))

retinue (ˈrɛtɪnjuː) *n.* band of followers or attendants

retire (rɪˈtaɪə) *vi.* **1.** give up office or work **2.** go away **3.** withdraw **4.** go to bed *—vt.* **5.** cause to retire **—reˈtired** *a.* that has retired from office *etc.* **—reˈtirement** *n.* **—reˈtiring** *a.* unobtrusive, shy **—retirement pension UK** weekly payment made by government to retired man over 65 or woman over 60

retort (rɪˈtɔːt) *vt.* **1.** reply **2.** repay in kind, retaliate **3.** hurl back (charge *etc.*) *—vi.* **4.** reply with countercharge *—n.* **5.** vigorous reply or repartee **6.** vessel with bent neck used for distilling

retouch (riːˈtʌtʃ) *vt.* touch up, improve by new touches, *esp.* of paint *etc.*

retrace (rɪˈtreɪs) *vt.* go back over (a route *etc.*) again

retract (rɪˈtrækt) *v.* draw back, recant **—reˈtractable** *or* **reˈtractible** *a.* **—reˈtractile** *a.* capable of being drawn in **—reˈtraction** *n.* drawing or taking back, *esp.* of statement *etc.* **—reˈtractor** *n.* **1.** muscle **2.** surgical instrument

retread (riːˈtrɛd) *vt.* **1.** renovate (worn rubber tyre) (**-ˈtreaded, -ˈtreading**) *—n.* (ˈriːtrɛd) **2.** renovated tyre (*also* **ˈremould**)

retreat (rɪˈtriːt) *vi.* **1.** move back from any position **2.** retire *—n.* **3.** act of, or military signal for, retiring, withdrawal **4.** place to which anyone retires **5.** refuge **6.** sunset call on bugle

retrench (rɪˈtrɛntʃ) *v.* **1.** reduce (expenditure), *esp.* by dismissing staff *—vt.* **2.** cut down **—reˈtrenchment** *n.*

retribution (rɛtrɪˈbjuːʃən) *n.* **1.** recompense, *esp.* for evil deeds **2.** vengeance **—retributive** (rɪˈtrɪbjʊtɪv) *a.*

retrieve (rɪˈtriːv) *vt.* **1.** fetch back again **2.** restore **3.** rescue from ruin **4.** recover, *esp.* information from computer **5.** regain **—reˈtrievable** *a.* **—reˈtrieval** *n.* **—reˈtriever** *n.* dog trained to retrieve game

retro- (*comb. form*) **1.** back; backwards, as in *retroactive* **2.** located behind, as in *retrochoir*

retroact (ˈrɛtrəʊækt) *vi.* **1.** react **2.** act in opposite direction **—retroˈactive** *a.* applying or referring to the past **—retroˈactively** *adv.*

retrochoir (ˈrɛtrəʊkwaɪə) *n.* space in large church or cathedral behind high altar

retrograde (ˈrɛtrəʊgreɪd) *a.* **1.** going backwards, reverting **2.** reactionary **—retroˈgress** *vi.* **1.** go back to earlier, *esp.* worse, condition; degenerate, deteriorate **2.** move backwards; recede **—retroˈgression** *n.* **—retroˈgressive** *a.*

retrorocket (ˈrɛtrəʊrɒkɪt) *n.* rocket engine to slow or reverse spacecraft *etc.*

retrospect (ˈrɛtrəʊspɛkt) *n.* looking back, survey of past **—retroˈspection** *n.* **—retroˈspective** *a.*

THESAURUS

retaliate even the score, exact retribution, get back at (*Inf.*), get even with (*Inf.*), get one's own back (*Inf.*), give as good as one gets (*Inf.*), give one a taste of one's own medicine, give tit for tat, make reprisal, pay one back in one's own coin, reciprocate, return like for like, strike back, take an eye for an eye, take revenge, wreak vengeance

retaliation an eye for an eye, a taste of one's own medicine, counterblow, counterstroke, reciprocation, repayment, reprisal, requital, retribution, revenge, tit for tat, vengeance

retard arrest, brake, check, clog, decelerate, defer, delay, detain, encumber, handicap, hinder, hold back *or* up, impede, obstruct, set back, slow down, stall

reticence quietness, reserve, restraint, secretiveness, silence, taciturnity, uncommunicativeness, unforthcomingness

reticent close-mouthed, mum, quiet, reserved, restrained, secretive, silent, taciturn, tight-lipped, uncommunicative, unforthcoming, unspeaking

retire 1. be pensioned off, (be) put out to grass (*Inf.*), give up work, stop working **2.** absent oneself, betake oneself, depart, exit, go away, leave, remove, withdraw **3.** go to bed, go to one's room, go to sleep, hit the sack (*Sl.*), kip down (*Brit. sl.*), turn in (*Inf.*) **4.** decamp, ebb, fall back, give ground, give way, pull back, pull out, recede, retreat, withdraw

retiring bashful, coy, demure, diffident, humble, meek, modest, quiet, reclusive, reserved, reticent, self-effacing, shrinking, shy, timid, timorous, unassertive, unassuming

retract 1. draw in, pull back, pull in, reel in, sheathe **2.** abjure, cancel, deny, disavow, disclaim, disown, recall, recant, renounce, repeal, repudiate, rescind, reverse, revoke, take back, unsay, withdraw

retreat *v.* **1.** back away, depart, draw back, ebb, fall back, give ground, go back, leave, pull back, recede, recoil, retire, shrink, turn tail, withdraw *~n.* **2.** departure, ebb, evacuation, flight, retirement, withdrawal **3.** asylum, den, haunt, haven, hideaway, privacy, refuge, resort, retirement, sanctuary, seclusion, shelter

retrench curtail, cut, cut back, decrease, diminish, economize, husband, lessen, limit, make economies, pare, prune, reduce, save, tighten one's belt, trim

retrenchment contraction, cost-cutting, curtailment, cut, cutback, economy, pruning, reduction, rundown, tightening one's belt

retribution an eye for an eye, compensation, justice, Nemesis, punishment, reckoning, recompense, redress, repayment, reprisal, requital, retaliation, revenge, reward, satisfaction, vengeance

retrieve fetch back, get back, recall, recapture, recoup, recover, redeem, regain, repair, repossess, rescue, restore, salvage, save, win back

retrospect afterthought, hindsight, recollection, reexamination, remembrance, reminiscence, review, survey

retroussé (rəˈtruːseɪ) *a.* (of nose) turned upwards, pug

retsina (rɛtˈsiːnə) *n.* Gr. wine

return (rɪˈtɜːn) *vi.* 1. go, come back —*vt.* 2. give, send back 3. report officially 4. elect —*n.* 5. returning, being returned 6. profit 7. official report 8. return ticket —**returning officer** officer conducting election —**return ticket** ticket allowing passenger to travel to and from a place

reunion (riːˈjuːnjən) *n.* gathering of people who have been apart

rev (rɛv) *inf. n.* 1. revolution (of engine) —*v.* 2. (*oft. with* up) increase speed of revolution (of) —**rev counter** UK *inf.* tachometer

Rev. 1. *Bible* Revelation 2. Reverend

revalue (riːˈvæljuː) *or U.S.* **revaluate** *v.* adjust exchange value of (currency) upwards —**revaluˈation** *n.*

revamp (riːˈvæmp) *vt.* renovate, restore

reveal (rɪˈviːl) *vt.* 1. make known 2. show —**revelation** (rɛvəˈleɪʃən) *n.*

reveille (rɪˈvælɪ) *n.* morning bugle call *etc.* to waken soldiers

revel (ˈrɛvᵊl) *vi.* 1. take pleasure (in) 2. make merry (-ll-) —*n.* 3. (*usu. pl.*) merrymaking —ˈ**reveller** *n.* —ˈ**revelry** *n.* festivity

revenge (rɪˈvɛndʒ) *n.* 1. retaliation for wrong done 2. act that satisfies this 3. desire for this —*vt.* 4. avenge 5. make retaliation for —*v.refl.* 6. avenge oneself —**reˈvengeful** *a.* 1. vindictive 2. resentful

revenue (ˈrɛvɪnjuː) *n.* income, *esp.* of state, as taxes *etc.* —**Inland Revenue** government department that administers and collects direct taxes, *eg* income tax

reverberate (rɪˈvɜːbəreɪt) *v.* echo, resound, throw back (sound *etc.*) —**reverberˈation** *n.*

revere (rɪˈvɪə) *vt.* hold in great regard or religious respect —**reverence** (ˈrɛvərəns) *n.* 1. revering 2. awe mingled with respect and esteem 3. veneration —**reverend** (ˈrɛvərənd) *a.* (*esp.* as prefix to clergyman's name) worthy of reverence —**reverent** (ˈrɛvərənt, ˈrɛvrənt) *a.* showing reverence —**reverential** (rɛvəˈrɛnʃəl) *a.* marked by reverence

reverie (ˈrɛvərɪ) *n.* daydream, absent-minded state

revers (rɪˈvɪə) *n.* part of garment which is turned back, *eg* lapel (*pl.* **-vers** (-ˈvɪəz))

reverse (rɪˈvɜːs) *v.* 1. (of vehicle) (cause to) move backwards —*vt.* 2. turn upside down or other way round 3. change completely —*n.* 4. opposite, contrary 5. side opposite, obverse 6. defeat 7. reverse gear —*a.* 8. opposite, contrary —**reˈversal** *n.* —**reˈversible** *a.* —**reverse charge** telephone call made at recipient's expense —**reverse gear** mechanism enabling vehicle to move backwards —**reversing light** light on rear of motor vehicle to provide illumination when reversing

revert (rɪˈvɜːt) *vi.* 1. return to former state 2. come back to subject 3. refer (to) a second time 4. turn backwards —**reˈversion** *n.* (of property) rightful passing to owner or designated heir *etc.* —**reˈverted** *a.* —**reˈvertible** *a.*

THESAURUS

return *v.* **1.** come back, come round again, go back, reappear, rebound, recoil, recur, repair, retreat, revert, turn back **2.** carry back, convey, give back, put back, re-establish, reinstate, remit, render, replace, restore, send, send back, take back, transmit **3.** give back, pay back, reciprocate, recompense, refund, reimburse, repay, requite **4.** choose, elect, pick, vote in **5.** announce, arrive at, bring in, come to, deliver, render, report, submit ~*n.* **6.** homecoming, reappearance, rebound, recoil, recrudescence, recurrence, retreat, reversion **7.** re-establishment, reinstatement, replacement, restoration **8.** account, form, list, report, statement, summary

reveal 1. announce, betray, broadcast, communicate, disclose, divulge, give away, give out, impart, leak, let on, let out, let slip, make known, make public, proclaim, publish, tell **2.** bare, bring to light, display, exhibit, expose to view, lay bare, manifest, open, show, uncover, unearth, unmask, unveil

revel *v.* **1.** *With* **in** bask, crow, delight, gloat, indulge, joy, lap up, luxuriate, rejoice, relish, savour, take pleasure, thrive on, wallow **2.** carouse, celebrate, go on a spree, live it up (*Inf.*), make merry, paint the town red (*Inf.*), push the boat out (*Brit. inf.*), rave (*Brit. sl.*), roister, whoop it up (*Inf.*) ~*n.* **3.** *Often plural* bacchanal, carousal, carouse, celebration, debauch, festivity, gala, jollification, merrymaking, party, saturnalia, spree

revelation announcement, betrayal, broadcasting, communication, disclosure, discovery, display, exhibition, exposé, exposition, exposure, giveaway, leak, manifestation, news, proclamation, publication, telling, uncovering, unearthing, unveiling

reveller carouser, celebrator, merrymaker, partygoer, pleasure-seeker, roisterer

revelry carousal, carouse, celebration, debauch, debauchery, festivity, fun, jollification, jollity, merrymaking, party, roistering, saturnalia, spree

revenge 1. *n.* an eye for an eye, reprisal, requital, retaliation, retribution, satisfaction, vengeance, vindictiveness **2.** *v.* avenge, even the score for, get one's own back for (*Inf.*), make reprisal for, repay, requite, retaliate, take an eye for an eye for, take revenge for, vindicate

revenue gain, income, interest, proceeds, profits, receipts, returns, rewards, takings, yield

reverberate echo, rebound, recoil, re-echo, resound, ring, vibrate

revere adore, be in awe of, defer to, exalt, have a high opinion of, honour, look up to, put on a pedestal, respect, reverence, think highly of, venerate, worship

reverence *n.* admiration, adoration, awe, deference, devotion, high esteem, homage, honour, respect, veneration, worship

reverent adoring, awed, decorous, deferential, devout, humble, loving, meek, pious, respectful, reverential, solemn, submissive

reverse *v.* **1.** invert, transpose, turn back, turn over, turn round, turn upside down, upend **2.** alter, annul, cancel, change, countermand, declare null and void, invalidate, negate, overrule, overset, overthrow, overturn, quash, repeal, rescind, retract, revoke, set aside, undo, upset **3.** back, backtrack, back up, go backwards, move backwards, retreat ~*n.* **4.** antithesis, contradiction, contrary, converse, inverse, opposite **5.** back, flip side, other side, rear, underside, verso, wrong side **6.** adversity, affliction, blow, check, defeat, disappointment, failure, hardship, misadventure, misfortune, mishap, repulse, reversal, setback, trial, vicissitude ~*adj.* **7.** back to front,

review (rɪˈvjuː) *vt.* **1.** examine **2.** look back on **3.** reconsider **4.** hold, make, write review of —*n.* **5.** general survey **6.** critical notice of book *etc.* **7.** periodical with critical articles **8.** inspection of troops —**reˈviewer** *n.* writer of reviews

revile (rɪˈvaɪl) *vt.* be viciously scornful of, abuse —**reˈviler** *n.*

revise (rɪˈvaɪz) *vt.* **1.** look over and correct **2.** restudy (work done previously) in preparation for examination **3.** change, alter —**reˈviser** *n.* —**revision** (rɪˈvɪʒən) *n.* **1.** re-examination for purpose of correcting **2.** revising of notes, subject for examination **3.** revised copy —**revisionism** (rɪˈvɪʒənɪzəm) *n.* **1.** (*sometimes* **R-**) moderate, nonrevolutionary version of Marxism developed in Germany around 1900 **2.** (*sometimes* **R-**) in Marxist-Leninist ideology, dangerous departure from true interpretation of Marx's teachings **3.** advocacy of revision of some political theory *etc.* —**revisionist** (rɪˈvɪʒənɪst) *n./a.* —**reˈvisory** *a.* of revision

revive (rɪˈvaɪv) *v.* bring, come back to life, vigour, use *etc.* —**reˈvival** *n.* reviving, *esp.* of religious fervour —**reˈvivalist** *n./a.*

revoke (rɪˈvəʊk) *vt.* **1.** take back, withdraw **2.** cancel —**revocable** (ˈrɛvəkəbᵊl) *a.* —**revocation** (rɛvəˈkeɪʃən) *n.* repeal

revolt (rɪˈvəʊlt) *n.* **1.** rebellion —*vi.* **2.** rise in rebellion **3.** feel disgust —*vt.* **4.** affect with disgust —**reˈvolting** *a.* disgusting, horrible

revolve (rɪˈvɒlv) *vi.* **1.** turn round, rotate **2.** be centred (on) —*vt.* **3.** rotate —**revolution** (rɛvəˈluːʃən) *n.* **1.** violent overthrow of government **2.** great change **3.** complete rotation, turning or spinning round —**revolutionary** (rɛvəˈluːʃənərɪ) *a./n.* —**revolutionize** *or* **-ise** (rɛvəˈluːʃənaɪz) *vt.* **1.** change considerably **2.** bring about revolution in —**revolving door** door that rotates about vertical axis, *esp.* with four leaves at right angles to each other

revolver (rɪˈvɒlvə) *n.* repeating pistol with revolving magazine

revue *or* **review** (rɪˈvjuː) *n.* theatrical entertainment with topical sketches and songs

revulsion (rɪˈvʌlʃən) *n.* **1.** sudden violent change of feeling **2.** marked repugnance or abhorrence

reward (rɪˈwɔːd) *vt.* **1.** pay, make return to (someone)

THESAURUS

backward, contrary, converse, inverse, inverted, opposite

revert backslide, come back, go back, hark back, lapse, recur, regress, relapse, resume, return, take up where one left off

review *v.* **1.** go over again, look at again, reassess, recapitulate, reconsider, re-evaluate, re-examine, rethink, revise, run over, take another look at, think over **2.** call to mind, look back on, recall, recollect, reflect on, remember, summon up **3.** assess, criticize, discuss, evaluate, examine, give one's opinion of, inspect, judge, read through, scrutinize, study, weigh, write a critique of ~*n.* **4.** analysis, examination, report, scrutiny, study, survey **5.** commentary, critical assessment, criticism, critique, evaluation, judgment, notice, study **6.** journal, magazine, periodical **7.** *Military* display, inspection, march past, parade, procession

reviewer arbiter, commentator, connoisseur, critic, essayist, judge

revise 1. alter, amend, change, correct, edit, emend, modify, reconsider, redo, re-examine, revamp, review, rework, rewrite, update **2.** go over, memorize, reread, run through, study, swot up (*Brit. inf.*)

revision 1. alteration, amendment, change, correction, editing, emendation, modification, re-examination, review, rewriting, updating **2.** homework, memorizing, rereading, studying, swotting (*Brit. inf.*)

revival awakening, quickening, reanimation, reawakening, rebirth, recrudescence, renaissance, renascence, renewal, restoration, resurgence, resurrection, resuscitation, revitalization, revivification

revive animate, awaken, breathe new life into, bring back to life, bring round, cheer, come round, comfort, invigorate, quicken, rally, reanimate, recover, refresh, rekindle, renew, renovate, restore, resuscitate, revitalize, rouse, spring up again

revoke abolish, abrogate, annul, call back, cancel, countermand, declare null and void, disclaim, invalidate, negate, nullify, quash, recall, recant, renounce, repeal, repudiate, rescind, retract, reverse, set aside, take back, withdraw

revolt *n.* **1.** defection, insurgency, insurrection, mutiny, putsch, rebellion, revolution, rising, sedition, uprising ~*v.* **2.** defect, mutiny, rebel, resist, rise, take to the streets, take up arms (against) **3.** disgust, give one the creeps (*Sl.*), make one's flesh creep, nauseate, offend, repel, repulse, shock, sicken, turn off (*Inf.*), turn one's stomach

revolting abhorrent, abominable, appalling, disgusting, distasteful, foul, horrible, horrid, loathsome, nasty, nauseating, nauseous, noisome, obnoxious, obscene, offensive, repellent, repugnant, repulsive, shocking, sickening

revolution *n.* **1.** coup, coup d'état, insurgency, mutiny, putsch, rebellion, revolt, rising, uprising **2.** drastic *or* radical change, innovation, metamorphosis, reformation, sea change, shift, transformation, upheaval **3.** circle, circuit, cycle, gyration, lap, orbit, rotation, round, spin, turn, wheel, whirl

revolutionary *n.* **1.** insurgent, insurrectionary, insurrectionist, mutineer, rebel, revolutionist ~*adj.* **2.** extremist, insurgent, insurrectionary, mutinous, radical, rebel, seditious, subversive **3.** avant-garde, different, drastic, experimental, fundamental, innovative, new, novel, progressive, radical, thoroughgoing

revolve circle, go round, gyrate, orbit, rotate, spin, turn, twist, wheel, whirl

revulsion abhorrence, abomination, aversion, detestation, disgust, distaste, loathing, recoil, repugnance, repulsion

reward 1. *n.* benefit, bonus, bounty, compensation, gain, honour, merit, payment, premium, prize, profit, recompense, remuneration, repayment, requital, return, wages **2.** *v.* compensate, honour, make it worth one's while, pay, recompense, remunerate, repay, requite

rewarding advantageous, beneficial, edifying, enriching, fruitful, fulfilling, gainful, gratifying, pleasing, productive, profitable, remunerative, satisfying, valuable, worthwhile

for service, conduct *etc.* —*n.* **2.** something given in return for a deed or service rendered —**re'warding** *a.* giving personal satisfaction, worthwhile

rewire (riː'waɪə) *vt.* provide (house *etc.*) with new wiring

RF radio frequency

R.F.C. Rugby Football Club

R.G.S. Royal Geographical Society

Rh **1.** *Chem.* rhodium **2.** rhesus (*esp. in* **Rh factor** (*see also* **rhesus factor** *at* RHESUS))

rhapsody ('ræpsədɪ) *n.* enthusiastic or high-flown (musical) composition or utterance —**rhapsodic** (ræp'sɒdɪk) *a.* —'**rhapsodist** *n.* —**rhapsodize** *or* **-ise** ('ræpsədaɪz) *v.*

rhea ('rɪə) *n.* S Amer. three-toed ostrich

rhebuck *or* **rhebok** ('riːbʌk) *n.* brownish-grey S Afr. antelope

rhenium ('riːnɪəm) *n.* dense silvery-white metallic element that has high melting point

rheostat ('rɪəstæt) *n.* instrument for regulating the value of the resistance in an electric circuit

rhesus ('riːsəs) *n.* small, long-tailed monkey of S Asia —**rhesus factor** feature distinguishing different types of human blood (*also* **Rh factor**)

rhetoric ('rɛtərɪk) *n.* **1.** art of effective speaking or writing **2.** artificial or exaggerated language —**rhe'torical** *a.* (of question) not requiring an answer —**rheto'rician** *n.*

rheum (ruːm) *n.* **1.** watery discharge, mucus **2.** catarrh —'**rheumy** *a.*

rheumatism ('ruːmətɪzəm) *n.* painful inflammation of joints or muscles —**rheu'matic** *a./n.* —'**rheumatoid** *a.* of, like rheumatism —**rheumatic fever** disease characterized by inflammation and pain in joints —**rheumatoid arthritis** chronic disease characterized by inflammation and swelling of joints

Rh factor *see* **rhesus factor** *at* RHESUS

rhinestone ('raɪnstəʊn) *n.* imitation gem made of paste

rhino ('raɪnəʊ) *n.* rhinoceros (*pl.* **-s**, '**rhino**)

rhino- *or before vowel* **rhin-** (*comb. form*) nose, as in *rhinology*

rhinoceros (raɪ'nɒsərəs, -'nɒsrəs) *n.* large thick-skinned animal with one or two horns on nose (**-es, -ros**)

rhizome ('raɪzəʊm) *n.* thick horizontal underground stem whose buds develop into new plants (*also* '**rootstock**, '**rootstalk**)

rho (rəʊ) *n.* 17th letter in Gr. alphabet (P, ρ) (*pl.* **-s**)

rhodium ('rəʊdɪəm) *n.* hard metal like platinum —'**rhodic** *a.*

rhododendron (rəʊdə'dɛndrən) *n.* any of various evergreen flowering shrubs

rhombus ('rɒmbəs) *n.* equilateral but not right-angled parallelogram, diamond-shaped figure (*pl.* **-es, -bi** (-baɪ)) —**rhombohedron** (rɒmbəʊ'hiːdrən) *n.* six-sided prism whose sides are parallelograms —'**rhomboid** *n./a.* —**rhom'boidal** *a.*

rhubarb ('ruːbɑːb) *n.* **1.** garden plant of which the fleshy stalks are cooked and used as fruit **2.** laxative from root of allied Chinese plant

rhumba ('rʌmbə, 'rʊm-) *n. see* RUMBA

rhumb line (rʌm) **1.** imaginary line on surface of sphere that intersects all meridians at same angle **2.** course navigated by vessel or aircraft that maintains uniform compass heading (*also* **rhumb**)

rhyme *or* **rime** (raɪm) *n.* **1.** identity of sounds at ends of lines of verse, or in words **2.** word or syllable identical in sound to another **3.** verse marked by rhyme —*vt.* **4.** use (word) to make rhymes —**rhymester, rimester** ('raɪmstə), '**rhymer** *or* '**rimer** *n.* poet, *esp.* one considered mediocre; poetaster, versifier —**rhyme scheme** pattern of rhymes used in piece of verse, usu. indicated by letters —**rhyming slang** slang in which word is replaced by word or phrase that rhymes with it

rhythm ('rɪðəm) *n.* measured beat or flow, *esp.* of words, music *etc.* —'**rhythmic(al)** *a.* —'**rhythmically** *adv.* —**rhythm-and-blues** *n.* kind of popular music derived from or influenced by blues —**rhythm method** method of contraception by restricting sexual intercourse to days in woman's menstrual cycle when conception is considered least likely to occur

RI Rhode Island

R.I. **1.** Regina et Imperatrix (*Lat.*, Queen and Empress) **2.** Rex et Imperator (*Lat.*, King and Emperor) **3.** Royal Institution **4.** religious instruction

ria ('rɪə) *n.* long narrow inlet of sea coast, being former valley submerged by sea

rib[1] (rɪb) *n.* **1.** one of curved bones springing from spine and forming framework of upper part of body **2.** cut of meat including rib(s) **3.** curved timber of framework of boat **4.** raised series of rows in knitting *etc.* —*vt.* **5.** furnish, mark with ribs **6.** knit to form rib pattern (**-bb-**) —'**ribbing** *n.*

rib[2] (rɪb) *vt. inf.* tease, ridicule (**-bb-**)

R.I.B.A. Royal Institute of British Architects

ribald ('rɪbᵊld) *a.* **1.** irreverent, scurrilous **2.** indecent —*n.* **3.** ribald person —'**ribaldry** *n.* vulgar, indecent talk

ribbon ('rɪbᵊn) *n.* **1.** narrow band of fabric used for trimming, tying *etc.* **2.** long strip or line of anything —**ribbon development** building of houses along main road leading out of town *etc.*

riboflavin *or* **riboflavine** (raɪbəʊ'fleɪvɪn) *n.* form of vitamin B

ribonucleic acid (raɪbəʊnjuː'kliːɪk, -'kleɪ-) *see* RNA

rice (raɪs) *n.* **1.** Eastern cereal plant **2.** its seeds as food —**rice paper** fine, edible Chinese paper

rich (rɪtʃ) *a.* **1.** wealthy **2.** fertile **3.** abounding **4.** valuable **5.** (of food) containing much fat or sugar **6.** mellow **7.** amusing —*n.* **8.** the wealthy classes —'**riches** *pl.n.* wealth —'**richly** *adv.*

THESAURUS

rhetoric **1.** eloquence, oratory **2.** bombast, fustian, grandiloquence, hot air (*Inf.*), hyperbole, magniloquence, pomposity, rant, verbosity, wordiness

rhyme **1.** *n.* ode, poem, poetry, song, verse **2.** *v.* chime, harmonize, sound like

rhythm accent, beat, cadence, flow, lilt, measure (*Prosody*), metre, movement, pattern, periodicity, pulse, swing, tempo, time

rhythmic, rhythmical cadenced, flowing, harmonious, lilting, melodious, metrical, musical, periodic, pulsating, throbbing

ribald bawdy, blue, broad, coarse, earthy, filthy, gross, indecent, licentious, naughty, near the knuckle

Richter scale (ˈrɪxtə) scale for expressing intensity of earthquake

rick[1] (rɪk) *n.* stack of hay *etc.*

rick[2] (rɪk) *vt./n.* sprain, wrench

rickets (ˈrɪkɪts) *n.* disease of children marked by softening of bones, bow legs *etc.*, caused by vitamin D deficiency —ˈ**rickety** *a.* **1.** shaky, insecure, unstable **2.** suffering from rickets

rickshaw (ˈrɪkʃɔː) *or* **ricksha** (ˈrɪkʃə) *n.* light two-wheeled man-drawn Asian vehicle

ricochet (ˈrɪkəʃeɪ, ˈrɪkəʃɛt) *vi.* **1.** (of bullet) rebound or be deflected by solid surface or water —*n.* **2.** bullet or shot to which this happens

rid (rɪd) *vt.* **1.** clear, relieve **2.** free **3.** deliver (**rid, ˈridding**) —ˈ**riddance** *n.* **1.** clearance **2.** act of ridding **3.** deliverance **4.** relief

ridden (ˈrɪdᵊn) *pp. of* RIDE

-ridden (*comb. form*) afflicted by, affected by, as in *disease-ridden*

riddle[1] (ˈrɪdᵊl) *n.* **1.** question made puzzling to test one's ingenuity **2.** enigma **3.** puzzling thing, person —*vi.* **4.** speak in, make riddles

riddle[2] (ˈrɪdᵊl) *vt.* **1.** pierce with many holes —*n.* **2.** coarse sieve for gravel *etc.* —**riddled with** full of, *esp.* holes

ride (raɪd) *v.* **1.** sit on and control or propel (horse, bicycle *etc.*) —*vi.* **2.** go on horseback or in vehicle **3.** lie at anchor **4.** be carried on or across —*vt.* **5.** travel over (**rode, ˈridden, ˈriding**) —*n.* **6.** journey on horse *etc.*, or in any vehicle **7.** riding track —ˈ**rider** *n.* **1.** one who rides **2.** supplementary clause **3.** addition to a document **4.** mathematical problem on given proposition —ˈ**riderless** *a.* —**riding crop** short whip with handle at one end for opening gates —**riding lamp** *or* **light** light on vessel showing it is at anchor

ridge (rɪdʒ) *n.* **1.** long, narrow hill **2.** long, narrow elevation on surface **3.** line of meeting of two sloping surfaces —*v.* **4.** form into ridges —ˈ**ridgepole** *n.* **1.** timber along ridge of roof, to which rafters are attached **2.** horizontal pole at apex of tent

ridiculous (rɪˈdɪkjʊləs) *a.* deserving to be laughed at; absurd, foolish —ˈ**ridicule** *n.* **1.** language or behaviour intended to humiliate or mock —*vt.* **2.** laugh at, deride

riding (ˈraɪdɪŋ) *n.* **1.** (**R-** *when part of name*) former administrative district of Yorkshire **2. C** parliamentary constituency

riesling (ˈriːzlɪŋ, ˈraɪz-) *n.* **1.** dry white wine **2.** type of grape used to make this wine

rife (raɪf) *a.* prevalent, common

riffle (ˈrɪfᵊl) *v.* flick through (pages *etc.*) quickly

riffraff (ˈrɪfræf) *n.* disreputable people, *esp.* collectively; rabble

rifle (ˈraɪfᵊl) *vt.* **1.** search and rob **2.** ransack **3.** make spiral grooves in (gun barrel *etc.*) —*n.* **4.** firearm with long barrel —ˈ**rifling** *n.* **1.** arrangement of grooves in gun barrel **2.** pillaging

rift (rɪft) *n.* crack, split, cleft —**rift valley** long narrow valley resulting from subsidence of land between two faults

rig (rɪg) *vt.* **1.** provide (ship) with spars, ropes *etc.* **2.** equip **3.** set up, *esp.* as makeshift **4.** arrange in dishonest way (**-gg-**) —*n.* **5.** way ship's masts and sails are arranged **6.** apparatus (for drilling for oil and gas) **7. US** articulated lorry —ˈ**rigger** *n.* —ˈ**rigging** *n.* ship's spars and ropes —ˈ**rigout** *n. inf.* person's clothing or costume, *esp.* bizarre outfit —**rig out 1.** (*oft. with* with) equip or fit out (with) **2.** dress or be dressed

right (raɪt) *a.* **1.** just **2.** in accordance with truth and

THESAURUS

(*Inf.*), obscene, off colour, Rabelaisian, racy, risqué, rude, scurrilous, smutty, vulgar

rich 1. affluent, filthy rich (*Inf.*), flush (*Inf.*), loaded (*Sl.*), made of money (*Inf.*), moneyed, opulent, propertied, prosperous, rolling (*Sl.*), stinking rich (*Inf.*), wealthy, well-heeled (*Sl.*), well-off, well-to-do **2.** abounding, full, productive, well-endowed, well-provided, well-stocked, well-supplied **3.** abounding, abundant, ample, copious, exuberant, fecund, fertile, fruitful, full, lush, luxurious, plenteous, plentiful, productive, prolific **4.** beyond price, costly, elaborate, elegant, expensive, exquisite, fine, gorgeous, lavish, palatial, precious, priceless, splendid, sumptuous, superb, valuable **5.** creamy, delicious, fatty, flavoursome, full-bodied, heavy, highly-flavoured, juicy, luscious, savoury, spicy, succulent, sweet, tasty **6.** deep, dulcet, full, mellifluous, mellow, resonant **7.** amusing, comical, funny, hilarious, humorous, laughable, ludicrous, ridiculous, risible, side-splitting

riches abundance, affluence, assets, fortune, gold, money, opulence, plenty, property, resources, richness, substance, treasure, wealth

richly elaborately, elegantly, expensively, exquisitely, gorgeously, lavishly, luxuriously, opulently, palatially, splendidly, sumptuously

rid clear, deliver, disabuse, disburden, disembarrass, disencumber, free, make free, purge, relieve, unburden

riddle brain-teaser (*Inf.*), Chinese puzzle, conundrum, enigma, mystery, poser, problem, puzzle, rebus

ride *v.* **1.** control, handle, manage, sit on **2.** be borne (carried, supported), float, go, journey, move, progress, sit, travel ~*n.* **3.** drive, jaunt, journey, lift, outing, spin (*Inf.*), trip, whirl (*Inf.*)

ridicule 1. *n.* banter, chaff, derision, gibe, irony, jeer, laughter, mockery, raillery, sarcasm, satire, scorn, sneer, taunting **2.** *v.* banter, caricature, chaff, deride, humiliate, jeer, lampoon, laugh at, laugh out of court, laugh to scorn, make a fool of, make fun of, make one a laughing stock, mock, parody, poke fun at, pooh-pooh, satirize, scoff, send up (*Brit. inf.*), sneer, take the mickey out of (*Inf.*), taunt

ridiculous absurd, comical, contemptible, derisory, farcical, foolish, funny, hilarious, incredible, laughable, ludicrous, nonsensical, outrageous, preposterous, risible, silly, stupid, unbelievable

rifle *v.* burgle, despoil, go through, gut, loot, pillage, plunder, ransack, rob, rummage, sack, strip

rift breach, break, chink, cleavage, cleft, crack, cranny, crevice, fault, fissure, flaw, fracture, gap, opening, space, split

rig *v.* **1.** accoutre, equip, fit out, furnish, kit out, outfit, provision, supply, turn out **2.** arrange, doctor, engineer, fake, falsify, fiddle with (*Inf.*), fix (*Inf.*), gerrymander, juggle, manipulate, tamper with, trump up ~*n.* **3.** accoutrements, apparatus, equipage, equipment, fitments, fittings, fixtures, gear, machinery, outfit, tackle

duty **3.** true **4.** correct **5.** proper **6.** of side that faces east when front is turned to north **7.** *Pol.* conservative or reactionary (*also* **right-wing**) **8.** straight **9.** upright **10.** of outer or more finished side of fabric —*vt.* **11.** bring back to vertical position **12.** put right—*vi.* **13.** come back to vertical position —*n.* **14.** claim, title *etc.* allowed or due **15.** what is right, just or due **16.** conservative political party **17.** *Boxing* punch, blow with right hand —*adv.* **18.** straight **19.** properly **20.** very **21.** on or to right side —**'rightful** *a.* —**'rightly** *adv.* —**right angle** angle of 90 degrees —**right-angled triangle** triangle one angle of which is right angle —**right-hand** *a.* **1.** of, located on or moving towards the right **2.** for use by right hand —**right-handed** *a.* **1.** using right hand with greater skill than left **2.** performed with right hand **3.** for use by right hand **4.** turning from left to right —**right-minded** *a.* holding opinions or principles that accord with what is right or with opinions of speaker —**Right Reverend** title of respect for bishop —**right whale** large, grey or black whalebone whale with large head and no dorsal fin —**right-hand man** most valuable assistant —**right of way** *Law* **1.** right to pass over someone's land **2.** path used (*pl.* **rights of way**)

righteous ('raɪtʃəs) *a.* **1.** just, upright **2.** godly **3.** virtuous **4.** good **5.** honest —**'righteousness** *n.*

rigid ('rɪdʒɪd) *a.* **1.** inflexible **2.** harsh, stiff —**ri'gidity** *n.*

rigmarole ('rɪgmərəʊl) *or* **rigamarole** ('rɪgəmərəʊl) *n.* **1.** meaningless string of words **2.** long, complicated procedure

rigor ('raɪgɔː, 'rɪgə) *n.* sudden coldness attended by shivering —**rigor mortis** ('rɪgə 'mɔːtɪs) stiffening of body after death

rigour *or U.S.* **rigor** ('rɪgə) *n.* **1.** harshness, severity, strictness **2.** hardship —**'rigorous** *a.* stern, harsh, severe

rile (raɪl) *vt. inf.* anger, annoy

rill (rɪl) *n.* small stream

rim (rɪm) *n.* **1.** edge, border, margin **2.** outer ring of wheel —**rimmed** *a.* bordered, edged

rime[1] (raɪm) *n.* hoarfrost —**'rimy** *a.*

rime[2] (raɪm) *n. see* RHYME

rind (raɪnd) *n.* outer coating of fruits *etc.*

rinderpest ('rɪndəpɛst) *n.* malignant infectious disease of cattle

ring[1] (rɪŋ) *n.* **1.** circle of gold *etc., esp.* for finger **2.** any circular band, coil, rim *etc.* **3.** people or things arranged so as to form circle **4.** group of people working together to advance their own interests **5.** enclosed area, *esp.* roped-in square for boxing —*vt.* **6.** put ring round **7.** mark (bird *etc.*) with ring —**'ringer** *n.* **1.** one who rings bells **2.** *sl.* person, thing apparently identical to another (*esp.* in **dead ringer**) —**'ringlet** *n.* curly lock of hair —**'ringbark** *v.* kill (tree) by cutting bark round trunk —**ring finger** third finger, *esp.* of left hand, on which wedding ring is worn —**'ringleader** *n.* instigator of mutiny, riot *etc.* —**ring main** domestic electrical supply in which outlet sockets are connected to mains supply through continuous closed circuit (**ring circuit**) —**'ringmaster** *n.* master of ceremonies in circus —**ring road** main road that bypasses a town (centre) —**'ringside** *n.* **1.** row of seats nearest boxing or wrestling ring **2.** any place affording close uninterrupted view —**'ringworm** *n.* fungal skin disease in circular patches

ring[2] (rɪŋ) *vi.* **1.** give out clear resonant sound, as bell **2.**

THESAURUS

right *adj.* **1.** equitable, ethical, fair, good, honest, honourable, just, lawful, moral, proper, righteous, true, upright, virtuous **2.** accurate, admissible, authentic, correct, exact, factual, genuine, precise, satisfactory, sound, spot-on (*Brit. inf.*), true, unerring, valid, veracious **3.** advantageous, appropriate, becoming, *comme il faut,* convenient, deserved, desirable, done, due, favourable, fit, fitting, ideal, opportune, proper, propitious, rightful, seemly, suitable **4.** conservative, reactionary, Tory ~*adv.* **5.** accurately, aright, correctly, exactly, factually, genuinely, precisely, truly **6.** appropriately, aptly, befittingly, fittingly, properly, satisfactorily, suitably **7.** directly, immediately, instantly, promptly, quickly, straight, straightaway, without delay **8.** bang, exactly, precisely, slap-bang (*Inf.*), squarely **9.** absolutely, all the way, altogether, completely, entirely, perfectly, quite, thoroughly, totally, utterly, wholly **10.** ethically, fairly, honestly, honourably, justly, morally, properly, righteously, virtuously ~*n.* **11.** authority, business, claim, due, freedom, interest, liberty, licence, permission, power, prerogative, privilege, title **12.** equity, good, goodness, honour, integrity, justice, lawfulness, legality, morality, propriety, reason, rectitude, righteousness, truth, uprightness, virtue ~*v.* **13.** compensate for, correct, fix, put right, rectify, redress, repair, settle, set upright, sort out, straighten, vindicate

righteous blameless, equitable, ethical, fair, good, honest, honourable, just, law-abiding, moral, pure, upright, virtuous

righteousness blamelessness, equity, ethicalness, faithfulness, goodness, honesty, honour, integrity, justice, morality, probity, purity, rectitude, uprightness, virtue

rigid adamant, austere, exact, fixed, harsh, inflexible, intransigent, invariable, rigorous, set, severe, stern, stiff, strict, stringent, unalterable, unbending, uncompromising, undeviating, unrelenting, unyielding

rigorous **1.** austere, challenging, demanding, exacting, firm, hard, harsh, inflexible, rigid, severe, stern, strict, stringent, tough **2.** bad, bleak, extreme, harsh, inclement, inhospitable, severe

rigour asperity, austerity, firmness, hardness, hardship, harshness, inflexibility, ordeal, privation, rigidity, sternness, strictness, stringency, suffering, trial

rig-out apparel, clobber (*Brit. sl.*), clothing, costume, dress, garb, gear (*Sl.*), get-up (*Inf.*), habit, outfit, raiment, togs

rig out **1.** accoutre, equip, fit, furnish, kit out, outfit, set up **2.** array, attire, clothe, costume, dress, kit out

rim border, brim, brink, circumference, edge, lip, margin, verge

rind crust, epicarp, husk, integument, outer layer, peel, skin

ring[1] *n.* **1.** band, circle, circuit, halo, hoop, loop, round **2.** arena, circus, enclosure, rink **3.** association, band, cabal, cartel, cell, circle, clique, combine, coterie, crew (*Inf.*), gang, group, junto, knot, mob, organization, syndicate ~*v.* **4.** circumscribe, encircle, enclose, encompass, gird, girdle, hem in, seal off, surround

resound —*vt.* **3.** cause (bell) to sound **4.** call (person) by telephone (**rang** *pt.*, **rung** *pp.*) —*n.* **5.** a ringing **6.** telephone call

rink (rɪŋk) *n.* **1.** sheet of ice for skating or curling **2.** floor for roller skating

rinkhals (ˈrɪŋkhaʊs) *n.* S Afr. ring-necked cobra

rinse (rɪns) *vt.* **1.** remove soap from (washed clothes, hair *etc.*) by applying clean water **2.** wash lightly —*n.* **3.** a rinsing **4.** liquid to tint hair

riot (ˈraɪət) *n.* **1.** tumult, disorder **2.** loud revelry **3.** disorderly, unrestrained disturbance **4.** profusion —*vi.* **5.** make, engage in riot —ˈ**riotous** *a.* unruly, rebellious, wanton

rip[1] (rɪp) *vt.* **1.** cut, tear away, slash, rend (**-pp-**) —*n.* **2.** rent, tear —ˈ**ripcord** *n.* cord pulled to open parachute —**rip-roaring** *a. inf.* characterized by excitement, intensity or boisterous behaviour —ˈ**ripsaw** *n.* handsaw with coarse teeth (used for cutting wood along grain) —**rip-off** *n. sl.* act of stealing, overcharging *etc.* —**rip off** *sl.* **1.** steal **2.** overcharge

rip[2] (rɪp) *n.* strong current, *esp.* one moving away from the shore

R.I.P. requiescat in pace

riparian (raɪˈpɛərɪən) *a.* of, on banks of river

ripe (raɪp) *a.* **1.** ready to be reaped, eaten *etc.* **2.** matured **3.** (of judgment *etc.*) sound —ˈ**ripen** *v.* **1.** make or grow ripe —*vi.* **2.** mature

riposte (rɪˈpɒst, rɪˈpəʊst) *n.* **1.** verbal retort **2.** counterstroke **3.** *Fencing* quick lunge after parry

ripple (ˈrɪpᵊl) *n.* **1.** slight wave, ruffling of surface **2.** sound like ripples of water —*vi.* **3.** flow, form into little waves **4.** (of sounds) rise and fall gently —*vt.* **5.** form ripples on

rise (raɪz) *vi.* **1.** get up **2.** move upwards **3.** appear above horizon **4.** reach higher level **5.** increase in value or price **6.** rebel **7.** adjourn **8.** originate; begin (**rose, risen** (ˈrɪzᵊn), ˈ**rising**) —*n.* **9.** rising **10.** slope upwards **11.** increase, *esp.* of wages —ˈ**riser** *n.* **1.** one who rises, esp. from bed **2.** vertical part of step —ˈ**rising** *n.* **1.** revolt —*a.* **2.** increasing in rank, maturity

risible (ˈrɪzɪbᵊl) *a.* **1.** inclined to laugh **2.** laughable —**risiˈbility** *n.*

risk (rɪsk) *n.* **1.** chance of disaster or loss —*vt.* **2.** venture **3.** put in jeopardy **4.** take chance of —ˈ**riskily** *adv.* —ˈ**risky** *a.* **1.** dangerous **2.** hazardous —**take** *or* **run a risk** proceed in an action regardless of danger involved

risotto (rɪˈzɒtəʊ) *n.* dish of rice cooked in stock and served with various other ingredients

risqué (ˈrɪskeɪ) *a.* suggestive of indecency

rissole (ˈrɪsəʊl) *n.* dish of fish or meat minced, coated with egg and breadcrumbs and fried

rite (raɪt) *n.* formal practice or custom, *esp.* religious —**ritual** (ˈrɪtjʊəl) *n.* **1.** prescribed order or book of rites **2.** regular, stereotyped action or behaviour —*a.* **3.** concerning rites —**ritualism** (ˈrɪtjʊəlɪzəm) *n.* practice of ritual —**ritualist** (ˈrɪtjʊəlɪst) *n.*

ritzy (ˈrɪtsɪ) *a. sl.* luxurious; elegant

rival (ˈraɪvᵊl) *n.* **1.** one that competes with another for

THESAURUS

ring[2] *v.* **1.** chime, clang, peal, resonate, resound, reverberate, sound, toll **2.** buzz (*Inf.*), call, phone, telephone ~*n.* **3.** chime, knell, peal **4.** buzz (*Inf.*), call, phone call

rinse 1. *v.* bathe, clean, cleanse, dip, splash, wash, wash out, wet **2.** *n.* bath, dip, splash, wash, wetting

riot *n.* **1.** anarchy, commotion, confusion, disorder, disturbance, donnybrook, fray, lawlessness, mob violence, quarrel, row, street fighting, strife, tumult, turbulence, turmoil, uproar **2.** boisterousness, carousal, excess, festivity, frolic, high jinks, jollification, merrymaking, revelry, romp **3.** display, extravaganza, flourish, show, splash ~*v.* **4.** fight in the streets, go on the rampage, raise an uproar, rampage, run riot, take to the streets **5.** carouse, cut loose, frolic, go on a binge *or* spree, make merry, paint the town red (*Inf.*), revel, roister, romp

riotous 1. anarchic, disorderly, insubordinate, lawless, mutinous, rampageous, rebellious, refractory, rowdy, tumultuous, ungovernable, unruly, uproarious, violent **2.** boisterous, loud, luxurious, noisy, orgiastic, rambunctious (*Inf.*), roisterous, rollicking, saturnalian, side-splitting, unrestrained, uproarious, wanton, wild

ripe 1. fully developed, fully grown, mature, mellow, ready, ripened, seasoned **2.** accomplished, complete, finished, in readiness, perfect, prepared, ready

ripen burgeon, come of age, come to fruition, develop, get ready, grow ripe, make ripe, mature, prepare, season

riposte answer, comeback (*Inf.*), rejoinder, repartee, reply, response, retort, return, sally

rise *v.* **1.** arise, get out of bed, get to one's feet, get up, rise and shine, stand up, surface **2.** arise, ascend, climb, enlarge, go up, grow, improve, increase, intensify, levitate, lift, mount, move up, soar, swell, wax **3.** advance, be promoted, climb the ladder, get on, get somewhere, go places (*Inf.*), progress, prosper, work one's way up **4.** appear, become apparent, crop up, emanate, emerge, eventuate, flow, happen, issue, occur, originate, spring, turn up **5.** mount the barricades, mutiny, rebel, resist, revolt, take up arms **6.** ascend, climb, get steeper, go uphill, mount, slope upwards ~*n.* **7.** advance, ascent, climb, improvement, increase, upsurge, upswing, upturn, upward turn **8.** advancement, aggrandizement, climb, progress, promotion **9.** acclivity, ascent, elevation, hillock, incline, rising ground, upward slope **10.** increment, pay increase, raise (*U.S.*)

risk 1. *n.* chance, danger, gamble, hazard, jeopardy, peril, possibility, speculation, uncertainty, venture **2.** *v.* chance, dare, endanger, expose to danger, gamble, hazard, imperil, jeopardize, put in jeopardy, take a chance on, venture

risky chancy (*Inf.*), dangerous, dicey (*Sl.*), dodgy (*Brit. inf.*), fraught with danger, hazardous, perilous, precarious, touch-and-go, tricky, uncertain, unsafe

rite act, ceremonial, ceremony, communion, custom, form, formality, liturgy, mystery, observance, ordinance, practice, procedure, ritual, sacrament, service, solemnity, usage

ritual *n.* **1.** ceremonial, ceremony, communion, liturgy, mystery, observance, rite, sacrament, service, solemnity **2.** convention, custom, form, formality, habit, ordinance, practice, prescription, procedure, protocol, red tape, routine, stereotype, usage ~*adj.* **3.** ceremonial, ceremonious, conventional, customary, formal, habitual, prescribed, procedural, routine, stereotyped

favour, success *etc.* —*vt.* 2. vie with (-ll-) —*a.* 3. in position of rival —ˈ**rivalry** *n.* keen competition

rive (raɪv) *v.* (*usu. as pp./a.* **riven**) 1. split asunder 2. tear apart (**rived** *pt.*, **rived**, ˈ**riven** *pp.*, ˈ**riving** *pr.p.*) —**riven** (ˈrɪvᵊn) *a.* split

river (ˈrɪvə) *n.* 1. large natural stream of water 2. copious flow —**river basin** area drained by river and its tributaries —ˈ**riverbed** *n.* channel in which river flows or has flowed

rivet (ˈrɪvɪt) *n.* 1. bolt for fastening metal plates, the end being put through holes and then beaten flat —*vt.* 2. fasten with rivets 3. cause to be fixed or held firmly, *esp.* (*fig.*) in surprise, horror *etc.* —ˈ**riveter** *n.*

rivulet (ˈrɪvjʊlɪt) *n.* small stream

R.L. Rugby League

rly. railway

R.M. 1. Royal Mail 2. Royal Marines 3. C Rural Municipality

R.M.A. Royal Military Academy (Sandhurst)

rms *or* **r.m.s.** root mean square

Rn *Chem.* radon

R.N. Royal Navy

RNA *Biochem.* ribonucleic acid; any of group of nucleic acids, present in all living cells, that play essential role in synthesis of proteins

R.N.(V.)R. Royal Naval (Volunteer) Reserve

roach (rəʊtʃ) *n.* European freshwater fish (*pl.* **roach, -es**)

road (rəʊd) *n.* 1. track, way prepared for passengers, vehicles *etc.* 2. direction, way 3. street —ˈ**roadster** *n.* 1. *obs.* touring car 2. kind of bicycle —ˈ**roadblock** *n.* barricade across road to stop traffic for inspection *etc.* —**road-fund licence UK** licence showing that tax payable in respect of motor vehicle has been paid —**road hog** selfish, aggressive driver —ˈ**roadholding** *n.* extent to which motor vehicle is stable and does not skid, *esp.* on sharp bends *etc.* —ˈ**roadhouse** *n.* public house, restaurant on country route —**road metal** broken stones used in macadamizing roads —**road sense** sound judgment in driving road vehicles —**road show** 1. *Rad.* live programme, usu. with audience participation, transmitted from radio van taking particular show on the road 2. group of entertainers on tour —ˈ**roadside** *n./a.* —ˈ**roadstead** *n. Naut.* partly sheltered anchorage (*also* **roads**) —**road test** test to ensure that vehicle is roadworthy, *esp.* after repair *etc.*, by driving it on roads —**road-test** *vt.* test (vehicle) in this way —ˈ**roadway** *n.* 1. surface of road 2. part of road used by vehicles —ˈ**roadworks** *pl.n.* repairs to road, *esp.* blocking part of road —ˈ**roadworthy** *a.* (of vehicle) mechanically sound —**hit the road** *sl.* start or resume travelling —**one for the road** a last alcoholic drink before leaving

roam (rəʊm) *v.* wander about, rove —ˈ**roamer** *n.*

roan (rəʊn) *a.* 1. (of horses) having coat in which main colour is thickly interspersed with another, *esp.* bay, sorrel or chestnut mixed with white or grey —*n.* 2. horse having such a coat

roar (rɔː) *vi.* 1. make or utter loud, deep, hoarse sound, as of lion —*v.* 2. (of people) utter (something) with loud deep cry, as in anger or triumph —*n.* 3. such a sound —ˈ**roaring** *a.* 1. *inf.* brisk and profitable —*adv.* 2. noisily

roast (rəʊst) *v.* 1. bake, cook in closed oven 2. cook by exposure to open fire 3. make, be very hot —*n.* 4. roasted joint —*a.* 5. roasted —ˈ**roaster** *n.* 1. oven *etc.* for roasting meat 2. chicken *etc.* suitable for roasting —ˈ**roasting** *n. inf.* severe criticism, scolding

rob (rɒb) *vt.* 1. plunder, steal from 2. pillage, defraud (-bb-) —ˈ**robber** *n.* —ˈ**robbery** *n.*

robe (rəʊb) *n.* 1. any long outer garment, oft. denoting rank or office —*vt.* 2. dress —*vi.* 3. put on robes, vestments

robin (ˈrɒbɪn) *n.* small brown bird with red breast (*also* **robin redbreast**)

robot (ˈrəʊbɒt) *n.* 1. automated machine, *esp.* performing functions in human manner 2. person of machinelike efficiency 3. **SA** traffic lights —**ro**ˈ**botic** *a.* of or like robot —**ro**ˈ**botics** *pl.n.* (*with sing. v.*) study of use of robots

robust (rəʊˈbʌst, ˈrəʊbʌst) *a.* sturdy, strong —**ro**ˈ**bustious** *a. obs.* 1. rough; boisterous 2. strong, robust, stout —**ro**ˈ**bustness** *n.*

roc (rɒk) *n.* monstrous bird of Arabian mythology

R.O.C. Royal Observer Corps

rock[1] (rɒk) *n.* 1. stone 2. large rugged mass of stone 3. hard sweet in sticks —ˈ**rockery** *n.* mound or grotto of stones or rocks for plants in garden —ˈ**rocky** *a.* 1. having many rocks 2. rugged —**rock bottom** lowest

THESAURUS

rival 1. *n.* adversary, antagonist, challenger, competitor, contender, contestant, emulator, opponent 2. *adj.* competing, competitive, conflicting, emulating, opposed, opposing 3. *v.* be a match for, bear comparison with, come up to, compare with, compete, contend, emulate, equal, match, measure up to, oppose, seek to displace, vie with

rivalry antagonism, competition, competitiveness, conflict, contention, contest, duel, emulation, opposition, struggle, vying

road avenue, course, direction, highway, lane, motorway, path, pathway, roadway, route, street, thoroughfare, track, way

roam drift, meander, peregrinate, prowl, ramble, range rove, stravaig (*Scot.*), stray, stroll, travel, walk, wander

roar 1. *v.* bawl, bay, bellow, clamour, crash, cry, howl, rumble, shout, thunder, vociferate, yell 2. *n.* bellow, clamour, crash, cry, howl, outcry, rumble, shout, thunder, yell

rob bereave, burgle, cheat, con (*Sl.*), defraud, deprive, despoil, dispossess, do out of (*Inf.*), gyp (*Sl.*), hold up, loot, pillage, plunder, raid, ransack, rifle, rip off (*Inf.*), sack, strip, swindle

robber bandit, brigand, burglar, cheat, con man (*Inf.*), fraud, highwayman, looter, pirate, plunderer, raider, stealer, swindler, thief

robbery burglary, depredation, embezzlement, filching, fraud, hold-up, larceny, pillage, plunder, raid, rapine, rip-off (*Inf.*), spoliation, stealing, stick-up (*U.S. sl.*), swindle, theft, thievery

robe 1. *n.* costume, gown, habit, vestment 2. *v.* apparel (*Archaic*), attire, clothe, drape, dress, garb

robot android, automaton, machine, mechanical man

robust able-bodied, athletic, brawny, fit, hale, hardy, healthy, hearty, husky (*Inf.*), in fine fettle, in good health, lusty, muscular, powerful, rude, rugged, sinewy, sound, staunch, stout, strapping, strong, sturdy, tough, vigorous, well

possible level —**rock-bound** *a.* hemmed in or encircled by rocks (*also* (*poet.*) **rock-girt**) —**rock cake** small cake containing dried fruit, with rough surface supposed to resemble rock —**rock crystal** transparent colourless quartz —**rock garden** garden featuring rocks or rockeries —**rock plant** plant that grows on rocks or in rocky ground —**rock rabbit SA** dassie, hyrax —**rock salmon** various food fishes, *esp.* dogfish —**rock salt** mineral consisting of sodium chloride in crystalline form, occurring in sedimentary beds *etc.*: important source of table salt (*also* ˈ**halite**)

rock[2] (rɒk) *v.* **1.** (cause to) sway to and fro **2.** reel or sway or cause (someone) to reel or sway, as with shock or emotion —*vi.* **3.** dance in rock-and-roll style —*n.* **4.** rocking motion **5.** rock-and-roll —ˈ**rocker** *n.* **1.** curved piece of wood *etc.* on which thing may rock **2.** rocking chair —ˈ**rocky** *a.* **1.** weak, unstable **2.** *inf.* (of person) dizzy; nauseated —**rock-and-roll** *or* **rock-'n'-roll** *n.* **1.** type of pop music of 1950s as blend of rhythm-and-blues and country-and-western **2.** dancing performed to such music —**rocking horse** toy horse mounted on rockers, on which child can rock to and fro in seesaw movement —**off one's rocker** *inf.* insane

rocket[1] (ˈrɒkɪt) *n.* **1.** self-propelling device powered by burning of explosive contents, used as firework, for display, signalling, line carrying, weapon *etc.* **2.** vehicle propelled by rocket engine, as weapon or carrying spacecraft —*vi.* **3.** move fast, *esp.* upwards, as rocket —ˈ**rocketry** *n.*

rocket[2] (ˈrɒkɪt) *n.* any of several kinds of flowering plant

rococo (rəˈkəʊkəʊ) *a.* (*oft.* **R-**) **1.** of furniture, architecture *etc.* having much conventional decoration in style of early 18th-cent. work in France **2.** tastelessly florid

rod (rɒd) *n.* **1.** slender cylinder of metal, wood *etc.* **2.** cane **3.** unit of length equal to 5½ yards

rode (rəʊd) *pt. of* RIDE

rodent (ˈrəʊdᵊnt) *n.* any gnawing animal, *eg* rat

rodeo (ˈrəʊdɪəʊ) *n.* **US, A** display of skills of cowboys, with bareback riding, cattle-handling techniques *etc.* (*pl.* **-s**)

rodomontade (rɒdəmɒnˈteɪd, -ˈtɑːd) *Lit. n.* **1.** boastful words or behaviour —*vi.* **2.** boast; rant

roe[1] (rəʊ) *n.* small species of deer

roe[2] (rəʊ) *n.* mass of eggs in fish

roentgen *or* **röntgen** (ˈrɒntgən, -tjən, ˈrɛnt-) *n.* measuring unit of radiation dose

rogation (rəʊˈgeɪʃən) *n.* (*usu. pl.*) *Christianity* solemn supplication, *esp.* in form of ceremony prescribed by Church —**Rogation Days** three days preceding Ascension Day

roger (ˈrɒdʒə) *interj.* **1.** *Telecomm. etc.* message received and understood **2.** expression of agreement

rogue (rəʊg) *n.* **1.** rascal, knave, scoundrel **2.** mischief-loving person, *oft.* child **3.** wild beast of savage temper, living apart from herd —ˈ**roguery** *n.* —ˈ**roguish** *a.* —**rogues' gallery** collection of portraits of known criminals kept by police for identification purposes

roister (ˈrɔɪstə) *vi.* **1.** be noisy or boisterous **2.** brag, bluster or swagger —ˈ**roisterer** *n.* reveller

role *or* **rôle** (rəʊl) *n.* **1.** actor's part **2.** specific task or function

roll (rəʊl) *v.* **1.** move by turning over and over —*vt.* **2.** wind round **3.** smooth out with roller —*vi.* **4.** move, sweep along **5.** undulate **6.** (of ship) swing from side to side **7.** (of aircraft) turn about a line from nose to tail in flight —*n.* **8.** act of rolling **9.** piece of paper *etc.* rolled up **10.** any object thus shaped, as *meat roll, swiss roll, etc.* **11.** official list or register, *esp.* of names **12.** bread baked into small oval or round **13.** continuous sound, as of drums, thunder *etc.* —ˈ**roller** *n.* **1.** cylinder of wood, stone, metal *etc.* used for pressing, crushing, smoothing, supporting thing to be moved, winding thing on *etc.* **2.** long wave of sea **3.** any of various Old World birds that have blue, green and brown plumage and erratic flight —ˈ**rolling** *a.* **1.** having gentle rising and falling slopes **2.** reverberating **3.** that may be turned up or down **4.** *sl.* extremely rich —*adv.* **5.** *sl.* swaying, staggering (*esp. in* **rolling drunk**) —**roll call** act, time of calling over list of names, as in schools or army —**rolled gold** metal coated with thin layer of gold —**roller bearings** bearings of hardened steel rollers —**roller coaster** *see* **big dipper** *at* BIG —**roller skate** skate with wheels instead of runner —**roller skating** —**roller towel** loop of towel on roller —**rolling mill 1.** mill or factory where ingots of heated metal are passed between rollers to produce sheets or bars of a required cross section and form **2.** machine used for this purpose —**rolling pin** cylindrical roller for pastry or dough —**rolling stock** locomotives, carriages *etc.* of railway —**rolling stone** restless or wandering person —ˈ**rollmop** *n.* herring fillet rolled, usu. around onion slices, and pickled in spiced vinegar —**roll-on** *a.* **1.** (of deodorant *etc.*) dispensed by means of revolving ball fitted into neck of container —*n.* **2.** woman's foundation garment —**roll-top** *a.* (of desk) with flexible lid sliding in grooves —**roll on UK** used to

THESAURUS

rock 1. lurch, pitch, reel, roll, sway, swing, toss, wobble **2.** astonish, astound, daze, dumbfound, jar, set one back on one's heels (*Inf.*), shake, shock, stagger, stun, surprise

rocky 1. boulder-strewn, craggy, pebbly, rough, rugged, stony **2.** adamant, firm, flinty, hard, rocklike, rugged, solid, steady, tough, unyielding

rod bar, baton, birch, cane, dowel, mace, pole, sceptre, shaft, staff, stick, switch, wand

rogue blackguard, charlatan, cheat, con man (*Inf.*), crook (*Inf.*), deceiver, devil, fraud, knave (*Archaic*), mountebank, ne'er-do-well, rapscallion, rascal, reprobate, scamp, scoundrel, sharper, swindler, villain

role 1. character, impersonation, part, portrayal, representation **2.** capacity, duty, function, job, part, position, post, task

roll *v.* **1.** elapse, flow, go past, go round, gyrate, pass, pivot, reel, revolve, rock, rotate, run, spin, swivel, trundle, turn, twirl, undulate, wheel, whirl **2.** bind, coil, curl, enfold, entwine, envelop, furl, swathe, twist, wind, wrap **3.** even, flatten, level, press, smooth, spread **4.** billow, lurch, reel, rock, sway, swing, toss, tumble, wallow, welter ~*n.* **5.** cycle, gyration, reel, revolution, rotation, run, spin, turn, twirl, undulation, wheel, whirl **6.** ball, bobbin, cylinder, reel, scroll, spool **7.** annals, catalogue, census, chronicle, directory, index, inventory, list, record, register, roster, schedule, scroll, table **8.** billowing, lurching, pitching, rocking, rolling, swell, tossing, undulation, wallowing, waves **9.** boom, drumming, growl, grumble, resonance, reverberation, roar, rumble, thunder express wish that eagerly anticipated event or date will come quickly —**roll up** *inf.* appear, turn up

rollick (ˈrɒlɪk) *vi.* **1.** behave in carefree or boisterous manner —*n.* **2.** boisterous or carefree escapade —ˈ**rollicking** *a.*

roly-poly (ˈrəʊlɪˈpəʊlɪ) *n.* **1.** pudding of suet pastry covered with jam and rolled up —*a.* **2.** round, plump

ROM (rɒm) *Comp.* read only memory

rom. *Print.* roman (type)

Rom. *Bible* Romans

Roman (ˈrəʊmən) *a.* of Rome or Church of Rome —**Roman alphabet** alphabet evolved by ancient Romans for writing of Latin and still used for writing most of languages of Western Europe —**Roman candle** firework that produces continuous shower of sparks punctuated by coloured balls of fire —**Roman Catholic** member of that section of Christian Church which acknowledges supremacy of the Pope —**Roman nose** nose having high prominent bridge —**Roman numerals** letters I, V, X, L, C, D, M used to represent numbers in manner of Romans —**roman type** plain upright letters, ordinary style of printing

romance (rəˈmæns, ˈrəʊmæns) *n.* **1.** love affair, *esp.* intense and happy one **2.** mysterious or exciting quality **3.** tale of chivalry **4.** tale with scenes remote from ordinary life **5.** literature like this **6.** picturesque falsehood —*vi.* (rəˈmæns) **7.** exaggerate, fantasize —**roˈmancer** *n.* —**roˈmantic** *a.* **1.** characterized by romance **2.** of or dealing with love **3.** (of literature *etc.*) preferring passion and imagination to proportion and finish —*n.* **4.** romantic person **5.** person whose tastes in art, literature *etc.* lie mainly in romanticism —**roˈmanticism** *n.* —**roˈmanticist** *n.* —**roˈmanticize** *or* **-cise** *v.*

Romance (rəˈmæns, ˈrəʊmæns) *a.* **1.** of vernacular language of certain countries, developed from Latin, as French, Spanish *etc.* —*n.* **2.** this group of languages

Romanesque (rəʊməˈnɛsk) *a./n.* (in) style of round-arched vaulted architecture of period between Classical and Gothic

Romany *or* **Rommany** (ˈrɒmənɪ, ˈrəʊ-) *n.* **1.** Gypsy **2.** Gypsy language —*a.* **3.** of the Gypsies or their language

romp (rɒmp) *vi.* **1.** run, play wildly, joyfully —*n.* **2.** spell of romping —ˈ**rompers** *pl.n.* child's one-piece garment consisting of trousers and bib with straps —**romp home** win easily

rondavel (rɒnˈdɑːvəl) *n.* **SA** circular building, oft. thatched

rondo (ˈrɒndəʊ) *n.* piece of music with leading theme to which return is continually made (*pl.* **-s**)

röntgen (ˈrɒntgən, -tjən, ˈrɛnt-) *n. see* ROENTGEN

roo (ruː) *n.* **A** *inf.* kangaroo

rood (ruːd) *n.* **1.** the Cross **2.** crucifix **3.** quarter of acre —**rood screen** screen separating nave from choir

roof (ruːf) *n.* **1.** outside upper covering of building **2.** top, covering part of anything —*vt.* **3.** put roof on, over —ˈ**roofing** *n.* **1.** material used to construct roof **2.** act of constructing roof —**roof rack** rack attached to roof of motor vehicle for carrying luggage *etc.* —ˈ**rooftree** *n. see* **ridgepole** *at* RIDGE —**hit** (*or* **raise** *or* **go through**) **the roof** *inf.* become extremely angry

rooibos (ˈrɔɪbɒs) *n.* S Afr. red-leafed tree

rooikat (ˈrɔɪkæt) *n.* S Afr. lynx

rook[1] (rʊk) *n.* **1.** bird of crow family —*vt.* **2.** *sl.* swindle, cheat —ˈ**rookery** *n.* colony of rooks

rook[2] (rʊk) *n.* chess piece (*also* ˈ**castle**)

rookie (ˈrʊkɪ) *n. inf.* recruit, *esp.* in army

room (ruːm, rʊm) *n.* **1.** space **2.** space enough **3.** division of house **4.** scope, opportunity —*pl.* **5.** lodgings —ˈ**roomy** *a.* spacious —ˈ**roommate** *n.* person with whom one shares room or lodging —**room service** service in hotel providing meals *etc.* in guests' rooms

roost (ruːst) *n.* **1.** perch for fowls —*vi.* **2.** perch —ˈ**rooster** *n.* **US** domestic cock —**come home to roost** have unfavourable repercussions

root (ruːt) *n.* **1.** part of plant that grows down into earth and conveys nourishment to plant **2.** plant with edible root, *eg* carrot **3.** vital part **4.** source, origin, original cause of anything **5.** *Anat.* embedded portion of tooth, nail, hair *etc.* **6.** primitive word from which other words are derived **7.** *Maths.* factor of a quantity which, when multiplied by itself the number of times indicated, gives the quantity —*v.* **8.** (cause to) take root —*vt.* **9.** pull by roots —*vi.* **10.** dig, burrow —ˈ**rootless** *a.* having no roots or ties —**root mean square** square root of average of squares of set of numbers —ˈ**rootstock** *n.* **1.** *see* RHIZOME **2.** *see* STOCK (sense 6) **3.** *Biol.* basic structure from which offshoots have developed —**root out** remove or eliminate completely

THESAURUS

rollicking *adj.* boisterous, carefree, cavorting, devil-may-care, exuberant, frisky, frolicsome, hearty, jaunty, jovial, joyous, lively, merry, playful, rip-roaring (*Inf.*), romping, spirited, sportive, sprightly, swashbuckling

roly-poly buxom, chubby, fat, overweight, plump, podgy, pudgy, rotund, rounded, tubby

romance *n.* **1.** affair, *affaire* (*du coeur*), affair of the heart, amour, attachment, intrigue, liaison, love affair, passion, relationship **2.** adventure, charm, colour, excitement, exoticness, fascination, glamour, mystery, nostalgia, sentiment **3.** fairy tale, fantasy, fiction, idyll, legend, love story, melodrama, novel, story, tale, tear-jerker (*Inf.*) **4.** absurdity, exaggeration, fabrication, fairy tale, falsehood, fiction, flight of fancy, invention, lie, tall story (*Inf.*), trumped-up story ~*v.* **5.** exaggerate, fantasize, let one's imagination run away with one, lie, make up stories, stretch the truth, tell stories

romantic *adj.* **1.** amorous, fond, lovey-dovey, loving, mushy (*Inf.*), passionate, sentimental, sloppy (*Inf.*), soppy (*Brit. inf.*), tender **2.** charming, colourful, exciting, exotic, fascinating, glamorous, mysterious, nostalgic, picturesque **3.** chimerical, exaggerated, extravagant, fabulous, fairy-tale, fanciful, fantastic, fictitious, idyllic, imaginary, imaginative, improbable, legendary, made-up, unrealistic, wild ~*n.* **4.** Don Quixote, dreamer, idealist, romancer, sentimentalist, utopian, visionary

rook bilk, cheat, clip (*Sl.*), defraud, diddle (*Inf.*), do (*Sl.*), fleece, gyp (*Sl.*), mulct, overcharge, rip off (*Sl.*), sting (*Inf.*), swindle

room **1.** allowance, area, capacity, compass, elbow-room, expanse, extent, latitude, leeway, margin, play, range, scope, space, territory, volume **2.** apartment, chamber, office **3.** chance, occasion, opportunity, scope

root for *inf.* cheer, applaud, encourage —**ˈrooter** *n.*

rope (rəʊp) *n.* **1.** thick cord —*vt.* **2.** secure, mark off with rope —**ˈropiness** *n.* —**ˈropy** *a.* **1.** *inf.* inferior, inadequate **2.** *inf.* not well **3.** (of liquid) sticky and stringy —**ˈropewalk** *n.* long narrow shed where ropes are made —**know the ropes** know details or procedures, as of job

ro-ro (ˈrəʊrəʊ) *a.* roll-on/roll-off: of cargo ship or ferry designed so that vehicles can be driven straight on and straight off

rorqual (ˈrɔːkwəl) *n.* whalebone whale with dorsal fin and series of grooves along throat and chest (*also* **ˈfinback**)

rosaceous (rəʊˈzeɪʃəs) *a.* **1.** of *Rosaceae,* family of plants typically having five-petalled flowers, including rose, strawberry *etc.* **2.** like rose, esp. rose-coloured

rosary (ˈrəʊzərɪ) *n.* **1.** *R.C.Ch.* series of prayers **2.** string of beads for counting these prayers as they are recited **3.** rose garden

rose[1] (rəʊz) *n.* **1.** shrub, climbing plant *usu.* with prickly stems and fragrant flowers **2.** the flower **3.** perforated flat nozzle for hose *etc.* **4.** pink colour —*a.* **5.** of this colour —**roseate** (ˈrəʊzɪeɪt) *a.* rose-coloured, rosy —**roˈsette** *n.* **1.** rose-shaped bunch of ribbon **2.** rose-shaped architectural ornament —**ˈrosy** *a.* **1.** flushed **2.** hopeful, promising —**rose-coloured** *a.* **1.** having colour of rose **2.** unwarrantably optimistic —**rose-water** *n.* **1.** scented water made by distillation of rose petals or by impregnation with oil of roses —*a.* **2.** elegant or delicate, *esp.* excessively so —**rose window** circular window with series of mullions branching from centre —**ˈrosewood** *n.* fragrant wood —**rose of Sharon** (ˈʃærən) low, spreading shrub with yellow flowers

rose[2] (rəʊz) *pt. of* RISE

rosé (ˈrəʊzeɪ) *n.* pink wine

rosemary (ˈrəʊzmərɪ) *n.* evergreen fragrant flowering shrub

Rosh Hashanah *or* **Rosh Hashana** (ˈrɒʃ həˈʃɑːnə; *Hebrew* ˈrɔʃ haʃaˈna) Jewish New Year

Rosicrucian (rəʊzɪˈkruːʃən) *n.* **1.** member of secret order devoted to occult beliefs —*a.* **2.** of the Rosicrucians or Rosicrucianism —**Rosiˈcrucianism** *n.*

rosin (ˈrɒzɪn) *n.* resin

ROSPA (ˈrɒspə) UK Royal Society for Prevention of Accidents

roster (ˈrɒstə) *n.* **1.** list or plan showing turns of duty —*vt.* **2.** place on roster

rostrum (ˈrɒstrəm) *n.* **1.** platform, stage, pulpit **2.** beak or bill of bird (*pl.* **-s, -tra** (-trə))

rot (rɒt) *v.* **1.** (cause to) decompose naturally —*vt.* **2.** corrupt (**-tt-**) —*n.* **3.** decay, putrefaction **4.** any disease producing decomposition of tissue **5.** *inf.* nonsense —**ˈrotten** *a.* **1.** decomposed, putrid **2.** corrupt —**ˈrotter** *n. sl., chiefly* UK worthless, unpleasant or despicable person

rota (ˈrəʊtə) *n.* roster, list

rotary (ˈrəʊtərɪ) *a.* **1.** (of movement) circular **2.** operated by rotary movement —**Roˈtarian** *n.* member of Rotary Club —**roˈtate** *v.* (cause to) move round centre or on pivot —**roˈtation** *n.* **1.** rotating **2.** regular succession —**ˈrotatory** *a.* —**ˈrotovate** *vt.* —**ˈrotovator** *n.* R mechanical cultivator with rotary blades —**Rotary Club** one of international association of businessmen's clubs

rote (rəʊt) *n.* mechanical repetition —**by rote** by memory

rotisserie (rəʊˈtɪsərɪ) *n.* (electrically-driven) rotating spit for cooking meat

rotor (ˈrəʊtə) *n.* revolving portion of a dynamo motor or turbine

rotten (ˈrɒtᵊn) *a. see* ROT

THESAURUS

roomy ample, broad, capacious, commodious, extensive, generous, large, sizable, spacious, wide

root *n.* **1.** radicle, radix, rhizome, stem, tuber **2.** base, beginnings, bottom, cause, core, crux, derivation, essence, foundation, fountainhead, fundamental, germ, heart, mainspring, nub, nucleus, occasion, origin, seat, seed, source, starting point ~*v.* **3.** anchor, become established, become settled, embed, entrench, establish, fasten, fix, ground, implant, moor, set, stick, take root

root out abolish, cut out, destroy, dig up by the roots, do away with, efface, eliminate, eradicate, erase, exterminate, extirpate, get rid of, remove, tear out by the roots, uproot, weed out

rope *n.* **1.** cable, cord, hawser, line, strand **2. know the ropes** be an old hand, be experienced, be knowledgeable, know all the ins and outs, know one's way around, know the score (*Inf.*), know what's what ~*v.* **3.** bind, fasten, hitch, lash, lasso, moor, pinion, tether, tie

roster agenda, catalogue, inventory, list, listing, register, roll, rota, schedule, scroll, table

rostrum dais, platform, podium, stage

rosy **1.** blooming, blushing, fresh, glowing, healthy-looking, reddish, roseate, rubicund, ruddy **2.** auspicious, bright, cheerful, encouraging, favourable, hopeful, optimistic, promising, reassuring, roseate, rose-coloured, sunny

rot *v.* **1.** corrode, corrupt, crumble, decay, decompose, degenerate, deteriorate, disintegrate, fester, go bad, moulder, perish, putrefy, spoil, taint **2.** decline, degenerate, deteriorate, languish, waste away, wither away ~*n.* **3.** blight, canker, corrosion, corruption, decay, decomposition, deterioration, disintegration, mould, putrefaction, putrescence **4.** balderdash, bosh (*Inf.*), bunk (*Inf.*), bunkum, claptrap (*Inf.*), codswallop (*Brit. sl.*), drivel, flapdoodle (*Sl.*), guff (*Sl.*), hogwash, moonshine, nonsense, poppycock (*Inf.*), rubbish, stuff and nonsense, tommyrot, tosh (*Inf.*), twaddle

rotary gyratory, revolving, rotating, rotational, rotatory, spinning, turning

rotate go round, gyrate, pirouette, pivot, reel, revolve, spin, swivel, turn, wheel

rotation **1.** gyration, orbit, pirouette, reel, revolution, spin, spinning, turn, turning, wheel **2.** alternation, cycle, interchanging, sequence, succession, switching

rotten **1.** bad, corroded, corrupt, crumbling, decayed, decaying, decomposed, decomposing, disintegrating, festering, fetid, foul, mouldering, mouldy, perished, putrescent, putrid, rank, sour, stinking, tainted, unsound **2.** bent (*Sl.*), corrupt, crooked (*Inf.*), deceitful, degenerate, dishonest, dishonourable, disloyal, faithless, immoral, mercenary, perfidious, treacherous, untrustworthy, venal, vicious

rotund (rəʊˈtʌnd) *a.* **1.** round **2.** plump **3.** sonorous —**roˈtundity** *n.*

rotunda (rəʊˈtʌndə) *n.* circular building or room, *esp.* with dome

rouble *or* **ruble** (ˈruːbᵊl) *n.* monetary unit of Soviet Union

roué (ˈruːeɪ) *n.* debauched or lecherous man; rake

rouge (ruːʒ) *n.* **1.** red powder, cream used to colour cheeks —*vt.* **2.** colour with rouge

rough (rʌf) *a.* **1.** not smooth, of irregular surface **2.** violent, stormy, boisterous **3.** rude **4.** uncivil **5.** lacking refinement **6.** approximate **7.** in preliminary form —*vt.* **8.** make rough **9.** plan out approximately **10.** (*with* it) live without usual comforts *etc.* —*n.* **11.** rough state or area **12.** sketch —**ˈroughage** *n.* unassimilated portion of food promoting proper intestinal action —**ˈroughen** *v.* —**ˈroughly** *adv.* —**rough-and-ready** *a.* **1.** crude, unpolished or hastily prepared, but sufficient for purpose **2.** (of person) without formality or refinement —**rough-and-tumble** *n.* **1.** fight or scuffle without rules —*a.* **2.** characterized by disorderliness and disregard for rules —**ˈroughcast** *a.* **1.** coated with mixture of lime and gravel —*n.* **2.** such mixture —*vt.* **3.** coat (wall *etc.*) with roughcast —**rough diamond** trustworthy but unsophisticated person —**rough-dry** *a.* **1.** (of clothes or linen) dried ready for pressing —*vt.* **2.** dry (clothes *etc.*) without ironing —**rough-hew** *vt.* shape roughly —**ˈroughhouse** *n. sl.* fight, row —**ˈroughshod** *a.* (of horse) shod with rough-bottomed shoes to prevent sliding —**ride roughshod over** treat harshly and without consideration

roulette (ruːˈlɛt) *n.* game of chance played with revolving wheel and ball

round (raʊnd) *a.* **1.** spherical **2.** cylindrical **3.** circular **4.** curved **5.** full, complete **6.** roughly correct **7.** large, considerable **8.** plump **9.** positive —*adv.* **10.** with circular or circuitous course —*n.* **11.** thing round in shape **12.** recurrent duties **13.** stage in competition **14.** customary course, as of milkman **15.** game (of golf) **16.** one of several periods in boxing match *etc.* **17.** cartridge for firearm **18.** rung **19.** movement in circle —*prep.* **20.** about **21.** on all sides of —*v.* **22.** make, become round —*vt.* **23.** move round —**ˈrounders** *n.* ball game —**ˈroundly** *adv.* **1.** plainly **2.** thoroughly —**ˈroundabout** *n.* **1.** revolving circular platform on which people ride for amusement **2.** road junction at which traffic passes round a central island —*a.* **3.** indirect; devious —**round dance 1.** dance in which dancers form circle **2.** ballroom dance in which couples revolve —**ˈRoundhead** *n. English hist.* supporter of Parliament against Charles I during Civil War —**round robin** petition signed with names in circle to conceal order —**round-shouldered** *a.* denoting faulty posture characterized by drooping shoulders and slight forward bending of back —**round table** meeting of parties or people on equal terms for discussion —**round-the-clock** *a.* throughout day and night —**round trip** trip to place and back again —**ˈroundup** *n.* **1.** act of gathering together cattle *etc.* for branding, counting or selling **2.** *inf.* any similar act of bringing together —**ˈroundworm** *n.* nematode worm that is common intestinal parasite of man and pigs —**round up 1.** drive (cattle) together **2.** collect and arrest criminals

roundel (ˈraʊndᵊl) *n.* **1.** rondeau **2.** small disc —**ˈroundelay** *n.* simple song with refrain

rouse (raʊz) *vt.* **1.** wake up, stir up, excite to action **2.** cause to rise —*vi.* **3.** waken

rout[1] (raʊt) *n.* **1.** overwhelming defeat, disorderly retreat **2.** noisy rabble —*vt.* **3.** scatter and put to flight

THESAURUS

rotter bad lot, blackguard, blighter (*Brit. inf.*), bounder (*Inf.*), cad (*Brit. inf.*), cur, louse (*Sl.*), rat (*Sl.*), stinker (*Sl.*), swine

rotund 1. bulbous, globular, orbicular, round, rounded, spherical **2.** chubby, corpulent, fat, fleshy, heavy, obese, plump, podgy, portly, roly-poly, rounded, stout, tubby **3.** full, grandiloquent, magniloquent, orotund, resonant, rich, round, sonorous

rough *adj.* **1.** broken, bumpy, craggy, irregular, jagged, rocky, rugged, stony, uneven **2.** agitated, boisterous, choppy, inclement, squally, stormy, tempestuous, turbulent, wild **3.** bearish, bluff, blunt, brusque, churlish, coarse, curt, discourteous, ill-bred, ill-mannered, impolite, inconsiderate, indelicate, loutish, rude, unceremonious, uncivil, uncouth, uncultured, ungracious, unmannerly, unpolished, unrefined, untutored **4.** boisterous, cruel, curt, drastic, extreme, hard, harsh, nasty, rowdy, severe, sharp, tough, unfeeling, unjust, unpleasant, violent **5.** arduous, austere, hard, rugged, spartan, tough, uncomfortable, unpleasant, unrefined **6.** basic, crude, cursory, formless, hasty, imperfect, incomplete, quick, raw, rough-and-ready, rough-hewn, rudimentary, shapeless, sketchy, unfinished, unpolished, unrefined, untutored **7.** crude, raw, rough-hewn, uncut, undressed, unhewn, unpolished, unprocessed, unwrought **8.** amorphous, approximate, estimated, foggy, general, hazy, imprecise, inexact, sketchy, vague ~*n.* **9.** draft, mock-up, outline, preliminary sketch, suggestion

rough-and-tumble 1. *n.* affray (*Law*), brawl, donnybrook, dust-up, (*Inf.*), fight, fracas, melee, punch-up (*Brit. sl.*), roughhouse (*Sl.*), scrap (*Inf.*), scuffle, struggle **2.** *adj.* boisterous, disorderly, haphazard, indisciplined, irregular, rough, rowdy, scrambled, scrambling

round *adj.* **1.** annular, ball-shaped, bowed, bulbous, circular, curved, curvilinear, cylindrical, discoid, disc-shaped, globular, orbicular, ring-shaped, rotund, rounded, spherical **2.** complete, entire, full, solid, unbroken, undivided, whole **3.** ample, bounteous, bountiful, considerable, generous, great, large, liberal, substantial **4.** ample, fleshy, full, full-fleshed, plump, roly-poly, rotund, rounded ~*n.* **5.** ball, band, circle, disc, globe, orb, ring, sphere **6.** division, lap, level, period, session, stage, turn **7.** ambit, beat, circuit, compass, course, routine, schedule, series, tour, turn **8.** bullet, cartridge, discharge, shell, shot ~*v.* **9.** bypass, circle, circumnavigate, encircle, flank, go round, skirt, turn

roundabout *adj.* circuitous, circumlocutory, devious, discursive, evasive, indirect, meandering, oblique, periphrastic, tortuous

round up assemble, bring together, collect, drive, gather, group, herd, marshal, muster, rally

rouse 1. arouse, awaken, call, get up, rise, wake, wake up **2.** agitate, anger, animate, arouse, bestir, disturb, excite, exhilarate, galvanize, get going, incite, in-

rout[2] (raʊt) *v.* **1.** dig over or turn up (something), *esp.* (of animal) with snout; root —*vt.* **2.** (*usu. with* out *or* up) find by searching **3.** (*usu. with* out) drive out **4.** (*oft. with* out) hollow or gouge out —*vi.* **5.** search, poke, rummage

route (ru:t) *n.* road, chosen way —**ˈroutemarch** *n.* **1.** *Mil.* long march undertaken for training purposes **2.** *inf.* any long exhausting walk

routine (ru:ˈti:n) *n.* **1.** regularity of procedure, unvarying round **2.** regular course —*a.* **3.** ordinary, regular

rove (rəʊv) *v.* wander, roam —**ˈrover** *n.* **1.** one who roves **2.** pirate

row[1] (rəʊ) *n.* **1.** number of things in a straight line **2.** rank **3.** file **4.** line

row[2] (raʊ) *inf. n.* **1.** dispute **2.** disturbance —*vi.* **3.** quarrel noisily

row[3] (rəʊ) *v.* **1.** propel (boat) by oars —*n.* **2.** spell of rowing —**rowing boat**

rowan (ˈrəʊən, ˈraʊ-) *n.* native Brit. tree producing bright red berries (*also* **(European) mountain ash**)

rowdy (ˈraʊdɪ) *a.* **1.** disorderly, noisy and rough —*n.* **2.** person like this

rowel (ˈraʊəl) *n.* small wheel with points on spur

rowlock (ˈrɒlək) *n.* appliance on gunwale of boat serving as point of leverage for oar

royal (ˈrɔɪəl) *a.* **1.** of, worthy of, befitting, patronized by, king or queen **2.** splendid —**ˈroyalist** *n.* supporter of monarchy —**ˈroyalty** *n.* **1.** royal dignity or power **2.** royal persons **3.** payment to owner of land for right to work minerals, or to inventor for use of his invention **4.** payment to author depending on sales —**Royal Air Force** air force of Great Brit. —**royal blue** (of) deep blue colour —**royal jelly** substance secreted by pharyngeal glands of worker bees and fed to all larvae when very young and to larvae destined to become queens throughout their development —**Royal Marines UK** corps of soldiers trained in amphibious warfare —**Royal Navy** navy of Great Brit. —**royal palm** palm tree of tropical Amer. having tall trunk with tuft of feathery pinnate leaves —**royal warrant** authorization to tradesman to supply goods to royal household

r.p.m. revolutions per minute

R.R. **1.** Right Reverend **2.** **C** Rural Route

R.S. **UK** Royal Society

R.S.A. **1.** Republic of South Africa **2.** Royal Scottish Academy **3.** Royal Scottish Academician **4.** Royal Society of Arts **5.** **NZ** Returned Services Association

RSFSR Russian Soviet Federated Socialist Republic

R.S.P.C.A. **UK** Royal Society for the Prevention of Cruelty to Animals

R.S.V. Revised Standard Version (of the Bible)

R.S.V.P. répondez s'il vous plaît (*Fr.*, please reply)

Rt. Hon. Right Honourable

Rt. Rev. Right Reverend

Ru *Chem.* ruthenium

R.U. Rugby Union

rub (rʌb) *vt.* **1.** apply pressure to with circular or backwards and forwards movement **2.** clean, polish, dry, thus **3.** pass hand over **4.** abrade, chafe **5.** remove by friction —*vi.* **6.** come into contact accompanied by friction **7.** become frayed or worn by friction (**-bb-**) —*n.* **8.** rubbing **9.** impediment —**ˈrubbing** *n.* impression taken of incised or raised surface by laying paper over it and rubbing with wax *etc.*

rubato (ru:ˈbɑ:təʊ) *Mus. n.* **1.** flexibility of tempo in performance (*pl.* **-s**) —*a./adv.* **2.** to be played with flexible tempo

rubber[1] (ˈrʌbə) *n.* **1.** coagulated sap of rough, elastic consistency, of certain tropical trees (*also* **India rubber, gum elastic, ˈcaoutchouc**) **2.** piece of rubber *etc.* used for erasing **3.** thing for rubbing **4.** person who rubs —*a.* **5.** made of rubber —**ˈrubberize** *or* **-ise** *vt.* coat, impregnate, treat with rubber —**ˈrubbery** *a.* —**rubber band** continuous loop of thin rubber, used to hold papers *etc.* together (*also* **elastic band**) —**ˈrubberneck** *sl. n.* **1.** person who gapes inquisitively **2.** sightseer, tourist —*vi.* **3.** stare in naive or foolish manner —**rubber plant** **1.** plant with glossy leathery leaves, cultivated as house plant in Europe and N Amer. **2.** any of several tropical trees, sap of which yields crude rubber —**rubber stamp** **1.** device for imprinting dates *etc.* **2.** automatic authorization

rubber[2] (ˈrʌbə) *n.* **1.** series of odd number of games or contests at various games **2.** two out of three games won

rubbish (ˈrʌbɪʃ) *n.* **1.** refuse, waste material **2.** anything worthless **3.** trash, nonsense —**ˈrubbishy** *a.* valueless

THESAURUS

flame, instigate, move, provoke, startle, stimulate, stir, whip up

rout **1.** *n.* beating, debacle, defeat, disorderly retreat, drubbing, headlong flight, hiding (*Inf.*), licking (*Inf.*), overthrow, overwhelming defeat, ruin, shambles, thrashing **2.** *v.* beat, chase, conquer, crush, cut to pieces, defeat, destroy, dispel, drive off, drub, lick (*Inf.*), overpower, overthrow, put to flight, put to rout, scatter, thrash, throw back in confusion, worst

route *n.* avenue, beat, circuit, course, direction, itinerary, journey, passage, path, road, round, run, way

routine **1.** *n.* custom, formula, grind (*Inf.*), groove, method, order, pattern, practice, procedure, programme, usage, way, wont **2.** *adj.* conventional, customary, everyday, familiar, habitual, normal, ordinary, standard, typical, usual, wonted, workaday

row[1] bank, column, file, line, queue, range, rank, sequence, series, string, tier

row[2] **1.** *n.* altercation, brawl, commotion, controversy, dispute, disturbance, falling-out (*Inf.*), fracas, fray, fuss, noise, quarrel, racket, ruckus (*Inf.*), ruction (*Inf.*), rumpus, scrap (*Inf.*), shouting match (*Inf.*), slanging match (*Brit.*), squabble, tiff, trouble, tumult, uproar **2.** *v.* argue, brawl, dispute, fight, scrap (*Inf.*), squabble, wrangle

rowdy **1.** *adj.* boisterous, disorderly, loud, loutish, noisy, obstreperous, rough, unruly, uproarious, wild **2.** *n.* brawler, hooligan, lout, rough (*Inf.*), ruffian, tearaway (*Brit.*), tough, troublemaker, yahoo

royal **1.** imperial, kinglike, kingly, monarchical, princely, queenly, regal, sovereign **2.** august, grand, impressive, magnificent, majestic, splendid, stately, superb, superior

rub *v.* **1.** abrade, caress, chafe, clean, fray, grate, knead, massage, polish, scour, scrape, shine, smooth, stroke, wipe ~*n.* **2.** caress, kneading, mas-

rubble (ˈrʌbᵊl) *n.* 1. fragments of stone *etc.* 2. builders' rubbish

rubella (ru:ˈbɛlə) *n.* mild contagious viral disease (*also* **German measles**)

rubicund (ˈru:bɪkənd) *a.* of reddish colour; ruddy

rubidium (ru:ˈbɪdɪəm) *n.* soft highly reactive radioactive element of alkali metal group

rubric (ˈru:brɪk) *n.* 1. title, heading 2. direction in liturgy 3. instruction

ruby (ˈru:bɪ) *n.* 1. precious red gem 2. its colour —*a.* 3. of this colour —**ruby wedding** fortieth wedding anniversary

ruche (ru:ʃ) *n.* strip of pleated or frilled lace *etc.* used to decorate blouses *etc.*

ruck[1] (rʌk) *n.* 1. crowd 2. common herd 3. rank and file 4. *Rugby* loose scrummage or maul

ruck[2] (rʌk) *n.* 1. crease —*v.* 2. make, become wrinkled

rucksack (ˈrʌksæk) *n.* pack carried on back, knapsack (*also* **back pack**)

ruction (ˈrʌkʃən) *n. inf.* noisy disturbance

rudder (ˈrʌdə) *n.* flat piece hinged to boat's stern or rear of aircraft used to steer

ruddy (ˈrʌdɪ) *a.* 1. of fresh or healthy red colour 2. rosy 3. florid

rude (ru:d) *a.* 1. impolite 2. coarse 3. vulgar 4. primitive 5. roughly made 6. uneducated 7. sudden, violent —ˈ**rudely** *adv.*

rudiments (ˈru:dɪmənts) *pl.n.* elements, first principles —**rudiˈmentary** *a.*

rue[1] (ru:) *v.* 1. grieve (for) —*vt.* 2. regret 3. deplore —*vi.* 4. repent —*n.* 5. *obs.* repentance —ˈ**rueful** *a.* 1. sorry 2. regretful 3. dejected 4. deplorable —ˈ**ruefully** *adv.*

rue[2] (ru:) *n.* plant with evergreen bitter leaves

ruff[1] (rʌf) *n.* 1. starched and frilled collar 2. natural collar of feathers, fur *etc.* on some birds and animals 3. type of shore bird —ˈ**ruffle** *vt.* 1. rumple, disorder 2. annoy, put out 3. frill, pleat —*n.* 4. frilled trimming

ruff[2] (rʌf) *n./v. Cards* trump

ruffian (ˈrʌfɪən) *n.* violent, lawless person —ˈ**ruffianism** *n.* —ˈ**ruffianly** *a.*

rufous (ˈru:fəs) *a.* reddish-brown

rug (rʌg) *n.* 1. small, *oft.* shaggy or thick-piled floor mat 2. thick woollen wrap, coverlet

rugby *or* **rugby football** (ˈrʌgbɪ) *n.* form of football in which the ball may be carried in the hands (*also* (*inf.*) ˈ**rugger**)

rugged (ˈrʌgɪd) *a.* 1. rough 2. broken 3. unpolished 4. harsh, austere

ruin (ˈru:ɪn) *n.* 1. decay, destruction 2. downfall 3. fallen or broken state 4. loss of wealth, position *etc.*

THESAURUS

sage, polish, shine, stroke, wipe 3. catch, difficulty, drawback, hindrance, hitch, impediment, obstacle, problem, snag, trouble

rubbish 1. debris, dregs, dross, flotsam and jetsam, garbage, junk, litter, lumber, offal, offscourings, refuse, scrap, trash, waste 2. balderdash, bosh (*Inf.*), bunkum, claptrap (*Inf.*), codswallop (*Brit. sl.*), drivel, flapdoodle (*Sl.*), gibberish, guff (*Sl.*), havers (*Scot.*), hogwash, moonshine, nonsense, piffle (*Inf.*), poppycock (*Inf.*), rot, stuff and nonsense, tommyrot, tosh (*Inf.*), twaddle

ruddy blooming, blushing, florid, flushed, fresh, glowing, healthy, red, reddish, rosy, rosy-cheeked, rubicund, sanguine, sunburnt

rude 1. abrupt, abusive, blunt, brusque, cheeky, churlish, curt, discourteous, disrespectful, ill-mannered, impertinent, impolite, impudent, inconsiderate, insolent, insulting, offhand, peremptory, short, uncivil, unmannerly 2. barbarous, boorish, brutish, coarse, crude, graceless, gross, ignorant, illiterate, loutish, low, oafish, obscene, rough, savage, scurrilous, uncivilised, uncouth, uncultured, uneducated, ungracious, unpolished, unrefined, untutored, vulgar 3. artless, crude, inartistic, inelegant, makeshift, primitive, raw, rough, rough-hewn, roughly-made, simple 4. abrupt, harsh, sharp, startling, sudden, unpleasant, violent

rudimentary basic, early, elementary, embryonic, fundamental, immature, initial, introductory, primary, primitive, undeveloped, vestigial

rudiments basics, beginnings, elements, essentials, first principles, foundation, fundamentals

rueful conscience-stricken, contrite, dismal, doleful, grievous, lugubrious, melancholy, mournful, penitent, pitiable, pitiful, plaintive, regretful, remorseful, repentant, sad, self-reproachful, sorrowful, sorry, woebegone, woeful

ruffian bruiser (*Inf.*), brute, bully, bully boy, hoodlum, hooligan, miscreant, rascal, rogue, rough (*Inf.*), roughneck (*Sl.*), rowdy, scoundrel, thug, tough, villain, wretch

ruffle 1. derange, disarrange, discompose, dishevel, disorder, mess up, rumple, tousle, wrinkle 2. agitate, annoy, confuse, disconcert, disquiet, disturb, fluster, harass, irritate, nettle, peeve (*Inf.*), perturb, put out, rattle (*Inf.*), shake up (*Inf.*), stir, torment, trouble, unsettle, upset, vex, worry

rugged 1. broken, bumpy, craggy, difficult, irregular, jagged, ragged, rocky, rough, stark, uneven 2. austere, crabbed, dour, gruff, hard, harsh, rough, rude, severe, sour, stern, surly 3. barbarous, blunt, churlish, crude, graceless, rude, uncouth, uncultured, unpolished, unrefined 4. arduous, demanding, difficult, exacting, hard, harsh, laborious, rigorous, stern, strenuous, taxing, tough, trying, uncompromising

ruin *n.* 1. bankruptcy, breakdown, collapse, crackup (*Inf.*), crash, damage, decay, defeat, destitution, destruction, devastation, disintegration, disrepair, dissolution, downfall, failure, fall, havoc, insolvency, nemesis, overthrow, ruination, subversion, the end, undoing, Waterloo, wreck, wreckage ~*v.* 2. bankrupt, break, bring down, bring to nothing, bring to ruin, crush, defeat, demolish, destroy, devastate, impoverish, lay in ruins, lay waste, overthrow, overturn, overwhelm, pauperize, raze, shatter, smash, wreak havoc upon, wreck 3. botch, damage, disfigure, injure, make a mess of, mangle, mar, mess up, spoil

ruinous 1. baleful, baneful (*Archaic*), calamitous, catastrophic, crippling, deadly, deleterious, destructive, devastating, dire, disastrous, extravagant, fatal, immoderate, injurious, murderous, noxious, pernicious, shattering, wasteful, withering 2. broken-down, decrepit, derelict, dilapidated, in ruins, ramshackle, ruined

—*pl.* **5.** ruined buildings *etc.* —*vt.* **6.** reduce to ruins **7.** bring to decay or destruction **8.** spoil **9.** impoverish —**ruiˈnation** *n.* —**ˈruinous** *a.* causing or characterized by ruin or destruction —**ˈruinously** *adv.*

rule (ruːl) *n.* **1.** principle **2.** precept **3.** authority **4.** government **5.** what is usual **6.** control **7.** measuring stick —*vt.* **8.** govern **9.** decide **10.** mark with straight lines **11.** draw (line) —**ˈruler** *n.* **1.** one who governs **2.** stick for measuring or ruling lines —**ˈruling** *n.* **1.** decision of someone in authority, such as judge **2.** one or more parallel ruled lines —*a.* **3.** controlling or exercising authority **4.** predominant —**rule of thumb** rough and practical approach, based on experience, rather than theory

rum (rʌm) *n.* spirit distilled from sugar cane

rumba *or* **rhumba** (ˈrʌmbə, ˈrum-) *n.* **1.** rhythmic dance, *orig.* Cuban **2.** music for it

rumble (ˈrʌmbəl) *vi.* **1.** make noise as of distant thunder, heavy vehicle *etc.* —*n.* **2.** such noise

rumbustious (rʌmˈbʌstjəs) *a.* boisterous, unruly

ruminate (ˈruːmɪneɪt) *vi.* **1.** chew cud **2.** ponder, meditate —**ˈruminant** *a./n.* cud-chewing (animal) —**rumiˈnation** *n.* quiet meditation and reflection —**ˈruminative** *a.*

rummage (ˈrʌmɪdʒ) *v.* **1.** search thoroughly —*n.* **2.** act of rummaging

rummy (ˈrʌmɪ) *or* **rum** *n.* card game

rumour *or U.S.* **rumor** (ˈruːmə) *n.* **1.** hearsay, common talk, unproved statement —*vt.* **2.** put round as, by way of, rumour

rump (rʌmp) *n.* **1.** hindquarters of mammal, not including legs **2.** person's buttocks

rumple (ˈrʌmpəl) *v./n.* crease, wrinkle

rumpus (ˈrʌmpəs) *n.* **1.** disturbance **2.** noise and confusion

run (rʌn) *vi.* **1.** move with more rapid gait than walking **2.** go quickly **3.** flow **4.** flee **5.** compete in race, contest, election **6.** revolve **7.** continue **8.** function **9.** travel according to schedule **10.** fuse **11.** melt **12.** spread **13.** have certain meaning —*vt.* **14.** cross by running **15.** expose oneself to (risk *etc.*) **16.** cause to run **17.** (of newspaper) print, publish **18.** land and dispose of (smuggled goods) **19.** manage **20.** operate (**ran** *pt.*, **run** *pp.*, **ˈrunning** *pr.p.*) —*n.* **21.** act, spell of running **22.** rush **23.** tendency, course **24.** period **25.** sequence **26.** heavy demand **27.** enclosure for domestic fowls, animals **28.** ride in car **29.** series of unravelled stitches, ladder **30.** score of one at cricket **31.** steep snow-covered course for skiing —**ˈrunner** *n.* **1.** racer **2.** messenger **3.** curved piece of wood on which sleigh slides **4.** any similar appliance **5.** slender stem of plant running along ground forming new roots at intervals **6.** strip of lace *etc.* placed on table for decoration **7.** strip of carpet —**ˈrunning** *a.* **1.** continuous **2.** consecutive **3.** flowing **4.** discharging **5.** effortless **6.** entered for race **7.** used for running —*n.* **8.** act of moving or flowing quickly **9.** management —**ˈrunny** *a.* tending to flow or exude moisture —**ˈrunabout** *n.* small light vehicle or aeroplane —**ˈrunaway** *n.* **1.** person or animal that runs away **2.** act or instance of running away —*a.* **3.** rising rapidly, as prices **4.** (of race *etc.*) easily won —**ˈrun-down** *n.* summary —**run-down** *a.* exhausted —**runner-up** *n.* contestant finishing race or competition in second place (*pl.* **runners-up**) —**running board** ledge beneath doors of old cars —**running commentary** commentary maintained continuously —**running head** *or* **title** *Print.* heading printed at top of every page of book —**running knot** knot that moves or slips easily —**running repairs** repairs that do not (greatly) interrupt operations —**run-of-the-mill** *a.* ordinary —**run-up** *n.* **1.** approach run by athlete for long jump, pole vault *etc.* **2.** preliminary or preparatory period —**ˈrunway** *n.* level stretch where aircraft take off and land —**run about** move busily from place to place —**run away 1.** take flight; escape **2.** go away; depart **3.** (of horse) gallop away uncontrollably —**run away with 1.** abscond or elope with **2.** make off with; steal **3.** escape from control of **4.** win easily or be assured of victory in (competition) —**run down 1.** stop working **2.** reduce **3.** exhaust **4.** denigrate —**run up 1.** amass; incur **2.** make by sewing together quickly **3.** hoist —**in the running** having a fair chance in a competition

THESAURUS

rule *n.* **1.** axiom, canon, criterion, decree, direction, guide, guideline, law, maxim, order, ordinance, precept, principle, regulation, ruling, standard, tenet **2.** administration, ascendancy, authority, command, control, direction, domination, dominion, empire, government, influence, jurisdiction, leadership, mastery, power, regime, reign, supremacy, sway **3.** condition, convention, custom, form, habit, order *or* way of things, practice, procedure, routine, wont ~*v.* **4.** administer, be in authority, be in power, be number one (*Inf.*), command, control, direct, dominate, govern, guide, hold sway, lead, manage, preside over, regulate, reign, wear the crown **5.** adjudge, adjudicate, decide, decree, determine, establish, find, judge, lay down, pronounce, resolve, settle

ruler 1. commander, controller, crowned head, emperor, empress, governor, head of state, king, leader, lord, monarch, potentate, prince, princess, queen, sovereign **2.** measure, rule, straight edge, yardstick

ruling *n.* **1.** adjudication, decision, decree, finding, judgment, pronouncement, resolution, verdict ~*adj.* **2.** commanding, controlling, dominant, governing, leading, regnant, reigning, upper **3.** chief, current, dominant, main, predominant, pre-eminent, preponderant, prevailing, prevalent, principal, regnant, supreme

ruminate brood, chew over, cogitate, consider, contemplate, deliberate, meditate, mull over, muse, ponder, reflect, revolve, think, turn over in one's mind

rumour 1. *n.* bruit (*Archaic or U.S.*), buzz, canard, gossip, hearsay, news, report, story, talk, tidings, whisper, word **2.** *v.* bruit (*Archaic or U.S.*), circulate, gossip, noise abroad, pass around, publish, put about, report, say, tell, whisper

run *v.* **1.** bolt, career, dart, dash, gallop, hare (*Brit. inf.*), hasten, hie, hotfoot, hurry, jog, leg it (*Inf.*), lope, race, rush, scamper, scramble, scud, scurry, speed, sprint **2.** abscond, beat a retreat, beat it (*Sl.*), bolt, clear out, cut and run (*Inf.*), decamp, depart, escape, flee, leg it (*Inf.*), make a run for it, make off, scarper (*Brit. sl.*), show a clean pair of heels, skedaddle (*Inf.*), take flight, take off (*Inf.*), take to one's heels **3.** course, glide, go, move, pass, roll, skim, slide **4.** go, operate, ply **5.** function, go, operate, perform, tick, work **6.** administer, be in charge of, boss (*Inf.*), carry on, conduct, control, coordinate, direct, head, lead, look after, manage, mastermind, operate, oversee, own, regulate, superintend, super-

rune (ru:n) *n.* **1.** character of earliest Germanic alphabet **2.** magic sign —ˈ**runic** *a.*

rung[1] (rʌŋ) *n.* crossbar or spoke, *esp.* in ladder

rung[2] (rʌŋ) *pp. of* RING[2]

runnel (ˈrʌnəl) *n.* **1.** gutter **2.** small brook or rivulet

running (ˈrʌnɪŋ) *see* RUN

runt (rʌnt) *n.* **1.** smallest young animal in litter **2.** *offens.* undersized person

rupee (ru:ˈpi:) *n.* monetary unit of India, Pakistan, Sri Lanka *etc.*

rupture (ˈrʌptʃə) *n.* **1.** breaking, breach **2.** hernia —*v.* **3.** break **4.** burst, sever

rural (ˈrʊərəl) *a.* **1.** of the country **2.** rustic —ˈ**ruralize** *or* **-ise** *v.* —**rural route C** mail service in rural area

rusbank (ˈrʊsbæŋk) *n.* **SA** wooden bench, settle

ruse (ru:z) *n.* stratagem, trick

rush[1] (rʌʃ) *vt.* **1.** impel, carry along violently and rapidly **2.** take by sudden assault —*vi.* **3.** cause to hurry **4.** move violently or rapidly —*n.* **5.** rushing, charge **6.** hurry **7.** eager demand **8.** heavy current (of air, water *etc.*) —*a.* **9.** done with speed **10.** characterized by speed —**rush hour** period at beginning and end of day when many people are travelling to and from work

rush[2] (rʌʃ) *n.* **1.** marsh plant with slender pithy stem **2.** the stems used as material for baskets —ˈ**rushy** *a.* full of rushes

rusk (rʌsk) *n.* kind of light biscuit

Russ. Russia(n)

russet (ˈrʌsɪt) *a.* **1.** reddish-brown —*n.* **2.** the colour

Russian (ˈrʌʃən) *n.* **1.** official language of Soviet Union: Indo-European language belonging to East Slavonic branch **2.** native or inhabitant of Russia or Soviet Union —*a.* **3.** of Russia or Soviet Union —**Russian roulette 1.** act of bravado in which each person in turn spins cylinder of revolver loaded with only one cartridge and presses trigger with barrel against his own head **2.** any foolish or potentially suicidal undertaking

rust (rʌst) *n.* **1.** reddish-brown coating formed on iron by oxidation **2.** disease of plants —*v.* **3.** contract, affect with rust —ˈ**rusty** *a.* **1.** coated with, affected by, or consisting of rust **2.** of rust colour **3.** out of practice —ˈ**rustproof** *a.*

rustic (ˈrʌstɪk) *a.* **1.** of or as of country people **2.** rural **3.** of rude manufacture **4.** made of untrimmed branches —*n.* **5.** countryman, peasant —ˈ**rusticate** *vt.*

THESAURUS

vise, take care of **7.** continue, extend, go, last, lie, proceed, range, reach, stretch **8.** cascade, discharge, flow, go, gush, issue, leak, move, pour, proceed, spill, spout, stream **9.** dissolve, fuse, go soft, liquefy, melt, turn to liquid **10.** be diffused, bleed, lose colour, mix, spread **11.** be current, circulate, climb, creep, go round, spread, trail **12.** display, feature, print, publish **13.** be a candidate, challenge, compete, contend, put oneself up for, stand, take part **14.** bootleg, deal in, ship, smuggle, sneak, traffic in ~*n.* **15.** dash, gallop, jog, race, rush, sprint, spurt **16.** drive, excursion, jaunt, journey, joy ride (*Inf.*), lift, outing, ride, round, spin (*Inf.*), trip **17.** chain, course, cycle, passage, period, round, season, sequence, series, spell, streak, stretch, string **18.** application, demand, pressure, rush **19.** ladder, rip, snag, tear **20.** course, current, direction, drift, flow, motion, movement, passage, path, progress, stream, tendency, tenor, tide, trend, way **21.** coop, enclosure, pen

runaway *n.* **1.** absconder, deserter, escapee, escaper, fugitive, refugee, truant ~*adj.* **2.** escaped, fleeing, fugitive, loose, out of control, uncontrolled, wild **3.** easily won, easy, effortless

run away 1. abscond, beat it (*Sl.*), bolt, clear out, cut and run (*Inf.*), decamp, do a bunk (*Brit. inf.*), escape, flee, make a run for it, run off, scarper (*Brit. sl.*), scram (*Inf.*), show a clean pair of heels, skedaddle (*Inf.*), take flight, take off, take to one's heels **2.** *With* **with a.** abscond, elope **b.** abscond, make off, pinch (*Inf.*), run off, snatch, steal **c.** romp home, walk it (*Inf.*), win by a mile (*Inf.*), win easily, win hands down

rundown briefing, outline, précis, recap (*Inf.*), résumé, review, run-through, sketch, summary, synopsis

run-down below par, debilitated, drained, enervated, exhausted, fatigued, out of condition, peaky, tired, under the weather (*Inf.*), unhealthy, weak, weary, worn-out

run down 1. curtail, cut, cut back, decrease, drop, pare down, reduce, trim **2.** debilitate, exhaust, sap the strength of, tire, undermine the health of, weaken **3.** belittle, criticize adversely, decry, defame, denigrate, disparage, knock (*Inf.*), revile, speak ill of, vilify

runner 1. athlete, harrier, jogger, miler, sprinter **2.** courier, dispatch bearer, errand boy, messenger **3.** offshoot, shoot, sprig, sprout, stem, stolon (*Bot.*), tendril

running *adj.* **1.** constant, continuous, incessant, in succession, on the trot (*Inf.*), perpetual, together, unbroken, unceasing, uninterrupted **2.** flowing, moving, streaming ~*n.* **3.** administration, charge, conduct, control, coordination, direction, leadership, management, organization, regulation, superintendency, supervision

run-of-the-mill average, common, commonplace, fair, mediocre, middling, modest, ordinary, passable, tolerable, undistinguished, unexceptional, unexciting, unimpressive

rupture *n.* **1.** breach, break, burst, cleavage, cleft, crack, fissure, fracture, rent, split, tear **2.** *Medical* hernia ~*v.* **3.** break, burst, cleave, crack, fracture, puncture, rend, separate, sever, split, tear

rural agrarian, agricultural, Arcadian, bucolic, countrified, country, pastoral, rustic, sylvan, upcountry

ruse artifice, blind, deception, device, dodge, hoax, imposture, manoeuvre, ploy, sham, stratagem, subterfuge, trick, wile

rush *v.* **1.** accelerate, bolt, career, dart, dash, dispatch, expedite, fly, hasten, hotfoot, hurry, hustle, lose no time, make haste, make short work of, press, push, quicken, race, run, scramble, scurry, shoot, speed, speed up, sprint, tear ~*n.* **2.** charge, dash, dispatch, expedition, haste, hurry, race, scramble, speed, surge, swiftness, urgency ~*v.* **3.** attack, capture, charge, overcome, storm, take by storm ~*n.* **4.** assault, charge, onslaught, push, storm, surge ~*adj.* **5.** brisk, cursory, emergency, expeditious, fast, hasty, hurried, prompt, quick, rapid, swift, urgent

rust *n.* **1.** corrosion, oxidation ~*v.* **2.** corrode, oxidize ~*n.* **3.** blight, mildew, mould, must, rot

1. banish from university —*vi.* **2.** live a country life —**rusti'cation** *n.* —**rus'ticity** *n.*

rustle[1] ('rʌs°l) *vi.* **1.** make sound as of blown dead leaves *etc.* —*n.* **2.** this sound

rustle[2] ('rʌs°l) *vt.* **US** steal (cattle) —'**rustler** *n.* **US** cattle thief

rut[1] (rʌt) *n.* **1.** furrow made by wheel **2.** settled habit or way of living **3.** groove —'**rutty** *a.*

rut[2] (rʌt) *n.* **1.** periodic sexual excitement among animals —*vi.* **2.** be under influence of this (**-tt-**)

ruthenium (ru:'θi:nɪəm) *n.* hard brittle white element of platinum metal group

ruthless ('ru:θlɪs) *a.* pitiless, merciless —'**ruthlessly** *adv.*

R.V. Revised Version (of the Bible)

-ry *(comb. form) see* -ERY

rye (raɪ) *n.* **1.** grain used for fodder and bread **2.** plant bearing it **3.** whisky made from rye —**rye bread** bread made entirely or partly from rye flour

rye-grass *n.* any of various kinds of grasses cultivated for fodder

THESAURUS

rustic *adj.* **1.** Arcadian, bucolic, countrified, country, pastoral, rural, sylvan, upcountry **2.** artless, homely, homespun, plain, simple, unaffected, unpolished, unrefined, unsophisticated ~*n.* **3.** boor, bumpkin, clod, clodhopper (*Inf.*), clown, country boy, country cousin, countryman, countrywoman, hillbilly, Hodge, peasant, son of the soil, swain (*Archaic*), yokel

rustle 1. *v.* crackle, crepitate, crinkle, susurrate (*Literary*), swish, whish, whisper, whoosh **2.** *n.* crackle, crepitation, crinkling, susurration *or* susurrus (*Literary*), rustling, whisper

rusty 1. corroded, oxidized, rust-covered, rusted **2.** chestnut, coppery, reddish, reddish-brown, russet, rust-coloured **3.** deficient, impaired, not what it was, out of practice, sluggish, stale, unpractised, weak

rut *n.* **1.** furrow, gouge, groove, indentation, pothole, score, track, trough, wheelmark **2.** dead end, groove, habit, humdrum existence, pattern, routine, system ~*v.* **3.** cut, furrow, gouge, groove, hole, indent, mark, score

ruthless adamant, barbarous, brutal, callous, cruel, ferocious, fierce, hard, hard-hearted, harsh, heartless, inexorable, inhuman, merciless, pitiless, relentless, remorseless, savage, severe, stern, unfeeling, unmerciful, unpitying, unrelenting, without pity

S

s *or* **S** (ɛs) *n.* **1.** 19th letter of English alphabet **2.** speech sound represented by this letter, either voiceless, as in *sit,* or voiced, as in *dogs* **3.** something shaped like S (*pl.* **s's, S's** *or* **Ss**)

S **1.** Society **2.** South(ern) **3.** *Chem.* sulphur **4.** *Phys.* entropy **5.** *Phys.* siemens **6.** *Phys.* strangeness

s. **1.** second (of time) **2.** shilling **3.** singular **4.** son **5.** succeeded

-'s (*comb. form*) **1.** forming possessive singular of nouns and some pronouns, as in *man's* **2.** forming possessive plural of nouns whose plurals do not end in *-s,* as in *children's* **3.** forming plural of numbers, letters, or symbols, as in *20's*

-s' (*comb. form*) forming possessive of plural nouns, and some singular nouns, ending in sounded *s,* as in *girls'; for goodness' sake*

S.A. **1.** Salvation Army **2.** South Africa **3.** South Australia **4.** *Sturmabteilung:* Nazi terrorist militia

Sabbath (ˈsæbəθ) *n.* **1.** Jewish and Christian day of worship and rest **2.** Sunday **—sabˈbatical** *a./n.* (denoting) leave granted to university staff *etc.* for study

sable (ˈseɪbᵊl) *n.* **1.** small weasellike Arctic animal **2.** its fur **3.** black (*pl.* **-s, ˈsable**) *—a.* **4.** black

sabot (ˈsæbəʊ) *n.* shoe made of wood, or with wooden sole

sabotage (ˈsæbətɑːʒ) *n.* **1.** intentional damage done to roads, machines *etc., esp.* secretly in war *—vt.* **2.** carry out sabotage on **3.** destroy, disrupt **—saboteur** (sæbəˈtɜː) *n.*

sabre *or U.S.* **saber** (ˈseɪbə) *n.* curved cavalry sword **—sabre rattling** menacing display of armed force

sac (sæk) *n.* pouchlike structure in an animal or vegetable body

saccharin (ˈsækərɪn) *n.* artificial sweetener **—saccharine** (ˈsækəriːn) *a. lit., fig.* excessively sweet

sacerdotal (sæsəˈdəʊtᵊl) *a.* of priests

sachet (ˈsæʃeɪ) *n.* small envelope or bag, *esp.* one holding liquid, as shampoo

sack[1] (sæk) *n.* **1.** large bag, *orig.* of coarse material **2.** pillaging **3.** *inf.* dismissal **4.** *sl.* bed *—vt.* **5.** pillage (captured town) **6.** *inf.* dismiss **—ˈsacking** *n.* material for sacks **—ˈsackcloth** *n.* coarse fabric used for sacks **—sackcloth and ashes** public display of extreme grief

sack[2] (sæk) *n. obs.* dry white wine from SW Europe

sacrament (ˈsækrəmənt) *n.* one of certain ceremonies of Christian Church, *esp.* Eucharist **—sacraˈmental** *a.*

sacred (ˈseɪkrɪd) *a.* **1.** dedicated, regarded as holy **2.** set apart, reserved **3.** inviolable **4.** connected with, intended for religious use **—ˈsacredly** *adv.* **—sacred cow** *inf.* person *etc.* held to be beyond criticism

sacrifice (ˈsækrɪfaɪs) *n.* **1.** giving something up for sake of something else **2.** act of giving up **3.** thing so given up **4.** making of offering to a god **5.** thing offered *—vt.* **6.** offer as sacrifice **7.** give up **8.** sell at very cheap price **—sacrificial** (sækrɪˈfɪʃəl) *a.*

sacrilege (ˈsækrɪlɪdʒ) *n.* misuse, desecration of something sacred **—sacrilegious** (sækrɪˈlɪdʒəs) *a.* **1.** profane **2.** desecrating

sacristan (ˈsækrɪstən) *or* **sacrist** (ˈsækrɪst, ˈseɪ-) *n.* official in charge of vestments and sacred vessels of church **—ˈsacristy** *n.* room where sacred vessels *etc.* are kept

sacrosanct (ˈsækrəʊsæŋkt) *a.* **1.** preserved by religious fear against desecration or violence **2.** inviolable **—sacroˈsanctity** *n.*

sacrum (ˈseɪkrəm) *n.* five vertebrae forming compound bone at base of spinal column (*pl.* **-cra** (-krə))

sad (sæd) *a.* **1.** sorrowful **2.** unsatisfactory, deplorable **—ˈsadden** *vt.* make sad

THESAURUS

sabotage **1.** *v.* cripple, damage, destroy, disable, disrupt, incapacitate, sap the foundations of, subvert, throw a spanner in the works (*Inf.*), undermine, vandalize, wreck **2.** *n.* damage, destruction, disruption, subversion, treachery, treason, wrecking

sack *v.* **1.** axe (*Inf.*), discharge, dismiss, fire (*Inf.*), give (someone) his cards, give (someone) his marching orders, give (someone) the boot (*Sl.*), kick out (*Inf.*) ~*n.* **2. the sack** discharge, dismissal, termination of employment, the axe (*Inf.*), the boot (*Sl.*), the chop (*Brit. sl.*), the push (*Sl.*) ~*v.* **3.** demolish, depredate (*Rare*), despoil, destroy, devastate, lay waste, loot, maraud, pillage, plunder, raid, ravage, rifle, rob, ruin, spoil, strip ~*n.* **4.** depredation, despoliation, destruction, devastation, looting, pillage, plunder, plundering, rape, rapine, ravage, ruin, waste

sackcloth and ashes compunction, contrition, grief, hair shirt, mortification, mourning, penitence, remorse, repentance

sacred **1.** blessed, consecrated, divine, hallowed, holy, revered, sanctified, venerable **2.** inviolable, inviolate, invulnerable, protected, sacrosanct, secure **3.** holy, religious, solemn

sacrifice **1.** *v.* forego, forfeit, give up, immolate, let go, lose, offer, offer up, surrender **2.** *n.* burnt offering, destruction, hecatomb, immolation, loss, oblation, renunciation, surrender

sacrilege blasphemy, desecration, heresy, impiety, irreverence, mockery, profanation, profaneness, profanity, violation

sad **1.** blue, cheerless, dejected, depressed, disconsolate, dismal, doleful, down, downcast, down in the dumps (*Inf.*), down in the mouth (*Inf.*), gloomy, glum, grief-stricken, grieved, heavy-hearted, low, low-spirited, lugubrious, melancholy, mournful, pensive, sick at heart, sombre, triste (*Archaic*), unhappy, wistful, woebegone **2.** calamitous, dark, depressing, disastrous, dismal, grievous, heart-rending, lachrymose, moving, pathetic, pitiable, pitiful, poignant, sorry, tearful, tragic, upsetting **3.** bad, deplorable, dismal, distressing, grave, lamentable, miserable, regrettable, serious, shabby, sorry, to be deplored, unfortunate, unhappy, unsatisfactory, wretched

sadden bring tears to one's eyes, cast a gloom upon, cast down, dash, deject, depress, desolate, dispirit, distress, grieve, make blue, make one's heart bleed, upset

saddle (ˈsædᵊl) *n.* **1.** rider's seat to fasten on horse, bicycle *etc.* **2.** anything resembling a saddle **3.** joint of mutton or venison **4.** ridge of hill —*vt.* **5.** put saddle on **6.** lay burden, responsibility on —*a.* **7.** resembling a saddle, as in *saddleback* —**ˈsaddler** *n.* maker of saddles *etc.* —**ˈsaddlery** *n.* —**ˈsaddlebag** *n.* small bag attached to saddle of bicycle *etc.* —**saddle soap** soft soap for preserving and cleaning leather —**ˈsaddletree** *n.* frame of saddle

Sadducee (ˈsædjʊsiː) *n. Judaism* member of ancient Jewish sect, denying resurrection of dead and validity of oral tradition

sadism (ˈseɪdɪzəm) *n.* form of (sexual) perversion marked by love of inflicting pain —**ˈsadist** *n.* —**sadistic** (səˈdɪstɪk) *a.* —**sadoˈmasochism** *n.* sadistic and masochistic elements in one person —**sadomasoˈchistic** *a.*

s.a.e. stamped addressed envelope

safari (səˈfɑːrɪ) *n.* (party making) overland (hunting) journey, *esp.* in Afr. (*pl.* **-s**) —**safari park** park where lions *etc.* may be viewed by public from cars

safe (seɪf) *a.* **1.** secure, protected **2.** uninjured, out of danger **3.** not involving risk **4.** trustworthy **5.** sure, reliable **6.** cautious —*n.* **7.** strong lockable container **8.** ventilated cupboard for meat *etc.* —**ˈsafely** *adv.* —**ˈsafety** *n.* —**safe-conduct** *n.* passport, permit to pass somewhere —**safe-deposit** *or* **safety-deposit** *n.* place with facilities for safe storage of money *etc.* —**ˈsafeguard** *n.* **1.** protection —*vt.* **2.** protect —**safety belt 1.** *see* **seat belt** *at* SEAT **2.** belt worn by person working at great height —**safety curtain** fireproof curtain that can be lowered to separate auditorium and stage —**safety glass** unsplinterable glass —**safety lamp** miner's oil lamp in which flame is surrounded by metal gauze to prevent it igniting combustible gas —**safety match** match that will light only when struck against prepared surface —**safety pin** spring clasp with covering catch, designed to shield point when closed —**safety razor** razor with guard over blade —**safety valve 1.** valve in pressure vessel that allows fluid to escape at excess pressure **2.** harmless outlet for emotion *etc.*

safflower (ˈsæflaʊə) *n.* thistlelike plant with flowers used for dye, oil

saffron (ˈsæfrən) *n.* **1.** crocus **2.** orange-coloured flavouring obtained from it **3.** the colour —*a.* **4.** orange

S.Afr. South Africa(n)

sag (sæg) *vi.* **1.** sink in middle **2.** hang sideways **3.** curve downwards under pressure **4.** give way **5.** tire **6.** (of clothes) hang loosely (**-gg-**) —*n.* **7.** droop

saga (ˈsɑːgə) *n.* **1.** legend of Norse heroes **2.** any long (heroic) story

sagacious (səˈgeɪʃəs) *a.* wise —**saˈgaciously** *adv.* —**sagacity** (səˈgæsɪtɪ) *n.*

sage[1] (seɪdʒ) *n.* **1.** very wise man —*a.* **2.** wise —**ˈsagely** *adv.*

sage[2] (seɪdʒ) *n.* aromatic herb

sagebrush (ˈseɪdʒbrʌʃ) *n.* aromatic plant of West N Amer.

Sagittarius (sædʒɪˈtɛərɪəs) *n.* (archer) 9th sign of zodiac, operative *c.* Nov. 22nd-Dec. 20th

sago (ˈseɪgəʊ) *n.* starchy cereal from powdered pith of sago palm

sahib (ˈsɑːhɪb) *n.* in India, form of address placed after man's name

said (sɛd) *pt./pp. of* SAY

sail (seɪl) *n.* **1.** piece of fabric stretched to catch wind for propelling ship *etc.* **2.** act of sailing **3.** journey upon the water **4.** ships collectively **5.** arm of windmill —*vi.* **6.** travel by water **7.** move smoothly **8.** begin voyage —*vt.* **9.** navigate —**ˈsailor** *n.* **1.** seaman **2.** one who sails —**ˈsailboard** *n.* floatable board, comprising sail, rudder and centreboard, used in windsurfing —**ˈsailcloth** *n.* **1.** fabric from which sails are made **2.** canvas-like cloth used for clothing *etc.*

saint (seɪnt; *unstressed* sənt) *n.* **1.** (title of) person formally recognized (*esp.* by R.C. Church) after death as having gained by holy deeds a special place in heaven **2.** exceptionally good person —**ˈsainted** *a.* **1.** canonized **2.** sacred —**ˈsaintliness** *n.* holiness —**ˈsaintly** *a.* —**Saint Bernard** large breed of dog with dense red-and-white coat —**Saint Leger** annual horse race run at Doncaster, England —**saintpaulia** (səntˈpɔːlɪə) *n.* Afr. violet —**Saint Swithin's Day** July 15th; if it rains on this day it is traditionally believed it will rain for the next forty days —**Saint Valentine's Day** Feb. 14th; observed as day for sending valentines —**Saint Vitus's dance** *Pathol. see* CHOREA

THESAURUS

saddle *v.* burden, charge, encumber, load, lumber (*Brit. inf.*), task, tax

sadistic barbarous, brutal, cruel, fiendish, perverse, perverted, ruthless, vicious

safe *adj.* **1.** free from harm, guarded, impregnable, in safety, intact, O.K. *or* okay (*Inf.*), out of danger, out of harm's way, protected, safe and sound, secure, undamaged, unharmed, unhurt, unscathed **2.** cautious, circumspect, conservative, dependable, discreet, on the safe side, prudent, realistic, reliable, sure, tried and true, trustworthy, unadventurous **3.** certain, impregnable, risk-free, riskless, secure, sound ~*n.* **4.** coffer, deposit box, repository, safe-deposit box, strongbox, vault

safeguard 1. *v.* defend, guard, look after, preserve, protect, screen, shield, watch over **2.** *n.* aegis, armour, bulwark, convoy, defence, escort, guard, protection, security, shield, surety

safely in one piece, in safety, safe and sound, securely, with impunity, without risk, with safety

safety assurance, cover, immunity, impregnability, protection, refuge, sanctuary, security, shelter

sage 1. *adj.* acute, canny, discerning, intelligent, judicious, learned, perspicacious, politic, prudent, sagacious, sapient, sensible, wise **2.** *n.* authority, elder, expert, guru, man of learning, master, Nestor, philosopher, pundit, savant, Solomon, Solon, wise man

sail *v.* **1.** cast *or* weigh anchor, embark, get under way, hoist the blue peter, put to sea, set sail **2.** captain, cruise, go by water, navigate, pilot, ride the waves, skipper, steer, voyage **3.** drift, float, fly, glide, scud, shoot, skim, skirr, soar, sweep, wing

sailor hearty (*Inf.*), Jack Tar, lascar, leatherneck (*Sl.*), marine, mariner, matelot (*Sl.*), navigator, salt, sea dog, seafarer, seafaring man, seaman, tar (*Inf.*)

saintly angelic, beatific, blameless, blessed, devout, full of good works, god-fearing, godly, holy, pious, religious, righteous, sainted, saintlike, sinless, virtuous, worthy

saithe (seɪθ) *n.* coalfish

sake[1] (seɪk) *n.* **1.** cause, account **2.** end, purpose **—for the sake of 1.** on behalf of **2.** to please or benefit

sake[2], **saké** *or* **saki** (ˈsɑːkɪ) *n.* Japanese alcoholic drink made of fermented rice

salaam (səˈlɑːm) *n.* **1.** bow of salutation, mark of respect in East *—vt.* **2.** salute

salacious (səˈleɪʃəs) *a.* excessively concerned with sex, lewd **—salacity** (səˈlæsɪtɪ) *n.*

salad (ˈsæləd) *n.* mixed vegetables, or fruit, used as food without cooking **—salad days** period of youth and inexperience **—salad dressing** oil, vinegar, herbs *etc.* mixed together as sauce for salad

salamander (ˈsæləmændə) *n.* **1.** variety of lizard **2.** mythical lizardlike fire spirit

salami (səˈlɑːmɪ) *n.* variety of highly-spiced sausage

salary (ˈsælərɪ) *n.* fixed regular payment to persons employed usu. in nonmanual work **—ˈsalaried** *a.*

salchow (ˈsɔːlkəʊ) *n. Figure skating* jump from inner backward edge of one foot with full turn in air, returning to outer backward edge of opposite foot

sale (seɪl) *n.* **1.** selling **2.** selling of goods at unusually low prices **3.** auction **—ˈsaleable** *or U.S.* **ˈsalable** *a.* capable of being sold **—sale of work** sale of articles, proceeds of which benefit charities **—ˈsaleroom** *n. chiefly* **UK** room where objects are displayed for sale, *esp.* by auction **—ˈsalesman** *n.* **1.** shop assistant **2.** one travelling to sell goods, *esp.* as representative of firm **—ˈsalesmanship** *n.* art of selling or presenting goods in most effective way **—sales talk** *or* **pitch** argument or other persuasion used in selling

salicin (ˈsælɪsɪn) *n.* substance obtained from poplars and used in medicine **—saliˈcylic** *a.* **—salicylic acid** white crystalline substance used in manufacture of aspirin, and as fungicide

salient (ˈseɪlɪənt) *a.* **1.** prominent, noticeable **2.** jutting out *—n.* **3.** salient angle, *esp.* in fortification **—ˈsalience** *or* **ˈsaliency** *n.*

saline (ˈseɪlaɪn) *a.* **1.** containing, consisting of a chemical salt, *esp.* common salt **2.** salty **—salinity** (səˈlɪnɪtɪ) *n.*

saliva (səˈlaɪvə) *n.* liquid which forms in mouth, spittle **—saˈlivary** *a.* **—salivate** (ˈsælɪveɪt) *v.* **—saliva test** test for use of drugs in athletes, racehorses *etc.*

Salk vaccine (sɔːlk) vaccine against poliomyelitis

sallow[1] (ˈsæləʊ) *a.* of unhealthy pale or yellowish colour

sallow[2] (ˈsæləʊ) *n.* tree or low shrub allied to the willow

sally (ˈsælɪ) *n.* **1.** rushing out, *esp.* by troops **2.** outburst **3.** witty remark *—vi.* **4.** rush **5.** set out (**ˈsallied, ˈsallying**)

Sally Lunn (lʌn) flat cake made from sweet yeast dough

salmagundi (sælməˈgʌndɪ) *n.* **1.** mixed salad dish of cooked meats, eggs, beetroot *etc.* **2.** miscellany

salmon (ˈsæmən) *n.* **1.** large silvery fish with orange-pink flesh valued as food **2.** colour of its flesh *—a.* **3.** of this colour **—salmon ladder** series of steps designed to enable salmon to move upstream to their breeding grounds

salmonella (sælməˈnɛlə) *n.* any of genus of bacteria causing disease, *esp.* food poisoning (*pl.* **-lae** (-liː))

salon (ˈsælɒn) *n.* **1.** (reception room for) guests in fashionable household **2.** commercial premises of hairdressers, beauticians *etc.*

saloon (səˈluːn) *n.* **1.** principal cabin or public room in passenger ship **2.** public room for specified use, *eg* billiards **3.** closed car with 2 or 4 doors and 4-6 seats **—saloon bar** first-class bar in hotel *etc.*

salpiglossis (sælpɪˈglɒsɪs) *n.* plant with bright funnel-shaped flowers

salsify (ˈsælsɪfɪ) *n.* purple-flowered plant with edible root

SALT (sɔːlt) Strategic Arms Limitation Talks *or* Treaty

salt (sɔːlt) *n.* **1.** white powdery or granular crystalline substance consisting mainly of sodium chloride, used to season or preserve food **2.** chemical compound of acid and metal **3.** wit *—vt.* **4.** season, sprinkle with, preserve with salt **—ˈsaltless** *a.* **—ˈsaltness** *n.* **—ˈsalty** *a.* of, like salt **—ˈsaltbush** *n.* shrub that grows in alkaline desert regions **—ˈsaltcellar** *n.* small vessel for salt at table **—salt lick** deposit, block of salt licked by game, cattle *etc.* **—ˈsaltpan** *n.* depression encrusted with salt after draining away of water **—saltpetre** *or U.S.* **saltpeter** (sɔːltˈpiːtə) *n.* potassium nitrate used in gunpowder **—ˈsaltwater** *a.* **—old salt** sailor **—salt away** *or* **down** hoard or save (money, valuables *etc.*) **—with a pinch, grain, of salt** allowing for exaggeration **—worth one's salt** efficient

saltant (ˈsæltənt) *a.* **1.** leaping **2.** dancing **—salˈtation** *n.* **—ˈsaltatory** *a.*

salubrious (səˈluːbrɪəs) *a.* favourable to health, beneficial **—saˈlubrity** *n.*

Saluki (səˈluːkɪ) *n.* tall hound with silky coat

salutary (ˈsæljʊtərɪ) *a.* wholesome, resulting in good **—ˈsalutarily** *adv.*

THESAURUS

sake 1. account, advantage, behalf, benefit, consideration, gain, good, interest, profit, regard, respect, welfare, wellbeing **2.** aim, cause, end, motive, objective, principle, purpose, reason

salary earnings, emolument, income, pay, remuneration, stipend

sale deal, disposal, marketing, selling, transaction, vending

salient arresting, conspicuous, important, jutting, marked, noticeable, outstanding, projecting, prominent, pronounced, protruding, remarkable, signal, striking

sallow anaemic, bilious, jaundiced-looking, pale, pallid, pasty, sickly, unhealthy, wan, yellowish

sally *v.* **1.** erupt, go forth, issue, rush, set out, surge *~n.* **2.** *Military* foray, incursion, offensive, raid, sortie, thrust **3.** *Fig.* bon mot, crack (*Inf.*), jest, joke, quip, retort, riposte, smart remark, wisecrack (*Inf.*), witticism

salt *n.* **1.** flavour, relish, savour, seasoning, taste **2. with a grain** *or* **pinch of salt** cynically, disbelievingly, doubtfully, sceptically, suspiciously, with reservations **3.** *Fig.* Attic wit, bite, dry humour, liveliness, piquancy, punch, pungency, sarcasm, sharpness, wit, zest, zip (*Inf.*)

salty brackish, briny, over-salted, saline, salt, salted

salubrious beneficial, good for one, healthful, health-giving, healthy, invigorating, salutary, wholesome

salutary 1. advantageous, beneficial, good, good for

salute (səˈluːt) *vt.* **1.** greet with words or sign **2.** acknowledge with praise —*vi.* **3.** perform military salute —*n.* **4.** word, sign by which one person greets another **5.** motion of arm as mark of respect to superior *etc.* in military usage **6.** firing of guns as military greeting of honour —**salutation** (sæljʊˈteɪʃən) *n.*

salvage (ˈsælvɪdʒ) *n.* **1.** act of saving ship or other property from danger of loss **2.** property so saved —*vt.* **3.** rescue, save from wreck or ruin

salvation (sælˈveɪʃən) *n.* (*esp.* of soul) fact or state of being saved —**Salvation Army** Christian body organized for evangelism and social work among poor

salve (sælv, sɑːv) *n.* **1.** healing ointment —*vt.* **2.** anoint with salve **3.** soothe

salver (ˈsælvə) *n.* (silver) tray for presentation of food, letters *etc.*

salvia (ˈsælvɪə) *n.* plant with blue or red flowers

salvo (ˈsælvəʊ) *n.* simultaneous discharge of guns *etc.* (*pl.* **-s, -es**)

sal volatile (sæl vɒˈlætɪlɪ) preparation of ammonia used to revive persons who faint *etc.*

SAM (sæm) surface-to-air missile

Sam. *Bible* Samuel

Samaritan (səˈmærɪtᵊn) *n.* **1.** native of ancient Samaria **2.** benevolent person

samarium (səˈmɛərɪəm) *n.* silvery metallic element of lanthanide series

samba (ˈsæmbə) *n.* **1.** dance of S Amer. origin **2.** music for it

same (seɪm) *a.* (*usu. with* the) **1.** identical, not different, unchanged **2.** uniform **3.** just mentioned previously —ˈ**sameness** *n.* **1.** similarity **2.** monotony

samite (ˈsæmaɪt) *n.* rich silk cloth

samovar (ˈsæməvɑː) *n.* Russian tea urn

Samoyed (səˈmɔɪed) *n.* dog with thick white coat and tightly curled tail

samp (sæmp) *n.* **SA** crushed maize used for porridge

sampan (ˈsæmpæn) *n.* small oriental boat

samphire (ˈsæmfaɪə) *n.* herb found on rocks by seashore

sample (ˈsɑːmpᵊl) *n.* **1.** specimen —*vt.* **2.** take, give sample of **3.** try **4.** test **5.** select —ˈ**sampler** *n.* beginner's exercise in embroidery —ˈ**sampling** *n.* **1.** the taking of samples **2.** sample

Samson (ˈsæmsən) *n.* **1.** *O.T.* judge of Israel, who performed herculean feats of strength until he was betrayed by his mistress Delilah **2.** any man of outstanding physical strength

samurai (ˈsæmʊraɪ) *n.* member of ancient Japanese warrior caste (*pl.* **-rai**)

sanatorium (sænəˈtɔːrɪəm) *or U.S.* **sanitarium** *n.* **1.** hospital, *esp.* for chronically ill **2.** health resort (*pl.* **-s, -ria** (-rɪə)) —ˈ**sanatory** *or* ˈ**sanative** *a.* curative

sanctify (ˈsæŋktɪfaɪ) *vt.* **1.** set apart as holy **2.** free from sin (**-fied, -fying**) —**sanctifiˈcation** *n.* —ˈ**sanctity** *n.* **1.** saintliness **2.** sacredness **3.** inviolability —ˈ**sanctuary** *n.* **1.** holy place **2.** part of church nearest altar **3.** formerly, place where fugitive was safe from arrest or violence **4.** place protected by law where animals *etc.* can live without interference —ˈ**sanctum** *n.* **1.** sacred place or shrine **2.** person's private room (*pl.* **-s, -ta**)

sanctimonious (sæŋktɪˈməʊnɪəs) *a.* making a show of piety, holiness —ˈ**sanctimony** *or* **sanctiˈmoniousness** *n.*

sanction (ˈsæŋkʃən) *n.* **1.** permission, authorization **2.** penalty for breaking law —*pl.* **3.** boycott or other coercive measure, *esp.* by one state against another regarded as having violated a law, right *etc.* —*vt.* **4.** allow, authorize, permit

sand (sænd) *n.* **1.** substance consisting of small grains of rock or mineral, *esp.* on beach or in desert —*pl.* **2.** stretches or banks of this, usu. forming seashore —*vt.* **3.** polish, smooth with sandpaper **4.** cover, mix with sand —ˈ**sander** *n.* power tool for smoothing surfaces

THESAURUS

one, helpful, practical, profitable, timely, useful, valuable **2.** healthful, healthy, salubrious, wholesome

salutation address, greeting, obeisance, salute, welcome

salute *v.* **1.** accost, acknowledge, address, doff one's cap to, greet, hail, kiss, pay one's respects to, salaam, welcome **2.** acknowledge, honour, pay tribute *or* homage to, present arms, recognize, take one's hat off to (*Inf.*) ~*n.* **3.** address, greeting, kiss, obeisance, recognition, salaam, salutation, tribute

salvage *v.* glean, recover, redeem, rescue, restore, retrieve, save

salvation deliverance, escape, lifeline, preservation, redemption, rescue, restoration, saving

same *adj.* **1.** aforementioned, aforesaid, selfsame, very **2.** alike, corresponding, duplicate, equal, equivalent, identical, indistinguishable, interchangeable, synonymous, twin **3.** changeless, consistent, constant, invariable, unaltered, unchanged, unfailing, uniform, unvarying

sameness identicalness, identity, indistinguishability, lack of variety, likeness, monotony, oneness, predictability, repetition, resemblance, similarity, standardization, tedium, uniformity

sample 1. *n.* cross section, example, exemplification, illustration, indication, instance, model, pattern, representative, sign, specimen **2.** *v.* experience, inspect, partake of, taste, test, try

sanctify absolve, anoint, bless, cleanse, consecrate, hallow, purify, set apart

sanctimonious canting, false, goody-goody (*Inf.*), holier-than-thou, hypocritical, pharisaical, pi (*Brit. sl.*), pietistic, pious, self-righteous, self-satisfied, smug, Tartuffian *or* Tartufian, too good to be true, unctuous

sanction *n.* **1.** allowance, approbation, approval, authority, authorization, backing, confirmation, countenance, endorsement, O.K. *or* okay (*Inf.*), ratification, stamp *or* seal of approval, support **2.** *Often plural* ban, boycott, coercive measures, embargo, penalty ~*v.* **3.** allow, approve, authorize, back, countenance, endorse, lend one's name to, permit, support, vouch for

sanctity 1. devotion, godliness, goodness, grace, holiness, piety, purity, religiousness, righteousness, sanctitude, spirituality **2.** inviolability, sacredness, solemnity

sanctuary 1. altar, church, Holy of Holies, sanctum, shrine, temple **2.** asylum, haven, protection, refuge, retreat, shelter **3.** conservation area, national park, nature reserve, reserve

—ˈ**sandy** *a.* **1.** like sand **2.** sand-coloured **3.** consisting of, covered with sand —ˈ**sandbag** *n.* bag filled with sand or earth, used as protection against gunfire, floodwater *etc.*, and as weapon —**sand bar** ridge of sand in river or sea, built up by action of tides *etc.* —ˈ**sandblast** *n.* **1.** jet of sand blown from a nozzle under pressure for cleaning, grinding *etc.* —*vt.* **2.** clean or decorate (surface) with sandblast —**sand castle** sand moulded into castle-like shape, *esp.* on seashore —ˈ**sandman** *n.* in folklore, magical person supposed to put children to sleep by sprinkling sand in their eyes —**sand martin** small brown European songbird with white underparts —ˈ**sandpaper** *n.* paper with sand stuck on it for scraping or polishing wood *etc.* —ˈ**sandpiper** *n.* shore bird —ˈ**sandpit** *n.* quantity of sand for children to play in —ˈ**sandshoes** *pl.n.* canvas shoes for beach wear *etc.* —ˈ**sandstone** *n.* rock composed of sand —ˈ**sandstorm** *n.* strong wind that whips up clouds of sand —**sand yacht** wheeled boat with sails, built to be propelled over sand

sandal (ˈsændᵊl) *n.* shoe consisting of sole attached by straps

sandalwood (ˈsændᵊlwʊd) *or* **sandal** *n.* sweet-scented wood

sanderling (ˈsændəlɪŋ) *n.* small sandpiper that frequents sandy shores

sandwich (ˈsænwɪdʒ, -wɪtʃ) *n.* **1.** two slices of bread with meat or other substance between —*vt.* **2.** insert between two other things —**sandwich board** one of two connected boards hung over shoulders in front of and behind person to display advertisements —**sandwich course** course consisting of alternate periods of study and industrial work —**sandwich man** man who carries sandwich board

sane (seɪn) *a.* **1.** of sound mind **2.** sensible, rational —**sanity** (ˈsænɪtɪ) *n.*

Sanforize *or* **-rise** (ˈsænfəraɪz) *vt.* **R** preshrink (fabric) using a patented process

sang (sæŋ) *pt. of* SING

sang-froid (*Fr.* sɑ̃ˈfrwa) *n.* composure; self-possession

Sangraal (sæŋˈgreɪl), **Sangrail** *or* **Sangreal** (ˈsæŋgrɪəl) *n. see* **Holy Grail** *at* HOLY

sangria (sæŋˈgriːə) *n.* Sp. drink of red wine and fruit juice, sometimes laced with brandy

sanguine (ˈsæŋgwɪn) *a.* **1.** cheerful, confident **2.** ruddy in complexion —ˈ**sanguinary** *a.* **1.** accompanied by bloodshed **2.** bloodthirsty

Sanhedrin (ˈsænɪdrɪn) *n. Judaism* supreme judicial, ecclesiastical, and administrative council of Jews in New Testament times

sanitary (ˈsænɪtərɪ) *a.* helping protection of health against dirt *etc.* —**saniˈtation** *n.* measures, apparatus for preservation of public health —**sanitary towel** *or esp. U.S.* **napkin** absorbent pad worn externally by women during menstruation

sank (sæŋk) *pt. of* SINK

sans (sænz) *prep.* without —**sans-culotte** (-kjʊˈlɒt) *n.* **1.** revolutionary of poorer class during French Revolution **2.** any revolutionary extremist

Sanskrit (ˈsænskrɪt) *n.* ancient language of India

Santa Claus (ˈsæntə klɔːz) legendary patron saint of children, who brings presents at Christmas (*also* **Father Christmas**)

sap[1] (sæp) *n.* **1.** moisture which circulates in plants **2.** energy —*vt.* **3.** drain of sap (**-pp-**) —ˈ**sapless** *a.* —ˈ**sapling** *n.* young tree

sap[2] (sæp) *vt.* **1.** undermine **2.** destroy insidiously **3.** weaken (**-pp-**) —*n.* **4.** trench dug in order to approach or undermine enemy position —ˈ**sapper** *n.* soldier in engineering unit

sap[3] (sæp) *n. inf.* gullible person —ˈ**sappy** *a.*

sapid (ˈsæpɪd) *a.* **1.** having pleasant taste **2.** agreeable or engaging —**saˈpidity** *n.*

sapient (ˈseɪpɪənt) *a.* (*usu. ironical*) wise, discerning, shrewd, knowing —ˈ**sapience** *n.*

saponify (səˈpɒnɪfaɪ) *Chem. v.* **1.** convert (fat) into soap by treatment with alkali —*vi.* **2.** undergo reaction in which ester is hydrolysed to acid and alcohol as result of treatment with alkali —**saponifiˈcation** *n.*

Sapphic (ˈsæfɪk) *a.* **1.** of Sappho, 6th-cent. B.C. Grecian poetess **2.** of metre associated with Sappho —*n.* **3.** Sapphic verse —ˈ**sapphism** *n.* lesbianism

sapphire (ˈsæfaɪə) *n.* **1.** (usu. blue) precious stone **2.** deep blue —*a.* **3.** of sapphire (blue) **4.** denoting 45th anniversary

saprophyte (ˈsæprəʊfaɪt) *n.* plant that lives on dead organic matter

saraband *or* **sarabande** (ˈsærəbænd) *n.* **1.** slow, stately Sp. dance **2.** music for it

Saracen (ˈsærəsᵊn) *n.* **1.** Arabian **2.** adherent of Mohammedanism in Syria and Palestine **3.** infidel —**Saracenic** (særəˈsɛnɪk) *a.*

sarcasm (ˈsɑːkæzəm) *n.* **1.** bitter or wounding ironic remark **2.** such remarks **3.** taunt; sneer **4.** irony **5.** use of such expressions —**sarˈcastic** *a.* —**sarˈcastically** *adv.*

sarcoma (sɑːˈkəʊmə) *n. Pathol.* usu. malignant tu-

THESAURUS

sane 1. all there (*Inf.*), *compos mentis*, in one's right mind, in possession of all one's faculties, lucid, mentally sound, normal, of sound mind, rational **2.** balanced, judicious, level-headed, moderate, reasonable, sensible, sober, sound

sanguine 1. animated, assured, buoyant, cheerful, confident, hopeful, in good heart, lively, optimistic spirited **2.** florid, red, rubicund, ruddy

sanitary clean, germ-free, healthy, hygienic, salubrious, unpolluted, wholesome

sanity 1. mental health, normality, rationality, reason, right mind (*Inf.*), saneness, stability **2.** common sense, good sense, judiciousness, level-headedness, rationality, sense, soundness of judgment

sap[1] *n.* animating force, essence, lifeblood, vital fluid

sap[2] *v.* bleed, deplete, devitalize, drain, enervate, erode, exhaust, rob, undermine, weaken, wear down

sap[3] *n. Inf.* charlie (*Brit. inf.*), chump (*Inf.*), drip (*Inf.*), fool, gull (*Archaic*), idiot, jerk (*Sl.*), muggins (*Brit. sl.*), nincompoop, ninny, nitwit, noddy, noodle, Simple Simon, simpleton, twit (*Inf.*), weakling, wet

sarcasm bitterness, causticness, contempt, cynicism, derision, irony, mockery, mordancy, satire, scorn, sneering

sarcastic acerbic, acrimonious, backhanded, biting, caustic, contemptuous, cutting, cynical, derisive, disparaging, ironical, mocking, mordant, sardonic, sarky (*Brit. inf.*), satirical, sharp, sneering, taunting

mour arising from connective tissue (*pl.* **-s, -mata** (-mətə)) **—sar'comatous** *a.*

sarcophagus (sɑːˈkɒfəgəs) *n.* stone coffin (*pl.* **-gi** (-gaɪ), **-es**)

sard (sɑːd) *or* **sardius** (ˈsɑːdɪəs) *n.* precious stone, variety of chalcedony

sardine (sɑːˈdiːn) *n.* small fish of herring family, usu. preserved in oil

sardonic (sɑːˈdɒnɪk) *a.* characterized by irony, mockery or derision

sardonyx (ˈsɑːdənɪks) *n.* gemstone, variety of chalcedony

sargassum (sɑːˈgæsəm) *n.* gulfweed, type of floating seaweed

sari (ˈsɑːrɪ) *n.* Hindu woman's robe (*pl.* **-s**)

sarong (səˈrɒŋ) *n.* skirtlike garment worn in Asian and Pacific countries

sarsaparilla (sɑːsəpəˈrɪlə) *n.* (flavour of) drink, *orig.* made from root of plant

sartorial (sɑːˈtɔːrɪəl) *a.* of tailor, tailoring or men's clothes

sash[1] (sæʃ) *n.* decorative belt or ribbon, wound around the body

sash[2] (sæʃ) *n.* wooden window frame opened by moving up and down in grooves

saskatoon (sæskəˈtuːn) *n.* Canad. shrub with purplish berries

sassafras (ˈsæsəfræs) *n.* laurel-like tree with aromatic bark used medicinally

Sassenach (ˈsæsənæx) *n. Scot.* English person

sat (sæt) *pt./pp. of* SIT

Sat. 1. Saturday 2. Saturn

Satan (ˈseɪtᵊn) *n.* the devil **—satanic(al)** (səˈtænɪk(ᵊl)) *a.* devilish, fiendish **—satanically** (səˈtænɪkəlɪ) *adv.* **—ˈSatanism** *n.* **1.** worship of Satan **2.** satanic disposition **—ˈSatanist** *n./a.*

satchel (ˈsætʃəl) *n.* small bag, *esp.* for school books

sate (seɪt) *vt.* satisfy (a desire or appetite) fully or excessively

sateen (sæˈtiːn) *n.* glossy linen or cotton fabric that resembles satin

satellite (ˈsætᵊlaɪt) *n.* **1.** celestial body or man-made projectile orbiting planet **2.** person, country *etc.* dependent on another

satiate (ˈseɪʃɪeɪt) *vt.* **1.** satisfy to the full **2.** surfeit **—ˈsatiable** *a.* **—satiˈation** *n.* **—satiety** (səˈtaɪɪtɪ) *n.* feeling of having had too much

satin (ˈsætɪn) *n.* fabric (of silk, rayon *etc.*) with glossy surface on one side **—ˈsatiny** *a.* of, like satin **—ˈsatinwood** *n.* any of various tropical trees that yield hard satiny wood

satire (ˈsætaɪə) *n.* **1.** composition in which vice, folly or foolish person is held up to ridicule **2.** use of ridicule or sarcasm to expose vice and folly **—satiric(al)** (səˈtɪrɪk(ᵊl)) *a.* **1.** of nature of satire **2.** sarcastic **3.** bitter **—satirist** (ˈsætərɪst) *n.* **—satirize** *or* **-rise** (ˈsætəraɪz) *vt.* **1.** make object of satire **2.** censure thus

satisfy (ˈsætɪsfaɪ) *vt.* **1.** content, meet wishes of **2.** pay **3.** fulfil, supply adequately **4.** convince (**-fied, -fying**) **—satisˈfaction** *n.* **—satisˈfactory** *a.*

satsuma (sætˈsuːmə) *n.* kind of small orange

saturate (ˈsætʃəreɪt) *vt.* **1.** soak thoroughly **2.** cause to absorb maximum amount **3.** *Chem.* cause (substance) to combine to its full capacity with another **4.** shell or bomb heavily **—satuˈration** *n.* act, result of saturating

Saturday (ˈsætədɪ) *n.* seventh day of week

Saturn (ˈsætɜːn) *n.* **1.** Roman god **2.** one of planets **—Saturnalia** (sætəˈneɪlɪə) *n.* **1.** ancient festival of Saturn **2.** (*also* **s-**) noisy revelry, orgy **—ˈsaturnine** *a.* **1.** gloomy **2.** sluggish in temperament, dull, morose

satyr (ˈsætə) *n.* **1.** woodland deity, part man, part goat **2.** lustful man **—satyric** (səˈtɪrɪk) *a.*

sauce (sɔːs) *n.* **1.** liquid added to food to enhance

THESAURUS

sardonic bitter, cynical, derisive, dry, ironical, jeering, malevolent, malicious, malignant, mocking, mordant, sarcastic, wry

Satan Apollyon, Beelzebub, Lord of the Flies, Lucifer, Mephistopheles, Old Nick, Prince of Darkness, The Devil, The Evil One

satanic accursed, black, demoniac, demoniacal, demonic, devilish, diabolic, evil, fiendish, hellish, infernal, inhuman, iniquitous, malevolent, malignant, wicked

satellite *n.* **1.** communications satellite, moon, sputnik **2.** *Fig.* attendant, dependant, follower, hanger-on, lackey, minion, parasite, retainer, sidekick (*Sl.*), sycophant, vassal

satiate 1. cloy, glut, gorge, jade, nauseate, overfill, stuff **2.** sate, satisfy, slake, surfeit

satire burlesque, caricature, irony, lampoon, parody, pasquinade, raillery, ridicule, sarcasm, send-up (*Brit. inf.*), skit, spoof (*Inf.*), takeoff (*Inf.*), travesty, wit

satirical, satiric biting, bitter, burlesque, caustic, censorious, cutting, cynical, incisive, ironical, mocking, mordant, pungent, Rabelaisian, sarcastic, sardonic, taunting

satirize abuse, burlesque, censure, criticize, deride, hold up to ridicule, lampoon, lash, parody, ridicule, send up (*Brit. inf.*), take off (*Inf.*), travesty

satisfaction 1. comfort, complacency, content, contentedness, contentment, ease, enjoyment, gratification, happiness, peace of mind, pleasure, pride, repletion, satiety, well-being **2.** achievement, appeasing, assuaging, fulfilment, gratification, resolution, settlement

satisfactory acceptable, adequate, all right, average, competent, fair, good enough, passable, sufficient, suitable, up to standard, up to the mark

satisfied at ease, complacent, content, contented, convinced, easy in one's mind, happy, like the cat that swallowed the canary (*Inf.*), pacified, positive, smug, sure

satisfy 1. appease, assuage, content, fill, gratify, indulge, mollify, pacify, please, quench, sate, satiate, slake, surfeit **2.** answer, be enough (adequate, sufficient), come up to expectations, do, fill the bill (*Inf.*), fulfil, meet, qualify, serve, serve the purpose, suffice **3.** assure, convince, dispel (someone's) doubts, persuade, put (someone's) mind at rest, quiet, reassure **4.** answer, comply with, discharge, fulfil, meet, pay (off), settle, square up

satisfying cheering, convincing, filling, gratifying, pleasing, pleasurable, satisfactory

saturate douse, drench, drouk (*Scot.*), imbue, impregnate, ret (*used of flax, etc.*), soak, souse, steep, suffuse, waterlog, wet through

flavour **2.** *inf.* impudence —*vt.* **3.** add sauce to **4.** *inf.* be cheeky, impudent to —**ˈsaucily** *adv.* —**ˈsaucy** *a.* impudent —**saucepan** (ˈsɔːspən) *n.* cooking pot with long handle

saucer (ˈsɔːsə) *n.* **1.** curved plate put under cup **2.** shallow depression

sauerkraut (ˈsauəkraut) *n.* Ger. dish of finely shredded and pickled cabbage

sauna (ˈsɔːnə) *n.* steam bath, *orig.* Finnish

saunter (ˈsɔːntə) *vi.* **1.** walk in leisurely manner, stroll —*n.* **2.** leisurely walk or stroll

-saur *or* **-saurus** (*comb. form*) lizard, as in *dinosaur*

saurian (ˈsɔːrɪən) *n.* one of the order of reptiles including the alligator, lizard *etc.*

sausage (ˈsɒsɪdʒ) *n.* minced meat enclosed in thin tube of animal intestine or synthetic material —**sausage roll** pastry cylinder filled with sausage

sauté (ˈsəuteɪ) *a.* fried quickly with little fat

Sauternes (səuˈtɜːn) *n.* sweet white Fr. wine

savage (ˈsævɪdʒ) *a.* **1.** wild **2.** ferocious **3.** brutal **4.** uncivilized, primitive —*n.* **5.** member of savage tribe, barbarian —*vt.* **6.** attack ferociously —**ˈsavagely** *adv.* —**ˈsavagery** *n.*

savanna *or* **savannah** (səˈvænə) *n.* extensive open grassy plain

savant (ˈsævənt) *n.* man of learning

save (seɪv) *vt.* **1.** rescue, preserve **2.** protect **3.** secure **4.** keep for future, lay by **5.** prevent need of **6.** spare **7.** except —*vi.* **8.** lay by money —*prep.* **9.** *obs.* except —*conj.* **10.** *obs.* but —**ˈsaving** *a.* **1.** frugal **2.** thrifty **3.** delivering from sin **4.** excepting **5.** compensating —*prep.* **6.** excepting —*n.* **7.** economy —*pl.* **8.** money, earnings put by for future use —**savings bank** bank that accepts savings of depositors and pays interest on them —**save as you earn** **UK** savings scheme in which monthly contributions earn tax-free interest

saveloy (ˈsævɪlɔɪ) *n.* type of smoked red sausage

saviour *or* *U.S.* **savior** (ˈseɪvjə) *n.* **1.** person who rescues another **2.** (**S-**) Christ

savoir-faire (ˈsævwɑːˈfɛə; *Fr.* savwarˈfɛːr) *n.* ability to do, say, the right thing in any situation

savory (ˈseɪvərɪ) *n.* aromatic herb used in cooking

savour *or* *U.S.* **savor** (ˈseɪvə) *n.* **1.** characteristic taste **2.** flavour **3.** odour **4.** distinctive quality —*vi.* **5.** have particular smell or taste **6.** (*with* of) have suggestion (of) —*vt.* **7.** give flavour to **8.** have flavour of **9.** enjoy, appreciate —**ˈsavoury** *or* *U.S.* **ˈsavory** *a.* **1.** attractive to taste or smell **2.** not sweet —*n.* **3.** savoury snack (before meal)

savoy (səˈvɔɪ) *n.* variety of cabbage

savvy (ˈsævɪ) *sl.* *v.* **1.** understand —*n.* **2.** wits, intelligence

saw[1] (sɔː) *n.* **1.** tool for cutting wood *etc.* by tearing it with toothed edge —*vt.* **2.** cut with saw —*vi.* **3.** make movements of sawing (**sawed, sawn, ˈsawing**) —**ˈsawyer** *n.* one who saws timber —**ˈsawbones** *n. sl.* surgeon or doctor —**ˈsawdust** *n.* fine wood fragments made in sawing —**ˈsawfish** *n.* fish armed with toothed snout —**ˈsawhorse** *n.* stand for supporting timber during sawing —**ˈsawmill** *n.* mill where timber is sawn into planks *etc.*

saw[2] (sɔː) *pt. of* SEE[1]

saw[3] (sɔː) *n.* wise saying, proverb

sawn (sɔːn) *pp. of* SAW[1]

sax (sæks) *inf.* saxophone

saxe (sæks) *n.* shade of blue

THESAURUS

sauce *n.* backchat (*Inf.*), brass (*Inf.*), cheek (*Inf.*), cheekiness, disrespectfulness, impertinence, impudence, insolence, lip (*Sl.*), nerve (*Inf.*), rudeness

saucy cheeky (*Inf.*), disrespectful, flip (*Inf.*), flippant, forward, fresh (*Inf.*), impertinent, impudent, insolent, pert, presumptuous, rude, smart-alecky (*Inf.*)

saunter **1.** *v.* amble, dally, linger, loiter, meander, mosey (*Inf.*), ramble, roam, rove, stravaig (*Scot. & Northern English dialect*), stroll, take a stroll, tarry, wander **2.** *n.* airing, amble, constitutional, promenade, ramble, stroll, turn, walk

savage *adj.* **1.** feral, rough, rugged, uncivilized, uncultivated, undomesticated, untamed, wild **2.** barbarous, beastly, bestial, bloodthirsty, bloody, brutal, brutish, cruel, devilish, diabolical, ferocious, fierce, harsh, inhuman, merciless, murderous, pitiless, ravening, ruthless, sadistic, vicious **3.** in a state of nature, nonliterate, primitive, rude, unspoilt ~*n.* **4.** autochthon, barbarian, heathen, indigene, native, primitive **5.** barbarian, bear, boor, roughneck (*Sl.*), yahoo, yobbo (*Brit. sl.*) ~*v.* **6.** attack, lacerate, mangle, maul, tear into (*Inf.*)

savagery barbarity, bestiality, bloodthirstiness, brutality, cruelty, ferocity, fierceness, inhumanity, ruthlessness, sadism, viciousness

save **1.** bail (someone) out, come to (someone's) rescue, deliver, free, liberate, recover, redeem, rescue, salvage, set free **2.** be frugal, be thrifty, collect, economize, gather, hide away, hoard, hold, husband, keep, keep up one's sleeve (*Inf.*), lay by, put aside for a rainy day, put by, reserve, retrench, salt away, set aside, store, tighten one's belt (*Inf.*), treasure up **3.** conserve, guard, keep safe, look after, preserve, protect, safeguard, screen, shield, take care of **4.** hinder, obviate, prevent, rule out, spare

saving **1.** *adj.* compensatory, extenuating, qualifying, redeeming **2.** *n.* bargain, discount, economy, reduction

savings fund, nest egg, provision for a rainy day, reserves, resources, store

saviour defender, deliverer, friend in need, Good Samaritan, guardian, knight in shining armour, liberator, preserver, protector, rescuer, salvation

Saviour Our *or* **The** Christ, Jesus, Messiah, Redeemer

savoir-faire accomplishment, address, diplomacy, discretion, finesse, poise, social graces, social knowhow (*Inf.*), tact, urbanity

savour *n.* **1.** flavour, piquancy, relish, smack, smell, tang, taste **2.** distinctive quality, excitement, flavour, interest, salt, spice, zest ~*v.* **3.** *Often with* **of** bear the hallmarks, be indicative, be suggestive, partake, show signs, smack, suggest, verge on **4.** appreciate, delight in, enjoy, enjoy to the full, gloat over, like, luxuriate in, partake, relish, revel in smack one's lips over

savoury agreeable, appetizing, dainty, delectable, delicious, full-flavoured, good, luscious, mouthwatering, palatable, piquant, rich, scrumptious (*Inf.*), spicy, tangy, tasty, toothsome

saw adage, aphorism, apophthegm, axiom, byword, dictum, gnome, maxim, proverb, saying

saxhorn (ˈsækshɔːn) *n.* instrument of trumpet class

saxifrage (ˈsæksɪfreɪdʒ) *n.* Alpine or rock plant

Saxon (ˈsæksən) *n.* **1.** member of West Germanic people who settled widely in Europe in the early Middle Ages —*a.* **2.** of this people or their language

saxophone (ˈsæksəfəʊn) *n.* keyed wind instrument

say (seɪ) *vt.* **1.** speak **2.** pronounce **3.** state **4.** express **5.** take as example or as near enough **6.** make a case for (**said** *pt./pp.*, ˈ**saying** *pr.p.*, **says** (sɛz) *3rd pers. sing. pres. ind.*) —*n.* **7.** what one has to say **8.** chance of saying it **9.** share in decision —ˈ**saying** *n.* maxim, proverb

S.A.Y.E. save as you earn

Sb *Chem.* antimony

Sc *Chem.* scandium

SC South Carolina

sc. **1.** scale **2.** scene **3.** science **4.** screw **5.** scruple (unit of weight)

s.c. *Print.* small capitals

S.C. **1.** A, NZ School Certificate **2.** Signal Corps **3.** C Social Credit

scab (skæb) *n.* **1.** crust formed over wound **2.** skin disease **3.** disease of plants **4.** *offens.* blackleg —ˈ**scabby** *a.*

scabbard (ˈskæbəd) *n.* sheath for sword or dagger

scabies (ˈskeɪbiːz) *n.* contagious skin disease —ˈ**scabious** *a.* having scabies, scabby

scabrous (ˈskeɪbrəs) *a.* **1.** having rough surface **2.** thorny **3.** indecent **4.** risky

scaffold (ˈskæfəld) *n.* **1.** temporary platform for workmen **2.** gallows —ˈ**scaffolding** *n.* (material for building) scaffold

scalar (ˈskeɪlə) *n./a.* (variable quantity, *eg* time) having magnitude but no direction

scalawag (ˈskæləwæg) *n. see* SCALLYWAG

scald (skɔːld) *vt.* **1.** burn with hot liquid or steam **2.** clean, sterilize with boiling water **3.** heat (liquid) almost to boiling point —*n.* **4.** injury by scalding

scale[1] (skeɪl) *n.* **1.** graduated table or sequence of marks at regular intervals used as reference or for fixing standards, as in making measurements, in music *etc.* **2.** ratio of size between a thing and a model or map of it **3.** (relative) degree, extent —*vt.* **4.** climb —*a.* **5.** proportionate —**scale up** *or* **down** increase or decrease proportionately in size

scale[2] (skeɪl) *n.* **1.** one of the thin, overlapping plates covering fishes and reptiles **2.** thin flake **3.** incrustation which forms in boilers *etc.* —*vt.* **4.** remove scales from —*vi.* **5.** come off in scales —ˈ**scaly** *a.* resembling or covered in scales

scale[3] (skeɪl) *n.* (*chiefly in pl.*) **1.** weighing instrument —*vt.* **2.** weigh in scales **3.** have weight of

scalene (ˈskeɪliːn) *a.* (of triangle) with three unequal sides

scallion (ˈskæljən) *n.* onion with small bulb and long leaves

scallop (ˈskɒləp, ˈskæl-) *n.* **1.** edible shellfish **2.** edging in small curves like edge of scallop shell —*vt.* **3.** shape like scallop shell **4.** cook in scallop shell or dish like one

scallywag (ˈskælɪwæg) *n. inf.* scamp, rascal (*also* ˈ**scalawag**, ˈ**scallawag**)

scalp (skælp) *n.* **1.** skin and hair of top of head —*vt.* **2.** cut off scalp of

scalpel (ˈskælpᵊl) *n.* small surgical knife

scamp (skæmp) *n.* **1.** mischievous person or child —*vt.* **2.** skimp

scamper (ˈskæmpə) *vi.* **1.** run about **2.** run hastily from place to place —*n.* **3.** act of scampering

scampi (ˈskæmpɪ) *n.* (*with sing. or pl. v.*) large prawns usu. eaten fried in batter

scan (skæn) *vt.* **1.** look at carefully, scrutinize **2.** measure or read (verse) by metrical feet **3.** examine, search by systematically varying the direction of a radar or sonar beam **4.** glance over quickly —*vi.* **5.** (of verse) conform to metrical rules (**-nn-**) —*n.* **6.** scanning —ˈ**scanner** *n.* device, *esp.* electronic, which scans —ˈ**scansion** *n.* analysis of metrical structure of verse

Scand. *or* **Scan.** Scandinavia(n)

scandal (ˈskændᵊl) *n.* **1.** action, event generally considered disgraceful **2.** malicious gossip —ˈ**scandalize** *or* **-ise** *vt.* shock —ˈ**scandalous** *a.* outrageous, dis-

THESAURUS

say *v.* **1.** add, affirm, announce, assert, come out with (*Inf.*), declare, give voice *or* utterance to, maintain, mention, pronounce, put into words, remark, speak, state, utter, voice **2.** answer, disclose, divulge, give as one's opinion, make known, reply, respond, reveal, tell **3.** communicate, convey, express, give the impression that, imply ~*n.* **4.** crack (*Inf.*), turn (chance, opportunity) to speak, voice, vote **5.** authority, clout (*Inf.*), influence, power, sway, weight

saying adage, aphorism, apophthegm, axiom, byword, dictum, gnome, maxim, proverb, saw

scale[1] *n.* **1.** calibration, degrees, gamut, gradation, graduated system, graduation, hierarchy, ladder, pecking order (*Inf.*), progression, ranking, register, seniority system, sequence, series, spectrum, spread, steps **2.** proportion, ratio **3.** degree, extent, range, reach, scope, way ~*v.* **4.** ascend, clamber, climb, escalade, mount, surmount **5.** adjust, proportion, prorate (*Chiefly U.S.*), regulate

scale[2] *n.* flake, lamina, layer, plate, squama (*Biol.*)

scaly flaky, furfuraceous (*Medical*), scabrous, scurfy, squamous *or* squamose (*Biol.*), squamulose

scamp devil, imp, knave (*Archaic*), mischief-maker, monkey, prankster, rascal, rogue, scallywag (*Inf.*), scapegrace, tyke (*Inf.*), wretch

scamper dart, dash, fly, hasten, hie (*Archaic*), hurry, romp, run, scoot, scurry, scuttle, sprint

scan check, con (*Archaic*), examine, glance over, investigate, look one up and down, look through, run one's eye over, run over, scour, scrutinize, search, size up (*Inf.*), skim, survey, sweep, take stock of

scandal **1.** crime, crying shame (*Inf.*), disgrace, embarrassment, offence, sin, wrongdoing **2.** abuse, aspersion, backbiting, dirt, dirty linen (*Inf.*), gossip, rumours, skeleton in the cupboard, slander, talk, tattle

scandalize affront, appal, cause a few raised eyebrows (*Inf.*), disgust, horrify, offend, outrage, shock

scandalous atrocious, disgraceful, disreputable, highly improper, infamous, monstrous, odious, opprobrious, outrageous, shameful, shocking, unseemly

graceful —ˈ**scandalmonger** *n.* person who spreads gossip *etc.*

Scandinavian (skændɪˈneɪvɪən) *a.* **1.** of Scandinavia, its inhabitants or their languages —*n.* **2.** native or inhabitant of Scandinavia

scandium (ˈskændɪəm) *n.* rare silvery-white metallic element occurring in numerous minerals

scant (skænt) *a.* barely sufficient or not sufficient —ˈ**scantily** *adv.* —ˈ**scanty** *a.*

scapegoat (ˈskeɪpgəʊt) *n.* person bearing blame due to others

scapegrace (ˈskeɪpgreɪs) *n.* mischievous person

scapula (ˈskæpjʊlə) *n.* shoulder blade (*pl.* **-lae** (-liː), **-s**) —ˈ**scapular** *a.* **1.** of scapula —*n.* **2.** part of habit of certain religious orders in R.C. Church

scar[1] (skɑː) *n.* **1.** mark left by healed wound, burn or sore **2.** change resulting from emotional distress —*v.* **3.** mark, heal with scar (**-rr-**)

scar[2] (skɑː) *n.* bare craggy rock formation

scarab (ˈskærəb) *n.* **1.** sacred beetle of ancient Egypt **2.** gem cut in shape of this

scarce (skɛəs) *a.* **1.** hard to find **2.** existing or available in insufficient quantity **3.** uncommon —ˈ**scarcely** *adv.* **1.** only just **2.** not quite **3.** definitely or probably not —ˈ**scarceness** *or* ˈ**scarcity** *n.*

scare (skɛə) *vt.* **1.** frighten —*n.* **2.** fright, sudden panic —ˈ**scary** *a.* —ˈ**scarecrow** *n.* **1.** thing set up to frighten birds from crops **2.** badly dressed or miserable-looking person —ˈ**scaremonger** *n.* one who spreads alarming rumours

scarf[1] (skɑːf) *n.* long narrow strip, large piece of material to put round neck, head *etc.* (*pl.* **-s, scarves**)

scarf[2] (skɑːf) *n.* **1.** part cut away from each of two pieces of timber to be jointed longitudinally **2.** joint so made (*pl.* **-s**) —*vt.* **3.** cut or join in this way —ˈ**scarfing** *n.*

scarify (ˈskɛərɪfaɪ, ˈskærɪ-) *vt.* **1.** scratch, cut slightly all over **2.** lacerate **3.** stir surface soil of **4.** criticize mercilessly (**-fied, -fying**) —**scarifiˈcation** *n.*

scarlatina (skɑːləˈtiːnə) *n.* scarlet fever

scarlet (ˈskɑːlɪt) *n.* **1.** brilliant red colour **2.** cloth or clothing of this colour, *esp.* military uniform —*a.* **3.** of this colour **4.** immoral, *esp.* unchaste —**scarlet fever** infectious fever with scarlet rash

scarp (skɑːp) *n.* **1.** steep slope **2.** inside slope of ditch in fortifications

scarper (ˈskɑːpə) *vi. sl.* depart in haste

scarves (skɑːvz) *n., pl. of* SCARF[1]

scat[1] (skæt) *vi. inf.* (*usu. imp.*) go away

scat[2] (skæt) *n. Jazz* singing characterized by improvised vocal sounds instead of words

scathe (skeɪð) (*usu. now as pp./a.* **scathed** & **unˈscathed**) *n.* **1.** injury, harm, damage —*vt.* **2.** injure, damage —ˈ**scathing** *a.* **1.** harshly critical **2.** cutting **3.** damaging

scatology (skæˈtɒlədʒɪ) *n.* **1.** scientific study of excrement, *esp.* in medicine and palaeontology **2.** preoccupation with obscenity, *esp.* in form of references to excrement —**scatoˈlogical** *a.*

scatter (ˈskætə) *vt.* **1.** throw in various directions **2.** put here and there **3.** sprinkle —*vi.* **4.** disperse —*n.* **5.** sprinkling —ˈ**scatterbrain** *n.* silly, careless person —ˈ**scatty** *a. inf.* silly, useless

scavenge (ˈskævɪndʒ) *v.* search for (anything usable), *usu.* among discarded material —ˈ**scavenger** *n.* **1.** person who scavenges **2.** animal, bird which feeds on refuse

Sc.D. Doctor of Science

S.C.E. Scottish Certificate of Education

scene (siːn) *n.* **1.** place of action of novel, play *etc.* **2.** place of any action **3.** subdivision of play **4.** view **5.** episode **6.** display of strong emotion —**scenario** (sɪˈnɑːrɪəʊ) *n.* summary of plot (of play *etc.*) or plan (*pl.* **-s**) —ˈ**scenery** *n.* **1.** natural features of district **2.** constructions of wood, canvas *etc.* used on stage to represent a place where action is happening —ˈ**scenic** *a.* **1.** picturesque **2.** of or on the stage

scent (sɛnt) *n.* **1.** distinctive smell, *esp.* pleasant one **2.** trail, clue **3.** perfume —*vt.* **4.** detect or track by or as if by smell **5.** suspect, sense **6.** fill with fragrance

THESAURUS

scant bare, barely sufficient, deficient, inadequate, insufficient, limited, little, minimal, sparse

scanty bare, deficient, exiguous, inadequate, insufficient, meagre, narrow, poor, restricted, scant, short, skimpy, slender, sparing, sparse, thin

scapegoat fall guy (*Inf.*), whipping boy

scar **1.** *n.* blemish, cicatrix, injury, mark, wound **2.** *v.* brand, damage, disfigure, mark

scarce at a premium, deficient, few, few and far between, infrequent, in short supply, insufficient, rare, seldom met with, uncommon, unusual, wanting

scarcely **1.** barely, hardly, only just, scarce (*Archaic*) **2.** by no means, definitely not, hardly, not at all, on no account, under no circumstances

scarcity dearth, deficiency, infrequency, insufficiency, lack, paucity, poverty, rareness, shortage, undersupply, want

scare **1.** *v.* affright (*Archaic*), alarm, daunt, dismay, frighten, give (someone) a fright, give (someone) a turn (*Inf.*), intimidate, panic, put the wind up (someone) (*Inf.*), shock, startle, terrify, terrorize **2.** *n.* alarm, alert, fright, panic, shock, start, terror

scathing belittling, biting, brutal, caustic, critical, cutting, harsh, mordant, sarcastic, scornful, searing, trenchant, withering

scatter **1.** broadcast, diffuse, disseminate, fling, litter, shower, sow, spread, sprinkle, strew **2.** disband, dispel, disperse, dissipate, disunite, put to flight, separate

scatterbrain bird-brain (*Inf.*), butterfly, featherbrain, flibbertigibbet, grasshopper mind, madcap

scenario master plan, outline, résumé, rundown, scheme, sequence of events, sketch, story line, summary, synopsis

scene **1.** area, locality, place, position, setting, site, situation, spot, whereabouts **2.** backdrop, background, location, *mise en scène*, set, setting **3.** act, division, episode, incident, part, stage **4.** carry-on (*Brit. inf.*), commotion, confrontation, display of emotion, exhibition, fuss, performance, row, tantrum, to-do, upset **5.** landscape, panorama, prospect, view, vista

scenery **1.** landscape, surroundings, terrain, view, vista **2.** *Theatre* backdrop, décor, flats, *mise en scène*, set, setting, stage set

scent *n.* **1.** aroma, bouquet, fragrance, odour, perfume, redolence, smell **2.** spoor, track, trail ~*v.* **3.** be

sceptic *or U.S.* **skeptic** (ˈskɛptɪk) *n.* **1.** one who maintains doubt or disbelief **2.** agnostic **3.** unbeliever —**ˈsceptical** *or U.S.* **ˈskeptical** *a.* —**ˈscepticism** *or U.S.* **ˈskepticism** *n.*

sceptre *or U.S.* **scepter** (ˈsɛptə) *n.* **1.** ornamental staff as symbol of royal power **2.** royal dignity

schedule (ˈʃɛdjuːl; *also, esp. U.S.* ˈskɛdʒuəl) *n.* **1.** plan of procedure for a project **2.** list **3.** timetable —*vt.* **4.** enter in schedule **5.** plan to occur at certain time —**on schedule** on time

schema (ˈskiːmə) *n.* overall plan or diagram (*pl.* **-mata** (-mətə)) —**scheˈmatic** *a.* presented as plan or diagram —**ˈschematize** *or* **-ise** *vt.*

scheme (skiːm) *n.* **1.** plan, design **2.** project **3.** outline —*v.* **4.** devise, plan, *esp.* in underhand manner —**ˈschemer** *n.*

scherzo (ˈskɛətsəʊ) *n. Mus.* light playful composition (*pl.* **-s, -zi** (-tsiː))

schism (ˈsɪzəm, ˈskɪz-) *n.* (group resulting from) division in political party, church *etc.* —**schisˈmatic** *n./a.*

schist (ʃɪst) *n.* crystalline rock which splits into layers —**ˈschistose** *a.*

schizanthus (skɪzˈænθəs) *n.* plant with divided leaves

schizo (ˈskɪtsəʊ) *inf. a.* **1.** schizophrenic —*n.* **2.** schizophrenic person (*pl.* **-s**)

schizo- *or before vowel* **schiz-** (*comb. form*) indicating cleavage, split, or division, as in *schizophrenia*

schizophrenia (skɪtsəʊˈfriːnɪə) *n.* mental disorder involving deterioration of, confusion about personality —**ˈschizoid** *a.* of schizophrenia —**schizoˈphrenic** *a./n.*

schmaltz *or* **schmalz** (ʃmælts, ʃmɔːlts) *n.* excessive sentimentality —**ˈschmaltzy** *a.*

schnapps *or* **schnaps** (ʃnæps) *n.* **1.** spirit distilled from potatoes **2.** *inf.* any strong spirit

schnitzel (ˈʃnɪtsəl) *n.* thin slice of meat, *esp.* veal

scholar (ˈskɒlə) *n. see* SCHOOL[1]

scholium (ˈskəʊlɪəm) *n.* **1.** marginal annotation **2.** note **3.** comment (*pl.* **-lia** (-lɪə)) —**ˈscholiast** *n.* **1.** commentator **2.** annotator

school[1] (skuːl) *n.* **1.** institution for teaching children or for giving instruction in any subject **2.** buildings of such institution **3.** group of thinkers, writers, artists *etc.* with principles or methods in common —*vt.* **4.** educate **5.** bring under control, train —**ˈscholar** *n.* **1.** learned person **2.** one taught in school **3.** one quick to learn —**scholarly** (ˈskɒləlɪ) *a.* learned, erudite —**scholarship** (ˈskɒləʃɪp) *n.* **1.** learning **2.** prize, grant to student for payment of school or college fees —**scholastic** (skəˈlæstɪk) *a.* **1.** of schools or scholars, or education **2.** pedantic —**ˈschooling** *n.* **1.** education, *esp.* when received at school **2.** training of animal, *esp.* of horse for dressage —**ˈschoolhouse** *n.* **1.** building used as school **2.** house attached to school —**ˈschoolman** *n.* medieval philosopher —**ˈschoolmarm** *n. inf.* **1.** woman schoolteacher **2.** woman considered old-fashioned or prim —**ˈschoolmaster** *or* **ˈschoolmistress** *n.* person who teaches in or runs a school

school[2] (skuːl) *n.* shoal (of fish, whales *etc.*)

schooner (ˈskuːnə) *n.* **1.** fore-and-aft rigged vessel with two or more masts **2.** tall glass

schottische (ʃɒˈtiːʃ) *n.* **1.** 19th-century German dance **2.** music for this

schwa *or* **shwa** (ʃwɑː) *n.* **1.** central vowel represented in International Phonetic Alphabet by (ə), *eg* 'a' in *around* **2.** symbol (ə) used to represent this sound

sciatica (saɪˈætɪkə) *n.* **1.** neuralgia of hip and thigh **2.** pain in sciatic nerve —**sciˈatic** *a.* **1.** of the hip **2.** of sciatica

science (ˈsaɪəns) *n.* **1.** systematic study and knowledge of natural or physical phenomena **2.** any branch of study concerned with observed material facts —**scienˈtific** *a.* **1.** of the principles of science **2.** systematic —**scienˈtifically** *adv.* —**ˈscientist** *n.* one versed in natural sciences —**science fiction** stories set in the future making imaginative use of scientific knowledge

Scientology (saɪənˈtɒlədʒɪ) *n.* religious cult based on belief that self-awareness is paramount

THESAURUS

on the track *or* trail of, detect, discern, get wind of, nose out, recognize, sense, smell, sniff, sniff out

sceptic agnostic, cynic, disbeliever, doubter, doubting Thomas, Pyrrhonist, scoffer

sceptical cynical, disbelieving, doubtful, doubting, dubious, hesitating, incredulous, mistrustful, questioning, quizzical, scoffing, unbelieving, unconvinced

scepticism cynicism, disbelief, doubt, incredulity, Pyrrhonism, suspicion

schedule 1. *n.* agenda, calendar, catalogue, inventory, itinerary, list, list of appointments, plan, programme, timetable **2.** *v.* appoint, arrange, be due, book, organize, plan, programme, time

scheme *n.* **1.** contrivance, course of action, design, device, plan, programme, project, proposal, strategy, system, tactics, theory **2.** arrangement, blueprint, chart, codification, diagram, disposition, draft, layout, outline, pattern, schedule, schema, system ~*v.* **3.** contrive, design, devise, frame, imagine, lay plans, plan, project, work out **4.** collude, conspire, intrigue, machinate, manoeuvre, plot, wheel and deal (*Inf.*)

schism breach, break, discord, disunion, division, rift, rupture, separation, splintering, split

scholar 1. academic, bookworm, egghead (*Inf.*), intellectual, man of letters, savant **2.** disciple, learner, pupil, schoolboy, schoolgirl, student

scholarly academic, bookish, erudite, intellectual, learned, lettered

scholarship 1. accomplishments, attainments, book-learning, education, erudition, knowledge, learning, lore **2.** bursary, exhibition, fellowship

scholastic 1. academic, bookish, learned, lettered, literary, scholarly **2.** pedagogic, pedantic, precise

school *n.* **1.** academy, alma mater, college, department, discipline, faculty, institute, institution, seminary **2.** adherents, circle, class, clique, denomination, devotees, disciples, faction, followers, following, group, pupils, sect, set ~*v.* **3.** coach, discipline, drill, educate, indoctrinate, instruct, prepare, prime, train, tutor, verse

schooling 1. book-learning, education, formal education, teaching, tuition **2.** coaching, drill, grounding, guidance, instruction, preparation, training

science body of knowledge, branch of knowledge, discipline

scientific accurate, controlled, exact, mathematical, precise, systematic

sci-fi (ˈsaɪˈfaɪ) *n. inf.* science fiction

scimitar (ˈsɪmɪtə) *n.* oriental curved sword

scintilla (sɪnˈtɪlə) *n. rare* minute amount

scintillate (ˈsɪntɪleɪt) *vi.* **1.** sparkle **2.** be animated, witty, clever —**scintilˈlation** *n.* —**scintillation counter** instrument for detecting and measuring intensity of high-energy radiation

scion (ˈsaɪən) *n.* **1.** descendant, heir **2.** slip for grafting

scission (ˈsɪʃən) *n.* act of cutting, dividing, splitting —**ˈscissile** *a.*

scissors (ˈsɪzəz) *pl.n.* **1.** cutting instrument of two blades pivoted together (*also* **pair of scissors**) —*n./a.* **2.** (with) scissorlike action of limbs in swimming, athletics *etc.*

sclerosis (sklɪəˈrəʊsɪs) *n.* a hardening of bodily organs, tissues *etc.* (*pl.* **-ses** (-siːz)) —**ˈsclera** *n.* firm white fibrous membrane that forms outer covering of eyeball —**sclerotic** (sklɪəˈrɒtɪk) *a.* **1.** of sclera **2.** of or having sclerosis —*n.* **3.** sclera

scoff[1] (skɒf) *vi.* **1.** (*oft. with* at) express derision (for) —*n.* **2.** derision **3.** mocking words —**ˈscoffer** *n.*

scoff[2] (skɒf) *v. sl.* eat rapidly

scold (skəʊld) *v.* **1.** find fault (with) —*vt.* **2.** reprimand, be angry with —*n.* **3.** one who does this

scollop (ˈskɒləp) *see* SCALLOP

sconce[1] (skɒns) *n.* bracket candlestick on wall

sconce[2] (skɒns) *n.* small protective fortification

scone (skəʊn, skɒn) *n.* small plain cake baked on griddle or in oven

scoop (skuːp) *n.* **1.** small shovel-like tool for ladling, hollowing out *etc.* **2.** *sl.* profitable deal **3.** *Journalism* exclusive news item —*vt.* **4.** ladle out **5.** hollow out, rake in with scoop **6.** make sudden profit **7.** beat (rival newspaper *etc.*)

scoot (skuːt) *vi. sl.* move off quickly —**ˈscooter** *n.* **1.** child's vehicle propelled by pushing on ground with one foot **2.** light motorcycle (*also* **motor scooter**)

scope (skəʊp) *n.* **1.** range of activity or application **2.** opportunity

-scope (*n. comb. form*) indicating instrument for observing or detecting, as in *microscope* —**-scopic** (*a. comb. form*)

scopolamine (skəˈpɒləmiːn) *n.* colourless viscous liquid alkaloid used in preventing travel sickness and as sedative and truth serum (*also* **ˈhyoscine**)

scorbutic (skɔːˈbjuːtɪk) *or* **scorbutical** *a.* of or having scurvy —**scorˈbutically** *adv.*

scorch (skɔːtʃ) *v.* **1.** burn, be burnt, on surface **2.** parch **3.** shrivel **4.** wither —*n.* **5.** slight burn —**ˈscorcher** *n. inf.* very hot day

score (skɔː) *n.* **1.** points gained in game, competition **2.** group of 20 **3.** (*esp. pl.*) a lot **4.** musical notation **5.** mark or notch, *esp.* to keep tally **6.** reason, account **7.** grievance —*v.* **8.** gain (points) in game —*vt.* **9.** mark **10.** (*with* out) cross out **11.** arrange music for —*vi.* **12.** keep tally of points **13.** succeed —**ˈscorecard** *n.* **1.** card on which scores are recorded **2.** card identifying players in sports match

scoria (ˈskɔːrɪə) *n.* **1.** solidified lava containing many cavities **2.** refuse obtained from smelted ore (*pl.* **-riae** (-rɪiː))

scorn (skɔːn) *n.* **1.** contempt, derision —*vt.* **2.** despise —**ˈscorner** *n.* —**ˈscornful** *a.* derisive —**ˈscornfully** *adv.*

Scorpio (ˈskɔːpɪəʊ) *n.* (scorpion) 8th sign of zodiac, operative *c.* Oct. 23rd - Nov. 21st

scorpion (ˈskɔːpɪən) *n.* small lobster-shaped animal with sting at end of jointed tail

Scot (skɒt) *n.* native of Scotland —**Scotch** *n.* whisky made in Scotland —**ˈScottish** *or* **Scots** *a.* —**Scotch broth UK** soup made from beef stock, vegetables, and pearl barley —**Scotch egg UK** hard-boiled egg en-

THESAURUS

scintillate coruscate, flash, give off sparks, gleam, glint, glisten, glitter, sparkle, twinkle

scoff belittle, deride, despise, flout, gibe, jeer, knock (*Inf.*), laugh at, make light of, make sport of, mock, poke fun at, pooh-pooh, revile, ridicule, scorn, scout (*Archaic*), sneer, taunt, twit

scold 1. *v.* bawl out (*Inf.*), berate, blame, bring (someone) to book, castigate, censure, chide, find fault with, give (someone) a dressing-down (row, talking-to) (*Inf.*), go on at (*Inf.*), haul (someone) over the coals (*Inf.*), have (someone) on the carpet (*Inf.*), lecture, nag, rate, rebuke, remonstrate with, reprimand, reproach, reprove, take (someone) to task, tell off (*Inf.*), tick off (*Inf.*), upbraid, vituperate **2.** *n.* nag, shrew, termagant (*Rare*), Xanthippe

scoop *n.* **1.** dipper, ladle, spoon **2.** exclusive, exposé, inside story, revelation, sensation ~*v.* **3.** bail, dig, dip, empty, excavate, gouge, hollow, ladle, scrape, shovel

scope area, capacity, compass, confines, elbowroom, extent, field of reference, freedom, latitude, liberty, opportunity, orbit, outlook, purview, range, reach, room, space, span, sphere

scorch blacken, blister, burn, char, parch, roast, sear, shrivel, singe, wither

score *n.* **1.** grade, mark, outcome, points, record, result, total **2.** *Plural* a flock, a great number, an army, a throng, crowds, droves, hosts, hundreds, legions, lots, masses, millions, multitudes, myriads, swarms, very many **3.** account, basis, cause, ground, grounds, reason **4.** a bone to pick, grievance, grudge, injury, injustice, wrong ~*v.* **5.** achieve, amass, chalk up (*Inf.*), gain, make, notch up (*Inf.*), win **6.** count, keep a tally of, keep count, record, register, tally **7.** crosshatch, cut, deface, gouge, graze, indent, mar, mark, nick, notch, scrape, scratch, slash **8.** *With* **out** cancel, cross out, delete, obliterate, put a line through, strike out **9.** *Music* adapt, arrange, orchestrate, set **10.** gain an advantage, go down well with (someone), impress, make a hit (*Inf.*), make an impact *or* impression, make a point, put oneself across, triumph

scorn 1. *n.* contempt, contemptuousness, contumely, derision, despite, disdain, disparagement, mockery, sarcasm, scornfulness, slight, sneer **2.** *v.* be above, consider beneath one, contemn, curl one's lip at, deride, disdain, flout, hold in contempt, look down on, make fun of, reject, scoff at, scout (*Archaic*), slight, sneer at, spurn, turn up one's nose at (*Inf.*)

scornful contemptuous, contumelious, defiant, derisive, disdainful, haughty, insolent, insulting, jeering, mocking, sarcastic, sardonic, scathing, scoffing, slighting, sneering, supercilious, withering

scornfully contemptuously, disdainfully, dismissively, scathingly, slightingly, with a sneer, with contempt, with disdain, witheringly, with lip curled

closed in layer of sausage meat and covered in breadcrumbs —**Scotch mist** 1. heavy wet mist 2. drizzle —ˈ**Scotsman** *n.* —**Scots pine** *or* **Scotch pine** 1. coniferous tree of Europe and W and N Asia 2. its wood —**Scottish Certificate of Education** Scottish examination equivalent to General Certificate of Education in England —**Scottish terrier** small long-haired breed of terrier

Scot. 1. Scotch (whisky) 2. Scotland 3. Scottish

scotch (skɒtʃ) *vt.* 1. put an end to 2. *obs.* wound

scoter (ˈskəʊtə) *n.* sea duck of northern regions

scot-free *a.* without harm or loss

Scotland Yard (ˈskɒtlənd) headquarters of police force of metropolitan London

Scottie *or* **Scotty** (ˈskɒtɪ) *n.* 1. Scottish terrier 2. *inf.* Scotsman

scoundrel (ˈskaʊndrəl) *n.* villain, blackguard —ˈ**scoundrelly** *a.*

scour[1] (skaʊə) *vt.* 1. clean, polish by rubbing 2. clear or flush out

scour[2] (skaʊə) *v.* move rapidly along or over (territory) in search of something

scourge (skɜːdʒ) *n.* 1. whip, lash 2. severe affliction 3. pest 4. calamity —*vt.* 5. flog 6. punish severely

Scouse (skaʊs) **UK** *inf. n.* 1. person from Liverpool 2. dialect of such person —*a.* 3. of or from Liverpool

scout (skaʊt) *n.* 1. one sent out to reconnoitre 2. (**S-**) member of **Scout Association**, organization to develop character and responsibility —*vi.* 3. go out, act as scout 4. reconnoitre —ˈ**scouter** *n.* leader of troop of scouts

scow (skaʊ) *n.* unpowered barge

scowl (skaʊl) *vi.* 1. frown gloomily or sullenly —*n.* 2. angry or gloomy expression

scrabble (ˈskræbᵊl) *vi.* 1. scrape with hands, claws in disorderly manner —*n.* 2. (**S-**) **R** word game

scrag (skræg) *n.* 1. lean person or animal 2. lean end of a neck of mutton —ˈ**scraggy** *a.* thin, bony

scraggly (ˈskræglɪ) *a.* untidy

scram (skræm) *vi. inf.* (*oft. imp.*) go away hastily, get out (**-mm-**)

scramble (ˈskræmbᵊl) *vi.* 1. move along or up by crawling, climbing *etc.* 2. struggle with others 3. (of aircraft, aircrew) take off hurriedly —*vt.* 4. mix up 5. cook (eggs) beaten up with milk 6. render (speech) unintelligible by electronic device —*n.* 7. scrambling 8. rough climb 9. disorderly proceeding 10. motorcycle race over rough ground —ˈ**scrambler** *n.* electronic device that renders speech unintelligible during transmission

scrap (skræp) *n.* 1. small piece or fragment 2. leftover material 3. *inf.* fight —*vt.* 4. break up, discard as useless —*vi.* 5. *inf.* fight (**-pp-**) —ˈ**scrappy** *a.* 1. unequal in quality 2. badly finished —ˈ**scrapbook** *n.* book in which newspaper cuttings *etc.* are kept —**scrap merchant** person dealing in scrap, *esp.* scrap metal

scrape (skreɪp) *vt.* 1. rub with something sharp 2. clean, smooth thus 3. grate 4. scratch 5. rub with harsh noise —*n.* 6. act, sound of scraping 7. *inf.* awkward situation, *esp.* as result of escapade —ˈ**scraper** *n.* 1. instrument for scraping 2. contrivance on which mud is scraped from shoes *etc.*

scratch (skrætʃ) *vt.* 1. score, make narrow surface wound on with claws, nails, or anything pointed 2. make marks on with pointed instruments 3. scrape (skin) with nails to relieve itching 4. remove, withdraw from list, race *etc.* —*vi.* 5. use claws or nails, *esp.* to relieve itching —*n.* 6. wound, mark or sound made by scratching 7. line or starting point —*a.* 8. got together at short notice 9. impromptu —ˈ**scratching** *n.* percussive effect obtained by rotating gramophone record manually: a disc-jockey technique —ˈ**scratchy** *a.*

THESAURUS

Scots Caledonian, Scottish

scoundrel blackguard, caitiff (*Archaic*), cheat, dastard (*Archaic*), good-for-nothing, heel (*Sl.*), incorrigible, knave (*Archaic*), miscreant, ne'er-do-well, rascal, reprobate, rogue, rotter (*Sl.*), scamp, scapegrace, vagabond, villain, wretch

scour[1] abrade, buff, burnish, clean, cleanse, flush, furbish, polish, purge, rub, scrub, wash, whiten

scour[2] beat, comb, forage, go over with a fine-tooth comb, hunt look high and low, rake, ransack, search

scourge *n.* 1. affliction, bane, curse, infliction, misfortune, penalty, pest, plague, punishment, terror, torment, visitation 2. cat, cat-o'-nine-tails, lash, strap, switch, thong, whip ~*v.* 3. beat, belt, cane, castigate, chastise, discipline, flog, horsewhip, lash, lather (*Inf.*), leather, punish, take a strap to, tan (someone's) hide (*Sl.*), thrash, trounce, wallop (*Inf.*), whale, whip

scout 1. *v.* case (*Sl.*), check out, investigate, make a reconnaissance, observe, probe, reconnoitre, see how the land lies, spy, spy out, survey, watch 2. *n.* advance guard, escort, lookout, outrider, precursor, reconnoitrer, vanguard

scowl 1. *v.* frown, glower, look daggers at, lower 2. *n.* black look, dirty look, frown, glower

scramble *v.* 1. clamber, climb, crawl, move with difficulty, push, scrabble, struggle, swarm 2. contend, hasten, jockey for position, jostle, look lively *or* snappy (*Inf.*), make haste, push, run, rush, strive, vie ~*n.* 3. climb, trek 4. commotion, competition, confusion, free-for-all (*Inf.*), hassle (*Inf.*), hustle, melee, muddle, race, rat race, rush, struggle, tussle

scrap *n.* 1. atom, bit, bite, crumb, fragment, grain, iota, mite, modicum, morsel, mouthful, part, particle, piece, portion, sliver, snatch, snippet, trace 2. junk, off cuts, waste ~*v.* 3. abandon, break up, demolish, discard, dispense with, ditch (*Sl.*), drop, get rid of, jettison, junk (*Inf.*), shed, throw away *or* out, throw on the scrapheap, toss out, write off ~*n.* 4. argument, battle, brawl, disagreement, dispute, dust-up (*Inf.*), fight, quarrel, row, scuffle, set-to (*Inf.*), squabble, tiff, wrangle ~*v.* 5. argue, bicker, come to blows, fall out (*Inf.*), fight, have a shouting match (*Inf.*), have words, row, squabble, wrangle

scrape *v.* 1. abrade, bark, graze, rub, scratch, scuff, skin 2. grate, grind, rasp, scratch, screech, set one's teeth on edge, squeak 3. clean, erase, file, remove, rub, scour ~*n.* 4. *Inf.* awkward *or* embarrassing situation, difficulty, dilemma, distress, fix (*Inf.*), mess, plight, predicament, pretty pickle (*Inf.*), tight spot (*Inf.*), trouble

scrappy bitty, disjointed, fragmentary, incomplete, perfunctory, sketchy, thrown together

scratch *v.* 1. claw, cut, damage, etch, grate, graze, incise, lacerate, make a mark on, mark, rub, score, scrape 2. annul, cancel, delete, eliminate, erase, pull

scrawl (skrɔːl) *vt.* **1.** write, draw untidily *—n.* **2.** thing scrawled **3.** careless writing

scrawny (ˈskrɔːnɪ) *a.* thin, bony

scream (skriːm) *vi.* **1.** utter piercing cry, *esp.* of fear, pain *etc.* **2.** be very obvious *—vt.* **3.** utter in a scream *—n.* **4.** shrill, piercing cry **5.** *inf.* very funny person or thing

scree (skriː) *n.* **1.** loose shifting stones **2.** slope covered with these

screech (skriːtʃ) *vi./n.* scream **—screech owl 1.** small N Amer. owl having reddish-brown or grey plumage **2.** UK any owl that utters screeching cry

screed (skriːd) *n.* **1.** long (tedious) letter, passage or speech **2.** thin layer of cement

screen (skriːn) *n.* **1.** device to shelter from heat, light, draught, observation *etc.* **2.** anything used for such purpose **3.** mesh over doors, windows to keep out insects **4.** white or silvered surface on which photographic images are projected **5.** windscreen **6.** wooden or stone partition in church *—vt.* **7.** shelter, hide **8.** protect from detection **9.** show (film) **10.** scrutinize **11.** examine (group of people) for presence of disease, weapons *etc.* **12.** examine for political motives **13.** *Elec.* protect from stray electric or magnetic fields **—ˈscreenplay** *n.* script for film, including instructions for sets and camera work **—screen process** *see* **silkscreen** *at* SILK **—the screen** cinema generally

screw (skruː) *n.* **1.** (nail-like device or cylinder with) spiral thread cut to engage similar thread or to bore into material (wood *etc.*) to pin or fasten **2.** anything resembling a screw in shape, esp. in spiral form **3.** propeller **4.** twist *—vt.* **5.** fasten with screw **6.** twist around **7.** *inf.* extort **—ˈscrewy** *a. inf.* crazy, eccentric **—ˈscrewball** US *sl. n.* **1.** eccentric person *—a.* **2.** odd; eccentric **—ˈscrewdriver** *n.* tool for turning screws **—screw top** bottle top that screws on to bottle, allowing bottle to be resealed after use **—screw-top** *a.* **—screw up 1.** distort **2.** *inf.* bungle

scribble (ˈskrɪbᵊl) *v.* **1.** write, draw carelessly *—vi.* **2.** make meaningless marks with pen or pencil *—n.* **3.** something scribbled **—ˈscribbly** *a.*

scribe (skraɪb) *n.* **1.** writer **2.** copyist *—v.* **3.** scratch a line on (a surface) with pointed instrument

scrimmage (ˈskrɪmɪdʒ) *n.* scuffle

scrimp (skrɪmp) *vt.* **1.** make too small or short **2.** treat meanly **—ˈscrimpy** *a.*

script (skrɪpt) *n.* **1.** (system or style of) handwriting **2.** written characters **3.** written text of film, play, radio or television programme **4.** answer paper in examination

scripture (ˈskrɪptʃə) *n.* **1.** sacred writings **2.** the Bible **—ˈscriptural** *a.*

scrofula (ˈskrɒfjʊlə) *n.* tuberculosis of lymphatic glands, *esp.* of neck **—ˈscrofulous** *a.*

scroll (skrəʊl) *n.* **1.** roll of parchment or paper **2.** list **3.** ornament shaped thus

Scrooge (skruːdʒ) *n.* miserly person

scrotum (ˈskrəʊtəm) *n.* pouch containing testicles (*pl.* **-ta** (-tə)) **—ˈscrotal** *a.*

scrounge (skraʊndʒ) *v. inf.* get (something) without cost, by begging **—ˈscrounger** *n.*

scrub[1] (skrʌb) *vt.* **1.** clean with hard brush and water **2.** scour **3.** *inf.* cancel, get rid of (**-bb-**) *—n.* **4.** scrubbing **—ˈscrubber** *n.* **1.** person or thing that scrubs **2.** apparatus for purifying gas **3.** *derogatory sl.* promiscuous girl

scrub[2] (skrʌb) *n.* **1.** stunted trees **2.** brushwood **—ˈscrubby** *a.* **1.** covered with scrub **2.** stunted **3.** *inf.* messy

scruff (skrʌf) *n.* nape (of neck)

scruffy (ˈskrʌfɪ) *a.* unkempt or shabby

scrum (skrʌm) *n.* **1.** *Rugby* restarting of play in which opposing packs of forwards push against each other to gain possession of the ball (*also* **ˈscrummage**) **2.** crush, crowd

scrump (skrʌmp) *v.* UK *dial.* steal (apples) from orchard or garden

THESAURUS

out, stand down, strike off, withdraw ~*n.* **3.** blemish, claw mark, gash, graze, laceration, mark, scrape ~*adj.* **4.** haphazard, hastily prepared, impromptu, improvised, rough, rough-and-ready

scrawl doodle, scrabble, scratch, scribble, squiggle

scream *v.* **1.** bawl, cry, holler (*Inf.*), screech, shriek, shrill, sing out, squeal, yell **2.** *Fig.* be conspicuous, clash, jar, shriek ~*n.* **3.** howl, outcry, screech, shriek, wail, yell, yelp **4.** *Inf.* card (*Inf.*), caution (*Inf.*), character (*Inf.*), comedian, comic, entertainer, hoot (*Brit. inf.*), joker, laugh, riot (*Sl.*), sensation, wit

screen *v.* **1.** cloak, conceal, cover, hide, mask, shade, shroud, shut out, veil **2.** defend, guard, protect, safeguard, shelter, shield **3.** cull, evaluate, examine, filter, gauge, grade, process, riddle, scan, sieve, sift, sort, vet **4.** broadcast, present, put on, show ~*n.* **5.** awning, canopy, cloak, concealment, cover, guard, hedge, mantle, shade, shelter, shield, shroud **6.** mesh, net, partition, room divider

screw *v.* **1.** tighten, turn, twist, work in **2.** *Inf. Often with* **out of** bleed, extort, extract, wrest, wring

scribble *v.* dash off, doodle, jot, pen, scratch, scrawl, write

scribe amanuensis, clerk, copyist, notary (*Archaic*), penman (*Rare*), scrivener (*Archaic*), secretary, writer

script 1. calligraphy, hand, handwriting, letters, longhand, penmanship, writing **2.** book, copy, dialogue, libretto, lines, manuscript, text, words

Scripture Holy Bible, Holy Scripture, Holy Writ, The Bible, The Book of Books, The Good Book, The Gospels, The Scriptures, The Word, The Word of God

scroll inventory, list, parchment, roll

Scrooge meanie (*Inf.*), miser, money-grubber (*Inf.*), niggard, penny-pincher (*Inf.*), skinflint, tightwad (*U.S. sl.*)

scrounge beg, bum (*Inf., chiefly U.S.*), cadge, forage for, freeload (*U.S. sl.*), hunt around (for), sorn (*Scot.*), sponge (*Inf.*), wheedle

scrounger cadger, freeloader (*U.S. sl.*), parasite, sorner (*Scot.*), sponger (*Inf.*)

scrub *v.* **1.** clean, cleanse, rub, scour **2.** *Inf.* abandon, abolish, call off, cancel, delete, discontinue, do away with, drop, forget about, give up

scruffy disreputable, draggletailed (*Archaic*), frowzy, ill-groomed, mangy, messy, ragged, run-down, scrubby (*Brit. inf.*), seedy, shabby, slatternly, slovenly, sluttish, squalid, tattered, ungroomed, unkempt, untidy

scrumptious ('skrʌmpʃəs) *a. inf.* very pleasing; delicious —'**scrumptiously** *adv.*

scrumpy ('skrʌmpɪ) *n.* rough dry cider

scrunch (skrʌntʃ) *v.* 1. crumple or crunch or be crumpled or crunched —*n.* 2. act or sound of scrunching

scruple ('skru:p'l) *n.* 1. doubt or hesitation about what is morally right 2. weight of 20 grains —*vi.* 3. hesitate —'**scrupulous** *a.* 1. extremely conscientious 2. thorough, attentive to small points

scrutiny ('skru:tɪnɪ) *n.* 1. close examination 2. critical investigation 3. official examination of votes *etc.* 4. searching look —**scruti'neer** *n.* examiner of votes —'**scrutinize** *or* **-nise** *vt.* examine closely

scuba ('skju:bə) *n./a.* (relating to) self-contained underwater breathing apparatus

scud (skʌd) *vi.* 1. run fast 2. run before the wind (**-dd-**)

scuff (skʌf) *vi.* 1. drag, scrape with feet in walking —*vt.* 2. scrape with feet 3. graze —*n.* 4. act, sound of scuffing —*pl.* 5. thong sandals —**scuffed** *a.* (of shoes) scraped or slightly grazed

scuffle ('skʌf'l) *vi.* 1. fight in disorderly manner 2. shuffle —*n.* 3. disorderly struggle

scull (skʌl) *n.* 1. oar used in stern of boat 2. short oar used in pairs —*v.* 3. propel, move by means of scull(s)

scullery ('skʌlərɪ) *n.* place for washing dishes *etc.* —'**scullion** *n.* 1. despicable person 2. *obs.* kitchen underservant

sculpture ('skʌlptʃə) *n.* 1. art of forming figures in relief or solid 2. product of this art —*vt.* 3. represent by sculpture —**sculpt** *v.* —'**sculptor** *n.* ('**sculptress** *fem.*) —'**sculptural** *a.* with qualities proper to sculpture

scum (skʌm) *n.* 1. froth or other floating matter on liquid 2. waste part of anything 3. vile person(s) or thing(s) —'**scummy** *a.*

scunner ('skʌnə) *dial., chiefly Scot. vt.* 1. produce feeling of aversion in —*n.* 2. strong aversion (*oft. in* **take a scunner**) 3. object of aversion

scupper ('skʌpə) *n.* 1. hole in ship's side level with deck to carry off water —*vt.* 2. *inf.* ruin, destroy, kill

scurf (skɜ:f) *n.* flaky matter on scalp, dandruff

scurrilous ('skʌrɪləs) *a.* coarse, indecently abusive —**scur'rility** *n.*

scurry ('skʌrɪ) *vi.* 1. run hastily ('**scurried**, '**scurrying**) —*n.* 2. bustling haste 3. flurry

scurvy ('skɜ:vɪ) *n.* 1. disease caused by lack of vitamin C —*a.* 2. mean, contemptible

scut (skʌt) *n.* short tail of hare or other animal

scuttle[1] ('skʌt'l) *n.* fireside container for coal

scuttle[2] ('skʌt'l) *vi.* 1. rush away —*n.* 2. hurried pace, run

scuttle[3] ('skʌt'l) *vt.* cause (ship) to sink by making holes in bottom

scythe (saɪð) *n.* 1. manual implement with long curved blade for cutting grass —*vt.* 2. cut with scythe

SD South Dakota

Se *Chem.* selenium

SE southeast(ern)

sea (si:) *n.* 1. mass of salt water covering greater part of earth 2. broad tract of this 3. waves 4. swell 5. large quantity 6. vast expanse —**sea anchor** *Naut.* device dragged in water to slow vessel —**sea anemone** sea animal with suckers like petals —'**seaboard** *n. chiefly* US coast —**sea cow** 1. dugong or manatee 2. *obs.* walrus —**sea dog** experienced or old sailor —'**seafaring** *a.* occupied in sea voyages —'**seafood** *n.* edible saltwater fish or shellfish —**sea-girt** *a. Lit.* surrounded by sea —**sea gull** gull —**sea horse** fish with bony plated body and horselike head —**sea kale** European coastal plant with edible asparagus-like shoots —**sea legs** *inf.* 1. ability to maintain one's balance on board ship 2. ability to resist seasickness —**sea level** level of surface of sea, taken to be mean level between high and low tide —**sea lion** kind of large seal —'**seaman** *n.* sailor —'**seamanship** *n.* skill in navigating, maintaining and operating vessel —'**seaplane** *n.* aircraft that lands on and takes off from water —**Sea Scout** Scout belonging to any of number of Scout troops whose main activities are sailing *etc.* —'**seashell** *n.* empty shell of marine mollusc —'**seasick** *a.* —'**seasickness** *n.* nausea caused by motion of ship —'**seaside** *n.* place, *esp.* holiday resort, on coast —**sea urchin** marine animal with globular body enclosed in rigid, spiny test —'**seaweed** *n.* plant growing in sea —'**seaworthy** *a.* in fit condition to put to sea

seal[1] (si:l) *n.* 1. device impressed on piece of wax *etc.*, fixed to letter *etc.* as mark of authentication 2. impression thus made 3. device, material preventing passage

THESAURUS

scrupulous careful, conscientious, exact, fastidious, honourable, meticulous, minute, moral, nice, painstaking, precise, principled, punctilious, rigorous, strict, upright

scrutinize analyse, dissect, examine, explore, inquire into, inspect, investigate, peruse, pore over, probe, scan, search, sift, study

scrutiny analysis, close study, examination, exploration, inquiry, inspection, investigation, perusal, search, sifting, study

scuffle 1. *v.* clash, come to blows, contend, exchange blows, fight, grapple, jostle, struggle, tussle 2. *n.* affray (*Law*), brawl, commotion, disturbance, fight, fray, ruck (*Sl.*), ruckus (*Inf.*), ruction (*Inf.*), rumpus, scrap (*Inf.*), set-to (*Inf.*), tussle

sculpture *v.* carve, chisel, cut, fashion, form, hew, model, mould, sculp, sculpt, shape

scum 1. algae, crust, dross, film, froth, impurities, offscourings, scruff 2. *Fig. canaille*, dregs of society, lowest of the low, rabble, ragtag and bobtail, riffraff, rubbish, trash (*Chiefly U.S.*)

scurrilous abusive, coarse, defamatory, foul, foul-mouthed, gross, indecent, infamous, insulting, low, obscene, offensive, Rabelaisian, ribald, salacious, scabrous, scandalous, slanderous, vituperative, vulgar

scurry 1. *v.* dart, dash, fly, hurry, race, scamper, scoot, scud, scuttle, skim, sprint, whisk 2. *n.* bustle, flurry, scampering, whirl

scuttle bustle, hare (*Brit. inf.*), hasten, hurry, run, rush, scamper, scoot, scramble, scud, scurry, scutter (*Brit. inf.*)

sea *n.* 1. main, ocean, the briny (*Inf.*), the deep, the drink (*Inf.*), the waves 2. *Fig.* abundance, expanse, mass, multitude, plethora, profusion, sheet, vast number

seafaring marine, maritime, nautical, naval, oceanic

of water, air, oil *etc.* (*also* **ˈsealer**) —*vt.* **4.** affix seal to **5.** ratify, authorize **6.** mark with stamp as evidence of some quality **7.** keep close or secret **8.** settle **9.** make watertight, airtight *etc.* —**sealing wax** hard material made of shellac and turpentine that softens when heated

seal[2] (siːl) *n.* **1.** amphibious furred carnivorous mammal with flippers as limbs —*vi.* **2.** hunt seals —**ˈsealer** *n.* man or ship engaged in sealing —**ˈsealskin** *n.* skin, fur of seals

seam (siːm) *n.* **1.** line of junction of two edges, *eg* of two pieces of cloth, or two planks **2.** thin layer, stratum —*vt.* **3.** mark with furrows or wrinkles —**ˈseamless** *a.* —**seamstress** (ˈsɛmstrɪs) *or* **sempstress** (ˈsɛmpstrɪs) *n.* woman who sews and makes clothes, *esp.* professionally —**ˈseamy** *a.* **1.** sordid **2.** marked with seams

seance (ˈseɪɒns) *n.* meeting of spiritualists

sear (sɪə) *vt.* **1.** scorch, brand with hot iron **2.** deaden

search (sɜːtʃ) *v.* **1.** look over or through (a place *etc.*) to find something —*vt.* **2.** probe into, examine —*n.* **3.** act of searching **4.** quest —**ˈsearcher** *n.* —**ˈsearching** *a.* **1.** keen **2.** thorough **3.** severe —**ˈsearchlight** *n.* powerful electric light with concentrated beam —**search warrant** legal document authorizing search of premises for stolen goods *etc.*

season (ˈsiːzᵊn) *n.* **1.** one of four divisions of year (spring, summer, autumn and winter), which have characteristic weather conditions **2.** period during which thing takes place, grows, is active *etc.* **3.** proper time —*vt.* **4.** flavour with salt, herbs *etc.* **5.** make reliable or ready for use **6.** make experienced —**ˈseasonable** *a.* **1.** appropriate for the season **2.** opportune **3.** fit —**ˈseasonal** *a.* depending on, varying with seasons —**ˈseasoning** *n.* flavouring —**season ticket** ticket for series of journeys, events *etc.* within a certain time

seat (siːt) *n.* **1.** thing for sitting on **2.** buttocks **3.** base **4.** right to sit (*eg* in council *etc.*) **5.** place where something is located, centred **6.** locality of disease, trouble *etc.* **7.** country house —*vt.* **8.** bring to or place on seat **9.** provide sitting accommodation for **10.** install firmly —**seat belt** belt worn in car, aircraft *etc.* to secure seated passenger (*also* **safety belt**)

SEATO (ˈsiːtəʊ) South East Asia Treaty Organization

sebaceous (sɪˈbeɪʃəs) *a.* **1.** of, pert. to fat **2.** secreting fat, oil

sec[1] (sɛk) *a.* **1.** (of wines) dry **2.** (of champagne) of medium sweetness

sec[2] (sɛk) *inf.* second (of time)

sec[3] (sɛk) secant

sec. **1.** second (of time) **2.** secondary **3.** secretary **4.** section **5.** sector

secant (ˈsiːkənt) *n. Maths.* **1.** (of angle) the reciprocal of its cosine **2.** line that intersects a curve

secateurs (ˈsɛkətəz) *pl.n.* small pruning shears

secede (sɪˈsiːd) *vi.* withdraw formally from federation, Church *etc.* —**secession** (sɪˈsɛʃən) *n.* —**secessionist** (sɪˈsɛʃənɪst) *n.*

seclude (sɪˈkluːd) *vt.* guard from, remove from sight, view, contact with others —**seˈcluded** *a.* **1.** remote **2.** private —**seˈclusion** *n.*

second[1] (ˈsɛkənd) *a.* **1.** next after first **2.** alternate **3.** additional **4.** of lower quality —*n.* **5.** person or thing coming second **6.** attendant **7.** sixtieth part of minute **8.** SI unit of time **9.** moment **10.** (*esp. pl.*) inferior goods —*vt.* **11.** support **12.** support (motion in meeting) so that discussion may be in order —**ˈseconder** *n.* —**ˈsecondly** *adv.* —**second-best** *a.* next to best —**second chamber** upper house of bicameral legislative assembly —**second class** class next in value *etc.* to first —**second-class** *a.* **1.** of grade next to best in quality *etc.* **2.** shoddy or inferior **3.** (of accommodation in hotel, on aircraft *etc.*) next in quality to first class **4.** UK (of letters) handled more slowly than first-class letters —*adv.* **5.** by second-class mail *etc.* —**Second Coming** *or* **Advent** *Christian theol.* prophesied return of Christ to earth at Last Judgment —**second cousin** child of first cousin of either of one's parents —**second fiddle** *inf.* **1.** second violin in string quartet **2.** person who has secondary status —**second generation** off-

THESAURUS

seal *v.* **1.** close, cork, enclose, fasten, make airtight, plug, secure, shut, stop, stopper, stop up, waterproof **2.** assure, attest, authenticate, confirm, establish, ratify, stamp, validate **3.** clinch, conclude, consummate, finalize, settle, shake hands on (*Inf.*) ~*n.* **4.** assurance, attestation, authentication, confirmation, imprimatur, insignia, notification, ratification, stamp

seam *n.* **1.** closure, joint, suture (*Surgery*) **2.** layer, lode, stratum, vein

search **1.** *v.* cast around, check, comb, examine, explore, ferret, frisk (*Inf.*), go over with a fine-tooth comb, inquire, inspect, investigate, leave no stone unturned, look, look high and low, probe, pry, ransack, rifle through, rummage through, scour, scrutinize, seek, sift, turn inside out, turn upside down **2.** *n.* examination, exploration, going-over (*Inf.*), hunt, inquiry, inspection, investigation, pursuit, quest, researches, rummage, scrutiny

searching *adj.* close, intent, keen, minute, penetrating, piercing, probing, quizzical, severe, sharp, thorough

season *n.* **1.** division, interval, juncture, occasion, opportunity, period, spell, term, time, time of year ~*v.* **2.** colour, enliven, flavour, lace, leaven, pep up, salt, salt and pepper, spice **3.** acclimatize, accustom, anneal, discipline, habituate, harden, inure, mature, prepare, toughen, train

seasonable appropriate, convenient, fit, opportune, providential, suitable, timely, welcome, well-timed

seasoning condiment, dressing, flavouring, relish, salt and pepper, sauce, spice

seat *n.* **1.** bench, chair, pew, settle, stall, stool **2.** axis, capital, centre, cradle, headquarters, heart, hub, location, place, site, situation, source, station **3.** base, bed, bottom, cause, footing, foundation, ground, groundwork **4.** abode, ancestral hall, house, mansion, residence **5.** chair, constituency, incumbency, membership, place ~*v.* **6.** accommodate, cater for, contain, have room *or* capacity for, hold, sit, take **7.** deposit, fix, install, locate, place, set, settle, sit

secede apostatize, break with, disaffiliate, leave, pull out, quit, resign, retire, separate, split from, withdraw

secluded cloistered, cut off, isolated, lonely, off the beaten track, out-of-the-way, private, reclusive, remote, retired, sequestered, sheltered, solitary, tucked away, unfrequented

seclusion concealment, hiding, isolation, privacy, remoteness, retirement, retreat, shelter, solitude

spring of parents born in a given country —**second-generation** *a.* of refined stage of development in manufacture —**second hand** pointer on face of timepiece that indicates seconds —**second-hand** *a.* 1. bought after use by another 2. not original 3. dealing in goods that are not new —*adv.* 4. not directly —**second lieutenant** officer holding lowest commissioned rank in armed forces of certain nations —**second nature** habit *etc.* long practised so as to seem innate —**second person** grammatical category of pronouns and verbs used when referring to individual(s) being addressed —**second-rate** *a.* 1. mediocre 2. second in importance *etc.* —**second sight** faculty of seeing events before they occur —**second thought** revised opinion on matter already considered —**second wind** 1. return of breath at normal rate, *esp.* following exertion 2. renewed ability to continue in effort —**come off second best** *inf.* be defeated in competition

second² (səˈkɒnd) *vt.* transfer (employee, officer) temporarily

secondary (ˈsɛkəndərɪ) *a.* 1. subsidiary, of less importance 2. developed from, or dependent on, something else —ˈ**secondarily** *adv.* —**secondary education** education of young people between ages of 11 and 18 —**secondary picketing** picketing by striking workers of distribution outlet *etc.* that supplies goods to or distributes goods from their employer

secret (ˈsiːkrɪt) *a.* 1. kept, meant to be kept from knowledge of others 2. hidden 3. private —*n.* 4. thing kept secret —ˈ**secrecy** *n.* keeping or being kept secret —ˈ**secretive** *a.* given to having secrets; uncommunicative, reticent —ˈ**secretiveness** *n.* —ˈ**secretly** *adv.* —**secret agent** person employed in espionage —**secret police** police force that operates secretly to check subversion —**secret service** government department that conducts intelligence or counterintelligence operations

secretary (ˈsɛkrətrɪ) *n.* 1. one employed by individual or organization to deal with papers and correspondence, keep records, prepare business *etc.* 2. head of a state department —**secreˈtarial** *a.* —**secreˈtariat** *n.* 1. body of secretaries 2. building occupied by secretarial staff —ˈ**secretaryship** *n.* —**secretary bird** large Afr. bird of prey

secrete (sɪˈkriːt) *vt.* 1. hide, conceal 2. (of gland *etc.*) collect and supply (particular substance in body) —**seˈcretion** *n.* —**seˈcretory** *a.*

sect (sɛkt) *n.* 1. group of people (within religious body *etc.*) with common interest 2. faction —**secˈtarian** *a.* 1. of a sect 2. narrow-minded

section (ˈsɛkʃən) *n.* 1. part cut off 2. division 3. portion 4. distinct part of city, country, people *etc.* 5. cutting 6. drawing of anything as if cut through 7. smallest military unit —ˈ**sectional** *a.*

sector (ˈsɛktə) *n.* 1. part, subdivision 2. part of circle enclosed by two radii and the arc which they cut off

secular (ˈsɛkjʊlə) *a.* 1. worldly 2. lay, not religious 3. not monastic 4. lasting for, or occurring once in, an age 5. centuries old —ˈ**secularism** *n.* —ˈ**secularist** *n.* one who believes that religion should have no place in civil affairs —**seculariˈzation** *or* **-riˈsation** *n.* —ˈ**secularize** *or* **-rise** *vt.* transfer from religious to lay possession or use

secure (sɪˈkjʊə) *a.* 1. safe 2. free from fear, anxiety 3. firmly fixed 4. certain 5. sure, confident —*vt.* 6. gain

THESAURUS

second *adj.* 1. following, next, subsequent, succeeding 2. additional, alternative, extra, further, other, repeated 3. inferior, lesser, lower, secondary, subordinate, supporting ~*n.* 4. assistant, backer, helper, supporter ~*v.* 5. advance, aid, approve, assist, back, encourage, endorse, forward, further, give moral support to, go along with, help, promote, support ~*n.* 6. flash, instant, jiffy (*Inf.*), minute, moment, sec (*Inf.*), split second, tick (*Brit. inf.*), trice, twinkling, twinkling of an eye, two shakes of a lamb's tail (*Inf.*)

secondary 1. derivative, derived, indirect, resultant, resulting, second-hand 2. consequential, contingent, inferior, lesser, lower, minor, second-rate, subordinate, unimportant 3. alternate, auxiliary, backup, extra, relief, reserve, second, subsidiary, supporting

second-class déclassé, indifferent, inferior, mediocre, outclassed, second-best, second-rate, undistinguished, uninspiring

second-hand 1. *adj.* handed down, hand-me-down (*Inf.*), nearly new, reach-me-down (*Inf.*), used 2. *adv.* at second-hand, indirectly, on the grapevine (*Inf.*)

secondly in the second place, next, second

second-rate cheap, cheap and nasty (*Inf.*), commonplace, inferior, low-grade, low-quality, mediocre, poor, rubbishy, shoddy, substandard, tacky (*Inf.*), tawdry

secrecy 1. concealment, confidentiality, huggermugger (*Rare*), mystery, privacy, retirement, seclusion, silence, solitude, surreptitiousness 2. clandestineness, covertness, furtiveness, secretiveness, stealth

secret *adj.* 1. backstairs, camouflaged, cloak-and-dagger, close, closet (*Inf.*), concealed, conspiratorial, covered, covert, disguised, furtive, hidden, hole-and-corner (*Inf.*), hush-hush (*Inf.*), reticent, shrouded, undercover, underground, under wraps, undisclosed, unknown, unpublished, unrevealed, unseen 2. hidden, out-of-the-way, private, retired, secluded, unfrequented, unknown ~*n.* 3. code, confidence, enigma, formula, key, mystery, recipe, skeleton in the cupboard

secretive cagey (*Inf.*), clamlike, close, cryptic, deep, enigmatic, playing one's cards close to one's chest, reserved, reticent, tight-lipped, uncommunicative, unforthcoming, withdrawn

secretly behind closed doors, behind (someone's) back, clandestinely, confidentially, covertly, furtively, in camera, in confidence, in one's heart, in one's inmost thoughts, in secret, on the q.t. (*Inf.*), on the sly, privately, quietly, stealthily, surreptitiously, unobserved

sect camp, denomination, division, faction, group, party, school, school of thought, splinter group, wing

sectarian bigoted, clannish, cliquish, doctrinaire, dogmatic, exclusive, factional, fanatic, fanatical, hidebound, insular, limited, narrow-minded, parochial, partisan, rigid

section *n.* 1. component, cross section, division, fraction, fragment, instalment, part, passage, piece, portion, sample, segment, slice, subdivision 2. *Chiefly U.S.* area, department, district, region, sector, zone

sector area, category, district, division, part, quarter, region, stratum, subdivision, zone

secular civil, earthly, laic, laical, lay, nonspiritual, profane, state, temporal, worldly

possession of 7. make safe 8. free (creditor) from risk of loss 9. make firm —**se'curely** *adv.* —**se'curity** *n.* 1. state of safety 2. protection 3. that which secures 4. assurance 5. anything given as bond, caution or pledge 6. one that becomes surety for another —**security risk** person deemed to be threat to state security

sedan (sɪ'dæn) *n.* **US** saloon car —**sedan chair** *Hist.* closed chair for one person, carried on poles by bearers

sedate[1] (sɪ'deɪt) *a.* 1. calm, collected 2. serious

sedate[2] (sɪ'deɪt) *vt.* make calm by sedative —**se'dation** *n.* —**sedative** ('sɛdətɪv) *a.* 1. having soothing or calming effect —*n.* 2. sedative drug

sedentary ('sɛdᵊntərɪ) *a.* 1. done sitting down 2. sitting much 3. (of birds) not migratory

sedge (sɛdʒ) *n.* plant like coarse grass growing in swampy ground —**sedge warbler** European songbird having streaked brownish plumage with white eye stripes

sedilia (sɛ'daɪlɪə) *n.* (*with sing. v.*) stone seats on south side of altar for priests

sediment ('sɛdɪmənt) *n.* 1. matter which settles to the bottom of liquid 2. matter deposited from water, ice or wind —**sedi'mentary** *a.*

sedition (sɪ'dɪʃən) *n.* speech or action threatening authority of a state —**se'ditious** *a.*

seduce (sɪ'dju:s) *vt.* 1. persuade to commit some (wrong) deed, *esp.* sexual intercourse 2. tempt 3. attract —**se'ducer** *n.* (**seductress** (sɪ'dʌktrɪs) *fem.*) —**seduction** (sɪ'dʌkʃən) *n.* —**seductive** (sɪ'dʌktɪv) *a.* 1. alluring 2. winning

sedulous ('sɛdjʊləs) *a.* 1. diligent 2. industrious 3. persevering, persistent —**se'dulity** *n.*

sedum ('si:dəm) *n.* rock plant

see[1] (si:) *vt.* 1. perceive with eyes or mentally 2. observe 3. watch 4. find out 5. consider 6. have experience of 7. interview 8. make sure 9. accompany —*vi.* 10. have power of sight 11. consider 12. understand (**saw, seen, 'seeing**) —**'seeing** *conj.* since, in view of the fact that

see[2] (si:) *n.* diocese, office or jurisdiction of bishop

seed (si:d) *n.* 1. reproductive germs of plants 2. one grain of this 3. such grains saved or used for sowing 4. origin 5. sperm 6. *obs.* offspring —*vt.* 7. sow with seed 8. arrange (draw for lawn tennis or other tournament) so that best players do not meet in early rounds —*vi.* 9. produce seed —**'seedling** *n.* young plant raised from seed —**'seedy** *a.* 1. shabby 2. (of plant) at seed-producing stage 3. *inf.* unwell, ill —**seed pearl** tiny pearl weighing less than a quarter of a grain

seek (si:k) *vt.* 1. make search or enquiry for —*vi.* 2. search (**sought, 'seeking**)

THESAURUS

secure *adj.* **1.** immune, impregnable, out of harm's way, protected, safe, sheltered, shielded, unassailable, undamaged, unharmed **2.** dependable, fast, fastened, firm, fixed, fortified, immovable, stable, steady, tight **3.** assured, certain, confident, easy, reassured, sure ~*v.* **4.** acquire, come by, gain, get, get hold of, land (*Inf.*), make sure of, obtain, pick up, procure, win possession of **5.** attach, batten down, bolt, chain, fasten, fix, lash, lock, lock up, make fast, moor, padlock, rivet, tie up **6.** assure, ensure, guarantee, insure

security **1.** asylum, care, cover, custody, immunity, preservation, protection, refuge, retreat, safekeeping, safety, sanctuary **2.** defence, guards, precautions, protection, safeguards, safety measures, surveillance **3.** assurance, certainty, confidence, conviction, ease of mind, freedom from doubt, positiveness, reliance, sureness **4.** collateral, gage, guarantee, hostage, insurance, pawn, pledge, surety

sedate calm, collected, composed, cool, decorous, deliberate, demure, dignified, earnest, grave, imperturbable, middle-aged, placid, proper, quiet, seemly, serene, serious, slow-moving, sober, solemn, staid, tranquil, unflappable (*Inf.*), unruffled

sedative **1.** *adj.* allaying, anodyne, calmative, calming, lenitive, relaxing, sleep-inducing, soothing, soporific, tranquillizing **2.** *n.* anodyne, calmative, downer *or* down (*Sl.*), narcotic, opiate, sleeping pill, tranquillizer

sedentary desk, desk-bound, inactive, motionless, seated, sitting, torpid

sediment deposit, dregs, grounds, lees, precipitate, residuum, settlings

sedition agitation, disloyalty, incitement to riot, rabble-rousing, subversion, treason

seditious disloyal, dissident, insubordinate, mutinous, rebellious, refractory, revolutionary, subversive, treasonable

seduce **1.** betray, corrupt, debauch, deflower, deprave, dishonour, ruin (*Archaic*) **2.** allure, attract, beguile, deceive, decoy, ensnare, entice, inveigle, lead astray, lure, mislead, tempt

seduction **1.** corruption, defloration, ruin (*Archaic*) **2.** allure, enticement, lure, snare, temptation

seductive alluring, attractive, beguiling, bewitching, captivating, come-hither (*Inf.*), enticing, flirtatious, inviting, irresistible, provocative, ravishing, sexy (*Inf.*), siren, specious, tempting

seductress Circe, enchantress, *femme fatale*, Lorelei, siren, temptress, vamp (*Inf.*)

see *v.* **1.** behold, catch a glimpse of, catch sight of, descry, discern, distinguish, espy, get a load of (*Sl.*), glimpse, heed, identify, lay *or* clap eyes on (*Inf.*), look, make out, mark, note, notice, observe, perceive, recognize, regard, sight, spot, view, witness **2.** appreciate, catch on (*Inf.*), comprehend, fathom, feel, follow, get, get the drift of, get the hang of (*Inf.*), grasp, know, make out, realize, take in, understand **3.** ascertain, determine, discover, find out, investigate, learn, make enquiries, refer to **4.** ensure, guarantee, make certain, make sure, mind, see to it, take care **5.** consider, decide, deliberate, give some thought to, judge, make up one's mind, mull over, reflect, think over **6.** confer with, consult, encounter, interview, meet, receive, run into, speak to, visit **7.** accompany, attend, escort, lead, show, usher, walk

seed **1.** egg, egg cell, embryo, germ, grain, kernel, ovule, ovum, spore **2.** *Fig.* children, descendants, heirs, issue, offspring, progeny, race, scions, spawn, successors

seedy **1.** crummy (*Sl.*), decaying, dilapidated, down at heel, faded, grubby, mangy, manky (*Scot. dialect*), old, run-down, scruffy (*Brit. inf.*), shabby, sleazy, slovenly, squalid, tatty, unkempt, worn **2.** *Inf.* ailing, ill, off colour, out of sorts, poorly (*Inf.*), sickly, under the weather (*Inf.*), unwell

seeing *conj.* as, inasmuch as, in view of the fact that, since

seem (siːm) *vi.* **1.** appear (to be or to do) **2.** look **3.** appear to one's judgment —ˈ**seeming** *a.* apparent but not real —ˈ**seemingly** *adv.*

seemly (ˈsiːmlɪ) *a.* becoming and proper —ˈ**seemliness** *n.*

seen (siːn) *pp. of* SEE[1]

seep (siːp) *vi.* trickle through slowly, as water, ooze

seer (sɪə) *n.* prophet

seersucker (ˈsɪəsʌkə) *n.* light cotton fabric with slightly crinkled surface

seesaw (ˈsiːsɔː) *n.* **1.** game in which children sit at opposite ends of plank supported in middle and swing up and down **2.** plank used for this —*vi.* **3.** move up and down

seethe (siːð) *vi.* **1.** boil, foam **2.** be very agitated **3.** be in constant movement (as large crowd *etc.*) (**seethed,** ˈ**seething**)

segment (ˈsɛgmənt) *n.* **1.** piece cut off **2.** section —*v.* (sɛgˈmɛnt) **3.** divide into segments —**seg**ˈ**mental** *a.* —**segmen**ˈ**tation** *n.*

segregate (ˈsɛgrɪgeɪt) *vt.* set apart from the rest —**segre**ˈ**gation** *n.*

seigneur (sɛˈnjɜː; *Fr.* sɛˈɲœːr) *n.* feudal lord, *esp.* in France —**sei**ˈ**gneurial** *a.* —ˈ**seigneury** *n.* estate of seigneur

seignior (ˈseɪnjə) *n.* **1.** *less common name for* seigneur **2.** in England, lord of seigniory —**sei**ˈ**gniorial** *a.* —ˈ**seigniory** *or* ˈ**signory** *n.* **1.** *less common names for* seigneury **2.** in England, fee or manor of seignior **3.** authority of seignior

seine (seɪn) *n.* type of large fishing net

seismic (ˈsaɪzmɪk) *a.* pert. to earthquakes —ˈ**seismograph** *n.* instrument that records earthquakes (*also* **seis**ˈ**mometer**) —**seismo**ˈ**logic(al)** *a.* pert. to seismology —**seis**ˈ**mologist** *n.* one versed in seismology —**seis**ˈ**mology** *n.* science of earthquakes

seismo- *or before vowel* **seism-** (*comb. form*) earthquake, as in *seismology*

seize (siːz) *vt.* **1.** grasp **2.** lay hold of **3.** capture —*vi.* **4.** (of mechanical parts) stick tightly through overheating —ˈ**seizable** *a.* —ˈ**seizure** *n.* **1.** act of taking, *esp.* by warrant, as goods **2.** sudden onset of disease

seldom (ˈsɛldəm) *adv.* not often, rarely

select (sɪˈlɛkt) *vt.* **1.** pick out, choose —*a.* **2.** choice, picked **3.** exclusive —**se**ˈ**lection** *n.* —**se**ˈ**lective** *a.* —**selec**ˈ**tivity** *n.* —**se**ˈ**lector** *n.*

selenium (sɪˈliːnɪəm) *n.* nonmetallic element with photoelectric properties —**se**ˈ**lenic** *a.*

self (sɛlf) *pron.* **1.** used reflexively or to express emphasis (*pl.* **selves**) —*a.* **2.** (of colour) same throughout, uniform —*n.* **3.** one's own person or individuality (*pl.* **selves**) —ˈ**selfish** *a.* **1.** concerned unduly over personal profit or pleasure **2.** lacking consideration for others **3.** greedy —ˈ**selfishly** *adv.* —ˈ**selfless** *a.* **1.** having no regard to self **2.** unselfish

self- (*comb. form*) of oneself or itself. See the list below

self-abnegation *n.* denial of one's own interests

self-abuse *n.* **1.** misuse of one's own abilities *etc.* **2.** *euphemistic* masturbation

self-aggrandizement *n.* act of increasing one's own power *etc.* —**self-aggrandizing** *a.*

self-assertion *n.* act of putting forward one's own opinions *etc.*, esp. in aggressive manner —**self-asserting** *a.* —**self-assertive** *a.*

self-assurance *n.* confidence in validity *etc.* of one's own opinions *etc.* —**self-assured** *a.*

self-conscious *a.* **1.** unduly aware of oneself **2.** conscious of one's acts or states

THESAURUS

seek 1. be after, follow, go gunning for, go in pursuit (quest, search) of, hunt, inquire, look for, pursue, search for **2.** ask, beg, entreat, inquire, invite, petition, request, solicit

seem appear, assume, give the impression, have the *or* every appearance of, look, look as if, look to be, pretend, sound like, strike one as being

seemly appropriate, becoming, befitting, *comme il faut*, decent, decorous, fit, fitting, in good taste, meet (*Archaic*), nice, proper, suitable, suited, the done thing

seer augur, predictor, prophet, sibyl, soothsayer

seesaw *v.* alternate, fluctuate, go from one extreme to the other, oscillate, pitch, swing, teeter

seethe 1. boil, bubble, churn, ferment, fizz, foam, froth **2.** be in a state (*Inf.*), be livid (furious, incensed), breathe fire and slaughter, foam at the mouth, fume, get hot under the collar (*Inf.*), rage, simmer, storm

segment bit, compartment, division, part, piece, portion, section, slice, wedge

segregate discriminate against, dissociate, isolate, separate, set apart, single out

segregation apartheid (*in South Africa*), discrimination, isolation, separation

seize 1. clutch, collar (*Inf.*), fasten, grab, grasp, grip, lay hands on, snatch, take **2.** apprehend, catch, get, grasp **3.** annex, appropriate, arrest, capture, commandeer, confiscate, hijack, impound, take by storm, take captive, take possession of

seizure 1. annexation, apprehension, arrest, capture, commandeering, confiscation, grabbing, taking **2.** attack, convulsion, fit, paroxysm, spasm

seldom hardly ever, infrequently, not often, occasionally, once in a blue moon (*Inf.*), rarely, scarcely ever

select *v.* **1.** choose, opt for, pick, prefer, single out, sort out ~*adj.* **2.** choice, excellent, first-class, first-rate, hand-picked, picked, posh (*Inf.*), preferable, prime, rare, recherché, selected, special, superior, topnotch (*Inf.*) **3.** cliquish, elite, exclusive, limited, privileged

selection choice, choosing, option, pick, preference

selective careful, discerning, discriminating, discriminatory, eclectic, particular

self-assurance assertiveness, confidence, positiveness, self-confidence

self-centred egotistic, inward looking, narcissistic, self-absorbed, selfish, self-seeking, wrapped up in oneself

self-confidence aplomb, confidence, high morale, nerve, poise, self-assurance, self-reliance, self-respect

self-confident assured, fearless, poised, secure, self-assured, self-reliant, sure of oneself

self-conscious affected, awkward, bashful, diffident,

self-determination *n.* the right of person or nation to decide for himself or itself

self-discipline *n.* disciplining of one's own feelings, desires *etc.* **—self-disciplined** *a.*

self-educated *a.* educated through one's own efforts without formal instruction

self-effacement *n.* act of making oneself, one's actions *etc.* inconspicuous **—self-effacing** *a.*

self-employed *a.* earning one's living in one's own business **—self-employment** *n.*

self-expression *n.* expression of one's own personality *etc.* as in painting *etc.* **—self-expressive** *a.*

self-government *n.* government of country *etc.* by its own people **—self-governed** *a.* **—self-governing** *a.*

selfheal ('sɛlfhiːl) *n.* European herbaceous plant reputedly having healing powers

self-important *a.* having unduly high opinion of one's own importance *etc.* **—self-importance** *n.*

self-improvement *n.* improvement of one's status, education *etc.* by one's own efforts

self-induced *a.* induced by oneself or itself

self-interest *n.* **1.** one's personal interest or advantage **2.** act of pursuing one's own interest

self-made *a.* having achieved wealth, status *etc.* by one's own efforts

self-opinionated *a.* **1.** having unduly high regard for oneself or one's own opinions **2.** clinging stubbornly to one's own opinions

self-possessed *a.* calm, composed **—self-possession** *n.*

self-propelled *a.* (of vehicle) provided with its own source of tractive power

self-raising *a.* (of flour) having raising agent already added

self-respect *n.* proper sense of one's own dignity and integrity

self-righteous *a.* smugly sure of one's own virtue

self-sacrifice *n.* sacrifice of one's own desires *etc.* for sake of well-being of others **—self-sacrificing** *a.*

selfsame ('sɛlfseɪm) *a.* very same

self-satisfied *a.* having or showing complacent satisfaction with oneself, one's own actions *etc.* **—self-satisfaction** *n.*

self-sealing *a.* (*esp.* of envelope) designed to become sealed by pressure only

self-seeking *n.* **1.** act of seeking one's own profit or interest *—a.* **2.** having exclusive preoccupation with one's own profit or interest **—self-seeker** *n.*

self-abasement
self-absorbed
self-absorption
self-addressed
self-adhesive
self-appointed
self-assurance
self-assured
self-catering
self-centred
self-confessed
self-confidence
self-confident
self-contained
self-control
self-deception
self-defeating
self-defence
self-delusion
self-denial
self-employed
self-esteem
self-evident
self-explanatory
self-help
self-indulgence
self-indulgent
self-inflicted
self-interest
self-knowledge
self-pity
self-portrait
self-preservation
self-raising
self-regard
self-reliance
self-reliant
self-reproach
self-restraint
self-sacrifice
self-satisfied
self-supporting

THESAURUS

embarrassed, ill at ease, insecure, nervous, out of countenance, shamefaced, sheepish, uncomfortable

self-control restraint, self-discipline, self-mastery, self-restraint, strength of mind *or* will, willpower

self-esteem *amour-propre*, confidence, faith in oneself, pride, self-assurance, self-regard, self-respect, vanity

self-evident axiomatic, clear, incontrovertible, inescapable, manifestly *or* patently true, obvious, undeniable, written all over (something)

self-government autonomy, home rule, independence, self-determination, self-rule, sovereignty

self-important arrogant, conceited, overbearing, pompous, presumptuous, pushy (*Inf.*), strutting, swaggering, swollen-headed

self-indulgence dissipation, excess, extravagance, incontinence, intemperance, self-gratification, sensualism

selfish egoistic, egoistical, egotistic, egotistical, greedy, looking out for number one (*Inf.*), mean, mercenary, narrow, self-centred, self-interested, self-seeking, ungenerous

selfless altruistic, generous, magnanimous, self-denying, self-sacrificing, ungrudging, unselfish

self-possessed collected, confident, cool, cool as a cucumber (*Inf.*), poised, self-assured, sure of oneself, together (*Sl.*), unruffled

self-reliant able to stand on one's own two feet (*Inf.*), capable, independent, self-sufficient

self-respect *amour-propre*, dignity, faith in oneself, morale, one's own image, pride, self-esteem

self-righteous complacent, goody-goody (*Inf.*), holier-than-thou, hypocritical, pharisaic, pi (*Brit. sl.*), pietistic, pious, priggish, sanctimonious, self-satisfied, smug, superior, too good to be true

self-sacrifice altruism, generosity, self-abnegation, self-denial, selflessness

self-satisfaction complacency, contentment, ease of mind, flush of success, glow of achievement, pride, self-approbation, self-approval, smugness

self-satisfied complacent, flushed with success, like

self-service *a./n.* (of) shop or restaurant where customers serve themselves
self-starter *n.* **1.** electric motor used to start internal-combustion engine **2.** switch that operates this motor
self-styled *a.* claiming to be of specified nature, profession *etc.*
self-sufficient *or* **self-sufficing** *a.* **1.** sufficient in itself **2.** relying on one's own powers
self-will *n.* **1.** obstinacy **2.** wilfulness **—self-willed** *a.* headstrong
self-winding *a.* (of wrist watch) winding automatically
sell (sɛl) *vt.* **1.** hand over for a price **2.** stock, have for sale **3.** make (someone) accept **4.** *inf.* betray, cheat —*vi.* **5.** find purchasers (**sold, ˈselling**) —*n. inf.* **6.** hoax —**ˈseller** *n.* **—selling race** *or* **plate** horse race in which winner must be offered for sale at auction —**ˈsellout** *n.* **1.** disposing of completely by selling **2.** betrayal
Sellotape (ˈsɛləteɪp) *n.* **1.** R type of adhesive tape —*vt.* **2.** seal using adhesive tape
Seltzer (ˈsɛltsə) *n.* aerated mineral water
selvage *or* **selvedge** (ˈsɛlvɪdʒ) *n.* finished, nonfraying edge of cloth
selves (sɛlvz) *n., pl. of* SELF
Sem. 1. Seminary **2.** Semitic
semantic (sɪˈmæntɪk) *a.* relating to meaning of words or symbols —**seˈmantics** *pl.n.* (*with sing. v.*) study of linguistic meaning
semaphore (ˈsɛməfɔː) *n.* **1.** post with movable arms for signalling **2.** system of signalling by human or mechanical arms
semblance (ˈsɛmbləns) *n.* **1.** (false) appearance **2.** image, likeness
semen (ˈsiːmɛn) *n.* **1.** fluid carrying sperm of male animals **2.** sperm
semester (sɪˈmɛstə) *n.* US half-year session in many universities, colleges
semi (ˈsɛmɪ) *inf.* semidetached house
semi- (*comb. form*) half, partly, not completely, as in *semicircle*
semiannual (sɛmɪˈænjʊəl) *a.* **1.** occurring every half-year **2.** lasting for half a year —**semiˈannually** *adv.*
semibreve (ˈsɛmɪbriːv) *n.* musical note half length of breve
semicircle (ˈsɛmɪsɜːkᵊl) *n.* half of circle —**semiˈcircular** *a.* **—semicircular canal** *Anat.* any of three looped fluid-filled membranous tubes that comprise labyrinth of ear
semicolon (sɛmɪˈkəʊlən) *n.* punctuation mark (;)
semiconductor (sɛmɪkənˈdʌktə) *n.* **1.** substance, as silicon, having electrical conductivity that increases with temperature **2.** device, as transistor, dependent on properties of such substance
semidetached (sɛmɪdɪˈtætʃt) *a./n.* (of) house joined to another on one side only
semifinal (sɛmɪˈfaɪnᵊl) *n.* match, round *etc.* before final
seminal (ˈsɛmɪnəl) *a.* **1.** capable of developing **2.** influential, important **3.** rudimentary **4.** of semen or seed
seminar (ˈsɛmɪnɑː) *n.* meeting of group (of students) for discussion
seminary (ˈsɛmɪnərɪ) *n.* college for priests
semiprecious (sɛmɪˈprɛʃəs) *a.* (of gemstones) having less value than precious stones
semiprofessional (sɛmɪprəˈfɛʃənᵊl) *a.* **1.** (of person) engaged in activity or sport part-time but for pay **2.** (of activity or sport) engaged in by semiprofessionals **3.** of person whose activities are professional in some respects —*n.* **4.** semiprofessional person
semiquaver (ˈsɛmɪkweɪvə) *n. Mus.* note having time value of one-sixteenth of semibreve
semiskilled (sɛmɪˈskɪld) *a.* partly skilled, trained but not for specialized work
Semite (ˈsiːmaɪt) *n.* member of race including Jews and Arabs **—Semitic** (sɪˈmɪtɪk) *a.* **1.** denoting a Semite **2.** Jewish
semitone (ˈsɛmɪtəʊn) *n.* musical halftone
semitrailer (sɛmɪˈtreɪlə) *n.* type of trailer that has wheels only at rear, front end being supported by towing vehicle
semivowel (ˈsɛmɪvaʊəl) *n. Phonet.* vowel-like sound that acts like consonant, as (w) in *well* and (j), represented as *y*, in *yell* (*also* **glide**)
semolina (sɛməˈliːnə) *n.* hard grains left after sifting of flour, used for puddings *etc.*
sempervivum (sɛmpəˈvaɪvəm) *n.* plant with ornamental rosettes of leaves
sempre (ˈsɛmprɪ) *adv. Mus.* always; consistently
S.E.N. State Enrolled Nurse
Sen. *or* **sen. 1.** senate **2.** senator **3.** senior
senate (ˈsɛnɪt) *n.* upper council of state, university *etc.* —**ˈsenator** *n.* —**senaˈtorial** *a.*
send (sɛnd) *vt.* **1.** cause to go or be conveyed **2.** dispatch **3.** transmit (by radio) (**sent, ˈsending**) —**ˈsendoff** *n. inf.* demonstration of good wishes to person about to set off on journey *etc.* **—send-up** *n.* UK parody or imitation **—send off 1.** cause to depart **2.** *Soccer, rugby etc.* (of referee) dismiss (player) from

THESAURUS

a cat that has swallowed the cream *or* the canary, pleased with oneself, proud of oneself, puffed up, self-congratulatory, smug, well-pleased
self-seeking *adj.* acquisitive, calculating, careerist, fortune-hunting, gold-digging, looking out for number one (*Inf.*), mercenary, on the make (*Sl.*), opportunistic, out for what one can get, self-interested, selfish, self-serving
sell 1. barter, dispose of, exchange, put up for sale, trade **2.** be in the business of, deal in, handle, hawk, market, merchandise, peddle, retail, stock, trade in, traffic in, vend **3.** *Inf. often with* **on** convert to, convince of, get (someone) hooked on (*Inf.*), persuade of, talk (someone) into, win (someone) over to **4.** betray, deliver up, give up, sell down the river (*Inf.*), sell out (*Inf.*), surrender
seller agent, dealer, merchant, rep, representative, retailer, salesman, saleswoman, shopkeeper, tradesman, traveller, vendor
send 1. communicate, consign, convey, direct, dispatch, forward, remit, transmit **2.** cast, deliver, fire, fling, hurl, let fly, propel, shoot
sendoff departure, farewell, going-away party, leave-taking, start, valediction

field of play for some offence —**send up** *sl.* 1. send to prison 2. UK make fun of, *esp.* by doing parody of

senescent (sɪˈnɛsᵊnt) *a.* 1. growing old 2. characteristic of old age —**seˈnescence** *n.*

senile (ˈsiːnaɪl) *a.* showing weakness of old age —**senility** (sɪˈnɪlɪtɪ) *n.*

senior (ˈsiːnjə) *a.* 1. superior in rank or standing 2. older —*n.* 3. superior 4. elder person —**seniˈority** *n.* —**senior aircraftman** rank in Royal Air Force comparable to that of private in army, though not lowest rank in Royal Air Force —**senior citizen UK, A, NZ,** *euphemistic* elderly person —**senior service UK** Royal Navy

senna (ˈsɛnə) *n.* 1. tropical plant 2. its dried leaves or pods, used as laxative

señor (sɛˈnjɔː; *Sp.* seˈɲor) *n.* Sp. title of respect, like Mr. (*pl.* **-s, -ñores** (*Sp.* -ˈɲores)) —**seˈñora** *n.* Mrs. —**señoˈrita** *n.* Miss

sensation (sɛnˈseɪʃən) *n.* 1. operation of sense, feeling, awareness 2. excited feeling, state of excitement 3. exciting event 4. strong impression 5. commotion —**senˈsational** *a.* 1. producing great excitement 2. melodramatic 3. of perception by senses —**senˈsationalism** *n.* 1. use of sensational language *etc.* to arouse intense emotional excitement 2. doctrine that sensations are basis of all knowledge

sense (sɛns) *n.* 1. any of bodily faculties of perception or feeling 2. sensitiveness of any or all of these faculties 3. ability to perceive, mental alertness 4. consciousness 5. meaning 6. coherence, intelligible meaning 7. sound practical judgment —*vt.* 8. perceive 9. understand —**ˈsenseless** *a.* —**ˈsenselessly** *adv.* —**sense organ** structure in animals that is specialized for receiving external stimuli and transmitting them to brain

sensible (ˈsɛnsɪbᵊl) *a.* 1. reasonable, wise 2. perceptible by senses 3. aware, mindful 4. considerable, appreciable —**sensiˈbility** *n.* ability to feel, *esp.* emotional or moral feelings —**ˈsensibly** *adv.*

sensitive (ˈsɛnsɪtɪv) *a.* 1. open to, acutely affected by, external impressions 2. easily affected or altered 3. easily upset by criticism 4. responsive to slight changes —**ˈsensitively** *adv.* —**sensiˈtivity** *or* **ˈsensitiveness** *n.* —**ˈsensitize** *or* **-tise** *vt.* make sensitive, *esp.* make (photographic film *etc.*) sensitive to light

sensor (ˈsɛnsə) *n.* device that responds to stimulus

sensory (ˈsɛnsərɪ) *or* **sensorial** (sɛnˈsɔːrɪəl) *a.* relating to organs, operation, of senses

sensual (ˈsɛnsjʊəl) *a.* 1. of senses only and not of mind 2. given to pursuit of pleasures of sense 3. self-indulgent 4. licentious —**ˈsensualism** *n.* —**ˈsensualist** *n.* —**sensuˈality** *n.*

sensuous (ˈsɛnsjʊəs) *a.* stimulating, or apprehended by senses, *esp.* in aesthetic manner

THESAURUS

senile decrepit, doddering, doting, failing, imbecile, in one's dotage, in one's second childhood

senior *adj.* elder, higher ranking, major (*Brit.*), older, superior

seniority eldership, longer service, precedence, priority, rank, superiority

sensation 1. awareness, consciousness, feeling, impression, perception, sense, tingle 2. agitation, commotion, crowd puller (*Inf.*), excitement, furore, hit (*Inf.*), scandal, stir, surprise, thrill, wow (*Sl., chiefly U.S.*)

sensational amazing, astounding, breathtaking, dramatic, electrifying, exciting, hair-raising, horrifying, lurid, melodramatic, revealing, scandalous, sensationalistic, shocking, spectacular, staggering, startling, thrilling, yellow (*of the press*)

sense *n.* 1. faculty, feeling, sensation, sensibility 2. appreciation, atmosphere, aura, awareness, consciousness, feel, impression, intuition, perception, premonition, presentiment, sentiment 3. definition, denotation, drift, gist, implication, import, interpretation, meaning, message, nuance, purport, significance, signification, substance 4. *Sometimes plural* brains (*Inf.*), clear-headedness, cleverness, common sense, discernment, discrimination, gumption (*Brit. inf.*), intelligence, judgment, mother wit, nous (*Brit. sl.*), quickness, reason, sagacity, sanity, sharpness, tact, understanding, wisdom, wit(s) ~*v.* 5. appreciate, apprehend, be aware of, discern, divine, feel, get the impression, grasp, have a feeling in one's bones (*Inf.*), have a funny feeling (*Inf.*), have a hunch, just know, notice, observe, perceive, pick up, realize, suspect, understand

senseless 1. absurd, asinine, crazy, daft (*Inf.*), fatuous, foolish, halfwitted, idiotic, illogical, imbecilic, inane, incongruous, inconsistent, irrational, ludicrous, mad, meaningless, mindless, moronic, nonsensical, pointless, ridiculous, silly, simple, stupid, unintelligent, unreasonable, unwise 2. anaesthetized, cold, deadened, insensate, insensible, numb, numbed, out, out cold, stunned, unconscious, unfeeling

sensibility 1. responsiveness, sensitiveness, sensitivity, susceptibility 2. *Often plural* emotions, feelings, moral sense, sentiments, susceptibilities 3. appreciation, awareness, delicacy, discernment, insight, intuition, perceptiveness, taste

sensible 1. canny, discreet, discriminating, down-to-earth, far-sighted, intelligent, judicious, matter-of-fact, practical, prudent, rational, realistic, reasonable, sagacious, sage, sane, shrewd, sober, sound, well-reasoned, well-thought-out, wise 2. *Usually with* **of** acquainted with, alive to, aware, conscious, convinced, mindful, observant, sensitive to, understanding 3. appreciable, considerable, discernible, noticeable, palpable, perceptible, significant, tangible, visible

sensitive 1. acute, delicate, easily affected, fine, impressionable, keen, perceptive, precise, reactive, responsive, sentient, susceptible 2. delicate, easily upset (hurt, offended), irritable, temperamental, tender, thin-skinned, touchy, umbrageous (*Rare*)

sensitivity delicacy, reactiveness, reactivity, receptiveness, responsiveness, sensitiveness, susceptibility

sensual 1. animal, bodily, carnal, epicurean, fleshly, luxurious, physical, unspiritual, voluptuous 2. erotic, lascivious, lecherous, lewd, libidinous, licentious, lustful, randy (*Sl.*), raunchy (*U.S. sl.*), sexual, sexy (*Inf.*), unchaste

sensuality animalism, carnality, eroticism, lasciviousness, lecherousness, lewdness, libidinousness, licentiousness, prurience, salaciousness, sexiness (*Inf.*), voluptuousness

sensuous epicurean, gratifying, hedonistic, lush, pleasurable, rich, sensory, sumptuous, sybaritic

sent (sɛnt) *pt./pp. of* SEND

sentence (ˈsɛntəns) *n.* **1.** combination of words, which is complete as expressing a thought **2.** judgment passed on criminal by court or judge —*vt.* **3.** pass sentence on, condemn —**senˈtential** *a.* of sentence —**senˈtentious** *a.* **1.** full of axioms and maxims **2.** pithy **3.** pompously moralizing —**senˈtentiously** *adv.* —**senˈtentiousness** *n.*

sentient (ˈsɛntɪənt) *a.* **1.** capable of feeling **2.** feeling **3.** thinking —**ˈsentience** *or* **ˈsentiency** *n.*

sentiment (ˈsɛntɪmənt) *n.* **1.** tendency to be moved by feeling rather than reason **2.** verbal expression of feeling **3.** mental feeling, emotion **4.** opinion —**sentiˈmental** *a.* **1.** given to indulgence in sentiment and in its expression **2.** weak **3.** sloppy —**sentiˈmentalist** *n.* —**sentimenˈtality** *n.* —**sentiˈmentalize** *or* **-lise** *v.*

sentinel (ˈsɛntɪnᵊl) *n.* sentry

sentry (ˈsɛntrɪ) *n.* soldier on watch —**sentry box** small shelter in which sentry may stand to be sheltered from weather

sepal (ˈsɛpᵊl) *n.* leaf or division of the calyx of a flower

separate (ˈsɛpəreɪt) *vt.* **1.** part **2.** divide **3.** sever **4.** put apart **5.** occupy place between —*vi.* **6.** withdraw, become parted —*a.* (ˈsɛprɪt, ˈsɛpərɪt) **7.** disconnected, apart **8.** distinct, individual —**ˈseparable** *a.* —**separately** (ˈsɛprɪtlɪ, ˈsɛpərɪtlɪ) *adv.* —**sepaˈration** *n.* **1.** disconnection **2.** *Law* living apart of married people without divorce —**ˈseparatism** *n.* —**ˈseparatist** *n.* person who advocates secession from organization, union *etc.* —**ˈseparator** *n.* **1.** that which separates **2.** apparatus for separating cream from milk —**separate school** C school for a large religious minority

sepia (ˈsiːpɪə) *n.* **1.** reddish-brown pigment made from a fluid secreted by the cuttlefish —*a.* **2.** of this colour

sepoy (ˈsiːpɔɪ) *n.* formerly, Indian soldier in service of Brit.

sepsis (ˈsɛpsɪs) *n.* presence of pus-forming bacteria in body

Sept. September

September (sɛpˈtɛmbə) *n.* 9th month

septennial (sɛpˈtɛnɪəl) *a.* lasting, occurring every seven years

septet (sɛpˈtɛt) *n.* **1.** music for seven instruments or voices **2.** group of seven performers

septic (ˈsɛptɪk) *a.* **1.** of, caused by, sepsis **2.** (of wound) infected —**septicaemia** *or* **septicemia** (sɛptɪˈsiːmɪə) *n.* blood poisoning —**septic tank** tank for containing sewage to be decomposed by anaerobic bacteria

septuagenarian (sɛptjuədʒɪˈnɛərɪən) *a.* **1.** aged between seventy and eighty —*n.* **2.** person of this age

Septuagesima (sɛptjuəˈdʒɛsɪmə) *n.* third Sunday before Lent

septum (ˈsɛptəm) *n. Biol., anat.* dividing partition between two tissues or cavities (*pl.* **-ta** (-tə))

septuple (ˈsɛptjupᵊl) *a.* **1.** seven times as much or many **2.** consisting of seven parts or members —*vt.* **3.** multiply by seven —**septuplicate** (sɛpˈtjuːplɪkət) *n./a.*

sepulchre *or U.S.* **sepulcher** (ˈsɛpəlkə) *n.* tomb, burial vault —**seˈpulchral** *a.* **1.** of burial, or the grave **2.** mournful **3.** gloomy —**ˈsepulture** *n.* burial

sequel (ˈsiːkwəl) *n.* **1.** consequence **2.** continuation, *eg* of story

sequence (ˈsiːkwəns) *n.* **1.** arrangement of things in successive order **2.** section, episode of film —**ˈsequent** *or* **seˈquential** *a.*

sequester (sɪˈkwɛstə) *vt.* **1.** separate **2.** seclude **3.** put aside —**seˈquestrate** *vt.* **1.** confiscate **2.** divert or appropriate income of (property) to satisfy claims against its owner —**sequestration** (siːkwɛˈstreɪʃən) *n.*

sequin (ˈsiːkwɪn) *n.* **1.** small ornamental metal disc on dresses *etc.* **2.** formerly, Venetian gold coin

sequoia (sɪˈkwɔɪə) *n.* giant Californian coniferous tree

THESAURUS

sentence 1. *n.* condemnation, decision, decree, doom, judgment, order, pronouncement, ruling, verdict **2.** *v.* condemn, doom, mete out justice to, pass judgment on, penalize

sententious 1. aphoristic, axiomatic, brief, compact, concise, epigrammatic, gnomic, laconic, pithy, pointed, short, succinct, terse **2.** canting, judgmental, moralistic, pompous, ponderous, preachifying (*Inf.*), sanctimonious

sentiment 1. emotion, sensibility, soft-heartedness, tender feeling, tenderness **2.** *Often plural* attitude, belief, feeling, idea, judgment, opinion, persuasion, saying, thought, view, way of thinking

sentimental corny (*Sl.*), dewy-eyed, drippy (*Inf.*), emotional, gushy (*Inf.*), impressionable, maudlin, mawkish, mushy (*Inf.*), nostalgic, overemotional, pathetic, romantic, schmaltzy (*Sl.*), simpering, sloppy (*Inf.*), slushy (*Inf.*), soft-hearted, tearful, tear-jerking (*Inf.*), tender, touching, weepy (*Inf.*)

sentimentality bathos, corniness (*Sl.*), emotionalism, gush (*Inf.*), mawkishness, mush (*Inf.*), nostalgia, play on the emotions, romanticism, schmaltz (*Sl.*), sloppiness (*Inf.*), slush (*Inf.*), sob stuff (*Inf.*), tenderness

separable detachable, distinguishable, divisible, scissile, severable

separate *v.* **1.** break off, cleave, come apart, come away, come between, detach, disconnect, disentangle, disjoin, divide, keep apart, remove, sever, split, sunder, uncouple **2.** discriminate between, isolate, put on one side, segregate, single out, sort out **3.** bifurcate, break up, disunite, diverge, divorce, estrange, go different ways, part, part company, set at variance *or* at odds, split up ~*adj.* **4.** detached, disconnected, discrete, disjointed, divided, divorced, isolated, unattached, unconnected **5.** alone, apart, autonomous, distinct, independent, individual, particular, single, solitary

separately alone, apart, independently, individually, one at a time, one by one, personally, severally, singly

separation 1. break, detachment, disconnection, disengagement, disjunction, dissociation, disunion, division, gap, segregation, severance **2.** break-up, divorce, estrangement, farewell, leave-taking, parting, rift, split, split-up

septic festering, infected, poisoned, pussy, putrefactive, putrefying, putrid, toxic

sepulchre burial place, grave, tomb, vault

sequel conclusion, consequence, continuation, development, end, follow-up, issue, outcome, payoff (*Inf.*), result, upshot

sequence arrangement, chain, course, cycle, order, procession, progression, series, succession

seraglio (sɛˈrɑːlɪəʊ) *or* **serail** (səˈraɪ) *n.* harem, palace, of Turkish sultan (*pl.* **-s**)

seraph (ˈsɛrəf) *n.* member of highest order of angels (*pl.* **-s, -aphim** (-əfɪm)) **—seˈraphic** *a.*

Serbian (ˈsɜːbɪən) *a.* **1.** of Serbia, its people or their dialect of Serbo-Croatian *—n.* **2.** dialect of Serbo-Croatian spoken in Serbia **3.** native or inhabitant of Serbia (*also* **Serb**) **—Serbo-Croatian** *or* **Serbo-Croat** *n.* **1.** chief official language of Yugoslavia *—a.* **2.** of this language

serenade (sɛrɪˈneɪd) *n.* **1.** sentimental piece of music or song of type addressed to woman by lover, *esp.* at evening *—v.* **2.** sing serenade (to)

serendipity (sɛrənˈdɪpɪtɪ) *n.* faculty of making fortunate discoveries by accident

serene (sɪˈriːn) *a.* **1.** calm, tranquil **2.** unclouded **3.** quiet, placid **—seˈrenely** *adv.* **—serenity** (sɪˈrɛnɪtɪ) *n.*

serf (sɜːf) *n.* one of class of medieval labourers bound to, and transferred with, land **—ˈserfdom** *or* **ˈserfhood** *n.*

serge (sɜːdʒ) *n.* strong hard-wearing twilled worsted fabric

sergeant (ˈsɑːdʒənt) *n.* **1.** noncommissioned officer in army **2.** police officer above constable **—sergeant major** highest noncommissioned officer in regiment **—sergeant at arms** parliamentary, court officer with ceremonial duties

series (ˈsɪəriːz) *n.* **1.** sequence **2.** succession, set (*eg* of radio, TV programmes with same characters, setting, but different stories) (*pl.* **-ries**) **—ˈserial** *n.* **1.** story or play produced in successive episodes or instalments **2.** periodical publication *—a.* **3.** of, in or forming a series **—ˈserialize** *or* **-lise** *vt.* publish, present as serial **—seriatim** (sɪərɪˈætɪm) *adv.* one after another

serif *or* **seriph** (ˈsɛrɪf) *n. Print.* small line finishing off stroke of letter

seriocomic (sɪərɪəʊˈkɒmɪk) *a.* mixing serious and comic elements **—serioˈcomically** *adv.*

serious (ˈsɪərɪəs) *a.* **1.** thoughtful, solemn **2.** earnest, sincere **3.** of importance **4.** giving cause for concern **—ˈseriously** *adv.*

sermon (ˈsɜːmən) *n.* **1.** discourse of religious instruction or exhortation spoken or read from pulpit **2.** any similar discourse **—ˈsermonize** *or* **-ise** *vi.* **1.** talk like preacher **2.** compose sermons

serpent (ˈsɜːpənt) *n. Lit.* snake **—ˈserpentine** *a.* **1.** like, shaped like, serpent *—n.* **2.** any of several kinds of green to black rock

serrate (ˈsɛrɪt, -eɪt) *a.* having notched, sawlike edge **—serˈrated** *a.* **—serˈration** *n.*

serried (ˈsɛrɪd) *a.* in close order, shoulder to shoulder

serum (ˈsɪərəm) *n.* watery animal fluid, *esp.* thin part of blood as used for inoculation or vaccination (*pl.* **-s, -ra** (-rə)) **—seˈrosity** *n.* **—ˈserous** *a.* of or producing serum

serval (ˈsɜːvᵊl) *n.* feline Afr. mammal

serve (sɜːv) *vt.* **1.** work for, under **2.** attend to (customers) in shop *etc.* **3.** provide **4.** provide (guests) with (food *etc.*) **5.** present (food *etc.*) in particular way **6.** provide with regular supply of **7.** pay homage to **8.** go through (period of service *etc.*) **9.** suit **10.** *Tennis etc.* put (ball) into play *—vi.* **11.** be member of military unit *—n.* **12.** *Tennis etc.* act of serving ball **—ˈservant** *n.* personal or domestic attendant **—ˈservice** *n.* **1.** the act of serving, helping, assisting **2.** system organized to provide for needs of public **3.** maintenance of vehicle **4.** use **5.** readiness, availability for use **6.** department of State employ **7.** employment of persons engaged in this **8.** set of dishes *etc.* **9.** form, session, of public worship *—pl.* **10.** armed forces *—vt.* **11.** overhaul **—ˈserviceable** *a.* **1.** in working order, usable **2.** durable **—ˈserving** *n.* portion of food or drink **—service area** place on motorway providing facilities as garage, restaurant *etc.* **—service charge** percentage of bill added to total to pay for service **—service flat** rented flat where landlord provides services such as cleaning *etc.* **—ˈserviceman** *n.* member of the armed forces **—service road** narrow road giving access to houses, shops *etc.* **—service station** place supplying fuel, oil, maintenance for motor vehicles **—service tree** Eurasian rosaceous tree with white flowers and brown edible apple-like fruits

THESAURUS

seraphic angelic, beatific, blissful, celestial, divine, heavenly, holy, pure, sublime

serene **1.** calm, composed, imperturbable, peaceful, placid, tranquil, undisturbed, unruffled, untroubled **2.** bright, clear, cloudless, fair, halcyon, unclouded

serenity **1.** calm, calmness, composure, peace, peacefulness, peace of mind, placidity, quietness, quietude, stillness, tranquillity **2.** brightness, clearness, fairness

series arrangement, chain, course, line, order, progression, run, sequence, set, string, succession, train

serious **1.** grave, humourless, long-faced, pensive, sedate, sober, solemn, stern, thoughtful, unsmiling **2.** deliberate, determined, earnest, genuine, honest, in earnest, resolute, resolved, sincere **3.** crucial, deep, difficult, far-reaching, fateful, grim, important, momentous, no laughing matter, of moment *or* consequence, pressing, significant, urgent, weighty, worrying **4.** acute, alarming, critical, dangerous, grave, severe

seriously **1.** all joking aside, earnestly, gravely, in all conscience, in earnest, no joking (*Inf.*), sincerely, solemnly, thoughtfully, with a straight face **2.** acutely, badly, critically, dangerously, distressingly, gravely, grievously, severely, sorely

sermon **1.** address, exhortation, homily **2.** dressing-down (*Inf.*), harangue, lecture, talking-to (*Inf.*)

servant attendant, domestic, drudge, help, helper, lackey, maid, menial, retainer, servitor (*Archaic*), slave, vassal

serve **1.** aid, assist, attend to, be in the service of, be of assistance, be of use, help, minister to, oblige, succour, wait on, work for **2.** act, attend, complete, discharge, do, fulfil, go through, observe, officiate, pass, perform **3.** answer, answer the purpose, be acceptable, be adequate, be good enough, content, do, do duty as, do the work of, fill the bill (*Inf.*), function as, satisfy, suffice, suit **4.** arrange, deal, deliver, dish up, distribute, handle, present, provide, set out, supply

service *n.* **1.** advantage, assistance, avail, benefit, help, ministrations, supply, use, usefulness, utility **2.** check, maintenance, overhaul, servicing **3.** business, duty, employ, employment, labour, office, work **4.** ceremony, function, observance, rite, worship *~v.* **5.** check, fine tune, go over, maintain, overhaul, recondition, repair, tune (up)

serviette (sɜːvɪˈɛt) *n.* table napkin

servile (ˈsɜːvaɪl) *a.* **1.** slavish, without independence **2.** cringing, fawning **3.** menial —**servility** (sɜːˈvɪlɪtɪ) *n.*

servitude (ˈsɜːvɪtjuːd) *n.* bondage, slavery

servomechanism (ˈsɜːvəʊmɛkənɪzəm) *n.* device for converting small mechanical force into larger force, *esp.* in steering mechanisms

servomotor (ˈsɜːvəʊməʊtə) *n.* motor that supplies power to servomechanism

sesame (ˈsɛsəmɪ) *n.* plant with seeds used as herbs and for making oil

sesqui- (*comb. form*) one and a half, as in *sesquicentennial*

sessile (ˈsɛsaɪl) *a.* **1.** (of flowers or leaves) having no stalk **2.** (of animals such as barnacle) permanently attached —**sessility** (sɛˈsɪlɪtɪ) *n.*

session (ˈsɛʃən) *n.* **1.** meeting of court *etc.* **2.** assembly **3.** continuous series of such meetings **4.** any period devoted to an activity **5.** school or university term or year

sestet (sɛˈstɛt) *n.* **1.** *Prosody* last six lines of sonnet **2.** *see* SEXTET (sense 1)

set (sɛt) *vt.* **1.** put or place in specified position or condition **2.** cause to sit **3.** fix **4.** point **5.** put up **6.** make ready **7.** establish **8.** prescribe, allot **9.** put to music **10.** (of hair) arrange while wet, so that it dries in position —*vi.* **11.** become firm or fixed **12.** (of sun) go down **13.** have direction (**set, ˈsetting**) —*a.* **14.** fixed, established **15.** deliberate **16.** formal **17.** arranged beforehand **18.** unvarying —*n.* **19.** act or state of being set **20.** bearing, posture **21.** *Rad., T.V.* complete apparatus for reception or transmission **22.** *Theat., cine.* organized settings and equipment to form ensemble of scene **23.** number of things, persons associated as being similar, complementary or used together **24.** *Maths.* group of numbers, objects *etc.* with at least one common property —**ˈsetback** *n.* anything that hinders or impedes —**set piece 1.** work of literature *etc.* intended to create impressive effect **2.** display of fireworks —**ˈsetscrew** *n.* screw that fits into coupling, cam *etc.* and prevents motion of part relative to shaft on which it is mounted —**set square** thin flat piece of plastic *etc.* in shape of right-angled triangle, used in technical drawing —**set-to** *n. inf.* brief disagreement or fight —**ˈsetup** *n.* **1.** position **2.** organization —**set to 1.** begin working **2.** start fighting —**set up** establish

sett *or* **set** (sɛt) *n.* badger's burrow

settee (sɛˈtiː) *n.* couch

setter (ˈsɛtə) *n.* any of various breeds of gun dog

setting (ˈsɛtɪŋ) *n.* **1.** background **2.** surroundings **3.** scenery and other stage accessories **4.** act of fixing **5.** decorative metalwork holding precious stone *etc.* in position **6.** tableware and cutlery for (single place at) table **7.** descending below horizon of sun **8.** music for song

settle[1] (ˈsɛtᵊl) *vt.* **1.** arrange, put in order **2.** establish, make firm or secure **3.** make quiet or calm **4.** decide upon **5.** end (dispute *etc.*) **6.** pay **7.** bestow (property) by legal deed —*vi.* **8.** come to rest **9.** subside **10.** become clear **11.** take up residence **12.** sink to bottom **13.** come to agreement —**ˈsettlement** *n.* **1.** act of settling **2.** place newly inhabited **3.** money bestowed legally **4.** subsidence (of building) —**ˈsettler** *n.* colonist

settle[2] (ˈsɛtᵊl) *n.* seat, usu. made of wood with high back and arms

THESAURUS

serviceable advantageous, beneficial, convenient, dependable, durable, efficient, functional, hard-wearing, helpful, operative, practical, profitable, usable, useful, utilitarian

session assembly, conference, discussion, get-together (*Inf.*), hearing, meeting, period, sitting, term

set *v.* **1.** aim, apply, deposit, direct, embed, fasten, fix, install, lay, locate, lodge, mount, park, place, plant, plonk, plump, position, put, rest, seat, situate, station, stick, turn **2.** agree upon, allocate, appoint, arrange, assign, conclude, decide (upon), designate, determine, establish, fix, fix up, name, ordain, regulate, resolve, schedule, settle, specify **3.** arrange, lay, make ready, prepare, spread **4.** adjust, coordinate, rectify, regulate, synchronize **5.** cake, condense, congeal, crystallize, gelatinize, harden, jell, solidify, stiffen, thicken **6.** allot, decree, impose, lay down, ordain, prescribe, specify **7.** decline, dip, disappear, go down, sink, subside, vanish ~*n.* **8.** attitude, bearing, carriage, fit, hang, position, posture, turn **9.** *mise-en-scène*, scene, scenery, setting, stage set, stage setting ~*adj.* **10.** agreed, appointed, arranged, customary, decided, definite, established, firm, fixed, prearranged, predetermined, prescribed, regular, scheduled, settled, usual **11.** artificial, conventional, formal, hackneyed, rehearsed, routine, standard, stereotyped, stock, traditional, unspontaneous ~*n.* **12.** band, circle, class, clique, company, coterie, crew (*Inf.*), crowd, faction, gang, group, outfit (*Inf.*), sect **13.** assemblage, assortment, batch, collection, compendium, coordinated group, kit, outfit, series

setback bit of trouble, blow, check, defeat, disappointment, hitch, hold-up, misfortune, rebuff, reverse, upset

setting backdrop, background, context, frame, locale, location, *mise en scène*, mounting, perspective, scene, scenery, set, site, surround, surroundings

settle 1. adjust, dispose, order, put into order, regulate, set to rights, straighten out, work out **2.** choose, clear up, complete, conclude, decide, dispose of, put an end to, reconcile, resolve **3.** *Often with* **on** *or* **upon** agree, appoint, arrange, choose, come to an agreement, confirm, decide, determine, establish, fix **4.** calm, compose, lull, pacify, quell, quiet, quieten, reassure, relax, relieve, sedate, soothe, tranquillize **5.** alight, bed down, come to rest, descend, land, light, make oneself comfortable **6.** dwell, inhabit, live, make one's home, move to, put down roots, reside, set up home, take up residence **7.** acquit oneself of, clear, discharge, liquidate, pay, quit, square (up) **8.** decline, fall, sink, subside

settlement 1. adjustment, agreement, arrangement, completion, conclusion, confirmation, disposition, establishment, resolution, termination, working out **2.** clearance, clearing, defrayal, discharge, liquidation, payment, satisfaction

settler colonist, colonizer, frontiersman, immigrant, pioneer, planter

set-to argument, argy-bargy (*Brit. inf.*), barney (*Inf.*), brush, disagreement, dust-up (*Inf.*), fight, quarrel, row, scrap (*Inf.*), slanging match (*Brit.*), spat, squabble, wrangle

setup arrangement, circumstances, conditions, organization, regime, structure, system

seven (ˈsɛvᵊn) *a./n.* cardinal number, next after six —ˈ**sevenˈteen** *a./n.* ten and seven —ˈ**seventh** *a.* ordinal number of seven —ˈ**seventy** *a./n.* ten times seven —**seven seas** all the oceans of the world —**seventh heaven 1.** final state of eternal bliss **2.** state of supreme happiness

sever (ˈsɛvə) *v.* **1.** separate, divide —*vt.* **2.** cut off —ˈ**severance** *n.* —**severance pay** compensation paid by a firm to employee for loss of employment

several (ˈsɛvrəl) *a.* **1.** some, a few **2.** separate; individual **3.** various **4.** different —*pron.* **5.** indefinite small number —ˈ**severally** *adv.* apart from others

severe (sɪˈvɪə) *a.* **1.** strict; rigorous **2.** hard to do **3.** harsh **4.** austere **5.** extreme —**seˈverely** *adv.* —**severity** (sɪˈvɛrɪtɪ) *n.*

Seville orange (səˈvɪl) **1.** orange tree grown for its bitter fruit, used *esp.* to make marmalade **2.** its fruit

sew (səʊ) *v.* **1.** join (pieces of fabric *etc.*) with needle and thread —*vt.* **2.** make by sewing (**sewed** *pt.*, **sewed, sewn** *pp.*, ˈ**sewing** *pr.p.*) —ˈ**sewing** *n.*

sewage (ˈsuːɪdʒ) *n.* refuse, waste matter, excrement conveyed in sewer —ˈ**sewer** *n.* underground drain to remove waste water and refuse —ˈ**sewerage** *n.* **1.** arrangement of sewers **2.** sewage —**sewage farm** place where sewage is treated, *esp.* for use as manure

sex (sɛks) *n.* **1.** state of being male or female **2.** males or females collectively **3.** sexual intercourse —*a.* **4.** concerning sex —*vt.* **5.** ascertain sex of —ˈ**sexism** *n.* discrimination on basis of sex —ˈ**sexist** *n./a.* —ˈ**sexless** *a.* **1.** having no sexual differentiation **2.** having no sexual appeal or desires —ˈ**sexual** *a.* —ˈ**sexually** *adv.* —ˈ**sexy** *a. inf.* provoking or intended to provoke sexual interest —**sex appeal** quality of attracting opposite sex —**sex change** change of sex, *esp.* involving medical or surgical treatment to alter sexual characteristics to those of opposite sex —**sex chromosome** either of chromosomes determining sex of animals —**sexual intercourse** act of procreation in which male's penis is inserted into female's vagina

sex- (*comb. form*) six, as in *sexcentenary*

sexagenarian (sɛksədʒɪˈnɛərɪən) *a./n.* (person) sixty years old

Sexagesima (sɛksəˈdʒɛsɪmə) *n.* the second Sunday before Lent

sexennial (sɛkˈsɛnɪəl) *a.* lasting, occurring every six years

sextant (ˈsɛkstənt) *n.* navigator's instrument for measuring elevations of heavenly body *etc.*

sextet *or* **sextette** (sɛksˈtɛt) *n.* **1.** (composition for) six singers or players **2.** group of six

sexton (ˈsɛkstən) *n.* official in charge of a church, oft. acting as gravedigger

sextuple (ˈsɛkstjʊpᵊl) *n.* **1.** quantity or number six times as great as another —*a.* **2.** six times as much or as many **3.** consisting of six parts or members —ˈ**sextuplet** *n.* **1.** one of six offspring born at one birth **2.** *Mus.* group of six notes played in time value of four

SF *or* **sf** science fiction

SFA Scottish Football Association

sforzando (sfɔːˈtsɑːndəʊ) *or* **sforzato** (sfɔːˈtsɑːtəʊ) *Mus. a./adv.* **1.** to be played with emphasis —*n.* **2.** symbol, mark *etc.* indicating this

S. Glam South Glamorgan

Sgt. Sergeant

sh (*spelling pron.* ʃʃʃ) *interj.* exclamation to request silence or quiet

shabby (ˈʃæbɪ) *a.* **1.** faded, worn, ragged **2.** poorly dressed **3.** mean, dishonourable **4.** stingy —ˈ**shabbily** *adv.* —ˈ**shabbiness** *n.*

shack (ʃæk) *n.* rough hut —**shack up** (*usu. with* with) *sl.* live (*esp.* with lover)

shackle (ˈʃækᵊl) *n.* (*oft. pl.*) **1.** metal ring or fastening for prisoner's wrist or ankle **2.** anything that confines —*vt.* **3.** fasten with shackles **4.** hamper

shad (ʃæd) *n.* herringlike fish

shade (ʃeɪd) *n.* **1.** partial darkness **2.** shelter, place sheltered from light, heat *etc.* **3.** darker part of anything **4.** depth of colour **5.** tinge **6.** ghost **7.** screen **8.** anything used to screen **9.** US windowblind —*pl.* **10.** US

THESAURUS

set up arrange, begin, compose, establish, found, initiate, install, institute, make provision for, organize, prearrange, prepare

several *adj.* assorted, different, disparate, distinct, divers (*Archaic*), diverse, indefinite, individual, many, particular, respective, single, some, sundry, various

severe 1. austere, cruel, Draconian, hard, harsh, inexorable, iron-handed, oppressive, pitiless, relentless, rigid, strict, unbending, unrelenting **2.** cold, disapproving, dour, flinty, forbidding, grave, grim, serious, sober, stern, strait-laced, tight-lipped, unsmiling **3.** acute, bitter, critical, dangerous, distressing, extreme, fierce, grinding, inclement, intense, violent **4.** ascetic, austere, chaste, classic, forbidding, functional, plain, restrained, simple, Spartan, unadorned, unembellished, unfussy **5.** arduous, demanding, difficult, exacting, fierce, hard, punishing, rigorous, stringent, taxing, tough, unrelenting **6.** astringent, biting, caustic, cutting, harsh, satirical, scathing, unsparing

severely 1. harshly, rigorously, sharply, sternly, strictly, with an iron hand, with a rod of iron **2.** acutely, badly, critically, dangerously, extremely, gravely, hard, sorely

severity austerity, gravity, hardness, harshness, plainness, rigour, seriousness, severeness, sternness, strictness, stringency, toughness

sex 1. gender **2.** *Inf.* coition, coitus, copulation, fornication, going to bed (with someone), intimacy, lovemaking, (sexual) intercourse, sexual relations

sexual 1. carnal, erotic, intimate, of the flesh, sensual **2.** genital, procreative, reproductive, sex, venereal

sexual intercourse carnal knowledge, coition, coitus, commerce (*Archaic*), congress, copulation, coupling, mating, union

sexy arousing, beddable, bedroom, come-hither (*Inf.*), cuddly, erotic, flirtatious, inviting, kissable, naughty, provocative, provoking, seductive, sensual, sensuous, slinky, suggestive, titillating, voluptuous

shabby 1. dilapidated, down at heel, faded, frayed, having seen better days, mean, neglected, poor, ragged, run-down, scruffy, seedy, tattered, tatty, the worse for wear, threadbare, worn, worn-out **2.** cheap, contemptible, despicable, dirty, dishonourable, ignoble, low, low-down (*Inf.*), mean, rotten (*Inf.*), scurvy, shameful, shoddy, ungentlemanly, unworthy

sl. sunglasses —*vt.* 11. screen from light, darken 12. represent (shades) in (drawing) —ˈ**shady** *a.* 1. shielded from sun 2. dim 3. dubious 4. dishonest 5. dishonourable

shadow (ˈʃædəʊ) *n.* 1. dark figure projected by anything that intercepts rays of light 2. patch of shade 3. slight trace 4. indistinct image 5. gloom 6. inseparable companion —*vt.* 7. cast shadow over 8. follow and watch closely —ˈ**shadowy** *a.* —**shadow cabinet** (in Brit. Parliament) members of opposition party, who would hold ministerial office if their party were in power

shaft (ʃɑːft) *n.* 1. straight rod, stem 2. handle 3. arrow 4. ray, beam (of light) 5. revolving rod for transmitting power 6. one of the bars between which horse is harnessed 7. entrance boring of mine

shag[1] (ʃæg) *n.* 1. matted wool or hair 2. long-napped cloth 3. coarse shredded tobacco —ˈ**shaggy** *a.* 1. covered with rough hair or wool 2. tousled, unkempt

shag[2] (ʃæg) *n.* any of various varieties of cormorant

shagreen (ʃæˈgriːn) *n.* 1. rough skin of certain sharks and rays 2. rough grainy leather made from certain animal hides

shah (ʃɑː) *n.* formerly, ruler of Iran

shake (ʃeɪk) *v.* 1. (cause to) move with quick vibrations 2. grasp the hand (of another) in greeting —*vi.* 3. tremble —*vt.* 4. upset 5. wave, brandish (**shook, ˈshaken**) —*n.* 6. act of shaking 7. vibration 8. jolt 9. *inf.* short period of time, jiffy —ˈ**shaker** *n.* 1. person or thing that shakes 2. container from which condiment is shaken 3. container in which ingredients of alcoholic drinks are shaken together —ˈ**shakily** *adv.* —ˈ**shaky** *a.* unsteady, insecure

shale (ʃeɪl) *n.* flaky, sedimentary rock

shall (ʃæl; *unstressed* ʃəl) *v. aux.* makes compound tenses or moods to express obligation, command, condition or intention (**should** *pt.*)

shallot (ʃəˈlɒt) *n.* kind of small onion

shallow (ˈʃæləʊ) *a.* 1. not deep 2. having little depth of water 3. superficial 4. not sincere —*n.* 5. shallow place —ˈ**shallowness** *n.*

shalom aleichem (ʃaˈlɔm aˈlexɛm) *Hebrew* peace be to you: used by Jews as greeting or farewell (*oft. also* **shaˈlom**)

sham (ʃæm) *a./n.* 1. imitation, counterfeit —*vi.* 2. pretend —*v.* 3. feign (-mm-)

shaman (ˈʃæmən) *n.* 1. priest of shamanism 2. medicine man of similar religion —ˈ**shamanism** *n.* religion of certain peoples of northern Asia, based on belief in good and evil spirits who can be controlled only by shamans

shamble (ˈʃæmbᵊl) *vi.* walk in shuffling, awkward way

shambles (ˈʃæmbᵊlz) *pl.n.* (*with sing. v.*) messy, disorderly thing or place

shame (ʃeɪm) *n.* 1. emotion caused by consciousness of guilt or dishonour in one's conduct or state 2. cause of disgrace 3. ignominy 4. pity, hard luck —*vt.* 5. cause to feel shame 6. disgrace 7. force by shame —ˈ**shameful** *a.* disgraceful —ˈ**shamefully** *adv.* —ˈ**shameless** *a.* 1. with no sense of shame 2. indecent —ˈ**shamefaced** *a.* ashamed

THESAURUS

shade *n.* 1. coolness, dimness, dusk, gloom, gloominess, obscurity, screen, semidarkness, shadiness, shadow, shadows 2. blind, canopy, cover, covering, curtain, screen, shield, veil 3. colour, hue, stain, tinge, tint, tone 4. apparition, ghost, manes, phantom, shadow, spectre, spirit ~*v.* 5. cast a shadow over, cloud, conceal, cover, darken, dim, hide, mute, obscure, protect, screen, shadow, shield, shut out the light, veil

shadow *n.* 1. cover, darkness, dimness, dusk, gathering darkness, gloaming, gloom, obscurity, protection, shade, shelter 2. hint, suggestion, suspicion, trace 3. ghost, image, phantom, remnant, representation, spectre, vestige 4. blight, cloud, gloom, sadness ~*v.* 5. cast a shadow over, darken, overhang, screen, shade, shield 6. dog, follow, spy on, stalk, tail (*Inf.*), trail

shadowy 1. crepuscular, dark, dim, dusky, gloomy, indistinct, murky, obscure, shaded, shady, tenebrious, tenebrous 2. dim, dreamlike, faint, ghostly, illusory, imaginary, impalpable, indistinct, intangible, nebulous, obscure, phantom, spectral, undefined, unreal, unsubstantial, vague, wraithlike

shady 1. bosky (*Literary*), bowery, cool, dim, leafy, shaded, shadowy, umbrageous 2. *Inf.* crooked, disreputable, dubious, fishy (*Inf.*), questionable, shifty, slippery, suspect, suspicious, unethical, unscrupulous, untrustworthy

shaft 1. handle, pole, rod, shank, stem, upright 2. beam, gleam, ray, streak

shaggy hairy, hirsute, long-haired, rough, unkempt, unshorn

shake *v.* 1. bump, fluctuate, jar, joggle, jolt, jounce, oscillate, quake, quiver, rock, shiver, shudder, sway, totter, tremble, vibrate, waver, wobble 2. brandish, flourish, wave 3. *Often with* **up** agitate, churn, convulse, rouse, stir 4. discompose, distress, disturb, frighten, intimidate, move, rattle (*Inf.*), shock, unnerve, upset ~*n.* 5. agitation, convulsion, disturbance, jar, jerk, jolt, jounce, pulsation, quaking, shiver, shock, shudder, trembling, tremor, vibration 6. *Inf.* instant, jiffy (*Inf.*), moment, second, tick (*Brit. inf.*), trice

shaky all of a quiver (*Inf.*), faltering, insecure, precarious, quivery, rickety, tottering, trembling, tremulous, unstable, unsteady, weak, wobbly

shallow 1. *adj. Fig.* empty, flimsy, foolish, frivolous, idle, ignorant, meaningless, puerile, simple, skin-deep, slight, superficial, surface, trivial, unintelligent 2. *n. Often plural* bank, flat, sandbank, sand bar, shelf, shoal

sham 1. *n.* counterfeit, feint, forgery, fraud, hoax, humbug, imitation, impostor, imposture, phoney (*Sl.*), pretence, pretender, pseud (*Sl.*), wolf in sheep's clothing 2. *adj.* artificial, bogus, counterfeit, ersatz, false, feigned, imitation, mock, phoney (*Sl.*), pretended, pseud (*Sl.*), pseudo (*Inf.*), simulated, spurious, synthetic 3. *v.* affect, assume, counterfeit, fake, feign, imitate, play possum, pretend, put on, simulate

shame *n.* 1. blot, contempt, degradation, derision, disgrace, dishonour, disrepute, ill repute, infamy, obloquy, odium, opprobrium, reproach, scandal, skeleton in the cupboard, smear 2. abashment, chagrin, compunction, embarrassment, humiliation, ignominy, loss of face, mortification, shamefacedness ~*v.* 3. abash, confound, disconcert, disgrace, embarrass, humble, humiliate, mortify, reproach, ridicule,

shammy (ˈʃæmɪ) *inf.* chamois leather

shampoo (ʃæmˈpuː) *n.* **1.** any of various preparations of liquid soap for washing hair, carpets *etc.* **2.** this process —*vt.* **3.** use shampoo to wash

shamrock (ˈʃæmrɒk) *n.* clover leaf, *esp.* as Irish emblem

shandy (ˈʃændɪ) *or U.S.* **shandygaff** (ˈʃændɪgæf) *n.* mixed drink, *esp.* beer diluted with soft drink

shanghai (ˈʃæŋhaɪ, ʃæŋˈhaɪ) *vt.* force, trick (someone) to do something

shank (ʃæŋk) *n.* **1.** lower leg **2.** shinbone **3.** stem of thing

shantung (ʃænˈtʌŋ) *n.* soft, natural Chinese silk

shanty[1] (ˈʃæntɪ) *n.* **1.** temporary wooden building **2.** crude dwelling

shanty[2] (ˈʃæntɪ) *n.* sailor's song with chorus

shape (ʃeɪp) *n.* **1.** external form or appearance **2.** mould, pattern **3.** *inf.* condition, *esp.* of physical fitness —*vt.* **4.** form, mould, fashion, make —*vi.* **5.** develop (**shaped, ˈshaping**) —**ˈshapeless** *a.* —**ˈshapely** *a.* well-proportioned

SHAPE (ʃeɪp) Supreme Headquarters Allied Powers Europe

shard (ʃɑːd) *or* **sherd** *n.* broken fragment, *esp.* of earthenware

share[1] (ʃɛə) *n.* **1.** portion, quota, lot **2.** unit of ownership in public company —*v.* **3.** give, take a share (of) **4.** join with others in doing, using (something) —**ˈshareholder** *n.*

share[2] (ʃɛə) *n.* blade of plough

shark (ʃɑːk) *n.* **1.** large usu. predatory sea fish **2.** person who cheats others

sharkskin (ˈʃɑːkskɪn) *n.* stiff rayon fabric

sharp (ʃɑːp) *a.* **1.** having keen cutting edge or fine point **2.** keen **3.** not gradual or gentle **4.** brisk **5.** clever **6.** harsh **7.** dealing cleverly but unfairly **8.** shrill **9.** strongly marked, *esp.* in outline —*adv.* **10.** promptly —*n.* **11.** *Mus.* note half a tone above natural pitch **12.** *sl.* cheat, swindler —**ˈsharpen** *vt.* make sharp —**ˈsharper** *n.* person who cheats or swindles —**ˈsharply** *adv.* —**ˈsharpness** *n.* —**sharp practice** dishonest dealings —**sharp-set** *a.* **1.** set to give acute cutting angle **2.** keenly hungry —**ˈsharpshooter** *n.* marksman —**sharp-witted** *a.* having or showing keen intelligence

shatter (ˈʃætə) *v.* **1.** break in pieces —*vt.* **2.** ruin (plans *etc.*) **3.** disturb (person) greatly

shave (ʃeɪv) *v.* **1.** cut close (*esp.* hair of face or head) —*vt.* **2.** pare away **3.** graze **4.** reduce (**shaved, ˈshaven, ˈshaving**) —*n.* **5.** shaving —**ˈshaver** *n.* **1.** person or thing that shaves **2.** electrical implement for shaving —**ˈshavings** *pl.n.* parings —**close** *or* **near shave** narrow escape

Shavian (ˈʃeɪvɪən) *a.* **1.** of or like George Bernard Shaw, his works, ideas *etc.* —*n.* **2.** admirer of Shaw or his works

shawl (ʃɔːl) *n.* piece of fabric to cover woman's shoulders or wrap baby

she (ʃiː) *pron.* 3rd person singular feminine pronoun

sheaf (ʃiːf) *n.* **1.** bundle, *esp.* corn **2.** loose leaves of paper (*pl.* **sheaves**)

shear (ʃɪə) *vt.* **1.** clip hair, wool from **2.** cut (through) **3.** fracture (**sheared** *pt.*, **shorn, sheared** *pp.*, **ˈshearing** *pr.p.*) —**ˈshearer** *n.* —**shears** *pl.n.* **1.** large pair of scissors **2.** any of various analogous cutting instruments

shearwater (ˈʃɪəwɔːtə) *n.* any of various sea birds

sheath (ʃiːθ) *n.* **1.** close-fitting cover, *esp.* for knife or sword **2.** scabbard **3.** condom (*pl.* **sheaths** (ʃiːðz)) —**sheathe** *vt.* put into sheath

sheave (ʃiːv) *n.* wheel with grooved rim, *esp.* one used as pulley

sheaves (ʃiːvz) *n., pl. of* SHEAF

shebang (ʃɪˈbæŋ) *n. sl.* situation, matter (*esp. in* **the whole shebang**)

shebeen *or* **shebean** (ʃəˈbiːn) *n.* **1.** *Irish, Scot.,* **SA**

THESAURUS

take (someone) down a peg (*Inf.*) **4.** blot, debase, defile, degrade, discredit, dishonour, smear, stain

shameful atrocious, base, dastardly, degrading, disgraceful, dishonourable, ignominious, indecent, infamous, low, mean, outrageous, reprehensible, scandalous, unbecoming, unworthy, vile, wicked

shameless abandoned, audacious, barefaced, brash, brazen, corrupt, depraved, dissolute, flagrant, hardened, immodest, improper, impudent, incorrigible, indecent, insolent, profligate, reprobate, unabashed, unashamed, unblushing, unprincipled, wanton

shape *n.* **1.** build, configuration, contours, cut, figure, form, lines, make, outline, profile, silhouette **2.** frame, model, mould, pattern **3.** appearance, aspect, form, guise, likeness, semblance **4.** condition, fettle, health, kilter, state, trim ~*v.* **5.** create, fashion, form, make, model, mould, produce **6.** accommodate, adapt, define, develop, devise, frame, guide, modify, plan, prepare, regulate, remodel

shapeless amorphous, asymmetrical, battered, embryonic, formless, indeterminate, irregular, misshapen, nebulous, undeveloped, unstructured

share 1. *v.* apportion, assign, distribute, divide, go Dutch (*Inf.*), go fifty-fifty (*Inf.*), go halves, parcel out, partake, participate, receive, split, use in common **2.** *n.* allotment, allowance, contribution, cut (*Inf.*), division, due, lot, part, portion, proportion, quota, ration, whack (*Inf.*)

sharp *adj.* **1.** acute, cutting, honed, jagged, keen, knife-edged, knifelike, pointed, razor-sharp, serrated, sharpened, spiky **2.** abrupt, distinct, extreme, marked, sudden **3.** alert, apt, astute, bright, clever, discerning, knowing, long-headed, observant, penetrating, perceptive, quick, quick-witted, ready, subtle **4.** artful, crafty, cunning, dishonest, fly (*Sl.*), shrewd, sly, smart, unscrupulous, wily **5.** clear, clear-cut, crisp, distinct, well-defined **6.** acrimonious, barbed, biting, bitter, caustic, cutting, harsh, hurtful, sarcastic, sardonic, scathing, severe, trenchant, vitriolic ~*adv.* **7.** exactly, on the dot, on time, precisely, promptly, punctually

sharpen edge, grind, hone, put an edge on, strop, whet

shatter 1. break, burst, crack, crush, crush to smithereens, demolish, explode, implode, pulverize, shiver, smash, split **2.** blast, blight, bring to nought, demolish, destroy, disable, exhaust, impair, overturn, ruin, torpedo, wreck **3.** break (someone's) heart, crush, devastate, dumbfound, knock the stuffing out of (someone) (*Inf.*), upset

shave *v.* **1.** crop, pare, plane, shear, trim **2.** brush, graze, touch

place where alcohol is sold illegally **2.** in S Afr., place where Black Afr. men engage in social drinking

shed[1] (ʃɛd) *n.* roofed shelter used as store or workshop

shed[2] (ʃɛd) *v.* **1.** (cause to) pour forth (*eg* tears, blood) —*vt.* **2.** cast off (**shed, ˈshedding**)

sheen (ʃiːn) *n.* gloss —**ˈsheeny** *a.*

sheep (ʃiːp) *n.* ruminant animal bred for wool and meat (*pl.* **sheep**) —**ˈsheepish** *a.* embarrassed, shy —**sheep-dip** *n.* (deep trough containing) solution in which sheep are immersed to kill vermin and germs in fleece —**ˈsheepdog** *n.* any of various breeds of dog, *orig.* for herding sheep —**ˈsheepfold** *n.* pen or enclosure for sheep —**ˈsheepshank** *n.* knot *etc.* made in rope to shorten it temporarily

sheer[1] (ʃɪə) *a.* **1.** perpendicular **2.** (of material) very fine, transparent **3.** absolute, unmitigated

sheer[2] (ʃɪə) *vi.* deviate from course, swerve, turn aside

sheet[1] (ʃiːt) *n.* **1.** large piece of cotton *etc.* to cover bed **2.** broad piece of any thin material **3.** large expanse —*vt.* **4.** cover with sheet —**sheet music** printed copy of short composition or piece

sheet[2] (ʃiːt) *n.* rope fastened in corner of sail —**sheet anchor** large anchor for emergency

sheik *or* **sheikh** (ʃeɪk) *n.* Arab chief

shekel (ˈʃɛkᵊl) *n.* **1.** Jewish weight and silver coin **2.** (*oft. pl.*) *inf.* money, cash

shelf (ʃɛlf) *n.* **1.** board fixed horizontally (on wall *etc.*) for holding things **2.** ledge (*pl.* **shelves**) —**shelf life** length of time packaged food *etc.* will last without deteriorating

shell (ʃɛl) *n.* **1.** hard outer case (*esp.* of egg, nut *etc.*) **2.** husk **3.** explosive projectile **4.** outer part of structure left when interior is removed —*vt.* **5.** take shell from **6.** take out of shell **7.** fire at with shells —**ˈshellfish** *n.* **1.** mollusc **2.** crustacean —**shell shock** nervous disorder caused by bursting of shells or bombs —**shell out** *inf.* pay up

shellac (ʃəˈlæk, ˈʃɛlæk) *n.* **1.** resin usu. produced in thin plates for use as varnish —*vt.* **2.** coat with shellac (**-ˈlacked, -ˈlacking**)

shelter (ˈʃɛltə) *n.* **1.** place, structure giving protection **2.** protection **3.** refuge; haven —*vt.* **4.** give protection to **5.** screen —*vi.* **6.** take shelter

shelve (ʃɛlv) *vt.* **1.** put on a shelf **2.** put off, defer indefinitely **3.** cease to employ —*vi.* **4.** slope gradually —**ˈshelving** *n.* **1.** material for making shelves **2.** set of shelves

shelves (ʃɛlvz) *n., pl. of* SHELF

shenanigan (ʃɪˈnænɪgən) *n. sl.* **1.** frolicking **2.** act of playing tricks *etc.*

shepherd (ˈʃɛpəd) *n.* **1.** man who tends sheep (**ˈshepherdess** *fem.*) —*vt.* **2.** guide, watch over —**shepherd's pie** *chiefly* **UK** dish of minced meat covered with mashed potato —**shepherd's-purse** *n.* plant with white flowers

sherbet (ˈʃɜːbət) *n.* fruit-flavoured effervescent powder, eaten as sweet or used in drinks

sherd (ʃɜːd) *n. see* SHARD

sheriff (ˈʃɛrɪf) *n.* **1.** US law enforcement officer **2.** in England and Wales, chief executive representative of the crown in a county **3.** in Scotland, chief judge of a district **4.** C municipal officer who enforces court orders *etc.* —**ˈsheriffdom** *n.*

Sherpa (ˈʃɜːpə) *n.* member of a Tibetan people (*pl.* **-s, ˈSherpa**)

sherry (ˈʃɛrɪ) *n.* fortified wine

Shetland pony (ˈʃɛtlənd) very small sturdy breed of pony

shewbread *or* **showbread** (ˈʃəʊbrɛd) *n.* unleavened bread used in Jewish ritual

shield (ʃiːld) *n.* **1.** piece of armour carried on arm **2.** any protection used to stop blows, missiles *etc.* **3.** any protective device **4.** sports trophy —*vt.* **5.** cover, protect

shieling (ˈʃiːlɪŋ) *n. chiefly Scot.* **1.** temporary shelter used by people tending cattle on high ground **2.** grazing ground

shift (ʃɪft) *v.* **1.** (cause to) move, change position —*n.* **2.** shifting **3.** relay of workers **4.** time of their working **5.** evasion **6.** expedient **7.** removal **8.** woman's underskirt or dress —**ˈshiftiness** *n.* —**ˈshiftless** *a.* lacking in resource or character —**ˈshifty** *a.* **1.** evasive **2.** of dubious character

THESAURUS

shed *v.* **1.** afford, cast, diffuse, drop, emit, give, give forth, pour forth, radiate, scatter, shower, spill, throw **2.** cast off, discard, exuviate, moult, slough

sheepish abashed, chagrined, embarrassed, foolish, mortified, self-conscious, shamefaced, silly, uncomfortable

sheer **1.** abrupt, headlong (*Archaic*), perpendicular, precipitous, steep **2.** absolute, arrant, complete, downright, out-and-out, pure, rank, thoroughgoing, total, unadulterated, unalloyed, unmitigated, unqualified, utter **3.** *Of fabrics* diaphanous, fine, gauzy, gossamer, seethrough, thin, transparent

sheet **1.** coat, film, folio, lamina, layer, leaf, membrane, overlay, pane, panel, piece, plate, slab, stratum, surface, veneer **2.** area, blanket, covering, expanse, stretch, sweep

shell *n.* **1.** carapace, case, husk, pod ~*v.* **2.** husk, shuck **3.** attack, barrage, blitz, bomb, bombard, strafe, strike ~*n.* **4.** chassis, frame, framework, hull, skeleton, structure

shelter **1.** *v.* cover, defend, guard, harbour, hide, protect, safeguard, seek refuge, shield, take in, take shelter **2.** *n.* asylum, cover, covert, defence, guard, haven, protection, refuge, retreat, roof over one's head, safety, sanctuary, screen, security, shiel (*Scot.*), umbrella

shelve defer, dismiss, freeze, hold in abeyance, hold over, lay aside, mothball, pigeonhole, postpone, put aside, put off, put on ice, table (*U.S.*)

shepherd *v.* conduct, convoy, guide, herd, marshal, steer, usher

shield *n.* **1.** buckler, escutcheon (*Heraldry*), targe (*Archaic*) **2.** aegis, bulwark, cover, defence, guard, protection, rampart, safeguard, screen, shelter, ward (*Archaic*) ~*v.* **3.** cover, defend, guard, protect, safeguard, screen, shelter, ward off

shift *v.* **1.** alter, budge, change, displace, fluctuate, move, move around, rearrange, relocate, remove, reposition, swerve, switch, transfer, transpose, vary, veer ~*n.* **2.** about-turn, alteration, change, displacement, fluctuation, modification, move, permutation, rearrangement, removal, shifting, switch, transfer, veering **3.** artifice, contrivance, craft, device, dodge,

shillelagh *or* **shillala** (ʃəˈleɪlə, -lɪ) *n.* in Ireland, cudgel

shilling (ˈʃɪlɪŋ) *n.* **1.** former Brit. coin, now 5p **2.** monetary unit in various countries

shillyshally (ˈʃɪlɪʃælɪ) *vi.* **1.** waver —*n.* **2.** wavering, indecision

shim (ʃɪm) *n.* **1.** thin washer used to adjust clearance for gears *etc.* —*vt.* **2.** modify clearance on (gear *etc.*) by use of shims (**-mm-**)

shimmer (ˈʃɪmə) *vi.* **1.** shine with quivering light —*n.* **2.** such light **3.** glimmer

shimmy (ˈʃɪmɪ) *n.* **1.** Amer. ragtime dance with much shaking of hips and shoulders **2.** abnormal wobbling motion in motor vehicle

shin (ʃɪn) *n.* **1.** front of lower leg —*v.* **2.** climb with arms and legs —*vt.* **3.** kick on shin (**-nn-**) —ˈ**shinbone** *n. see* TIBIA

shindig (ˈʃɪndɪg) *or* **shindy** (ˈʃɪndɪ) *n. inf.* row; noisy disturbance

shine (ʃaɪn) *vi.* **1.** give out, reflect light **2.** perform very well, excel —*vt.* **3.** cause to shine by polishing (**shone, ˈshining**) —*n.* **4.** brightness, lustre **5.** polishing —ˈ**shiner** *n.* **1.** something that shines, such as polishing device **2.** small N Amer. freshwater cyprinid fish **3.** *inf.* black eye —ˈ**shiny** *a.*

shingle[1] (ˈʃɪŋgᵊl) *n.* **1.** wooden roof tile —*vt.* **2.** cover with shingles

shingle[2] (ˈʃɪŋgᵊl) *n.* mass of pebbles

shingles (ˈʃɪŋgᵊlz) *n.* disease causing inflammation along a nerve

Shinto (ˈʃɪntəʊ) *n.* native Japanese religion —ˈ**Shintoism** *n.*

shinty (ˈʃɪntɪ) *n.* **1.** simple form of hockey played with ball and sticks curved at lower end **2.** stick used in this game

ship (ʃɪp) *n.* **1.** large seagoing vessel —*vt.* **2.** put on or send by ship —*vi.* **3.** embark **4.** take service in ship (**-pp-**) —ˈ**shipment** *n.* **1.** act of shipping **2.** goods shipped —ˈ**shipper** *n.* company *etc.* in business of shipping freight —ˈ**shipping** *n.* **1.** freight transport business **2.** ships collectively —ˈ**shipboard** *a.* taking place, used, or intended for use aboard ship —ˈ**shipmate** *n.* sailor who serves on same ship as another —ˈ**shipshape** *a.* orderly, trim —ˈ**shipwreck** *n.* **1.** destruction of ship through storm, collision *etc.* —*vt.* **2.** cause to undergo shipwreck —ˈ**shipwright** *n.* artisan skilled in tasks required to build vessels —ˈ**shipyard** *n.* place for building and repair of ships

-ship (*comb. form*) **1.** state, condition, as in *fellowship* **2.** rank, office, position, as in *lordship* **3.** craft, skill, as in *scholarship*

shire (ʃaɪə) *n.* county —**shire horse** large heavy breed of carthorse

shirk (ʃɜːk) *vt.* evade, try to avoid (duty *etc.*)

shirr (ʃɜː) *vt.* **1.** gather (fabric) into parallel rows —*n.* **2.** series of gathered rows decorating dress *etc.*

shirt (ʃɜːt) *n.* garment for upper part of body —ˈ**shirty** *a. sl.* annoyed —**shirt-tail** *n.* part of shirt that extends below waist —ˈ**shirtwaister** *or U.S.* ˈ**shirtwaist** *n.* woman's dress with bodice resembling shirt

shish kebab (ˈʃiːʃ kəˈbæb) *see* KEBAB

shiver[1] (ˈʃɪvə) *vi.* **1.** tremble, usu. with cold or fear; shudder; vibrate —*n.* **2.** act, state of shivering

shiver[2] (ˈʃɪvə) *v.* **1.** splinter, break in pieces —*n.* **2.** splinter

shoal[1] (ʃəʊl) *n.* **1.** stretch of shallow water **2.** sandbank, sandbar —*v.* **3.** make, become shallow

shoal[2] (ʃəʊl) *n.* **1.** large number of fish swimming together —*vi.* **2.** form shoal

shock[1] (ʃɒk) *vt.* **1.** horrify, scandalize —*n.* **2.** violent or damaging blow **3.** emotional disturbance **4.** state of weakness, illness, caused by physical or mental shock **5.** paralytical stroke **6.** collision **7.** effect on sensory nerves of electric discharge —ˈ**shocker** *n.* person or thing which shocks or distresses —ˈ**shocking** *a.* **1.** causing shock, disgust *etc.* **2.** *inf.* very bad or terrible —**shock absorber** device, *esp.* in cars, to absorb shocks —**shock therapy** *or* **treatment** treatment of certain psychotic conditions by injecting drugs or by passing electric current through brain

shock[2] (ʃɒk) *n.* group of corn sheaves placed together

shock[3] (ʃɒk) *n.* **1.** mass of hair —*a.* **2.** shaggy —ˈ**shock-headed** *a.*

THESAURUS

equivocation, evasion, expedient, move, resource, ruse, stratagem, subterfuge, trick, wile

shifty contriving, crafty, deceitful, devious, duplicitous, evasive, fly-by-night (*Inf.*), furtive, scheming, slippery, tricky, underhand, unprincipled, untrustworthy, wily

shimmer 1. *v.* dance, gleam, glisten, phosphoresce, scintillate, twinkle **2.** *n.* diffused light, gleam, glimmer, glow, incandescence, iridescence, lustre, phosphorescence, unsteady light

shine *v.* **1.** beam, emit light, flash, give off light, glare, gleam, glimmer, glisten, glitter, glow, radiate, scintillate, shimmer, sparkle, twinkle **2.** be conspicuous (distinguished, outstanding, pre-eminent), excel, stand out, stand out in a crowd, star **3.** brush, buff, burnish, polish, rub up ~*n.* **4.** brightness, glare, gleam, lambency, light, luminosity, radiance, shimmer, sparkle **5.** glaze, gloss, lustre, patina, polish, sheen

shining 1. beaming, bright, brilliant, effulgent, gleaming, glistening, glittering, luminous, radiant, resplendent, shimmering, sparkling **2.** *Fig.* brilliant, celebrated, conspicuous, distinguished, eminent, glorious, illustrious, leading, outstanding, splendid

shiny agleam, bright, burnished, gleaming, glistening, glossy, lustrous, nitid (*Poetic*), polished, satiny, sheeny

shirk avoid, dodge, duck (out of) (*Inf.*), evade, get out of, scrimshank (*Brit. military sl.*), shun, sidestep, skive (*Brit. sl.*), slack

shiver *v.* break, crack, fragment, shatter, smash, smash to smithereens, splinter

shock *v.* **1.** agitate, appal, astound, disgust, disquiet, give (someone) a turn (*Inf.*), horrify, jar, jolt, nauseate, numb, offend, outrage, paralyse, revolt, scandalize, shake, shake out of one's complacency, shake up (*Inf.*), sicken, stagger, stun, stupefy, traumatize, unsettle ~*n.* **2.** blow, bolt from the blue, bombshell, breakdown, collapse, consternation, distress, disturbance, prostration, state of shock, stupefaction, stupor, trauma, turn (*Inf.*), upset **3.** blow, clash, collision, encounter, impact, jarring, jolt

shocking abominable, appalling, atrocious, detestable, disgraceful, disgusting, disquieting, distress-

shod (ʃɒd) *pt./pp. of* SHOE

shoddy (ˈʃɒdɪ) *a.* **1.** worthless, trashy **2.** second-rate **3.** made of poor material

shoe (ʃuː) *n.* **1.** covering for foot, not enclosing ankle **2.** metal rim or curved bar put on horse's hoof **3.** any of various protective plates or undercoverings *—vt.* **4.** protect, furnish with shoe or shoes (**shod** *pt./pp.*, **ˈshoeing** *pr.p.*) —**ˈshoehorn** *n.* curved plastic or metal implement, inserted at back of shoe, used to ease in heel —**ˈshoestring** *a./n.* very small (amount of money *etc.*) —**ˈshoetree** *n.* wooden or metal block inserted into shoe to preserve shape

shone (ʃɒn; *U.S.* ʃəʊn) *pt./pp. of* SHINE

shoo (ʃuː) *interj.* **1.** go away *—vt.* **2.** drive away

shook (ʃʊk) *pt. of* SHAKE

shoot (ʃuːt) *vt.* **1.** hit, wound, kill with missile fired from weapon **2.** send, slide, push rapidly *—v.* **3.** discharge (weapon) **4.** photograph, film *—vi.* **5.** hunt **6.** sprout (**shot, ˈshooting**) *—n.* **7.** young branch, sprout **8.** shooting competition **9.** hunting expedition —**ˈshooter** *n.* —**shooting brake UK** estate car —**shooting star** *inf.* meteor —**shooting stick** device resembling walking stick, having spike at one end and folding seat at other

shop (ʃɒp) *n.* **1.** place for retail sale of goods and services **2.** workshop, works building *—vi.* **3.** visit shops to buy *—vt.* **4.** *sl.* inform against (**-pp-**) —**shop floor 1.** part of factory housing machines **2.** workers in factory —**ˈshopkeeper** *n.* person who owns or manages shop —**ˈshoplifter** *n.* one who steals from shop —**shopping centre 1.** area of town where most of shops are situated **2.** complex of stores, restaurants *etc.* with adjoining car park —**ˈshopsoiled** *a.* faded *etc.* from being displayed in shop —**shop steward** trade union representative of workers in factory *etc.* —**ˈshoptalk** *n.* conversation concerning one's work, *esp.* outside business hours —**ˈshopwalker** *n.* overseer who directs customers *etc.* —**talk shop** talk of one's business *etc.* at unsuitable moments

shore[1] (ʃɔː) *n.* edge of sea or lake

shore[2] (ʃɔː) *vt.* (*oft. with* up) prop (up)

shorn (ʃɔːn) *pp. of* SHEAR

short (ʃɔːt) *a.* **1.** not long **2.** not tall **3.** brief, hasty **4.** not reaching quantity or standard required **5.** wanting, lacking **6.** abrupt, rude **7.** friable *—adv.* **8.** suddenly, abruptly **9.** without reaching end *—n.* **10.** drink of spirits, as opposed to beer *etc.* **11.** short film *—pl.* **12.** short trousers —**ˈshortage** *n.* deficiency —**ˈshorten** *v.* —**ˈshortening** *n.* butter, lard or other fat, used in cake mixture *etc.* to make pastry light —**ˈshortly** *adv.* **1.** soon **2.** briefly —**ˈshortcake** *or* **ˈshortbread** *n.* sweet, brittle cake made of butter, flour and sugar —**short-change** *vt.* **1.** give less than correct change to **2.** *sl.* cheat, swindle —**short circuit** faulty connection between two points in electric circuit, establishing path of low resistance through which excessive current can flow —**short-circuit** *v.* **1.** develop or cause to develop short circuit *—vt.* **2.** bypass (procedure *etc.*) —**ˈshortcoming** *n.* failing, defect —**short cut 1.** shorter route than usual one **2.** means of saving time or effort —**short-cut** *vi.* use short cut —**ˈshortfall** *n.* failure to meet requirement —**ˈshorthand** *n.* method of rapid writing by signs or contractions —**short-handed** *a.* lacking the usual or necessary number of workers, helpers —**ˈshorthorn** *n.* short-horned breed of cattle with several regional varieties —**short list** selected list of candidates (*esp.* for job) from which final selection will be made —**short-lived** *a.* living or lasting only for a short time —**short-range** *a.* of limited extent in time or distance —**short shrift** summary treatment —**short-sighted** *a.* **1.** relating to or suffering from myopia **2.** lacking foresight —**short-tempered** *a.* easily moved to anger —**short-term** *a.* **1.** extending over limited period **2.** *Fin.* extending over or maturing within short period of time —**short ton US** ton (2000 lbs.) —**short wave** radio wave between 10 and 50 metres —**short-winded** *a.* **1.** tending to run out of breath, *esp.* after exertion **2.** (of speech or writing) abrupt

shot (ʃɒt) *n.* **1.** act of shooting **2.** missile **3.** lead in small pellets **4.** marksman, shooter **5.** try, attempt **6.** photograph **7.** short film sequence **8.** dose **9.** *inf.* injection *—a.* **10.** woven so that colour is different, according to angle of light *—v.* **11.** *pt./pp. of* SHOOT —**ˈshotgun** *n.* **1.** firearm with unrifled bore used mainly for hunting small game *—a.* **2.** *chiefly* **US** involving coercion or duress —**shot put** athletic event in which contestants hurl heavy metal ball as far as possible

THESAURUS

ing, dreadful, foul, frightful, ghastly, hideous, horrible, horrifying, loathsome, monstrous, nauseating, odious, offensive, outrageous, repulsive, revolting, scandalous, sickening, stupefying, unspeakable

shoddy cheap-jack (*Inf.*), inferior, junky, poor, rubbishy, second-rate, slipshod, tacky (*Inf.*), tatty, tawdry, trashy

shoot *v.* **1.** bag, blast (*Sl.*), bring down, hit, kill, open fire, pick off, plug (*Sl.*), pump full of lead (*Sl.*), zap (*Sl.*) **2.** discharge, emit, fire, fling, hurl, launch, let fly, project, propel *~n.* **3.** branch, bud, offshoot, scion, slip, sprig, sprout, twig *~v.* **4.** bud, burgeon, germinate, put forth new growth, sprout

shore beach, coast, foreshore, lakeside, sands, seaboard (*Chiefly U.S.*), seashore, strand (*Poetic*), waterside

short *adj.* **1.** abridged, brief, compendious, compressed, concise, curtailed, laconic, pithy, sententious, succinct, summary, terse **2.** diminutive, dumpy, little, low, petite, small, squat, wee **3.** brief, fleeting, momentary, short-lived, short-term **4.** *Often with* **of** deficient, inadequate, insufficient, lacking, limited, low (on), meagre, poor, scant, scanty, scarce, short-handed, slender, slim, sparse, tight, wanting **5.** abrupt, blunt, brusque, crusty, curt, discourteous, gruff, impolite, offhand, sharp, terse, testy, uncivil **6.** *Of pastry* brittle, crisp, crumbly, friable *~adv.* **7.** abruptly, by surprise, suddenly, unaware, without warning

shortage dearth, deficiency, deficit, failure, inadequacy, insufficiency, lack, leanness, paucity, poverty, scarcity, shortfall, want

shortcoming defect, drawback, failing, fault, flaw, frailty, imperfection, weakness, weak point

shorten abbreviate, abridge, curtail, cut, cut back, cut down, decrease, diminish, dock, lessen, reduce, trim, turn up

short-sighted 1. myopic, near-sighted **2.** careless, ill-advised, ill-considered, impolitic, impractical, improvident, imprudent, injudicious, unthinking

short-tempered choleric, fiery, hot-tempered, impa-

should (ʃʊd) *pt. of* SHALL

shoulder (ˈʃəʊldə) *n.* **1.** part of body to which arm or foreleg is attached **2.** anything resembling shoulder **3.** side of road —*vt.* **4.** undertake **5.** bear (burden) **6.** accept (responsibility) **7.** put on one's shoulder —*vi.* **8.** make way by pushing —**shoulder blade** shoulder bone

shout (ʃaʊt) *n.* **1.** loud cry —*v.* **2.** utter (cry *etc.*) with loud voice

shove (ʃʌv) *vt.* **1.** push **2.** *inf.* put —*n.* **3.** push —**shove off** *inf.* go away

shovel (ˈʃʌvᵊl) *n.* **1.** instrument for scooping, lifting earth *etc.* —*vt.* **2.** lift, move (as) with shovel (**-ll-**) —ˈ**shoveler** *n.* duck with spoon-shaped bill

show (ʃəʊ) *vt.* **1.** expose to view **2.** point out **3.** display, exhibit **4.** explain; prove **5.** guide **6.** accord (favour *etc.*) —*vi.* **7.** appear **8.** be noticeable (**showed, shown,** ˈ**showing**) —*n.* **9.** display, exhibition **10.** spectacle **11.** theatrical or other entertainment **12.** indication **13.** competitive event **14.** ostentation **15.** semblance **16.** pretence —ˈ**showily** *adv.* —ˈ**showy** *a.* **1.** gaudy **2.** ostentatious —**show business** entertainment industry (*also* (*inf.*) **show biz**) —ˈ**showcase** *n.* **1.** glass case used for displaying and protecting objects in museum *etc.* **2.** setting in which anything may be displayed to best advantage —ˈ**showdown** *n.* **1.** confrontation **2.** final test —ˈ**showjumping** *n.* horse-riding competition to demonstrate skill in jumping obstacles —ˈ**showman** *n.* **1.** one employed in, or owning, show at fair *etc.* **2.** one skilled at presenting anything in effective way —**show-off** *n.* —ˈ**showpiece** *n.* **1.** anything exhibited **2.** anything prized as fine example of its type —**show off 1.** exhibit to invite admiration **2.** behave in such a way as to make an impression —**show up 1.** reveal **2.** expose **3.** *inf.* embarrass **4.** *inf.* arrive

shower (ˈʃaʊə) *n.* **1.** short fall of rain **2.** anything coming down like rain **3.** kind of bath in which person stands while being sprayed with water **4. US** party to present gifts to a person, such as a prospective bride —*vt.* **5.** bestow liberally —*vi.* **6.** take bath in shower —ˈ**showery** *a.*

shrank (ʃræŋk) *pt. of* SHRINK

shrapnel (ˈʃræpnᵊl) *n.* **1.** shell filled with pellets which scatter on bursting **2.** shell splinters

shred (ʃrɛd) *n.* **1.** fragment, torn strip **2.** small amount —*vt.* **3.** cut, tear to shreds (**shred** *or* ˈ**shredded,** ˈ**shredding**)

shrew (ʃruː) *n.* **1.** animal like mouse **2.** bad-tempered woman **3.** scold —ˈ**shrewish** *a.* nagging

shrewd (ʃruːd) *a.* **1.** astute, intelligent **2.** crafty

shriek (ʃriːk) *n.* **1.** shrill cry **2.** piercing scream —*v.* **3.** screech

shrift (ʃrɪft) *n.* **1.** confession **2.** absolution

shrike (ʃraɪk) *n.* bird of prey

shrill (ʃrɪl) *a.* **1.** piercing, sharp in tone —*v.* **2.** utter (words *etc.*) in such tone —ˈ**shrilly** *adv.*

shrimp (ʃrɪmp) *n.* **1.** small edible crustacean **2.** *inf.* undersized person —*vi.* **3.** fish for shrimps

shrine (ʃraɪn) *n.* place (building, tomb, alcove) of worship, usu. associated with saint

shrink (ʃrɪŋk) *vi.* **1.** become smaller **2.** retire, flinch, recoil —*vt.* **3.** make smaller (**shrank** *pt.,* ˈ**shrunken, shrunk** *pp.,* ˈ**shrinking** *pr.p.*) —*n.* **4.** *sl.* psychiatrist —ˈ**shrinkage** *n.* —**shrink-wrap** *vt.* package (product) in flexible plastic wrapping designed to shrink about its contours

shrivel (ˈʃrɪvᵊl) *vi.* shrink and wither (**-ll-**)

THESAURUS

tient, irascible, peppery, quick-tempered, ratty (*Brit. sl.*), testy, touchy

shot *n.* **1.** discharge, lob, pot shot, throw **2.** ball, bullet, lead, pellet, projectile, slug **3.** *Inf.* attempt, chance, conjecture, crack (*Inf.*), effort, endeavour, essay, go, guess, opportunity, stab, surmise, try, turn

shoulder *v.* **1.** accept, assume, bear, be responsible for, carry, take on, take upon oneself **2.** elbow, jostle, press, push, shove, thrust

shout 1. *n.* bellow, call, cry, roar, scream, yell **2.** *v.* bawl, bay, bellow, call (out), cry (out), holler (*Inf.*), hollo, raise one's voice, roar, scream, yell

shove *v.* crowd, drive, elbow, impel, jostle, press, propel, push, shoulder, thrust

shovel *v.* convey, dredge, heap, ladle, load, move, scoop, shift, spoon, toss

show *v.* **1.** appear, be visible, disclose, display, divulge, evidence, evince, exhibit, indicate, make known, manifest, present, register, reveal, testify to **2.** assert, clarify, demonstrate, elucidate, evince, explain, instruct, point out, present, prove, teach **3.** accompany, attend, conduct, escort, guide, lead **4.** accord, act with, bestow, confer, grant ~*n.* **5.** array, demonstration, display, exhibition, expo (*Inf.*), exposition, fair, manifestation, pageant, pageantry, parade, representation, sight, spectacle, view **6.** affectation, air, appearance, display, illusion, likeness, ostentation, parade, pose, pretence, pretext, profession, semblance **7.** entertainment, presentation, production

showdown breaking point, clash, climax, confrontation, crisis, culmination, exposé, moment of truth

shower 1. *n. Fig.* barrage, deluge, fusillade, plethora, rain, stream, torrent, volley **2.** *v.* deluge, heap, inundate, lavish, load, pour, rain, spray, sprinkle

showman entertainer, impresario, performer, publicist, stage manager

show off 1. advertise, demonstrate, display, exhibit, flaunt, parade, spread out **2.** boast, brag, make a spectacle of oneself, shoot a line (*Inf.*), swagger

show up 1. expose, highlight, lay bare, pinpoint, put the spotlight on, reveal, unmask **2.** *Inf.* embarrass, let down, mortify, put to shame, shame, show in a bad light **3.** *Inf.* appear, arrive, come, make an appearance, put in an appearance, turn up

shred *n.* **1.** bit, fragment, piece, rag, ribbon, scrap, sliver, snippet, tatter **2.** *Fig.* atom, grain, iota, jot, particle, scrap, trace, whit

shrewd acute, artful, astute, calculated, calculating, canny, clever, crafty, cunning, discerning, discriminating, far-seeing, far-sighted, fly (*Sl.*), intelligent, keen, knowing, long-headed, perceptive, perspicacious, sagacious, sharp, sly, smart, wily

shriek *v./n.* cry, howl, scream, screech, squeal, wail, whoop, yell

shrill acute, ear-piercing, ear-splitting, high, high-pitched, penetrating, piercing, piping, screeching, sharp

shrink 1. contract, decrease, deflate, diminish, drop off, dwindle, fall off, grow smaller, lessen, narrow, shorten, shrivel, wither, wrinkle **2.** cower, cringe,

shroud (ʃraʊd) *n.* 1. sheet, wrapping, for corpse 2. anything which covers, envelops like shroud —*pl.* 3. set of ropes to masthead —*vt.* 4. put shroud on 5. screen, veil 6. wrap up

Shrovetide (ˈʃrəʊvtaɪd) *n.* the three days preceding Lent —**Shrove Tuesday** day before Ash Wednesday

shrub (ʃrʌb) *n.* bushy plant —ˈ**shrubbery** *n.* plantation, part of garden, filled with shrubs

shrug (ʃrʌg) *vi.* 1. raise shoulders, as sign of indifference, ignorance *etc.* —*vt.* 2. move (shoulders) thus 3. (*with* off) dismiss as unimportant (**-gg-**) —*n.* 4. shrugging

shrunk (ʃrʌŋk) *pp. of* SHRINK

shuck (ʃʌk) *n.* shell, husk, pod

shudder (ˈʃʌdə) *vi.* 1. shake, tremble violently, *esp.* with horror —*n.* 2. shuddering, tremor

shuffle (ˈʃʌfˀl) *vi.* 1. move feet without lifting them 2. act evasively —*vt.* 3. mix (cards) 4. (*with* off) evade, pass to another —*n.* 5. shuffling 6. rearrangement —ˈ**shuffler** *n.*

shun (ʃʌn) *vt.* 1. avoid 2. keep away from (**-nn-**)

shunt (ʃʌnt) *vt.* 1. push aside 2. divert 3. move (train) from one line to another

shush (ʃʊʃ) *interj.* 1. be quiet, hush —*vt.* 2. silence or calm by saying 'shush'

shut (ʃʌt) *v.* 1. close —*vt.* 2. bar 3. forbid entrance to (**shut**, ˈ**shutting**) —ˈ**shutter** *n.* 1. movable window screen, usu. hinged to frame 2. device in camera admitting light as required to film or plate —ˈ**shuteye** *n. sl.* sleep —**shut down** close or stop (factory, machine *etc.*)

shuttle (ˈʃʌtˀl) *n.* 1. instrument which threads weft between threads of warp in weaving 2. similar appliance in sewing machine 3. plane, bus *etc.* travelling to and fro over short distance —ˈ**shuttlecock** *n.* small, light cone with cork stub and fan of feathers used as a ball in badminton

shy[1] (ʃaɪ) *a.* 1. awkward in company 2. timid, bashful 3. reluctant 4. scarce, lacking (*esp.* in card games, not having enough money for bet *etc.*) —*vi.* 5. start back in fear 6. show sudden reluctance (**shied**, ˈ**shying**) —*n.* 7. start of fear by horse —ˈ**shyly** *adv.* —ˈ**shyness** *n.*

shy[2] (ʃaɪ) *vt./n.* throw (**shied**, ˈ**shying**)

Shylock (ˈʃaɪlɒk) *n.* heartless or demanding creditor

shyster (ˈʃaɪstə) *n. sl.* dishonest, deceitful person

si (siː) *n. Mus. see* TE

Si *Chem.* silicon

SI *Fr.* Système International (d'Unités), international system of units of measurement based on units of ten

Siamese (saɪəˈmiːz) *a.* of Siam, former name of Thailand —**Siamese cat** breed of cat with blue eyes —**Siamese twins** twins born joined to each other by some part of body

sibilant (ˈsɪbɪlənt) *a.* 1. hissing —*n.* 2. speech sound with hissing effect

sibling (ˈsɪblɪŋ) *n.* person's brother or sister

sibyl (ˈsɪbɪl) *n.* woman endowed with spirit of prophecy —**sibylline** (ˈsɪbɪlaɪn) *a.* occult

sic (sɪk) *Lat.* thus: oft. used to call attention to a quoted mistake

sick (sɪk) *a.* 1. inclined to vomit, vomiting 2. not well or healthy, physically or mentally 3. *inf.* macabre, sadistic, morbid 4. *inf.* bored, tired 5. *inf.* disgusted —ˈ**sicken** *v.* 1. make, become sick —*vt.* 2. disgust; nauseate —ˈ**sickening** *a.* 1. causing sickness or revulsion 2. *inf.* extremely annoying —ˈ**sickly** *a.* 1. unhealthy, weakly 2. inducing nausea —ˈ**sickness** *n.* —ˈ**sickbay** *n.* place set aside for treating sick people, *esp.* in ships

sickle (ˈsɪkˀl) *n.* reaping hook —**sickle cell anaemia** inherited form of anaemia in which large number of red blood cells become sickle-shaped

THESAURUS

draw back, flinch, hang back, quail, recoil, retire, shy away, wince, withdraw

shrivel dehydrate, desiccate, dwindle, shrink, wilt, wither, wizen, wrinkle

shroud *v.* 1. blanket, cloak, conceal, cover, envelop, hide, screen, swathe, veil ~*n.* 2. cerecloth, cerement, covering, grave clothes, winding sheet 3. cloud, mantle, pall, screen, veil

shudder 1. *v.* convulse, quake, quiver, shake, shiver, tremble 2. *n.* convulsion, quiver, shuddering, spasm, trembling, tremor

shuffle 1. drag, scrape, scuff, scuffle, shamble 2. confuse, disarrange, disorder, intermix, jumble, mix, rearrange, shift 3. *Usually with* **off** *or* **out of** beat about the bush, beg the question, cavil, dodge, equivocate, evade, gloss over, hedge, prevaricate, pussyfoot (*Inf.*), quibble

shun avoid, cold-shoulder, elude, eschew, evade, fight shy of, give (someone *or* something) a wide berth, have no part in, keep away from, shy away from, steer clear of

shut bar, close, draw to, fasten, push to, seal, secure, slam

shut down cease, cease operating, close, discontinue, halt, shut up, stop, switch off

shy 1. *adj.* backward, bashful, cautious, chary, coy, diffident, distrustful, hesitant, modest, mousy, nervous, reserved, reticent, retiring, self-conscious, self-effacing, shrinking, suspicious, timid, wary 2. *v. Sometimes with* **off** *or* **away** balk, buck, draw back, flinch, quail, rear, recoil, start, swerve, take fright, wince

shyness bashfulness, diffidence, lack of confidence, modesty, mousiness, nervousness, reticence, self-consciousness, timidity, timidness, timorousness

sick 1. green around the gills (*Inf.*), ill, nauseated, puking (*Sl.*), qualmish, queasy 2. ailing, diseased, feeble, indisposed, laid up (*Inf.*), on the sick list (*Inf.*), poorly (*Inf.*), under the weather (*Inf.*), unwell, weak 3. *Inf.* black, ghoulish, macabre, morbid, sadistic 4. *Inf. Often with* **of** blasé, bored, disgusted, displeased, fed up, jaded, revolted, satiated, tired, weary

sicken 1. disgust, make one's gorge rise, nauseate, repel, revolt, turn one's stomach 2. be stricken by, contract, fall ill, go down with (*Brit.*), show symptoms of, take sick

sickening disgusting, distasteful, foul, loathsome, nauseating, nauseous, noisome, offensive, putrid, repulsive, revolting, stomach-turning (*Inf.*), vile

sickly 1. ailing, bilious, bloodless, delicate, faint, feeble, indisposed, infirm, in poor health, lacklustre, languid, pallid, peaky, pining, unhealthy, wan, weak,

side (saɪd) *n.* **1.** one of the surfaces of object, *esp.* upright inner or outer surface **2.** either surface of thing having only two **3.** part of body that is to right or left **4.** region nearer or farther than, or right or left of, dividing line *etc.* **5.** region **6.** aspect or part **7.** one of two parties or sets of opponents **8.** sect, faction **9.** line of descent traced through one parent **10.** *sl.* swank, conceit —*a.* **11.** at, in the side **12.** subordinate, incidental —*vi.* **13.** (*usu. with* with) take up cause (of) —**ˈsiding** *n.* short line of rails on which trains or wagons are shunted from main line —**side arms** weapons carried on person, by belt or holster, such as sword, pistol *etc.* —**ˈsideboard** *n.* piece of furniture for holding dishes *etc.* in dining room —**ˈsideboards** *pl.n.* **UK** man's whiskers grown down either side of face in front of ears (*also* **US ˈsideburns**) —**ˈsidecar** *n.* small car attached to side of motorcycle —**ˈsidekick** *n. sl., chiefly* **US** close friend or follower —**ˈsidelight** *n.* either of two small lights on front of motor vehicle —**ˈsideline** *n.* **1.** *Sport* boundary of playing area **2.** subsidiary interest or activity —**ˈsidelong** *a.* **1.** lateral, not directly forward —*adv.* **2.** obliquely —**side-saddle** *n.* riding saddle orig. designed for women riders in skirts, who sit with both legs on near side of horse —**ˈsideshow** *n.* **1.** small show offered in conjunction with larger attraction, as at circus **2.** subordinate event —**ˈsideslip** *n.* skid —**ˈsidesman** *n. Anglican Ch.* man elected to help parish churchwarden —**side-splitting** *a.* **1.** producing great mirth **2.** (of laughter) very hearty —**ˈsidestep** *v.* **1.** step aside from or out of way of (something) —*vt.* **2.** dodge —**side step** movement to one side, as in boxing *etc.* —**ˈsidetrack** *v.* **1.** distract or be distracted from main topic —*n.* **2.** digression —**ˈsidewalk** *n.* **US** footpath beside road —**ˈsideways** *adv.* **1.** to or from the side **2.** laterally

sidereal (saɪˈdɪərɪəl) *a.* relating to, fixed by, stars

sidle (ˈsaɪdᵊl) *vi.* **1.** move in furtive or stealthy manner **2.** move sideways

SIDS sudden infant death syndrome

siege (siːdʒ) *n.* besieging of town or fortified place

siemens (ˈsiːmənz) *n.* derived SI unit of electrical conductance

sienna (sɪˈɛnə) *n.* (pigment of) brownish-yellow colour

sierra (sɪˈɛərə) *n.* range of mountains with jagged peaks

siesta (sɪˈɛstə) *n.* rest, sleep in afternoon

sieve (sɪv) *n.* **1.** device with network or perforated bottom for sifting —*vt.* **2.** sift **3.** strain

sift (sɪft) *vt.* **1.** separate (*eg* with sieve) coarser portion from finer **2.** examine closely

sigh (saɪ) *vi./n.* (utter) long audible breath —**sigh for** yearn for, grieve for

sight (saɪt) *n.* **1.** faculty of seeing **2.** seeing **3.** thing seen **4.** view **5.** glimpse **6.** device for guiding eye **7.** spectacle **8.** *inf.* pitiful or ridiculous object **9.** *inf.* large number, great deal —*vt.* **10.** catch sight of **11.** adjust sights of (gun *etc.*) —**ˈsightless** *a.* —**sight-read** *v.* play, sing (music) without previous preparation —**ˈsight-screen** *n. Cricket* white screen placed near boundary behind bowler to help batsman see ball —**ˈsightsee** *v.* visit (place) to look at interesting sights —**ˈsightseeing** *n.*

sigma (ˈsɪgmə) *n.* **1.** 18th letter in Gr. alphabet (Σ, σ or, when final, ς), consonant, transliterated as *S* **2.** *Maths.* symbol Σ, indicating summation

sign (saɪn) *n.* **1.** mark, gesture *etc.* to convey some meaning **2.** (board, placard bearing) notice, warning *etc.* **3.** symbol **4.** omen **5.** evidence —*vt.* **6.** put one's signature to **7.** ratify —*vi.* **8.** make sign or gesture **9.** affix signature —**sign language** any system of communication by signs, *esp.* used by deaf —**ˈsignpost** *n.* **1.** post bearing sign that shows way, as at roadside **2.** something that serves as indication —*vt.* **3.** mark with signposts

THESAURUS

weakly **2.** bilious (*Inf.*), cloying, mawkish, nauseating, revolting (*Inf.*), syrupy (*Inf.*)

sickness **1.** nausea, queasiness, (the) collywobbles (*Sl.*), vomiting **2.** affliction, ailment, bug (*Inf.*), complaint, disease, disorder, illness, indisposition, infirmity, malady

side *n.* **1.** border, boundary, division, edge, limit, margin, part, perimeter, periphery, rim, sector, verge **2.** aspect, face, facet, flank, hand, part, surface, view **3.** camp, cause, faction, party, sect, team **4.** *Brit. sl.* airs, arrogance, insolence, pretentiousness ~*adj.* **5.** flanking, lateral **6.** ancillary, incidental, indirect, lesser, marginal, minor, oblique, roundabout, secondary, subordinate, subsidiary ~*v.* **7.** *Usually with* **with** ally with, associate oneself with, befriend, favour, go along with (*Inf.*), join with, second, support, take the part of, team up with (*Inf.*)

sidelong *adj.* covert, indirect, lateral, oblique, sideways

sidestep avoid, bypass, circumvent, dodge, duck (*Inf.*), elude, evade, skip, skirt

sidetrack deflect, distract, divert, lead off the subject

sideways crabwise, edgeways, laterally, obliquely, sidelong, sidewards, to the side

siesta catnap, doze, forty winks (*Inf.*), nap, rest, sleep, snooze (*Inf.*)

sieve **1.** *n.* colander, riddle, screen, sifter, strainer, tammy cloth **2.** *v.* bolt, remove, riddle, separate, sift, strain

sift **1.** bolt, filter, pan, part, riddle, separate, sieve **2.** analyse, examine, fathom, go through, investigate, pore over, probe, screen, scrutinize

sigh *v.* **1.** breathe, complain, grieve, lament, moan, sorrow, sough, suspire (*Archaic*) **2.** *Often with* **for** grieve, languish, long, mourn, pine, yearn

sight *n.* **1.** eye, eyes, eyesight, seeing, vision **2.** appearance, apprehension, eyeshot, field of vision, ken, perception, range of vision, view, viewing, visibility **3.** display, exhibition, pageant, scene, show, spectacle, vista **4.** *Inf.* blot on the landscape (*Inf.*), eyesore, fright (*Inf.*), mess, monstrosity, spectacle ~*v.* **5.** behold, discern, distinguish, make out, observe, perceive, see, spot

sign *n.* **1.** clue, evidence, gesture, giveaway, hint, indication, manifestation, mark, note, proof, signal, spoor, suggestion, symptom, token, trace, vestige **2.** board, notice, placard, warning **3.** badge, character, cipher, device, emblem, ensign, figure, logo, mark, representation, symbol **4.** augury, auspice, foreboding, forewarning, omen, portent, presage, warning, writing on the wall ~*v.* **5.** autograph, endorse, initial, inscribe, set one's hand to, subscribe **6.** beckon, gesticulate, gesture, indicate, signal, use sign language, wave

signal ('sɪgn°l) *n.* **1.** sign to convey order or information, *esp.* on railway **2.** that which in first place impels any action **3.** *Rad. etc.* sequence of electrical impulses transmitted or received —*a.* **4.** remarkable, striking —*vt.* **5.** make signals to —*vi.* **6.** give orders *etc.* by signals (**-ll-**) —'**signalize** *or* **-lise** *vt.* make notable —'**signally** *adv.* —**signal box 1.** building containing signal levers for railway lines **2.** control point for large area of railway system —'**signalman** *n.* railway employee in charge of signals

signatory ('sɪgnətərɪ) *n.* one of those who sign agreements, treaties

signature ('sɪgnɪtʃə) *n.* **1.** person's name written by himself **2.** act of writing it —**signature tune** tune associated with particular programme, person *etc.*

signet ('sɪgnɪt) *n.* small seal —**signet ring** finger ring bearing signet

significant (sɪg'nɪfɪkənt) *a.* **1.** revealing **2.** designed to make something known **3.** important —**sig'nificance** *n.* **1.** import, weight **2.** meaning —**sig'nificantly** *adv.* —**signifi'cation** *n.* meaning —**significant figures 1.** figures of number that express magnitude to specified degree of accuracy **2.** number of such figures

signify ('sɪgnɪfaɪ) *vt.* **1.** mean **2.** indicate **3.** denote **4.** imply —*vi.* **5.** be of importance ('**signified**, '**signifying**)

signor *or* **signior** ('si:njɔ:; *It.* siɲ'ɲo:r) *n.* It. title of respect, like Mr. (*pl.* **-s, -gnori** (*It.* -'ɲo:ri)) —**signora** (si:n'jɔ:rə; *It.* siŋ'ŋo:ra) *n.* Mrs. (*pl.* **-s, -re** (*It.* -re)) —**signorina** (si:njɔ:'ri:nə; *It.* siŋŋo'ri:na) *n.* Miss (*pl.* **-s, -ne** (*It.* -ne))

Sikh (si:k) *n.* member of Indian religious sect

silage ('saɪlɪdʒ) *n.* fodder crop harvested while green and stored in state of partial fermentation

silence ('saɪləns) *n.* **1.** absence of noise **2.** refraining from speech —*vt.* **3.** make silent **4.** put a stop to —'**silencer** *n.* device to reduce noise of engine exhaust, firearm —'**silent** *a.*

silhouette (sɪlu:'ɛt) *n.* **1.** outline of object seen against light **2.** profile portrait in black

silica ('sɪlɪkə) *n.* naturally occurring dioxide of silicon —**siliceous** *or* **silicious** (sɪ'lɪʃəs) *a.* —**sili'cosis** *n.* lung disease caused by inhaling silica dust over a long period

silicon ('sɪlɪkən) *n.* brittle metalloid element found in sand, clay, stone, widely used in chemistry, industry —'**silicone** *n.* large class of synthetic substances, related to silicon and used in chemistry, industry and medicine —**silicon chip** *see* CHIP (sense 4)

silk (sɪlk) *n.* **1.** fibre made by larvae (**silkworm**) of certain moth **2.** thread, fabric made from this —'**silken** *a.* **1.** made of, like silk **2.** soft **3.** smooth **4.** dressed in silk —'**silkily** *adv.* —'**silkiness** *n.* —'**silky** *a.* —**silk hat** man's top hat covered with silk —**silk-screen** *n.* stencil process of printing a design through screen of fine mesh cloth

sill (sɪl) *n.* **1.** ledge beneath window **2.** bottom part of door or window frame

sillabub ('sɪləbʌb) *n. see* SYLLABUB

silly ('sɪlɪ) *a.* **1.** foolish **2.** trivial **3.** feeble-minded —*n.* **4.** person who is silly —'**silliness** *n.* —**silly billy** silly person —**silly season** time during hot summer months when journalists fill space reporting on frivolous events and activities

silo ('saɪləʊ) *n.* **1.** pit, tower for storing fodder or grain **2.** underground missile launching site (*pl.* **-s**)

silt (sɪlt) *n.* **1.** mud deposited by water —*v.* **2.** fill, be choked with silt —**sil'tation** *n.* —'**silty** *a.*

Silurian (saɪ'luərɪən) *a.* **1.** of or formed in third period of Palaeozoic era, during which fishes first appeared —*n.* **2.** Silurian period or rock system

silvan ('sɪlvən) *a. see* SYLVAN

silver ('sɪlvə) *n.* **1.** white precious metal **2.** things made of it **3.** silver coins **4.** cutlery —*a.* **5.** made of silver **6.** resembling silver or its colour **7.** having pale lustre, as moon **8.** soft, melodious, as sound **9.** bright —*vt.* **10.** coat with silver —'**silvery** *a.* —**silver birch** tree having silvery-white peeling bark —**silver jubilee** 25th anniversary —**silver lining** hopeful aspect of otherwise desperate situation —**silver plate 1.** thin layer of silver deposited on base metal **2.** articles, *esp.* tableware, made of silver plate —**silver-plate** *vt.* coat (metal *etc.*) with silver —**silver screen** *inf.* **1.** films collectively **2.** screen on to which films are projected —'**silverside** *n.* **UK** cut of beef below aitchbone and above leg —'**silversmith** *n.* craftsman who makes articles of silver —**silver wedding** 25th wedding anniversary

THESAURUS

signal 1. *n.* beacon, cue, gesture, go-ahead (*Inf.*), green light, indication, indicator, mark, sign, token **2.** *adj.* conspicuous, distinguished, eminent, exceptional, extraordinary, famous, memorable, momentous, notable, noteworthy, outstanding, remarkable, significant, striking **3.** *v.* beckon, communicate, gesticulate, gesture, give a sign to, indicate, motion, nod, sign, wave

significance 1. force, implication(s), import, meaning, message, point, purport, sense, signification **2.** consequence, consideration, importance, impressiveness, matter, moment, relevance, weight

significant 1. denoting, eloquent, expressing, expressive, indicative, knowing, meaning, meaningful, pregnant, revealing, suggestive **2.** critical, important, material, momentous, noteworthy, serious, vital, weighty

signify 1. announce, be a sign of, betoken, communicate, connote, convey, denote, evidence, exhibit, express, imply, indicate, intimate, matter, mean, portend, proclaim, represent, show, stand for, suggest, symbolize **2.** *Inf.* be of importance *or* significance, carry weight, count, matter

silence *n.* **1.** calm, hush, lull, noiselessness, peace, quiescence, quiet, stillness **2.** dumbness, muteness, reticence, speechlessness, taciturnity, uncommunicativeness ~*v.* **3.** cut off, cut short, deaden, extinguish, gag, muffle, quell, quiet, quieten, stifle, still, strike dumb, subdue, suppress

silent 1. hushed, muted, noiseless, quiet, soundless, still, stilly (*Poetic*) **2.** dumb, mum, mute, nonvocal, not talkative, speechless, struck dumb (*Inf.*), taciturn, tongue-tied, uncommunicative, unspeaking, voiceless, wordless

silhouette delineation, form, outline, profile, shape

silky silken, sleek, smooth, velvety

silly absurd, asinine, brainless, childish, fatuous, feeble-minded, foolhardy, foolish, frivolous, giddy, idiotic, immature, imprudent, inane, inappropriate, irresponsible, meaningless, pointless, preposterous, puerile, ridiculous, senseless, stupid, trivial, unwise, witless

silviculture ('sɪlvɪkʌltʃə) *n.* branch of forestry concerned with cultivation of trees

simian ('sɪmɪən) *a.* of, like apes

similar ('sɪmɪlə) *a.* resembling, like **—simi'larity** *n.* likeness, close resemblance

simile ('sɪmɪlɪ) *n.* comparison of one thing with another, using *as* or *like, esp.* in poetry

similitude (sɪ'mɪlɪtju:d) *n.* **1.** outward appearance, likeness **2.** guise

simmer ('sɪmə) *v.* **1.** keep or be just bubbling or just below boiling point *—vi.* **2.** be in state of suppressed anger or laughter

simnel cake ('sɪmnᵊl) UK fruit cake covered with layer of marzipan

simper ('sɪmpə) *v.* **1.** smile, utter in silly or affected way *—n.* **2.** simpering smile

simple ('sɪmpᵊl) *a.* **1.** not complicated **2.** plain **3.** not combined or complex **4.** ordinary, mere **5.** guileless **6.** stupid **—'simpleton** *n.* foolish person **—sim'plicity** *n.* **1.** simpleness **2.** clearness **3.** artlessness **—simplifi'cation** *n.* **—'simplify** *vt.* make simple, plain or easy (**-plified, -plifying**) **—sim'plistic** *a.* very simple, naive **—'simply** *adv.* **—simple fraction** fraction in which both the numerator and the denominator are integers **—simple fracture** fracture in which broken bone does not pierce skin **—simple interest** interest paid on principal alone **—simple-minded** *a.* **1.** stupid; feeble-minded **2.** mentally defective **3.** unsophisticated **—simple-mindedness** *n.* **—simple sentence** sentence consisting of single main clause

simulate ('sɪmjuleɪt) *vt.* **1.** make pretence of **2.** reproduce, copy (*esp.* conditions of particular situation) **—simu'lation** *n.* **—'simulator** *n.*

simultaneous (sɪməl'teɪnɪəs) *a.* occurring at the same time **—simultaneity** (sɪmәltə'ni:ɪtɪ) *or* **simul'taneousness** *n.* **—simul'taneously** *adv.*

sin[1] (sɪn) *n.* **1.** transgression of divine or moral law, *esp.* committed consciously **2.** offence against principle or standard *—vi.* **3.** commit sin (**-nn-**) **—'sinful** *a.* **1.** of nature of sin **2.** guilty of sin **—'sinfully** *adv.* **—'sinner** *n.* **—sin bin C** *sl.* penalty box used in ice hockey

sin[2] *Maths.* sine

SIN C Social Insurance Number

since (sɪns) *prep.* **1.** during or throughout period of time after *—conj.* **2.** from time when **3.** because *—adv.* **4.** from that time

sincere (sɪn'sɪə) *a.* **1.** not hypocritical, actually moved by or feeling apparent emotions **2.** true, genuine **3.** unaffected **—sin'cerely** *adv.* **—sincerity** (sɪn'sɛrɪtɪ) *n.*

sine (saɪn) *n.* mathematical function, *esp.* ratio of length of hypotenuse to opposite side in right-angled triangle

sinecure ('saɪnɪkjʊə) *n.* office with pay but minimal duties

THESAURUS

silver 1. *adj.* argent (*Poetic*), pearly, silvered, silvery **2.** *n.* silver plate, silverware

similar alike, comparable, congruous, corresponding, in agreement, like, much the same, resembling, uniform

similarity affinity, agreement, analogy, closeness, comparability, concordance, congruence, correspondence, likeness, point of comparison, relation, resemblance, sameness, similitude

simmer *Fig.* be angry (agitated, tense, uptight (*Inf.*)), boil, burn, fume, rage, seethe, smart, smoulder

simple 1. clear, easy, elementary, intelligible, lucid, manageable, plain, straightforward, uncomplicated, understandable, uninvolved **2.** classic, clean, natural, plain, Spartan, unadorned, uncluttered, unembellished, unfussy **3.** elementary, pure, single, unalloyed, unblended, uncombined, undivided, unmixed **4.** artless, childlike, frank, green, guileless, ingenuous, innocent, naive, natural, sincere, unaffected, unpretentious, unsophisticated **5.** bald, basic, direct, frank, honest, naked, plain, sincere, stark, undeniable, unvarnished **6.** brainless, credulous, dense, dumb (*Inf.*), feeble, feeble-minded, foolish, half-witted, moronic, obtuse, shallow, silly, slow, stupid, thick

simple-minded 1. a bit lacking (*Inf.*), addle-brained, backward, brainless, dead from the neck up (*Sl.*), dim-witted, feeble-minded, foolish, idiot, idiotic, moronic, retarded, simple, stupid **2.** artless, natural, unsophisticated

simpleton blockhead, booby, dolt, dope (*Sl.*), dullard, dunce, fool, goose (*Inf.*), greenhorn (*Inf.*), idiot, imbecile (*Inf.*), jackass, moron, nincompoop, ninny, numskull, Simple Simon, stupid (*Inf.*), twerp (*Inf.*)

simplicity 1. absence of complications, clarity, clearness, ease, easiness, elementariness, obviousness, straightforwardness **2.** clean lines, lack of adornment, modesty, naturalness, plainness, purity, restraint **3.** artlessness, candour, directness, guilelessness, innocence, lack of sophistication, naivety, openness

simplify abridge, decipher, disentangle, facilitate, make intelligible, reduce to essentials, streamline

simply 1. clearly, directly, easily, intelligibly, modestly, naturally, plainly, straightforwardly, unaffectedly, unpretentiously, without any elaboration **2.** just, merely, only, purely, solely

simultaneous at the same time, coincident, coinciding, concurrent, contemporaneous, synchronous

simultaneously all together, at the same time, concurrently, in chorus, in concert, in the same breath, in unison, together

sin 1. *n.* crime, damnation, error, evil, guilt, iniquity, misdeed, offence, sinfulness, transgression, trespass, ungodliness, unrighteousness, wickedness, wrong, wrongdoing **2.** *v.* err, fall, fall from grace, go astray, lapse, offend, transgress, trespass (*Archaic*)

sincere artless, bona fide, candid, earnest, frank, genuine, guileless, heartfelt, honest, natural, no-nonsense, open, real, serious, straightforward, true, unaffected, unfeigned, wholehearted

sincerely earnestly, genuinely, honestly, in all sincerity, in good faith, really, seriously, truly, wholeheartedly

sincerity artlessness, bona fides, candour, frankness, genuineness, good faith, guilelessness, honesty, probity, seriousness, straightforwardness, truth, wholeheartedness

sinecure cushy number (*Sl.*), gravy train (*Sl., chiefly U.S.*), money for jam *or* old rope (*Inf.*), soft job (*Inf.*), soft option

sine die (ˈsaɪnɪ ˈdaɪɪ) *Lat.* with no date, indefinitely postponed

sine qua non (ˈsaɪnɪ kweɪ ˈnɒn) *Lat.* essential condition or requirement

sinew (ˈsɪnjuː) *n.* **1.** tough, fibrous cord joining muscle to bone —*pl.* **2.** muscles, strength —ˈ**sinewy** *a.* **1.** stringy **2.** muscular

sing (sɪŋ) *vi.* **1.** utter musical sounds **2.** hum, whistle, ring —*vt.* **3.** utter (words) with musical modulation **4.** celebrate in song or poetry (**sang, sung,** ˈ**singing**) —ˈ**singer** *n.* —ˈ**singsong** *n.* **1.** informal singing session —*a.* **2.** monotonously regular in tone, rhythm

singe (sɪndʒ) *vt.* **1.** burn surface of (**singed,** ˈ**singeing**) —*n.* **2.** act or effect of singeing

Singh (sɪŋ) *n.* title assumed by Sikh on becoming full member of community

single (ˈsɪŋgˀl) *a.* **1.** one only **2.** alone, separate **3.** unmarried **4.** for one **5.** formed of only one part, fold *etc.* **6.** denoting ticket for train *etc.* valid for outward journey only **7.** whole-hearted, straightforward —*n.* **8.** single thing **9.** gramophone record with one short item on each side **10.** single ticket —*vt.* **11.** (*with* out) pick (out) —ˈ**singleton** *n.* **1.** *Bridge etc.* original holding of one card only in suit **2.** single object as distinguished from pair or group **3.** *Maths.* set containing only one member —ˈ**singly** *adv.* —**single-breasted** *a.* (of garment) overlapping only slightly and with one row of fastenings —**single entry** *Book-keeping* entered in one account only —**single file** persons, things arranged in one line —**single-handed** *a./adv.* without assistance —**single-minded** *a.* having but one aim or purpose —**single-mindedness** *n.*

singlet (ˈsɪŋglɪt) *n.* sleeveless undervest

singular (ˈsɪŋgjʊlə) *a.* **1.** remarkable **2.** unusual **3.** unique **4.** denoting one person or thing —**singuˈlarity** *n.* something unusual —ˈ**singularly** *adv.* **1.** particularly **2.** peculiarly

Sinhalese (sɪnhəˈliːz) *or* **Singhalese** (sɪŋəˈliːz) *n.* **1.** member of people living chiefly in Sri Lanka **2.** language of this people —*a.* **3.** of this people or their language

sinister (ˈsɪnɪstə) *a.* **1.** threatening **2.** evil-looking **3.** wicked **4.** unlucky **5.** *Her.* on left-hand side

sink (sɪŋk) *vi.* **1.** become submerged (in water) **2.** drop, give way **3.** decline in value, health *etc.* **4.** penetrate —*vt.* **5.** cause to sink **6.** make by digging out **7.** invest (**sank** *pt.*, **sunk,** ˈ**sunken** *pp.*, ˈ**sinking** *pr.p.*) —*n.* **8.** receptacle with pipe for carrying away waste water **9.** cesspool **10.** place of corruption, vice —ˈ**sinker** *n.* weight for fishing line —**sinking fund** money set aside at intervals for payment of particular liability at fixed date

Sinn Fein (ˈʃɪn ˈfeɪn) Irish republican political movement

Sino- (*comb. form*) Chinese, of China, as in *Sino-Tibetan*

Sinology (saɪˈnɒlədʒɪ) *n.* study of Chinese history, language, culture *etc.* —**Sinological** (saɪnəˈlɒdʒɪkˀl) *a.* —**Siˈnologist** *n.*

sinuous (ˈsɪnjʊəs) *a.* **1.** curving **2.** devious **3.** lithe —ˈ**sinuate** *a.* —**sinuˈosity** *n.*

sinus (ˈsaɪnəs) *n.* cavity, *esp.* any of air passages in bones of skull —**sinuˈsitis** *n.* inflammation of sinus

Sion (ˈsaɪən) *n. see* ZION

sip (sɪp) *v.* **1.** drink in very small portions (**-pp-**) —*n.* **2.** small drink

siphon *or* **syphon** (ˈsaɪfˀn) *n.* **1.** device, *esp.* bent tube, which uses atmospheric or gaseous pressure to draw liquid from container —*vt.* **2.** draw off thus **3.** draw off in small amounts

sir (sɜː) *n.* **1.** polite term of address for a man **2.** (**S-**) title of knight or baronet

sire (saɪə) *n.* **1.** male parent, *esp.* of horse or domestic animal **2.** term of address to king —*vt.* **3.** beget

siren (ˈsaɪərən) *n.* **1.** device making loud wailing noise, *esp.* giving warning of danger **2.** legendary sea nymph who lured sailors to destruction **3.** alluring woman

Sirius (ˈsɪrɪəs) *n.* brightest star in sky, lying in constellation Canis Major (*also* **Dog Star**)

sirloin (ˈsɜːlɔɪn) *n.* prime cut of loin of beef

THESAURUS

sinful bad, corrupt, criminal, depraved, erring, guilty, immoral, iniquitous, irreligious, morally wrong, ungodly, unholy, unrighteous, wicked

sing 1. carol, chant, chirp, croon, make melody, pipe, trill, vocalize, warble, yodel **2.** buzz, hum, purr, ring, whine, whistle

singe burn, char, scorch, sear

singer chanteuse (*Fem.*), chorister, crooner, minstrel, songster, vocalist

single *adj.* **1.** distinct, individual, lone, one, only, particular, separate, singular, sole, solitary, unique **2.** free, unattached, unmarried, unwed **3.** exclusive, individual, separate, simple, unblended, uncompounded, undivided, unmixed, unshared ~*v.* **4.** *Usually with* **out** choose, cull, distinguish, fix on, pick, pick on *or* out, put on one side, select, separate, set apart, winnow

single-minded dedicated, determined, dogged, fixed, monomaniacal, steadfast, stubborn, tireless, undeviating, unswerving, unwavering

singly individually, one at a time, one by one, separately

singular 1. conspicuous, eminent, exceptional, noteworthy, outstanding, prodigious, rare, remarkable, uncommon, unique, unparalleled **2.** atypical, curious, eccentric, extraordinary, odd, out-of-the-way, peculiar, puzzling, queer, strange, unusual **3.** individual, separate, single, sole

sinister dire, disquieting, evil, injurious, malevolent, malign, malignant, menacing, ominous, threatening

sink *v.* **1.** cave in, decline, descend, dip, disappear, droop, drop, drown, ebb, engulf, fall, founder, go down, go under, lower, merge, plummet, plunge, sag, slope, submerge, subside **2.** abate, collapse, drop, fall, lapse, relapse, retrogress, slip, slump, subside **3.** decay, decline, decrease, degenerate, depreciate, deteriorate, die, diminish, dwindle, fade, fail, flag, go downhill (*Inf.*), lessen, weaken, worsen **4.** bore, dig, drill, drive, excavate, lay, put down

sinner evildoer, miscreant, offender, reprobate, transgressor, trespasser (*Archaic*), wrongdoer

sip 1. *v.* sample, sup, taste **2.** *n.* drop, swallow, taste, thimbleful

siren charmer, Circe, *femme fatale*, Lorelei, seductress, temptress, vamp (*Inf.*), witch

sirocco (sɪˈrɒkəʊ) *n.* hot oppressive wind beginning in N Afr. and reaching S Europe (*pl.* **-s**)

sisal (ˈsaɪsᵊl) *n.* (fibre of) plant used in making ropes

siskin (ˈsɪskɪn) *n.* small olive-green bird of finch family

sissy (ˈsɪsɪ) *a./n.* weak, cowardly (person)

sister (ˈsɪstə) *n.* **1.** daughter of same parents **2.** woman fellow-member, *esp.* of religious body **3.** senior nurse —*a.* **4.** closely related, similar —ˈ**sisterhood** *n.* **1.** relation of sister **2.** order, band of women —ˈ**sisterly** *a.* —**sister-in-law** *n.* **1.** sister of husband or wife **2.** brother's wife

sit (sɪt) *vi.* **1.** adopt posture or rest on buttocks, thighs **2.** perch **3.** (of bird) cover eggs to hatch them **4.** pose for portrait **5.** occupy official position **6.** hold session **7.** remain **8.** keep watch over baby *etc.* —*vt.* **9.** take (examination) (**sat**, ˈ**sitting**) —ˈ**sitter** *n.* **1.** person or animal that sits **2.** person who is posing for portrait **3.** *see* **baby-sitter** *at* BABY —ˈ**sitting** *n.* **1.** continuous period of being seated **2.** in canteen *etc.*, such period during which one of two or more meals is served **3.** meeting, *esp.* of official body **4.** incubation period of bird's eggs during which mother sits on them —**sit-down** *a.* (of meal *etc.*) eaten while sitting down at table —**sit-down strike** strike in which employees refuse to leave their place of employment —**sit-in** *n.* protest involving refusal to move from place —**sitting duck** *inf.* person or thing in defenceless position —**sitting tenant** tenant already occupying flat *etc.* —**sit down 1.** adopt sitting posture **2.** (*with* under) suffer (insults *etc.*) without protest —**sit in** protest by sit-in

sitar (sɪˈtɑː) *n.* stringed musical instrument, *esp.* of India

site (saɪt) *n.* **1.** place, location **2.** space for, with, a building —*vt.* **3.** locate in specific place

situate (ˈsɪtjʊeɪt) *vt.* place, locate —**situˈation** *n.* **1.** place, position **2.** state of affairs **3.** employment, post —**situation comedy** comedy based on humorous situations that could arise in day-to-day life

six (sɪks) *a./n.* cardinal number one more than five —ˈ**sixˈteen** *n./a.* six and ten —**sixth** *a.* **1.** ordinal number of six —*n.* **2.** sixth part —ˈ**sixty** *n./a.* six times ten —**six-shooter** *n.* US *inf.* revolver with six chambers —**sixth sense** any supposed means of perception, such as intuition

size[1] (saɪz) *n.* **1.** bigness, dimensions **2.** one of series of standard measurements of clothes *etc.* **3.** *inf.* state of affairs —*vt.* **4.** arrange according to size —ˈ**sizable** *or* ˈ**sizeable** *a.* quite large —**size up** *inf.* assess (person, situation *etc.*)

size[2] (saɪz) *n.* **1.** gluelike sealer, filler —*vt.* **2.** coat, treat with size

sizzle (ˈsɪzᵊl) *vi./n.* (make) hissing, spluttering sound, as of frying —ˈ**sizzler** *n. inf.* hot day

SJA Saint John's Ambulance (Brigade *or* Association)

SK Saskatchewan

skate[1] (skeɪt) *n.* **1.** steel blade attached to boot, for gliding over ice —*vi.* **2.** glide as on skates —ˈ**skateboard** *n.* small board mounted on roller-skate wheels

skate[2] (skeɪt) *n.* large marine ray

skean-dhu (skiːənˈduː) *n.* dagger worn in stocking as part of Highland dress

skedaddle (skɪˈdædᵊl) *vi. inf.* scamper off

skein (skeɪn) *n.* **1.** quantity of yarn, wool *etc.* in loose knot **2.** flight of wildfowl

skeleton (ˈskɛlɪtən) *n.* **1.** bones of animal **2.** bones separated from flesh and preserved in their natural position **3.** very thin person **4.** outline, draft, framework **5.** nucleus —*a.* **6.** reduced to a minimum **7.** drawn in outline **8.** not in detail —ˈ**skeletal** *a.* —**skeleton key** key filed down so as to open many different locks

skeptic (ˈskɛptɪk) *n.* US *see* SCEPTIC

skerry (ˈskɛrɪ) *n.* rocky island or reef

sketch (skɛtʃ) *n.* **1.** rough drawing **2.** brief account **3.** essay **4.** short humorous play —*v.* **5.** make sketch (of) —ˈ**sketchy** *a.* **1.** omitting detail **2.** incomplete **3.** inadequate

skew (skjuː) *vi.* **1.** move obliquely —*a.* **2.** slanting **3.** crooked —ˈ**skewˈwhiff** *a. inf.* **1.** aslant **2.** crooked

skewbald (ˈskjuːbɔːld) *a.* (*esp.* of horse) white and any other colour (except black) in patches

skewer (ˈskjʊə) *n.* **1.** pin to fasten meat together —*vt.* **2.** pierce or fasten with skewer

ski (skiː) *n.* **1.** long runner fastened to foot for sliding over snow or water (*pl.* **-s, ski**) —*vi.* **2.** slide on skis (**skied**, ˈ**skiing**) —**ski jump** ramp overhanging slope from which skiers compete to make longest jump —**ski-jump** *vi.*

skid (skɪd) *v.* **1.** (cause (*esp.* vehicle) to) slide (sideways) out of control with wheels not revolving (**-dd-**) —*n.* **2.** instance of this **3.** device to facilitate sliding, *eg* in moving heavy objects —ˈ**skidpan** *n.* area made slippery so that drivers can practise controlling skids —**skid row** *or* **road** *sl., chiefly* US dilapidated section of city inhabited by vagrants *etc.*

skidoo (ˈskɪduː) *n.* C snowmobile

skiff (skɪf) *n.* small boat

THESAURUS

sit 1. be seated, perch, rest, settle, take a seat, take the weight off one's feet **2.** assemble, be in session, convene, deliberate, meet, officiate, preside

site 1. *n.* ground, location, place, plot, position, spot **2.** *v.* install, locate, place, position, set, situate

sitting *n.* consultation, get-together (*Inf.*), hearing, meeting, period, session

situation 1. locale, locality, location, place, position, seat, setting, site, spot **2.** ball game (*Inf.*), case, circumstances, condition, kettle of fish (*Inf.*), plight, state, state of affairs, status quo, the picture (*Inf.*) **3.** berth (*Inf.*), employment, job, office, place, position, post

size amount, bigness, bulk, dimensions, extent, greatness, hugeness, immensity, largeness, magnitude, mass, measurement(s), proportions, range, vastness, volume

size up appraise, assess, evaluate, get (something) taped (*Brit. inf.*), get the measure of, take stock of

sizzle crackle, frizzle, fry, hiss, spit, splutter

skeleton *Fig.* bare bones, bones, draft, frame, framework, outline, sketch, structure

sketch 1. *v.* block out, delineate, depict, draft, draw, outline, paint, plot, portray, represent, rough out **2.** *n.* delineation, design, draft, drawing, outline, plan, skeleton

sketchy bitty, cobbled together, crude, cursory, inadequate, incomplete, outline, perfunctory, rough,

skill (skɪl) *n.* practical ability, cleverness, dexterity —ˈ**skilful** *or U.S.* ˈ**skillful** *a.* expert, masterly, adroit —ˈ**skilfully** *or U.S.* ˈ**skillfully** *adv.* —**skilled** *a.* having, requiring knowledge, united with readiness and dexterity

skillet (ˈskɪlɪt) *n.* small frying pan

skim (skɪm) *vt.* **1.** remove floating matter from surface of (liquid) **2.** glide over lightly and rapidly **3.** read thus —*vi.* **4.** move thus (**-mm-**) —**skim** *or* **skimmed milk** milk from which cream has been removed

skimp (skɪmp) *v.* **1.** give short measure (on) **2.** do (thing) imperfectly —ˈ**skimpy** *a.* **1.** meagre **2.** scanty

skin (skɪn) *n.* **1.** outer covering of vertebrate body, lower animal or fruit **2.** animal skin used as material or container **3.** film on surface of cooling liquid *etc.* **4.** complexion —*vt.* **5.** remove skin of (**-nn-**) —ˈ**skinless** *a.* —ˈ**skinned** *a.* **1.** stripped of skin **2.** having skin of specified kind —ˈ**skinner** *n.* **1.** dealer in hides **2.** furrier —ˈ**skinny** *a.* thin —**skin-deep** *a.* **1.** superficial **2.** slight —**skin diving** underwater swimming using breathing apparatus —**skin flick** film containing much nudity and explicit sex scenes —ˈ**skinflint** *n.* miser, niggard —**skin graft** transplant of piece of healthy skin to wound to form new skin —ˈ**skin**ˈ**tight** *a.* fitting close to skin —**keep one's eyes skinned** watch carefully

skint (skɪnt) *a. sl.* without money

skip[1] (skɪp) *vi.* **1.** leap lightly **2.** jump a rope as it is swung under one —*vt.* **3.** pass over, omit (**-pp-**) —*n.* **4.** act of skipping —**skipping-rope** *n.* **UK** cord that is held in hands and swung round so that holder or others can jump over it

skip[2] (skɪp) *n.* **1.** large open container for builders' rubbish *etc.* **2.** large bucket, container for transporting men, materials in mines *etc.*

skipper (ˈskɪpə) *n.* **1.** captain of ship, plane or team —*vt.* **2.** captain

skirl (skɜːl) *n.* sound of bagpipes

skirmish (ˈskɜːmɪʃ) *n.* **1.** fight between small parties, small battle —*vi.* **2.** fight briefly or irregularly

skirt (skɜːt) *n.* **1.** woman's garment hanging from waist **2.** lower part of woman's dress, coat *etc.* **3.** outlying part **4.** *sl.* woman —*vt.* **5.** border **6.** go round —ˈ**skirting** *n.* **1.** vertical board round margin of floor (*also* **skirting board**) **2.** material for women's skirts

skit (skɪt) *n.* satire, *esp.* theatrical burlesque

skittish (ˈskɪtɪʃ) *a.* frisky, frivolous

skittles (ˈskɪtʼlz) *pl.n.* ninepins

skive (skaɪv) *v.* evade (work or responsibility)

skivvy (ˈskɪvɪ) *n.* female servant who does menial work

skokiaan (ˈskɔːkɪɑːn) *n.* **SA** potent alcoholic beverage

skua (ˈskjuːə) *n.* large predatory gull

skulduggery *or U.S.* **skullduggery** (skʌlˈdʌgərɪ) *n. inf.* trickery

skulk (skʌlk) *vi.* **1.** sneak out of the way **2.** lurk

skull (skʌl) *n.* bony case that encloses brain —**skull and crossbones** picture of human skull above two crossed thighbones, used as warning of danger or death —ˈ**skullcap** *n.* close-fitting cap

skunk (skʌŋk) *n.* **1.** small N Amer. animal which emits evil-smelling fluid **2.** *sl.* mean person

sky (skaɪ) *n.* **1.** apparently dome-shaped expanse extending upwards from the horizon **2.** outer space **3.** heavenly regions (*pl.* **skies**) —*vt.* **4.** hit (cricket ball) high —ˈ**skydiving** *n.* parachute jumping with delayed opening of parachute —**sky-high** *a./adv.* **1.** at or to unprecedented level —*adv.* **2.** high into air —ˈ**skyjack** *vt.* hijack (an aircraft) —ˈ**skylark** *n.* **1.** lark, noted for singing while hovering at great height —*vi.* **2.** *inf.* romp or play jokes —ˈ**skylight** *n.* window in roof or ceiling —ˈ**skyline** *n.* **1.** line at which earth and sky appear to meet **2.** outline of trees *etc.* seen against sky —ˈ**skyscraper** *n.* very tall building —**blow sky-high** destroy

THESAURUS

scrappy, skimpy, slight, superficial, unfinished, vague

skilful able, accomplished, adept, adroit, apt, clever, competent, dexterous, experienced, expert, handy, masterly, practised, professional, proficient, quick, ready, skilled, trained

skill ability, accomplishment, adroitness, aptitude, art, cleverness, competence, dexterity, experience, expertise, expertness, facility, finesse, handiness, ingenuity, intelligence, knack, proficiency, quickness, readiness, skilfulness, talent, technique

skilled able, accomplished, a dab hand at (*Brit. inf.*), experienced, expert, masterly, practised, professional, proficient, skilful, trained

skim **1.** cream, separate **2.** brush, coast, dart, float, fly, glide, sail, soar **3.** *Usually with* **through** glance, run one's eye over, scan, skip (*Inf.*), thumb *or* leaf through

skimp be mean with, be niggardly, be sparing with, pinch, scamp, scant, scrimp, stint, withhold

skin *n.* **1.** fell, hide, integument, pelt, tegument **2.** casing, coating, crust, film, husk, membrane, outside, peel, rind ~*v.* **3.** abrade, bark, excoriate, flay, graze, peel, scrape

skinny emaciated, lean, scraggy, skeletal, skin-and-bone (*Inf.*), thin, twiggy, undernourished

skip *v.* **1.** bob, bounce, caper, cavort, dance, flit, frisk, gambol, hop, prance, trip **2.** eschew, give (something) a miss, leave out, miss out, omit, pass over, skim over

skirmish **1.** *n.* affair, affray (*Law*), battle, brush, clash, combat, conflict, contest, dust-up (*Inf.*), encounter, engagement, fracas, incident, scrap (*Inf.*), scrimmage, set-to (*Inf.*), spat, tussle **2.** *v.* clash, collide, come to blows, scrap (*Inf.*), tussle

skirt *v.* **1.** border, edge, flank, lie alongside **2.** *Often with* **around** *or* **round** avoid, bypass, circumvent, detour, evade, steer clear of ~*n.* **3.** *Often plural* border, edge, fringe, hem, margin, outskirts, periphery, purlieus, rim

skit burlesque, parody, sketch, spoof (*Inf.*), takeoff (*Inf.*), travesty, turn

skulk creep, lie in wait, loiter, lurk, pad, prowl, slink, sneak

sky azure (*Poetic*), empyrean (*Poetic*), firmament, heavens, upper atmosphere, vault of heaven, welkin (*Archaic*)

slab chunk, hunk, lump, piece, portion, slice, wedge, wodge (*Brit. inf.*)

Skye terrier (skaɪ) short-legged breed of terrier with long wiry hair

slab (slæb) *n.* thick, broad piece

slack[1] (slæk) *a.* 1. loose 2. sluggish 3. careless, negligent 4. not busy —*n.* 5. loose part, as of rope —*vi.* 6. be idle or lazy —ˈ**slacken** *v.* 1. make or become looser 2. make or become slower —ˈ**slacker** *n.* person who evades work —ˈ**slackly** *adv.* —**slack water** period of still water around turn of tide

slack[2] (slæk) *n.* coal dust, small pieces of coal

slacks (slæks) *pl.n.* informal trousers worn by men or women

slag (slæg) *n.* 1. refuse of smelted metal 2. *sl.* coarse woman —**slag heap** hillock of waste matter from coal-mining *etc.*

slain (sleɪn) *pp. of* SLAY

slake (sleɪk) *vt.* 1. satisfy (thirst, desire *etc.*) 2. combine (lime) with water to produce calcium hydroxide

slalom (ˈslɑːləm) *n.* race over winding course in skiing *etc.*

slam (slæm) *v.* 1. shut noisily 2. bang —*vt.* 3. hit 4. dash down 5. *inf.* criticize harshly (-**mm**-) —*n.* 6. (noise of) this action —**grand slam** *Cards* winning of all tricks

slander (ˈslɑːndə) *n.* 1. false or malicious statement about person —*v.* 2. utter such statement (about) —ˈ**slanderer** *n.* —ˈ**slanderous** *a.*

slang (slæŋ) *n.* 1. colloquial language —*vt.* 2. *sl.* scold, abuse violently

slant (slɑːnt) *v.* 1. slope —*vt.* 2. put at angle 3. write, present (news *etc.*) with bias —*n.* 4. slope 5. bias, point of view 6. idea —*a.* 7. sloping, oblique —ˈ**slantwise** *or* ˈ**slantways** *adv.*

slap (slæp) *n.* 1. blow with open hand or flat instrument —*vt.* 2. strike thus 3. *inf.* put (on, down) carelessly or messily (-**pp**-) —ˈ**slapdash** *a.* careless and abrupt —ˈ**slaphappy** *a. inf.* 1. cheerfully irresponsible 2. dazed as if from repeated blows —ˈ**slapstick** *n.* boisterous knockabout comedy —**slap-up** *a.* **UK** *inf.* (*esp.* of meals) lavish

slash (slæʃ) *vt.* 1. gash 2. lash 3. cut, slit 4. criticize unmercifully —*n.* 5. gash 6. cutting stroke

slat (slæt) *n.* narrow strip of wood or metal as in blinds *etc.*

slate (sleɪt) *n.* 1. kind of stone which splits easily in flat sheets 2. piece of this for covering roof or, formerly, for writing on —*vt.* 3. cover with slates 4. abuse —ˈ**slating** *n.* severe reprimand

slater (ˈsleɪtə) *n.* woodlouse

slattern (ˈslætən) *n.* slut —ˈ**slatternly** *a.* slovenly, untidy

slaughter (ˈslɔːtə) *n.* 1. killing —*vt.* 2. kill —ˈ**slaughterous** *a.* —ˈ**slaughterhouse** *n.* place for killing animals for food

Slav (slɑːv) *n.* member of any of peoples of E Europe or Soviet Asia who speak Slavonic language —**Sla**ˈ**vonic** *or* ˈ**Slavic** *n.* 1. branch of Indo-European family of languages, including Bulgarian, Russian, Polish, Czech *etc.* —*a.* 2. of this group of languages

slave (sleɪv) *n.* 1. captive, person without freedom or personal rights 2. one dominated by another or by a habit *etc.* —*vi.* 3. work like slave —ˈ**slaver** *n.* person, ship engaged in slave traffic —ˈ**slavery** *n.* —ˈ**slavish** *a.* servile —**slave-driver** *n.* 1. *esp.* formerly, person forcing slaves to work 2. employer demanding excessively hard work from employees

THESAURUS

slack *adj.* **1.** baggy, easy, flaccid, flexible, lax, limp, loose, not taut, relaxed **2.** asleep on the job (*Inf.*), easy-going, idle, inactive, inattentive, lax, lazy, neglectful, negligent, permissive, remiss, tardy **3.** dull, inactive, quiet, slow, slow-moving, sluggish ~*n.* **4.** excess, give (*Inf.*), leeway, looseness, play, room ~*v.* **5.** dodge, flag, idle, neglect, relax, shirk, skive (*Brit. sl.*), slacken

slacken (off) abate, decrease, diminish, drop off, ease (off), lessen, let up, loosen, moderate, reduce, relax, release, slack off, slow down, tire

slacker dodger, do-nothing, gold brick (*U.S. sl.*), good-for-nothing, idler, loafer, passenger, scrimshanker (*Brit. military sl.*), shirker, skiver (*Brit. sl.*)

slam 1. bang, crash, dash, fling, hurl, smash, throw, thump **2.** *Sl.* attack, castigate, criticize, damn, excoriate, lambaste, pan (*Inf.*), pillory, shoot down (*Inf.*), slate (*Inf.*), vilify

slander 1. *n.* aspersion, backbiting, calumny, defamation, detraction, libel, misrepresentation, muckraking, obloquy, scandal, smear **2.** *v.* backbite, blacken (someone's) name, calumniate, decry, defame, detract, disparage, libel, malign, muckrake, slur, smear, traduce, vilify

slanderous abusive, calumnious, damaging, defamatory, libellous, malicious

slang *v.* abuse, berate, call names, hurl insults at, insult, inveigh against, malign, rail against, revile, scold, vilify, vituperate

slant *v.* **1.** angle off, bend, bevel, cant, incline, lean, list, shelve, skew, slope, tilt ~*n.* **2.** camber, declination, diagonal, gradient, incline, pitch, rake, ramp, slope, tilt ~*v.* **3.** angle, bias, colour, distort, twist, weight ~*n.* **4.** angle, attitude, bias, emphasis, leaning, one-sidedness, point of view, prejudice, viewpoint

slap *n.* **1.** bang, blow, clout (*Inf.*), cuff, smack, spank, wallop (*Inf.*), whack ~*v.* **2.** bang, clap, clout (*Inf.*), cuff, hit, spank, strike, whack **3.** *Inf.* daub, plaster, plonk, spread

slapdash abrupt, careless, clumsy, disorderly, haphazard, hasty, hurried, last-minute, messy, negligent, perfunctory, slipshod, sloppy (*Inf.*), slovenly, thoughtless, thrown together, untidy

slash 1. *v.* cut, gash, hack, lacerate, rend, rip, score, slit **2.** *n.* cut, gash, incision, laceration, rent, rip, slit

slate *v.* abuse, berate, blame, castigate, censure, criticize, haul over the coals (*Inf.*), lambaste, lay into (*Inf.*), pan (*Inf.*), pitch into, rail against, rap (someone's) knuckles (*Inf.*), rebuke, roast (*Inf.*), scold, slam (*Sl.*), slang, take to task, tear (someone) off a strip (*Inf.*)

slaughter 1. *n.* blood bath, bloodshed, butchery, carnage, extermination, killing, liquidation, massacre, murder, slaying **2.** *v.* butcher, destroy, do to death, exterminate, kill, liquidate, massacre, murder, put to the sword, slay

slaughterhouse abattoir, butchery, shambles

slave 1. *n.* bondservant, bondsman, drudge, scullion (*Archaic*), serf, servant, skivvy, slavey (*Brit. inf.*), vassal, villein **2.** *v.* drudge, grind (*Inf.*), skivvy (*Brit.*), slog, toil, work one's fingers to the bone

slaver (ˈslævə) *vi.* **1.** dribble saliva from mouth **2.** fawn —*n.* **3.** saliva running from mouth

slaw (slɔː) *n. chiefly* US *short for* COLESLAW

slay (sleɪ) *vt.* **1.** kill **2.** *inf.* impress, *esp.* by being very funny (**slew, slain, ˈslaying**)

sleazy (ˈsliːzɪ) *a.* sordid

sledge[1] (slɛdʒ) *or* (*esp. U.S.*) **sled** (slɛd) *n.* **1.** carriage on runners for sliding on snow **2.** toboggan —*v.* **3.** convey, travel by sledge

sledge[2] (slɛdʒ) *n.* heavy hammer with long handle (*also* **ˈsledgehammer**)

sleek (sliːk) *a.* glossy, smooth, shiny

sleep (sliːp) *n.* **1.** unconscious state regularly occurring in man and animals **2.** slumber, repose **3.** *inf.* dried particles *oft.* found in corners of eyes after sleeping —*vi.* **4.** take rest in sleep, slumber (**slept, ˈsleeping**) —**ˈsleeper** *n.* **1.** one who sleeps **2.** beam supporting rails of railway **3.** railway sleeping car —**ˈsleepily** *adv.* —**ˈsleepiness** *n.* —**ˈsleepless** *a.* —**ˈsleepy** *a.* —**sleeping bag** large well-padded bag for sleeping in, *esp.* outdoors —**sleeping car** railway car fitted with compartments containing bunks for sleeping in —**sleeping partner** partner in business who does not play active role (*also* **silent partner**) —**sleeping policeman** protuberance built across roads to deter motorists from speeding —**sleeping sickness** Afr. disease spread by tsetse fly —**ˈsleepwalk** *vi.* walk while asleep

sleet (sliːt) *n.* rain and snow or hail falling together

sleeve (sliːv) *n.* **1.** part of garment which covers arm **2.** case surrounding shaft **3.** gramophone record cover —*vt.* **4.** furnish with sleeves —**sleeved** *a.* —**ˈsleeveless** *a.* —**have (something) up one's sleeve** have (something) prepared secretly for emergency

sleigh (sleɪ) *n.* sledge

sleight (slaɪt) *n.* **1.** dexterity **2.** trickery **3.** deviousness —**sleight of hand 1.** (manual dexterity in) conjuring, juggling **2.** legerdemain

slender (ˈslɛndə) *a.* **1.** slim, slight **2.** feeble

slept (slɛpt) *pt./pp. of* SLEEP

sleuth (sluːθ) *n.* **1.** detective **2.** tracking dog (*also* **ˈsleuthhound**) —*vt.* **3.** track

slew[1] (sluː) *pt. of* SLAY

slew[2] *or esp. U.S.* **slue** (sluː) *v.* swing round

slice (slaɪs) *n.* **1.** thin flat piece cut off **2.** share **3.** flat culinary tool —*vt.* **4.** cut into slices **5.** cut cleanly **6.** hit (ball) with bat *etc.* at angle

slick (slɪk) *a.* **1.** smooth **2.** smooth-tongued **3.** flattering **4.** superficially attractive **5.** sly —*vt.* **6.** make glossy, smooth —*n.* **7.** slippery area **8.** patch of oil on water

slide (slaɪd) *vi.* **1.** slip smoothly along **2.** glide, as over ice **3.** deteriorate morally —*v.* **4.** pass imperceptibly (**slid** (slɪd) *pt.*, **slid, slidden** (ˈslɪdᵊn) *pp.*, **ˈsliding** *pr.p.*) —*n.* **5.** sliding **6.** surface, track for sliding **7.** sliding part of mechanism **8.** piece of glass holding object to be viewed under microscope **9.** photographic transparency **10.** ornamental clip to hold hair in place, hair slide —**slide rule** mathematical instrument of two parts, one of which slides upon the other, for rapid calculations —**sliding scale** schedule for automatically varying one thing (*eg* wages) according to fluctuations of another (*eg* cost of living)

slight (slaɪt) *a.* **1.** small, trifling **2.** not substantial, fragile **3.** slim, slender —*vt.* **4.** disregard **5.** neglect —*n.* **6.** indifference **7.** act of discourtesy —**ˈslightly** *adv.*

slim (slɪm) *a.* **1.** thin **2.** slight —*v.* **3.** make or become slim by diet and exercise (**-mm-**)

slime (slaɪm) *n.* greasy, thick, liquid mud or similar substance —**ˈslimy** *a.* **1.** like slime **2.** fawning

THESAURUS

slavery bondage, captivity, enslavement, serfdom, servitude, subjugation, thraldom, thrall, vassalage

slavish abject, base, cringing, despicable, fawning, grovelling, low, mean, menial, obsequious, servile, submissive, sycophantic

slay 1. annihilate, assassinate, butcher, destroy, dispatch, do away with, eliminate, exterminate, kill, massacre, mow down, murder, rub out (*U.S. sl.*), slaughter **2.** *Inf.* amuse, be the death of (*Inf.*), impress, make a hit with (*Inf.*), wow (*Sl., chiefly U.S.*)

sleek glossy, lustrous, shiny, smooth, well-fed, well-groomed

sleep 1. *v.* be in the land of Nod, catnap, doze, drop off (*Inf.*), drowse, hibernate, nod off (*Inf.*), rest in the arms of Morpheus, slumber, snooze (*Inf.*), snore, take a nap, take forty winks (*Inf.*) **2.** *n.* beauty sleep (*Inf.*), dormancy, doze, forty winks (*Inf.*), hibernation, nap, repose, rest, shuteye (*Sl.*), siesta, slumber(s), snooze (*Inf.*)

sleepiness doziness, drowsiness, heaviness, lethargy, somnolence, torpor

sleepless disturbed, insomniac, restless, unsleeping, wakeful

sleepy drowsy, dull, heavy, inactive, lethargic, sluggish, slumbersome, somnolent, torpid

slender 1. lean, narrow, slight, slim, svelte, sylphlike, willowy **2.** faint, feeble, flimsy, fragile, poor, remote, slight, slim, tenuous, thin, weak

sleuth detective, dick (*U.S. sl.*), gumshoe (*U.S. sl.*), private eye (*Inf.*), (private) investigator, sleuthhound (*Inf.*), tail (*Inf.*)

slice 1. *n.* cut, helping, piece, portion, segment, share, sliver, wedge **2.** *v.* carve, cut, divide, sever

slick 1. *adj.* glib, meretricious, plausible, polished, smooth, sophistical, specious **2.** *v.* make glossy, plaster down, sleek, smarm down (*Brit. inf.*), smooth

slide *v.* coast, glide, glissade, skim, slip, slither, toboggan, veer

slight *adj.* **1.** feeble, inconsiderable, insignificant, insubstantial, meagre, minor, modest, negligible, paltry, scanty, small, superficial, trifling, trivial, unimportant, weak **2.** delicate, feeble, fragile, lightly-built, slender, slim, small, spare ~*v.* **3.** affront, cold-shoulder, despise, disdain, disparage, give offence *or* umbrage to, ignore, insult, neglect, scorn, show disrespect for, snub, treat with contempt ~*n.* **4.** affront, contempt, discourtesy, disdain, disregard, disrespect, inattention, indifference, insult, neglect, rebuff, slap in the face (*Inf.*), snub, (the) cold shoulder

slightly a little, marginally, on a small scale, somewhat, to some extent *or* degree

slim *adj.* **1.** lean, narrow, slender, slight, svelte, sylphlike, thin, trim **2.** faint, poor, remote, slender, slight ~*v.* **3.** diet, lose weight, reduce, slenderize (*Chiefly U.S.*)

slimy 1. clammy, glutinous, miry, mucous, muddy,

sling (slɪŋ) *n.* **1.** strap, loop with string attached at each end for hurling stone **2.** bandage for supporting wounded limb **3.** rope, belt *etc.* for hoisting, carrying weights —*vt.* **4.** throw **5.** hoist, swing by rope (**slung, ˈslinging**) —**ˈslingback** *n.* shoe with strap instead of full covering for heel

slink (slɪŋk) *vi.* move stealthily, sneak (**slunk, ˈslinking**) —**ˈslinky** *a.* **1.** sinuously graceful **2.** (of clothes *etc.*) figure-hugging

slip[1] (slɪp) *v.* **1.** (cause to) move smoothly, easily, quietly **2.** pass out of (mind *etc.*) **3.** (of motor vehicle clutch) engage partially, fail —*vi.* **4.** lose balance by sliding **5.** fall from person's grasp **6.** (*usu. with* up) make mistake **7.** decline in health, morals —*vt.* **8.** put on or take off easily, quickly **9.** let go (anchor *etc.*) **10.** dislocate (bone) (**-pp-**) —*n.* **11.** act or occasion of slipping **12.** mistake **13.** petticoat **14.** small piece of paper **15.** plant cutting **16.** launching slope on which ships are built **17.** *Cricket* (fieldsman in) position offside and a little behind wicket **18.** covering for pillow —**ˈslippy** *a.* **1.** *see* SLIPPERY (sense 1) **2. UK** *inf.* alert —**ˈslipknot** *n.* knot tied so that it will slip along rope round which it is made (*also* **running knot**) —**slip-on** *a.* **1.** (of garment or shoe) easily put on or removed —*n.* **2.** slip-on garment or shoe —**slipped disc** *Pathol.* herniated intervertebral disc, oft. resulting in pain due to pressure on spinal nerves —**slip road** narrow road giving access to motorway *etc.* —**ˈslipshod** *a.* slovenly, careless —**ˈslipstream** *n. Aviation* stream of air driven astern by engine —**slip-up** *n. inf.* mistake or mishap —**ˈslipway** *n.* incline for launching ships —**slip up** *inf.* blunder

slip[2] (slɪp) *n.* clay mixed with water to creamy consistency, used for decorating ceramic ware

slipper (ˈslɪpə) *n.* light shoe for indoor use

slippery (ˈslɪpərɪ, -prɪ) *a.* **1.** so smooth as to cause slipping or to be difficult to hold or catch **2.** changeable **3.** unreliable **4.** crafty, wily

slit (slɪt) *vt.* **1.** make long straight cut in **2.** cut in strips (**slit, ˈslitting**) —*n.* **3.** long narrow cut or opening

slither (ˈslɪðə) *vi.* slide unsteadily (down slope *etc.*)

sliver (ˈslɪvə) *n.* **1.** thin small piece torn off something **2.** splinter

slob (slɒb) *n. inf.* stupid, coarse person

slobber (ˈslɒbə) *or* **slabber** (ˈslæbə) *vi.* **1.** slaver **2.** be weakly and excessively demonstrative —*n.* **3.** running saliva **4.** maudlin speech —**ˈslobbery** *or* **ˈslabbery** *a.*

slob ice C sludgy masses of floating ice

sloe (sləʊ) *n.* blue-black, sour fruit of blackthorn —**sloe-eyed** *a.* having dark slanted or almond-shaped eyes

slog (slɒg) *vt.* **1.** hit vigorously, *esp.* at cricket —*vi.* **2.** work or study with dogged determination **3.** move, work with difficulty (**-gg-**) —*n.* **4.** tiring walk **5.** long exhausting work **6.** heavy blow

slogan (ˈsləʊgən) *n.* distinctive phrase (in advertising *etc.*)

sloop (slu:p) *n.* **1.** small one-masted vessel **2.** *Hist.* small warship

sloot (slu:t) *n.* **SA** ditch for irrigation or drainage

slop (slɒp) *vi.* **1.** spill —*vt.* **2.** spill, splash (**-pp-**) —*n.* **3.** liquid spilt **4.** liquid food **5.** dirty liquid —*pl.* **6.** liquid refuse —**ˈsloppy** *a.* **1.** careless, untidy **2.** sentimental **3.** wet, muddy

slope (sləʊp) *vt.* **1.** place slanting —*vi.* **2.** lie in, follow an inclined course **3.** go furtively —*n.* **4.** slant **5.** upward, downward inclination

slosh (slɒʃ) *n.* **1.** watery mud, snow *etc.* **2.** *sl.* heavy blow —*v.* **3.** splash —*vt.* **4.** hit —**sloshed** *a. sl.* drunk

slot (slɒt) *n.* **1.** narrow hole or depression **2.** slit for coins —*vt.* **3.** put in slot **4.** sort **5.** *inf.* place in series, organization (**-tt-**) —**slot machine** automatic machine worked by insertion of coin

sloth (sləʊθ) *n.* **1.** sluggish S Amer. animal **2.** sluggishness —**ˈslothful** *a.* lazy, idle

THESAURUS

oozy, viscous **2.** creeping, grovelling, obsequious, oily, servile, smarmy (*Brit. inf.*), soapy (*Sl.*), sycophantic, toadying, unctuous

sling *v.* **1.** cast, chuck (*Inf.*), fling, heave, hurl, lob (*Inf.*), shy, throw, toss **2.** dangle, hang, suspend, swing

slink creep, prowl, pussyfoot (*Inf.*), skulk, slip, sneak, steal

slip *v.* **1.** glide, skate, slide, slither **2.** fall, lose one's balance, miss *or* lose one's footing, skid, trip (over) **3.** conceal, creep, hide, insinuate oneself, sneak, steal **4.** *Sometimes with* **up** blunder, boob (*Brit. sl.*), err, go wrong, make a mistake, miscalculate, misjudge, mistake ~*n.* **5.** bloomer (*Brit. inf.*), blunder, boob (*Brit. sl.*), error, failure, fault, imprudence, indiscretion, mistake, omission, oversight, slip of the tongue, slip-up (*Inf.*)

slippery **1.** glassy, greasy, icy, lubricious (*Rare*), perilous, skiddy (*Inf.*), slippy (*Inf.*), smooth, unsafe, unstable, unsteady **2.** crafty, cunning, devious, dishonest, duplicitous, evasive, false, foxy, shifty, sneaky, treacherous, tricky, two-faced, unpredictable, unreliable, untrustworthy

slipshod careless, loose, slapdash, sloppy (*Inf.*), slovenly, unsystematic, untidy

slit **1.** *v.* cut (open), gash, knife, lance, pierce, rip, slash, split open **2.** *n.* cut, fissure, gash, incision, opening, rent, split, tear

slither *v.* glide, skitter, slide, slink, slip, snake, undulate

slog *v.* **1.** hit, hit for six, slosh (*Brit. sl.*), slug, sock (*Sl.*), strike, thump, wallop (*Inf.*) **2.** apply oneself to, labour, peg away at, persevere, plod, plough through, slave, toil, tramp, trek, trudge, work ~*n.* **3.** effort, exertion, hike, labour, struggle, tramp, trek, trudge

slogan catchword, jingle, motto, rallying cry

slope *v.* **1.** drop away, fall, incline, lean, pitch, rise, slant, tilt ~*n.* **2.** brae (*Scot.*), declination, declivity, descent, downgrade (*Chiefly U.S.*), gradient, inclination, incline, ramp, rise, scarp, slant, tilt ~*v.* **3.** *With* **off, away,** *etc.* creep, make oneself scarce, skulk, slink, slip, steal

sloppy **1.** muddy, sludgy, slushy, splashy, watery, wet **2.** *Inf.* amateurish, careless, clumsy, hit-or-miss (*Inf.*), inattentive, messy, slipshod, slovenly, unkempt, untidy, weak **3.** banal, gushing, mawkish, mushy (*Inf.*), overemotional, sentimental, slushy (*Inf.*), soppy (*Brit. inf.*), trite, wet (*Brit. inf.*)

slot **1.** *n.* aperture, channel, groove, hole, slit **2.** *v.* adjust, assign, fit, fit in, insert, pigeonhole

slouch (slaʊtʃ) *vi.* **1.** walk, sit *etc.* in lazy or ungainly, drooping manner —*n.* **2.** drooping bearing **3.** incompetent or slovenly person —*a.* **4.** (of hat) with wide, flexible brim

slough[1] (slaʊ) *n.* **1.** bog **2.** (slu:) C hole where water collects

slough[2] (slʌf) *n.* **1.** skin shed by snake —*v.* **2.** shed (skin) —**slough off** cast off (cares *etc.*)

sloven (ˈslʌvᵊn) *n.* dirty, untidy person —**ˈslovenly** *a.* **1.** untidy **2.** careless **3.** disorderly —*adv.* **4.** in slovenly manner

slow (sləʊ) *a.* **1.** lasting a long time **2.** moving at low speed **3.** behind the true time **4.** dull —*v.* **5.** (cause to) decrease in speed —**ˈslowly** *adv.* —**ˈslowness** *n.* —**ˈslowcoach** *n.* person slow in moving, acting, deciding *etc.* —**slow-motion** *a.* (of film) showing movement greatly slowed down

slowworm (ˈsləʊwɜːm) *n.* small legless lizard, blindworm

sludge (slʌdʒ) *n.* **1.** slush, ooze **2.** sewage

slue[1] (slu:) *v. esp.* US *see* SLEW[2]

slue[2] (slu:) *n. see* SLOUGH[1] (sense 2)

slug[1] (slʌg) *n.* **1.** land snail with no shell **2.** bullet —**ˈsluggard** *n.* lazy, idle person —**ˈsluggish** *a.* **1.** slow **2.** lazy, inert **3.** not functioning well

slug[2] (slʌg) *vt.* **1.** hit, slog (**-gg-**) —*n.* **2.** heavy blow **3.** portion of spirits —**ˈslugger** *n.* hard-hitting boxer, slogger

sluice (slu:s) *n.* **1.** gate, door to control flow of water —*vt.* **2.** pour water over, through

slum (slʌm) *n.* **1.** squalid street or neighbourhood —*vi.* **2.** visit slums (**-mm-**)

slumber (ˈslʌmbə) *vi./n.* sleep —**ˈslumberer** *n.*

slump (slʌmp) *vi.* **1.** fall heavily **2.** relax ungracefully **3.** decline suddenly in value, volume or esteem —*n.* **4.** sudden decline **5.** (of prices *etc.*) sharp fall **6.** depression

slung (slʌŋ) *pt./pp. of* SLING

slunk (slʌŋk) *pt./pp. of* SLINK

slur (slɜː) *vt.* **1.** pass over lightly **2.** run together (words, musical notes) **3.** disparage (**-rr-**) —*n.* **4.** slight, stigma **5.** *Mus.* curved line above or below notes to be slurred

slurp (slɜːp) *v. inf.* eat, drink noisily

slurry (ˈslʌrɪ) *n.* muddy liquid mixture, such as cement, mud *etc.*

slush (slʌʃ) *n.* **1.** watery, muddy substance **2.** excess sentimentality —**slush fund** US fund for financing bribery, corruption

slut (slʌt) *n.* dirty (immoral) woman —**ˈsluttish** *a.* —**ˈsluttishness** *n.*

sly (slaɪ) *a.* **1.** cunning, wily, knowing **2.** secret, deceitful —**ˈslyly** *or* **ˈslily** *adv.* —**ˈslyness** *n.*

Sm *Chem.* samarium

smack[1] (smæk) *n.* **1.** taste, flavour **2.** *sl.* heroin —*vi.* (*with* of) **3.** have taste (of) **4.** be suggestive (of)

smack[2] (smæk) *vt.* **1.** slap **2.** open and close (lips) with loud sound —*n.* **3.** smacking slap **4.** crack **5.** such sound **6.** loud kiss —*adv.* **7.** *inf.* squarely; directly —**ˈsmacker** *n. sl.* **1.** loud kiss **2.** pound note or dollar bill

smack[3] (smæk) *n.* small sailing vessel, usu. for fishing

small (smɔːl) *a.* **1.** little **2.** unimportant; petty **3.** short **4.** weak **5.** mean —*n.* **6.** small slender part, *esp.* of the back —*pl.* **7.** *inf.* personal laundry, underwear —**ˈsmallness** *n.* —**small beer** *inf., chiefly* UK people or things of no importance —**small change 1.** coins, *esp.* those of low value **2.** *rare* person or thing of little importance —**ˈsmallholding** *n.* small area of farming land —**small hours** hours just after midnight —**small-minded** *a.* having narrow views; petty —**ˈsmallpox** *n.*

THESAURUS

sloth faineance, idleness, inactivity, indolence, inertia, laziness, slackness, slothfulness, sluggishness, torpor

slothful do-nothing (*Inf.*), fainéant, idle, inactive, indolent, inert, lazy, skiving (*Brit. inf.*), slack, sluggish, torpid, workshy

slouch *v.* droop, loll, slump, stoop

slovenly careless, disorderly, heedless, loose, negligent, slack, slapdash, slatternly, slipshod, sloppy (*Inf.*), unkempt, untidy

slow *adj.* **1.** creeping, dawdling, deliberate, easy, lackadaisical, laggard, lagging, lazy, leaden, leisurely, loitering, measured, plodding, ponderous, slow-moving, sluggardly, sluggish, tortoise-like, unhurried **2.** backward, behind, behindhand, delayed, dilatory, late, long-delayed, tardy, unpunctual **3.** gradual, lingering, long-drawn-out, prolonged, protracted, time-consuming **4.** behind the times, boring, conservative, dead, dead-and-alive (*Brit.*), dull, inactive, one-horse (*Inf.*), quiet, slack, sleepy, sluggish, stagnant, tame, tedious, uneventful, uninteresting, unproductive, unprogressive, wearisome **5.** blockish, bovine, dense, dim, dull, dull-witted, dumb (*Inf.*), obtuse, retarded, slow on the uptake (*Inf.*), slow-witted, stupid, thick, unresponsive ~*v.* **6.** *Often with* **up** *or* **down** brake, check, curb, decelerate, delay, detain, handicap, hold up, lag, reduce speed, rein in, relax, restrict, retard, slacken (off), spin out

slowly at a snail's pace, at one's leisure, by degrees, gradually, inchmeal, in one's own (good) time, leisurely, ploddingly, steadily, taking one's time, unhurriedly, with leaden steps

sluggish dull, heavy, inactive, indolent, inert, lazy, lethargic, lifeless, listless, phlegmatic, slothful, slow, slow-moving, torpid, unresponsive

slumber *v.* be inactive, doze, lie dormant, nap, repose, sleep, snooze (*Inf.*)

slump *v.* **1.** collapse, crash, decline, deteriorate, fall, fall off, go downhill (*Inf.*), plummet, plunge, reach a new low, sink, slip ~*n.* **2.** collapse, crash, decline, depreciation, depression, downturn, failure, fall, falling-off, low, recession, reverse, stagnation, trough ~*v.* **3.** bend, droop, hunch, loll, sag, slouch

slur *n.* affront, aspersion, blot, brand, calumny, discredit, disgrace, innuendo, insinuation, insult, reproach, smear, stain, stigma

slut drab (*Archaic*), slattern, sloven, trollop

sly 1. artful, astute, clever, conniving, covert, crafty, cunning, devious, foxy, furtive, guileful, insidious, scheming, secret, shifty, stealthy, subtle, underhand, wily **2.** arch, impish, knowing, mischievous, roguish

smack 1. *v.* box, clap, cuff, hit, pat, slap, sock (*Sl.*), spank, strike, tap **2.** *n.* blow, crack, slap **3.** *adv. Inf.* directly, exactly, plumb, point-blank, precisely, right, slap (*Inf.*), squarely, straight

contagious disease —**small-scale** *a.* 1. of limited size 2. (of map *etc.*) giving small representation of something —**small talk** light, polite conversation —**small-time** *a.* *inf.* insignificant —**small-timer** *n.*

smarm (smɑːm) *vi.* *inf.* fawn —ˈ**smarmy** *a.* *inf.* unpleasantly suave; fawning

smart (smɑːt) *a.* 1. astute 2. brisk 3. clever, witty 4. impertinent 5. trim, well dressed 6. fashionable 7. causing stinging pain —*v.* 8. feel, cause pain —*n.* 9. sharp pain —ˈ**smarten** *v.* —ˈ**smartly** *adv.* —ˈ**smartness** *n.* —**smart aleck** (ˈælɪk) *or* ˈ**smarty** *inf.* conceited person, know-all

smash (smæʃ) *vt.* 1. break violently 2. strike hard 3. ruin 4. destroy —*vi.* 5. break 6. dash violently —*n.* 7. heavy blow 8. collision (of vehicles *etc.*) 9. total financial failure 10. *inf.* popular success —**smashed** *a.* *sl.* very drunk or affected by drugs —ˈ**smasher** *n.* *inf.* attractive person, thing —ˈ**smashing** *a.* *inf., chiefly* UK excellent —**smash-and-grab** *a.* *inf.* of robbery in which shop window is broken and contents removed

smattering (ˈsmætərɪŋ) *n.* slight superficial knowledge

smear (smɪə) *vt.* 1. rub with grease *etc.* 2. smudge, spread with dirt, grease *etc.* —*n.* 3. mark made thus 4. sample of secretion for medical examination 5. slander

smell (smɛl) *vt.* 1. perceive by nose 2. *fig.* suspect —*vi.* 3. give out odour 4. use nose (**smelt** *or* **smelled,** ˈ**smelling**) —*n.* 5. faculty of perceiving odours by nose 6. anything detected by sense of smell —ˈ**smelly** *a.* with strong (unpleasant) smell —**smelling salts** preparation of ammonium carbonate that has stimulant action when sniffed in cases of faintness *etc.*

smelt[1] (smɛlt) *vt.* extract (metal) from (ore) —ˈ**smeltery** *n.*

smelt[2] (smɛlt) *n.* fish of salmon family

smew (smjuː) *n.* type of duck

smilax (ˈsmaɪlæks) *n.* 1. climbing shrub having slightly lobed leaves and berry-like fruits 2. much branched vine of S Afr. with glossy green foliage

smile (smaɪl) *n.* 1. curving or parting of lips in pleased or amused expression —*vi.* 2. wear, assume a smile 3. (*with* on) approve, favour

smirch (smɜːtʃ) *vt.* 1. dirty, sully 2. disgrace, discredit —*n.* 3. stain 4. disgrace

smirk (smɜːk) *n.* 1. smile expressing scorn, smugness —*vi.* 2. give such smile

smite (smaɪt) *vt.* 1. strike 2. attack 3. afflict 4. affect, *esp.* with love or fear (**smote,** ˈ**smitten,** ˈ**smiting**)

smith (smɪθ) *n.* worker in iron, gold *etc.* —**smithy** (ˈsmɪðɪ) *n.* blacksmith's workshop

smithereens (smɪðəˈriːnz) *pl.n.* small bits

smitten (ˈsmɪtᵊn) *pp. of* SMITE

smock (smɒk) *n.* 1. loose outer garment —*vt.* 2. gather by sewing in honeycomb pattern

smog (smɒg) *n.* mixture of smoke and fog

smoke (sməʊk) *n.* 1. cloudy mass of suspended particles that rises from fire or anything burning 2. spell of tobacco smoking —*vi.* 3. give off smoke 4. inhale and expel tobacco smoke —*vt.* 5. use (tobacco) by smoking 6. expose to smoke (*esp.* in curing fish *etc.*) —ˈ**smoker** *n.* —ˈ**smokily** *adv.* —ˈ**smoky** *a.* —**smoke screen** 1. *Mil.* cloud of smoke produced to obscure movements 2. something said or done to conceal truth —ˈ**smokestack** *n.* chimney that conveys smoke into air

smolt (sməʊlt) *n.* young salmon at stage when it migrates from fresh water to sea

smooch (smuːtʃ) *vi./n.* *inf.* kiss, cuddle

smooth (smuːð) *a.* 1. not rough, even of surface or texture 2. sinuous 3. flowing 4. calm, soft, soothing 5. suave, plausible 6. free from jolts —*vt.* 7. make smooth 8. quieten —ˈ**smoothly** *adv.* —**smooth-spoken** *a.* speaking in gently persuasive manner —**smooth-tongued** *a.* suave or persuasive in speech

THESAURUS

small 1. diminutive, immature, little, mini, miniature, minute, petite, pint-sized (*Inf.*), pocket-sized, puny, slight, tiny, undersized, wee, young 2. insignificant, lesser, minor, negligible, paltry, petty, trifling, trivial, unimportant 3. base, grudging, illiberal, mean, narrow, petty, selfish

small-minded bigoted, envious, grudging, hidebound, intolerant, mean, narrow-minded, petty, rigid, ungenerous

smart *adj.* 1. acute, adept, agile, apt, astute, bright, brisk, canny, clever, ingenious, intelligent, keen, nimble, quick, quick-witted, ready, sharp, shrewd 2. chic, elegant, fashionable, fine, modish, natty (*Inf.*), neat, snappy, spruce, stylish, trim, well dressed, well turned out 3. clever, effective, impertinent, nimble-witted, pointed, ready, saucy, smart-alecky (*Inf.*), witty 4. brisk, cracking (*Inf.*), jaunty, lively, quick, spanking, spirited, vigorous ~*v.* 5. burn, hurt, pain, sting, throb, tingle ~*adj.* 6. hard, keen, painful, piercing, resounding, sharp, stinging ~*n.* 7. burning sensation, pain, pang, smarting, soreness, sting

smash *v.* 1. break, collide, crash, crush, demolish, disintegrate, pulverize, shatter, shiver ~*n.* 2. accident, collision, crash, pile-up (*Inf.*), smash-up (*Inf.*) ~*v.* 3. defeat, destroy, lay waste, overthrow, ruin, wreck ~*n.* 4. collapse, defeat, destruction, disaster, downfall, failure, ruin, shattering

smashing excellent, exhilarating, fab (*Sl.*), fabulous (*Inf.*), fantastic (*Inf.*), first-class, first-rate, great (*Inf.*), magnificent, marvellous, out of this world (*Inf.*), sensational, stupendous, super (*Inf.*), superb, superlative, terrific (*Inf.*), wonderful

smear *v.* 1. bedaub, bedim, besmirch, blur, coat, cover, daub, dirty, patch, plaster, rub on, smudge, soil, spread over, stain, sully ~*n.* 2. blot, blotch, daub, smudge, splotch, streak 3. calumny, defamation, libel, mudslinging, slander, vilification, whispering campaign

smell *n.* 1. aroma, bouquet, fragrance, odour, perfume, redolence, scent, whiff ~*v.* 2. get a whiff of (*Brit. sl.*), nose, scent, sniff ~*n.* 3. fetor, pong (*Brit. inf.*), stench, stink ~*v.* 4. be malodorous, hum (*Sl.*), pong (*Brit. inf.*), reek, stink, stink to high heaven (*Inf.*), whiff (*Brit. sl.*)

smirk *n.* grin, leer, simper, smug look, sneer

smitten 1. afflicted, beset, laid low, plagued, struck 2. beguiled, bewitched, bowled over (*Inf.*), captivated, charmed, enamoured, infatuated, swept off one's feet

smoky begrimed, black, caliginous (*Archaic*), grey, grimy, hazy, murky, reeky, smoke-darkened, sooty, thick

smooth *adj.* 1. even, flat, flush, horizontal, level, plain, plane, unwrinkled 2. glossy, polished, shiny,

smorgasbord (ˈsmɔːgəsbɔːd) *n.* buffet meal of assorted dishes

smote (sməʊt) *pt. of* SMITE

smother (ˈsmʌðə) *vt.* **1.** suffocate **2.** envelop **3.** suppress —*vi.* **4.** be suffocated

smoulder *or U.S.* **smolder** (ˈsməʊldə) *vi.* **1.** burn slowly without flame **2.** (of feelings) exist in suppressed state

smudge (smʌdʒ) *vt.* **1.** make smear, stain, dirty mark on —*n.* **2.** smear or dirty mark

smug (smʌg) *a.* self-satisfied, complacent

smuggle (ˈsmʌgᵊl) *vt.* **1.** import, export without paying customs duties **2.** conceal, take secretly

smut (smʌt) *n.* **1.** piece of soot, particle of dirt **2.** lewd or obscene talk *etc.* **3.** disease of grain —*vt.* **4.** blacken, smudge (**-tt-**) —ˈ**smutty** *a.* **1.** soiled with smut, soot **2.** obscene, lewd

Sn *Chem.* tin

snack (snæk) *n.* light, hasty meal —**snack bar** bar at which snacks are served

snaffle (ˈsnæfᵊl) *n.* **1.** light bit for horse —*vt.* **2.** *sl.* appropriate, scrounge **3.** put snaffle on

snag (snæg) *n.* **1.** difficulty **2.** sharp protuberance **3.** hole, loop in fabric caused by sharp object **4.** obstacle (*eg* tree branch *etc.* in river bed) —*vt.* **5.** catch, damage on snag (**-gg-**)

snail (sneɪl) *n.* **1.** slow-moving mollusc with shell **2.** slow, sluggish person —**snail-like** *a.* —**snail's pace** very slow rate

snake (sneɪk) *n.* **1.** long scaly limbless reptile, serpent —*vi.* **2.** move like snake —ˈ**snaky** *a.* of, like snakes —**snake charmer** entertainer who appears to charm snakes by playing music —**snakes and ladders** board game in which tossed dice determine how far counters move either to climb up ladders or slide down snakes

snap (snæp) *v.* **1.** break suddenly **2.** (cause to) make cracking sound **3.** bite (at) suddenly **4.** speak (words) suddenly, angrily (**-pp-**) —*n.* **5.** act of snapping **6.** fastener **7.** *inf.* snapshot **8.** *inf.* easy task **9.** brief period, *esp.* of cold weather —*a.* **10.** sudden, unplanned, arranged quickly —ˈ**snapper** *n.* perchlike fish —ˈ**snappy** *a.* **1.** irritable **2.** *sl.* quick **3.** *sl.* well dressed, fashionable —ˈ**snapdragon** *n.* plant with flowers that can be opened like a mouth —**snap fastener** press stud —ˈ**snapshot** *n.* photograph

snare[1] (snɛə) *n.* **1.** (noose used as) trap —*vt.* **2.** catch with one

snare[2] (snɛə) *n. Mus.* set of gut strings wound with wire fitted across bottom of drum to increase vibration —**snare drum** *Mus.* cylindrical double-headed drum with snares

snarl (snɑːl) *n.* **1.** growl of angry dog **2.** tangle, knot —*vi.* **3.** utter snarl **4.** grumble —**snarl-up** *n. inf.* confusion, obstruction, *esp.* traffic jam

snatch (snætʃ) *vt.* **1.** make quick grab or bite at **2.** seize, catch —*n.* **3.** grab **4.** fragment **5.** short spell

snazzy (ˈsnæzɪ) *a. inf.* stylish, flashy

sneak (sniːk) *vi.* **1.** slink **2.** move about furtively **3.** act in mean, underhand manner —*n.* **4.** mean, treacherous person **5.** petty informer —ˈ**sneaking** *a.* secret but persistent —**sneak thief** person who steals articles from premises which he enters through open windows *etc.*

sneakers (ˈsniːkəz) *pl.n. chiefly* **US** flexible, informal sports shoes

sneer (snɪə) *n.* **1.** scornful, contemptuous expression or remark —*vi.* **2.** assume scornful expression —*v.* **3.** speak or utter contemptuously

THESAURUS

silky, sleek, soft, velvety **3.** calm, equable, glassy, mirror-like, peaceful, serene, tranquil, undisturbed, unruffled **4.** agreeable, bland, mellow, mild, pleasant, soothing **5.** facile, glib, ingratiating, persuasive, plausible, silky, slick, smarmy (*Brit. inf.*), suave, unctuous, urbane **6.** easy, effortless, flowing, fluent, frictionless, regular, rhythmic, steady, unbroken, uneventful, uniform, uninterrupted, untroubled, well-ordered ~*v.* **7.** flatten, iron, level, plane, polish, press **8.** allay, alleviate, appease, assuage, calm, ease, extenuate, facilitate, iron out the difficulties of, mitigate, mollify, palliate, pave the way, quieten, soften

smother 1. choke, extinguish, snuff, stifle, strangle, suffocate **2.** conceal, hide, keep back, muffle, repress, stifle, suppress **3.** be swimming in, cocoon, cover, envelop, heap, inundate, overwhelm, shower, shroud, surround

smoulder *Fig.* be resentful, boil, burn, fester, fume, rage, seethe, simmer, smart under

smug complacent, conceited, holier-than-thou, priggish, self-opinionated, self-righteous, self-satisfied, superior

snack bite, bite to eat, break, elevenses (*Brit. inf.*), light meal, nibble, refreshment(s), titbit

snag 1. *n.* catch, complication, difficulty, disadvantage, drawback, hitch, inconvenience, obstacle, problem, stumbling block, the rub **2.** *v.* catch, hole, rip, tear

snap *v.* **1.** break, come apart, crack, give way, separate **2.** bite, bite at, catch, grip, nip, seize, snatch **3.** bark, flare out, flash, fly off the handle at (*Inf.*), growl, jump down (someone's) throat (*Inf.*), lash out at, retort, snarl, speak sharply **4.** click, crackle, pop ~*n.* **5.** bite, grab, nip ~*adj.* **6.** abrupt, immediate, instant, on-the-spot, sudden, unplanned, unpremeditated

snappy 1. apt to fly off the handle (*Inf.*), cross, edgy, hasty, irritable, like a bear with a sore head (*Inf.*), quick-tempered, snappish, tart, testy, touchy, waspish **2.** chic, dapper, fashionable, modish, natty (*Inf.*), smart, stylish, trendy (*Brit. inf.*), up-to-the-minute, well dressed

snare 1. *v.* catch, entrap, net, seize, springe, trap, trepan (*Archaic*), wire **2.** *n.* catch, gin, net, noose, pitfall, springe, trap, wire

snarl *v.* complain, growl, grumble, mumble, murmur, show its teeth (*of an animal*)

snarl-up confusion, entanglement, muddle, obstruction, tangle, (traffic) jam

snatch 1. *v.* clutch, gain, grab, grasp, grip, make off with, pluck, pull, rescue, seize, take, win, wrench, wrest **2.** *n.* bit, fragment, part, piece, smattering, snippet, spell

sneak 1. *v.* cower, lurk, pad, sidle, skulk, slink, slip, smuggle, spirit, steal **2.** *n.* informer, snake in the grass, telltale

sneaking 1. hidden, private, secret, suppressed, unavowed, unconfessed, undivulged, unexpressed, un-

sneeze (sni:z) *vi.* **1.** emit breath through nose with sudden involuntary spasm and noise —*n.* **2.** sound or act of sneezing

snick (snɪk) *n.* **1.** small cut or notch, nick —*vt.* **2.** cut; clip; nick

snicker (ˈsnɪkə) *see* SNIGGER

snide (snaɪd) *a.* malicious, supercilious

sniff (snɪf) *vi.* **1.** inhale through nose with sharp hiss **2.** (*with* at) express disapproval *etc.* by sniffing —*vt.* **3.** take up through nose **4.** smell —*n.* **5.** act or sound of sniffing —**ˈsniffle** *vi.* sniff noisily through nose, *esp.* when suffering from a cold in the head, snuffle

snifter (ˈsnɪftə) *n.* **1.** pear-shaped glass with bowl that narrows towards the top so that aroma of brandy *etc.* is retained **2.** *inf.* small alcoholic drink

snigger (ˈsnɪgə) *n.* **1.** sly, disrespectful laugh, *esp.* partly stifled —*vi.* **2.** utter such laugh

snip (snɪp) *v.* **1.** cut (bits off) (**-pp-**) —*n.* **2.** act, sound of snipping **3.** bit cut off **4.** *inf.* bargain **5.** *inf.* certainty —**ˈsnippet** *n.* shred, fragment, clipping —**snips** *pl.n.* tool for cutting

snipe (snaɪp) *n.* **1.** wading bird —*v.* **2.** shoot at (enemy) from cover **3.** (*with* at) criticize, attack (person) slyly —**ˈsniper** *n.*

snitch (snɪtʃ) *inf. vt.* **1.** steal —*vi.* **2.** inform on someone —*n.* **3.** telltale

snivel (ˈsnɪvᵊl) *vi.* **1.** sniffle to show distress **2.** whine (**-ll-**)

snob (snɒb) *n.* one who pretentiously judges others by social rank *etc.* —**ˈsnobbery** *n.* —**ˈsnobbish** *a.* of, like snob —**ˈsnobbishly** *adv.*

snoek (snʊk) *n.* **SA** barracouta

snood (snu:d) *n.* **1.** pouchlike hat, worn at back of head to hold woman's hair **2.** *Scot.* headband, *esp.* formerly worn by young unmarried women

snook (snu:k) *n.* **UK** rude gesture, made by putting one thumb to nose with fingers outstretched (*esp. in* **cock a snook at**)

snooker (ˈsnu:kə) *n.* **1.** game played on billiard table —*vt.* **2.** leave (opponent) in unfavourable position **3.** place (someone) in difficult situation

snoop (snu:p) *vi.* **1.** pry, meddle **2.** peer —*n.* **3.** one who acts thus **4.** act or instance of snooping

snooty (ˈsnu:tɪ) *a. sl.* haughty

snooze (snu:z) *vi.* **1.** take short sleep, be half asleep —*n.* **2.** nap

snore (snɔ:) *vi.* **1.** breathe noisily when asleep —*n.* **2.** noise of snoring

snorkel (ˈsnɔ:kᵊl) *n.* **1.** tube for breathing underwater —*vi.* **2.** swim, fish using this (**-ll-**)

snort (snɔ:t) *vi.* **1.** make (contemptuous) noise by driving breath through nostrils —*n.* **2.** such noise

snot (snɒt) *n. vulg.* mucus from nose

snout (snaʊt) *n.* animal's nose

snow (snəʊ) *n.* **1.** frozen vapour which falls in flakes **2.** *sl.* cocaine —*v.* **3.** fall, sprinkle as snow —*vt.* **4.** let fall, throw down like snow **5.** cover with snow —**ˈsnowy** *a.* **1.** of, like snow **2.** covered with snow **3.** very white —**ˈsnowball** *n.* **1.** snow pressed into hard ball for throwing —*vi.* **2.** increase rapidly in importance *etc.* **3.** play, fight with snowballs —**ˈsnowberry** *n.* shrub with small pink flowers and white berries —**snow blindness** temporary blindness due to brightness of snow —**ˈsnowdrift** *n.* bank of deep snow —**ˈsnowdrop** *n.* small, white, bell-shaped spring flower —**ˈsnowfall** *n.* **1.** fall of snow **2.** *Met.* amount of snow received in specified place and time —**snow fence C** fence erected in winter beside exposed road —**ˈsnowflake** *n.* **1.** one of mass of ice crystals that fall as snow **2.** any of various European plants that have white bell-shaped flowers —**snow goose** white N Amer. goose —**snow-in-summer** *n.* rock plant with white flowers —**snow line** elevation above which snow does not melt —**ˈsnowman** *n.* figure shaped out of snow —**ˈsnowmobile** *n.* **C** motor vehicle with caterpillar tracks and front skis —**ˈsnowplough** *n.* implement or vehicle for clearing away snow —**ˈsnowshoes** *pl.n.* shoes like rackets for travelling on snow —**snow under 1.** cover and block with snow **2.** *fig.* overwhelm

SNP Scottish National Party

snub (snʌb) *vt.* **1.** insult (*esp.* by ignoring) intentionally (**-bb-**) —*n.* **2.** snubbing, rebuff —*a.* **3.** short and blunt

snuff[1] (snʌf) *n.* powdered tobacco for inhaling through nose —**snuff-dipping** *n.* absorbing nicotine by holding in mouth, between cheek and gum, a small amount of tobacco

snuff[2] (snʌf) *vt.* extinguish (*esp.* light from candle) —**ˈsnuffer** *n.* **1.** cone-shaped implement for extinguishing candles —*pl.* **2.** instrument resembling scissors for trimming wick of candle —**snuff it** *sl.* die

THESAURUS

voiced **2.** intuitive, nagging, niggling, persistent, uncomfortable, worrying

sneer 1. *v.* curl one's lip, deride, disdain, gibe, hold in contempt, hold up to ridicule, jeer, laugh, look down on, mock, ridicule, scoff, scorn, sniff at, snigger, turn up one's nose (*Inf.*) **2.** *n.* derision, disdain, gibe, jeer, mockery, ridicule, scorn, snidery, snigger

sniff *v.* breathe, inhale, smell, snuff, snuffle

snigger giggle, laugh, smirk, sneer, snicker, titter

snip *v.* **1.** clip, crop, cut, nick, nip off, notch, shave, trim ~*n.* **2.** bit, clipping, fragment, piece, scrap, shred, snippet **3.** *Inf.* bargain, giveaway, good buy

snivel blubber, cry, girn (*Dialect*), gripe (*Inf.*), grizzle (*Inf.*), mewl, moan, sniffle, snuffle, weep, whimper, whine, whinge (*Inf.*)

snobbery airs, arrogance, condescension, pretension, pride, side (*Brit. sl.*), snobbishness, snootiness (*Inf.*), uppishness (*Brit. inf.*)

snobbish arrogant, condescending, high and mighty (*Inf.*), high-hat (*Inf., chiefly U.S.*), hoity-toity (*Inf.*), patronizing, pretentious, snooty (*Inf.*), stuck-up (*Inf.*), superior, toffee-nosed (*Sl.*), uppish (*Brit. inf.*)

snoop interfere, poke one's nose in (*Inf.*), pry, spy

snooze 1. *v.* catnap, doze, drop off (*Inf.*), drowse, kip (*Brit. sl.*), nap, nod off (*Inf.*), take forty winks (*Inf.*) **2.** *n.* catnap, doze, forty winks (*Inf.*), kip (*Brit. sl.*), nap, siesta

snub 1. *v.* cold-shoulder, cut (*Inf.*), cut dead (*Inf.*), give (someone) the brush-off (*Sl.*), give (someone) the cold shoulder, humble, humiliate, mortify, rebuff, shame, slight **2.** *n.* affront, brushoff (*Sl.*), humiliation, insult, put-down, rebuff, slap in the face, snubbing

snug comfortable, comfy (*Inf.*), cosy, homely, intimate, sheltered, warm

snuggle cuddle, nestle, nuzzle

snuffle (ˈsnʌfˈl) *vi.* breathe noisily or with difficulty

snug (snʌg) *a.* warm, comfortable —**ˈsnuggle** *v.* lie close to, for warmth or affection —**ˈsnugly** *adv.*

snye (snaɪ) *n.* C side channel of river

so[1] (səʊ) *adv.* **1.** to such an extent **2.** in such a manner **3.** very **4.** the case being such **5.** accordingly —*conj.* **6.** therefore **7.** in order that **8.** with the result that —*interj.* **9.** well —**so-and-so** *n. inf.* **1.** person whose name is forgotten or ignored **2.** *euphemistic* person or thing regarded as unpleasant —**so-called** *a.* called by but doubtfully deserving the name —**so long** *interj.* **1.** *inf.* farewell; goodbye —*adv.* **2.** SA *sl.* in the meantime, for the time being

so[2] (səʊ) *n. Mus. see* SOH

So. south(ern)

soak (səʊk) *v.* **1.** steep —*vt.* **2.** (*with* up) absorb **3.** drench —*vi.* **4.** lie in liquid —*n.* **5.** soaking **6.** *sl.* habitual drunkard

soap (səʊp) *n.* **1.** compound of alkali and oil used in washing —*vt.* **2.** apply soap to —**ˈsoapy** *a.* —**ˈsoapbox** *n.* crate used as platform for speech-making —**soap opera** radio or television serial of domestic life —**ˈsoapstone** *n.* massive compact variety of talc, used for making hearths *etc.* (*also* **ˈsteatite**)

soar (sɔː) *vi.* **1.** fly high **2.** increase, rise (in price *etc.*)

sob (sɒb) *vi.* **1.** catch breath, *esp.* in weeping (**-bb-**) —*n.* **2.** sobbing —**sob story** tale of personal distress told to arouse sympathy

sober (ˈsəʊbə) *a.* **1.** not drunk **2.** temperate **3.** subdued **4.** dull, plain **5.** solemn —*v.* **6.** make, become sober —**ˈsoberly** *adv.* —**soˈbriety** *n.* state of being sober

sobriquet *or* **soubriquet** (ˈsəʊbrɪkeɪ) *n.* **1.** nickname **2.** assumed name

Soc. *or* **soc.** Society

soccer (ˈsɒkə) *n.* game of football played with spherical ball

sociable (ˈsəʊʃəbˈl) *a.* **1.** friendly **2.** convivial —**sociaˈbility** *n.* —**ˈsociably** *adv.*

social (ˈsəʊʃəl) *a.* **1.** living in communities **2.** relating to society **3.** sociable —*n.* **4.** informal gathering —**ˈsocialite** *n.* member of fashionable society —**socialiˈzation** *or* **-liˈsation** *n.* —**ˈsocialize** *or* **-lise** *v.* —**ˈsocially** *adv.* —**social contract** *or* **compact** agreement entered into by individuals, that results in formation of state and entails surrender of some personal liberties —**social science** study of society and of relationship of individual members within society, including economics, history, psychology *etc.* —**social security** state provision for the unemployed, aged *etc.* —**social services** welfare activities organized by state —**social studies** (*with sing. v.*) study of how people live and organize themselves in society, embracing geography, economics *etc.* —**social work** work to improve welfare of others

socialism (ˈsəʊʃəlɪzəm) *n.* political system which advocates public ownership of means of production, distribution and exchange —**ˈsocialist** *n./a.* —**sociaˈlistic** *a.*

society (səˈsaɪətɪ) *n.* **1.** living associated with others **2.** those so living **3.** companionship **4.** company **5.** association **6.** club **7.** fashionable people collectively

socio- (*comb. form*) denoting social or society, as in *socioeconomic*

socioeconomic (səʊsɪəʊiːkəˈnɒmɪk) *a.* of or involving both economic and social factors

sociology (səʊsɪˈɒlədʒɪ) *n.* study of societies

sociopolitical (səʊsɪəʊpəˈlɪtɪkˈl) *a.* of or involving both political and social factors

sock[1] (sɒk) *n.* cloth covering for foot

sock[2] (sɒk) *sl. vt.* **1.** hit —*n.* **2.** blow

socket (ˈsɒkɪt) *n.* hole or recess for something to fit into

Socratic (sɒˈkrætɪk) *a.* of, like Gr. philosopher Socrates

sod (sɒd) *n.* **1.** lump of earth with grass **2.** *sl.* person considered obnoxious **3.** *sl.* person, as specified

THESAURUS

soak *v.* **1.** bathe, damp, drench, immerse, infuse, marinate (*Cookery*), moisten, penetrate, permeate, saturate, steep, wet **2.** *With* **up** absorb, assimilate, drink in, take up *or* in

soar 1. ascend, fly, mount, rise, tower, wing **2.** climb, escalate, increase, rise, rocket, shoot up

sob *v.* bawl, blubber, boohoo, cry, greet (*Dialect*), howl, shed tears, snivel, weep

sober *adj.* **1.** abstemious, abstinent, moderate, on the wagon (*Inf.*), temperate **2.** calm, clear-headed, cold, composed, cool, dispassionate, grave, level-headed, lucid, peaceful, practical, rational, realistic, reasonable, sedate, serene, serious, solemn, sound, staid, steady, unexcited, unruffled **3.** dark, drab, plain, quiet, severe, sombre, subdued ~*v.* **4.** *Usually with* **up** bring (someone) back to earth, calm down, clear one's head, come *or* bring to one's senses, give (someone) pause for thought, make (someone) stop and think

sobriety 1. abstemiousness, abstinence, moderation, nonindulgence, self-restraint, soberness, temperance **2.** calmness, composure, coolness, gravity, level-headedness, reasonableness, restraint, sedateness, seriousness, solemnity, staidness, steadiness

so-called alleged, ostensible, pretended, professed, self-styled, *soi-disant*, supposed

sociability affability, companionability, congeniality, conviviality, cordiality, friendliness, gregariousness, neighbourliness

sociable accessible, affable, approachable, companionable, conversable, convivial, cordial, familiar, friendly, genial, gregarious, neighbourly, outgoing, social, warm

social *adj.* **1.** collective, common, communal, community, general, group, organized, public, societal **2.** companionable, friendly, gregarious, neighbourly, sociable ~*n.* **3.** do (*Inf.*), gathering, get-together (*Inf.*)

socialize be a good mixer, entertain, fraternize, get about *or* around, get together, go out, mix

society 1. civilization, culture, humanity, mankind, people, population, social order, the community, the general public, the public, the world at large **2.** camaraderie, companionship, company, fellowship, friendship **3.** association, brotherhood, circle, club, corporation, fellowship, fraternity, group, guild, institute, league, organization, sisterhood, union **4.** beau monde, elite, gentry, *haut monde*, high society, polite society, the country set, the nobs (*Sl.*), the smart set, the swells (*Inf.*), the toffs (*Brit. sl.*), the top drawer, upper classes, upper crust (*Inf.*)

soda (ˈsəudə) *n.* **1.** compound of sodium **2.** soda water —**soda fountain** US **1.** counter that serves drinks, snacks *etc.* **2.** apparatus dispensing soda water —**soda water** water charged with carbon dioxide

sodden (ˈsɒdᵊn) *a.* **1.** soaked **2.** drunk **3.** heavy and doughy

sodium (ˈsəudɪəm) *n.* metallic alkaline element —**sodium bicarbonate** white crystalline soluble compound used in baking powder *etc.* (*also* **bicarbonate of soda**) —**sodium carbonate** soluble crystalline compound used in manufacture of glass, ceramics, soap and paper, and as cleansing agent —**sodium chloride** common table salt

Sodom (ˈsɒdəm) *n.* **1.** *O.T.* city that, with Gomorrah, traditionally typifies depravity **2.** this city as representing homosexuality **3.** any place notorious for depravity

sodomy (ˈsɒdəmɪ) *n.* anal intercourse —ˈ**sodomite** *n.*

sofa (ˈsəufə) *n.* upholstered seat with back and arms, for two or more people

soft (sɒft) *a.* **1.** yielding easily to pressure **2.** mild **3.** easy **4.** subdued **5.** quiet, gentle **6.** (too) lenient **7.** oversentimental **8.** feeble-minded **9.** (of water) containing few mineral salts **10.** (of drugs) not liable to cause addiction —**soften** (ˈsɒfᵊn) *v.* **1.** make, become soft or softer —*vt.* **2.** mollify **3.** lighten **4.** mitigate **5.** make less loud —ˈ**softly** *adv.* gently, quietly —ˈ**softy** *or* ˈ**softie** *n. inf.* person who is sentimental, weakly foolish or lacking in physical endurance —**soft-boiled** *a.* (of egg) boiled for a short time so that yolk remains soft —**soft drink** drink that is nonalcoholic —**soft furnishings** curtains, rugs *etc.* —**softˈhearted** *a.* easily moved to pity —**soft palate** posterior fleshy portion of roof of mouth —**soft-pedal** *vt.* **1.** mute tone of (piano) **2.** *inf.* make (something) less obvious by deliberately failing to emphasize it —**soft pedal** foot-operated lever on piano that causes fewer of strings to sound —**soft sell** *chiefly* US method of selling based on indirect suggestion or inducement —**soft shoe** (of tap dancing) done without metal taps on shoes —**soft soap** flattery —**soft spot** sentimental fondness —ˈ**software** *n.* computer programs, tapes *etc.* for a particular computer system —ˈ**softwood** *n.* wood of coniferous tree

SOGAT (ˈsəugæt) UK Society of Graphical and Allied Trades

soggy (ˈsɒgɪ) *a.* **1.** soaked with liquid **2.** damp and heavy

soh *or* **so** (səu) *n. Mus.* in tonic sol-fa, name used for fifth note or dominant of any scale

soigné *or* (*fem.*) **soignée** (ˈswɑːnjeɪ) *a.* well-groomed

soil[1] (sɔɪl) *n.* **1.** earth, ground **2.** country, territory

soil[2] (sɔɪl) *v.* **1.** make, become dirty —*vt.* **2.** tarnish, defile —*n.* **3.** dirt **4.** sewage **5.** stain

soiree (ˈswɑːreɪ) *n.* private evening party, *esp.* with music

sojourn (ˈsɒdʒɜːn, ˈsʌdʒ-) *vi.* **1.** stay for a time —*n.* **2.** short stay —ˈ**sojourner** *n.*

sol (sɒl) *n. Mus. see* SOH

solace (ˈsɒlɪs) *n./vt.* comfort in distress

solar (ˈsəulə) *a.* of the sun —**solariˈzation** *or* **-iˈsation** *n.* —ˈ**solarize** *or* **-ise** *vt.* affect by sunlight —**solar cell** cell that produces electricity from sun's rays —**solar plexus** (ˈplɛksəs) network of nerves at pit of stomach —**solar system** system containing sun and heavenly bodies held in its gravitational field

solarium (səuˈlɛərɪəm) *n.* **1.** room built mainly of glass to give exposure to sun **2.** (place with) bed for acquiring suntan by artificial means

sold (səuld) *pt./pp. of* SELL

solder (ˈsɒldə; *U.S.* ˈsɒdər) *n.* **1.** easily-melted alloy used for joining metal —*vt.* **2.** join with solder —**soldering iron**

soldier (ˈsəuldʒə) *n.* **1.** one serving in army —*vi.* **2.** serve in army **3.** (*with* on) persist doggedly —ˈ**soldierly** *a.* —ˈ**soldiery** *n.* troops —**soldier of fortune** man who seeks money or adventure as soldier

sole[1] (səul) *a.* **1.** one and only, unique **2.** solitary —ˈ**solely** *adv.* **1.** alone **2.** only **3.** entirely

sole[2] (səul) *n.* **1.** underside of foot **2.** underpart of boot *etc.* —*vt.* **3.** fit with sole

sole[3] (səul) *n.* small edible flatfish

solecism (ˈsɒlɪsɪzəm) *n.* breach of grammar or etiquette

THESAURUS

sodden boggy, drenched, drookit (*Scot.*), marshy, miry, saturated, soaked, soggy, sopping, waterlogged

soft 1. creamy, cushioned, cushiony, doughy, elastic, gelatinous, pulpy, quaggy, spongy, squashy, swampy, yielding **2.** bendable, ductile (*of metals*), elastic, flexible, impressible, malleable, mouldable, plastic, pliable, supple **3.** downy, feathery, fleecy, flowing, fluid, furry, like a baby's bottom (*Inf.*), rounded, silky, smooth, velvety **4.** balmy, bland, caressing, delicate, diffuse, dim, dimmed, dulcet, faint, gentle, light, low, mellifluous, mellow, melodious, mild, murmured, muted, pale, pastel, pleasing, quiet, restful, shaded, soft-toned, soothing, subdued, sweet, temperate, twilight, understated, whispered **5.** compassionate, gentle, kind, pitying, quiet, sensitive, sentimental, sympathetic, tender, tenderhearted **6.** easy-going, indulgent, lax, lenient, liberal, overindulgent, permissive, spineless, weak **7.** *Inf.* comfortable, cushy (*Sl.*), easy, undemanding **8.** *Inf.* a bit lacking (*Inf.*), daft (*Inf.*), feeble-minded, foolish, silly, simple, soft in the head (*Inf.*), soppy (*Brit. inf.*)

soften abate, allay, alleviate, appease, assuage, calm, cushion, diminish, ease, lessen, lighten, lower, melt, mitigate, moderate, modify, mollify, muffle, palliate, quell, relax, soothe, still, subdue, temper, tone down, turn down

softhearted charitable, compassionate, generous, indulgent, kind, sentimental, sympathetic, tender, tenderhearted, warm-hearted

soil[1] *n.* **1.** clay, dirt, dust, earth, ground, loam **2.** country, land, region, terra firma, territory

soil[2] *v.* bedraggle, befoul, begrime, besmirch, defile, dirty, foul, maculate (*Literary*), muddy, pollute, smear, spatter, spot, stain, sully, tarnish

solace 1. *n.* alleviation, assuagement, comfort, consolation, relief **2.** *v.* allay, alleviate, comfort, console, mitigate, soften, soothe

soldier enlisted man (*U.S.*), fighter, GI (*U.S. inf.*), man-at-arms, military man, redcoat, serviceman, squaddy (*Brit. inf.*), Tommy (*Brit.*), trooper, warrior

sole alone, exclusive, individual, one, one and only, only, single, singular, solitary

solecism blunder, boo-boo (*Inf.*), breach of etiquette,

solemn ('sɒləm) *a.* **1.** serious **2.** formal **3.** impressive —**solemnity** (sə'lɛmnɪtɪ) *n.* —**solemnization** *or* **-isation** (sɒləmnaɪ'zeɪʃən) *n.* —**solemnize** *or* **-ise** ('sɒləmnaɪz) *vt.* **1.** celebrate, perform **2.** make solemn —'**solemnly** *adv.*

solenoid ('səʊlɪnɔɪd) *n.* coil of wire as part of electrical apparatus

sol-fa ('sɒl'fɑː) *n. Mus.* system of syllables sol, fa *etc.* sung in scale

solicit (sə'lɪsɪt) *vt.* **1.** request **2.** accost **3.** urge **4.** entice —**solici'tation** *n.* —**so'licitor** *n.* lawyer who prepares documents, advises clients, but represents them in lower courts only —**so'licitous** *a.* **1.** anxious **2.** eager **3.** earnest —**so'licitude** *n.* —**Solicitor General UK** law officer of Crown ranking next to Attorney General

solid ('sɒlɪd) *a.* **1.** not hollow **2.** compact **3.** composed of one substance **4.** firm **5.** massive **6.** reliable, sound —*n.* **7.** body of three dimensions **8.** substance not liquid or gas —**soli'darity** *n.* **1.** unity of interests **2.** united state —**solidifi'cation** *n.* —**so'lidify** *v.* **1.** make, become solid or firm **2.** harden (**-ified, -ifying**) —**so'lidity** *n.* —'**solidly** *adv.* —**solid geometry** branch of geometry concerned with solid geometric figures —**solid-state** *a.* (of electronic device) consisting chiefly of semiconductor materials and controlled by means of their electrical properties

solidus ('sɒlɪdəs) *n.* short stroke (/) used in text to separate items (*pl.* **-di** (-daɪ))

soliloquy (sə'lɪləkwɪ) *n. esp.* in drama, thoughts spoken by person while alone —**so'liloquize** *or* **-ise** *v.*

solipsism ('sɒlɪpsɪzəm) *n.* doctrine that self is the only thing known to exist —'**solipsist** *n.*

solitary ('sɒlɪtərɪ, -trɪ) *a.* **1.** alone, single —*n.* **2.** hermit —**soli'taire** *n.* **1.** game for one person played with pegs set in board **2.** single precious stone, *esp.* diamond, set by itself —'**solitude** *n.* **1.** state of being alone **2.** loneliness —**solitary confinement** isolation imposed on prisoner

solo ('səʊləʊ) *n.* **1.** music for one performer (*pl.* **-s, -li** (-liː)) **2.** card game like whist (*pl.* **-s**) —*a.* **3.** not concerted **4.** unaccompanied, alone **5.** piloting aeroplane alone —'**soloist** *n.*

solstice ('sɒlstɪs) *n.* either shortest (winter) or longest (summer) day of year —**solstitial** (sɒl'stɪʃəl) *a.*

solve (sɒlv) *vt.* **1.** work out, explain **2.** find answer to —**solubility** (sɒljʊ'bɪlɪtɪ) *n.* —**soluble** ('sɒljʊbᵊl) *a.* **1.** capable of being dissolved in liquid **2.** able to be solved or explained —**so'lute** *n.* **1.** substance dissolved in solution —*a.* **2.** *Bot.* unattached —**solution** (sə'luːʃən) *n.* **1.** answer to problem **2.** dissolving **3.** liquid with something dissolved in it —'**solvable** *a.* —'**solvency** *n.* —'**solvent** *a.* **1.** able to meet financial obligations —*n.* **2.** liquid with power of dissolving

Som. Somerset

somatic (səʊ'mætɪk) *a.* **1.** of the body, as distinct from the mind **2.** of animal body or body wall as distinct from viscera, limbs and head

sombre *or U.S.* **somber** ('sɒmbə) *a.* dark, gloomy

sombrero (sɒm'brɛərəʊ) *n.* wide-brimmed hat (*pl.* **-s**)

some (sʌm; *unstressed* səm) *a.* **1.** denoting an indefinite number, amount or extent **2.** one or other **3.** amount of **4.** certain **5.** approximately —*pron.* **6.** portion, quantity —'**somebody** *pron.* **1.** some person —*n.* **2.** important person —'**somehow** *adv.* by some means unknown —'**someone** *pron.* some person —'**something** *pron.* **1.** thing not clearly defined **2.** indefinite amount, quantity or degree —'**sometime** *adv.* **1.** formerly **2.** at some (past or future) time —*a.* **3.** former —'**sometimes** *adv.* **1.** occasionally **2.** now and then —'**somewhat** *adv.* to some extent, rather —'**somewhere** *adv.*

THESAURUS

cacology, faux pas, gaffe, gaucherie, impropriety, incongruity, indecorum, lapse, mistake

solely alone, completely, entirely, exclusively, merely, only, single-handedly, singly

solemn 1. earnest, glum, grave, portentous, sedate, serious, sober, staid, thoughtful **2.** august, awe-inspiring, ceremonial, ceremonious, dignified, formal, grand, grave, imposing, impressive, majestic, momentous, stately

solemnity earnestness, grandeur, gravity, impressiveness, momentousness, portentousness, sacredness, sanctity, seriousness

solemnize celebrate, commemorate, honour, keep, observe

solicit ask, beg, beseech, canvass, crave, entreat, implore, importune, petition, plead for, pray, seek, supplicate

solicitous anxious, apprehensive, attentive, careful, caring, concerned, eager, earnest, troubled, uneasy, worried, zealous

solicitude anxiety, attentiveness, care, concern, considerateness, consideration, regard, worry

solid *adj.* **1.** compact, concrete, dense, firm, hard, massed, stable, strong, sturdy, substantial, unshakable **2.** genuine, good, pure, real, reliable, sound **3.** agreed, complete, continuous, unalloyed, unanimous, unbroken, undivided, uninterrupted, united, unmixed **4.** constant, decent, dependable, estimable, law-abiding, level-headed, reliable, sensible, serious, sober, trusty, upright, upstanding, worthy

solidarity accord, camaraderie, cohesion, community of interest, concordance, esprit de corps, harmony, like-mindedness, singleness of purpose, soundness, stability, team spirit, unanimity, unification, unity

solidify cake, coagulate, cohere, congeal, harden, jell, set

solitary 1. *adj.* alone, lone, single, sole **2.** *n.* hermit, introvert, loner (*Inf.*), lone wolf, recluse

solitude isolation, loneliness, privacy, reclusiveness, retirement, seclusion

solution 1. answer, clarification, elucidation, explanation, explication, key, resolution, result, solving, unfolding, unravelling **2.** blend, compound, emulsion, mix, mixture, solvent, suspension (*Chem.*) **3.** disconnection, dissolution, dissolving, liquefaction, melting

solve answer, clarify, clear up, crack, decipher, disentangle, elucidate, explain, expound, get to the bottom of, interpret, resolve, unfold, unravel, work out

sombre dark, dim, dismal, doleful, drab, dull, dusky, funereal, gloomy, grave, joyless, lugubrious, melancholy, mournful, obscure, sad, sepulchral, shadowy, shady, sober

somebody *n.* big noise (*Brit. sl.*), big shot (*Sl.*), big wheel (*Sl.*), bigwig (*Sl.*), celebrity, dignitary, heavyweight (*Inf.*), household name, luminary, name, no-

somersault *or* **summersault** (ˈsʌməsɔːlt) *n.* tumbling head over heels

somnambulist (sɒmˈnæmbjʊlɪst) *n.* sleepwalker —**somˈnambulism** *n.* —**somnambuˈlistic** *a.*

somnolent (ˈsɒmnələnt) *a.* **1.** drowsy **2.** causing sleep —**ˈsomnolence** *or* **ˈsomnolency** *n.*

son (sʌn) *n.* male child —**ˈsonny** *n.* familiar term of address to boy or man —**son-in-law** *n.* daughter's husband

sonar (ˈsəʊnɑː) *n.* device like echo sounder

sonata (səˈnɑːtə) *n.* piece of music in several movements —**sonatina** (sɒnəˈtiːnə) *n.* short sonata

son et lumière (ˈsɒn eɪ ˈluːmɪɛə) *Fr.* entertainment staged at night at famous place, building, giving dramatic history of it with lighting and sound effects

song (sɒŋ) *n.* **1.** singing **2.** poem *etc.* for singing —**ˈsongster** *n.* **1.** singer **2.** songbird (**ˈsongstress** *fem.*)

sonic (ˈsɒnɪk) *a.* pert. to sound waves —**sonic barrier** *see* **sound barrier** *at* SOUND[1] —**sonic boom** explosive sound caused by aircraft travelling at supersonic speed

sonnet (ˈsɒnɪt) *n.* fourteen-line poem with definite rhyme scheme —**sonneˈteer** *n.* writer of this

sonorous (səˈnɔːrəs, ˈsɒnərəs) *a.* giving out (deep) sound, resonant —**sonority** (səˈnɒrɪtɪ) *n.* —**soˈnorously** *adv.*

soon (suːn) *adv.* **1.** in a short time **2.** before long **3.** early, quickly

soot (sʊt) *n.* black powdery substance formed by burning of coal *etc.* —**ˈsooty** *a.* of, like soot

sooth (suːθ) *n.* truth —**ˈsoothsayer** *n.* one who foretells future, diviner

soothe (suːð) *vt.* **1.** make calm, tranquil **2.** relieve (pain *etc.*)

sop (sɒp) *n.* **1.** piece of bread *etc.* soaked in liquid **2.** concession, bribe —*vt.* **3.** steep in water *etc.* **4.** soak (up) (**-pp-**) —**ˈsopping** *a.* completely soaked —**ˈsoppy** *a. inf.* oversentimental

sophist (ˈsɒfɪst) *n.* fallacious reasoner, quibbler —**ˈsophism** *n.* specious argument —**soˈphistical** *a.* —**ˈsophistry** *n.*

sophisticate (səˈfɪstɪkeɪt) *vt.* **1.** make artificial, spoil, falsify, corrupt —*n.* (səˈfɪstɪkeɪt, -kɪt) **2.** sophisticated person —**soˈphisticated** *a.* **1.** having refined or cultured tastes, habits **2.** worldly-wise **3.** superficially clever **4.** complex —**sophistiˈcation** *n.*

sophomore (ˈsɒfəmɔː) *n.* US student in second year at college

-sophy (*n. comb. form*) indicating knowledge or intellectual system, as in *philosophy* —**-sophic** *or* **-sophical** (*a. comb. form*)

soporific (sɒpəˈrɪfɪk) *a.* **1.** causing sleep (*esp.* by drugs) —*n.* **2.** drug or other agent that induces sleep

soprano (səˈprɑːnəʊ) *n.* **1.** highest voice in women and boys **2.** singer with this voice **3.** musical part for it (*pl.* **-s**)

sorbet (ˈsɔːbɪt, -beɪ) *n.* (fruit-flavoured) water ice

sorcerer (ˈsɔːsərə) *or* (*fem.*) **sorceress** (ˈsɔːsərɪs) *n.* magician —**ˈsorcery** *n.* witchcraft, magic

sordid (ˈsɔːdɪd) *a.* **1.** mean, squalid **2.** ignoble, base —**ˈsordidly** *adv.* —**ˈsordidness** *n.*

sore (sɔː) *a.* **1.** painful **2.** causing annoyance **3.** severe **4.** distressed **5.** annoyed —*adv.* **6.** *obs.* grievously, intensely —*n.* **7.** sore place, ulcer, boil *etc.* —**ˈsorely** *adv.* **1.** grievously **2.** greatly

sorghum (ˈsɔːgəm) *n.* kind of grass cultivated for grain

THESAURUS

table, personage, person of note, public figure, star, superstar, V.I.P.

somehow by fair means or foul, by hook or (by) crook, by some means or other, come hell or high water (*Inf.*), come what may, one way or another

sometimes at times, every now and then, every so often, from time to time, now and again, now and then, occasionally, off and on, once in a while, on occasion

somnolent comatose, dozy, drowsy, half-awake, heavy-eyed, nodding off (*Inf.*), sleepy, soporific, torpid

song air, anthem, ballad, canticle, canzonet, carol, chant, chorus, ditty, hymn, lay, lyric, melody, number, pop song, psalm, shanty, strain, tune

soon anon (*Archaic*), any minute now, before long, betimes (*Archaic*), in a little while, in a minute, in a short time, in the near future, shortly

soothe allay, alleviate, appease, assuage, calm, calm down, compose, ease, hush, lull, mitigate, mollify, pacify, quiet, relieve, settle, smooth down, soften, still, tranquillize

soothsayer augur, diviner, foreteller, prophet, seer, sibyl

sophisticated **1.** blasé, citified, cosmopolitan, cultivated, cultured, jet-set, refined, seasoned, urbane, worldly, worldly-wise, world-weary **2.** advanced, complex, complicated, delicate, elaborate, highly-developed, intricate, multifaceted, refined, subtle

sophistication finesse, poise, savoir-faire, *savoir-vivre*, urbanity, worldliness, worldly wisdom

sophistry casuistry, fallacy, quibble, sophism

soporific **1.** *adj.* hypnotic, sedative, sleep-inducing, sleepy, somniferous (*Rare*), somnolent, tranquillizing **2.** *n.* anaesthetic, hypnotic, narcotic, opiate, sedative, tranquillizer

soppy corny (*Inf.*), daft (*Inf.*), drippy (*Inf.*), gushy (*Inf.*), lovey-dovey, mawkish, overemotional, oversentimental, schmaltzy (*Sl.*), sentimental, silly, slushy (*Inf.*), soft (*Inf.*), weepy (*Inf.*)

sorcerer enchanter, mage (*Archaic*), magician, magus, necromancer, sorceress, warlock, witch, wizard

sorcery black art, black magic, charm, divination, enchantment, incantation, magic, necromancy, spell, witchcraft, witchery, wizardry

sordid **1.** dirty, filthy, foul, mean, seamy, seedy, sleazy, slovenly, slummy, squalid, unclean, wretched **2.** backstreet, base, debauched, degenerate, degraded, despicable, disreputable, ignoble, low, shabby, shameful, vicious, vile

sore *adj.* **1.** angry, burning, chafed, inflamed, irritated, painful, raw, reddened, sensitive, smarting, tender **2.** annoying, distressing, grievous, harrowing, severe, sharp, troublesome **3.** acute, critical, desperate, dire, extreme, pressing, severe, urgent **4.** afflicted, aggrieved, angry, annoyed, grieved, hurt, irked, irritated, pained, peeved (*Inf.*), resentful, stung, upset, vexed ~*n.* **5.** abscess, boil, chafe, gathering, inflammation, ulcer

sorority (səˈrɒrɪtɪ) *n. chiefly* **US** social club or society for university women

sorrel (ˈsɒrəl) *n.* **1.** plant **2.** reddish-brown colour **3.** horse of this colour —*a.* **4.** of this colour

sorrow (ˈsɒrəʊ) *n.* **1.** pain of mind, grief, sadness —*vi.* **2.** grieve —**ˈsorrowful** *a.*

sorry (ˈsɒrɪ) *a.* **1.** feeling pity or regret **2.** distressed **3.** miserable, wretched **4.** mean, poor —**ˈsorrily** *adv.* —**ˈsorriness** *n.*

sort (sɔːt) *n.* **1.** kind or class —*vt.* **2.** classify

sortie (ˈsɔːtɪ) *n.* sally by besieged forces

SOS **1.** international code signal of distress **2.** call for help

so-so *a. inf.* mediocre

sostenuto (sɒstəˈnuːtəʊ) *a./adv. Mus.* in smooth sustained manner

sot (sɒt) *n.* habitual drunkard

sotto voce (ˈsɒtəʊ ˈvəʊtʃɪ) *It.* in an undertone

sou (suː) *n.* **1.** former French coin **2.** small amount of money

soubrette (suːˈbrɛt) *n.* **1.** minor female role in comedy **2.** any flirtatious girl

soufflé (ˈsuːfleɪ) *n.* dish of eggs beaten to froth, flavoured and baked

sough (saʊ) *n.* low murmuring sound as of wind in trees

sought (sɔːt) *pt./pp. of* SEEK

souk (suːk) *n.* open-air marketplace, *esp.* in N Afr. and Middle East

soul (səʊl) *n.* **1.** spiritual and immortal part of human being **2.** example, pattern **3.** person —**ˈsoulful** *a.* full of emotion or sentiment —**ˈsoulless** *a.* **1.** mechanical **2.** lacking sensitivity or nobility **3.** heartless, cruel —**soul-destroying** *a.* (of occupation *etc.*) monotonous —**soul food** *inf.* food, as yams *etc.*, traditionally eaten by U.S. Negroes —**soul mate** person for whom one has deep affinity —**soul music** type of Black music resulting from addition of jazz and gospel to urban blues style —**soul-searching** *n.* deep or critical examination of one's motives, actions *etc.*

sound[1] (saʊnd) *n.* **1.** what is heard **2.** noise —*vi.* **3.** make sound **4.** seem **5.** resonate with a certain quality —*vt.* **6.** cause to sound **7.** utter —**sound barrier** large increase in resistance encountered by aircraft approaching speed of sound —**sound effect** sound artificially produced to create theatrical effect, as in plays, films *etc.* —**sounding board 1.** thin wooden board in violin *etc.* designed to reflect sound **2.** person *etc.* used to test new idea *etc.* —**sound track** recorded sound accompaniment of film *etc.* —**sound wave** wave that propagates sound

sound[2] (saʊnd) *a.* **1.** in good condition **2.** solid **3.** of good judgment **4.** legal **5.** solvent **6.** thorough **7.** effective **8.** watertight **9.** deep —**ˈsoundly** *adv.* thoroughly

sound[3] (saʊnd) *vt.* **1.** measure depth of (well, sea *etc.*) **2.** probe —**ˈsoundings** *pl.n.* measurements taken by sounding —**sound out** ascertain views of

sound[4] (saʊnd) *n.* channel, strait

soup (suːp) *n.* liquid food made by boiling meat, vegetables *etc.* —**ˈsoupy** *a.* **1.** like soup **2.** murky **3.** sentimental —**soup kitchen 1.** place where food, *esp.* soup, is served to destitute people **2.** *Mil.* mobile kitchen

soupçon (supˈsɔ̃) *Fr.* small amount

sour (saʊə) *a.* **1.** acid **2.** gone bad **3.** rancid **4.** peevish **5.** disagreeable —*v.* **6.** make, become sour —**ˈsourly** *adv.* —**ˈsourness** *n.* —**sour grapes** attitude of despising something because one cannot have it oneself —**ˈsourpuss** *n.* sullen, sour-faced person

THESAURUS

sorrow 1. *n.* affliction, anguish, distress, grief, heartache, heartbreak, misery, mourning, regret, sadness, unhappiness, woe **2.** *v.* agonize, bemoan, be sad, bewail, grieve, lament, moan, mourn, weep

sorrowful affecting, afflicted, dejected, depressed, disconsolate, distressing, doleful, grievous, heartbroken, heart-rending, heavy-hearted, lamentable, lugubrious, melancholy, miserable, mournful, painful, piteous, rueful, sad, sick at heart, sorry, tearful, unhappy, woebegone, woeful, wretched

sorry 1. apologetic, conscience-stricken, contrite, guilt-ridden, in sackcloth and ashes, penitent, regretful, remorseful, repentant, self-reproachful, shamefaced **2.** disconsolate, distressed, grieved, melancholy, mournful, sad, sorrowful, unhappy **3.** commiserative, compassionate, full of pity, moved, pitying, sympathetic **4.** abject, base, deplorable, dismal, distressing, mean, miserable, paltry, pathetic, piteous, pitiable, pitiful, poor, sad, shabby, vile, wretched

sort 1. *n.* brand, breed, category, character, class, denomination, description, family, genus, group, ilk, kind, make, nature, order, quality, race, species, stamp, style, type, variety **2.** *v.* arrange, assort, catalogue, categorize, choose, class, classify, distribute, divide, file, grade, group, order, put in order, rank, select, separate, systematize

soul 1. animating principle, essence, intellect, life, mind, psyche, reason, spirit, vital force **2.** being, body, creature, individual, man, mortal, person, woman **3.** embodiment, essence, example, incarnation, pattern, personification, quintessence, type

sound[1] *n.* **1.** din, noise, report, resonance, reverberation, tone, voice ~*v.* **2.** echo, resonate, resound, reverberate **3.** appear, give the impression of, look, seem, strike one as being **4.** announce, articulate, declare, enunciate, express, pronounce, signal, utter

sound[2] *adj.* **1.** complete, entire, firm, fit, hale, hale an hearty, healthy, intact, perfect, robust, solid, sturdy, substantial, undamaged, unhurt, unimpaired, uninjured, vigorous, well-constructed, whole **2.** correct, fair, just, level-headed, logical, orthodox, proper, prudent, rational, reasonable, reliable, responsible, right, right-thinking, sensible, true, trustworthy, valid, well-founded, well-grounded, wise **3.** established, orthodox, proven, recognized, reliable, reputable, safe, secure, solid, solvent, stable, tried-and-true **4.** deep, peaceful, unbroken, undisturbed, untroubled

sound[3] *v.* **1.** fathom, plumb, probe **2.** examine, inspect, investigate, probe, test

sound out canvass, examine, probe, pump, question, see how the land lies

sour *adj.* **1.** acetic, acid, acidulated, bitter, pungent, sharp, tart, unpleasant **2.** bad, curdled, fermented, gone off, rancid, turned, unsavoury, unwholesome **3.** acrid, acrimonious, churlish, crabbed, cynical, disagreeable, discontented, embittered, grouchy (*Inf.*),

source (sɔːs) *n.* **1.** origin, starting point **2.** spring

souse (saʊs) *v.* **1.** plunge, drench or be drenched **2.** pickle —*n.* **3.** sousing **4.** brine for pickling

soutane (suːˈtæn) *n.* priest's cassock

south (saʊθ) *n.* **1.** cardinal point opposite north **2.** region, part of country *etc.* lying to that side —*a./adv.* **3.** (that is) towards south —**southerly** (ˈsʌðəlɪ) *a.* **1.** towards south —*n.* **2.** wind from the south —**southern** (ˈsʌðən) *a.* in south —ˈ**Southerner** *n.* (*sometimes* **s-**) native or inhabitant of south of any specified region —ˈ**southwards** *adv.* —ˈ**Southdown** *n.* breed of sheep —**southˈeast** *n.* **1.** point of compass midway between south and east —*a.* **2.** (*sometimes* **S-**) denoting southeastern part of specified country *etc.* **3.** in, towards or facing southeast —*adv.* **4.** in, to, towards or (*esp.* of wind) from southeast —**Southˈeast** *n.* (*usu. with* the) southeastern part of Britain —**Southern Cross** small constellation in S hemisphere whose four brightest stars form cross —**southern hemisphere** (*oft.* **S- H-**) that half of earth lying south of equator —**southern lights** aurora australis —ˈ**southpaw** *inf. n.* **1.** any left-handed person, *esp.* a boxer —*a.* **2.** of or relating to southpaw —**South Pole** southernmost point on earth's axis —**South Seas** seas south of equator —**south-southeast** *n.* **1.** point on compass midway between southeast and south —*a./adv.* **2.** in, from or towards this direction —**south-southwest** *n.* **1.** point on compass midway between south and southwest —*a./adv.* **2.** in, from or towards this direction —**southˈwest** *n.* **1.** point on compass midway between west and south —*a.* **2.** (*sometimes* **S-**) of or denoting southwestern part of specified country *etc.* **3.** in or towards southwest —*adv.* **4.** in, to, towards or (*esp.* of wind) from southwest —**Southˈwest** *n.* (*usu. with* the) southwestern part of Britain

souvenir (suːvəˈnɪə, ˈsuːvənɪə) *n.* keepsake, memento

sou'wester (saʊˈwɛstə) *n.* waterproof hat

sovereign (ˈsɒvrɪn) *n.* **1.** king, queen **2.** former Brit. gold coin worth 20 shillings —*a.* **3.** supreme **4.** efficacious —ˈ**sovereignty** *n.* **1.** supreme power and right to exercise it **2.** dominion **3.** independent state

soviet (ˈsəʊvɪət, ˈsɒv-) *n.* **1.** elected council at various levels of government in U.S.S.R. **2.** (**S-**) citizen of U.S.S.R. —*a.* **3.** (**S-**) of U.S.S.R., its people or its government —ˈ**sovietism** *n.*

sow[1] (səʊ) *vi.* **1.** scatter, plant seed —*vt.* **2.** scatter, deposit (seed) **3.** spread abroad (**sowed** *pt.*, **sown** *or* **sowed** *pp.*, ˈ**sowing** *pr.p.*)

sow[2] (saʊ) *n.* female adult pig

soya bean (ˈsɔɪə) *or U.S.* **soybean** (ˈsɔɪbiːn) *n.* edible bean used as meat substitute, in making soy sauce *etc.* —**soy sauce** (sɔɪ) salty, dark brown sauce made from fermented soya beans, used *esp.* in Chinese cookery (*also* **soya sauce**)

sozzled (ˈsɒzəld) *a. sl.* drunk

sp. **1.** special **2.** species (*pl.* **spp.**) **3.** specific **4.** specimen **5.** spelling

spa (spɑː) *n.* **1.** medicinal spring **2.** place or resort with such a spring

space (speɪs) *n.* **1.** extent **2.** room **3.** period **4.** empty place **5.** area **6.** expanse **7.** region beyond earth's atmosphere —*vt.* **8.** place at intervals —**spacious** (ˈspeɪʃəs) *a.* roomy, extensive —**space age** period in which exploration of space has become possible —**space-age** *a.* ultramodern —ˈ**spacecraft** *or* ˈ**spaceship** *n.* vehicle for travel beyond earth's atmosphere —ˈ**spaceman** *n.* —**space shuttle** vehicle designed to carry men and materials to space stations *etc.* —**space station** any manned artificial satellite designed to orbit earth and provide base for scientific research in space —ˈ**spacesuit** *n.* sealed, pressurized suit worn by astronaut —**space-time** *n. Phys.* continuum having three spatial coordinates and one time coordinate that together specify location of particle or event (*also* **space-time continuum**)

spade[1] (speɪd) *n.* tool for digging —ˈ**spadework** *n.* arduous preparatory work

spade[2] (speɪd) *n.* leaf-shaped black symbol on playing card

spadix (ˈspeɪdɪks) *n.* spike of small flowers on fleshy stem, whole being enclosed in spathe (*pl.* **spadices** (speɪˈdaɪsiːz))

spaghetti (spəˈgɛtɪ) *n.* pasta in form of long strings

Spam (spæm) *n.* **R** kind of tinned luncheon meat

span (spæn) *n.* **1.** space from thumb to little finger as measure **2.** extent, space **3.** stretch of arch *etc.* **4.** distance from wingtip to wingtip (*also* ˈ**wingspan**) —*vt.* **5.** stretch over **6.** measure with hand (**-nn-**)

spangle (ˈspæŋgˀl) *n.* **1.** small shiny metallic ornament —*vt.* **2.** decorate with spangles

THESAURUS

grudging, ill-natured, ill-tempered, jaundiced, peevish, tart, ungenerous, waspish ~*v.* **4.** alienate, disenchant, embitter, envenom, exacerbate, exasperate, turn off (*Inf.*)

source author, begetter, beginning, cause, commencement, derivation, fountainhead, origin, originator, rise, spring, starting point, wellspring

souse drench, dunk, immerse, marinate (*Cookery*), pickle, soak, steep

souvenir keepsake, memento, relic, remembrancer (*Archaic*), reminder, token

sovereign *n.* **1.** chief, emperor, empress, king, monarch, potentate, prince, queen, ruler, shah, supreme ruler, tsar ~*adj.* **2.** absolute, chief, dominant, imperial, kingly, monarchal, paramount, predominant, principal, queenly, regal, royal, ruling, supreme, unlimited **3.** effectual, efficacious, efficient, excellent

sovereignty ascendancy, domination, kingship, primacy, supremacy, supreme power, suzerainty, sway

sow broadcast, disseminate, implant, inseminate, lodge, plant, scatter, seed

space **1.** amplitude, capacity, elbowroom, expanse, extension, extent, leeway, margin, play, room, scope, spaciousness, volume **2.** blank, distance, gap, interval, lacuna, omission **3.** duration, interval, period, span, time, while

spaceman astronaut, cosmonaut

spacious ample, broad, capacious, comfortable, commodious, expansive, extensive, huge, large, roomy, sizable, uncrowded, vast

spadework donkeywork, groundwork, labour, preparation

span **1.** *n.* amount, distance, extent, length, reach, spread, stretch **2.** *v.* arch across, bridge, cover, cross, extend across, link, range over, traverse, vault

spaniel (ˈspænjəl) *n.* breed of dog with long ears and silky hair

Spanish (ˈspænɪʃ) *n.* **1.** official language of Spain, Mexico and most countries of S and Central Amer., except Brazil —*a.* **2.** of Spanish language or its speakers **3.** of Spain or Spaniards —ˈ**Spaniard** *n.* native or inhabitant of Spain —**Spanish America** parts of America colonized by Spaniards and now chiefly Spanish-speaking —**Spanish fly 1.** European blister beetle, the dried bodies of which yield cantharides **2.** cantharides —**Spanish Main 1.** mainland of Spanish America **2.** Caribbean Sea

spank (spæŋk) *vt.* **1.** slap with flat of hand, *esp.* on buttocks —*n.* **2.** one or series of these slaps —ˈ**spanking** *n.* **1.** series of spanks —*a.* **2.** quick, lively **3.** large, fine

spanner (ˈspænə) *n.* tool for gripping nut or bolt head

spanspek (ˈspænspɛk) *n.* **SA** sweet melon

spar[1] (spɑː) *n.* pole, beam, *esp.* as part of ship's rigging

spar[2] (spɑː) *vi.* **1.** box **2.** dispute, *esp.* in fun (**-rr-**) —*n.* **3.** sparring —**sparring partner** person who practises with boxer during training

spar[3] (spɑː) *n.* any of various kinds of crystalline mineral

spare (spɛə) *vt.* **1.** leave unhurt **2.** show mercy **3.** abstain from using **4.** do without **5.** give away —*a.* **6.** additional **7.** in reserve **8.** thin, lean **9.** scanty —*n.* **10.** spare part (for machine) —ˈ**sparing** *a.* economical, careful —ˈ**sparerib** *n.* cut of pork ribs with most of meat trimmed off —**spare tyre UK** *sl.* roll of fat just above waist

spark (spɑːk) *n.* **1.** small glowing or burning particle **2.** flash of light produced by electrical discharge **3.** vivacity, humour **4.** trace **5.** in internal-combustion engines, electric spark (in sparking plug) which ignites explosive mixture in cylinder —*vi.* **6.** emit sparks —*vt.* **7.** (*oft. with* off) kindle, excite —**sparking plug** device screwed into cylinder head of internal-combustion engine to ignite explosive mixture by means of electric spark (*also* **spark plug**)

sparkle (ˈspɑːkᵊl) *vi.* **1.** glitter **2.** effervesce **3.** scintillate —*n.* **4.** small spark **5.** glitter **6.** flash **7.** lustre —ˈ**sparkler** *n.* **1.** type of firework that throws out sparks **2.** *inf.* sparkling gem

sparrow (ˈspærəʊ) *n.* small brownish bird —**sparrow hawk** hawk that hunts small birds

sparse (spɑːs) *a.* thinly scattered

Spartan (ˈspɑːtᵊn) *a.* **1.** of ancient Gk. city of Sparta, its inhabitants or their culture **2.** (*sometimes* **s-**) very strict or austere **3.** (*sometimes* **s-**) possessing courage and resolve

spasm (ˈspæzəm) *n.* **1.** sudden convulsive (muscular) contraction **2.** sudden burst of activity *etc.* —**spasˈmodic** *a.* occurring in spasms

spastic (ˈspæstɪk) *a.* **1.** affected by spasms, suffering cerebral palsy —*n.* **2.** person who has cerebral palsy

spat[1] (spæt) *pt./pp. of* SPIT[1]

spat[2] (spæt) *n.* short gaiter

spat[3] (spæt) *n.* slight quarrel

spate (speɪt) *n.* **1.** rush, outpouring **2.** flood

spathe (speɪð) *n.* large sheathlike leaf enclosing flower cluster

spatial *or* **spacial** (ˈspeɪʃəl) *a.* of, in space

spatter (ˈspætə) *vt.* **1.** splash, cast drops over —*vi.* **2.** be scattered in drops —*n.* **3.** slight splash **4.** sprinkling

spatula (ˈspætjʊlə) *n.* utensil with broad, flat blade used for various purposes

spawn (spɔːn) *n.* **1.** eggs of fish or frog **2.** *oft. offens.* offspring —*vi.* **3.** (of fish or frog) cast eggs —*vt.* **4.** produce, engender

spay (speɪ) *vt.* remove ovaries from (animal)

speak (spiːk) *vi.* **1.** utter words **2.** converse **3.** deliver discourse —*vt.* **4.** utter **5.** pronounce **6.** express **7.** communicate in (**spoke, ˈspoken, ˈspeaking**) —ˈ**speakable** *a.* —ˈ**speaker** *n.* **1.** one who speaks **2.** one who specializes in speech-making **3.** (*oft.* **S-**) official chairman of many legislative bodies **4.** loudspeaker —ˈ**speakeasy** *n.* **US** place where alcoholic drink was sold illicitly during Prohibition —**speaking clock UK** telephone service giving verbal statement of time

THESAURUS

spank *v.* belt (*Sl.*), cuff, give (someone) a hiding (*Inf.*), put (someone) over one's knee, slap, slipper (*Inf.*), smack, tan (*Sl.*), wallop (*Inf.*)

spar *v.* argue, bicker, dispute, exchange blows, fall out (*Inf.*), have a tiff, lead a cat-and-dog life, scrap (*Inf.*), skirmish, spat (*U.S.*), squabble, wrangle, wrestle

spare *adj.* **1.** additional, emergency, extra, free, going begging (*Inf.*), in excess, in reserve, leftover, odd, over, superfluous, supernumerary, surplus, unoccupied, unused, unwanted **2.** gaunt, lank, lean, meagre, slender, slight, slim, thin, wiry **3.** economical, frugal, meagre, modest, scanty, sparing ~*v.* **4.** afford, allow, bestow, dispense with, do without, give, grant, let (someone) have, manage without, part with, relinquish **5.** be merciful to, deal leniently with, go easy on (*Inf.*), have mercy on, leave, let off (*Inf.*), pardon, refrain from, release, relieve from, save from

sparing careful, chary, cost-conscious, economical, frugal, money-conscious, prudent, saving, thrifty

spark *n.* **1.** flare, flash, flicker, gleam, glint, scintillation, spit **2.** atom, hint, jot, scintilla, scrap, trace, vestige ~*v.* **3.** *Often with* **off** animate, excite, inspire, kindle, precipitate, provoke, set in motion, set off, start, stimulate, stir, touch off, trigger (off)

sparkle *v.* **1.** beam, coruscate, dance, flash, gleam, glint, glisten, glister (*Archaic*), glitter, glow, scintillate, shimmer, shine, spark, twinkle, wink **2.** bubble, effervesce, fizz, fizzle ~*n.* **3.** brilliance, coruscation, dazzle, flash, flicker, gleam, glint, glitter, lustre, radiance, spark, twinkle

spartan 1. abstemious, ascetic, austere, bleak, disciplined, extreme, frugal, plain, rigorous, self-denying, severe, stern, strict, stringent **2.** bold, brave, courageous, daring, dauntless, doughty, fearless, hardy, heroic, intrepid, resolute, unflinching, valorous

spasm 1. contraction, convulsion, paroxysm, throe (*Rare*), twitch **2.** access, burst, eruption, fit, frenzy, outburst, seizure

spasmodic convulsive, erratic, fitful, intermittent, irregular, jerky, sporadic

spate deluge, flood, flow, outpouring, rush, torrent

speak 1. articulate, communicate, converse, discourse, enunciate, express, make known, pronounce, say, state, talk, tell, utter, voice **2.** address, argue, declaim, deliver an address, descant, discourse, ha-

spear (spɪə) *n.* **1.** long pointed weapon **2.** slender shoot, as of asparagus —*vt.* **3.** transfix, pierce, wound with spear —**ˈspearhead** *n.* **1.** leading force in attack, campaign —*vt.* **2.** lead, initiate (attack, campaign *etc.*)

spearmint (ˈspɪəmɪnt) *n.* type of mint

spec (spɛk) *n. inf.* speculation, gamble (*esp. in* **on spec**)

spec. 1. special **2.** specification **3.** speculation

special (ˈspɛʃəl) *a.* **1.** beyond the usual **2.** particular, individual **3.** distinct **4.** limited —**ˈspecialism** *n.* —**ˈspecialist** *n.* one who devotes himself to special subject or branch of subject —**speciˈality** *n.* special product, skill, characteristic *etc.* —**specialiˈzation** *or* **-iˈsation** *n.* —**ˈspecialize** *or* **-ise** *vi.* **1.** be specialist —*vt.* **2.** make special —**ˈspecially** *adv.* —**Special Branch UK** department of police force concerned with political security —**special constable** person recruited for temporary police duties, *esp.* in time of emergency —**special delivery** delivery of mail outside time of scheduled delivery —**special licence UK** licence permitting marriage to take place without usual legal conditions

specie (ˈspiːʃiː) *n.* coined, as distinct from paper, money

species (ˈspiːʃiːz; *Lat.* ˈspiːʃiiːz) *n.* **1.** sort, kind, *esp.* of animals *etc.* **2.** class **3.** subdivision (*pl.* **-cies**)

specific (spɪˈsɪfɪk) *a.* **1.** definite **2.** exact in detail **3.** characteristic of a thing or kind —**speˈcifically** *adv.* —**specifiˈcation** *n.* detailed description of something to be made, done —**ˈspecify** *vt.* state definitely or in detail (**-ified, -ifying**) —**specific gravity** ratio of density of substance to that of water

specimen (ˈspɛsɪmɪn) *n.* **1.** part typifying whole **2.** individual example **3.** *Med.* sample of tissue, urine *etc.* taken for diagnostic examination

specious (ˈspiːʃəs) *a.* deceptively plausible, but false —**ˈspeciously** *adv.* —**ˈspeciousness** *n.*

speck (spɛk) *n.* **1.** small spot, particle —*vt.* **2.** spot —**ˈspeckle** *n./vt.* speck

specs (spɛks) *pl.n. inf.* spectacles

spectacle (ˈspɛktəkᵊl) *n.* **1.** show **2.** thing exhibited **3.** ridiculous sight —*pl.* **4.** pair of lenses for correcting defective sight —**specˈtacular** *a.* **1.** impressive **2.** showy **3.** grand **4.** magnificent —*n.* **5.** lavishly produced performance —**specˈtator** *n.* one who looks on

spectra (ˈspɛktrə) *n., pl. of* SPECTRUM

spectre *or U.S.* **specter** (ˈspɛktə) *n.* **1.** ghost **2.** image of something unpleasant —**ˈspectral** *a.* ghostly

spectrum (ˈspɛktrəm) *n.* band of colours into which beam of light can be decomposed, *eg* by prism (*pl.* **-tra**) —**ˈspectroscope** *n.* instrument for producing, examining spectra —**specˈtroscopist** *n.* —**specˈtroscopy** *n.* study of spectra by use of spectroscopes *etc.*

speculate (ˈspɛkjʊleɪt) *vi.* **1.** guess, conjecture **2.** engage in (risky) commercial transactions —**specuˈlation** *n.* —**ˈspeculative** *a.* given to, characterized by speculation —**ˈspeculator** *n.*

speculum (ˈspɛkjʊləm) *n.* **1.** mirror **2.** reflector of polished metal, *esp.* in reflecting telescopes (*pl.* **-la** (-lə), **-s**) —**ˈspecular** *a.*

sped (spɛd) *pt./pp. of* SPEED

speech (spiːtʃ) *n.* **1.** act, faculty of speaking **2.** words, language **3.** conversation **4.** discourse **5.** (formal) talk given before audience —**ˈspeechify** *vi.* make speech, *esp.* long and tedious one (**-ified, -ifying**) —**ˈspeech-**

THESAURUS

rangue, hold forth, lecture, plead, speechify, spiel (*Inf.*)

speaker lecturer, mouthpiece, orator, public speaker, spieler (*Inf.*), spokesman, spokesperson, spokeswoman, word-spinner

spearhead *v.* be in the van, blaze the trail, head, initiate, launch, lay the first stone, lead, lead the way, pioneer, set in motion, set off

special 1. distinguished, especial, exceptional, extraordinary, festive, gala, important, memorable, momentous, out of the ordinary, red-letter, significant, uncommon, unique, unusual **2.** appropriate, certain, characteristic, distinctive, especial, individual, particular, peculiar, precise, specialized, specific

specialist authority, connoisseur, consultant, expert, master, professional

speciality claim to fame, distinctive *or* distinguishing feature, forte, *pièce de résistance*, special, specialty

species breed, category, class, collection, description, group, kind, sort, type, variety

specific 1. clear-cut, definite, exact, explicit, express, limited, particular, precise, unambiguous, unequivocal **2.** characteristic, distinguishing, especial, peculiar, special

specification condition, detail, item, particular, qualification, requirement, stipulation

specify be specific about, cite, define, designate, detail, enumerate, indicate, individualize, itemize, mention, name, particularize, spell out, stipulate

specimen copy, embodiment, example, exemplar, exemplification, exhibit, individual, instance, model, pattern, proof, representative, sample, type

specious casuistic, deceptive, fallacious, misleading, plausible, sophistic, sophistical, unsound

speck 1. blemish, blot, defect, dot, fault, flaw, fleck, mark, mote, speckle, spot, stain **2.** atom, bit, dot, grain, iota, jot, mite, modicum, particle, shred, tittle, whit

spectacle 1. display, event, exhibition, extravaganza, pageant, parade, performance, show, sight **2.** curiosity, laughing stock, marvel, phenomenon, scene, sight, wonder

spectacular 1. *adj.* breathtaking, daring, dazzling, dramatic, eye-catching, fantastic (*Inf.*), grand, impressive, magnificent, marked, remarkable, sensational, splendid, staggering, striking, stunning (*Inf.*) **2.** *n.* display, extravaganza, show, spectacle

spectator beholder, bystander, eyewitness, looker-on, observer, onlooker, viewer, watcher, witness

speculate 1. cogitate, conjecture, consider, contemplate, deliberate, guess, hypothesize, meditate, muse, scheme, suppose, surmise, theorize, wonder **2.** gamble, have a flutter (*Inf.*), hazard, play the market, risk, take a chance with, venture

speculation 1. conjecture, consideration, contemplation, deliberation, guess, guesswork, hypothesis, opinion, supposition, surmise, theory **2.** gamble, gambling, hazard, risk

speculative 1. abstract, academic, conjectural, hypothetical, notional, suppositional, tentative, theoretical **2.** chancy (*Inf.*), dicey (*Sl.*), hazardous, risky, uncertain, unpredictable

less *a.* **1.** dumb **2.** at a loss for words —**speech day UK** in schools, annual prize-giving day at which speeches are made

speed (spi:d) *n.* **1.** swiftness **2.** rate of progress **3.** degree of sensitivity of photographic film **4.** *sl.* amphetamine —*vi.* **5.** move quickly **6.** drive vehicle at high speed **7.** *obs.* succeed —*vt.* **8.** further **9.** expedite (**sped** *or* **ˈspeeded** *pt./pp.*) —**ˈspeedily** *adv.* —**ˈspeeding** *n.* driving (vehicle) at high speed, *esp.* over legal limit —**ˈspeedo** *n. inf.* speedometer (*pl.* **-s**) —**ˈspeedy** *a.* **1.** quick **2.** rapid **3.** nimble **4.** prompt —**ˈspeedboat** *n.* light, fast motorboat —**speed limit** maximum permitted speed at which vehicle may travel on certain roads —**speedˈometer** *n.* instrument to show speed of vehicle —**ˈspeedway** *n.* track for motorcycle racing —**ˈspeedwell** *n.* plant with small, *usu.* blue flowers

spek (spɛk) *n.* **SA** bacon

speleology *or* **spelaeology** (spi:lɪˈɒlədʒɪ) *n.* study, exploring of caves —**speleoˈlogical** *or* **spelaeoˈlogical** *a.*

spell[1] (spɛl) *vt.* **1.** give letters of in order **2.** read letter by letter **3.** indicate, result in (**spelled** *or* **spelt** *pt./pp.*, **ˈspelling** *pr.p.*) —**ˈspelling** *n.* —**spell out** make explicit

spell[2] (spɛl) *n.* **1.** magic formula **2.** enchantment —**ˈspellbound** *a.* enchanted, entranced

spell[3] (spɛl) *n.* (short) period of time, work

spelt (spɛlt) *pt./pp. of* SPELL[1]

spend (spɛnd) *vt.* **1.** pay out **2.** pass (time) on activity *etc.* **3.** use up completely (**spent** *pt./pp.*, **ˈspending** *pr.p.*) —**ˈspender** *n.* —**spent** *a.* used up, exhausted —**ˈspendthrift** *n.* wasteful person

sperm (spɜ:m) *n.* **1.** male reproductive cell **2.** semen —**spermaceti** (spɜ:məˈsɛtɪ, -ˈsi:tɪ) *n.* white, waxy substance obtained from oil from head of sperm whale —**sperˈmatic** *a.* of sperm —**spermatozoon** (spɜ:mətəʊˈzəʊɒn) *n.* any of male reproductive cells released in semen during ejaculation (*pl.* **-zoa** (-ˈzəʊə)) (*also* **sperm, ˈzoosperm**) —**ˈspermicide** *n.* drug *etc.* that kills sperm —**sperm whale** large, toothed whale hunted for sperm oil, spermaceti and ambergris (*also* **ˈcachalot**)

spew (spju:) *v.* vomit

sphagnum (ˈsfægnəm) *n.* moss that grows in bogs

sphere (sfɪə) *n.* **1.** ball, globe **2.** range **3.** field of action **4.** status **5.** position **6.** province —**spherical** (ˈsfɛrɪkᵊl) *a.* —**ˈspheroid** *n.* **1.** geometric surface produced by rotating ellipse about one of its two axes —*a.* **2.** shaped like but not exactly a sphere

sphincter (ˈsfɪŋktə) *n.* ring of muscle surrounding opening of hollow bodily organ

sphinx (sfɪŋks) *n.* **1.** statue in Egypt with lion's body and human head **2.** (**S-**) monster with woman's head and lion's body **3.** enigmatic person (*pl.* **-es, sphinges** (ˈsfɪndʒi:z))

spice (spaɪs) *n.* **1.** aromatic or pungent vegetable substance **2.** spices collectively **3.** anything that adds flavour, relish, piquancy, interest *etc.* —*vt.* **4.** season with spices, flavour —**ˈspicily** *adv.* —**ˈspicy** *a.* **1.** flavoured with spices **2.** *inf.* slightly indecent, risqué

spick-and-span *or* **spic-and-span** (ˈspɪkənˈspæn) *a.* **1.** neat, smart **2.** new-looking

spider (ˈspaɪdə) *n.* small eight-legged creature which spins web to catch prey —**ˈspidery** *a.* —**spider plant** hardy house plant with long thin leaves

THESAURUS

speech **1.** communication, conversation, dialogue, discussion, intercourse, talk **2.** address, discourse, disquisition, harangue, homily, lecture, oration, spiel (*Inf.*) **3.** articulation, dialect, diction, enunciation, idiom, jargon, language, lingo (*Inf.*), parlance, tongue, utterance, voice

speechless dumb, inarticulate, mum, mute, silent, tongue-tied, unable to get a word out (*Inf.*), wordless

speed *n.* **1.** acceleration, celerity, expedition, fleetness, haste, hurry, momentum, pace, precipitation, quickness, rapidity, rush, swiftness, velocity ~*v.* **2.** belt (along) (*Sl.*), bomb (along), bowl along, career, dispatch, exceed the speed limit, expedite, flash, gallop, get a move on (*Inf.*), go hell for leather (*Inf.*), go like a bat out of hell (*Inf.*), go like the wind, hasten, hurry, lose no time, make haste, press on, put one's foot down (*Inf.*), quicken, race, rush, sprint, step on it (*Inf.*), tear, urge, zoom **3.** advance, aid, assist, boost, expedite, facilitate, further, help, impel, promote

speedy expeditious, express, fast, fleet, fleet of foot, hasty, headlong, hurried, immediate, nimble, precipitate, prompt, quick, rapid, summary, swift, winged

spell[1] *v.* amount to, augur, herald, imply, indicate, mean, point to, portend, presage, promise, result in, signify, suggest

spell[2] *n.* **1.** abracadabra, charm, conjuration, exorcism, incantation, sorcery, witchery **2.** allure, bewitchment, enchantment, fascination, glamour, magic, trance

spell[3] *n.* bout, course, interval, patch, period, season, stint, stretch, term, time, tour of duty, turn

spellbound bemused, bewitched, captivated, charmed, enchanted, enthralled, entranced, fascinated, gripped, hooked (*Inf.*), mesmerized, possessed, rapt, transfixed, transported, under a spell

spelling orthography

spell out clarify, elucidate, make clear *or* plain, make explicit, specify

spend **1.** disburse, expend, fork out (*Sl.*), lay out, pay out, shell out (*Inf.*), splash out (*Brit. inf.*) **2.** blow (*Sl.*), consume, deplete, dispense, dissipate, drain, empty, exhaust, fritter away, run through, squander, use up, waste **3.** fill, occupy, pass, while away

spendthrift big spender, prodigal, profligate, spender, squanderer, waster, wastrel

spent *adj.* **1.** all in (*Sl.*), burnt out, bushed (*U.S. inf.*), dead beat (*Inf.*), debilitated, dog-tired (*Inf.*), done in *or* up (*Inf.*), drained, exhausted, fagged (out) (*Inf.*), knackered (*Sl.*), played out (*Inf.*), prostrate, ready to drop (*Inf.*), shattered (*Inf.*), tired out, weakened, wearied, weary, whacked (*Brit. inf.*), worn out **2.** consumed, expended, finished, gone, used up

sphere **1.** ball, circle, globe, globule, orb **2.** capacity, compass, department, domain, employment, field, function, pale, province, range, rank, realm, scope, station, stratum, territory, walk of life

spherical globe-shaped, globular, orbicular, rotund, round

spice *n.* **1.** relish, savour, seasoning **2.** colour, excitement, gusto, kick (*Inf.*), pep, piquancy, tang, zap (*Sl.*), zest, zip (*Inf.*)

spiel (ʃpiːl) *inf. n.* **1.** glib (sales) talk —*vi.* **2.** deliver spiel, recite —ˈ**spieler** *n.*

spigot (ˈspɪgət) *n.* peg, plug

spike (spaɪk) *n.* **1.** sharp point **2.** sharp pointed object **3.** long flower cluster with flowers attached directly to the stalk —*vt.* **4.** pierce, fasten with spike **5.** render ineffective **6.** add alcohol to (drink) —ˈ**spiky** *a.* —ˈ**spikenard** *n.* **1.** aromatic Indian plant with rose-purple flowers **2.** aromatic ointment obtained from this plant

spill[1] (spɪl) *v.* **1.** (cause to) pour, flow over, fall out, *esp.* unintentionally **2.** upset —*vi.* **3.** be lost or wasted (**spilt** (spɪlt) *or* **spilled** *pt./pp.*) —*n.* **4.** fall **5.** amount spilt —ˈ**spillage** *n.*

spill[2] (spɪl) *n.* thin strip of wood, twisted paper *etc.* for lighting fires *etc.*

spin (spɪn) *v.* **1.** (cause to) revolve rapidly **2.** whirl —*vt.* **3.** twist into thread **4.** (*with* out) prolong **5.** *inf.* tell (a story) —*vi.* **6.** fish with lure (**spun,** *obs.* **span** (spæn) *pt.,* **spun** *pp.,* ˈ**spinning** *pr.p.*) —*n.* **7.** spinning **8.** (of aircraft) descent in dive with continued rotation **9.** rapid run or ride **10.** in skating, rapid turning on the spot **11.** angular momentum of elementary particle —ˈ**spinner** *n.* **1.** person or thing that spins **2.** *Cricket* ball that is bowled with spinning motion; spin bowler **3.** fishing lure with fin or wing that revolves —ˈ**spinneret** *n.* any of several organs in spiders *etc.* through which silk threads are exuded —ˈ**spinning** *n.* act, process of drawing out and twisting into threads, as wool, cotton, flax *etc.* —**spin bowler** *Cricket* bowler who specializes in bowling balls with spinning motion —**spin-dry** *vt.* spin (clothes) in spin-dryer —**spin-dryer** *n.* device that extracts water from clothes *etc.* by spinning them in perforated drum —**spinning jenny** early type of spinning frame with several spindles —**spinning wheel** household machine with large wheel turned by treadle for spinning wool *etc.* into thread —**spin-off** *n.* any product or development derived incidentally from application of existing knowledge or enterprise

spina bifida (ˈspaɪnə ˈbɪfɪdə) congenital condition in which meninges of spinal cord protrude through gap in backbone

spinach (ˈspɪnɪdʒ, -ɪtʃ) *n.* **1.** annual plant with edible leaves **2.** the leaves, eaten boiled as vegetable

spindle (ˈspɪndᵊl) *n.* rod, axis for spinning —ˈ**spindly** *a.* **1.** long and slender **2.** attenuated —ˈ**spindlelegs** *or* ˈ**spindleshanks** *pl.n.* **1.** long thin legs **2.** person who has such legs

spindrift (ˈspɪndrɪft) *or* **spoondrift** (ˈspuːndrɪft) *n.* spray blown along surface of sea

spine (spaɪn) *n.* **1.** backbone **2.** thin spike, *esp.* on fish *etc.* **3.** ridge **4.** back of book —ˈ**spinal** *a.* —ˈ**spineless** *a.* **1.** lacking spine **2.** cowardly —ˈ**spiny** *a.* **1.** (of animals) having or covered with quills or spines **2.** (of plants) covered with spines **3.** troublesome —**spinal column** series of contiguous bony segments that surround spinal cord (*also* **spine, vertebral column**) —**spinal cord** cord of nerve tissue within spinal canal, which together with brain forms central nervous system —**spine-chiller** *n.* film *etc.* that arouses terror

spinet (spɪˈnɛt, ˈspɪnɪt) *n.* keyboard instrument like harpsichord

spinnaker (ˈspɪnəkə; *Naut.* ˈspæŋkə) *n.* large yacht sail

spinney (ˈspɪnɪ) *n.* small wood

spinster (ˈspɪnstə) *n.* unmarried woman

spiracle (ˈspaɪərəkᵊl, ˈspaɪrə-) *n. Zool.* opening for breathing

spiraea *or esp. U.S.* **spirea** (spaɪˈrɪə) *n.* any of various plants with small white or pink flower sprays

spiral (ˈspaɪərəl) *n.* **1.** continuous curve drawn at ever-increasing distance from fixed point **2.** anything resembling this —*a.* **3.** having shape of spiral —ˈ**spirally** *adv.*

spirant (ˈspaɪrənt) *a.* **1.** *Phonet. see* FRICATIVE —*n.* **2.** fricative consonant

spire (spaɪə) *n.* **1.** pointed part of steeple **2.** pointed stem

spirit (ˈspɪrɪt) *n.* **1.** life principle animating body **2.** disposition **3.** liveliness **4.** courage **5.** frame of mind **6.** essential character or meaning **7.** soul **8.** ghost **9.** liquid got by distillation, alcohol —*pl.* **10.** emotional state **11.** strong alcoholic drink, *eg* whisky —*vt.* **12.** (*usu. with* away *or* off) carry away mysteriously —ˈ**spirited** *a.* lively —ˈ**spiritless** *a.* listless, apathetic —ˈ**spiritual** *a.* **1.** given to, interested in things of the spirit —*n.* **2.** Negro sacred song, hymn —ˈ**spiritualism** *n.* belief that spirits of the dead communicate with the living —ˈ**spiritualist** *n.* —**spirituˈality** *n.* —ˈ**spiritually** *adv.* —ˈ**spirituous** *a.* alcoholic —**spirit gum** glue made from gum dissolved in ether —**spirit lamp** lamp that burns methylated or other spirits —**spirit level** glass tube containing bubble in liquid, used to check horizontal, vertical surfaces —**spirits of salts** hydrochloric acid

THESAURUS

spike *n.* **1.** barb, point, prong, spine ~*v.* **2.** impale, spear, spit, stick **3.** block, foil, frustrate, render ineffective, thwart

spill **1.** *v.* discharge, disgorge, overflow, overturn, scatter, shed, slop over, spill *or* run over, throw off, upset **2.** *n. Inf.* accident, cropper (*Inf.*), fall, tumble

spin *v.* **1.** gyrate, pirouette, reel, revolve, rotate, turn, twirl, twist, wheel, whirl **2.** concoct, develop, invent, narrate, recount, relate, tell, unfold **3.** be giddy, be in a whirl, grow dizzy, reel, swim, whirl ~*n.* **4.** gyration, revolution, roll, twist, whirl **5.** *Inf.* drive, hurl (*Scot.*), joy ride (*Inf.*), ride, turn, whirl

spine **1.** backbone, spinal column, vertebrae, vertebral column **2.** barb, needle, quill, rachis, ray, spike, spur

spineless cowardly, faint-hearted, feeble, gutless (*Inf.*), inadequate, ineffective, irresolute, lily-livered, soft, spiritless, squeamish, submissive, vacillating, weak, weak-kneed (*Inf.*), weak-willed, without a will of one's own, yellow (*Inf.*)

spiral **1.** *adj.* circular, cochlear, cochleate (*Biol.*), coiled, corkscrew, helical, scrolled, voluted, whorled, winding **2.** *n.* coil, corkscrew, curlicue, gyre (*Literary*), helix, screw, volute, whorl

spirit *n.* **1.** air, breath, life, life force, psyche, soul, vital spark **2.** attitude, character, complexion, disposition, essence, humour, outlook, quality, temper, temperament **3.** animation, ardour, backbone, courage, dauntlessness, earnestness, energy, enterprise, enthusiasm, fire, force, gameness, grit, guts (*Inf.*), life, liveliness, mettle, resolution, sparkle, spunk (*Inf.*), stoutheartedness, vigour, warmth, zest **4.** atmosphere, feeling, gist, humour, tenor, tone **5.** es-

spirt (spɜːt) *see* SPURT

spit[1] (spɪt) *vi.* **1.** eject saliva —*vt.* **2.** eject from mouth (**spat, spit** *pt./pp.*, **ˈspitting** *pr.p.*) —*n.* **3.** spitting, saliva —**ˈspittle** *n.* saliva —**spitˈtoon** *n.* vessel to spit into —**ˈspitfire** *n.* person with fiery temper —**spitting image** *inf.* person who bears physical resemblance to another —**spit and polish** *inf.* punctilious attention to neatness, discipline *etc.*, esp. in armed forces

spit[2] (spɪt) *n.* **1.** sharp rod to put through meat for roasting **2.** sandy point projecting into the sea —*vt.* **3.** thrust through (**-tt-**)

spite (spaɪt) *n.* **1.** malice —*vt.* **2.** thwart spitefully —**ˈspiteful** *a.* —**ˈspitefully** *adv.* —**in spite of** regardless of; notwithstanding

spiv (spɪv) *n.* smartly dressed man, *esp.* one who makes living by shady dealings

splake (spleɪk) *n.* type of hybrid Canad. trout

splash (splæʃ) *v.* **1.** scatter (liquid) about, on or over (something) —*vt.* **2.** print, display prominently —*n.* **3.** sound of water being scattered **4.** patch, *esp.* of colour **5.** (effect of) extravagant display **6.** small amount —**ˈsplashdown** *n.* **1.** controlled landing of spacecraft on water **2.** time scheduled for this event —**splash down**

splat (splæt) *n.* wet, slapping sound

splatter (ˈsplætə) *v./n.* spatter

splay (spleɪ) *a.* **1.** spread out **2.** slanting **3.** turned outwards —*v.* **4.** spread out **5.** twist outwards —*n.* **6.** slant surface **7.** spread —**ˈsplayfooted** *a.* flat and broad (of foot)

spleen (spliːn) *n.* **1.** organ in abdomen **2.** anger **3.** irritable or morose temper —**splenetic** (splɪˈnɛtɪk) *a.* —**ˈspleenwort** *n.* any of various ferns

splendid (ˈsplɛndɪd) *a.* **1.** magnificent **2.** brilliant **3.** excellent —**ˈsplendidly** *adv.* —**ˈsplendour** *or U.S.* **ˈsplendor** *n.*

splice (splaɪs) *vt.* **1.** join by interweaving strands **2.** join (wood) by overlapping **3.** *sl.* join in marriage —*n.* **4.** spliced joint

spline (splaɪn) *n.* narrow groove, ridge, strip, *esp.* joining wood *etc.*

splint (splɪnt) *n.* rigid support for broken limb *etc.*

splinter (ˈsplɪntə) *n.* **1.** thin fragment of glass, wood *etc.* —*v.* **2.** break into fragments, shiver —**splinter group** group that separates from main party, organization, *oft.* after disagreement

split (splɪt) *v.* **1.** break asunder **2.** separate **3.** divide —*vi.* **4.** *sl.* depart; leave (**split, ˈsplitting**) —*n.* **5.** crack, fissure **6.** dessert of fruit and ice cream —**ˈsplitting** *a.* **1.** (of headache) acute **2.** (of head) assailed by overpowering unbearable pain —**split infinitive** in English grammar, infinitive used with another word between *to* and verb —**split-level** *a.* (of house *etc.*) having floor level of one part about half storey above floor level of adjoining part —**split pea** pea dried and split and used in soups *etc.* —**split personality 1.** tendency to change rapidly in mood or temperament **2.** schizophrenia —**split second** infinitely small period of time —**split-second** *a.* made or arrived at in infinitely short time

THESAURUS

sence, intent, intention, meaning, purport, purpose, sense, substance **6.** *Plural* feelings, frame of mind, humour, mood, morale **7.** apparition, ghost, phantom, shade (*Literary*), shadow, spectre, spook (*Inf.*), sprite, vision ~*v.* **8.** *With* **away** *or* **off** abduct, abstract, carry, convey, make away with, purloin, remove, seize, snaffle (*Brit. inf.*), steal, whisk

spirited active, animated, ardent, bold, courageous, energetic, game, high-spirited, lively, mettlesome, plucky, sparkling, sprightly, spunky (*Inf.*), vigorous, vivacious

spit 1. *v.* discharge, eject, expectorate, hiss, spew, splutter, sputter, throw out **2.** *n.* dribble, drool, saliva, slaver, spittle, sputum

spite *n.* **1.** animosity, bitchiness (*Sl.*), gall, grudge, hate, hatred, ill will, malevolence, malice, malignity, pique, rancour, spitefulness, spleen, venom **2. in spite of** despite, in defiance of, notwithstanding, regardless of ~*v.* **3.** annoy, discomfit, gall, harm, hurt, injure, needle (*Inf.*), nettle, offend, pique, provoke, put out, put (someone's) nose out of joint (*Inf.*), vex

spiteful barbed, bitchy (*Inf.*), catty (*Inf.*), cruel, ill-disposed, ill-natured, malevolent, malicious, malignant, rancorous, snide, splenetic, venomous, vindictive

splash *v.* **1.** bespatter, shower, slop, slosh (*Inf.*), spatter, splodge, spray, spread, sprinkle, squirt, strew, wet **2.** blazon, broadcast, flaunt, headline, plaster, publicize, tout, trumpet ~*n.* **3.** burst, dash, patch, spattering, splodge, touch **4.** *Inf.* display, effect, impact, sensation, splurge, stir

spleen acrimony, anger, animosity, animus, bad temper, bile, bitterness, gall, hatred, hostility, ill humour, ill will, malevolence, malice, malignity, peevishness, pique, rancour, resentment, spite, spitefulness, venom, vindictiveness, wrath

splendid 1. admirable, brilliant, exceptional, glorious, grand, heroic, illustrious, magnificent, outstanding, rare, remarkable, renowned, sterling, sublime, superb, supreme **2.** costly, dazzling, gorgeous, imposing, impressive, lavish, luxurious, magnificent, ornate, resplendent, rich, sumptuous, superb **3.** excellent, fantastic (*Inf.*), fine, first-class, glorious, great (*Inf.*), marvellous, wonderful **4.** beaming, bright, brilliant, glittering, glowing, lustrous, radiant, refulgent

splendour brightness, brilliance, ceremony, dazzle, display, effulgence, glory, gorgeousness, grandeur, lustre, magnificence, majesty, pomp, radiance, refulgence, renown, resplendence, richness, show, solemnity, spectacle, stateliness, sumptuousness

splice *v.* braid, entwine, graft, interlace, intertwine, intertwist, interweave, join, knit, marry, mesh, plait, unite, wed, yoke

splinter 1. *n.* chip, flake, fragment, needle, paring, shaving, sliver **2.** *v.* break into smithereens, disintegrate, fracture, shatter, shiver, split

split *v.* **1.** bifurcate, branch, break, break up, burst, cleave, come apart, come undone, crack, disband, disunite, diverge, fork, gape, give way, go separate ways, open, part, pull apart, rend, rip, separate, slash, slit, snap, splinter **2.** allocate, allot, apportion, carve up, distribute, divide, divvy up (*Inf.*), dole out, halve, parcel out, partition, share out, slice up ~*n.* **3.** breach, crack, damage, division, fissure, gap, rent, rip, separation, slash, slit, tear ~*adj.* **4.** bisected, broken, cleft, cracked, divided, dual, fractured, ruptured, twofold

splotch (splɒtʃ) *or* **splodge** (splɒdʒ) *n./vt.* splash, daub —ˈ**splotchy** *or* ˈ**splodgy** *a.*

splurge (splɜːdʒ) *v.* **1.** spend (money) extravagantly —*n.* **2.** ostentatious display, *esp.* of wealth **3.** bout of unrestrained extravagance

splutter (ˈsplʌtə) *vi.* **1.** make hissing, spitting sounds —*vt.* **2.** utter incoherently with spitting sounds —*n.* **3.** process or noise of spluttering **4.** spluttering incoherent speech

spode (spəʊd) *n.* (*sometimes* **S-**) china or porcelain manufactured by Josiah Spode, English potter, or his company

spoil (spɔɪl) *vt.* **1.** damage, injure **2.** damage manners or behaviour of (*esp.* child) by indulgence **3.** pillage —*vi.* **4.** go bad (**spoiled** *or* **spoilt** *pt./pp.*, ˈ**spoiling** *pr.p.*) —*n.* **5.** booty **6.** waste material, *esp.* in mining (*also* ˈ**spoilage**) —ˈ**spoiler** *n.* slowing device on aircraft wing *etc.* —ˈ**spoilsport** *n. inf.* one who spoils pleasure of other people —**spoiling for** eager for

spoke[1] (spəʊk) *pt. of* SPEAK —ˈ**spoken** *pp. of* SPEAK —ˈ**spokesman** *n.* one deputed to speak for others

spoke[2] (spəʊk) *n.* radial bar of wheel

spoliation (spəʊlɪˈeɪʃən) *n.* **1.** act of spoiling **2.** robbery **3.** destruction

spondee (ˈspɒndiː) *n.* metrical foot consisting of two long syllables (¯ ¯)

sponge (spʌndʒ) *n.* **1.** marine animal **2.** its skeleton, or a synthetic substance like it, used to absorb liquids **3.** type of light cake —*vt.* **4.** wipe with sponge —*vi.* **5.** live meanly at expense of others —*v.* **6.** cadge —ˈ**sponger** *n. sl.* one who cadges or lives at expense of others —ˈ**spongy** *a.* **1.** spongelike **2.** wet and soft —**sponge bag** small bag usu. made of plastic that holds toilet articles

sponsor (ˈspɒnsə) *n.* **1.** one promoting, advertising something **2.** one who agrees to give money to a charity on completion of specified activity by another **3.** one taking responsibility (*esp.* for welfare of child at baptism, *ie* godparent) **4.** guarantor —*vt.* **5.** act as sponsor for —ˈ**sponsorship** *n.*

spontaneous (spɒnˈteɪnɪəs) *a.* **1.** voluntary **2.** natural **3.** not forced **4.** produced without external force —**spontaneity** (spɒntəˈniːɪtɪ, -ˈneɪ-) *n.* —**sponˈtaneously** *adv.* —**sponˈtaneousness** *n.* —**spontaneous combustion** ignition of substance as result of internal oxidation processes

spoof (spuːf) *n.* **1.** mild satirical mockery **2.** trick, hoax

spook (spuːk) *n.* ghost —ˈ**spooky** *a.*

spool (spuːl) *n.* reel, bobbin

spoon (spuːn) *n.* **1.** implement with shallow bowl at end of handle for eating or serving food *etc.* —*vt.* **2.** lift with spoon —ˈ**spoonful** *n.* —ˈ**spoonbill** *n.* any of several wading birds having long horizontally flattened bill —**spoon-feed** *vt.* **1.** feed with spoon **2.** spoil **3.** provide (person) with ready-made opinions *etc.*

spoonerism (ˈspuːnərɪzəm) *n.* amusing transposition of initial consonants, *eg* 'half-warmed fish' for 'half-formed wish'

spoor (spʊə, spɔː) *n.* **1.** trail of wild animals —*v.* **2.** follow spoor (of)

sporadic (spəˈrædɪk) *or* **sporadical** *a.* **1.** intermittent **2.** scattered —**spoˈradically** *adv.*

spore (spɔː) *n.* minute reproductive organism of some plants and protozoans

sporran (ˈspɒrən) *n.* pouch worn in front of kilt

sport (spɔːt) *n.* **1.** game, activity for pleasure, competition, exercise **2.** enjoyment **3.** mockery **4.** cheerful person, good loser —*vt.* **5.** wear, *esp.* ostentatiously **6.** (*with* with) play —*vi.* **7.** frolic —ˈ**sportiness** *n.* —ˈ**sporting** *a.* **1.** of sport **2.** behaving with fairness, generosity —ˈ**sportive** *a.* playful —ˈ**sporty** *a.* **1.** stylish, loud or gay **2.** relating to or appropriate to sportsman —**sporting chance** sufficient prospect of success to justify the attempt —**sports car** fast (open) car —**sports jacket** man's casual jacket —ˈ**sportsman** *n.* **1.** one who engages in sport **2.** good loser

spot (spɒt) *n.* **1.** small mark, stain **2.** blemish **3.** pimple **4.** place **5.** (difficult) situation **6.** *inf.* small quantity —*vt.* **7.** mark with spots **8.** detect **9.** observe (-tt-) —ˈ**spotless** a. **1.** unblemished **2.** pure —ˈ**spotlessly** *adv.* —ˈ**spotty** *a.* **1.** with spots **2.** uneven —**spot check** random examination —ˈ**spotlight** *n.* **1.** powerful light illuminating small area **2.** centre of attention —**spot-on** *a.* **UK** *inf.* absolutely correct —**spotted dick** *or* **dog** **UK** steamed or boiled suet pudding containing dried fruit —**spot-weld** *vt.* **1.** join (two pieces of metal) by electrically generated heat —*n.* **2.** weld so formed

THESAURUS

spoil *v.* **1.** blemish, damage, debase, deface, destroy, disfigure, harm, impair, injure, mar, mess up, ruin, upset, wreck **2.** baby, cocker (*Rare*), coddle, cosset, indulge, kill with kindness, mollycoddle, overindulge, pamper, spoon-feed **3.** addle, become tainted, curdle, decay, decompose, go bad, go off (*Brit. inf.*), mildew, putrefy, rot, turn **4. spoiling for** bent upon, desirous of, eager for, enthusiastic about, keen to, looking for, out to get (*Inf.*), raring to

spoilsport damper, dog in the manger, kill-joy, misery (*Brit. inf.*), party-pooper (*U.S. sl.*), wet blanket (*Inf.*)

spoken expressed, oral, phonetic, put into words, said, told, unwritten, uttered, verbal, viva voce, voiced, by word of mouth

spongy absorbent, cushioned, cushiony, elastic, light, porous, spongelike, springy

sponsor **1.** *n.* angel (*Inf.*), backer, godparent, guarantor, patron, promoter **2.** *v.* back, finance, fund, guarantee, lend one's name to, patronize, promote, put up the money for, subsidize

spontaneous extempore, free, impromptu, impulsive, instinctive, natural, unbidden, uncompelled, unconstrained, unforced, unpremeditated, unprompted, voluntary, willing

spontaneously extempore, freely, impromptu, impulsively, instinctively, off one's own bat, off the cuff (*Inf.*), of one's own accord, on impulse, quite unprompted, voluntarily

sporadic infrequent, intermittent, irregular, isolated, occasional, on and off, random, scattered, spasmodic

sport *n.* **1.** amusement, diversion, enjoyment, entertainment, exercise, game, pastime, physical activity, play, recreation **2.** buffoon, butt, derision, fair game, game, laughing stock, mockery, plaything, ridicule ~*v.* **3.** *With* **with** amuse oneself, dally, flirt, play, take advantage of, toy, treat lightly *or* cavalierly, trifle **4.** *Inf.* display, exhibit, show off, wear **5.** caper, disport, frolic, gambol, play, romp

sporting fair, game (*Inf.*), gentlemanly, sportsmanlike

spouse (spaʊs, spaʊz) *n.* husband or wife —**spousal** (ˈspaʊzᵊl) *n.* marriage

spout (spaʊt) *v.* **1.** pour out —*vi.* **2.** *sl.* speechify —*n.* **3.** projecting tube or lip for pouring liquids **4.** copious discharge —**up the spout** *sl.* **1.** ruined; lost **2.** pregnant

SPQR Senatus Populusque Romanus (*Lat.*, the Senate and people of Rome)

sprain (spreɪn) *n./vt.* wrench or twist (of muscle *etc.*)

sprang (spræŋ) *pt. of* SPRING

sprat (spræt) *n.* small sea fish

sprawl (sprɔːl) *vi.* **1.** lie or sit about awkwardly —*v.* **2.** spread in rambling, unplanned way —*n.* **3.** sprawling

spray[1] (spreɪ) *n.* **1.** (device for producing) fine drops of liquid —*vt.* **2.** sprinkle with shower of fine drops —**spray gun** device that sprays fluid in finely divided form by atomizing it in air jet

spray[2] (spreɪ) *n.* **1.** branch, twig with buds, flowers *etc.* **2.** floral ornament, brooch *etc.* like this

spread (sprɛd) *v.* **1.** extend **2.** stretch out **3.** open out **4.** scatter **5.** distribute or be distributed **6.** unfold —*vt.* **7.** cover (**spread, ˈspreading**) —*n.* **8.** extent **9.** increase **10.** ample meal **11.** food which can be spread on bread *etc.* —**spread-eagle** *a.* with arms and legs outstretched (*also* **spread-eagled**)

spree (spriː) *n.* **1.** session of overindulgence **2.** romp

sprig (sprɪg) *n.* **1.** small twig **2.** ornamental design like this **3.** small nail

sprightly (ˈspraɪtlɪ) *a.* lively, brisk —**ˈsprightliness** *n.*

spring (sprɪŋ) *vi.* **1.** leap **2.** shoot up or forth **3.** come into being **4.** (*with* up) appear **5.** grow **6.** become bent or split —*vt.* **7.** produce unexpectedly **8.** set off (trap) (**sprang, sprung, ˈspringing**) —*n.* **9.** leap **10.** recoil **11.** piece of coiled or bent metal with much resilience **12.** flow of water from earth **13.** first season of year —**ˈspringy** *a.* elastic —**spring balance** device in which object to be weighed is attached to end of helical spring, extension of which indicates weight on calibrated scale —**ˈspringboard** *n.* flexible board for diving —**spring-clean** *v.* clean (house) thoroughly —**spring-cleaning** *n.* —**springer spaniel** breed of spaniel with silky coat, used for flushing or springing game —**spring onion** immature onion cultivated for its tiny bulb and long green leaves which are eaten in salads *etc.* —**spring tide** high tide at new or full moon

springbok *or* **springbuck** (ˈsprɪŋbʌk) *n.* **1.** S Afr. antelope **2.** (**S-**) South African national sportsman

sprinkle (ˈsprɪŋkᵊl) *vt.* scatter small drops on, strew —**ˈsprinkler** *n.* —**ˈsprinkling** *n.* small quantity or number

sprint (sprɪnt) *vi.* **1.** run short distance at great speed —*n.* **2.** such run, race

sprit (sprɪt) *n.* small spar set diagonally across fore-and-aft sail in order to extend it —**spritsail** (ˈsprɪtseɪl; *Naut.* ˈsprɪtsəl) *n.* sail extended by sprit

sprite (spraɪt) *n.* fairy, elf

sprocket (ˈsprɒkɪt) *n.* **1.** projection on wheel or

THESAURUS

spot *n.* **1.** blemish, blot, blotch, daub, discoloration, flaw, mark, pimple, plook (*Scot.*), pustule, smudge, speck, stain, taint **2.** locality, location, place, point, position, scene, site, situation **3.** *Inf.* bit, little, morsel, splash **4.** *Inf.* difficulty, mess, plight, predicament, quandary, trouble ~*v.* **5.** catch sight of, descry, detect, discern, espy, identify, make out, observe, pick out, recognize, see, sight **6.** besmirch, blot, dirty, dot, fleck, mark, mottle, soil, spatter, speckle, splodge, splotch, stain, sully, taint, tarnish

spotless above reproach, blameless, chaste, faultless, flawless, gleaming, immaculate, innocent, irreproachable, pure, shining, snowy, unblemished, unimpeachable, unstained, unsullied, untarnished, virgin, virginal, white

spotlight *n. Fig.* attention, fame, interest, limelight, notoriety, public attention, public eye

spouse better half (*Inf.*), companion, consort, helpmate, husband, mate, partner, wife

spout *v.* **1.** discharge, emit, erupt, gush, jet, shoot, spray, spurt, squirt, stream, surge **2.** *Inf.* declaim, expatiate, go on (*Inf.*), hold forth, orate, pontificate, rabbit on (*Brit. sl.*), ramble (on), rant, speechify, spiel (*Inf.*), talk

sprawl *v.* flop, loll, lounge, ramble, slouch, slump, spread, straggle, trail

spray[1] *v.* **1.** atomize, diffuse, scatter, shower, sprinkle ~*n.* **2.** drizzle, droplets, fine mist, moisture, spindrift, spoondrift **3.** aerosol, atomizer, sprinkler

spray[2] *n.* bough, branch, corsage, floral arrangement, shoot, sprig

spread *v.* **1.** be displayed, bloat, broaden, dilate, expand, extend, fan out, open, open out, sprawl, stretch, swell, unfold, unfurl, unroll, widen **2.** escalate, multiply, mushroom, proliferate **3.** advertise, blazon, broadcast, bruit, cast, circulate, cover, diffuse, disseminate, distribute, make known, make public, proclaim, promulgate, propagate, publicize, publish, radiate, scatter, shed, strew, transmit **4.** arrange, array, cover, furnish, lay, prepare, set ~*n.* **5.** advance, advancement, development, diffusion, dispersion, dissemination, escalation, expansion, increase, proliferation, spreading, suffusion, transmission **6.** compass, extent, period, reach, span, stretch, sweep, term **7.** *Inf.* array, banquet, blowout (*Sl.*), feast, repast

spree bacchanalia, bender (*Inf.*), binge (*Inf.*), carouse, debauch, fling, jag (*Sl.*), junketing, orgy, revel, romp, splurge

sprightly active, agile, airy, alert, animated, blithe, brisk, cheerful, energetic, frolicsome, gay, jaunty, joyous, lively, nimble, perky, playful, spirited, sportive, spry, vivacious

spring *v.* **1.** bounce, bound, hop, jump, leap, rebound, recoil, vault **2.** *Often with* **from** arise, be derived, be descended, come, derive, descend, emanate, emerge, grow, issue, originate, proceed, start, stem **3.** *With* **up** appear, burgeon, come into existence *or* being, develop, mushroom, shoot up ~*n.* **4.** bound, buck, hop, jump, leap, saltation, vault **5.** bounce, bounciness, buoyancy, elasticity, flexibility, give (*Inf.*), recoil, resilience, springiness

sprinkle *v.* dredge, dust, pepper, powder, scatter, shower, spray, strew

sprinkling admixture, dash, dusting, few, handful, scatter, scattering, smattering, sprinkle

sprint *v.* dart, dash, go at top speed, hare (*Brit. inf.*), hotfoot, put on a burst of speed, race, scamper, shoot, tear, whiz (*Inf.*)

sprite apparition, brownie, dryad, elf, fairy, goblin, imp, leprechaun, naiad, nymph, pixie, spirit, sylph

capstan for engaging chain **2.** wheel with sprockets (*also* **sprocket wheel**)

sprout (spraut) *v.* **1.** put forth (shoots) —*vi.* **2.** spring up —*n.* **3.** shoot

spruce[1] (spru:s) *n.* variety of fir

spruce[2] (spru:s) *a.* neat in dress

sprung (sprʌŋ) *pp. of* SPRING

spry (spraɪ) *a.* nimble, vigorous

spud (spʌd) *n. inf.* potato

spume (spju:m) *n./vi.* foam, froth

spun (spʌn) *pt./pp. of* SPIN

spunk (spʌŋk) *n.* courage, spirit

spur (spɜ:) *n.* **1.** pricking instrument attached to horseman's heel **2.** incitement **3.** stimulus **4.** projection on cock's leg **5.** projecting mountain range **6.** railway branch line or siding —*vt.* **7.** ride hard (**-rr-**)

spurious (ˈspjʊərɪəs) *a.* not genuine

spurn (spɜ:n) *vt.* reject with scorn, thrust aside

spurt *or* **spirt** (spɜ:t) *v.* **1.** send, come out in jet —*vi.* **2.** rush suddenly —*n.* **3.** jet **4.** short sudden effort, *esp.* in race

sputnik (ˈsputnɪk, ˈspʌt-) *n.* any of series of Russian satellites

sputter (ˈspʌtə) *v.* splutter

sputum (ˈspju:təm) *n.* spittle (*pl.* **-ta** (-tə))

spy (spaɪ) *n.* **1.** one who watches (*esp.* in rival countries, companies *etc.*) and reports secretly —*vi.* **2.** act as spy —*vt.* **3.** catch sight of (**spied, ˈspying**) —**ˈspyglass** *n.* small telescope

Sq. 1. Square 2. Squadron

squab (skwɒb) *n.* **1.** young unfledged bird, *esp.* pigeon **2.** short fat person **3.** well-stuffed cushion —*a.* **4.** (of birds) unfledged **5.** short and fat

squabble (ˈskwɒbᵊl) *vi.* **1.** engage in petty, noisy quarrel, bicker —*n.* **2.** petty quarrel

squad (skwɒd) *n.* small party, *esp.* of soldiers —**ˈsquadron** *n.* division of cavalry regiment, fleet or air force —**squadron leader** officer holding commissioned rank, between flight lieutenant and wing commander in air forces of Brit. and certain other countries

squalid (ˈskwɒlɪd) *a.* mean and dirty —**ˈsqualor** *n.*

squall (skwɔ:l) *n.* **1.** harsh cry **2.** sudden gust of wind **3.** short storm —*vi.* **4.** yell

squander (ˈskwɒndə) *vt.* spend wastefully, dissipate

square (skwɛə) *n.* **1.** equilateral rectangle **2.** area of this shape **3.** in town, open space (of this shape) **4.** product of a number multiplied by itself **5.** instrument for drawing right angles —*a.* **6.** square in form **7.** honest **8.** straight, even **9.** level, equal **10.** denoting a measure of area **11.** *inf.* old-fashioned, conservative —*vt.* **12.** make square **13.** find square of **14.** pay **15.** bribe —*vi.* **16.** fit, suit —**ˈsquarely** *adv.* —**square-bashing** *n.* **UK** *Mil. sl.* drill on barrack square —**square dance** any of various formation dances in which couples form squares —**square-dance** *vi.* perform such dance —**square deal** any transaction *etc.* that is honest and fair —**square leg** *Cricket* **1.** fielding position on on side approximately at right angles to batsman **2.** person who fields in this position —**square measure** unit or system of units for measuring areas —**square metre** *etc.* area equal to that of square with sides one metre *etc.* long —**square root** number that, multiplied by itself, gives number of which it is factor

squash (skwɒʃ) *vt.* **1.** crush flat **2.** pulp **3.** suppress **4.**

THESAURUS

sprout *v.* bud, develop, germinate, grow, push, shoot, spring, vegetate

spruce as if one had just stepped out of a bandbox, dainty, dapper, elegant, natty (*Inf.*), neat, smart, trig (*Archaic*), trim, well-groomed, well turned out

spry active, agile, alert, brisk, nimble, nippy (*Brit. inf.*), quick, ready, sprightly, supple, vigorous

spur *v.* **1.** animate, drive, goad, impel, incite, press, prick, prod, prompt, stimulate, urge ~*n.* **2.** goad, prick, rowel **3.** impetus, impulse, incentive, incitement, inducement, motive, stimulus

spurious artificial, bogus, contrived, counterfeit, deceitful, fake, false, feigned, forged, imitation, mock, phoney (*Sl.*), pretended, pseudo (*Inf.*), sham, simulated, specious, unauthentic

spurn cold-shoulder, contemn, despise, disdain, disregard, rebuff, reject, repulse, scorn, slight, snub, turn one's nose up at (*Inf.*)

spurt **1.** *v.* burst, erupt, gush, jet, shoot, spew, squirt, surge **2.** *n.* access, burst, fit, rush, spate, surge

spy *n.* **1.** double agent, fifth columnist, foreign agent, mole, secret agent, secret service agent, undercover agent ~*v.* **2.** *Usually with* **on** follow, keep under surveillance, keep watch on, shadow, tail (*Inf.*), trail, watch **3.** catch sight of, descry, espy, glimpse, notice, observe, set eyes on, spot

squabble **1.** *v.* argue, bicker, brawl, clash, dispute, fall out (*Inf.*), fight, have words, quarrel, row, scrap (*Inf.*), wrangle **2.** *n.* argument, barney (*Inf.*), difference of opinion, disagreement, dispute, fight, quarrel, row, scrap (*Inf.*), set-to (*Inf.*), spat, tiff

squad band, company, crew, force, gang, group, team, troop

squalid broken-down, decayed, dirty, disgusting, fetid, filthy, foul, low, nasty, poverty-stricken, repulsive, run-down, seedy, sleazy, slovenly, slummy, sordid, unclean

squalor decay, filth, foulness, meanness, sleaziness, slumminess, squalidness, wretchedness

squander be prodigal with, blow (*Sl.*), consume, dissipate, expend, fritter away, frivol away, lavish, misspend, misuse, run through, scatter, spend, spend like water, throw away, waste

square *Fig. v.* **1.** *Often with* **with** accord, agree, conform, correspond, fit, harmonize, match, reconcile, suit, tally, **2.** *Sometimes with* **up** balance, clear (up), discharge, liquidate, make even, pay off, quit, satisfy, settle **3.** accommodate, adapt, adjust, align, even up, level, regulate, suit, tailor, true (up) **4.** *Sl.* bribe, buy off, corrupt, fix (*Inf.*), rig, suborn ~*adj.* **5.** aboveboard, decent, equitable, ethical, fair, fair and square, genuine, honest, just, on the level (*Inf.*), straight, straightforward, upright **6.** *Inf.* behind the times (*Inf.*), bourgeois, conservative, conventional, old-fashioned, out of date, straight (*Sl.*), strait-laced, stuffy

squash *v.* **1.** compress, crush, distort, flatten, mash, pound, press, pulp, smash, stamp on, trample down **2.** annihilate, crush, humiliate, put down (*Sl.*), put (someone) in his (*or* her) place, quash, quell, silence, sit on (*Inf.*), suppress humiliate —*n.* 5. juice of crushed fruit 6. crowd 7. game played with rackets and soft balls in walled court 8. marrowlike plant

squat (skwɒt) *vi.* 1. sit on heels 2. act as squatter (-tt-) —*a.* 3. short and thick —ˈ**squatter** *n.* one who settles on land or occupies house without permission

squaw (skwɔː) *n.* N Amer. Indian woman

squawk (skwɔːk) *n.* 1. short harsh cry, *esp.* of bird —*vi.* 2. utter this cry

squeak (skwiːk) *vi./n.* (make) short shrill sound

squeal (skwiːl) *n.* 1. long piercing squeak —*vi.* 2. make one 3. *sl.* confess information (about another)

squeamish (ˈskwiːmɪʃ) *a.* 1. easily made sick 2. easily shocked 3. overscrupulous

squeegee (ˈskwiːdʒiː) *or* **squilgee** (ˈskwɪldʒiː) *n.* 1. tool with rubber blade for clearing water (from glass *etc.*), spreading wet paper *etc.* —*vt.* 2. press, smooth with squeegee

squeeze (skwiːz) *vt.* 1. press 2. wring 3. force 4. hug 5. subject to extortion —*n.* 6. act of squeezing 7. period of hardship, difficulty caused by financial weakness

squelch (skwɛltʃ) *vi.* 1. make, walk with wet sucking sound, as in walking through mud —*n.* 2. squelching sound

squib (skwɪb) *n.* 1. small firework that hisses before exploding 2. insignificant person

squid (skwɪd) *n.* type of cuttlefish

squiffy (ˈskwɪfɪ) *a.* UK *inf.* slightly drunk

squiggle (ˈskwɪgᵊl) *n.* 1. wavy, wriggling mark —*vi.* 2. wriggle 3. draw squiggle

squill (skwɪl) *n.* 1. Mediterranean plant of lily family 2. its bulb, used medicinally as expectorant

squint (skwɪnt) *vi.* 1. have the eyes turned in different directions 2. glance sideways —*n.* 3. this eye disorder 4. glance —*a.* 5. having a squint

squire (skwaɪə) *n.* country gentleman

squirm (skwɜːm) *vi.* 1. wriggle 2. be embarrassed —*n.* 3. squirming movement

squirrel (ˈskwɪrəl) *n.* small graceful bushy-tailed tree animal

squirt (skwɜːt) *v.* 1. force (liquid) or (of liquid) be forced through narrow opening —*n.* 2. jet 3. *inf.* short or insignificant person

Sr *Chem.* strontium

Sr. *or* **Sr** 1. Senior 2. Sister

S.R.C. UK Science Research Council

S.R.N. State Registered Nurse

SS 1. Saints 2. paramilitary organization within Nazi party that provided Hitler's bodyguard, security forces, concentration camp guards *etc.* 3. (*also* S.S.) steamship

SSE south-southeast

SSR Soviet Socialist Republic

S.S.R.C. UK Social Science Research Council

SSW south-southwest

st. stone (weight)

St. *or* **St** 1. Saint 2. Strait 3. Street

stab (stæb) *v.* 1. pierce, strike (at) with pointed weapon (-bb-) —*n.* 2. blow, wound so inflicted 3. sudden sensation, *eg* of fear 4. attempt

stabilize *or* **-ise** (ˈsteɪbɪlaɪz) *vt.* make steady, restore to equilibrium, *esp.* of money values, prices and wages —**stabiliˈzation** *or* **-iˈsation** *n.* —ˈ**stabilizer** *or* **-iser** *n.* device to maintain equilibrium of ship, aircraft *etc.*

stable[1] (ˈsteɪbᵊl) *n.* 1. building for horses 2. racehorses of particular owner, establishment 3. such establishment —*vt.* 4. put into stable

stable[2] (ˈsteɪbᵊl) *a.* 1. firmly fixed 2. steadfast, resolute —**stability** (stəˈbɪlɪtɪ) *n.* 1. steadiness 2. ability to resist change of any kind —ˈ**stably** *adv.*

staccato (stəˈkɑːtəʊ) *a.* 1. *Mus.* with notes sharply separated 2. abrupt

stack (stæk) *n.* 1. ordered pile, heap 2. chimney —*vt.* 3. pile in stack 4. control (aircraft waiting to land) so that they fly at different altitudes

stadium (ˈsteɪdɪəm) *n.* open-air arena for athletics *etc.* (*pl.* **-s, -dia** (-dɪə))

staff (stɑːf) *n.* 1. body of officers or workers employed by a company *etc.*; personnel (*pl.* **-s**) 2. pole (*pl.* **-s, staves**) 3. set of five lines on which music is written (*pl.* **-s, staves**) —*vt.* 4. supply with personnel —**staff nurse** qualified nurse ranking immediately below sister —**staff sergeant** *Mil.* 1. UK noncommissioned officer holding sergeant's rank and carrying out certain special duties 2. US noncommissioned officer who ranks: in Army, above sergeant and below sergeant first class; in Air Force, above airman first class and below technical sergeant; in Marine Corps, above sergeant and below gunnery sergeant

THESAURUS

squawk *v.* cackle, crow, cry, hoot, screech, yelp

squeak *v.* peep, pipe, shrill, squeal, whine, yelp

squeal *n.* **1.** scream, screech, shriek, wail, yell, yelp, yowl ~*v.* **2.** scream, screech, shout, shriek, shrill, wail, yelp **3.** *Sl.* betray, blab, grass (*Brit. sl.*), inform on, peach (*Sl.*), rat on, sell (someone) down the river (*Inf.*), sing (*Sl.*), snitch (*Sl.*)

squeamish **1.** delicate, fastidious, finicky, nice (*Rare*), particular, prissy (*Inf.*), prudish, punctilious, scrupulous, strait-laced **2.** nauseous, qualmish, queasy, queer, sick, sickish

squeeze *v.* **1.** clutch, compress, crush, grip, nip, pinch, press, squash, wring **2.** cram, crowd, force, jam, jostle, pack, press, ram, stuff, thrust, wedge **3.** clasp, cuddle, embrace, enfold, hold tight, hug **4.** bleed (*Inf.*), bring pressure to bear on, extort, lean on (*Inf.*), milk, oppress, pressurize, put the screws on (*Inf.*), put the squeeze on (*Inf.*), wrest ~*n.* **5.** clasp, embrace, handclasp, hold, hug

squirm agonize, fidget, flounder, shift, twist, wiggle, wriggle, writhe

stab *v.* **1.** bayonet, cut, gore, injure, jab, knife, pierce, puncture, run through, spear, stick, thrust, transfix, wound ~*n.* **2.** gash, incision, jab, puncture, rent, thrust, wound **3.** ache, pang, prick, twinge

stability constancy, durability, firmness, permanence, solidity, soundness, steadfastness, steadiness, strength

stable abiding, constant, deep-rooted, durable, enduring, established, fast, firm, fixed, immutable, invariable, lasting, permanent, reliable, resolute, secure, sound, steadfast, steady, strong, sturdy, sure, unalterable, unchangeable, unwavering, well-founded

stack **1.** *n.* clamp (*Brit. agriculture*), cock, heap,

Staffs. (stæfs) Staffordshire

stag (stæg) *n.* 1. male deer —*a.* 2. for men only

stage (steɪdʒ) *n.* 1. period, division of development 2. raised floor or platform 3. (platform of) theatre 4. scene of action 5. stopping-place on road, distance between two of them 6. separate unit of space rocket that can be jettisoned —*vt.* 7. put (play) on stage 8. arrange, bring about —ˈ**staging** *n.* any temporary structure used in building, *esp.* platforms supported by scaffolding —ˈ**stagy** *a.* theatrical —ˈ**stagecoach** *n.* formerly, four-wheeled horse-drawn vehicle used to carry passengers *etc.* on regular route —**stage fright** panic that may beset person about to appear in front of audience —ˈ**stagehand** *n.* person who sets stage, moves props *etc.* in theatrical production —**stage-manage** *v.* 1. work as stage manager for (play *etc.*) —*vt.* 2. arrange or supervise from behind the scenes —**stage manager** person who supervises stage arrangements of theatrical production —**stage-struck** *a.* infatuated with glamour of theatrical life —**stage whisper** loud whisper intended to be heard by audience

stagflation (stægˈfleɪʃən) *n.* inflationary economic situation characterized by decline in industrial output

stagger (ˈstægə) *vi.* 1. walk unsteadily —*vt.* 2. astound 3. arrange in overlapping or alternating positions, times 4. distribute over a period —*n.* 5. act of staggering —*pl.* 6. form of vertigo 7. disease of horses —ˈ**staggering** *a.* astounding

stagnate (stægˈneɪt) *vi.* cease to flow or develop —ˈ**stagnant** *a.* 1. sluggish 2. not flowing 3. foul, impure —**stagˈnation** *n.*

staid (steɪd) *a.* of sober and quiet character, sedate —ˈ**staidly** *adv.* —ˈ**staidness** *n.*

stain (steɪn) *vt.* 1. spot, mark 2. apply liquid colouring to (wood *etc.*) 3. bring disgrace upon —*n.* 4. spot, mark, discoloration 5. moral taint —ˈ**stainless** *a.* —**stainless steel** rustless steel alloy

stairs (stɛəz) *pl.n.* set of steps, *esp.* as part of house —ˈ**staircase** *or* ˈ**stairway** *n.* 1. structure enclosing stairs 2. stairs —ˈ**stairwell** *n.* vertical shaft that contains staircase

stake (steɪk) *n.* 1. sharpened stick or post 2. money wagered or contended for —*vt.* 3. secure, mark out with stakes 4. wager, risk —**stake out US** *sl.* keep under surveillance

stalactite (ˈstæləktaɪt) *n.* lime deposit like icicle on roof of cave

stalagmite (ˈstæləgmaɪt) *n.* lime deposit like pillar on floor of cave

stale (steɪl) *a.* 1. old, lacking freshness 2. hackneyed 3. lacking energy, interest through monotony —ˈ**stalemate** *n.* 1. *Chess* draw through one player being unable to move 2. deadlock, impasse

stalk[1] (stɔːk) *n.* 1. plant's stem 2. anything like this

stalk[2] (stɔːk) *v.* 1. follow, approach (game *etc.*) stealthily —*vi.* 2. walk in stiff and stately manner —*n.* 3. stalking —**stalking-horse** *n.* pretext

stall (stɔːl) *n.* 1. compartment in stable *etc.* 2. erection for display and sale of goods 3. seat in chancel of church 4. finger sheath —*pl.* 5. area of seats on ground floor of theatre or cinema, nearest to orchestra pit or screen —*vt.* 6. put in stall 7. hinder 8. stick fast —*v.* 9. delay 10. stop unintentionally (motor engine) 11. lose flying speed (of aircraft) —*vi.* 12. prevaricate

stallion (ˈstæljən) *n.* uncastrated male horse, *esp.* one used for breeding

stalwart (ˈstɔːlwət) *a.* 1. strong 2. brave 3. staunch —*n.* 4. stalwart person

stamen (ˈsteɪmɛn) *n.* male organ of flowering plant (*pl.* **-s, stamina** (ˈstæmɪnə))

stamina (ˈstæmɪnə) *n.* power of endurance, vitality

THESAURUS

hoard, load, mass, mound, mountain, pile 2. *v.* accumulate, amass, assemble, bank up, heap up, load, pile, stockpile

staff *n.* 1. employees, lecturers, officers, organization, personnel, teachers, team, workers, work force 2. cane, pole, prop, rod, stave, wand

stage 1. *n.* division, juncture, lap, leg, length, level, period, phase, point, step 2. *v.* arrange, bring about, do, engineer, give, lay on, mount, orchestrate, organize, perform, play, present, produce, put on

stagger *v.* 1. falter, hesitate, lurch, reel, sway, teeter, totter, vacillate, waver, wobble 2. amaze, astonish, astound, bowl over (*Inf.*), confound, dumbfound, flabbergast, give (someone) a shock, nonplus, overwhelm, shake, shock, strike (someone) dumb (*Inf.*), stun, stupefy, surprise, take (someone) aback, take (someone's) breath away, throw off balance 3. alternate, overlap, step, zigzag

stagnant brackish, motionless, quiet, sluggish, stale, standing, still

stagnate decay, decline, deteriorate, fester, go to seed, idle, languish, lie fallow, rot, rust, stand still, vegetate

staid calm, composed, decorous, demure, grave, quiet, sedate, self-restrained, serious, sober, solemn, steady

stain *v.* 1. blemish, blot, colour, dirty, discolour, dye, mark, soil, mark, spot, tarnish, tinge 2. besmirch, blacken, contaminate, corrupt, defile, deprave, disgrace, drag through the mud, sully, taint ~*n.* 3. blemish, blot, discoloration, dye, mark, spot, tint 4. blemish, blot on the escutcheon, disgrace, dishonour, infamy, reproach, shame, slur, stigma

stake *n.* 1. pale, paling, picket, pole, post, spike, stave, stick ~*v.* 2. brace, prop, secure, support, tether, tie up 3. *Often with* **out** define, delimit, demarcate, lay claim to, mark out, outline, reserve ~*n.* 4. ante, bet, chance, hazard, peril, pledge, risk, venture, wager 5. claim, concern, interest, investment, involvement, share ~*v.* 6. bet, chance, gamble, hazard, imperil, jeopardize, pledge, put on, risk, venture, wager

stale 1. decayed, dry, faded, fetid, flat, fusty, hard, insipid, musty, old, sour, stagnant, tasteless 2. antiquated, banal, cliché-ridden, common, commonplace, drab, effete, flat, hackneyed, insipid, old hat, overused, platitudinous, repetitious, stereotyped, threadbare, trite, unoriginal, worn-out

stalk *v.* 1. creep up on, follow, haunt, hunt, pursue, shadow, tail (*Inf.*), track 2. flounce, march, pace, stride, strut

stalwart athletic, beefy (*Inf.*), brawny, daring, dependable, hefty (*Inf.*), husky (*Inf.*), indomitable, intrepid, lusty, manly, muscular, redoubtable, robust, rugged, sinewy, staunch, stout, strapping, strong, sturdy, valiant, vigorous

stamina energy, force, grit (*Inf.*), indefatigability,

stammer (ˈstæmə) *v.* **1.** speak, say with repetition of syllables, stutter —*n.* **2.** habit of so speaking —**ˈstammerer** *n.*

stamp (stæmp) *vi.* **1.** put down foot with force —*vt.* **2.** impress mark on **3.** affix postage stamp to **4.** fix (in memory) **5.** reveal, characterize —*n.* **6.** stamping with foot **7.** imprinted mark **8.** appliance for marking **9.** piece of gummed paper printed with device as evidence of postage *etc.* **10.** character —**stamping ground** habitual meeting or gathering place

stampede (stæmˈpiːd) *n.* **1.** sudden frightened rush, *esp.* of herd of cattle **2.** headlong rush of a crowd **3.** C rodeo —*vi.* **4.** cause, take part in stampede

stance (stæns, stɑːns) *n.* **1.** manner, position of standing **2.** attitude **3.** point of view

stanch (stɑːntʃ) *vt. see* STAUNCH

stanchion (ˈstɑːnʃən) *n.* **1.** upright bar, support —*vt.* **2.** support

stand (stænd) *v.* **1.** have, take, set in upright position —*vi.* **2.** remain **3.** be situated **4.** remain firm or stationary **5.** cease to move **6.** adhere to principles **7.** offer oneself as a candidate **8.** (*with* for) be symbol *etc.* (of) —*vt.* **9.** endure **10.** *inf.* provide free, treat to (**stood, ˈstanding**) —*n.* **11.** holding firm **12.** position **13.** halt **14.** something on which thing may be placed **15.** structure from which spectators watch sport *etc.* **16.** stop made by pop group *etc.* —**ˈstanding** *n.* **1.** reputation, status **2.** duration —*a.* **3.** erect **4.** permanent, lasting **5.** stagnant **6.** performed from stationary position, as in *standing jump* —**stand-by** *n.* person or thing that is ready for use or can be relied on in emergency —**stand-in** *n.* person, thing that acts as substitute —**standing order 1.** instruction to bank by depositor to pay stated amount at regular intervals **2.** rule governing procedure *etc.* of legislative body **3.** *Mil.* one of number of orders which have long-term validity —**standˈoffish** *a.* reserved or aloof —**ˈstandstill** *n.* complete cessation of movement —**stand by 1.** be available and ready to act if needed **2.** be present as onlooker **3.** be faithful to —**stand in** deputize —**stand over 1.** watch closely **2.** postpone

standard (ˈstændəd) *n.* **1.** accepted example of something against which others are judged **2.** degree, quality **3.** flag **4.** weight or measure to which others must conform **5.** post **6.** SA school form or grade —*a.* **7.** usual, regular **8.** average **9.** of recognized authority, competence **10.** accepted as correct —**standardiˈzation** *or* **-iˈsation** *n.* —**ˈstandardize** *or* **-ise** *vt.* regulate by a standard —**standard-bearer** *n.* **1.** man who carries a standard **2.** leader of party *etc.* —**standard gauge** railway track with distance of 56½ inches between lines —**standard-gauge** *or* **standard-gauged** *a.* of or denoting railway with standard gauge —**standard lamp** electric light fixed to tall support standing on floor —**standard time** official local time of region or country determined by distance from Greenwich of line of longitude passing through area —**standard of living** level of subsistence or material welfare of community, person *etc.*

standpoint (ˈstændpɔɪnt) *n.* **1.** point of view, opinion **2.** mental attitude

stank (stæŋk) *pt. of* STINK

stannary (ˈstænərɪ) *n.* place or region where tin is mined or worked

stannous (ˈstænəs) *a.* of, containing tin

stanza (ˈstænzə) *n.* group of lines of verse

staple (ˈsteɪpˀl) *n.* **1.** U-shaped piece of wire used to fasten papers, cloth *etc.* **2.** short length of stiff wire formed into U-shape with pointed ends, used for holding hasp to post, securing electrical cables *etc.* **3.** main product **4.** fibre **5.** pile of wool *etc.* —*a.* **6.** principal **7.** regularly produced or made for market —*vt.* **8.** fasten with staple **9.** sort, classify (wool *etc.*) according to length of fibre —**ˈstapler** *n.* small device for fastening papers together

star (stɑː) *n.* **1.** celestial body, seen as twinkling point of light **2.** asterisk (*) **3.** celebrated player, actor *etc.* **4.** medal, jewel *etc.* of apparent shape of star —*vt.* **5.**

THESAURUS

lustiness, power, power of endurance, resilience, resistance, staying power, strength, vigour, vitality

stammer *v.* falter, hem and haw, hesitate, pause, splutter, stumble, stutter

stamp *v.* **1.** beat, crush, trample **2.** engrave, fix, impress, imprint, inscribe, mark, mould, print **3.** betray, brand, categorize, characterize, exhibit, identify, label, mark, pronounce, reveal, show to be, typecast ~*n.* **4.** brand, cast, earmark, hallmark, imprint, mark, mould, signature **5.** breed, cast, character, cut, description, fashion, form, kind, sort, type

stampede *n.* charge, flight, rout, rush, scattering

stance 1. bearing, carriage, deportment, posture **2.** attitude, point of view, position, stand, standpoint, viewpoint

stand *v.* **1.** be upright, be vertical, erect, mount, place, position, put, rank, rise, set **2.** be in force, belong, be situated *or* located, be valid, continue, exist, halt, hold, obtain, pause, prevail, remain, rest, stay, stop **3.** abide, allow, bear, brook, cope with, countenance, endure, experience, handle, put up with (*Inf.*), stomach, submit to, suffer, support, sustain, take, thole (*Dialect*), tolerate, undergo, wear (*Brit. sl.*), weather, withstand ~*n.* **4.** halt, rest, standstill, stay, stop, stopover **5.** attitude, determination, firm stand, opinion, position, stance, standpoint **6.** base, booth, bracket, dais, frame, grandstand, place, platform, rack, rank, stage, staging, stall, stance (*Chiefly Scot.*), support, table

standard *n.* **1.** average, benchmark, canon, criterion, example, gauge, grade, guide, guideline, measure, model, norm, pattern, principle, requirement, rule, sample, specification, touchstone, type, yardstick ~*adj.* **2.** accepted, average, basic, customary, normal, orthodox, popular, prevailing, regular, set, staple, stock, typical, usual **3.** approved, authoritative, classic, definitive, established, official, recognized ~*n.* **4.** banner, colours, ensign, flag, pennant, pennon, streamer

standardize assimilate, bring into line, institutionalize, mass-produce, regiment, stereotype

stand by 1. back, befriend, be loyal to, champion, defend, stick up for (*Inf.*), support, take (someone's) part, uphold **2.** be prepared, wait, wait in the wings

standing *n.* **1.** condition, credit, eminence, estimation, footing, position, rank, reputation, repute, station, status **2.** continuance, duration, existence, experience ~*adj.* **3.** fixed, lasting, permanent, perpetual, regular, repeated **4.** erect, perpendicular, rampant (*Heraldry*), upended, upright, vertical

standpoint angle, opinion, point of view, position, post, stance, station, vantage point, viewpoint

adorn with stars **6.** mark (with asterisk) **7.** feature as star performer *—vi.* **8.** play leading role (in film *etc.*) (-rr-) *—a.* **9.** leading, most important, famous **—'stardom** *n.* **—'starlet** *n.* young actress who is projected as potential star **—'starry** *a.* covered with stars **—star-crossed** *a.* dogged by ill luck **—'starfish** *n.* small star-shaped sea creature **—'stargaze** *vi.* **1.** observe stars **2.** daydream **—'stargazing** *n./a.* **—starry-eyed** *a.* given to naive wishes, judgments *etc.* **—Star-Spangled Banner 1.** national anthem of the United States **2.** Stars and Stripes **—star-studded** *a.* featuring large proportion of well-known performers **—Star of David** emblem symbolizing Judaism, consisting of six-pointed star formed by superimposing one equilateral triangle upon another **—Stars and Stripes** national flag of the United States, consisting of 50 white stars and seven red and six white horizontal stripes

starboard ('stɑːbəd, -bɔːd) *n.* **1.** right-hand side of ship, looking forward *—a.* **2.** of, on this side

starch (stɑːtʃ) *n.* **1.** substance forming the main food element in bread, potatoes *etc.*, and used mixed with water, for stiffening linen *etc.* *—vt.* **2.** stiffen thus **—'starchy** *a.* **1.** containing starch **2.** stiff **3.** formal **4.** prim

stare (stɛə) *vi.* **1.** look fixedly **2.** gaze with wide-open eyes *—n.* **3.** staring, fixed gaze **—stare one in the face** be obvious or visible to one **—stare out** abash by staring at

stark (stɑːk) *a.* **1.** blunt, bare **2.** desolate **3.** absolute *—adv.* **4.** completely

starling ('stɑːlɪŋ) *n.* glossy black speckled songbird

start (stɑːt) *vt.* **1.** begin **2.** set going *—vi.* **3.** begin, *esp.* journey **4.** make sudden movement *—n.* **5.** beginning **6.** abrupt movement **7.** advantage of a lead in a race **—'starter** *n.* **1.** electric motor starting car engine **2.** competitor in, supervisor of, start of race

startle ('stɑːtᵊl) *vt.* surprise, frighten or alarm suddenly

starve (stɑːv) *v.* (cause to) suffer or die from hunger **—star'vation** *n.*

stash (stæʃ) *vt. inf.* put away, hide

-stat (*comb. form*) device that causes something to remain stationary or constant, as in *thermostat*

state (steɪt) *n.* **1.** condition **2.** place, situation **3.** politically organized people **4.** government **5.** rank **6.** pomp *—vt.* **7.** express in words **—'stated** *a.* **1.** fixed **2.** regular **3.** settled **—'stateless** *a.* **1.** without nationality **2.** without state or states **—'stately** *a.* dignified, lofty **—'statement** *n.* **1.** expression in words **2.** account **—State Enrolled Nurse** nurse who has passed examinations enabling him or her to perform many nursing services **—stately home UK** large mansion, *esp.* one open to public **—state-of-the-art** *a.* (of hi-fi equipment *etc.*) up-to-the-minute **—State Registered Nurse** nurse who has passed examinations enabling him or her to perform all nursing services **—'stateroom** *n.* **1.** private cabin on ship **2.** large room in palace, mansion, used for ceremonial occasions **—state school** any school maintained by the state **—'statesman** *n.* respected political leader

static ('stætɪk) *a.* **1.** motionless, inactive **2.** pert. to bodies at rest or in equilibrium **3.** *Comp.* (of a memory) not needing its contents refreshed periodically *—n.* **4.** electrical interference in radio reception *—pl.* **5.** (*with sing. v.*) branch of physics **—'statically** *adv.*

station ('steɪʃən) *n.* **1.** place where thing stops or is placed **2.** stopping place for railway trains **3.** local office for police force, fire brigade *etc.* **4.** place equipped for radio or television transmission **5.** bus garage **6.** post, employment **7.** status **8.** position in life *—vt.* **9.** put in position **—'stationary** *a.* **1.** not moving, fixed **2.** not changing **—station wagon** estate car

THESAURUS

star 1. *n.* celebrity, draw (*Inf.*), idol, lead, leading man *or* lady, luminary, main attraction, name **2.** *adj.* brilliant, celebrated, famous, illustrious, leading, major, paramount, principal, prominent, talented, well-known

stare *v.* gape, gawk, gawp (*Brit. sl.*), gaze, goggle, look, rubberneck (*Sl.*), watch

stark *adj.* **1.** absolute, arrant, bald, bare, blunt, consummate, downright, entire, flagrant, out-and-out, palpable, patent, pure, sheer, simple, unalloyed, unmitigated, utter **2.** austere, bare, barren, bleak, cold, depressing, desolate, drear (*Literary*), dreary, forsaken, grim, harsh, plain, severe, solitary, unadorned ~*adv.* **3.** absolutely, altogether, clean, completely, entirely, quite, utterly, wholly

start *v.* **1.** appear, arise, begin, come into being, come into existence, commence, depart, first see the light of day, get on the road, get under way, go ahead (*Inf.*), hit the road (*Inf.*), issue, leave, originate, pitch in (*Inf.*), sally forth, set off, set out **2.** activate, embark upon, engender, enter upon, get going, initiate, instigate, kick off (*Inf.*), make a beginning, open, originate, put one's hand to the plough (*Inf.*), set about, set in motion, start the ball rolling, take the first step, take the plunge (*Inf.*), turn on **3.** begin, create, establish, father, found, inaugurate, initiate, institute, introduce, launch, lay the foundations of, pioneer, set up **4.** blench, flinch, jerk, jump, recoil, shy, twitch ~*n.* **5.** beginning, birth, commencement, dawn, first step(s), foundation, inauguration, inception, initiation, kickoff (*Inf.*), onset, opening, outset **6.** advantage, edge, head start, lead **7.** convulsion, jar, jump, spasm, twitch

startle agitate, alarm, amaze, astonish, astound, frighten, give (someone) a turn (*Inf.*), make (someone) jump, scare, shock, surprise, take (someone) aback

state *v.* **1.** affirm, articulate, assert, asseverate, aver, declare, enumerate, explain, expound, express, present, propound, put, report, say, specify, voice ~*n.* **2.** case, category, circumstances, condition, mode, pass, plight, position, predicament, shape, situation, state of affairs **3.** ceremony, dignity, display, glory, grandeur, majesty, pomp, splendour, style **4.** body politic, commonwealth, country, federation, government, kingdom, land, nation, republic, territory

stately august, ceremonious, deliberate, dignified, elegant, grand, imperial, imposing, impressive, lofty, majestic, measured, noble, pompous, regal, royal, solemn

statement account, announcement, communication, communiqué, declaration, explanation, proclamation, recital, relation, report, testimony, utterance

static changeless, constant, fixed, immobile, inactive, inert, motionless, stagnant, stationary, still, unmoving, unvarying

station *n.* **1.** base, depot, headquarters, location, place, position, post, seat, situation **2.** appointment, business, calling, employment, grade, occupation,

stationer (ˈsteɪʃənə) *n.* dealer in writing materials *etc.* —**ˈstationery** *n.*

statistics (stəˈtɪstɪks) *pl.n.* **1.** numerical facts collected systematically and arranged **2.** (*with sing. v.*) the study of them —**staˈtistical** *a.* —**staˈtistically** *adv.* —**statisˈtician** *n.* one who compiles and studies statistics

statue (ˈstætjuː) *n.* solid carved or cast image of person, animal *etc.* —**ˈstatuary** *n.* statues collectively —**statuesque** (stætjʊˈɛsk) *a.* **1.** like statue **2.** dignified —**statuˈette** *n.* small statue

stature (ˈstætʃə) *n.* **1.** bodily height **2.** greatness

status (ˈsteɪtəs) *n.* **1.** position, rank **2.** prestige **3.** relation to others —**status quo** (kwəʊ) existing state of affairs —**status symbol** possession regarded as proof of owner's wealth *etc.*

statute (ˈstætjuːt) *n.* written law —**ˈstatutory** *a.* enacted, defined or authorized by statute

staunch (stɔːntʃ) *vt.* **1.** stop flow of (blood) (*also* **stanch**) —*a.* **2.** trustworthy, loyal

stave (steɪv) *n.* **1.** one of the pieces forming barrel **2.** verse, stanza **3.** *Mus.* staff —*vt.* **4.** (*usu. with* in) burst or force (hole in something) **5.** (*with* off) ward (off) (**stove, staved** *pt./pp.*, **ˈstaving** *pr.p.*)

staves (steɪvz) *n., pl. of* STAFF, STAVE

stay[1] (steɪ) *vi.* **1.** remain **2.** sojourn **3.** pause **4.** wait **5.** endure —*vt.* **6.** stop **7.** hinder **8.** postpone (**stayed, ˈstaying**) —*n.* **9.** remaining, sojourning **10.** check **11.** restraint **12.** deterrent **13.** postponement —**stay-at-home** *a./n.* (person) enjoying quiet and unadventurous use of leisure —**staying power** endurance

stay[2] (steɪ) *n.* **1.** support, prop **2.** rope supporting mast *etc.* —*pl.* **3.** formerly, laced corsets

S.T.D. subscriber trunk dialling

stead (stɛd) *n. rare* place —**stand (someone) in good stead** be useful or of good service to (someone)

steady (ˈstɛdɪ) *a.* **1.** firm **2.** regular **3.** temperate **4.** industrious **5.** reliable —*vt.* **6.** make steady —**ˈsteadily** *adv.* —**ˈsteadiness** *n.* —**ˈsteadfast** *a.* firm, fixed, unyielding —**ˈsteadfastly** *adv.* —**steady state** *Phys.* condition of system when some or all of quantities describing it are independent of time —**steady (on)** be careful

steak (steɪk) *n.* **1.** thick slice of meat, *esp.* beef **2.** slice of fish

steal (stiːl) *v.* **1.** take (something) without right or leave —*vi.* **2.** move silently (**stole, ˈstolen, ˈstealing**)

stealth (stɛlθ) *n.* secret or underhand procedure, behaviour —**ˈstealthily** *adv.* —**ˈstealthy** *a.*

steam (stiːm) *n.* **1.** vapour of boiling water **2.** *inf.* power, energy —*vi.* **3.** give off steam **4.** rise in vapour **5.** move by steam power —*vt.* **6.** cook or treat with steam —**ˈsteamer** *n.* **1.** steam-propelled ship **2.** vessel for cooking or treating with steam —**ˈsteamy** *a.* **1.** of, full of, or covered with steam **2.** *inf.* lustful —**steam-engine** *n.* engine worked or propelled by steam —**steam iron** electric iron that emits steam to facilitate pressing and ironing —**ˈsteamroller** *n.* **1.** large roller, *orig.* moved by steam, for levelling road surfaces *etc.* **2.** any great power used to crush opposition —*vt.* **3.** crush

stearin *or* **stearine** (ˈstɪərɪn) *n.* **1.** colourless crystalline ester, present in fats and used in soap and candles (*also* **triˈstearin**) **2.** fat in its solid form

steatite (ˈstɪətaɪt) *n.* soapstone

steed (stiːd) *n. Poet.* horse

steel (stiːl) *n.* **1.** hard and malleable metal made by mixing carbon in iron **2.** tool, weapon of steel **3.** C railway track, line —*vt.* **4.** harden —**ˈsteely** *a.* —**steel band** type of band consisting mainly of percussion instruments made from oildrums —**steel wool** woven mass of fine steel fibres, used for cleaning or polishing

steelyard (ˈstiːljɑːd) *n.* kind of balance with unequal arms

steep[1] (stiːp) *a.* **1.** rising, sloping abruptly **2.** precipitous **3.** *inf.* difficult **4.** (of prices) very high or exorbitant **5.** *inf.* unreasonable —**ˈsteepen** *v.* —**ˈsteeply** *adv.*

THESAURUS

position, post, rank, situation, sphere, standing, status ~*v.* **3.** assign, establish, fix, garrison, install, locate, post, set

stationary at a standstill, fixed, inert, moored, motionless, parked, standing, static, stock-still, unmoving

status condition, consequence, degree, distinction, eminence, grade, position, prestige, rank, standing

stay *v.* **1.** abide, continue, delay, establish oneself, halt, hang around (*Inf.*), hover, linger, loiter, pause, put down roots, remain, reside, settle, sojourn, stand, stay put, stop, tarry, wait **2.** *Often with* **at** be accommodated at, lodge, put up at, sojourn, visit **3.** adjourn, defer, discontinue, hold in abeyance, hold over, prorogue, postone, put off, suspend **4.** *Archaic* arrest, check, curb, delay, detain, hinder, hold, impede, obstruct, prevent ~*n.* **5.** holiday, sojourn, stop, stopover, visit **6.** deferment, delay, halt, pause, postponement, remission, reprieve, stopping, suspension

steadfast constant, dedicated, dependable, established, faithful, fast, firm, fixed, intent, loyal, persevering, reliable, resolute, single-minded, stable, staunch, steady, unfaltering, unflinching, unswerving, unwavering, unyielding

steady *adj.* **1.** firm, fixed, immovable, safe, stable, substantial, unchangeable, uniform **2.** balanced, calm, dependable, equable, having both feet on the ground, imperturbable, level-headed, reliable, sedate, sensible, serene, serious-minded, settled, sober, staid, steadfast **3.** ceaseless, confirmed, consistent, constant, continuous, even, faithful, habitual, incessant, nonstop, persistent, regular, rhythmic, unbroken, unfaltering, unfluctuating, uninterrupted, unremitting, unvarying, unwavering ~*v.* **4.** balance, brace, secure, stabilize, support **5.** compose *or* calm oneself, cool down, sober (up), get a grip on oneself (*Inf.*)

steal **1.** appropriate, be light-fingered, embezzle, filch, half-inch (*Inf.*), heist (*U.S. sl.*), lift (*Inf.*), misappropriate, nick (*Sl.*), peculate, pilfer, pinch (*Inf.*), pirate, plagiarize, poach, prig (*Brit. sl.*), purloin, shoplift, snitch (*Sl.*), swipe (*Sl.*), take, thieve, walk *or* make off with **2.** creep, flit, insinuate oneself, slink, slip, sneak, tiptoe

stealing embezzlement, larceny, misappropriation, pilferage, pilfering, plagiarism, robbery, shoplifting, theft, thievery, thieving

stealth furtiveness, secrecy, slyness, sneakiness, stealthiness, surreptitiousness, unobtrusiveness

stealthy clandestine, covert, furtive, secret, secretive, skulking, sly, sneaking, sneaky, surreptitious, underhand

steep[2] (stiːp) *vt.* **1.** soak, saturate —*vi.* **2.** be soaked —*n.* **3.** act or process of steeping **4.** the liquid used for this purpose

steeple (ˈstiːpᵊl) *n.* church tower with spire —**ˈsteeplechase** *n.* **1.** horse race with ditches and fences to jump **2.** foot race with hurdles *etc.* to jump —**ˈsteeplejack** *n.* one who builds, repairs chimneys, steeples *etc.*

steer[1] (stɪə) *vt.* **1.** guide, direct course of (vessel, motor vehicle *etc.*) —*vi.* **2.** direct one's course —**ˈsteerage** *n.* **1.** effect of a helm **2.** formerly, cheapest accommodation on ship —**steering committee** committee set up to prepare topics to be discussed, order of business *etc.* for legislative assembly *etc.* —**steering gear, wheel** *etc.* mechanism for steering —**ˈsteersman** *n.* helmsman of vessel

steer[2] (stɪə) *n.* castrated male ox

stein (staɪn) *n.* earthenware beer mug

stele (ˈstiːlɪ, stiːl) *n.* ancient carved stone pillar or slab (*pl.* **stelae** (ˈstiːliː), **steles** (ˈstiːlɪz, stiːlz))

stellar (ˈstɛlə) *a.* of stars

stem[1] (stɛm) *n.* **1.** stalk, trunk **2.** long slender part, as in tobacco pipe **3.** part of word to which inflections are added **4.** foremost part of ship

stem[2] (stɛm) *vt.* check, stop, dam up (**-mm-**)

stench (stɛntʃ) *n.* offensive smell

stencil (ˈstɛnsᵊl) *n.* **1.** thin sheet of plastic or metal pierced with pattern, which is brushed over with paint or ink, leaving pattern on surface under it **2.** pattern produced by this process —*vt.* **3.** mark (surface) with stencil (**-ll-**)

Sten gun (stɛn) light sub-machine-gun

stenography (stəˈnɒgrəfɪ) *n.* shorthand writing —**steˈnographer** *n.* —**stenoˈgraphic** *a.*

stentorian (stɛnˈtɔːrɪən) *a.* (of voice) very loud

step (stɛp) *vi.* **1.** move and set down foot **2.** proceed (in this way) —*vt.* **3.** measure in paces (**-pp-**) —*n.* **4.** act of stepping **5.** sound made by stepping **6.** mark made by foot **7.** manner of walking **8.** series of foot movements forming part of dance **9.** gait **10.** pace **11.** measure, act, stage in proceeding **12.** board, rung *etc.* to put foot on **13.** degree in scale **14.** mast socket **15.** promotion —*pl.* **16.** stepladder (*also* **pair of steps**) —**ˈstepladder** *n.* four-legged ladder having broad flat steps —**stepping stone 1.** one of series of stones acting as footrests for crossing streams *etc.* **2.** circumstance that assists progress towards some goal

stepchild (ˈstɛptʃaɪld) *n.* child of husband or wife by former marriage —**ˈstepbrother** *n.* —**ˈstepfather** *n.* —**ˈstepmother** *n.* —**ˈstepsister** *n.*

stephanotis (stɛfəˈnəʊtɪs) *n.* climbing shrub with fragrant waxy flowers

steppe (stɛp) *n.* (*oft. pl.*) extensive treeless plain in European and Asiatic Russia

-ster (*comb. form*) **1.** indicating person who is engaged in certain activity, as in *prankster* **2.** indicating person associated with or being something specified, as in *mobster, youngster*

stere (stɪə) *n.* cubic metre

stereo- *or sometimes before vowel* **stere-** (*comb. form*) three-dimensional quality or solidity, as in *stereoscope*

stereophonic (stɛrɪəˈfɒnɪk, stɪər-) *a.* (of sound reproduction) using two or more separate microphones to feed two or more loudspeakers through separate channels in order to give spatial effect to sound —**ˈstereo** *a./n.* (of, for) stereophonic gramophone *etc.*

stereoscope (ˈstɛrɪəskəʊp, ˈstɪər-) *n.* optical instrument for viewing two-dimensional pictures, giving illusion of depth and relief —**stereoscopic** (stɛrɪəˈskɒpɪk, stɪər-) *a.*

stereotype (ˈstɛrɪətaɪp, ˈstɪər-) *n.* **1.** metal plate for printing cast from set-up type **2.** something (monotonously) familiar, conventional, predictable —*vt.* **3.** make stereotype of —**ˈstereotyped** *a.* **1.** lacking originality or individuality **2.** reproduced from or on stereotype printing plate

sterile (ˈstɛraɪl) *a.* **1.** unable to produce fruit, crops, young *etc.* **2.** free from (harmful) germs —**sterility** (stɛˈrɪlɪtɪ) *n.* —**sterilization** *or* **-isation** (stɛrɪlaɪˈzeɪʃən) *n.* process or act of making sterile —**sterilize** *or* **-ise** (ˈstɛrɪlaɪz) *vt.* render sterile

sterling (ˈstɜːlɪŋ) *a.* **1.** genuine, true **2.** of solid worth, dependable **3.** in British money —*n.* **4.** British money

stern[1] (stɜːn) *a.* severe, strict

stern[2] (stɜːn) *n.* rear part of ship

sternum (ˈstɜːnəm) *n.* breastbone (*pl.* **-na** (-nə), **-s**)

sterols (ˈstɛrɒlz) *pl.n.* class of complex organic alcohols, including ergosterol, cholesterol —**ˈsteroid** *n.* *Biochem.* any of group of organic compounds including sterols, bile acids, many hormones, and D vitamins

THESAURUS

steep *adj.* **1.** abrupt, headlong, precipitous, sheer **2.** *Inf.* excessive, exorbitant, extortionate, extreme, high, overpriced, stiff, uncalled-for, unreasonable

steer *v.* be in the driver's seat, conduct, control, direct, govern, guide, pilot

stem[1] *n.* axis, branch, peduncle, shoot, stalk, stock, trunk

stem[2] *v.* bring to a standstill, check, contain, curb, dam, hold back, oppose, resist, restrain, stanch, stay (*Archaic*), stop, withstand

step *n.* **1.** footfall, footprint, footstep, gait, impression, pace, print, stride, trace, track, walk **2.** act, action, deed, expedient, manoeuvre, means, measure, move, procedure, proceeding **3.** advance, advancement, move, phase, point, process, progression, stage **4.** degree, level, rank, remove **5.** doorstep, round, rung, stair, tread ~*v.* **6.** move, pace, tread, walk

stereotype 1. *n.* formula, mould, pattern, received idea **2.** *v.* categorize, conventionalize, dub, pigeonhole, standardize, take to be, typecast

sterile 1. abortive, bare, barren, dry, empty, fruitless, infecund, unfruitful, unproductive, unprofitable, unprolific **2.** antiseptic, aseptic, disinfected, germ-free, sterilized

sterilize autoclave, disinfect, fumigate, purify

sterling authentic, excellent, first-class, genuine, pure, real, sound, standard, substantial, superlative, true

stern austere, authoritarian, bitter, cruel, flinty, forbidding, frowning, grim, hard, harsh, inflexible, relentless, rigid, rigorous, serious, severe, steely, strict, unrelenting, unsparing, unyielding

stertorous (ˈstɜːtərəs) *a.* **1.** with sound of heavy snoring **2.** breathing in this way

stet (stɛt) *Lat.*, let it stand (proofreader's direction to cancel alteration previously made)

stethoscope (ˈstɛθəskəʊp) *n.* instrument for listening to action of heart, lungs *etc.*

stetson (ˈstɛtsᵊn) *n.* type of broad-brimmed felt hat

stevedore (ˈstiːvɪdɔː) *n.* one who loads or unloads ships

stew (stjuː) *n.* **1.** food cooked slowly in closed vessel **2.** state of excitement, agitation or worry —*v.* **3.** cook by stewing —**stewed** *a.* **1.** (of fish *etc.*) cooked by stewing **2.** UK (of tea) bitter through having been left to infuse for too long **3.** *sl.* drunk

steward (ˈstjuəd) *n.* **1.** one who manages another's property **2.** official managing race meeting, assembly *etc.* **3.** attendant on ship's or aircraft's passengers (**ˈstewardess** *fem.*)

stick (stɪk) *n.* **1.** long, thin piece of wood **2.** anything shaped like a stick **3.** *inf.* person, as in *good stick* —*vt.* **4.** pierce, stab **5.** place, fasten, as by pins, glue **6.** (*with* out) protrude **7.** *inf.* tolerate, abide —*vi.* **8.** adhere **9.** come to stop, jam **10.** remain **11.** be fastened **12.** (*with* out) protrude (**stuck** *pt./pp.*) —**ˈsticker** *n.* adhesive label, poster —**ˈsticky** *a.* **1.** covered with, like adhesive substance **2.** (of weather) warm, humid **3.** *inf.* difficult, unpleasant —**sticking plaster** thin cloth with adhesive substance on one side, used for covering slight wounds —**stick insect** insect that resembles a twig —**stick-in-the-mud** *n. inf.* person who lacks initiative or imagination —**stick-up** *n. sl., chiefly* US robbery at gunpoint —**sticky wicket 1.** cricket pitch rapidly dried by sun after rain and particularly conducive to spin **2.** *inf.* difficult situation —**stick up** *sl., chiefly* US rob, *esp.* at gunpoint —**stick up for** *inf.* support or defend

stickleback (ˈstɪkᵊlbæk) *n.* small fish with sharp spines on back

stickler (ˈstɪklə) *n.* (*usu. with* for) person who insists on something

stiff (stɪf) *a.* **1.** not easily bent or moved **2.** rigid **3.** awkward **4.** difficult **5.** thick, not fluid **6.** formal **7.** stubborn **8.** unnatural **9.** strong or fresh, as breeze **10.** *inf.* excessive —*n.* **11.** *sl.* corpse —**ˈstiffen** *v.* —**ˈstiffly** *adv.* —**ˈstiffness** *n.* —**stiff-necked** *a.* obstinate, stubborn

stifle (ˈstaɪfᵊl) *vt.* smother, suppress

stigma (ˈstɪgmə) *n.* distinguishing mark, *esp.* of disgrace (*pl.* **-s, stigmata** (ˈstɪgmətə, stɪgˈmɑːtə)) —**ˈstigmatism** *n.* —**ˈstigmatize** *or* **-ise** *vt.* mark with stigma

stile (staɪl) *n.* arrangement of steps for climbing a fence

stiletto (stɪˈlɛtəʊ) *n.* **1.** small dagger **2.** small boring tool **3.** very high heel on woman's shoe, tapering to very narrow tip (*pl.* **-s**) —*a.* **4.** thin, pointed like stiletto

still[1] (stɪl) *a.* **1.** motionless **2.** noiseless **3.** at rest —*vt.* **4.** quiet —*adv.* **5.** to this time **6.** yet **7.** even —*n.* **8.** photograph, *esp.* of film scene —**ˈstillness** *n.* —**ˈstillborn** *a.* born dead —**still life** painting of inanimate objects

still[2] (stɪl) *n.* apparatus for distilling —**still room** pantry, storeroom in large house

stilt (stɪlt) *n.* **1.** pole with footrests for walking raised from ground **2.** long post supporting building *etc.* **3.** shore bird similar to avocet but having straight bill —**ˈstilted** *a.* stiff in manner, pompous —**ˈstiltedly** *adv.*

Stilton (ˈstɪltən) *n.* either of two rich cheeses, blue-veined or white

stimulus (ˈstɪmjʊləs) *n.* **1.** something that rouses to activity **2.** incentive (*pl.* **-uli** (-julaɪ, -juliː)) —**ˈstimulant**

THESAURUS

stick *n.* **1.** baton, birch, cane, pole, rod, staff, stake, switch, twig, wand ~*v.* **2.** adhere, affix, attach, bind, bond, cement, cleave, cling, fasten, fix, fuse, glue, hold, hold on, join, paste, weld **3.** dig, gore, insert, jab, penetrate, pierce, pin, poke, prod, puncture, spear, stab, thrust, transfix **4.** *With* **out** bulge, extend, jut, obtrude, poke, project, protrude, show **5.** be bogged down, become immobilized, be embedded, catch, clog, come to a standstill, jam, lodge, snag, stop **6.** linger, persist, remain, stay **7.** *Sl.* abide, bear up under, endure, get on with, stand, stomach, take, tolerate **8. stick up for** *Inf.* champion, defend, stand up for, support, take the part *or* side of, uphold

sticky 1. adhesive, claggy (*Dialect*), clinging, gluey, glutinous, gooey (*Inf.*), gummy, syrupy, tacky, tenacious, viscid, viscous **2.** *Inf.* awkward, delicate, difficult, discomforting, embarrassing, hairy (*Sl.*), nasty, painful, thorny, tricky, unpleasant **3.** clammy, close, humid, muggy, oppressive, sultry, sweltering, warm

stiff 1. brittle, firm, hard, hardened, inelastic, inflexible, rigid, solid, solidified, taut, tense, tight, unbending, unyielding **2.** artificial, austere, ceremonious, chilly, cold, constrained, forced, formal, laboured, mannered, pompous, priggish, prim, punctilious, standoffish, starchy (*Inf.*), stilted, uneasy, unnatural, unrelaxed, wooden **3.** arthritic, awkward, clumsy, creaky (*Inf.*), crude, graceless, inelegant, jerky, rheumaticky (*Inf.*), ungainly, ungraceful, unsupple **4.** arduous, difficult, exacting, fatiguing, formidable, hard, laborious, tough, trying, uphill **5.** brisk, fresh, powerful, strong, vigorous

stiffen brace, coagulate, congeal, crystallize, harden, jell, reinforce, set, solidify, starch, tauten, tense, thicken

stifle 1. asphyxiate, choke, smother, strangle, suffocate **2.** check, choke back, cover up, curb, extinguish, hush, muffle, prevent, repress, restrain, silence, smother, stop, suppress

still 1. *adj.* at rest, calm, hushed, inert, lifeless, motionless, noiseless, pacific, peaceful, placid, quiet, restful, serene, silent, smooth, stationary, stilly (*Poetic*), tranquil, undisturbed, unruffled, unstirring **2.** *v.* allay, alleviate, appease, calm, hush, lull, pacify, quiet, quieten, settle, silence, smooth, smooth over, soothe, subdue, tranquillize **3.** *adv.* but, even, for all that, however, nevertheless, notwithstanding, yet

stilted artificial, bombastic, constrained, forced, grandiloquent, high-flown, high-sounding, inflated, laboured, pedantic, pompous, pretentious, stiff, unnatural, wooden

stimulant analeptic, bracer (*Inf.*), energizer, excitant, pep pill (*Inf.*), pick-me-up (*Inf.*), restorative, reviver, tonic, upper (*Sl.*)

stimulate animate, arouse, encourage, fan, fire, foment, goad, impel, incite, inflame, instigate, prompt, provoke, quicken, rouse, spur, turn on (*Inf.*), urge, whet

stimulating exciting, exhilarating, galvanic, inspiring, intriguing, provocative, provoking, rousing, stirring, thought-provoking

n. drug *etc.* acting as a stimulus —ˈ**stimulate** *vt.* rouse up, spur —ˈ**stimulating** *a.* acting as stimulus —**stimuˈlation** *n.* —ˈ**stimulative** *a./n.*

sting (stɪŋ) *vt.* **1.** thrust sting into **2.** cause sharp pain to **3.** *sl.* impose upon by asking for money **4.** overcharge —*vi.* **5.** feel sharp pain (**stung,** ˈ**stinging**) —*n.* **6.** (wound, pain, caused by) sharp pointed organ, oft. poisonous, of certain insects and animals —ˈ**stingray** *n.* ray having whiplike tail bearing serrated venomous spine capable of inflicting painful weals

stingy (ˈstɪndʒɪ) *a.* **1.** mean **2.** avaricious **3.** niggardly —ˈ**stingily** *adv.* —ˈ**stinginess** *n.*

stink (stɪŋk) *vi.* **1.** give out strongly offensive smell **2.** *sl.* be abhorrent (**stank, stunk,** ˈ**stinking**) —*n.* **3.** such smell, stench **4.** *inf.* fuss, bother —ˈ**stinker** *n. sl.* **1.** difficult or unpleasant person or thing **2.** something of very poor quality —**stink bomb** small bomb containing liquid with offensive smell

stint (stɪnt) *v.* **1.** be frugal, miserly to (someone) with (something) —*n.* **2.** allotted amount of work or time **3.** limitation, restriction

stipend (ˈstaɪpend) *n.* salary, *esp.* of clergyman —**stiˈpendiary** *a.* receiving stipend

stipple (ˈstɪpᵊl) *vt.* **1.** engrave, paint in dots —*n.* **2.** this process

stipulate (ˈstɪpjuleɪt) *vt.* specify in making a bargain —**stipuˈlation** *n.* proviso, condition —ˈ**stipulator** *n.*

stipule (ˈstɪpjuːl) *n.* small paired outgrowth occurring at base of leaf or its stalk —ˈ**stipular** *a.*

stir[1] (stɜː) *v.* **1.** (begin to) move —*vt.* **2.** set, keep in motion **3.** excite; rouse **4.** (*with* up) cause (trouble) (-rr-) —*n.* **5.** commotion, disturbance —ˈ**stirring** *a.* **1.** exciting emotions; stimulating **2.** active or busy

stir[2] (stɜː) *n.* **1.** *sl.* prison **2.** NZ *sl.* noisy party —**stir-crazy** *a.* US *sl.* mentally disturbed as result of being in prison

stirk (stɜːk) *n.* **1.** heifer of 6 to 12 months old **2.** yearling heifer or bullock

stirrup (ˈstɪrəp) *n.* metal loop hung from strap for supporting foot of rider on horse (*also* **stirrup iron**) —**stirrup cup** cup containing alcoholic drink offered to horseman ready to depart —**stirrup pump** hand-operated pump, base of cylinder of which is placed in bucket of water: used in fighting fires

stitch (stɪtʃ) *n.* **1.** movement of needle in sewing *etc.* **2.** its result in the work **3.** sharp pain in side **4.** least fragment (of clothing) —*vt.* **5.** sew, fasten *etc.* with stitches

stoat (stəʊt) *n.* small mammal with brown coat and black-tipped tail

stock (stɒk) *n.* **1.** goods, material stored, *esp.* for sale or later use **2.** reserve, fund **3.** financial shares in, or capital of, company *etc.* **4.** standing, reputation **5.** farm animals, livestock **6.** plant, stem from which cuttings are taken **7.** handle of gun, tool *etc.* **8.** liquid broth produced by boiling meat *etc.* **9.** flowering plant **10.** lineage —*pl.* **11.** *Hist.* frame to secure feet, hands (of offender) **12.** frame to support ship during construction —*a.* **13.** kept in stock **14.** standard, hackneyed —*vt.* **15.** keep, store **16.** supply with livestock, fish *etc.* —ˈ**stockist** *n.* dealer who maintains stocks of specified product —ˈ**stocky** *a.* thickset —ˈ**stockbreeder** *n.* person who breeds livestock as occupation —ˈ**stockbroker** *n.* agent for buying, selling shares in companies —**stock car** ordinary car strengthened and modified for a form of racing in which cars often collide —**stock exchange** institution for buying and selling shares —ˈ**stockjobber** *n.* dealer on a stock exchange —ˈ**stockman** *n.* man experienced in driving, handling cattle, sheep —**stock market** stock exchange —ˈ**stockpile** *v.* acquire and store large quantity of (something) —**stock-still** *a.* motionless —ˈ**stocktaking** *n.* examination, counting and valuing of goods in shop *etc.* —ˈ**stockyard** *n.* yard with pens or covered buildings where farm animals are assembled, sold *etc.* —**stock in trade 1.** goods necessary for carrying on business **2.**

THESAURUS

stimulus encouragement, fillip, goad, incentive, incitement, inducement, provocation, shot in the arm (*Inf.*), spur

sting *v.* **1.** burn, hurt, pain, smart, tingle, wound **2.** *Inf.* cheat, defraud, do (*Sl.*), fleece, overcharge, rip off (*Sl.*), swindle, take for a ride (*Inf.*)

stint 1. *n.* assignment, bit, period, quota, share, shift, spell, stretch, term, time, tour, turn **2.** *v.* begrudge, be sparing (frugal, mingy (*Brit. inf.*), parsimonious), economize, hold back, save, scrimp, skimp on, spoil the ship for a ha'porth of tar, withhold

stipulate agree, contract, covenant, engage, guarantee, insist upon, lay down, lay down *or* impose conditions, make a point of, pledge, postulate, promise, require, settle, specify

stipulation agreement, clause, condition, contract, engagement, precondition, prerequisite, provision, proviso, qualification, requirement, restriction, settlement, *sine qua non*, specification, term

stir *v.* **1.** agitate, beat, disturb, flutter, mix, move, quiver, rustle, shake, tremble **2.** *Often with* **up** animate, arouse, awaken, cause, excite, incite, inflame, instigate, kindle, prompt, provoke, quicken, raise, spur, stimulate, urge **3.** affect, electrify, excite, fire, inspire, move, rouse, thrill, touch **4.** bestir, be up and about (*Inf.*), budge, exert oneself, get a move on (*Inf.*), get moving (*Inf.*), hasten, look lively (*Inf.*), make an effort, mill about, move, shake a leg (*Inf.*) ~*n.* **5.** activity, ado, agitation, bustle, commotion, disorder, disturbance, excitement, ferment, flurry, fuss, movement, to-do, tumult, uproar

stirring animating, dramatic, emotive, exciting, exhilarating, heady, impassioned, inspiring, intoxicating, lively, moving, rousing, spirited, stimulating, thrilling

stock *n.* **1.** array, assets, assortment, cache, choice, commodities, fund, goods, hoard, inventory, merchandise, range, reserve, reservoir, selection, stockpile, store, supply, variety, wares **2.** *Animals* beasts, cattle, domestic animals, farm animals, flocks, herds, horses, livestock, sheep **3.** ancestry, background, breed, descent, extraction, family, forebears, house, line, lineage, line of descent, parentage, pedigree, race, strain, type, variety **4.** *Money* capital, funds, investment, property ~*adj.* **5.** banal, basic, commonplace, conventional, customary, formal, hackneyed, ordinary, overused, regular, routine, run-of-the-mill, set, standard, staple, stereotyped, traditional, trite, usual, worn-out ~*v.* **6.** deal in, handle, keep, sell, supply, trade in **7.** *With* **up** accumulate, amass, buy up, gather, hoard, lay in, put away, replenish, save, store (up), supply **8.** equip, fill, fit out, furnish, kit out, provide with, provision, supply

anything constantly used by someone as part of his occupation, trade *etc.*

stockade (stɒˈkeɪd) *n.* enclosure of stakes, barrier

stockinet (stɒkɪˈnɛt) *n.* machine-knitted elastic fabric

stocking (ˈstɒkɪŋ) *n.* one of pair of close-fitting coverings for legs and feet —**ˈstockinged** *a.*

stodgy (ˈstɒdʒɪ) *a.* (*esp.* of food) heavy, dull —**stodge** *n.* heavy, solid food

stoep (stuːp) *n.* **SA** veranda

stoic (ˈstəʊɪk) *a.* **1.** capable of much self-control, great endurance without complaint —*n.* **2.** stoical person —**ˈstoical** *a.* —**stoicism** (ˈstəʊɪsɪzəm) *n.*

stoke (stəʊk) *v.* feed, tend (fire or furnace) —**ˈstoker** *n.* —**ˈstokehold** *n. Naut.* **1.** coal bunker for ship's furnace **2.** hold for ship's boilers; fire room —**ˈstokehole** *n.* **1.** stokehold **2.** hole in furnace through which it is stoked

stole[1] (stəʊl) *pt. of* STEAL —**ˈstolen** *pp. of* STEAL

stole[2] (stəʊl) *n.* long scarf or shawl

stolid (ˈstɒlɪd) *a.* **1.** hard to excite **2.** heavy, slow, apathetic —**stoˈlidity** *n.* —**ˈstolidly** *adv.*

stoma (ˈstəʊmə) *n.* **1.** *Bot.* epidermal pore in plant leaves, that controls passage of gases through plant **2.** *Zool., anat.* mouth or mouthlike part (*pl.* **stomata** (ˈstəʊmətə, ˈstɒm-, stəʊˈmɑːtə))

stomach (ˈstʌmək) *n.* **1.** sac forming chief digestive organ in any animal **2.** appetite **3.** desire, inclination —*vt.* **4.** put up with —**stomach pump** *Med.* suction device for removing stomach contents —**stomach upset** slight digestive disorder

stomp (stɒmp) *vi. inf.* stamp

stone (stəʊn) *n.* **1.** (piece of) rock **2.** gem **3.** hard seed of fruit **4.** hard deposit formed in kidneys, bladder **5.** weight, 14 lbs. —*vt.* **6.** throw stones at **7.** free (fruit) from stones —**stoned** *a. sl.* stupefied by alcohol or drugs —**ˈstonily** *adv.* —**ˈstony** *or* **ˈstoney** *a.* **1.** of, like stone **2.** hard **3.** cold —**Stone Age** period in human culture identified by use of stone implements —**stone-blind** *a.* completely blind —**ˈstonechat** *n.* black songbird with reddish-brown breast —**stone-cold** *a.* completely cold —**stone-cold sober** completely sober —**ˈstonecrop** *n.* N temperate plant having fleshy leaves and typically red, yellow or white flowers —**stone deaf** completely deaf —**ˈstonemason** *n.* person skilled in preparing stone for building —**stone's throw** short distance —**stoneˈwall** *vi.* **1.** obstruct business **2.** play slow game, *esp.* in cricket —**ˈstoneware** *n.* heavy common pottery —**ˈstonewashed** *a.* (of clothes or fabric) given a faded look by being subjected to abrasive action of many small pieces of pumice —**stony-broke** *a. sl.* with no money left

stood (stʊd) *pt./pp. of* STAND

stooge (stuːdʒ) *n.* **1.** *Theat. etc.* performer who is always the butt of another's jokes **2.** *sl.* one taken advantage of by another

stook (stuːk) *n.* group of sheaves set upright in field to dry

stool (stuːl) *n.* **1.** backless chair **2.** excrement —**stool ball** game resembling cricket —**stool pigeon 1.** living or dummy pigeon used as decoy **2.** police informer

stoop (stuːp) *vi.* **1.** lean forward or down, bend **2.** swoop **3.** abase, degrade oneself —*n.* **4.** stooping carriage of the body

stop (stɒp) *vt.* **1.** check, bring to halt **2.** prevent **3.** interrupt **4.** suspend **5.** desist from **6.** fill up (an opening) —*vi.* **7.** cease, come to a halt **8.** stay (-pp-) —*n.* **9.** stopping or becoming stopped **10.** punctuation mark, *esp.* full stop **11.** any device for altering or regulating pitch **12.** set of pipes in organ having tones of a distinct quality —**ˈstoppage** *n.* —**ˈstopper** *n.* plug for closing bottle *etc.* —**ˈstopcock** *n.* valve to control or stop flow of fluid in pipe —**ˈstopgap** *n.* temporary substitute —**ˈstopoff** *or* **ˈstopover** *n.* short break in journey —**stop press** news put into a newspaper at the last minute —**ˈstopwatch** *n.* watch which can be stopped for exact timing of race

THESAURUS

stocky chunky, dumpy, mesomorphic, solid, stubby, stumpy, sturdy, thickset

stodgy 1. filling, heavy, leaden, starchy, substantial **2.** boring, dull, dull as ditchwater, formal, fuddy-duddy (*Inf.*), heavy going, laboured, staid, stuffy, tedious, turgid, unexciting, unimaginative, uninspired

stoical calm, cool, dispassionate, impassive, imperturbable, indifferent, long-suffering, philosophic, phlegmatic, resigned, stoic, stolid

stoicism acceptance, calmness, dispassion, fatalism, forbearance, fortitude, impassivity, imperturbability, indifference, long-suffering, patience, resignation, stolidity

stolid apathetic, bovine, doltish, dull, heavy, lumpish, obtuse, slow, stupid, unemotional, wooden

stomach *n.* **1.** abdomen, belly, breadbasket (*Sl.*), gut (*Inf.*), inside(s) (*Inf.*), paunch, pot, potbelly, spare tyre (*Inf.*), tummy (*Inf.*) **2.** appetite, desire, inclination, mind, relish, taste ~*v.* **3.** abide, bear, endure, put up with (*Inf.*), reconcile *or* resign oneself to, submit to, suffer, swallow, take, tolerate

stony *Fig.* adamant, blank, callous, chilly, cold, expressionless, frigid, hard, heartless, hostile, icy, indifferent, inexorable, merciless, obdurate, pitiless, unfeeling, unforgiving, unresponsive

stoop *v.* **1.** be bowed *or* round-shouldered, bend, bow, crouch, descend, duck, hunch, incline, kneel, lean, squat **2.** *Often with* **to** abase oneself, condescend, degrade oneself, deign, demean oneself, descend, lower oneself, resort, sink, vouchsafe ~*n.* **3.** bad posture, droop, round-shoulderedness, sag, slouch, slump

stop *v.* **1.** be over, break off, bring *or* come to a halt, bring *or* come to a standstill, call it a day (*Inf.*), cease, come to an end, conclude, cut out (*Inf.*), cut short, desist, discontinue, draw up, end, finish, halt, leave off, pack in (*Brit. inf.*), pause, peter out, pull up, put an end to, quit, refrain, run down, run its course, shut down, stall, terminate **2.** arrest, bar, block, break, check, close, forestall, frustrate, hinder, hold back, impede, intercept, interrupt, obstruct, plug, prevent, rein in, repress, restrain, seal, silence, staunch, stem, suspend **3.** break one's journey, lodge, put up, rest, sojourn, stay, tarry ~*n.* **4.** cessation, conclusion, discontinuation, end, finish, halt, standstill **5.** break, rest, sojourn, stay, stopover, visit

stopgap improvisation, makeshift, resort, shift, substitute, temporary expedient

stoppage abeyance, arrest, close, closure, cutoff, deduction, discontinuance, halt, hindrance, lay-off, shutdown, standstill, stopping

store (stɔː) *vt.* **1.** stock, furnish, keep —*n.* **2.** shop **3.** abundance **4.** stock **5.** department store **6.** place for keeping goods **7.** warehouse —*pl.* **8.** stocks of goods, provisions —ˈ**storage** *n.* —**storage battery** *esp.* US accumulator —**storage heater** electric device which accumulates and radiates heat generated by off-peak electricity —**store cattle** cattle bought lean to be fattened for market

storey *or U.S.* **story** (ˈstɔːrɪ) *n.* horizontal division of a building

stork (stɔːk) *n.* large wading bird

storm (stɔːm) *n.* **1.** violent weather with wind, rain, hail, sand, snow *etc.* **2.** assault on fortress **3.** violent outbreak, discharge —*vt.* **4.** assault **5.** take by storm —*vi.* **6.** rage —ˈ**stormy** *a.* **1.** like storm **2.** (emotionally) violent —**storm centre 1.** centre of cyclonic storm *etc.* where pressure is lowest **2.** centre of disturbance or trouble —**storm door** additional door outside ordinary door, providing extra insulation against wind *etc.* —**storm-trooper** *n.* **1.** member of Nazi S.A. **2.** member of force of shock troops —**stormy petrel 1.** any of various small petrels typically having dark plumage and paler underparts **2.** person who brings trouble

story (ˈstɔːrɪ) *n.* **1.** (book, piece of prose *etc.*) telling about events, happenings **2.** *inf.* lie **3.** US *see* STOREY —ˈ**storybook** *n.* book containing stories, *esp.* for children

stoup *or* **stoop** (stuːp) *n.* small basin for holy water

stout (staʊt) *a.* **1.** fat **2.** sturdy **3.** resolute —*n.* **4.** kind of beer —ˈ**stoutly** *adv.* —ˈ**stoutness** *n.* —**stoutˈhearted** *a.* brave

stove[1] (stəʊv) *n.* apparatus for cooking, heating *etc.* —ˈ**stovepipe** *n.* **1.** pipe that serves as flue to stove **2.** man's tall silk hat

stove[2] (stəʊv) *pt./pp. of* STAVE

stow (stəʊ) *vt.* pack away —ˈ**stowage** *n.* —ˈ**stowaway** *n.* one who hides in ship to obtain free passage

strabismus (strəˈbɪzməs) *n.* abnormal parallel alignment of one or both eyes, characterized by turning inwards or outwards from nose (*also* **squint**)

straddle (ˈstræd'l) *vt.* **1.** bestride —*vi.* **2.** spread legs wide —*n.* **3.** act or position of straddling

Stradivarius (strædɪˈvɑːrɪəs) *n.* violin manufactured in Italy by Antonio Stradivari or his family

strafe (streɪf, strɑːf) *vt.* attack (*esp.* with bullets, rockets) from air

straggle (ˈstræg'l) *vi.* stray, get dispersed, linger —ˈ**straggler** *n.*

straight (streɪt) *a.* **1.** without bend **2.** honest **3.** level **4.** in order **5.** (of spirits) undiluted, neat **6.** expressionless **7.** (of drama, actor *etc.*) serious **8.** *sl.* heterosexual —*n.* **9.** straight state or part —*adv.* **10.** direct —ˈ**straighten** *v.* —**straightaˈway** *adv.* immediately (*also* **straight away**) —**straight face** serious facial expression, *esp.* one that conceals impulse to laugh —**straight-faced** *a.* —**straightˈforward** *a.* **1.** open, frank **2.** simple **3.** honest —**straightˈforwardly** *adv.* —**straight man** subsidiary actor who acts as stooge to comedian

strain[1] (streɪn) *vt.* **1.** stretch tightly **2.** stretch to full or to excess **3.** filter —*vi.* **4.** make great effort —*n.* **5.** stretching force **6.** violent effort **7.** injury from being strained **8.** burst of music or poetry **9.** great demand **10.** (condition caused by) overwork, worry *etc.* **11.** tone of speaking or writing —**strained** *a.* —ˈ**strainer** *n.* filter, sieve

THESAURUS

store *v.* **1.** accumulate, deposit, furnish, garner, hoard, husband, keep, keep in reserve, lay by *or* in, lock away, put aside, put aside for a rainy day, put by, put in storage, reserve, salt away, save, stash (*Inf.*), stock, stockpile ~*n.* **2.** abundance, accumulation, cache, fund, hoard, lot, mine, plenty, plethora, provision, quantity, reserve, reservoir, stock, stockpile, supply, wealth **3.** chain store, department store, emporium, market, mart, outlet, shop, supermarket **4.** depository, repository, storehouse, storeroom, warehouse

storm *n.* **1.** blast, blizzard, cyclone, gale, gust, hurricane, squall, tempest, tornado, whirlwind **2.** *Fig.* agitation, anger, clamour, commotion, disturbance, furore, hubbub, outbreak, outburst, outcry, passion, roar, row, rumpus, stir, strife, tumult, turmoil, violence ~*v.* **3.** assail, assault, beset, charge, rush, take by storm ~*n.* **4.** assault, attack, blitz, blitzkrieg, offensive, onset, onslaught, rush ~*v.* **5.** bluster, complain, fly off the handle (*Inf.*), fume, rage, rant, rave, scold, thunder

stormy blustering, blustery, boisterous, dirty, foul, gusty, raging, rough, squally, tempestuous, turbulent, violent, wild, windy

story 1. account, anecdote, chronicle, fictional account, history, legend, narration, narrative, novel, recital, record, relation, romance, tale, version, yarn **2.** *Inf.* falsehood, fib, fiction, lie, untruth, white lie **3.** article, feature, news, news item, report, scoop

stout 1. big, bulky, burly, corpulent, fat, fleshy, heavy, obese, on the large *or* heavy side, overweight, plump, portly, rotund, substantial, tubby **2:** able-bodied, athletic, beefy (*Inf.*), brawny, hardy, hulking, husky (*Inf.*), lusty, muscular, robust, stalwart, strapping, strong, sturdy, substantial, tough, vigorous **3.** bold, brave, courageous, dauntless, doughty, fearless, gallant, intrepid, lion-hearted, manly, plucky, resolute, valiant, valorous

straggle drift, lag, linger, loiter, ramble, range, roam, rove, spread, stray, string out, trail, wander

straight *adj.* **1.** direct, near, short, undeviating, unswerving **2.** aligned, erect, even, horizontal, in line, level, perpendicular, plumb, right, smooth, square, true, upright, vertical **3.** blunt, candid, forthright, frank, honest, outright, plain, point-blank, straightforward, unqualified **4.** above board, accurate, authentic, decent, equitable, fair, fair and square, honest, honourable, just, law-abiding, reliable, respectable, trustworthy, upright **5.** arranged, in order, neat, orderly, organized, put to rights, shipshape, sorted out, tidy **6.** neat, pure, unadulterated, undiluted, unmixed ~*adv.* **7.** as the crow flies, at once, direct, directly, immediately, instantly

straightaway at once, directly, immediately, instantly, now, on the spot, right away, straightway (*Archaic*), there and then, this minute, without any delay, without more ado

straighten arrange, neaten, order, put in order, set *or* put to rights, smarten up, spruce up, tidy (up)

straightforward 1. above board, candid, direct, forthright, frank, genuine, guileless, honest, open, sincere, truthful **2.** clear-cut, easy, elementary, routine, simple, uncomplicated, undemanding

strain[1] *v.* **1.** distend, draw tight, extend, stretch,

strain[2] (streın) *n.* **1.** breed or race **2.** *esp. Biol.* type **3.** trace, streak

strait (streıt) *n.* **1.** channel of water connecting two larger areas of water —*pl.* **2.** position of difficulty or distress —*a.* **3.** narrow **4.** strict —**ˈstraiten** *vt.* **1.** make strait, narrow **2.** press with poverty —**ˈstraitjacket** *or* **ˈstraightjacket** *n.* jacket to confine arms of violent person —**strait-laced** *a.* **1.** austere, strict **2.** puritanical

strand[1] (strænd) *v.* **1.** run aground **2.** leave, be left helpless or in difficulties —*n.* **3.** *Poet.* shore

strand[2] (strænd) *n.* one of individual fibres or threads of string, wire *etc.*

strange (streındʒ) *a.* **1.** odd, queer **2.** unaccustomed **3.** foreign **4.** uncommon **5.** wonderful **6.** singular —**ˈstrangely** *adv.* —**ˈstrangeness** *n.* —**ˈstranger** *n.* **1.** unknown person **2.** foreigner **3.** (*with* to) one unaccustomed (to)

strangle (ˈstræŋgᵊl) *vt.* **1.** kill by squeezing windpipe **2.** suppress —**stranguˈlation** *n.* strangling —**ˈstranglehold** *n.* **1.** wrestling hold in which wrestler's arms are pressed against opponent's windpipe **2.** complete control over person or situation

strap (stræp) *n.* **1.** strip, *esp.* of leather —*vt.* **2.** fasten, beat with strap (**-pp-**) —**ˈstrapping** *a.* tall and well-made —**ˈstraphanger** *n.* in bus, train, one who has to stand, steadying himself with strap provided for this

strata (ˈstrɑːtə) *n., pl. of* STRATUM

stratagem (ˈstrætıdʒəm) *n.* plan, trick —**strategic(al)** (strəˈtiːdʒık(ᵊl)) *a.* —**straˈtegically** *adv.* —**ˈstrategist** *n.* —**ˈstrategy** *n.* **1.** art of war **2.** overall plan

strathspey (stræθˈspeı) *n.* type of Scottish dance with gliding steps

stratosphere (ˈstrætəsfıə) *n.* upper part of the atmosphere, approx. 11 kms above earth's surface

stratum (ˈstrɑːtəm) *n.* **1.** layer, *esp.* of rock **2.** class in society (*pl.* **-s, -ta**) —**stratifiˈcation** *n.* —**ˈstratify** *v.* form, deposit in layers (**-ified, -ifying**)

stratus (ˈstreıtəs) *n.* grey layer cloud (*pl.* **-ti** (-taı))

straw (strɔː) *n.* **1.** stalks of grain **2.** single stalk **3.** long, narrow tube used to suck up liquid —**strawberry** (ˈstrɔːbərı, -brı) *n.* **1.** creeping plant producing red, juicy fruit **2.** the fruit —**strawberry blonde** (of hair) reddish blonde —**strawberry mark** soft vascular red birthmark

stray (streı) *vi.* **1.** wander **2.** digress **3.** get lost —*a.* **4.** strayed **5.** occasional, scattered —*n.* **6.** stray animal

streak (striːk) *n.* **1.** long line or band **2.** element, trace —*vt.* **3.** mark with streaks —*vi.* **4.** move fast **5.** *inf.* run naked in public —**ˈstreaky** *a.* **1.** having streaks **2.** striped —**streaky bacon** bacon having alternating strips of fat and lean meat

stream (striːm) *n.* **1.** flowing body of water or other liquid **2.** steady flow **3.** class, division of schoolchildren grouped together because of similar ability —*vi.* **4.** flow **5.** run with liquid **6.** float, wave in the air —*vt.* **7.** group (schoolchildren) in streams —**ˈstreamer** *n.* **1.** (paper) ribbon **2.** narrow flag —**stream of consciousness 1.** *Psychol.* continuous flow of ideas, feelings *etc.* forming content of individual's consciousness **2.** literary technique that reveals flow of thoughts and feelings of characters through long passages of soliloquy

THESAURUS

tauten, tighten **2.** drive, exert, fatigue, injure, overexert, overtax, overwork, pull, push to the limit, sprain, tax, tear, tire, twist, weaken, wrench **3.** endeavour, go all out for (*Inf.*), labour, make a supreme effort, strive, struggle **4.** filter, percolate, purify, riddle, screen, seep, separate, sieve, sift ~*n.* **5.** effort, exertion, force, injury, pull, sprain, struggle, tautness, tension, tensity (*Rare*), wrench **6.** anxiety, burden, pressure, stress, tension **7.** *Often plural* air, lay, measure (*Poetic*), melody, song, theme, tune

strain[2] *n.* **1.** ancestry, blood, breed, descent, extraction, family, lineage, pedigree, race, stock **2.** streak, suggestion, suspicion, tendency, trace, trait

strained artificial, awkward, constrained, difficult, embarrassed, false, forced, laboured, put on, self-conscious, stiff, tense, uncomfortable, uneasy, unnatural, unrelaxed

strait-laced austere, moralistic, narrow, narrow-minded, of the old school, old-maidish (*Inf.*), overscrupulous, prim, proper, prudish, puritanical, strict, Victorian

straits *n.* **1.** crisis, difficulty, dilemma, distress, embarrassment, emergency, extremity, hardship, hole (*Sl.*), mess, pass, perplexity, plight, predicament, pretty *or* fine kettle of fish (*Inf.*) **2.** *Sometimes singular* channel, narrows, sound

strand *n.* fibre, filament, length, lock, rope, string, thread, tress, twist

strange 1. abnormal, astonishing, bizarre, curious, eccentric, exceptional, extraordinary, fantastic, funny, irregular, marvellous, mystifying, odd, out-of-the-way, peculiar, perplexing, queer, rare, remarkable, singular, unaccountable, uncanny, uncommon, unheard of, weird, wonderful **2.** alien, exotic, foreign, new, novel, outside one's experience, remote, unexplored, unfamiliar, unknown, untried **3.** *Often with* **to** a stranger to, ignorant of, inexperienced, new to, unaccustomed, unpractised, unseasoned, unused, unversed in

stranger alien, foreigner, guest, incomer, new arrival, newcomer, outlander, unknown, visitor

strangle 1. asphyxiate, choke, garrotte, smother, strangulate, suffocate, throttle **2.** gag (*Inf.*), inhibit, repress, stifle, suppress

strap *n.* **1.** belt, leash, strip, thong, tie ~*v.* **2.** bind, buckle, fasten, lash, secure, tie, truss **3.** beat, belt, flog, lash, scourge, whip

stratagem artifice, device, dodge, feint, intrigue, manoeuvre, plan, plot, ploy, ruse, scheme, subterfuge, trick, wile

strategic calculated, deliberate, diplomatic, planned, politic

strategy approach, grand design, manoeuvring, plan, planning, policy, procedure, programme, scheme

stray *v.* **1.** deviate, digress, diverge, get off the point, get sidetracked, go off at a tangent, ramble **2.** be abandoned *or* lost, drift, err, get lost, go astray, lose one's way, meander, range, roam, rove, straggle, wander ~*adj.* **3.** abandoned, homeless, lost, roaming, strayed, vagrant **4.** accidental, chance, erratic, freak, occasional, odd, random, scattered

streak *n.* **1.** band, layer, line, slash, smear, strip, stripe, stroke, vein **2.** dash, element, strain, touch, trace, vein ~*v.* **3.** band, daub, fleck, slash, smear, striate, stripe **4.** dart, flash, fly, hurtle, move like greased lightning (*Inf.*), speed, sprint, sweep, tear, whistle, whiz (*Inf.*), zoom

streamlined (ˈstriːmlaɪnd) *a.* (of car, plane *etc.*) built so as to offer least resistance to air

street (striːt) *n.* road in town or village, usu. lined with houses —**street credibility** a command of style, knowledge *etc.* associated with urban counterculture (*also* **street cred**) —**street-credible** *a.* —**ˈstreet-walker** *n.* prostitute —**ˈstreetwise** *a.* adept at surviving in urban, poor and oft. criminal environment

strength (strɛŋθ) *n.* **1.** quality of being strong **2.** power **3.** capacity for exertion or endurance **4.** vehemence **5.** force **6.** full or necessary number of people —**ˈstrengthen** *v.* make or become stronger —**on the strength of 1.** relying on **2.** because of

strenuous (ˈstrɛnjʊəs) *a.* **1.** energetic **2.** earnest —**ˈstrenuously** *adv.*

streptomycin (strɛptəʊˈmaɪsɪn) *n.* antibiotic drug

stress (strɛs) *n.* **1.** emphasis **2.** strain **3.** impelling force **4.** effort **5.** tension —*vt.* **6.** emphasize **7.** accent **8.** put mechanical stress on

stretch (strɛtʃ) *vt.* **1.** extend **2.** exert to utmost **3.** tighten, pull out **4.** reach out —*vi.* **5.** reach **6.** have elasticity —*n.* **7.** stretching, being stretched, expanse **8.** spell —**ˈstretcher** *n.* **1.** person, thing that stretches **2.** appliance on which ill, wounded or dead person is carried

strew (struː) *vt.* scatter over surface, spread (**strewed** *pt.*, **strewn** *or* **strewed** *pp.*, **ˈstrewing** *pr.p.*)

strewth (struːθ) *interj.* expression of surprise or dismay

stria (ˈstraɪə) *n.* small channel or threadlike line in surface of shell or other object (*pl.* **striae** (ˈstraɪiː)) —**striate** (ˈstraɪɪt) *a.* **1.** streaked, furrowed, grooved (*also* **striˈated**) —*vt.* (ˈstraɪeɪt) **2.** mark with streaks **3.** score —**striˈation** *n.*

stricken (ˈstrɪkən) *a.* **1.** seriously affected by disease, grief, famine **2.** afflicted —*v.* **3.** *pp. of* STRIKE

strict (strɪkt) *a.* **1.** stern, not lax or indulgent **2.** defined **3.** without exception

stricture (ˈstrɪktʃə) *n.* **1.** critical remark **2.** constriction

stride (straɪd) *vi.* **1.** walk with long steps (**strode, stridden** (ˈstrɪdᵊn), **ˈstriding**) —*n.* **2.** single step **3.** its length **4.** regular pace

strident (ˈstraɪdᵊnt) *a.* **1.** harsh in tone **2.** loud **3.** urgent

strife (straɪf) *n.* **1.** conflict **2.** quarrelling

strike (straɪk) *v.* **1.** hit (against) **2.** ignite **3.** (of snake) bite **4.** (of plants) (cause to) take root **5.** attack **6.** hook (fish) **7.** sound (time) as bell in clock *etc.* —*vt.* **8.** affect **9.** arrive at, come upon **10.** enter mind of **11.** discover (gold, oil *etc.*) **12.** dismantle, remove **13.** make (coin) —*vi.* **14.** cease work as protest or to make demands (**struck** *pt.*, **ˈstricken, struck** *pp.*, **ˈstriking** *pr.p.*) —*n.* **15.** act of striking —**ˈstriker** *n.* —**ˈstriking** *a.* noteworthy, impressive —**ˈstrikebreaker** *n.* person who

THESAURUS

stream 1. *n.* beck, brook, burn, course, creek (*U.S.*), current, drift, flow, freshet, outpouring, rill, river, rivulet, run, rush, surge, tide, torrent, tributary **2.** *v.* cascade, course, emit, flood, flow, glide, gush, issue, pour, run, shed, spill, spout

streamlined efficient, modernized, organized, rationalized, sleek, slick, smooth, smooth-running, time-saving, well-run

street avenue, boulevard, lane, road, roadway, row, terrace, thoroughfare

strength 1. backbone, brawn, brawniness, courage, firmness, fortitude, health, lustiness, might, muscle, robustness, sinew, stamina, stoutness, sturdiness, toughness **2.** cogency, concentration, effectiveness, efficacy, energy, force, intensity, potency, power, resolution, spirit, vehemence, vigour, virtue (*Archaic*)

strengthen 1. animate, brace up, consolidate, encourage, fortify, give new energy to, harden, hearten, invigorate, nerve, nourish, rejuvenate, restore, stiffen, toughen **2.** bolster, brace, build up, buttress, confirm, corroborate, enhance, establish, give a boost to, harden, heighten, increase, intensify, justify, reinforce, steel, substantiate, support

strenuous active, bold, determined, eager, earnest, energetic, persistent, resolute, spirited, strong, tireless, vigorous, zealous

stress *n.* **1.** emphasis, force, importance, significance, urgency, weight **2.** anxiety, burden, hassle (*Inf.*), nervous tension, oppression, pressure, strain, tautness, tension, trauma, worry **3.** accent, accentuation, beat, emphasis ~*v.* **4.** accent, accentuate, belabour, dwell on, emphasize, harp on, lay emphasis upon, point up, repeat, rub in, underline, underscore

stretch *v.* **1.** cover, extend, put forth, reach, spread, unfold, unroll **2.** distend, draw out, elongate, expand, inflate, lengthen, pull, pull out of shape, rack, strain, swell, tighten ~*n.* **3.** area, distance, expanse, extent, spread, sweep, tract **4.** bit, period, run, space, spell, stint, term, time

strict 1. austere, authoritarian, firm, harsh, no-nonsense, rigid, rigorous, severe, stern, stringent **2.** accurate, close, defined, exact, faithful, meticulous, particular, precise, religious, scrupulous, true **3.** absolute, complete, perfect, total, utter

strident clamorous, clashing, discordant, grating, harsh, jangling, jarring, rasping, raucous, screeching, shrill, stridulant, stridulous, unmusical, vociferous

strife animosity, battle, bickering, clash, clashes, combat, conflict, contention, contest, controversy, discord, dissension, friction, quarrel, rivalry, row, squabbling, struggle, warfare, wrangling

strike *v.* **1.** bang, beat, box, buffet, chastise, clobber (*Sl.*), clout (*Inf.*), clump (*Sl.*), cuff, hammer, hit, knock, lay a finger on (*Inf.*), pound, punish, slap, smack, smite, sock (*Sl.*), thump, wallop (*Inf.*) **2.** be in collision with, bump into, clash, collide with, come into contact with, dash, hit, knock into, run into, smash into, touch **3.** affect, come to, come to the mind of, dawn on *or* upon, hit, impress, make an impact on, occur to, reach, register (*Inf.*), seem **4.** *Sometimes with* **upon** come upon *or* across, discover, encounter, find, happen *or* chance upon, hit upon, light upon, reach, stumble upon *or* across, turn up, uncover, unearth **5.** affect, assail, assault, attack, deal a blow to, devastate, fall upon, hit, invade, set upon, smite **6.** achieve, arrange, arrive at, attain, effect, reach **7.** down tools, mutiny, revolt, walk out

striking astonishing, conspicuous, dazzling, extraordinary, forcible, impressive, memorable, noteworthy, noticeable, out of the ordinary, outstanding, stunning (*Inf.*), wonderful

tries to make strike ineffectual by working —ˈ**strikebreaking** *n./a.* —**strike pay** allowance paid by trade union to members on strike —**strike off** remove

Strine (straɪn) *n.* humorous transliteration of Australian pronunciation

string (strɪŋ) *n.* **1.** (length of) thin cord or other material **2.** strand, row **3.** series **4.** fibre in plants —*pl.* **5.** conditions —*vt.* **6.** provide with, thread on string **7.** form in line, series (**strung,** ˈ**stringing**) —**stringed** *a.* (of musical instruments) furnished with strings —ˈ**stringer** *n.* **1.** *Archit.* horizontal timber beam used for structural purposes **2.** *Naut.* longitudinal structural brace for strengthening hull of vessel **3.** part-time journalist retained by newspaper to cover particular area —ˈ**stringy** *a.* **1.** like string **2.** fibrous —**string course** *Archit.* ornamental projecting band or continuous moulding along wall (*also* ˈ**cordon**) —**string vest** undergarment made from large-meshed material

stringent (ˈstrɪndʒənt) *a.* strict, rigid, binding —ˈ**stringency** *n.* severity —ˈ**stringently** *adv.*

strip (strɪp) *vt.* **1.** lay bare, take covering off **2.** dismantle **3.** deprive —*vi.* **4.** undress (**-pp-**) —*n.* **5.** long, narrow piece **6.** act of undressing or performing striptease —ˈ**stripper** *n.* —**strip cartoon** *see* **comic strip** *at* COMIC —**strip lighting** electric lighting by means of long glass tubes that are fluorescent lamps —ˈ**striptease** *n.* cabaret or theatre act in which person undresses

stripe (straɪp) *n.* **1.** narrow mark, band **2.** chevron as symbol of military rank —ˈ**stripy** *a.*

stripling (ˈstrɪplɪŋ) *n.* youth

strive (straɪv) *vi.* try hard, struggle, contend (**strove, striven** (ˈstrɪvᵊn), ˈ**striving**)

strobe (strəʊb) *n.* apparatus which produces high-intensity flashing light

stroboscope (ˈstrəʊbəskəʊp) *n.* **1.** instrument producing intense flashing light **2.** similar device synchronized with shutter of camera so that series of still photographs can be taken of moving object —**strobo**ˈ**scopic(al)** *a.*

strode (strəʊd) *pt. of* STRIDE

stroke (strəʊk) *n.* **1.** blow **2.** sudden action, occurrence **3.** apoplexy **4.** mark of pen, pencil, brush *etc.* **5.** chime of clock **6.** completed movement in series **7.** act, manner of striking (ball *etc.*) **8.** style, method of swimming **9.** rower sitting nearest stern setting the rate of rowing **10.** act of stroking —*vt.* **11.** set stroke for (rowing crew) **12.** pass hand lightly over

stroll (strəʊl) *vi.* **1.** walk in leisurely or idle manner —*n.* **2.** leisurely walk

strong (strɒŋ) *a.* **1.** powerful **2.** robust **3.** healthy **4.** difficult to break **5.** noticeable **6.** intense **7.** emphatic **8.** not diluted **9.** having a certain number —ˈ**strongly** *adv.* —**strong-arm** *inf. a.* **1.** of or involving physical force or violence —*vt.* **2.** show violence towards —ˈ**strongbox** *n.* box or safe in which valuables are locked for safety —**strong drink** alcoholic drink —ˈ**stronghold** *n.* fortress —**strong language** swearing —ˈ**strongroom** *n.* specially designed room for storing valuables

strontium (ˈstrɒntɪəm) *n.* silvery-white chemical element —**strontium 90** radioactive isotope of strontium present in fallout of nuclear explosions

strop (strɒp) *n.* **1.** leather for sharpening razors —*vt.* **2.** sharpen on strop (**-pp-**) —ˈ**stroppy** *a. sl.* angry, awkward

strophe (ˈstrəʊfɪ) *n.* division of ode —**strophic** (ˈstrɒfɪk, ˈstrəʊ-) *a.*

strove (strəʊv) *pt. of* STRIVE

struck (strʌk) *pt./pp. of* STRIKE

structure (ˈstrʌktʃə) *n.* **1.** (arrangement of parts in)

THESAURUS

string *n.* **1.** cord, fibre, twine **2.** chain, file, line, procession, queue, row, sequence, series, strand, succession ~*v.* **3.** festoon, hang, link, loop, sling, stretch, suspend, thread

stringent binding, demanding, exacting, inflexible, rigid, rigorous, severe, strict, tight, tough

strings *Fig.* catches (*Inf.*), complications, conditions, obligations, prerequisites, provisos, qualifications, requirements, stipulations

strip *v.* **1.** bare, denude, deprive, despoil, dismantle, divest, empty, gut, lay bare, loot, peel, pillage, plunder, ransack, rob, sack, skin, spoil **2.** disrobe, unclothe, uncover, undress ~*n.* **3.** band, belt, bit, fillet, piece, ribbon, shred, slip, swathe, tongue

stripling adolescent, boy, fledgling, hobbledehoy (*Archaic*), lad, shaver (*Inf.*), young fellow, youngster, youth

strive attempt, compete, contend, do all one can, do one's best, do one's utmost, endeavour, exert oneself, fight, go all out (*Inf.*), labour, leave no stone unturned, make every effort, strain, struggle, toil, try, try hard

stroke *n.* **1.** accomplishment, achievement, blow, feat, flourish, hit, knock, move, movement, pat, rap, thump **2.** apoplexy, attack, collapse, fit, seizure, shock ~*v.* **3.** caress, fondle, pat, pet, rub

stroll 1. *v.* amble, make one's way, mooch (*Inf.*), mosey (*Inf.*), promenade, ramble, saunter, stooge (*Inf.*), stretch one's legs, take a turn, toddle, wander **2.** *n.* airing, breath of air, constitutional, excursion, promenade, ramble, turn, walk

strong 1. athletic, beefy (*Inf.*), brawny, burly, capable, hale, hardy, healthy, Herculean, lusty, muscular, powerful, robust, sinewy, sound, stalwart, stout, strapping, sturdy, tough, virile **2.** acute, dedicated, deep, deep-rooted, eager, fervent, fervid, fierce, firm, intense, keen, severe, staunch, vehement, violent, zealous **3.** clear, clear-cut, cogent, compelling, convincing, distinct, effective, emphatic, formidable, great, marked, overpowering, persuasive, potent, powerful, redoubtable, sound, telling, trenchant, unmistakable, urgent, weighty, well-established, well-founded **4.** durable, hard-wearing, heavy-duty, on a firm foundation, reinforced, sturdy, substantial, well-armed, well-built, well-protected **5.** bold, bright, brilliant, dazzling, glaring, intense, loud, stark **6.** biting, concentrated, heady, highly-flavoured, highly-seasoned, hot, intoxicating, piquant, pungent, pure, sharp, spicy, undiluted

stronghold bastion, bulwark, castle, citadel, fastness, fort, fortress, keep, refuge

structure *n.* **1.** arrangement, configuration, conformation, construction, design, fabric, form, formation, interrelation of parts, make, make-up, organization **2.** building, construction, edifice, erection, pile ~*v.* **3.** arrange, assemble, build up, design, organize, put together, shape

construction, building *etc.* **2.** form **3.** organization *—vt.* **4.** give structure to **—ˈstructural** *a.*

strudel (ˈstruːdᵊl) *n.* thin sheet of dough usu. filled with apple and baked

struggle (ˈstrʌgᵊl) *vi.* **1.** contend **2.** fight **3.** proceed, work, move with difficulty and effort *—n.* **4.** act of struggling

strum (strʌm) *v.* strike strings of (guitar *etc.*) (**-mm-**)

strumpet (ˈstrʌmpɪt) *n. obs.* promiscuous woman

strung (strʌŋ) *pt./pp. of* STRING

strut (strʌt) *vi.* **1.** walk affectedly or pompously (**-tt-**) *—n.* **2.** brace **3.** rigid support, usu. set obliquely **4.** strutting gait

strychnine (ˈstrɪkniːn) *n.* poison obtained from nux vomica seeds **—ˈstrychnic** *a.*

stub (stʌb) *n.* **1.** remnant of anything, *eg* pencil, cigarette *etc.* **2.** counterfoil of cheque *etc.* *—vt.* **3.** strike (toes) against fixed object **4.** extinguish by pressing against surface (**-bb-**) **—ˈstubby** *a.* short, broad

stubble (ˈstʌbᵊl) *n.* **1.** stumps of cut grain after reaping **2.** short growth of beard

stubborn (ˈstʌbᵊn) *a.* unyielding, obstinate

stucco (ˈstʌkəʊ) *n.* plaster (*pl.* **-s, -es**) **—ˈstuccoed** *a.*

stuck (stʌk) *pt./pp. of* STICK **—stuck-up** *a. inf.* conceited; snobbish

stud[1] (stʌd) *n.* **1.** nail with large head **2.** removable double-headed button **3.** vertical wall support *—vt.* **4.** set with studs (**-dd-**)

stud[2] (stʌd) *n.* set of animals, *esp.* horses, kept for breeding **—ˈstudbook** *n.* book giving pedigree of noted or thoroughbred animals, *esp.* horses **—stud farm**

studio (ˈstjuːdɪəʊ) *n.* **1.** workroom of artist, photographer *etc.* **2.** building, room where film, television or radio shows are made, broadcast (*pl.* **-s**) **—studio couch** upholstered couch that can be converted into double bed

study (ˈstʌdɪ) *vi.* **1.** be engaged in learning *—vt.* **2.** make study of **3.** try constantly to do **4.** consider **5.** scrutinize (**ˈstudied, ˈstudying**) *—n.* **6.** effort to acquire knowledge **7.** subject of this **8.** scrutiny **9.** room to study in **10.** book, report *etc.* produced as result of study **11.** sketch **—student** (ˈstjuːdᵊnt) *n.* one who studies, *esp.* at university *etc.* **—ˈstudied** *a.* carefully designed, premeditated **—studious** (ˈstjuːdɪəs) *a.* **1.** fond of study **2.** thoughtful **3.** painstaking **4.** deliberate

stuff (stʌf) *vi.* **1.** eat (large amount) *—vt.* **2.** pack, cram, fill (completely) **3.** fill with seasoned mixture **4.** fill (animal's skin) with material to preserve lifelike form *—n.* **5.** material, fabric **6.** any substance **—ˈstuffing** *n.* material for stuffing, *esp.* seasoned mixture for inserting in poultry *etc.* before cooking **—ˈstuffy** *a.* **1.** lacking fresh air **2.** *inf.* dull, conventional **—do your stuff** *inf.* do what is required or expected of you

stultify (ˈstʌltɪfaɪ) *vt.* make ineffectual (**-ified, -ifying**) **—stultifiˈcation** *n.*

stumble (ˈstʌmbᵊl) *vi.* **1.** trip and nearly fall **2.** falter *—n.* **3.** act of stumbling **—stumbling block** obstacle

stump (stʌmp) *n.* **1.** remnant of tree, tooth *etc.* when main part has been cut away **2.** one of uprights of wicket in cricket *—vt.* **3.** confuse, puzzle **4.** break wicket of (batsman out of his ground in playing ball)

THESAURUS

struggle *v.* **1.** exert oneself, go all out (*Inf.*), labour, make every effort, strain, strive, toil, work, work like a Trojan ~*n.* **2.** effort, exertion, grind (*Inf.*), labour, long haul, pains, scramble, toil, work ~*v.* **3.** battle, compete, contend, fight, grapple, lock horns, scuffle, wrestle ~*n.* **4.** battle, brush, clash, combat, conflict, contest, encounter, hostilities, skirmish, strife, tussle

strut *v.* parade, peacock, prance, stalk, swagger

stub *n.* butt, counterfoil, dog-end (*Inf.*), end, fag end (*Inf.*), remnant, stump, tail, tail end

stubborn bull-headed, contumacious, cross-grained, dogged, dour, fixed, headstrong, inflexible, intractable, mulish, obdurate, obstinate, opinionated, persistent, pig-headed, recalcitrant, refractory, self-willed, stiff-necked, tenacious, unbending, unmanageable, unshakable, unyielding, wilful

stuck cemented, fast, fastened, firm, fixed, glued, joined

student apprentice, disciple, learner, observer, pupil, scholar, undergraduate

studied calculated, conscious, deliberate, intentional, planned, premeditated, purposeful, well-considered, wilful

studio atelier, workshop

studious academic, assiduous, attentive, bookish, careful, diligent, eager, earnest, hard-working, intellectual, meditative, reflective, scholarly, sedulous, serious, thoughtful

study *v.* **1.** apply oneself (to), bone up (on) (*Inf.*), burn the midnight oil, cogitate, con (*Archaic*), consider, contemplate, cram (*Inf.*), examine, go into, hammer away at, learn, lucubrate (*Rare*), meditate, mug up (*Brit. sl.*), ponder, pore over, read, read up, swot (up) (*Brit. inf.*) **2.** analyse, deliberate, examine, investigate, look into, peruse, research, scrutinize, survey ~*n.* **3.** academic work, application, book work, cramming (*Inf.*), learning, lessons, reading, research, school work, swotting (*Brit. inf.*), thought **4.** analysis, attention, cogitation, consideration, contemplation, examination, inquiry, inspection, investigation, review, scrutiny, survey

stuff *v.* **1.** compress, cram, crowd, fill, force, jam, load, pack, pad, push, ram, shove, squeeze, stow, wedge **2.** gobble, gorge, gormandize, guzzle, make a pig of oneself (*Inf.*), overindulge, sate, satiate ~*n.* **3.** cloth, fabric, material, raw material, textile **4.** essence, matter, pith, quintessence, staple, substance

stuffing 1. filler, kapok, packing, quilting, wadding **2.** farce, farcemeat, forcemeat

stuffy 1. airless, close, fetid, frowsty, fuggy, heavy, muggy, oppressive, stale, stifling, suffocating, sultry, unventilated **2.** conventional, deadly, dreary, dull, fusty, humourless, musty, old-fashioned, old-fogyish, pompous, priggish, prim, prim and proper, staid, stilted, stodgy, strait-laced, uninteresting

stumble 1. blunder about, come a cropper (*Inf.*), fall, falter, flounder, hesitate, lose one's balance, lurch, reel, slip, stagger, trip **2.** falter, fluff (*Inf.*), stammer, stutter

stump *v.* **1.** baffle, bewilder, bring (someone) up short, confound, confuse, dumbfound, flummox, foil, mystify, outwit, perplex, puzzle, stop, stymie **2.** clomp, clump, lumber, plod, stamp, stomp (*Inf.*), trudge

—*vi.* **5.** walk heavily, noisily —**'stumpy** *a.* short and thickset

stun (stʌn) *vt.* **1.** knock senseless **2.** amaze (**-nn-**) —**'stunner** *n. inf.* person or thing of great beauty, quality *etc.* —**'stunning** *a.*

stung (stʌŋ) *pt./pp. of* STING

stunk (stʌŋk) *pp. of* STINK

stunt[1] (stʌnt) *vt.* check growth of, dwarf —**'stunted** *a.* **1.** underdeveloped **2.** undersized

stunt[2] (stʌnt) *n.* **1.** feat of dexterity or daring **2.** anything spectacular, unusual, done to gain publicity —**stunt man** professional acrobat substituted for actor when dangerous scenes are filmed

stupefy ('stju:pɪfaɪ) *vt.* **1.** make insensitive, lethargic **2.** astound (**-efied, -efying**) —**stupe'faction** *n.*

stupendous (stju:'pɛndəs) *a.* **1.** astonishing, amazing **2.** huge

stupid ('stju:pɪd) *a.* **1.** slow-witted **2.** silly **3.** dazed or stupefied

stupor ('stju:pə) *n.* **1.** dazed state **2.** insensibility

sturdy ('stɜ:dɪ) *a.* **1.** robust **2.** strongly built **3.** vigorous —**'sturdily** *adv.* —**'sturdiness** *n.*

sturgeon ('stɜ:dʒən) *n.* fish yielding caviar and isinglass

stutter ('stʌtə) *v.* **1.** speak (word *etc.*) with difficulty **2.** stammer —*n.* **3.** act or habit of stuttering

sty[1] (staɪ) *n.* **1.** place in which pigs are kept **2.** hovel, dirty place

sty[2] *or* **stye** (staɪ) *n.* inflammation on edge of eyelid

Stygian ('stɪdʒɪən) *a.* **1.** of river Styx in Hades **2.** gloomy **3.** infernal

style (staɪl) *n.* **1.** manner of writing, doing *etc.* **2.** designation **3.** sort **4.** elegance, refinement **5.** superior manner, quality **6.** design —*vt.* **7.** shape, design **8.** adapt **9.** designate —**'stylish** *a.* fashionable —**'stylishly** *adv.* —**'stylist** *n.* **1.** one cultivating style in literary or other execution **2.** designer **3.** hairdresser —**sty'listic** *a.* —**'stylize** *or* **-ise** *vt.* give conventional stylistic form to

stylus ('staɪləs) *n.* **1.** writing instrument **2.** in record-player, tiny point running in groove of record (*pl.* **-li** (-laɪ), **-es**)

stymie *or* **stymy** ('staɪmɪ) *vt.* hinder, thwart

styptic ('stɪptɪk) *a./n.* (designating) a substance that stops bleeding

styrene ('staɪri:n) *n.* colourless liquid used in making synthetic rubber, plastics

suave (swɑ:v) *a.* smoothly polite, affable, bland —**'suavity** *n.*

sub (sʌb) *n.* **1.** subeditor **2.** submarine **3.** subscription **4.** substitute **5.** *inf.* advance payment of wages, salary —*vi.* **6.** *inf.* serve as substitute —*v.* **7.** *inf.* grant or receive (advance payment) —*vt.* **8.** subedit (**-bb-**)

sub- (*comb. form*) under, less than, in lower position, subordinate, forming subdivision, as in *subaqua, subeditor, subheading, subnormal, subsoil.* Such words are not given here where the meaning may be easily inferred from the simple word

subaltern ('sʌbᵊltən) *n.* army officer below rank of captain

subcommittee (sʌbkə'mɪtɪ) *n.* section of committee functioning separately from main body

subconscious (sʌb'kɒnʃəs) *a.* **1.** acting, existing without one's awareness —*n.* **2.** *Psychol.* that part of human mind unknown, or only partly known, to possessor

THESAURUS

stun *Fig.* amaze, astonish, astound, bewilder, confound, confuse, daze, dumbfound, flabbergast (*Inf.*), hit (someone) like a ton of bricks (*Inf.*), knock out, knock (someone) for six (*Inf.*), overcome, overpower, shock, stagger, strike (someone) dumb (*Inf.*), stupefy, take (someone's) breath away

stunt *n.* act, deed, exploit, feat, feature, gest (*Archaic*), *tour de force*, trick

stunted diminutive, dwarfed, dwarfish, little, small, tiny, underdeveloped, undersized

stupefaction amazement, astonishment, awe, wonder, wonderment

stupefy amaze, astound, bewilder, confound, daze, dumbfound, knock senseless, numb, shock, stagger, stun

stupendous amazing, astonishing, astounding, breathtaking, colossal, enormous, fabulous (*Inf.*), fantastic (*Inf.*), gigantic, huge, marvellous, mind-blowing (*Sl.*), mind-boggling (*Inf.*), out of this world (*Inf.*), overwhelming, phenomenal, prodigious, staggering, stunning (*Inf.*), superb, surpassing belief, surprising, tremendous (*Inf.*), vast, wonderful

stupid **1.** Boeotian, brainless, cretinous, deficient, dense, dim, doltish, dopey (*Sl.*), dozy (*Brit. inf.*), dull, dumb (*Inf., chiefly U.S.*), foolish, gullible, half-witted, moronic, naive, obtuse, simple, simple-minded, slow, slow on the uptake (*Inf.*), slow-witted, sluggish, stolid, thick, thickheaded, unintelligent, witless, woodenheaded (*Inf.*) **2.** crackbrained, futile, half-baked (*Inf.*), idiotic, ill-advised, imbecilic, inane, indiscreet, irrelevant, irresponsible, laughable, ludicrous, meaningless, mindless, nonsensical, pointless, puerile, rash, senseless, short-sighted, silly, trivial, unintelligent, unthinking **3.** dazed, groggy, in a daze, insensate, punch-drunk, semiconscious, senseless, stunned, stupefied

sturdy athletic, brawny, built to last, determined, durable, firm, flourishing, hardy, hearty, lusty, muscular, powerful, resolute, robust, secure, solid, stalwart, staunch, steadfast, stouthearted, substantial, vigorous, well-built, well-made

stutter *v.* falter, hesitate, speak haltingly, splutter, stammer, stumble

style *n.* **1.** cut, design, form, hand, manner, technique **2.** design, fashion, mode, rage, trend, vogue **3.** approach, custom, manner, method, mode, way **4.** *bon ton*, chic, cosmopolitanism, dash, dressiness (*Inf.*), élan, elegance, fashionableness, flair, grace, panache, polish, refinement, savoir-faire, smartness, sophistication, stylishness, taste, urbanity **5.** affluence, comfort, ease, elegance, gracious living, grandeur, luxury **6.** appearance, category, characteristic, designation, genre, kind, pattern, sort, spirit, strain, tenor, tone, type, variety **7.** diction, expression, mode of expression, phraseology, phrasing, treatment, turn of phrase, vein, wording ~*v.* **8.** adapt, arrange, cut, design, dress, fashion, shape, tailor **9.** address, call, christen, denominate, designate, dub, entitle, label, name, term

stylish à la mode, chic, classy (*Sl.*), dapper, dressy

subcontinent (sʌbˈkɒntɪnənt) *n.* large land mass that is distinct part of continent —**subcontiˈnental** *a.*

subcontract (sʌbˈkɒntrækt) *n.* **1.** subordinate contract under which supply of materials or labour is let out to someone other than party to main contract —*vi.* (sʌbkənˈtrækt) **2.** (*oft. with* for) enter into subcontract —*vt.* (sʌbkənˈtrækt) **3.** let out (work) on subcontract —**subconˈtractor** *n.*

subculture (ˈsʌbkʌltʃə) *n.* subdivision of national culture with distinct integrated network of behaviour, beliefs and attitudes

subcutaneous (sʌbkjuːˈteɪnɪəs) *a.* under the skin

subdivide (sʌbdɪˈvaɪd, ˈsʌbdɪvaɪd) *vt.* divide again —**subdivision** (ˈsʌbdɪvɪʒən) *n.*

subdominant (sʌbˈdɒmɪnənt) *Mus. n.* **1.** fourth degree of major or minor scale **2.** key or chord based on this —*a.* **3.** of the subdominant

subdue (səbˈdjuː) *vt.* **1.** win control over; conquer **2.** overcome **3.** render less intense or less conspicuous (**-ˈdued, -ˈduing**)

subfusc (ˈsʌbfʌsk) *a.* devoid of brightness; drab, dull or dark

subject (ˈsʌbdʒɪkt) *n.* **1.** theme, topic **2.** that about which something is predicated **3.** conscious self **4.** one under power of another —*a.* **5.** owing allegiance **6.** subordinate **7.** dependent **8.** liable —*vt.* (səbˈdʒɛkt) **9.** cause to undergo **10.** make liable **11.** subdue —**subˈjection** *n.* act of bringing, or state of being, under control —**subˈjective** *a.* **1.** based on personal feelings, not impartial **2.** of the self **3.** existing in the mind **4.** displaying artist's individuality —**subjecˈtivity** *n.*

subjoin (sʌbˈdʒɔɪn) *vt.* add to end of something written *etc.*

sub judice (ˈdʒuːdɪsɪ) *Lat.* under judicial consideration

subjugate (ˈsʌbdʒʊgeɪt) *vt.* **1.** force to submit **2.** conquer —**subjuˈgation** *n.* —**ˈsubjugator** *n.*

subjunctive (səbˈdʒʌŋktɪv) *Gram. n.* **1.** mood used mainly in subordinate clauses expressing wish, possibility —*a.* **2.** in, of that mood

sublease (ˈsʌbliːs) *n.* **1.** lease of property made by lessee of that property —*v.* (sʌbˈliːs) **2.** grant sublease of (property); sublet

sublet (sʌbˈlɛt) *vt.* (of tenant) let whole or part of what he has rented to another

sublieutenant (sʌbləˈtɛnənt) *n.* most junior commissioned officer in Royal Navy and certain other navies —**sublieuˈtenancy** *n.*

sublimate (ˈsʌblɪmeɪt) *vt.* **1.** *Psychol.* direct energy (*esp.* sexual) into activities considered more socially acceptable **2.** refine —*n.* **3.** *Chem.* material obtained when substance is sublimed —**subliˈmation** *n.*

sublime (səˈblaɪm) *a.* **1.** elevated **2.** eminent **3.** majestic **4.** inspiring awe **5.** exalted —*v.* **6.** *Chem.* (cause to) change from solid to vapour —**subˈlimely** *adv.* —**sublimity** (səˈblɪmɪtɪ) *or* **suˈblimeness** *n.*

subliminal (sʌbˈlɪmɪnᵊl) *a.* resulting from processes of which the individual is not aware

sub-machine-gun *n.* portable automatic gun with short barrel

submarine (ˈsʌbməriːn, sʌbməˈriːn) *n.* **1.** (war)ship which can travel (and attack from) below surface of sea and remain submerged for long periods —*a.* **2.** below surface of sea

submerge (səbˈmɜːdʒ) *or* **submerse** (səbˈmɜːs) *v.* place, go under water —**subˈmergence** *or* **subˈmersion** *n.* —**subˈmersible** *or* **subˈmergible** *a.* **1.** able to be submerged **2.** capable of operating under water *etc.* —*n.* **3.** warship designed to operate under water

submit (səbˈmɪt) *vt.* **1.** surrender **2.** put forward for consideration —*vi.* **3.** surrender **4.** defer (**-tt-**) —**subˈmission** *n.* —**subˈmissive** *a.* meek, obedient

subordinate (səˈbɔːdɪnɪt) *a.* **1.** of lower rank or less importance —*n.* **2.** inferior **3.** one under order of another —*vt.* (səˈbɔːdɪneɪt) **4.** make, treat as subordi-

THESAURUS

(*Inf.*), fashionable, in fashion, in vogue, modish, natty (*Inf.*), polished, smart, snappy, snazzy (*Inf.*), trendy (*Brit. inf.*), urbane, voguish, well turned-out

subconscious *adj.* hidden, inner, innermost, intuitive, latent, repressed, subliminal, suppressed

subdue 1. beat down, break, conquer, control, crush, defeat, discipline, gain ascendancy over, get the better of, get the upper hand over, get under control, humble, master, overcome, overpower, overrun, put down, quell, tame, trample, triumph over, vanquish **2.** check, control, mellow, moderate, quieten down, repress, soften, suppress, tone down

subdued dim, hushed, low-key, muted, quiet, shaded, sober, soft, subtle, toned down, unobtrusive

subject *n.* **1.** affair, business, field of enquiry *or* reference, issue, matter, object, point, question, subject matter, substance, theme, topic **2.** citizen, dependant, liegeman, national, subordinate, vassal ~*adj.* **3.** at the mercy of, disposed, exposed, in danger of, liable, open, prone, susceptible, vulnerable **4.** conditional, contingent, dependent **5.** answerable, bound by, captive, dependent, enslaved, inferior, obedient, satellite, subjugated, submissive, subordinate, subservient ~*v.* **6.** expose, lay open, make liable, put through, submit, treat

subjective biased, emotional, idiosyncratic, instinctive, intuitive, nonobjective, personal, prejudiced

sublime elevated, eminent, exalted, glorious, grand, great, high, imposing, lofty, magnificent, majestic, noble, transcendent

submerge deluge, dip, drown, duck, dunk, engulf, flood, immerse, inundate, overflow, overwhelm, plunge, sink, swamp

submission 1. acquiescence, assent, capitulation, giving in, surrender, yielding **2.** compliance, deference, docility, meekness, obedience, passivity, resignation, submissiveness, tractability, unassertiveness **3.** argument, contention, proposal **4.** entry, handing in, presentation, submitting, tendering

submissive abject, accommodating, acquiescent, amenable, biddable, bootlicking (*Inf.*), compliant, deferential, docile, dutiful, humble, ingratiating, lowly, malleable, meek, obedient, obeisant, obsequious, passive, patient, pliant, resigned, subdued, tractable, uncomplaining, unresisting, yielding

submit 1. accede, acquiesce, agree, bend, bow, capitulate, comply, defer, endure, give in, hoist the white flag, knuckle under, lay down arms, put up with (*Inf.*), resign oneself, stoop, succumb, surrender, throw in the sponge, toe the line, tolerate, yield **2.** commit, hand in, present, proffer, put forward, refer, table, tender **3.** advance, argue, assert, claim, contend, move, propose, propound, put, state, suggest, volunteer

nate —**sub'ordinately** *adv.* —**subordi'nation** *n.* —**subordinate clause** *Gram.* clause with adjectival, adverbial or nominal function, rather than one that functions as separate sentence in its own right

suborn (sə'bɔːn) *vt.* bribe to do evil —**subornation** (sʌbɔː'neɪʃən) *n.* —**sub'orner** *n.*

subplot ('sʌbplɒt) *n.* subordinate plot in novel, film *etc.*

subpoena (səb'piːnə) *n.* **1.** writ requiring attendance at court of law —*vt.* **2.** summon by such order (**-naed, -naing**)

sub rosa ('rəuzə) in secret

subscribe (səb'skraɪb) *vt.* **1.** pay, promise to pay (contribution) —*v.* **2.** write (one's name) at end of document —**sub'scriber** *n.* —**subscription** (səb'skrɪpʃən) *n.* **1.** subscribing **2.** money paid —**subscriber trunk dialling UK** service by which telephone subscribers can obtain trunk calls by dialling direct without aid of operator

subscript ('sʌbskrɪpt) *a.* **1.** *Print.* (of character) printed below base line —*n.* **2.** subscript character (*also* **sub'index**)

subsection (sʌb'sɛkʃən) *n.* division of a section

subsequent ('sʌbsɪkwənt) *a.* later, following or coming after in time —**'subsequence** *n.*

subservient (səb'sɜːvɪənt) *a.* submissive, servile —**sub'servience** *n.*

subset ('sʌbsɛt) *n.* mathematical set contained within larger set

subside (səb'saɪd) *vi.* **1.** abate, come to an end **2.** sink **3.** settle **4.** collapse —**subsidence** (səb'saɪdᵊns, 'sʌbsɪdᵊns) *n.*

subsidiary (səb'sɪdɪərɪ) *a.* **1.** supplementing **2.** secondary **3.** auxiliary —*n.* **4.** subsidiary person or thing

subsidize *or* **-ise** ('sʌbsɪdaɪz) *vt.* **1.** help financially **2.** pay grant to —**'subsidy** *n.* money granted

subsist (səb'sɪst) *vi.* exist, sustain life —**sub'sistence** *n.* **1.** the means by which one supports life **2.** livelihood

subsonic (sʌb'sɒnɪk) *a.* concerning speeds less than that of sound

substance ('sʌbstəns) *n.* **1.** matter **2.** particular kind of matter **3.** chief part, essence **4.** wealth —**sub'stantial** *a.* **1.** considerable **2.** of real value **3.** solid, big **4.** important **5.** really existing —**substanti'ality** *n.* —**sub'stantially** *adv.* —**sub'stantiate** *vt.* bring evidence for, confirm, prove —**substanti'ation** *n.* —**'substantive** *a.* **1.** having independent existence **2.** real, fixed —*n.* **3.** noun

substitute ('sʌbstɪtjuːt) *v.* **1.** put, serve in exchange (for) —*n.* **2.** thing, person put in place of another **3.** deputy —**substi'tution** *n.*

substratum (sʌb'strɑːtəm, -'streɪ-) *n.* **1.** that which is laid or spread under **2.** layer of earth lying under another **3.** basis (*pl.* **-ta** (-tə), **-s**)

subsume (səb'sjuːm) *vt.* incorporate (idea, case *etc.*) under comprehensive heading, classification

subtenant (sʌb'tɛnənt) *n.* person who rents property from tenant —**sub'tenancy** *n.*

subtend (səb'tɛnd) *vt.* *Geom.* be opposite to and delimit

THESAURUS

subordinate 1. *adj.* dependent, inferior, junior, lesser, lower, minor, secondary, subject, subservient **2.** *n.* aide, assistant, attendant, dependant, inferior, junior, second, subaltern, underling

subordination inferior *or* secondary status, inferiority, servitude, subjection, submission

subscribe chip in (*Inf.*), contribute, donate, give, offer, pay, pledge, promise

subscription annual payment, contribution, donation, dues, gift, membership fee, offering

subsequent after, consequent, consequential, ensuing, following, later, succeeding, successive

subside 1. abate, decrease, de-escalate, diminish, dwindle, ease, ebb, lessen, let up, level off, melt away, moderate, peter out, quieten, recede, slacken, wane **2.** cave in, collapse, decline, descend, drop, ebb, lower, settle, sink

subsidence 1. decline, descent, ebb, settlement, settling, sinking **2.** abatement, decrease, de-escalation, diminution, easing off, lessening, slackening

subsidiary aiding, ancillary, assistant, auxiliary, contributory, cooperative, helpful, lesser, minor, secondary, serviceable, subordinate, subservient, supplemental, supplementary, useful

subsidize finance, fund, promote, put up the money for, sponsor, support, underwrite

subsidy aid, allowance, assistance, contribution, financial aid, grant, help, subvention, support

subsist be, continue, eke out an existence, endure, exist, keep going, last, live, make ends meet, remain, stay alive, survive, sustain oneself

subsistence aliment, existence, food, keep, livelihood, living, maintenance, provision, rations, support, survival, sustenance, upkeep, victuals

substance 1. body, element, fabric, material, stuff, texture **2.** burden, essence, gist, gravamen (*Law*), import, main point, matter, meaning, pith, significance, subject, sum and substance, theme **3.** affluence, assets, estate, means, property, resources, wealth

substantial 1. ample, big, considerable, generous, goodly, important, large, significant, sizable, tidy (*Inf.*), worthwhile **2.** bulky, durable, firm, hefty, massive, solid, sound, stout, strong, sturdy, well-built **3.** actual, existent, material, positive, real, true, valid, weighty

substantially essentially, in essence, in essentials, in substance, in the main, largely, materially, to a large extent

substantiate affirm, attest to, authenticate, bear out, confirm, corroborate, establish, prove, support, validate, verify

substitute *v.* **1.** change, commute, exchange, interchange, replace, swap (*Inf.*), switch **2.** *With* **for** act for, be in place of, cover for, deputize, double for, fill in for, hold the fort for, relieve, stand in for, take over ~*n.* **3.** agent, depute (*Chiefly Scot.*), deputy, equivalent, expedient, locum, locum tenens, makeshift, proxy, relief, replacement, representative, reserve, stand-by, stopgap, sub, supply, surrogate, temp (*Inf.*), temporary

substitution change, exchange, interchange, replacement, swap (*Inf.*), switch

subterfuge artifice, deception, deviousness, dodge, duplicity, evasion, excuse, machination, manoeuvre, ploy, pretence, pretext, quibble, ruse, shift, stall, stratagem, trick

subterfuge (ˈsʌbtəfjuːdʒ) *n.* trick, lying excuse used to evade something

subterranean (sʌbtəˈreɪnɪən) *a.* underground (*also* **subterˈrestrial**)

subtitle (ˈsʌbtaɪtᵊl) *n.* **1.** secondary title of book **2.** (*oft. pl.*) written translation of film dialogue superimposed on film

subtle (ˈsʌtᵊl) *a.* **1.** not immediately obvious **2.** ingenious, acute **3.** crafty **4.** intricate **5.** delicate **6.** making fine distinctions —**ˈsubtlety** *n.* —**ˈsubtly** *adv.*

subtonic (sʌbˈtɒnɪk) *n. Mus.* seventh degree of major or minor scale

subtract (səbˈtrækt) *vt.* take away, deduct —**subˈtraction** *n.*

subtrahend (ˈsʌbtrəhɛnd) *n.* number to be subtracted from another number (**minuend**)

subtropical (sʌbˈtrɒpɪkᵊl) *a.* of regions bordering on the tropics

suburb (ˈsʌbɜːb) *n.* (*often pl.*) residential area on outskirts of city —**subˈurban** *a./n.* —**subˈurbia** *n.* **1.** suburbs or people living in them considered as an identifiable community or class in society **2.** life, customs *etc.* of suburban people

subvention (səbˈvɛnʃən) *n.* subsidy

subvert (səbˈvɜːt) *vt.* **1.** overthrow **2.** corrupt —**subˈversion** *n.* —**subˈversive** *a.*

subway (ˈsʌbweɪ) *n.* **1.** underground passage **2.** underground railway

succeed (səkˈsiːd) *vi.* **1.** accomplish purpose **2.** turn out satisfactorily **3.** follow —*vt.* **4.** follow, take place of —**success** (səkˈsɛs) *n.* **1.** favourable accomplishment, attainment, issue or outcome **2.** successful person or thing —**successful** (səkˈsɛsful) *a.* —**successfully** (səkˈsɛsfəlɪ) *adv.* —**succession** (səkˈsɛʃən) *n.* **1.** following **2.** series **3.** succeeding —**successive** (səkˈsɛsɪv) *a.* following in order, consecutive —**successively** (səkˈsɛsɪvlɪ) *adv.* —**successor** (səkˈsɛsə) *n.*

succinct (səkˈsɪŋkt) *a.* terse, concise

succour *or U.S.* **succor** (ˈsʌkə) *vt./n.* help in distress

succubus (ˈsʌkjʊbəs) *n.* female demon fabled to have sexual intercourse with sleeping men (*pl.* **-bi** (-baɪ))

succulent (ˈsʌkjʊlənt) *a.* **1.** juicy, full of juice **2.** (of plant) having thick, fleshy leaves —*n.* **3.** such plant —**ˈsucculence** *or* **ˈsucculency** *n.*

succumb (səˈkʌm) *vi.* **1.** yield, give way **2.** die

such (sʌtʃ) *a.* **1.** of the kind or degree mentioned **2.** so great, so much **3.** so made *etc.* **4.** of the same kind —**such and such** particular thing that is unspecified —**ˈsuchlike** *inf. a.* **1.** such —*pron.* **2.** other such things

suck (sʌk) *vt.* **1.** draw into mouth **2.** hold, dissolve in mouth **3.** draw in —*n.* **4.** sucking —**ˈsucker** *n.* **1.** person, thing that sucks **2.** organ, appliance which adheres by suction **3.** shoot coming from root or base of stem of plant **4.** *inf.* person easily deceived or taken in

suckle (ˈsʌkᵊl) *v.* feed from the breast —**ˈsuckling** *n.* unweaned infant

sucrose (ˈsjuːkrəʊz, -krəʊs) *n.* sugar

THESAURUS

subtle **1.** acute, deep, delicate, discriminating, ingenious, intricate, nice, penetrating, profound, refined, sophisticated **2.** delicate, faint, implied, indirect, insinuated, slight, understated **3.** artful, astute, crafty, cunning, designing, devious, intriguing, keen, Machiavellian, scheming, shrewd, sly, wily

subtlety **1.** acumen, acuteness, cleverness, delicacy, discernment, fine point, intricacy, nicety, refinement, sagacity, skill, sophistication **2.** artfulness, astuteness, craftiness, cunning, deviousness, guile, slyness, wiliness

subtract deduct, detract, diminish, remove, take away, take from, take off, withdraw

suburbs dormitory area (*Brit.*), environs, faubourgs, neighbourhood, outskirts, precincts, purlieus, residential areas, suburbia

subversive destructive, incendiary, inflammatory, insurrectionary, overthrowing, perversive, riotous, seditious, treasonous, underground, undermining

subvert **1.** demolish, destroy, invalidate, overthrow, overturn, raze, ruin, sabotage, undermine, upset, wreck **2.** confound, contaminate, corrupt, debase, demoralize, deprave, pervert, poison, vitiate

succeed **1.** arrive (*Inf.*), be successful, come off (*Inf.*), do all right for oneself (*Inf.*), do the trick (*Inf.*), flourish, gain one's end, get to the top (*Inf.*), make good, make it (*Inf.*), prosper, thrive, triumph, turn out well, work **2.** be subsequent, come next, ensue, follow, result, supervene **3.** *Usually with* **to** accede, assume the office of, come into, come into possession of, enter upon, follow, inherit, replace, take over

success **1.** ascendancy, eminence, fame, favourable outcome, fortune, happiness, hit (*Inf.*), luck, prosperity, triumph **2.** best seller, big name, celebrity, hit (*Inf.*), market leader, sensation, smash hit (*Inf.*), somebody, star, V.I.P., winner

successful acknowledged, at the top of the tree, best-selling, booming, efficacious, favourable, flourishing, fortunate, fruitful, lucky, lucrative, moneymaking, out in front (*Inf.*), paying, profitable, prosperous, rewarding, thriving, top, unbeaten, victorious, wealthy

successfully famously (*Inf.*), favourably, in triumph, swimmingly, victoriously, well, with flying colours

succession **1.** chain, continuation, course, cycle, flow, order, procession, progression, run, sequence, series, train **2.** accession, assumption, elevation, entering upon, inheritance, succeeding, taking over

successive consecutive, following, in a row, in succession, sequent, succeeding

succinct brief, compact, compendious, concise, condensed, gnomic, in a few well-chosen words, laconic, pithy, summary, terse, to the point

succour **1.** *v.* aid, assist, befriend, comfort, encourage, foster, give aid and encouragement to, help, minister to, nurse, relieve, render assistance to, support **2.** *n.* aid, assistance, comfort, help, relief, support

succulent juicy, luscious, lush, mellow, moist, mouthwatering, rich

succumb capitulate, die, fall, fall victim to, give in, give way, go under, knuckle under, submit, surrender, yield

sucker butt, cat's paw, dupe, easy game *or* mark (*Inf.*), fool, mug (*Sl.*), pushover (*Sl.*), sap (*Sl.*), sitting duck (*Inf.*), victim

suction (ˈsʌkʃən) *n.* **1.** drawing or sucking of air or fluid **2.** force produced by difference in pressure

Sudanese (suːdəˈniːz) *a.* **1.** of Sudan, in NE Afr. —*n.* **2.** native or inhabitant of Sudan

sudden (ˈsʌdən) *a.* **1.** done, occurring unexpectedly **2.** abrupt, hurried —ˈ**suddenly** *adv.* —ˈ**suddenness** *n.* —**sudden infant death syndrome** unexplained death of infant during sleep

sudorific (sjuːdəˈrɪfɪk) *a.* **1.** causing perspiration —*n.* **2.** medicine that produces sweat

suds (sʌdz) *pl.n.* froth of soap and water, lather

sue (sjuː, suː) *vt.* **1.** prosecute **2.** seek justice from **3.** beseech —*vi.* **4.** make application or entreaty (**sued, ˈsuing**)

suede (sweɪd) *n.* leather with soft, velvety finish

suet (ˈsuːɪt, ˈsjuːɪt) *n.* hard animal fat from sheep, ox *etc.*

suffer (ˈsʌfə) *v.* **1.** undergo, endure, experience (pain *etc.*) —*vt.* **2.** *obs.* allow —ˈ**sufferable** *a.* —ˈ**sufferance** *n.* toleration —ˈ**sufferer** *n.*

suffice (səˈfaɪs) *v.* be adequate, satisfactory (for) —**sufficiency** (səˈfɪʃənsɪ) *n.* adequate amount —**sufficient** (səˈfɪʃənt) *a.* enough, adequate

suffix (ˈsʌfɪks) *n.* **1.** letter or word added to end of word —*vt.* (ˈsʌfɪks, səˈfɪks) **2.** add, annex to the end

suffocate (ˈsʌfəkeɪt) *v.* **1.** kill, be killed by deprivation of oxygen **2.** smother —**suffoˈcation** *n.*

suffrage (ˈsʌfrɪdʒ) *n.* vote or right of voting —ˈ**suffragist** *n.* one claiming a right of voting (**suffraˈgette** *fem.*)

suffuse (səˈfjuːz) *vt.* well up and spread over —**sufˈfusion** *n.*

sugar (ˈʃʊgə) *n.* **1.** sweet crystalline vegetable substance —*vt.* **2.** sweeten, make pleasant (with sugar) —ˈ**sugary** *a.* —**sugar beet** variety of common beet grown for sugar —**sugar cane** plant from whose juice sugar is obtained —**sugar daddy** *sl.* wealthy (elderly) man who pays for (*esp.* sexual) favours of younger person —**sugar loaf** conical mass of hard refined sugar

suggest (səˈdʒɛst) *vt.* **1.** propose **2.** call up the idea of —**suggestiˈbility** *n.* —**sugˈgestible** *a.* easily influenced —**sugˈgestion** *n.* **1.** hint **2.** proposal **3.** insinuation of impression, belief *etc.* into mind —**sugˈgestive** *a.* containing, open to suggestion, *esp.* of something indecent

suicide (ˈsuːɪsaɪd, ˈsjuː-) *n.* **1.** act or instance of killing oneself intentionally **2.** person who does this —**suiˈcidal** *a.*

suit (suːt, sjuːt) *n.* **1.** set of clothing **2.** garment worn for particular event, purpose **3.** one of four sets in pack of cards **4.** action at law —*v.* **5.** make, be fit or appropriate (for) **6.** be acceptable (to) —**suitaˈbility** *n.* —ˈ**suitable** *a.* **1.** fitting, proper **2.** convenient **3.** becoming —ˈ**suitably** *adv.* —ˈ**suitcase** *n.* flat rectangular travelling case

suite (swiːt) *n.* **1.** matched set, *esp.* of furniture **2.** set of rooms **3.** retinue

suitor (ˈsuːtə, ˈsjuːt-) *n.* **1.** wooer **2.** one who sues **3.** petitioner

sulk (sʌlk) *vi.* **1.** be silent, resentful, *esp.* to draw

THESAURUS

sudden abrupt, hasty, hurried, impulsive, quick, rapid, rash, swift, unexpected, unforeseen, unusual

suddenly abruptly, all at once, all of a sudden, on the spur of the moment, out of the blue (*Inf.*), unexpectedly, without warning

sue **1.** *Law* bring an action against (someone), charge, have the law on (someone) (*Inf.*), indict, institute legal proceedings against (someone), prefer charges against (someone), prosecute, summon, take (someone) to court **2.** appeal for, beg, beseech, entreat, petition, plead, solicit, supplicate

suffer **1.** ache, agonize, be affected, be in pain, be racked, feel wretched, go through a lot (*Inf.*), grieve, have a thin *or* bad time, hurt **2.** bear, endure, experience, feel, go through, put up with (*Inf.*), support, sustain, tolerate, undergo **3.** *Archaic* allow, let, permit

suffice answer, be sufficient (adequate, enough, satisfactory), content, do, fill the bill (*Inf.*), meet requirements, satisfy, serve

sufficient adequate, competent, enough, enow (*Archaic*), satisfactory

suffocate asphyxiate, choke, smother, stifle, strangle

suffuse bathe, cover, flood, imbue, infuse, mantle, overspread, permeate, pervade, spread over, steep, transfuse

suggest **1.** advise, advocate, move, offer a suggestion, propose, put forward, recommend **2.** bring to mind, connote, evoke, put one in mind of

suggestion **1.** motion, plan, proposal, proposition, recommendation **2.** breath, hint, indication, insinuation, intimation, suspicion, trace, whisper

suggestive bawdy, blue, immodest, improper, indecent, indelicate, off colour, provocative, prurient, racy, ribald, risqué, rude, smutty, spicy (*Inf.*), titillating, unseemly

suit *v.* **1.** agree, agree with, answer, be acceptable to, become, befit, be seemly, conform to, correspond, do, go with, gratify, harmonize, match, please, satisfy, tally **2.** accommodate, adapt, adjust, fashion, fit, modify, proportion, tailor ~*n.* **3.** *Law* action, case, cause, lawsuit, proceeding, prosecution, trial **4.** clothing, costume, dress, ensemble, habit, outfit

suitability appropriateness, aptness, fitness, opportuneness, rightness, timeliness

suitable acceptable, applicable, apposite, appropriate, apt, becoming, befitting, convenient, cut out for, due, fit, fitting, in character, in keeping, opportune, pertinent, proper, relevant, right, satisfactory, seemly, suited

suite **1.** apartment, collection, furniture, rooms, series, set **2.** attendants, entourage, escort, followers, retainers, retinue, train

suitor admirer, beau, follower (*Obsolete*), swain (*Archaic*), wooer

sulk be in a huff, be put out, brood, have the hump (*Brit. inf.*), look sullen, pout

sulky aloof, churlish, cross, disgruntled, ill-humoured, in the sulks, moody, morose, perverse, petulant, put out, querulous, resentful, sullen, vexed

sullen brooding, cheerless, cross, dismal, dull, gloomy, glowering, heavy, moody, morose, obstinate, out of humour, perverse, silent, sombre, sour, stubborn, surly, unsociable

attention to oneself —*n.* **2.** sulky mood —**ˈsulkily** *adv.* —**ˈsulky** *a.*

sullen (ˈsʌlən) *a.* **1.** unwilling to talk or be sociable; morose **2.** dismal, dull —**ˈsullenly** *adv.*

sully (ˈsʌlɪ) *vt.* stain, tarnish, disgrace (**ˈsullied, ˈsullying**)

sulpha drug (ˈsʌlfə) sulphonamide used to treat bacterial infections

sulphate (ˈsʌlfeɪt) *n.* salt formed by sulphuric acid in combination with any base

sulphonamide (sʌlˈfɒnəmaɪd) *n.* any of group of drugs used as internal germicides in treatment of many bacterial diseases

sulphur *or U.S.* **sulfur** (ˈsʌlfə) *n.* pale yellow nonmetallic element —**ˈsulphide** *n.* compound of sulphur with more electropositive element —**ˈsulphite** *n.* salt or ester of acid —**sulphitic** (sʌlˈfɪtɪk) *a.* —**sulphuric** *or U.S.* **sulfuric** (sʌlˈfjʊərɪk) *a.* —**ˈsulphurous** *a.* —**sulphur dioxide** colourless soluble pungent gas used in manufacture of sulphuric acid, preservation of foodstuffs, bleaching and disinfecting —**sulphuric acid** colourless oily corrosive liquid used in manufacture of fertilizers, dyes and explosives

sultan (ˈsʌltən) *n.* ruler of Muslim country —**sulˈtana** *n.* **1.** sultan's wife **2.** kind of raisin —**ˈsultanate** *n.* **1.** territory or country ruled by sultan **2.** office, rank or jurisdiction of sultan

sultry (ˈsʌltrɪ) *a.* **1.** (of weather) hot, humid **2.** (of person) looking sensual

sum (sʌm) *n.* **1.** amount, total **2.** problem in arithmetic —*v.* **3.** add up **4.** (*with* up) make summary of (main parts) (**-mm-**) —**summing-up** *n.* summary of main points of speech *etc.* —**sum total 1.** total obtained by adding up sum or sums **2.** everything included

sumach *or U.S.* **sumac** (ˈsuːmæk, ˈʃuː-) *n.* shrub with clusters of green flowers and red hairy fruits

summary (ˈsʌmərɪ) *n.* **1.** abridgment or statement of chief points of longer document, speech *etc.* **2.** abstract —*a.* **3.** done quickly —**ˈsummarily** *adv.* **1.** speedily **2.** abruptly —**ˈsummarize** *or* **-ise** *vt.* **1.** make summary of **2.** present briefly and concisely —**sumˈmation** *n.* adding up

summer (ˈsʌmə) *n.* **1.** second, warmest season —*vi.* **2.** pass the summer —**ˈsummery** *a.* —**ˈsummerhouse** *n.* small building in garden or park, used for shade in summer —**summer school** academic course *etc.* held during summer —**summer solstice 1.** time at which sun is at its northernmost point in sky; June 21st **2.** *Astron.* point on celestial sphere at which ecliptic is furthest north from celestial equator —**ˈsummertime** *n.* daylight-saving time, *ie* time shown by clocks *etc.* put forward one hour during certain period of year

summit (ˈsʌmɪt) *n.* top, peak —**summit conference** meeting of heads of governments

summon (ˈsʌmən) *vt.* **1.** demand attendance of **2.** call on **3.** bid (witness) appear in court **4.** gather up (energies *etc.*) —**ˈsummons** *n.* **1.** call **2.** authoritative demand

sump (sʌmp) *n.* place or receptacle (*esp.* as oil reservoir in engine) where fluid collects

sumptuous (ˈsʌmptjʊəs) *a.* **1.** lavish, magnificent **2.** costly —**ˈsumptuary** *a.* pert. to or regulating expenditure —**ˈsumptuously** *adv.* —**ˈsumptuousness** *n.*

sun (sʌn) *n.* **1.** luminous body round which earth and other planets revolve **2.** its rays —*vt.* **3.** expose to sun's rays (**-nn-**) —**ˈsunless** *a.* —**ˈsunny** *a.* **1.** like the sun **2.** warm **3.** cheerful —**ˈsunbathing** *n.* exposure of whole or part of body to sun's rays —**ˈsunbeam** *n.* ray of sun —**ˈsunburn** *n.* inflammation of skin due to excessive exposure to sun —**ˈsundial** *n.* device indicating time during hours of sunlight by means of pointer that casts shadow on to surface marked in hours —**ˈsundown** *n.* sunset —**ˈsunfish** *n.* sea fish with large rounded body —**ˈsunflower** *n.* plant with large golden flowers —**ˈsunglasses** *pl.n.* glasses with darkened or polarizing lenses that protect eyes from sun's glare —**sun-god** *n.* sun considered as personal deity —**sun lamp** lamp that generates ultraviolet rays —**ˈsunrise** *n.* **1.** daily appearance of sun above horizon **2.** atmospheric phenomena accompanying this appearance **3.** time at which sun rises at particular locality —**sunrise industry** any of the high-technology industries, such as electronics, that hold promise of future development —**ˈsunset** *n.* **1.** daily disappearance of sun below horizon **2.** atmospheric phenomena accompanying this disappearance **3.** time at which sun sets at particular locality —**ˈsunshade** *n.* device, *esp.* parasol or awning, serving to shade from sun —**ˈsunshine** *n.* **1.** light or warmth received directly from sun **2.** lighthearted term of affection —**ˈsunshiny** *a.* —**ˈsunspot** *n.* dark patch appearing temporarily on sun's surface —**ˈsunstroke** *n.* illness caused by prolonged exposure to intensely hot sun —**ˈsuntan** *n.* colouring of skin by exposure to sun

Sun. Sunday

THESAURUS

sultry 1. close, hot, humid, muggy, oppressive, sticky, stifling, stuffy, sweltering **2.** come-hither (*Inf.*), erotic, passionate, provocative, seductive, sensual, sexy (*Inf.*), voluptuous

sum aggregate, amount, entirety, quantity, reckoning, score, sum total, tally, total, totality, whole

summarily arbitrarily, at short notice, expeditiously, forthwith, immediately, on the spot, peremptorily, promptly, speedily, swiftly, without delay, without wasting words

summarize abridge, condense, encapsulate, epitomize, give a rundown of, give the main points of, outline, précis, put in a nutshell, review, sum up

summary 1. *n.* abridgment, abstract, compendium, digest, epitome, essence, extract, outline, précis, recapitulation, résumé, review, rundown, summing-up, synopsis **2.** *adj.* arbitrary, brief, compact, compendious, concise, condensed, cursory, hasty, laconic, perfunctory, pithy, succinct

summit acme, apex, crown, crowning point, culmination, head, height, peak, pinnacle, top, zenith

summon 1. arouse, assemble, bid, call, call together, cite, convene, convoke, invite, rally, rouse, send for **2.** *Often with* **up** call into action, draw on, gather, invoke, mobilize, muster

sumptuous costly, dear, de luxe, expensive, extravagant, gorgeous, grand, lavish, luxurious, magnificent, opulent, plush (*Inf.*), posh (*Inf.*), rich, ritzy (*Sl.*), splendid, superb

sun 1. *n.* daystar (*Poetic*), eye of heaven, Helios (*Greek myth*), Phoebus (*Greek myth*), Phoebus Apollo (*Greek myth*), Sol (*Roman myth*) **2.** *v.* bake, bask, sunbathe, tan

sundae (ˈsʌndiː, -deɪ) *n.* ice cream topped with fruit *etc.*

Sunday (ˈsʌndɪ) *n.* **1.** first day of week **2.** Christian Sabbath —**Sunday best** one's best clothes —**Sunday school** school for religious instruction of children

sunder (ˈsʌndə) *vt.* separate, sever

sundry (ˈsʌndrɪ) *a.* several, various —**ˈsundries** *pl.n.* odd items not mentioned in detail

sung (sʌŋ) *pp. of* SING

sunk (sʌŋk) *pp. of* SINK

sup (sʌp) *vt.* **1.** take by sips —*vi.* **2.** take supper (**-pp-**) —*n.* **3.** mouthful of liquid

sup. **1.** above **2.** superior **3.** *Gram.* superlative **4.** supplement **5.** supplementary **6.** supply

super (ˈsuːpə, ˈsjuːpə) *a. inf.* very good

super- (*comb. form*) above, greater, exceeding(ly), as in *superhuman, superman, superstore, supertanker.* Such compounds are not given here where the meaning may be inferred from the simple word

superable (ˈsuːpərəbˈl, ˈsjuː-) *a.* **1.** capable of being overcome **2.** surmountable

superannuate (suːpərˈænjʊeɪt, sjuː-) *vt.* **1.** pension off **2.** discharge or dismiss as too old —**superˈannuated** *a.* —**superannuˈation** *n.* **1.** pension given on retirement **2.** contribution by employee to pension

superb (sʊˈpɜːb, sjʊ-) *a.* **1.** splendid **2.** grand **3.** impressive —**suˈperbly** *adv.*

supercargo (suːpəˈkɑːgəʊ, sjuː-) *n.* officer on merchant ship in charge of cargo

supercharge (ˈsuːpətʃɑːdʒ, ˈsjuː-) *vt.* charge, fill to excess —**ˈsupercharged** *a.* —**ˈsupercharger** *n.* in internal-combustion engine, device to ensure complete filling of cylinder with explosive mixture when running at high speed

supercilious (suːpəˈsɪlɪəs, sjuː-) *a.* displaying arrogant pride, scorn, indifference

superconductivity (suːpəkɒndʌkˈtɪvɪtɪ, sjuː-) *n.* *Phys.* property of certain substances that have almost no electrical resistance at temperatures close to absolute zero —**superconˈductive** *or* **superconˈducting** *a.* —**superconˈductor** *n.*

supercool (suːpəˈkuːl, sjuː-) *v.* *Chem.* cool without freezing or crystallization to temperature below that at which freezing or crystallization should occur

superego (suːpərˈiːgəʊ, -ˈɛgəʊ, sjuː-) *n.* *Psychoanal.* that part of the unconscious mind that acts as conscience for the ego

supererogation (suːpərɛrəˈgeɪʃən, sjuː-) *n.* **1.** performance of work in excess of that required **2.** *R.C.Ch.* prayers, devotions *etc.* beyond those prescribed as obligatory

superficial (suːpəˈfɪʃəl, sjuː-) *a.* **1.** of or on surface **2.** not careful or thorough **3.** without depth, shallow —**superficiˈality** *n.*

superfluous (suːˈpɜːflʊəs, sjuː-) *a.* **1.** extra, unnecessary **2.** excessive **3.** left over —**superˈfluity** *n.* **1.** superabundance **2.** unnecessary amount —**suˈperfluously** *adv.*

supergrass (ˈsuːpəgrɑːs) *n.* person who acts as police informer on a large scale

superheat (suːpəˈhiːt, sjuː-) *vt.* **1.** heat (vapour, *esp.* steam) to temperature above its saturation point for given pressure **2.** heat (liquid) to temperature above its boiling point without boiling occurring **3.** overheat —**superˈheater** *n.*

superheterodyne receiver (suːpəˈhɛtərədaɪn, sjuː-) radio receiver that combines two radio-frequency signals by heterodyne action to produce signal above audible frequency limit

superimpose (suːpərɪmˈpəʊz, sjuː-) *vt.* **1.** set or place on or over something else **2.** (*usu. with* on *or* upon) add (to) —**superimpoˈsition** *n.*

superintend (suːpərɪnˈtɛnd, sjuː-) *vt.* **1.** have charge of **2.** overlook **3.** supervise —**superinˈtendence** *n.* —**superinˈtendent** *n.* senior police officer

superior (suːˈpɪərɪə, sjuː-) *a.* **1.** greater in quality or quantity **2.** upper, higher in position, rank or quality **3.** showing consciousness of being so —**superiˈority** *n.* quality of being higher, greater or more excellent

THESAURUS

sundry assorted, different, divers (*Archaic*), miscellaneous, several, some, varied, various

sunless bleak, cheerless, cloudy, dark, depressing, gloomy, grey, hazy, overcast, sombre

sunny **1.** bright, brilliant, clear, fine, luminous, radiant, summery, sunlit, sunshiny, unclouded, warm, without a cloud in the sky **2.** *Fig.* beaming, blithe, buoyant, cheerful, cheery, genial, happy, joyful, light-hearted, optimistic, pleasant, smiling

sunrise aurora (*Poetic*), break of day, cockcrow, dawn, daybreak, daylight, dayspring (*Poetic*), sunup

sunset close of (the) day, dusk, eventide, gloaming, nightfall, sundown

superb admirable, breathtaking, choice, excellent, exquisite, fine, first-rate, gorgeous, grand, impressive, magnificent, marvellous, of the first water, splendid, superior, unrivalled

supercilious arrogant, condescending, contemptuous, disdainful, haughty, high and mighty (*Inf.*), hoity-toity (*Inf.*), imperious, insolent, lofty, lordly, overbearing, patronizing, proud, scornful, snooty (*Inf.*), stuck-up (*Inf.*), toffee-nosed (*Sl.*), uppish (*Brit. inf.*), vainglorious

superficial **1.** exterior, external, on the surface, peripheral, shallow, skin-deep, slight, surface **2.** casual, cosmetic, cursory, desultory, hasty, hurried, inattentive, nodding, passing, perfunctory, sketchy, slapdash **3.** empty, empty-headed, frivolous, lightweight, shallow, silly, trivial **4.** apparent, evident, ostensible, outward, seeming

superficiality emptiness, lack of depth, lack of substance, shallowness, triviality

superfluous excess, excessive, extra, in excess, left over, needless, on one's hands, pleonastic (*Rhetoric*), redundant, remaining, residuary, spare, superabundant, supererogatory, supernumerary, surplus, surplus to requirements, uncalled-for, unnecessary, unneeded, unrequired

superintend administer, control, direct, inspect, look after, manage, overlook, oversee, run, supervise

superintendence care, charge, control, direction, government, guidance, inspection, management, supervision, surveillance

superior **1.** better, grander, greater, higher, more advanced (expert, extensive, skilful), paramount, predominant, preferred, prevailing, surpassing, unrivalled **2.** airy, condescending, disdainful, haughty, lofty, lordly, patronizing, pretentious, snobbish, stuck-up (*Inf.*), supercilious

superlative (su:ˈpɜːlətɪv, sju:-) *a.* 1. of, in highest degree or quality 2. surpassing 3. *Gram.* denoting form of adjective, adverb meaning 'most' —*n.* 4. *Gram.* superlative degree of adjective or adverb

supermarket (ˈsu:pəmɑːkɪt, ˈsju:-) *n.* large self-service store selling chiefly food and household goods

supernatural (su:pəˈnætʃərəl, sju:-) *a.* 1. being beyond the powers or laws of nature 2. miraculous —**superˈnaturally** *adv.*

supernova (su:pəˈnəʊvə, sju:-) *n.* star that explodes and is for a few days up to one hundred million times brighter than sun (*pl.* **-vae** (-vi:), **-s**)

supernumerary (su:pəˈnju:mərərɪ, sju:-) *a.* 1. in excess of normal number, extra —*n.* 2. extra person or thing

superphosphate (su:pəˈfɒsfeɪt, sju:-) *n.* chemical fertilizer

superpose (su:pəˈpəʊz, sju:-) *vt. Geom.* place (one figure) upon another so that their perimeters coincide

superpower (ˈsu:pəpaʊə, ˈsju:-) *n.* 1. an extremely powerful state, such as U.S.A. 2. extremely high power, *esp.* electrical —**ˈsuperpowered** *a.*

superscribe (su:pəˈskraɪb, sju:-) *vt.* write (inscription *etc.*) above, on top of or outside —**superscription** (su:pəˈskrɪpʃən, sju:-) *n.*

superscript (ˈsu:pəskrɪpt, ˈsju:-) *n./a.* (character) printed, written above the line

supersede (su:pəˈsi:d, sju:-) *vt.* 1. take the place of 2. set aside, discard, supplant —**supersession** (su:pəˈsɛʃən, sju:-) *n.*

supersonic (su:pəˈsɒnɪk, sju:-) *a.* denoting speed greater than that of sound

superstition (su:pəˈstɪʃən, sju:-) *n.* religion, opinion or practice based on belief in luck or magic —**superˈstitious** *a.* —**superˈstitiously** *adv.*

superstructure (ˈsu:pəstrʌktʃə, ˈsju:-) *n.* 1. structure above foundations 2. part of ship above deck

supertax (ˈsu:pətæks, ˈsju:-) *n.* tax on large incomes in addition to usual income tax

supervene (su:pəˈvi:n, sju:-) *vi.* happen, as an interruption or change —**supervention** (su:pəˈvɛnʃən, sju:-) *n.*

supervise (ˈsu:pəvaɪz, ˈsju:-) *vt.* 1. oversee 2. direct 3. inspect and control 4. superintend —**supervision** (su:pəˈvɪʒən, sju:-) *n.* —**ˈsupervisor** *n.* —**ˈsupervisory** *a.*

supine (su:ˈpaɪn, sju:-; ˈsu:paɪn, ˈsju:-) *a.* 1. lying on back with face upwards 2. indolent —*n.* (ˈsu:paɪn, ˈsju:-) 3. Latin verbal noun

supper (ˈsʌpə) *n.* (light) evening meal

supplant (səˈplɑ:nt) *vt.* 1. take the place of, *esp.* unfairly 2. oust —**supˈplanter** *n.*

supple (ˈsʌpəl) *a.* 1. pliable 2. flexible 3. compliant —**ˈsupply** *or* **ˈsupplely** *adv.*

supplement (ˈsʌplɪmənt) *n.* 1. thing added to fill up, supply deficiency, *esp.* extra part added to book *etc.* 2. additional number of periodical, usu. on special subject 3. separate, oft. illustrated section published periodically with newspaper —*vt.* (ˈsʌplɪmɛnt) 4. add to 5. remedy deficiency of —**suppleˈmentary** *a.* additional —**supplementary angle** either of two angles whose sum is 180° —**supplementary benefit** UK allowance paid to various groups of people by state to bring their incomes up to minimum levels established by law

suppliant (ˈsʌplɪənt) *a.* 1. petitioning —*n.* 2. petitioner

supplicate (ˈsʌplɪkeɪt) *v.* 1. beg humbly —*vt.* 2. entreat —**suppliˈcation** *n.* —**ˈsupplicatory** *a.*

supply (səˈplaɪ) *vt.* 1. furnish 2. make available 3. provide (**supˈplied, supˈplying**) —*n.* 4. supplying, substitute 5. stock, store

support (səˈpɔːt) *vt.* 1. hold up 2. sustain 3. assist 4. corroborate —*n.* 5. supporting, being supported 6. means of support —**supˈportable** *a.* —**supˈporter** *n.* adherent —**supˈporting** *a.* (of film *etc.* role) less important —**supˈportive** *a.*

THESAURUS

superiority advantage, ascendancy, excellence, lead, predominance, pre-eminence, preponderance, prevalence, supremacy

superlative *adj.* consummate, crack (*Sl.*), excellent, greatest, highest, magnificent, matchless, of the first water, of the highest order, outstanding, peerless, supreme, surpassing, transcendent, unparalleled, unrivalled, unsurpassed

supernatural abnormal, dark, ghostly, hidden, miraculous, mysterious, mystic, occult, paranormal, phantom, preternatural, psychic, spectral, supranatural, uncanny, unearthly, unnatural

supervise administer, be on duty at, be responsible for, conduct, control, direct, handle, have *or* be in charge of, inspect, keep an eye on, look after, manage, oversee, preside over, run, superintend

supervision administration, auspices, care, charge, control, direction, guidance, instruction, management, oversight, stewardship, superintendence, surveillance

supervisor administrator, boss (*Inf.*), chief, foreman, inspector, manager, overseer, steward, superintendent

supervisory administrative, executive, managerial, overseeing, superintendent

supplant displace, oust, overthrow, remove, replace, supersede, take over, take the place of, undermine, unseat

supple bending, elastic, flexible, limber, lithe, plastic, pliable, pliant

supplement 1. *n.* added feature, addendum, addition, appendix, codicil, complement, extra, insert, postscript, pull-out, sequel 2. *v.* add, augment, complement, extend, fill out, reinforce, supply, top up

supplementary accompanying, additional, ancillary, auxiliary, complementary, extra, secondary, supplemental

suppliant 1. *adj.* begging, beseeching, craving, entreating, imploring, importunate, on bended knee, petitioning 2. *n.* applicant, petitioner, suitor, supplicant

supplication appeal, entreaty, invocation, petition, plea, pleading, prayer, request, solicitation, suit

supply 1. *v.* afford, cater to *or* for, come up with, contribute, endow, fill, furnish, give, grant, minister, outfit, produce, provide, purvey, replenish, satisfy, stock, store, victual, yield 2. *n.* cache, fund, hoard, quantity, reserve, reservoir, source, stock, stockpile, store

support *v.* 1. bear, bolster, brace, buttress, carry,

suppose (səˈpəʊz) *vt.* **1.** assume as theory **2.** take for granted **3.** accept as likely **4.** (in passive) be expected, obliged **5.** (in passive) ought —**supposed** (səˈpəʊzd, -ˈpəʊzɪd) *a.* —**supposedly** (səˈpəʊzɪdlɪ) *adv.* —**suppoˈsition** *n.* **1.** assumption **2.** belief without proof **3.** conjecture —**suppoˈsitious** *or* **supposititious** (səpɒzɪˈtɪʃəs) *a.* sham, spurious, counterfeit

suppository (səˈpɒzɪtərɪ, -trɪ) *n.* medication (in capsule) for insertion in orifice of body

suppress (səˈprɛs) *vt.* **1.** put down, restrain **2.** crush, stifle **3.** keep or withdraw from publication —**supˈpression** *n.*

suppurate (ˈsʌpjʊreɪt) *vi.* fester, form pus —**suppuˈration** *n.*

supra- (*comb. form*) above, over, as in *supranational.* Such words are not given here where the meaning may easily be inferred from the simple word

supreme (sʊˈpriːm, sjʊ-) *a.* **1.** highest in authority or rank **2.** utmost —**supremacy** (sʊˈprɛməsɪ, sjʊ-) *n.* position of being supreme —**suˈpremely** *adv.* —**suˈpremo** *n.* person with overall authority (*pl.* **-s**) —**Supreme Being** God

Supt. *or* **supt.** superintendent

sur-[1] (*comb. form*) over, above; beyond, as in *surcharge*

sur-[2] (*comb. form*) *see* SUB-

surcease (sɜːˈsiːs) *v.* **1.** (cause to) cease —*n.* **2.** cessation

surcharge (ˈsɜːtʃɑːdʒ) *n.* **1.** additional charge —*vt.* (sɜːˈtʃɑːdʒ, ˈsɜːtʃɑːdʒ) **2.** subject to additional charge

surd (sɜːd) *n.* **1.** *Maths.* sum containing one or more irrational roots of numbers **2.** *Phonet.* voiceless consonant —*a.* **3.** of or relating to surd

sure (ʃʊə, ʃɔː) *a.* **1.** certain **2.** trustworthy **3.** without doubt —*adv.* **4.** *inf.* certainly —**ˈsurely** *adv.* —**surety** (ˈʃʊətɪ, ˈʃʊərɪtɪ) *n.* one who makes himself responsible for another's obligations —**sure-fire** *a. inf.* certain to succeed or meet expectations —**sure-footed** *a.* **1.** unlikely to fall, slip or stumble **2.** not likely to err or fail

surf (sɜːf) *n.* **1.** waves breaking on shore —*vi.* **2.** swim in, ride surf —**ˈsurfer** *n.* —**ˈsurfboard** *n.* board used in sport of riding over surf

surface (ˈsɜːfɪs) *n.* **1.** outside face of body **2.** exterior **3.** plane **4.** top, visible side **5.** superficial appearance, outward impression —*a.* **6.** involving the surface only **7.** going no deeper than surface —*v.* **8.** (cause to) come to surface —*vt.* **9.** put a surface on —**surface tension** property of liquids caused by intermolecular forces near surface leading to apparent presence of surface film

surfeit (ˈsɜːfɪt) *n.* **1.** excess **2.** disgust caused by excess —*vt.* **3.** feed to excess

THESAURUS

hold, hold up, prop, reinforce, shore up, sustain, underpin, uphold **2.** be a source of strength to, buoy up, cherish, finance, foster, fund, keep, look after, maintain, nourish, provide for, strengthen, subsidize, succour, sustain, take care of, underwrite **3.** advocate, aid, assist, back, boost (someone's) morale, champion, defend, forward, go along with, help, promote, second, side with, stand behind, stand up for, stick up for (*Inf.*), take (someone's) part, take up the cudgels for, uphold **4.** attest to, authenticate, bear out, confirm, corroborate, document, endorse, lend credence to, substantiate, verify ~*n.* **5.** abutment, back, brace, foundation, lining, pillar, post, prop, shore, stanchion, stay, stiffener, underpinning **6.** aid, approval, assistance, backing, blessing, championship, comfort, encouragement, friendship, furtherance, help, loyalty, moral support, patronage, protection, relief, succour, sustenance **7.** keep, livelihood, maintenance, subsistence, sustenance, upkeep

supporter adherent, advocate, ally, apologist, champion, co-worker, defender, fan, follower, friend, helper, patron, sponsor, upholder, well-wisher

suppose 1. assume, calculate (*U.S. dialect*), conjecture, dare say, expect, guess (*Inf.*), imagine, infer, judge, opine, presume, presuppose, surmise, take as read, take for granted, think **2.** believe, conceive, conclude, conjecture, consider, fancy, hypothesize, imagine, postulate, pretend

supposed 1. accepted, alleged, assumed, hypothetical, presumed, presupposed, professed, putative, reputed, rumoured **2.** *With* **to** expected, meant, obliged, ought, required

supposedly allegedly, at a guess, avowedly, by all accounts, hypothetically, ostensibly, presumably, professedly, purportedly, theoretically

supposition assumption, conjecture, doubt, guess, guesswork, hypothesis, idea, notion, postulate, presumption, speculation, surmise, theory

suppress 1. beat down, check, clamp down on, conquer, crack down on, crush, drive underground, extinguish, overpower, overthrow, put an end to, quash, quell, quench, snuff out, stamp out, stop, subdue, trample on **2.** censor, conceal, contain, cover up, curb, hold in *or* back, hold in check, keep secret, muffle, muzzle, repress, restrain, silence, smother, stifle, withhold

suppression check, clampdown, crackdown, crushing, dissolution, elimination, extinction, inhibition, prohibition, quashing, smothering, termination

supremacy absolute rule, ascendancy, dominance, domination, dominion, lordship, mastery, paramountcy, predominance, pre-eminence, primacy, sovereignty, supreme authority, sway

supreme cardinal, chief, crowning, culminating, extreme, final, first, foremost, greatest, head, highest, incomparable, leading, matchless, paramount, peerless, predominant, pre-eminent, prevailing, prime, principal, sovereign, superlative, surpassing, top, ultimate, unsurpassed, utmost

sure 1. assured, certain, clear, confident, convinced, decided, definite, free from doubt, persuaded, positive, satisfied **2.** accurate, dependable, effective, foolproof, honest, indisputable, infallible, neverfailing, precise, reliable, sure-fire (*Inf.*), tried and true, trustworthy, trusty, undeniable, undoubted, unerring, unfailing, unmistakable, well-proven **3.** assured, bound, guaranteed, ineluctable, inescapable, inevitable, irrevocable

surely assuredly, beyond the shadow of a doubt, certainly, come what may, definitely, doubtlessly, for certain, indubitably, inevitably, inexorably, undoubtedly, unquestionably, without doubt, without fail

surface 1. *n.* covering, exterior, façade, face, facet, outside, plane, side, skin, superficies (*Rare*), top, veneer **2.** *adj.* apparent, exterior, external, outward,

surge (sɜːdʒ) *n.* 1. wave 2. sudden increase 3. *Elec.* sudden rush of current in circuit —*vi.* 4. move in large waves 5. swell, billow

surgeon (ˈsɜːdʒən) *n.* medical expert who performs operations —**ˈsurgery** *n.* 1. medical treatment by operation 2. doctor's, dentist's consulting room —**ˈsurgical** *a.* —**ˈsurgically** *adv.* —**surgical spirit** methylated spirit

surly (ˈsɜːlɪ) *a.* 1. gloomily morose 2. ill-natured 3. cross and rude —**ˈsurlily** *adv.* —**ˈsurliness** *n.*

surmise (sɜːˈmaɪz) *v./n.* guess, conjecture

surmount (sɜːˈmaʊnt) *vt.* get over, overcome —**surˈmountable** *a.*

surname (ˈsɜːneɪm) *n.* family name

surpass (sɜːˈpɑːs) *vt.* 1. go beyond 2. excel 3. outstrip —**surˈpassable** *a.* —**surˈpassing** *a.* 1. excellent 2. exceeding others

surplice (ˈsɜːplɪs) *n.* loose white vestment worn by clergy and choristers

surplus (ˈsɜːpləs) *n.* what remains over in excess

surprise (səˈpraɪz) *vt.* 1. cause surprise to 2. astonish 3. take, come upon unexpectedly 4. startle (someone) into action thus —*n.* 5. what takes unawares 6. something unexpected 7. emotion aroused by being taken unawares

surrealism (səˈrɪəlɪzəm) *n.* movement in art and literature emphasizing expression of the unconscious —**surˈreal** *a.* —**surˈrealist** *n./a.*

surrender (səˈrɛndə) *vt.* 1. hand over, give up —*vi.* 2. yield 3. cease resistance 4. capitulate —*n.* 5. act of surrendering

surreptitious (sʌrəpˈtɪʃəs) *a.* 1. done secretly or stealthily 2. furtive —**surrepˈtitiously** *adv.*

surrogate (ˈsʌrəgɪt) *n.* 1. deputy, *esp.* of bishop 2. substitute

surround (səˈraʊnd) *vt.* 1. be, come all round, encompass 2. encircle 3. hem in —*n.* 4. border, edging —**surˈroundings** *pl.n.* conditions, scenery *etc.* around a person, place, environment

surtax (ˈsɜːtæks) *n.* additional tax

surveillance (sɜːˈveɪləns) *n.* close watch, supervision —**surˈveillant** *a./n.*

survey (sɜːˈveɪ, ˈsɜːveɪ) *vt.* 1. view, scrutinize 2. inspect, examine 3. measure, map (land) —*n.* (ˈsɜːveɪ) 4. a surveying 5. inspection 6. report incorporating results of survey —**surˈveyor** *n.*

survive (səˈvaɪv) *vt.* 1. outlive 2. come through alive —*vi.* 3. continue to live or exist —**surˈvival** *n.* continuation of existence of persons, things *etc.* —**surˈvivor** *n.* one left alive when others have died —**survival of the fittest** natural selection

sus (sʌs) *n. sl.* 1. suspect 2. suspicion

susceptible (səˈsɛptəbᵊl) *a.* 1. yielding readily 2. capable 3. impressionable —**susceptiˈbility** *n.*

THESAURUS

superficial **3.** *v.* appear, come to light, come up, crop up (*Inf.*), emerge, materialize, rise, transpire

surfeit 1. *n.* excess, glut, overindulgence, plethora, satiety, superabundance, superfluity **2.** *v.* cram, fill, glut, gorge, overfeed, overfill, satiate, stuff

surge 1. *v.* billow, eddy, gush, heave, rise, roll, rush, swell, swirl, tower, undulate, well forth **2.** *n.* billow, breaker, efflux, flood, flow, gush, intensification, outpouring, roller, rush, swell, uprush, upsurge, wave

surly bearish, brusque, churlish, crabbed, cross, crusty, curmudgeonly, grouchy (*Inf.*), gruff, ill-natured, morose, perverse, sulky, sullen, testy, uncivil, ungracious

surmise 1. *v.* come to the conclusion, conclude, conjecture, consider, deduce, fancy, guess, hazard a guess, imagine, infer, opine, presume, speculate, suppose, suspect **2.** *n.* assumption, conclusion, conjecture, deduction, guess, hypothesis, idea, inference, notion, possibility, presumption, speculation, supposition, suspicion, thought

surmount conquer, exceed, get over, master, overcome, overpower, overtop, pass, prevail over, surpass, triumph over, vanquish

surpass beat, best, eclipse, exceed, excel, go beyond, go one better than (*Inf.*), outdo, outshine, outstrip, override, overshadow, top, tower above, transcend

surpassing excellent, exceptional, extraordinary, incomparable, matchless, outstanding, phenomenal, rare, supreme, transcendent, unrivalled

surplus balance, excess, remainder, residue, superabundance, superfluity, surfeit

surprise *v.* **1.** amaze, astonish, astound, bewilder, bowl over (*Inf.*), confuse, disconcert, flabbergast (*Inf.*), leave open-mouthed, nonplus, stagger, stun, take aback **2.** burst in on, catch in the act *or* red-handed, catch napping, catch unawares *or* off-guard, come down on like a bolt from the blue, discover, spring upon, startle ~*n.* **3.** amazement, astonishment, bewilderment, incredulity, stupefaction, wonder **4.** bolt from the blue, bombshell, eye-opener (*Inf.*), jolt, revelation, shock, start (*Inf.*)

surrender *v.* **1.** abandon, cede, concede, deliver up, forego, give up, hand over, part with, relinquish, renounce, resign, waive, yield **2.** capitulate, give in, give oneself up, give way, lay down arms, quit, show the white flag, submit, succumb, throw in the towel, yield ~*n.* **3.** capitulation, delivery, relinquishment, renunciation, resignation, submission, yielding

surreptitious clandestine, covert, fraudulent, furtive, secret, sly, sneaking, stealthy, unauthorized, underhand, veiled

surround close in on, encircle, enclose, encompass, envelop, environ, fence in, girdle, hem in, ring

surroundings background, environment, environs, location, milieu, neighbourhood, setting

surveillance care, control, direction, inspection, observation, scrutiny, superintendence, supervision, vigilance, watch

survey *v.* **1.** contemplate, examine, inspect, look over, observe, reconnoitre, research, review, scan, scrutinize, study, supervise, view **2.** appraise, assess, estimate, map, measure, plan, plot, prospect, size up, take stock of, triangulate ~*n.* **3.** examination, inquiry, inspection, overview, perusal, random sample, review, scrutiny, study

survive be extant, endure, exist, hold out, keep body and soul together (*Inf.*), last, live, live on, outlast, outlive, pull through, remain alive, subsist

susceptibility liability, predisposition, proneness, propensity, responsiveness, sensitivity, suggestibility, vulnerability, weakness

suspect (səˈspɛkt) *vt.* **1.** doubt innocence of **2.** have impression of existence or presence of **3.** be inclined to believe **4.** mistrust —*a.* (ˈsʌspɛkt) **5.** of suspected character —*n.* (ˈsʌspɛkt) **6.** suspected person

suspend (səˈspɛnd) *vt.* **1.** hang up **2.** cause to cease for a time **3.** debar from an office or privilege **4.** keep inoperative **5.** sustain in fluid —**susˈpenders** *pl.n.* straps for supporting stockings —**suspended animation** temporary cessation of vital functions —**suspended sentence** prison sentence that is not served by offender unless he commits further offence during its currency —**suspender belt** belt with suspenders hanging from it to hold up women's stockings

suspense (səˈspɛns) *n.* **1.** state of uncertainty, *esp.* while awaiting news, an event *etc.* **2.** anxiety, worry —**susˈpension** *n.* **1.** state of being suspended **2.** springs on axle of body of vehicle —**susˈpensory** *a.* —**suspension bridge** bridge suspended from cables that hang between two towers and are anchored at both ends

suspicion (səˈspɪʃən) *n.* **1.** suspecting, being suspected **2.** slight trace —**susˈpicious** *a.*

suss (sʌs) *vt. sl.* **1.** suspect **2.** (*oft. with* out) investigate, find (out)

sustain (səˈsteɪn) *vt.* **1.** keep, hold up **2.** endure **3.** keep alive **4.** confirm —**susˈtainable** *a.* —**sustenance** (ˈsʌstənəns) *n.* food

suture (ˈsuːtʃə) *n.* **1.** act of sewing **2.** sewing up of a wound **3.** material used for this **4.** a joining of the bones of the skull —**ˈsutural** *a.*

suzerain (ˈsuːzəreɪn) *n.* **1.** sovereign with rights over autonomous state **2.** feudal lord —**suzerainty** (ˈsuːzərəntɪ) *n.*

svelte (svɛlt, sfɛlt) *a.* **1.** lightly built, slender **2.** sophisticated

SW *or* **S.W.** southwest(ern)

Sw. **1.** Sweden **2.** Swedish

swab (swɒb) *n.* **1.** mop **2.** pad of surgical wool *etc.* for cleaning, taking specimen *etc.* **3.** *sl.* low or unmannerly fellow —*vt.* **4.** clean with swab (**-bb-**) —**ˈswabber** *n.*

swaddle (ˈswɒdˀl) *vt.* swathe —**swaddling clothes** *Hist.* long strips of cloth for wrapping newborn baby

swag (swæg) *n.* **1.** *sl.* stolen property **2.** A *inf.* bag carried by swagman —**ˈswagman** *n.* A itinerant tramp

swagger (ˈswægə) *vi.* **1.** strut **2.** boast —*n.* **3.** strutting gait **4.** boastful, overconfident manner —**swagger stick** *or esp. U.K.* **swagger cane** short cane or stick carried on occasion by army officers

Swahili (swɑːˈhiːlɪ) *n.* **1.** Bantu language widely used as lingua franca throughout E and central Afr. **2.** member of people speaking this language (*pl.* **-s, -li**) —**Swaˈhilian** *a.*

swain (sweɪn) *n.* rustic lover

swallow[1] (ˈswɒləʊ) *vt.* **1.** cause, allow to pass down gullet **2.** engulf **3.** suppress, keep back **4.** *inf.* believe gullibly —*n.* **5.** act of swallowing

swallow[2] (ˈswɒləʊ) *n.* migratory bird with forked tail and skimming manner of flight —**swallow dive** dive in which diver arches back, keeping his legs straight and his arms outstretched —**ˈswallowtail** *n.* **1.** butterfly having tail-like extension of each hind wing **2.** forked tail of swallow or similar bird

swam (swæm) *pt. of* SWIM

swami (ˈswɑːmɪ) *n.* in India, title of respect for Hindu saint or religious teacher (*pl.* **-es, -s**)

swamp (swɒmp) *n.* **1.** bog —*vt.* **2.** entangle in swamp **3.** overwhelm **4.** flood —**ˈswampy** *a.*

THESAURUS

susceptible **1.** *Usually with* **to** disposed, given, inclined, liable, open, predisposed, prone, subject, vulnerable **2.** alive to, easily moved, impressionable, receptive, responsive, sensitive, suggestible, tender

suspect *v.* **1.** distrust, doubt, harbour suspicions about, have one's doubts about, mistrust, smell a rat (*Inf.*) **2.** believe, conclude, conjecture, consider, fancy, feel, guess, have a sneaking suspicion, hazard a guess, speculate, suppose, surmise, think probable ~*adj.* **3.** doubtful, dubious, fishy (*Inf.*), open to suspicion, questionable

suspend **1.** append, attach, dangle, hang, swing **2.** adjourn, arrest, cease, cut short, debar, defer, delay, discontinue, hold off, interrupt, lay aside, pigeonhole, postpone, put off, shelve, stay, withhold

suspense anticipation, anxiety, apprehension, doubt, expectancy, expectation, indecision, insecurity, irresolution, tension, uncertainty, wavering, worry

suspension abeyance, adjournment, break, breaking off, deferment, delay, disbarment, discontinuation, interruption, moratorium, postponement, remission, respite, stay

suspicion **1.** bad vibes (*Inf.*), chariness, distrust, doubt, funny feeling (*Inf.*), jealousy, lack of confidence, misgiving, mistrust, qualm, scepticism, wariness **2.** conjecture, guess, gut feeling (*Inf.*), hunch, idea, impression, notion, supposition, surmise **3.** glimmer, hint, shade, shadow, *soupçon*, strain, streak, suggestion, tinge, touch, trace

suspicious **1.** apprehensive, distrustful, doubtful, jealous, mistrustful, sceptical, suspecting, unbelieving, wary **2.** doubtful, dubious, fishy (*Inf.*), funny, irregular, of doubtful honesty, open to doubt *or* misconstruction, queer, questionable, shady (*Inf.*), suspect

sustain **1.** bear, carry, hold up, keep from falling, keep up, support, uphold **2.** bear, bear up under, endure, experience, feel, suffer, undergo, withstand **3.** aid, assist, comfort, foster, help, keep alive, nourish, nurture, provide for, relieve **4.** approve, confirm, continue, keep alive, keep going, keep up, maintain, prolong, protract, ratify **5.** confirm, endorse, uphold, validate, verify

sustenance aliment, comestibles, daily bread, eatables, edibles, food, nourishment, provender, provisions, rations, refection, refreshments, victuals

swagger **1.** *v.* bluster, boast, brag, bully, gasconade (*Rare*), hector, parade, prance, show off (*Inf.*), strut, swank (*Inf.*) **2.** *n.* arrogance, bluster, braggadocio, display, gasconade (*Rare*), ostentation, pomposity, show, showing off (*Inf.*), swank (*Inf.*), swashbuckling

swallow *v.* **1.** absorb, consume, devour, down (*Inf.*), drink, eat, gulp, ingest, swig (*Inf.*), swill, wash down **2.** *Often with* **up** absorb, assimilate, consume, engulf, envelop, overrun, overwhelm, use up, waste **3.** choke back, hold in, keep back, repress, suppress **4.** *Inf.* accept, believe, buy (*Inf.*), fall for

swamp *n.* **1.** bog, everglade(s) (*U.S.*), fen, marsh, mire, morass, moss (*Scot., & northern English dialect*), quagmire, slough ~*v.* **2.** capsize, drench, engulf, flood, inundate, overwhelm, sink, submerge,

swan (swɒn) *n.* **1.** large, webfooted water bird with graceful curved neck —*vi.* **2.** *inf.* stroll idly (**-nn-**) —**ˈswannery** *n.* —**swan's-down** *n.* **1.** fine soft down feathers of swan, used to trim clothes *etc.* **2.** thick soft fabric of wool with silk, cotton or rayon **3.** cotton fabric with heavy nap —**swan song 1.** fabled song of a swan before death **2.** last act *etc.* before death —**swan-upping** *n.* **UK** practice of marking nicks in swans' beaks as sign of ownership

swank (swæŋk) *vi. sl.* **1.** swagger **2.** show off —**ˈswanky** *a. sl.* **1.** smart **2.** showy

swap *or* **swop** (swɒp) *n./v. inf.* **1.** exchange **2.** barter (**-pp-**)

sward (swɔːd) *or* **swarth** (swɔːθ) *n.* green turf

swarm[1] (swɔːm) *n.* **1.** large cluster of insects **2.** vast crowd —*vi.* **3.** (of bees) be on the move in swarm **4.** gather in large numbers

swarm[2] (swɔːm) *v.* climb (rope *etc.*) by grasping with hands and knees

swarthy (ˈswɔːðɪ) *a.* dark-complexioned

swashbuckler (ˈswɒʃbʌklə) *n.* swaggering daredevil person —**ˈswashbuckling** *a.*

swastika (ˈswɒstɪkə) *n.* form of cross with arms bent at right angles, used as badge by Nazis

swat (swɒt) *vt.* **1.** hit smartly **2.** kill, *esp.* insects (**-tt-**)

swatch (swɒtʃ) *n.* **1.** sample of cloth or other material **2.** a number of such samples, usu. fastened together in book form

swathe (sweɪð) *vt.* cover with wraps or bandages

sway (sweɪ) *v.* **1.** swing unsteadily **2.** (cause to) vacillate in opinion *etc.* —*vt.* **3.** influence opinion *etc.* of —*n.* **4.** control **5.** power **6.** swaying motion

swear (swɛə) *vt.* **1.** promise on oath **2.** cause to take an oath —*vi.* **3.** declare **4.** curse (**swore, sworn, ˈswearing**) —**ˈswearword** *n.* socially taboo word of a profane, obscene or insulting character

sweat (swɛt) *n.* **1.** moisture oozing from, forming on skin, *esp.* in humans —*v.* **2.** (cause to) exude sweat —*vi.* **3.** toil **4.** *inf.* worry —*vt.* **5.** employ at wrongfully low wages (**sweat** *or* **ˈsweated** *pt./pp.*, **ˈsweating** *pr.p.*) —**ˈsweaty** *a.* —**ˈsweatband** *n.* **1.** band of material set in hat to protect it from sweat **2.** piece of cloth tied around forehead to keep sweat out of eyes or around wrist to keep hands dry, as in sports —**sweat shirt** long-sleeved knitted cotton sweater —**ˈsweatshop** *n.* workshop where employees work long hours for low wages

sweater (ˈswɛtə) *n.* woollen jersey

Swede (swiːd) *n.* **1.** native of Sweden **2.** (**s-**) variety of turnip —**ˈSwedish** *a.* **1.** of Sweden, its people or their language —*n.* **2.** official language of Sweden

sweep (swiːp) *vi.* **1.** effect cleaning with broom **2.** pass quickly or magnificently **3.** extend in continuous curve —*vt.* **4.** clean with broom **5.** carry impetuously (**swept, ˈsweeping**) —*n.* **6.** act of cleaning with broom **7.** sweeping motion **8.** wide curve **9.** range **10.** long oar **11.** one who cleans chimneys —**ˈsweeping** *a.* **1.** wide-ranging **2.** without limitations, reservations —**sweep** *or* **ˈsweepstake** *n.* gamble in which winner takes stakes contributed by all

sweet (swiːt) *a.* **1.** tasting like sugar **2.** agreeable **3.** kind, charming **4.** fresh, fragrant **5.** in good condition **6.** tuneful **7.** gentle, dear, beloved —*n.* **8.** small piece of sweet food **9.** sweet course served at end of meal —**ˈsweeten** *v.* —**ˈsweetener** *n.* **1.** sweetening agent, *esp.* one that is sugar-free **2.** *sl.* bribe —**ˈsweetish** *a.* —**ˈsweetly** *adv.* —**ˈsweetbread** *n.* animal's pancreas used as food —**ˈsweetbrier** *n.* wild rose —**sweet corn** variety of maize whose kernels are rich in sugar and eaten as vegetable when young —**ˈsweetheart** *n.* lover —**ˈsweetmeat** *n.* sweetened delicacy, *eg* small cake, sweet —**sweet pea** plant of pea family with bright flowers —**sweet potato 1.** trailing plant **2.** its edible, sweetish, starchy tubers —**sweet-talk** *vt. inf.* coax, flatter —**sweet tooth** strong liking for sweet foods —**sweet william** (ˈwɪljəm) garden plant with flat flower clusters

THESAURUS

swallow up, upset, wash over, waterlog **3.** beset, besiege, deluge, flood, inundate, overload, overwhelm, snow under

swampy boggy, fenny, marish (*Obsolete*), marshy, miry, quaggy, waterlogged, wet

swap, swop *v.* bandy, barter, exchange, interchange, switch, trade, traffic

swarm 1. *n.* army, bevy, concourse, crowd, drove, flock, herd, horde, host, mass, multitude, myriad, shoal, throng **2.** *v.* congregate, crowd, flock, mass, stream, throng

swarthy black, brown, dark, dark-complexioned, dark-skinned, dusky, swart (*Archaic*), tawny

swashbuckling bold, daredevil, dashing, flamboyant, gallant, mettlesome, roisterous, spirited, swaggering

swastika fylfot

swathe bandage, bind, bundle up, cloak, drape, envelop, enwrap, fold, furl, lap, muffle up, sheathe, shroud, swaddle, wrap

sway *v.* **1.** bend, fluctuate, incline, lean, lurch, oscillate, rock, roll, swing, wave **2.** affect, control, direct, dominate, govern, guide, induce, influence, persuade, prevail on, win over ~*n.* **3.** ascendency, authority, clout (*Inf.*), command, control, dominion, government, influence, jurisdiction, power, predominance, rule, sovereignty

swear 1. affirm, assert, attest, avow, declare, depose, give one's word, pledge oneself, promise, state under oath, take an oath, testify, vow, warrant **2.** be foul-mouthed, blaspheme, curse, cuss (*Inf.*), imprecate, take the Lord's name in vain, turn the air blue, utter profanities

sweat *n.* **1.** diaphoresis (*Medical*), exudation, perspiration, sudor (*Medical*) ~*v.* **2.** moisture, glow, perspire **3.** *Inf.* agonize, be on pins and needles (*Inf.*), be on tenterhooks, chafe, fret, lose sleep over, suffer, torture oneself, worry

sweaty clammy, drenched (bathed, soaked) in perspiration, glowing, perspiring, sticky, sweating

sweep *v.* **1.** brush, clean, clear, remove **2.** career, flounce, fly, glance, glide, hurtle, pass, sail, scud, skim, tear, zoom ~*n.* **3.** arc, bend, curve, gesture, move, movement, stroke, swing **4.** compass, extent, range, scope, span, stretch, vista

sweeping 1. all-embracing, all-inclusive, bird's-eye, broad, comprehensive, extensive, global, radical, thoroughgoing, wide, wide-ranging **2.** across-the-board, blanket, exaggerated, indiscriminate, overdrawn, overstated, unqualified, wholesale

swell (swɛl) *v.* **1.** expand *—vi.* **2.** be greatly filled with pride, emotion **(swelled, ˈswollen, ˈswelling)** *—n.* **3.** act of swelling or being swollen **4.** wave of sea **5.** mechanism in organ to vary volume of sound **6.** *sl.* person of high social standing *—a.* **7.** *sl.* smart, fine **—swelled head** *or* **swollen head** *inf.* inflated view of one's own worth

swelter (ˈswɛltə) *vi.* be oppressed with heat

swept (swɛpt) *pt./pp. of* SWEEP **—ˈsweptwing** *a.* (of aircraft *etc.*) having wings swept backwards

swerve (swɜːv) *vi.* **1.** swing round, change direction during motion **2.** turn aside (from duty *etc.*) *—n.* **3.** swerving

swift (swɪft) *a.* **1.** rapid, quick, ready *—n.* **2.** bird like a swallow **—ˈswiftly** *adv.*

swig (swɪg) *n.* **1.** large swallow of drink *—v.* **2.** drink thus **(-gg-)**

swill (swɪl) *v.* **1.** drink greedily *—vt.* **2.** pour water over or through *—n.* **3.** liquid pig food **4.** greedy drinking **5.** rinsing

swim (swɪm) *vi.* **1.** support and move oneself in water **2.** float **3.** be flooded **4.** have feeling of dizziness *—vt.* **5.** cross by swimming **6.** compete in by swimming **(swam, swum, ˈswimming)** *—n.* **7.** spell of swimming **—ˈswimmer** *n.* **—ˈswimmingly** *adv.* successfully, effortlessly **—swimming pool** artificial pool for swimming **—ˈswimsuit** *n.* woman's one-piece swimming garment

swindle (ˈswɪndᵊl) *n./v.* cheat **—ˈswindler** *n.*

swine (swaɪn) *n.* **1.** pig **2.** contemptible person (*pl.* **swine**) **—ˈswinish** *a.* **—swine fever** infectious viral disease of pigs **—ˈswineherd** *n.*

swing (swɪŋ) *v.* **1.** (cause to) move to and fro **2.** (cause to) pivot, turn **3.** hang **4.** arrange, play (music) with (jazz) rhythm *—vi.* **5.** be hanged **6.** hit out (at) **(swung** *pt./pp.*) *—n.* **7.** act, instance of swinging **8.** seat hung to swing on **9.** fluctuation (*esp.* in voting pattern) **10. C** train of freight sleighs, canoes **—ˈswinger** *n. inf.* person regarded as modern, lively **—ˈswingboat** *n.* piece of fairground equipment consisting of boat-shaped carriage for swinging in

swingeing (ˈswɪndʒɪŋ) *a.* **1.** severe **2.** huge

swipe (swaɪp) *v.* **1.** (*sometimes with* at) strike with wide, sweeping or glancing blow *—vt.* **2.** *sl.* steal

swirl (swɜːl) *v.* **1.** (cause to) move with eddying motion *—n.* **2.** such motion

swish (swɪʃ) *v.* **1.** (cause to) move with audible hissing sound *—n.* **2.** the sound *—a.* **3.** *inf.* fashionable, smart

Swiss (swɪs) *n.* **1.** native of Switzerland *—a.* **2.** of Switzerland **—swiss roll** type of rolled-up sponge cake

switch (swɪtʃ) *n.* **1.** mechanism to complete or interrupt electric circuit *etc.* **2.** abrupt change **3.** flexible stick or twig **4.** tufted end of animal's tail **5.** tress of false hair *—vi.* **6.** shift, change **7.** swing *—vt.* **8.** affect (current *etc.*) with switch **9.** change abruptly **10.** strike with switch **—ˈswitchback** *n.* road, railway with steep rises and descents **—ˈswitchboard** *n.* installation for establishing or varying connections in telephone and electric circuits

THESAURUS

sweet *adj.* **1.** cloying, honeyed, luscious, melting, saccharine, sugary, sweetened, syrupy, toothsome **2.** affectionate, agreeable, amiable, appealing, attractive, beautiful, charming, delightful, engaging, fair, gentle, kind, lovable, sweet-tempered, taking, tender, unselfish, winning, winsome **3.** beloved, cherished, darling, dear, dearest, pet, precious, treasured **4.** aromatic, balmy, clean, fragrant, fresh, new, perfumed, pure, redolent, sweet-smelling, wholesome **5.** dulcet, euphonic, euphonious, harmonious, mellow, melodious, musical, silver-toned, silvery, soft, sweet-sounding, tuneful ~*n.* **6.** afters (*Brit. inf.*), dessert, pudding, sweet course **7.** *Usually plural* bonbon, candy (*U.S.*), confectionery, sweetie, sweetmeats

sweeten honey, sugar, sugar-coat

sweetheart admirer, beau, beloved, boyfriend, darling, dear, flame (*Inf.*), follower (*Obsolete*), girlfriend, inamorata, inamorato, love, lover, steady (*Inf.*), suitor, swain (*Archaic*), sweetie (*Inf.*), truelove, valentine

swell *v.* **1.** balloon, become bloated *or* distended, become larger, be inflated, belly, billow, bloat, bulge, dilate, distend, enlarge, expand, extend, fatten, grow, increase, protrude, puff up, rise, round out, tumefy, well up ~*n.* **2.** billow, rise, surge, undulation, wave **3.** *Inf.* beau, blade (*Archaic*), cockscomb (*Inf.*), dandy, fashion plate, fop, nob (*Sl.*), toff (*Brit. sl.*) ~*adj.* **4.** *Inf.* de luxe, exclusive, fashionable, fine, grand, plush *or* plushy (*Inf.*), posh (*Inf.*), ritzy (*Sl.*), smart, stylish

swerve *v.* bend, deflect, depart from, deviate, diverge, incline, sheer off, shift, skew, stray, swing, turn, turn aside, veer, wander, wind

swift abrupt, expeditious, express, fast, fleet, fleet-footed, flying, hurried, nimble, nippy (*Brit. inf.*), prompt, quick, rapid, ready, short, short-lived, spanking, speedy, sudden, winged

swiftly as fast as one's legs can carry one, (at) full tilt, double-quick, fast, hotfoot, hurriedly, in less than no time, nippily (*Brit. inf.*), posthaste, promptly, rapidly, speedily, without losing time

swill *v.* **1.** consume, drain, drink (down), gulp, guzzle, imbibe, pour down one's gullet, quaff, swallow, swig (*Inf.*), toss off **2.** *Often with* **out** drench, flush, rinse, sluice, wash down, wash out ~*n.* **3.** hogwash, mash, mush, pigswill, scourings, slops, waste

swindle 1. *v.* bamboozle (*Inf.*), bilk (of), cheat, con (*Sl.*), deceive, defraud, diddle (*Inf.*), do (*Sl.*), dupe, fleece, hornswoggle (*Sl.*), overcharge, pull a fast one (on someone) (*Inf.*), put one over on (someone) (*Inf.*), rip (someone) off (*Sl.*), rook (*Sl.*), take (someone) for a ride (*Inf.*), take to the cleaners (*Inf.*), trick **2.** *n.* cheat, con trick (*Inf.*), deceit, deception, double-dealing, fiddle (*Brit. inf.*), fraud, imposition, knavery, racket, rip-off (*Sl.*), roguery, sharp practice, swizz (*Brit. inf.*), swizzle (*Brit. inf.*), trickery

swindler charlatan, cheat, confidence man, con man (*Sl.*), fraud, impostor, knave (*Archaic*), mountebank, rascal, rogue, rook (*Sl.*), shark, sharper, trickster

swing *v.* **1.** be pendent, be suspended, dangle, hang, move back and forth, suspend **2.** fluctuate, oscillate, rock, sway, vary, veer, vibrate, wave **3.** *Usually with* **round** curve, pivot, rotate, swivel, turn, turn on one's heel, wheel ~*n.* **4.** fluctuation, oscillation, stroke, sway, swaying, vibration

swirl *v.* agitate, boil, churn, eddy, spin, surge, twirl, twist, whirl

switch *v.* **1.** change, change course, deflect, deviate, divert, exchange, interchange, rearrange, replace by, shift, substitute, swap (*Inf.*), trade, turn aside ~*n.*

swither (ˈswɪðə) *Scot. dial. vi.* **1.** hesitate; be perplexed —*n.* **2.** hesitation; perplexity; agitation

swivel (ˈswɪvᵊl) *n.* **1.** mechanism of two parts which can revolve the one on the other —*v.* **2.** turn (on swivel) (**-ll-**)

swizzle (ˈswɪzᵊl) *n.* **1.** an alcoholic drink containing gin or rum **2.** *inf.* **UK** swindle or disappointment (*also* **swizz**) —**swizzle stick** small rod used to agitate effervescent drink to facilitate escape of carbon dioxide

swob (swɒb) *see* SWAB

swollen (ˈswəulən) *pp. of* SWELL

swoon (swuːn) *vi./n.* faint

swoop (swuːp) *vi.* **1.** dive, as hawk —*n.* **2.** act of swooping **3.** sudden attack

swoosh (swuʃ) *vi.* **1.** make rustling, swirling sound, *esp.* when moving, pouring out —*n.* **2.** swirling, rustling sound or movement

swop (swɒp) *see* SWAP

sword (sɔːd) *n.* weapon with long blade for cutting or thrusting —**sword dance** dance in which performers dance nimbly over swords on ground or brandish them in the air —ˈ**swordfish** *n.* fish with elongated sharp upper jaw, like sword —ˈ**swordplay** *n.* **1.** action or art of fighting with sword **2.** verbal sparring —**sword swallower** person who swallows or appears to swallow swords, in a circus *etc.*

swore (swɔː) *pt. of* SWEAR —**sworn** *pp. of* SWEAR

swot (swɒt) *inf. v.* **1.** study hard (**-tt-**) —*n.* **2.** one who works hard at lessons or studies

swum (swʌm) *pp. of* SWIM

swung (swʌŋ) *pt./pp. of* SWING

sybarite (ˈsɪbəraɪt) *n.* person who loves luxury —**sybaritic** (sɪbəˈrɪtɪk) *a.*

sycamore (ˈsɪkəmɔː) *n.* tree allied to plane tree and maple

sycophant (ˈsɪkəfənt) *n.* one using flattery to gain favours —ˈ**sycophancy** *n.* —**sycoˈphantic** *a.*

syllable (ˈsɪləbᵊl) *n.* division of word as unit for pronunciation —**sylˈlabic** *a.* —**sylˈlabify** *vt.*

syllabub *or* **sillabub** (ˈsɪləbʌb) *n.* **1.** sweet frothy dish of cream, sugar and wine **2.** something insubstantial

syllabus (ˈsɪləbəs) *n.* **1.** outline of a course of study **2.** programme, list of subjects studied on course (*pl.* **-es, -bi** (-baɪ))

syllogism (ˈsɪlədʒɪzəm) *n.* form of logical reasoning consisting of two premisses and conclusion —**sylloˈgistic** *a.*

sylph (sɪlf) *n.* **1.** slender, graceful woman **2.** sprite —ˈ**sylphlike** *a.*

sylvan *or* **silvan** (ˈsɪlvən) *a.* of forests, trees

sym- *see* SYN-

symbiosis (sɪmbɪˈəusɪs) *n.* living together of two organisms of different kinds, *esp.* to their mutual benefit —**symbiotic** (sɪmbɪˈɒtɪk) *a.*

symbol (ˈsɪmbᵊl) *n.* **1.** sign **2.** thing representing or typifying something —**symˈbolic** *a.* —**symˈbolically** *adv.* —ˈ**symbolism** *n.* **1.** use of, representation by symbols **2.** movement in art holding that work of art should express idea in symbolic form —ˈ**symbolist** *n./a.* —ˈ**symbolize** *or* **-ise** *v.*

symmetry (ˈsɪmɪtrɪ) *n.* **1.** proportion between parts **2.** balance of arrangement between two sides **3.** order —**symˈmetrical** *a.* **1.** having due proportion in parts **2.** harmonious **3.** regular

sympathy (ˈsɪmpəθɪ) *n.* **1.** feeling for another in pain *etc.* **2.** compassion, pity **3.** sharing of emotion, interest, desire *etc.* **4.** fellow feeling —**sympaˈthetic** *a.* —**sympaˈthetically** *adv.* —ˈ**sympathize** *or* **-ise** *vi.* —**sympathetic magic** type of magic in which it is sought to produce large-scale effect by performing some small-scale ceremony resembling it, as pouring of water on altar to induce rainfall

symphony (ˈsɪmfənɪ) *n.* **1.** composition for full orchestra **2.** harmony of sounds —**symphonic** (sɪmˈfɒnɪk) *a.* —**symˈphonious** *a.* harmonious —**symphonic poem** extended orchestral composition, based on nonmusical material, such as work of literature or folk tale —**symphony orchestra** large orchestra comprising strings, brass, woodwind, harp and percussion

THESAURUS

2. about-turn, alteration, change, change of direction, exchange, reversal, shift, substitution, swap (*Inf.*) ~*v.* **3.** lash, swing, swish, twitch, wave, whip

swollen bloated, distended, dropsical, enlarged, inflamed, puffed up, puffy, tumescent, tumid

swoop 1. *v.* descend, dive, pounce, rush, stoop, sweep **2.** *n.* descent, drop, lunge, plunge, pounce, rush, stoop, sweep

sword blade, brand (*Archaic*), trusty steel

syllabus course of study, curriculum

symbol badge, emblem, figure, image, logo, mark, representation, sign, token, type

symbolic allegorical, emblematic, figurative, representative, significant, token, typical

symbolize betoken, body forth, connote, denote, exemplify, mean, personify, represent, signify, stand for, typify

symmetrical balanced, in proportion, proportional, regular, well-proportioned

symmetry agreement, balance, correspondence, evenness, form, harmony, order, proportion, regularity

sympathetic 1. affectionate, caring, commiserating, compassionate, concerned, condoling, feeling, interested, kind, kindly, pitying, responsive, supportive, tender, understanding, warm, warm-hearted **2.** *Often with* **to** agreeable, approving, encouraging, favourably disposed, friendly, in sympathy with, pro, well-disposed **3.** agreeable, appreciative, companionable, compatible, congenial, friendly, like-minded, responsive, well-intentioned

sympathetically appreciatively, feelingly, kindly, perceptively, responsively, sensitively, understandingly, warm-heartedly, warmly, with compassion, with feeling, with interest

sympathize 1. bleed for, commiserate, condole, empathize, feel for, feel one's heart go out to, grieve with, have compassion, offer consolation, pity, share another's sorrow **2.** agree, be in accord, be in sympathy, go along with, identify with, side with, understand

sympathy 1. commiseration, compassion, condolence(s), empathy, pity, tenderness, thoughtfulness, understanding **2.** affinity, agreement, congeniality, correspondence, fellow feeling, harmony, rapport, union, warmth

symposium (sɪmˈpəʊzɪəm) *n.* **1.** conference, meeting **2.** discussion, writings on a given topic (*pl.* **-s, -sia** (-zɪə))

symptom (ˈsɪmptəm) *n.* **1.** change in body indicating its state of health or disease **2.** sign, token —**sympto'matic** *a.*

syn- *or* **sym-** (*comb. form*) with, together, alike

synagogue (ˈsɪnəgɒg) *n.* (place of worship of) Jewish congregation

synchromesh (ˈsɪŋkrəʊmɛʃ) *a.* (of gearbox) having device that synchronizes speeds of gears before they engage

synchronize *or* **-ise** (ˈsɪŋkrənaɪz) *vt.* **1.** make agree in time —*vi.* **2.** happen at same time —**'synchronism** *n.* —**synchroni'zation** *or* **-i'sation** *n.* —**'synchronous** *a.* simultaneous

synchrotron (ˈsɪŋkrətrɒn) *n.* device for acceleration of stream of electrons

syncopate (ˈsɪŋkəpeɪt) *vt.* accentuate (weak beat in bar of music) —**synco'pation** *n.*

syndicate (ˈsɪndɪkɪt) *n.* **1.** body of people, delegates associated for some enterprise —*vt.* (ˈsɪndɪkeɪt) **2.** form into syndicate **3.** publish in many newspapers at the same time —**'syndicalism** *n.* economic movement aiming at combination of workers in all trades to enforce demands of labour

syndrome (ˈsɪndrəʊm) *n.* **1.** combination of several symptoms in disease **2.** symptom, set of symptoms or characteristics

synod (ˈsɪnəd, ˈsɪnɒd) *n.* **1.** church council **2.** convention

synonym (ˈsɪnənɪm) *n.* word with same meaning as another —**syno'nymity** *n.* —**synonymous** (sɪˈnɒnɪməs) *a.*

synopsis (sɪˈnɒpsɪs) *n.* summary, outline (*pl.* **-ses** (-siːz)) —**syn'optic** *a.* **1.** of, like synopsis **2.** having same viewpoint

syntax (ˈsɪntæks) *n.* part of grammar treating of arrangement of words in sentence —**syn'tactic** *a.* —**syn'tactically** *adv.*

synthesis (ˈsɪnθɪsɪs) *n.* putting together, combination (*pl.* **-theses** (-θɪsiːz)) —**'synthesize** *or* **-ise** *v.* (cause to) combine into a whole —**'synthesizer** *n.* **1.** *see* MOOG SYNTHESIZER **2.** person or thing that synthesizes —**synthetic** (sɪnˈθɛtɪk) *a.* **1.** artificial **2.** of synthesis

syphilis (ˈsɪfɪlɪs) *n.* contagious venereal disease —**syphi'litic** *a.*

Syrian (ˈsɪrɪən) *a.* **1.** of Syria, republic in W. Asia, its people or their dialect of Arabic —*n.* **2.** native or inhabitant of Syria

syringe (ˈsɪrɪndʒ, sɪˈrɪndʒ) *n.* **1.** instrument for drawing in liquid by piston and forcing it out in fine stream or spray **2.** squirt —*vt.* **3.** spray, cleanse with syringe

syrup (ˈsɪrəp) *n.* **1.** thick solution obtained in process of refining sugar **2.** any liquid like this, *esp.* in consistency —**'syrupy** *a.*

system (ˈsɪstəm) *n.* **1.** complex whole, organization **2.** method **3.** classification —**syste'matic** *a.* methodical —**syste'matically** *adv.* —**'systematize** *or* **-ise** *vt.* **1.** reduce to system **2.** arrange methodically —**systemic** (sɪˈstɛmɪk, -ˈstiː-) *a.* affecting entire body or organism —**systems analysis** analysis of methods involved in scientific and industrial operations, usu. with computer so that improved system can be designed

systole (ˈsɪstəlɪ) *n.* contraction of heart and arteries for expelling blood and carrying on circulation —**systolic** (sɪˈstɒlɪk) *a.* **1.** contracting **2.** of systole

THESAURUS

symptom expression, indication, mark, note, sign, syndrome, token, warning

symptomatic characteristic, indicative, suggestive

synthesis 1. amalgamation, coalescence, combination, integration, unification, welding **2.** amalgam, blend, combination, composite, compound, fusion, union

synthetic artificial, ersatz, fake, man-made, manufactured, mock

system 1. arrangement, classification, combination, coordination, organization, scheme, setup (*Sl.*), structure **2.** fixed order, frame of reference, method, methodology, modus operandi, practice, procedure, routine, technique, theory, usage **3.** definite plan, logical process, method, methodicalness, orderliness, regularity, systematization

systematic businesslike, efficient, methodical, orderly, organized, precise, standardized, systematized, well-ordered

T

t *or* **T** (tiː) *n.* **1.** 20th letter of English alphabet **2.** speech sound represented by this letter **3.** something shaped like T (*pl.* **t's, T's** *or* **Ts**) **—to a T** in every detail; perfectly

t 1. tense **2.** ton

T 1. absolute temperature **2.** *Chem.* tritium **3.** surface tension **4.** tablespoon

ta (tɑː) *interj.* **UK** *inf.* thank you

Ta *Chem.* tantalum

TA Territorial Army

Taal (tɑːl) *n.* **SA** language, *esp.* Afrikaans

tab[1] (tæb) *n.* tag, label, short strap **—keep tabs on** *inf.* keep watchful eye on

tab[2] (tæb) **1.** tabulator **2.** tablet

tabard (ˈtæbəd) *n.* (herald's) short tunic open at sides

tabby (ˈtæbɪ) *n./a.* (cat) with markings of stripes *etc.* on lighter background

tabernacle (ˈtæbənækᵊl) *n.* **1.** portable shrine of Israelites **2.** *R.C.Ch.* receptacle containing consecrated Host **3.** place of worship not called a church

table (ˈteɪbᵊl) *n.* **1.** piece of furniture consisting of flat board supported by legs **2.** food **3.** set of facts, figures arranged in lines or columns *—vt.* **4.** lay on table **5.** submit (motion *etc.*) for consideration by meeting **6.** suspend discussion of (bill *etc.*) indefinitely **—ˈtablecloth** *n.* cloth for covering table **—ˈtableland** *n.* plateau, high flat area **—table licence** licence authorizing sale of alcoholic drinks with meals only **—ˈtablespoon** *n.* spoon used for serving food *etc.* **—table tennis** ball game played on table with small bats and light hollow ball

tableau (ˈtæbləʊ) *n.* **1.** group of persons, silent and motionless, arranged to represent some scene **2.** dramatic scene (*pl.* **-leaux** (-ləʊ, -ləʊz))

table d'hôte (ˈtɑːbᵊl ˈdəʊt) *Fr.* (meal) with limited choice of dishes, at a fixed price

tablet (ˈtæblɪt) *n.* **1.** pill of compressed powdered medicinal substance **2.** flattish cake of soap *etc.* **3.** slab of stone, wood *etc., esp.* used formerly for writing on

tabloid (ˈtæblɔɪd) *n.* illustrated popular small-sized newspaper with terse, sensational headlines

taboo *or* **tabu** (təˈbuː) *a.* **1.** forbidden; disapproved of *—n.* **2.** prohibition resulting from social conventions *etc.* **3.** thing prohibited *—vt.* **4.** place under taboo

tabor *or* **tabour** (ˈteɪbə) *n.* small drum, used *esp.* in Middle Ages, struck with one hand while other held pipe

tabular (ˈtæbjʊlə) *a.* shaped, arranged like a table **—ˈtabulate** *vt.* arrange (figures, facts *etc.*) in tables **—tabuˈlation** *n.* **—ˈtabulator** *n.* **1.** device for setting stops that locate column margins on typewriter **2.** *Comp.* machine that reads data from punched cards *etc.*, producing lists, tabulations or totals

tacho- (*comb. form*) speed, as in *tachometer*

tachograph (ˈtækəgrɑːf) *n.* device for recording speed and distance travelled by lorries

tachometer (tæˈkɒmɪtə) *n.* device for measuring speed, *esp.* of revolving shaft (in car) and hence revolutions per minute

tacit (ˈtæsɪt) *a.* **1.** implied but not spoken **2.** silent **—ˈtacitly** *adv.* **—ˈtaciturn** *a.* **1.** talking little **2.** habitually silent **—taciˈturnity** *n.*

tack[1] (tæk) *n.* **1.** small nail **2.** long, loose, temporary stitch **3.** *Naut.* course of ship obliquely to windward **4.** course, direction **5.** *inf.* food *—vt.* **6.** nail with tacks **7.** stitch (garment) with long, loose temporary stitches **8.** append, attach *—v.* **9.** sail to windward **—on the wrong tack** under false impression

tack[2] (tæk) *n.* riding harness for horses

tackies (ˈtækɪz) *pl.n.* **SA** plimsolls

tackle (ˈtækᵊl) *n.* **1.** equipment, apparatus, *esp.* lifting appliances with ropes **2.** *Sport* physical challenge of opponent *—vt.* **3.** take in hand **4.** grapple with **5.** challenge

tacky[1] (ˈtækɪ) *a.* sticky, not quite dry **—ˈtackiness** *n.*

tacky[2] (ˈtækɪ) *a.* **US** *inf.* **1.** shabby, shoddy **2.** ostentatious and vulgar **3.** (of person) eccentric; crazy

tact (tækt) *n.* **1.** skill in dealing with people or situations **2.** delicate perception of the feelings of others **—ˈtactful** *a.* **—ˈtactfully** *adv.* **—ˈtactless** *a.* **—ˈtactlessly** *adv.*

THESAURUS

table *n.* **1.** bench, board, counter, slab, stand **2.** board, diet, fare, food, spread (*Inf.*), victuals **3.** agenda, catalogue, chart, diagram, digest, graph, index, inventory, list, plan, record, register, roll, schedule, synopsis, tabulation *~v.* **4.** enter, move, propose, put forward, submit, suggest

tableau picture, representation, scene, spectacle

taboo 1. *adj.* anathema, banned, beyond the pale, disapproved of, forbidden, frowned on, not allowed, not permitted, outlawed, prohibited, proscribed, ruled out, unacceptable, unmentionable, unthinkable **2.** *n.* anathema, ban, disapproval, interdict, prohibition, proscription, restriction

tabulate arrange, catalogue, categorize, chart, classify, codify, index, list, order, range, systematize, tabularize

tacit implicit, implied, inferred, silent, taken for granted, undeclared, understood, unexpressed, unspoken, unstated, wordless

taciturn aloof, antisocial, close-lipped, cold, distant, dumb, mute, quiet, reserved, reticent, silent, tight-lipped, uncommunicative, unforthcoming, withdrawn

tack *n.* **1.** drawing pin, nail, pin, staple, thumbtack (*U.S.*), tintack **2.** approach, bearing, course, direction, heading, line, method, path, plan, procedure, tactic, way *~v.* **3.** affix, attach, fasten, fix, nail, pin, staple **4.** baste, stitch **5.** add, annex, append, attach, tag

tackle *n.* **1.** accoutrements, apparatus, equipment, gear, implements, outfit, paraphernalia, rig, rigging, tools, trappings **2.** block, challenge, stop *~v.* **3.** apply oneself to, attempt, begin, come *or* get to grips with, deal with, embark upon, engage in, essay, get stuck into (*Inf.*), have a go at (*Inf.*), set about, take on, try, turn one's hand to, undertake **4.** block, bring down, challenge, clutch, confront, grab, grasp, halt, intercept, seize, stop, take hold of, throw

tact address, adroitness, consideration, delicacy, diplomacy, discretion, finesse, judgment, perception,

tactics (ˈtæktɪks) *n.* (*usu. pl.*) **1.** art of handling troops, ships in battle **2.** adroit management of a situation **3.** plan(s) for this —ˈ**tactical** *a.* —**tacˈtician** *n.* —**tactical voting** (in election) casting vote not for party of one's choice but for second strongest contender in consitituency, in order to defeat likeliest winner

tactile (ˈtæktaɪl) *a.* of the sense of touch

tadpole (ˈtædpəʊl) *n.* immature frog, in its first state before gills and tail are absorbed

taffeta (ˈtæfɪtə) *n.* smooth, stiff fabric of silk, rayon *etc.*

taffrail (ˈtæfreɪl) *n.* **1.** rail at stern of ship **2.** flat ornamental part of stern

Taffy (ˈtæfɪ) *n. sl.* Welshman

tag[1] (tæg) *n.* **1.** label identifying or showing price of something **2.** ragged, hanging end **3.** pointed end of shoelace *etc.* **4.** trite quotation **5.** any appendage —*vt.* **6.** append, add (on) —*vi.* **7.** (*usu. with* on *or* along) trail behind (**-gg-**)

tag[2] (tæg) *n.* **1.** children's game where one being chased becomes the chaser upon being touched by chaser —*vt.* **2.** touch (**-gg-**) —**tag wrestling** wrestling match for teams of two, where one partner may replace the other upon being touched on hand

tagetes (tæˈdʒiːtiːz) *n.* plant with yellow or orange flowers

tail (teɪl) *n.* **1.** flexible prolongation of animal's spine **2.** lower or inferior part of anything **3.** appendage **4.** rear part of aircraft **5.** *inf.* person employed to follow and spy on another —*pl.* **6.** reverse side of coin **7.** *inf.* tail coat —*vt.* **8.** remove tail of **9.** *inf.* follow closely, trail —**tailed** *a.* —ˈ**tailings** *pl.n.* waste left over from some (*eg* industrial) process —ˈ**tailless** *a.* —ˈ**tailback** *n.* queue of traffic stretching back from an obstruction —ˈ**tailboard** *n.* removable or hinged rear board on lorry *etc.* —**tail coat** man's evening dress jacket —**tail end** last part —**tail gate** gate used to control flow of water at lower end of lock —ˈ**tailgate** *n.* **1.** *esp.* **US** tailboard —*v.* **2. US** drive very close behind (vehicle) —ˈ**taillight** *or* ˈ**taillamp** *n.* light at rear of vehicle —ˈ**tailpiece** *n.* **1.** extension or appendage that lengthens or completes something **2.** decorative design at foot of page *etc.* **3.** piece of wood to which strings of violin *etc.* are attached at lower end **4.** short beam or rafter with one end embedded in wall —ˈ**tailpipe** *n.* pipe from which exhaust gases are discharged, *esp.* at rear of motor vehicle —ˈ**tailplane** *n.* stabilizing surface at rear of aircraft —ˈ**tailspin** *n.* spinning dive of aircraft —ˈ**tailwind** *n.* wind blowing in same direction as course of aircraft or ship —**tail off** diminish gradually, dwindle —**turn tail** run away

tailor (ˈteɪlə) *n.* maker of outer clothing, *esp.* for men —ˈ**tailored** *a.* **1.** having simple lines, as some women's garments **2.** specially fitted —ˈ**tailorbird** *n.* tropical Asian warbler that builds nest by sewing together large leaves using plant fibres —**tailor-made** *a.* **1.** made by tailor **2.** well-fitting **3.** appropriate —*n.* **4.** *inf.* factory-made cigarettes

taint (teɪnt) *v.* **1.** affect or be affected by pollution *etc.* —*n.* **2.** defect, flaw **3.** infection, contamination

take (teɪk) *vt.* **1.** grasp, get hold of **2.** get, receive **3.** assume **4.** adopt **5.** accept **6.** understand **7.** consider **8.** carry, conduct **9.** use **10.** capture **11.** consume **12.** require —*vi.* **13.** be effective **14.** please **15.** go (**took,** ˈ**taken,** ˈ**taking**) —*n.* **16.** *esp. Cine.* (recording of) scene, sequence photographed without interruption —ˈ**taking** *a.* charming —ˈ**takings** *pl.n.* earnings, receipts —ˈ**takeaway UK, A, NZ** *a.* **1.** sold for consumption away from premises **2.** selling food for consumption away from premises —*n.* **3.** shop or restaurant that sells such food —**take-home pay** remainder of one's pay after all income tax and other compulsory deductions have been made —**take-off** *n.* **1.** instant at which aircraft becomes airborne **2.** commencement of flight **3.** *inf.* act of mimicry —ˈ**takeover** *n.* act of assuming power, control *etc.* —**take after** resemble in appearance or character —**take down 1.** write down **2.** dismantle **3.** humiliate —**take in 1.** understand **2.** make (garment *etc.*) smaller **3.** deceive —**take in vain 1.** blaspheme **2.** mention (person's name) —**take off 1.** (of aircraft) leave ground **2.** *inf.* go away **3.** *inf.* mimic —**take over 1.** assume control or management (of) **2.** *Print.* move (copy) to next line —**take to** become fond of

THESAURUS

savoir-faire, sensitivity, skill, thoughtfulness, understanding

tactful careful, considerate, delicate, diplomatic, discreet, judicious, perceptive, polished, polite, politic, prudent, sensitive, subtle, thoughtful, understanding

tactic 1. approach, course, device, line, manoeuvre, means, method, move, ploy, policy, scheme, stratagem, tack, trick, way **2.** *Plural* campaign, generalship, manoeuvres, plans, strategy

tactical adroit, artful, clever, cunning, diplomatic, politic, shrewd, skilful, smart, strategic

tactician brain (*Inf.*), campaigner, coordinator, director, general, mastermind, planner, strategist

tactless blundering, boorish, careless, clumsy, discourteous, gauche, harsh, impolite, impolitic, imprudent, inconsiderate, indelicate, indiscreet, inept, injudicious, insensitive, maladroit, rough, rude, sharp, thoughtless, uncivil, undiplomatic, unfeeling, unkind, unsubtle

tail 1. *n.* appendage, conclusion, empennage, end, extremity, rear end, tailpiece, train **2.** *v. Inf.* dog the footsteps of, follow, keep an eye on, shadow, stalk, track, trail

tail off decrease, die out, diminish gradually, drop, dwindle, fade, fall away, peter out, wane

tailor clothier, costumier, couturier, dressmaker, garment maker, outfitter, seamstress

taint *v.* **1.** adulterate, blight, contaminate, corrupt, dirty, foul, infect, poison, pollute, soil, spoil **2.** besmirch, blacken, blemish, blot, brand, damage, defile, disgrace, dishonour, muddy, ruin, shame, smear, stain, stigmatize, sully, tarnish, vitiate ~*n.* **3.** black mark, blemish, blot, blot on one's escutcheon, defect, disgrace, dishonour, fault, flaw, shame, smear, spot, stain, stigma **4.** contagion, contamination, infection, pollution

take *v.* **1.** abduct, acquire, arrest, capture, carry off, catch, clutch, ensnare, entrap, gain possession of, get, get hold of, grasp, grip, have, help oneself to, lay hold of, obtain, receive, secure, seize, win **2.** abstract, appropriate, carry off, filch, misappropriate, nick (*Brit. sl.*), pinch (*Inf.*), pocket, purloin, run off with, steal, swipe (*Sl.*), walk off with **3.** consume, drink, eat, imbibe, ingest, inhale, swallow **4.** accept,

talc (tælk) *n.* 1. soft mineral of magnesium silicate 2. talcum powder —**talcum powder** powder, *usu.* scented, to absorb body moisture, deodorize *etc.*

tale (teɪl) *n.* 1. story, narrative, report 2. fictitious story —**tell tales** 1. tell fanciful lies 2. report malicious stories *etc., esp.* to someone in authority

talent (ˈtælənt) *n.* 1. natural ability or power 2. ancient weight or money 3. *inf.* (*esp.* attractive) members of opposite sex —ˈ**talented** *a.* gifted —**talent scout** person whose occupation is searching for talented sportsmen, performers *etc.* for engagement as professionals

talisman (ˈtælɪzmən) *n.* 1. object supposed to have magic power 2. amulet (*pl.* -**s**) —**talisˈmanic** *a.*

talk (tɔːk) *vi.* 1. express, exchange ideas *etc.* in words 2. spread rumours or gossip —*vt.* 3. express in speech, utter 4. discuss —*n.* 5. speech, lecture 6. conversation 7. rumour —ˈ**talkative** *a.* fond of talking —ˈ**talker** *n.* —**talking book** recording of book, designed to be used by blind —**talking head** (on television) person, shown only from shoulders up, who speaks without illustrative material —**talking-to** *n. inf.* reproof —**talk back** answer boldly or impudently —**talk into** persuade to by talking —**talk out of** dissuade from by talking

tall (tɔːl) *a.* 1. high, of great stature 2. incredible, untrue (*esp. in* **tall story**) —ˈ**tallboy** *n.* high chest of drawers —**tall order** demand which is difficult to accomplish

tallow (ˈtæləʊ) *n.* 1. melted and clarified animal fat —*vt.* 2. smear with this

tally (ˈtælɪ) *vi.* 1. correspond one with the other 2. keep score (-**lied**, -**lying**) —*n.* 3. record, account, total number —ˈ**tallier** *n.*

tally-ho (tælɪˈhəʊ) *interj.* huntsman's cry to urge on hounds

Talmud (ˈtælmʊd) *n.* body of Jewish law —**Talˈmudic** *a.*

talon (ˈtælən) *n.* claw

tamarind (ˈtæmərɪnd) *n.* 1. tropical tree 2. its pods containing sour brownish pulp

tamarisk (ˈtæmərɪsk) *n.* ornamental, evergreen tree or shrub with slender branches, very small leaves and spiky flowers

tambour (ˈtæmbʊə) *n.* 1. *Real tennis* sloping buttress on one side of receiver's end of court 2. embroidery frame consisting of two hoops over which fabric is stretched while being worked 3. embroidered work done on such frame 4. sliding door on desks *etc.*, made of thin strips of wood glued on to canvas backing 5. *Archit.* wall that is circular in plan, *esp.* supporting

THESAURUS

adopt, assume, enter upon, undertake 5. assume, believe, consider, deem, hold, interpret as, perceive, presume, receive, regard, see as, think of as, understand 6. bear, bring, carry, cart, convey, ferry, fetch, haul, tote (*Inf.*), transport 7. accompany, bring, conduct, convoy, escort, guide, lead, usher 8. attract, become popular, captivate, charm, delight, enchant, fascinate, please, win favour 9. call for, demand, necessitate, need, require

take down 1. make a note of, minute, note, put on record, record, set down, transcribe, write down 2. demolish, disassemble, dismantle, level, raze, take apart, take to pieces, tear down 3. deflate, humble, humiliate, mortify, put down (*Sl.*)

take in 1. absorb, assimilate, comprehend, digest, grasp, understand 2. *Inf.* bilk, cheat, con (*Inf.*), deceive, do (*Sl.*), dupe, fool, gull (*Archaic*), hoodwink, mislead, pull the wool over (someone's) eyes (*Inf.*), swindle, trick

take-off 1. departure, launch, liftoff 2. *Inf.* caricature, imitation, lampoon, mimicry, mocking, parody, satire, send-up (*Brit. inf.*), spoof (*Inf.*), travesty

take off 1. become airborne, leave the ground, lift off, take to the air 2. *Inf.* beat it (*Sl.*), decamp, depart, disappear, go, hit the road (*Sl.*), leave, set out, split (*Sl.*), strike out 3. *Inf.* caricature, hit off, imitate, lampoon, mimic, mock, parody, satirize, send up (*Brit. inf.*), spoof (*Inf.*), travesty

take over assume control of, become leader of, come to power, gain control of, succeed to, take command of

take to become friendly, be pleased by, be taken with, conceive an affection for, get on with, like, warm to

taking 1. *adj.* attractive, beguiling, captivating, charming, compelling, delightful, enchanting, engaging, fascinating, fetching (*Inf.*), intriguing, pleasing, prepossessing, winning 2. *n. Plural* earnings, gain, gate, income, pickings, proceeds, profits, receipts, returns, revenue, take, yield

tale 1. account, anecdote, *conte*, fable, fiction, legend, narration, narrative, novel, relation, report, romance, saga, short story, story, yarn (*Inf.*) 2. cock-and-bull story (*Inf.*), fabrication, falsehood, fib, lie, rigmarole, rumour, spiel (*Inf.*), tall story (*Inf.*), untruth

talent ability, aptitude, bent, capacity, endowment, faculty, flair, forte, genius, gift, knack, parts, power

talented able, artistic, brilliant, gifted, well-endowed

talk *v.* 1. articulate, chat, chatter, communicate, converse, crack (*Scot.*), express oneself, gab (*Inf.*), give voice to, gossip, natter, prate, prattle, rap (*Sl.*), say, speak, utter, verbalize, witter (*Inf.*) 2. chew the rag (*Inf.*), confabulate, confer, have a confab (*Inf.*), hold discussions, negotiate, palaver, parley ~*n.* 3. address, discourse, disquisition, dissertation, harangue, lecture, oration, sermon, speech 4. blather, blether, chat, chatter, chitchat, conversation, crack (*Scot.*), gab (*Inf.*), gossip, hearsay, jaw (*Sl.*), natter, rap (*Sl.*), rumour, tittle-tattle 5. colloquy, conclave, confab (*Inf.*), confabulation, conference, consultation, dialogue, discussion, meeting, negotiation, palaver, parley, seminar, symposium

talkative big-mouthed (*Sl.*), chatty, effusive, gabby (*Inf.*), garrulous, gossipy, long-winded, loquacious, mouthy, prolix, verbose, voluble, wordy

talker conversationalist, lecturer, orator, speaker, speechmaker

talking-to criticism, dressing-down (*Inf.*), lecture, rap on the knuckles (*Inf.*), rebuke, reprimand, reproach, reproof, row, scolding, slating (*Inf.*), telling-off (*Inf.*), ticking-off (*Inf.*), wigging (*Brit. sl.*)

tall 1. big, elevated, giant, high, lanky, lofty, soaring, towering 2. *Inf.* absurd, embellished, exaggerated, far-fetched, implausible, incredible, overblown, preposterous, steep (*Brit. inf.*), unbelievable

tally *v.* 1. accord, agree, coincide, concur, conform, correspond, fit, harmonize, jibe (*Inf.*), match, parallel, square, suit 2. compute, count up, keep score, mark, reckon, record, register, total ~*n.* 3. account, count, mark, reckoning, record, running total, score, total

dome or surrounded by colonnade 6. drum —*v.* 7. embroider on tambour

tambourine (tæmbəˈriːn) *n.* flat half-drum with jingling discs of metal attached

tame (teɪm) *a.* 1. not wild, domesticated 2. subdued 3. uninteresting —*vt.* 4. make tame —**ˈtamely** *adv.* 1. in a tame manner 2. without resisting —**ˈtamer** *n.*

Tamil (ˈtæmɪl) *n.* 1. member of a people of S India and Sri Lanka 2. language of this people (*pl.* **-s, ˈTamil**) —*a.* 3. of this people

tam-o'-shanter (tæməˈʃæntə) *n.* Scottish brimless wool cap with bobble in centre

tamp (tæmp) *vt.* pack, force down by repeated blows

tamper (ˈtæmpə) *vi.* (*usu. with* with) interfere improperly, meddle

tampon (ˈtæmpɒn) *n.* plug of lint, cotton *etc.* inserted in wound, body cavity, to stop flow of blood, absorb secretions *etc.*

tan[1] (tæn) *a./n.* 1. (of) brown colour of skin after long exposure to rays of sun *etc.* —*v.* 2. (cause to) go brown —*vt.* 3. (of animal hide) convert to leather by chemical treatment 4. *inf.* beat, flog (**-nn-**) —**ˈtanner** *n.* —**ˈtannery** *n.* place where hides are tanned —**ˈtannic** *a.* of tan, tannin or tannic acid —**ˈtannin** *n.* vegetable substance used as tanning agent —**ˈtanbark** *n.* bark of certain trees, yielding tannin —**tannic acid** astringent derived from oak bark *etc.*, used in tanning *etc.*

tan[2] (tæn) *Trig.* tangent

tanager (ˈtænədʒə) *n.* any of family of Amer. songbirds having short thick bill and, in male, brilliantly coloured plumage

tandem (ˈtændəm) *n.* bicycle for two riders, one behind the other

tandoori (tænˈdʊərɪ) *n.* Indian method of cooking meat or vegetables on a spit in clay oven

tang (tæŋ) *n.* 1. strong pungent taste or smell 2. trace, hint 3. spike, barb —**ˈtangy** *a.*

tangent (ˈtændʒənt) *n.* 1. line that touches a curve without cutting 2. divergent course 3. *Trig.* ratio of side opposite given acute angle in right-angled triangle to adjacent side —*a.* 4. touching, meeting without cutting —**tanˈgential** *a.* —**tanˈgentially** *adv.*

tangerine (tændʒəˈriːn) *n.* 1. Asian citrus tree 2. its fruit, a variety of orange 3. reddish-orange colour

tangible (ˈtændʒəbᵊl) *a.* 1. that can be touched 2. definite 3. palpable; concrete —**tangiˈbility** *n.*

tangle (ˈtæŋgᵊl) *n.* 1. confused mass or situation —*vt.* 2. twist together in muddle —*vi.* 3. contend

tango (ˈtæŋgəʊ) *n.* dance of S Amer. origin (*pl.* **-s**)

tank (tæŋk) *n.* 1. storage vessel for liquids or gas 2. armoured motor vehicle moving on tracks 3. cistern 4. **UK, US** *dial.* reservoir —**ˈtanker** *n.* ship, lorry *etc.* for carrying liquid in bulk —**tank farming** *see* HYDROPONICS —**tank up** *chiefly* **UK** *sl.* imbibe large quantity of alcoholic drink

tankard (ˈtæŋkəd) *n.* 1. large drinking cup of metal or glass 2. its contents, *esp.* beer

tanner (ˈtænə) *n.* **UK** *inf.* sixpence

tannin (ˈtænɪn) *n. see* TAN[1]

Tannoy (ˈtænɔɪ) *n.* **R** type of public-address system

tansy (ˈtænzɪ) *n.* yellow-flowered aromatic herb

tantalize *or* **-ise** (ˈtæntəlaɪz) *vt.* torment by appearing to offer something desired, tease —**ˈtantalus** *n.* **UK** case in which bottles may be locked with their contents visible

tantalum (ˈtæntələm) *n.* hard greyish-white metallic element

tantamount (ˈtæntəmaʊnt) *a.* 1. equivalent in value or signification 2. equal, amounting

tantrum (ˈtæntrəm) *n.* childish outburst of temper

Taoism (ˈtɑːəʊɪzəm) *n.* system of religion and philosophy based on teachings of Lao-tse, Chinese philosopher, and advocating simple, honest life and noninterference with course of natural events —**ˈTaoist** *n./a.* —**Taoˈistic** *a.*

tap[1] (tæp) *v.* 1. strike lightly but with some noise (**-pp-**) —*n.* 2. slight blow, rap —**tap dance** step dance in which performer makes makes sharp, loud taps of the foot, toe or heal on stage as he dances —**tap-dance** *vi.* perform tap dance —**tap-dancer** *n.* —**tap-dancing** *n.*

tap[2] (tæp) *n.* 1. valve with handle to regulate or stop flow of fluid in pipe *etc.* 2. stopper, plug permitting liquid to be drawn from cask *etc.* 3. steel tool for forming internal screw threads —*vt.* 4. put tap in 5. draw off (as) with tap 6. make secret connection to (telephone wire) to overhear conversation on it 7. make connection to (pipe, drain *etc.*) 8. form internal threads in 9. **UK** *sl.* ask (someone) for money; obtain (money) from someone (**-pp-**) —**ˈtaproom** *n.* bar, as in hotel or pub

THESAURUS

tame *adj.* 1. amenable, broken, cultivated, disciplined, docile, domesticated, gentle, obedient, tractable 2. compliant, docile, manageable, meek, obedient, spiritless, subdued, submissive, unresisting 3. bland, boring, dull, flat, humdrum, insipid, lifeless, prosaic, tedious, unexciting, uninspiring, uninteresting, vapid, wearisome ~*v.* 4. break in, domesticate, gentle, house-train, make tame, pacify, train 5. break the spirit of, bridle, bring to heel, conquer, curb, discipline, enslave, humble, master, repress, subdue, subjugate, suppress

tamper alter, damage, fiddle (*Inf.*), fool about (*Inf.*), interfere, intrude, meddle, mess about, monkey around, muck about (*Brit. sl.*), poke one's nose into (*Inf.*), tinker

tangible actual, concrete, corporeal, definite, discernible, evident, manifest, material, objective, palpable, perceptible, physical, positive, real, solid, substantial, tactile, touchable

tangle *n.* 1. coil, confusion, entanglement, jam, jungle, knot, mass, mat, mesh, snarl, twist, web 2. complication, entanglement, fix (*Inf.*), imbroglio, labyrinth, maze, mess, mix-up ~*v.* 3. coil, confuse, entangle, interlace, interlock, intertwist, interweave, jam, kink, knot, mat, mesh, snarl, twist 4. *Often with* **with** come into conflict, come up against, contend, contest, cross swords, dispute, lock horns

tantalize baffle, balk, disappoint, entice, frustrate, keep (someone) hanging on, lead on, make (someone's) mouth water, provoke, taunt, tease, thwart, titillate, torment, torture

tantamount as good as, commensurate, equal, equivalent, synonymous, the same as

tantrum fit, flare-up, hysterics, ill humour, outburst, paddy (*Brit. inf.*), storm, temper, wax (*Inf.*)

tape (teɪp) *n.* **1.** narrow long strip of fabric, paper *etc.* **2.** magnetic recording of music *etc.* —*vt.* **3.** record (speech, music *etc.*) —**tape deck** platform supporting spools *etc.* of tape recorder, incorporating motor and playback, recording and erasing heads —**tape machine** telegraphic device that records current stock quotations electronically or on ticker tape —**tape measure** tape of fabric or metal, marked off in centimetres, inches *etc.* —**tape recorder** apparatus for recording sound on magnetized tape and playing it back —**tape recording 1.** act of recording on magnetic tape **2.** magnetized tape used for this **3.** music *etc.* so recorded —**ˈtapeworm** *n.* long flat worm parasitic in animals and man —**have (someone) taped** *inf.* have (someone) sized up, have measure of (someone)

taper (ˈteɪpə) *vi.* **1.** become gradually thinner towards one end —*n.* **2.** thin candle **3.** long wick covered with wax; spill **4.** a narrowing

tapestry (ˈtæpɪstrɪ) *n.* fabric decorated with designs in colours woven by needles, not in shuttles —**ˈtapestried** *a.*

tapioca (tæpɪˈəʊkə) *n.* beadlike starch made from cassava root, used *esp.* in puddings

tapir (ˈteɪpə) *n.* Amer. animal with elongated snout, allied to pig

tappet (ˈtæpɪt) *n.* in internal-combustion engine, short steel rod conveying movement imparted by the lift of a cam to the valve stem

taproot (ˈtæpruːt) *n.* large single root growing straight down

tar[1] (tɑː) *n.* **1.** thick black liquid distilled from coal *etc.* —*vt.* **2.** coat, treat with tar (**-rr-**)

tar[2] (tɑː) *n. inf.* sailor

tarantella (tærənˈtɛlə) *n.* **1.** lively It. dance **2.** music for it

tarantula (təˈræntjʊlə) *n.* any of various large (poisonous) hairy spiders (*pl.* **-s, -lae** (-liː))

tarboosh (tɑːˈbuːʃ) *n.* felt brimless cap, usu. red and oft. with silk tassel, worn by Muslim men

tardy (ˈtɑːdɪ) *a.* **1.** slow **2.** late —**ˈtardily** *adv.*

tare[1] (tɛə) *n.* **1.** weight of wrapping or container for goods **2.** unladen weight of vehicle

tare[2] (tɛə) *n.* **1.** vetch **2.** weed

target (ˈtɑːgɪt) *n.* **1.** mark to aim at in shooting *etc.* **2.** thing aimed at **3.** object of criticism **4.** butt —**target language** language into which text *etc.* is translated

tariff (ˈtærɪf) *n.* **1.** tax levied on imports *etc.* **2.** list of charges **3.** method of charging for supply of services, *eg* electricity

Tarmac (ˈtɑːmæk) *n.* **R** mixture of tar, bitumen and crushed stones rolled to give hard, smooth surface *esp.* as used for road, airport runway *etc.* (*also* **Tarmaˈcadam**)

tarn (tɑːn) *n.* small mountain lake

tarnish (ˈtɑːnɪʃ) *v.* **1.** (cause to) become stained, lose shine or become dimmed or sullied —*n.* **2.** discoloration, blemish

taro (ˈtɑːrəʊ) *n.* **1.** plant of Pacific islands **2.** its edible roots

tarot (ˈtærəʊ) *n.* one of special pack of cards now used mainly in fortune-telling

tarpaulin (tɑːˈpɔːlɪn) *n.* (sheet of) heavy hard-wearing waterproof fabric

tarragon (ˈtærəgən) *n.* aromatic herb

tarry (ˈtærɪ) *vi.* **1.** linger, delay **2.** stay behind (**-ried, -rying**)

tarsier (ˈtɑːsɪə) *n.* nocturnal tree-dwelling mammal of Indonesia *etc.*

tarsus (ˈtɑːsəs) *n.* **1.** bones of ankle and heel collectively **2.** corresponding part in other mammals *etc.* **3.** connective tissue supporting free edge of each eyelid (*pl.* **-si** (-saɪ)) —**ˈtarsal** *a.* **1.** of tarsus or tarsi —*n.* **2.** tarsal bone

tart[1] (tɑːt) *n.* **1.** pie or flan filled with fruit, jam *etc.* **2.** *inf., offens.* promiscuous woman, *esp.* prostitute —**tart up UK** *sl.* **1.** dress and make (oneself) up in provocative or promiscuous way **2.** reissue or decorate in cheap and flashy way

tart[2] (tɑːt) *a.* **1.** sour, bitter **2.** sharp

tartan (ˈtɑːtᵊn) *n.* **1.** woollen cloth woven in pattern of coloured checks, *esp.* in colours, patterns associated with Scottish clans **2.** such pattern

tartar[1] (ˈtɑːtə) *n.* **1.** crust deposited on teeth **2.** deposit formed during fermentation of wine —**tarˈtaric** *a.* —**tartaric acid** colourless crystalline acid found in many fruits

tartar[2] (ˈtɑːtə) *n.* vicious-tempered person, difficult to deal with

Tartar (ˈtɑːtə) *see* TATAR

tartar sauce mayonnaise sauce mixed with chopped herbs, capers *etc.*

tartrazine (ˈtɑːtrəziːn, -zɪn) *n.* artificial dye that produces yellow colour: used as food additive, in drugs *etc.*

THESAURUS

tap[1] **1.** *v.* beat, drum, knock, pat, rap, strike, touch **2.** *n.* beat, knock, light blow, pat, rap, touch

tap[2] *n.* **1.** faucet (*U.S.*), spigot, spout, stopcock, valve **2.** bung, plug, spile, stopper ~*v.* **3.** bleed, broach, drain, draw off, open, pierce, siphon off, unplug **4.** bug (*Inf.*), eavesdrop on, listen in on

tape 1. *n.* band, ribbon, strip **2.** *v.* record, tape-record, video

taper come to a point, narrow, thin

target 1. aim, ambition, bull's-eye, end, goal, intention, mark, object, objective **2.** butt, quarry, scapegoat, victim

tariff 1. assessment, duty, excise, impost, levy, rate, tax, toll **2.** bill of fare, charges, menu, price list, schedule

tarnish 1. *v.* befoul, blacken, blemish, blot, darken, dim, discolour, drag through the mud, dull, lose lustre *or* shine, rust, soil, spot, stain, sully, taint **2.** *n.* blackening, black mark, blemish, blot, discoloration, rust, spot, stain, taint

tarry abide, bide, dally, dawdle, delay, dwell, hang around (*Inf.*), linger, lodge, loiter, lose time, pause, remain, rest, sojourn, stay, take one's time, wait

tart[1] **1.** flan, pastry, pie, tartlet **2.** call girl, fallen woman, *fille de joie*, floozy (*Sl.*), harlot, hooker (*U.S. sl.*), loose woman, prostitute, slut, streetwalker, strumpet, trollop, whore, woman of easy virtue

tart[2] **1.** acid, acidulous, astringent, bitter, piquant, pungent, sharp, sour, tangy, vinegary **2.** acrimonious, astringent, barbed, biting, caustic, crusty, cutting, harsh, nasty, scathing, sharp, short, snappish, testy, trenchant, wounding

Tas. Tasmania

task (tɑːsk) *n.* **1.** piece of work (*esp.* unpleasant or difficult) set or undertaken —*vt.* **2.** assign task to **3.** exact —**task force** naval or military unit dispatched to carry out specific undertaking —**ˈtaskmaster** *n.* overseer —**take to task** reprove

Tasmanian devil (tæzˈmeɪnɪən) small, ferocious, carnivorous marsupial of Tasmania

Tass (tæs) *n.* principal news agency of Soviet Union

tassel (ˈtæsᵊl) *n.* **1.** ornament of fringed knot of threads *etc.* **2.** tuft

taste (teɪst) *n.* **1.** sense by which flavour, quality of substance is detected by the tongue **2.** this act or sensation **3.** (brief) experience of something **4.** small amount **5.** preference, liking **6.** power of discerning, judging **7.** discretion, delicacy —*v.* **8.** observe or distinguish the taste of (a substance) **9.** take small amount of (food *etc.*) into mouth —*vt.* **10.** experience —*vi.* **11.** have specific flavour —**ˈtasteful** *a.* **1.** in good style **2.** with, showing good taste —**ˈtastefully** *adv.* —**ˈtasteless** *a.* —**ˈtaster** *n.* **1.** person who samples food or drink for quality **2.** device used in tasting or sampling **3.** *esp.* formerly, person employed to taste food and drink prepared for king *etc.* to test for poison —**ˈtasty** *a.* pleasantly or highly flavoured —**taste bud** small organ of taste on tongue

tat[1] (tæt) *v.* make (something) by tatting (-tt-) —**ˈtatter** *n.* —**ˈtatting** *n.* type of handmade lace

tat[2] (tæt) *n.* **1.** ragged, shoddy article **2.** tattiness

ta-ta (tæˈtɑː) *interj.* UK *inf.* goodbye; farewell

Tatar *or* **Tartar** (ˈtɑːtə) *n.* **1.** member of Mongoloid people who established powerful state in central Asia in 13th century **2.** descendant of this people, now scattered throughout Soviet Union **3.** Turkic language or dialect spoken by this people —*a.* **4.** of Tatars

tater (ˈteɪtə) *n. dial.* potato

tatter (ˈtætə) *v.* **1.** make or become ragged, worn to shreds —*n.* **2.** ragged piece

tattle (ˈtætᵊl) *vi./n.* gossip, chatter —**ˈtattletale** *chiefly* US *n.* **1.** scandalmonger, gossip —*a.* **2.** telltale

tattoo[1] (tæˈtuː) *n.* **1.** formerly, beat of drum and bugle call **2.** military spectacle or pageant

tattoo[2] (tæˈtuː) *vt.* **1.** mark (skin) in patterns *etc.* by pricking and filling punctures with indelible coloured inks (-ˈ**tooed**, -ˈ**tooing**) —*n.* **2.** mark so made

tatty (ˈtætɪ) *a.* shabby, worn-out —**ˈtattiness** *n.*

tau (tɔː, taʊ) *n.* 19th letter in Gr. alphabet (T, τ)

taught (tɔːt) *pt./pp. of* TEACH

taunt (tɔːnt) *vt.* **1.** provoke, deride with insulting words *etc.* **2.** tease; tantalize —*n.* **3.** instance of this

taupe (təʊp) *n.* brownish-grey colour

Taurus (ˈtɔːrəs) *n.* (bull) 2nd sign of zodiac, operative *c.* Apr. 21st-May 20th

taut (tɔːt) *a.* **1.** drawn tight **2.** under strain —**ˈtauten** *vt.* make tight or tense

tauto- *or before vowel* **taut-** (*comb. form*) identical, same, as in *tautology*

tautology (tɔːˈtɒlədʒɪ) *n.* repetition of same thing in other words in same sentence —**tautoˈlogical** *a.*

tavern (ˈtævən) *n.* inn, public house

tawdry (ˈtɔːdrɪ) *a.* showy, but cheap and without taste, flashy —**ˈtawdrily** *adv.* —**ˈtawdriness** *n.*

tawny (ˈtɔːnɪ) *a./n.* (of) light (yellowish) brown —**tawny owl** European owl having reddish-brown plumage and round head

tawse *or* **taws** (tɔːz) *n.* in Scotland, leather strap used *esp.* formerly by schoolteacher to punish pupils

tax (tæks) *n.* **1.** compulsory payments by wage earners, companies *etc.* imposed by government to raise revenue **2.** heavy demand (on something) —*vt.* **3.** impose tax on **4.** strain **5.** accuse, blame —**ˈtaxable** *a.* —**taxˈation** *n.* levying of taxes —**tax-deductible** *a.* legally deductible from income before tax assessment —**tax exile** person who lives abroad to avoid paying high taxes —**tax-free** *a.* exempt from taxation —**ˈtaxpayer** *n.* —**tax return** statement of personal income for tax purposes

THESAURUS

task *n.* **1.** assignment, business, charge, chore, duty, employment, enterprise, exercise, job, labour, mission, occupation, toil, undertaking, work **2. take to task** blame, censure, criticize, lecture, reprimand, reproach, reprove, scold, tell off (*Inf.*), upbraid ~*v.* **3.** assign to, charge, entrust

taste *n.* **1.** flavour, relish, savour, smack, tang **2.** bit, bite, dash, drop, morsel, mouthful, nip, sample, sip, *soupçon*, spoonful, swallow, titbit, touch **3.** appetite, bent, desire, fancy, fondness, inclination, leaning, liking, palate, partiality, penchant, predilection, preference, relish **4.** appreciation, cultivation, culture, discernment, discrimination, elegance, grace, judgment, perception, polish, refinement, style **5.** correctness, decorum, delicacy, discretion, nicety, politeness, propriety, restraint, tact, tactfulness ~*v.* **6.** differentiate, discern, distinguish, perceive **7.** assay, nibble, relish, sample, savour, sip, test, try **8.** have a flavour of, savour of, smack **9.** come up against, encounter, experience, feel, have knowledge of, know, meet with, partake of, undergo

tasteful aesthetically pleasing, artistic, beautiful, charming, cultivated, cultured, delicate, discriminating, elegant, exquisite, fastidious, graceful, handsome, harmonious, in good taste, polished, refined, restrained, smart, stylish

tasteless 1. bland, boring, dull, flat, flavourless, insipid, mild, stale, tame, thin, uninspired, uninteresting, vapid, watered-down, weak **2.** cheap, coarse, crass, crude, flashy, garish, gaudy, graceless, gross, impolite, improper, indecorous, indelicate, indiscreet, inelegant, low, rude, tactless, tawdry, uncouth, unseemly, vulgar

tasty appetizing, delectable, delicious, flavourful, flavoursome, full-flavoured, good-tasting, luscious, palatable, sapid, savoury, scrumptious (*Inf.*), toothsome, yummy (*Sl.*)

taunt 1. *v.* deride, flout, gibe, guy (*Inf.*), insult, jeer, mock, provoke, reproach, revile, ridicule, sneer, tantalize, tease, torment, twit, upbraid **2.** *n.* barb, censure, cut, derision, dig, gibe, insult, jeer, provocation, reproach, ridicule, sarcasm, teasing

taut flexed, rigid, strained, stressed, stretched, tense, tight

tavern alehouse (*Archaic*), bar, boozer (*Brit. inf.*), hostelry, inn, pub (*Brit. inf.*), public house

tawdry brummagem, cheap, cheap-jack (*Inf.*), flashy, gaudy, gimcrack, glittering, meretricious, plastic

taxi (ˈtæksɪ) *n.* **1.** motor vehicle for hire with driver (*pl.* **-s**) (*also* **cab, ˈtaxicab**) —*vi.* **2.** (of aircraft) run along ground under its own power **3.** go in taxi (**ˈtaxied** *pt./pp.*, **ˈtaxying, ˈtaxiing** *pr.p.*) —**ˈtaximeter** *n.* meter fitted to taxi to register fare, based on length of journey —**taxi rank** place where taxis wait to be hired

taxidermy (ˈtæksɪdɜːmɪ) *n.* art of stuffing, mounting animal skins to give them lifelike appearance —**taxiˈdermal** *or* **taxiˈdermic** *a.* —**ˈtaxidermist** *n.*

taxonomy (tækˈsɒnəmɪ) *n.* science, practice of classification, *esp.* of biological organisms

Tb *Chem.* terbium

T.B. *or* **t.b.** tuberculosis

T-bone steak steak cut from sirloin of beef, containing T-shaped bone

tbs. *or* **tbsp.** tablespoon(ful)

Tc *Chem.* technetium

tch *interj./n.* **1.** clicking sound made with tongue, to express disapproval *etc.* —*vi.* **2.** utter tch's

te *or* **ti** (tiː) *n. Mus.* in tonic sol-fa, syllable used for seventh note or subtonic of any scale

Te *Chem.* tellurium

tea (tiː) *n.* **1.** dried leaves of plant cultivated *esp.* in (sub)tropical Asia **2.** infusion of it as beverage **3.** any of various herbal infusions **4.** tea, cakes *etc.* as light afternoon meal **5.** main evening meal —**tea bag** small porous bag of paper containing tea leaves —**tea ball** *chiefly* **US** perforated metal ball filled with tea leaves and used to make tea —**ˈteacake** *n.* **UK** flat bun, usu. eaten toasted and buttered —**tea-chest** *n.* square wooden box lined with foil for exporting tea *etc.* —**tea cosy** covering for teapot to keep contents hot —**ˈteacup** *n.* **1.** cup out of which tea may be drunk **2.** amount teacup will hold, about four fluid ounces (*also* **ˈteacupful**) —**ˈteahouse** *n.* restaurant, *esp.* in Japan or China, where tea and light refreshments are served —**tea leaf 1.** dried leaf of tea shrub, used to make tea **2.** (*usu. pl.*) shredded parts of these leaves, *esp.* after infusion —**tea party** social gathering at which tea is served —**ˈteapot** *n.* container with lid, spout and handle, in which tea is made —**ˈtearoom** *n.* **UK** restaurant where tea and light refreshments are served (*also* **ˈteashop**) —**ˈteaspoon** *n.* small spoon for stirring tea *etc.* —**tea tree** Aust., N.Z. tree

teach (tiːtʃ) *vt.* **1.** instruct **2.** educate **3.** train **4.** impart knowledge of —*vi.* **5.** act as teacher (**taught, ˈteaching**) —**ˈteacher** *n.* —**ˈteaching** *n.* —**teaching machine** machine that presents information and questions to user, registers answers, and indicates whether these are correct or acceptable

teak (tiːk) *n.* **1.** E Indian tree **2.** very hard wood obtained from it

teal (tiːl) *n.* **1.** type of small duck **2.** greenish-blue colour

team (tiːm) *n.* **1.** set of animals, players of game *etc.* associated in activity —*v.* **2.** (*usu. with* up) (cause to) make a team —**ˈteamster** *n.* driver of team of draught animals —**team-mate** *n.* fellow member of team —**team spirit** subordination of individual desire for good of team —**ˈteamwork** *n.* cooperative work by team acting as unit

tear[1] (tɪə) *n.* drop of fluid appearing in and falling from eye —**ˈtearful** *a.* **1.** inclined to weep **2.** involving tears —**ˈtearless** *a.* —**ˈteardrop** *n.* —**tear gas** irritant gas causing abnormal watering of eyes and temporary blindness —**tear-jerker** *n. inf.* excessively sentimental film *etc.*

tear[2] (tɛə) *vt.* **1.** pull apart, rend —*vi.* **2.** become torn **3.** rush (**tore, torn, ˈtearing**) —*n.* **4.** hole, cut; split —**ˈtearaway** *n.* **UK** reckless impetuous person —**tear away** persuade (oneself or someone else) to leave

tease (tiːz) *vt.* **1.** tantalize, torment, irritate, bait **2.** pull apart fibres of —*n.* **3.** one who teases —**ˈteaser** *n.* annoying or puzzling problem —**ˈteasing** *a.*

teasel, teazel, *or* **teazle** (ˈtiːzəl) *n.* plant with prickly leaves and head

teat (tiːt) *n.* **1.** nipple of female breast **2.** rubber nipple of baby's feeding bottle

tech (tɛk) *a./n. inf.* technical (college)

tech. 1. technical **2.** technology

technetium (tɛkˈniːʃɪəm) *n.* silvery-grey metallic element, artificially produced by bombardment of molybdenum by deuterons

technical (ˈtɛknɪkəl) *a.* **1.** of, specializing in industrial, practical or mechanical arts and applied sciences **2.** skilled in practical and mechanical arts **3.** belonging to particular art or science **4.** according to letter of the law —**techniˈcality** *n.* **1.** point of procedure **2.** state of being technical —**ˈtechnically** *adv.* —**techˈnician** *n.* one skilled in technique of an art —**technique** (tɛkˈniːk) *n.* **1.** method of performance in an art **2.** skill required for mastery of subject —**technical college** higher educational institution, with courses in art, technology *etc.* —**technical drawing** drawing done

THESAURUS

(*Sl.*), raffish, showy, tacky, tasteless, tatty, tinsel, tinselly, vulgar

tax *n.* **1.** assessment, charge, contribution, customs, duty, excise, imposition, impost, levy, rate, tariff, tithe, toll, tribute **2.** burden, demand, drain, load, pressure, strain, weight ~*v.* **3.** assess, charge, demand, exact, extract, impose, levy a tax on, rate, tithe **4.** burden, drain, enervate, exhaust, load, make heavy demands on, overburden, push, put pressure on, sap, strain, stretch, task, try, weaken, wear out, weary, weigh heavily on **5.** accuse, arraign, blame, charge, impeach, impugn, incriminate, lay at one's door

teach advise, coach, demonstrate, direct, discipline, drill, edify, educate, enlighten, give lessons in, guide, impart, implant, inculcate, inform, instil, instruct, school, show, train, tutor

teacher coach, dominie (*Scot.*), don, educator, guide, guru, instructor, lecturer, master, mentor, mistress, pedagogue, professor, schoolmaster, schoolmistress, schoolteacher, trainer, tutor

team *n.* **1.** band, body, bunch, company, crew, gang, group, line-up, set, side, squad, troupe **2.** pair, span, yoke ~*v.* **3.** *Usually with* **up** band together, cooperate, couple, get together, join, link, unite, work together, yoke

tear *v.* **1.** claw, divide, lacerate, mangle, mutilate, pull apart, rend, rip, rive, run, rupture, scratch, sever, shred, split, sunder **2.** belt (*Sl.*), bolt, career, charge, dart, dash, fly, gallop, hurry, race, run, rush, shoot, speed, sprint, zoom ~*n.* **3.** cut, hole, laceration, mutilation, rent, rip, run, rupture, scratch, split

tease aggravate (*Inf.*), annoy, badger, bait, bedevil, chaff, gibe, goad, guy (*Inf.*), irritate, lead on, mock, needle, pester, plague (*Inf.*), provoke, rag, rib (*Inf.*), ridicule, tantalize, taunt, torment, twit, vex, worry

with T-squares, scales *etc.* —**technical knockout** *Boxing* judgment of knockout given when boxer is in referee's opinion too badly beaten to continue

Technicolor (ˈtɛknɪkʌlə) *n.* **R** colour photography, *esp.* in cinema

techno- (*comb. form*) **1.** craft; art, as in *technology, technography* **2.** technological; technical, as in *technocracy*

technocracy (tɛkˈnɒkrəsɪ) *n.* **1.** government by technical experts **2.** group of these experts

technology (tɛkˈnɒlədʒɪ) *n.* **1.** application of practical, mechanical sciences to industry, commerce **2.** technical methods, skills, knowledge —**technoˈlogical** *a.* —**techˈnologist** *n.*

tectonic (tɛkˈtɒnɪk) *a.* of construction or building —**tecˈtonics** *pl.n.* (*with sing. v.*) art, science of building

ted (tɛd) *inf.* teddy boy

teddy bear (ˈtɛdɪ) child's soft toy bear (*also* **ˈteddy**)

teddy boy **1. UK** *esp.* in mid-1950s, one of cult of youths who wore mock Edwardian fashions **2.** any tough or delinquent youth

Te Deum (tiː ˈdiːəm) **1.** ancient Latin hymn in rhythmic prose **2.** musical setting of this hymn **3.** service of thanksgiving in which recital of this hymn forms central part

tedious (ˈtiːdɪəs) *a.* causing fatigue or boredom, monotonous —**ˈtedium** *n.* monotony

tee (tiː) *n.* **1.** *Golf* slightly raised ground from which first stroke of hole is made **2.** small peg supporting ball for this stroke **3.** target in some games (*eg* quoits) —**tee off** make first stroke of hole in golf

teem (tiːm) *vi.* **1.** abound, swarm, be prolific **2.** pour, rain heavily

teens (tiːnz) *pl.n.* years of life from 13 to 19 —**ˈteenage** *a.* —**ˈteenager** *n.* young person between 13 and 19 —**ˈteenybopper** *n. sl.* young teenager, usu. girl, who avidly follows fashions

teeny (ˈtiːnɪ) *a.* extremely small; tiny (*also* **teeny-weeny** (ˈtiːnɪˈwiːnɪ), **teensy-weensy** (ˈtiːnzɪˈwiːnzɪ))

teepee (ˈtiːpiː) *n. see* TEPEE

tee shirt *see* T-SHIRT

teeter (ˈtiːtə) *vi.* **1.** seesaw or make similar movements **2.** vacillate

teeth (tiːθ) *n., pl. of* TOOTH —**teethe** (tiːð) *vi.* (of baby) grow first teeth —**teething ring** hard ring on which babies may bite while teething —**teething troubles** problems, difficulties at first stage of something

teetotal (tiːˈtəʊtᵊl) *a.* pledged to abstain from alcohol —**teeˈtotalism** *n.* —**teeˈtotaller** *n.*

Teflon (ˈtɛflɒn) *n.* **R** polymer used to make nonstick coatings on cooking utensils

tel. **1.** telegram **2.** telegraph(ic) **3.** telephone

tel- (*comb. form*) *see* TELE-

tele- (*comb. form*) at a distance, from far off, as in *telescope*

telecast (ˈtɛlɪkɑːst) *vi./n.* (broadcast) television programme

telecommunications (tɛlɪkəmjuːnɪˈkeɪʃənz) *pl.n.* (*with sing. v.*) science and technology of communications by telephony, radio, television *etc.*

telegram (ˈtɛlɪgræm) *n.* message sent by telegraph

telegraph (ˈtɛlɪgræf) *n.* **1.** electrical apparatus for transmitting messages to a distance **2.** any signalling device for transmitting messages —*v.* **3.** communicate by telegraph —*vt.* **4. C** cast (votes) illegally by impersonating registered voters —**teleˈgraphic** *a.* —**teleˈgraphically** *adv.* —**teˈlegraphist** *n.* one who works telegraph —**teˈlegraphy** *n.* **1.** science of telegraph **2.** use of telegraph

telekinesis (tɛlɪkaɪˈniːsɪs) *n.* **1.** movement of a body caused by thought or willpower **2.** ability to cause such movement —**telekinetic** (tɛlɪkɪˈnɛtɪk) *a.*

teleology (tɛlɪˈɒlədʒɪ, tiːlɪ-) *n.* **1.** doctrine of final causes **2.** belief that things happen because of the purpose or design that will be fulfilled by them —**teleoˈlogic(al)** *a.*

telepathy (tɪˈlɛpəθɪ) *n.* action of one mind on another at a distance —**teleˈpathic** *a.* —**teleˈpathically** *adv.*

telephone (ˈtɛlɪfəʊn) *n.* **1.** apparatus for communicating sound to hearer at a distance —*v.* **2.** communicate, speak by telephone —**telephonic** (tɛlɪˈfɒnɪk) *a.* —**teˈlephonist** *n.* person operating telephone switchboard —**teˈlephony** *n.* —**telephone box** soundproof enclosure from which paid telephone call can be made (*also* **telephone kiosk, telephone booth**) —**telephone directory** book listing names, addresses and telephone numbers of subscribers in particular area

telephoto (ˈtɛlɪfəʊtəʊ) *a.* (of lens) producing magnified image of distant object —**telephoˈtography** *n.* process or technique of photographing distant objects using telephoto lens

teleprinter (ˈtɛlɪprɪntə) *n.* apparatus like typewriter, by which typed messages are sent and received by wire

THESAURUS

technique **1.** approach, course, fashion, manner, means, method, mode, modus operandi, procedure, style, system, way **2.** address, adroitness, art, artistry, craft, craftsmanship, delivery, execution, facility, knack, know-how (*Inf.*), performance, proficiency, skill, touch

tedious annoying, banal, boring, deadly dull, drab, dreary, dull, fatiguing, humdrum, irksome, laborious, lifeless, long-drawn-out, monotonous, prosaic, prosy, soporific, tiring, unexciting, uninteresting, vapid, wearisome

tedium banality, boredom, deadness, drabness, dreariness, dullness, ennui, lifelessness, monotony, routine, sameness, tediousness, the doldrums

teem abound, be abundant, bear, be crawling with, be full of, be prolific, brim, bristle, burst at the seams, overflow, produce, pullulate, swarm

teenager adolescent, boy, girl, juvenile, minor, youth

teetotaller abstainer, nondrinker, Rechabite

telegram cable, radiogram, telegraph, telex, wire (*Inf.*)

telegraph *n.* **1.** tape machine (*Stock Exchange*), teleprinter, telex **2.** cable, radiogram, telegram, telex, wire (*Inf.*) ~*v.* **3.** cable, send, telex, transmit, wire (*Inf.*)

telepathy mind-reading, sixth sense, thought transference

telephone **1.** *n.* blower (*Inf.*), handset, line, phone **2.** *v.* buzz (*Inf.*), call, call up, dial, get on the blower (*Inf.*), give (someone) a buzz (*Inf.*), give (someone) a call, give (someone) a ring (*Brit.*), give someone a tinkle (*Brit. inf.*), phone, put a call through to, ring (*Brit.*)

Teleprompter (ˈtɛlɪprɒmptə) *n.* **R** *T.V.* device to enable speaker to refer to his script out of sight of the cameras

telesales (ˈtɛlɪseɪlz) *pl.n.* selling of commodity or service by salesperson who makes initial approach by telephone

telescope (ˈtɛlɪskəʊp) *n.* **1.** optical instrument for magnifying distant objects —*v.* **2.** slide or drive together, *esp.* parts designed to fit one inside the other **3.** make smaller, shorter —**telescopic** (tɛlɪˈskɒpɪk) *a.*

teletext (ˈtɛlɪtɛkst) *n.* electronic system which shows information, news on subscribers' television screens

television (ˈtɛlɪvɪʒən) *n.* **1.** system of producing on screen images of distant objects, events *etc.* by electromagnetic radiation **2.** device for receiving this transmission and converting it to optical images **3.** programmes *etc.* viewed on television set —**ˈtelevise** *vt.* **1.** transmit by television **2.** make, produce as television programme

telex (ˈtɛlɛks) *n.* **1.** international telegraph service using teleprinters —*v.* **2.** transmit (message) to (person *etc.*) by telex

tell (tɛl) *vt.* **1.** let know **2.** order, direct **3.** narrate, make known **4.** discern **5.** distinguish **6.** count —*vi.* **7.** give account **8.** be of weight, importance **9.** *inf.* reveal secrets (**told, ˈtelling**) —**ˈteller** *n.* **1.** narrator **2.** bank cashier —**ˈtelling** *a.* effective, striking —**ˈtelltale** *n.* **1.** sneak **2.** automatic indicator —*a.* **3.** revealing

tellurian (tɛˈlʊərɪən) *a.* of the earth —**telˈluric** *a.* —**telˈlurium** *n.* nonmetallic bluish-white element —**tellurous** (ˈtɛljʊrəs, tɛˈlʊərəs) *a.*

telly (ˈtɛlɪ) *inf.* television (set)

temerity (tɪˈmɛrɪtɪ) *n.* boldness, audacity

temp (tɛmp) *inf. n.* **1.** one employed on temporary basis —*vi.* **2.** work as temp

temp. **1.** temperature **2.** temporary

temper (ˈtɛmpə) *n.* **1.** frame of mind **2.** anger, oft. noisy **3.** mental constitution **4.** degree of hardness of steel *etc.* —*vt.* **5.** restrain, qualify, moderate **6.** harden **7.** bring to proper condition —**ˈtempered** *a.* having temper or temperament as specified, as in *ill-tempered*

tempera (ˈtɛmpərə) *n.* emulsion used as painting medium

temperament (ˈtɛmpərəmənt) *n.* **1.** natural disposition **2.** excitability; moodiness; anger —**temperaˈmental** *a.* **1.** given to extremes of temperament, moody **2.** of, occasioned by temperament **3.** *inf.* working erratically and inconsistently; unreliable —**temperaˈmentally** *adv.*

temperate (ˈtɛmpərɪt) *a.* **1.** not extreme **2.** showing, practising moderation —**ˈtemperance** *n.* **1.** moderation **2.** abstinence, *esp.* from alcohol —**ˈtemperately** *adv.* —**Temperate Zone** parts of earth's surface lying between Arctic Circle and tropic of Cancer and between Antarctic Circle and tropic of Capricorn

temperature (ˈtɛmprɪtʃə) *n.* **1.** degree of heat or coldness **2.** *inf.* (abnormally) high body temperature

tempest (ˈtɛmpɪst) *n.* violent storm —**temˈpestuous** *a.* **1.** turbulent **2.** violent, stormy —**temˈpestuously** *adv.*

template *or* **templet** (ˈtɛmplɪt) *n.* mould, pattern. to help shape something accurately

temple[1] (ˈtɛmpᵊl) *n.* **1.** building for worship **2.** shrine

THESAURUS

telescope **1.** *n.* glass, spyglass **2.** *v.* abbreviate, abridge, compress, condense, consolidate, contract, curtail, cut, shorten, shrink, trim, truncate

television gogglebox (*Brit. sl.*), idiot box (*Sl.*), receiver, small screen (*Inf.*), telly (*Brit. inf.*), the box (*Brit. inf.*), the tube (*Sl.*), TV, TV set

tell *v.* **1.** acquaint, announce, apprise, communicate, confess, disclose, divulge, express, impart, inform, let know, make known, mention, notify, proclaim, reveal, say, speak, state, utter **2.** authorize, bid, call upon, command, direct, enjoin, instruct, order, require, summon **3.** chronicle, depict, describe, give an account of, narrate, portray, recount, rehearse, relate, report **4.** comprehend, discern, discover, make out, see, understand **5.** differentiate, discern, discriminate, distinguish, identify **6.** carry weight, count, have *or* take effect, have force, make its presence felt, register, take its toll, weigh **7.** calculate, compute, count, enumerate, number, reckon, tally

telling considerable, decisive, effective, effectual, forceful, forcible, impressive, influential, marked, potent, powerful, significant, solid, striking, trenchant, weighty

temper *n.* **1.** attitude, character, constitution, disposition, frame of mind, humour, mind, mood, nature, temperament, tenor, vein **2.** bad mood, fit of pique, fury, paddy (*Brit. inf.*), passion, rage, tantrum, wax (*Inf.*) **3.** anger, annoyance, heat, hot-headedness, ill humour, irascibility, irritability, irritation, passion, peevishness, petulance, resentment, surliness ~*v.* **4.** abate, admix, allay, assuage, calm, lessen, mitigate, moderate, mollify, palliate, qualify, restrain, soften, soft-pedal (*Inf.*), soothe, tone down **5.** anneal, harden, strengthen, toughen

temperament **1.** bent, cast of mind, character, complexion, constitution, disposition, frame of mind, humour, make-up, mettle, nature, outlook, personality, quality, soul, spirit, stamp, temper, tendencies, tendency **2.** anger, excitability, explosiveness, hot-headedness, impatience, mercurialness, moodiness, moods, petulance, volatility

temperamental **1.** capricious, easily upset, emotional, erratic, excitable, explosive, fiery, highly strung, hot-headed, hypersensitive, impatient, irritable, mercurial, moody, neurotic, passionate, petulant, sensitive, touchy, volatile **2.** erratic, inconsistent, undependable, unpredictable, unreliable

temperance **1.** continence, discretion, forbearance, moderation, restraint, self-control, self-discipline, self-restraint **2.** abstemiousness, abstinence, prohibition, sobriety, teetotalism

temperate **1.** agreeable, balmy, calm, clement, cool, fair, gentle, mild, moderate, pleasant, soft **2.** calm, composed, dispassionate, equable, even-tempered, mild, moderate, reasonable, self-controlled, self-restrained, sensible, stable **3.** abstemious, abstinent, continent, moderate, sober

tempest cyclone, gale, hurricane, squall, storm, tornado, typhoon

tempestuous **1.** agitated, blustery, boisterous, breezy, gusty, raging, squally, stormy, turbulent, windy **2.** agitated, boisterous, emotional, excited, feverish, furious, heated, hysterical, impassioned,

temple[2] (ˈtɛmpˀl) *n.* flat part on either side of forehead

tempo (ˈtɛmpəʊ) *n.* rate, rhythm, *esp.* in music (*pl.* **-s, -pi** (-piː))

temporal[1] (ˈtɛmpərəl) *a.* **1.** of time **2.** of this life or world, secular **3.** *Gram.* of tense or linguistic expression of time —**tempoˈrality** *n.*

temporal[2] (ˈtɛmpərəl) *a. Anat.* of temple or temples —**temporal bone** either of two compound bones forming sides of skull

temporary (ˈtɛmpərərɪ) *a.* lasting, used only for a time —**ˈtemporarily** *adv.*

temporize *or* **-ise** (ˈtɛmpəraɪz) *vi.* **1.** use evasive action; hedge; gain time by negotiation *etc.* **2.** conform to circumstances —**ˈtemporizer** *or* **-iser** *n.*

tempt (tɛmpt) *vt.* **1.** try to persuade, entice, *esp.* to something wrong or unwise **2.** dispose, cause to be inclined —**tempˈtation** *n.* **1.** act of tempting **2.** thing that tempts —**ˈtempter** *n.* (**ˈtemptress** *fem.*) —**ˈtempting** *a.* attractive, inviting

tempus fugit (ˈtɛmpəs ˈfjuːdʒɪt) *Lat.* time flies

ten (tɛn) *n./a.* cardinal number next after nine —**tenth** *a./n.* ordinal number —**ten-gallon hat US** cowboy's broad-brimmed felt hat with high crown —**tenpin bowling** (ˈtɛnpɪn) bowling game in which bowls are rolled down lane to knock over ten target pins (*also* (*esp.* **US**) **ˈtenpins**) —**the Ten Commandments** *O.T.* commandments summarizing basic obligations of man towards God and his fellow men

ten. *Mus.* **1.** tenor **2.** tenuto

tenable (ˈtɛnəbˀl) *a.* able to be held, defended, maintained

tenacious (tɪˈneɪʃəs) *a.* **1.** holding fast **2.** retentive **3.** stubborn —**tenacity** (tɪˈnæsɪtɪ) *n.*

tenant (ˈtɛnənt) *n.* one who holds lands, house *etc.* on rent or lease —**ˈtenancy** *n.* —**ˈtenantry** *n.* body of tenants —**tenant farmer** person who farms land rented from another, rent usu. taking form of crops *etc.*

tench (tɛntʃ) *n.* freshwater game fish

tend[1] (tɛnd) *vi.* **1.** be inclined **2.** be conducive **3.** go or move (in particular direction) —**ˈtendency** *n.* inclination, bent —**tenˈdentious** *or* **tenˈdencious** *a.* having, showing tendency or bias, controversial

tend[2] (tɛnd) *vt.* take care of, watch over —**ˈtender** *n.* **1.** small boat carried by yacht or ship **2.** carriage for fuel and water attached to steam locomotive **3.** one who tends, *eg* bar tender

tender[1] (ˈtɛndə) *a.* **1.** not tough or hard **2.** easily hurt **3.** gentle, loving, affectionate **4.** delicate, soft —**ˈtenderize** *or* **-ise** *vt.* soften (meat) by pounding or by treating with substance made for this purpose —**ˈtenderly** *adv.* —**ˈtenderness** *n.* —**ˈtenderfoot** *n.* newcomer, *esp.* to ranch *etc.* —**ˈtenderloin** *n.* tender cut of pork *etc.* from between sirloin and ribs

tender[2] (ˈtɛndə) *vt.* **1.** offer —*vi.* **2.** make offer or estimate —*n.* **3.** offer **4.** offer or estimate for contract to undertake specific work **5.** what may legally be offered in payment

THESAURUS

intense, passionate, stormy, turbulent, uncontrolled, violent, wild

temple church, holy place, place of worship, sanctuary, shrine

temporarily briefly, fleetingly, for a little while, for a moment, for a short time, for a short while, for the moment, for the time being, momentarily, pro tem

temporary brief, ephemeral, evanescent, fleeting, fugacious, fugitive, here today and gone tomorrow, impermanent, interim, momentary, passing, pro tem, *pro tempore*, provisional, short-lived, transient, transitory

tempt allure, appeal to, attract, coax, decoy, draw, entice, inveigle, invite, lead on, lure, make one's mouth water, seduce, tantalize, whet the appetite of, woo

temptation allurement, appeal, attraction, attractiveness, bait, blandishments, coaxing, come-on (*Inf.*), decoy, draw, enticement, inducement, invitation, lure, pull, seduction, snare, tantalization

tempting alluring, appetizing, attractive, enticing, inviting, mouthwatering, seductive, tantalizing

tenable arguable, believable, defendable, defensible, justifiable, maintainable, plausible, rational, reasonable, sound, viable

tenacious **1.** clinging, fast, firm, forceful, iron, strong, tight, unshakable **2.** retentive, unforgetful **3.** adamant, determined, dogged, firm, inflexible, intransigent, obdurate, obstinate, persistent, pertinacious, resolute, staunch, steadfast, strong-willed, stubborn, sure, unswerving, unyielding

tenacity **1.** fastness, firmness, force, forcefulness, power, strength **2.** firm grasp, retention, retentiveness **3.** application, determination, diligence, doggedness, firmness, inflexibility, intransigence, obduracy, obstinacy, perseverance, persistence, pertinacity, resoluteness, resolution, resolve, staunchness, steadfastness, strength of purpose, strength of will, stubbornness

tenancy holding, lease, occupancy, occupation, possession, renting, residence

tenant holder, inhabitant, leaseholder, lessee, occupant, occupier, renter, resident

tend[1] **1.** be apt, be biased, be disposed, be inclined, be liable, be likely, gravitate, have a leaning, have an inclination, have a tendency, incline, lean, trend **2.** aim, bear, be conducive, conduce, contribute, go, head, influence, lead, make for, move, point

tend[2] attend, care for, cater to, control, cultivate, feed, guard, handle, keep, keep an eye on, look after, maintain, manage, minister to, nurse, nurture, protect, see to, serve, take care of, wait on, watch, watch over

tendency bent, disposition, inclination, leaning, liability, partiality, penchant, predilection, predisposition, proclivity, proneness, propensity, readiness, susceptibility

tender[1] **1.** breakable, delicate, feeble, fragile, frail, soft, weak **2.** affectionate, amorous, benevolent, caring, compassionate, considerate, fond, gentle, humane, kind, loving, merciful, pitiful, sentimental, softhearted, sympathetic, tenderhearted, warm, warm-hearted **3.** aching, acute, bruised, inflamed, irritated, painful, raw, sensitive, smarting, sore

tender[2] *v.* **1.** estimate, extend, give, hand in, offer, present, proffer, propose, put forward, submit, suggest, volunteer ~*n.* **2.** bid, estimate, offer, proffer, proposal, submission, suggestion **3.** currency, medium, money, payment, specie

tenderness **1.** delicateness, feebleness, fragility, frailness, sensitiveness, sensitivity, softness, vulner-

tendon (ˈtɛndən) *n.* sinew attaching muscle to bone *etc.*

tendril (ˈtɛndrɪl) *n.* **1.** slender curling stem by which climbing plant clings to anything **2.** curl, as of hair

tenement (ˈtɛnəmənt) *n.* building divided into separate flats (*also* **tenement building**)

tenet (ˈtɛnɪt, ˈtiːnɪt) *n.* doctrine, belief

tenner (ˈtɛnə) *inf.* ten-pound note

tennis (ˈtɛnɪs) *n.* game in which ball is struck with racket by players on opposite sides of net, lawn tennis —**tennis elbow** strained muscle as a result of playing tennis —**tennis shoe** rubber-soled canvas shoe tied with laces

tenon (ˈtɛnən) *n.* tongue put on end of piece of wood *etc.* to fit into a mortise —**tenon saw**

tenor (ˈtɛnə) *n.* **1.** male voice between alto and bass **2.** music for, singer with this **3.** saxophone *etc.* intermediate between alto and baritone or bass **4.** general course, meaning

tense[1] (tɛns) *n.* modification of verb to show time of action

tense[2] (tɛns) *a.* **1.** stretched tight, strained; taut **2.** emotionally strained —*v.* **3.** make, become tense —ˈ**tensile** *a.* **1.** of tension **2.** capable of being stretched —ˈ**tension** *n.* **1.** stretching **2.** strain when stretched **3.** emotional strain or excitement **4.** hostility **5.** suspense **6.** *Elec.* voltage —**tensile strength** measure of ability of material to withstand longitudinal stress

tent (tɛnt) *n.* portable shelter of canvas —**tent stitch** *see* **petit point** *at* PETIT

tentacle (ˈtɛntəkəl) *n.* elongated, flexible organ of some animals (*eg* octopus) used for grasping, feeding *etc.*

tentative (ˈtɛntətɪv) *a.* **1.** done as a trial **2.** experimental, cautious —ˈ**tentatively** *adv.*

tenterhooks (ˈtɛntəhʊks) *pl.n.* —**on tenterhooks** in anxious suspense

tenuous (ˈtɛnjʊəs) *a.* **1.** flimsy, uncertain **2.** thin, fine, slender —**teˈnuity** *n.*

tenure (ˈtɛnjʊə, ˈtɛnjə) *n.* (length of time of) possession, holding of office, position *etc.*

tenuto (tɪˈnjuːtəʊ) *a./adv. Mus.* (of note) to be held for or beyond its full time value

tepee *or* **teepee** (ˈtiːpiː) *n.* N Amer. Indian cone-shaped tent of animal skins

tepid (ˈtɛpɪd) *a.* **1.** moderately warm, lukewarm **2.** half-hearted

tequila (tɪˈkiːlə) *n.* Mexican alcoholic spirit

ter. **1.** terrace **2.** territory

terbium (ˈtɜːbɪəm) *n.* rare metallic element

tercel (ˈtɜːsəl) *or* **tiercel** *n.* male falcon or hawk, *esp.* as used in falconry

tercentenary (tɜːsɛnˈtiːnərɪ) *or* **tercentennial** *a./n.* (of) three hundredth anniversary

tergiversate (ˈtɜːdʒɪvəseɪt) *vi.* **1.** change sides or loyalties **2.** be evasive or ambiguous —**tergiverˈsation** *n.*

term (tɜːm) *n.* **1.** word; expression **2.** limited period of time **3.** period during which courts sit, schools are open *etc.* **4.** limit, end —*pl.* **5.** conditions **6.** mutual relationship —*vt.* **7.** name, designate —**terms of reference** specific limits of responsibility that determine activities of investigating body *etc.* —**terms of trade UK** *Econ.* ratio of export prices to import prices

termagant (ˈtɜːməgənt) *n. rare* shrewish woman; scold

terminal (ˈtɜːmɪnəl) *a.* **1.** at, forming an end **2.** pert. to, forming a terminus **3.** (of disease) ending in death —*n.* **4.** terminal part or structure **5.** extremity **6.** point where current enters, leaves electrical device (*eg* battery) **7.** device permitting operation of computer at some distance from it —**terminal velocity 1.** constant maximum velocity reached by body falling under gravity through fluid, *esp.* atmosphere **2.** velocity of missile or projectile when it reaches target **3.** maximum velocity attained by rocket *etc.* flying in parabolic flight path **4.** maximum velocity that aircraft can attain

terminate (ˈtɜːmɪneɪt) *v.* bring, come to an end —ˈ**terminable** *a.* —**termiˈnation** *n.*

THESAURUS

ability, weakness **2.** affection, amorousness, attachment, benevolence, care, compassion, consideration, devotion, fondness, gentleness, humaneness, humanity, kindness, liking, love, mercy, pity, sentimentality, softheartedness, sympathy, tenderheartedness, warm-heartedness, warmth **3.** ache, aching, bruising, inflammation, irritation, pain, painfulness, rawness, sensitiveness, sensitivity, smart, soreness

tense *adj.* **1.** rigid, strained, stretched, taut, tight **2.** anxious, apprehensive, edgy, fidgety, jittery (*Inf.*), jumpy, keyed up, nervous, on edge, overwrought, restless, strained, strung up (*Inf.*), under pressure, uptight (*Sl.*), wound up (*Inf.*), wrought up ~*v.* **3.** brace, flex, strain, stretch, tauten, tighten

tension **1.** pressure, rigidity, stiffness, straining, stress, stretching, tautness, tightness **2.** anxiety, apprehension, edginess, hostility, ill feeling, nervousness, pressure, restlessness, strain, stress, suspense, the jitters (*Inf.*), unease

tentative **1.** conjectural, experimental, indefinite, provisional, speculative, unconfirmed, unsettled **2.** backward, cautious, diffident, doubtful, faltering, hesitant, timid, uncertain, undecided, unsure

tepid **1.** lukewarm, slightly warm, warmish **2.** apathetic, cool, half-hearted, indifferent, lukewarm, unenthusiastic

term *n.* **1.** appellation, denomination, designation, expression, locution, name, phrase, title, word **2.** duration, interval, period, season, space, span, spell, time, while **3.** course, session **4.** bound, boundary, close, conclusion, confine, culmination, end, finish, fruition, limit, terminus ~*v.* **5.** call, denominate, designate, dub, entitle, label, name, style

terminal *adj.* **1.** bounding, concluding, extreme, final, last, limiting, ultimate, utmost **2.** deadly, fatal, incurable, killing, lethal, mortal ~*n.* **3.** boundary, end, extremity, limit, termination, terminus **4.** depot, end of the line, station, terminus

terminate abort, bring *or* come to an end, cease, close, complete, conclude, cut off, discontinue, end, expire, finish, issue, lapse, put an end to, result, run out, stop, wind up

termination abortion, cessation, close, completion, conclusion, consequence, cut-off point, discontinuation, effect, end, ending, expiry, finale, finis, finish, issue, result, wind-up (*Inf.*)

terminology (tɜːmɪˈnɒlədʒɪ) *n.* **1.** set of technical terms or vocabulary **2.** study of terms —**terminoˈlogical** *a.*

terminus (ˈtɜːmɪnəs) *n.* **1.** finishing point **2.** farthest limit **3.** railway station, bus station *etc.* at end of long-distance line (*pl.* **-ni** (-naɪ), **-es**)

termite (ˈtɜːmaɪt) *n.* insect, some species of which feed on and damage wood (*also* **white ant**)

tern (tɜːn) *n.* sea bird like gull

ternary (ˈtɜːnərɪ) *a.* **1.** consisting of three **2.** proceeding in threes

Terpsichore (tɜːpˈsɪkərɪ) *n.* Muse of dance and choral song —**Terpsichorean** (tɜːpsɪkəˈrɪən, -ˈkɔːrɪən) *oft. jocular a.* **1.** of dancing (*also* **Terpsichoˈreal**) —*n.* **2.** dancer

Terr. **1.** Terrace **2.** Territory

terrace (ˈtɛrəs) *n.* **1.** raised level place **2.** level cut out of hill **3.** row, street of houses built as one block **4.** (*oft. pl.*) unroofed tier for spectators at football stadium —*vt.* **5.** form into, furnish with terrace

terra cotta (ˈtɛrə ˈkɒtə) **1.** hard unglazed pottery **2.** its colour, brownish red

terra firma (ˈfɜːmə) *Lat.* firm ground; dry land

terrain (təˈreɪn) *n.* area of ground, *esp.* with reference to its physical character

terra incognita (ɪnˈkɒgnɪtə) *Lat.* unexplored or unknown area

terrapin (ˈtɛrəpɪn) *n.* type of aquatic tortoise

terrazzo (tɛˈrætsəʊ) *n.* floor, wall finish of chips of stone set in mortar and polished

terrene (tɛˈriːn) *a.* **1.** of earth; worldly; mundane **2.** *rare* of earth; earthy —*n.* **3.** land **4.** *rare* earth

terrestrial (təˈrɛstrɪəl) *a.* **1.** of the earth **2.** of, living on land

terrible (ˈtɛrəbᵊl) *a.* **1.** serious **2.** dreadful, frightful **3.** excessive **4.** causing fear —ˈ**terribly** *adv.*

terrier (ˈtɛrɪə) *n.* small dog of various breeds, *orig.* for following quarry into burrow

terrific (təˈrɪfɪk) *a.* **1.** very great **2.** *inf.* good, excellent **3.** terrible, awe-inspiring

terrify (ˈtɛrɪfaɪ) *vt.* fill with fear, dread

terrine (tɛˈriːn) *n.* **1.** oval earthenware cooking dish **2.** food cooked or served in such dish, *esp.* paté

territory (ˈtɛrɪtərɪ) *n.* **1.** region **2.** geographical area under control of a political unit, *esp.* a sovereign state **3.** area of knowledge —**terriˈtorial** *a.* of territory —**Territorial Army** locally recruited volunteer force —**territorial waters** waters over which nation exercises jurisdiction

terror (ˈtɛrə) *n.* **1.** great fear **2.** *inf.* troublesome person or thing —ˈ**terrorism** *n.* **1.** use of violence, intimidation to achieve ends **2.** state of terror —ˈ**terrorist** *n./a.* —ˈ**terrorize** *or* **-ise** *vt.* force, oppress by fear, violence

terry (ˈtɛrɪ) *n./a.* (pile fabric) with the loops uncut

terse (tɜːs) *a.* **1.** expressed in few words, concise **2.** abrupt

tertiary (ˈtɜːʃərɪ) *a.* **1.** third in degree, order *etc.* **2.** (**T-**) of Tertiary period or rock system —*n.* **3.** (**T-**) geological period before Quaternary

Terylene (ˈtɛrəliːn) *n.* **R** **1.** synthetic yarn **2.** fabric made of it

tessellate (ˈtɛsɪleɪt) *vt.* **1.** make, pave, inlay with mosaic of small tiles **2.** (of identical shapes) fit together exactly —ˈ**tessellated** *a.* —**tesselˈlation** *n.* —**tessera** (ˈtɛsərə) *n.* stone used in mosaic (*pl.* **-ae** (-iː))

test (tɛst) *vt.* **1.** try, put to the proof **2.** carry out test(s) on —*n.* **3.** critical examination **4.** means of trial —ˈ**testing** *a.* difficult —**test case** lawsuit viewed as means of establishing precedent —**test match** one of series of international sports contests, *esp.* cricket —**test paper** **1.** *Chem.* paper impregnated with indicator for chemical tests **2.** question sheet of test **3.** paper completed by test candidate —**test pilot** pilot who flies aircraft of new design to test performance in air —**test tube** narrow cylindrical glass vessel used in scientific experiments —**test-tube baby** baby conceived in artificial womb

THESAURUS

terminology argot, cant, jargon, language, lingo (*Inf.*), nomenclature, patois, phraseology, terms, vocabulary

terminus **1.** boundary, close, end, extremity, final point, goal, limit, target, termination **2.** depot, end of the line, garage, last stop, station

terms **1.** conditions, particulars, premises (*Law*), provisions, provisos, qualifications, specifications, stipulations **2.** charges, fee, payment, price, rates

terrible **1.** bad, dangerous, desperate, extreme, serious, severe **2.** *Inf.* abhorrent, awful, bad, beastly (*Inf.*), dire, dreadful, duff (*Brit. sl.*), foul, frightful, hateful, hideous, loathsome, obnoxious, odious, offensive, poor, repulsive, revolting, rotten (*Inf.*), unpleasant, vile **3.** appalling, awful, dread, dreaded, dreadful, fearful, frightful, gruesome, harrowing, horrendous, horrible, horrid, horrifying, monstrous, shocking

terribly awfully (*Inf.*), decidedly, desperately, exceedingly, extremely, gravely, greatly, much, seriously, thoroughly, very

terrific **1.** awesome, awful, dreadful, enormous, excessive, extreme, fearful, fierce, gigantic, great, harsh, horrific, huge, intense, monstrous, severe, terrible, tremendous **2.** *Inf.* ace (*Inf.*), amazing, breathtaking, excellent, fabulous (*Inf.*), fantastic (*Inf.*), fine, great (*Inf.*), magnificent, marvellous, outstanding, sensational (*Inf.*), smashing (*Inf.*), stupendous, super (*Inf.*), superb, very good, wonderful

terrify alarm, appal, awe, dismay, fill with terror, frighten, frighten out of one's wits, horrify, intimidate, make one's blood run cold, make one's flesh creep, make one's hair stand on end, petrify, put the fear of God into, scare, scare to death, shock, terrorize

territory area, bailiwick, country, district, domain, land, province, region, sector, state, terrain, tract, zone

terror **1.** alarm, anxiety, awe, consternation, dismay, dread, fear, fear and trembling, fright, horror, intimidation, panic, shock **2.** bogeyman, bugbear, devil, fiend, monster, scourge

terrorize browbeat, bully, coerce, intimidate, menace, oppress, strong-arm (*Inf.*), threaten

terse **1.** aphoristic, brief, clipped, compact, concise, condensed, crisp, elliptical, epigrammatic, gnomic, incisive, laconic, neat, pithy, sententious, short, succinct, summary, to the point **2.** abrupt, brusque, curt, short, snappy

test **1.** *v.* analyse, assay, assess, check, examine,

testament (ˈtɛstəmənt) *n.* **1.** *Law* will **2.** testimony **3.** (T-) one of the two main divisions of the Bible —**testaˈmentary** *a.*

testate (ˈtɛsteɪt, ˈtɛstɪt) *a.* having left a valid will —**ˈtestacy** *n.* state of being testate —**tesˈtator** *n.* maker of will (**tesˈtatrix** *fem.*)

testicle (ˈtɛstɪkᵊl) *n.* either of two male reproductive glands

testify (ˈtɛstɪfaɪ) *v.* **1.** declare **2.** bear witness (to) (**-fied, -fying**)

testimony (ˈtɛstɪmənɪ) *n.* **1.** affirmation **2.** evidence —**testiˈmonial** *n.* **1.** certificate of character, ability *etc.* **2.** tribute given by person expressing regard for recipient —*a.* **3.** of testimony or testimonial

testis (ˈtɛstɪs) *n.* testicle (*pl.* **testes** (ˈtɛstiːz)) —**tesˈtosterone** *n.* hormone secreted mainly by testes

testy (ˈtɛstɪ) *a.* irritable, short-tempered —**ˈtestily** *adv.*

tetanus (ˈtɛtənəs) *n.* acute infectious disease producing muscular spasms, contractions (*also* **ˈlockjaw**)

tetchy (ˈtɛtʃɪ) *a.* cross, irritable, touchy —**ˈtetchiness** *n.*

tête-à-tête (teɪtəˈteɪt) *n.* **1.** private conversation between two people **2.** small sofa for two people, *esp.* S-shaped (*pl.* **-s, -tête**) —*adv.* **3.** intimately; in private

tether (ˈtɛðə) *n.* **1.** rope or chain for fastening (grazing) animal —*vt.* **2.** tie up with rope —**be at the end of one's tether** have reached limit of one's endurance

tetra- *or before vowel* **tetr-** (*comb. form*) four, as in *tetrameter*

tetrad (ˈtɛtræd) *n.* group or series of four

tetraethyl lead (tɛtrəˈiːθaɪl lɛd) colourless oily insoluble liquid used in petrol to prevent knocking

tetragon (ˈtɛtrəgɒn) *n.* figure with four angles and four sides —**teˈtragonal** *a.* —**tetraˈhedron** *n.* solid contained by four plane faces

tetralogy (tɛˈtrælədʒɪ) *n.* series of four related works, as in drama or opera

tetrameter (tɛˈtræmɪtə) *n.* *Prosody* **1.** line of verse consisting of four metrical feet **2.** verse composed of such lines

Teuton (ˈtjuːtən) *n.* **1.** member of ancient Germanic people from Jutland who migrated to S Gaul in 2nd century B.C. **2.** member of any Germanic-speaking people, *esp.* German —*a.* **3.** Teutonic —**Teuˈtonic** *a.* **1.** German **2.** of ancient Teutons

text (tɛkst) *n.* **1.** (actual words of) book, passage *etc.* **2.** passage of Scriptures *etc., esp.* as subject of discourse —**ˈtextual** *a.* of, in a text —**ˈtextbook** *n.* book of instruction on particular subject —**textual criticism 1.** scholarly study of manuscripts, *esp.* of Bible, to establish original text **2.** literary criticism emphasizing close analysis of text

textile (ˈtɛkstaɪl) *n.* **1.** any fabric or cloth, *esp.* woven —*a.* **2.** of (the making of) fabrics

texture (ˈtɛkstʃə) *n.* **1.** surface of material, *esp.* as perceived by sense of touch **2.** character, structure **3.** consistency —*vt.* **4.** give distinctive texture to

T.G.W.U. Transport and General Workers' Union

Th *Chem.* thorium

-th[1] (*comb. form*) **1.** action or its consequence, as in *growth* **2.** quality, as in *width*

-th[2] *or* **-eth** (*comb. form*) forming ordinal numbers, as in *fourth, thousandth*

Thai (taɪ) *a.* **1.** of Thailand —*n.* **2.** native of Thailand (*pl.* **-s, Thai**) **3.** language of Thailand

thalidomide (θəˈlɪdəmaɪd) *n.* drug formerly used as sedative, but found to cause abnormalities in developing foetus

thallium (ˈθælɪəm) *n.* highly toxic metallic element —**ˈthallic** *a.*

than (ðæn; *unstressed* ðən) *conj.* introduces second part of comparison

thane *or* **thegn** (θeɪn) *n.* *Hist.* nobleman holding lands in return for certain services

thank (θæŋk) *vt.* **1.** express gratitude to **2.** say thanks to **3.** hold responsible —**ˈthankful** *a.* grateful, appreciative —**ˈthankless** *a.* **1.** having, bringing no thanks **2.** unprofitable —**thanks** *pl.n.* words of gratitude —**Thanksgiving Day** public holiday in Canad. and U.S.A.

that (ðæt; *unstressed* ðət) *a.* **1.** demonstrates or particularizes (*pl.* **those**) —*demonstrative pron.* **2.** particular thing meant (*pl.* **those**) —*adv.* **3.** as —*relative pron.* **4.** which, who —*conj.* **5.** introduces noun or adverbial clauses

thatch (θætʃ) *n.* **1.** reeds, straw *etc.* used as roofing material —*vt.* **2.** roof (a house) with reeds, straw *etc.* —**ˈthatcher** *n.*

thaw (θɔː) *v.* **1.** melt **2.** (cause to) unfreeze **3.** defrost —*vi.* **4.** become warmer or more genial —*n.* **5.** a melting (of frost *etc.*)

THESAURUS

experiment, investigate, prove, put to the proof, put to the test, try, try out, verify **2.** *n.* analysis, assessment, attempt, catechism, check, evaluation, examination, investigation, ordeal, probation, proof, trial

testament 1. last wishes, will **2.** attestation, demonstration, earnest, evidence, exemplification, proof, testimony, tribute, witness

testify affirm, assert, attest, bear witness, certify, corroborate, declare, depone (*Scots Law*), depose (*Law*), evince, give testimony, show, state, swear, vouch, witness

testimonial certificate, character, commendation, credential, endorsement, recommendation, reference, tribute

testimony 1. affidavit, affirmation, attestation, avowal, confirmation, corroboration, declaration, deposition, evidence, information, profession, statement, submission, witness **2.** corroboration, demonstration, evidence, indication, manifestation, proof, support, verification

text 1. body, contents, main body, matter **2.** wording, words **3.** *Bible* paragraph, passage, sentence, verse **4.** reader, reference book, source, textbook

texture character, composition, consistency, constitution, fabric, feel, grain, make, quality, structure, surface, tissue, weave

thank express gratitude, say thank you, show gratitude, show one's appreciation

thankful appreciative, beholden, grateful, indebted, obliged, pleased, relieved

thankless 1. fruitless, unappreciated, unprofitable, unrequited, unrewarding, useless **2.** inconsiderate, unappreciative, ungracious, ungrateful, unmindful, unthankful

Th.D. Doctor of Theology

the (*stressed or emphatic* ðiː; *unstressed before consonant* ðə; *unstressed before vowel* ðɪ) the definite article

theatre *or U.S.* **theater** (ˈθɪətə) *n.* **1.** place where plays *etc.* are performed **2.** drama, dramatic works generally **3.** large room with (tiered) seats, used for lectures *etc.* **4.** surgical operating room —**theatrical** (θɪˈætrɪkᵊl) *a.* **1.** of, for the theatre **2.** exaggerated, affected —**theatrically** (θɪˈætrɪkəlɪ) *adv.* —**theatricals** (θɪˈætrɪkᵊlz) *pl.n.* amateur dramatic performances

thee (ðiː) *pron. obs.* objective and dative of THOU[1]

theft (θɛft) *n.* stealing

their (ðɛə) *a.* belonging to them —**theirs** *pron.* something or someone belonging to them

theism (ˈθiːɪzəm) *n.* belief in creation of universe by one god —ˈ**theist** *n.* —**theˈistic(al)** *a.*

them (ðɛm; *unstressed* ðəm) *pron.* **1.** objective case of THEY **2.** those persons or things —**themˈselves** *pron.* emphatic and reflexive form of THEY

theme (θiːm) *n.* **1.** main idea or topic of conversation, book *etc.* **2.** subject of composition **3.** recurring melody in music —**theˈmatic** *a.*

then (ðɛn) *adv.* **1.** at that time **2.** next **3.** that being so

thence (ðɛns) *adv.* from that place, point of reasoning *etc.*

theo- *or before vowel* **the-** (*comb. form*) God; gods, as in *theology*

theocracy (θɪˈɒkrəsɪ) *n.* government by a deity or a priesthood —**theoˈcratic** *a.*

theodolite (θɪˈɒdəlaɪt) *n.* surveying instrument for measuring angles

theology (θɪˈɒlədʒɪ) *n.* systematic study of religion(s) and religious belief(s) —**theologian** (θɪəˈləʊdʒɪən) *n.* —**theoˈlogical** *a.* —**theoˈlogically** *adv.*

theorem (ˈθɪərəm) *n.* proposition which can be demonstrated by argument —**theoreˈmatic** *or* **theoˈremic** *a.*

theory (ˈθɪərɪ) *n.* **1.** supposition to account for something **2.** system of rules and principles **3.** rules and reasoning *etc.* as distinguished from practice —**theoˈretic(al)** *a.* **1.** based on theory **2.** speculative, as opposed to practical —**theoˈretically** *adv.* —**theoreˈtician** *n.* student or user of theory rather than practical aspects of subject —ˈ**theorist** *n.* —ˈ**theorize** *or* **-ise** *vi.* form theories, speculate

theosophy (θɪˈɒsəfɪ) *n.* any of various religious, philosophical systems claiming possibility of intuitive insight into divine nature

therapy (ˈθɛrəpɪ) *n.* healing treatment (*usu.* in *comb. forms* as *radiotherapy*) —**therapeutic** (θɛrəˈpjuːtɪk) *a.* **1.** of healing **2.** serving to improve or maintain health —**therapeutics** (θɛrəˈpjuːtɪks) *pl.n.* (*with sing. v.*) art of healing —ˈ**therapist** *n.*

there (ðɛə) *adv.* **1.** in that place **2.** to that point —ˈ**thereabouts** *or* ˈ**thereabout** *adv.* near that place, time *etc.* —**thereˈafter** *adv.* from that time on; after that time —**thereˈby** *adv.* by that means —ˈ**therefore** *adv.* in consequence, that being so —**thereˈin** *adv. Formal, law* in or into that place *etc.* —**thereˈof** *adv. Formal, law* **1.** of or concerning that or it **2.** from or because of that —**thereˈto** *adv.* **1.** *Formal, law* to that or it **2.** *obs.* in addition to that —**thereˈunder** *adv. Formal, law* **1.** in documents *etc.*, below that or it; subsequently in that; thereafter **2.** under terms or authority of that —**thereuˈpon** *adv.* at that point, immediately afterwards —**thereˈwith** *or* **therewithˈal** *adv.* **1.** *Formal, law* with or in addition to that **2.** *rare* thereupon **3.** *obs.* by means of or on account of that

therm (θɜːm) *n.* unit of measurement of heat —ˈ**thermal** *or* ˈ**thermic** *a.* **1.** of, pert. to heat **2.** hot, warm (*esp.* of spring *etc.*) **3.** (of garments) specially made so as to have exceptional heat-retaining qualities

thermion (ˈθɜːmɪən) *n. Phys.* ion emitted by incandescent body —**thermiˈonic** *a.* pert. to thermion —**thermionic valve** electronic valve in which electrons are emitted from a heated rather than a cold cathode

thermo- *or before vowel* **therm-** (*comb. form*) related to, caused by or producing heat, as in *thermopile*

thermocouple (ˈθɜːməʊkʌpᵊl) *n.* **1.** device for measuring temperature consisting of pair of wires of different metals joined at both ends **2.** similar device with only one junction between two dissimilar metals

thermodynamics (θɜːməʊdaɪˈnæmɪks) *pl.n.* (*with sing. v.*) the science that deals with the interrelationship and interconversion of different forms of energy

thermoelectricity (θɜːməʊɪlɛkˈtrɪsɪtɪ) *n.* electricity developed by the action of heat —**thermoeˈlectric(al)** *a.* **1.** of conversion of heat energy to electrical energy **2.** of conversion of electrical energy

thermometer (θəˈmɒmɪtə) *n.* instrument to measure temperature —**thermoˈmetric** *a.*

THESAURUS

thanks acknowledgment, appreciation, credit, gratefulness, gratitude, recognition, thanksgiving

thaw defrost, dissolve, liquefy, melt, soften, unfreeze, warm

theatrical **1.** dramatic, dramaturgic, melodramatic, scenic, Thespian **2.** affected, artificial, ceremonious, dramatic, exaggerated, hammy (*Inf.*), histrionic, mannered, ostentatious, overdone, pompous, showy, stagy, stilted, unreal

theft embezzlement, fraud, larceny, pilfering, purloining, rip-off (*Sl.*), robbery, stealing, swindling, thievery, thieving

theme **1.** argument, burden, idea, keynote, matter, subject, subject matter, text, thesis, topic **2.** leitmotiv, motif, recurrent image, unifying idea **3.** composition, dissertation, essay, exercise, paper

theological divine, doctrinal, ecclesiastical, religious

theorem deduction, dictum, formula, hypothesis, principle, proposition, rule, statement

theoretic, theoretical abstract, academic, conjectural, hypothetical, ideal, impractical, pure, speculative

theorize conjecture, formulate, guess, hypothesize, project, propound, speculate, suppose

theory **1.** assumption, conjecture, guess, hypothesis, presumption, speculation, supposition, surmise, thesis **2.** philosophy, plan, proposal, scheme, system

therapeutic ameliorative, analeptic, beneficial, corrective, curative, good, healing, remedial, restorative, salubrious, salutary, sanative

therapy cure, healing, remedial treatment, remedy, treatment

therefore accordingly, as a result, consequently, ergo, for that reason, hence, so, then, thence, thus, whence

thermonuclear (θɜːməʊˈnjuːklɪə) *a.* involving nuclear fusion

thermoplastic (θɜːməʊˈplæstɪk) *n.* **1.** plastic that retains its properties after being melted and solidified —*a.* **2.** (of plastic *etc.*) becoming soft when heated and rehardening on cooling without appreciable change of properties

Thermos *or* **Thermos flask** (ˈθɜːməs) *n.* **R** vacuum flask

thermosetting (θɜːməʊˈsɛtɪŋ) *a.* (of material, *esp.* synthetic plastic) hardening permanently after one application of heat and pressure

thermostat (ˈθɜːməstæt) *n.* apparatus for automatically regulating temperature —**thermoˈstatic** *a.*

thesaurus (θɪˈsɔːrəs) *n.* **1.** book containing lists of synonyms and sometimes antonyms **2.** dictionary of selected words, topics (*pl.* **-es, -ri** (-raɪ))

these (ðiːz) *pron., pl. of* THIS

thesis (ˈθiːsɪs) *n.* **1.** written work submitted for degree, diploma **2.** theory maintained in argument (*pl.* **theses** (ˈθiːsiːz))

Thespian (ˈθɛspɪən) *a.* **1.** theatrical —*n.* **2.** actor, actress

Thess. *Bible* Thessalonians

theta (ˈθiːtə) *n.* eighth letter in Gr. alphabet (Θ, θ)

they (ðeɪ) *pron.* the third person plural pronoun

thick (θɪk) *a.* **1.** having great thickness, not thin **2.** dense, crowded **3.** viscous **4.** (of voice) throaty **5.** *inf.* stupid, insensitive **6.** *inf.* friendly (*esp. in* **thick as thieves**) —*n.* **7.** busiest, most intense part —**ˈthicken** *v.* **1.** make, become thick —*vi.* **2.** become more involved, complicated —**ˈthickening** *n.* **1.** something added to liquid to thicken it **2.** thickened part or piece —**ˈthicket** *n.* thick growth of small trees —**ˈthickly** *adv.* —**ˈthickness** *n.* **1.** dimensions of anything measured through it, at right angles to length and breadth **2.** state of being thick **3.** layer —**ˈthickhead** *n.* **1.** stupid or ignorant person; fool **2.** Aust. or SE Asian songbird —**thickˈheaded** *a.* —**thickˈheadedness** *n.* —**thickˈset** *a.* **1.** sturdy and solid of body **2.** set closely together —**thick-skinned** *a.* insensitive to criticism or hints; not easily upset or affected

thief (θiːf) *n.* one who steals (*pl.* **thieves** (θiːvz)) —**thieve** *v.* steal —**ˈthievish** *a.*

thigh (θaɪ) *n.* upper part of leg

thimble (ˈθɪmbᵊl) *n.* cap protecting end of finger when sewing

thin (θɪn) *a.* **1.** of little thickness **2.** slim, lean **3.** of little density **4.** sparse; fine **5.** loose, not close-packed **6.** *inf.* unlikely —*v.* **7.** make, become thin (**-nn-**) —**ˈthinner** *n.* —**ˈthinness** *n.* —**thin-skinned** *a.* sensitive to criticism or hints; easily upset or affected

thine (ðaɪn) *pron./a.* (thing) belonging to thee

thing (θɪŋ) *n.* **1.** material object **2.** any possible object of thought **3.** preoccupation, obsession (*esp. in* **have a thing about**) —**thingumabob** *or* **thingamabob** (ˈθɪŋəməbɒb) *n. inf.* a person or thing the name of which is unknown, temporarily forgotten or deliberately overlooked (*also* **ˈthingumajig, ˈthingamajig** *or* **ˈthingummy**)

think (θɪŋk) *vi.* **1.** have one's mind at work **2.** reflect, meditate **3.** reason **4.** deliberate **5.** imagine **6.** hold opinion —*vt.* **7.** conceive, consider in the mind **8.** believe **9.** esteem (**thought, ˈthinking**) —**ˈthinkable** *a.* able to be conceived, considered, possible, feasible —**ˈthinker** *n.* —**ˈthinking** *a.* reflecting, reasoning —**think-tank** *n.* group of experts studying specific problems

THESAURUS

thesis 1. composition, disquisition, dissertation, essay, monograph, paper, treatise **2.** contention, hypothesis, idea, line of argument, opinion, proposal, proposition, theory, view

thick *adj.* **1.** broad, bulky, deep, fat, solid, substantial, wide **2.** close, clotted, coagulated, compact, concentrated, condensed, crowded, deep, dense, heavy, impenetrable, opaque **3.** abundant, brimming, bristling, bursting, chock-a-block, chock-full, covered, crawling, frequent, full, numerous, packed, replete, swarming, teeming **4.** blockheaded, brainless, dense, dim-witted (*Inf.*), dopey (*Sl.*), dull, insensitive, moronic, obtuse, slow, slow-witted, stupid, thickheaded **5.** dense, heavy, impenetrable, soupy **6.** distorted, guttural, hoarse, husky, inarticulate, indistinct, throaty **7.** *Inf.* chummy (*Inf.*), close, confidential, devoted, familiar, friendly, hand in glove, inseparable, intimate, matey (*Brit. inf.*), on good terms, pally (*Inf.*), well in (*Inf.*) ~*n.* **8.** centre, heart, middle, midst

thicken cake, clot, coagulate, condense, congeal, deepen, gel, inspissate (*Archaic*), jell, set

thickset 1. beefy (*Inf.*), brawny, bulky, burly, heavy, muscular, powerfully built, stocky, strong, stubby, sturdy, well-built **2.** closely packed, dense, densely planted, solid, thick

thick-skinned callous, case-hardened, hard-boiled (*Inf.*), hardened, impervious, insensitive, stolid, tough, unfeeling, unsusceptible

thief bandit, burglar, cheat, cracksman (*Sl.*), crook (*Inf.*), embezzler, housebreaker, larcenist, mugger (*Inf.*), pickpocket, pilferer, plunderer, purloiner, robber, shoplifter, stealer, swindler

thieve cheat, embezzle, filch, half-inch (*Inf.*), knock off (*Sl.*), lift (*Inf.*), misappropriate, nick (*Brit. sl.*), peculate, pilfer, pinch (*Inf.*), plunder, poach, purloin, rip off (*Sl.*), rob, run off with, snitch (*Sl.*), steal, swindle, swipe (*Sl.*)

thin *adj.* **1.** attenuate, attenuated, fine, narrow, threadlike **2.** delicate, diaphanous, filmy, fine, flimsy, gossamer, seethrough, sheer, translucent, transparent, unsubstantial **3.** bony, emaciated, lank, lanky, lean, light, meagre, scraggy, scrawny, skeletal, skinny, slender, slight, slim, spare, spindly, thin as a rake, undernourished, underweight **4.** deficient, meagre, scanty, scarce, scattered, skimpy, sparse, wispy **5.** dilute, diluted, rarefied, runny, watery, weak, wishy-washy (*Inf.*) **6.** feeble, flimsy, inadequate, insufficient, lame, poor, scant, scanty, shallow, slight, superficial, unconvincing, unlikely, unsubstantial, weak ~*v.* **7.** attenuate, cut back, dilute, diminish, emaciate, prune, rarefy, reduce, refine, trim, water down, weaken, weed out

thing 1. affair, article, being, body, circumstance, concept, entity, fact, matter, object, part, portion, something, substance **2.** apparatus, contrivance, device, gadget, implement, instrument, machine, means, mechanism, tool **3.** aspect, detail, facet, factor, feature, item, particular, point, statement,

thio- *or before vowel* **thi-** (*comb. form*) sulphur, *esp.* denoting replacement of oxygen atom with sulphur atom, as in *thiol, thiosulphate*

thiopentone sodium (θaɪəʊˈpɛntəʊn) *or* **thiopental sodium** (θaɪəʊˈpɛntæl) barbiturate drug used as intravenous general anaesthetic (*also* **sodium pentothal**)

third (θɜːd) *a.* **1.** ordinal number corresponding to *three* —*n.* **2.** third part —**third degree** *see* DEGREE —**third dimension** dimension of depth by which solid object may be distinguished from two-dimensional drawing or picture of it —**third man** *Cricket* fielding position on off side near boundary behind batsman's wicket —**third party** *Law, insurance etc.* person involved by chance or only incidentally in legal proceedings *etc.* —**third person** grammatical category of pronouns and verbs used when referring to objects or individuals other than speaker or his addressee(s) —**third-rate** *a.* mediocre, inferior —**Third World** developing countries of Afr., Asia, Latin Amer.

thirst (θɜːst) *n.* **1.** desire to drink **2.** feeling caused by lack of drink **3.** craving, yearning —*vi.* **4.** feel lack of drink —ˈ**thirstily** *adv.* —ˈ**thirsty** *a.*

thirteen (ˈθɜːˈtiːn) *n./a.* three plus ten —ˈ**thirty** *n./a.* three times ten

this (ðɪs) *demonstrative a./pron.* denotes thing, person near, or just mentioned (*pl.* **these**)

thistle (ˈθɪsˈl) *n.* prickly plant with dense flower heads —ˈ**thistledown** *n.* mass of feathery plumed seeds produced by thistle

thither (ˈðɪðə) *or* **thitherward** *adv. obs.* to or towards that place

thixotropic (θɪksəˈtrɒpɪk) *a.* (of certain liquids, as paints) having property of thickening if left undisturbed but becoming less viscous when stirred

tho *or* **tho'** (ðəʊ) US, *poet. see* THOUGH

thole[1] (θəʊl) *or* **tholepin** (ˈθəʊlpɪn) *n.* wooden pin set upright in gunwale of rowing boat to serve as fulcrum in rowing

thole[2] (θəʊl) *vt.* **1.** *dial.* put up with; bear **2.** suffer

thong (θɒŋ) *n.* **1.** narrow strip of leather, strap **2.** *chiefly* **US, A, NZ** flip-flop (sandal)

thorax (ˈθɔːræks) *n.* part of body between neck and belly —**thoracic** (θɔːˈræsɪk) *a.*

thorium (ˈθɔːrɪəm) *n.* radioactive metallic element

thorn (θɔːn) *n.* **1.** prickle on plant **2.** spine **3.** bush noted for its thorns **4.** *fig.* anything which causes trouble or annoyance (*esp. in* **thorn in one's side** *or* **flesh**) —ˈ**thorny** *a.*

thorough (ˈθʌrə) *a.* **1.** careful, methodical **2.** complete, entire —ˈ**thoroughly** *adv.* —ˈ**thoroughbred** *a.* **1.** of pure breed —*n.* **2.** purebred animal, *esp.* horse —ˈ**thoroughfare** *n.* **1.** road or passage open at both ends **2.** right of way —ˈ**thoroughgoing** *a.* **1.** extremely thorough **2.** absolute; complete

those (ðəʊz) *pron., pl. of* THAT

thou[1] (ðaʊ) *pron. obs.* the second person singular pronoun (*pl.* **ye, you**)

thou[2] (θaʊ) *n.* **1.** thousandth of inch **2.** *inf.* thousand (*pl.* **-s, thou**)

though (ðəʊ) *conj.* **1.** in spite of the fact that, even if —*adv.* **2.** nevertheless

thought (θɔːt) *n.* **1.** process of thinking **2.** what one

THESAURUS

thought **4.** *Inf.* attitude, bee in one's bonnet, fetish, fixation, hang-up (*Inf.*), *idée fixe*, mania, obsession, phobia, preoccupation, quirk

think *v.* **1.** believe, conceive, conclude, consider, deem, determine, esteem, estimate, hold, imagine, judge, reckon, regard, suppose, surmise **2.** brood, cerebrate, chew over (*Inf.*), cogitate, consider, contemplate, deliberate, have in mind, meditate, mull over, muse, ponder, reason, reflect, revolve, ruminate, turn over in one's mind, weigh up **3.** anticipate, envisage, expect, foresee, imagine, plan for, presume, suppose

thinker brain (*Inf.*), intellect (*Inf.*), mastermind, philosopher, sage, theorist, wise man

thinking contemplative, cultured, intelligent, meditative, philosophical, ratiocinative, rational, reasoning, reflective, sophisticated, thoughtful

thin-skinned easily hurt, hypersensitive, quick to take offence, sensitive, soft, susceptible, tender, touchy, vulnerable

third-rate bad, duff (*Brit. sl.*), indifferent, inferior, low-grade, mediocre, poor, poor-quality, ropy (*Brit. inf.*), shoddy

thirst *n.* **1.** craving to drink, drought, dryness, thirstiness **2.** appetite, craving, desire, eagerness, hankering, hunger, keenness, longing, lust, passion, yearning, yen (*Inf.*)

thirsty 1. arid, dehydrated, dry, parched **2.** athirst, avid, burning, craving, desirous, dying, eager, greedy, hankering, hungry, itching, longing, lusting, thirsting, yearning

thorn 1. barb, prickle, spike, spine **2.** affliction, annoyance, bane, bother, curse, irritant, irritation, nuisance, pest, plague, scourge, torment, torture, trouble

thorny 1. barbed, bristling with thorns, bristly, pointed, prickly, sharp, spiky, spinous, spiny **2.** awkward, difficult, harassing, hard, irksome, problematic, sticky (*Inf.*), ticklish, tough, troublesome, trying, unpleasant, upsetting, vexatious, worrying

thorough, thoroughgoing 1. all-embracing, all-inclusive, assiduous, careful, complete, comprehensive, conscientious, efficient, exhaustive, full, in-depth, intensive, leaving no stone unturned, meticulous, painstaking, scrupulous, sweeping **2.** absolute, arrant, complete, downright, entire, out-and-out, perfect, pure, sheer, total, unmitigated, unqualified, utter

thoroughbred blood, full-blooded, of unmixed stock, pedigree, pure-blooded, purebred

thoroughfare access, avenue, highway, passage, passageway, road, roadway, street, way

thoroughly 1. assiduously, carefully, completely, comprehensively, conscientiously, efficiently, exhaustively, from top to bottom, fully, inside out, intensively, leaving no stone unturned, meticulously, painstakingly, scrupulously, sweepingly, through and through, throughout **2.** absolutely, completely, downright, entirely, perfectly, quite, totally, to the full, utterly, without reservation

though 1. *conj.* albeit, allowing, although, despite the fact that, even if, even supposing, granted, notwithstanding, while **2.** *adv.* all the same, for all that, however, nevertheless, nonetheless, notwithstanding, still, yet

thinks **3.** product of thinking **4.** meditation —*v.* **5.** *pt./pp. of* THINK —**'thoughtful** *a.* **1.** considerate **2.** showing careful thought **3.** engaged in meditation **4.** attentive —**'thoughtless** *a.* inconsiderate, careless, heedless —**thought transference** *Psychol. see* TELEPATHY

thousand ('θauzənd) *n./a.* cardinal number, ten hundred

thrall (θrɔːl) *n.* **1.** slavery **2.** slave, bondsman —*vt.* **3.** enslave —**'thralldom** *or* **'thraldom** *n.* bondage

thrash (θræʃ) *vt.* **1.** beat, whip soundly **2.** defeat soundly **3.** thresh —*vi.* **4.** move, plunge, *esp.* arms, legs in wild manner —**thrash out 1.** argue about from every angle **2.** solve by exhaustive discussion

thread (θrɛd) *n.* **1.** fine cord **2.** yarn **3.** ridge cut spirally on screw **4.** theme, meaning —*vt.* **5.** put thread into **6.** fit film, magnetic tape *etc.* into (machine) **7.** put on thread **8.** pick (one's way *etc.*) —**'threadbare** *a.* **1.** worn, with nap rubbed off **2.** meagre **3.** shabby

threat (θrɛt) *n.* **1.** declaration of intention to harm, injure *etc.* **2.** person or thing regarded as dangerous —**'threaten** *vt.* **1.** utter threats against **2.** menace

three (θriː) *n./a.* cardinal number, one more than two —**'threesome** *n.* group of three —**three-D** *or* **3-D** *n.* three-dimensional effect —**three-dimensional** *a.* **1.** having three dimensions **2.** simulating the effect of depth —**three-legged race** race in which pairs of competitors run with adjacent legs tied together —**threepenny bit** *or* **thrupenny bit** ('θrʌpnɪ, -ənɪ, 'θrɛp-) former twelve-sided Brit. coin valued at three old pence —**three-ply** *a.* having three layers (as wood) or strands (as wool) —**three-point turn** complete turn of motor vehicle using forward and reverse gears —**three-quarter** *a.* **1.** being three quarters of something **2.** being of three quarters the normal length —*n.* **3.** *Rugby* any of players between full back and forwards —**'three'score** *n./a. obs.* sixty

threnody ('θrɛnədɪ, 'θriː-) *or* **threnode** ('θriːnəʊd, 'θrɛn-) *n.* ode, song or speech of lamentation, *esp.* for dead —**'threnodist** *n.*

thresh (θrɛʃ) *v.* **1.** beat, rub (wheat, *etc.*) to separate grain from husks and straw **2.** thrash

threshold ('θrɛʃəʊld, 'θrɛʃhəʊld) *n.* **1.** bar of stone or wood forming bottom of doorway **2.** entrance **3.** starting point **4.** point at which a stimulus is perceived, or produces a response

threw (θruː) *pt. of* THROW

thrice (θraɪs) *adv.* three times

thrift (θrɪft) *n.* **1.** saving, economy **2.** genus of plant, sea pink —**'thrifty** *a.* economical, frugal, sparing

thrill (θrɪl) *n.* **1.** sudden sensation of excitement and pleasure —*v.* **2.** (cause to) feel a thrill —*vi.* **3.** vibrate, tremble —**'thriller** *n.* book, film *etc.* with story of mystery, suspense —**'thrilling** *a.* exciting

thrips (θrɪps) *n.* small slender-bodied insect that feeds on plant sap (*pl.* **thrips**)

thrive (θraɪv) *vi.* **1.** grow well **2.** flourish, prosper (**throve, thrived** *pt.*, **thriven** ('θrɪvᵊn), **thrived** *pp.*, **'thriving** *pr.p.*)

THESAURUS

thought 1. brainwork, cerebration, cogitation, consideration, contemplation, deliberation, introspection, meditation, musing, reflection, regard, rumination, thinking **2.** assessment, belief, concept, conception, conclusion, conjecture, conviction, estimation, idea, judgment, notion, opinion, thinking, view

thoughtful 1. attentive, caring, considerate, helpful, kind, kindly, solicitous, unselfish **2.** astute, canny, careful, cautious, circumspect, deliberate, discreet, heedful, mindful, prudent, wary, well thought-out **3.** contemplative, deliberative, in a brown study, introspective, lost in thought, meditative, musing, pensive, rapt, reflective, ruminative, serious, studious, thinking, wistful

thoughtless 1. impolite, inconsiderate, indiscreet, insensitive, rude, selfish, tactless, uncaring, undiplomatic, unkind **2.** absent-minded, careless, foolish, heedless, ill-considered, imprudent, inadvertent, inattentive, injudicious, mindless, neglectful, negligent, rash, reckless, regardless, remiss, silly, stupid, unmindful, unobservant, unthinking

thrash 1. beat, belt, birch, cane, chastise, drub, flagellate, flog, give (someone) a (good) hiding (*Inf.*), hide (*Inf.*), horsewhip, lambaste, leather, paste (*Sl.*), punish, scourge, spank, take a stick to, tan (*Sl.*), whip **2.** beat, beat (someone) hollow (*Brit. inf.*), clobber (*Brit. sl.*), crush, defeat, drub, hammer (*Inf.*), maul, overwhelm, paste (*Sl.*), rout, slaughter (*Inf.*), trounce, wipe the floor with (*Inf.*) **3.** flail, heave, jerk, plunge, squirm, thresh, toss, toss and turn, writhe

thrash out argue out, debate, discuss, have out, resolve, settle, solve, talk over

thread *n.* **1.** cotton, fibre, filament, line, strand, string, yarn **2.** course, direction, drift, motif, plot, story line, strain, tenor, theme, train of thought ~*v.* **3.** ease, inch, loop, meander, pass, pick (one's way), squeeze through, string, wind

threadbare down at heel, frayed, old, ragged, scruffy, shabby, tattered, tatty, used, worn, worn-out

threat 1. commination, intimidatory remark, menace, threatening remark, warning **2.** danger, hazard, menace, peril, risk

threaten 1. endanger, imperil, jeopardize, put at risk, put in jeopardy **2.** browbeat, bully, cow, intimidate, lean on (*Sl.*), make threats to, menace, pressurize, terrorize, warn

threesome triad, trilogy, trine, trinity, trio, triple, triplet, triplex, triptych, triumvirate, triune, troika

threshold 1. door, doorsill, doorstep, doorway, entrance, sill **2.** beginning, brink, dawn, inception, opening, outset, start, starting point, verge

thrift carefulness, economy, frugality, good husbandry, parsimony, prudence, saving, thriftiness

thrifty careful, economical, frugal, parsimonious, provident, prudent, saving, sparing

thrill *n.* **1.** adventure, buzz (*Sl.*), charge (*Sl.*), flush of excitement, glow, kick (*Inf.*), pleasure, sensation, stimulation, tingle, titillation **2.** flutter, fluttering, quiver, shudder, throb, tremble, tremor, vibration ~*v.* **3.** arouse, electrify, excite, flush, get a charge (*Sl.*), get a kick (*Inf.*), glow, move, send (*Sl.*), stimulate, stir, tingle, titillate **4.** flutter, quake, quiver, shake, shudder, throb, tremble, vibrate

thrilling electrifying, exciting, gripping, hair-raising, rip-roaring (*Inf.*), riveting, rousing, sensational, stimulating, stirring

thrive advance, bloom, boom, burgeon, develop, do well, flourish, get on, grow, grow rich, increase, prosper, succeed, wax

thro' *or* **thro** (θruː) *Poet. see* THROUGH

throat (θrəʊt) *n.* **1.** front of neck **2.** either or both of passages through it —**ˈthroaty** *a.* (of voice) hoarse

throb (θrɒb) *vi.* **1.** beat, quiver strongly, pulsate (**-bb-**) —*n.* **2.** pulsation, beat; vibration

throes (θrəʊz) *pl.n.* condition of violent pangs, pain *etc.* —**in the throes of** *inf.* in the process of

thrombosis (θrɒmˈbəʊsɪs) *n.* formation of clot of coagulated blood in blood vessel or heart

throne (θrəʊn) *n.* **1.** ceremonial seat, powers and duties of king or queen —*vt.* **2.** place on throne, declare king *etc.*

throng (θrɒŋ) *n./v.* crowd

throstle (ˈθrɒsᵊl) *n.* thrush

throttle (ˈθrɒtᵊl) *n.* **1.** device controlling amount of fuel entering engine and thereby its speed —*vt.* **2.** strangle **3.** suppress **4.** restrict (flow of liquid *etc.*)

through (θruː) *prep.* **1.** from end to end, from side to side of **2.** between the sides of **3.** in consequence of **4.** by means or fault of —*adv.* **5.** from end to end **6.** to the end —*a.* **7.** completed **8.** *inf.* finished **9.** continuous **10.** (of transport, traffic) not stopping —**throughˈout** *adv./prep.* in every part (of) —**ˈthroughput** *n.* quantity of material processed, *esp.* by computer —**through ticket** ticket for whole of journey —**through train, bus** *etc.* train, bus *etc.* which travels whole (unbroken) length of long journey —**carry through** accomplish

throve (θrəʊv) *pt. of* THRIVE

throw (θrəʊ) *vt.* **1.** fling, cast **2.** move, put abruptly, carelessly **3.** give, hold (party *etc.*) **4.** cause to fall **5.** shape on potter's wheel **6.** move (switch, lever *etc.*) **7.** *inf.* baffle, disconcert (**threw, thrown, ˈthrowing**) —*n.* **8.** act or distance of throwing —**ˈthrowaway** *a.* **1.** *chiefly* **UK** said incidentally, *esp.* for rhetorical effect; casual —*n.* **2.** anything that can be thrown away or discarded **3.** *chiefly* **US** handbill —**throw away 1.** get rid of; discard **2.** fail to make good use of; waste —**ˈthrowback** *n.* **1.** one who, that which reverts to character of an ancestor **2.** this process

thrum (θrʌm) *v.* **1.** strum rhythmically but without expression on (musical instrument) —*vi.* **2.** drum incessantly (**-mm-**) —*n.* **3.** repetitive strumming

thrush[1] (θrʌʃ) *n.* songbird

thrush[2] (θrʌʃ) *n.* **1.** fungal disease of mouth, *esp.* in infants **2.** vaginal infection caused by same fungus **3.** foot disease of horses

thrust (θrʌst) *vt.* **1.** push, drive —*v.* **2.** (make a) stab —*vi.* **3.** push one's way (**thrust, ˈthrusting**) —*n.* **4.** lunge, stab with pointed weapon *etc.* **5.** cutting remark **6.** propulsive force or power

thud (θʌd) *n.* **1.** dull heavy sound —*vi.* **2.** make thud (**-dd-**)

thug (θʌg) *n.* brutal, violent person —**ˈthuggery** *n.* —**ˈthuggish** *a.*

thuja *or* **thuya** (ˈθuːjə) *n.* any of various coniferous trees of N Amer. and E Asia

thulium (ˈθjuːlɪəm) *n.* malleable ductile silvery-grey element

thumb (θʌm) *n.* **1.** first, shortest, thickest finger of hand —*vt.* **2.** handle, dirty with thumb **3.** signal for (lift in vehicle) **4.** flick through (pages of book *etc.*) —**thumb index** series of indentations cut into fore-edge of book to facilitate quick reference —**thumb-index** *vt.* furnish with thumb index —**ˈthumbnail** *n.* **1.** nail of thumb —*a.* **2.** concise and brief —**ˈthumbscrew** *n.* **1.** instrument of torture that pinches or crushes thumbs **2.** screw with projections on head enabling it to be turned by thumb and forefinger

thump (θʌmp) *n.* **1.** dull heavy blow **2.** sound of one —*vt.* **3.** strike heavily —*vi.* **4.** throb, beat or pound violently —**ˈthumping** *a. sl.* huge; excessive

THESAURUS

thriving blooming, booming, burgeoning, developing, doing well, flourishing, going strong (*Inf.*), growing, healthy, prosperous, successful, wealthy, well

throb 1. *v.* beat, palpitate, pound, pulsate, pulse, thump, vibrate **2.** *n.* beat, palpitation, pounding, pulsating, pulse, thump, thumping, vibration

throng 1. *n.* assemblage, concourse, congregation, crowd, crush, horde, host, jam, mass, mob, multitude, pack, press, swarm **2.** *v.* bunch, congregate, converge, cram, crowd, fill, flock, hem in, herd, jam, mill around, pack, press, swarm around, troop

throttle *v.* **1.** choke, garrotte, strangle, strangulate **2.** control, gag (*Inf.*), inhibit, silence, stifle, suppress

through *prep.* **1.** between, by, from end to end of, from one side to the other of, in and out of, past **2.** as a consequence *or* result of, because of, by means of, by virtue of, by way of, using, via, with the help of ~*adj.* **3.** completed, done, ended, finished, terminated, washed up (*Inf.*)

throughout all over, all the time, all through, during the whole of, everywhere, for the duration of, from beginning to end, from end to end, from start to finish, from the start, over the length and breadth of, right through, the whole time, through the whole of

throw *v.* **1.** cast, chuck (*Inf.*), fling, heave, hurl, launch, lob (*Inf.*), pitch, project, propel, put, send, shy, sling, toss **2.** *Inf.* astonish, baffle, confound, confuse, disconcert, dumbfound, put one off one's stroke, throw off, throw one off one's stride, throw out **3.** bring down, dislodge, fell, floor, hurl to the ground, overturn, unseat, upset ~*n.* **4.** cast, fling, heave, lob (*Inf.*), pitch, projection, put, shy, sling, toss

throw away 1. cast off, discard, dispense with, dispose of, ditch (*Sl.*), dump (*Inf.*), get rid of, jettison, reject, scrap, throw out **2.** blow (*Sl.*), fail to exploit, fritter away, lose, make poor use of, squander, waste

thrust *v.* **1.** butt, drive, elbow *or* shoulder one's way, force, impel, jam, plunge, poke, press, prod, propel, push, ram, shove, urge **2.** jab, lunge, pierce, stab, stick ~*n.* **3.** drive, lunge, poke, prod, push, shove, stab **4.** impetus, momentum, motive force, motive power, propulsive force

thud *n./v.* clonk, clump, clunk, crash, knock, smack, thump, wallop (*Inf.*)

thug assassin, bandit, bruiser (*Inf.*), bully boy, cutthroat, gangster, hooligan, killer, mugger (*Inf.*), murderer, robber, ruffian, tough

thumb *n.* **1.** pollex ~*v.* **2.** hitch (*Inf.*), hitchhike **3.** *Often with* **through** browse through, flick through, flip through, glance at, leaf through, riffle through, run one's eye over, scan the pages of, skim through, turn over **4.** dog-ear, finger, handle, mark

thump 1. *n.* bang, blow, clout (*Inf.*), clunk, crash, knock, rap, smack, thud, thwack, wallop (*Inf.*), whack **2.** *v.* bang, batter, beat, belabour, clout (*Inf.*), crash, hit, knock, lambaste (*Sl.*), pound, rap, smack,

thunder (ˈθʌndə) *n.* 1. loud noise accompanying lightning —*vi.* 2. rumble with thunder 3. make noise like thunder —*vt.* 4. utter loudly —ˈ**thundering** *a. sl.* very great; excessive —ˈ**thunderous** *a.* —ˈ**thundery** *a.* sultry —ˈ**thunderbolt** *or* ˈ**thunderclap** *n.* 1. lightning flash followed by peal of thunder 2. anything totally unexpected and unpleasant —ˈ**thundercloud** *n.* electrically charged cumulonimbus cloud associated with thunderstorms —ˈ**thunderstorm** *n.* storm with thunder and lightning and usu. heavy rain or hail —ˈ**thunderstruck** *a.* amazed

thurible (ˈθjʊərɪbᵊl) *n. see* CENSER

Thurs. Thursday

Thursday (ˈθɜːzdɪ) *n.* fifth day of week

thus (ðʌs) *adv.* 1. in this way 2. therefore

thwack (θwæk) *vt./n.* whack

thwart (θwɔːt) *vt.* 1. foil, frustrate —*adv.* 2. *obs.* across —*n.* 3. seat across a boat

thy (ðaɪ) *a.* belonging to thee —**thy**ˈ**self** *pron.* emphatic form of THOU[1]

thyme (taɪm) *n.* aromatic herb

thymol (ˈθaɪmɒl) *n.* white crystalline substance obtained from thyme and used as antiseptic *etc.*

thymus (ˈθaɪməs) *n.* small ductless gland in upper part of chest (*pl.* **-es, -mi** (-maɪ))

thyroid (ˈθaɪrɔɪd) *a.* 1. of thyroid gland 2. of largest cartilage of larynx —*n.* 3. thyroid gland 4. preparation of thyroid gland of certain animals, used to treat hypothyroidism —**thyroid gland** endocrine gland controlling body growth, situated (in man) at base of neck

ti (tiː) *n. Mus. see* TE

Ti *Chem.* titanium

tiara (tɪˈɑːrə) *n.* jewelled head ornament, coronet

tibia (ˈtɪbɪə) *n.* inner and thicker of two bones of the leg below the knee (*pl.* **-biae** (-bɪiː), **-s**) —ˈ**tibial** *a.*

tic (tɪk) *n.* spasmodic twitch in muscles, *esp.* of face

tick[1] (tɪk) *n.* 1. slight tapping sound, as of watch movement 2. small mark (✓) 3. *inf.* moment —*vt.* 4. mark with tick —*vi.* 5. make ticking sound —ˈ**ticker** *n.* 1. *sl.* heart 2. *sl.* watch 3. person or thing that ticks 4. US tape machine —**ticker tape** continuous paper ribbon —ˈ**ticktack** *n.* 1. UK system of sign language, mainly using hands, by which bookmakers transmit their odds to each other at racecourses 2. US ticking sound —ˈ**ticktock** *n.* 1. ticking sound as made by clock —*vi.* 2. make ticking sound —**tick off** 1. mark off 2. reprimand —**tick over** 1. (of engine) idle 2. continue to function smoothly

tick[2] (tɪk) *n.* small insectlike parasite living on and sucking blood of warm-blooded animals

tick[3] (tɪk) *n.* mattress case —ˈ**ticking** *n.* strong material for mattress covers

tick[4] (tɪk) *n. inf.* credit, account

ticket (ˈtɪkɪt) *n.* 1. card, paper entitling holder to admission, travel *etc.* 2. label 3. summons served for parking or traffic offence 4. US list of candidates of one party for election —*vt.* 5. attach label to 6. issue tickets to

tickle (ˈtɪkᵊl) *vt.* 1. touch, stroke, poke (person, part of body *etc.*) to produce laughter *etc.* 2. please, amuse (*oft. in* **tickle one's fancy**) —*vi.* 3. be irritated, itch —*n.* 4. act, instance of this 5. C narrow strait —ˈ**ticklish** *a.* 1. sensitive to tickling 2. requiring care or tact

tiddler (ˈtɪdlə) *n. inf.* very small fish *etc.* —ˈ**tiddly** *a.* tiny

tiddly (ˈtɪdlɪ) *a. inf.* slightly drunk

tiddlywinks (ˈtɪdlɪwɪŋks) *pl.n.* game of trying to flip small plastic discs into cup

tide (taɪd) *n.* 1. rise and fall of sea happening twice each lunar day 2. stream 3. season, time —ˈ**tidal** *a.* of, like tide —**tidal wave** great wave, *esp.* produced by earthquake —ˈ**tidemark** *n.* 1. mark left by highest or lowest point of tide 2. *chiefly* UK mark showing level reached by liquid 3. *inf., chiefly* UK dirty mark on skin, indicating extent to which someone has washed

THESAURUS

strike, thrash, throb, thud, thwack, wallop (*Inf.*), whack

thumping colossal, enormous, excessive, exorbitant, gargantuan, gigantic, great, huge, impressive, mammoth, massive, monumental, terrific, thundering (*Sl.*), titanic, tremendous, whopping (*Inf.*)

thunder *n.* **1.** boom, booming, cracking, crash, crashing, detonation, explosion, pealing, rumble, rumbling ~*v.* **2.** blast, boom, clap, crack, crash, detonate, explode, peal, resound, reverberate, roar, rumble **3.** bark, bellow, declaim, roar, shout, yell

thunderous booming, deafening, ear-splitting, loud, noisy, resounding, roaring, tumultuous

thunderstruck aghast, amazed, astonished, astounded, bowled over (*Inf.*), dazed, dumbfounded, flabbergasted (*Inf.*), floored (*Inf.*), knocked for six (*Inf.*), left speechless, nonplussed, open-mouthed, paralysed, petrified, rooted to the spot, shocked, staggered, struck dumb, stunned, taken aback

thus **1.** as follows, in this fashion (manner, way), like so, like this, so, to such a degree **2.** accordingly, consequently, ergo, for this reason, hence, on that account, so, then, therefore

thwart baffle, balk, check, defeat, foil, frustrate, hinder, impede, obstruct, oppose, outwit, prevent, stop, stymie

tick[1] *n.* **1.** clack, click, clicking, tap, tapping, ticktock **2.** *Brit. inf.* flash, half a mo (*Brit. inf.*), instant, jiffy (*Inf.*), minute, moment, sec (*Inf.*), second, shake (*Inf.*), split second, trice, twinkling, two shakes of a lamb's tail (*Inf.*) **3.** dash, mark, stroke ~*v.* **4.** clack, click, tap, ticktock **5.** check off, choose, indicate, mark, mark off, select

tick[2] account, credit, deferred payment, the slate (*Brit. inf.*)

ticket **1.** card, certificate, coupon, paper, pass, slip, token, voucher **2.** card, docket, label, marker, slip, sticker, tab, tag

tickle *Fig.* amuse, delight, divert, entertain, excite, gratify, please, thrill, titillate

ticklish awkward, critical, delicate, difficult, nice, risky, sensitive, thorny, touchy, tricky, uncertain, unstable, unsteady

tick off **1.** check off, mark off, put a tick at **2.** *Inf.* berate, censure, chide, haul over the coals (*Inf.*), lecture, rebuke, reprimand, reproach, reprove, scold, take to task, tear off a strip (*Inf.*), tell off (*Inf.*), upbraid

tide course, current, ebb, flow, stream

tide over aid, assist, bridge the gap, help, keep one going, keep one's head above water, keep the wolf from the door, see one through

—**tide someone over** help someone for a while, *esp.* by loan *etc.*

tidings ('taɪdɪŋz) *pl.n.* news

tidy ('taɪdɪ) *a.* **1.** orderly, neat **2.** *inf.* of fair size —*vt.* **3.** put in order

tie (taɪ) *vi.* **1.** make an equal score —*vt.* **2.** fasten, bind, secure **3.** restrict (**tied, 'tying**) —*n.* **4.** that with which anything is bound **5.** restriction, restraint **6.** long, narrow piece of material worn knotted round neck **7.** bond, link **8.** drawn game, contest **9.** match, game in eliminating competition —**tied** *a.* **1.** (of public house) obliged to sell beer *etc.* of only one brewer **2.** (of cottage *etc.*) rented to tenant only as long as he is employed by owner —**tie-dyeing** *n.* way of dyeing cloth in patterns by tying sections tightly so they will not absorb dye —**'tiepin** *n.* ornamental pin used to pin ends of tie to shirt —**tie-up** *n.* **1.** link, connection **2.** *chiefly* **US** standstill **3.** *chiefly* **US** *inf.* traffic jam —**tie up 1.** bind securely (as if) with string *etc.* **2.** moor (vessel) **3.** engage attentions of **4.** conclude (organization of something) **5.** come or bring to complete standstill **6.** commit (funds *etc.*) and so make unavailable for other uses **7.** subject (property) to conditions that prevent sale *etc.*

tier (tɪə) *n.* row, rank, layer

tiercel ('tɪəsᵊl) *n. see* TERCEL

tiff (tɪf) *n.* petty quarrel

tiffin ('tɪfɪn) *n.* in India, light meal, *esp.* at midday

tiger ('taɪgə) *n.* large carnivorous feline animal —**'tigress** *n.* **1.** female tiger **2.** fierce, cruel or wildly passionate woman —**tiger lily** lily plant cultivated for its flowers, which have black-spotted orange petals —**tiger moth** moth with wings conspicuously marked with stripes and spots —**tiger's-eye** *or* **'tigereye** *n.* semiprecious golden-brown stone

tight (taɪt) *a.* **1.** taut, tense **2.** closely fitting **3.** secure, firm **4.** not allowing passage of water *etc.* **5.** cramped **6.** *inf.* mean **7.** *inf.* drunk —**'tighten** *v.* —**'tightly** *adv.* —**tights** *pl.n.* one-piece clinging garment covering body from waist to feet —**tight'fisted** *a.* mean; miserly —**tight'knit** *a.* **1.** closely integrated **2.** organized carefully —**tight-lipped** *a.* **1.** secretive; taciturn **2.** with lips pressed tightly together, as through anger —**'tightrope** *n.* rope stretched taut above the ground, on which acrobats perform

tigon ('taɪgən) *or* **tiglon** ('tɪglɒn) *n.* offspring of tiger and lioness

tike (taɪk) *n. see* TYKE

tiki ('tiːkiː) *n.* amulet, figurine of Maori cultures

tilde ('tɪldə) *n.* diacritical mark (˜) placed over letter to indicate nasal sound, as in Sp. *señor*

tile (taɪl) *n.* **1.** flat piece of ceramic, plastic *etc.* material used for roofs, walls, floors, fireplaces *etc.* —*vt.* **2.** cover with tiles —**tiled** *a.* —**'tiling** *n.* —**on the tiles** *inf.* on a spree, *esp.* of drinking or debauchery

till¹ (tɪl) *prep.* **1.** up to the time of —*conj.* **2.** to the time that

till² (tɪl) *vt.* cultivate —**'tillage** *n.* —**'tiller** *n.*

till³ (tɪl) *n.* **1.** drawer for money in shop counter **2.** cash register

tiller ('tɪlə) *n.* lever to move rudder of boat

tilt (tɪlt) *v.* **1.** incline, slope, slant **2.** tip up —*vi.* **3.** take part in medieval combat with lances **4.** thrust, aim —*n.* **5.** slope, incline **6.** *Hist.* combat for mounted men with lances, joust

tilth (tɪlθ) *n.* **1.** tilled land **2.** condition of soil

Tim. *Bible* Timothy

timber ('tɪmbə) *n.* **1.** wood for building *etc.* **2.** trees suitable for the sawmill —**'timbered** *a.* **1.** made of wood **2.** covered with trees —**timber limit 1. C** area to which rights of cutting trees are limited **2.** timber line —**timber line** geographical limit beyond which trees will not grow

THESAURUS

tidings advice, bulletin, communication, greetings, information, intelligence, message, news, report, word

tidy *adj.* **1.** businesslike, clean, cleanly, methodical, neat, ordered, orderly, shipshape, spick-and-span, spruce, systematic, trim, well-groomed, well-kept, well-ordered **2.** *Inf.* ample, considerable, fair, generous, good, goodly, handsome, healthy, large, largish, respectable, sizable, substantial ~*v.* **3.** clean, groom, neaten, order, put in order, put in trim, put to rights, spruce up, straighten

tie *v.* **1.** attach, bind, connect, fasten, interlace, join, knot, lash, link, make fast, moor, rope, secure, tether, truss, unite **2.** bind, confine, hamper, hinder, hold, limit, restrain, restrict **3.** be even, be neck and neck, draw, equal, match ~*n.* **4.** band, bond, connection, cord, fastening, fetter, joint, knot, ligature, link, rope, string **5.** affiliation, allegiance, bond, commitment, connection, duty, kinship, liaison, obligation, relationship **6.** encumbrance, hindrance, limitation, restraint, restriction **7.** dead heat, deadlock, draw, stalemate **8.** *Brit.* contest, fixture, game, match

tier bank, echelon, file, layer, level, line, order, rank, row, series, storey, stratum

tie up 1. attach, bind, pinion, restrain, tether, truss **2.** lash, make fast, moor, rope, secure **3.** engage, engross, keep busy, occupy **4.** bring to a close, conclude, end, finish off, settle, terminate, wind up, wrap up (*Inf.*)

tight 1. close, close-fitting, compact, constricted, cramped, fast, firm, fixed, narrow, rigid, secure, snug, stiff, stretched, taut, tense **2.** hermetic, impervious, proof, sealed, sound, watertight **3.** close, grasping, mean, miserly, niggardly, parsimonious, penurious, sparing, stingy, tightfisted **4.** *Inf.* drunk, half cut (*Brit. sl.*), half seas over (*Brit. inf.*), inebriated, in one's cups, intoxicated, pickled (*Inf.*), pie-eyed (*Sl.*), plastered (*Sl.*), smashed (*Sl.*), sozzled (*Inf.*), stewed (*Sl.*), stoned (*Sl.*), three sheets in the wind (*Sl.*), tiddly (*Brit. sl.*), tipsy, under the influence (*Inf.*)

tighten close, constrict, cramp, fasten, fix, narrow, rigidify, screw, secure, squeeze, stiffen, stretch, tauten, tense

till¹ cultivate, dig, plough, turn over, work

till² cash box, cash drawer, cash register

tilt *v.* **1.** cant, incline, lean, list, slant, slope, tip **2.** attack, break a lance, clash, contend, cross swords, duel, encounter, fight, joust, overthrow, spar ~*n.* **3.** angle, cant, inclination, incline, list, pitch, slant, slope **4.** *Medieval history* clash, combat, duel, encounter, fight, joust, lists, set-to (*Inf.*), tournament, tourney

timber beams, boards, forest, logs, planks, trees, wood

timbre ('tımbə, 'tæmbə) *n.* **1.** *Mus.* quality of sound **2.** *Phonet.* tone differentiating one vowel *etc.* from another

time (taım) *n.* **1.** existence as a succession of states **2.** hour **3.** duration **4.** period **5.** point in duration **6.** opportunity **7.** occasion **8.** leisure **9.** tempo —*vt.* **10.** choose time for **11.** note time taken by —'**timeless** *a.* **1.** unaffected or unchanged by time; ageless **2.** eternal —'**timely** *a.* at opportune or appropriate time —'**timer** *n.* person, device for recording or indicating time —'**timing** *n.* regulation of actions or remarks in relation to others to produce best effect, as in theatre *etc.* —**time and motion study** analysis of industrial or work procedures to determine most efficient methods of operation (*also* **time and motion, time study, motion study**) —**time bomb** bomb designed to explode at prearranged time —**time clock** clock which records, by punching or stamping **timecards** inserted into it, time of arrival or departure of employees —**time exposure 1.** exposure of photographic film for a relatively long period, usu. a few seconds **2.** photograph produced by such exposure —**time-honoured** *a.* respectable because old —**time-lag** *n.* period of time between cause and effect —**time off** period when one is absent from work for holiday, through sickness *etc.* —**time-out** *n. chiefly* **US 1.** *Sport* interruption in play during which players rest, discuss tactics *etc.* **2.** period of rest; break —'**timepiece** *n.* watch or clock —'**timeserver** *n.* person who compromises and changes his opinions *etc.* to suit current fashions —**time sharing 1.** system by which users at different terminals of computer can apparently communicate with it at same time **2.** system of part-ownership of holiday home, whereby each participant owns property for particular period every year for specified number of years —**time signature** *Mus.* sign, usu. consisting of two figures, one above other, after key signature, indicating tempo —'**timetable** *n.* plan showing hours of work, times of arrival and departure *etc.* —'**timeworn** *a.* **1.** showing adverse effects of overlong use or of old age **2.** hackneyed; trite —**time zone** region throughout which same standard time is used —**Greenwich Mean Time** world standard time, time as settled by passage of sun over the meridian at Greenwich —**time and a half** rate of pay equalling one and a half times normal rate, oft. for overtime

timid ('tımıd) *a.* **1.** easily frightened **2.** lacking self-confidence —**ti'midity** *or* '**timidness** *n.* —'**timidly** *adv.* —'**timorous** *a.* **1.** timid **2.** indicating fear

timpani *or* **tympani** ('tımpənı) *pl.n.* set of kettledrums —'**timpanist** *or* '**tympanist** *n.*

tin (tın) *n.* **1.** malleable metal **2.** container made of tin or tinned iron —*vt.* **3.** put in tin, *esp.* for preserving (food) **4.** coat with tin (**-nn-**) —'**tinny** *a.* **1.** (of sound) thin, metallic **2.** cheap, shoddy —'**tin'foil** *n.* **1.** thin foil made of tin or alloy of tin and lead **2.** thin foil made of aluminium; used for wrapping foodstuffs —**tin god 1.** self-important person **2.** person erroneously regarded as holy or venerable —**tin lizzie** ('lızı) *inf.* old or decrepit car —**tin plate** thin steel sheet coated with layer of tin that protects steel from corrosion —**tin-plate** *vt.* coat with layer of tin —'**tinpot** *a. inf.* inferior, worthless —'**tinsmith** *n.* person who works with tin or tin plate

tincture ('tıŋktʃə) *n.* **1.** solution of medicinal substance in alcohol **2.** colour, stain —*vt.* **3.** colour, tint

tinder ('tındə) *n.* dry, easily-burning material used to start fire —'**tinderbox** *n.* **1.** formerly, box for holding tinder, *esp.* one fitted with flint and steel **2.** touchy or explosive person or thing

tine (taın) *n.* tooth, spike of fork, antler, harrow *etc.*

tinea ('tınıə) *n.* fungal skin disease

ting (tıŋ) *n.* **1.** sharp sound, as of bell **2.** tinkling —*vi.* **3.** tinkle —**ting-a-ling** *n.* sound of small bell

tinge (tındʒ) *n.* **1.** slight trace, flavour —*vt.* **2.** colour, flavour slightly

tingle ('tıŋgᵊl) *vi.* **1.** feel thrill or pricking sensation —*n.* **2.** sensation of tingling

tinker ('tıŋkə) *n.* **1.** formerly, travelling mender of pots and pans —*vi.* **2.** fiddle, meddle (*eg* with machinery), oft. inexpertly —**tinker's damn** *or* **cuss** *sl.* slightest heed (*esp. in* **not give a tinker's damn** *or* **cuss**)

tinkle ('tıŋkᵊl) *v.* **1.** (cause to) give out series of light sounds like small bell —*n.* **2.** this sound or action

tinsel ('tınsəl) *n.* **1.** glittering, metallic substance for decoration **2.** anything sham and showy

tint (tınt) *n.* **1.** colour **2.** shade of colour **3.** tinge —*vt.* **4.** dye, give tint to

tintinnabulation (tıntınæbjʊ'leıʃən) *n.* act or instance of ringing or pealing of bells

tiny ('taını) *a.* very small, minute

THESAURUS

time 1. age, chronology, date, duration, epoch, era, generation, hour, interval, period, season, space, span, spell, stretch, term, while **2.** instance, juncture, occasion, point, stage **3.** allotted span, day, duration, life, life span, lifetime, season **4.** heyday, hour, peak **5.** *Mus.* beat, measure, metre, rhythm, tempo

timeless abiding, ageless, ceaseless, changeless, deathless, endless, enduring, eternal, everlasting, immortal, immutable, imperishable, indestructible, lasting, permanent, persistent, undying

timely appropriate, at the right time, convenient, judicious, opportune, prompt, propitious, punctual, seasonable, suitable, well-timed

timetable agenda, calendar, curriculum, diary, list, order of the day, programme, schedule

timid afraid, apprehensive, bashful, cowardly, coy, diffident, faint-hearted, fearful, irresolute, modest, mousy, nervous, pusillanimous, retiring, shrinking, shy, timorous

timorous afraid, apprehensive, bashful, cowardly, coy, diffident, faint-hearted, fearful, frightened, irresolute, mousy, nervous, pusillanimous, retiring, shrinking, shy, timid, trembling

tinge *n.* **1.** cast, colour, dye, shade, stain, tincture, tint, wash **2.** bit, dash, drop, pinch, smack, smattering, *soupçon*, sprinkling, suggestion, touch, trace ~*v.* **3.** colour, dye, imbue, shade, stain, suffuse, tinge, tint

tingle 1. *v.* have goose pimples, itch, prickle, sting, tickle **2.** *n.* goose pimples, itch, itching, pins and needles (*Inf.*), prickling, quiver, shiver, stinging, thrill, tickle, tickling

tinker *v.* dabble, fiddle (*Inf.*), meddle, mess about, monkey, muck about (*Brit. sl.*), play, potter, toy

tint *n.* **1.** cast, colour, hue, shade, tone **2.** dye, rinse, stain, tincture, tinge, wash **3.** hint, shade, sugges-

-tion (*comb. form*) state, condition, action, process, result, as in *election, prohibition*

tip[1] (tɪp) *n.* **1.** slender or pointed end of anything **2.** piece of metal, leather *etc.* protecting an extremity —*vt.* **3.** put a tip on (**-pp-**) —**ˈtipstaff** *n.* **1.** court official **2.** metal-tipped staff formerly used as symbol of office

tip[2] (tɪp) *n.* **1.** small present of money given for service rendered **2.** helpful piece of information **3.** warning, hint —*vt.* **4.** give tip to (**-pp-**) —**ˈtipster** *n.* one who sells tips about races —**tip-off** *n.* warning or hint, *esp.* given confidentially and based on inside information —**tip off**

tip[3] (tɪp) *vt.* **1.** tilt, upset **2.** touch lightly —*vi.* **3.** topple over (**-pp-**) —*n.* **4.** place where rubbish is dumped

tippet (ˈtɪpɪt) *n.* covering for the neck and shoulders

tipple (ˈtɪpᵊl) *v.* **1.** drink (alcohol) habitually, *esp.* in small quantities —*n.* **2.** alcoholic drink —**ˈtippler** *n.*

tipsy (ˈtɪpsɪ) *a.* (slightly) drunk

tiptoe (ˈtɪptəʊ) *vi.* **1.** walk on ball of foot and toes **2.** walk softly

tiptop (tɪpˈtɒp) *a.* of the best quality or highest degree

TIR Transports Internationaux Routiers (*Fr.*, International Road Transport)

tirade (taɪˈreɪd) *n.* long speech, generally vigorous and hostile, denunciation

tire[1] (taɪə) *vt.* **1.** reduce energy of, *esp.* by exertion **2.** bore **3.** irritate —*vi.* **4.** become tired, wearied, bored —**tired** *a.* **1.** weary; fatigued **2.** no longer fresh; hackneyed —**ˈtireless** *a.* unable to be tired —**ˈtirelessly** *adv.* —**ˈtiresome** *a.* wearisome, irritating, tedious —**ˈtiring** *a.*

tire[2] (taɪə) *n.* US tyre

tiro (ˈtaɪrəʊ) *n. see* TYRO

tissue (ˈtɪsjuː, ˈtɪʃuː) *n.* **1.** substance of animal body, plant *etc.* **2.** fine, soft paper, *esp.* used as handkerchief *etc.* **3.** fine woven fabric

tit[1] (tɪt) *n.* any of numerous small, active Old World songbirds *esp.* bluetit, tomtit *etc.*

tit[2] (tɪt) *n.* **1.** *vulg. sl.* female breast **2.** *sl.* despicable, stupid person

Tit. *Bible* Titus

titan (ˈtaɪtᵊn) *n.* person of great strength or size —**tiˈtanic** *a.* huge, epic

titanium (taɪˈteɪnɪəm) *n.* rare metal of great strength and rust-resisting qualities

titbit (ˈtɪtbɪt) *or esp. U.S.* **tidbit** (ˈtɪdbɪt) *n.* **1.** tasty morsel of food **2.** pleasing scrap (of scandal *etc.*)

tit for tat blow for blow, retaliation

tithe (taɪð) *n.* **1.** *esp. Hist.* tenth part of agricultural produce paid for the upkeep of the clergy or as tax —*vt.* **2.** exact tithes from —**tithe barn** formerly, large barn where agricultural tithe of parish was stored

Titian red (ˈtɪʃən) *a.* (of hair) reddish-gold, auburn

titillate (ˈtɪtɪleɪt) *vt.* tickle, stimulate agreeably —**titilˈlation** *n.* —**ˈtitillator** *n.*

titivate *or* **tittivate** (ˈtɪtɪveɪt) *v.* dress or smarten up —**titiˈvation** *or* **tittiˈvation** *n.*

title (ˈtaɪtᵊl) *n.* **1.** name of book **2.** heading **3.** name **4.** appellation denoting rank **5.** legal right or document proving it **6.** *Sport* championship —**ˈtitled** *a.* of the aristocracy —**title deed** legal document as proof of ownership —**ˈtitleholder** *n.* person who holds title, *esp.* sporting championship —**title page** page in book that gives title, author, publisher *etc.* —**title role** role of character after whom play *etc.* is named

titration (taɪˈtreɪʃən) *n.* operation in which measured amount of one solution is added to known quantity of another solution until reaction between the two is complete —**ˈtitrate** *vt.* measure volume or concentration of (solution) by titration

titter (ˈtɪtə) *vi.* **1.** laugh in suppressed way —*n.* **2.** such laugh

THESAURUS

tion, tinge, touch, trace ~*v.* **4.** colour, dye, rinse, stain, tincture, tinge

tiny diminutive, dwarfish, infinitesimal, insignificant, Lilliputian, little, microscopic, mini, miniature, minute, negligible, petite, pint-sized (*Inf.*), puny, pygmy, slight, small, trifling, wee

tip[1] **1.** *n.* apex, cap, crown, end, extremity, head, peak, point, summit, top **2.** *v.* cap, crown, finish, surmount, top

tip[2] *n.* **1.** baksheesh, gift, gratuity, perquisite, *pourboire* **2.** *Also* **tip-off** clue, forecast, gen (*Brit. inf.*), hint, information, inside information, pointer, suggestion, warning, word, word of advice ~*v.* **3.** remunerate, reward **4.** *Also* **tip off** advise, caution, forewarn, give a clue, give a hint, suggest, tip (someone) the wink (*Brit. inf.*), warn

tip[3] **1.** *v.* cant, capsize, incline, lean, list, overturn, slant, spill, tilt, topple over, upend, upset **2.** *n. Brit.* dump, midden (*Dialect*), refuse heap, rubbish heap

tipple 1. *v.* bend the elbow (*Inf.*), drink, imbibe, indulge (*Inf.*), quaff, swig, take a drink, tope **2.** *n.* alcohol, booze (*Inf.*), drink, John Barleycorn, liquor, poison (*Inf.*)

tire 1. drain, droop, enervate, exhaust, fag (*Inf.*), fail, fatigue, flag, jade, knacker (*Sl.*), sink, take it out of (*Inf.*), wear down, wear out, weary, whack (*Brit. inf.*) **2.** annoy, bore, exasperate, harass, irk, irritate, weary

tired 1. all in (*Sl.*), asleep *or* dead on one's feet, dead beat (*Inf.*), dog-tired (*Inf.*), done in (*Inf.*), drained, drooping, drowsy, enervated, exhausted, fagged (*Inf.*), fatigued, flagging, jaded, knackered (*Sl.*), ready to drop, sleepy, spent, weary, whacked (*Brit. inf.*), worn out **2.** clichéd, conventional, corny (*Inf.*), familiar, hackneyed, old, outworn, stale, stock, threadbare, trite, well-worn

tireless determined, energetic, indefatigable, industrious, resolute, unflagging, untiring, unwearied, vigorous

tiresome annoying, boring, dull, exasperating, flat, irksome, irritating, laborious, monotonous, tedious, trying, uninteresting, vexatious, wearing, wearisome

tiring arduous, demanding, enervative, exacting, exhausting, fatiguing, laborious, strenuous, tough, wearing, wearying

tissue 1. fabric, gauze, mesh, structure, stuff, texture, web **2.** paper, paper handkerchief, wrapping paper

titbit *bonne bouche*, choice item, dainty, delicacy, goody (*Inf.*), juicy bit, morsel, scrap, snack, treat

title 1. caption, heading, inscription, label, legend, name, style **2.** appellation, denomination, designation, epithet, handle (*Sl.*), moniker (*Inf.*), name, nickname, nom de plume, pseudonym, sobriquet, term **3.** championship, crown, laurels **4.** claim, entitlement, ownership, prerogative, privilege, right

tittle (ˈtɪtᵊl) *n.* whit, detail

tittle-tattle *n./vi.* gossip

titular (ˈtɪtjʊlə) *a.* **1.** pert. to title **2.** nominal **3.** held by virtue of a title

tizzy (ˈtɪzɪ) *n. inf.* state of confusion, anxiety

Tl *Chem.* thallium

Tm *Chem.* thulium

TN Tennessee

tn. ton(s)

TNT trinitrotoluene

to (tuː; *unstressed* tʊ, tə) *prep.* **1.** towards, in the direction of **2.** as far as **3.** used to introduce a comparison, ratio, indirect object, infinitive mood *etc.* —*adv.* **4.** to the required or normal state or position —**to and fro** *a./adv.* **1.** back and forth **2.** here and there —**toing and froing**

toad (təʊd) *n.* animal like large frog —**toad-in-the-hole** *n.* sausages baked in batter

toadflax (ˈtəʊdflæks) *n.* perennial plant having yellow-orange flowers (*also* **butter-and-eggs**)

toadstool (ˈtəʊdstuːl) *n.* fungus like mushroom, but usu. poisonous

toady (ˈtəʊdɪ) *n.* **1.** one who flatters, ingratiates himself —*vi.* **2.** do this (**ˈtoadied, ˈtoadying**)

toast[1] (təʊst) *n.* **1.** slice of bread crisped and browned on both sides by heat —*vt.* **2.** crisp and brown (as bread) **3.** dry or warm at fire —**ˈtoaster** *n.* electrical device for toasting bread —**toast-rack** *n.* small, partitioned stand of metal *etc.* for serving toasted bread

toast[2] (təʊst) *n.* **1.** tribute, proposal of health, success *etc.* made by company of people and marked by drinking together **2.** person toasted —*vt.* **3.** drink toast to —**ˈtoastmaster** *n.* person who introduces speakers, proposes toasts *etc.* at public dinners (**ˈtoastmistress** *fem.*)

tobacco (təˈbækəʊ) *n.* **1.** plant with leaves used for smoking **2.** the prepared leaves (*pl.* **-s, -es**) —**toˈbacconist** *n.* one who sells tobacco products

toboggan (təˈbɒgən) *n.* **1.** sledge for sliding down slope of snow —*vi.* **2.** slide on toboggan

toby jug (ˈtəʊbɪ) mug in form of stout, seated man

toccata (təˈkɑːtə) *n.* rapid piece of music for keyboard instrument

tocsin (ˈtɒksɪn) *n.* alarm signal, bell

today (təˈdeɪ) *n.* **1.** this day —*adv.* **2.** on this day **3.** nowadays

toddle (ˈtɒdᵊl) *vi.* **1.** walk with unsteady, short steps **2.** *inf.* stroll —*n.* **3.** toddling —**ˈtoddler** *n.* child beginning to walk

toddy (ˈtɒdɪ) *n.* sweetened mixture of alcoholic spirit, hot water *etc.*

to-do *n. inf.* fuss, commotion (*pl.* **-s**)

toe (təʊ) *n.* **1.** digit of foot **2.** anything resembling toe in shape or position —*vt.* **3.** reach, touch or kick with toe —**ˈtoecap** *n.* reinforced covering for toe of shoe —**ˈtoehold** *n.* **1.** small foothold to facilitate climbing **2.** any means of gaining access, support *etc.* **3.** wrestling hold in which opponent's toe is held and leg twisted —**toe the line** conform

toff (tɒf) *n. sl.* well-dressed or upper-class person

toffee *or* **toffy** (ˈtɒfɪ) *n.* chewy sweet made of boiled sugar *etc.* —**toffee-apple** *n.* apple fixed on stick and coated with toffee —**toffee-nosed** *a. sl., chiefly* **UK** pretentious; supercilious; snobbish

tofu (ˈtəʊfuː) *n.* unfermented soya bean curd

tog (tɒg) *n.* unit of measurement of warmth of continental quilts *etc.* —**tog rating** *or* **value**

toga (ˈtəʊgə) *n.* loose outer garment worn by ancient Romans

together (təˈgɛðə) *adv.* **1.** in company **2.** simultaneously —*a./adv.* **3.** *inf.* (well) organized —**toˈgetherness** *n.* feeling of closeness or affection from being united with other people

toggle (ˈtɒgᵊl) *n.* **1.** small wooden, metal peg fixed crosswise on cord, wire *etc.* and used for fastening as button **2.** any similar device —**toggle joint** device consisting of two arms pivoted at common joint and at outer ends, and used to apply pressure by straightening angle between two arms —**toggle switch** electric switch having projecting lever that is manipulated in particular way to open or close circuit

togs (tɒgz) *pl.n. inf.* clothes

toil (tɔɪl) *n.* **1.** heavy work or task —*vi.* **2.** labour —**ˈtoilsome** *or* **ˈtoilful** *a.* laborious —**ˈtoilworn** *a.* **1.** weary with toil **2.** hard and lined

toilet (ˈtɔɪlɪt) *n.* **1.** lavatory **2.** process of washing, dressing **3.** articles used for this —**ˈtoiletry** *n.* object or cosmetic used in making up *etc.* —**toilet paper** *or* **tissue** thin absorbent paper, oft. wound in roll round cardboard cylinder (**toilet roll**), used for cleaning oneself after defecation or urination —**toilet training** training of young child to use toilet when he needs to discharge bodily waste —**toilet water** form of liquid perfume lighter than cologne

THESAURUS

titter chortle (*Inf.*), chuckle, giggle, laugh, snigger, tehee

toady 1. *n.* apple polisher (*U.S. sl.*), bootlicker (*Inf.*), crawler (*Sl.*), creep (*Sl.*), fawner, flatterer, flunkey, groveller, hanger-on, jackal, lackey, lickspittle, minion, parasite, spaniel, sycophant, truckler, yes man **2.** *v.* be obsequious to, bow and scrape, butter up, crawl, creep, cringe, curry favour with, fawn on, flatter, grovel, kiss the feet of, kowtow to, lick the boots of (*Inf.*), suck up to (*Inf.*)

toast[1] *v.* brown, grill, heat, roast, warm

toast[2] *n.* **1.** compliment, drink, health, pledge, salutation, salute, tribute **2.** darling, favourite, heroine ~*v.* **3.** drink to, drink (to) the health of, pledge, salute

together *adv.* **1.** as a group, as one, cheek by jowl, closely, collectively, hand in glove, hand in hand, in a body, in concert, in cooperation, in unison, jointly, mutually, shoulder to shoulder, side by side **2.** all at once, as one, at one fell swoop, at the same time, concurrently, contemporaneously, en masse, in unison, simultaneously, with one accord **3.** *Inf.* arranged, fixed, ordered, organized, settled, sorted out, straight, to rights ~*adj.* **4.** *Sl.* calm, composed, cool, stable, well-adjusted, well-balanced, well-organized

toil 1. *n.* application, donkey-work, drudgery, effort, elbow grease (*Inf.*), exertion, graft (*Inf.*), hard work, industry, labour, pains, slog, sweat, travail **2.** *v.* drag oneself, drudge, graft (*Inf.*), grind (*Inf.*), grub, knock oneself out, labour, push oneself, slave, slog, strive, struggle, sweat (*Inf.*), work, work like a dog, work like a Trojan, work one's fingers to the bone

token (ˈtəukən) *n.* **1.** sign or object used as evidence **2.** symbol **3.** disc used as money **4.** gift card, voucher exchangeable for goods of a certain value —*a.* **5.** nominal, slight —ˈ**tokenism** *n.* practice of making only token effort or doing no more than minimum, *esp.* to comply with law

tokoloshe (tɒkɒˈlɒʃ, -ˈlɒʃɪ) *n.* **SA** malevolent imp in Bantu folklore

told (təuld) *pt./pp. of* TELL

tolerate (ˈtɒləreɪt) *vt.* **1.** put up with **2.** permit —ˈ**tolerable** *a.* **1.** bearable **2.** fair, moderate —ˈ**tolerably** *adv.* —ˈ**tolerance** *n.* (degree of) ability to endure stress, pain, radiation *etc.* —ˈ**tolerant** *a.* **1.** disinclined to interfere with others' ways or opinions **2.** forbearing **3.** broad-minded —ˈ**tolerantly** *adv.* —**toleˈration** *n.*

toll[1] (təul) *vt.* **1.** make (bell) ring slowly at regular intervals **2.** announce death thus —*vi.* **3.** ring thus —*n.* **4.** tolling sound

toll[2] (təul, tɒl) *n.* **1.** tax, *esp.* for the use of bridge or road **2.** loss, damage incurred through accident, disaster *etc.*

tollie (ˈtɒlɪ) *n.* **SA** steer calf

toluene (ˈtɒljuiːn) *n.* colourless volatile flammable liquid obtained from petroleum and coal tar

tom (tɒm) *n.* male of some animals, *esp.* cat

tomahawk (ˈtɒməhɔːk) *n.* **1.** fighting axe of N Amer. Indians —*vt.* **2.** strike, kill with tomahawk

tomato (təˈmɑːtəu) *n.* **1.** plant with red fruit **2.** the fruit, used in salads *etc.* (*pl.* **-es**)

tomb (tuːm) *n.* **1.** grave **2.** monument over grave —ˈ**tombstone** *n.* gravestone

tombola (tɒmˈbəulə) *n.* lottery with tickets drawn to win prizes

tomboy (ˈtɒmbɔɪ) *n.* girl who acts, dresses in boyish way

Tom, Dick, and (or) Harry ordinary, undistinguished or common person (*esp. in* **every Tom, Dick, and Harry; any Tom, Dick, or Harry**)

tome (təum) *n.* large book or volume

tomfoolery (tɒmˈfuːlərɪ) *n.* nonsense, silly behaviour

tommy (ˈtɒmɪ) *n. sl.* private soldier in Brit. army —**Tommy gun** type of sub-machine-gun —ˈ**tommyrot** *n.* utter nonsense

tomorrow (təˈmɒrəu) *adv./n.* (on) the day after today

tom-tom *or* **tam-tam** *n.* drum associated with N Amer. Indians or with Asia

ton (tʌn) *n.* **1.** measure of weight, 1016 kg (2240 lbs) (*also* **long ton**) **2. US** measure of weight, 907 kg (2000 lbs) (*also* **short ton**) —ˈ**tonnage** *n.* **1.** carrying capacity **2.** charge per ton **3.** ships collectively —**ton-up UK** *inf. a.* **1.** (*esp.* of motorcycle) capable of speeds of a hundred miles per hour or more **2.** liking to travel at such speeds —*n.* **3.** person who habitually rides at such speeds

tone (təun) *n.* **1.** quality of musical sound **2.** quality of voice, colour *etc.* **3.** general character, style **4.** healthy condition —*vt.* **5.** give tone to —*v.* **6.** blend, harmonize —ˈ**tonal** *a.* —**toˈnality** *n.* —**tone-deaf** *a.* unable to distinguish subtle differences in musical pitch —**tone deafness** —**tone poem** orchestral work based on story, legend *etc.*

tong (tɒŋ) *n.* formerly, secret society of Chinese Americans

tongs (tɒŋz) *pl.n.* large pincers, *esp.* for handling coal, sugar

THESAURUS

toilet 1. ablutions (*Military inf.*), bathroom, bog (*Brit. sl.*), closet, convenience, gents (*Brit. inf.*), ladies' room, latrine, lavatory, loo (*Brit. inf.*), outhouse, powder room, privy, urinal, washroom, water closet, W.C. **2.** ablutions, bathing, dressing, grooming, toilette

token 1. *n.* badge, clue, demonstration, earnest, evidence, expression, index, indication, manifestation, mark, note, proof, representation, sign, symbol, warning **2.** *adj.* hollow, minimal, nominal, perfunctory, superficial, symbolic

tolerable 1. acceptable, allowable, bearable, endurable, sufferable, supportable **2.** acceptable, adequate, all right, average, fair, fairly good, fair to middling, good enough, indifferent, mediocre, middling, not bad (*Inf.*), O.K. (*Inf.*), ordinary, passable, run-of-the-mill, so-so (*Inf.*), unexceptional

tolerance endurance, fortitude, hardiness, hardness, resilience, resistance, stamina, staying power, toughness

tolerant 1. broad-minded, catholic, charitable, fair, forbearing, latitudinarian, liberal, long-suffering, magnanimous, open-minded, patient, sympathetic, unbigoted, understanding, unprejudiced **2.** complaisant, easy-going, free and easy, indulgent, kind-hearted, lax, lenient, permissive, soft

tolerate abide, accept, admit, allow, bear, brook, condone, countenance, endure, indulge, permit, pocket, put up with (*Inf.*), receive, sanction, stand, stomach, submit to, suffer, swallow, take, thole (*Scot.*), turn a blind eye to, undergo, wink at

toleration acceptance, allowance, condonation, endurance, indulgence, permissiveness, sanction, sufferance

toll[1] *v.* **1.** chime, clang, knell, peal, ring, sound, strike **2.** announce, call, signal, summon, warn ~*n.* **3.** chime, clang, knell, peal, ring, ringing, tolling

toll[2] **1.** assessment, charge, customs, demand, duty, fee, impost, levy, payment, rate, tariff, tax, tribute **2.** cost, damage, inroad, loss, penalty

tomb burial chamber, catacomb, crypt, grave, mausoleum, sepulchre, vault

tombstone gravestone, headstone, marker, memorial, monument

tome book, volume, work

tomfoolery 1. buffoonery, childishness, clowning, fooling around (*Inf.*), foolishness, horseplay, idiocy, larks (*Inf.*), messing around (*Inf.*), shenanigans (*Inf.*), silliness, skylarking (*Inf.*), stupidity **2.** balderdash, baloney (*Inf.*), bilge (*Inf.*), bosh (*Inf.*), bunk (*Inf.*), bunkum, claptrap (*Inf.*), hogwash, hooey (*Sl.*), inanity, nonsense, poppycock (*Inf.*), rot, rubbish, stuff and nonsense, tommyrot, tosh, trash, twaddle

tone *n.* **1.** accent, emphasis, force, inflection, intonation, modulation, pitch, strength, stress, timbre, tonality, volume **2.** air, approach, aspect, attitude, character, drift, effect, feel, frame, grain, manner, mood, note, quality, spirit, style, temper, tenor, vein **3.** cast, colour, hue, shade, tinge, tint ~*v.* **4.** blend, go well with, harmonize, match, suit

tongue (tʌŋ) *n.* **1.** muscular organ inside mouth, used for speech, taste *etc.* **2.** various things shaped like this **3.** language; speech; voice —**tongue-and-groove joint** joint made by means of tongue along edge of one board that fits into groove along edge of another board —**tongue-lash** *vt.* reprimand severely; scold —**tongue-lashing** *n./a.* —**tongue-tie** *n.* congenital condition in which tongue has restricted mobility as result of abnormally short fold of skin under tongue —**tongue-tied** *a.* **1.** speechless, *esp.* with embarrassment or shyness **2.** having condition of tongue-tie —**tongue twister** sentence or phrase difficult to articulate clearly and quickly

tonic (ˈtɒnɪk) *n.* **1.** medicine to improve bodily tone or condition **2.** *Mus.* first keynote of scale —*a.* **3.** invigorating, restorative **4.** of tone —**tonic sol-fa** method of teaching music, by which syllables are used as names for notes of major scale in any key —**tonic water** *or* **tonic** *n.* mineral water oft. containing quinine

tonight (təˈnaɪt) *n.* **1.** this night **2.** the coming night —*adv.* **3.** on this night

tonne (tʌn) *n.* metric ton, 1000 kg

tonsil (ˈtɒnsəl) *n.* gland in throat —ˈ**tonsillar** *a.* —**tonsilˈlectomy** *n.* surgical removal of tonsils —**tonsilˈlitis** *n.* inflammation of tonsils

tonsorial (tɒnˈsɔːrɪəl) *a. oft. jocular* of barbering or hairdressing

tonsure (ˈtɒnʃə) *n.* **1.** shaving of part of head as religious or monastic practice **2.** part shaved —*vt.* **3.** shave thus

too (tuː) *adv.* **1.** also, in addition **2.** in excess, overmuch

took (tʊk) *pt. of* TAKE

tool (tuːl) *n.* **1.** implement or appliance for mechanical operations **2.** servile helper **3.** means to an end —*vt.* **4.** work on with tool **5.** indent design on (leather book cover *etc.*) —ˈ**tooling** *n.* **1.** decorative work **2.** setting up *etc.* of tools, *esp.* for machine operation

toot (tuːt) *v.* **1.** (cause to) give short blast, hoot or whistle —*n.* **2.** short sound of horn, trumpet *etc.*

tooth (tuːθ) *n.* **1.** bonelike projection in gums of upper and lower jaws of vertebrates **2.** various pointed things like this **3.** prong, cog (*pl.* **teeth**) —ˈ**toothsome** *a.* of delicious or appetizing appearance, flavour or smell —ˈ**toothy** *a.* having or showing numerous, large or projecting teeth —ˈ**toothache** *n.* pain in or about tooth —ˈ**toothbrush** *n.* small brush, usu. with long handle, for cleaning teeth —**tooth-comb** *n.* small comb with teeth close together —ˈ**toothpaste** *n.* paste for cleaning teeth, applied with toothbrush —ˈ**toothpick** *n.* small sharp sliver of wood *etc.* for extracting pieces of food from between teeth

tootle (ˈtuːtᵊl) *inf. v.* **1.** toot —*n.* **2.** soft hoot or series of hoots

top[1] (tɒp) *n.* **1.** highest part, summit **2.** highest rank **3.** first in merit **4.** garment for upper part of body **5.** lid, stopper of bottle *etc.* **6.** platform on ship's mast —*vt.* **7.** cut off, pass, reach, surpass top of **8.** provide top for (**-pp-**) —ˈ**topless** *a.* (of costume, woman) with no covering for breasts —ˈ**topmost** *a.* **1.** supreme **2.** highest —ˈ**topper** *n.* **1.** *inf.* top hat **2.** person or thing that tops or excels —ˈ**topping** *n.* **1.** something that tops something else, *esp.* sauce or garnish for food —*a.* **2.** high or superior in rank, degree *etc.* **3.** **UK** *sl.* excellent; splendid —**top brass** *inf.* **1.** high-ranking army officers **2.** important officials —ˈ**topcoat** *n.* outdoor coat worn over suit *etc.* —**top dog** *inf.* leader or chief of group —**top-drawer** *a.* of highest standing, *esp.* socially —**top-dress** *vt.* spread soil, fertilizer *etc.* on surface of (land) —**top dressing** —**top-flight** *a.* of superior or excellent quality —**topgallant** (tɒpˈgælənt; *Naut.* təˈgælənt) *n.* **1.** mast on square-rigger above topmast or extension of topmast **2.** sail set on yard of topgallant mast —*a.* **3.** of topgallant —**top gear 1.** highest forward ratio of gearbox in motor vehicle **2.** highest speed, greatest energy *etc.* (*also* **top**) —**top hat** man's hat with tall cylindrical crown —**top-heavy** *a.* **1.** unbalanced **2.** with top too heavy for base —**top-hole** *interj./a.* **UK** *inf.* excellent; splendid —ˈ**topknot** *n.* **1.** crest, tuft, chignon *etc.* on top of head **2.** European flatfish —**top-level** *a.* of those on highest level of influence or authority —**topmast** (ˈtɒpmɑːst; *Naut.* ˈtɒpməst) *n.* mast next above lower mast on sailing vessel —ˈ**topˈnotch** *a.* excellent, first-class —**topsail** (ˈtɒpseɪl; *Naut.* ˈtɒpsəl) *n.* square sail carried on yard set on topmast —**top-secret** *a.* needing highest level of secrecy, security —ˈ**topside** *n.* **1.** uppermost side **2.** **UK** lean cut of beef from thigh, containing no bone **3.** (*oft. pl.*) part of ship's sides above waterline **4.** (*oft. pl.*) part of ship above decks —ˈ**topsoil** *n.* surface layer of soil

top[2] (tɒp) *n.* toy which spins on tapering point

topaz (ˈtəʊpæz) *n.* precious stone of various colours

tope[1] (təʊp) *v.* consume (alcoholic drink) as regular habit, usu. in large quantities —ˈ**toper** *n.*

tope[2] (təʊp) *n.* small grey shark of European coastal waters

topee *or* **topi** (ˈtəʊpiː, -pɪ) *n.* lightweight hat made of pith (*pl.* **-s**)

topiary (ˈtəʊpɪərɪ) *a.* **1.** (of shrubs) shaped by cutting or pruning, made ornamental by trimming or training —*n.* **2.** topiary work **3.** topiary garden —ˈ**topiarist** *n.*

topic (ˈtɒpɪk) *n.* subject of discourse, conversation *etc.* —ˈ**topical** *a.* **1.** up-to-date, having news value **2.** of topic

THESAURUS

tongue 1. argot, dialect, idiom, language, lingo (*Inf.*), parlance, patois, speech, talk, vernacular **2.** articulation, speech, utterance, verbal expression, voice

tongue-tied at a loss for words, dumb, dumbstruck, inarticulate, mute, speechless, struck dumb

tonic analeptic, boost, bracer (*Inf.*), cordial, fillip, livener, pick-me-up (*Inf.*), refresher, restorative, roborant, shot in the arm (*Inf.*), stimulant

too 1. also, as well, besides, further, in addition, into the bargain, likewise, moreover, to boot **2.** excessively, exorbitantly, extremely, immoderately, inordinately, over-, overly, unduly, unreasonably, very

tool *n.* **1.** apparatus, appliance, contraption, contrivance, device, gadget, implement, instrument, machine, utensil **2.** agency, agent, intermediary, means, medium, vehicle, wherewithal **3.** cat's-paw, creature, dupe, flunkey, hireling, jackal, lackey, minion, pawn, puppet, stooge (*Sl.*) ~*v.* **4.** chase, cut, decorate, ornament, shape, work

top *n.* **1.** acme, apex, apogee, crest, crown, culmination, head, height, high point, meridian, peak, pinnacle, summit, vertex, zenith **2.** cap, cork, cover, lid, stopper **3.** first place, head, highest rank, lead ~*v.* **4.** cap, cover, crown, finish, garnish, roof, tip **5.** ascend, climb, crest, reach the top of, scale, surmount **6.** beat, best, better, eclipse, exceed, excel, go beyond, outdo, outshine, outstrip, surpass, transcend

topography (təˈpɒgrəfɪ) *n.* (description of) surface features of a place —**toˈpographer** *n.* —**topoˈgraphic** *a.* —**topoˈgraphically** *adv.*

topology (təˈpɒlədʒɪ) *n.* **1.** branch of mathematics concerned with generalization of concepts of continuity, limit *etc.* **2.** branch of geometry describing properties of figure that are unaffected by continuous distortion **3.** *Maths.* family of subsets of given set *S*, such that *S* is topological space **4.** study of topography of given place **5.** anatomy of any specific bodily area, structure or part —**topoˈlogic(al)** *a.* —**toˈpologist** *n.*

topple (ˈtɒpᵊl) *v.* (cause to) fall over, collapse

topsy-turvy (ˈtɒpsɪˈtɜːvɪ) *a.* **1.** upside down **2.** in confusion

toque (təʊk) *n.* **1.** small round hat **2.** C knitted cap

tor (tɔː) *n.* high, rocky hill

Torah (ˈtəʊrə) *n.* **1.** the Pentateuch **2.** scroll on which this is written **3.** whole body of Jewish sacred writings and tradition, including oral expositions of the Law

torch (tɔːtʃ) *n.* **1.** portable hand light containing electric battery and bulb **2.** burning brand *etc.* **3.** any apparatus burning with hot flame (*eg* for welding) —**ˈtorchbearer** *n.* —**torch singer** —**torch song** sentimental song, usu. sung by woman —**carry a torch for** be in love with, *esp.* unrequitedly

tore (tɔː) *pt. of* TEAR[2] —**torn** *pp. of* TEAR[2]

toreador (ˈtɒrɪədɔː) *n.* bullfighter

torment (tɔːˈmɛnt) *vt.* **1.** torture in body or mind **2.** afflict **3.** tease —*n.* (ˈtɔːmɛnt) **4.** suffering, torture, agony of body or mind —**torˈmentor** *n.*

tornado (tɔːˈneɪdəʊ) *n.* **1.** whirlwind **2.** violent storm (*pl.* **-es, -s**)

torpedo (tɔːˈpiːdəʊ) *n.* **1.** cylindrical, self-propelled underwater missile with explosive warhead, fired *esp.* from submarine (*pl.* **-es**) —*vt.* **2.** strike, sink with, as with, torpedo

torpid (ˈtɔːpɪd) *a.* sluggish, apathetic —**torˈpidity** *or* **ˈtorpidness** *n.* —**ˈtorpor** *n.* torpid state

torque (tɔːk) *n.* **1.** collar, similar ornament of twisted gold or other metal **2.** *Mech.* any rotating or twisting force

torr (tɔː) *n.* unit of pressure equal to one millimetre of mercury (133.322 newtons per square metre)

torrent (ˈtɒrənt) *n.* **1.** rushing stream **2.** downpour —**torˈrential** *a.* **1.** resembling a torrent **2.** overwhelming

torrid (ˈtɒrɪd) *a.* **1.** parched, dried with heat **2.** highly emotional —**torˈridity** *or* **ˈtorridness** *n.* —**Torrid Zone** land between tropics

torsion (ˈtɔːʃən) *n.* twist, twisting

torso (ˈtɔːsəʊ) *n.* **1.** (statue of) body without head or limbs **2.** trunk (*pl.* **-s, -si** (-sɪ))

tort (tɔːt) *n. Law* private or civil wrong

tortilla (tɔːˈtiːə) *n.* thin Mexican pancake

tortoise (ˈtɔːtəs) *n.* four-footed reptile covered with shell of horny plates —**ˈtortoiseshell** *n.* **1.** mottled brown shell of hawksbill turtle used commercially —*a.* **2.** of yellowish-brown mottled colour **3.** made of tortoiseshell

tortuous (ˈtɔːtjʊəs) *a.* **1.** winding, twisting **2.** involved, not straightforward —**tortuˈosity** *n.*

torture (ˈtɔːtʃə) *n.* **1.** infliction of severe pain —*vt.* **2.** subject to torture —**ˈtorturer** *n.* —**torture chamber**

Tory (ˈtɔːrɪ) *n.* **1.** member of Brit., Canad. conservative party **2.** politically reactionary person

toss (tɒs) *vt.* **1.** throw up, about —*vi.* **2.** be thrown, fling oneself about —*n.* **3.** act of tossing —**toss-up** *n.* **1.** instance of tossing up coin **2.** *inf.* even chance or risk —**toss up** spin (coin) in air to decide between alternatives by guessing which side will fall uppermost

tot[1] (tɒt) *n.* **1.** very small child **2.** small quantity, *esp.* of drink

tot[2] (tɒt) *v.* (*with* up) total; add (**-tt-**)

total (ˈtəʊtᵊl) *n.* **1.** whole amount **2.** sum, aggregate —*a.* **3.** complete, entire, full, absolute —*v.* **4.** (*some-*

THESAURUS

topic issue, matter, point, question, subject, subject matter, text, theme, thesis

topical contemporary, current, newsworthy, popular, up-to-date, up-to-the-minute

topmost dominant, foremost, highest, leading, loftiest, paramount, principal, supreme, top, upper, uppermost

topple capsize, collapse, fall, fall headlong, fall over, keel over, knock down, knock over, overbalance, overturn, tip over, totter, tumble, upset

topsy-turvy chaotic, confused, disarranged, disorderly, disorganized, inside-out, jumbled, messy, mixed-up, untidy, upside-down

torment *v.* **1.** afflict, agonize, crucify, distress, excruciate, harrow, pain, rack, torture **2.** annoy, bedevil, bother, chivvy, devil (*Inf.*), harass, harry, hound, irritate, nag, persecute, pester, plague, provoke, tease, trouble, vex, worry ~*n.* **3.** agony, anguish, distress, hell, misery, pain, suffering, torture

torn cut, lacerated, ragged, rent, ripped, slit, split

tornado cyclone, gale, hurricane, squall, storm, tempest, twister (*U.S. inf.*), typhoon, whirlwind, windstorm

torpor accidie, acedia, apathy, dormancy, drowsiness, dullness, inactivity, inanition, indolence, inertia, inertness, languor, laziness, lethargy, listlessness, numbness, passivity, sloth, sluggishness, somnolence, stagnancy, stupor, torpidity

torrent cascade, deluge, downpour, effusion, flood, flow, gush, outburst, rush, spate, stream, tide

tortuous **1.** bent, circuitous, convoluted, crooked, curved, indirect, mazy, meandering, serpentine, sinuous, twisted, twisting, winding, zigzag **2.** ambiguous, complicated, convoluted, cunning, deceptive, devious, indirect, involved, mazy, misleading, roundabout, tricky

torture **1.** *v.* afflict, agonize, crucify, distress, excruciate, harrow, lacerate, martyr, pain, persecute, put on the rack, rack, torment **2.** *n.* affliction, agony, anguish, distress, hell, laceration, martyrdom, misery, pain, pang(s), persecution, rack, suffering, torment

toss *v.* **1.** cast, chuck (*Inf.*), fling, flip, hurl, launch, lob (*Inf.*), pitch, project, propel, shy, sling, throw **2.** agitate, disturb, jiggle, joggle, jolt, rock, roll, shake, thrash, tumble, wriggle, writhe **3.** heave, labour, lurch, pitch, roll, wallow ~*n.* **4.** cast, fling, lob (*Inf.*), pitch, shy, throw

tot[1] *n.* **1.** baby, child, infant, little one, mite, toddler, wean (*Scot.*) **2.** dram, finger, measure, nip, shot (*Inf.*), slug, snifter (*Inf.*), toothful

tot[2] *v.* add up, calculate, count up, reckon, sum (up), tally, total

times with to) amount —*vt.* **5.** add up (**-ll-**) —**to'tality** *n.* —**'totalizator, 'totalizer** *or* **'totalisator, 'totaliser** *n.* machine to operate system of betting on racecourse in which money is paid out to winners in proportion to their stakes —**total allergy syndrome** combination of symptoms produced by allergic reaction to various elements of modern everyday life

totalitarian (təʊtælɪ'tɛərɪən) *a.* of dictatorial, one-party government

tote[1] (təʊt) totalizator

tote[2] (təʊt) *vt.* haul, carry —**tote bag** large handbag or shopping bag

totem ('təʊtəm) *n.* tribal badge or emblem —**to'temic** *a.* —**totem pole** post carved, painted with totems, *esp.* by Amer. Indians

totter ('tɒtə) *vi.* **1.** walk unsteadily **2.** begin to fall

toucan ('tu:kən) *n.* tropical Amer. bird with large bill

touch (tʌtʃ) *n.* **1.** sense by which qualities of object *etc.* are perceived by touching **2.** characteristic manner or ability **3.** touching **4.** slight blow, stroke, contact, amount *etc.* —*vt.* **5.** come into contact with **6.** put hand on **7.** reach **8.** affect emotions of **9.** deal with, handle **10.** eat, drink **11.** *inf.* (try to) borrow from —*vi.* **12.** be in contact **13.** (*with* on) refer (to) —**touched** *a.* **1.** moved to sympathy or emotion **2.** showing slight insanity —**'touching** *a.* **1.** emotionally moving —*prep.* **2.** concerning —**'touchy** *a.* easily offended, sensitive —**'touchdown** *n.* **1.** moment at which landing aircraft or spacecraft comes into contact with landing surface **2.** *Rugby* act of placing or touching ball on ground behind goal line, as in scoring try **3.** *American football* scoring play for six points achieved by being in possession of ball in opponents' end zone —**touch judge** one of two linesmen in rugby —**'touchline** *n.* side line of pitch in some games —**'touchpaper** *n.* paper soaked in saltpetre for firing gunpowder —**'touchstone** *n.* criterion —**touch-type** *vi.* type without looking at keyboard —**touch-typist** *n.* —**'touchwood** *n.* tinder —**touch and go** precarious (situation) —**touch down 1.** (of aircraft *etc.*) land **2.** *Rugby* place ball behind goal line, as when scoring try

touché (tu:'ʃeɪ) *interj. orig.* in fencing, acknowledgment that blow, witty remark *etc.* has been successful

tough (tʌf) *a.* **1.** strong, resilient, not brittle **2.** sturdy **3.** able to bear hardship, strain **4.** difficult **5.** needing effort to chew **6.** *sl.* rough, uncivilized, violent **7.** *inf.* unlucky, unfair —*n.* **8.** *inf.* rough, violent person —**'toughen** *v.* —**'toughness** *n.*

toupee ('tu:peɪ) *n.* hairpiece

tour (tʊə) *n.* **1.** travelling round **2.** journey to one place after another **3.** excursion —*v.* **4.** make tour (of) —**'tourism** *n.* **1.** tourist travel **2.** this as an industry —**'tourist** *n.* one who travels for pleasure —**'touristy** *a. inf., oft. derogatory* abounding in or designed for tourists

tour de force (tur də 'fɔrs) *Fr.* brilliant stroke, achievement

tourmaline ('tʊəməli:n) *n.* crystalline mineral used for optical instruments and as gem

tournament ('tʊənəmənt) *n.* **1.** competition, contest

THESAURUS

total 1. *n.* aggregate, all, amount, entirety, full amount, mass, sum, totality, whole **2.** *adj.* absolute, all-out, complete, comprehensive, consummate, downright, entire, full, gross, integral, out-and-out, outright, perfect, sheer, sweeping, thorough, thoroughgoing, unconditional, undisputed, undivided, unmitigated, unqualified, utter, whole **3.** *v.* add up, amount to, come to, mount up to, reach, reckon, sum up, tot up

totalitarian authoritarian, despotic, dictatorial, monolithic, one-party, oppressive, tyrannous, undemocratic

totter falter, lurch, quiver, reel, rock, shake, stagger, stumble, sway, teeter, tremble, walk unsteadily, waver

touch *n.* **1.** feel, feeling, handling, palpation, physical contact, tactility **2.** blow, brush, caress, contact, fondling, hit, pat, push, stroke, tap **3.** bit, dash, detail, drop, hint, intimation, jot, pinch, smack, small amount, smattering, *soupçon*, speck, spot, suggestion, suspicion, taste, tincture, tinge, trace, whiff **4.** approach, characteristic, handiwork, manner, method, style, technique, trademark, way **5.** ability, adroitness, art, artistry, command, deftness, facility, flair, knack, mastery, skill, virtuosity ~*v.* **6.** brush, caress, contact, feel, finger, fondle, graze, handle, hit, lay a finger on, palpate, pat, push, strike, stroke, tap **7.** abut, adjoin, be in contact, border, brush, come together, contact, converge, graze, impinge upon, meet **8.** affect, disturb, get through to, get to (*Inf.*), have an effect on, impress, influence, inspire, make an impression on, mark, melt, move, soften, stir, strike, upset **9.** be a party to, concern oneself with, consume, deal with, drink, eat, get involved in, handle, have to do with, partake of, use, utilize **10.** *With* **on** allude to, bring in, cover, deal with, mention, refer to, speak of **11.** arrive at, attain, come to, reach

touching affecting, emotive, heartbreaking, melting, moving, pathetic, piteous, pitiable, pitiful, poignant, sad, stirring, tender

touchstone criterion, guage, measure, norm, standard, yardstick

touchy bad-tempered, captious, crabbed, cross, easily offended, grouchy, grumpy, irascible, irritable, oversensitive, peevish, pettish, petulant, querulous, quick-tempered, sensitive, splenetic, surly, testy, tetchy, thin-skinned, ticklish

tough *adj.* **1.** cohesive, durable, firm, hard, inflexible, leathery, resilient, resistant, rigid, rugged, solid, stiff, strong, sturdy, tenacious **2.** brawny, fit, hard as nails, hardened, hardy, resilient, seasoned, stalwart, stout, strapping, strong, sturdy, vigorous **3.** hard-bitten, pugnacious, rough, ruffianly, ruthless, uncivilized, vicious, violent **4.** arduous, baffling, difficult, exacting, exhausting, hard, intractable, irksome, knotty, laborious, perplexing, puzzling, strenuous, thorny, troublesome, uphill **5.** *Inf.* bad, hard cheese (*Brit. sl.*), hard lines (*Brit. inf.*), hard luck, lamentable, regrettable, too bad (*Inf.*), unfortunate, unfair, unlucky ~*n.* **6.** bravo, bruiser (*Inf.*), brute, bully, bully boy, hooligan, rough (*Inf.*), roughneck (*Sl.*), rowdy, ruffian, thug

tour *n.* **1.** excursion, expedition, jaunt, journey, outing, peregrination, progress, trip **2.** circuit, course, round ~*v.* **3.** explore, go on the road, go round, holiday in, journey, sightsee, travel round, travel through, visit

tourist excursionist, globetrotter, holiday-maker, journeyer, sightseer, traveller, tripper, voyager

usu. with several stages to decide overall winner **2.** *Hist.* contest between knights on horseback —**ˈtourney** *n. Hist.* knightly tournament

tourniquet (ˈtʊənɪkeɪ) *n. Med.* bandage, surgical instrument to constrict artery and stop bleeding

tousle (ˈtaʊzᵊl) *vt.* **1.** tangle, ruffle **2.** treat roughly —*n.* **3.** disorderly, tangled or rumpled state **4.** dishevelled or disordered mass, *esp.* of hair

tout (taʊt) *vi.* **1.** solicit custom (usu. in undesirable fashion) **2.** obtain and sell information about racehorses —*n.* **3.** one who touts

tow[1] (təʊ) *vt.* **1.** drag along behind, *esp.* at end of rope —*n.* **2.** towing or being towed **3.** vessel, vehicle in tow —**ˈtowage** *n.* —**ˈtowbar** *n.* metal bar attached to car for towing caravan *etc.* —**ˈtowpath** *n.* path beside canal, river, orig. for towing —**ˈtowrope** *n.* rope or cable used for towing vehicle or vessel (*also* **ˈtowline**)

tow[2] (təʊ) *n.* fibre of hemp, flax —**tow-headed** *a.* with pale-coloured or rumpled hair

towards (təˈwɔːdz, tɔːdz) *prep.* **1.** in direction of **2.** with regard to **3.** as contribution to (*also* **toˈward**)

towel (ˈtaʊəl) *n.* **1.** cloth for wiping off moisture after washing —*vt.* **2.** dry or wipe with towel (**-ll-**) —**ˈtowelling** *n.* material used for making towels —**throw in the towel** give up completely

tower (ˈtaʊə) *n.* **1.** tall strong structure oft. forming part of church or other large building **2.** fortress —*vi.* **3.** stand very high **4.** loom —**ˈtowering** *a.* **1.** very tall; lofty **2.** outstanding, as in importance or stature **3.** very intense —**tower block** a building of many storeys, as for offices or flats

town (taʊn) *n.* collection of dwellings *etc.*, larger than village and smaller than city —**ˈtownship** *n.* **1.** small town **2.** C land-survey area —**town clerk** chief administrative officer of town —**town crier** formerly, person employed to make public announcements in streets —**town hall** chief building in which municipal business is transacted, oft. with hall for public meetings —**town planning** comprehensive planning of physical and social development of town —**ˈtownspeople** *pl.n.*

toxic (ˈtɒksɪk) *a.* **1.** poisonous **2.** due to poison —**toxaemia** *or U.S.* **toxemia** (tɒkˈsiːmɪə) *n.* blood poisoning —**toxˈicity** *n.* strength of a poison —**toxiˈcology** *n.* study of poisons —**ˈtoxin** *n.* poison of bacterial origin

toy (tɔɪ) *n.* **1.** something designed to be played with **2.** (miniature) replica —*a.* **3.** very small —*vi.* **4.** act idly, trifle —**toy boy** very young male lover of older woman

trace[1] (treɪs) *n.* **1.** track left by anything **2.** indication **3.** minute quantity —*vt.* **4.** follow course, track of **5.** find out **6.** make plan of **7.** draw or copy exactly, *esp.* using tracing paper —**ˈtracer** *n.* **1.** person or thing that traces **2.** ammunition that can be observed when in flight by burning of chemical substances in base of projectile **3.** *Med.* radioactive isotope introduced into body to study metabolic processes *etc.* by following its progress with Geiger counter or other detector **4.** investigation to trace missing cargo *etc.* —**ˈtracery** *n.* interlaced ornament, *esp.* stonework of Gothic window —**ˈtracing** *n.* traced copy of drawing —**trace element** chemical element occurring in very small quantity in soil *etc.* —**tracer bullet** bullet which leaves visible trail so that aim can be checked —**tracing paper** transparent paper placed over drawing, map *etc.* to enable exact copy to be taken

trace[2] (treɪs) *n.* **1.** chain, strap by which horse pulls vehicle **2.** *Angling* short piece of gut, nylon attaching hook or fly to line

trachea (trəˈkiːə) *n.* windpipe (*pl.* **tracheae** (trəˈkiːiː)) —**traˈcheal** *or* **traˈcheate** *a.* —**tracheˈotomy** *n.* surgical incision into trachea

track (træk) *n.* **1.** mark, line of marks, left by passage of anything **2.** path, rough road **3.** course **4.** railway line **5.** distance between two road wheels on one axle **6.** circular jointed metal band driven by wheels as on tank, bulldozer *etc.* **7.** course for running or racing **8.** separate section on gramophone record —*vt.* **9.** follow trail or path of **10.** (*with* down) find thus —**track events** athletic sports held on a track —**track record** past accomplishments of person, company *etc.* —**track shoe** light running shoe fitted with steel spikes for better grip —**ˈtracksuit** *n.* warm, two-piece garment worn *esp.* by athletes

tract[1] (trækt) *n.* **1.** wide expanse, area **2.** *Anat.* system of organs *etc.* with particular function

tract[2] (trækt) *n.* treatise or pamphlet, *esp.* religious one —**ˈtractate** *n.* short tract

THESAURUS

tournament **1.** competition, contest, event, match, meeting, series **2.** *Medieval* joust, the lists, tourney

tow *v.* drag, draw, haul, lug, pull, trail, trawl, tug

towards **1.** en route for, for, in the direction of, in the vicinity of, on the road to, on the way to, to **2.** about, concerning, for, regarding, with regard to, with respect to

tower *n.* **1.** belfry, column, obelisk, pillar, skyscraper, steeple, turret **2.** castle, citadel, fort, fortification, fortress, keep, refuge, stronghold ~*v.* **3.** ascend, be head and shoulders above, dominate, exceed, loom, mount, overlook, overtop, rear, rise, soar, surpass, top, transcend

toxic baneful (*Archaic*), deadly, harmful, lethal, noxious, pernicious, pestilential, poisonous, septic

toy **1.** *n.* doll, game, plaything **2.** *v.* amuse oneself, dally, fiddle (*Inf.*), flirt, play, sport, trifle, wanton

trace *n.* **1.** evidence, indication, mark, record, relic, remains, remnant, sign, survival, token, vestige **2.** bit, dash, drop, hint, iota, jot, shadow, *soupçon*, suggestion, suspicion, tincture, tinge, touch, trifle, whiff **3.** footmark, footprint, footstep, path, slot, spoor, track, trail ~*v.* **4.** ascertain, detect, determine, discover, ferret out, find, follow, hunt down, pursue, search for, seek, shadow, stalk, track, trail, unearth **5.** chart, copy, delineate, depict, draw, map, mark out, outline, record, show, sketch

track *n.* **1.** footmark, footprint, footstep, mark, path, scent, slot, spoor, trace, trail, wake **2.** course, flight path, line, orbit, path, pathway, road, track, trajectory, way **3.** line, permanent way, rail, rails ~*v.* **4.** chase, dog, follow, follow the trail of, hunt down, pursue, shadow, stalk, tail (*Inf.*), trace, trail

tract[1] area, district, estate, expanse, extent, lot, plot, quarter, region, stretch, territory, zone

tract[2] booklet, brochure, disquisition, dissertation, essay, homily, leaflet, monograph, pamphlet, tractate, treatise

tractable **1.** amenable, biddable, compliant, controllable, docile, governable, manageable, obedient, persuadable, submissive, tame, willing, yielding **2.** ductile, fictile, malleable, plastic, pliable, pliant, tractile, workable

tractable ('træktəbᵊl) *a.* easy to manage, docile, amenable

traction ('trækʃən) *n.* action of drawing, pulling —**traction engine** steam-powered locomotive used, *esp.* formerly, for drawing heavy loads along roads or over rough ground

tractor ('træktə) *n.* motor vehicle for hauling, pulling *etc.*

trad (træd) *n.* **1.** *chiefly* UK traditional jazz —*a.* **2.** traditional

trade (treɪd) *n.* **1.** commerce, business **2.** buying and selling **3.** any profitable pursuit **4.** those engaged in trade —*vi.* **5.** engage in trade —*vt.* **6.** buy and sell **7.** barter **8.** exchange (one thing) for another —'**trader** *n.* —**trade-in** *n.* used article given in part payment for new —'**trademark** *or* **trade name** *n.* distinctive mark (secured by legal registration) on maker's goods —**trade price** price of commodities as sold by wholesalers to retailers —**trade secret** secret formula, process *etc.* known and used to advantage by only one manufacturer —'**tradesman** *n.* **1.** shopkeeper **2.** skilled worker —**Trades Union Congress** major association of British trade unions —**trade union** *or* **trades union** society of workers for protection of their interests —**trade wind** wind blowing constantly towards equator in certain parts of globe —**trading estate** *chiefly* UK large area in which a number of commercial or industrial firms are situated —**trading stamp** stamp given by some retail organizations to customers, redeemable for merchandise or cash

tradescantia (trædɛs'kænʃɪə) *n.* widely cultivated plant with striped variegated leaves

tradition (trə'dɪʃən) *n.* **1.** unwritten body of beliefs, facts *etc.* handed down from generation to generation **2.** custom, practice of long standing **3.** process of handing down —**tra'ditional** *a.* —**tra'ditionally** *adv.*

traduce (trə'dju:s) *vt.* slander

traffic ('træfɪk) *n.* **1.** vehicles passing to and fro in street, town *etc.* **2.** (illicit) trade —*vi.* **3.** trade, *esp.* in illicit goods (*eg* drugs) ('**trafficked,** '**trafficking**) —'**trafficker** *n.* trader —**traffic island** *see* ISLAND (sense 2) —**traffic lights** set of coloured lights at road junctions *etc.* to control flow of traffic —**traffic warden** one employed to supervise road traffic, parking *etc.*

tragedy ('trædʒɪdɪ) *n.* **1.** sad or calamitous event **2.** dramatic, literary work dealing with serious, sad topic and with ending marked by (inevitable) disaster —**tra'gedian** *n.* actor in, writer of tragedies (**tragedi'enne** *fem.*) —'**tragic** *a.* **1.** of, in manner of tragedy **2.** disastrous **3.** appalling —'**tragically** *adv.* —**tragi'comedy** *n.* play with both tragic and comic elements

trail (treɪl) *vt.* **1.** drag behind one —*vi.* **2.** be drawn behind **3.** hang, grow loosely —*n.* **4.** track, trace **5.** thing that trails **6.** rough, ill-defined track in wild country —'**trailer** *n.* **1.** vehicle towed by another vehicle **2.** *Cine.* advertisement of forthcoming film **3.** trailing plant —'**trailblazer** *n.* **1.** pioneer in particular field **2.** person who blazes trail

train (treɪn) *vt.* **1.** educate, instruct, exercise **2.** cause to grow in particular way **3.** aim (gun *etc.*) —*vi.* **4.** follow course of training, *esp.* to achieve physical fitness for athletics —*n.* **5.** line of railway vehicles joined to locomotive **6.** succession, *esp.* of thoughts, events *etc.* **7.** procession of animals, vehicles *etc.* travelling together **8.** trailing part of dress **9.** body of attendants —**trai'nee** *n.* one training to be skilled worker, *esp.* in industry —'**trainer** *n.* **1.** person who trains athletes **2.** piece of equipment employed in training, such as simulated aircraft cockpit **3.** person who schools racehorses —'**training** *n.* —'**trainbearer** *n.* attendant who holds up train of dignitary's robe —**train spotter** person who collects numbers of railway locomotives

THESAURUS

traction adhesion, drag, draught, drawing, friction, grip, haulage, pull, pulling, purchase, resistance

trade *n.* **1.** barter, business, buying and selling, commerce, dealing, exchange, traffic, transactions, truck **2.** avocation, business, calling, craft, employment, job, line, line of work, métier, occupation, profession, pursuit, skill **3.** clientele, custom, customers, market, patrons, public ~*v.* **4.** bargain, barter, buy and sell, deal, do business, exchange, have dealings, peddle, traffic, transact, truck **5.** barter, exchange, swap, switch

trader broker, buyer, dealer, marketer, merchandiser, merchant, seller

tradesman **1.** dealer, merchant, retailer, seller, shopkeeper, vendor **2.** artisan, craftsman, journeyman, skilled worker, workman

tradition convention, custom, customs, established practice, folklore, habit, institution, lore, praxis, ritual, unwritten law, usage

traditional accustomed, ancestral, conventional, customary, established, fixed, folk, historic, long-established, old, oral, time-honoured, transmitted, unwritten, usual

traffic *n.* **1.** coming and going, freight, movement, passengers, transport, transportation, vehicles **2.** barter, business, buying and selling, commerce, communication, dealing, dealings, doings, exchange, intercourse, peddling, relations, trade, truck ~*v.* **3.** bargain, barter, buy and sell, deal, do business, exchange, have dealings, have transactions, market, peddle, trade, truck

tragedy adversity, affliction, calamity, catastrophe, disaster, grievous blow, misfortune

tragic anguished, appalling, awful, calamitous, catastrophic, deadly, dire, disastrous, doleful, dreadful, fatal, grievous, heartbreaking, heart-rending, ill-fated, ill-starred, lamentable, miserable, mournful, pathetic, pitiable, ruinous, sad, shocking, sorrowful, unfortunate, woeful, wretched

trail *v.* **1.** dangle, drag, draw, hang down, haul, pull, stream, tow **2.** dangle, droop, extend, hang, straggle ~*n.* **3.** footprints, footsteps, mark, marks, path, scent, spoor, trace, track, wake **4.** beaten track, footpath, path, road, route, track, way **5.** appendage, stream, tail, train

train *v.* **1.** coach, discipline, drill, educate, guide, improve, instruct, prepare, rear, rehearse, school, teach, tutor **2.** exercise, improve, prepare, work out **3.** aim, bring to bear, direct, focus, level, line up, point ~*n.* **4.** chain, concatenation, course, order, progression, sequence, series, set, string, succession **5.** caravan, column, convoy, file, procession **6.** appendage, tail, trail **7.** attendants, cortege, court, entourage, followers, following, household, retinue, staff, suite

training **1.** coaching, discipline, education, ground-

traipse *or* **trapes** (treɪps) *vi. inf.* walk wearily

trait (treɪt, treɪ) *n.* characteristic feature

traitor (ˈtreɪtə) *n.* one who betrays or is guilty of treason —**ˈtraitorous** *a.* **1.** disloyal **2.** guilty of treachery —**ˈtraitorously** *adv.*

trajectory (trəˈdʒɛktərɪ) *n.* line of flight, (curved) path of projectile

tram (træm) *n.* vehicle (*esp.* electrically driven and for public transport) running on rails laid on roadway (*also* **ˈtramcar**) —**ˈtramway** *n.* rails for trams in street

trammel (ˈtræməl) *n.* **1.** anything that restrains or holds captive **2.** type of compasses —*vt.* **3.** restrain, hinder (**-ll-**)

tramp (træmp) *vi.* **1.** travel on foot, *esp.* as vagabond or for pleasure **2.** walk heavily —*n.* **3.** (homeless) person who travels about on foot **4.** walk **5.** tramping **6.** vessel that takes cargo wherever shippers desire **7.** *sl., chiefly* US prostitute; promiscuous woman

trample (ˈtræmpᵊl) *v.* tread (on) and crush under foot

trampoline (ˈtræmpəlɪn, -liːn) *n.* tough canvas sheet stretched horizontally with elastic cords *etc.* to frame, for gymnastic, acrobatic use

trance (trɑːns) *n.* **1.** unconscious or dazed state **2.** state of ecstasy or total absorption

trannie *or* **tranny** (ˈtrænɪ) *inf.* transistor radio

tranquil (ˈtræŋkwɪl) *a.* calm, quiet, serene —**tranˈquillity** *or U.S.* (*sometimes*) **tranˈquility** *n.* —**ˈtranquillize, -ise** *or U.S.* **ˈtranquilize** *vt.* make calm —**ˈtranquillizer** *or* **-iser** *n.* drug which induces calm, tranquil state —**ˈtranquilly** *adv.*

trans. **1.** transaction **2.** transferred **3.** transitive **4.** translated **5.** translator **6.** transport(ation) **7.** transverse

trans- (*comb. form*) across, through, beyond, on the other side, as in *transatlantic*

transact (trænˈzækt) *vt.* **1.** carry through **2.** negotiate **3.** conduct (affair *etc.*) —**transˈaction** *n.* **1.** performing of any business **2.** that which is performed **3.** single sale or purchase —*pl.* **4.** proceedings **5.** reports of a society

transatlantic (trænzətˈlæntɪk) *a.* **1.** on or from the other side of the Atlantic **2.** crossing the Atlantic

transceiver (trænˈsiːvə) *n.* combined radio transmitter and receiver

transcend (trænˈsɛnd) *vt.* **1.** rise above **2.** exceed, surpass —**tranˈscendence** *n.* —**tranˈscendent** *a.* —**transcenˈdental** *a.* **1.** surpassing experience **2.** supernatural **3.** abstruse —**transcenˈdentalism** *n.* —**transcendental meditation** technique, based on Hindu traditions, for relaxing and refreshing mind and body through silent repetition of mantra

transcribe (trænˈskraɪb) *vt.* **1.** copy out **2.** transliterate, translate **3.** record for later broadcast **4.** arrange (music) for different instrument —**ˈtranscript** *n.* copy —**tranˈscription** *n.* **1.** act or instance of transcribing or state of being transcribed **2.** something transcribed **3.** representation in writing of actual pronunciation of word *etc.* using phonetic symbols

transducer (trænzˈdjuːsə) *n.* any device that converts one form of energy into another

transept (ˈtrænsɛpt) *n.* **1.** transverse part of cruciform church **2.** either of its arms

transfer (trænsˈfɜː) *v.* **1.** move, send from one person, place *etc.* to another (**-rr-**) —*n.* (ˈtrænsfɜː) **2.** removal of person or thing from one place to another **3.** design which can be transferred from one surface to another by pressure, heat *etc.* —**transˈferable** *or* **transˈferrable** *a.* —**transference** (ˈtrænsfərəns) *n.* transfer

THESAURUS

ing, guidance, instruction, schooling, teaching, tuition, tutelage, upbringing **2.** body building, exercise, practice, preparation, working-out

trait attribute, characteristic, feature, idiosyncrasy, lineament, mannerism, peculiarity, quality, quirk

traitor apostate, back-stabber, betrayer, deceiver, defector, deserter, double-crosser (*Inf.*), fifth columnist, informer, Judas, miscreant, quisling, rebel, renegade, snake in the grass (*Inf.*), turncoat

trajectory course, flight, flight path, line, path, route, track

tramp *v.* **1.** footslog, hike, march, ramble, range, roam, rove, slog, trek, walk, yomp **2.** march, plod, stamp, stump, toil, traipse (*Inf.*), trudge, walk heavily ~*n.* **3.** derelict, dosser (*Brit. sl.*), down-and-out, drifter, hobo (*Chiefly U.S.*), vagabond, vagrant **4.** hike, march, ramble, slog, trek

trample crush, flatten, run over, squash, stamp, tread, walk over

trance abstraction, daze, dream, ecstasy, hypnotic state, muse, rapture, reverie, spell, stupor, unconsciousness

tranquil at peace, calm, composed, cool, pacific, peaceful, placid, quiet, restful, sedate, serene, still, undisturbed, unexcited, unperturbed, unruffled, untroubled

tranquillity ataraxia, calm, calmness, composure, coolness, equanimity, hush, imperturbability, peace, peacefulness, placidity, quiet, quietness, quietude, repose, rest, restfulness, sedateness, serenity, stillness

tranquillize calm, compose, lull, pacify, quell, quiet, relax, sedate, settle one's nerves, soothe

tranquillizer barbiturate, bromide, downer (*Sl.*), opiate, red (*Sl.*), sedative

transact accomplish, carry on, carry out, conclude, conduct, discharge, do, enact, execute, handle, manage, negotiate, perform, prosecute, see to, settle, take care of

transaction **1.** action, affair, bargain, business, coup, deal, deed, enterprise, event, matter, negotiation, occurrence, proceeding, undertaking **2.** *Plural* affairs, annals, doings, goings-on (*Inf.*), minutes, proceedings, record

transcend eclipse, exceed, excel, go above, go beyond, leave behind, leave in the shade (*Inf.*), outdo, outrival, outshine, outstrip, outvie, overstep, rise above, surpass

transcendent consummate, exceeding, extraordinary, incomparable, matchless, peerless, pre-eminent, second to none, sublime, superior, transcendental, unequalled, unique, unparalleled, unrivalled

transcribe **1.** copy out, engross, note, reproduce, rewrite, set out, take down, transfer, write out **2.** interpret, render, translate, transliterate **3.** record, tape, tape-record

transcript carbon, carbon copy, copy, duplicate,

transfigure (træns'fɪgə) *vt.* alter appearance of —**transfiguration** (trænsfɪgjʊ'reɪʃən) *n.*

transfix (træns'fɪks) *vt.* **1.** astound, stun **2.** pierce

transform (træns'fɔːm) *vt.* change shape, character of —**transfor'mation** *n.* —**trans'former** *n. Elec.* apparatus for changing voltage of alternating current

transfuse (træns'fjuːz) *vt.* convey from one vessel to another, *esp.* blood from healthy person to one injured or ill —**trans'fusion** *n.*

transgress (trænz'grɛs) *vt.* **1.** break (law) —*vi.* **2.** sin —**trans'gression** *n.* —**trans'gressor** *n.*

tranship (træn'ʃɪp) *v. see* TRANSSHIP

transient ('trænzɪənt) *a.* fleeting, not permanent —'**transience** *n.*

transistor (træn'zɪstə) *n.* **1.** *Electron.* small, semiconducting device used to amplify electric currents **2.** portable radio using transistors —**tran'sistorize** *or* **-ise** *v.* **1.** convert to use or manufacture of transistors and other solid-state components —*vt.* **2.** equip with transistors and other solid-state components

transit ('trænsɪt, 'trænz-) *n.* passage, crossing —**transition** (træn'zɪʃən) *n.* change from one state to another —**transitional** (træn'zɪʃən°l) *a.* —'**transitive** *a.* (of verb) requiring direct object —'**transitory** *a.* not lasting long, transient —**transit camp** camp in which refugees *etc.* live temporarily

translate (træns'leɪt, trænz-) *vt.* **1.** turn from one language into another **2.** explain —**trans'lation** *n.* —**trans'lator** *n.*

transliterate (trænz'lɪtəreɪt) *vt.* write in the letters of another alphabet —**transliter'ation** *n.*

translucent (trænz'luːs°nt) *a.* letting light pass through, semitransparent —**trans'lucence** *n.*

transmigrate (trænzmaɪ'greɪt) *vi.* (of soul) pass into another body —**transmi'gration** *n.*

transmit (trænz'mɪt) *vt.* **1.** send, cause to pass to another place, person *etc.* **2.** communicate **3.** send out (signals) by means of radio waves **4.** broadcast (radio, television programme) (-tt-) —**trans'mission** *n.* **1.** transference **2.** gear by which power is communicated from engine to road wheels —**trans'mitter** *n.* **1.** person or thing that transmits **2.** equipment used for generating and amplifying radio-frequency carrier, modulating carrier with information and feeding it to aerial for transmission **3.** microphone in telephone that converts sound waves into audio-frequency electrical signals **4.** device that converts mechanical movements into coded electrical signals transmitted along telegraph circuit

transmogrify (trænz'mɒgrɪfaɪ) *vt. inf.* change completely *esp.* into bizarre form

transmute (trænz'mjuːt) *vt.* change in form, properties or nature —**transmu'tation** *n.*

transom ('trænzəm) *n.* **1.** crosspiece **2.** lintel

THESAURUS

manuscript, note, notes, record, reproduction, transcription, translation, transliteration, version

transfer 1. *v.* carry, change, consign, convey, displace, hand over, make over, move, pass on, relocate, remove, shift, translate, transmit, transplant, transport, transpose, turn over **2.** *n.* change, displacement, handover, move, relocation, removal, shift, transference, translation, transmission, transposition

transfix 1. engross, fascinate, halt *or* stop in one's tracks, hold, hypnotize, mesmerize, paralyse, petrify, rivet the attention of, root to the spot, spellbind, stop dead, stun **2.** fix, impale, pierce, puncture, run through, skewer, spear, spit, transpierce

transform alter, change, convert, make over, metamorphose, reconstruct, remodel, renew, revolutionize, transfigure, translate, transmogrify (*Jocular*), transmute

transformation alteration, change, conversion, metamorphosis, radical change, renewal, revolution, revolutionary change, sea change, transfiguration, transmogrification (*Jocular*), transmutation

transgress break, break the law, contravene, defy, disobey, do *or* go wrong, encroach, err, exceed, fall from grace, go astray, go beyond, infringe, lapse, misbehave, offend, overstep, sin, trespass, violate

transgression breach, contravention, crime, encroachment, error, fault, infraction, infringement, iniquity, lapse, misbehaviour, misdeed, misdemeanour, offence, sin, trespass, violation, wrong, wrongdoing

transgressor criminal, culprit, delinquent, evildoer, felon, lawbreaker, malefactor, miscreant, offender, sinner, trespasser, villain, wrongdoer

transient brief, ephemeral, evanescent, fleeting, flying, fugacious, fugitive, here today and gone tomorrow, impermanent, momentary, passing, short, short-lived, short-term, temporary, transitory

transit carriage, conveyance, crossing, motion, movement, passage, portage, shipment, transfer, transport, transportation, travel, traverse

transition alteration, change, changeover, conversion, development, evolution, flux, metamorphosis, metastasis, passage, passing, progression, shift, transit, transmutation, upheaval

transitional changing, developmental, fluid, intermediate, passing, provisional, temporary, transitionary, unsettled

transitory brief, ephemeral, evanescent, fleeting, flying, fugacious, here today and gone tomorrow, impermanent, momentary, passing, short, short-lived, short-term, temporary, transient

translate 1. construe, convert, decipher, decode, interpret, paraphrase, render, transcribe, transliterate **2.** elucidate, explain, make clear, paraphrase, put in plain English, simplify, spell out, state in layman's language

translation 1. construction, decoding, gloss, interpretation, paraphrase, rendering, rendition, transcription, transliteration, version **2.** elucidation, explanation, paraphrase, rephrasing, rewording, simplification

translator interpreter, linguist, metaphrast, paraphrast

transmission carriage, communication, conveyance, diffusion, dispatch, dissemination, remission, sending, shipment, spread, transfer, transference, transport

transmit 1. bear, carry, communicate, convey, diffuse, dispatch, disseminate, forward, hand down, hand on, impart, pass on, remit, send, spread, take, transfer, transport **2.** broadcast, disseminate, put on the air, radio, relay, send, send out

transparent (trænsˈpærənt) *a.* **1.** letting light pass without distortion **2.** that can be seen through distinctly **3.** obvious —**transˈparence** *n.* —**transˈparency** *n.* **1.** quality of being transparent **2.** photographic slide **3.** picture made visible by light behind it —**transˈparently** *adv.*

transpire (trænˈspaɪə) *vi.* **1.** become known **2.** *inf.* happen **3.** (of plants) give off water vapour through leaves —**transpiration** (trænspəˈreɪʃən) *n.*

transplant (trænsˈplɑːnt) *vt.* **1.** move and plant again in another place **2.** transfer (organ) surgically from one body to another —*n.* (ˈtrænsplɑːnt) **3.** surgical transplanting of organ **4.** anything transplanted —**transplanˈtation** *n.*

transponder (trænˈspɒndə) *n.* radio or radar transmitter-receiver that transmits signals automatically when it receives predetermined signals

transport (trænsˈpɔːt) *vt.* **1.** convey from one place to another **2.** *Hist.* banish, as criminal, to penal colony **3.** enrapture —*n.* (ˈtrænspɔːt) **4.** (means of) conveyance **5.** ships, aircraft *etc.* used in transporting stores, troops *etc.* **6.** a ship *etc.* so used **7.** ecstasy, rapture or any powerful emotion —**transporˈtation** *n.* **1.** transporting **2.** *Hist.* deportation to penal colony —**transport café UK** inexpensive eating place on main route, used mainly by long-distance lorry drivers

transpose (trænsˈpəʊz) *vt.* **1.** change order of, interchange **2.** put (music) into different key —**transˈposal** *n.* —**transpoˈsition** *n.*

transsexual (trænzˈsɛksjʊəl) *n.* **1.** person who is completely identified with opposite sex **2.** person who has undergone medical procedures to alter sexual characteristics to those of opposite sex

transship (trænsˈʃɪp) *or* **tranship** *v.* move from one ship, train *etc.* to another

transubstantiation (trænsəbstænʃɪˈeɪʃən) *n.* doctrine that substance of bread and wine changes into substance of Christ's body when consecrated in Eucharist

transuranic (trænzjʊˈrænɪk), **transuranian** (trænzjʊˈreɪnɪən), *or* **transuranium** *a.* **1.** (of element) having atomic number greater than that of uranium **2.** of behaviour of transuranic elements

transverse (trænzˈvɜːs) *a.* **1.** lying across **2.** at right angles

transvestite (trænzˈvɛstaɪt) *n.* person seeking sexual pleasure by wearing clothes normally worn by opposite sex

trap[1] (træp) *n.* **1.** snare, device for catching game *etc.* **2.** anything planned to deceive, betray *etc.* **3.** arrangement of pipes to prevent escape of gas **4.** movable opening, *esp.* through ceiling *etc.* **5.** *Hist.* two-wheeled carriage **6.** *sl.* mouth —*vt.* **7.** catch, ensnare (**-pp-**) —**ˈtrapper** *n.* one who traps animals for their fur —**trap door** door in floor or roof

trap[2] (træp) *vt.* (*oft. with* out) dress, adorn (**-pp-**)

trapeze (trəˈpiːz) *n.* horizontal bar suspended from two ropes for use in gymnastics, acrobatic exhibitions *etc.*

trapezium (trəˈpiːzɪəm) *n.* quadrilateral figure with only two sides parallel (*pl.* **-s, -zia** (-zɪə)) —**ˈtrapezoid** *n.* quadrilateral with no parallel sides

trappings (ˈtræpɪŋz) *pl.n.* equipment, ornaments

Trappist (ˈtræpɪst) *n.* member of Cistercian order of monks who observe strict silence

trash (træʃ) *n.* **1.** *chiefly* **US** rubbish **2.** nonsense —**ˈtrashy** *a.* worthless, cheap

trauma (ˈtrɔːmə) *n.* **1.** nervous shock **2.** injury (*pl.* **-ta** (-tə), **-s**) —**trauˈmatic** *a.* of, causing, caused by trauma

travail (ˈtræveɪl) *vi./n.* labour, toil

travel (ˈtrævᵊl) *vi.* **1.** go, move from one place to another (**-ll-**) —*n.* **2.** act of travelling, *esp.* as tourist **3.** *Machinery* distance component is permitted to move

THESAURUS

transparency **1.** clarity, clearness, diaphaneity, diaphanousness, filminess, gauziness, limpidity, limpidness, pellucidity, pellucidness, sheerness, translucence, translucency, transparence **2.** apparentness, distinctness, explicitness, obviousness, patentness, perspicuousness, plainness, unambiguousness, visibility **3.** photograph, slide

transparent **1.** clear, crystal clear, crystalline, diaphanous, filmy, gauzy, limpid, lucent, lucid, pellucid, seethrough, sheer, translucent, transpicuous **2.** apparent, as plain as the nose on one's face (*Inf.*), distinct, easy, evident, explicit, manifest, obvious, patent, perspicuous, plain, recognizable, unambiguous, understandable, undisguised, visible

transpire **1.** *Inf.* arise, befall, chance, come about, come to pass (*Archaic*), happen, occur, take place, turn up **2.** become known, be disclosed, be discovered, be made public, come out, come to light, emerge

transplant displace, relocate, remove, resettle, shift, transfer, uproot

transport *v.* **1.** bear, bring, carry, convey, fetch, haul, move, remove, run, ship, take, transfer **2.** banish, deport, exile, sentence to transportation **3.** captivate, carry away, delight, electrify, enchant, enrapture, entrance, move, ravish, spellbind ~*n.* **4.** conveyance, transportation, vehicle **5.** carriage, conveyance, removal, shipment, shipping, transference, transportation **6.** cloud nine (*Inf.*), enchantment, euphoria, heaven, rapture, seventh heaven **7.** bliss, delight, ecstasy, happiness, ravishment

transpose alter, change, exchange, interchange, move, rearrange, relocate, reorder, shift, substitute, swap (*Inf.*), switch, transfer

transverse athwart, crossways, crosswise, diagonal, oblique

trap *n.* **1.** ambush, gin, net, noose, pitfall, snare, springe, toils **2.** ambush, artifice, deception, device, ruse, stratagem, subterfuge, trick, wile ~*v.* **3.** catch, corner, enmesh, ensnare, entrap, snare, take **4.** ambush, beguile, deceive, dupe, ensnare, inveigle, trick

trappings accoutrements, adornments, decorations, dress, equipment, finery, fittings, fixtures, fripperies, furnishings, gear, livery, ornaments, panoply, paraphernalia, raiment (*Archaic*), things, trimmings

trash **1.** balderdash, drivel, foolish talk, hogwash, inanity, nonsense, rot, rubbish, tripe (*Inf.*), trumpery, twaddle **2.** dregs, dross, garbage, junk, litter, offscourings, refuse, rubbish, sweepings, waste

trashy brummagem, catchpenny, cheap, cheap-jack (*Inf.*), flimsy, inferior, meretricious, rubbishy, shabby, shoddy, tawdry, thrown together, tinsel, worthless

traumatic agonizing, damaging, disturbing, hurtful, injurious, painful, scarring, shocking, upsetting, wounding

—*pl.* **4.** (account of) travelling —**ˈtraveller** *n.* —**ˈtravelogue** *or U.S.* (*sometimes*) **ˈtravelog** *n.* film *etc.* about travels —**travel agency** *or* **bureau** agency that arranges and negotiates holidays *etc.* for travellers —**travel agent** —**traveller's cheque** cheque sold by bank *etc.* to bearer, who signs it on purchase and can cash it abroad by signing it again —**travelling salesman** salesman who travels within assigned territory to sell merchandise or solicit orders for commercial enterprise he represents by direct personal contact with (potential) customers

traverse (ˈtrævɜːs) *vt.* **1.** cross, go through or over —*vi.* **2.** (of gun) move laterally —*n.* **3.** anything set across **4.** partition **5.** *Mountaineering* face, steep slope to be crossed from side to side —*a.* **6.** being, lying across

travesty (ˈtrævɪstɪ) *n.* **1.** farcical, grotesque imitation **2.** mockery —*vt.* **3.** make, be a travesty of (**-estied, -estying**)

trawl (trɔːl) *n.* **1.** net dragged at deep levels behind special boat, to catch fish —*vi.* **2.** fish with one —**ˈtrawler** *n.* trawling vessel

tray (treɪ) *n.* **1.** flat board, usu. with rim, for carrying things **2.** any similar utensil

treachery (ˈtrɛtʃərɪ) *n.* deceit, betrayal —**ˈtreacherous** *a.* **1.** disloyal **2.** unreliable, dangerous —**ˈtreacherously** *adv.*

treacle (ˈtriːkᵊl) *n.* thick syrup produced when sugar is refined —**ˈtreacly** *a.*

tread (trɛd) *vt.* **1.** set foot on **2.** trample —*vi.* **3.** walk **4.** (*sometimes with* on) repress (**trod** *pt.*, **ˈtrodden** *or* **trod** *pp.*, **ˈtreading** *pr.p.*) —*n.* **5.** treading **6.** fashion of walking **7.** upper surface of step **8.** part of rubber tyre in contact with ground —**ˈtreadmill** *n.* **1.** *Hist.* cylinder turned by treading on steps projecting from it **2.** dreary routine *etc.*

treadle (ˈtrɛdᵊl) *n.* lever worked by foot to turn wheel

treason (ˈtriːzᵊn) *n.* **1.** violation by subject of allegiance to sovereign or state **2.** treachery; disloyalty —**ˈtreasonable** *or* **ˈtreasonous** *a.* constituting treason —**ˈtreasonably** *adv.*

treasure (ˈtrɛʒə) *n.* **1.** riches **2.** stored wealth or valuables —*vt.* **3.** prize, cherish **4.** store up —**ˈtreasurer** *n.* official in charge of funds —**ˈtreasury** *n.* **1.** place for treasure **2.** (**T-**) government department in charge of finance —**treasure-trove** *n.* treasure found hidden with no evidence of ownership

treat (triːt) *n.* **1.** pleasure, entertainment given —*vt.* **2.** deal with, act towards **3.** give medical treatment to **4.** give (someone) gift, food *etc.* at one's own expense —*vi.* **5.** negotiate **6.** (*with* of) discourse (on) —**ˈtreatment** *n.* **1.** method of counteracting a disease **2.** act or mode of treating **3.** manner of handling an artistic medium

treatise (ˈtriːtɪz) *n.* book discussing a subject, formal essay

treaty (ˈtriːtɪ) *n.* signed contract between states *etc.*

THESAURUS

travel *v.* **1.** cross, go, journey, make a journey, make one's way, move, proceed, progress, ramble, roam, rove, take a trip, tour, traverse, trek, voyage, walk, wander, wend **2.** be transmitted, carry, get through, move ~*n.* **3.** *Usually plural* excursion, expedition, globetrotting, journey, movement, passage, peregrination, ramble, tour, touring, trip, voyage, walk, wandering

traveller excursionist, explorer, globetrotter, gypsy, hiker, holiday-maker, journeyer, migrant, nomad, passenger, tourist, tripper, voyager, wanderer, wayfarer

traverse bridge, cover, cross, cut across, go across, go over, make one's way across, negotiate, pass over, ply, range, roam, span, travel over, wander

travesty **1.** *n.* burlesque, caricature, distortion, lampoon, mockery, parody, perversion, send-up (*Brit. inf.*), sham, spoof (*Inf.*), takeoff (*Inf.*) **2.** *v.* burlesque, caricature, deride, distort, lampoon, make a mockery of, make fun of, mock, parody, pervert, ridicule, send up (*Brit. inf.*), sham, spoof (*Inf.*), take off (*Inf.*)

treacherous **1.** deceitful, disloyal, double-crossing (*Inf.*), double-dealing, duplicitous, faithless, false, perfidious, recreant (*Archaic*), traitorous, treasonable, unfaithful, unreliable, untrue, untrustworthy **2.** dangerous, deceptive, hazardous, icy, perilous, precarious, risky, slippery, slippy (*Inf.*), tricky, unreliable, unsafe, unstable

treachery betrayal, deceit, disloyalty, double-cross (*Inf.*), double-dealing, duplicity, faithlessness, infidelity, perfidiousness, perfidy, stab in the back, treason

tread *v.* **1.** hike, march, pace, plod, stamp, step, stride, tramp, trudge, walk **2.** crush underfoot, squash, trample **3.** bear down, crush, oppress, quell, repress, ride roughshod over, subdue, subjugate, suppress **4.** footfall, footstep, gait, pace, step, stride, walk

treason disaffection, disloyalty, duplicity, lese-majesty, mutiny, perfidy, sedition, subversion, traitorousness, treachery

treasonable disloyal, false, mutinous, perfidious, seditious, subversive, traitorous, treacherous, treasonous

treasure *n.* **1.** cash, fortune, funds, gold, jewels, money, riches, valuables, wealth ~*v.* **2.** adore, cherish, dote upon, esteem, hold dear, idolize, love, prize, revere, value, venerate, worship **3.** accumulate, cache, collect, garner, hoard, husband, lay up, salt away, save, stash (away) (*Inf.*), store up

treasury bank, cache, hoard, repository, store, storehouse, vault

treat *n.* **1.** banquet, celebration, entertainment, feast, gift, party, refreshment **2.** delight, enjoyment, fun, gratification, joy, pleasure, satisfaction, surprise, thrill ~*v.* **3.** act towards, behave towards, consider, deal with, handle, look upon, manage, regard, use **4.** apply treatment to, attend to, care for, doctor, medicate, nurse **5.** buy for, entertain, feast, foot *or* pay the bill, give, lay on, pay for, provide, regale, stand (*Inf.*), take out, wine and dine **6.** *With* **of** be concerned with, contain, deal with, discourse upon, discuss, go into, touch upon **7.** bargain, come to terms, confer, have talks, make terms, negotiate, parley

treatise disquisition, dissertation, essay, exposition, monograph, pamphlet, paper, study, thesis, tract, work, writing

treatment **1.** care, cure, healing, medication, medicine, remedy, surgery, therapy **2.** action towards,

treble (ˈtrɛbᵊl) *a.* **1.** threefold, triple **2.** *Mus.* high-pitched —*n.* **3.** soprano voice **4.** part of music for it **5.** singer with such voice —*v.* **6.** increase threefold —ˈ**trebly** *adv.* —**treble chance** method of betting in football pools in which chances of winning are related to number of draws and number of home and away wins forecast by competitor —**treble clef** *Mus.* clef that establishes G fifth above middle C as being on second line of staff

tree (triː) *n.* **1.** large perennial plant with woody trunk **2.** beam **3.** anything (*eg* genealogical chart) resembling tree or tree's structure —*vt.* **4.** force, drive up tree —**tree creeper** small songbird

trefoil (ˈtrɛfɔɪl) *n.* **1.** plant with three-lobed leaf, clover **2.** carved ornament like this

trek (trɛk) *n.* **1.** long difficult journey, *esp.* on foot **2.** SA journey or stage of journey, *esp.* migration by ox wagon —*vi.* **3.** make a trek (**-kk-**) —ˈ**trekker** *n.*

trellis (ˈtrɛlɪs) *n.* **1.** lattice or grating of light bars fixed crosswise —*vt.* **2.** screen, supply with one

tremble (ˈtrɛmbᵊl) *vi.* **1.** quiver, shake **2.** feel fear, anxiety —*n.* **3.** involuntary shaking, quiver, tremor —ˈ**trembler** *n.* trembling spring that makes electrical contact when shaken

tremendous (trɪˈmɛndəs) *a.* **1.** vast, immense **2.** *inf.* exciting, unusual **3.** *inf.* excellent

tremolo (ˈtrɛmələʊ) *n.* quivering or vibrating effect in singing or playing (*pl.* **-s**)

tremor (ˈtrɛmə) *n.* **1.** quiver **2.** shaking **3.** minor earthquake

tremulous (ˈtrɛmjʊləs) *a.* **1.** quivering slightly **2.** timorous, agitated

trench (trɛntʃ) *n.* **1.** long narrow ditch, *esp.* as shelter in war —*vt.* **2.** cut grooves or ditches in —**trench coat** double-breasted waterproof coat

trenchant (ˈtrɛntʃənt) *a.* cutting, incisive, biting

trencher (ˈtrɛntʃə) *n.* *Hist.* wooden plate on which food was served —ˈ**trencherman** *n.* person who enjoys food; hearty eater

trend (trɛnd) *n.* **1.** direction, tendency, inclination, drift **2.** fashion; mode —ˈ**trendiness** *n.* —ˈ**trendy** *a./n.* *inf.* consciously fashionable (person) —ˈ**trendsetter** *n.* person or thing that creates or may create new fashion —ˈ**trendsetting** *a.*

trephine (trɪˈfiːn) *or* **trepan** (trɪˈpæn) *n.* **1.** instrument for cutting circular pieces, *esp.* from skull —*vt.* **2.** remove circular section of bone, *esp.* from skull, of (someone)

trepidation (trɛpɪˈdeɪʃən) *n.* fear, anxiety

trespass (ˈtrɛspəs) *vi.* **1.** intrude (on property *etc.* of another) **2.** transgress, sin —*n.* **3.** wrongful entering on another's land **4.** wrongdoing —ˈ**trespasser** *n.*

tress (trɛs) *n.* long lock of hair

trestle (ˈtrɛsᵊl) *n.* board fixed on pairs of spreading legs and used as support

trews (truːz) *pl.n.* close-fitting trousers, orig. of tartan

tri- (*comb. form*) three, as in *trisect*

triad (ˈtraɪæd) *n.* **1.** group of three **2.** *Chem.* element, radical with valency of three

trial (ˈtraɪəl, traɪl) *n.* **1.** act of trying, testing **2.** experimental examination **3.** *Law* investigation of case before judge **4.** thing, person that strains endurance or patience —**trial and error** method of discovery *etc.* based on practical experiment and experience rather than theory —**trial balance** *Book-keeping* statement of all debit and credit balances in ledger of double-entry system

THESAURUS

behaviour towards, conduct, dealing, handling, management, manipulation, reception, usage

treaty agreement, alliance, bargain, bond, compact, concordat, contract, convention, covenant, entente, pact

trek **1.** *n.* expedition, footslog, hike, journey, long haul, march, odyssey, slog, tramp **2.** *v.* footslog, hike, journey, march, plod, range, roam, rove, slog, traipse (*Inf.*), tramp, trudge, yomp

tremble **1.** *v.* oscillate, quake, quiver, rock, shake, shake in one's shoes, shiver, shudder, teeter, totter, vibrate, wobble **2.** *n.* oscillation, quake, quiver, shake, shiver, shudder, tremor, vibration, wobble

tremendous **1.** appalling, awesome, awful, colossal, deafening, dreadful, enormous, fearful, formidable, frightful, gargantuan, gigantic, great, huge, immense, mammoth, monstrous, prodigious, stupendous, terrible, terrific, titanic, towering, vast, whopping (*Inf.*) **2.** *Inf.* ace (*Inf.*), amazing, excellent, exceptional, extraordinary, fabulous (*Inf.*), fantastic (*Inf.*), great, incredible, marvellous, super (*Inf.*), terrific (*Inf.*), wonderful

tremor **1.** agitation, quaking, quaver, quiver, quivering, shake, shaking, shiver, tremble, trembling, trepidation, vibration, wobble **2.** earthquake, quake (*Inf.*), shock

trench channel, cut, ditch, drain, earthwork, entrenchment, excavation, fosse, furrow, gutter, pit, trough, waterway

trenchant acerbic, acid, acidulous, acute, astringent, biting, caustic, cutting, hurtful, incisive, keen, mordant, penetrating, piquant, pointed, pungent, sarcastic, scathing, severe, sharp, tart

trend **1.** bias, course, current, direction, drift, flow, inclination, leaning, tendency **2.** craze, fad (*Inf.*), fashion, look, mode, rage, style, thing, vogue

trepidation agitation, alarm, anxiety, apprehension, blue funk (*Inf.*), butterflies (*Inf.*), cold feet (*Inf.*), cold sweat (*Inf.*), consternation, dismay, disquiet, disturbance, dread, emotion, excitement, fear, fright, jitters (*Inf.*), nervousness, palpitation, perturbation, quivering, shaking, the heebie-jeebies (*Sl.*), trembling, tremor, uneasiness, worry

trespass *v.* **1.** encroach, infringe, intrude, invade, obtrude, poach **2.** *Archaic* offend, sin, transgress, violate, wrong ~*n.* **3.** encroachment, infringement, intrusion, invasion, poaching, unlawful entry, wrongful entry **4.** breach, crime, delinquency, error, evildoing, fault, infraction, iniquity, injury, misbehaviour, misconduct, misdeed, misdemeanour, offence, sin, transgression, wrongdoing

trespasser **1.** infringer, interloper, intruder, invader, poacher, unwelcome visitor **2.** *Archaic* criminal, delinquent, evildoer, malefactor, offender, sinner, transgressor, wrongdoer

tress braid, curl, lock, plait, ringlet

triad threesome, trilogy, trine, trinity, trio, triple, triplet, triptych, triumvirate, triune

trial **1.** assay, audition, check, dry run (*Inf.*), examination, experience, experiment, probation, proof,

triangle (ˈtraɪæŋgˀl) *n.* **1.** figure with three angles **2.** percussion musical instrument —**triˈangular** *a.* —**triangulate** (traɪˈæŋgjʊleɪt) *vt.* **1.** survey by method of triangulation **2.** calculate trigonometrically **3.** divide into triangles **4.** make triangular —*a.* (traɪˈæŋgjʊlɪt, -leɪt) **5.** marked with or composed of triangles —**trianguˈlation** *n.* method of surveying in which area is divided into triangles, one side and all angles of which are measured and lengths of other lines calculated trigonometrically

Triassic (traɪˈæsɪk) *a.* **1.** of first period of Mesozoic era —*n.* **2.** Triassic period or rock system (*also* **ˈTrias**)

tribe (traɪb) *n.* **1.** race **2.** subdivision of race of people —**ˈtribal** *a.*

tribulation (trɪbjʊˈleɪʃən) *n.* **1.** misery, trouble, affliction, distress **2.** cause of this

tribune (ˈtrɪbjuːn) *n.* person or institution upholding public rights —**tribunal** (traɪˈbjuːnˀl, trɪ-) *n.* **1.** lawcourt **2.** body appointed to inquire into and decide specific matter **3.** seat of judge

tributary (ˈtrɪbjʊtərɪ) *n.* **1.** stream flowing into another —*a.* **2.** auxiliary **3.** contributory **4.** paying tribute

tribute (ˈtrɪbjuːt) *n.* **1.** sign of honour or recognition **2.** tax paid by one state to another

trice (traɪs) *n.* moment —**in a trice** instantly

triceps (ˈtraɪsɛps) *n.* muscle having three heads, *esp.* one that extends forearm (*pl.* **-es, -ceps**)

trichina (trɪˈkaɪnə) *n.* minute parasitic worm (*pl.* **-nae** (-niː)) —**trichinosis** (trɪkɪˈnəʊsɪs) *n.* disease caused by this

trichromatic (traɪkrəʊˈmætɪk) *or* **trichromic** (traɪˈkrəʊmɪk) *a.* **1.** involving combination of three primary colours **2.** of normal colour vision **3.** having three colours —**triˈchromatism** *n.*

trick (trɪk) *n.* **1.** deception **2.** prank **3.** mannerism **4.** illusion **5.** feat of skill or cunning **6.** knack **7.** cards played in one round **8.** spell of duty —*vt.* **9.** cheat, hoax, deceive —**ˈtrickery** *n.* —**ˈtrickster** *n.* —**ˈtricky** *a.* **1.** difficult, needing careful handling **2.** crafty

trickle (ˈtrɪkˀl) *v.* (cause to) run, flow, move in thin stream or drops

tricolour *or U.S.* **tricolor** (ˈtrɪkələ, ˈtraɪkʌlə) *a.* **1.** three-coloured —*n.* **2.** tricolour flag (*eg* of France)

tricot (ˈtrɪkəʊ, ˈtriː-) *n.* **1.** thin rayon or nylon fabric knitted or resembling knitting **2.** ribbed dress fabric

tricycle (ˈtraɪsɪkˀl) *n.* three-wheeled cycle

trident (ˈtraɪdˀnt) *n.* three-pronged fork or spear

triennial (traɪˈɛnɪəl) *a.* happening every, or lasting, three years

trifle (ˈtraɪfˀl) *n.* **1.** insignificant thing or matter **2.** small amount **3.** pudding of sponge cake, whipped cream *etc.* —*vi.* **4.** toy **5.** act, speak idly —**ˈtrifler** *n.* —**ˈtrifling** *a.* **1.** insignificant, petty **2.** frivolous; idle

trig. **1.** trigonometry **2.** trigonometrical —**trig station** *or* **point** landmark which surveyor uses

trigger (ˈtrɪgə) *n.* **1.** catch which releases spring, *esp.* to fire gun —*vt.* **2.** (*oft. with* off) start, set in action *etc.* —**trigger-happy** *a.* tending to irresponsible, ill-considered behaviour, *esp.* in use of firearms

trigonometry (trɪgəˈnɒmɪtrɪ) *n.* branch of math-

THESAURUS

test, testing, test-run **2.** contest, hearing, judicial examination, litigation, tribunal **3.** attempt, crack (*Inf.*), effort, endeavour, go, shot (*Inf.*), stab, try, venture, whack (*Inf.*) **4.** adversity, affliction, burden, cross to bear, distress, grief, hardship, hard times, load, misery, ordeal, pain, suffering, tribulation, trouble, unhappiness, vexation, woe, wretchedness **5.** bane, bother, hassle (*Inf.*), irritation, nuisance, pain in the neck (*Inf.*), pest, plague (*Inf.*), thorn in one's flesh, vexation

tribe blood, caste, clan, class, division, dynasty, ethnic group, family, gens, house, people, race, seed, sept, stock

tribulation adversity, affliction, bad luck, blow, burden, care, cross to bear, curse, distress, grief, heartache, ill fortune, misery, misfortune, ordeal, pain, reverse, sorrow, suffering, trial, trouble, unhappiness, vexation, woe, worry, wretchedness

tribunal bar, bench, court, hearing, judgment seat, judicial examination, trial

tribute **1.** accolade, acknowledgment, applause, commendation, compliment, encomium, esteem, eulogy, gift, gratitude, honour, laudation, panegyric, praise, recognition, respect, testimonial **2.** charge, contribution, customs, duty, excise, homage, impost, offering, payment, ransom, subsidy, tax, toll

trick *n.* **1.** artifice, con (*Sl.*), deceit, deception, device, dodge, feint, fraud, gimmick, hoax, imposition, imposture, manoeuvre, ploy, ruse, stratagem, subterfuge, swindle, trap, wile **2.** antic, cantrip (*Scot.*), caper, device, feat, frolic, gag (*Sl.*), gambol, jape, joke, juggle, legerdemain, leg-pull (*Brit. inf.*), practical joke, prank, put-on (*Sl.*), sleight of hand, stunt **3.** art, command, craft, device, expertise, gift, hang (*Inf.*), knack, know-how (*Inf.*), secret, skill, technique **4.** characteristic, crotchet, foible, habit, idiosyncrasy, mannerism, peculiarity, practice, quirk, trait ~*v.* **5.** bamboozle (*Inf.*), cheat, con (*Sl.*), deceive, defraud, delude, dupe, fool, gull (*Archaic*), have (someone) on, hoax, hoodwink, impose upon, mislead, pull the wool over (someone's) eyes, put one over on (someone) (*Inf.*), swindle, take in (*Inf.*), trap

trickery cheating, chicanery, con (*Sl.*), deceit, deception, dishonesty, double-dealing, fraud, funny business, guile, hanky-panky (*Inf.*), hoax, imposture, jiggery-pokery (*Inf.*), monkey business (*Inf.*), pretence, skulduggery (*Inf.*), swindling

trickle *v.* crawl, creep, dribble, drip, drop, exude, ooze, percolate, run, seep, stream

tricky **1.** complicated, delicate, difficult, knotty, problematic, risky, sticky (*Inf.*), thorny, ticklish, touch-and-go **2.** artful, crafty, cunning, deceitful, deceptive, devious, foxy, scheming, slippery, sly, subtle, wily

trifle *n.* **1.** bagatelle, bauble, child's play, gewgaw, knick-knack, nothing, plaything, toy, triviality **2.** bit, dash, drop, jot, little, pinch, spot, touch, trace ~*v.* **3.** amuse oneself, coquet, dally, dawdle, flirt, fritter, idle, mess about, palter, play, toy, wanton, waste, waste time

trifling empty, frivolous, idle, inconsiderable, insignificant, minuscule, negligible, paltry, petty, piddling (*Inf.*), puny, shallow, silly, slight, small, tiny, trivial, unimportant, valueless, worthless

trigger *v.* activate, bring about, cause, elicit, generate, give rise to, produce, prompt, provoke, set in motion, set off, spark off, start

ematics dealing with relations of sides and angles of triangles —**trigono'metrical** *a.*

trike (traɪk) tricycle

trilateral (traɪ'lætərəl) *a.* having three sides —**tri'laterally** *adv.*

trilby ('trɪlbɪ) *n.* man's soft felt hat

trill (trɪl) *vi.* **1.** sing with quavering voice **2.** sing lightly **3.** warble —*n.* **4.** such singing or sound

trillion ('trɪljən) *n.* **1.** one million million million, 10^{18} **2.** US one million million, 10^{12}

trilobite ('traɪləbaɪt) *n.* extinct marine arthropod abundant in Palaeozoic times, having segmented exoskeleton divided into three parts —**trilobitic** (traɪlə'bɪtɪk) *a.*

trilogy ('trɪlədʒɪ) *n.* series of three related (literary) works

trim (trɪm) *a.* **1.** neat, smart **2.** slender **3.** in good order —*vt.* **4.** shorten slightly by cutting, prune **5.** decorate **6.** adjust **7.** put in good order **8.** adjust balance of (ship, aircraft) (**-mm-**) —*n.* **9.** decoration **10.** order, state of being trim **11.** haircut that neatens existing style **12.** upholstery, accessories in car **13.** edging material, as inside woodwork round doors, windows *etc.* —**'trimming** *n.* (*oft. pl.*) decoration, addition

trimaran ('traɪməræn) *n.* three-hulled vessel

trinitrotoluene (traɪnaɪtrəʊ'tɒljuiːn) *or* **trinitrotoluol** (traɪnaɪtrəʊ'tɒljʊɒl) *n.* a high explosive derived from toluene

trinity ('trɪnɪtɪ) *n.* **1.** the state of being threefold **2.** (**T-**) the three persons of the Godhead —**trini'tarian** *n./a.* —**Trinity Sunday** Sunday after Whit Sunday

trinket ('trɪŋkɪt) *n.* small ornament, trifle —**'trinketry** *n.*

trio ('triːəʊ) *n.* **1.** group of three **2.** music for three parts (*pl.* **-s**)

triode ('traɪəʊd) *n. Electron.* three-electrode valve

trip (trɪp) *n.* **1.** (short) journey for pleasure **2.** stumble **3.** switch **4.** *inf.* hallucinatory experience caused by drug —*v.* **5.** (*oft. with* up) (cause to) stumble **6.** (cause to) make false step, mistake —*vi.* **7.** run lightly; skip; dance **8.** *inf.* take hallucinatory drugs —*vt.* **9.** operate (switch) (**-pp-**) —**'tripper** *n.* tourist

tripartite (traɪ'pɑːtaɪt) *a.* having, divided into three parts

tripe (traɪp) *n.* **1.** stomach of cow *etc.* prepared for food **2.** *inf.* nonsense

triplane ('traɪpleɪn) *n.* aeroplane with three wings one above another

triple ('trɪpᵊl) *a.* **1.** threefold —*v.* **2.** treble —**'triplet** *n.* **1.** three of a kind **2.** one of three offspring born at one birth —**'triply** *adv.* —**triple jump** athletic event in which competitor has to perform hop, step and jump in continuous movement —**triple point** *Chem.* temperature and pressure at which three phases of substance are in equilibrium

triplicate ('trɪplɪkɪt) *a.* **1.** threefold —*vt.* ('trɪplɪkeɪt) **2.** make threefold —*n.* **3.** state of being triplicate **4.** one of set of three copies —**tripli'cation** *n.*

tripod ('traɪpɒd) *n.* stool, stand *etc.* with three feet

tripos ('traɪpɒs) *n.* degree examination at Cambridge University

triptych ('trɪptɪk) *n.* carving, set of pictures, *esp.* altarpiece, on three panels hinged side by side

trireme ('traɪriːm) *n.* ancient Gr. galley with three banks of oars on each side

trisect (traɪ'sɛkt) *vt.* divide into three (equal) parts —**tri'section** *n.*

trite (traɪt) *a.* hackneyed, banal

tritium ('trɪtɪəm) *n.* radioactive isotope of hydrogen

triumph ('traɪəmf) *n.* **1.** great success **2.** victory **3.**

THESAURUS

trim *adj.* **1.** compact, dapper, natty (*Inf.*), neat, nice, orderly, shipshape, smart, soigné, soignée, spick-and-span, spruce, tidy, well-groomed, well-ordered, well turned-out **2.** fit, shapely, sleek, slender, slim, streamlined, svelte, willowy ~*v.* **3.** barber, clip, crop, curtail, cut, cut back, dock, even up, lop, pare, prune, shave, shear, tidy **4.** adorn, array, beautify, bedeck, deck out, decorate, dress, embellish, embroider, garnish, ornament, trick out **5.** adjust, arrange, balance, distribute, order, prepare, settle ~*n.* **6.** adornment, border, decoration, edging, embellishment, frill, fringe, garnish, ornamentation, piping, trimming **7.** condition, fettle, fitness, form, health, order, repair, shape (*Inf.*), situation, state **8.** clipping, crop, cut, pruning, shave, shearing, tidying up, trimming

trimming **1.** adornment, border, braid, decoration, edging, embellishment, frill, fringe, garnish, ornamentation, piping **2.** *Plural* accessories, accompaniments, appurtenances, extras, frills, garnish, ornaments, paraphernalia, trappings

trinity threesome, triad, trilogy, trine, trio, triple, triplet, triptych, triumvirate, triune

trinket bagatelle, bauble, bibelot, gewgaw, gimcrack, kickshaw, knick-knack, nothing, ornament, piece of bric-a-brac, toy, trifle

trio threesome, triad, trilogy, trine, trinity, triple, triplet, triptych, triumvirate, triune

trip *n.* **1.** errand, excursion, expedition, foray, jaunt, journey, outing, ramble, run, tour, travel, voyage **2.** blunder, boob (*Brit. sl.*), error, fall, false move, false step, faux pas, indiscretion, lapse, misstep, slip, stumble ~*v.* **3.** blunder, boob (*Brit. sl.*), err, fall, go wrong, lapse, lose one's balance, lose one's footing, make a false move, make a faux pas, miscalculate, misstep, slip, slip up (*Inf.*), stumble, tumble **4.** catch out, confuse, disconcert, put off one's stride, throw off, trap, unsettle **5.** caper, dance, flit, frisk, gambol, hop, skip, spring, tread lightly **6.** *Inf.* get high (*Inf.*), get stoned (*Sl.*), take drugs, turn on (*Sl.*) **7.** activate, engage, flip, pull, release, set off, switch on, throw, turn on

tripe balderdash, bunkum, claptrap (*Inf.*), drivel, foolish talk, garbage, guff (*Sl.*), hogwash, inanity, nonsense, poppycock (*Inf.*), rot, rubbish, trash, trumpery, twaddle

triple **1.** *adj.* threefold, three times as much, three-way, tripartite **2.** *v.* increase threefold, treble, triplicate

triplet threesome, triad, trilogy, trine, trinity, trio, triple, triumvirate, triune

tripper excursionist, holiday-maker, journeyer, sightseer, tourist, voyager

trite banal, bromidic, clichéd, common, commonplace, corny (*Sl.*), dull, hack, hackneyed, ordinary, pedestrian, routine, run-of-the-mill, stale, stereotyped, stock, threadbare, tired, uninspired, unoriginal, worn

exultation —*vi.* **4.** achieve great success or victory **5.** exult —**tri'umphal** *a.* —**tri'umphant** *a.* **1.** victorious **2.** exultant

triumvirate (traɪˈʌmvɪrɪt) *n.* joint rule by three persons

trivalent (traɪˈveɪlənt, ˈtrɪvələnt) *a. Chem.* **1.** having valency of three **2.** having three valencies (*also* **ter'valent**) —**tri'valency** *n.*

trivet (ˈtrɪvɪt) *n.* metal bracket or stand for pot or kettle

trivia (ˈtrɪvɪə) *pl.n.* petty, unimportant things, details —**'trivial** *a.* **1.** of little consequence **2.** commonplace —**trivi'ality** *n.*

trochee (ˈtrəukiː) *n.* in verse, foot of two syllables, first long and second short —**tro'chaic** *a.*

trod (trɒd) *pt. of* TREAD —**'trodden** *or* **trod** *pp. of* TREAD

troglodyte (ˈtrɒglədaɪt) *n.* cave dweller

troika (ˈtrɔɪkə) *n.* **1.** Russian vehicle drawn by three horses abreast **2.** three horses harnessed abreast **3.** triumvirate

Trojan (ˈtrəudʒən) *n./a.* **1.** (inhabitant) of ancient Troy **2.** steadfast or persevering (person) —**Trojan Horse 1.** *Gr. myth.* hollow wooden figure of horse left outside Troy by Greeks and dragged inside by Trojans. Men concealed inside opened city to final Greek assault **2.** trap intended to undermine enemy

troll[1] (trəul) *vt.* fish for by dragging baited hook or lure through water

troll[2] (trəul) *n.* supernatural being in Scandinavian mythology and folklore

trolley (ˈtrɒlɪ) *n.* **1.** small wheeled table for food and drink **2.** wheeled cart for moving goods *etc.* **3.** US tram —**trolley bus** bus deriving power from overhead electric wire but not running on rails

trollop (ˈtrɒləp) *n.* promiscuous or slovenly woman

trombone (trɒmˈbəun) *n.* deep-toned brass wind instrument with sliding tube —**trom'bonist** *n.*

troop (truːp) *n.* **1.** group or crowd of persons or animals **2.** unit of cavalry —*pl.* **3.** soldiers —*vi.* **4.** move in a troop, flock —**'trooper** *n.* cavalry soldier

trope (trəup) *n.* figure of speech

trophy (ˈtrəufɪ) *n.* **1.** prize, award, as shield, cup **2.** memorial of victory, hunt *etc.*

-trophy (*n. comb. form*) certain type of nourishment or growth, as in *dystrophy* —**-trophic** (*a. comb. form*)

tropic (ˈtrɒpɪk) *n.* **1.** either of two lines of latitude at 23½° N (**tropic of Cancer**) or 23½° S (**tropic of Capricorn**) —*pl.* **2.** area of earth's surface between these lines —**'tropical** *a.* **1.** pert. to, within tropics **2.** (of climate) very hot —**'tropicbird** *n.* tropical aquatic bird having long tail feathers and white plumage with black markings

tropism (ˈtrəupɪzəm) *n.* response of organism, *esp.* plant, to external stimulus by growth in direction determined by stimulus

troposphere (ˈtrɒpəsfɪə) *n.* lowest atmospheric layer, in which air temperature decreases normally with height at about 6.5° C per km

trot (trɒt) *vi.* **1.** (of horse) move at medium pace, lifting feet in diagonal pairs **2.** (of person) run easily with short strides (-tt-) —*n.* **3.** trotting, jog —**'trotter** *n.* **1.** horse trained to trot in race **2.** foot of certain animals, *esp.* pig

Trot (trɒt) *n. inf.* follower of Trotsky; Trotskyite

troth (trəuθ) *n. obs.* fidelity, truth

Trotskyism (ˈtrɒtskɪɪzəm) *n.* theory of communism of Leon Trotsky, Russian revolutionary and writer, in which he called for immediate worldwide revolution by proletariat —**'Trotskyite** *or* **'Trotskyist** *n./a.*

troubadour (ˈtruːbəduə) *n.* one of school of early poets and singers

trouble (ˈtrʌbᵊl) *n.* **1.** state or cause of (mental) distress, pain, inconvenience *etc.* **2.** care, effort —*vt.* **3.** be trouble to —*vi.* **4.** be inconvenienced, concerned **5.** be agitated **6.** take pains; exert oneself —**'troublesome** *a.* —**'troubleshooter** *n.* person who locates cause of trouble and removes or treats it, as in running of machine —**'troubleshooting** *n./a.*

THESAURUS

triumph *n.* **1.** elation, exultation, happiness, joy, jubilation, pride, rejoicing **2.** accomplishment, achievement, ascendancy, attainment, conquest, coup, feat, hit (*Inf.*), mastery, sensation, smash (*Inf.*), smash-hit (*Inf.*), success, *tour de force*, victory, walkover (*Inf.*) ~*v.* **3.** *Often with* **over** best, carry the day, come out on top (*Inf.*), dominate, flourish, get the better of, overcome, overwhelm, prevail, prosper, subdue, succeed, take the honours, thrive, vanquish, win **4.** celebrate, crow, exult, gloat, glory, jubilate, rejoice, revel, swagger

triumphant boastful, celebratory, cock-a-hoop, conquering, dominant, elated, exultant, glorious, jubilant, proud, rejoicing, successful, swaggering, triumphal, undefeated, victorious, winning

trivia details, minutiae, petty details, trifles, trivialities

trivial commonplace, everyday, frivolous, incidental, inconsequential, inconsiderable, insignificant, little, meaningless, minor, negligible, paltry, petty, puny, slight, small, trifling, trite, unimportant, valueless, worthless

triviality 1. frivolity, inconsequentiality, insignificance, littleness, meaninglessness, negligibility, paltriness, pettiness, slightness, smallness, triteness, unimportance, valuelessness, worthlessness **2.** detail, no big thing, no great matter, nothing, petty detail, technicality, trifle

troop *n.* **1.** assemblage, band, body, bunch (*Inf.*), company, contingent, crew (*Inf.*), crowd, drove, flock, gang, gathering, group, herd, horde, multitude, pack, squad, swarm, team, throng, unit **2.** *Plural* armed forces, army, fighting men, men, military, servicemen, soldiers, soldiery ~*v.* **3.** crowd, flock, march, parade, stream, swarm, throng, traipse (*Inf.*)

trophy award, bays, booty, cup, laurels, memento, prize, souvenir, spoils

tropical hot, humid, lush, steamy, stifling, sultry, sweltering, torrid

trot 1. *v.* canter, go briskly, jog, lope, run, scamper **2.** *n.* brisk pace, canter, jog, lope, run

trouble *n.* **1.** agitation, annoyance, anxiety, disquiet, distress, grief, heartache, irritation, misfortune, pain, sorrow, suffering, torment, tribulation, vexation, woe, worry **2.** agitation, bother (*Inf.*), commotion, discontent, discord, disorder, dissatisfaction, disturbance, row, strife, tumult, unrest **3.** ailment, complaint, defect, disability, disease, disorder, fail-

trough (trɒf) *n.* 1. long open vessel, *esp.* for animals' food or water 2. narrow channel 3. *Met.* area of low pressure

trounce (traʊns) *vt.* beat thoroughly, thrash

troupe (tru:p) *n.* company of performers —**'trouper** *n.* 1. member of troupe 2. dependable worker or associate

trousers ('traʊzəz) *pl.n.* two-legged outer garment with legs reaching to the ankles

trousseau ('tru:səʊ) *n.* bride's outfit of clothing (*pl.* **-seaux** (-səʊz), **-s**)

trout (traʊt) *n.* freshwater sport and food fish

trowel ('traʊəl) *n.* small tool like spade for spreading mortar, lifting plants *etc.*

troy weight *or* **troy** (trɔɪ) *n.* system of weights used for gold, silver and gems

truant ('tru:ənt) *n.* 1. one absent without leave, *esp.* child so absenting himself or herself from school —*a.* 2. being or relating to truant —**'truancy** *n.*

truce (tru:s) *n.* 1. temporary cessation of fighting 2. respite, lull

truck[1] (trʌk) *n.* wheeled (motor) vehicle for moving goods

truck[2] (trʌk) *n.* 1. barter 2. dealing (*esp. in* **have no truck with**) 3. payment of workmen in goods 4. *inf.* rubbish

truckle ('trʌk°l) *vi.* yield weakly

truckle bed low bed on wheels, stored under larger bed

truculent ('trʌkjʊlənt) *a.* aggressive, defiant

trudge (trʌdʒ) *vi.* 1. walk laboriously —*n.* 2. laborious or wearisome walk

true (tru:) *a.* 1. in accordance with facts 2. faithful 3. exact, correct 4. genuine —**'truism** *n.* self-evident truth —**'truly** *adv.* 1. exactly 2. really 3. sincerely —**truth** *n.* 1. state of being true 2. something that is true —**'truthful** *a.* 1. accustomed to speak the truth 2. accurate, exact —**'truthfully** *adv.* —**true-blue** *a.* unwaveringly or staunchly loyal —**true blue** *chiefly* UK staunch royalist or conservative

truffle ('trʌf°l) *n.* 1. edible fungus growing underground 2. sweet resembling this

trug (trʌg) *n.* long shallow basket used by gardeners

truism ('tru:ɪzəm) *n. see* TRUE

trump[1] (trʌmp) *n.* 1. card of suit temporarily ranking above others —*v.* 2. play trump card on (plain suit) —**trump up** invent, concoct —**turn up** *or* **out trumps** turn out (unexpectedly) well, successfully

trump[2] (trʌmp) *n.* 1. trumpet 2. blast on trumpet —**the last trump** final trumpet call on Day of Judgment

trumpery ('trʌmpərɪ) *a.* 1. showy but worthless —*n.* 2. worthless finery 3. trash, rubbish

THESAURUS

ure, illness, malfunction, upset **4.** bother, concern, danger, difficulty, dilemma, dire straits, hot water (*Inf.*), mess, nuisance, pest, pickle (*Inf.*), predicament, problem, scrape (*Inf.*), spot (*Inf.*) **5.** attention, bother, care, effort, exertion, inconvenience, labour, pains, struggle, thought, work ~*v.* **6.** afflict, agitate, annoy, bother, discompose, disconcert, disquiet, distress, disturb, fret, grieve, harass, inconvenience, pain, perplex, perturb, pester, plague, sadden, torment, upset, vex, worry **7.** be concerned, bother, burden, discomfort, discommode, disturb, impose upon, incommode, inconvenience, put out **8.** exert oneself, go to the effort of, make an effort, take pains, take the time

troublesome 1. annoying, arduous, bothersome, burdensome, demanding, difficult, harassing, hard, importunate, inconvenient, irksome, irritating, laborious, oppressive, pestilential, plaguy (*Inf.*), taxing, tiresome, tricky, trying, upsetting, vexatious, wearisome, worrisome, worrying **2.** disorderly, insubordinate, rebellious, recalcitrant, refractory, rowdy, turbulent, uncooperative, undisciplined, unruly, violent

trough 1. crib, manger, water trough **2.** canal, channel, depression, ditch, duct, flume, furrow, gully, gutter, trench, watercourse

trounce beat, clobber (*Brit. sl.*), crush, defeat heavily *or* utterly, drub, give a hiding (*Inf.*), give a pasting (*Sl.*), hammer (*Inf.*), lick (*Inf.*), make mincemeat of, overwhelm, paste (*Sl.*), rout, slaughter (*Inf.*), thrash, walk over (*Inf.*), wipe the floor with (*Inf.*)

troupe band, cast, company

trouper actor, artiste, entertainer, performer, player, theatrical, thespian

truancy absence, absence without leave, malingering, shirking, skiving (*Brit. sl.*)

truant 1. *n.* absentee, delinquent, deserter, dodger, malingerer, runaway, shirker, skiver (*Brit. sl.*), straggler **2.** *adj.* absent, absent without leave, A.W.O.L., missing, skiving (*Brit. sl.*)

truce armistice, break, ceasefire, cessation, cessation of hostilities, intermission, interval, let-up (*Inf.*), lull, moratorium, peace, respite, rest, stay, treaty

truck barter, business, buying and selling, commerce, communication, connection, contact, dealings, exchange, relations, trade, traffic

truculent aggressive, antagonistic, bad-tempered, bellicose, belligerent, combative, contentious, cross, defiant, fierce, hostile, ill-tempered, itching *or* spoiling for a fight (*Inf.*), obstreperous, pugnacious, scrappy (*Inf.*), sullen, violent

trudge 1. *v.* clump, drag oneself, footslog, hike, lumber, march, plod, slog, stump, traipse (*Inf.*), tramp, trek, walk heavily, yomp **2.** *n.* footslog, haul, hike, march, slog, traipse (*Inf.*), tramp, trek, yomp

true 1. accurate, actual, authentic, bona fide, correct, exact, factual, genuine, legitimate, natural, precise, pure, real, right, truthful, valid, veracious, veritable **2.** confirmed, constant, dedicated, devoted, dutiful, faithful, fast, firm, honest, honourable, loyal, pure, sincere, staunch, steady, true-blue, trustworthy, trusty, unswerving, upright **3.** accurate, correct, exact, on target, perfect, precise, proper, spot-on (*Brit. inf.*), unerring

truism axiom, bromide, cliché, commonplace, platitude, stock phrase, trite saying

truly 1. accurately, authentically, beyond doubt, beyond question, correctly, exactly, factually, genuinely, in actuality, in fact, in reality, in truth, legitimately, precisely, really, rightly, truthfully, veraciously, veritably, without a doubt **2.** confirmedly, constantly, devotedly, dutifully, faithfully, firmly, honestly, honourably, loyally, sincerely, staunchly, steadily, with all one's heart, with dedication, with devotion **3.** exceptionally, extremely, greatly, indeed, of course, really, to be sure, verily, very

trumpet (ˈtrʌmpɪt) *n.* **1.** metal wind instrument like horn —*vi.* **2.** blow trumpet **3.** make sound like one, as elephant —*vt.* **4.** proclaim, make widely known

truncate (trʌŋˈkeɪt, ˈtrʌŋkeɪt) *vt.* cut short —ˈ**truncated** *a.* **1.** (of cone *etc.*) having apex or end removed by plane intersection **2.** shortened (as if) by cutting off (*also* ˈ**truncate**)

truncheon (ˈtrʌntʃən) *n.* **1.** short thick club or baton **2.** staff of office or authority —*vt.* **3.** cudgel

trundle (ˈtrʌndᵊl) *vt.* roll, as a thing on little wheels

trunk (trʌŋk) *n.* **1.** main stem of tree **2.** person's body without or excluding head and limbs **3.** box for clothes *etc.* **4.** elephant's proboscis —*pl.* **5.** man's swimming costume —**trunk call** long-distance telephone call —**trunk line** main line of railway, canal, telephone *etc.* —**trunk road** main road

truss (trʌs) *vt.* **1.** (*oft. with* up) fasten, tie —*n.* **2.** support **3.** medical device of belt *etc.* to hold hernia in place **4.** package, bundle (of hay *etc.*) **5.** cluster of flowers at end of single stalk

trust (trʌst) *n.* **1.** confidence **2.** firm belief **3.** reliance **4.** combination of producers to reduce competition and keep up prices **5.** care, responsibility **6.** property held for another —*vt.* **7.** rely on **8.** believe in **9.** consign for care —*v.* **10.** expect, hope —**trusˈtee** *n.* one legally holding property on another's behalf —**trusˈteeship** *n.* —ˈ**trustful** *a.* **1.** inclined to trust **2.** credulous —ˈ**trustworthy** *a.* **1.** reliable, dependable, honest **2.** safe —ˈ**trusty** *a.* **1.** faithful **2.** reliable —**trust fund** money, securities *etc.* held in trust

truth (tru:θ) *n. see* TRUE

try (traɪ) *vi.* **1.** attempt, endeavour —*vt.* **2.** attempt **3.** test **4.** make demands upon **5.** investigate (case) **6.** examine (person) in court of law **7.** purify; refine (as metals) (**tried, ˈtrying**) —*n.* **8.** attempt, effort **9.** *Rugby* score gained by touching ball down over opponent's goal line —**tried** *a.* **1.** proved **2.** afflicted —ˈ**trying** *a.* **1.** upsetting, annoying **2.** difficult —**try-on** *n.* UK *inf.* something done to test out person's tolerance *etc.* —ˈ**tryout** *n.* —**trysail** (ˈtraɪseɪl; *Naut.* ˈtraɪsᵊl) *n.* small fore-and-aft sail set on sailing vessel in foul weather to help keep her head to wind —**try on 1.** put on (garment) to find out whether it fits *etc.* **2.** *inf.* attempt to deceive or fool (*esp. in* **try it on**) —**try out 1.** test; put to experimental use **2.** (*usu. with* for) US (of actor *etc.*) undergo test; submit (actor *etc.*) to test to determine suitability for role *etc.*

tryst (trɪst, traɪst) *n.* **1.** appointment to meet **2.** place appointed

tsar, tzar, *or* **czar** (zɑ:) *n.* emperor, king, *esp* of Russia 1547-1917 —**tsaˈritsa, czaˈrina,** *or* **czaˈritsa** *n.* wife of tsar

tsetse fly *or* **tzetze fly** (ˈtsɛtsɪ) Afr. bloodsucking

THESAURUS

trumpery *n.* **1.** balderdash, bilge (*Inf.*), bunkum, claptrap (*Inf.*), drivel, foolishness, foolish talk, garbage, guff (*Sl.*), hogwash, idiocy, inanity, nonsense, poppycock (*Inf.*), rot, rubbish, stuff, trash, tripe (*Inf.*), twaddle **2.** bagatelle, bauble, gewgaw, kickshaw, knick-knack, toy, trifle, trinket ~*adj.* **3.** brummagem, cheap, flashy, meretricious, nasty, rubbishy, shabby, shoddy, tawdry, trashy, trifling, useless, valueless, worthless

trumpet 1. *n.* bugle, clarion, horn **2.** *v.* advertise, announce, broadcast, extol, noise abroad, proclaim, publish, shout from the rooftops, sound loudly, tout (*Inf.*)

trump up concoct, contrive, cook up (*Inf.*), create, fabricate, fake, invent, make up

truncate abbreviate, clip, crop, curtail, cut, cut short, lop, pare, prune, shorten, trim

truncheon baton, club, cudgel, staff

trunk 1. bole, stalk, stem, stock **2.** body, torso **3.** proboscis, snout **4.** bin, box, case, chest, coffer, crate, kist (*Scot.*), locker, portmanteau

truss *v.* **1.** bind, bundle, fasten, make fast, pack, pinion, secure, strap, tether, tie ~*n.* **2.** beam, brace, buttress, joist, prop, shore, stanchion, stay, strut, support **3.** *Medical* bandage, support **4.** bale, bundle, package, packet

trust *n.* **1.** assurance, belief, certainty, certitude, confidence, conviction, credence, credit, expectation, faith, hope, reliance **2.** duty, obligation, responsibility **3.** care, charge, custody, guard, guardianship, protection, safekeeping, trusteeship ~*v.* **4.** assume, believe, expect, hope, presume, suppose, surmise, think likely **5.** bank on, believe, count on, depend on, have faith in, lean on, pin one's faith on, place confidence in, place one's trust in, place reliance on, rely upon, swear by, take at face value **6.** assign, command, commit, confide, consign, delegate, entrust, give, put into the hands of, sign over, turn over

trustful confiding, credulous, gullible, innocent, naive, optimistic, simple, unguarded, unsuspecting, unsuspicious, unwary

trustworthy dependable, ethical, honest, honourable, level-headed, mature, principled, reliable, responsible, righteous, sensible, steadfast, to be trusted, true, trusty, truthful, upright

trusty dependable, faithful, firm, honest, reliable, responsible, solid, staunch, steady, straightforward, strong, true, trustworthy, upright

truth 1. accuracy, actuality, exactness, fact, factuality, factualness, genuineness, legitimacy, precision, reality, truthfulness, validity, veracity, verity **2.** candour, constancy, dedication, devotion, dutifulness, faith, faithfulness, fidelity, frankness, honesty, integrity, loyalty, naturalism, realism, uprightness **3.** axiom, certainty, fact, law, maxim, proven principle, reality, truism, verity

try *v.* **1.** aim, attempt, do one's best, do one's damnedest (*Inf.*), endeavour, essay, exert oneself, have a go (crack, shot, stab, whack), make an attempt, make an effort, seek, strive, struggle, undertake **2.** appraise, check out, evaluate, examine, experiment, inspect, investigate, prove, put to the test, sample, taste, test **3.** afflict, annoy, inconvenience, irk, irritate, pain, plague, strain, stress, tax, tire, trouble, upset, vex, weary **4.** adjudge, adjudicate, examine, hear ~*n.* **5.** attempt, crack (*Inf.*), effort, endeavour, essay, go, shot (*Inf.*), stab, whack (*Inf.*)

trying aggravating (*Inf.*), annoying, arduous, bothersome, difficult, exasperating, fatiguing, hard, irksome, irritating, stressful, taxing, tiresome, tough, troublesome, upsetting, vexing, wearisome

try out appraise, check out, evaluate, experiment with, inspect, put into practice, put to the test, sample, taste, test

tsar autocrat, despot, emperor, head, leader, overlord, ruler, sovereign, tyrant

fly whose bite transmits various diseases to man and animals

T-shirt *or* **tee-shirt** *n.* informal (short-sleeved) sweater, *usu.* of cotton

tsp. teaspoon

T-square *n.* T-shaped ruler for drawing parallel lines, right angles *etc.*

TT *or* **T.T.** 1. teetotal 2. Tourist Trophy 3. tuberculin tested

tub (tʌb) *n.* 1. open wooden vessel like bottom half of barrel 2. small round container 3. bath 4. *inf.* old, slow ship *etc.* —**ˈtubby** *a.* 1. plump 2. shaped like tub

tuba (ˈtju:bə) *n.* valved brass wind instrument of low pitch

tube (tju:b) *n.* 1. long, narrow, hollow cylinder 2. flexible cylinder with cap to hold liquids, pastes 3. (*sometimes* T-) underground electric railway, *esp.* in London 4. *sl., chiefly* US television set —**ˈtubing** *n.* 1. tubes collectively 2. length of tube 3. system of tubes 4. fabric in form of tube —**ˈtubular** *a.* like tube

tuber (ˈtju:bə) *n.* fleshy underground stem of some plants, *eg* potato —**ˈtuberous** *a.*

tubercle (ˈtju:bəkˀl) *n.* 1. any small rounded nodule on skin *etc.* 2. small lesion of tissue, *esp.* produced by tuberculosis —**tuˈbercular** *a.* —**tuˈberculin** *n.* extraction from bacillus used to test for and treat tuberculosis —**tubercuˈlosis** *n.* communicable disease, *esp.* of lungs —**tuberculin tested** (of milk) produced by cows certified as free of tuberculosis

T.U.C. Trades Union Congress

tuck (tʌk) *vt.* 1. push, fold into small space 2. gather, stitch in folds 3. draw, roll together —*n.* 4. stitched fold 5. *inf.* food —**ˈtucker** *n.* strip of linen or lace formerly worn across bosom by women —**tuck-in** *n.* UK *inf.* meal, *esp.* large —**tuck shop** *chiefly* UK shop, *esp.* near school, where cakes and sweets are sold —**tuck in** 1. put to bed and make snug 2. thrust loose ends or sides of (something) into confining space 3. *inf.* eat, *esp.* heartily

Tudor (ˈtju:də) *a.* 1. of the English royal house ruling 1485-1603 2. in, resembling style of this period, *esp.* of architecture

Tues. Tuesday

Tuesday (ˈtju:zdɪ) *n.* third day of week

tufa (ˈtju:fə) *n.* porous rock formed as deposit from springs *etc.*

tuff (tʌf) *n.* hard volcanic rock consisting of consolidated fragments of lava

tuffet (ˈtʌfɪt) *n.* small mound or seat

tuft (tʌft) *n.* bunch of feathers, threads *etc.*

tug (tʌg) *vt.* 1. pull hard or violently 2. haul 3. jerk forward (**-gg-**) —*n.* 4. violent pull 5. ship used to tow other vessels —**tug of war** contest in which two teams pull against one another on a rope

tuition (tju:ˈɪʃən) *n.* 1. teaching, instruction 2. private coaching —**tuˈitional** *a.*

tulip (ˈtju:lɪp) *n.* plant with bright cup-shaped flowers

tulle (tju:l) *n.* kind of fine thin silk or lace

tullibee (ˈtʌləbi:) *n.* Canad. whitefish

tumble (ˈtʌmbˀl) *v.* 1. (cause to) fall, roll, twist *etc.*, *esp.* in play —*vt.* 2. rumple, disturb —*n.* 3. fall 4. somersault —**ˈtumbler** *n.* 1. stemless drinking glass 2. acrobat 3. spring catch in lock —**tumble-down** *a.* dilapidated —**tumble drier** *or* **tumbler drier** machine that dries clothes *etc.* by tumbling in warm air —**tumble to** *inf.* realize, understand

tumbrel *or* **tumbril** (ˈtʌmbrəl) *n.* open cart for taking victims of French Revolution to guillotine

tumefy (ˈtju:mɪfaɪ) *v.* (cause to) swell —**tuˈmescence** *n.* —**tuˈmescent** *a.* (becoming) swollen

tummy (ˈtʌmɪ) *n. inf. childish word for* stomach

tumour *or U.S.* **tumor** (ˈtju:mə) *n.* abnormal growth in or on body

tumult (ˈtju:mʌlt) *n.* violent uproar, commotion —**tuˈmultuous** *a.*

tumulus (ˈtju:mjʊləs) *n.* burial mound, barrow (*pl.* **-li** (-laɪ))

tun (tʌn) *n.* 1. large cask 2. measure of liquid

tuna (ˈtju:nə) *n. see* TUNNY

tundra (ˈtʌndrə) *n.* vast treeless zone between icecap and timber line of N Amer. and Eurasia

tune (tju:n) *n.* 1. melody 2. quality of being in pitch 3. adjustment of musical instrument 4. concord 5. frame of mind —*vt.* 6. put in tune 7. adjust (machine) to obtain most efficient running 8. adjust (radio circuit) —**ˈtuneful** *a.* —**ˈtunefully** *adv.* —**ˈtuner** *n.* —**tune-up** *n.* adjustments to engine to improve performance —**tuning fork** two-pronged metal fork that when struck produces pure note of constant specified pitch —**tune in** adjust (radio, television) to receive (a station, programme) —**tune up** 1. adjust (musical instrument) to particular pitch 2. tune (instruments) to common pitch 3. adjust (engine) in (car *etc.*) to improve performance

THESAURUS

tuck *v.* **1.** fold, gather, insert, push ~*n.* **2.** fold, gather, pinch, pleat **3.** *Inf.* comestibles, eats (*Sl.*), food, grub (*Sl.*), nosh (*Sl.*), scoff (*Sl.*), victuals

tuck in 1. bed down, enfold, fold under, make snug, put to bed, swaddle, wrap up **2.** eat heartily, get stuck in (*Sl.*)

tug 1. *v.* drag, draw, haul, heave, jerk, lug, pull, tow, wrench, yank **2.** *n.* drag, haul, heave, jerk, pull, tow, traction, wrench, yank

tuition education, instruction, lessons, schooling, teaching, training, tutelage, tutoring

tumble 1. *v.* drop, fall, fall end over end, fall headlong, fall head over heels, flop, lose one's footing, pitch, plummet, roll, stumble, topple, toss, trip up **2.** *n.* collapse, drop, fall, flop, headlong fall, plunge, roll, somersault, spill, stumble, toss, trip

tumble-down crumbling, decrepit, dilapidated, disintegrating, falling to pieces, ramshackle, rickety, ruined, shaky, tottering

tumour cancer, carcinoma (*Medical*), growth, lump, neoplasm (*Medical*), sarcoma (*Medical*), swelling

tumult ado, affray (*Law*), agitation, altercation, bedlam, brawl, brouhaha, clamour, commotion, din, disorder, disturbance, excitement, fracas, hubbub, hullabaloo, outbreak, pandemonium, quarrel, racket, riot, row, ruction (*Inf.*), stir, strife, turmoil, unrest, upheaval, uproar

tumultuous agitated, boisterous, clamorous, confused, disorderly, disturbed, excited, fierce, hectic, irregular, lawless, noisy, obstreperous, passionate, raging, restless, riotous, rowdy, rumbustious,

tungsten (ˈtʌŋstən) *n.* greyish-white metal, used in lamp filaments, some steels *etc.*

tunic (ˈtjuːnɪk) *n.* **1.** close-fitting jacket forming part of uniform **2.** loose hiplength or kneelength garment

tunnel (ˈtʌnᵊl) *n.* **1.** underground passage, *esp.* as track for railway line **2.** burrow of a mole *etc.* —*vt.* **3.** make tunnel through —*vi.* **4.** (*with* through, under *etc.*) make or force a way (through or under something) (**-ll-**) —**ˈtunneller** *n.*

tunny (ˈtʌnɪ) *n.* large marine food and game fish

tup (tʌp) *n.* male sheep, ram

tupik (ˈtuːpək) *n.* C tent used as summer shelter by Eskimos

tuppence (ˈtʌpəns) *n. see* **twopence** *at* TWO

tuque (tuːk) *n.* C knitted cap with tapering end

turban (ˈtɜːbᵊn) *n.* **1.** in certain countries, man's headdress, made by coiling length of cloth round head or a cap **2.** woman's hat like this

turbid (ˈtɜːbɪd) *a.* **1.** muddy, not clear **2.** disturbed —**turˈbidity** *or* **ˈturbidness** *n.*

turbine (ˈtɜːbɪn, -baɪn) *n.* rotary engine driven by steam, gas, water or air playing on blades

turbo- (*comb. form*) of, relating to, or driven by a turbine, as in *turbofan*

turbofan (tɜːbəʊˈfæn) *n.* **1.** bypass engine in which large fan driven by turbine forces air rearwards around exhaust gases to increase propulsive thrust **2.** aircraft driven by turbofans **3.** fan in such engine

turbojet (tɜːbəʊˈdʒɛt) *n.* **1.** turbojet engine **2.** aircraft powered by turbojet engines, in which exhaust gasses provide propulsion

turboprop (tɜːbəʊˈprɒp) *n.* **1.** gas turbine for driving aircraft propeller **2.** aircraft powered by turboprops

turbot (ˈtɜːbət) *n.* large European flatfish

turbulent (ˈtɜːbjʊlənt) *a.* **1.** in commotion **2.** swirling **3.** riotous —**ˈturbulence** *n. Met.* instability of atmosphere causing gusty air currents *etc.*

tureen (təˈriːn) *n.* serving dish for soup

turf (tɜːf) *n.* **1.** short grass with earth bound to it by matted roots **2.** grass, *esp.* as lawn (*pl.* **-s, turves**) —*vt.* **3.** lay with turf —**turf accountant** bookmaker —**the turf 1.** horse racing **2.** racecourse —**turf out** *inf.* dismiss, throw out

turgid (ˈtɜːdʒɪd) *a.* **1.** swollen, inflated **2.** bombastic —**turˈgescent** *a.* —**turˈgidity** *n.*

turkey (ˈtɜːkɪ) *n.* large bird reared for its flesh

Turkish (ˈtɜːkɪʃ) *a.* of, pert. to Turkey, the Turks —**Turk** *n.* **1.** native of Turkey **2.** native speaker of any Turkic language **3.** brutal or domineering person —**ˈTurkic** *n.* branch of Altaic family of languages, including Turkish —**Turkish bath** steam bath —**Turkish coffee** very strong black coffee —**Turkish delight** gelatin flavoured and coated with powdered sugar —**Turkish towel** rough, loose-piled towel

turmeric (ˈtɜːmərɪk) *n.* **1.** Asian plant **2.** powdered root of this used as dye, medicine and condiment

turmoil (ˈtɜːmɔɪl) *n.* confusion and bustle, commotion

turn (tɜːn) *v.* **1.** move around, rotate **2.** change, reverse, alter position or direction (of) —*vi.* **3.** (*oft. with* into) change in nature, character *etc.* **4.** (of milk) become rancid or sour —*vt.* **5.** make, shape on lathe —*n.* **6.** act of turning **7.** inclination **8.** period, spell **9.** turning **10.** short walk **11.** (part of) rotation **12.** performance —**ˈturner** *n.* —**ˈturning** *n.* road, path leading off main route —**ˈturnabout** *n.* **1.** act of turning so as to face different direction **2.** reversal of opinion *etc.* —**ˈturncoat** *n.* one who forsakes his party or principles —**turning circle** smallest circle in which vehicle can turn —**turning point 1.** moment when course of events is changed **2.** point at which there is change in direction or motion —**ˈturnkey** *n. obs.* keeper of keys, *esp.* in prison; warder, jailer —**turn-off** *n.* **1.** road *etc.* branching off from main thoroughfare **2.** something or someone that turns one off —**turn-on** *n.* something or someone that turns one on —**ˈturnout** *n.* **1.** number of people appearing for some purpose, occasion **2.** way in which person is dressed, equipped —**ˈturnover** *n.* **1.** total sales made by business over certain period **2.** rate at which staff leave and are replaced **3.** small pasty —**ˈturnpike** *n. Hist.* (gate across) road where toll was paid —**ˈturnstile** *n.* revolving gate for controlling admission of people —**ˈturnstone** *n.* shore bird that lifts up stones in search of food —**ˈturntable** *n.* revolving platform, *esp.* on record-player —**turn-up** *n.* **1.** turned-up fold at bottom of trouser leg **2.** unexpected or chance occurrence —**turn down** refuse —**turn off 1.** leave (road *etc.*) **2.** (of road *etc.*) deviate from (another road *etc.*) **3.** cause (something) to cease operating by turning knob *etc.* **4.** *inf.* cause (person *etc.*) to feel dislike or distaste for (something) —**turn on 1.** cause (something) to operate by turning knob *etc.* **2.** depend or hinge on **3.** become hostile; retaliate **4.** *inf.* produce (charm *etc.*) suddenly or automatically **5.** *sl.* arouse emotionally or sexually **6.** *sl.* take or become intoxicated by drugs **7.** *sl.* introduce to drugs *etc.* —**turn up 1.** appear **2.** be found **3.** increase (flow, volume)

THESAURUS

stormy, turbulent, unrestrained, unruly, uproarious, violent, vociferous, wild

tune *n.* **1.** air, melody, melody line, motif, song, strain, theme **2.** agreement, concert, concord, consonance, euphony, harmony, pitch, sympathy, unison **3.** attitude, demeanour, disposition, frame of mind, mood ~*v.* **4.** adapt, adjust, attune, bring into harmony, harmonize, pitch, regulate

tuneful catchy, consonant (*Music*), easy on the ear (*Inf.*), euphonious, harmonious, mellifluous, melodic, melodious, musical, pleasant, symphonic

tunnel 1. *n.* burrow, channel, hole, passage, passageway, shaft, subway, underpass **2.** *v.* burrow, dig, dig one's way, excavate, mine, penetrate, scoop out, undermine

turbulent 1. agitated, blustery, boiling, choppy, confused, disordered, foaming, furious, raging, rough, tempestuous, tumultuous, unsettled, unstable **2.** agitated, anarchic, boisterous, disorderly, insubordinate, lawless, mutinous, obstreperous, rebellious, refractory, riotous, rowdy, seditious, tumultuous, unbridled, undisciplined, ungovernable, unruly, uproarious, violent, wild

turf 1. clod, divot, grass, green, sod, sward **2. the turf** horse-racing, racecourse, racetrack, racing, the flat

turmoil agitation, bedlam, brouhaha, bustle, chaos, commotion, confusion, disorder, disturbance, ferment, flurry, hubbub, noise, pandemonium, row, stir, strife, trouble, tumult, turbulence, uproar, violence

turn *v.* **1.** circle, go round, gyrate, move in a circle, pivot, revolve, roll, rotate, spin, swivel, twirl, twist,

turnip (ˈtɜːnɪp) *n.* plant with globular root used as food

turpentine (ˈtɜːpᵊntaɪn) *n.* **1.** resin got from certain trees **2.** oil, spirits made from this

turpitude (ˈtɜːpɪtjuːd) *n.* depravity

turps (tɜːps) turpentine

turquoise (ˈtɜːkwɔɪz, -kwɑːz) *n.* **1.** bluish-green precious stone **2.** this colour —*a.* **3.** bluish-green

turret (ˈtʌrɪt) *n.* **1.** small tower **2.** revolving armoured tower for guns on warship, tank *etc.*

turtle (ˈtɜːtᵊl) *n.* sea tortoise —ˈ**turtleneck** *n.* **1.** round high close-fitting neck on sweater **2.** sweater itself

turtledove (ˈtɜːtᵊldʌv) *n.* **1.** Old World dove having brown plumage with speckled wings and long dark tail **2.** gentle or loving person

tusk (tʌsk) *n.* long pointed side tooth of certain animals (*eg* elephant, wild boar *etc.*) —ˈ**tusker** *n.* animal with tusks fully developed

tussle (ˈtʌsᵊl) *n./vi.* fight, wrestle, struggle

tussock (ˈtʌsək) *n.* **1.** clump of grass **2.** tuft —ˈ**tussocky** *a.*

tutelage (ˈtjuːtɪlɪdʒ) *n.* act, office of tutor or guardian —ˈ**tutelary** *or* ˈ**tutelar** *a.*

tutor (ˈtjuːtə) *n.* **1.** one teaching individuals or small groups —*v.* **2.** teach thus —**tuˈtorial** *n.* period of instruction with tutor

tutti (ˈtʊtɪ) *a./adv. Mus.* to be performed by whole orchestra, choir *etc.*

tutti-frutti (ˈtuːtɪˈfruːtɪ) *n.* **1.** ice cream or confection containing small pieces of candied or fresh fruits **2.** preserve of chopped mixed fruits **3.** flavour like that of many fruits combined

tutu (ˈtuːtuː) *n.* short, stiff skirt worn by ballerinas

tu-whit tu-whoo (təˈwɪt təˈwuː) imitation of sound made by owl

tuxedo (tʌkˈsiːdəʊ) *n.* **US** dinner jacket (*pl.* **-s**)

TV television

twaddle (ˈtwɒdᵊl) *n.* silly talk

twain (tweɪn) *n. obs.* two —**in twain** asunder

twang (twæŋ) *n.* **1.** vibrating metallic sound **2.** nasal speech —*v.* **3.** (cause to) make such sounds

tweak (twiːk) *vt.* **1.** pinch and twist or pull —*n.* **2.** a tweaking

twee (twiː) *a. inf.* excessively sentimental, sweet, pretty

tweed (twiːd) *n.* **1.** rough-surfaced cloth used for clothing —*pl.* **2.** suit of tweed —ˈ**tweedy** *a.* **1.** of tweed **2.** showing fondness for hearty outdoor life, usu. associated with wearers of tweeds

tweet (twiːt) *n./vi.* chirp —ˈ**tweeter** *n.* loudspeaker reproducing high-frequency sounds

tweezers (ˈtwiːzəz) *pl.n.* small forceps or tongs

twelve (twɛlv) *n./a.* cardinal number two more than ten —**twelfth** *a./n.* ordinal number —**Twelfth Day** Jan. 6th, twelfth day after Christmas; feast of Epiphany —**twelve-tone** *a.* of type of serial music which uses as musical material tone row formed by 12 semitones of chromatic scale

twenty (ˈtwɛntɪ) *n./a.* cardinal number, twice ten —ˈ**twentieth** *a./n.* ordinal number

THESAURUS

wheel, whirl **2.** change course, change position, go back, move, return, reverse, shift, swerve, switch, veer, wheel **3.** arc, come round, corner, go round, negotiate, pass, pass around, take a bend **4.** adapt, alter, become, change, convert, divert, fashion, fit, form, metamorphose, mould, mutate, remodel, shape, transfigure, transform, transmute **5.** become rancid, curdle, go bad, go off (*Brit. inf.*), go sour, make rancid, sour, spoil, taint **6.** fashion, frame, make, mould, shape ~*n.* **7.** bend, change, circle, curve, cycle, gyration, pivot, reversal, revolution, rotation, spin, swing, turning, twist, whirl **8.** bias, direction, drift, heading, tendency, trend **9.** bend, change of course, change of direction, curve, departure, deviation, shift **10.** chance, crack (*Inf.*), fling, go, opportunity, period, round, shift, shot (*Inf.*), spell, stint, succession, time, try, whack (*Inf.*) **11.** airing, circuit, constitutional, drive, excursion, jaunt, outing, promenade, ride, saunter, spin (*Inf.*), stroll, walk **12.** affinity, aptitude, bent, bias, flair, gift, inclination, knack, leaning, propensity, talent

turn down decline, rebuff, refuse, reject, repudiate, say no to, spurn, throw out

turning bend, crossroads, curve, junction, side road, turn, turn-off

turning point change, climacteric, crisis, critical moment, crossroads, crux, decisive moment, moment of decision, moment of truth

turn off 1. branch off, change direction, depart from, deviate, leave, quit, take another road, take a side road **2.** cut out, kill, put out, shut down, stop, switch off, turn out, unplug **3.** *Inf.* alienate, bore, disenchant, disgust, displease, irritate, lose one's interest, nauseate, offend, put off, repel, sicken

turn on 1. activate, energize, ignite, put on, set in motion, start, start up, switch on **2.** balance, be contingent on, be decided by, depend, hang, hinge, pivot, rest **3.** assail, assault, attack, fall on, lose one's temper with, round on **4.** *Sl.* arouse, arouse one's desire, attract, excite, please, stimulate, thrill, titillate, work up **5.** *Sl.* get high (*Inf.*), get stoned (*Sl.*), take drugs, trip (*Inf.*) **6.** *Sl.* expose, get one started with, inform, initiate, introduce, show

turnover 1. business, flow, output, outturn (*Rare*), production, productivity, volume, yield **2.** change, coming and going, movement, replacement

turn up 1. appear, arrive, attend, come, put in an appearance, show (*Sl.*), show one's face, show up (*Inf.*) **2.** appear, become known, be found, bring to light, come to light, come to pass, come up with, crop up (*Inf.*), dig up, disclose, discover, expose, find, pop up, reveal, transpire, unearth **3.** amplify, boost, enhance, increase, increase the volume of, intensify, make louder, raise

tussle 1. *v.* battle, brawl, contend, fight, grapple, scrap (*Inf.*), scuffle, struggle, vie, wrestle **2.** *n.* battle, bout, brawl, competition, conflict, contention, contest, fight, fracas, fray, punch-up (*Inf.*), scrap (*Inf.*), scuffle, set-to (*Inf.*), struggle

tutor 1. *n.* coach, educator, governor, guardian, guide, guru, instructor, lecturer, master, mentor, preceptor, schoolmaster, teacher **2.** *v.* coach, direct, discipline, drill, edify, educate, guide, instruct, lecture, school, teach, train

tutorial individual instruction, lesson, seminar

tweak *v./n.* jerk, nip, pinch, pull, squeeze, twist, twitch

twerp *or* **twirp** (twɜːp) *n. inf.* silly person

twice (twaɪs) *adv.* two times

twiddle (ˈtwɪdᵊl) *v.* **1.** fiddle —*vt.* **2.** twist

twig[1] (twɪg) *n.* small branch, shoot

twig[2] (twɪg) *v. inf.* notice; understand (**-gg-**)

twilight (ˈtwaɪlaɪt) *n.* soft light after sunset —ˈ**twilit** *a.* —**twilight zone 1.** inner-city area where houses have become dilapidated **2.** any indefinite or transitional condition or area

twill (twɪl) *n.* fabric woven so as to have surface of parallel ridges

twin (twɪn) *n.* **1.** one of pair, *esp.* of two children born together —*a.* **2.** being a twin —*v.* **3.** pair, be paired —**twin-set** *n.* **UK** matching jumper and cardigan —**twin town UK** town that has civic associations with foreign town

twine (twaɪn) *v.* **1.** twist, coil round —*n.* **2.** string, cord

twinge (twɪndʒ) *n.* **1.** momentary sharp, shooting pain **2.** qualm

twinkle (ˈtwɪŋkᵊl) *vi.* **1.** shine with dancing or quivering light, sparkle —*n.* **2.** twinkling **3.** flash **4.** gleam of amusement in eyes —ˈ**twinkling** *n.* very brief time

twirl (twɜːl) *v.* **1.** turn or twist round quickly **2.** whirl —*vt.* **3.** twiddle —*n.* **4.** rotating; being rotated; whirl, twist **5.** something wound around or twisted; coil **6.** written flourish

twist (twɪst) *v.* **1.** make, become spiral, by turning with one end fast **2.** distort, change **3.** wind —*n.* **4.** thing twisted **5.** dance popular in 1960s, in which dancers vigorously twist the hips —ˈ**twister** *n. inf.* swindler —ˈ**twisty** *a.*

twit (twɪt) *n.* **1.** *inf.* foolish person —*vt.* **2.** taunt (**-tt-**)

twitch (twɪtʃ) *v.* **1.** give momentary sharp pull or jerk (to) —*n.* **2.** such pull or jerk **3.** spasmodic jerk, spasm

twitter (ˈtwɪtə) *vi.* **1.** (of birds) utter succession of tremulous sounds —*n.* **2.** such succession of notes

two (tuː) *n./a.* cardinal number, one more than one —ˈ**twofold** *a./adv.* —ˈ**twosome** *n.* **1.** two together, *esp.* two people **2.** match between two people —**two-edged** *a.* **1.** having two cutting edges **2.** (*esp.* of remark) having two interpretations —**two-faced** *a.* **1.** double-dealing, deceitful **2.** with two faces —**twopence** *or* **tuppence** (ˈtʌpəns) *n.* **UK 1.** sum of two pennies **2.** something of little value (*esp. in* **not care** *or* **give twopence**) **3.** formerly, Brit. silver coin —**twopenny** *or* **tuppenny** (ˈtʌpənɪ) *a. chiefly* **UK 1.** cheap, tawdry (*also* **twopenny-halfpenny**) **2.** worth two pence —**two-ply** *a.* **1.** made of two layers, strands *etc.* —*n.* **2.** two-ply knitting yarn *etc.* —**two-step** *n.* **1.** ballroom dance in duple time **2.** music for such dance —**two-stroke** *a.* (of internal combustion engine) making one explosion to every two strokes of piston —**two-time** *v. inf.* deceive (someone, *esp.* lover) by carrying on relationship with another —**two-timer** *n.*

TX Texas

-ty[1] (*comb. form*) multiple of ten, as in *sixty, seventy*

-ty[2] (*comb. form*) state, condition, quality, as in *cruelty*

tycoon (taɪˈkuːn) *n.* powerful, influential businessman

tyke *or* **tike** (taɪk) *n.* **1.** *inf.* small, cheeky child **2.** small (mongrel) dog

tympani (ˈtɪmpənɪ) *pl.n. see* TIMPANI

tympanum (ˈtɪmpənəm) *n.* **1.** cavity of middle ear **2.** tympanic membrane **3.** any diaphragm resembling that in middle ear in function **4.** *Archit.* recessed space, *esp.* triangular, bounded by cornices of pediment **5.** recessed space bounded by arch and lintel of doorway or window below it **6.** *Mus.* drum **7.** scoop wheel for raising water (*pl.* **-s, -na** (-nə)) —**tym**ˈ**panic** *a.* —**tympanic membrane** thin membrane separating external ear from middle ear

Tynwald (ˈtɪnwəld, ˈtaɪn-) *n.* Parliament of Isle of Man

type (taɪp) *n.* **1.** class, sort **2.** model; pattern **3.** characteristic build **4.** specimen **5.** block bearing letter used for printing **6.** such pieces collectively —*vt.* **7.** print with typewriter **8.** typify **9.** classify —ˈ**typist** *n.* one

THESAURUS

twig branch, offshoot, shoot, spray, sprig, stick, withe

twilight dimness, dusk, evening, gloaming (*Scot.*), half-light, sundown, sunset

twin 1. *n.* clone, corollary, counterpart, double, duplicate, fellow, likeness, lookalike, match, mate, ringer (*Sl.*) **2.** *adj.* corresponding, double, dual, duplicate, geminate, identical, matched, matching, paired, parallel, twofold **3.** *v.* couple, join, link, match, pair, yoke

twine *n.* **1.** cord, string, yarn ~*v.* **2.** braid, entwine, interlace, interweave, knit, plait, splice, twist, twist together, weave **3.** bend, coil, curl, encircle, loop, meander, spiral, surround, twist, wind, wrap, wreathe

twinge bite, gripe, pain, pang, pinch, prick, sharp pain, spasm, stab, stitch, throb, throe (*Rare*), tic, tweak, twist, twitch

twinkling flash, instant, jiffy (*Inf.*), moment, second, shake (*Inf.*), split second, tick (*Inf.*), trice, twinkle, two shakes of a lamb's tail (*Inf.*)

twirl *v.* **1.** gyrate, pirouette, pivot, revolve, rotate, spin, turn, turn on one's heel, twiddle, twist, wheel, whirl, wind ~*n.* **2.** gyration, pirouette, revolution, rotation, spin, turn, twist, wheel, whirl **3.** coil, spiral, twist

twist *v.* **1.** coil, corkscrew, curl, encircle, entwine, intertwine, screw, spin, swivel, twine, weave, wind, wrap, wreathe, wring **2.** contort, distort, screw up **3.** alter, change, distort, falsify, garble, misquote, misrepresent, pervert, warp ~*n.* **4.** coil, curl, spin, swivel, twine, wind **5.** braid, coil, curl, hank, plug, quid, roll **6.** arc, bend, convolution, curve, meander, turn, undulation, zigzag **7.** defect, deformation, distortion, flaw, imperfection, kink, warp

twister cheat, con man (*Inf.*), crook (*Inf.*), deceiver, fraud, rogue, swindler, trickster

twit ass, blockhead, chump (*Inf.*), clown, dope (*Sl.*), fool, halfwit, idiot, juggins (*Brit. inf.*), nincompoop, ninny, nitwit, silly-billy (*Inf.*), simpleton, twerp (*Inf.*)

twitch 1. *v.* blink, flutter, jerk, jump, pluck, pull, snatch, squirm, tug, yank **2.** *n.* blink, flutter, jerk, jump, pull, spasm, tic, tremor, twinge

two-edged ambiguous, ambivalent, backhanded, double-edged, equivocal

two-faced deceitful, deceiving, dissembling, double-dealing, duplicitous, false, hypocritical, insincere, Janus-faced, perfidious, treacherous, untrustworthy

tycoon baron, big cheese (*Sl.*), big noise (*Sl.*), capitalist, captain of industry, fat cat (*Sl.*), financier, industrialist, magnate, merchant prince, mogul, plutocrat, potentate, wealthy businessman

who operates typewriter —ˈ**typo** *n. inf.* error in typing —ˈ**typecast** *vt.* cast (actor) in same kind of role continually —ˈ**typeface** *n.* **1.** printing surface of any type character **2.** style or design of character on type (*also* **face**) —ˈ**typescript** *n.* typewritten document or copy —ˈ**typesetter** *n.* **1.** person who sets type; compositor **2.** typesetting machine —ˈ**typewrite** *v.* —ˈ**typewriter** *n.* keyed writing machine

-type (*comb. form*) **1.** type, form, as in *archetype* **2.** printing type; photographic process, as in *collotype*

typhoid (ˈtaɪfɔɪd) *n.* **1.** acute infectious disease, affecting *esp.* intestines —*a.*, *also* **tyˈphoidal** **2.** resembling typhus —ˈ**typhus** *n.* infectious disease

typhoon (taɪˈfuːn) *n.* violent tropical storm or cyclone —**typhonic** (taɪˈfɒnɪk) *a.*

typical (ˈtɪpɪkᵊl) *or* **typic** *a.* **1.** true to type **2.** characteristic —ˈ**typically** *adv.*

typify (ˈtɪpɪfaɪ) *vt.* serve as type or model of (**-ified, -ifying**)

typography (taɪˈpɒgrəfɪ) *n.* **1.** art of printing **2.** style of printing —**tyˈpographer** *n.* —**typoˈgraphical** *a.*

tyrannosaur (tɪˈrænəsɔː) *or* **tyrannosaurus** (tɪrænəˈsɔːrəs) *n.* large carnivorous two-footed dinosaur common in N Amer. in Upper Jurassic and Cretaceous times

tyrant (ˈtaɪrənt) *n.* **1.** oppressive or cruel ruler **2.** one who forces his will on others cruelly and arbitrarily —**tyrannical** (tɪˈrænɪkᵊl) *a.* **1.** despotic **2.** ruthless —**tyrannically** (tɪˈrænɪkəlɪ) *adv.* —**tyrannicide** (tɪˈrænɪsaɪd) *n.* **1.** slayer of tyrant **2.** his deed —**tyrannize** *or* **-ise** (ˈtɪrənaɪz) *v.* exert ruthless or tyrannical authority (over) —**tyrannous** (ˈtɪrənəs) *a.* —**tyranny** (ˈtɪrənɪ) *n.* despotism

tyre *or U.S.* **tire** (taɪə) *n.* **1.** (inflated) rubber ring over rim of road vehicle **2.** metal band on rim of cart wheel

Tyrian (ˈtɪrɪən) *n.* **1.** native of ancient Tyre, port in S Lebanon and centre of ancient Phoenician culture —*a.* **2.** of ancient Tyre

tyro *or* **tiro** (ˈtaɪrəʊ) *n.* novice, beginner (*pl.* **-s**)

tzar (zɑː) *n. see* TSAR

tzetze fly (ˈtsɛtsɪ) *see* TSETSE FLY

THESAURUS

type 1. breed, category, class, classification, form, genre, group, ilk, kidney, kind, order, sort, species, strain, subdivision, variety **2.** case, characters, face, fount, print, printing **3.** archetype, epitome, essence, example, exemplar, model, original, paradigm, pattern, personification, prototype, quintessence, specimen, standard

typhoon cyclone, squall, storm, tempest, tornado, tropical storm

typical archetypal, average, characteristic, classic, conventional, essential, illustrative, in character, indicative, in keeping, model, normal, orthodox, representative, standard, stock, true to type, usual

typify characterize, embody, epitomize, exemplify, illustrate, incarnate, personify, represent, sum up, symbolize

tyrannical absolute, arbitrary, authoritarian, autocratic, coercive, cruel, despotic, dictatorial, domineering, high-handed, imperious, inhuman, magisterial, oppressive, overbearing, overweening, peremptory, ruthless, severe, tyrannous, unjust, unreasonable

tyranny absolutism, authoritarianism, autocracy, coercion, cruelty, despotism, dictatorship, harsh discipline, high-handedness, imperiousness, oppression, peremptoriness, reign of terror, unreasonableness

tyrant absolutist, authoritarian, autocrat, bully, despot, dictator, Hitler, martinet, oppressor, slave-driver

tyro apprentice, beginner, catechumen, greenhorn (*Inf.*), initiate, learner, neophyte, novice, novitiate, pupil, student, trainee

U

u *or* **U** (juː) *n.* **1.** 21st letter of English alphabet **2.** any of several speech sounds represented by this letter, as in *mute, cut* or *minus* **3.** something shaped like U (*pl.* **u's, U's** *or* **Us**)

U **1.** united **2.** unionist **3.** university **4.** UK universal (used to describe category of film certified as suitable for viewing by anyone) **5.** *Chem.* uranium

U.A.E. United Arab Emirates

UB40 *n.* UK **1.** registration card issued by Department of Employment to person registering as unemployed **2.** *inf.* person registered as unemployed

ubiquitous (juːˈbɪkwɪtəs) *a.* **1.** everywhere at once **2.** omnipresent —**uˈbiquity** *n.*

U-boat *n.* German submarine

u.c. *Print.* upper case

udder (ˈʌdə) *n.* milk-secreting organ of cow *etc.*

UDI Unilateral Declaration of Independence

UEFA (juːˈeɪfə, ˈjuːfə) Union of European Football Associations

UFO (*sometimes* ˈjuːfəʊ) unidentified flying object

ugh (ʊx, ʊh, ʌh) *interj.* exclamation of disgust, annoyance *etc.*

ugly (ˈʌglɪ) *a.* **1.** unpleasant or repulsive to the sight, hideous **2.** ill-omened **3.** threatening —**ˈuglify** *v.* —**ˈugliness** *n.* —**ugly duckling** person or thing, initially ugly or unpromising, that changes into something beautiful or admirable

UHF ultrahigh frequency

UHT ultra heat treated

U.K. United Kingdom

ukase (juːˈkeɪz) *n.* in imperial Russia, edict of Czar

Ukrainian (juːˈkreɪnɪən) *a.* **1.** of Ukraine —*n.* **2.** East Slavonic language of Ukrainians **3.** native or inhabitant of Ukraine

ukulele *or* **ukelele** (juːkəˈleɪlɪ) *n.* small four-stringed guitar, *esp.* of Hawaii

ulcer (ˈʌlsə) *n.* open sore on skin, mucous membrane that is slow to heal —**ˈulcerate** *v.* make, form ulcer(s) —**ˈulcerated** *a.* —**ulceˈration** *n.* —**ˈulcerous** *a.*

ulna (ˈʌlnə) *n.* longer of two bones of forearm (*pl.* **ulnae** (ˈʌlniː), **-s**)

ulster (ˈʌlstə) *n.* man's heavy double-breasted overcoat

ult. **1.** ultimate **2.** ultimo

ulterior (ʌlˈtɪərɪə) *a.* **1.** lying beneath, beyond what is revealed or evident (*eg* motives) **2.** situated beyond

ultimate (ˈʌltɪmɪt) *a.* **1.** last **2.** highest **3.** most significant **4.** fundamental —**ˈultimately** *adv.* —**ultimatum** (ʌltɪˈmeɪtəm) *n.* **1.** final proposition **2.** final terms offered (*pl.* **-s, -ta** (-tə)) —**ˈultimo** *adv.* in last month

ultra (ˈʌltrə) *a.* **1.** extreme, *esp.* in beliefs or opinions —*n.* **2.** extremist

ultra- (*comb. form*) beyond, excessive(ly), extreme(ly) as in *ultramodern*

ultrahigh frequency (ˈʌltrəhaɪ) (band of) radio waves of very short wavelength

ultramarine (ʌltrəməˈriːn) *n.* blue pigment

ultrasonic (ʌltrəˈsɒnɪk) *a.* of sound waves beyond the range of human ear —**ultraˈsonics** *pl.n.* (*with sing. v.*) branch of physics concerned with ultrasonic waves (*also* **superˈsonics**)

ultrasound (ʌltrəˈsaʊnd) *n.* ultrasonic waves, used in cleaning metallic parts, echo sounding, medical diagnosis *etc.*

ultraviolet (ʌltrəˈvaɪəlɪt) *a.* of electromagnetic radiation, *eg* of sun *etc.*, beyond limit of visibility at violet end of spectrum

ululate (ˈjuːljʊleɪt) *vi.* howl, wail —**ˈululant** *a.* —**uluˈlation** *n.*

umbel (ˈʌmbᵊl) *n.* umbrellalike flower cluster with stalks springing from central point —**umbelˈliferous** *a.*

umber (ˈʌmbə) *n.* dark brown pigment

umbilical (ʌmˈbɪlɪkᵊl, ʌmbɪˈlaɪkᵊl) *a.* of (region of) navel —**umˈbilicus** *n.* **1.** *Biol.* hollow structure, such as cavity at base of gastropod shell **2.** *Anat.* navel (*pl.* **-bilici** (-ˈbɪlɪsaɪ, -bəˈlaɪsaɪ)) —**umbilical cord** **1.** cordlike structure connecting foetus with placenta of mother **2.** cord joining astronaut to spacecraft *etc.*

umbra (ˈʌmbrə) *n.* **1.** region of complete shadow due to obstruction of light by opaque object, *esp.* shadow cast by moon onto earth during solar eclipse **2.** darker inner region of sunspot (*pl.* **-brae** (-briː), **-s**) —**ˈumbral** *a.*

umbrage (ˈʌmbrɪdʒ) *n.* offence, resentment (*esp.* in **give** *or* **take umbrage**)

umbrella (ʌmˈbrɛlə) *n.* **1.** folding circular cover of nylon *etc.* on stick, carried in hand to protect against rain, heat of sun **2.** anything shaped or functioning like an umbrella

THESAURUS

ubiquitous all-over, ever-present, everywhere, omnipresent, pervasive, universal

ugly **1.** hard-favoured, hard-featured, homely (*Chiefly U.S.*), ill-favoured, misshapen, not much to look at, plain, unattractive, unlovely, unprepossessing, unsightly **2.** disagreeable, disgusting, distasteful, frightful, hideous, horrid, monstrous, objectionable, offensive, repugnant, repulsive, revolting, shocking, terrible, unpleasant, vile **3.** dangerous, forbidding, menacing, ominous, sinister, threatening

ulcer abscess, boil, fester, gathering, gumboil, peptic ulcer, pustule, sore

ulterior concealed, covert, hidden, personal, secondary, secret, selfish, undisclosed, unexpressed

ultimate *adj.* **1.** conclusive, decisive, end, eventual, extreme, final, furthest, last, terminal **2.** extreme, greatest, highest, maximum, most significant, paramount, superlative, supreme, topmost, utmost **3.** basic, elemental, fundamental, primary, radical

ultimately after all, at last, basically, eventually, finally, fundamentally, in due time, in the end, sooner or later

umbrage anger, chagrin, displeasure, grudge, high dudgeon, huff, indignation, offence, pique, resentment, sense of injury

umbrella brolly (*Brit. inf.*), gamp (*Brit. inf.*)

umiak *or* **oomiak** (ˈuːmɪæk) *n.* Eskimo boat made of skins

umlaut (ˈʊmlaʊt) *n.* **1.** mark (¨) placed over vowel in some languages, such as German **2.** *esp.* in Germanic languages, change of vowel within word caused by assimilating influence of vowel or semivowel in preceding or following syllable

umpire (ˈʌmpaɪə) *n.* **1.** person chosen to decide question, or to decide disputes and enforce rules in a game —*v.* **2.** act as umpire in or for (game *etc.*)

umpteen (ʌmpˈtiːn) *a. inf.* many —**umpˈteenth** *n./a.*

UN *or* **U.N.** United Nations

un- (*comb. form*) not, contrary to, opposite of, reversal of an action, removal from, release, deprivation. See the list below

unaccountable (ʌnəˈkaʊntəbˀl) *a.* that cannot be explained

unaffected[1] (ʌnəˈfɛktɪd) *a.* unpretentious, natural, sincere —**unafˈfectedly** *adv.*

unaffected[2] (ʌnəˈfɛktɪd) *a.* not affected

unanimous (juːˈnænɪməs) *a.* **1.** in complete agree-

unaˈbated
unaˈbridged
unacˈceptable
unacˈcompanied
unacˈcustomed
unacˈknowledged
unacˈquainted
unaˈdorned
unaˈdulterated
unadˈventurous
unaˈfraid
unˈaided
unalˈloyed
unˈalterable
unamˈbiguous
unˈanswerable
unapˈpealing
unˈappetizing
unapˈpreciated
unapˈproachable
unˈarmed
unaˈshamed
unˈasked
unatˈtainable
unatˈtended
unatˈtractive
unˈauthorized
unaˈvailable
unˈbalanced
unˈbearable
unˈbeaten
unbeˈcoming
unbeˈlievable
unbeˈliever
unbeˈlieving
unˈbias(s)ed
unˈbind
unˈblemished
unˈblinking
unˈblock
unˈbolt
unˈborn
unˈbreakable
unˈbroken
unˈbuckle
uncared-for
unˈceasing
unˈcensored
unˈcensured
unˈcertain
unˈchallenged
uncharacteˈristic
unˈcharitable
unˈchecked
unˈchristian
unˈcircumcized
unˈcivil
unˈclaimed
unˈclear
unˈclothe
unˈcluttered
unˈcoil
unˈcombed

THESAURUS

umpire 1. *n.* adjudicator, arbiter, arbitrator, judge, moderator, ref (*Inf.*), referee **2.** *v.* adjudicate, arbitrate, call (*Sport*), judge, moderate, referee

unabridged complete, full-length, uncondensed, uncut, unexpurgated, unshortened, whole

unacceptable disagreeable, displeasing, distasteful, improper, inadmissible, insupportable, objectionable, offensive, undesirable, unpleasant, unsatisfactory, unwelcome

unaccompanied a cappella (*Music*), alone, by oneself, lone, on one's own, solo, unescorted

unaccountable baffling, incomprehensible, inexplicable, inscrutable, mysterious, odd, peculiar, puzzling, strange, unexplainable, unfathomable, unintelligible

unaccustomed 1. *With* **to** a newcomer to, a novice at, green, inexperienced, not given to, not used to, unfamiliar with, unpractised, unused to, unversed in **2.** new, out of the ordinary, remarkable, special, strange, surprising, uncommon, unexpected, unfamiliar, unprecedented, unusual, unwonted

unaffected[1] artless, genuine, honest, ingenuous, naive, natural plain, simple, sincere, straightforward, unassuming, unpretentious, unsophisticated, unspoilt, unstudied, without airs

unaffected[2] aloof, impervious, not influenced, proof, unaltered unchanged, unimpressed, unmoved, unresponsive, unstirred, untouched

unafraid confident, daring, dauntless, fearless, intrepid, unfearing, unshakable

unalterable fixed, fixed as the laws of the Medes and the Persians, immutable, invariable, permanent, steadfast, unchangeable, unchanging

unanimity accord, agreement, chorus, concert, concord, concurrence, consensus, harmony, like-mindedness, one mind, unison, unity

unanimous agreed, agreeing, at one, common, concerted, concordant, harmonious, in agreement, in complete accord, like-minded, of one mind, united

unanimously by common consent, nem. con., unitedly, unopposed, with one accord, without exception, without opposition

unanswerable insoluble, insolvable, unascertainable, unexplainable, unresolvable

unappetizing distasteful, insipid, off-putting (*Brit. inf.*), tasteless, unappealing, unattractive, uninteresting, uninviting, unpalatable, unpleasant, unsavoury, vapid

unapproachable 1. aloof, chilly, cool, distant, frigid, offish (*Inf.*), remote, reserved, standoffish, unfriendly, unsociable, withdrawn **2.** inaccessible, out of reach, out-of-the-way, remote, un-get-at-able (*Inf.*), unreachable

unarmed assailable, defenceless, exposed, helpless, open, open to attack, unarmoured, unprotected, weak, weaponless, without arms

ment **2.** agreed by all —**una'nimity** *n.* —**u'nanimously** *adv.*

unassailable (ʌnə'seɪləbᵊl) *a.* **1.** able to withstand attack **2.** irrefutable —**unas'sailably** *adv.*

unassuming (ʌnə'sju:mɪŋ) *a.* not pretentious, modest

unattached (ʌnə'tætʃt) *a.* **1.** not connected with any specific thing, group *etc.* **2.** not engaged or married

unavailing (ʌnə'veɪlɪŋ) *a.* useless, futile

unaware (ʌnə'wɛə) *a.* not aware, uninformed —**una'wares** *adv.* **1.** without previous warning **2.** unexpectedly

unbend (ʌn'bɛnd) *v.* **1.** release or be released from restraints of formality **2.** *inf.* relax (mind) or (of mind) become relaxed **3.** make or become straight from original bent shape (-**'bent,** -**'bending**) —**un'bending** *a.* **1.** rigid, inflexible **2.** characterized by sternness or severity

unbidden (ʌn'bɪdᵊn) *a.* **1.** not commanded; voluntary, spontaneous **2.** not invited

un'comfortable
uncom'mitted
un'common
uncom'municative
uncom'plaining
un'complicated
uncompli'mentary
uncon'cerned
uncon'ditional
uncon'firmed
uncon'nected
un'conquered
uncon'trollable
uncon'trolled
uncontro'versial
uncon'ventional
uncon'vincing
unco'operative
unco'ordinated
un'cork
uncor'roborated
un'couple
un'critical
un'crowned
un'cultivated
un'cultured
un'curbed
un'curl
un'damaged
un'daunted
unde'cided
unde'feated
unde'fended
unde'manding
undemo'cratic
unde'monstrative
unde'niable
under'bid *v.*
'underbid *n.*
'underclothes
under'do
under'done
underem'ployed
under'foot
'undergarment
under'lie
under'manned
under'nourish
under'paid
'underpants
'underpart
under'priced
under'sea
under'sexed
'undershirt
under'sized
'underskirt
under'staffed
under'state
under'value
under'water
under'weight
unde'served

THESAURUS

unassailable 1. impregnable, invincible, invulnerable, secure, well-defended **2.** absolute, conclusive, incontestable, incontrovertible, indisputable, irrefutable, positive, proven, sound, undeniable

unassuming diffident, humble, meek, modest, quiet, reserved, retiring, self-effacing, simple, unassertive, unobtrusive, unostentatious, unpretentious

unattached 1. autonomous, free, independent, nonaligned, unaffiliated, uncommitted **2.** a free agent, available, by oneself, footloose and fancy-free, not spoken for, on one's own, single, unengaged, unmarried

unattended abandoned, disregarded, ignored, left alone, not cared for, unguarded, unwatched

unauthorized illegal, unapproved, unconstitutional, unlawful, unofficial, unsanctioned, unwarranted

unavailing abortive, bootless, fruitless, futile, idle, ineffective, ineffectual, of no avail, pointless, to no purpose, unproductive, unsuccessful, useless, vain

unaware heedless, ignorant, incognizant, oblivious, unconscious, unenlightened, uninformed, unknowing, unmindful, unsuspecting

unawares aback, abruptly, by surprise, off guard, on the hop (*Brit. inf.*), suddenly, unexpectedly, unprepared, without warning

unbalanced asymmetrical, irregular, lopsided, not balanced, shaky, unequal, uneven, unstable, unsymmetrical, wobbly

unbearable insufferable, insupportable, intolerable, oppressive, too much (*Inf.*), unacceptable, unendurable

unbeaten triumphant, unbowed, undefeated, unsubdued, unsurpassed, unvanquished, victorious, winning

unbecoming 1. ill-suited, inappropriate, incongruous, unattractive, unbefitting, unfit, unflattering, unsightly, unsuitable, unsuited **2.** discreditable, improper, indecorous, indelicate, offensive, tasteless, unseemly

unbelievable astonishing, beyond belief, far-fetched, implausible, impossible, improbable, inconceivable, incredible, outlandish, preposterous, questionable, staggering, unconvincing, unimaginable, unthinkable

unbeliever agnostic, atheist, disbeliever, doubting Thomas, infidel, sceptic

unbending 1. aloof, distant, formal, inflexible, reserved, rigid, stiff, uptight (*Sl.*) **2.** firm, hard-line, intractable, resolute, severe, strict, stubborn, tough, uncompromising, unyielding

unbiased disinterested, dispassionate, equitable, even-handed, fair, impartial, just, neutral, objective, open-minded, unprejudiced

unbidden 1. free, spontaneous, unforced, unprompted, voluntary, willing **2.** unasked, uninvited, unwanted, unwelcome

unbind free, loosen, release, set free, unchain, undo,

unbosom (ʌnˈbʊzəm) *vt.* tell or reveal (one's secrets *etc.*)

unbounded (ʌnˈbaʊndɪd) *a.* having no boundaries or limits —**unˈboundedly** *adv.*

unbridled (ʌnˈbraɪdˀld) *a.* **1.** with all restraints removed **2.** (of horse *etc.*) wearing no bridle

unburden (ʌnˈbɜːdˀn) *vt.* **1.** remove load or burden from **2.** relieve, make free (one's mind, oneself *etc.*) of worry *etc.* by revelation or confession

uncalled-for *a.* unnecessary; unwarranted

uncanny (ʌnˈkænɪ) *a.* weird, mysterious

uncial (ˈʌnsɪəl) *a.* **1.** of majuscule letters, as used in Greek and Latin manuscripts of third to ninth centuries, that resemble modern capitals but are more rounded —*n.* **2.** uncial letter or manuscript —**ˈuncially** *adv.*

uncle (ˈʌŋkˀl) *n.* **1.** brother of father or mother **2.** husband of aunt

undeˈserving
undeˈsirable
undeˈtected
undeˈterred
undeˈveloped
undiˈminished
unˈdisciplined
undisˈcovered
undisˈputed
undisˈturbed
unˈdying
unˈearned
unecoˈnomic
unˈeducated
uneˈmotional
unˈending
unˈequal
unˈequalled
uneˈquivocal
unˈethical
unˈeven
uneˈventful
unexˈpected
unexˈplained
unˈfailing
unˈfair
unˈfaithful
unfaˈmiliar
unˈfashionable
unˈfavourable
unˈfeeling
unˈfeigned
unˈfinished
unˈfit
unˈflinching
unˈfold
unforeˈseen
unforˈgettable
unforˈgivable
unˈfortunate
unˈfounded
unˈfurl
unˈgodly
unˈgovernable
unˈgracious
ungramˈmatical
unˈgrateful
unˈhallowed
unˈhappy
unˈharmed
unˈhealthy
unˈheard
unheard-of
unˈheated
unˈheeded
unˈhelpful
unˈhurried
unˈhurt
unhyˈgienic
uniˈdentified
uniˈmaginable
uniˈmaginative
unimˈpaired

THESAURUS

unfasten, unfetter, unloose, unshackle, untie, unyoke

unblemished flawless, immaculate, perfect, pure, spotless, unflawed, unspotted, unstained, unsullied, untarnished

unbounded absolute, boundless, endless, immeasurable, infinite, limitless, unbridled, unchecked, unconstrained, uncontrolled, unlimited, unrestrained, vast

unbreakable armoured, durable, indestructible, infrangible, lasting, nonbreakable, resistant, rugged, shatterproof, solid, strong, toughened

unbridled excessive, intemperate, licentious, rampant, riotous, unchecked, unconstrained, uncontrolled, uncurbed, ungovernable, ungoverned, unrestrained, unruly, violent, wanton

unbroken **1.** complete, entire, intact, solid, total, unimpaired, whole **2.** ceaseless, constant, continuous, endless, incessant, progressive, serried, successive, uninterrupted, unremitting

unburden **1.** disburden, discharge, disencumber, ease the load, empty, lighten, relieve, unload **2.** come clean (*Inf.*), confess, confide, disclose, get (something) off one's chest (*Inf.*), lay bare, make a clean breast of, reveal, tell all, unbosom

uncalled-for gratuitous, inappropriate, needless, undeserved, unjust, unjustified, unnecessary, unprovoked, unwarranted, unwelcome

uncanny creepy (*Inf.*), eerie, eldritch (*Poetic*), mysterious, preternatural, queer, spooky (*Inf.*), strange, supernatural, unearthly, unnatural, weird

unceasing ceaseless, constant, continual, continuing, continuous, endless, incessant, never-ending, nonstop, perpetual, persistent, unending, unfailing, unremitting

uncertain **1.** ambiguous, chancy, conjectural, doubtful, incalculable, indefinite, indeterminate, indistinct, questionable, risky, speculative, undetermined, unforeseeable, unpredictable **2.** ambivalent, doubtful, dubious, hazy, in two minds, irresolute, unclear, unconfirmed, undecided, undetermined, unfixed, unresolved, unsettled, unsure, up in the air, vacillating, vague

uncharitable cruel, hardhearted, insensitive, mean, merciless, stingy, unchristian, unfeeling, unforgiving, unfriendly, ungenerous, unkind, unsympathetic

uncivil bad-mannered, bearish, boorish, brusque, churlish, discourteous, disrespectful, gruff, ill-bred, ill-mannered, impolite, rude, surly, uncouth, unmannerly

uncomfortable awkward, causing discomfort, cramped, disagreeable, hard, ill-fitting, incommodious, irritating, painful, rough, troublesome

uncommitted floating, free, free-floating, neutral, nonaligned, nonpartisan, not involved, (sitting) on the fence, unattached, uninvolved

uncommon **1.** bizarre, curious, few and far between, infrequent, novel, odd, out of the ordinary, peculiar, queer, rare, scarce, singular, strange, unfamiliar, unusual **2.** distinctive, exceptional, extraordinary, incomparable, inimitable, notable, noteworthy, out-

uncompromising (ʌnˈkɒmprəmaɪzɪŋ) *a.* not prepared to compromise —**unˈcompromisingly** *adv.*

unconscionable (ʌnˈkɒnʃənəbˀl) *a.* **1.** unscrupulous, unprincipled **2.** excessive

unconscious (ʌnˈkɒnʃəs) *a.* **1.** insensible **2.** not aware **3.** not knowing **4.** (of thoughts, memories *etc.*) of which one is not normally aware —*n.* **5.** these thoughts —**unˈconsciously** *adv.* —**unˈconsciousness** *n.*

uncounted (ʌnˈkaʊntɪd) *a.* **1.** innumerable **2.** not counted

uncouth (ʌnˈku:θ) *a.* **1.** clumsy, boorish **2.** without ease or polish

unimˈportant
unimˈpressed
uninˈformed
uninˈhabited
uninˈhibited
unˈinjured
uninˈspired
uninˈsured
uninˈtelligent
uninˈtelligible
uninˈtended
uninˈtentional
unˈinteresting
uninterˈrupted
uninˈvited
uninˈviting
unˈjustified
unˈkind
unˈknown
unˈlabelled
unˈladylike
unˈlawful
unˈlearned
unˈleash
unˈlettered
unˈlike
unˈlikely
unˈlimited
unˈlined
unˈload
unˈlock
unlooked-for
unˈlucky
unˈmade
unˈmake
unˈmanageable
unˈmanned
unˈmannerly
unˈmarked
unˈmarried
unˈmask
unˈmentionable
unˈmerciful
unˈmerited
unmisˈtak(e)able
unˈmoved
unˈmusical
unˈnamed
unˈnatural
unˈnecessary
unˈnoticed
unobˈservant
unobˈserved
unobˈtainable
unobˈtrusive
unˈoccupied
unofˈficial
unˈopened
unopˈposed
unˈorganized
unˈorthodox
unˈpack
unˈpaid

THESAURUS

standing, rare, remarkable, singular, special, superior, unparalleled, unprecedented

uncommunicative close, curt, guarded, reserved, reticent, retiring, secretive, short, shy, silent, taciturn, tight-lipped, unforthcoming, unresponsive, unsociable, withdrawn

uncompromising decided, firm, hard-line, inexorable, inflexible, intransigent, obdurate, obstinate, rigid, steadfast, strict, stubborn, tough, unbending, unyielding

unconcerned 1. aloof, apathetic, cool, detached, dispassionate, distant, incurious, indifferent, oblivious, uninterested, uninvolved, unmoved, unsympathetic **2.** blithe, carefree, careless, easy, insouciant, nonchalant, not bothered, relaxed, serene, unperturbed, unruffled, untroubled, unworried

unconditional absolute, categorical, complete, downright, entire, explicit, full, out-and-out, outright, plenary, positive, thoroughgoing, total, unlimited, unqualified, unreserved, unrestricted, utter

unconnected detached, disconnected, divided, independent, separate

unconscionable 1. amoral, criminal, unethical, unfair, unjust, unprincipled, unscrupulous **2.** excessive, exorbitant, extravagant, extreme, immoderate, inordinate, outrageous, preposterous, unreasonable

unconscious 1. blacked out (*Inf.*), comatose, dead to the world, insensible, knocked out, numb, out, out cold, senseless, stunned **2.** blind to, deaf to, heedless, ignorant, in ignorance, lost to, oblivious, unaware, unknowing, unmindful, unsuspecting **3.** automatic, gut (*Inf.*), inherent, innate, instinctive, involuntary, latent, reflex, repressed, subconscious, subliminal, suppressed, unrealized

uncontrollable beside oneself, carried away, frantic, furious, irrepressible, irresistible, like one possessed, mad, strong, ungovernable, unmanageable, unruly, violent, wild

uncontrolled boisterous, furious, lacking self-control, out of control, out of hand, rampant, riotous, running wild, unbridled, unchecked, uncurbed, undisciplined, ungoverned, unrestrained, unruly, unsubmissive, untrammelled, violent

unconventional atypical, bizarre, bohemian, different, eccentric, far-out (*Sl.*), freakish (*Inf.*), idiosyncratic, individual, individualistic, informal, irregular, nonconformist, odd, offbeat, original, out of the ordinary, uncustomary, unorthodox, unusual, way-out (*Inf.*)

unconvincing dubious, feeble, fishy (*Inf.*), flimsy, hard to believe, implausible, improbable, inconclusive, lame, questionable, specious, suspect, thin, unlikely, unpersuasive, weak

uncounted countless, infinite, innumerable, legion, multitudinous, myriad, numberless, unnumbered, untold

uncouth awkward, barbaric, boorish, clownish, clumsy, coarse, crude, gawky, graceless, gross, ill-mannered, loutish, lubberly, oafish, rough, rude, rustic, uncivilized, uncultivated, ungainly, unrefined, unseemly, vulgar

uncover 1. bare, lay open, lift the lid, open, show, strip, take the wraps off, unwrap **2.** bring to light, disclose, discover, divulge, expose, lay bare, make known, reveal, unearth, unmask

uncover (ʌnˈkʌvə) *vt.* **1.** remove cover, top *etc.* from **2.** reveal, disclose *—v.* **3.** take off (one's head covering), *esp.* as mark of respect

unction (ˈʌŋkʃən) *n.* **1.** anointing **2.** excessive politeness **3.** soothing words or thoughts —ˈ**unctuous** *a.* **1.** slippery, greasy **2.** oily in manner, ingratiating

undeceive (ʌndɪˈsiːv) *vt.* reveal truth to (someone mistaken, misled)

under (ˈʌndə) *prep.* **1.** below, beneath **2.** bound by, included in **3.** less than **4.** subjected to **5.** known by **6.** in the time of *—adv.* **7.** in lower place or condition *—a.* **8.** lower —**under way 1.** in progress **2.** *Naut.* in motion in direction headed

under- (*comb. form*) beneath, below, lower, too little, as in *underground, underbid.* Such words are not given where the meaning can be deduced from the meaning(s) of the simple word

underage (ʌndərˈeɪdʒ) *a.* below required age, *esp.* below legal age for voting or drinking

undercarriage (ˈʌndəkærɪdʒ) *n.* landing gear of aircraft

undercoat (ˈʌndəkəʊt) *n.* coat of paint applied before top coat

undercover (ʌndəˈkʌvə) *a.* done or acting in secret

undercurrent (ˈʌndəkʌrənt) *n.* **1.** current that lies beneath another current **2.** opinion, emotion *etc.* lying beneath apparent feeling or meaning (*also* ˈ**underflow**)

undercut (ʌndəˈkʌt) *v.* **1.** charge less than (competitor) in order to obtain trade **2.** cut away under part of (something) **3.** *Sport* hit (ball) in such a way as to impart backspin *—n.* (ˈʌndəkʌt) **4.** act of cutting underneath **5.** tenderloin of beef **6.** *Sport* stroke that imparts backspin to ball

underdeveloped (ʌndədɪˈvɛləpt) *a.* **1.** immature;

unˈpardonable
unˈpick
unˈpin
unˈpleasant
unˈpleasing
unˈplumbed
unˈpopular
unˈpractised
unˈprecedented
unpreˈdictable
unpreˈpared
unpreposˈsessing
unpreˈtentious
unˈprintable
unproˈductive
unproˈfessional
unˈprofitable
unˈpromising
unproˈpitious
unproˈtected
unproˈvoked
unˈqualified
unˈquestionable
unˈreal
unreaˈlistic
unˈreasonable
unˈregistered
unreˈlenting
unreˈliable
unreˈpentant
unrepreˈsentative
unreˈquited
unreˈserved
unreˈsolved
unreˈstrained
unˈrighteous
unˈripe
unˈrivalled
unˈruffled
unˈsaddle
unˈsafe
unˈsaid
unˈsaleable
unsatisˈfactory
unˈscathed
unˈscheduled
unscienˈtific
unˈscramble
unˈscrew
unˈscrupulous
unˈseasonable
unˈseat
unˈseemly
unselfˈconscious
unˈselfish
unˈsettle
unˈshak(e)able
unˈsheathe
unˈskilful
unˈskilled
unˈsociable
unˈsocial
unsoˈlicited

THESAURUS

undeceive be honest with, correct, disabuse, disillusion, enlighten, open (someone's) eyes (to), put (someone) right, set (someone) straight, shatter (someone's) illusions

undecided 1. ambivalent, dithering, doubtful, dubious, hesitant, in two minds, irresolute, swithering (*Scot.*), torn, uncertain, uncommitted, unsure, wavering **2.** debatable, indefinite, in the balance, moot, open, pending, tentative, unconcluded, undetermined, unsettled, up in the air, vague

undefended defenceless, exposed, naked, open to attack, unarmed, unfortified, unguarded, unprotected, vulnerable, wide open

undemonstrative aloof, cold, contained, distant, formal, impassive, reserved, restrained, reticent, stiff, stolid, unaffectionate, uncommunicative, unemotional, unresponsive, withdrawn

undeniable beyond (a) doubt, beyond question, certain, clear, evident, incontestable, incontrovertible, indisputable, indubitable, irrefutable, manifest, obvious, patent, proven, sound, sure, unassailable, undoubted, unquestionable

under *prep.* **1.** below, beneath, on the bottom of, underneath **2.** belonging to, comprised in, included in, subsumed under *~adv.* **3.** below, beneath, down, downward, lower, to the bottom

underclothes lingerie, smalls (*Inf.*), underclothing, undergarments, underlinen, underthings (*Inf.*), underwear, undies (*Inf.*)

undercover clandestine, concealed, confidential, covert, hidden, hush-hush (*Inf.*), intelligence, private, secret, spy, surreptitious, underground

undercurrent 1. crosscurrent, rip, rip current, riptide, underflow, undertow **2.** atmosphere, aura, drift, feeling, flavour, hidden feeling, hint, murmur, overtone, sense, suggestion, tendency, tenor, tinge, trend, undertone, vibes (*Inf.*), vibrations

undercut 1. sacrifice, sell at a loss, sell cheaply, undercharge, underprice, undersell **2.** cut away, cut out, excavate, gouge out, hollow out, mine, undermine

undersized **2.** relating to societies lacking economical and industrial development necessary to advance **3.** *Photog.* (of film *etc.*) processed in developer for less than required time

underdog (ˈʌndədɒg) *n.* **1.** losing competitor in contest *etc.* **2.** person in position of inferiority

underestimate (ʌndərˈɛstɪmeɪt) *vt.* **1.** make too low an estimate of **2.** think insufficiently highly of *—n.* (ʌndərˈɛstɪmɪt) **3.** too low an estimate **—underestiˈmation** *n.*

underexpose (ʌndərɪkˈspəʊz) *vt.* **1.** *Photog.* expose (film *etc.*) for too short a period or with insufficient light **2.** fail to subject to appropriate publicity **—underexˈposure** *n.*

undergo (ʌndəˈgəʊ) *vt.* experience, endure, sustain (**-ˈwent, -ˈgone, -ˈgoing**)

undergraduate (ʌndəˈgrædjʊɪt) *n.* student member of university or college who has not taken degree

underground (ˈʌndəgraʊnd) *a.* **1.** under the ground **2.** secret *—adv.* (ʌndəˈgraʊnd) **3.** under earth's surface **4.** secretly *—n.* **5.** secret but organized resistance to government in power **6.** railway system under the ground

undergrowth (ˈʌndəgrəʊθ) *n.* small trees, bushes *etc.* growing beneath taller trees in wood or forest

underhand (ˈʌndəhænd) *a.* **1.** secret, sly **2.** *Sport* underarm

underlay (ʌndəˈleɪ) *vt.* **1.** place (something) under or beneath **2.** support by something laid beneath (**-ˈlaid, -ˈlaying**) *—n.* (ˈʌndəleɪ) **3.** lining, support *etc.* laid underneath something else **4.** felt, rubber *etc.* laid beneath carpet to increase insulation

underline (ʌndəˈlaɪn) *vt.* **1.** put line under **2.** emphasize

underling (ˈʌndəlɪŋ) *n.* subordinate

underlying (ʌndəˈlaɪɪŋ) *a.* **1.** concealed but detectable **2.** fundamental; basic **3.** lying under

undermine (ʌndəˈmaɪn) *vt.* **1.** wear away base, support of **2.** weaken insidiously

underneath (ʌndəˈniːθ) *adv.* **1.** below *—prep.* **2.** under *—a.* **3.** lower *—n.* **4.** lower part, surface *etc.*

unˈsolved
unsoˈphisticated
unˈsound
unˈsparing
unˈspecified
unˈspoken
unˈsporting
unˈstable
unˈsteady
unˈstinted
unsubˈstantiated
unsucˈcessful
unˈsuitable
unˈsure
unsurˈpassed
unsusˈpected
unsusˈpecting
unˈsweetened
unsympaˈthetic
unsysteˈmatic
unˈtainted
unˈtamed
unˈtangle
unˈtapped
unˈtaught
unˈtaxed
unˈthinking
unˈthrone
unˈtidy
unˈtimely
unˈtrained
unˈtroubled
unˈtrue
unˈtrustworthy
unˈtruthful
unˈtutored
unˈtwist
unˈtypical
unˈusable
unˈused
unˈusual
unˈutterable
unˈveil
unˈverified
unˈvoiced
unˈwanted
unˈwarranted
unˈwary
unˈwashed
unˈwavering
unˈwelcome
unˈwholesome
unˈwilling
unˈwind
unˈwise
unˈworkable
unˈworldly
unˈworn
unˈworthy
unˈwrap
unˈwritten
unˈyielding
unˈzip

THESAURUS

underdog fall guy (*Inf.*), little fellow (*Inf.*), loser, victim, weaker party

underestimate belittle, hold cheap, minimize, miscalculate, misprize, not do justice to, rate too low, sell short (*Inf.*), set no store by, think too little of, underrate, undervalue

undergo bear, be subjected to, endure, experience, go through, stand, submit to, suffer, sustain, weather, withstand

underground *adj.* **1.** below ground, below the surface, buried, covered, subterranean **2.** clandestine, concealed, covert, hidden, secret, surreptitious, undercover *~n.* **the underground 3.** the metro, the subway, the tube (*Brit.*) **4.** the Maquis, partisans, the Resistance

undergrowth bracken, brambles, briars, brush, brushwood, scrub, underbrush, underbush, underwood

underhand clandestine, crafty, crooked (*Inf.*), deceitful, deceptive, devious, dishonest, dishonourable, fraudulent, furtive, secret, secretive, sly, sneaky, stealthy, surreptitious, treacherous, underhanded, unethical, unscrupulous

underline 1. italicize, mark, rule a line under, underscore **2.** accentuate, bring home, call *or* draw attention to, emphasize, give emphasis to, highlight, point up, stress

underling flunky, hireling, inferior, lackey, menial, minion, nonentity, retainer, servant, slave, subordinate, understrapper

underlying 1. concealed, hidden, latent, lurking, veiled **2.** basal, basic, elementary, essential, fundamental, intrinsic, primary, prime, root

undermine 1. dig out, eat away at, erode, excavate, mine, tunnel, undercut, wear away **2.** debilitate, disable, impair, sabotage, sap, subvert, threaten, weaken

underpass ('ʌndəpɑːs) *n.* section of road passing under another road, railway line *etc.*

underpin (ʌndə'pɪn) *vt.* **1.** support from beneath, *esp.* by prop **2.** give corroboration or support to (**-nn-**)

underprivileged (ʌndə'prɪvɪlɪdʒd) *a.* lacking rights and advantages of other members of society

underseal ('ʌndəsiːl) *n.* UK coating of tar *etc.*, applied to underside of motor vehicle to retard corrosion

underside ('ʌndəsaɪd) *n.* bottom or lower surface

understand (ʌndə'stænd) *v.* **1.** know and comprehend **2.** realize —*vt.* **3.** infer **4.** take for granted (**-'stood, -'standing**) —**under'standable** *a.* —**under'standably** *adv.* —**under'standing** *n.* **1.** intelligence **2.** opinion **3.** agreement —*a.* **4.** sympathetic

understudy ('ʌndəstʌdɪ) *n.* **1.** one prepared to take over theatrical part from performer if necessary —*vt.* **2.** act as understudy (to) or learn (part) thus

undertake (ʌndə'teɪk) *vt.* **1.** make oneself responsible for **2.** enter upon **3.** promise (**-'took, -'taken, -'taking**) —**'undertaker** *n.* one who arranges funerals —**'undertaking** *n.* **1.** that which is undertaken **2.** project **3.** guarantee

undertone ('ʌndətəʊn) *n.* **1.** quiet, dropped tone of voice **2.** underlying tone or suggestion

undertow ('ʌndətəʊ) *n.* **1.** backwash of wave **2.** current beneath surface moving in different direction from surface current

underwear ('ʌndəwɛə) *n.* garments worn next to skin (*also* **'underclothes**)

underworld ('ʌndəwɜːld) *n.* **1.** criminals and their associates **2.** *Myth.* abode of the dead

underwrite ('ʌndəraɪt, ʌndə'raɪt) *vt.* **1.** agree to pay **2.** accept liability in (insurance policy) (**-'wrote, -'written, -'writing**) —**'underwriter** *n.* **1.** one that underwrites **2.** agent for insurance company who assesses risks

undies ('ʌndɪz) *pl.n. inf.* women's underwear

undo (ʌn'duː) *vt.* **1.** untie, unfasten **2.** reverse **3.** cause downfall of (**-'did, -'done, -'doing**) —**un'doing** *n.* —**un'done** *a.* **1.** ruined **2.** not performed

THESAURUS

underprivileged badly off, deprived, destitute, disadvantaged, impoverished, in need, in want, needy, poor

undersized atrophied, dwarfish, miniature, pygmy, runtish, runty, small, squat, stunted, tiny, underdeveloped, underweight

understand **1.** appreciate, apprehend, be aware, catch on (*Inf.*), comprehend, conceive, cotton on (*Inf.*), discern, fathom, follow, get, get the hang of (*Inf.*), get to the bottom of, grasp, know, make head or tail of (*Inf.*), make out, penetrate, perceive, realize, recognize, savvy (*Sl.*), see, take in, tumble to (*Inf.*), twig (*Brit. inf.*) **2.** assume, be informed, believe, conclude, gather, hear, infer, learn, presume, suppose, take it, think

understanding *n.* **1.** appreciation, awareness, comprehension, discernment, grasp, insight, intelligence, judgment, knowledge, penetration, perception, sense **2.** belief, conclusion, estimation, idea, interpretation, judgment, notion, opinion, perception, view, viewpoint **3.** accord, agreement, common view, gentlemen's agreement, meeting of minds, pact ~*adj.* **4.** accepting, compassionate, considerate, discerning, forbearing, forgiving, kind, kindly, patient, perceptive, responsive, sensitive, sympathetic, tolerant

understood **1.** implicit, implied, inferred, tacit, unspoken, unstated **2.** accepted, assumed, axiomatic, presumed, taken for granted

understudy *n.* double, fill-in, replacement, reserve, stand-in, sub, substitute

undertake **1.** agree, bargain, commit oneself, contract, covenant, engage, guarantee, pledge, promise, stipulate, take upon oneself **2.** attempt, begin, commence, embark on, endeavour, enter upon, set about, tackle, take on, try

undertaker funeral director, mortician (*U.S.*)

undertaking **1.** affair, attempt, business, effort, endeavour, enterprise, game, operation, project, task, venture **2.** assurance, commitment, guarantee, pledge, promise, solemn word, vow, word, word of honour

undertone **1.** low tone, murmur, subdued voice, whisper **2.** atmosphere, feeling, flavour, hint, suggestion, tinge, touch, trace, undercurrent

undervalue depreciate, hold cheap, look down on, make light of, minimize, misjudge, misprize, set no store by, underestimate, underrate

underwater submarine, submerged, sunken, undersea

under way afoot, begun, going on, in motion, in operation, in progress, started

underwear lingerie, smalls (*Inf.*), underclothes, underclothing, undergarments, underlinen, undies (*Inf.*), unmentionables

underweight half-starved, puny, skin and bone, skinny, undernourished, undersized

underworld **1.** criminal element, criminals, gangland (*Inf.*), gangsters, organized crime **2.** abode of the dead, Hades, hell, infernal region, nether regions, nether world, the inferno

underwrite back, finance, fund, guarantee, insure, provide security, sponsor, subsidize

undesirable disagreeable, disliked, distasteful, dreaded, objectionable, obnoxious, offensive, out of place, repugnant, (to be) avoided, unacceptable, unattractive, unpleasing, unpopular, unsavoury, unsuitable, unwanted, unwelcome, unwished-for

undeveloped embryonic, immature, inchoate, in embryo, latent, potential, primordial (*Biol.*)

undisciplined disobedient, erratic, fitful, obstreperous, uncontrolled, unpredictable, unreliable, unrestrained, unruly, unschooled, unsteady, unsystematic, untrained, wayward, wild, wilful

undisputed accepted, acknowledged, beyond question, certain, conclusive, freely admitted, incontestable, incontrovertible, indisputable, irrefutable, not disputed, recognized, sure, unchallenged, uncontested, undeniable, undoubted, unquestioned

undisturbed **1.** not moved, quiet, uninterrupted, untouched, without interruption **2.** calm, collected, composed, equable, even, motionless, placid, serene, tranquil, unagitated, unbothered, unperturbed, unruffled, untroubled

undo **1.** disengage, disentangle, loose, loosen, open, unbutton, unfasten, unlock, untie, unwrap **2.** annul, cancel, invalidate, neutralize, nullify, offset, reverse,

undoubted (ʌnˈdaʊtɪd) *a.* certain; indisputable —**unˈdoubtedly** *adv.*

undue (ʌnˈdjuː) *a.* **1.** excessive **2.** improper; illegal —**unˈduly** *adv.* immoderately

undulate (ˈʌndjʊleɪt) *v.* move up and down like waves —**unduˈlation** *n.* —**ˈundulatory** *a.*

unearth (ʌnˈɜːθ) *vt.* **1.** dig up **2.** discover

unearthly (ʌnˈɜːθlɪ) *a.* **1.** ghostly; eerie **2.** heavenly; sublime **3.** ridiculous or unreasonable (*esp. in* **unearthly hour**) —**unˈearthliness** *n.*

uneasy (ʌnˈiːzɪ) *a.* **1.** anxious **2.** uncomfortable

unemployed (ʌnɪmˈplɔɪd) *a.* having no paid employment, out of work —**unemˈployment** *n.*

unerring (ʌnˈɜːrɪŋ) *a.* **1.** not missing the mark **2.** consistently accurate

UNESCO (juːˈnɛskəʊ) United Nations Educational, Scientific and Cultural Organization

unexceptionable (ʌnɪkˈsɛpʃənəbˀl) *a.* beyond criticism or objection —**unexˈceptionably** *adv.*

unexceptional (ʌnɪkˈsɛpʃənˀl) *a.* **1.** ordinary or normal **2.** subject to or allowing no exceptions —**unexˈceptionally** *adv.*

THESAURUS

wipe out **3.** bring to naught, defeat, destroy, impoverish, invalidate, mar, overturn, quash, ruin, shatter, subvert, undermine, upset, wreck

undoing collapse, defeat, destruction, disgrace, downfall, humiliation, overthrow, overturn, reversal, ruin, ruination, shame

undone incomplete, left, neglected, not completed, not done, omitted, outstanding, passed over, unattended to, unfinished, unfulfilled, unperformed

undoubted acknowledged, certain, definite, evident, incontrovertible, indisputable, indubitable, obvious, sure, undisputed, unquestionable, unquestioned

undoubtedly assuredly, beyond a shadow of (a) doubt, beyond question, certainly, definitely, doubtless, of course, surely, undeniably, unmistakably, unquestionably, without doubt

undue disproportionate, excessive, extravagant, extreme, immoderate, improper, inordinate, intemperate, needless, overmuch, too great, too much, uncalled-for, undeserved, unnecessary, unseemly, unwarranted

unduly disproportionately, excessively, extravagantly, immoderately, improperly, inordinately, out of all proportion, overly, overmuch, unjustifiably, unnecessarily, unreasonably

undying constant, continuing, deathless, eternal, everlasting, immortal, imperishable, indestructible, inextinguishable, infinite, perennial, permanent, perpetual, sempiternal (*Literary*), undiminished, unending, unfading

unearth **1.** dig up, disinter, dredge up, excavate, exhume **2.** bring to light, discover, expose, ferret out, find, reveal, root up, turn up, uncover

unearthly **1.** eerie, eldritch (*Poetic*), ghostly, haunted, nightmarish, phantom, spectral, spooky (*Inf.*), strange, uncanny, weird **2.** ethereal, heavenly, not of this world, preternatural, sublime, supernatural **3.** abnormal, absurd, extraordinary, ridiculous, strange, ungodly (*Inf.*), unholy (*Inf.*), unreasonable

uneasy **1.** agitated, anxious, apprehensive, discomposed, disturbed, edgy, ill at ease, impatient, jittery (*Inf.*), nervous, on edge, perturbed, restive, restless, troubled, uncomfortable, unsettled, upset, worried **2.** awkward, constrained, insecure, precarious, shaky, strained, tense, uncomfortable, unstable

uneconomic loss-making, nonpaying, non-profit-making, nonviable, unprofitable

uneducated ignorant, illiterate, unlettered, unread, unschooled, untaught

unemotional apathetic, cold, cool, impassive, indifferent, listless, passionless, phlegmatic, reserved, undemonstrative, unexcitable, unfeeling, unimpressionable, unresponsive

unemployed idle, jobless, laid off, on the dole (*Brit. inf.*), out of a job, out of work, redundant, resting (*of an actor*), workless

unending ceaseless, constant, continual, endless, eternal, everlasting, incessant, interminable, never-ending, perpetual, unceasing, unremitting

unequal **1.** different, differing, disparate, dissimilar, not uniform, unlike, unmatched, variable, varying **2.** asymmetrical, disproportionate, ill-matched, irregular, unbalanced, uneven

unequivocal absolute, certain, clear, clear-cut, decisive, definite, direct, evident, explicit, incontrovertible, indubitable, manifest, plain, positive, straight, unambiguous, uncontestable, unmistakable

unethical dirty, dishonest, dishonourable, disreputable, illegal, immoral, improper, shady (*Inf.*), underhand, unfair, unprincipled, unprofessional, unscrupulous, wrong

uneven **1.** bumpy, not flat, not level, not smooth, rough **2.** disparate, ill-matched, one-sided, unequal, unfair

uneventful boring, commonplace, dull, humdrum, monotonous, ordinary, quiet, routine, tedious, unexceptional, unexciting, uninteresting, unmemorable, unremarkable, unvaried

unexceptional common or garden (*Inf.*), commonplace, conventional, insignificant, mediocre, normal, ordinary, pedestrian, run-of-the-mill, undistinguished, unimpressive, unremarkable, usual

unexpected abrupt, accidental, astonishing, chance, fortuitous, not bargained for, out of the blue, startling, sudden, surprising, unanticipated, unforeseen, unlooked-for, unpredictable

unfair **1.** arbitrary, biased, bigoted, discriminatory, inequitable, one-sided, partial, partisan, prejudiced, unjust **2.** crooked (*Inf.*), dishonest, dishonourable, uncalled-for, unethical, unprincipled, unscrupulous, unsporting, unwarranted, wrongful

unfaithful **1.** deceitful, disloyal, faithless, false, false-hearted, perfidious, recreant (*Archaic*), traitorous, treacherous, treasonable, unreliable, untrustworthy **2.** adulterous, faithless, fickle, inconstant, two-timing (*Inf.*), unchaste, untrue

unfamiliar **1.** alien, curious, different, little known, new, novel, out-of-the-way, strange, unaccustomed, uncommon, unknown, unusual **2.** *With* **with** a stranger to, inexperienced in, unaccustomed to, unacquainted, unconversant, uninformed about, uninitiated in, unpractised in, unskilled at, unversed in

unfashionable antiquated, behind the times, dated, obsolete, old-fashioned, old hat, out, outmoded, out of date, out of fashion, passé, unpopular

unfavourable **1.** adverse, bad, contrary, disadvanta-

unfortunate (ʌnˈfɔːtʃənɪt) *a.* **1.** causing or attended by misfortune **2.** unlucky or unhappy **3.** regrettable; unsuitable *—n.* **4.** unlucky person **—unˈfortunately** *adv.*

unfounded (ʌnˈfaʊndɪd) *a.* **1.** (of ideas, allegations *etc.*) baseless **2.** not yet established **—unˈfoundedly** *adv.*

unfrock (ʌnˈfrɒk) *vt.* deprive (person in holy orders) of ecclesiastical status

ungainly (ʌnˈgeɪnlɪ) *a.* awkward, clumsy

unguarded (ʌnˈgɑːdɪd) *a.* **1.** unprotected; vulnerable **2.** open; frank **3.** incautious

unguent (ˈʌŋgwənt) *n.* ointment

ungulate (ˈʌŋgjʊlɪt, -leɪt) *n.* any of large group of mammals all of which have hooves

unhinge (ʌnˈhɪndʒ) *vt.* **1.** remove (door *etc.*) from its hinges **2.** unbalance (person, his mind *etc.*)

unholy (ʌnˈhəʊlɪ) *a.* **1.** not holy or sacred **2.** immoral or depraved **3.** *inf.* outrageous; unnatural

uni- (*comb. form*) one, as in *unicorn, uniform.* Such words are not given here where the meanings may easily be inferred from the simple word

UNICEF (ˈjuːnɪsɛf) United Nations International Children's Emergency Fund

unicellular (juːnɪˈsɛljʊlə) *a.* (of organisms and certain algae) consisting of single cell **—unicelluˈlarity** *n.*

unicorn (ˈjuːnɪkɔːn) *n.* mythical horselike animal with single long horn

THESAURUS

geous, hostile, ill-suited, infelicitous, inimical, low, negative, poor, unfortunate, unfriendly, unsuited **2.** inauspicious, inopportune, ominous, threatening, unlucky, unpromising, unpropitious, unseasonable, untimely, untoward

unfeeling 1. apathetic, callous, cold, cruel, hardened, hardhearted, heartless, inhuman, insensitive, pitiless, stony, uncaring, unsympathetic **2.** insensate, insensible, numb, sensationless

unfinished deficient, half-done, imperfect, incomplete, in the making, lacking, unaccomplished, uncompleted, undone, unfulfilled, wanting

unfit 1. ill-equipped, inadequate, incapable, incompetent, ineligible, no good, not cut out for, not equal to, not up to, unprepared, unqualified, untrained, useless **2.** ill-adapted, inadequate, inappropriate, ineffective, not designed, not fit, unsuitable, unsuited, useless **3.** debilitated, decrepit, feeble, flabby, in poor condition, out of kelter, out of shape, out of trim, unhealthy

unflinching bold, constant, determined, firm, resolute, stalwart, staunch, steadfast, steady, unfaltering, unshaken, unshrinking, unswerving, unwavering

unfold disentangle, expand, flatten, open, spread out, straighten, stretch out, undo, unfurl, unravel, unroll, unwrap

unforeseen abrupt, accidental, out of the blue, startling, sudden, surprise, surprising, unanticipated, unexpected, unlooked-for, unpredicted

unforgettable exceptional, extraordinary, fixed in the mind, impressive, memorable, never to be forgotten, notable

unforgivable deplorable, disgraceful, indefensible, inexcusable, shameful, unjustifiable, unpardonable, unwarrantable

unfortunate 1. adverse, calamitous, disastrous, ill-fated, ill-starred, inopportune, ruinous, unfavourable, untoward **2.** cursed, doomed, hapless, hopeless, luckless, out of luck, poor, star-crossed, unhappy, unlucky, unprosperous, unsuccessful, wretched **3.** deplorable, ill-advised, inappropriate, infelicitous, lamentable, regrettable, unbecoming, unsuitable

unfounded baseless, fabricated, false, groundless, idle, spurious, trumped up, unjustified, unproven, unsubstantiated, vain, without basis, without foundation

ungainly awkward, clumsy, gangling, gawky, inelegant, loutish, lubberly, lumbering, slouching, uncoordinated, uncouth, ungraceful

ungodly blasphemous, corrupt, depraved, godless, immoral, impious, irreligious, profane, sinful, vile, wicked

ungovernable rebellious, refractory, uncontrollable, unmanageable, unrestrainable, unruly, wild

ungracious bad-mannered, churlish, discourteous, ill-bred, impolite, offhand, rude, uncivil, unmannerly

ungrateful heedless, ingrate (*Archaic*), selfish, thankless, unappreciative, unmindful, unthankful

unguarded 1. careless, foolhardy, heedless, ill-considered, impolitic, imprudent, incautious, indiscreet, rash, thoughtless, uncircumspect, undiplomatic, unthinking, unwary **2.** defenceless, open to attack, undefended, unpatrolled, unprotected, vulnerable **3.** artless, candid, direct, frank, guileless, open, straightforward

unhappy blue, crestfallen, dejected, depressed, despondent, disconsolate, dispirited, down, downcast, gloomy, long-faced, melancholy, miserable, mournful, sad, sorrowful

unharmed in one piece (*Inf.*), intact, safe, safe and sound, sound, undamaged, unhurt, uninjured, unscarred, unscathed, untouched, whole, without a scratch

unhealthy 1. ailing, delicate, feeble, frail, infirm, in poor health, invalid, poorly (*Inf.*), sick, sickly, unsound, unwell, weak **2.** deleterious, detrimental, harmful, insalubrious, insanitary, noisome, noxious, unwholesome

unheard-of 1. little known, obscure, undiscovered, unfamiliar, unknown, unregarded, unremarked, unsung **2.** inconceivable, never before encountered, new, novel, singular, unbelievable, undreamed of, unexampled, unique, unprecedented, unusual

unhinge 1. confound, confuse, craze, derange, disorder, distemper (*Archaic*), drive out of one's mind, madden, unbalance, unsettle **2.** detach, disconnect, disjoint, dislodge, remove

unholy 1. base, corrupt, depraved, dishonest, evil, heinous, immoral, iniquitous, irreligious, profane, sinful, ungodly, vile, wicked **2.** *Inf.* appalling, awful, dreadful, horrendous, outrageous, shocking, unearthly, ungodly (*Inf.*), unnatural, unreasonable

unhurried calm, deliberate, easy, easy-going, leisurely, sedate, slow, slow and steady, slow-paced

unidentified anonymous, mysterious, nameless, un-

uniform (ˈjuːnɪfɔːm) *n.* **1.** identifying clothes worn by members of same group, *eg* soldiers, nurses *etc.* —*a.* **2.** not changing, unvarying **3.** regular, consistent **4.** conforming to same standard or rule —**uniˈformity** *n.* sameness —**ˈuniformly** *adv.*

unify (ˈjuːnɪfaɪ) *v.* make or become one (**-ified, -ifying**) —**unifiˈcation** *n.* —**Unification Church** religious sect founded by Rev. Sun Myung Moon, S Korean industrialist and religious leader

unilateral (juːnɪˈlætərəl) *a.* **1.** one-sided **2.** (of contract) binding one party only —**uniˈlaterally** *adv.*

unimpeachable (ʌnɪmˈpiːtʃəbᵊl) *a.* unquestionable as to honesty, truth *etc.*

union (ˈjuːnjən) *n.* **1.** joining into one **2.** state of being joined **3.** result of being joined **4.** federation, combination of societies *etc.* **5.** trade union —**ˈunionism** *n.* —**ˈunionist** *n.* supporter of union —**ˈunionize** *or* **-nise** *v.* organize (workers) into trade union —**Union Jack** national flag of United Kingdom

unique (juːˈniːk) *a.* **1.** being only one of its kind **2.** unparalleled

unisex (ˈjuːnɪsɛks) *a.* of clothing, hair style, hairdressers *etc.* that can be worn or used by either sex

unison (ˈjuːnɪsᵊn) *n.* **1.** *Mus.* singing *etc.* of same note as others **2.** agreement, harmony, concord

unit (ˈjuːnɪt) *n.* **1.** single thing or person **2.** standard quantity **3.** group of people or things with one purpose —**Uniˈtarian** *n.* member of Christian body that denies doctrine of the Trinity —**Uniˈtarianism** *n.* —**ˈunitary** *a.* —**unit trust UK** investment trust that issues units for public sale, holders of which are creditors with their interests represented by independent trust company

unite (juːˈnaɪt) *vt.* **1.** join into one, connect **2.** associate **3.** cause to adhere —*vi.* **4.** become one **5.** combine —**ˈunity** *n.* **1.** state of being one **2.** harmony **3.** agreement, uniformity **4.** combination of separate parts into connected whole **5.** *Maths.* the number one —**United Empire Loyalist** American colonist who settled in Canada in War of Amer. Independence from loyalty to Britain —**United Kingdom** island of Great Britain together with Northern Ireland —**United Nations Organization** organization formed in 1945 to promote peace and international cooperation

THESAURUS

classified, unfamiliar, unknown, unmarked, unnamed, unrecognized, unrevealed

unification alliance, amalgamation, coalescence, coalition, combination, confederation, federation, fusion, merger, union, uniting

uniform *n.* **1.** costume, dress, garb, habit, livery, outfit, regalia, regimentals, suit ~*adj.* **2.** consistent, constant, equable, even, regular, smooth, unbroken, unchanging, undeviating, unvarying **3.** alike, equal, identical, like, same, selfsame, similar

uniformity constancy, evenness, homogeneity, invariability, regularity, sameness, similarity

unify amalgamate, bind, bring together, combine, confederate, consolidate, federate, fuse, join, merge, unite

unimaginable beyond one's wildest dreams, fantastic, impossible, inconceivable, incredible, indescribable, ineffable, mind-boggling (*Inf.*), unbelievable, unheard-of, unthinkable

unimaginative barren, commonplace, derivative, dry, dull, hackneyed, lifeless, matter-of-fact, ordinary, pedestrian, predictable, prosaic, routine, tame, uncreative, uninspired, unoriginal, unromantic, usual

unimpeachable above reproach, beyond criticism, beyond question, blameless, faultless, impeccable, irreproachable, perfect, unassailable, unblemished, unchallengeable, unexceptionable, unquestionable

unimportant immaterial, inconsequential, insignificant, irrelevant, low-ranking, minor, not worth mentioning, nugatory, of no account, of no consequence, of no moment, paltry, petty, slight, trifling, trivial, worthless

uninhabited abandoned, barren, desert, deserted, desolate, empty, unoccupied, unpopulated, unsettled, untenanted, vacant, waste

uninhibited **1.** candid, frank, free, free and easy, informal, instinctive, liberated, natural, open, relaxed, spontaneous, unrepressed, unreserved, unselfconscious **2.** free, unbridled, unchecked, unconstrained, uncontrolled, uncurbed, unrestrained, unrestricted

uninspired commonplace, dull, humdrum, indifferent, ordinary, prosaic, stale, stock, unexciting, unimaginative, uninspiring, uninteresting, unoriginal

unintelligent brainless, dense, dull, empty-headed, foolish, gormless (*Brit. inf.*), obtuse, slow, stupid, thick, unreasoning, unthinking

unintelligible double Dutch (*Brit. inf.*), illegible, inarticulate, incoherent, incomprehensible, indecipherable, indistinct, jumbled, meaningless, muddled, unfathomable

unintentional accidental, casual, fortuitous, inadvertent, involuntary, unconscious, undesigned, unintended, unpremeditated, unthinking, unwitting

uninteresting boring, commonplace, drab, dreary, dry, dull, flat, humdrum, monotonous, tedious, tiresome, unenjoyable, uneventful, unexciting, uninspiring, wearisome

uninterrupted constant, continual, continuous, nonstop, peaceful, steady, sustained, unbroken, undisturbed, unending

uninvited not asked, not invited, unasked, unbidden, unwanted, unwelcome

uninviting disagreeable, offensive, off-putting (*Brit. inf.*), repellent, repulsive, unappealing, unappetizing, unattractive, undesirable, unpleasant, untempting, unwelcoming

union **1.** amalgam, amalgamation, blend, combination, conjunction, fusion, junction, mixture, synthesis, uniting **2.** alliance, association, Bund, coalition, confederacy, confederation, federation, league

unique **1.** lone, one and only, only, single, solitary, sui generis **2.** incomparable, inimitable, matchless, nonpareil, peerless, unequalled, unexampled, unmatched, unparalleled, unrivalled, without equal

unison accord, accordance, agreement, concert, concord, cooperation, harmony, unanimity, unity

unit **1.** assembly, detachment, entity, group, section, system, whole **2.** component, constituent, element, item, member, module, part, piece, portion, section, segment **3.** measure, measurement, module, quantity

Univ. University

univalent (juːnɪˈveɪlənt; juːˈnɪvələnt) *a.* **1.** (of chromosome during meiosis) not paired with its homologue **2.** *Chem. see* MONOVALENT **—uniˈvalency** *n.*

universe (ˈjuːnɪvɜːs) *n.* **1.** all existing things considered as constituting systematic whole **2.** the world **—uniˈversal** *a.* **1.** relating to all things or all people **2.** applying to all members of a community **—universˈality** *n.* **—uniˈversally** *adv.* **—universal joint** *or* **coupling** form of coupling between two rotating shafts allowing freedom of movement in all directions

university (juːnɪˈvɜːsɪtɪ) *n.* educational institution for study, examination and conferment of degrees in various branches of learning

unjust (ʌnˈdʒʌst) *a.* not in accordance with accepted standards of justice; unfair **—unˈjustly** *adv.*

unkempt (ʌnˈkɛmpt) *a.* of rough or uncared-for appearance

unless (ʌnˈlɛs) *conj.* except under the circumstances that

unloose (ʌnˈluːs) *or* **unloosen** *vt.* **1.** release **2.** loosen (hold, grip *etc.*) **3.** unfasten, untie

unman (ʌnˈmæn) *vt.* **1.** cause to lose nerve *etc.* **2.** make effeminate **3.** remove men from (**-nn-**)

unmitigated (ʌnˈmɪtɪgeɪtɪd) *a.* not diminished in intensity, severity *etc.*

unnatural (ʌnˈnætʃərəl) *a.* **1.** abnormal **2.** not in accordance with accepted standards of behaviour **3.** uncanny; supernatural **4.** affected, forced **5.** inhuman, monstrous **—unˈnaturally** *adv.*

unnerve (ʌnˈnɜːv) *vt.* cause to lose courage, confidence *etc.*

U.N.O. United Nations Organization

THESAURUS

unite 1. amalgamate, blend, coalesce, combine, confederate, consolidate, couple, fuse, incorporate, join, link, marry, merge, unify, wed **2.** ally, associate, band, close ranks, club together, cooperate, join forces, join together, league, pool, pull together

unity 1. entity, integrity, oneness, singleness, undividedness, unification, union, wholeness **2.** accord, agreement, concord, concurrence, consensus, harmony, peace, solidarity, unanimity

universal all-embracing, catholic, common, ecumenical, entire, general, omnipresent, total, unlimited, whole, widespread, worldwide

universality all-inclusiveness, completeness, comprehensiveness, entirety, generality, generalization, totality, ubiquity

universally always, everywhere, in all cases, in every instance, invariably, uniformly, without exception

universe cosmos, creation, everything, macrocosm, nature, the natural world

unjust biased, inequitable, one-sided, partial, partisan, prejudiced, undeserved, unfair, unjustified, unmerited, wrong, wrongful

unkind cruel, hardhearted, harsh, inconsiderate, inhuman, insensitive, malicious, mean, nasty, spiteful, thoughtless, uncaring, uncharitable, unchristian, unfeeling, unfriendly, unsympathetic

unknown 1. alien, concealed, dark, hidden, mysterious, new, secret, strange, unrecognized, unrevealed, untold **2.** anonymous, nameless, uncharted, undiscovered, unexplored, unidentified, unnamed

unlawful actionable, against the law, banned, criminal, forbidden, illegal, illegitimate, illicit, outlawed, prohibited, unauthorized, unlicensed

unlike contrasted, different, dissimilar, distinct, divergent, diverse, ill-matched, incompatible, not alike, opposite, unequal, unrelated

unlikely 1. doubtful, faint, improbable, not likely, remote, slight, unimaginable **2.** implausible, incredible, questionable, unbelievable, unconvincing

unlimited boundless, countless, endless, extensive, great, illimitable, immeasurable, immense, incalculable, infinite, limitless, unbounded, vast

unload disburden, discharge, dump, empty, off-load, relieve, unburden, unlade, unpack

unlock free, let loose, open, release, unbar, unbolt, undo, unfasten, unlatch

unlucky cursed, disastrous, hapless, luckless, miserable, unfortunate, unhappy, unsuccessful, wretched

unmanageable 1. awkward, bulky, cumbersome, difficult to handle, inconvenient, unhandy, unwieldy **2.** difficult, fractious, intractable, obstreperous, out of hand, refractory, stroppy (*Brit. sl.*), uncontrollable, unruly, wild

unmannerly badly behaved, bad-mannered, discourteous, disrespectful, ill-bred, ill-mannered, impolite, misbehaved, rude, uncivil, uncouth

unmarried bachelor, celibate, maiden, single, unattached, unwed, unwedded, virgin

unmask bare, bring to light, disclose, discover, expose, lay bare, reveal, show up, uncloak, uncover, unveil

unmerciful brutal, cruel, hard, heartless, implacable, merciless, pitiless, relentless, remorseless, ruthless, uncaring, unfeeling, unsparing

unmistakable certain, clear, conspicuous, decided, distinct, evident, glaring, indisputable, manifest, obvious, palpable, patent, plain, positive, pronounced, sure, unambiguous, unequivocal

unmitigated grim, harsh, intense, oppressive, persistent, relentless, unabated, unalleviated, unbroken, undiminished, unmodified, unqualified, unredeemed, unrelieved

unmoved 1. fast, firm, in place, in position, steady, unchanged, untouched **2.** cold, dry-eyed, impassive, indifferent, unaffected, unfeeling, unimpressed, unresponsive, unstirred, untouched

unnatural 1. aberrant, abnormal, anomalous, irregular, odd, perverse, perverted, unusual **2.** bizarre, extraordinary, freakish, outlandish, queer, strange, supernatural, unaccountable, uncanny **3.** affected, artificial, assumed, contrived, factitious, false, feigned, forced, insincere, laboured, mannered, phoney (*Sl.*), self-conscious, stagy, stiff, stilted, strained, studied, theatrical

unnecessary dispensable, expendable, inessential, needless, nonessential, redundant, supererogatory, superfluous, surplus to requirements, uncalled-for, unneeded, unrequired, useless

unnerve confound, daunt, demoralize, disarm, disconcert, discourage, dishearten, dismay, dispirit, fluster, frighten, intimidate, rattle (*Inf.*), shake, throw off balance, unhinge, unman, upset

unparalleled (ʌnˈpærəlɛld) *a.* unmatched; unequalled

unprincipled (ʌnˈprɪnsɪpᵊld) *a.* lacking moral principles

unquote (ʌnˈkwəʊt) *interj.* expression used parenthetically to indicate that preceding quotation is finished

unravel (ʌnˈrævᵊl) *vt.* undo, untangle (-ll-)

unread (ʌnˈrɛd) *a.* **1.** (of book *etc.*) not yet read **2.** (of person) having read little

unregenerate (ʌnrɪˈdʒɛnərɪt) *a.* **1.** unrepentant; unreformed **2.** obstinately adhering to one's own views —**unreˈgeneracy** *n.* —**unreˈgenerately** *adv.*

unremitting (ʌnrɪˈmɪtɪŋ) *a.* never slackening or stopping

unrest (ʌnˈrɛst) *n.* troubled or rebellious state, discontent

THESAURUS

unnoticed disregarded, ignored, neglected, overlooked, undiscovered, unheeded, unobserved, unperceived, unrecognized, unremarked, unseen

unobtrusive humble, inconspicuous, keeping a low profile, low-key, meek, modest, quiet, restrained, retiring, self-effacing, subdued, unassuming, unnoticeable, unostentatious, unpretentious

unoccupied **1.** empty, tenantless, uninhabited, untenanted, vacant **2.** at leisure, disengaged, idle, inactive, unemployed

unofficial informal, personal, private, unauthorized, unconfirmed, wildcat

unorthodox abnormal, heterodox, irregular, unconventional, uncustomary, unusual, unwonted

unpaid **1.** due, not discharged, outstanding, overdue, owing, payable, unsettled **2.** honorary, unsalaried, voluntary

unparalleled beyond compare, consummate, exceptional, incomparable, matchless, peerless, rare, singular, superlative, unequalled, unique, unmatched, unprecedented, unrivalled, unsurpassed, without equal

unpardonable deplorable, disgraceful, indefensible, inexcusable, outrageous, scandalous, shameful, unforgivable, unjustifiable

unpleasant abhorrent, bad, disagreeable, displeasing, distasteful, ill-natured, irksome, nasty, objectionable, obnoxious, repulsive, troublesome, unattractive, unlikable, unlovely, unpalatable

unpopular avoided, detested, disliked, not sought out, out in the cold, out of favour, rejected, shunned, unattractive, undesirable, unloved, unwanted, unwelcome

unprecedented abnormal, exceptional, extraordinary, freakish, new, novel, original, remarkable, singular, unexampled, unheard-of, unparalleled, unrivalled, unusual

unpredictable chance, changeable, doubtful, erratic, fickle, fluky (*Inf.*), iffy, inconstant, random, unforeseeable, unreliable, unstable, variable

unprepared **1.** half-baked (*Inf.*), ill-considered, incomplete, not thought out, unfinished, unplanned **2.** caught napping, caught on the hop (*Brit. inf.*), surprised, taken aback, taken off guard, unaware, unready, unsuspecting **3.** ad-lib, extemporaneous, improvised, off the cuff (*Inf.*), spontaneous

unpretentious homely, honest, humble, modest, plain, simple, straightforward, unaffected, unassuming, unimposing, unobtrusive, unostentatious, unspoiled

unprincipled amoral, corrupt, crooked, deceitful, devious, dishonest, immoral, tricky, unconscionable, underhand, unethical, unprofessional, unscrupulous

unproductive **1.** bootless, fruitless, futile, idle, ineffective, inefficacious, otiose, unavailing, unprofitable, unremunerative, unrewarding, useless, vain, valueless, worthless **2.** barren, dry, fruitless, sterile, unprolific

unpromising adverse, discouraging, doubtful, gloomy, inauspicious, infelicitous, ominous, unfavourable, unpropitious

unprotected defenceless, exposed, helpless, naked, open, open to attack, pregnable, unarmed, undefended, unguarded, unsheltered, unshielded, vulnerable

unqualified **1.** ill-equipped, incapable, incompetent, ineligible, not equal to, not up to, unfit, unprepared **2.** categorical, downright, outright, unconditional, unmitigated, unreserved, unrestricted, without reservation

unquestionable absolute, beyond a shadow of doubt, certain, clear, conclusive, definite, faultless, flawless, incontestable, incontrovertible, indisputable, indubitable, irrefutable, manifest, patent, perfect, self-evident, sure, undeniable, unequivocal, unmistakable

unravel disentangle, extricate, free, separate, straighten out, undo, unknot, untangle, unwind

unreal **1.** chimerical, dreamlike, fabulous, fanciful, fictitious, illusory, imaginary, make-believe, phantasmagoric, storybook, visionary **2.** hypothetical, immaterial, impalpable, insubstantial, intangible, mythical, nebulous **3.** artificial, fake, false, insincere, mock, ostensible, pretended, seeming, sham

unrealistic non-naturalistic, unauthentic, unlifelike, unreal

unreasonable **1.** excessive, exorbitant, extortionate, extravagant, immoderate, steep (*Brit. inf.*), too great, uncalled-for, undue, unfair, unjust, unwarranted **2.** absurd, far-fetched, foolish, illogical, irrational, mad, nonsensical, preposterous, senseless, silly, stupid

unregenerate **1.** godless, impious, profane, sinful, unconverted, unreformed, unrepentant, wicked **2.** hardened, intractable, obdurate, obstinate, recalcitrant, refractory, self-willed, stubborn

unreliable **1.** disreputable, irresponsible, not conscientious, treacherous, undependable, unstable, untrustworthy **2.** deceptive, delusive, erroneous, fake, fallible, false, implausible, inaccurate, mistaken, specious, uncertain, unconvincing, unsound

unrepentant abandoned, callous, hardened, impenitent, incorrigible, not contrite, obdurate, shameless, unregenerate, unremorseful, unrepenting

unreserved demonstrative, extrovert, forthright, frank, free, open, open-hearted, outgoing, outspoken, uninhibited, unrestrained, unreticent

unresolved doubtful, moot, open to question, pending, problematical, unanswered, undecided, undetermined, unsettled, unsolved, up in the air, vague, yet to be decided

unroll (ʌnˈrəʊl) *v.* **1.** open out (something rolled or folded) or (of something rolled *etc.*) become unwound —*vi.* **2.** become visible or apparent, *esp.* gradually

unruly (ʌnˈruːlɪ) *a.* badly behaved, ungovernable, disorderly

unsaturated (ʌnˈsætʃəreɪtɪd) *a.* **1.** not saturated **2.** (of chemical compound, *esp.* organic compound) containing one or more double or triple bonds and thus capable of undergoing addition reactions —**unsatuˈration** *n.*

unsavoury *or U.S.* **unsavory** (ʌnˈseɪvərɪ) *a.* distasteful, disagreeable

unsightly (ʌnˈsaɪtlɪ) *a.* ugly

unspeakable (ʌnˈspiːkəbᵊl) *a.* **1.** incapable of expression in words **2.** indescribably bad or evil **3.** not to be uttered —**unˈspeakably** *adv.*

unstructured (ʌnˈstrʌktʃəd) *a.* without formal or systematic organization

unstrung (ʌnˈstrʌŋ) *a.* **1.** emotionally distressed **2.** (of stringed instrument) with strings detached

unstudied (ʌnˈstʌdɪd) *a.* **1.** natural **2.** (*with* in) without knowledge or training

THESAURUS

unrest 1. agitation, disaffection, discontent, discord, dissatisfaction, dissension, protest, rebellion, sedition, strife, tumult, turmoil **2.** agitation, anxiety, disquiet, distress, perturbation, restlessness, uneasiness, worry

unrestrained abandoned, boisterous, free, immoderate, inordinate, intemperate, natural, unbounded, unbridled, unchecked, unconstrained, uncontrolled, unhindered, uninhibited, unrepressed

unrivalled beyond compare, incomparable, matchless, nonpareil, peerless, supreme, unequalled, unexcelled, unmatched, unparalleled, unsurpassed, without equal

unruly disobedient, disorderly, fractious, headstrong, insubordinate, intractable, lawless, mutinous, obstreperous, rebellious, refractory, riotous, rowdy, turbulent, uncontrollable, ungovernable, unmanageable, wayward, wild, wilful

unsafe dangerous, hazardous, insecure, perilous, precarious, risky, threatening, treacherous, uncertain, unreliable, unsound, unstable

unsaid left to the imagination, tacit, undeclared, unexpressed, unspoken, unstated, unuttered, unvoiced

unsatisfactory deficient, disappointing, displeasing, inadequate, insufficient, mediocre, not good enough, not up to par, not up to scratch (*Inf.*), poor, unacceptable, unsuitable, unworthy, weak

unsavoury 1. distasteful, nasty, objectionable, obnoxious, offensive, repellent, repugnant, repulsive, revolting, unpleasant **2.** disagreeable, distasteful, nauseating, sickening, unappetizing, unpalatable

unscrupulous conscienceless, corrupt, crooked (*Inf.*), dishonest, dishonourable, exploitative, immoral, improper, knavish, roguish, ruthless, unconscientious, unconscionable, unethical, unprincipled

unseemly discreditable, disreputable, improper, inappropriate, indecorous, indelicate, in poor taste, out of keeping, out of place, unbecoming, unbefitting, undignified, unrefined, unsuitable

unselfish altruistic, charitable, devoted, disinterested, generous, humanitarian, kind, liberal, magnanimous, noble, self-denying, selfless, self-sacrificing

unsettle agitate, bother, confuse, discompose, disconcert, disorder, disturb, fluster, perturb, rattle (*Inf.*), ruffle, throw (*Inf.*), throw into confusion (disorder, uproar), throw off balance, trouble, unbalance, upset

unshakable absolute, constant, firm, fixed, resolute, staunch, steadfast, sure, unassailable, unswerving, unwavering, well-founded

unsightly disagreeable, hideous, horrid, repulsive, revolting (*Inf.*), ugly, unattractive, unpleasant, unprepossessing

unskilled amateurish, inexperienced, uneducated, unprofessional, unqualified, untalented, untrained

unsociable chilly, cold, distant, hostile, inhospitable, introverted, reclusive, retiring, standoffish, uncongenial, unforthcoming, unfriendly, unneighbourly, unsocial, withdrawn

unsolicited free-will, gratuitous, spontaneous, unasked for, uncalled-for, unforced, uninvited, unrequested, unsought, unwelcome, voluntary, volunteered

unsophisticated 1. artless, childlike, guileless, inexperienced, ingenuous, innocent, naive, natural, unaffected, untutored, unworldly **2.** plain, simple, straightforward, uncomplex, uncomplicated, uninvolved, unrefined, unspecialized

unsound 1. ailing, defective, delicate, deranged, diseased, frail, ill, in poor health, unbalanced, unhealthy, unhinged, unstable, unwell, weak **2.** defective, erroneous, fallacious, false, faulty, flawed, ill-founded, illogical, invalid, shaky, specious, unreliable, weak **3.** flimsy, insecure, not solid, rickety, shaky, tottering, unreliable, unsafe, unstable, unsteady, wobbly

unspeakable 1. beyond description, beyond words, inconceivable, indescribable, ineffable, inexpressible, overwhelming, unbelievable, unimaginable, unutterable, wonderful **2.** abominable, appalling, awful, bad, dreadful, evil, execrable, frightful, heinous, horrible, loathsome, monstrous, odious, repellent, shocking, too horrible for words

unspoken 1. assumed, implicit, implied, left to the imagination, not put into words, not spelt out, tacit, taken for granted, undeclared, understood, unexpressed, unspoken, unstated **2.** mute, silent, unsaid, unuttered, voiceless, wordless

unstable 1. insecure, not fixed, precarious, rickety, risky, shaky, tottering, unsettled, unsteady, wobbly **2.** capricious, changeable, erratic, fitful, fluctuating, inconsistent, inconstant, irrational, unpredictable, unsteady, untrustworthy, vacillating, variable, volatile

unsteady 1. infirm, insecure, precarious, reeling, rickety, shaky, tottering, treacherous, unsafe, unstable, wobbly **2.** changeable, erratic, flickering, flighty, fluctuating, inconstant, irregular, unreliable, unsettled, vacillating, variable, volatile, wavering

unsubstantiated open to question, unattested, unconfirmed, uncorroborated, unestablished, unproven, unsupported

unsuccessful 1. abortive, bootless, failed, fruitless, futile, ineffective, unavailing, unproductive, useless,

unsung (ʌnˈsʌŋ) *a.* 1. not acclaimed or honoured 2. not yet sung

untenable (ʌnˈtɛnəbᵊl) *a.* (of theories *etc.*) incapable of being maintained, defended

unthinkable (ʌnˈθɪŋkəbᵊl) *a.* 1. out of the question 2. inconceivable 3. unreasonable

untie (ʌnˈtaɪ) *v.* 1. unfasten or free (knot or something that is tied) or (of knot *etc.*) become unfastened —*vt.* 2. free from restriction (**-ˈtied, -ˈtying**)

until (ʌnˈtɪl) *conj.* 1. to the time that 2. (with a negative) before —*prep.* 3. up to the time of

unto (ˈʌntuː) *prep. obs.* to

untold (ʌnˈtəʊld) *a.* 1. incapable of description 2. incalculably great in number or quantity 3. not told

untouched (ʌnˈtʌtʃt) *a.* 1. not touched 2. not harmed —**unˈtouchable** *a.* 1. not able to be touched —*n.* 2. *esp.* formerly, non-caste Hindu, forbidden to be touched by one of caste

untoward (ʌntəˈwɔːd) *a.* awkward, inconvenient

unutterable (ʌnˈʌtərəbᵊl) *a.* incapable of being expressed in words —**unˈutterably** *adv.*

THESAURUS

vain 2. balked, defeated, foiled, frustrated, hapless, ill-starred, losing, luckless, unfortunate, unlucky

unsuitable improper, inapposite, inappropriate, inapt, incompatible, incongruous, ineligible, infelicitous, out of character, out of keeping, out of place, unacceptable, unbecoming, unbefitting, unfitting, unseasonable, unseemly, unsuited

unsure 1. insecure, lacking in confidence, unassured, unconfident 2. distrustful, doubtful, dubious, hesitant, in a quandary, irresolute, mistrustful, sceptical, suspicious, unconvinced, undecided

unsurpassed consummate, exceptional, incomparable, matchless, nonpareil, paramount, peerless, second to none, superlative, supreme, transcendent, unequalled, unexcelled, unparalleled, unrivalled, without an equal

unsuspecting confiding, credulous, gullible, inexperienced, ingenuous, innocent, naive, off guard, trustful, trusting, unconscious, unsuspicious, unwarned, unwary

unsympathetic apathetic, callous, cold, compassionless (*Rare*), cruel, hard, harsh, heartless, indifferent, insensitive, soulless, stony-hearted, uncompassionate, unconcerned, unfeeling, unkind, unmoved, unpitying, unresponsive

untamed barbarous, feral, fierce, not broken in, savage, unbroken, uncontrollable, undomesticated, untameable, wild

untangle clear up, disentangle, explain, extricate, solve, straighten out, unravel, unsnarl

untenable fallacious, flawed, groundless, illogical, indefensible, insupportable, shaky, unreasonable, unsound, unsustainable, weak

unthinkable 1. absurd, illogical, impossible, improbable, not on (*Inf.*), out of the question, preposterous, unlikely, unreasonable 2. beyond belief, beyond the bounds of possibility, implausible, inconceivable, incredible, insupportable, unbelievable, unimaginable

unthinking careless, heedless, impulsive, inadvertent, instinctive, mechanical, negligent, oblivious, rash, senseless, unconscious, unmindful, vacant, witless

untidy bedraggled, chaotic, cluttered, disorderly, higgledy-piggledy (*Inf.*), jumbled, littered, messy, muddled, muddly, mussy (*U.S. inf.*), rumpled, slatternly, slipshod, sloppy (*Inf.*), slovenly, topsy-turvy, unkempt

untie free, loosen, release, unbind, undo, unfasten, unknot, unlace

untimely awkward, badly timed, early, ill-timed, inappropriate, inauspicious, inconvenient, inopportune, mistimed, premature, unfortunate, unseasonable, unsuitable

untold 1. indescribable, inexpressible, undreamed of, unimaginable, unspeakable, unthinkable, unutterable 2. countless, incalculable, innumerable, measureless, myriad, numberless, uncountable, uncounted, unnumbered 3. hidden, private, secret, undisclosed, unknown, unpublished, unrecounted, unrelated, unrevealed

untouched intact, safe and sound, undamaged, unharmed, unhurt, uninjured, unscathed, without a scratch

untoward annoying, awkward, disastrous, ill-timed, inconvenient, inimical, irritating, troublesome, unfortunate, vexatious

untrained amateur, green, inexperienced, raw, uneducated, unpractised, unqualified, unschooled, unskilled, untaught, untutored

untroubled calm, composed, cool, peaceful, placid, serene, steady, tranquil, unagitated, unconcerned, undisturbed, unflappable (*Inf.*), unflustered, unperturbed, unruffled, unstirred, unworried

untrue 1. deceptive, dishonest, erroneous, fallacious, false, inaccurate, incorrect, lying, misleading, mistaken, sham, spurious, untruthful, wrong 2. deceitful, disloyal, faithless, false, forsworn, inconstant, perfidious, traitorous, treacherous, two-faced, unfaithful, untrustworthy

untrustworthy capricious, deceitful, devious, dishonest, disloyal, fair-weather, faithless, false, fickle, fly-by-night (*Inf.*), not to be depended on, slippery, treacherous, tricky, two-faced, undependable, unfaithful, unreliable, untrue, untrusty

untruthful crooked (*Inf.*), deceitful, deceptive, dishonest, dissembling, false, fibbing, hypocritical, lying, mendacious

unusual abnormal, atypical, bizarre, curious, different, exceptional, extraordinary, odd, out of the ordinary, phenomenal, queer, rare, remarkable, singular, strange, surprising, uncommon, unconventional, unexpected, unfamiliar, unwonted

unutterable beyond words, extreme, indescribable, ineffable, overwhelming, unimaginable, unspeakable

unwanted *de trop*, going begging, outcast, rejected, superfluous, surplus to requirements, unasked, undesired, uninvited, unneeded, unsolicited, unwelcome, useless

unwary careless, hasty, heedless, imprudent, incautious, indiscreet, rash, reckless, thoughtless, uncircumspect, unguarded, unwatchful

unwavering consistent, dedicated, determined, resolute, single-minded, staunch, steadfast, steady, un-

unwell (ʌnˈwɛl) *a.* not well, ill

unwieldy (ʌnˈwiːldɪ) *a.* **1.** awkward, big, heavy to handle **2.** clumsy

unwitting (ʌnˈwɪtɪŋ) *a.* **1.** not knowing **2.** not intentional

up (ʌp) *prep.* **1.** from lower to higher position **2.** along —*adv.* **3.** in or to higher position, source, activity *etc.* **4.** indicating completion (**ˈupper** *comp.*, **ˈuppermost** *sup.*) —**ˈupward** *a./adv.* —**ˈupwards** *or* **ˈupward** *adv.* —**up-and-coming** *a.* promising continued or future success; enterprising —**ˈupˈhill** *a.* **1.** inclining; sloping **2.** requiring protracted effort —*adv.* **3.** up incline or slope **4.** against difficulties —*n.* **5.** rising incline —**up time** time during which computer *etc.* actually operates —**up-to-date** *a.* modern; fashionable —**upwardly mobile** (of person or social group) moving or aspiring to move to higher class or status —**upward mobility** —**up against** confronted with

up- (*comb. form*) up, upper, upwards as in *uproot, upgrade.* Such words are not given here where the meaning may easily be inferred from the simple word

upbeat (ˈʌpbiːt) *n.* **1.** *Mus.* unaccented beat; upward gesture of conductor's baton indicating this —*a.* **2.** *inf.* cheerful; optimistic

upbraid (ʌpˈbreɪd) *vt.* scold, reproach

upbringing (ˈʌpbrɪŋɪŋ) *n.* rearing and education of children

update (ʌpˈdeɪt) *vt.* bring up to date

upfront (ˈʌpˈfrʌnt) *a.* **1.** open and frank —*adv./a.* **2.** (of money) paid out at beginning of business arrangement

upgrade (ʌpˈgreɪd) *vt.* **1.** promote to higher position **2.** improve

upheaval (ʌpˈhiːvᵊl) *n.* sudden or violent disturbance

uphold (ʌpˈhəʊld) *vt.* **1.** maintain **2.** support (**upˈheld, upˈholding**)

upholster (ʌpˈhəʊlstə) *vt.* fit springs, padding and coverings on (chairs *etc.*) —**upˈholsterer** *n.* —**upˈholstery** *n.*

upkeep (ˈʌpkiːp) *n.* act, process or cost of keeping something in good repair

upland (ˈʌplənd) *n.* high land

uplift (ʌpˈlɪft) *vt.* **1.** raise aloft **2.** *Scot.,* **NZ** collect; pick up (documents *etc.*) —*n.* (ˈʌplɪft) **3.** a lifting up **4.** mental, social or emotional improvement —*a.* (ˈʌplɪft) **5.** designating brassiere for lifting and supporting breasts

upon (əˈpɒn) *prep.* on

upper (ˈʌpə) *a. comp. of* UP **1.** higher, situated above —*n.* **2.** upper part of boot or shoe —**ˈuppermost** *a. sup. of* UP —**upper-case** *a.* of or relating to capital letters used in setting or production of printed or typed matter —**ˈuppercut** *n.* short-arm upward blow —**the upper hand** position of control

THESAURUS

deviating, unfaltering, unflagging, unshakable, unshaken, unswerving, untiring

unwelcome excluded, rejected, unacceptable, undesirable, uninvited, unpopular, unwanted, unwished for

unwell ailing, ill, indisposed, in poor health, off colour, out of sorts, poorly (*Inf.*), sick, sickly, under the weather (*Inf.*), unhealthy

unwholesome 1. deleterious, harmful, insalubrious, junk (*Inf.*), noxious, poisonous, tainted, unhealthy, unnourishing **2.** bad, corrupting, degrading, demoralizing, depraving, evil, immoral, perverting, wicked

unwieldy 1. awkward, burdensome, cumbersome, inconvenient, unhandy, unmanageable **2.** bulky, clumsy, hefty, massive, ponderous, ungainly, weighty

unwilling averse, demurring, disinclined, grudging, indisposed, laggard (*Rare*), loath, not in the mood, opposed, reluctant, resistant, unenthusiastic

unwind disentangle, slacken, uncoil, undo, unravel, unreel, unroll, untwine, untwist

unwise foolhardy, foolish, ill-advised, ill-considered, ill-judged, impolitic, improvident, imprudent, inadvisable, indiscreet, injudicious, irresponsible, rash, reckless, senseless, short-sighted, silly, stupid

unwitting 1. ignorant, innocent, unaware, unconscious, unknowing, unsuspecting **2.** accidental, chance, inadvertent, involuntary, undesigned, unintended, unintentional, unmeant, unplanned

unworldly 1. abstract, celestial, metaphysical, nonmaterialistic, religious, spiritual, transcendental **2.** ethereal, extraterrestrial, otherworldly, unearthly

unworthy 1. *With* **of** beneath the dignity of, improper, inappropriate, out of character, out of place, unbecoming, unbefitting, unfitting, unseemly, unsuitable **2.** base, contemptible, degrading, discreditable, disgraceful, dishonourable, disreputable, ignoble, shameful **3.** ineligible, not deserving of, not fit for, not good enough, not worth, undeserving

unwritten oral, unrecorded, vocal, word-of-mouth

unyielding adamant, determined, firm, hardline, immovable, inexorable, inflexible, intractable, obdurate, obstinate, relentless, resolute, rigid, staunch, steadfast, stubborn, tough, unbending, uncompromising, unwavering

upbringing breeding, bringing-up, care, cultivation, education, nurture, raising, rearing, tending, training

upgrade advance, ameliorate, better, elevate, enhance, improve, promote, raise

upheaval cataclysm, disorder, disruption, disturbance, eruption, overthrow, revolution, turmoil, violent change

uphill *adj.* **1.** ascending, climbing, mounting, rising **2.** arduous, difficult, exhausting, gruelling, hard, laborious, punishing, Sisyphean, strenuous, taxing, tough, wearisome

uphold advocate, aid, back, champion, defend, encourage, endorse, hold to, justify, maintain, promote, stand by, support, sustain, vindicate

upkeep 1. conservation, keep, maintenance, preservation, repair, running, subsistence, support, sustenance **2.** expenditure, expenses, oncosts (*Brit.*), operating costs, outlay, overheads, running costs

uplift 1. *v.* elevate, heave, hoist, lift up, raise **2.** *n.* advancement, betterment, cultivation, edification, enhancement, enlightenment, enrichment, improvement, refinement

upper high, higher, loftier, top, topmost

upper hand advantage, ascendancy, control, dominion, edge, mastery, superiority, supremacy, sway, whip hand

uppermost highest, loftiest, most elevated, top, topmost, upmost

uppish (ˈʌpɪʃ) *a. inf.* **1.** self-assertive **2.** arrogant **3.** affectedly superior

upright (ˈʌpraɪt) *a.* **1.** erect **2.** honest, just —*adv.* **3.** vertically —*n.* **4.** thing standing upright, *eg* post in framework **5.** upright piano —**upright piano** piano with rectangular vertical case

uprising (ˈʌpraɪzɪŋ, ʌpˈraɪzɪŋ) *n.* rebellion, revolt

uproar (ˈʌprɔː) *n.* tumult, disturbance —**upˈroarious** *a.* rowdy —**upˈroariously** *adv.*

uproot (ʌpˈruːt) *vt.* **1.** pull up by or as if by the roots **2.** displace (person or persons) from native or habitual surroundings

upset (ʌpˈsɛt) *vt.* **1.** overturn **2.** distress **3.** disrupt **4.** make ill (**upˈset, upˈsetting**) —*n.* (ˈʌpsɛt) **5.** unexpected defeat **6.** confusion **7.** trouble **8.** overturning

upshot (ˈʌpʃɒt) *n.* outcome, end

upside down (ˈʌpsaɪd) **1.** turned over completely; inverted **2.** in disorder or chaos

upsilon (ˈʌpsɪlɒn) *n.* 20th letter in Gr. alphabet (Υ, υ), vowel transliterated as *y* or *u*

upstage (ˈʌpˈsteɪdʒ) *a.* **1.** of back of stage —*vt.* **2.** *inf.* draw attention away from (another) to oneself

upstanding (ʌpˈstændɪŋ) *a.* **1.** of good character **2.** upright and vigorous in build

upstart (ˈʌpstɑːt) *n.* one suddenly raised to wealth, power *etc.*

uptake (ˈʌpteɪk) *n.* **1.** shaft *etc.* used to convey smoke or gases, *esp.* one that connects furnace to chimney **2.** lifting up —**quick** (*or* **slow**) **on the uptake** *inf.* quick (or slow) to understand or learn

uptight (ʌpˈtaɪt) *a. inf.* **1.** displaying tense nervousness, irritability **2.** repressed

upturn (ʌpˈtɜːn) *v.* **1.** turn or cause to turn over or upside down —*vt.* **2.** create disorder in **3.** direct upwards —*n.* (ˈʌptɜːn) **4.** upward trend or improvement

uranium (jʊˈreɪnɪəm) *n.* white radioactive metallic element, used as chief source of nuclear energy

urban (ˈɜːbᵊn) *a.* relating to town or city —**ˈurbanize** *or* **-nise** *vt.* change (countryside) to residential or industrial area

urbane (ɜːˈbeɪn) *a.* elegant, sophisticated —**urbanity** (ɜːˈbænɪtɪ) *n.*

urchin (ˈɜːtʃɪn) *n.* mischievous, unkempt child

Urdu (ˈʊədu:, ˈɜː-) *n.* official language of Pakistan, belonging to Indic branch of Indo-European family of languages, closely related to Hindi

urea (ˈjʊərɪə) *n.* substance occurring in urine

ureter (jʊˈriːtə) *n.* tube that conveys urine from kidney to urinary bladder or cloaca —**uˈreteral** *or* **ureteric** (jʊərɪˈtɛrɪk) *a.*

urethra (jʊˈriːθrə) *n.* canal conveying urine from bladder out of body (*pl.* **-thrae** (-θriː), **-s**)

urge (ɜːdʒ) *vt.* **1.** exhort earnestly **2.** entreat **3.** drive on —*n.* **4.** strong desire —**ˈurgency** *n.* —**ˈurgent** *a.* **1.** pressing **2.** needing attention at once —**ˈurgently** *adv.*

THESAURUS

uppish affected, arrogant, conceited, high and mighty (*Inf.*), hoity-toity (*Inf.*), overweening, presumptuous, putting on airs, self-important, snobbish, stuck-up (*Inf.*), supercilious, toffee-nosed (*Sl.*), uppity (*Inf.*)

upright **1.** erect, on end, perpendicular, straight, vertical **2.** *Fig.* above board, conscientious, ethical, faithful, good, high-minded, honest, honourable, incorruptible, just, principled, righteous, straightforward, true, trustworthy, unimpeachable, virtuous

uprising disturbance, insurgence, insurrection, mutiny, outbreak, putsch, rebellion, revolt, revolution, rising, upheaval

uproar brawl, brouhaha, clamour, commotion, confusion, din, furore, hubbub, hullabaloo, hurly-burly, mayhem, noise, outcry, pandemonium, racket, riot, ruckus (*Inf.*), ruction (*Inf.*), rumpus, turbulence, turmoil

uproarious clamorous, confused, disorderly, loud, noisy, riotous, rowdy, tempestuous, tumultuous, turbulent, wild

upset *v.* **1.** capsize, knock over, overturn, spill, tip over, topple over **2.** change, disorder, disorganize, disturb, mess up, mix up, put out of order, spoil, turn topsy-turvy **3.** agitate, bother, discompose, disconcert, dismay, disquiet, distress, disturb, fluster, grieve, perturb, ruffle, throw (someone) off balance, trouble ~*n.* **4.** defeat, reverse, shake-up (*Inf.*), sudden change, surprise **5.** agitation, bother, discomposure, disquiet, distress, disturbance, shock, trouble, worry ~*adj.* **6.** capsized, overturned, spilled, tipped over, toppled, tumbled, upside down **7.** disordered, disturbed, gippy (*Sl.*), ill, poorly (*Inf.*), queasy, sick **8.** agitated, bothered, confused, disconcerted, dismayed, disquieted, distressed, disturbed, frantic, grieved, hurt, overwrought, put out, ruffled, troubled, worried **9.** at sixes and sevens, chaotic, confused, disordered, in disarray *or* disorder, messed up, muddled, topsy-turvy **10.** beaten, conquered, defeated, overcome, overthrown, vanquished

upshot conclusion, consequence, culmination, end, end result, event, finale, issue, outcome, payoff (*Inf.*), result

upside down **1.** bottom up, inverted, on its head, overturned, upturned, wrong side up **2.** *Inf.* chaotic, confused, disordered, higgledy-piggledy (*Inf.*), in confusion (chaos, disarray, disorder), jumbled, muddled, topsy-turvy

upstanding **1.** ethical, good, honest, honourable, incorruptible, moral, principled, true, trustworthy, upright **2.** firm, hale and hearty, hardy, healthy, robust, stalwart, strong, sturdy, upright, vigorous

upstart arriviste, nobody, *nouveau riche*, parvenu, social climber, status seeker

up-to-date all the rage, current, fashionable, in, in vogue, modern, newest, now (*Inf.*), stylish, trendy (*Brit. inf.*), up-to-the-minute, with it (*Inf.*)

urban city, civic, inner-city, metropolitan, municipal, oppidan (*Rare*), town

urbane civil, civilized, cosmopolitan, courteous, cultivated, cultured, debonair, elegant, mannerly, polished, refined, smooth, sophisticated, suave, well-bred, well-mannered

urbanity charm, civility, courtesy, culture, elegance, grace, mannerliness, polish, refinement, sophistication, suavity, worldliness

urchin brat, gamin, guttersnipe, mudlark (*Sl.*), ragamuffin, street Arab, waif, young rogue

urge *v.* **1.** appeal to, beg, beseech, entreat, exhort, implore, plead, press, solicit **2.** advise, advocate, champion, counsel, insist on, push for, recommend, support **3.** compel, constrain, drive, egg on, encourage, force, goad, hasten, impel, incite, induce, insti-

urine (ˈjʊərɪn) *n.* fluid excreted by kidneys to bladder and passed as waste from body —**ˈuric** *a.* —**urinal** (jʊˈraɪnᵊl, ˈjʊərɪ-) *n.* (place with) sanitary fitting(s) used by men for urination —**ˈurinary** *a.* —**ˈurinate** *vi.* discharge urine —**uriˈnation** *n.*

urn (ɜːn) *n.* **1.** vessel like vase, *esp.* for ashes of the dead **2.** large container with tap for making and dispensing tea, coffee *etc.*

urogenital (jʊərəʊˈdʒɛnɪtᵊl) *or* **urinogenital** *a.* of urinary and genital organs and their functions (*also* **genitoˈurinary**)

Ursa Major (ˈɜːsə ˈmeɪdʒə) extensive conspicuous constellation in N hemisphere. The seven brightest stars form Plough (*also* **the Great Bear, the Bear**)

Ursa Minor (ˈɜːsə ˈmaɪnə) small faint constellation, brightest star of which is Pole Star (*also* **the Little Bear, the Bear**)

ursine (ˈɜːsaɪn) *a.* of, like a bear

us (ʌs) *pron. pl.* the objective case of WE

U.S. United States (of America)

use (juːz) *vt.* **1.** employ, avail oneself of **2.** exercise **3.** exploit **4.** consume —*n.* (juːs) **5.** employment, application to a purpose **6.** need to employ **7.** serviceableness **8.** profit **9.** habit —**ˈusable** *or* **ˈuseable** *a.* fit for use —**usage** (ˈjuːsɪdʒ, -zɪdʒ) *n.* **1.** act of using **2.** custom **3.** customary way of using —**used** *a.* second-hand, not new —**useful** (ˈjuːsfʊl) *a.* **1.** of use **2.** helpful **3.** serviceable —**usefully** (ˈjuːsfəlɪ) *adv.* —**usefulness** (ˈjuːsfʊlnɪs) *n.* —**useless** (ˈjuːslɪs) *a.* —**uselessly** (ˈjuːslɪslɪ) *adv.* —**uselessness** (ˈjuːslɪsnɪs) *n.* —**user-friendly** *a.* (*esp.* of computer system) easily operated and understood —**used to** (juːst) *a.* **1.** accustomed to —*vt.* **2.** did so formerly

usher (ˈʌʃə) *n.* **1.** doorkeeper, one showing people to seats *etc.* (**usheˈrette** *fem.*) —*vt.* **2.** introduce, announce **3.** inaugurate

U.S.S.R. Union of Soviet Socialist Republics

usual (ˈjuːʒʊəl) *a.* habitual, ordinary —**ˈusually** *adv.* **1.** as a rule **2.** generally, commonly

usurp (juːˈzɜːp) *vt.* seize wrongfully —**usurˈpation** *n.* violent or unlawful seizing of power —**uˈsurper** *n.*

usury (ˈjuːʒərɪ) *n.* **1.** lending of money at excessive interest **2.** such interest —**ˈusurer** *n.* money lender —**uˈsurious** *a.*

UT Utah

utensil (juːˈtɛnsəl) *n.* vessel, implement, *esp.* in domestic use

uterus (ˈjuːtərəs) *n.* womb (*pl.* **uteri** (ˈjuːtəraɪ)) —**uterine** (ˈjuːtəraɪn) *a.* of the uterus

utilidor (juːˈtɪlədə; *Canad.* -dɒr) *n.* **C** above-ground insulated casing for pipes

utility (juːˈtɪlɪtɪ) *n.* **1.** usefulness **2.** benefit **3.** useful thing —*a.* **4.** made for practical purposes —**utiliˈtarian** *a.* **1.** useful rather than beautiful **2.** of utilitarianism —*n.* **3.** believer in utilitarianism —**utiliˈtarianism** *n.* doctrine that morality of actions is to be tested by their utility, *esp.* that the greatest good of the greatest number should be the sole end of public action —**utiliˈzation** *or* **-liˈsation** *n.* —**ˈutilize** *or* **-lise** *vt.* make use of —**utility room** room used for storage, laundry *etc.*

THESAURUS

gate, press, propel, push, spur, stimulate ~*n.* **4.** compulsion, desire, drive, fancy, impulse, itch, longing, wish, yearning, yen (*Inf.*)

urgency exigency, extremity, gravity, hurry, imperativeness, importance, importunity, necessity, need, pressure, seriousness, stress

urgent compelling, critical, crucial, immediate, imperative, important, instant, not to be delayed, pressing, top-priority

urinate leak (*Sl.*), make water, micturate, pass water, pee (*Sl.*), spend a penny (*Brit. inf.*), tinkle (*Brit. inf.*), wee (*Inf.*), wee-wee (*Inf.*)

usable at one's disposal, available, current, fit for use, functional, in running order, practical, ready for use, serviceable, utilizable, valid, working

usage **1.** control, employment, handling, management, operation, regulation, running, treatment, use **2.** convention, custom, form, habit, matter of course, method, mode, practice, procedure, regime, routine, rule, tradition, wont

use *v.* **1.** apply, avail oneself of, bring into play, employ, exercise, find a use for, make use of, operate, ply, practise, profit by, put to use, turn to account, utilize, wield, work **2.** act towards, behave towards, deal with, exploit, handle, manipulate, misuse, take advantage of, treat **3.** consume, exhaust, expend, run through, spend, waste ~*n.* **4.** application, employment, exercise, handling, operation, practice, service, treatment, usage, wear and tear **5.** advantage, application, avail, benefit, good, help, mileage (*Inf.*), point, profit, service, usefulness, utility, value, worth **6.** custom, habit, practice, usage, way, wont **7.** call, cause, end, necessity, need, object, occasion, point, purpose, reason

used cast-off, hand-me-down (*Inf.*), nearly new, not new, reach-me-down (*Inf.*), second-hand, shopsoiled, worn

used to accustomed to, at home in, attuned to, familiar with, given to, habituated to, hardened to, in the habit of, inured to, tolerant of, wont to

useful advantageous, all-purpose, beneficial, effective, fruitful, general-purpose, helpful, of help, of service, of use, practical, profitable, salutary, serviceable, valuable, worthwhile

useless bootless, disadvantageous, fruitless, futile, hopeless, idle, impractical, ineffective, ineffectual, of no use, pointless, profitless, unavailing, unproductive, unworkable, vain, valueless, worthless

usher **1.** *n.* attendant, doorkeeper, escort, guide, usherette **2.** *v. Usually with* **in** bring in, herald, inaugurate, initiate, introduce, launch, open the door to, pave the way for, precede, ring in

usual accustomed, common, constant, customary, everyday, expected, familiar, fixed, general, habitual, normal, ordinary, regular, routine, standard, stock, typical, wonted

usually as a rule, as is the custom, as is usual, by and large, commonly, for the most part, generally, habitually, in the main, mainly, mostly, most often, normally, on the whole, ordinarily, regularly, routinely

utility advantageousness, avail, benefit, convenience, efficacy, fitness, point, practicality, profit, service, serviceableness, use, usefulness

utilize appropriate, avail oneself of, employ, have recourse to, make the most of, make use of, profit by, put to use, resort to, take advantage of, turn to account, use

—**utility truck** **A, NZ** small truck with open body and low sides

utmost (ˈʌtməʊst) *or* **uttermost** *a.* **1.** to the highest degree **2.** extreme, furthest —*n.* **3.** greatest possible amount

Utopia (juːˈtəʊpɪə) *n.* (*sometimes* **u-**) imaginary state with perfect political and social conditions or constitution —**Uˈtopian** *a.* (*sometimes* **u-**) ideally perfect but impracticable

utter[1] (ˈʌtə) *vt.* **1.** express, emit audibly, say **2.** put in circulation (forged banknotes, counterfeit coin) —**ˈutterance** *n.* **1.** act of speaking **2.** expression in words **3.** spoken words

utter[2] (ˈʌtə) *a.* complete, total, absolute —**ˈutterly** *adv.*

uttermost (ˈʌtəməʊst) *see* UTMOST

U-turn *n.* **1.** U-shaped turn by vehicle in order to go in opposite direction **2.** reversal of political policy

U.V. ultraviolet

uvula (ˈjuːvjʊlə) *n.* pendent fleshy part of soft palate (*pl.* **-lae** (-liː), **-s**) —**ˈuvular** *a.*

uxorious (ʌkˈsɔːrɪəs) *a.* excessively fond of one's wife

THESAURUS

utmost *adj.* **1.** chief, extreme, greatest, highest, maximum, paramount, pre-eminent, supreme **2.** extreme, farthest, final, last, most distant, outermost, remotest, uttermost ~*n.* **3.** best, greatest, hardest, highest, most

utter[1] *v.* articulate, enunciate, express, pronounce, put into words, say, speak, verbalize, vocalize, voice

utter[2] *adj.* absolute, arrant, complete, consummate, downright entire, out-and-out, perfect, sheer, stark, thorough, thoroughgoing, total, unmitigated, unqualified

utterly absolutely, completely, entirely, extremely, fully, perfectly, thoroughly, totally, to the core, wholly

V

v *or* **V** (viː) *n.* **1.** 22nd letter of English alphabet **2.** speech sound represented by this letter, as in *vote* **3.** something shaped like V (*pl.* **v's, V's** *or* **Vs**)

v volt

V *Chem.* vanadium

v. 1. verb **2.** verso **3.** versus **4.** very **5.** vide

V-1 *n.* flying robot bomb invented by Germans in World War II (*also* **ˈdoodlebug, ˈbuzzbomb**)

VA Virginia

V.A. 1. Vicar Apostolic **2.** (Order of) Victoria and Albert

vacant (ˈveɪkənt) *a.* **1.** without thought, empty **2.** unoccupied —**ˈvacancy** *n.* **1.** state of being unoccupied **2.** unfilled post, accommodation *etc.* —**ˈvacantly** *adv.*

vacate (vəˈkeɪt) *vt.* quit, leave empty —**vaˈcation** *n.* **1.** time when universities and law courts are closed **2.** US holidays **3.** act of vacating

vaccinate (ˈvæksɪneɪt) *vt.* inoculate with vaccine as protection against a specific disease —**vacciˈnation** *n.* —**ˈvaccinator** *n.* —**vaccine** (ˈvæksiːn) *n.* any substance used for inoculation against disease

vacillate (ˈvæsɪleɪt) *vi.* **1.** fluctuate in opinion **2.** waver **3.** move to and fro —**vacilˈlation** *n.* **1.** indecision **2.** wavering **3.** unsteadiness

vacuum (ˈvækjʊəm) *n.* **1.** place, region containing no matter and from which all or most air, gas has been removed (*pl.* **-s, -ua** (-jʊə)) —*v.* **2.** clean with vacuum cleaner —**vaˈcuity** *n.* —**ˈvacuous** *a.* **1.** vacant **2.** expressionless **3.** unintelligent —**vacuum cleaner** apparatus for removing dust by suction —**vacuum flask** double-walled flask with vacuum between walls, for keeping contents of inner flask at temperature at which they were inserted —**vacuum-packed** *a.* packed in airtight container to maintain freshness *etc.* —**vacuum pump** pump for producing low gas pressure —**vacuum tube** *or* **valve** *see* VALVE (sense 3)

vade mecum (ˈvɑːdɪ ˈmeɪkʊm) handbook *etc.* carried on person for immediate use when needed

vagabond (ˈvægəbɒnd) *n.* **1.** person with no fixed home **2.** wandering beggar or thief —*a.* **3.** like a vagabond

vagary (ˈveɪgərɪ, vəˈgɛərɪ) *n.* **1.** something unusual, erratic **2.** whim

vagina (vəˈdʒaɪnə) *n.* passage from womb to exterior —**vaˈginal** *a.*

vagrant (ˈveɪgrənt) *n.* **1.** vagabond, tramp —*a.* **2.** wandering, *esp.* without purpose —**ˈvagrancy** *n.*

vague (veɪg) *a.* **1.** indefinite, uncertain **2.** indistinct **3.** not clearly expressed **4.** absent-minded

vain (veɪn) *a.* **1.** conceited **2.** worthless, useless **3.** unavailing **4.** foolish —**ˈvainly** *adv.*

vainglory (veɪnˈglɔːrɪ) *n.* boastfulness, vanity —**vainˈglorious** *a.*

valance (ˈvæləns) *n.* short curtain round base of bed *etc.*

vale (veɪl) *n. Poet.* valley

valediction (vælɪˈdɪkʃən) *n.* farewell —**valeˈdictory** *n.* **1.** farewell address —*a.* **2.** parting, farewell

valency (ˈveɪlənsɪ) *or esp. U.S.* **valence** (ˈveɪləns) *n. Chem.* combining power of element or atom

valentine (ˈvæləntaɪn) *n.* (one receiving) card, gift, expressing affection on Saint Valentine's Day, Feb. 14th

valet (ˈvælɪt, ˈvæleɪ) *n.* gentleman's personal servant

valetudinarian (vælɪtjuːdɪˈnɛərɪən) *or* **valetudinary** (vælɪˈtjuːdɪnərɪ) *a.* **1.** sickly **2.** infirm —*n.* **3.** person obliged or disposed to live the life of an invalid

valiant (ˈvæljənt) *a.* brave, courageous

valid (ˈvælɪd) *a.* **1.** sound **2.** capable of being justified **3.** of binding force in law —**vaˈlidity** *n.* **1.** soundness **2.** power to convince **3.** legal force —**ˈvalidate** *vt.* make valid

THESAURUS

vacancy job, opening, opportunity, position, post, room, situation

vacant 1. available, disengaged, empty, free, idle, not in use, to let, unemployed, unengaged, unfilled, unoccupied, untenanted, void **2.** absent-minded, abstracted, blank, dreaming, dreamy, expressionless, idle, inane, incurious, vacuous

vacuum emptiness, free space, gap, nothingness, space, vacuity, void

vagabond 1. *n.* beggar, bum (*U.S. inf.*), down-and-out, hobo (*U.S.*), itinerant, knight of the road, migrant, nomad, outcast, rascal, rover, tramp, vagrant, wanderer, wayfarer **2.** *adj.* destitute, down and out, drifting, fly-by-night (*Inf.*), footloose, homeless, idle, itinerant, journeying, nomadic, rootless, roving, shiftless, vagrant, wandering

vagrant 1. *n.* beggar, bird of passage, bum (*U.S. inf.*), hobo (*U.S.*), itinerant, person of no fixed address, rolling stone, tramp, wanderer **2.** *adj.* itinerant, nomadic, roaming, rootless, roving, unsettled, vagabond

vague amorphous, blurred, dim, doubtful, fuzzy, generalized, hazy, ill-defined, imprecise, indefinite, indeterminate, indistinct, lax, loose, nebulous, obscure, shadowy, uncertain, unclear, unknown, unspecified, woolly

vain 1. arrogant, bigheaded (*Inf.*), cocky, conceited, egotistical, inflated, narcissistic, ostentatious, overweening, peacockish, pleased with oneself, proud, self-important, stuck-up (*Inf.*), swaggering, swanky (*Inf.*), swollen-headed (*Inf.*), vainglorious **2.** abortive, empty, fruitless, futile, hollow, idle, nugatory, pointless, senseless, time-wasting, trifling, trivial, unavailing, unimportant, unproductive, unprofitable, useless, worthless

valedictory *adj.* farewell, final, parting

valiant bold, brave, courageous, dauntless, doughty, fearless, gallant, heroic, indomitable, intrepid, lionhearted, plucky, redoubtable, stouthearted, valorous, worthy

valid 1. binding, cogent, conclusive, convincing, efficacious, efficient, good, just, logical, powerful, sound, substantial, telling, weighty, well-founded, well-grounded **2.** authentic, bona fide, genuine, in force, lawful, legal, legally binding, legitimate, official

validity 1. cogency, force, foundation, grounds, point, power, soundness, strength, substance, weight **2.** authority, lawfulness, legality, legitimacy, right

valise (vəˈliːz) *n.* travelling bag

valley (ˈvælɪ) *n.* 1. low area between hills 2. river basin

valour *or U.S.* **valor** (ˈvælə) *n.* bravery —**ˈvalorous** *a.*

value (ˈvæljuː) *n.* 1. worth 2. utility 3. equivalent 4. importance —*pl.* 5. principles, standards —*vt.* 6. estimate value of 7. hold in respect 8. prize —**ˈvaluable** *a.* 1. precious 2. worthy 3. capable of being valued —*n.* 4. (*usu. pl.*) valuable thing —**valuˈation** *n.* estimated worth —**ˈvalued** *a.* 1. estimated; appraised 2. highly thought of —**ˈvalueless** *a.* worthless —**ˈvaluer** *n.* —**value added tax** tax on difference between cost of basic materials and cost of article made from them —**value judgment** subjective assessment based on one's own values or those of one's class

valve (vælv) *n.* 1. device to control passage of fluid *etc.* through pipe 2. *Anat.* part of body allowing one-way passage of fluids 3. part of radio or television which controls flow of current 4. any of separable parts of shell of mollusc 5. *Mus.* device on brass instrument for lengthening tube —**ˈvalvular** *a.* of, like valves

vamoose (vəˈmuːs) *vi. sl.* depart quickly

vamp[1] (væmp) *inf. n.* 1. woman who deliberately allures men —*v.* 2. exploit (man) as vamp

vamp[2] (væmp) *n.* 1. something patched up (*also* **reˈvamp**) 2. front part of shoe upper —*vt.* 3. patch up, rework

vampire (ˈvæmpaɪə) *n.* in folklore, corpse that rises from dead to drink blood of the living —**vampire bat** bat that sucks blood of animals

van[1] (væn) *n.* 1. covered vehicle, *esp.* for goods 2. railway carriage for goods and use of guard

van[2] (væn) *n.* vanguard

vanadium (vəˈneɪdɪəm) *n.* metallic element used in manufacture of hard steel

vandal (ˈvændᵊl) *n.* one who wantonly and deliberately damages or destroys —**ˈvandalism** *n.* —**ˈvandalize** *or* **-lise** *vt.*

Vandyke beard (ˈvændaɪk) short pointed beard (*also* **ˈVandyke**)

vane (veɪn) *n.* 1. weathercock 2. blade of propeller 3. fin on bomb *etc.* 4. sight on quadrant

vanguard (ˈvæŋgɑːd) *n.* leading, foremost group, position *etc.*

vanilla (vəˈnɪlə) *n.* 1. tropical climbing orchid 2. its seed(pod) 3. essence of this for flavouring

vanish (ˈvænɪʃ) *vi.* 1. disappear 2. fade away —**vanishing cream** cosmetic cream that is colourless once applied, used as foundation or cleansing cream —**vanishing point** 1. point to which parallel lines appear to converge 2. point at which something disappears

vanity (ˈvænɪtɪ) *n.* 1. excessive pride or conceit 2. ostentation —**vanity case** *or* **box** woman's small hand case for carrying cosmetics *etc.*

vanquish (ˈvæŋkwɪʃ) *vt.* 1. subdue in battle 2. conquer, overcome —**ˈvanquishable** *a.* —**ˈvanquisher** *n.*

vantage (ˈvɑːntɪdʒ) *n.* advantage

vapid (ˈvæpɪd) *a.* flat, dull, insipid —**vaˈpidity** *n.*

vapour *or U.S.* **vapor** (ˈveɪpə) *n.* 1. gaseous form of a substance more familiar as liquid or solid 2. steam, mist 3. invisible moisture in air —**ˈvaporize** *or* **-rise** *v.* convert into, pass off in, vapour —**ˈvaporizer** *or* **-riser** *n.* —**ˈvaporous** *a.*

variable (ˈvɛərɪəbᵊl) *see* VARY

varicose (ˈværɪkəʊs) *a.* (of vein) swollen, twisted

variegate (ˈvɛərɪgeɪt) *vt.* diversify by patches of different colours —**ˈvariegated** *a.* streaked, spotted, dappled —**varieˈgation** *n.*

variety (vəˈraɪɪtɪ) *n.* 1. state of being varied or various 2. diversity 3. varied assortment 4. sort, kind

THESAURUS

valley coomb, cwm (*Welsh*), dale, dell, depression, dingle, glen, hollow, strath (*Scot.*), vale

valuable *adj.* 1. costly, dear, expensive, high-priced, precious 2. beneficial, cherished, esteemed, estimable, held dear, helpful, important, prized, profitable, serviceable, treasured, useful, valued, worthwhile, worthy ~*n.* 3. *Usually plural* heirloom, treasure(s)

value *n.* 1. cost, equivalent, market price, monetary worth, rate 2. advantage, benefit, desirability, help, importance, merit, profit, serviceableness, significance, use, usefulness, utility, worth 3. *Plural* code of behaviour, ethics, (moral) standards, principles ~*v.* 4. account, appraise, assess, compute, estimate, evaluate, price, put a price on, rate, set at, survey 5. appreciate, cherish, esteem, hold dear, hold in high regard *or* esteem, prize, regard highly, respect, set store by, treasure

valued cherished, dear, esteemed, highly regarded, loved, prized, treasured

valueless miserable, no good, of no earthly use, of no value, unsaleable, useless, worthless

vanguard advance guard, forefront, forerunners, front, front line, front rank, leaders, spearhead, trailblazers, trendsetters, van

vanish become invisible, be lost to sight, die out, disappear, disappear from sight *or* from the face of the earth, dissolve, evanesce, evaporate, exit, fade (away), melt (away)

vanity affected ways, airs, arrogance, bigheadedness (*Inf.*), conceit, conceitedness, egotism, narcissism, ostentation, pretension, pride, self-admiration, self-love, showing off (*Inf.*), swollen-headedness (*Inf.*), vainglory

vanquish beat, conquer, crush, defeat, get the upper hand over, master, overcome, overpower, overwhelm, put down, put to flight, put to rout, quell, reduce, repress, rout, subdue, subjugate, triumph over

vapour breath, dampness, exhalation, fog, fumes, haze, miasma, mist, smoke, steam

variable capricious, chameleonic, changeable, fickle, fitful, flexible, fluctuating, inconstant, mercurial, mutable, protean, shifting, temperamental, unstable, unsteady, vacillating, wavering

variance difference, difference of opinion, disagreement, discord, discrepancy, dissension, dissent, divergence, inconsistency, lack of harmony, strife, variation

variant 1. *adj.* alternative, derived, different, divergent, exceptional, modified 2. *n.* alternative, derived form, development, modification, sport (*Biol.*), variation

variation alteration, break in routine, change, departure, departure from the norm, deviation, difference,

various (ˈvɛərɪəs) *a.* manifold, diverse, of several kinds

varlet (ˈvɑːlɪt) *n.* formerly, menial servant; rascal

varmint (ˈvɑːmɪnt) *n. inf.* obnoxious person or animal

varnish (ˈvɑːnɪʃ) *n.* **1.** resinous solution put on a surface to make it hard and shiny —*vt.* **2.** apply varnish to

varsity (ˈvɑːsɪtɪ) *n.* **UK** *inf.* university

vary (ˈvɛərɪ) *v.* (cause to) change, diversify, differ, deviate (**ˈvaried, ˈvarying**) —**variaˈbility** *n.* —**ˈvariable** *a.* **1.** changeable **2.** unsteady; fickle —*n.* **3.** something subject to variation —**ˈvariance** *n.* state of discord, discrepancy —**ˈvariant** *a.* **1.** different —*n.* **2.** difference in form **3.** alternative form or reading —**variˈation** *n.* **1.** alteration **2.** extent to which thing varies **3.** modification —**variˈational** *a.* —**ˈvaried** *a.* **1.** diverse **2.** modified **3.** variegated

vas (væs) *n. Anat.* vessel, tube carrying bodily fluid (*pl.* **vasa** (ˈveɪsə)) —**vas deferens** (ˈdɛfərɛnz) duct within each testis that conveys spermatozoa to ejaculatory duct (*pl.* **vasa deferentia** (dɛfəˈrɛnʃɪə))

vascular (ˈvæskjʊlə) *a.* of, with vessels for conveying sap, blood *etc.*

vase (vɑːz) *n.* vessel, jar as ornament or for holding flowers

vasectomy (væˈsɛktəmɪ) *n.* contraceptive measure of surgical removal of part of vas bearing sperm from testicle

Vaseline (ˈvæsɪliːn) *n.* **R** jellylike petroleum product

vassal (ˈvæsəl) *n.* **1.** holder of land by feudal tenure **2.** dependant —**ˈvassalage** *n.*

vast (vɑːst) *a.* very large —**ˈvastly** *adv.* —**ˈvastness** *n.*

vat (væt) *n.* large tub, tank

VAT (*sometimes* væt) value added tax

Vatican (ˈvætɪkən) *n.* **1.** Pope's palace **2.** papal authority

vaudeville (ˈvəʊdəvɪl, ˈvɔː-) *n.* theatrical entertainment with songs, juggling acts, dance *etc.*

vault[1] (vɔːlt) *n.* **1.** arched roof **2.** arched apartment **3.** cellar **4.** burial chamber **5.** place for storing valuables —*vt.* **6.** build with arched roof —**ˈvaulting** *n.* one or more vaults in building or such structures collectively

vault[2] (vɔːlt) *v.* **1.** spring, jump over (object) with the hands resting on something —*n.* **2.** such jump —**ˈvaulting** *a.* **1.** excessively confident **2.** used to vault

vaunt (vɔːnt) *v./n.* boast

vb. verb

V.C. **1.** Vice Chairman **2.** Vice Chancellor **3.** Victoria Cross **4.** Viet Cong

VCR **1.** video cassette recorder **2.** visual control room (at airfield)

VD venereal disease

VDU visual display unit

veal (viːl) *n.* calf flesh as food

vector (ˈvɛktə) *n.* **1.** quantity (*eg* force) having both magnitude and direction **2.** disease-carrying organism, *esp.* insect **3.** compass direction, course

V-E Day day marking Allied victory in Europe in World War II (May 8th, 1945)

veer (vɪə) *vi.* **1.** change direction **2.** change one's mind

vegan (ˈviːgən) *n.* strict vegetarian, who does not eat animal products

vegetable (ˈvɛdʒtəbəl) *n.* **1.** plant, *esp.* edible one **2.** *inf.* person who has lost use of his mental faculties, limbs *etc.* **3.** *inf.* dull person —*a.* **4.** of, from, concerned with plants —**vegetable marrow** plant with long, green-striped fruit, eaten as vegetable —**vegetable oil** any of group of oils obtained from plants

vegetarian (vɛdʒɪˈtɛərɪən) *n.* **1.** one who does not eat meat —*a.* **2.** not eating meat; without meat —**vegeˈtarianism** *n.*

vegetate (ˈvɛdʒɪteɪt) *vi.* **1.** (of plants) grow, develop **2.** (of person) live dull, unproductive life —**vegeˈtation**

THESAURUS

discrepancy, diversification, diversity, innovation, modification, novelty, variety

varied assorted, different, diverse, heterogeneous, miscellaneous, mixed, motley, sundry, various

variety **1.** change, difference, discrepancy, diversification, diversity, many-sidedness, multifariousness, variation **2.** array, assortment, collection, cross section, intermixture, medley, miscellany, mixture, multiplicity, range **3.** brand, breed, category, class, kind, make, order, sort, species, strain, type

various assorted, different, differing, disparate, distinct, divers (*Archaic*), diverse, diversified, heterogeneous, many, many-sided, miscellaneous, several, sundry, varied, variegated

varnish *v.* adorn, decorate, embellish, gild, glaze, gloss, japan, lacquer, polish, shellac

vary alter, alternate, be unlike, change, depart, differ, disagree, diverge, diversify, fluctuate, intermix, modify, permutate, reorder, transform

varying changing, different, distinct, distinguishable, diverse, fluctuating, inconsistent

vast astronomical, boundless, colossal, enormous, extensive, gigantic, great, huge, illimitable, immeasurable, immense, limitless, mammoth, massive, measureless, monstrous, monumental, never-ending, prodigious, sweeping, tremendous, unbounded, unlimited, vasty (*Archaic*), voluminous, wide

vault[1] *n.* **1.** arch, ceiling, roof, span **2.** catacomb, cellar, crypt, mausoleum, tomb, undercroft **3.** depository, repository, strongroom

vault[2] *v.* bound, clear, hurdle, jump, leap, spring

vaunt boast about, brag about, crow about, exult in, flaunt, give oneself airs about, make a display of, make much of, parade, prate about, show off, talk big about (*Inf.*)

veer be deflected, change, change course, change direction, sheer, shift, swerve, tack, turn

vegetate **1.** be inert, deteriorate, exist, go to seed, idle, languish, loaf, moulder, stagnate **2.** burgeon, germinate, grow, shoot, spring, sprout, swell

vehemence ardour, eagerness, earnestness, emphasis, energy, enthusiasm, fervency, fervour, fire, force, forcefulness, heat, impetuosity, intensity, keenness, passion, verve, vigour, violence, warmth, zeal

vehement ardent, eager, earnest, emphatic, enthusiastic, fervent, fervid, fierce, forceful, forcible, impassioned, impetuous, intense, passionate, powerful, strong, violent, zealous

n. **1.** plants collectively **2.** plants growing in a place **3.** process of plant growth —**vegetative** (ˈvɛdʒɪtətɪv) *a.*

vehement (ˈviːɪmənt) *a.* **1.** marked by intensity of feeling **2.** vigorous **3.** forcible —ˈ**vehemence** *n.* —ˈ**vehemently** *adv.*

vehicle (ˈviːɪkəl) *n.* **1.** means of conveying **2.** means of expression **3.** medium —**vehicular** (vɪˈhɪkjʊlə) *a.*

veil (veɪl) *n.* **1.** light material to cover face or head **2.** mask, cover —*vt.* **3.** cover with, as with, veil —**veiled** *a.* disguised —**take the veil** become a nun

vein (veɪn) *n.* **1.** tube in body taking blood to heart **2.** rib of leaf or insect's wing **3.** fissure in rock filled with ore **4.** streak **5.** distinctive trait, strain *etc.* **6.** mood —*vt.* **7.** mark with streaks —ˈ**veiny** *a.* —**venation** (viːˈneɪʃən) *n.* **1.** arrangement of veins in leaf *etc.* **2.** such veins collectively —ˈ**venous** *a.* of veins

Velcro (ˈvɛlkrəʊ) *n.* **R** fastening consisting of two strips of nylon fabric, one having tiny hooked threads and the other a coarse surface, that form strong bond when pressed together

veld *or* **veldt** (fɛlt, vɛlt) *n.* elevated grassland in S Afr. —**veldskoen** (ˈfɛltskʊn, ˈvɛlt-) *n.* **SA** ankle-length boot *orig.* of raw hide

veleta *or* **valeta** (vəˈliːtə) *n.* ballroom dance in triple time

vellum (ˈvɛləm) *n.* **1.** parchment of calfskin used for manuscripts or bindings **2.** paper resembling this

velocipede (vɪˈlɒsɪpiːd) *n.* early form of bicycle

velocity (vɪˈlɒsɪtɪ) *n.* **1.** rate of motion in given direction, *esp.* of inanimate things **2.** speed

velodrome (ˈviːlədrəʊm, ˈvɛl-) *n.* area with banked track for cycle racing

velours *or* **velour** (vɛˈlʊə) *n.* fabric with velvety finish

velum (ˈviːləm) *n.* **1.** *Zool.* membranous covering or organ **2.** soft palate (*pl.* **vela** (ˈviːlə))

velvet (ˈvɛlvɪt) *n.* silk or cotton fabric with thick, short pile —**velveˈteen** *n.* cotton fabric resembling velvet —ˈ**velvety** *a.* **1.** of, like velvet **2.** soft and smooth

vena cava (ˈviːnə ˈkeɪvə) either of two large veins that convey oxygen-depleted blood to heart (*pl.* **venae cavae** (ˈviːniː ˈkeɪviː))

venal (ˈviːnəl) *a.* **1.** guilty of taking, prepared to take, bribes **2.** corrupt —**veˈnality** *n.*

vend (vɛnd) *vt.* sell —ˈ**vendible** *a.* **1.** saleable, marketable —*n.* **2.** (*usu. pl.*) *rare* saleable object —ˈ**vendor** *n.* —**vending machine** machine that automatically dispenses goods when money is inserted

vendetta (vɛnˈdɛtə) *n.* bitter, prolonged feud

veneer (vɪˈnɪə) *n.* **1.** thin layer of fine wood **2.** superficial appearance —*vt.* **3.** cover with veneer

venerable (ˈvɛnərəbəl) *a.* worthy of reverence —ˈ**venerate** *vt.* look up to, respect, revere —**venerˈation** *n.*

venereal (vɪˈnɪərɪəl) *a.* **1.** (of disease) transmitted by sexual intercourse **2.** infected with venereal disease **3.** of genitals or sexual intercourse

venery[1] (ˈvɛnərɪ, ˈviː-) *n. obs.* pursuit of sexual gratification

venery[2] (ˈvɛnərɪ, ˈviː-) *n. Hist.* art, practice of hunting

Venetian (vɪˈniːʃən) *a.* **1.** of Venice, port in NE Italy —*n.* **2.** native or inhabitant of Venice —**Venetian blind** window blind made of thin horizontal slats arranged to turn so as to admit or exclude light

vengeance (ˈvɛndʒəns) *n.* **1.** revenge **2.** retribution for wrong done —ˈ**vengeful** *a.*

venial (ˈviːnɪəl) *a.* pardonable

venison (ˈvɛnɪzən, -sən) *n.* flesh of deer as food

venom (ˈvɛnəm) *n.* **1.** poison **2.** spite —ˈ**venomous** *a.* poisonous

venous (ˈviːnəs) *a. see* VEIN

vent[1] (vɛnt) *n.* **1.** small hole or outlet —*vt.* **2.** give outlet to **3.** utter **4.** pour forth

vent[2] (vɛnt) *n.* vertical slit in garment, *esp.* at back of jacket

ventilate (ˈvɛntɪleɪt) *vt.* **1.** supply with fresh air **2.** bring into discussion —**ventiˈlation** *n.* —ˈ**ventilator** *n.*

ventral (ˈvɛntrəl) *a.* abdominal

ventricle (ˈvɛntrɪkəl) *n.* cavity, hollow in body, *esp.* in heart or brain —**venˈtricular** *a.*

THESAURUS

vehicle *Fig.* apparatus, channel, means, means of expression, mechanism, medium, organ

veil **1.** *v.* cloak, conceal, cover, dim, disguise, hide, mantle, mask, obscure, screen, shield **2.** *n.* blind, cloak, cover, curtain, disguise, film, mask, screen, shade, shroud

veiled concealed, covert, disguised, hinted at, implied, masked, suppressed

vein **1.** blood vessel, course, current, lode, seam, stratum, streak, stripe **2.** dash, hint, strain, streak, thread, trait **3.** attitude, bent, character, faculty, humour, mode, mood, note, style, temper, tenor, tone, turn

venal bent (*Sl.*), corrupt, corruptible, crooked (*Inf.*), dishonourable, grafting, mercenary, prostituted, purchasable, rapacious, simoniacal, sordid, unprincipled

vendetta bad blood, blood feud, feud, quarrel

veneer *n. Fig.* appearance, façade, false front, finish, front, gloss, guise, mask, pretence, semblance, show

venerable august, esteemed, grave, honoured, respected, revered, reverenced, sage, sedate, wise, worshipped

venerate adore, esteem, hold in awe, honour, look up to, respect, revere, reverence, worship

veneration adoration, awe, deference, esteem, respect, reverence, worship

vengeance an eye for an eye, avenging, lex talionis, reprisal, requital, retaliation, retribution, revenge, settling of scores

venial allowable, excusable, forgivable, insignificant, minor, pardonable, slight, trivial

venom **1.** bane, poison, toxin **2.** acidity, acrimony, bitterness, gall, grudge, hate, ill will, malevolence, malice, maliciousness, malignity, rancour, spite, spitefulness, spleen, virulence

venomous baneful (*Archaic*), envenomed, mephitic, noxious, poison, poisonous, toxic, virulent

vent **1.** *n.* aperture, duct, hole, opening, orifice, outlet, split **2.** *v.* air, come out with, discharge, emit, empty, express, give expression to, give vent to, pour out, release, utter, voice

ventilate *Fig.* air, bring out into the open, broadcast, debate, discuss, examine, make known, scrutinize, sift, talk about

ventriloquist (vɛnˈtrɪləkwɪst) *n.* one who can so speak that the sounds seem to come from some other person or place —**venˈtriloquism** *n.*

venture (ˈvɛntʃə) *vt.* **1.** expose to hazard **2.** risk —*vi.* **3.** dare **4.** have courage (to do something or go somewhere) —*n.* **5.** risky undertaking **6.** speculative commercial undertaking —**ˈventuresome** *or* **ˈventurous** *a.*

venue (ˈvɛnjuː) *n.* **1.** *Law* district in which case is tried **2.** meeting place **3.** location

Venus (ˈviːnəs) *n.* **1.** Roman goddess of love **2.** planet between earth and Mercury —**Venus's flytrap** insect-eating plant

veracious (vɛˈreɪʃəs) *a.* **1.** truthful **2.** true —**veracity** (vɛˈræsɪtɪ) *n.*

veranda *or* **verandah** (vəˈrændə) *n.* open or partly enclosed porch on outside of house

verb (vɜːb) *n.* part of speech used to express action or being —**ˈverbal** *a.* **1.** of, by, or relating to words spoken rather than written **2.** of, like a verb —**ˈverbalism** *n.* **1.** verbal expression; phrase; word **2.** exaggerated emphasis on importance of words **3.** statement lacking real content —**ˈverbalize** *or* **-lise** *vt.* **1.** put into words —*vi.* **2.** speak —**ˈverbally** *adv.* —**verbatim** (vɜːˈbeɪtɪm) *adv./a.* word for word, literal(ly) —**verbal noun** noun derived from verb

verbascum (vɜːˈbæskəm) *n.* perennial garden plant

verbena (vɜːˈbiːnə) *n.* **1.** genus of fragrant, beautiful plants **2.** their characteristic scent

verbiage (ˈvɜːbɪɪdʒ) *n.* excess of words —**verbose** (vɜːˈbəʊs) *a.* wordy, long-winded —**verbosity** (vɜːˈbɒsɪtɪ) *n.*

verdant (ˈvɜːdᵊnt) *a.* green and fresh —**ˈverdure** *n.* **1.** greenery **2.** freshness —**ˈverdurous** *a.*

verdict (ˈvɜːdɪkt) *n.* **1.** decision of a jury **2.** opinion reached after examination of facts

verdigris (ˈvɜːdɪgrɪs) *n.* green film on copper

verdure (ˈvɜːdʒə) *n. see* VERDANT

verge (vɜːdʒ) *n.* **1.** edge **2.** brink **3.** grass border along a road —*vi.* **4.** (*with* on) come close (to) **5.** (*sometimes with* on) be on the border (of)

verger (ˈvɜːdʒə) *n.* **1.** caretaker and attendant in church **2.** bearer of wand of office

verify (ˈvɛrɪfaɪ) *vt.* **1.** prove, confirm truth of **2.** test accuracy of (**-ified, -ifying**) —**ˈverifiable** *a.* —**verifiˈcation** *n.*

verily (ˈvɛrɪlɪ) *adv. obs.* **1.** truly **2.** in truth

verisimilitude (vɛrɪsɪˈmɪlɪtjuːd) *n.* **1.** appearance of truth **2.** likelihood —**veriˈsimilar** *a.* probable; likely

veritable (ˈvɛrɪtəbᵊl) *a.* actual, true, genuine —**ˈveritably** *adv.*

verity (ˈvɛrɪtɪ) *n.* **1.** truth **2.** reality **3.** true assertion

verkrampte (fəˈkramtə) *n.* **SA** Afrikaner Nationalist opposed to liberal trends in government policy, particularly those related to race

verligte (fəˈləxtə) *n.* **SA** member of any white political party who supports more liberal trends in government policy

vermi- (*comb. form*) worm, as in *vermicide, vermiform, vermifuge*

vermicelli (vɜːmɪˈsɛlɪ, -ˈtʃɛlɪ) *n.* **1.** pasta in fine strands, used in soups **2.** tiny chocolate strands used to coat cakes *etc.*

vermicide (ˈvɜːmɪsaɪd) *n.* substance to destroy worms —**verˈmicular** *a.* **1.** resembling form, motion or tracks of worms **2.** of worms —**ˈvermiform** *a.* shaped like a worm (*eg* **vermiform appendix**)

vermilion (vəˈmɪljən) *a./n.* (of) bright red colour or pigment

vermin (ˈvɜːmɪn) *n.* (*with pl. v.*) injurious animals, parasites *etc.* —**ˈverminous** *a.*

vermouth (ˈvɜːməθ) *n.* wine flavoured with aromatic herbs *etc.*

vernacular (vəˈnækjʊlə) *n.* **1.** commonly spoken language or dialect of particular country or place —*a.* **2.** of vernacular **3.** native

vernal (ˈvɜːnᵊl) *a.* of spring

vernier (ˈvɜːnɪə) *n.* sliding scale for obtaining fractional parts of subdivision of graduated scale

veronica (vəˈrɒnɪkə) *n.* genus of plants including speedwell

verruca (vɛˈruːkə) *n.* wart, *esp.* on foot

versatile (ˈvɜːsətaɪl) *a.* **1.** capable of or adapted to many different uses, skills *etc.* **2.** liable to change —**versatility** (vɜːsəˈtɪlɪtɪ) *n.*

verse (vɜːs) *n.* **1.** stanza or short subdivision of poem or the Bible **2.** poetry **3.** line of poetry —**versifiˈcation**

THESAURUS

venture *v.* **1.** chance, endanger, hazard, imperil, jeopardize, put in jeopardy, risk, speculate, stake, wager **2.** advance, dare, dare say, hazard, make bold, presume, stick one's neck out (*Inf.*), take the liberty, volunteer ~*n.* **3.** adventure, chance, endeavour, enterprise, fling, gamble, hazard, jeopardy, project, risk, speculation, undertaking

verbal literal, oral, spoken, unwritten, verbatim, word-of-mouth

verbally by word of mouth, orally

verbatim exactly, precisely, to the letter, word for word

verbose circumlocutory, diffuse, garrulous, long-winded, periphrastic, pleonastic, prolix, tautological, windy, wordy

verbosity garrulity, logorrhoea, long-windedness, loquaciousness, prolixity, rambling, verbiage, verboseness, windiness, wordiness

verdict adjudication, conclusion, decision, finding, judgment, opinion, sentence

verge **1.** *n.* border, boundary, brim, brink, edge, extreme, limit, lip, margin, roadside, threshold **2.** *v.* approach, border, come near

verification authentication, confirmation, corroboration, proof, substantiation, validation

verify attest, attest to, authenticate, bear out, check, confirm, corroborate, prove, substantiate, support, validate

vernacular **1.** *adj.* colloquial, common, indigenous, informal, local, mother, native, popular, vulgar **2.** *n.* argot, cant, dialect, idiom, jargon, native language, parlance, patois, speech, vulgar tongue

versatile adaptable, adjustable, all-purpose, all-round, flexible, functional, handy, many-sided, multifaceted, protean, resourceful, variable

versed accomplished, acquainted, competent, conversant, experienced, familiar, knowledgeable, practised, proficient, qualified, seasoned, skilled, well informed, well up in (*Inf.*)

n. —ˈ**versify** *v.* turn (something) into verse (**-ified, -ifying**) —**versed in** skilled in

version (ˈvɜːʃən) *n.* **1.** description from certain point of view **2.** translation **3.** adaptation

verso (ˈvɜːsəʊ) *n.* back of sheet of printed paper, left-hand page (*pl.* **-s**)

versus (ˈvɜːsəs) *prep.* against

vertebra (ˈvɜːtɪbrə) *n.* single section of backbone (*pl.* **-brae** (-briː), **-s**) —ˈ**vertebral** *a.* of the spine —ˈ**vertebrate** *n.* **1.** animal with backbone —*a.* **2.** having a backbone

vertex (ˈvɜːtɛks) *n.* summit (*pl.* **-es, vertices** (ˈvɜːtɪsiːz))

vertical (ˈvɜːtɪkᵊl) *a.* **1.** at right angles to the horizon **2.** upright **3.** overhead

vertigo (ˈvɜːtɪgəʊ) *n.* giddiness (*pl.* **-es, vertigines** (vɜːˈtɪdʒɪniːz)) —**vertiginous** (vɜːˈtɪdʒɪnəs) *a.* dizzy

vertu (vɜːˈtuː) *n. see* VIRTU

verve (vɜːv) *n.* **1.** enthusiasm **2.** spirit **3.** energy, vigour

very (ˈvɛrɪ) *a.* **1.** exact, ideal **2.** same **3.** complete **4.** actual —*adv.* **5.** extremely, to great extent —**very high frequency** radio frequency or band lying between 300 and 30 megahertz —**very low frequency** radio frequency band or radio frequency lying between 30 and 3 kilohertz

vesicle (ˈvɛsɪkᵊl) *n.* small blister, bubble or cavity —**veˈsicular** *a.*

vespers (ˈvɛspəz) *n.* **1.** evening church service **2.** evensong

vessel (ˈvɛsᵊl) *n.* **1.** any object used as container, *esp.* for liquids **2.** ship, large boat **3.** tubular structure conveying liquids (*eg* blood) in body

vest (vɛst) *n.* **1.** undergarment for the trunk —*vt.* **2.** place **3.** bestow **4.** confer **5.** clothe —ˈ**vestment** *n.* robe or official garment —**vested interest** strong personal interest in particular state of affairs

vestal (ˈvɛstᵊl) *a.* pure, chaste —**vestal virgin** in ancient Rome, one of virgin priestesses whose lives were dedicated to Vesta and to maintaining sacred fire in her temple

vestibule (ˈvɛstɪbjuːl) *n.* entrance hall, lobby

vestige (ˈvɛstɪdʒ) *n.* small trace, amount —**vesˈtigial** *a.*

vestry (ˈvɛstrɪ) *n.* room in church for keeping vestments, holding meetings *etc.*

vet (vɛt) *n.* **1.** veterinary surgeon —*vt.* **2.** examine **3.** check (**-tt-**)

vet. **1.** veteran **2.** veterinary

vetch (vɛtʃ) *n.* plant of bean family

veteran (ˈvɛtərən) *n.* **1.** one who has served a long time, *esp.* in fighting services —*a.* **2.** long-serving —**veteran car UK** car constructed before 1919, *esp.* before 1905

veterinary (ˈvɛtərɪnərɪ) *a.* of, concerning the health of animals —**veterinary surgeon** surgeon qualified to treat animal ailments

veto (ˈviːtəʊ) *n.* **1.** power of rejecting piece of legislation or preventing it from coming into effect **2.** any prohibition (*pl.* **-es**) —*vt.* **3.** enforce veto against **4.** forbid with authority

vex (vɛks) *vt.* **1.** annoy **2.** distress —**vexˈation** *n.* **1.**

THESAURUS

version account, adaptation, exercise, interpretation, portrayal, reading, rendering, side, translation

vertical erect, on end, perpendicular, upright

vertigo dizziness, giddiness, light-headedness, loss of equilibrium, swimming of the head

verve animation, brio, dash, élan, energy, enthusiasm, force, get-up-and-go (*Inf.*), gusto, life, liveliness, punch (*Inf.*), sparkle, spirit, vigour, vim (*Sl.*), vitality, vivacity, zeal, zip (*Inf.*)

very **1.** *adv.* absolutely, acutely, awfully (*Inf.*), decidedly, deeply, eminently, exceedingly, excessively, extremely, greatly, highly, jolly (*Brit.*), noticeably, particularly, profoundly, really, remarkably, superlatively, surpassingly, terribly, truly, uncommonly, unusually, wonderfully **2.** *adj.* actual, appropriate, exact, express, identical, perfect, precise, real, same, selfsame, unqualified

vessel **1.** barque (*Poetic*), boat, craft, ship **2.** container, pot, receptacle, utensil

vest *v.* **1.** *With* **in** *or* **with** authorize, be devolved upon, bestow, confer, consign, empower, endow, entrust, furnish, invest, lodge, place, put in the hands of, settle **2.** apparel, bedeck, clothe, cover, dress, envelop, garb, robe

vestibule anteroom, entrance hall, foyer, hall, lobby, porch, portico

vestige evidence, glimmer, hint, indication, relic, remainder, remains, remnant, residue, scrap, sign, suspicion, token, trace, track

vet *v.* appraise, check, check out, examine, give (someone *or* something) the once-over (*Inf.*), investigate, look over, pass under review, review, scan, scrutinize, size up (*Inf.*)

veteran **1.** *n.* master, old hand, old stager, old-timer, past master, past mistress, pro (*Inf.*), trouper, warhorse (*Inf.*) **2.** *adj.* adept, battle-scarred, expert, long-serving, old, proficient, seasoned

veto **1.** *v.* ban, disallow, forbid, give the thumbs down to, interdict, kill (*Inf.*), negative, prohibit, put the kibosh on (*Sl.*), refuse permission, reject, rule out, turn down **2.** *n.* ban, embargo, interdict, nonconsent, prohibition

vex afflict, aggravate (*Inf.*), agitate, annoy, bother, bug (*Inf.*), displease, distress, disturb, exasperate, fret, gall, grate on, harass, irritate, molest, needle (*Inf.*), nettle, offend, peeve (*Inf.*), perplex, pester, pique, plague, provoke, put out, rile, tease, torment, trouble, upset, worry

vexation **1.** aggravation (*Inf.*), annoyance, displeasure, dissatisfaction, exasperation, frustration, irritation, pique **2.** bother, difficulty, headache (*Inf.*), irritant, misfortune, nuisance, problem, thorn in one's flesh, trouble, upset, worry

vexatious afflicting, aggravating (*Inf.*), annoying, bothersome, burdensome, disagreeable, disappointing, distressing, exasperating, harassing, irksome, irritating, nagging, plaguy (*Archaic*), provoking, teasing, tormenting, troublesome, trying, unpleasant, upsetting, worrisome, worrying

vexed **1.** afflicted, aggravated (*Inf.*), agitated, annoyed, bothered, confused, displeased, distressed, disturbed, exasperated, fed up, harassed, irritated, miffed (*Inf.*), nettled, out of countenance, peeved (*Inf.*), perplexed, provoked, put out, riled, ruffled, tormented, troubled, upset, worried **2.** contested, controversial, disputed, moot, much debated

cause of irritation 2. state of distress —**vex'atious** *a.* —**vexed** *a.* 1. cross, annoyed 2. much discussed

VHF *or* **vhf** very high frequency

V.I. Vancouver Island

via ('vaɪə) *prep.* by way of

viable ('vaɪəb'l) *a.* 1. practicable 2. able to live and grow independently —**via'bility** *n.*

viaduct ('vaɪədʌkt) *n.* bridge over valley for a road or railway

vial ('vaɪəl) *n. see* PHIAL

viands ('viːəndz) *pl.n.* food

viaticum (vaɪ'ætɪkəm) *n.* 1. Holy Communion as administered to person dying or in danger of death 2. *rare* provisions or travel allowance for journey (*pl.* **-ca** (-kə), **-s**)

vibes (vaɪbz) *pl.n. inf.* 1. vibrations 2. vibraphone

vibraphone ('vaɪbrəfəʊn) *n.* musical instrument like xylophone, but with electronic resonators, that produces a gentle vibrato

vibrate (vaɪ'breɪt) *v.* 1. (cause to) move to and fro rapidly and continuously 2. give off (light or sound) by vibration —*vi.* 3. oscillate 4. quiver —**'vibrant** *a.* 1. throbbing 2. vibrating 3. appearing vigorous, lively —**vi'bration** *n.* 1. a vibrating —*pl.* 2. *inf.* instinctive feelings about a place, person *etc.* —**vibrato** (vɪ'brɑːtəʊ) *n.* vibrating effect in music (*pl.* **-s**) —**vi'brator** *n.* —**'vibratory** *a.*

viburnum (vaɪ'bɜːnəm) *n.* subtropical shrub with white flowers and berrylike fruits

Vic. A Victoria (state)

vicar ('vɪkə) *n.* clergyman in charge of parish —**'vicarage** *n.* vicar's house —**vicarial** (vɪ'kɛərɪəl) *a.* of vicar —**vicar apostolic** *R.C. Ch.* titular bishop having jurisdiction in missionary countries —**vicar general** official appointed to assist bishop of diocese in administrative or judicial duties (*pl.* **vicars general**) —**Vicar of Christ** *R.C.Ch.* the Pope

vicarious (vɪ'kɛərɪəs, vaɪ-) *a.* 1. obtained, enjoyed or undergone at second hand through sympathetic participation in another's experiences 2. suffered, done *etc.* as substitute for another —**vi'cariously** *adv.*

vice[1] (vaɪs) *n.* 1. evil or immoral habit or practice 2. criminal immorality, *esp.* prostitution 3. fault, imperfection —**vice squad** police division which deals with enforcement of gaming and prostitution laws

vice[2] *or U.S.* (*oft.*) **vise** (vaɪs) *n.* appliance with screw jaw for holding things while working on them

vice[3] (vaɪs) *n. inf.* person who serves as deputy to another

vice- (*comb. form*) in place of, second to, as in *vice-chairman, viceroy.* Such compounds are not given here where meaning may be inferred from simple word

vice admiral commissioned officer of flag rank in certain navies, junior to admiral and senior to rear admiral

vicegerent (vaɪs'dʒɛrənt) *n.* 1. person appointed to exercise all or some of authority of another 2. *R.C.Ch.* representative of God or Christ on earth, such as pope —*a.* 3. invested with or characterized by delegated authority —**vice'gerency** *n.*

vice president officer ranking immediately below president and serving as his deputy —**vice-presidency** *n.*

viceroy ('vaɪsrɔɪ) *n.* ruler acting for king in province or dependency (**vicereine** (vaɪs'reɪn) *fem.*) —**vice'regal** *a.* of viceroy —**vice'royalty** *n.*

vice versa ('vaɪsɪ 'vɜːsə) *Lat.* conversely, the other way round

vichy water ('vɪʃɪ) 1. (*sometimes* **V-**) mineral water from Vichy in France, reputed to be beneficial to health 2. any sparkling mineral water resembling this

vicinage ('vɪsənɪdʒ) *n. rare* 1. residents of particular neighbourhood 2. vicinity

vicinity (vɪ'sɪnɪtɪ) *n.* neighbourhood

vicious ('vɪʃəs) *a.* 1. wicked, cruel 2. ferocious, dangerous 3. leading to vice —**'viciously** *adv.* —**vicious circle** 1. situation in which attempt to resolve one problem creates new problems that lead back to original situation 2. *Logic* invalid form of reasoning in which conclusion is derived from premiss orig. deduced from same conclusion 3. *Logic* circular definition

vicissitude (vɪ'sɪsɪtjuːd) *n.* 1. change of fortune —*pl.* 2. ups and downs of fortune —**vicissi'tudinous** *a.*

victim ('vɪktɪm) *n.* 1. person or thing killed, injured *etc.* as result of another's deed, or accident, circumstances *etc.* 2. person cheated 3. sacrifice —**victimi'zation** *or* **-mi'sation** *n.* —**'victimize** *or* **-mise** *vt.* 1. punish unfairly 2. make victim of

victor ('vɪktə) *n.* 1. conqueror 2. winner —**vic'torious**

THESAURUS

viable applicable, feasible, operable, practicable, usable, within the bounds of possibility, workable

vibrant 1. aquiver, oscillating, palpitating, pulsating, quivering, trembling 2. alive, animated, colourful, dynamic, electrifying, full of pep (*Inf.*), responsive, sensitive, sparkling, spirited, vivacious, vivid

vibrate fluctuate, judder (*Inf.*), oscillate, pulsate, pulse, quiver, resonate, reverberate, shake, shiver, sway, swing, throb, tremble, undulate

vibration juddering (*Inf.*), oscillation, pulsation, pulse, quiver, resonance, reverberation, shaking, throb, throbbing, trembling, tremor

vice 1. corruption, degeneracy, depravity, evil, evildoing, immorality, iniquity, profligacy, sin, venality, wickedness 2. blemish, defect, failing, fault, imperfection, shortcoming, weakness

vicinity area, district, environs, locality, neck of the woods (*Inf.*), neighbourhood, precincts, propinquity, proximity, purlieus

vicious abandoned, abhorrent, atrocious, bad, barbarous, corrupt, cruel, dangerous, debased, degenerate, degraded, depraved, diabolical, ferocious, fiendish, foul, heinous, immoral, infamous, monstrous, profligate, savage, sinful, unprincipled, vile, violent, wicked, worthless, wrong

victim 1. casualty, fatality, injured party, martyr, sacrifice, scapegoat, sufferer 2. dupe, easy prey, fall guy (*Inf.*), gull (*Archaic*), innocent, sitting target, sucker (*Sl.*)

victimize discriminate against, have a down on (someone) (*Inf.*), have it in for (someone) (*Inf.*), have one's knife into (someone), persecute, pick on

victor champ (*Inf.*), champion, conquering hero, conqueror, first, prizewinner, top dog (*Inf.*), vanquisher, winner *a.* **1.** winning **2.** triumphant —ˈ**victory** *n.* winning of battle *etc.*

victoria (vɪkˈtɔːrɪə) *n.* **1.** four-wheeled horse-drawn carriage with folding hood **2. UK** large sweet plum, red and yellow in colour (*also* **victoria plum**)

Victorian (vɪkˈtɔːrɪən) *a.* **1.** of Victoria, queen of Great Brit. and Ireland, or period of her reign **2.** exhibiting characteristics popularly attributed to Victorians, *esp.* prudery *etc.* **3.** of Victoria (state in Aust. or any of the cities) —*n.* **4.** person who lived during reign of Queen Victoria **5.** inhabitant of Victoria (state or any of the cities) —**Victoria Cross** highest decoration for gallantry in face of enemy awarded to Brit. and Commonwealth armed forces —**Victoria Day** Monday preceding May 24th: national holiday in Canad. in commemoration of Queen Victoria's birthday

victual (ˈvɪtᵊl) *n.* **1.** (*usu. pl.*) food —*v.* **2.** supply with or obtain food (**-ll-**) —ˈ**victualler** *n.*

vicuña (vɪˈkjuːnə, -ˈkuːnjə) *n.* **1.** S Amer. animal like llama **2.** fine, light cloth made from its wool

vide (ˈvaɪdɪ) *Lat.* see —**vide infra** see below —**vide supra** see above

videlicet (vɪˈdiːlɪsɛt) *Lat.* namely

video (ˈvɪdɪəʊ) *a.* **1.** relating to or used in transmission or production of television image —*n.* **2.** film recorded on video cassette **3.** video cassette (recorder) (*pl.* **videos**) —*v.* **4.** record (television programme *etc.*) on video cassette recorder (ˈ**videoed,** ˈ**videoing**) —**video cassette** cassette containing video tape —**video cassette recorder** tape recorder for vision and sound signals using magnetic tape in closed plastic cassettes: used for recording and playing back television programmes and films —**video disc** *or* ˈ**videodisc** *n.* disc stored with information, which one plays like a gramophone record, the result being translated, in sound and vision, on to TV set —**video nasty** film, usu. specially made for video, that is explicitly horrific and pornographic —ˈ**videophone** *n.* telephonic device in which there is both verbal and visual communication between parties —**video tape** magnetic tape on which to record television programme

vie (vaɪ) *vi.* (*with* with *or* for) contend, compete (against or for someone, something) (**vied,** ˈ**vying**)

Vietnamese (vjɛtnəˈmiːz) *a.* **1.** of Vietnam, in SE Asia —*n.* **2.** native of Vietnam (*pl.* **-ese**) **3.** language of Vietnam

view (vjuː) *n.* **1.** survey by eyes or mind **2.** range of vision **3.** picture **4.** scene **5.** opinion **6.** purpose —*vt.* **7.** look at **8.** survey **9.** consider —ˈ**viewer** *n.* **1.** one who views **2.** one who watches television **3.** optical device to assist viewing of photographic slides —ˈ**viewfinder** *n.* device on camera enabling user to see what will be included in photograph —ˈ**viewpoint** *n.* **1.** way of regarding a subject **2.** position commanding view of landscape

viewdata (ˈvjuːdeɪtə) *n.* *see* TELETEXT

vigil (ˈvɪdʒɪl) *n.* **1.** a keeping awake, watch **2.** eve of feast day —ˈ**vigilance** *n.* —ˈ**vigilant** *a.* watchful, alert —**vigilance committee US** self-appointed body of citizens organized to maintain order *etc.*

vigilante (vɪdʒɪˈlæntɪ) *n.* one, *esp.* as member of group, who unofficially takes it upon himself to enforce law

vignette (vɪˈnjɛt) *n.* **1.** short literary essay, sketch **2.** photograph or portrait with the background shaded off

vigour *or U.S.* **vigor** (ˈvɪgə) *n.* **1.** force, strength **2.** energy, activity —ˈ**vigorous** *a.* **1.** strong **2.** energetic **3.** flourishing —ˈ**vigorously** *adv.*

Viking (ˈvaɪkɪŋ) *n.* medieval Scandinavian seafarer, raider, settler

vile (vaɪl) *a.* **1.** very wicked, shameful **2.** disgusting **3.** despicable —ˈ**vilely** *adv.* —ˈ**vileness** *n.* —**vilification** (vɪlɪfɪˈkeɪʃən) *n.* —**vilify** (ˈvɪlɪfaɪ) *vt.* **1.** speak ill of **2.** slander (**-ified, -ifying**)

THESAURUS

victorious champion, conquering, first, prizewinning, successful, triumphant, vanquishing, winning

victory conquest, laurels, mastery, success, superiority, the palm, the prize, triumph, win

victuals bread, comestibles, eatables, eats (*Sl.*), edibles, food, grub (*Sl.*), meat, nosh (*Sl.*), provisions, rations, stores, supplies, viands, vittles (*Obsolete*)

view *n.* **1.** aspect, landscape, outlook, panorama, perspective, picture, prospect, scene, spectacle, vista **2.** range *or* field of vision, sight, vision **3.** *Sometimes plural* attitude, belief, conviction, feeling, impression, judgment, notion, opinion, point of view, sentiment, thought, way of thinking **4.** contemplation, display, examination, inspection, look, scan, scrutiny, sight, survey, viewing ~*v.* **5.** behold, contemplate, examine, explore, eye, gaze at, inspect, look at, observe, regard, scan, spectate, stare at, survey, watch, witness **6.** consider, deem, judge, look on, regard, think about

viewer observer, one of an audience, onlooker, spectator, TV watcher, watcher

viewpoint angle, frame of reference, perspective, point of view, position, slant, stance, standpoint, vantage point, way of thinking

vigilant alert, Argus-eyed, attentive, careful, cautious, circumspect, keeping one's eyes peeled *or* skinned (*Inf.*), on one's guard, on one's toes, on the alert, on the lookout, on the qui vive, on the watch, sleepless, unsleeping, wakeful, watchful, wide awake

vigorous active, brisk, dynamic, effective, efficient, energetic, enterprising, flourishing, forceful, forcible, full of energy, hale, hale and hearty, hardy, healthy, intense, lively, lusty, powerful, red-blooded, robust, sound, spanking, spirited, strenuous, strong, virile, vital, zippy (*Inf.*)

vigorously all out, eagerly, energetically, forcefully, hammer and tongs, hard, like mad (*Sl.*), lustily, strenuously, strongly, with a vengeance, with might and main

vigour activity, animation, dash, dynamism, energy, force, forcefulness, gusto, health, liveliness, might, oomph (*Inf.*), pep, power, punch (*Inf.*), robustness, snap (*Inf.*), soundness, spirit, strength, verve, vim (*Sl.*), virility, vitality, zip (*Inf.*)

vile **1.** abandoned, abject, appalling, bad, base, coarse, contemptible, corrupt, debased, degenerate, degrading, depraved, despicable, disgraceful, evil, humiliating, ignoble, impure, loathsome, low, mean, miserable, nefarious, perverted, shocking, sinful, ugly, vicious, vulgar, wicked, worthless, wretched **2.** disgusting, foul, horrid, loathsome, nasty, nauseating, noxious, offensive, repellent, repugnant, repulsive, revolting, sickening

vilify abuse, asperse, bad-mouth (*U.S. sl.*), berate,

villa (ˈvɪlə) *n.* **1.** large, luxurious, country house **2.** detached or semidetached suburban house

village (ˈvɪlɪdʒ) *n.* small group of houses in country area —ˈ**villager** *n.*

villain (ˈvɪlən) *n.* **1.** wicked person **2.** *inf.* mischievous person —ˈ**villainous** *a.* **1.** wicked **2.** vile —ˈ**villainy** *n.*

villein (ˈvɪlən) *n.* in medieval Europe, peasant personally bound to his lord, to whom he paid dues and services in return for land —ˈ**villeinage** *n.*

vim (vɪm) *n. inf.* force, energy

vinaigrette (vɪneɪˈgrɛt) *n.* **1.** small bottle of smelling salts **2.** type of salad dressing

vinculum (ˈvɪŋkjʊləm) *n.* **1.** line drawn above group of mathematical terms, used as sign of aggregation in mathematical expressions, as in $\overline{x+y}$ **2.** *Anat.* bandlike structure, *esp.* uniting two or more parts (*pl.* **-la** (-lə))

vindicate (ˈvɪndɪkeɪt) *vt.* **1.** clear of charges **2.** justify **3.** establish the truth or merit of —ˈ**vindicable** *a.* capable of being vindicated; justifiable —**vindiˈcation** *n.* —ˈ**vindicator** *n.* —ˈ**vindicatory** *a.*

vindictive (vɪnˈdɪktɪv) *a.* **1.** revengeful **2.** inspired by resentment

vine (vaɪn) *n.* climbing plant bearing grapes —ˈ**vinery** *n.* **1.** hothouse for growing grapes **2.** vineyard **3.** vines collectively —**vinosity** (vɪˈnɒsɪtɪ) *n.* distinctive and essential quality and flavour of wine —**vintage** (ˈvɪntɪdʒ) *n.* **1.** gathering of the grapes **2.** the yield **3.** wine of particular year **4.** time of origin —*a.* **5.** best and most typical —**vintner** (ˈvɪntnə) *n.* dealer in wine —**vintage car** *chiefly* **UK** old car, *esp.* constructed between 1919 and 1930 —**vineyard** (ˈvɪnjəd) *n.* plantation of vines

vinegar (ˈvɪnɪgə) *n.* acid liquid obtained from wine and other alcoholic liquors —ˈ**vinegary** *a.* **1.** like vinegar **2.** sour **3.** bad-tempered

vingt-et-un (vẽteˈœ̃) *Fr. see* PONTOON[2]

vini- *or before vowel* **vin-** (*comb. form*) wine, as in *viniculture*

viniculture (ˈvɪnɪkʌltʃə) *n.* process or business of growing grapes and making wine

vinyl (ˈvaɪnɪl) *n.* plastic material with variety of domestic and industrial uses

viol (ˈvaɪəl) *n.* early stringed instrument preceding violin —ˈ**violist** *n.* person who plays viol

viola[1] (vɪˈəʊlə) *n. see* VIOLIN

viola[2] (ˈvaɪələ, vaɪˈəʊ-) *n.* single-coloured variety of pansy

violate (ˈvaɪəleɪt) *vt.* **1.** break (law, agreement *etc.*), infringe **2.** rape **3.** outrage, desecrate —ˈ**violable** *a.* —**vioˈlation** *n.* —ˈ**violator** *n.*

violent (ˈvaɪələnt) *a.* **1.** marked by, due to, extreme force, passion or fierceness **2.** of great force **3.** intense —ˈ**violence** *n.* —ˈ**violently** *adv.*

violet (ˈvaɪəlɪt) *n.* **1.** plant with small bluish-purple or white flowers **2.** the flower **3.** bluish-purple colour —*a.* **4.** of this colour

violin (vaɪəˈlɪn) *n.* small four-stringed musical instrument —**viˈola** *n.* large violin with lower range —**vioˈlinist** *n.* —**violoncello** (vaɪələnˈtʃɛləʊ) *n. see* CELLO —**viola da gamba** (vɪˈəʊlə də ˈgæmbə) second largest and lowest member of viol family

V.I.P. very important person

viper (ˈvaɪpə) *n.* venomous snake

virago (vɪˈrɑːgəʊ) *n.* abusive woman (*pl.* **-es, -s**)

virgin (ˈvɜːdʒɪn) *n.* **1.** one who has not had sexual

THESAURUS

calumniate, debase, decry, defame, denigrate, disparage, malign, pull to pieces (*Inf.*), revile, run down, slander, smear, speak ill of, traduce, vilipend (*Rare*), vituperate

villain 1. blackguard, caitiff (*Archaic*), criminal, evildoer, knave (*Archaic*), libertine, malefactor, miscreant, profligate, rapscallion, reprobate, rogue, scoundrel, wretch **2.** devil, monkey, rascal, rogue, scallywag (*Inf.*), scamp

villainous atrocious, bad, base, blackguardly, criminal, cruel, debased, degenerate, depraved, detestable, diabolical, evil, fiendish, hateful, heinous, ignoble, infamous, inhuman, mean, nefarious, outrageous, ruffianly, scoundrelly, sinful, terrible, thievish, vicious, vile, wicked

villainy atrocity, baseness, crime, criminality, delinquency, depravity, devilry, iniquity, knavery, rascality, sin, turpitude, vice, wickedness

vindicate 1. absolve, acquit, clear, defend, do justice to, exculpate, excuse, exonerate, free from blame, justify, rehabilitate **2.** advocate, assert, establish, maintain, support, uphold

vindication apology, assertion, defence, exculpating, exculpation, excuse, exoneration, justification, maintenance, plea, rehabilitation, substantiation, support

vindictive full of spleen, implacable, malicious, malignant, rancorous, relentless, resentful, revengeful, spiteful, unforgiving, unrelenting, vengeful, venomous

vintage 1. *n.* collection, crop, epoch, era, generation, harvest, origin, year **2.** *adj.* best, choice, classic, mature, prime, rare, ripe, select, superior, venerable

violate 1. break, contravene, disobey, disregard, encroach upon, infract, infringe, transgress **2.** abuse, assault, befoul, debauch, defile, desecrate, dishonour, invade, outrage, pollute, profane, rape, ravish

violation 1. abuse, breach, contravention, encroachment, infraction, infringement, transgression, trespass **2.** defilement, desecration, profanation, sacrilege, spoliation

violence 1. bestiality, bloodshed, bloodthirstiness, brutality, brute force, cruelty, destructiveness, ferocity, fierceness, fighting, force, frenzy, fury, murderousness, passion, rough handling, savagery, strong-arm tactics (*Inf.*), terrorism, thuggery, vehemence, wildness **2.** boisterousness, power, raging, roughness, storminess, tumult, turbulence, wildness **3.** abandon, acuteness, fervour, force, harshness, intensity, severity, sharpness, vehemence

violent 1. berserk, bloodthirsty, brutal, cruel, destructive, fiery, forcible, furious, headstrong, homicidal, hot-headed, impetuous, intemperate, maddened, maniacal, murderous, passionate, powerful, raging, riotous, rough, savage, strong, uncontrollable, ungovernable, unrestrained, vehement, vicious, wild **2.** blustery, boisterous, devastating, full of force, gale force, powerful, raging, ruinous, strong, tempestuous, tumultuous, turbulent, wild **3.** acute, agonizing, biting, excruciating, extreme, harsh, inordinate, intense, outrageous, painful, severe, sharp

intercourse —*a.* **2.** without experience of sexual intercourse **3.** unsullied, fresh **4.** (of land) untilled —ˈ**virginal** *a.* **1.** of, like virgin —*n.* **2.** (*oft. pl.*) type of spinet —**vir**ˈ**ginity** *n.* —**Virgin Birth** doctrine that Jesus Christ was conceived solely by direct intervention of Holy Spirit so that Mary remained a virgin after his birth —**Virgin Mary** Mary, mother of Christ (*also* **the Virgin**)

Virginia creeper (vəˈdʒɪnɪə) climbing plant that turns red in autumn

Virgo (ˈvɜːgəʊ) *n.* (virgin) 6th sign of the zodiac operative c. Aug. 22nd-Sept. 21st

virgule (ˈvɜːgjuːl) *n. Print. see* SOLIDUS

virile (ˈvɪraɪl) *a.* **1.** (of male) capable of copulation or procreation **2.** strong, forceful —**virility** (vɪˈrɪlɪtɪ) *n.*

virology (vaɪˈrɒlədʒɪ) *n. see* VIRUS

virtu *or* **vertu** (vɜːˈtuː) *n.* **1.** taste or love for curios or works of fine art **2.** such objects collectively **3.** quality of being appealing to connoisseur (*esp. in* **articles of virtu, objects of virtu**)

virtual (ˈvɜːtʃʊəl) *a.* so in effect, though not in appearance or name —ˈ**virtually** *adv.* practically, almost

virtue (ˈvɜːtjuː) *n.* **1.** moral goodness **2.** good quality **3.** merit **4.** inherent power —ˈ**virtuous** *a.* **1.** morally good **2.** chaste —ˈ**virtuously** *adv.*

virtuoso (vɜːtjʊˈəʊzəʊ) *n.* one with special skill, *esp.* in a fine art (*pl.* **-s, -si** (-ziː)) —**virtuosity** (vɜːtjʊˈɒsɪtɪ) *n.* great technical skill, *esp.* in a fine art, as music

virulent (ˈvɪrʊlənt) *a.* **1.** very infectious, poisonous *etc.* **2.** malicious

virus (ˈvaɪrəs) *n.* any of various submicroscopic organisms, some causing disease —ˈ**viral** *a.* of virus —**vi**ˈ**rology** *n.* study of viruses

visa (ˈviːzə) *n.* endorsement on passport permitting the bearer to travel into country of issuing government —ˈ**visaed** *a.*

visage (ˈvɪzɪdʒ) *n.* face

vis-à-vis (viːzɑːˈviː) *Fr.* **1.** in relation to, regarding **2.** opposite to

Visc. Viscount

viscera (ˈvɪsərə) *pl.n.* large internal organs of body, *esp.* of abdomen (*sing.* **viscus** (ˈvɪskəs)) —ˈ**visceral** *a.*

viscid (ˈvɪsɪd) *a.* sticky, of a consistency like treacle —**vis**ˈ**cidity** *n.*

viscose (ˈvɪskəʊs) *n.* (substance used to produce) synthetic fabric

viscount (ˈvaɪkaʊnt) *n.* Brit. nobleman ranking below earl and above baron (ˈ**viscountess** *fem.*)

viscous (ˈvɪskəs) *a.* thick and sticky —**vis**ˈ**cosity** *n.*

visible (ˈvɪzɪbᵊl) *a.* that can be seen —**visi**ˈ**bility** *n.* degree of clarity of atmosphere, *esp.* for navigation —ˈ**visibly** *adv.*

vision (ˈvɪʒən) *n.* **1.** sight **2.** insight **3.** dream **4.** phantom **5.** imagination —ˈ**visionary** *a.* **1.** marked by vision **2.** impractical —*n.* **3.** mystic **4.** impractical person

visit (ˈvɪzɪt) *v.* **1.** go, come and see, stay temporarily with (someone) —*n.* **2.** stay **3.** call at person's home *etc.* **4.** official call —ˈ**visitant** *n.* **1.** ghost; apparition **2.** visitor or guest, usu. from far away **3.** migratory bird that is present in particular region only at certain

THESAURUS

virgin 1. *n.* damsel (*Archaic*), girl, maid (*Archaic*), maiden (*Archaic*), vestal, virgo intacta **2.** *adj.* chaste, fresh, immaculate, maidenly, modest, new, pristine, pure, snowy, uncorrupted, undefiled, unsullied, untouched, unused, vestal, virginal

virile forceful, lusty, macho, male, manlike, manly, masculine, potent, red-blooded, robust, strong, vigorous

virility machismo, manhood, masculinity, potency, vigour

virtual essential, implicit, implied, in all but name, indirect, potential, practical, tacit, unacknowledged

virtually as good as, effectually, for all practical purposes, in all but name, in effect, in essence, nearly, practically, to all intents and purposes

virtue 1. ethicalness, excellence, goodness, high-mindedness, incorruptibility, integrity, justice, morality, probity, quality, rectitude, righteousness, uprightness, worth, worthiness **2.** advantage, asset, attribute, credit, good point, good quality, merit, plus (*Inf.*), strength

virtuosity brilliance, éclat, expertise, finish, flair, mastery, panache, polish, skill

virtuoso *n.* artist, genius, maestro, magician, master, master hand

virtuous 1. blameless, ethical, excellent, exemplary, good, high-principled, honest, honourable, incorruptible, moral, praiseworthy, pure, righteous, upright, worthy **2.** celibate, chaste, clean-living, innocent, pure, spotless, virginal

virulent 1. baneful (*Archaic*), deadly, infective, injurious, lethal, malignant, pernicious, poisonous, septic, toxic, venomous **2.** acrimonious, bitter, envenomed, hostile, malevolent, malicious, rancorous, resentful, spiteful, splenetic, venomous, vicious, vindictive

visible anywhere to be seen, apparent, clear, conspicuous, detectable, discernible, discoverable, distinguishable, evident, in sight, in view, manifest, not hidden, noticeable, observable, obvious, palpable, patent, perceivable, perceptible, plain, to be seen, unconcealed, unmistakable

vision 1. eyes, eyesight, perception, seeing, sight, view **2.** breadth of view, discernment, farsightedness, foresight, imagination, insight, intuition, penetration, prescience **3.** castle in the air, concept, conception, daydream, dream, fantasy, idea, ideal, image, mental picture, pipe dream **4.** apparition, chimera, delusion, ghost, hallucination, illusion, mirage, phantasm, phantom, revelation, spectre, wraith

visionary *adj.* **1.** dreaming, dreamy, idealistic, quixotic, romantic, starry-eyed, with one's head in the clouds **2.** chimerical, delusory, fanciful, fantastic, ideal, idealized, illusory, imaginary, impractical, prophetic, speculative, unreal, unrealistic, unworkable, utopian ~*n.* **3.** daydreamer, Don Quixote, dreamer, enthusiast (*Archaic*), idealist, mystic, prophet, romantic, seer, theorist, utopian, zealot

visit 1. *v.* be the guest of, call in, call on, drop in on (*Inf.*), go to see, inspect, look (someone) up, pay a call on, pop in (*Inf.*), stay at, stay with, stop by, take in (*Inf.*) **2.** *n.* call, sojourn, stay, stop

visitation 1. examination, inspection, visit **2.** bane, blight, calamity, cataclysm, catastrophe, disaster, infliction, ordeal, punishment, scourge, trial

visitor caller, company, guest, visitant

times (*also* **ˈvisitor**) —**visiˈtation** *n.* **1.** formal visit or inspection **2.** affliction or plague —**ˈvisitor** *n.*

visor *or* **vizor** (ˈvaɪzə) *n.* **1.** front part of helmet made to move up and down before face **2.** eyeshade, *esp.* on car **3.** peak on cap

vista (ˈvɪstə) *n.* view, *esp.* distant view

visual (ˈvɪʒʊəl, -zjʊ-) *a.* **1.** of sight **2.** visible —**visualiˈzation** *or* **-liˈsation** *n.* —**ˈvisualize** *or* **-lise** *vt.* form mental image of —**visual aids** devices, such as films, slides *etc.*, that display in visual form material to be understood or remembered

vital (ˈvaɪtˀl) *a.* **1.** necessary to, affecting life **2.** lively, animated **3.** essential **4.** highly important —**viˈtality** *n.* life, vigour —**ˈvitalize** *or* **-lise** *vt.* **1.** give life to **2.** lend vigour to —**ˈvitally** *adv.* —**ˈvitals** *pl.n.* vital organs of body —**vital statistics 1.** data concerning human life or conditions affecting it, such as death rate **2.** *inf.* measurements of woman's bust, waist and hips

vitamin (ˈvɪtəmɪn, ˈvaɪ-) *n.* any of group of substances occurring in foodstuffs and essential to health

vitiate (ˈvɪʃɪeɪt) *vt.* **1.** spoil **2.** deprive of efficacy **3.** invalidate —**vitiˈation** *n.*

viticulture (ˈvɪtɪkʌltʃə) *n.* **1.** science, art or process of cultivating grapevines **2.** study of (growing of) grapes —**vitiˈculturist** *n.*

vitreous (ˈvɪtrɪəs) *a.* **1.** of glass **2.** glassy —**vitrifiˈcation** *n.* —**ˈvitrify** *v.* convert or be converted into glass, or glassy substance (**-ified, -ifying**) —**vitreous humour** *or* **body** transparent gelatinous substance that fills eyeball between lens and retina

vitriol (ˈvɪtrɪɒl) *n.* **1.** sulphuric acid **2.** caustic speech —**vitriˈolic** *a.*

vituperate (vɪˈtjuːpəreɪt) *vt.* abuse in words, revile —**vituperˈation** *n.* —**viˈtuperative** *a.*

viva (ˈviːvə) *interj.* long live; up with (specified person or thing)

vivace (vɪˈvɑːtʃɪ) *a./adv.* *Mus.* to be performed in brisk lively manner

vivacious (vɪˈveɪʃəs) *a.* lively, gay, sprightly —**vivacity** (vɪˈvæsɪtɪ) *n.*

vivarium (vaɪˈvɛərɪəm) *n.* place where animals are kept under natural conditions for study *etc.* (*pl.* **-s, -ia** (-ɪə))

viva voce (ˈvaɪvə ˈvəʊtʃɪ) *Lat. adv.* **1.** by word of mouth —*n.* **2.** oral examination (*oft.* **ˈviva**)

vivid (ˈvɪvɪd) *a.* **1.** bright, intense **2.** clear **3.** lively, animated **4.** graphic —**ˈvividly** *adv.*

vivify (ˈvɪvɪfaɪ) *vt.* animate, inspire (**-ified, -ifying**)

viviparous (vɪˈvɪpərəs) *a.* bringing forth young alive

vivisection (vɪvɪˈsɛkʃən) *n.* dissection of, or operating on, living animals —**ˈvivisect** *v.* subject (animal) to vivisection —**viviˈsectionist** *n.* —**ˈvivisector** *n.*

vixen (ˈvɪksən) *n.* **1.** female fox **2.** spiteful woman —**ˈvixenish** *a.*

viz. videlicet

vizier (vɪˈzɪə) *n.* high official in some Muslim countries

V-J Day day marking Allied victory over Japan in World War II (Aug. 15th, 1945)

V.L. Vulgar Latin

VLF *or* **vlf** *Rad.* very low frequency

V neck neck on garment resembling shape of letter 'V' —**V-neck** *or* **V-necked** *a.*

voc. *or* **vocat.** vocative

vocable (ˈvəʊkəbˀl) *n.* word regarded as sequence of letters or spoken sounds

vocabulary (vəˈkæbjʊlərɪ) *n.* **1.** list of words, usu. in alphabetical order **2.** stock of words used in particular language *etc.*

vocal (ˈvəʊkˀl) *a.* **1.** of, with, or giving out voice **2.** outspoken, articulate —*n.* **3.** piece of popular music that is sung —**ˈvocalist** *n.* singer —**ˈvocalize** *or* **-ise** *vt.* utter with voice —**ˈvocally** *adv.* —**vocal cords** either of two pairs of membranous folds in larynx

vocalic (vəʊˈkælɪk) *a.* of vowel(s)

vocation (vəʊˈkeɪʃən) *n.* (urge, inclination, predisposition to) particular career, profession *etc.* —**voˈcational** *a.* —**vocational guidance** guidance service based on psychological tests and interviews to find out what career may best suit person

THESAURUS

visual 1. ocular, optic, optical **2.** discernible, observable, perceptible, visible

visualize conceive of, conjure up a mental picture of, envisage, imagine, picture, see in the mind's eye

vital 1. basic, cardinal, essential, fundamental, imperative, indispensable, necessary, requisite **2.** critical, crucial, decisive, important, key, life-or-death, significant, urgent **3.** animated, dynamic, energetic, forceful, full of the joy of living, lively, spirited, vibrant, vigorous, vivacious, zestful

vitality animation, energy, exuberance, go (*Inf.*), life, liveliness, lustiness, pep, robustness, sparkle, stamina, strength, vigour, vim (*Sl.*), vivaciousness, vivacity

vitriolic *Fig.* acerbic, acid, bitchy (*Sl.*), bitter, caustic, destructive, dripping with malice, envenomed, sardonic, scathing, venomous, virulent, withering

vituperation abuse, billingsgate, blame, castigation, censure, fault-finding, flak (*Inf.*), invective, obloquy, rebuke, reprimand, reproach, scurrility, tongue-lashing, vilification

vivacious animated, bubbling, cheerful, ebullient, effervescent, frolicsome, full of life, gay, high-spirited, jolly, light-hearted, lively, merry, scintillating, sparkling, spirited, sportive, sprightly, vital

vivacity animation, ebullience, effervescence, energy, gaiety, high spirits, life, liveliness, pep, quickness, sparkle, spirit, sprightliness

vivid 1. bright, brilliant, clear, colourful, glowing, intense, rich **2.** distinct, dramatic, graphic, highly-coloured, lifelike, memorable, powerful, realistic, sharp, sharply-etched, stirring, strong, telling, true to life **3.** active, animated, dynamic, energetic, expressive, flamboyant, lively, quick, spirited, striking, strong, vigorous

vixen *Fig.* fury, harpy, harridan, hellcat, scold, shrew, spitfire, termagant (*Rare*), virago, Xanthippe

vocabulary dictionary, glossary, language, lexicon, wordbook, word hoard, words, word stock

vocal *adj.* **1.** articulate, articulated, oral, put into words, said, spoken, uttered, voiced **2.** articulate, blunt, clamorous, eloquent, expressive, forthright, frank, free-spoken, noisy, outspoken, plain-spoken, strident, vociferous

vocation business, calling, career, employment, job, life's work, life work, métier, mission, office, post, profession, pursuit, role, trade

vocative (ˈvɒkətɪv) *n.* in some languages, case of nouns used in addressing a person

vociferate (vəʊˈsɪfəreɪt) *v.* exclaim, cry out —**vociferˈation** *n.* —**voˈciferous** *a.* shouting, noisy

vodka (ˈvɒdkə) *n.* Russian spirit distilled from grain, potatoes *etc.*

vogue (vəʊg) *n.* **1.** fashion, style **2.** popularity

voice (vɔɪs) *n.* **1.** sound given out by person in speaking, singing *etc.* **2.** quality of the sound **3.** expressed opinion **4.** (right to) share in discussion **5.** verbal form proper to relation of subject and action —*vt.* **6.** give utterance to, express —**ˈvoiceless** *a.* —**voice-over** *n.* voice of unseen commentator heard during film *etc.* —**ˈvoiceprint** *n.* graphic representation of person's voice recorded electronically

void (vɔɪd) *a.* **1.** empty **2.** destitute **3.** not legally binding —*n.* **4.** empty space —*vt.* **5.** make ineffectual or invalid **6.** empty out

voile (vɔɪl) *n.* light semitransparent fabric

vol. volume

volatile (ˈvɒlətaɪl) *a.* **1.** evaporating quickly **2.** lively **3.** fickle, changeable —**volatility** (vɒləˈtɪlɪtɪ) *n.* —**volatilization** *or* **-lisation** (vɒlætɪlaɪˈzeɪʃən) *n.* —**volatilize** *or* **-lise** (vɒˈlætɪlaɪz) *v.* (cause to) evaporate

vol-au-vent (*Fr.* vɔloˈvã) *n.* small, light pastry case with savoury filling

volcano (vɒlˈkeɪnəʊ) *n.* **1.** hole in earth's crust through which lava, ashes, smoke *etc.* are discharged **2.** mountain so formed (*pl.* **-es, -s**) —**volcanic** (vɒlˈkænɪk) *a.* —**volcanology** (vɒlkəˈnɒlədʒɪ) *or* **vulcaˈnology** *n.* study of volcanoes and volcanic phenomena

vole (vəʊl) *n.* small rodent

volition (vəˈlɪʃən) *n.* **1.** act, power of willing **2.** exercise of the will —**voˈlitional** *a.*

volley (ˈvɒlɪ) *n.* **1.** simultaneous discharge of weapons or missiles **2.** rush of oaths, questions *etc.* **3.** *Sport* kick, stroke *etc.* at moving ball before it touches ground —*v.* **4.** discharge or be discharged —*vt.* **5.** utter **6.** fly, strike *etc.* in volley —**ˈvolleyball** *n.* team game where large ball is hit by hand over high net

volt (vəʊlt) *n.* unit of electric potential —**ˈvoltage** *n.* electric potential difference expressed in volts —**ˈvoltmeter** *n.*

voltaic (vɒlˈteɪɪk) *a.* *see* GALVANIC (sense 1)

volte-face (ˈvɒltˈfɑːs) *Fr. n.* complete reversal of opinion or direction (*pl.* **volte-face**)

voluble (ˈvɒljubˀl) *a.* talking easily, readily and at length —**voluˈbility** *n.* —**ˈvolubly** *adv.*

volume (ˈvɒljuːm) *n.* **1.** space occupied **2.** bulk, mass **3.** amount **4.** power, fullness of voice or sound **5.** control on radio *etc.* for adjusting this **6.** book **7.** part of book bound in one cover —**voluˈmetric** *a.* pert. to measurement by volume —**voluminous** (vəˈluːmɪnəs) *a.* bulky, copious

voluntary (ˈvɒləntərɪ) *a.* **1.** having, done by free will **2.** done without payment **3.** supported by freewill contributions **4.** spontaneous —*n.* **5.** organ solo in church service —**ˈvoluntarily** *adv.* —**volunˈteer** *n.* **1.** one who offers service, joins force *etc.* of his own free will —*v.* **2.** offer oneself or one's services

voluptuous (vəˈlʌptjʊəs) *a.* of, contributing to pleasures of the senses —**voˈluptuary** *n.* one given to luxury and sensual pleasures

vomit (ˈvɒmɪt) *v.* **1.** eject (contents of stomach) through mouth —*n.* **2.** matter vomited

voodoo (ˈvuːduː) *n.* **1.** practice of black magic, *esp.* in W Indies, witchcraft —*vt.* **2.** affect by voodoo

voracious (vɒˈreɪʃəs) *a.* greedy, ravenous —**voˈraciously** *adv.* —**voracity** (vɒˈræsɪtɪ) *n.*

THESAURUS

vociferous clamant, clamorous, loud, loudmouthed (*Inf.*), noisy, obstreperous, ranting, shouting, strident, uproarious, vehement

vogue *n.* **1.** craze, custom, *dernier cri*, fashion, last word, mode, style, the latest, the rage, the thing (*Inf.*), trend, way **2.** acceptance, currency, fashionableness, favour, popularity, prevalence, usage, use

voice *n.* **1.** articulation, language, power of speech, sound, tone, utterance, words **2.** decision, expression, part, say, view, vote, will, wish ~*v.* **3.** air, articulate, assert, come out with (*Inf.*), declare, divulge, enunciate, express, give expression *or* utterance to, put into words, say, utter, ventilate

void *adj.* **1.** bare, clear, drained, emptied, empty, free, tenantless, unfilled, unoccupied, vacant **2.** *With* **of** destitute, devoid, lacking, without **3.** dead, ineffective, ineffectual, inoperative, invalid, nonviable, nugatory, null and void, unenforceable, useless, vain, worthless ~*n.* **4.** blank, blankness, emptiness, gap, opening, space, vacuity, vacuum ~*v.* **5.** discharge, drain, eject, eliminate (*Physiol.*), emit, empty, evacuate **6.** abnegate, cancel, invalidate, nullify, rescind

volatile airy, changeable, erratic, explosive, fickle, flighty, gay, giddy, inconstant, lively, mercurial, sprightly, unsettled, unstable, unsteady, up and down (*Inf.*), variable, whimsical

volition choice, choosing, determination, discretion, election, free will, option, preference, purpose, resolution, will

volley *n.* barrage, blast, bombardment, burst, cannonade, discharge, explosion, fusillade, hail, salvo, shower

volubility fluency, garrulity, gift of the gab (*Inf.*), glibness, loquaciousness, loquacity

voluble articulate, blessed with the gift of the gab (*Inf.*), fluent, forthcoming, glib, loquacious, talkative

volume **1.** aggregate, amount, body, bulk, capacity, compass, cubic content, dimensions, mass, quantity, total **2.** book, publication, tome, treatise

voluminous ample, big, billowing, bulky, capacious, cavernous, copious, full, large, massive, prolific, roomy, vast

voluntarily by choice, freely, of one's own accord, of one's own free will, on one's own initiative, willingly, without being asked, without prompting

voluntary discretional, free, gratuitous, honorary, intended, intentional, optional, spontaneous, uncompelled, unconstrained, unforced, unpaid, volunteer, willing

volunteer *v.* let oneself in for (*Inf.*), need no invitation, offer, offer one's services, put oneself at (someone's) disposal, step forward

voluptuous epicurean, hedonistic, licentious, luxurious, pleasure-loving, self-indulgent, sensual, sybaritic

-vorous (*a. comb. form*) feeding on; devouring, as in *carnivorous* **—-vore** (*n. comb. form*)

vortex (ˈvɔːtɛks) *n.* **1.** whirlpool **2.** whirling motion (*pl.* **-es, vortices** (ˈvɔːtɪsiːz))

votary (ˈvəʊtərɪ) *n.* one vowed to service or pursuit (**ˈvotaress** *fem.*) **—ˈvotive** *a.* given, consecrated by vow

vote (vəʊt) *n.* **1.** formal expression of choice **2.** individual pronouncement **3.** right to give it, in question or election **4.** result of voting **5.** that which is given or allowed by vote **—***v.* **6.** express, declare opinion, choice, preference *etc.* by vote **7.** authorize, enact *etc.* by vote **—ˈvoter** *n.*

vouch (vaʊtʃ) *vi.* (*usu. with* for) guarantee, make oneself responsible (for) **—ˈvoucher** *n.* **1.** document proving correctness of item in accounts, or to establish facts **2.** ticket as substitute for cash **—vouchˈsafe** *vt.* condescend to grant or do

vow (vaʊ) *n.* **1.** solemn promise, *esp.* religious one **—***vt.* **2.** promise, threaten by vow

vowel (ˈvaʊəl) *n.* **1.** any speech sound pronounced without stoppage or friction of the breath **2.** letter standing for such sound, as *a, e, i, o, u*

vox (vɒks) *n.* voice; sound (*pl.* **voces** (ˈvəʊsiːz)) **—vox populi** (ˈpɒpjʊlaɪ) voice of the people; popular or public opinion

voyage (ˈvɔɪɪdʒ) *n.* **1.** journey, *esp.* long one, by sea or air **—***vi.* **2.** make voyage **—ˈvoyager** *n.* **—voyageur** (vwɑːjɑːˈʒɜː; *Fr.* vwajaˈʒœːr) *n.* C guide, trapper in N regions

voyeur (vwaɪˈɜː) *n.* one obtaining sexual pleasure by watching sexual activities of others

vs. versus

V-sign *n.* **1.** UK offensive gesture made by sticking up index and middle fingers with palm of hand inwards **2.** similar gesture with palm outwards meaning victory or peace

V.S.O. Voluntary Service Overseas

V.S.O.P. very superior old pale

VT Vermont

VTOL (ˈviːtɒl) vertical takeoff and landing

VTR video tape recorder

vulcanize *or* **-nise** (ˈvʌlkənaɪz) *vt.* treat (rubber) with sulphur at high temperature to increase its durability **—ˈvulcanite** *n.* rubber so hardened **—vulcaniˈzation** *or* **-niˈsation** *n.* **—vulcaˈnology** *n. see* **volcanology** *at* VOLCANO

vulgar (ˈvʌlgə) *a.* **1.** offending against good taste **2.** coarse **3.** common **—vulgarian** (vʌlˈgɛərɪən) *n.* vulgar (rich) person **—ˈvulgarism** *n.* coarse, obscene word, phrase **—vulgarity** (vʌlˈgærɪtɪ) *n.* **—vulgariˈzation** *or* **-riˈsation** *n.* **—ˈvulgarize** *or* **-rise** *vt.* make vulgar or too common **—ˈvulgarly** *adv.* **—vulgar fraction** simple fraction **—Vulgar Latin** any of dialects of Latin spoken in Roman Empire other than classical Latin

Vulgate (ˈvʌlgeɪt, -gɪt) *n.* fourth-century Latin version of the Bible

vulnerable (ˈvʌlnərəbˀl) *a.* **1.** capable of being physically or emotionally wounded or hurt **2.** exposed, open to attack, persuasion *etc.* **—vulneraˈbility** *n.*

vulpine (ˈvʌlpaɪn) *a.* **1.** of foxes **2.** foxy

vulture (ˈvʌltʃə) *n.* large bird which feeds on carrion **—ˈvulturine** *or* **ˈvulturous** *a.* **1.** of vulture **2.** rapacious

vulva (ˈvʌlvə) *n.* external genitals of human female

v.v. vice versa

vying (ˈvaɪɪŋ) *pr.p. of* VIE

THESAURUS

vomit *v.* belch forth, be sick, bring up, disgorge, eject, emit, heave, puke (*Sl.*), regurgitate, retch, sick up (*Inf.*), spew out *or* up, throw up (*Inf.*)

voracious avid, devouring, gluttonous, greedy, hungry, insatiable, omnivorous, prodigious, rapacious, ravening, ravenous, uncontrolled, unquenchable

vote 1. *n.* ballot, franchise, plebiscite, poll, referendum, right to vote, show of hands, suffrage **2.** *v.* ballot, cast one's vote, elect, go to the polls, opt, return

vouch *Usually with* **for** affirm, answer for, assert, asseverate, attest to, back, certify, confirm, give assurance of, go bail for, guarantee, stand witness, support, swear to, uphold

vouchsafe accord, cede, condescend to give, confer, deign, favour (someone) with, grant, yield

vow 1. *v.* affirm, consecrate, dedicate, devote, pledge, promise, swear, undertake solemnly **2.** *n.* oath, pledge, promise, troth (*Archaic*)

voyage *n.* crossing, cruise, journey, passage, travels, trip

vulgar blue, boorish, cheap and nasty, coarse, common, crude, dirty, flashy, gaudy, gross, ill-bred, impolite, improper, indecent, indecorous, indelicate, low, nasty, naughty, off colour, ribald, risqué, rude, suggestive, tasteless, tawdry, uncouth, unmannerly, unrefined

vulgarity bad taste, coarseness, crudeness, crudity, gaudiness, grossness, indecorum, indelicacy, lack of refinement, ribaldry, rudeness, suggestiveness, tastelessness, tawdriness

vulnerable accessible, assailable, defenceless, exposed, open to attack, sensitive, susceptible, tender, thin-skinned, unprotected, weak, wide open

w *or* **W** (ˈdʌbəljuː) *n.* **1.** 23rd letter of English alphabet **2.** speech sound represented by this letter, usu. bilabial semivowel, as in *web* (*pl.* **w's, W's** *or* **Ws**)

W **1.** *Chem.* tungsten **2.** watt **3.** Wednesday **4.** west(ern)

w. **1.** week **2.** weight **3.** width

W. **1.** Wales **2.** Welsh

WA Washington

W.A. **1.** West Africa **2.** Western Australia

WAAC (wæk) *n.* **1.** Women's Army Auxiliary Corps **2.** member of this corps (*also* **waac**)

WAAF (wæf) *n.* **1.** Women's Auxiliary Air Force **2.** member of this force (*also* **Waaf**)

wacky (ˈwækɪ) *a. sl.* eccentric or unpredictable

wad (wɒd) *n.* **1.** small pad of fibrous material **2.** thick roll of banknotes **3.** sum of money —*vt.* **4.** line, pad, stuff *etc.* with wad (**-dd-**) —ˈ**wadding** *n.* stuffing

waddle (ˈwɒdəl) *vi.* **1.** walk like duck —*n.* **2.** this gait

wade (weɪd) *vi.* **1.** walk through something that hampers movement, *esp.* water **2.** proceed with difficulty —ˈ**wader** *n.* **1.** person or bird that wades —*pl.* **2.** angler's high waterproof boots

wafer (ˈweɪfə) *n.* **1.** thin, crisp biscuit **2.** thin slice of anything

waffle[1] (ˈwɒfəl) *n.* kind of pancake with deep indentations on both sides —**waffle iron** utensil for cooking waffles, having two flat, studded plates hinged together

waffle[2] (ˈwɒfəl) *inf. vi.* **1.** speak, write in vague wordy manner —*n.* **2.** vague speech *etc.* **3.** nonsense

waft (wɑːft, wɒft) *vt.* **1.** convey smoothly through air or water —*n.* **2.** breath of wind **3.** odour, whiff

wag (wæg) *v.* **1.** (cause to) move rapidly from side to side (**-gg-**) —*n.* **2.** instance of wagging **3.** *inf.* humorous, witty person —ˈ**waggish** *a.* —ˈ**wagtail** *n.* small bird with wagging tail

wage (weɪdʒ) *n.* **1.** (*oft. pl.*) payment for work done —*vt.* **2.** engage in

wager (ˈweɪdʒə) *n./v.* bet

waggle (ˈwægəl) *v.* wag —ˈ**waggly** *a.*

Wagnerian (vɑːgˈnɪərɪən) *a.* pert. to German composer Richard Wagner, his music or his theories

wagon *or* **waggon** (ˈwægən) *n.* **1.** four-wheeled vehicle for heavy loads **2.** railway freight truck —ˈ**wagoner** *or* ˈ**waggoner** *n.* —**wagoˈnette** *or* **waggoˈnette** *n.* four-wheeled horse-drawn vehicle with two lengthwise seats facing each other behind driver's seat

waif (weɪf) *n.* homeless person, *esp.* child

wail (weɪl) *v.* **1.** cry out —*vt.* **2.** lament —*n.* **3.** mournful cry

wainscot (ˈweɪnskət) *n.* **1.** wooden lining of walls of room —*vt.* **2.** line thus

waist (weɪst) *n.* **1.** part of body between hips and ribs **2.** various narrow central parts —ˈ**waistband** *n.* encircling band of material to finish and strengthen skirt *etc.* at waist —**waistcoat** (ˈweɪskəʊt) *n.* sleeveless garment worn under jacket or coat —ˈ**waistline** *n.* line, size of waist (of person, garment)

wait (weɪt) *v.* **1.** stay in one place, remain inactive in expectation (of something) **2.** be prepared (for something) **3.** delay —*vi.* **4.** serve in restaurant *etc.* —*n.* **5.** act or period of waiting —*pl.* **6.** street musicians, carol singers —ˈ**waiter** *n.* **1.** attendant on guests at hotel, restaurant *etc.* (ˈ**waitress** *fem.*) **2.** one who waits —**waiting game** postponement of action in order to gain advantage —**waiting list** list of people waiting to obtain some object, treatment *etc.*

waive (weɪv) *vt.* **1.** forgo **2.** not insist on —ˈ**waiver** *n.* (written statement of) this act

THESAURUS

wad ball, block, bundle, chunk, hunk, lump, mass, plug, roll

wadding filler, lining, packing, padding, stuffing

waddle rock, shuffle, sway, toddle, totter, wobble

wade **1.** ford, paddle, splash, walk through **2.** *With* **through** drudge, labour, peg away, plough through, toil, work one's way

waffle **1.** *v.* blather, jabber, prate, prattle, rabbit on (*Brit. sl.*), verbalize, witter on (*Inf.*) **2.** *n.* blather, jabber, padding, prating, prattle, prolixity, verbiage, verbosity, wordiness

waft **1.** *v.* bear, be carried, carry, convey, drift, float, ride, transmit, transport **2.** *n.* breath, breeze, current, draught, puff, whiff

wag **1.** *v.* bob, flutter, nod, oscillate, quiver, rock, shake, stir, vibrate, waggle, wave, wiggle **2.** *n.* bob, flutter, nod, oscillation, quiver, shake, toss, vibration, waggle, wave, wiggle

wage **1.** *n. Also* **wages** allowance, compensation, earnings, emolument, fee, hire, pay, payment, recompense, remuneration, reward, stipend **2.** *v.* carry on, conduct, engage in, practise, proceed with, prosecute, pursue, undertake

wager **1.** *n.* bet, flutter (*Brit. inf.*), gamble, pledge, punt, stake, venture **2.** *v.* bet, chance, gamble, hazard, lay, pledge, punt, put on, risk, speculate, stake, venture

waggle *v.* flutter, oscillate, shake, wag, wave, wiggle, wobble

waif foundling, orphan, stray

wail **1.** *v.* bemoan, bewail, cry, deplore, grieve, howl, keen, lament, ululate, weep, yowl **2.** *n.* complaint, cry, grief, howl, keen, lament, lamentation, moan, ululation, weeping, yowl

wait **1.** *v.* abide, bide one's time, cool one's heels, dally, delay, hang fire, hold back, hold on (*Inf.*), linger, mark time, pause, remain, rest, stand by, stay, tarry **2.** *n.* delay, halt, hold-up, interval, pause, rest, stay

waiter, waitress attendant, server, steward, stewardess

waive abandon, defer, dispense with, forgo, give up, postpone, put off, refrain from, relinquish, remit, renounce, resign, set aside, surrender

waiver abandonment, abdication, disclaimer, giving up, relinquishment, remission, renunciation, resignation, setting aside, surrender

wake[1] (weɪk) *v.* **1.** rouse from sleep **2.** stir (up) (**woke, ˈwoken, ˈwaking**) —*n.* **3.** vigil **4.** watch beside corpse **5.** (*oft. pl.*) annual holiday in parts of N England —**ˈwakeful** *a.* —**ˈwaken** *v.* wake

wake[2] (weɪk) *n.* track or path left by anything that has passed, as track of turbulent water behind ship

wale (weɪl) *n.* **1.** raised mark left on skin after stroke of whip **2.** weave of fabric, such as ribs in corduroy **3.** *Naut.* ridge of planking along rail of ship —*v.* **4.** raise wales (on) by striking **5.** weave with wale

walk (wɔːk) *v.* **1.** (cause, assist to) move, travel on foot at ordinary pace —*vt.* **2.** cross, pass through by walking **3.** escort, conduct by walking —*n.* **4.** act, instance of walking **5.** path or other place or route for walking **6.** manner of walking **7.** occupation, career —**ˈwalker** *n.* —**ˈwalkabout** *n.* informal walk among crowd by royalty *etc.* —**walkie-talkie** *or* **walky-talky** *n.* portable radio set containing both transmission and receiver units —**walking stick** stick, cane carried to assist walking —**walk-on** *n.* small part in play *etc.*, *esp.* one without lines —**ˈwalkout** *n.* **1.** strike **2.** act of leaving as a protest —**ˈwalkover** *n.* unopposed or easy victory

wall (wɔːl) *n.* **1.** structure of brick, stone *etc.* serving as fence, side of building *etc.* **2.** anything resembling this —*vt.* **3.** enclose with wall **4.** block up with wall —**ˈwallboard** *n.* thin board made of materials, such as compressed wood fibres or gypsum plaster, used to cover walls *etc.* —**ˈwallflower** *n.* **1.** garden flower, oft. growing on walls **2.** woman who remains seated at dance *etc.* for lack of partner —**ˈwallpaper** *n.* paper, usu. patterned, to cover interior walls

wallaby (ˈwɒləbɪ) *n.* Aust. marsupial similar to and smaller than kangaroo

wallet (ˈwɒlɪt) *n.* small folding case, *esp.* for paper money, documents *etc.*

walleyed (ˈwɔːlaɪd) *a.* **1.** squinting **2.** having eyes with pale irises

Walloon (wɒˈluːn) *n.* **1.** member of French-speaking people living chiefly in S and SE Belgium **2.** French dialect of Belgium —*a.* **3.** of Walloons or their dialect

wallop (ˈwɒləp) *inf. vt.* **1.** beat soundly **2.** strike hard —*n.* **3.** stroke or blow —**ˈwalloper** *n. inf.* one who wallops —**ˈwalloping** *inf. n.* **1.** thrashing —*adv.* **2.** very, greatly —*a.* **3.** great

wallow (ˈwɒləʊ) *vi.* **1.** roll (in liquid or mud) **2.** revel —*n.* **3.** act or instance of wallowing **4.** muddy place where animals wallow

Wall Street street in New York, where Stock Exchange and major banks are situated

wally (ˈwɒlɪ) *n. sl.* stupid person

walnut (ˈwɔːlnʌt) *n.* **1.** large nut with crinkled shell splitting easily into two halves **2.** the tree **3.** its wood

walrus (ˈwɔːlrəs, ˈwɒl-) *n.* large sea mammal with long tusks (*pl.* **-es, -rus**)

waltz (wɔːls) *n.* **1.** ballroom dance **2.** music for it —*v.* **3.** dance or lead (someone) in or as in a waltz

wampum (ˈwɒmpəm) *n.* beads made of shells, formerly used by N Amer. Indians as money and for ornament

wan (wɒn) *a.* pale, sickly complexioned, pallid

wand (wɒnd) *n.* stick, usu. straight and slender, *esp.* as carried by magician *etc.*

wander (ˈwɒndə) *v.* **1.** roam, ramble —*vi.* **2.** go astray, deviate —*n.* **3.** stroll —**ˈwanderer** *n.* —**ˈwanderlust** *n.* irrepressible urge to wander or travel

wane (weɪn) *vi./n.* **1.** decline **2.** (of moon *etc.*) decrease in size

THESAURUS

wake[1] *v.* **1.** arise, awake, awaken, bestir, come to, get up, rouse, rouse from sleep, stir **2.** activate, animate, arouse, awaken, enliven, excite, fire, galvanize, kindle, provoke, quicken, stimulate, stir up ~*n.* **3.** deathwatch, funeral, vigil, watch

wake[2] aftermath, backwash, path, track, trail, train, wash, waves

wakeful insomniac, restless, sleepless, unsleeping

waken activate, animate, arouse, awake, awaken, be roused, come awake, come to, enliven, fire, galvanize, get up, kindle, quicken, rouse, stimulate, stir

walk *v.* **1.** advance, amble, foot it, go, go by shanks's pony (*Inf.*), go on foot, hike, hoof it (*Sl.*), march, move, pace, perambulate, promenade, saunter, step, stride, stroll, traipse (*Inf.*), tramp, travel on foot, trek, trudge **2.** accompany, convoy, escort, take ~*n.* **3.** constitutional, hike, march, perambulation, promenade, ramble, saunter, stroll, traipse (*Inf.*), tramp, trek, trudge, turn **4.** carriage, gait, manner of walking, pace, step, stride **5.** aisle, alley, avenue, esplanade, footpath, lane, path, pathway, pavement, promenade, sidewalk, trail **6.** area, arena, calling, career, course, field, line, métier, profession, sphere, trade, vocation

walker footslogger, hiker, pedestrian, rambler, wayfarer

walkout industrial action, protest, stoppage, strike

walkover child's play (*Inf.*), doddle (*Brit. sl.*), easy victory, picnic (*Inf.*), piece of cake (*Inf.*), pushover (*Sl.*), snap (*Inf.*)

wall **1.** divider, enclosure, panel, partition, screen **2.** barricade, breastwork, bulwark, embankment, fortification, palisade, parapet, rampart, stockade **3.** barrier, block, fence, hedge, impediment, obstacle, obstruction

wallet case, holder, notecase, pocketbook, pouch, purse

wallow **1.** lie, roll about, splash around, tumble, welter **2.** bask, delight, glory, indulge oneself, luxuriate, relish, revel, take pleasure

wan anaemic, ashen, bloodless, cadaverous, colourless, discoloured, ghastly, livid, pale, pallid, pasty, sickly, washed out, waxen, wheyfaced, white

wand baton, rod, sprig, stick, twig, withe, withy

wander *v.* **1.** cruise, drift, knock about, knock around, meander, mooch around (*Sl.*), peregrinate, ramble, range, roam, rove, straggle, stravaig (*Scot.*), stray, stroll, traipse (*Inf.*) **2.** depart, deviate, digress, divagate (*Rare*), diverge, err, get lost, go astray, go off at a tangent, go off course, lapse, lose concentration, lose one's train of thought, lose one's way, swerve, veer ~*n.* **3.** cruise, excursion, meander, peregrination, ramble, traipse (*Inf.*)

wanderer bird of passage, drifter, gypsy, itinerant, nomad, rambler, ranger, rolling stone, rover, stroller, traveller, vagabond, vagrant, voyager

wane **1.** *v.* abate, atrophy, decline, decrease, die out, dim, diminish, draw to a close, drop, dwindle, ebb, fade, fade away, fail, lessen, sink, subside, taper off, weaken, wind down, wither **2.** *n.* abatement, atro-

wangle (ˈwæŋgəl) *inf. vt.* **1.** manipulate, manage in skilful way —*n.* **2.** intrigue, trickery, something obtained by craft

Wankel engine (ˈwæŋkəl) type of rotary four-stroke internal-combustion engine without reciprocating parts

want (wɒnt) *v.* **1.** desire —*vt.* **2.** lack —*n.* **3.** desire **4.** need **5.** deficiency —ˈ**wanted** *a.* being sought, *esp.* by the police —ˈ**wanting** *a.* **1.** lacking **2.** below standard

wanton (ˈwɒntən) *a.* **1.** dissolute **2.** without motive, thoughtless **3.** unrestrained —*n.* **4.** wanton person *esp.* woman

war (wɔː) *n.* **1.** fighting between nations **2.** state of hostility **3.** conflict, contest —*vi.* **4.** make war (-rr-) —ˈ**warlike** *a.* **1.** of, for war **2.** fond of war —ˈ**warrior** *n.* fighter —**war crime** crime committed in wartime in violation of accepted customs of war —**war cry 1.** cry used by attacking troops in war **2.** distinctive word, phrase used by political party *etc.* —ˈ**warfare** *n.* hostilities —**war game 1.** notional tactical exercise for training military commanders, in which no military units are actually deployed **2.** game in which model soldiers are used to create battles in order to study tactics —ˈ**warhead** *n.* part of missile *etc.* containing explosives —ˈ**warhorse** *n.* **1.** horse used in battle **2.** *inf.* veteran soldier or politician —**war memorial** monument to those who die in war —ˈ**warmonger** *n.* one fostering, encouraging war —**war paint 1.** painted decoration of face and body applied by certain N Amer. Indians before battle **2.** *inf.* cosmetics —ˈ**warpath** *n.* route taken by N Amer. Indians on warlike expedition —ˈ**warship** *n.* vessel armed, armoured for naval warfare —**on the warpath** *inf.* in a state of anger

War. Warwickshire

warble (ˈwɔːbəl) *v.* sing with trills —ˈ**warbler** *n.* **1.** person or bird that warbles **2.** kind of small songbird

ward (wɔːd) *n.* **1.** division of city, hospital *etc.* **2.** minor under care of guardian **3.** guardianship **4.** bar in lock, groove in key that prevents incorrectly cut key opening lock —ˈ**warder** *n.* jailer (ˈ**wardress** *fem.*) —ˈ**wardship** *n.* **1.** office of guardian **2.** state of being under guardian —ˈ**wardroom** *n.* senior officers' mess on warship —**ward off** avert, repel

-ward (*comb. form*) **1.** indicating direction towards, as in *backward step* **2.** *esp.* US *see* -WARDS

warden (ˈwɔːdən) *n.* person, officer in charge of building, institution, college *etc.*

wardrobe (ˈwɔːdrəʊb) *n.* **1.** piece of furniture for hanging clothes in **2.** person's supply of clothes **3.** costumes of theatrical company

-wards *or* **-ward** (*comb. form*) indicating direction towards, as in *step backwards*

ware (wɛə) *n.* **1.** goods **2.** articles collectively —*pl.* **3.** goods for sale **4.** commodities **5.** merchandise —ˈ**warehouse** *n.* storehouse for goods prior to distribution and sale

warlock (ˈwɔːlɒk) *n.* wizard, sorcerer

warm (wɔːm) *a.* **1.** moderately hot **2.** serving to maintain heat **3.** affectionate **4.** ardent **5.** earnest **6.** hearty **7.** (of colour) having yellow or red base —*v.* **8.**

THESAURUS

phy, decay, declension, decrease, diminution, drop, dwindling, ebb, fading, failure, fall, falling off, lessening, sinking, subsidence, tapering off, withering

want *v.* **1.** covet, crave, desire, feel a need for, hanker after, have a fancy for, have a yen for (*Inf.*), hunger for, long for, need, pine for, require, thirst for, wish, yearn for **2.** be able to do with, be deficient in, be short of, be without, call for, demand, fall short in, have need of, lack, miss, need, require, stand in need of ~*n.* **3.** appetite, craving, demand, desire, fancy, hankering, hunger, longing, necessity, need, requirement, thirst, wish, yearning, yen (*Inf.*) **4.** absence, dearth, default, deficiency, famine, insufficiency, lack, paucity, scantiness, scarcity, shortage

wanting 1. absent, incomplete, lacking, less, missing, short, shy **2.** defective, deficient, disappointing, faulty, imperfect, inadequate, inferior, leaving much to be desired, not good enough, not up to expectations, not up to par, patchy, poor, sketchy, substandard, unsound

wanton *adj.* **1.** abandoned, dissipated, dissolute, fast, immoral, lecherous, lewd, libertine, libidinous, licentious, loose, lustful, of easy virtue, promiscuous, rakish, shameless, unchaste **2.** arbitrary, cruel, evil, gratuitous, groundless, malevolent, malicious, motiveless, needless, senseless, spiteful, uncalled-for, unjustifiable, unjustified, unprovoked, vicious, wicked, wilful **3.** careless, devil-may-care, extravagant, heedless, immoderate, intemperate, lavish, outrageous, rash, reckless, unrestrained, wild ~*n.* **4.** Casanova, debauchee, Don Juan, harlot, lecher, libertine, loose woman, profligate, prostitute, rake, roué, slut, strumpet, tart (*Inf.*), trollop, voluptuary, whore, woman of easy virtue

war 1. *n.* armed conflict, battle, bloodshed, combat, conflict, contention, contest, enmity, fighting, hostilities, hostility, strife, struggle, warfare **2.** *v.* battle, campaign against, carry on hostilities, clash, combat, conduct a war, contend, contest, fight, make war, strive, struggle, take up arms, wage war

war cry battle cry, rallying cry, slogan, war whoop

ward 1. area, district, division, precinct, quarter, zone **2.** apartment, cubicle, room **3.** charge, dependant, minor, protégé, pupil **4.** care, charge, custody, guardianship, keeping, protection, safekeeping

warden administrator, caretaker, curator, custodian, guardian, janitor, keeper, ranger, steward, superintendent, warder, watchman

warder, wardress custodian, gaoler, guard, jailer, keeper, prison officer, screw (*Sl.*), turnkey (*Archaic*)

ward off avert, avoid, beat off, block, deflect, fend off, forestall, keep at arm's length, keep at bay, parry, repel, stave off, thwart, turn aside, turn away

wardrobe 1. closet, clothes cupboard, clothes-press **2.** apparel, attire, clothes, collection of clothes, outfit

warehouse depository, depot, stockroom, store, storehouse

wares commodities, goods, lines, manufactures, merchandise, produce, products, stock, stuff

warfare armed conflict, armed struggle, arms, battle, blows, campaigning, clash of arms, combat, conflict, contest, discord, fighting, hostilities, passage of arms, strategy, strife, struggle, war

warlike aggressive, bellicose, belligerent, bloodthirsty, combative, hawkish, hostile, inimical, jingoistic, martial, militaristic, military, pugnacious, sabre-rattling, unfriendly, warmongering

make, become warm —ˈ**warmly** *adv.* —**warmth** *n.* **1.** mild heat **2.** cordiality **3.** vehemence, anger —**warm-blooded** *a.* ardent —**warm-bloodedness** *n.* —**warm front** *Met.* boundary between warm air mass and cold air above

warn (wɔːn) *vt.* **1.** put on guard **2.** caution, admonish **3.** give advance information to **4.** notify authoritatively —ˈ**warning** *n.* **1.** hint of harm *etc.* **2.** admonition **3.** advance notice

warp (wɔːp) *v.* **1.** (cause to) twist (out of shape) **2.** pervert or be perverted —*n.* **3.** state, condition of being warped **4.** lengthwise threads on loom

warrant (ˈwɒrənt) *n.* **1.** authority **2.** document giving authority —*vt.* **3.** guarantee **4.** authorize, justify —**warranˈtee** *n.* person given warranty —ˈ**warrantor** *n.* person, company giving warranty —ˈ**warranty** *n.* **1.** guarantee of quality of goods **2.** security —**warrant officer** officer in certain armed services who holds a rank between those of commissioned and noncommissioned officers.

warren (ˈwɒrən) *n.* (burrows inhabited by) colony of rabbits

wart (wɔːt) *n.* small hard growth on skin —**wart hog** kind of Afr. wild pig

wary (ˈwɛərɪ) *a.* watchful, cautious, alert

was (wɒz; *unstressed* wəz) *pt.* first and third person sing. of BE

wash (wɒʃ) *v.* **1.** clean (oneself, clothes *etc.*), *esp.* with water, soap *etc.* **2.** move, be moved by water —*vi.* **3.** be washable **4.** *inf.* be able to be proved true —*vt.* **5.** flow, sweep over, against —*n.* **6.** act of washing **7.** clothes washed at one time **8.** sweep of water, *esp.* set up by moving ship **9.** thin coat of colour —ˈ**washable** *a.* capable of being washed without damage *etc.* —ˈ**washer** *n.* **1.** one who, that which, washes **2.** ring put under a nut —ˈ**washing** *n.* clothes to be washed —ˈ**washy** *a.* **1.** dilute **2.** watery **3.** insipid —ˈ**washboard** *n.* **1.** board having surface, usu. of corrugated metal, on which, *esp.* formerly, clothes are scrubbed **2.** *Naut.* planklike shield fastened to gunwales of boat to prevent water from splashing over side —**wash drawing** pen-and-ink drawing that has been lightly brushed over with water —**washing-up** *n.* **UK 1.** washing of dishes, cutlery *etc.* after meal **2.** dishes, cutlery *etc.* waiting to be washed up —**wash leather** piece of leather, usu. chamois, used for washing windows *etc.* —ˈ**washout** *n. inf.* complete failure —**washed out 1.** faded or colourless **2.** exhausted, pale

wasp (wɒsp) *n.* striped stinging insect resembling bee —ˈ**waspish** *a.* irritable, snappish —**wasp waist** very small waist

Wasp *or* **WASP** (wɒsp) *n.* **US** *usu. derogatory* person descended from N European Protestant stock

wassail (ˈwɒseɪl) *n.* **1.** formerly, toast made to person at festivities **2.** festivity when much drinking takes place **3.** alcoholic drink drunk at such festivity, *esp.* spiced beer —*v.* **4.** drink health of (person) at wassail —*vi.* **5.** go from house to house singing carols at Christmas

waste (weɪst) *vt.* **1.** expend uselessly, use extravagantly **2.** fail to take advantage of **3.** lay desolate —*vi.*

THESAURUS

warm *adj.* **1.** balmy, heated, lukewarm, moderately hot, pleasant, sunny, tepid, thermal **2.** affable, affectionate, amiable, amorous, cheerful, cordial, friendly, genial, happy, hearty, hospitable, kindly, loving, pleasant, tender **3.** animated, ardent, cordial, earnest, effusive, emotional, enthusiastic, excited, fervent, glowing, heated, intense, keen, lively, passionate, spirited, stormy, vehement, vigorous, violent, zealous ~*v.* **4.** heat, heat up, melt, thaw, warm up

warm-blooded ardent, earnest, emotional, enthusiastic, excitable, fervent, impetuous, lively, passionate, rash, spirited, vivacious

warmonger belligerent, hawk, jingo, militarist, sabre-rattler

warmth 1. heat, hotness, warmness **2.** animation, ardour, eagerness, earnestness, effusiveness, enthusiasm, excitement, fervency, fervour, fire, heat, intensity, passion, spirit, transport, vehemence, vigour, violence, zeal, zest **3.** affability, affection, amorousness, cheerfulness, cordiality, happiness, heartiness, hospitableness, kindliness, love, tenderness

warn admonish, advise, alert, apprise, caution, forewarn, give fair warning, give notice, inform, make (someone) aware, notify, put one on one's guard, summon, tip off

warning *n.* admonition, advice, alarm, alert, augury, caution, caveat, foretoken, hint, notice, notification, omen, premonition, presage, sign, signal, threat, tip, tip-off, token, word, word to the wise

warrant *n.* **1.** assurance, authority, authorization, carte blanche, commission, guarantee, licence, permission, permit, pledge, sanction, security, warranty ~*v.* **2.** affirm, answer for, assure, attest, avouch, certify, declare, guarantee, pledge, secure, stand behind, underwrite, uphold, vouch for **3.** approve, authorize, call for, commission, demand, empower, entitle, excuse, give ground for, justify, license, necessitate, permit, require, sanction

warrior champion, combatant, fighter, fighting man, man-at-arms, soldier

wary alert, attentive, cagey (*Inf.*), careful, cautious, chary, circumspect, distrustful, guarded, heedful, leery (*Sl.*), on one's guard, on the lookout, on the qui vive, prudent, suspicious, vigilant, watchful, wide-awake

wash *v.* **1.** bath, bathe, clean, cleanse, launder, moisten, rinse, scrub, shampoo, shower, wet **2.** *With* **away** bear away, carry off, erode, move, sweep away, wash off **3.** *Inf.* bear scrutiny, be convincing, be plausible, carry weight, hold up, hold water, stand up, stick ~*n.* **4.** ablution, bath, bathe, cleaning, cleansing, laundering, rinse, scrub, shampoo, shower, washing **5.** ebb and flow, flow, roll, surge, sweep, swell, wave **6.** coat, coating, film, layer, overlay, screen, stain, suffusion

washed out 1. blanched, bleached, colourless, etiolated, faded, flat, lacklustre, mat, pale **2.** all in (*Sl.*), dead on one's feet, dog-tired (*Inf.*), done in (*Inf.*), drained, drawn, exhausted, fatigued, haggard, knackered (*Sl.*), pale, spent, tired-out, wan, weary, worn-out

washout 1. disappointment, disaster, dud (*Inf.*), failure, fiasco, flop (*Inf.*), mess **2.** failure, incompetent, loser

waspish bad-tempered, cantankerous, captious, crabbed, crabby, cross, crotchety (*Inf.*), fretful, grumpy, ill-tempered, irascible, irritable, peevish, peppery, pettish, petulant, snappish, splenetic, testy, touchy, waxy (*Brit. sl.*)

4. dwindle **5.** pine away —*n.* **6.** act of wasting **7.** what is wasted **8.** refuse **9.** desert —*a.* **10.** worthless, useless **11.** desert **12.** wasted —**ˈwastage** *n.* **1.** loss by use or decay **2.** reduction in numbers, *esp.* of workforce —**ˈwasteful** *a.* extravagant —**ˈwastefully** *adv.* —**ˈwasting** *a.* reducing vitality, strength, or robustness of body —**ˈwastrel** *n.* wasteful person, idler —**ˈwasteland** *n.* barren or desolate area of land

watch (wɒtʃ) *vt.* **1.** observe closely **2.** guard —*vi.* **3.** wait expectantly **4.** be on watch —*n.* **5.** portable timepiece for wrist, pocket *etc.* **6.** state of being on the lookout **7.** guard **8.** spell of duty —**ˈwatchful** *a.* —**ˈwatchfully** *adv.* —**ˈwatchdog** *n.* **1.** dog trained to guard property **2.** person or group that acts as protector against inefficiency *etc.* —**ˈwatchmaker** *n.* one skilled in making and repairing watches —**ˈwatchman** *n.* man guarding building *etc., esp.* at night —**watch night** in Protestant churches, service held on night of Dec. 31st, to mark passing of old year —**ˈwatchword** *n.* **1.** password **2.** rallying cry

water (ˈwɔːtə) *n.* **1.** transparent, colourless, odourless, tasteless liquid, substance of rain, river *etc.* **2.** body of water **3.** river **4.** lake **5.** sea **6.** tear **7.** urine —*vt.* **8.** put water on or into **9.** irrigate, provide with water —*vi.* **10.** salivate **11.** (of eyes) fill with tears **12.** take in or obtain water —**ˈwatery** *a.* —**water bed** waterproof mattress filled with water —**water biscuit** thin crisp plain biscuit —**ˈwaterbuck** *n.* Afr. antelope —**water buffalo** oxlike Asian animal —**water butt** barrel with one end open, used for collecting and storing rainwater —**water chestnut** floating aquatic plant of Asia, having edible nutlike fruits —**water closet** sanitary convenience flushed by water —**ˈwatercolour** *or U.S.* **ˈwatercolor** *n.* **1.** pigment mixed with water **2.** painting in this —**ˈwatercourse** *n.* stream —**ˈwatercress** *n.* plant growing in clear ponds and streams —**ˈwaterfall** *n.* perpendicular descent of waters of river —**ˈwaterfront** *n.* area of town alongside body of water, such as harbour —**water gauge** instrument that indicates presence or quantity of water in tank *etc.* (*also* **water glass**) —**water glass 1.** syrupy solution of sodium silicate dissolved in water, used as preservative, *esp.* for eggs **2.** water gauge —**water hole** depression, such as pool, containing water, *esp.* one used by animals as drinking place —**water ice** ice cream made from frozen sugar syrup flavoured with fruit juice *etc.* —**watering place 1.** place where drinking water may be obtained **2.** UK spa **3.** UK seaside resort —**water jump** ditch over which athletes or horses must jump, as in steeplechase —**water lily** plant that floats on surface of fresh water —**water line 1.** line marked at level around vessel's hull to which vessel will be immersed when afloat **2.** line marking level reached by body of water —**ˈwaterlogged** *a.* saturated, filled with water —**water main** principal supply pipe in arrangement of water pipes —**ˈwatermark** *n.* faint translucent design stamped on substance of sheet of paper —**water meadow** meadow that remains fertile due to periodic flooding by stream —**ˈwatermelon** *n.* large edible fruit which has hard green rind and sweet watery reddish flesh —**water pistol** toy pistol that squirts stream of water —**water power 1.** power latent in dynamic or static head of water as used to drive machinery **2.** source of such power, such as drop in level of river *etc.* —**ˈwaterproof** *a.* **1.** not letting water through —*vt.* **2.** make waterproof —*n.* **3.** waterproof garment —**water rate** charge levied for use of public water supply —**water-repellent** *a.* (of garments *etc.*) having water-resistant finish —**ˈwatershed** *n.* **1.** line separating two river systems **2.** divide —**water-ski** *n.* **1.** type of ski used for gliding over water —*vi.* **2.** ride over water on water-skis, while holding rope towed by speedboat —**ˈwaterspout** *n.* **1.** *Met.* tornado occurring over water, that forms column of water and mist; sudden heavy rainfall **2.** pipe or channel through which water is discharged —**water table** level below which ground is saturated with water —**ˈwatertight** *a.* **1.** so fitted as to prevent water entering or escaping **2.** with no loopholes or weak points —**water tower** storage tank mounted on towerlike structure so that water can be distributed at uniform pressure —**water vapour** water in gaseous state, *esp.* when due to evaporation at temperature below boiling point —**water wheel 1.** water-driven turbine consisting of wheel having vanes set axially across its rim, used to drive machinery **2.** wheel with buckets attached to its rim

THESAURUS

waste *v.* **1.** blow (*Sl.*), dissipate, fritter away, frivol away (*Inf.*), lavish, misuse, run through, squander, throw away **2.** atrophy, consume, corrode, crumble, debilitate, decay, decline, deplete, disable, drain, dwindle, eat away, ebb, emaciate, enfeeble, exhaust, fade, gnaw, perish, sap the strength of, sink, undermine, wane, wear out, wither **3.** despoil, destroy, devastate, lay waste, pillage, rape, ravage, raze, ruin, sack, spoil, wreak havoc upon ~*n.* **4.** dissipation, expenditure, extravagance, frittering away, loss, lost opportunity, misapplication, misuse, prodigality, squandering, unthriftiness, wastefulness **5.** desolation, destruction, devastation, havoc, ravage, ruin **6.** debris, dregs, dross, garbage, leavings, leftovers, litter, offal, offscourings, refuse, rubbish, scrap, sweepings, trash **7.** desert, solitude, void, wasteland, wild, wilderness ~*adj.* **8.** leftover, superfluous, supernumerary, unused, unwanted, useless, worthless **9.** bare, barren, desolate, devastated, dismal, dreary, empty, uncultivated, uninhabited, unproductive, wild

wasteful extravagant, improvident, lavish, prodigal, profligate, ruinous, spendthrift, thriftless, uneconomical, unthrifty

wastrel 1. prodigal, profligate, spendthrift, squanderer **2.** drone, good-for-nothing, idler, layabout, loafer, loser, malingerer, ne'er-do-well, shirker, waster

watch *v.* **1.** contemplate, eye, gaze at, look, look at, look on, mark, note, observe, pay attention, peer at, regard, see, stare at, view **2.** attend, be on the alert, be on the lookout, be vigilant, be wary, be watchful, keep an eye open (*Inf.*), look out, take heed, wait **3.** guard, keep, look after, mind, protect, superintend, take care of, tend ~*n.* **4.** chronometer, clock, pocket watch, timepiece, wristwatch **5.** alertness, attention, eye, heed, inspection, lookout, notice, observation, supervision, surveillance, vigil, vigilance, watchfulness

watchdog 1. guard dog **2.** custodian, guardian, inspector, monitor, protector, scrutineer

watchful alert, attentive, circumspect, guarded, heedful, observant, on one's guard, on the lookout, on the qui vive, on the watch, suspicious, vigilant, wary, wide awake

watchman caretaker, custodian, guard, security guard, security man

for raising water from pond *etc.* **—water wings** inflatable rubber device, placed under arms of person learning to swim **—ˈwaterworks** *pl.n.* **1.** (*with sing. v.*) establishment for storing, purifying, and distributing water for community supply **2.** (*with pl. v.*) display of water in movement, as in fountains **3.** (*with pl. v.*) *sl.* crying; tears

Watergate (ˈwɔːtəgeɪt) *n.* political scandal when agents employed by U.S. President Richard Nixon's re-election organization were caught breaking into Democratic Party headquarters in Watergate building, Washington, D.C.; exacerbated by attempts to conceal the fact that White House officials had approved the burglary

Waterloo (wɔːtəˈluː) *n.* **1.** town in Belgium, site of battle where Napoleon met his final defeat **2.** total or crushing defeat (*esp. in* **meet one's Waterloo**)

watt (wɒt) *n.* unit of electric power **—ˈwattage** *n.* electric power expressed in watts

wattle (ˈwɒtˀl) *n.* **1.** frame of woven branches *etc.* as fence **2.** fleshy pendent lobe of neck of certain birds, *eg* turkey **—wattle and daub** form of wall construction consisting of interwoven twigs plastered with mixture of clay and water

waul *or* **wawl** (wɔːl) *vi.* cry or wail plaintively like cat

wave (weɪv) *v.* **1.** move to and fro, as hand in greeting or farewell **2.** signal by waving **3.** give, take shape of waves (as hair *etc.*) *—n.* **4.** ridge and trough on water *etc.* **5.** act, gesture of waving **6.** vibration, as in radio waves, of electric and magnetic forces alternating in direction **7.** prolonged spell of something **8.** upsurge **9.** wavelike shape in the hair *etc.* **—ˈwavy** *a.* **—ˈwaveband** *n.* range of wavelengths or frequencies used for particular type of radio transmission **—ˈwavelength** *n.* distance between same points of two successive sound waves

waver (ˈweɪvə) *vi.* **1.** hesitate, be irresolute **2.** be, become unsteady **—ˈwaverer** *n.*

wax[1] (wæks) *n.* **1.** yellow, soft, pliable material made by bees **2.** this or similar substance used for sealing, making candles *etc.* **3.** waxy secretion of ear *—vt.* **4.** put wax on **—ˈwaxen** *a.* **1.** made of, treated with, or covered with wax **2.** resembling wax in colour or texture **—ˈwaxy** *a.* like wax **—ˈwaxbill** *n.* Afr. finchlike weaverbird **—wax paper** paper coated with wax or paraffin to make it waterproof **—ˈwaxwing** *n.* small songbird **—ˈwaxwork** *n.* lifelike figure, *esp.* of famous person, reproduced in wax

wax[2] (wæks) *vi.* grow, increase

way (weɪ) *n.* **1.** manner **2.** method, means **3.** track **4.** direction **5.** path **6.** passage **7.** course **8.** route **9.** progress **10.** state or condition **—ˈwaybill** *n.* document attached to goods in transit specifying their nature, point of origin, destination and rate to be charged **—ˈwayfarer** *n.* traveller, *esp.* on foot **—wayˈlay** *vt.* lie in wait for and accost, attack (**-ˈlaid, -ˈlaying**) **—way-out** *a. inf.* **1.** extremely unconventional or experimental **2.** excellent or amazing **—ˈwayside** *n.* **1.** side or edge of a road *—a.* **2.** situated by the wayside **—ˈwayward** *a.* capricious, perverse, wilful **—ˈwaywardly** *adv.* **—ˈwaywardness** *n.* **—ways and means 1.** revenues and methods of raising revenues needed for functioning of state *etc.* **2.** methods and resources for accomplishing some purpose

-ways (*comb. form*) indicating direction or manner, as in *sideways*

Wb *Phys.* weber

w.b. **1.** water ballast **2.** waybill (*also* **W/B, W.B.**) **3.** westbound

W.C. *or* **WC** water closet

we (wiː) *pron.* first person plural pronoun

weak (wiːk) *a.* **1.** lacking strength **2.** feeble **3.** fragile **4.** defenceless **5.** easily influenced **6.** faint **—ˈweaken** *v.* **—ˈweakling** *n.* feeble creature **—ˈweakly** *a.* **1.** weak **2.** sickly *—adv.* **3.** in a weak or feeble manner **—ˈweakness** *n.* **—weak-kneed** *a. inf.* yielding readily to force, intimidation *etc.*

THESAURUS

waterfall cascade, cataract, chute, fall, force (*Northern Brit.*), linn (*Scot.*)

watertight **1.** sound, waterproof **2.** airtight, firm, flawless, foolproof, impregnable, incontrovertible, sound, unassailable

watery aqueous, damp, fluid, humid, liquid, marshy, moist, soggy, squelchy, wet

wave *v.* **1.** brandish, flap, flourish, flutter, move to and fro, oscillate, quiver, ripple, shake, stir, sway, swing, undulate, wag, waver, wield **2.** beckon, direct, gesticulate, gesture, indicate, sign, signal *~n.* **3.** billow, breaker, comber, ridge, ripple, roller, sea surf, swell, undulation, unevenness **4.** current, drift, flood, ground swell, movement, outbreak, rash, rush, stream, surge, sweep, tendency, trend, upsurge

waver **1.** be indecisive, be irresolute, be unable to decide, be unable to make up one's mind, blow hot and cold (*Inf.*), dither, falter, fluctuate, hesitate, hum and haw, seesaw, shillyshally (*Inf.*), swither (*Scot.*), vacillate **2.** flicker, fluctuate, quiver, reel, shake, sway, totter, tremble, undulate, vary, wave, weave, wobble

wax *v.* become fuller, become larger, develop, dilate, enlarge, expand, fill out, get bigger, grow, increase, magnify, mount, rise, swell

way **1.** approach, course of action, fashion, manner, means, method, mode, plan, practice, procedure, process, scheme, system, technique **2.** access, avenue, channel, course, direction, highway, lane, path, pathway, road, route, street, thoroughfare, track, trail **3.** distance, journey, length, stretch, trail **4.** advance, approach, journey, march, passage, progress **5.** characteristic, conduct, custom, habit, idiosyncrasy, manner, nature, personality, practice, style, trait, usage, wont **6.** *Inf.* circumstance, condition, fettle, shape (*Inf.*), situation, state, status **7.** forward motion, headway, movement, passage, progress

wayfarer bird of passage, globetrotter, Gypsy, itinerant, journeyer, nomad, rover, traveller, trekker, voyager, walker, wanderer

wayward capricious, changeable, contrary, contumacious, cross-grained, disobedient, erratic, fickle, flighty, froward, headstrong, inconstant, incorrigible, insubordinate, intractable, mulish, obdurate, obstinate, perverse, rebellious, refractory, self-willed, stubborn, undependable, ungovernable, unmanageable, unpredictable, unruly, wilful

weak **1.** anaemic, debilitated, decrepit, delicate, effete, enervated, exhausted, faint, feeble, fragile, frail, infirm, languid, puny, shaky, sickly, spent, tender, unsound, unsteady, wasted, weakly **2.** cowardly,

weal[1] (wi:l) *n.* streak left on flesh by blow of stick or whip

weal[2] (wi:l) *n. obs.* prosperity or wellbeing (*esp. in* **the public weal, common weal**)

weald (wi:ld) *n. obs.* forested country

wealth (wɛlθ) *n.* **1.** riches **2.** abundance —**ˈwealthiness** *n.* —**ˈwealthy** *a.*

wean (wi:n) *vt.* **1.** accustom to food other than mother's milk **2.** win over, coax away

weapon (ˈwɛpən) *n.* **1.** implement to fight with **2.** anything used to get the better of an opponent

wear (wɛə) *vt.* **1.** have on the body **2.** show **3.** produce (hole *etc.*) by rubbing *etc.* **4.** harass; weaken **5.** *inf.* allow, tolerate —*vi.* **6.** last **7.** become impaired by use **8.** (*with* on) (of time) pass slowly (**wore, worn, ˈwearing**) —*n.* **9.** act of wearing **10.** things to wear **11.** damage caused by use **12.** ability to resist effects of constant use —**ˈwearer** *n.* —**wear and tear** depreciation or loss resulting from ordinary use

weary (ˈwɪərɪ) *a.* **1.** tired, exhausted, jaded **2.** tiring **3.** tedious —*v.* **4.** make, become weary (**ˈwearied, ˈwearying**) —**ˈwearily** *adv.* —**ˈweariness** *n.* —**ˈwearisome** *a.* causing weariness

weasel (ˈwi:zᵊl) *n.* small carnivorous mammal with long body and short legs

weather (ˈwɛðə) *n.* **1.** day-to-day meteorological conditions, *esp.* temperature, cloudiness *etc.* of a place —*a.* **2.** towards the wind —*v.* **3.** affect or be affected by weather —*vt.* **4.** endure **5.** resist **6.** come safely through **7.** sail to windward of —**ˈweathering** *n.* mechanical and chemical breakdown of rocks by action of rain, cold *etc.* —**weather-beaten** *a.* showing signs of exposure to weather —**ˈweatherboard** *n.* timber boards used as external cladding of house —**weather-bound** *a.* (of vessel, aircraft *etc.*) delayed by bad weather —**ˈweathercock** *n.* revolving vane to show which way wind blows —**weather eye 1.** vision of person trained to observe changes in weather **2.** *inf.* alert or observant gaze —**weather house** model house, usu. with two human figures, one that enters to foretell bad weather and one that enters to foretell good weather —**weather strip** thin strip of metal, felt *etc.* fitted between frame of door or window and opening part to exclude draughts and rain —**weather vane** vane designed to indicate direction in which wind is blowing

weave (wi:v) *vt.* **1.** form into texture or fabric by interlacing, *esp.* on loom **2.** fashion, construct —*vi.* **3.** practise weaving **4.** make one's way, *esp.* with side to side motion (**wove** *or* **weaved, ˈwoven** *or* **weaved, ˈweaving**) —**ˈweaver** *n.*

THESAURUS

impotent, indecisive, ineffectual, infirm, irresolute, namby-pamby, powerless, soft, spineless, timorous, weak-kneed (*Inf.*) **3.** distant, dull, faint, imperceptible, low, muffled, poor, quiet, slight, small, soft **4.** deficient, faulty, inadequate, lacking, poor, substandard, under-strength, wanting **5.** feeble, flimsy, hollow, inconclusive, invalid, lame, pathetic, shallow, slight, unconvincing, unsatisfactory **6.** defenceless, exposed, helpless, unguarded, unprotected, unsafe, untenable, vulnerable, wide open

weaken abate, debilitate, depress, diminish, droop, dwindle, ease up, enervate, fade, fail, flag, give way, impair, invalidate, lessen, lower, mitigate, moderate, reduce, sap, sap the strength of, soften up, temper, tire, undermine, wane

weakling coward, doormat (*Sl.*), drip (*Inf.*), jellyfish (*Inf.*), milksop, mouse, sissy, wet (*Brit. inf.*), wimp (*Inf.*)

weakness 1. debility, decrepitude, enervation, faintness, feebleness, fragility, frailty, impotence, infirmity, irresolution, powerlessness, vulnerability **2.** Achilles heel, blemish, chink in one's armour, defect, deficiency, failing, fault, flaw, imperfection, lack, shortcoming

wealth 1. affluence, assets, capital, cash, estate, fortune, funds, goods, lucre, means, money, opulence, pelf, possessions, property, prosperity, resources, riches, substance **2.** abundance, bounty, copiousness, cornucopia, fullness, plenitude, plenty, profusion, richness, store

wealthy affluent, comfortable, filthy rich (*Sl.*), flush (*Inf.*), in the money (*Inf.*), loaded (*Sl.*), made of money (*Inf.*), moneyed, on easy street (*Sl.*), opulent, prosperous, quids in (*Sl.*), rich, rolling in it (*Sl.*), stinking rich (*Sl.*), well-heeled (*Sl.*), well-off, well-to-do

wear *v.* **1.** bear, be clothed in, be dressed in, carry, clothe oneself, don, dress in, have on, put on, sport **2.** display, exhibit, fly, show **3.** abrade, consume, corrode, deteriorate, erode, fray, grind, impair, rub, use, wash away, waste **4.** bear up, be durable, endure, hold up, last, stand up **5.** annoy, drain, enervate, exasperate, fatigue, harass, irk, pester, tax, undermine, vex, weaken, weary **6.** *Brit. sl.* accept, allow, brook, countenance, fall for, permit, put up with (*Inf.*), stand for, stomach, swallow (*Inf.*), take ~*n.* **7.** apparel, attire, clothes, costume, dress, garb, garments, gear, habit, outfit, things **8.** abrasion, attrition, corrosion, damage, depreciation, deterioration, erosion, friction, use, wear and tear

weariness drowsiness, enervation, exhaustion, fatigue, languor, lassitude, lethargy, listlessness, prostration, tiredness

wearing exasperating, exhausting, fatiguing, irksome, oppressive, taxing, tiresome, tiring, trying, wearisome

wearisome annoying, boring, bothersome, burdensome, dull, exasperating, exhausting, fatiguing, humdrum, irksome, monotonous, oppressive, pestilential, prosaic, tedious, troublesome, trying, uninteresting, vexatious, wearing

weary *adj.* **1.** all in (*Sl.*), asleep *or* dead on one's feet (*Inf.*), dead beat (*Inf.*), dog-tired (*Inf.*), done in (*Inf.*), drained, drooping, drowsy, enervated, exhausted, fagged (*Inf.*), fatigued, flagging, jaded, knackered (*Sl.*), ready to drop, sleepy, spent, tired, wearied, whacked (*Brit. inf.*), worn out **2.** arduous, enervative, irksome, laborious, taxing, tiresome, tiring, wearing, wearisome **3.** bored, browned-off (*Inf.*), discontented, fed up, impatient, indifferent, jaded, sick (*Inf.*), sick and tired (*Inf.*) ~*v.* **4.** burden, debilitate, drain, droop, enervate, fade, fag (*Inf.*), fail, fatigue, grow tired, sap, take it out of (*Inf.*), tax, tire, tire out, wear out **5.** annoy, become bored, bore, exasperate, have had enough, irk, jade, make discontented, plague, sicken, try the patience of, vex

weather 1. *n.* climate, conditions **2.** *v.* bear up against, brave, come through, endure, get through, live through, make it (*Inf.*), overcome, pull through,

web (wɛb) *n.* **1.** woven fabric **2.** net spun by spider **3.** membrane between toes of waterfowl, frogs *etc.* —ˈ**webbing** *n.* strong fabric woven in strips

weber (ˈveɪbə) *n.* SI unit of magnetic flux

wed (wɛd) *v.* **1.** marry —*vt.* **2.** unite closely (ˈ**wedded, wed** *pt./pp.*, ˈ**wedding**) —ˈ**wedding** *n.* act of marrying, nuptial ceremony —ˈ**wedlock** *n.* marriage

Wed. Wednesday

wedge (wɛdʒ) *n.* **1.** piece of wood, metal *etc.*, thick at one end, tapering to a thin edge —*vt.* **2.** fasten, split with wedge **3.** stick by compression or crowding

Wedgwood (ˈwɛdʒwʊd) *n.* **R** kind of pottery with ornamental reliefs

Wednesday (ˈwɛnzdɪ) *n.* fourth day of week

wee (wiː) *a.* small, little

weed (wiːd) *n.* **1.** plant growing where undesired **2.** *inf.* tobacco **3.** *inf.* marijuana **4.** *inf.* thin, sickly person, animal —*vt.* **5.** clear of weeds —ˈ**weedy** *a.* **1.** full of weeds **2.** *inf.* thin, weakly —**weed out** remove, eliminate what is unwanted

weeds (wiːdz) *pl.n.* (widow's) mourning clothes

week (wiːk) *n.* **1.** period of seven days, *esp.* one beginning on Sunday and ending on Saturday **2.** hours, days of work in seven-day period —ˈ**weekly** *a./adv.* **1.** (happening, done, published *etc.*) once a week —*n.* **2.** newspaper or magazine issued every week —ˈ**weekday** *n.* any day of week except Sunday and *usu.* Saturday —**weekˈend** *n.* Saturday and Sunday, *esp.* considered as rest period

weep (wiːp) *v.* **1.** shed (tears) **2.** grieve (**wept**, ˈ**weeping**) —ˈ**weepy** *a.* —**weeping willow** willow with drooping branches

weevil (ˈwiːvɪl) *n.* small beetle harmful to grain *etc.*

weft (wɛft) *n.* cross threads in weaving, woof

weigh (weɪ) *vt.* **1.** find weight of **2.** consider **3.** raise (anchor) —*vi.* **4.** have weight **5.** be burdensome —**weight** *n.* **1.** measure of the heaviness of an object **2.** quality of heaviness **3.** heavy mass **4.** object of known mass for weighing **5.** unit of measurement of weight **6.** importance, influence —*vt.* **7.** add weight to —ˈ**weightily** *adv.* —ˈ**weighting** *n.* additional allowance payable in particular circumstances —ˈ**weightlessness** *n.* having little or no weight, experienced *esp.* at great distances from earth because of reduced gravitational attraction (*also* **zero gravity**) —ˈ**weighty** *a.* **1.** heavy **2.** onerous **3.** important **4.** momentous —ˈ**weighbridge** *n.* machine for weighing vehicles *etc.* by means of metal plate set into road —ˈ**weightlifting** *n.* sport of lifting barbells of specified weights in prescribed manner —**weight training** physical exercise using heavy or light weights, to improve muscle performance

weir (wɪə) *n.* river dam

weird (wɪəd) *a.* **1.** unearthly, uncanny **2.** strange, bizarre

welch (wɛlʃ) *vi. see* WELSH

welcome (ˈwɛlkəm) *a.* **1.** received gladly **2.** freely

THESAURUS

resist, ride out, rise above, stand, stick it out (*Inf.*), suffer, surmount, survive, withstand

weave 1. blend, braid, entwine, fuse, incorporate, interlace, intermingle, intertwine, introduce, knit, mat, merge, plait, twist, unite 2. build, construct, contrive, create, fabricate, make, make up, put together, spin 3. crisscross, move in and out, weave one's way, wind, zigzag

web 1. cobweb, spider's web 2. interlacing, lattice, mesh, net, netting, network, screen, tangle, toils, weave, webbing

wed 1. become man and wife, be married to, espouse, get hitched (*Inf.*), get married, join, make one, marry, splice (*Inf.*), take as one's husband, take as one's wife, take to wife, tie the knot (*Inf.*), unite 2. ally, blend, coalesce, combine, commingle, dedicate, fuse, interweave, join, link, marry, merge, unify, unite, yoke

wedding espousals, marriage, marriage ceremony, nuptial rite, nuptials, wedlock

wedge 1. *n.* block, chock, chunk, lump, wodge (*Brit. inf.*) 2. *v.* block, cram, crowd, force, jam, lodge, pack, ram, split, squeeze, stuff, thrust

wedlock marriage, matrimony

weed out dispense with, eliminate, eradicate, extirpate, get rid of, remove, root out, separate out, shed, uproot

weekly by the week, every week, hebdomadal, hebdomadally, hebdomadary, once a week

weep bemoan, bewail, blub (*Sl.*), blubber, boohoo, complain, cry, greet (*Dialect*), keen, lament, moan, mourn, shed tears, snivel, sob, ululate, whimper, whinge (*Inf.*)

weigh 1. have a weight of, measure the weight of, put on the scales, tip the scales at (*Inf.*) 2. consider, contemplate, deliberate upon, evaluate, examine, give thought to, meditate upon, mull over, ponder, reflect upon, study, think over 3. be influential, carry weight, count, cut any ice (*Inf.*), have influence, impress, matter, tell 4. bear down, burden, oppress, prey

weight *n.* 1. avoirdupois, burden, gravity, heaviness, heft (*Inf.*), load, mass, poundage, pressure, tonnage 2. ballast, heavy object, load, mass 3. greatest force, main force, onus, preponderance 4. authority, clout (*Inf.*), consequence, consideration, efficacy, emphasis, impact, import, importance, influence, moment, persuasiveness, power, significance, substance, value ~*v.* 5. add weight to, ballast, charge, freight, increase the load on, increase the weight of, load, make heavier

weighty 1. burdensome, cumbersome, dense, heavy, hefty (*Inf.*), massive, ponderous 2. consequential, considerable, critical, crucial, forcible, grave, important, momentous, portentous, serious, significant, solemn, substantial 3. backbreaking, burdensome, crushing, demanding, difficult, exacting, onerous, oppressive, taxing, worrisome, worrying

weird bizarre, creepy (*Inf.*), eerie, eldritch (*Poetic*), far-out (*Sl.*), freakish, ghostly, grotesque, mysterious, odd, outlandish, queer, spooky (*Inf.*), strange, supernatural, uncanny, unearthly, unnatural

welcome *adj.* 1. acceptable, accepted, agreeable, appreciated, delightful, desirable, gladly received, gratifying, pleasant, pleasing, pleasurable, refreshing, wanted 2. at home, free, invited, under no obligation ~*n.* 3. acceptance, entertainment, greeting, hospitality, reception, salutation ~*v.* 4. accept gladly, bid welcome, embrace, greet, hail, meet, offer hospitality to, receive, receive with open arms, roll out the red carpet for, usher in permitted —*n.* **3.** kindly greeting —*vt.* **4.** greet with pleasure **5.** receive gladly (**-comed, -coming**)

weld (wɛld) *vt.* **1.** unite (metal) by softening with heat **2.** unite closely —*n.* **3.** welded joint —**ˈwelder** *n.* **1.** tradesman who welds **2.** machine used in welding

welfare (ˈwɛlfɛə) *n.* wellbeing —**welfare state** system in which the government takes responsibility for the social, economic *etc.* security of its citizens

well[1] (wɛl) *adv.* **1.** in good manner or degree **2.** suitably **3.** intimately **4.** fully **5.** favourably, kindly **6.** to a considerable degree —*a.* **7.** in good health **8.** suitable (**ˈbetter** *comp.*, **best** *sup.*) —*interj.* **9.** exclamation of surprise, interrogation *etc.* —**well-appointed** *a.* well equipped or furnished —**well-balanced** *a.* **1.** having good balance or proportions **2.** sane or sensible —**ˈwellˈbeing** *n.* state of being well, happy, or prosperous —**well-connected** *a.* having influential or important relatives or friends —**well-disposed** *a.* inclined to be friendly, kindly (towards) —**well-done** *a.* **1.** (of food, *esp.* meat) cooked thoroughly **2.** accomplished satisfactorily —**well-grounded** *a.* **1.** well instructed in basic elements of subject **2.** based on good reasons —**well-heeled** *a. sl.* rich; wealthy —**well-intentioned** *a.* having benevolent intentions, usu. with unfortunate results —**well-mannered** *a.* having good manners —**well-nigh** *adv. poet.* nearly; almost —**well-off** *a.* fairly rich —**well-read** *a.* having read much —**well-spoken** *a.* speaking fluently, graciously, aptly —**well-to-do** *a.* moderately wealthy —**well tried** proved to be satisfactory by long experience —**well-wisher** *n.* person who shows benevolence towards person, cause *etc.* —**well-wishing** *a./n.* —**well-worn** *a.* **1.** so much used as to be affected by wear **2.** hackneyed

well[2] (wɛl) *n.* **1.** hole sunk into the earth to reach water, gas, oil *etc.* **2.** spring **3.** any shaft like a well **4.** space in a lawcourt where solicitors sit —*vi.* **5.** spring, gush —**ˈwellhead** *n.* **1.** source of well or stream **2.** source, fountainhead or origin —**ˈwellspring** *n.* **1.** source of spring or stream **2.** source of abundant supply

Wellington boots (ˈwɛlɪŋtən) high waterproof boots (*also* **ˈWellingtons, ˈwellies**)

welsh *or* **welch** (wɛlʃ) *vi.* fail to pay debt or fulfil obligation —**ˈwelsher** *or* **ˈwelcher** *n.*

Welsh (wɛlʃ) *a.* **1.** of Wales —*n.* **2.** language, natives or inhabitants of Wales —**Welsh rabbit** *or* **rarebit** savoury dish of melted cheese on toast —**Welsh terrier** wire-haired breed of terrier with black-and-tan coat

welt (wɛlt) *n.* **1.** raised, strengthened seam **2.** weal —*vt.* **3.** provide with welt **4.** thrash

welter (ˈwɛltə) *vi.* **1.** roll or tumble —*n.* **2.** turmoil, disorder

welterweight (ˈwɛltəweɪt) *n.* **1.** professional boxer weighing 140-147 lbs (63.5-66.5 kg); amateur boxer weighing 63.5-67 kg (140-148 lbs) **2.** wrestler weighing usu. 154-172 lbs (70-78 kg)

wen (wɛn) *n.* cyst, *esp.* on scalp

wench (wɛntʃ) *n. now oft. facetious* young woman

wend (wɛnd) *v.* go, travel

wendigo (ˈwɛndɪgɒ) *n.* **C** *see* SPLAKE

wensleydale (ˈwɛnzlɪdeɪl) *n.* **1.** type of white cheese with flaky texture **2.** breed of sheep with long woolly fleece

went (wɛnt) *pt. of* GO

wept (wɛpt) *pt./pp. of* WEEP

were (wɜː; *unstressed* wə) imperfect indicative plural and subjunctive sing. and pl. of BE

werewolf (ˈwɪəwʊlf, ˈwɛə-) *n.* in folklore, human being turned into wolf

Wesleyan (ˈwɛzlɪən) *a.* **1.** pert. to English preacher, John Wesley (1703-91), who founded Methodism **2.** of Methodism, *esp.* in its original form —*n.* **3.** follower of John Wesley **4.** member of Methodist Church —**ˈWesleyanism** *n.*

west (wɛst) *n.* **1.** part of sky where sun sets **2.** part of country *etc.* lying to this side **3.** occident —*a.* **4.** that is toward or in this region —*adv.* **5.** to the west —**ˈwesterly** *a.* —**ˈwestern** *a.* **1.** of, in the west —*n.* **2.** film, story *etc.* about cowboys or frontiersmen in western U.S. —**ˈwesternize** *or* **-ise** *vt.* influence with customs, practices *etc.* of West —**ˈwestward** *a./adv.* —**ˈwestwards** *adv.* towards the west —**western hemisphere** (*oft.* **W-H-**) that half of the globe containing N and S Amer. —**go west** *inf.* **1.** disappear **2.** die **3.** be lost —**the West Country** southwest of England, *esp.* Cornwall, Devon and Somerset —**the West End** part of W central London containing main shopping and entertainment areas

Westminster (ˈwɛstmɪnstə) *n.* British Houses of Parliament

wet (wɛt) *a.* **1.** having water or other liquid on a

THESAURUS

welfare advantage, benefit, good, happiness, health, interest, profit, prosperity, success, wellbeing

well[1] *adv.* **1.** agreeably, capitally, famously (*Inf.*), happily, in a satisfactory manner, nicely, pleasantly, satisfactorily, smoothly, splendidly, successfully **2.** ably, adeptly, adequately, admirably, conscientiously, correctly, effectively, efficiently, expertly, proficiently, properly, skilfully, with skill **3.** correctly, easily, fairly, fittingly, in all fairness, justly, properly, readily, rightly, suitably **4.** closely, completely, deeply, fully, intimately, personally, profoundly, thoroughly **5.** approvingly, favourably, glowingly, graciously, highly, kindly, warmly **6.** abundantly, amply, completely, considerably, fully, greatly, heartily, highly, substantially, sufficiently, thoroughly, very much ~*adj.* **7.** able-bodied, fit, hale, healthy, hearty, in fine fettle, in good health, robust, sound, strong, up to par **8.** advisable, agreeable, bright, fine, fitting, flourishing, fortunate, good, happy, lucky, pleasing, profitable, proper, prudent, right, satisfactory, thriving, useful

well[2] *n.* **1.** fountain, pool, source, spring, waterhole **2.** bore, hole, pit, shaft **3.** fount, mine, repository, source, wellspring ~*v.* **4.** flow, gush, jet, ooze, pour, rise, run, seep, spout, spring, spurt, stream, surge, trickle

well-balanced 1. graceful, harmonious, proportional, symmetrical, well-proportioned **2.** judicious, level-headed, rational, reasonable, sane, sensible, sober, sound, together (*Sl.*), well-adjusted

well-nigh all but, almost, just about, more or less, nearly, next to, practically, virtually

well-off affluent, comfortable, flush (*Inf.*), loaded (*Sl.*), moneyed, prosperous, rich, wealthy, well-heeled (*Sl.*), well-to-do

well-to-do affluent, comfortable, flush (*Inf.*), loaded (*Sl.*), moneyed, prosperous, rich, wealthy, well-heeled (*Sl.*), well-off

surface or being soaked in it **2.** rainy **3.** not yet dry (paint, ink *etc.*) **4.** *inf.* (of person) feeble, dull *etc.* (**ˈwetter** *comp.*, **ˈwettest** *sup.*) —*vt.* **5.** make wet (**wet, ˈwetted** *pt./pp.*, **ˈwetting** *pr.p.*) —*n.* **6.** moisture, rain 7. (*oft.* **W-**) UK *inf.* Conservative politician who is not a hardliner —**wet blanket** *inf.* one depressing spirits of others —**wet dream** erotic dream accompanied by emission of semen —**wetland** (ˈwɛtlənd) *n.* (*sometimes pl.*) area of marshy land, *esp.* considered as part of ecological system —**wet nurse** woman suckling another's child —**wet suit** close-fitting rubber suit worn by divers *etc.*

wether (ˈwɛðə) *n.* castrated ram

W. Glam. West Glamorgan

whack (wæk) *vt.* **1.** strike with sharp resounding blow —*n.* **2.** such blow **3.** *inf.* share **4.** *inf.* attempt —**whacked** *a.* exhausted —**ˈwhacking** *a. inf.* big, enormous

whale (weɪl) *n.* large fish-shaped sea mammal —**ˈwhaler** *n.* man, ship employed in hunting whales —**ˈwhaling** *n.* work or industry of hunting and processing whales for food, oil *etc.* —**ˈwhalebone** *n.* horny elastic substance from projections of upper jaw of certain whales

wham (wæm) *n.* **1.** forceful blow or sound produced by it —*v.* **2.** strike or cause to strike with great force (**-mm-**)

wharf (wɔːf) *n.* platform at harbour, on river *etc.* for loading and unloading ships (*pl.* **wharves** (wɔːvz), **-s**)

what (wɒt; *unstressed* wət) *pron.* **1.** which thing **2.** that which **3.** request for statement to be repeated —*a.* **4.** which **5.** as much as **6.** how great, surprising *etc.* —*interj.* 7. exclamation of surprise, anger *etc.* —**whatˈever** *pron.* **1.** anything which **2.** of what kind it may be —**whatsoˈever** *a.* **1.** at all: used as intensifier with indefinite pronouns and determiners such as *none, anybody etc.* —*pron.* **2.** *rare* whatever —**ˈwhatnot** *n.* **1.** *inf.* person, thing whose name is unknown, forgotten *etc.* **2.** small stand with shelves

wheat (wiːt) *n.* cereal plant with thick four-sided seed spikes of which bread is chiefly made —**ˈwheaten** *a.* —**ˈwheatear** *n.* small songbird —**wheat germ** embryo of wheat kernel —**ˈwheatmeal** *n.* wholemeal flour made from wheat

wheedle (ˈwiːdᵊl) *v.* coax, cajole

wheel (wiːl) *n.* **1.** circular frame or disc (with spokes) revolving on axle **2.** anything like a wheel in shape or function **3.** act of turning **4.** steering wheel —*v.* **5.** (cause to) turn as if on axis **6.** (cause to) move on or as if on wheels **7.** (cause to) change course, *esp.* in opposite direction —**ˈwheelbarrow** *n.* barrow with one wheel —**ˈwheelbase** *n.* distance between front and rear hubs of vehicle —**ˈwheelchair** *n.* chair mounted on large wheels, used by people who cannot walk —**ˈwheelhouse** *n.* enclosed structure on vessel's bridge for steersman —**ˈwheelspin** *n.* revolution of wheels without full grip of road —**ˈwheelwright** *n.* person who makes or mends wheels as trade

wheeze (wiːz) *vi.* **1.** breathe with difficulty and whistling noise —*n.* **2.** this sound **3.** *inf.* trick, idea, plan —**ˈwheezy** *a.*

whelk (wɛlk) *n.* sea snail, *esp.* edible variety

whelp (wɛlp) *n.* **1.** young of certain animals, *esp.* of wolf or dog **2.** *disparaging* youth **3.** *jocular* child —*v.* **4.** give birth to (whelps)

when (wɛn) *adv.* **1.** at what time —*conj.* **2.** at the time that **3.** although **4.** since —*pron.* **5.** at which (time) —**whenˈever** *adv./conj.* at whatever time —**whensoˈever** *conj./adv. rare* whenever

whence (wɛns) *adv./conj. formal* **1.** from what place or source **2.** how

where (wɛə) *adv./conj.* **1.** at what place **2.** at or to the place in which —**ˈwhereabouts** *adv./conj.* **1.** in what, which place —*n.* **2.** present position —**whereˈas** *conj.* **1.** considering that **2.** while, on the contrary —**whereˈby** *conj.* by which —**ˈwherefore** *adv. obs.* **1.** why **2.** consequently —**whereˈof** *obs., formal adv.* **1.** of what or which person or thing? —*pron.* **2.** of which (person or thing) —**whereuˈpon** *conj.* at which point —**wherˈever** *adv.* at whatever place —**ˈwherewithal** *n.* necessary funds, resources *etc.*

whet (wɛt) *vt.* **1.** sharpen **2.** stimulate (**-tt-**) —**ˈwhetstone** *n.* stone for sharpening tools

whether (ˈwɛðə) *conj.* introduces the first of two alternatives, of which the second may be expressed or implied

whew (hwjuː) *interj.* exclamation expressing relief, delight *etc.*

whey (weɪ) *n.* watery part of milk left after separation of curd in cheese making

which (wɪtʃ) *a.* **1.** used in requests for a selection from alternatives —*pron.* **2.** which person or thing **3.** the thing 'who' —**whichˈever** *pron.*

THESAURUS

wet *adj.* **1.** aqueous, damp, dank, drenched, dripping, humid, moist, moistened, saturated, soaked, soaking, sodden, soggy, sopping, waterlogged, watery, wringing wet **2.** clammy, dank, drizzling, humid, misty, pouring, raining, rainy, showery, teeming **3.** *Brit. inf.* effete, feeble, foolish, ineffectual, irresolute, namby-pamby, silly, soft, spineless, timorous, weak, weedy (*Inf.*) ~*n.* **4.** clamminess, condensation, damp, dampness, humidity, liquid, moisture, water, wetness **5.** damp weather, drizzle, rain, rains, rainy season, rainy weather ~*v.* **6.** damp, dampen, dip, douse, drench, humidify, irrigate, moisten, saturate, soak, splash, spray, sprinkle, steep, water

wharf dock, jetty, landing stage, pier, quay

wheedle butter up, cajole, charm, coax, court, draw, entice, flatter, inveigle, persuade, talk into, worm

wheel **1.** *n.* circle, gyration, pivot, revolution, roll, rotation, spin, turn, twirl, whirl **2.** *v.* circle, gyrate, orbit, pirouette, revolve, roll, rotate, spin, swing, swivel, turn, twirl, whirl

wheeze *v.* **1.** breathe roughly, catch one's breath, cough, gasp, hiss, rasp, whistle ~*n.* **2.** cough, gasp, hiss, rasp, whistle **3.** *Brit. sl.* expedient, idea, plan, ploy, ruse, scheme, stunt, trick, wrinkle (*Inf.*)

whereabouts location, position, site, situation

wherewithal capital, equipment, essentials, funds, means, money, ready (*Inf.*), ready money, resources, supplies

whet **1.** edge, file, grind, hone, sharpen, strop **2.** animate, arouse, awaken, enhance, excite, incite, increase, kindle, pique, provoke, quicken, rouse, stimulate, stir

whiff *n.* **1.** aroma, blast, breath, draught, gust, hint, odour, puff, scent, smell, sniff ~*v.* **2.** breathe, inhale, puff, smell, smoke, sniff, waft **3.** *Brit. sl.* hum (*Sl.*), pong (*Brit. inf.*), reek, stink

whiff (wɪf) *n.* **1.** brief smell or suggestion of **2.** puff of air —*vt.* **3.** smell

Whig (wɪg) *n.* member of British political party that preceded the Liberal Party

while (waɪl) *conj.* **1.** in the time that **2.** in spite of the fact that, although **3.** whereas —*vt.* **4.** pass (time, usu. idly) —*n.* **5.** period of time —**whilst** *conj.* while

whim (wɪm) *n.* sudden, passing fancy —**ˈwhimsical** *a.* **1.** fanciful **2.** full of whims —**whimsiˈcality** *n.* —**ˈwhimsy** *or* **ˈwhimsey** *n.* **1.** whim **2.** caprice —*a.* **3.** quaint, comical or unusual, oft. in tasteless way

whimper (ˈwɪmpə) *vi.* **1.** cry or whine softly **2.** complain in this way —*n.* **3.** such cry or complaint

whin (wɪn) *n.* gorse

whine (waɪn) *n.* **1.** high-pitched plaintive cry **2.** peevish complaint —*vi.* **3.** utter this

whinge (wɪndʒ) *inf. vi.* **1.** whine, complain —*n.* **2.** complaint

whinny (ˈwɪnɪ) *vi.* **1.** neigh softly (**ˈwhinnied, ˈwhinnying**) —*n.* **2.** gentle neigh

whip (wɪp) *vt.* **1.** strike with whip **2.** thrash **3.** beat (cream, eggs) to a froth **4.** lash **5.** *inf.* pull, remove, insert *etc.* quickly **6.** *inf.* steal —*vi.* **7.** dart (**-pp-**) —*n.* **8.** lash attached to handle for urging or punishing **9.** one who enforces attendance of political party **10.** call made on members of Parliament to attend for important divisions **11.** elastic quality permitting bending in mast, fishing rod *etc.* **12.** whipped dessert —**ˈwhipping** *n.* **1.** thrashing with whip or similar implement **2.** cord used for binding or lashing **3.** binding formed by wrapping rope *etc.* with cord or twine —**ˈwhipcord** *n.* **1.** strong worsted fabric with diagonally ribbed surface **2.** hard twisted cord used for lashes of whips *etc.* —**whip hand** (*usu. with* the) **1.** in driving horses *etc.*, hand holding whip **2.** advantage or dominating position —**ˈwhiplash** *n.* quick lash of whip or like that of whip —**whiplash injury** injury to neck as result of sudden jerking of unsupported head —**ˈwhippersnapper** *n.* insignificant but pretentious or cheeky person, oft. young one. (*also* **ˈwhipster**) —**whipping boy** scapegoat —**whip-round** *n. inf.* collection of money

whippet (ˈwɪpɪt) *n.* racing dog like small greyhound

whir *or* **whirr** (wɜː) *v.* **1.** (cause to) fly, spin *etc.* with buzzing or whizzing sound —*vi.* **2.** bustle —*n.* **3.** this sound **4.** bustle

whirl (wɜːl) *v.* **1.** swing rapidly round **2** drive or be driven at high speed —*vi.* **3.** move rapidly in a circular course —*n.* **4.** whirling movement **5.** confusion, bustle, giddiness —**ˈwhirligig** *n.* **1.** spinning toy **2.** merry-go-round —**ˈwhirlpool** *n.* circular current, eddy —**ˈwhirlwind** *n.* **1.** wind whirling round while moving forwards —*a.* **2.** rapid or sudden —**ˈwhirlybird** *n. inf.* helicopter

whisk (wɪsk) *vt.* **1.** brush, sweep, beat lightly **2.** beat to a froth —*v.* **3.** move, remove, quickly —*n.* **4.** light brush **5.** egg-beating implement

whisker (ˈwɪskə) *n.* **1.** long stiff hair at side of mouth of cat or other animal **2.** any of hairs on a man's face —**by a whisker** *inf.* only just

whisky (ˈwɪskɪ) *n.* spirit distilled from fermented cereals (*Irish*, **C, US** **ˈwhiskey**)

whisper (ˈwɪspə) *v.* **1.** speak in soft, hushed tones, without vibration of vocal cords **2.** rustle —*n.* **3.** such speech **4.** trace or suspicion **5.** rustle

whist (wɪst) *n.* card game

whistle (ˈwɪsᵊl) *vi.* **1.** produce shrill sound by forcing breath through rounded, nearly closed lips —*vt.* **2.** utter, summon *etc.* by whistle —*n.* **3.** such sound **4.** any similar sound **5.** instrument to make it —**ˈwhistler** *n.* —**whistle stop 1. US** minor railway station where trains stop only on signal; small town having such a station **2.** brief appearance in town, *esp.* by political candidate

whit (wɪt) *n.* jot, particle (*esp. in* **not a whit**)

white (waɪt) *a.* **1.** of the colour of snow **2.** pale **3.** light in colour **4.** having a light-coloured skin —*n.* **5.** colour of snow **6.** white pigment **7.** white part **8.** clear fluid

THESAURUS

whim caprice, conceit, craze, crotchet, fad (*Inf.*), fancy, freak, humour, impulse, notion, passing thought, quirk, sport, sudden notion, urge, vagary, whimsy

whimper 1. *v.* blub (*Sl.*), blubber, cry, grizzle (*Inf.*), mewl, moan, pule, snivel, sob, weep, whine, whinge (*Inf.*) **2.** *n.* moan, snivel, sob, whine

whimsical capricious, chimerical, crotchety, curious, droll, eccentric, fanciful, fantastic, fantastical, freakish, funny, mischievous, odd, peculiar, playful, quaint, queer, singular, unusual, waggish, weird

whine *n.* **1.** cry, moan, plaintive cry, sob, wail, whimper **2.** beef (*Sl.*), complaint, gripe (*Inf.*), grouse, grumble, moan ~*v.* **3.** beef (*Sl.*), bellyache (*Sl.*), carp, complain, cry, gripe (*Inf.*), grizzle (*Inf.*), grouse, grumble, moan, sob, wail, whimper, whinge (*Inf.*)

whip *v.* **1.** beat, birch, cane, castigate, flagellate, flog, give a hiding (*Inf.*), lash, leather, punish, scourge, spank, strap, switch, tan (*Sl.*), thrash **2.** exhibit, flash, jerk, produce, pull, remove, seize, show, snatch, whisk **3.** *Inf.* dart, dash, dive, flit, flounce, fly, rush, shoot, tear, whisk **4.** beat, whisk ~*n.* **5.** birch, bullwhip, cane, cat-o'-nine-tails, crop, horsewhip, knout, lash, rawhide, riding crop, scourge, switch, thong

whipping beating, birching, caning, castigation, flagellation, flogging, hiding (*Inf.*), lashing, leathering, punishment, spanking, tanning (*Sl.*), the strap, thrashing

whirl *v.* **1.** circle, gyrate, pirouette, pivot, reel, revolve, roll, rotate, spin, swirl, turn, twirl, twist, wheel ~*n.* **2.** birl (*Scot.*), circle, gyration, pirouette, reel, revolution, roll, rotation, spin, swirl, turn, twirl, twist, wheel **3.** confusion, daze, dither, flurry, giddiness, spin **4.** flurry, merry-go-round, round, series, succession **5.** agitation, bustle, commotion, confusion, flurry, hurly-burly, stir, tumult, uproar

whirlwind 1. *n.* dust devil, tornado, waterspout **2.** *adj.* hasty, headlong, impetuous, impulsive, lightning, quick, rapid, rash, short, speedy, swift

whisk *v.* **1.** brush, flick, sweep, whip, wipe **2.** dart, dash, fly, hasten, hurry, race, rush, shoot, speed, sweep, tear **3.** beat, fluff up, whip ~*n.* **4.** brush, flick, sweep, whip, wipe **5.** beater

whisky barley-bree (*Scot.*), bourbon, John Barleycorn, malt, rye, Scotch, usquebaugh

whisper *v.* **1.** breathe, murmur, say softly, speak in hushed tones, utter under the breath **2.** hiss, murmur, rustle, sigh, sough, susurrate (*Literary*), swish ~*n.* **3.** hushed tone, low voice, murmur, soft voice, undertone **4.** hiss, murmur, rustle, sigh, sighing, soughing, susurration *or* susurrus (*Literary*), swish **5.** breath, fraction, hint, shadow, suggestion, suspicion, tinge, trace, whiff

round yolk of egg **9.** **(W-)** white person —**ˈwhiten** *v.* —**ˈwhiteness** *n.* —**ˈwhitish** *a.* —**white ant** termite —**ˈwhitebait** *n.* small edible fish —**white blood cell** *see* LEUCOCYTE —**ˈwhitecap** *n.* wave with white broken crest —**white-collar** *a.* denoting nonmanual salaried workers —**white dwarf** one of class of small faint stars of enormous density —**white elephant** useless, unwanted, gift or possession —**white feather** symbol or mark of cowardice —**ˈwhitefish** *n.* **1.** food fish having large silvery scales and small head **2.** in Brit. fishing industry, any edible marine fish or invertebrate excluding herrings but including trout, salmon and all shellfish —**white flag** white banner or cloth used as signal of surrender or truce —**ˈwhitefly** *n.* insect typically having body covered with powdery wax —**white friar** Carmelite friar, so called because of white cloak that forms part of habit of this order —**white gold** white lustrous alloy containing gold together with platinum and palladium and sometimes smaller amounts of silver, nickel, or copper —**white goods** **1.** household linen such as sheets, tablecloths *etc.* **2.** large household appliances, such as refrigerators *etc.* —**white heat** **1.** intense heat characterized by emission of white light **2.** *inf.* state of intense excitement or activity —**white hope** one expected to bring honour or glory to his group, team *etc.* —**white horse** **1.** outline of horse carved into side of chalk hill **2.** wave with white broken crest —**white-hot** *a.* **1.** at such high temperature that white light is emitted **2.** *inf.* in state of intense emotion —**white lead** (lɛd) **1.** white solid usu. regarded as mixture of lead carbonate and lead hydroxide used in paint and in making putty and ointments for treatment of burns **2.** either of two similar white pigments based on lead sulphate or lead silicate —**white lie** minor, unimportant lie —**white matter** whitish tissue of brain and spinal cord, consisting mainly of nerve fibres —**white meat** any meat that is light in colour, such as veal —**white noise** sound or electrical noise that has relatively wide continuous range of frequencies of uniform intensity —**white paper** government report on matter recently investigated —**white pepper** condiment made from husked dried beans of pepper plant —**white sale** sale of household linens at reduced prices —**white sauce** thick sauce made from flour, butter, seasonings, and milk or stock —**white slave** woman, child forced or enticed away for purposes of prostitution —**white spirit** colourless liquid obtained from petroleum, used as substitute for turpentine —**white tie** **1.** white bow tie worn as part of man's formal evening dress **2.** formal evening dress for men —**ˈwhitewash** *n.* **1.** substance for whitening walls *etc.* —*vt.* **2.** apply this to **3.** cover up, gloss over, suppress —**white whale** small white toothed whale of northern waters (*also* **beˈluga**) —**ˈwhitewood** *n.* **1.** tree with light-coloured wood, such as the tulip tree **2.** its wood —**show the white feather** act in cowardly manner —**the White House** **1.** official Washington residence of president of U.S. **2.** U.S. presidency —**White man's burden** supposed duty of White race to bring education and Western culture to non-White inhabitants of their colonies

Whitehall (waɪtˈhɔːl) *n.* **1.** street in London where main government offices are situated **2.** British Government

whither (ˈwɪðə) *adv. Poet.* **1.** to what place **2.** to which

whiting (ˈwaɪtɪŋ) *n.* edible sea fish

whitlow (ˈwɪtləʊ) *n.* abscess on finger, *esp.* round nail

Whitsun (ˈwɪtsᵊn) *n.* week following **Whit Sunday**, seventh Sunday after Easter

whittle (ˈwɪtᵊl) *vt.* **1.** cut, carve with knife **2.** pare away —**whittle down** reduce gradually, wear (away)

whiz *or* **whizz** (wɪz) *n.* **1.** loud hissing sound **2.** *inf.* person skilful at something —*vi.* **3.** move with or make such sound **4.** *inf.* move quickly —**whiz kid, whizz kid,** *or* **wiz kid** *inf.* person who is outstandingly successful for his or her age

who (huː) *pron.* relative and interrogative pronoun, always referring to persons —**whodunit** *or* **whodunnit** (huːˈdʌnɪt) *n. inf.* detective story —**whoˈever** *pron.* who, any one or every one that —**whosoˈever** *pron. formal* whoever

W.H.O. World Health Organization

whoa (wəʊ) *interj.* command used, *esp.* to horses, to stop or slow down

whole (həʊl) *a.* **1.** complete **2.** containing all elements or parts **3.** entire **4.** not defective or imperfect **5.** healthy —*n.* **6.** complete thing or system —**ˈwholly** *adv.* —**ˈwholesome** *a.* producing good effect, physically or morally —**wholeˈhearted** *a.* **1.** sincere **2.** enthusiastic —**ˈwholemeal** *a.* of, pert. to flour which contains the whole of the grain —**whole number** **1.** integer **2.** natural number —**ˈwholesale** *n.* **1.** sale of goods by large quantities to retailers —*a.* **2.** dealing by wholesale **3.** extensive —**ˈwholesaler** *n.* —**on the whole** **1.** taking everything into consideration **2.** in general

THESAURUS

white ashen, bloodless, ghastly, grey, pale, pallid, pasty, wan, waxen, wheyfaced

white-collar clerical, executive, nonmanual, office, professional, salaried

whiten blanch, bleach, blench, etiolate, fade, go white, pale, turn pale

whitewash *v.* camouflage, conceal, cover up, extenuate, gloss over, make light of, suppress

whole *adj.* **1.** complete, entire, full, in one piece, integral, total, unabridged, uncut, undivided **2.** faultless, flawless, good, in one piece, intact, inviolate, mint, perfect, sound, unbroken, undamaged, unharmed, unhurt, unimpaired, uninjured, unmutilated, unscathed, untouched **3.** able-bodied, better, cured, fit, hale, healed, healthy, in fine fettle, in good health, recovered, robust, sound, strong, well ~*n.* **4.** aggregate, all, everything, lot, sum total, the entire amount, total **5.** ensemble, entirety, entity, fullness, piece, totality, unit, unity **6. on the whole a.** all in all, all things considered, by and large, taking everything into consideration **b.** as a rule, for the most part, generally, in the main, in general, mostly, predominantly

wholehearted committed, complete, dedicated, determined, devoted, earnest, emphatic, enthusiastic, genuine, heartfelt, hearty, real, sincere, true, unfeigned, unqualified, unreserved, unstinting, warm, zealous

wholesale *adj.* all-inclusive, broad, comprehensive, extensive, far-reaching, indiscriminate, mass, sweeping, wide-ranging

wholesome **1.** beneficial, good, healthful, health-giving, healthy, helpful, hygienic, invigorating, nourishing, nutritious, salubrious, salutary, sanitary, strengthening **2.** clean, decent, edifying, ethical, exemplary, honourable, improving, innocent, moral,

whom (huːm) *pron.* objective case of WHO

whoop (wuːp) *n.* shout or cry expressing excitement *etc.*

whoopee (wʊˈpiː) *n. inf.* gay, riotous time —**make whoopee 1.** participate in wild noisy party **2.** make love

whooping cough (ˈhuːpɪŋ) infectious disease of mucous membrane lining air passages, marked by convulsive coughing with loud whoop or indrawing of breath

whoops (wʊps) *interj.* exclamation of surprise or of apology

whopper (ˈwɒpə) *n. inf.* **1.** anything unusually large **2.** monstrous lie —ˈ**whopping** *a.*

whore (hɔː) *n.* prostitute —ˈ**whorehouse** *n.* brothel

whorl (wɜːl) *n.* **1.** ring of leaves or petals **2.** turn of spiral **3.** anything forming part of circular pattern, *eg* lines of human fingerprint

whortleberry (ˈwɜːtᵊlbɛrɪ) *n.* small Eurasian shrub of erica genus with edible sweet blackish berries (*also* ˈ**bilberry,** ˈ**huckleberry, (UK)** ˈ**blaeberry**)

whose (huːz) *pron.* possessive case of WHO and WHICH

why (waɪ) *adv.* for what cause or reason

WI Wisconsin

W.I. 1. West Indian **2.** West Indies **3. UK** Women's Institute

wick (wɪk) *n.* strip of thread feeding flame of lamp or candle with oil, grease *etc.*

wicked (ˈwɪkɪd) *a.* **1.** evil, sinful **2.** very bad **3.** mischievous —ˈ**wickedly** *adv.* —ˈ**wickedness** *n.*

wicker(work) (ˈwɪkə(wɜːk)) *n.* woven cane *etc.*, basketwork

wicket (ˈwɪkɪt) *n.* **1.** small gate **2.** *Cricket* set of three stumps and bails **3.** cricket pitch —ˈ**wicketkeeper** *n.* *Cricket* player on fielding side positioned directly behind wicket

wide (waɪd) *a.* **1.** having a great extent from side to side, broad **2.** having considerable distance between **3.** spacious **4.** liberal **5.** vast **6.** far from the mark **7.** opened fully —*adv.* **8.** to the full extent **9.** far from the intended target —*n.* **10.** *Cricket* ball bowled out of batsman's reach —ˈ**widely** *adv.* —ˈ**widen** *v.* —**width** (wɪdθ) *or* ˈ**wideness** *n.* breadth —**wide-angle lens** lens system on camera that can cover angle of view of 60° or more —**wide-eyed** *a.* innocent or credulous —ˈ**widespread** *a.* **1.** extending over a wide area **2.** common

widow (ˈwɪdəʊ) *n.* **1.** woman whose husband is dead and who has not married again —*vt.* **2.** make a widow of —ˈ**widower** *n.* man whose wife is dead and who has not married again —ˈ**widowhood** *n.*

wield (wiːld) *vt.* **1.** hold and use **2.** brandish **3.** manage

wife (waɪf) *n.* a man's partner in marriage, married woman (*pl.* **wives**) —ˈ**wifely** *a.*

wig (wɪg) *n.* artificial hair for the head

wigeon *or* **widgeon** (ˈwɪdʒən) *n.* Eurasian duck of marshes, swamps *etc.*

wigging (ˈwɪgɪŋ) *n.* UK *sl.* reprimand

wiggle (ˈwɪgᵊl) *v.* **1.** (cause to) move jerkily from side to side —*n.* **2.** such movement —ˈ**wiggly** *a.*

wigwam (ˈwɪgwæm) *n.* N Amer. Indian's hut or tent

wilco (ˈwɪlkəʊ) *interj.* expression in telecommunications *etc.* indicating that message just received will be complied with

wild (waɪld) *a.* **1.** not tamed or domesticated **2.** not cultivated **3.** savage **4.** stormy **5.** uncontrolled **6.** random **7.** excited **8.** rash **9.** frantic **10.** *inf.* (of party *etc.*) rowdy, exciting —ˈ**wildly** *adv.* —ˈ**wildness** *n.* —ˈ**wildcat** *n.* **1.** undomesticated European and Amer. feline animal **2.** *inf.* wild, savage person —*a.* **3.** unsound, irresponsible **4.** sudden, unofficial, unauthorized —**wild-goose chase** futile pursuit —ˈ**wildlife** *n.* wild animals and plants collectively —**wild oats** *sl.* indiscretions of youth, *esp.* dissoluteness before settling down (*esp. in* **sow one's wild oats**) —**Wild West**

THESAURUS

nice, pure, respectable, righteous, uplifting, virtuous, worthy

wholly all, altogether, completely, comprehensively, entirely, fully, heart and soul, in every respect, one hundred per cent (*Inf.*), perfectly, thoroughly, totally, utterly

whore brass (*Sl.*), call girl, cocotte, courtesan, demimondaine, demirep (*Rare*), fallen woman, *fille de joie*, harlot, hooker (*U.S. sl.*), hustler (*U.S. sl.*), lady of the night, loose woman, prostitute, streetwalker, strumpet, tart (*Inf.*), trollop, woman of easy virtue, woman of ill repute

wicked 1. abandoned, abominable, amoral, atrocious, bad, black-hearted, corrupt, debased, depraved, devilish, dissolute, egregious, evil, fiendish, flagitious, foul, guilty, heinous, immoral, impious, iniquitous, irreligious, nefarious, scandalous, shameful, sinful, unprincipled, unrighteous, vicious, vile, villainous, worthless **2.** arch, impish, incorrigible, mischievous, naughty, rascally, roguish **3.** acute, agonizing, awful, crashing, destructive, dreadful, fearful, fierce, harmful, injurious, intense, mighty, painful, severe, terrible

wide *adj.* **1.** ample, broad, catholic, comprehensive, distended, encyclopedic, expanded, expansive, extensive, far-reaching, general, immense, inclusive, large, sweeping, vast **2.** away, distant, off, off course, off target, remote **3.** dilated, distended, expanded, fully open, outspread, outstretched **4.** ample, baggy, capacious, commodious, full, loose, roomy, spacious ~*adv.* **5.** as far as possible, completely, fully, right out, to the furthest extent **6.** astray, nowhere near, off course, off target, off the mark, out

wide-eyed credulous, green, impressionable, ingenuous, innocent, naive, simple, trusting, unsophisticated, unsuspicious, wet behind the ears (*Inf.*)

widen broaden, dilate, enlarge, expand, extend, open out *or* up, open wide, spread, stretch

widespread broad, common, epidemic, extensive, far-flung, far-reaching, general, pervasive, popular, prevalent, rife, sweeping, universal, wholesale

width breadth, compass, diameter, extent, girth, measure, range, reach, scope, span, thickness, wideness

wield 1. brandish, employ, flourish, handle, manage, manipulate, ply, swing, use **2.** apply, be possessed of, command, control, exercise, exert, have, have at one's disposal, hold, maintain, make use of, manage, possess, put to use, utilize

wife better half (*Humorous*), bride, helpmate, helpmeet, little woman (*Inf.*), mate, old lady (*Inf.*), old woman (*Inf.*), partner, spouse, (the) missis *or* missus (*Inf.*), woman (*Inf.*)

western U.S., *esp.* with reference to its frontier lawlessness

wildebeest (ˈwɪldɪbiːst, ˈvɪl-) *n.* gnu

wilderness (ˈwɪldənɪs) *n.* **1.** desert, waste place **2.** state of desolation or confusion

wildfire (ˈwaɪldfaɪə) *n.* **1.** raging, uncontrollable fire **2.** anything spreading, moving fast

wile (waɪl) *n.* (*usu. pl.*) trick —ˈ**wily** *a.* crafty, sly

wilful *or U.S.* **willful** (ˈwɪlfʊl) *a.* **1.** obstinate, self-willed **2.** intentional —ˈ**wilfully** *or U.S.* ˈ**willfully** *adv.*

will (wɪl) *v. aux.* **1.** forms moods and tenses indicating intention or conditional result (**would** *pt.*) —*vi.* **2.** have a wish —*vt.* **3.** wish **4.** intend **5.** leave as legacy —*n.* **6.** faculty of deciding what one will do **7.** purpose **8.** volition **9.** determination **10.** wish **11.** directions written for disposal of property after death —ˈ**willing** *a.* **1.** ready **2.** given cheerfully —ˈ**willingly** *adv.* —ˈ**willingness** *n.* —ˈ**willpower** *n.* ability to control oneself, one's actions, impulses

willies (ˈwɪlɪz) *pl.n. sl.* nervousness, jitters, or fright (*esp. in* **give** (*or* **get**) **the willies**)

will-o'-the-wisp (wɪləðəˈwɪsp) *n.* **1.** brief pale flame or phosphorescence sometimes seen over marshes **2.** elusive person or hope

willow (ˈwɪləʊ) *n.* **1.** tree, such as the weeping willow with long thin flexible branches **2.** its wood —ˈ**willowy** *a.* lithe, slender, supple —ˈ**willowherb** *n.* tall plant with mauve flowers

willy-nilly (ˈwɪlɪˈnɪlɪ) *adv./a.* (occurring) whether desired or not

wilt (wɪlt) *v.* (cause to) become limp, drooping or lose strength *etc.*

Wilts. (wɪlts) Wiltshire

wimp (wɪmp) *n. inf.* feeble ineffective person —ˈ**wimpish** *or* ˈ**wimpy** *a.*

wimple (ˈwɪmpᵊl) *n.* garment worn by nun, around face

win (wɪn) *vi.* **1.** be successful, victorious —*vt.* **2.** get by labour or effort **3.** reach **4.** allure **5.** be successful in **6.** gain the support, consent *etc.* of (**won**, ˈ**winning**) —*n.* **7.** victory, *esp.* in games —ˈ**winner** *n.* —ˈ**winning** *a.* charming —ˈ**winnings** *pl.n.* sum won in game, betting *etc.*

wince (wɪns) *vi.* **1.** flinch, draw back, as from pain *etc.* —*n.* **2.** this act

winceyette (wɪnsɪˈɛt) *n.* cotton fabric with raised nap

winch (wɪntʃ) *n.* **1.** machine for hoisting or hauling using cable wound round drum —*vt.* **2.** move (something) by using a winch

wind[1] (wɪnd) *n.* **1.** air in motion **2.** breath **3.** flatulence

THESAURUS

wild 1. feral, ferocious, fierce, savage, unbroken, undomesticated, untamed **2.** free, indigenous, native, natural, uncultivated **3.** desert, deserted, desolate, empty, godforsaken, trackless, uncivilized, uncultivated, uninhabited, unpopulated, virgin **4.** barbaric, barbarous, brutish, ferocious, fierce, primitive, rude, savage, uncivilized **5.** boisterous, chaotic, disorderly, impetuous, lawless, noisy, riotous, rough, rowdy, self-willed, turbulent, unbridled, uncontrolled, undisciplined, unfettered, ungovernable, unmanageable, unrestrained, unruly, uproarious, violent, wayward **6.** blustery, choppy, furious, howling, intense, raging, rough, tempestuous, violent **7.** at one's wits' end, berserk, beside oneself, crazed, crazy, delirious, demented, excited, frantic, frenzied, hysterical, irrational, mad, maniacal, rabid, raving **8.** extravagant, fantastic, flighty, foolhardy, foolish, giddy, ill-considered, impracticable, imprudent, madcap, outrageous, preposterous, rash, reckless

wilderness 1. desert, jungle, waste, wasteland, wild **2.** clutter, confused mass, confusion, congeries, jumble, maze, muddle, tangle, welter

wildlife flora and fauna

wile *Usually plural* artifice, contrivance, device, dodge, imposition, lure, manoeuvre, ploy, ruse, stratagem, subterfuge, trick

wilful 1. adamant, bull-headed, determined, dogged, froward, headstrong, inflexible, intractable, intransigent, mulish, obdurate, obstinate, persistent, perverse, pig-headed, refractory, self-willed, stubborn, uncompromising, unyielding **2.** conscious, deliberate, intended, intentional, purposeful, volitional, voluntary, willed

will *n.* **1.** choice, decision, determination, discretion, option, prerogative, volition **2.** declaration, last wishes, testament **3.** choice, decision, decree, desire, fancy, inclination, mind, pleasure, preference, wish **4.** aim, determination, intention, purpose, resolution, resolve, willpower ~*v.* **5.** choose, desire, elect, opt, prefer, see fit, want, wish **6.** bequeath, confer, give, leave, pass on, transfer

willing agreeable, amenable, compliant, consenting, content, desirous, disposed, eager, enthusiastic, favourable, game (*Inf.*), happy, inclined, in favour, in the mood, nothing loath, pleased, prepared, ready, so-minded

willingly by choice, cheerfully, eagerly, freely, gladly, happily, of one's own accord, of one's own free will, readily, voluntarily, with all one's heart, without hesitation, with pleasure

willingness agreeableness, agreement, consent, desire, disposition, enthusiasm, favour, good will, inclination, volition, will, wish

willpower determination, drive, firmness of purpose *or* will, fixity of purpose, force *or* strength of will, grit, resolution, resolve, self-control, self-discipline, single-mindedness

wilt 1. become limp *or* flaccid, droop, sag, shrivel, wither **2.** diminish, dwindle, ebb, fade, fail, flag, languish, lose courage, melt away, sag, sink, wane, weaken, wither

wily arch, artful, astute, cagey (*Inf.*), crafty, crooked, cunning, deceitful, deceptive, designing, fly (*Sl.*), foxy, guileful, intriguing, scheming, sharp, shifty, shrewd, sly, tricky, underhand

win *v.* **1.** achieve first place, achieve mastery, be victorious, carry all before one, carry the day, come first, conquer, finish first, gain victory, overcome, prevail, succeed, take the prize, triumph **2.** accomplish, achieve, acquire, attain, bag (*Inf.*), catch, collect, come away with, earn, gain, get, net, obtain, pick up, procure, receive, secure **3.** *Often with* **over** allure, attract, bring *or* talk round, carry, charm, convert, convince, disarm, induce, influence, persuade, prevail upon, sway ~*n.* **4.** *Inf.* conquest, success, triumph, victory

wince 1. *v.* blench, cower, cringe, draw back, flinch, quail, recoil, shrink, start **2.** *n.* cringe, flinch, start

4. idle talk **5.** hint or suggestion **6.** scent borne by air —*vt.* **7.** render short of breath, *esp.* by blow *etc.* **8.** get the scent of —**ˈwindward** *n.* side against which wind is blowing —**ˈwindy** *a.* **1.** exposed to wind **2.** flatulent **3.** *sl.* nervous, scared **4.** *inf.* talking too much —**ˈwindbag** *n.* *sl.* voluble person who has little of interest to communicate —**ˈwindbreak** *n.* fence, line of trees *etc.* serving as protection from wind —**ˈwindcheater** *n.* warm jacket, usu. with close-fitting knitted neck, cuffs and waistband —**wind-chill** *n.* serious chilling effect of wind and low temperature: measured on scale from hot to fatal to life (*esp. in* **wind-chill factor**) —**ˈwindfall** *n.* **1.** unexpected good luck **2.** fallen fruit —**wind gauge 1.** *see* ANEMOMETER **2.** *Mus.* device for measuring wind pressure in bellows of organ —**wind instrument** musical instrument played by blowing or air pressure —**ˈwindjammer** *n.* large merchant sailing ship —**windmill** (ˈwɪndmɪl, ˈwɪnmɪl) *n.* wind-driven apparatus with fanlike sails for raising water, crushing grain *etc.* —**ˈwindpipe** *n.* passage from throat to lungs —**ˈwindscreen** *n.* protective sheet of glass *etc.* in front of driver or pilot —**windscreen wiper UK** electrically operated blade with rubber edge that wipes windscreen clear of rain *etc.* —**ˈwindsock** *n.* cone of material flown on mast at airfield to indicate wind direction —**wind tunnel** chamber for testing aerodynamic properties of aircraft *etc.* in which current of air can be maintained at constant velocity

wind² (waɪnd) *vi.* **1.** twine **2.** meander —*vt.* **3.** twist, coil **4.** wrap **5.** make ready for working by tightening spring (**wound, ˈwinding**) —*n.* **6.** act of winding **7.** single turn of something wound **8.** a turn, curve —**winding sheet** sheet in which corpse is wrapped for burial; shroud —**wind-up** *n. inf., chiefly* **US 1.** act of concluding **2.** end —**wind down 1.** lower or move down by cranking **2.** (of clock spring) become slack **3.** diminish gradually in force or power —**wind up 1.** bring to or reach a conclusion **2.** tighten spring of (clockwork mechanism) **3.** *inf.* make nervous, tense *etc.* **4.** *inf. see* LIQUIDATE (sense 2) **5.** *inf.* end up (in specified state)

windlass (ˈwɪndləs) *n.* winch, *esp.* simple one worked by a crank

window (ˈwɪndəʊ) *n.* **1.** hole in wall (with glass) to admit light, air *etc.* **2.** anything similar in appearance or function **3.** area for display of goods behind glass of shop front —**window box** long narrow box, placed on windowsill, in which plants are grown —**window-dressing** *n.* **1.** arrangement of goods in a shop window **2.** deceptive display —**ˈwindowpane** *n.* sheet of glass in window —**window-shop** *vi.* look at goods in shop windows without buying them (**-pp-**) —**ˈwindowsill** *n.* sill below window

Windsor chair (ˈwɪnzə) simple wooden chair, usu. having shaped seat, splayed legs, and back of many spindles

wine (waɪn) *n.* fermented juice of grape *etc.* —**ˈwino** *n.* person who habitually drinks wine as means of getting drunk —**ˈwinepress** *n.* apparatus for extracting juice from grape —**ˈwineskin** *n.* skin of sheep or goat sewn up and used as holder for wine

wing (wɪŋ) *n.* **1.** feathered limb a bird uses in flying **2.** one of organs of flight of insect or some animals **3.** main lifting surface of aircraft **4.** lateral extension **5.** side portion of building projecting from main central portion **6.** one of sides of a stage **7.** flank corps of army on either side **8.** part of car body that surrounds wheels **9.** *Sport* (player on) either side of pitch **10.** faction, *esp.* of political party —*pl.* **11.** insignia worn by qualified aircraft pilot **12.** sides of stage —*vi.* **13.** fly **14.** move, go very fast —*vt.* **15.** disable, wound slightly —**winged** *a.* having wings —**wing chair** chair having wings on each side of back —**wing commander** officer holding commissioned rank in certain air forces, such as Royal Air Force: junior to group captain and senior to squadron leader —**wing nut** threaded nut tightened by hand by means of two flat wings projecting from central body (*also* **butterfly nut**)

wink (wɪŋk) *v.* **1.** close and open (an eye) rapidly, *esp.* to indicate friendliness or as signal —*vi.* **2.** twinkle —*n.* **3.** act of winking

winkle (ˈwɪŋkᵊl) *n.* shellfish, periwinkle —**winkle-pickers** *pl.n.* shoes or boots with very pointed narrow toes —**winkle out** extract

THESAURUS

wind¹ *n.* **1.** air, air-current, blast, breath, breeze, current of air, draught, gust, zephyr **2.** *Inf.* clue, hint, inkling, intimation, notice, report, rumour, suggestion, tidings, warning, whisper **3.** babble, blather, bluster, boasting, empty talk, gab (*Inf.*), hot air, humbug, idle talk, talk, verbalizing **4.** breath, puff, respiration **5.** *Inf.* flatulence, flatus, gas

wind² *v.* **1.** coil, curl, encircle, furl, loop, reel, roll, spiral, turn around, twine, twist, wreathe **2.** bend, curve, deviate, meander, ramble, snake, turn, twist, zigzag ~*n.* **3.** bend, curve, meander, turn, twist, zigzag

windfall bonanza, find, godsend, jackpot, manna from heaven, stroke of luck

winding 1. *n.* bend, convolution, curve, meander, turn, twist, undulation **2.** *adj.* anfractuous, bending, circuitous, convoluted, crooked, curving, flexuous, indirect, meandering, roundabout, serpentine, sinuous, spiral, tortuous, turning, twisting

wind up 1. bring to a close, close, close down, conclude, end, finalize, finish, liquidate, settle, terminate, tie up the loose ends (*Inf.*), wrap up **2.** *Inf.* excite, make nervous, make tense, put on edge, work up **3.** *Inf.* be left, end one's days, end up, find oneself, finish up

windy 1. blowy, blustering, blustery, boisterous, breezy, gusty, squally, stormy, tempestuous, wild, windswept **2.** boastful, bombastic, diffuse, empty, garrulous, long-winded, loquacious, meandering, pompous, prolix, rambling, turgid, verbose, wordy **3.** *Sl.* afraid, chicken (*Sl.*), cowardly, fearful, frightened, nervous, scared, timid

wing *n.* **1.** organ of flight, pennon (*Poetic*), pinion (*Poetic*) **2.** arm, branch, circle, clique, coterie, faction, group, grouping, section, segment, set, side **3.** adjunct, annexe, ell, extension ~*v.* **4.** fly, glide, soar **5.** fleet, fly, hasten, hurry, race, speed, zoom **6.** clip, hit, nick, wound

wink *v.* **1.** bat, blink, flutter, nictate, nictitate **2.** flash, gleam, glimmer, sparkle, twinkle ~*n.* **3.** blink, flutter, nictation **4.** flash, gleam, glimmering, sparkle, twinkle

winkle out dig out, dislodge, draw out, extract, extricate, force out, prise out, smoke out, worm out

winner champ (*Inf.*), champion, conquering hero, conqueror, first, master, vanquisher, victor

winnow (ˈwɪnəʊ) *vt.* **1.** blow free of chaff **2.** sift, examine

winsome (ˈwɪnsəm) *a.* charming, winning

winter (ˈwɪntə) *n.* **1.** the coldest season —*vi.* **2.** pass, spend the winter —ˈ**wintry** *or* ˈ**wintery** *a.* **1.** of, like winter **2.** cold —ˈ**wintergreen** *n.* evergreen shrub, *esp.* subshrub of E N Amer., which has white, bell-shaped flowers and edible red berries —**winter solstice** time at which sun is at its southernmost point in sky appearing at noon at its lowest altitude above horizon. It occurs about Dec. 22nd. —**winter sports** sports held in open air on snow or ice —**oil of wintergreen** aromatic compound, formerly made from the shrub but now synthesized: used medicinally and for flavouring

wipe (waɪp) *vt.* **1.** rub so as to clean —*n.* **2.** wiping —ˈ**wiper** *n.* **1.** one that wipes **2.** automatic wiping apparatus (*esp.* **windscreen wiper**) —**wipe out 1.** erase **2.** annihilate **3.** *sl.* kill

wire (waɪə) *n.* **1.** metal drawn into thin, flexible strand **2.** something made of wire, *eg* fence **3.** telegram —*vt.* **4.** provide, fasten with wire **5.** send by telegraph —ˈ**wiring** *n.* system of wires —ˈ**wiry** *a.* **1.** like wire **2.** lean and tough —**wire-gauge** *n.* **1.** flat plate with slots in which standard wire sizes can be measured **2.** standard system of sizes for measuring diameters of wires —**wire-haired** *a.* (of various breeds of dog) with short stiff hair —ˈ**wiretap** *v.* tap (telephone wire *etc.*) to obtain information secretly —**wire wool** mass of fine wire, used *esp.* to clean kitchen articles

wireless (ˈwaɪəlɪs) *n.* **1.** *old-fashioned term for* radio, radio set —*a.* **2.** of or for radio

wise[1] (waɪz) *a.* **1.** having intelligence and knowledge **2.** sensible —**wisdom** (ˈwɪzdəm) *n.* **1.** (accumulated) knowledge, learning **2.** erudition —ˈ**wisely** *adv.* —ˈ**wiseacre** *n.* one who wishes to seem wise —**wisdom tooth** third molar usu. cut about 20th year

wise[2] (waɪz) *n. obs.* manner

-wise (*comb. form*) **1.** indicating direction or manner, as in *clockwise, likewise* **2.** with reference to, as in *businesswise*

wisecrack (ˈwaɪzkræk) *n. inf.* flippant, (would-be) clever remark

wish (wɪʃ) *vi.* **1.** have a desire —*vt.* **2.** desire —*n.* **3.** desire **4.** thing desired —ˈ**wishful** *a.* **1.** desirous **2.** too optimistic —ˈ**wishbone** *n.* V-shaped bone above breastbone of fowl —**wishful thinking** erroneous belief that one's wishes are in accordance with reality

wishy-washy (ˈwɪʃɪwɒʃɪ) *a. inf.* **1.** lacking in substance, force, colour *etc.* **2.** watery; thin

wisp (wɪsp) *n.* **1.** light, delicate streak, as of smoke **2.** twisted handful, usu. of straw *etc.* **3.** stray lock of hair —ˈ**wispy** *a.*

wisteria (wɪˈstɪərɪə) *n.* climbing shrub with usu. mauve flowers

wistful (ˈwɪstfʊl) *a.* **1.** longing, yearning **2.** sadly pensive —ˈ**wistfully** *adv.*

wit[1] (wɪt) *n.* **1.** ingenuity in connecting amusingly incongruous ideas **2.** person gifted with this power **3.** sense **4.** intellect **5.** understanding **6.** ingenuity **7.** humour —ˈ**witless** *a.* foolish —ˈ**witticism** *n.* witty remark —ˈ**wittily** *adv.* —ˈ**wittingly** *adv.* **1.** on purpose **2.** knowingly —ˈ**witty** *a.*

wit[2] (wɪt) *v. obs.* be or become aware of (something) —**to wit** that is to say; namely

witch (wɪtʃ) *n.* **1.** person, usu. female, believed to practise, practising, or professing to practise (black) magic, sorcery **2.** ugly, wicked woman **3.** fascinating woman —ˈ**witchery** *n.* —ˈ**witchcraft** *n.* —**witch doctor** in certain societies, man appearing to cure or cause injury, disease by magic —**witch-hunt** *n.* rigorous campaign to expose dissenters on pretext of safeguarding public welfare —**witch-hunting** *n./a.*

THESAURUS

winning 1. alluring, amiable, attractive, bewitching, captivating, charming, delectable, delightful, disarming, enchanting, endearing, engaging, fascinating, fetching, lovely, pleasing, prepossessing, sweet, taking, winsome **2.** conquering, successful, triumphant, victorious

winnings booty, gains, prize(s), proceeds, profits, spoils, takings

winnow comb, cull, divide, fan, part, screen, select, separate, separate the wheat from the chaff, sift, sort out

wintry brumal, chilly, cold, freezing, frosty, frozen, harsh, hibernal, hiemal, icy, snowy

wipe *v.* **1.** brush, clean, dry, dust, mop, rub, sponge, swab **2.** clean off, erase, get rid of, remove, rub off, take away, take off ~*n.* **3.** brush, lick, rub, swab

wipe out annihilate, blot out, destroy, efface, eradicate, erase, expunge, exterminate, extirpate, kill to the last man, massacre, obliterate

wiry 1. lean, sinewy, strong, tough **2.** bristly, kinky, stiff

wisdom astuteness, circumspection, comprehension, discernment, enlightenment, erudition, foresight, insight, intelligence, judgment, judiciousness, knowledge, learning, penetration, prudence, reason, sagacity, sapience, sense, sound judgment, understanding

wise aware, clever, discerning, enlightened, erudite, informed, intelligent, judicious, knowing, perceptive, politic, prudent, rational, reasonable, sagacious, sage, sapient, sensible, shrewd, sound, understanding, well-advised, well-informed

wisecrack *n.* barb, funny (*Inf.*), gag (*Sl.*), jest, jibe, joke, pithy remark, quip, sardonic remark, smart remark, witticism

wish *v.* **1.** aspire, covet, crave, desiderate, desire, hanker, hope, hunger, long, need, set one's heart on, sigh for, thirst, want, yearn **2.** ask, bid, command, desire, direct, instruct, order, require ~*n.* **3.** aspiration, desire, hankering, hope, hunger, inclination, intention, liking, longing, thirst, urge, want, whim, will, yearning **4.** bidding, command, desire, order, request, will

wistful contemplative, disconsolate, dreaming, dreamy, forlorn, longing, meditative, melancholy, mournful, musing, pensive, reflective, sad, thoughtful, yearning

wit 1. badinage, banter, drollery, facetiousness, fun, humour, jocularity, levity, pleasantry, raillery, repartee, wordplay **2.** card (*Inf.*), comedian, epigrammatist, *farceur*, humorist, joker, punster, wag **3.** acumen, brains, cleverness, common sense, comprehension, discernment, ingenuity, insight, intellect, judgment, mind, nous (*Brit. sl.*), perception, practical intelligence, reason, sense, understanding, wisdom

witch- (*comb. form*) *see* WYCH-

witch hazel *or* **wych-hazel** *n.* **1.** any of genus of trees and shrubs of N Amer. having medicinal properties **2.** astringent medicinal solution containing extract of bark and leaves of one of these shrubs, applied to treat bruises, *etc.*

with (wɪð, wɪθ) *prep.* **1.** in company or possession of **2.** against **3.** in relation to **4.** through **5.** by means of —**withal** (wɪˈðɔːl) *adv.* also, likewise —**within** (wɪˈðɪn) *prep./adv.* in, inside —**without** (wɪˈðaʊt) *prep.* **1.** lacking **2.** *obs.* outside

withdraw (wɪðˈdrɔː) *v.* draw back or out (**-ˈdrew, -ˈdrawn, -ˈdrawing**) —**withˈdrawal** *n.* —**withˈdrawn** *a.* reserved, unsociable

withe (wɪθ, wɪð, waɪð) *n.* **1.** strong flexible twig, *esp.* of willow, suitable for binding things together —*vt.* **2.** bind with withes

wither (ˈwɪðə) *v.* (cause to) wilt, dry up, decline —**ˈwithering** *a.* (of glance *etc.*) scornful

withers (ˈwɪðəz) *pl.n.* ridge between a horse's shoulder blades

withhold (wɪðˈhəʊld) *vt.* **1.** restrain **2.** keep back **3.** refrain from giving (**-ˈheld, -ˈholding**) —**withˈholder** *n.*

withstand (wɪðˈstænd) *vt.* oppose, resist, *esp.* successfully (**-ˈstood, -ˈstanding**)

withy (ˈwɪðɪ) *n.* **1.** *see* WITHE (sense 1) **2.** willow tree

witness (ˈwɪtnɪs) *n.* **1.** one who sees something **2.** testimony **3.** one who gives testimony —*vi.* **4.** give testimony —*vt.* **5.** see **6.** attest to genuineness of **7.** see and sign as having seen —**witness box** *or esp. U.S.* **stand** place in court of law in which witnesses stand to give evidence

wives (waɪvz) *n., pl. of* WIFE —**old wives' tale** superstitious tradition

wizard (ˈwɪzəd) *n.* **1.** sorcerer, magician **2.** expert —**ˈwizardry** *n.*

wizened (ˈwɪzˀnd) *or* **wizen** *a.* shrivelled, wrinkled

wk. 1. week (*pl.* **wks.**) **2.** work

WNW west-northwest

woad (wəʊd) *n.* blue dye from plant

wobble (ˈwɒbˀl) *vi.* **1.** move unsteadily, sway —*n.* **2.** an unsteady movement —**ˈwobbliness** *n.* —**ˈwobbly** *a.* shaky, unstable, unsteady —**throw a wobbly** *sl.* become very angry or excited

woe (wəʊ) *n.* grief —**ˈwoebegone** *a.* looking sorrowful —**ˈwoeful** *a.* **1.** sorrowful **2.** pitiful **3.** wretched —**ˈwoefully** *adv.*

wog (wɒg) *n. sl. offens.* foreigner, *esp.* one who is not White

wold (wəʊld) *n.* open downs, moorland

wolf (wʊlf) *n.* **1.** wild predatory doglike animal of northern countries **2.** *inf.* man who habitually tries to seduce women (*pl.* **wolves** (wʊlvz)) —*vt.* **3.** eat ravenously —**ˈwolfhound** *n.* largest breed of dog, used

THESAURUS

witch enchantress, magician, necromancer, occultist, sorceress

witchcraft enchantment, incantation, magic, necromancy, occultism, sorcery, sortilege, spell, the black art, the occult, voodoo, witchery, witching, wizardry

withdraw 1. draw back, draw out, extract, pull out, remove, take away, take off **2.** absent oneself, back out, depart, detach oneself, disengage, drop out, fall back, go, leave, make oneself scarce (*Inf.*), pull back, pull out, retire, retreat, secede

withdrawal 1. extraction, removal **2.** departure, disengagement, exit, exodus, retirement, retreat, secession

withdrawn aloof, detached, distant, introverted, quiet, reserved, retiring, shrinking, shy, silent, taciturn, timorous, uncommunicative, unforthcoming

wither blast, blight, decay, decline, desiccate, disintegrate, droop, dry, fade, languish, perish, shrink, shrivel, wane, waste, wilt

withering blasting, blighting, devastating, humiliating, hurtful, mortifying, scornful, snubbing

withhold check, conceal, deduct, hide, hold back, keep, keep back, keep secret, refuse, repress, reserve, resist, restrain, retain, sit on (*Inf.*), suppress

withstand 1. bear, brave, combat, confront, cope with, defy, endure, face, grapple with, hold off, hold out against, oppose, put up with (*Inf.*), resist, stand up to, suffer, take, take on, thwart, tolerate, weather **2.** endure, hold *or* stand one's ground, hold out, remain firm, stand, stand fast, stand firm

witness *n.* **1.** beholder, bystander, eyewitness, looker-on, observer, onlooker, spectator, viewer, watcher **2.** attestant, corroborator, deponent, testifier ~*v.* **3.** attend, be present at, look on, mark, note, notice, observe, perceive, see, view, watch **4.** attest, authenticate, bear out, bear witness, confirm, corroborate, depone, depose, give evidence, give testimony, testify **5.** countersign, endorse, sign

witticism bon mot, clever remark, epigram, one-liner (*Sl.*), play on words, pleasantry, pun, quip, repartee, riposte, sally, witty remark

witty amusing, brilliant, clever, droll, epigrammatic, facetious, fanciful, funny, gay, humorous, ingenious, jocular, lively, original, piquant, sparkling, waggish, whimsical

wizard 1. conjurer, enchanter, mage (*Archaic*), magician, magus, necromancer, occultist, shaman, sorcerer, thaumaturge (*Rare*), warlock, witch **2.** ace (*Inf.*), adept, expert, genius, hotshot (*Inf.*), maestro, master, prodigy, star, virtuoso, whiz (*Inf.*), whizz kid (*Inf.*), wiz (*Inf.*)

wizened dried up, gnarled, lined, sere (*Archaic*), shrivelled, shrunken, withered, worn, wrinkled

wobble 1. *v.* quake, rock, seesaw, shake, sway, teeter, totter, tremble, vibrate, waver **2.** *n.* quaking, shake, tremble, tremor, unsteadiness, vibration

woe adversity, affliction, agony, anguish, burden, curse, dejection, depression, disaster, distress, gloom, grief, hardship, heartache, heartbreak, melancholy, misery, misfortune, pain, sadness, sorrow, suffering, trial, tribulation, trouble, unhappiness, wretchedness

woeful 1. afflicted, agonized, anguished, calamitous, catastrophic, cruel, deplorable, disastrous, disconsolate, distressing, doleful, dreadful, gloomy, grieving, grievous, heartbreaking, heart-rending, lamentable, miserable, mournful, pathetic, piteous, pitiable, pitiful, plaintive, sad, sorrowful, tragic, unhappy, wretched **2.** appalling, awful, bad, deplorable, disappointing, disgraceful, dreadful, duff (*Brit. sl.*), feeble, hopeless, inadequate, lousy (*Inf.*), mean, miserable, paltry, pathetic, pitiable, pitiful, poor, rotten (*Inf.*), shocking, sorry, terrible, wretched

formerly to hunt wolves —**wolf whistle** whistle by man expressing admiration for a woman —**cry wolf** raise false alarm

wolfram (ˈwʊlfrəm) *n.* tungsten

wolverine (ˈwʊlvəriːn) *n.* carnivorous mammal inhabiting Arctic regions

woman (ˈwʊmən) *n.* **1.** adult human female **2.** women collectively (*pl.* **women** (ˈwɪmɪn)) —ˈ**womanhood** *n.* —ˈ**womanish** *a.* effeminate —ˈ**womanize** *or* **-ise** *vi. inf.* (of a man) indulge in many casual affairs with women —ˈ**womanizer** *or* **-iser** *n.* —ˈ**womankind** *n.* —ˈ**womanly** *a.* of, proper to woman —**Women's Institute** in Commonwealth countries, society for women interested in engaging in craft and cultural activities —**Women's Liberation** movement for removal of attitudes, practices that preserve social, economic *etc.* inequalities between women and men (*also* **women's lib**)

womb (wuːm) *n.* female organ of conception and gestation, uterus

wombat (ˈwɒmbæt) *n.* Aust. burrowing marsupial with heavy body, short legs and dense fur

won (wʌn) *pt./pp. of* WIN

wonder (ˈwʌndə) *n.* **1.** emotion excited by amazing or unusual thing **2.** marvel, miracle —*vi.* **3.** be curious **4.** feel amazement —ˈ**wonderful** *a.* **1.** remarkable **2.** very fine —ˈ**wonderfully** *adv.* —ˈ**wonderment** *n.* surprise —ˈ**wondrous** *a.* **1.** inspiring wonder **2.** strange

wonky (ˈwɒŋkɪ) *a. inf.* **1.** shaky, unsteady **2.** groggy **3.** askew **4.** unreliable

wont (wəʊnt) *n.* **1.** custom —*a.* **2.** accustomed —ˈ**wonted** *a.* habitual, established

woo (wuː) *vt.* court, seek to marry —ˈ**wooer** *n.* suitor

wood (wʊd) *n.* **1.** substance of trees, timber **2.** firewood **3.** tract of land with growing trees —ˈ**wooded** *a.* having (many) trees —ˈ**wooden** *a.* **1.** made of wood **2.** obstinate **3.** without expression —ˈ**woody** *a.* —ˈ**woodbine** *n.* honeysuckle —ˈ**woodcarver** *n.* —ˈ**woodcarving** *n.* **1.** act of carving wood **2.** work of art produced by carving wood —ˈ**woodchuck** *n.* Amer. burrowing marmot —ˈ**woodcock** *n.* game bird —ˈ**woodcut** *n.* **1.** engraving on wood **2.** impression from this —**woodland** (ˈwʊdlənd) *n.* woods, forest —ˈ**woodlark** *n.* Old World lark similar to skylark —ˈ**woodlouse** *n.* small grey land crustacean with seven pairs of legs (*pl.* **-lice**) —ˈ**woodpecker** *n.* bird which searches tree trunks for insects —**wood pigeon** large Eurasian pigeon —ˈ**woodpile** *n.* heap of firewood —**wood pulp** finely pulped wood that has been digested by chemical, such as caustic soda, used in making paper —ˈ**woodruff** *n.* plant, *esp.* sweet woodruff, which has small sweet-scented white flowers, used to flavour wine and in perfumery —**wood sorrel** Eurasian plant having trefoil leaves, underground creeping stem and white purple-veined flowers —**woodwind** (ˈwʊdwɪnd) *a./n.* (of) wind instruments of orchestra, *orig.* made of wood —ˈ**woodwork** *n.* **1.** art or craft of making things in wood **2.** components made of wood, such as doors *etc.* —ˈ**woodworm** *n.* insect larva that bores into wood

woof[1] (wuːf) *n.* the threads that cross the warp in weaving

woof[2] (wʊf) *interj.* **1.** imitation of bark of dog —*vi.* **2.** (of dog) bark

woofer (ˈwuːfə) *n.* loudspeaker for reproducing low-frequency sounds

wool (wʊl) *n.* **1.** soft hair of sheep, goat *etc.* **2.** yarn spun from this —ˈ**woollen** *or U.S.* ˈ**woolen** *a.* —ˈ**woolly** *or U.S.* (*oft.*) ˈ**wooly** *a.* **1.** of wool **2.** vague, muddled —*n.* **3.** knitted woollen garment —ˈ**woolgathering** *a./n.* daydreaming —ˈ**woolsack** *n.* Lord Chancellor's seat in British House of Lords

woozy (ˈwuːzɪ) *a. inf.* **1.** dazed or confused **2.** experiencing dizziness, nausea *etc.* as result of drink —ˈ**woozily** *adv.* —ˈ**wooziness** *n.*

Worcs. (wɜːks) Worcestershire

word (wɜːd) *n.* **1.** unit of speech or writing regarded by users of a language as the smallest separate meaningful unit **2.** term **3.** message **4.** brief remark **5.** information **6.** promise **7.** command —*vt.* **8.** express in

THESAURUS

wolf 1. *n. Inf.* Casanova, Don Juan, lady-killer, lecher, Lothario, philanderer, seducer, womanizer **2.** *v. With* **down** bolt, cram, devour, gobble, gollop, gorge, gulp, pack away (*Inf.*), scoff (*Sl.*), stuff

woman bird (*Sl.*), chick (*Sl.*), dame (*Sl.*), female, girl, lady, lass, lassie, maid (*Archaic*), maiden (*Archaic*), miss, she

womanizer Casanova, Don Juan, lady-killer, lecher, Lothario, philanderer, seducer, wolf (*Inf.*)

womanly female, feminine, ladylike, matronly, motherly, tender, warm

wonder *n.* **1.** admiration, amazement, astonishment, awe, bewilderment, curiosity, fascination, stupefaction, surprise, wonderment **2.** curiosity, marvel, miracle, nonpareil, phenomenon, portent, prodigy, rarity, sight, spectacle, wonderment ~*v.* **3.** ask oneself, be curious, be inquisitive, conjecture, cudgel one's brains (*Inf.*), doubt, inquire, meditate, ponder, puzzle, query, question, speculate, think **4.** be amazed (astonished, awed, dumbstruck), be flabbergasted (*Inf.*), boggle, gape, gawk, marvel, stand amazed, stare

wonderful 1. amazing, astonishing, astounding, awe-inspiring, awesome, extraordinary, fantastic, incredible, marvellous, miraculous, odd, peculiar, phenomenal, remarkable, staggering, startling, strange, surprising, unheard-of, wondrous **2.** ace (*Inf.*), admirable, brilliant, excellent, fabulous (*Inf.*), fantastic (*Inf.*), great (*Inf.*), magnificent, marvellous, outstanding, sensational, smashing (*Inf.*), stupendous, super (*Inf.*), superb, terrific, tiptop, tremendous

woo chase, court, cultivate, importune, pay court to, pay one's addresses to, pay suit to, press one's suit with, pursue, seek after, seek the hand of, seek to win, solicit the good will of, spark (*Rare*)

wood 1. coppice, copse, forest, grove, thicket, trees, woodland **2.** planks, timber

wooded forested, sylvan (*Poetic*), timbered, tree-clad, tree-covered, woody

wooden 1. ligneous, made of wood, of wood, timber, woody **2.** blank, colourless, deadpan, dull, emotionless, empty, expressionless, glassy, lifeless, spiritless, unemotional, unresponsive, vacant **3.** inflexible, obstinate, rigid, stiff, unbending, unyielding

wool fleece, hair, yarn

woolly *adj.* **1.** fleecy, flocculent, hairy, made of wool, shaggy, woollen **2.** blurred, clouded, confused, foggy, fuzzy, hazy, ill-defined, indefinite, indistinct, muddled, nebulous, unclear, vague

words, *esp.* in particular way —'**wordily** *adv.* —'**wording** *n.* choice and arrangement of words —'**wordy** *a.* using more words than necessary, verbose —**word blindness** *see* ALEXIA, DYSLEXIA —**word-perfect** *or U.S.* **letter-perfect** *a.* 1. correct in every detail 2. (of speaker *etc.*) knowing one's speech *etc.* perfectly —**word processing** storage and organization of language by electronic means, *esp.* for business purposes —**word processor** installation for word processing, typically consisting of key-board and VDU incorporating microprocessor, storage and processing capabilities —**word wrapping** *Comp.* automatic shifting of word at end of line to new line in order to keep within preset margins

wore (wɔː) *pt. of* WEAR

work (wɜːk) *n.* 1. labour 2. employment 3. occupation 4. task 5. toil 6. something made or accomplished 7. production of art or science 8. book 9. needlework —*pl.* 10. factory 11. total of person's deeds, writings *etc.* 12. *inf.* everything, full or extreme treatment 13. mechanism of clock *etc.* —*vt.* 14. cause to operate 15. make, shape —*vi.* 16. apply effort 17. labour 18. operate 19. be engaged in trade, profession *etc.* 20. turn out successfully 21. ferment —'**workable** *a.* —'**worker** *n.* —'**working** *n.* 1. operation or mode of operation of something 2. act or process of moulding something pliable 3. (*oft. pl.*) part of mine or quarry that is being or has been worked —*a.* 4. of or concerned with person or thing that works 5. concerned with, used in, or suitable for work 6. capable of being operated or used —'**workaday** *a.* 1. ordinary 2. suitable for working days —**worka'holic** *n.* person obsessively addicted to work —**work force** 1. total number of workers employed by company on specific project *etc.* 2. total number of people who could be employed —'**workhouse** *n. Hist.* institution offering food, lodgings for unpaid menial work —**work-in** *n.* form of industrial action in which factory threatened with closure is occupied and run by its workers —**working class** social class consisting of wage earners, *esp.* manual —**working-class** *a.* —**working party** advisory committee studying specific problem, question —'**workman** *n.* manual worker —'**workmanlike** *or* '**workmanly** *a.* appropriate to or befitting a good workman —'**workmanship** *n.* 1. skill of workman 2. way thing is finished 3. style —**work-out** *n.* session of physical exercise, *esp.* for training or practice —'**workshop** *n.* place where things are made —'**workshy** *a.* not inclined to work —**work station** area in office *etc.* where one person works —**work in** 1. insert or become inserted 2. find space for —**work of art** 1. piece of fine art, as painting, sculpture 2. something that may be likened to piece of fine art, *esp.* in beauty *etc.* —**work out** 1. accomplish by effort 2. solve by reasoning or calculation 3. devise or formulate 4. prove satisfactory 5. happen as specified 6. take part in physical exercise, as in training 7. remove all mineral in (mine *etc.*) that can be profitably exploited —**work to rule** adhere strictly to all

THESAURUS

word *n.* **1.** brief statement, comment, declaration, expression, remark, utterance **2.** expression, locution, name, term, vocable **3.** account, advice, bulletin, communication, communiqué, dispatch, gen (*Brit. inf.*), information, intelligence, intimation, message, news, notice, report, tidings **4.** command, go-ahead (*Inf.*), green light, order, signal **5.** affirmation, assertion, assurance, guarantee, oath, parole, pledge, promise, solemn oath, solemn word, undertaking, vow, word of honour **6.** bidding, command, commandment, decree, edict, mandate, order, ukase (*Rare*), will ~*v.* **7.** couch, express, phrase, put, say, state, utter

wordy diffuse, discursive, garrulous, long-winded, loquacious, pleonastic, prolix, rambling, verbose, windy

work *n.* **1.** drudgery, effort, elbow grease (*Inf.*), exertion, grind (*Inf.*), industry, labour, slog, sweat, toil, travail (*Literary*) **2.** business, calling, craft, duty, employment, job, line, livelihood, métier, occupation, office, profession, pursuit, trade **3.** assignment, chore, commission, duty, job, stint, task, undertaking **4.** achievement, composition, creation, handiwork, *oeuvre*, opus, performance, piece, production **5.** art, craft, skill, workmanship ~*v.* **6.** drudge, exert oneself, labour, peg away, slave, slog (away), sweat, toil **7.** be employed, be in work, do business, earn a living, have a job **8.** act, control, direct, drive, handle, manage, manipulate, move, operate, ply, use, wield **9.** function, go, operate, perform, run **10.** fashion, form, handle, knead, make, manipulate, mould, process, shape

workable doable, feasible, possible, practicable, practical, viable

workaday common, commonplace, everyday, familiar, humdrum, mundane, ordinary, practical, prosaic, routine

worker artisan, craftsman, employee, hand, labourer, proletarian, tradesman, wage earner, working man, working woman, workman

working *n.* **1.** action, functioning, manner, method, mode of operation, operation, running **2.** *Plural* diggings, excavations, mine, pit, quarry, shaft ~*adj.* **3.** active, employed, in a job, in work, labouring **4.** functioning, going, operative, running **5.** effective, practical, useful, viable

workman artificer, artisan, craftsman, employee, hand, journeyman, labourer, mechanic, operative, tradesman, worker

workmanlike, workmanly adept, careful, efficient, expert, masterly, painstaking, professional, proficient, satisfactory, skilful, skilled, thorough

workmanship art, artistry, craft, craftsmanship, execution, expertise, handicraft, handiwork, manufacture, skill, technique, work

work out **1.** accomplish, achieve, attain, win **2.** calculate, clear up, figure out, find out, puzzle out, resolve, solve **3.** arrange, construct, contrive, develop, devise, elaborate, evolve, form, formulate, plan, put together **4.** be effective, flourish, go as planned, go well, prosper, prove satisfactory, succeed **5.** come out, develop, evolve, go, happen, pan out (*Inf.*), result, turn out **6.** do exercises, drill, exercise, practise, train, warm up

works **1.** factory, mill, plant, shop, workshop **2.** canon, *oeuvre*, output, productions, writings **3.** actions, acts, deeds, doings **4.** action, guts (*Sl.*), innards (*Inf.*), insides (*Inf.*), machinery, mechanism, movement, moving parts, parts, workings

workshop atelier, factory, mill, plant, shop, studio, workroom, works

working regulations to reduce rate of work as form of protest

world (wɜːld) *n.* **1.** the universe **2.** the planet earth **3.** sphere of existence **4.** mankind, people generally **5.** society —**ˈworldly** *a.* **1.** earthly **2.** mundane **3.** absorbed in the pursuit of material gain, advantage **4.** carnal —**World Bank** international organization established in 1945 to assist economic development, by advance of loans guaranteed by member governments (official name: **International Bank for Reconstruction and Development**) —**world-beater** *n.* person or thing that surpasses all others in its category; champion —**World Cup** international association football championship competition held every four years between national teams selected through preliminary tournaments —**world-shaking** *a.* of enormous significance; momentous —**world war** war involving many countries

worm (wɜːm) *n.* **1.** small limbless creeping snakelike creature **2.** anything resembling worm in shape or movement **3.** *inf.* weak, despised person —*pl.* **4.** (disorder caused by) infestation of worms, *esp.* in intestines —*vi.* **5.** crawl —*vt.* **6.** work (oneself) in insidiously **7.** extract (secret) craftily **8.** rid of worms —**ˈwormy** *a.* —**ˈwormcast** *n.* coil of earth excreted by earthworm —**worm-eaten** *a.* **1.** full of holes gnawed by worms **2.** old, antiquated —**worm gear 1.** device consisting of threaded shaft (**worm**) that mates with gear wheel (**worm wheel**) so that rotary motion can be transferred between two shafts at right angles to each other **2.** gear wheel driven by threaded shaft or worm (*also* **worm wheel**)

wormwood (ˈwɜːmwʊd) *n.* **1.** bitter herb **2.** bitterness

worn (wɔːn) *pp. of* WEAR —**worn-out** *a.* **1.** worn or used until threadbare, valueless or useless **2.** exhausted

worry (ˈwʌrɪ) *vi.* **1.** be (unduly) concerned —*vt.* **2.** trouble, pester, harass **3.** (of dog) seize, shake with teeth (**ˈworried, ˈworrying**) —*n.* **4.** (cause of) anxiety, concern —**ˈworrier** *n.* —**ˈworrisome** *a.* **1.** causing worry **2.** tending to worry —**worry beads** string of beads that when played with supposedly relieves nervous tension

worse (wɜːs) *a./adv.* **1.** *comp. of* BAD *or* BADLY —*n.* **2.** inferior or less good person, thing or state —**ˈworsen** *v.* **1.** make, grow worse —*vt.* **2.** impair —*vi.* **3.** deteriorate —**worst** *a./adv.* **1.** *sup. of* BAD *or* BADLY —*n.* **2.** least good or most inferior person, part or thing

worship (ˈwɜːʃɪp) *vt.* **1.** show religious devotion to **2.** adore **3.** love and admire (**-pp-**) —*n.* **4.** act of worshipping **5.** title used to address mayor, magistrate *etc.* —**ˈworshipful** *a.* —**ˈworshipper** *n.*

worsted (ˈwʊstɪd) *n.* **1.** woollen yarn —*a.* **2.** made of woollen yarn **3.** spun from wool

wort (wɜːt) *n.* **1.** *obs.* plant, herb **2.** infusion of malt before fermentation

worth (wɜːθ) *a.* **1.** having or deserving to have value specified **2.** meriting —*n.* **3.** excellence **4.** merit, value **5.** virtue **6.** usefulness **7.** price **8.** quantity to be had for a given sum —**worthily** (ˈwɜːðɪlɪ) *adv.* —**worthiness** (ˈwɜːðɪnɪs) *n.* —**ˈworthless** *a.* useless —**worthy** (ˈwɜːðɪ) *a.* **1.** virtuous **2.** meriting —*n.* **3.** one of eminent worth

THESAURUS

world 1. earth, earthly sphere, globe **2.** everybody, everyone, humanity, humankind, human race, man, mankind, men, the public, the race of man **3.** cosmos, creation, existence, life, nature, universe **4.** area, domain, environment, field, kingdom, province, realm, sphere, system

worldly 1. carnal, earthly, fleshly, lay, mundane, physical, profane, secular, sublunary, temporal, terrestrial **2.** avaricious, covetous, grasping, greedy, materialistic, selfish, worldly-minded

worn frayed, ragged, shabby, shiny, tattered, tatty, the worse for wear, threadbare

worn-out 1. broken-down, clapped-out (*Brit. inf.*), decrepit, done, frayed, on its last legs, ragged, rundown, shabby, tattered, tatty, threadbare, used, used-up, useless, worn **2.** all in (*Sl.*), dead *or* out on one's feet (*Inf.*), dog-tired (*Inf.*), done in (*Inf.*), exhausted, fatigued, fit to drop, jiggered (*Dialect*), knackered (*Brit. sl.*), played-out, prostrate, spent, tired, tired out, weary

worried afraid, anxious, apprehensive, bothered, concerned, distracted, distraught, distressed, disturbed, fearful, fretful, frightened, ill at ease, nervous, on edge, overwrought, perturbed, tense, tormented, troubled, uneasy, unquiet, upset

worry *v.* **1.** agonize, annoy, badger, be anxious, bother, brood, disquiet, distress, disturb, feel uneasy, fret, harass, harry, hassle (*Inf.*), hector, importune, irritate, make anxious, perturb, pester, plague, tantalize, tease, torment, trouble, unsettle, upset, vex **2.** attack, bite, gnaw at, go for, harass, harry, kill, lacerate, savage, tear ~*n.* **3.** annoyance, care, irritation, pest, plague, problem, torment, trial, trouble, vexation **4.** annoyance, anxiety, apprehension, care, concern, disturbance, fear, irritation, misery, misgiving, perplexity, torment, trouble, unease, vexation, woe

worsen aggravate, damage, decay, decline, degenerate, deteriorate, exacerbate, get worse, go downhill (*Inf.*), go from bad to worse, retrogress, sink, take a turn for the worse

worship 1. *v.* adore, adulate, deify, exalt, glorify, honour, idolize, laud, love, praise, pray to, put on a pedestal, respect, revere, reverence, venerate **2.** *n.* adoration, adulation, deification, devotion, exaltation, glorification, glory, homage, honour, laudation, love, praise, prayer(s), regard, respect, reverence

worth 1. aid, assistance, avail, benefit, credit, desert(s), estimation, excellence, goodness, help, importance, merit, quality, usefulness, utility, value, virtue, worthiness **2.** cost, price, rate, valuation, value

worthless futile, ineffectual, insignificant, inutile, meaningless, miserable, no use, nugatory, paltry, pointless, poor, rubbishy, trashy, trifling, trivial, unavailing, unimportant, unusable, useless, valueless, wretched

worthwhile beneficial, constructive, gainful, good, helpful, justifiable, productive, profitable, useful, valuable, worthy

worthy 1. *adj.* admirable, commendable, creditable, decent, dependable, deserving, estimable, excellent, good, honest, honourable, laudable, meritorious, praiseworthy, reliable, reputable, respectable, righteous, upright, valuable, virtuous, worthwhile **2.** *n.* big shot (*Sl.*), bigwig (*Sl.*), dignitary, luminary, notable, personage

4. (local) notable —**worth'while** *a.* worth the time, effort *etc.* involved

would (wʊd; *unstressed* wəd) *v. aux.* 1. expressing wish, intention, probability —*v.* 2. *pt. of* WILL —**would-be** *a.* wishing, pretending to be

wound[1] (wu:nd) *n.* 1. injury, hurt from cut, stab *etc.* —*vt.* 2. inflict wound on, injure 3. pain

wound[2] (waʊnd) *pt./pp. of* WIND[2]

wove (wəʊv) *pt. of* WEAVE

woven ('wəʊvᵊn) *pp. of* WEAVE

wow (waʊ) *interj.* 1. exclamation of astonishment, admiration *etc.* —*n.* 2. *inf.* object of astonishment, admiration *etc.* 3. variation, distortion in pitch in record player *etc.*

w.p.m. words per minute

W.R.A.C. Women's Royal Army Corps

wrack *or* **rack** (ræk) *n.* seaweed

W.R.A.F. Women's Royal Air Force

wraith (reɪθ) *n.* 1. apparition of a person seen shortly before or after death 2. spectre

wrangle ('ræŋgᵊl) *vi.* 1. quarrel (noisily) 2. dispute 3. US, C herd cattle —*n.* 4. noisy quarrel 5. dispute —'**wrangler** *n.* US, C cowboy

wrap (ræp) *vt.* 1. cover, *esp.* by putting something round 2. put round (-pp-) —**wrap** *or* '**wrapper** *n.* 1. loose garment 2. covering —'**wrapping** *n.* material used to wrap —'**wrapover,** '**wraparound** *or* '**wrap-round** *a.* (of garment, *esp.* skirt) not sewn up at one side, but worn wrapped round body and fastened so that open edges overlap

wrasse (ræs) *n.* type of sea fish

wrath (rɒθ) *n.* anger —'**wrathful** *a.*

wreak (ri:k) *vt.* 1. inflict (vengeance) 2. cause

wreath (ri:θ) *n.* something twisted into ring form, *esp.* band of flowers *etc.* as memorial or tribute on grave *etc.* —**wreathe** *vt.* 1. form into wreath 2. surround 3. wind round

wreck (rɛk) *n.* 1. destruction of ship 2. wrecked ship 3. ruin 4. something ruined —*vt.* 5. cause the wreck of —'**wreckage** *n.* —'**wrecker** *n.* 1. person or thing that destroys, ruins 2. one whose job is to demolish houses, dismantle old cars *etc.*

wren (rɛn) *n.* kind of small songbird

Wren (rɛn) *n.* member of Women's Royal Naval Service

wrench (rɛntʃ) *vt.* 1. twist 2. distort 3. seize forcibly 4. sprain —*n.* 5. violent twist 6. tool for twisting or screwing 7. spanner 8. sudden pain caused *esp.* by parting

wrest (rɛst) *vt.* 1. take by force 2. twist violently

wrestle ('rɛsᵊl) *vi.* 1. fight (*esp.* as sport) by grappling and trying to throw down 2. strive 3. struggle —*n.* 4. struggle, tussle —'**wrestler** *n.* —'**wrestling** *n.*

wretch (rɛtʃ) *n.* 1. despicable person 2. miserable creature —**wretched** ('rɛtʃɪd) *a.* 1. miserable, unhappy 2. worthless —**wretchedly** ('rɛtʃɪdlɪ) *adv.* —**wretchedness** ('rɛtʃɪdnɪs) *n.*

wrick (rɪk) *n./vt.* strain; sprain

wriggle ('rɪgᵊl) *vi.* 1. move with twisting action, as worm 2. squirm —*n.* 3. this action

wright (raɪt) *n. obs.* workman; maker; builder

wring (rɪŋ) *vt.* 1. twist 2. extort 3. pain 4. squeeze out

THESAURUS

wound *n.* **1.** cut, damage, gash, harm, hurt, injury, laceration, lesion, slash **2.** anguish, distress, grief, heartbreak, injury, insult, offence, pain, pang, sense of loss, shock, slight, torment, torture, trauma ~*v.* **3.** cut, damage, gash, harm, hit, hurt, injure, irritate, lacerate, pierce, slash, wing **4.** annoy, cut (someone) to the quick, distress, grieve, hurt, hurt the feelings of, mortify, offend, pain, shock, sting, traumatize

wrangle 1. *v.* altercate, argue, bicker, brawl, contend, disagree, dispute, fall out (*Inf.*), fight, have words, quarrel, row, scrap, squabble **2.** *n.* altercation, angry exchange, argy-bargy (*Brit. inf.*), barney (*Inf.*), bickering, brawl, clash, contest, controversy, dispute, falling-out (*Inf.*), quarrel, row, set-to (*Inf.*), slanging match (*Brit.*), squabble, tiff

wrap 1. *v.* absorb, bind, bundle up, cloak, cover, encase, enclose, enfold, envelop, fold, immerse, muffle, pack, package, roll up, sheathe, shroud, surround, swathe, wind **2.** *n.* cape, cloak, mantle, shawl, stole

wrapper case, cover, envelope, jacket, packaging, paper, sheath, sleeve, wrapping

wrath anger, choler, displeasure, exasperation, fury, indignation, ire, irritation, passion, rage, resentment, temper

wrathful angry, beside oneself with rage, displeased, enraged, furious, incensed, indignant, infuriated, irate, on the warpath (*Inf.*), raging, wroth (*Archaic*)

wreath band, chaplet, coronet, crown, festoon, garland, loop, ring

wreathe adorn, coil, crown, encircle, enfold, entwine, envelop, enwrap, festoon, intertwine, interweave, surround, twine, twist, wind, wrap, writhe

wreck *v.* **1.** break, dash to pieces, demolish, destroy, devastate, mar, play havoc with, ravage, ruin, shatter, smash, spoil ~*n.* **2.** derelict, hulk, shipwreck, sunken vessel **3.** desolation, destruction, devastation, disruption, mess, overthrow, ruin, undoing

wreckage debris, fragments, hulk, pieces, remains, rubble, ruin, wrack

wrench *v.* **1.** force, jerk, pull, rip, tear, tug, twist, wrest, wring, yank **2.** distort, rick, sprain, strain ~*n.* **3.** jerk, pull, rip, tug, twist, yank **4.** sprain, strain, twist **5.** ache, blow, pain, pang, shock, upheaval, uprooting **6.** adjustable spanner, shifting spanner, spanner

wrestle battle, combat, contend, fight, grapple, scuffle, strive, struggle, tussle

wretch 1. blackguard, cur, good-for-nothing, miscreant, outcast, profligate, rascal, rat (*Inf.*), rogue, rotter (*Sl.*), ruffian, scoundrel, swine, vagabond, villain, worm **2.** poor thing, unfortunate

wretched 1. abject, brokenhearted, cheerless, comfortless, crestfallen, dejected, deplorable, depressed, disconsolate, distressed, doleful, downcast, forlorn, gloomy, hapless, hopeless, melancholy, miserable, pathetic, pitiable, pitiful, poor, sorry, unfortunate, unhappy, woebegone, woeful, worthless **2.** calamitous, deplorable, inferior, miserable, paltry, pathetic, poor, sorry, worthless

wriggle *v.* **1.** jerk, jiggle, squirm, turn, twist, wag, waggle, wiggle, writhe **2.** crawl, slink, snake, twist and turn, worm, zigzag ~*n.* **3.** jerk, jiggle, squirm, turn, twist, wag, waggle, wiggle

(**wrung, ˈwringing**) —**ˈwringer** *n.* machine consisting of two rollers between which wet clothes are run to squeeze out the water

wrinkle[1] (ˈrɪŋkᵊl) *n.* **1.** slight ridge or furrow on surface **2.** crease in the skin **3.** fold **4.** pucker —*v.* **5.** make, become wrinkled, pucker —**ˈwrinklies** *pl.n. inf., offens.* old people —**ˈwrinkly** *a.*

wrinkle[2] (ˈrɪŋkᵊl) *n. inf.* (useful) trick, hint

wrist (rɪst) *n.* joint between hand and arm —**ˈwristlet** *n.* band worn on wrist

writ (rɪt) *n.* written command from law court or other authority

write (raɪt) *vi.* **1.** mark paper *etc.* with the symbols which are used to represent words or sounds **2.** compose **3.** send a letter —*vt.* **4.** set down in words **5.** compose **6.** communicate in writing (**wrote, written** (ˈrɪtᵊn), **ˈwriting**) —**ˈwriter** *n.* **1.** one who writes **2.** author —**write-off** *n. inf.* something damaged beyond repair —**write-up** *n.* written (published) account of something

writhe (raɪð) *vi.* **1.** twist, squirm in or as in pain *etc.* **2.** be acutely embarrassed (**writhed** *pt.*, **writhed,** *Poet.* **writhen** (ˈrɪðᵊn) *pp.*, **ˈwrithing** *pr.p.*)

W.R.N.S. Women's Royal Naval Service

wrong (rɒŋ) *a.* **1.** not right or good **2.** not suitable **3.** wicked **4.** incorrect **5.** mistaken **6.** not functioning properly —*n.* **7.** that which is wrong **8.** harm **9.** evil —*vt.* **10.** do wrong to **11.** think badly of without justification —**ˈwrongful** *a.* —**ˈwrongfully** *adv.* —**ˈwrongly** *adv.* —**ˈwrongdoer** *n.* one who acts immorally or illegally —**wrong-foot** *vt. Tennis etc.* play shot in such a way as to cause (one's opponent) to be off balance —**wrong-headed** *a.* **1.** constantly wrong in judgment **2.** foolishly stubborn

wrote (rəʊt) *pt. of* WRITE

wrought (rɔːt) *v.* **1.** *pt./pp. of* WORK —*a.* **2.** (of metals) shaped by hammering or beating —**wrought iron** pure form of iron used *esp.* in decorative railings *etc.*

wrung (rʌŋ) *pt./pp. of* WRING

W.R.V.S. Women's Royal Voluntary Service

wry (raɪ) *a.* **1.** turned to one side, contorted, askew **2.** sardonic, dryly humorous —**ˈwryneck** *n.* type of woodpecker

WSW west-southwest

wt. weight

WV West Virginia

WWI World War One

WWII World War Two

WX women's extra (size)

WY Wyoming

wych- *or* **witch-** (*comb. form*) (of tree) with pliant branches

wych-elm *or* **witch-elm** (ˈwɪtʃɛlm) *n.* **1.** Eurasian elm tree, having rounded shape, longish pointed leaves, clusters of small flowers and winged fruits **2.** wood of this tree

wynd (waɪnd) *n.* in Scotland, narrow lane, alley

THESAURUS

wring 1. coerce, extort, extract, force, screw, squeeze, twist, wrench, wrest **2.** distress, hurt, lacerate, pain, pierce, rack, rend, stab, tear at, wound

wrinkle[1] **1.** *n.* corrugation, crease, crinkle, crow's-foot, crumple, fold, furrow, gather, line, pucker, rumple **2.** *v.* corrugate, crease, crinkle, crumple, fold, furrow, gather, line, pucker, ruck, rumple

wrinkle[2] device, dodge, gimmick, idea, plan, ploy, ruse, scheme stunt, tip, trick, wheeze (*Brit. sl.*)

writ court order, decree, document, summons

write author (*Nonstandard*), commit to paper, compose, copy, correspond, create, draft, draw up, indite, inscribe, jot down, pen, put down in black and white, put in writing, record, scribble, set down, take down, tell, transcribe

writer author, columnist, essayist, hack, littérateur, man of letters, novelist, penman, penny-a-liner (*Rare*), penpusher, scribbler, scribe, wordsmith

writhe contort, distort, jerk, squirm, struggle, thrash, thresh, toss, twist, wiggle, wriggle

wrong *adj.* **1.** erroneous, fallacious, false, faulty, inaccurate, incorrect, in error, mistaken, off beam (*Inf.*), off target, out, unsound, untrue, wide of the mark **2.** bad, blameworthy, criminal, crooked, dishonest, dishonourable, evil, felonious, illegal, illicit, immoral, iniquitous, reprehensible, sinful, unethical, unfair, unjust, unlawful, wicked, wrongful **3.** funny, improper, inappropriate, inapt, incongruous, incorrect, indecorous, infelicitous, malapropos, not done, unacceptable, unbecoming, unconventional, undesirable, unfitting, unhappy, unseemly, unsuitable **4.** amiss, askew, awry, defective, faulty, not working, out of commission, out of order ~*n.* **5.** abuse, bad *or* evil deed, crime, error, grievance, immorality, inequity, infraction, infringement, iniquity, injury, injustice, misdeed, offence, sin, sinfulness, transgression, trespass, unfairness, wickedness ~*v.* **6.** abuse, cheat, discredit, dishonour, harm, hurt, ill-treat, ill-use, impose upon, injure, malign, maltreat, misrepresent, mistreat, oppress, take advantage of

wrongdoer criminal, culprit, delinquent, evildoer, lawbreaker, malefactor, miscreant, offender, sinner, transgressor, trespasser (*Archaic*)

wrongful blameworthy, criminal, dishonest, dishonourable, evil, felonious, illegal, illegitimate, illicit, immoral, improper, reprehensible, unethical, unfair, unjust, unlawful, wicked

wry 1. askew, aslant, awry, contorted, crooked, deformed, distorted, off the level, twisted, uneven, warped **2.** droll, dry, ironic, mocking, pawky (*Scot.*), sarcastic, sardonic

XYZ

x *or* **X** (ɛks) *n.* **1.** 24th letter of English alphabet **2.** speech sound sequence represented by this letter, pronounced as *ks* or *gz* or, in initial position, *z*, as in *xylophone* (*pl.* **x's, X's** *or* **Xs**)

x *Maths.* unknown quantity

X 1. Christ **2.** Christian **3.** Cross **4.** Roman numeral, 10 **5.** mark indicating something wrong, a choice, a kiss, signature *etc.* **6.** unknown, mysterious person, factor

xanthine (ˈzænθiːn, -θaɪn) *n.* **1.** crystalline compound found in urine, blood and certain plants **2.** any of three substituted derivatives of xanthine, which act as stimulants and diuretics

***x*-axis** *n.* reference axis, usu. horizontal, along which *x*-coordinate is measured

X-chromosome *n.* sex-determining chromosome that occurs in pairs in homologically paired cells of females of many animals and as one of pair with Y-chromosome in those of males

Xe *Chem.* xenon

xeno- *or before vowel* **xen-** (*comb. form*) something strange, different or foreign, as in *xenogamy*

xenogamy (zɛˈnɒgəmɪ) *n.* **1.** pollination from another plant **2.** cross-fertilization —**xeˈnogamous** *a.*

xenon (ˈzɛnɒn) *n.* colourless, odourless gas occurring in very small quantities in air

xenophobia (zɛnəˈfəʊbɪə) *n.* dislike, hatred, fear, of strangers or aliens

xerography (zɪˈrɒgrəfɪ) *n.* photocopying process —**Xerox** (ˈzɪərɒks) *n.* **R** xerographic copying process, machine

xi (zaɪ, saɪ, ksaɪ, ksiː) *n.* 14th letter in Gr. alphabet (Ξ, ξ) (*pl.* **-s**)

Xmas (ˈɛksməs, ˈkrɪsməs) Christmas

x-ray *or* **X-ray** *n.* **1.** radiation of very short wavelengths, capable of penetrating solid bodies, and printing on photographic plate shadow picture of objects not permeable by rays —*vt.* **2.** photograph by x-rays

xylem (ˈzaɪləm, -lɛm) *n.* plant tissue that conducts water and mineral salts from roots to other parts

xylene (ˈzaɪliːn) *n.* aromatic hydrocarbon existing in three isomeric forms, all three being colourless flammable volatile liquids used as solvents *etc.*

xylograph (ˈzaɪləgrɑːf) *n.* **1.** wood engraving **2.** impression from wood block

xyloid (ˈzaɪlɔɪd) *a.* **1.** pert. to wood **2.** woody, ligneous

xylophone (ˈzaɪləfəʊn) *n.* musical instrument of wooden bars which sound when struck

xylose (ˈzaɪləʊz, -ləʊs) *n.* white crystalline sugar found in wood and straw and used in dyeing, tanning, diabetic food *etc.*

y *or* **Y** (waɪ) *n.* **1.** 25th letter of English alphabet **2.** speech sound represented by this letter, usu. semivowel, as in *yawn*, or vowel, as in *symbol, shy* **3.** something shaped like Y (*pl.* **y's, Y's** *or* **Ys**)

y *Maths.* **1.** *y*-axis or coordinate measured along *y*-axis in Cartesian coordinate system **2.** algebraic variable

Y 1. any unknown or variable factor, number or thing **2.** *Chem.* yttrium

-y[1] *or* **-ey** (*comb. form*) **1.** characterized by; consisting of; filled with; resembling, as in *sunny, sandy, smoky, classy* **2.** tending to; acting or existing as specified, as in *leaky, shiny*

-y[2], **-ie,** *or* **-ey** (*comb. form*) *inf.* **1.** denoting smallness and expressing affection and familiarity, as in *doggy, Jamie* **2.** person or thing concerned with or characterized by being, as in *groupie, goalie, fatty*

-y[3] (*comb. form*) **1.** act of doing what is indicated by verbal element, as in *inquiry* **2.** state, condition, quality, as in *geography, jealousy*

yacht (jɒt) *n.* vessel propelled by sail or power, used for racing, pleasure *etc.* —**ˈyachtsman** *n.*

yahoo (jəˈhuː) *n.* crude, coarse person

yak[1] (jæk) *n.* shaggy-haired, long-horned ox of Central Asia

yak[2] (jæk) *sl. n.* **1.** noisy, continuous, trivial talk —*vi.* **2.** chatter or talk in this way (**-kk-**)

Yale lock (jeɪl) **R** cylinder lock using flat serrated key

yam (jæm) *n.* **1.** tropical root vegetable **2.** sweet potato

Yang (jæŋ) *n. see* YIN AND YANG

yank (jæŋk) *vt.* **1.** jerk, tug; pull quickly —*n.* **2.** quick tug

Yank (jæŋk) *a./n. sl.* American

yap (jæp) *vi.* **1.** bark (as small dog) **2.** talk idly; gossip (**-pp-**) —*n.* **3.** sharp bark

yarborough (ˈjɑːbərə, -brə) *n. Bridge, whist* hand of 13 cards with no card higher than nine

yard[1] (jɑːd) *n.* **1.** unit of length, 0.915 metre **2.** spar slung across ship's mast to extend sails —**ˈyardstick** *n.* formula or standard of measurement or comparison

yard[2] (jɑːd) *n.* piece of enclosed ground, oft. attached to or adjoining building and used for some specific purpose, as garden, storage, holding livestock *etc.* —**ˈyardage** *n.* **1.** use of yard **2.** charge made for this

yarmulke (ˈjɑːməlkə) *n. Judaism* man's skullcap worn at prayer, and by strongly religious Jews at all times

yarn (jɑːn) *n.* **1.** spun thread **2.** tale —*vi.* **3.** tell a tale

yarrow (ˈjærəʊ) *n.* plant with flat white flower clusters

yashmak *or* **yashmac** (ˈjæʃmæk) *n.* face veil worn by Muslim women

yaw (jɔː) *vi.* **1.** (of aircraft *etc.*) turn about vertical axis **2.** (of ship *etc.*) deviate temporarily from course

THESAURUS

X-rays Röntgen rays (*Old name*)

yank *v./n.* hitch, jerk, pull, snatch, tug, wrench

yardstick benchmark, criterion, gauge, measure, standard, touchstone

yarn *n.* **1.** fibre, thread **2.** *Inf.* anecdote, cock-and-bull story (*Inf.*), fable, story, tale, tall story

yearly annual, annually, every year, once a year, per annum

yearn ache, covet, crave, desire, hanker, have a yen for (*Inf.*), hunger, itch, languish, long, lust, pant, pine, set one's heart upon

yawl (jɔːl) *n.* two-masted sailing vessel

yawn (jɔːn) *vi.* **1.** open mouth wide, *esp.* in sleepiness **2.** gape —*n.* **3.** a yawning

yaws (jɔːz) *pl.n.* contagious tropical skin disease

y-axis *n.* reference axis of graph or two- or three-dimensional Cartesian coordinate system along which *y*-coordinate is measured

Yb *Chem.* ytterbium

Y-chromosome *n.* sex chromosome that occurs as one of pair with X-chromosome in homologically paired cells of males of many animals

yd *or* **yd.** yard (measure)

ye (jiː, *unstressed* jɪ) *pron. obs.* you

yea (jeɪ) *interj. obs.* yes

year (jɪə) *n.* **1.** time taken by one revolution of earth round sun, about 365 days **2.** twelve months —**ˈyearling** *n.* animal one year old —**ˈyearly** *adv.* **1.** every year, once a year —*a.* **2.** happening *etc.* once a year —**ˈyearbook** *n.* reference book published annually and containing details of events of previous year

yearn (jɜːn) *vi.* **1.** feel longing, desire **2.** be filled with pity, tenderness —**ˈyearning** *n.*

yeast (jiːst) *n.* substance used as fermenting agent, *esp.* in raising bread —**ˈyeasty** *a.* **1.** of, like yeast **2.** frothy, fermenting

yell (jɛl) *v.* **1.** cry out in loud shrill tone **2.** *inf.* call —*n.* **3.** loud shrill cry **4.** *inf.* call

yellow (ˈjɛləʊ) *a.* **1.** of the colour of lemons, gold *etc.* **2.** *inf.* cowardly —*n.* **3.** yellow colour —**yellow fever** acute infectious disease of (sub)tropical climates —**ˈyellowhammer** *n.* small European bunting —**yellow pages** classified telephone directory or section of directory that lists subscribers by business or service provided —**yellow streak** cowardly trait —**ˈyellowwood** *n.* SA **1.** type of conifer **2.** its rich yellow wood used *esp.* for furniture and building

yelp (jɛlp) *vi./n.* (produce) quick, shrill cry

yen[1] (jɛn) *n.* Japanese monetary unit (*pl.* **yen**)

yen[2] (jɛn) *n. inf.* longing, craving

yeoman (ˈjəʊmən) *n.* **1.** *Hist.* farmer cultivating his own land **2.** assistant, subordinate —**ˈyeomanry** *n.* **1.** yeomen collectively **2.** Brit. volunteer cavalry force, organized in 1761 for home defence —**yeoman of the guard** member of ceremonial bodyguard (**Yeomen of the Guard**) of British monarch

yes (jɛs) *interj.* affirms or consents, gives an affirmative answer —**yes man** weak person willing to agree to anything

yesterday (ˈjɛstədɪ, -deɪ) *n.* **1.** day before today **2.** recent time —*adv.* **3.** on the day before today

yet (jɛt) *adv.* **1.** now **2.** still **3.** besides **4.** hitherto **5.** nevertheless —*conj.* **6.** but, at the same time, nevertheless

yeti (ˈjɛtɪ) *n. see* **abominable snowman** *at* ABOMINATE

yew (juː) *n.* **1.** evergreen tree with dark leaves **2.** its wood

Y.H.A. UK Youth Hostels Association

Yiddish (ˈjɪdɪʃ) *a./n.* (of, in) dialect of mixed German and Hebrew used by many Jews in Europe —**yid** *n. sl. offens.* Jew

yield (jiːld) *vt.* **1.** give or return as food **2.** produce **3.** provide **4.** concede **5.** give up, surrender —*vi.* **6.** submit **7.** (*with* to) comply (with) **8.** surrender, give way —*n.* **9.** amount produced, result **10.** return, profit

Yin and Yang (jɪn) two complementary principles of Chinese philosophy: Yin is negative, dark and feminine; Yang is positive, bright and masculine

Y.M.C.A. Young Men's Christian Association

yob (jɒb) *or* **yobbo** (ˈjɒbəʊ) *n. sl.* aggressive, surly youth (*pl.* **-s**)

yodel (ˈjəʊdˀl) *v.* **1.** warble in falsetto tone (**-ll-**) —*n.* **2.** falsetto warbling as practised by Swiss mountaineers

yoga (ˈjəʊgə) *n.* Hindu philosophical system aiming at spiritual, mental and physical wellbeing by means of certain physical and mental exercises —**yogi** (ˈjəʊgɪ) *n.* one who practises yoga (*pl.* **-s, -gin** (-gɪn))

yoghurt *or* **yogurt** (ˈjɒgət) *n.* thick, custardlike preparation of curdled milk

THESAURUS

yell **1.** *v.* bawl, holler (*Inf.*), howl, scream, screech, shout, shriek, squeal **2.** *n.* cry, howl, scream, screech, shriek, whoop

yet **1.** as yet, so far, thus far, until now, up to now **2.** however, nevertheless, notwithstanding, still **3.** additionally, as well, besides, further, in addition, into the bargain, moreover, over and above, still, to boot **4.** already, just now, now, right now, so soon

yield *v.* **1.** afford, bear, bring forth, bring in, earn, furnish, generate, give, net, pay, produce, provide, return, supply ~*n.* **2.** crop, earnings, harvest, income, output, produce, profit, return, revenue, takings ~*v.* **3.** abandon, abdicate, admit defeat, bow, capitulate, cave in (*Inf.*), cede, cry quits, give in, give up the struggle, give way, knuckle under, lay down one's arms, part with, raise the white flag, relinquish, resign, resign oneself, submit, succumb, surrender, throw in the towel **4.** accede, agree, allow, bow, comply, concede, consent, go along with, grant, permit

yoke *n.* **1.** bond, chain, coupling, ligament, link, tie **2.** bondage, burden, domination, enslavement, helotry, oppression, serfdom, service, servility, servitude, slavery, thraldom, vassalage ~*v.* **3.** bracket, connect, couple, harness, hitch, join, link, tie, unite

yokel boor, bucolic, clodhopper (*Inf.*), (country) bumpkin, country cousin, countryman, hick (*Inf., chiefly U.S.*), hillbilly, hind (*Obsolete*), peasant (*Inf.*), rustic

young *adj.* **1.** adolescent, callow, green, growing, immature, infant, in the springtime of life, junior, juvenile, little, unfledged, youthful **2.** at an early stage, early, fledgling, new, newish, not far advanced, recent, undeveloped ~*n.* **3.** babies, brood, family, issue, litter, little ones, offspring, progeny

youngster boy, cub, girl, juvenile, kid (*Inf.*), lad, lass, pup (*Inf.*), teenager, teenybopper (*Sl.*), urchin, young adult, young hopeful, young person, young shaver (*Inf.*), young 'un (*Inf.*), youth

youth **1.** adolescence, boyhood, early life, girlhood, immaturity, juvenescence, salad days, young days **2.** adolescent, boy, kid (*Inf.*), lad, shaveling (*Archaic*), stripling, teenager, young man, young shaver (*Inf.*), youngster **3.** teenagers, the rising generation, the young, younger generation, young people

youthful **1.** boyish, childish, girlish, immature, inexperienced, juvenile, pubescent, puerile, young **2.** active, fresh, spry, vigorous, young at heart, young looking

yoicks (haɪk; *spelling pron.* jɔɪks) *interj.* cry used by fox-hunters to urge on hounds

yoke (jəʊk) *n.* **1.** wooden bar put across necks of two animals to hold them together and to which plough *etc.* may be attached **2.** various objects like a yoke in shape or use **3.** fitted part of garment, *esp.* round neck, shoulders **4.** bond, tie **5.** domination —*vt.* **6.** put a yoke on **7.** couple, unite

yokel (ˈjəʊkᵊl) *n. disparaging term for* (old-fashioned) country dweller

yolk (jəʊk) *n.* **1.** yellow central part of egg **2.** oily secretion of skin of sheep

Yom Kippur (jɒm ˈkɪpə; *Hebrew* jɔm kiˈpur) Jewish holiday celebrated as day of fasting, when prayers of penitence are recited in synagogue (*also* **Day of Atonement**)

yon (jɒn) *a. obs., dial.* that or those over there —ˈ**yonder** *a.* **1.** yon —*adv.* **2.** over there, in that direction

yoo-hoo (ˈjuːhuː) *interj.* call to attract attention

YOP (jɒp) Youth Opportunities Programme

yore (jɔː) *n. Poet.* the distant past

yorker (ˈjɔːkə) *n. Cricket* ball that pitches directly under bat —**york** *vt. Cricket* bowl (batsman) by pitching ball under or just beyond bat

Yorks. (jɔːks) Yorkshire

Yorkshire pudding (ˈjɔːkʃɪə) savoury baked batter eaten with roast beef —**Yorkshire terrier** very small terrier with long straight coat

you (juː; *unstressed* jʊ) *pron.* referring to person(s) addressed, or to unspecified person(s)

young (jʌŋ) *a.* **1.** not far advanced in growth, life or existence **2.** not yet old **3.** immature **4.** junior **5.** recently formed **6.** vigorous —*n.* **7.** offspring —ˈ**youngster** *n.* child

your (jɔː,. jʊə; *unstressed* jə) *a.* belonging to you —**yours** *pron.* —**your**ˈ**self** *pron.* (*pl.* **your**ˈ**selves**)

youth (juːθ) *n.* **1.** state or time of being young **2.** state before adult age **3.** young man **4.** young people —ˈ**youthful** *a.* —**youth hostel** inexpensive lodging place *esp.* for young people travelling cheaply (*also* ˈ**hostel**)

yowl (jaʊl) *vi./n.* (produce) mournful cry

yo-yo (ˈjəʊjəʊ) *n.* toy consisting of a spool attached to a string, by which it can be spun out and reeled in while attached to the finger (*pl.* **-s**)

Y.S.T. US, C Yukon Standard Time

Y.T. C Yukon Territory

ytterbium (ɪˈtɜːbɪəm) *n.* silvery element of lanthanide series of metals, used to improve mechanical properties of steel

yttrium (ˈɪtrɪəm) *n.* silvery metallic element used in various alloys

yucca (ˈjʌkə) *n.* tropical plant with stiff lancelike leaves

Yugoslav *or* **Jugoslav** (ˈjuːgəʊslɑːv) *n.* **1.** native of Yugoslavia, federal republic in SE Europe **2.** Serbo-Croatian (language) —*a.* **3.** of Yugoslavia

yule (juːl) *n.* (*sometimes* **Y-**) the Christmas festival or season

Yuppie (ˈjʌpɪ) (*sometimes* **y-**) *n.* **1.** young urban (*or* upwardly mobile) professional —*a.* **2.** designed for or appealing to Yuppies

Y.W.C.A. Young Women's Christian Association

z *or* **Z** (zɛd; *U.S.* ziː) *n.* **1.** 26th letter of English alphabet **2.** speech sound represented by this letter **3.** something shaped like Z (*pl.* **z's, Z's** *or* **Zs**)

z *Maths.* **1.** *z*-axis or coordinate measured along *z*-axis in Cartesian or cylindrical coordinate system **2.** algebraic variable

zany (ˈzeɪnɪ) *a.* comical, funny in unusual way

zeal (ziːl) *n.* **1.** fervour **2.** keenness, enthusiasm —**zealot** (ˈzɛlət) *n.* **1.** fanatic **2.** enthusiast —**zealous** (ˈzɛləs) *a.* **1.** ardent **2.** enthusiastic **3.** earnest —**zealously** (ˈzɛləslɪ) *adv.*

zebra (ˈzɛbrə, ˈziːbrə) *n.* striped Afr. animal like a horse —**zebra crossing** pedestrian crossing marked by stripes on road

zebu (ˈziːbuː) *n.* humped Indian ox or cow

Zen (zɛn) *n. Buddhism* Japanese school teaching contemplation, meditation

zenith (ˈzɛnɪθ) *n.* **1.** point of the heavens directly above an observer **2.** point opposite nadir **3.** summit, peak **4.** climax —ˈ**zenithal** *a.*

zephyr (ˈzɛfə) *n.* soft, gentle breeze

zeppelin (ˈzɛpəlɪn) *n.* large, cylindrical, rigid airship

zero (ˈzɪərəʊ) *n.* **1.** nothing **2.** figure 0 **3.** point on graduated instrument from which positive and negative quantities are reckoned **4.** the lowest point (*pl.* **-s, -es**) —**zero hour 1.** *Mil.* time set for start of attack *etc.* **2.** *inf.* critical time —**zero option** (in international nuclear arms negotiations) offer to remove all shorter-range nuclear missiles if other side will do same —**zero-rated** *a.* denoting goods on which buyer pays no value-added tax —**zero-zero option** (in international nuclear arms negotiations) offer to remove all intermediate-range nuclear missiles if other side will do same

zest (zɛst) *n.* **1.** enjoyment **2.** excitement, interest, flavour **3.** peel of orange or lemon

zeta (ˈziːtə) *n.* sixth letter in Gr. alphabet (Ζ, ζ)

zigzag (ˈzɪgzæg) *n.* **1.** line or course characterized by sharp turns in alternating directions —*vi.* **2.** move along in zigzag course (**-zagged** *pt./pp.*, **-zagging** *pr.p.*)

zinc (zɪŋk) *n.* bluish-white metallic element with wide variety of uses, *esp.* in alloys as brass *etc.* —ˈ**zinco-**

THESAURUS

zeal ardour, devotion, eagerness, earnestness, enthusiasm, fanaticism, fervency, fervour, fire, gusto, keenness, militancy, passion, spirit, verve, warmth, zest

zealot bigot, enthusiast, extremist, fanatic, fiend (*Inf.*), maniac, militant

zealous afire, ardent, burning, devoted, eager, earnest, enthusiastic, fanatical, fervent, fervid, impassioned, keen, militant, passionate, rabid, spirited

zenith acme, apex, apogee, climax, height, high noon, high point, meridian, peak, pinnacle, summit, top, vertex

zero 1. cipher, naught, nil, nothing, nought **2.** bottom, lowest point *or* ebb, nadir, nothing, rock bottom

zero hour appointed hour, crisis, moment of decision, moment of truth, turning point, vital moment

zest 1. appetite, delectation, enjoyment, gusto, keenness, relish, zeal, zing (*Inf.*) **2.** charm, flavour, interest, kick (*Inf.*), piquancy, pungency, relish, savour, smack, spice, tang, taste

graph *n.* —**zin'cographer** *n.* —**zin'cography** *n.* art or process of engraving zinc to form printing plate —**zinc ointment** medicinal ointment of zinc oxide, petrolatum and paraffin —**zinc oxide** white insoluble powder used as pigment in paints, cosmetics, glass *etc.* (*also* **flowers of zinc**)

zing (zɪŋ) *n. inf.* **1.** short high-pitched buzzing sound **2.** vitality; zest —*vi.* **3.** make or move with high-pitched buzzing sound

zinnia ('zɪnɪə) *n.* plant with daisylike, brightly-coloured flowers

Zion ('zaɪən) *or* **Sion** *n.* **1.** hill on which Jerusalem stands **2.** Judaism **3.** Christian Church **4.** heaven —**'Zionism** *n.* movement to found, support Jewish homeland in Palestine —**'Zionist** *n./a.*

zip (zɪp) *n.* **1.** device for fastening with two rows of flexible metal or nylon teeth, interlocked and opened by a sliding clip (*also* **'zipper, zip fastener**) **2.** short whizzing sound **3.** energy, vigour —*vt.* **4.** fasten with zip —*vi.* **5.** move with zip (**-pp-**)

zircon ('zɜːkɒn) *n.* mineral used as gemstone and in industry —**zir'conium** *n.* greyish-white metallic element, occurring chiefly in zircon, that is exceptionally corrosion-resistant and has low neutron absorption

zither ('zɪðə) *n.* flat stringed instrument

zloty ('zlɒtɪ) *n.* Polish coin (*pl.* **-s, 'zloty**)

Zn *Chem.* zinc

zodiac ('zəʊdɪæk) *n.* imaginary belt of the heavens along which the sun, moon, and chief planets appear to move, divided crosswise into twelve equal areas, called **signs of the zodiac,** each named after a constellation —**zodiacal** (zəʊ'daɪəkəl) *a.*

zombie *or* **zombi** ('zɒmbɪ) *n.* **1.** person appearing lifeless, apathetic *etc.* **2.** corpse supposedly brought to life by supernatural spirit

zone (zəʊn) *n.* **1.** region with particular characteristics or use **2.** any of the five belts into which tropics and arctic and antarctic circles divide the earth —**'zonal** *a.*

zoo (zuː) *n.* place where wild animals are kept, studied, bred and exhibited (*in full* **zoological gardens**)

zoo- *or before vowel* **zo-** (*comb. form*) animals, as in *zooplankton*

zoogeography (zəʊədʒɪ'ɒgrəfɪ) *n.* science of geographical distribution of animals

zoography (zəʊ'ɒgrəfɪ) *n.* descriptive zoology —**zo'ographer** *or* **zo'ographist** *n.* —**zoo'graphic(al)** *a.*

zooid ('zəʊɔɪd) *n.* **1.** independent animal body, such as individual of coelenterate colony **2.** cell or body capable of spontaneous motion, produced by organism

zool. **1.** zoological **2.** zoology

zoology (zəʊ'ɒlədʒɪ, zuː-) *n.* **1.** scientific study of animals **2.** characteristics of particular animals or of fauna of particular area —**zoo'logical** *a.* —**zo'ologist** *n.*

zoom (zuːm) *v.* **1.** (cause to) make loud buzzing, humming sound **2.** (cause to) go fast or rise, increase sharply —*vi.* **3.** (*with* in *or* out) use camera lens of adjustable focal length to make subject appear closer or further away —**zoom lens** lens used in this way

zoophyte ('zəʊəfaɪt) *n.* plantlike animal, *eg* sponge —**zoophytic** (zəʊə'fɪtɪk) *a.*

Zoroastrianism (zɒrəʊ'æstrɪənɪzəm) *or* **Zoroastrism** *n.* dualistic religion founded by Persian prophet Zoroaster, based on concept of continuous struggle between Ormazd, god of creation, light and goodness, and his archenemy, Ahriman, spirit of evil and darkness

Zr *Chem.* zirconium

Zulu ('zuːlʊ, -luː) *n.* member, language of native S Afr. tribes

zygote ('zaɪgəʊt, 'zɪg-) *n.* fertilized egg cell

THESAURUS

zone area, belt, district, region, section, sector, sphere

SUPPLEMENTS

PUNCTUATION MARKS AND OTHER SYMBOLS

,	comma
;	semicolon
:	colon
.	full stop
—	dash
!	exclamation mark
?	interrogation or doubt
-	hyphen, as in *knick-knack*
'	apostrophe, as in *Queen's English*
( )	parentheses
[ ]	brackets
}	brace, to enclose two or more lines
´	acute accent, as in *blasé*
\`	grave accent } as in *tête-à-tête*
^	circumflex } as in *tête-à-tête*
~	tilde, used over *n* in certain Spanish words to denote the sound of *ny*, as in *señor*
¸	cedilla, to denote that *c* is pronounced soft, as in *façade*
" "	quotation marks
' '	quotation marks, when used within a quotation, as in *"He said, 'I will go at once' and jumped into the car."*
¯	macron, to mark length of sound, as in *cōbra*
˘	breve, marking a short sound, as in *lĭnen*
¨	diaeresis, as in *daïs*
¨	in German, used to denote modification of the vowel sound, as in *Köln* (Cologne)
‸	caret, marking a word or letter to be inserted in the line
* *	* .. .. .. — or - - - - ellipsis to indicate a break in a narrative, or an omission
⁂	or ⁂ asterism, used to call attention to a particular passage
. . .	. . or - - - - leaders, to direct the eye to a certain point
¶	paragraph
*	star, asterisk (1) a reference mark (2) used in philology to denote forms assumed to have existed though not recorded
†	dagger, obelisk (1) a reference mark (2) obsolete or dead
‡	double dagger, a reference mark
²	superior figure, used (1) as a reference mark (2) to indicate a homonym
ᵃ	superior letter
§	section mark
‖	parallel mark
☛	index, hand, fist
#	number; space
"	ditto
&	ampersand, and
&c	et cetera
@	at
℘	per
%	per cent, per hundred
©	copyright
®	registered, registered trademark
♂	male
♀	female.

PUNCTUATION MARKS AND THE USE OF CAPITAL LETTERS

apostrophe The sign ('), used to indicate possession. In the singular -'s is used (eg *day's end*); in the plural the apostrophe is added to the end of the word (eg *the neighbours' dog*). Plurals that do not end in -s also take -'s (eg *sheep's eyes*). Except for a few traditional exceptions (like *Jesus'*, *Keats'*) proper names ending in -s take -'s at the end (eg *Thomas's, the Jones's*).

brackets These serve to isolate part of a sentence which could be omitted and still leave an intelligible statement. Punctuation of the rest of the sentence should run as if the bracketed portion were not there, eg *That house over there* (*with the blue door*) *is ours.* Square brackets are used where the writer inserts his own information into a quotation, eg *I knew Pitt* [*the Younger*] *as a boy.*

capital letters These are used at the beginning of a sentence or quoted speech, and for proper names and titles of people and organizations, eg *Mr. Robertson, Dr. Smith, South America, British Rail.* They are not used when speaking of a general topic like *the pay of miners, the manufacture of cosmetics.* If an initial *the* is included in a title it has a capital, eg *We went to see The Tempest.*

colons and semicolons The function of these is to provide more of a break than a comma, and less than a full stop. The colon is used to make an abrupt break between two related statements, eg *Take it or leave it: the choice is yours.* It is also used to introduce a list, quotation, or summary and may be followed by a dash if the following matter begins on a separate line. Semicolons can be used instead of conjunctions to link two sentences or parts of them, eg *Two of the lights were working; two were out.*

commas 1. These make divisions or slight pauses in sentences, eg *She stormed out, slamming the door behind her.*

2. Commas are used to divide units in a series of nouns, adjectives, or phrases, eg *The cupboard was full of pots, pans, and crockery.* In such a series the last comma (ie before 'and' or 'or') is optional. It is not usual to place a comma between the last of a series of adjectives and the noun, eg *It was a long, hot, humid day.*

3. Commas also serve to mark off a word or phrase in a sentence which can stand grammatically complete on its own, as can dashes and brackets. Commas give the lightest degree of separation, dashes produce a jerky effect, and brackets cut off part of a sentence most firmly, eg *He hurried home, taking a short cut, but still arrived too late. It's a long time — over two years — since last we met. They both went to Athens* (*unaware of each other's plans*) *and stayed in the same hotel.*

4. When two phrases are linked by a conjunction a comma is used if there is a contrast, eg *She was dark, but her brother was fair.*

5. When addressing a person, commas are used before and after the person's name or title, eg *Well, Mrs. Smith, how are you today?*

exclamation marks These should only be used after genuine exclamations and not after ordinary statements.

full stops These are used at the end of a complete sentence containing a main verb, except in reported speech and where a passage takes the form of an argument, eg *You may think you can get away with it. Not a chance.* Full stops are also often used after abbreviations and initial letters standing for the whole word (as in *fig., a.m., R.C.*) but for abbreviations which include the first and last letters of a word (*Dr., Mr., ft.*) it is equally acceptable to omit the stop (*Dr, Mr, ft*). It is also usual to write titles, like *BBC, USA, TUC,* without stops. As usage varies the above should be taken only as a guide to common practice.

PUNCTUATION AND THE USE OF CAPITAL LETTERS (*cont.*)

hyphens Compound words, like *lay-by* or *manor house*, or words with a prefix, like *unpick*, may or may not contain a hyphen. It is generally used when the compound is new and dropped as it becomes familiar. When a compound adjective comes before a noun it should be hyphenated to stress that the constituent parts are not to be used independently, eg *He has a half-Italian wife.*

inverted commas (**quotation marks, quotes**) 1. These are used for direct quotation, not for indirect speech. It is usual to have a comma before and after a quotation if the sentence is resumed, eg *He said, "Follow me", and set off down the street.*
2. Single quotation marks can be used to indicate a title or quotation within a speech, eg *"I loved 'War and Peace'," she said, "but it took so long to read."*

question marks These are used at the end of direct questions, but not after reported ones.

PLURALS OF NOUNS

Plurals are formed by adding -s except in the following cases.

1. When a word ends in -ch, -s, -sh, -ss, or -x the plural is formed by adding -es (eg *benches, gases, dishes, crosses, taxes*).

2. When a word ends in -y preceded by a consonant the plural form is -ies (eg *parties, bodies, policies*). When a word ends in -y preceded by a vowel the plural is formed by adding -s (eg *trays, joys, keys*).

3. When a word ends in -o the more common plural ending is -oes (eg *cargoes, potatoes, heroes, goes*). In many less familiar words when the final -o is preceded by a vowel the plural ending is -os (eg *avocados, armadillos, studios, cameos*).

4. When a word ends in -f the plural is formed either by adding -s (eg *beliefs, cuffs, whiffs*) or by changing the -f to -v and adding -es (eg *wives, thieves, loaves*). Some words may take both forms (eg *scarf, hoof, wharf*).

5. When a word ends in -ex or -ix the more formal plural ending is -ices. In more general contexts -es is used (eg *appendices, appendixes; indices, indexes*).

6. When a word from Latin ends in -is the plural form is -es (eg *crises, analyses*).

With compound words (like *court-martial*) it is usually the most important part which is pluralized (eg *courts-martial, lord-justices, mothers-in-law*).
In certain cases the plural form of a word is the same as the singular (eg *deer, sheep, grouse*) and in some words both forms end in -s (eg *measles, corps, mews*).

There are two main types of plural which take either singular or plural verbs:

a. words like *media* and *data*. These are in common use as singular nouns although, strictly, this is incorrect.

b. words ending in -ics. Generally, these are treated as plural when the word relates to an individual person or thing (eg *his mathematics are poor; the hall's acoustics are good*) and as singular when it is regarded more strictly as a science (eg *mathematics is an important subject*).

CHEMICAL SYMBOLS

Each element is placed in alphabetical order of its symbol and is followed by its atomic number.

Ac actinium, 89
Ag silver, 47
Al aluminium, 13
Am americium, 95
Ar argon, 18
As arsenic, 33
At astatine, 85
Au gold, 79
B boron, 5
Ba barium, 56
Be beryllium, 4
Bi bismuth, 83
Bk berkelium, 97
Br bromine, 35
C carbon, 6
Ca calcium, 20
Cd cadmium, 48
Ce cerium, 58
Cf californium, 98
Cl chlorine, 17
Cm curium, 96
Co cobalt, 27
Cr chromium, 24
Cs caesium, 55
Cu copper, 29
Dy dysprosium, 66
Er erbium, 68
Es einsteinium, 99
Eu europium, 63
F fluorine, 9
Fe iron, 26
Fm fermium, 100
Fr francium, 87
Ga gallium, 31
Gd gadolinium, 64
Ge germanium, 32
H hydrogen, 1
Ha hahnium, 105
He helium, 2
Hf hafnium, 72
Hg mercury, 80
Ho holmium, 67
I iodine, 53
In indium, 49
Ir iridium, 77
K potassium, 19
Kr krypton, 36
La lanthanum, 57
Li lithium, 3
Lr lawrencium, 103
Lu lutetium, 71
Md mendelevium, 101
Mg magnesium, 12
Mn manganese, 25
Mo molybdenum, 42
N nitrogen, 7
Na sodium, 11
Nb niobium, 41
Nd neodymium, 60
Ne neon, 10
Ni nickel, 28
No nobelium, 102
Np neptunium, 93
O oxygen, 8
Os osmium, 76
P phosphorus, 15
Pa protactinium, 91
Pb lead, 82
Pd palladium, 46
Pm promethium, 61
Po polonium, 84
Pr praseodymium, 59
Pt platinum, 78
Pu plutonium, 94
Ra radium, 88
Rb rubidium, 37
Re rhenium, 75
Rf rutherfordium, 104
Rh rhodium, 45
Rn radon, 86
Ru ruthenium, 44
S sulphur, 16
Sb antimony, 51
Sc scandium, 21
Se selenium, 34
Si silicon, 14
Sm samarium, 62
Sn tin, 50
Sr strontium, 38
Ta tantalum, 73
Tb terbium, 65
Tc technetium, 43
Te tellurium, 52
Th thorium, 90
Ti titanium, 22
Tl thallium, 81
Tm thulium, 69
U uranium, 92
V vanadium, 23
W tungsten, 74
Xe xenon, 54
Y yttrium, 39
Yb ytterbium, 70
Zn zinc, 30
Zr zirconium, 40

COUNTRIES, RELATED NOUNS AND ADJECTIVES, CURRENCIES, AND CAPITALS

Country	Noun/ Adjective	Currency Unit	Capital
Afghanistan	Afghan	afghani	Kabul
Albania	Albanian	lek	Tirana
Algeria	Algerian	dinar	Algiers
Andorra	Andorran	franc/peseta	Andorra la Vella
Angola	Angolan	kwanza	Luanda
Argentina	Argentine *or* Argentinian	austral	Buenos Aires
Australia	Australian	dollar	Canberra
Austria	Austrian	schilling	Vienna
Bahamas	Bahamian	dollar	Nassau
Bahrain	Bahraini	dinar	Manama
Bangladesh	Bangladeshi	taka	Dhaka
Barbados	Barbadian	dollar	Bridgetown
Belgium	Belgian	franc	Brussels
Benin	Beninese	franc	Porto Novo
Bermuda	Bermudan	dollar	Hamilton
Bolivia	Bolivian	peso	La Paz
Botswana		pula	Gaborone
Brazil	Brazilian	cruzeiro	Brasilia
Bulgaria	Bulgarian	lev	Sofia
Burma	Burmese	kyat	Rangoon
Burundi	Burundian	franc	Bujumbura
Cambodia	Cambodian	riel	Phnom Penh
Cameroon	Cameroonian	franc	Yaoundé
Canada	Canadian	dollar	Ottawa
Central African Rep.		franc	Bangui
Chad	Chadian	franc	Ndjamena
Chile	Chilean	peso	Santiago
China	Chinese	yuan	Peking
China (Taiwan)	Chinese	dollar	Taipei
Colombia	Colombian	peso	Bogotá
Congo	Congolese	franc	Brazzaville
Costa Rica	Costa Rican	colon	San José
Cuba	Cuban	peso	Havana
Cyprus	Cypriot	pound	Nicosia
Czechoslovakia	Czech, Czechoslovak, *or* Czechoslovakian	crown	Prague
Denmark	Dane; Danish	krone	Copenhagen
Djibouti		franc	Djibouti
Dominica	Dominican	dollar	Roseau
Dominican Republic	Dominican	peso	Santo Domingo
Ecuador	Ecuadorean	sucre	Quito
Egypt	Egyptian	pound	Cairo
El Salvador	Salvadorean	colon	San Salvador
Equatorial Guinea		franc	Malabo
Ethiopia	Ethiopian	birr	Addis Ababa
Fiji	Fijian	dollar	Suva
Finland	Finn; Finnish	markka	Helsinki
France	Frenchman, -woman; French	franc	Paris
Gabon	Gabonese	franc	Libreville
Gambia	Gambian	dalasi	Banjul
Germany	German	deutschmark	Berlin
Ghana	Ghanaian	cedi	Accra
Greece	Greek	drachma	Athens
Grenada	Grenadian	dollar	St George's

COUNTRIES, RELATED NOUNS AND ADJECTIVES, CURRENCIES, AND CAPITALS (*cont.*)

Country	Noun/ Adjective	Currency Unit	Capital
Guatemala	Guatemalan	quetzal	Guatemala City
Guinea	Guinean	franc	Conakry
Guinea-Bissau		peso	Bissau
Guyana	Guyanese	dollar	Georgetown
Haiti	Haitian	gourde	Port-au-Prince
Honduras	Honduran	lempira	Tegucigalpa
Hungary	Hungarian	forint	Budapest
Iceland	Icelander; Icelandic	krona	Reykjavik
India	Indian	rupee	New Delhi
Indonesia	Indonesian	rupiah	Jakarta
Iran	Iranian	rial	Tehran
Iraq	Iraqi	dinar	Baghdad
Ireland, Republic of	Irishman, -woman; Irish	punt	Dublin
Israel	Israeli	shekel	Jerusalem
Italy	Italian	lira	Rome
Ivory Coast		franc	Yamoussoukro
Jamaica	Jamaican	dollar	Kingston
Japan	Japanese	yen	Tokyo
Jordan	Jordanian	dinar	Amman
Kenya	Kenyan	shilling	Nairobi
Korea, North	North Korean	won	Pyongyang
Korea, South	South Korean	won	Seoul
Kuwait	Kuwaiti	dinar	Kuwait
Laos	Laotian	kip	Vientiane
Lebanon	Lebanese	pound	Beirut
Lesotho		loti	Maseru
Liberia	Liberian	dollar	Monrovia
Libya	Libyan	dinar	Tripoli
Liechtenstein		franc	Vaduz
Luxembourg		franc	Luxembourg
Madagascar	Madagascan	franc	Antananarivo
Malawi	Malawian	kwacha	Lilongwe
Malaysia	Malaysian	ringgit	Kuala Lumpur
Maldives	Maldivian	rufiyaa	Malé
Mali	Malian	franc	Bamako
Malta	Maltese	pound	Valletta
Mauritania	Mauritanian	franc	Nouakchott
Mauritius	Mauritian	rupee	Port Louis
Mexico	Mexican	peso	Mexico City
Monaco	Monegasque	franc	Monaco
Mongolian People's Republic	Mongolian	tugrik	Ulan Bator
Morocco	Moroccan	dirham	Rabat
Mozambique	Mozambican	escudo	Maputo
Namibia	Namibian	rand	Windhoek
Nauru	Nauruan	dollar	Nauru
Nepal	Nepalese	rupee	Katmandu
Netherlands	Dutchman, -woman, Netherlander; Dutch	guilder	Amsterdam
New Zealand	New Zealander	dollar	Wellington
Nicaragua	Nicaraguan	cordoba	Managua
Niger		franc	Niamey
Nigeria	Nigerian	naira	Lagos
Norway	Norwegian	krone	Oslo
Oman	Omani	rial	Muscat

COUNTRIES, RELATED NOUNS AND ADJECTIVES, CURRENCIES, AND CAPITALS (*cont.*)

Country	Noun/ Adjective	Currency Unit	Capital
Pakistan	Pakistani	rupee	Islamabad
Panama	Panamanian	balboa	Panama City
Papua New Guinea	Papuan	kina	Port Moresby
Paraguay	Paraguayan	guarani	Asunción
Peru	Peruvian	inti	Lima
Philippines	Filipino *or* Philippine	peso	Manila
Poland	Pole; Polish	zloty	Warsaw
Portugal	Portuguese	escudo	Lisbon
Qatar	Qatari	riyal	Doha
Romania	Romanian	leu	Bucharest
Rwanda	Rwandan	franc	Kigali
San Marino	San Marinese *or* Sammarinese	lira	San Marino
Saudi Arabia	Saudi Arabian	riyal	Riyadh
Senegal	Senegalese	franc	Dakar
Sierra Leone	Sierra Leonean	leone	Freetown
Singapore	Singaporean	dollar	Singapore
Somalia	Somalian	shilling	Mogadiscio
South Africa	South African	rand	Cape Town (legislative) Pretoria (administrative)
Spain	Spaniard; Spanish	peseta	Madrid
Sri Lanka	Sri Lankan	rupee	Colombo
Sudan	Sudanese	pound	Khartoum
Surinam	Surinamese	guilder	Paramaribo
Swaziland	Swazi	emalangeni	Mbabane
Sweden	Swede; Swedish	krona	Stockholm
Switzerland	Swiss	franc	Bern
Syria	Syrian	pound	Damascus
Tanzania	Tanzanian	shilling	Dodoma
Thailand	Thai	baht	Bangkok
Togo	Togolese	franc	Lomé
Tonga	Tongan	pa'anga	Nuku'alofa
Trinidad and Tobago	Trinidadian, Tobagan	dollar	Port-of-Spain
Tunisia	Tunisian	dinar	Tunis
Turkey	Turk; Turkish	lira	Ankara
Uganda	Ugandan	shilling	Kampala
United Arab Emirates		dirham	Abu Dhabi
United Kingdom	Briton; British	pound	London
Uruguay	Uruguayan	peso	Montevideo
USA	American	dollar	Washington D.C.
USSR	Russian *or* Soviet	rouble	Moscow
Vatican City		lira	Vatican City
Venezuela	Venezuelan	bolivar	Caracas
Vietnam	Vietnamese	dong	Hanoi
Western Samoa	Samoan	tala	Apia
Yemen	Yemeni	riyal; dinar	Sanaa
Yugoslavia	Yugoslav *or* Yugoslavian	dinar	Belgrade
Zaïre	Zaïrean	zaïre	Kinshasa
Zambia	Zambian	kwacha	Lusaka
Zimbabwe	Zimbabwean	dollar	Harare